Jane's
Urban Transport
Systems
2009-2010

Editor: Mary Webb
Contributing Editor: Jackie Clarke

Twenty-eighth Edition

ISBN 978 0 7106 2903 6
"Jane's" is a registered trademark

Contents

Jane's Urban Transport Systems website: juts.janes.com

Front cover image: New Optara Rapta double-deck bus, introduced at EuroBus Expo 2008, available with an optional Enova Hybrid drive system (Optare PLC)

1374733

How to use Jane's Urban Transport Systems

Content

This title provides information on the systems, manufacturers and consultants within the global public transport market. Details are given for the world's major public transport systems, including details of both current operations and future plans. Traffic statistics are given for all operations wherever they are available, together with fleet lists and numbers in service. Key contact details are also provided.

Also within the title are many of the manufacturers involved in the urban transport industry. Data includes contact details, background to the companies, companies' product lines, contracts gained and future plans/R&D. The product also covers numerous consultancy services associated with the industry.

Structure

This publication is divided into three main sections— Urban Transport Systems and Operators, Manufacturers and Consultancy Services.

The Urban Transport Systems and Operators section is a listing of major cities, arranged alphabetically within country, describing the characteristics of their various modes of public transport. After a brief résumé of the range of services offered and the organisational basis on which they are provided, there are entries for the principal transport authorities, operators and modes. The range of information varies. Bus and trolleybus systems, metros and light rail/tramways generally have detailed tabular data on their physical and operating characteristics, fare structures, provision of facilities for elderly and disabled people, signalling and control systems, integration with other modes of transport, and farebox recovery rates. Commuter railways, ferries, paratransit and other operations are covered in a less detailed format which nevertheless aims to show their main characteristics. The political background to public transport provision is often covered, as are current and future plans for investment.

Traffic statistics (passenger journeys/boardings, vehicle-km) are shown for all operations wherever possible. There has been much confusion over use of the terms 'linked' and 'unlinked' journeys, and we have banished them. Instead the term 'boardings' is used wherever we have a clear indication that unlinked trips are involved; 'journeys' continues to refer to linked trips (one or more boardings on one or more modes).

Dates given with the traffic statistics indicate the financial year to which they apply, generally the most recent. While some other data may have been culled from that year's annual report (for example, the fleet lists) most information will generally be more up-to-date.

Fleet lists are also shown for all modes wherever possible, and may include class designation, builder and manufacturer of principal components (for example, bus chassis and bodywork), year of build and/or delivery, when rebuilt or refurbished and the numbers in service. For rail vehicles, the letters M and T indicate powered (motor) and unpowered (trailer) cars.

The Manufacturers section lists equipment builders and suppliers to the urban transport industry under fourteen main headings, several of which cover both road and rail equipment. The aim is to list product ranges, new developments and recent contracts.

Similarly, the final section details the capabilities and recent activities in the areas of Consultancy Services.

Record Structure

Urban Transport Systems and Operators

The following main headings are used within each record:
Contact details Includes address, telephone and fax numbers, e-mail address and Web address, followed by the Key personnel.
Systems data One or more tabular section/s throughout the record, giving useful statistics, such as passenger journeys, fleet listings, operating costs, subsidies, financing for new vehicles etc.
Background Provides a brief history.
Current situation Existing services.
Developments Recent improvements or additions to existing services/infrastructure etc, and information on future developments proposed/planned or already under way.

Manufacturers and Consultancy Services

The following main headings are used within each record.
Contact details The following main headings are used within each record.
Other offices Subsidiaries and worldwide offices.
Background Brief company history.
Products/Services Outline of products and services.
Range More detailed information on particular products and services.
Projects Details of current involvement.
Production Latest information of annual production figures and export data.
Contracts Details of most recent and/or major contracts won.
Developments Current R&D and joint ventures, for example.

Images

Photographs are provided for equipment wherever possible, as are maps in the Urban Transport Systems and Operators section. Images are annotated with a seven digit number which uniquely identifies them in Jane's image database.

Other information

For Definitions of Terms and Currency Standards information, please see the Glossary.

Please visit juts.janes.com to view the list of latest updates that have been added to the online version of Jane's Urban Transport Systems subsequent to this print edition.

Other products available from Jane's

defence

Aero-Engines
Aircraft Component Manufacturers
Aircraft Upgrades
Air-Launched Weapons
All the World's Aircraft
Ammunition Handbook
Amphibious and Special Forces
Armour and Artillery
Armour and Artillery Upgrades
Avionics
C4I Systems
Defence Equipment & Technology Intelligence Centre
Defence Equipment Library
Defence Forecasts – Combat Vehicle Programmes
Defence Forecasts – Military Aircraft Programmes
Defence Forecasts – Military Vessel Programmes
Defence Industry
Defence Industry & Markets Intelligence Centre
Defence Magazines Library
Defence Weekly
Electronic Mission Aircraft
Electro-Optic Systems
Explosive Ordnance Disposal
Fighting Ships
Helicopter Markets and Systems
High-Speed Marine Transportation
Infantry Weapons
International ABC Aerospace Directory
International Defence Directory
International Defence Review
Land-Based Air Defence
Marine Propulsion
Market Intelligence Library
Military Communications
Military Intelligence Library
Military Vehicles and Logistics
Mines and Mine Clearance
Missiles and Rockets
Naval Construction and Retrofit Markets
Naval Weapon Systems
Navy International
Nuclear, Biological and Chemical Defence
Radar & Electronic Warfare Systems
Simulation & Training Systems
Space Systems and Industry
Strategic Weapon Systems

defence, cont.

Underwater Warfare Systems
Unmanned Aerial Vehicles & Targets
Unmanned Ground Vehicles and Systems
Unmanned Maritime Vehicles and Systems
World Air Forces
World Armies
World Defence Industry
World Navies

law enforcement

The Beat Officer's Companion
Part 1 Promotion Crammer for Sergeants and Inspectors
Part 2 Pass for Promotion for Sergeants and Inspectors
Police & Homeland Security Equipment
Police Review
The Scottish Beat Officer's Companion
The Traffic Officer's Companion

security

Country Risk Daily Report
Foreign Report
Homeland Security & Resilience Monitor (RUSI/Jane's)
Intelligence Digest
Intelligence Review
Islamic Affairs Analyst
Military & Security Assessments Intelligence Centre
Security Library
Sentinel Country Risk Assessments
Sentinel Library
Terrorism & Insurgency Centre
Terrorism & Security Monitor
Terrorism Watch Report
World Insurgency & Terrorism

transport

Air Traffic Control
Airport Review
Airports and Handling Agents
Airports, Equipment and Services
Locomotives and Rolling Stock Forecasts
Merchant Ships
Transport Finance
Transport Library
Urban Transport Systems
World Railways

discover more

Jane's Information Group

Asia	Europe and Africa	North/Central/South America
Tel: +65 6576 5300	Tel: +44 (0) 20 8700 3750	Tel: +1 (800) 824 0768

Jane's
An IHS Company
Intelligence and Insight You Can Trust

Glossary

ABS	Anti-lock Braking System
ADA	Americans with Disabilities Act
AFC	Automated Fare Collection
AGT	Automated Guided Transit
ANPR	Automatic Number Plate Recognition
ATC	Automatic Train Control
ATO	Automatic Train Operation
ATP	Automatic Train Protection
ATS	Automatic Train Supervision
AVL	Automatic Vehicle Location
AVO	Automatic Vehicle Operation
AVP	Automatic Vehicle Protection
AVS	Automatic Vehicle Supervision
BOT	Build, Operate and Transfer
BRT	Bus Rapid Transit
CAG	Computer-Aided Gear changing
CCTV	Closed Circuit Television
CKD	Completely Knocked Down
CMS	Control and Management/Monitoring System
CNG	Compressed Natural Gas
CTC	Centralised Traffic Control
DBOM	Design, Build, Operate, Maintain
demu	diesel-electric multiple-unit
dmu	diesel multiple-unit
DOT	Double-O-Tube (tunnel construction)
DPTAC	Disabled Persons Transport Advisory Committee (accessible buses)
DTC	Direct Train Control
EEV	Enhanced Environmental Vehicle
EGS	Easy Gear Shift
E&M	Engineering & Maintenance
emu	electric multiple-unit
Euro-1, Euro-2, Euro-3	European Exhaust Emission Standards
FFGA	Full Funding Grant Agreement
GLT	Guided Light Transit
GPS	Global Positioning System
GRP	Glass-Reinforced Plastic
GTO	Gate Turn-Off
gvw	Gross Vehicle Weight
HEV	Hybrid-Electric Vehicle
HOV	High-Occupancy Vehicle
HVAC	Heating, Ventilation and Air Conditioning
ICMU	Interference Current Monitoring Unit
IGBT	Insulated Gate Bipolar Transistor
LHD	Left-Hand Drive
LNG	Liquefied Natural Gas
LPG	Liquefied Petroleum Gas
LRT	Light Rapid Transit
LRV	Light Rail Vehicle
M	Motor
MO.MO	Modular Metro concept
MSS	Maintenance Support System
OTRB	Over-the-Road Bus (bus characterised by an elevated passenger deck located over a baggage compartment) (US)
PHEV	Plug-in Hybrid Electric Vehicle
PPD	Passengers Per Day
PRT	Personal Rapid Transit
PTE	Passenger Transport Executive
RER	*Réseau Express Régional*
RHD	Right-Hand Drive
S-Bahn	High frequency heavy rail suburban passenger service (Austria, Germany & Switzerland)
SCR	Selective Catalytic Reduction
SLF	Super Low Floor
SPV/SPE	Special Purpose Vehicle/Entity
T	Trailer
TETRA	TErrestrial Trunked RAdio
TGV	*Train à Grande Vitesse*
TPT	Train Positioning and Tracking
U-Bahn	Underground metro system (Austria and Germany)
UITP	the International Union of Public Transport
ULT	Ultra Light Transit
VLRS	Variable Level Rail System
VVVF	Variable Voltage Variable Frequency
WAP	Wireless Application Protocol

Definitions of terms

The following definitions have been included to assist with understanding certain terminology used in this publication.

Proposed:	System proposal, usually prior to any funding application/agreement.
Planned:	System with study/ies being undertaken or completed and/or funding application and/or approval.
Under construction:	Civil works and/or system construction work being undertaken.
Light rail:	Lightweight vehicles, running on lightweight track, often using bus-derived technology and simple supporting infrastructure, such as stops/stations and civil works and frequent street-running.
Metro:	Heavy-rail-based, usually frequent passenger service, sometimes operating on existing and shared track, with heavier infrastructure and vehicles, often subterranean.
Trolleybus:	Rubber-tyred, passenger transport powered by overhead supply. (Not to be confused with US 'trolley', which is often referred to as 'streetcar', which is either a tram or a Light Rail V ehicle (LRV) system.)
Tram:	Europe and elsewhere. LRV, usually street-running. In the US, small, rubber-tyred passenger-carrying vehicle, often articulated or linked, in specialised situations, such as airport transport and leisure/tourist activities, sometimes park-and-ride operations.

Currency standards

In our continuing effort to improve consistency, ISO 4217 currency codes are being adopted for the use of currency values within content. A full list of these codes can be obtained from the International Organization for Standardization at www.iso.org.

Jane's Users' Charter

This publication is brought to you by Jane's Information Group, a global company with more than 100 years of innovation and an unrivalled reputation for impartiality, accuracy and authority.

Our collection and output of information and images is not dictated by any political or commercial affiliation. Our reportage is undertaken without fear of, or favour from, any government, alliance, state or corporation.

We publish information that is collected overtly from unclassified sources, although much could be regarded as extremely sensitive or not publicly accessible.

Our validation and analysis aims to eradicate misinformation or disinformation as well as factual errors; our objective is always to produce the most accurate and authoritative data.

In the event of any significant inaccuracies, we undertake to draw these to the readers' attention to preserve the highly valued relationship of trust and credibility with our customers worldwide.

If you believe that these policies have been breached by this title, you are invited to contact the editor.

A copy of Jane's Information Group's Code of Conduct for its editorial teams is available from the publisher.

janes.com

Intelligence and Insight You Can Trust

Quality Policy

Jane's Information Group is the world's leading unclassified information integrator for military, government and commercial organisations worldwide. To maintain this position, the Company will strive to meet and exceed customers' expectations in the design, production and fulfilment of goods and services.

Information published by Jane's is renowned for its accuracy, authority and impartiality, and the Company is committed to seeking ongoing improvement in both products and processes.

Jane's will at all times endeavour to respond directly to market demands and will also ensure that customer satisfaction is measured and employees are encouraged to question and suggest improvements to working practices.

Jane's will continue to invest in its people through training and development to meet the Investor in People standards and changing customer requirements.

janes.com

Intelligence and Insight You Can Trust

EDITORIAL AND ADMINISTRATION

Group Publishing Director: Sean Howe, e-mail: sean.howe@janes.com

Publisher: Chris Bridge, e-mail: chris.bridge@janes.com

Compiler/Editor: Welcomes information and comments from users who should send material to:
Information Collection
Jane's Information Group, Sentinel House, 163 Brighton Road, Coulsdon, Surrey CR5 2YH, UK
Tel: (+44 20) 87 00 37 00 Fax: (+44 20) 87 00 39 00
e-mail: yearbook@janes.com

SALES OFFICES

Europe and Africa
Jane's Information Group Limited, Sentinel House, 163 Brighton Road, Coulsdon, Surrey CR5 2YH, UK
Tel: (+44 20) 87 00 37 50 Fax: (+44 20) 87 00 37 51
e-mail: customer.servicesuk@janes.com

North/Central/South America
Jane's Information Group Inc, 110 N Royal Street, Suite 200, Alexandria, Virginia 22314, US
Tel: (+1 703) 683 37 00 Fax: (+1 703) 836 02 97
Tel: (+1 800) 824 07 68 Fax: (+1 800) 836 02 97
e-mail: customer.servicesus@janes.com

Asia
Jane's Information Group Asia, 78 Shenton Way, #12–01, Singapore 079120
Tel: (+65) 65 76 53 00 Fax: (+65) 62 26 11 85
e-mail: asiapacific@janes.com

Oceania
Jane's Information Group, Level 3, 33 Rowe Street, Eastwood NSW 2122, Australia
Tel: (+61 2) 98 04 12 00 Fax: (+61 2) 98 04 02 00
e-mail: oceania@janes.com

Middle East
Jane's Information Group, PO Box 502138, Dubai, United Arab Emirates
Tel: (+971 4) 390 23 36 Fax: (+971 4) 390 88 48
e-mail: mideast@janes.com

Japan
Jane's Information Group, CERA51 Bldg. 1-21-8 Ebisu, Shibuya-ku, Tokyo 150-0013, Japan
Tel: (+81 3) 57 91 96 63 Fax: (+81 3) 54 20 64 02
e-mail: japan@janes.com

ADVERTISEMENT SALES OFFICES

Head Office
Jane's Information Group
Sentinel House, 163 Brighton Road, Coulsdon, Surrey CR5 2YH, UK
Tel: (+44 20) 87 00 37 00 Fax: (+44 20) 87 00 38 59/37 44
e-mail: transadsales@janes.com

Janine Boxall, Global Advertising Sales Director
Tel: (+44 20) 87 00 38 52 Fax: (+44 20) 87 00 38 59/37 44
e-mail: janine.boxall@janes.com

Mat Stevens, Advertising Sales Manager, Transport
Tel: (+44 20) 87 00 37 41 Fax: (+44 20) 87 00 37 44
e-mail: mat.stevens@janes.com

Kevin Lyons, Advertising Sales Consultant, Transport
Tel: (+44 20) 87 00 37 27 Fax: (+44 20) 87 00 37 44
e-mail: kevin.lyons@janes.com

US/Canada
Jane's Information Group
110 N Royal St. Suite 200, Alexandria, Virginia 22314, US
Tel: (+1 703) 683 37 00 Fax: (+1 703) 836 55 37
e-mail: transadsales@janes.com

Janet Berta, US Advertising Sales Director
Tel: (+1 703) 836 24 10 Fax: (+1 703) 836 55 37
e-mail: janet.berta@janes.com

Sean Fitzgerald, Southeast Region Advertising Sales Manager
Tel: (+1 703) 836 24 46 Fax: (+1 703) 836 55 37
e-mail: sean.fitzgerald@janes.com

Linda Hewish, Northeast Region Advertising Sales Manager
Tel: (+1 703) 836 24 13 Fax: (+1 703) 836 55 37
e-mail: linda.hewish@janes.com

Janet Murphy, Central Region Advertising Sales Manager
Tel: (+1 703) 836 31 39 Fax: (+1 703) 836 55 37
e-mail: janet.murphy@janes.com

Australia: Richard West *(UK Head Office)*

Benelux: Kevin Lyons *(UK Head Office)*

China and Hong Kong: Mat Stevens *(UK Head Office)*

France: Mat Stevens *(UK Head Office)*

Germany and Austria: Key accounts: *MCW Media and Consulting Wehrstedt*
Tel: (+49 34) 74 36 20 90 Fax: (+49 34) 74 36 20 91
e-mail: info@wehrstedt.org

Israel: *Oreet International Media*
Tel: (+972 3) 570 65 27 Fax: (+972 3) 570 65 26
e-mail: liat_h@oreet-marcom.com

Italy and Switzerland: *Ediconsult Internazionale Srl*
Tel: (+39 010) 58 36 84 Fax: (+39 010) 56 65 78
e-mail: genova@ediconsult.com

Middle East: Mat Stevens *(UK Head Office)*

Russia and Ukraine: Mat Stevens *(UK Head Office)*

Scandinavia: *The Falsten Partnership*
23, Walsingham Road, Hove, East Sussex, BN41 2XA, UK
Tel: (+44 1273) 77 10 20 Fax: (+ 44 1273) 77 00 70
e-mail: sales@falsten.com

Singapore: Mat Stevens *(UK Head Office)*

South Africa: Richard West *(UK Head Office)*

South Korea: *JES Media Inc*
Contact: Young-Seoh Chinn
Tel: (+82 2) 481 34 11/13 Fax: (+82 2) 481 34 14
e-mail: jesmedia@unitel.co.kr

Spain: *Via Exclusivas SL*
e-mail: viaexclusivas@viaexclusivas.com

UK: Kevin Lyons *(UK Head Office)*

For all other areas, contact Mat Stevens *(UK Head Office)*

ADVERTISING COPY
Kate Gibbs *(UK Head Office)*
Tel: (+44 20) 87 00 37 42 Fax: (+44 20) 87 00 38 59/37 44
e-mail: kate.gibbs@janes.com

For North America, South America and Caribbean only:
Jane's US address
Tel: (+1 703) 683 37 00 Fax: (+1 703) 836 55 37
e-mail: us.ads@janes.com

Executive Overview

Financial

In the current economic climate, combined with high oil prices during 2008, is it possible for public transport operators to become bankrupt, and what would happen if they did? There is no doubt that these two factors have hit public transport operators hard. High oil prices, and the resultant higher operating costs, have forced some to increase fares, sometimes at rates much higher than could ever have been anticipated (Phoenix, Arizona, US, being just one example, where some fares could increase by as much as 40 per cent) but high oil-based fuel prices and the economic downturn have also encouraged passengers to use public transport rather than their own cars, increasing operating costs again. A 'double-whammy.'

It seems unlikely that any government, certainly in the West, would allow a city's public transport system to fail completely, but some operators, especially in the US, are already considering reducing services (see St Louis below) or have done so. In the end it will be the travelling public that has to cover the operator's shortfalls, either by increased ticket prices or by taxation - so nothing new there.

The banking crisis has also had its effect. One example of this is the St Louis, US operator, Metro. Under complicated financial instruments, known as structured lease transaction, Metro sold vehicles and maintenance facilities and then leased them back, using them as collateral. However, the contracts for these transactions stipulate that Metro's insurers, Ambac and FSA, must be AAA rated. The drop in ratings of the two companies has resulted in Metro being compelled to find new, AAA-rated insurers, which at the time of writing it had been unable to do.

Metro's bankers have agreed to a short extension to find replacement insurers, and the operator is asking the US Congress to back the insurance companies.

As a result of the drop in the ratings, Metro may be forced to take money from its reserves. There is currently a shortfall of some USD50 million in its budget, which would cause it to make cutbacks in services.

Big bus registration defies economic gloom

Surprisingly, the latest registration data from the Society of Motor Manufacturers and Traders (SMMT) in the UK shows that 2008 was very positive for big buses, however was not for coaches. In summary:

- Positive trend for big buses held through to Q4 2008 led by double-deckers;
- Large coaches saw a big fall in 2008, but total still above the 2000–2005 average;
- Significant structural and spending shifts in bus and coach demand since 2003.

A recent press release announced: "December's data registrations raised a note of caution over the recent strong growth in double-deck bus registrations," said Paul Everitt, SMMT Chief Executive. "The trend held for most of the year and growth hit 122 per cent after demand had reached an atypically low level in 2007. Big bus demand will be hit by the abrupt recession but may prove more resilient than coach demand has been. Given stable funding and passenger numbers, the growing use of buses in urban and remote rural areas should support the market."

Security

Security initiatives include: the introduction by transport operators of best practise measures including security briefings to staff; 'alert' posters and the introduction of 'security tours' by managers. In the UK, through investment by Transport for London (TfL) and with the support of the Mayor of London, there will be 2,700 uniformed officers dedicated to policing the transport system in London by June 2009.

First Group, one of the UK's largest transport operators, has introduced Secure Station Status, a scheme managed by the Department for Transport, in partnership with the British Transport Police (BTP) and the crime prevention charity Crime Concern. It requires stations to meet stringent standards in their design, management, security and passenger safety. The company has secured the services of a Police Inspector from BTP on a year's secondment to help with the approach to security.

Attention is also being paid to the review of security technology such as the continued development of IP-based (Internet Protocol-based) security systems, with the benefits of integrated systems such as Closed Circuit Television (CCTV) cameras, alarm and announcement systems and information points, which can all be managed from a central control room.

A key company in this area of security technology is Bosch Security Systems Inc (www.boschsecurity.us), part of the Bosch Group. The company is responsible for the IP CCTV technology at the new St Pancras International station in London, UK, which opened in November 2007. The entire CCTV system is integrated into the station's other management systems, including: intruder systems, electronic access control, station management and help points. Bosch's integrated IP Network Video System provides St Pancras International with secure access to real-time and recorded video from anywhere on the network and also offers the ability to support multiple viewers at any one time.

Integrated products from the Bosch Security range include its recently launched Videojet 8008, a multi-stream Video-over IP CCTV network-based video surveillance encoder. The system delivers high quality, real-

time video with a hardware engine that produces 25 images per second of MPEG-4 video to DVD quality. The high-quality output video signals allow video to be viewed on any standard PC, using Bosh's VIDOS video management software or a web browser.

Helping London Transport improve its customer services and security announcements, Interalia (www.interalia.com), which offers design and manufacture of digital voice-announcement solutions, has partnered with UK-based Installation Project Services Ltd (IPS Ltd) (www.ips-ltd.co.uk) in the installation of the former's Commander Platform and Station Digital Announcement System at Borough and Kennington Underground stations. The system delivers a variety of platform messages to London Underground passengers, ranging from emergency messages to customer information. It has already been fitted by the company at more than 30 London Underground stations including the network's largest and most complex stations, Oxford Circus and Bank/Monument. The system can also be triggered in large stations where an incident calls for the evacuation of part of the station.

London Underground has specified the system to provide a foreign language message capability with around 20 general public information messages studio-recorded in French, German, Spanish, Italian and Japanese.

CCTV systems provide bus and coach operators with a powerful tool to combat crime on buses and reduce fraudulent insurance claims and Stagecoach, one of the UK's largest bus operators, signed a GBP1.5 million contract in 2008 for the supply, installation and maintenance of CCTV on its new buses. The 12-month deal will ensure all new buses ordered by Stagecoach in 2008-09 are fitted with digital CCTV systems from LOOK CCTV (www.lookcctv.com), a subsidiary of AIM-listed Quadnetics Group plc. Stagecoach already makes extensive use of CCTV technology throughout its bus fleet across the UK.

Recently in the Netherlands, an increase in violent incidents against bus drivers and vehicles has resulted in two routes in Arnhem being changed to avoid certain areas. Gouda town council will install cameras in buses that travel through the Oosterwei district, as drivers have been threatened there.

Similar surveillance technology is employed on railway services and UK-based First ScotRail has installed another 116 CCTV cameras under its commitment to make stations as safe as possible for its customers. The cameras have been provided at three stations – 47 at Inverness, 46 at Motherwell and 23 at Glasgow Queen Street Low Level. The GBP350,000 investment also includes eight CCTV Help Points on platforms at the three stations, providing additional reassurance for passengers as well as an extra information service operating both day and night. The train operator now manages a total of 3,950 cameras and 441 CCTV Help Points at 241 stations across Scotland.

A national passenger survey by Passenger Focus, the UK consumer watchdog, put customer satisfaction with First ScotRail's personal security at stations at 72 per cent - up nine percentage points year on year.

Live mobile video streaming

In November 2008, Swedish company Icomera AB (www.icomera.com), a provider of cellular broadband gateways, was selected to provide real-time communications for a major trial of live CCTV on London buses. As the first stage of a major initiative to offer live mobile video streaming technology to municipalities and transport operators for public safety applications, 21st Century Crime Prevention Services Ltd (21st Century CCTV) (www.21stcenturycctv.com), a subsidiary of TG21 plc (www.tg21plc.com), has equipped 21 double-deck buses in North London with the technology This allows live images to be transmitted to a central control centre shared by officers from TfL and the Metropolitan Police's Transport Operational Command Unit.

The LIVEview system installed on each bus comprises a ProGuard Digital Video Recorder (DVR), developed by 21st Century CCTV, connected to Icomera's Moovbox™ M200 mobile broadband gateway and cameras fitted both inside and outside of the bus which record images continuously to disk. The Moovbox™ enables the driver to activate a high-speed link to allow operators to view live or recorded footage in real time.

The six month trial, on behalf of Transport for London (TfL), will monitor and analyse the use of the technology to decide whether it can help deal with incidents.

In February 2009, Icomera announced the installation of free Internet access and real-time vehicle tracking on the Green Line express coach service between Luton International Airport and Central London. The fleet of buses has been equipped with Icomera's Moovbox™ M Series mobile broadband gateway, providing Wi-Fi connectivity whilst mobile. The technology also enables Arriva staff to monitor and track the fleet's vehicles in real-time.

Icomera previously announced free Wi-Fi Internet access on FirstGroup plc's RailAir coach service linking Heathrow Airport with Reading, also utilising the Moovbox™ M Series.

Body scanning technology

Although body scanning technology is advancing and new security screening measures have been trialled in the UK both at Luton and Heathrow airports, and also at Paddington railway station, UK Government surveys have revealed that the travelling public would be unlikely to accept major delays to journeys at this time. The BTP is said to be enhancing its existing stop and search capabilities through the use of X-ray equipment for the screening of bags and through the deployment of more sniffer dogs.

In the US, the Transportation Security Administration (TSA) is going to install see-through body scanners at 10 of the busiest airports for security purposes. The new scanners have been tested at Melbourne Airport alongside 'next generation' baggage X-ray machines that can detect explosives in luggage.

The controversial see-through body scanning equipment uses a low energy X-ray to reveal any objects, metal or otherwise, under a person's clothing, including body features. The testing of the scanners will include monitoring the affect of the flow of passengers through the security point; a scenario that does impact on its use in other environments such as public transport systems where currently aviation-style security is not so viable.

Explosives detection on rapid transit

Detection of explosives is not easy to install on rapid transit networks, but in the UK, London Underground Ltd (LUL) carried out a trial with 3DX-RAY Ltd's (www.3dx-ray.com) TPXi-Flatscreen x-ray bomb and threat detection system. This portable, flat-screen, digital system was developed in collaboration with the British Transport Police (BTP).

K9 protection in the US

Working in combination with the Department of Homeland Security, other federal agencies and industry experts, the Transportation Security Administration (TSA) prepares dogs and handlers as part of its National Explosives Detection Canine Team Program. Operating as mobile teams, they can quickly locate and identify dangerous materials which may pose a threat to the transport system. They can also be used to rule out the presence of dangerous materials in unattended packages, structures or vehicles, which ultimately helps to maintain an efficient flow of passengers.

The TSA runs an Explosives Detection Canine Handler Course at Lackland Air Force Base in San Antonio, Texas. Law enforcement officers from across the US attend the course where they are paired with one of TSA's canine team-mates. After dog and handler are paired up, the new team completes a rigorous 10-week course to learn how to locate and identify a wide variety of dangerous materials while working as an effective unit. This training includes search techniques for aircraft, baggage, vehicles and transportation structures, as well as procedures for identifying dangerous materials and alerting the handler when these materials are present.

The TSA states that: Federal Air Marshals, surface transportation, canine teams, and advanced screening technology working as Visible Intermodal Protection Response, or VIPR Teams, offer the ability to raise the level of security in any mode of transportation anywhere in the country quickly and effectively.

Explosives detection canine teams provide strong detection and deterrent capabilities and can be sent quickly to key junction points across systems, stations, terminals or other facilities.

The TSA also states that: through the Surface Transportation Security Inspection Program, or STSI, it has deployed 100 inspectors assigned to 18 field offices across the US, to provide support to the nation's largest mass transit systems.

K9 security in action

In April 2008, Amtrak announced the deployment of its new specialised Amtrak Mobile Security Team to patrol stations and trains and randomly inspect passenger baggage. The Mobile Security Team supplements ongoing patrols already in place by Amtrak to enhance the safety and security of passenger rail travel. The deployment of the Mobile Security Team and the launch of random baggage inspection are further steps in Amtrak's ongoing efforts to strengthen rail security as a means to minimise the risk of terrorist threats. The Mobile Security Teams will ultimately be deployed nationwide.

The mobile security team's squads may consist of armed specialised Amtrak police, explosives detecting K9 units and armed counter-terrorism special agents in tactical uniforms. They will screen passengers, randomly inspect baggage and patrol stations. These squads may also sweep through trains using K9 units.

Other developments

A project at the University of California, Riverside, has been awarded nearly USD1 million in grants to develop an electronic 'nose' that could be used to identify tiny amounts of explosives in high-traffic, high-risk areas. This technology has the potential to work as well as sniffer dogs, and can have advantages over its canine counterparts in that it could operate for seven days a week without the need to go off duty for rest breaks. The sensor has the potential for many applications.

Scientists from the University of New South Wales (UNSW) and University of Sydney have developed e-nose technology, which has drawn interest from NSW rail corporations and has potential uses in emissions monitoring and the security industry.

The device has advantages over traditional security measures in that it is cheaper than a 24-hour security team. It can also help prevent the high cost of graffiti vandalism by literally sniffing out the culprits with the 'electronic nose' that can detect paint and alert security officers. The electronic nose is a simple device, which contains a number of sensors that can each respond to the reaction of substances with oxygen by a change in electrical resistance. It is the pattern of these responses that creates a 'fingerprint' of the smell.

The technology could be used to supplement sniffer dogs and other security measures and can be used to detect hundreds of different odours.

Further information on this technology can be found at E-Nose Pty Ltd (www.e-nose.info).

Bus lane security/enforcement

In December 2008, APT Security Systems (www.aptcontrols.co.uk/apt-security-systems/), a division of APT Controls Ltd, announced that it had designed and installed a new system of four bi-folding gates to prevent unauthorised access to a new dedicated bus lane in Swansea, UK.

"The installations of these gates illustrates our commitment to providing effective infrastructure that gives public transport priority and reduces journey times for those using it," said John Hague, Cabinet Member for the Environment.

APT Security Systems' bi-fold gates, installed in Swansea, UK to prevent unauthorised vehicles from using the new Express Way dedicated bus lane
(APT Security Systems)   1375198

Greenstuff

In January 2009, LaFrance Industries (www.mvmills.com/lafrance industries/), a division of Mount Vernon Mills Inc, announced that BC Transit, British Columbia, will use its new eco-friendly seating fabric in a planned 115-bus procurement during 2009. The fabric is created using 100 per cent recycled Repreve® yarn. The company manufactures fabrics for the transit bus, motorcoach and rail markets.

Ethanol

With some people expressing concern about the production of ethanol from corn, in late 2008, Algenol Biofuels Inc (www.algenolbiofuels.com), a privately owned company founded in early 2006 and headquartered in Naples, Florida, US, announced that it will be producing ethanol for commercial sale in 2009 in Sonora, Mexico.

The difference with Alegonol is that its Direct to Ethanol™ process does not use food, farmland or fresh water. Instead, the process links photosynthesis with natural enzymes to produce ethanol from individual algae cells.

Algenol states that its prototype production strains are producing ethanol at a rate of 6,000 gallons/acre/year and this is expected to improve to 10,000 gallons/acre/year by the end of 2009. With further refinement, the algae cells have the potential to increase production rates to 12,000 to 40,000 gallons/acre/year in the future. The company also states that it only uses algae strains that do not produce human toxins and that the specific algae cells used cannot live in the environment found outside their Capture Technology™ contained sealed bioreactor.

In Reading, UK, the main transport operator, Reading Buses, is putting an ethanol-powered hybrid bus into service. It is already using ethanol-powered technology and the Scania ethanol-hybrid double-deck bus uses series hybrid technology, charging super capacitors.

Scania ethanol-hybrid bus with capacitor storage (Scania)   1375402

AutoTram®

The Fraunhofer Institute for Transportation and Infrastructure Systems IVI, Dresden, Germany (www.ivi.fraunhofer.de), in co-operation with vehicle construction, engineering, energy-storage systems, fuel-cell and diesel set partners, is developing the AutoTram®, a people-mover system on 'virtual rails'. Based on light vehicle construction, the AutoTram® runs on rubber tyres over conventional concrete and asphalt surfaces.

Aims for the systems include; hybrid and zero-emission propulsion technology, optical guidance, safety concept with mechanical 'fall-back' system; multi-axles and all-wheel steering, including a modular vehicle concept.

Currently, the AutoTram® is in its testing phase, with a new development project scheduled to start in early 2009.

Light rail development

Light rail continues to expand with several new tramways being announced.

Cities introducing LRT/city metros for the first time include Algiers and Constantine, Algeria; Santo Domingo, Dominican Republic (metro); Goa, India (Skybus Metro); Firenze, Italy; Madrid and Zaragoza, Spain, and Antalya, Turkey (LRT).

Catenary-free and contactless operating tram

In January 2009, Bombardier Transportation introduced the Bombardier PRIMOVE™ tram on the test track at Bombardier's Bautzen, Germany site. The contactless and catenary-free vehicle does not require third rail power supply or have high-roof equipment, with the result that it will be suitable for operations in historic city centres, where aesthetics are important and in smaller tunnel profiles.

Electric power components are 'hidden' in the vehicle and beneath the track. The technology works in the following manner: the electrical primary and secondary circuits are separated from each other, a principle also used in transformers. Creating a magnet field, the primary circuit is built into the infrastructure. The secondary circuit in the vehicle transforms this energy field into electricity for the tram's operation. The cable of the primary circuit can be easily integrated in between the tracks. The vehicle is equipped with pick-up coils underneath the vehicle, which are connected to the tram's traction system through a cable. In addition, connected segments in the ground ensure a safe operation as they are only fully energised when completely covered by the vehicle. Therefore, the system can also be integrated in pedestrian zones.

An additional benefit of the system is the integration of the MITRAC™ Energy Saver, which is mounted on the roof of a light rail vehicle. The capacitors of the system store the energy released each time a vehicle brakes and re-use it during acceleration or operation. Applied to light rail vehicles, the system has (during testing in Mannheim since 2003) been reported to save up to 30 per cent of energy, thus reducing emissions as well as costs. The technology can also be used as a performance booster by adding extra power to the vehicle during acceleration. The system has double-layer capacitor technology (also known as ultracapacitors), a smartly designed storage device charged with the electrical energy released when the brakes are used.

Benefits for rail operators include completely invisible power supply, easy installation and the fact that weather conditions do not affect the system. In addition, the contactless and safe energy transfer system is said to reduce wear on parts, limiting equipment lifecycle costs. The system's electrical drive operates with lower noise levels and eliminates emissions.

Further information can be found at http://www.bombardier.com/en/transportation/sustainability/technology/primove-catenary-free-operation.

Bombardier's new PRIMOVE system enables trams to operate catenary-free
(Bombardier Transportation)   1375862

Technology for less-able passengers

Travel Assistant Device (TAD) to aid transit riders with special needs

Researchers at the National Center for Transit Research at the Center for Urban Transportation Research (CURT), University of South Florida (USF) have prepared a report, in co-operation with the State of Florida Department of Transportation and the US Department of Transportation, on a Travel Assistant Device (TAD) to aid transit riders with special needs, such as those with brain injures and other cognitive impairments.

The travel assistant device (TAD) developed for this project is a prototype software system that can be installed on off-the-shelf, Global Positioning System (GPS)-enabled mobile/cell phones. The TAD software provides various informational prompts such as playing the recorded audio messages 'Get ready' and 'Pull the cord now!', vibrating to alert the rider to pull the cord to tell the driver to stop. These prompts are delivered to the rider in a just-in-time method. The real-time location of the rider can be viewed by the travel trainer or family member through a web page. TAD utilizes stop and route data provided by transit agencies. TAD was designed for use by cognitively-disabled transit riders, but can be used by any transit user.

The device with the proof-of-concept TAD software has been field tested in the Tampa area on Hillsborough Area Regional Transit (HART), Florida, US, transit bus routes.

New London Underground maps

London's Mayor and London Underground (LU) have launched two new Tube maps, a Tube Toilet map and a new Step-free Tube Guide.

The Tube Toilet map shows which stations have male, female and accessible toilets for wheelchair users, whether they are inside or outside the ticket gates and whether they have baby changing facilities.

The Step-free Tube Guide gives information about the step and gap between the train and platform at step-free stations, and gives information about the stations where you can change between lines without encountering steps or escalators.

As well as wheelchair users, this guide will also help older passengers, those with heavy luggage and/or with children's buggies/prams.

Currently, London Underground has 54 step-free stations and 25 per cent of stations will be step-free by 2010.

The Rehabilitation Engineering Research Center on Accessible Public Transportation (RERC-APT)

The Rehabilitation Engineering Research Center on Accessible Public Transportation (RERC-APT), a partnership between the Robotics Institute at Carnegie Mellon University and the IDEA Center at State University of New York (SUNY), Buffalo, US, will research and develop methods to empower consumers and service providers in the design and evaluation of accessible transportation equipment, information services and physical environments. The Center has been awarded a grant of some USD948,000 from the United States Department of Education through the National Institute on Disability and Rehabilitation Research.

Partners and associated centres are: the United Spinal Association; Gillig Corporation; the RERC on Universal Design and the Built Environment; the Quality of Life Technologies Engineering Research Center and Grimshaw-Architects and the collaborating transportation providers are the Niagara Frontier Transportation Authority (NFTA) and the Port Authority of Allegheny County.

Current research projects are: Empowering the User to Improve the Travel Chain and Human Factors of Boarding and Disembarking Vehicles, with the development projects being Open Information System Tools and Improved Vehicle Interiors, An Industry Partnership Project.

Gillig Corporation will incorporate, at their own expense, the modifications designed by the centre into a new bus, whilst the Niagara Frontier Transportation Authority (NFTA), Buffalo and the Port Authority of Allegheny County, Pittsburgh will assist researchers, especially in the design and access of interiors of buses.

Further information can be found at www.rercapt.org

Fuel-cell buses

In December 2008, Ballard Power Systems announced that the pre-production fuel cell bus, manufactured by New Flyer Industries Canada ULC, ISE Corporation and Ballard consortium, successfully completed its field trial and Notice to Proceed has now been authorised for the manufacture of 20 fuel cell buses for BC Transit's hydrogen fuel cell demonstration fleet. Ballard began delivery of its HD6 fuel cell bus modules in December 2008 with the remaining modules being delivered through mid-2009.

During the evaluation period, the pre-production bus operated up to 16 hours per day in Victoria and Whistler, and accumulated over 575 hours of on-road testing. The fuel cell buses have a driving range of approximately 450 km along with a stated electrical efficiency of 57 per cent at rated power, more than double the efficiency of an internal combustion engine.

The bus powertrain is based on a hybrid fuel-cell/battery architecture with an electric drive, which enables higher vehicle efficiency and improved fuel cell durability. This is the first time that Ballard's bus fuel cell products have been integrated into a hybrid drive. The 150 kW HD6 fuel-cell bus module is designed to be robust and durable in harsh motive conditions. The HD6 fuel cell bus module is comprised of two stack modules connected in series to provide a gross power output of 150 kW.

These buses will be delivered to BC Transit by the end of 2009 and will be in use during and after the 2010 Olympic and Paralympic Winter Games in the Resort Municipality of Whistler. When delivery is completed, the BC Transit fleet of 20 buses will be the largest fleet of fuel cell buses in the world.

Hybrid buses

By the end of 2009, the number of hybrid buses in London, UK, will have more than quadrupled to 56 buses and confirm London's position as the home of the largest fleet of hybrid buses in the UK. A further 300 hybrid buses are expected be in operation by 2011.

Both TfL and the Mayor say they are committed to the introduction of hybrid technology and by 2012, TfL has committed itself to a longer-term programme that will see a further 300 new hybrid buses joining the fleet by the end of March 2011, after which it is expected that all new buses entering service in London will be hybrid.

The Mayor has also specified that the 'New Bus for London' Routemaster replacement should run on a hybrid engine (see further information on the new Routemaster below).

EXECUTIVE OVERVIEW

This Wrightbus StreetCar RTV for Las Vegas has a hybrid transmission
(The Wright Group)   1375966

The roll-out of hybrids will contribute to the Mayor's target of a 60 per cent reduction in emissions across London by 2025.

All hybrid buses have an energy storage system and a motor/generator to recharge it. But there are two configurations that manufacturers are offering:

- The parallel hybrid is driven by the diesel engine or the electric motor or by both. There is a direct link between the engine and wheels with the option of electric assistance for climbing hills or for maximum acceleration;
- The series hybrid features a small diesel engine charging the batteries, which in turn power an electric motor. There is no direct transmission link between the engine and the wheels. It is also possible to operate in purely electric mode - at bus stops, for example, to minimise local air quality emissions in sensitive areas; the bus can pull away from the bus stop in quiet electric mode and engage diesel power as required by the system for maintaining battery charge.

With both systems, normal braking can drive the motor unit in alternator mode to achieve regenerative braking/energy recovery to charge the battery and reduce fuel consumption.

Hybrid technology was placed firmly on the map at the UK's Euro Bus Expo, the coach and bus exhibition held at Birmingham in November 2008. One large UK manufacturer, Optare, made a bold statement about hybrids with a Hybrid Electric Vehicle (HEV) Optare Solo and HEV technology on a Tempo single-decker. It also announced a new double-deck bus, the Rapta, which will have the option of hybrid technology.

Optare worked with Enova Systems Inc (www.enovasystems.com), California, US, to produce an innovative option for the Solo+. Enova Systems is a supplier of digital power components and systems products. Also at Euro Bus Expo, HEV technology was displayed on a Tempo single-decker to TfL specification. It is one of five entering service in London, UK, with operator Metroline, a further five are on order for the operator East London. As its conventional power unit, the Tempo uses a Cummins 250Hp ISBE unit operating to Euro 5 standards with Selective Catalytic Reduction (SCR) technology. The Allison EP40 parallel hybrid drive system has been specified with nickel metal hydride batteries.

On the Bus Rapid Transit (BRT) front, the new Wrightbus StreetCar articulated Rapid Transit Vehicles (RTVs) for Las Vegas operate with hybrid technology. A total of 50 were being delivered during 2008/2009 to the Regional Transportation Commission (RTC) of Southern Nevada. The 'ACE Downtown Connector' service will introduce a high speed transit connection from downtown Las Vegas. Each of the 18.7 m long StreetCar RTVs is powered by a hybrid electric drive system developed in conjunction with the ISE Corporation and Siemens. With a modular driveline, the Siemens (ISE) Electric Hybrid Drive System includes a Cummins ISL engine, features water-cooled nickel metal hydride batteries, and also incorporates for the very first time in transit buses a Siemens permanent-magnet motor.

Volvo Bus have been at the forefront of hybrid technology with the launch of its new hybrid bus programme in 2008 with the new Volvo B5TL double-deck bus in the UK and the Volvo 7700 hybrid in mainland Europe. Volvo says that with a hybrid solution that is largely based on standard products and with fuel savings of up to 30 per cent, customers can achieve payback on the incremental capital costs far quicker than was previously the case. The technology also substantially lowers the exhaust emissions and noise levels.

This Wrightbus double-deck bus is going into service in London and has a hybrid transmission (The Wrigth Group)   1375967

In the UK, Volvo has introduced the B5L Hybrid, a double-deck bus, due to enter series production in 2009, and deliveries of complete production double deck vehicles will commence early in 2010. There are some early production vehicles on the road in 2009. The chassis layout follows the same principles as the Volvo 7700 Hybrid, which was recently launched at the IAA in Hanover, with a rear offset driveline. The battery energy storage unit is installed under two of the seats in the lower saloon, just behind the front axle, to achieve the minimum intrusion into the gangway and to optimise the weight distribution. The first vehicle produced has Gemini bodywork, from Wrightbus in Ballymena, Northern Ireland. With an overall length of 10.4 m, the vehicle offers 66 seats (45 upper saloon, 21 lower saloon) and space for up to 20 further passengers standing. It uses Valence lithium phosphate batteries. Valence Technology Inc (www.valence.com) is an international specialist in the development of lithium phosphate energy storage solutions.

Also at the show was Alexander Dennis's Enviro 400H hybrid double-deck bus with lithium ion batteries that do not need mains recharging during their extended life cycle. The 10.8-m version (single door) seats 32, plus one wheelchair on the lower deck and 41 on the upper deck. The engine is a 4.5 litre Cummins four-cylinder turbocharged and intercooled, certified to Euro 4 emission levels. The BAE Systems HybriDrive driveline incorporates a 120 kW compact permanent magnet generator and 185 kW compact oil-cooled motor. The storage system uses lithium Ion nano-phosphate technology.

Driving the auxiliary systems with electric motors also saves energy because the load can be delivered when needed most, as with power steering where the most power is needed at low speeds, so matching the demand avoids wasteful operation.

The next step will be the in-service operation of six double-deckers in London, UK, and a single-deck bus in Sweden. As well as defining the best control strategies for the vehicles to deliver the best results, this operation will also give operators, drivers and maintenance staff the practical experience needed ahead of volume introduction.

BAE Systems, Isuzu and Itochu Corporation are introducing low-emission hybrid buses in Japan in 2009. BAE Systems' HybriDrive propulsion system will be demonstrated and tested on Isuzu buses. Isuzu will install the HybriDrive system on two buses, evaluating their performance at Isuzu's proving grounds and in passenger service. The system consists of a generator, an electric motor and an energy storage system managed by computerised controls. A diesel engine that powers the generator operates independently of the electric drive motor, running at a nearly consistent speed. BAE Systems' HybriDrive systems have been fitted in more than 1,500 buses in cities such as New York, San Francisco, Toronto and will be fitted in London in the near future.

Other new-technology propulsion systems include hydrogen-based systems. Hydrogen has returned as a promising fuel source, but not employing fuel-cell technology. In 2008, Air Products and Chemicals Inc (www.airproducts.com) signed a deal with TfL to provide it with hydrogen technology for a fleet of buses. The company will supply the hydrogen fuel and a dedicated fuelling station for 10 buses in London's transport system. The buses produce substantially fewer emissions of carbon dioxide and other pollutants than diesel buses, in the case of fuel-cell buses, they produce no pollution at all at the point of use. It is expected that the buses will be on London roads by 2010. The UK-based Environmental Transport Association has welcomed this clean technology, but says there have been three fuel cell buses operating in London since 2005, so it's disappointing that three years later there are only a further ten being added – that's out of a London bus fleet of 8,000 vehicles.

With biofuels, the UK Government is taking a more cautious approach, as part of its response to concerns about the indirect environmental and social impacts of producing them. It says that biofuels will only have a role to play if they are sustainably produced. It is to invest GBP27 million in the development of biofuels that can be produced without competing with food crops (see also the section on Ethanol above). It also wants to see two new eligible fuels - biobutanol and hydrogenated renewable diesel - added to the list of acceptable renewable fuels that are eligible.

UK-based Stagecoach has signed a contract to source most of its electricity requirement for its UK bus operations from renewables. Electricity generated from mostly small-scale hydro, as well as on-shore wind and biomass, will provide more than 70 per cent of the company's required supply, with the remainder coming from cleaner, low-carbon sources. Smart meters are also being installed to help cut energy use as part of the GBP3.5 million contract with Opus Energy. The two-year contract, which will dramatically decrease CO_2 emissions, covers electricity supply to around 240 UK sites.

Stagecoach is testing biofuelled-buses, which run on 100 per cent biodiesel. The biofuel is manufactured by Argent Energy (UK) Limited (www.argentenergy.com) from used cooking oil and other food industry by-products, which are from sustainable sources that do not involve the destruction of natural habitats or compete with the human food chain. The environmental project also allows customers to exchange used cooking oil for discounted bus travel. Since the initiative was launched in October 2007, it has cut CO_2 emissions from the buses by 80 per cent, saving 550 tonnes of carbon, and more than 21 tonnes of used cooking oil have been recycled.

Energy storage does not necessarily have to involve an electric battery. A UK company, Flybrid Systems LLP (www.flybridsystems.com), has developed an entirely mechanical, high-speed, flywheel-based energy storage and recovery system. It is powerful, small and light, giving a better power to weight ratio than existing automotive hybrid technology. This

Alexander Dennis Enviro400H double-deck hybrid bus for London (ADL)   1375548

higher power makes it possible to store more energy during short braking periods, dramatically increasing system effectiveness. The system is also said to be very efficient, with up to 70 per cent of braking energy being returned to the wheels to drive the vehicle back up to speed. The device is readily recycled and relatively inexpensive to make as it can be made entirely from conventional materials.

Hybrid-electric shuttle bus

In January 2009, Azure Dynamics Corporation (www.azuredynamics.com) announced that its Balance™ Hybrid Electric shuttle bus had been certified by Altoona testing, on the Ford E-450 chassis, which will enable purchasers to apply for financial assistance from the federal government. The completion of testing qualifies the shuttle buses for Federal Transit Authority (FTA) programmes of up to 80 per cent funding when purchased by public transit agencies in the US. In addition to the FTA programmes, the vehicle may qualify for up to USD3,000 US Federal tax credit and/or individual state and agency programmes. These incentives, plus reported 40 per cent fuel savings, 30 per cent greenhouse gas emissions savings and reduced vehicle maintenance costs, should encourage agencies and operators to consider hybrid-electric vehicles as a cost-effective option for shuttle services.

Battery technology

Axeon Holdings plc (www.axeon.com), a UK-based independent supplier of lithium-ion battery solutions, says that lithium-ion batteries have displaced lead-acid technology with an improved storage and safety record. Combined with an effective battery management system both battery-electric (EV) and HEV technology has now become feasible. The EV, with batteries only, needs a large battery pack. With the HEV, hybrid technology uses an internal combustion engine as the main propulsion and batteries provide extra propulsion when needed. The hybrid battery is smaller and has a different charging regime, with on-board charging which tops up the battery. The range of an EV is about 208 km (130 miles) with overnight charging from an external charger. That of a hybrid is 640 km (400 miles).

On the horizon is a new battery technology called lithium polymer. These are the batteries in mobile phones and computers, using a gel electrolyte. Economies of scale make these an attractive possibility if some of the technical issues can be resolved. At present the two technologies are nickel metal hydride with a storage capacity of up to 100 watt hours per kg and lithium-ion and lithium iron phosphate with around 130 watt hours per kg. The new-technology batteries have a similar power-to-weight ratio as the sodium-sulphur battery, hailed in the 90s as the way forward. Sodium-sulphur batteries have to be kept hot, as the electrolyte is molten. Both nickel and lithium technology batteries have a cost advantage over sodium sulphur.

MODURBAN - Modular Urban Guided Rail System

MODURBAN is a European Union (EU) research project jointly funded (50:50) by the EU and major rail industry stakeholders under the sixth EU Framework Programme. The project started in January 2005 and ended in March 2009. It has a total budget of some EUR20 million. The aim of the project is to provide common functional specifications (Functional Requirement Specifications (FRS) for operators and a common technical architecture for manufacturers for urban guided public transport systems. Project management has been undertaken by UNIFE – the Association of the European Rail Industry (www.unife.org).

In December 2008, some of the key MODURBAN results were shown on the Metro de Madrid network. The FRS is a complete set of 'ready-to-use' requirements, suitable for all urban rail operators, covering systems ranging from manually driven trains to fully driverless operations. These commonly agreed requirements clarify the roles and responsibilities between the operators and the suppliers.

Another development of the MODURBAN project is the success in defining a commonly agreed Fault-tolerant Data Communications System, where one network supports all applications (train control, video, passenger

information, etc), and where this Data Communications System is interoperable/interchangeable between the different suppliers.

On the Metro de Madrid, MODURBAN demonstrated a selection of results, namely:
- The Intelligent Driving concept;
- Interchangeable Data Communication System operation;
- Passenger Information System and Video onboard and wayside operation;
- Light Weight Materials (prototype development of light weight grab rail).

For further information, please visit www.modurban.org.

European Bus System of the Future (EBSF)

The European Bus System of the Future (EBSF) is one of the largest surface transport R&D projects ever undertaken by the European Union with a consortium of 47 partners and a total budget of EUR26 million (funds of EUR16 million). The EBSF aims to increase the attractiveness and raise the image of bus systems in urban areas, by means of developing new vehicles and infrastructure technologies, in combination with operational best practices. The project will build upon state-of-the-art clean vehicular technologies and concentrate on improving the bus system as a whole. Seven European cities will test and validate the project headways: Bremerhaven, Budapest, Gothenburg, Lyon, Madrid, Rome and Rouen. The project was launched in September 2008 and is planned to run for four years.

The development of the new generation urban bus system will, hopefully, stimulate European cities to deploy new bus lines, making public transport more attractive. The new 'European Bus System' concept stemming from the project will also help European manufacturers to maintain or improve their competitive position.

EBSF is an initiative of the European Commission under the 7th Framework Programme for R&D. The project is co-ordinated by the International Association of Public Transport (UITP).

The EBSF will carry out analysis of the needs of today and tomorrow of the main stakeholders of Bus Systems: users, operators and authorities. The project will also identify all requirements of Bus Systems and their components (vehicle, infrastructure, operation).

Prototypes of sub-systems, demonstrator buses and infrastructures, and new operations will be tested and validated in the seven participating European cities.

EBSF will demonstrate the full potential of the new 'European Bus System' bus concept, producing a final handbook, 'EBSF Vision', to guide and recommend authorities and operators, giving crucial keys on implementing the new generation of bus networks.

For further information, please see www.ebsf.eu.

Communications/Information Systems

An exciting new development in urban transport is an initiative and trial in Reading, UK, which started in 2008 and is exploring the use of WiMAX™ with enhanced communications to improve the reliability and efficiency of existing transport management services provided by Reading Borough Council (RBC), including traffic control and congestion. This is the first project in Europe to prove the viability and flexibility of WiMAX™, combined with Wi-Fi and Global Positioning System (GPS) technology, for tackling congestion and making public transport easier to use in an urban environment. WiMAX™ (Worldwide Interoperability for Microwave Access), is a telecommunications technology (based on the IEEE 802.16 standard) that provides wireless transmission of data using a variety of transmission modes.

Currently, GPS and satellite navigation (satnav) technology can interact with travel cameras on motorways to suggest better routes when there is travel congestion, but satnav isn't sufficiently accurate in urban locations. Local authorities now spend a lot of money on telephony. It costs RBC some GBP400,000 per year to communicate with its buses/ traffic lights / CCTV and travel cameras.

From a security perspective, currently, information from CCTV cameras on buses are captured and downloaded at the end of the day, but with WiMAX™ and Wi-Fi technology, images can be sent direct to a live transport data hub. Instead of being restricted by possibly overloaded mobile phone systems, WiMAX™ technology means that local authorities can operate their own transmitters and receivers, subject to the UK government releasing MoD frequencies (a decision was expected in early 2009).

The initiative and trial are part-funded by the South East England Development Agency (SEEDA), the UK Government-funded agency responsible for the sustainable economic development and regeneration of the South East of England. SEEDA has put GBP900,000 into a GBP1.8 million transport research project co-ordinated by UK consultancy Peter Brett Associates and co-funded by a consortium including businesses, the University of Southampton's Transportation Research Group and RBC. This project is one of the first from the UK Government's new Innovation Platforms.

For further information on the initiative and trial, please see www.readingseedaproject.co.uk.

Another UK development has taken place at Southampton, UK airport. UK-based consultants Mott MacDonald and airport operator British Airports Authority (BAA) have launched what is claimed to be the first live, integrated travel system to be used at a UK airport. Passengers arriving at Southampton Airport benefit from an integrated travel display system, designed by Mott MacDonald to provide live updates on transport networks across the south of England. Five screens located throughout the airport's main terminal building help passengers as they embark upon their onward journeys by giving them the latest bus, rail, ferry and road information, including incident alerts. Mott MacDonald was appointed as system designer and project manager for the scheme after BAA identified a need to enhance the accessibility and level of information available to its passengers.

The travel information is drawn from several disparate sources, including Highways Agency CCTV and Southampton Airport Parkway train station timetables. The GBP50,000 system uses proprietary software to obtain live data feeds through the internet from the Highways Agency, South West Trains and the Red Funnel ferry service to the Isle of Wight, acquiring information for local bus services from the city's ROMANSE system, which then automatically updates the information on the screens. (ROMANSE is the joint Hampshire County Council and Southampton City Council traffic and travel control centre.)

But passengers continue to appreciate traditional information provision. In the UK, Nottingham City Transport (NCT) bus passengers in the Arnold area are now benefiting from improved bus stop information, thanks to GBP130,000 investment in new infrastructure by Nottinghamshire County Council.

New bus stops are being installed at 200 stops across the Arnold area and will significantly increase timetable availability for NCT services there when the latest phase is completed in early 2009. Many of the new stops will be installed at sites which previously did not have a timetable case at the stop.

Recent research on accessing information about bus times showed that 79 per cent of NCT passengers used information at the bus stop to find out about their service and just under half of all passengers stated it was the source they used the most.

Climate change and emissions

An important change to increase the chance of railways when competing with road transport was called for in 2008. While aimed at freight, it does have implications for all modes. The revision of the Eurovignette Directive will put an end to the privileged situation of road transport, which politicians and experts agreed at a high level event hosted by the European rail sector in Strasbourg in November 2008. Currently, Member States are legally prevented from charging trucks the true costs of their environmental impact. This distorts competition in the transport sector, as other modes, such as rail, can already be charged for their external costs, in addition to track access charges. Within the EU-27, transport currently produces 27 per cent of all CO_2 emissions, of which road transport is responsible for a massive 72 per cent - a fact that makes firm actions on reducing CO_2 emissions from road vehicles extremely urgent.

Saïd El Khadraoui, the European Parliament's rapporteur on the revision of the Eurovignette Directive, is calling for the Directive to encompass a broader range of external costs: "In addition to costs of congestion, local air pollution and noise as proposed by the Commission, the revised Eurovignette directive should also allow Member States to charge trucks for their CO_2 emissions," he said.

In China, Pirelli won a pilot project in 2008, launched ahead of the Beijing Olympic Games, to cut particulate emissions from diesels by over 95 per cent. The Italian Ministry for the Environment and the Municipality of Beijing ran a pilot project in the Chinese capital to test particulate filter technology developed by Pirelli Eco Technology. This is being trialled on buses and later on trucks, snowploughs and tractors used by the local public transport company. This is part of a wider Sino-Italian deal on environmental protection, that began in 2000, which has led to more than 80 projects.

UK-based Stagecoach has reported that consumer concerns about the environment and health are helping drive a shift from car travel to greener public transport. Stagecoach research reveals a 10 per cent change in travel habits in three years, with nearly a third of respondents switching transport mode for health or environmental reasons. Buses are seeing the biggest increase in usage due to the growing trend of more intelligent car use and one in three consumers are prepared to pay more for greener public transport. Stagecoach found that of those who had previously used the car, 36 per cent had switched to the bus, 30 per cent now walked and five per cent now travelled by train. This study of more than 4,000 consumers revealed that 12 per cent of respondents had changed mode as a result of environmental considerations, whilst 20 per cent cited health reasons. Some 47 per cent of respondents said they were using their car less, with 36 per cent stating an increased use of buses and 19 per cent more use of trains.

The research also found that:
- 62 per cent were more likely to travel with a company whose ethics supported the environment;
- 32 per cent would be prepared to pay more for public transport that is environmentally sustainable;
- eight per cent said they would switch from the car to the bus if it was fuelled by biodiesel.

In London, UK, Heathrow Express, which operates an intensive rail service between London and Heathrow Airport, reports that over the decade it has been operating it has regenerated enough energy to have boiled 400 million kettles. The service was launched in June 1998 and is operated by BAA.

Heathrow Express's friendly approach to the environment began with the purchase of carbon-efficient electric trains (class 332 Electrical Multiple Units - emus) which were fitted with electrical regenerative brakes.

In 2008, a new UK and Ireland network was launched to encourage innovation and promote sustainable, clean and efficient transport in our towns and cities. The initiative includes walking and cycling projects as well as work towards developing cleaner fuel and more efficient vehicles.

CIVITAS - which stands for CIty-VITAlity-Sustainability - is a European initiative aiming to bring cleaner and more efficient transport to cities by promoting integrated, sustainable transport strategies. A total of 36 cities across Europe are members of the scheme, including Preston, Norwich, Winchester, Bristol in the UK and Cork, Ireland. The new CIVITAS UK and Ireland Network will see local authorities working closely with representatives of the Department for Transport, the Irish Ministry of Transport and the European Commission to share best practice and experiences.

The key results of the scheme in Preston have been to:
- Improve road safety;
- Provide a safe and attractive environment for residents and students;
- Enhance the University campus;
- Reduce the impact of traffic;
- Encourage feelings of safety;
- Improve connections to the area from the city centre;
- Encourage use of public transport.

The Sustainable Travel Towns initiative in Darlington has seen nine per cent fewer car driver trips, with a 15 per cent increase in walking, a two per cent increase in public transport use and a 65 per cent increase in cycling since 2004.

Similarly, Peterborough has seen a 10 per cent reduction in car driver trips, an 11 per cent increase in walking, a 22 per cent increase in cycling and a 13 per cent increase in public transport use.

Worcester has shown a 12 per cent reduction in car driver trips, a 19 per cent increase in walking, a 30 per cent increase in cycling and a 13 per cent increase in public transport use since 2004.

For further information on the CIVITAS initiative, please see www.civitas-initiative.org.

Bus Rapid Transit (BRT)

Bus Rapid Transit (BRT) is becoming more of an acceptable alternative to light rail as well as being seen as an intermediary between trams and buses.

Istanbul is expanding its BRT transport system with the acquisition in 2009 of 250 Mercedes-Benz CapaCity buses. The Turkish transport operator Istanbul Elektrik Tramvay ve Tünel Isletmeleri (IETT) is using the buses on specially constructed busways, running from the suburb of Avcilar to the inner city of Istanbul. The BRT concept, which began in 2007, has proved so popular with passengers that the originally 17-km long route has been extended to 29 km. The introduction of the Mercedes-Benz CapaCity buses has significantly reduced daily journey times for many passengers, whilst noticeably relieving traffic congestion in the inner city. For example, a journey that once took 1.5 hours has been shortened to 40 minutes. Today the BRT system carries 530,000 passengers on a daily basis, which means 70,000 to 80,000 fewer individual journeys in the dense traffic of this major Turkish city. Accordingly, plans are now being made to extend the BRT line across the Bosphorus, to the Asian area of the city.

One challenge for BRT systems is that they have been regarded as not suitable for running through pedestrian zones in city centres. But the UK trial running in the historic market town of Boston has shown that specially adapted buses can operate safely. During a trial started in 2008, local operator Brylaine Travel Limited started operating the Optare SlimLine Solo buses, each fitted with a special sensor. The sensor automatically reduces the speed of the buses to walking pace as they enter the pedestrian zone. It then activates the four-way hazard warning lights and triggers an audible warning alarm to alert people during its progress through the zone.

These 2.33 m wide buses, slightly narrower than the standard 2.5-m wide Solo and with a seating capacity of 30 plus additional standees, are a suitable size for high-frequency town services. The vehicles are operating on the new Boston Into Town branded service, which is being run by Brylaine on behalf of Lincolnshire County Council, which owns the vehicles. The network covers three routes, in a three-mile radius around Boston, on a 30-minute cycle working from 07.00 until 19.00, six days a week. The routes have been designed to take in local schools as well as linking employment, health, leisure and shopping facilities across the town.

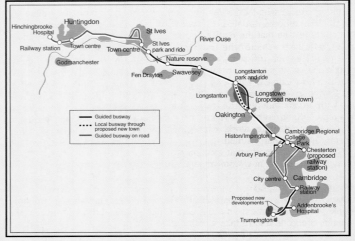

The Cambridge Guided Busway runs partly over a former railway line and will provide a bus rapid transit service linking Cambridge, St Ives and Huntingdon 1336000

It is not just trams that can be acceptable in pedestrianised areas. This Optare Solo bus is specially adapted to operate in such areas (Optare plc)   1375964

Could this be the type of rapid transit favoured in the UK? – an Optare 100-seat Olympus bus to coach specification (Optare plc)   1375965

Also in the UK, the Cambridge Guided Busway (www.cambridgeshire.gov.uk/transport/guided/) is now due to open in mid-2009. The 25.1-km guided busway, linking Cambridge with Huntingdon, partly uses a disused railway. A peak time, guided bus frequency of 10 minutes is planned and the service will run from 06.00 until 24.00, with specially adapted buses which will be supplied and operated by two operators.

In 2008, Volvo supplied 41 buses for a new BRT system in Mexico. The city of Guadalajara started its first BRT line using Volvo 7300 articulated buses on the Volvo B12M chassis. Guadalajara is Mexico's second largest city with slightly more than four million inhabitants and the financial centre for the country's western region. Like many big cities, Guadalajara suffers from increasing road congestion, air pollution and an obsolete transit system. But, as is the case with several cities, Guadalajara has chosen to invest in BRT. The system has been named Macrobús and commenced in December 2008. The first bus corridor connects the northern part of the city to the southern part. The route is 16 km long and has 27 stops. Each bus seats 160 passengers, who can rapidly board and leave the bus due to the raised floor, which is on the same level as the floor in the specially built bus stops. This is the first of three BRT corridors planned for 2008-2012 in the city. The complete project will cover 77 km and require many more articulated buses. The BRT system will be complemented with feeder services, state-of-the-art telecommunications and information technology and urban improvement works.

Whilst the UK is constructing what is proposed to be the largest busway in the world (Cambridge), other cities have also decided to stay with the bus. Following a change in administration in London, BRT and light rail projects have been cancelled, in favour of heavy rail and conventional bus-based systems. The UK public has traditionally favoured vehicles with a high proportion of seating, as opposed to 'standee' vehicles. In Leeds in the early 1950s, single-deck standee tramcars were virtually boycotted by the travelling public, who let the vehicles pass by virtually empty, preferring to wait for a traditional double-deck tram with many seats.

It could just be that the British public may prefer a bus with many seats to a rapid-transit vehicle with few seats. UK bus manufacturer Optare has built two Olympus 100-seat double-deck buses based on the Volvo B9TL tri-axle chassis, which have entered service with Buckinghamshire company Soul Brothers Limited with a second in-build at Optare's Blackburn plant. The Olympus was ordered primarily for use on a private school contract but also with private hire opportunities in mind. It has already been put into use on a regular Saturday shuttle run for a local university and is being marketed for other private hire work, especially school trips for which its high capacity is particularly suited.

The company reports that customers and the children who travel on it have commented on how comfortable and well-equipped it is.

Bus passes in the UK

In the UK, a new concessionary bus travel scheme was announced in 2008. People aged 60 and over, and eligible disabled, whose principle residence is England, are now able to take advantage of free off-peak, local bus travel anywhere in England. Off-peak is 09.30 to 23.00 on weekdays and anytime at weekends and Bank Holidays. The new statutory entitlement applies to up to 11 million eligible people. It does not cover national coach travel or other

modes of transport. However, individual Travel Concession Authorities (TCAs) are able to extend the travel benefits (such as to tubes, trains and all day travel) at their own discretion, as has happened in London. Other schemes are running in Scotland and Wales.

The UK Government is providing additional funding of GBP212 million a year from April 2008 to fund the England-wide bus concession.

Road-rail operation

The possibility of a bus being able to run on rails has been investigated since the 1930s. Road-rail technology is well established in the railway track maintenance field and passenger-carrying road-rail vehicles transport staff to remote locations as well as carrying out maintenance work. In the early 1980s, a UK university carried out a demonstration project on the privately-owned West Somerset Railway. It designed a single-deck bus that was able to run on the railway and go back onto the road at a level-crossing. The project was successful and members of the transport press were able to ride on the bus in both rail and road modes. Experiments were carried out in Japan recently with similar road-rail technology. Japanese Railways Hokkaido installed a dual wheel train-tyre system on midibuses so that they can be used as both road and light rail transport. The use of the vehicles on congestion-free railway tracks makes rail transport far more viable as JR Hokkaido points out, with the cost of remodelling a midibus being approximately 10 per cent of the cost for ordinary train cars and as weight is also around 10 per cent, railway tracks require less maintenance. Commercial systems were planned for market by 2007, but have yet to be unveiled.

New Routemaster for London?

A design for a new version of the Routemaster bus by sports car maker Aston Martin and architect Norman Foster is joint winner of the New Bus for London design competition, being run by Boris Johnson. One of Mayor Johnson's election pledges was to phase out 'bendy buses' (articulated buses) and replace them with a new design of double-decker bus. The Aston Martin-Foster design is for a zero-emissions vehicle, with solar panels built into a glass roof, full accessibility and, in keeping with the original Routemaster, warm lighting and wooden floors.

The other wining design by Alan Ponsford, on behalf of vehicle manufacturer Capoco Design Limited (pictured below), features a Routemaster-style front engine and familiar styling, and has a low floor to allow easy access. The original Routemaster did not allow access for wheelchair users.

A spokesperson for the Environmental Transport Association (ETA) said: "Whichever of the designs is chosen, the new Routemaster will not only be greener and more accessible than the original, but just as importantly for the promotion of public transport, it will be a design of which we can be proud of ."

The final design could be on the road in three years.

One design that did not win deserves a mention for being a hybrid in another way - it can carry freight or passengers. Hugh Frost, an industrial designer, submitted the Freight*BUS. It features advanced technology and the ability to adapt to varying numbers of passengers and freight. This flexibility is in part due to ceiling-suspended pairs of seats, which can be completely folded out of the way. At night, or during off-peak times of day, Frost envisages his Freight*BUS being utilised to carry goods around the city, with a capacity of the equivalent to 35 standard 'europallets'. To aid loading and unloading, Frost has designed a palletless system.

The Freight*BUS is designed for several possible propulsion systems, including batteries that are automatically recharged when the bus stops and the potential for fuel-cell operation in the future. Thanks to in-wheel electric motors, the bus can manoeuvre into tight bus stops in a 'crab-like' movement. Although the Freight*BUS did not win Boris Johnson's competition, Frost is looking for partners to fund development of his concept further.

For further information, please see www.onroutebus.co.uk.

One of the winning Routemaster designs, submitted by Capoco Design Limited (Capoco Design Limited)   1375970

MARY WEBB

Mary Webb has been an employee of Jane's Information Group for more than 19 years. Having started her employment in the defence sector, she was involved at a managerial level in a number of the transport publications, both for existing products and in New Product Development, before being appointed as Managing Editor (ME), Transport, in 1994. After an illness, she stepped down as ME, Transport, and accepted the opportunity to take over the Editorship of *Jane's Road Traffic Management and ITS* in March 2001, having commissioned and championed the first edition of the title in 1997. Mary took over the Editorship of *Jane's Urban Transport Systems* in April 2002.

Mary has wide experience in the transport market, and also has an excellent appreciation and understanding of the aspirations, objectives and goals of Jane's Information Group, its working processes and the expectations of its customers.

Mary Webb (Peter Roelofs)   1375974

JACKIE CLARKE

Jackie Clarke has been an employee of Jane's Information Group since 1989, working within the Transport portfolio of titles. Jackie has remained within this market area of the company as it continues to evolve from a traditional publishing organisation to an e-business provider of intelligence and analysis. During this time, Jackie has worked in the various capacities of Assistant Editor for the titles *International ABC Aerospace Directory*, *Jane's Airports and Handling Agents*, *Jane's Road Traffic Management* and *Jane's World Airlines* and currently as Contributing Editor, Manufacturers and Services for *Jane's World Railways* and sister title, *Jane's Urban Transport Systems*. Over this time Jackie has gained a wide experience of the transport market and continues to champion this business sector for Jane's Information Group.

Jackie Clarke   1342328

Acknowledgements

There are many thanks to be extended to the contributors and correspondents who have helped me during the last annual cycle of *Jane's Urban Transport Systems*, which results in this, the hard copy format of the title. These individuals regularly provide information to ensure that the continuously updated online and other electronic versions are kept as up to date as possible.

My first acknowledgements go equally to my Contributing Editor, Manufacturers — Jackie Clarke — who not only ensures that the entries for those organisations are maintained, but who also continues to provide new entries and additional information, and to Tony Pattison, a major contributor of data and images and whose support is greatly appreciated. Ken Harris, Editor of *Jane's World Railways*, our 'sister' publication, whose knowledge, especially in the field of commuter rail, is invaluable to me and who completes the partnership which allows the two titles to provide co-ordinated information across our area of the land transport market.

I would also like to thank Roger Carvell, who has continued to apply his many skills and attention to detail in the updating of the maps in the title.

Of all of the many people involved in the production of the title at the Jane's main office, without whom the title in all its formats would not be produced, some deserve special mention for their dedication and conscientious work: Hannah Leech, Senior Content Editor, Transport Desk, who manages the copy flow, Heather Swift, Gabriella Cordeiro and Chantel Watkins, and all of the team who are involved with the gathering and distribution of updated information for the title.

My thanks also go to Adam Harding, Managing Editor, Transport and the Management Team at Jane's Coulsdon office, for their help and support throughout the year and their continued drive to assist me with the suggested improvements to the title.

I must also acknowledge *Jane's Transport Finance* as being an excellent source of material.

The list of people who have sent images and news for publication is extensive, and all of these are appreciated for their time and effort. Those who stand out as having provided exceptional contributions: Bill Luke, Steve Morgan, Peter Roelofs and Quintus Vosman.

As well as all of the above, my appreciation is also extended to the companies, organisations and authorities for their co-operation in providing information for inclusion to ensure that the data we provide is as comprehensive as possible.
Mary Webb, Editor, February 2009

As Contributing Editor to both *Jane's Urban Transport Systems* and also our 'sister' title, *Jane's World Railways*, my role is to oversee the coverage of the companies that appear in the sections contained within the Manufacturers and Services 'umbrella'. This year has included the additional challenges of learning the new system by which the Jane's titles are now being produced and this in itself has taken us a step further toward providing our customers with a product that will reflect improvements in structure, access to information and enhanced continuity.

The task of updating the high numbers of entries contained within our titles is very much aided by the valuable contribution from our contacts at the companies featured, who diligently supply us with their editorial amendments and new developments from around the world. I am always very grateful to the individuals who take time to collate, in many cases, large volumes of information, often from within different divisions of their company, in order for us to reflect such timely and comprehensive content. It is as important as ever to be included on company press release distribution and to continue to receive new images to enhance the content of our coverage.

Also assisting me within the editorial team are Kate Hainsworth, who has helped with the data-gathering effort and research and who has recently commenced work on editorial processing, Ken Harris, Editor of *Jane's World Railways*, who provides great help and guidance, and Mary Webb, as Editor of *Jane's Urban Transport Systems*, who provides continuous support and input throughout the editing process.
Jackie Clarke, Contributing Editor, February 2009

Alphabetical list of advertisers

URBAN TRANSPORT SYSTEMS

* Metro in operation   † Metro under contruction or in design

WORLD URBAN TRAM AND LIGHT RAIL SYSTEMS

(excluding museum, rural and purely interurban lines)

Some 350 light rail and tramway systems are operating in cities and towns worldwide, some serving urban areas too small to be covered in the following pages. Below is a comprehensive list of all major urban LRT and tramway systems. We are indebted to *Tramways & Urban Transit* magazine and the Light Rail Transit Association for compilation of this list.

* indicates a system built new since 1978 (not noted for systems identified as 'T' herein, as it applies to the majority of those)
† indicates a system extending or extended (including tunnel construction) recently
‡ indicates operations suspended
(T) indicates a heritage tramway operated primarily for tourist purposes
(2) indicates two (or more) separate operations
(R) indicates a rubber-tyred system
Systems in italics are steel-wheeled, automated (mostly), fully segregated lines

ARGENTINA
Buenos Aires * (2 also T)

ARMENIA
Yerevan

AUSTRALIA
Adelaide †
Ballarat (T)
Bendigo (T)
Melbourne †
Sydney *† (also T)
Victor Harbour (T)

AUSTRIA
Gmunden
Graz †
Innsbruck †
Linz †
Salzburg
Vienna †

AZERBAIJAN
Baku

BELARUS
Masyr *
Minsk
Navapolatsk *
Vitsyebsk

BELGIUM
Antwerp †
Brussels †
Charleroi
Ghent †
Ostend

BOSNIA-HERZEGOVINA
Sarajevo

BRAZIL
Belém (T)
Campos do Jordão
Macapa (Ultra Light Rail)
Rio de Janeiro
Santos (T)

BULGARIA
Sofia †

CANADA
Calgary *†
Edmonton *†
Nelson (T)
Ottawa *
Toronto (2)
Vancouver*† (also T)

CHILE
Iquique (T)

CHINA
Anshan ‡
Changchun †
Dalian
Hong Kong *(2)
Tianjin (R)

CROATIA
Osijek
Zagreb †

CZECH REPUBLIC
Brno †

Liberec
Most
Olomouc
Ostrava
Plzen †
Prague †

EGYPT
Alexandria
Cairo
Heliopolis
Helwan *

ESTONIA
Tallinn

FINLAND
Helsinki †

FRANCE
Bordeaux *†
Caen (R)
Clermont-Ferrand * (R)
Grenoble *†
Le Mans *
Lille
Lyons (Lyon) *†
Marseille †
Montpellier *†
Mulhouse*†
Nancy (R)
Nantes *†
Nice
Orleans *†
Paris *† (2)
Rouen *
St Etienne
Strasbourg *†
Valenciennes *†

GERMANY
Augsburg †
Bad Schandau
Berlin †
Bielefeld †
Bochum-Gelsenkirchen †
Bonn †
Brandenburg
Braunschweig †
Bremen †
Chemnitz †
Cologne †
Cottbus
Darmstadt †
Dessau †
Dortmund †
Dresden
Düsseldorf †
Duisburg †
Erfurt †
Essen †
Frankfurt Am Main †
Frankfurt/Oder
Freiburg/Breisgau †
Gera †
Görlitz †
Gotha
Halberstadt
Halle †
Hannover †
Heidelberg †
Heilbronn *†
Jena †

Karlsruhe †
Kassel †
Krefeld †
Leipzig †
Ludwigshafen
Magdeburg †
Mainz †
Mannheim-Ludwigshafen Heidelberg†
Mülheim/Ruhr †
Munich (München) †
Naumburg (T)
Nordhausen †
Nuremburg (Nürnberg) †
Oberhausen *†
Plauen
Potsdam †
Rostock †
Saarbrücken *†
Schöneiche
Schwerin
Strausberg
Stuttgart †
Ulm †
Woltersdorf
Wuppertal
Würzburg †
Zwickau †

GREECE
Athens *

HUNGARY
Budapest †
Debrecen
Miskolc
Szeged

INDIA
Calcutta (Kolkata)

IRELAND
Dublin *

ITALY
Cagliari *
Genoa *†
Messina *
Milan †
Naples
Padua (R)
Rome (2)†
Sassari *
Trieste
Turin †

JAPAN
Enoshima
Fukui
Fukuoka
Hakodate
Hiroshima †
Kagoshima
Kochi
Kumamoto
Kyoto
Matsuyama
Nagasaki
Okayama
Osaka
Sapporo

Takaoka
Tokyo
Toyama
Toyohashi

KAZAKHSTAN
Almaty
Oskemen
Pavlodar
Temirtau

KOREA, NORTH
Chongjin *
Pyongyang *(2)

LATVIA
Daugavpils
Liepaya
Riga

MALAYSIA
*Kuala Lumpur**

MEXICO
Guadalajara *
Mexico City
Monterrey *†

NETHERLANDS
Amsterdam †
The Hague †
Houten *
Rotterdam †
Utrecht *

NEW ZEALAND
Christchurch (T)

NORWAY
Bergen (T)
Oslo
Trondheim

PERU
Lima (T)

PHILIPPINES
Manila *†(2)

POLAND
Bydgoszcz
Czestochowa
Elblag †
Gdansk
Gorzow
Grundziadz
Katowice †
Krakow †
Lódź
Poznan †
Szczecin
Torun
Warsaw †
Wroclaw †

PORTUGAL
Lisbon
Oporto (Porto) *† (also T)
Sintra (T)
Sul do Tejo (Almada/Seixal) *

ROMANIA
Arad
Botoşani *
Braila
Bucharest †
Cluj *
Constanta *
Craiova *
Galati
Iasi
Oradea
Ploiesti *
Reşiţa *
Sibiu
Timişoara †

RUSSIAN FEDERATION
Achinsk
Angarsk
Arkhangelsk

Barnaul
Biysk
Chelyabinsk
Cherepovets
Dzerzhinsk
Irkutsk
Ivanovo
Izhevsk
Kaliningrad
Kazan
Kemerovo
Kharbarovsk
Kolomna
Komsomolsk-na-Amure
Krasnoarmeisk
Krasnodar
Krasnoturinsk
Krasnoyarsk
Kursk
Lipetsk
Magnitogorsk †
Moscow
Naberezhnye Chelny
Nizhnekamsk
Nizhny Novgorod
Nizhniy-Tagil
Noginsk
Novocherkassk
Novokuznetsk
Novosibirsk
Novotroitsk
Omsk
Orel
Orsk (2)
Osinniki
Perm
Prokopyevsk
Pyatigorsk
Rostov-on-Don
Ryazan
Salavat
Samara
Saratov
Smolensk
Stary Oskol *
St Petersburg
Taganrog
Tomsk
Tula
Tver
Ufa
Ulan-Ude
Ulyanovsk
Usolye-Sibirskoye
Ust-Ilimsk *
Ust-Katav
Vladikavkaz
Vladivostok
Volchansk
Volgograd
Volzhskiy
Voronezh
Yaroslavl
Yekaterinburg
Zlatoust

SERBIA
Belgrade

SLOVAKIA
Bratislava
Kosice
Trencianske Teplice

SOUTH AFRICA
Kimberley (T)

SPAIN
Alicante *†
Barcelona * (also T)
Bilbao *†
La Coruna (T)
Madrid *
Murcia * (Demonstration tramway, with plans
to operate a full service on an extended line)
Parla *
Seville *†
Soller

Tenerife *
Valencia *†
Vélez-Málaga *

SWEDEN
Gothenburg †
Norrköping †
Stockholm † (2) (also T)

SWITZERLAND
Basle (2)
Bern (2)
Geneva † (2)
Glattal *
Lausanne *
Neuchâtel
Zürich † (2)

TUNISIA
Tunis *†

TURKEY
Ankara *†
Antalya *
Bursa *
Eskisehir *
Istanbul *†(2) (also T)
Izmir *†
Konya *†

UKRAINE
Avdiyivka
Dniprodzerzhinsk
Dnipropetrovsk †
Donetsk
Druzhkivka
Horlivka
Kharkov
Kiev †
Konotop
Konstantinovka
Kostyatinivka ‡
Kramatorsk
Kriviy Rih (2*)
Lugansk
Lviv
Makiyivka
Mariupol
Molochne *
Nikolayiv
Odessa
Vinnitsya
Yenakiyeve
Yevpatoriya
Zaporizhzhya
Zhitomir

UNITED KINGDOM
Birkenhead (T)
Birmingham-Wolverhampton *
Blackpool
Croydon *
Douglas (T)
London†
Manchester *†
Newcastle Upon Tyne *†
Nottingham *
Sheffield *

UNITED STATES
Baltimore *†
Boston
Buffalo *
Charlotte *†
Cleveland
Dallas *† (also T)
Denver *†
*Detroit**
Galveston (T)
Houston *
Jersey City *†
Kenosha (T)
Las Vegas
Little Rock (T)†
Long Beach (T)
Los Angeles *† (also T)
Lowell (T)
Memphis *(T)†
*Miami**
Minneapolis *

SYSTEMS

Newark †
New Orleans †
Philadelphia †
Pittsburgh †
Portland *†(2)
Sacramento *†
Salt Lake City *†

San Diego *†
San Francisco †
San Jose *†
Seattle *
St Louis *†
Tacoma *
Tampa (T)

Trenton Camden *
Tucson (T)

UZBEKISTAN
Tashkent

SYSTEMS UNDER CONSTRUCTION

ALGERIA
Algiers
Constantine
Oran

BRAZIL
Crato—Juazeiro do Norte

CHINA
Suzhou

FRANCE
Angers
Reims
Toulon

IRAN
Mashad

ISRAEL
Jerusalem
Tel Aviv

ITALY
Bergamo
Florence
L'Aquila (R)
Perugia

KOREA, SOUTH
Busan
Seoul
Yong-In

MOROCCO
Rabat

NIGERIA
Abuja

NORWAY
Bergen

SPAIN
Granada
Málaga
Vitoria-Gasteiz

TURKEY
Adana

UNITED STATES
Norfolk
Phoenix
Seattle (2nd)

VENEZUELA
Maracaibo

SYSTEMS PLANNED

ARGENTINA
Mendoza

AUSTRALIA
Gold Coast

BELGIUM
Hasselt (to Maastricht)

CANADA
Montreal
Vancouver

CHINA
Macau

DENMARK
Copenhagen

ECUADOR
Quito

FRANCE
Brest
La Rochelle
Le Havre
Saint Denis (Réunion)
Tours

GREECE
Thessalonika

INDIA
Kochi

ISRAEL
Haifa—Nazareth

ITALY
Palermo
Venice-Mestre (R)

JORDAN
Amman

LUXEMBOURG
Luxembourg

MOROCCO
Rabat

NETHERLANDS
Arnhem (T)
Dordrecht-Geldermalsen
Gouda-Leiden
Groningen
Maastricht (to Hasselt)

NEW ZEALAND
Auckland
Wellington

NIGERIA
Calabar
Lagos

PAKISTAN
Karachi

SAUDI ARABIA
Jeddah
Riyadh

SENEGAL
Dakar

SOUTH AFRICA
Durban

SPAIN
Cadiz
Zaragoza

SRI LANKA
Colombo

TAIWAN
Kaohsiung

TURKEY
Kayseri

UNITED KINGDOM
Bristol (Ultra Light Rail)
Edinburgh
Glasgow
London (2)

UNITED STATES
Atlanta
Bayonne (T)
Birmingham (T)
Cincinnati
Grand Rapids
Irvine
Lancaster
Miami
Roanoke
Washington, DC
Winston-Salem

VIETNAM
Hanoi
Ho Chi Minh City

WORLD URBAN TROLLEYBUS SYSTEMS

Around 340 trolleybus systems are operating in cities and towns worldwide some serving urban areas too small to be covered in the following pages. Below is a comprehensive list of all urban trolleybus systems known to be operating.

* SYSTEM CURRENTLY NOT OPERATING

ARGENTINA
Córdoba
Mendoza
Rosario

ARMENIA
Yerevan

AUSTRIA
Linz
Salzburg

AZERBAIJAN
Baku
Gyandzha
Mingechaur

BELARUS
Bobruisk
Brest-Litovsk
Gomel
Grodno
Minsk
Mogilev
Vitebsk

BELGIUM
Ghent

BOSNIA
Sarajevo

BRAZIL
Santos
São Paulo (2 systems)

BULGARIA
Burgas
Dobrich
Gabrovo
Khaskovo
Pazardzhik
Pernik
Pleven
Plovdiv
Ruse
Sliven
Sofia
Stara Zagora
Varna
Veliko Turnovo
Vratsa

CANADA
Edmonton
Vancouver

CHILE
Valparaíso

CHINA
Beijing
Dalian
Guangzhou
Hangzhou
Harbin
Jinan
Lanzhou *
Luoyang
Nanchang
Qingdao
Qiqihar
Shanghai
Taiyuan
Wuhan (2 systems)
Xi'an
Xingtai
Zhengzhou

CZECH REPUBLIC
Brno
České Budějovice

Chomutov
Hrádec Králové
Jihlava
Mariánské Lázně
Opava
Ostrava
Pardubice
Plzeň
Teplice
Ústí nad Labem
Zlín

ECUADOR
Quito

ESTONIA
Tallinn

FRANCE
Limoges
Lyons
Nancy
St Etienne

GEORGIA
Chiatura
Gori
Kutaisi
Ozurgeti
Poti
Rustavi
Sukhumi
Zugdidi

GERMANY
Eberswalde
Esslingen
Solingen

GREECE
Athens

HUNGARY
Budapest
Debrecen
Szeged

IRAN
Tehran

ITALY
Ancona
Bologna
Cagliari
Chieti *
Genoa
La Spezia
Milan
Modena
Naples (2 systems)
Parma
Rimini
Rome
San Remo

KAZAKHSTAN
Aqtöbe
Almaty
Astana
Karaganda
Kustanai
Petropavlovsk
Taraz

KOREA, NORTH
Anju
Chongjin
Haeju
Hamhung
Kanggye
Kimchaek
Nampo

Phyongsong
Pyongyang
Sinuiju
Sunchon
Tokchon
Wonsan

KYRGYZSTAN
Bishek
Naryn
Osh

LATVIA
Riga

LITHUANIA
Kaunas
Vilnius

MEXICO
Guadalajara
Mexico City

MOLDOVA
Balţi
Bendery
Chişinău
Tiraspol

MONGOLIA
Ulaan Baatar

NEPAL
Kathmandu *

NETHERLANDS
Arnhem

NEW ZEALAND
Wellington

NORWAY
Bergen

POLAND
Gdynia
Lublin
Tychy

PORTUGAL
Coimbra

ROMANIA
Baia Mare
Braşov
Bucharest
Cluj
Constanţa
Galaţi
Mediaş
Piatra Neamţ
Ploieşti
Sibiu
Târgu Jiu
Timişoara
Vaslui

RUSSIAN FEDERATION
Abakan
Almetyevsk
Archangelsk *
Armavir
Astrakhan
Balakovo
Barnaul
Belgorod
Berezniki
Blagoveshchensk
Bratsk
Bryansk
Cheboksary
Chelyabinsk

SYSTEMS

Cherkessk
Chita
Dzerzhinsk
Engels
Irkutsk
Ivanovo
Izhevsk
Kaliningrad
Kaluga
Kamensk-Uralskiy
Kazan
Kemerovo
Khabarovsk
Khimki
Kirov
Kostroma
Kovrov
Krasnodar
Krasnoyarsk
Kurgan
Kursk
Leninsk-Kuznetskiy
Lipetsk
Maikop
Makhachkala
Miass
Moscow
Murmansk
Nalchik
Nizhny Novgorod
Novgorod
Novocheboksarsk
Novokuybyshevsk
Novokuznetsk
Novorossiysk
Novosibirsk
Omsk
Orel
Orenburg
Penza
Perm
Petrozavodsk
Podolsk
Rostov-on-Don
Rubtsovsk
Ryazan
Rybinsk
Samara
Saransk
Saratov
Smolensk
Stavropol
Sterlitamak
St Petersburg
Syzran
Taganrog
Tambov
Tolyatti

Tomsk
Tula
Tver
Tyumen
Ufa
Ulyanovsk
Vidnoye
Vladikavkaz
Vladimir
Vladivostok
Volgodonsk
Volgograd
Vologda
Yaroslavl
Yekaterinburg
Yoshkar-Ola

SERBIA
Belgrade

SLOVAKIA
Banská Bystrica
Bratislava
Košice
Prešov
Žilina

SPAIN
Castellón

SWEDEN
Landskrona

SWITZERLAND
Bern
Biel
La Chaux-de-Fonds
Fribourg
Geneva
Lausanne
Lucerne
Montreux-Vevey
Neuchâtel
Schaffhausen
St Gallen
Winterthur
Zürich

TAJIKISTAN
Dushanbe

TURKMENISTAN
Ashgabat

UKRAINE
Alchevsk
Antratsit
Artyemivsk
Bila Tserkov
Cherkasy

Chernigiv
Chernivtsi
Dnipropetrovsk
Dobropilya
Donetsk
Horlivka
Ivano-Frankivsk
Kerch
Kharkov
Khartsyzsk
Kherson
Khmelnitsky
Kiev
Kirovograd
Kramatorsk
Krasnodon
Kremenchuk
Kriviy Rih
Lisichansk
Lugansk
Lutsk
Lviv
Makiyivka
Mariupol
Mikolayiv
Odessa
Poltava
Rivne
Sevastopol
Severodonetsk
Simferopol
Slavyansk
Stakhanov
Sumy
Ternopol
Vinnitsya
Vuglegirsk
Yalta
Zaporizhzhya
Zhitomir

UNITED STATES
Boston
Dayton
Philadelphia
San Francisco
Seattle

UZBEKISTAN
Almalyk
Bukhoro *
Jizzax (formerly Dzhizakh)
Namangan
Tashkent
Urgench

VENEZUELA
Mérida

SYSTEMS UNDER CONSTRUCTION (*) OR ACTIVE DEVELOPMENT

ETHIOPIA
Addis Ababa

ITALY
Avellino *
Bari *
Biella
Lecce *

Pescara *
Verona

PORTUGAL
Amadora

RUSSIAN FEDERATION
Gatchina *

VENEZUELA
Barquisimeto *

URBAN TRANSPORT SYSTEMS AND OPERATORS

URBAN TRANSPORT SYSTEMS AND OPERATORS

Algeria

Algiers

Population: City 1.2 million, metropolitan area 3.5 million (estimates)

Public transport

Bus services mostly provided by state-run undertaking (l'Enterprise de Transport Urbains et Suburbains d'Alger (ETUSA)) serving the city, suburbs and coastal area and which is also responsible for two public elevators and a funicular. Suburban railway operated by Algerian National Railways (SNTF); light rail/tramway and metro under construction. Further funiculars and cable cars are planned. Taxi sharing extensive. Much company-sponsored transport provided privately.

The organisation which is responsible for public transport in Algiers is:

Ministère des Transports

119 rue, Didouche Mourad, 16001 Alger-Centre, Algiers, Algeria
Tel: (+213 21) 74 06 81   Fax: (+213 21) 74 76 24

Société Nationale des Transports Ferroviaires (SNTF) – Algerian National Railways

21–23 Boulevard Mohamed V, Algiers, Algeria
Tel: (+213 21) 71 15 10   Fax: (+213 21) 63 32 98
e-mail: dg-snt@sntf.dz
Web: www.sntf.dz

Key personnel

Director General: Abdelhamid Lalaimia
Regional Director, Algiers: Kerdel Ramdane
External Relations Manager: Ms Houriadib

Type of operation: Suburban heavy rail

Passenger journeys: (2004) 27.3 million (all operations)
Train-km: Not currently available

Current situation

Service provided on routes from Algiers Maritime to Blida (50 km) and Thenia (54 km) using 228 diesel-hauled push-pull cars.

For further information on SNTF, please see *Jane's World Railways*.

Developments

In 2004, SNTF awarded ALSTOM a contract to electrify the Algiers suburban network, using the 25 kV AC 50 Hz system. Covering some 300 track-km, the project covers the El Harrach-El Affroun, Oued Smar-Gué de Constantine and Algiers-Thénia sections.

In 2006, SNTF placed an order with Stadler for 64 four-car Fast Light Innovative Regional Train (FLIRT) articulated emus to served Algiers suburban network, electrification of which is in progress. Delivery of the trains will extend from 2008 to the end of 2010. The contract includes the supply of a driver training simulator and the provision of maintenance services for a 10-year period.

Entreprise Metro d'Alger (EMA)

170 rue Hassiba Ben Bouali, Algiers, Algeria
Tel: (+213 21) 66 17 34/47
Fax: (+213 21) 66 17 57
e-mail: contact@metroalger-dz.com
Web: www.metroalger-dz.com

Key personnel

President: Abdelkader Mekrebi
Director-General: H Bellil
Assistant General Manager: Tayeb Zendaoui
 Staff: Not currently available

Light rail

Type of operation: Light rail (under construction)

Current situation

In 2006, a consortium of SYSTRA and RATP-Développement was awarded the contract to manage construction of the priority section of the eastern line of the Algiers tramway. This section, between Carrefour du Ruisseau and Bordj el Kiffan, will be 16.3 km long with 30 stops. A depot and control centre is due to be built at Bordj el Kiffan.

The total length of the line will be some 23 km with 38 stops. Ridership is estimated at 150,000 passengers per day and service is currently scheduled to start in early 2009.

Alstom will supply 29 *Citadis* trams for the line.

Metro

Type of operation: Metro (under construction)

Current situation

In 2006, a consortium led by Siemens Transportation Systems was awarded the contract for the construction of Line 1 of the Algiers metro network. CAF will supply 14 six car metro trains and the ticketing system will be supplied by Thales. The latter will be a combined system, using magnetic tickets and a contactless card.

The first phase of Line 1, mostly in tunnel, will be 9 km long with 10 stations and is currently scheduled to come into operation in 2008.

A 3-line total network is envisaged, with a total length in excess of 60 km and with some 60 stations.

Argentina

Buenos Aires

Population: City 2.78 million, metropolitan area 12.4 million (estimates)

Public transport

Bus services provided by route associations of independent 'colectivo' mini and midibus owners and operators under general direction of national transport authority. Municipally owned metro, with light rail extensions, and state-owned suburban railways, all run by private operators on a concessionary basis; also privately owned suburban light rail line. Light rail/tramway being demonstrated in the Puerto Madero district.

Comisión Nacional de Regulación del Transporte (CNRT)

Maipú 88, CP-Buenos Aires, Argentina
Tel: (+54 11) 48 19 31 66/7
e-mail: dgtransito@buenosaires.gov.ar
Web: www.cnrt.gov.ar

Current situation

The Comisión Nacional de Regulación del Transporte (CNRT) was established in 1996, and combines the operations of the previous Comisión Nacional de Transporte Automotor (CONTA), the Comisión Nacional de Transporte Ferroviario (CNTF) and incorporates the Unidad de Coordinación del Programa de Reestructuración Ferroviario (UNCPRF).

The CNRT is responsible for the control and operation of public transport services.

Bus/minibus
Current situation

There are more than 190 urban bus lines, operated by private companies.

'Colectivo' minibuses and midi-buses, operating scheduled services, account for some 80 per cent of all public transport trips and 54 per cent of total trips.

Metrovías SA

Bartolomé Mitre 3342, Buenos Aires 1201, Argentina
Tel: (+54 11) 49 59 68 00
Fax: (+54 11) 48 66 30 37
e-mail: info@metrovias.com.ar
Web: www.metrovias.com.ar

Key personnel

Chief Executive Officer: Alberto Verra

Current situation

Metrovías is the concessionaire of the metros of Buenos Aires, the pre-metro LRT service and the Urquiza suburban line. Metrovías is part of the Roggio Group, a large Argentine construction organisation, which has a 55.3 per cent shareholding. The company receives the technical assistance of Belgian consultants Transurb Consult SC. As part of that group, Metrovías took over overall operation of the metro and pre-metro light rail systems and the Urquiza line with 70 km of route and 103 stations, handling an annual ridership of 300 million passengers.

Metro

Staff: 2,500

Type of operation: Full metro, first line opened 1913

Passenger journeys: (2000) 256.3 million
(2001) 238.6 million
(2002) 219.3 million

Route length: 39.5 km
Number of lines: 5
Number of stations: 67 (all in tunnel)
Gauge: 1,435 mm
Track: 44 kg/m or 45.5 kg/m rail on timber sleepers on stone ballast; concrete sleepers on new sections
Tunnel: All double-track; Line A, cut-and-cover; others bored
Electrification: Line A, 1.1 kV DC, overhead; Line B, 550 V DC, third rail; Lines C, D and E, 1.5 kV DC, overhead

Service: Peak 3–6 min, off-peak 10–12 min
Fare structure: Flat, with free transfer
Fare collection: Manual; token to turnstile
Operating costs financed by: Fares 67 per cent, other commercial sources 5 per cent, subsidy/grants 28 per cent

Rolling stock: 497 cars
La Brugeoise, Line A (1913/24, 12 rebuilt 1987) M105
Siemens/O&K, Lines C, D, E

(1934)	M29 T28
(1941)	M9 T9
(1944)	M14
Baseler, Lines C, D, E (1954) | T13 |
Fab Militares/Siemens, Line B (1978) | M20 |
Nat Movil y Const/GEE, Lines C, D, E (1964) | M30 |
Fab Militares, Lines C, D, E (1964) | T30 |
Fab Militares/GE, Line B (1965) | M20 |
Materfer/Fab Militares/Siemens,
Lines C, D E (1980) | M30 T30 |
Ex-Tokyo Line B | M100 |
Ex-Nagoya Line D (1996/97) | 30 |

On order: 80 ALSTOM vehicles ordered in 2001

Light rail
Passenger journeys: (1991) 2.8 million

Current situation
The 7.4 km light rail line from Line E at Plaza de los Virreyes to Gen Savio opened in 1987; electrified 750 V DC; 13 stations. Further construction in progress to create a loop at the line's outer end. Plans exist for Line E1 to link Plaza de los Virreyes with the national airport.

Rolling stock: 17 cars
Fab Militares/Siemens LRV (1988)   M17

Suburban rail
Passenger journeys: (2003) 26.6 million
(2004) 28.3 million
(2005) 27.7 million

Current situation
In January 1994, the Metrovías consortium commenced a 20-year concession to run electric suburban services on the Urquiza suburban line running west of the Argentinian capital.

Metrovías Urquiza line services link Buenos Aires Frederico Lacrose terminal with General Lemos, serving 23 stations.

Developments
Improvements undertaken by Metrovías or in progress include track renewal, level crossing safety work and measure to enhance passenger accessibility.

Rolling stock: 108 emu cars, usually in three two-car trainsets (Urquiza line)

Ferrovías SAC
Avenida Ramos Mejía 1430, 1430 Buenos Aires, Argentina
Tel: (+54 11) 43 14 14 44
Fax: (+54 11) 43 11 80 02
e-mail: atencionalpasajero@ferrovias.com.ar
Web: www.ferrovias.com

Key personnel
President: Roman Aldao

Tram
A demonstration tramway has been set up by Alstom in the Perto Madero district. It is being operated temporarily with two 5-car *Citadis* trams (to be called *Celeris* in Buenos Aires), from Mulhouse. Upon completion of the 2 km project, which is estimated to cost some ARS46 million, Ferrovías will operate the system.

Suburban rail
Passenger journeys: (Annual) 40 million (estimate)
Route length: 54.3 km
Number of stations: 22
Gauge: 1,000 mm

Map of Buenos Aires metro and light rail   1115203

Current situation
On 3 February 1994, a 10-year operating contract was signed by government and Ferrovías for the former Belgrano North route from Buenos Aires Retiro station west to Villa Rosa. Operations began on 30 April 1994. In 2001, Ferrovías renegotiated its concession to obtain a 20-year extension in return for extensive investment.

Trains are operated as six-car formations, with a 10-minute frequency at peak periods. A limited stop express service using refurbished rolling stock was introduced between Retiro and Los Polvorines in May 2006, running four times a day in each direction.

Developments
Infrastructure has been refurbished and upgraded over the whole line and 18 km of track between Retiro and Carapachay has been completely relaid. Further track renewals were in progress or planned in 2006. Ferrovías has also undertaken a refurbishment programme covering the 22 stations it serves, financed by its own resources.

Under the terms of a re-negotiated concession, Ferrovías plans eventually to electrify the 54 km Retiro-Villa Rosa line, on the Belgrano North system, reconstructing all 22 stations and providing a fleet of new emus. Electrification is projected in three phases (Retiro-Grand Bourg, Grand Bourg-Del Viso and Del Viso-Villa Rosa), using the 25 kV AC system.

In 2005, the government agreed the purchase of 17 Class 9600 two-car dmus from Trains of Portugal to replace older equipment. Refurbishment of these was in progress in Argentina in 2006. A modernisation programme of coaching stock was also in progress in 2006, including provision of automatic doors.

Rolling stock: 20 locomotives plus 120 coaches
GM G22 CU diesel-electric
locomotives   20

Nuevo Tren de la Costa SA
Juan B de la Salle 653 (Piso 1), San Isidro, 1642 Buenos Aires, Argentina
Tel: (+54 11) 40 02 60 43
Fax: (+54 11) 40 02 60 63
e-mail: info@trendelacosta.com.ar
Web: www.trendelacosta.com.ar

Key personnel
President: Matias M Brea
  Staff: 180

Type of operation: Light rail, opened 1994

Passenger boardings: (2005) 1.8 million

Current situation
This 15 km, 1,435 mm gauge light rail line with 11 stations, built on the formation of an abandoned railway, links Maipú and Delta in the northern suburbs. It is electrified at 1.5 kV DC overhead; fares cover 80 per cent of operating costs. The line serves a number of new commercial and leisure developments.

Service: 20 min
Fare collection: Single ride, 12-ride tickets, monthly pass; discounts for residents

Rolling stock: 8 cars
CAF (1994)   M8

Trenes de Buenos Aires SA (TBA)
Avenida Ramos Mejía 1358 – piso 2°, 1104 Buenos Aires, Argentina
Tel: (+54 11) 43 17 44 0009
Fax: (+54 11) 43 17 44
Web: www.tbanet.com.ar

Key personnel
President: Marcelo Calderó
Vice-President and General Manager:
  Jorge Alvarez

Director of Planning and Investment:
Marcos Chicote
Head of Administration and Finance: Daniel Rubio
Head of Contract Administration: Francisco Pafumi
Head of Legal Affairs: Walter Iglesias
Head of Institutional Relations and Communications:
Gustavo Gago
Manager, Mitre Line: Ernesto Limardo
Manager, Sarmiento Line: Guillermo D'Abenigno
Head of Centralised Transport: Antonio Mazzaglia
Staff: 3,732 (2006)

Type of operation: Suburban rail

Passenger journeys: (Both lines)
(2003) 165.9 million
(2004) 174.7 million
(2005) 180.6 million

Current situation
TBA holds a concession to operate the Mitre and
Sarmiento suburban lines serving Buenos Aires.
For further information on TBA, please see
Jane's World Railways.

Union de Gestacion Operative Ferroviaria de Emergencia SA (UGOFE)

Linea San Martín (LSM)
Avenida Ramos Mejía 1552, Hal Central Estación
Retiro, C1104AJP Buenos Aires, Argentina

Tel: (+54 11) 43 11 92 07
e-mail: info@ugofe.com.ar
Web: www.ugofe.com.ar

Type of operation: Commuter rail

Passenger journeys: (2003/04) 77.7 million
(2004/05) 74.2 million
(2005/06) 83.9 million

Background
The UGOFE consortium, formed by Ferrovías,
Metrovías and Trenes de Buenos Aires, took over
the concession for suburban services on the
former Ferrocarril General San Martín in January
2005.

Current situation
UGOFE operates a high-frequency diesel-
operated commuter service between Buenos
Aires Retiro station and Pilar, northwest of the
capital. Services are branded Linea San Martín
(LSM).
For further information on LSM, please see
Jane's World Railways.

Developments
As part of the Argentinian government's
National Rail Recovery Plan (Plan Nacional
de Recuperación Ferroviaria), investments of
ARS1,118 million in the San Martín system were
planned during the period 2004–10.

In 2006, a new service was launched between
the district of Retiro and the city of Hurlingham,
which is part of the part of the Gran Buenos Aires
metropolitan area.

Rolling stock/fleet
In 2006, the fleet comprised some 20
locomotives and around 120 coaches. While
many of the locomotives have been refurbished
with government funding, they include Alco
units dating from the 1950s. To strengthen
the fleet, in 2006 LSM acquired two English
Electric Class 1400 diesel-electric locomotives
from Trains of Portugal (CP). The first of these
put to use on the Retiro Hurlingham service.
CP was also the source of 10 second-hand
coaches introduced in 2006. Coaches in the
existing fleet have also been refurbished and
modernised.
In 2006, the Argentinian government signed a
USD123 million contract with Chinese industry
covering the supply of 24 diesel-electric
locomotives and 160 coaches to modernise the
LSM fleet. Deliveries were expected to start in
2007.

Córdoba
Population: 3.1 million (estimated)

Public transport
Bus and trolleybus services provided by
municipal transport department.

Municipalidad de Córdoba
Transport Department
Palacio Municipal 6 de Julio, Caseros y Marcelo T
de Alvear, Córdoba, Argentina
Tel: (+54 35) 428 56 37 ext. 1465
Web: www.cordobaciudad.gov.ar

Key personnel
Secretary for Transport: Walter Montenegro
Director, General: Carlos Fúnes
Director, Transport: Carlos Ferrario
Assistant Director, Transport: Flavio Araoz

Current situation
This authority supervises all public transport in
Córdoba, which is provided by private operators.
An exception has been the trolleybus network,
which has variously been in private and
municipal hands. Public transport co-operatives
were merged by the municipal authorities in 1970
into 13 route associations. Excessive competition
between members led in 1980 to reorganisation
of services by route-corridor, which were then
put out to tender.

Bus
Current situation
There are 50 routes concentrated along nine
corridors, plus three radial and 12 other routes.
Mergers and takeovers have reduced the number
of operators to six, employing some 3,400. These
are: Dr Belgrano, Ciudad de Córdoba, El Coniferal,
Union 12 de Octubre, America and Konfort.

Developments
An air conditioned express network of 12
midibus routes has been set up, run in part by
new operator Konfort and using Mercedes LO709
and Toyota Coaster vehicles.
A new fare collection system is planned to
replace the existing clipcard/token arrangements.

Number of routes: 65
Route length: 2,123 km

Fleet: 1,025 vehicles, mainly Mercedes midibuses
but with some Brazilian-bodied Mercedes buses
and an increasing number of El Detalle OA101s;
there are also some Fiat-Iveco AU130s and re-
engined Zanellos, both built locally; the Express
network is operated by Mercedes LO710/OF1215
and Toyota Coasters.
Ciudad de Córdoba has bought 23 Scania
buses. Air-conditioned minibuses run on some
routes.

Fare collection: Prepurchase ticket or token to driver
Fare structure: Flat, with transfer permitted to two
orbital routes
Average peak-hour speed: 16 km/h

Trolleybus
**Transporte Automotor Municipal Sociedad del
Estado (TAMSE)**
División de Trolebuses

Current situation
A trolleybus system opened in stages between
1989 and 1994, and now comprises four routes
with a total route-length of about 30 km.
The infrastructure and vehicles are owned by the
municipality, while operation and maintenance
have usually been carried out by a private
company under contract. However, operations
have been hampered by difficulties, with the

municipality taking over from the three private
companies that have so far attempted to run the
system. In 1997 the operating concession was
again granted to a private company, Trolecor, a
new partnership between local businessmen and
Norinco of China. New vehicles were promised
as part of the agreement with city officials.
Trolecor announced that 50 Norinco-built two-
axle trolleybuses were to be supplied to replace
all of the ZIU vehicles, and 16 were delivered
in 1999 and 2000 and entered service in 2000.
However, the vehicles were deemed to be
unreliable and of poor quality, sufficiently so for
the remainder of the order to be cancelled. Many
of the ZIU vehicles were given a light overhaul to
extend their useful lives, until other new vehicles
could be ordered.

Developments
Various options for acquiring new vehicles were
explored, but none came to fruition. Meanwhile,
the number of serviceable trolleybuses declined
from about 50 to 30. In July 2004, the municipal
government revoked Trolecor's contract, citing
poor maintenance of both infrastructure and
vehicles and other management problems. The
system is now operated by a city agency named
Transporte Automotor Municipal Sociedad del
Estrado (TAMSE). and, more specifically, by
that agency's División de Trolebuses. TAMSE
has begun to attend to the neglected wiring
and substations and to rehabilitate some of the
derelict trolleybuses, with a goal of increasing
the number of serviceable vehicles to 50 by early
2005.

Fleet: 56 trolleybuses (only some 30 serviceable as
at mid-2004)

ZIU 682 (1989/93)	29
ZIU 683 articulated (1990/92)	11
Norinco SYWG100 (1999)	16

Mendoza
Population: 1.58 million (2001 Census)

Public transport
'Colectivo' bus and minibus services are provided
by private operators and groups operating through
an association and are supervised by the provincial
transport department. Trolleybus services are run by
the Province-owned corporation.

Dirección de Vias y Medios de Transporte
Alberdi 250, 5519 San José, Guaymallen,
Mendoza, Argentina
Tel: (+54 261) 432 33 79
Fax: (+54 261) 431 07 15
e-mail: comunicacionviasytransporte@mendoza.
gov.ar
Web: www.transporte.mendoza.gov.ar

Key personnel
Director: Andrés Da Rold
Staff: Not available currently

Current situation
The provincial Dirección de Vias y Medios de
Transportes is in charge of co-ordinating and
regulating the *colectivo* bus operations of the
city's 10 main groupings of private operators and

co-operatives, each franchised for one or more specific routes. There are about 50 routes, many of which started as branches of the original 10-route core network but are now numbered and operated separately. The principal operators are: El Trapiche, El Plumerillo, Antartida Argentina, Paso de los Andes and TAC.

In 1990, consultants BVC carried out traffic management studies, which were expected to lead to improved operating conditions for buses.

The Dirección de Vias y Medios de Transportes is also in charge of regulating city and regional taxi services, as well as the Taxi-Flet public-hire freight pick-ups, which charge by the hour.

Passenger journeys: Approx 70 million (annual)
Vehicle-km: Approx 20 million (annual)

Number of routes: 40
Route length: 560 km

Fleet: Approx 500 vehicles, including Mercedes LO1114, OF1214, OH1314 and OH1419 types, El Detalle OA101 and Zanello, many bodied by local companies

Fare structure: Urban, flat; suburban, distance-related
Fare collection: Payment to driver

Empresa Provincial de Transportes de Mendoza (EPTM)

Calle Perú 2592, Mendoza 5500, Argentina
Tel: (+54 261) 425 17 33
Fax: (+54 261) 438 06 50

e-mail: eptm@mendoza.gov.ar
Web: www.obras.mendoza.gov.ar/Paginas/troles.htm

Key personnel
General Director: Héctor Salcedo
    Staff: Approx 200

Trolleybus
Passenger journeys: Approx 15 million (annual)

Number of routes: 5
Route length: 90 km (round trip; most routes are one-way loops)

Fleet: 95 trolleybuses (of which, about 70 serviceable)
Tokyu/Nissan/Toshiba
    (1962, refurbished 1996) (in store)   1
Uritsky ZIU9 (1984)   16
Krupp (ex-Solingen) some stored   78
In peak service: Approx 60
Most intensive service: 7–10 min
One-person operation: 100 per cent
Fare structure: Flat, higher in late evening
Fare collection: Payment to driver

Background
Empresa Provincial de Transportes de Mendoza (EPTM) is a public agency of the government of Mendoza province, under the Ministry of Environment and Public Works. It was created in 1958.

Current situation
Work on a sixth trolleybus route, running westwards from the city centre to Universidad

Nacional de Cuyo, began in July 2004. This new route, which had a round-trip length of 13.5 km, opened in October 2005. Although initially terminating in the city centre, it is to be through-routed with another route, 'Villa Nueva', as soon as wiring renewal work on that route is completed. As of early 2009, this had still not been completed, and the route remains 'temporarily' bus-operated. For this reason, the total number of routes continues to be five and not six.

Developments
Further expansion of the system is still planned, but progress has been very slow.

Under an agreement finalised in August 2008, 80 second-hand trolleybuses have been purchased from TransLink of Vancouver, BC, Canada. The Flyer E901A/E902 vehicles were built in 1982–4 and were withdrawn from service in Vancouver in 2007 and 2008. All 80 trolleybuses were transported by ship in November 2008 to Chile, from where they were taken by road to Mendoza. They are expected to begin entering service in early 2009, gradually replacing most, or all, of the ex-Solingen vehicles. Some will be used only as sources of parts.

Rosario
Population: 1 million (estimated)

Public transport
Bus and minibus services provided by private companies under concessions supervised by municipal transport authority. Remaining trolleybus route reopened 1994 and now operated by municipal transport authority.

Dirección General de Transporte (DGT)
Secretaría de Servicios Públicos, Municipalidad de Rosario
Avenida Pellegrini 2808 PB, 2000 Rosario, Argentina
Tel: (+54 341) 430 99 76

Key personnel
Secretary of Public Services: Clara García

Current situation
This is the municipal transport authority, responsible for allocation and supervision of operating concessions for the city's public transport.

Developments
All buses (but not trolleybuses) were equipped with ticket validating machines by early 1995, but they were unused until DGT ordered their commissioning late in the year. But with three incompatible systems installed, there were severe mechanical problems and passenger confusion, and the operator successfully petitioned DGT to allow temporary resumption of fare collection by drivers or conductors.

In early 1997, DGT selected the British Wayfarer ticketing system as the citywide standard and required all city bus companies to equip their fleets with validators for this system, and to discontinue driver collection of fares. Trolleybus operator Ecobus was the last to comply, in May 1997.

The Ovidio Lagos UTE joint venture has ended and for the next round of tenders a minimum fleet size of 100 will be necessary.

Trolleybus
Sociedad del Estado Municipal para el Transporte Urbano de Rosario (Semtur)
Avenida Provincias Unidas 2520, Rosario, Argentina
Tel: (+54 341) 459 01 80, 480 76 91, 480 76 98
e-mail: semtur@rosario.gov.ar

Key personnel
President: Clara García

Number of routes: 1
Route length: 12.8 km

Current situation
After refurbishment and extension by about 1 km at each end, Route K reopened in 1994 and has been commercially successful. Its fleet of 20 trolleybuses was built for the system planned in Belo Horizonte, but never used.

Route K was extended westwards by about 500 m to Bulevar Wilde in July 2003.

Developments
In October 2004, the municipal transport authority cancelled private operator Ecobus's concession to operate the trolleybus system and operation has been taken over by the city. Ecobus was only the second private operator to run the system since 1994, but the city's officials had become increasingly dissatisfied with the company's performance, citing, among other reasons, poor vehicle maintenance and financial mismanagement, the latter provoking the company's employees to strike for three days over non-payment of wages.

The city also took legal possession of the fleet of 20 trolleybuses. The depot and all other fixed infrastructure have always been municipally owned. All drivers and maintenance personnel

were hired by the city, to allow the service to continue without interruption.

All 20 trolleybuses were painted in new livery in 2005.

Fleet: 20 trolleybuses
Volvo/Marcopolo/Powertronics (1987/88, but stored unused until 1993/94)   20

Rosario Bus SA
Gral Jose de San Martín 2690, Rosario, Santa Fe, Argentina
Tel: (+54 341) 480 82 35
Fax: (+54 341) 480 82 32
e-mail: info@rosariobus.com.ar
Web: www.rosariobus.com.ar

Passenger journeys: (2007) 151.2 million (estimate)
Vehicle-km: Not available currently

Number of routes: 23 (estimate)
Length of routes: Not available currently

Current situation
The company provides bus services in and around Rosario with an estimated fleet of around 500 vehicles.

Developments
The company is planning to introduce vehicle location, using GPS and the Internet, security technology, such as CCTV, contactless ticketing and more environmentally friendly vehicles.

Fleet: Not available currently
On order: Not available currently
Average age of fleet: 5 years (2005 estimate)
Fare structure: Flat (zonal on interurban routes)
Fare collection: 2- and 6-trip tickets, prepaid paper card with magnetic strip; single ticket by cash from machine

Armenia

Yerevan

Population: 1.1 million (estimate)

Public transport
The majority of public transport services are provided by overcrowded minivans ('marshrutka') and taxis, although there are limited bus and trolleybus services. Tram operations ceased in early 2004, after funds to repair the route and vehicles were not forthcoming. Metro.

Yerevan Metro
76 Marshal Bagramanian Avenue, Yerevan 375033, Armenia
Tel: (+374 2) 27 45 43　Fax: (+374 2) 15 13 95

Key personnel
Chairman: Areg A Barseghyan
Director: Vaagn V Akopyan
　Staff: 1,198

Type of operation: Full metro; initial route opened 1981

Passenger journeys: (2004) 12.1 million

Route length: 12.1 km
Number of lines: 1

Number of stations: 10
Gauge: 1,520 mm
Track: 50 kg/m rail on timber or concrete sleepers
Max gradient: 4%
Minimum curve radius: 250 m
Tunnel: Bored and cut-and-cover
Electrification: 825 V, third rail

Service: Peak 5 min, off-peak 10 min
First/last train: 06.30/23.00
Fare structure: Flat
Fare collection: Manual

Operating costs financed by: Fares and other revenues 45 per cent, government subsidy 55 per cent (2002)

Rolling stock: 13 two-car trains
81-717　　　　　　　　　　　　　　　M26

Current situation
No work is currently being undertaken on the metro. Work on the northwest extension has been suspended.

Developments
There are long-term plans for two more lines.

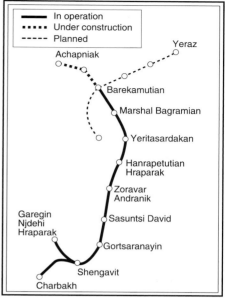
Map of Yerevan metro　　　　　1115281

Australia

Adelaide
Population: City 1.1 million (2001 estimate), urban area 1.2 million (2001 estimate)

Public transport
Bus (including guided busway service), tram and suburban rail services administered by the Department for Transport, Energy and Infrastructure's Public Transport Division (PTD) and operated by state government authority. Private operators, including Torrens Transit, Transitplus and Southlink, operate all of the metropolitan bus services within the Adelaide metropolitan area. TransAdelaide maintains the rail contract for suburban rail which includes train and tram services.

Department for Transport, Energy and Infrastructure (DTEI)
Public Transport Division (PTD)
PO Box 1, Walkerville, South Australia 5081, Australia
Tel: (+61 8) 83 03 08 22　Fax: (+61 8) 83 03 08 28
Web: www.adelaidemetro.com.au
　www.dtup.sa.gov.au

Key personnel
Executive Director: Heather Webster

Current situation
The Public Transport Division (PTD) was established by the state government in May 2005, as part of the Department for Transport, Energy and Infrastructure (DTEI). It replaces the former Passenger Transport Board (PTB). The PTD is responsible for administration and regulation of passenger transport throughout South Australia, including taxis, hire cars, charter bus operators (100 routes) and both country and metropolitan bus, train and tram services. The PTD is charged with the responsibility for overall integration of public transport in terms of services and ticketing. The PTD may not operate services itself.

For the history of the PTB, please see previous editions of *Jane's Urban Transport Systems.*

New FLEXITY *and old H Class trams at Victoria Square terminus in the city centre*　　　1321967

Class 3000 rail car approaching Adelaide Railway station　　　1321966

TransAdelaide

GPO Box 2351, Adelaide, South Australia 5001, Australia
Tel: (+61 8) 82 18 22 00   Fax: (+61 8) 82 18 22 06
e-mail: info@transadelaide.sa.gov.au
Web: www.transadelaide.com.au

Street address

136 North Terrace, Adelaide, South Australia 5001, Australia

Key personnel

General Manager: Bob Stobbe
Executive Manager, Rail Systems: Vacant
Executive Manager, Infrastructure: Vi Nguyen
Executive Manager, Organisational development: Fiona Kidd
Executive Manager, Corporate Services: Shaun Matters
Executive Manager, Planning & Development: Randall Barry
Executive Manager, Trams: James Hall
Marketing & Business Development Manager: Bill Holmes
Security Manager: Harry Carbone
Staff: 560

Passenger journeys: (All modes)
(2005/06) 13.8 million
(2006/07) 13.9 million

Current situation

TransAdelaide is a Government business entity which operates metropolitan passenger rail services (train and tram). The organisation operates approximately 1,500 train services a week and maintains over AUD600 million worth of infrastructure (tracks, stations and train fleet).

TransAdelaide operate metropolitan passenger rail services as a contractor to the Passenger Transport Division (PTD) of the Department of Transport Energy and Infrastructure (DTEI), which promotes the public transport system under the brand of Adelaide Metro.

This year's State Budget announced the biggest single investment in Adelaide's public transport system ever by the South Australian State Government. Rail Revitalisation forms the centrepiece of this AUD2 billion investment and will transform the metropolitan passenger rail network by delivering a number of rail initiatives including:
- Concrete re-sleepering of the metropolitan passenger rail network;
- Electrification of the Noarlunga (including Tonsley), Outer Harbor (including Grange) and Gawler lines;
- Gauge standardisation of the rail network;
- Interchange, station and Park 'n' Ride infrastructure upgrades.

Other elements of the Public Transport Blueprint include:
- Extension of the tram line to the Adelaide Entertainment Centre;
- Construction of new light rail links to West Lakes, Semaphore and Port Adelaide;
- Conversion of existing diesel rail cars to electric;
- Procurement of new electric rail cars, trams and tram-train (dual-voltage) vehicles;
- Introduction of a new integrated ticketing system;
- Procurement of new buses, improved services as well as investigating bus priority options in the city and suburbs.

Revitalisation of the rail network is a large and complex project, which requires a significant amount of detailed planning with many factors to consider such as:
- Developing and assessing options to minimise the disruption to commuters and the surrounding community;
- Analysing options for alternative passenger services during construction;
- The staging of construction works, as well as the complicated technical and engineering aspects.

The recent budget announcement for revitalisation of the public transport network follows the release of the Strategic Infrastructure Plan for South Australia in 2005. This plan provided a long-term, state-wide framework for

the planning and delivery of infrastructure by the government and the private sector.

Tramway

Staff: Not currently available

Type of operation: Conventional tramway

Passenger journeys: (2002/03) 2.07 million
(2003/04) 2.15 million
(2004/05) 2.09 million
(2005/06) 2.07 million
(2006/07) 2.36 million
Car-km: (Annual) 0.8 million

Developments

Following the opening of the tram line extension to City West in October 2007, four new stops have been added to the line; the number of timetabled stops on the line is now 24. There is also one special event stop at the Racecourse at Morphettville.

Significantly, the tram line extension not only links the light rail tram to the heavy rail train network with the tram stop at Adelaide Railway Station, it also provides a platform for the further extension of the tram line planned to the Adelaide Entertainment Centre.

The tram line from City West to Moseley Square is 12.3 km long and the trams are powered by 600 V DC overhead wire.

Rolling stock: 16 cars

Pengelley Class H (1929)	M5
Bombardier *FLEXITY* Classic (2005/06)	M11
In peak service:	10

Route length: 12.3 km
Number of lines: 1
Number of stops: 24
Gauge: Standard
Track: 50 kg/m concrete sleepers on ballast, sleepers on concrete on road areas
Electrification: 600 V DC, overhead

Service: Peak 10 min, off-peak 15 min
First/last car: 05 35/23 50
Fare structure: Metro-ticket

Suburban railway

Staff: Not currently available

Type of operation: Suburban heavy rail

Passenger journeys: (2003/04) 11.19 million
(2003/04) 11.1 million
(2004/05) 11.2 million
(2005/06) 11.7 million
(2006/07) 11.6 million
Train-km: Not currently available

Current situation

Services provided on five suburban rail routes serving 84 stations to termini at Outer Harbor (22 km), Gawler (41 km), Noarlunga (30 km), Grange (13 km) and Belair (22 km), providing 30-minute off-peak/20-minute peak frequency railcar services.

The Passenger Transport Division continues to encourage passengers to purchase tickets 'off-board' from licensed ticket vendors, though onboard ticket vending machines are available. Only seven stations are staffed.

For further information, please see *Jane's World Railways.*

Developments

Major works on the Bakewell Underpass have had an impact on rail patronage figures, being a significant contributor to the small decrease in patronage as opposed to the previous year's increase. Nonetheless, it is understood that such infrastructure work is absolutely necessary for transport needs. The next four years will also prove challenging with the concrete re-sleepering of the Belair and Noarlunga lines, but the benefits are anticipated to be worth the short-term disruption. When completed, the new rail will not only provide a smoother ride but

will enable TransAdelaide to achieve improved on-time running.

Rolling stock: 99 railcars

2000 class	M11
2100 class	M18
3000 class	M30
3100 class	M40
In peak service: 93	

Fare evasion control: Passenger service assistants on duty during operating hours and security staff after 19:00

Torrens Transit

Mile End Depot
PO Box 331, Marleston, South Australia 5033, Australia
Tel: (+61 8) 82 92 81 00
Fax: (+61 8) 82 92 81 55
e-mail: mileend@torrenstransit.co.au
Web: www.torrenstransit.com.au

Street address

71 Richmond Road (off Railway Terrace), Mile End, South Australia 5031, Australia

Key personnel

Contact: Doug Lamont
  Staff: 700+

Number of routes: 145+

Background

Torrens Transit, a member of the Transit Systems Australia group, commenced operations in the Adelaide metropolitan area on 23 April 2000.

Current situation

The company provides services from Modbury in the north to Glenelg in the south and from Aludana in the east to the Lefevre Peninsula in the west, and also operates the Circle Line and the Adelaide Free service.

The company is certified to ISO 9001:2000 standards.

Depots, including maintenance facilities, are located at Mile End, Camden Park, Newton, Port Adelaide, Hendon, Morphettville, St Agnes and Edinburgh.

In June 2002, a Torrens Transit MAN bus began on-road trials using biodiesel fuel produced from canola oil.

Developments

In April 2005, the company gained new contract areas, North South from Gepps Cross to Happy Valley and Outer North East from Klemzig to Golden Grove (O-Bahn).

Fleet: 660 vehicles

MAN SL200	72
MAN SL202 CNG	40
MAN SL202 diesel	4
MAN NL202 diesel	408
MAN NL202G CNG	24
MAN SG280	17
MAN NL202G (Adelaide Free)	11
Dennis Dart SLF single-door	2
MAN 11.190	34
MAN NL232 CNG	27
MAN 18-280	15
Scania Combo articulated L94A6X212	6

Adelaide O-Bahn

Passenger journeys: In excess of 7 million annually

Current situation

The guided bus O-Bahn provides high-speed (100 km/h) service on the 12 km corridor from Modbury in the northeastern suburbs to Gilberton just outside Adelaide's central business district. See *Jane's Urban Transport Systems 1988* for history and description. In total, 113 Mercedes-Benz buses (standard and articulated) are equipped with lateral guidewheels for busway operations.

SouthLink

PO Box 165, 21 Krawarri Street, Lonsdale, South
Australia 5160, Australia
Tel: (+61 8) 81 86 28 88
Fax: (+61 8) 81 86 29 99
e-mail: info@southlink.com.au
Web: www.southlink.com.au

Key personnel
Managing Director: Ashley Barnes

Background
A subsidiary of the Australian Transit Enterprises
group of companies, the company was
established in 2000.

Current situation
The company operates bus services in the
southern suburbs of the metropolitan area of
Adelaide on more than 70 routes.

Including the new operations in the north
of the city, the company provides services to
Smithfield, Elizabeth, Salisbury, Mawson Lakes,
Marion, Hallett Cove, Woodcroft, Noarlunga
Centre, Aldinga and Sellicks Beach.

Developments
SouthLink won a five year contract to operate
Adelaide metro bus services in the outer north
area of Adelaide, which was previously operated
by Serco. SouthLink commenced these new
operations in April 2005.

Transitplus

PO Box 227, Aldgate, South Australia 5154,
Australia
Tel: (+61 8) 83 39 75 44   Fax: (+61 8) 83 39 76 11
e-mail: info@transitplus.com.au
Web: www.transitplus.com.au

Key personnel
General Manager: Mark Dunlop
Business Manager: Grant Elsworthy

Current situation
Transitplus, a joint venture between
TransAdelaide and Australian Transit Enterprises
Pty Ltd (ATE), was formed in 2000 and won a
contract to operate Metroticket Bus Services in
the Adelaide Hills area.

Fleet: The fleet includes: MAN SG280 articulated,
Scania L94UB, Scania L94UB6X2, Scania
L94UA6X2/2, Scania L94UB4X2, Volvo B 10M,
Volvo B 10M Fuji articulated and Mitsubishi Rosa.

Brisbane

Population: 751,000, metropolitan area 1.78 million
(2004 estimated)

Public transport
Bus and ferry services provided by municipal
undertaking, with all ferry and some bus services
operated under contract. Suburban trains by
Queensland Rail. Some suburbs served exclusively
by private bus and ferry operators. Heavy rail link
to airport from city and some suburbs.

Brisbane Transport
Brisbane City Council
GPO Box 1434, Brisbane, Queensland 4001,
Australia
Tel: (+61 7) 34 03 88 88   Fax: (+61 7) 34 03 69 05
Web: www.brisbane.qld.gov.au;
　　　www.translink.com.au

Key personnel
Bus Operations
Divisional Manager: Alan Warren
Financial Manager: Roger Wimsett
Bus Operations Manager: Alan Geyer
Network Operations Manager: Sherry Clarke
Major Projects Manager: Peter King
Quality, Risk & Systems Manager: Craig Evans
Human Resource Manager: Greg Newman
Operations Support Manager: Paul Chicoteau
Workshops Manager: Martin Peake
Network Scheduling Manager: Roman Gafa
Network Planning Manager: Brian Bothwell
Staff: Not currently available

Ferry Operations
Manager, Transport & Traffic: Brendan Sowry
Principal Public Transport: Gail Davies
*Senior Co-ordinator, City Cat & River Ferry
　Operations:* Gaylene Vivian
　Staff: Not currently available

Background
Brisbane Transport is a business unit of Brisbane
City Council.

Current situation
Brisbane Transport provides bus services in
Brisbane and the surrounding areas. Brisbane
City Council – Transport and Traffic provides ferry
services from the suburbs along the Brisbane
River.

Developments
Brisbane Transport has experienced record
patronage growth of over 273 per cent in the last
three financial years.
　The public have been provided with a more
seamless transport system with integrated
ticketing available on bus, rail and ferry services,
throughout south east Queensland.
　TransLink Transport Authority is the Queensland
State Government entity responsible for

integrating and managing the major transport
operators into one network, covering south
east Queensland from Gympie North/Noosa to
Coolangatta and west to Helidon.
　TransLink's contact details are as follows:
　GPO Box 50, Brisbane, Queensland 4001,
Australia
　Tel: (+61 7) 13 12 30
　Web: www.translink.com.au
　Under integrated ticketing stage two, a 'Go
Card' smartcard has been introduced which
allows full integration of public transport services
throughout South-East Queensland.

Bus
Passenger journeys: (2003/04) 48.1 million
(2004/05) 53.1 million
(2005/06) 59.8 million
(2006/07) 63.5 million
(2007/08) 67.6 million
Vehicle-km: (2003/04) 42.1 million
(2004/05) 44.9 million
(2005/06) 47.1 million
(2006/07) 50.0 million
(2007/08) 53.6 million

Number of Network routes: 231
Route length: 3,861 km

Number of School routes: 206
Route length: 2,762 km

Current situation
The Loop
The Loop is a free, council bus service that circles
Brisbane's central business district. The Loop
stops at several destinations including Central

Station, Queen Street Mall, City Botanic Gardens,
Riverside Centre, QUT and King George Square.
　The service regularly carries 23,000 passengers
per week.
　Planning is underway to extend the service,
by providing a second, free loop service to cater
for patrons accessing hospitals and medical
specialists in the Spring Hill area. This service
was expected to commence in late October
2008.

Developments
Brisbane Transport Bus Build workshop currently
has a contract with Volgren Australia to build
MAN gas-powered buses. This contract provides
for 180 buses over three years commencing
in the 2005/06 fiscal year. A further contract
provides for 125 rigid equivalent buses to be
delivered in 2008/09.
　In October 2008, Brisbane City Council
announced the formation of a commercial
partnership with Volgren Australia to build a
minimum of 60 buses per year over the next
10 years. A 'state of the art' facility is to be
developed in the new industrial precinct of Eagle
Farm in Brisbane, and will have a build capacity
of 150 buses per annum.
　In March 2006, the Toowong Bus Depot
Compressed Natural Gas (CNG) facility was
opened. This now brings the total number of
depot sites fitted with CNG filling stations to
three. As at June 2008, CNG gas buses represent
50 per cent of the total fleet. As more gas buses
are delivered in 2008/09, the gas bus fleet
percentage will increase. Depots fitted with CNG
filling stations still retain a small diesel fleet.
Construction of the new Willawong Depot in the

A section of the South East Busway, running over Victoria Bridge (Mary Webb)　　　0585180

southwest of Brisbane is well under way, with completion expected by March/April 2009. When completed, the depot will be the fourth with CNG refuelling. The depot capacity will be 200 buses, with the majority of these being CNG.

Bus Upgrade Zones (BUZ)
The Bus Upgrade Zone (BUZ) programme is a multi-million dollar investment that is making bus travel around Brisbane easier. The BUZ programme is delivering high-frequency, 'no timetable needed' services along the major transport corridors across the city. They operate 18 hours per day, seven days per week, every 5–10 minutes during peak hours and every 10–15 minutes off-peak. These services have more than doubled off-peak patronage.

Since January 2004, nine BUZ routes have been introduced: Route 111 (Eight Mile Plains), Route 130 (Parkinson), Route 150 (Browns Plains), Route 199 (New Farm – West End), Route 200 (Carindale), Route 333 (Chermside), Route 345 (Aspley), Route 385 (The Gap) and Route 444 (Moggill).

Fleet: 926 vehicles (includes contractor South Western, but excludes Hornibrook 11 leased buses)

Scania U94LB gas	216
MAN 18310 gas	212
MAN 18310 diesel	15
MAN A24 313F gas articulated	29
MAN SL200	22
Volvo B10M	319 (excludes Hornibrook 11 leased buses)
Volvo B10L	59
Mercedes-Benz 500LE	40
Volvo B6BLE	2
Volvo/Volgren B10M articulated	12

In peak service: 828 (includes contractors)

Most intensive service: 5–10 mins during peak and 10–15 mins off peak on BUZ, Busway routes 111 and 160 services
One-person operation: All routes
Fare collection: Payment on boarding (change given), prepurchase or multi-trip tickets, which are being phased out by 31 December 2008
Fare structure: Zonal (5 zones); 50 per cent discount for children, seniors and pensioners; bus/rail day ticket
Fares collected on board: 27 per cent
Fare evasion control: Random inspection and driver control; spot fines
Integration with other modes: Integration with other bus, rail and ferry services controlled by TransLink
Operational control: By Network co-ordination and depot staff
Average distance between stops: 250–300 m (more than 1 km on Cityxpress/Great Circle routes)
Average peak-hour speed: 16 km/h (50 km/h on Busway services)
Bus priority: Two dedicated Busway Ways 16 km (South East) and 5 km (Inner North) in length. A 2 km section under the City Centre opened in May 2008, linking two new bus stations at Roma Street and King George Square. The Eleanor Schonell Bridge (previously known as the Green Bridge) (bus/cycle/pedestrian) over Brisbane River at the University of Queensland opened in December 2006. A 2-km Busway linking this bridge with the main Busway network is currently nearing completion, and work has commenced on the Northern Busway.
Operating costs financed by: TransLink contract fee, Council CSO and other commercial sources
Subsidy from: Council pays a Community Service Obligation (CSO) of approximately 26 per cent of total operating costs
New vehicles financed by: Loans and funding through Queensland Treasury Corporation and Queensland Government and self-funding through council sinking fund

Ferry
There are three river transport services operated by Brisbane City Council, the Inner City and Cross River (both monohull ferry) services and CityCat.

One of Brisbane's CityCat ferries, an important part of the city's commuter services   1326683

One of Brisbane's monohull ferries   1326682

Passenger journeys: (2003/04) 3.7 million
(2004/05) 5.0 million
(2005/06) 5.7 million
(2006/07) 6.0 million
(2007/08) 6.1 million

Ferry fleet: 21

Operating hours: (2003/04) 73,338
(2004/05) 74,489
(2005/06) 79,690
(2006/07) 84,037
(2007/08) 92,227 (estimated)

QR Citytrain
GPO Box 1429, Brisbane, Queensland 4001, Australia
Tel: (+61 7) 32 35 22 22 (general enquiries); 32 35 31 59
Fax: (+61 7) 32 35 12 95
e-mail: webmaster@qr.com.au
Web: www.citytrain.com.au; www.qr.com.au

Street address
305 Edward Street, Brisbane, Queensland 4000, Australia

Key personnel
Group General Manager, Passenger Services: Michael Scanlan

Type of operation: Suburban and interurban heavy rail

Passenger journeys: (2000/01) 44.7 million
(2001/02) 45.4 million
(2002/03) 46.2 million
(2003/04) 48.1 million
(2004/05) 48.6 million (estimate, as Translink now has an integrated ticketing system)
(2005/06) 53.1 million (estimate, as Translink now has an integrated ticketing system)

Route-km: Suburban: 208.8 km; interurban: 186.8 km

Background
QR is a government-owned corporation established under the state Queensland Transport Infrastructure Act. All shares are held on behalf of the state by the State Treasurer and the Minister for Transport and Main Roads. A nine-member government-appointed board guides the management team.

Current situation
Suburban/interurban services are provided over a network of 395 km on seven routes with 143 stations, electrified at 25 kV 50 Hz, with a 1,067 mm gauge. Trains run every 10 to 15 minutes at peak times or every 15 to 30 minutes off-peak; zonal fares.

The ticketing system has been taken over by Translink, a Division of Queensland Transport.

The system is zonal and is integrated between Citytrain rail service and bus services provided by a number of bus operators throughout South East Queensland. At present, the system is paper-based, with a Smartcard system being developed.

For further information on QR, please see *Jane's World Railways.*

Developments
A major system expansion and upgrade programme is currently under way. This is a long-term programme, which will deliver increased capacity on a number of lines, additional rolling stock, upgraded stations (including access for the disabled), upgraded intermodal facilities and improved safety and security. The programme will also provide system expansion with several rail line extensions proposed.

Rolling stock: 449 cars

Three-car suburban emus (EMU)	87
Three-car interurban emus (IMU)	14
Two-car InterCity Express (ICE) units	8 plus 4 trailers
Three-car suburban emus (SMU)	42

In peak service: 95 per cent

Brisbane
Type of operation: Private bus

Current situation
Private bus lines provide services in the metropolitan area, mostly to the suburbs. Some of these, including Hornibrook Bus Lines (www.hornibrook.com.au), Kangaroo Bus Lines (www.kangaroobuslines.com.au) and National Bus Company (www.natbusqld.com.au), are business partners in the TransLink integrated smartcard system (see entry for Brisbane Transport). Responsibility of State Department of Transport, which also supervises some longer-distance ferry operations.

Airtrain Citylink Limited – Brisbane Airtrain
PO Box 66, Pinkenba, Brisbane, Queensland 4008, Australia
Tel: (+61 7) 32 16 33 08
Fax: (+61 7) 32 16 33 61
e-mail: info@airtrain.com.au
Web: www.airtrain.com.au

Key personnel
General Manager: Chris Basche

QR service and South East Busway interchange at South Bank station (Mary Webb)   0585182

QR Citytrain units, Brisbane   1143177

Sales Manager: Alison Lake
Passenger journeys: (2004/05) 1.12 million

Background
Airtrain is owned and operated by Airtrain Citylink Limited, a private company, without government subsidy.

Current situation
Airtrain commenced operations in mid-2001, using QR trains, and is totally integrated with the QR station network.

The system is neither a monorail nor a light rail system – 8.5 km of conventional heavy rail elevated track was constructed for the services. City bound services run from the airport approximately every 15 minutes during peak hours to five stations. A separate service, the Gold Coast/Robina service, leaves from the airport approximately every 30 minutes and stops at South Brisbane and South Bank stations. Tickets can be purchased at stations.

For further information, please see *Jane's World Railways.*

Canberra
Population: 332,500 (2006 estimate)

Public transport
Bus services provided by state-controlled organisation, with some independent operations.

Australian Capital Territory Internal Omnibus Network (ACTION Buses)
Department of Territory and Municipal Services
GPO Box 158, Canberra ACT 2601, Australia
Tel: (+61 2) 62 07 80 00
Fax: (+61 2) 62 07 80 80
e-mail: action@act.gov.au
Web: www.action.act.gov.au

Street address
12 Wattle Street, Lyneham 2602, Australian Capital Territory, Australia

Key personnel
General Manager: Tom Elliot
  Staff: 700

Background
ACTION Buses provides public passenger transport services to the ACT. It provides scheduled route, school and special needs transport services.

Current situation
ACTION's operating environment is unusual in that Canberra has the highest average income and single- and two-car ownership in Australia, and a very large 'Y'-shaped geographical area with minimal traffic congestion, abundant, relatively cheap car parking and low-density housing. ACTION's challenge is to provide public transport travel times that are competitive with travel by car and at a cost less than pay car parking.

To meet this challenge, ACTION has 700 staff, two depots, a corporate office and four interchanges to provide more than 2,500 services a day. ACTION has a fleet of 379 route buses, including 106 easy-access buses, and 18 minibuses that are used for special needs transport.

Developments
Supporting the Canberra Plan is the ACT government's Sustainable Transport Plan (STP),

which was released in April 2004. The Sustainable Transport Plan reflects the ACT government's commitment to achieving a sustainable transport system for the ACT over 25 years. ACTION Authority is a major participant in the plan, with its share of public transport (defined as adult journey-to-work trips) targeted to increase from 6.7 per cent in 2002 to 16 per cent in 2026. The first key milestone has been set for 2011, with a target of nine per cent. ACTION Buses is on track to meet this target.

In 2001/02, the ACT government allocated AUD17.2 million over five years for the acquisition of 42 new CNG buses. In 2005/06, the remaining nine buses of the 2001/02 funding were delivered. In addition, in the 2005/06 Budget, the ACT government has provided to ACTION AUD4.84 million to purchase 11 additional buses, bringing the total to 63 buses.

Express services
In September 2004, ACTION introduced substantial new express route peak-hour services, called *Xpresso*. *Xpresso* services provide ACTION's customers with reduced travel times, services that are more direct to work, multiple

ACTION easy access bus with extendable ramp

1172297

ACTION Scania L94UB CB60 low-floor CNG bus

1172296

departures on each route and a wider choice of services from the outer areas of Canberra.

flexibus

Demand responsive evening services, branded as *flexibus* were introduced in April 2005. *flexibus* was designed to complement the ACT government's Sustainable Transport Plan, to combat low patronage on evening services and create a more efficient and responsive service for customers. Eight main bus routes have been retained in the evening; all other evening bus routes now provide an 'on demand and flexible' customer responsive service. Customers are dropped off closer to their destination. This is a variation from the traditional services provided by a fixed bus route. For travel departing from any point other than a bus interchange, where buses still depart to a public timetable, customers are able to book their pick-up at their closest bus stop by phoning ACTION's Customer Service Centre. A trial of evening *flexibus* services, which provides a door-to-door service to two suburbs, Kambah and Gungahlin, in ACTION's smaller wheelchair-accessible minibuses, also commenced in April 2005.

Bus

Passenger boardings: (Annual) 17.0 million (estimate)
Vehicle-km: (Annual) 23.4 million (estimate)

Number of routes: 114
Route length: Not currently available

Fleet: 379 vehicles

Irisbus Agoraline CB60 low-floor diesel (2002/03)	20
Scania L94UB CB60 low-floor CNG (2004/06)	64
Dennis Dart SLF diesel midibus (1997)	25
Renault PR180.2 MkI articulated (1987/89)	27
Renault PR180.2 MkII articulated (1993)	7
Renault PR100.2 MkI (1987/90)	109
Renault PR100.2 MkII (1990/93)	113
Renault PR100.3 diesel (1993/96, 1994, 1995)	33
Renault PR100.3 NGV (1993/94)	2
Renault PR100.3A diesel (easy access) (1994/96)	7
Hino AC 140 (1987/89)	14
Mitsubishi Rosa (2004)	4

In peak service: Not currently available

Most intensive service: 4–7 min, intertown express
One-person operation: All routes
Fare collection: Cash to driver, or prepurchase magnetic tickets via ACTION ticket agents or online
Fare structure: Flat fare on boarding for cash payers; pre-purchase 10 single-ride, daily, weekly and monthly magnetic tickets; shoppers off-peak daily ticket; reduced fares for students; free travel for children under five years and not attending school; transfer option available at no extra charge on some tickets
Fares collected on board: 20 per cent
Operational control: Route and ticket inspectors; two-way radio; movements monitored through all interchanges

Arrangements for elderly/disabled: Concession fares with reimbursement provided by ACT government. New buses built to low-floor design with ramp and carefully placed handrails for ease of entry and exit; bell push-buttons placed low down; raised bay numerals at interchanges assist blind people; reserved bus seating identified by upholstery colour.

ACTION's bus fleet includes more than 106 easy access wheelchair-accessible buses for people with reduced mobility. 'Easy access' means there are no steps, so getting into and out of the bus is easier and safer for customers. Each of these buses is equipped with an extendable ramp, a wide front entrance, and space in the bus to accommodate wheelchairs or prams. All Intertown buses (300 series), Routes 34 (seven days a week) and 84 (Monday to Friday) are serviced by easy access buses.
Average distance between stops: 300 m
Average peak-hour speed: Local feeder buses 30 km/h, express 35 km/h
Bus priority: All interchanges are bus-only areas; 13.7 km of bus-only lanes on arterial roads; priority sections of road and/or priority traffic signals at some intersections; additional bus-only lanes planned
Subsidy from: ACT government
New vehicles financed by: Grant and loan funding

Hobart

Population: 202,200 (2004 estimate)

Public transport

Bus services are provided by a state government business enterprise. Private operators run services to some suburbs.

Metro Tasmania Pty Ltd – Metro

PO Box 61, 212 Main Road, Moonah 7009, Tasmania, Australia
Tel: (+61 3) 62 33 42 32   Fax: (+61 3) 62 72 87 70
e-mail: correspondence@metrotas.com.au
Web: www.metrotas.com.au

Key personnel

Chief Executive Officer: Tony Sim
Manager, Strategic Planning: Peter Kruup
Manager, Business Development: Nicole Brigg
   Staff: 451

Background

Metro Tasmania Pty Ltd is a state-owned company established in February 1998. The company trades as Metro and operates bus services in Hobart, Launceston and Burnie. Metro is the largest passenger transport company in Tasmania.

Current situation

In the last decade, the composition of the Metro fleet has changed so that there are now buses with varying passenger capacities. The four main buses are standard rigid buses (about 42 seats), articulated buses (about 70 seats), long rigid buses (14.5 m – 55 seats) and midibuses (29 seats). The range of bus sizes enables Metro to better match buses with demand compared to a fleet containing buses of only one size.

Hobart

Metro currently operates some 1,580 scheduled trips in Hobart per day, including Express and dedicated school services. In general, operation

on these routes Monday to Thursday commences after 6.30 am and finishes by 10.30 pm. An additional 95 services run later on Fridays to around midnight. On Saturdays, services commence operation at around 7.30 am. Most routes cease operating by 12.10 am. On some routes, Sunday and public holiday services are not provided whilst on others, services start at 9.00 am or later and finish by 8.00 pm.

Launceston

In Launceston, Metro operates some 600 scheduled trips per day as well as dedicated school services. In general, operation on these routes Monday to Friday commences after 7.00 am and finishes by 10.00 pm. On Saturdays, services travelling inward commence operation at around 8.30 am (outward at around 9.00 am). Most routes cease operating by 10.00 pm. On some routes, Sunday and public holiday services are not provided while on others, services start at 10.00 am or later and finish by 17:30.

Burnie

In Burnie and its surrounding area, including Wynyard and Ulverstone, Metro operates some 140 scheduled trips per day. These generally operate between the hours of 07.30 and 18.00 on weekdays and between 09.00 and 17.00 on Saturdays.

Developments

In September 2007, Metro increased the number of services to Southern Suburbs of Kingston and Blackmans Bay. A new combined route, known as the Southern Connector, was introduced and services the University of Tasmania and major southern shopping centres and suburbs.

In November 2007, all services were changed in Launceston on new routes and timetables. The alterations featured significantly improved weekend services on core routes, as well as the reintroduction of night services to most suburbs from Monday to Saturday.

Bus

Passenger journeys: (2003/04) 9.6 million
(2004/05) 9.7 million
(2005/06) 9.9 million
(2006/07) 9.9 million
Vehicle-km: (2003/04) 10.2 million
(2004/05) 10.5 million
(2005/06) 9.9 million
(2006/07) 10.0 million

Number of routes: 275
Route length: (One way) 360 km

Fleet: 211 vehicles
MAN midibuses	20
Scania 14.5 m	3
Scania standard accessible buses	39
Scania standard buses	130
Volvo articulated	19

In peak service: 188
Average age of fleet: 11.9 years

Most intensive service: 5 min
One-person operation: All routes
Fare collection: Payment to driver for single and daily multitrip tickets; prepurchase 10-trip, 10-day and monthly tickets
Fare structure: Sections; 20 per cent discount for prepurchase multitickets; flat fare for children and concession travellers
Fares collected on board: 46 per cent
Fare evasion control: Electronic warning on ticket validator; inspectors
Operational control: Supervisors/mobile radio
Arrangements for elderly/disabled: All buses have kneeling capability, accessible buses are being introduced progressively
Average peak-hour speed: 23.2 km/h
Average distance between stops: 400 m

Scania 12.5 m accessible bus in central Burnie, undertaking a Saturday service, following the reintroduction of Saturday services after a 15-year gap, when no services operated   1310670

Operating costs financed by: Fares 26 per cent, other commercial sources five per cent, government contract payment 69 per cent
Subsidy from: No subsidy. Government contracts for services under a net contract
New vehicles financed by: Own resources

The above statistics relate to the metropolitan areas of Hobart, Launceston and Burnie and include the regional towns of Ulverstone and Wynyard.

Hobart
Other operators
Current situation

Two private operators are licensed to provide service within Metro's operating area: Tasmanian Redline Coaches and Tassielink Coaches. There is no common ticketing with Metro.

Redline Coaches

199 Collins Street, Hobart 7000, Tasmania
Tel: (+61 3) 63 36 14 46
e-mail: redline@tasredline.com.au
Web: www.redlinecoaches.com.au

Current situation
Tasmanian Redline Coaches operates two routes providing service within Metro's operating area.

Tigerline Travel Tasmania – Tassielink Coaches

Hobart Bus Terminal, 64 Brisbane Street, Hobart 7000, Tasmania
Tel: (+61 3) 62 30 89 00   Fax: (+61 3) 62 31 60 90
e-mail: info@tassielink.com.au
Web: www.tassielink.com.au

Key personnel
Key personnel details have been removed at the company's request. The main contacts are the customer service consultants at the telephone and e-mail details given above.

Background
In 1997, the company purchased and amalgamated TRC Travel and TigerLine Coaches with Tasmanian Wilderness Travel. In 1999, the Port Arthur, West Coast, East Coast and Huon Services were added from Hobart Coaches. Later acquisitions include the service between Cressy, Longford and Launceston (October 2005).

Current situation
In 2006, Tigerline Coaches and Tassielink Coaches merged their fleets and now operate as Tassielink Coaches.

Tassielink Coaches provide regular passenger services to Huon Valley-Richmond, Campania-Swansea, East Coast-Hobart, Launceston, Devonport-West Coast, including connections to the Overland Track-Cressy, Longford-Port Arthur.

Melbourne
Population: 3.7 million (estimate)

Public transport
All bus, tram, light and heavy rail services in the metropolitan area are administered by the Department of Infrastructure's (DOI) Public Transport Division and operated by contracted transport operators.

A new integrated smartcard ticketing system for public transport in Victoria is currently being developed, 'Myki' (www.myki.com.au), with a pilot scheduled for 2007 and roll-out continuing into 2008.

Department of Infrastructure (DOI)
Public Transport Division
GPO Box 2797, Melbourne, Victoria 3001, Australia
Tel: (+61 3) 96 55 33 33   Fax: (+61 3) 96 55 64 26

e-mail: DOI-ODCS-PA-Internet_Mail_Database-Transport@doi.vic.gov.au
Web: www.doi.vic.gov.au

Key personnel
Minister for Transport: Peter Batchelor
Director of Public Transport: Jim Betts

Background
The Public Transport Division was established in 1998 (as the Office of the Director of Public Transport) as the Victoria government agency responsible for public transport services. It has assumed the planning and performance management functions from the former Public Transport Corporation. Contracted transport operators are now responsible for the delivery of public transport services and the Division has a contract management role and liaises closely with public transport operators, local government and other state government agencies to ensure that Victoria has an efficient, reliable and integrated transport system that meets the needs of everyone in the community.

Current situation
The Division's functions include ensuring that accessible transport is available for those who need it, contract management, performance monitoring, planning for future transport needs, the safety of passengers on the transport network, transport for special events, regulation of taxis, and the co-ordination of Victoria's ticketing systems and fare structures.

Transport Ticketing Authority (TTA)
PO Box 18023, Collins Street East, Melbourne, Victoria 8003, Australia
Tel: (+61 3) 96 51 81 11   Fax: (+61 3) 96 51 75 78
e-mail: smartcard@doi.vic.gov.au

Street address
Level 38 55 Collins Street, Melbourne, Victoria 3000, Australia

Key personnel
Chief Executive: Vivian Miners

Background
The Transport Ticketing Authority (TTA) was established in June 2003 as a state body with a dual role; to oversee Victoria's current public transport ticketing system contract and to procure and manage the new ticketing solution for Victoria.

Developments
In mid-2005, Kamco, an international consortium with its headquarters based in Melbourne, was selected to work with the Transport Ticketing Authority (TTA) to provide Victoria's next generation of public transport ticketing. The contract was valued at AUD494 million and the smartcard system is scheduled to begin to be rolled out in 2007.

National Bus Company Pty Ltd (NBC)
PO Box 387, Clifton Hill, Victoria 3068, Australia
Tel: (+61 3) 94 88 21 00   Fax: (+61 3) 94 82 25 59
e-mail: reception@natbusco.com.au
Web: www.nationalbus.com.au

Current situation
National Bus Company commenced operating in 1993, having been selected as the Victoria government's first privatisation franchise public transport provider. It operates 44 public transport routes in Melbourne with a fleet of more than 260 buses, including 84 low-floor wheelchair-accessible buses.

Yarra Trams
Head Office
GPO Box 5231, Melbourne, Victoria 3001, Australia
Tel: (+61 3) 96 19 32 00   Fax: (+61 3) 96 19 32 17
Freephone: (1 800) 80 01 66 (Australia only)
Web: www.yarratrams.com.au

Street address
Level 23, 500 Collins Street, Melbourne, Victoria 3000, Australia

Key personnel
Chief Executive Officer: Dennis Cliche
Chief Financial Officer: Raymond O'Flaherty
Director, Operations: Paulo Correa
Manager, Rail Safety: Trent Wavish
Manager, Human Resources: Des Davies
Manager, Marketing and Metlink Relations: Paul Matthews
Manager, Technical Services: Rod Beet
Manager, Network Strategy and Development: Andy Wood
Manager, Operations: Dennis Griffiths
Manager, Customer Service: Trevor Greer
Manager, Corporate Affairs: Florence Forzy-Raffard
Manager, Information Technology: Andre Socha
Staff: 1,800

Type of operation: Tram

Passenger journeys: (2005) 145 million
(2006) 150 million
(2007) 155 million
Vehicle-km: (2006) 26 million
(2007) 22.5 million

Number of routes: 27
Route length: 249 km (double-track)
Number of stops: 1,806, including 289 platform tram stops

Background
Yarra Trams is owned and operated by the Metrolink Victoria Pty Ltd, a joint-venture partnership. Metrolink is made up of engineering and infrastructure company Transfield Pty Ltd, Australia and Transdev, France, which is a private tram operator and one of France's largest

public transport operators. Transfield provides operations, maintenance asset and project management services to a range of industries such as mining, roads, rail and public transport, water, power, telecommunications, facilities management and defence. Transdev specialises in the development and operation of mass transit systems, including bus, metro/underground, light rail and modern tramway networks.

Current situation
Yarra Trams has been operating the entire tram network since 2004. The current franchise agreement with the Government of Victoria will expire in November 2009.

The trams operate in and around Melbourne between 5 am and 1 am Mondays to Thursdays. In 2006, late-night services were introduced on Fridays and Saturdays. Yarra Trams operates from eight tram depots (Brunswick, Camberwell, East Preston, Essendon, Glenhuntly, Kew, Malvern and Southbank).

Yarra Trams also operates a free service for tourists, the City Circle tram.

Developments
Think Tram Program
The Think Tram Program is a Government of Victoria initiative to improve tram travel times, reliability and safety along the busiest parts of Melbourne's tram network. As part of the programme, a range of road-based improvements such as tram stop upgrades, right turn bans and traffic light sequence changes have been implemented.

Accessible Tram Stop Program
The Accessible Tram Stop Program is a Government of Victoria programme committed to making public transport more accessible and aims to construct 180 additional accessible tram stops across Melbourne's tram network. Yarra Trams is responsible for managing the development and delivery of the programme.

St Kilda Road Project
A strategy is being implemented to improve tram infrastructure on St Kilda Road, the busiest and most important section of Melbourne's tram network. The nine routes that travel along St Kilda Road carry almost one third of all tram patrons. The upgrade will address the current operational issues and will meet the objective of providing a safe, modern and reliable tram service while enhancing the streetscape of the Melbourne Boulevard. The project is being implemented in stages. The first stage, near the Arts Centre, included tram stop and track upgrade and was completed in June 2008.

Fleet: 499 trams

A-class	70
B-class	132
C-class low-floor Citadis	36
D-class three-section low-floor Combino	38
D-class five-section low-floor Combino	21
C2-class five-section low-floor Citadis (leased)	5 (by the end of 2008)
W-class heritage trams	52
Z-class	145

Fares structure: Coin-only ticket machines on board sell 2-hour, daily, City Saver and 60 plus Metcards for zones 1 and 2; onboard validation; discounted prepurchase
Fare evasion control: More than 250 staff patrol trams
Integration with other modes: The Metcard can be used on any tram, train or bus within the metropolitan area
Average speed: 16 km/h (11 km/h within the CBD)

Veolia Transport Australia (VTA)
Connex Melbourne
GPO Box 5092BB, Melbourne, Victoria 3001, Australia
Tel: (+61 3) 96 10 24 00
Fax: (+61 3) 96 10 26 00
e-mail: info@veoliatransport.com.au
Web: www.veoliatransport.com.au
www.connexmelbourne.com.au

Key personnel
Chief Executive Officer: Bruce Hughes
Chief Operating Officer: Mark Paterson
Staff: In excess of 3,000 (including maintenance staff)

Type of operation: Heavy rail

Passenger journeys: (2003/04) 133 million
(2004/05) 135 million
(2005/06) 163 million
(2006/07) 187.4 million
Train-km: (2006/07) 32.5 million

Current situation
Connex operates services on 15 electrified lines with a total length of 372 km (excluding the Stony Point service) with 211 stations. These are radial in nature and extend from the city centre to Melbourne's eastern, northeastern, southeastern, bayside, northern and western suburbs. Trains also operate to Melbourne's Showgrounds and Flemington racecourse when required. Connex also operates a diesel-hauled service between Frankston and Stony Point.

From mid-October 2006, Connex Melbourne is operating 1,877 services on Mondays–Thursdays, 1,879 services on Fridays, 1,472 on Saturdays and 1,172 on Sundays.

More than 25,000 free parking spaces are provided at stations.

For further information, please see *Jane's World Railways*.

Connex Melbourne Comeng three-car train　　　　　1194946

Developments
In February 2004, the government awarded Connex the franchise to operate the entire Melbourne train network for at least the following five years and the company became sole operator of the network on 18 April 2004. The contract provides for a government subsidy.

Connex and the State Government have announced a three-stage timetable and operating improvement programme. The first stage, which will introduce 105 new services a week, was scheduled to start in late April 2008,

focusing on creating additional capacity for the evening peak period as well as the running of six-carriage trains until at least 19.00 on all lines (except the Williamstown and Alamein shuttles, which will still operate in three-car configuration between the peak hours and after about 18.00) to create more space for customers. It will also see an upgraded train and a completely revamped timetable for the Stony Point line.

The second stage is due to commence in November 2008, which will change the way train services use the city loop.

The third stage will see further timetable changes and improvements in early 2009 to enhance frequency between the peak periods and to enable the arrival of new trains from late 2009.

Rolling stock: 331 three-car units

Comeng three-car sets (refurbished)	187
ALSTOM X'Trapolis three-car emu	58
Siemens three-car emu	72
Hitachi	14

Perth

Population: 1.51 million (2006 estimated)

Public transport
Bus, suburban rail and ferry services in Perth's metropolitan area are provided by private (bus and ferry) and public (suburban rail) operators, co-ordinated and monitored by the Public Transport Authority (PTA), a statutory authority of the state government. The PTA was established in July 2004 to administer all public transport within Western Australia.

Transperth
Level 1, Public Transport Centre, West Parade, Perth, Western Australia 6000, Australia
Tel: (+61 8) 93 26 22 77 Fax: (+61 8) 93 26 24 87
e-mail: enquire@pta.wa.gov.au
Web: www.pta.wa.gov.au

Key personnel
Chief Executive Officer, PTA: Reece Waldock
Executive Director, Finance and Contracts, PTA: Peter King
Director, Transperth: Mark Burgess
General Manager, Transperth Train Operations: Pat Italiano
Manager, Corporate Communications, PTA: Richard Barrett
Staff: 55

Passenger boardings: (Bus, suburban rail and ferry – including transfers)
(2002/03) 88.1 million
(2003/04) 90.6 million
(2004/05) 95.0 million
(2005/06) 98.5 million
(2006/07) 100.9 million
Total annual vehicle-km (all modes): (2004/05) 55.8 million
(2005/06) 57.3 million
(2006/07) 58.4 million

Current situation
Transperth is an arm of the Public Transport Authority (PTA) which co-ordinates the provision of public transport services for metropolitan Perth. Rolling stock is owned by the Government of Western Australia. All public transport services are provided under contractual arrangements with service providers that may be government, or privately owned as follows:
- Train services are provided by Transperth Train Operations (PTA).
- Passenger information services are provided by Serco Australia Pty. Common user infrastructure services are managed by Transperth, employing a number of different contractors.
- Ferry services are operated by a private company, Captain Cook Cruises.
- Bus services are provided by three private companies – PATH Transit (Australian Transport Enterprises), Swan Transit (independent) and Southern Coast Transit (Veolia Environment) – that operate within a total of 10 contract areas of varying sizes.
- Central Area Transit – CAT Services. The Red, Blue and Yellow free CAT services are operated on behalf of Perth City Council in Central Perth. Real-time stop information on the CAT services is available at all stops.

- In Fremantle, one free CAT service operates, jointly funded by Transperth and Fremantle city council.
- A free CAT service within the city of Joondalup was introduced in January 2006. It is jointly funded by Transperth, the City of Joondalup and a local university.

Developments
An extension of the 4 km Northern Suburbs Railway, from Currambine to Clarkson, opened in October 2004. The station has connecting bus

services and car parking for 800 cars. A new park-and-ride station at Greenwood, between Warwick and Whitfords on the Northern Suburbs Railway, opened in December 2004, with accommodation for 600 cars. A master plan for another extension north from Clarkson is being prepared.

A new 1.4 km single-line branch from the existing Armadale Line at Cannington to Thornlie opened in August 2005. Bus routes in the area were rerouted to feed the new station, which has parking spaces for 650 cars.

A Transperth Mercedes-Benz O500LE bus, powered by CNG, working one of the free CAT services in central Perth (Alan Mortimer)
1330384

The first test train in the new Perth City Tunnel at Esplanade Station, opened in October 2007. The full line opened in December 2007 (Courtesy of New Metro Rail)
1330394

State Government policy requires that future bus deliveries should be powered by Compressed Natural Gas (CNG). Delivery of Mercedes-Benz O500LE vehicles, powered by CNG, commenced in August 2004 and by September 2007, 225 had been delivered. The three Mercedes Citaro hydrogen fuel cell buses, run experimentally as part of a worldwide comparative 2-year trial, were withdrawn in September 2007.

Smartcard fare collection for the Transperth network, named Smartrider, was fully introduced in April 2007. The successful contractor for the project is Delairco Bartrol, a division of Downer EDI, using Wayfarer, UK ticketing technology. The system provides for a tag-on and tag-off facility on each vehicle/station and includes a transfer period. The 12 busiest suburban railway stations are fitted with closed barriers, with the others having free-standing validators.

In September 2007, Transperth was about to commence a 3-year trial with three CNG-powered articulated buses, from Iveco, MAN and Scania.

The main rail line from Mandurah and Rockingham (Southern Suburbs Railway) to Perth opened in December 2007. The line runs through the city of Perth in a 770 m twin-bored tunnel and 930 m of open dive and cut-and-cover tunnel sections, which will include two stations. This line will connect with the Northern Suburbs Railway, opened in 1993. The project involved the construction of 72 km of new electrified railway with 10 stations.

Number of routes: Bus – 289; suburban rail – 5 lines; ferry – 1

Unduplicated route length: Bus 2,200 km, suburban train 166.7 km, ferry 1.3 km

Number of stops: 12,613 (May 2008)

Most intensive service frequency: 3 min

One-person operation: All routes/modes

Operating costs (including capital charges): Financed 20.0 per cent fares, advertising and service contributions (CAT services and a few ordinary services are jointly funded) and 80.0 per cent subsidies

Fare-collection method: Smartcards used to 'tag on' and 'tag off' on buses, ferries and at all stations – 58 per cent, cash fares on board buses & ferries and at railway station ticket machines – 42 per cent

Fare structure: 9 fare zones, with 120 min or 180 min transfer period, depending on distance travelled; ticket integration with all other modes – bus, train, ferry

Operational control: Bus Company radio, Global Positioning System (GPS) for Perth CAT Services, Transperth Train Control for suburban railways; Transperth inspectors monitor service performance and fare evasion

Bus priority: Bus lanes. There is a continuing improvement group to develop priority at traffic lights, queue-jump lanes as well as further bus lanes

New vehicles financed by: Western Australian State Government

Bus fleet: 1,129 buses

MAN 11.190 HOCL (1996)	1
MAN SG 292H articulated (1988)	7
Mercedes-Benz O305 CNG (1985/86)	2
Mercedes-Benz O305 diesel (1979–86)	60
Mercedes-Benz O305G articulated (1979/80/87)	30
Mercedes-Benz O405 CNG (1991)	15
Mercedes-Benz O405 diesel (1990–92)	34
Mercedes-Benz O405NH CNG (2001–03)	48
Mercedes-Benz O405NH diesel (1999–2002)	351
Mercedes-Benz OC500LE CNG (2003–05)	279
Renault PR 100-2 CNG (1987)	9
Renault PR 100-2 diesel (1986/87)	225
Renault PR 100-3 CNG (1993)	1
Renault PR 180-2 articulated (1988/89)	65
Scania CNG articulated	1
MAN CNG articulated	1

New vehicles required each year: 72

On order: 649 out of a total current order for 896 Mercedes-Benz buses have been delivered

Average age of fleet: 10.8 years (at mid-2008)

Canning bridge Station, 7 km from the City, on the new Southern Suburbs Railway (opened in December 2007) (Alan Mortimer)   1330383

One of the newest Mercedes-Benz O500LE buses working in Kings Park, close to the City of Perth (Alan Mortimer)   1198712

A new three-car Bombardier train leaving the park-and-ride station at Greenwood (Alan Mortimer)   1115153

Train fleet:
Rolling stock: 68 cars
Walkers-ABB 2-car units (1991/92) 21
Walkers-ABB 2-car units (1992/93) 22
Walkers-Adtranz 2-car units (1998/99) 5
EDI-Bombardier 3-car units (2004/06) 31
New rolling stock: 15 additional 3-car trains have been ordered from EDI-Bombardier for delivery by 2010.
Peak requirements: At November 2006, 905 buses, 46 two-car trains, 30 three-car trains, 1 ferry

Ferry
Current situation
Two vessels: *Shelley Taylor Smith*, 148 seats (1998); *Princess*, 100 seats (1991).

Ferry 'Shelley Taylor Smith' crossing from Perth City to South Perth, the short ferry route
(Alan Mortimer)
1198713

Sydney
Population: 3.5 million (2001 Census)

Public transport
Bus and ferry/catamaran services serving central urban area and Sydney harbour provided by State Transit Authority. The Department of Planning (NSW) exercises overall responsibility for planning and co-ordination of all public transport including privately run bus, ferry, taxi and hire car services. RailCorp provides extensive suburban rail services. Private bus operators serve suburban and outer areas. Monorail serves the Darling Harbour redevelopment; light rail serves Darling Harbour and City West (Ultimo) areas.

Department of Planning (NSW)
Information Centre
GPO Box 39, Sydney, New South Wales 2001, Australia
Tel: (+61 2) 92 28 63 33   Fax: (+61 2) 92 28 65 55
e-mail: information@dipnr.nsw.gov.au
Web: www.planning.nsw.gov.au

Street address
22-33 Bridge Street, Sydney, Australia

Head office
GPO Box 39, Sydney, New South Wales 2001, Australia
Tel: (+61 2) 92 28 61 11   Fax: (+61 2) 92 28 64 55
e-mail/Web: as above

State Transit Authority of New South Wales (State Transit)
Head Office
PO Box 2557, Strawberry Hills, New South Wales 2012, Australia
Tel: (+61 2) 92 45 57 77
Tel: (+61 2) 92 45 57 79 (Customer Relations and Communications)
Fax: (+61 2) 92 45 56 10
Fax: (+61 2) 92 45 57 71 (Customer Relations and Communications)
Web: www.sta.nsw.gov.au

Street address
Level 1, 219-241 Cleveland Street, Strawberry Hills, New South Wales 2010, Australia

Key personnel
Acting Chief Executive: Peter Rowley
General Manager, Customer Relations and Communications: Ms Frier Bentley
Staff: 4,500+ (2006)
(All modes)

Passenger journeys: (2002/03) 212.3 million
(2003/04) 198 million
(2004/05) 199.36 million
(2005/06) 199.38 million

Vehicle-km: (2002/03) 90.0 million
(2003/04) 88 million (estimate)
(2004/05) 86 million (estimate)
(2005/06) 91 million (estimate)

Background
State Transit's structure was reorganised at the start of 1993 to meet the government's requirement for a new and accountable business-like culture in the public sector, capable of meeting minimum service levels set by the Department of Transport.

Current situation
A smaller corporate head office now oversees eight major business units and three satellite depots, plus Sydney Ferries and a further business unit responsible for operations in Newcastle (180 km north). There are 25 operating contracts within State Transit's area.
State Transit is the government-owned authority responsible for the operation of Sydney Buses, Newcastle Bus & Ferry Services and Western Sydney Buses.
The Sydney bus system serves a population of some 1.7 million and covers an area of 645 km².

Developments
Western Sydney Buses was incorporated in July 2002, under the Transport Administration Act 1988, as a public subsidiary corporation of State Transit and commenced operations in February 2003. It operates the bus services along the Bus Rapid Transitway (BRT) from Liverpool to Parramatta, known as the T-way service.
In 2006, some 38 per cent of the vehicles in the fleet were fully accessible for wheelchair users, 43 per cent are low-floor, 21 per cent are CNG-powered and 31 per cent comply with Euro 3 emissions standards.
State Transit's business management systems are certified to ISO 9001:2000 standards.
A total of 505 new buses are on order, of which 250 are Euro 5 vehicles.

Fleet: In excess of 1,991 vehicles (June 2007)
Mercedes-Benz 0305 MkII diesel (1978–80) 50
Mercedes-Benz 0305 MkIII diesel (1981–83) 167
Mercedes-Benz 0305G articulated diesel (1981, 1983/84) 14
Mercedes-Benz 0305 MkIV (1983–87) 352
Mercedes-Benz 0405 MkV diesel/CNG (1987–90) 257
MAN SL202 diesel (1989) 50
Mercedes-Benz 0405 PMC160 diesel (1990–91) 11
Scania L113CRB – Ansair Commuter CNG (1992) 2
Scania L113TRBL diesel (1993–94) 50
Scania L113CRB CNG (1994–95) 100
Scania L113CRL diesel (1994, 1996–98) 156
Mercedes-Benz 0405N CNG n/a
MAN 11.220 HOCL diesel (1996–97) 17
Volvo B10B diesel (1996 (acquired by Sydney Buses 1999)) 4

Volvo B10BLE diesel (1997–2000) 124
Mercedes-Benz 0405 – Custom Coaches '516' diesel (1998 (acquired by Sydney Buses 1999)) 4
Mercedes-Benz 0405NH CNG (1999–2002) 300
Volvo B12BLE – Custom Coaches CB60 diesel (2003–2007) 170
Volvo B12BLE – Volgren diesel (2005) 50
Volvo B12BLE articulated diesel (2005–2006) 80
Volve B12BLE – diesel (Euro 5) (2007) 33
On order: 250 Volve B12BLE – diesel (Euro 5) buses, delivery started in 2007; 255 Mercedes-Benz CNG buses
Average age of vehicles: Not currently available

Sydney Buses
State Transit Authority of New South Wales (State Transit)
PO Box 2557, Strawberry Hills, New South Wales 2010, Australia
Tel: (+61 2) 92 45 57 77   Fax: (+61 2) 92 45 57 10
Web: www.sydneybuses.nsw.gov.au

Street address
Level 1, 219-241 Cleveland Street, Strawberry Hills, New South Wales 2010, Australia

Passenger journeys: (2002/03) 187.3 million
Vehicle-km: (2002/03) 79.7 million
(2003/04) 80 million (estimate)
(2004/05) 78 million (estimate)
(2005/06) 83 million (estimate)

Number of routes: More than 300
Route length: 946 km

Developments
Sydney Buses is accredited to ISO 9001:2000 standards.
For developments, please see main entry for State Transit.

Fleet:
Breakdown of fleet is not currently available, but please see main entry for State Transit for total operating fleet
In peak service: Not currently available
Average age of fleet: 12.2 years
Most intensive service: 3 min
One-person operation: All routes
Fare collection: Payment to driver, or cancellation of prepurchase multitrip tickets or pass
Fare structure: Stage; multitrip tickets; quarterly and annual 'Travelpass' intermodal passes; off-bus multitrip tickets for use with onboard cancelling machines
Fares collected on board: 25 per cent
Integration with other modes: Timed interchange with suburban rail services and ferries; intermodal 'Travelpass'; airport express bus
Bus priority: Peak-hour bus lanes and priority when joining traffic flow; priority traffic signals

Operational control: Route inspectors/mobile radio; two-way radio in all vehicles; central radio control room

Arrangements for elderly/disabled: Ultra-low-floor buses have ramp and space for two wheelchairs; half fare for elderly, with low-cost day tickets for unlimited bus/train/ferry travel after 09.00. Ministry of Transport subsidises taxi service for disabled; wheelchair users have specially modified vehicles, others use standard taxis and all pay half metered fare, state government subsidising remainder

Operating costs financed by: Fares 55 per cent, other commercial sources 4.6 per cent, subsidy/grants 40.4 per cent

Subsidy from: State government contract payment

New vehicles financed by: Internal funds

Veolia Transport NSW Pty Ltd

33-39 Bay Road, Taren Point, New South Wales 2229, Australia
Tel: (+61 2) 95 40 22 77, 87 00 05 55
Fax: (+61 2) 95 40 17 20, 87 00 05 90
e-mail: businfo@veoliatransportnsw.com.au
Web: www.veoliatransportnsw.com.au

Key personnel
Managing Director: Morris Caputi
General Manager, Operations: Len Kidd
Maintenance Manager: Mark Harbridge
Finance Manager: Rod Draper
Commercial Manager: Ian Gaffney
Group Operations Manager: Graham Richards
   Staff: 485 (2007)

Passenger journeys: (2006) 8.8 million (estimate)
Vehicle-km: (2006) 13.4 million (estimate)

No of routes: 56 (estimate)
Route length: Not currently available

Current situation
Veolia Transport NSW Pty Ltd (previously known as Connex NSW), is a subsidiary of Veolia Transport Australia Ltd. The company provides bus services, including school and charter services, centred on Sydney's southern, southwestern and western suburbs. The company is contracted to operate these services until 2012.

Developments
In May 2006, a 9.5-km bus corridor, using bus priority, was opened between Miranda and Hurstville in southern Sydney.
   In early 2007, the company acquired the operations of Transit First.

Fleet: 263 vehicles
Breakdown of fleet is not currently available

Bus & Coach Association (NSW)

Locked Bag 13, North Parramatta, New South Wales 1750, Australia
Tel: (+61 2) 88 39 95 00
Fax: (+61 2) 96 83 14 65
e-mail: bca@bcansw.com.au
Web: www.bcansw.com.au

Street address
27 Villiers Street, North Parramatta, New South Wales 2151, Australia

Key personnel
President: Stephen Rowe
Metropolitan Vice-President: Steve Scott
Country Vice-Presidents: Frank D'Apuzzo
Executive Director: Darryl Mellish
Marketing: Matt Threlkeld

Background
The Bus & Coach Association (BCA) was formed in 1942 and represents the private bus industry in New South Wales and the owners of the New South Wales coach fleet. It also liaises with its

national body, the Bus Industry Confederation (BIC), to formulate policy to increase public transport use.

Current situation
Some 700 members operate approximately 7,000 buses throughout the New South Wales area, including Wollongong, Blue Mountains, Central Coast and the Greater Sydney metropolitan area, carrying more than 100 million passengers per year.
   BCA also organises seminars and training courses on a number of topics, including bus priority and bus reform.

Metro Transport Sydney Pty Limited

190 Pyrmont Street, Pyrmont, New South Wales 2009, Australia
Tel: (+61 2) 85 84 52 50   Fax: (+61 2) 96 60 46 95
e-mail: info@metrolightrail.com.au
Web: www.metrolightrail.com.au

Key personnel
Chief Executive Officer: Kevin Warrell
Commercial Manager: Vacant
Marketing Director: Michelle Silberman

Operator:
Veolia Transport Sydney

220 Pyrmont Street, Pyrmont, New South Wales 2009, Australia
Tel: (+61 2) 85 84 52 88   Fax: (+61 2) 96 60 09 55
e-mail: reception@veoliatransportsydney.com.au
Web: www.veoliatransportsydney.com.au

Light rail
Key personnel
Contact: Warwick Horsely
   Staff: 75

Type of operation: Light rail, initial route opened 1997

Passenger journeys: (2006) 3.5 million (estimate)
Vehicle-km: (2006) 0.74 million (includes monorail)

Route length: 7.2 km
dedicated right-of-way: 5.7 km
Number of routes: 1
Number of stops: 14
Gauge: 1,435 mm
Track: Conventional ballasted track, continuously welded 53 kg/m; rubber-mounted concrete slab in sensitive areas; on-street section: independent concrete slabs, with grooved head rail embedded in elastomeric compound
Minimum curve radius: 20 m
Maximum gradient: 8.5 %
Electrification: 750 V DC overhead

Current situation
Veolia (previously Connex) has a management contract to operate the light rail line until 2008. Extensions are under consideration.

Developments
In May 2004, Metro Transport Sydney submitted a proposal to extend the system from Central station to Circular Quay to the Department of Infrastructure, Planning and Natural Resources (DIPNR). The proposal includes two route options and would be served by 13 trams operating between 06.00 and 24.00 with a headway of 2.5 minutes in peak hours. Included in the plans is a new bus/tram interchange at Central station and an integrated ticketing system with buses and trains. The cost of the project is estimated at AUD180 million, to be funded by a combination of public and private investment. It is estimated ridership would be some 40,000 per day.

Rolling stock: 7 five-car vehicles
Adtranz Variotram LRV (1997)   M7

Service: 8 to 10 min (06.00 to 24.00), 30 min (24.00 to 06.00)
First/last train: 24 hour operation
Fare structure: Zonal; reduced fare for pensioners and children (4 to 15 years); Day Pass, Commuter and Weekly tickets; group discounts
Signalling/control: Relay-based interlocking system; Automatic Train Protection (ATP) system; Operations Control centre with a Supervisory Control and Data Acquisition (SCADA) system
Integration with other modes: Tramlink is a combined CityRail and Metro Light Rail ticket for travel on both systems
Arrangements for elderly/disabled: Fully accessible
Surveillance/security: CCTV at all stops

Monorail
Key personnel
Marketing Director: Michelle Silberman
   Staff: 75

Type of operation: Straddle monorail, opened 1988

Passenger journeys: (2006) 2.5 million (estimate)
Vehicle-km: (2006) 0.74 million (includes light rail)

Route length:
Number of stops: 8

Current situation
An automated loop line with eight stations connects the city centre with Darling Harbour; electrified 500 V AC. Privately developed by TNT, the link is a fully commercial operation. The company was acquired by Metro Transport

Passengers boarding one of Sydney's light rail vehicles at the Convention Centre, Darling Harbour (Peter Roelofs)
0585200

in 1998 and is operated under a management contact by Veolia (Previously Connex) until 2008.

Developments
In December 2006, a new monorail station, Chinatown, was opened.

Rolling stock: 6 seven-car trainsets
Service: 3 to 5 min; 24 hours per day, 364 days per year (closed Christmas Day)
First/last train: 07.00/22.00 (Mon-Thurs), 07.00/24.00 (Fri & Sat), 08.00/22.00 (Sun)
Fare structure: Standard (1 loop); Supervoucher Pass (unlimited travel day-pass); reduced fare for pensioners, war widows and senior citizens; METROcard rechargeable discount card for frequent users; group discounts

Rail Corporation New South Wales (RailCorp)
PO Box K349, Haymarket, New South Wales 1238, Australia
Tel: (+61 2) 82 02 20 00   Fax: (+61 2) 82 02 21 11
e-mail: feedback@railcorp.nsw.gov.au
Web: www.railcorp.nsw.gov.au

Street address
18 Lee Street, Chippendale, New South Wales 2008

Key personnel
Chairman: Ross Bunyon
Chief Executive Officer: Rob Mason
General Manager, Marketing: Ann Combe
   Staff: 13,800 (2007 estimate)

Type of operation: Suburban and interurban rail

Passenger journeys: (2004/05) 270.3 million (CityRail)
(2004/05) 1.77 million (CountryLink)
(2005/06) 273.7 million (CityRail)
(2005/06) 1.74 million (CountryLink)
(2006/07) 281.3 million (CityRail)
(2006/07) 1.61 million (CountryLink)

Background
Rail Corporation New South Wales (RailCorp) is a state-owned corporation, which primarily focuses on the provision of safe, clean and reliable passenger train and coach services throughout New South Wales.

Current situation
RailCorp provides passenger train transport throughout New South Wales via its CityRail (www.cityrail.info) and CountryLink (www.countrylink.info) services and is responsible for the safe operation, crewing and maintenance of passenger trains and stations. It also owns and maintains the metropolitan rail network and provides access to freight operators in the metropolitan area.
   RailCorp operates an extensive suburban and intercity rail network totalling 1,700 km with 302 stations, mostly electrified 1.5 kV DC. The network extends well beyond the Sydney suburban area and includes intercity trains to the Hunter Valley, Central Coast, Blue Mountains, South Coast and Southern Highlands.
   For further information on CityRail and CountryLink, please see *Jane's World Railways*.

Developments
RailCorp intends to replace the existing non air-conditioned rolling stock with modern, air-conditioned trains through a Public-Private-Partnership (PPP).

Waverton substation project
The company is increasing the electrical capacity of the network by upgrading and constructing new and existing electrical substations across the metropolitan area. In total, 25 substations will be constructed or upgraded over the next five years. A new substation will be constructed at Waverton Station.

Sydney's elevated monorail weaves its way around, and sometimes through, buildings in the city centre (Peter Roelofs)
0585199

Epping to Chatswood Rail Line
Currently under way, this project will increase capacity on the CityRail network and provide direct rail access for the growing North Ryde/Macquirie Park area of the city. The line will be 12 km long with three new stations and Epping Station and the Chatswood Transport Interchange are being upgraded.
   The line is currently scheduled to open in mid-2009.

South West Rail Link (SWRL)
There is a proposal for a new 13-km twin-track rail line from Glenfield to Leppington via Edmonson Park. The Transport Infrastructure Development Corporation (TIDC) will deliver the project on behalf of the NSW Government by 2014.

Sydney Ferries Corporation
PO Box R1799, Royal Exchange, New South Wales 1225, Australia
Tel: (+61 2) 92 46 83 00   Fax: (+61 2) 92 46 83 61
e-mail: mail@sydneyferries.info
Web: www.sydneyferries.info

Head Office street address
3/35 Pitt Street, Sydney, New South Wales 2000, Australia

Key personnel
Acting Chair: Geoff Ashton
Chief Executive Officer: Suzanne Sinclair
   Staff: Approximately 600 (2004/05)

Passenger journeys: (2000/01) 14.9 million
(2001/02) 13.6 million
(2002/03) 13.3 million
(2003/04) 14.0 million (estimate)
(2004/05) 14.1 million

Vehicle-km: (2000/01) 1.3 million
(2001/02) 1.4 million
(2002/03) 1.3 million
(2003/04) 1.3 million
(2004/05) 1.3 million

Number of routes: 8
Route length: 37 km
Number of stops: 41 wharves

Current situation
Sydney Ferries operates important commuter, leisure and tourist ferry services across Sydney Harbour and along the Parramatta River. Ferries provide an important link between Sydney Harbour residential suburbs and the major bus/rail interchange at Circular Quay. Cruise and charter services also operate.
   The eight routes operated from Circular Quay are:
Parramatta/Rydalmere;
Balmain/Woolwich;
Darling Harbour;
Neutral Bay;
Mosman;
Taronga Zoo;
Eastern Suburbs;
Manly.
   All wharves have CCTV installed, which is currently being improved.
   All ferries are wheelchair accessible and about half of the wharves are accessible.

Developments
In July 2004, Sydney Ferries Corporation was formed, as a state-owned corporation independent of the State Transit Authority.
   In 2004/05, approximately 49 per cent of total patronage was for commuter travel.

A grant was provided by the NSW Greenhouse Office to trial an alternative non-fossil fuel, known as biodiesel. The trial took place in 2005/06, which assessed the differential impact of diesel, biodiesel and blended diesel/biodiesel fuels (20 per cent and 80 per cent biodiesel) on the engine of the First Fleet Class vessel Borrowdale over a 3-month period. The trial includes testing of gas and air emissions.

Recent service improvements include:
Additional peak hour services to Cabarita on the Parramatta River to better service the new Breakfast Point development;
Services to Garden Island every day;
Additional services to Rose Bay and Watsons Bay on weekends, reducing waiting times and doubling service frequency.

Service: Services are operated 18 hours a day, 7 days a week
Fare structure: DayTripper all-day bus, train and ferry ticket, FerryTen 10-ride ferry ticket, weekly TravelPass
Operating costs financed by: Fares 64 per cent, other commercial sources 10 per cent, subsidy/grants 26 per cent

Sydney Ferries provide important commuter links to central Sydney. Here, a Freshwater Class ferry on the Manly service (Peter Roelofs)　　　　　0585131

Austria

Graz
Population: 287,723 (2006)

Public transport
Bus, tramway and funicular services operated by municipal undertaking, part of public utility trading company responsible also for gas, electricity and water services; commuter rail services provided by private company.

GRAZ-AG Stadtwerke für kommunale Dienste Verkehrsbetriebe
Steyrergasse 114, A-8010 Graz, Austria
Tel: (+43 316) 88 74 01
Fax: (+43 316) 88 77 88
e-mail: a.scholz@grazag.at
Web: www.grazag.at, www.gvb.at

Key personnel
Chair: Dr Wolfgang Messner
Directors: Dr Wolfgang Messner, Wolfgang Malik
Manager of Verkehrsbetriebe:
　Prok Dr Antony Scholz
　Staff: 798 (transport 469) (2007)

Background
In 1997 a total of 58 operators in Steiermark joined in formation of the Verkehrsverbund Steiermark tariff region, extending a uniform zonal fare structure to a population of some 1.2 million. Finance comes from the national government, the province of Steiermark and the city of Graz.

Passenger journeys: (All modes)
(2003) 91.7 million
(2004) 94.5 million
(2005) 98.2 million
(2006) 91.9 million*
(2007) 92.7 million*
*New method of calculation

Fare collection: Ticket purchase on buses and tramways, from shops or machines at main stations; validating equipment on board
Fare structure: Zonal, flat within zones; prepurchase 10-zone and zonal 24 h, weekly and monthly passes, annual tickets
Fares collected on board: 11.78 per cent (2007)
Operating costs financed by: Fares 81 per cent, other commercial sources (cross-subsidy) 12 per cent, subsidy 7 per cent (2006)
Subsidy from: Government and city (7 per cent) (2006)

Bus
Staff: 306 (operating) (2007)

Passenger journeys: (2003) 38.6 million
(2004) 40.8 million
(2005) 44.5 million
(2006) 43.3 million
(2007|) 41.5 million
Vehicle-km: (2003) 10.4 million
(2004) 10.2 million
(2005) 9.7 million
(2006) 9.7 million
(2007) 9.7 million

Number of routes: 25 (plus 8 night lines Friday and Saturday)
Number of stops: 649
Route length: (One way) 191.68 km
On priority right-of-way: 13.2 km

Fleet: 136 buses
Mercedes-Benz O530 N3L Citaro	34
Mercedes-Benz O530 N3 Citaro GB	17
Mercedes-Benz O405 N2 (Solo)	9
Mercedes-Benz O530 N3 Citaro	63
MAN NG272	8
Mercedes O405 GN2	4
Steyr City SC 6F 58	1

In peak service: 115
On order: None

Most intensive service: 6 min
One-person operation: All routes
Fare evasion control: Inspectors
Operational control: Route inspectors/mobile radio with computerised online monitoring
Arrangements for elderly/disabled: Reduced rate monthly and annual passes for unrestricted travel on weekdays after 08.15 and at weekends
Average distance between stops: 378.4 m
Average peak-hour speed: 20.51 km/h

Tramway
Staff: 163

Type of operation: Conventional tramway

Passenger journeys: (2003) 52.3 million
(2004) 53.1 million
(2005) 53.1 million
(2006) 48.1 million
(2007) 50.5 million
Car-km: (2003) 9.5 million
(2004) 9.5 million
(2005) 9.7 million
(2006) 8.8 million
(2007) 9.5 million

Graz trams, with 651 in the foreground on a Route 6 service to Hauptbahnhof (John C Baker)　　　　　1115241

Route length: 61.22 km
Number of lines: 9
Number of stops: 177
Gauge: 1,435 mm
Track: 60.5 kg/m Ri60 rail on concrete
Electrification: 600 V DC, overhead

Service: Peak 5 min, off-peak 10 min
First/last car: 04.30/00.30
One-person operation: All cars
Average distance between stops: 344.9 m
Average peak-hour speed: 16.32 km/h

Rolling stock: 72 cars
SGP 260 (1963)	M5
Lohner Wien 260 (1965)	M2
Duewag 520 (1971)	M15
SGP 500 (1978)	M10
SGP 600 (1986)	M12
GVB 580 (581–584)	M4
BW5 650 low-floor tram	M18
Lohner 260 (262)	1
S6P 250 (251, 252)	2
Siemens Duewag 290 (291–293)	M3

In peak service: 54
On order: 45 Stadler low-floor trams

Developments
The city council plans further expansion of the system.

Funicular

Current situation
The Schlossbergbahn Funicular carries 0.27 million passengers annually. The Schlossberglifs carries 0.41 million passengers annually.

Light rail (proposed)

Current situation
A regional light rail network has been proposed for the greater Graz area, sharing existing ÖBB and local railway alignments.

Graz-Köflacher Bahn und Busbetrieb GmbH (GKB) – Graz-Köflach Railway and Bus Ltd

Köflacher Gasse 35-41, A-8020 Graz, Austria
Tel: (+43 316) 598 70
Fax: (+43 316) 59 87 16
e-mail: office@gkb.at
Web: www.gkb.at

Key personnel
Managing Director: Franz Weintögl
Marketing & Public Relations: Peter Stoessl
    Staff: 420

Type of operation: Commuter bus and rail

Passenger journeys: (2003) 3.1 million (train)
(2003) 5.9 million (bus)
(2004) 6 million (bus – approximate)
(2004) 4.1 million (rail – approximate)

Background
Founded in 1856 to transport coal. First passenger service commenced in 1873. The railway, which is operated as an autonomous entity, heads south from its own station at Graz to Lieboch, where it branches northwest to Köflach and south to Wies-Eibiswald. In addition, the company operates 27 bus routes in Western Styria.

Current situation
GKB operates diesel railcar and commuter push-pull services at approximately hourly intervals.
    For further information, please see entry in *Jane's World Railways.*

Developments
Extension plans to the Graz system might see trams on the GKB rail line from Wetzelsdorf to Seiersberg and Premstätten Tolebad (7.3 km).

Rolling stock: 15 diesel locomotives, 15 double-deck coaches, 13 dmus and 7 'nostalgic' carriages

Fleet: 42 buses

Linz

Population: City 189,000, Greater Linz 271,000 (2007 estimates)

Public transport

Bus, trolleybus, tramway and local rail line operated by municipally owned company also responsible for other public utilities.

Linz AG Linien

Wiener Strasse 151, Postfach 1300, A-4021 Linz, Austria
Tel: (+43 732) 340 00   Fax: (+43 732) 34 00 74 87
e-mail: linien@linzag.at
Web: www.linzag.at

Key personnel
Chairman: Jürgen Himmelbauer
General Manager: Walter Rathberger
Operating Manager: Albert Waldhör
    Staff: 505 (full time)

Passenger journeys: (All modes)
(2002/03) 88.3 million
(2003/04) 89.8 million
(2004/05) 91.0 million
(2005/06) 93.5 million
(2006/07) 94.5 million

Operating costs financed by: Fares 72.1 per cent, internal cross-subsidy 27.9 per cent

Current situation
Profits from the electricity and district heating trading divisions help support the public transport operation.

Developments
CNG buses have been in use since October 2007.

Bus and trolleybus

Passenger journeys: (2002/03) Bus 37.1 million, trolleybus 14.4 million
(2003/04) Bus 37.7 million, trolleybus 14.6 million
(2004/05) Bus 30.8 million, trolleybus 16.4 million
(2005/06) Bus 28.6 million, trolleybus 15.3 million
(2006/07) Bus 28.9 million, trolleybus 15.5 million
Vehicle-km: (2002/03) Bus 3.9 million, trolleybus 1.3 million
(2003/04) Bus 4.0 million, trolleybus 1.4 million
(2004/05) Bus 4.0 million, trolleybus 1.3 million
(2005/06) Bus 4.0 million, trolleybus 1.3 million
(2006/07) Bus 4.3 million, trolleybus 1.1 million

Number of routes: Bus 21, trolleybus 4
Route length: Bus 138.1 km, trolleybus 19.1 km

Fleet: 89 buses
MAN NG 272 (1993/96)	14
MAN NG 262 (1997/99)	23
Volvo B7 LA (Leihbus) (1999)	7
Steyr Volvo SN12 HUA 285 (B10L) (1994)	1
Steyr Volvo SN12 HUA 245 (B10L) (1996/97)	22
Volvo B7L (2000)	2
Mercedes-Benz Citaro 0530-G-CNG	20

In peak service: 71

Fleet: 19 trolleybuses
Volvo B7 LA-Trolley (2000/01)	19

In peak service: 19

Most intensive service: 5 min
One-person operation: All routes
Fare collection: Prepurchase, and automatic machines for ticket issuing and cancellation at all stops
Fare structure: MINI, MIDI and MAXI ticketcards, passes (weekly, monthly and annual)
Fares collected on board: None
Fare evasion control: Random inspection
Operational control: Route inspectors/mobile radio/Rechnergesteuertes Betriebsleitsystem (RBL)

Average peak-hour speed: Bus 19.1 km/h, trolleybus 18.9 km/h, tram 20.2 km/h
New vehicles financed by: Free financing and credit

Tramway

Type of operation: Conventional tramway and Cityrunner (Niederflurstrassenbahnen)

Passenger journeys: (2001/02) 35.1 million
(2002/03) 36.4 million
(2003/04) 37.1 million
(2004/05) 47.6 million
(2005/06) 49.1 million
(2006/07) Not yet available
Car-km: (2005/06) 2.3 million

Route length: 21.1 km
Number of lines: 3
Number of stops: 51
Gauge: 900 mm
Max gradient: 4%
Minimum curve radius: 17 m
Electrification: 600 V DC, overhead

Service: Peak 4–6 min, off-peak 6–15 min
First/last car: 04.00/23.47

Cityrunner Bombardier tram in Ebelsberg   1176842

Fare collection: Prepurchase and automatic machines for ticket issuing and cancellation at all stops
One-person operation: All vehicles

Rolling stock: 49 cars
Bombardier-Rotax GTW10 (1977, 1985/86)   M28
Bombardier NSTRB8 (2003/04)   M21
In peak service: 40

Local railway (Bergbahn)
Current situation
The company also operates the Bergbahn, a 2.9-km railway with eight stations running from Bergbahnhof at the tramway Line 3 terminal to Pöstlingberg, operating on 600 V DC catenary. It carries about 500,000 passengers a year.

Developments
The Bergbahn closed at the end of March 2008 for about one year for the rebuilding, which, in addition to the re-gauging from 1,000 mm to 900 mm and an extension from the Bergbahnhof Talstation to Haptplatz station, will also include renewal and modification of the overhead wiring to accommodate pantograph current-collection in place of trolley poles.

To work the new through service, three new low-floor, air-conditioned trams have been ordered from Bombardier for delivery in early 2009. There is an option for a fourth car. Most of the existing fleet, which dates from 1948–60, will be withdrawn, but Vossloh-Kiepe will rebuild three of the existing cars for continued use as needed.

The Bergbahn is expected to re-open in March/April 2009.

Linz 003 on Route 2 service from Universität to solarCity (John C Baker)   1124811

Vienna
Population: 1.63 million (2005 estimate)

Public transport
Bus, metro, light rail and tramway services provided by municipal undertaking. Suburban rail services operated by Federal Railway (ÖBB) and Wiener Lokalbahnen (WLB). Some privately operated bus routes. Fares integrated throughout the conurbation, under Verkehrsverbund Ost-Region (VOR).

Verkehrsverbund Ost-Region GmbH (VOR)
PO Box 360, Mariahilfer Strasse 77–79, A-1060 Vienna, Austria
Tel: (+43 1) 526 604 80
Fax: (+43 1) 526 604 81 06
e-mail: office@vor.at
Web: www.vor.at

Key personnel
Director General: Alexandra Reinagl, Wolfgang Schroll
Staff: 75

Passenger journeys: (2002) 843 million
(2005) 805 million
(2006) 832.1 million

Background
In 2002, the federal government withdrew from VOR's Board of Directors. The new shareholder percentages are shown below. At that time, it was decided that VOR would provide services to an area of 23,500 km² and a population of around 3.2 million.

Current situation
VOR was created in 1984 to integrate public transport within the Vienna-Eastern Austria region, an area of 8,400 km². Shareholders in VOR are the *Länder* Vienna (44 per cent), Niederösterreich (44 per cent), and Burgenland (12 per cent). The area covered, including operations in satellite towns, has a total population in excess of 2.7 million, and is served by five metro lines, 36 regional and suburban railway lines, 32 tramway routes and 264 bus routes.

A common fares policy was adopted throughout the area, covering all operations of Wiener Linien, the private and regional bus lines, the suburban bus and rail services of ÖBB and the WLB Vienna-Baden local railway.

In 2006, some 25 per cent of all trips made in the region were by public transport.

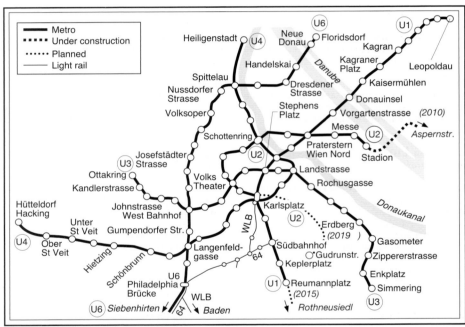

Vienna's metro and light rail systems   1298726

Wiener Linien GmbH & Co KG
PO Box 63, Erdbergstrasse 202, A-1031 Vienna, Austria
Tel: (+43 1) 790 90
Fax: (+43 1) 790 91 49
e-mail: post@wienerlinien.at
Web: www.wienerlinien.at

Key personnel
Directors: Walter Andrie, Günter Steinbauer, Michael Lichtenegger
Operating Manager, Bus: Fritz Machala
Staff: 7,772 (2007)

Passenger journeys: (All modes)
(2003) 721.8 million
(2004) 735.3 million
(2005) 746.8 million
(2006) 772.1 million
(2007) 793.0 million

Operating costs financed by: Fares 45.63 per cent, other commercial sources 0.39 per cent, subsidy/grants 53.98 per cent (2007)
Subsidy from: City authorities

Bus
Passenger journeys: (2003) 108.4 million
(2004) 110.5 million
(2005) 111.7 million
(2006) 117.5 million
(2007) 116.0 million
Vehicle-km: (2003) 29.3 million
(2004) 29.6 million
(2005) 29.4 million
(2006) 29.1 million
(2007) 28.8 million

Number of routes: 83 (including 23 night)
Route length: Not available

Fleet: 478 vehicles (2007)
ÖAF-Gräf & Stift low-floor   283
ÖAF-Gräf & Stift low-floor   183
ÖAF-Gräf & Stift minibus   12
In peak service: 396 (2007)
New vehicles required each year: Renewal of six-eight per cent of fleet

One-person operation: All services
Fare collection: Driver issues tickets; prepurchase multitickets and passes

Wien 662 on Route 43 service to Neuwaldegg
(John C Baker)   0585162

Wiener Linien at left, 4743 & 1269 on Line 21. At right, 681 on Line 2 (Quintus Vosman)   1208955

Fare structure: Flat (lower rate for short rides); prepurchase multitickets; eight-day, 24-hour and 72-hour tourist passes; free transfer; free travel for children up to 19 on Sundays and holidays

Fare evasion control: Uniformed and non-uniformed inspectors; penalty fare

Average distance between stops: 400.5 m

Average peak-hour speed: In mixed traffic, 17.0 km/h

Integration with other modes: Tickets valid on all modes for through journeys involving transfers (tickets valid on, but not sold by, private bus lines)

Operating costs financed by: Fares 26.62 per cent, other commercial sources 0.32 per cent, subsidy/grants 73.06 per cent

New vehicles financed by: Loans raised by city

Metro

Type of operation: Full metro (U-Bahn), initial route opened 1976

Passenger journeys: (2003) 299.9 million
(2004) 309.7 million
(2005) 315.4 million
(2006) 337.8 million
(2007) 363.3 million
Train-km: (2003) 43.5 million
(2004) 44.9 million
(2005) 45.0 million
(2006) 48.2 million
(2007) 51.9 million

Route length: 52.4 km
  in tunnel: 35.0 km (estimate)
Number of lines: 4
Number of stations: 71
  in tunnel: 48
Gauge: 1,435 mm
Track: Flat-bottomed S 48-U, 48.33 kg/m rail; timber sleepers on ballast bed and soundproofed superstructure with synthetic sleepers
Max gradient: 45%
Minimum curve radius: 300 m
Tunnel: Partly single-track bored; partly double-track cut-and-cover
Electrification: 750 V DC, third rail

Rolling stock: 612 cars, including 504 cars in two-car sets; 108 cars Modular Metro (MO.MO)
Simmering-Graz-Pauker (1972 on)   M252 T252
Siemens AG Österreich V/v   M72 T36
On order 25 MO.MO Siemens trains for delivery in 2008, a further 15 trains by the end of 2011
In peak service: 436 (2007)

Service: Peak 2½–5 min, off-peak 4–7½ min
First/last train: 04.15/00.53
Fare structure: Flat
Operating costs financed by: Fares 63.18 per cent, other commercial sources 0.51 per cent, subsidy/grants 36.31 per cent
Fare-evasion control: Uniformed and non-uniformed inspectors
One-person operation: All services
Signalling: Continuous automatic train running control, with centralised control
Surveillance: CCTV on all platforms

Developments

The northwards extension of U1 to Leopoldau was completed in September 2006.

In 2003, the construction of the eastwards extension of U2 to Aspern started. The first part to the station 'Stadion' opened in May 2008.

The following extensions (Phase 4) have also been approved:

U2 Aspernstrasse – Flugfeld Aspern: 4.5 km, elevated/at grade, four stations (Schanzen, Hausfeldstrasse, two at Flugfeld Aspern to be named), 2013;

U1 Reumannplatz – Rothneusiedl: 4.7 km, with intermediate stations at Trostgasse (underground), Altes Landgut (underground), Alaudagasse, Donauländebahn and Oberlaaer Strasse, 2015;

U2 Karlsplatz – Gudrunstrasse: 4.6 km (all underground, with intermediate stations at Schwarzenbergplatz, Rennweg, St Marx and Arsenal), 2019 (planned to become part of a future U5 in the long term).

There are further long-term extensions proposed for U6, U4, U2 and a new line U5, although none of these has yet received approval.

Light rail

Passenger journeys: (2003) 109.8 million
(2004) 110.4 million
(2005) 112.0 million
(2006) 112.1 million
(2007) 113.1 million
Car-km: (2003) 14.4 million
(2004) 14.6 million
(2005) 14.4 million
(2006) 14.5 million
(2007) 15.1 million

Route length: 17.4 km
  in tunnel: 7 km
  elevated: 10.4 km
Number of lines: 1
Number of stations: 24
Electrification: 750 V DC, overhead

Rolling stock: 170 cars
Bombardier-Rotax E6 (1979)   M46
Bombardier-Rotax C6 (1979)   T46
Bombardier-Rotax T low-floor (1993/94/95) M78

In peak service: 148 (2007)
On order: 46 low-floor Bombardier LRVs for line U6, 26 of which have already been delivered with the remainder due to be delivered by April 2009

Service: Peak 2½–5 min, off-peak 4–7½ min
First/last car: 04.16/01.04

Wiener Linien Type E1 tram (Neil Grace)   1180348

Fare structure: Flat
Operating costs financed by: Fares 59.57 per cent, other commercial sources 0.08 per cent, subsidy/grants 40.35 per cent
Signalling: Magnetic train control

Tramway

Type of operation: Conventional tramway

Passenger journeys: (2003) 203.7 million
(2004) 204.7 million
(2005) 207.7 million
(2006) 204.7 million
(2007) 200.4 million
Car-km: (2003) 39.4 million
(2004) 39.0 million
(2005) 38.2 million
(2006) 37.0 million
(2007) 35.9 million

Route length: 179.0 km
  in tunnel: 3.8 km
  elevated: 2.2 km
Number of lines: 32
Number of stops: 1,128
Gauge: 1,435 mm
Track: 59.7 kg/m grooved rail on rubber base or gravel and long concrete sleeper; some Vignole rail on timber sleepers in ballast bed
Max gradient: 6.5%
Minimum curve radius: 18–20 m
Electrification: 600 V DC, overhead

Developments

In June 2004, 150 ultra-low-floor (ULF) trams were ordered from Siemens Transportation Systems (TS) and its consortium partner Elin EBG, Austria. There is also an option for a further 150 vehicles. The first trams were delivered in 2006.

Rolling stock: 826 cars (2006)
Bombardier-Rotax/SGP E1 (1967)	M237
Bombardier-Rotax/SGP E2 (1977)	M121
Bombardier-Rotax c3 (1959)	T88
Bombardier-Rotax c4 (1974)	T73
Bombardier-Rotax c5 (1977)	T117
SGP A ultra-low-floor (1994)	M51
SGP B ultra-low-floor (1994)	M101
SGP A1 ultra-low-floor (2007)	M16
In peak service: 626 (2007)
On order: 80 A1ultra-low-floor and 70 B1 ultra-low-floor Siemens trams, delivery of 27 A1 trams has already taken place with the remaining vehicles due to be delivered by 2014

Service: Peak 2½–6 min, off-peak 3½–15 min
First/last car: 04.23/01.27
Fare structure: Flat
Operating costs financed by: Fares 37.28 per cent, other commercial sources 0.44 per cent, subsidy/grants 62.28 per cent

Österreichische Bundesbahnen (ÖBB) – Austrian Federal Railways

ÖBB-Holding AG
Twin Tower, Wienerbergstrasse 11, A1100 Vienna, Austria
Tel: (+43 1) 93 00 00
Fax: (+43 1) 93 00
e-mail: holding@oebb.at
Web: www.oebb.at

Key personnel

Chairman of the Board, ÖBB-Holding AG: Peter Klugar
Members of the Board of Management, ÖBB-Holding AG: Gustav Poschalko, Erich Sölinger
  Staff: 43,000

Passenger services

ÖBB-Personenverkehr AG
IZD-Tower, Wagramerstrasse 17-19, A-1220 Vienna, Austria
Tel: (+43 1) 93 00 00
e-mail: service@pv.oebb.at

Class 4024 Talent emu at Wolfsthal forming a Vienna S-Bahn Line S7 service (Quintus Vosman)
1129905

Key personnel

Members of the Board of Management: Ms Gabriele Lutter, Josef Halbmayr

Type of operation: S-Bahn and conventional suburban/regional rail, bus

Passenger journeys: (2006) 196 million

Background

In 2005, as a result of the Federal Railways Structure Act 2003, ÖBB-Holding AG was established as a state-owned enterprise, overseeing several individual stock and limited liability companies. ÖBB-Personenverkehr AG is responsible for passenger operations.

Current situation

Some information has been removed at the company's request.
  For further information on the ÖBB Group, please see *Jane's World Railways.*

City Airport Train (CAT)

City Air Terminal BetriebsgmbH
Office Park, PO Box 1, A-1300 Wien-Flughafen, Austria
Tel: (+43 1) 252 50
e-mail: info@cityairporttrain.at
Web: www.cityairporttrain.com

Key personnel

Chief Executive Officers: Mrs Doris Pulker-Rohrhofer,
  Ms Elizabeth Landrichter

Current situation

Some information has been removed at the company's request,

Fleet

Traction and rolling stock is provided by ÖBB. Services are operated using three three-car, push-pull formations of double-deck stock which carries 'CAT' livery and branding. Initially, similarly painted Class 1014 electric locomotives were used as traction but poor reliability led to more general use of Class 1016 machines.

Ostbahn-Vienna Airport link

Developments
A line from Götzendorf, on the Ostbahn international route east from Vienna to the city's airport, is to be built by 2015, having been deferred for financial reasons. The line will connect the airport to Austria's main line rail network. Estimated cost of the project is EUR145 million.

Wiener Lokalbahnen AG (WLB)

AG der Wiener Lokalbahnen AG
Eichenstrasse 1, A-1120 Vienna, Austria
Tel: (+43 1) 90 44 40   Fax: (+43 1) 90 44 43 50
e-mail: office@wlb.at
  bus-reisen@wlb.at
Web: www.wlb.at

Key personnel

General Manager: Dr Harald Brock
  Staff: 300 (estimate)

Wien 119 & 126 at Guntramsdorf on the local service from Baden to Vienna (John C Baker)   0585163

Passenger journeys: (2005) 8.76 million
(2006) 9,35 million

Current situation
WLB, 96 per cent owned by the city of Vienna,
operates one interurban rail line and seven
feeder bus routes.

Operating costs financed by: Not currently
available
Subsidy from: Government, and Vienna and
Niederösterreich Land administrations

Interurban/light rail
Passenger journeys: (Annual) 10 million (estimate)

Current situation
This 30.4 km light rail line (1,435 mm gauge,
electrified 850 V DC) runs from Vienna Opera over
tram tracks and the tram subway on to private
right-of-way to Baden.

Developments
In July 2004, Bombardier Transportation was
awarded a contract to build four three-car LRVs,
type TW 400. The contract was valued at some
€12 million and the vehicles were delivered in
2006.

Rolling stock: 36 trams
Duewag SGP T6 (1979/87/92/93)   M26

BWS TW 400 3-section low-floor (2000/06)   M10
dmus (1976, 2001/02)   M6
On order: Not currently available

Bus
Number of routes: 3
Route length: 81 km

Fleet: 48 buses
MAN   3
Gräf & Stift SL200/202/UH240 (1984/87/88/90)   15
Gräf & Stift NL202 (1991/92/93)   14
Steyr City-bus   3
Steyr SL12UHA (1992/93)   6
Setra S130/140 (1983)   4
Coaches   3

Azerbaijan

Baku

Population: City: 2.1 million, metropolitan area 3
million (estimates)

Public transport
Bus and trolleybus/tramway and funicular
services operated by municipal authority; metro;
suburban/commuter rail services provided by
Azerbaijani Railways (ADDY) (www.addy.gov.az)
(for further information, please see *Jane's World
Railways*); shared taxis – 'marshrut/marsrut'.

Administration for Municipal Public Transport
29 Aghasadykh Garaybeyli Street, Baku, AZ-1108,
Azerbaijan
Tel: (+994 12) 62 15 94; 62 28 65; 62 18 33

Bus
Upravlenie Passajirskogo Transporta

Route length: 1,512 km

Fleet: 605 vehicles, including some articulated

One-person operation: All routes
Fare collection: Conductors
Fare structure: Flat
Average peak-hour speed: 18 km/h

Tramvaino-Trolleibusnoe Upravlenie
Trolleybus
Route length: 175 km

Fleet: 340 vehicles
Skoda 9Tr
Skoda 14Tr   230
ZIU9

One-person operation: All routes
Fare collection: Conductors
Fare structure: Flat
Average peak-hour speed: 17 km/h

Tramway
Type of operation: Conventional tramway

Route length: 71 km
Gauge: 1,524 mm
Fare structure: Flat
Fare collection: Conductors
One-person operation: All routes

Rolling stock: 90 cars
RVZ6   M40
KTM5   M50

Current situation
Trams were eliminated from the city centre after
opening of the metro, but their use as feeders
continues and further extensions are planned
into areas where traffic density would not support
a metro line.

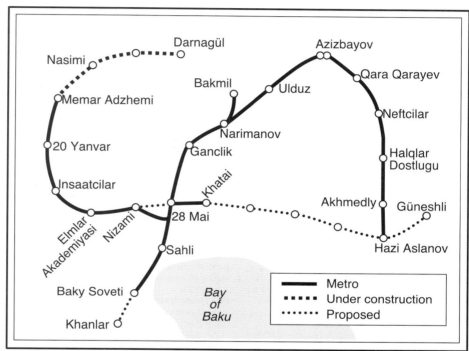

Map of Baku metro   0589905

Baki Metropoliteni – Baku Metro (BM)
H Javid avenue 33A, 370602 Baku, Azerbaijan
Tel: (+994 12) 490 00 25
e-mail: mail@metro.gov.az
Web: www.metro.gov.az:8101/eng/index.htm

Key personnel
Head of Metro: T M Akhmedov
Chief Engineer: E E Muradov
  Staff: 4,100

Type of operation: Full metro, first line opened
1967

Passenger journeys: (2003) 0.4 million (estimate)

Route length: 31.5 km
Number of lines: 2
Number of stations: 20
Gauge: 1,520 mm
Max gradient: 6%
Minimum curve radius: 300 m
Tunnel: Baku chamber method developed to
counter poor geological conditions; stations mostly
cut-and-cover and closed
Electrification: 825 V DC, third rail

Service: 2 min
First/last train: 05.30/24.00
Fare structure: Flat; smartcard
Fare collection: Automatic barriers

Signalling: Automatic train stop; radio-telephone
communication between trains and central
control

Rolling stock: 185 cars
E/Ex
Breakdown not currently available
Ex3 (1975)
Breakdown not currently available
Others
Breakdown not currently available

Current situation
In 2002, a short extension was completed
between Ahmedli and Hazi Asianov, which will
eventually link to the extension of the line from
Khatai to Gunashli.

Developments
A 4.1 km extension with three stations
and a further 10.2 km extension with five
stations, from Khatai to Gunashli, are under
construction. However, works on these have
ceased and there are no proposed dates for
completion. An eventual network of 3 lines is
envisaged.
  In 2006, payment for fares were changed to
pre-paid smartcard.

Belarus

Minsk

Population: 1.83 million (2008 estimate)

Public transport

Public transport services; bus, tramway, trolleybus and metro (the latter with extensions under construction and planned) are provided by government-owned company, MinskTrans. Suburban rail services provided by Belarussian Railways (BC) (www.rw.by) (please see *Jane's World Railways* for further information).

'MinskTrans' Public Transport Department

Varvasheny Street 2, Minsk 220770, Belarus
Tel: (+375 17) 219 86 01, 284 31 29
Fax: (+375 17) 222 94 84
e-mail: info@minsktrans.by
Web:www.minsktrans.by

Key personnel

General Manager: Leontiy Papenok

Developments

At the end of 2003, there was a restructuring of the public transport in Minsk. Previously known as Minskgarelektrotrans, the division responsible for trolleybus and tram operations became part of the Minsk City Executive Committee and is now known as 'MinskTrans' Public Transport Department. The department now also oversees bus and metro operations.

Bus

Passenger journeys: (2005) 259.8 million
Vehicle-km: Not currently available

Number of routes: 170
Route length: 2,102.8 km

Current situation

Bus operations are based on five depots.
Passengers are advised of the next stop/s by the loudspeaker system.

Fleet: 1,900 vehicles
MAZ-103 12 m low-floor	103
MAZ-104 12 m	210
MAZ-105 18 m middle floor articulated	180
Ikarus 260, 280	Approximately 400
LAZ	270
'Sprinter' 20-seat midibuses	200
Coaches, including Ikarus 250, 256 and MAZ-152	Approximately 200
Other, regional buses 'Neman' and LiAZ	Approximately 100

In peak service: 920
On order: 80 MAZ-103 and 80 MAZ-105 buses, delivery due by the end of 2006

Fare structure: Flat for city routes, km-based for regional and interurban routes; single, 10-day and monthly passes for city routes; 50 per cent discount for senior citizens and students and free travel for some citizens on city and regional buses
Fare collection: Semi-automatic on board for single paper tickets, prepaid paper passes and single trip tickets, cash to driver
Fare evasion control: Ticket inspectors
Operational control: Automatic System of Dispatcher Direction (ASDU-A) between 'technical points' on routes and a central dispatch officer, using telephone communication
Arrangements for elderly/disabled: Reduced fare for senior passengers and students, some disabled passengers travel free

Trolleybus

Passenger journeys: (2005) 200.6 million
Vehicle-km: Not currently available

Number of routes: 67
Route length: 713.2 km

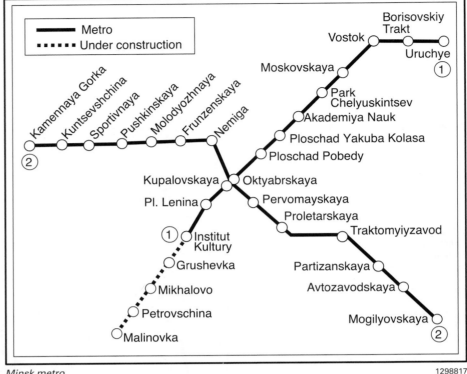

Minsk metro   1298817

Current situation

Minsk's trolleybus system serves some 28 per cent of the total annual public transport passenger journeys. The system has four depots and 83 power substations.

Fleet: 1,030 vehicles, including:
BelCommuneMach Model 333, low-floor 18 m articulated	one1
BelCommuneMach Model 321, low-floor 12 m	19
MAZ/BelCommuneMach Model 221, low-floor	105
BelCommuneMach Model 213, three-axle articulated	70
Other three-axle articulated units including ZiU-683, TrolZa-6205, YuMZ T1 and K11	16
Others (mainly ZiU-682)	some 800

In peak service: 790
On order: At least 26 MAZ/BelCommuneMach Model 221 low-floor will be delivered by the end of 2006 and at least 26 BelCommuneMach Model 213, 3-axle articulated, will also be delivered by the end of 2006

Tramway

Tel/Fax: (+375 17) 294 13 76
e-mail: tram@minsktrans.by

Key personnel

Director: Yurenya Rostislav Stanislavovich
Staff: 1,039

Type of operation: Conventional tramway

Passenger journeys: (2005) 34.6 million
Vehicle-km: Not currently available

Route length: 97.1 km
Number of lines: 10

Developments

From 2000, BelCommuneMach began assembly of Model 601-02 four-axle trams with thyristor-pulse control system and in 2002, BelCommuneMach assembled three-section, six-axle, mid-section low-floor, 26 m trams Model 743, also with thyristor-pulse control system.

Rolling stock: 157 cars
Full breakdown of fleet is not currently available, but is believed to include:

BelCommuneMach Model 743, three-section, six-axle, 26 m (2002)	M1
BelCommuneMach 601-02, four-axle	M31
ČKD Tatra T3M (T6B5)	M24
Duewag GT-8D three-section, eight-axle (ex-Karlsruhe, converted to run on the 1,524 mm routes)	M10
Riga RVZ-6M/2	Approximately M80

In peak service:118
On order: At least eight BelCommuneMach 601-02 four-axle were due to be delivered by the end of 2006

Metro

Nezavisimosti Avenue 6, Minsk 220030, Belarus
Tel: (+375 17) 219 50 09   Fax: (+375 17) 200 51 22
e-mail: metro@minkstrans.by

Key personnel

Head of Metro: Nikolay Abdreev Trofimovich
Staff: 3,576

Type of operation: Full metro, initial route opened 1984

Passenger journeys: (2004) 261.2 million
(2005) 250.4 million
(2006) Not currently available
(2007) 262 million (estimate)
Train-km: Not currently available

Route length: 30.3 km
Number of lines: two
Number of stations: 25
Gauge: 1,520 mm
Max gradient: four per cent
Min curve radius: 400 m
Electrification: 825 V DC, third rail

Developments

In late 2007, a 2.7 km extension to Line 1 was opened, with two new stations.
An extension to Line 1, southwest to Petrovshchina with four stations, is under construction.
There are also tentative plans for Lines 3 and 4.

Rolling stock: 223 cars from Mytischi and St Petersburg plants (Line 1: 23 five-car trains, Line 2: 27 four-car trains)

On order: None
Service: Peak 2 (Line 1), 2½ (Line 2) min, off-peak 4–10 min

First/last trains: 05.30/01.00
Fare collection: Token and magnetic card; 10-day and monthly passes; discount for students

Revenue control: Validators for magnetic cards and tokens

Belgium

Antwerp

Population: 461,500 (2006 estimate), metropolitan area 1.2 million (estimate)

Public transport
Bus and tramway/pre-metro services operated by publicly owned regional undertaking. An independent company operates five bus routes under contract. Suburban rail services operated by State railway.

De Lijn Antwerpen
Vlaamse Vervoermaatschappij (VVM)
Grotehondstraat 58, B-2018 Antwerp, Belgium
Tel: (+32 3) 218 14 11   Fax: (+32 3) 218 15 00
e-mail: antwerp@delijn.be
Web: www.delijn.be

Key personnel
Managing Director: Lode De Kesel
   Staff: 2,606 (as at December 2007)

Passenger journeys: (All modes)
(2005) 172.4 million
(2006) 175.1 million
(2007) 182.2 million

Operating costs financed by: Fares 15 per cent, subsidy/grants 85 per cent (for entire VVM) (2007)

Current situation
In 1991, control of urban and regional public transport in the Vlaanderen region passed to VVM, known as De Lijn, which took over the former urban and national (SNCV) networks in the area. VVM is responsible for all operations of the former National Bus Company (NMBV/SNCV) and urban operators MIVG and MIVA in Flemish-speaking regions.

De Lijn Antwerpen is one of five divisions of VVM, operating public transport in and around the Antwerp, Mechelen and Turnhout regions, with a total population of 1.67 million. The following data refers to the entire operation.

Bus
Passenger journeys: (2005) 91.8 million
(2006) 91.2 million
(2007) 92.6 million
Vehicle-km: (2006) 49.1 million
(2007) 49.6 million

Number of routes: 255
Route length: Approximately 880 km

Fleet: 565 vehicles
Standard (high-floor)	86
Standard low-floor	236
Articulated (high-floor)	6
Articulated low-floor	191
City bus	34
Microbus	12

In peak service: Not currently available

Most intensive service: 10 min
One-person operation: All routes
Fare collection: Payment to driver or prepurchase with validation/cancellation machines onboard

De Lijn Van Hool bus   1373454

Fare structure: Zonal; multitickets; monthly passes; transfer surcharge; zonal system of three cities and several suburban zones; passes for several zones or whole city system
Fare-evasion control: Random inspection
Integration with other modes: Prepurchase zonal tickets and passes also valid on other services under national integrated zonal ticket system
Operational control: Route inspectors/mobile radio
Average peak-hour speed: Urban routes: 20.67 km/h; regional routes: 33.50 km/h

Tramway
Type of operation: Conventional tramway

Passenger journeys: (2005) 80.6 million
(2006) 83.9 million
(2007) 89.6 million
Car-km: (2005) 8.6 million
(2006) 9.0 million
(2007) 9.4 million

Route length: 66.68 km
Number of routes: 12
Number of stations: 324
Electrification: 600 V DC, overhead

Developments
The following extensions have opened or are scheduled to open:
Western extension to Zwijndrecht (2000);
Southern extension to Bolivarplaats – Antwerp (2006);
Extension Eksterlaar – Silsburg (2009);
Eastern extension to Boechout (2009/10) and Eastern extension to Wijnegem (2009/10).

Rolling stock: 225 cars
PCC 1	M50
PCC 2	M105
Siemens low-floor	M70

On order: 1 detached coastal tram
Service: Peak 6 min, off-peak 10–15 min

Fare structure: As for bus
Revenue control: Prepurchase of tickets encouraged by discount; cancelling machines on board
Integration with other modes: As bus
One-person operation: All tram lines

Société Nationale des Chemins de fer Belges (SNCB)/Nationale Maatschappij der Belgische Spoorwegen (NMBS) (Belgian National Railway)
NMBS-Holding
North-East District
Koningin Astridplein 27, B-2018 Antwerp, Belgium
Tel: (+32 3) 204 20 02
Fax: (+32 3) 204 29 00
e-mail: districtsdirecteurno@b-holding.be
Web: www.b-rail.be

Key personnel
District Director: Walter Valaert
   Staff: 37,185 (total in Belgium, of which 7,928 in the North-East District)

Type of operation: Suburban heavy rail

Passenger journeys: (Total operations)
(2003) 169.3 million
(2004) 178.3 million
(2005) 186.6 million
(2006) 197.5 million
(2007) 206.5 million

Current situation
Services through the provinces of Antwerpen, Limburg and Vlaams-Brabant.

For further information on Société Nationale des Chemins de fer Belges (SNCB)/Nationale Maatschappij der Belgische Spoorwegen (NMBS), please see *Jane's World Railways*.

Brussels

Population: Capital region: 1 million (2005 estimate), metropolitan area 1.9 million (estimate)

Public transport
Bus, tramway, metro and pre-metro services provided by statutory undertaking with supervisory board of state, city and other representatives and under overall control of the Capital Region Ministry of Communications. Bus services also provided by regional operators TEC and De Lijn in city and suburbs, and suburban rail services by State railway SNCB/NMBS.

Société des Transports Intercommunaux de Bruxelles – Maatschappij voor het Intercommunaal Vervoer te Brussel (STIB-MIVB)

Avenue de la Toison d'Or 15, B-1050 Brussels, Belgium
Tel: (+32 2) 515 20 07   Fax: (+32 2) 515 32 84
Web: www.stib.irisnet.be

Key personnel
President: Eric Varrept
Director General: Alain Flausch
Deputy Director General: K Lauwers
Communications and Public Relations: J P Alvin
Commercial Directorate: A Carle
Human Resources Directorate: P Lenaerts
Finance Administration and Logistics Directorate: B Delvosal
Transport Supply: L H Sermeus
Operations, Tram: M Carême
Operations, Bus: S Cormer
Operations, Metro: L Bioul
Operations, Special Services: D Dumont
    Staff: 5,893 (2005) (all modes)

Current situation
STIB operations cover the 19 communes of the city and other suburban areas. Following devolution of powers to the regions in 1989, STIB is now funded solely by the Brussels regional government, which is also the overall planning authority. A five-year management contract agreed with the authority in 1991 gives STIB firm financial targets accompanied by more secure sources of finance.

The new administration voted in 1989 to give greater priority to public transport, and has been improving frequencies as well as completing current metro projects, studying further tramway extensions and segregation schemes, and expanding park-and-ride facilities.

STIB is also responsible for the Poelaert lift, which transports pedestrians from the upper and lower town, and the Cambio car-sharing scheme.

Developments
In June 2005, STIB signed the UITP charter for sustainable development.

During 2005, STIB and the Region began studying the possibility of providing shared taxi services for evening and night time operations.

STIB has plans for improvements to the surface network. These include high-performance tram routes, increased frequency of trams, extension of existing and creation of new tram lines, new bus links, new rolling stock, exclusive lanes and remote control of traffic lights.

Passenger journeys: (All modes)
(2001) 182.6 million
(2002) 204.3 million
(2003) 220.4 million
(2004) 239.2 million
(2005) 254.8 million

Operating costs financed by: (All modes) fares 33 per cent, other commercial sources 5 per cent, subsidy/grants 62 per cent
Subsidy from: Regional government

Bus
Staff: 1,193

Passenger journeys:
(2001) 47.1 million
(2002) 50.1 million
(2003) 54.4 million
(2004) 67.3 million
(2005) 71.5 million

Number of routes: 44
Route length: 305 km

Fleet: 571 vehicles
Fleet breakdown not currently available
In peak service: 425

Most intensive service: 5 min
One-person operation: All routes
Fare collection: Prepurchase multitickets or passes with validation and cancelling machines on board or payment to driver; over 90 per cent hold passes or multijourney cards
Fare structure: Flat, discount for ticketcards, passes. Free transfers within 60 min
Fare evasion control: Roving inspectors
Operational control: Central control of all modes has radio contact with bus fleet and traffic management monitoring facilities; sophisticated real-time monitoring of all surface vehicles
Arrangements for elderly/disabled: Special minibus service provided; all buses are now low-floor; on-request service for the disabled with 18 minibuses, with ridership estimated at 40,000 per year.
Average peak-hour speed: 17.2 km/h
Integration with other modes: MTB annual or monthly season tickets valid on all STIB services, De Lijn/TEC and NMBS/SNCB lines within Brussels area

Current situation
The bus fleet is now 100 per cent low-floor. Of the fleet of 571 vehicles, 20 are CNG, 12 are hybrid-electric and, by the end of 2006, 269 diesel buses were due to be equipped with particle filters.

Developments
140 older buses were due to be replaced in 2006 with new diesel buses which meet Euro-4 standards.

Tramway/pre-metro
Drivers: 690

Type of operation: Conventional tramway with 2 pre-metro city-centre tunnels

Passenger journeys:
(2001) 51.8 million
(2002) 57.6 million
(2003) 63.5 million
(2004) 66.4 million
(2005) 68.8 million
Car-km: Not currently available

Route length: 133.6 km
  in tunnel: 12.1 km
  reserved track: 63.7 km
Number of routes: 15, including 2 pre-metro
Number of stations: Pre-metro 17 (4 joint with metro)
Gauge: 1,435 mm
Electrification: 600 V DC, overhead

Service: Peak 3 min in city centre, off-peak 4 or 5 cars per hour on most routes
First/last car: 05.00/00.34
Fare structure: As bus
Fare collection: As bus
One-person operation: All cars
Automatic control: All light rail and pre-metro cars to be equipped with 'Greenwave' equipment for priority traffic light control

Rolling stock: 292 cars
Fleet breakdown not currently available
In peak service: 224
On order: 46 bidirectional Bombardier FLEXITY Outlook trams (27 T3000 32 m trams and 19 T4000 42 m trams), delivery between June 2005 and February 2007. A further order for 22 T3000 trams was made in 2005

Metro
Drivers: 172

Type of operation: Full metro, first line opened 1976

Passenger journeys:
(2001) 83.7 million
(2002) 96.6 million
(2003) 102.5 million
(2004) 105.5 million
(2005) 114.5 million

Route length: 33.9 km
Number of lines: 3

Number of stations: 52
Gauge: 1,435 mm
Electrification: 900 V DC, third rail

Service: Peak 7 min
First/last train: 05.00/01.00
Fare structure: Flat
Security: Metro and pre-metro have some 730 colour surveillance cameras which cover the entire network, plus 940 cameras on-board vehicles. Other cameras cover STIB's installations

Rolling stock: 192 cars, in three- and five-car sets

BN Series 100 (1975/76)	M90
BN Series 200 (1980/81)	M70
BN (1991/92)	M32

In peak service: 151 cars
On order: 15 CAF 94 m 'Boas' trains ordered in February 2004. Delivery commenced at the end of 2006

Current situation
A 60 km metro was planned, based on diversion of existing tramways into tunnel in a 'pre-metro' stage. Construction difficulties and political problems slowed development, but 1985 saw completion of metro Line 1, on which dedicated trains first ran in 1976. Two sections of pre-metro continue to carry tram services in the city centre (see above).

The extension of Line 1A to Baudouin/Boudewijn was opened in August 1998.

Developments
The extension of Line 2 to Delacroix was opened in September 2006. The remaining section from Delacroix to Gare de l'Oest is due to be completed in 2008. When the latter is completed, the network is due to be restructured.

A new depot is under construction, between Delacroix and Gare de l'Oeust stations, scheduled to be completed in 2008.

De Lijn Vlaams-Brabant
Vlaamse Vervoermaatschappij (VVM)
Martelarenplein 19, B-3000 Leuven, Belgium
Tel: (+32 16) 31 37 11   Fax: (+32 16) 31 37 12
e-mail: vlbrab@delijn.be
Web: www.delijn.be

TEC Brabant Wallon
Place Henri Berger 6, B-1300 Wavre, Belgium
Tel: (+32 10) 23 53 53
Fax: (+32 10) 23 53 10
e-mail: infotec@tecbw.com
Web: www.tecbw.com; www.infotec.be

Current situation
Separate organisations are responsible for urban and regional operations in the two language-based areas of the country: Vlaamse Vervoermaatschappij (VVM) operates in Flemish-speaking areas as De Lijn, and Société Régionale Wallonne du Transport Public (SRWT) operates in French-speaking areas as TEC. These substantial bus operations in and around Brussels reflect the former tramway system serving outer areas now swallowed up in the metropolitan area. Services are closely integrated with those of STIB-MIVB.

Société Nationale des Chemins de fer Belges (SNCB)/Nationale Maatschappij der Belgische Spoorwegen (NMBS) (Belgian National Railway)

NMBS-Holding
Central District
Avenue Fonsnylaan 47B, B-1060 Brussels, Belgium
Tel: (+32 2) 224 53 00
Fax: (+32 2) 224 79 89
Web: www.b-rail.be

Type of operation: Suburban and interurban heavy rail

Passenger journeys: (Total operations)
(2003) 169.3 million
(2004) 178.3 million
(2005) 186.6 million

Current situation
Suburban and longer-distance interurban services run at least hourly on 10 routes radiating from Brussels. Most trains run through from Nord to Midi or vice versa, providing frequent cross-city link through Centrale station. Also 20 min service to the National airport. Electrified 3 kV DC.

For further information on Société Nationale des Chemins de fer Belges (SNCB)/Nationale Maatschappij der Belgische Spoorwegen (NMBS), please see *Jane's World Railways*.

Charleroi

Population: 201,300 (2006 estimate), urban area: 500,000 (estimate)

Public transport
Bus and tramway/light rail services provided by regional publicly owned undertaking. Suburban rail services by state railway (SNCB).

Société de Transport en Commun de Charleroi (TEC Charleroi)

Place des Tramways 9, B-6000 Charleroi, Belgium
Tel: (+32 71) 23 41 15   Fax: (+32 71) 23 42 09
e-mail: contact@tec-wl.be
Web: www.infotec.be

Key personnel
Director General: Gilbert Delva
   Staff: 1,047

Passenger journeys: (Both modes)
(2002) 23.547 million
(2003) 24.081 million
(2004) 24.096 million
(2005) 25.007 million
(2006) 26.812 million

Current situation
TEC was created in 1991 under the reorganisation of local transport that saw control pass to the new regional body Société Regionale Wallonne du Transport. TEC replaced the former operators STIC and SNCV and brought public transport in Charleroi under single management. It serves a total of 20 towns covering an area of some 1,100 km². Four longer-distance bus routes are run by private operators.

Part of the former network of interurban tramways in Charleroi and the surrounding area has been converted into a light rail system. Services feed into an 8- km City-centre line, mostly elevated, which may eventually form a loop. The initial section was opened in 1976, though subsequent progress has been intermittent.

A further section to Janson and Parc opened in 1996, when two new routes were introduced.

Bus
Number of routes: 70
Route length: 1,819.2 km

Fleet: 283 vehicles (as at March 2007)

Van Hool A120	10
Van Hool/DAF	17
Van Hool/ MAN A500	20
Van Hool/MAN A600	10
EMI/RVI	40
BKF/DAF	3
Van Hool/DAF A508	2
Van Hool/Cat A500	85
QBS/PSA	1
Van Hool/MAN A330	16
Van Hool/MAN A508 SEAG	4
Van Hool/MAN A508	4
IRB/IVE	60
JKR/DAF Transit 2000	3
JKR/MAN Transit 2000	4

One-person operation: All routes
Fare collection: Payment to driver or pre-purchase
Fare structure: Zonal; ticket cards; various passes; free transfers; national system of common zonally valid multi-journey strip tickets

TEC-Charleroi buses at Sud station   1323682

TEC-Chareroi LRVs/trams at depot   1323680

Fares collected on board: 29 per cent (increasing, due to mobility advertising campaign)
Fare evasion control: Inspectors; penalty
Operational control: Route inspectors/mobile radio
Arrangements for elderly/disabled: Passes at reduced rates
Average distance between stops: 700 m
Average peak-hour speed: In mixed traffic, 15 km/h
Operating costs financed by: Fares 28.4 per cent, other commercial sources 3.6 per cent, subsidy/grants 68 per cent
Subsidy from: Regional government
New vehicles financed by: Loans

Tramway/light rail
Type of operation: Conventional tramway/light rail

Route length: 19.7 km
Number of stations: 20

Gauge: 1,000 mm
Track: 50 kg/m rail on 'Angleur' tie-plates inclined 1/20; 20/40 ballast
Electrification: 600 V DC, overhead

Rolling stock: 40 articulated cars
BN/ACEC (1980)   M40

Service: Peak 5 min, off-peak 30 min
First/last car: 05.00/20.00
Fare structure: Zonal
Fare collection: Pre- purchase tickets, or cash to driver
Fare evasion control: Roving inspectors, spot fines
Integration with other services: Bus feeders at many stations
Operating costs financed by: Fares 15.3 per cent, subsidy/grants 84.7 per cent

Société Nationale des Chemins de fer Belges (SNCB)/Nationale Maatschappij der Belgische Spoorwegen (NMBS)(Belgian National Railways)

SNCB-Holding
South-West District
Quai de la Gare du Sud 1, B-6000 Charleroi, Belgium

Tel: (+32 71) 60 25 00   Fax: (+32 71) 60 23 91
Web: www.b-rail.be

Key personnel
District Director: J M Delannoy
Type of operation: Suburban heavy rail

Passenger journeys: (Total operations)
(2003) 169.3 million
(2004) 178.3 million
(2005) 186.6 million

Current situation
Services operate about hourly on seven routes out of Charleroi Sud station, electrified 3 kV DC.

For further information, please see *Jane's World Railways.*

Ghent

Population: 233,100 (2006 estimate)

Public transport
Bus, trolleybus and tramway services are provided by a publicly owned regional undertaking. Suburban rail services are by the state railway SNCB/NMBS.

De Lijn Oost-Vlaanderen

Vlaamse Vervoermaatschappij (VVM)
Brusselsesteenweg 361, B-9050 Ghentbrugge, Belgium
Tel: (+32 9) 210 93 11   Fax: (+32 9) 210 93 16
e-mail: ovl@delijn.be
Web: www.delijn.be

Key personnel
Managing Director: Vacant
   Staff: 1,441 (as at May 2007)

Passenger journeys: (All modes)
(2002) 65.4 million
(2004) 85.0 million
(2005) 92.2 million
(2006) 95.5 million

Operating costs financed by: Fares 15 per cent, subsidy/grants 85 per cent (for entire VVM) (2005)

Current situation
In 1991, control of urban and regional public transport in the Vlaanderen region passed to VVM, known as De Lijn, which took over the former urban and national (SNCV) networks in the area. De Lijn is responsible for all operations of the former National Bus Company (NMVB/SNCV) and urban operators MIVG and MIVA in Flemish-speaking regions.

De Lijn Oost-Vlaanderen is one of five divisions of VVM, operating public transport in and around Ghent, and in the Dender and Waasland regions, with a total population of 1.36 million. The following data refers to the entire operation, including bus routes operated by licences operators.

Bus

Vehicle-km: (2005) 19.2 million
(2006) 36.9 million

Number of routes: 200
Route length: 2,906 km

Fleet: 371 vehicles

Standard	36
Standard low-floor	171
Articulated	66
Articulated low-floor	66
City buses	28
Microbuses	4

Most intensive service: 15 min
One-person operation: All routes
Fare collection: Payment to driver or pre- purchase with validation/cancellation machines on board
Fare structure: Zonal; multi-tickets; monthly passes; transfer surcharge; zonal system of three city and several suburban zones; passes for several zones or whole city system
Fare-evasion control: Random inspection
Operational control: Route inspectors/mobile radio

De Lijn Van Hool trolleybus   1067796

De Lijn Siemens tram at Flanders Expo (Marcel Vleugels)   1115283

Integration with other modes: Pre-purchase zonal tickets and passes also valid on other services under national integrated zonal ticket system
Average peak-hour speed: Urban routes: 21.1 km/h; regional routes: 29.26 km/h

Tramway

Type of operation: Conventional tramway
Car-km: (2002) 2.8 million
(2003) 2.9 million
(2004) 2.9 million
(2005) 2.9 million
(2006) 3.1 million

Route length: 34.7 km
Number of routes: 3
Number of stops: 169
Electrification: 600 V DC, overhead

Service: Peak 4–10 min; off-peak 15–30 min
Fare structure: As bus

Rolling stock: 77 cars

PCC 1	24
PCC 2	22
Siemens low-floor	31

On order: Four Siemens NGT6 low-floor trams due to come into operation in 2007

Developments
Opening of the southern extension to Zwijnaarde took place in 2000.

Opening of the southwestern extension to St Danus-Westrem took place in 2004.

Opening of the southwest extension to the exhibition hall Flanders Expo took place in April 2005. There are 300 park-and-ride places at the new terminus.

Trolleybus

Vehicle-km: (2002) 710,000
(2003) 538,000
(2004) Not currently available
(2005) Not currently available
(2006) 563,692

Route length: 8.3 km
Number of routes: 1

Fleet: 18 trolleybuses	
ACEC/Van Hool (1988)	18

Société Nationale des Chemins de fer Belges (SNCB)/Nationale Maatschappij der Belgische Spoorwegen (NMBS) (Belgian National Railways)

NMBS-Holding
North-West District
Koningin Maria-Hendrikaplein 2, B-9000 Ghent, Belgium

Tel: (+32 9) 241 23 00   Fax: (+32 9) 241 21 07
Web: www.b-rail.be

Key personnel
PR Officer: Geert Dierckx

Type of operation: Suburban heavy rail

Passenger journeys: (Total operations)
(2003) 169.3 million
(2004) 178.3 million
(2005) 186.6 million

Current situation
Nine routes converge on Ghent's St Pieters station, with trains at least hourly.

For further information on Société Nationale des Chemins de fer Belges (SNCB)/Nationale Maatschappij der Belgische Spoorwegen (NMBS), please see *Jane's World Railways*.

Liège

Population: 185,500, metropolitan area 600,000 (2005 estimates)

Public transport
Urban bus services for city and province provided by publicly owned regional undertaking. Suburban rail services by State railway (SNCB).

Société Régionale Wallonne des Transports (SRWT)

Transport En Commun (TEC) Liège-Verviers
Avenue Gouverneur Bovesse 96, B-5100 Jambes (Namur), Belgium
Tel: (+32 81) 32 27 11
e-mail: info@tec-wl.be
Web: www.infotec.be

Key personnel
Chair: Hector Magotte
  Director General: Freddy Joris
  Staff: 1,636

Current situation
TEC was created in 1991 under the reorganisation of local transport that saw control pass to the new regional body Société Regionale Wallonne du Transport. TEC replaced three former operators, STIL, STIV and SNCV; it serves a total population of 997,000 throughout the province of Liège. About 25 per cent of routes are contracted out, mainly in rural areas.

Developments
Magnetic ticketing introduced 1994. Minibus services for mobility-impaired passengers introduced 1996.

Bus

Passenger journeys: (Total operations, including contracted)
(1995) 77.5 million
(1996) 74.8 million
(1997) 75.1 million

Vehicle-km: (1995) 31.2 million
(1996) 31.5 million
(1997) 34.8 million

Number of routes: 191, of which 49 Liège urban
Route length: (One way) 4,062 km
On priority right-of-way: 16.6 km

Fleet: 1,107 vehicles
Liège urban

Volvo B59 (1976/77)	4
Van Hool/MAN A120/20/50/051/60 (1978/80/81/82/90)	164
Van Hool/DAF A120/3 (1978/79/80/81)	33
Van Hool/MAN AG280 (1981/84/86)	40
Van Hool/DAF AG280/3 (1986)	11
Van Hool/MAN AG700 (1993)	7
Van Hool/MAN A600 (1991/92)	90
Van Hool/DAF A600 (1991)	18
Van Hool/MAN A500PL (1993)	41
Renault R312 (1994/95/96)	138
Renault Agora-PMR	5
Mercedes TPMR minibus (1996)	3
MAN minibus (1988)	1
Van Hool/MAN A508 midibus	2
Regional fleet	
Standard	488
Articulated	58
Midibus	2
Minibus	2

In peak service: 450 (Liège urban)

Most intensive service: 2 min
One-person operation: All routes
Fare collection: Single tickets, multijourney cards, monthly and annual passes
Fare structure: Stage
Arrangements for elderly/disabled: Trials being made with lift-equipped buses on a city-centre route
Average distance between stops: 378 m
Average peak-hour speed: 24 km/h
Bus priority: Bus lanes total 16.6 km, of which 10.6 km are physically separated

Integration with other modes: Combined road-rail tickets available; several interchanges between rail and interurban bus
Operational control: Radio-telephone enables controller to call drivers individually or in groups; 400 buses at the main Robermont depot are linked to a computer which programmes departures into service and checks and maintains battery charging, preheating and fuel levels
Operating costs financed by: Fares 31.4 per cent, other commercial sources (advertising) 3.8 per cent, regional subsidy/grants 64.8 per cent
New vehicles financed by: Loans

Société Nationale des Chemins de fer Belges (SNCB)/Nationale Maatschappij der Belgische Spoorwegen (NMBS) (Belgian National Railway)

NMBS-Holding
South-East District
Place des Guillemins 2/002, B-4000 Liège, Belgium
Tel: (+32 4) 229 26 53
Web: www.b-rail.be

Type of operation: Suburban heavy rail

Passenger journeys: (Total operations)
(2003) 169.3 million
(2004) 178.3 million
(2005) 186.6 million

Current situation
Hourly services run on six routes out of Guillemins station.

For further information on Société Nationale des Chemins de fer Belges (SNCB)/Nationale Maatschappij der Belgische Spoorwegen (NMBS), please see *Jane's World Railways*.

Brazil

Belo Horizonte

Population: City: 2.4 million (2006), metropolitan area 4.35 million (estimate)

Public transport
Bus services for the city are provided by independent operators and co-ordinated by the municipally controlled BHTrans. Interurban bus services within the metropolitan area are the responsibility of the Minas Gerais state government (DER-MG), which also manages urban bus operations in other municipalities making up the Belo Horizonte metropolitan area. Metro and suburban rail services operated by state company.

Empresa de Transporte e Trânsito de Belo Horizonte S/A (BHTrans)

Avenida Engenheiro Carlos Goulart, N° 900, Bairro Buritis, Belo Horizonte, CEP 30.455.902, Minas Gerais, Brazil

Tel: (+53 31) 32 77 65 00   Fax: (+53 31) 33 79 56 60
Web: www.bhtrans.pbh.gov.br

Key personnel
Director – President: Ricardo Medanha Ladeira
Operations Manager: Alexandre A C Meirelles

Current situation
BHTrans replaced the similar authority Transmetro in 1993 with a remit to plan, manage, co-ordinate, execute, delegate and oversee provision of public transport service in the Belo Horizonte municipality. BHTrans is responsible for the planning and implementation of traffic operations and the city's road system as well as controlling the public collective and school transport operators and taxis. Approximately 1.4 million passenger journeys are carried out each day.

Bus operations are carried out by private companies, under contract to BHTrans. Some routes include segregated busways and bus lanes, in total approximately 21 km in length.

Developments
After years of delays, the project to integrate the public transport systems of Belo Horizonte is being implemented (BHBUS).

A centralised traffic management system (CIT) has been installed to monitor vehicles, regulate traffic lights in real time and send electronic messages to the drivers. As well as improving traffic flow in the city centre, it has also reduced vehicle accidents and improved pedestrian safety. Once the system is installed fully, the reduction in 'stop and go' movements is expected to speed up buses, lower fuel consumption and reduce vehicle emissions and noise. Further improvements include the installation of two air pollution monitors and the design of an inspection and maintenance programme for vehicles.

Currently, the company is in the process of further integrating private bus operations with the metro system. In mid-2006, the World Bank produced a report on the integration of the two systems and the restructuring of the municipal bus system

(BHBUS). With the Bank's financial assistance, in the way of a loan, the number of integrated bus lines has risen from 155 to 170. Some 60 per cent of the demand for metro services has been integrated and fare integration between the two systems is now by smartcard. Inter-municipal bus service integration is carried out via paper tickets. However, full integration is being delayed due to concerns by the private bus owners in relation to loss of income should inter-municipality services be integrated fully with the new system.

Seven minibus lines have been set up, with reduced fares, to serve disadvantaged areas.

There are plans to increase the number of busways/bus lanes, starting with the Avenue Antonio Carlos, one of the busiest corridors in the city.

Private bus
Number of routes: Not currently available
Route length: City 7,800 km, including metropolitan region: 16,157 km

Fleet: 2,900 vehicles (estimate)
Breakdown of fleet not currently available

In peak service: 2,500 (estimate)
Average age of fleet: Not currently available

Operating costs financed by: Fares 100 per cent

Metrô de Belo Horizonte (Metrô BH)
Superintendência de Trens Urbanos de Belo Horizonte (STU-BH)
Rua Januária, 181 Floresta, Belo Horizonte, CEP 31.110-060, Brasil
Tel: (+53 31) 32 50 39 00
e-mail: stu-bh@cbtu.gov.br
Web: www.metrobh.gov.br

Central administration
Companhia Brasileira de Trens Urbanos (CBTU)
Estrada Velha da Tijuca 77, Usina, Rio de Janeiro, CEP 20.531-080, Brazil
Tel: (+53 21) 25 75 31 74
e-mail: imprensa@cbtu.gov.br
Web: www.cbtu.gov.br

Key personnel
Superintendent of Projects Implementation: Bernardo Galvão Medeiros
Staff: 763

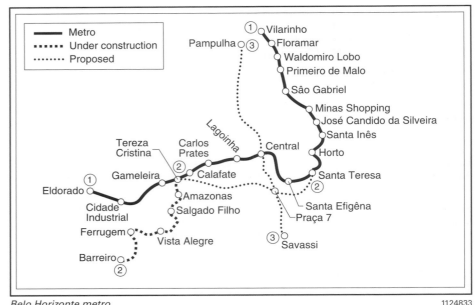

Belo Horizonte metro   1124833

Type of operation: Regional metro, opened 1986

Passenger journeys: (2004) 29.4 million
(2005) 32.0 million
(2006) 35.6 million
(2007) 39.5 million

Route length: 28.2 km
Number of lines: 1
Number of stations: 19
Gauge: 1,600 mm
Track: Conventional ballast
Electrification: 3 kV DC, overhead

Current situation
The Companhia Brasileira de Trens Urbanos (CBTU) is a federal government company, responsible for the operation of the train systems in five Brazilian metropolitan regions: Belo Horizonte, Recife, Natal, João Pessoa and Maceió
The subdivision of Belo Horizonte (Superintendência de Trens Urnanos de Belo Horizonte (STU-BH)), known as Metrô BH, is served by metro Line 1, which is 28.2 km long and runs from Eldorado to Vilarinho.
Trains run every 4 min (peak) or 16 min (off-peak) from 05.45 to 23.00. Flat fare system

with bus/rail transfers and integration on some routes. There is interchange with bus routes, which generates approximately 60 per cent of demand at an integrated tariff.

Developments
Two additional lines are projected: Linha 2 (9.3 km), running west-east to connect Barreiro and Hospitais; and Linha 3 (10.3 km), running north-south to connect Pampulha and Savassi.

Rolling stock: 25 four-car emus
Francorail TCO/Cobrasma (1985)   M20 T20
CCTU (1997/2001)   M30 T30

Service: 4 min (peak)
First/last train: 05.45/23.00
Integration with other modes: 56 bus routes provide feeder services; interchange with suburban rail
Operating costs financed by:
Fares cover 55 per cent of operating costs; central government subsidy 45 per cent

---

Brasilia
Population: City: 198,422 (2000 Census), including satellite cities: 2.3 million (estimate)

Public transport
Bus services supervised by public transport department of the district government (DETRAN-DF). Metro.

Departamento de Trânsito do Distrito Federal (DETRAN-DF)
SAM Lote A Bloco B, Ed Sede DETRAN/DF, CEP 70.620- 230, Brasilia, Brazil
Tel: (+55 61) 33 42 25 99
Fax: Not currently available
Web: www.detran.df.gov.br

Key personnel
Director General: Délio Cardoso Cézar da Silva
Assistant to the Director General: Jorge Cézar de Araújo Caldas
Director, Transit Security: Dalmo Rebello Silveira

Current situation
Services of state-owned Transportes Colectivo de Brasilia (TCB) (www.tcb.df.gov.br) (145 vehicles). Provides services on some 22 routes, mainly centred on the 'Plano Pilot' – the downtown

area of Brasilia. DETRAN-DF is responsible for licensing other operators, and planning and supervising of all services.

Companhia do Metropolitano do Distrito Federal – Metrô-DF
Avenida Jequitibá, Lote 155, Águas Claras, CEP 71.929-540, Brasilia DF, Brazil
Tel: (+55 61) 33 53 70 00   Fax: (+55 61) 33 53 14 72
e-mail: pre@metro.df.gov.br, gab@metro.df.gov.br
Web: www.metro.df.gov.br

Key personnel
Director President: José Gaspar de Souza

Type of operation: Conventional metro

Route length: 40.4 km
  in tunnel: 10.4 km
Number of lines: 2
Number of stations: 21 (total will be 29)
Gauge: 1,600 mm
Track: Surface, ballasted; in tunnels, concrete slab; 57 kg/m rail
Minimum curve radius: 250 m
Electrification: 750 V DC, third rail

Current situation
The Green Line connects the Metrô-DF Central station, located in Brasília's downtown bus

station, to the Águas Claras station, and extends to the Ceilândia Sul station, in the satellite city of Ceilândia.
The Orange Line also begins in downtown Brasilia, at the downtown central bus station, and continues, on tracks parallel to the Green Line, up to the Águas Claras station, then onwards to the Samambaia station.
The two lines are shaped like a 'Y' and follow the two main axes of urban population travel.
The metro lines travel both underground and on the surface. Surface stretches run along trenches, landfills, ditches and level ground sections. There are no elevated sections, only some overpasses above roads and streams.

Developments
Metrô-DF's total project includes 40.4 km of track from downtown Brasília and the satellite cities of Samambaia, Ceilândia, Taguatinga, Águas Claras and Guará.
The 108 Sul and Ceilândia Sul-Ceilândia stations were commissioned in April 2008. This section services Guariroba, Ceilândia Centro and Ceilândia Norte stations. The 102 Sul and 112 Sul stations are already being built, together with Guará station. The 102 Sul and 112 Sul stations are scheduled to be ready in April 2009 and Guará station in 2010. The Estrada Parque station has already been completed, but has not yet been

opened to the public as part of the company's operational strategy.

104 Sul, 106 Sul, and 110 Sul stations only need internal finishing, decoration and operational equipment, as well as access ramps to the underground facilities. No date has yet been set for their commissioning, nor for Onoyama station.

Rolling stock: 80 cars (20 four-car emus)
Mafersa (1993/94)   M40 T40

Service: Peak 6 min 10 sec, off-peak 7 min 15 sec–10 min
First/last train: 06.00/23.30 (Monday-Friday), 07.00/19.00 (Saturday, Sunday and holidays)
Fare structure: Flat
Integration with other modes: Planned
Signalling: Full ATC
Surveillance: Planned

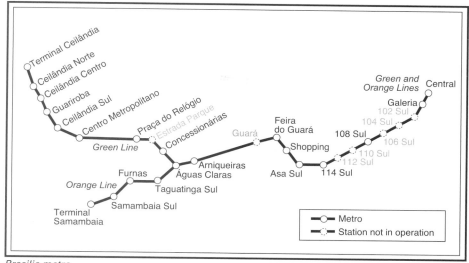

Brasilia metro   1168314

Curitiba

Population: 1.59 million (2000 Census)

Public transport
Integrated Transport Network operated by URBS, a publicly-administrated, privately-funded company, which is responsible for provision of system of busways and terminals and setting of fares and service levels.

Urbanização de Curitiba S/A (URBS)
Empresa Gerenciadora do Transporte Coletivo, Prefeitura Municipal de Curitiba
PO Box 17017, Av Presidente Affonso Camargo 330, CP 80060-090, Curitiba, Paraná, Brazil
Tel: (+55 41) 322 48 46   Fax: (+55 41) 232 94 75
Web: www.curitiba.pr.gov.br

Key personnel
Chief of Division: Luiz Filla
Head of Press Relations: Janaína Cássia

Background
Publicly administered, privately funded company founded in 1963.

Current situation
Curitiba's collective transportation system has collected a series of international awards. The most recent was granted by the English Building and Social Housing Foundation.

Begun in the 1970s with the aim of prioritising mass transport, the system aims to combine low operational costs with quality service. Around two million passengers are transported daily with a 89 per cent user satisfaction rate, according to a survey by URBS, which runs the system.

The most significant edge within Curitiba's transportation scheme is the availability of an integrated tariff, which allows commuters throughout the whole city for a single fare. Each user can make his or her own intinerary, since the system is integrated by means of terminals and tube-stations.

Terminals are integration points located at the end of structural axes. Users who live in nearby areas arrive at one of the existing 20 terminals by means of the feeder routes. From there they can choose any itinerary, paying a single fare. Express bus routes complete the trip downtown. The remaining points in Curitiba can be reached with the interdistrict and 'speedy' bus routes.

Tube stations, of which there are 351, are loading and unloading platforms, at the same height as the doors of the Direct Route (also called 'speedy') buses. Fares are paid beforehand, at the station itself, making a fare collector inside the bus unnecessary. Vehicles spend less time commuting between the tube stations, located

Bi-articulated bus on busway, Curitiba (Bill Luke)   0126408

Bi-articulated bus at Barbarosa terminal, Curitiba (Bill Luke)   0126406

an average of 800 m apart. Paying fares in advance saves riders up to 60 minutes daily and, if compared to a conventional system, saves up to 18 per cent of operating costs, URBS reports.

In total, 251 tube stations are equipped with lifts for disabled users.

Those commuting long distances, which is the case in most low-income populations, are subsidised by those making shorter trips. It is estimated that around 80 per cent of users have benefited by this integration.

In 2001, the Integrated Transport Network operated with 1,902 buses, making about 14,000 journeys daily, totalling 316,000 km every 24 hours.

The system is integrated with several metropolitan area municipalities, serving eight cities within Greater Curitiba: Almirante Tamandaré, Colombo, Pinhais, São José dos Pinhais, Araucária, Fazenda Rio Grande, Campo Magro and Campo Largo. Integration is supported by conventional bus routes, metropolitan buses, expresses and ligeirinho (speedy) buses transporting about 250,000 passengers daily who either live or work in the neighbouring cities.

Trinitarian system
From 1974 onward, an express bus system – called the 'surface subway' – has been operational in Curitiba. It consists of a revolutionary solution for linking downtown to the neighbourhoods through exclusive traffic lanes. The trinitarian system of lanes was therefore created, flanking an 'express bus only' middle lane with two outer lanes for slower traffic. The express lanes enable a considerably higher average bus speed without jeopardising passenger safety.

There are now 72 km of exclusive lanes which cross the city along its north, south, east, west and southwest axes. The main axes are complemented by 270 km of feeder routes and 185 km of interdistrict routes, servicing about 65 per cent of the urban area. If added to the conventional routes, Curitiba's urban transportation system covers the entire municipal area.

Fare structure: Flat; set by city. Double for executive midibus services and lower for city centre and neighbourhood routes. Free transfers authorised
Fare collection: By driver or prepurchase from roadside ticket machines on main routes
Fares collected on board: 60 per cent
Operational control: Route inspectors

Arrangements for elderly/disabled: Free travel for over-65s/blind persons, disabled people from low-income families and retired people with low incomes
Average speed: On reserved lanes 20 km, direct line 32 km/h, other 16 km/h
Average distance between stops: 500 m on exclusive lanes, with terminals (transfer stations) every 4 km; direct line 3.2 km
Bus priority: 72 km of busways and bus lanes under city pro-public transport policy (see below), and priority at junctions by bus actuations or area traffic control
Operating costs financed by: Fares 100 per cent
New vehicles financed by: Municipality, with fares recovery element

---

Fortaleza
Population: 2.38 million (estimate as at July 2005)

Public transport
Bus services regulated by ETTUSA and operated by private companies. Regional metro system being developed from suburban rail lines.

Empresa de Transporte Urbano de Fortaleza SA (ETUFOR)
Avenida dos Expedicionários, 5677 – Vila União, Fortaleza/Ceará, CEP 60410-411, Brazil
Tel: (+55 85) 34 52 93 01
e-mail: ettusa@ettusa.ce.gov.br
Web: www.etufor.ce.gov.br

Key personnel
President: José Ademar Gondim
Technical Director: Daniel Lustosa
Director, Administration, Finance and Commerce: José Livino Lopes
Head of Communications: Kerla Alencar

Passenger journeys: (2005) 260 million (approximate)

Current situation
ETUFOR is a public/private partnership which, on behalf of the Fortaleza municipality, regulates all plans , municipal bus transport, taxis, mototaxis, vans and school transport.
Currently, there are 25 companies that operate bus services in Fortaleza, with a total fleet of approximately 1,623 buses and an average vehicle age of 5.4 years. These companies provide integrated services on more than 200 routes under the Integrated System of Transport (SIT).

Companhia Cearense de Transportes Metropolitanos – Metrofor (Metropolitan Transport Company of Ceará)
Rua 24 de Maio, No 60 – Centro, Fortaleza, CE/CEP 60.020-001, Brazil

Tel: (+55 85) 31 01 71 00
Fax: (+55 85) 31 01 47 44
Freephone: 0800 85 55 58
e-mail: metrofor@metrofor.ce.gov.br
Web: www.metrofor.ce.gov.br

Key personnel
Assistant to the President: Fernando Mota

Type of operation: Suburban heavy rail

Background
Metrofor is a semi-state company, whose major participant is the State of Ceará Government. Created in May 1977, the company co-ordinates and carries out the implementation of the Metrofor Project in Fortaleza and metropolitan area.

Passenger journeys: (1995) 7.6 million

Current situation
Two separate metre-gauge routes (43 km, 17 stations) have been upgraded and resignalled to form the first stage of a commuter railway/metro. Fares cover 18 per cent of operating costs.

Developments
The Metrofor Project consists of three stages, with an estimated total cost of USD590 million. The aim of the project is to modernise the existing railway system through electrification of the Fortaleza Metropolitan Region (FMR) main lines, the acquisition of new rolling stock (totalling 18 trains), the installation of modern signalling and communications systems and new and improved stations. The projected number of passengers carried on the completed system is given as 344,000 per day.

First Stage
Construction of the South line, which links João Felipe Station, in Fortaleza, with Vila das Flores, in the municipality of Pacatuba. Work includes

duplication of the tracks and separation of the passenger transport system from the cargo transportation system.
Some 24 km of duplicated track for passenger transport will be implemented, 3.8 km of which will be underground and 2.8 km being elevated between Couto Fernandes and Vila Perry.
There is an estimated requirement for 10 new trains for this stage.

Second Stage
Interconnection from Caucaia to Fortaleza (João Felipe) with construction of 19 km of passenger line and a further eight trains. This includes electrification and communications systems.

Third Stage
Full integration of the Metrofor system with urban and metropolitan buses and private vehicles. There will also be a study to examine the possible need for further stations and rolling stock on the Maracanaú-Fortaleza-Caucaia passenger line.
A branch from Conjunto Jereissati, at Maracanaú, to the city of Maranguape is also envisaged, with diesel traction trains operating on this route.
Metrofor has placed a turnkey order with Alstom for the metro system. The order covers 10 four-car trainsets, which incorporate the ONIX 3000 drive system, and the signalling system. In addition, Alstom is responsible for the management of the project and the integration and installation of the complete electrical and mechanical system. The overall system will be manufactured by Alstom's factories in São Paulo, with traction equipment supplied by Alstom's plant in Tarbes, France.

Rolling stock: 6 diesel locomotives, 45 coaches

Porto Alegre
Population: 1.44 million (2006 estimate), metropolitan area 3.8 million (2005 estimate)

Public transport
Bus and minibus services provided by private operators holding concessions and organised into consortia, and fixed-route shared-taxi system, supervised by municipal administration which has established a busway system. Suburban rail (please see entry for CPTM in *Jane's World Railways*). Metro, with extension planned.

Companhia Carris Porto-Alegrense (Carris)
Rua Albion 385, Bairro São José, Porto Alegre-RS, Brazil
Tel: (+55 51) 32 89 21 00
e-mail: sacc@carris.com.br
Web: www.carris.com.br

Passenger boardings: (2006) 24 million (estimate)
Vehicle-km: (2006) 73 million (estimate)

Number of routes: 26
Route length: Not currently available

Key personnel
Director President: Anotnio Lorenzi
Director of Finance: Regis Leal
Director of Technology: Hélio Flores Mendes
Manager, Administration/Finance: Marco Antonio Silva
Manager, Operations: Julio César Gomes dos Santos
Manager, Maintenance: Antenor Forlin
Co-ordinator, Communications and Marketing: Luzia Lindenbaum
Public Relations: Ana Otto
Staff: 1,600 (estimate)

Background
Carris is the city council's public transport service and has been operating for more than 130 years.

Current situation
Companhia Carris Porto-Alegrense (Carris) is the city council's public transport bus service operator – the Prefeitura de Port Alegre has 99.9 per cent ownership.
Bus fares are integrated with Trensurb metro services.

Fleet: 335 vehicles
Full fleet breakdown is not currently available, but includes:

Air-conditioned buses	142
Automatic buses	244
Accessible buses	127

Empresa Pública de Transporte e Circulação (EPTC)

Secretaria Municipal da Mobilidade Urbana (SMMU)
Rua João Neves da Fontoura 7, Porto Alegre, RS, Brazil
Tel: (+55 51) 32 89 43 50
Fax: (+55 51) 32 89 43 24
e-mail: eptc@eptc.prefpoa.com.br
Web: www.eptc.com.br

Key personnel
Secretary of Transport and President-Director, EPTC: Luiz Afonso dos Santos Senna
Contact: Emilio Merino Dominguez

Current situation
The Empresa Pública de Transporte e Circulação (EPTC) was created in 1998 in order to implement the new Código Brasileiro de Trânsito (Brazilian Traffic Code) compiled by the federal government. The Code was set up to improve transportation throughout the country.

Urban services are provided by 14 companies organised into three operational consortia, which operate in three geographical areas of the city, and a public company, Companhia Carris Porto-Alegrense (Carris), which operates circular routes in the downtown area and is also responsible for co-operation between the three consortia. There are some 300 bus routes with a total fleet of some 1,430 vehicles carrying an average of 1.17 million passengers per day.

The metropolitan bus system is managed by the state government of Rio Grande do Sul, with daily passenger journeys of more than 350,000.

There is also a fleet of more than 400 21-seater minibuses, permitted to carry seated passengers only, which operate as a taxi-shuttle service. These cater for 80,000 daily journeys.

Busway
Current situation
The first mass public transport corridors in Porto Alegre were created in the 1980s, with 28 km of bus lanes built along central reservations. Although overtaking is prohibited, the lanes built resulted in increased speed and shortened travel times, with fleet and operational resources being optimised.

In 2001, construction work began at Terceira Perimetral Avenue, the latest and largest investment in Porto Alegre's road network. This transverse route, the primary axis between the southern and northern areas of the city, includes a two-lane central platform, will be 11 km in length, will have 19 stations and four interchange points and will connect up to 20 city neighbourhoods.

Bus-only lanes in the centre of major roads and eight lanes (total length 51 km, with a total of 85 stops) are used by both urban services and those originating outside the city, and some bus flows exceed 350 per hour. The Comonor convoy system is used to maximise the capacity of the lanes which are up to 9.1 km long. Buses to and from various destinations are held at lane entry points to travel as a unit halting in unison at each stop, enabling volumes of up to 20,000 passengers per hour to be carried at speeds of more than 20 km/h, including stops. Buses serve protected 'stations', though passengers generally must cross the outer (general) traffic lanes to reach them. SMT staff assist in this by undertaking traffic control.

Interchange Protasio Alves on the Corredor Terceira Perimetral 1137310

Empresa de Trens Urbanos de Porto Alegre SA (Trensurb)

Rua Ernesto Neugebauer 1985, Bairro Humaitá, CEP 90.250-140 Porto Alegre, RS, Brazil
Tel: (+55 51) 21 29 80 00
Fax: (+55 51) 21 29 81 66
e-mail: seapobib@trensurb.com.br
Web: www.trensurb.com.br

Key personnel
Director and President: Marco Arildo Prates da Cunha
Director, Administration and Financial: Paulo Roberto Cardoso Thimóteo
Director, Operations: Luiz Carlos De Cesaro
Expansion and Development Superintendent: Humberto Kasper
Staff: 1,123 (as at December 2003)

Type of operation: Regional metro, opened 1985

Passenger journeys: (2002) 41.29 million
(2003) 44.68 million
(2004) 48.98 million
(2005) 47.25 million
(2006) 45.78 million

Route length: 34.5 km
Number of routes: 1
Number of stations: 17
Gauge: 1,600 mm
Track: Conventional ballasted, twin-block concrete sleepers with 57 kg/m welded rail
Electrification: 3 kV DC, overhead

Background
Trensurb was established in 1980 to develop a high-capacity regional metro from the existing federal railway system, RFFSA, suburban line from Porto Alegre downtown to Novo Hamburgo, an important development corridor. The line was opened from Mercado to Sapucaia do Sul in 1985, extended by 3.9 km to Unisinos in São Leopoldo in 1997 and by a further 2.4 km elevated section to São Leopoldo in 2001.

Current situation
Although Trensurb is not a part of the Companhhia Brasileira de Trens Urbanso – Brazilian Urban Trains Company (CBTU), the company is managed directly by the federal government. Transfer to local state control has been discussed, but without an effective conclusion.

In December 2003, the three institutional levels – federal, state and municipal – signed an agreement to study an integrated network of medium- and high-capacity public transport in the Porto Alegre Metropolitan Region, and Transurb will participate in this project.

Under the agreement, a study is being carried out for a second line.

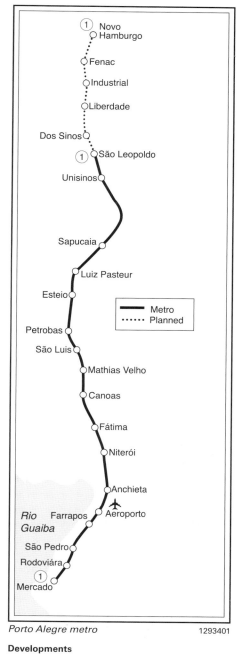
Porto Alegre metro 1293401

Developments
A 9.3 km four-station extension to Line 1, northwards from São Leopoldo to Novo Hamburgo, is planned.

Projects for future new lines will be defined by the studies under way by the work group under the above mentioned agreement.

Rolling stock: 25 four-car trains
Nippon Sharyo/Hitachi/Kawasaki (1984)   M100
In peak service: 19 trains

Service: Peak 5 min, off-peak 10 min
First/last train: 05.15/23.20
Fare structure: Flat
Operational control/communications: CTC, ATC with ATS and cab signalling
Integration with other modes: Transfer to 142 bus routes feeding 16 Trensurb stations
Operating costs financed by: Fares 32.6 per cent, other commercial sources 4.7 per cent, subsidy/grants 62.7 per cent

---

Recife

Population: City 1.52 million, metropolitan area 3.65 million (estimates)

Public transport
Bus services provided by private companies, with busways regulated by municipally owned undertakings. Metro and suburban railway operated by state company.

Empresa Metropolitana de Transportes Urbanos (EMTU)

Cais de Santa Rita s/n São José, 50020-360 Recife, Brazil
Tel: (+55 81) 34 19 10 01, 34 19 10 02
Fax: (+55 81) 32 24 06 10
e-mail: emtu@emtu.pe.gov.br
Web: www.emtu.pe.gov.br

Key personnel
President: Dilson Peixote
Head of Planning: Maurício Renato Pina Moreira
Staff: 300+

Current situation
EMTU was created in 1980 to eliminate conflict between public transport operators licensed by the federal, state and municipal authorities.

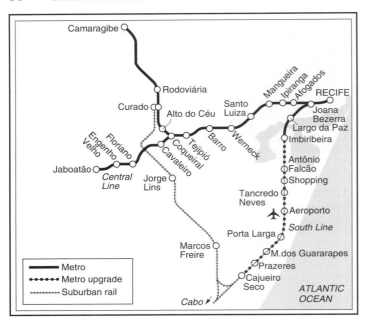

Map of Recife metro
1115206

EMTU supervises a network of 359 conventional bus and 18 minibus routes, operated by 17 different companies.

Developments
In 2006, the fleet underwent a major upgrade with the purchase of 442 new buses.

Recife
Private bus/minibus
Current situation
Operations of some 17 private companies carry approximately 420 million passengers annually.

Fleet: 2,79 9 vehicles	
Two-axle, full-size buses	2,616
Articulated buses	55
Minibuses	51
Microbuses	77

Metrorec
Superintendência de Trens Urbanos de Recife (STU-REC)
Rua José Natario 478, Areias, Recife, CEP 50.900-000, Brazil
Tel: (+55 81) 32 52 61 00

Central administration
Companhia Barsileira de Trens Urbanos (CBTU)
Estrada Velha da Tijuca 77, Usina, Rio de Janeiro, CEP 20.531-080, Brazil
Tel: (+55 21) 25 75 31 74
e-mail: imprensa@cbtu.gov.br
Web: www.cbtu.gov.br

Key personnel
Staff: 1,477

Type of operation: Regional metro, first line opened 1985; suburban rail

Passenger journeys: (2004) 53.7 million
(2005) 54.3 million
(2006) 57.2 million
(2007) 56.6 million

Route length: 68.8 km (Central Line 24.4 km, South Line 13.4 km, Diesel Line 31 km)
Number of lines: 3
Number of stations: 27
Gauge: 1,600 mm and 1,000 mm
Track: Conventional ballasted
Electrification: 3 kV DC, overhead 37.8 km Metrorec line

Current situation
The Companhia Brasileira de Trens Urbanos (CBTU) is a federal government company, responsible for the operation of the train systems in five Brazilian metropolitan regions: Belo Horizonte, Recife, Natal, João Pessoa and Maceió.

The Recife subdivision, known as Metrorec, is served by two lines, the Central Line (Recife-Camaragibe/Jaboatão) and the South Line (Recife-Cabo) and the diesel-worked suburban service South Line, linking Cabo to the Central Line, (31 km long, gauge 1,000 mm).

Trains on the Central Line run every 6 min (peak) or 7½ min (off-peak) from 05.30 to 23.00. Flat fare system, with bus/rail transfers and integration on some routes. There is interchange with bus routes which generates approximately 50 per cent of demand at an integrated tariff.

Trains on the Diesel Line run every 60 min (peak) or 65 min (off-peak) from 05.30 to 20.00.

Developments
There are plans for a light rail system (31.9 km), linking Cajueiro-Seco to Curado.

Rolling stock: 25 four-car emus, 4 diesel locomotives, 21 coaches
Service: Peak 6 min
First/last train: 05.00/23.00
Integration with other modes: 56 bus routes provide feeder services; interchange with suburban rail
Operating costs financed by: Fares 20 per cent, central government subsidy 80 per cent

---

Rio De Janeiro
Population: City 6.1 million, metropolitan area (including Niterói and 13 other cities) 12.6 million (2006 estimates)

Public transport
Bus services provided in part by state-controlled public company and in part by independent operators and co-operatives, which provide all services in adjoining city of Niterói and also operate a number of premium express services across conurbation. Metro franchised to private-sector company; ferries across Guanabara Bay; suburban railways controlled by regional/state authorities.

Superintêndencia Municipal de Transportes Urbanos (SMTU)
Secretaria Municipal de Transportes – SMTR
Av Presidente Vargas, 817/ 23°, CEP: 20071-004, Rio de Janeiro, Brazil
Tel: (+55 21) 25 07 47 48, 25 07 17 88
Fax: (+55 21) 22 24 49 73
Web:www.rio.rj.gov.br/smtr
www.rio.rj.gov.br/smtu

Key personnel
Secretary, Municipal Transport: Arolde de Oliveira

Background
Private buses are licensed and supervised by the SMTU.

Current situation
Following collapse of the municipally owned bus company CTC-RJ, services are provided by

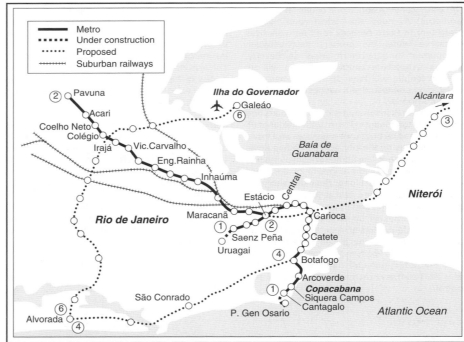

Map of Rio de Janeiro metro and suburban rail system
1124822

33 independent bus operators under licences issued by the municipality for the operation of defined services at set fares levels, though the level of supervision is low. Services include all-seated premium express commuter links with air conditioned coaches aimed particularly at

private car commuters, and microbuses. SMTU also licenses the city's 20,000 legal taxis.

Developments
A funicular railway was due to open in October 2000 linking the top station of the Corcovado rack

Daimler-Benz midibus of BrasoLis at Copacabana   0009713

Buses of two private operators on Av President Vargas   0009712

line and the foot of the Christ statue overlooking the city.

Fare collection: Payment to conductor seated at turnstile near rear entrance

Fare structure: Flat in city

Operating costs financed by: Fares 100 per cent; Vale Transporte tickets subsidised by employers up to 6 per cent of wage levels

Other bus operators

Current situation

In addition to the licensed operations described above, there are estimated to be some 2,000 buses and 5,000 vans which operate illegally. Unlicensed paratransit vans originally provided late-evening shuttle services from the city centre to the suburbs, but they now run regular commuter services to the north and west of the city, and also to Niterói. Vehicles range from Kombis to imported 14-seater Topics with air conditioning, music and reclining seats. Some operators offer free drinks and sweets.

Some vans shadow regular bus routes, calling at the same stops and poaching passengers, while others demand references from prospective passengers to avoid police surveillance. SMTU's lack of staff cannot keep pace with the spread of illegal operations, and in any case, attempts to close them down have led to violent confrontations between passengers and the authorities. Surveys by the illegal operators apparently show that 85 per cent of their passengers are car owners attracted by the fast and comfortable services, even though fares are higher than on regular routes.

Tramway

Type of operation: Conventional tramway

Current situation

Two routes totalling 8.2 km survive to serve the hilly suburb of Santa Teresa, operated with vintage rolling stock, partly as a tourist attraction. The Carioca tramway has survived due to its unique central area access across a broad valley

on a single track atop an arched stone aqueduct. Trams run half-hourly from 06.00 to 23.30; fares revenue covers only the cost of the electricity required to run the service.

Rolling stock: 17 cars
St Louis Car/General Electric (1909)   M17

Opportrans Concessão Metroviária SA (Metrô Rio)

Av Presidente Vargas 2000, Centro, CEP 20201-031 Rio de Janeiro, Brazil
Tel: (+55 21) 516 11 23
Fax: (+55 21) 516 51 35, 32 11 64 64
Web: www.metrorio.com.br

Type of operation: Full metro and light rail, first line opened 1979

Passenger journeys: (Annual) 182.5 million (estimate)

Route length: Metro (Line 1) 15.7 km, all in tunnel; light rail/pre-metro (Line 2) 21.7 km
Number of lines: 2
Number of stations: 33
Gauge: 1,600 mm
Max gradient: 4%
Minimum curve radius: 500 m
Tunnel: Mainly cut-and-cover; various techniques, including diaphragm walls up to 1.2 m thick, used to prevent soil subsidence and property damage due to high water table
Electrification: 750 V DC, third rail

Current situation
Six-car trains are used on Line 1 and four-car trains on Line 2.

Developments
In early 2007, a 1.2-km extension of Line 1 opened, from Siqueira Campos to Cantagalo.

In a partnership between Metrô Rio and Rio Ônibus, bus and metro services have been integrated.

There are plans for a further extension of Line 1 southwards to Praca General Osório and a 1-km shuttle line, to be operated by four-car trains, from Saens Peña to a new station, Uruguai, is under construction.

Other plans include a new 22-km Line 6, which will link the international airport with Barra de Tijuca and provide transfers to Line 2 and suburban rail services and a new Line 3, running from Carioca station to Niterol and São Gonçalo.

Rolling stock: 210 cars

Mafersa A cab cars	M82
Cobrasma B	M100
Cobrasma/BN LRV	M28

Service: Mon-Sat: Line 1 4–7 min, Line 2 5–10 min
First/last train: Mon-Sat: 05.00/24.00, Sun and holidays: 07.00/23.00
Fare structure: Flat, with combined bus/rail ticket for some journeys
Revenue control: Automatic fare collection
Integration with other modes: Suburban rail, ferries, and some bus
Automatic control: Automatic pilot system

SuperVia Concessionária de Transportes Ferroviários SA (SuperVia)

Rua da América 210, Centro, Rio de Janeiro RJ, CEP 20210-590, Brazil
Tel: (+55 21) 21 11 95 27, 21 11 95 78, 21 11 94 94
Fax: (+55 21) 21 11 95 42
Web: www.supervia.com.br

Key personnel
Director, Operations: Joao Gouveia
Head of Corporate Communications: Ivone Malta
    Staff: 3,416

Type of operation: Suburban heavy rail

Passenger journeys: (2006) 145 million (estimate)
Train-km: Not currently available

Current situation
Previously operated by Flumitrens. In November 1998, the Supervia private consortium, comprising Bolsa 2000, CAF and RENFE, took over operations under a 25-year concession.

SuperVia Concessionária de Transportes Ferroviários SA (SuperVia) operates five lines, totalling 225 km in length with 89 stations, serving 11 municipalities in the metropolitan area of Rio de Janeiro.

For further information on SuperVia, please see *Jane's World Railways*.

Developments
SuperVia plans to develop its exiting lines into a surface metro network, which would allow the company to substantially increase its passengers per day. This will require replacement of signalling and power supplies, the purchase of new vehicles and the refurbishment of some existing trains. The plan is dependant upon funding being available from the government for the new vehicles.

In early 2006, the first of 20 new four-car Rotem/Toshiba trains were delivered and 18 trains were being rebuilt. Station upgrades are also under way. Some trains have been increased from eight to nine cars to handle peak traffic.

Rolling stock: 159 trains, some air-conditioned
Breakdown of fleet is not currently available

In peak service: Not currently available

Barcas SA

Rua Miguel de Lemos 80, Ponta D'Areia, Niterói – RJ, CEP-24040-260, Brazil
Tel: (+55 21) 40 04 31 13
e-mail: sac@barcas-sa.com.br
Web: www.barcas-sa.com.br

Passenger journeys: (Annual) 25.5 million (estimate)
Vessel-km: Not currently available

Ferry
Current situation
Barcas SA was formed from the privatisation of the former Compania de Navigacao do Estado do Rio de Janeiro (CONERJ) government-owned ferry operator in 1998. The company provides services between Rio-Niterói and Praça XV-Charitas. Services on the Rio-Niterói route run every 20 min (every 12 minutes in peak hours).

The fleet comprises 22 vessels. The full breakdown is not currently available, but includes vessels built by Rodriquez Cantieri Navali Do Brazil: three catamarans and three 29 m City Cat

Ferries, the former built in 2004 and the latter delivered in 2002.

Aerobarcos do Brasil, Transportes Maritimos e Turismo SA (Transtur)
Praça Iaia Garcia 3, Ribeira, Rio de Janeiro RJ, CEP-21930-040, Brazil
Tel: (+55 21) 33 96 85 41   Fax: (+55 21) 33 96 39 65
e-mail: transtur@ism.com.br
Web: www.transtur.com.br

Key personnel
Director of Administration: Hamilton Amarante Carvalho
Staff: 207

Passenger journeys: Not currently available
Vessel-km: Not currently available

Ferry
Current situation
Operates between Rio and Niterói, every 10 min from 06.15 to 20.15, and between Rio and Paquetá Island every two hours weekdays and hourly at weekends and holidays. The fleet includes hydrofoils and catamarans. Fares cover 100 per cent of costs.

For full breakdown of fleet, please see Jane's High-Speed Marine Transportation.

Salvador
Population: City 2.65 million (2006 Census), metropolitan area 3.4 million (estimate)

Public transport
Bus services in the city and 17 administrative areas are provided by franchised private groups supervised by a municipal organisation. Ferry service, funiculars and public elevator; metro under construction.

Superintendência de Transporte Público (STP)
Avenida Vale dos Barris 501, Estacionamento São Raimundo, Barris, Salvador, Bahia, CEP 40.070-055, Brazil
Tel: (+55 71) 21 09 36 00   Fax: (+55 71) 21 09 37 33
e-mail: stpnet@pms.ba.gov.br
Web: www.stp.salvador.ba.gov.br

Key personnel
Secretary of Transport and Infrastructure: Almir Melo
Superintendent of Public Transport: Matheus Lima Moura
Information Manager: Paulo Coqueijo Viana
Staff: 590

Bus
Current situation
Organising the provision of bus services is the responsibility of STP, set up in 1992 as successor to the former SETRAM organisation. STP coordinates and supervises the services of 18 private bus operators (for which SMTU is the holding company) working under franchises issued by the municipality (see below for list of private operators and their fleets). It also operates the major Lapa and Pirajá bus stations and plans bus priority and promotional measures. STP oversees planning of bus services, sets fare levels and supervises the franchises.

Developments
Bids are being evaluated for construction of an 11.9 km automated metro from Lapa to Pirajá.

Passenger journeys: (All operators)
(2003) 454.7 million
(2005) 457.6 million
(2007) 459.9 million
Vehicle-km: (All operators)
(2003) 213.2 million
(2005) 215.4 million
(2007) 212.2 million

Number of routes: 453 (28 of which are 'pooled'; includes 12 executive)
Route length: Roads covered 1,461 km
Operating costs financed by: Fares 100 per cent

Private bus
Current situation
There are 18 franchised companies (see below) with a total fleet of 2,594 vehicles (as at December 2007), which operate a total of 465 regular bus routes, including 21 'pooled' routes.

Bus in Salvador   1323792

Bus at Iguatemi shopping mall   1323790

Total fleet: 2,594 buses
In peak service: 2,214
Average age of fleet: 4.85 years

Private bus operators

Axé Transportes Urbanos Ltda
Rua General Labutat, 48E – Est. Pirajá, Salvador – Bahia, CEP 41.290-460, Brazil
Tel: (+55 71) 33 92 56 08
Fax: (+55 71) 33 92 72 26
e-mail: cpdaxe@svn.com.bt

Developments
Axé Transportes Urbanos Ltda acquired 13 vehicles in 2005 and 12 in 2006.
Staff: 733

Number of routes: 26 (regular)

Fleet: 150

Bahia Transportes Urbanos Ltda (BTU)
Avenida Santiago de Compostela s/nº, Brotas, Salvador – Bahia, CEP 40.275-700, Brazil
Tel: (+55 71) 34 80 77 77   Fax: (+55 71) 34 50 80 80
e-mail: btu@svn.com.br

Developments
Bahia Transportes Urbanos Ltda (BTU) acquired 41 vehicles in 2005 and another five in 2006.
Staff: 991

Number of routes: 40 (regular)

Fleet: 214

Viação Senhor do Bomfim (Barramar)
Rua Matiniano do Bomfim 744 – Retrio, Salvador-Bahia, CEP 40.330-650, Brazil
Tel: (+55 71) 33 81 17 95   Fax: (+55 71) 33 82 17 95
e-mail: barramar@svn.com.br

Developments
Viação Senhor do Bomfim (Barramar) acquired 21 vehicles in 2005 and 36 in 2006.
Staff: 1,130

Number of routes: 36 (regular)

Fleet: 214

Boa Viagem Transportes Ltda
Avenida Afranio Peixoto 901, Paripe, Salvador, CEP 40.750-010, Brazil
Tel: (+55 71) 35 21 13 44
Fax: (+55 71) 35 21 31 60
e-mail: boaviagem@atarde.com

Developments
Boa Viagem Transportes Ltda acquired 10 vehicles in 2005 and four in 2006.
Staff: 673

Number of routes: 22 (regular)

Fleet: 137

Central Salvador Transportes
Avenida Otávio Mangabeira 17399 – São Cristovão, Salvador, CEP 41.500-020, Brazil
Tel: (+55 71) 33 77 51 54
Fax: (+55 71) 33 77 39 85
e-mail: tondina@terra.com.br

Developments
Central Salvador Transportes acquired 16 vehicles in 2006.
Staff: 654

Number of routes: 35 (regular)

Fleet: 137

Ilha Tropical Transportes Ltda (ITT)
Parque S S Schindler Q-G, s/nº – S Caetano, Salvador, CEP 40.395-550, Brazil
Tel: (+55 71) 33 04 00 46
Fax: (+55 71) 33 04 17 10
e-mail: ilhatropical@bol.com
Staff: 187

Developments
Ilha Tropical Transportes Ltda acquired three vehicles in 2006.

Number of routes: five (regular)

Fleet: 30

Empresa de Transportes Joevanza SA (Joevanza)
Rua Thomas Gonzaga 43, Pernamnués, Salvador, CEP 41.100-000, Brazil
Tel: (+55 71) 34 80 00 06   Fax: (+55 71) 34 80 00 29
e-mail: joevanza@terra.com.br

Developments
Empresa de Transportes Joevanza SA (Joevanza) acquired two vehicles in 2005 and 17 in 2006.
Staff: 319

Number of routes: 10 (regular)

Fleet: 63

Transportes Ondina Ltda
Avenida Vasco da Gama 347 – Rio Vermelho, Salvador, CEP 40.240-090, Brazil
Tel: (+55 71) 32 45 63 66   Fax: (+55 71) 32 45 10 69
e-mail: tondina@terra.com.br

Terminal at Rodoviária station, with Praia Grande articulated bus in the foreground   1328453

Rio Vermelho bus   1328454

Developments
Transportes Ondina Ltda acquired seven vehicles in 2005 and four in 2006.
Staff: 263

Number of routes: 13 (regular)

Fleet: 73

Praia Grande Transportes Ltda
Avenida Afranio Peixoto s/nº – Praia Grande, Salvador, CEP 40.713-580, Brazil
Tel: (+55 71) 33 98 04 78   Fax: (+55 71) 33 98 09 87
e-mail: pgfin@atarde.com.br

Developments
Praia Grande Transportes Ltda acquired 45 vehicles in 2005 and 12 in 2006.
Staff: 1,124

Number of routes: 29 (regular)

Fleet: 239

Viação Rio Vermelho Ltda
Avenida Dorival Caymmi 18270 – São Cristovão, Salvador, CEP 41.500-000, Brazil
Tel: (+55 71) 33 77 25 87   Fax: (+55 71) 33 77 02 50
e-mail: vrv@svn.com.br

Developments
Viação Rio Vermelho Ltda acquired 25 vehicles in 2006.
Staff: 745

Number of routes: 35 (regular)

Fleet: 177

Coletivos São Cristovão Ltda
G II – Estrada Velha de Ipitanga s/nº – Km 1.5, Salvador, CEP 41.280-520, Brazil
Tel: (+55 71) 33 92 15 92   Fax: (+55 71) 33 92 18 93
e-mail: scrissa@terra.com.br

Developments
Coletivos São Cristovão Ltda acquired three vehicles in 2005 and 31 in 2006.
Staff: 530

Number of routes: 269 (regular)

Fleet: 123

Transportes Sol SA (Transol)
Avenida San Martin s/nº, Retiro, Salvador, CEP 40.360-010, Brazil
Tel: (+55 71) 32 56 22 99   Fax: (+55 71) 32 56 22 10
e-mail: solbraga@svn.com.br

Developments
Transportes Sol SA (Transol) acquired nine vehicles in 2005 and 20 in 2006.
Staff: 645

Number of routes: 28 (regular)

Fleet: 144

Empresa de Transportes União Ltda

Rua Tio Juca 84 E, Jd. Eldorado – IAPI, Salvador, CEP 40.310-120
Tel: (+55 71) 32 33 22 93   Fax: (+55 71) 33 89 13 16
e-mail: transuniao@e-net.com.br

Developments
Empresa de Transportes União Ltda acquired 21 vehicles in 2006.
Staff: 1,089

Number of routes: 41 (regular)

Fleet: 197

Transportes Verdemar Ltda

Avenida Vasco da Gama 850 – Rio Vermelho, Salvador, CEP 40.230-730, Brazil
Tel: (+55 71) 33 34 10 22   Fax: (+55 71) 33 34 12 52
e-mail: verdemar@svn.com.br

Developments
Transportes Verdemar Ltda acquired 13 vehicles in 2005 and 14 in 2006.
Staff: 525

Number of routes: 32 (regular)

Fleet: 120

Violeta Transportes Ltda (Vitral)

Rua Thomas Gonzaga 43, Pernambués, Salvador, CEP 41.100-000, Brazil
Tel: (+55 71) 34 80 66 33   Fax: (+55 71) 34 80 37 97
e-mail: cpd@vitral.com.br

Developments
Violeta Transportes Ltda (Vitral) acquired 12 vehicles in 2005 and 20 in 2006.
Staff: 525

Number of routes: 23 (regular)

Fleet: 119

Capital Transportes Urbanos Ltda

Avenida Aliomar Baleeiro s/nº – Lote 1 – Pirajá, Salvador, CEP 41.590-190, Brazil
Tel: (+55 71) 33 04 00 46   Fax: (+55 71) 33 04 17 10

Developments
Capital Transportes Urbanos Ltda acquired four vehicles in 2005 and 50 in 2006.
Staff: 824

Number of routes: 35 (regular)

Fleet: 217

Modelo Transporte Urbanos Ltda

Avenida Tiradentes 142 – Caminho de Areia, Salvador, CEP 40.440-000, Brazil
Tel: (+55 71) 33 12 00 25   Fax: (+55 71) 33 12 00 25

Developments
Modelo Transporte Urbanos Ltda acquired two vehicles in 2006.
Staff: 335

Plano Inclinado Liberdade-Calçada   1328458

Plano Inclinado Gonçalves   1328456

Number of routes: 18 (regular)

Fleet: 80

Expresso Vitória Bahia

Estrada de Lobato 62, Campinas Piraja, Salvador, CEP 40.330-201, Brazil
Tel: (+55 71) 34 32 75 00   Fax: (+55 71) 32 46 41 88

Developments
Expresso Vitória Bahia acquired 36 vehicles in 2005 and five in 2006.
Staff: 757

Number of routes: 27 (regular)

Fleet: 152

Elevador Lacerda
1323789

Funiculars
Current situation
The Plano Inclinado Liberdade-Calçada carries approximately 3.6 million passengers a year, a second funicular, the Gonçalves, carries around 1.5 million and the Plano Inclinado Pilar carries some 93,000 passengers per year.

Elevator
Current situation
The Elevador Lacerda provides a lift service of four cars between the upper and lower town areas, used by more than 9.4 million passengers a year.

Ferry
Current situation
Cross-harbour ferries and catamarans carry about 1.8 million passengers (including foot passengers) a year and 331,000 motor vehicles.

Taxis
There are two co-operative taxi companies in Salvador and 23 other taxi organisations providing service to the area, with a total of about 7,260 vehicles.

Companhia De Transporte de Salvador (CTS)
CTS/Diretoria de Planejamento, No Canteiro de Obras do Metrô de Salvador na Rótula do Abacaxi, CEP-40.330-600, Salvador, Bahia, Brazil
Tel: (+55) 71 33 27 11 55
e-mail: ctsdaf@salvador.ba.gov.br
Web: www.metro.salvador.ba.gov.br

Type of operation: Metro (under construction)

Current situation
Construction of metro Line 1 began in 2000 and is being carried out by a consortium of Camargo Corrêa, Andrade Cutierrez and Siemens. The 11.9 km (1.4 km in tunnel, 4.8 km elevated) double-track line will run from Lapa-Pirajá (Salvador downtown) with eight stations with 3 kV DC overhead electrification.

The vehicles will be supplied by Siemens and the system will be operated privately for a 25-year period.

Developments
Line 1 was scheduled to open some time in 2008.

There are plans for possible extensions to Line 1 and a second Line 2, which will run east-west. There are also plans to extend Line 2.

In early 2006, the World Bank announced that, having assisted with Phase 1 of the project, it may also assist with Phase 2.

Taxi rank in Salvador
1328460

São Paulo

Population: City 11 million, metropolitan area 18.3 million (2006 estimates)

Public transport

Bus services in the metropolitan area are run mostly by private operators, while São Paulo city bus and trolleybus services are entirely provided by private companies through service contracts with São Paulo Transporte SA (SPTrans), the municipal transit agency which supervises operations on behalf of the Secretaria dos Transportes Metropolitanos (São Paulo State Secretariat for Metropolitan Transport) (STM). The metro is operated by a company jointly owned by city, state and federal governments, with a major stake held by state government, and is supervised by the STM. The STM also supervises interurban metropolitan rail and bus services, provided respectively by the State Metropolitan Railways (CPTM) and Metropolitan Bus Transit Agency (EMTU). About 50 per cent of the 20 million daily trips in the metropolitan area are made by public transport, 75 per cent of those being by bus.

Secretaria Municipal dos Transportes (SMT)

R. Barão de Itapetininga, 18 – 14° andar, República, São Paulo 01042-000, Brazil
Tel: (+55 11) 31 20 99 99
e-mail: smt@prefeitura.sp.gov.br
Web: www6.prefeitura.sp.gov.br/secretarias/
    transportes, www.stm.sp.gov.br

Key personnel

Secretary: Frederico Bussinger

Current situation

SMT is responsible for city traffic and transport management. The transit department (DTP) deals with buses, taxis and related matters. São Paulo Transporte (SPTrans) acts on behalf of SMT/DTP with respect to bus transport activities and registration/inspection of taxis and paratransit vans.

São Paulo Transporte SA – SPTrans

Rua Treze de Maio 1376, An 1, Bela Vista, São Paulo, SP, 01327-002, Brazil
Tel: (+55 11) 32 83 09 33   Fax: (+55 11) 35 58 58
e-mail: sptrans@sptrans.com.br
Web: www.sptrans.com.br

Key personnel

President: Ulrich Hoffmann
General Manager, Technology and Engineering: José Carlos Nunes Martinelli
Operations Director: Carlos Albert Tavares Carmona

Current situation

For history of bus operations see earlier editions. By 1992, the former CMTC (Companhia Municipal de Transporte Colectivos), which had begun to authorise private operators to help cope with demand, was operating only 25 per cent of services. A total of 31 private operators, licensed by the Municipal Transport Secretariat through CMTC, was responsible for the rest. As concessions expired, CMTC was once again designated exclusive operator, but with the power to contract out services which it did not wish to operate.

In January 1999 the number of passengers carried had fallen to 88.3 million, the lowest figure for the last 15 years and 27.7 per cent below the figure for January 1998. This development is attributed to the increasing competition from private minibuses (see below). In 2000, 44 out of the 71 groups of routes were due for retendering, the remainder in 2004. Companies from outside São Paulo and even foreign companies may participate in the bidding.

Articulated bus at Av Ibirapuera for SPTrans (William A Luke)   0126469

At the end of 1998, 71 service contracts were being fulfilled by 53 private operators with staff totalling 54,165 and a total of 10,800 buses and 550 trolleybuses, in fleets ranging from 35 to 440 vehicles. All those contracts terminated by 2001, and SPTrans was considering alternative contract-out procedures.

Alternative fuels

Three battery-powered buses are undergoing tests. The 56 lead acid batteries develop 57 kW and provide a range of 100 km. It is expected these buses will start revenue service in early 2000. Within a period of two years it is planned to develop a hydrogen-powered bus. Fuel cells developed jointly by Ballard and DaimlerChrysler will be employed. It is expected that the bus will have a range of 200 km.

Busways

Growing traffic congestion and changing demand patterns forced the city to look for alternatives to its mostly radial bus network which was based on routes of the former tramway system. A trunk/feeder concept was adopted using bus-only corridors placed on central reservation. The Paes de Barros (1975) and Santo Amaro (1983) corridors feature stops on offset islands located to the right of the bus flow in both directions. On Vila Nova Cachoeirinha corridor (1991) buses run in the extreme left lane of each carriageway nearest to the median strip. Stops at raised islands allow level access to buses, thereby reducing dwell time, and all vehicles must have extra doors on the left side. Such has been the success of this latter scheme that it became the model for all future projects. A further three corridors – Itapecerica, Rio Bonito and Guarapiranga – were due to be operational before the end of 2000, and four more are planned.

Trunk routes are served by larger vehicles, including trolleybuses, articulated and double-articulated buses, and standard Padron commuter buses. In addition, part of the original radial bus network has been revamped to act as feeders, although some routes have survived to cater for specific flows. Fare-free interchange between trunk and feeder routes is only possible at terminals, but a smartcard time-based fare system is being developed to allow free interchange anywhere, between any two bus routes, within a time interval to be specified.

In addition to the bus corridor scheme, a 102 km network of fully segregated busways known as VLP had been proposed, of which an 8.5 km section between Parque Dom Pedro II terminal and Sacomã was due to be the first to open. Although this first section was publicly funded, operation was intended to be entirely private. An O-Bahn style guided system was to be adopted, with different guide rail and overhead options being tried on a 1.2 km test track.

The new concept bus has the formal name of VLP (Veícolo Leve Sobre Pneus or Light

Vehicle on Tyres) but the official 'nickname' 'Fura-Fila' (Queue Jumper) is most commonly used. It features high platform loading and four double-doors on each side. It carries up to 270 passengers. The vehicle has air conditioning, a sound system, padded seats and a computerised driver's console. There is space for wheelchairs.

A prototype three-section double-articulated guided trolleybus was supplied by Volvo/Marcopolo in early 1998 and trial running without passengers began on a 900 m section of the route in September 1998. At that time, a 4.5 km section was expected to open with limited service 'within a few months'. However, progress was slowed considerably by various difficulties, including construction problems and funding shortfall. It was not until September 2000 that the first passenger service was inaugurated and this was only a demonstration/trial service for a few months – a 2.8 km route section which was served only for two hours per day, three days per week and between 11.30 and 15.30 and by just three vehicles; the prototype vehicle and the only two other articulated trolleybuses from the SPTrans fleet. The latter had been retrofitted with offside doors for use on the Fura-Fila demonstration/trial service.

In November 2000, all construction on the first line was suspended, initially due to the thefts of considerable lengths of newly strung trolleybus wiring and a dispute between SPTrans and the contractor. Local elections also added to the delays.

In 2001, the new mayor announced that the first line would be completed but that no further sections would be built. Delays and changes to the plan continued. Costs had risen far above the original estimate, and one change adopted in an effort to reduce costs was the decision that the vehicles would use hybrid bus technology, rather than be trolleybuses. The prototype vehicle was placed in storage in early 2001, and remains stored in 2005.

In March 2002, the project was renamed 'Paulistão', although it is still referred to as the Fura-Fila.

Construction resumed in late 2002/early 2003, but costs continue to escalate again slowing progress. By the end of 2004, about two-thirds of the line (approx 6–7 km) had been largely completed, but construction was again suspended in January 2005, with another change of government.

Work resumed again in November 2005, but the estimated opening day has been given as the end of 2008. The length of the route has been increased from 8.5 km to 30 km, extending eastwards to Cidade Tiradentes to increase demand. The extended portion of the route will be built as segregated lanes on existing roads, which will help to keep costs down. The new section, whilst it will have priority signalling, will not be guided.

Trolleybus network

The trolleybus overhead and electrification systems are owned by the utility Eletropaulo. As of about 1998, the system comprised 25 routes, operated by a fleet of 55 of which 439 were on lease from the municipality and 111 belonged to the operators.

Subsequently, there has been a considerable reduction in the size of the system. Between 2000 and mid-2004, the number of trolleybus routes declined from about 25 to 14 and the size of the network went from 310 km to about 200 km, with several sections being closed and dismantled and a few closed but kept intact. The number of trolleybuses still in use under SPTrans' jurisdiction went from 552 vehicles to 227. Most route closures were in the northern and western areas of the city, but to the south the Santo Amaro corridor, a busway that had been operating with a fleet of 96 trolleybuses, was converted to bus in September 2003.

Among the factors which have led to this decline was a nationwide electricity shortage in 2001, large increases in the cost of electricity, the withdrawal of government subsidies for the purchase and operation of electric vehicles, and changes to the way in which SPTrans allocated routes to prospective operators in any given city zone. The condition of the infrastructure also deteriorated in some areas, following the 1998 privatisation of Eletropaulo, the state agency responsible for the maintenance of all overhead wiring and substations.

Developments

Conversion of the whole bus fleet to driver-only operation, supported by magnetic ticketing and smartcards, was expected to be completed in 1999. SPTrans has authorised operators to introduce new vehicle types, including double-articulated diesels for corridor operation. Studies have indicated a need to cater for market segmentation, and future contracts will allow for greater diversity of service standards.

In September 2003, the then-mayor announced a new policy to phase out all SPTrans trolleybus operations. Some of the newer trolleybuses were to be converted to hybrid propulsion. The Santo Amaro corridor ceased to be trolleybus-operated in that month and several more routes closed in the following months, with the last closure being Route 9300 to Case Verde in June 2004.

The policy to withdraw all trolleybus operations was retracted in early 2005 by a new administration. SPTrans has now been directed to study the feasibility of reinstating a few of the closed routes where the infrastructure has not been dismantled and of refurbishing and returning to service some of the trolleybuses which were withdrawn in late 2004.

As of mid-2005, there are 14 routes in operation.

Bus and trolleybus

Passenger boardings: (1998) 4.7 million daily
Vehicle-km: (1998) 2 million daily

Number of routes: Bus 825 (approx), trolleybus 14
Route length: Bus 21,240 km, trolleybus 200 km

Fleet: 12,353

Conventional bus	9,912
Padron type	385
Articulated	356
Double articulated	21
Trolleybus (active, of which two articulated)	227
Trolleybus 2-axle (stored)	167
Gas-powered	240
Executive service	112
Neighbourhood service bus	928
Hybrid (converted from trolleybus)	5

In peak service: 10,700
Average age of fleet: 4.5 years

Most intensive service: 2 min
One-person operation: Three central ring routes; all routes by the end of 1999
Fare collection: Electronic ticketing is to be introduced systemwide. In February 1999 only

Ibirapuera shopping bus on Route 846-M for SPTrans (William A Luke)　　0126471

Circular Central trolley bus en route for Bandeira Terminal (William A Luke)　　0126470

688 buses were thus equipped. A cost saving of between 15 and 20 per cent is expected
Fare structure: Flat; elderly and disabled and some government employees free
Fare evasion control: Checks by driver; all routes operate front entry
Operational control: Route inspectors/automatic vehicle monitoring system
Arrangements for elderly/disabled: 200 routes have at least one lift-equipped bus; 100 lift-equipped vans operate demand-response service to eligible patrons
Bus priority: 60 km of reserved lanes for both trolleybuses and buses, plus a 37 km segregated suburban busway (see separate entry for EMTU) and 230 km of bus/trolleybus priority lanes
Integration with other modes: Bus and trolleybus services partially integrated; 45 per cent of routes feed metro or suburban rail stations
Operating costs financed by: Fares 82 per cent (1998)
New vehicles financed by: Government financial agencies/local private institutions

Private minibus

The number of private minibuses, locally known as Peruas (turkeys), has increased considerably in recent years. It is estimated they carry 3 million passengers monthly. Due to non-stop running over given routes they are faster than buses. It has been reported that the Peruas charge the same fares as Spartans. SMT intends to freeze the number of Peruas at 2,700 vehicles.

Companhia Paulista de Trens Metropolitanos (CPTM)

Rua Boa Vista, 185 9º andar, 01014-001 São Paulo – SP, Brazil
Tel: (+55 11) 32 93 44 45　Fax: (+55 11) 32 93 45 46
e-mail: mbandeira@cptm.sp.gov.br
Web: www.cptm.sp.gov.br

Key personnel

President: Mário Manuel Seabra Rodrigues Bandeira*
Directors:
　Operation/Maintenance: José Luiz Lavorente
　Administration and Finance: Antônio Kanji Hoshikawa
　Engineering: Stanislav Feriancic
　Staff: 5,573 (December 2004)
*Also responsible for Planning

Type of operation: Suburban heavy rail

Passenger journeys: (2001) 311.7 million
(2002) 345.4 million
(2003) 353.8 million
(2004) 368.8 million

Background

CPTM was created by the São Paulo state government in May 1992, to operate the city's suburban passenger services, and started operations of the former FEPSA's routes in August 1993. In May 1994, CPTM took over the former operations of Companhia Brasileira de

Trens Urbanos (CBTU) and thus integrated suburban rail and metro services.

Current situation
The network now comprises six routes totalling 270 km (192 km of 1,600 mm gauge, 60 km dual-gauge, and 18 km metre-gauge), serving 95 stations and electrified at 3 kV DC. Trains run every 4-14 minutes at peak times.

The six routes are:

Line A: (Luz-Jundiaí, 60.5 km), comprising 17 stations with metro and Line B interchange at Barra Funda

Line B: (Júlio Prestes-Amador Bueno, 42 km), comprising 24 stations with Line C interchange at Osasco and Presidente Altino

Line C: (Osasco-Jurubatuba, 24.3 km), comprising 15 stations

Line D: (Luz-Rio Grande da Serra, 37.2 km), comprising 14 stations

Line E: (Luz-Estudantes, 50 km), comprising 15 stations with metro interchanges at three

Line F: (Brás-Calmon Viana, 38.8 km), comprising 10 stations with Line E interchanges at Brás, Tatuapé and Calmon Viana.

Modernisation of the network has been under way since 1985, financed by the World Bank and the Brazilian National Development Bank. On Lines A, D, E and F (the former CBTU routes) to Jundiaí, Paranapiacaba, Estudantes and Calmon Viana, the state government has also provided funds for upgrading of track, power supply and stations, as well as installation of ATC and CTC, and refurbishment of the emus. To augment the fleet, 30 four-car emus were bought from an ALSTOM/Adtranz/CAF consortium and 48 three-car emus were purchased second-hand from Spain's national railway RENFE, delivery starting in February 1998.

In early 1998, CPTM took delivery of the first of 48 refurbished ex-Spanish National Railways (RENFE) Class 440 emus. These became CPTM Class 2100.

For further information on CPTM, please see *Jane's World Railways*.

Developments
Improvements to existing lines
East Project – Expresso Leste
The East region is one of the most populous of the São Paulo metropolitan area, with the daily demand for transportation to the central region of São Paulo city at some 2.5 million trips. To satisfy demand, the 'Expresso Leste' service was created on Line E, connecting Guaianazes to Luz station and stopping at six stations en route.

South Project
This project aims to transform this railway line into one with the characteristics of a surface subway, integrating with the subway system at Pinheiros station (future Line 4) and Santo Amaro (Line 5), connecting the southern and west regions to the downtown area.

'Integração Centro' Project
The 'Integração Centro' Project will link CPTM's six lines at Barra Funda, Luz and Brás terminals and also integrate with the subway system. Work commenced in 2001 and includes the construction and upgrade of 7 km of permanent way, the installation and refurbishment of aerial overhead, construction of a unified control centre for all of CPTM's system, and the upgrading and modernisation of the Brás and Luz stations, providing access with escalators and elevators and support equipment for disabled passengers.

This project is estimated to require investments of some USD95.1 million and will allow passengers to travel from east to west of the São Paulo metropolitan area.

Line 5
CPTM finished the Line 5 – Lilac works in 2002, and transferred the responsibility of operation and maintenance to the subway company Companhia do Metropolitano de São Paulo (CMSP) – please see separate entry.

New lines
Airport Line
In 2004, CPTM will propose a rail link from Barra Funda to Gov André Franco Montoro airport in Guarulhos. The 31 km line would comprise 17 km of surface alignment, 8 km underground and 8 km elevated. CPTM plans to award a DBOT (Design/Build/Operate and Transfer) concession for the project.

On the same line, a high-quality service called 'Trem de Guarulhos' will be implemented between the two biggest cities of the São Paulo metropolitan area, São Paulo and Guarulhos. In Guarulhos there will be a bus interchange terminal and a new station placed in the future São Paulo University.

Traction and rolling stock
In 2000, CPTM received the last of 30 new Class 2000 emus for Line 6 in a transaction financed through a Eurobond issue. The new trainsets were built by a Franco-Spanish consortium (including CAF, GEC Alstom and Adtranz) known as COFESBRA, to a design similar to the Class 447 for RENFE of Spain. Also that year, deliveries commenced of 10 new emus from Siemens for Line C modernisation.

In 2004, the company received a further three refurbished emus. Two more are due to be delivered by 2005.

Fleet Modernisation Project
The fleet modernisation programme continues, with 109 cars having been refurbished and nine others due to be delivered in 2004.

Rolling stock: 256 emus, 18 dmus in three- or four-car sets

Companhia do Metropolitano de São Paulo – METRÔ (CMSP)
Rua Boa Vista 175, CEP 01014-001, São Paulo, Brazil
Tel: (+55 11) 32 91 28 62
Fax: (+55 11) 32 91 28 68
Web: www.metro.sp.gov.br

Key personnel
President (Temporary): José Jorge Fagali
Operations Director: Conrado Grava de Souza
Planning and Expansion Director: Marcos Kassab
Engineering and Construction Director: Luiz Carlos Pereira Grillo
Financial Director: José Jorge Fagali
Corporate Affairs Director: Sérgio Corrêa Brasil
Staff: 7,520 (December 2007)

Type of operation: Full metro, initial route opened 1974

Passenger journeys: (2003) 507 million
(2004) 503 million
(2005) 513 million
(2006) 564 million
(2007) 612 million
Car-km: (2003) 85.9 million
(2004) 86.5 million
(2005) 88.0 million
(2006) 92.2 million
(2007) 99.6 million

Route length: 61.3 km
  in tunnel: 32.8 km
  elevated: 14.7 km
Number of lines: 4
Line 1 – Blue, Line 2 – Green, Line 3 – Red, Line 4 – Yellow is under construction and Line 5 – Lilac.
Number of stations: 55
  in tunnel: 29
  elevated: 15
Gauge: 1,600 mm (Line 1, Line 2 and Line 3)
  1,435 mm (Line 5)
Track: 57 kg/m rail on continuous concrete beams in tunnels and on elevated sections; concrete sleepers on surface (Line 1, Line 2 and Line 3) and UIC 60 (Line 5)
Maximum gradient: 4%
Minimum curve radius: 300 m

Tunnel: Double-track cut-and-cover; single-track shield-driven bore
Electrification: 750 V DC, third rail (Line 1, Line 2 and Line 3); 1,500 V DC, pantograph (Line 5)

Current situation
Companhia do Metropolitano de São Paulo – METRÔ (CMSP) operates four lines of a network of 61.3 km. The operation and the maintenance processes are certified to NBR ISO 9001:2000 standards.

In 2006, Metro of São Paulo implemented the Occupational Health and Safety Management System – SGSSO, to became the first public transport company in Brazil to be OHSAS 18001:1999 certified.

Developments
Line 2 – Green
In March 2004, construction commenced on the Line 2 expansion, including the first 3.7 km of the line and three new stations. In 2006, two of these stations became operational – Chácara Klabin and Imigrantes, and the third station, Alto do Ipiranga, was put into operation in June 2007.

Currently, Line 2 is 10.7 km long with 11 stations.

Also under construction is a 4-km extension to this line, with 3 new stations, that it scheduled to be put into operation in 2010.

Line 4 – Yellow
The Line 4, on which construction started in March 2004, will connect the central area of São Paulo city to Vila Sonia, an area in the western part of the city. This line will have a total length of 12.8 km and 11 stations, all underground, and it is planned to be implemented in 2 phases. When complete, Line 4 will allow direct connection with Line 1, Line 2 and Line 3. It will also provide connection with 4 lines of the Metropolitan Train operated by Companhia Paulista de Trens Metropolitanos – CPTM, a commuter urban railway that serves the metropolitan area of São Paulo. The line will be operated by a Concessionaire named VIAQUATRO, a private company contracted on a Public Private Partnership (PPP) basis. This company is responsible for providing the trains and the signalling system, as well as other items. This concession was granted by the Government of State of São Paulo for a period of 30 years. The line is due to start partial operation in early 2010.

Accessibility
Metro of São Paulo is improving the existing trains and stations to give accessibility to elderly and disabled passengers. The improvements include the installation of new lifts/elevators, improvement of visual and tactile communications, improvements to the audio system, continuous training of the staff on mobility issues, orientation campaigns on metro use, users' manuals and guides, Braille language and special typology guides for sight-impaired passengers, reserved seats in stations and trains and locations for wheelchair on trains.

Smartcard
In 2006, the municipal bus smartcard fare collection system was implemented on the metro network.

The company is currently in the process of requesting bids for a new Communications-Based Train Control (CBTC) technology signalling system for Lines 1, 2 and 3, and thus may be able to reduce the headways on these lines.

Metro of São Paulo is also inviting bids for 16 new trains for Line 2, 17 new trains for Lines 1 and 3 and the modernisation of all 98 trains of Lines 1 and 3.

Rolling stock: 702 cars, formed into six-car trains

Line 1 – Blue	
Mafersa (1974)	M306
Line 2 – Green	
Alstom Transporte/Adtranz (now Bombardier) Spain (1998/99)	M66
Line 3 – Red	
Mafersa/Cobrasma (1982 onwards)	M282

Line 5 – Lilac
Alsthom (2002)   M48
In peak service: 630

On order:
Service: Peak: Line 1: 109 s; Line 2: 149 s; Line 3: 101 s, Line 5: 307 s
   Off-peak Line 1: 147 s; Line 2: 221 s; Line 3: 143 s, Line 5: 507 s (December 2007.)
First/last train: 04.40/00.35
Fare structure: Flat, integrated tickets with discount available for Metro-Bus with smartcard; free integration for some connections to urban railway (CPTM); free travel for the elderly, disabled and unemployed; half-fare for students, one-way ticket for Line 5 only
Fare collection: Magnetic ticket; smartcard
Arrangements for elderly/disabled: The company is improving existing trains and stations to be accessible. These improvements include the installation of new lifts (elevators), improvements to the visual and tactile communications, improvements to the audio system, continuous training of staff on mobility impaired users, orientation campaigns on metro use, users' manuals and guides, Braille language and specific typology guide for blind users, reserved seats in trains and on stations, locations for wheelchairs in trains and adequate toilet facilities for mobility impaired users.
Integration with other modes: CMSP has taken a lead in integration through development of feeder suburban rail, bus and trolleybus services
Revenue control: Microprocessor-controlled electronic turnstiles for access control and data collection; central processing for fare-collection system
Signalling: ATS – automatic train supervision for routing, terminal departing and turn-around and line regulation, accomplished by two control centres, one for Lines 1, 2 and 3 and a separate control centre for Line 5; ATO – Automatic train operation to perform the functions of door control, programmed stop at stations, performance level control between stations; ATP – Automatic train protection for traffic safety.
Operating costs financed by: Fares: 76.7 per cent, other commercial revenue: 6.8 per cent, concessionaire fare support: 13.9 per cent, other operating revenue support: 2.6 per cent.

Empresa Metropolitana de Transportes Urbanos de São Paulo SA (EMTU/SP)

Rua Joaquim Casemiro 290, Barrio Planalto, São Bernardo do Campo SP, 09890-050, Brazil
Tel: (+55 800) 19 00 88   Fax: (+55 11) 43 41 11 20
Web: www.emtu.sp.gov.br

Key personnel
Director President: José Ignácio Sequeira de Almeida
Director, Corporate: José Eduardo Marques Cupertino
Director, Operations: Antônio Carlos de Moraes
   Staff: 17,735 (including those of franchised operators)

Passenger journeys: 479 million annually, including 65 million by Metra
Vehicle-km: 307 million annually

Current situation
Empresa Metropolitana de Transportes Urbanos de São Paulo (EMTU/SP), which is under jurisdiction of Secretaria de Estado dos Transportes Metropolitanos (STM – São Paulo State Government Secretariat for Metropolitan Transportation), has the objective of providing low- and medium-capacity public transit services in the São Paulo State metropolitan areas. EMTU is responsible for managing and supervising transit services in the metropolitan areas, including scheduled, chartered and special inter-city bus services. It also manages and supervises the privately operated São Mateus-

Sumaré Station – Line 2 – Green   1326750

Villa as Belezas Station – Line 5 – Lilac   1326753

Jabaquara Metropolitan Corridor (Corredor ABD – São Mateus-Jabaquara), a segregated busway. EMTU is responsible for the planning of low- and medium-capacity transit services and for the interconnection of high capacity modes. Co-ordination and region-wide dialogue with city government authorities comprising the metropolitan regions have been fundamental for the feasibility of EMTU initiatives and achievements.

EMTU is an anonymous society ruled through mixed economy and joint stock company structures. Its mission is to promote and to manage the low- and medium-capacity transportation system in the São Paulo State Metropolitan Regions.

EMTU oversees and regulates intermunicipal bus operations among 39 suburban municipalities lying outside the city of São Paulo but within the metropolitan area. Its principal divisions are identified as 'Regular' (ordinary bus operations comprising 50 private operators serving 489 routes with a combined fleet of some 3,950 buses), 'Aeroporto' (special bus services which connect Guarulhos and Congonhas airports with various locations in São Paulo city), 'Fretamento' (charter/private hire bus companies – nearly 600

individual operators with a combined fleet of 5,654 buses and minibuses), and the 'Corredor Metropolitano São Mateus/Jabaquara' (a 33 km network of busways in the southeastern part of the metropolitan area, much of which is operated with trolleybuses). The final division is franchised to Metra until 2017.

Developments
Under the guidelines established by both the Strategic Planning 2007–2010 and the Expansion Plan 2007–2010, EMTU has developed a number of strategic projects which will help the accomplishment of its mission and its vision. Some of those projects, in brief, are:

Brazilian Hydrogen Fuel Bus
The project entails the assembly of the first Brazilian bus prototype powered by hydrogen fuel cells. Developed through a partnership with the Ministério das Minas e Energia (Brazilian Federal Ministry of Mining and Energy), with sponsorship by the following institutions: UN Development Programme – UNPD, Global Environment Facility – GEF and FINEP – Financiadora de Estudos e Projetos (Research and Projects Financing). The bus prototypes are

intended to be tested during 2008, on the São Mateus – Jabaquara Metropolitan Corridor.

The proposed benefits of the project are: zero emission (non pollutant) transportation system (the only residue being water vapour); dissemination of an innovative technological knowledge on a worldwide basis; establishment of a new transportation market by means of partnership between bus operating companies, manufactures and universities and the development of a Brazilian specification for bus powered by hydrogen fuel cells.

Integrated Ticket – CPTM/Metropolitan Bus Corridor

The Integrated Ticket will allow integration of the terminals of CPTM's line D (railway system) and the São Mateus – Jabaquara Metropolitan Corridor's terminals (bus/trolleybus system), sharing the same fare. The passengers will save 30 cents, resulting in a seven per cent saving with a return/two-way ticket.

Guarulhos – São Paulo Bus Corridor

The Guarulhos – São Paulo Bus Corridor is a corridor built to link the two cities as a main axis of public transportation. The project includes exclusive lanes, advanced technology vehicles and public transportation priority.

Northwest Metropolitan Bus Corridor

The Northwest Metropolitan Bus Corridor has been built in the Campinas Metropolitan Region, including the following municipalities: Hortolândia, Sumaré, Monte Mor, Nova Odessa, Americana, Campinas and Santa Bárbara D'Oeste. The Northwest Metropolitan Bus Corridor allows the integration of both municipal and inter-municipal bus lines.

The benefits of the project are: 32.7 km of preferential bus lanes, integration of metropolitan terminals; transfer stations as well as modernisation of bus stops and vehicles; number of users estimated: up to 3.5 million passengers per month; modern vehicles with low pollutant emissions and improvement of environmental conditions for the Metropolitan

Campinas Region (reduction of kilometres travelled by buses as well as renovation of the bus fleet).

Metropolitan Integration System

The Metropolitan Integration System (Sistema Integrado Metropolitano – SIM) is the structuring of metropolitan public transportation system in the Baixada Santista Metropolitan Region. The project comprises the building of the Expresso da Baixada (Baixada Express) light rail transit system along a 14-km route.

The benefits of the project are: reduction of the fleet used, resulting in higher efficiency; 10 per cent reduction in CO_2 emissions and reduction of up to 30 minutes of trip time.

Sistema Metropolitani de Transportes Ltda (Metra)

Address as above
Tel: (+55 11) 42 90 38 00   Fax: (+55 11) 43 41 65 92
Web: www.metra.com

Key personnel

Director: Fernando José Vicenzo

Passenger journeys: Approx 65 million (annual)

Number of routes: Bus 6 (of which 2 minibus), trolleybus 6
Route length: Bus 82 km (of which 62 km minibus), trolleybus 67 km (total lengths, including duplication/overlap)

Current situation

CMSP was authorised to build and operate a feeder trolleybus network outside the city's boundaries. Electrification of one 10.4 km section was never completed, resulting in the initially 'temporary' inclusion of some buses in the fleet becoming permanent. EMTU later took over operations, but CMSP remains as the construction authority. Four routes in the southern suburbs were opened in 1988/90, known as the Medium Capacity Network. These total 33 km and run from Ferrazopolis and Piraporinha to Jabaquara metro station, Santo

André station on the suburban rail system and the São Mateus terminal of the SPTrans trolleybus operation, and five other interchanges, on routes provided with segregated lanes. Bus-only lanes comprise all but 3 km of the 33 km and 22 km are equipped for trolleybuses.

Operation and maintenance of EMTU's system was transferred to private-sector operator Metra in 1997 under a 20-year contract.

Developments

In August 2000, Metra introduced services between Diadema and Brooklin, the first completely new route section added since completion of the initial 33 km system in 1990. However, this new 15 km section is operated by minibuses, without segregation from the other traffic. It is not known whether plans for construction of busway lanes along this section are still being pursued.

In 2001, Metra took over from EMTU responsibility for maintenance of the busway roads and related infrastructure.

Since 2002, Metra has gradually been withdrawing the 46 Cobrasma trolleybuses that opened the system in 1988 and replacing them with new low-floor trolleybuses, the first in South America, but recycling the electrical equipment from the old vehicles into the new ones. The propulsion equipment is refurbished by Eletra before being installed in new 'Urbanuss Pluss LF' model body shell/chassis supplied by Busscar.

Fleet: Bus 134 (of which 30 articulated and 3 hybrid), minibuses 25

Conventional 2-axle, diesel	101
Articulated diesel	30
Hybrid 2-axle	3

Fleet: 61 trolleybuses

Cobrasma/Tectronic (1986/90)	18
Scania/Marcopolo/Powertronics ex-Belo Horizonte	22
Marcopolo/Volvo articulated (1998)	10
Busscar/Mercedes-Benz/Eletra partially low-floor (2001)	1
Busscar/Eletra low-floor (2002/05)	10

Bulgaria

Sofia

Population: City 1.25 million, metropolitan area 1.4 million (2006 estimates)

Public transport

Bus, trolleybus, tramway and metro services are provided by subsidiaries of a wholly municipally owned limited liability company.

Public Transport Company Sofia Ltd (SKGT- Sofia EOOD)

84 Knyaginya Maria Louisa Boulevard, 1202 Sofia, Bulgaria
Tel: (+359 2) 831 90 75   Fax: (+359 2) 831 90 75
e-mail: skgt@skgt-bg.com
Web: www.skgt-bg.com

Key personnel

General Manager: Nikolay Kostov

Current situation

In January 2003, Sofia Public Transport Company – Holding EAD (joint stock company) became Public Transport Company Sofia Ltd (SKGT-Sofia EOOD) (sole proprietor limited liability company) with the following activities:

- Organisation, management, supervision and finance of the Sofia public transport as an integrated process;
- Issuing of transportation documents and collection of the transportation revenues;
- Unified transport operations planning in Sofia, vehicle movement timetables, routes optimisation;

- Operation of information-management system for monitoring and supervision of the traffic, based on GPS-identification;
- Operation of unified automated fare collection system (ticketing system);
- Advertising and information services in public transport;
- Infrastructure maintenance, repairing and construction, including: railways, contact and cable nets, rectifier stations and outdoor equipment.

The company is 100 per cent municipally owned and executes the functions of a Public Transport Authority (PTA).

From 1 January 2003, public transport operations were assigned to:
- Four municipal-owned joint-stock transport companies.
- Stolichen Autotransport EAD (Metropolitan Bustransport), operating buses;
- Stolichen Elektrotransport EAD (Metropolitan Electrotransport), operating trams and trolleybuses;
- Metropoliten EAD, operating one metro line;
- Vuzeni linii EAD (Cableways), operating two lines of cable cars.
- Six private bus operators;
- Tramcar EAD, responsible for repairs to tram bodies.

A unified fare collection system covers all transport modes. There are single tickets, one-day, five-day, monthly and three-monthly passes, reduced fares for pensioners, students and disabled people, free travel for war veterans

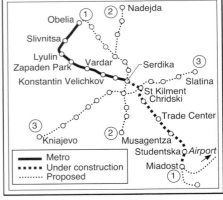

Sofia's metro   1298722

and disabled service personnel. The tickets and passes are issued by SKGT-Sofia EOOD which also collects and distributes revenue. The public transport operators are paid on the base of km covered. The fares revenues are 59.5 per cent of the public transport budget, with the remaining 40.5 per cent coming from subsidies and compensations from the state budget.

Developments

In early 2007, SKGT awarded a contract to MIKROELEKTRONIKA spol sro as the main supplier of a new electronic fare collection system. The system will include a contactless smart card system. Initially, the tram and trolleybus fleet will be equipped with the system, with buses being equipped at a later date. The system was first implemented in September 2008.

Bus
Stolichen Autotransport EAD
21 Zhitnitza Str, 1618 Sofia, Bulgaria
Tel: (+359 2) 955 90 20

Passenger journeys: (Annual) 242 million
Vehicle-km: (Annual) 33.3 million

Number of routes: 78
Route length (one-way): 1,210 km

Key personnel
Executive Director: Asen Dobranov
   Staff: 3,223

Current situation
Stolichen Autotransport EAD operates buses from three garages, providing city, urban and 'hiking' lines.

Fleet: 616 buses
Articulated buses:

Ikarus 280 articulated	107
Mercedes-Benz O305 G articulated	115
Mercedes-Benz O345 G articulated	41
Mercedes-Benz O345 G Konecto	50
MAN SG262 articulated	30
Chavdar 141 articulated	25

Standard buses:

BMC 220 SLF	61
Mercedes-Benz O305	74
Mercedes-Benz O405	10
Mercedes-Benz O302 T	25
Mercedes-Benz O345 S	6
Mercedes-benz O345 S Konecto	30
MAN SL232	21
MAN SL200	4
Ikarus Solo	17

On order: Not currently available
In peak service: 431
First/last bus: 05.00/23.00
One-person operation: All routes
Fare collection: See above
Fare structure: See above
Fare evasion control: Not currently available
Bus priority: 35 km of bus lanes
Average peak-hour speed: 19.6 km/h
Operating costs financed by: Fares: 59.5 per cent; subsidies and compensation: 40.5 per cent

Private operators
Vehicle-km: (Annual) 10.1 million

Number of routes: 16

Current situation
Six private operators operate 16 routes.

Fleet: 123 buses

Mercedes-Benz O305	13
Mercedes-Benz O345 S	37

Den Oudsten	17
Neoplan	3
MAN 202	16
MAN 232	7
BMC 220 SLF	30

On order: Not currently available
In peak service: Not currently available
First/last bus: 05.00/23.00

Tram and trolleybus
Stolichen Elektrotransport EAD
193 Knyaginya Maria Louisa Boulevard, 1233 Sofia, Bulgaria
Tel: (+359 2) 931 80 85   Fax: (+359 2) 931 61 84
e-mail: elektrodir@dir.bg
System data

Passenger journeys: (Annual) 184 million
Tram: 124.4 million
Trolleybus: 59.6 million
Vehicle-km: Not currently available

Operating costs financed by: Fares 59.5 per cent, subsidies and compensation 40.5 per cent

Key personnel
Executive Director: Yordan Vasilev
   Staff: 2,300

Current situation
Stolichen Elektrotransport EAD is responsible for the tram and trolleybus services. Vehicles are distributed between three tram and two trolleybus depots and one garage. A separate department, Transenergo, is responsible for the power supply, including substations, catenary and cables.

Tram
Type of operation: Conventional tramway, initial route opened 1901

Number of lines: 16
Route length: 214.5 km (169 km single track with gauge 1,009 mm, 34.5 km single track with gauge 1,435 mm and 5.5 km of three-rail track which serves both type of track gauges)
Gauge: 1,009 mm (14 routes) 1,435 mm (two routes)
Electrification: 600 V DC, overhead

Developments
In early 2006, a contract was awarded to the Inekon Group, in conjunction with Tramcar EAD, for the complete modernisation of 18 trams. The double-articulated trams will be upgraded to triple-articulated, with a low-floor middle section. The project was scheduled to be completed by the end of 2008.

Fleet: 293 trams
1,009 mm gauge (229 cars)

T8M-300 BG 1300 eight-axle	M24
T8M-900 eight-axle	M39
T8M-503 eight-axle	M1
T6M-400 (Sofia 100) six-axle	M38

T6M-700 (Sofia) six-axle	M36
T8M-700 IT	M18
T4D four-axle	M16
T6A2 four-axle	M40
T6AT SF	M17

1,435 mm gauge (64 cars)

T6MD-1000M	M1
T6B5 four-axle	M37
T4-205 Duewag four-axle	M9
T6-231 Duewag six-axle	M10
T8-401 Duewag eight-axle	M7

In peak service: 176
One-person operation: All routes
Average peak-hour speed: 12.5 km/h

Trolleybus
Number of routes: nine
Route length: 207 km (plus 50 km at depots)

Fleet: 153 trolleybuses

Ikarus-Ganz 280T articulated	141
Kobra 272-2002	1
Kobra 272-2005	2
TK-130	1
MAN	8

In peak service: 99

First/last trolleybus: 05.00/23.00
Average peak-hour speed: 14 km/h

Metro
Metropoliten EAD
121 Knyaz Boris I Street, 1000 Sofia, Bulgaria
Tel: (+359 2) 921 20 01   Fax: (+359 2) 987 22 44
e-mail: metro@metropolitan.bg
Web: www.metropolitan.bg

Passenger journeys: (Annual) 25,929
Vehicle-km: Not currently available

Number of lines: one
Route length: 9.9 km
Number of stations: eight
Gauge: 1,435 mm
Electrification: 825 V DC, third rail

Key personnel
Executive Director: Stoyan Bratoev
   Staff: Not currently available

Current situation
Two further lines are planned, with the total planned network extending to 52 km with 47 stations.

Developments
The extension to Line 1, running southeast from Serdika, is under construction and is currently scheduled to be completed in early 2009.

Fleet: Not currently available, but 48 Russian-built cars have been delivered
First/last train: 05.00/23.00
Average peak-hour speed: 40.9 km/h

Canada

Calgary
Population: City: 988,193, metropolitan area: 1.1 million (2006 Census)

Public transport
Bus services and light rail system operated by municipal government.

Calgary Transit (CT)
928 32nd Avenue Northeast Connector, PO Box 2100, Postal Station M, Calgary, Alberta T2P 2M5, Canada

Tel: (+1 403) 537 77 11   Fax: (+1 403) 537 77 37
e-mail: scott.hale@calgary.ca
Web: www.calgarytransit.com

Key personnel
Director: Fred Wong
Finance Leader: Tim Johnson
Manager, Operations: Bill Thompson
Manager, LRT: Russell Davies
Manager, Bus and Auxiliary Vehicles: Dragon Vasic
Manager, Accessible Transportation Services:
   Karim Rayani
Manager, Service Design: Doug Morgan

Manager, Transit Planning: Neil McKendrick
Manager, Facilities: Peter Enslen
Manager, Business Strategies: Koji Miyaji
   Staff: 2,505

Current situation
In 2007, Calgary Transit experienced an increase in ridership of 9.6 per cent over 2006. Accessible transport is now provided on 76 of Calgary Transit's 162 routes and at all of its light rail stations.

The Community Shuttle service, using 105 minibuses each seating 21, continues to expand as the service grows to serve developing suburban areas. The less expensive Community Shuttle continues to replace larger service buses on routes that do not meet the minimum performance of 20 passengers per operating hour.

CT provides services to a population of more than 1,019,000.

Developments

Accessible service is now provided at all of the 37 light rail stations.

Passenger journeys: (All modes)
(2003) 78 million
(2004) 80.6 million
(2005) 81.95 million
(2006) 89.92 million
(2007) 90.2 million
Route-km: (2003) 4,338
(2004) 4,553
(2005) 4,571
(2006) 4,530
(2007) 4,471

Operating costs financed by: Fares 47.1 per cent, other commercial sources 0.9 per cent, provincial grants 1.2 per cent, municipal support (tax levy) 50.8 per cent

Bus

Passenger journeys: (2003) 46.8 million
(2004) 45.9 million
(2005) 45.9 million
(2006) 50.3 million
(2007) 44.5 million
Vehicle-km: (2003) 43.2 million
(2004) 44.1 million
(2005) 43.9 million
(2006) 45.7 million
(2007) 46.0 million

Number of routes: 162, including Community Shuttle
Route length: (One-way) 4,698 km
On priority right-of-way: 2 km shared with light rail

Fleet: 863 vehicles
Standard motor bus	261
Low-floor bus	491
Articulated bus	6
Community Shuttle (minibus)	105
In peak service: 664

Most intensive service: 2 min
One-person operation: All routes
Fare collection: Exact fare to farebox, pre-purchase tickets, day/monthly passes, transfers
Fare structure: Flat
Fares collected on board: 20.6 per cent (adult – 2007)
Fare-evasion control: By driver and inspectors (Protective Services Officers)

Integration with other modes: Bus and light rail routes integrated; feeder and main line buses serve stations; park-and-ride (1,821 spaces on bus routes, 12,305 at stations)
Operational control: Supervisors/radio control
Arrangements for elderly/disabled: Low-floor accessible service on 76 routes; reduced-rate annual pass for seniors depending on income
Average distance between stops: 300 m
Average peak-hour speed: 24 km/h
New vehicles financed by: Municipal property tax revenues and provincial fuel-tax rebate; some federal funds expected

Light rail (CTrain)

Type of operation: Light rail, initial route opened 1981, extended 1985, 1987, 1990, 2001, 2003, 2004 and 2007

Passenger journeys: (2003) 31.2 million
(2004) 34.7 million
(2005) 36.1 million
(2006) 39.5 million
(2007) 45.7 million
Train-km: (2003) 3.30 million
(2004) 3.64 million
(2005) 3.79 million
(2006) 4.02 million
(2007) 3.71 million

Route length: 44.9 km
  in tunnel: 2.9 km
Number of routes: 2 (3 legs)
Number of stations: 37
Gauge: 1,435 mm
Track: 60 kg/m Ri-60 girder rail on ballasted concrete sleepers, 50 kg/m ARA 100T welded rail on concrete slab in tunnel and city-centre sections
Max gradient: 6%
Electrification: 600 V DC, overhead

Current situation

In 2001 and 2003, Calgary Transit took delivery of 32 SD160 LRVs featuring AC and IGBT propulsion technology. The SD160 is based on the SD100 LRV. The six-axle vehicle is 23 m (76 ft) long and can carry up to 200 passengers. With eight sliding doors it can operate from platforms or kerbside. Calgary has ordered 117 vehicles from Siemens for its light rail system.

In December 2003, the 2.7 km extension of the Northwest Line to Dalhousie opened.

Developments

The extension of the Northwest Line to Crowfoot is scheduled for 2008.

According to the planned capital requirements during the period 2014-23, the replacement of 50 U2 LRVs, the purchase of 25 LRVs, and the refurbishment of existing LRVs have been identified.

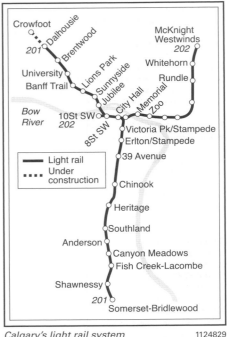

Calgary's light rail system   1124829

In 2007, Calgary Transit received an additional 27 SD160 LRVs for a total of 149 LRVs. A further seven SD160s are expected in early 2008.

In December 2007, the 2.8-km extension to McKnight Westwinds was opened for revenue service.

Rolling stock: 149 cars
Siemens-Duewag U2 (1981)	26
Siemens-Duewag U2 (1983/85)	56
Siemens-Duewag U2 AC propulsion	2
Siemens SD160 AC propulsion	65
On order: 7 Siemens SD160 LRVs due for delivery in 2008
In peak service: 120

Service: Peak 5 min, midday 10 min, off-peak 15 min
Fare structure: Flat, as bus; free fare zone on 2 km downtown section of Seventh Avenue
Fare collection: Self-service ticket dispensers and prepaid ticket cancellers on platforms; monthly passes; transfer from bus
Integration with other modes: Feeder buses at most stations; park-and-ride (12,305 spaces)
Fare evasion control: Roving inspectors (Protective Services Officers)
One-person operation: 100 per cent
Signalling: Automatic block with interlockings at all junctions and terminals; auto-switching and station signs controlled by onboard VETAG in transit mall; all train movements monitored at radio control centre

---

Edmonton

Population: City: 730,372 (2006 estimate), metropolitan area: 1.03 million (2006 Census)

Public transport

Bus, trolleybus and light rail services operated by municipal undertaking with two small suburban bus systems.

Edmonton Transit System (ETS)

Suite 500, Scotia Place, 10060 Jasper Avenue, Edmonton, Alberta T5J 3R8, Canada
Tel: (+1 780) 496 57 40   Fax: (+1 780) 496 42 44
Web: www.edmonton.ca/transit
    www.TakeETS.com

Key personnel

Manager of Transit: Charles A Stolte
Director, LRT: Dave Geake
Director, ETS Security, Service Support and Safety: Ron Gabruck

Director, Community Relations: Dennis Nowicki
Director, Business Development: Patricia Waisman
Director, Bus Operations: Wes Brodhead
Director, Service Development: Ken Koropeski
Director, Disabled Adult Transit System (DATS): Lorna Stewart
Director, Fleet and Facilities: John Sirovyak
Staff: 1,616 full-time, 461 part-time

Current situation

Edmonton's public transport operation functions as a branch of the Municipal Transportation Department, reporting to the General Manager.

ETS operates 163 bus routes, 262 school routes and one light rail transit line, carrying approximately 61.9 million passengers per annum. The Disabled Adult Transportation System (DATS) is run with a combination of city-owned/operated vehicles and contracted service, and carries just under one million passengers annually.

In 2008, Edmonton Transit celebrated its 100th anniversary.

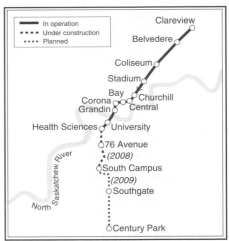

Map of Edmonton's light rail system   1115295

Developments

The City of Edmonton has embarked on an evaluation of 13 clean-diesel and hybrid buses. All of the units were used in regular service and underwent special testing. The evaluation included purchase and operating costs, reliability, fuel efficiency, noise generation and environmental impact. Results will be compared to the 2006 diesel vehicles and current trolleys. The University of Alberta co-ordinated the testing. A preliminary report was produced in early 2008.

In early 2009, four trolleybus routes were still in operation, with 24 trolleybuses in peak service. The trolley fleet and overhead network will be dismantled by early 2010. Additional diesel-electric hybrid buses will be purchased to replace the trolleys.

Passenger journeys: (All modes)
(2003) 46.04 million
(2004) 53.05 million
(2005) 54.41 million
(2006) 57.45 million
(2007) 61.90 million

Operating costs financed by: Fares 40 to 45 per cent, other commercial sources five per cent, tax levy 50 per cent

Bus and trolleybus

Vehicle-km: (2003) 31.36 million
(2004) 34.58 million
(2005) 37.17 million
(2006) 38.73 million
(2007) 35.32 million

Number of routes: Bus 156, trolleybus four
Route length: Bus 4,048 km, trolleybus not available currently

Fleet: 905 buses
GMC	42
New Flyer low-floor	765
New Flyer low-floor articulated	13
Community buses (includes 26 ELF and 13 Glaval)	42
GMC-Brown Boveri (1981/82) trolleybuses	40
Orion VII hybrid bus	two
New Flyer/Allison hybrid bus	two
New Flyer/ISE hybrid bus	two

In peak service: 685 (2007)

Most intensive service: five min
One-person operation: All routes
Fare collection: Exact fare payment to farebox; prepurchase multitickets or monthly pass
Fare structure: Flat; monthly passes, 10-journey discount multitickets, free 90 min transfers; ETS tickets and passes valid on suburban operators' buses within city limits
Arrangements for elderly/disabled: Discounted annual senior passes and discounted monthly seniors' passes. Door-to-door Disabled Adult Transportation System (DATS) operated with special vehicles; low-floor buses available for service on routes with kneeling capability, hydraulic ramp and two wheelchair positions. Programme offering discounted passes to recipients of Assured Income for the Severely Handicapped (AISH)
Integration with other modes: Common fare for buses and LRT, free transfers apply; cycle racks are currently used on three routes (Routes 1, 4 and 9)

Developments

In 2007, Edmonton Transit trialled a 'Family Fare', where using a Day Pass, a family (one adult and up to four children, ages 12 and under) are able to travel on ETS (bus and LRT) all day, any day of the week.

Initiated an Employ-E Discounted Pass Program, where ETS has partnered with employers to provide a minimum employee discount of 24 per cent off the regular Adult Monthly pass fare.

Light Rail Transit (LRT)

Type of operation: Light rail, initial route opened 1978

Health Sciences station, in the university district, is the terminus of a 2006 extension of Edmonton's light rail system. The first segment of an extension further southwards was due to open in early 2009 (Steve Morgan)   1375712

A 1982 GM/BBC trolleybus on ETS route 135, followed by a New Flyer D40LF diesel bus on route 52, in the city centre (Steve Morgan)   1375710

Car-km: (2003) 2.7 million
(2004) 2.7 million
(2005) 2.7 million
(2006) 2.85 million
(2007) 3.01 million

Route length: 13.7 km
Number of lines: one
Number of stations: 11
Gauge: 1,435 mm
Tunnel: Cut-and-cover and bored
Electrification: 600 V DC, overhead

Current situation

Light rail line extends from Clareview in northeast Edmonton to Health Sciences Station near the University of Alberta, comprising 13.7 km of track and 11 stations.

Developments

Construction continues on the eight km extension to the Century Park Station.

Rolling stock: 37 articulated cars
Duewag/Siemens (1978)	M14
Duewag/Siemens (1979)	M3
Duewag/Siemens (1982)	M20

In peak service: 31
On order: 26 Siemens SD160 two-section high-floor LRT cars for delivery in 2008/09, due to enter service in 2009

Service: five min
First/last car: 05.30/01.31

Integration with other modes: Common fare systems on bus and LRT; cycles carried off-peak

Edmonton
Other operators
Current situation

Operators in the adjacent localities of St Albert and Sherwood Park run services through to downtown Edmonton, and issue passes valid on ETS services.

St Albert Transit

235 Carnegie Drive, St Albert, Alberta T8N 5A7, Canada
Tel: (+1 780) 418 60 60 (Monday to Friday)
Fax: (+1 780) 459 40 50
e-mail: transit@st-albert.net
Web: www.ridestat.ca

Key personnel

Planning & Customer Service Manager: Ian Sankey

Current situation

St Albert Transit provides public transit service in the City of St Albert and into the adjacent City of Edmonton.

The company operates 49 buses of which 18 are 18 m articulated buses, with the remaining 31 buses either 12 m low-floor or nine m low-floor accessible vehicles. They travel a total of 2.0 million km each year and carry over 1.1 million riders annually.

Service operates on weekdays and Saturdays from approximately 06.00 to 01.00 and on Sundays from 08.00 to 19.00.

The company also operates Dial-a-bus and Handibus (paratransit) services.

Fares are duo-zonal – local and commuter – with multiride tickets, local and commuter monthly passes available. There are reduced fares for juniors, students and seniors.

Strathcona County Transit
2001 Sherwood Drive, Sherwood Park, Alberta T8A 3W7, Canada
Tel: (+1 780) 417 71 80   Fax: (+1 780) 417 71 76
e-mail: info@strathcona.ab.ca,
  muir@strathcona.ab.ca
Web: www.strathcona.ab.ca

Office address
200 Streambank Avenue, Sherwood Park, Alberta T8H 1N1, Canada

Current situation
Strathcona County Transit operates weekday and weekend routes, plus school services and a

St Albert Transit bus 811, a New Flyer D60LF, in Downtown Edmonton, starting a journey on route 201 (Steve Morgan)   1375713

dial-a-bus service. There are two park-and-ride facilities. Two cash fares – local and commuter – with monthly passes and multi-ride tickets

available. Annual passes for seniors are also available and there are fare reductions for students and seniors.

Halifax
Population: Halifax Regional Municipality (HRM) 372,679 (2006 Census), metropolitan area 404,807 (2006)

Public transport
Bus services, including Bus Rapid Transit (BRT), and ferry services provided by undertaking under the control of regional authority.

Halifax Regional Municipality (HRM) – Metro Transit
Transit Services, 200 Ilsley Avenue, Dartmouth, Nova Scotia B3B 1V1, Canada
Tel: (+1 902) 490 66 14   Fax: (+1 902) 490 66 88
e-mail: contactHRM@halifax.ns.ca
  Web: www.halifax.ca

Key personnel
Acting General Manager: Patricia Soanes
Manager, Transit Planning and Development: Edward Robar
  Staff: 571 (2008)

Background
The former Metropolitan Transit Commission, established in 1981 to bring together separate Halifax and Dartmouth transit undertakings, was absorbed in 1986 by its parent body, the Metropolitan Authority. In 1996, Metro Transit became part of the Halifax Regional Municipality (HRM) under the amalgamation of four municipal units as a single regional authority.

Current situation
Metro Transit operates 54 fixed routes and schedules in and around Halifax and three ferries on two routes between Dartmouth and Halifax. An Access-a-Bus service uses 24 vehicles and taxis specially for people with mobility problems. The bus and ferry service is now part of a larger Regional Operations Department, which also covers municipal engineering and public works.

Developments
Metro Transit introduced the U-Pass to Saint Mary's University in September 2003, Dalhousie University in January 2006 and Mount Saint Vincent University and NSCAD University in September 2007. All eligible full-time students who are registered on three or more courses pay for the U-Pass as part of their student fee. The U-Pass is valid from 1 September to 30 April with unlimited use on the conventional transit system including the ferry.

HRM developed the MetroLink service in response to Transport Canada's Urban Transportation Showcase Program, established in order to promote effective strategies to reduce greenhouse gas emissions by attracting commuters to public transit. This included the construction of two new bus terminals in 2005. The Portland Hills Terminal, Dartmouth, opened in May 2005 and the Sackville Terminal, Lower Sackville, opened in November 2005.

In August 2005, Metro Transit introduced Phase 1 of MetroLink, a limited-stop fully accessible (ALF) Bus Rapid Transit (BRT) direct service on the new Route 159 Portland Hills Link and Route 165 Woodside Link. Phase II of the MetroLink began in February 2006 with the introduction of the new Route 185 Sackville Link from the new Sackville Terminal.

Passenger journeys (both modes): (2002/03) 17.6 million
(2003/04) 18.6 million
(2004/05) 19.7 million
(2005/06) 21.5 million
(2006/07) 22.5 million
Vehicle-km (both modes): (2002/03) 8.9 million
(2003/04) 10.2 million
(2004/05) 10.5 million
(2005/06) 11.6 million
(2006/07) 13.0 million

Bus
Number of routes: 54
Route length: (One way) 900 km (approximate)

Fleet: 257 vehicles

MCI Classic	15
Nova Bus (1993/96)	31
Nova Bus (ALF)	15
GMC	3
Articulated	14
New Flyer (ALF)	162
New Flyer 30 ft	3
Paratransit vehicles	24

In peak service: 184

Most intensive service: 10 min
Fare collection: Prepurchase or exact fare to farebox
Fare structure: Flat; prepurchase adult, senior and children's tickets; monthly passes; U-Pass integration with other modes; 13 park-and-ride locations
Fares collected on board: 62 per cent
Integration with other modes: Free transfer to ferry; routes serve carpool areas and 13 park-and-ride lots
Operational control: Route inspectors/mobile radio/AVL computers
Arrangements for elderly/disabled: 24 lift-equipped vehicles; 168,271 trips in 2006/07; funded 94 per cent by municipality
Average peak-hour speed: Not currently available
Operating costs financed by: Not currently available
New vehicles financed by: Halifax Regional Municipality/Federal Government Transit Program

Ferry
Number of routes: Two

Background
Originally known as the Dartmouth Ferry, operations on this service began in 1752.

Current situation
Services between Halifax and Dartmouth and Halifax and Woodside are provided every 15 minutes at peak times. More than 3,500 commuters use the service daily.

There are bus connections at both Woodside and the Halifax ferry terminal.

Fleet: Three vessels

Mississauga
Population: 668,549 (2006 Census)

Public transport
Bus services provided by city municipal undertaking. Local commuter rail and shuttle bus services run by Government of Ontario Transit (GO Transit). Three adjacent municipal systems (Brampton, Oakville and TTC Toronto) operate into peripheral Mississauga bus terminals.

Mississauga Transit
975 Central Parkway West, Mississauga, Ontario L5C 3B1, Canada
Tel: (+1 905) 615 46 36
Fax: (+1 905) 615 38 33
e-mail: transit.info@city.mississauga.on.ca
Web: www.mississaugatransit.com;
  www.city.mississauga.on.ca

Key personnel
Transit Director: Geoff Marinoff
  Staff: 780 (estimate)

Current situation
Started privately in 1968 with six buses and two routes; the City of Mississauga purchased the transit system in 1974. Development has been rapid, serving an area adjacent to Toronto where population has more than doubled in 20 years.

Mississauga Transit provides fixed-route and accessible bus services.

Developments

An exclusive Bus Rapid Transit (BRT) route with 12 stations is planned, running east-west across Mississauga. The BRT Project is currently at design stage, with a detailed design phase and start of construction scheduled for 2008. The City of Mississauga will lead the design and construction of the BRT East (City Centre to Renforth) segment, at an estimated cost of CAD259 million, whilst GO Transit will lead the design and construction of the BRT West (Winston Churchill to Erin Mills) segment. A total of 15 60 ft BRT buses will be required for the route.

During 2008, feasibility and Environmental assessment studies will be carried out for the Hurontario Corridor rapid transit project.

Mississauga Transit plans to introduce an electronic smartcard system (Presto). The system will cover the whole of the Greater Toronto Area (GTA) and will include the TTC and GO Transit (see separate entries) and the complete system is scheduled to be operational in 2008/09.

Mississauga Transit also plans to implement Smartbus technology. This will include Global Positioning System (GPS), Automatic Passenger Counter (APC) and Traffic Signal Priority (TSP) technology.

Mississauga Transit intends to add 18 buses to its fleet during 2008.

The Transit Central Parkway Campus Expansion & Refurbishment project is under way.

Bus

Passenger journeys: Not currently available
Vehicle-km: Not currently available

Number of routes: 62 + 2 shuttle bus routes
Route length: (One way) 1,080 km

Fleet: 327 vehicles

Orion I 35 ft (1984)	15
Orion I 40 ft (1985/86/88)	36
Orion II 26 ft (1997)	12
Orion V 40 ft (1989/90/91/92/93/97)	142
Orion VI 40ft (1998)	42
Orion VII 40 ft (2001)	14
New Flyer articulated (1993/97/2001)	66

In peak service: 275

Most intensive service: 7½ min
One-person operation: All routes
Fare collection: Exact fare to farebox, or prepurchase ticket or pass
Fare structure: Flat; prepurchase 10-ticket books; weekly passes and add-on rate for GO Transit rail passes
Operational control: Route supervisors; all vehicles radio equipped, central control
Integration with other modes: Connections with TTC Toronto, Brampton Transit, Oakville Transit and GO Transit; services to Toronto International Airport
Arrangements for elderly/disabled: Over-65s can buy reduced rate annual pass; blind persons and pre-school children travel free; accessible buses, ramp-equipped and with two wheelchair/scooter securement areas, are available on 24 routes
Operating costs financed by: Fares 66 per cent, City 34 per cent (2000)
New vehicles financed by: City 100%

Greater Toronto Transit Authority (GTTA) (GO Transit)

20 Bay Street, Suite 600, Toronto, Ontario, M5J 2W3, Canada
Tel: (+1 416) 869 36 00   Fax: (+1 416) 869 35 25
Web: www.gotransit.com

Key personnel

Chairman: Peter Smith
Vice-Chairman: Stephen Smith
Managing Director and Chief Executive Officer: Gary W McNeil
Acting Director, Corporate Services: Stephen Martin
Director, Financial Services: Frances Chung
Staff: 1,493 (2007)

Bus

For fleet information, statistics and other information, please see the entry under Toronto.

Current situation

GO (originally an abbreviation of Government of Ontario) Transit serves a territory of over 8,000 km² with a growing population of five million. It runs an integrated bus and rail passenger network with a total 2007 ridership of more than 50.9 million, of which 43.4 million were by rail, a 5.3 per cent increase over 2006.

GO now operates seven lines (taking into account that the Lakeshore line has been split into East and West lines) and 58 stations, with Toronto's Union station as the system's hub. In addition to 181 trains run daily, in 2008 GO Transit will operate 1,814 bus trips each day. Train and directly related bus services carry an average of 205,000 passengers each weekday.

Train services are run under contract over mostly Canadian National (in six corridors) and Canadian Pacific Railway tracks (one corridor) – by CN and CPR crews to GO Transit specification.

GO Transit connects with all of the municipal transit systems in the Greater Toronto Area, including the Toronto Transit Commission (TTC).

GO riders with valid tickets or passes pay CAD0.60 exact cash per ride to travel on Mississauga Transit to and from Long Branch, Port Credit, Clarkson, Dixie, Cooksville, Erindale, Streetsville, Meadowvale, Lisgar and Malton GO stations. A CAD23.00 monthly sticker is also available to GO monthly pass holders. The sticker is sold at the stations mentioned previously, plus Union station, Hamilton GO Centre, Burlington, Appleby and Oakville GO stations.

Mississauga Transit also runs a shuttle bus service to and from Cooksville and Meadowvale GO stations.

Developments

There are plans to build a Bus Rapid Transit (BRT) line, known as the Mississauga Transitway, to be used by GO Transit and Mississauga city buses. However, federal funding is still awaited for this project.

Montréal

Population: City 1.62 million, urban area 3.32 million, metropolitan area 3.64 million (2006 estimates)

Public transport

Bus and metro services on Montreal island operated by urban transport corporation responsible to Montreal Urban Community, overseen by regional transport authority (AMT) which also operates suburban rail services. Other bus operators STL and RTL serve north and south shore areas respectively.

l'Agence Métropolitaine de Transport (AMT)

500 Place d'Armes, Suite 2525, Montreal, Québec H2Y 2W2, Canada
Tel: (+1 514) 287 24 64   Fax: (+1 514) 287 24 60
e-mail: tram@amt.qc.ca
Web: www.amt.qc.ca

Key personnel

Chief Executive Officer: Joël Gauthier
Vice-Presidents
Administration and Finance: Louis Champagne
Communications and Marketing: Marie Gendron
Planning and Development: Robert Olivier
Commuter Rail/Trains: Nancy Frechette
Real Estate Corporate Executive Secretary: Michel Fortier
Projects Management: Jean Hardy
Metropolitan Equipment: Nancy Frechette (Interim)
Safety and Security: Daniel Randall
Director, Commuter Trains: Louis Machado

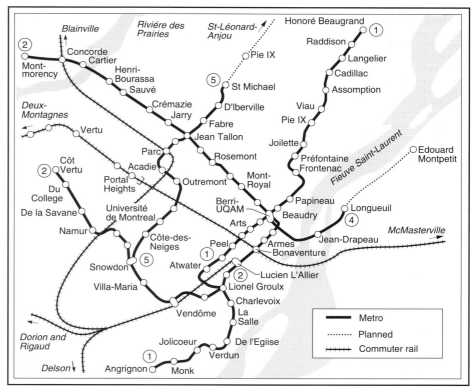

Map of Montreal's metro and commuter rail network

1168064

Current situation

AMT was created in 1996 by the government of Quebec. Its remit is to support, develop, co-ordinate and promote public transportation throughout 83 local municipalities with a population of 3.2 million in an area covering 5,000 km².

AMT took over Montreal's commuter rail operations in 1996 with the objectives of improving, developing and extending suburban train services. It is the planning authority for regional transit services (regional and express bus, reserved lanes and metropolitan termini) and manages a multimodal regional fare structure based on distance – monthly passes that can be used on all networks.

AMT also owns and operates certain infrastructure deemed as strategic to the development of transport corridors – 31 reserved bus lanes (totalling 85 km), 15 regional bus terminals and 62 parking lots (with total spaces for 27,000 vehicles). As patronage grows in these corridors, AMT may consider funding infrastructure improvements to provide increased capacity.

Funding for AMT's activities comes from various taxes – on fuel (1.5 per cent), on car registration fee (CAD30 per car) and on real estate (1 cent per CAD100 of property value) – plus municipal contribution to commuter rail services (40 per cent of expenses).

Suburban/commuter rail
Passenger journeys: (2005) 14.6 million
(2006) 15.1 million
(2007) 15.8 million

Current situation
The electrified former CN route from Montreal Central station to Deux-Montagnes (30 km, 12 stations) was recommissioned in 1995 after a three-year modernisation project. Diesel push-pull services are operated on four routes: Montreal (Lucien-L'Allier station) to Dorion-Rigaud (64 km, 19 stations); Montreal (Lucien-L'Allier station) to Blainville-Saint-Jérôme (60 km, 13 stations); Montreal (Central station) to Mont-Saint-Hilaire (35 km, seven stations); Montreal (Lucien-L'Allier station) to Delson-Candiac (23 km, eight stations).

Under the stewardship of AMT, the Montreal commuter rail network has grown from two to five lines, with additions and extensions planned.

Developments
AMT plans to add a new train line in 2010. The project consists of a 51 km line, linking Montreal (Central station) and the northeast of the metropolitan area (Repentigny, Terrebonne and Mascouche), that will serve 11 new stations, with trains using the Deux-Montagnes line as far as Mont-Royal station. Ridership is estimated at 5,500 every morning.

In January 2007, a 16 km extension of the Montreal/Blainville line to Saint-Jérôme opened, with one additional station.

In 2006 and 2007, four new stations were built – Chabanel, Vimont, Saint-Jérôme and de la Concorde.

AMT has received 22 new bilevel cars built by Bombardier in 2004, which are currently operating on the Montreal/Dorion-Rigaud and Montreal-Blainville-Saint-Jérôme lines. The Montreal-Deux-Montagnes line is served by 29 electric two-car MR90s, also built by Bombardier in 1994. The other lines are served by diesel vehicles, with 135 cars and 21 locomotives.

AMT will receive 160 new multi-level cars, built by Bombardier, between 2009 and 2012.

Rolling stock: 29 two-car emus, 135 push-pull cars, 21 locomotives, 22 bilevel cars
F-40PH GML diesel locomotives
  (1974 – rented)   M5
GP-9-GC418 GML diesel locomotives
  (1959)   M4
F-59PH-I GMC diesel locomotives
  (1999–2000)   M11
MR-90 Bombardier two-car emu
  (1995)   M29 T29
Push-pull cars (various)   T135
Bombardier bilevel cars (2004)   T22
In peak service: Not currently available
On order: 160 Bombardier multi-level cars for delivery between 2009 and 2012

Bombardier 2000 bilevel commuter cars introduced on the Montreal/Dorion-Rigaud and the Montreal/Blainville/Saint-Jérôme lines   1141811

Bombardier's Multilevel cars for AMT, Montréal, Québec, Canada (artistic rendering)
(Bombardier Transportation)   1342237

Société de Transport de Montréal (STM) – Montreal Transit Corp (MTC)
800 De La Gauchetière Street West, Montréal, Québec H5A 1J6, Canada
Tel: (+1 514) 786 46 36   Fax: (+1 514) 280 56 66
Web: www.stm.info

Key personnel
Chairman of the Board: Claude Trudel
Director General: Yves Devin
Executive Director, Operations: Carl Desrosiers
Executive Director, Planning, Marketing and Communications: Denise Vaillancourt
Executive Director, Commercial and Government Affairs: Pierre Rocray
Executive Director, Strategic Planning: Céline Desmarteau
Executive Director, Human Resources: Alain Brière
Executive Director, Shared Services: Alain Savard
Executive Director, Major Metro Projects Management: Pierre Vézina
Executive Director, Major Bus Projects Management: Peirre Dauphinais
Staff: 7,606 (2007)

Passenger journeys: (2006) 448.9 million (estimate) (2007) 447.6 million (unlinked passenger trips)

Operating costs financed by: Fares 48.3 per cent, City 35.6 per cent, Government of Quebec 6.5 per cent, other (including AMT) 9.6 per cent
Subsidy from: City of Montreal 35.6 per cent, Quebec provincial government 6.5 per cent, AMT 6.2 per cent, cities outside Montreal 0.5 per cent

Current situation
The Commission de Transport de la Communauté Urbaine de Montréal (CTCUM) was established in 1970 to widen the role of its predecessor. In 1980 it became responsible for bus services in the West Island and an extensive regional area, acquiring assets from private firms. In 1983, some of these routes were relinquished following decisions of the communities served, and in 1984 regional routes were returned to private ownership. In 1982, the city's two remaining suburban rail services were taken over from CN and CP, and these were transferred to AMT (see separate entry) in 1996.

In 1985, the authority was restyled as STCUM, and as a public corporation made directly responsible to the metropolitan authority, the Montreal Urban Community. In January 2001, owing to the formation of the City of Montréal, STCUM became the Société de Transport de Montréal (STM). It provides services in 29 municipalities with a total population of two million.

STM has entered a five-year partnership, Reno-Systems, with Dessau-Soprin Inc as part of the Montreal subway asset preservation programme. The first phase is to identify the size of grant needed to meet the cost of replacement or renovation of non-rolling stock and report to the government of Québec. The partnership will plan and manage projects assisted by SODETEG, France.

In 2007, STM provided some 85 per cent of all public transportation in the metropolitan area and some 75 per cent of all trips throughout the province.

Developments

Two long-planned metro extensions are to go ahead (see below), and three alignments are being studied as possible routes for light rail.

Light rail feasibility studies are being carried out along three corridors: east-west along the north edge of the island, north-south along Park Avenue, and east-west from Boucherville to Brossard, with a direct link to Montreal city centre by way of Highway 10.

In April 2005, STM carried out road-testing trials of articulated buses as part of its 2008–10 procurement programme.

In May 2005, the Board agreed to add CAD1 million to the budget for paratransit services. The contract with 12 taxi companies to provide these services was renewed, ending in 2006.

STM is in the process of introducing a smart card payment system. The new system is operational in one sector of the city. Full implementation will follow, with the system scheduled to be fully installed by June 2009.

STM was awarded CAD3.6 million by the federal government to improve security across the system. There are plans to utilise the funds to add 240 more video cameras top the existing 1,200 already installed.

There are long-term plans for bus and metro vehicles, which, if approved, would see more than 1,000 new buses in the fleet and the replacement of the MR063 metro cars.

Bus

Passenger journeys:
(2006) 193.4 million (estimate)
(2007) 224.1 million (unlinked passenger trips)
Vehicle-km: (2006) 77.5 million (estimate)
(2007) 70.1 million

Number of routes: 192 (20 night routes)
Route length: 4,420 km
On priority right-of-way: 44 km

Developments

During 2007, 1,500 electronic fare control boxes for buses were deployed in order to counteract fraud.

In November 2007, STM chose B5 biodiesel for it bus fleet.

NovaBus was selected to supply 202 articulated buses and the vehicles are due to enter service in late 2009.

Fleet: 1,594 vehicles (plus 101 paratransit vehicles) (2007)
Full fleet breakdown is not currently available, but comprises:

Standard buses	496
Low-floor buses	1094
City minibuses	4

In peak service: 1,243
On order: 202 NovaBus articulated buses, scheduled to enter service in 2009

Most intensive service: 3–15 min
One-person operation: All routes

Nova bus of STM (Bill Luke)　　　　　　　　　0554798

Fare collection: Exact fare; monthly and weekly passes, ticket or cash to driver, or transfer; ticket machines issue transfer from metro
Fare structure: Flat, with 1.5 h free transfer; monthly passes and six-ticket strips sold through over 700 outlets; monthly regional all-modes travelcard also valid on STL and STRSM. Cart Touristique (Tourist Card) one- and three-day tickets valid on STM services.
Fares collected on board: 9 per cent
Integration with other modes: Fully integrated with metro; Metrobus peak-hour express feeder services, also integrated fares with commuter services and suburban buses
Operational control: Route operations chiefs/mobile radio with central control room
Arrangements for elderly/disabled: Fleet of 101 adapted minibuses and special arrangements with 18 taxi firms provide services within the standard fare structure, carrying more than two million passengers in 2007
Average distance between stops: 225 m
Average peak-hour speed: In mixed traffic 16–20 km/h
New vehicles financed by: Subsidy from provincial government (50 per cent); STM (50 per cent)

Metro

Type of operation: Rubber-tyred full metro, first line opened 1966

Passenger journeys: (2006) 255.5 million (estimate)
(2007) 223.5 million (unlinked passenger trips)
Car-km: (2006) 69 million (estimate)
(2007) 64.8 million

Route length: 71 km
Number of lines: 4 (Line 1 – Green, Line 2 – Orange, Line 4 – Yellow, Line 5 – Blue)
Number of stations: 68
Gauge: 1,435 mm
Track: 35 kg/m security rails flanked by 254 mm wide concrete running tracks and lateral guide bars
Max gradient: 6.5%
Min curve radius: 140 m
Tunnel: About 30 per cent cut-and-cover
Electrification: 750 V DC

Current situation

There are longer-term plans for further extensions to the Blue and Yellow Lines.

Developments

The extension of Line 2 (Orange Line) from Henri-Bourassa to Montmornecy (5.2 km, three stations) opened in April 2007.

In June 2007, service on the Blue Line was improved by having six-car trains available at all times.

In August 2007, STM introduced an on-call public taxi service between Phillips Avenue and the Sainte-Anne-de-Bellevue commuter train station during peak hours only.

The MR-73 cars are undergoing refitting.

Rolling stock: 759 cars

MR063 Canadian Vickers (1960s)	336
MR-73 Bombardier (1970s)	423

Service: Peak 3–4 min (Green and Orange Lines)
4–6 min (Yellow Line) 5–6 min (Blue Line)

Off-peak 7–12 min (Green and Orange Lines)
10 min (Yellow Line) 7–11 min (Blue Line)
First/last train: 05.30/01.00
One-person operation: On Lines 1, 2 and 5
Stations: No pavement entrances to stations: access through small off-street structures and through commercial buildings
Fare structure: Zonal
Revenue collection: Magnetic pass-readers installed at all stations; implementation of new Opus smartcard fare-collection system April 2008 to June 2009
Security: 132 police officers patrol the network
Signalling: Cab signalling with ATC and ATO

Société de transport de Laval (STL)

2250 avenue Francis-Hughes, Laval, Québec H7S 2C3, Canada
Tel: (+1 450) 662 54 00　Fax: (+1 450) 662 54 59
Web: www.stl.laval.qc.ca

Key personnel

General Manager: Pierre Giard
　Staff: 678 (including 457 drivers)

Passenger journeys: (2001) 17.7 million
(2004) 18.7 million
Vehicle-km: (2001) 13.6 million
(2004) 14.0 million

Operating costs financed by: Fares 29 per cent, town of Laval 55.4 per cent, government subsidy 8.4 per cent, Metropolitan Transport Agency 4.6 per cent, other sources 2.6 per cent

Current situation

STL, which was created in 1984, runs buses in the city of Laval on Montreal's north shore, serving an area of 247 km^2 with a population of nearly 364,800. Its 34 routes extend to 641 km, operated with a fleet of 229 buses (2005). Accessible service is provided with 22 minibuses operated by 9062-5948 Québec Inc and Coop-Taxi vehicles. Paratransit ridership is currently more than 250,000 trips per year (2005).

Réseau de Transport de Longueuil (RTL)

1150 boulevard Marie-Victorin, Longueuil, Québec J4G 2M4, Canada
Tel: (+1 450) 442 86 00　Fax: (+1 450) 463 10 43
Web: www.rtl-longueuil.qc.ca

Key personnel

President: Claude Gladu
General Manager: Pierre del Fante
　Staff: 900

Passenger journeys: (1997) 26.9 million

Current situation

RTL serves an area of 273.92 km^2 and a population of some 385,000. There are 70 bus routes served by a fleet of 347 vehicles. RTL also provides paratransit, shared taxi and school services. Paratransit services ridership is more than 230,000 per year.

Ottawa

Population: City 859,000, metropolitan area 1.1 million (estimates)

Public transport

Public transit services in the city of Ottawa are provided by OC Transpo. City council sets transit policies and guides the implementation of service. The Director of Transit Services is responsible for operating the transit system within the set policies and budgets, and reports to the Deputy City Manager, Public Works and Services (PWS), who in turn reports to Transportation Committee and Council. Nine members of the Council are appointed to the Transportation Committee.

OC Transpo

Transit Services Branch, City of Ottawa
1500 St Laurent Boulevard, Ottawa, Ontario
K1G 0Z8, Canada
Tel: (+1 613) 741 64 40   Fax: (+1 613) 741 73 59
Web: www.octranspo.com

Key personnel

Chair of Transit Committee: Alex Cullen
Transit Services Director: Alain Mercier
   Staff: 2,198

Background

Established in 1972, OC Transpo has exclusive rights to operate within the area of the regional municipality of Ottawa-Carleton, serving the communities of Ottawa, Nepean, Vanier, Rockcliffe, Gloucester, Kanata and Orleans with a population of 865,600.

Current situation

As of 1 January 2001, OC Transpo became a Branch of the City of Ottawa and has exclusive rights to operate within the city boundaries.

A policy established in the 1970s determined that the majority of growth in demand should be accommodated by public transport. A key feature is the 31 km bus Transit-way in three main corridors with 25 'stations' and central area bus priority access. This was completed in 1996. The average number of Transit-way weekday passengers is 200,000.

The system has been extended by the addition of 23 km (includes both directions) of exclusive bus shoulder lanes on the freeway. The last section of this was added in 2001 and currently there are 38 stations. Widespread use has been made of other transit priority measures, such as traffic signal pre-emption and bus bypass lanes.

In October 2001, OC Transpo began operation of a light rail network using single-operator train units and a shared track that crosses two other active rail lines. The 8 km line uses existing Canadian Pacific track and carries 9,090 passengers daily. The O-Train is fully integrated with bus services.

Transit service was expanded to rural communities of Ottawa in September 2002. This development was accompanied by the introduction of fare zones, with a premium attached to express trips to and from rural areas.

OC Transpo has a fare system offering considerable discounts for payments other than cash. Monthly, annual and semester passes are available and are supplemented by discounted tickets and Day Passes that become Family passes on Sundays and statutory holidays.

An automated passenger information system is in operation. Telephone information is provided relating to the timetable of services from any bus stop, operated by dialling 560-1000 plus a unique four-digit bus stop number. Electronic displays at main departure points in Transit-way stations and in shopping centres provide bus departure times. Automatic vehicle and location operates for all buses, and it is to be integrated with the 560 system to provide real-time information to passengers at each stop.

An automatic trip planning service is available on OC Transpo's website (see above).

OC Transpo New Flyer articulated bus on the Transitway at Train station (Bill Luke)   1115125

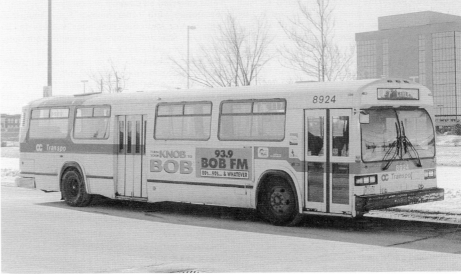
OC Transpo Nova Bus Classic low-floor bus (Bill Luke)   1115127

Developments

GPS is currently being installed on the whole transit fleet. It will allow for automatic vehicle location to be integrated with the 560 system (see above) to provide real-time information for passengers at each stop.

In March 2006, a new discounted transit pass became available to Ottawa residents who receive benefits under the Ontario Disability Support Progam (ODSP). The Community Pass is a one-year pilot project and replaces the previous policy of free fares for transit customers who use a mobility aid.

Bus

Passenger journeys: (2001) 84.7 million
(2002) 86.8 million
(2003) 87.9 million
(2004) 88.8 million
(2005) 89.6 million
Vehicle-km: (2001) 52.3 million
(2002) 52.9 million
(2003) 54.2 million
(2004) 53.9 million
(2005) 53.2 million

Number of routes: 225 (all routes) (2005)
Route length: (One way) 2,950 km (2004)
On priority right-of-way: 34.2 km

Fleet: 911 vehicles (2005)

New Flyer articulated 60LF	224
Orion/GM/MCI Nova Bus 40 ft	311
Flyer 40 ft	82
Orion low-floor 40 ft	138
Nova Bus low-floor 40 ft	20
Flyer 40 ft low-floor	135
Ford van	1

In peak service: 765 (2005)
Average age of fleet: 7.8 years (2005)

Most intensive service: 3 min
One-person operation: All routes
Fare collection: Exact fare to Duncan farebox or pre-purchase tickets; Day Passes or monthly passes
Fare structure: Zonal; free transfer; monthly, annual or semester passes; Day Passes; Regular, Express or rural Express fares; child's fare (age 11 and under)
Fares collected on board: 5.2 per cent (73.2 per cent of passengers use passes, 19.6 per cent use prepurchase tickets) (2004)
Operational control: Central radio control, plus route inspectors/mobile radio, with automatic vehicle monitoring being developed
Security: Transit Law Enforcement Officers
Arrangements for elderly/disabled: Two private companies provide three services under contract using a fleet of minivans, taxis and cars. See separate section below for more details. Some 57 per cent of the conventional fleet is fully accessible (2005) and this was due to rise to 65 per cent by 2006. As of January 2006, there were 62 bus routes which were designated as accessible, although many other routes are served by low-floor vehicles. A one-year pilot project for a new Community Pass started in March 2006.
Integration with other modes: 18 park-and-ride sites; Sportworks bike racks on 337 buses (2005)
Average distance between stops: 250 m
Average peak-hour speed: In mixed traffic, 27.4 km/h

Bus priority: 12.5 km of exclusive bus lanes on city streets; 11.5 km bus lane on Provincial highway; exclusive bus Transitways (see below)

Operating costs financed by: Fares 51.1 per cent, other commercial sources 1.2 per cent, subsidy/grants 47.7 per cent (2004)

Subsidy from: City (by property taxes) 47.7 per cent (2004)

New vehicles financed by: Reserve 66.7 per cent, provincial subsidy 33.3 per cent, development charges 0.0 per cent (2004)

Busway (Transitway)
Current situation

The Transitway is fully grade-separated. It penetrates the central area using bus lanes for 2 km on two one-way streets, while several reserved bus lanes provide priority access to the Transitway in suburban areas.

Ramp access is provided to the Transitway so express routes may operate direct from residential areas if the demand is sufficient for frequent service; otherwise feeder service is provided, with passengers transferring to Transitway services at stations.

Developments

A new Transitway station and adjoining park-and-ride site opened in January 2007, named Strandherd.

Para Transpo

In July 2002, three separate contracts were awarded to two private contractors for the operation of the Para Transpo services. One of the contractors was awarded two contracts, one for small bus services and the other for sedan services. This contractor has a fleet of 91 lift-equipped minivans and 37 cars. The third contract was awarded to a taxi company, which uses up to 30 vehicles to provide a dedicated service.

In total, 770,000 passengers were carried on the Para Transpo services in 2005. The services are funded 92.9 per cent by the municipality and 7.1 per cent by fares, with 0.0 per cent reserves.

Light rail
O-Train

Transit Services Branch, City of Ottawa
1500 St Laurent Boulevard, Ottawa, Ontario K1G 0Z8, Canada

Tel: (+1 613) 741 64 40   Fax: (+1 613) 741 73 59
Web: www.octranspo.com

Most intensive service: 15 min

Current situation

A light rail diesel project opened in October 2001 on an 8 km section of existing CP Rail freight line between Bayview and Greenboro.

The service is operated by three Bombardier Talent BR643 dmus, each seating 135 with 150 standing. Each unit is 48 m long and 2.9 m wide, weighs 72,000 kg and has a top speed of 120 km/h.

The service runs on single track, with five stations and a passing track at Carleton station, the midway point on the line.

The average daily weekday ridership is 9,090.

Developments

This pilot project was the first step towards a citywide light rail system. After voting in December 2006 to terminate the north-south light rail transit project, city councillors are considering other viable rapid transit alternatives.

Québec

Population: City: 491,142, metropolitan area: 715,515 (2006 Census)

Public transport

Bus services provided by transport commission responsible to urban municipal authority.

Réseau de Transport de la Capitale (RTC)

720 rue des Rocailles, Québec G2J 1A5, Canada
Tel: (+1 418) 627 23 51   Fax: (+1 418) 641 67 05
Web: www.rtcquebec.ca

Key personnel

President: Gilles Marcotte
General Manager: Normand Carrier
Director of Operations: Denis Andlauer
Director of Research and Marketing: Pierre Bouvier
Communications Director: Claude Lévesque
Operations Directorate Co-ordinator: Denis Andlauer
   Staff: 1,349

Current situation

RTC was created in 1969 and acquired the buses and services of seven companies which had previously served the 600 km² area and one municipality in and around the city.

RTC also provides paratransit transport services with the Societé de Transport Adapté de Quebec (STAQ).

Developments

In February 2007, an electric minibus started trials in the city.

A smartcard payment system is due to be installed, starting in 2008.

RTC is examining the possibility of introducing tram/light rail to Quebec.

Bus

Passenger journeys: (2006) 40 million
(2007) Not currently available
(2008) 43 million
Vehicle-km: (2006) 23.5 million
(2007) Not currently available
(2008) 24 million

Number of routes: 97
Route length: 600 km
Number of stops: 4,402

Fleet: 546 vehicles

GM Canada New Look (1971–82)	43
GM/MCI/Nova Bus Classic (1983–95)	140
MCI Classic articulated (1992)	2
Orion II 24 ft (1994)	4
Nova Bus LFS low-floor (1996–2003)	357

In peak service: 450
Average age of fleet: 9.2 years

Most intensive service: 5 min
One-person operation: All services
Fare collection: Payment to driver or prepurchase pass
Fare structure: Flat; exact fare; monthly passes
Operational control: Inspectors, radio
Bus priority: 39.7 km peak-hour bus lanes
Average peak-hour speed: 20 km/h
Operating costs financed by: Fares 36 per cent, subsidy/grants 64 per cent
Subsidy from: Province and one city

Toronto

Population: City 2.5 million, urban area 4.75 million, metropolitan area 5.6 million (2006 estimates)

Public transport

Bus, metro, tramway and advanced light rail services provided by Transit Commission, responsible to the City of Toronto; bus and rail regional commuter services run by GO Transit.

Toronto Transit Commission (TTC)

Marketing and Public Affairs Department
1900 Yonge Street, Toronto M4S 1Z2, Canada
Tel: (+1 416) 393 40 00   Fax: (+1 416) 488 61 98
Web: www.ttc.ca

Key personnel

Chair: Adam Giambrone
Vice-Chair: Joe Mihevc
Chief General Manager: Gary Webster
General Managers
   Operations: Rick Cornacchia
   Engineering and Construction: John Sepulis
   Executive and General Secretary: Vincent Rodo
   Manager, Materials and Procurement:
   A Chocorlan
   Chief Marketing Officer (Acting): Alice Smith
   Corporate Communications Assistant:
   Michael DeToma
   Staff: 10,930

Passenger journeys: (2001) 420 million
(2002) 415.5 million
(2004) 418.1 million
(2005) 431.2 million
Vehicle-km: (2004) 195.7 million
(2005) 196.6 million

Operating costs financed by: Fares 75 per cent, subsidy/grants 25 per cent
Subsidy from: City of Toronto Council; Province of Ontario

Background

Constituted in its present form in 1954, TTC serves the 632 km² City of Toronto area in co-ordination with a number of neighbouring systems including York Region Transit, Brampton Transit, Mississauga Transit, Durham Region Transit and the GO Transit commuter system (see separate entries in Systems section).

The TTC is made up of nine commissioners, all elected city councillors.

Current situation

TTC provides bus, metro and light rail/tramway services in and around the Toronto area, with late night (Blue Night Network) services for bus and light rail/tramway on most major routes. TTC also provides Community Bus services in the Lawrence Manor, Parkdale, East York, Etobicoke and South Don Mills areas and the Wheel-Train service for passengers with disabilities.

The Sheppard Subway extension (6.4 km, five stations), forecast to add 30 million journeys annually, opened in November 2002.

Developments

TTC's Toronto Transit City – Light Rapid Transit Plan is a 120 km network of dedicated and fully accessible rapid transit lines. Estimated cost: CAD6 billion. Projected to carry 175 million riders.

Spadina Extension from Downsview Station to Steeles Avenue. Length: 6.2 km with four stations: Sheppard West, Finch West, York University and Steeles West.

Bus

Passenger journeys: (2002) 248 million
Vehicle-km: (2004) 100.7 million
(2005) 102.8 million
Number of routes: 167 (103 accessible)
Route length: (Round-trip) 6,934.1 km

Fleet: 1,491 buses (805 accessible)
GM/MCI New Look/Classic T6H-53707N (1975/83)
                   Not currently available
Flyer various models (1977/81/85/86)
                   Not currently available
OBI Orion II low-floor (Wheel-Trans)
                   Not currently available

OBI Orion V 40 ft
Not currently available
OBI Orion V CNG-powered
Not currently available
OBI Orion 60 ft
Not currently available
Overland Elf (Wheel-Trans)
Not currently available
Nova RTS 40 ft
Not currently available
Orion VI CNG-powered
Not currently available
In peak service: Not currently available
Average age of fleet: Not currently available
On order: 180 Orion Cummins ISL-powered buses and 180 ISB hybrid buses, delivery was scheduled to commence in March 2006

Most intensive service: 2–3 min
One-person operation: All routes
Fare collection: Pay-as-you-enter, pay-as-you-board with seamless connections between buses, trams/light rail and the subway/metro. Entry is by cash, ticket, token, valid pass or valid transfer. Exact fare is required on buses and trams/light rail
Fare structure: Flat; free transfers; prepurchase multitickets and tokens; daily, weekly and monthly passes
Fare evasion control: Visual check by drivers, route supervisors and security staff
Integration with other modes: 242 timed connections at metro/ICTS stations during the morning peak; connections with GO Transit trains; numerous connections with other local transit authorities, without fare integration; 26 park-and-ride lots
Operational control: AVLC via computerised communications and information system, with control from seven divisions through onboard communications and data exchange system (TRUMP) fitted to all vehicles
Arrangements for qualified elderly/disabled, based on physical function mobility: 103 routes accessible; Wheel-Trans door-to-door service uses 145 low-floor buses, plus 73 sedan/taxis and 32 wheelchair-accessible taxis operated by private contractors. Wheel-Trans staff handle reservations, despatching and scheduling; fares match regular TTC. Five community bus routes link seniors' centres, shopping areas, medical and community facilities
New vehicles financed by: Subsidy: Province 33 per cent, City of Toronto 67 per cent

Current situation
In 2006, Wheel-Trans, a door-to-door service for people with physical disabilities who have the most difficulty using conventional transit service, carried 1.89 million passenger trips with a fleet of 270 paratransit vehicles (includes Community Buses and contracted taxis). Community Bus services carried 95,286 passenger trips with five vehicles on five routes.

Developments
In June 2006, more than 1,700 TTC and Wheel-Trans buses were using bio-fuel, a soy-diesel blend known as B5.

Metro
Type of operation: Full metro, first line opened 1954

Passenger journeys: (2002) 163.4 million
Car-km: (2002) 76.3 million
(2004) 78.4 million
(2005) 77.7 million

Route length: 61.9 km
Number of lines: 3
Number of stations: 64
Gauge: 1,495 mm
Track: 57.5 kg/m T-rail; open cut, conventional sleepers on ballast and concrete sleepers (on new sections) on ballast; bored tunnel, rail laid on concrete bed; and rail laid on double concrete sleepers on resilient rubber pads
Tunnel: Cut-and-cover sections, steel-reinforced poured concrete box structures; bored tunnels, shield driven precast concrete or cast-iron linings
Electrification: 600 V DC, third rail

Developments
Acess to 28 major stations is being improved via the installation of lifts. The new T1 cars are fully accessible, with wider doors, clear centre aisles and lock-in positions for wheelchairs. Currently 19 stations are fully accessible.

All subway trains (and Scarborough RT trains) can be boarded by people with wheelchairs, scooters and other mobility devices. The TTC has 372 T-1 accessible subway cars (more than 50 per cent of the subway car fleet). These cars have a wheelchair/scooter position. T-1 trains run on all three subway lines: Bloor-Danforth, Yonge-University-Spadina and Sheppard. The TTC has ordered 234 new, fully accessible cars scheduled for delivery beginning in 2009.

The TTC has ordered 234 new, fully accessible cars scheduled for delivery beginning in 2009. These cars will have new security features, such as an open layout, built-in ramps for easier evacuation, on-board LCD information screens and security cameras as well as a passenger alarm intercom system. Delivery will start in 2009 and be completed before the end of 2011.

The platform at Union Station will be extended and a second platform is being constructed. Construction began in 2008, after a sewer has been relocated. The cost of the project is estimated at CAD90 million and is scheduled to be completed in 2011.

Rolling stock: 722 cars

Hawker Siddeley Canada H4 (1974/75)	M88
Hawker Siddeley Canada H5 (1976/79)	M136
UTDC/Can-Car Rail H6 (1986/89)	M126
Bombardier T1 (1995/1999)	M372

In peak service: 556
On order: 39 six-car Bombardier metro trains

Service: Peak 2½ –5½ min, off-peak 4–5½ min
First/last train: 05.31/02.14
Fare structure: Flat with free transfers to surface system
Revenue control: Conventional and wheelchair-accessible turnstiles; token and monthly pass activate turnstiles; high-gate turnstiles at automatic entry areas
Integration with other modes: Free transfer with surface systems at 36 stations; free paper transfer at 28 stations
Arrangements for elderly/disabled: Programme under way to improve access at 23 stations (see below); 19 stations are fully accessible currently
One-person operation: None
Signalling: Automatic block and interlocking signals and wayside signals
Centralised control: Centralised train despatch and control system; similar system installed on Scarborough ICTS line (see below)
Surveillance: Designated waiting areas at all stations consisting of well-lit location monitored by CCTV cameras and with voice intercom system

Tramway/light rail
Type of operation: Conventional tramway, light rail

Passenger journeys: (2002) 40.6 million
Car-km: (2002) 11.3 million
(2004) 12.2 million
(2005) 11.8 million

Route length: 190.0 km
Number of lines: 11
Gauge: 1,495 mm
Track: 50 kg/m T-rail
Electrification: 600 V DC, overhead

Service: Peak 2½–10 min, off-peak 5–20 min
Fare structure: As bus
Fare collection: As bus; proof-of-payment on Queen Street Line
One-person operation: All cars

Rolling stock: 248 cars

UTDC/Swiss Industrial L1 (1977/78)	M6
UTDC/Hawker Siddeley Canada L2 (1979/81)	M190
UTDC/Can-Car Rail L3 (1987/89)	M52

In peak service: 200

Developments
To start the Toronto Transit City 120 km expansion plan, and to ensure that the TTC's popular existing tram/light rail routes continue to run into the future, the TTC is starting the process of acquiring new LRVs for Toronto. The first LRV prototype is scheduled to arrive in Toronto by 2010 – and will be accessible.

Scarborough RT (Intermediate Capacity Transit System)
Type of operation: Intermediate capacity advanced light metro transit system, opened 1985

Passenger journeys: (2002) 4.1 million
Car-km: (2002) 4.3 million
(2004) 4.4 million
(2005) 4.3 million

Route length: 6.4 km
elevated: 2.3 km
Number of routes: 1
Number of stations: 6
Gauge: 1,435 mm
Track: 115 lb/yd continuously welded T-rail fixed to concrete base with rubber insulation pads
Max gradient: 5.2%
Minimum curve radius: 35 m normal, 18 m minimum
Electrification: 600 V DC, ungrounded, collection from two power rails and reaction rail

Service: Peak 3½ min, off-peak 5½ min
Fare structure: Flat, free transfers

Bombardier's subway cars for Toronto, Canada (artistic rendering) (Bombardier Transportation)
1330338

Revenue collection: Conventional and token and monthly pass-activated turnstiles; visual inspection

Integration with other modes: Fully integrated with rest of TTC system

One-person operation: None

Automatic control: Fully automatic with manual over-ride, manual door operation

Signalling: Moving block; centralised control and dispatch

Rolling stock: 28 cars
UTDC/VentureTrans S1 (1984/85)   M28
In peak service: 24

Current situation

This fully automated system linking Scarborough with Kennedy metro station has cars powered by Linear Induction Motors (LIMs) running on conventional steel-rail track.

Developments

A study has identified three possible options which would replace this ageing system: Replacing existing vehicles with larger ones and expanding stations/platforms; Constructing a light rail system; Constructing a new metro/ subway line.

Greater Toronto Transit Authority (GTTA) (GO Transit)

20 Bay Street, Suite 600, Toronto, Ontario M5J 2W3, Canada
Tel: (+1 416) 869 36 00   Fax: (+1 416) 869 35 25
e-mail: ems@gotransit.com
Web: www.gotransit.com

Key personnel

Chairman: Peter Smith
Vice-Chairman: Stephen Smith
Managing Director and Chief Executive Officer:
  Gary W McNeil
Acting Director, Corporate Services: Stephen Martin
Director, Financial Services: Frances Chung
  Staff: 1,493 (2007)

Passenger journeys: (Both modes)
(2005) 46.8 million
(2006) Not currently available
(2007) 50.9 million
Vehicle-km: Not currently available

Operating costs financed by: Revenue (mostly fares) 89.4 per cent

Background

GO Transit is the provincially funded, inter-regional public transit service for the Greater Toronto Area (GTA) and its surrounding areas. Created in 1967 by the province of Ontario, GO has grown from a single rail line along Lake Ontario's shoreline into an integrated network of trains and buses connecting downtown Toronto with the surrounding communities. In a transfer of responsibilities, the Province handed over the funding of GO to the GTA municipalities at the beginning of 1998. In January 2002, the Province of Ontario took back responsibility of GO Transit. Legally known as the Greater Toronto Transit Authority, GO is once again a crown agency of the province of Ontario.

Current situation

GO (originally an abbreviation of Government of Ontario) Transit serves a territory of over 8,000 km² with a growing population of more than five million. It runs an integrated bus and rail passenger network with a total 2007 ridership of more than 50.9 million, of which 43.4 million were by rail, a 5.3 per cent increase over 2006.

GO now operates seven lines (taking into account that the Lakeshore line has been split into East and West lines) and 58 stations, with Toronto's Union station as the system's hub. In addition to 181 trains run daily, in 2008 GO Transit

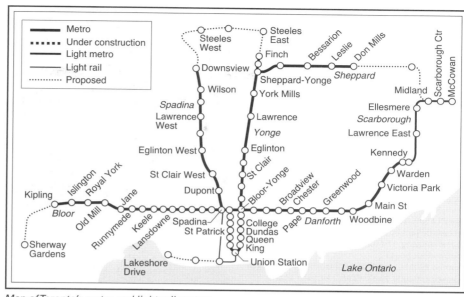

Map of Toronto's metro and light rail system   1115267

will operate 1,814 bus trips each day. Train and directly related bus services carry an average of 205,000 passengers each weekday.

Train services are run under contract over mostly Canadian National (in six corridors) and Canadian Pacific Railway tracks (one corridor) – by CN and CPR crews to GO Transit specification.

GO Transit connects with all of the municipal transit systems in the Greater Toronto Area, including the Toronto Transit Commission (TTC).

Developments

In May 2004, a new stream of funding for improvements to GO infrastructure was announced jointly by the Ontario and Federal governments. CAD1.05 billion is to be made available to fund a 10-year expansion programme, comprising 12 major projects. These include improvements to Toronto's Union Station, 36 km of three-tracking on the Lakeshore East and West lines to eliminate bottlenecks and raise capacity for expansion of GO Train services, 33 km of new track on the Georgetown route, improvements to the Milton, Bradford and Stouffville lines and new buses and park-and-ride stations to expand the GO Bus network to serve Peterborough, Cambridge, Niagara Falls and the Guelph-Kitchener-Waterloo area.

In December 2004, the province of Ontario became GO's official agent to supply a common fare collection system for the GTA Farecard, which will enable seamless, integrated transit across the Greater Toronto Area. The new farecard was

introduced in August 2007, with the completion across the GTA set for 2010.

GO has opened six new train stations since late 2004. East Gwillimbury on the Bradford line opened in November 2004. Mount Pleasant opened in February 2005 on the Georgetown line. GO opened Kennedy Station on the Stouffville line in June 2005. Milliken Station was relocated in September 2005. This new station is bigger, accessible and has parking. Lisgar Station opened in September 2007 on the Milton line. Barrie Sout, an extension of what was the Bradford line and is now the Barrie line, opened in December 2007.

In recent years, stairways, elevators and new passenger information signs have been added at Union Station. Major construction projects include rehabilitation of the roof over the train platforms, a new platform for tracks 13 and 14 and a second GO concourse, in the west end of the building. GO will also be replacing the tracks and modernising the signal system to allow more trains to run. When completed, all of this will improve service for customers.

Several other large projects are being undertaken across the GO network. These fall under the GO Transit Rail Improvement Program (GO TRIP), with the Government of Canada, the Province of Ontario and the municipal governments in the Greater Toronto Area all playing a role in the funding. The projects include adding new track on the Lakeshore and Georgetown lines to allow for better train service, underpasses or overpasses that will separate

GO Transit bus (Brian Main, GO Transit)   1158909

GO Train service from CPR or CN freight traffic on the Georgetown, Bradford, and Stouffville lines and improvements to allow GO Train service to extend north to Barrie.

Bus (GO Buses)

Passenger journeys: (2005) 7.1 million
(2006) Not currently available
(2007) 7.5 million
Vehicle-km: Not currently available

Route length: (One way) 2,429 km
Terminals: 14

Fleet: 316 buses
MCI 102C3 40 ft (1993)	12
Prevost XL40 40 ft (1999)	20
Orion V Suburban 40 ft (2001–04)	30
MCI DL4500 45 ft (2001–07)	254

On order: Planned from March 2008: 12 MCI DL4500 45 ft (replacing 12 MCI 102C3 40 ft), 12 Enviro 500 double-deck buses
Planned for May 2008: 20 MCI DL4500 45 ft
Planned for June 2008: 15 MCI DL4500 45 ft
Planned for September 2008: 7 MCI DL4500 45 ft, 2 hybrid buses

Average age of fleet: 4 years
Fare collection: Prepurchased ticket or pass
Fare evasion control: Inspection by driver, transit enforcement officer or customer attendant
Arrangements for disabled: Many buses kneel. Several GO Bus routes are wheelchair accessible on some or all trips. Companions and/or a specially trained dog for assistance to disabled people and visually impaired passengers ride free on some services
Operating costs financed by: Fares 89.4 per cent

Suburban rail (GO Trains)

Passenger journeys: (2004) 38.2 million
(2005) 39.6 million
(2006) 41.2 million
(2007) 43.4 million
Train-km: Not currently available

Number of lines: 7
Number of stations: 58
Route length: 390 km

Current situation
Diesel-hauled suburban service operated under contract. Lakeshore route Aldershot-Toronto-Oshawa runs all day, with peak hour extension from Aldershot to Hamilton. Other routes to Stouffville, Richmond Hill, Milton, Bradford and Georgetown. Total 390 km, 1,435 mm gauge, zonal fares.

Developments
Design work has started on a multiyear improvement programme, with provincial environmental assessment approval being granted for the Milton, Lakeshore East, Bradford and Stouffville corridor expansions. The Burlington portion of the Lakeshore West corridor expansion has also been given the

GO Transit train (Brian Main, GO Transit)   1158910

Bombardier BiLevel *commuter cars operated by GO Transit* (Bombardier Transportation)   0580215

same approvals and construction of new track has commenced. This expansion is due to be completed by 2012.

A contract was awarded to Wabtec subsidiary MotivePower Inc covering the supply of 27 new MP40 locomotives for delivery in 2007–08, with an option to procure a further 26.

GO Transit has also placed a contract with Bombardier for the supply of 35 additional Bi Level coaches, delivery of which should start in late 2008.

In late 2007, Siemens Transportation Systems (TS) was awarded a contract to upgrade the entire signalling and communication system in and around Toronto's Union Station and the traffic control centre as part of the GO Transit Rail Improvement Program (GO TRIP). The contract

was valued at some CAD280 million. The upgrade will take place during 2008.

Also in late 2007, Bombardier Transportation was awarded a five-year contract to supply fleet operations services for GO Transit. The contract was valued at some CAD130 million and includes options for up to 15 additional years. Should GO Transit exercise all available options, the contract could reach an estimated value of CAD483 million. Under the contract, Bombardier will be responsible for train operations, from June 2008, and well as management of train crews on six of the seven commuter lines.

Rolling stock: 45 diesel-electric locomotives in 38 trainsets, 417 bi-level commuter coaches
GM/EMD F59PH	45

Vancouver

Population: City 612,000, metropolitan area 2.25 million (2007 estimates)

Public transport

Bus, trolleybus and ferry (SeaBus) and automated light rapid transit (SkyTrain) are owned by and operated for the South Coast British Columbia Transportation Authority (SCBCTA, operating as Translink), a regional corporation which assumed responsibility for public transport within Greater Vancouver from BC Transit on 1 April 1999.

The SCBCTA was known as the Greater Vancouver Transportation Authority (GVTA) from 1999 to late 2007, when new legislation changed the name, governance and potential geographic scope.

Translink plans, funds and owns the assets of the public transportation system, with subsidiary companies and contractors providing the service.

West Coast Express, a GVTA subsidiary company, provides commuter rail service.

South Coast British Colombia Transportation Authority (SCBCTA) (TransLink)

TransLink
1600-4720 Kingsway, Burnaby, British Columbia V5H 4N2, Canada
Tel: (+1 604) 453 45 00   Fax: (+1 604) 453 46 26
e-mail: info@translink.bc.ca
Web: www.translink.bc.ca

Key personnel
Chair: Dale Parker
Chief Executive Officer: Pat Jacobsen
Corporate Secretary: Carol Lee

Passenger journeys: (all modes, unlinked)
(2003) 255.5 million
(2004) 273.7 million
(2005) 275.7 million
(2006) 282.8 million
(2007) 294.0 million

Current situation
The South Coast British Colombia Transportation Authority (SCBCTA, operating name TransLink) is responsible for all public transport, a regional major road network, transportation demand management and vehicle emissions testing

within Metro Vancouver. The authority's legal name was changed and governance revised in late 2007. The Board of Directors now consists of nine appointed members, replacing the previous board structure of elected municipal representatives. A Mayors' Council consisting of the mayors of all 21 municipalities in the service area appoints the board and is responsible for approving transportation and funding plans, including borrowing limits. The Mayors' Council may also appoint a Regional Transportation Commissioner who approves any cash fare increases above inflation, customer satisfaction, complaint procedures and any sales of major assets. The 2007 governance change also allows for future expansion of the service area to the north and east if adjacent municipalities wish to opt-in.

Bus and trolleybus services are provided by Coast Mountain Bus Company, a wholly owned subsidiary of the SCBCTA, and by four contract operators. SeaBus, a harbour ferry service, is also provided by Coast Mountain Bus Company. Two separate operating subsidiaries of the SCBCTA provide SkyTrain (automated light rapid transit) and West Coast Express (commuter rail) service.

The SCBCTA opened the Millennium Line, a 20 km extension of the SkyTrain automated light rapid transit system, in August 2002. A 1 km extension to the new VCC-Clark station, the line's thirteenth station, opened in January 2006. All stations are fully integrated with the surface bus and trolleybus systems. The SkyTrain network now carries 230,000 passengers (unlinked trips) on a weekday.

Developments

A 19 km north-south rapid transit line (Canada Line) between Richmond, Vancouver international airport and downtown Vancouver is under construction as a Public/Private Partnership (PPP or P3). The Canada Line, which will cost more than CAD2 billion, is expected to open in late 2009, in time for the 2010 Winter Olympic Games. The system will operate underground within the City of Vancouver and mainly at elevation in the City of Richmond and the airport. The line will have 16 stations and is projected to carry more than 100,000 passengers per weekday after opening. A consortium, InTransitBC, led by SNC-Lavalin, is designing, building and partially financing the line and will operate and maintain it for a 35-year period (five year construction and 30 year operation). Construction started in late 2005. 40 automated rail cars in two-car sets (20 trains) are being delivered by Hyundai Rotem, a division of Hyundai Motor Group, South Korea. The Canada Line will be fully integrated with the other bus, trolleybus, rail and ferry services provided by TransLink.

In February 2006, Alcatel was awarded a EUR25 million contract by SNC-Lavalin Inc, to provide a Communications-Based Train Control (CBTC) system for the Canada Line.

In February 2008, the authority and Province announced that SkyTrain would be the preferred technology to connect the Millennium Line to Coquitlam city centre in the northeast sector of the region. The planned 11 km route will have up to 10 stations and will be fully integrated with bus and other rail services provided by TransLink. Subject to securing funding, the planned completion date is 2014. The estimated cost of the line, which includes a 2 km tunnel, is CAD1.4 billion. In addition, 48 SkyTrain cars are on order from Bombardier for 2008-09 delivery to increase passenger capacity on the existing SkyTrain network.

The Province of British Columbia announced a transit plan in January 2008 that includes two additional light rail extensions, both planned to be in operation by 2020. First is a 12 km, CAN2.8 billion line from Broadway/Commercial SkyTrain station to UBC. Secondly, a 6 km extension of the existing SkyTrain line is to be built in north Surrey as part of a CAN3.1 billion package of SkyTrain capacity improvements.

The Authority is also working on the development of two Busway projects in the

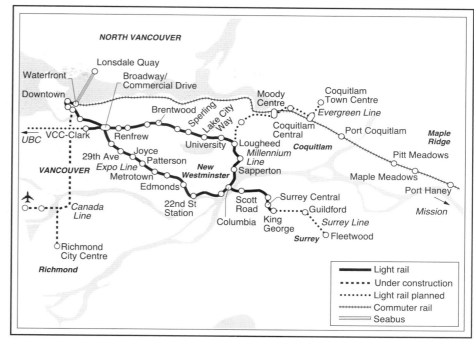

Map of Vancouver's transit system

1124835

eastern suburbs. The King George Busway between Surrey City Centre and Newton is to be completed in 2013 at a cost of CAD 200 million. The busway could be converted to Light Rail in the future. A second busway using dedicated bus ramps and median HOV lanes on Highway #1 will connect Langley with Lougheed Town Centre Station. This facility is being developed as part of a Provincial Highway improvement.

In mid-2007, armed transit police started patrolling on buses, to reduce non-payment of fares and assaults on bus drivers.

Operating costs financed by: Fares: 53 per cent. The remainder is paid by a petrol (gasoline) tax, property tax, residential hydro levy and parking sales tax.
Subsidies: SCBCTA locally controlled taxes and taxes transferred from provincial government.

Bus and trolleybus
Background
TransLink bus services are delivered by Coast Mountain Bus Company, a subsidiary of the SCBCTA, and by four contracted operators.

Coast Mountain Bus Company
13401 108th Avenue, Surrey, British Columbia V3T 5T4, Canada
Tel: (+1 604) 953 30 00   Fax: (+1 604) 953 31 51
Web: www.coastmountainbus.com

Key personnel
President and Chief Executive Officer:
    Denis Clements
    Staff: 3,800

Passenger journeys: (bus, trolleybus and community shuttle)
(2003) 186.9 million
(2004) 201.8 million
(2005) 202.3 million
(2006) 205.8 million
(2007) 214.9 million
Vehicle-km: (bus, trolleybus and community shuttle)
(2003) 68.8 million
(2004) 71.9 million
(2005) 75.1 million
(2006) 79.3 million
(2007) 83.7 million

Number of routes: 200
On priority right-of-way: 115 km of bus and High Occupancy Vehicle (HOV) lanes
Trolleybus electrification: 600 V DC

Current situation
TransLink bus services are delivered under four brand names: B-Line, Express Coach, Bus, and Community Shuttle. Over 96 per cent of services are provided by the Coast Mountain Bus Company, a wholly owned subsidiary of SCBCTA, while four per cent are delivered by contracted operators.

Contracted operators include West Vancouver Municipal Transit (Blue Bus), Bowen Island Community Transit, Metro Shuttle and DW Services Ltd.

Three-door passenger loading procedure is used on articulated buses at all stops on the #99 B-Line between the University of BC and Broadway Station and on articulated buses at four busy terminals to speed up boarding times. All buses in the system are designated as fare paid zones and customers must show proof of payment while on board buses.

In 2008, front-mounted bicycle racks were provided on all buses.

Developments
Replacement of the electric trolleybus fleet with low-floor New Flyer Industries Ltd vehicles, with Vossloh Kiepe electrics, was largely completed in 2007. The new fleet consists of 188 40 ft trolleybuses and 40 60 ft trolleybuses. The articulated trolleys entered service in 2008.

A new bus communications system, with GPS features, was introduced in 2008 to improve communications. This includes visual and audible next stop announcements and supports the introduction of real-time next bus information at stops, through electronic communications.

There are 75 Orion V suburban buses with high-back seats and air conditioning operating on eight longer-distance routes connecting the southern suburbs with Vancouver using the Highway #99 corridor, where buses use bus-only and HOV lanes. These routes will be truncated to connect with the Canada Line at Bridgeport station in 2009.

Community Shuttle minibuses have been introduced for use on lower-traffic routes and during lower demand periods across the region. There are currently 157 Community Shuttle buses, 19 of which are operated by the three private-sector operators, three by West Vancouver Blue Bus, and 135 by Coast Mountain Bus Company, under contract to TransLink.

Bus ridership increased by 4.4 per cent in 2007, mainly as a result of service improvements and regional economic growth. A current initiative is to expand the Frequent Bus Network, the key routes in the region that provide service at least every 15 minutes, 15 hours per day, seven days per week.

A new 417-vehicle maintenance and operations facility for TransLink's Vancouver routes opened in September 2006, replacing a facility on West 41st Avenue which had been in use since 1948.

Trolleybus route #15 closed in September 2005, to make way for the start of construction of the Canada Line rapid transit line, which will be underground along Cambie Street. TransLink proposes to replace the #15 trolley with conventional buses when the Canada Line opens, due to reduced ridership. Trolley overhead line extensions totalling 5.8 km are being built in 2008–9 to integrate trolley routes with the Canada Line, improve service coverage and increase operating efficiency.

Bus ridership (unlinked) increased by 4.4 per cent in 2007 and is projected to grow by 2.5 per cent in 2008.

Fleet: 1,237 buses and minibuses (total excluding trolleybus, all operators) (2007)

MCI Classic 12 m	22
Flyer D40 12 m high-floor	148
Flyer D60 18 m high-floor	21
Orion I 12 m high-floor	9
New Flyer D40 12 m low-floor	447
New Flyer D60 18 m low-floor	131
Nova Bus 12 m low-floor	127
Orion V Suburban 12 m high-floor	75
New Flyer 12 m CNG low-floor	75
New Flyer, 12 m CNG high-floor – converted to diesel	25
Minibuses (various makes, models)	157

Fleet: 228 trolleybuses (as at end 2008)

New Flyer E40LFR 40 ft low-floor (2005–07)	188
New Flyer E60LFR 60 ft Low-floor articulated (2006-07)	40

In peak service: 1,184 (all buses)

On order: 16 low-floor diesel articulated buses, nine highway coaches, 126 diesel low-floor buses to be delivered in 2007. An additional 34 articulated New Flyer trolleybuses are also due for delivery in 2009, along with 66 NovaBus LFS buses. 141 NovaBus hybrid buses are on order for 2009 delivery.

Most intensive service: 2–3 min

Hours of operation: 04.00–03.00 every day (NightBus service every night on 12 routes)

One-person operation: All routes

Fare collection: All buses and trolleybuses have Cubic electronic fareboxes. Fare system on buses and trolleybuses is integrated with SkyTrain, SeaBus and West Coast Express fares

Fare structure: Time and distance based; three zones apply on weekdays (04.00–18.30). After 18.30 on weekdays and all day Saturday, Sunday and holidays a single fare zone is in effect; free transfers are issued on board, valid for 90 minutes of travel in any direction; monthly passes (FareCards), tickets (FareSavers) in books of 10; day passes; low-cost annual passes for low-income senior residents; Universal pass (U-Pass) for 63,000 post-secondary students

Fare-evasion control: Verification of cash, tickets and transfers and U-Passes by electronic farebox and verification of monthly and annual passes through visual inspection by operator. All buses are designated as fare paid zones and customers must retain proof of payment on board or are subject to fines. Articulated buses on route #99 B-Line have all-door loading at all stops along the route and articulated buses use all-door loading at four major terminals.

Operational control: All conventional vehicles are radio-equipped, whilst community shuttle vehicle operators use mobile/cell phones; 28 vehicles assigned to one rapid bus route (#98 B-Line) have automated vehicle location systems. TransLink will introduce a new integrated automated vehicle location and communications system on all buses in 2008.

Integration with other modes: All fares the same for bus, trolleybus, SkyTrain and SeaBus. These fares are accepted as partial credit towards fares on West Coast Express. Free transfer between modes

Average distance between stops: 200 m for local service

New Flyer B-Line bus in Richmond, with Canada Line guideway under construction in the background   1343283

One of 188 New Flyer low-floor trolleybuses, with which SCBCTA renewed most of its trolleybus fleet during 2006/7   1343282

Nova LFS 12.2 m low-floor bus, 126 of which were ordered from Nova Bus in late 2006 (Volvo Bus Corporation)   1327541

Number of bus stops: 8,000 (87 per cent of regional population is within 450 m walk of a bus stop)

Average peak hour speed: 20 km/h

Number of buses with outside bike racks: 90 per cent

Arrangements for elderly/disabled: By early 2008, all buses will be equipped to handle wheelchairs; all newer buses, with the exception of long-distance suburban buses, are low-floor

Custom transit service for disabled: A door-to-door service is provided for persons with disabilities in addition to the conventional bus service. The custom transit system, known as HandyDART, has 315 vehicles and is operated by seven private contractors under eight sub-regional contracts. There were 1.22 million passengers carried during 2007, with 1.35 million boardings projected for 2008.

West Vancouver Municipal Transit (Blue Bus)

221 Lloyd Avenue, North Vancouver, British Columbia, V7P 3M2, Canada
Tel: (+1 604) 985 77 77   Fax: (+1 604) 985 86 91
e-mail: bluebusinfo@westvancouver.cat
Web: www.westvancouver.ca

Key personnel
Director of Engineering and Transportation:
  Emil Barth
Transit Manager: Greg Curry
Manager of Public Works & Transportation:
  Brent Dozzi
  Staff: 117 (Transit Department)

Passenger journeys (unlinked): (West Vancouver Bus)
(2002) 3.1 million
(2003) 3.2 million
(2005) 7.61 million
(2006) 7.85 million
(2007) 8.3 million
Vehicle-km: (2007) 2.31 million

Number of routes: 11

Current situation
Provides 'Blue Bus' service for West Vancouver including Downtown Vancouver, the University of British Columbia (UBC), the Village of Lions Bay and to the mid Lonsdale/Lions Gate Hospital and Lynn Valley in North Vancouver. Express services are also provided to Horseshoe Bay and the BC Ferry Terminal which services Vancouver Island, Sunshine Coast and Bowen Island. The transit department operates as a contractor under the South Coast British Columbia Transportation Authority (SCBCTA) through an Annual Operating Agreement. TransLink owns the buses and maintenance facility and determines routes, service levels and fares. Buses are identified by a blue motif, with the West Vancouver Municipal crest attached to the centre-front roof line, which is different from the livery used elsewhere.

The entire fleet is either low-floor or lift-equipped and all buses have bike racks.

Fleet: 49 buses
Orion I (1992)	9
Flyer G40 low-floor (1995)	17
Flyer D40 low-floor (1999)	10
Flyer D60 articulated (1991)	3
Nova 40 low-floor	6
Community Shuttle 24-seat	4
In peak service: 35	

Fare structure: 3-zone, discounted fares after 18.30, weekends and holidays; cash, monthly FareCards, FareSaver tickets and DayPasses

British Columbia Rapid Transit Company Ltd (SkyTrain)
Rapid Transit
6800 14th Avenue, Burnaby, British Columbia V3N 4S7, Canada
Tel: (+1 604) 520 36 41
Web: www.translink.bc.ca

Key personnel
President: Doug Kelsey
  Staff: 540

Type of operation: Automated intermediate-capacity metro (light rail transit), opened in 1986 with extensions in 1990, 1994 and 2002. A further 1 km extension opened in January 2006

Background
Operated by BC Rapid Transit Company, a subsidiary company of South Coast British Colombia Transportation Authority (SCBCTA).

Passenger journeys: (2003) 62.0 million
(2004) 65.0 million
(2005) 66.3 million
(2006) 69.5 million
(2007) 71.2 million
Car-km: (2003) 33.5 million
(2004) 33.7 million
(2005) 36.0 million
(2006) 35.4 million
(2007) 34.9 million

Number of lines: 2 (Expo Line and Millennium Line)
Route length: 50 km
  in tunnel: 2.5 km
  elevated: 43.5 km
  at grade: 3 km
Number of stations: 33
Gauge: 1,435 mm
Track: Mainly lightweight, pre-stressed concrete elevated guideways; 47.7 kg/m rail fixed direct to concrete track bed

Electrification: 600 V DC collected by brushes from side rails (2 in vertical series) and fed to linear induction motors through variable-voltage variable-frequency converter

Current situation
Cars are lightweight, are powered by linear induction motors, and have steerable bogies to reduce noise, vibration and wheel and track wear.

Mark I cars normally operate in four-car sets (capacity 300) and Mark II cars mostly operate in two-car sets (capacity 260), with some four-car Mark II trains operated in weekday peak periods (capacity 520).

The Millennium Line opened in August 2002. The CAD1.2 billion project, financed by the Province of British Columbia, increased the length of the system from 29 km to 49 km and added 11 new stations. A twelfth station, located mid-route, opened in November 2003 and in January 2006 the line was extended to a thirteenth station. Sixty Mark II cars, built by Bombardier, were introduced in 2002 to provide the service on the new line and increase capacity on the old line, now known as the Expo Line.

Service is operated as two lines, with the common section from Waterfront station to Columbia station used by all trains. Two morning peak short-turn trains between Broadway and Waterfront were added in 2007 to help alleviate crowding on the inner portion of the line, where passenger volume exceeds 10,500 passengers/hour/direction.

A two-car Mark II train heading eastbound from Joyce-Collngwood   1343284

A Bombardier Mark II train departs Braid station on the Millennium Line   0572145

Developments

A 1 km extension of the Millennium Line from Commercial Drive station to VCC-Clark station opened in January 2006.

In late 2006, Bombardier won a contract to supply 34 Advanced Rapid Transit (ART) MKII cars for the existing SkyTrain system. The contract was valued at some EUR77 million and includes options for a further 38 vehicles. Approval to exercise the first option for 14 additional vehicles was received in late 2007. Delivery of the vehicles is scheduled for the first late 2008 through to 2009.

Also in late 2006, the SkyTrain system was made fully accesssible with the installation of elevators at the last station without them, Granville Station.

Rolling stock: 210 cars

UTDC (Mark I) (1985/89/94)	150
Bombardier (Mark II) (2002)	60

In peak service: 192
On order: 48 Bombardier Advanced Rapid Transit (ART) MKII cars

Service: 2–5 min during peak, 3–8 min off-peak
First/last trains: Weekdays: 05.00–02.00; Saturday: 06.00–02.00; Sunday and holidays: 07.00–01.00
Integration with other modes: All fares the same for bus, trolleybus, SkyTrain and SeaBus. Free transfer between modes. All stations but one have connecting bus routes
Fare collection: Self-serve ticket vending machines accept cash, credit and debit cards at all stations.
Fare structure: Same as bus, trolleybus and SeaBus
Fare evasion control: Proof of payment, enforced by roving police force. Fine for failure to produce proof of purchase whilst in fare paid zones in stations and on board trains
Signalling: Seltrac system with central computer control; all trains are driverless, with roving staff on trains and at stations
Arrangements for elderly/disabled: All trains equipped to handle wheelchairs. All stations are accessible to people with disabilities
Accommodation for bicycles: Two bicycles per train allowed at all times, with the exception of weekday peak periods in the peak direction of travel

West Coast Express Limited (WCE)

Suite 295, 601 West Cordova Street, Vancouver, British Columbia V6B 1G1, Canada
Tel: (+1 604) 488 89 06, (+1 800) 570 72 45
Fax: (+1 604) 689 38 96
Web: www.westcoastexpress.com

Key personnel
President and Chief Executive Officer:
  Doug Kelsey
  Staff: 13

Type of operation: Commuter rail service using locomotives and bilevel cars on existing railway track opened in 1995. Additional bus services (TrainBus) also provided.

Background
West Coast Express, a subsidiary of South Coast British Colombia Transportation Authority (SCBCTA), provides commuter rail and coach services. The company contracts with Canadian Pacific Railway for train operations and with Gray Line for coach services.

Passenger journeys: (2003) 1.9 million
(2004) 2.0 million
(2005) 2.1 million
(2006) 2.3 million
(2007) 2.5 million
Car-km: (2002) 1.1 million
(2003) 1.1 million
(2004) 1.2 million
(2005) 1.2 million
(2006) 1.2 million

Millennium Line train in cutting at Commercial Drive station, with the elevated Expo Line in the background
0572146

Bombardier's Advanced Rapid Transit (ART) MKII vehicles for the SkyTrain system (Bombardier Transportation)
1327543

Number of lines: 1
Route length: 65 km
Number of stations: 8
Gauge: 1,435 mm

Current situation
The West Coast Express commuter rail service between Mission and Vancouver (65 km) was inaugurated in 1995, using Canadian Pacific Railway tracks. Service consists of five trains each day during the morning and afternoon peak periods, Monday-Friday, in the direction of peak flow only.

In 2003, WCE extended its operating hours with a coach-bus service known as TrainBus, operated by a private contractor. A coach-bus departs from Waterfront station each evening, calling at every WCE station. An additional TrainBus service, launched in September 2003, starts after the last train leaves Mission in the morning. Three additional Monday-Friday TrainBus trips were introduced in September 2007, and five weekend round trips were introduced in January 2008.

Developments
One additional station is proposed for 2010, at Albion.

A sixth locomotive has been procured and delivered, providing the system with a back-up vehicle.

Rolling stock: 6 locomotives and 37 bilevel Bombardier passenger cars

Service: 5 trains westbound in the am peak and 5 eastbound in the pm peak Monday-Friday. Five one-way coach trips Monday-Friday, three round trips on Saturday and two round trips on Sunday.
Integration with other modes: Premium fare system with five zones. West Coast Express tickets and passes good for transfer onto all city

West Coast Express commuter train at Port Haney Station
1175466

buses, SkyTrain and SeaBus. Transfer from other modes given credit for West Coast Express fares. All West Coast Express stations are served by connecting bus routes. Downtown terminal at Waterfront Station is integrated with SkyTrain, SeaBus and bus routes; more than 2,000 Park-and-Ride spaces at six stations.

Fare collection: Self-serve ticket vending machines at all stations

Fare evasion control: Proof of payment, enforced by roving security force. Fine for failure to provide proof of payment

Arrangements for elderly/disabled: All trains equipped to handle wheelchairs

SeaBus
Ferry
Coast Mountain Bus Company
13401 108th Avenue, Surrey, British Columbia V3T 5T4, Canada
Tel: (+1 604) 953 30 00   Fax: (+1 604) 953 31 51
e-mail: info@coastmountainbus.com
Web: www.coastmountainbus.com
    www.translink.bc.ca
    Staff: 80

Type of operation: Catamaran ferry, operating on 3 km cross-harbour route.

Background
The service opened in 1977.
    Ferry services are marketed under the brand name of SeaBus. The service is operated by Coast Mountain Bus Company, a subsidiary of the GVTA.

Passenger journeys: (2003) 4.6 million
(2004) 4.9 million
(2005) 5.0 million
(2006) 5.2 million
(2007) 5.4 million (preliminary figure)

A SeaBus passenger ferry departs from the Lonsdale Quay terminal in North Vancouver bound for Waterfront station in downtown Vancouver   0572144

Vessel-km: (2003) 142,350
(2004) 142,350
(2005) 142,121
(2006) 141,900
(2007) 142,000 (preliminary figure)

Number of routes: 1
Route length: 3 km
Number of stops: 2

Current situation
The SeaBus passenger ferry service operates across Burrard Inlet, connecting downtown Vancouver with North Vancouver.
    Two SeaBus catamaran ferries, each with a capacity of 400 persons, operate every 15 minutes during the daytime Monday–Saturday during the summer months and every 30 minutes

at night and on Sundays, connecting with buses and SkyTrain.

Developments
The GVTA has completed a study of other possible ferry routes connecting the North Shore of Burrard Inlet with downtown Vancouver. One additional route, connecting Waterfront station in Vancouver with Ambleside in West Vancouver is under consideration for pilot service demonstrations in 2008 or later.
    The GVTA has approved the acquisition of a new SeaBus for the North Vancouver to Waterfront Station route in 2009, in time for the 2010 Winter Olympics. Peak services will be increased to every 10 minutes, and evening/Sunday services to every 15 minutes in 2010.

Winnipeg
Population: City 633,451, metropolitan area 694,668 (2006 Census)

Public transport
Bus services provided by municipal undertaking.

City of Winnipeg Transit Department
421 Osborne Street, Winnipeg, Manitoba R3L 2A2, Canada
Tel: (+1 204) 986 57 17   Fax: (+1 204) 986 68 63
e-mail: transit@winnipeg.ca
Web: www.winnipegtransit.ca

Key personnel
Acting Chief Administration Officer: Alex Robinson
Director of Transit: Dave Wardrop
Manager of Operators: Keith D Martin
Manager of Plant and Equipment: Tony Dreolini
Manager of Handi-Transit: Catherine Caldwell
Customer Services:
    Tel: (+1 204) 986 56 94
    e-mail: transit@winnipeg.ca
    Staff: 1,270

Current situation
The public transit service became the responsibility of Winnipeg's Transit Department in 1972, under the newly uniformed City of Winnipeg. The Department provides:
    Regular Transit – scheduled, fixed-route service consisting of cross-town routes, downtown routes (service terminating in the city centre), express routes and feeder routes (suburban area service only).
    Handi-Transit – service for people who are legally blind or unable to use regular services because of a physical disability.
    Handi-Transit is funded by a municipal grant. In June 1997, Handi-Transit services were contracted out to 11 private operating companies. Winnipeg

Transit maintains all administrative functions, including registration, booking and scheduling. In 2005, 584,205 passengers were carried.
    The company also provides Chartered Bus and Special Events Transit services.

Developments
The city council established a Rapid Transit Task Force to recommend a long-term rapid transit plan for the City of Winnipeg. The task force is made up of three city councillors and six representatives from within the community. In January 2005, workshops were held to gather public feedback about the future of rapid transit in Winnipeg, the final plan for which is scheduled to be submitted to the Executive Policy Committee by June 2005.
    In 2007, Winnipeg Transit took possession of 12 New Flyer D40i Invero design low-floor buses as well as 30 D40LF low-floor design buses.

With the arrival of these new buses, Winnipeg Transit's low-floor bus compliment rose to 305 vehicles, allowing accessible bus services on all routes at weekends and most routes during non-peak services on week days.
    The EcoPass programme continues to expand and amongst the participating companies' employees monthly bus pass sales have increased by more than 400 per cent. Transit usage has increased by approximately 45 per cent and there are now 23 participating organisations.
    The Navigo Trip Planner, which was introduced on a trial basis in December 2002, has won the 2004 Canadian Urban Transit Association award for Innovation in Technology and Customer Service. Navigo allows users to obtain travel times, schematic maps, walking distances and walking/transfer directions. Navigo processes over 3,000 trip requests per day.

Winnipeg Transit New Flyer 30 ft low-floor bus (Brian Keller, Winnipeg Transit)   1135737

Work has begun on a Bus Radio System Replacement Project. The company will be replacing the current radio system with several Advanced Transit System technologies, such as new state-of-the-art control-centre computer software and communication tools, as well as several on-vehicle improvements like GPS locating devices, real-time passenger information, and real-time service adjustments. These improvements will increase safety and efficiency while providing better information to drivers, control-room supervisors and passengers.

During 2008, Winnipeg Transit is scheduled to receive 30 New Flyer D40LF low-floor buses with air conditioning. With the arrival of these new buses, Winnipeg Transit's low-floor bus compliment will rise to 335 vehicles.

Winnipeg Transit New Flyer Invero 40 ft low-floor bus (Brian Keller, Winnipeg Transit)   1135739

Bus

Passenger journeys (unlinked): (2002) 52.2 million
(2003) 53.2 million
(2004) 55.6 million
Vehicle-km: (2002) 25.7 million
(2003) 26.0 million
(2004) 26.4 million

Number of routes: 85
Number of stops: 4,900
Route length: (One way) 594 km

Fleet: 535 vehicles (breakdown of vehicle types and numbers not available currently)
Number of vehicles required for peak level service: 452
New vehicles required each year: 30
Average age of fleet: 9.2 years

Most intensive service: 2–6 min
One-person operation: All routes
Fare collection: Cleveland Farebox

Fare structure: Flat; discount 10-journey tickets, monthly pass, Max 5 weekday pass, 7-day Superpass, reduced-fare Superpass, Post Secondary Monthly pass; free Downtown Spirit Shuttle
Fares collected on board: 50 per cent
Fare evasion control: Driver control
Operational control: Mobile radio
Arrangements for elderly/disabled: Handi-Transit provides a parallel transit service, for those with disabilities and limited mobility that prevents them from using regular transit. In 2004, Handi-Transit vehicles, a combination of designated taxis, vans and buses carried 546,000 passengers; 290 low-floor accessible buses, that kneel, have extendable ramps and room for two wheelchairs
Average distance between stops: 200–250 m
Average peak-hour speed: In mixed traffic, 19.4 km/h
Bus priority: 'Diamond Lane' – 5 km of bus lanes reserved in peak hours; transit priority signals – nine signals throughout city; Graham Transit Mall – 1 km bus/pedestrian mall; suburban transit terminals – 8 terminals

Winnipeg Transit New Flyer 40 ft low-floor bus (Brian Keller, Winnipeg Transit)   1135738

Operating costs financed by: Fares 49 per cent, other commercial sources 3 per cent, subsidy/grants 48 per cent
Subsidy from: City of Winnipeg 65 per cent, Province of Manitoba 35 per cent
New vehicles financed by: Provincial government grant; debt financing and transit bus replacement

Chile

Santiago De Chile
Population: 5.5 million (2002 estimate)

Public transport
Bus services provided by ten private operators under government regulation. Minibus ('Liebre') and fixed-route shared taxi services. Government-owned metro.

Transantiago
Nueva York 19, piso 10, Santiago de Chile, Chile
Tel: (+56 2) 428 79 00   Fax: (+56 2) 428 79 26
e-mail: info@transantiago.cl
Web: www.transantiago.cl

Contracted bus
Background
Supervised by the Ministry of Transport and Telecommunications (www.mtt.cl).

Current situation
Transantiago, the governments' public transportation modernisation plan, is currently being implemented. The new system will improve the efficiency of the bus system and integrate the bus and metro networks. It also aims to reduce pollution in the city.

In 2004, some 7,500 privately owned buses operated throughout Santiago. These services were not linked to the metro system. Having started in October 2005, private companies are now being appointed to operate the bus network, and have already introduced some 1,100 new, low-floor, Euro-3 buses, mostly articulated, built by Volvo in Brazil. These are currently operating alongside older vehicles, but the intention is that the latter will gradually be withdrawn and replaced by 2010, by which time ten operators will have been appointed and the total number of

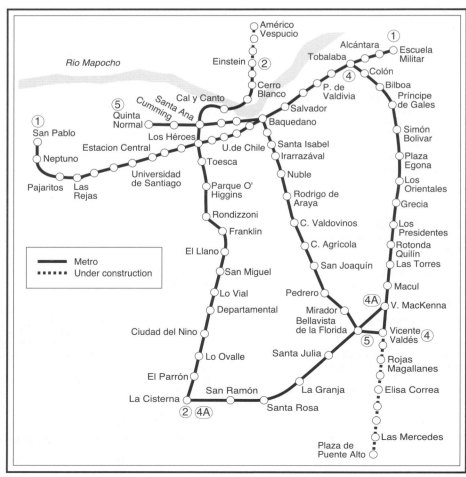

Map of Santiago de Chile metro   1115290

buses will have been reduced to approximately 5,000, some 1,800 of those being new.

There are plans to divide the bus network into two sub-systems – main and local lines. Both will act as feeders to the metro system.

Routing of the newly regulated system will be monitored and co-ordinated by a new Transantiago Management and Information Center.

The bus system will be integrated with the metro system. The Multivia contactless prepaid electronic payment/smartcard, already in use on the metro system, will also be implemented on the bus system in due course. There are also plans for a passenger information system.

Volvo B9SALF articulated buses, which started operating on the Santiago Bus Rapid Transit (BRT) Transantiago system in October 2005 (Volvo Bus Corporation)
1115229

Empresa de Transporte de Pasajeros Metro SA (Metro de Santiago)

Av Libertador Bernardo O'Higgins 1414, Santiago de Chile, Chile
Tel: (+56 2) 250 30 00; 671 31 19
(+56 2) 250 31 90 (Information Department)
Fax: (+56 2) 699 24 75
Web: www.metrosantiago.cl

Key personnel
President: Fernando Bustamante H
General Manager: Rodrigo Azócar H
Operating Manager: Jorge Inostroza S
Staff: 1,344

Type of operation: Full metro, rubber-tyred system, opened 1975

Passenger journeys: (Annual) 328 million (estimate)

Route length: 57.2 km
 in tunnel: 74.2 km
Number of lines: 5
Number of stations: 89
 in tunnel: n/a
Gauge: 1,435 mm
Track: Concrete surface with 40 kg/m guide rail for rubber-tyred operation
Max gradient: 4.8%
Minimum curve radius: 205 m
Tunnel: Cut-and-cover
Electrification: 750 V DC, collected from 2 lateral guide rails

Developments
Various extensions to Lines 1, 2 and 5 have opened in the last two years and in late 2005, the first two sections of Line 4 also opened.

In March 2006, the linking section of Line 4 opened, from Grecia to Vicente Valdés.

Line 4A, from Vicuña MacKenna to La Cisterna, opened in August 2006.

La Cisterna is to become a major transit interchange under the Transantiago programme,

with the construction of dedicated bus lanes and a second interchange at Quinta Normal.

A further extension to Line 2, running northwards from Cerro Blanco to Américo Vespucio, is partly complete, with the remaining 2.4 km section due to open in late 2006.

In February 2007, the Multivia smartcard ticketing is to be introduced across the whole city and its transport operators.

Plans for an extension from Quinta Normal to Maipú have been announced. This would run to the west of the city, some 13.5 km in length with 13 stations.

There is another proposal to extend Line 1 from Escuela Militar eastwards for 4 km with four stations by 2009.

Other proposals for future extensions and a new line would ultimately result in a network with a total length of some 104 km and 108 stations, possibly by 2009.

Rolling stock: Not currently available
Alsthom-Atlantique (1975–80)

M	Not currently available
N	Not currently available
P/R	Not currently available
Concarril NS88 (1990)	Not currently available
GEC Alsthom (1996)	Not currently available
Alstom (1999/2000)	Not currently available
Alstom METROPOLIS	Not currently available

In peak service: Not currently available
On order: Not currently available

Service: Peak 2–3 min, off-peak 4–8 min
First/last train: 06.30/22.30
Fare structure: Differential fares (high, medium and low) on each line according to day and time, non-working days rate medium fare; ticket buys 1 or 2 journeys, or attracts discount, according to time of day; stored-fare pass; through fares to suburban rail and some taxi-route feeders; scholars travel free
Revenue control: Magnetic ticket control at all stations; stored fare tickets (Multivia)
Integration with other modes: Feeder buses on 20 routes run to 5 stations

One-person operation: All trains; full ATC
Signalling: Centralised control system
Operating costs financed by: Fares 90.3 per cent, other commercial sources 9.7 per cent

Empresa de los Ferrocarriles del Estado (EFE) – Chilean State Railways

Ferrocarriles Suburbanos SA (Metrotren)
Avenida Liberatador Bernado O'Higgins 3170, Estación Central, Santiago de Chile, Chile
Tel: (+56 2) 779 07 07   Fax: (+56 2) 776 26 09
e-mail: contacto@efe.cl
Web: www.efe.cl

Key personnel
President: Guillermo Díaz Silva
General Manager: Eduardo Castillo Aguirre
Manager, Infrastructure: Jorge Sepúlveda Haran
Manager, Administration and Finance: Jorge Letelier De la Cruz
Manager, Planning: Dario Farren

Type of operation: Suburban heavy rail

Passenger journeys: (2000) 3.53 million
(2001) 5.33 million
(2002) 5.31 million
(2003) 2.39 million
(2004) 7.58 million

Current situation
Suburban passenger services are operated in the Santiago area by Ferrocarriles Suburbanos SA (Suburban Railways Ltd) and marketed as 'Metrotren'.

There are currently 94 daily services on the route between Santiago de Chile and San Fernando. There are 18 intermediate stations.

For further information on EFE, please see *Jane's World Railways*.

Developments
Metrotren currently operates 13 refurbished Class UT-440 emus.

Valparaiso
Population: City 275,442, region 1.7 million (2007 estimates)

Public transport
Bus and trolleybus services operated by private firms; municipal and privately owned funiculars and elevators; metro, operated by subsidiary of the state railway system.

Trolebuses de Chile SA
Chacabuco No 2998, Valparaiso, Chile
Tel: (+56 32) 21 04 08
e-mail: trolebuses@entelchile.net

Representative office
Avenida Argentina 271, 3° Piso, Valparaiso, Chile
Tel: (+56 32) 249 30 30

Key personnel
President: Pedro Heimpell
Representative: Alexis Bustos Cáceres

Current situation
In 2003, ETCE's Pullman-Standard trolleybuses, which are the oldest trolleybuses still in service anywhere in the world, were declared a National Monument by the Chilean Government.

After the Empresa de Transportes Colectivos Eléctricos (ETCE) suffered financial difficulties,

operation of the two remaining trolleybus routes was taken over by Trolebuses de Chile SA.

Developments
The service has struggled to remain profitable due mainly to considerable competition from 'micro' diesel minibuses.

Trolleybus
Number of routes: 2 (one currently suspended)
Route length: 5 km

Fleet: 73 trolleybuses (of which about 25 serviceable)
Pullman (1952)	6
Pullman (1947/48, rebodied 1987/88)	4

For details of the latest updates to *Jane's Urban Transport Systems* online and to discover the additional information available exclusively to online subscribers please visit
juts.janes.com

Pullman (1947/48, 3 slightly rebuilt 1988/89)	4
Pullman (1947/52, rebodied 1991/92 for Santiago) (most stored)	18
FBW/SWS/MFO articulated (1959/64, ex-Zürich)	6
FBW/R&J/BBC articulated (1974, ex-Zürich)	1
Berna/SWS/SAAS articulated (1965, ex-Geneva) (most stored (13 of 16))	16
FBW/Hess/BBC articulated (1975, ex-Geneva)	2
Berna 2-axle (1966, ex-Schaffhausen)	1
Berna articulated (1966, ex-Schaffhausen)	2
Saurer/Hess/BBC (1970/75, ex-St Gallen, in store)	5
Shenfeng (1991, ex-Santiago) (most stored (6 of 8))	8

In peak service: 15 (approx)

Most intensive service: 3 min
One-person operation: All vehicles
Fare collection: Payment to driver
Fare structure: Flat
Operating costs financed by: Fares 100 per cent

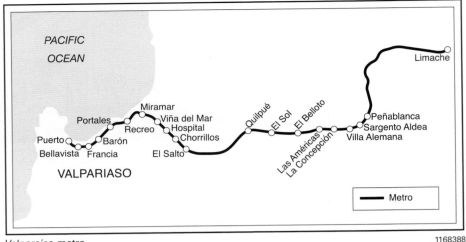

Valparaiso metro   1168388

Ministerio de Transportes y Telecomunicaciones

Edificio Esmeralda, 6° Piso, Valparaiso, Chile
Tel: (+56 32) 59 46 89, 90   Fax: (+56 32) 23 41 88
e-mail: seremitt-05@Mtt.cl
Web: www.mtt.cl

Key personnel
General Manager: Mauricio Candia Llancas
Staff: Not currently available

Private bus

Passenger journeys: Not currently available
Vehicle-km: Not currently available

Current situation
Bus services in Valparaiso and adjacent resort of Viña del Mar, as elsewhere in Chile, are wholly operated by private firms. No details are available for private bus vehicles and passenger volumes in Valparaíso.

Funiculars/Elevators

Current situation
There are 24 ancient funiculars (Ascensors), of which 16 are currently in operation, serving the many hills which ring Valparaíso Bay. Five are municipally owned; the remainder are private, but with fares and service levels regulated by

the city. They carry about 500,000 passengers annually. There are also a number of public lifts, of which three are believed to be working.

Metro Regional de Valparaíso SA (MERVAL) – Valparaiso Regional Metro Ltd

Viana 1685, Viña del Mar, V Región, Chile
Tel: (+56 32) 252 75 00   Fax: (+56 32) 252 75 09
e-mail: merval@merval.cl
Web: www.merval.cl

Key personnel
President: Sergio Solis Mateluna
Director General: Mansa Kausel Contador
Deputy Director General and Head of Operations: José Miguel Obando Neira
Head of Development: Alvaro Valenzuela Alcalde
Head of Administration and Finance: José Morales Vielma
Head of Marketing and Sales: Manuel Aranguiz Alonson
Staff: 160 (estimate)

Type of operation: Suburban railway/metro

Passenger boardings: (2006) 7.95 million
(2007) 11.35 million
(2008) 11.98 million (projected)

Vehicle-km: (2006) 2.67 million
(2007) 2.43 million

Type of operation: Metro, opened November 2005

Route length: 45 km
 in tunnel: 5 km
Number of stations: 20
 in tunnel: 4

Background
MERVAL (Metro Regional de Valparaíso SA) is a subsidiary of Empresa de los Ferrocarriles del Estados (EFE) – Chilean State Railways and was established in 1987 with a remit to create a regional commuter railway based on an existing route.

Current situation
Service is operated by MERVAL between Puerto and Limache (45 km, 20 stations), electrified at 3 kV DC.
  Bus services are also provided as shuttle services to some train stations.

Fleet: 54 cars
Alstom X'Trapolis two-car trains (2005)   27

Service: 6 to 12 mins peak hours, 12 to 18 mins off-peak
First/last train: 06.30/23.00
Fare structure: Zonal (five zones)

China

Beijing

Population: Urban area: 13.33 million, municipality: 15.81 million (2007 estimates)

Public transport

Bus and trolleybus services operated by state-owned enterprise. Metro network with some light rail, being extensively expanded.

Beijing Public Transport Holdings Ltd (BPT)

No 29 Lian Hua Chi Xi Li, Fengtai District, Beijing 100161, China
Tel: (+86 10) 63 96 00 88
Fax: (+86 10) 63 96 20 03
e-mail: bptc@bjbus.com
Web: www.bjbus.com

Key personnel
President: Zheng Shusen
Staff: 104,452

Passenger journeys: (2007) 4,096 million
Vehicle-km: (2007) 1,668 million

Number of routes: 823 (bus and trolleybus)
Route length: Not currently available

Current situation
At the end of 2007, BPT operated 823 routes (621 bus including 15 trolleybus, 18 tourist and 184 long-distance) with a fleet of 25,368 vehicles, providing local and suburban passenger transportation services in the Beijing area and long-distance services to other destinations. Fares are flat for local routes and stage for suburban routes. Since January 2007 some of the monthly passes have ceased.
  BPT consists of 29 subordinate units, including 14 branch companies, share-holding subsidiaries and four affiliated institutions.
  BPT services account for about 84 per cent of all transit mode journeys in Beijing.
  In 2007 BPT carried 4.096 billion passengers, an increase of 20 per cent from 2006.

Developments
BPT continues to pursue a campaign to reduce pollution, and by the end of 2000, nearly 80 per cent of all of its vehicles were powered by CNG and LNG engines. Since April 2007 BPT started to

operate low sulphur diesel (or Europe IV diesel) for Euro IV standard engines on all of its diesel powered fleet.
  In 2006 BPT planned a CNY2.8 billion investment in 3,485 new type buses, including 1,485 new and 2,000 replacements. By 2008 BPT plans to further retire 1,721 old buses and add 1,950 new.
  In June 2006, three Mercedes-Benz Citaro fuel-cell buses were introduced as demonstration models. The project ran until October 2007.

Fleet: 25,368 (2008)
Breakdown of fleet is not currently available

In peak service: Not currently available
On order: Not currently available
Average age of fleet: Not currently available

Service: Not currently available
First/last bus: Not currently available
One person operation: Not currently available
Fare collection: Cash and smartcard.
Fare structure: Smartcard customers receive a discount of 60 per cent for adults and 80 per cent for students.

Bus Rapid Transit (BRT) (Southern Axis BRT Line One)

No 29 Lian Hua Chi Xi Li, Fengtai District, Beijing 100161, China
Tel: (+86 10) 63 96 00 88
Fax: (+86 10) 63 96 20 03
e-mail: bptc@bjbus.com
www.bjbus.com

Beijing BRT Company Ltd
Vice-President: Yan Yabin

Background
The Beijing BRT Company is majority owned by the state-owned Beijing General Bus Company and by other shareholders, some of which are private companies. Revenue from the BRT is collected by the company.

Current situation
The first phase of the BRT corridor, 5.5 km long, opened in late 2004. In early 2006, the corridor was extended to 16 km with 17 stops. In March 2006, ridership was reported at approximately 75,000 per day.

In July 2008 Line 2 (16 km) serving Chaoyangmen-Yangzha and Line 3 (22.95 km) which serves Andingmen-Hongruyuan Xiaoqu, commenced operations. Line 3 also has a 21.85 km diversion route with 22 stations. A fleet of 60 articulated buses operate on the route, with regular buses also operating in the corridor at peak time.

Developments
An additional 40–50 articulated buses have been ordered.

Fleet: 40 buses CBC-Iveco 18 m low-floor articulated buses
Jinhua Neoplan 18 m low-floor articulated buses
On order: An additional 40–50 articulated buses

Beijing Subway Group Limited – Beijing Subway

2 Xi Zhi Men Wai Da Jie, 100044 Beijing, China
Tel: (+86 10) 68 34 56 78
e-mail: dtservice@bjsubway.com
Web: www.bjsubway.com

Key personnel
General Manager, Operations: Xie Zhengguang
Chief Engineer: Yao Jingdi
Staff: 10,000 including 1,600 engineers and technicians

Metro
Type of operation: Full metro, first line opened 1969

Passenger journeys: not currently available

Route length: 200 km
Number of lines: 8
Number of stations: 123
Gauge: 1,435 mm
Track: Concrete slab, 50 kg/m welded rail, elastic fastenings
Max gradient: 3%
Minimum curve radius: 250 m
Tunnel: Cut-and-cover, 4.1 m wide, 4.35 m high
Electrification: 750 V DC, third rail

Current situation
Three new lines were opened in July 2008 ahead of the 2008 Olympic Games. BS now operates 8 lines including Line 1, Line 2, Line 5, Line 8 (Olympic Line), Line 10 (Phase 1), Line 13, Batong Line and Airport Line with 123 stations. The total length is 200 km.

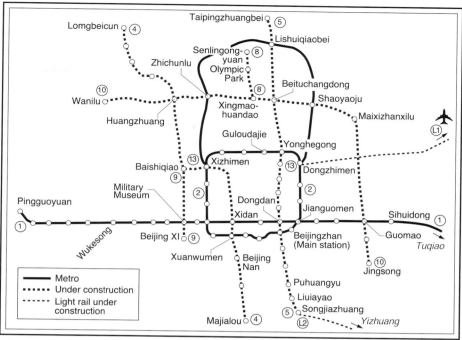
Map of Beijing's metro and light rail network

1115270

- **Line 1:** The line runs east-west, 31 km long with 23 stations. It has interchange stations with Line 2, Line 5 and Line 10.
- **Line 2:** The line runs in a loop service, 23 km with 18 stations. It has interchange stations with Line 1, Line 13, Line 5 and Airport Line.
- **Line 5:** The line runs north-south, 27.6 km with 23 stations. It has interchange stations with Line 1, Line 2, Line 10 and Line 13.
- **Line 13:** Opened in two stages, the western sector in 2002 and the eastern section in 2003 – The line runs 41 km long with 16 stations. It has interchange stations with Line 2, Line 5 and Line 10.
- **Batong Line:** The line is an extension to Line 1. It runs east-west, 19 km with 13 stations.
- **Line 8 (Olympic Line):** The line is part of Line 8 development. It runs north-south, 4.5 km with 4 stations. It has interchange stations with Line 10.
- **Line 10 (Phase 1):** The line has interchange stations with Line 1, Line 5, Line 8, Line 13 and Airport Line.
- **Airport Line:** The line serves as a link between the city centre and Beijing Capital International Airport. 28 km long with 4 stations.

In 2007 BS adjusted its fare structure and introduced a flat fare.

Developments
With three new lines opened in July 2008, by 2015, BS aims to expand its network from its current 10 lines to 19 lines with 561 km of tracks.

In April 2006, ALSTOM, as part of a consortium, was awarded a contract for the supply of the renovation of the Line 2 signalling system and the supply of a Communications-Based Train Control (CBTC) system. The contract was valued at in excess of EUR28 million and the work was scheduled to be completed in mid-2008.

Originally introduced in 2003, since May 2006 the Yikatong contactless smartcard can be used on the whole of the metro system and buses and taxis.

The company will purchase 84 new metro trains and update 60 existing vehicles for Lines 1 and 2 by May 2008.

Singapore Technologies and a local partner will provide an integrated Traffic Command Centre (TTC) for the metro network, to be operational before the start of the Summer Olympic Games.

The contract value is estimated at USD15.9 million.

The following lines are currently under construction or are planned:
- **Line 4:** 29 km long, the majority of which is underground, running north-west-south from Longbeicun to Majialou with 24 stations (23 underground). In December 2004, MTR Corporation signed the Principle Agreement to form a PPP with Beijing Infrastructure Investment Co Ltd (BIIC) and Beijing Capital Group (BCG) for the investment, construction and operation of Line 4. The Joint Venture (JV) Agreement was signed in late 2005 and the business licence for the company was granted in January 2006. Construction commenced in 2004 and the line is due to open in September 2009.
- **Line 9:** This line is planned to be constructed in two phases. The first will run north–south from Baishiqiao to Beijing West Railway Station and is due to open in 2010. There are plans then to extend the line to Beijing World Park. The line will be 18.3 km long with 15 stations.
- **Line L2 (Yizhuang light rail):** This line will serve the southeast area of the city, 19.5 km long with 10 stations.

Service: Peak 3–4 min, off-peak 8 min
First/last train: 05.10/23.40
Line 1: 05.10/23.15
Line 2: 05.09/22.55
Line 5. 04:59/23.10
Line 8: 05.15/23.36
Line 10: 05.05/23.45
Line 13: 05.35/23.45
Airport Line: 06.00/23.10
Batong Line: 06.00/23.15
Fare structure: Flat
Fare collection: Ticket or Yikatong contactless smartcard
Signalling: Automatic block with 3-aspect colourlights and CTC; control-to-driver FM radio on Line 2. Modernisation will permit trains to run at 2 min headways, and Line 1 is being equipped with ATS/ATP/ATO
Arrangements for elderly/disabled: Only part of the system is accessible, but facilities are gradually being introduced

Rolling stock: Not currently available

Changchun

Population: City: 3.58 million, metropolitan area: 7.46 million (2007 estimates)

Public transport

A single municipal company operates bus, minibus and tram services; light rail with extensions under construction and planned.

Changchun Public Transport Group Company Ltd (CCGJG)

49 Dajing Road, Nanguan District, 130041 Changchun City, People's Republic of China
Tel: (+86 431) 580 81 12
Fax: (+86 431) 580 81 12
e-mail: ccptg@tom.com

Key personnel
President and General Manager: Cui Shusen
Vice-General Manager: Zhu Shengli
    Staff: 11,000 (2008)

Passenger journeys: (2008) 40 million
Vehicle-km: Not currently available

Current situation

Established in 2001, Changchun Public Transport Group Company Ltd is a state-owned enterprise providing public transport services in urban and suburban areas of Changhun.

In 2008, the company had a total fleet of 2,713 vehicles and 106 routes (one of which is a tram route), totalling 1,885 km. Annual passenger journeys are approximately 40 million and profit for 2004 is estimated at USD1.6 million.

Fares are paid in cash, on a distance-based tariff.

Number of routes: 106 (bus and tram)
Route length: 1,885 km

Developments

In October 2008 the Ghangchun Government announced an extension project for Tram Line 54, which will see the line extend from Xi'an Road through Qingzhou Road to Yanghua Road. The construction will include 1.393 km track extension and enlargement of one parking facility.

Bus

Fleet: 2,713
Breakdown of fleet is not currently available
In peak service: Not currently available
On order: Not currently available
Average age of fleet: Not currently available
Service: Not currently available
First/last bus: Not currently available
One person operation: Not currently available
Fare collection: Cash
Fare structure: Distance-based tariff

Tramway

Type of operation: One route operated
Passenger journeys: Not currently available
Route length: Not currently available
Number of stations: Not currently available
Number of routes: 1
Number of stops: Not currently available
Gauge: Not currently available
Track: Not currently available
Electrification: Not currently available

Changchun City Rail Transit LLC

1305 Anda Street, Changchun City, 130061 Changchun, China
Tel: (+86 431) 619 68 68   Fax: (+86 431) 619 68 18

Key personnel
President: Wang Chengren
General Manager: Yao Hongwei

Type of operation: Light rail/metro

Passenger journeys: Not currently available

Route length: 14.6 km
    in tunnel: 1 km (approximate)
    elevated: 1 km (approximate)
Number of lines: 1
Number of stations: 17

Current situation

Phase 1 (Line 3) of the light rail/metro network was completed in December 2001 and commenced its trial operation in October 2002. The 14.6 km line has 17 stations. Phase 2 (Line 3 extension) started its trial operation in December 2006. The 17 km line has 16 stations.

Developments

There are further plans for the network. Phase 3, at planning stage, would see a new Line 4, 17 km with 15 stations, to be served by 42 vehicles. Construction on Phase 3 officially commenced in October 2008. Two other new lines are planned, Line 1, running north-south, and Line 2, running east-west. The whole project is scheduled to be completed by 2010, when 52 km of light rail service will be in operation.

First/last train: 06.00/21.00
Most intensive service: 5 minutes
Fare structure: Flat

Chengdu

Population: Urban area: 11.12 million (2008 estimate)

Public transport

Bus services are supplemented by large numbers of private minibuses; metro under construction.

Chengdu Metro Limited Liability Company

Chengdu Metro Building, 158 Suhan Road, Chengdu 610031, China
Tel: (+86 28) 87 56 40 43
Fax: (+86 28) 87 67 91 60
e-mail: cddt@cdmetro.cn
Web: www.cdmetro.cn

Key personnel
General Manager: Wu Yong
Vice General Manager: Xiao Zhongping
Chief Engineer: Yu Bo

Type of operation: Metro (under construction)

Current situation

In 2005, construction started in Line 1 of the Chengdu Metro. When completed, this line will have 23 stations (5 elevated) on a total length of 31.6 km (22.4 in tunnel). The first phase of Line 1 will be 16 km long with 15 stations and is currently scheduled for opening in late 2010.

Planned rolling stock for the initial line is 22 three-car Changchún Car Co trains, with the possibility of increasing train lengths to five-car in the future.

Chengdu Metro Limited Liability Company will operate the network.

Developments

The following lines are currently under construction or are planned:
- **Line 2:** In December 2007 construction was started on Line 2, which will be 50.65 km long (17.45 km underground) with 26 stations

(11 elevated and 15 underground), with an expected completion date of 2012.

There are plans for a further five lines: 3, 4, 5, 6 and 7.
- **Line 3:** The line will be 49.28 km long (15.59 km underground) with 22 stations (11 elevated and 11 underground).
- **Line 4:** The line will be 38.9 km long (20.21 km underground) with 19 stations (8 elevated and 11 underground).
- **Line 5:** The line will be 24.63 km long (17.9 km underground) with 13 stations (2 elevated and 11 underground).
- **Line 6A:** The line will be 2.05 km long (15.5 km underground) with 13 stations (2 elevated and 11 underground).
- **Line 6B:** The line will be 15.11 km long (5.52 km underground) with 8 stations (4 elevated and 4 underground).
- **Line 7:** The line will be 41.93 km long (29.63 km underground) with 22 stations (5 elevated and 17 underground).

Chongqing

Population: 28.08 million (includes urban population of 13.11 million and rural area of 14.97 million (2007 estimates)

Public transport

Local and interurban bus services; monorail; Bus Rapid Transit (BRT) planned.

Three types of bus service are provided within the city including: public trolleybus (five lines), new type bus (more than 90 lines) and mini bus (27 lines). The fare structure is flat. Other main transport modes within the city include: city cable car, elevator and river cableway to accommodate the geographical condition.

Chongqing Urban Mass Transit Corporation

Tel: (+86 23) 68 00 22 22
e-mail: cqmetro@cta.cq.cn
Web: www.cqmetro.cn

Key personnel
Staff: 1,900

Type of operation: Monorail, opened 2005

Passenger journeys: Not currently available

No of lines: 1
Route length: 19.2 km
No of stations: 18

Background

The Chongqing Urban Mass Transit Corporation was established in 1992 to oversee the building of the monorail line, which started in 2000.

Current situation
The first stage of the line (Line 2) was opened in 2005, with a further stage opening in 2006.

Developments
There are plans for a further three lines to form a network, comprising light rail, monorail and metro, with a total length of some 130 km, although construction is unlikely to commence before 2010.

Rolling stock: 21 four-car trainsets
CNR Type QKZ2 monorail car   84
Service: 8–9 min peak, 12 min off-peak
First/last train: 07.00/22.00
Fare structure: Zonal

CNR Type QKZ2 monorail car
for Chongqing (CNR)
1135825

Dalian

Population: 6.08 million, urban area 3.368 million, municipal area 2.414 million (2008 estimates)

Public transport
Bus, trolleybus and tram/light rail services overseen by municipal authority, with services provided by state-owned, joint-venture and co-operative enterprises; limited local rail service; paratransit operations.

Dalian Municipal Communications & Port Administrative Bureau
Road Transportation Administrative Office of Dalian
401 Zhongshan Road, Shahekou District, People's Republic of China
Tel: (+86 411) 84 30 58 23
e-mail: jt_bgs@dl.gov.cn
Web: www.jt.dl.gov.cn
Staff: 13,826

Key personnel
President: Yao Zainlin

Current situation
Public transport is provided by four state-owned enterprises (Dalian Mordern Track Transportation Co Ltd (tram/trolleybus/LRT), Dalian No1 Bus Co, Dalian No 2 Bus Co and Dalian Bus Joint Co), two joint ventures (Tongheng Co and Tongli Co) and two co-operative enterprises (Guanzhong Co and Ganghao Co).

There are 109 lines in total, a light rail transport line, three tram lines, one trolleybus line, 72 standard bus lines and 28 minibus lines.

Bus
Passenger journeys: Not currently available

Number of routes: 104
Route length: Not currently available

Fleet: 3,700 (estimate)

Fare collection: Payment to seated conductor, monthly passes available for all modes, electronic card
Fare structure: Flat

Integration with other modes: Convenient interchange between modes at nodal points. Monthly passes

Dalian Modern Track Transportation Co Ltd
No 7 Liberation Square, Shahekou District, Dalian 116012, People's Republic of China
Tel: (+86 411) 84 64 07 78
Fax: (+86 411) 84 59 06 03

Key personnel
President: Sui Yuejia
Staff: 4,256

Light rail
Type of operation: Light rail, first line opened 2003

Passenger journeys: 50,000 daily (estimate)

Route length: 49.15 km
Number of stations: 11 (mostly elevated)

Rolling stock: Four-car vehicles, total fleet and breakdown not currently available

Current situation
The light rail line was built to link the original urban area with a new development zone, or 'new city', which includes a Technology Development Zone, the port and the resort area of Golden Pebble Beach. The total construction cost for the project is estimated as USD232 million.

Developments
An extension, connecting the Dalian development area with Jinzhou, is under construction. It will be some 14 km long with nine stations.

CNR Model DL6WA light rail vehicle for Dalian LRT (China Northern Locomotive and Rolling Stock Industry (Group) Corporation (CNR))
1135829

Trolleybus

Passenger journeys: (1996) 85,000 daily

Number of routes: 101
Route length: 14.5 km
Number of stops: 22

Fleet: 125 trolleybuses, Dalian DL661/DLD72C and Shenyang SY561
First/last car: 04.05-23-25/04-25-23-50
Fare collection: Payment to seated conductor, monthly passes, JC card
Fare structure: Flat
Most intensive service: Every few minutes
Integration with other modes: Convenient interchange between modes at nodal points. Monthly passes

Tramway

Type of operation: Conventional tramway, first line opened 1907

Passenger journeys: Over 600,000 daily

Route length: 14.7 km
Number of routes: 3

Trolleybus, tram and minibus in central Dalian   0009930

Number of stops: 29
Gauge: 1,435 mm
Track: Railway type on side reservation and in centre of street
Electrification: Overhead

Service: 1 min
First/last car: (201)04.10.23:45/(202)05:30-21:50/(203) 04:30-00:05

Fare collection: Payment to seated conductor, monthly passes; JC card
Fare structure: Flat
Integration with other modes: Convenient interchange between modes at nodal points. Monthly passes available for all modes

Rolling stock: About 100 motored cars including up to 21 articulated, all built locally

---

Guangzhou

Population: City 7.4 million (2004), metropolitan area 12.5 million (estimate)

Public transport

Bus, trolleybus and ferry services provided by state/municipal enterprises with separate bus companies (two of which are now part-privately owned), a trolleybus company, a ferry company, minibus and taxi companies; metro (extending). Light rail link to Zhuhai under construction.

Communications Commission of Guangzhou Municipality

No1 Fuqian Road, Guangzhou, PC 510032, People's Republic of China
Tel: (+86 20) 83 12 59 10, 83 12 58 10
Web: http://english.gz.gov.cn, www.gz.gov.cn

Key personnel

Head of Municipal Communications Commission: Xiang Weixiong
Staff: Not currently available

Current situation

The Bureau is responsible for planning and management of Guangzhou's public transport, both urban and inter-urban.

Subsidiaries include the Guangzhou City No 1, No 2 and No 3 Bus Companies, the Guangzhou City Trolleybus Company, passenger ship company, Guangzhou Taxi Company, Baiyun Taxi and Minibus Company and the Bureau oversees the state's involvement in joint venture bus operations.

Manufacturing subsidiaries assemble and overhaul buses. Fleet numbers are issued in blocks to the various public and private bus companies, each has an appropriate prefix so that No 2 Bus Co is prefixed 1-, Trolleybus Company D (*dien che* – electric car), and similar.

There are also a number of privately operated bus services.

The total fleet number is not currently available (but estimated at 7,500 in early 2007). All vehicles are Chinese-built, either by State or joint venture companies.

Developments

No 1 and No 2 Bus Company are now both part-privately owned: No 1 Bus Company, now known as Guangzhou No 1 Bus Shareholding Company (with a fleet of an estimated 1,700 vehicles), is owned 50 per cent by Guangzhou Hangjia Wieye Development Co Ltd. Guangzhou No 2 Bus Company is now 60.63 per cent owned by

New World First Bus Services (China) Limited and is now operated as a joint venture, formed in December 2006, known as Guangzhou New World Bus Services Limited. The joint venture period for the latter is 30 years.

In 2006, the Commission announced that the city is implementing an Intelligent Transport System, which includes a computerised dispatch system for buses. Some 1,591 buses and trolleybuses on 89 routes have had the necessary equipment installed and the project is due to be completed by the end of 2007. Public information display boards are also being installed, with some 1,600 due to be in operation by the end of 2007.

The city is also promoting the use of LPG in buses and taxis, and there are plans to add 20 bus terminals and 305 bus stops in the period 2006–2010.

There is a World Bank-assisted Guangzhou City Center Transport Project under way, which includes the development of a bus lane network, the institutional reform of public transport and construction of a maintenance depot.

In early 2007, some 86 per cent of the bus fleet (an estimated 6,430 vehicles) was using LPG.

Guangzhou Metro Corporation

16/F CTS Center, 219 Zhongshan Wu Road, Guangzhou 510030, China
Tel: (+86 20) 83 10 66 66   Fax: (+86 20) 83 10 66 11
e-mail: zhangchunhai@gzmtr.com
Web: www.gzmtr.com

Key personnel

President and General Manager: Lu Guanglin
Vice-Presidents:
  He Lin
  Chen Shaozhang
  Liang Qiaoming
  Ding Jianlong
Project Manager: Jin Feng
Deputy Chief Engineer: Ning Zi Rong
Public Relations Department: Jane Li
Manager, Enterprise Division: Zhang Chunhai
Staff: 6,312

Passenger journeys: (2003) 116 million
(2004) 164 million
Train-km: (2003) 17.6 million

Route length: 96.67 km
  in tunnel: 93.12 km
Number of lines: 4
Number of stations: 62
  at grade: 2

Background

The Guangzhou Metro Corporation was incorporated in 1992 to oversee construction of Line 1 of the city's metro, which began in early 1994 after a complicated bidding process. A German consortium headed by Siemens and Adtranz (now Bombardier) provided the rolling stock, power supply equipment and other items, while Balfour Beatty Power Construction of the UK provided the catenary.

Current situation

Currently, four lines are in operation with a number of extensions and new lines under construction.

Developments

In December 2005, the following openings took place: Line 2 – Pazhou-Wanshengwei; first section of Line 3 – Kecun-Guangzhou Dongzhan; Line 4 Phase 1 – Wanshengwei-Xinzao.

In December 2006, the Line 3 extensions from Kecun to Panyu Square and Tianhe Keyunzhan to Tiyu Xilu opened and Line 4 was extended from Xinzao to Huangge.

Future projects are as follows:
- Line 2 – north extension: Construction started mid-2006, scheduled for opening in 2009;
- Line 2 – south extension: Construction started mid-2005, scheduled for opening in 2009;
- Line 3 – north extension: Construction started mid-2006, scheduled for opening in 2009;
- Line 4 – Phase 2: first section opened in December 2006, further sections due for opening in 2007 and 2010;
- Line 5: Construction started in 2004, scheduled for opening in 2007 and 2008;
- Line 6: Construction started mid-2005, scheduled for opening in 2008 and 2010;
- Guangfo Line: Construction started in 2002, scheduled for opening in 2010;
- Guangzhu Line: Construction started in 2005, scheduled for opening in 2008.

In May 2003, Siemens Transportation Systems announced that it is to supply, in co-operation with Chinese railcar manufacturer Zhuzhou Electric Locomotive Works (ZELW), 40 three-car units for the new Line 3. The first trainsets were delivered in 2005, with deliveries being completed by mid-2007.

In December 2003, Bombardier Transportation officially handed over the first six-car *Movia*™ metro trainset for Line 2. This delivery is part of a 26 six-car (156 cars) order.

The Guangzhou municipal government has approved an additional seven trains (total 42 cars) for Line 1 and the installation of the 'shield door' system at stations. The door installation started in December 2004 and the project is due to be completed in 2008. The vehicles will be manufactured by Bombardier/Changchun Car Company and are due to be delivered by late 2006.

The corporation is also overseeing the construction of the Guanfo metro line. This new line will connect with Line 3 at Lijiao station.

By 2010, Guangzhou Track Traffic Construction Plan proposes a total of nine lines, 255 km in length and with 105 stations.

In 2004, the headway on both lines was reduced substantially.

Also in 2004, the operational business of the corporation obtained ISO 9001:2000 certification.

In October 2004, Bombardier Transportation received an order, through its joint venture, Changchun Bombardier Railway Vehicles Co Ltd, for the supply of 48 *Movia*™ metro cars (eight six-car trainsets) for use on Lines 1 and 2. Delivery was due to commence in early 2005 and last until late 2006. In January 2005, the company also received an order for 200 bogies and 400 bogie kits from a Chinese/Japanese consortium for Lines 4 and 5. Deliveries began in December 2005 and and are due to last until the end of 2010.

Service: Peak: Line 1: 4½ min, Line 2: 4 min 35 sec
Fare structure: Zonal
Fare collection: Tickets at stations, stored-value, 'Yang Cheng Tong Transportation Card' contactless smartcard
Integration with other modes: Smartcard can also be used on buses, ferries and taxis

Bombardier Transportation Movia™ *train (Bombardier Transportation)* 1115112

Fleet: Line 1: 21 six-car trains; Line 2: 26 six-car trains. See also below
Vehicles on order: Line 3: 40 three-car Siemens trainsets, delivery commenced in 2005 and be completed by mid-2007; eight six-car Bombardier trainsets for Lines 1 and 2 – delivery 2006

Guangzhou Passenger Ship Company

Binjiang West Road, Haizhuang Matou, Haizhu District, Guangzhou, China
Tel: (+86 20) 84 41 35 27

Key personnel
Contact: Guohui He

Current situation
The company is mainly responsible for ferry services across the Pearl River, but also serves tourist needs.

Fleet: Not currently available

Hangzhou
Population: Metropolitan area 6.4 million (includes urban population of 3.9 million (estimate) (2003)

Public transport
Bus and trolleybus services provided by municipal agency; metro system planned, with construction scheduled to start in 2006.

Hangzhou Public Transport Group Co Ltd (HZPTC)
1 ChaoHui Road, Hangzhou 310004, Zhejiang Province, People's Republic of China
Tel: (+86 571) 85 19 38 63
Fax: (+86 571) 85 19 46 96
e-mail: hzjinling@gmail.com
Web: www.hzbus.com.cn

Key personnel
General Manager: Jiang Tianron
Chief Engineer: Jin Ling

Current situation
A citywide bus network is operated using two-axle buses, articulated buses and double-deckers, all made in China, supplemented by trolleybus routes. In the city, 3,847 vehicles operate on 345 urban routes.

Developments
A 3G (GPS, GPRS, GIS) + ADSL fleet management control has been installed, involving 2,500 buses and 208 trolleybuses on 130 routes.

Bus
Staff: 9,000 (2004)

Vehicle-km: (2001) 126.2 million
(2002) 204.7 million
(2004) 215.6 million

Number of routes: 336 (2004)
Route length: 4,438 km (2004)

Fleet: 3,639 vehicles, including 112 articulated, 120 double-deck, 689 minibuses and 1,920 air-conditioned vehicles

Fare collection: Cash to onboard machines; contactless smartcard ticketing (monthly passes)

Air-conditioned bus, Hangzhou 1175473

City bus, Hangzhou 1175474

Trolleybus
Staff: 800 (2004)

Vehicle-km: (2001) 15.4 million
(2002) 10.5 million
(2004) 12.5 million

Number of routes: 9 (2004)
Route length: 102.9 km (2004)

Fleet: 208 trolleybuses, including 102 articulated,
106 two-axle and 31 air-conditioned vehicles

Fare collection: Cash to onboard machines;
contactless smartcard ticketing (monthly passes)

Articulated trolleybus in Hangzhou
1175476

Harbin

Population: Metropolitan area 3.3 million, region
9.5 million (2005 estimates)

Public transport
Bus, minibus and trolleybus services; metro
planned.

Harbin Municipal People's Government
Subway Construction Office
412 Xidazhi Street, Nangang District, Harbin
150800, China
Tel: (+86 451) 87 51 58 11
Fax: (+86 451) 87 51 58 11

e-mail: hrbgdb@vip.sina.com
Web: www.harbin.gov.cn

Key personnel
Contact: Liu Peitao

Type of operation: Metro (planned)

Current situation
The first phase of Line 1 of a metro network
has been planned, with a length of 14.4 km and
16 stations. The line will run from Harbin East
Railway station to the Second Affiliated Hospital
of Harbin Medical University in west of the city.
The cost of this phase is estimated at USD643
million.

Developments
The State Council has approved the current
plan. Construction of the first phase of Line 1
is scheduled to commence shortly and be
completed in 2008, with the service starting in
2009.
Future plans include:
- The second phase of Line 1, from the Second
  Affiliated Hospital of Harbin Medical University
  to Harbin South Railway Station (3.07 km);
- The first phase of ring line Line 3 from Hexing
  Road Station to Turbine Factory (7.1 km);
- A second phase of Line 3 (20.95 km with 17
  stations).

Hong Kong

Hong Kong Special Administrative Region of The People's Republic of China
Population: 6.99 million (2208 estimate)

Public transport
Over 11 million passenger journeys are made
daily on Hong Kong's multimodal public transport
system. Franchised bus services accounted for
3.94 million daily passenger journeys in 2007,
with rail services carrying 4.21 million. Minibuses,
taxis, ferries and paratransit services accounted
for the remaining percentage.

The Transport Bureau of the HKSAR
government controls policy, with advice from a
Transport Advisory Committee. All operations
except railways and tramways are under the
direct supervision of the Transport Department.
In 1999, the government published the Final
Report of the *Third Comprehensive Transport
Study*. This maintained the previous policies of
expanding transport infrastructure, expanding and
improving public transport and managing road
use. More specifically, stress is now placed on
better integrating transport and land use planning,
making better use of railways as the backbone of
the public transport system, enhancing public
transport services and facilities, exploiting
the use of advanced technologies in transport
management and upgrading environmental
protection.

The Mass Transit Railway (MTR) and Kowloon-
Canton Railway systems have been merged
since 2 December 2007. The integrated system
is operated and managed by the semi-privatised
MTR Corporation Limited. The MTR Corporation
Limited operates a coordinated railway network
in the urban areas, New Territories and Lantau
Island as well as an express connection to Hong
Kong International Airport. It also provides light
rail services in the Northwest New Territories

and feeder buses to the light rail system.
Private sector companies operate electric
trams and a funicular railway on Hong Kong
Island.

In pursuit of expanding the railway system,
the government published its second *Railway
Development Strategy* in 2000. This involves the
completion of six new passenger railway projects,
subject to traffic growth and project interfaces. The
six new passenger railways are:

- Kowloon Southern Link (KSL) – an extension of
  West Rail from its Nam Cheong Station to the
  East Rail East Tsim Sha Tsui Station. The works
  for the KSL have commenced
- Shatin to Central Link (SCL) – a new rail corridor
  from Tai Wai to Central which comprises the East
  Kowloon Line, Tai Wai to Diamond Hill Link and
  the Fourth Rail Harbour Crossing
- West Island Line (WIL) – an extension of the
  MTR from Sheung Wan to Kennedy Town

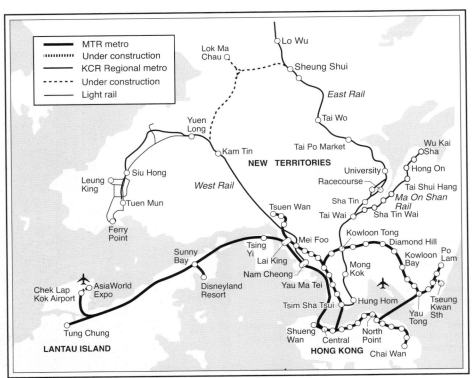

Map of Hong Kong's metro and rail
1290988

- South Island Line (SIL) – an extension of the MTR to Southern District
- North Hong Kong Island Line (NIL) – an additional rail corridor along the new north shore of Hong Kong Island between the MTR Hong Kong Station and Fortress Hill Station
- Northern Link/ Hong Kong Section of the Guangzhou-Shenzhen-Hong Kong Express Rail Link (NOL/ERL) – the NOL will connect the West Rail Kam Sheung Road Station to the Lok Ma Chau boundary crossing, the ERL runs from a new terminus at West Kowloon to the boundary at Lok Ma Chau for connection with the Mainland section of the ERL.

The railway system is the largest passenger carrying mode. Five operators have been granted franchises to operate bus services in the territory.

Most major operators have now adopted the 'Octopus' smartcard system. Octopus facilitated the application of composite fares (interchange discounts) for connecting routes and the development of 'bus-to-bus' interchanges during 2000 while, from early 2001 and late 2003 onwards, the former MTR Corporation and Kowloon-Canton Railway Corporation began to experiment with train-to-bus and train-to-minibus composite fares respectively.

Government-licensed 16-seat 'Public Light Buses' and taxis provide supplementary public transport services, while 'Residents' Services' are licensed to serve specific housing developments.

In measures to improve air quality, the government requires all newly registered vehicles to meet Euro 4 emission standards, with effect from October 2006. Since February 2001, all franchised bus operators have converted to using ultra-low-sulphur diesel fuel in their vehicles. New taxis have to be LPG-fuelled since 2001.

Commissioner for Transport
Transport Department
41st Floor Immigration Tower, 7 Gloucester Road, Wan Chai, Hong Kong SAR
Tel: (+852) 28 04 26 00
Fax: (+852) 28 24 04 33
e-mail: tdenq@td.gov.hk
Web: www.td.gov.hk

Key personnel
Commissioner: Alan Wong Chi-kong
Deputy Commissioner, Transport Services and Management: Ms Carolina Yip Lai-ching
Deputy Commissioner, Planning and Technical Services: Lau Ka-keung
Assistant Commissioner for Transport, Administration and Licensing: Miss Ying Lui
Assistant Commissioner for Transport, Bus and Railway: Albert Yuen Lap-pun
Assistant Commissioner for Transport, Management and Paratransit: Don Ho Yue-man
Assistant Commissioner for Transport, Urban: Anthony Loo Khim-chung
Assistant Commissioner for Transport, New Territories: Miss Cindy Law
Assistant Commissioner, Planning: To Kam-biu
Assistant Commissioner for Transport, Technical Services: Tsang King-man

Current situation
The Transport Department of Hong Kong is organised as follows:
Commissioner for Transport;
Two Deputy Commissioners, responsible for:
Transport Services and Management – responsible for the following branches: Administration and Licensing; Bus and Railway and Management and Paratransit, as well as joint management of the Urban Regional Office and the New Territories Regional Office with the Deputy Commissioner for:
Planning and Technical Services – responsible for the Planning and Technical Services branches.

The Transport Advisory Committee advises on transport policy, and the Transport Tribunal reviews the decisions of the Commissioner.

Developments
The 3.3 km Disneyland Resort Line operates as a single-track railway providing a shuttle service between Disneyland Resort Station and Sunny Bay Station, where passengers can interchange with the existing Tung Chung Line. The rail line opened in August 2005 prior to the opening of the Hong Kong Disneyland theme park in September 2005.

The Kowloon Motor Bus Co (1933) Ltd (KMB)
9 Po Lun Street, Lai Chi Kok, Kowloon, Hong Kong, China
Tel: (+852) 27 86 88 88   Fax: (+852) 27 45 03 00
Web: www.kmb.hk

Key personnel
Chairman: Sir S Y Chung
Managing Director: Edmond T M Ho
Executive Director: Ms Winnie Ng
Operations Director: Tim Ip
Commercial Director: James C Louey
Finance and Administration Director: William S K Ho
Corporate Affairs Director: Ms Winnie W Y Ho
Company Secretary: Ms Lana Woo
Staff: 12,000 (2007)

Background
A wholly owned subsidiary of Transport International Holdings Limited.

Current situation
Operations are in Kowloon and the New Territories. In addition, services are operated through the three cross-harbour tunnels to Hong Kong Island.

KMB is Hong Kong's largest public transport operator, having been first granted a franchise in 1933. In January 2006, this franchise was extended to July 2017.

Population increase, particularly in the New Towns of the New Territories, continues, and further routes are introduced to meet demand. Air-conditioned double-deckers have gained general acceptance, and further air conditioned routes are being introduced to meet demand for higher quality services.

Smartcard (Octopus) is now in use on all vehicles.

All new KMB buses are super-low-floor and are equipped with Euro-3 engines. Also, all KMB buses are powered by ultra-low-sulphur diesel, and the programme to equip earlier buses with catalytic converters has been completed.

Developments
KMB installed the first 'Cyber Bus Stop' in Hong Kong. A built-in computer with touchscreens allows passengers access to the company's website to obtain bus routes and other information.

In 2006, 2 Euro 4 prototype vehicles were under evaluation (one Volvo B9TL and one Trident Enviro 500)

During 2006, 39 Trident Enviro 500 and 12 Volvo B9TL Enviro 500 buses were licenced for service, bringing the total to 271 Trident Enviro 500 and 13 BT9L Enviro 500 vehicles as at the end of 2006.

KMB 'super intelligent' bus, which has a fully integrated network system for improved monitoring and maintenance   1147015

Wrightbus 12 m double-deck bus, on Volvo B9TL chassis, for KMB   1180209

In 2006, 57 Wright buses were licensed for service, making a total of 164 as at the end of 2006.

In 2006, KMB placed orders with Volvo for 38 B9TL 12 m double-deck buses with Wright bodies, 85 B9TL 12 m double-deck buses with Enviro 500 bodies with delivery scheduled for 2006–7 and two Scania Caetano Euro 4 prototype buses, to be delivered in 2006–7.

In 2006, KMB introduced the first Euro 4 double-deck buses in Asia.

In 2007, 53 Volvo B9TL Enviro 500 buses were licensed for service, bringing the total number of these vehicles to 66 as at the end of that year.

Also in 2007, the third Euro 4 double-deck bus in the KMB fleet, a Scania Caetano prototype bus, was licensed.

Passenger boardings: (2003) 1,061 million
(2004) 1,064 million
(2005) 1,010 million
(2006) 1,008 million
(2007) 1,008 million
Vehicle-km: (2003) 383 million
(2004) 379 million
(2005) 374 million
(2006) 371 million
(2007) 365 million

No of routes: Approx 400

Fleet: 4,047 vehicles, of which 3,806 are air conditioned (as at the end of 2007)
Double-deck
Volvo Olympian 3-axle — 30
Leyland Olympian 3-axle — 69
Dennis Dragon 3-axle — 142
Volvo Olympian 3-axle air conditioned — 878
Dennis Dragon 3-axle air conditioned — 760
Dennis Trident 3-axle air conditioned — 541
Leyland Olympian 3-axle air conditioned — 149
Scania 3-axle air conditioned — 22
Neoplan Centroliner 3-axle air conditioned — 161
Volvo Super Olympian 3-axle air conditioned — 592
MAN 3-axle air conditioned — 47
Dennis Trident Enviro 500 3-axle
air conditioned — 271
Volvo Wrightbus 3-axle air conditioned — 100
NeoMAN 3-axle air conditioned — 1
Volvo B9TL Enviro 500 3-axle air conditioned — 66
Volvo B9TL Wrightbus 3-axle air conditioned — 64
Volvo B9TL Volgren 3-axle air conditioned — 1
Dennis Trident Enviro 500 (Euro 4) 3-axle
air conditioned — 1
Scania Caetano (euro 4) 3-axle air-conditioned — 1
Single-deck
Dennis Dart air conditioned — 57
Dennis Lance air conditioned — 15
Mitsubishi air conditioned — 79
On order: Scania Caetano (Euro 4)

One-person operation: All services
Fare collection: Payment to farebox on board or smartcard (Octopus)
Fare structure: Sectional and flat
Fares collected on board: 100 per cent
Fare evasion control: Bus captains and inspectors
Operational control: Terminus supervisors, inspectors/mobile radio
Arrangements for the elderly/disabled: Reserved seats, more handholds, coloured and textured stanchions, half-fare for over 65s; flat fare of HKD2.00 or half of the standard adult fare if this comes to less than HKD2.00 on Sundays & public holidays for the elderly; free rides for the Elderly on 'Senior Citizens' Day', and free rides for disabled persons on the 'International Day of the Disabled Persons'. More low-floor buses for mobility handicapped.
Average speed: 21 km/h (approximate)
Bus priority: On the congested Lion Rock Tunnel Road, Tuen Mun Road, Tate's Cairn Highway, Nathan Road and other smaller scale measures in conjunction with Transport Department
Integration with other modes: Smartcard (Octopus) valid with other major operators; bus routes to MTR stations; intermodal Octopus bus-bus and bus-rail interchange schemes with MTR, New World First Bus and Citybus

KMB Euro 4 three-axle double-deck bus 1330382

Operating costs financed by: Fares 99 per cent; other commercial sources 1 per cent
New vehicles financed by: Shareholders' funds and loans from banks

Sun Bus Limited

Sun Bus Holdings Limited (SBH)
9 Po Lun Street, Lai Chi Kok, Kowloon, Hong Kong
Tel: (+852) 23 71 23 45
Fax: (+852) 27 44 54 62
Web: www.kmb.hk

Key personnel
General Manager: Benjamin Wong

Passenger journeys: Not currently available
Vehicle-km: Not currently available

Background
A wholly owned subsidiary of Transport International Holdings Limited.

Current situation
The SBH Group is one of the leading operators in Hong Kong's non-franchised bus industry. It has 13 business units which provide bus services to specific markets, including large residential estates and shopping malls, major employers, theme parks, hotels, local travel agents and schools, as well as the general public through chartered hire services.

Developments
The SBH Group has continued to expand to meet market demand for non-franchised services. Its fleet grew to 356 buses by the end of 2007.

The SBH Group intends to take delivery of not less than 30 new buses for fleet upgrade in 2008.

Fleet: 356 buses (2007)
Breakdown of fleet is not currently available
In peak service: Not currently available
On order: Not currently available

Long Win Bus Co Ltd (LWBC)

9 Po Lun Street, Lai Chi Kok, Kowloon, Hong Kong, China
Tel: (+852) 27 86 60 35
Fax: (+852) 27 45 67 79
Web: www.kmb.hk

Key personnel
Chairman: Sir S Y Chung
Managing Director: Edmond Ho Tat Man
General Manager: Kenrick Fok
Staff: 443

Background
A wholly owned subsidiary of Transport International Holdings Limited, which is listed on the Hong Kong Stock Exchange.

Current situation
This subsidiary of Transport International Holdings Limited holds a franchise to operate 18 routes serving the international airport at Chek Lap Kok, Tung Chung New Town and the Hong Kong Disneyland Resort and services to the major New Towns in the New Territories. LWBC started operations with a fleet of brand new low-floor double-decks. Environmental protection includes Euro-2 or above engines in all new buses and water purification measures at depots to prevent contaminated waste entering the drainage system.

Developments
In June 2003, the company commenced a new 10-year franchise for its airport and North Lantau bus networks.

Passenger boardings (2003) 19.3 million
(2004) 22.3 million
(2005) 24.3 million
(2006) 26.5 million
(2007) 27.7 million
Vehicle-km: (2003) 22.7 million
(2004) 23.5 million
(2005) 23.8 million
(2006) 24.5 million
(2007) 24.9 million

Number of routes: 18

Fleet: 155 buses
Dennis Trident low-floor — 136
Dennis Trident Enviro 500 — 16
Dennis Lance — 3
In peak service: Not currently available
Average age of fleet: Not currently available

One-person operation: All services
Fare collection: Sectional and flat
Fares collected on board: 100 per cent
Fare evasion control: Bus captains and service co-ordinators
Operational control: Control centre, service co-ordinators/mobile radio
Arrangements for elderly/disabled: All double-deck buses fully accessible to wheelchairs; reserved seats, more handholds, coloured and textured stanchions; half-fare for over-65s; 152 buses have had Bus Stop Announcement Systems installed
Average speed: 32.7 km/h
Bus priority: None
Integration with other modes: Smartcard (Octopus) valid with other major operators; Octopus joint bus-bus interchange schemes with New Lantao Bus and Citybus Limited; Octopus bus-bus interchange

schemes between Airbus routes, shuttle routes and recreational routes
Operating costs financed by: Fares 100 per cent
New vehicles financed by: Loans from banks and Export Credit Guarantee

New World First Bus Services Limited (NWFB)
8 Chong Fu Road, Chai Wan, Hong Kong
Tel: (+852) 21 36 21 40
Fax: (+852) 21 47 36 11
e-mail: bus_ideas@nwfb.com.hk
Web: www.nwfb.com.hk

Key personnel
Managing Director: Samuel Cheng
Head of Operations and Planning: William Chung
Head of Operations and Engineering: Paul Li

Passenger boardings: (2006/07187.3 million (estimate) 184.35 million
Vehicle-km: Not currently available

Number of routes: 94

Background
In 2002, the Government renewed the franchise of the Company until 2013.

In March 2004, NWFB became a member company of Merryhill Group Limited, a comprehensive transport services provider jointly formed by Chow Tai Fook Enterprises Limited and NWS Holdings Limited. In December 2004, Merryhill Group Limited was renamed as NWS Transport Services Limited. The renaming aimed to establish the corporate image of the Group's transport businesses following its restructuring, as well as reflecting its business perspectives.

Current situation
New World First Bus (NWFB) is jointly owned by Chow Tai Fook Enterprises Limited and NWS Holdings Limited (NWS Holdings, Stock code: 0659.HK). NWS Holdings, the infrastructure and service entity of the New World Development Company (Stock code: 0017.HK), embraces a diversified range of businesses in Hong Kong, Mainland China and Macau.

New World First Bus Limited (NWFB) currently operates 94 routes throughout Hong Kong Island and the New Territories. Its fleet of vehicles is fully air-conditioned.

Developments
The company commissioned a new environmentally friendly depot – Chong Fu Road Depot – which opened in 2002.

In 2007, NWFB invested HKD65 million to acquire 18 new UK Dennis Trident Euro 4 double deck buses.

Fleet: 695 (as at June 2007)
Fleet breakdown is not currently available
Average age of fleet: 8.8 years (as at June 2007)

New Lantao Bus Co (1973) Ltd (NLB)
Head office
3/F, 8 Chong Fu Road, Chai Wan, Hong Kong
Tel: (+852) 25 78 11 78, 28 07 13 83
Fax: (+852) 28 11 00 62, 27 94 91 43
e-mail: info@newlantaobus.com
Web: www.newlantaobus.com

Field office
G/F, Unit D, Silver centre, Silvermine Bay, Lantau, Hing Kong
Tel: (+852) 29 84 83 61
Fax: (+852) 29 84 88 12; 27 94 91 43

Key personnel
Executive Director: Peter Mok

Background
A 99.99 per cent owned subsidiary of Kwoon Chung Motors Co Ltd (KCM), which is a wholly

Dennis Trident Euro 4 double deck bus
1367180

owned subsidiary of Kwoon Chung Bus Holdings Limited (KCBH). KCBH is listed on the Hong Kong Stock Exchange (Stock Code: 0306) and has operations in Hong Kong and more than 10 major cities in mainland China, including Shanghai, Chongqing and Guangzhou.

Current situation
New Lantao Bus was formed in 1973 by an amalgamation of smaller companies. It operates 22 routes on Lantao Island. Its previous franchise expired on 21 March 2007, and has been renewed for nine years and 11 months as from 1 April 2007. Daily ridership is estimated at approximately 39,000.

Number of routes: 22 (as at March 2007)

Passenger boardings: (FY2007) 14.2 million
Vehicle-km: (FY2007) 4.9 million

Fleet: 101 buses (all single-deck) (as at 30 September 2007)

Kwoon Chung Bus Holdings Limited (Kwoon Chung)
Unit 1205 Eastern Harbour Centre, 28 Hoi Chak Street, Quarry Bay, Hong Kong
Tel: (+852) 25 78 11 78
Fax: (+852) 25 63 23 32; 25 61 17 78
e-mail: contact@kcm.com.hk
Web: www.kcm.com.hk

Key personnel
Chairman: Thomas Wong Chung-pak
Executive Director: Peter Mok
Managing Director: Matthew Wong Leung-pak

Background
Incorporated in Bermuda with limited liability, and listed on the Hong Kong Stock Exchange (1996).

Current situation
Through its subsidiaries, namely Kwoon Chung Motors Co Ltd, Tai Fung Coach Co Ltd, Good Fund Services Ltd and Trade Travel (Hong Kong) Ltd, Kwoon Chung is the largest non-franchised public bus company in Hong Kong, in terms of fleet size. This was 581 buses as at 31 March 2002.

Kwoon Chung also has operations in 10 cities in China, the largest being in Shanghai: Shanghai Pudong Kwoon Chung Co with 711 buses, Shanghai Wu Qi Kwoon Chung Co (No 5 Bus) with 1,023 buses and 81 taxis. The combined fleet size in China was 3,413 with 15,825 employees (as at 31 March 2002).

In Hong Kong, the company has maintained its position as the leading school-bus provider and has a strong position in resident and employee services.

The network was extended during 1998 to the new Hong Kong International Airport at Chek Lap Kok, where Kwoon Chung is also the holding company of the New Lantao Bus Co (1973) Ltd, the franchised bus operator in Lantau.

The acquisition of Tai Fung Coach Co Ltd and Trade Travel (Hong Kong) Ltd (operating as Holiday Rental) in April 1997, has enabled the company to become the biggest provider, in terms of fleet size, of tour buses and coaches to hotels and tour operators in Hong Kong.

Coaches are also provided under contract by Tai Fung Coach Co Ltd to the Mass Transit Railway for use on Airport Express shuttle bus services.

Citybus Limited
Corporate Communications Department
8 Ching Fu Road, Chai Wan, Hong Kong SAR, China
Tel: (+852) 29 63 48 88
Fax: (+852) 28 57 61 79
e-mail: webmaster@citybus.com.hk
Web: www.citybus.com.hk

Key personnel
Managing Director: Samuel Cheng
Head of Operations and Planning: William Chung
Head of Operations and Engineering: Paul Li
  Staff: 2,800 (estimate)

Current situation
Citybus is jointly owned by Chow Tai Fook Enterprises Limited and NWS Holdings Limited ('NWS Holdings', Stock code: 0659.HK). NWS Holdings, the infrastructure and service flagship of New World Development Company Limited (Stock code: 0017.HK), embraces a diversified range of businesses in Hong Kong, Mainland China and Macau.

The company provides franchised bus service on Hong Kong Island and for Hong Kong International Airport and Tung Chung new town with a fleet of air-conditioned buses.

Citybus also runs contract and private hire services. It provides staff shuttle bus services for organisations such as Hong Kong Television Broadcasts Limited, as well as a variety of single-deck, double-deck and open top buses for private hire.

Developments
In pursuit of improving the bus fleet's maintenance standard and operational efficiency,

Citybus has invested over HKD300 million in the commissioning of a 'smart' and environmentally friendly depot, on a site area of 10,000 m² in Chai Wan. With cutting-edge technologies and innovative environmentally friendly initiatives, the central engineering workshop handles major units overhaul, such as engines, gearboxes and air-conditioning systems, as well as different maintenance procedures, for the bus fleet. Citybus has developed the Environmental Management Plan and Environmental Management Systems, which conform to international standards, specifically for the construction and operation of the depot. In addition, Environmental Management and Audit requirements have been identified for monitoring environmental impacts on the surroundings adjacent to the depot.

Environmentally-friendly initiatives include:

- Construction of 3 m high sound barriers on the roof to minimise the noise generated from the depot's operation
- Double-skinned underground fuel tanks are installed with lead detection to reduce risk of land contamination caused by leakage
- Landscaping for visual and air quality enhancements
- Use of Pozilock refuelling system to avoid spillage of diesel during bus fuelling
- Use of recycled water in computerised drive-through bus cleaning machines to reduce resource requirements
- Use of lighting and air-conditioning systems with pre-set timers to reduce energy consumption
- Powerful mechanical ventilation system is available to improve air quality
- Each bus bay at the depot is equipped with an exhaust extraction pipe that is directly connected to the exhaust pipe of a bus for filtering and displacing exhaust air before emitting outside the depot, in order to reduce the emission of exhaust air as well as being environmentally friendly
- Segregation and storage of all chemicals under the Dangerous Goods Ordinance in classifying dangerous goods
- Use of environmentally friendly goods, such as refrigerants used in chiller plants, where possible
- Installation of state-of-the-art equipment, such as collection of waste oil to centralised tanks by pipe-work, to improve waste management

In 2007, Citybus invested HKD35 million to acquire 10 new Dennis Trident Euro 4 3-axle double-deck buses, which started serving Citybus Shenzhen West Express Routes B3 and B3X in December 2007.

Bus

Passenger boardings: (2006) 624,000 daily average
(2007) 586,000 daily average
Vehicle-km: Not currently available

Number of routes: 110 (Hong Kong Island 92, Airport and North Lantau Island 18) (June 2007)

Fleet: 914 buses (Hong Kong Island services 743, Airport and North Lantau Island 171 plus private hire vehicles) (June 2007)

A comprehensive breakdown is not currently available, but the fleet includes:
Single-deck

Dennis Dart/Carlyle 9.8 m (ex- New World First Bus) (2003)	10
Volvo B6LE/ Jit Luen low-floor 10.6 m	28
MAN NL262/R 11.8 m	75
Jiangsu Flxible Corporation 11.7 m[1]	32
King Long 11.4 m[2]	18
Volvo/Van Hool Alizee B10M-60 coach (1990, 1992)	6

Double-deck

AEC/Park Royal Routemaster R2RH open-top 8.4 m[3]	2
Leyland/ECW Olympian 11.2 m (1987)	1
Leyland/Roe Olympian 9.7 m	3
Leyland/Alexander Olympian 11.2 m 3-axle (refurbished 2001)	41
Leyland/Alexander Olympian 10.5 m 3-axle[4]	34
Volvo/Alexander Olympian 10.5 m 3-axle[4]	10

Dennis Trident Euro 4 3-axle double-deck bus – Citybus's new 'Green Bus' 1343554

Leyland/Alexander Olympian 12 m 3-axle[5]	16
Volvo/Alexander Olympian 12 m 3-axle	2
Volvo/Alexander Olympian 12 m 3-axle	70
Leyland/Alexander Olympian 12 m 3-axle[6]	55
Volvo/Alexander Olympian 12 m 3-axle[6]	31
Volvo/Alexander Olympian 12 m 3-axle	58
Volvo/Plaxton Olympian 12 m 3-axle	20
Volvo/Alexander Olympian 12 m 3-axle (1996)[7]	6
Volvo/Alexander Olympian 12 m 3-axle (1996)	90
Volvo/Plaxton Olympian 12 m 3-axle	35
Dennis/Duple Metsec Dragon 10.4 m 3-axle (1994)[8]	39
Dennis/Duple Metsec Dragon 12 m 3-axle (1994/95/96)[9]	80
Volvo/Alexander Olympian 11.3 m 3-axle (1995, 1997/98)	140
Volvo/Alexander Olympian 11.3 m 3-axle (2001)	2
Dennis/Duple Metsec Trident 12 m 3-axle	51
Dennis/Alexander Trident 12 m 3-axle	11
Dennis/Alexander Trident 12 m 3-axle	1
Dennis/Duple Metsec Trident 12 m 3-axle	1
Dennis/Duple Metsec Trident 12 m 3-axle	60
Dennis/Duple Metsec Trident 12 m 3-axle	40
MAN/Volgren 12 m 3-axle	1
Dennis/Duple Metsec Trident 10.7 m 3-axle	1
Scania/Volgren 12 m 3-axle Euro-3	1
Dennis/Alexander Trident 12 m 3-axle (ex-New World First Bus) (2003)	9
Dennis Trident Euro 4 3-axle double-deck	10

Average age of fleet:
Hong Kong Island services: 10.6 years, Airport and North Lantau Island services: 8.8 years (June 2007)

Most intensive service: 3 min
One-person operation: 100 per cent
Fare collection: Farebox on board, mobile fareboxes on selected routes in peak hours to allow boarding through centre doors. Smartcard equipment is fitted to all buses.
Fare structure: Stage/flat fare
Operational control: Inspectors with patrol cars and mobile radio. Route regulators.
Arrangements for elderly/disabled: 50 per cent concession fare for elderly. All new buses are low-floor, and most have space for a wheelchair. All buses have most DiPTAC features.

[1] In use on Beijing routes
[2] In use on Tianjin routes
[3] One of which is currently in storage.
[4] Currently being refurbished.
[5] To be refurbished.
[6] Refurbishment completed in 2000.
[7] Refurbishment completed in 2002.
[8] Refurbishment started in 2002.
[9] Refurbishment started in 2001.

Hongkong Tramways Limited

Whitty Street Tram Depot, Connaught Road West, Western District, Hong Kong, China
Tel: (+852) 21 18 63 38   Fax: (+852) 21 18 60 38
e-mail: enquiry@hktramways.com
Web: www.hktramways.com

Key personnel
General Manager: Johnny T H Leung
Operations Manager: David C K Wong
Senior Engineering Manager: Steven S Y Chan
Personnel and Administration Manager: Jeremy W M Yam
Permanent Way Maintenance Engineer: Kelvin K K Koo
Staff: 700 (estimate)

Background
A wholly owned subsidiary of Wharf (Holdings) Ltd.

Type of operation: Street tramway, opened 1904

Passenger boardings: (2002) 87.1 million
(2003) 81.7 million
(2004) 84.9 million
(2005) 84.2 million
(2006) 83.9 million
Car-km: (2002) 6.1 million
(2003) 6.0 million
(2004) 6.1 million
(2005) 6.3 million
(2006) 6.0 million

Route length: 30 km
Number of routes: 6
Number of depots: 2 (Whitty Street and Sai Wan Ho)
Number of stops: 123
Gauge: 1,067 mm
Track: Ri60 grooved 60.6 kg/m rail directly fixed to concrete slab embedded in road surface (some special work Ri59)
Electrification: 500 V DC, overhead
Current collection: Trolley pole

Current situation
The service area covered is between Shau Kei Wan, Happy Valley and Kennedy Town.

The tram fleet has been upgraded by a rewiring programme and the replacement of the standard controllers by Siemens Programmable Logic Controllers. At the end of 2000, two new trams were constructed with aluminium-alloy bodies and chopper control.

Also in 2000, Hongkong Tramways introduced the three alloy aluminium metal body trams which were designed and manufactured by its engineering team. The trams were upgraded with different facilities and equipment in order to ensure safety and improve comfort. The changes included a replacement of rotary controllers with electronic speed controllers or a DC chopper control system, incorporating 'Deadman's handles', and rewiring with Low Smoke & Fume (LSF) cabling and fitted with traction grade convertors.

During 2001, all trams (except two antique trams and one heritage tram) had rotary controllers replaced by electronic speed controllers.

Developments
It is envisaged that all of the standard trams will be replaced by trams of the new design, albeit with recycled trucks from the present fleet.

Rolling stock: 163 double-deck cars, including two antique tramcars, built by local contractors and Hongkong Tramway's workshop

Two-axle standard cars (1986 design, built 1987–91)	M160
Two-axle heritage car (replica 1949 design, built 1991)	M1
Two-axle open-balcony car for tours/hires (1953/55, modified)	M1
Two-axle aluminium-bodied prototypes (2000 design)	M2

In peak service: 155

Service: Peak 1.5 min, 2–6 min off-peak
First/last car: 05.07/00.40
Fare structure: Flat fare, pay on exit; by cash or Octopus card; monthly tickets; tourist tickets (joint with 'Star' Ferry Co) and seniors' concessionary fare
Average distance between stops: 250 m
Operating costs financed by: Fares 84 per cent. Other commercial sources 16 per cent
One-person operation: 100 per cent

MTR Corporation Limited (MTR)
MTR Headquarters Building, Telford Plaza, PO Box 9916, Kowloon Bay, Hong Kong, China
Tel: (+852) 29 93 21 11   Fax: (+852) 27 98 88 22
Web: www.mtr.com.hk

Key personnel
Chairman: Raymond K F Ch'ien
Chief Executive Officer: C K Chow
Operations Director: Andrew McCusker
Project Director: Russell Black
China and International Business Director: Francis Lung
Finance Director: Lincoln Leong
Property Director: Thomas Ho
Human Resources Director: William Chan
Legal Director and Secretary: Leonard Turk
   Staff: Approximately 12,400 (as at 31 December 2007)

Type of operation: Full metro, light rail and intercity railway, first line opened 1979

Passenger journeys: (2003) 777 million
(2004) 842 million
(2005) 866 million
(2006) 876 million
(2007) 945 million
Car-km: (2003) 128 million
(2004) 130 million
(2005) 132 million
(2006) 136 million
(2007) 149 million

Route length: 211.6 km
   in tunnel: 77.2 km
   elevated or at gradient: 134.1 km
Number of lines: 11
Number of stations: 150
Gauge: 1,432 mm on KTL/TWL/ISL/TKL/TCL/DRL/AEL
   1,435 mm on ERL/MOL/WRL/LRL
Track: BS 90A 45 kg/m is used on KTL and TWL; UIC60 60 kg/m is used on ISL/TKL/TCL/DRL/MOL/WRL/AEL and ERL (East Tsim Sha Tsui to Hung Hom; Sheung Shui to Lok Ma Chau); UIC54 54 kg/m is used on ERL (Hung Hom to Lo Wu) and LRL Ri60 is used on LRL

Maximum gradient: 6.5% (LRL)
Minimum curve radius: 300 m
Tunnel: Bored single-track, bored double-track and cut-and-cover and drill and blast
Electrification: 1.5 kV DC, overhead for KTL/TWL/ISL/TKL/TCL/DRL; 25 kV AC, overhead for ERL/WRL/MOL; 720 V DC for LRL

Background
Previously known as The Mass Transit Railway Corporation, established in 1975 to build and operate Hong Kong's metro system.

In June 2000, it was reconstituted as the MTR Corporation Limited and partially privatised on a public share offering on 5 October 2000, which left the government owning 76.68 per cent of the company's shares (as at 31st December 2006). The company has an exclusive franchise for 50 years (which may be extended) from 30 June 2000.

Current situation
MTR operates nine main commuter lines – Kwun Tong Line (KTL), Tsuen Wan Line (TWL), Island Line (ISL), Tseung Kwan O Line (TKL), Tung

MTR fleet   1180327

MTR Alexander Dennis Enviro 500 tri-axle bus   1303283

MTR ktt intercity train   1303284

Chung Line (TCL), Disneyland Resort Line (DRL), East Rail Line (ERL), Ma On Shan Line (MOL) and West Rail Line (WRL) and a Light Rail Line (LRL) in the New Territories. MTR also operates the Airport Express Line (AEL) linking the Hong Kong International Airport and the central business district areas, and intercity services to Beijing, Shanghai and major cities of Guangdong Province in the Mainland of China. MTR also provides feeder bus services to and from many MTR stations in the New Territories.

Developments
The Corporation merged with the government-owned rail operator, the Kowloon-Canton Railway Corporation, on 2 December 2007 to operate the merged rail network in Hong Kong.

Rolling stock:
KTL/TWL/ISL/TKL/TCL/DRL: 994 cars
AEL: 88 cars
EAL: 444 cars
WRL: 154 cars
MOL: 64 cars
LRL: 119 cars
Intercity Train: 2 electric locos + 12 cars
Full breakdown is not currently available, but includes:

Metro-Cammell (1979/81)	M210
Metro-Cammell (1981/84)	M238 T124
Metro-Cammell (1984)	M20
Metro-Cammell (1986)	T28
Comeng Phase I LRV (1987)	n/a
Metro-Cammell K01 (1987)	n/a
Metro-Cammell (1989)	M40 T11
Metro-Cammell K03/K05 (1991)	n/a
Kawasaki Phase II LRV (1992)	n/a
GEC Alsthom (1994/95)	M66 T22
United Group Phase III LRV (1997)	n/a
GEC Alsthom (1997/98)	T3
Adtranz/CAF Airport Express (1997)	M66 T22
Adtranz/CAF Lantau (1997)	M72 T24
Itochu/Kinki Sharyo/Kawasaki (IKK) SP1900 (2000/01)	n/a
Mitsubishi-Rotem Consortium (2002)	M78 T26
Itochu/Kinki Sharyo/Kawasaki (IKK) SP1950 (2003)	n/a
Itochu/Kinki Sharyo/Kawasaki (IKK) SP1900 emu (T1-T22) (2003)	n/a
Mitsubishi-Rotem Consortium (2006)	M24 T8
Itochu/ABB Consortium intercity train	n/a

In peak service: KTL/TWL/ISL/TKL/TCL/DRL/AEL: 952 cars
EAL: 384 cars
WRL: 126 cars
MOL: 52 cars
LRL: 117 cars

Service: Peak 2 min, off-peak 4–12 min
First/last train: 06.00/01.00
Fare structure: Distance-based, with single and Octopus smartcard stored-value tickets
Integration with other modes: Octopus ticket is also valid for travel on Citybus, New World buses and ferries, the 'Star' Ferry, KMB bus routes, green minibus routes and some red minibus routes
Revenue control: AFC at all stations
Operating costs financed by: Fares 67 per cent, other commercial sources 33 per cent
One-person operation: All trains except DRL trains
Automatic control: All lines except in depots
Surveillance: CCTV on platforms and concourses
Platform screen doors: Full-height platform screen doors are installed at all underground stations with air conditioning. Half-height platform edge gates are installed at Sunny Bay Station and Disneyland Resort Station and are built above ground with natural ventilation

Airport Express
Type of operation: Dedicated express rail link to Hong Kong International Airport, commenced 6 July 1998

Route length: 35.2 km
  in tunnel: 7.6 km
  elevated: 9.4 km
  ground level: 18.2 km

MTR Itochu/Kinki Sharyo/Kawasaki (IKK) SP1900 train   1303285

MTR Metro-Cammell emu   1303286

MTR Comeng LRV   1303287

Number of lines: 1
Number of stations: 5
Integration with other modes: In conjunction with its Airport Express service, the MTR operates a fleet of shuttle buses under contract, connecting major hotels with its Hong Kong and Kowloon stations. These are operated free of charge but are strictly for Airport Express passengers only.

Disneyland Resort Line
Current situation
The 3.4 km Disneyland Resort Line, connecting to the Disney theme park, is the newest extension that started operation in August 2005. This two-station line, operated with three four-car trains, is the first extension in the MTR system to employ fully automatic train operations technology.

Kowloon-Canton Railway Corporation (KCRC)

KCRC House, 9 Lok King Street, Fo Tan, Sha Tin, New Territories, Hong Kong, China
Tel: (+852) 26 88 13 33   Fax: (+852) 26 88 09 83
Web: www.kcrc.com

Key personnel

Chairman: Michael Tien
Directors
   Chief Executive Officer: James Blake
   Senior Director, Transport: Y T Li
   Senior Director, Capital Projects: K K Lee
   Director, Finance: Lawrence Li
   Director, Property: Daniel Lam
   Director, Human Resources: Mimi Cunningham
   Staff: 6.080 (September 2006) – Transport: 4,539;
Capital Projects: 746; Property: 132; Corporate and other services: 663

Current situation

KCRC is wholly owned by the Hong Kong Special Administrative Region Government. It operates three rail systems. The first is the 35 km East Rail, a suburban mass transit railway with 14 stations, which links Kowloon with Shenzhen in mainland China and branches off to Ma On Shan at Tai Wai. This line began as a single-track system in 1910 and was completely electrified and upgraded to double-track in 1983.

The second is the 30.5 km West Rail, a new railway line which opened in December 2003, and which provides service between the North West New Territories (NWNT) and urban areas of Kowloon.

The third railway, which operates in the North West New Territories, is the Light Rail system, linking the towns of Yuen Long, Tuen Mun and Tin Shui Wai. This system also provides a feeder service for West Rail.

Additionally, KCRC runs feeder buses, freight and intercity passenger services to major cities in mainland China.

Other services provided by KCRC include property development and related commercial activities.

Developments

To meet future transport requirements, KCRC is constructing and planning new railway lines that will more than double its existing network. These are: the Lok Ma Chau Spur Line and the Kowloon Southern Link. Three other projects are at planning stage: the Northern Link, the Express Rail Link and the Sha Tin to Central Link.

The Ma On Shan Rail and the Tsim Sha Tsui Extension were completed in 2004, whilst the Lok Ma Chau Spur Line was completed in 2007.

On 2 December 2007, MTR Corporation Limited (MTR) merged with the Kowloon-Canton Railway Corporation to operate the merged rail network in Hong Kong.

East Rail

Type of operation: Regional metro line/suburban mass transit railway, opened 1910. East Rail serves 14 stations along a 35.1 km route and Ma On Shan Rail serves eight stations along a 11.5 route

Passenger journeys: (2001) 292 million
(2002) 296 million
(2003) 278 million
(2004) 292 million
(2005) 325 million
Passenger-km: (2001) 4,487 million
(2002) 4,540 million
(2003) 4,183 million
(2004) 4,385 million
(2005) 4,731 million

Route length: 35.1 km (East Rail), 11.5 km (Ma On Shan Rail)
Number of lines: 2
Number of stations: 22
Gauge: 1,435 mm
Track: 54 kg/m rail on concrete sleepers
Max gradient: 1%
Minimum curve radius: 270 m
Electrification: 25 kV 50 Hz, overhead

Signalling and telecommunications

East Rail operates an integrated computer-based signalling and telecommunications system, designed to comply with the Automatic Train Protection (ATP) and Automatic Train Operation (ATO) systems. It comprises a Train Control System (TCS), a Centralised Solid State Interlocking System (CSSI), a Power Control System (PCS) and an Integrated Control and Communications System (ICCS).

Operated on screen-based workstations, the TCS provides a complete range of train control, regulation and monitoring functions. The signalling system is centralised at the East Rail Control Centre, which provides manual and automatic route settings and allows bidirectional working on both the up and down lines. The PCS system controls and monitors the 25 kV AC power supply to the trains and the ICCS allows effective station control and voice communications between operation parties by employing Synchronous Digital Hierarchy (SDH) and Fibre Optics Transmission Network.

Developments

An extension of 7.4 km, Lok Ma Chau Spur Line running from Sheung Shui to a new station at Lok Ma Chau, will provide rail crossing to mainland China to alleviate congestion at the Lo Wu boundary crossing. At Lok Ma Chau there would be a pedestrian connection with the planned Shenzen metro. The target opening date for this extension is 2007.

Rolling stock: 444 emu cars (East Rail), 72 emu cars (Ma On Shan Rail), 12 diesel locomotives (for freight operations and maintenance)

Service: Peak 2.7–3 min; off-peak 5–6 min
First/last train: 05.28/01.08
Fare structure: Zonal/Monthly pass as a temporary promotional activity
Revenue collection: Automatic machines and entrance/exit barriers
Integration with other modes: MTR, KCR feeder buses, other buses and minibuses
Operation financed by: Fares

West Rail

Type of operation: Heavy rail/mass transit railway, first phase opened December 2003. West Rail serves nine stations along the 30.5 km route

Passenger journeys: (2004) 48 million
(2005) 65 million
Passenger-km: (2004) 661 million
(2005) 897 million

Route length: 30.5 km
Number of lines: 1
Number of stations: 9
   elevated: 13.4 km
   in tunnel: 11.5 km

Current situation

West Rail is a 30.5 km twin-track passenger railway with nine stations, linking Sham Shui Po in West Kowloon, via Kwai Tsing and Tsuen Wan with Yuen Long and Tuen Mun in the North West New Territories.

Signalling and telecommunications

West Rail has one of the most advanced signalling systems in the world. The SELTRAC system, using tested and proven technology, will manage the location and destination of each train on the West Rail system. The route will be automatically set according to the train schedule so that trains can be operated with minimal human intervention. The system will maintain frequent and regular data communication with the trains, making it possible to schedule train service as frequently as one train per direction every 105 seconds. The Operations Control Centre, having a wide array of equipment, is housed inside the West Rail Building. A giant display screen feeds duty officers with real-time operational data, such as train locations, status of traction power system and tunnel ventilation system.

Rolling stock: 154 Itochu-Kinki-Kawasaki (IKK) emu cars, currently in seven-car trains
Itochu-Kinki-Kawasaki (IKK) emu cars (2002/03)   154
In peak service: 22 seven-car trains

Service: Peak 3.5 min; off-peak 5–8 min
First/last train: 05.45/12.45
Fare structure: Zonal
Revenue collection: Automatic machines and entrance/exit barriers
Integration with other modes: MTR, LR, KCR buses, cross-boundary direct buses, other buses, minibuses and taxis
Operation financed by: Fares

Light Rail

Key personnel
Director: Jonathan Yu

Type of operation: Light rail; first line opened 1988

Passenger journeys: (2001) 117 million
(2002) 114 million
(2003) 106 million
(2004) 132 million
(2005) 136 million
Passenger-km: (2001) 501 million
(2002) 503 million
(2003) 498 million
(2004) 458 million
(2005) 442 million

Route length: 36.2 km
   reserved track: 28 km
Number of routes: 11
Number of stops: 68
Gauge: 1,435 mm
Track: UIC54 kg/m flat bottom on concrete sleepers and some grooved rail; 3 km paved track in concrete
Max gradient: 6.1%
Minimum curve radius: 20 m
Electrification: 750 V DC, overhead

Background

The Light Rail system was established in 1998 to provide local passenger transport within the North West New Territories (NWNT).

Current situation

The Light Rail system provides service to approximately one million residents in the rapidly growing new towns in the NWNT. The system operates largely at grade with some 80 junctions that integrate with other road traffic.

In 2003, Light Rail changed from being a stand-alone provider of light rail services in the NWNT to also provide a feeder service for West Rail.

Light rail had a 51.3 per cent share of the internal public transport market in the NWNT in 2005.

Developments

KCRC is spending more than HKD2.3 billion to improve and expand the light rail system. These projects include the construction of two new extensions in Tin Shui Wai; upgrading or modification of four light rail stops to provide an interchange service for West Rail; the installation of a new signalling system for the two new extensions; grade separation of several busy light rail/road junctions. The last project in the improvement scheme, the Tsing Lun Road Footbridge, was completed in July 2005.

KCRC has also restructured its light rail services to tie in with the opening of West Rail, so that residents of the NWNT can make the best use of the improved public transport infrastructure.

Rolling stock: 119 cars
Comeng (1987/88)   M69
Kawasaki (1992/93)   M20 T10
Goninan (1997/98)   M20
In peak service: 111

Service: Peak 5–9 min, off-peak 7–13 min
First/last car: 05.11/01.00
Fare structure: Five zones for single-ride tickets; number of stops travelled for Octopus card holders
Revenue control: Ticket vending machines on all platforms, inspectors, spot penalty

Integration with other modes: WR, KCR buses, other buses, minibuses, taxis and ferries

Other lines

Lok Ma Chau Spur Line

The government of the Hong Kong Special Administrative Region endorsed the corporation's construction of the Lok Ma Chau Spur Line in June 2002. Construction started in January 2003, and the project is scheduled for completion in 2007.

The Lok Ma Chau Spur Line will be the second railway link between Hong Kong and mainland China, relieving congestion at Lo Wu station. The 7.4 km alignment will run from East Rail's Sheung Shui station to Lok Ma Chau station.

Kowloon Southern Link (KSL)

The Kowloon Southern Link (KSL), 3.8 km in length, will extend West Rail from Nam Cheong station at Sham Shui Po to East Rail's Tsim Sha Tsui East station. By joining East Rail with West Rail, it will provide passengers with a direct point of transfer between the two, forming a unified network.

In September 2002, the government of Hong Kong SAR invited the KCRC to proceed with the detailed planning and design of the KSL Project. The scheme was initially gazetted on 26 March 2004, whilst the proposed amendments to minimise disruption to the public during the construction and operation of the KSL were gazetted on 7 January 2005. Construction work commenced in October 2005 and the expected completion date is 2009. Upon completion of the KSL, it will take only 30 minutes to travel from Tsin Shui Wai to Tsim Sha Tsui East.

The Northern Link

The Northern Link will join East Rail and West Rail at the northern section. It will provide a railway corridor between the northeast and northwest districts of the New Territories, as well as linking West Rail to Lok Ma Chau for cross-boundary passengers.

Sha Tin to Central Link

The corporation won the bid to plan, build and operate the Sha Tin to Central Link in 2002. In view of the possible merger of KCRC and the MTR Corporation, the final design and implementation of the Link are subject to the decision of the government.

KCRC Bus

Passenger journeys: (2001) 21 million
(2002) 26 million
(2003) 26 million
(2004) 20 million
(2005) 27 million
Vehicle-km: (2001) 6.2 million
(2002) 6.78 million
(2003) 7.7 million
(2004) 6.95 million
(2005) 5.92 million

Fleet: 143 buses

Current situation

KCRC's integrated fare system allows East Rail, West Rail and Light Rail Octopus passengers the use of a free feeder bus service that connects housing estates to East Rail stations, West Rail stations and Light Rail stops. Passengers who do not use the rail network at the end of the bus journey are required to pay fares.

The corporation operates a total of 15 routes, as at the end of 2005, including West Rail and Light Rail feeder bus services, residential routes and express routes, but excluding feeder routes which are operated under a KMB franchise.

The fleet operates service for 19 hours each day.

The 'Star' Ferry Company Limited

16F Ocean Centre, Harbour City, Canton Road, Kowloon, Hong Kong
Tel: (+852) 21 18 62 23   Fax: (+852) 21 18 60 28
e-mail: sf@starferry.com.hk
Web: www.starferry.com.hk

Star Ferry Company's MV Shining Star *at TST Pier*   1143612

Key personnel

General Manager: Johnny T H Leung
Staff: 336

Passenger journeys: (2002) 28.7 million
(2003) 27.3 million
(2004) 29.5 million
(2005) 28.8 million
(2006) 28.9 million

Current situation

Operates two franchised cross-harbour passenger routes from Tsim Sha Tsui to Central and to Wanchai, and three licensed services from Central to Hung Hom, from Wanchai to Hung Hom and a harbour tour service within Victoria Harbour, with a fleet of 12 vessels.

New World First Ferry Services Limited (NWFF)

New World First Ferry Services (Macau) Limited (NWFFM)
71 Hing Wah Street West, Lai Chi Kok, Kowloon, Hong Kong
Tel: (+825) 21 31 81 81   Fax: (+852) 21 31 88 77
Web: www.nwff.com.hk

Key personnel

Director and General Manager: John C Y Hui

Passenger journeys: Approximately 18 million per year

Number of routes: 5 (in Hong Kong waters) + 1 Macau route

Current situation

New World First Ferry Services Limited (NWFF), a member of Chow Tai Fook Enterprises and NWS Holdings, took over ferry service licences for routes which had been previously operated by the Hongkong & Yaumati Ferry Company. The associate company New World First Ferry Services (Macau) Limited (NWFFM) operates ferry services between Tsim Sha Tsui and Macau.

Developments

First Ferry has invested HKD500 million in acquiring a fleet of new high-speed catamarans since 2000. These new vessels are double-decked and have a capacity of more than 400 passengers with speeds ranging from 27 to 43.5 knots.

Fleet: 30 vessels

The fleet comprises five double-deckers, six triple-deckers and 19 high-speed double-deck catamarans.

For further details of the fleet vessels, please see *Jane's High-Speed Marine Transportation*.

Hong Kong
Licensed ferries
Current situation

Since April 1999, most of the ferry services have been provided by licensed ferry operators. There are currently 11 ferry operators providing 26 regular, licensed passenger ferry services to outlying islands and across the harbour, as at 1 April 2008. There are two franchised ferry services operated by 'Star' Ferry plying between Central and Tsim Sha Tsui as well as between Wan Chai and Tsim Sha Tsui. The licensed and franchised ferry services are supplemented by 'kaitos' which are licensed to serve remote coastal settlements.

In 2007, ferry passengers amounted to 54 million.

For further information on ferry services, please see www.td.gov.hk/transport_in_hong_kong/public_transport/ferries/index.htm.

Peak Tramways Company Limited

1 Lugard Road, The Peak, Hong Kong
Tel: (+852) 28 49 76 54
Fax: (+852) 28 49 62 37
e-mail: info@thepeak.com.hk
Web: www.thepeak.com.hk

Key personnel

Head of Engineering and Operations:
Joseph Sin

Background

A wholly owned subsidiary of The Hongkong & Shanghai Hotels Limited.

Type of operation: Funicular railway, opened 1888

Passenger journeys: (2002) 3.7 million
(2003) 3.0 million
(2004) 4.1 million
(2005) 3.9 million
(2006) 4.4 million
Car-km: (2002) 103,000
(2003) 88,934
(2004) 97,056
(2005) 91,700
(2006) 94,496

Route length: 1.4 km
Number of lines: 1
Number of stations: 6
Gauge: 1,524 mm

Current situation

The Peak Tramway was completely rebuilt in 1989. The Peak Tower, the Upper Terminus, was redeveloped in 1997 as a commercial and entertainment complex.

In November 2003, Peak Tramways was granted an extension to the operating rights of the tramway for a further 10 years, commencing 1 January 2004.

Developments

The signalling system was upgraded in 2005.

The Peak Tower has recently undergone substantial revitalisation.

The Peak Tram Historical Gallery in the Lower terminus was opened in September 2007.

Fare structure: Single and return tickets, reductions for children and seniors

Rolling stock: 2 cars built by Gangloff AG (Von Roll) in 1989

One of Peak Tramways'
Von Roll cars
0530138

Nanjing

Population: 6 million (estimate)

Public transport

Bus services provided by municipal authority; metro.

Nanjing Metro Corporation

Nanjing, Jiangsu Province, People's Republic of China
Web: www.nj-dt.com

Type of operation: Metro, trial running started in mid-2005

Route length: 17 km
   in tunnel: 10.6 km
Number of lines: 1
Number of stations: 19

Background

Plans for a north-south metro line were put forward in 1990. This is Line 1 of what is now proposed as a four-line network totalling 121 km. Approval was granted in late 1994 and construction started in late 2000.

The initial route will run 17 km from Maigaoqiao in the north via an interchange with the city's main railway station to Xiaohang in the southwest. Some 10.2 km in the city centre will be in cut-and-cover tunnel, with the remainder elevated. A fleet of six-car trains will take power from a bottom-contact 750 V DC third rail.

Current situation

In April 2002 the Nanjing Metro Co Ltd selected Alstom, in partnership with the Nanjing Puzhen Rolling Stock Works, to supply 20 six-car metro trains for the north-south line. The contract is valued at approximately EUR160 million. Delivery was due to commence in May 2004 and should be completed in June 2006.

Developments

In May 2005, Line 1 of the metro was completed and under test running, with three of the trainsets in operation. Full service was expected to start in August or September 2005 and construction on Line 2 was expected to start in late 2005.

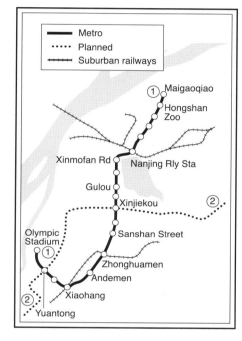

Nanjing metro
1115132

Shanghai

Population: City/municipality 18.5 million (2007 estimate), metropolitan area in excess of 20.0 million (estimate)

Public transport

Bus and trolleybus services provided by municipally owned company; bus services also provided by private companies; metro; light rail; maglev; cross-river ferries, but bus routes and one trolleybus route run through the two under-river tunnels, and bus routes also cross the Huangpu bridge.

Shanghai Public Utility Administration Bureau

34 Yanan Road East, Shanghai 200002, China
Tel: (+86 21) 63 21 76 16; 12 00

Key personnel
Director: Jin Xin
General Manager: Li Gansheng
   Staff: 74,000

Shanghai Transit (ST)
Operating costs financed by: Fares 100 per cent

Current situation

The Bureau is responsible for planning and management of Shanghai's public transport, water transport, water and gas supply and other utilities. It oversees the activities of state and private bus and trolleybus operations in the Municipal Region of Shanghai.

There is serious overcrowding on both modes, which cater for some 15 million daily journeys. Traffic congestion is exacerbated by six million or so cycles. Despite constant route expansion and congestion relief measures, severe short-term capacity problems remain and a computerised urban traffic control system is being developed. The long-planned metro, the first short section of which is in operation, is seen as a means of relieving pressure on the busiest corridors.

Staggering of commuting hours has also been effective in reducing congestion, with some 684,000 employees working staggered shifts. As an inducement, ST offers chartered buses which may deviate from fixed routes.

The bus network serves urban areas and the suburbs well beyond the limits of trolleybus operation. Most of the fleet is articulated, but is to designs built for many years and is fitted mostly with petrol rather than diesel engines.

Bus

Number of routes: 368 (26 all-night)
Route length: 18,407 km

Fleet: 5,341 buses, more than 70 per cent articulated, including:
2-axle Shanghai SK640, SK640J
Articulated: Shanghai SK661, SK661F, SK661P, SK662, SK670
MAN diesel articulated   100
Some vehicles of older types still in use

Most intensive service: Less than 1 min on some routes at peak times
One-person operation: None
Fare collection: Payment to seated conductors, monthly passes
Fare structure: Stage
Average distance between stops: 798 m in urban area, 1,472 m in suburbs
Integration with other modes: Bus and trolleybus networks form integrated transport system

Current situation

To alleviate congestion during peak hours over 500 vehicles have been assigned to 23 bus routes for express journeys and short workings. Some 179 buses form a contingency fleet with radio

Newly built trolleybus on Route 21 with other buses and trolleybuses in Shanghai city centre (Patric Cunnane)   0103481

Articulated trolleybus on Route 20 in Shanghai city centre (Patric Cunnane)   0103482

communication to cope with unusual passenger flows and special mother-and-baby buses have been introduced on about 20 routes to ease the problems of nursing mothers in peak-hour conditions.

Developments
Diesel engines are being tested and a number of diesel buses are expected to be imported from Europe.

Automatic vehicle monitoring installed in a small fleet of buses as a pilot project.

Trolleybus
Number of routes: 12
Route length: 186 km

Fleet: 923 trolleybuses, all articulated with chopper control

Most intensive service: 1 min
One-person operation: None
Fare collection: Payment to seated conductors, monthly passes
Fare structure: Stage
Operational control: Emergency turning circles just outside city centre provided on trolleybus routes to allow vehicles to turn short if required. Parallel wiring or passing loops at a number of locations where routes share wiring
Average peak-hour speed: 17 km/h
Average distance between stops: 567 m, extended to over 1 km in central area during peak hours

Current situation
The network is currently operating near to capacity with traffic flows of 13,000 passengers/h on some sections, vehicles running at less than 1 min headways on some routes (requiring tight

dispatching) and 178-passenger trolleybuses proving inadequate. The busiest trolleybus routes are supplemented by petrol bus shuttles over their peak sections. Technically the system is the most advanced in China.

Kwoon Chung Bus Holdings Limited
Unit 1205, Eastern Harbour Centre, 28 Hoi Chak Street, Quarry Bay, Hong Kong, China
Tel: (+852) 25 78 11 78   Fax: (+852) 25 62 33 99
e-mail: contact@kcm.com.hk
Web: www.kcm.com.hk

Key personnel
Chairman: Thomas Wong Chung Pak
Managing Director: Matthew Wong Leung Pak

Current situation
Through two joint venture companies, the Kwoon Chung group, based in Hong Kong, operates more than 1,600 buses in Shanghai; 672 with Shanghai Pudong Kwoon Chung and 1,023 with Shanghai Wu Qi Kwoon Chung Public Transport Companies. These two subsidiaries also provide taxi services.

Shanghai Pudong Kwoon Chung Public Transport Co Ltd
Current situation
Formed in 1992, Shanghai Pudong Kwoon Chung Public Transport Co Ltd was one of the earliest Co-operative Joint Ventures (CJV) between a Hong Kong company and mainland interests and is now a 51.5 per cent subsidiary of the Kwoon Chung group, operating a large fleet of buses and taxis, mainly in the Pudong area of Shanghai.

Number of routes: 32

Fleet: 672 buses + 25 taxis

Shanghai Wu Qi Kwoon Chung Public Transport Co Ltd
Current situation
This joint venture was set up in June 1998 in conjunction with the state-owned Shanghai No 5 Bus Co and is the largest Sino-Foreign joint venture to operate public buses in the PRC. The Company is a 50.09 per cent subsidiary of the Kwoon Chung group and operates public bus and taxi services, mainly in the Puxi area of Shanghai.

Number of routes: 38

Fleet: 1,023 buses + 81 taxis

Shanghai Metro Operation Co Ltd
12 Heng Shan Road, 200031 Shanghai, People's Republic of China
Tel: (+86 21) 64 31 24 60   Fax: (+86 21) 64 33 95 98

Key personnel
Chief General Manager: Zhou Huai
Vice-General Manager: Zhou Qinghao
Staff: 2,700

Type of operation: Full metro, first line opened 1993

Route length: 65.6 km
  in tunnel: 13.4 km
Number of lines: 4 (extension to Line 1 is known as Line 5)
Number of stations: 49
Gauge: 1,435 mm
Track: 60 kg/m rail; concrete sleepers in ballast on surface sections, concrete trackbed in tunnels
Max gradient: 3.2%
Minimum curve radius: 300 m
Electrification: 1.5 kV DC, overhead

Current situation
Shanghai Metro Operation Co Ltd operates Lines 1-4 of the Shanghai metro system. Line 5 (Xinmin Line) is operated by the Shanghai Rail Transit Co Ltd.

The 6.6 km southern portion of Line 1 opened in 1993 prior to inauguration of full public service in December 1994. Construction of Line 2 was carried out by the German Shanghai Metro Group joint venture of Adtranz and Siemens – the same group that equipped Line 1. Trial running on Line 2 started in September 1999, and it opened throughout in mid-2000.

A further 35 six-car trains were supplied for Line 2. These are similar to the Line 1 cars, but have AC traction motors, more powerful air conditioning and wider doors to assist in handling peak-hour loads of 60,000 passengers/h in each direction.

Developments
Line 3 (Pearl Line) opened in mid-2001 and Line 5 (Xinmin Line) opened in late 2003.

Some 180 km of new lines have been approved for construction under the latest Five-Year Plan. Included in these plans are:
Extension of Line 1 northwards (due to be completed in 2003);
Westward extension of Line 2 to Hongqiao Airport (scheduled to open in 2005), with further extensions both east and west;
Second Phase of the Pearl Line (M4, currently under construction), forming a circle with the existing Pearl Line (scheduled for completion by the end of 2004);
Line 7 (M7) to the northwest, linking with M4 (planned completion in 2006), with further extensions north and southeast;
Line 8 (M8, Yanpu Line), scheduled to start operations in 2005; 28 six-car Metropolis trains have been ordered from ALSTOM, with a value of approximately €184 million. Delivery due to start

in October 2005 and be completed by the end of 2007;

Puding Light Rail (L4), expected to be operational in 2005;

Shensong Line – first phase of the regional express line R4, scheduled for completion in 2005.

Rolling stock:
Line 1: 96 cars
AEG/Siemens (1992/93)   M64 T32
On order: 10 six-car trainsets (Bombardier), (signalling system by Casco Signal Ltd), delivery scheduled between June 2004 and May 2005.
Line 2: 210 cars
Consortium, including Adtranz/Siemens
(6-car trainsets) (2000)   210
Line 3 (Pearl Line): 168 cars
ALSTOM Metropolis (6-car trainsets) (2002)   168
Option: 10 trains
Line 5 (Xinmin Line): 152 cars
ALSTOM Metropolis (4-car trainsets) (2003)   152

Service: Peak 4.5–5 min (Line 1), 7 min (Line 2), 11.5 min (Pearl Line)
First/last train: 05.00/23.00
One-person operation: None
Fare structure: Flat

Fare collection: Manual; AFC planned
Signalling: ATC, ATS and ATO
Surveillance: CCTV at stations

Shanghai Maglev Transportation Development Co Ltd (SMTDC)
2520 Long Yang Road, Pudong, Shanghai, China
Tel: (+86 21) 28 90 71 00   Fax: (+86 21) 28 90 71 81
e-mail: webmaster@smtdc.com
Web: www.smtdc.com

Type of operation: Magnetic levitation system (Maglev), opened for public services January 2004

Route length: 30 km (double-track)
Number of stations: 2

Background
German consortium Transrapid, which included Siemens, ThyssenKrupp and Transrapid International, which itself is a jointly owned company of Siemens and ThyssenKrupp, obtained its first commercial contract to build a high-speed magnetic levitation system connecting the Shanghai financial centre in Lujiazui (Longyang Road) with the Pudong international airport. The consortium was responsible for the provision of the vehicles, power supply, propulsion and operational control systems. Construction on the guideway started in 2001, with the aim that the 30 km journey would take less than 8 minutes.

Current situation
The Shanghai Maglev Transportation Development Company (SMTDC) is responsible for the guideway infrastructure and the stations, as well as for operating the system.

Possible extensions are an initial extension of the track to the old airport at Shanghai, Hongqiao Airport (34 km), followed by a further phase extending the line to the city of Hangzhou.

Fleet: Currently 3 Transrapid trains with 5 sections

First/last train: 06.45/21.30

Service: Headway: 15 mins; Journey time: 7 min 20 secs
Maximum speed: 431 km/h
Fare structure: Single and return tickets; discount for airline passengers with proof of purchase of airline ticket; one-way VIP ticket available

---

Shenyang
Population: 7 million (2006)

Public transport
Bus and trolleybus services provided by municipal agencies; metro under construction.

Shenyang ComfortDelGro Anyun Bus Co Ltd
No 8 Hua Hai Road, Shenyang Jing Ji Ji, Shu Kai Fa District, Shentang, Liaoning, People's Republic of China
Tel: (+86 24) 25 37 64 41   Fax: (+86 24) 25 37 65 36
e-mail: choopy@comfortdelgro.com
Web: www.comfortdelgro.com.sg

Key personnel
General Manager, North-East China: Choo Peng Yen
   Staff: Not currently available

Passenger journeys: Not currently available
Vehicle-km: Not currently available

Current situation
Shenyang ComfortDelGro Anyun Bus Co Ltd began operations in 2005, and provides scheduled bus services in the Shenyang area.

Developments
In October 2005, the company announced that it had acquired the operating rights to 50 bus routes, 1,218 buses and other assets from Shenyang Passenger Transport Group.

Bus
Number of routes: 62 (estimate)
Route length: Not currently available

Fleet: 1,600 buses (estimate)
Fleet breakdown is not currently available

Fare structure: Stage
Fare collection: Payment to seated conductors, monthly passes
Operating costs financed by: Not currently available

Shenyang Metro Co Ltd
28-3 Dongbinhe Road, Shenhe District, Shenyang City 110011, Liaoning Province, People's Republic of China
Tel: (+86 24) 24 08 51 01   Fax: (+86 24) 24 08 41 66
e-mail: symtc@163.com
Web: www.symtc.com

Key personnel
Director, Shenyang Subway Construction Office: Tong Jingshi

Type of operation: Metro (under construction)

Current situation
After many years of planning and proposals, construction has begun on the Shenyang metro network. Long-term plans envisage a five-line system with a total length of some 182 km.

The local government will carry out the first phase of the project from 2005 to 2012.

Developments
Construction on Line 1 began in late 2005. The line will run east-west across the city, with a length of 22.2 km and 18 stations. Current expectations are for completion in late 2009.

Work on Line 2, running north-south, 19.3 km long (all underground) with 17 stations, is due to start in late 2006. Completion is scheduled before 2013.

The estimated investment required for Lines 1 and 2 is some USD2.11 billion.

Tianjin
Population: Metropolitan area 5.0 million (estimate), Municipal area 10.2 million (2004 estimate)

Public transport
Bus services operated by municipal company and metro run by separate agency, with extensions planned; light rail.

Tianjin Public Transportation Group
Tianjin, China
Tel: (+86 22) 26 29 32 24
Fax: (+86 22) 26 29 32 25
Web: www.tjbus.com

Current situation
Public company, responsible for providing public transportation services and operates bus and taxi operations.

In 2004, there were approximately 400 bus lines.

Tianjin Metro General Corporation
97 Jie-Fang-Bei Road, He-ping, 300041 Tianjin, China
Tel: (+86 22) 39 98 15   Fax: (+86 22) 23 39 61 94
Web: www.tjdt.cn,
   www.ditie.cc

Key personnel
General Manager: Wang Yu-ji

Type of operation: Full metro, initial route opened 1980, re-opened for trial running 2006

Route length: 22.2 km
Number of lines: 1
Number of stations: 22
Gauge: 1,435 mm
Track: 50 kg/m rail laid on concrete sleepers
Max gradient: 3%
Minimum curve radius: 300 m
Tunnel: Cut-and-cover
Electrification: 750 V DC, third rail

Service frequency: 12 min peak, 15–20 min off-peak
First/last train: 05.30/22.30
Fare structure: Distance related
Fare collection: Manual sale from booking offices

For details of the latest updates to *Jane's Urban Transport Systems* online and to discover the additional information available exclusively to online subscribers please visit

juts.janes.com

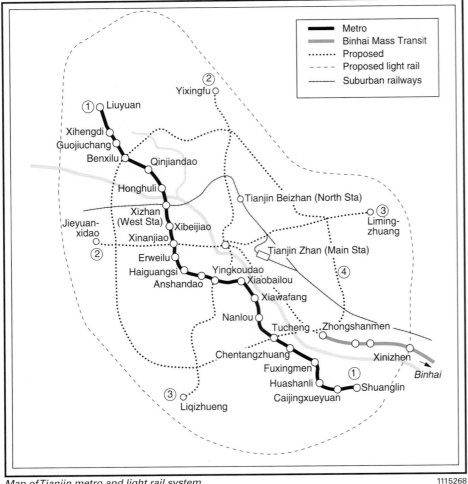

Map of Tianjin metro and light rail system   1115268

Tianjin Binhai Mass Transit Development Co Ltd (BMT)

No 99 Seventh Street, TEDA, Tianjin, China
Tel: (+86 22) 65 70 10 23, 12 80
Fax: (+86 22) 65 70 10 43
Web: www.ctbmt.cn

Type of operation: Light rail, opened for trial running in 2004

Passenger journeys: Not currently available

Gauge: 1,435 mm
Track: 60 kg/m
Electrification: 1,500 V DC

Background

Tianjin Binhai Mass Transit Development Co Ltd (BMT) was established in January 2001. The company was jointly invested and established by the Tianjin Economic and Technological Development Area, Tianjin Port Free Trade Zone, Tianjin Harbour and Tianjin Tanggu District.

Construction on the light rail system commenced in 2001 and was completed in 2003. The completed Binhai LRT Line is 45.4 km long and runs between downtown Tianjin and the Tianjin Economic Development Area (TEDA) with 19 stations. Headways for the completed system is 3½ minutes and hours of operation are 06.30–21.30. The project cost around USD783 million.

In October 2002 a contract was signed by the Beijing Hua-Tie Information Technology Development Company with Union Switch and Signal Inc, US, for the design and delivery of an Automatic Train Control (ATC) system for the Binhae New Development Area Rail Rapid Transit Light Rail Transit (LRT) line.

In February 2003, Motorola was awarded a contract to supply TErrestrial Trunked RAdio (TETRA) digital radio and communications system for the whole of the system.

Developments

Trial operations began on the eastern section of the line in March 2004. The western part of the line is scheduled to open later in 2006.

Trial operations are being served by eight four-car trains.

Fleet: 116 vehicles (planned)

CNR, stainless steel LRT vehicles   116

Integration with other modes: Because of limited rolling stock, passengers are not yet encouraged to use the metro instead of other public transport
Signalling: Automatic block

Rolling stock: 24 cars, former Beijing prototypes
Changchun BJ-111   M24
On order: A fleet of cars similar to those running in Beijing is being built

Current situation

The metro closed in October 2001 for reconstruction and expansion.

Seven lines are planned, with a total length of 154 km.

Developments

In June 2006, **Line 1** opened for trial operations, running from 09.00–16.00 with five minute headways. The contactless ticketing system was supplied by Telvent and the TErrestrial Trunked RAdio (TETRA) digital radio system by Motorola Inc.

Line 2: Planning and design completed. The line will be 22.5 km long, with 20.3 km and 18 of the 20 stations underground. Construction is due to start in 2006.

Line 3: Planning and design completed. Total length will be 28.4 km, with 2.2 km at grade and 6.2 km elevated and 22 stations. Construction is due to start later in 2006.

Wuhan

Population: 4.45 million (2001 Census), conurbation 7 million

Public transport

Wuhan is the capital of Hubei Province and has an area of some 8,500 km². It comprises three towns – Wuchang, Hankou, and Hanyang.

Bus and trolleybus services are operated by municipal agencies throughout the area, and by state-owned steel and iron enterprise in the housing area adjacent to the steelworks. Ferries provide most direct link between the two largest component cities of the conurbation which are separated by the Yangzi river. Chinese Railways operates a few suburban trains; light rail and metro lines proposed.

Wuhan City Bus Company

Wuhan, Hubei Province, China

Number of routes: Approx 60 (including suburban)

Current situation

An expanding network covers all areas. Routes are operated wholly within each of the cities of Wuchang, Hankou and Hanyang which make up the conurbation, and also across the Han river bridges which connect Hankou and Hanyang, and the Yangzi river bridge which links Hanyang and Wuchang.

Fleet: Locally built buses, mainly articulated. Types include Wuhan WG 661, WG 670 (both articulated), WG 645 and others

Fare collection: Cash payment to seated conductor; monthly passes

Wuhan City Trolleybus

Bus

Current situation

About 40 articulated Wuhan buses are used alongside the trolleybus fleet on the cross-river trolleybus routes.

Trolleybus

Current situation

The system is expanding slowly and now comprises two trunk routes crossing both rivers from Hankou to Wuchang via Hanyang, three routes wholly within Hankou and two wholly within Wuchang.

Number of routes: 7

Fleet: Approx 220 trolleybuses (over 90 per cent articulated), almost all built locally; 12 old Beijing BK540 were bought second-hand from Beijing around 1986 but may now have been replaced by more modern vehicles

Fare collection: Cash payment to seated conductor; monthly passes

Wuhan Steel & Iron Company

Current situation

The suburb of Wuchang, housing most of the labour force of the Wuhan steelworks, is served by bus and trolleybus routes operated by a department of the steelworks enterprise. This network is separate from that of the Wuhan municipality's agencies and there is no physical connection between the two trolleybus systems, which are several km apart. There is one basic trolleybus route, although wiring permits an alternative, and the fleet is estimated at 50 articulated trolleybuses (Wuhan and Shengyan types) and 100 buses (Wuhan, Xiangtan and Ikarus). Services run throughout the day, but are most frequent at shift-change times at the steelworks.

Wuhan
Light rail/metro (proposed)
Current situation
Although there have been reports of proposed light rail and metro systems in Wuhan and that bids had been invited for a metro line between Gutian Yilu and Fujiapo and a system of six light

rail lines, the latter in 2000, no progress on either project has been forthcoming.

Xi'an
Population: City 3.2 million, metropolitan area 7.9 million (estimates)

Public transport
An extensive network of bus and trolleybus services provided by municipal agencies covers the city and inner suburbs. The trolleybus system includes an interurban route to a satellite town. Minibuses. A few suburban trains are run by Chinese Railways. Metro under construction.

Xi'an Municipal Government
Transportation Bureau
No.68, Mid-section of Huanchengnan Road, Xi'an, Shaanxi Province, People's Republic of China
Tel: (+86 29) 87 86 26 37
Fax: (+86 29) 87 85 32 88
Web: www.xa.gov.cn

Bus
Current situation
In 2003, the estimated fleet for public transport services was 2,720 vehicles and in 2000 some 23 per cent of daily trips were carried out by bus.

Most bus routes also support minibus services run in parallel, providing more comfort for a higher fare.

Number of routes: 159
Route length: 3,141 km

Fleet: Approx 500 buses, including many articulated. Types are mainly Xi'an two-axle and articulated, and Beijing BK663 articulated, but there are also small batches of Chengdu, Siping, Jianyu and Tianjin buses, and Daimler Fleetline double-deck ex-KMB of Hong Kong

Fare collection: Stage fares paid to seated conductor, two conductors on articulated vehicles; monthly passes

Trolleybus
Number of routes: 5

Fleet: Over 100, all articulated. Most are type Shanghai SK561, but latest deliveries are Beijing BD562

Metro
Current situation
Construction of the first part of Line 2 (1.5 km demonstration line) started in early 2007. Line 2 will eventually have a length of 26.4 km (23.5 km in tunnel) and will run on a north-south alignment with 20 stations. Completion is currently scheduled for 2011. A 19.7 km line could start in 2002 and be completed in 2006. If the foreign investment is forthcoming, the remainder of the money will be raised from government funds, the issue of bonds and public fund raising.

A further 23.9 km line (Line 1) is planned, running east-west. Construction on this line is due to commence when Line 2 is due to begin operations.

There are long-term plans for a total of six lines with a total length of 251.8 km.

Colombia

Bogota
Population: 6.8 million (2000 estimate)

Public transport
Bus Rapid Transit (BRT) system and feeder service provided by private companies, under contract to public corporation. Expansion to BRT system planned.

Empresa Distrital de Transporte del Tercer Milenio – TransMilenio SA
Avenue El Dorado #66-63, Bogotá DC, Colombia
Tel: (+57 1) 275 70 00; 220 30 00
Fax: (+57 1) 324 98 70, 80; 221 53 83, 53 23
Web: www.transmilenio.gov.co

Key personnel
General Manager Advisor: Augusto Hernández

Background
Formed in 1999, TransMilenio is a state stock company of Bogotá's mayor's office and is responsible for managing the new mass transit/Bus Rapid Transit (BRT) system which carries the same name. The system is based on dedicated busways operated by high-capacity buses – all of them articulated, during the first stage – with large loading terminals and modern bus stops, all of them with raised platforms at the same level as the bus floor and automated ticketing. The system is operated like a modern light rail system, with new stations, platforms, approach bridges for passengers, underground pathways and new garages.

Current situation
TransMilenio operates two types of 'trunk' service- normal and 14 express. Feeder bus services, on green non-articulated buses, connect to the TransMilenio routes and are provided in the western areas of Colsubsidio, Bolivia, Garcés Navas, Villas del Dorado, Villas de Granada, Quirigua, Bochica and El Cortijo.

TransMilenio articulated bus at Las Aguas station 1137518

TransMilenio station, showing platform doors 1137517

Volvo do Brasil has supplied the majority of the articulated vehicles for the system. The vehicles were built in Curitiba and shipped CKD to Colombia, where they were reassembled and delivered to TransMilenio.

Both the trunk and the feeder services are operated by private companies under contract to TransMilenio. These companies are responsible for operations, acquisition of vehicles, recruitment of drivers, maintenance etc. Compensation is awarded to the companies according to miles of service provided.

Passenger journeys: (2002) 373.5 million (feeder routes: 151.3 million)
Vehicle-km: (2002) 71.3 million

Number of routes: 39
Route length: 42 km
Length of feeder routes: 309 km
Number of stops: 61

Fleet: 470 vehicles (241 vehicles total on feeder routes)

Volvo (articulated)	about 300
Other	about 170

Service: Normal service: 5 min; Express service: 4 min
First/last bus: 05.00/23.00
Fare: Flat

Fare collection: Prepaid contactless smartcard system, operated by private company contracted to TransMilenio
Integration with other modes: Fare covers transfer from feeder services to main TransMilenio routes
Average speed: 26.2 km/h

Developments
There are 10 proposed extensions planned for the period 2001–2006, totalling some 131 km. The 15-year development plan projects approximately 388 km of new routes serving a population of 5.5 million potential passengers.

Phase II of the system includes three trunk corridors: Calle 13-Americas, NQS, and Suba,

with a total length of 43 km. These are scheduled to be operational by the end of 2005. Projected ridership once the six routes are all operational is 1.4 million passengers per day and it is estimated that a fleet of some 850 buses will be needed for the services.

As well as providing much-improved public transport services and reduced fares for the population, the new system has resulted in the reduction of traffic accident casualties and of emissions.

Bogota
Private bus/minibus
Current situation
With the 'TransMilenio' project (see separate entry for TransMilenio SA), bus services throughout Bogotá were completely reorganised. Almost all of the private companies already providing services became associated with the new plan and system, to deliver trunk and feeder services for the city under contract.

Medellín
Population: City 2.4 million (2005), metropolitan area 3.6 million (estimate)

Public transport
Bus, minibus and metro services, supplemented by cablecar operations (Metrocable), provided by private companies. Bus Rapid Transit (BRT) (Metroplus) route under construction.

Secretaria de Transportes y Tránsito de Medellín
Carrera 64C, No 72–58, Barrio Caribe, Medellin, Antioquia, Colombia
Tel: (+57 4) 444 41 44
e-mail: sugerenciasyreclamos@medellin.gov.co
Web:alcaldia.medellin.gov.co/transito/

Passenger boardings: Not currently available

Current situation
Bus services are operated by private companies and co-operatives on concessions awarded by the Secretaria de Transportes y Tránsito de Medellín, initially for a year and then for progressively longer periods after review.

A fleet of more than 4,200 vehicles runs some 200 routes.

Bus Rapid Transit (BRT) (Metroplus)
Metroplús SA
Carrera 46, No 52-82, Edificio de la Cultura, Piso 3 y 4, Cámara de Commercio de Medellin, Medellin, Antioquia, Colombia
Tel: (+57 4) 576 37 30   Fax: (+57 4) 293 33 67
Web: www.metroplus.gov.co

Key personnel
Director, Metropolitan Area: Oscar José Mesa Sánchez
Staff: Not currently available

Type of operation: Bus Rapid Transit (BRT) (under construction)

Current situation
Metroplús SA is a limited company, established in 2005 to develop a flexible transportation system which will be integrated with the services and fares of the existing Metro and Metrocable network.

The company has the following participants: Municipio de Medellín (55 per cent), Metro de Medellín (25 per cent), Municipio de Envigado (10 per cent), Municipio de Itagüí (five per cent), Terminales de Transporte (four per cent) and Instituto para el Desarrollo de Antioquia (one per cent).

The project is a 12.5-km Bus Rapid Transit (BRT) system (Metroplus), which will run from the Belén

sector to the University of Medellín. The busway will be segregated and will have 21 stations/stops. Vehicles will be CNG-powered. Currently under construction, the route is scheduled to be operational in 2008.

Developments
There are plans, at design stage, for expansion of the network, totalling some 11 km with 19 stations, along the Avenida del Poblado and the Avenida Guayabal.

Metro de Medellín Ltda
Calle 44, No 46 – 001, Bello, Antioquia, Colombia
Tel: (+57 4) 454 88 88
Fax: (+57 4) 452 44 50
e-mail: metro@metrodemedellin.org.co
Web: www.metrodemedellin.org.co

Key personnel
General Manager: Ramiro Márquez Ramirez
Staff: 815

Type of operation: Full metro, opened 1995

Passenger journeys: Not currently available
Vehicle-km: Not currently available

Background
Formed in 1979.

Current situation
The metro was opened in three stages in 1995/96.

Metro de Medellín is certified to ISO 9001:2000 standards.

Developments
An extension northwards to Hatillo (21 km, two new stations) on Line A is under construction. It will use existing track to Cisneros.

Route length: 31 km (including link line)
   elevated: 9 km
Number of lines: 2 (plus link line between Niquía and San Javier during peak periods)
Number of stations: 25
Gauge: 1,435 mm
Electrification: 1.5 kV DC, overhead

Service: Peak 5 min, off-peak 10 min
First/last train: 05.00/23.00
Fare structure: Flat; tickets for 1, 2 and 10 trips; discounts for some trips made using Civica smartcard
Fare collection: Turnstiles; Civica smartcard
Operating costs financed by: Fares 92 per cent, other commercial sources 8 per cent

Medellín metro   0573994

Rolling stock: 126 cars, in three-car sets
MAN/Ateinsa/Siemens   M84 T42

Metrocable
Type of system: Aerial cable transit system, inaugurated July 2004

Passenger journeys: Not currently available
Route length: Not currently available
Number of lines: 2
Number of stations: 9 (of which 4 are transfer stations to the Metro)

Current situation
Two lines are currently in service, with Line J serving the districts of Juan XXIII, Vallejuelos and La Aurora and Line K, opened in 2008, serving Andalucia, Popular and Santo Domingo Savio.

Developments
A further line, Line S, is under construction and is scheduled to open in 2009. It will run from Santo Domingo Savio Station to El Tambro, with no intermediate stations.

Côte d'Ivoire

Abidjan

Population: Metropolitan area 3.6 million (2005 estimate)

Public transport
Bus and lagoon boat services in the metropolitan area and inner suburbs provided under concession from government by 'mixed economy' company part owned by vehicle manufacturer and responsible to Ministry. Substantial numbers of privately owned 'Gbaka' minibuses and taxis serve suburbs and outer areas.

Société des Transports Abidjanais (SOTRA)
BP 2009, Abidjan 01, Côte d'Ivoire, Africa
Tel: (+225) 21 75 71 00
Fax: (+225) 21 25 97 21
Web: www.sotra-ci.com

Key personnel
President: Albert Dago Dadie
Director General: Philippe Attey
  Staff: 3,955 (as at March 2006)

Current situation
SOTRA was created in 1960. A 39.8 per cent stake is held by the French manufacturer Renault, 60.13 per cent by the state and 0.07 per cent by the Ville d'Abidjan. SOTRA's council of administration comprises the President, six members appointed by the state, three by Renault and one by the city of Abidjan.

SOTRA operates over some 108,188 km with 65 urban routes, 12 express routes, three ferry lines and two Taxi-Bagages services, which cater for passengers to and from the city's markets. Special school and workplace services are also provided. Approximately 700,000 passengers are carried daily.

SOTRA is awaiting the outcome of studies into proposals for its privatisation.

Plans to set up a privately owned bus company, Société des Transports Urbains (SOTU), to operate principally in the densely populated areas of Yopougon and Abobo, have not progressed.

Bus
Fleet: 756 buses, of which 447 in service
In peak service: 415

Other operators
Current situation
Private minibuses known as Gbakas, with 14-32 seats (usually 18 seats), operate both legally and illegally to all districts of the city.

There are also extensive taxis operations, both private city taxis ('woro-woros' – usually four-seater cars) and private metered taxis.

Ferry
Current situation
19 'lagoon buses' ferry approximately 30,000 passengers per day to and from work.

Croatia

Zagreb

Population: City: 784,900, metropolitan area 1.1 million (2007 estimates)

Public transport
Bus, tramway and funicular services provided by municipal undertaking. Suburban rail services provided by state railway, Hrvatske Zeljeznice doo (HZ) (please see *Jane's World Railways* for further information).

Zagreb City Holding Ltd – Zagreb Electrical Tramway (ZET)
Ozaljska 105, HR-10110 Zagreb, Croatia
Tel: (+385 1) 365 15 55   Fax: (+385 1) 364 05 20
e-mail: javnost@zet.hr
Web: www.zet.hr

Key personnel
General Manager: Ivan Tolić
Executive Director, Traffic: Drago Marić
Executive Director, Tram: Zvonko Pečeić
Executive Director, Bus: Stjepan Smolčić
Executive Director, Development: Siniša Uglik
Director, Economy: Ljuba Žgela
  Staff: 4,262

Passenger journeys: (All modes)
(2003) 268.9 million
(2004) 253.7 million
(2005) 256 million
(2006) 259 million
(2007) 316 million

Operating costs financed by: Fares 23.76 per cent, other commercial sources 17.20 per cent, subsidy/grants 59.03 per cent

Current situation
The municipal area of Zagreb is some 641.33 km². ZET operates within this area and neighbouring municipalities covering a total of 1,192.63 km², having separately contracted arrangements with each in regard to service levels and fares. Trams provide the main city-centre penetration, with buses generally acting as feeders. Many suburban bus routes now terminate at interchange points with trams or articulated buses providing frequent trunk services to the city centre, with express journeys operating in peak hours.

At the end of 1994, ZET ceased to operate bus services outside the city limits, these operations being tendered for by private companies.

Type TMK 2200 Koncar/TZV Gredlj low-floor tram for ZET (Toma Bacic)   1129938

Tendering for city services started in 1995, with the aim of reducing operating costs.

Bus
Passenger journeys: (2003) 84.5 million
(2004) 79.7 million
(2005) 80.4 million
(2006) 82 million
(2007) 99 million
Vehicle-km: (2003) 261. million
(2004) 26.1 million
(2005) 26 million
(2006) 25.5 million
(2007) 26.2 million

Number of routes: 124 plus 4 night
Route length: (One way) 1,389 km

Fleet: 325 buses	
TAM standard	2
MARBUS	2
MAN standard	74
MAN low-floor	54
MAN articulated	19
MAN low-floor articulated	44
Mercedes-Benz standard	15
Mercedes-Benz low-floor	53
Mercedes-Benz articulated	25
Mercedes-Benz low-floor articulated	37
In peak service: 263	

Most intensive service: 5 min
One-person operation: All routes
Fare collection: Prepurchase or payment to driver, with cancelling machines on board
Fare structure: Zones covering Zagreb (Zagreb City is Zone 1) and each neighbouring municipality; single tickets; monthly and yearly passes valid in Zagreb only, or individual municipalities plus Zagreb City; free transfer between bus and tram in direction of journey; free travel for students (elementary and secondary school and university) and unemployed from Zagreb City area
Fare-evasion control: Ticket inspectors
Operational control: Mobile route inspectors in radio contact with supervisors at terminal points and with central control on UKW system, new supervision and control system

Arrangements for elderly/disabled: Free travel for disabled and those over 65, funded by Zagreb City; 8 buses equipped to carry wheelchairs; 5 buses equipped to carry children with development difficulties

Average peak-hour speed: 20.42 km/h

Tramway
Type of operation: Conventional tramway

Passenger journeys: (2003) 183.7 million
(2004) 173.3 million
(2005) 175 million
(2006) 176 million
(2007) 216 million
Car-km: (2003) 22.5 million
(2004) 22.3 million
(2005) 22.2 million
(2006) 21 million
(2007) 18.6 million

Route length: 205 km
Number of lines: 15, plus 4 night
Number of stops: 256
Gauge: 1,000 mm
Max gradient: 4.5%
Minimum curve radius: 18 m
Electrification: 600 V DC, overhead

Developments
Seventy low-floor trams were ordered in 2002 from a consortium – CROTRAM – of Koncar and TZV Gredelj.

Other recent developments include new supervision and control system, equipment for onboard selling and cancellation of tickets and for selling tickets at stations, equipment for the sale of prepurchase memory cards, a project for a depot for the 200 new low-floor trams and bidding for 209 new low-floor buses, 60 of which would be CNG vehicles.

Rolling stock: 403 cars

Duro Dakovic 101 2-axle	M10
2100 articulated (refurbished)	M16
2200 low-floor articulated	M70
201 4-axle	M18
TP1Z trailer	T46
CKD Tatra 301 articulated	M51
401 4-axle	M87
B4 trailer	T73
TMK900	M1
Duewag ex-Mannheim	M16

In peak service: 316
On order: 70 Type TMK 2200 low-floor CROTAM (Koncar/TZV Gredlj) trams, ordered in 2002

Service: Peak 6–7 min, off-peak 7–8 min
First/last car: (Day service) 04.01/00.05

ZET's funicular service 0043285

Fare structure: Monthly and yearly passes, single tickets, day tickets
One-person operation: On all routes
Fare evasion control: Roving inspectors
Centralised control: New supervision and control system
Average peak-hour speed: 13.27 km/h

Cable car/funicular
Current situation
The 4 km tourist cable car, which used to run to the summit of Mount Medvednica, is no longer in operation. A 66 m funicular links the upper old town with the city centre. It carried 715,948 passengers in 2007.

Cyprus

Nicosia
Population: 206,200 (2001)

Public transport
Bus services provided for city and suburbs by private company supervised by Ministry of Transport.

Leoforeia Leikosias (Nicosia Buses Co Ltd)
8 Heroes Street, PO Box 23641, Nicosia, Cyprus
Tel: (+357 2) 77 88 41; 66 58 14
Fax: (+357 2) 77 33 23
e-mail: nic_bus@spidernet.com.cy
Web: www.nicosiabuses.com.cy

Key personnel
Chair: Stefos Kaloyeros
Operating Manager: Costas Christodoulou
  Staff: 103

Current situation
The Nicosia Bus Company was founded in 1971 and is the largest bus transport company in Cyprus, with a fleet of over 100 buses and coaches. Nicosia Buses operate services on 15 routes connecting Nicosia with its suburbs. Intercity bus routes connect Nicosia with Limassol. Buses also run to places of interest and hotels and transfer tourists on scheduled excursions on a request basis. Special bus routes for students and transportation of company personnel on a contract basis within Nicosia area.

Bus
Number of routes: 15 (plus two intercity routes)
Route length: (One way) 234 km

Fleet: 102 vehicles
Tourist

Air conditioned coaches (22–57 seats)	51
Bus	
Mercedes	7
Renault	4
Isuzu	6
Hino	11
Toyota	23

All buses are equipped with wireless communication and some have portable telephones.

Most intensive service: Peak 10–15 min, off-peak 20–30 min
One-person operation: All routes
Fare collection: Payment to driver/prepurchase
Fare structure: Zonal (two types of tickets). Monthly passes
Fares collected on board: 70 per cent
Fare evasion control: Spot checks by inspectors; penalty
Operational control: Route inspectors with radio
Average distance between stops: 250 m
Average peak-hour speed: In mixed traffic, 16 km/h
Operating costs financed by: Fares 100 per cent, other commercial sources four per cent
New vehicles financed by: Long-term bank loans

Czech Republic

Brno
Population: City 366,680, metropolitan area 729.510 (estimates)

Public transport
Bus, trolleybus, tramway and boat services provided by municipal undertaking.

Dopravní podnik města Brna as (DPMB as)
Hlinky 151, CZ-656 46 Brno, Czech Republic
Tel: (+420 543) 17 11 11 (exchange)
(+420 543) 17 43 17 (Information)
Fax: (+420 542) 21 63 75
e-mail: dpinfo@dpmb.cz
Web: www.dpmb.cz

Key personnel
President: Petr Zbytek
General Manager: Bedøich Proke
Economic Manager: Mrs Marie Marhanová

Technical Manager: Rudolf John
Operations Manager: Jiøí Valníèek
  Staff: 2,928

Current situation
The system includes bus, trolleybus and tramway operations and a fleet of seven ships operating on the Brno-dam.

Developments
New trolleybus depot opened 1997, presaging reinstatement of Route 140 which had been bus-operated.

Passenger journeys: 338.99 million (2004/5)

Operating costs financed by: Fares 35 per cent, subsidy/grants 65 per cent
Subsidy from: State and city council

Bus and trolleybus
Number of routes: Bus 47, trolleybus 13

Route length: Bus 637.9 km, trolleybus not currently available

Fleet: 299 buses

Karosa B731	22
B931	56
B732	124
City bus	20
Karosa B741 articulated	28
B941	33
B961	16

In peak service: 246

Fleet: 149 trolleybuses

Skoda 14Tr	90
Skoda 15Tr articulated (1990/91)	8
Skoda T21Tr low-floor (1999/2002)	43
Skoda 22Tr low-floor articulated (2003/04)	8

In peak service: 112
On order: 21 Skoda 25Tr low-floor articulated trolleybuses for 2007/09 delivery

Most intensive service: 4 min
One-person operation: All routes
Fare collection: Prepurchase with onboard cancellation
Fare structure: Time and 3 zones
Fares collected on board: 29 per cent
Fare evasion control: Random inspection
Operational control: Route inspectors/mobile radio
Arrangements for elderly/disabled: Pensioners over 70 and disabled free

Tramway

Type of operation: Conventional tramway

Passenger journeys: (1997) 188 million
(1999) 186 million

Route length: 137.5 km
Number of lines: 13
Gauge: 1,435 mm
Electrification: 600 V DC, overhead

Rolling stock: 327 cars

CKD Tatra K2/K2R articulated (1973/83)	M98
CKD Tatra T3 (1967/90)	M144
CKD Tatra KT8 articulated (1986/93)	M30
CKD KT8 articulated, low-floor centre section (2000)	M7
CKD Tatra T6A5 (1995)	M20
CKD RT6N1 low-floor articulated (1997)	M4
CKD K3R-N articulated, rebuilt from K2 with new low-floor section (2006/7)	M1
Skoda Astra/Anitra 03T low-floor articulated (2003/05)	M17
Krnov/Pragoimex low-floor (2006)	T4
Skoda 13T low-floor articulated (2007)	M2

In peak service: 298
On order: 18 Skoda 13T partially low-floor articulated trams, for delivery 2008

Developments
Extension of Line 8 to Brno-Venkov opened in May 1998.

Skoda 14Tr trolleybus, Brno (Milan Šrámek) 1115146

A Skoda 03T tram (Milan Šrámek) 1115148

Ostrava

Population: City 318,726 (2007), metropolitan area 1.2 million (estimate)

Public transport

Bus, trolleybus and tramway services operated by municipal authority.

Dopravní podnik Ostrava AS

Poděbradova 494/2, CZ-701 71 Ostrava 1, Czech Republic
Tel: (+420 59) 740 11 11   Fax: (+420 59) 740 10 95
e-mail: dpored@dpo.cz
infoservis@dpo.cz
Web: www.dpo.cz

Key personnel
Director: František Vaštik
Head of Marketing: Miroslav Albrecht
Staff: 2,900

Passenger journeys: (All modes)
Not currently available

Fare collection: Prepurchase with validation/cancelling machines on board
Fare structure: Flat fare for each route
Fare evasion control: Roving inspectors
Operating costs financed by: Fares 33.8 per cent, other commercial sources 5 per cent, subsidy/grants 60.7 per cent, tax levy 0.6 per cent

Bus and trolleybus

Passenger journeys: Not currently available
Vehicle-km: Not currently available

Number of routes: Bus 65, trolleybus 10
Route length: Not currently available

Fleet: 322 buses
Fleet breakdown is not currently available
In peak service: 313

Fleet: 65 trolleybuses

Skoda 14Tr (1985/92)	26
Skoda 15Tr articulated (1990/91)	9
Skoda 21Tr low-floor (1997/2002)	15
Solaris Trollino 12AC (2003/06)	10
Solaris Trollino 15AC 3-axle rigid (2004/06)	4
Solaris Trollino 18AC articulated (2005)	1

In peak service: 52

Most intensive service: 1–2 min
One-person operation: All routes
Average peak-hour speed: In mixed traffic, bus 26.6 km/h, trolleybus 18.5 km/h

Tramway

Type of operation: Conventional tramway

Passenger journeys: Not currently available
Car-km: Not currently available

Route length: 254 km
Number of lines: 19
Number of stops: 98
Gauge: 1,435 mm
Electrification: 600 V DC, overhead

Service: Peak 10 min
First/last car: 24 h service

Rolling stock: 294 cars (excluding work and museum cars)

CKD Tatra T3 (1968/86)	M103
CKD Tatra T3G, modernised with GTO control (1983/97)	M46
CKD Tatra T3R, modernised with IGBT control (1982/87)	M44
CKD Tatra T3R.EVN, rebodied and low-floor section added	M12
CKD Tatra T6A5 (1994/98)	M38
CKD Tatra K2 articulated (1966/83)	M9
CKD Tatra KT8 articulated (1989)	M6
CKD Tatra KT8 articulated, (1984/89) (rebuilt with low-floor central section 2004/06)	M10
Skoda Astra 03T low-floor articulated (1998/2001)	M14
Inekon 01 Trio low-floor articulated (2002/04)	M9
Pargoimex Vario LF3 low-floor articulated	M1
Pragoimex VV60LF low-floor	T2

In peak service: Not currently available

Prague

Population: 1.17 million (2005 estimate)

Public transport

Bus, tramway and metro services provided by municipally owned corporation, some bus services contracted from private operators. Suburban services by state-owned Czech Railways and private bus operators.

Dopravní podnik hlavního města Prahy, akciová společnost – Prague Public Transit Co Inc

Sokolovská 217/42, CZ-190 22 Prague 9, Czech Republic
Tel: (+420 2) 96 19 20 00
Fax: (+420 2) 96 19 20 03
e-mail: Vrancikovam@dpp.cz (Marketing Department)
Web: www.dpp.cz

Key personnel

General Manager: Tomáš Jílek
Metro Operations Unit Manager: Ladislav Urbánek
Metro Rolling Stock Management Unit Manager: Josef Němeček
Metro Wayside Unit Manager: Jaroslav Šubert
Tram Operation Unit Manager: Petr Hloch
Tram Rolling Stock Management Unit Manager: Jan Doubek
Tram Wayside Unit Manager: Jan Founě
Bus Operation Unit Manager: Václav Jelínek
Bus Fleet Management Unit Manager: Jiřá Pilař
    Staff: 12,594 (as at 31 December 2006)

Passenger journeys: (2001) 1,104 million
(2002) 1,116 million
(2003) 1,130 million
(2004) 1,161 million
(2005) 1,147 million

Current situation

The company is currently aiming to improve services in suburban areas as the city grows. New tramways and metro lines are under construction with others planned. The fleet, in particular the bus fleet, is being renewed to give better access for people with reduced mobility.

Developments

In 2003, a newly developed tram line was opened, connecting the city centre with a densely populated residential area in the southwestern part of the city, formerly serviced only by overloaded buses.
    An extension with three stations (Střížkov-Prosek-Letňay) and 4.6 km of track is being developed from the current temporary terminus (Ládví). The project is scheduled to be completed at the beginning of 2008.

Fare structure: Flat rate for single tickets valid for 15 min (no transfer) and 90 min (with transfer) within Prague inner and outer zones P and 0; 24 h, 3- and 15-day, monthly, 3-monthly and yearly passes and season tickets with optional commencement of validity period; concessions for children, students, elderly and military
Fare collection: Prepurchase tickets with electronic validation on buses, metro and trams; most passengers use passes
Fare evasion control: Inspectors on board and in paid station areas
Arrangements for elderly/disabled: Some special bus services; 25 per cent of the bus fleet is low-floor; electronic information system for blind persons
Operating costs financed by: Fares 25 per cent, other sources 6 per cent, subsidy/grants 69 per cent

Bus
Staff: 3,640

Passenger journeys: (2001) 329 million
(2002) 341 million
(2003) 337 million
(2004) 322 million
(2005) 293 million
Vehicle-km: (2001) 63 million
(2002) 65 million
(2003) 65 million
(2004) 62 million
(2005) 62 million

Number of routes: 193 (14 night routes)
Route length: 2,084 km

Fleet: 1,248 vehicles (as at 31 December 2006)

Karosa B731	80
Karosa B951	131
Karosa B732, B732R	158
Karosa B732 accessible	7
Karosa B741 articulated	69
Karosa B961	31
Karosa B931	198
Karosa B941 articulated	175
Karosa C734/C734R	7
Karosa C934	1
Karosa Citybus	330
Karosa Citybus articulated	53
Neoplan N-4014	2
Ikarus midi E91	6
In peak service: 946	

Most intensive service: Peak 2.4 min
One-person operation: All routes
Arrangements for disabled/elderly: As of 31 December 2005, the total number of low-floor buses was 374, all of them equipped with holding ramps at central door to enable access for wheelchairs.
Average peak-hour speed: 26.1 km/h

Metro
Staff: 3,814

Type of operation: Full metro, initial route opened 1974

Passenger journeys: (2001) 442 million
(2002) 416 million
(2003) 459 million
(2004) 496 million
(2005) 515 million

Route length: 54.7 km
Number of lines: 3
Number of stations: 54
Gauge: 1,435 mm
Tunnel: Cut-and-cover and bored; over the Nusle valley metro tunnel incorporated beneath highway on Nusle bridge, 43 m above ground
Electrification: 750 V DC, bottom-contact third rail

Current situation

Construction on the extension from Ládví to Letňay on Line C started in 2004, with completion scheduled for 2008. The extension will be 4.6 km long with three new stations.

Developments

In May 2006, an extension to Line A, from Skalka to the Depo Hostivař station, was opened. The new station has park-and-ride facilities.
    Security on the metro network is to be improved, including CCTV, turnstiles, pass and ticket scanners to detect explosives and air monitors for toxic gases.
    Long-term plans include a new Line D, to link Náměstí Míru and Nové Dvory, a semi-circular Line E and extensions at both ends of Line A.

Rolling stock: 741 trains

Mytischy 81-71	251
Mytischy 81-71 (reconstructed by Škoda)	250
Siemens M1	240
In peak service: Not currently available	
On order: None	

Service: Peak 2 min
First/last train: 05.00/24.00
Signalling: Automatic block; ATP
Centralised control: Radio communication with trains individually or en masse

Tramway
Staff: 3,343

Type of operation: Conventional tramway, with new light rail sections

Passenger journeys: (2001) 332 million
(2002) 358 million
(2003) 335 million
(2004) 335 million
(2005) 340 million
Car-km: (2001) 46 million
(2002) 49 million
(2003) 48 million
(2004) 49.7 million
(2005) 49 million

Irisbus and Karosa buses on Route 130 at Plzenska (Ken Harris)   0585170

Newly completed Type M1 metro car at the Siemens SKV plant, Prague (Ken Harris)   0585171

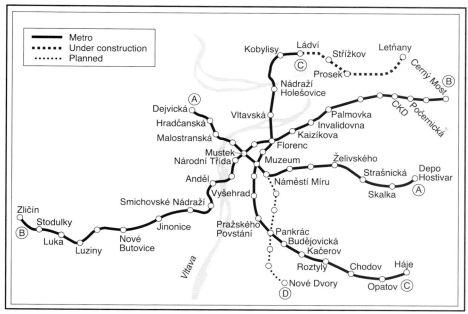

Map of Prague metro   1115286

Tram on Route 9 in front of the National Theatre, Prague   0530140

Number of lines: 35 (nine night)
Route length: 559 km
Number of stops: 628
Gauge: 1,435 mm
Electrification: 600 V DC, overhead

Service: Peak 4–12 min
First/last car: 04.30/24.00 (day service); night service runs every 30 min with timed transfers at interchanges
One-person operation: All cars

Developments
An extension to the Barrandov housing estate in the southwestern suburbs was opened in 2003 (3.5 km, six stations).

In early 2004, Škoda was awarded a contract to deliver 20 14T trams starting in 2005. There is an option for a further 40 vehicles.

In early 2005, some of the T3 vehicles were rebuilt.

In late 2005, Pars Komponenty sro (previously Pars Holding sro Sumperk) was awarded a nine-year contract to refurbish the fleet of Tatra KT8 trams, including the replacement of the centre sections with low-floor sections.

Under a programme started in 2006, some of the Tatra T3 cars are being retrofitted with a low-floor area at the centre doorway.

Rolling stock: 972 cars

Tatra T3, T3R.P, T3PLF	M366
Tatra T3M	M95
Tatra T3SU	M289
Tatra KT8D5, KT8N2	M47
Tatra T6A5	M151
Tatra RT6N	M4
Škoda 14T	M20

On order: There is an option for a further 40 Skoda 30 m five-section low-floor 14T trams
In peak service: Not currently available

Funicular climbing Petrin Hill   0530142

Funicular
Current situation
The 510 m funicular which climbs Petrin Hill carries 1.3 million passengers annually.

České Dráhy as (ČD)
Nábřeží Ludvíka Svobody 1222/12, CZ-110
15 Prague 1, Czech Republic
Tel: (+420 972) 21 11 11; 23 29 99
Fax: (+420 972) 23 20 81
e-mail: press@cd.cz
Web: www.cd.cz

Key personnel
Chairman, Steering Committee: Antonin Tesarik
Chairman, Supervisory Board: Vojtech Kocourek
Chairman and Director General: Petr Kousal
First Deputy Director General: Josef Bazala
Deputy Director General, Economy: Ivan Foltyn
Deputy Director General, Transport and Operations: Jiri Kloutvor
Deputy Director General, Infrastructure: Vlastimil Nesetril
Director, Passenger Transport: Jiri Kafka

Type of operation: Suburban heavy rail

Current situation
Services provided on eight routes, partially electrified, to a distance of about 60 km. Regular services are provided every 30 minutes in peak hours and every 60 minutes off-peak.

Developments
Improved service is to be offered on the line to Kladno (37.5 km), which is to be upgraded and electrified by a private company, PRAK. Two branches are proposed for construction, to Ruzyne international airport and Kladno town centre.

On 1 January 2003, the company was restructured and became the Czech Railways joint stock company (100 per cent owned by the state). The company operates regional passenger transport under contract to the regional authorities.

Denmark

Aarhus
Population: City 296,300, metropolitan area 739,000 (2006 estimates)

Public transport
Bus services provided by municipal undertaking; limited local and regional train service provided by Danske Statsbaner (DSB) – Danish State Railways.

Midttrafik
Søren Nymarks Vey 3, DK-8270 Høbjerg, Denmark

Tel: (+45) 87 40 82 00
Fax: (+45) 87 40 82 01
e-mail: midttrafik@midttrafik.dk
Web: www.midttrafik.dk

Key personnel
Director: Jens Erik Sørensen

Vice-Director: Ms Mette Julbo
Staff: 120 (estimate)

Current situation
Since January 2007, Midttrafik, formed by a merger of Aarhus Sporveje and two other public transport operators, has co-ordinated bus operations in the Midtjylland region. Services cover 19 municipalities and a population of some 1.2 million, including Aarhus.

As well as local, regional and express fixed route operations, the organisation also provides paratransit services, with an estimated 146,000 trips in 2007.

Midttrafik also co-ordinates the operations of Midtjyske Jernbaner A/S, two local railways, Odderbanen (www.odderbanen.dk), connecting Aarhus and Odder and Lemvigbanen (www.lemvigbanen.dk), connecting Holstebro-Lemvig-Thyborøn. For further information, please see *Jane's World Railways.*

Developments
Midttrafik plans to introduce new ticketing machines.

Bus
Passenger journeys: (2007) 90 million (estimate)
Vehicle-km: (2007) Not currently available

Number of routes: 400 (estimate)
Route length: Not currently available

Fleet: 1,161 vehicles
Breakdown of fleet is not currently available
In peak service: Not currently available
On order: Not currently available

Most intensive service: 7 to 8 min
One-person operation: All routes
Fare collection: Self-service with Autelca B-20 ticket vending machines, Almex M canceller, all on board

Fare structure: Zonal, with single and multitickets and season cards; 'klippekort' 10-ride ticket; free transfer to local trains and regional buses and free transfer from regional trains; reduced fare for those under 16
Fares collected on board: 9.6 per cent (68.6 per cent of passengers use passes, 21.8 per cent multitickets)
Fare evasion control: 24 inspectors (plus two in flexible jobs, partly inspectors/bus drivers)
Operational control: Mobile radio
Arrangements for elderly/disabled: Price reduction on season cards financed under social law
Average distance between stops: 500 m
Average peak-hour speed: In mixed traffic, 27.02 km/h
Bus priority: 9.3 km bus lanes
Operating costs financed by: Fares 33.1 per cent, other commercial sources 1.5 per cent, subsidy/grants 65.4 per cent
Subsidy from: Local council taxation
New vehicles financed by: Operating budget

Danske Statsbaner (DSB) – Danish State Railways
DSB Communications
Sølvgade 40, DK-1349 Copenhagen K, Denmark
Tel: (+45) 33 14 04 00
Fax: (+45) 33 54 42 40
e-mail: molsted@dsb.dk
dsbkomm@dsbkomm.dsb.dk
Web: www.dsb.dk

Key personnel
President and Chief Executive Officer: Søren Eriksen
Division Directors:
  Main-Line and Regional Trains: Frank Olesen
Commercial: Mogens Jønck
  Staff: 9,200 (Group total)

Type of operation: Suburban and regional services (plus long-distance services)

Background
On 1 January 1997, DSB was split in two: infrastructure was allocated to a new company, Banestyrelsen, while DSB continues to operate trains. Since the sale of its freight division to the Railion Group in 2001, DSB has been entirely a passenger operator and accounts for 80 per cent of total Danish passenger traffic; the remainder is carried by smaller 'local' railway companies and by Arriva Tog.

Since January 2000, private companies have been able to provide passenger services in competition with DSB, subject to capacity. There are two types of passenger transport carried out as a public service: 'negotiated' transport and 'tendered' transport. All services not offered for tender are handled as negotiated transport.

Since 1 January 1999, DSB has been an independent publicly owned corporation which operates services under contract to the Ministry of Transport. DSB receives no other public funds: costs and investment are financed from operating income and loans.

A contract covering a 10-year period starting in 2005 was agreed between DSB and the Ministry of Transport in late 2003. DSB will receive DKK2.4 billion a year compared with DKK2.8 billion in 2005. There will be a rise in train-km of 26 per cent but provision has been made to allow franchises to be sought for up to one third of regional services.

For further information on DSB, please see main entry under Copenhagen in *Jane's Urban Transport Systems* and in *Jane's World Railways.*

Current situation
Provides limited suburban services around Aarhus (Århus).

Copenhagen
Population: City 656,582; Metropolitan area 2.8 million (2008 estimates)

Public transport
All bus services and six local railways in the metropolitan area are planned and co-ordinated by the public authority Trafikselskabet Movia – Movia Public Transport (previously Hovedstadens Udviklingsråd (HUR) – the Greater Copenhagen Authority). The area is also served by local and regional trains of Danish State Railways (DSB). The common fare system allows for transfer between buses and trains throughout the region. Metro.

Rejsekort AS – The Travel Card Ltd
Borgergade 14, 3. 1300 Copenhagen K, Denmark
Tel: (+45) 33 43 24 00
e-mail: REKO@rejsekort.dk
Web: www.rejsekort.dk

Key personnel
Project Manager: Thomas Boe Bramsen

Background
Danish transport authorities, including Trafikselskabet Movia, Danish State Railways (DSB), and Ørestad Development Corporation – The Metro (Ørestadsselskabet), together with a number of county transport companies, are pursuing a project to introduce a smartcard-based integrated transit fare collection system, known as Rejsekort, which is intended to cover the whole of Denmark, starting with the Greater Copenhagen region, in 2009.

In 2003, Rejsekort AS (The Travel Card Ltd) was founded by the transport organisations listed above. The company will be responsible for carrying out the tender process for the system,

entering into a single contract with the system supplier, being the formal travel card issuer and entering into a participation contract with the individual participating transport companies (the users).

Trafikselskabet Movia – Movia Public Transport
Gammel Køge Landevej 3, DK-2500 Valby, Denmark
Tel: (+45) 36 13 14 00   Fax: (+45) 36 13 20 97
e-mail: moviatrafik@moviatrafik.dk
Web: www.moviatrafik.dk

Key personnel
Chairman, Movia Public Transport: Finn Aaberg
Vice-Chairmen, Movia Public Transport: Knud Larsen
Executive Director: Johannes Sloth
  Staff: 328

Background
Movia Public Transport is a politically governed organisation responsible for the planning and tendering of bus, local train and disabled (paratransit) services in the two regions covering the eastern part of Denmark (the Capital Region and the Zeeland Region).

The two regions cover the costs of Movia's administration expenses and the deficit for local train and regional bus services. The level of service is decided by the regions.

The 45 municipalities in the Movia area cover the deficit for local bus services. The level of service is decided by each municipality.

Movia is governed by a nine-member board, seven members of which represent municipalities and two who represent the regions.

Regional, including S-trains, and national trains are the responsibility of the Danish State

Railways, whilst the Copenhagen metro is the responsibility of the Metro company.

Current situation
Movia Public Transport provides services in a metropolitan area of some 1.8 million people and some 3,000 km².

Developments
Movia Public Transport, in collaboration with DSB, the Metro company and the Danish counties, is planning to replace the existing ticket system with a smartcard system in 2009. The new stored-value cards will be valid anywhere in the country.

Bus
Current situation
Bus services are subject to tender and are run by 11 private operators.

Principal operators:

Arriva Skandinavien AS
Skøjtevej 26, DK-2770 Kastrup, Denmark
Tel: (+45) 72 30 25 00
Fax: (+45) 72 30 25 01
Web: www.arriva.co.uk

Key personnel
Managing Director: Johnny Hansen

Background
In 1997 Arriva acquired Unibus, which ran scheduled bus routes in Copenhagen, school bus services and transport services for people with disabilities. This was followed with the purchase of Silkeborg Bybusser and in March 1999, Arriva acquired Bus Danmark, one of the country's largest bus operators.

Now with around a third of the bus market, Arriva is the largest provider of bus services in Denmark.

City-Trafik AS

Thorvald Borgsgade 2-4, DK-2300 Copenhagen S, Denmark
Tel: (+45) 32 96 19 16   Fax: (+45) 32 96 21 16

Developments
In March 2004, City-Trafic won a six-year contract, with a two-year option, to operate six bus routes.

De Hvide Busser AS

Portusvej 6c, DK-3490 Kvistgård, Denmark
Tel: (+45) 45 86 28 86   Fax: (+45) 45 76 69 76
e-mail: hil@dhb.dk
Web: www.dhb.dk

Fjordbus AS

Fabriksvangen 25, Postboks 109, DK-3550 Slangerup, Denmark
Tel: (+45) 47 38 02 00   Fax: (+45) 47 38 02 82
e-mail: fjordbus@fjordbus.dk
Web: www.fjordbus.dk

Netbus AS

Stamholmen 217, DK-2650 Hvidovre, Denmark
Tel: (+45) 70 10 00 40   Fax: (+45) 33 21 03 04
e-mail: mail@netbus.dk
Web: www.netbus.dk

Partner Bus AS

Industrivej 22, DK-4050 Skibby, Denmark
Tel: (+45) 47 52 88 32   Fax: (+45) 47 52 79 35

Østtrafik AS

Stationsvej 2, Hårlev Street, DK-4652 Hårlev, Denmark
Tel: (+45) 70 10 60 23   Fax: (+45) 56 29 31 01
e-mail: post@oesttrafik.dk
Web: www.oesttrafik.dk

Managing Director: Bent M Larsen
Fleet: Approx 40 buses

Da Blå Omnibusser AS

Skovlytoften 36, DK-2840 Holte, Denmark
Tel: (+45) 45 42 01 77
Fax: (+45) 45 42 30 38

Dito Bus AS

KP Danøsvej 2, DK-4300 Holbæk, Denmark
Tel: (+45) 59 44 07 86

Kruse AS

Skydebanevej 2, DK-4900 Nakskov, Denmark
Tel: (+45) 45 76 69 76

Anchars Rute AS

Østre Teglgade 2, DK-2450 Copenhagen SV, Denmark
Tel: (+45) 38 88 10 50
Fax: (+45) 38 88 10 51

Concordia Bus Danmark AS

Swebus AB, Storg Varugatan 1, SE-2119 Malmo, Sweden
Tel: (+46) 40 10 72 81

Summary of Movia Public Transport (previously HUR) information

Passenger journeys:(2004) 238 million
(2005) 235 million
(2006) 236 million
(2007) 225 million
Vehicle-km: Not currently available

Number of routes: 590
Route length: 12,372 km
Bus hours: (2007) 4.1 million

Fleet: 1,351 buses
12 m single-deck	1,042
13.7 m single-deck	243
Articulated	4
Double-deck	19
Tele-bus vehicles	26
Harbour bus	2
Service bus (9–10 m)	17

In peak service: Not currently available
Average age of fleet: 6.5 years

Most intensive service: 3 min
One-person operation: All services
Fare collection: Preprinted tickets issued by driver with manually operated ticket machine; 10-clip cards and monthly passes sold at approximately 700 outlets. Monthly passes only available in a limited number of outlets.
Fare structure: Zonal; all tickets valid for free transfer between buses and between bus and rail; cash tickets, 10-clip cards and monthly passes exist. Tourist cards including bus and rail travel and admissions to attractions
Allocation of sales: 69 per cent of all sales are made from the trains sales organisation (train stations), 27 per cent from the buses sales organisation and four per cent from the metro sales organisation (metro stations)
Fares collected on board: 51 per cent of all single ticket income is generated on board buses
Fare evasion control: On-the-spot penalty payment to inspectors (Fine: EUR80)
Operational control: Route inspectors/mobile radio/traffic centre
Arrangements for elderly/disabled: Three month off-peak hour passes at approximately one-tenth of the normal adult price for persons over the age of 65; special fare scheme for the disabled
Operating costs financed by: Fares and public funds

Local/regional rail services

Lokalbanen AS

e-mail: kundeservice@lokalbanen.dk
Web: www.lokalbanen.dk

Background
Lokalbanen AS is a wholly owned subsidiary of Movia Public Transport and is the operating company responsible for the eight local/regional railways, for which Movia Public Transport assumed responsibility in 2002. These include the Frederiksværkbanen, Gribskovbanen (two lines), Hornbækbanen, Nærumbanen, Lille Nord and Østbanen.

The company responsible for the infrastructure is Hovedstadens Lokalbaner AS (HL).

Developments
In late 2005, the company awarded a EUR77 million contract to Alstom for 27 transit trainsets to be used in the greater Copenhagen region. The first delivery took place in late 2006, and the final delivery took place in late 2007.

Banedanmark – Rail Net Denmark

Amerika Plads 15, DK-2100 Copenhagen Ø, Denmark
Tel: (+45) 82 34 00 00   Fax: (+45) 82 34 45 72
e-mail: banedanmark@bane.dk
Web: www.banedanmark.dk

Key personnel
Chief Executive Officer: Jesper Hansen
Chief Operating Officer: Susan Münster
Chief Financial Officer: Søren Stahlfest Møller
Deputy Director of Human Resources: Charlotte Smidt
Deputy Director of Contracting: Søren Horn Petersen
Safety and Quality Manager: Ole Christensen
Manager, Management Secretariat: Kirsten Hestbæk Berthelsen
Public Relations Manager: Inger Petersen Thalund
Resignalling Project Manager: Morten Søndergaard
Strategy Manager: Per Lindholm Larsen
Internal Auditor: Henning H Larsen
Staff: 2,060 (total employees as at 31 December 2007)

Regional and suburban rail
Background
As a result of legislation in the Danish parliament, DSB (Danish State Railways) was split in two on 1 January 1997: DSB continued to operate trains (please see separate entry), while the newly formed Banestyrelsen (now Banedanmark) took over responsibility for the infrastructure, traffic control, capacity management and planning. From 1 January 1999, freight operators have been allowed 'open access' to the national network and similar rights have been available to passenger operators to compete with DSB since 1 January 2000.

Banedanmark is required to seek tenders for work on the infrastructure throughout the network from outside companies. The contracting division is at 'arms' length' from the main company in order for it to be able to compete for contracts and has its own sales staff.

In 2003, Banestyrelsen's Strategic Planning Unit was transferred to the National Rail Authority and on 1 March 2004 Banestyrelsen was renamed Banedanmark.

Current situation
Regional services link Copenhagen with northwestern, western and southern Zealand via Roskilde (three routes). Suburban services link Copenhagen with Roskilde, Helsingør and Copenhagen Airport, Kastrup. Another service links Roskilde with Copenhagen Airport, Kastrup. Local services link Roskilde with Næstved via Køge.

The 169 route-km Copenhagen suburban S-Train system operates on 1.5 kV DC overhead supply.

On 2 July 2000, service began on The Øresund fixed link together with a common ticketing system, covering train and bus in the region. After delivery of all the ordered 27 purpose-built emus in 2001, an integrated local service in the Øresund region was inaugurated on the 17 June 2001, consisting of a traffic system combining the suburban services from Helsingør to Malmö every 20 minutes.

For further information, please see full entry in *Jane's World Railways.*

Developments
On the S-Train network, doubling of the Frederikssund line was completed in 2002 and a new interchange opened at Flintholm in January 2004. The Copenhagen Ring Line was extended south from Flintholm to a temporary terminus in January 2005 and reached its eventual terminus at Ny Ellebjerg in 2007. Work to increase train speeds throughout the S-Train network is also in progress. Construction of a fourth S-Train line westwards out of Copenhagen Central station started in September 2008 and is expected to be completed by the end of 2010.

Østerport station, Copenhagen, where, in 2005, Banedanmark completed improvements to facilities for terminating services. Featured in this view is a Bombardier-built push-pull set powered by a DSB Class ME diesel-electric locomotive (Ken Harris)
1122869

A new traffic control centre for the Copenhagen S-Train was opened in 2007.

In late 2008, Banedanmark is expected to present a proposal for total replacement of the signalling system on the S-Train system by 2020 to the Danish Government. The system is most likely to use a standard communications-based train control system.

Danske Statsbaner (DSB) – Danish State Railways

DSB Communications
Sølvgade 40, Copenhagen K, DK-1349, Denmark
Tel: (+45) 33 14 04 00
Fax: (+45) 33 14 04 40
e-mail: molsted@dsb.dk
    dsbkomm@dsbkomm.dsb.dk
Web: www.dsb.dk

Key personnel

President and Chief Executive Officer: Søren Eriksen
    Staff: 9,200 (Group total)

Passenger journeys: (All passenger operations)
(2005) 153 million
(2006) 157 million
(2007) 158 million
Train-km: Not currently available

Background

On 1 January 1997 the Danish State Railways organisation (DSB) was split in two: infrastructure was allocated to a new company, Banestyrelsen, while DSB retained operation of the trains. Since the sale of its freight division to the Railion Group in 2001, DSB has been entirely a passenger operator and accounts for 80 per cent of total Danish passenger traffic; the remainder is carried by smaller 'local' railway companies and by Arriva Tog.

Since January 2000, private companies have been able to provide passenger services in competition with DSB, subject to capacity. There are two types of passenger transport carried out as a public service: 'negotiated' transport and 'tendered' transport. All services not offered for tender are handled as negotiated transport.

Since 1 January 1999, DSB has been an independent publicly owned corporation which operates services under contract to the Ministry of Transport. DSB S-Train has been a wholly owned subsidiary of DSB since 1 January 1999 and its services are covered by a separate contract. DSB receives no other public funds: costs and investment are financed from operating income and loans.

A contract covering a 10-year period starting in 2005 was agreed between DSB and the Ministry of Transport in late 2003. DSB will receive DKK2.4 billion a year compared with DKK2.8 billion in 2005. There will be a rise in train-km of 26 per cent but provision has been made to allow franchises to be sought for up to one-third of regional services.

For further information on DSB, please see *Jane's World Railways.*

DSB S-tog a/s (S-Train)

Address as above
e-mail: s-tog@s-tog.dsb.dk
Web: www.dsb.dk/stog

Key personnel

Division Director and Managing Director, DSB S-tog a/s: Gert Frost
    Staff: 1,829 (2007)

Type of operation: Suburban rail (S-Train)

Passenger journeys: (2004) 89.6 million
(2005) 89.7 million
(2006) 90.4 million
(2007) 88.6 million
Train-km: (2006) 15.5 million
(2007) 15.0 million

S-Train emus at Copenhagen Central station (Ken Harris)   1156478

Operating costs financed by: Fares 59.7 per cent, other commercial sources three per cent, national subsidies 37.3 per cent

Current situation

DSB S-tog a/s (S-Train) is a wholly-owned subsidiary of DSB that provides suburban passenger services over 172 km, 1,435 mm gauge of independent 1.5 kV DC lines in the Greater Copenhagen area. Operation of the Hillerød-Helsingør 'Lille Nord' line passed to the local railway at the beginning of 2007. Fare levels are set by regional traffic authority Movia.

A 10-year contract for provision of S-Train services for the period 2005-14 contains targets for service levels and punctuality; it will also see an increase in train-km of 13 per cent. The contract specifies the amount of support to be paid by the Ministry of Transport and Power. In 2007 this was DKK1,422 million, but it will fall to around DKK800 million by 2014. A pre-tax profit of DKK188 million was made in 2007.

Developments

In January 2007, the Ring Line was completed when the final terminus at Ny Ellebjerg in the south of the city was completed. The project started in 1998 and consists of a double-track line that connects with other S-Train lines at Hellerup, Ryparken, Flintholm, Danshøj and Ny Ellebjerg. It also connects with the Copenhagen Metro at Flintholm.

The timetable was reorganised in September 2007 and is based on six routes with a 10-minute interval service in the daytime on weekdays and a 20-minute interval service at other times.

The upgrading of Copenhagen Central Station continues with investments in buildings, stations and maintenance of trains.

Rolling stock: 104 eight-car and 31 four-car emus
ALSTOM-LHB/Siemens SA/SB/SC/SD
    (1995)   M624T208
ALSTOM/Siemens SE/SF/SG/SH (2005)   M93T31

Current situation

The system is operated by 104 eight-car single-axle articulated emus and 31 similar four-car emus delivered 1995-2006 by ALSTOM (formerly Linke-Hoffmann-Busch) and Siemens: one eight-car set has been withdrawn.

Ørestadsselskabet – Ørestad Development Corporation

Arne Jacobsen Alle 17, DK-2300 Copenhagen S, Denmark
Tel: (+45) 33 11 17 00   Fax: (+45) 33 11 23 01
e-mail: info@m.dk, orestad@orestad.dk
Web: www.m.dk, www.orestad.dk

Key personnel

Manager of Planning: Lene Skytte

Type of operation: Metro, first line opened October 2002

Passenger journeys: (2005) 44 million (estimate)

No of lines:	2
Route length:	16.8 km
in tunnel:	9 km
No of stations:	17
in tunnel:	9

Electrification: 750 V DC, third rail

Current situation

Phase 1, between Nørreport and Vestamager/Lergravsparken, has been operational since October 2002. Two further sections have been opened – Nørreport to Frederiksberg (May 2003) and Frederiksberg to Vanløse (October 2003).

The Copenhagen metro is a fully automated high-frequency train system that operates around the clock. Underground stations have platform screen doors.

Developments

The next phase is to be a link between Lerravsparken and the airport (Lufthavn) (Østamagerbanen), which is due to open in late 2007. When this phase is completed, the system will extend to 21 km (9 km in tunnel) with 22 stations, nine of which are underground. Ansaldo Trasporti will operate the system for the first five years.

The metro was developed simultaneously with a new urban development – Ørestad – an area close to Copenhagen's international airport on Amager island.

Two further lines, M3 and M4, have been proposed to create a City Ring circle line. These new lines would be fully-automated and run in tunnel. Daily ridership is predicted to be some 275,000 per day. The project is scheduled to be completed in 2017.

Vestamager-bound service approaching Universitete station on Line M1 (Ken Harris)   1158682

The Rejsekort, a new integrated electronic smartcard system, is expected to be tested during 2007, with full implementation nationwide by 2009.

Rolling stock: 34 three-car Ansaldo trains

Most intensive service: 2 min (peak); 15 min (night)

Fare structure: Zonal; 10-trip, daily, weekly and monthly passes

Arrangements for disabled/elderly:
Trains are fully accessible. All stations have a lift
Centralised control: Control and Maintenance Centre (CMC); ATP; ATO; ATS

Ecuador

Quito

Population: City 1.5 million (2005 estimate), metropolitan area 1.8 million (2001 Census)

Public transport
Bus, including Ecovía and Metrobús BRT systems, and minibus services mostly provided by independent operators forming route or area associations and co-operatives, supervised by the municipality. Municipal services also operate some routes; trolleybus routes. Light rail planned.

Empresa Metropolitana de Servicios y Administración del Transporte (EMSAT)
Avenida 10 de Agosto N35-108 e Ignacio San María, Quito, Ecuador
Tel: (+593 2) 224 20 26, 243 26 27, 225 67 67
Fax: (+593 2) 243 26 43, 246 28 32
e-mail: emsat@quito.gov.ec
Web: www.quito.gov.ec

Key personnel
General Manager: Ms Cecilia Gárante Correa
Director of Administration and Finance: Mariana Bravo de Aguirre
Contact: Ms Yadira Helou
   Staff: Not currently available

Passenger journeys: (Metropolitan District figures) 1.4 million (daily estimate)
Vehicle-km: Not currently available

Background
The city of Quito set up the Empresa Metropolitana de Servicios y Administración del Transporte (EMSAT) through Municipal By-Law No. 055 of 13 July 2001.

Current situation
The Metropolitan Company is responsible for the management, co-ordination, administration, implementation and auditing of the traffic and transport system in the Metropolitan District of Quito, and is supported by a highly professional and experienced technical team in order to guarantee the continuous improvement of mobility conditions for the population, in conjunction with the active participation of the players involved.

The City of Quito is characterised by complex geographical and topographical contours which result in limited available road capacity and which, together with a vast increase in the number of motor vehicles and the poor operational structure of the public transport system, with excessive travelling times, high-cost operations, congestion and air pollution, generate serious mobility and accessibility problems for the population.

Confronted with this situation, the current city administration, led by Mayor Paco Moncayo, established from the year 2000 onwards a policy to prioritise the use of public transport, in view of the fact that 78 per cent of journeys are made using this system.

The strategic planning for the field of mobility is outlined in the Plan Equinoccio 21 (Equinox 21 Plan – a strategic development plan for the city up to 2025), in the Plan General de Desarrollo Territorial (PGDT) (General Plan for Territorial Development), in the Plan de Uso y Ocupación del Suelo (PUOS) (Plan for the use and occupation

of land) and in the Plan Maestro de Transporte y Vialidad (PMTV) (Master Plan for Transport and Traffic), which are due to be rolled out in the next 20 years in the Metropolitan District of Quito, which will, it is estimated, have some 3,300,000 inhabitants.

The axis that provides the city's mobility is the Integrated Public Transport System, MetrobusQ.

The MetrobusQ system is Quito's Integrated Public Transport Network made up of high capacity trunk feeder corridors, both in the central urban area and in the metropolitan zones. The network also has a system of pre-established stops, transfer stations and terminals, forming part of an operation that is integrated both physically and in terms of its fare system.

The system has been implemented progressively from 1995 onwards, with the operation of the Central Trolleybus Corridor (Green Line), with a passenger base of approximately 240,000. In 2002, the north-east Ecovía corridor (Red Line) went into operation, moving 96,000 passengers, and in 2005, operations began on the central corridor Norte América-Prensa-Diego de Vásquez, (Blue Line), serving 270,000 passengers, including services on the Metropolitan corridor Mitad del Mundo and the sub-trunk feeder route Amazonas.

The MetrobusQ System transports approximately 600,000 passengers per day. Its extension and modernisation have been the priority task in the present administration, achieving improvement through a process of incorporating new systems of fare collection, journey recording, scheduling and operations control.

The Council has thus achieved sustained and constant work on mobility and transport, with two key themes: extension and improvement of roads and integration of the transport systems. The objective is to encourage the use of quality public transport, thus reducing congestion and pollution and reclaiming the streets for pedestrians.

For the first time in history, the city of Quito will have an integrated system in that citizens will be able to use feeders and exclusive corridors such as the MetrobusQ. It is currently being implemented, under the guidelines and policies established in the Transport Master Plan. The plan envisages implementation of longitudinal trunk routes and transverse sub-trunk routes in the southern sector of the city, from the sector Seminario Mayor in the west and la Marín in the East, to the southern limit of the DMQ (Metropolitan District of Quito), operating in exclusive lanes, with pre-established stops and operated by articulated buses on trunk routes and type I and II buses on feeder services.

Implementation of the MetrobusQ system began in December 1995 using the Avenida 10 de Agosto corridor, as a trolleybus system with 13 articulated units (capacity: 180 people), and in 1996, 77 trolleybuses were incorporated into the system and the service route was extended until, in May 2000, the route from the extreme north to the south of the district was completed, giving a length of 16.2 km of trunk route and 90 conventional units in 16 feeder routes.

Within the same scheme, operations began in 2001 on the Ecovía corridor from the Avenida 6 de Diciembre, with a length of 9.4 km on its trunk axis. The service is provided by 42 articulated buses and 35 feeder buses on about seven routes.

In November 2004, the central north corridor began operations, in addition to the América

corridor, with a fleet of 17 articulated buses, and the process of increasing the high capacity units continued until June 2006 when the fleet was completed. This major road corridor currently operates with 74 articulated vehicles and 17 feeder lines are run using 136 conventional units. The process of restructuring the system is continuing with the implementation of new feeder routes and extension of the service.

Developments
In August 2007, operations were due to start on the Sustainable System of the South, this being made up in its operational structure of the following corridors: south east (Guamaní-Maldonado-Seminario), south central (Quitumbe-Centro Histórico-Seminario), south west (Quitumbe-Mariscal Sucre-Seminario) and eastern peripheral (Guamaní-Simón Bolívar-Marín Valle); the sub-trunk feeder routes Alonso de Angulo and Rodrigo de Chávez; the system is also provided by transversal services, feeders and local services, which feed into and integrate with the various transfer stations, interchange stops and stops for trunk routes.

The population involved is 900,000 people and there are 12,492 urban hectares containing, among other things, infrastructure and relevant instances of land use: 530 industries, 500 educational establishments, 56 supply centres and 120 medical centres. The estimated coverage of demand is on average 1,370,000 journeys per day.

There are 32 public transport operators taking part in the project and they will be participating in a process of modernisation for the centralised management of operations using business management and administration mechanisms. A progressive implementation of the services on the Sustainable System of the South is planned, starting at the beginning of the second half of 2007 and running until the first half of 2010.

For it to operate effectively, there are plans to implement complementary traffic management systems which will make it possible to give priority to the circulation of public transport and of the main traffic axis in general and also to its immediate area of influence.

They will be equipped with a new centralised traffic signal system, which will guarantee efficient traffic operations, minimising delays at intersections, above all for public transport.

A horizontal and vertical traffic signal system has also been designed, together with the appropriate road safety infrastructure along the whole of the extension of the corridors and roads on which the feeder buses run in order to maintain control of the flow of vehicles and pedestrians.

In addition to the various fixtures on the corridors, such as stops and transfer stations, there will be an information system (signage) which will help to provide orientation and information to public transport users.

This system will run on three circuits initially. The advantages are:
• Increased coverage and improved quality of transport services;
• New route structure with integrated services;
• Microregional Terminals connecting Quito to the valleys (Rio Coca, La Marín, La Ofelia);
• Shorter journey times;
• More regular and more reliable services;
• Improvement of the quality of the environment with the introduction of high capacity

environment-friendly buses using new technology;
- Modernisation of transport companies;
- Fewer effects on traffic.

EMSAT also administers other commercial public transport services, such as taxis, schools transport, light commercial vehicles, institutional and tourist transport, which complement the Metropolitan Public Transport System. The management achieves this by issuing licences, operating permits and adhesive municipal registration discs, subject to compliance with the requirements that guarantee an adequate transport service to users.

EMSAT's aim is to provide a decent and reliable public transport system by processing and regulating commercial transport services, such as taxis, light commercial vehicles, school and tourist services, which, added to the vast Integrated Public Transport System, Metrobus-Q, allow the community to achieve mobility and generate productivity.

Studies of the supply and demand for the public transport service are being undertaken on about 115 conventional routes, which serve 612 sectors, and this coverage is extending as new conventional transport systems are implemented, as is the case with transport between local districts and freight transport.

Technical investigations by employees of the organisation, in conjunction with the Escuela Politécnica Nacional del Ecuador (National Polytechnic of Ecuador) and the Escuela Politécnica del Ejército (National Polytechnic for the Military) are making it possible to generate management plans for mechanical inspections of public and conventional transport, in addition to the compulsory vehicle checks, twice a year for units, an exercise that is being carried out in collaboration with CORPAIRE.

The system also includes the administration of the Microregional Terminals (La Marín, El Girón, Río Coca y La Ofelia) which link up the Integrated Public Transport System with the inter-district system, covering a demand from 90,000 users. The Transition Plan for the operation of the Interprovincial Terminals at Quitumbe and Carapungo, envisaged by the Transport Master Plan, will go into effect.

The Conventional Transport service network is made up of a fleet of 2,628 urban buses, belonging to 54 operators and 500 inter-district units, with 17 operators, which together generate 1,384,000 daily journeys in the Metropolitan District of Quito. Like all public transport units in the Metropolitan district, this fleet undergoes Vehicle Inspections twice a year in the CORPAIRE workshops, thus guaranteeing the optimum technical and mechanical conditions for the provision of the service.

As far as the infrastructure for the road network is concerned, EMSAT, in conjunction with the Dirección Metropolitana de Transporte (DMT) (Metropolitan Transport Office) and the Empresa Metropolitana de Obras Públicas (EMOPQ) (Metroplitan Company for Public Works), has planned and structured 'Geometrical Reforms' (of road layout), which will allow substantial improvement of the city's road network through the introduction of lanes for vehicles waiting to turn, modifying the road layout, for instance in terms of the layout of highways, flower beds, traffic islands, pavements, to which will be added traffic control facilities such that a safe, convenient and efficient flow of pedestrians and vehicles can be achieved, mainly at intersections and high-demand road sections where there are significant instances of accidents, congestion and conflicts.

The removal of the roundabouts will lead to a substantial improvement in the movement of vehicles and passengers in sectors that were the source of continual conflicts.

As a measure to optimise vehicle flow, a Contraflow system was applied. This allowed light commercial vehicles to use a Contraflow lane, so that there are three lanes in one direction (either north-south or south-north) and one lane in the opposite direction during the period assigned for contraflow, thus reducing traffic congestion

in critical sectors, especially at peak times in the morning and evening, achieving an increase in the speed of traffic flow and shortening journey times for users.

The introduction of contraflows requires the carrying out of traffic studies, the installation of horizontal and vertical signage for purposes of restriction, prevention and information provision, as well as coordination for their control by the National Police, which is the body responsible for traffic control in the District.

The signalling system controls and administers the intersections especially in the road corridors such as the exclusive trolleybus lane, the exclusive Ecovia lane, areas of influence and the central north corridor, which was recently incorporated in EMSAT. The city of Quito has around 690 traffic signal intersections, 350 of which are operated and controlled by EMSAT. In the future, all the intersections will be improved and will be incorporated in a modern Centralised Traffic Signal System for the Metropolitan district.

EMSAT is carrying out work on horizontal and vertical signing, to facilitate and direct the interaction of vehicle flows in accordance with traffic standards.

In co-ordination with the National Police, EMSAT annually carries out horizontal and vertical signing on the main intersections and road corridors in the city and in the districts of the DMQ (Metropolitan District of Quito), with the aim of providing road safety for drivers and pedestrians.

The work consists of installing road direction arrows, zebra crossings (pedestrian crossings), lane division lines, identification of bus stops, among other things with the main focus on pedestrian crossings and traffic light intersections.

At district level, the auditing of the public transport system and of the road network and its infrastructure falls within EMSAT's remit.

Auditing makes it possible to check compliance with what was set out in the operating permits as well as technical standards and regulations issued by EMSAT, which make it possible to evaluate the quality of service in the traffic and transport systems in the Metropolitan District of Quito.

In this context, the auditing exercises that are carried out in collaboration with other organisations and offices in the public sector linked or related to mobility establish guidelines and corrective measures that regulate the city's traffic and transport system.

Auditing of the public transport system includes:
- Checking compliance with the Operating Permit;
- Monitoring of operations: fleet, route, intervals/frequencies, stops, checking the demand;
- Supervision of the service Coordinating with the National Police to control vehicles that are illegally providing the transport service in the DMQ
- Co-ordinating with the Metropolitan Office for the Environment, CORPAIRE and the National Police to control environmental pollution generated by the transport system.

So that the system for auditing the management of public transport has positive results, a 'Base Line Phase' was implemented by putting in place electronic devices known as GPSs (Global Positioning Systems) in public transport units, an exercise which began in 2007.

Through these devices, the technical experts in the Auditing Office obtain in real time all the information relating to the operation of these public transport units from software installed in the organisation's central offices.

The installation of this software has resulted in a number of benefits for users and operators. Thus, users will be guaranteed departure and arrival timetables for the units, defined routes, stopping times, operating speed; number of buses per operator; location of the units, information on the operator, etc.

Operators will be able to rely on information on departure and arrival timetables at each station and stop in the system, on the speed at which they must run between each station and stop, stopping time, the distance covered by the

vehicle, excessive delays, stops that have not been made.

Furthermore, from the Operations Centre in which the screens and keyboards are located, it will be possible to send all the information about these factors, through a voice communication device with the driver, in order to inform and reassure users. The aim is to improve the public transport service substantially, guaranteeing the user a fast, safe and comfortable journey as well as ensuring that operators achieve adequate and correct operation of their unit that enables them to save on fuel, tyres and brakes and other vehicle components.

With this new technology consisting of on board diagnostics (OBD); Global Positioning Systems (GPS) and the Geographic Information System (GIS), EMSAT will in future be able to monitor all modes of transport that currently operate in the DMQ, that is: urban, inter-district, taxis, light commercial vehicles, school and tourist services, with the aim of guaranteeing a better service to the municipality.

Unidad Operadora del Sistema Trolebús (UOST) – Compañía Trolebus Quito SA

Avenida Maldonado s/n y Miguel Carrión, Sector El Recreo, Quito, Ecuador
Tel: (+593 2) 266 50 16, 18, 19, 22
Fax: (+593 2) 266 50 19
Web: www.trolebus.gov.ec

Key personnel
General Manager: Fuad M Tutillo
Staff: Not currently available

Type of operation: Bus and trolleybus

Passenger journeys: Not currently available
Vehicle-km: Not currently available

Number of routes: 16 (plus 6 trolleybus)
Route length: 16.2 km (El Trole)

Trolleybus electrification: 750 V DC

Current situation
The trolleybus system, the Ecovia system and some feeder bus routes, are operated by UOST. The unique trolleybus system, called El Trole, has been described as a rubber-tyred light rail line; light rail was rejected only on the grounds that vibration might harm historic buildings in the city centre. The route is entirely segregated and forms the city's central trunk route.

All passenger boarding and alighting is at high-platform enclosed 'stations', which give stepless access to the vehicles. New traffic signals were installed at 140 intersections along the route, with detectors beneath the road surface. All fare collection takes place off the vehicles, tickets being issued either on board the feeder buses or from vending machines and sales staff at the stations, which also have security personnel. Access to the 'platforms' is by turnstiles which accept the prepurchased tokens or tickets.

The estimated lifespan for the trolleybuses was originally projected to be 17 years, but the fleet has been used much more heavily that originally anticipated that UOST has shortened this to 15 years. This would indicate that the 54 oldest vehicles will be due for replacement in 2010.

Conversion of the entire line to light rail, in 2009, has now been proposed. This new system, Tren Rápido de Quito (TRAQ), would be 29.2 km long with 22 stations.

Fleet: 113 trolleybuses, semi- or fully dual-mode
Mercedes-Benz/Hispano Carrocera/AEG articulated, with auxiliary diesel engines (1995/96)   54
Mercedes-Benz/Hispano Carrocera/Adtranz articulated, dual-mode (1999/2000)   59
In peak service: 87

Most intensive service: Peak 1–1.5 min; off-peak 3–5 min
Operating costs financed by: Fares, 100 per cent

Egypt

Alexandria

Population: 4 million (estimate)

Public transport

Bus, light rail and tram services provided by Transport Authority responsible to Governor of Alexandria; suburban rail service run by state railway (ER); metro proposed.

Alexandria Passenger Transport Authority

PO Box 466, 3 Aflaton Street, El Shatby, 21111 Alexandria, Egypt
Tel: (+20 3) 597 52 23   Fax: (+20 3) 597 11 87
e-mail: apta@cns-egypt.com

Key personnel

Chairman: Medhat Hafez
Tel: (+20 3) 591 18 10; 592 52 23
    Staff: 8,754 (all modes)

Current situation

Two distinct tramway systems are operated – a network of street-running conventional lines in the west and south of the city and three light rail routes running into a terminus at Ramleh Square from the east.

Passenger journeys: (All modes)

(1999/2000) 293.9 million
(2000/01) 278.5 million
(2001/02) 275.8 million

Operating costs financed by: (All modes)

Fares 46 per cent, other commercial sources 6 per cent, subsidy/grants from government 48 per cent

Bus

Key personnel

Managing Director: Ahmed Abd Al-Khalek
General Managers: Mohamed Kamis
    Mortda Mohammed
    Ahmed Abo Hiba
    Atef Gurguis
    Staff: 3,982

Passenger journeys: (1999/2000) 122.1 million

(2000/01) 115.7 million
(2001/02) 118.6 million
Vehicle-km: (1999/2000) 51.5 million
(2000/01) 50.2 million
(2001/02) 45.9 million

Number of routes: 113
Route length: 2,383 km

Fleet: 684 vehicles

Nasr Man 976/1	225
Scania CLB 113	32
Volvo Kastor K315 B7	36
Renault Kastor K315 R12	30
Nasr 811	15
Man K 315 Kastor (air conditioned)	35
GM Egypt (mini)	43
Kastor K309 Deutz	59
Nasr 974/942 (mini)	76
Kastor K 309 Deutz (air conditioned)	15
MAN K309 (mini)	24
MAN K309 (midi)	4
Iveco	50
Cargo	39
Daewoo	1

New vehicles required each year: 75–100

One-person operation: On all minibus routes
Fare collection: Mostly conductors (seated)
Fare structure: Flat, with one class
Fare evasion control: Roving inspectors
Average peak-hour speed: 19 km/h
New vehicles financed by: State investments

Tram

Key personnel

Managing Director: Salah Mosa
General Manager, City Tramway: Mahasen Rami

Type of operation: Conventional tramway

Passenger journeys: (1999/2000) 94.1 million
(2000/01) 69.1 million
(2001/02) 66.4 million
Car-km: (1999/2000) 59.2 million
(2000/01) 59.5 million
(2001/02) 59.4 million

Route length: 28 km
Number of lines: 17
Gauge: 1,435 mm
Electrification: 600 V DC, overhead

Rolling stock: 151 cars

Duewag articulated (1966 ex-Copenhagen)	M91
Kinki/Toshiba	M15 T15
Ganz-Mávag/Duewag (1986)	M15 T15

Light rail (Ramleh lines)

Key personnel

General Manager: Mahmoud Ismail

Type of operation: Light rail, mostly on segregated route

Passenger journeys: (1999/2000) 77.7 million
(2000/01) 93.6 million
(2001/02) 90.8 million
Car-km: 22 million (annual)

Route length: 16 km
Number of lines: 3
Gauge: 1,435 mm
Electrification: 600 V DC, overhead

Rolling stock: 42 three-car sets

Kinki Sharyo/Toshiba (1976)	108
Kinki Sharyo double-deck (1994)	MC6
SEMAF (1995)	M12

Developments

Modernisation of track and catenary has been completed, along with installation of electronic signalling. New depot and workshops planned.
It is planned to upgrade the Ramleh lines to urban metro standards.

Egyptian National Railways (ENR)

PO Box 466, Station Building, Ramses Square, 11794 Cairo, Egypt
Tel: (+20 2) 574 29 68   Fax: (+20 2) 574 29 50
e-mail: enr@egyptrail.gov.eg
Web: www.egyptrail.gov.eg

Key personnel

Chairman: Eid Abd El Kader Metwalli Awad
Deputy Chairman, Operations and Commercial Affairs: Mahmoud Ahmed Kassem

Type of operation: Suburban heavy rail

Current situation

Frequent commuter services are operated to Abou Kir, east of Alexandria, and some commuter use made of other main lines. Services on the Abou Kir line run at 15 min intervals.

National Authority for Tunnels (NAT)

Ministry of Transport
PO Box 466, Ramses Building, Ramses Square, Cairo 11794, Egypt
Tel: (+20 2) 574 29 68   Fax: (+20 2) 574 29 50
e-mail: InfoC@nat.org.eg (Information centre)
Web: www.nat.org.eg

Key personnel

Chairman: Eng Atta A ElSherbiny

Type of operation: Metro (proposed)

Background

The National Authority for Tunnels (NAT) was established in 1983 as part of the Ministry of Transport. NAT is responsible for the design and construction of tunnels for the metro or roads.

Current situation

A study for the Alexandria Regional metro was undertaken in 1986 and a further major study was completed in 2000. The line will have a total length of 43 km, running from Abou Kir in the east to Km 21 on the Marsa Matrouh road in the west. The conceptual design for the whole line as well as the design of the first section, from Abou Kir to Misr Station, about 21.5 km, have been prepared.
The planning and construction authority for the line is the National Authority for Tunnels (NAT) (see also entry in, Urban Transport Systems and Operators, Egypt, Cairo section).

Cairo

Population: City 6.8 million, metropolitan area 17.9 million (2006 estimates)

Public transport

Bus services provided by government-owned transport authority, which also operates tramway networks in Cairo and Heliopolis, and cross-Nile ferries. Other extensive fixed-route shared-taxi/minibus services by private operators. Suburban rail and metro (currently being expanded) operated by state railway. Metro Line 3 under construction.

Cairo Transport Authority (CTA)

El Gabel elahmer, Imtdad Ramsis, Cairo, Egypt
Tel: (+20 2) 684 57 05; 683 19 60
Fax: (+20 2) 685 52 11

Key personnel

Planning and Technical Research: Ashraf Hamed
    Staff: 40,499

Passenger journeys: 1,144 million (annual)

Current situation

CTA operates buses, minibuses, river buses, trams and a surface metro taken over from the Heliopolis Company in 1992.
CTA operates four central bus maintenance and repair workshops, a steel moulding factory, and three training centres for management, operational and technical training.
Greater Cairo Bus Company (GCBC) is a subsidiary of CTA.
Tramway operation is now on routes 9 (Port Said depot to Shoubra-el-Kheima) and 12 (Port Said depot to El Matariya) only.

Developments

In 2004, the GCBC ordered its second set of 50 CNG bus engines, bringing the total in use to 100. CTA and GCBC will use these engines in transit buses under the Cairo Air Improvement Project, which aims at changing from diesel vehicles to low-emissions buses.

Bus

Staff: 29,860

Passenger journeys: 952.5 million (annual)
Vehicle-km: 188.5 million (annual)

Number of routes: 338
Route length: 1,450 km
Average speed: 17.5 km/h

Fleet: 1,788 vehicles, including Nasr/Iveco, Iveco, Mercedes O302, Mercedes minibus, Iveco minibus

One-person operation: None
Fare collection system: Payment to conductor
Fare structure: City area, flat; elsewhere, distance-related
Fare evasion control: Roving inspectors

Minibus
Staff: 3,740

Passenger journeys: 121 million (annual)
Vehicle-km: 42 million (annual)

Number of routes: 62

Fleet: 499 minibuses

Average speed: 15.2 km/h

Current situation
Minibuses seat 25.

Tramway (Cairo city lines)
Staff: 3,527

Type of operation: Conventional tramway

Passenger journeys: 49.6 million
Train-km: 5 million

Route length: 54 km
Number of lines: 16
Average speed: 13.2 km/h
Gauge: 1,000 mm

Fare structure: Flat; monthly seasons
Fare evasion control: Roving inspectors
Fare collection: Coin to conductor

Rolling stock: 68 two-car sets

Developments
Infrastructure improvements, including provision of some extensions on reserved track, and re-equipment of the rolling stock fleet, have helped to overcome the effects of a long period of underinvestment, but chaotic traffic conditions and poor trackwork still hamper operations on city-centre streets. Such sections will probably close when the urban metro lines are completed (see below). CTA took over operation of the Heliopolis tramway network in 1993. There has been some rationalisation of routes and fleets.

Tramway (Helwan Line)
Current situation
A 16 km route opened in 1981 links Helwan with El Tibbeen, with a branch (8 km) to May 15 City (opened 1984). It runs mostly on reserved track and is operated by Kinki Sharyo or Semaf wide-bodied cars.

LRT (surface metro)
Staff: 2,941

Passenger journeys: 17.8 million (annual)
Train-km: 1.3 million (annual)
Number of routes: 6
Average speed: 17.4 km/h

Fleet: 18 three-car sets

Current situation
The former Heliopolis system was taken over by CTA in 1992. It is still worked on as a separate system, referred to locally as the surface metro.

Riverbus
Staff: 435

Passenger journeys: 3.1 million
Boat-km: 765,533

Number of routes: 9

Average speed: 9.3 km/h

Fleet: 20 boats

Current situation
A fleet of cross-Nile ferries is operated. Small launches are used on one main route (2 km) between the central business area and the old city.

Egyptian National Railways (ENR)
Station Building, Ramses Square, 11794 Cairo, Egypt
Tel: (+20 2) 575 10 00   Fax: (+20 2) 574 00 00
e-mail: enr@egyptrail.gov.eg
Web: www.egyptrail.gov.eg

Key personnel
Chairman: Eid Abd El Kader Metwalli Awad
Deputy Chairman, Operations and Commercial Affairs: Mahmoud Ahmed Kassem
General Manager, Metro: Magdy El Azzab

Type of operation: Suburban heavy rail, regional and urban metro

Current situation
ENR operates the regional metro Line 1, the urban metro Line 2 and three conventional suburban routes (diesel-operated). Frequent cross-city service provided between El Marg, Cairo (Mubarak) and Helwan (42 km, 33 stations, electrified 1.5 kV DC). This upgraded suburban line is known as Line 1 of the metro.

For further information on ENR's mainline operations, please see *Jane's World Railways.*

Developments
The Line 2 extension from Um Elmassreen to El Mounib (2.6 km) opened in January 2005.

A third line, the Greater Cairo Metro Line 3 (GCML3), is under construction and will provide a third cross-city connection, connecting Imbaba and Mohandeseen in the west with Cairo International Airport in the extreme east.

It will be 34.2 km long (30.3 km in tunnel) with 29 stations (27 underground). Current plans are to construct the line in four phases. Construction has started on Phase 1 of Line 3, which will run from Attaba to Abbassia and will be 4.3 km long with five underground stations. The National Authority for Tunnels (NAT) has contracted 24 international contractors and 11 consultants covering all aspects of the works. Please see entry for NAT for further information on Line 3.

There are long-term plans for a further three metro lines.

Metro (Line 1)
Type of operation: Full metro, opened in two phases in 1987 and 1989

Passenger journeys: Approx 1.2 million per day

Route length: 44 km
  in tunnel: 4.7 km
Number of lines: one
Number of stations: 35 (five underground)

Rolling stock: 43 nine-car trains

Metro (Line 2)
Type of operation: Full metro, first phase opened 1996 (five phases)

Passenger journeys:
Approx 1.2 million per day

Route length: 21.6 km
  in tunnel: 13 km
  elevated: eight km
Number of lines: one
Number of stations: 20 (12 underground, two elevated, six at grade)
Gauge: 1,435 mm

Current situation
The first section of urban metro Line 2, the eight km from Shobra-el-Kheima to an

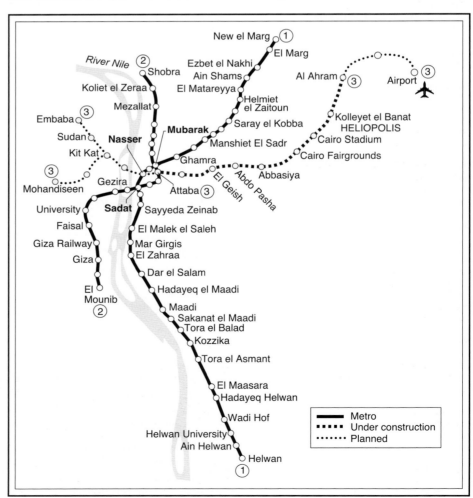

Cairo's metro and regional lines   1168389

interchange with Line 1 at Mubarak (Ramses Square), opened in 1996. The National Authority for Tunnels (NAT) (see separate entry) is the planning and construction authority.

Phase IIA of Line 2 was a 5.1 km route with three stations from Tahrir Square to Cairo university; this opened in April 1999. Phase IIB was a further extension to an interchange with ER's Upper Egypt Line at El Giza (2.5 km, three stations), which opened in 2000.

Developments
The fifth phase of Line 2, a 2.6 km surface extension from Giza suburbs to El Mounib station, was inaugurated in January 2005.

Rolling stock: 35 eight-car trains
Mitsubishi (1994/95) M140 T140

First/last train: 05.00/24.00 (Line 1); 05.00/00.15 (Line 2)
Service: Peak two min 45 secs
Fare structure: Distance-related; weekly and quarterly season tickets; discounted tickets for police, armed forces, children (four to 10 years) and for the blind and their companions
Arrangements for elderly/disabled: Elevators at most Line 2 stations (not Sadat, Mubarak, El Mazallet and Shubra El-Khelma)

National Authority for Tunnels (NAT)
Ministry of Transport
PO Box 466, Ramses Building, Ramses Square, Cairo 11794, Egypt
Tel: (+20 2) 574 29 68   Fax: (+20 2) 574 29 50

e-mail: InfoC@nat.org.eg (Information Centre)
Web: www.nat.org.eg

Key personnel
Chairman: Eng Atta A ElSherbiny

Background
The National Authority for Tunnels (NAT) was established in 1983 as an affiliate organisation of the Egyptian Ministry of Transport. NAT is responsible for the studies and research for and the design and construction of tunnels for metro or roads.

Since 1983, about 66 km of metro network have been constructed, in two lines. For map, please see separate entry for Egyptian National Railways (ENR).

Current situation
Line 1: Connects New El Marg with Helwan. Inaugurated in two phases in 1987 and 1989, with an extension in 1999.

Passenger journeys:
(Daily) 1.2 million (approximate)
Train-km:
Not currently available

Route length: 44 km
  in tunnel: 4.7 km
Number of stations: 35
  in tunnel: 5
Gauge: 1,435 mm

Line 2: Links Shobra-el-Kheima in the north with El-Monib in the south. Opened in five phases. The fifth phase, from Um-El Masrrien station to El-Monib station, was inaugurated in January 2005.

Passenger journeys:
(Daily) 1.2 million (approximate)
Train-km:
Not currently available

Route length: 21.6 km
  in tunnel: 13 km
Number of stations: 20
  in tunnel: 12
  elevated: 2

Developments
Greater Cairo Metro Line No 3 (GCML3)
The NAT is proceeding with the construction of the Greater Cairo Metro Line No 3, which will connect Imbaba in the west of the City with Cairo international airport in the east. It will be approximately 34.2 km in length and will be constructed in four phases. There will be 29 stations, 27 of which will be underground.

Construction has started on the Greater Cairo Metro Line No 3 Phase 1, which extends from Attaba to Abbasia. It is 4.3 km long with 5 stations, all in tunnel, and this phase also includes the construction of a high-voltage substation and a light repair shop for rolling stock. The construction work is being carried out by a consortium that includes international and local companies.

The NAT is awaiting offers for the execution of Phase 2, which will run from Abbasia to Heliopolis, 7.12 km long with 4 underground stations. Work on diverting public utilities along the route has started.

Preparations have started for the study and basic design stages for Phase 3 (approximately 17 km long) and Phase 4 (approximately 14 km long).

Estonia

Tallinn
Population: 400,200 (2007 estimate)

Public transport
Bus, trolleybus and tramway services operated by two separate municipal undertakings managed by the city government's Department of Transport; suburban rail.

Tallinna Trammi-ja Trollibussikoondise AS (TTTK) – Tallinn Tram & Trolleybus Company Ltd
Paldiski Mnt 48A, EE-10614 Tallinn, Estonia
Tel: (+372 6) 97 61 00
Fax: (+372 6) 72 19 59
e-mail: tttk@tttk.ee
Web: www.tttk.ee

Key personnel
Chairman: Toomas Sepp
  Staff: 865 (as at 31 March 2008)

Fare structure: Flat
Fare collection: On board or prepurchase and validation; 30-day and monthly passes
Arrangements for elderly/disabled: Reduced-rate passes; over-65s travel free
Operating costs financed by: Fares 41 per cent, other commercial sources 5 per cent, subsidy/grants 54 per cent

Trolleybus
Staff: 247 (as at 31 March 2008)

Passenger journeys: (2003) 40.4 million
Vehicle-km: (2003) 6.7 million
(2004) 6.7 (estimate)

Route length: 134.3 km
Number of routes: 8

Fleet: 128 vehicles	
Skoda 14Tr (1983/90)	79
Skoda 15Tr articulated (1989/91)	24
Ikarus 280-T ex-Hoyerswerda (1989)	4
Ikarus 415T (1992)	1
Ikarus 412T (1999)	5
Ganz-Solaris 12 (2002/03)	10
Ganz-Solaris 18 (2003)	5

In peak service: 98 (23 articulated + 75 normal trolleybuses)

Current situation
All trolleybuses are accessible.

Tramway
Staff: 171 (as at 31 March 2008)

Type of operation: Conventional tramway

Passenger journeys: (2003) 31.1 million
Vehicle-km: (2003) 3.7 million
(2004) 3.7 million (estimate)

Route length: 66 km
Number of routes: 4
Gauge: 1,067 mm

Rolling stock: 113 cars

Tatra KT6 tram with low-floor middle section, renovated by TTTK in 2001   1036644

Tatra T4 (1973/80)   34
Tatra KT4 articulated, some ex-Gera (1980/90)   77
Tatra KT6 low-floor middle section,
renovated by TTTK (2001)   2

In peak service: 68 (52 articulated KT4 + 16 2-car
T4 or KT6 units)

Service: 4–5 min (peak)

Current situation
Two trams routes have accessible vehicles with
low-floor sections.

Tallinna Autobussikoondise AS (TAK) – Tallinn Bus Company Ltd

Kadaka tee 62 A, EE-12618 Tallinn, Estonia
Tel: (+372 6) 50 95 00   Fax: (+372 6) 50 95 09
e-mail: tak@tak.ee
Web: www.tak.ee

Key personnel
Chairman of the Management Board: Mati Mägi
Member of the Management Board, Traffic & Buses:
   Hugo Linholm
Member of the Management Board, Finance: Jüri
   Nõmmsalu
   Staff: 1,072 (May 2003)

Current situation
In 1993 the former state-owned bus undertaking
became a limited liability company owned
by the Tallinn city government. Formerly an
urban-only operation, the company began
expansion into the suburbs in 1993, with three
routes.
   Tallinn Bus is one of three transport companies
operating in Tallin.

Developments
A new concept has been introduced with the
coupling of trailers to 15 Scania buses during
rush hours, increasing capacity to some 200. The
trailer is made of aluminium alloy.

Bus
Passenger boardings: (1995) 87.1 million
(1996) 81.4 million
(1997) 77.3 million
Vehicle-km: (1995) 18.6 million
(1996) 17.6 million
(1997) 18.9 million

Number of routes: 47
Route length: 522.1 km

Fleet: 335 vehicles
Ikarus 260 (1982/89)   About 50
Ikarus 280 (1981/88)   About 60

Ganz-Solaris 18 trolleybus of TTTK   1036643

Volvo/Scania (1979/96)   156
BaltScan Scania L113CLB city bus (1995/97)   45

In peak service: 302
Most intensive service: 6 min
One-person operation: 50 per cent of routes
Fare structure: Common with other modes; single
tickets and 30-day pass
Fare collection: Ticket vending machines on
board
Arrangements for elderly/disabled: Discount single
tickets and three day passes for children, students
and retired people up to the age of 65; free services
for those ages 65 and older
Average peak-hour speed: 17.5 km/h
Operating costs financed by: Fares 43 per cent,
subsidy/grants and other commercial sources 57
per cent

Elektriraudtee Aktsiaselts (Elektriraudtee AS)

Vabaduse pst 176, EE-10917 Tallinn, Estonia
Tel: (+372 6) 73 74 06
Fax: (+372 6) 73 74 00
e-mail: info@elektriraudtee.ee
Web: www.elektriraudtee.ee

Key personnel
Supervisory Board:
Chairman: Ardo Ojasalu
Members: Ivan Kappanen; Heiki Kivimaa,
   Aap Tänav, Alar Urm
Managing Director: Tarmo Olgo

Managers: Alar Kaup, Rein Riisalu
   Staff: 215 (2001)

Type of operation: Suburban rail
Passenger boardings: (2001) 3.56 million
Vehicle-km: (2001) 1.2 million

Background
Elektriraudtee AS was established as a wholly
owned subsidiary of Estonian Railways. It
began operations as an independent business
in January 1999 following the approval of rail
privatisation legislation in parliament in 1997.

Current situation
As of 31 December 2001, Elektriraudtee AS
is wholly owned by the Republic of Estonia,
represented by the Ministry of Transportation
and Communications. It provides public
transportation on suburban commuter services
on six electrified lines. The total length of the
network is 131.8 km, with 36 stations/stops,
around Tallinn and in Harju County. The 1,520 mm
gauge track is electrified at 3 kV DC and the
service runs a fleet of 69 emu cars (as at the end
of 2001) built by Riga, in Latvia. Fares are zonal.

Developments
Refurbishment of the existing rolling stock has
commenced and there have been repairs made
to the maintenance and repair depot facilities.
   In 2001, the company introduced two-car units
during the summer months, when demand is
reduced.

Ethiopia

Addis Ababa

Population: 2.9 million (estimated)

Public transport
Bus services operated by public transport division
of government-controlled Public Transport
Corporation, operating both urban and intercity
services. Shared taxi and 'Wee Eeut' minivan use
is extensive and peak-only midibuses operate.
A trolleybus system has been proposed.

Addis Ababa City Administration Transport Authority

Addis Ababa City Bus Services
PO Box 8639, Addis Ababa, Ethiopia
Tel: (+251 1) 61 46 90

Fax: (+251 1) 61 47 02
e-mail: a.a.tcb@telecom.net.et
Web: www.telecom.net.et/~aata/

Key personnel
General Manager: Ziemedkun Girma

Bus
Number of routes: 40
Route length: (One way) 150 km

Current situation
The city bus system operates under a number
of constraints, including vehicle shortages,
poor terminal and garage facilities, lack of an
operations control system and a proliferation of
short and duplicated routes running over very
poor roads. Lack of capital hampers provision of
spare parts and new vehicles.

Developments
A trolleybus system has been proposed for the city.

Fleet: Approximately 200 buses, all single-deck
standard length, comprising 160 Mercedes OF1621/
Jonckheere, plus about 25 Volvo B7F with Italian
Borsani bodies and a few Fiat 331A/Borsani. A
small batch of 15 Mercedes was reported as having
arrived in early 1995.

Most intensive service: 5 min
Fare structure: Flat, higher for suburban journeys
Fare collection: Conductors on board in fixed location
Average peak-hour speed: 14.4 km/h
Operating costs financed by: Fares 88 per cent,
subsidy/grants 12 per cent
Subsidy from: Government; PTC is exempted from
government duties and taxes on fuel, spare parts,
vehicles and workshop equipment and tools

Finland

Helsinki

Population: City 565,186, urban area 1.0 million, metropolitan area 1.3 million (2006 estimates)

Public transport
Bus, metro and tramway services operated by city transport undertaking, under overall policy of City Council. Five private bus companies provide services under contract. Ferry services to the Suomenlinna islands run by SLL, jointly owned by the city and state; privately operated waterbuses run summer only. Suburban services provided by State Railways (VR). Regional services and transport within Espoo, Vantaa and Kauniainen, which form an integrated metropolitan area wit Helsinki, are overseen by the Helsinki Metropolitan Area Council (YTV) (www.ytv.fi/eng).

Helsingin kaupungin liikennelaitos (HKL)/Helsingfors Stads Trafikverk (HST) – Helsinki City Transport (HKL)
PO Box 1400, FIN-00099, City of Helsinki, Finland
Tel: (+358 9) 47 21
Fax: (+358 9) 472 37 01
Web: www.hkl.fi, www.hel.fi/HKL

Key personnel
Managing Director: Matti Lahdenranta
Staff: 1,066 (2006 average)

Passenger boardings (in millions): (All modes)

Year	HKL services	Regional services (including all trains)	Region total
2003	197.1	110.6	307.7
2004	194.0	110.6	304.6
2005	192.4	111.8	304.2
2006	189.5	112.2	301.7

Operating costs financed by: (All modes) Helsinki: Fares 52.7 per cent, subsidy/grants 47.3 per cent (2006); Whole region: Fares 56.3 per cent, subsidy/grants 43.7 per cent (2006)
Subsidy from: Municipal taxes
Fare structure: Paper single tickets and reloadable contactless travel cards and single-use contact cards for visitors' tickets; flat fare within each municipality and three regional fares for different combinations of municipalities
Ticketing system: Single tickets can be bought from drivers, as a text message by mobile phone or from vending machines (in central areas). A project to renew the contactless travel card system is under way.
Fares collected on board: 25.8 per cent of total revenue
Fare evasion control: Roving inspectors for all modes; spot fine. Tickets must be presented on boarding, for buses.

Current situation
The Helsinki region covers four cities and an area of 1,463 km². In Helsinki the responsible body is Helsinki City Transport (HKL). The internal services of the other cities and regional services are the responsibility of a regional body, Helsinki Metropolitan Area Council (YTV). The authorities plan and decide the routes, the timetables and the fares and buy the transport services from the operators. All revenues are passed to the authorities.

All bus services have been tendered, while regional trains are run by the State Railways under a direct contract with YTV. Tram and metro services are produced and provided by HKL. The contracts are based on gross contract schemes, where the operators receive revenues

Helsingin Bussiliikenne Oy Scania E94 bus on Route 23 service at Pasila Böle (Ken Harris)   1166446

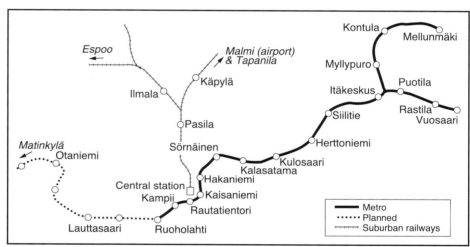

Helsinki metro and suburban rail   1124820

based on vehicles in use, kilometres driven and hours driven. Incentives, based on passenger interviews, count for 0 to 4 per cent of the basic contract sum.

In 2000 HKL introduced 300 city bikes as an additional form of public transport. These can be used by anybody for a deposit of EUR2.

A new ticketing system, based on contactless smartcard technology was introduced in 2001 and put into full use in late 2002. See above for more details, under Ticketing system.

Developments
A westward extension of the metro to Espoo has been approved in principle and is in the detailed planning stage with construction starting by 2010. General plans for a second metro line, The Töölö line, are being updated.

A new tram line 9 will open in the autumn of 2008. Further extensions to new residential areas close to the city centre are planned. 42 6-axle articulated trams from 1983-1987 will be extended to 8-axle trams with low floor centre sections and an initial order for 40 new trams is planned for 2008.

A new traffic light priority and passenger information system based on Internet technology is being piloted. This system is also used to provide passengers with wireless Internet connections on some vehicles.

A project to renew the contactless travel cards is under way. Distribution of new cards will begin in 2009 and the whole system will be updated by 2014. A new fare structure may be implemented simultaneously with the new ticketing system.

Bus
(Helsinki internal routes only)
Passenger boardings: (2003) 83.6 million*
(2004) 80.6 million*
(2005) 79.4 million*
(2006) 78.5 million*
Vehicle-km: (2003) 33.05 million
(2004) 31.38 million
(2005) 31.05 million
(2006) 30.71 million
*A new counting system based on travel card has been introduced for buses. These figures are therefore incomplete.

Number of routes: 79 day/peak routes, 9 late night routes and 19 service routes

Fleet: 447 full size vehicles 21 midibuses needed for peak service. All vehicles owned by the five private operators.
One-person operation: All routes
Average distance between stops: 400 m
Average peak-hour speed: 26.8 km/h
Bus priority: 42 km of bus lanes
Integration with other modes: Full integration of fares and services

Operational control: Mobile radio or mobile phones in all vehicles depending on operator. Limited control room and radio patrol cars.
New vehicles financed by: Operating companies

Private bus companies
All bus services are operated by private companies. These are:
Helsingin Bussiliikenne Oy (www.helb.fi);
Oy Pohjolan Kaupunkiliikenne Ab (www.pohjolanliikenne.fi);
Concordia Bus Finland Oy (www.concordiabus.fi);
Veolia Transport Finland Oy (www.veolia-transport.fi);
Etelä-Suomen Linjaliikenne Oy (www.savonlinja.fi).

Metro
Type of operation: Full metro, initial route opened 1982

Passenger boardings: (2003) 55.4 million
(2004) 55.4 million
(2005) 56.0 million
(2006) 56.8 million
Car-km: (2003) 12.9 million
(2004) 13.0 million
(2005) 13.2 million
(2006) 13.1 million

Route length: 21.2 km*
  in tunnel: 6.5 km
Number of stations: 17
  in tunnel: 7
Gauge: 1,524 mm
Max gradient: 3.5%
Minimum curve radius: 300 m
Electrification: 750 V DC, third rail
*Length of double-track infrastructure.

Service: 4–10 min
First/last train: 05.25/23.26

Rolling stock: 54 two-car sets
Valmet Oy/Strömberg Oy   M84
Bombardier Transportation DWA   M24

Current situation
The line is the first of a planned network agreed by the city council in 1969. A 4 km branch from Itäkeskus to Vuosaari with three stations was opened in 1998.

Developments
In Jan 2007, Kalasatama station opened.
  A westward extension of the metro to Espoo has been approved in principle and is in the detailed planning stage with construction starting by 2010. General plans for a second metro line, the Töölö line, are being updated.

Tramway
Type of operation: Conventional tramway

Passenger boardings: (2003) 56.8 million
(2004) 56.6 million
(2005) 55.6 million
(2006) 52.8 million
Car-km: (2003) 5.5 million
(2004) 5.3 million
(2005) 5.3 million
(2006) 5.2 million

Route length: 84.5 km*
  on reserved track: 53.8 km
Number of lines: 11
*Total track length.

Max gradient: 8%
Minimum curve radius: 15 m
Electrification: 600 V DC, overhead

Service: Peak 4 min
First/last car: 05.30/01.30
One-person operation: All routes

Rolling stock: 131 cars
Karia/Valmet 4-axle (1959)   5
Düweg/BBC 6-axle articulated (1970)   4
Valmet 6-axle articulated
  (1973/75 and 1983/87)   81

HKL Bombardier-built Variotram on Route 7A service in Messuakio (Ken Harris)   1166448

Extended Valmet 8-axle articulated
  (1984/2006)   1
Bombardier Transportation (1998/2004)   40

In peak service: 90 (2003), 91 (2004), 87 (2005), 87 (2006)
On order:

VR Ltd – Finnish State Railways
VR-Yhtymä Oy
PO Box 488, Vilhonkatu 13, FIN-00101 Helsinki, Finland
Tel: (+358 9) 307 10   Fax: (+358 9) 30 72 23 30
Web: www.vr.fi

Key personnel
Managing Director: Tapio Simos
Passenger Services Director: Ikka Seppänen
Technical Director: Markku Pesonen
Operations Director: Tapio Myllymäki
Director, Corporate Marketing: Martti Mäkinen
  Staff: 5,599 (rail services) (2006)

Type of operation: Suburban heavy rail

Passenger journeys: (All passenger operations)
(2003) 59.9 million
(2004) 60.1 million
(2005) 63.5 million
(2006) 65.0 million

Current situation
VR-Group Ltd is wholly owned by the Finnish state, whose voting rights are exercised by the Ministry of Transport and Communications. The Ministry is responsible for railway licensing. It also purchases passenger services from VR. Since 1 July 1995, the Finnish State Railways (Valtionrautatiet, VR) has been a limited-liability company, with all shares owned by the state. On the same date ownership of rail infrastructure was transferred to the Finnish Rail Administration.
  Rail services are provided by two principal subsidiaries, transport operator VR Ltd (VR Osakeyhtiö) and VR-Track Ltd (Oy VR-Rata Ab).
  VR operates suburban trains on three routes out of Helsinki: to Karjaa, Vantaankoski and Riihimäki, totalling 173 km, 52 stations, electrified 25 kV 50 Hz. Minimum one or two trains per hour (four trains peak hours, every 5 minutes between Helsinki and Tikkurila); zonal fares.
  In the Helsinki metropolitan area, VR has an agreement with the Helsinki Metropolitan Area Council (YTV) regarding provision of suburban service, under which tickets issued by the participating municipalities are valid on VR trains. Outside the metropolitan area only VR's zonal tickets are valid. The traffic figures above apply to the whole Helsinki suburban operation.
  For further information on VR-Group Ltd, please see *Jane's World Railways*.

Finnish Railways (VR) Class Sm4 emu leaving Pasila station for Helsinki (Ken Harris)   1166447

Developments

In October 2005, VR Ltd signed a contract with Helsinki Metropolitan Area Council (YTV) for the provision of services within its administrative area. Valued at around EUR46 million annually, the contract covers the period 2006–17. In 2005, 40.9 million passenger journeys were made within the YTV-administered zone, an increase of 7 per cent, while in the Greater Helsinki area as a whole, 51 million journeys were made (up by 6.2 per cent). This new contract, more detailed than previous agreements between the two parties, enables VR to make longer-term service plans and takes into account the planned procurement of new rolling stock by Junakalusto Oy, established jointly by VR Group Ltd and the communities of Helsinki, Espoo, Kauniainen and Vantaa.

In 2006, a new Z-commuter service started operating between Helsinki and Lahti.

Rolling stock

In 2001, VR placed an order with CKD Vagónka to supply 16 single-unit railcars for regional lines. The 63-seat vehicles are equipped for driver-only operation and up to three units can be operated in multiple. By mid-2006 all were in service. The contract included an option for an additional 20 similar vehicles.

The last of 30 Class Sm4 emus ordered from Fiat Ferroviaria (now ALSTOM), for Helsinki suburban services, had been delivered by mid-2005. In 2006, refurbishment was in progress of the 50 aluminium-bodied Class Sm2 emus.

Steps to further modernise the Helsinki suburban fleet were taken at the end of August 2006, when Junakalusto Oy placed an order with Stadler for 32 four-car FLIRT emus to replace existing Class Sm1 units. Junakalusto Oy is a company established by the communities of Helsinki, Espoo, Kauniainen and Vantaa together with VR Group Ltd to undertake the procurement and leasing of rail vehicles to be used for regional services administered by Helsinki Metropolitan Area Council. (YTV). Delivery of the units is due in 2009–10.

France

Bordeaux

Population: City 229,000 (2004 estimate), metropolitan area 925,253 (1999 Census)

Public transport

Bus and light rail services operated under contract to local authority consortium for 27 towns of the Communauté Urbaine de Bordeaux (CUB) and three adjoining towns.

Société Nationale des Chemins de Fer Français (SNCF) – French National Railways

SNCF Proximites
34 rue du Commandant Mouchotte, F-75699, Paris Cedex 14, France
Tel: (+33 1) 53 25 60 00   Fax: (+33 1) 53 25 88 15
Web: www.sncf.fr

Key personnel
Business Director, Transport Public: Jean-Pierre Farandou

Type of operation: Suburban heavy rail

Background
SNCF is divided into four businesses, each of which has its own budget and bottom-line responsibility: Long-Distance Passenger (Voyageurs France-Europe); Urban and Regional Passenger (Transport Public – TP); Infrastructure; and Freight (Fret SNCF). Each Business Director contracts with the other departments for the means of production and back-up services. Each of the 20 geographical regions has its own director, who has control of local passenger services and reports directly to the President. Regional and Paris Region passenger services are heavily subsidised while other activities are required to break even.

Current situation
Suburban services around Bordeaux on six routes, including the busiest to Arcachon (60 km).

Rolling stock is mainly CORAIL-hauled trains with two-car Z2 emus and two-car X.TER dmus.

All services are financed by the Aquitaine and Poitou-Charentes Regions.

Developments
Modernisation of several lines: Bordeaux-Pointe de Grave and Libourne-Bergerac in Aquitaine, Niort-Saintes and La Rochelle-Rochefort in Poitou-Charentes.

Construction of a new bridge over the Garonne river, with four tracks. Development of new services.

Veolia Transport Bordeaux

25 rue du Commandant Marchand, F-33 082 Bordeaux Cedex, France
Tel: (+33 5) 57 57 88 00
Fax: (+33 5) 57 57 88 01
e-mail: infotbc@tbc-connex.fr
Web: www.infotbc.com

Key personnel
Director: Benoît Meugniot
Staff: 2,017 (all modes December 2007)

Current situation
Veolia Transport Bordeaux is part of the Véolia Transport group of companies, the transport division of Véolia Environnement.

Connex Bordeaux operates in a region which covers 861.85 km² and a metropolitan urbanised population of 0.74 million. The company's service area is 552 km² and has a population of some 0.67 million.

Currently, 87.4 per cent of the company's fleet is low-floor.

An electric shuttlebus service, 'Navette Electrique', runs in the city centre and some communities are served by the 'Créabus' on-demand service.

Bus

Passenger journeys: (2004) 59.1 million
(2005) 34.9
(2006) 34.1 million
(2007) 34.1 million
Vehicle-km: (2004) 25.0 million
(2005) 22.3 million
(2006) 21.9 million
(2007) 21.3 million

Number of routes: 70 daytime routes (of which 6 are express line) and 14 night lines, plus one electrical shuttle and three transport on demand
Number of stops: 3,214
Route length: (One way) 974.1 km
On priority right-of-way: 15.6 km

Current situation
There are 143 CNG buses in the fleet.

Fleet: 507 vehicles

MAN NG262 low-floor articulated	20
MAN NG272 low-floor articulated	22
Renault PR180-2 articulated	21
Heuliez low-floor GNV	152
MAN NL222 low-floor	75
RVI AGORA low-floor	53

Alstom Citadis LRV in Bordeaux using the Alimentation Par le Sol (APS) current supply system. The current is supplied via a third rail between the tracks, energised only when the tram is over it. The system was installed at the request of Bordeaux city council to avoid unsightly overhead wires (Tony Pattison)
1183513

Heuliez GX127	12
Renault PR112	18
Mercedes-Benz 0100 City	7
Irisbus Agora low-floor articulated GNV	25
Irisbus Citelis low-floor articulated GNV	96
Oreos electrical vehicles	6

In peak service: 377
On order: Not currently available
Average age of fleet: 6.9 years

Most intensive service: 8 min
One-person operation: All services
Fare collection: Automatic fare collection system, with compulsory onboard cancellation of tickets or passes onboard
Fare structure: Flat, multitickets, free transfers on buses and tramway within 1 h; weekly, monthly/annual passes; 1-day, 2-day and 3-day ride-at-will tickets, single route passes
Fares collected on board: Not available
Fare evasion control: Inspectors
Operational control: 65 route inspectors/mobile radio
Arrangements for elderly/disabled: Reduced or free fares financed by city
Average distance between stops: 300 m
Average commercial speed: 15.9 km/h
Bus priority: Bus lanes totalling 15.6 km, of which 4.6 km physically separated and 0.6 km contraflow
Operating costs financed by: Fares 26.9 per cent, other commercial sources 2.1 per cent, subsidy/grants 70.99 per cent
Subsidy from: Dedicated payroll tax ('versement') and transport authority grant
New vehicles financed by: CUB

Tramway
Passenger journeys: (2004) 17.9 million
(2005) 33.9 million
(2006) 41.3 million
(2007) 41.3 million
Vehicle-km: (2004) 1.4 million
(2005) 2.1 million
(2006) 2.4 million
(2007) 3.01 million

Number of routes: 3
Number of stops: 149
Route length: (One way) 37.2 km
On priority right-of-way: 37.2 km
Average commercial speed: 18.2 km/h

Current situation
The first phase of construction on the three tramway routes, with a total length of 24.5 km and 53 stations, has been completed and the first sections entered service in December 2003. Three lines are now in operation and serve the areas of Bordeaux as follows:
Line A: St Augustin-Cenon La Moriette;
Line B: Pessac Bougnard-Quinconces;
Line C: Quinconces-Gare St Jean.
Construction work, track, track surfacing work, APS ground-based electrical supply system and supply of trainsets were undertaken by a consortium led by Alstom. Alstom will supply a total of 74 *Citadis* low-floor trainsets for the completed system and has an option for the total maintenance of the supplied equipment.
The first of the Citadis trainsets was delivered in August 2002.

The second phase of construction is proposed to extend the system by a further 18.8 km (total length of 43.3 km) and 31 stations (total 84 stations) with 70 vehicles. This phase proposes to be completed by 2008.

Developments
Construction has commenced on Phase 2 of the project. This will see:
Line A extended from Cenon La Moriette to Floirac (February 2007)
Line B extension from Pessac Bougnard to Pessac Centre (May 2007)
Extension of Line A from Saint Augustin to Mérignac Centre (June 2007)
Extension of Line B from Quinconces to Bassin Flot (July 2007)
Line C extension from Quinconces to Grand Parc (November 2007)
Line C extension from Grand Parc to Aubiers (February 2008);
Line C extension from Gare St Jean to Bègles Terres Neuves (February 2008)
Line A extension from Lormont to Carbon Blanc (May 2008)
Line B extension from Bassin Flot to Cité Claveau (October 2008).

Fleet: 67 vehicles

Alstom *Citadis 402* low-floor	55
Alstom *Citadis 302* low-floor	12

On order: Not currently available

In peak service: 67
Average age of fleet: Not currently available
Most intensive service: 4–5 min

Grenoble
Population: City 157,500 (2005 estimate), metropolitan area 514,559 (1999 Census), area served 370,000

Public transport
Bus services mostly provided under contract concession by company formed by 26 local authorities in the city region with almost 17 per cent provided by arrangement by VFD (www.vfd.fr) and private company Grindler (www.autocars-grindler.com). Light rail network.

Société d'Economie Mixte des Transports en Commun de l'Agglomération Grenobloise (SEMITAG)
PO Box 258, F-38044 Grenoble Cedex 9, France
Tel: (+33 4) 76 20 66 11
Fax: (+33 4) 76 20 66 99
e-mail: allotag@semitag.fr
Web: www.semitag.com

Key personnel
Chairman: Jacques Chiron
Director General: Joël Pitrel
Staff: 1,423

Passenger journeys: (All modes)
(2002) 60.761 million
(2003) 63.761 million
(2004) 68.503 million
(2005) 69.877 million
(2006) 71.593 million

Operating costs financed by: Fares 34.4 per cent, other commercial sources 2.1 per cent, subsidy/grants 63.5 per cent
Subsidy from: Consortium of local authorities owning SEMITAG, and through 1.80 per cent payroll tax on employers

Current situation
SEMITAG (marketed as TAG) operates as a 'mixed economy' company responsible to the Syndicat Mixte des Transports en Commun (SMTC)

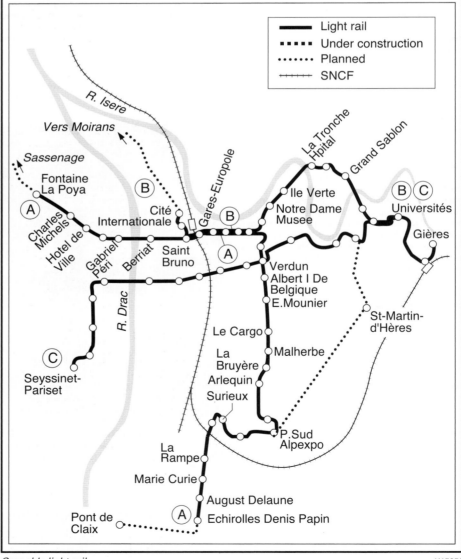

Grenoble light rail

1115256

representing 26 local authorities in the city region. SEMITAG is 65 per cent owned by SMTC, 27 per cent by TRANSDEV. The network is 83 per cent operated by SEMITAG directly, with the remainder mostly provided under contract by VFD and Grindler. Figures below include both operations.

The light rail network has been an unqualified success, and has become the model for many recent light rail projects worldwide. Two core routes have replaced the city's busiest bus routes, around which other bus lines have been replanned as feeders. Light rail now accounts for more than 53 per cent of all public transport trips. Many city-centre streets traversed by the trams have been pedestrianised, and several new car parks have been built at the fringes of the central area. Removal of street traffic has also permitted restoration of the historic city-centre area.

Bus

Passenger journeys: (2002) 30.4 million
(2003) 31.9 million
(2004) 34.8 million
(2005) 36.2 million
(2006) 33.5 million
Vehicle-km: (2002) 12.4 million
(2003) 12.5 million
(2004) 13.4 million
(2005) 13.6 million
(2006) 12.5 million

Number of routes: 25 (of which 5 operated by VFD)
Route length: (One way) 281 km
On priority right-of-way: 39.6 km

Fleet: 310 buses (as at 31/12/2006)
Standard buses
Irisbus Agora S	56
Irisbus Agora GNV	72
Heuliez GX 317	70
Citelis	30
Articulated	
Irisbus Agora L	22
Heuliez GX 187	18
Renault PR 180/182	2
Mercedes-Benz Citaro	8
Minibus/Midibus	
Gruau MG 36 (plus CEA)	6
Evobus Cito	6
Heuliez GX 117	9
Other	
Renault Master/Traffic	8
Peugeot Boxer	3

In peak service: 250

Fleet: In 1999, all trolleybuses were replaced by conventional buses due to their advanced age.

Most intensive service: 3 min
One-person operation: All services
Fare collection: Prepurchase carnets or daily/weekly/monthly passes, or payment to driver; validation on board buses and on LRT platforms
Fare structure: Flat; single ticket gives free transfer within 1 h; carnets/passes
Fares collected on board: 9.5 per cent (2006)
Fare evasion control: Inspectors
Operational control: Route inspectors/mobile radio

Arrangements for elderly/disabled: 11 minibuses operate services for disabled; free or reduced-rate travel for over-60s and invalids
Integration with other modes: Park-and-ride at 13 stops (more than 2,000 car places)
Average distance between stops: 300 m
Bus priority: On-vehicle traffic-light control by Philips VETAG; plus SAE central control and reporting system
New vehicles financed by: SMTC

Light rail

Type of operation: Light rail, initial route opened 1987

Passenger journeys: (2002) 30.4 million
(2003) 31.9 million
(2004) 33.7 million
(2005) 33.7 million
(2006) 38.1 million
Car-km: (2002) 2.6 million
(2003) 2.6 million
(2004) 2.6 million
(2005) 2.6 million
(2006) 3.4 million

Route length: 31.2 km
Number of lines: 3 (plus one under construction)
Number of stops: 63
Gauge: 1,435 mm
Track: 55 kg/m Type 35G grooved rail on twin-block sleepers with elastic fastenings, resting on rubber pads and mounted in concrete slab
Electrification: 750 V DC, overhead
Service: Peak 3 min, off-peak 6–10 min
First/last car: 04.34/01.36
Fare structure: As bus

Integration with other modes: 3 major city-centre interchanges; bus routes replanned as feeders; park-and-ride at 13 stops; full access for wheelchairs

Rolling stock: 88 cars
Alsthom-Francorail (1986/87), Alsthom-Francorail (1989), GEC Alsthom (1996)
  six-axle low-floor articulated   M53
Alstom Citadis bi-directional low-floor
  (2005/06)   M35
In peak service: 72
On order: None

Current situation
Line A was extended 3.4 km southwest from Grand' Place to Echirolles Delaune, opening in two sections in 1995 and 1996. Line A was further extended 0.5 km from Echirolles to Village II, a dense housing development, in December 1997.

A 1,150 m northwards extension of Line B opened to Palais de Justice in November 1999 and a further 500 m section to Europole opened in February 2001.

Developments
Line B was extended to Gières station in March 2006 and the new Line C (9.6 km, 19 stations) was inaugurated in May 2006.

There are plans for a north-south line, Line D, at St Martin d'Hères, also joining Line B.

There are also plans for a 1.5 km extension to Line B to the international scientific area MINATEC to open in 2009.

Bus line 1 is planned to become a 'BHNS line' (Bus Rapid Transit) in 2009.

SEMITAG Citadis LRV
(SEMITAG – P Crochard 2007)
1322678

Lille/Roubaix/Tourcoing

Population: City 226,800 (2004 estimate), Metropolitan area 1.7 million (2000 estimate)

Public transport

Bus, tram and automated metro services for conurbation of Lille/Roubaix/Tourcoing, operated by private company contracted to the Lille Metropole Communauté Urbaine (LMCU), comprising 87 towns, with private companies contracted to operate suburban bus routes. Suburban rail services by SNCF.

Transports en Commun de la Métropole Lilloise (Transpole)

BP 1009, 908 avenue de la République, F-59701 Marcq-en-Baroeul Cedex, France
Tel: (+33 3) 20 81 43 43; 20 40 40 40
Fax: (+33 3) 20 81 43 14
Web: www.transpole.fr

Key personnel

President and General Manager: Dany Mariotte
Operations Manager, Bus: Christian Bleux
Operations and Maintenance Manager, Metro and Tram: Jean Wildemersch
   Staff: 2,000

Current situation

Transpole is a private company (part of KEOLIS) linked by a 'high risk' contract to a 'syndicat mixte' involving the city of Lille and the département du Nord, with overall policy and financial responsibility for the bus, tram and VAL automated metro operations.

Suburban bus services are operated by private firms under contract to Transpole; their operations are fully integrated into the conurbation's fares and ticketing system.

Transpole is to assume responsibility for co-ordination of transport for disabled people within the LMCU area.

Lille was the first city in the world to introduce an automatic metro and since its introduction usage of the public transport network has doubled. The authorities aim to double usage again by 2015.

Passenger journeys: (All modes)
(2001) 103.7 million
(2002) 110.6 million
(2003) 117.0 million
(2004) 120.2 million
(2005) 123.3 million

Fare collection: Single tickets from driver on buses and machines on trams and metro stations, free transfer within 1 hour; monthly passes or carnets prepurchased and cancelled on board
Fare structure: Urban and suburban tariffs; 10-journey carnets for single journeys; monthly and weekly passes; 'Ticket Plus' offers unlimited travel on all modes including SNCF trains; also cross-frontier tickets to Mouscron, Waasten, Wervik, Komen and Herseaux in Belgium
Fares collected on board: 10.2 per cent on buses, 22.5 per cent from station machines
Fare evasion control: Inspectors
Arrangements for elderly/disabled: Fare reductions for over-65s and unemployed within LMCU area

Operating costs financed by: Fares 60 per cent, concessionary fares compensation 11 per cent, subsidy/grants 28.9 per cent

Contracted bus and suburban bus

Passenger journeys: (2005) 38 million
Vehicle-km: (2005) 17 million

Number of routes: 89
Route length: (One way) 1,150 km

Fleet: 500 buses (including suburban buses)

Integration with other modes: Services and fares integrated with Transpole bus, tram and metro

Current situation

Transpole retains responsibility for planning, network changes, management and information provision, while standard fares and ticket systems apply.

Tramway (Le Mongy)

Type of operation: Conventional tramway

Passenger journeys: (2001) 6.2 million
(2002) 6.3 million
(2003) 7.0 million
(2004) 7.5 million
(2005) 7.3 million
Car-km: (2005) 1.3 million

Route length: 22 km
Number of routes: 2
Number of stations: 36
Gauge: 1,000 mm
Electrification: 750 V DC, overhead

Service: 3–4 min on common route
First/last car: 05.15/01.30

Rolling stock: 24 cars
Breda LRV (1993/94)   M24
In peak service: 21

Current situation

The tramway known as Le Mongy links central Lille with Roubaix and Tourcoing, running mostly on reserved track from an underground interchange with VAL at Gares.

Metro (VAL)

Type of operation: Fully automated (unmanned) metro (rubber-tyred), VAL system, opened 1983

Passenger journeys: (2001) 61.0 million
(2002) 65.3 million
(2003) 70.7 million
(2004) 74.2 million
(2005) 78.0 million
Car-km: (2005) 10 million

Route length: 45 km
Number of lines: 2
Number of stations: 60
Gauge: 2,060 mm between H-type guide bars also used for power supply
Track: Precast concrete longitudinal sleepers, with track heating provided by cables embedded in sleepers. Track equipment specific to system's automatic controls includes 170 mm wide strip carrying transmission lines; aluminium plate contacts used for command and control and regulation of traffic; ultra-sonic transceiver at the entry and exit to every station
Electrification: 750 V DC, collected by shoes from guide bars

Service: Peak 1 min, off-peak 3–6 min
First/last train: 05.12/00.12
Fare structure: Flat, common tariff for all modes
Fare collection: Automatic ticket machines with touch-screens and accepting credit cards, validating machines at entrance to all platforms
Integration with other modes: At several stations, including connection with Le Mongy tramway at Gares; bus feeders; 5 park-and-ride stations offering 1,150 parking spaces
Control: VAL was Europe's first fully automated driverless metro; in normal operation VAL stations are unmanned too. Surveillance is provided by 444 CCTV cameras linked to 24 TV monitors in the control room. For full description see *Jane's Urban Transport Systems 1987.*

Rolling stock: 143 two-car sets
CIMT	M88
Alsthom VAL 206	M78
Matra/Siemens VAL 208	M120

Current situation

Line 1 from Chr B Calmette via Lille Flandre station and the longer Line 2 from St Philbert to C H Dron via Lille Flandre and Lille Europe stations, Croix Centre, Roubaix and Tourcoing, with interchange between the two at Porte des Postes.

The frequency is every minute (peak) and the operating speed is 40 km/h. The manufacturer Matra reports that the VAL system accounts for 50 per cent of trips using public transport while representing 33 per cent of overall public transport costs.

Line 2 was extended in three stages to Tourcoing Hopital Dron by October 2000.

Société Nationale des Chemins de Fer Français (SNCF) – French National Railways

Direction du Transport Public, Division Information et Relation Client
209/211 rue de Bercy, F-75585, Paris Cedex 12, France
Tel: (+33 3) 20 87 31 10   Fax: (+33 3) 20 87 35 12
Web: www.sncf.fr

Key personnel

Business Director, Public Transport: Bernard Sinou
Director of Communications: Bernard Emsellem
Type of operation: Suburban heavy rail

Current situation

Limited suburban services provided on seven routes, that to Tourcoing (13 km) served about hourly, the rest intermittently, mainly by a fleet of 65 three-car RIB push-pull trains.

For further information on SNCF, please see *Jane's World Railways.*

Lyons (Lyon)

Population: City 470,000, metropolitan area 1.78 million (2007 estimates)

Public transport

Bus, trolleybus, metro and two funicular services operated under contract for Lyon local transport authority Sytral, comprising representatives of the Département du Rhône and the Communauté Urbain. Suburban rail services operated by French National Railways (SNCF).

Société Lyonnaise des Transport en Commun (TCL)

'Le Lyonnais' Headquarter Building, PO Box 3167, 19 boulevard Vivier Merle, F-69212 Lyons Cedex 3, France
Tel: (+33 4) 78 71 80 80   Fax: (+33 4) 72 33 84 62
e-mail: tcl@tcl.fr
Web: www.tcl.fr

Key personnel

President: Michel Cornil
Director General: Jean Marie Sévin
   Staff: 4,300 (all transport services)

Passenger boardings: (All modes)
(2002) 250 million
(2003) 270 million
(2004) 290 million

Operating costs financed by: Fares 41.6 per cent, subsidy/grants 58.4 per cent
Subsidy from: 'Versement' employee payroll tax 60 per cent, local authority contributions 40 per cent

Current situation

Public transport for the conurbation, the second largest in France, is provided by a private company (a subsidiary of KEOLIS) under the commercial name TCL. TCL is franchised to operate a network determined by the Syndicat Mixte des Transports Urbains de l'Agglomération Lyonnaise (Sytral), a local transport authority set up in 1983. It comprises 16 representatives of the 62 districts making up the Lyons urban community and 10 from the Département du Rhône. Current policy involves reducing bus penetration of the city centre in favour of metro, with strengthened suburban bus services.

As well as the standard 'versement' employee payroll tax to assist public transport, the balance of operating costs is financed by contributions from a local income tax raised 85 per cent by the urban community and 15 per cent by the département.

Developments

The local transport plan is based mainly on the development of 11 surface 'main lines' operated with either trolleybus or light rail. New light rail Lines 1 and 2 were opened in January 2001.

Bus and trolleybus

Vehicle-km: (2003) Bus 31.4 million, trolleybus 3.3 million
(2004) Bus 32.4 million, trolleybus 2.7 million

Number of routes: Bus 104, minibus 15, trolleybus 6
Route length: (One way) Bus 1,275 km, trolleybus 26 km
On priority right-of-way: 68 km

Current situation

A further 1.1 million vehicle-km are run by private contractors.

From 1996, 22 suburban routes in the Rhône département were opened to TCL ticket holders within the Lyons urban area.

In 1999, Sytral received seven new Kiepe Type NMT 222/A53 trolleybuses for steep Line 6. By 2001, the trolleybus fleet had been completed, with the addition of 55 12 m and 12–18 m Irisbus vehicles. New trolleybus lines will be created. At present trolleybus routes represent 8 per cent of the network but 19 per cent of journeys.

Developments

Further trolleybus routes are under study.

Fleet: 885 buses
Renault R312	313
Heuliez GX317	5
Agora	461
Articulated	76
Gruau minibus and Oreos	30

In peak service: 770
Average age of fleet: 8 years
New vehicles required each year: 56

Fleet: 102 trolleybuses
Kiepe NMT 222/A53	7
Irisbus 12 m	69
Irisbus 18 m	26

Average age of fleet: 2 years
Trolleybus electrification: 600 V DC

Most intensive service: 5 min
One-person operation: All routes
Fare collection: On buses or prepurchase from agencies and metro stations
Fare structure: Flat; individual journey tickets with free transfers between all modes within 1 h; carnets of 10 single-journey tickets; monthly all-mode passes; monthly zonal passes including TCL/SNCF or TCL/suburban buses; family and student passes; tourist day passes; passengers can pay for monthly passes by direct debit, with the 11th month free; single tickets and carnets account for 46 per cent of revenue, passes 54 per cent
Fares collected on board: 11 per cent
Fare evasion control: Inspection patrols; penalty
Operational control: Comprehensive system of radio monitoring; buses linked to area control rooms (centralised at night and weekends) and to roving inspectors

ALSTOM Citadis tram at Porte des Alpes, Lyons (note feature extension) (David Haydock)   0104717

Renault Agora bus at Part-Dieu, Lyons (David Haydock)   0104719

Renault PR180 articulated bus crossing the River Rhône, Lyons (David Haydock)   0104718

Arrangements for elderly/disabled: Reduced price or free monthly pass for over-65s who pay no income tax and invalids; 'Optibus' prereserved door-to-door on-demand service operated by a private company, Interhône, contracted by Sytral, using 20 minibuses plus taxis
Integration with other modes: Full integration between bus, trolleybus, funicular and metro services; tickets interavailable, some include SNCF rail
Average distance between stops: 400 m
Average peak-hour speed: In mixed traffic 19.7 km/h
Bus priority: 68 km of reserved bus lanes, of which 23.5 km are contraflow, 33.1 km protected and 1.1 km in pedestrianised streets
New vehicles financed by: Sytral

Tram

Operated by TCL (address as above).
Type of operation: Conventional tramway. Two routes opened January 2001.

Route length: 23.2 km
Number of lines: 2
Number of stations: 49
Gauge: 1,435 mm
Electrification: 750 V DC overhead
Service: 3 min peak
First/last car: 04.30/00.00
Fare structure: As bus/metro
Revenue collection: Automatic vending machines at stations, validators on board

Integration with other modes: Bus feeders, 400-space car park at Porte des Alpes

Current situation
On 2 January 2001, 8.7 km Line T1 and 10 km Line T2 opened. Line T1 runs north from Perrache station, serving Part-Dieu station, to the university campus at La Doua. Line T2 runs east from Perrache to the Porte des Alpes shopping centre, serving two major hospitals en route. Each was expected to carry 50,000 passengers per day by 2003.

Developments
Line T2 was extended 4.5 km, with nine stations, to Saint Priest in 2003. Extension of Line T2 from Perrache to Montrochet is under construction. Two more new lines are under study. In addition, Sytral will decide on the use of the former Est de Lyon heavy rail line from Part-Dieu to Décines-Meyzieu for a light rail line with an extension to Saint Exupéry airport.

Rolling stock: 47 vehicles
ALSTOM Citadis five-section (2000/2001)   M47

Metro
Operated by TCL (address as above).

Type of operation: Rubber-tyred full metro, initial route opened 1978, automated Line D opened 1992; plus Line C incorporating long-established rack railway

Passenger journeys: (2003) 190 million
Car-km: (2003) 14.9 million
(2004) 14.5 million

Route length: 29.1 km, including rack railway 2.3 km
   in tunnel: 28.8 km
Number of lines: 4
Number of stations: 42
Gauge: 1,435 mm (for security rails)
Track: Pneumatic rubber tyres run on 68 kg/m metal plates, with lateral guide bars; security rails on RS-type concrete sleepers; polyester insulating sleepers support guide rail, which carries power supply; entire track system bedded in Stedef-type concrete slab; Line C is steel wheel on steel rail
Max gradient: 6.5%; 20% on rack Line C
Minimum curve radius: 100 m; 80 m on Line C
Tunnel: Mostly cut-and-cover
Electrification: 750 V DC, collection from lateral bars; overhead on Line C

Current situation
Line D, which is fully automated on the Maggaly system, opened in stages during 1991/92. In contrast to Lille, platform screens and doors are not provided. Instead, an infra-red beam system detects an obstruction or a person falling on to the track. Train doors have sensitive edges so that passengers' clothing does not become trapped.
   Line B was extended 2.4 km with three new stations from Jean Macé to Stade de Gerland in September 2000.

Developments
At present, there are no more extensions planned to the metro network, work being concentrated on new tram/trolleybus routes, except one new

Lyons
metro and
light rail
0585148

station in La Soie on Line A, connected to the future light rail system.

Service: Peak 2.5–5 min, off-peak 3–7 min, evenings 6–11 min
First/last train: 05.00/00.20
Fare structure: Flat
Integration with other modes: As bus
Signalling: CTC, ATC and ATO

Rolling stock: 178 cars
Alstom Lines A and B   M64 T32
Alstom Rack Line C   M10
GEC Alsthom Line D (1991)   M72
In peak service: 130 cars

Funiculars
Route length: 1.2 km
Number of lines: 2
Number of stations: 5
Number of cars: 6

Société Nationale des Chemins de fer Français (SNCF) – French National Railways
Rhône-Alpes Region
Public Transport, Marketing Department, 209/211 rue de Bercy, Cedex 12, FR-75585, Paris, France
Tel: (+33 1) 53 25 60 00
Web: www.sncf.com

Rhône-Alpes Regional Branch
78, rue de la Villette, Cedex 03, FR-69425, Lyon, France
Tel: (+33 4) 72 84 65 72

Key personnel
Business Director, Transport Public: Jean-Pierre Franadou
Press Service: Joëlle Tournebize
Tel: (+33 1) 53 25 86 09
Regional Director, Rhône-Alpes Region: Philippe De Mester

Type of operation: Suburban heavy rail

Passenger journeys: (Rhône-Alpes region)
Not currently available
Train-km: Not currently available

Current situation
Suburban services provided on seven Train Express Régional (TER) routes, carrying about one million passengers a year. The local regional council is gradually increasing service frequencies and promoting cross-city services. Karlsruhe-style light rail service, with on-street running, is under development for Lyons.
   There are plans for the modernisation of the network to the west of Lyon, improvements to the Lton-Bourg-en-Bresse line and track modernisation between Lyon and Roanne and Saint-Gervais-Chamonix-Vallorcine.
   For further information on SNCF, please see *Jane's World Railways.*

Developments
From December 2007, TER services in the Rhône-Alpes region began running at regular intervals and connections with bus and other train services have been improved.
   The OùRA smartcard was introduced into the region in late 2005, and e-ticketing for the whole region is planned to be implemented by late 2009.

Marseille
Population: 807,000 (1999 Census), area served 881,000

Public transport
Bus, trolleybus, tramway and metro services provided by municipal undertaking supervised by the City of Marseille and Bouches du Rhône Département, with separate metro construction authority operating the metro. Bus routes run to adjoining suburbs of Aubagne, La Penne, Allauch and Plan de Cuques. Limited suburban rail services operated by French National Railways (SNCF). Private cars are used for more than half of all journeys within the city and

for 91 per cent of journeys between Marseille and the metropolitan area. On 1 January 2001 an urban community was created between 18 municipalities with a population of 92,000. Aix-en-Provence and Aubagne chose not to join.

Régie des Transports de Marseille (RTM)
PO Box 334, F-13271 Marseille Cedex 8, France
Tel: (+33 4) 91 10 55 55   Fax: (+33 4) 91 10 53 09
e-mail: enligne@rtm.fr
Web: www.rtm.fr

Key personnel
Director General: Alain Gille
   Staff: 3,000

Passenger boardings: (All modes)
(1995) 148.2 million
(1996) 126 million
(1998) 139.3 million

Operating costs financed by: Fares and other commercial sources 43 per cent; compensation for concessionary fares 18 per cent; subsidy 39 per cent
Subsidy from: City council and Bouches du Rhône département

Bus

Passenger journeys: (1995) Bus 85.4 million, trolleybus 6.6 million
(2000) 81 million (combined)
Vehicle-km: (1995) Bus 21.6 million, trolleybus 0.8 million

Number of routes: Bus 78, including 13 night
Route length: Bus 575 km
On priority right-of-way: 24.1 km

Fleet: 542 buses

Berliet PR100	168
Heuliez GX113	293
Mercedes O405N	37
Heuliez GX77 narrow-body	27
Van Hool AU138 narrow/short wheelbase	16
Renault R312	1

In peak service: 460
Average age of fleet: 9.4 years

Most intensive service: 5 min
One-person operation: All routes
Fare collection: Magnetically coded cards used exclusively
Fare structure: Flat, weekly/monthly passes and multitickets/carnets including transfers; single tickets do not allow interchange
Fares collected on board: 17 per cent
Fare evasion control: Roving inspectors
Arrangements for elderly/disabled: Reduced fares or free travel for over-65s and invalids
Bus priority: Two main corridors into city centre from north and south equipped with bus-activated traffic lights; also some bus lanes on busiest route, Line 21
Operational control: Electronic bus monitoring; all buses, trams and metro cars equipped with radio
Average peak-hour speed: Bus 15.5 km/h

Developments

The 10 busiest stops of Route 21 are equipped with Alphabus displays, showing next bus waiting times. Five bus/metro interchanges are equipped with Topbus displays giving next bus departure times; a buzzer warns passengers of imminent departure.

In 1996 RTM introduced the Carte Réseau Libertés, a magnetic card which can be used to pay for all modes of public transport, plus car parks, parking meters and tolls. The card allows a one-hour journey including transfers and, unusually, a return journey if required. There are three versions: single journey, fixed-value and rechargeable.

The trolleybus system closed in 2004.

Metro

Régie des Transports de Marseille (RTM)

44 avenue Alexandre Dumas, F-13272 Marseille Cedex 8, France
Tel: (+33 4) 91 23 25 25
Fax: (+33 4) 91 71 05 87

Key personnel
Director General: Michel Croc

Background
Operated by: RTM. Construction authority: Société du Métro de Marseille (SMM)

Current situation
Line 1 is to be extended from La Timone via La Blancarde to La Fourragere (2.7 km with four stations). Work was due to begin in 2003 for completion in 2006.

A park-and-ride site is to be created at La Fourragere with 500 spaces.

Line 2 is to be extended from Sainte-Marguerite-Dromel to Saint-Loup in 2007 but the line has still to be finalised.

Northwards extension of Line 1 from La Rose to Chateau-Gombert is planned for 2010–2015.

Type of operation: Rubber-tyred full metro, initial route opened 1978

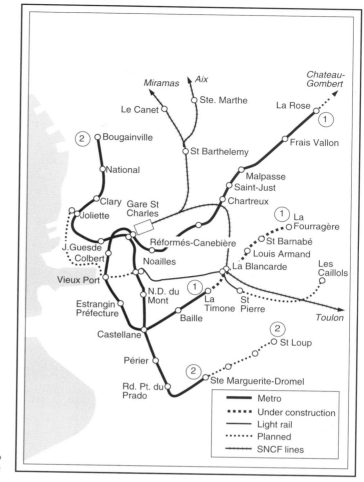

Marseille metro
0533802

Passenger boardings: (2000) 56 million

Route length: 19.5 km
Number of lines: 2
Number of stations: 24
Track: 2 steel guideways (2,000 mm gauge) for train's pneumatic tyres; 2 steel guidance rails fixed outside running guideways; 2 conventional rails for running in case of tyre punctures and guiding through sections without guidance rails
Tunnel: Bored or blasted
Electrification: 750 V DC, collected by side shoe from guidance rail

Service: Peak 3 min, off-peak 5–10 min
First/last train: 05.00/21.00
Fare structure: Flat
Integration with other modes: Ticket integration with bus services. Monthly ticket for unlimited travel on metro, tramway, trolleybus and bus; also monthly 'Carte Azur' ticket allowing in addition travel on SNCF trains within RTM area
Fare collection: Automatic ticket machines
Signalling: Cab signalling; continuous speed display to drivers; automatic operation with monitored manual drive
Centralised control: Traffic control station or computer ensures regulation of traffic by modifying inter-station speeds and calculating stopping times at stations
Surveillance: CCTV on stations

Rolling stock: 144 cars, in four-car sets

CIMT Series A (1977)	M42 T21
CIMT Series B (1984)	M30 T15
CIMT Series N (1985/86)	M36

In peak service: 116 cars

Tramway (Metro Tramway Marseille)

Web: www.metro-tramway-marseille.com

Type of operation: Conventional tramway

Passenger journeys: (1995) 4.6 million
(2000) 3.3 million
Car-km: (1995) 0.5 million

Background
Operated by: RTM.

Current situation
A three-line tramway system is currently being developed, the first sections of which are scheduled to become operational in 2006/07.

Developments
In June 2004, Bombardier Transportation began the development of a new bidirectional *FLEXITY*™ Outlook tram for the Marseille tramway network. An order for 25 to 30 of the new vehicles is expected shortly.

Rolling stock: 19 cars, operated as 9 two-car sets

PCC	M16
BN (1984)	M3

In peak service: 16 cars

Régie Départementale des Transports des Bouches du Rhône (RDT 13) – Cartreize

Rue Ernest Prados, F-13090, Marseille, Aix en Provence, France
Tel: (+33 4) 42 93 59 00
Fax: (+33 4) 42 93 59 01

Current situation
An extensive network of suburban and regional bus services is provided under the Cartreize brand name by several private and one local authority-owned operator under the auspices of the Département des Bouches-du-Rhône.

Société Nationale des Chemins de fer Français (SNCF) – French National Railways

Marseille Division, Provence-Alpes-Côte d'Azur
Esplanade St-Charles, F-13232 Marseille, France
Tel: (+33 4) 91 95 11 10
Fax: (+33 4) 91 95 10 01
e-mail: webpr@sncf.fr
Web: www.sncf.com.fr

Current situation
Limited suburban services are provided on SNCF lines out of Marseille St Charles station. Busiest routes are to Aix-en-Provence (37 km)

and Toulon (67 km), each with about 18 return trips daily.
A third track is to be laid between Marseille and Aubagne. The Aix-en-Provence line is to be

partly double-tracked. Both projects should be complete by late 2006.

Nancy
Population: City 105,000, Metropolitan area 420,000 (estimates)

Public transport
Bus and Guided Light Transit (GLT) services are operated under franchise on behalf of the Communauté Urbaine du Grand Nancy (CUGN).

Communauté Urbaine du Grand Nancy (CUGN)
22-24 viaduc Kennedy, CO No 36, F-54035 Nancy Cédex, France
Tel: (+33 3) 83 91 83 91   Fax: (+33 3) 83 91 83 96
Web: www.grand-nancy.org

Key personnel
President and Mayor of Nancy: André Rossinot

Type of operation: Bus and Guided Light Transit (GLT)

Operated by:

Connex Nancy SA – Service de Transport de l'Agglomération Nancéienne (STAN)
59 Rue Marcel Brot, BP 20347, F-54006 Nancy Cédex, France
Tel: (+33 3) 83 30 86 00
Fax: (+33 3) 83 36 21 61
e-mail: reseau-stan@connexnancy.fr
Web: www.reseau-stan.com

Key personnel
Director: Guy Pierron
  Staff: 690

Current situation
Connex Nancy, operating as Service de Transport de l'Agglomeration Nanceienne (STAN), holds the franchise for operation of the urban bus and GLT operations for a consortium of 19 suburban local authorities, the CUGN and 11 others.
STAN also operates on-demand-transport, MobiStan and has three park-and-ride facilities.
Nancy was the first city to use a Guided Light Transit system (bus guided by a central rail), the Bombardier Transport sur Voie Réservée (TVR), marketed as a rubber-tyred tramway (tram-on-tyres).
The TVR route is 11.5 km long, 8.7 km of which is on a 'reserved way' with 29 stops. There are plans for two more lines to be added, creating a 25 km network capable of carrying 100,000 passengers a day.
Bombardier has supplied 25 TVR vehicles. The TVR was chosen because it can climb the 12 per cent gradients on the Vandoeuvres section.

Developments
A new short length of reserved track was added to the TVR route in October 2007 in the Vélodrome area, replacing on-street running.

Bus and GLT
Passenger journeys: (2006) 21.9 million (estimate)
Vehicle-km: (2006) 8.6 million (estimate)

Number of routes: Bus 27 (includes MobiStan (1), minibus (1) and P'tit Stan (3)), GLT 1
Route length: Bus: Not currently available, trolleybus 11 km (estimate)
On priority right-of-way: 9.3 km
Trolleybus electrification: 750 V DC

Fleet: 183 buses (plus 12 minibuses)
Complete breakdown of fleet is not currently available

Bombardier GLT tram-on-tyres for Nancy, France (Bombardier Transportation)   0585138

One of Nancy's double-articulated Bombardier TVR vehicles in guided mode, running on Route T1 northbound approaching Division de Fer stop (Steve Morgan)   1341651

Average age of fleet: 8 years
Fleet: 25 rubber-tyred trams
Bombardier double-articulated TVR vehicles   25

Most intensive service: 5 min
One-person operation: All routes
Fare structure: Flat in urban area central zone, plus three outer zones for suburban routes; reduced rate for 10-trip and 20-trip ticket; higher fares for journeys after 21.35 on 3 routes; weekly and monthly passes; one-way unlimited transfer within 1 h; bus/rail pass
Fare collection: Payment to driver or prepurchase multijourney tickets or passes; magnetic tickets and passes must be validated on every boarding
Operational control: Computerised vehicle monitoring system based on monitoring of distance run/stops made by vehicles and display of this information to both drivers and central controllers, as well as analysis by computer
Bus priority: Traffic signal control gives bus priority. Pedestrianised bus-only precinct along 1 km of central area street served by trolleybus routes; original 5.8 km of bus lanes extended to 9 km
Average peak-hour speed: In mixed traffic, 13.2 km/h
Operating costs financed by: Fares 47.5 per cent, other commercial sources 5.7 per cent, subsidy/grants 46.8 per cent
Subsidy from: District

Societe Nationale des Chemins der Fer Français (SNCF) – French National Railways
34 rue de Commandant Mouchotte, F-75699, Paris Cedex 14, France
Tel: (+33 3) 53 25 60 00
Web: www.sncf.com

Type of operation: Suburban/interurban rail

Passenger journeys: Not currently available
Train-km: Not currently available

Key personnel
Director of Communications:
  Bernard Emseellem
Head of Press Service: Jean-Paul Boulet
Business Director, SNCF Proximites:
  Jean-Pierre Farandou
Press Service, Transport Public:
  Joëlle Tournebize

Current situation
Limited service on nine routes.
  For further information on SNCF, please see *Jane's World Railways.*

Nantes

Population: City 280,000 (2004 estimate), urban area 545,000, metropolitan area 711,000 (1999 estimates)

Public transport

Bus services provided in conurbation and environs by SEMITAN (TAN), a semi-public undertaking controlled (and 65 per cent owned) by 'Le District' consortium of 21 regional local authorities through representative board and supervised by Transport Commission of the member authorities. Private firms operate routes under contract. Light rail. Ferry shuttle services.

SEMITAN (TAN)

PO Box 64605, 3 rue Bellier, F-44046 Nantes Cedex 1, France
Tel: (+33 2) 51 81 77 00
Fax: (+33 2) 51 81 77 70
e-mail: semitan@tan.fr
Web: www.tan.fr

Key personnel
President: Albert Mahé
Vice-President: Camille Durand
Director General: Alain Boeswillwald
External Communications: Murielle Bréheret
   e-mail: mbreheret@tan.fr
   Staff: 1,590 (2007)

Passenger journeys: (All modes)
(2003) 90.5 million
(2006) 104.4 million
(2007) 109.5 million

Operating costs financed by: Fares 41.1 per cent, other commercial sources 5.8 per cent, subsidy/grants 53.1 per cent

Current situation
Passenger traffic on the routes of SEMITAN (marketed as TAN) and its contract operators has increased substantially under a pro-public transport policy established by the controlling district local authority consortium, now Nantes Metropole.

The tramway had a striking effect on the city's public transport (see earlier editions of *Jane's Urban Transport Systems*), accounting for more than 40 per cent of the daily journeys to the centre of the urban area at peak hours by public transport, and 15 per cent of total daily travel, some 472,500 trips. The bus network has been restructured to act largely as a feeder to the tramway; 80 per cent of bus routes serve at least one tram stop.

In 2000, SEMITAN was awarded ISO 9002 certification for its maintenance procedures and, since 2002, NF Services, for two bus lines, Nos 32 and 25. In 2007, 21 lines (bus and tram) were certified and some 80 per cent of customers now travel on certified lines.

Developments
Line 4, from the city centre of Nantes, the Commercial area, to Vertou in the south, opened in November 2006. The 6.7 km route is served by 20 buses running a 'deluxe' service on their own right-of-way. Peak service is at 4 minute intervals.

A new ferry service was launched in mid-2005. The ferry, with a capacity of 100 passengers, makes six stops between the south railway station and the universities. Another ferry commenced a river-crossing from mid-2005.

Bus (SEMITAN direct operations)
Passenger journeys: Not currently available
Vehicle-km: (2005) 18.2 million
(2006) 18.3 million
(2007) 19.0 million

Number of routes: 61 (including 26 chartered lines)
Route length: 624 km

Fleet: 382 vehicles + 4 ferries

Standard bus	245
Articulated bus	110

LRV at Le Cardo station on tram line 2 1329017

Mercedes-Benz Citaro CNG articulated bus on the BusWay (Line 4) 1322727

Midibus	3
Minibuses for disabled service	23
Electric minibus	1
Ferries	4

On order: Not currently available
In peak service: Not currently available
Most intensive service: 4 min
One-person operation: All routes
Fare collection: Payment to driver, or prepurchase multitickets or passes with cancellation on board; single tickets valid 1 h, 'Passeport' (annual pass)
Fare structure: Flat. Various passes/multitickets
Fares collected on board: 15 per cent
Arrangements for elderly/disabled: Minibuses adapted to take wheelchairs. System administered for SEMITAN by a local disablement research body. Free travel for blind people and escorts, free/reduced for persons over 65 provided by communities participating in SEMITAN
Average speed: 20 km/h

Bus (contracted)
Services operated under contract by several private transport companies.

Passenger journeys: Not currently available
Vehicle-km: (2003) 4.3 million
(2005) 4.3 million
(2007) 4.7 million

Light rail
Type of operation: Light rail, initial route opened 1985

Passenger journeys: (2003) 40.7 million
(2005) 57.2 million
(2007) 63.5 million

Car-km: (2003) 3.6 million
(2005) 4 million
(2006) 4.3 million
(2007) 4.5 million

Route length: 40 km
Number of routes: 3
Number of stops: 84
Gauge: 1,435 mm
Track: Ri60 grooved rail on street sections, conventional ballasted track with UIC50 rail elsewhere
Electrification: 750 V DC, overhead

Developments
Line 3 was extended to the south from the Hotel Dieu station to Gare de Pont-Rousseau in Rezé, a new tramway terminal, in 2007.

In 2009, Line 3 will be extended to the north (one new station and park-and-ride) and Lines 1 and 2 will be connected to the north in 2010.

Rolling stock: 79 trainsets

Alsthom articulated (1984/88/94)	M46
Bombardier low-floor	M33

On order: None

Service: Peak 2½–6 min, off-peak 6–7 min
First/last car: 04.30/00.30
Fare structure: As bus

Revenue collection: Automatic ticket vending machines, validators on board
Integration with other modes: 19 park-and-ride sites

Société Nationale des Chemins de fer Français (SNCF) – French National Railways

Nantes Division
2 boulevard de Stalingrad, F-44401 Nantes, France

Tel: (+33 2) 40 74 45 94
Fax: (+33 2) 40 08 16 03
e-mail: terpaysdelaloire@sncf.fr
Web: www.sncf.fr

Type of operation
Suburban heavy rail.

Current situation
Local trains, mostly dmus refurbished with funds from the Pays de la Loire region, serve four routes.

Developments
LRT services over SNCF lines are planned for an extension of tram line 1 from Haluchere to Sucé-sur-Erdre and a cross-city line from Carquefou to Bouaye.

Orleans

Population: City 115,000, metropolitan area 275,000 (estimates)

Public transport
Bus and tram services provided in a conurbation of 22 towns by SEMTAO, a semi-public undertaking, of which TRANSDEV has a 20 per cent share, but controlled and owned by the Communauté des Communes de l'Agglomération Orléannaise, a grouping of local towns.

Société d'Economie Mixte des Transports de l'Agglomération Orléannaise (SETAO) (SEMTAO)

64 rue Pierre Louguet, F-45800 Saint-Jean-de-Braye, France
Tel: (+33 2) 38 71 98 38   Fax: (+33 2) 38 71 98 39
Web: www.semtao.fr

Key personnel
Director General: A Magnon-Pujo
    Staff: 684

Current situation
The Société d'Economie Mixte des Transports de l'Agglomération Orléannaise (SETAO) (SEMTAO), a public undertaking in which TRANSDEV holds a 20 per cent stake, provides bus, tram and on-demand services to 22 local towns/communes.

Passenger journeys: (All modes)
(2006) 23.4 million (estimate)
Vehicle-km: (All modes)
(2006) 11 million (estimate)

Bus
Passenger journeys: Not currently available
Vehicle-km: Not currently available

Number of routes: 30 (plus 3 shuttles and 8 on-demand routes)
Route length: Not currently available

Current situation
Bus services were restructured in December 2000 to reduce parallel running with, and to feed into, the tramway. Services were divided into main lines, tram feeders and orbitals. All routes were

given numbers instead of letters. Bus-km rose by 6.6 per cent and commercial speed was expected to rise by 3.3 per cent. A trial with on-demand minibus services in four towns was expanded to cover three more towns in 2000. An evening service network until 00.30 was introduced at the same time as the tram. SEMTAO is buying around 10 new low-floor buses per year and refurbishing others to extend life by 10 years.

Fleet: 201 vehicles
Full breakdown of fleet is not currently available

In peak service: 150 buses (estimate)
Average age of fleet: 7 years

Most intensive service: 8 min
One-person operation: All routes
Fare collection: Payment to driver, or prepurchase multitickets or passes with cancellation on board
Fare structure: Flat. Various passes and multitickets
Fares collected on board: 20 per cent
Arrangements for elderly/disabled: Special dial-a-bus services for disabled
Average speed: 20 km/h
Operating costs financed by: Tickets and other sources 45.2 per cent, subsidy 54.8 per cent

Tram
Type of operation: Conventional tramway, initial route opened November 2000

Passenger journeys: Not currently available
Car-km: (Annual) 1.1 million (estimate)

Route length: 18 km
Number of routes: 1
Number of stops: 24
Gauge: 1,435 mm
Track: Type GP35 grooved rail for street sections, UIC50 rail elsewhere
Electrification: 750 V DC, overhead

Current situation
North-south Line 1 opened in November 2000.

Developments
In September 2006, Alstom was selected to provide the second tram line for the city. The new contract, valued at some EUR108 million,

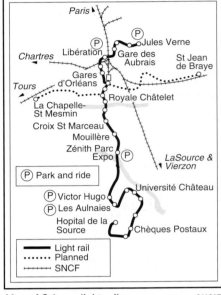

Map of Orleans light rail   0110151

includes the design and manufacture of the entire system and the supply of 21 Citadis 302 low-floor trams, with an option for a further 6 vehicles. The line will connect St-Jean-de Braye with La Chapelle St-Mesmin via the city centre, where the line will be equipped with the APS surface current collection system. The 12.3-km long line will have 26 stops and is currently scheduled to enter service in 2011.

Rolling stock: 22 cars
Alstom Citadis 301   M22

On order: 21 Alstom Citadis 302 low-floor trams, with an option for a further 6 vehicles

Service: 6 min peak
First/last car: 04.10/01.30
Fare collection: Automatic ticket vending machines at each station, validation on board
Fare structure: As bus
Integration with other modes: Six park-and-ride car parks totalling 900 spaces. Bus feeders

---

Paris

Population: City 2.14 million (2005 estimate), region 11.2 million (estimate)

Public transport
Bus, metro, light rail and a funicular operated by Paris Transport Authority (RATP) under overall control of a board (syndicat) consisting of government and local authority representatives (STIF). STIF also supervises operation of regional cross-city metro (RER) shared by RATP with French National Railways (SNCF), and SNCF's extensive suburban services. Some suburban bus lines operated by private firms are also integrated under STIF.

Syndicat des Transports d'Ile-de-France (STIF)

9-11 Avenue de Villars, F-75007 Paris, France
Tel: (+33 1) 47 53 28 00
Fax: (+33 1) 47 05 11 05
e-mail: stif@stif-idf.fr
Web: www.stif-idf.fr

Key personnel
President: Jean-Paul Huchon
Director General: Sophie Mougard
Press Contact: Marie-France Villedieu

Background
The Syndicat des Transports d'Ile-de-France (STIF), formerly the Syndicat des Transports Parisiens (STP), has responsibility for organising public transport in the Ile-de-France. A public

body created in 1959, it includes representatives of the Ile de France Region and of the eight Ile-de-France départements under the President of the Region Ile de France.

Current situation
Has overall responsibility for policy and co-ordination of urban and suburban transport provision in the greater Paris area (Ile-de-France region) with a population of about 11 million in the 12,000 km² Ile de France Region.
    The network includes 211 km of metro, 14 lines, 380 stations; 580 km RER, jointly run by RATP and SNCF-IDF, 5 lines, 58 RATP, 165 SNCF-IDF stations, 7 jointly run stations (RATP and SNCF-IDF); 1,286 km SNCF-IDF lines, 5,000 trains, 208 stations not including RER; 18,417 km bus routes, 1,254 lines, 7,400 buses.

Its powers have been strengthened under recent government devolution moves to include organisation of transport services, special school bus services, on-demand services, the ability to raise funds and borrow money, to be responsible for work to public transport infrastructure and to delegate to local authorities, except for fare policy. The body, with representatives of départements, Paris itself and the Île-de-France region brings together the operations of RATP, SNCF and private bus operators, and is responsible for authorising provision of transport, overseeing the level of service and setting fares. STIF is responsible for authorising major projects, and has administered the very substantial investment in public transport facilities, including RER development, electrification of suburban railways, improved bus fleet, better orbital networks, bus lane and shelter provision and information developments.

STIF administers a range of contractual arrangements with private bus operators for provision of suburban services. All give the operator a local monopoly but this may be in the form of own risk operation, guaranteed receipts, a contracted price or a management contract.

Developments

In October 2001, STIF introduced the 'Navigo' electronic smart card, which will gradually replace the existing magnetic tickets. The first stage (2001-2003) saw the existing 1 million yearly passes transferred onto the news system, and the second phase (2006) the 2.5 million monthly passes will be replaced.

IF is currently working on the implementation of the 2000-2006 Masterplan of investments, agreed between the national government and the Region. This programme led to investments of EUR3.6 billion into the public transport systems within the Ile de France Region. The main focus is to improve suburban-to-suburban links, through new orbital rail lines and tramway routes. The metro routes, which often stop at the administrative boundaries of Paris, will be extended into the suburbs.

In January 2004, STIF signed a new wave of contracts with the two main transport operators (RATP and SNCF) for four years. Under this new framework, the two companies have committed themselves to agreed levels of services with a defined level of quality. Under the contracts, STIF commits itself to paying the companies the agreed compensation and the financial incentives linked to agreed quality of service. The previous system of automatic payment of losses of companies has thus been replaced by a more dynamic approach.

In late 2005, STIF issued an EU tender for rolling stock funding options as well as financial and legal advisers.

Régie Autonome des Transports Parisiens (RATP)

LAC B916, 54 Quai de la Rapée ou 189, Rue de Bercy, F-75599 Paris Cedex 12, France
Tel: (+33 8) 92 68 77 14   Fax: (+33 1) 58 76 16 50
Web: www.ratp.fr

Key personnel

President and Director General: Anne-Marie Idrac
Director of Development: Philippe Ventejol
   Staff: 44,860

Passenger journeys: (Annual) 2,600 million

Operating costs financed by: Fares 41.8 per cent, subsidy/grants 58.2 per cent
Subsidy from: Compensation for 'social fares' reductions (17.3 per cent), Indemnité Compensatrice (33 per cent), employers ('versement'), national and local government

Background

RATP, established in 1949, is controlled by a board composed of representatives of central government, local authorities, staff and transport professionals. Central area public transport is based on a dense metro network with closely

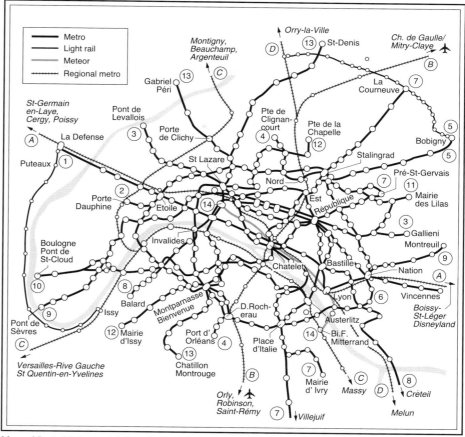

Map of Paris Metro and light rail system

1115259

spaced stations. Express metro (Réseau Express Régional, RER) routes traverse the conurbation and serve large areas of the suburbs.

Government policy has involved encouraging the use of public transport, establishing a dedicated employee tax (the 'versement') for operating support. Legislation, introduced in 1982, allowed for employers to become liable for paying part of the cost of commuters' season tickets.

To relieve RER Line A, a new fully automated metro line known as Météor (Metro Rapide Est-Ouest) from Tolbiac to Gare de Lyon and Madeleine, was opened in 1998.

Current situation

RATP provides bus, metro, tram and RER services throughout the Ile de France region.

Developments

From May 2006, the existing Carte Orange weekly and monthly tickets were replaced by Navigo contactless travel cards supplied by ASK.

Long-term plans exist for a major programme of new light rail lines, which would create a 'ring line' to provide services for the city's suburbs. New lines would total some 50 km and existing lines would be extended by nearly 19 km.

Bus

Staff: 12,398, plus 2,801 maintenance staff

Passenger journeys: (1998) 850 million
Vehicle-km: (1997) 142 million

Number of routes: 322
Route length: (One way) 2,650 km; urban 559 km, suburban 2,103 km (plus 118 km local)
On priority right-of-way: 304 km in city, 173 km in suburbs

Most intensive service: 3–4 min
One-person operation: All routes
Fare collection: Tickets validated by machine on board, passes shown to driver
Fare structure: 8 zones; multiticket carnets, and weekly, monthly and yearly all-mode passes (Carte Orange), zonal day tickets
Fares collected on board: 33 per cent; over 50 per cent of passengers use zonal passes

Fare evasion control: Roving inspectors in teams, plus radio
Operational control: All buses fitted with radio; other methods include centralised despatching by route controllers, now covering 131 routes, initiating terminal departures. A system of computerised monitoring linked to 'next bus' information at stops, known as ALEXIS and introduced on Trans Val-de-Marne and the tramway, is being tested on routes 26 and 29
Bus priority: 'Ligne Pilote' routes use extensive system of bus lanes; one route also equipped for experimental on-board traffic light control. Now 40 per cent of route-km in central area operate over bus lanes, covering 214 route-km (32 km of busway), with further 173.5 route-km in suburbs. Extensive system of reserved busways proposed for suburbs; Trans Val-de-Marne segregated busway. Further plans for city-centre busways and control of traffic congestion
Integration with other modes: Multitickets valid for use on buses, metro and RER; zonal passes valid on all modes; buses timed to meet trains at certain interchange stations
Average distance between stops: Urban 320 m; suburban 420 m
Average peak-hour speed: Urban 9.9 km/h; suburban 13.9 km/h
New vehicles financed by: Capital budget investments

Metro

Staff: 9,250, plus maintenance staff (see RER below)

Type of operation: Full metro, first line opened 1900

Passenger journeys: (Including funicular) (1998) 1,157 million
Car-km: (1997) 199.4 million

Route length: 201.5 km
Number of lines: 16 (includes 2 'bis' lines)
Number of stations: 297
Gauge: 1,435 mm
Electrification: 750 V DC, third rail

Service: 1 min 35 s to 3 min minimum
Operating times: 05.30–01.15
Fare structure: Flat

Fare collection: Automatic machines with change-giving facility or carnets of 10 tickets at reduced price, entrance gates at all stations, exit gates at RER stations; roving inspectors

Integration with other modes: Greater Paris area divided into seven zones. Monthly pass (Navigo – previously Carte Orange) and tourist passes for unlimited journeys within valid zones on metro, buses, RER, suburban SNCF lines and coach lines; used by more than 60 per cent of RATP passengers

Signalling: All lines linked to central control and monitoring post (PCC) which receives all data on train movements and locations, issues appropriate instructions, and remotely controls all trackside equipment; ATO on all lines

Rolling stock: 3,532 cars

MP55 (1956/57)	M48 T16
CIMT MP59 (1966/67)	M405 T202
CIMT MP73 (1974)	M245
CIMT/B&L MF67 (1967/76)	M904 T581
Franco-Belge/Alsthom MF77 (1978/86)	M708 T270
GEC Alstom/Bombardier-ANF MF88 (1992)	M10 T5
GEC Alstom MP89 (1996)	M90
Météor MP89CA (1998)	M48

MP cars are rubber-tyred, MF steel-wheeled.

New-generation metro trains have steerable axles with independent wheels and full-width gangways between cars.

On order: 45 five-car MF2000 trains for Line 2 to be manufactured between mid-2007 and the end of 2009. These vehicles are by a consortium which includes Alstom, Bombardier and Areva TA.

Developments

The extension of the automated Line 14 (Météor) to Gare Saint-Lazare was opened in December 2003.

Extensions to the metro are due to open in 2007: Line 4: Porte d'Orléans-Bagneux; Line 8: Créteil Préfecture-Parc des Sports; Line 12: Porte de la Chapelle-Mairie d'Aubervillers and Line 14: Bibliothéque-Olympiades.

Regional metro (RER)

Operated jointly by RATP and SNCF (see below)
Staff: 2,896, plus 2,735 maintenance staff shared with metro

Type of operation: Regional express metro

Passenger journeys: (RATP lines)
(1998) 368 million

SNCF line figures included in suburban rail total, see below

Route length: 366 km, of which 115 km operated by RATP and 251 km by SNCF
Number of lines: Four with numerous branches (Lines A and B jointly operated, Lines C and D SNCF only)
Number of stations: 158 (RATP 64, SNCF 94)
Gauge: 1,435 mm
Electrification: 1.5 kV DC and 25 kV 50 Hz, overhead

Rolling stock: RATP, 376 Type MS61 cars, 273 MI79 cars (see SNCF entry also), 65 M12N cars

Developments

SNCF intends to refurbish existing suburban rolling stock and possibly order new single-deck emus.

Funicular
Current situation
The 102 m Funiculaire de Montmartre was built in 1901 as a water balance system and electrified in 1935. It has an incline of 36 per cent. After refurbishment, it reopened in 1991 with new cars offering capacity of 2,000 passengers/h in each direction.

Light rail
Type of operation: Light rail, initial route opened 1992
Passenger journeys: (1998) 19.8 million

RATP Irisbus articulated bus on the Val du Marne busway (Bill Luke)   1115260

Citadis 302 LRV on RATP's T2 line (Milan Šrámek)   1115261

Route length: 20.4 km
Number of lines: 2
Number of stops: 34
Gauge: 1,435 mm
Electrification: 750 V DC, overhead
Service: Peak 5 min, off-peak 8 min
First/last car: 05.00/23.59
Fare structure: As bus
Fare collection: Automatic vending machines, onboard validators

Rolling stock: 39 articulated vehicles

GEC Alstom (1991/92)	M17
GEC Alstom (1996)	M22

Current situation

Light rail line T1 links St Denis and Bobigny in the northeast suburbs. Most of the route is on-street private right-of-way; there are 28 bus feeders. A second 11.3 km light rail route, T2, opened in 1997, running over a former SNCF line from La Defense to Issy Val-de-Seine. The T2 runs in the right-of-way of SNCF's last third-rail suburban railway from Puteaux to Issy Val-de-Seine, closed in 1993, with a northern extension from Puteaux to La Défense. Daily ridership had reached 30,000 by the end of 1997, 20 per cent better than forecasts for 2000.

Developments

Line 3, which will run from Pont du Garigliano-Boulevard via Porte de Versailles to Port d'Ivry, is under construction and scheduled to open in late 2006.

In October 2005, the first of the 22 *Citadis* trams for Line 3 was tested.

RATP has ordered 49 six-car rubber-tyred MP05 metro trains from Alstom to re-equip Line 1. The vehicles will be delivered from mid-2008 until the end of 2010. The contract was valued at EUR474 million and includes an option for an additional 10 trainsets.

People mover (OrlyVAL)
Passenger journeys: (1995) 1.6 million

Current situation

A 7.2 km automated people mover with three stations opened in 1991 between Orly airport and Antony station on RER Line B. A 4 min interval service is operated. RATP undertook the project jointly with Matra using VAL technology; the scheme was funded with contributions from Air Inter and a number of banks.

Rolling stock: Eight two-car trains

Société Nationale des Chemins de Fer Français (SNCF) – French National Railways

34 rue du Commandant Mouchotte, F-75699, Paris Cedex 14, France
Tel: (+33 1) 53 25 60 00
Fax: (+33 1) 53 25 88 15
Web: www.sncf.com
www.transilien.com

Key personnel

Business Director, Ile de France Passenger: Thierry Mignaux
Staff: 174,755 (2003 group total)

Type of operation: Suburban heavy rail

Passenger journeys: (Paris suburban)
(2001) 560 million

Route length: Suburban lines, 1,263 km; RER-SNCF lines, 274 km
Number of lines: Suburban, 37; RER-SNCF, 4 (Lines A and B operated jointly with RATP, Lines C and D SNCF only)
Number of stations: 382
Electrification: 25 kV AC, overhead (654 km); 1.5 kV DC, overhead (512 km)

Fare structure: 67 per cent of passengers use the zonal Carte Integrale (annual pass) or Carte Orange (monthly or weekly pass); remainder use graduated-fare tickets (15 per cent), weekly workers' passes or student passes. Zonal system is increasing its share
Integration with other modes: Carte Integrale and Carte Orange valid on SNCF, RATP and private bus services; other combined passes available (including day and monthly passes for all modes), SNCF-RER/RATP or Metro/RATP
Fare evasion control: Automatic turnstiles, roving inspectors
Operating costs financed by: Fares 43 per cent, employers' tax (versement transport) 40 per cent, other commercial sources 1 per cent, subsidy 16 per cent. Subsidy provided by state (70 per cent) and local authorities (30 per cent)
One-person operation: Totally on RER and partially on other suburban lines, except trains out of Paris Est (planned for introduction when EOLE opens)
Rolling stock: 3,505 cars, formed as emus or 6-car to 8-car push-pull sets hauled by electric locomotives. Many of both types of train comprise double-deck cars (1,491 total). SNCF is aiming for 100 per cent double-deck operation by 2005; 53 five-car double-deck sets for EOLE were delivered by the end of 1999
On order: 32 four-car double-deck emus for outer suburban services. This stock is a shared SNCF/RATP design with three doorways per side and all axles motored

Current situation

SNCF is divided into four businesses, each of which has its own budget and bottom-line responsibility: Long-Distance Passenger (Voyageurs France-Europe); Urban and Regional Passenger (Transport Public – TP); Paris Region Passenger (Ile de France) (which now comes under TP); and Freight (Fret SNCF). Each Business Director contracts with the other departments for

Class Z 22500 double-deck emu for Ile de France services (ALSTOM) 0554548

the means of production and back-up services. Each of the 20 geographical regions has its own director, who has control of local passenger services and reports directly to the President. Regional and Paris Region passenger services are heavily subsidised while other activities are required to break even.

SNCF services in the Paris region are now marketed under the name Transilien. Services have achieved about 10 billion passenger-km since 1991, despite extensions to the RER system.

Transport provision in the Paris region is governed by five-year contracts (contrats de plan) between the Ile de France region and the state.

In the same way that responsibility for rail transport was transferred to regional councils in 2002, a similar transfer was to be made in July 2005 to the Syndicat des Transports d'Ile-de-France (STIF).

Major developments of the Paris network centre on the RER (Regional Express) network, started in 1969, which links suburban lines across the centre of the city. The network consists of five lines, A, B, C, D and E. The RER is operated by the SNCF, in the case of Lines A and B jointly with the Paris transport authority RATP; SNCF now has 1,282 route-km of suburban operation in the region. All are electrified.

Three-quarters of Paris region traffic is with discounted fares. Operating costs are met 40 per cent by fares (but employers pay half the cost of their employees' annual tickets or Navigo monthly/weekly tickets); 40 per cent by the Versement Transport, the payroll tax levied from employers; and 20 per cent by public authorities (the state, 70 per cent; departmental authorities, 30 per cent).

For further information on SNCF, please see *Jane's World Railways.*

Developments

Plans for a rail link between Paris and Charles de Gaulle airport are under consideration. The CDG Express, also known as 'Virgule', proposed by SNCF, RFF and ADP, would operate from Gare de l'Est with 15 minute headway and would be 32 km long (23 km on existing track) with 1.7 km in tunnel.

Fleet

Following difficulties in supplying enough locomotives for the freight activity, SNCF divided the main line locomotive fleet by activity sector at the beginning of 1999. 141 electric locomotives were allocated to Ile de France. Transport Public locomotives and rolling stock are now nominally allocated region by region and are increasingly based closer to their area of operation.

SNCF Paris suburban rolling stock at the start of 2003 totalled 2,992 emu cars (751 sets) and 1,125 push-pull trainset cars. Of the combined fleet, 2,513 cars were double-deck.

SNCF has ordered 60 ALSTOM Prima electric locomotives for Paris suburban services. These are designated Class BB 27300 and will be identical to Fret SNCF's BB 27000 except for being equipped to operate passenger trains. They will replace older classes powering double-deck stock in push-pull mode.

In mid-2005 SNCF was expected shortly to place a large order for 330 four- or five-car single-deck suburban emus, known as Nouvelle Automotrice Transilien (NAT), which will replace the last remaining stainless-steel emus dating from the 1960s.

Rennes

Population: City 209,000, metropolitan area 588,000 (estimates)

Public transport

Bus services provided by franchised operators under control of a semi-public company representing 37 towns; VAL automated metro.

Société d'Economie Mixte des Transports Collectifs de l'Agglomération Rennaise (SEMTCAR)

1 rue Geneviève de Gaulle Anthonioz, CS80827, F-35208, Rennes Cedex 02, France
Tel: (+33 2) 99 85 89 30
Fax: (+33 2) 99 65 11 51
e-mail: info@semtcar.fr
Web: www.semtcar.fr

Key personnel

President and Director General: Daniel Delaveau
Director General: Guy Malbrancke
Director, Communications: T Courau
Staff: 20

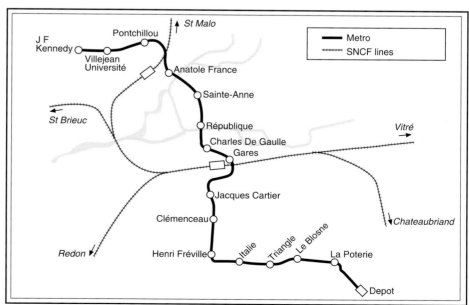
Map of Rennes VAL line a and suburban rail network 0568961

Siemens/Matra VAL 208 vehicle on the Rennes VAL metro   1033558

Background
Created in 1992, SEMTCAR is a semi-public limited company whose capital is held by Rennes Métropole (68.7 per cent) and Transdev (30 per cent).

Current situation
SEMTCAR is responsible for the construction of the metro a and b lines.

The company is also making its experience and expertise in project management available to other French and foreign projects (see separate entry in Consultancy services section).

Metro
For detail of the metro, please see separate entry for Service de Transport de l'Agglomération Rennaise (STAR) – Rennes Metropole Transport Service.

Current situation
Line 1 (Line a) of the VAL automated metro, with 15 stations, was opened in March 2002. The line runs from J F Kennedy to La Poterie, mostly underground.

Developments
SEMTCAR is carrying out studies for a proposed second line (Line b) running northeast from the southwest of the city and intersecting the current line at Gares and Ste Anne stations.

Service de Transport de l'Agglomération Rennaise' (STAR) – Rennes District Transport Service
Rue Jean-Marie Huchet, PO Box 94001, F-35040 Rennes Cedex, France
Tel: (+33 2) 99 27 40 00   Fax: (+33 2) 99 27 40 27
e-mail: contact@star.fr
Web: www.star.fr

Key personnel
Director General: François Xavier Gelin
Operating Manager: Bruno Loy
Project Manager, Metro: Roland Clavel
   Staff: 701

Passenger journeys (both modes): Not currently available

Current situation
STAR is the public transport network for Rennes and 37 communities, the largest of these being Cesson-Sévigné and Bruz. Known as Rennes Métropole, this area has some 390,000 inhabitants. The system comprises bus and automated metro services.

The network is operated by Keolis Rennes, a subsidiary of the Keolis Group, which was awarded the operations contract in 2006 and which will run services for seven years.

Suburban lines and school transport is subcontracted to Kelis Emeraude, Keolis Armot, TIV, Jollivet, Cars Morand and Cars Orain.

Paratransit services, HANDISTAR, are carried out by SRTS.

Bus
Passenger journeys: Not currently available
Vehicle-km: Not currently available

Number of routes: 15 urban, 28 suburban, 11 express, 5 community
Route length: Not currently available
On priority right-of-way: 20 km

Developments
A further six bus lines will be accessible by the end of 2008.

Fleet: 246 vehicles, plus 80 hired for suburban services	
Renault SC10	26
Renault R312	76
Renault PR180	59
Heuliez GX187	13
Van Hool AG300 low-floor articulated	62
Van Hool A300 low-floor articulated	10

In peak service: 216
Average age of fleet: 10.2 years
Most intensive service: Peak 4 min, off-peak 7 min
One-person operation: All routes
Fare structure: Flat, reduced-rate carnets of 10 tickets or 6 return journeys; single tickets valid 1 h; weekly and monthly passes; day rover ticket; 1-hour bus/metro ticket ('Ticket Unité'); KorriGo prepaid smartcard
Fare collection: Tickets sold by approved vendors and drivers; cancellers on board
Fares collected on board: 22 per cent
Fare evasion control: Inspectors
Average peak-hour speed: Urban 14 km/h, suburban 24 km/h

Arrangements for elderly/disabled: Special services operated by Handistar with 14 minibuses; free travel for invalids; 6 bus lines are accessible
Integration with other modes: Bus and Metro are fully integrated
Operating costs financed by: Fares 38 per cent, subsidy/grants 62 per cent
Subsidy from: District
New vehicles financed by: District

Metro
Type of operation: Light rail – Véhicule Automatique Léger (VAL). First line opened March 2002.

Route length: 9.4 km
   in tunnel: 3.7 km
   elevated: 1 km
Number of lines: 1
Number of stops: 15
   in tunnel: 13

Current situation
Line 1 (Line a) of the VAL automated metro, with 15 stations, was opened in March 2002. The line runs from J F Kennedy to La Poterie, mostly underground.

There are four park-and-ride locations.

Developments
SEMTCAR is carrying out studies for a proposed second line (Line b) running northeast from the city centre and intersecting the current line at Gares station. There may also be extensions to both ends of the existing line.

Rolling stock: 16 two-car vehicles
Siemens/Matra VAL 208 (2000)	16

Service: Peak: 2½ min; daytime: 3–5 min, off-peak: 7–10 min
First/last car: 05.15/00.40 (weekdays); 07.30/00.40 (weekend)
Fare structure: Single, 10-trip, daily tickets; weekly and monthly passes
Integration with other modes: Metro and bus are fully integrated
Arrangements for elderly/disabled: All stations are accessible

Société Nationale des Chemins de fer Français (SNCF) – French National Railways
Rennes Region
22 boulevard de Beaumont, F-35040 Rennes, France
Tel: (+33 2) 99 29 11 10   Fax: (+33 2) 99 29 12 18
e-mail: webbr@sncf.fr
Web:www.sncf.com

Train Express Régional (TER)
Region Bretagne
BP 90527, F-35 005 Rennes Cedex, France
Web: www.ter-sncf.com/bretagne

Current situation
Limited suburban services operate on five routes.

For further information on SNCF, please see *Jane's World Railways.*

Developments
The KorriGo prepaid smartcard is now available for all transport modes in the Rennes commuter area.

Rouen
Population: City 109,000 (estimate), metropolitan area 541,400 (2007 estimate)

Public transport
Bus, including BRT, and light rail services provided by private company under concession from the Agglomération Rouennaise.

Transports en Commun de l'Agglomération Rouennaise (TCAR)/Veolia Transport
Les Deux Rivières, 15 rue de la Petite Chartreuse, BP 99, F-76002 Rouen Cedex 1, France
Tel: (+33 2) 35 52 52 00   Fax: (+33 2) 35 52 52 38
e-mail: tcar.communication@veolia-transport.fr

Web: www.tcar.fr
   www.veolia-transport.com

Key personnel
President: Raymond Hue
International Relations Manager: Werner Kutil
   Staff: 1,103 (as at 31 December 2007)

Background
TCAR is a subsidiary of the Veolia Environment group (Veolia Transport).

Current situation
TCAR operates a light rail system and regular bus lines (Métrobus network) and, since February 2001, the Bus Rapid Transit system TEOR (three lines) in the Rouen metropolitan area, covering some 448 km², to 45 communes and a population of 411,435. There are also school bus services, taxi services and services for people with reduced mobility.

Some interurban services are operated by subcontractors.

Operating costs financed by: Fares approximately 30 per cent, plus unspecified contribution (lump sum payment) by the organising authority (financed mostly via transport tax and financial fiscal contributions from the member municipalities) plus some commercial revenue (percentage not specified)

Bus (not including TEOR)
Passenger boardings (unlinked): (2007) 41.38 million
Vehicle-km: (2007) 13.59 million

Number of routes: 29 regular plus 24 school routes and 15 shared taxi routes
Route length: 522.9 km (excluding school routes)
On priority right-of-way: Not currently available

Developments
Since 2005, 106 new buses have been purchased. New Agora vehicles are biodiesel fuelled and have particulate filters, CCTV and air-conditioning and are accessible.

Fleet: TCAR: 191 Irisbus AGORA standard and articulated, Evobus O 405 N standard and articulated and Heuliez GX 117 L standard vehicles; subcontracted: Not currently available
TCAR/Veolia: *Full breakdown of TCAR/Veolia fleet vehicles is not currently available, but comprises:*
Standard bus	145
Articulated bus	30
Midibus	16
Subcontracted: *Breakdown of subcontracted fleet is not currently available*
Average age of fleet: Not currently available

Most intensive service: five min
One-person operation: All routes
Fare structure: Flat, one h unlimited travel; 10-journey tickets for single journeys; monthly and one to three-day, seven-day, 31-day passes and annual subscription; free tickets for unemployed and reductions for others
Fare collection: Magnetic tickets sold in three main ticket offices, by approved vendors/agents, automatic vending machines (in light rail stations); bus drivers sell only single tickets (one h); validators on board
Fare evasion control: Inspectors
Arrangements for elderly/disabled: Reduced fares; taxi or minibus provision by appointment
Average commercial speed: 17.55 km/h
Subsidy from: Not currently available
New vehicles financed by: Not currently available

TEOR
Developments
Line T1 and T3 have been extended to the Haut de Rouen, Bihorel and Darnéta with effect from January 2007.

Passenger boardings (unlinked): (2007) 9.98 million
Vehicle-km: (2007) 2.49 million

Number of lines: three
Route length: 37.19 km
On priority right-of-way: Not currently available

Fleet: 64 vehicles
Irisbus Agora articulated low-floor	36
Irisbus Citelis articulated low-floor	28
Average age of TEOR fleet: Not currently available

Fare structure: As for bus

TEOR bus in-station   1368792

TEOR Agora articulated bus on segregated busway   1368791

Métro light rail vehicle crossing the River Seine   1368790

Light rail (Métro)

Current situation

In the five years since introduction, the number of passengers on the TCAR network grew by 60 per cent and ticket revenue by 68 per cent; 26 per cent of light rail passengers did not use public transport before.

Type of operation: Light rail, first line opened December 1994

Passenger journeys (unlinked): (2007) 15.75 million
Car-km: (2007) 1.41 million

Route length: 18.3 km
  in tunnel: 1.7 km (total underground: 2.2 km)
Number of lines: two
Number of stops: 31
  in tunnel: five
Gauge: 1,435 mm
Max gradient: seven per cent
Minimum curve radius: 25 m
Electrification: 750 V DC, overhead

Rolling stock: 28 cars
GEC Alstom (1993/94)   M28

Service: Daytime 6–9 min (three min in peak on central/common trunk), evening 15–20 min
First/last car: 05.00/23.30
Fare structure: As for bus
Fare collection: As for bus
Average commercial speed: 19.02 km/h

Rouen light rail network
1168386

Rouen light rail network

St Etienne

Population: City 177,000 (2004 estimate), Metropolitan area: 321,000 (estimate)

Public transport

Bus, trolleybus and tramway services provided by franchised company STAS for the Department of Urban Transport of Saint-Etienne Métropole, a 'syndicat' grouping of 15 towns.

Société des Transports Urbains de l'Agglomération Stéphanoise (STAS)

Avenue Pierre Mendès France, BP 90055, F-42272 Saint-Priest-en-Jarez Cedex, France
Tel: (+33 4) 77 92 82 00   Fax: (+33 4) 77 92 82 01
e-mail: stas@stas.tm.fr
Web: www.stas.tm.fr

Key personnel

Director General: Not currently available
Operating Manager: Not currently available
  Staff: 694

Passenger journeys: (All modes)
Not currently available

Operating costs financed by: Fares 61 per cent, other commercial sources 6 per cent, subsidy/grants 33 per cent
Subsidy from:
New vehicles financed by:
One-person operation: All routes

Fare structure: Flat; single tickets valid 1 h from cancellation; multi-trip, daily, weekly, weekend and monthly passes
Fare collection: Single tickets sold on bus and trolleybus; automatic machines at tram stops; 135 approved vendors; cancellers on board
Fare evasion control: Inspectors

Arrangements for elderly/disabled: Special services on demand; low-floor buses and trams; stops specially designed for ease of access

Current situation

STAS, part of the Veolia Transportation group, holds the franchise for operation of urban transport from the Department of Urban Transport of Saint-Etienne Métropole, which is a grouping of St Etienne and 15 neighbouring towns.

Developments

A second 2 km tramway line, from Châteaucreux station to downtown Place du Peuple, is under construction. It is scheduled for opening in late 2006.

A total of 2 km of the existing tramway line, beyond Place du Peuple, is being restructured.

Bus and trolleybus

Vehicle-km: Not currently available

Number of routes: Bus 43, trolleybus 3
Route length: Not currently available
On private right-of-way: Not currently available
Average speed: 14.1 km/h

Fleet: Not currently available
In peak service: Not currently available
Average age of fleet: 8 years

Fleet: 41 trolleybuses
Renault ER100R/ER100H (1977/82, some refurbished
  2003/05) (6 ex-Grenoble)   31
Irisbus Cristalis ETB12 low-floor (2003)   11

In peak service: Not currently available
Average age of fleet:
New vehicles financed by:

Contracted bus

Vehicle-km: Not currently available

Tramway

Type of operation: Conventional tramway
Car-km: Not currently available

Route length: 9.3 km
Number of routes: 1
Number of stops: 31
Gauge: 1,000 mm
Electrification: 600 V DC, overhead

Rolling stock: 35 tramcars
GEC Alsthom articulated (1994)   M15
GEC Alsthom/Vevey articulated (1997/98)   M20
In peak service: 31 cars
First/last tram: 04.30/24.00

Most intensive service: Peak 3 min
Integration with other modes: Connection to SNCF services

Société Nationale des Chemins de Fer Français (SNCF) – French National Railways

Lyons Region
Address: 10 Cours de Verdun, F-69286 Lyons, France
Tel: (+33 4) 72 40 11 10   Fax: (+33 4) 72 40 10 16

Type of operation: Suburban heavy rail

Current situation

Limited service on three lines, half hourly off-peak, 10 minutes in peak periods, hourly or better to Lyons.

Developments

As part of the PDU plan, the 14 km St Etienne Carnot-Firminy line will be electrified at 1,500 V DC, stations will be relocated or modernised and a 15 minute peak and 30 minute off-peak service introduced. Bus services and trolleybus Route 1, St Etienne Bellevue-Firminy, will be remodelled to feed into stations. In a later stage, bus services in the Gier valley towards Lyons will be restructured to feed into rail stations and new feeders created.

Strasbourg

Population: City 270,00, urban area 420,000, metropolitan area 702,000 (estimates)

Public transport
Bus and light rail services provided by franchised company CTS, owned mainly by the Communauté Urbaine de Strasbourg (CUS) (52 per cent) and Bas-Rhin Département (26 per cent), also operating regional routes. CTS is administered by a board which includes representatives from the city and CUS; suburban rail.

Compagnie des Transports Strasbourgeois SA (CTS)
14 rue de la Gare aux Marchandises, BP2, F-67035 Strasbourg Cedex 2, France
Tel: (+33 3) 88 77 70 11   Fax: (+33 3) 88 77 70 98-9
e-mail: info@cts-strasbourg.fr
Web: www.cts-strasbourg.fr

Key personnel
President: Roland Ries
Director General: Jean-Françoise Soulet
Operating Manager: Jean-Louis Metzger
Project Director: Alain Giesi
   Staff: 1,519 (as at December 2007)

Passenger boardings: (both modes, unlinked trips)
(2007) 89.25 million

Current situation
Service started on the first tram route (Line A) in November 1994. Traffic levels on Line A have surpassed all forecasts, running at 77,000 passengers daily in 1999 and reaching more than 110,000 on some Saturdays. Lines B, C and D had been added by late 2000. Between 1992 and 2003, public transport use rose by more than 84 per cent overall.

Strasbourg has enforced severe restrictions on car traffic; the city centre is pedestrianised and cars cannot drive from one side to the other. Their only access is to four 'loops' which extend to the edge of the central area. The result has been a 17 per cent drop in city-centre car traffic.

Contactless ticketing was introduced in 2004.

Bus
Passenger journeys: (Urban)
(2007) 41.75 million
Vehicle-km: (Urban)
(2007) 11.04 million

Number of routes: 30 urban, 11 interurban
Route length: Urban 318 km, interurban 359 km
On priority right-of-way: 7 km

Fleet: 313 vehicles
Urban fleet

Heuliez GX317	2
Heuliez GX327 GNV	41
Agora Standard	70
Agora GNV (CNG)	55
Agora articulated	28
Heuliez GX57	5
Van Hool AG300 low-floor articulated	34
Heuliez GX87	7
Irisbus Citélis CNG	13
Interurban fleet	
Renault Tracer	2
Setra standard	22
Setra 15 m	8
Setra articulated	5
Heuliez GX87	8
Heuliez GX57	7
Heuliez GX317	3
ARES	3

In peak service: Urban 221, interurban 55
Average age of fleet: 7 years

Most intensive service: 4 min
One-person operation: All routes
Fare structure: Urban, flat; interurban, zonal
Fare collection: Single and Return tickets from driver, valid up to one hour, with free transfer, or prepurchase carnets with validation on board; weekly, monthly and annual passes; car parking plus return tram tickets; Alsaplus pass for CTS/SNCF journeys; Badgeo pre-paid contactless smartcard.
Arrangements for elderly/disabled: Some 95.3 per cent of bus fleet is low-floor; special minibus services; reduced rate tickets and monthly passes for over-65s and invalids
Operating costs financed by: Fares 68 per cent, subsidy/grants 32 per cent
Subsidy from: CUS (urban) and Bas-Rhin Département (interurban)

Light rail
Type of operation: Light rail, initial route opened 1994

Passenger journeys: (2007) 47.5 million
Car-km: (2007) 3.75 million

Route length: 53 km
Number of lines: 5
Number of stations: 66
Gauge: 1,435 mm
Electrification: 750 V DC, overhead

Service: Peak 2½ min
First/last car: 04.30/00.30
Fare structure/collection: As bus

Integration with other modes: Nine park-and-ride sites with 4,190 car parking spaces. Bus routes restructured to feed into tram routes.

Rolling stock: 94 LRVs

Bombardier Eurotram (1994)	M53
Alstom Citadis (2005)	M41

On order: None

Developments
In August 2007, Line C was extended from the Esplanade to Neuhof and Line D from Etoile Polygon to Aristide Briand. Line E opened, running from Baggersee Robertsau Boecklin to the Homme de Fer station.

In November 2007, three new stations were added to Line E.

In January and May 2008, Line B was extended to Lingolsheim Tergaertel.

All stops have electronic displays, showing the destination of the next vehicle and waiting times.

Société Nationale des Chemins de Fer Français (SNCF) – French National Railways
Strasbourg Region
3 boulevard du Président Wilson, F-67803 Strasbourg, France
Tel: (+33 3) 88 32 56 33   Fax: (+33 3) 88 75 41 39
Web: www.sncf.com

Train Express Régional (TER)
Region Alsace
JL Laffond 10, Avenue Du General Leclerc, F-68053 Mulhouse, France
Web: www.ter-sncf.com/alsace

Current situation
Limited local services operate. The Alsace region has financed a half-hourly peak, hourly off-peak 200 km/h local service to Mulhouse. At the end of 1999 a company covering an area up to 30 km from the city – Société d'Intermodanité du Bassin de Strasbourg (SIBS) – was created by CTS (25 per cent), Transdev (25 per cent) and SNCF (50 per cent). It is proposed to link tram Line B from Strasbourg's central station to Gresswiller and Obernai over SNCF lines to Molsheim by 2008/09, with a new section of track serving the city's airport.

For further information on SNCF, please see *Jane's World Railways.*

Toulouse

Population: City 435,000 (2004), metropolitan area 917,000 (1999 Census)

Public transport
Urban bus services and metro are organised in the conurbation and its environs by the Syndicat Mixte des Transports en Commun de l'Agglomération Toulousaine (SMTC), which comprises Toulouse and 83 surrounding municipalities.

The SMTC is formed of the Greater Toulouse Authority, the Sicoval Public Authority and the SITPRT Syndicate. The SMTC manages the operation of the public transport network (régie) and sets transport policies and fares levels.

The operator for buses and metro is Tisséo Réseau Urbain (from the 1st of January 2006).

Tisséo-SMTC also manages the airport shuttle service and a specific service for disabled people (Mobibus).

There are also some limited suburban rail services provided by the French National Railway (SNCF) in the agglomeration. Lines C and D are standard rail services, which are integrated into the urban tariff area.

An 10.9 km light rail line with 18 stations, Line E, will be built from Les Arènes station to Beauzelle. An extension to Saint-Orleans is planned.

Syndicat Mixte des Transports en Commun de l'Agglomération Toulousaine (SMTC)
7, Esplanade Compans – Caffarelli, BP 61, F-31902 Toulouse Cedex 9, France
Tel: (+33 5) 67 77 80 80   Fax: (+33 5) 67 77 80 01
e-mail: smtcat@smtcat.fr
Web: www.tisseo.fr

Tisséo-SMTC
9 rue Michel Labrousse, F-31081 Toulouse Cedex 1, France
Tel: (+33 5) 61 41 70 70   Fax: (+33 5) 62 11 26 20
Web: www.tisseo.fr

Key personnel
President: Jean-Luc Moudenc
Vice-President: Georges Beyney
Director General of Services: Alexandre Murat
Assistant Director General: Jean-Paul Mazabrard
Secretary: Sébastien Clermont
Director of Finance: Christian Amiel
Director of Public Affairs: Sylvain Zalateu
Director of Development: François Barbier
Director of Communications: Guy Claverie
Director of Network: Vincent Gerojon
   Staff: 1,900 (estimate)

Current situation
Operator of bus and metro from 1 January 2006.

Overall use of the network has increased by 48.5 per cent since the metro opened, with interchange rising from 12 to 25 per cent.

Fare collection: Ticket sales by approved vendors on bus and from change-giving machines on metro stations; cancellers on board buses and in metro stations
Fare structure: Flat in each of 2 zones, inner covering Toulouse, Balma and Blagnac, and outer extending to 50 neighbouring towns; day, weekly and monthly passes; 10-journey and 12-journey tickets
Fare evasion control: Penalty payment

Bus
Passenger journeys: (2003) 46.0 million
(2004) 47.7 million

Number of routes: Urban 64
Route length: Urban 652 km
On priority right-of-way: 9 km

Current situation
Tisséo-Aéroport provides shuttles services, at 20 minute intervals, between Toulouse Blagnac airport and Toulouse Matabiau station.

Fleet: 528 vehicles
Mercedes-Benz/Evobus O405 CNG,
   articulated   23
Heuliez GX107   142
Heuliez GX317   276
Renault SC 10 R 044   61
Renault SC 10 R 444   2
Renault PR 180, articulated   2
Mercedes-Benz/Evobus Cito, midibus   17
Midibus MREOS   5
In peak service: Urban 425
Average age of fleet: 7.1 years

Most intensive service: 3–4 min
One-person operation: All routes
Average distance between stops: 300–400 m
Average peak-hour speed: In mixed traffic, 8 km/h; in bus lanes (city-centre only), 14 km/h
Bus priority: Bus lanes, dedicated traffic signals, bus priority at intersections; 9 km reserved
Operational control: All buses have radios
Arrangements for elderly/disabled: 5 buses equipped for disabled riders; on-demand service in co-operation with city authorities and SETRAS (*Service de Transport Spécialisé*); free transfer
Operating costs financed by: *Urban* – fares 47 per cent, other commercial sources 3 per cent, subsidy/grants 50 per cent
Subsidy from: Employers' payroll tax (versement) 28 per cent, local councils 22 per cent
New vehicles financed by: Loans and proceeds of employers' tax

Metro
Type of operation: Fully automated (unmanned) rubber-tyred metro, VAL system, opened 1993

Passenger journeys: (2003) 34 million
(2004) 39.9 million

Route length: 12 km
  in tunnel: 9 km
Number of lines: 1
Number of stations: 18
  in tunnel: 16
Gauge: 2,060 mm between H-type guide bars
Electrification: 750 V DC, collection by shoes from guide bars

Current situation
EUR100 million was lent by the European Investment Bank to extend Toulouse metro's Line A, which has been in operation since 1993. The money was chiefly for the extension of Line A but was also to pay for three stations and the acquisition of eight trainsets. The overall project includes building a second 15 km metro line (Line B) from Ramonville to Borderouge with 20 stations, expanding Jean-Jaures station, and the purchase of more rolling stock.
    In December 2003, the extension of Line A was completed from Joliment to Balma Gramont, 2.3 km in length, with three stations.

Toulouse metro train   1323750

Developments
The 15 km north-south Line B was confirmed in 1996 and construction began in 2002. It will be completely underground, with 20 stations, and will link Borderouge with Ramonville via Rangeuil university campus, providing interchange with Line A at Jeane-Jaures in the city centre. The line is due to be completed in mid-2007.
    A total of 35 Siemens VAL 208 trains have been ordered for the network, most scheduled to operate on Line B.
    A southern extension to Line B is planned.

Rolling stock: 43 two-car trains
GEC Alstom VAL 206 (1993)   M58
Siemens VAL 208   M28
In peak service: Not currently available
On order: 35 Siemens VAL 208 trains

Service: Peak 1 min 40 sec
First/last train: 05300/00.30
Integration with other modes: Feeder buses serve five stations

Tram
Current situation
An 10.9 km light rail line with 18 stations, Line E, will be built from Les Arènes station to Beauzelle. An extension to Saint-Orleans is planned.
    Construction is under way, with the project scheduled for completion by 2010.
    A contract, worth EUR65.7 million, was awarded to ALSTOM, comprising a fixed portion for design studies and the production of a

full-scale model (due to be available in late 2007) as well as four other parts for the supply and maintenance of 18 CITADIS trams, with an option for a further six cars. The first tram is scheduled to be delivered by the end of 2008.

Société Nationale des Chemins de Fer Français (SNCF) – French National Railways
Toulouse Region
Boulevard Marengo 9, BP 5209, F-31079 Toulouse, France
Tel: (+33 5) 61 10 11 10
Fax: (+33 5) 61 10 15 45
Web: www.sncf.fr
   www.ter-sncf.com

Type of operation: Suburban heavy rail

Passenger journeys: Not currently available
Train-km: Not currently available

Current situation
Limited suburban services provided on six routes into Toulouse Matabiau station, with 10 stations within the city limits and a further 15 in the conurbation.
    With opening of metro Line A in 1993, urban tickets became valid over the SNCF line (Line C) to Colomiers. A further line (Line D) provides standard rail services and is also integrated into the urban tariff area.

Georgia

Tbilisi
Population: 1.25 million (estimate)

Public transport
Bus services and funicular, operated by municipal undertaking; private fixed-route minibus and taxi operations; metro.

Tbilisis Metropoliteni (Tbilisi Metro)
Ploshchad Vokzalnaya 2, Tbilisi 380012, Georgia

Key personnel
Director General: Zurab Kikalishvili

Type of operation: Full metro, first line opened 1966

Passenger journeys: (2005) 105 million (estimate)

Route length: 26.4 km
  in tunnel: 16.4 km

Number of lines: 2
Number of stations: 22
Gauge: 1,524 mm
Max gradient: 4%
Minimum curve radius: 400 m
Electrification: 825 V DC, third rail

Developments
The Metro is currently being upgraded, including the stations and the trains, and this is due to be completed by 2007.

Line 1 is being extended to the University and a third line is planned or under construction. No completion dates are known for these projects.

Rolling stock: 186 cars, mostly in 3- and 4-car sets
Mytischy/Tbilisi E60   M186
Service: Peak 2½ min, off-peak 4 min
First/last train: 06.00/01.00
Fare structure: Flat
Revenue control: Open passage automatically controlled by photoelectric cell
One-person operation: None
Signalling: Automatic train stop; radio communication between trains and central control

Map of the Tbilisi
Metro
1115272

Germany

Aachen
Population: City 258,000, district 308,000 (estimates), region served 1,097,062 (AVV area, 2006)

Public transport
Bus services provided by publicly owned transport and electricity company. Fares and services co-ordinated with DB rail services on two lines, regional bus services of RVE, an associated company of DB and other operators within the framework of Aachener Verkehrsverbund GmbH (AVV). Also joint cross-border services run in conjunction with Belgian and Dutch operators.

Aachener Verkehrsverbund GmbH (AVV)
Neuköllner Strasse 1, D-52068 Aachen, Germany
Tel: (+49 241) 96 89 70
Fax: (+49 241) 968 97 20
e-mail: info@avv.de
Web: www.avv.de

Key personnel
General Manager: H J Sistenich

Current situation
Regional transit authority co-ordinates the bus and train services of eight operators:
Aachener Strassenbahn und Energieversorgungs AG (ASEAG);
DB Regio NRW GmbH Geschäftsbereich Rheinland (DB);
Dürener Kreisbahn GmbH (DKB);
Regionalverkehr Euregio Maas-Rhein GmbH (RVE);
Rurtalbahn GmbH (RTB);
TAETER Aachen, Veolia Verkehr Rheinland GmbH (TAETER Aachen);
WestEnergie und Verkehr GmbH & Co KG (west);
APV Linienverkehr GmbH & Co KG (APV).
Cross-border co-operation with:
Société Nationale des Chemins de Fer Belges (SNCB), Belgium;
Société de Transport en Commun Liège-Verviers (TEC), Belgium;

De Lijn Limburg (De Lijn), Belgium;
Nederlandse Spoorwegen Reizigers (NS), Netherlands;
Veolia Transport Limburg (Veolia), Netherlands.

Passenger journeys: (2002) 96.8 million
(2003) 99.4 million
(2004) 101.0 million
(2005) 101.2 million
(2006) 102.0 million

Aachener Strassenbahn und Energieversorgungs-AG (ASEAG)
Neuköllner Strasse 1, D-52068 Aachen, Germany
Tel: (+49 241) 168 80
Fax: (+49 241) 168 82 36
e-mail: anregungen@aseag.de
Web: www.aseag.de

Key personnel
General Manager: Dipl-Ing Hans-Peter Appel
Commercial Director: Dr Joachim Duttenhofer
Administration Manager: Uwe Peifer
Commercial Manager: Klaus Reinartz
Head of Corporate Communications: Eva Wussing
Spokesperson: Anne Linden
Staff: Not currently available

Current situation
ASEAG provides fixed route, express and shuttle services for events.

Developments
The company is fitting particulate filters to its existing fleet of buses and is introducing Euro 5 vehicles to its fleet.

Bus
Passenger journeys: (2007) 62 million (estimate)
Vehicle-km: Not currently available

Number of routes: 63 (7 night routes at weekends)
Route length: (One way) 1,148 km (estimate)
On priority right-of-way: 12 km

Fleet: 268 vehicles, plus 84 contracted	
Mercedes O305 (1982/85)	32
MAN SL200 (1979/85)	46
Mercedes O405 (1988)	12
MAN SL202 (1987/89)	31
Mercedes O405N low-floor (1991/92)	12
MAN NL202 low-floor (1991/93)	27
Mercedes O305G articulated (1983/84)	6
Mercedes O405G articulated (1987/88)	6
MAN SG242 articulated (1986/88/92)	47
Van Hool A508 midibus (1990)	10
MAN NG272 articulated (1993)	7
Mercedes O405 N2 (1998)	25
Mercedes O405 GN2 articulated (1998)	7
In peak service: 314	
New vehicles required: 20 annually	

Most intensive service: 7 min
One-person operation: All routes
Fare collection: Prepurchase or payment to driver
Fare structure: Stages, single and multitickets, weekly and transferable monthly passes; day tickets
Fares collected on board: 26 per cent (74 per cent hold passes)
Fare evasion control: Roving inspectors
Arrangements for elderly/disabled: Free travel for disabled, reimbursed by federal government
Operational control: All buses radio-equipped
Average peak-hour speed: 20.5 km/h
Operating costs financed by: Fares 77 per cent, subsidy/grants 23 per cent
Subsidy from: National 80 per cent and state 20 per cent governments
New vehicles financed by: Depreciation and subsidy.

DB Regio NRW GmbH
Region Nordrhein-Westfalen, Geschäftsbereich Rheinland
Dompropst-Ketzer Strasse 1-9, D-50667 Cologne, Germany
Tel: (+49 221) 14 14 33 04
Fax: (+49 221) 141 24 42
Web: www.bahn.de/nordrhein-westfalen

Key personnel
Head of Region: Stefan Kühn

Type of operation: Suburban heavy rail

Passenger journeys: (whole Rheinland area)
Approx 76 million per year

Current situation
Regional rail service from Aachen to Düren (and onwards to Cologne) and Aachen to Mönchengladbach (and onwards to Düsseldorf). Each line is served by two trains per hour and most run with double-deck coaches.

In 2001, the Euregiobahn, a diesel-operated cross-border rail service between Stolberg Alstadt, Aachen and Heerlen (Netherlands), was created. A second line of the Euregiobahn, connecting Weisweiler, Aachen and Herzogenrath, was due to start operations in 2004.

In co-operation with Belgian National Railways (SNCB), a regional cross-border service between Aachen, Vervier and Liège commenced operations in December 2002.

The AVV joint tariff scheme gives access not only to regional trains but also to all city buses in Aachen and to the buses of the whole of the AVV region.

Most intensive service: 30 min peak, 60 min off-peak; more frequent on overlapping sections; additional peak-hour trains

Rolling stock: 26 diesel railcars, double-deck coaches, locomotives

Dürener Kreisbahn GmbH (DKB)

Postfach 10 04 62, D-52304 Düren, Germany
Tel: (+49 2421) 390 10   Fax: (+49 2421) 39 01 88
e-mail: service@dkb-dn.de
Web: www.dkb-dn.de

Street address
Kölner Landstrasse 271, D-52351 Düren, Germany

Key personnel
General Managers: Bernd Böhnke, Guido Edmunds
Staff: 125

Passenger journeys: (2007) 10.8 million (estimate)
Vehicle-km: Not currently available
Number of routes: 31 (plus night routes)
Route length: 710 km

Current situation
County council-owned operator providing urban and rural bus services in and around Düren.

Fleet: 77 buses
Breakdown of fleet is not currently available
In peak service: Not currently available
On order: Not currently available

Regionalverkehr Euregio Maas-Rhein GmbH (RVE)

Neuköllner Strasse 1, D-52068 Aachen, Germany
Tel: (+49 241) 91 28 90
Fax: (+49 241) 912 89 12
e-mail info@rve-aachen.de
Web: www.rve-aachen.de

Key personnel
Managing Directors: Andree Bach, Siegfried Dargatz

Current situation
Bus company owned by DB provides suburban and rural services covering the Aachen area.

Fleet: 43 buses

Mercedes-Benz Citaro G articulated (2005)	1
Setra SG 221 UL articulated (1992)	2

MAN Lion's City (NÜ 263) (2006)	2
Setra S 415 NF (2007/08)	8
Setra S3 315 UL (2004)	1
Setra S 315 NF (1996/97, 2000/02/03/04)	10
Den Oudsten B 96 DL 595 (2000/01)	10
Den Oudsten B 96 DL 595 (1997)	4
MAN NÜ 263 (1998)	1
Mercedes-Benz O 408 (1994)	2
Mercedes-Benz 313 CDI (Sprinter) (2003/04)	2

In peak service: Not currently available
On order: Not currently available.

Rurtalbahn GmbH

Kölner Landstrasse 271, D-52351 Düren, Germany
Tel: (+49 2421) 39 01 42
Fax: (+49 2421) 39 01 35
e-mail: info@rurtalbahn.de
Web: www.rurtalbahn.de

Key personnel
General Managers: Guido Edmunds, Hans-Peter Niessen, Achim Schmitz
Staff: Not currently available

Type of operation: Heavy rail

Passenger journeys: Not currently available
Train-km: Not currently available
Number of routes: 3
Route length: 75 km (passenger operations)

Current situation
Passenger services ar operated from Düren to Linnich (26 km), south to Heombach (30 km) and southeast to Zülpich (19 km)

For further information on Rurtalbahn, please see *Jane's World Railways.*

Fleet: 17 railcars

Siemens Duewag RegioSprinter	17.

Augsburg

Population: 269,500 (2006 estimate), district 507,500 (estimate)

Public transport
Bus and tramway services provided by municipal authority. DB Regio AG provides commuter services. Suburban bus services provided by regional bus company and independent operators. Regional transit authority (AVV) integrates urban and suburban services.

Augsburger Verkehrsverbund GmbH (AVV)

Prinzregentenstrasse 2, D-86150 Augsburg, Germany
Tel: (+49 821) 34 37 70   Fax: (+49 821) 34 37 71 07
e-mail: info@avv-augsburg.de
Web: www.avv-augsburg.de

Key personnel
Managing Director: Helmut Hofmann

Passenger journeys: (2000) 74.4 million
(2001) 76.5 million
(2002) 76.0 million
(2003) 76.9 million
(2004) Not yet available

Current situation
AVV, the regional transit authority, was created in 1985 by the city of Augsburg and surrounding local authorities to co-ordinate public transport in the region. The scheme includes six rail lines (158 km) radiating from Augsburg and 101 regional bus routes operated by 19 companies with a route length of 2,220 km. Full integration of these was completed in 1992. As at July 2005, there were 1,821 park-and ride places and 1,804

bike-and-ride spaces at 21 stations, with a further 1,297 park-and-ride and 790 bike-and-ride spaces planned.

Urban services in Augsburg were fully integrated into AVV during 1995.

Operating costs financed by: Fares 52.4 per cent, other commercial sources 19.2 per cent, local authority subsidies 28.4 per cent (2003)

DB Regio AG

Regio Bayerisch-Schwaben
Victoriastrasse1, D-86150, Augsburg, Germany
Tel: (+49 821) 503 23 70
Fax: (+49 821) 503 24 78
e-mail: hans-juergen.ziegler@bahn.de
Web: www.bahn.de/bayern

Key personnel
Managers: Hans-Jürgen Ziegler
Antonia von Bassewitz

Current situation
Commuter services are operated on six lines totalling 158 km, integrated into AVV (see separate entry). Frequencies are irregular.

For further information on DB, please see *Jane's World Railways.*

Regionalbus Augsburg GmbH (RBA)

Eichleitnerstrasse 17, D-86199 Augsburg, Germany
Tel: (+49 821) 50 21 50   Fax: (+49 821) 502 15 88
e-mail: info@rba-bus.de
Kontakt@rba-nus.de
Web: www.rba-bus.de

Key personnel
Managing Directors: Walter Jägle, Josef Zeiselmair
Staff: 283

Passenger journeys: (2007) 27 million (estimate)
Vehicle-km: Not currently available

Current situation
Formerly owned by DB, this regional bus company was sold to a group of private bus operators in 1992. There are 156 local and regional routes operated, extending well beyond the AVV area, totalling 5,369 km, with a fleet of some 166 buses, plus 395 subcontracted.

Stadtwerke Augsburg Verkehrs-GmbH + Augsburger Verkehrsgesellschaft

Postfach 10 24 40, D-86014 Augsburg, Germany
Tel: (+49 821) 65 00 57 00
Freephone: 0800 65 00 32 40
Fax: (+49 821) 65 00 57 04
e-mail: stadtwerke-augsburg@stawa.de
Web: www.stawa.de

Street address
Hoher Weg 1, D-86152 Augsburg, Germany

Key personnel
General Managers: Dr Claus Gebhardt, Norbert Walter
Operating Manager: Dipl-Ing Herbert Stepputat
Staff: 773

Passenger journeys: (2003) 53.35 million
(2004) 53.63 million
(2005) 54.95 million
(2006) 54.22 million
(2007) 54.02 million

Operating costs financed by: Not currently available
Subsidy from: City

Current situation
In order to improve the attractiveness of public transport in the region, frequency on bus and tram routes has been improved, and there are plans for more reserved rights-of-way for both buses and trams. Four suburban routes are served by shared taxis, operating to fixed schedule but on request by phone or radio-call from driver of connecting tram or bus.

Bus
Vehicle-km: (2003) 5.74 million
(2004) 5.73 million
(2005) 5.51 million
(2006) 5.52 million
(2007) 5.49 million

Number of routes: 18
Route length: (One way) 164.1 km
On priority right-of-way: 2 km

Developments
Stadtwerke Augsburg Verkehrs-GmbH operates its own CNG filling station, which is also available to other users.

Fleet: 100 vehicles
MAN NG low-floor   16
MAN NL CNG-powered   15
MAN NG low-floor CNG-powered   69
In peak service: 82
On order: Not currently available

Most intensive service: 10 min
One-person operation: All routes

Fare collection: Payment to driver or pre-purchase with validation/cancellation machines on board
Fare structure: Zonal, multitickets, day and period passes, annual subscription
Fares collected on board: 6 per cent (58 per cent hold passes)
Fare-evasion control: Random inspection with penalty (EUR40)
Operational control: Mobile radio, BRL
Arrangements for elderly/disabled: Free travel for disabled, reimbursed by government

Tramway
Type of operation: Conventional tramway

Passenger journeys: (2003) 35.2 million
(2004) 35.4 million
(2005) 36.3 million
(2006) Not currently available
(2007) 35.5 million
Car-km: (2002) 3.53 million
(2003) 3.68 million
(2004) 3.9 million
(2005) 3.97 million
(2006) 3.95 million
(2007) 3.97 million

Route length: 38.5 km
Number of routes: 4 (all cross-town)
Number of stops: 91
Gauge: 1,000 mm
Electrification: 600 V DC, overhead

Developments
A new route (5) is being planned from Burgermeister Ackermann Strasse to Zentralklinikum and Neusäss.

A further new route (6) has been built from Königsplatz to Chippenhamring (near Friedberg).

Plans also exist to divert Route 3 underground at Hbf to give a direct connection from tram to main line platforms. Most tramway stops have been equipped with dynamic passenger information systems.

Rolling stock: 76 cars
MAN GT8 (1976)   M12
Duewag/MAN M8C (1985)   M12
AEG GT6M low-floor (1995/96)   M11
Siemens NF8 Combino (2000/02/04)   M41
In peak service: 64

On order: 24 40 m 7-section Bombardier *FLEXITY* Outlook low-floor trams for delivery 2009/10
Service: All day 5 min
Fare structure: Zonal, as bus

Stadtwerke Gersthofen (STWG)
Rathausplatz 1, D-86368 Gersthofen, Germany
Tel: (+49 821) 249 10
e-mail: info@stadt-gersthofen.de
Web: www.stadt-gersthofen.de

Key personnel
Operating Manager: Hans Baumer

Current situation
Local authority operator runs a service between Gersthofen and Augsburg, and other local services, with a fleet of 24 buses.

Berlin
Population: Regional area 3.39 million (2004 estimate)

Public transport
Municipal authority provides metro, tram, bus and ferry services. Regional metro (S-Bahn) service provided by a subsidiary company of national railway DB and outer-suburban rail services by DB. Some local suburban tramways link with BVG, also tram and bus services run by municipal authority in neighbouring city of Potsdam. A regional transport authority (VBB) oversees public transport operations in the Berlin-Brandenburg area, including an integrated ticketing system.

Berliner Verkehrsbetriebe (BVG) AöR
Potsdamer Strasse 188, D-10783 Berlin, Germany
Tel: (+49 30) 25 60   Fax: (+49 30) 216 41 86
e-mail: info@bvg.de
Web: www.bvg.de

Key personnel
General Manager: Andreas Sturmowski
Operations Manager: Thomas Necker
Personnel Manager: Lothar Zweiniger
Division Manager, Metro: Hans-Christian Kaiser
Division Manager, Tram: Klaus-Dietrich Matschke
Division Manager, Bus: Johannes Müller
   Staff: 10,928 (2006)

Passenger journeys: (All modes)
(2002) 799 million
(2004) 906 million
(2005) 907 million
(2006) 914 million

Operating costs financed by: Fares and other commercial sources, subsidy/grants
Subsidy from: Berlin

Current situation
Formed in 1929, BVG is a municipal authority operating two separate metro systems (large

and small profile), an extensive bus network, tramways and ferries. BVG had been responsible for operation of S-Bahn services in west Berlin (taken over from the eastern authorities in 1984), but these were transferred to the DB subsidiary S-Bahn Berlin GmbH in 1994. BVG assumed management responsibility for the east Berlin operator BVB in 1990, and full merger of the two systems took place in 1992.

A number of through bus services to surrounding country areas have been inaugurated jointly with regional transport operators. All

metro stations have been reopened on the routes previously passing beneath East Berlin without stops. A uniform route-numbering scheme now encompasses all routes in the VBB region.

A major upgrading of the metro is in progress under the U-Bahn 2000 scheme (see below).

A new subsidiary, Berlin Transport GmbH, started operation in 1999, employing staff on different conditions from BVG itself. The objective is to improve competitiveness when bidding for contracted local services.

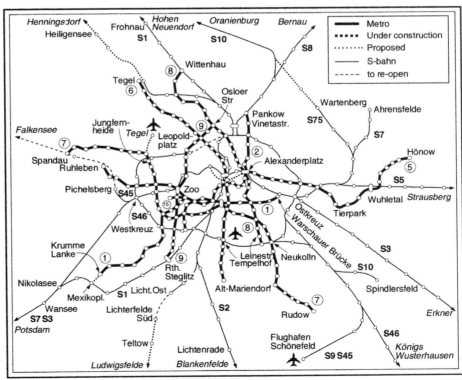

Map of Berlin's metro

0137307

Bus

Passengers journeys: (2002) 361.3 million
(2004) 407 million
(2005) 404.7 million
Vehicle-km: (2000) 95.7 million

Number of routes: 151 (night 54)
Number of stops: 2,611 (night 1,505)
Route length: 1,626 km (night 750 km)
On priority right-of-way: 101.92 km

Developments

Part of the bus network is subcontracted to private operators, following contracts for the first routes let in 1992. Door-to-door service is provided by contracted taxis on some of the all-night routes.

In October 2006, BVG, along with six other public transport operators, signed a Memorandum of Understanding (MoU) with regard to the purchase and use of hydrogen buses.

In early 2007, BVG began testing a Mercedes-Benz Citaro LE low-floor bus.

Fleet: 1,328 vehicles, plus 197 contracted

Double-deck	357
Single-deck	395
Articulated	459
Special vehicles	117

On order: None

Most intensive service: 2 min
One-person operation: All services
Fare collection: Single tickets sold on buses and at ticket offices on U-Bahn stations; daily, weekly and monthly passes; senior citizen passes; free daily travel for disabled. Automatic ticket vending machines for single and multi-tickets at U-Bahn stations. Transfers on single tickets within 2 h. Cancellation by machine or driver
Fare structure: Flat, with short-distance ticket
Fare evasion control: Inspectors with spot penalty (EUR60)
Operational control: Bus radio link to control centre
Arrangements for elderly/disabled: Accessible buses in operation on almost all routes (145 of 146). Separate 'Telebus' network of low-floor wheelchair-accessible midibuses operated by special agency on request (see separate entry)
Integration with other modes: Full integration with tram, U-Bahn and S-Bahn services; transfers available; multimodal passes
Bus priority: 101.92 km network of city-centre bus lanes; long-term objective to secure 156 km of bus lanes
Average distance between stops: 514 m
Average speed: 19.56 km/h

Metro

Type of operation: Full metro, first line opened 1902

Passenger journeys: (2002) 400 million
(2004) 457 million
(2005) 464 million
(2006) 466.4 million
Car-km: (2002) 136.5 million
(2005) 123.5 million
(2006) 122.1 million

Route length: 144.2 km
  in tunnel: 119.8 km
  elevated: 10.2 km
Number of lines: 9
Number of stations: 170
Gauge: 1,435 mm
Track: 41 kg/m S 41 rail, conventional sleepers on ballast
Max gradient: 4%
Minimum curve radius: 74 m
Tunnel: Mainly cut-and-cover
Electrification: 750 V DC, third rail; bottom contact on large-profile lines

Developments

Trial running on new line U55 took place in October 2006.

Modernised CKD Tatra KTD4 tram of BVG (Quintus Vosman)   0554783

Rolling stock: 1,278 cars (formed in 506 sets)

Small profile (2.3 m wide) 506 cars	O&K A364
(1964)	M2T2
O&K A3L67 (1967/68)	M39T39
O&K A3L71 (1971/73)	M66T66
O&K/DWM A3L/A3E	M79T79
LEW GI/1	M39T39
LEW GI/1E	M12T12
Waggon Union A3L82/83	M8T8
Bombardier HK2000 (2001)	M8T8
Large profile (2.65 m wide) 772 cars	O&K F74
(1973/75)	M28T28
O&K/Waggon Union F76 (1976/78)	M39T39
O&K/Waggon Union F79 (1980/81)	M36T36
Waggon Union F84 (1984/85)	M39T39
Waggon Union F87 (1986/87)	M21T21
ABB F90 (1990/92)	M30T30
ABB F92 (1992/93)	M55T55
Adtranz H95 (1995/97)	M6T6
Adtranz H97 (1999/2000)	M72T72
Bombardier H01 (2001/02)	M60T60

On order: 20 4-car Bombardier metro trainsets, Class HK. Delivery is scheduled for 2007.

Service: Peak 3 min, off-peak 5-10 min
First/last train: 04.00/0.30 (weekdays)
Fare structure: Flat, as bus
Integration with other modes: Fully integrated with bus, tram and S-Bahn
One-person operation: All trains
Signalling: Electromagnetic, Siemens
Surveillance: CCTV at all stations and in 20 trains, H type; trains also equipped with radio and radio telephone

Tramway

Type of operation: Conventional tramway

Passenger journeys: (2002) 142.5 million
(2004) 171.3 million
(2005) 167.5 million
(2006) 173.5 million
Car-km: (2002) 33.8 million
(2005) 27.8 million
(2006) 27.2 million

Route length: 189.4 km
Number of lines: 22 (9 for 24-hour service)
Number of stops: 377
Gauge: 1,435 mm
Electrification: 600 V DC, overhead

Current situation

After the merger of the two public transport operations, expansion of the tramway network into the western part of the city was proposed. The first such route, a 2.7 km extension of Route 23 along Osloer Strasse to Louise Schroeder Platz, was opened in 1995, and was further extended by 2.8 km along Seestrasse to Klinikum Rudolf Virchow. In December 1998, the first part of the route to Alexanderplatz was opened (extension to Greifswalder Strasse route, along the Alexanderplatz to Hackescher Markt). A short extension from Revaler Strasse to Warschauer Strasse U-Bahn opened in May 2000, and the

section from Buchholz Kirche to Buchholz West (1.7 km) opened in October 2000.

Developments

The new Berlin government, established in late 2001, approved plans for further tramway extensions, but the worsening economic situation has resulted in only two existing projects, to be completed by the end of the decade:

Invalidenstrasse-Hauptbahnhof   Lehrter Bahnhof;

Eberswalder Strasse-Nordbahnhof.

The modernisation of the existing network is almost completed, including renewal of track and overhead, and depot and power supply modernisation. Refurbishment of Tatra tramcars has been completed, while a new fleet of low-floor cars has been delivered.

Traffic management measures have been completed, resulting in priority for trams at almost all traffic lights/signals and the average operating speed has increased to 24.6 km/h.

In mid-2006, BVG signed a letter of intent to purchase new trams from Bombardier Transportation, to replace the existing Tatra trams. Prototype vehicles are scheduled to be delivered in 2007/8.

In late 2006, 21 Tatra trams were sold to Szczecin, Poland.

Rolling stock: 574 cars

CKD Tatra KTD4 (1980/87) modernised	M249
CKD Tatra T6A2 (1988/90) modernised	M118T57
AEG Adtranz GT6N low-floor (1994/98)	M105
Adtranz GT 6-98ZR (double ended)	M15
Adtranz GT 6-99ZR (double ended)	M30

Service: Peak 3–5 min; 10–20 min; night service at 30 min on five lines
First/last tram: 04.30/00.30 (daytime tram routes)
Arrangements for elderly/disabled: 150 low-floor cars are accessible
Average speed: 19.3 km/h

Ferry

Passenger journeys: Not currently available

Current situation

Six vessels ply six routes with a total length of 6.9 km. Three routes operate throughout the year and three more are operational in spring and summer.

Two of the ferries are accessible for disabled passengers and bicycles are carried on all vessels.

DB Regio AG

Regionalbereich Berlin/Brandenburg
Babelsberger Strasse 18, D-14473 Potsdam, Germany
Tel: (+49 331) 235 67 01
Fax: (+49 331) 235 67 09
e-mail: RAN-Berlin-Brandenburg@bahn.de
Web: www.bahn.de/brandenburg

Key personnel
Chairman: Dr-Ing Joachim Trettin
Manager, Marketing and Finance: Peter Buchner
Manager, Production and Technical: Karsten Preissel
Manager, Personnel: Andreas Zylka
Type of operation: Regional rail

Passenger journeys: Not currently available

Current situation
Part of the Region Nordost, DB Regio AG's Berlin/
Brandenberg services cover a network of 2,121 km
and serve 296 stations and halts, with some 1,938
million passenger-km recorded annually. Services
are fully integrated with the joint VBB tariff.
    For further information on DB, please see
Jane's World Railways.

Developments
In mid-2006, the new Berlin Hauptbahnhof main
station was opened.

SRS tram

1113688

Havelbus Verkehrsgesellschaft mbH (HVG)

Johannsenstrasse 12-17, D-14482 Potsdam,
Germany
Tel: (+49 331) 749 13 00 Fax: (+49 331) 70 51 61
e-mail: mail@havelbus.de
info@havelbus.de
Web: www.onlinefahrausweise.de

Key personnel
General Manager: Dieter Schäfer
    Staff: 500 (estimate)

Passenger journeys: (2003) 18.6 million

Current situation
Regional bus company formed in 1992 by
Potsdam and Nauen county councils to take over
the regional bus services previously operated
by ViP (see separate entry in Urban Transport
Systems and Operators). Several routes extend
into the outskirts of Berlin, where they link with
BVG services.

Bus
Vehicle-km: (2003) 12.5 million
Number of routes: 90
Route length: 2,442 km

Fleet: 200 (estimate)
*Full fleet breakdown is not currently available, but
includes:*

Mercedes-Benz 530 Citaro	n/a
Mercedes-Benz 405N/GN	n/a
Mercedes-Benz Integro	n/a
Mercedes-Benz Integro O 550-19	n/a
Mercedes-Benz Cito	n/a
Mercedes-Benz O 530 U/MU	n/a
MAN NG 313 articulated	n/a
MAN SG 312 articulated	n/a
MAN NL 202	n/a

S-Bahn Berlin GmbH

Invalidenstrasse 19, D-10115 Berlin, Germany
Tel: (+49 30) 29 74 33 33 Fax: (+49 30) 28 44 53 63 33
e-mail: kundenbetreuung@s-bahn-berlin.de
Web: www.s-bahn-berlin.de

Key personnel
Directors
Marketing and Management Spokesman:
Dr Tobias Heinemann
Operations: Ulrich Thon
Commercial: Thomas Prechtl
Personnel: Olaf Hagenauer
    Staff: 3,075 (2007)

Type of operation: S-Bahn

Passenger journeys: (2005) 356.8 million
(2006) 375.8 million
(2007) 70.5 million

Train-km: Not currently available
Number of stations: 166
Route length: 332 km
Gauge: 1,435 mm
Electrification: 800 V DC, third rail

Current situation
This subsidiary of DB took over operation of
the S-Bahn network at the beginning of 1995.
Service is provided on 15 routes. Fares are
fully integrated with other modes. Peak-hour
frequency on the busiest section is 2 minutes.
Off-peak services run every 5–10 minutes; trains
run from about 04.00 to 01.00; 20 minute service
to Schönefeld airport.

Rolling stock: 1,364 (in two-car sets) (2007)

Class 480	156
Class 481	984
Class 485	224

In peak service: Not currently available
Average age of fleet: 8.8 years (2007)
Fare structure: Zonal (3 zones)
Fare collection: Day, group, 4-trip, 7-day and multi-
modal 48- or 72-hour tickets from machines at stations;
validation on board vehicles; reduced fare for children
from 6 to 14, free travel for children under 6

Schöneicher-Rüdersdorfer Strassenbahn GmbH (SRS GmbH)

Dorfstrasse 15, D-15566 Schöneiche bei Berlin,
Germany
Tel: (+49 30) 65 48 68 33 Fax: (+49 30) 65 48 68 44
e-mail: info@srs-tram.de
Web: www.srs-tram.de

Key personnel
General Manager: Detlef Bröcker
Operations Manager: Reinhold Schröter
    Staff: 28

Type of operation: Suburban tramway

Passenger journeys: (2003) 1.05 million
(2004) 1.00 million
(2005) 1.00 million
(2006) 1.00 million
(2007) 1.00 million

Route length: 14 km
No of stops: 20
Gauge: 1,000 mm
Electrification: 600 V AC overhead

Background
Public-private ownership (70 per cent owned by
Veolia Transportation).

Current situation
Metre-gauge tramway providing S-Bahn feeder
service over the Rüdersdorf-Schöneiche-
Friedrichshagen route (14 km). All cars are
maintained at SRS workshops.

Developments
The eastern section of the line is currently being
rebuilt and the terminus in Friedrichshagen is to
be built in front of the S-Bahn station entrance.
Tram stops will also be equipped with real-time
passenger information displays.

Fleet: 7 cars for revenue service (plus heritage cars)

Tatra KT4D 4-axle trams	2
Düwag GT6 6-axle trams	5

Most intensive service: Mon-Friday 20 min
Fare structure: Zonal, 10-ride tickets, monthly passes
Fare collection: From driver and ticket machines
Integration with other modes: Integrated into VBB
tariff system
Average speed: 28 km/h

Strausberger Eisenbahn Gmbh

c/o Stadtwerke Strausberg GmbH
Kastanienallee 38, D-15344 Strausberg,
Germany
Tel: (+49 33) 41 34 51 00
Fax: (+49 33) 41 34 54 10
e-mail: ste@strausberger-eisenbahn.de
Web: www.strausberger-eisenbahn.de

Key personnel
Managing Director: Andreas Gagel

Type of operation: Suburban tramway

Passenger journeys: (2007) 1.46 million (estimate)
Vehicle-km: Not currently available

Current situation
Standard-gauge 6 km tramway with 9 stops,
connecting the town of Strausberg with S-Bahn
line S5 at Strausberg station. Fleet of six cars
with two trailers.

For details of the latest updates to *Jane's Urban Transport Systems* online and to discover the
additional information available exclusively to online subscribers please visit
juts.janes.com

Verkehrsbetrieb Potsdam GmbH (ViP)

PO Box 60 14 54, D-14414 Potsdam, Germany
Tel: (+49 331) 661 40   Fax: (+49 331) 661 42 79
e-mail: info@vip-potsdam.de
Web: www.stadtwerke-potsdam.de

Street address
Fritz-Zubeil-Strasse 96, D-14482 Potsdam, Germany

Key personnel
General Manager: Georg Dukiewicz
   Staff: 516

Passenger journeys: (1998) 26 million
(1999) 25 million
(2000) 23.1 million

Current situation
Potsdam is a neighbouring city to the southwest of Berlin, with a population of 135,000. Bus and tramway services are provided by the municipal authority. Connections and through ticketing with BVG as part of VBB.

Developments
Short tramway extension opened 1997, between Robert Baberske Strasse and Kirchsteigfeld (1.3 km). Under proposals announced in January 1997, extensions over DB tracks from Potsdam Stern to Teltow, and Potsdam to Beelitz, are planned, while within Potsdam a link between Babelsberg and Stern is being considered. A 2.9 km extension of the current Route 92 from Kappellenberg to Bornstedter Feld opened at the end of 1999.

The tram fleet for years consisted exclusively of Tatra KT4D articulated cars, all extensively renovated recently. In addition, a new fleet of 48 low-floor Combino LRVs has been ordered from Siemens, of which 44 are five-section and the remainder seven-section. Delivery of the outstanding vehicles has been deferred by request of ViP and is due to recommence in 2005.

A new bus and tram depot at Babelsberg opened in 2001. It replaces four existing facilities.

In 2000, most bus routes were withdrawn from the city centre and converted to tramway feeders. This has led to a loss of passengers and the resultant loss of revenue exceeds the cost savings.

Bus

Vehicle-km: (1998) 3.5 million
(1999) 3.46 million
(2000) 3.4 million

Number of routes: 10
Route length: 138.4 km

Fleet: 48 buses

Mercedes O405N	39
Mercedes O405GN articulated	9

Tramway

Vehicle-km: (1998) 4.4 million
(1999) 4.1 million
(2000) 3.8 million

Number of routes: 8
Route length: 28 km (on private right-of-way: 70%)
Gauge: 1,435 mm

Fleet: 94 cars

ČKD Tatra KT4DM modernised	M78
Siemens Combino (1998/99)	M16

Verkehrsverbund Berlin-Brandenburg GmbH (VBB)

Hardenbergplatz 2, D-10623 Berlin, Germany
Tel: (+49 30) 25 41 40   Fax: (+49 30) 25 41 41 12
e-mail: info@vbbonline.de
Web: www.vbbonline.de

Siemens Combino tram at ViP's new depot, Potsdam (Tony Pattison)   0109543

Siemens Combino tram at Potsdam railway station (Oubeck.com)   0126396

Key personnel
Managing Director: Hans-Werner Franz

Background
This regional transport authority started operations in 1999, taking over the role of the former Verkehrsgemeinschaft Berlin-Brandenburg which had been formed as a precursor. Its activities comprise joint promotion of all public transport services in Berlin and much of Brandenburg. A new unified tariff system was introduced in April 1999.

Current situation
Ownership of VBB is one-third by the state of Berlin, one-third by the state of Brandenburg, and one-third by cities within Brandenburg state. It covers an area of 30,000 km² and serves 5.9 million inhabitants, and is thus the biggest Verkehrsverbund (in terms of area) in Germany.

The VBB is responsible for the planning and co-ordination of 45 public and private transport companies' transport services, the unified tariff system and marketing, customer information, sales co-ordination and the apportioning of revenues to the transport enterprises.

Developments
VBB is participating in a pilot project, known as 'Anspruchsvolle Umweltstandards im ÖPNVWettbewerb' (high-quality environmental standards in local public passenger transport competition). The project, supported by the German Federal Ministry for the Environment, makes use of innovative technology and demonstrates how the strict air quality and noise targets of the future can be met by buses, trains and communities at large.

VBB and its partners are developing and implementing a new integrated concept of varied, flexible transport services under the research project 'Impuls 2005', a research project backed by the Federal Ministry for Research. The project is examining the changes taking place in rural areas, improving region-wide coverage with public passenger transport. The project's elements include innovative services, such as extended information services covering 'Call Buses', capacity management for transport providers, an adapted vehicle communications system and reliable connections to scheduled services.

VBB will be building a cross-border transport management system with its Polish partners. In the future, this will enable passengers to cross the German-Polish border by bus and train on combined routes with a single ticket.

Woltersdorfer-Strassenbahn GmbH

Vogelsdorfer Strasse 1, D-15569 Woltersdorf, bei Berlin, Germany
Tel: (+49 33) 62 88 12 30
Fax: (+49 33) 62 88 12 44
e-mail: service@woltersdorfer-strassenbahn.de
Web: www.woltersdorfer-strassenbahn.com

Key personnel
Contact: Monika Viktor
   Staff: 20

Type of operation: Suburban tramway

Passenger journeys: (2007) 630,000 (estimate)
Vehicle-km: Not currently available

Current situation
Standard-gauge tramway providing S-Bahn feeder service over Woltersdorf-Rahnsdorf route (5.6 km). Fleet of 11 cars (plus 6 historic vehicles).

Bielefeld

Population: 327,131 (2005)

Public transport

Urban and regional transport co-ordinated by the regional authority OWL. Bus and tramway services provided by subsidiary company for municipal authority and bus services by subsidiary of DB.

BVO Busverkehr Ostwestfalen GmbH

Am Bahnhof 6, D-33602 Bielefeld, Germany
Tel: (+49 521) 52 07 00
Fax: (+49 521) 520 70 70
e-mail: info@bvo-bielefeld.de
Web: www.bvo-bielefeld.de

Key personnel

Managing Directors: Andree Bach
    Ulrich Jaeger

Background

BVO Busverkehr Ostwestfalen GmbH is part of DB's Nordrhein-Westfalen region.

Current situation

Railway-associated bus company providing suburban and regional bus services to a population of some 2 million in the Ostwestfalen-Lippe region.

Number of routes: Not currently available
Route length (whole region): 7,910 km

Fleet (whole region): 598 vehicles
Fleet breakdown not currently available

moBiel GmbH

PO Box 21 90 46, D-33697 Bielefeld, Germany
Tel: (+49 521) 51 40 19   Fax: (+49 521) 51 41 41
e-mail: info@moBiel.de
Web: www.moBiel.de

Street address

Otto-Brenner-Strasse 242, 33604 Bielefeld, Germany

Key personnel

Technical and Operating Manager: Dipl-Ing Kai-Uwe Steinbrecher
Operating Manager: Hans-Jürgen Krain
Commercial Manager: Wolfgang Brinkmann
    Staff: 401 (at 31 December 2006)

Passenger journeys: (All modes)
(2002) 36 million
(2003) 37.2 million
(2004) 38.8 million
(2005) 39.1 million
(2006) 40.3 million

Operating costs financed by: Fares 77.5 per cent, other commercial sources 1.7 per cent, subsidy/grants 20.8 per cent

Bus

Vehicle-km: (2002) 5.2 million
(2003) 5.4 million
(2004) 5.6 million
(2005) 5.5 million
(2006) 5.5 million

Number of routes: 36
Route length: 390 km

Fleet: 73 buses, plus 26 contracted
MAN A76 midi	3
Neoplan N4009 midi	3
MAN NL202 (222) low-floor solo	5
MAN NG313 low-floor articulated	7
Mercedes-Benz O530G articulated	36
Mercedes-Benz O530N	19
In peak service: 63 (59 + 4 midibuses)
On order: 5 vehicles

Duewag LRV at Bielefeld town hall (Oubeck.com)   0081782

Most intensive service: 10 min
One-person operation: All routes
Fare collection: Payment to driver or by ticket dispensing machines
Arrangements for elderly/disabled: Free travel for disabled, reimbursed by government

Current situation

Shared taxi/dial-a-ride service runs in place of certain bus routes at off-peak periods (after 8 pm), at supplementary fare. Some 22 per cent of bus mileage is provided by subcontractors.

Tramway/light rail

Type of operation: Conventional tramway upgraded to Stadtbahn, with tunnel section in central area

Car-km: (2002) 4.7 million
(2003) 4.7 million
(2004) 4.9 million
(2005) 5.0 million
(2006) 5.0 million

Route length: 37 km
    in tunnel: 6 km
Number of routes: 4
Number of stops: 62
    in tunnel: 7
Gauge: 1,000 mm
Track: S41 rail on sleepers in ballast (new S49)
Electrification: 750 V DC, overhead

Service: Peak 5 min, off-peak 10 min, night 30 min
First/last car: 04.30/01.00
Fare structure: Zonal
Fare collection: Prepurchase from self-service machines or agencies
Control: Siemens ZUB 100 from central control room
Surveillance: CCTV on underground platform and university

Rolling stock: 81 cars
Duewag M8C	M40
Duewag Stadtbahn M8D (1994/95)	M20
Duewag Stadtbahn M8D (1998/99)	M16
MB4	T5
In peak service: 72 + 4 trailers

Current situation

Patronage on the light rail lines has increased by up to 95 per cent since 1990 and two-car sets now run on weekdays on all routes. New cars have only one driving cab, with the small fleet of trailers being used coupled between pairs of Stadtbahn cars. Line 4 to University opened in April 2000, and was completed in 2002, with the opening of the Lohmannshof extension.

Doubling of the northern end of Route 3 in Babenhausen was completed at the end of 1996.

Developments

Extensions of Route 2 to Milse-Ost and Route 3 to Theesen are planned. The extension in Riponbarracks has been cancelled.

OWL Verkehr GmbH

PO Box 10 20 70, D-33520 Bielefeld, Germany
Tel: (+49 521) 557 66 60
Fax: (+49 521) 55 76 66 67
e-mail: info@owlverkehr.de
Web: www.owlverkehr.de

Street address

Willy-Brandt-Platz 2, D-33602 Bielefeld, Germany

Key personnel

Chairman of the Board: Ulrich Jaeger (Busverkehr Ostwestfalen)
Directors: Hans-Jürgen Krain (moBiel GmbH)
    Günter Krückemeier (Minden-Herforder-Verkehrs-Service GmbH)

Current situation

OWL Verkehr GmbH was founded in May 2004, as a non-competitive combination of 35 local transportation companies and Deutsche Bahn AG, as well as two additional private railway companies (Eurobahn and Nordwestbahn), which operate buses and train routes. They are responsible for route planning and timetables, ticket distribution and direct customer services.

At the OWL Verkehr GmbH, the focus is on the management of the local public transport within the operating area 'Ostwestfalen', in particular:
Implementation and development of tariffs and tickets;
Apportioning the resultant return on sales between the participating transport enterprises;
Further development of ticket distribution systems;
Marketing and public relations;
Organisation and co-ordination of urban route planning and timetables, quality and service of the local public transport;
Implementation and development of capabilities for economisation.

Bochum-Gelsenkirchen

Population: Bochum 382.087 (2005 estimate), Gelsenkirchen 269,972 (2006 estimate)

Public transport
Bus and tramway/light rail services in Bochum, Gelsenkirchen and adjoining cities provided by public corporation within framework of Verkehrsverbund Rhein-Ruhr (VRR) (please see entry for Rhein-Ruhr). Underground sections of tramway in both Bochum and Gelsenkirchen; standard-gauge Stadtbahn line U35 links Bochum and Herne. Area also served by DB S-Bahn.

Bochum-Gelsenkirchener Strassenbahnen AG (Bogestra)
Universitätsstrasse 58, D-44789 Bochum, Germany
Tel: (+49 234) 30 30
Fax: (+49 234) 303 23 00
e-mail: info@bogestra.de
Web: www.bogestra.de

Key personnel
Marketing and Operations Manager: Dr Burkhard Rüberg
Personnel, Communications and Infrastructure Manager: Gisbert Schlotzhauer
Staff: 2,181

Passenger journeys: (All modes)
(2005) 137.4 million (estimate)

Operating costs financed by: (All modes) fares 28.2 per cent, other commercial sources 7.6 per cent, subsidy/grants 64.2 per cent
Subsidy from: State (*Land*) and municipal government

Current situation
Bochum-Gelsenkirchener Strassenbahnen AG (Bogestra) is a joint venture between the cities of Bochum and Gelsenkirchen. The company's fare policies are regulated and overseen by the Verkehrsverbund Rhein-Rhur GmbH (VRR) (see entry for Rhein-Ruhr) Bogestra provides services in the Ruhr area.

Bus
Vehicle-km: (2005) 18.1 million (estimate)

Number of routes: 66
Route length: 1,002.4 km
On priority right-of-way: 4 km shared with tramway

Fleet: 250
MAN SL202 standard (1984/88)
Breakdown of fleet not currently available
Neoplan N416SL standard (1983/87)
MAN SG242H/242 articulated (1986/88)
Mercedes O405G articulated (1987/90)
MAN NL202 low-floor (1989/94)
Neoplan N4016 low-floor (1989)
MAN NG272 low-floor articulated (1992/94)
Mercedes O405GN low-floor articulated (1995/98)
MAN NG312 low-floor articulated (1995)
MAN NL223 low-floor (1998)
MAN NL263 low-floor (1999)
MAN NG313 low-floor articulated (1999)
Other
In peak service: Not currently available
On order: Not currently available

Most intensive service: 10 min
One-person operation: All routes
Fare collection: Prepurchase monthly or weekly pass or multitickets with cancellers, cash to driver
Fare structure: Zonal (VRR)
Fare evasion control: Roving inspectors
Average speed: Weekdays 22 km/h

Tramway/pre-metro
Type of operation: Conventional tramway with underground sections in city centre
Car-km: (2000) 8.2 million

Route length: 109.7 km
On private right-of-way: 63.4 km, reserved track 10.4 km, in tunnel 4.9 km with 6 stations
Number of lines: 7
Number of stops: 196

Gauge: 1,000 mm
Electrification: 600 V DC, overhead

Fare structure: Zonal (VRR)
Fare collection: Prepurchase, payment to driver; roving inspectors
One-person operation: All routes

Rolling stock: 93 cars

Duewag M65 6-axle (1976/77)	M29
Duewag M6C 6-axle (1981/82)	M22
Duewag/Siemens MGT6D 6-axle low-floor (1992/94)	M42

In peak service: 85

Developments
The tram subway under Bochum town centre opened in early 2006.

Light rail
Type of operation: U-Bahn/Stadtbahn with high platforms

Car-km: (1997) 2.4 million
(1998) 2.4 million

Route length: 16.5 km
    in tunnel: 10.7 km
Number of lines: 1
Number of stations: 21
Gauge: 1,435 mm
Tunnel: Cut-and-cover and bored
Electrification: 750 V DC, overhead

Service: Peak 5 min, off-peak 10–15 min
First/last train: 04.03/00.33
Surveillance: CCTV, emergency telephones
Operational control: Fully automated (microprocessor)

Rolling stock: 25 cars

Duewag/Siemens B80D (1989/93)	M25

In peak service: 11

Regional bus
Current situation
Bogestra provides joint and/or connecting services with all neighbouring operators – Essen, Recklinghausen (Vestische), Herne, Dortmund and Wuppertal.

DB Regio AG
DB Regio NRW GmbH
Region Nordrhein-Westfalen, Geschäftsbereich Rhein-Ruhr
Hollestrasse 3, D-45127 Essen, Germany
Tel: (+49 201) 175 25 07   Fax: (+49 201) 175 23 02
Web: www.bahn.de/nordrhein-westfahlen

Key personnel
Head of Region: Thorsten Siggelkow

Type of operation: Suburban/regional rail and S-Bahn

Current situation
Extensive suburban, regional and S-Bahn services to other cities in Rhein-Ruhr.

Bonn

Population: 313, 600 (estimate)

Public transport
Bus and tramway/Stadtbahn services operated by subsidiary company of municipal authorities under common directorate. Some other bus services. All public transport in Cologne/Bonn area co-ordinated by Verkehrsverbund Rhein-Sieg (VRS) (see Cologne entry).

Stadtwerke Bonn Verkehrs-GmbH (SWBV)
SWB Bus und Bahn
Postfach 2651, D-53016 Bonn, Germany
Tel: (+49 228) 71 11
Fax: (+49 228) 711 27 7048 49
e-mail: info@stadtwerke-bonn.de
Web: www.stadtwerke-bonn.de

Key personnel
Directors: Prof Dr Ing Hermann Zemlin, Heinz Jürgen Reining
Staff: 876

Passenger journeys: (All modes)
(2000) 74.4 million
(2001) 74.9 million
(2002) 76.8 million
(2003) 77.5 million
(2004) 88.3 million

Operating costs financed by: Not currently available

Current situation
SWB Bus and Bahn is a partner of the Verkehrsverbund Rhein-Sieg (VRS), a partnership between the public transportation systems of nine cities and districts in the Cologne/Bonn area. The partnership provides a joint tariff and timetable scheme.

Since January 2004, SWBV GmbH has been responsible for the management of the Elektrischen Bahnen der Stadt Bonn und des Rhein-Sieg-Kreises (SSB).

Bus
Vehicle-km: (2000) 12.6 million
(2001) 12.0 million
(2002) 11.8 million
(2003) 11.4 million
(2004) 16.7 million

Number of routes: 84 (and eight nightbus lines) (2004)
Route length: (One way) 1,993.8 km

Fleet: 191 vehicles, plus 279 hired (approx 81 per cent low-floor)

Standard buses	147
Articulated buses	44

Most intensive service: 5 min
One-person operation: All routes
Fare collection: Prepurchase with validation and cancelling machines or cash to driver; ticket dispensers installed in buses in 1999
Fare structure: Zonal; prepurchase carnets or weekly, monthly, and annual passes
Fares collected on board: 13 per cent
Fare evasion control: Roving inspectors with penalty
Operational control: Route inspectors/mobile radio
Average peak-hour speed: 21.3 km/h
New vehicles financed by: Depreciation, subsidy and loans

Tramway/light rail
Type of operation: Stadtbahn and conventional tramway

Car-km: (2000) 7.1 million
(2001) 7.2 million
(2002) 7.3 million
(2003) 7.1 million
(2004) 7.3 million

Route length: 125.4 km (2004)
Number of routes: 9 (3 tram, 6 LRT)
Number of stops: 82
Gauge: 1,435 mm
Electrification: 750 V DC, overhead

Rolling stock: SSB 22 cars, SWB 75 cars
Duewag Stadtbahn B100C/S 6-axle
    articulated   M75
Dueweg R1 6-axle low-floor (1994/95)   M22

Current situation
Network comprises three routes of urban tramway
and four of Stadtbahn, 1,435 mm gauge. Routes
16 and 18 to Cologne, over former Cologne-Bonn
railway, are operated jointly with KVB Cologne.
Routes 66 (Bad Honnef, Bonn, Siegburg), 67
(Bad Godesberg, Siegburg) and 68 (Ramersdorf,
Bornheim) are operated with Elektrischen Bahnen
der Stadt Bonn und des Rhein-Sieg-Kreises
(SSB). Route 63 (Bad Godesberg Tannenbusch) is
operated by the City of Bonn.

Rhein-Sieg Verkehrsgesellschaft mbH (RSVG)

Steinstrasse 31, D-53844 Troisdorf-Sieglar,
Germany
Tel: (+49 2241) 49 90   Fax: (+49 2241) 49 92 98
e-mail: Info@RSVG.de
Web: www.rsvg.de

Key personnel
Managing Directors: Herbert Lutz
    Dr-Ing Lothar Franz
    Staff: 364

Passenger journeys: (1997) 16.8 million
(1998) 16.4 million
(1999) 16.7 million
Vehicle-km: (1997) 9.4 million
(1998) 9.6 million
(1999) 9.8 million

Fleet: 178 buses, plus 41 on hire

Current situation
Local authority-owned regional bus company
providing services in the area around Bonn,
especially on the right bank of the Rhine, and
urban services in Siegburg, plus through routes
to Bonn, as part of the VRS network.

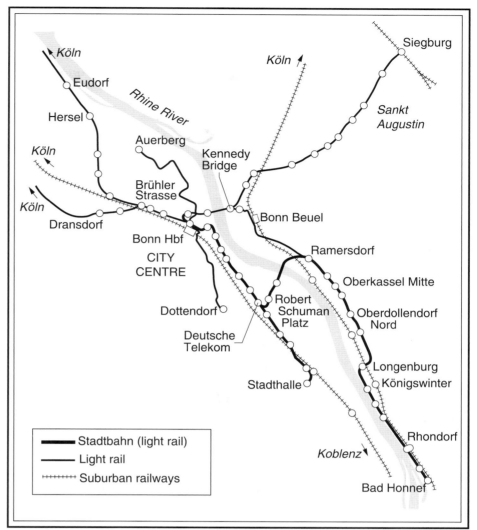

Map of Bonn's light and suburban rail system   1115265

Bremen

Population: 545,000 (2005 estimate)

Public transport
Bus and tramway services operated by Bremer
Strassenbahn AG (BSAG). Suburban rail services
operated by DB. Bus services also run by private
operators. Services co-ordinated by regional
transit authority VBN.

Verkehrsverbund Bremen/ Niedersachsen GmbH (VBN)

Willy-BrandtBrand-Platz 7, D-28215 Bremen,
Germany
Tel: (+49 421) 596 00   Fax: (+49 421) 596 01 99
e-mail: info@vbn.de
Web: www.vbn.de

Key personnel
Managing Director: Wolfgang Müller

Passenger journeys: (2003) 125.1 million
(2004) 128.9 million
(2005) 131.5 million
(2006) 132.0 million
(2007) 132.5 million

Fare structure: Zonal

Current situation
Set up in 1989, this regional transit authority
embraces the cities of Bremen, Bremerhaven,
Oldenburg and Delmenhorst and surrounding
areas within a radius of 50–70 km from Bremen,
covering 8,500 km² with a population of about
1.9 million. VBN co-ordinates services provided
by BSAG (see separate entry) with suburban

rail services of DB and suburban and regional
bus services provided by 36 public and private
operators with a network of 470 routes. A uniform
zonal tariff allows free transfers between modes
and operators.

Bremer Strassenbahn AG (BSAG)

Flughafendamm 12, D-28199 Bremen, Germany
Tel: (+49 421) 559 60
Fax: (+49 421) 559 63 02
e-mail: info@bsag.de
Web: www.bsag.de

Key personnel
Managing Director: Dipl Ing Georg Drechsler
    Personnel Director: Michael Hünig
Finance Director: Peter Hofmann
Manager, Corporate Planning: Markus Hallenkamp
Manager, Traffic Planning: Volker Arndt
Manager, Commercial: Horst Rehberg
Manager, Engineering: Gerd Spanjer
    Staff: 2,036 (2006)

Passenger journeys: (All modes)
(2002) 95.7 million
(2003) 96.6 million
(2004) 96.9 million
(2005) 97.5 million
(2006) 97.2 million
Vehicle-km: (2004) 22.1 million
(2005) 21.9 million
(2006) 21.93 million

Fare collection: Payment to driver, prepurchase
multitickets or pass; validation and cancelling
machines on board; electronic chipcards.

Fare structure: Zonal (area divided into 91
numbered zones); single tickets and day passes
obtainable from driver; four and 10 multi-journey
tickets or weekly/monthly passes from booking
offices; monthly/day passes transferable; a second
person and up to four children may ride free after
19.00 and at weekends; football admission tickets
valid for travel to and from stadium
Fares collected on board: 10.7 per cent
Operating costs financed by: (All modes) Fares
47 per cent, other commercial sources 8 per cent,
subsidy/grants 45 per cent; some subsidies made
directly in respect of certain routes
Subsidy from: Deficits made good by Bremer
Versorgungs und Verkehrsgesellschaft mbH as
parent company. Part of the funds available for
support come under Federal legislation providing
for larger states to compensate smaller ones,
like Bremen, for greater burden of providing
local services. Contributions also received from
neighbouring Lower Saxony municipalities

Bus
Vehicle-km: Not currently available

Number of routes: 44
Route length: 554.6 km

Fleet: 221 vehicles
*Full breakdown of fleet is not currently available,
but includes:*
Neoplan Type N 4021 articulated
    (1994/95, 1999)   79
Evobus 0 405 GN2 articulated (1997)   30
MAN NG 313 articulated (2002)   30
Solaris Urbino 18 articulated (2006)   1
Solaris Urbino 18 EEV articulated (2006)   9
Mercedes-Benz 0 405 N standard (1990/92)   n/a

Mercedes-Benz 0 405 N2 standard
(1994, 97, 98)   n/a
MAN NL 202 standard (1992, 94)   n/a
Mini- and midibus   3

Most intensive service: 5 min
One-person operation: All routes
Operational control: Traffic controllers on each route with mobile radio; computer-based control
Average distance between stops: 594 m
Average peak-hour speed: 22.3 km/h
New vehicles financed by: Leasing

Developments
Solaris Bus & Coach have been awarded a contract to supply a total of 40 new buses, 22 Solaris Urbino 18 three-axle articulated buses, 16 Solaris Urbino 12 two-axle buses and two Solaris midibuses. All of these vehicles will be powered by Enhanced Environmental Vehicle (EEV) engines.

Tramway
Type of operation: Conventional tramway
Car-km: Not currently available

Route length: 110.7 km
Number of lines: 8
Number of stops: 131
Gauge: 1,435 mm
One-person operation: All routes

Rolling stock: 121 cars
Full breakdown of fleet is not currently available, but includes:
Wegmann 4-axle articulated   n/a
AEG/Kiepe GT8N 8-axle low-floor
(1993/95/96)   77
Bombardier/Vossloh Kiepe
FLEXITY GT8N1 (2005/7)   M30
On order: 14 Bombardier/Vossloh Kiepe *FLEXITY* GT8N1, delivery to commence in February 2008. Option for a further 9 vehicles

Current situation
Eight-route network upgraded to Stadtbahn standards in suburbs, with street running maintained in city centre.

Developments
Expansion plans include two extensions to Route 1, an extension to Route 8 and two extensions to Routes 2 and 10. These are due to be completed between 2010 and 2011. An extension to Route 4 is also in development.

Weser-Ems Busverkehr GmbH
Friedrich-Rauers-Strasse 9, D-28195 Bremen, Germany
Tel: (+49 421) 30 89 70
Fax: (+49 421) 308 97 15
e-mail: info@weser-ems-bus.de
Web: www.weser-ems-bus.de

Key personnel
Managing Directors: Herbert Schlienkamp, André Pieperjohanns
Staff: 449

Number of routes: 400
Number of bus stops: 7,500

Current situation
Regional bus company owned by DB provides suburban and rural services on routes within VOS, VEJ and VBN areas.

Fleet: 163 vehicles, including MAN, Mercedes-Benz Citaro, Kässbohrer and Neoplan

Wolters Linienverkehrsbetriebe GmbH (Wolters)
Bremer Strasse 49, D-28816 Stuhr-Brinkum, Germany
Tel: (+49 421) 949 94 13
Fax: (+49 421) 949 94 29
e-mail: info@wolters-buslinien.de
Web: www.wolters-buslinien.de

Key personnel
Director: Herr Langhof

Passenger journeys: (2006) 1.1 million (estimate)
Vehicle-km: (2006) 1.86 million (estimate)

Current situation
Independent bus operator providing suburban services, on 11 routes and school services, with a fleet of 24 buses, to the south of Bremen.

Fleet: 24 buses
Setra 215 UL and 315 NF   15
MAN A10   2
EvoBus Citaro   4
Mercedes-Benz O 405   1
Mercedes-Benz O 405G   2

In peak service: Not currently available
On order: Not currently available

Delbus GmbH & Co KG
Bahnhofstrasse 22, D-27749 Delmenhorst, Germany
Tel: (+49 4221) 919 20   Fax: (+49 4221) 91 92 20
e-mail: info@delbus.de
Web: www.delbus.de

Key personnel
Managing Director and Operating Manager: Carsten Hoffmann

Passenger journeys: (2006/07) 3.7 million
Vehicle-km: (2006/07) 1.8 million

Current situation
Subsidiary company of BSAG providing local bus service over 15 routes in Delmenhorst (population 79,000), with a fleet of 30 buses. Connection with BSAG services at two points; through ticketing.

DB Regio AG
Region Nord
Ernst-August-Platz 10, D-30159 Hannover, Germany
Tel: (+49 511) 286 46 11   Fax: (+49 511) 286 21 80
e-mail: Maria.Osang@bahn.de
Web: www.bahn.de/bremen

Key personnel
Head of Region: Dr Wolfram von Fritsch
Transport Manager: Peter Büsing
Marketing Manager: Guido Verhoefen
Commercial Manager: Günther Köhnke

Type of operation: Suburban heavy rail

Passenger journeys: Not currently available

Current situation
Services operated on six routes radiating from Bremen Hauptbahnhof, totalling 473 km with 32 stations, under VBN tariff (see separate entry), carrying about 10 million passengers annually. The route from Bremen Hauptbahnhof to Vegesack (17 km) and Verden (Aller) (35 km) has been upgraded to City Bahn standards with fixed interval service (15 minutes peak, 30 minutes off-peak).
Regional services are operated over a network of 2,960 km in Lower Saxony and the Bremen area, serving 367 stations and halts.
For further information on DB Regio AG, please see other entries in *Jane's Urban Transport Systems* and *Jane's World Railways.*

Chemnitz
Population: 246,110 (2006 estimate)

Public transport
Bus and tramway services provided by municipal company, some suburban rail services (CBC) and regional bus company Autobus Sachsen. Light rail over freight lines.

Autobus GmbH Sachsen
Postfach 411169, D-09025, Chemnitz, Germany
Tel: (+49 371) 380 81 12
Fax: (+49 371) 380 81 38
e-mail: info@autobus-sachsen.de
Web: www.autobus-sachsen.de

Street address
Zwickauer Strasse 58, D-09112 Chemnitz, Germany

Key personnel
General Manager: Jens Meiwald
Staff: 306 (2008)

Passenger journeys: (2003) 9.4 million
(2004) 9.4 million
(2005) 9.8 million

CVAG Mercedes-Benz Citaro low-floor bus (Quintus Vosman)   1168212

(2006) 9.7 million
(2007) 8.9 million
Vehicle-km: (2003) 6.1 million
(2004) 6.1 million
(2005) 6.08 million
(2006) 5.95 million
(2007) 5.92 million

Current situation
Local government-owned bus company providing regional services in the area around Chemnitz.

Fleet: 133 buses, including 7 buses for tourist activities.
Full breakdown of fleet is not available currently

Chemnitzer Verkehrs-Aktiengesellschaft (CVAG)

PO Box 114, D-09001 Chemnitz, Germany
Tel: (+49 371) 237 00   Fax: (+49 371) 237 06 00
e-mail: kontakt@cvag.de
Web: www.cvag.de

Street address

Carl-von-Ossietzky-Strasse 186, D-09127,
Chemnitz, Germany

Key personnel

Directors: Andreas Rasemann, Karl Gerhard Degrief
Managers: Regina Vogl, Heiko Wolf,
   Dr Reinhart Seidel, Stefan Tschök
Product Manager, Marketing: Steffen Kuss
   Staff: 564

Passenger journeys: (2002) 42.3 million
(2003) 42.4 million
(2006) 42 million (estimate)

Current situation

CVAG serves an area of 118 km². The bus system
is more extensive than in many eastern German
cities as the former 925 mm gauge tram network
was replaced largely by buses rather than total
conversion to 1,435 mm gauge. Conversion was
completed in 1988.

Developments

Bus routes are being replanned as feeders to
an extended tram network, including new light
rail routes into surrounding areas, some of
which may take over existing DB routes. Tram
service now replaced by buses at times of low
demand.
Operating costs financed by: Fares 29.1 per cent,
subsidy/grants 60 per cent, other 10.9 per cent (bus
and tram combined)

Bus

Vehicle-km: (2003) 7.7 million
(2006) 6.3 million

Number of routes: 30 (2006)
Route length: 385 km including duplication,
unduplicated 326 km (2006)
On priority right-of-way: 1.1 km

Fleet: 86 vehicles

Mercedes-Benz Sprinter (2001)	2
Mercedes-Benz O405N low-floor (1991–93)	18
Mercedes-Benz O530N Citaro low-floor	13
Mercedes O405GN low-floor articulated (1993–97)	19
Mercedes-Benz O530GN Citaro low-floor articulated (2001–04)	24
MAN NG313	4
MAN NG313CNG low-floor articulated gas-driven (2000)	2
Volvo V7000 low-floor articulated (2001)	2
Others	2

In peak service: Not currently available
Average age of fleet: 8.6 years

Most intensive service: 10 min
One-person operation: All routes
Operational control: Computer-based system
planned
Fare structure: Time-based single or multiride
tickets; daily, weekly and monthly passes, annual
subscription
Fare collection: Prepurchase and onboard ticket
vending machines, onboard validation
Fare evasion control: Roving inspectors
Average distance between stops: 600 m
Average speed: 21.54 km/h
Operating costs financed by: Fares 32 per cent,
subsidy/grants 68 per cent
Subsidy from: City of Chemnitz 100 per cent

Tramway

Type of operation: Conventional tramway

Passenger journeys: Not currently available
Car-km: (2003) 1.9 million
(2006) 1.6 million

CVAG Variobahn tram (Quintus Vosman)   1168211

Number of routes: 5 (2006)
Number of stops: 62
Route length: 39.97 km including duplication,
unduplicated 28.73 km (2006)
On priority right-of-way: More than 90 per cent
Gauge: 1,435 mm
Electrification: 600 V DC, overhead

Service: Peak 7 min
Average distance between stops: 450 m
Average speed: 18.8 km/h
Type of rail: Ri60 (60.5 kg/m); S49 (49.1 kg/m)
Max gradient: 6.6%
Min curve radius: 27 m
Fare evasion control: Roving inspectors
Operating costs financed by: Fares 41 per cent,
subsidy/grants 59 per cent

Rolling stock: 64 cars (plus 6 special) (2006)

CKD Tatra T3D/B3D 4-axle modernised (1981–88)	M30 T11
Adtranz/Bombardier 6NGT-LDE 6-axle low-floor articulated (1993, 1999/2000)	M13
Adtranz/Bombardier 6NGT'LDZ 6-axle low-floor articulated bidirectional (1998/2000)	M10
Special cars	6

In peak service: 29
Average age of fleet: 13 years

Most intensive service: 10 min
One-person operation: All routes
Operational control: Computer-based system
planned

City-Bahn Chemnitz GmbH (CBC)

Postfach 114, D-09001 Chemnitz, Germany
Tel: (+49 371) 495 79 52 22
Fax: (+49 371) 495 79 52 41
e-mail: kontakt@city-bahn.de
Web: www.city-bahn.de

Street address

Krenkelstrasse 6, D-09120 Chemnitz, Germany

Key personnel

Managers: Herr Leonhardt, Herr Meiwald

Passenger journeys: (2003) 1.86 million
(2004) 1.95 million
(2005) 2.17 million
(2006) 2.37 million
(2007) 2.39 million
Vehicle-km: (2003) 1.2 million
(2004) 1.25 million
(2005) 1.29 million
(2006) 1.46 million
(2007) 1.45 million

Current situation

Company founded in 1997 jointly by CVAG
(currently 60 per cent) and Autobus GmbH
Sachsen (currently 40 per cent) for planning of
the light rail line from Stollberg to Chemnitz
(23 km), using tram tracks from Altchemnitz to
Chemnitz Central station and rail tracks from
Altchemnitz to Stollberg.
   First section opened in 1998 with leased diesel
railcars. Double-ended versions of the 'Variobahn'
(Variotram) are being used on this route; six
were ordered from Adtranz/Bombardier at the
end of 1999 and the light rail system opened in
December 2002.
   Currently, five routes are in operation:
Chemnitz-Stollberg, Chemnitz-Limbach-
Oberfrohna, Chemnitz-Hainichen, Stollberg-
Glauchau-Zwickau and Chemnitz-Burgstädt.
The last three routes will not be electrified, but
the use of dual-mode vehicles is envisaged,
with a new connection between the tram and
rail systems planned at the main station. The
conversion of the main station is scheduled to be
completed in 2013.

Developments

The Stollberg-Glauchau and Chemnitz-Hainichen
routes have recently been upgraded, with seven
new stations and a reduction in the journey time
on both.
   Proposed future developments include
integration of the system with other modes.
   The Chemnitz-Limbach-Oberfrohna route is
temporarily in bus operation.

Zweckverband Verkehrsverbund Mittelsachsen (ZVMS)

c/o Verkehrsverbund Mittelsachsen GmbH
Am Rathaus 2, D-09111 Chemnitz, Germany
Tel: (+49 371) 40 00 80
Fax: (+49 371) 400 08 99
e-mail: post@vms-mobil.de
Web: www.vms-mobil.de

Key personnel

Chairman: Dr Peter Seifert
Chief Executive Officer: Dr Harald Neuhaus

Current situation

Regional transit authority created in 1998 to
co-ordinate public transport in the regions of
Chemnitz, Mittweida, Freiberg, Erzgebirge,
Zwickau and West-Sachsen (Saxony), an area of
4,683 km² with a population of 1.3 million.
   Responsible for integrated fares, tickets,
schedules and passenger information. Co-
ordination of 29 public and private transport
companies.

Cologne

Population: 986,168 (2006), area served 1.3 million
(3.2 million in VRS area)

Public transport

Bus, tramway and light rail services provided
by municipal authority, co-ordinated under the
Verkehrsverbund Rhein-Sieg (VRS) to provide
integrated local transport throughout the region.
Tramway being upgraded to Stadtbahn; S-Bahn
and regional rail services provided by DB.

DB Region NRW GmbH

Region Nordrhein-Westfalen, Geschäftsbereich
Rheinland
Dompropst-Ketzer Strasse 1-9, D-50667 Cologne,
Germany
Tel: (+49 221) 141 433 04
Fax: (+49 221) 141 24 42
Web: www.bahn.de/nordrhein-westfalen

Key personnel
Head of Region: Stefan Kühn

Type of operation: S-Bahn and regional rail

Passenger journeys: (total Rheinland region)
Approximately 76 million annually

Current situation
S-Bahn service is now provided on three cross-
city routes from Düsseldorf-Gerresheim to
Bergisch Gladbach through Cologne Hbf; Rhein-
Ruhr S-Bahn Route S6 Essen via Düsseldorf-
Langenfeld to Cologne Hansaring, created a
second link between the Rhein-Ruhr and Cologne
(Rhein-Sieg) S-Bahn systems; and Cologne-
Troisdorf-Siegburg-Aug (Sieg).

City-Bahn regional rail service in operation
between Cologne and Gummersbach in the east,
to Horrem in the west, and to Euskirchen in the
southwest. Construction of a dedicated pair of
tracks on the route to Horrem and onwards to
Düren (42 km) started in 1999, for line S13, which
was opened at the end of 2002. An S-Bahn line
to Cologne/Bonn airport is planned in connection
with the new high-speed line from Cologne to
Frankfurt. The 15 km line was expected to be
completed in June 2004.

For further information on DB, please see
Jane's World Railways.

Rolling stock: 59 electric railcars (ET 423, ET425),
82 double-deck coaches, 203 other coaches, 59
locomotives
Most intensive service: 15–20 min (peak), 3–60 min
(off-peak)

Bombardier tram at Frechen station (Oubeck.com)   0126404

Bombardier tram at new underground terminus in Bensberg (Oubeck.com)   0126405

Kölner Verkehrs-Betriebe AG (KVB)

Scheidtweilerstrasse 38, D-50933 Cologne
(Braunsfeld), Germany
Tel: (+49 221) 54 70   Fax: (+49 221) 547 31 25
e-mail: info@kvb-koeln.de
Web: http://www.kvb-koeln.de

Key personnel
Executive committee: Werner Böllinger
    Walter Reinarz
    Edith Wurbs
    Hubert Kämmerling
Directors:
    Bus and Light Rail: Dr Erhard Schrameyer
    Infrastructure and Maintenance: Dr Wolfgang
    Meyer
    Finance: Edith Wurbs
    Personnel: Mr Kammerling
    Media Contact: Franz Wolf Ramien
Staff: 3,272

Current situation
Kölner Verkehrs-Betriebe AG was founded in 1877
and is 90 per cent owned by Cologne City Works
Group and 10 per cent by the City of Cologne.

The company had a turnover of DM3,126 in 1999.
The Köln and Bonn transport companies are to
be merged into a new company, Köln-Bonner-
Verkehrsunternehman AG (KBV). The merger will
be effected in several stages until 2003. The bus
company, RVK, may also be included.

Passenger journeys: (All modes)
(1998) 225.3 million
(1999) 230 million
(2000) 230 million

Operating costs financed by: Fares 58 per cent,
subsidy/grants 42 per cent

Developments
The Cologne-Bonn interurban railway KBE, which
also operated its own fleet of 34 buses, was
merged with KVB in 1992. In recognition of KVB's
contribution to the life of the city, the authorities
have approved an annual grant of 25 per cent of
tramway track maintenance costs. KVG took over
responsibility for the cable car between Cologne
Zoo and Rheinpark in 1998.

Bus

Vehicle-km: (1998) 20.9 million
(1999) 20.9 million
(2000) 21.0 million

Number of routes: 42
Route length: 455 km
Number of stops: 648

Fleet: 213 vehicles, plus 81 contracted	
Mercedes O405N low-floor (1991/2000)	55
Neoplan N4021 articulated (1989)	4
Neoplan N4021 low-floor articulated (1992)	10
Neoplan N4014NF low-floor (1992/93)	52
Volvo Steyr SC6F58 (1993)	5
MAN NG272 low-floor articulated (1994/95)	65
Mercedes O405 GN2 (2000)	5
Others	17

Most intensive service: 10 min
One-person operation: All routes
Fare collection: Vending machines on board or
prepurchase multitickets or pass; validation and
cancelling machines on board

Fare evasion control: Roving inspectors; DM60 penalty

Operational control: Mobile radio, computer-based system (RBL) introduced in 1998 on five bus and two rail routes (to be extended)

Average peak-hour speed: 21.4 km/h

Tramway/Stadtbahn

Type of operation: Conventional tramway and Stadtbahn

Car-km: (1998) 31.9 million
(1999) 32.1 million
(2000) 132.2 million

Route length: 191 km
Number of routes: 15
Number of stations: 32 (in tunnel)
Gauge: 1,435 mm
Max gradient: 5%
Min curve radius: 60 m
Electrification: 750 V DC, overhead
Average speed: 26.1 km/h

Service: Peak 4 min, off-peak 20 min
First/last car: 04.20/02.00

Rolling stock: 339 cars

Duewag B80D 6-axle Stadtbahn (1987–92)	M40
Waggon Union B80D 6-axle Stadtbahn (1987/90)	M10
Bombardier K4000 6-axle articulated (1995/97/98/99)	M120
Waggon Union B80D 6-axle Stadtbahn (1987/90)	M10
Bombardier K4000 6-axle articulated (1995/97/ 98/99)	M120

On order: 4 further K4000 for 2002 delivery; 55 K5000 Stadtbahn (option for further 91), all from Bombardier

Current situation

The upgraded tramway system in Cologne now operates largely with modern LRVs, either high-floor Stadtbahn types (in particular on the joint interurban lines to Bonn), or more recent low-floor trams which predominate on the 'Gürtel' (belt) and east-west links. Underground sections continued to be opened and the Mülheim east-west section (3.9 km, four stations) opened in 1997.

Developments

Construction started in 1999 on a 2.2 km extension of tram Route 1 from Junkersdorf to Weiden, for opening in May 2002. At the other end of the route, a 600 m underground extension to Bensberg-Zentrum opened in May 2000. Work also started on the first 0.8 km extension of existing Line 3 from Bocklemünd to Ollenhauerring (ultimately to Mengenich) for 2002 opening. Sections of the KBE Vorgebirgsbahn (Route 18), currently single track, are being doubled, with completion by 2002. Route 12 is planned for conversion to Stadtbahn operation from 2002. Plans have now been finalised for a new direct north-south line from Köln Hauptbahnhof, which would allow direct connection to the former KBE Rheinuferbahn to Bonn. Construction of the first of three phases (Breslauer Platz-Raderberg Marktstrasse) was expected to start in late 2001 for final opening in 2011.

The east-west routes are now operated exclusively with low-floor LRVs. These routes will become a largely separate system and only three stations on the belt line are shared with the high-platform LRT network. Ultimately, a fleet of some 400 cars is planned for the two systems.

A new generation of high-floor Stadtbahn cars, the K5000, has been developed, with 55 ordered from Bombardier Transportation in February 2000 for delivery starting June 2001 and an option for a further 91.

A new depot is planned at Ossendorf, as is a computer-based control system for the Bruck and Bocklemund tram routes.

Interurban rail
Current situation
The KBE lines, now merged into KVB and SWB Bonn, total 58.5 km with 40 stations, electrified 750 V DC overhead.

Kraftverkehr Wupper-Sieg AG (KWS)

PO Box 30 09 53, D-51338 Leverkusen, Germany
Tel: (+49 2171) 500 70
Fax: (+49 2171) 500 71 77
e-mail: info@wupsi.de
Web: www.wupsi.de

Street address
Borsigstrasse 18, D-51381 Leverkusen, Germany

Key personnel
Director: Dr Gerd Wasser
  Staff: 315

Current situation

Local government owned bus operator serving Leverkusen and Bergisch Gladbach and adjoining rural area, population 527,000.

Developments

Following formation of VRS, several routes were cut back to act as rail feeders. KVB bus routes outside Cologne city limits have been taken over by KWS in compensation.

Passenger journeys: (1997) 21.7 million
(1998) 20.6 million
(2000) 20.8 million
Vehicle-km: (1996) 9.7 million
(1998) 9.8 million
(2000) 9.8 million
(2002) 9.6 million

Number of routes: 153
Route length: 497 km

Fleet: 144 buses, plus 53 contracted
Fare structure: As VRS

Regio-Bus-Rheinland GmbH (RBR)

Godesberger Allee 120, D-53175 Bonn, Germany
Tel: (+49 228) 96 77 50
e-mail: info@rbr-online.de
Web: www.rbr-online.de

Key personnel
Public Relations: Sabine Fusshoell er
  Staff: 104

Current situation

Formed in 1999 as a joint venture of Regionalverkehr Köln GmbH (RVK) (51 per cent) and independent Univers Reisen of Bonn (49 per cent). Since 2001, RBR has been 100 per cent owned by RVK (see separate entry). RBR does not hold any traffic rights and scheduled services are exclusively operated under contract to other operators. Commercial matters are handled by RVK.

Fleet: 32 vehicles, subcontracted from RVK

Regionalverkehr Köln GmbH (RVK)

Theodor-Heuss-Ring 38-40, D-50668 Cologne, Germany
Tel: (+49 221) 163 70
Fax: (+49 221) 163 72 39
e-mail: rvk-office@rvk.de
Web: www.rvk.de

Key personnel
Managing Director: Eugen Puderbach
Public Relations: Sabine Fusshoeller
  Staff: 763

Current situation

This regional bus company, formerly controlled by DB and Deutsche Bündespost, was taken over by eight local government owned transport companies (including KVB and SWB) in 1996. It provides suburban, interurban and rural bus services.

Passenger journeys: (2000) 34.7 million
(2004) 25.3 million
Vehicle-km: (2000) 19.5 million
(2004) 14.7 million

Fleet: 353 buses, plus 319 contracted out to independent operators

Fare structure: VRS within area; separate km-based tariff beyond
Operating costs financed by: Fares 99.2 per cent

Verkehrsverbund Rhein-Sieg GmbH (VRS)

Krebsgasse 5-11, D-50667 Cologne, Germany
Tel: (+49 221) 20 80 80
Fax: (+49 221) 208 08 40
e-mail: info@vrsinfo.de
Web: www.vrsinfo.de

Key personnel
Managing Directors: Wilhelm Schmidt-Freitag
  Norbert Reinkober
Manager, Communications: Claudia Dillenhöfer

Passenger journeys: Approx 500 million annually

Current situation

Formed in 1987 and covering an area of 5,150 km² with a population of 3.2 million, VRS territory extends from Gummersbach in the east to Düren and Euskirchen in the west, from Langenfeld/Monheim in the north to Bonn/Linz in the south. VRS co-ordinates all public transport services by road and rail within its area, including regional rail services of DB. A uniform tariff scheme with free transfers, irrespective of mode or operator, is applied.

Services are provided by Stadtwerke Bonn (SWB, and its associate SSB), Kölner Verkehrs Betriebe (KVB), Regionalverkehr Köln (RVK), Kraftverkehr Wupper-Sieg (KWS), Rhein-Sieg Verkehrsgesellschaft (RSVG), Oberbergische Verkehrsgesellschaft (OVAG), Bahnen der Stadt Monheim (BSM), the independent bus operators Verkehrsbetrieb Hüttebräucker at Leichlingen, Kraftverkehr Gebr Wiedenhoff at Solingen and Rhein-Erft Verkehrsgesellschaft (REVG), whose services are operated by RVK under contract, and DB. Local services in Euskirchen, Hürth and Dormagen are also included. Stadtwerke Brühl and Stadtwerke Wesseling GmbH joined VRS in 1998.

One of the first measures taken by VRS was to cut back regional bus routes into Cologne at the outer termini of the city's tramways where passengers now have to change. Throughout the VRS area, some 20 per cent of commuters use public transport, rising to 27 per cent in the core cities.

Developments

DB won a 15-year concession, starting in 1998, to operate three local rail lines in the VRS area - Cologne-Gummersbach, Euskirchen-Jünkenrath and Bonn-Euskirchen-Bad Münstereifel. The deal involved purchase of 45 three-car Talent dmus from Talbot.

Fare structure: Zonal; single, day and multiride tickets, weekly and monthly passes (non-transferable), transferable monthly passes (not valid before 09.00); free transfer within area, irrespective of mode or operator; 7 per cent of passengers use passes
Operating costs financed by: Fares 44 per cent, contractual grants 11 per cent, subsidy 45 per cent

Dortmund

Population: 586,000 (2006 estimate), area served 668,000

Public transport

Bus and tramway services provided by municipal company, also responsible for other public utilities, operating as part of Rhein-Ruhr Verkehrsverbund, co-ordinating fares and services with regional rail (S-Bahn); people mover.

Dortmunder Stadtwerke AG (DSW21)

Deggingstrasse 40, D-44141 Dortmund, Germany
Tel: (+49 231) 955 00   Fax: (+49 231) 955 33 00
e-mail: posteingang@dsw.de
welcome@dsw21.de
Web: www.dsw21.de, www.bus-und-bahn.de

Key personnel
Directors: Guntram Pehlke (Chair and Chief Executive Officer)
Karl-Heinz Faust
Hubert Jung
Technical/Transport Manager: Udo Griebsch
Operating and Marketing Manager: Dr-Jug Heinz-Josef Pohlmann
Legal Affairs Manager: Petra Bohle
Finance and Accounting Manager: Peter Becker
Data Processing Manager: Bernd-Michael Schnider
Way and Works Manager: Kürt Otto
Administration Manager/Personnel: Joachim Basista
Press and Information: Wolfgang Herbrand, Bernd Winkelmann, Thomas Steffen
Staff: 1,866

Passenger journeys: (All modes)
(2002) 116.7 million
(2003) 122.7 million

Fare structure: Zonal; as Rhein-Ruhr, plus various special fares
Operating costs financed by: Fares 30 per cent, other commercial sources 5.3 per cent, subsidy/grants 24.4 per cent including cross-subsidy from gas and water supply, remainder as deficit
Source of subsidy: Region 91.7 per cent, local 8.3 per cent

Bus

Vehicle-km: (2000) 13.3 million
Number of routes: 56
Route length: (One way) 761.2 km

Fleet: 163 vehicles, plus 73 contracted
MAN SL200 standard (1983/85)	9
MAN SG242H articulated (1987/88)	31
MAN NG272 low-floor articulated (1989/94)	41
MAN NL202 low-floor (1991/93)	36
Van Hool AG300 articulated (1994)	2
Van Hool A360 low-floor (1996)	6
Mercedes O405N low-floor (1997)	6
MAN NG312 low-floor articulated (1997)	2
MAN NL223 low-floor (1999)	8
MAN NG263 low-floor articulated (1998)	9
MAN NM223 low-floor midi (1999)	8
Other	5

In peak service: 130

Most intensive service: 10 min
One-person operation: All routes
Fare collection: Pre-purchase pass (chip card) or multi-tickets with validation and cancelling machines; payment to driver; in January 1999 ticket sales via the Internet were introduced (ticket2print)
Fare evasion control: Roving inspectors

Integration with other modes: At passenger's request, bus and tram drivers may summon a taxi to any stop
Average speed: 22 km/h
Operating costs financed by: Fares 32.2 per cent, other commercial sources 5.6 per cent, subsidy/grants 27.2 per cent, remainder as deficit

Tramway/light rail

Type of operation: Conventional tramway largely on reserved track with six routes upgraded under the Rhein-Ruhr Stadtbahn project with city-centre tunnels

Passenger journeys: (2000) 60 million
Vehicle-km: (2000) 8.6 million

Route length: 90.9 km, of which 44.8 km Stadtbahn
   reserved track: 50.6 km
   in tunnel: 13.7 km
Number of routes: 3 tramway, 6 light rail
Number of stops: 124, of which 67 on Stadtbahn network
Gauge: 1,435 mm
Electrification: 600 V DC, overhead

Rolling stock: 118 cars
Duewag N8C articulated (1978/80/82)	M52
Duewag B6 6-axle articulated (1986/93)	M43
Duewag B8 8-axle articulated (1994)	M11

In peak service: 102
On order: Plans for 47 low-floor cars for the east-west tunnel routes, delivery starting in 2005

Current situation
Under the Rhein-Ruhr Stadtbahn plan, which comprises four stages, 10 branches of the tramway network are being linked by three cross-city tunnels to create a light rail system of 41 km, with 59 stations, of which 20 km will be in tunnel. The remainder will be upgraded tramway, though much of the present system is already at or close to Stadtbahn standards (see under Rhein-Ruhr).

DB Regio AG

DB Regio NRW GmbH
Region Nordrhein-Westfalen, Geschäftsbereich Rhein-Ruhr
Hollestrasse 3, D-45127 Essen, Germany
Tel: (+49 201) 175 25 07,   Fax: (+49 201) 175 23 02
Web: www.bahn.de/nordrhein-westfahlen

Key personnel
Head of Region: Thorsten Siggelkow

Type of operation: Regional metro (S-Bahn).

Current situation
A 9 km extension of Rhein-Ruhr Line S1 from Bochum-Langengreer serves Dortmund Hbf with a 20 min service. Route S4 links Lütgendortmund with Unna and Herne via Dortmund-Stadthaus, and in 1994 S5 was opened from Dortmund to Witten and Hagen with trains every 30 min (see Rhein-Ruhr entry). Other local services operate on five routes out of Dortmund Hbf.

Separate tracks are under construction for S4 between Dortmund and Herne, including a 1.4 km tunnel section.

H-Bahn Gesellschaft Dortmund mbH (H-Bahn)

Emil-Figge-Strasse 71d, D-44227 Dortmund, Germany
Tel: (+49 231) 757 55   Fax: (+49 231) 75 92 46
e-mail: info@h-bahn21.de
Web: www.h-bahn21.de

Key personnel
Director: Dipl Ing Rolf Schupp
Operations Manager: Dipl-Ing Wolfgang Schlotmann
Technical Manager: Dipl-Ing Rolf Schupp
Staff: 10, plus 17 part-time

Type of operation: People mover (H-Bahn – now known as Sipem, Siemens People Mover) – suspended monorail (first route opened 1984)

Passenger journeys: (2004) 1.5 million
(2006) 1.6 million
Route length: 3.9 km
Number of lines: 1 (plus branch)
Number of stations: 5

Operating costs financed by: Fares 71 per cent, other commercial sources 1 per cent, subsidy/grants 18 per cent
Subsidy from: City 100 per cent (through DSW)

Current situation
Currently, there are two routes with a 3.9 km route length on 2.8 km track length. One route links a residential area with Dortmund University and the S-Bahn station, while the other connects the north and south campuses. Three cars with top speed of 50 km/h provide capacity of up to 1,620 passengers/h.

In 1996, H-Bahn became a wholly owned subsidiary of Dortmunder Stadtwerke, and it has been agreed to keep the line in operation at least until 2020.

Developments
Plans are being developed to extend the line in stages: the 1.2 km extension of Line 1 to Technologiezentrum opened in December 2003.

H-Bahn links university and S-Bahn station

0113542

Dresden

Population: City 504,635 (2006), urban area 1.25 million, metropolitan area 3.5 million (estimates)

Public transport

Central area served mainly by tramways operated by municipal company which also operates bus services, ferries across the River Elbe and two funiculars. Suburban rail services run by German Rail (DB); suburban/regional bus services by regional bus company. All transport services in Dresden and surrounding area are co-ordinated by Regional Transit Authority (VVO).

DB Regio AG

Verkehrsbetrieb Sachsen
Hansastrasse 4, D-01097 Dresden, Germany
Tel: (+49 351) 461 86 00
Fax: (+49 351) 461 86 06
Web: www.bahn.de/sachsen

Key personnel

Contact: Klaus-Dieter Martini

Type of operation: Suburban heavy rail and narrow-gauge local railways.

Passenger journeys: Not currently available

Current situation

Part of the Region Südost, DB Regio AG's Sachsen services covers a network of 1,364 km centred on Dresden and Leipzig and serves 320 stations and halts, with some 986 million passenger-km recorded annually.

For further information on DB, please see *Jane's World Railways.*

Dresdner Verkehrsbetriebe AG (DVB AG)

Trachenberger Strasse 40, D-01129 Dresden, Germany
Tel: (+49 351) 85 70
Fax: (+49 351) 857 10 10
e-mail: postoffice@dvbag.de
Web: www.dvbag.de

Key personnel

Directors
Traffic and Personnel: Hans-Juergen Credé
Technical and Commercial: Reiner Zieschank
Press Officer: Falk Lösch
Staff: 1,681 (2007)

Passenger journeys: (All modes)
(2004) 137.6 million
(2005) 137.9 million
(2006) 139.5 million
(2007) 142.0 million

Subsidiaries

Dresdner Verkehrsservicegesellschaft mbH (DVS), a low-cost carrier which competes for work tendered by the parent company. Founded in 1996;

VerkehrsConsult Dresden-Hamburg GmbH (VCDH), a consultancy for the participation in international and national traffic projects;

TEATER-TOURS GmbH, a private-public-partnership carrier in the bus sector;

Verkehrsgesellschaft Meissen mbH, a regional bus company;

Dresden-IT GmbH (dd it), offering services in information technology.

Developments

In 2004, DVB bought 74.1 per cent of the regional bus company Verkehrsgesellschaft Meissen mbH.

Operating costs covered by: Fares and other sources 66 per cent, loss assumption 34 per cent
Subsidy from: Local sources 100 per cent

Bus

Vehicle-km: (2004) 13.8 million
(2005) 14.3 million
(2006) 13.4 million
(2007) 13.3 million

Number of routes: 28
Route length: 294 km
Number of stops: 427

Fleet: 145 buses
Full breakdown of fleet is not currently available, but comprises:
Articulated kneeling buses:
MAN   14
Mercedes-Benz   7
Solaris   16
Low-floor buses:
MAN   32
Mercedes-Benz   41
Solaris   34
Solaris hybrid   1
In peak service: 105

Most intensive service: 7.5 min
One-person operation: All routes
Fare collection: Tickets from kiosks, machines (including on board) or driver, with cancelling machines on board; over 80 per cent use passes
Fare structure: See VVO (separate entry in)
Fare evasion control: Roving inspectors; penalty fare
Average speed: 21.3 km/h
Average distance between stops: 460 m

Developments

Subcontractors provide 38.3 per cent of vehicle-km.

Tramway

Type of operation: Conventional tramway and light rail
Vehicle-km: (2004) 12.3 million
(2005) 11.9 million
(2006) 12.5 million
(2007) 13.0 million

Route length: 130.2 km
    reserved track: 54.7 km
Number of lines: 12
Number of stops: 153
Number of stops used by both bus and tram: 99
Average distance between stops: 476 m
Average speed: 20.3 km/h
Gauge: 1,450 mm
Electrification: 600 V DC, overhead

Rolling stock: 267 cars
ČKD Tatra T4D/B4D (1971/84) modernised   M101
Siemens/DWA NGT 6   M60
Bombardier NGT 8   M23
Siemens NGT D8   M23
Bombardier NGT D12   M60

On order: 10 Bombardier NGT D8 five-car, low-floor trams for delivery in 2008/09

Current situation

An extension from Gorbitz to Gompitz is under construction and was scheduled to be completed in 2008.

In connection with the opening of a Volkswagen luxury car factory in Strassburger Platz, a freight service (CarGoTram) over DVB lines was introduced to serve the new works in March 2001. Schalker Eisenhütte has constructed two 20-axle five-section bidirectional vehicles, each 59.4 m long, plus two reserve intermediate modules.

Funicular/monorail

Current situation

A funicular, built in 1895, links the suburb of Loschwitz on the right bank of the Elbe with the hillside residential areas of Weisser Hirsch, 94 m higher. It is 547 m long, of metre gauge, and has a maximum gradient of 28 per cent.

The 274 m suspended monorail which links Loschwitz with Oberloschwitz has now been fully

restored. It also works on the funicular principle and climbs 84 m with a maximum gradient of 40 per cent.

Ferry

Current situation

DVB operates three passenger ferries and the Kleinzschachwitz-Pillnitz vehicular ferry across the river Elbe.

Regionalverkehrs Dresden GmbH (RVD)

Ammonstrasse 25, D-01067 Dresden, Germany
Tel: (+49 351) 49 21 30   Fax: (+49 351) 495 40 33
e-mail: service@rvd.de
Web: www.rvd.de

Key personnel

Directors: Dieter Unger, Gisela Mühle
Staff: 336

Passenger journeys: (1997) 13.2 million
(1998) 12.3 million
(2000) 14.2 million
(2003) 13.8 million
Vehicle-km: (1997) 9.5 million
(1998) 9.9 million
(2000) 10.3 million
(2003) 8.9 million

Current situation

This bus company is owned by the county councils of Weisseritzkreis and Meissen. Regional services are operated from Dresden to surrounding towns with a fleet of 97 Mercedes, MAN, Setra and Renault buses plus 90 contracted, on 69 regional and eight urban (Freital and Dippoldiswalde) routes extending to 2,060 km, from depots in Dresden, Dippoldiswalde, Freital and Radeberg. School children account for 55 per cent of passengers.

Verkehrsverbund Oberelbe GmbH (VVO)

Elbcenter Dresden
Leipziger Strasse 120, D-01127 Dresden, Germany
Tel: (+49 351) 85 26 50   Fax: (+49 351) 852 65 13
e-mail: info@vvo-online.de
Web: www.vvo-online.de

Key personnel

Chair: Arndt Steinbach
Managing Director: Knut Ringat
Project Management: Doreen Kahrs

Passenger journeys: (2000) 191 million
(2003) 194 million
(2004) 196 million

Current situation

Established in 1998, VVO comprises the city of Dresden, five neighbouring counties and the town of Hoyerswerda, an area of 4,869 km² with a population share of 1.2 million. Initially there are 207 regional bus routes, 12 tramway routes, 66 urban bus routes and 18 ferries and funiculars. The small trolleybus system in Hoyerswerda closed at the end of 1994. DB-operated lines are also part of the system.

VVO is a political body with its own administration and planning unit. Actual services are provided by existing operators as contractors.

The transport system will be centrally planned and will favour rail services. Bus services duplicating railway lines will be withdrawn step-by-step. Bus services connecting rural areas and Dresden are serviced at modern interchanges. All services operate to a synchronised timetable. A uniform tariff allowing free intermodal transfers will apply.

Fare structure: Zonal, single and daily tickets, season tickets (weekly, monthly and annual), concessions for children, students and apprentices (reduced fares for monthly tickets valid from 9 am)

Duisburg

Population: 502,522 (2005)

Public transport

Bus and tramway services provided by municipally owned company operating as part of Rhein-Ruhr Verkehrsverbund, co-ordinating fares and services. DB S-Bahn services wholly integrated with urban services.

Duisburger Verkehrsgesellschaft AG (DVG)

Bungerstrasse 27, D-47053 Duisburg, Germany
Tel: (+49 203) 60 40
Fax: (+49 203) 604 29 00
e-mail: info@dvv.de
Web: www.dvv.de/dvg/

Key personnel
Directors:
Chairman: Dr Hermann Janning
Technical: Dr Ing Edmund Baer
Personnel: Klaus Siewor
 Staff: 1,045 (2001)

Passenger journeys: (All modes)
(2000) 46 million

Operating costs financed by: Fares 47 per cent, other commercial sources 7 per cent, subsidy/grants 46 per cent
Subsidy from: Duisburger Versorgungs- und Verkehrsgesellschaft mbH, city of Duisburg 90 per cent and state Nordrhein-Westfalen (public grants) 10 per cent

Bus

Passenger journeys: (2001) 23.3 million
Vehicle-km: (2001) 8.99 million

Number of routes: 33
Route length: 484.5 km

Fleet: 162 vehicles, plus 9 contracted	
Mercedes O405 (1992)	17
Van Hool AG300 articulated (1996)	11
Neoplan N4020/3 (1997)	1
Mercedes O405N low-floor (1997)	4
MAN NL263 low-floor (1998/2001)	17
Mercedes O530 Citaro (1999)	108
Others	4

On order: None

Most intensive service: 10–20 min
One-person operation: All routes
Fare collection: Payment to driver or prepurchase pass or multitickets with validation and cancelling machines
Fare structure: Zonal; as Rhein-Ruhr
Fare evasion control: Roving inspectors with penalty
Operational control: Route inspectors/mobile radio
Arrangements for elderly/disabled: 1 minibus operating on demand; free travel for disabled, reimbursed by government
Average speed: 20.6 km/h

Tramway/light rail

Type of operation: Light rail/upgraded tramway (Stadtbahn), conventional tramway

Passenger journeys: (2001) 23.7 million
Car-km: (1999) 4.4 million
(2000) 4.6 million
(2001) 4.96 million

Route length: 56.6 km
 in tunnel: 8.5 km
Number of routes: 2 tram, 1 Stadtbahn joint with Rheinbahn Düsseldorf
Number of stations/stops: 90/180
 in tunnel: 7/16

Max gradient: 6%
Min curve radius: 18 m
Gauge: 1,435 mm
Electrification: 750 V DC, overhead

Service: Peak 10 min, off-peak 30 min
First/last car: 04.00/24.00
One-person operation: All cars
Fare evasion control: Roving inspectors

Rolling stock: 65 cars	
Duewag B80C Stadtbahn 6-axle articulated	
(1983/85)	M18
Duewag GT10NC-DU 10-axle articulated	M46
(1986/93, rebuilt with low-floor section 1996/97)	
Adtranz Variobahn 6NGT 6-axle (1996)	M1

Current situation
A former tram route, now upgraded to LRT standards as Route U79, runs to Düsseldorf and is jointly operated (see under Rhein-Ruhr).

DB Regio AB

DB Regio NRW GmbH
Region Nordrhein-Westfalen, Geschäftsbereich Rhein-Ruhr
Hollestrasse 3, D-45127 Essen, Germany
Tel: (+49 201) 175 25 07   Fax: (+49 201) 175 23 02
Web: www.bahn.de/nordrhein-westfahlen

Key personnel
Head of Region: Thorsten Siggelkow
Type of operation: Regional metro (S-Bahn)

Current situation
Duisburg is served by Line S1 (Dortmund-Duisburg-Düsseldorf) of the Rhein-Ruhr S-Bahn, and other suburban and regional services of DB.

Düsseldorf

Population: 581,858 (2006)

Public transport

Bus, tramway, light rail and leisure ferry services provided in city and surrounding area by municipal company and suburban rail services by DB and Regiobahn, all operating as part of Rhein-Ruhr Verkehrsverbund (VRR), co-ordinating fares and services. See also Rhein-Ruhr entry.

Düsseldorf

Regional bus
Current situation
Regional bus services provided by Busverkehr Rheinland (BVR), an associated company of DB. For full details see under Rhein-Ruhr entry.

DB Regio AG

DB Regio NRW GmbH
Region Nordrhein-Westfalen, Geschäftsbereich Rhein-Ruhr
Hollestrasse 3, D-45127 Essen, Germany
Tel: (+49 201) 175 25 07,
Fax: (+49 201) 175 23 02
Web: www.bahn.de/nordrhein-westfahlen

Key personnel
Head of Region: Thorsten Siggelkow

Type of operation: Regional metro (S-Bahn)

Current situation
Düsseldorf is served by four lines of the Rhein-Ruhr S-Bahn (see under Rhein-Ruhr), and by other (non-S-Bahn) suburban services of DB.

Developments
The DB freight line Düsseldorf-Ratingen West-Duisburg will be reactivated for passenger service. Operations were due to start in 2005 and put out to tender.

Flughafen Düsseldorf GmbH (SkyTrain)

Postfach 30 03 63, D-40403 Düsseldorf, Germany
Tel: (+49 211) 42 10
Fax: (+49 211) 421 66 66
Web: www.duesseldorf-international.de

Street address
Flughafenstrasse 120, D-40474 Düsseldorf, Germany

Key personnel
Chairman of the Supervisory Board: Lord Mayor Dirk Elbers
Chief Executive Officer: Christoph Blume
Managing Director: Thomas Schnalke

Type of operation: Suspended monorail

Passenger boardings: Not currently available
Vehicle-km: Not currently available

Length of system: 2.5 km
Number of stations: Four

Current situation
A 2.5 km fully automated suspended monorail (SkyTrain) started operation between Düsseldorf airport and the closest main line railway station (Düsseldorf airport rail station) in July 2002. It has a capacity of 2,000 passengers/hour. Headway is one minute (peak).

Developments
Siemens Transportation operates and maintains the system.

In September 2006, SkyTrain resumed passenger service after the control technology, vehicles and accelerated station clearance were revised.

Rolling stock: Six suspended two-car articulated monorail vehicles.

The SkyTrain at Düsseldorf international airport (Siemens AG)   1115214

Regionale Bahngesellschaft Kaarst-Neuss-Düsseldorf-Erkrath-Mettmann-Wuppertal mbH (Regiobahn GmbH)

An der Regiobahn 15, D-40822 Mettmann, Germany
Tel: (+49 2104) 30 50 Fax: (+49 2104) 30 51 05
e-mail: info@regio-bahn.de
Web: www.regio-bahn.de, www.regiobahn.de

Key personnel
Managing Directors: Joachim Korn
    Wolfgang Teubner

Passenger journeys: 18,600 daily

Current situation
Founded by various local authorities, this company took over operation from DB of the Kaarst-Neuss and Düsseldorf-Mettmann lines (total 34.2 km, of which 16.5 km over DB tracks, 18 stations) in late 1999; an extension to Wuppertal-Vohwinkel is planned. Operation has been contracted to Rheinisch-Bergische Eisenbahn, a subsidiary of Veolia Verkehr Rheinland GmbH.

Developments
Four more Bombardier Talent dmus have been delivered.

Rolling stock: 12 dmus (Bombardier Talent)
In peak service: 10

Rheinbahn AG

PO Box 10 42 63, D-40033 Düsseldorf (Oberkassel), Germany
Tel: (+49 211) 582 01 Fax: (+49 211) 582 19 66
e-mail: rheinbahn@rheinbahn.de
Web: www.rheinbahn.de

Street address
Hansaallee 1, D-40549, Düsseldorf, Germany

Key personnel
Directors: Peter Ackermann
    Dirk Biesenbach
Infrastructure Manager: Jürgen Breuer
Operations Manager: Dirk Langensiepen
Marketing and Sales Manager: Bernhard Herrmann
Finance Manager: Norbert Tabke
    Staff: 2,828 (2006)

Passenger journeys: (2002) 207.0 million
(2003) 208.2 million
(2004) 209.1 million
(2005) 210.2
(2006) 212.1
Vehicle-km: (All modes)
(2003) 46.6 million
(2004) 46.5 million
(2005) 46.8 million
(2006) 46.7 million

Operating costs financed by: Fares 81 per cent, subsidy/grants 19 per cent (2005)

Current situation
The company is owned by Düsseldorf Stadwerke Gesellschaft für Beteiligungen mbH (95 per cent) and Stadt Düsseldorf (5 per cent). It is a member of the Verkehrsverbund Rhein-Ruhr (VRR) partnership.
    Rheinbahn AG serves Düsseldorf, Meerbusch and Kreis Mettmann with an area of some 569 km² and a population in excess of 998,000.

Bus
Vehicle-km: (2002) 28.2 million
(2003) 27.9 million
(2004) 28.2 million
(2005) 28.2 million
(2006) 28.4 million

Number of routes: 91
Route length: 1,324.0 km

Bombardier Talent dmu of Regiobahn (Michael Wittwer)   0567068

Rheinbahn NF10 tram   1115115

Fleet: 443 vehicles
Full breakdown of fleet is not currently available, but includes:

Mercedes-Benz O 405 GN GS (1993/98) articulated	26
Mercedes-Benz O405 N SL-A (1994)	2
Mercedes-Benz O 530 GN 3 Citaro (1999–2004)	74
MAN NL 263/E3 SL-A (2001, 2008)	4
MAN 202 SL-A (1993/96)	1
MAN 222 SL-A (1999)	12
MAN 223-2 (1999-2000)	29
MAN NL 263-2 (2001/02)	85
MAN NL283 (A 37) (2006/08)	77
Solaris Urbino 12 (2005)	21
MAN NG 272 PL articulated (1992, 1994)	7
MAN NG 262 6/3 T articulated (1997)	32
MAN NG 313/E3 (A 23) articulated (2001)	15
MAN NG 313/E3 (A 23) articulated (2001)	36
Neoplan N4411 midi (1999/2001)	12
Neoplan N4407 (2000)	4
Others	6

On order: Not currently available
In peak service: 352

Most intensive service: 10 min
One-person operation: All routes
Fare collection: Prepurchase tickets or pass with validation and cancelling machines; payment to driver
Fare structure: Zonal; prepurchase multiride tickets, weekly and monthly passes, Jobticket (see below)
Fares collected on board: 16 per cent
Fare evasion control: Roving inspectors
Arrangements for elderly/disabled: Free travel for disabled, reimbursed by government
Operational control: Route inspectors/mobile radio
Average peak-hour speed: 19 km/h

Developments
A full 100 per cent share of Reisechenst Maassen GmbH was purchased in 2006.

Tramway/light rail
Type of operation: Stadtbahn and conventional tramway

Car-km: (Tram and Stadtbahn)
(2002) 19.5 million
(2003) 18.7 million
(2004) 18.4 million
(2005) 18.6 million
(2006) 18.3 million

Route length: Tramway 85.3 km, Stadtbahn 61.2 km (in tunnel 6 km)
Number of lines: 20 (Tramway 13, Stadtbahn 7)
Number of stops: 277

Current situation
Plans envisage a four-line Stadtbahn network of some 68 km, of which 15 km will be in tunnel. Under the Rhein-Ruhr Stadtbahn scheme, the existing tramway is being upgraded. Tunnels now extend to 6 km and are used by five routes, including the interurbans to Neuss, Krefeld and Duisburg. At Hbf there is interchange with the S-Bahn. Buffet facilities are available on the interurban services to Krefeld; those to Duisburg were suspended in 1998 and are awaiting a new contractor.

Developments
Construction of an east-west light rail line from Grafenberg to Bilk (7.4 km), with a tunnel (6.7 km) in the city centre, which was approved in 1991 for opening in 1994/96, will not now be ready before 2008, though the section to Oberbilk S-Bahn may be operative before then.

A new line is also planned between Werhahn (S-Bahn station) and Uni-Kliniken (3.6 km, eight stops), which will be served by standard low-floor trams. A further range of extensions to both Stadtbahn and tramway were announced in the 'Public Transport Expansion Plan 2004' in mid-1999.

Rolling stock: 318 cars
Stadtbahn
Duewag B80D 6-axle
articulated Stadtbahn (1981/93)   M103
Duewag GT8 8-axle articulated   M25
Tramway
GT8   M57
GT NF6   M48

GT NF8   M15
GT NF10   M36
Duewag 4-axle (1955/66)   T29
Siemens NF8 (2006)   M5
On order: 15 Siemens NF84 CGTNF8 trams are being delivered

Rhein-Bus Verkehrsbetrieb GmbH (Rhein-Bus)

Lierenfelder Strasse 40, D-40231 Düsseldorf, Germany
Tel: (+49 211) 97 15 00   Fax: (+49 211) 971 50 50
e-mail: rhein-bus@rhein-bus.de
Web: www.rhein-bus.de

Passenger journeys: Not currently available
Vehicle-km: Not currently available

Current situation
This low-cost bus company was formed as a joint venture between Rheinbahn and independent operator Taeter of Aachen. Rhein-Bus operates services under contract to Rheinbahn.

Fleet: 29
Mercedes-Benz (1986)   1
Volvo (1996)   11
MAN (1997)   6
Mercedes-Benz (1988)   2
Mercedes-Benz articulated (1996)   6
MAN articulated (1997)   3

Essen

DB Regio AG
DB Regio NRW GmbH
Region Nordrhein-Westfalen, Geschäftsbereich Rhein-Ruhr
Hollestrasse 3, D-45127 Essen, Germany
Tel: (+49 201) 175 25 07
Fax: (+49 201) 175 23 02
Web: www.bahn.de/nordrhein-westfahlen

Key personnel
Head of Region: Thorsten Siggelkow

Type of operation: Regional metro (S-Bahn)

Current situation
Essen is served by Lines S1, S3 and S6 of the Rhein-Ruhr S-Bahn (see under Rhein-Ruhr), and by other DB suburban services. DB associated company Busverkehr Rheinland (BVR) provides some suburban bus services.

Essen
Population: City 581,400, metropolitan area 5.3 million (estimates)

Public transport
Bus, Stadtbahn, tramway and bus/guided bus services operated by municipal company and suburban rail and bus services by DB, both operating as part of Rhein-Ruhr Verkehrsverbund co-ordinating fares and services. See also under Rhein-Ruhr.

Essener Verkehrs-AG (EVAG)
Zweigertstrasse 34, D-45130 Essen, Germany
Tel: (+49 201) 82 60
Fax: (+49 201) 826 10 00
Web: www.evag.de

Key personnel
Directors: Wolfgang Meyer
   Johannes Werner Schmidt
Marketing Manager: Helmut Kanand
Personnel Manager: Wolfgang Daub
Infrastructure Manager: Michael Mertin
   Staff: 2,118

Passenger journeys: (All modes)
(2006) 109.5 million (estimate)

Operating costs financed by: Fares 47 per cent, other commercial sources 10 per cent, subsidy/grants 43 per cent
Subsidy from: Federal government and state Nordrhein-Westfalen for tunnel construction; from state and city for operations

Current situation
Essener Verkehrs-AG (EVAG) provides bus, tram and light rail services to all parts of the city and to the neighbouring cities of Mülheim and Gelsenkirchen.

EVAG Essen former Docklands Light Rail London LHB LRV at Messewest Süd Grüba (Oubeck.com)
0104657

Bus
Vehicle-km: Not currently available

Number of routes: 46
Route length: 495 km

Fleet: 233 vehicles, plus 21 subcontracted	
Mercedes O405 standard (1987)	5
Mercedes O405N low-floor (1990/96/99)	91
Mercedes O405GN low-floor articulated (1993/97/99)	79
MAN NL202 low-floor (1993/97)	37
MAN NG272 articulated (1998)	21

Most intensive service: 5 min
One-person operation: All services
Fare collection: By driver or prepurchase at vending machines and from newspaper kiosks; cancelling equipment on all vehicles
Fare structure: Zonal with multiride tickets and weekly and monthly passes standardised under Rhein-Ruhr Verkehrsverbund
Fares collected on board: 8 per cent
Fare evasion control: Roving inspectors
Integration with other modes: Integrated transit system for all modes in Rhein-Ruhr Verkehrsverbund
Operational control: Mobile radio; computer-aided control system under implementation
Arrangements for elderly/disabled: Free travel for disabled, reimbursed by government; most buses are low-floor vehicles
Average distance between stops: 542 m
Average peak-hour speed: On separate right-of-way 25–35 km/h; in mixed traffic, 20 km/h
New vehicles financed by: 30–40 per cent from state funds

Tramway/light rail
Type of operation: Light rail (U-Stadtbahn), conventional tramway
Car-km: Not currently available

Route length: Tram 54.2 km, Stadtbahn 16.1 km
U-Stadtbahn (1,435 mm gauge): 16.1 km (in tunnel 5.3 km, segregated 4.7 km, on street 1.8 km)
(mixed gauge): 1.9 km (in tunnel)
Tramway (1,000 mm gauge): 54.2 km (in tunnel 5.1 km, segregated 5 km, on street 42.2 km)
Number of lines: 3 Stadtbahn, 9 tramway
Number of stops: 116
Gauge: U-Stadtbahn 1,435 mm; tramway 1,000 mm
Track: S49, Ri59, Ri59N, Ri60, Ri60N rail, conventional sleepers on ballast
Tunnel: Cut-and-cover; bored single track; bored stations
Electrification: 750 V DC, overhead

First/last car: 04.30/00.15
Fare collection: Cancelling equipment on all cars
Fare evasion control: Travelling inspectors
One-person operation: All services
Average speed: Stadtbahn 28 km/h; tramway 20.4 km/h
Average distance between stops: Stadtbahn 683 m, tramway 548 m

Rolling stock: 145 cars; also operates and maintains 7 B80 LRVs owned by Mülheim for use on joint routes	
Standard-gauge	
Duewag LRV B80 (1976/85)	M24
LHB P86/P89 ex-London Docklands (1986/89)	M21
Metre-gauge	
Duewag M8S 8-axle articulated (1975/76)	M18

Duewag M8C 8-axle articulated (1979/90)   M57
Duewag 8-axle articulated (1960/66)   M5
DWA/Adtranz M8DNF low-floor (1999/2000) M20
On order: Further 14 M8DNF low-floor trams

Current situation
Essen's Stadtbahn lines are part of the much larger Rhein-Ruhr development. Tunnel sections (1.5 km) to Westendstrasse opened in 1991, further section of U11 between Karlsplatz and Altenessen (2.5 km) opened in 1998. Metre-gauge operation beyond Altenessen to Gelsenkirchen-Horst ceased in 1998, pending conversion of the remainder of the route to standard-gauge; approximately 2.5 km

in tunnel and another 4 km on surface is under construction for 2001 opening.

There is joint operation of Stadtbahn Line U18 to Mülheim, and tram routes to Mülheim and Gelsenkirchen, the latter being operated entirely by EVAG.

Introduction of tram priority at traffic lights in progress, along with computerised data transmission radio. Job creation programme for information and passenger service personnel under way at major stations.

In contrast to the activities of the last few years, in 1999 EVAG announced a plan to open a new tram line on the surface in the city

centre and Hauptbahnhof, linking with existing Line 109 which currently runs through the city underground tunnel. Stadtbahn Line U17, currently being rebuilt with high platforms on the surface section, is likely to be extended to a new terminus at Hatzperstrasse in Bredeney.

Developments
A computerised passenger information system FIS (*Fahrgast Informations System*) has been introduced experimentally on the Stadtbahn route in northern Essen. It provides information on real-time arrivals, transfer possibilities, delays and breakdowns.

Frankfurt Am Main
Population: City 648,328 (2005 estimate), urban area 1.5 million (estimate); RMV area 5 million

Public transport
Bus, tramway, Stadtbahn (light rail) and administrative services provided by municipal companies operating as part of Rhein-Main Verkehrsverbund (RMV), co-ordinating fares and services with regional bus and rail services provided by DB and other operators.

Rhein-Main-Verkehrsverbund GmbH (RMV)
Alte Bleiche 5, D-65719 Hofheim, Germany
Tel: (+49 6192) 29 40   Fax: (+49 6192) 29 49 00
e-mail: rmv@rmv.de
Web: www.rmv.de

Key personnel
Chief Executive Officer: Volker Sparmann
General Manager: Hansjörg Röhrich

Passenger journeys: (All modes)
(2004) 634 million
(2005) 640 million
(2006) 645 million

Current situation
The regional transit authority RMV was set up in 1994; it became operational in 1995 as successor to Frankfurter Verkehrsverbund (FVV). It is one of the largest regional transit authorities in Germany, covering an area of 14,000 km² with a population of 5 million. Extending from Marburg in the north to Erbach in the south and from Limburg in the west to Fulda in the east, the area includes the cities of Darmstadt, Frankfurt, Offenbach and Wiesbaden, seven other cities and 15 rural authorities.

RMV is responsible for implementation of decisions taken by politicians at state, county or city level, and for management of services which are provided by both public and private operators. It is mainly aimed at regional transit, while purely local services remain the responsibility of cities and counties.

RMV is formed by local authorities and buys in services from existing operators. RMV embraces about 50 rail routes (1,450 km plus 279 km S-Bahn) and 950 bus routes (12,000 km) run by more than 140 operators. There are over 350 ticket sales outlets.

In 2006 there were 1.9 million daily journeys made in the RMV area.

Developments
The success of a pilot scheme with electronic chip cards, called 'getin', in Hanau lead to a general adoption by RMV, as a step towards implementing electronic ticketing.

Seventeen multimodal mobility and transport information centres have been opened in the RMV area. Information and services are provided for urban transport, DB rail, airport, road traffic situation, cycling, taxi, hire cars and car sharing. The authority's website (see above) also provides a successful information service.

Fare structure: Zonal; single tickets (reduced fares during off-peak hours), passes (weekly/monthly/annual), day tickets. Short-distance tickets and other special offers; all ordinary passes transferable; no ticket sales on board rail vehicles, but vending machines at every station/stop; free transfers

traffiQ – Lokale Nahverkehrgesellschaft Frankfurt am Main mbH
Stiftstrasse 9-17, D-60313 Frankfurt am Main, Germany
Tel: (+49 69) 21 22 44 24
Fax: (+49 69) 21 22 44 30
e-mail: info@traffiQ.de
Web: www.traffiQ.de

Key personnel
Managing Director: Hans-Jörg v Berlepsch
Project Manager: Rolf Valussi
Communications Manager: Klaus Linek
Finance and Planning Manager: Dorothea Kalleicher
Customer and Market Research Manager: Johannes Theissen
Services and Administration Manager: Thomas Etges

Current situation
The company was founded on 1 September 2001 and is wholly owned by the city of Frankfurt am Main. *traffiQ* was formed to take over administrative functions hitherto carried out by VGF (see separate entry) which, in turn, will become a pure operating and infrastructure company.

In accordance with EU regulations, *traffiQ* is responsible for issuing and awarding tenders, quality control, public transportation planning, marketing, customer relations and similar tasks.

Bus routes currently operated by VGF will be put out to tender in five groups between 2005 and 2010. Metro and tramway franchises of VGF are still valid until 2011.

Developments
Seventeen lines were put out to tender in December 2005. The contract was awarded to Inder-City-Bus GmbH, a subsidiary of VGF.

A further 12 lines were put out to tender in December 2006. The contract was awarded to Alpina Bad Homburg GmbH, a subsidiary of the Veolia Group (formerly known as Connex).

Nine lines were put out to tender in December 2007. The contract was awarded to Autobus Sippel GmbH, a subsidiary of Arriva.

Seven lines will be put out for tender in December 2009.

Stadwerke Verkehrsgesellschaft Frankfurt am Main mbH (VGF)
D-60276 Frankfurt am Main, Germany
Tel: (+49 69) 213 03   Fax: (+49 69) 21 32 27 40
e-mail: info@vgf-ffm.de
Web: www.vgf-ffm.de

Street address
Kurt-Schumacher-Strasse 10, D-60311 Frankfurt am Main, Germany

Key personnel
Directors: Werner Röhre, Michael Budig
   Staff: 2,234 (2006)

Passenger journeys: (All modes)
(2002) 156.7 million
(2003) 152.5 million
(2004) 152.5 million
(2005) 153.1 million
(2006) 154.2 million

Operating costs financed by: Fares and others 82.7 per cent, subsidy/grants 17.3 per cent
Subsidy from: Holding budget

Background
In 1996, the municipal transport authority was transformed into a commercial company (GmbH), entirely owned by the city of Frankfurt. Most central area services are provided by Stadtbahn (in Frankfurt confusingly labelled U-Bahn) and tram, with buses acting as feeders and serving suburban areas. Surface tramways have largely been eliminated from the city centre, leaving the Stadtbahn and S-Bahn as the main means of cross-city-centre transport, but in 1999 the first new surface tramway for decades were opened along Konrad-Adenauer-Strasse to link Route 12 with the last remaining cross-city line.

Current situation
VGF operates Frankfurt's bus and tram routes and the Stadtbahn.

In 1996 the city agreed a rail transport plan (GVP) that would commit DM640 million to Stadtbahn and tramway improvements. Proposals include a further 11 km of Stadtbahn and 10 km of tramway, plus two new S-Bahn stations.

VGF is a partner in the Rhein-Main Verkehrsverbund (RMV) regional association.

Arrangements for elderly/disabled: Several tram and seven urban bus routes served by lift-equipped low-floor vehicles; installation of lifts at metro stations in progress. A large fleet of low-floor trams and buses has entered service in the last few years.

Bus
Passenger journeys: (2002) 36.9 million
(2003) 35.3 million
(2004) 35.3 million
(2005) 35.6 million
(2006) 36.8 million
Vehicle-km: (2002) 112.9 million
(2003) 112.0 million
(2004) 112.0 million
(2005) 113.3 million
(2006) 111.3 million

Number of routes: 49
Route length: 307.64 km

Developments
Introduction of bus priority lanes under study. Passengers may leave buses other than at

designated stops after 20.00, except in the central area.

The workshops at Rebstock have been reorganised and now also undertake work for outside customers.

Fleet: 204 buses

Mercedes-Benz O405N low-floor	43
EvoBus O530 GN3 Citaro	36
EvoBus 0530 Citaro	125

In peak service: 168
On order: From mid-2007, 37 new EvoBus Citaro vehicles are due to be delivered

Most intensive service: 5 min
One-person operation: All routes
Fare structure: Zonal (see RMV)
Fare evasion control: Roving inspectors; penalty fare of EUR40
Average speed: 18–20 km/h

Light rail (Stadtbahn)

Type of operation: Light rail (Stadtbahn) runs underground (23 km) in the city centre, but largely on converted tram routes in the suburbs; initial route opened 1968

Passenger journeys: (2002) 97.3 million
(2003) 95.3 million
(2004) 95.3 million
(2005) 95.4 million
(2006) 95.1 million
Car-km: (2002) 345.3 million
(2003) 338.2 million
(2004) 338.2 million
(2005) 338.9 million
(2006) 338.2 million

Route length: 61.16 km
  in tunnel: 23 km
Number of lines: 7
Number of stations: 84
Gauge: 1,435 mm
Tunnel: Box section
Electrification: 600 V DC, overhead

Current situation
The extension of the underground station Ostbahnhof (75 m underground) with access to Hanauer Landstrasse, was scheduled to open in early 2007.

Developments
In mid-2006, an order was placed for 146 new high-floor Bombardier *Flexity* LRVs. Delivery is scheduled for 2008–2013. The contract was valued for an estimated figure of EUR300 million and there is an option for up to a further 24 vehicles. These new LRVs will replace the older Type Ptb, Type U2e and Type U2h Duewag vehicles.

There will be an extension to Frankfurt Riedberg and onward to Nieder-Eschbach, with construction due to start in 2007 and service starting in 2009.

Constrcution on new line U41, from Nieder-Eschbach to Nordwest Zentrum, will start in 2007.

Rolling stock: 223 cars

Duewag Type Ptb	M59
Duewag Type U2e	M36
Duewag Type U2h	M62
Duewag Type U3	M27
Duewag Type U4	M39

On order: 146 new high-floor Bombardier *Flexity* LRVs (Type U5) for delivery between 2008 and 2013

Service: Peak 2 min
Fare structure: Zonal (see RMV)
Integration with other modes: Common tariff structure throughout RMV area

Tramway

Passenger journeys: (2002) 44.3 million
(2003) 43.2 million
(2004) 43.2 million

Artist's impression of the Bombardier FLEXITY Swift *Light Rail Vehicle for VGF, Frankfurt/Main, Germany* (Bombardier Transportation)
1323577

(2005) 43.5 million
(2006) 43.6 million
Car-km: (2002) 138.0 million

Route length: 63.55 km
Number of routes: 8

Developments
Construction of a new double track tram route, Line 18, from the junction of Rohrbachstrasse, Friedberger Landstrasse and Glauburgstrasse via Friedberger Landstrasse to the new Frankfurter Bogen estate, will be built from 2007 and scheduled to open by the end of 2009.

Fleet: 108 vehicles (plus 8 trailers)

Duewag/Crede Type K	M4 T6
Duewag Type L	M1 T1
Duewag Type M	M1 T1
Duewag Type N	M1
Duewag Type O	M2
Duewag Type Pt	M11
Duewag Type R	M38
Bombardier Type S (2003/07)	M60

On order: The remaining vehicles from the order for 65 new Type S Bombardier Transportation trams are due for delivery by March 2007

Verkehrsgesellschaft mbH Untermain (VU)

Mainzer Landstrasse 181, D-60327 Frankfurt am Main, Germany
Tel: (+49 69) 758 09 50
Fax: (+49 69) 75 80 95 60
e-mail: info@vu-gmbh.de
Web: www.bahn.de

Key personnel
Directors: Siegfried Dargatz
  Jost Knebel
  Staff: 59 (2005)

Current situation
Subsidiary of DB. Regional bus company operating services within the RMV area and in adjacent parts of Bavaria with a fleet of Mercedes buses, plus contracted buses.

Developments
The number of low-floor buses in the fleet is increasing. All vehicles (own and contractors) are radio-controlled.

In early 2005, a contract for four bus lines in the Frankfurt area was awarded to VU by *traffiQ.*

Bus

Passenger journeys: Not currently available
Vehicle-km: Not currently available

Number of routes: Not currently available

Hessische Landesbahn GmbH (HLB)

Mannheimer Strasse 15, D-60329 Frankfurt, Germany
Tel: (+49 69) 242 52 40
Fax: (+49 69) 24 25 24 60
e-mail: mail@hlb-online.de
Web: www.hlb-online.de

Key personnel
Managing Directors: P Berking
  Veit Salzmann
Marketing and Corporate Communications: Christina Schloter

Passenger journeys: (Both modes, Frankfurt area) Not currently available

Background
In 2006, Frankfurt-Königsteiner Eisenbahn AG (FKE) (www.fke-online.de), a state-owned local railway, came under the management of HLB Basis AG, in which Hessische Landesbahn GmbH (HLB) has an 84.65 per cent stake, with responsibility for infrastructure and rolling stock maintenance. Train operations are undertaken by another wholly owned subsidiary, HLB Hessenbahn GmbH, while the group's bus operations are managed by HLB Hessenbus GmbH.

For further information on Hessische Landesbahn GmbH (HLB), please see *Jane's World Railways.*

Bus

Vehicle-km: (2000) 5.4 million
Number of routes: 45
Route length: Not currently available

Fleet: 122 vehicles
Full breakdown of fleet is not currently available, but includes

Mercedes-Benz EvoBus Citaro low-floor single-deck	12

Local railway

Current situation
This is a local railway operating diesel railcars between Frankfurt-Höchst and Königstein (25 km), the Höchst-Bad Soden line (part of S3 taken over from DB in 1992), total 46 km, the HLB-owned Taunusbahn (TSB), from Friedrichsdorf to Brandoberndorf and local bus feeder services in the Frankfurt-Höchst/Kelkheim/Hofheim/Königstein area. It connects with S-Bahn at Höchst, but during peak hours some trains continue over main line tracks to Frankfurt Hauptbahnhof.

Car-km: (2000) 1.9 million

Rolling stock: 25 diesel railcars

Offenbacher Verkehrs-Betriebe GmbH (OVB)

Heberstrasse 14, D-63065 Offenbach am Main, Germany
Tel: (+49 69) 80 05 80   Fax: (+49 69) 80 05 81 90
e-mail: info@ovb-of.de
Web: www.ovb-tickets.de

Key personnel

Managing Director: Volker Lampmann
    Staff: 260

Current situation

Municipally owned company provides bus service in the city of Offenbach and Frankfurt.
    OVB co-ordinates its operations with the train lines operating within the Rhein-Main Transport Association area.
    The entire fleet of buses is low-floor.

Bus

Passenger journeys: (Annual) 12.5 million (estimate)
Vehicle-km: Not currently available

Number of routes: 8
Route length: 235 km
Fleet: 57 (all operations)
Full breakdown of fleet is not currently available, but is believed to include:
Mercedes-Benz
MAN
VW/Auwärter
Average age of fleet: 3.6 years

Service: 10–15 min (daytime weekdays), 30 min (evenings and weekends)

DB Regio AG

Regionalverkehr Hessen
Mannheimer Strasse 81, D-60327 Frankfurt am Main, Germany
Tel: (+49 69) 26 53 51 00, 26 51 50 10
Fax: (+49 69) 26 53 50 02, 26 53 50 04
e-mail: Thomas.Schare@bahn.de
Web: www.bahn.de/hessen

Key personnel

Chair of Region/Marketing: Charlott Lutterbeck
Production and Regional Spokesman: Thomas Schare
Manager, Finance: Wolfgang Pollety

Current situation

Rhein-Main services cover a network of 536 km centred on Frankfurt am Main and Limburg and serve 135 stations and halts.
    For further information on DB, please see *Jane's World Railways.*

Regional metro

Type of operation: Regional metro (S-Bahn)
Passenger journeys: Not currently available

S-Bahn Rhein-Main

Gutleutstrasse 163-167, D-60327 Frankfurt am Main, Germany
Tel: (+49 69) 26 54 25 00   Fax: (+49 69) 26 54 25 09
e-mail: Hans-Hugo.Schnöring@bahn.de
Web: www.bahn.de

Key personnel

Spokesman: Hans-Hugo Schnöring

Current situation

The S-Bahn Rhein-Main network is centred on Frankfurt am Main, and covers a network of 300 km serving 109 stations and halts and recording some 14 million passenger-km annually.

Rolling stock: 102 ET 420 plus 71 ET 423, 175 double-deck coaches, 639 other coaches, 34 diesel railcars

Most intensive service: 15 min peak, 30-60 min off-peak (more frequent on overlapping sections)

ESWE Verkehrsgesellschaft mbH (ESWE)

Gartenfeldstrasse 18, D-65189, Wiesbaden, Germany
Tel: (+49 611) 780 23 50   Fax: (+49 611) 780 21 99
Web: www.eswe.com

Key personnel

Chair: Dr Gerhard Heunemann
Managing Director: Hans Rauwolf
Marketing Director: Frank Beucker
Technical Director: Rainer Merz
Commercial Director: Uwe Cramer
Operations Director: Bernd Jakob
    Staff: 639

Bus

Passenger journeys: (2000) 51.3 million
(2001) 53.2 million
(2002) 50.6 million
Vehicle-km: (2000) 11.8 million

Number of routes: 42
Route length: (One way) 588 km
On priority right-of-way: 12 km

Fleet: 176 vehicles, plus 52 contracted
Mercedes O405 (1987/89)	39
Mercedes O405G articulated (1988/92)	41
Mercedes O405N low-floor (1990/94)	49
Mercedes O405GN low-floor articulated (1997)	12
MAN NL202 low-floor (1993)	23
Mercedes-Benz Citaro articulated (1999)	12
In peak service: 183

Most intensive service: 5 min
One-person operation: All routes
Fare structure: As RMV
Fares collected on board: 35.7 per cent
Operational control: Route inspectors/mobile radio. Computer-based bus control system RBL with infra-red beacons along routes activated by onboard equipment; activation of traffic signals for bus priority
Arrangements for elderly/disabled: Disabled travel free, partly funded by government; low-floor buses have wheelchair ramp at centre door
Integration with other modes: Cross-river routes to Mainz operated jointly with Stadtwerke Mainz
Average peak-hour speed: 20.1 km/h
Operating costs financed by: Fares 42.5 per cent, other commercial sources 28.6 per cent, subsidy/grants 28.9 per cent

Subsidy from: In part by cross-subsidy from other municipal enterprises which are part of the company (electricity, gas, water etc) and in part from city and state

Funicular

ESWE also operates a 500 m funicular with two cars.

HEAG mobilo GmbH (HEAG)

Klappacher Strasse 172, D-64285 Darmstadt, Germany
Tel: (+49 6151) 709 40 00
Fax: (+49 6151) 709 41 46
e-mail: info@heagmobilo.de
Web: www.heagmobilo.de, www.heag.de

Key personnel

Managing Directors: Harald Fiedler, Matthias Kalbfuss
    Staff: Not currently available

Passenger journeys: Not currently available

Background

In 1999 HEAG took over independent operator Glück & Seitz.

Current situation

Municipally owned company provides bus and tramway services in Darmstadt and the surrounding area.

Developments

In January 2005, the company restructured. HEAG mobiTram GmbH & Co KG in Gründing is responsible for tramway operations and HEAG mobiBus GmbK & Co KG for bus operations. The latter also provides services to Frankfurt Airport.

Bus

HEAG mobiBus GmbH & Co KG
Bickenbacher Strasse 50, D-64342 Seeheim-Jugenheim, Germany
Tel: (+49 6257) 20 68   Fax: (+49 6257) 636 91
e-mail: info@heagmobibus.de
Web: www.heagmobibus.de

Route length: Not currently available

Fleet: Not currently available

Tramway

HEAG mobiTram GmbH & Co KG in Gründing
Klappacher Strasse 172, D-64285 Darmstadt, Germany
Tel: (+49 6151) 709 40 00
Fax: (+49 6257) 70 94 14 61
e-mail: info@heagmobitram.de
Web: www.heagmobitram.de

Car-km: Not currently available

Route length: Not currently available
Number of routes: Not currently available
Gauge: 1,000 mm
Electrification: 600 V DC, overhead

Rolling stock: Not currently available

Halle

Population: 238, 014 (2005)

Public transport

Tramway and bus services provided by municipal company. German Railways (DB) runs local and regional metro (S-Bahn) services.

Mitteldeutscher Verkehrsverbund (MDV)

Current situation

This is the regional transit authority for the Halle/Leipzig region. For details see Leipzig entry.

Hallesche Verkehrs-AG (HAVAG)

Postfach 20 06 58, D-06007 Halle/Saale, Germany
Tel: (+49 345) 58 10
Fax: (+49 345) 581 57 77
e-mail: post@havag.com
Web: www.havag.com

Street address
Freiimfelder Strasse 74, D-06112 Halle (Saale), Germany

Key personnel
Technical Director: René Pietsch
Commercial Director: Dipl Ing/Dipl Wirtsch-Ing François Girard
Technical and Maintenance Manager: Gerd Blumenau
Permanent Way Manager: Erhard Krüger
  Staff: 870 (2007)

Passenger journeys: (2003) 58.0 million
(2005) 60.6 million
(2006) 59.0 million
(2007) 57.4 million

Operating costs financed by: Fares 38.8 per cent, other commercial sources 25.3 per cent, subsidy/grants 35.9 per cent
Subsidy from: Regional government 13 per cent, local government 69 per cent, other 18 per cent

Current situation
HAVAG provides tramway and feeder bus services in the Halle/Merseburg area, serving a total population of 287,728. Bus services in Halle-Neustadt were taken over from Omnibusbetrieb Saalekreis GmbH when the latter town was incorporated into Halle in 1991. A regional transit authority co-ordinates the services of HAVAG, the S-Bahn and regional bus companies.

Bus
Vehicle-km: (2003) 5.3 million
(2004) 5.0 million
(2005) 5.1 million
(2006) 4.2 million
(2007) 3.7 million

Number of routes: 24
Route length: 221.7 km
On private right-of-way: 1.8 km

Fleet: 43 vehicles

Merecedes-Benz O 407	2
Mercedes-Benz O 405 G articulated	7
Mercedes-Benz O 405 GN2 CNG articulated	5
Mercedes-Benz O 530 N Citaro	23
Mercedes-Benz O 530 G Citaro	5
Mercedes-Benz O 405 NF:	1

In peak service: 24

Most intensive service: 15 min
One-person operation: All routes
Fare collection: Fare to driver or prepurchase; 77 per cent of passengers use passes; 3 sales outlets plus vending machines
Fare structure: Flat, single and multijourney tickets, short-distance ticket valid 4 stops; off-peak/daily/monthly passes; annual subscription
Integration with other modes: Joint fare scheme with HAVAG and DB S-Bahn
Arrangements for elderly/disabled: Reduced fares for disabled
Average distance between stops: 493 m

Tramway
Type of operation: Conventional tramway

Passenger journeys: Not currently available

Car-km: (2003) 10.1 million
(2004) 9.7 million
(2005) 9.0 million
(2006) 7.7 million
(2007) 7.5 million

Number of routes: 15
Route length: 86.1 km
Number of stops: 329
Average distance between stops: 460 m
Gauge: 1,000 mm
Electrification: 600 V DC, overhead

Developments
In October 2006, the Nuestadt-Hbf link was completed. Also in that month, the section of route 3 between Trotha and Südstadt was reintroduced.
  In October 2007, the tram link between Heide and Kröllwitz was completed.

Rolling stock: 213 cars

Duewag MGT6D 6-axle low-floor (1992/2001)	M62
Bombardier MGTK	M30
ČKD T4D-C	M80
ČKD B4D-C	M41

In peak service: Not currently available
On order: Not currently available
Service: Peak 15 min

DB Regio AG
Verkehrsbetrieb Sachsen-Anhalt
Volkmannstrasse 38, D-06112 Halle (Saale), Germany
Tel: (+49 345) 215 27 00
Fax: (+49 345) 215 27 47
Web: www.bahn.de/sachsen-anhalt

Key personnel
Spokesman: Thomas Hoffmann
Manager, Finance: Stephen Georg Wigger

Current situation
Part of the Region Südost, DB Regio AG's Sachsen-Anhalt services cover a network of 1,602 km centred on Halle and serve 293 stations and halts, with some 852 million passenger-km recorded annually.
  Burgenlandbahn GmbH (www.burgenlandbahn.de) services cover a network of 161 km centred on Halle, Merseburg and Naumburg and serve 47 stations and halts, with some 14.4 million passenger-km recorded annually.
  For further information on DB, please see *Jane's World Railways.*

S-Bahn
Type of operation: Regional suburban rail (S-Bahn)

Passenger journeys: Not currently available

Current situation
S-Bahn services on line S7 run over a U-shaped loop from Halle-Trotha in the north-east via Halle (Saale) Hbf and Halle-Neustadt to Halle Nietleben in the north- west. Most intensive service is every 20 min, provided by seven push-pull sets of double-deck cars hauled by electric locomotives.
  Service is also provided on line S10 from Halle (Saale) Hbf to Leipzig.

Hamburg
Population: 1.75 million (2006 estimate), area served 2.6 million (estimate)

Public transport
All public transport in Hamburg and the adjoining metropolitan area is co-ordinated by a public transit authority, Hamburger Verkehrsverbund GmbH (HVV). Bus and metro services are provided by city transport company, ferry services by city shipping company, urban and regional rail (S-Bahn) by DB Regio AG and DB subsidiary respectively, other regional services by three bus companies and a local railway (AKN), and park-and-ride facilities by a separate company.

Hamburger Verkehrsverbund GmbH (HVV)
Steinstrasse 7, D-20095 Hamburg, Germany
Tel: (+49 40) 325 77 50   Fax: (+49 40) 32 57 75 20
e-mail: info@hvv.de
Web: www.hvv.com

Key personnel
Managing Directors: Peter Kellermann, Lutz Aigner
Press and Media Relations: Gisela Becker
Legal Affairs/Co-operation with other Transport Associations: Dr Gerrit Landsberg, Helen Kassner
Director, Office Management: Tom Vogel
Director, Market Communication: Christian Gontard
Director, Fares/Marketing and Sales: Matthias Wiarda
Director, Rail Service/Strategic Planning: Wolfgang Märtens
Director, Bus and Ferry Services: Joachim Wiucha
Director, Procurement by Tender: Andreas Trostmann
Director, PTA/Transport Operator Financing: Jens Renken

Passenger journeys: (All modes)
(2000) 494 million
(2001) 502 million
(2002) 504 million
(2003) 512 million (projected)

Fare collection: Single tickets (payment to driver or from vending machine), day tickets, weekly or monthly passes, annual subscription, bulk sales of passes to employers at reduced rates; Card+Ride introduced in 1994; onboard sales (bus only) 19 per cent. As an experiment, 50 HHA ticket machines have been adapted to accept payment by a smartcard which also serves as a telephone card
Fare structure: Zonal, transfers free, premium for express bus or first class on S-Bahn; reduced price passes for off-peak travel
Fare evasion control: Random inspection; penalty
Arrangements for elderly/disabled: Reduced rate passes for disabled, paid by government
Operating costs financed by: Fares 52 per cent, contractual grants 7 per cent, subsidy 41 per cent

Current situation
HVV, which was formerly a co-ordinating body of transport operators in the conurbation, was restructured in 1996. It is currently controlled by: The Free and Hanseatic City of Hamburg (85 per cent), the Regional State of Schleswig-Holstein (3 per cent), Landesnahverkehrsgesellschaft Niedersachsen mbH (2 per cent), Kreis[1] Herzogtum Lauenburg (1.5 per cent), Kreis Pinneberg (1.5 per cent), Kreis Segeberg (1.5 per cent), Kreis Stormarn (1.5 per cent), Landkreis Harburg (1 per cent), Landkreis Stade (1 per cent) and Landkreis Lüneburg (1.5 per cent).
  The HVV service area covers some 8,700 km² and provides service for 3.32 million residents. In Hamburg, approximately 25 per cent of all journeys are made by public transport, and 33 per cent of commuter traffic is carried by HVV operators. In the wider city area, HVV services account for 67 per cent of all trips made.
  HVV has established a zonal ticket system allowing free intermodal transfer and integrated services with an overall passenger information system. Park-and-ride sites total 94 with 14,720 spaces, and about 300 cycle lockers were introduced at 32 bike-and-ride sites in 1998.
Kreis: political and administrative borough or council.

Developments
A substantial extension of the HVV area, to include the four Schleswig-Holstein boroughs to the north of Hamburg, was implemented in 2002. In December 2004, the boroughs to the south were also included – Harburg, Lüneburg and Stade. In this extended area, transport services are currently provided by 38 public transport operators co-operating with HVV.

Hamburger Hochbahn AG (HOCHBAHN)

Steinstrasse 20, D-20095 Hamburg, Germany
Tel: (+49 40) 328 80 Fax: (+49 40) 32 88 45 62
Web: www.hochbahn.de

Key personnel
Board of Directors:
 Chairman of the Board: Dipl Econ Günter Elste
 Vice-Chairman of the Board: Dr Ulf Lange
 Directors, Bus (Temporary): Dipl Econ Günter Elste
  Dipl-Ing Ulrich Sieg
 Operating Manager, Bus: Vacant
 Director, Metro: Dipl-Ing Ulrich Sieg
 Operating Manager, Metro: Dr Christoph Levin
  Staff: 4,398 (2007)

Passenger numbers: (All modes)
(2003) 364.4 million (reconciliation)
(2004) 365.9 million (reconciliation)
(2005) 368.8 million
(2006) 375.4 million
(2007) 383.3 million

Operating costs covered by: (All modes) Fares 54 per cent, other commercial sources 11 per cent, subsidy/grants 13 per cent, other revenue 22 per cent
Subsidy from: State and city

Current situation
HOCHBAHN provides services both directly and through more than 20 subsidiary companies and associated or affiliated divisions. These include the shipping lines HADAG (see separate entry) and ATG Alster-Touristik, the bus undertaking Jasper, the central bus station, the cleaning company TEREG, a staff accommodation service and a security company. HOCHBAHN also operates the vehicle research and development company FFG and has a consulting subsidiary Hamburg-Consult.

Developments
At the beginning of 2007, all HOCHBAHN bus and rail subsidiaries outside Hamburg were brought together in the BeNEX GmbH holding (for further information, please see *Jane's World Railways.*

In 2008, BeNEX was awarded two rail tenders in the Federal State of Bavaria totalling approximately 10 million rail-km per annum.

Arrangements for elderly/disabled: All future bus purchases will be of low-floor types with wheelchair ramp; 100 per cent of the fleet is currently accessible. Lifts have been installed at 34 U-Bahn stations; guidelines being installed in platform floors for visually impaired and blind people.

Bus
Passenger journeys: (2005) 192 million
(2006) 195.6 million
(2007) 199.7 million
Vehicle-km: (2003) 45.9 million
(2004) 45.0 million (reconciliation)
(2005) 44.3 million
(2006) 43.7 million
(2007) 45.0 million

Number of routes: 112
Route length: 1,492 km
On priority right-of-way: 21 km
Average distance between stops: 697 m

Fleet: 704 vehicles

Mercedes-Benz O405N low-floor (1991/97)	203
Mercedes-Benz O405GN low-floor articulated (1992/93)	40
Mercedes-Benz Citaro (1997/2005)	269
Mercedes-Benz Citaro articulated (2000/2005)	90
MAN NG 313 (1999/2004)	28
MAN articulated (2000/2004)	19
Van Hool double-articulated	25
Mercedes-Benz Citaro fuel cell	9
Others	7

On order: Not currently available

In peak service: 588
New vehicles required each year: 67
Average age of fleet: 7.4 years

Most intensive service: 3 min
One-person operation: All routes
Fares collected on board: 26 per cent
Operational control: Computer-aided control system RBL
Integration with other modes: Tickets interchangeable between all modes; single ticket covers any journey by any combination of modes. Computerised passenger information system provides personalised optimal travel details. Many stations have bus feeders, with other main corridors served by express buses to the city centre; park-and-ride encouraged. At several metro/bus interchanges, signals have been installed to warn bus drivers of late running of metro trains so they may wait for transferring passengers
Average speed: 19.7 km/h

Current situation
There are five bus depots, with managers who since 1996 have taken over a wide range of responsibilities formerly vested in head office, including staffing, vehicles, infrastructure and subcontracting.

In 2004 bus operational control was centralised and some digital bus stop displays were installed, providing GPS-based real-time bus schedules.

Developments
Testing of a hydrogen fuel cell-powered bus and of a double-articulated Van Hool AGG300 was carried out in 2004 and 2005, and testing of fuel cell technology will continue throughout 2008.

HOCHBAHN LHB DT4 trainset at Hafenviadukt (HOCHBAHN)   1174283

Mock-up of the new DT5 trainset (HOCHBAHN)   1374850

HOCHBAHN Line U1 crossing the river Alster (HOCHBAHN)   1197824

There are 25 double-articulated buses are in operation.

HOCHBAHN is retrofitting its existing buses with CRT in order to reduce emissions.

The installation of video cameras in 450 buses was completed by the end of 2007.

Metro

Staff: 1,512 (2007)

Type of operation: Full metro, first line opened 1912

Passenger journeys: (2005) 177 million
(2006) 179.8 million
(2007) 183.6 million
Car-km: (2003) 71.6 million
(2004) 71.7 million
(2005) 72.8 million
(2006) 74.0 million
(2007) 72.9 million

Route length: 100.7 km
  In tunnel: 41.5 km
  Elevated: 9 km
Number of lines: 3
Number of stations: 89
Gauge: 1,435 mm
Track: 49 kg/m S49 rail, sleepers on ballast
Maximum gradient: 5%
Minimum curve radius: 70 m
Tunnel: Bored single-track, concrete caisson, bored double-track
Electrification: 750 V DC, third rail

Current situation

'Trainscreen' visual information system installed in metro cars provides service information, news, entertainment and commercials. LCD flat screens and wireless data transfer technology is used.

Technology permits 'self dispatch' of trains by drivers.

Developments

A new line, U4, is due to open in 2011. The line will be approximately 4 km in length, with two new stops. It will link the new residential and business quarters in the HafenCity Harbour area of Hamburg to the city centre.

Starting in 2009, HOCHBAHN will replace all DT2 and DT3 units with new trainsets. The DT5 trainsets consist of three compartments, provide higher levels of passenger comfort, areas for wheelchairs and prams and a modern passenger information system. DT2 trainsets are only used for additional (non-regular) peak services or backup. All regular services are run by types DT3 and DT4.

The new DT5 trainsets were ordered from a consortium of Alstom and Bombardier in December 2006. The contract was valued at a total of EUR240 million. Delivery is scheduled to begin in 2009 and continue until 2013. There is an option for a minimum of a further 40 vehicles.

Rolling stock: 744 cars (total, 738 in use) in 212 sets of two, three and four cars

DT1 two-car sets	6 (3 sets)
LHB DT2 two-car sets (1962/66)	30 (15 sets)
LHB DT3 three-car sets (1968/71) (modernised)	204 (in 68 sets)
LHB/Alstom DT4 four-car sets (1989–2004)	504 (in 126 sets)

On order: 27 Alstom/Bombardier DT5 three-car sets

Service: Peak 2.5–5 min, off-peak 5–10 min
First/last train: 04.01/01.15 weekdays, non-stop service on Fridays and Saturdays
Surveillance: CCTV on all platforms and in all cars type DT3 and DT4
Fare evasion control: Random inspection, penalty fare

Deutsche Bahn AG

S-Bahn Hamburg GmbH (SBHG)
Museumstrasse 39, D-22765 Hamburg, Germany
Tel: (+49 40) 39 18 43 85   Fax: (+49 40) 39 18 21 84
e-mail: S-Bahn.Hamburg@bahn.de
Web: www.s-bahn-hamburg.de

HOCHBAHN Mercedes-Benz fuel cell bus (HOCHBAHN)   1374851

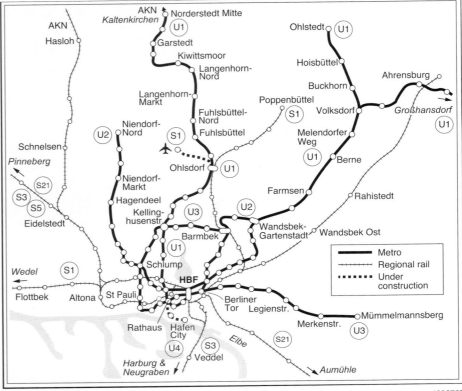

Hamburg's metro and S-Bahn network   1298727

Key personnel

Managing and Marketing Director: Kay Uwe Arnecke
Commercial Director: Arne Voss
Technical Director: Michael Dirmeier
  Staff: 930

Type of operation: Urban heavy rail

Passenger journeys: (2004) 176 million
(2006) 184 million

Current situation

The Hamburg S-Bahn comprises a 145-km six-line network serving 68 stations. The core network is electrified using a 1.2 kV DC third rail system but some services operate, since December 2007, over routes employing the standard German main line 15 kV AC overhead system.

For a map of Hamburg's metro and S-Bahn, please see the separate entry for Hamburger Hochbahn AG (HOCHBAHN).

Developments

In 2001, work began on the 3-km branch line from Ohlsdorf to Hamburg Airport, which opened in December 2008. An estimated 70 per cent of the line is in tunnel.

The Stade project: Existing emus are equipped for 15 kV 16⅔ Hz AC and used as dual-power trains on the existing S-Bahn line from Hamburg City to Hamburg-Neugraben and the DB line up to Buxtehude and Stade. Passenger service commenced in 2007. Nine new emus (Series 474.3) and 33 retrofits to existing Series 474 vehicles have been contracted to a consortium of ALSTOM LHB and Bombardier Transportation. These emus are equipped with roof-mounted pantographs and lateral current collectors. The value of the contract is approximately EUR90 million.

Long-term plans include an extension of third-rail or dual-power lines beyond present terminals: Elmshorn/Itzehoe, Quickborn/Kaltenkirchen and Ahrensburg/Bad Oldesloe.

In 2007, a 10 year operating contract was concluded between DB and Hamburg Land.

In 2007, the fleet comprised 52 Class 472 and 112 Class 474 units, all three-car.

The Class 472 units, built in the 1970s and 1980s, have been refurbished and modernised.

Number of stations: 68
Operational control: CCTV on platforms
Fare evasion control: Roving inspectors

Rolling stock: 164 three-car units

Series 472	M156
Series 474	336

On order: None

VHH PVG Group

Georgsplatz 1, D-20099 Hamburg, Germany
Tel: (+49 40) 72 59 41 40
Fax: (+49 40) 72 59 41 56
e-mail: info@vhhpvg.de
Web: www.vhhpvg.de

Key personnel
Executive Committee: Ralf-Dieter Pemöller, Philip Cramer
Staff: 1,560

Bus

Passenger journeys: (Annual) 91 million (estimate)
Vehicle-km: (Annual) 37 million (estimate)

Number of routes: 159
Route length: 600 km

Current situation
PVG, majority-owned by the city of Hamburg, provides local bus services in the western part of Hamburg and Pinneberg region (both within and outside the HVV area), and in the western part of Hamburg on behalf of HHA.

Fleet: 600 vehicles (estimate)
Fleet breakdown is not currently available

KVG Stade GmbH & Co KG (KVG)

Harburger Strasse 96, D-21680 Stade, Germany
Tel: (+49 4141) 52 50   Fax: (+49 4141) 52 51 05
e-mail: info@kvg-bus.de
Web: www.kvg-bus.de

Key personnel
Managing Director: Heinz-Dieter Pohl

Bus

Passenger journeys: Not currently available
Vehicle-km: Not currently available

Fleet: 30 buses (estimate)

Current situation
Regional bus company, formerly associated with DB. The company, which was taken over by local government in 1996, provides rural and urban transit in area south of River Elbe from Cuxhaven in north to Luneburg in south. Partner company in HVV.

AKN Eisenbahn AG

Rudolf-Diesel-Strasse 2, D-24568, Kaltenkirchen, Germany
Tel: (+49 4191) 93 39 33
Fax: (+49 4191) 93 31 18
e-mail: info@akn.de
Web: www.akn.de

Key personnel
Director: Dipl-Ing Johannes Kruszynski
Staff: 345

Type of operation: Local rail

Passenger journeys: (2004) 12.5 million
(2005) 13.5 million
(2006) 14.4 million
Passenger-km: (2006) 141.4 million
Train-km: Not currently available

Background
Founded in 1883 as the Altona-Kaltenkirchener Eisenbahngesellschaft.

Current situation
Formed by the merger of several local government-owned lines in and around Hamburg, three of which totalling 117 km, run within the Hamburger Verkehrsverbund (HVV) area. AKN also operates passenger trains over the Neumünster-Heide-Büsum line (Schleswig-Holstein-Bahn, 87 km) and over VGN's Norderstedt Mitte-Süd line.

Jointly with Hamburger Hochbahn (HOCHBAHN) formed the NBE Nordbahn Eiesenbahn, to take over operation of the 45-km Neumünster-Bad Oldesloe line.

Developments
Since December 2004, AKN has extended existing Route A1 to Hamburg Hbf, with AKN electro-diesel dmus running over S-Bahn lines.

Rolling stock: 39 dmu cars

P+R-Betriebsgesellschaft mbH

Steinstrasse 20, D-20095 Hamburg, Germany
Tel: (+49 40) 32 88 25 53
Fax: (+49 40) 32 88 28 74
e-mail: info@p-und-r.com

Key personnel
Managing Director: Dipl-Ing Axel von Knobloch

Background
P+R, a management company for park-and-ride facilities, was founded in 1969 and took over its first multistorey car park in 1975. It is controlled by the City of Hamburg commercial holding, HGV (Hamburger Gesellschaft für Vermögens- und Beteiligungsmanagement mbH), with the German Automobile Club, ADAC (Allgemeiner Deutscher Automobilclub), having a five per cent shareholding.

The company is funded by the HGV and central government. When private investors are unable to provide as many car parking spaces as are demanded by building regulations, they are required to pay the city compensation for every parking space which is not built. These funds are then invested in P+R facilties.

Current situation
P+R operates sites at nine U-Bahn and 11 S-Bahn stations with a total of more than 7,350 car parking spaces, including car parks and P+R facilities. There are also 695 bicycle boxes available for hire. An existing car park has been enlarged by 200 spaces. There are a further two car parks, with 500 and 250 spaces, at the planning stage.

There are no charges for the use of P+R facilities and public transport users have priority allocation of spaces. Any operating loss by P+R is balanced by the HGV.

DB Regio AG

Region Nord
Regionalbahn Schleswig-Holstein
Alte Lübecker Chaussee 15, D-24114 Kiel, Germany

Tel: (+49 431) 247 91 23
Fax: (+49 431) 247 94 93
e-mail: Robert.Guggenberger@bahn.de
Web: www.bahn.de/schleswig-holstein

Key personnel
Head of Region: Dr Wolfram von Fritsch
Managing Director: Edward Jendretzki
Transport Manager: Dirk Fischer
Marketing Manager: Torsten Reh
Personnel Manager: Nils Schaper

Type of operation: Suburban heavy rail

Passenger journeys: Not currently available

Current situation
The RegionalBahn Schleswig-Holstein is part of the Region Nord of DB Regio AG. Amongst other services, it runs outer-suburban trains in the HVV area over 38 route-km serving 12 stations.

In total there are 875 route-km in the Hamburg and Schleswig-Holstein area.

For further information on DB Regio AG, please see other entries in *Jane's Urban Transport Systems* and *Jane's World Railways*.

Rolling stock: Single- or double-deck push-pull trains propelled by main line AC electric or diesel locomotives

HADAG Seetouristik und Fährdienst AG

St Pauli Fischmarkt 28, D-20359 Hamburg, Germany
Tel: (+49 40) 311 70 70   Fax: (+49 40) 31 17 07 10
e-mail: info@hadag.de
Web: www.hadag.de

Key personnel
Director: Jens Wrage
Staff: 85

Ferry

Passenger journeys: (2003) 4.2 million
(2004) 5.1 million
(2005) 5.6 million
(2006) 6.4 million

Route length: 27.6 km
No of piers served: 21

Current situation
This subsidiary of HHA operates 21 vessels on eight routes in the harbour and on the River Elbe, with a total route length of 27.6 km and a frequency of 15 minutes (at peak times). Local cruises are also operated.

HADAG vessel 'Övelgönne'

1197871

Hannover
Population: 515,559 (2006)

Public transport
Light rail and bus services provided by municipally controlled companies, and regional rail services by DB, both operating as part of Grossraum-Verkehr Hannover transport association.

Grossraum-Verkehr Hannover (GVH)
c/o üstra Hannoversche Verkehrsbetriebe AG
PO Box 2540, Am Hohen Ufer 6, D-30159 Hannover, Germany
Tel: (+49 511) 16 68 30 00
Fax: (+49 511) 366 14 52
e-mail: info@gvh.de
Web: www.gvh.de

Key personnel
Directors: Wilhelm Lindenberg (Üstra)
   Wolfgang Stack (RegioBus)

Passenger journeys: (Annual) 174 million

Background
After HVV Hamburg, Grossraum-Verkehr Hannover (GVH) (the Greater Hannover Transport Association) is the second oldest regional transit authority in Germany, having been established in 1970. In March of that year, the common fare system, with a standard tariff, came into force.

Current situation
The GVH provides services to 22 cities and communities and a population of approximately 1.1 million residents in the Hannover region and surrounding areas.
   The integrated system comprises:
   üstra Hannoversche Verkehrsbetriebe AG, with trams and buses in Hannover city and some neighbouring towns and communities;
   RegioBus Hannover GmbH, with bus services, especially in the areas around Hannover but also into the city centre;
   DB Regio AG, German Rail's fast connections in the region with its regional and local rapid transit network.
   Suburban rail services of DB were upgraded to S-Bahn standard in 2000. Tickets allow free transfer between üstra services as well as to regional bus and DB rail services; üstra carries about 77 per cent of all passengers in the Grossraum area. Regional bus services are provided by RegioBus Hannover GmbH. Dial-a-bus (Ruf-Bus) and Call-a-Taxi, taxi-sharing and car-sharing services operate in several communities mainly during weekends and evening hours.
   Region Hannover, a political entity uniting the city and county of Hannover, is a partner in GVH.

Fare structure: Zonal, multiple-ride tickets at reduced fare, daily/monthly passes, annual subscription, free intermodal transfers, first class available on DB trains, special fares (including 50 per cent discount offer to employers who buy annual subscriptions for all their staff); 70 per cent of passengers use passes, which are transferable
Operating costs financed by: Not currently available

üstra Hannoversche Verkehrsbetriebe AG (üstra)
Postfach 25 40, D-30025 Hannover, Germany
Tel: (+49 511) 166 80   Fax: (+49 511) 16 68 26 22
e-mail: info@uestra.de
Web: www.uestra.de

Street address
Am Hohen Ufer 6, D-30159 Hannover, Germany

Key personnel
Chairman of the Board of Directors: André Neiss

Hauptbahnhof, where light rail, buses and main line rail converge   0585101

Two of üstra's silver TW 2000 LRVs, which have been part of the fleet since 1997 (üstra)   0585102

Head of Public Relations and Press Spokesperson:
   Udo Iwannek
   Staff: 928 (transport employees)

Passenger journeys: (All modes)
(2005) 150.8 million
(2006) 151.9 million
Vehicle-km: (2005) 37.4 million
(2006) 37.9 million

Operating costs financed by: Fares 68.8 per cent, subsidy/grants 31.2 per cent (2006)
Subsidy from: Kommunalverband Grossraum Hannover (regional authority formed by city and county) for operating costs; federal and state grants for new investment

Background
Originally established in 1892 as the Strassenbahn Hannover AG.
   In 1998 üstra was the first European transport company with buses and LRVs to be awarded the environmental audit certificate in accordance with the environmental audit law.
   Some 98.38 per cent of üstra's shares are held by the Versorgungs- und Verkehrsgesellschaft Hannover mbH (VVG), which is owned by the City of Hannover and the Region of Hannover.
   The üstra group also operates a consulting subsidiary, TransTec, which advises municipalities and public transport operators worldwide in the fields of research and project management.

Current situation
Operations serve approximately 750,000 people. Conversion of tramways to form a light rail system with city-centre sections entirely in tunnel was completed in 1992, and the last pure tram route (16) closed in 1996.

Bus
Vehicle-km: (2002) 12.7 million
(2003) 12.7 million
(2005) 13.5 million
(2006) 13.6 million

Number of routes: 39
Route length: 495.3 km

Developments
In 2006, üstra updated its bus fleet with 11 new Solaris Urbino vehicles. Another 11 buses followed in 2007.

Fleet: 135 vehicles (2006)

Most intensive service: 3 min
One-person operation: All routes
Fare collection: Fare to driver or prepurchase tickets/passes with validation and cancelling machines on board; some roadside vending machines
Fares collected on board: 12 per cent
Fare evasion control: Roving inspectors; spot fine
Operational control: Operation supervisors/mobile voice radio on all vehicles. BON computerised operating control system with centralised online monitoring in operation for all buses and LRT vehicles (see earlier editions of *Jane's Urban Transport Systems*). All fleet to be included, providing permanent voice and datalink
Average peak-hour speed: 21.6 km/h
Bus priority: Bus lanes and vehicle-activated traffic signals by inductive loop and computer-controlled system
New vehicles financed by: Internal resources and subsidies
Operating costs financed by: Income 98 per cent, subsidy/grants 2 per cent (2002)

Light rail
Type of operation: Light rail with city-centre underground sections

Car-km: (2002) 24.1 million
(2003) 24.5 million
(2005) 23.9 million
(2006) 24.4 million

Route length: 119.69 km
   in tunnel: 18.6 km
Number of lines: 12
Number of stops: 195
   in tunnel: 19
Gauge: 1,435 mm
Electrification: 600 V DC, overhead

Developments

In June 2006, the 4.6 km extension of Route 3 from Lahe to Altwarmbüchen was opened.

An 1.5 km branch to Misburg/Nord is scheduled to open in late 2008 and a further 1.7 km extension to Misburg/Meyers is currently planned for 2011.

There are plans to extend Route 6 from Messe/Ost.

Rolling stock: 311 cars

Stadtbahnwagen Series 6000 (1974–1993)	167
Stadtbahnwagen TW 2000 (1997–1999)	48
Stadtbahnwagen TW 2500 (1997–1999)	96

In peak service: 247

Service: Peak 4 min

Fare collection: Vending machines at all LRT stations and in TW2000 LRVs

Fare evasion control: As bus

One-person operation: All routes

Centralised control: Priority at traffic lights; BON system (see above)

Operating costs financed by: Fares 80 per cent, subsidy/grants 20 per cent

RegioBus Hannover GmbH

Georgstrasse 54, D-30159 Hannover, Germany
Tel: (+49 511) 36 88 80
Fax: (+49 511) 36 88 87 99
e-mail: info@regiobus.de
Web: www.regiobus.de

Key personnel

Director: Wolfgang Stack
   Staff: 682 (2006)

Passenger journeys: (2001) 27.3 million
(2002) 28.3 million
(2004) 30.0 million

Vehicle-km: (2001) 24.3 million
(2002) 24.2 million
(2004) 24.6 million

Current situation

Regional bus company formed in 1998 by the merger of management company B.U.S. with bus operators RVH, VB and StMB. The main shareholders are regional and local authorities with 88.5 per cent and Verkehrsbetriebe Bachstein (VB), a private bus company, with 11.5 per cent.

Under the trademark 'RegioBus Sprinter' a through bus service has been introduced on three lines from Pattensen, Gehrden and Lohnde/Wunstorf to central Hannover, avoiding a change of mode at the railhead. This reverses a trend prevalent in Germany for at least two decades.

At the weekends, the 'RegioBus NightLiners' run as a continuation of the üstra buses and light rail (see separate entry) and the local DB Regio trains to the furthest regions of the fare area.

Developments

Since 2001, RegioBus has successfully run the citybus service in the town of Nienburg (Weser). All four bus routes meet simultaneously at the city's central station to allow passengers to change buses easily.

Route length: 2,012 km

Fleet: 246, plus 140 contracted (2002)
Fleet includes MAN A 20, MAN Midi, Setra 315 NF, Setra 215 UL and Mercedes-Benz Citaro

New vehicles required each year: 25
Average age of fleet: 6 years

Most intensive service: 10 min
Operating costs financed by: Fares 33.1 per cent, grants 9.2 per cent, subsidy 57.5 per cent

DB Regio AG

Region Nord
Ernst-August-Platz 10, D-30159 Hannover, Germany

'RegioBus Sprinter' Mercedes-Benz Citaro low-floor bus (Henning Scheffen)   0572169

MAN low-floor buses of RegioBus on citybus route in Nienburg (Weser) (Tolga Otkun)   0572172

Tel: (+49 511) 286 46 11
Fax: (+49 511) 286 21 80
e-mail: Maria.Osang@bahn.de
Web: www.bahn.de/niedersachsen

Key personnel

Head of Region: Dr Wolfram von Fritsch
Transport Manager: Peter Büsing
Marketing Manager: Guido Verhoefen
Commercial Manager: Günther Köhnke

Type of operation: Regional metro (S-Bahn) and suburban heavy rail

Passenger journeys: Not currently available

Background

The S-Bahn system in Hannover was established to handle the traffic for the Expo2000 Hannover World Exposition.

Current situation

Today's five S-Bahn-routes operate with 46 emus of the ET424 or ET425 series, providing service for short- and middle-distance suburban traffic.

Regional services are operated over a network of 2,960 km in the Lower Saxony and Bremen area and serve 367 stations and stops.

The S-Bahn trains can be used with GVH tickets, the integrated transport system in the greater Hannover area.

For further information on DB Regio AG, please see other entries in *Jane's Urban Transport Systems* and *Jane's World Railways*.

Developments

Extension of two routes to Hildesheim and another route to Celle are planned.

In early 2006, a contract, estimated at EUR500 million, was signed for DB Regio AG to continue to operate the S-Bahn system until 2014.

Karlsruhe

Population: City 285,800 (2006 estimate)

Public transport

Bus and light rail/tramway services provided by municipal undertaking also responsible for other public utilities; suburban services provided by AVG interurban railway and DB, sharing tracks on certain routes. Regional transit authority.

Karlsruher Verkehrsverbund GmbH (KVV)

Postfach 1140, D-76001, Karlsruhe, Germany
Tel: (+49 721) 610 70   Fax: (+49 721) 61 07 50 09
e-mail: info@kvv.karlsruhe.de
Web: www.kvv.de

Street address
Tullastrasse 71, D-76131 Karlsruhe, Germany

Key personnel
Managing Director: Dr Walter Casazza

Passenger journeys: (2003) 156.5 million
(2004) 159.7 million
(2005) 163.2 million
(2006) 167.2 million
(2007) 169.6 million

Current situation

This regional transport authority was set up in 1994 by the cities of Karlsruhe and Baden-Baden and the counties of Karlsruhe, Germersheim and Rastatt, with a total population of about 1.3 million.

Services are provided by VBK/AVG, DB and RVS (see separate entries for each operator), and also by the municipal bus companies of Rastatt and Baden-Baden, SWEG (a regional railway and bus company), and 15 other bus operators over a network of 12 rail, 11 light rail and seven tram lines, and 186 bus routes.

Verkehrsbetriebe Karlsruhe GmbH (VBK)

Tullastrasse 71, D-76131 Karlsruhe, Germany
Tel: (+49 721) 610 70   Fax: (+49 721) 61 07 50 09
e-mail: info@vbk.karlsruhe.de
Web: www.karlsruhe.de/kvv

Key personnel
Operating Director: Dr Walter Casazza
Commercial Director: Wolfgang Weiss
Technical Director: Siegfried Lorenz
  Staff: 1,125 (2007)

Passenger journeys: (All modes)
(2003) 99.8 million (plus AVG 57.3 million)
(2004) 102.0 million (plus AVG 61.0 million)
(2005) 104.5 million (plus AVG 63.0 million)
(2006) 108.1 million (plus AVG 65.4 million)
(2007) 109.3 million (plus AVG 65.4 million)

Operating costs financed by: Fares 57.1 per cent, other commercial sources 25.0 per cent, subsidy/grants 17.9 per cent
Subsidy from: Internal cross-subsidy from overall municipal trading activities including electricity generating

Bus

Vehicle-km: (2003) 3.6 million
(2004) 3.8 million
(2005) 3.9 million
(2006) 3.9 million
(2007) 3.9 million

Number of routes: 23
Route length: 141.7 km, plus school and contract services

Fleet: 50 buses, plus 27 subcontracted
Mercedes-Benz O405N (1993/95)	7
Mercedes-Benz O405GN (1996/97)	8
Mercedes-Benz O405NKF (1997/98)	9
Mercedes-Benz O530N (2001)	22
SETRA S315NF (2002)	2
Mercedes-Benz O530GN	2

In peak service: Not currently available
On order: Not currently available

New vehicles required each year: 5

One-person operation: All routes
Fare collection: Monthly and annual tickets sold in kiosks; vending machines at bus stops and in trams/LRVs; drivers sell single and 24 h tickets
Fare structure: Zonal, 7 zones; monthly tickets or annual subscription, various special offers
Fare evasion control: Ticket inspection
Integration with other modes: Fully integrated with light rail/tramway and regional bus services

Average distance between stops: 542 m (approximate)
Average peak-hour speed: In mixed traffic, 24 km/h (approximate)

Light rail/tramway

Type of operation: Light rail/conventional tramway, including operation over DB main line tracks

Car-km: (2001) 7.8 million (VBK), 10.9 million (AVG)
(2002) 7.8 million (VBK), 12.0 million (AVG)
(2003) 7.9 million (VBK), 13.4 million (AVG)
(2004) 7.9 million (VBK), 14.2 million (AVG)
(2005) 8.1 million (VBK), 15.7 million (AVG)
(2006) 8.9 million (VBK), 17.3 million (AVG)
(2007) 9,0 million (VBK), 18.2 million (AVG)

Low-floor tram GT8-70D/N (VBK GmbH)   1346145

Mercedes-Benz O530N low-floor and low-floor articulated buses in new fleet colours (VBK GmbH)
1346146

Type GT8-100D/2S two-systems tram/LRV in the Murgtal, operating at 15 kV AC (VBK GmbH)
1346147

Route length: VBK 65.2 km, AVG 515.2 km including DB lines

Number of lines: 7 tram, plus 10 light rail (AVG)

Number of stops: 340 (approximate)

Gauge: 1,435 mm

Track: Grooved NP 4/40 rail; flat-bottomed S 41/10 rail conventional sleepers on ballast; sleepers on concrete

Max gradient: 6%

Minimum curve radius: 21 m

Electrification: 750 V DC, overhead; 15 kV AC on DB tracks

Rolling stock: 283 cars plus one diesel car (pool includes AVG fleet and 4 DB LRVs)

Tramway

DWM/WU 8-axle articulated (1966/78)	M31
Duewag GT6-70D/N 6-axle low-floor articulated (1995/96)	M45
Duewag GT8-70D/N 8-axle low-floor (1999/2000)	M25

Stadtbahn

Waggon Union GT6-80C 6-axle (1983/84)	M20
Duewag GT8-80C 8-axle (1987/91)	M40
Duewag GT8-100C/2S 8-axle dual-voltage (1991/95)	M36
Adtranz/Siemens GT8-100D/MSY 8-axle dual-voltage (1997/99/2000)	M85
Diesel cars	M1

On order: None

Service: Peak 5 min (central section on Kaiserstrasse 1 min), off-peak 10 min

First/last car: 03.50/03.31 (continuous service at weekends)

Fare structure: Zonal

Integration with other modes: Through running to and common fare system with AVG and with DB lines (see below); through ticketing with regional bus services

One-person operation: All routes

Current situation

A 68 km wide tram network operated by the Verkehrsbetriebe Karlsruhe (VBK) and a 580 km wide light rail network connecting the city of Karlsruhe with rural areas, mostly by TramTrains operated by Albtal-Verkehrs-Gesellschaft (AVG) marks the public transport in Karlsruhe. Both companies are city owned.

Karlsruhe has pioneered the concept of through-running between city-centre tram tracks and DB main lines. Today this transport mode is known as TramTrain operation or the Karlsruhe model.

Developments

In May 2006, a new 3.1 km double-track tramline into the north of the city was opened. The VBK decided to replace the bus with a tram system and connect the 10,000 inhabitants directly to the tram network. The extension is running on segregated tracks, mostly on green tracks to reduce noise and vibration. Six stops provide level entrance into the vehicles and fulfil the requirements of handicapped people.

Also in 2006, route S2 was extended by 6.8 km, double-track, from to Stutensee-Spöck.

At present, most of the tram and TramTrain lines run through the pedestrian precinct along Kaiserstrasse. This causes a bottleneck. Now the State Government of Baden-Württemberg has ensured public funding for a light rail tunnel in Karlsruhe by signing an outline agreement with the City council. By 2016, all trams currently using the pedestrian precinct will travel through a tunnel. The total budget for this combined solution is about EUR500 million. EUR300 million will be funded by the federal government, EUR100 million by the state and EUR100 million by the City. The planning phase (German TWA (Planfeststellungsbeschluss)) is nearing completion and works should start by 2009.

A new tram depot will be inaugurated in December 2008. It will replace the old depot in the east of the city. New storage facilities became necessary because of the growing fleet of 2.65 m

LRV on Line 2 to Rheinstetten (Mike McBride)   1162452

wide low-floor trams. The old depot was only fitted for the older 2.40 m tram vehicles and the conversion of the existing building for wider trams was not technically possible. The new depot will also accommodate a common radio control centre (ITCS) for the urban tram network and the regional TramTrain services.

Currently, a new 1.8 km tram line is planned for the southeast district of Karlsruhe. A cost-benefit calculation has outlined the benefit of the new infrastructure. Construction works should start by 2011.

VBK and AVG have been making considerable efforts to adapt the network to the needs of disabled people. The next project will improve the station forecourt in Karlsruhe, which will have level access to trams, TramTrains and buses and to offer step-free interchanges between all transport modes.

In 2008, AVG signed a contract to adapt the existing railway route between Wörth-Germersheim, in the state of Rhineland-Palatinate, to TramTrain operation. Operation will be taken over by DB from 2010 onwards.

Albtal-Verkehrs-Gesellschaft mbH (AVG) – Albtalbahn

Postfach 1140, D-76001 Karlsruhe, Germany
Tel: (+49 721) 610 70   Fax: (+49 721) 61 07 50 09
e-mail: info@avgkarlsruhe.de
Web: www.albtalbahn.de

Street address

Tullastrasse 71, D-76131 Karlsruhe, Germany

Key personnel

Managing Director: Dr Walter Casazza
Operating Director: Dr Walter Casazza
Infrastructure Manager: Dipl-Ing Siegfried Lorenz
Commercial Manager: Wolfgang D Weiss
    Staff: 606

Passenger journeys: (2002) 54.1 million
(2003) 57.3 million
(2004) 61.0 million
(2005) 63.0 million
(2006) 65.4 million

Background

Company with same ownership and management as Verkehrsbetriebe Karlsruhe GmbH (VBK), but different legal status and operating to railway rather than tramway regulations. AVG originally operated electric interurban railway from Karlsruhe southwards via Ettlingen to Bad Herrenalb and Ittersbach. This line has now been fully integrated with LRT operations of VBK. The Neureut-Leopoldshafen LRT line, a converted DB freight line which is legally a railway, is also owned by AVG.

Since 1994, AVG has taken over operation of several DB routes, replacing or supplementing DB trains. More trains are operated than under

DB, and the number of passengers has more than doubled over certain sections.

In 1994, AVG acquired the regional railway lines from Bruchsal to Menzingen and Odenheim from SWEG. Electric traction was introduced between Bruchsal and Menzigen in 1996, with the branch to Odenheim following in 1997. For further developments, see separate entry for Verkehrsbetriebe Karlsruhe GmbH (VBK) in Urban Transport Systems and Operators section.

Current situation

AVG also operates a small bus network based on Ettlingen, serving as a feeder to the interurban rail line and catering for local needs. The 22 plus some 50 subcontracted buses ran 3.5 million km in 2006.

For further information on AVG, please see *Jane's World Railways.*

Developments

Further extensions of the suburban routes S2 to Stutensee (a suburb of Karlsruhe) and S4 to Öhringen have been completed.

A 3 km tunnel is planned to relieve LRT congestion in the centre of Karlsruhe.

The new tramline to Nordstadt opened in early 2006.

Line 2 has been extended to Spöck and the extension on Line S41 was completed in December 2006.

Fleet: 181 electric LRVs, owned by AVG, VBK and DB, are operated in a pool. Of these, 121 are equipped for dual-voltage operation. Other vehicles are included in the fleet listing in the separate entry for Verkehrsbetriebe Karlsruhe GmbH (VBK).

RVS Regionalbusverkehr Südwest GmbH (SüdwestBus)

Gartenstrasse 78, D-76135 Karlsruhe, Germany
Tel: (+49 721) 840 60
Fax: (+49 721) 840 62 20
e-mail: info@suedwestbus.de
Web: www.suedwestbus.de

Key personnel

Directors: Uwe Loeschmann
        Frank Klingenhöfer
    Staff: 500 (approximate)

Passenger journeys: (2002) 30 million (approximate)
Vehicle-km: (2002) 27 million (approximate)

Current situation

Suburban and regional bus services operated by SüdwestBus, a DB subsidiary. All routes which previously ran through to Karlsruhe have been cut back to feed the LRT lines of VBK/AVG. Statistics apply to the whole SüdwestBus operation, not just services within the KVV area.

Fleet: Over 500 vehicles

DB Regio AG

Region RheinNeckar
Am Victoria-Turn 2, D-68163, Mannheim, Germany
Tel: (+49 621) 830 15 00
Fax: (+49 621) 830 15 09

e-mail: ran.rhein-neckar@bahn.de
Web: www.bahn.de/s-bahn-rheinneckar

Key personnel
Head of Region: Andreas Schilling
Transport Manager: Maik Dreser

Commercial Manager: Jürgen Bank
Personnel Manager: Winfried Nessel

Type of operation: Regional rail and metro (S-Bahn)

For further information, please see under Mannheim and in *Jane's World Railways.*

Leipzig

Population: 504,000 (2006 estimate)

Public transport

Central area served almost entirely by tramways operated by municipal company which also owns suburban bus company; suburban rail services by German Rail (DB Regio AG).

Mitteldeutscher Verkehrsverbund (MDV) GmbH

Karl-Liebknecht-Strasse 8, D-04107 Leipzig, Germany
Tel: (+49 341) 868 43 10   Fax: (+49 341) 868 43 98 9
e-mail: post@mdv.de
Web: www.mdv.de

Key personnel
Managing Director: Werner Meier
Press Speaker: Matthias Neumann

Current situation
The MDV was founded in 2001. There are a total of 28 transport companies integrated under the MDV.
The authority comprises the cities of Halle and Leipzig and and six adjacent counties with a total area of 7,900 km²

Passenger journeys: (2007) 710 million

Leipziger Verkehrsbetriebe (LVB) GmbH

Karl-Liebknecht-Strasse 12, D-04107 Leipzig, Germany
Tel: (+49 341) 49 20   Fax: (+49 341) 492 10 05
e-mail: info@lvb.de
Web: www.lvb.de

Key personnel
Directors: Wilhelm Hanss (Chair, Personnel)
Technical: Ronald Juhrs
Finance: Klaus Heininger
  Staff: 1,005 (2006)

Passenger journeys: (2003) 107.1 million*
(2004) 111.3 million*
(2005) 123.3 million**
(2006) 123.3 million**
(2007) 124.1 million

*Includes subsidiary RVL.
**Not comparable to previous years, due to change in counting method.

Current situation
The former state-owned company is now 100 per cent owned by LVV Leipziger Versorgungs- und Verkehrsbetriebe mbH. LVV is a holding company entirely owned by the city of Leipzig, combining three public companies for water, energy and transport.
Within the last few years LVB was transformed into a group of companies, with seven subsidiaries. These subsidiaries were former departments of LVB, with responsibilities including infrastructure maintenance, vehicle maintenance, consulting and vehicles services. The aim of outsourcing these areas is to increase competitiveness and flexibility of the companies in preparation for competition in the liberalised European transport market.

Bus

Passenger journeys: (2003) 27.7 million
(2004) 23.4 million*

(2005) 23.7 million*
(2006) 23.5 million*
(2007) 23.8 million*
Vehicle-km: (2003) 11.2 million
(2004) 11.2 million*
(2005) 10.8 million*
(2006) 10.8 million*
(2007) 10.7 million*
*Includes subsidiary RVL.

Number of routes: 60
Route length: 1,115.8 km
Includes subsidiary RVL.

Fleet: 110 vehicles (2007)

MAN NL202 (1994)	23
MAN NL223 (1998)	3
Mercedes O405GN (1992/95)	19
Mercedes-Benz O530	30
Mercedes-Benz Cito midibus	5
Solaris Urbino 12	28
Other	2

In peak service: 130

Most intensive service: 10 min
One-person operation: All routes
Fare collection: Prepurchase single and multi-ride tickets from kiosks, cancelled on board; day tickets, weekly and monthly passes; 64 per cent of passengers use passes
Fare structure: Time- and zone-based
Fare evasion control: Roving inspectors
Integration with other modes: Since 2001, members of the MDV (Mitteldeutcher Verkehrsverbund) and a further 26 public transport companies' tickets/fares are all valid within the MDV region
Average peak-hour speed: 24.36 km/h (2007)

Tramway

Type of operation: Conventional tramway

Passenger journeys: (2003) 79.2 million
(2004) 99.9 million
(2005) 99.6 million
(2006) 101.6 million
(2007) 100.3 million
Car-km: (2003) 27.0 million
(2004) 27.0 million
(2005) 26.5 million
(2006) 24.1 million
(2007) 21.4 million

Number of routes: 13 (2007)
Route length: 211.8 km
On private right-of-way: 82.5 km
Number of stops: 515
Gauge: 1,458 mm

Rolling stock: 338 cars (2007)

ČKD Tatra T4D/B4D (1969/83)	M30 T18
ČKD Tatra T4DM/B4DM (1969/86)	M153 T44
Siemens/Duewag/ABB/Bautzen NGT8 (1994/97)	M56
Bombardier low-floor NB4 (2000)	T38
Bombardier Classix XXL (2006)	M24
FBL Leoliner	M23*

On order: * Total of 30 Leoliner trams for delivery. Built by LVB subsidiary Leoliner Fahrzeug-Bau Leipzig GmbH (FBL)
In peak service: 151 sets (2007)

Regionalverkehr Leipzig GmbH (RVL)

Pegauer Strasse 124, D-04442 Zwenkau, Germany
Tel: (+49 342) 036 00   Fax: (+49 342) 036 01 05
e-mail: info@rvl.de
Web: www.rvl.de/leipzig/index.html

Key personnel
Directors: Gerd Hartmann, Uwe Rössler

Current situation
RVL was created in 1992 out of the former state-owned Kraftverkehr Leipzig. It operates suburban and regional bus services, school transport services and vehicles for hire.

Developments
In 2002, the company became 100 per cent owned by LVG (see separate entry).

Passenger journeys: Not currently available
Vehicle-km: Not currently available

Number of routes: 29
Fleet: Not currently available

Eilenburger Busverkehr GmbH (SaxBus)

Gustav-Adolf-Ring 2, D-04838 Eilenburg, Germany
Tel: (+49 3423) 700 60
Fax: (+49 3423) 70 06 25
e-mail: info@saxbus.de
  michaela.wilde@saxbus.de
Web: www.connex-gruppe.de/seiten/saxbus/

Key personnel
Managing Director: Klaus Beyer
  Staff: 78

Passenger journeys: Approx 1.5 million annually

Background
Originally a private company, founded in 1993, SaxBus provides services in Leipzig, Eilenburg and Bad Düben.

Current situation
Part of the Connex Group and a member of the MDV partnership. The company is also associated with Taeter Aachen GmbH & Co KG.

Fleet
SaxBus's fleet of some 40 vehicles includes MAN, Setra and Mercedes-Benz buses and coaches.

Auto-Webel GmbH

Hallesche Strasse 70, D-04509 Delitzsch, Germany
Tel & Fax : (+49 342) 025 21 88

Key personnel
Managing Director: Wolfgang Webel

Current situation
This family-owned company was reprivatised in 1991. It operates most regional bus services in the county of Delitzsch, north of Leipzig, with a fleet of 22 buses.
The company is part of the MDV partnership.

DB Regio AG

Verkehrsbetrieb Sachsen
Hansstrasse 4, D-01097 Dresden, Germany
Tel: (+49 351) 461 86 00
Fax: (+49 351) 461 86 06
Web: www.bahn.de/sachsen

Key personnel
Contact: Klaus-Dieter Martini

Type of operation: Suburban heavy rail

Current situation
Part of the Region Südost, DB Regio AG's Sachsen services cover a network of 1,364 km centred on Dresden and Leipzig and serve 320 stations and halts, with some 986 million passenger-km recorded annually .

For further information on DB, please see *Jane's World Railways.*

Magdeburg
Population: 228,515 (2005)

Public transport
Bus, tramway and ferry services provided by municipal company; S-Bahn operated by DB; regional bus services.

Magdeburger Verkehrsbetriebe GmbH (MVB)
Otto-von-Guericke Strasse 25, D-39104 Magdeburg, Germany
Tel: (+49 391) 54 80 Fax: (+49 391) 543 00 46
e-mail: Info@mvbnet.de
Web: www.mvbnet.de

Key personnel
Directors: Dr-Ing Herbert Preil (Commercial)
  Hans-Dieter Hakke (Technical)
  Staff: 959

Passenger journeys: (1998) 55.7 million
(1999) 59.0 million
(2000) 58.1 million

Operating costs financed by: Fares 48 per cent, subsidy/grants 52 per cent

Developments
A co-operation agreement concluded between MVB, DB and bus operators from four surrounding counties in 1996 envisages introduction of joint timetables and tariffs. Discussions have taken place about the possibility of creating a regional transport authority (verkehrsverbund) for Magdeburg and its surrounding local authorities.

In September 1998, the first step towards a common fare system was taken with the mutual recognition of season tickets for tram and bus journeys in the greater Magdeburg area.

Bus
Vehicle-km: (1998) 3.4 million
(1999) 3.4 million
(2000) 13.5 million

Number of routes: 11
Route length: 144 km

Fleet: 61 buses
MAN NL202 low-floor	12
MAN NG272 low-floor articulated	10
Mercedes O405N low-floor	24
Mercedes O405GN low-floor articulated	13
Others	2

In peak service: 47

Most intensive service: 10 min
One-person operation: All routes
Fare collection: By driver
Fare structure: Flat transferable daily, weekly, monthly and annual passes, also valid in certain other cities by mutual agreement; reduced price for passes after 09.00; surcharge for onboard tickets
Arrangements for elderly/disabled: Free travel for disabled, reimbursed by government
Integration with other modes: Through-ticketing (passes only) with DB regional services and connecting urban buses in Burg, Genthin and Haldensleben
Average distance between stops: 570 m
Average speed: 20.7 km/h

Developments
A new central bus station (ZOB) in Maybachstrasse opened in August 2000.

Tramway
Type of operation: Conventional tramway

Alstom LHB NGT8D low-floor tram outside Magdeburg railway station (Tony Pattison)   0109544

ČKD Tatra modernised cars in Magdeburg in overall advertising livery (Tony Pattison)   0109545

Car-km: (1998) 10.7 million
(1999) 11.0 million
(2000) 9.7 million

Number of routes: 9
Route length: 59 km
Number of stops: 116
Gauge: 1,435 mm
Minimum curve radius: 30 m
Electrification: 600 V DC, overhead

Service: Peak 10 min
First/last car: 04.15/23.00
Average distance between stops: 540 m
Average speed: 19.2 km/h

Rolling stock: 162 cars
ČKD Tatra T4D/B4D 4-axle (1968/86)	
(modernised 1991/94)	M77 T5
ČKD Tatra T6A2 4-axle	
(modernised 1995/97)	M11 T6
LHB NGT8D 8-axle low-floor articulated	
(1994/95)	M53
Others	10

In peak service: 227
On order: 19 NGT8D for delivery in 2002.

Current situation
New workshops opened in 1999. Tatra cars are now programmed to remain in service until 2015, as fewer new cars were ordered than originally planned. Similarly, the use of trailer cars is being progressively abandoned.

Several tram stops have been fitted with real-time information displays showing the actual arrival time of the next tram. The existing reverser at Diesdorf (route 6) was replaced by a 300 m extension and new turning circle, with park and ride places, in October 2000.

Developments
Construction started in October 2000 of the first stage of a new north-south link. Work will take place in seven phases and will involve new construction along Europaring, Wienerstrasse and Raiffeisenstrasse (future route 11 from Olvenstedt to Leipziger Chaussee), from Reform to Bördepark, and from Breiter Weg to Kannenstieg via Neustädter Feld. The first section was expected to be completed by the end of 2003.

DB Regio AG
Verkehrsbetrieb Sachsen-Anhalt
Volkmannstrasse 38, D-06112 Halle (Saale), Germany
Tel: (+49 345) 215 27 00
Fax: (+49 345) 215 27 47
Web: www.bahn.de/sachsen-anhalt

Key personnel
Spokesman: Thomas Hoffmann
Finance: Stephen Georg Wigger

Current situation
Part of the Region Südost, Sachsen-Anhalt services cover a network of 1,602 km centred on Halle and serving 293 stations and halts, with some 852 million passenger-km recorded annually.

For further information on DB, please see *Jane's World Railways.*

Mannheim-Ludwigshafen Heidelberg

Population: Mannheim 307,640 (2005), Ludwigshafen 167,410 (2004 estimate), metropolitan region 2.4 million (estimate), Heidelberg 142,889 (2004)

Public transport

Bus tramway/light rail services provided under a central organisation, Rhein-Neckar-Verkerh GmbH (RNV), which was formed by the merger of five previous operators: MVV, MVV OEG, VBL, RHB and HSB. Further bus services provided by wholly owned subsidiary of DB. S-Bahn services. A regional transit authority (VRN) covers the whole Rhein-Neckar region, including Heidelberg.

Verkehrsverbund Rhein-Neckar GmbH (VRN)/ Unternehmensgesellschaft Verkehrsverbund Rhein-Neckar GmbH (URN)

B1, 3-5, D-68159 Mannheim, Germany
Tel: (+49 621) 107 70 60
Fax: (+49 621) 107 70 69
e-mail: info@vrn.de, h.kummerow@urn.de
Web: www.vrn.de, www.urn.de

Key personnel

Managing Director, VRN: Werner Schreiner
Managing Director, URN: Horst Kummerow

Passenger journeys: (All modes)
(2000) 231.5 million

Current situation

Regional transit authority for the entire Rhein-Neckar region, comprising 300 cities and towns with a total population of 2.5 million, established 1989. Services are now amalgamated under the Rhein-Neckar-Verkehr GmbH (please see separate entry in *Jane's Urban Transport Systems*), plus other municipal bus and associated operators, a state-owned local railway and bus company, a Rhein ferry, and German Railway (DB).

In 1996 VRN became a political body formed by three states and 19 cities. URN is an association of transport operators. Both associations work in close co-operation with one another and are managed from the same address.

Rhein-Neckar-Verkehr GmbH (RNV)

Möhlstrasse 27, D-68165 Mannheim, Germany
Tel: (+49 621) 46 54 93
Fax: (+49 621) 46 54 90
e-mail: kontakt@rnv-online.de
Web: www.rnv-online.de

Key personnel

Directors: Andreas Kerber
  Günther Quass
  Staff: 1,800

Passenger journeys: (All modes)
(2005) 150 million (estimated)
(2006) 162 million

Operating costs financed by: The five member companies
Subsidy from: Subsidies are allocated to the five member companies

Current situation

In 2005, a new public transport company, Rhein-Neckar-Verkehr GmbH (RNV), was formed by the merger of the five companies that had previously provided services in the Mannheim/Ludwigshafen/Heidelberg area: MVV Verkehr AG (35.13 per cent), MVV OEG AG (16.26 per cent), VBL (18.36 per cent), RHB (2.42 per cent) and HSB (27.83 per cent).

RNV subsidiaries:
V-Bus GmbH
Goethestrasse 12, D-68519 Viernheim, Germany
Tel: (+49 6204) 971 05
Fax: (+49 6204) 97 10 65
e-mail: info@v-bus.de
Web: www.rnv-online/vbus

Key personnel

Director: Stefan Prüfer

Background

Subsidiary of RNV GmbH, owned 99 per cent by RNV and 1 per cent by the city of Viernheim.

Omnibusbetriebe Beth GmbH

Wormer Strasse 84, D-68623 Lampertheim, Germany
Tel: (+49 6206) 929 20
Fax: (+49 6206) 92 92 61
e-mail: a-beth@t-online.de

Background

Subsidiary of RNV GmbH, owned 100 per cent by RNV.

Key personnel

Director: Stefan Prüfer

RNV bus data (all operations):
Developments
An 800 m guided bus-way has been built in Feudenheim, integrated with an existing tramway reservation. This allows buses to bypass a traffic bottleneck and gain four minutes per journey; 13 buses have been fitted with guide-wheels.

Vehicle-km: (2006) 11.97 million
Number of routes: 74
Route length: 560.6 km

Fleet: 158
Breakdown of fleet is not currently available
In peak service: Not currently available

Most intensive service: 10 min
One-person operation: All routes
Fare collection: Pre-purchase passes or tickets, with validation and cancelling machines on board, or payment to driver; 87 per cent of passengers use passes
Fare structure: Flat; pre-purchase weekly/monthly and annual passes, and multijourney tickets
Fare evasion control: Roving inspectors inspect 1 per cent of all passengers
Average peak-hour speed: 25.2 km/h

RNV tramway data (all operations):
Type of operation: Conventional tramway
Car-km: (2006) 12.2 million

Route length: 301.8 km
On private right-of-way: 75 per cent
Number of lines: 21
Number of stops: Not currently available

Gauge: 1,000 mm
Electrification: 600 V DC, overhead

Developments
In June 2006, 600 m of new track was opened for route 4.
  There are 10 Bombardier trams on order for RNV operations.

Rolling stock: 217 trams
Fleet breakdown is not currently available
In peak service: 206
On order: 10 vehicles

Service: Peak 10 min, off-peak 10–30 min
First/last car: 04.30/03.00
Fare structure: Flat
Fare collection: Pre-purchase tickets or pass; validation and cancelling machines on board; roving inspectors inspect 1 per cent of all passengers
Arrangements for elderly/disabled: Tramway and bus stops being modified to improve accessibility

Busverkehr Rhein-Neckar GmbH (BRN)

Willy-Brandt-Platz 7, D-68161 Mannheim, Germany
Tel: (+49 621) 12 00 30   Fax: (+49 621) 120 03 60
e-mail: omnibus@brn.de
Web: www.brn.de

Key personnel

Directors: Uwe Loeschmann
  Bernhard Krämer
  Staff: 314

Passenger journeys: (2005) 44 million (estimate)
Vehicle-km: (2005) 25 million (estimate)

Current situation

Regional bus company, owned by DB, providing suburban and regional services to some 2.4 million people over 107 routes, total 2,988 km, with a fleet of 250 buses plus 270 subcontracted.

DB Regio AG

Region RheinNeckar
Am Victoria-Turn 2, D-68163, Mannheim, Germany
Tel: (+49 621) 830 15 00
Fax: (+49 621) 830 15 09
e-mail: ran.rhein-neckar@bahn.de
Web: www.bahn.de/s-bahn-rheinneckar

Key personnel

Head of Region: Andreas Schilling
Transport Manager: Maik Dreser
Commercial Manager: Jürgen Bank
Personnel Manager: Winfried Nessel

Type of operation: Regional rail and S-Bahn

S-Bahn ET 425 emu (Manfred Rinderspacher)   1196012

Current situation

DB Regio AG – Region RheinNeckar is one of nine self-contained management units of DB Regio AG in Germany, which serves the Rhein-Neckar region in the border triangle Rheinland-Pfalz, Baden-Württemberg and Hessen. DB Regio RheinNeckar runs a fleet of 170 trains covering a total route network of 805 km supported by about 1,000 employees. Trains travel some 20 million train-km each year and serve 278 stations.

Whereas on electrified lines EMU's class ET 425 (Total: 75) are particularly employed, most of the trains on diesel lines are being operated by class VT 628 (Total: 63) and VT 612 (Total: 12). The few locomotive-driven trains are hauled by class BR 218 (Total: 16).

The S-Bahn RheinNeckar forms the backbone of public transport in the Rhein-Neckar region. It serves the cities of Heidelberg, Mannheim and Ludwigshafen and connects with the surrounding region. The S-Bahn network, with its four lines, covers 290 km and serves 73 stations and stopping points of the DB Regio RheinNeckar region and is suitable for the mobility-impaired throughout. The four S-Bahn lines Homburg (Saar) – Kaiserslautern – Osterburken (S1), Kaiserslautern – Eberbach/Mosbach (S2), Germersheim – Speyer – Karlsruhe (S3), and Germersheim – Speyer – Bruchsal (S4) are served at hourly intervals. About EUR280 million have been invested in upgrading the S-Bahn infrastructure and stations, and an additional amount of some EUR190 million has been spent on procuring rolling stock – 40 low-floor EMU's ET 425. The EMU's are serviced at a new S-Bahn workshop in Ludwigshafen. The new workshop hall, covering an area of about 4,700 m² and costing some EUR16 million, was built as an annexe to existing DB Regio workshop facilities in Ludwigshafen. Following this extension, the Ludwigshafen depot now offers a total workshop capacity for servicing up to 95 electric multiple units on a shift system.

The rate of increase in passengers is about 30 per cent since December 2003 and the average punctuality rate is 98 per cent every year.

As well as the operation of the S-Bahn system, DB Regio AG – Region RheinNeckar also provides the regional transport services (RB, RE), which serve the surrounding area of Heidelberg, Mannheim and Ludwigshafen not covered by S-Bahn. These transport services amounts to 14 million train-km each year.

Developments

The administration union (Zweckverband Verkehrsverbund Rhein-Neckar) of the Rhein-Neckar transport association passed a guideline for further extension of the S-Bahn RheinNeckar, including routes to Biblis, Mainz, Darmstadt and Sinsheim/Eppingen.

Mönchengladbach

Population: 263,000 (2002)

Public transport

Bus services in Mönchengladbach and surrounding towns provided by municipal operator. Rail links to neighbouring cities provided by DB Regionalbahn Rheinland GmbH. Bus and rail services are fully integrated (free intermodal transfers) and co-ordinated by Verkehrsverbund Rhein-Ruhr GmbH (VRR).

Niederrheinische Versorgong und Verkehr AG (NVV) – MöBus

PO Box 200951, D-41209 Mönchengladbach, Germany
Tel: (+49 2166) 68 80   Fax: (+49 2166) 688 24 45
e-mail: info@nvv-ag.de
Web: www.nvv-ag.de

Street address

Odenkirchener Str. 201, D-41236 Mönchengladbach, Germany

Key personnel

Directors: Friedhelm Kirchhartz (Chair)
  Rainer Hellekes
  Eberhard Metzner
Communications: Daniel Plezer
Press Contact: Helmut Marmann
  Staff: 452

Bus

Passenger journeys: (1998) 35.8 million
(2000) 35.8 million
(2002) 39.4 million
Vehicle-km: (1998) 11 million
(2000) 11.8 million
(2002) 12.2 million

Number of routes: 48
Route length: (One way) 865 km

Fleet: 201 vehicles plus 24 contracted

Mercedes O405 (1985/90)	29
Mercedes O405G articulated (1988)	5
MAN SL202 (1985/92)	35
MAN NL202 (1990/93) low floor	6
MAN NG272 low-floor articulated (1993/94)	16
Mercedes O405N2 (1990/97) low floor	51
MAN NL222/223 (1996/99) low floor	40
Others	19
In peak service: 187	

Most intensive service: 10 min
One-person operation: All routes
Fare collection: Prepurchase or driver-issued
Fare structure: Zonal; single tickets, multiride cards, daily, weekly and monthly passes (VRR scheme)
Integration with other modes: Fully integrated under VRR scheme with S-Bahn services and with neighbouring municipal operators
Operational control: Computer-based (RBL) system introduced in 1999.
Average distance between stops: 505 m

Average peak-hour speed: 22.7 km/h
Operating costs financed by: Fares 36 per cent, other commercial sources 6 per cent, subsidy/grants and deficit 58 per cent
Subsidy from: City (including cross-subsidy from other public utilities) and state

Developments

New bus station adjacent to main railway station opened in 2000. 200 traffic lights to be equipped for bus priority in the near future.

DB Regio AG

DB Regio NRW GmbH
Region Nordrhein-Westfalen, Geschäftsbereich Rhein-Ruhr
Hollestrasse 3, D-45127 Essen, Germany
Tel: (+49 201) 175 25 07
Fax: (+49 201) 175 23 02
Web: www.bahn.de/nordrhein-westfahlen

Key personnel

Head of Region: Thorsten Siggelkow

Type of operation: S-Bahn and regional rail

Current situation

Extensive suburban services connect Mönchengladbach with other cities in the Rhein-Ruhr.

Munich (München)

Population: 1.3 million (2005 estimate), MVV service area 2.5 million (2005)

Public transport

Bus, tramway and metro services provided by city undertaking under policy of Münchner Verkehrs- und Tarifverbund GmbH (MVV). Suburban rail services (S-Bahn) operated by S-Bahn München GmbH (a DB Group company) and suburban bus services by 56 operators under MVV. Airport shuttle Maglev proposed.

Münchner Verkehrs- und Tarifverbund GmbH (MVV)

Thierschstrasse 2, D-80538 Munich, Germany
Tel: (+49 89) 21 03 30   Fax: (+49 89) 21 03 32 82
e-mail: info@mvv-muenchen.de
Web: www.mvv-muenchen.de

Key personnel

Directors: Alexander Freitag, Klaus Wergles

Passenger journeys: (2000) 546.9 million
(2003) 554.9 million
(2004) 558 million
(2005) 580.7 million

Munich tram on route 20 (Patrick Allen)

1345819

Fare structure: Zonal, free intermodal transfers
Fare collection: Single tickets; multiride tickets; season tickets and passes; transferable pass for off-peak travel; day ticket

Background

All public transport in Munich and surrounding area of 5,500 km², covering eight rural areas, 175 local authorities and a population of some

2.5 million, is co-ordinated and fully integrated by the regional transport authority Münchner Verkehrs- und Tarifverbund GmbH (MVV). MVV is responsible for future transport planning, marketing, tariffs and recommendations concerning headways and capacity.

Current situation

Regional bus services are provided by some 56 operators, tram, bus and U-Bahn by Münchner Verkehrsgesellschaft mbH (MVG) (see separate entry) and S-Bahn by S-Bahn München (part of the Deutsche Bahn Gruppe).

A total of 24,500 park-and-ride spaces and 46,200 bike-and-ride spaces were available in the MVV area in 2005.

Regional bus

Passenger journeys: (2001) 32.3 million

Vehicle-km: (2001) 21.3 million
(2002) 22.8 million
(2003) 24.0 million
(2004) 23.3 million
(2005) 23.9 million

Current situation

Regional bus services are provided by 56 private operators, all integrated with MVV. There are 209 routes, operated by 545 buses (peak requirement).

Münchener Verkehrsgesellschaft mbH (MVG)

Emmy-Noether-Strasse 2, D-80287 Munich, Germany
Tel: (+49 89) 219 10 (Switchboard)
Fax: (+49 89) 21 91 24 49
e-mail: privatkunden@swm.de
Web: www.mvg-mobil.de

Key personnel

Chairman, MVG, Vice-Chairman and General Manager Transportation, SWM: Herbert König
Staff: 2,699 (2007)

Passenger journeys: (All modes)
(2004) 442.2 million
(2005) 460 million
(2006) 475 million
(2007) 482 million

Operating costs financed by: Fares 51 per cent, subsidy/grants 49 per cent
Subsidy from: Contributions made through cross-subsidy from other municipal enterprises, city of Munich, state and federal government

Background

This wholly owned subsidiary of Stadtwerke München GmbH (SWM) took over operations with effect from 1 January 2002. Staff and infrastructure remain with SWM and are leased to MVG as required.

Current situation

MVG serves an area of 401 km², including the district municipalities of Grünwald, Gräfeling, Garching, Neubiberg, Planegg, Unterföhring and Karlsfeld, and a total population of 1.39 million.

Bus

Passenger journeys: (2004) 156.1 million
(2005) 162 million
(2006) 165 million
(2007) 166 million
Vehicle-km: Not currently available

Number of routes: 67 (8 night service routes)
Number of stops: 889
Route length: 458 km (unduplicated)
On priority right-of-way: 21 km

Fleet: 229 vehicles, plus 186 contracted
Standard bus   166
Articulated bus   246
Minibuses   3
In peak service: 464

Most intensive service: 10 min
One-person operation: All routes
Fare collection: Pre-purchase tickets or passes with validation and cancelling machines on board, or payment to driver
Fare structure: Zonal (MVV)
Fare evasion control: Roving inspectors
Average distance between stops: 515 m
Average peak-hour speed: 18.1 km/h
Operational control: Computer-based automatic data transmission between buses and control room

Tramway

Type of operation: Conventional tramway

Passenger journeys: (2004) 83.4 million
(2005) 87 million
(2006) 89 million
(2007) 91 million
Car-km: Not currently available

Route length: 71.2 km
On priority right-of-way: 47 km
Number of lines: 10 (4 night service routes)
Number of stops: 148
Gauge: 1,435 mm
Max gradient: 4%
Minimum curve radius: 15 m
Electrification: 650 V DC, overhead (change to 750 V planned)

Current situation

There are now 301 real-time passenger information display units.

Developments

Planning approval has been received for the new Route 23 (3 km). Work is currently scheduled to start in 2007, with the route becoming operational in 2009.

Four new Stadler low-floor trams have been ordered.

Rolling stock: 92 cars (2007)
Fleet breakdown is not currently available
In peak service: 83
On order: Options for 27 single articulated cars

Service: Peak 5 min, off-peak 10 min
First/last car: 05.00/01.00
One-person operation: All cars; since 1999 drivers have not sold tickets
Fare structure: Zonal (MVV)
Fare evasion control: Roving inspectors
Average distance between stops: 481 m
Average speed: 20.2 km/h

Metro

Type of operation: Full metro (U-Bahn), first line opened 1971

Passenger journeys: (2004) 307.2 million
(2005) 324 million
(2006) 330 million
(2007) 336 million
Car-km: Not currently available

Route length: 93 km
  in tunnel: 83 km
Number of lines: 6
Number of stations: 94
Gauge: 1,435 mm
Tunnel: Shield driven 5.74 m diameter, conventional tunnelling and cut-and-cover
Electrification: 750 V DC, third rail

Current situation

Basic network of three main lines comprises six routes (U1/2, U3/6, U4/5).

Developments

An extension of U6 from Garching-Hohbrüch to Garching-Forschungszentrum (two stations, 4.4 km) opened in October 2006.

Construction has started on the U3 extension to Moosach S-Bahn station and is scheduled to be completed in 2010. The first section from Olympiazentrum to OEZ is due to be completed in 2007.

Several other extensions are at the planning stage: U4-east Arabellapark-Engschalking (1.9 km) (although this may be substituted by a tram line), U5-west Laimer Platz-Pasing (3.6 km), U6 from Grosshadern to Martinsried (1.3 km). The system will eventually extend to some 110 km.

Rolling stock: 580 cars
Type A   Not currently available
Type B   Not currently available
Type C (six-car trains)
  (2002/06)   Not currently available
In peak service: Not currently available
On order:
Service: Peak 2–3 min, off-peak 10 min
Fare structure: Zonal (MVV)
Arrangements for elderly/disabled: 85 stations are wheelchair accessible
Signalling: ATC; SpDrL77 signalling and train control equipment with track circuits
Integration with other modes: Interchange with S-Bahn at 9 stations
Average speed: 36.7 km/h

Regionalverkehr Oberbayern GmbH (RVO)

Hirtenstrasse 24, D-80335 Munich, Germany
Tel: (+49 89) 55 16 40   Fax: (+49 89) 55 16 41 99
e-mail: auskunft@rvo-bus.de
Web: www.rvo-bus.de

Key personnel

Managers: Veit Bodenschatz, Peter Heider
Finance: Karlheinz Prokop
Marketing: Nicolaj Eberlein
Production/Technical: Veit Bodenschatz
  Staff: 574

Current situation

This associated company of DB operates extensive suburban and rural bus services both within and outside the MVV area, some under contract.

Bus

Number of routes: 355, of which 70 within MVV
Route length: 12,406 km, of which 1,675.8 km within MVV

Fleet: 307 buses, including Kässbohrer, Mercedes and MAN, plus 335 hired

DB Regio AG

S-Bahn München
Orleansplatz 9a, D-81667 Munich, Germany
Tel: (+49 89) 13 08 46 75
Fax: (+49 89) 13 08 29 91
e-mail: Heinrich.Beckmann@bahn.de
Web: www.s-bahn-muenchen.de

Key personnel

Managing Director and Spokesman: Heinrich Beckmann
Manager: Michael Wuth
  Staff: 1,100 (estimate)

Type of operation: Regional metro (S-Bahn)

Passenger journeys: (Annual) 218 million (estimate)
Train-km: (Annual) 19 million (estimate)

Current situation

S-Bahn service is operated over 10 lines totalling 442 km, with a 4 km city-centre tunnel section; 1,435 mm gauge, electrified at 15 kV 16⅔ Hz AC; 147 stations and recording 2,260 million passenger-km annually. Trains run every 20 minutes peak, 40 minutes off-peak, combining in the city centre to provide a 2–4 minute interval service; some lines have a 10 minute service during rush hours and this frequency is to be extended throughout the network over the next few years. Zonal fare structure (see under MVV). Operating costs are financed by fares (54.5 per cent), with the balance coming from federal government and Munich city subsidy.

For further information on DB, please see *Jane's World Railways*.

Rolling stock: 234 four-car trains
ET 423   M468 T468
In peak service: Not currently available

Munich Airport Maglev

Type of operation: Airport shuttle Maglev (project cancelled)

Background
A Transrapid fully automatic Maglev project to link Munich Central Station to link to Munich Airport.

Developments
In March 2008, the German Government cancelled the project, due to increasing costs.

DB class 423 train on München S-Bahn line 2, Petershausen to Erding (Quintus Vosman)   1289704

Nuremberg (Nürnberg)

Population: 500,000 (2005 estimate), region 1.7 million (estimate)

Public transport
Bus, tramway and metro services operated in Nuremberg and on behalf of the municipality of Erlangen by VAG, a subsidiary of municipally owned utilities holding company Städtische Werke Nürnberg GmbH. Regional S-Bahn services operated by German Railways (DB). All public transport in area around Nuremberg, including local bus services in Schwabach and regional bus services, are co-ordinated by the regional transit authority VGN.

Verkehrsverbund Grossraum Nürnberg GmbH (VGN)
Rothenburger Strasse 9, D-90443 Nüremberg, Germany
Tel: (+49 911) 27 07 50   Fax: (+49 911) 270 75 50
e-mail: info@vgn.de
Web: www.vgn.de

Key personnel
Directors: Jürgen Haasler, Prof Dr Willi Weisskopf

Passenger journeys: (All modes and operators)
(2003) 216.0 million
(2004) 217.5 million
(2005) 218.5 million
(2006) 223.7 million (Bus 34.69 per cent, tram 12.29 per cent, metro 38.99 per cent, regional rail 14.03 per cent)
(2007) 224.5 million (Bus 34.66 per cent, tram 12.29 per cent, metro 38.97 per cent, regional rail 14.09 per cent)

Fare structure: Zonal, free transfer between all modes and operators
Fare collection: Season tickets (63.82 per cent), multiride tickets (17.80 per cent), single tickets (12.62 per cent), others (5.77 per cent); vending machines at metro stations and all tram stops, sales by driver only on buses
Operating costs financed by: Fares 44 per cent, subsidy/grants 56 per cent
Subsidy from: State 63 per cent, local 37 per cent

Current situation
Regional transit authority founded by city of Nuremberg and 17 other local authorities, with the Bavarian state government, to co-ordinate public transport in Nuremberg and the surrounding area. Federal government participation ended in 1996. Fare structures have been standardised, allowing free transfer between modes and operators. Schedules have been co-ordinated to reduce travelling time. Revenues are pooled between operators and local authorities provide subsidy. All planning and marketing is undertaken by VGN.

Developments
In 2006, the service area was enlarged, by the addition of another part of a rural district, to 11,620 km².
In December 2007, the area was again enlarged and is currently 11,750 km².

infra fürth verkehr GmbH
Leyher Strasse 69, D-90763 Fürth, Germany
Tel: (+49 911) 970 42 11   Fax: (+49 911) 970 46 07
e-mail: dialog@infra-fuerth.de
   verkehrsbetriebe@infar-fuerth.de
Web: www.infra-fuerth.de

Key personnel
Director: Dr Hans Partheimüller
Operating Manager: Klaus Dieregswiler
Marketing Manager: Vacant

Bus
Passenger journeys: (2000) 17.3 million*
(2002) 17.7 million*
(2003) 16.9 million*
(2004) 28.1 million
(2005) 29.0 million
*Without metro
Vehicle-km: (2000) 3.7 million
(2003) 3.8 million
(2004) 3.2 million
(2005) 3.1 million

Number of routes: 12
Route length: 103.3 km

Current situation
The former Fürth municipal operator, whose operations are conducted in close co-operation with VAG Nuremberg. Buses are purchased by Fürth, but operated on its behalf by VAG Nuremberg (now included with Nuremberg figures).

Fleet: 46 (25 standard and 21 articulated) plus 20 on hire

Metro
Current situation
Metro operated by VAG Nuremberg on behalf of infra fürth (see separate entry).

Erlanger Stadwerke AG (ESTW)
Äussere Brucker Strasse 33, D-91052 Erlangen, Germany
Tel: (+49 9131) 82 30   Fax: (+49 9131) 823 44 57
e-mail: kaufmaennischerBereich@estw.de
Web: www.estw.de

Key personnel
Directors: Wolfgang Geus
   Matthias Exner
Marketing Manager: Helmut Kandra

Bus
Passenger journeys: Not currently available
Vehicle-km: Not currently available

Route length: 28 km (estimate)

Current situation
Twelve services operated by VAG Nuremberg (www.vag.de) on behalf of ESTW.

Omnibusverkehr Franken GmbH (OVF)
Sandstrasse 38-40, D-90443 Nuremberg, Germany
Tel: (+49 911) 43 05 70
Fax: (+49 911) 43 05 71 99
e-mail: info@ovf.de
Web: www.ovf.de

Key personnel
Managers: Peter Heider
   Karl-Heinz Winkler
   Staff: 690 (estimate)

Passenger journeys: (Annual) 50 million (estimate)
Vehicle-km: (Annual) 46.7 million (estimate)

Current situation
Regional bus company, owned by DB Regio AG, providing suburban and rural services to a population of some 3.6 million and recording some 794 million passenger-km annually. Total route length is some 16,819 km.
   The company's fleet totals some 1,350 buses, of which 258 are own by OVF and 1,090 vehicles are owned by subcontractors. The full breakdown is not currently available, but includes MAN, Setra, Mercedes-Benz and Neoplan buses.

Gesellschaft Privater Verkehrsunternehmen im VGN mbH (GPV)
Postfach 2911, D-90013 Nuremberg, Germany
Tel: (+49 911) 21 46 77 37
Fax: (+49 911) 21 46 77 31
e-mail: info@gpv-nuernberg.de
Web: www.gpv-nuernberg.de

Street address
Hallplatz 2, D-90402, Nuremberg, Germany

Key personnel
Managers: Werner Reck, Werner Geiger

Current situation

Association representing 20 out of the 80 independent bus operators providing regional services as associate members of VGN.

Developments

Services in outlying areas are to be improved, especially feeders to rail stations.

DB Regio AG

Regio Mittelfranken
Hinterm Bahnhof 33, D-90459 Nuremburg, Germany

Tel: (+49 911) 219 38 82
Fax: (+49 911) 219 25 84
e-mail: Hilmar.Laug@bahn.de
Web: www.bahn.de/bayern

Key personnel

Manager and Spokesman: Hilmar Laug
Manager: Anja Seidl
    Staff: 2,870 (estimate)

Suburban railway

Type of operation: Suburban heavy rail

Passenger boardings: Not currently available

Current situation

Part of the Region Bayern, Mittelfranken services cover a network of 688 km centred on Nuremberg, serving 157 stations and halts and recording 881 million passenger-km annually.

DB operates suburban and rural services within the VGN area on S-Bahn and other regional routes. Lines radiating from Nuremberg are being upgraded to form an S-Bahn (regional metro) network under a public-transport-orientated, Total Traffic Plan limiting highway construction.

Services are operated by three- and five-car push-pull trainsets with electric locomotives running at 20 minute intervals during peak hours, and every 40 minutes off-peak.

Rhein-Ruhr

Population: 11.7 million (2005 estimate)

Public transport

The Rhein-Ruhr conurbation, covering an area between Düsseldorf and Dortmund, also encompasses the major centres of Duisburg, Mülheim, Essen, Bochum, Krefeld and Wuppertal and many smaller towns. Bus, express bus, trolleybus, tram, Stadtbahn (light rail) and S-Bahn (regional metro) services, provided by various local authority undertakings and German Railways (DB), are co-ordinated at a regional level by VRR. For local transport in main towns see individual entries.

Verkehrsverbund Rhein-Ruhr AöR (VRR)

Augustastrasse 1, D-45879 Gelsenkirchen, Germany
Tel: (+49 209) 158 40
Fax: (+49 209) 239 67
e-mail: info@vrr.de
Web: www.vrr.de

Key personnel

Chairman of the Administrative Board: Herbert Napp
Directorate: Martin Husmann,
    Klaus Vorgang

Current situation

VRR is responsible for co-ordinating public transport for the region. Its remit extends to marketing, planning, integration of services and operation of a common tariff system and public relations. After more than 25 years as a limited liability company, VRR became an institution under public law in September 2006 to ensure a more efficient organisation.

Public transport is organised according to a scheme consisting of three levels:

Political level: Communes and districts delegate their representatives to the board of association and the administrative board;

Management level: As an institution under public law, Europe's largest public transport authority has optimised its management to prepare it for coming challenges.

Operations level: Communal and regional transport companies (responsible for operating bus and tram lines) as well as commuter rail companies have signed co-operation agreements with VRR. These companies are also included in the decision making process.

The following transport companies are affiliated with VRR:

Abellio Rail NRW GmbH
Bahnen der Stadt Monheim GmbH
Bochum-Gelsenkirchener Strassenbahnen AG
Busverkehr Rheinland GmbH
DB Regio NRW GmbH
DSW21
Duisburger Verkehrsgesellschaft AG
Essener Verkehrs AG (EVAG)

Flughafen Düsseldorf GmbH
Hagener Strassenbahn AG
Kreisverkehrsgesellschaft Mettmann mbH
Mülheimer Verkehrsgesellschaft mbH
Niederrheinische Verkehrsbetriebe AG
Niederrheinische Versorgung und Verkehr AG
Niederrheinwerke Viersen mobil GmbH
NordWestBahn GmbH
Prignitzer Eisenbahn GmbH
Regiobahn GmbH
Regionalverkehr Niederrhein GmbH
Rheinbahn AG
StadtBus Dormagen GmbH
Stadtwerke Neuss GmbH
Stadtwerke Oberhausen AG
Stadtwerke Remscheid GmbH
Stadtwerke Solingen GmbH
Strassenbahn Herne-Castrop-Rauxel GmbH (HCR)
SWK Mobil GmbH
Verkehrsgesellschaft der Stadt Velbert mbH
Verkehrsgesellschaft Ennepe-Ruhr mbH
Verkehrsgesellschaft Hilden GmbH
Vestische Strassenbahnen GmbH
Wuppertaler Stadtwerke AG

Within the VRR area, the transport companies provide service on a total of 897 routes. An integrated interurban light rail (Stadtbahn) network is in operation and designed to complement the S-Bahn. There is also an extensive network of DB local and suburban rail routes, some of which form part of the S-Bahn network.

The following service concept has been implemented by VRR:

Regional Express Railway – hourly limited stop trains for intercity travel within the region;

Regional metro (S-Bahn);

LRT (Stadtbahn) – accelerated tramway and accelerated bus services promoted jointly as Express Bus (SchnellBus);

Urban services – by local tram and bus;

Night Express – late night services at weekends.

Vestische Strassenbahnen GmbH

Westerholter Strasse 550, D-45701 Herten, Germany
Tel: (+49 2366) 18 61 86, 18 60
Fax: (+49 2366) 18 64 44
e-mail: info@vestische.de
Web: www.vestische.de

Key personnel

Managing Director: Martin Schmidt
    Staff: 1,000 (estimate)

Bus

Passenger journeys: (2006) 50 million (estimate)
Vehicle-km: (2006) 20 million (estimate)

Route length: 1,279 km

Fleet: 237 vehicles

Neoplan N 4014 SB (1991)	7
Neoplan N 4014 Stadt (1992/3)	33
MAN NL 202 CE (1992)	7
Neoplan N 4021 (1992/3)	11
Neoplan N 4014CE (1993, 1996)	8
MAN NL 202 Stadt (1994)	13
MAN 222 CE (1996)	4
Neoplan N 4114 (1996)	3
Neoplan N 4020 (1997)	5
MAN NG 313 (1999)	12
Neoplan N4416 (2000/1/2)	43
Neoplan N 4407 midibus (2001)	7
Neoplan N 4421 (2002)	11
EvoBus Citaro (2003/4/6)	60
MAN NL 263 (2004)	11

Current situation

Local authority-owned bus company (formerly tramway) providing service in Recklinghausen and Bottrop and the densely populated area between and around these cities with a population of some one million residents.

Busverkehr Rheinland GmbH (BVR)

Worringer Strasse 34-42, D-40211 Düsseldorf, Germany
Tel: (+49 211) 16 99 00
Fax: (+49 211) 169 90 66
e-mail: info@bvr-gmbh.de
Web: www.bvr-online.de

Key personnel

Managing Director: Andree Bach
    Staff: 461

Passenger journeys: (1997) 40.7 million
(1998) 32.2 million
(2000) 32.5 million
Vehicle-km: (1997) 29.4 million
(1998) 26.3 million
(2000) 25.2 million

Fleet: 203 buses, plus 541 hired

Current situation

Regional bus company associated with DB, providing suburban and regional bus services on some 66 routes within VRR area and others beyond. Figures above apply to all BVR operations.

DB Regio NRW GmbH

Web: www.bahn.de
Type of operation: Regional metro (S-Bahn)

S-Bahn
Current situation

The S-Bahn Rhein-Ruhr network covers the area of the Ruhr valley (including Essen and Duisburg), parts of the Rhineland (Düsseldorf and Cologne) and parts of Westphalia (Dortmund and Unna).

Further information has been removed at the request of DB.

Stuttgart

Population: City 591,528 (2006), region 2.7 million (estimate)

Public transport

Bus, tramway/light rail, rack railway and funicular services provided by company with majority ownership by the city of Stuttgart, developing S-Bahn and associated feeder buses operated by German Railway (DB), other bus services by independent operators, all co-ordinated under Stuttgart Verkehrs- und Tarifverbund (VVS).

Verkehrs- und Tarifverbund Stuttgart GmbH (VVS)

Rotebühlstrasse 121, D-70178 Stuttgart, Germany
Tel: (+49 711) 660 60
Fax: (+49 711) 660 62 57, 66 06 24 00
e-mail: kontakt@vvs.de
Web: www.vvs.de

Key personnel

Directors: Witgar Weber
Thomas Hachenberger

Passenger boardings: (All modes)
(Annual) 305 million (estimate)

Number of lines/routes: Regional rail 17, commuter rail 6, tram/light rail 11, bus/trolleybus 352

Current situation

Regional bus and rail developments, fares and services, publicity and planning in an area in excess of 2,590 km² surrounding Stuttgart are all co-ordinated by a Verkehrsverbund formed in 1978 by Stuttgarter Strassenbahnen and DB to provide finance for and co-ordination of the developing Stadtbahn and urban bus network operated by SSB and the regional metro (S-Bahn) and associated feeder bus services operated by DB. The area includes the city of Stuttgart and 141 other towns and neighbourhoods, including Esslingen, Böblingen, Ludwigsburg and Rems-Murr-Kreis, with a total population of some 2.4 million. The only partners in VVS are SSB and DB, although 40 other transport operators are now associated with VVS.

The Verkehrsverbund is controlled by a board of representatives of SSB, DB and local authorities, including the Baden-Württemberg Land government. Tariff standardisation applies to an inner area centred on Stuttgart comprising four zones. There is integrated ticketing for the region.

There are currently approximately 16,000 parking spaces at park-and-ride facilities at rail stations.

Developments

In July 2005, the 1.75 km-long section of the U2 line was opened. Further improvements are under construction or planned for the S-Bahn network. Please see separate entry.

Also in 2005, a flexible monthly season ticket was introduced.

Fare structure: Zonal, single and multiride tickets; daily, weekly and monthly passes; annual subscription, discounted sales to employers who buy passes for all their staff; off-peak passes at reduced fares; first class available on S-Bahn; free transfers between modes and operators
Operating costs financed by: Fares 46 per cent, subsidy/grants 54 per cent
Subsidy from: Federal and state governments, city of Stuttgart, four surrounding counties

Stuttgarter Strassenbahnen AG (SSB)

Schockenriedstrasse 50, D-70565 Stuttgart, Germany
Tel: (+49 711) 788 50   Fax: (+49 711) 78 85 23 06
e-mail: service@mail.ssb-ag.de
Web: www.ssb-ag.de

Key personnel

Marketing/Administration: Dr Martell Beck
Tel: (+49 711) 78 85 24 27
e-mail: martell.beck@mail.ssb-ag.de
Legal Matters: Dr Harald Eberlein
Tel: (+49 711) 78 85 26 39
e-mail: harald.eberlein@mail.ssb-ag.de
Sales, Purchasing: Wolfgang Müllner
Tel: (+49 711) 78 85 27 51
e-mail: wolfgang.müllner@mail.ssb-ag.de
Corporate Planning: Dr Volker Christiani
Tel: (+49 711) 78 85 25 97
e-mail: volker.christiani@mail.ssb-ag.de
Staff: 2,740

Passenger journeys: (All modes)
(2006) 187.4 million
(2007) 187.2 million

Operating costs financed by: Fares 51.3 per cent, grants 20.0 per cent, subsidy 7.5 per cent and other revenue 21.1 per cent
Subsidy from: Local authority subsidy; federal and state grants for new investment

Current situation

SSB's majority shareholder is the city of Stuttgart. Operations extend outside the city to serve a total population of 970,000, with co-ordination on a regional level with DB under VVS.

Fare collection: Prepurchase from offboard ticket-issuing machines and ticket offices, or driver on buses only; cancellation/validation machines on board
Fare structure: Zonal; single, day and multiride tickets; weekly, monthly and annual passes; 61 per cent use passes
Integration with other modes: Free transfer in VVS areas with Stadtbahn, S-Bahn and regional rail and bus services

Bus

Passenger journeys: (2007) Not currently available
Vehicle-km: (2007) 14.9 million

Number of routes: 54
Route length: 674 km
On priority right-of-way: 14.9 km

Developments

In accordance with the INVK (Integrated Local Transport Planning) strategy, bus services in parts of the city and region are being restructured. Parallel with development of the LRT network, buses act mainly as feeders for the light rail and S-Bahn lines, and duplication of rail services is avoided.

Bus flow improvements in progress include provision of more bus lanes, projecting kerbs at stops, traffic signal priority and integration in computer-based monitoring. Special service of 10 night bus routes operates on Friday and Saturday nights.

Fleet: 265 vehicles

Mercedes-Benz O 405 (1995/96)	23
Mercedes-Benz O 405 G articulated (1992/95)	48
Mercedes-Benz O 530 (2003/07)	36
Mercedes-Benz O 530 G (2000/07)	114
Mercedes-Benz O 53GL articulated	4
MAN NL 313 (2001)	30
MAN NL 363 (2002)	10

In peak service: Not currently available
Average age of fleet: 6.8 years

Most intensive service: Peak 7½ min
One-person operation: All routes
Average distance between stops: 534 m
Average speed: 22.7 km/h

Tramway/light rail

Type of operation: Conventional metre-gauge tramway completely replaced by 1,435 mm gauge Stadtbahn (LRT) by the end of 2007, with mixed 1,435/1,000 mm gauge operation on two sections only for museum vehicles.

Passenger journeys: (2007) Not currently available
Car-km: (2003) Stadtbahn 10.2 million, tram 1.2 million
(2004) Stadtbahn 12.1 million, tram 1.2 million
(2005) Not currently available
(2006) Not currently available
(2007) 13.5 million (Stadtbahn and tram)

Route length: Stadtbahn 123 km, rack 2.2 km
  reserved track: 123 km (Stadtbahn)
  in tunnel: 23.5 km
Number of lines: Stadtbahn 16
Number of stops: 196
Gauge: 1,435 mm (Stadtbahn) and 1,000 mm (rack railway)
Max gradient: 8.5%
Minimum curve radius: 50 m
Electrification: 750 V DC, overhead

Current situation

The conversion from metre-gauge tramway to standard-gauge light rail (Stadtbahn) was completed in December 2007. There is 23.5 km of tunnel in the city centre. Dual Gauge tracks remain on some routes and are used for historic tram operations.

Developments

The northern branch of U15 to Stammheim is scheduled to be finished by 2010.

The building works for an extension of U6 to Fasanenhof started in 2008. A further extension of the line to the new exhibition centre at Stuttgart International Airport is at planning stage.

A new line LRT-line U12 is at the planning stage, as a result of the Stuttgart 21-Project of Deutsche Bahn AG. The S21-project aims to convert the terminus-main station in Stuttgart into an underground through-station.

Rolling stock: 169 cars

Duewag DT8.4-9 Stadtbahn (1985/93/96)	M114
Adtranz/Siemens DT8.10-11 (1999/2005)	M50
MAN/SLM rack-Stadtbahn (1982)	M3
Funicular	2

On order: 20 DT8.13 (60 DT8 cars have been rebuilt)

Service: Peak 6–7½–10 min, off-peak 10–12 min
First/last car: 04.45/00.15
Arrangements for elderly/disabled: 174 of the 183 high-platform stations are accessible by ramp or lift
One-person operation: All routes
Operational control: Computer-based monitoring also provides passenger information

Rack railway/funicular
Current situation

A 2.2 km rack line on the Riggenbach-Lamelle system links Marienplatz with Degerloch, metre-gauge, 18 per cent maximum gradient, 680 V DC overhead, three cars with bicycle trailers.

Regional Bus Stuttgart GmbH (RBS)

PO Box 10 39 37, D-70034 Stuttgart
Tel: (+49 711) 66 60 70   Fax: (+49 711) 66 60 79 99
e-mail: info@rbs-bus.de
Web: www.rbs-bus.de

Key personnel

Managing Director: Manfred Hovenjürgen
  Staff: Not currently available

Current situation

Regional bus company owned by DB runs a network of routes as feeders to the S-Bahn, carrying about 49 million passengers a year on services over a total area of approximately 11,841 km².

Fleet: 304 buses, plus 412 contracted

DB Regio AG

Regionalverkehr Württemberg
Ehmannstrasse 56, D-70191 Stuttgart, Germany
Tel: (+49 711) 20 92 71 60   Fax: (+49 711) 20 92 71 86
e-mail: ran-baden-wuerttemberg@bahn.de
Web: www.bahn.de/baden-wuerttemberg

Key personnel
Commercial Manager: Peter Rumpf
Technical Manager: Frank Buermeyer
   Staff: 797

Current situation
Part of the Region Baden-Württemberg, Württemberg services cover a network of 920 km centred on Stuttgart and serve 143 stations and halts.
   For further information on DB, please see *Jane's World Railways.*

S-Bahn Stuttgart
Presselstrasse 17, D-10191 Stuttgart, Germany
Tel: (+49 711) 20 92 70 87   Fax: (+49 69) 26 52 05 99
e-mail: S-Bahn.Stuttgart@bahn.de

Key personnel
Commercial Manager and Spokesman:
   Hans-A Krause
Technical Manager: Werner Faulhaber
   Staff: 550 (estimate)

Type of operation: Regional metro (S-Bahn)

Passenger journeys: (Annual) 120 million (estimate)

Current situation
S-Bahn trains run over six routes with a total length of 177 km serving 10 stations, electrified 15 kV 16⅔ Hz overhead. Peak-hour trains every 15 min, off-peak 30 min. Suburban trains also run on 12 non-S-Bahn routes with a route length of 375 km. Operations co-ordinated under VVS.

Developments
There are plans for an extension of line S1 to Wendlingen and Kirchheim.
   Expansion of the single-track section from Freiberg to Benningen to double-track is under way, with construction currently scheduled to be completed in 2008.

Rolling stock: 90 ET 420 and 58 ET 423 three-car trains
On order: None

Wuppertal
Population: 363,522 (2002), area served 465,400

Public transport
Bus and monorail services provided by municipal company also responsible for other public utilities, under overall policy control of city and co-ordinated by Verkehrsverbund Rhein-Ruhr (VRR). City also served by DB rail services as part of Rhein-Ruhr network.

Wuppertaler Stadtwerke AG (WSW)
Bromberger Strasse 39-41, D-42281 Wuppertal, Germany
Tel: (+49 202) 56 90
Fax: (+49 202) 569 45 90

e-mail: wsw@wsw-online.de
Web: www.wsw-online.de

Key personnel
Supervisory Board Chairman: Peter Jung
Executive Committee: Claudia Fischer,
   Rainer Hübner, Heinz-Werner Thissen
   Further information has been removed at the company's request.

DB Regio AG
DB Regio NRW GmbH
Region Nordrhein-Westfalen, Geschäftsbereich Rhein-Ruhr
Hollestrasse 3, D-45127 Essen, Germany
Tel: (+49 201) 175 25 07   Fax: (+49 201) 175 23 02
Web: www.bahn.de/nordrhein-westfahlen

Key personnel
Head of Region: Thorsten Siggelkow

Type of operation: Suburban heavy rail

Current situation
Extensive suburban services including express routes (SB) link Wuppertal with other cities in the Rhein-Ruhr. The city's S-Bahn route is the east-west line from Hagen through Wuppertal to Düsseldorf, Neuss and Mönchengladbach, opened in 1988 as S8 (see Rhein-Ruhr entry).

Greece

Athens
Population: City 745,500, urban area 3.1 million, Greater Athens metropolitan area 3.8 million (estimates)

Public transport
State-owned company OASA is responsible for overall planning of public transport under the supervision and control of the Ministry of Transport and Communications. OASA is also responsible for the financial support of three operating companies: ETHEL (Thermal Bus Corporation) and ILPAP (Athens-Piraeus Area Electric Buses), which operate buses and trolleybuses, and ISAP, which operates suburban rail services. Suburban bus services also provided by a private company, KTEL N Attikis. Two new metro lines operating since February 2000; metro expansion under construction. Tram operations by public company, an affiliate of Attiko Metro SA, under the Ministry of Transport & Communications, started operations in 2004.

Attiko Metro SA
191-193 Messogion Avenue, GR-115 25 Athens, Greece
Tel: (+30 210) 679 23 99
(+30 210) 679 20 30 (Public Relations Division)
Fax: (+30 210) 672 61 26
(+30 210) 679 20 93 (Public Relations Division)
e-mail: info@ametro.gr
Web: www.ametro.gr

Key personnel
Chairman: George Yannis
Vice-Chairman: Emmanouil Drakakis
General Manager and Board Member: Theodoros
   Kontogiannopoulos
   Staff: 420

Type of operation: Full metro; first commissioned in January 2000

Athens metro and suburban rail network

1124830

Current situation
Attiko Metro SA was founded in 1991 by the Greek State to design, construct and operate the Athens Metro.

Attiko Metro awarded Bechtel Company a contract for the provision of technical services and technical support for the period 1991–2002.

Metro train at Halandri Station   1149667

Sections of Lines 2 and 3 of the metro system were commissioned in January 2000. The Athens-Piraeus Railway, designated Metro Line 1, continues to be managed and operated separately (see separate entry for ISAP), however, both systems are being marketed jointly as Metro.

Developments
The Line 3 extension from Ethiniki Amyna to Doukissis Plakentias and Athens Airport was also commissioned in August 2004. This extension consists of an underground section of 5.9 km and an overhead section of 20.7 km (used by both Attiko Metro and the Suburban Railway). During the first phase of its operation, this extension had three stations – Halandri, Doukissis Plakentias and Airport, whilst, during the second phase of this extension, Pallina, Kantza and Koropi stations were added on the shared network. In March 2007, the contract was signed for the construction of Holargos, Nomismatokopio and Aghia Paraskevi Stations, to complete the initial line.

Seven new trains with a maximum speed of 120 km/h (fully air-conditioned and with special areas for luggage) connect the centre of the city (Syntagma) with the airport in approximately 30 minutes.

The first phase of the extensions was completed with the opening of the Line 3 extension from Monastiraki to Egaleo (4.3 km with three stations) in June 2007.

The second phase of the extensions includes (estimated dates of completion, up to 2009):
- Line 2 extension from Aghios Antonios to Anthoupoli (2 km, two stations, 2009);
- Line 2 extension from Aghios Dimitrios to Elliniko (5.5 km, four stations, 2009);
- Three intermediate stations on Line 3 extension from D Plakentias to the Airport (2009);
- Line 3 extension from Egaleo to Haidari (1.5 km, one station, 2009).

Further extensions include:
- Line 3 extension from Haidari to Piraeus (7.5 km, six stations, put out to tender in June 2006, to be completed in 2013 (estimate));
- Line 4, a new Metro line, which will have a total length of 20.9 km and 20 stations (funds not yet secured).

Hanwa Rotem has delivered 21 new trains (126 cars), 14 of which will be used on Lines 2 and 3 and the remainder (dual-voltage, air-conditioned vehicles) will be used on the airport service.

In November 2007, a contract was signed for the installation of an air-conditioning system in the 14 trains for Lines 1 and 2.

The resources required for the purchase of 17 new trains have been secured, and the relevant procurement process commenced in April 2008.

Operating costs financed by: Fares 80 per cent, other sources 20 per cent

Passenger boardings: (2004) 600,000 daily (including the sections commissioned in 2004)
(2005) 600,000 daily
(2006) 650,000 daily
(2007) 650,000 daily

Route length: 30 km
Number of lines: 2
Number of stations (all in tunnel): 27
Gauge: 1,435 mm
Electrification: 750 V DC, third rail

Service: Peak 3 min, off-peak 6–10 min
Integration with other modes: Interchange with ISAP Line 1 at Attiki, Omonia and Monastiraki Stations
Surveillance: CCTV, public address and emergency telephones at all stations
Rolling stock: 49 six-car trains
ALSTOM (1998/99)   M84 84
Rotem (2003/04)   M126

ETHEL SA – Thermal Bus Company
6 Parnassou Street, GR-182 33 Athens, Greece
Tel: (+30 210) 493 30 02; 491 87 88
Fax: (+30 210) 492 21 55
e-mail: ethel@ethel.gr
Web: www.ethel.gr

Parent organisation
OASA (please see separate entry in).

Key personnel
President of the Board: Vassilis Spanakis
Managing Director: George Stergiou (tentative appointment)
Staff: 6,950 (of which 70 per cent drivers, 3 per cent dispatchers/supervisors, 12 per cent technicians/mechanics, 15 per cent executive/administrative/other)

Background
ETHEL was established in 1994 pursuant to Law 2175/1993 as one of OASA's subsidiary companies, responsible for providing transportation with thermal buses within the area of OASA's operation, a service which until then was under the jurisdiction of an independent OASA Division.

In 1996, ETHEL's Articles of Association were adjusted to the provisions of Law 2414/1996 concerning Modernisation of Public Corporations and Organisations. Improvement works were implemented at existing Depots, the Repair Base and the Central Offices.

Current situation
The reconstruction of 1,100 new slots and four fuel supply boxes was implemented at the Anthousa depot. Mechanical equipment was purchased at the existing Depots and Repair Base. The preliminary architectural study was completed for the construction of the new Anthousa depot. The tender documents were completed for the integrated technical fleet maintenance and materials' management IT system.

Developments
The investments scheduled for 2007 were:
- Construction of a new depot on land owned by ETHEL at Anthousa. The design of the project has been completed and put out to tender.
- Renovation and modernisation projects on existing depots and central offices.
- Preliminary steps required to construct the Thriasio Plain Depot (administrative authorisation) on a 120,000 m² plot (formerly the Liosis Army Camp) in the Ano Liosion area.

The procurement of 520 new buses has been tendered and the contract is expected to be signed by the end of the year (2007). Specifically, the tender refers to the procurement of 100 18 m articulated buses, 220 8.6 m micro-buses and 200 CNG buses. The project has been included in the 3rd CSF Railways, Airports and Urban Transport Operational Programme.

Bus
Passenger boardings: (2002) 369 million
(2003) 379 million
(2004) 379 million (estimate)
(2005) 362 million
(2006) 358 million
Vehicle-km: (2002) 100.2 million

Number of routes: 324
Route length: (Both directions) 7,546 km
Depots: 8

Current situation
Most buses feature low kneeling floor, air conditioning and noise insulation. 700 buses have special equipment for invalid person's accessible trips. All diesel buses comply with EURO 4 specifications for gas emissions.

Mercedes-Benz Elbo 0405GN articulated bus   1330361

Den Oudsten Alliance City bus 1330360

Fleet: 2,093 vehicles
Standard buses: Van Hool A 300, Ikarus, Den
Oudsten, Neoplan N 4016, Renault Agora (416 CNG
buses), Irisbus Agora S, MRC Elvo O405N C93 &
C97, Mercedes-Benz 1,531
Articulated buses: Volvo B7L, Volvo
B10M, MRC Elvo O405 GN C97 338
Mini-Midibuses: Midi Neoplan,
Van Hool A 507 224
In peak service: 1,900 vehicles

Most intensive service: 5 min
One-person operation: 100 per cent
Fare collection: Validation machines, tickets sold at
kiosks
Fare structure: Flat; annual, monthly, weekly, daily
passes
Fare evasion control: Roving inspectors
Average peak-hour speed: 16 km/h
Operational control: 300 bus controllers;
telematics-assisted computer monitoring for CNG
buses currently in operation (planned extension to
cover entire fleet)
Operating costs financed by: Fares 35 per cent,
other sources (mainly loans), subsidies/grants
62 per cent

Ilektriki Sidirodromi Athinon-Pireos SA (ISAP) – Athens-Piraeus Electric Railways Company SA

67 Athinas Street, GR-105 52 Athens, Greece
Tel: (+30 210) 324 83 11-17
Fax: (+30 210) 322 39 35
Web: www.isap.gr

Key personnel
Managing Director: Nicolaos Papathanassis
General Technical Manager: Nickolaos Skoulariotis
Staff: 1,270 (April 2006)

Operating costs financed by: (2005) Fares 41 per
cent, subsidies/grants 19 per cent, lending
40 per cent

Background
Athens-Piraeus Electric Railways SA is a
company which was established by the 10-
12/2.1976 legislative act and was ratified by Law
352/1976. ISAP SA is a Legal Entity of Private
Law and operates as a Société Anonyme. ISAP
SA is a subsidiary company of OASA SA (Athens
Urban Transportation Organisation) as per Law
2669/1998.

Current situation
ISAP operates the 750 V DC Athens-Piraeus
Electric Railway linking Kifissia in the north with
Athens and Piraeus, which is now designated
Line 1 of the metro system. For a map of the
Athens metro system please see the entry for
Attiko Metro.

During the period 2000–03, 120 new vehicles
(Adtranz/Siemens/Hellenic Shipyards) were
delivered.

Developments
Modernisation of the Athens-Piraeus line has
been carried out. Capacity has increased from
17,000 to 22,000 passengers per hour and
direction. The daily capacity is estimated to
increase by 25 per cent from 400,000 to 500,000.
This is being achieved by increasing and renewing
the rolling stock and by the improvements to
the track and traffic signalling system. A new
state-of-the-art control centre further assists the
primary goal by guaranteeing the required safety
levels for the enhanced operation.
In addition, reconstruction and renovation
work has taken place at all of the stations to
improve the system's appeal and passenger
safety. All stations are now accessible to disabled
and elderly passengers.
Service has already been inaugurated in all of
the renovated stations. ISAP Metro Line 1 was a
major transport service for spectators during the
Athens 2004 Olympic Games. It provided direct
connection between the two most important
venue sites – Athens Olympic Sports Complex
and Faliro Coastal Zone Sports Complex – and
the city centre, while providing transfers to all
the other modes (metro lines, Olympic Express
Buslines, suburban railway and tram lines).
A new station, Neratziotissa, was built, located
between Marousi and Irini stations, to link Line 1
with the Elefsina-Spata airport motorway (Attiki
Odos) and suburban railway.
All trains are now air-conditioned.

ISAP – Metro Line 1
Type of operation: Metro

Passenger boardings: (2003) 105 million
(2004) 110 million
(2005) 117 million
(2006) 125 million
(2007) 132 million

Route length: 26.5 km (double track)
in tunnel: 3 km
Number of lines: 1
Number of stations: 24
in tunnel: 3
Gauge: 1,435 mm
Track: Timber and concrete sleepers on ballast
Max gradient: 4%
Minimum curve radius: 145 m
Tunnel: Cut-and-cover
Electrification: 750 V DC, third rail

Rolling stock: 243 cars, 44 trains
MAN/Siemens (1985–95), 5-car trains 123
Adtranz/Siemens/Hellenic Shipyards
(2000–03), 6-car trains 120
In peak service: 175

Service: Peak 3½ min
Integration with other modes: Interchange with
Line 2 at Attiki and Omonia stations and with
Line 3 at Monastiraki station; interchange with
suburban rail (PROASTIAKOS) at Neratziotissa
station; interchange with tram line at Faliro
station
First/last train: 05.00/01.00
Fare collection: Tickets from manned kiosks and
vending machines at all stations; ticket validation
machines at entry
Fare structure: Annual, monthly, daily passes
Surveillance: CCTV at all stations
Arrangements for elderly/disabled: Access at all
stations (since mid-2004)

ILPAP SA – Athens-Piraeus Area Electric Buses
Kirkis & Achaias Street, New Philadelphia, GR-
143 42 Athens, Greece
Tel: (+30 210) 258 33 00-06
Fax: (+30 210) 253 30 50
e-mail: grammatia@athens-trolley.gr
Web: www.athens-trolley.gr

Key personnel
Managing Director: Avraam Gounaris
Staff: 1,497

Background
Founded in 1970 and is a subsidiary of OASA SA.

Neoplan articulated trolleybus, Model N6221, in special livery 0583927

Current situation

ILPAP operates one of the largest trolleybus fleets in the European Union. Environmental advantages favour trolleybuses; accordingly most of the routes serve the central business district.

Two new trolley lines replaced existing bus trunk lines with environmentally friendly services. One more is under final approval. Reallocation of scheduled trips in the existing lines was performed.

The company has modernised its fleet; 366 (315 standard 12 m and 51 articulated) new anti-polluting, air conditioned low-kneeling-floor vehicles are already in operation. All new vehicles are equipped with a hybrid diesel engine for flexibility in case of road blockages and operational capacity during electric power failures.

Developments

A new depot for parking, maintenance and repair of the fleet vehicles will be constructed in the Rouf area. In this way, 'dead' mileage is to be reduced and, as a result, a decline in the operating costs is anticipated.

Trolleybus

Passenger journeys: (2002) 85.2 million
(2003) 78 million
(2004) 77 million
(2005) 77.2 million
(2006) 80 million
Vehicle-km: 29,833 (daily average)

Number of routes: 22
Route length (both directions): 348 km

Fleet: 366 trolleybuses, Van Hool, Neoplan and Elvo/Sfakianakis

Van Hool/Alstom/Sfakianakis	112
Neoplan/Kiepe/Elvo	254

In peak service: 300

Most intensive service: 7 min
One-person operation: 100 per cent
Fare collection: Prepurchase ticket, monthly or annual pass at kiosks; validation machines on board
Fare structure: Flat; monthly passes
Fare-evasion control: Random inspection
Operational control: Route inspectors; mobile radio
Average peak-hour speed: 14.2 km/h
Operating costs financed by: Fares 30.2 per cent, other sources (mainly loans) and subsidies/grants 69.8 per cent
New vehicles financed by: Loans, government grants for investment EEC (ETPA)

KTEL N Attikis

Kotsika 2, Pedion Areos, Athens 10434, Greece
Tel: (+30 210) 884 29 73

Type of operation: Suburban bus

Current situation

KTEL N Attikis provides frequent suburban bus services from three terminals in central Athens to various points within the surrounding Attica prefecture.

OASA SA – Athens Urban Transport Organization

15 Metsovou Street, GR-106 82 Athens, Greece
Tel: (+30 210) 820 09 59; 884 27 16-19
Fax: (+30 210) 821 05 08
e-mail: oasa@oasa.gr
Web: www.oasa.gr

Key personnel

President of the Board: Dimitris Tsaboulas
Managing Director: Konstantinos Matalas (in transition to) Abram Gounaris (by tentative appointment)

General Director, Transportation Department: Panagiotis Kontogiannis
General Director, Finance and Commercial Division: Spyridon Giannakopoulos
Staff: 174

Key budget figures for Athens Public Transportation System (all modes)

2006
Revenues from fares: EUR264 million (187 single tickets, 74 monthly passes, 3.75 annual passes)
Revenues from subsidies: EUR130.00 million
Revenues from other sources (compensation for concessionary tickets): EUR15 million
Operating expenses: EUR632 million
Total expenses: EUR798 million
Total Investments: EUR61.6 million
Older loan payment: EUR157 million
New loans: EUR489 million (in corporate bonds)

Operating costs financed by: (2005) Fares and concessions 43 per cent

Key Annual Ridership Figures

2006
Bus: 357 million
Trolleybus: 81 million
Metro: 304 million
Tram: 14.5 million
Total (including suburban railway): 758 million

Background

OASA was established in 1993 as successor to the similar body OAS (first founded in 1977). Its legal framework is set in the 2669/98 Public Transport Act. The Administrative body and the Managing Director are responsible for the company's management. Apart from its mission as the main authority for public transportation throughout the city, it is also responsible for organising management, financial support, marketing and promotion of three operating companies, established as subsidiaries under the same law. OASA's three affiliates are ETHEL SA, created in 1994 to operate all bus services, ILPAP SA, established in 1970, which provides all trolleybus services and ISAP SA, established in 1976, which is responsible for Line 1 of the Athens metro. Law 3297/2004 provided that urban public transport is to be carried out exclusively by OASA's subsidiary operators (ETHEL, ISAP, ILPAP) and transportation providers: AMEL, which is responsible for Lines 2 & 3 of Athens Metro; TRAM which is responsible for tramway lines; PROASTIAKOS which is responsible for suburban rail; and with which OASA is contracted. Please see separate entries for each of these companies.

Current situation

The Athens Urban Transport Organisation (OASA) is a Legal Entity of Private Law. It is totally owned by the Greek State, applying the principles of private economy and performing for public benefit under the supervision and the control of the Ministry of Transport and Communications. OASA is responsible for planning, control and co-ordination, implementation and operation of all public transport modes in the Greater Athens area.

• A Restructuring Plan was planned and implemented in the Municipalities and Communities of areas under OASA's jurisdiction. This includes:
• A network of local and inter-municipal bus lines was developed for the efficient feeding of track-guided means of transport, especially in the areas where new metro stations have been established;
• A series of supplementary actions were implemented (introduction of 14 new bus lines, extension or changes to 57 existing lines, amendment of routes to 35 lines);
• Additional night bus service on certain main corridors;
• Reducing and/or completely removing bus terminals from particularly busy points in the centre of Athens and setting up bus and interchange stations;
• Transport services to support development of the Olympic Village in the Municipalities of

Acharnes and Thrakomakedones were extended. Furthermore, a study by OASA, and in co-operation with the Municipality of Ano Liosia, lead to the reorganisation of the area's transport network.

• The Athens Sightseeing Public Bus Line service is now offered throughout the year, connecting various places of tourist interest (museums, archeological sites) with central hotel establishments and the central business district.
• Implementation and/or authorisation of new bus-priority lanes on several main avenues (4 km in total) and studies for additional lanes in Athens and Piraeus central districts (5 km in total). Bus priority measures now includes busways, with-flow bus priority lanes and contra-flow (including bus lanes in the middle of the street) for a total length of 51 km. In addition, pavement extensions are installed at 335 central bus stops to stop illegal parking. Bus stop lighting systems are installed, powered by solar energy.
• Productivity enhancements to the operation of the 15 crane vehicles towing illegally parked cars and thus preventing intersection blocking with the use of GPS receivers and the implementation of central management. 24-hour and weekend operation has been established. Further procurement of five additional cranes is under way. Increased numbers of monitoring cameras for the enforcement of bus lanes restrictions in most major road arteries.
• The General Planning Study for Athens Transportation System is in progress. The total allocated budget is in the range of EUR4.7 million, and is funded partially by European Union (Third Community Support Framework). The object of the study is the development and the compilation of a strategic plan for the Transportation Network of Attica for the next decade, aiming at optimising the operation and performance of the Public Transportation System. A series of surveys (household survey, passenger private modes, traffic counts, transit ridership) have already been conducted in 2006 in order to feed an update of the Origin-Destination matrices for the entire Attica region. An adjunct study was also conducted for the Port of Piraeus greater area with the purpose of evaluating alternatives for fixed-guided mass transit. Additional budget is allocated in the development of modelling and forecasting tools for immediate, short-term and long-term planning. The current studies are scheduled to be completed by the end of 2008, which will lead to the compilation of a medium- to long-term Transportation Master Plan for Attica.
• A fare-use study is been conducted as a prerequisite for the proportional allocation of the combined fare revenues among the operating companies. The study will evaluate ridership in the several available public transport modes in relation to the type of fare utilised.
• Hiring to fill 52 new staff positions is in the final stage. Half of the new positions are allocated in the formation of a new ticket evasion/control team, whereas the rest include various scientific positions (transportations engineers, economists, health professionals etc) in addition to administrative staff.

Developments

Projects and further developments currently being undertaken or under consideration, include:
• A custom trip-planner system was developed in-house to assist the call centre clerks. An Internet based trip-planner was developed in addition to the in-house application. The system is fed with a slightly more compact (lighter) version of the transportation services database, which is currently updated once per month. The web-page, which has been online since the end of 2005, is currently hosted under an external research consultant and was created through a pilot project financed by the Ministry of Development. There is a plan to commit to a formal maintenance contract in the future, which will include the provision for several info-kiosks in central locations. Further

extensions of the current systems will include feeds from the telematics infrastructure that is gradually implemented across the fleet of buses and trolleys.

- **Automatic Fare Collection System:** The project for the procurement and implementation of the Automatic Fare Collection System (AFCS) with a total budget of EUR28.8 million relates to replacement of yearly and monthly paper coupons and cards and those coupons/cards issued to special categories of passengers with 'smart' tickets. The tender for the project was published in October 2006 and at the current stage (April 2007) it is at the phase of technical evaluation of offers. The completion of the tender and execution of the contract are expected to be completed during 2007. The project's completion is expected within 20 months from the execution of the Contract.
- **New Telematics System:** The project refers to the 'Procurement, Installation and Maintenance of the OASA Telematics System' and is implemented on behalf of OASA, ETHEL and ILPAP. The project's objective is the development of an integrated system for the supervision of 2,200 ETHEL buses and 366 ILPAP trolleys and dynamic information to passengers at 150 smart stations.
- The Public Transport Observatory's research program was issued with the purpose of collecting various transport data. Studies were conducted for passenger traffic, fare types, route times and speed in public transportation means, congestion signs at crucial network points, traffic and transit composition as well as measurements of offences in bus lanes. Furthermore, the combined operation of the Observatory and THEPEK (Crisis and Emergency Weather Condition Management Centre) has made it possible to calculate specific quantitative indicators to evaluate the transport services offered. The Observatory appointment is now re-extended.

Organismos Sidirodromon Ellados (OSE) – Hellenic Railways Organisation

1-3 Karolou Street, GR-10437 Athens, Greece
Tel: (+30 210) 524 75 41   Fax: (+30 210) 524 32 90
Web: www.ose.gr

Key personnel
President: Nikolaos Baltas
Managing Director: Dionysios P Chionis
Director, Passenger: Christos Toubanakis
    Staff: Not currently available

Type of operation: Suburban rail

Passenger journeys: (All operations)
(2003) 8.9 million
(2004) 9.4 million
(2005) 9.9 million
Train-km: Not currently available

Background
The Hellenic Railways Organisation (OSE) was formed in January 1970 to integrate, organise

and develop Greek rail transport. It is wholly state-owned and has a number of subsidiaries.

OSE operates passenger services on its standard gauge main trunk line north from the capital, Athens, to Thessaloníki.

For further information on OSE, please see *Jane's World Railways.*

Trenose SA
Key personnel
President: Aggelos Androulidakis
Managing Director: Panagiotis Ktenidis
    Staff: Not currently available

Current situation
Trenose SA is the operator of OSE's passenger and freight services, as well as the railway's telecommunications network.

Developments
Major work is in progress in Athens to create a standard gauge suburban network with some electrification. By 2011 it is expected to extend to 281 km. This includes a line from the port of Piraeus via Athens Larissa station and an interchange known as SKA (Acharnes Transportation Centre), in the north of the city, to Eleftherios Venizelos (EV) airport in the east. This section of the project was completed in time for the Olympic Games in August 2004, albeit using diesel traction. It involved construction of 20 km of new line and the upgrading of an existing 10 km. Between Plakentia and the airport, the line is shared by OSE and metro trains. The line provides a 30-minute journey time between Larissa station and EV.

Subsequent stages of the project provided for a new double-track line from SKA to west to Corinth and on to Kiato, including a new bridge over the Corinth Canal. This section was due to open in 2007. Gauge conversion of the metre-gauge line from Corinth to Xylokastro is to be completed by 2009. Extension of the system south from EV to the port of Lavrio (33 km), mainly using the alignment of an abandoned metre-gauge line, was at the environmental impact stage in 2007, with completion projected for 2012. North of SKA suburban trains will use the existing line to Inoi, Thiva and Khalkis.

TRAM SA – Athens Tram

Aeroporias Street, Helliniko, Greece
Tel: (+30 210) 997 80 00   Fax: (+30 210) 991 15 43
e-mail: info@tramsa.gr
    commercial@tramsa.gr
Web: www.tramsa.gr

Key personnel
President: Alexandros Vrachnos*
Managing Director: Christos Anastassopoulos*
General Manager: Vacant*
Chief Communications Officer: Lilly Gallis
    Staff: 500

*These three positions are currently being reviewed by the Minister of Transport & Communications.

Type of operation: Tram network, opened July 2004

Passenger journeys: Approx 65,000 per day
Vehicle-km: Not currently available

Gauge: 1,435 mm
Electrification: 750 v DC, overhead/pantograph
Number of routes: 3
Route length: (Both directions) 56 km
Number of stops: 48
Scheduled itineraries: 400 daily trips

Background
TRAM SA – Athens Tram is a public company under the Ministry of Transport & Communications and a subsidiary of Attiko Metro SA. The company was founded in 2001 for the planning, development, construction and operation of the tram network.

Current situation
Three tram lines have been in operation since July 2004 (before the beginning of the Athens Olympic Games). Passenger traffic amounts to 65,000 on all 400 itineraries per day.

Developments
A further extension of the current network to the central port of Piraeus has been approved by both the Minister of Transportation and the Piraeus Mayor and is now under study with the aim for the extended network to be fully operational during 2009. The network extension from Glyfada to Voula has been completed and is due to start commercial operations in October 2007.

A new depot for parking, maintenance and repair of the fleet vehicles was constructed in the area occupied previously by Athens old airport field at Helliniko.

A complete overhaul of the intersection traffic lights has been carried out in order to reduce accident rates and to increase operating speeds by pre-emption and other priority measures.

Fleet: 35 five-car tramcars
Ansaldobreda Sirio low-floor LRV (2003–4)   35
In peak service: 30

Most intensive service: 7$\frac{1}{2}$ min
One-person operation: 100 per cent
Fare collection: ATMs at all stops; Tram kiosks at all major stops; validation machines on/off board
Fare structure: Zonal; short-distance tickets; monthly passes; discounted fare
Fare-evasion control: Random inspection
Operational control: Operational Control centre (OCC); route inspectors via cameras; Global Inspection System (GIS) and mobile radio
Average peak-hour speed: 23 km/h

Hungary

Budapest
Population: 1.77 million (2001)

Public transport
Bus, trolleybus, tramway, rack railway, suburban railways and metro operated by former municipal undertaking; river ferries; commuter rail services by Hungarian State Railways.

Transport matters are overseen by the following authority:

Ministry of Economy and Transport
Pf 111, H-1880 Budapest, Hungary

Street address
V Honvéd utca 13-15, H-1055 Budapest V ker, Hungary
Tel: (+36 1) 374 27 00
Fax: (+36 1) 302 23 94
e-mail: ugyfelszolgalat@gkm.gov.hu
Web: www.gkm.gov.hu

Key personnel
Minister of Economy and Transport: Janos Koka
Deputy State Secretary for Transport: Csaba Zsolt Horvath
Railways Department: Istvan Pakozdi

Budapest Transport Privately Held Corporation (BKV Ltd)
Akácfa u 15, H-1072 Budapest, Hungary
Tel: (+36 1) 461 65 00   Fax: (+36 1) 461 65 71
e-mail: ugyfelszolgalat@bkv.hu
Web: www.bkv.hu

Key personnel
Chief Executive Director: Attila Antal
Deputy Chief Executive Officer for Transport: László Somodi
Deputy Chief Executive Officer for Technology: Zsolt Balogh

Deputy Chief Executive Officer for Finance:
Norbert Tóth
Deputy Chief Executive Officer of Sales and Communications: Miklós Regöczi
Human Resources Director: Dr Eleonóra Szilágyi Szalai
Strategic Director: Gyula Bosnyák
Metro Line 4 Project Directorate:
Staff: 13,822 (12,817 full time) (2006)

Passenger boardings (All modes): (2003) 1,400 million (estimate)
(2006) 1,300 million (approximate)
Vehicle-km: (2006) 179 million

Operating costs financed by: Fares 40.4 per cent, price supplement 26.4 per cent, other commercial sources 5.4 per cent, municipal grants 27.8 per cent.

Current situation
BKV Ltd provides services under contract to the Municipality of Budapest. It operates the city's bus, trolleybus, tram, metro, funicular and suburban railways.

The company is currently undergoing structural change, details of which are not yet available.

In 2006, BKV Ltd's turnover was some HUF107.287 billion.

Developments
In 2006, investment by the Municipality of Budapest totalled HUF65.12 billion, of which HUF120.55 million was a subsidy in the form of capital reconstruction by the general Assembly of the Municipal Council.

Bus and trolleybus
Passenger journeys: (2006) Bus: 532.8 million, trolleybus: 75.7 million
Vehicle-km: Not currently available

Number of routes: Not currently available
Route length: Bus: 796.9 km, trolleybus: 66.3 km (2006)
Number of stops: Bus: 3,702, trolleybus: 280 (2006)

Developments
In 2006, 50 low-floor articulated Volvo buses were added to the fleet.

Fleet: Bus: 1,438 (2006), trolleybus: 165 (2006)
Bus
Full breakdown of fleet is not currently available, but includes:
IK 260
IK 415
IK 412
IK 405
IK 280 articulated
IK 435 articulated
Volvo 7700A 60 ft articulated (2004–06)   150
Trolleybus
Full breakdown of fleet is not currently available, but includes:
ZiU-9 35 ft
IK-280T
IK-435T
IK-411/412T
Solaris Trollino

On order: Some Solaris Trollino trolleybuses are still to be delivered

Most intensive service: Bus: 3–30 min peak, 6–60 min off-peak; trolleybus: 2–12 min peak, 7–15 min off-peak
One-person operation: All routes
Average distance between stops: Bus: 440 m; trolleybus: 340 m
Fare structure: Flat, pre-purchase tickets or passes, day and weekly tickets, monthly and annual passes. Unified pass system (BEB)
Fare evasion control: Random inspection
Arrangements for elderly/disabled: Accessible buses on 17 routes; reduced fares for monthly and annual passes
Operational control: Route inspectors/mobile radio with computerised monitoring under development
Average speed: Bus: 16.5 km/h, trolleybus: 11.9 km/h

Metro
Type of operation: Full metro, including one small-profile line opened in 1896

Passenger journeys: (2006) 280.1 million
Car-km: Not currently available

Route length: 31.4 km
Number of lines: 3 (including small-profile Millennium Line 1)
Number of stations: 78
Gauge: 1,435 mm
Max gradient: 4%
Minimum curve radius: 300 m
Tunnel: Bored single-track
Electrification: 825 V DC, third rail; Millennium Line, 600 V DC overhead
Operating fleet: 392 cars (23 articulated cars on the Millennium Line) (2006)

Service: Peak 2–3 min, off-peak 4–9 min
First/last train: 04.30/23.10
Fare structure: Flat, prepurchase; day, weekly and monthly and annual tickets issued for other modes also valid on metro; discount booklets for 10 or 20 trips. Unified pass system (BEB)
Revenue control: Cancellers at inwards gates
Signalling: CTC; ATC with driver-only operation installed on Line 3
Surveillance: CCTV on platforms and escalators
Average speed: 23.9 km/h

Developments
In 2005, BKV awarded a contract to Siemens Transportation Systems (TS) for the supply of a new control, signalling and safety system for Line 2, which is currently being reconstructed. The contract was valued at EUR 26 million and the system is due to go into operation in June 2008.

In 2006, BKV ordered 170 Metropolis metro cars from an Alstom-led consortium, Budapest Metropolis Consortium. The contract was valued at some EUR247 million. The order comprises of 15 four-car train sets for use on Line 4 when it is completed and 22 five-car sets to replace the existing stock on Line 2. The contract includes three years maintenance of the new vehicles and an option for a further seven four-car sets for a planned extension to Line 4.

There are plans for a new Line 5, construction on which is due to start in late 2007. Longer-term plans include extensions to Line 3 and Line 1.

During 2006, a number of improvements were made to Metro Line 2. These included renewal of two stations, rail replacement in two tunnels and renovations of maintenance and storage facilities.

Metro Line 4 project (proposed)

DBR Metro Project Directorate
Kéthly Anna tér 1. 3 emelet (Greenpoint 7 irodaház), H-1077, Budapest, Hungary
Tel: (+36 1) 411 30 50
Fax: (+36 1) 411 30 51
e-mail: info@metro4.hu
Web: www.metro4.hu

Key personnel
Deputy Chief Executive Officer for Metro Line 4:
Ferenc Olti
Project Director: Árpád Balogh

Background
The General Assembly of the Capital City established DBR Metro Ltd in 1997 (under the BKV Public Transport Company's authority) with the purpose of preparing and co-ordinating the metro project development. Since February 1999 the organisation has been operating under the name of BKV Rt DBR Metro Project Directorate (BKV Rt DBR Metró Projekt Igazgatóság).

The scope of the activities of this organisation includes investment tasks, the central co-ordination of project progress, assignment of the tasks to be carried out (implementation is a duty of the consultation companies selected by tender procedures), as well as the management of project financing.

Current situation
Construction is under way, but the project is now unlikely to be completed before 2010.

Light rail/tramway
Type of operation: Light rail and conventional tramway

Passenger journeys: (2006) 334.9 million
Car-km: Not currently available
Figures include passenger journey for cogwheel railway

Route length: 237.7 km (2006 – unduplicated)
Number of lines: 33
Number of stops: 678
Gauge: 1,435 mm
Track: Vignole 48.5 kg/m, Phoenix 59 kg/m rail. About 75 km to light rail standards
Electrification: 600 V DC, overhead

Operating fleet: 718 vehicles (2006)
Fleet breakdown is not currently available, but includes:
ICS 27 m high-floor double-articulated
Tatra T5C 40 ft
TW 6000 80 ft (ex-Hannover)
Siemens Combino Plus (2006/07)   38
On order:

Service: Peak 3–10 min, off-peak 5–15 min
First/last car: 04.00/23.45
Fare structure: Flat; day, weekly and monthly tramway season tickets valid on suburban railway, metro and trolleybuses, but not on buses, rack railway or river buses. Unified pass system (BEB)
Integration with other modes: Full integration, with buses acting as feeders for light rail and metro services
One-person operation: All routes
Average speed: 13.4 km/h

Developments
In 2006, 26 new Combino trams were added to the fleet and the Hungaria tram depot was reconstructed. Platforms have been adjusted for the new low-floor trams, and modern shelters have been built. Modernisation of the Grand Boulevard power supply system was also carried out.

Rack railway/chair lift/funicular
Current situation
The Varosmajor-Szechenyihegy rack line, 3.7 km, 1,435 mm gauge, is electrified at 1.5 kV DC. It carried 2.8 million passengers in 1996. There is also a chair lift linking Janoshegy and Zugliget (1 km), and the Buda Castle funicular.

Rolling stock: seven two-car sets
SGP (1973)   M7 T7

Suburban railway (HÉV)
Type of operation: Suburban rail

Passenger journeys: (2006) 57.5 million
Vehicle-km: Not currently available
Track length: 239.5 km
Number of stops: 139
Average speed: 22.4 km/h

Operating fleet: 294 cars (196 four-axle locomotives/motorcars + 98 four-axle coaches/trailers)

Current situation
Fourteen routes are served from five main lines, total 230.5 km with 139 stations, 1,435 mm gauge, electrified 1.1 kV DC. Trains run every 5–15 min at peak times, 10–60 min off-peak, all one-man operated. Flat fare within city boundaries, zonal elsewhere. The HÉV lines are owned jointly by the municipalities of Budapest and the districts served.

BKV Hajózási Szolgáltató Kft
Zsilip Utca 11-13, H-1131 Budapest, Hungary
Tel: (+36 6) 209 55 33   Fax: (+36 1) 369 13 59
e-mail: kulonjarat@bpship.hu
Web: www.ship-bp.hu

Type of operation: River ferries

Current situation
A fleet of 17 vessels operates a 20 min service on four routes (one summer only), carrying 204,000 passengers in 1995.

MÁV Co Ltd – Hungarian State Railways Co Ltd
Magyar Államvasutak Rt, Andrássy út 73-75, H-1940, Budapest, Hungary
Tel: (+36 1) 322 06 60   Fax: (+36 1) 342 85 96
e-mail: mail@mav.hu
Web: www.mav.hu

Key personnel
Chairman: Dr László Udvari
General Manager: Zoltán Mándoki
Special Director, Passenger Services: Ferenc Vizsy
Infrastructure: Dr Tibor Zsákai
Assistant General Managers:
  Economics: Annamaria Benczédi
  Personnel: Dr Flórián Kugler
  Chief of International Affairs Department: József Lovas

Type of operation: Suburban heavy rail

Background
MÁV Co Ltd was originally established in June 1993.

Current situation
From 1997, new InterPici services began, running over distances of 30 to 60 km and feeding into MÁV's InterCity network. In 2002, these provided 31 train-pairs over 13 routes. They employ refurbished dmus to provide connections with smaller communities at distances of up to 50 km from main centres and offer a standard of travel close to that of intercity services.

Developments
Plans to develop a 23 km rail link between Budapest Nyugati station and the city's Ferihegy airport have been proposed. If adopted, the scheme would be implemented by a joint venture company in which MÁV would hold a share. A study commissioned by MÁV and property developer TriGranit, which reported in early 2001, found that the link could be completed at a cost of US$80 million. Some private sector funding would be required to complete the scheme. Around one-third of the line's route would entail new construction, including a 650 m tunnel to provide access to the airport terminal. A journey time of 19 minutes is foreseen, with a service frequency of three trains an hour.
For further information on MÁV, please see *Jane's World Railways.*

India

Ahmedabad
Population: City 3.7 million, metropolitan area 5.1 million (2006 estimates)

Public transport
Bus services provided by municipally owned undertaking. Metro proposed.

Ahmedabad Municipal Transport Service (AMTS)
Transport House, PO Box 142, outside Jamalpur Gate, Ahmedabad 380022, India
Tel: (+91 79) 25 39 18 81; 86   Fax: (+91 79) 25 35 45 68
e-mail: contact@amts.in
Web: www.amts.in

Key personnel
Transport Manager: T G Jhalawadia
  Staff: 3,838

Developments
AMTS has adopted route rationalisation to minimise bus transfers, reduce congestion inside major terminals and increase route lengths for enhanced crew utilisation.

Bus
Passenger journeys: (2003/04) 127.6 million
(2004/05) 127.6 million
(2005/06) 211.4 million
(2006/07) 271.7 million
Vehicle-km: (2004/05) 29.57 million
(2005/06) Not available
(2006/07) 33 million

Number of routes: 180

Route length: 2,219 km

Fleet: 892 vehicles
Full breakdown of fleet is not currently available, but includes:
Ashok-Leyland single-deck
Others
Average number of buses on the road: 727
Average age of fleet: 9.86 years

Most intensive service: 10 min
Fare collection: Conductor
Fare structure: Stage
Fare evasion control: Random inspection with penalty
Average peak-hour speed: 18.3 km/h
Operating costs financed by: (2006/07) Fares 79.6 per cent, other commercial sources 5.4 per cent
Operating ratio: (2006/07) 125.6 per cent

Ahmedabad
Metro (proposed)
The Delhi Metro Rail Corporation (DMRC) prepared a detailed project report for metro corridors for Ahmedabad and submitted this to the state government in June 2005.
The proposed system is for two lines. Line 1 would run from Aksardham to Vasage (32.65 km) and Line 2 to Thartej (10.9 km) with a total length of 43.55 km. The cost of the project is estimated at INR42 billion.

Bangalore
Population: 6.7 million (estimate)

Public transport
Bus services provided by Metropolitan Transport Corporation; privately owned buses and minibuses and auto-rikshaws; metro and suburban rail systems proposed.

Bangalore Metropolitan Transport Corporation (BMTC)
Central Office, KH House, Shanthinagar, Bangalore 560027, India
Tel: (+91 80) 295 25 01   Fax: (+91 80) 295 24 01
e-mail: bmtc@bgl.vsnl.net.in
Web: www.bmtcinfo.com

Key personnel
Managing Director: U Tripathy
Director, technical: O Hemaraju
  Staff: 20,582

Current situation
Before 1997, bus services in Bangalore were provided by two divisions of Karnataka State Road Transport Corporation (KSRTC) – BTS (North) and BTS (South). At that time Bangalore city operations were separated from KSRTC and placed under an independent government-owned corporation: Bangalore Metropolitan Transport Corporation (BMTC). It now has 30 depots, four

Buses in Bangalore   1136459

major bus stations, 31 sub bus stations and one central workshop. Each depot's holding is around 125 buses. BMTC has managed to prove that urban transport can be a financially viable activity, as it makes profit.
During 2006/07, BMTC made a profit of INR2,074 million.

Developments
The number of depots is being increased to 24 to improve control. Until four years ago there were only 13 depots. There have been 348 new buses added to the fleet and 127 buses removed. Some buses connect villages in the areas surrounding the city with the main routes, indicating the

One of the first of the new Volvo city buses to go into service in Bangalore (Volvo Bus Corporation)
1208968

BMTC low-floor bus (K K Gupta)   1115189

BMTC single-deck articulated (vestibule) bus (K K Gupta)   1115190

difference on red boards. Paid monthly passes of different types are being introduced for the convenience of the public. Passengers with impaired vision travel free. Several benefits are being offered to these pass holders. In addition to the purchase of these passes at counters established by BMTC, customers can now also purchase passes on the Internet. A bus tracking system based on GPS and GIS (Geographical Information System) was installed on 1,100 vehicles of BMTC for monitoring of operations.

In early 2006, the first of 25 Volvo low-floor city buses started operation in the city. The city bus is built using the B7RLE chassis and the bodywork is based on the Volvo 8700. As well as low entry, the buses have wheelchair ramps and air conditioning. A new call centre has been opened.

Bus

Passenger journeys: (2003/04) 976.8 million
(2004/05) 1,086.6 million
(2006/07) 1,277.5 million
Vehicle-km: (2003/04) 260 million
(2004/05) 306.3 million
(2006/07) 346.9 million

Number of routes: 1,383

Fleet: 4,859 vehicles
Full breakdown of fleet is not currently available, but is believed to include:
Tata
Ashok Leyland
Volvo B7RLE
Minibuses
Hired buses

On order: 25 Volvo B7RLE buses have been received and assembly has been carried out in Bangalore
Average age of fleet: 4.31 years

Most intensive service: 5 min
One-person operation: 189 point-to-point services
Fare collection: By conductor on vehicle, through computerised booking at Shivaji bus stand, through sale of monthly passes, or exact fares in coinbox
Fare structure: Distance-related
Fares collected on board: 95.4% (2.6% by concession passes, 2% by street conductors)
Fare evasion control: Inspectors
Operating costs financed by: Fares 119.5 per cent, 21.3 per cent by other sources of revenue
Operating ratio: (2006/07) 83.64 per cent

Bangalore Metro Rail Corporation Ltd (BMRCL)

3rd Floor, BMTC Complex, KH Road, Shantinagar, Bangalore 560 027, India
Tel: (+91 80) 22 96 93 00
Fax: (+91 80) 22 96 92 22
e-mail: bmrcl@dataone.in
Web: www.bmrc.co.in

Key personnel

Managing Director: N Sivasailam
Director (Rolling Stock, Signalling & Electrical): D D Phauja
Director (Project & Planning): B S Sudhir Chandra
Chief Engineer (Design & Underground): N P Sharma
Chief Engineer (Reach 3): Arvind Kumar
Chief Engineer (Reach 1): Dani Thomas
Chief Engineer (Extensions & Depot): Captain Doddihal
Chief Engineer (Reach 2): P N Nayak
Chief Engineer (Reach 4): H S Prakash Kumar
Chief Engineer (Traction & General Services): R K Roy
Chief Engineer (Signalling & Telecommunications): A S Shanker
General Manager (Accounts) & Company Secretary: Anil B Shedbal
Environmental Officer & General Manager (Administration): C Jayaram
Chief Public Relations Officer & Deputy Chief Engineer, Electrical: B L Yashavanth Chavan
Staff: Not currently available

Type of operation: Mass rapid transit system (under construction)

Current situation

The Bangalore Metro Rail system has been designed to support an integrated public transport system.

The metro, branded the Namma Metro, will run through the commercial and residential areas of the city. It will consist of two lines, electrified (750 v DC, third rail), the North-South and East-West Corridors, covering a total length of 41.8 km. The East-West corridor will be 18.1 km long and the North-South corridor will be 23.7 km long. Of the total 41.8 km, 6.8 km. will be underground and the rest will be elevated.

The frequency of the Metro trains will initially be every four minutes reducing to three minutes,

based on demand. The travel time from end to end on the East-West corridor will be 33 minutes, and on the North-South corridor 44 minutes. The system is designed for a maximum train speed of 80 km/h. The commercial speed is 32 km/h. The tracks will be standard gauge (1.435 m). The Bangalore Metro has been designed for a capacity of 40,000 Peak Hour Peak Direction Trips (PHPDT). The number of passengers expected to travel on the metro every day are projected at 10.20 lakhs (1.02 million) in 2011 and 16.10 lakhs (1.61 million) in 2021.

Developments

Construction work on the first elevated section from Baiyappanahalli to Mahatma Gandhi Road (7 km – Reach 1) began in January 2007 and commercial operation of this section is expected to commence by December 2010. The full network is expected to be commissioned by September 2012.

The total project outlay envisaged is INR6,395 crores/million, which is proposed to be financed by way of equity (30 per cent); the debt is financed by the shareholders to the extent of 25 per cent subordinated debt to the senior term debt of 45 per cent. 60 per cent of senior debt is funded by Japan International Cooperation Agency (JICA) and the remainder from local banks.

Project status as at October 2008
Utility Diversion

Diversions of utilities, such as moving water and sewerage pipes, electricity lines, lamp posts, traffic signal posts, telephone cables etc, are at various stages of implementation.

Environment

15,000 saplings have been planted and are being nurtured in lieu of 1,500 trees to be pruned or removed. An environmental base-line monitoring survey has been conducted. A noise and vibration study near archaeological monuments has been undetaken under the auspices of the National Physical Laboratory, New Delhi. A hydrological survey has been conducted by IISc, Bangalore for underground tunnelling works.

Elevated Section Viaduct works
The contract for the construction of a viaduct in Reach-1 (Baiyappanahalli to Cricket Stadium) has been awarded and has been in progress since April 2007.

Work relating to the construction of piers and the casting of segments (in casting yard) is in progress.

Detailed Design Consultants (DDC) of viaducts in Reach 2 and 3 appointed and the work of design and preparation of BOQ/drawings is complete.

The tender for construction of viaducts in Reach 2 and Reach 3 is finalised and the Letter of Agreement (LOA) will be issued shortly.

The tender for the construction of a viaduct in Reach 4 has been issued and will be opened shortly.

Underground Section
Pre-qualification documents for stations, tunnels (including Ventilation and Air-Conditioning (VAC)) approved by JICA. Seven consortia have participated. They are under evaluation. Main tender likely to be issued by end October 2008.

Depots
Baiyappanahalli in Reach 1: yard works, such as levelling, road and boundary wall works, in progress. For depot works, tender documents have been issued.

Peenya in Reach 3: survey of land completed. Tender document for Package – I works, such as levelling, internal roads and boundary walls, issued.

Rolling Stock
The rolling stock suppliers' technical documents for the tender bids are under evaluation.

Signalling & Telecommunications
Five pre-qualification tenders have been shortlisted after a global tender. Main tenders have been issued to the five pre-qualified bidders.

Electric Traction
Main tender document issued.

Automatic Fare Collection
Eleven companies/consortia have been pre-qualified for the automatic fare collection system. Main tender under preparation for issue to the pre-qualified contractors.

Escalators & Lifts
Pre-qualification tender bids for the elevators are being invited.

Five companies have been pre-qualified to participate in the main tender.

Operation Control Centre
Tender document issued as part of Baiyappanahally Depot Package – II.

South Western Railways
Divisional Office, 560023, Bangalore, India
Tel: (+91 80) 287 14 98
e-mail: cpro@southwesternrailway.in
Web: www.southwesternrailway.in

Key personnel
General Manager: T N Perti
Chief Public Relations Officer: B S Dashrathi

Type of operation: Local/commuter rail services

Current situation
Suburban services operate over several routes into Bangalore City station.

Double-tracking is in progress, with dmu services proposed.

Bombay (Mumbai)
Population: Conurbation 15.4 million, metropolitan area 17.7 million (2001 Census)

Public transport
Bus and ferry services provided by municipal undertaking, and by state road transport corporation in suburban areas. Intensively used suburban rail network of Central and Western railways. Extensive use of taxis and autorickshaws and private company and school buses. Metro under construction.

Brihan Mumbai Electric Supply & Transport Undertaking (BEST)
Best Bhavan, Best Marg, PO Box 192, Mumbai (Bombay) 400001, India
Tel: (+91 22) 22 85 62 62
Fax: (+91 22) 22 85 12 44
e-mail: transport@bestundertaking.com
Web: www.bestundertaking.com

Key personnel
General Manager: Uttamrao Khobragade
Assistant General Manager: G R Jagtap
Public Relations Officer: A S C Tamboli
  Staff: 30,905 (2008)

Passenger journeys: (2003/04) 1,610 million
(2004/05) 1,636 million
(2006/07) 1,503 million
(2007/08) 1,553 million
Vehicle-km: (2003/04) 241.3 million
(2004/05) 239.0 million
(2006/07) 237.3 million
(2007/08) 226.4 million
Number of routes: 387
Route length: (One way) 5,824.2 km

Current situation
BEST has 25 Depots and the total service area is divided into five zones. The primary role of BEST is to supplement the suburban railway system. The Undertaking has a well-equipped training school for the traffic staff. Midibuses are run in those areas where it is not possible to operate standard buses, due to the narrowness of the roads. 'Ladies first' buses run at various points, where ladies are given priority.

BEST's losses are subsidised by its Electricity Supply Division.

Developments
Bus Pass Scheme: The scheme was introduced by BEST Undertaking with effect from 2 January 2007. The Bus Passes are in the form of a contactless smart card with a built-in electronic chip that stores information of the validity period of the bus pass, the destinations of travel permitted on the pass, value of the bus pass, passenger's identity card number etc. The bus passes are issued to the commuters through various Service Delivery Points (SDPs) spread across the operational area. On-board bus conductors and field inspectors, posted for checking passenger tickets, validate these bus passes with the help of a Hand Held Terminal (HHT).

Grab Handles: BEST has appointed an advertising company to replace existing grab handles with those of international design and standard. The space on the grab handles will be sold by the company as advertising space and the revenue will be shared with BEST on a fixed income per bus per month basis.

Installation of Drop Boxes in buses by M/s Vodafone: M/s Vodafone Ltd has installed Drop Boxes in BEST buses. One drop box is installed per bus behind the driver's cabin area. Their customers drop their payment cheques in these boxes and BEST receives non-operating revenue towards fixed rental charges and cheques collection charges per bus every month.

Installation of Surveillance System on BEST Buses: Closed Circuit Television (CCTV) equipment, comprising two cameras (one each at the entry and exit) and a four channel digital video/audio recorder, are being installed on all buses. The system will be financed, installed and maintained by M/s EMNET SAMSARA on a Build, Own and Operate (BOO) basis. Under this project, two LCD Screens will also be installed in every bus. These LCD screens are capable of displaying advertisement, entertainment and/or public information messages.

Fleet: 3,884 (2008)
Full breakdown of fleet is not available currently, but comprises:

Single-deck (diesel)	2,022
Single-deck (CNG)	762
Double-deck	178
Midibus (diesel)	63
Midibus (CNG)	112
Air conditioned	72
Mumbai Urban Transport Project (MUTP)	644
Low-floor	31

In peak service: 3,727 (2008)

Average age of fleet: 5.54 (2008)
Most intensive service: 1 min
One-person operation: 5 routes
Fare collection: Conductors issue pre-printed tickets; pre-paid smartcard

Fare structure: Distance-related/telescopic
Fare evasion control: Organised checking system
Operating costs financed by: Fares 93 per cent; 7 per cent by other sources of revenue
New vehicles financed by: Internal resources and loans from financial institutions

Maharashtra State Road Transport Corporation (MSRT)
Maharashtra Vahatuk Bhavan, Dr Anandrao Nair Marg, Mumbai (Bombay) 400008, India
Tel: (+91 22) 23 02 29 00   Fax: (+91 22) 23 08 69 52
e-mail: mstnsk@bomb6.vsnl.net.in (Mumbai Division)

Key personnel
Vice-Chairman and Managing Director: O P Gupta
Secretary: B G Punckar
  Staff: 102,299 (2006/07)

Passenger journeys: (2004/05) 2,140.7 million
(2006/07) 2,167.3 million
Vehicle-km: (2004/05) 1,814 million
(2006/07) 1,751 million

Current situation
MSRT operates extensive services throughout Maharashtra State. In 2006/07 the average size of the fleet was 15,352. The average age was 5.09 years.

MSRT provides service in the Thane, Raigad and Palghar divisions of the Bombay metropolitan region, though its city operations account for less than five per cent of the total.

Developments
The Corporation has recently started air-conditioned bus services on selected routes and has also changed the design of its standard buses, making them more comfortable and attractive. It has also advertised recently that it wishes to hire 25 new 45-seater Volvo/King Long buses.

Delhi Metro Rail Corporation (DMRC)
C-14&15, Bandra-Kurla Complex, Bandra East, Mumbai (Bombay) 400 051, India
Tel: (+91 22) 26 59 00 01 – 26 59 00 08 (eight lines)
Fax:(+91 22) 26 59 12 64
e-mail: mmrda@giasbm01.vsnl.net.in
Web: www.mmrdamumbai.org

Key personnel
Metropolitan Commissioner: T Chandra Shekhar
Director, MRTS: G R Menon
  Tel: (+91 22) 26 59 41 44   Fax: (+91 22) 26 59 12 64
  e-mail: pdmutp@vsnl.net

Type of operation: Metro (under construction)

Current situation
In 2003, the Mumbai Metropolitan Region Development Authority (MMRDA) appointed the Delhi Metro Rail Corporation (DMRC) to prepare the master plan for the Mumbai metro. This was duly accepted by the Government of Maharashtra. The DMRC subsequently submitted Detailed Project Reports (DPRs) for two routes: Versova-Andheri-Ghatkopar (total length 11 km, all elevated, with 12 stations) and Colaba-Charkop (36 km). It is proposed to build a complete metro network of 146 km in three phases to cover the areas not connected by the existing suburban rail network. In phase one, the Varsova-Andheri-Ghatkopar, Colaba-Mahim-Charkop and Bandra-Kurla Mankhurd sections (62.44 km) will be built.

Developments
In June 2006, the Prime Minister laid the foundation stone for the The Versova-Andheri-Ghatkopar (VAG) corridor. It has a projected ridership of 475,000 passengers per day by 2009–10 (at commencement of operations) and is proposed to be operated by four-car air-conditioned vehicles. There will be three-aspect automatic signalling and a central control centre. Stations will have an automatic fare collection system installed and there will be lifts for less-able passengers. The new system will be integrated with bus, taxi and rickshaw services and there will be interchanges with suburban railway at two stations. The total estimated capital cost, at 2003 prices, is INR9,703 million.

Journey time over VAG will take 21 minutes and frequency of trains will initially be 5 minutes, reducing to 3.5 minutes during peak hours. Track will be standard gauge (1,435 mm) with ballastless track.

A depot and Operations Control Centre (OCC) will be located at D N Nagar.

A Special Purpose Vehicle (SPV), MUMBAI METRO ONE PVT Ltd, has been set up by the government to implement the VAG corridor. This is a Joint Venture Company consisting of MMRDA, Reliance Energy Pvt Ltd and Veolia Transport, France. MMRDA is the nodal agency for the development of Metro system and is also the concessioning authority for the VAG corridor.

Construction of Mumbai's metro was formally inaugurated on 4 October 2006. The MMRDA is to take a 26 per cent equity stake in the project which is to be built under a 35-year BOOT concession. Completion of Line 1 is expected in 2009 and will provide interchanges to both the Central Railway's Harbour line at Mankhurd and Bandra on the Western Railway.

Detailed planning was approved for Line 2 in September 2006. Line 2 will interchange with Line 1 at Bandra, which will also see construction of Line 3, an underground route to Colaba. Line 2 is scheduled to open in 2011 when ridership is forecast at 1.2 million passengers per day. MMRDA will also take a 26 per cent stake in Line 2 when bidding is completed for the 35-year Build-Own-Operate-Transfer (BOOT) concession. The Maharashtra State Government has agreed to provide Rs16 billion towards construction of Line 2.

Western Railway (WR)
Churchgate, Mumbai 400020, India
Tel: (+91 22) 22 09 75 65; 76 19
Fax: (+91 22) 22 01 76 31
e-mail: gm@wr.railnet.gov.in
Web: www.wr.indianrail.gov.in

Type of operation: Suburban heavy rail

Passenger journeys: (2003/2004) Not available
(2004/2005) 1,146 million
(2005/06) 1,104 million

Background
Western Railway in its present form came into existence in November 1951, with the merger of the Bombay, Baroda and Central India Railway (BB&CI), with other State Railways – Saurashtra, Rajputana and Jaipur. In 1964, the railway was extended to Mumbai.

Current situation
Extremely heavy traffic is carried on WR's electrified suburban route between Bombay's Churchgate station and Virar (60.6 km, 28 stations). The suburban section has now been extended by another 64 km to Dahanu Road. 1,043 suburban trains run daily on the Churchgate and Virar section. Coupon validation machines have helped to reduce the queue length at suburban station ticket windows.

Developments
It has not been possible to increase the number of trains in proportion to the growth in patronage, but many trains have been extended from nine to 12 cars. At present 511 services are operated by 12-car trains. This has enabled an increase in capacity in excess of 33 per cent. With the completion of the quadrupling of track on the Borivali -Virar section, 20 new trains have been added in that section.

Tracks, signalling and traction systems are being improved to permit augmentation of services. A INR330 million train management system has been installed on the suburban network. Provision of automatic signalling on the Virar-Dahanu Road section, and the balance of the work of providing a fifth line from Andheri to Borivali, have been completed.

The work of converting the existing 1.5 kV DC system to the more efficient 25 kV AC traction is now also being carried out by MRVC on both Western and Central railways due to limitations of the DC system. VVVF-controlled three-phase drive equipments are being provided on the emus for dual-voltage operation during the transition. First AC/DC emu rake was introduced on the suburban section in June 2001.

The work to quadruple the track between Borivali and Virar was completed in July 2007.

Rolling stock: 971 emu cars M430, T541

Central Railway (CR)
Chatrapati Shivaji Terminus, Mumbai 400001, India
Tel: (+91 22) 22 62 12 30   Fax: (+91 22) 22 62 45 55
e-mail: gm@cr.railnet.gov.in
Web: www.centralrailwayonline.com

Key personnel
General Manager: S B Ghosh Dastidar
Chief Public Relations Officer: Sunil Jain
    Staff: Not currently available

Type of operation: Suburban heavy rail

Passenger journeys: (2003/2004) 1,100 million
(2005/06) 1,155 million

Current situation
CR now operates the most extensive suburban network in the country. It provides 1,236 services daily from Chatrapati Shivaji terminus to Khopoli (115 km), Kasara (121 km) on the main line, and to Panvel (50 km), Andheri (21 km) on the Harbour branch, and associated lines.

It carries nearly 3.4 million passengers daily, serving 73 stations.

For further information on CR, please see *Jane's World Railways.*

Developments
The existing infrastructure of the suburban railway system has reached its limit of performance and CR has devised short-term and planned long-term measures to augment capacity. Some of the short-term measures taken in the recent past are operating 12-car emus, respacing of signals to reduce headways, strengthening of track structures and augmentation of power supply, together allowing an improvement in frequency from 5 to 3.5 minutes. As a long-term solution, provision of an independent corridor is essential for operation of suburban services. As a part of this, construction of a third pair of tracks between Diva and Kalyan is in progress. The work of conversion of DC to AC traction is presently being undertaken by MRVC.

During 2006/07, the traction system from Kasara to Titwala was made suitable for 25 kv AC. Due to this, 13 AC/DC emu rakes were introduced for service. This enabled increase in speeds to 00 kmph and the conversion of nine to 12-car rakes on nine services. Buzzer facility was provided to indicate to the handicapped persons the position of their coach at 33 suburban stations. For increased security, 73 CCTVs have been installed at 37 stations. The railway is also developing a pilot project for a smart card ticketing system which will greatly help in reducing queues for tickets and the handling of cash.

The World Bank has approved a loan of INR16.13 billion for the Mumbai suburban sections of the Central Railway and the Western Railway.

Rolling stock: M382, T759

Mumbai Railway Vikas Corporation Ltd (MRVC Ltd)
2nd Floor, Churchgate Railway Station Building, Mumbai 400 020, India
Tel: (+91 22) 22 08 00 15, 22 01 46 23
Fax: (+91 22) 22 09 69 72
e-mail: commrvc@vsnl.net
Web: www.mrvc.indianrail.gov.in

Key personnel
Managing Director: P C Sehgal
Chief Public Relations Officer: Prakash Rao Vazalwar
    Staff: Not currently available

Current situation
MRVC was incorporated in July 1999 and became operational in April 2000 with an equity capital of INR250 million subscribed by IR and the government of Maharashtra. MRVC is executing suburban rail projects identified in the Mumbai Urban Transport Project (MUTP) (www.mmrdamumbai.org/projects_mutp.htm) for augmentation and optimisation of the Mumbai suburban rail system. The MUTP, when completed, aims to bring down the passenger number per nine car train to 3,000 (as against the existing 5,000).

The rail component of Phase I of the MUTP consists of:
5th & 6th Lines Kurla – Thane;
Optimisation of Central Railway;
Optimisation of Harbour line;
5th line Mahim – Santacruz;
Quadrupling of Borivali-Virar section;
Optimisation of Western Railway;
DC to AC conversion (1,500 V DC to 25 kV AC);
emu procurement & manufacture;
Stabling lines for emus;
Maintenance facilities for emus;
Virar car shed;
Track machines;
Institutional strengthening & studies;
Resettlement & rehabilitation.

Infrastructure components comprise: Addition of 93 track km – base figure 790 km (excluding loop line and yards) (34 km in Thane-Turbhe-Vashi section and 53 km in Virar-Borivali section under MUTP have since been added); introduction of dual-voltage 101 new nine car rakes. 51 on additional account and 50 on conversion account; resettlement & rehabilitation of approximately 15,000 Project Affected households; Operation of 12-car rakes on all lines (excluding Harbour line) by lengthening of all platforms; achieving three minutes headway on all the lines (re-spacing of signalling to be carried out); DC to AC conversion in all suburban sections except Thane-CSTM section (to be taken up in Phase II).

Phase II of the MUTP consists of:
5th & 6th lines CSTM – Kurla;
5th & 6th lines Thane – Diwa;
6th line Borivali – Mumbai Central;
Extension of Harbour Line from Andheri to Goregaon;

DC to AC conversion (1,500 V DC to 25 kV AC) (CSTM –Thane section); Station Improvement and Trespassing Control Scheme; Resettlement & Rehabilitation; emu procurement & manufacture; Maintenance facilities for emus; Stabling lines for emus; Technical assistance & institutional strengthening.

Infrastructure components comprise: Addition of 88 track km – existing 790 km and 93 km being added in MUTP Phase I; 96 new nine car rakes; DC to AC conversion in Thane – CSTM section (172 Track km), completing the DC-AC conversion on Mumbai Suburban system; Resettlement & rehablitation of approximately 3,000 Project Affected households.

In this phase 800 new trains will be added (an increase of 30 per cent more than Phase I).

Bombay (Mumbai)
Private bus/taxi
Current situation
Significant numbers of private taxis, autorickshaws and private buses operate, with transport for schools and factories often provided by contracted services.

Calcutta (Kolkata)
Population: City 4.6 million, metropolitan area 14.7 million (estimates)

Public transport
Bus services provided in part by state-owned undertaking and also by substantial groupings of private bus and minibus owner-operators. State-owned tramway. Suburban rail and metro services provided by Indian Railways.

Calcutta State Transport Corporation (CSTC)
45 Ganesh Chandra Avenue, First Floor, Kolkata (Calcutta) 700 013, India
Tel: (+91 33) 25 53 17 96; 14 39
Fax: (+91 33) 25 53 30 17
e-mail: casttrco@yahoo.co.in

Key personnel
Managing Director: D H Sahoo
Director of Operations: S N Mandal
Public Relations Officer: S K Mukerjee
Staff: 7,282

Current situation
CSTC operates urban services in Calcutta and longer distance routes in the state of West Bengal. Its urban services face strong competition from private operators and have been affected by changing travel patterns; in addition, high operating costs and inefficiency have hampered attempts to boost patronage. These problems are being addressed by the RITES consultancy, which has drawn up an operational, technical and financial improvement programme designed to bring CSTC to financial viability.

Great effort has been put into raising productivity, with the staff:bus (on road) ratio cut from 22 in 1984 to 10.95 in 2004/2005. During the same period the number of daily kilometres run per employee increased to 19.81. Measures such as optimal fleet utilisation to reduce fuel consumption, fare evasion controls and better scheduling have also helped improve performance.

Bus
Passenger journeys: (2003/2004) Not available
(2004/2005) Not available
(2006/07) 187.7 million
Vehicle-km: (2003/2004) Not available
(2004/2005) 58.6 million
(2006/07) 53.6 million

Number of routes: 89 urban, 122 long-distance
Route length: 23,332 km

Fleet: 1,159 vehicles (635 on road)
Full breakdown of fleet is not currently available, but includes:
　Ashok-Leyland single-deck
　Ashok-Leyland semi-articulated double-deck
　Tata single-deck

Average age of fleet: 6.65 years
Most intensive service: 5 min
Fare collection: Payment to one or two conductors
Fare structure: Stage
Fare evasion control: Roving inspectors, penalty
Average peak-hour speed: 8 km/h
Operating costs financed by: Fares 39.7 per cent, other commercial sources 1 per cent, state government subsidy 59.3 per cent
Operating ratio: 251.91%

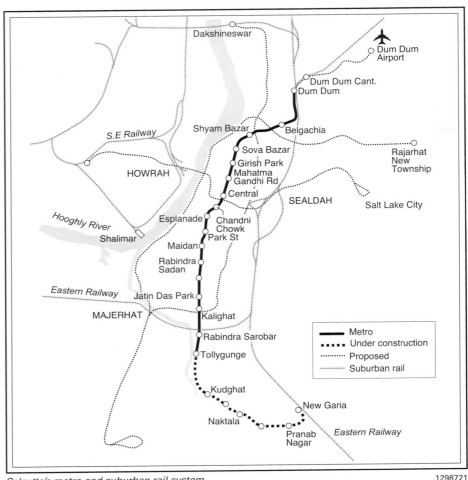

Calcutta's metro and suburban rail system　　　　1298721

Calcutta Tramways Company (1978) Limited (CTC)
12 R N Mukherjee Road, Kolkata (Calcutta) 700 001, India
Tel: (+91 33) 248 80 23　Fax: (+91 33) 248 32 77
e-mail: tramways@cal3.vsnl.net.in
Web: www.calcuttatramways.com

Key personnel
Chairman and Managing Director:
　P K Chattapadhyay
Chief Operating Manager: A K Patra
Works Manager: S S Gosh
Staff: 8,300 (estimate)

Type of operation: Conventional tramway and bus

Passenger journeys: (All modes)
(Annual) 58 million (estimate)

Tram
Passenger journeys: Not currently available
Vehicle-km: Not currently available

Bus
Passenger journeys: Not currently available
Vehicle-km: Not currently available

Number of routes: 37 (including 10 express routes)
Number of depots: 4

Current situation
Tram operations are severely affected by traffic congestion and passengers have been moving to faster modes of transport. CTC started operating buses in 1992, to cut down losses in parallel with some tram routes.

Developments
There has been little recent investment or modernisation of the tram system.

Tramway
Number of routes: 37
Route length: 68 km
in reserved right-of-way: 25 km
Number of lines: 29
Number of stops: 447
Number of depots: 7
Gauge: 1,435 mm
Electrification: 550 V DC, overhead

Rolling stock: 319 trams (239 operational)
In peak service: 180

Service: Peak 4 min
First/last car: 04.15/23.40
Fare structure: Graduated but telescopic
Operating costs financed by: Fares 30 per cent, other commercial sources 3 per cent, state government subsidy 67 per cent

Metro Railway – Metro Rail Bhavan
33/1 JL Nehru Road, Kolkata (Calcutta) 700 071, India
Tel: (+91 33) 22 26 39 59　Fax: (+91 33) 22 26 39 59

e-mail: metrorly@cal.vsnl.net.in
gm@mtp.railnet.gov.in
Web: www.kolmetro.com

Key personnel
General Manager: Ravindra Nath Verma
Chief Operations Manager: J K Mitra
Chief Engineer: Neeraj Jain
Chief Electrical Engineer: D C Pattanayak
Chief Engineer/CON: V K Gupta
Senior Public Relations Officer: P Dutta
Staff: Not available currently

Type of operation: Full metro, opened 1984

Passenger journeys: (2005/06) 107.87 million
(2006/07) 114.81 million
(2007/08) 120.62 million

Route length: 16.45 km
  elevated: 1.6 km
Number of lines: one
Number of stations: 17
  in tunnel: 15
Gauge: 1,676 mm
Track: UIC 60 kg/m rail; ballastless track with reinforced concrete bed
Max gradient: two per cent
Min curve radius: 300 m
Electrification: 750 V DC, third rail

Current situation
Through service on the entire section from Tollyganj to Dum Dum was introduced in 1995 but the ridership on the system was low. There were problems with maintenance and disruption in services. An action plan was prepared for almost every aspect of metro working. This has resulted in an increasze in ridership and earnings.

Currently, the main reason for underutilisation is the running of a number of bus and minibus routes along the metro corridor. For this, route rationalisation and linking of metro stations by bus and tram routes along the east-west arterial roads has to be carried out.

Developments
An extension from Tollygunge to Garia (8.5 km) was sanctioned in 1999/2000 at a sanctioned cost of INR9,076.9 million and is currently under construction. A third of the project cost will be borne by the Government of West Bengal. The section will mostly be on an elevated structure and the alignment will run along the Tolly's Nullah. There will be six stations along the route. This extension will link the South 24 Parganas District with Kolkata's Central Business area and reduce the pressure on Sealdah's South Suburban Section.

The Railway Board approved a preliminary survey on a 6.74-km extension – Dum Dum-Baranagar-Dakshineshwar. The survey was recently completed.

A preliminary survey for Integration of the Airport line with Kolkata Metro and an extension to the Airport Terminal (approximately six km) has also been approved. Survey work is in progress.

In late 2007, the West Bengal government sanctioned INR1,220 million for the 13.77-km, standard gauge East-West Metro project (eight km in-tunnel, 5.77 km elevated; 12 stations, six in-tunnel). The completion cost is estimated at INR46,760 million. The project is to be executed through a Joint Venture Company to be formed by the Central Government and the State Government. The route will run from Howrah Station to Salt Lake Sector V. Work will be carried out in two phases and the project is currently scheduled to start in early 2009.

Rolling stock: 144 cars
ICF A   M108
ICF B   T36
On order: Seven new, eight-car trains are to be ordered from ICF

Service: Peak 7–8 min, off-peak 10–15 min
First/last train: Weekdays 07.00/21.45, Sunday 14.00/21.45
Fare structure: three zones; single and two-ride tickets, discounted 12-, 40- and 80-ride tickets, group tickets; discount for smartcard users
Fare collection: Magnetic tickets; stored-value, contactless smartcard
Fare evasion control: AFC with magnetically encoded tickets and microprocessor-controlled entry/exit gates
Integration with other modes: Partially available. Total phased and dedicated bus services for metro passengers to be provided
Signalling: Colourlights (two aspect); CATC system is partially implemented. The system is designed for train frequency of 4.5 min.
Surveillance: CCTV and security personnel
One-person operation: None; all cars suitable (except eight cars under refurbishment)
Arrangements for elderly/disabled: 24 seats in each train for disabled passengers, 14 seats in each coach for women

Eastern Railway (ER)
17 Netaji Subhas Road, Kolkata (Calcutta) 700 001, India
Tel: (+91 33) 222 71 20   Fax: (+91 33) 248 03 70
Web: www.easternrailway.gov.in

Key personnel
General Manager: N K Goel
Chief Public Relations Officer: Deepak Kumar Jha

Type of operation: Suburban heavy rail

Passenger journeys: (2003/2004) 590 million
(2005/06) 721 million

Current situation
Some 1.8 million daily journeys are made on the Calcutta suburban network.

Developments
The new Kolkata terminal located in the northern part of the city was inaugurated in January 2006. This relieves the saturated Howrah and Sealdah terminals.

Rolling stock: M430, T913
emus   1,003

South Eastern Railway (SER)
11 Garden Reach, Kidderpore, Kolkata (Calcutta) 700 043, India
Tel: (+91 33) 24 39 12 81   Fax: (+91 33) 24 39 78 26
Web: www.serailway.gov.in

Key personnel
General Manager: V K Raina
Chief Operating Manager: P Sengupta
Chief Public Relations Officer: D Chandra

Type of operation: Suburban heavy rail

Passenger journeys: (2003/2004) 79 million
(2005/06) 86 million

Rolling stock: M113, T246

Current situation
Two major terminals serve the city – Sealdah and Howrah – to the east and west of the central business district. Sealdah is served by ER trains and Howrah by both ER and SER services; together they handle about 900 daily suburban trains. At peak times, emus are overcrowded heavily in excess of crush loads. Most routes are electrified at 25 kV, 1,676 mm gauge. Both railways are now operating dmu services on several non-electrified sections and main line emus on several main line electrified sections.

Developments
The ER Circular Railway is now in operation from Dum Dum to Majerhat, with the section from Princep Ghat to Majerhat having been completed. The stations of the Circular Railway are being upgraded. The work to provide connection to Dum Dum airport is also completed. In view of the problem which commuters face in changing from metro to the suburban system at Dum Dum, the entire stretch of circular railway has been electrified for introduction of direct emu services to the northern suburbs. The work to extend platforms to accommodate 12-coach emu trains is in progress on the Ballygunge-Diamond Harbour and Bandel-Bardhman sections.

On SER, 19 new emu trains were introduced during 2000/2001. Work on several projects for augmentation of line capacity in the suburban sections is under way. Construction of a new coaching terminal at Shalimar has been in progress for some time to ease the congestion at Howrah. Phase I of this work was completed in November 1999 and land acquisition for Phase II is in progress. Some trains already reach Shalimar by a link from SER's main suburban route at Santragachi, some 7 km from Howrah.

The Howrah-Amta and Tamluk-Digha lines have also been completed and these two projects have helped the local populations' commuters. A 12-car emu train was introduced for the first time in Sealdah Division. More of these were subsequently introduced in the Howrah and Sealdah divisions.

Calcutta (Kolkata)
Private bus/minibus
Current situation
Private bus operations account for about half of the public transport trips and two-thirds of bus trips in the city – around 1,000 million journeys annually. Route associations, generally one for each route, have developed. Owners retain control over operations and retain fares but the associations govern relationships between members and set operating standards. Private bus crews are paid a percentage of the fares, which keeps fare evasion below the high levels suffered by CSTC, and are allotted to individual vehicles, improving maintenance responsibility.

The state regional transport authority allocates licences for private buses and minibuses, as well as taxis.

Fleet: Over 2,200; full-size buses are all Tata, whilst the minibuses comprise Tata, Toyota and Hindustan.

Calcutta (Kolkata)
Ferry services
Ferry services provide easy access to trans-river traffic and carry about 0.25 million passengers on an average weekday.

Delhi
Population: City 13.8 million (2001 Census), metropolitan area 21.5 million (estimate)

Public transport
Bus services provided by the Delhi Government's Transport Corporation, Delhi Metro (Lines 1, 2 & 3) and private bus and minibus services granted permits by State Transport Authority. Limited suburban rail services by Northern Railway. Monorail proposed.

Delhi Transport Corporation (DTC)
Indraprastha Estate, New Delhi 110002, India
Tel: (+91 11) 23 37 02 36   Fax: (+91 11) 23 37 08 77

e-mail: cmddtc@bol.net.in
Web: www.dtc.nic.in

Key personnel
Chairman/Managing Director: A Prakash
Public Relations Manager: Swatantra Dua
Staff: 29,200

Current situation

DTC handles extremely large passenger volumes and experiences severe overcrowding, although the Delhi Metro, private bus and minibus services now account for a good proportion of total demand. Substantial deficits have been incurred due to factors such as concession and free passes to various categories of passengers, surplus staff and increased operating costs. Losses amount to INR3,000 million annually, excluding interest on loans and depreciation costs.

Apart from normal passenger traffic, DTC is also operating a daily Delhi sightseeing tour and interstate services to six states. As per a directive of the supreme court, all buses are now CNG-powered. About 200 buses have a GPS-based automatic vehicle tracking system.

Developments

The state government is planning to ensure that the existing modes of transport and the Delhi Metro will complement one another. Six high-capacity buses are on order. On arrival, these buses will be deployed on Central Secretariat-CGO and Shivaji Stadium-Hari Nagar routes. Prior to the Commonwealth games they will be deployed on planned routes.

DTC has also introduced 22 low-floor buses and plans to have a total of 525 of these buses in the fleet in due course. The maintenance of these buses will be outsourced to the manufacturers.

DTC has issued bids for the design, development and installation of automatic ticket machines in 1,000 buses on a Build-Operate-Transfer (BOT) basis and for GPS-enabled Automatic Vehicle Tracking and monitoring, with a passenger information system.

Bus

Passenger journeys: (2003/2004) 963.8 million (2004/2005) 1,056.8 million
Vehicle-km: (2003/2004) 251.1 million (2004/2005) 262.0 million

Number of routes: 814 (plus interstate routes)

Fleet: Over 3,105 vehicles, including privately operated vehicles. The fleet includes:
Full fleet breakdown is not currently available, but includes:
Ashok Leyland single-deck
Tata
High-capacity buses
Average age of fleet: 2.9 years

Most intensive service: 5–10 min
One-person operation: None
Fare collection: Payment to conductors; passes
Fare structure: Distance-related for ordinary services; fixed fare on other services; various passes
Fare evasion control: Checking staff, field officers and mobile courts
Integration with other modes: Some bus routes feed electric rail services and the Metro, but common ticketing is not yet in place
Average distance between stops: 500 m
Operating costs financed by: (2004/2005) Fares 59.8 per cent, other commercial sources 5.67 per cent. Operating ratio in 2004/2005: 167.12 per cent
New vehicles financed by: Interest-bearing loans and funds from the government

Delhi
Private bus/minibus
Current situation

Heavy pressure on the public transport system has encouraged the growth of private bus and minibus services, which now account for a substantial part of the traffic.

There are over 4,000 private buses granted licences by the state government under various schemes popularly known as Blue Line, Suvidha and White Line, chartered buses and minibuses on specified routes. As the buses operate on main routes only, autorickshaws (or manually operated cycle rickshaws) at bus stops near residential areas provide a convenient means for the commuters to travel to and from their homes to these bus stops.

Developments

The state government is trying to ensure that the private bus operators provide safe and reliable public transport but with little success. Therefore it has been revamping the state-owned DTC system so that it caters for a larger share of commuter traffic.

There are plans to increase the DTC's fleet from 3,470 to 4,500 buses.

Delhi Metro Rail Corporation Ltd (DMRC)

13 Fire Brigade Lane, Barakhamba Road, New Delhi 110001, India
Tel: (+91 11) 23 41 79 10/12
Fax: (+91 11) 23 41 79 21
e-mail: anuj@delhimetrorail.com (Public Relations)
Web: www.delhimetrorail.com

Key personnel

Managing Director: E Sreedharan
Director, Electrical: Satish Kumar
Director, Finance: R N Joshi
Director, Operations: Raj Kumar
Director, Works: Mangu Singh
Director, Projects: Vijay Anand
Director, Rolling Stock: Harjit Singh Anand
Chief Public Relations Officer: Anuj Dayal
  e-mail: anuj@delhimetrorail.com

Type of operation: Metro, (Phase I, consisting of Lines 1, 2 & 3, completed in November 2006; first line of Phase II completed in June 2008, Phase II due to be completed fully in 2010)

Passenger journeys: 2.6 million per day (projected by the end of 2011)

Route length: 68.2 km (Line 1: 25.1 km, Line 2: 11 km, Line 3: 32.1 km)
  in tunnel: 13.17 km (Line 2: 11 km, Line 3: 2.17 km)
  elevated: 50.53 km (Line 1: 20.6 km, Line 3: 29.93 km)
  at grade: 4.5 km (Line 1)
Number of lines: 3
Number of stations: 62
Gauge: 1,676 mm

Current situation

Delhi Metro Rail Corporation Ltd (DMRC) was registered in May 1995 with equal equity participation of the Government of India and the Government of the National Capital Territory of Delhi. DMRC is a special purpose organisation vested with autonomy and powers to execute this project, involving many technical complexities, under a difficult urban environment and within a very limited time frame. Phase I was completed in seven years and nine months, against the original target of 10 years, and within the estimated cost of USD2.1 billion. The last section of Phase I was opened to the public in November 2006.

Phase I consisted of three lines:

At present, DMRC operates 70 train sets of four coaches each. Automatic Train Protection (ATP) and Automatic Train Operation (ATO) systems have been installed. Trains are available every three and a half to four minutes on all the three lines. Kashmere Gate and Rajiv Chowk serve as interchange stations between Lines 1 and 2 and Lines 2 and 3 respectively.

Ticketing and passenger control is through an Automatic Fare Collection (AFC) system. Special facilities have been provided for less able passengers.

Developments
Phase II (operational)

On 4 June 2008, the first line of Phase II was opened to the public, seven months ahead of schedule. This line, a 3.1 km elevated section from Shahdara to Dilshad Garden, is an extension of Line 1 and has three stations as detailed in table one.

Phase II (under construction)

After completing Phase I of the Delhi Metro nearly three years ahead of schedule, DMRC has now started construction of the second phase of the project. The detailed project report of Phase II has finalised routes with a total length of 128.06 km. Of this, 3.1 km from Shahdara to Dilshad Garden has already been completed, while one corridor linking Jahangirpuri to Badli covering 3.42 km is awaiting government approval. The entire Phase II needs to be completed by 2010 before the Commonwealth Games scheduled to be held in Delhi.

Of the total, some 4.10 km will be at grade, 94.13 km will be elevated and 29.83 km will be underground. Three of these corridors (Airport Express Link, Central Secretariat-Badarpur and Inderlok-Mundka) will be standard gauge, whilst the rest will be broad gauge.

The success of the Delhi Metro has encouraged other Indian cities to attempt the introduction of metro systems. DMRC has already been appointed

Line Number	Total length (km)	Length in tunnel (km)	Length, elevated (km)	Length, at grade (km)
Line 1: Shahdara-Rithala (18 stations)	22.0	0.0	17.5	4.5
Line 2: Vishwavidyalaya-Central Secretariat (10 stations)	11.0	11.0	0.0	0.0
Line 3: Indraprastha-Barakhamba Road-Dwarka Sub-City (31 stations)	32.1	2.17	29.93	0.0
Total	65.10	13.17	47.43	4.5

Table 1

Line Number 1	Total length (km)	In tunnel (km)	Elevated (km)	At grade (km)
Shahdara – Dilshad Garden (3 stations)	3.1	0.0	3.1	0.0

Section Number	Route	Length (km)	Number of stations
1	Central Secretariat-Green Park	6.6	6
2	Green Park-Qutub Minar	5.92	4
3	Qutub Minar-Gurgaon extension	14.77	9
4	Vishwavidyalaya-Jahangirpuri	6.36	5
5	Indraprastha-New Ashok Nagar	8.07	5
6	New Ashok Nagar – NOIDA	7.0	6
7	Yamuna Bank-Anand Vihar ISBT	6.17	5
8	Anand Vihar-Vaishali, Ghaziabad	2.57	2
9	Inderlok/Kirtinagar-Mundka	18.46	16
10	Central Secretariat-Lajpat Nagar	6.51	5
11	Lajpat Nagar-Badarpur	13.65	11
12	Airport Link (New Delhi-Airport)	19.20	5
13	Airport Link (Airport-Dwarka S.21)	3.5	1
14	Dwarka Sec.9 to 21	2.76	2
Total		121.54	82

Metro train leaving Tis Hazari station on Line 1 (Peter Roelofs)   1115103

CAF, Spain has been awarded the concession for the installation of all systems, including rolling stock, overhead electrification, track, signalling and telecommunications, ventilation and air-conditioning, automatic fare collection, baggage check-in and handling, depot and other facilities and for operating the system for 30 years.

In October 2007, Bombardier Transportation was awarded a contract, valued at some EUR30 million, for the supply, installation, test and commissioning of its *Bombardier CityFlo 350* train control and signalling system on Lines 5 and 6.

Rolling stock: At present, 280 broad gauge coaches are available with DMRC. The corporation has awarded contracts for supply of 496 coaches for Phase II. Of these, 340 broad gauge coaches will be supplied by a consortium of Bombardier Transportation GmbH, Germany, and Bombardier Transportation, India, whilst 156 standard gauge coaches will be supplied by a consortium of Mitsubishi Corporation, ROTEM, Mitsubishi Electric Corporation and Bharat Earth Movers Limited, India. In addition, an order for 60 more broad gauge coaches for Phase I has been placed with Mitsubishi Corporation, ROTEM and Mitsubishi Electric Corporation.

Service: Peak: 3.5 min

Fare collection: Distance-related; single-ride and return token, contactless rechargeable smartcard (discounted fare) and single-ride, contactless smart token

Revenue control: Automated fare collection machines and turnstile gates

Security: Central Industrial Security Force and Delhi Metro Police

Elevated Line 1 passing over Maharana Pratap bus terminus (Peter Roelofs)   1115104

Northern Railway (NR)

Public Relations Office
NOCR Building, State Entry Road, New Delhi, India
Tel: (+91 11) 23 74 70 84
Fax: (+91 11) 23 36 34 69
e-mail: cpro@nr.railnet.gov.in
Web: www.nr.indianrail.gov.in

Key personnel
General Manager: S Prakash

Type of operation: Suburban heavy rail

Passenger journeys: (2003/2004) 2.77 million (2005/06) 2.81 million

Current situation
Limited emu services provided on ring railway (35 km, 21 stations), with seven trains clockwise and eight trains anti-clockwise, and on Delhi-Mathura Jn/Palwal, New Delhi-Shakurbasti and Delhi-Gaziabad routes. Main line emu services are provided between Delhi and Aligarh (122 km) and Delhi and Kurukshetra/Panipat (156/89 km).

Existing Ring Railway service is at present much under-utilised. To attract more commuters, it is necessary to increase frequency of emu trains, to make stations more accessible and secure and to provide integration with bus services.

However, the Ring Rail was commissioned primarily to carry freight, bypassing Delhi main station, and was not intended as an urban transport mode.

Developments
The metre gauge track from Delhi to Rewari has been converted to broad gauge and two trains have started commuter services between these cities.

Northern Railway is providing third and fourth lines from Sahibabad to Anand Vihar and is developing a new terminal at Anand Vihar.

During 2005/06, the number of emu coaches has been increased.

Rolling stock: M134, T461

the Prime Consultant for Kochi Metro and is the in-house consultant for Mumbai Metro. DMRC has also submitted Detailed Project Reports (DPRs) for metro systems in Bangalore, Kolkata (East-West Line), Mumbai, Ahmedabad and Chennai. Work has already begun on the Bangalore Metro. DPRs are also under preparation for Pune and high-speed metro links from the new airport at Bangalore to the city centre.

On the international front, DMRC has completed its first international consultancy

assignment for a Special Assistance on Project Implementation (SAPI) study for the Jakarta Mass Rapid Transit (MRT) System in Indonesia. Other countries that have shown interest in Delhi Metro include Pakistan, Sri Lanka, Bangladesh, Ireland and Vietnam.

DMRC is constructing a high-speed underground Airport line, linking the heart of the city with the Indira Ghandhi International Airport. The civil work on the line, to be carried out by DMRC, has started. A consortium of Reliance Energy and

Delhi
Monorail (proposed)

Monorail Malaysia Technology Sdn Bhd (MMT), a Kuala Lumpur-based company, has entered into a joint venture with Ircon International of India to undertake the first stages of the MYR1.12 billion (USD300 million) Delhi Public-Private Partnership (PPP) monorail project. The 50:50 joint venture with the Indian government-linked company will begin with a feasibility study to assess the best approach for the feeder service to the main Delhi Metro railway system that is currently under construction.

MMT and Ircon signed a Memorandum Of Agreement (MOA) in early August 2005 that starts this monorail PPP project.

The Ircon-MMT joint venture has proposed that an initial 15 km of monorail route will begin as a pilot project – the work to be undertaken on the basis of a PPP project – with the Indian Government and the National Capital Territory of Delhi Government contributing towards capital costs. This pilot project is expected to take up to three years.

The Delhi monorail project's pre-feasibility study for the 60 km route and the detailed feasibility study for the pilot project are expected to be submitted within two months of the receipt of the project report from the government of the National Capital Territory of Delhi.

Hyderabad/Secunderabad

Population: 7 million (with Secunderabad) (estimate)

Public transport

Bus services provided by State Road Transport Corporation with additional private buses, minibuses and autorickshaws. Suburban services of South Central Railway. Metro proposed.

Andhra Pradesh State Road Transport Corporation (APSRT)

Mushirabad, Hyderabad 500020, India
Tel: (+91 40) 23 44 33 33, 27 61 75 71
Fax: (+91 40) 27 61 71 35
e-mail: pro@apsrtc.gov.in
        rmhcr@apsrtc.gov.in
Web: http://apsrtc.gov.in

Key personnel

Vice-Chairman and Managing Director: V Dinsh Reddy
Staff: (statewide total) 115,676

Current situation

Provides services throughout Andhra Pradesh with a fleet of 19,692 buses (including 1,673 hired); total of 4,601 million passengers carried in 2006/07. City services account for only about 12 per cent of vehicle-km.

Losses in 2006/07 were INR1,118 million.

Hyderabad City Region

Jubilee Bus Station, Secunderabad 500003, India
Tel: (+91 40) 23 44 33 33
     (+91 984) 804 85 87 (mobile)
Fax: (+91 40) 23 44 33 44

Key personnel

Regional Manager: C Panduranga Murthy
Staff: 16,401

Developments

These include construction of additional bus shelters, bus bays and stations, setting up of a quick response cell, passenger guidance scheme and passenger educational programme, plus the introduction of circular and telescopic routes.

A guide book has been published to help passengers understand the system.

Bus

Vehicle-km: (2004/05) 273.3 million

Number of routes: 914
Route length: (One way) 14,624 km

Fleet: 2,841 vehicles, including six double-deck and 14 Metro Liner luxury coaches

Ashok Leyland	2,827
Eicher	9
Tata	5
Volvo	14

Most intensive service: 2 min
Fare collection: Payment to conductor or prepurchase pass
Average peak-hour speed: Ordinary services, 20 km/h; express, 24 km/h

Ashok Leyland bus on service in Hyderabad (Peter Roelofs)   1341105

Fare evasion control: Random checks, with penalty
Operational control: Route inspectors
Arrangements for elderly/disabled: Free travel for disabled; cost borne by operator
Operating costs financed by: Realised from fares and passes, INR3,669.6 million, and other commercial sources INR408 million
New vehicles financed by: IBDI and other financial institutions

South Central Railway (SCR)

Railnilayam, Secunderabad 500371, India
Tel: (+91 40) 27 83 34 20   Fax: (+91 40) 27 83 32 03
e-mail: gm@scr.railnet.gov
Web: http://scrailway.gov.in/web

Key personnel

General Manager: H K Padhee
Deputy Regional Manager, Hyderabad: Vishnoi Rajiv

Passenger journeys: (Ligampalli-Hyderabad-Secunderabad-Falaknuma)
(2003/04) 162 million (estimate)
Train-km: Not currently available

Route length: 43 km
Number of lines: 2
Number of stations: 26

Current situation

Multi-modal services are operated on Secunderabad-Falaknuma (14.54 km) and Secunderabad-Hyderabad-Lingapalli (33 km). 84 services are provided daily by ICF emus.

For further information on SCR, please see *Jane's World Railways.*

Developments

19 additional services were provided from early 2007.

There are proposals for Phase II of the system. This may include services from Bhongir to Secunderabad, Secunderabad to Manoharabad and one section from Falaknuma to Shamshabad. The Tellapur to Patancheru line may also be revived.

There are plans for an integrated train/bus ticketing system.

Fare structure: Distance-based

Mass Rapid Transit System (MRTS)

Office of Project Directors MMTS
Municipal Complex, Tank Bund Road, Hyderabad 500 063, India
Tel: (+91 40) 23 22 08 48

Type of operation: Metro (proposed)

Current situation

The DMRC has prepared a Detailed Project Report (DPR) for a metro rail system, with proposed corridors for high population density areas' connectivity to the heart of the city, where central business and the seat of the government are located. The MRTS will cover three corridors; Miyapur-Chaitanya puri (26 km), Tarnaka-Hitech City (20 km) and Secundrabad-Falaknuma. The Andhra Pradesh Government has invited bids for the evaluation of technologies/systems proposed by the developers.

Developments

In August 2005, the Andhra Pradesh Government invited a global expression of interest/request for qualification for the design, development, construction, financing, operation and maintenance of the elevated project on a Build-Operate-Transfer (BOT) basis.

Jaipur

Population: 3.3 million (estimate)

Public transport

Bus services provided by State Road Transport Corporation; auto rickshaws, tempos and minibuses operated by private companies. Bus Rapid Transit (BRT) system planned.

Rajasthan State Road Transport Corporation (RSRTC)

PO Box 210, Parivahan Marg, Jaipur 302001, India
Tel: (+91 141) 237 30 43   Fax: (+91 141) 511 60 21
e-mail: info@rajasthanroadways.com
Web: www.rsrtc.gov.in

Key personnel

Managing Director: A Jain
   Staff: (statewide total) 21,798

Current situation

Provides services throughout Rajasthan with a total fleet of 4,519 vehicles in 2006/07.

The present bus service in Jaipur is inadequate for the rapidly growing population, and much of the city's transport is provided by private operators.

Bus

(Jaipur city service only)

Passenger journeys: 30 million (annual)
Vehicle-km: 5 million (annual)

Number of routes: 40
Route length: 250 km

Fleet: 170 buses, including Ashok Leyland, Tata and hired buses

Fare collection: Floating or seated conductor
Fare structure: Stage – based on km travelled

Jaipur
Minibus
Current situation
Private minibuses seating about 20 passengers, three-wheelers seating about 12, and cycle rickshaws provide much of the city's public transport. These are considered wasteful of road space, and congestion on city streets is increasing rapidly.

Jaipur
Bus Rapid Transport (BRT) (planned)
Current situation
The Jaipur Development Authority (JDA) has prepared a project for the development of Bus Rapid Transit (BRT) system with a total length of 42 km. The corridors will run North-South and East-West across the city, with Government Hostel as the central hub. The Central Government has approved the project and the JDA has invited bids for these corridors. The project is to be implemented through a Special Purpose Vehicle (SPV) on a Private-Public-Partnership (PPP) basis. In addition, a ring road is also planned in Jaipur.

Previous plans for a light rail system have not been progressed.

Kanpur

Population: 4.1 million (2001 Census)

Public transport

UP State Road Transport Corporation (www.upsrtc.com) buses, some CNG-powered, private bus, auto rickshaws, 'tempo taxi' operations and cycle rickshaws provide most of the city's public transport needs; limited local trains of Northern Central and North Eastern Railways.

Regional Transport Office

Sarvodaya Nagar, Kanpur 208005, India

Type of operation: Private bus operators

Background

Buses are licensed by the Regional Transport Office.

Current situation

Private operators licensed by the Regional Transport Office run 43 bus routes. In the absence of adequate mass transport system, use of low-capacity vehicles is increasing, which is resulting in growing congestion and pressure on the limited transport infrastructure.

Developments

Some CNG-powered buses have been introduced.

Fleet: 264 buses, mainly Tata, Eicher, DCM and Swaraj Mazda; 2,163 'tempo taxis', mainly Bajaj Auto and Vikram and 850 autos

Fare structure: Stage
Fare collection: Cash to conductor on buses, to driver on 'tempo taxis'

Northern, North Central and North Eastern Railways

Station Superintendent, Kanpur Central Railway Station, Kanpur, India
Tel: (+91 512) 232 81 57

Current situation

Northern Railway (www.nr.indianrail.gov.in) runs 11 return main line emu services at commuting times between Kanpur and Lucknow (72 km), in addition to one pair of local trains, one pair of main line emu trains between Kanpur and Etawah and two pairs of local trains.

North Central Railway (www.ncr.railnet.gov.in) runs one pair of main line emu trains between Kanpur and Etawah and two pairs of local trains to Fatehpur.

North Eastern Railway (www.nerailway.gov.in) runs several local trains to nearby towns.

Developments

A study by RITES has recommended provision of 58.7 km of mass transport network comprising four corridors. Three of these corridors will be rail-based and the fourth corridor will be dedicated busway. However, the state government has taken no decision on this so far.

Lucknow

Population: 2.8 million (estimate)

Public transport

UP State Road Transport buses and minibus services operated by private companies, supplemented by auto rickshaws, cycle rickshaws and paratransit 'tempo taxi' operations; limited local rail services.

U P State Road Transport Corporation

Parivahan Bhavan, Tehri Kothi, Lucknow 226 001, India
Tel: (+91 522) 222 23 63
Fax: (+91 522) 227 45 78
e-mail: upsrtc@sacharnet.in
Web: www.upsrtc.com

Key personnel

Managing Director: K S Atoria

Current situation

Bus services operated by the Uttar Pradesh State Road Transport Corp declined in the face of extensive competition from eight-seater 'tempo taxis' which had catered for most journeys for many years. Private bus services were permitted in 1993. Private buses, minibuses and cycle rickshaws now handle the majority of the city's transport needs. However, there is considerable congestion, delay and rising incidence of accidents.

UPSRTC currently has six bus depots in Lucknow.

Developments

To provide a better city bus service in Lucknow, the state government is giving several concessions and facilities to the city bus service operators.

The state government commissioned a study by RITES to suggest means of augmenting the transport system in Lucknow, who had proposed a Light Rail Transit (LRT) system (63.76 km in length), to be provided in two phases at a total cost of INR34.5 billion. To date, no decision has yet been made on these proposals.

Recently, the government decided to start bus services by the State Road Transport Corporation in the city again, with 50 buses on five routes. Later it is planned to introduce its bus services in the entire city on about 50 routes.

Number of routes: 5

Fleet: 50 buses

Fare structure: Stage
Fare collection: Cash to conductor

Scooters India Ltd

Lucknow-Kanpur Road, Sarojini Nagar, Lucknow 226008, India
Tel: (+91 522) 243 62 42; 65 70
Web: www.scootersindia.com

Key personnel

Managing Director: P Muthusamy
Director, Technical: P P Sarkar
Chief Marketing Manager: S Gagdani

Type of operation: Taxis

Background

Scooters India Ltd, a Lucknow manufacturer of two- and three-wheelers, is manufacturing pollution-free battery-operated three-wheeler tempo taxis.

Current situation

These battery operated vehicles are in operation in 'pollution-free zones' such as the Taj Mahal and hospital areas.

Developments

The government has declared certain areas as 'pollution-free zones' and permits only the operation of these vehicles in those areas.

Fare collection: Cash to driver on tempo taxis

Northern Railway

Divisional Railway Manager
Hazratgunj, Lucknow 226001, India
Tel: (+91 522) 222 60 18
e-mail: cpro@nr.railnet.gov.in
Web: www.nr.indianrail.gov.in

North Eastern Railway

Lucknow Division
7 Ashok Marg, Lucknow 226001, India
Tel: (+91 522) 222 83 09   Fax: (+91 522) 262 83 09
e-mail: gm@ner.railnet.gov.in;
    drm@ljn.railnet.gov.in
Web: www.nerailway.gov.in

Key personnel
Divisional General Manager: Ashima Singh

Type of operation: Suburban rail

Current situation
NR operates seven pairs of main line emu (memu) trains between Lucknow and Kanpur (72 km) and two pairs of local trains, while North Eastern Railway runs three trains between Lucknow and Sitapur.

Developments
In June 2002, suburban main line emu services were inaugurated by the Prime Minister on the Lucknow Ring Railway. The service consists of eight emu trains in each direction, four pairs by Northern Railway and four by North Eastern Railway. It involved electrification of 38 route-km. Lucknow is the first non-metropolitan city in India to have an electrified suburban railway network.

Subsequently, in October 2002, electrification and main line emu services were extended from Lucknow to Barabanki (14.36 km).

Madras (Chennai)

Population: City 4.34 million (2001 Census), metropolitan area 7.5 million (estimate)

Public transport

Most public transport needs are met by bus services provided by the metropolitan division of the State Transport Corporation. Suburban rail service is provided by Indian Railways on three routes, and on an initial 9.2 km section of regional metro completed in 1997. Metro extending.

Metropolitan Transport Corporation (Chennai) Limited (MTC)

Pallavan House, Anna Salai, Chennai 600002, India
Tel: (+91 44) 23 45 58 01   Fax: (+91 44) 23 45 58 30
e-mail: mtc.chennai@vsnl.net
Web: www.mtcbus.org

Key personnel
Managing Director: M Ramasubramaniam
    Staff: 17,522

Background
Under a reorganisation scheme, Pallavan Transport Corporation has been renamed Metropolitan Transport Corporation (Chennai Division) Ltd. The Metropolitan Transport II amalgamated with Metropolitan Transport I and functions as one corporation under the name of 'Metropolitan Transport Corporation (Chennai) Ltd' with effect from 1 March 2001.

Current situation
Metropolitan Transport Corporation (Chennai) Limited is a Government of Tamil Nadu Undertaking. It is governed by a Board of Directors appointed by the Government of Tamil Nadu.

Over the past 20 years various infrastructure works have been carried out by the Metropolitan Development Authority, with World Bank loans. The company has augmented its fleet by 1,441 vehicles over a 10-year period. There are currently 25 depots.

Feeder services are provided from Chennai central station complex to Egmore railway station and Tambaram station.

Developments
There is a move towards the introduction of more low-floor, lighter and more efficient buses.

A Global Positioning System (GPS) for buses is currently undergoing a pilot trial. It is to provide feeder services to MRTS stations and a train/bus link ticket and a smartcard ticketing system, MTC has extended its route length from 40 to 50 km.

During 2007 (up to October 2007), 512 buses were added to the fleet, limited-stop services on all main routes have been introduced and other improvements have been made.

Bus (metropolis services)
Passenger journeys: (2003/2004) 1,231.3 million
(2004/2005) 1,320.5 million
(2006/07) 3.958 million (daily average)
Vehicle-km: (2003/2004) 214.6 million
(2004/2005) 215.6 million
(2006/07) 215.1 million

Number of routes: 544
Route lengths: 4 to 50 km

Fleet: 2,803 vehicles
Ashok Leyland single-deck	2,363
Tata	378
Double-deck	10
Articulated/trailer (vestibule) bus	42
Low-floor buses	10

In peak service: 2,660
Average age of fleet: 7.83 years

Most intensive service: 3 min
One-person operation: None
Fare collection: Payment to conductor
Fare structure: Stages; monthly season tickets; tokens
Fare evasion control: Random inspection; penalty
Operational control: Over 245 route inspectors (checking and timekeeping); over 80 sets of mobile radio
Arrangements for elderly/disabled: Some seats reserved; free passes for blind and disabled at operator's cost
Operating costs financed by: (2004/05) Fares 106.1 per cent, other commercial sources 2.4 per cent
Operating ratio (2004/05): 94.5 per cent – the transport corporation is a separate corporate entity formed under the Companies Act 1956. The operating cost is met out of the revenue generated only

Chennai Metro Rail Limited

11/6 Seethammal Road, Alwarpet, Chennai 600 018, India
Tel: (+91 44) 24 31 33 22   Fax: (+91 44) 24 31 24 30
e-mail: chennaimetrorail@gmail.com
Web: www.chennaimetrorail.gov.in

Key personnel
Chairman: Thiru S M Hoda
Managing Director: T V Somanathan
    Staff: Not currently available

Type of operation: Metro (proposed)

Current situation
Chennai Metro Rail Limited is a Special Purpose Vehicle (SPV), created in December 2007 by the Tamil Nadu Government to implement the Chennai Metro Rail Project.

A Detailed Project Report (DPR) has been prepared by the Delhi Metro Rail Corporation Limited (DMRC), which proposes a two-line initial phase for the system. The Government of Tamil Nadu has approved the first two lines in principle. Currently, the project costs of some RS146,000 million is expected to be funded in part by the Central and State Governments (some 40 per cent of costs), with the remainder coming from the Japan Bank for International Cooperation (JBIC).

The two proposed corridors in Phase I are:
1. Washermenpet to Chennai Airport (23.085 km, 8.785 km elevated and 14.3 km in tunnel, 18 stations (seven elevated, 11 in tunnel);
2. Chennai Central to St Thomas Mount (21.961 km, 12.266 km elevated and 9.695 km in tunnel), 18 stations (nine elevated, nine in tunnel).

The proposed Metro system would be operated at 750 V DC third rail electrification. Continuous Automatic Train Control (CATC) system with Automatic Train Protection (ATP), Automatic Train Operation (ATO), Fiber Optic Transmission System (FOTS), Automatic Fare Collection (AFC) System and Automatic Train Supervision System (ATSS) are planned for the network.

Developments
The Government of India approved the Chennai Metro Rail Project Phase I on 28th January 2009.

Tentatively, the project is programmed for completion in FY2014/15.

Madras Railway Transport System (MRTS)
Regional metro (RTS)

Regional Metro, Periar EVR High Road, Chennai 600008, India
Tel: (+91 44) 25 32 24 86

Type of operation: Mass Rapid Transit System (MRTS); first section opened 1997

Passenger journeys: Not currently available
Train-km: Not currently available

Route length: 27 km
Number of lines: 1
Number of stations: 17
Track: Ballastless track on elevated sections; some track on PSC girders

Current situation
The initial section of a city circle route from Chennai Beach to Luz (now Thirumalai) became fully operational in October 1997 with opening of the Chepauk-Luz portion. The 2.75 km from Beach to Park Town with three stations is on surface and the remaining 6.2 km with five stations is elevated; electrification is at 25 kV. One more elevated station has been completed, along with commissioning of the extension work.

MRTS services have been rationlised, frequency increased and three-car rakes have been introduced. These measures have been widely welcomed by commuters.

Developments
Extension of the line by 10.8 km (3.2 km on surface and 7.6 km elevated) from Thirumalai to Velachery, at a cost of INR6.9 billion, was taken up by SR in co-ordination with Tamil Nadu state government, which bore two-thirds of the cost, besides providing government land available along the alignment free of cost. This extension was inaugurated in November 2007.

An extension from Velachery to St Thomas (5 km, three stations) is under way. The work is expected to be completed by December 2010.

DMRC prepared a feasibility report for a three-line metro rail system for Madras/Chennai and submitted it to the state government in

May 2004. Two further lines are planned, one from Beach to Koyambedu (13.5 km) and the second from Tiruvotriyur to Chennai International Airport (31.5 km).

Fleet: 6-car trains
Breakdown of fleet is not currently available
First/last train: 06.00/21.30

Service: 10 min peak, 20 min off-peak
Fare structure: Distance-based; single and return tickets, monthly and 3-month passes, reduced fare for children and students.
Fare collection: Cash, paper tickets; integrated ticketing proposed
Integration with other modes: All stations have bus links

Southern Railway (SR)

Park Town, Chennai 600 003, India
Tel: (+91 44) 25 35 34 55
Fax: (+91 44) 25 34 18 00
e-mail: cpro@sr.railnet.gov.in
Web: www.southernrailway.gov.in

Key personnel
General Manager: Rakesh Chopra
Chief Public Relations Officer: Ms Neenu Ittyerah
  Staff: Not currently available

Type of operation: Suburban heavy rail

Passenger journeys: (2003/2004) BG* 123 million, MG**: 118 million (In July 2004, the gauge conversion to BG was completed and MG services ceased)
(2005/06) 260 million
(2007/08) 326 million

*BG = Broad Gauge – 1.676 m wide
**MG = Metre Gauge – 1 m wide

Current situation
Apart from the Madras Railway Transport System (MRTS) (see separate entry), SR runs suburban services over three routes electrified at 25 kV 50 Hz, out of Chennai Central and Beach stations on the following sections:
1. Chennai Central/Moore Market Complex to Gummidipundi (46 km);
2. Chennai Central/Moore Market Complex to Tiruvallur (42 km);
3. Chennai Beach – Tambaram – Chengalpattu (60 km).
   Principal traffic is on the section to Tambaram (29 km), which carries 447,000 passengers daily.
   Some 669 broad-gauge suburban emu trains run daily.
   For further information on SR, please see *Jane's World Railways*.

Developments
Following a pilot project on the Chennai Central-Gummidipundi and Chennai Beach-Gummidipundi sections, SR will implement a Train Protection Warning System (TPWS) in its Chennai division.

Rolling stock: 669 emu cars (as at March 2008)
Breakdown of fleet is not currently available

Pune

Population: 3.76 million (2001 Census)

Public transport
Bus services provided by municipal undertaking operating within the urban and suburban area, with some longer-distance routes running into the service area of a second municipal operator serving the twin city of Pimpri-Chinchwad (population 516,000). Extensive taxi and autorickshaw services; interdistrict and state routes operated by the Maharasthra State Road Transport Corporation.

Pune Municipal Transport (PMT)

Swargate, Pune 411037, India
Tel: (+91 20) 24 44 04 17
Fax: (+91 20) 24 44 54 90

Key personnel
General Manager: C A Pathak
  Staff: 6,913

Bus

Passenger journeys: (2002/03) 179.3 million
(2003/04) Not available
(2004/05) 228.2 million
Vehicle-km: (2002/03) 59.0 million
(2003/04) Not available
(2004/05) 61 million

Number of routes: 185
Route length: 3,515 km

Fleet: 927 vehicles
Tata
Ashok Leyland single-deck
Ashok Leyland double-deck
Others
In peak service: 662
Average age of fleet: 8.23 years

Most intensive service: 5 min
One-person operation: None
Fare collection: Conductors
Fare structure: Stage; higher fare for night and express services; monthly passes
Fares collected on board: 92 per cent
Arrangements for elderly/disabled: Concessional fare
Average peak-hour speed: 20 km/h
Operating costs financed by: Fares 95.7 per cent, tax levy 3.6 per cent, subsidy/grants 0.6 per cent

Developments
Study for a high-capacity mass transit for the city has been carried out by RITES.

Pimpri-Chinchwad Municipal Transport (PCMT)

Sector 23, Transport Nagar, Nigdi, Pune 411044, India
Tel: (+91 20) 27 65 36 82
Fax: (+91 20) 27 47 99 99

Key personnel
General Manager: A K Pawar
Transport Manager: N N Bothe
  Staff: 1,895

Current situation
Competes with PMT on some busy routes, but is the sole provider in some areas of Pune's twin city Pimpri-Chinchwad. Has introduced high-quality minibus services at premium fares.

A seven to eight-seat three-wheeler auto – a very popular mode of transport (K K Gupta) 0126461

Ashok Leyland bus of PMT (K K Gupta) 0126462

Bus

Passenger journeys: (2002/03) 21.6 million
(2003/04) Not available
(2004/05) 30.35 million
Vehicle-km: (2002/03) 11.7 million
(2003/04) Not available
(2004/05) 12.4 million

Number of routes: 55
Route length: 1,463 km

Fleet: 212 vehicles
Ashok Leyland single-deck
Ashok Leyland double-deck
Tata
Others
Average age of fleet: 8.62 years

Operating costs financed by: Fares 74 per cent,
other commercial sources 8.7 per cent
Operating ratio in 2004/2005: 139.94 per cent

Central Railway (CR)

Division office, 411001 Pune, India
Tel: (+91 212) 263 74 00

Current situation
CR operates 16 pairs of suburban trains to Lonavla,
one pair to Taligan, six pairs of intercity trains to
Mumbai (including well known Deccam Queen)
and a Shatabdi Express for daily commuters.

Indonesia

Jakarta

Population: 8.4 million (2000 Census); latest
estimate nearly 10 million, metropolitan area
approximately 16 million (2006 estimate),
Jabotabek region 16–18 million (estimate)

Public transport

Three government-owned busways are the main
mode of transportation within the city. Private
bus operations. Taxi operations, also three-
wheeled scooters ('bajaj') and motorcycle taxis
('ojek'). State railway Persero provides suburban
service, being upgraded to regional metro;
monorail under construction.

Pemerintah Propinsi DKI Jakarta – The Jakarta City Administration

Public Transportation Department
Jalan Medan, Merdeka Selatan 8-9, Blok G, Lantai
3, Jakarta, Indonesia
Tel: (+62 21) 344 70 09 ext 3158
Fax: (+62 21) 384 88 50; 344 66 34
e-mail: arezaf68@yahoo.com;
  dkiweb@jakarta.go.id
Web: www.jakarta.go.id;
  www.dephub.go.id/english

Passenger journeys: (All modes)
(1990) 1,379 million

Current situation

This city government authority is responsible
for co-ordination and licensing of all public road
transport. It also operates 14 bus terminals and
maintains bus shelters. Three of the terminals
serve as interchange points between urban and
interurban buses, the latter not permitted to
penetrate the central area.

Bus

Web: http://trans.jakarta.go.id

Current situation

Three guided busways runs through the city
centre on elevated alignment. Line 1 runs from
Blok M Bus Station in the suburb of Kebayoran
Baru to Kota Station in the central business
district. Line 2 runs from Kalideres to Harmoni
and Line 3 runs from Pulogadung to Harmoni.

Lines 2 and 3 are currently operating with
24 vehicles instead of the planned 80 and the
terminal at Harmoni is still under construction.
Full service is scheduled to be in operation in
mid-2006.

Busways run in dedicated lanes and
station announcements and LED displays are
provided.

One-person operation: None
Fare collection: Two conductors per vehicle; no
tickets issued
Fare structure: Flat; surcharge for express (100 per
cent) and air conditioned (300 per cent) services;
free transfers between busway lines
Fares collected on board: 100 per cent
Arrangements for elderly/disabled: None

Average peak-hour speed: Urban 8 km/h;
suburban 17 km/h
Bus priority: Bus lanes along some main routes,
not always respected by other vehicles
Integration with other modes: Interchange with
interurban buses at three terminals

Minibus
Current situation

Co-operatives operate minibus services within
Jakarta. Metro Mini was founded in 1962 and
originally restricted to vehicles of not more
than 15 seats, but was reorganised in 1977 and
authorised to operate vehicles with up to 25
seats. Kopaja was founded in 1980, and two
other co-operatives (Koantas Bima and Kopami
Jaya) came into being more recently. Together
they operate more than 4,000 vehicles, mainly
Mitsubishi, Isuzu and Daihatsu with local
bodywork.

All vehicles carry conductors and charge fares
20 per cent higher than ordinary city buses.

Mikrolet
Current situation

Two co-operatives, Koperasi and APK, operate
Mikrolets (vehicles with 10–15 seats) on regular
routes, one within the city and the other mainly
on suburban routes. Their combined fleets total
more than 8,000 vehicles. Mikrolets do not
operate into the central business district.

Vehicles are either owned by their drivers or by
investors and hired out on a daily basis. The city
government specifies a number of types which
are eligible for Mikrolet operation, which may
then be further restricted by the co-operative.
City government also defines a uniform livery
and lettering.

Bemo
Current situation

Public service vehicles with fewer than 10
seats are officially referred to as Bemos. These
are not licensed by the city government, but
by the various districts. They operate on short
intra-neighbourhood routes which may change
frequently according to demand. There are a total
of 1,096 three-wheel scooters with longitudinal
seats for six passengers, also known locally as
Toyokos. It is estimated that each carries some
35 passengers a day, amounting to around 14
million annual journeys.

PT Kereta Api (Persero) – The Indonesian Railways

Jalan Perintis Kemerdekaan No 1, Bandung
40117, Java Barat, Indonesia
Tel: (+62 22) 424 13 70, 423 00 31 ext. 13300,
13310
Fax: (+62 22) 424 13 70
e-mail: info@kereta-api.com
Web: www.kereta-api.com

Key personnel
Chief Executive Officer: Saiful Imam
Contact: Akhmad Sujadi

Type of operation: Suburban heavy rail

Background
Previously known as Perum Keteta Api
(Perumka), the company was renamed PT Kereta
Api (Persero) in 1999.

Current situation
Services operate on a 30-km city railway
network, over four lines and nine routes with
23 city stations, connecting the city centre with
the regions of Tangerang, Bekasi, Bojonggede,
Bogor and Serpong. There are two types of
service: air conditioned, limited-stop and non air
conditioned, economy. There are some weekend
special services.

There are plans by the central government
to develop the existing suburban/commuter
rail network to serve the Jabotabek planning
region, a 6,000 km² area covering Jakarta and its
satellite towns of Bogor, Tangerang and Bekasi.
Improvements would include double-tracking on
the Serpong-Tanah Abang line, one new line and
access to the bus network.

Rolling stock: Not currently available

PT Jakarta Monorail

c/o Indonesian Transit Central (ITC)
Gedung Victoria 3rd floor, Suite 304, Jl Sultan
Hasanuddin Kav 47-51, Kebayoran Baru, Jakarta
Selatan 12160, Indonesia
e-mail: info@i-transitcentral.co.id
Web: www.i-transircentral.co.id

Key personnel
President Director, ITC: Ruslan Diwirjo
  Director, ITC: Sukmawaty Syukur
  Director, ITC: Mubarak Nahdi
  Chairman, ITC: Saiful Imam

Type of operation: Elevated monorail

Background
PT Jakarta Monorail is a consortium that includes
PT Indonesian Transit Central and the Omnico
Consortium.

Current situation
The new elevated monorail system is planned
to be formed of two lines, the Green Line
(14.8 km with 17 stations) and the Blue Line
(12.2 km with 12 stations), serving two areas of
the city, the business district and a suburban
line linking areas to the east and west of
the city. There are planned interchanges with
standard bus and rail/commuter rail services
and with the Bus Rapid Transit (BRT) system.
It is estimated ridership will be up to 250,000
per day.

The project is estimated to cost in excess
of USD600 million and was scheduled to be
completed in 2007.

PT Jakarta Monorail will build and operate the
system.

Developments
A groundbreaking ceremony was held in
June 2004 to mark the start of construction.
However, financial constraints may have delayed
completion.

Iran

Tehran

Population: City 7.79 million, metropolitan area 13.4 million (2006 estimates)

Public transport

Bus and trolleybus services provided by government authority, which also supervises bus services in other cities and private minibus operations. Metro and suburban rail operational, with extensions under construction.

Union of City Bus Organizations (UCBO)

No 15 Naderi Avenue, Keshavarz Boulevard, 14166 Tehran, Iran
Tel: (+98 21) 897 79 16/8   Fax: (+98 21) 897 79 19
e-mail: info@iri-ucbo.com
    Taraffo@iri-ucbo.com

Key personnel

Managing Director: M A Taraffo
    Staff: 16, 587 (2005)

Current situation

As well as operating the extensive bus network and the new trolleybus route, UCBO supervises the declining minibus service.

Currently, the metro service operates three lines, with others being brought into service in phases. The bus lines are currently being redesigned, to complement the developing metro system.

Developments

As part of a nationwide environmental movement, UCBO has started conversion from diesel to LPG- and CNG-powered engines, with 1,329 buses re-equipped initially. UCBO has increased the fleet with locally manufactured urban buses – the modified Mercedes-Benz 355 and 457.

The company plans to increase the fleet by as many as 2,000 units by the end of 2005, along with the development of supporting infrastructure, such as depots and repair shops.

Bus

Passenger journeys: (2001/2002) 1,500 million (2004/05) 1,500 million

Number of routes: 256
Route length: 2,214 km

Fleet: 6,680 buses

Mercedes-Benz O302	616
Mercedes-Benz O305	13
Mercedes-Benz modified O355	3,018
Mercedes-Benz O305G articulated	2
Mercedes-Benz 457	928
Ikarus 260	182
Ikarus 280 articulated	461
MAN articulated	964
Volvo B10M	200
Renault 350	250
Other	46

One-person operation: All routes
Fare collection: Prepurchase at ticket booths
Fare structure: Flat
Operational control: Route inspectors
Bus priority: Bus lanes extend to 66 km
Operating costs financed by: Fares 20 per cent, subsidy/grants 80 per cent
Subsidy from: National government and municipality of Tehran

Trolleybus

Current situation

A 7 km trolleybus route opened in the east of the city in 1992 following an agreement under which Skoda installed the infrastructure and supplied vehicles. A fleet of 25 articulated bimode 15Tr trolleybuses was delivered for the start of service, with a further 40 supplied later. Trolleybuses carry about 75,000 passengers daily.

The total network length in 2005 was 14.1 km, comprising five routes, of which two are limited-stop express services that otherwise duplicate other routes. Most sections include two sets of wires in each direction, for stopping and express services. All routes start at Emam Hossein metro station. Routes 1 and 2 run east for 7 km in a segregated median busway, shared with buses, whilst routes 3 to 5 run southwards and are not segregated from other road traffic.

Passenger journeys: (Daily) approx 75,000
Vehicle-km: (1997/98) 1.7 million

Fleet: 66 trolleybuses

Skoda 15Tr (articulated)	65
Volvo B10M ex-diesel 2 -axle bus	1

Minibus

Current situation

Private operators run minibus services on 114 routes. The minibuses are privately owned and operate under special contract between each individual owner and UCBO.

In addition to minibuses, there are vehicles operating under similar conditions on 113 routes carrying around 2 million passengers annually.

Fleet: 3,125

Fiat	2,226
Mercedes	385
Iveco	511
Other	3

Tehran Urban & Suburban Railway Company (TUSRC)

PO Box 15878-4661, 37 Miremad Avenue, Tehran 15878-13113, Iran
Tel: (+98 21) 88 74 01 10/13
Fax: (+98 21) 88 74 01 14/15
e-mail: info@tehranmetro.com
Web: www.tehranmetro.com

Key personnel

Chairman and Managing Director (TUSRC): Mohsen Hashemi
Managing Director, Tehran Urban & Suburban Railway Operation Co (TUSROC): Jafar Rabiee
    PO Box 11155-994, No 956 Hafez Cross, Enghelab Street, Tehran 1131813131, Iran
    Tel: (+98 21) 66 74 79 01, 02
    Fax: (+98 21) 66 74 79 00
    e-mail: rabiee@tehranmetro.com
Executive Manager, Line 6: Mohammad Montazeri

Tehran's metro and rail network

1124831

Manager, Public Relations & International Affairs (TUSRC): Koorosh Mirzadeh
Public Relations & International Affairs (TUSROC): Mohsen Mohammadian
Staff: 3,535

Type of operation: Metro, first section opened 2000

Background
The Tehran Urban & Suburban Railway Company (TUSRC) was established to develop and construct an urban rail network serving the Iranian capital, including a 41.5 km electrified suburban heavy rail system that forms Line 5.
TUSRC is controlled by Tehran's municipality.

Passenger journeys: (2003) 199.79 million
(2004) 209.55 million
(2005) 253.44 million
(2006) 300.54 million
(2007) 415.61 million
Train-km: Not currently available

Gauge: 1,435 mm
Electrification: 750 V DC third rail
Route length: 90.0 km
    in tunnel: 53.6 km
Number of lines: 3 (including Line 5)
Number of stations: 49 (3 under construction)
(including Line 5)

Current situation
Line 1, a 28.1-km north-southern line with 22 stations, operates for 17½ hours per day with peak hour headway of 3 minutes. Line 2 is a 20-km west-eastern line with 19 stations with operating hours and peak hour headway as for Line 1.
Line 5 is a 41.5-km suburban line with eight stations (with three more under construction) with operating hours as for Line 1 and headway of 10 minutes during peak hours.

Developments
Work is under way to extend Line 1 by approximately 7.8 km further north with seven more stations. The headway is expected to be reduced to two minutes in the future. A southwards extension to the airport is also under consideration.
Work is under way to extend line 2 some 4 km further eastwards with four more stations. Headway is expected to be reduced as per Line 1 in the future.
Tenders for two more urban Lines, 3 and 4, have been carried out, the winners have been selected, contracts have been drawn up and construction has begun.
The future programme for the Tehran metro network foresees nine urban and four express lines with a total length of some 430 km. The express lines will connect Karaj in the west with Pakdasht in the east, Parand and the international airport to northern Tehran, Pardis in the east to the national railway in the south and northern Tehran to the city of Varamin.
In May 2004, the contract for Line 4 was awarded to NORINCO. Line 4 will run west-east across the city. It will be 21 km in length with 22 stations and will link Ekbatan to Shahid Kolahdooz Square. It will have interchanges with Line 1 at Darvazeh Dolat station and with Line 2 at Azadi and Darvazeh Shemiran stations. The line will be introduced in two phases and will be operated using 161 metro cars.
In May 2005, it was announced that new cars were to be added to the fleet. Some 300 cars were ordered from China in 2003.
In February 2006, seven new metro cars, manufactured by Arak Pars Wagon Company, were being tested for use on the metro. Arak Pars Wagon Company, together with Tehran Wagon Manufacturing Company, have delivered several locally built metro cars for use on the urban lines.
In 2007, TUSRC was restructured as a holding company, with affiliated but independent companies responsible for functions such as operation, construction, procurement, rolling stock manufacture and station management.

Trains in station on Line 1 of the Tehran Metro   1179774

Tehran metro train on Line 1   1179773

Double-deck passenger coaches on TUSRC's suburban Line 5   1114597

In July 2007, the head of Tehran's Subway Company, Mohsen Hashemi, and the Managing Director of Bank of Industry and Mine, Mehdi Razavi, signed a contract to provide USD100 million to start the executive operation of Tehran Subway's Line Three. Line 3 is to include 23 underground stations over a distance of about 24 kilometres, and seven ground-level stations over a length of 11 kilometres. The project is to be completed in five phases by 2014. Executive work on the first phase extending over 7 km and involving 1,100 m of tunnel has started and is due to be operational in 2009. The line runs from the southern-most part in Islamshahr and, after passing through Chahardangeh, Rah-Ahan, Monirieh and Vali-e Asr squares, will reach Shahid Beheshti Street and then cross Resalat, Majidieh streets and Imam Ali-Shahid Zeinuddin Intersection to terminate in Lashgarak. The total cost of the line has been estimated at EUR770 million.

Rolling stock: 518 metro cars (74 seven-car trains) (Line 1 and 2)
Changchun Railway Car Works
   Currently not available

Tehran Wagon Co
   Currently not available

Service: 06.00–23.30
Fare structure: Zonal: urban (Lines 1 and 2); contactless smartcards (CSC) with discount; weekly and monthly tickets
Automatic control: Traffic Control Centre (TCC); Interlocking signalling system; Automatic Train Protection system; Automatic Train Control TVM300 equipment (CS Transport)
Surveillance: CCTV in ticket hall, corridors and platforms

Tehran-Karaj-Mehrshahr Express Line (Line 5)
Type of operation: Commuter surface line, opened 1999
Gauge: 1,435 mm
Electrification: 25 kV 50 Hz overhead/catenary

Route length: 41.5 km
Number of lines: 1
Number of stations: 8 (3 under construction)

Current situation
Running west from the centre of Tehran at Sadeghieh, where interchange is made with Line 2 of the Tehran metro system, Line 5 provides connections to the satellite cities of Karaj and Mehr-Shahr. Services on the initial section to Karaj began in 1999.

It is being constructed and equipped by the China International Trust, Investment and International Co-operation Corporation, the China National Technical Import and Export Corporation and the China North Industry Corporation.

Developments
Construction is in progress of a 1.4 km extension to Line 5, which will serve depot facilities at the line's western end.

Rolling stock: 24 electric locomotives, 88 double-deck coaches, eight cars per train

Zhuzhou Electric Locomotives Works	
Class TM1	12
Zhuzhou Electric Locomotives Works	
Class TM2 (2005)	12
Changchun Railway Car Works	
double-deck coaches	88

Ireland

Dublin

Population: City 505,739, urban area 1.1 million, region 1.2 million, Greater Dublin Area 1.7 million (2006 Census)

Public transport
Bus and suburban rail services are operated by autonomous divisions of state transport responsible to the Department of Public Enterprise; light rail with extension/s planned/proposed, DART (Dublin Area Rapid Transit) services provided between Greystones, Bray, Howth and Malahide.

Current situation
The Greater Dublin Authority oversees strategic planning including land use and regulation of transportation. Suburban services operated by Bus Eireann, with some independent operators running commercial services in the Greater Dublin area.

Dublin Bus/Bus Atha Cliath
59 Upper O'Connell Street, Dublin 1, Ireland
Tel: (+353 1) 872 00 00   Fax: (+353 1) 873 11 95
e-mail: info@dublinbus.ie
Web: www.dublinbus.ie

Key personnel
Chairman: Dr John Lynch
Chief Executive: Joe Meagher
Directors: David Egan,
   William McCamley, John Moloney,
   Arnold O'Byrne, Tom Coffey, Peter Webster
Chief Financial Officer: Richard O'Farrell
Chief Engineer: Shane Doyle
Business Development Manager: Paddy Doherty
Human Resources Manager: Gerry Maguire
Operations Manager: Mick Matthews
Marketing & Information Manager: Dawn Bailey
   Staff: 3,840 (as at October 2008)

Current situation
Dublin Bus, which is a wholly owned subsidiary of the state-owned Coras Iompar Eireann Group, currently operates almost all commercial routes in the Greater Dublin area. It is the main public transport provider for the Greater Dublin Area (extending as far as Newcastle in County Wicklow, Balbriggan in north County Dublin, Dunboyne in County Meath and Kilcock in County Kildare). Carrying 150 million customers a year, Dublin Bus provides an extensive range of bus services – Radial, Cross City, Orbital, DART Feeder, Airlink, express limited stop commuter services, Nitelink, Schoolink and Sightseeing tours.

Dublin Bus employs 3,840 full time members of staff and has a fleet of 1,148 buses. Due to investment, more than 70 per cent of its buses is low-floor wheelchair accessible with plans to a fully accessible fleet by 2012. As part of the Governments Transport 21 programme of sustained investment in public transport, Dublin Bus is expanding services and improving frequencies on key bus corridors.

There are approximately 190 km of bus lanes (Quality Bus Corridors) in the Dublin Metropolitan Area.

Developments
Dublin Bus has applied for planning permission to develop a new bus depot at Grange Castle in the western suburbs of the city.

Contactless Smartcard Ticketing was introduced in 2008.

The company is currently beginning an Automated Vehicle Location (AVL) and a Real Time Passenger Information (RTPI) Project, which will be implemented over the next two to three years.

Under the Transport 21 Investment Programme, the aim is to expand the bus network in the Dublin area and to achieve an increase in passenger carrying capacity through new and replacement bus acquisition. In 2007, the company received 100 extra buses, and has used these to implement new routes which offer a more comprehensive service across the city.

Bus
Passenger journeys: (2003) 149.8 million
(2004) 149.8 million
(2005) 145.7 million
(2006) 146.3 million
(2007) 148.0 million
Vehicle-km: (2003) 56.6 million
(2004) 57.0 million
(2005) 57.9 million
(2006) 59.2 million
(2007) 63.2 million

Number of routes: 222
Route length: (One way) 3,347 km
On priority right-of-way: Bus-lane km (on-street, dedicated or mixed): 184.9 km
Bus-only road-km (separate dedicated road): 1.7 km
Traffic signals with bus priority: four per cent

Fleet: 1,148 vehicles (as at September 2008), includes:
Standard:

Volvo B10L 9 m	four
Double-deck:	
Volvo Olympian (Volvo engine)	304
Volvo B7LDD	441
Alexander Dennis Trident 2	10
Volvo B7LDD (Mk II)	200
Volvo B9TL Tri-axle	70
Volvo B9TL Two-axle	50
Articulated:	
Volvo B7LA	20
Mini/Midibus:	
Volvo B6BLE	49

Average age of fleet: 5.7 years

Most intensive service: 4–8 min
One-person operation: 100 per cent
Fare structure: Stage-based; daily, weekly, monthly and annual commuter tickets; two-journey tickets for the different stages; arrangements for through ticketing on feeder services to DART trains
Fare collection: Wayfarer electronic ticket machines and magnetic card validators on all vehicles; contactless smartcard ticketing introduced in 2008; exact-fare fareboxes on all routes
Fares collected on board: 67 per cent
Fare evasion control: A dedicated Revenue Control Unit which undertakes random spot checks on all Dublin Bus services on a daily basis to prevent revenue fraud
Integration with other modes: Plans for small city-centre transport interchanges; feeder buses to DART rail services
Operational control: Currently beginning an Automated Vehicle Location (AVL) and a Real Time Passenger Information (RTPI) Project, which will be implemented over the next two to three years
Arrangements for elderly/disabled: Free travel at all times for those with disabilities and those aged 66 years and over (paid for by relevant government departments); 73 per cent of the fleet now fully accessible (Since September 2008)
Average peak-hour speed: In peak, 12.95 km/h; in bus lanes, off-peak 15.4 km/h
Bus priority: Substantial system of Quality Bus Corridors (bus lanes) – approximately 190 km
Operating costs financed by: Fares and other commercial sources 72 per cent, subsidy/grants 28 per cent
Subsidy from: Central government subvention
New vehicles financed by: Transport 21 and own resources

Dualway Coaches Ltd
Keatings Park, Rathcoole, Co Dublin, Ireland
Tel: (+353 1) 458 00 54   Fax: (+353 1) 458 08 08
e-mail: info@dualwaycoaches.com
Web: www.dualwaycoaches.com

Key personnel
Managing Director: Anthony McConn
General Manager: David McConn
Operations Manager: Kevin Tyrrell

Current situation
Dualway Coaches is the largest independent operator in the Dublin area, and the only Irish Coach Operator to be accredited with the Optimus Ireland's Best Service Excellence Award.

Dualway operate scheduled, sightseeing and private charter services in the city. Scheduled services include the Village Link from Newcastle to Tallaght, and Route 505 from Rathcoole to Dublin city centre.

Fleet: 49 vehicles

AEC-Park Royal Routemaster double-deck	2
AEC-Park Royal Routemaster open-top double-deck	1
Daimler Fleetline/MCW open-top double-deck	7
Leyland Atlantean/East Lancs double-deck	3
Leyland Atlantean open-top double-deck	13
Leyland Olympian	3
Volvo Olympian/East Lancs double-deck	3
Volvo Olympus/East Lancs double-deck	1
Volvo Visionaire/East Lancs double-deck	1
Plaxton coach	4
DAF coach	2
Mercedes-Benz coach	1
Mercedes-Benz minicoach	8

Bus Éireann
Broadstone, Dublin 7, Ireland
Tel: (+353 1) 830 22 22   Fax: (+353 1) 830 93 77
e-mail: info@buseireann.ie
Web: www.buseireann.ie

Key personnel
Chief Executive: Tim Hayes
Chief Operating Officer: Martin Nolan
Chief Mechanical Engineer: Joe Neiland
Manager, Human Resources: Des Tallon
Manager, Media and Public Relations:
Andrew McLindon
Staff: Not available currently

Current situation
Bus Éireann is Ireland's national bus company, formed in 1987 as a subsidiary of CIÉ (Córas Iompair Éireann) to provide bus services throughout Ireland with the exception of Dublin city. The company operates Expressway interurban coach services, Eurolines coach services to Britain and Europe, city bus services in Cork, Limerick, Galway and Waterford, commuter services in the greater Dublin area, local and rural bus services, school bus services on behalf of the Department of Education and ancillary services including coach and bus hire.

High-frequency commuter routes operated in the greater Dublin area, with departures every 15 minutes during peak hours on routes serving towns up to 50 km from Dublin. Off-peak services depart every 30 minutes to hourly. The increased frequency has generated increased patronage with a daily average of 6,000 commuters compared with 3,500 three years ago. Hourly express routes have been introduced on a number of long-distance interurban routes.

Developments
In 2008, Wrightbus supplied 48 12 m Urban Eclipse single-deck buses, on Volvo B7RLE chasis, to Bus Eireann. Each bus carries 45 seated and 28 standing passengers.

Fleet: 1,366 coaches and buses (656 of which are allocated to school transport)

Dublin
Other operators
A number of smaller independent operators undertake contract work in the city including Alan Martin Coaches. Mortons Coaches, Dublin, runs Circle Line Bus Service commuter routes

Bus Éireann commuter coach enters Dublin coach station near LUAS tram terminus at Dublin Connolly station (Tony Pattison)   0585189

Bus Éireann Scania bus   1194941

Setra Aircoach at Dublin international airport (Stephen Morris)   1115162

and a feeder service to Luas between Tallaght and CityWest Business Park. Aircoach operates express coaches from the airport to city-centre hotels.

Dublin Area Rapid Transit (DART)
Iarnród Éireann (Irish Rail)
Connolly Station, Dublin 1, Ireland
Tel: (+353 1) 836 33 33
Fax: (+353 1) 836 47 60
Web: www.irishrail.ie

Key personnel
Chief Executive: Dick Fearn
General Manager, DART: Tom Devoy
Staff: 291

Type of operation: Suburban rail (metro)

Passenger journeys: (All Dublin suburban)
(2004) 23.1 million
(2006) 32.7 million
(2007) 34.1 million
Train-km: Not available currently

Current situation

Frequent suburban service (approximately 15 minutes off-peak) operated over single route Howth/Malahide-Dublin-Greystones (52 km) known as DART, 30 stations, 1,600 mm gauge, electrified at 1.5 kV DC overhead.

Stations are manned, but with ticket-controlled turnstiles.

Developments

Iarnród Éireann have announced plans to construct a 5.2 km underground line beneath Dublin that will link Docklands with Heuston station. Known as the DART Underground Interconnector, the new DART line will run directly beneath the city centre. This new development is part of the government's 10-year transport investment plan to integrate Luas, Metro, DART, commuter and mainline services in the Greater Dublin area. The line will increase capacity from the existing 33 million journeys per annum throughout the Dublin area to 100 million by 2015.

The line will diverge from the existing DART Northern Line at Clontarf Road, diving underground to reach Docklands station in the west of the city. Here it will connect with an extension of the Luas Red Line. From Docklands, the DART line will continue to Pearse, with DART connections and mainline services south to Bray and Rosslare, before running beneath the city centre to St Stephen's Green, linking with Luas Green line and future connections northwards to the airport. The Interconnector will then run to High Street and Heuston stations, offering interchange facilities with Luas Red Line and intercity and commuter services. There are also plans for DART services to be extended to Maynooth and Hazelhatch in the west and Balbriggan in the north. In recent years, population growth has increased in these locations. It will also offer increased DART travel possibilities northwards from Bray and Greystones in the south. The DART Underground Interconnector is expected to be complete by 2015.

A new DART station is also planned at Clongriffin in North Dublin, opening in late 2009.

Rolling stock: 154 vehicles (emu)

Linke-Hofmann-Busch emu 8100 Class (1983/84)	M38 T38
ALSTOM 8200 Class (2000)	M5 T5
Mitsui/Tokyu 8500 Class (2000)	M8 T8
Mitsui/Tokyu 8510 Class (2002)	M6 T6
Mitsui/Tokyu 8520 Class (2004)	M20 T20

Commuter rail
Iarnród Éireann (Irish Rail)

Key personnel

General Manager, Intercity and Commuter Networks: Cal Carmichael

Current situation

Diesel suburban service between Dublin and Maynooth (26 km, nine stations), and on other lines outside the DART area to Drogheda, Dundalk, Gorey and Kildare, total 201 km.

Developments

Capacity on the Kildare commuter routes will be increased when a rail upgrade is completed by 2010. The upgrade will allow an increased frequency of commuter trains into Heuston station. This involves quadrupling about 10 km of track between Hazelhatch and Dublin. This will separate the commuter lines from the express lines allowing the number of train paths to increase. Two new stations will be built at Adamstown in north Dublin and Kishoge near Lucan.

A new station for Docklands has already been built on the Maynooth-Dublin commuter line.

A new 7.5 km line is proposed from Clonsilla to Dunboyne in County Meath by 2010.

Dublin Area Rapid Transit Mitsui-built emu at Bray station (Tony Pattison)   0585190

CAF-built suburban dmu at Connolly station, with preserved steam locomotive on special service (Tony Pattison)   0585191

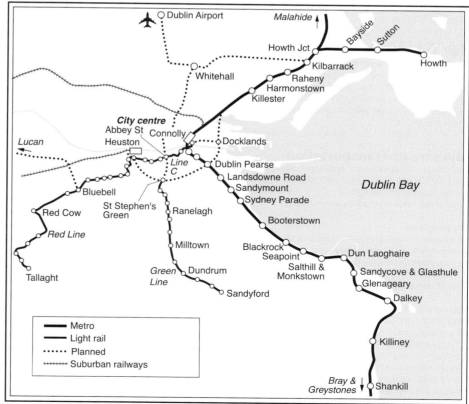

Map of Dublin's metro and light rail and suburban rail network   1115291

Fleet: 180 vehicles (dmu)
Mitsui/Tokyu 2600 Class (1994)   M17
ALSTOM 2700 Class (1998)   M27*
Mitsui/Tokyu 2800 Class (2000)   M20
CAF 2900 Class (2003)   M116
*25 single-cab vehicles, 2 twin-cab vehicles

Luas

Veolia Transport
Luas Depot, Red Cow Roundabout, Clondalkin,
Dublin 22, Ireland
Tel: (+353 1) 461 49 10
e-mail: info@luas.ie
Web: www.luas.ie

Key personnel
Manager, Strategic Planning and Public Relations:
  Brian Brennan

Type of operation: Light rail, first line opened 2004

Passenger journeys: (2005) 20 million
(2006) 26 million
(2007) 28 million
Vehicle-km: Not currently available

Route length: 23 km
Gauge: 1,435 mm
Electrification: 750 V DC overhead

Current situation
Veolia Transport, which operates the Luas system,
changed its name from Connex Transport in
2006.
  The Green Line (opened in June 2004), runs
from St Stephen's Green, near Dublin city
centre, to Sandyford via the Dundrum shopping
complex, claimed to be the largest in Europe.
Much of the alignment is on former railway line
and speeds are high.
  The Red Line, from Dublin Connolly railway
station to Tallaght, runs via Dublin Heuston
station and Red Cow. It opened in September
2004. Much of this alignment is street-based.
  In the first year of operation around 20
million passengers were carried, exceeding
expectations. In 2007, 28 million passengers were
carried.

Luas newly-extended LRV in Dublin   1368748

Developments
The 7.5 km extension of Line B1, from Sandyford
to Cherrywood was agreed in 2007, and the line
is due to open in 2010.
  Alstom is supplying 18 Citadis trams starting in
2008. They are for the Red, Green and Docklands
extension.
  Consultation started in 2007 on the 1.5-km
extension of the Red Line eastwards from
Connolly Station terminus to the Point Depot,
designated Line C1. The Point Depot is a large
entertainment complex.
  In 2007, lengthening of each car on the Red
Line by two sections was implemented.

Fleet:
Alstom Citadis LRV   40
On order: 18 Alstom Citadis trams, delivery starting
in 2008

Rolling stock
The basic tram can were extended in 2007/08
to 40 m, by adding modules to respond to
additional capacity requirements. All 40 trams
are now 40 m long. The height of each tram is
3.27 m excluding pantograph.

Service: 3 min (peak), 10 min daytime, 15 min
evenings
First/last train: Mon-Fri: 05.30–00.30, Sat: 06.30–00.30,
Sun: 07.00–23.30
Fare structure: Ticket machines at each stop
(prepurchase necessary); ticket agents, selling 1-,
7- and 30-day tickets
Revenue control: Roving customer service officers
to help passengers and check tickets
Surveillance: CCTV at stops and on trams
Arrangements for elderly/disabled: Low-floor
trams and ramps at all stations
One-person operations: All services
Maximum speed: 70 km/h

Israel

Jerusalem
Population: 732,100 (estimate)

Public transport
Most bus services provided by local members of
national transport co-operative society; light rail
under construction.

Ministry of Transportation
Clal Center, 97 Jaffa Road, Jerusalem, Israel
Tel: (+972 2) 622 82 11   Fax: (+972 2) 622 86 93
e-mail: tammy_r@jtmt.gov.il
Web: www.rakevetkala-jerusalem.org.il

Key personnel
Minister of Transportation: Avigdor Liberman
Public Relations: Ovadia Avner
e-mail: pniot@mot.gov.il

Type of operation: Light rail (under construction)

Current situation
This initial light rail line will be 13.8 km long with
23 stations, 1,435 mm gauge, electrification 750
V DC overhead, running from Pisgat Ze'ev, in the
north of the city, via Jaffa Road to Mount Herzl.
Bus services are to be reorganised to complement,
rather than compete with, the new line, and Jaffa
Road in the city centre will be pedestrianised.
  Tickets will be purchased in advance of
boarding at stops, with on-board validation

and integrated ticketing with the bus system is
proposed. There will be roving ticket inspectors.
There will also be terminals at stops and on the
vehicles displaying schedule information.
  Park-and-Ride facilities will be built to reduce
city centre congestion.

Developments
In early 2004, an agreement was signed between
the state and the CityPass consortium (www.
citypass.co.il), headed by ALSTOM and including
two Israeli companies, Ashtrom and Polar
Investments. The concession is to build and
operate the first light rail line for 30 years. The line
is scheduled to begin operation in 2010 with a fleet
of 23 ALSTOM Citadis Type 302 low-floor LRVs.
  There are further plans to expand the system,
including extending and adding branches to the
initial line, to a total of eight lines 54 km in length
and with 75 stations. The Ministry of Transport
and the city council plan to carry out and operate
the scheme in stages, financed and run by the
private sector.

Egged Transportation Co-operative Society Ltd (Egged)
142 Menachem Begin Road, Tel Aviv 64921, Israel
PO Box 33091, Tel Aviv 61330
Tel: (+972 3) 692 22 11
Fax: (+972 3) 692 27 33
Web: www.egged.co.il

Key personnel
Chairman of the Board and Chief Financial Officer:
  Arik Feldman
  Staff: 8,400 (national total)

Current situation
The Jerusalem Region is the smallest of Egged's
three divisions, extending from Beit Shemesh
to the Jordan Valley. For details of Egged's
operations, please see the Tel Aviv entry in
section.

Bus
(Jerusalem Region operations only)
  Staff: 1,760

Passenger journeys: Specific figures not available

Fleet: 667 buses

One-person operation: All routes
Fare collection: Manually by driver from ticket
board
Fare structure: Flat
Fares collected on board: 100 per cent
Fare evasion control: Inspectors
Average peak-hour speed: In bus lanes, 20 km/h; in
mixed traffic, 18.6 km/h
Bus priority: 3.9 km of bus lanes; further 4.8 km
planned
Subsidy from: Government

Tel Aviv – Jaffa (Yafo)

Population: City 384,600, metropolitan area 3.2 million (estimates)

Public transport

Bus services mainly provided by one co-operative with some private company services. Suburban rail services; light rail under construction.

Dan Public Transport Company Limited

39 Shaul Hamelech Blvd, PO Box 33038, Tel Aviv, Israel
Tel: (+972 3) 693 44 44   Fax: (+972 3) 693 35 50
e-mail: information@dan.co.il
Web: www.dan.co.il

Key personnel

Chair: Yoram Sharabi
Executive Traffic Director: Barkochva Yimini
   Staff: 3,500

Current situation

The DAN bus co-operative is the largest provider of bus services in Tel Aviv and its metropolitan area. Its operating territory covers the most densely populated areas, comprising the Tel Aviv metropolitan area and seven surrounding cities, with a population of 2.5 million.

Developments

Originally established as a co-operative, Dan was restructured in 2002 as a commercial company.

The company is introducing GPS-based location systems for its bus fleet, and information displays on board the vehicles and at bus stops for passengers. More accessible buses are to be added to the fleet.

Bus

Passenger journeys: (Annual) 204 million (estimate)

Number of routes: 112
Bus priority: 43 km bus lanes
Route length: (One way) 2,820 km

Fleet: 1,340 vehicles

MAN SL200	973
MAN articulated	244
Coaches	96
Minibuses	27

In peak service: 94 per cent of the fleet
New vehicles required each year: 95
On order: 15 minibuses and 80 standard MAN buses per year

Most intensive service: 5 min
One-person operation: 100 per cent
Fare collection: Payment to driver, prepaid cards
Fare structure: Zonal, 'FreeMonthly' cards, 'Free Daily' cards
Arrangements for elderly/disabled: Reduced fees for elderly passengers, accessible buses on several routes, with more planned
Integration with other modes: Dan co-operates with the Israel Railway to offer a range of joint tickets for bus and train travel, with discounts on daily and monthly travel cards
Average peak-hour speed: 17.0 km/h
Operating costs financed by: Fares 72 per cent, government subsidy/grants 28 per cent

Egged Transportation Co-operative Society Ltd (Egged)

142 Menachem Begin Road, Tel Aviv 64921, Israel
PO Box 33091, Tel Aviv 61330
Tel: (+972 3) 692 22 11   Fax: (+972 3) 692 27 33
Web: www.egged.co.il

Key personnel

Chairman of the Board and Chief Financial Officer: Arik Feldman
   Staff: 8,400 (national total)

Current situation

Egged's Northern Region provides part of the Tel Aviv area bus services. It also runs services in most other parts of Israel, including city areas, and at regional and interurban level. The co-operative has about 5,800 members and some 3,200 additional hired staff. The total passenger carryings are about 1 million daily, with a 3,250 vehicle fleet operating some 1,034 urban and suburban routes. The figures for Tel Aviv are approximations and reflect some regional as well as city services.

Bus

Passenger journeys: Approx 100 million (annual)
Vehicle-km: Approx 40 million (annual)

Number of routes: 25

Fleet: 400 buses, including Mercedes-Benz, MAN and Volvo

Most intensive service: 5-10 min
One-person operation: All routes
Fare collection: Tickets sold by driver from rack or prepurchased with cancellation by driver. Manual machines
Fare structure: Zonal
Fare evasion control: Inspectors
Average peak-hour speed: 17.2 km/h
Bus priority: 15.4 km of bus lanes in 7 sections in central area

NTA – Metropolitan Mass Transit System Ltd

53 Yigal Alon Street, Tel Aviv 617891, Israel
Tel: (+972 3) 689 30 00   Fax: (+972 3) 689 30 01
e-mail: nta@nta.co.il
Web: www.nta.co.il

Key personnel

Chairman: Benny Vaknin
General Manager: Yishai Dotan
   Staff: Not currently available

Current situation

In 1998, NTA completed a comprehensive feasibility study for a mass transit in metropolitan Tel Aviv and subsequently prepared a master plan, in which it has defined the initial implementation phase.

The master plan was approved as a national statutory plan that details the rail alignments planned for Tel Aviv.

The Master Plan includes:
Red Line – a 22 km light rail pre-metro line that is partially at-grade and partially underground. There will be 31 stations/stops, 10 in tunnel. The line runs from Bat Yam in the south, through Jerusalem Boulevard in Jaffa to the Arlosoroff Terminal in Tel Aviv, then along Jabotinsky Street to Petach-Tikva.

Green Line – a light rail system covering 14 km of alignment, from Rishon Lezion, through Holon to central Tel Aviv, then to the Arlosoroff terminal.
Yellow Line: – mostly overground, 26 km long connecting seven cities with 48 stations, all at grade. This is currently at design stage.

The tunnelled section of the Red Line runs beneath Tel Aviv's central business district. Whereas surface sections would have a headway of 3 minutes, a shuttle service in the tunnel section would allow headways of 90 seconds. The double frequency of service along this section would accommodate 15,000 to 20,000 passengers in the peak hour, in the peak direction.

Developments

Preparatory work has started for the Red Line.

In May 2007, the Metro Transportation Solution (MTS) group, comprising Africa Israel, Siemens, Germany, the Egged bus co-operative, CCECC, China, Da Costa Soares, Portugal and HTM, Netherlands, signed a concession agreement with the state. The line will be built on a Build, Operate, Transfer (BOT) basis, with MTS operating the line for 32 years. However, the financial arrangements are not yet completed.

Completion of the Red Line is currently scheduled for 2013, should the work commence in early 2008 as planned.

There are also plans for a fourth line, the Purple Line.

Israel Railways (IR)

Central Station, PO Box 18085, Tel Aviv 61180, Israel
Tel: (+972 3) 693 74 01   Fax: (+972 3) 693 74 80
Web: www.israrail.org.il

Key personnel

Director General: Yossi Snir
Deputy General Director, Traffic: Harel Even
Director, Passenger Traffic: (vacant)
Public Relations and Spokesman: Benny Naor

Current situation

Cross-city service was inaugurated by Israel Railways in 1993 with completion of a 4.5 km double-track connection between IR's South and Central stations. Diesel-hauled suburban trains link Herzliyya in the north with Lod in the south. Two new stations on the cross-city line opened in late 1995.

Developments

In the Tel Aviv area IR plans several lines as part of a developing suburban network, and electrification of some routes is proposed. Projects include: a new 19 km line from Tel Aviv South to Rishon Le-Zion West, due for completion in 2007 and eventually to be extended to Ashdod; a 9 km branch from the Tel Aviv-Lod line to Ben Gurion International Airport, which was due to open in March 2004.

Plans to build two new stations on the cross-Tel Aviv 'Ayalon Railway', at Hahagana and University, were implemented in 2001. In November 2001, a third track was commissioned between University and Savidor (Tel Aviv Central) on the Ayalon Railway, increasing capacity by 50 per cent. Work to provide a third track on other sections of the Ayalon Railway was in progress in 2003.

For further information on IR, please see *Jane's World Railways*.

Italy

Bologna

Population: 380,000, conurbation 908,000 (estimated)

Public transport

Bus, trolleybus and local railway services provided by regional authority which operates both urban area and regional services. Tram and metro planned. Some suburban rail services by

Trenitalia SpA – Regionale and a local railway Ferrovia Bologna-Porto Maggiore.

ATC spa – Trasporti Pubblici Bologna – Bologna Public Transport Authority

Via Saliceto 3, I-40128 Bologna BO, Italy

Tel: (+39 051) 35 01 17
Fax: (+39 051) 35 01 06
e-mail: atcitta@atc.bo.it
Web: www.atc.bo.it

Key personnel

General Manager: Claudio Claroni
   Staff: Approximately 2,000 (of which 1,300 are drivers)

Current situation

ATC spa runs the public transport system in the Bologna catchment area operating urban and suburban services and transporting about 106 million passengers annually over a network covering 4,600 km. Total annual vehicle-km is in the region of 36 million. ATC also controls traffic planning, both public and private, in the city and suburban areas and manages parking on behalf of Bologna municipality. Trolleybuses returned to this city in 1991 after closure in 1982; some 40 km of wiring had been retained on a care and maintenance basis. Reintroduction coincided with new restrictions on motor car access to the city centre on environmental grounds. Route 13 runs west to southeast via the city centre, from Borgo Panigale to San Ruffillo.

City-centre circular route 32/33 was converted in October 2002, following complete renewal of most of the wiring (left in place since the withdrawal of trolleybuses from that route in 1979), and two further route reopenings are planned. Much wiring renewal work has taken place on the western half of Route 14 and on Route 20, both formerly trolleybus routes, and work is under way to electrify the present eastern section of Route 14, which was not previously a trolleybus route. The infrastructure along Route 14 for trolleybuses was completed in 2007, except for a new section added to the project's scope only recently, to extend the new wiring from Largo Mattei to ATC's Due Madonne depot. However, additional vehicles are needed before service can be introduced.

ATC runs a number of special services, including the Videobus, which runs to a regular timetable but requires prebooking by passengers, and the Freebus demand-response service which features stops equipped with 'call bus' buttons.

Interurban routes are being integrated with the local rail network. One line, Bologna-Galliere, offers through fares to feeder buses at several stations en route, and timetables have been revised to ensure better connections at interchanges.

The company also manages the local railway line Bologna-Vignola.

Developments

An 800 m extension of Route 13 in San Ruffillo, from Ponte Savena to Via Pavese, opened in September 2007. The project included the addition of a new substation.

ATC has developed an Automated Vehicle Management system (AVM), using GPS technology, for the whole of the fleet.

ATC-Bologna has successfully participated in the following European projects:
- VESTA (Thermie programme):
  optimisation of the public transport service by setting up a centralised network control system to manage the service in real time and to gather service data.
- CERERE (Thermie programme):
  creation of on-demand public transport services both on fixed and variable routes in low-demand areas in order to rationalise the service and save energy.
- GAUDI (Drive programme):
  the participation of several European cities has allowed the addressing of a number of highly important topics both in the area of public transport services and of transport in general. The main objectives of the project included experimental applications in the fields of automatic control of access to limited traffic zones, integrated fare management.
- ANTARES (Thermie programme):
  the activities carried out within this programme aimed at creating the first modules for the global urban mobility management system. The system developed: traffic light management for bus priority, variable message signs for private and public transport.
- CENTAUR (Clean & Efficient New Transport Approach for Urban Rationalisation):
  the project has introduced and developed a fleet of four innovative technology-based hybrid buses.

- TOSCA (Technological & Operational Support for Car shAring):
  door-to-door alternative to the traditional public transport concept. Car sharing is a modern idea of mobility, which provides the use of a car without owning one. This service, though having the private car flexibility, gives a higher economic and ecological efficiency.
- MOBISERVICE: this project has investigated multimodal systems and services provided by the leading Mobility Service Centres in Europe and has identified the 'best practice' adopted.
- ALTAIR: this ongoing project foresees a feasibility study and a trial for the implementation of a multilinguistic application for online information and ticketing purchase and payment via mobile phone.

Other current projects include:
- Real-time information for blind people:
  85 bus stops have been equipped with a radio transmitter device able to communicate via radio with a pocket radio receiver allowing blind people to get real-time information while waiting at the bus stops.
- Hellobus: ATC has developed an information system, which allows real-time buses information by using a GSM mobile phone. The user gets the required information about bus running times at a specified bus stop, directly from his/her mobile phone just by selecting a short message (SMS), which contains the bus stop predefined code number and the number of the line desired. The message is then forwarded to the ATC operative centre through the mobile provider. This latter, receiver of the message, provides, through a forecast algorithm, the estimated time of bus arrival at the specified bus stop and sends back as an answer a short message with the forecast time of arrival.
- Onboard audio video information: about 200 devices (WOB-Welcome On Board) have been installed on the vehicles for onboard information. Such devices display next bus stop real-time information thanks to the GPS-based monitoring system. The WOB system also provides general information on the service as well as breaking news, sports, video clips, trailers etc.
- (DirettATC): ATC, aware of the growing need of citizens to have improved personal safety and security at bus stops, has created an interactive customer information and assistance system (DirettATC). The service allows the user to get in direct contact with the call centre operators in order to receive information related to the service or for any other emergency request. The system consists of a central station located at ATC and some multimedia kiosks positioned under the bus shelters. Kiosks are simply provided with a red push button

through which the customer connects to the operators.
- Car sharing: as a result of the European project TOSCA, ATC is involved in the ICS network for national car sharing management. In Bologna, the service includes 20 vehicles, 12 pick-up points, 520 users.
- Demand-responsive transport (Prontobus): a demand-response service specifically designed to satisfy the requests of inhabitants of low-density areas in the northern countryside of Bologna. The service operates on request only and only for the booked route, unlike a standard bus service. The service is operated only if at least one reservation is made.
- Solar panels: 30 photovoltaic panels have been installed. This solution provides lighting for those bus stops for which electrical connections is not possible or would be very expensive.
- Installation of natural gas refuelling stations at depots:
  the installation enables refuelling times comparable to diesel vehicles.
- Limited traffic zones automatic control (RITA):
  five gates for the automatic control of reserved lanes have already been installed. The system allows the number plates of private non-authorised vehicles running in these areas to be read and identified and fines to be imposed.
- Tram: the project for rubber-wheel vehicles with constrained guidance will soon be operational. The vehicle adopted will be an 18 m Civis from Irisbus and will run along the Bologna San Lazzaro to the city centre.
- Rapid transit system (metro): will be completed soon and will cover the areas Fair district-railway station-Borgo Panigale.
- STIMER: the new ticketing system involving the Emilia Romagna region will start by 2005–06. It will be based on zoning criteria and will adopt smartcard contactless technology.

In late 2003, ATC signed a contract, with a partnership of Irisbus and Consorzio Cooperativee Costruzioni, for the construction of and rolling stock for a new network of guided trolleybus lines that is planned to extend to more than 25 km over several years. This will be in addition to the existing network of non-guided trolleybus routes, but the two will be fully compatible with regard to overhead power supply. The contract includes the supply of 49 Irisbus Cristalis, 18 m articulated trolleybuses, the first example of which was delivered in early 2005. The new network will use the Civis system of optical guidance. The start of the infrastructure work was delayed until September 2007, due to major changes to the plans after the contracts had been signed, but agreed to by the contractors in late 2004, mostly as a result of local political factors. The first route is to run eastwards from the city centre to San Lazzaro, but

MAN/Autodromo trolleybus of ATC Bologna entering the new extension of Route 13 to Via Pavese, in San Ruffillo (Steve Morgan)   1341742

a predicted opening date has not been given. Two or three additional routes are planned. Owing to the delays in the infrastructure construction, no further Irisbus trolleybuses have been delivered and those that have been completed are being stored at the Irisbus factory.

Bus and trolleybus
(Urban area services only)

Passenger journeys: 104 million per year
Vehicle-km: Not currently available

Number of routes: Bus 50, trolleybus 2
Route length: Bus 565 km, trolleybus 18.6 km
On priority right-of-way: 40 km

Fleet: Approx 500 buses
Fiat 480.12.21
Fiat 490.12.22
Fiat 409/Menarini
Fiat 421/A/Menarini
Fiat 421/AL/Menarini
Breda/Menarini M221/1 LU
Fiat 490E18mt
Menarini 201/LU
Fiat minibus
Fiat minibus for disabled service
BredaMenarinibus 230/1MU
MAN NL202 FU CAM low-floor
Iveco 491.12.22
BredaMenarinibus M321U
In peak service: Approx 333
On order: 10 Pollicino battery-powered, 20 Carvin A9SE12 7.7 m, 4 low-floor suburban, 6 Cacciamali TCM890 urban, 21 Mercedes O405 12 m suburban and 20 Van Hool AG300 low-floor

Fleet: 55 dual-mode trolleybuses

Menarini M220 LU/4P (1990)	10
Breda 4001.12 (1990)	9
MAN NGT240 18 m low-floor (1998/2000)	35
Irisbus Cristalis low-floor articulated (2005)	1

On order: A further 48 Irisbus Cristalis articulated trolleybuses for delivery 2008/9

Most intensive service: 3 min
One-person operation: All routes
Fare collection: Tickets from machines and authorised vendors (newspaper kiosks, tobacconists, bars)
Fare structure: Flat, with time ticket (1 h), daily, transferable monthly and annual season tickets valid on all urban lines at varying rates for ordinary passengers, workers and students
Fare evasion control: Random inspection with penalty
Operational control: Inspectors/mobile radio
Arrangements for elderly/disabled: Reduced fares for persons on minimum pensions and disabled paid for by local authorities and included in subsidy provision below
Average distance between stops: 350 m
Average peak-hour speed: In mixed traffic, 15.4 km/h
Operating costs financed by: Fares 38.1%, other commercial sources 5%, subsidy/grants 56.9% (including concessionary fares reimbursement)
Subsidy from: Region 97.6%, national government 1.4%, local and other sources 1%
New vehicles financed by: Internal resources, with contribution from national transport fund

Suburban rail

Società Suburbana FBV
Via S Donato 25, Bologna, Italy
Tel: (+39 051) 421 79 11   Fax: (+39 051) 421 79 30
e-mail: info@suburbanafbv.it
Web: www.suburbanafbv.it

Key personnel
President: Claudio Claroni
Administration: Roberto Soffrittie
Director, Operations: Fabio Formentin

Current situation
In September 2003, the Bologna-Vignola railway line became operational. The 17 stations are equipped with real-time information panels and a GPS monitoring system. Supporting bus routes are also equipped with these systems to provide intermodal link information. The route is operated with two diesel locomotives.

Trenitalia SpA
Direzione Regionale – Emilia Romagna (Bologna)
P le Medaglie d'oro, 4 scala C, I-40121 Bologna, Italy
Tel: (+39 051) 630 33 85
Fax: (+39 051) 630 34 05
e-mail: rapclientela.er@trenitalia.it
Web: www.trenitalia.com
  www.trenitalia.it

Type of operation: Suburban heavy rail

Background
In 2000, FS Holding Sp (FS) split off its operating division as Trenitalia SpA. Trentitalia's Business Unit – Passeggeri Locale (Local Passengers) operates local passenger services including city suburban.

Current situation
Irregular services provided on six routes. Upgrading and integration planned under a scheme approved in 1986.

Developments
In 2005, Trenitalia launched sms2go, a new service which provides travel information via SMS.

Florence
Population: City 367,000, Province 958,000 (2004 estimate)

Public transport
Bus services provided by undertaking belonging to consortium of local authorities serving region as well as city, with some additional privately owned regional services. Suburban services by Trenitalia SpA – Regionale. Tramway under construction.

Azienda Trasporti Area Fiorentina spa (ATAF)
CP 4140, Viale dei Mille 115, I-50131 Florence, Italy
Tel: (+39 055) 565 01   Fax: (+39 055) 565 02 09
e-mail: segreteria@ataf.fi.it
Web: www.ataf.net

Key personnel
President: Aldo Frango
Administrative Council: Luigi Di Renzo, Stafno Marmugi, Salvatire Quarta, Fabrizio Signorini
Director General: Renzo Brunetti
Lines Director: Piero Sassoli
Technical Director: Massimo Ruini
  Staff: 1,416

Background
Azienda Trasporti Area Fiorentina spa (ATAF) represents a consortium of nine municipalities: Bagno a Ripoli, Calenzano, Campi Bisenzio, Fiesole, Florence, Impruneta, Scandicci, Sesto Fiorentino and Vaglia. These cover a total territorial surface area of 538 km² with a population of some

ATAF's Iveco CNG low-floor bus   0038774

600,000. ATAF controls all local public transport in the Florentine area.

Developments
There are now four 'Blue Line' routes operated by Gulliver electric minibuses serving the historic city centre. Route 16 (FS-Scandicci) has joined the airport bus (Route 62) as ATAF's second 'direct' service running on reserved right-of-way and with limited stops. ATAF also operates dial-a-bus in some parts of the city, with both the stop and time specified by the caller.

A fleet of 50 low-floor buses has been delivered, and trials with gas-powered buses were made in 1997.

ATAF's legal status changed in 1996, bringing the undertaking greater autonomy and more responsibility for its financial performance.

ATAF now has a contract with the Comune (city council) for provision of service.

Bus
Passenger journeys: (1997) 77.3 million
Vehicle-km: (1997) 19.8 million

Number of routes: 69
Route length: 630 km
On priority right-of-way: 24 km

Fleet: 506 vehicles

Fiat, Menarini and Inbus standard	301
Fiat, Menarini and Inbus low-floor	35
Fiat 412 double-deck	1
Fiat 470.18.24 and Iveco articulated	51
Fiat 470.18.24 and Iveco articulated low-floor	51
Various small/minibuses	33

For details of the latest updates to *Jane's Urban Transport Systems* online and to discover the additional information available exclusively to online subscribers please visit
juts.janes.com

ATAF's Technobus electric low-floor bus in the centre of Florence (D Burns)　　　0104659

ATAF's ticket machine in central Florence
(D Burns)　　　0104658

Technobus electric minibuses	20
Iveco CNG low-floor (1996)	14

In peak service: 382
On order: 50 buses a year

Most intensive service: 2 min
One-person operation: All single-deck routes
Fare collection: Coin to farebox or prepurchase passes with cancelling machine on bus
Fare structure: Mainly flat; time-tickets, multitickets, monthly passes
Fare evasion control: Roving inspectors
Integration with other modes: Several lines terminate at rail stations
Operational control: Mobile radio
Arrangements for elderly/disabled: Half and free fares
Average distance between stops: 292 m
Average peak-hour speed: 15.9 km/h
Operating costs financed by: Fares 39.8 per cent, other commercial sources 3.3 per cent, subsidy/grants 56.9 per cent
Subsidy from: National government 88 per cent, local taxes 12 per cent
New vehicles financed by: National transport fund and local authorities

Tramway (under construction)
Gauge: 1,435 mm
Min curve radii: 25 m

Max gradient: 7 per cent (approx)
Electrification: 750 V DC

Current situation
Construction of the first of three tram lines began in December 2004. The line will be 7.5 km long with 15 stops and will run from Florence S Maria Novella (Florence railway station) to Scandicci. The route will be almost entirely segregated and will have priority signalling. There will be a workshop depot at Villa Costanza. Service is foreseen at three minutes and opening is scheduled for early 2008. Seventeen Ansaldobreda Sirio trams are on order for this line. RATP won the concession to build and operate this line in December 2004.

A 30-year contract for the construction of lines 2 (7.5 km) and 3 (first phase, 4.5 km. A second phase of 8.5 km is planned to be built at a later stage) was signed with RATP/ALSTOM in June 2005. Construction is expected to begin in the second half of 2006, with opening in 2009/10.

Trenitalia SpA – Regionale
Divisione Trasporto Regionale (Florence)
Piazza della Croce Rossa, I-10061 Rome, Italy
Tel: (+39 02) 63 71 79 45; 63 71 79 47; 63 71 79 39
Fax: (+39 02) 63 71 79 87
Web: www.trenitalia.com;
　www.regionale.trenitalia.it

Type of operation: Suburban heavy rail

Background
In 2000, FS Holding Sp (FS) split off its operating division as Trenitalia SpA. Trentitalia Regionale operates local passenger services including city suburban.

Current situation
Trains run frequently between Florence and Pisa airport, Pistoia and Arezzo; irregular services on other routes. Electrified 3 kV DC, 1,435 mm gauge.

Developments
Track quadrupling is to be undertaken between Florence and both Prato and Empoli to permit segregation of suburban and long-distance services. When completed, trains will run every 10/20 minutes to Prato, and 20/30 minutes to Empoli and Pisa airport. The Faentina Line is also to be rehabilitated.

An integrated ticketing system known as the Orange Card has been introduced experimentally in daily, weekly and monthly versions; it can be used on FS, ATAF and Co-operativa Autolinee Pratesi buses.

Genoa
Population: 604,732 (2003)

Public transport
Urban and suburban bus, trolleybus and regional networks operated by municipal undertakings, 10 elevators, two funiculars and one rack railway, and a light rail route.

Azienda Mobilita e Trasporti Genova spa (AMT)
Via L Montaldo 2, CP 1756, I-16137 Genoa, Italy
Tel: (+39 010) 55 81 14
Fax: (+39 010) 558 24 00
e-mail: amt.spa@amt.genova.it
Web: www.amt.genova.it

Key personnel
Principal Officers: Ing Sordini, Dott Pesci (General Manager), Rag Lepera, Sig Cecchini, Ing Figone, Ing Galanti, Dott Ravera
Staff: 2,174 (as at 1/1/2005)

Passenger journeys: (2004) 148.1 million

An Ansaldobreda trolleybus turning at Foce, the eastern terminus of Genoa's trolleybus route
(Steve Morgan)　　　0533772

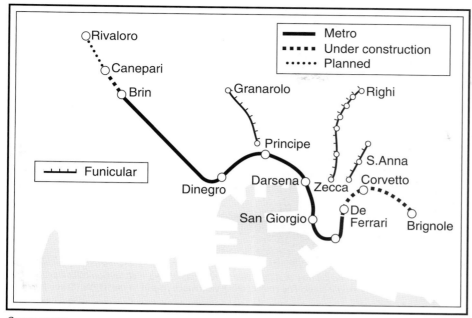

Genoa metro   1127070

Current situation

Urban route networks are operated.

Initial section of metro opened in 1990, but planned expansion has been slower than originally anticipated.

The first route of a planned three-route trolleybus network opened in 1997, the 7 km Route 30, between Foce and Via Francia.

Developments

In 1999, the company became an SpA. In 2002, the suburban services were relinquished to ALI SpA (www.provincia.genova.it/ali/). In 2004, the integrated ticketing responsibility was passed to AMI SpA (www.amibus.it).

From February 2005, the metro was extended to De Ferrari.

In July 2005, an order was placed with Van Hool/Kiepe for the supply of 17 articulated trolleybuses, with an option for a further three vehicles. These are to be used for the planned conversion of bus route 20 to trolleybus in 2008. Delivery of these trolleybuses began in late 2007, but as at the end of that year, none had entered service.

Bus and trolleybus (urban operations only)

Passenger journeys: (2004) 148.1 million
Vehicle-km: (2004) 29.1 million

Number of routes: Bus 135, trolleybus 1
Route length: 937 km

Fleet: 827 buses

Fiat 316 (1979/90)	44
Fiat 418 (1973/75)	4
Fiat 470 (1987)	4
Fiat 471 (1985/87)	38
Fiat 480 (1991)	15
Inbus 210 (1984)	36
Fiat 3471 (1985/88)	18
Fiat 490E (1996/98)	46
Fiat 491E (1999/2000)	54
Fiat VS 880 (1982/1984)	13
Pollicino (1997/2001)	14
Breda 2001 (1989/91)	69
Breda M230 (1996/1999)	66
Breda M231 (2000)	20
Breda M321 (1997/2000)	69
Siccar 181C (1979/91)	20
Irisbus 491E.18 (2002/03)	23
Iveco 490EEY (1994/1999)	18
Iveco 491E (2000/01)	61
Scania CN (2002/04)	50
Menarini 201 (1984/1988)	40
Autodromo 7.7 (2002/04)	28
Autodromo Tango	30
Cacciamali TCC (2002/04)	33
Mercedes-Benz 214K (2002/04)	9
Mercedes-Benz Evobus (2003)	5

In peak service: 602
Average age of fleet: 9.03 years

Fleet: 20 trolleybuses

Breda/Ansaldo F15 (1997/98)	20

On order: 17 Van Hool/Kiepe articulated low-floor trolleybuses for delivery in 2007/08

Most intensive service: 3–10 min
One-person operation: All routes
Fare collection: Automatic issuing machines or roadside points of sale
Fare structure: 90 min period tickets, passes; passes
Fare evasion control: Inspectors
Fares collected on board: 0 per cent
Number of stops: 2,484
Operational control: Radio and inspectors
Average distance between stops: 250 m
Average peak-hour speed: 15 km/h
Operating costs financed by: Fares and other commercial sources 32.9 per cent, subsidy/grants 67.7 per cent
Subsidy from: City, region and province; balance as deficit

Elevators
Current situation

Public lifts are operated to serve areas built on steeply sloping hillsides.

Developments

In December 2004, a new lift opened at Montegalletto.

Funiculars/rack railway
Current situation

Two funiculars (Righi – 1.4 km and Sant'Anna – 358 m) and a 1.1 km rack tramway from Principe to Granarolo are operated; two cars serve each route. In 1990, proposals to upgrade the rack line were accepted by the municipality, but lack of funds prevented their implementation. Now the work is to be undertaken in a four year programme.

Metro
Type of operation: Metro, opened 1990

Car-km: (2004) 0.6 million

Route length: Approx 5 km
Number of routes: 1
Number of stations: 6

Gauge: 1,435 mm
Electrification: 750 V DC, overhead

Service interval: 4 min (peak), 10 min (off-peak)
First/last car: 06.30/21.00

Rolling stock: 18 vehicles

Firema (1989)	M6
Firema (1992–95)	M12

Current situation

Initial section between Brin and Principe in operation utilising an existing tunnel and right-of-way of former tramway system. The extension from Dinegro to Principe opened 1992.

The extension from Principe to San Giorgio was officially opened in July 2003, with passenger services starting in August.

Developments

A further extension from San Giorgio to Brignole is under construction.

The next extension, which has received approval, will run from Brignole towards Staglieno with a branch from Terralba to the San Martino Hospital with four stations.

A possible future project would be an extension from Dinegro westwards towards Sampierdarena.

In February 2005, the line was extended from San Giorgio to De Ferarri station (5.2 km). The intermediate station is not yet opened.

Trenitalia SpA

Direzione Regionale – Liguria
Via Andrea Doria 5, I-16126 Genoa, Italy
Tel: (+39 010) 25 25 77   Fax: (+39 010) 274 34 17
e-mail: rapclienela.li@trenitalia.it
Web: www.trenitalia.com

Type of operation: Suburban heavy rail

Passenger journeys: 36.5 million (estimate)
Train-km: 7.2 million (estimate)

Background

In 2000, FS Holding Sp (FS) split off its operating division as Trenitalia SpA. Trenitalia Local Passengers Business Unit operates local passenger services including city suburban.

Current situation

Services run on several cross-city routes with major flows concentrated on the coastal route from Voltri in the west to Nervi/Borgio F in the east. Train frequency is often every 10 min. Less busy routes to Acqui terme and Ronco Scrivia have half-hourly service. There are 19 stations within the urban area.

In 1993, a new mostly underground alignment was introduced linking Sampierdarena in the east with Brignole in the west, making it possible to segregate suburban services on the congested central section between Porta Principe and Brignole, where trains run every five to seven minutes. A new underground suburban station at Porta Principe links with buses and metro as well as FS long-distance trains. Brignole is a major bus interchange.

Trenitalia has standardised tariffs on regional services in Liguria, with the same fare charged on routes regardless of mode. An integrated timetable covers all operators, and unnecessary duplication of services eliminated. An hourly ticket gives free transfer to ATM bus and metro services for incoming commuters. In addition, there are new monthly passes valid on both trains and buses throughout the region.

In 2004, local services accounted for some 35 per cent of the local passenger transport journeys.

Developments

Modernisation of vehicles is ongoing. Real-time information is available at stations.

Rolling stock: 53 vehicles

Milan

Population: City 1.31 million, urban area 4.3 million, metropolitan area 7.4 million (estimates)

Public transport

Bus, trolleybus, tramway and metro services provided by municipal undertaking now serving neighbouring communities and also operating suburban and interurban services. Suburban rail services operated by national and regionally owned railways, being upgraded to regional metro.

Azienda Trasporti Milanesi spa (ATM)

Foro Buonaparte 61, I-20121 Milan, Italy
Tel: (+39 02) 805 58 41
Fax: (+39 02) 86 46 37 95
Web: www.atm-mi.it

Key personnel

President and Chief Executive Officer:
   Bruno Soresina
Board of Administration: Francesco Tofoni, Michele Battiato, Umberto Bertelè, Franco Caron, Giuseppe Frattini, Massimo Ferrari
Director General: Roberto Massetti
Director, Personnel: Giuseppe Pinna
Director, Commercial: Pierluigi Silvestri
Director, Logistics: Francesco Lipari
Director, Finance: Dr C di Nella
Manager, Surface Routes: Bruno Decio
Manager, Metro and Tram: Valerio Cocucci
   Staff: 8,511

Current situation

ATM is responsible for bus, trolleybus, tram and metro services within the Milan city boundaries, and for metro, bus and tram routes in an area extending to about 30 km from the city centre. It provides services to a population of some 2.9 million in an area of 1,052 km². In the suburban region, there are three extensions of metro in the northeast, tram routes to Limbiate and Carate, and 45 bus routes.

Since 1985 ATM has staffed parking areas at metro park-and-ride stations, and in 1988 took over control of many city-centre parking meters. Areawide integrated fares structure implemented in 1991 covering ATM and private operators' services, based on urban and interurban zones.

Developments

Plans to extend the metro further into the suburbs have been temporarily halted, but tramway upgrading and segregation is continuing. In an attempt to curb traffic congestion, park-and-ride sites are planned with a total of 35,000 spaces.

In 2006, all shelters will be replaced and will include variable message displays.

Activation of a magnetic and electronic ticketing system is scheduled to take place shortly.

Passenger boardings: (All modes)
(2004) 590.5 million
Vehicle-km: (All modes)
(2004) 138.5 million

Operating costs financed by: (Bus and trolleybus) Fares 37.3 per cent, other commercial sources 3.3 per cent, subsidy/grants 59.4 per cent
Subsidy from: Regional and local government

Bus and trolleybus

Passenger boardings: (1996) Bus 253.5 million urban, 44.2 million suburban; trolleybus 47.4 million
(1997) Bus 251.4 million urban, 43.4 million suburban; trolleybus 44.5 million
Vehicle-km: (1996) Bus 34.8 million urban, 20.3 million suburban; trolleybus 4.7 million

Number of routes: Bus 93 (50 urban, 43 suburban), trolleybus 3
Route length: Bus 417.9 km urban, 622.8 km suburban; trolleybus 40.4 km

A three-car tramset in Varedo on one of ATM's two remaining northern suburban tramway/light rail lines, which are mostly single-track. The rolling stock was modernised in the 1980s (Steve Morgan)
0533779

Fleet: 1,603 buses

Standard Fiat 421/418/INBUS 210	800
Fiat 471 Effeuno (1984/88)	266
Fiat 571-12 (1982)	5
Iveco Turbocity (1990)	92
Iveco-Macchi 580 (1989)	80
Iveco	50
Bredabus (1991)	71
Menarini NU201/1 (1981)	62
Lancia 718-441 (1973)	2
Lancia 703-08 (1962)	3
Mauri Turbo 5500-5529 (1991)	2
Others	140
Disabled service	30

In peak service: 715 urban, 471 suburban

Fleet: 145 trolleybuses

Fiat 2470/Socimi (1983)	70
Bredabus 200-232 articulated (1991)	33
Socimi/Macchi articulated (1994/95)	33
MAN/Autodromo low-floor articulated (1998–2000)	8
Irisbus Cristalis low-floor articulated (2005)	10

On order: Between 55 and 80 Van Hool trolleybuses, all articulated for delivery 2009/10. The contract was signed in mid-2007, establishing the value, but the exact number of vehicles is yet to be determined, dependant upon the proportion, if any, of two-axle vehicles. The first vehicle was delivered in November 2008.
In peak service: 120
Trolleybus electrification: 600 V DC

Most intensive service: 5 min
One-person operation: All routes
Fare collection: Prepurchase with cancellation on board, or passes
Fare structure: Urban, flat; interurban, zonal; multitickets; prepurchase tickets and multitickets sold through machines and shops; weekly, monthly and annual passes
Fares collected on board: None
Fare evasion control: Random inspection with penalty
Operational control: Inspectors; computerised monitoring system being evaluated on one route
Arrangements for elderly/disabled: Fleet of lift-equipped midibuses
Average distance between stops: Interurban 580 m, urban 288 m
Average peak-hour speed: Bus urban 12.9 km/h, suburban 18.4 km/h; trolleybus 12.2 km/h
Bus priority: Reserved trolleybus lanes provided for part of city circular route (6.9 km) on central reserved alignment originally intended for tramway operation; priority measures to be completed for whole route
New vehicles financed by: Regional grants

Tramway

Type of operation: Conventional tramway

Passenger boardings: (1996) 177.4 million
(1997) 172.3 million urban, 4.3 million suburban
Car-km: (1996) 24 million

One of ATM's Ansaldobredo Sirio trams westbound on Via Emanueli on new Line 7, which opened in December 2002 as the first of four new 'Metrotramvie' (Steve Morgan)
0567225

Route length: 259.1 urban, 25.0 km suburban
Number of lines: 20 (18 urban, two suburban)
Number of stops: 600 urban, 55 suburban
Gauge: 1,445 mm
Track: 52 kg/m grooved and 50 kg/m standard rail, conventional sleepers on ballast
Max gradient: 5 per cent
Min curve radius: 20 m
Electrification: 600 V DC, overhead

Service: Peak 2–5 min, off-peak 5–12 min
First/last car: 05.00/01.30
Fare structure: Flat
Fare evasion control: Travelling inspectors
One-person operation: All routes

Rolling stock: 661 cars

1500 4-axle (1928)	M320
4600/4700 6-axle articulated (1955/56/84)	M29
4800 8-axle (1973)	M44
Marelli/Asgen 8-axle 4900 (1976)	M100
Suburban fleet	M38 T73
Bombardier Eurotram low-floor 7000 (1999–2002)	M26
Ansaldobreda Sirio 7100 Series 35 m (2002–04)	M26
Ansaldobreda Sirio 7500 Series 25 m (2003/04)	M5

In peak service: 367
On order: A further 26 Ansaldobreda Sirio 7100 Series and 30 (of a total order for 35) Ansaldobreda Sirio 7500 Series 25 m are in the process of being delivered

Current situation
Also operated are two remaining suburban tram lines totalling 40.4 km.

Developments
Current policy is for modernisation and strengthening of the electrification equipment, along with construction of two extensions and four new light rail lines (Metrotramvie). Line 24 is being extended from Via Noto to the municipal boundary at Via Selvanesco.

The first of the light rail schemes to open, in December 2002, was the initial section of the Precotto Line, to Largo Mattei in the Biccoca district. This incorporates a new branch of about 2 km and service is provided as new Route 7.

The Sud (South) Line involved new construction as far as Piazza Abbiategrasso and was opened in December 2003.

The Nord (North) Line to Parco Nord (7.1 km) is essentially a complete rebuilding of the section within the city of Milan of the suburban tram line to Desio, which was cut back to the city limits in 1999 and 2001/02 to permit work, including the replacement of single track with double track, to be carried out. It was opened in December 2003 and is served by an extension of Route 4 and new Route 5. The suburban tram route to Desio now has its Milan terminus adjacent to the new Parco Nord terminus of urban tram lines 4 and 5 and has not been re-extended into Milan.

The fourth line runs from Piazza Lagosta northwards to Cinisello Balsamo (8.5 km), of which the 3 km section between Lagosta and Bicocca uses the existing tracks of Route 7. Construction began in March 2004 and the new line opened in January 2009, as route 31.

Further extensions proposed are from Precotto to Cascina Gobba and a branch off the Nord Line running from Piazza Maciachini to Certosa FS station, incorporating a part of the existing tram route 3.

Metro
Background
Operated by ATM. Construction authority: Metropolitana Milanese SpA (see separate entry).

Type of operation: Full metro, first line opened 1964

Passenger boardings: (1996) 345.7 million (1997) 307.1 million urban, 31.9 million suburban
Car-km: (1996) 52.7 million

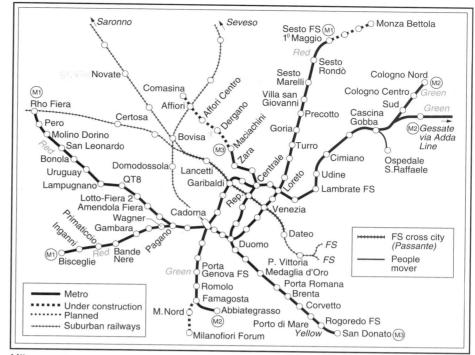

Milan metro

1115205

Route length: 74 km
  in tunnel: 51 km
Number of lines: three
Number of stations: 87
  in tunnel: 72
Gauge: 1,435 mm
Track: 50 kg/m UNI rail; ballasted and slab-track
Electrification: Red Line: 750 V DC, third-rail collection and fourth-rail return, conversion to 1.5 kV overhead planned; Green and Yellow Lines: 1.5 kV DC, overhead

Service: Peak Red Line 2–2½ min, off-peak five min
First/last train: 05.56/00.20
Fare structure: Flat, integrated with surface transport systems for urban lines; zonal for interurban line
Revenue control: Automatic entry barriers
Automatic control: Wayside and cab signalling, automatic block with automatic train stop, and CTC; ATO, ATP and ATS on Line 3 from new computerised control centre
Surveillance: Remote control of all stations by CCTV with voice/video datalinks

Rolling stock: 714 cars

Marelli Line 1 (1962–89)	M126
Asgen Line 1 (1962–88)	M122 T82
Ansaldo/Breda/OMS Line 2 (1970–87)	M176 T88
Socimi/Fiat/Breda/OMS Line 3 (1989/90)	M80 T40

In peak service: 558

Developments
In March 2005, the extension of Line 3 from Famagosta to Abbiategrasso (1.3 km) opened.

The extension of Line 1 to Rho Fiera opened in September 2005 (2.1 km), with the intermediate station at Pero opening in December 2005.

Current projects are an expansion of Line 3 northwards from Machiachini to Comasina (4.5 km, four stations), due to open in 2007, and an extension of Line 2 from Famagosta to Milanofiori Forum (4.7 km, two stations), scheduled for opening in 2006.

Future projects include an extension of Line 1 from Sesto FS to Monza Bettola (3.3 km, four stations) – financing has been approved for this extension and it is scheduled to open in 2007.

Trenitalia SpA
Divisione Passeggeri Regionale
Direzione Regional – Lombardia
Piazza S Freud 1, I-20154 Milano, Italy
Tel: (+39 02) 63 71 63 48   Fax: (+39 02) 63 71 74 87
e-mail: rapclientela.lo@trenitalia.it
Web: www.trenitalia.com

Type of operation: Suburban heavy rail

Current situation
Services provided on routes into five Milan city terminals, electrified 3 kV DC; 20 minute interval service to Malpensa airport.

For further information on Trenitalia SpA, please see *Jane's World Railways.*

Ferrovie Nord Milano SpA (FNM) – North Milan Railway
Piazzale Cadorna 14, I-20123 Milan, Italy
Tel: (+39 02) 851 11   Fax: (+39 02) 851 17 08
e-mail: infocare@ferrovienord.it
Web: www.fnmgroup.it

Key personnel
President: Norberto Achille
Director General: Marco Piuri
Director, Operations: Angelo Colzani
  Staff: 2,931 (2004)

Type of operation: Interurban railway

Passenger journeys: (2004) 50.47 million
(2005) 52.34 million

Background
FNM is by far the largest train operator in Italy after Trenitalia and has traditionally been owned by the Lombardia region, which still holds 58 per cent of its capital. FS now holds 15 per cent of its capital.

Current situation
LeNORD serves the northern suburbs of Milan with a main four-track route to Saronno, where it forks to Como and to Laveno on Lake Maggiore. The latter is single track beyond Malnate. Also from Saronno a single-track branch heads west to Novara, and a freight-only branch east to Seregno. A further double-track route runs from Bovisa to Seveso, beyond which single track extends to Canzo-Asso. In 1993 FNM took over operation of the 108 km non-electrified Brescia North Railway, linking Edolo with Rovato and Brescia.

As well as operating conventional suburban services, FNM's VieNord provides a dedicated link to Milan's Malpensa airport. The company launched its 'Malpensa Express' from Cadorna terminus in Milan in May 1999, shortly after the airport began to handle scheduled international flights. In 2004, Malpensa Express services carried 1.5 million passengers.

TAF double-deck emu forming a Malpensa Express service at Saronno (David Haydock)   0583013

For further information on FNM, please see *Jane's World Railways*.

Developments
In May 2006, FNM revealed a new corporate image and changes to subsidiaries, with the following brand names created: LeNORD, for local passenger transport; VieNord, for Malpensa Express; FerrovieNord, for infrastructure manager FNM Esercizio; Nord-Ing, for infrastructure planning and NordCargo for freight services.

The 4 km from LeNORD's present Milan terminus to Bovisa carries over 500 trains a day, two-thirds of which continue to Saronno. This section is being widened from two to four tracks. Quadrupling beyond Bovisa to Cadorna will enable separation of fast and slow services. This is scheduled for completion by the end of 2006. In May 2003 FNM opened a new station at Milano Nord Domodossola on this section, replacing the facility at Milano Nord Bullona.

The first phase of a EUR237 million scheme to serve Milan's Malpensa airport, by doubling 20.5 km of the Saronno-Novara branch as far as Bivio Sacconago and constructing from there a 13 km airport link, was completed in 1999. Track doubling from Bivio Sacconago to Vanzaghello went out to tender in early 2004.

In 2004, the Italian Government granted EUR74.5 million for upgrading and electrification of the 15 km Saronno-Seregno line, including doubling 10 route-km and construction of seven stations. The line is part of a putative Bergamo-Malpensa Airport line.

Completion of these projects, including the Passante, is forecast to boost LeNORD daily train working to almost 700 services.

Rolling stock: (2006 – all operations) 31 electric locomotives, 20 diesel locomotives, 110 emu power cars, 15 diesel railcars, 270 trailer vehicles and passenger coaches and 96 freight wagons. The fleet includes many double-deck coaches, which often operate with Class E750 single-deck railcars.

Metropolitana Milanese SpA (MM)

Head Office
Strutture ed Infrastrutture del Territorio
Via del Vecchio Politecnico 8, I-20121 Milan, Italy
Tel: (+39 02) 774 71   Fax: (+39 02) 78 00 33
e-mail: info@metropolitanamilanese.it
Web: www.metropolitanamilanese.it

Key personnel
Chairman and Managing Director: Giulio Burchi
Board of Directors: Antonio Acerbo, Saverio Bratta, Sergio Galimberti, Laura Girard, Roberto Massetti, Giovanni Paramithiotti, Domenico Scarcella, Maria Elisabetta Serr, i Livio Torio, Benedetto Tusa

Marketing: Brunello Salvadori
Legal and Corporate Affairs: Mario Martino
Technical: Bruno Cavagna
Project Management: Ignazio Carbone
Construction: Enrico Arini
Transport Engineering: Marco Broglia

Type of operation: Regional metro (under construction)

Background
Metropolitana Milanese SpA (MM) is the construction authority for the regional metro.

Current situation
A 9 km underground line opened at the beginning of 1998, bringing FNM and FS lines from the north into a new city-centre station at Porta Venezia. This forms the first stage of a cross-city link which will see the line extended to Porta Vittoria in 2004, allowing through running to several FS routes in the east and south. All lines are or will be electrified at 3 kV DC.

The first section comprises a link from FNM lines at Bovisa, through new stations at Lancetti, P Garibaldi and Repubblica, to Venezia. All four stations are major bus and/or metro interchanges. At Lancetti, a link comes in from FS lines at Certosa, allowing all suburban trains from the north and west to use the cross-city line.

For the start of services, a joint FS/FNM fleet of 50 four-car double-deck trains has been supplied by a consortium of Ansaldo, Breda, Firema and Adtranz. When the entire route is completed, a further batch of some 120 trains will be needed to operate eight routes and provide a three minute service through the cross-city tunnel.

For further information on Milan metro, please see separate entry for Azienda Trasporti Milanesi spa (ATM).

Developments
In March 2005, the extension of Line 3 from Famagosta to Abbiategrasso (1.3 km) opened.

The extension of Line 1 to Rho Fiera opened in September 2005 (2.1 km), with the intermediate station at Pero opening in December 2005.

Current projects are an expansion of Line 3 northwards from Machiachini to Comasina (4.5 km, four stations), due to open in 2007, and an extension of Line 2 from Famagosta to Milanofiori Forum (4.7 km, two stations), scheduled for opening in 2006.

Future projects include an extension of Line 1 from Sesto FS to Monza Bettola (3.3 km, four stations) – financing has been approved for this extension and it is scheduled to open in 2007.

Naples

Population: City 1 million, metropolitan area in excess of 3 million (estimates)

Public transport
Bus, trolleybus, tramway and funicular services provided by municipal undertaking with further suburban bus, trolleybus and local railway undertaking, and private suburban bus operators. Suburban trains on Circumvesuviana and other local railways, and on Italian Railways (FS) (now Trenitalia). Metro.

Azienda Napoletana Mobilità SpA (ANM)

Via GB Marino 1, I-80125 Naples, Italy
Tel: (+39 081) 763 11 11
Fax: (+39 081) 763 20 70
Web: www.anm.it

Key personnel
President: Antonio Simeone
Vice-President: Giuseppina Mengano Amarelli
Director General: Renato Muratore

ANM Ansaldobreda F19 low-floor trolleybus on Route 254R (Steve Morgan)   0567194

Directors:
Operations: Fabrizio Cicala
Personnel and Organisational: Sabato Carotenuto
Mobility Planning: Giulio Pasanisi
Technical and Infrastructure: Roberto Pensa
Staff: 3,339

Passenger boardings: (2005) 175 million (estimate)

Operating costs financed by: Fares 13 per cent, other commercial sources two per cent, subsidy/grants 85 per cent

Current situation
ANM is an independent subsidiary of the municipality of Naples.

An all-modes 'Napolipass' was introduced in 1994 for the transit services within the city boundaries. Initially, two suburban rail operators, SEPSA and Circumvesuviana, did not join the pass scheme, but eventually did so in 1997. In October 2000, a new zone-and distance-based fare structure called Unico Compania was introduced, which extended the system to the province of Naples, and later, in October 2001, the system was further extended to cover the entire region. The consortium that manages the system is the Consorzio UnicoCampania (website: www.unicocampania.it).

A programme to expand the use of trolleybuses was adopted in the late 1990s, under which it was planned to renew or renovate the wiring of routes which were withdrawn between 1975 and about 1984. New sections were built to address the conversion of many two-way street sections to one-way traffic. For this programme, 75 new low-floor trolleybuses were ordered from Breda (now Ansaldobreda), subsequently increased to 87, to replace the existing vehicles. The first new trolleybuses entered service in October 2000, and all of the old vehicles were withdrawn by March 2001.

The plans for infrastructure renewal have proceeded very slowly, with no routes having been reactivated as at late 2003. The expansion focus has been changed to the planned introduction of two new trolleybus routes, 201-2, in the city centre. The total number of trolleybuses currently required is about 39. In addition, a planned conversion of an existing bus depot to trolleybus used to accommodate all 87 of the new vehicles has been delayed, and this has resulted in only 63 of the 87 new vehicles being delivered, with 12 more being stored at Ansaldobreda's Napoli plant and a further 12 at the company's Pistoia plant.

Developments
A fleet of hybrid buses was introduced as part of the European Union Centaur/THERMIE programme. Other facets of the Centaur programme include AVIT (Automatic Vehicles Identification Technology) and introductions of wheelchair lifts for disabled people.

Work to electrify the city-centre bus route 201 and conversion to trolleybus took place in June 2004.

In April 2006, ANM opened new central-area trolleybus route 202, replacing identical bus route C55.

Conversion of additional motorbus routes to trolleybus is planned.

Bus and trolleybus
Passenger boardings: Not currently available
Vehicle-km: Not currently available

Number of routes: Bus 143, trolleybus 5
Route length: (One way) bus 1,796 km, trolleybus approx 60 km

Fleet: 1,016 buses
In peak service: 485

Fleet: 63 trolleybuses
Ansaldobreda F19 low-floor (2000/02)   63
On order: A further 24 identical vehicles, of which 12 have already been completed and delivered (but which are temporarily stored at the local

AnsaldoBreda Sirio tram of ANM in unsegregated kerbside street running in the San Giovanni district, on route 4 (Steve Morgan)
1341746

Ansaldobreda plant, due to lack of space at the operator's trolleybus depot)
In peak service: 39

Fare collection: Multiride tickets and passes with validation and cancelling machines on board, or payment to driver or farebox
Fare structure: Stages (three rates); monthly passes, multiride all-mode and all-operator tickets
Fare evasion control: Roving inspectors
Average peak-hour speed: Bus 13.6 km/h, trolleybus 11.8 km/h

Developments
Trolleybus routes 254 and 254R were combined as one route, 254, in July 2007.

Tramway
Type of operation: Conventional tramway

Passenger boardings: Not currently available
Vehicle-km: Not currently available

Route length: 19 km
Number of routes: 3

Gauge: 1,435 mm
Electrification: 600 V DC, overhead

Rolling stock: 51 cars
Meridionali (1933/35) rebodied by
  Fiore/SOFER (1976/80)   M29
Ansaldobreda Sirio low-floor 18.5 m
  (2004/06)   M22
On order: None

Current situation
The section of tramway between Piazzale Tecchio and Bagnoli was closed in October 1998. A further closure of the section between Piazza Vittoria and Piazzale Tecchio took place in December 2000, and as a result of this trams Route 1 was cut back to Piazza Vittoria and Route 2 was withdrawn.

Developments
There are plans to raise the voltage of the tram network to 750 V at some stage.

All tram services were suspended from August 2003 to January 2004 in order to permit some track re-laying and modification of all of the overhead wiring, to accommodate pantographs in place of trolley poles. This was made very complex by the existence of numerous tram-crossings and trolleybus wires on this system. 29 trams have been fitted with pantographs.

The first of 22 new Ansaldobreda Sirio low-floor 18.5 m trams entered service in December 2004 and by mid-2005 15 of these vehicles had entered service (of 16 received). These are the first all-new trams to enter service on this system since the 1940s, although the older cars

in the present fleet have been heavily rebuilt/modernised since they first entered service.

Funicular
Current situation
Three funiculars are operated (total 2.6 km) with 14 cars, carrying about 1.5 million passengers a year. Annual vehicle-km in 1997 was 42,500.

Developments
A modernisation programme has been carried out and is now almost completed.

Circumvesuviana Srl – Circumvesuviana Railway
Corso Garibaldi 387, I-80142 Naples, Italy
Tel: (+39 081) 772 21 11
Fax: (+39 081) 772 24 50
e-mail: circum@vesuviana.it
Web: www.vesuviana.it

Key personnel
General Manager: Fernando Rigo
General Director: Antonio Sarnataro
Rail Operations Director: Gennaro Acampora
  Staff: 1,800 (2008)

Type of operation: Suburban railway

Passenger journeys: (2007) 38.1 million
Train-km: Not currently available

Current situation
This busy suburban network links Naples with Nola, Baiano, Sarno and Sorrento, together with a circuit of Mount Vesuvius. Total 144 km on four routes with 96 stations, 950 mm gauge, electrified 1.5 kV DC.

For further information on Circumvesuviana Railway, please see *Jane's World Railways.*

Developments
In March 2003 a new double-track line opened from Napoli Collegamento to Casalnuovo, doubling capacity on the Baiano Line. A branch from Volla to San Giorgio a Cremano enables a service to be run from San Giorgio to Casalnuovo. Other plans include: double-tracking of the Sorrento branch between Torre Annunziata and Castellamare di Stabia; double-tracking and realignment of the Sarno branch west of Scafati, a total of 14.5 km. Further extensions, double-tracking and realignments have been statutorily authorised, including a new line from Alfa Sud to Acerra.

Rolling stock: 118 articulated three-car emus, three diesel shunting locomotives, four Bo-Bo electric locomotives, two coaches and 26 wagons

Compagnia Trasporti Pubblici SpA (CTP)

Via Sannio 19, I-80146 Naples, Italy
Tel: (+39 081) 700 11 11 (Central number)
Fax: (+39 081) 700 51 01 (Central number)
e-mail: info@ctpn.it
Web: www.ctpn.na.it

Key personnel
President: Ferdinando Scotto
Director General: Marcello Turrini
Director of Personnel: Alberto Salvatore
Director of Planning and Quality: Giuseppe
  Fiorentino
  Staff: 1,517

Passenger journeys: (2004) 33.7 million
(2006) 33.5 million
(2007) 33.5 million

Current situation
CTP is a Public Transport Company (TPL) owned
50 per cent by the province and 50 per cent by
the Naples municipality. It operates a network of
suburban and interurban bus services, mainly
in extra-urban territory, serving 72 communities
between Naples and Caserta. CTP manages
bus services in the Vesuvian area through
participating companies, plus tourist services in
Naples and Sorrento. It operates a self-contained
trolleybus system from Naples to Aversa.
  CTP provides consulting services and manages
a methane filling station.

Developments
Ten new low-floor vehicles were ordered from
Solaris/Ganz in October 2003, and these entered
service in April 2005.
  New trolleybus route M11 was introduced in
June 2005, connecting Piscinola-Scampia metro
station with Teverola and Aversa. This mostly
followed previous route M13.
  In May 2003, during the UITP World Congress
and Mobility & City Transport Exhibition, CTP
signed the Charter on Sustainable Development,
agreeing to adhere to its social, environmental
and economic principles, and to integrate these
into its own strategic objectives. To this purpose,
50 new buses powered by methane and 10
trolleybuses have entered service. Another of the
company's aims has been the implementation of
a photovoltaic system to generate electricity.

Bus and trolleybus
Vehicle-km: (2005) 21.5 million
(2006) 18.3 million

Number of routes: Bus 140, trolleybus 2
Route length: 2,300 km

Fleet: 506 buses	
Urban	98
Suburban	279
Interurban	129

Fleet: 13 trolleybuses	
Ansaldobreda F19 low-floor (2000)	3
Solaris/Ganz Trollino 12T low-floor (2005)	10

Consorzio UnicoCampania

Piazza Matteotti 7, I-80133, Italy
Tel: (+39 081) 551 31 09; 420 12 85
Fax: (+39 081) 551 44 14
e-mail: info@unicocampania.it
Web: www.unicocampania.it

Key personnel
General Manager: Antonietta Sannion

Background
The Consorzio UnicoCampania was founded on
19 December 1994, as the Napolipass Consortium
with the aim of promoting and improving
public transport in the city of Naples, with the
introduction of the 'GiraNapoli' combined tariff.
  From 12 December 2002 the consortium
became the regionally based 'Consorzio

UnicoCampania', which includes the following
associated companies and thus integrates all the
551 towns of the Campania Region, with a total
of some 5.8 million residents.

Associated companies
Company	Areas served
ACMS	Caserta and its Province
AIR	Provinces of Naples and Avellino
AMTS	Benevento
ANM	Naples and its Province
Circumvesuviana	Naples and Provinces of NA, AV and SA
CSTP	Salerno and its Province
CTI/ATI	Avellino and its Province
CTP	Naples, Provinces of Naples and Caserta
MetroCampania Nord-Est	Provinces of Naples, Caserta and Benevento
MetroNapoli	Metro network
SEPSA	Naples and its Province
SITA	Provinces of Naples, Avellino and Salerno
Trenitalia	Regional railway network

Current situation
Consorzio UnicoCampania is a consortium of
13 public transport companies, which manages
tariff integration in Campania.

Metrocampania Nord-Est srl

Formerly Ferrovia Alifana e Benevento Napoli Srl
(Alifana Railway)
Via Don Bosco (ex-scalo merci), I-80141 Naples,
Italy
Tel: (+39 081) 789 71 11
Fax: (+39 081) 789 72 92
e-mail: info@metrocampanianordest.it;
  seg.napoli@metrocampanianordest.it
Web: www.metrocampanianordest.it

Key personnel
Director General: G Racioppi
Director, Alifana Railway: A Marescotti
Director, Benevento-Naples Railway:
  G de Iudicibus

Type of operation: Suburban railways

Passenger journeys: (FABN)
(2002) 1.6 million

Current situation
MetroCampania Nord-Est srl, formerly Ferrovie
Alifana e Benevento-Napoli (FABN), comprises
the former Alifana Railway (FA) Piedmonte
Matese-Santa Maria Capua Vetere line (41 km)
and the Benevento-Naples Railway (FBN)
(49 km). Trains on both lines run through to
Naples over FS tracks. MetroCampania Nord
Est srl also operates buses. The ex-FA line
is now being modernised and electrified at
3 kV DC. FA also owns a 35 km direct line from
Santa Maria Capua Vetere to Naples via Aversa
but this has not operated since 1976. In 1996
the government agreed to fund 50 per cent of
the cost of converting this line from 950 mm
to standard-gauge and taking it from Piscinola
to Capodichino airport, with the municipality
providing an additional EUR155 million to extend
tracks to Garibaldi/Centrale in central Naples. The
Piscinola-Garibaldi line, which will be electrified
at 1.5 kV DC, will be shared with the Naples
metro. Work began in 1997.

Developments
Tenders were called in 2004 to build the 3.3 km
Piscinola-Capodichino Aeroporto section. The
12 km section from Aversa to Piscinola has
already been rebuilt underground but the tunnel,
ready since 1990, still awaits track and overhead
power supply equipment. Conversion from Santa
Maria Capua Vetere to Aversa is still under study.
The Piscinola-Mugnano section was due to open
in 2005 and Mugnano-Aversa in 2006, electrified
at 1.5 kV DC and operated by Naples metro

trains. The ex-FBN line is already fully electrified.
Plans exist to build a cut-off to reduce the line's
length by 7 km, eliminate level crossings and
raise speeds from 70 km/h to between 100 and
140 km/h.
  In 2003–04 the FA line received three refurbished
railcars, former FS Class 668.1400 units. In 2004,
the Campania region allocated EUR31.7 million
for eight emus for the FA line.

Rolling stock:
FA	16 diesel railcars, three trailers
FBN	Five electric railcars, one two-car emu, three three-car emus

MetroNapoli SpA

Via Ponte dei Francesi 37/d, I-80146, Naples, Italy
Tel: (+39 081) 559 42 00
Fax: (+39 081) 559 42 94
Freephone: 800 56 88 66
e-mail: info@metro.na.it
Web: www.metro.na.it

Current situation
In 2000, Italian railways were liberalised on EU
lines and any licensed operator can now operate
over FS tracks and use its passenger and freight
facilities. FS licensed its own operating arm
under the name Trenitalia. It operates long-
distance passenger, regional passenger and
freight services. FS retains exclusive rights to
infrastructure management.
  In 2001 MetroNapoli SpA, one of the new
companies licensed to operate over the national
rail network, took over staff and rolling stock of
the (then) 8.3 km Vanvitelli-Piscinola conventional
metro line (Line 1, also called the Metropolitana
Collinare), the 17 km FS Napoli Gianturco-
Pozzuoli Solfatara line (Line 2, formerly known
as 'Metropolitana FS') and the four funiculars:
Centrale, Chiaia, Mergellina and Montesanto.
  During the period 1 February 2001 to 31
October 2005, Trenitalia SpA held 38 per cent
of the MetroNapoli SpA shares, ANM SpA held
11 per cent and Naples Municipality held 51
per cent.
  In November 2005, Trenitalia SpA left the
company and its shares were bought by Naples
Municipality. Since November 2005, Trenitalia
SpA has been operating Line 2.
  As at December 2005, Naples Municipality held
99 per cent and ANM one per cent of the shares.

Developments
The transport plan for the City of Naples includes
the extension of Line 1 to form a circular route,
which will link upper Vomero with the old
town centre and the business centre at Centro
Direzionale. It will also link to the national rail
network (FS) and Capodichino airport.

Metro Line 1
Passenger journeys: (2005) 28.64 million
(2006) 28.9 million
Train-km: (2005) 981,874
(2006) 871,598

Route length: 13.5 km
  in tunnel: 9 km
Number of lines: 2 (for Line 6 information, see
below)
Number of stations: 14
Gauge: 1,435 mm
Electrification: 1.5 kV DC, overhead

Current situation
The line in operation is 13.3 km long, linking
Piscinola to piazza Dante and serving a total of
14 stations: Piscinola; Chiaiano; Frullone; Colli
Aminei; Policlinico; Rione Alto; Montedonzelli;
Medaglie d'Oro; Vanvitelli; Quattro Giornate;
Salvator Rosa; Materdei; Museo; Dante. It's a
particularly demanding line with gradients of
55 per thousand in some stretches, extremely
tight bends (up to 160 m radius) and a maximum
height difference of 235 m. Mean distance
between any two adjacent stations is 850 m,

with some stations lying at considerable depths (Salvator Rosa at 47 m; Rione Alto at 42 m). Two thirds of the track is underground (almost completely double-tunnel); the rest is above ground, mainly on viaducts (from Colli Aminei to Piscinola).

All of the stations have been designed to modern safety standards, with no barriers to access and special access for visually impaired people. A staff-controlled box is present at each station equipped with alarms for all internal systems (lifts, escalators, lights), a loudspeaker system, phone extensions and an emergency intercom for the lifts. The stations are equipped with a total of 84 escalators and 53 lifts. The line currently operates from 06:00 to 23:45.

Rolling stock: 76 cars (in four- and six-car sets)
Fiore/SOFER (1991–2001)   M36
Firema (1990–2000)   M40
First/last train: 06.00/23.45

Service: 6 min
Arrangements for elderly/disabled: Special access for visually impaired passengers

Line 6
Passenger journeys: n/a
Train-km: n/a

Route length: 2.3 km
in tunnel: 2.3 km
Number of stations: 4
Gauge: 1,435 mm
Electrification: 750 V DC, overhead

Current situation
The retained section of the original project comprises 5.8 km and nine stations, from Mostra to Municipio, and will be entirely underground. The LFR name was not revived and the line was designated Line 6 (Linea 6) of the metro system in 1997.

Construction resumed in about 1999 and the previously completed section is being renovated and also upgraded to improve facilities for the disabled.

Work is due to recommence on the outstanding six vehicles, and an order for a further six cars has been placed, of a completely new but compatible design.

The electrification is at 750 V DC, overhead.

Developments
Since February 2007, Linea 6 has been operating with four stations (Mostra, Augusto, Lala and Mergellina). The remaining section from Mergellina to Municipio should open in 2009, except for the intermediate stations on that section which will be not be completed and opened until 2011.

Rolling stock: 2 vehicles
Firema (1990/91)   M2

First/last train: 06.00/21.19
Service: 10 min
Arrangements for elderly/disabled: Special access for visually impaired passengers

Funiculars
Passenger journeys: (2005) 13.03 million
(2006) 15.4 million
Train-km: (2005) 139,104
(2006) 175,664

Route length: 3.12 km (total)
Number of lines: 4
Number of stations: 16
Electrification: 500 V DC

Current situation
There are four funiculars operating in Naples: Centrale, Chiaia, Montesanto and Mergellina.

The Centrale Funicular links the Vomero area (piazza Fuga) to the San Ferdinando area (via Toledo). There are four stops: Piazza Fuga, Corso Vittorio Emanuele, Petraio and Piazza Augusteo.

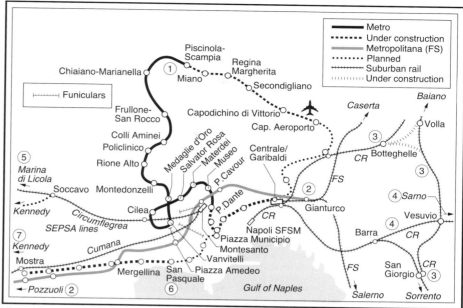
Map of Naples metro and light rail
1115257

Salvator Rosa station
1179465

The line is 1.235 m long with a mean gradient of 12 per cent. There are two 'trains', each made up of three carriages. Each train can hold up to 450 passengers.

The Chiaia Funicular links the Vomero (Via Cimarosa) to the Chiaia area (Parco Margherita). There are four stops: Cimarosa, Vittorio Emanuele, Palazzolo and Amedeo. The line is 500 m long with a continuous gradient of 29.18 per cent. There are two trains with two carriages per train. Each train can hold up to 300 passengers.

The Mergellina Funicular links Posillipo to Mergellina. There are five stops: Manzoni, Parco Angelina, S. Gioacchino, S. Antonio and Mergellina. The line is 550 m long with a mean gradient of 16.87 per cent. There are two single-carriage trains. Each train can hold up to 60 passengers.

The Montesanto Funicular links the Vomero (Via Morghen) with Montesanto (piazzetta Montesanto). There are three stops: Morghen, Vittorio Emanuele, Montesanto. The line is 824 m with a mean gradient of 20.84 per cent. There are two trains each with two carriages. Each train can hold up to 300 passengers.

All funicular stations (except Mergellina) provide access for disabled people and are equipped with lifts for wheelchair users and/or lifts.

Società per l'Esercizio di Pubblici Servizi SpA (SEPSA)
General Headquarters
Via Cisterna dell'Olio 44, I-80134 Naples, Italy
Tel: (+39 081) 542 92 05   Fax: (+39 081) 552 29 77
e-mail: sepsa@sepsa.it
Web: www.sepsa.it

Key personnel
President: Nicola Martino
General Manager: Raffaello Bianco
    Staff: 800 (rail operations, estimate)

Other offices
Railway Operations Division
Piazzetta Cumana 100, I-80125 Naples, Italy
Tel: (+39 081) 735 41 11   Fax: (+39 081) 735 42 92
e-mail: direzione.ferro@sepsa.it

Vehicle Operations Division
Via Vuova Agnano 9/d, I-80125 Naples, Italy
Tel: (+39 081) 542 97 84
Fax: (+39 081) 542 97 85
e-mail: direzione.auto@sepsa.it

Administrative Division
Via Vuova Agnano 9/d, I-80125 Naples, Italy
Tel: (+39 081) 542 91 11
Fax: (+39 081) 542 99 68; 99 83
e-mail: direzione.amm@sepsa.it

Background
SEPSA was formed in 1883, to construct and operate a rail service from Naples to Pozzuoli (Cumana Railway).

Current situation
SEPSA currently manages the rail service from Naples to Pozzuoli (Cumana Railway) and the Circumflegrea Railway as well as bus routes between Naples and the Phlegrean Littoral and through the islands of Ischia and Procida. The company provides rail services to the towns of Naples, Pozzuoli, Bacoli, Quarto and Giugliano. Bus lines serve the towns of Naples, Pozzuoli, Bacoli, Monte Di Procida, Procida and all municipalities on the island of Ischia and to a total population of some 1.4 million.

Suburban rail
Staff: 800 (2007 estimate)

Passenger boardings: (2007) 19 million
Vehicle-km: (2007) 1.6 million

Current situation
Operates two busy lines out of Montesanto station serving the western suburbs, the Cumana Railway (20 km) and the Circumflegrea Railway, also known as Ferrovia Cumana-Circumflegrea Autolinee, (27 km), running to Torregaveta by two routes; 1,435 mm gauge, electrified at 3 kV DC. Fares cover an estimated 20 per cent of operating costs.

There are three operational divisions under the supervision of the General Manager: Railway Operations, Vehicle Operations and Administration.

The company is certified to UNI EN ISO 9002 Quality Control standards.

Developments
Doubling is in progress on both lines. In 1996, the government allocated SEPSA EUR75 million towards the EUR108 million cost of a new line to serve the university at Monte Angelo. Work started in 2001 on a 5.5 km connection with three new stations between Kennedy on the Cumana line and Soccavo on the Circumflegrea line. A new station is to be built at Cilea in order to provide interchange with the Naples metro system. Plans also exist for a new line from Licola, on the Circumflegrea, to Mondragone, and for a line linking the Circumflegrea and FS lines north of Naples with a new airport at Grazzanise.

In December 2007, SEPSA ordered twelve two-car emus from Firema Trasporti for delivery in 2008. The Campania region has tendered for the refurbishment of thirteen Type ET.400 two-car emus.

Rolling stock
Fleet: 30 two-car emus, three diesel locomotives, 10 wagons
Further breakdown of fleet is not currently available
On order: 12 two-car Firema Trasporti emus, for delivery in 2008

Bus
Tel: (+39 081) 542 97 91
Fax: (+39 081) 542 97 89
e-mail: auto.napoli@sepsa.it
    Staff: Not currently available

Passenger boardings: (2007) 8.5 million
Vehicle-km: (2007) 8.3 million

Current situation
Also operates 21 Naples area bus routes (94 buses over 179 km) and four in Isola di Procida (14 buses over 33 km), and a separate network in Isola d'Ischia (78 buses over 211 km).

Fleet: 186 vehicles (urban and suburban operation)
Full breakdown of fleet is not currently available, but it is believed to include:
Breda 2001
Fiat 316E 8 18
Iribus U150
Irisbus 203E.9.24/U87
Iveco 200E.10.20/U94
Pollicino
Cito 520/U57AC-10/4
Fiat 315E 8 18
Fiat 370 12 L25
Fiat 370E.9.27.1 Orlandi
Fiat 671 12 24 L84
Iveco bus 380 12 35 P L71
Citaro 530/S98/AC-4/E3
Fiat 471 12 20 115 3P
Fiat 570 12 20
Fiat 571 12 20 100
Fiat 590E 12 22 96 3P V
Iveco bus 200E.10.20/S75
Breda Menarini MU230
Fiat 242 18 D F5
Fiat 316E 8 18
Fiat 470 10 20 105
Fiat 470 12 20 P122
Fiat 480.10.21 105
Fiat 571 10 20 100
Fiat 400-10.1 W/L-3.2
Fiat 49.10.1-N-3,6
Fiat A70.14

In peak service: Not currently available
On order: Not currently available

Trenitalia SpA – Passeggeri Locale
Direzione Regionale – Campania
C so Novara 10, Palazzo FS 17° piano, I-80142 Naples, Italy
Tel: (+39 081) 567 41 53
Fax: (+39 081) 567 44 12
e-mail: rapclientela.cm@trenitalia.it
Web: www.trenitalia.com

Head Office
Trenitalia SpA
Passenger Division
No 1 Piazza della Croce Rossa, I-10061 Rome, Italy

Type of operation: Suburban heavy rail

Passenger journeys: (Compania region) 98,000 (daily, approximate)
Train-km: (Compania region) (Annual) 11 million (approximate)

Background
In 2000, FS Holding Sp (FS) split off its operating division as Trenitalia SpA.

Trenitalia's Passeggeri Locale business unit operates local passenger services including city suburban.

Current situation
Suburban rail services run on a number of lines into Centrale and Piazza Garibaldi stations.

Developments
Since January 2003, an integrated tariff system has been in operation across the region.

Improvements in the region include the installation of air conditioning on trains and a real-time passenger information system.

Since November 2005, Trenitalia SpA has been operating Line 2 of the Naples Metro.

Metro Line 2 (Passante)
Route length: 16.5 km
Number of lines: 1
Number of stations: 11
Gauge: 1,435 mm
Electrification: 3 kV DC, overhead
Service: Peak 7–8 min; other times 9–10 min

Rolling stock: 80 cars (operated in four-car sets)
Breda, class ALe.724 emu (1983)   M40 T40

Palermo
Population: City: 675,500 (2006 estimate), Province: 1.24 million (2004 estimate)

Public transport
Bus services provided by municipal company, tramway under construction. Suburban train services.

AMAT Palermo SpA (Azienda Municipalizzata Autotrasporti)
Via Roccazzo 77, (Passo Di Rigano), I-90135 Palermo, Italy
Tel: (+39 091) 35 01 11   Fax: (+39 091) 22 45 63
e-mail: amat@amat.pa.it
Web: www.amat.pa.it

Key personnel
President: Sergio Rodi
Vice-President: Vincenzo Cannatella
Director General: Domenico Drago
    Staff: 2,050 (estimate)

Current situation
In addition to operation of the urban bus service, AMAT is now also responsible for the following

activities: operation of a car-sharing club; operation of paid parking for 3,000 cars in the city centre; tow-away service for illegally parked cars; maintenance of road signs; planning of future tramway services and operation of a campsite for mobile homes.

Developments
In 2005, AMAT became a public limited company.

Construction of a three-line, 15.3-km tram Light Rail Transit system is under way. The first two lines are expected to enter service in late 2009, with the third line becoming operational in 2010. It is expected the trams will carry 77,000 passengers daily.

Under a EUR192 million contract led by SIS, AMAT has ordered 17 bi-directional *Bombardier Flexity* Outlook, 32 m low-floor trams for the system, with the vehicles scheduled for delivery in 2009. Each tram will consist of five modules. Bombardier will also supply a *Bombardier CITYFLO* 150 traffic management system and has a four year maintenance contract for the fleet.

Bus
Passenger journeys: (Annual) 36.5 million (estimate)
Route length: 324 km
No of routes: 100+

Fleet: 350 (estimate)
Breakdown of fleet is not currently available

Average age of fleet: less than seven years

Most intensive service: 4 min
One-person operation: All routes
Fare collection: Prepurchase, on board sales against supplement
Fare structure: 90 min period tickets with free transfers, multi-ride tickets, various passes
Integration with other modes: Free transfers to suburban trains (Metro)

Trenitalia SpA
Passegeri Regionale
Direzione Regionale Sicilia
Via Roma 19, I-90133 Palermo, Italy
Tel: (+39 91) 617 02 24
Fax: (+39 91) 617 66 91
e-mail: rapclientela.si@trenitalia.it
Web: www.trenitalia.com

Type of operation: Suburban heavy rail, locally referred to as 'Metro'

Background
Trentitalia's Passegeri Regionale business unit operates local passenger services including city suburban.

Current situation
Frequent trains run at irregular intervals over two routes with a total length of 20 km, serving 13 stations.

For further information on Trenitalia, please see *Jane's World Railways*.

Rome

Population: 2.55 million (2001 Census)

Public transport
Bus, tramway, trolleybus, metro, suburban railway and suburban bus services operated by municipal authorities. Other suburban rail services by Trenitalia SpA – Regionale.

Agenzia per I Trasporti Autoferrotranviari del Comune di Roma (ATAC)
Via Volturno 65, I-00185 Rome, Italy
Tel: (+39 06) 46 95 20 27; 20 80
Fax: (+39 06) 46 95 20 87; 22 84; 469 51;
e-mail: clienti@atac.roma.it
Web: www.atac.roma.it

Key personnel
President: Mario di Carlo
General Manager: Domenico Mazzamurro
Operating Manager: Ottavio Mirabelli
  Staff: 12,691

Operating costs financed by: Fares 23 per cent, other commercial sources 2.5 per cent, subsidy/grants 74.5 per cent

Current situation
Under this regime, the two municipal companies which had run all urban transport, ATAC and Cotral, came under common management in 1994. A further reorganisation in 2000 saw creation of Metroferro, now Met.Ro (see separate entry), as operator of the metro and the three suburban railways formerly run by Cotral. ATAC continues to oversee the operation of the bus network and the tramway.

A new city government elected in 1993 had as one of its principal aims a dramatic improvement in public transport provision, and several new tram routes in the historic city centre and extensions have been proposed. There are to be more interchanges and park-and-ride, designed to encourage more drivers to leave their cars at home.

An all-modes integrated tariff system known as Metrebus was introduced throughout the Lazio region in 1994, covering some 378 municipalities and believed to be the largest scheme of its type in Europe. ATAC, Cotral and FS bus and train services are involved in the system, which is based on zones. A five per cent increase in patronage was recorded in the first few months; the ultimate goal is to raise public transport's market share by 25 per cent by the end of the century.

ATAC now is responsible for planning and investment and owns the depots and vehicles. Trambus SpA is responsible for operation and maintenance of the bus and tram network.

A new operator is Assoziazione Temporanea di Imprese (ATI), a group of private companies which are taking over bus services from ATAC. These are divided into four groups, totalling 30 million km/year. The first group of 21 routes in the east of Rome is managed by an ATI consisting of APM Perugia, ARPA Chieti, SITA and French company Transdev.

Bus & Trolleybus (Trambus network)

Trambus SpA
Via Prenestina 45, I-00176 Rome, Italy
Tel: (+39 06) 469 51 (Main number)
Tel: (+39 06) 46 95 39 76 (Marketing & Communications)
Fax: (+39 06) 46 95 39 75
e-mail: relazioni.esterne@trambus.com
Web: www.trambus.com

A Solaris/Ganz trolleybus inbound at Piazza Sempione on route 90 Express, the first route in Rome's 2005-opened trolleybus system (Steve Morgan)
1341741

Key personnel
President: Raffaele Morese
Chief Executive Officer: Filippo Allegra
Commercial Director: Alfredo Fratalocchi
External Relations, Marketing and Communications:
  Cynthia Orlandi
  Staff: 8,581

Passenger journeys: (2006) 1,200 million (estimate)

Number of routes: Bus 257 (22 night routes), trolleybus 1
Route length: (One way) 2,726 km
On priority right-of-way: 66 km
Trolleybus electrification: 750 V DC

Developments
The first of several planned trolleybus routes opened in March 2005. It is a conversion of the former diesel bus route 90 Express, which connects Termini railway station with Largo Labia, in Fidene, and uses segregated lanes over most of its length. The route is 11.5 km in length and the majority of it is powered at 750 v from overhead wiring, but the 500 m section of the route closest to the city centre is unwired, for aesthetic reasons, and the vehicles use electric battery power to operate over that section.

Although Trambus operates the trolleybus service, the construction of the route and the supply of the vehicles was the responsibility of ATAC. Conversion of several more bus routes to trolleybus is planned, but has been delayed, and several changes have been made. Electrification of routes 60-Express and 30-Express has been postponed indefinitely. Instead, it was expected that tenders would be invited in 2008 for the construction of a network of five shorter dual-mode trolleybus routes in the EUR district, in the southern part of the city, feeding the metro stations EUR-Palasport, EUR-Fermi and Laurentina.

Fleet: 2,374 buses
In peak service: 77 per cent of fleet

Fleet: 30 trolleybuses
Solaris/Ganz Trollino 18T articulated
  bimodal (2004/05)   30
In peak service: 77 per cent of fleet

Most intensive service: 2 min
One-person operation: 99 per cent
Fare collection: Prepurchase from machines; cancelling machines on board

Fare structure: Flat; prepurchase multitickets; weekly and monthly passes; ticket with 90 min time limit; combined ATAC/Acotral/FS passes
Fares collected on board: 71 percent of passengers hold passes; onboard ticket sales confined to three daytime routes and all night services
Fare evasion control: Inspectors
Integration with other modes: Connections with two metro lines; flat fare and passes for all modes
Operational control: Route inspectors; mobile radio with computerised online monitoring
Arrangements for elderly/disabled: 121 lift-equipped minibuses
Average distance between stops: 250–350 m
Average peak-hour speed: In mixed traffic, 15.44 km/h

Tramway
Type of operation: Conventional tramway

Passenger journeys: (1999) 81 million

Route length: 51.3 km
Number of lines: 6
Gauge: 1,445 mm
Max gradient: 8 per cent
Minimum curve radius: 18 m
Track: Conventional sleepers on ballast
Electrification: 600 V DC, overhead

Service: Peak 3 min, off-peak 9 min
First/last car: 05.00/24.00
Fare structure: Flat
One-person operation: On most cars
Centralised control: Radio-telephone

Rolling stock: 179 cars
Stanga (1948/52)	M58
MRS	M8
Socimi Type T8000 (1990/92)	M41
Alstom/Fiat Cityway Type 1 31 m (1997/99)	M28
Alstom/Fiat Cityway Type 2 33 m (1999/2001)	M50
Alstom/Fiat Cityway Type 2 44 m (2000)	M2

Metropolitana di Roma SpA (Met.Ro)
Via Tiburtina 770, I-00159 Rome, Italy
Tel: (+39 06) 57 53 30 38
Fax: (+39 06) 57 53 30 85
e-mail: info@metroroma.it
Web: www.metroroma.it

Key personnel
President: Stefano Bianchi
Managing Director: Roberto Cavalieri
Operations Manager: Gennaro Antonio Maranzano
Manager, Roma-Lido: Renzo Rea
Manager, Roma-Pantano: Gaetano Barberio
Manager, Roma-Viterbo: Umberto Montanari
  Staff: Approx 2,700

Current situation
Met.Ro was created in 2000 to run the metro and the three former Cotral suburban lines.

Metro
Staff: 2,700+

Type of operation: Full metro, first line opened 1955

Passenger journeys: Approx 1 million daily

Route length: 36.6 km
  in tunnel: 27.5 km
Number of lines: 2
Number of stations: 49 (Line A – 27 stations, Line B – 22 stations)
Gauge: 1,435 mm
Track: Line A, 50 kg/m 50 UNI; Line B, 46 or 50 kg/m rail; Line A, indirect fastenings to timber sleepers on ballast. Rail laid directly onto concrete on Tiber Bridge and other short sections
Max gradient: 4 per cent
Minimum curve radius: 100 m
Tunnel: Line A, cut-and-cover and closed tunnel excavation
Electrification: 1.5 kV DC, overhead

Current situation
Metroferro SpA, formerly Cotral, is responsible for operation of the metro and heavy rail network. Metroferro was renamed Met.Ro SpA on 1 March 2001.
  Metro Line A was extended from Valle Aurelia to Battistini in 2000. Linee Laziali SpA, formerly part of Cotral, operates regional buses in the Lazio region. Linee Laziali was renamed Cotral SpA on 1 March 2001.

Developments
Quintiliani station on Line B opened in June 2003.
  The Italian Government has approved Line B1 (4.5 km, three stations), a branch of Line B, from Bologna to Jonio. This branch will possibly open in 2010.
  There are further plans for an extension to Line B beyond Rebibbia and the Cotral line will be converted to Line C, with a northward extension also planned. There are also plans for a Line D.

Rolling stock: 377 cars
Breda Line A   M152 T37
Breda Line B   M188
On order: 10 six-car trains being delivered for opening of the Line A extension; a further 11 six-car trains ordered

Service: Peak: Line A – 3½ min, Line B – 4 min
Integration with other modes: Bus feeder services. Season tickets for metro and commuter lines or whole urban transport network
Fare collection: Ticket-issuing machines incorporating cancelling machines

Fare structure: Flat, single and return tickets, monthly passes, annual pass
Signalling: Coded-current track circuits for continuous signal aspect repetition on board; central control system includes train number recognition
Surveillance: CCTV at stations and in other areas, roving security staff travel on trains, some stations have a permanent security presence
Operating costs financed by: Fares 24.9 per cent

Suburban railway
Staff: 1,310

Passenger journeys: Approx 200,000 daily

Current situation
Operates three suburban networks, Rome-Viterbo (102 km, 1,435 mm gauge, electrified 3 kV DC), Rome-Pantano (18.4 km, 950 mm gauge, electrified 1.5 kV DC), and Rome-Ostia Lido (29 km, 1,435 mm gauge, electrified 1.5 kV DC), which shares the tracks of metro Line B into the centre.

Developments
The Rome Piazzale Flaminio-Prima Porta section of the Viterbo route (Line F) has been upgraded and doubled. Doubling is in progress on the line to Montebello. The rest of the Viterbo line is to be modernised at a cost of EUR103 million. The Pantano Borghese route is to be rebuilt to standard gauge on its inner section to become semi-metro Line G, connecting with metro Lines A and B at Termini via a new city-centre tunnel. From Torre Angela to Pantano the line is being doubled and rebuilt to metro standards with segregated tracks to become part of metro Line C in 2011. The line from Grotte Celoni (12.6 km from Rome) to Pantano reopened in March 2006 after being closed for 10 years.
  On the Lido di Ostia route (Line E), a tender for construction of an 18 km single-track extension from Lido di Ostia to Tor Vaianica was launched in mid-2005. A further line could be built from Tor Vaiancica to Pomezia on the FS Roma-Formia line.

Rolling stock: 74 cars (Viterbo route), 34 vehicles (Pantano Borghese route) and 162 cars (Lido di Ostia route)

Trenitalia SpA – Regionale
Divisione Trasporto Regionale (Rome)
Piazza della Croce Rossa, I-10061 Rome, Italy
Tel: (+39 02) 63 71 79 45; 63 71 79 47; 63 71 79 39
Fax: (+39 02) 63 71 79 87
Web: www.trenitalia.com
  www.regionale.trenitalia.it

Type of operation: Suburban heavy rail

Background
In 2000, FS Holding Sp (FS) split off its operating division as Trenitalia SpA. Trentitalia Regionale operates local passenger services including city suburban.

Current situation
Extensive suburban services operated on routes out of Rome Termini and other city stations, extending to some 450 route-km with 79 stations. A 2 km branch, opened 1990, serves Fiumicino international airport. Under construction is a 17 km orbital route through the northern and western suburbs utilising in part an 11 km alignment already completed. Completion of this route awaits funding.

Developments
Five new routes are proposed. Services being rebranded as FM (Ferrovia Metropolitana), with a regular interval timetable and more trains.
  Double-tracking and electrification is in progress of the St Peter's-La Storta section of the Viterbo line. The Avezzano line is also being doubled, along with quadrupling of the Ciampino line. Completion of quadrupling over the northern portion of the city ring line will allow separation of suburban trains from long-distance and freight services. Investment totalling Lit1,700 billion is planned over the next 10 years.

Trenitalia Class 464 engine and double-deck carriages, Rome (Quintus Vosman)   0126546

Turin
Population: City 910,400 (2008 estimate), Metropolitan area 2.2 million (estimate)

Public transport
Public transport services operated by Gruppo Torinese Trasporti (GTT) – urban and suburban bus and tramway networks, regional bus and local railways; suburban rail services provided by Italian Railways (Trenitalia); VAL-type metro.

Gruppo Torinese Trasporti SpA (GTT)
Corso Turati 19/6, I-10128 Turin, Italy
Tel: (+39 011) 576 41   Fax: (+39 011) 576 43 30
e-mail: gtt@gtt.to.it
Web: www.comune.torino.it/gtt/

Key personnel
President: Giancarlo Guiati
Managing Director: Tommaso Panero

Operating Director: Antonio Ardissone
  Staff: 5,240

Passenger journeys: (All modes)
(Annual) 190 million
Vehicle-km: (Annual) 53.1 million

Operating costs financed by: Fares 25 per cent, other commercial sources 5 per cent, subsidy/grants 70 per cent

Alsthom Series 6000 Citiway tram (Marcel Vleugels)   1115238

Subsidy from: Regional government 81 per cent, municipalities of Turin and surrounding area 19 per cent

Current situation
Gruppo Torinese Trasporti (GTT) was formed in January 2003 by the merger of Azienda Torinesi Mobilité SpA (ATM) and Societa per Azioni Torinese Trasporti Intercomunali – Satti.

The company is organised into four divisions: Holding; Local Public Transit; Railways; Infrastructures and Engineering.

GTT manages the city and suburban networks of Turin (eight tram lines, 100 bus lines, 100 km tram network, 1,000 km bus network); intercity network (73 bus lines, of 3,600 km); railway network (two lines, concession, of 82 km, one managed line on behalf of Trenitalia of 24 km). These services provide public transit to the city and the suburban areas of Turin and to 25 other municipalities (29 municipalities for train services).

ATM operates the urban and suburban bus networks and tram routes, two of which are on segregated right-of-way. It serves the city of Turin and 220 towns in the provinces of Turin and Alessandria, Asti and Cuneo.

Bus
Passenger journeys: Not available currently
Vehicle-km: (2008) 53.1 million (estimate)

Number of routes: 100
Route length: 1,000 km
On priority right-of-way: (Tram and bus) 62 km

Fleet: 1,006 vehicles

Iveco 471 Viberti (1985/88)	47
Iveco 580 TurboCity-S (1990)	30
Iveco 571 S-Euffeno (1988)	15
Bredabus 3001.12LL (1989)	20
Iveco 471 U-Euffeno (1985/88)	100
Iveco 480 TurboCity-U (1989/91)	118
Iveco 480 Viberti (1989/91)	152
Fiat 421 (1973/83)	302
Bredabus BB3001 08AC (1992)	5
Inbus AU280FT De Simon (1991)	30
Iveco 490 Altrobus dual-mode (1994)	2
Iveco 490 Viberti (1994)	45
Iveco 490 (1994)	19
Iveco 490E TurboCity UR-Green (1994)	100
Iveco 480 18.29 Viberti (1994)	21

In peak service: 790

Most intensive service: Peak 4–7 min, off-peak 6–13 min
One-person operation: All routes
Fare collection: Prepurchase passes and multitickets from automatic machines and shops
Fare structure: Flat within urban and suburban zones; tickets with time validity, passes and 10-journey multitickets (urban only); integrated 'Formula' weekly/monthly passes allow all modes travel within specified zones
Fare evasion control: Roving inspectors
Average peak-hour speed: 17.8 km/h
Integration with other modes: Bus and tram services integrated and connect with rail stations and outer-suburban termini; fares integration between ATM, Satti and FS started in 1996 (passes only)

Tramway/light rail
Type of operation: Conventional tramway/light rail

Passenger journeys: Not available currently
Car-km: Not available currently

Route length: 104.8 km, plus light rail 19.2 km
Number of lines: eight tramway, two light rail
Gauge: 1,445 mm
Track: Part conventional sleepers on ballast
Max gradient: 5.8%
Minimum curve radius: 15 m
Electrification: 580 V DC, overhead

Service: Peak 4–7 min, off-peak 6–10 min
First/last car: 04.30/01.00
Fare structure: As bus
Fare collection: As bus

One-person operation: All cars
Signalling: Centralised control; priority at traffic lights in operation on Routes 3, 4, 9, 10, 16

Rolling stock: 246 cars

2800 (1958/60, rebuilt 1979/82)	M102
Fiat/Ansaldo/OMS 7000 LRV (1982/86)	M35
Fiat/Ansaldo/OMS 5000 LRV low-floor (1989/92)	M53
Restaurant tram (1958, rebuilt 1968)	M1
Citiway Class 6000 LRV (2003/04)	M55

In peak service: Not currently available
On order: None

Suburban bus
Background
Previously operated by Societa per Azioni Torinese Trasporti Intercomunali – Satti. Satti had responsibility for outer suburban and commuter bus services, serving the provinces of Turin, Cuneo, Asti and Alessandria, and the urban and suburban bus services of the city of Ivrea.

The company also provided regional rail services: Chieri-Turin-Pont Canavese and Turin-Turin airport-Ceres.

Satti also provided special, school and shuttle services.

Passenger journeys: (2008) 18.6 million (estimate)
Vehicle-km: (2008) 13.1 million (estimate)

Number of routes: 73
Route length: (One way) 3,600 km

Fleet: More than 300 buses, mostly Fiat

Local railways
Passenger journeys: (2008) 4.4 million (estimated)
Car-km: (2008) 1.2 million (estimated)

GTT BredaMenarinibus articulated bus (Ken Harris)   0580934

GTT Fiat/Ansaldo/OMS Series 5000 (5033) low-floor tram (Marcel Vleugels)   1115194

Current situation
GTT operates local services over two routes, Turin-Ceres (43 km, electrified as far as Germagnano) and Turin-Rivarolo-Pont Canavese (38 km) and one line managed on behalf of the Italian Railway company, Trenitalia, covering 24 km.

Developments
Rebuilding after a landslip plus re-electrification on the Germagnano-Ceres section is continuing, with reopening expected in late 2008.

In 2005–06 GTT received 10 ALSTOM Minuetto three-car emus. An option for nine additional units was taken up in 2007, with delivery due to run from September 2009. In 2007 GTT was refurbishing and re-engining its dmu fleet.

Rolling stock: Not available currently

Metro – MetroTorino
e-mail: infometrotorino@gtt.to.it
Web: www.metrotorino.it

Type of operation: VAL-type metro, first section opened February 2006

Number of lines: 1
Route length: 9.6 km
Number of stations: 14

Current situation
The 7.5 km VAL system between Porta Susa and Collegno, with 11 stations, opened in February 2006.

Developments
The 2 km extension from Porta Susa to Porta Nuova, with a further three stations (the fourth station, Porta Susa, is currently still under construction, but works are 95 per cent completed), opened in October 2007.

The second stage of the system, which will run from Porta Nuova to Lingotto (with six stations), is under construction, with a further 2-km extension (two stations) to Piazza Begnasi planned.

Line 2 is at planning stage, with 26 stations proposed.

Rolling stock: 46 Siemens VAL 208 trainsets

First/last train: 05.30/23.30 (Mon-Fri); 05.30/01.10 (Sat); 08.00/22.00 (Sun)
Fare collection: Magnetic strip paper tickets from retailers and ATMs, contactless smartcard, single trip and season tickets available, including multi-modal passes
Fare structure: Flat

Venice
Population: City 62,000, municipality 269,780, province 832,326 (2006 estimates)

Public transport
Bus and boat services in city, Lido and surrounding areas provided by authority owned by consortium of Province of Venice and 21 local authorities. Suburban rail services operated by state and regional railways.

Azienda Consorzio Trasporti Veneziano SpA (Actv SpA)
Isola Nova del Tronchetto 32, I-30135 Venice, Italy
Tel: (+39 041) 272 21 11   Fax: (+39 041) 520 71 35
e-mail: direzione@actv.it
Web: www.actv.it

Key personnel
President: Marcello Panettoni
Director General: M Castagna
Administration and Finance Director: G Paolo Marella
Public Relations Director: M Moro

Operating costs financed by: Fares 43.3 per cent, other commercial sources 7.2 per cent, regional and national subsidies 49.5 per cent

Developments
Since April 1997, the ferry routes linking San Marco with Lido, Murano and the airport, and Piazzale Roma with Murano, have been contracted to a private operator. Fares and timetables are integrated with Actv services.

Actv is currently undertaking a project for the introduction of a single electronic fare payment card for all existing transport and parking services in the Venice area, with the prospect of extending this to use on trams/metro in the future.

Bus
Passenger journeys: (2003) 90.9 million
(2004) 91.6 million
(2005) 95.3 million
(2006) 96.1 million
Vehicle-km: (2003) 31.6 million
(2004) 31.9 million
(2005) 32.2 million
(2006) 32.4 million

Number of routes: Urban 49, suburban 35
Route length: 707 km

Fleet: 600 vehicles
In peak service: Urban 256, suburban 223
On order: Not currently available

Most intensive service: 10 min
One-person operation: All routes
Fare collection: Payment to farebox or prepurchase with validation and cancelling machines on board
Fare structure: Urban, stage or flat rate for each hour's travel, day and three day tickets; suburban/interurban, stage
Fare evasion control: Random inspection
Average peak-hour speed: Urban 21.6 km/h

Boat
Passenger journeys: (2003) 96.3 million
(2004) 98.0 million
(2005) 101.5 million
(2006) 104.2 million

Number of routes: 18
Route length: 192 km

Fleet: 152 vessels, including 58 larger water buses, 49 smaller water buses, single-agent water buses, 15 offshore motorboats, 13 foot-passenger ferries and seven car ferries
In peak service: 96

Light rail (under construction)
In March 2001 the City Council chose Actv Spa to run tram services on the route Favaro-Mestre-Venice and Mestre-Margehera. The cost of construction for these two services was approximated at Lit300 billion, with 60 per cent provided by the Ministry of Transport and the remaining funds sourced by Actv Spa.

The Translohr light-rail urban tram system has been chosen and is under construction in the Mestre district.

Venice
Private boat
Current situation
Private gondolas provide a ferry service at various locations, as well as operating on a private taxi basis.

Trenitalia SpA
Direzione Regionale (Veneto)
Via Decorati al valor civile 90, I-30171 Venezia Mestre, Italy
Tel: (+39 041) 369 62 34
Fax: (+39 041) 369 62 32
e-mail: direzione.veneto@trenitalia.it
Web: www.trenitalia.com

Type of operation: Suburban heavy rail

Trenitalia SpA – Regionale
Direzione Piemonte
Via Nizza 8 bis, I-10125 Torino, Italy
Tel: (+39 011) 669 94 36
Fax: (+39 011) 665 20 00
e-mail: direzione.piemonte@trenitalia.it
Web: www.trenitalia.com

Type of operation: Suburban heavy rail

Passenger journeys: (Piemonte region)
(Annual) 71.5 million (estimate)
Train-km: (Piemonte region)
(Annual) 19.9 million (estimate)

Background
In 2000, FS Holding Sp (FS) split off its operating division as Trenitalia SpA. Trenitalia Regionale operates local passenger services including city suburban.

Current situation
Frequent service provided on five routes, electrified 3 kV DC.

For further information on Trenitalia, please see *Jane's World Railways.*

Background
In 2000, FS Holding Sp (FS) split off its operating division as Trenitalia SpA.

The regional and local passenger activities are managed by the Passegeri Regionale division, which is further divided according to type of service provided. The Suburbano and Metropolitano businesses, which oversee suburban services, are structured as 21 local management units.

Trenitalia Regionale operates local passengers services, including city suburban.

Current situation
Main line and suburban trains link Venice Santa Lucia to the mainland station at Mestre (9 km), every 4 min peak, 10 min off-peak. Local services run on four routes: to S Donna di Piave, Treviso (30 km), Bassano and Padua (37 km).

Developments
An intensive service is operated between Santa Lucia and Mestre. An integrated tariff system has been introduced covering Trenitalia trains, urban buses and boat services.

Sistemi Territoriali SpA (ST)
Viale degli Alpini 23, I-35028 Piove di Sacco, Italy
Tel: (+39 049) 584 02 65   Fax: (+39 049) 970 29 95
e-mail: ferroviaadriamestre@sistemiterritorialispa.it
Web: www.sistemiterritorialispa.it

Key personnel
President: Gian Michele Gambato

Type of operation: Suburban heavy rail

Passenger journeys: Not currently available

Current situation
Formerly Ferrovie Venete, ST is majority-owned by the Veneto region. It operates local services on the diesel-operated 58 km Ferrovia Adria-Mestre line, serving Venezia Mestre and Venezia Santa Lucia stations. Up to 10 services per day are operated between Adria and Venezia Santa Lucia, with some additional trains originating/terminating at Piove di Sacco. Since 2007, integrated tariffs have been available covering ST/Trenitalia and ST/ACTV services.

Developments
A EUR21 million track renewal and modernisation programme started in 2007. Work also included elimination of level crossings.

Rolling stock
Fleet: 12 diesel railcars and three driving trailers

Japan

Chiba

Population: City: 924,353, Prefecture: 6.1 million (preliminary Census figures 2005)

Public transport

Situated 40 km to the east of central Tokyo, Chiba has seen recent large-scale commercial and residential development and a rapid increase in population, many of whom commute to Tokyo. JR and private rail services; monorail operated by third-sector company; privately operated bus services, including Chiba City Bus, Chiba Chuo Bus, Chiba Flower Bus, Chiba Green Bus, Chiba Kaihin Kotsu, Chiba Nairiku Bus Co Ltd, Chiba Rainbow Bus (www.chiba-rainbow-bus.jp) and Chibakotsu Co Ltd (www.chibakotsu.co.jp).

The PASMO rechargeable contactless smartcard ticketing system is being introduced throughout the region. The Chiba Urban Monorail is scheduled to introduce the system from 2009, and the bus companies will follow in due course.

Keisei Electric Railway Co Ltd

1-10-3 Oshiage, Sumida-ku, Tokyo 131-8555, Japan
Tel: (+81 3) 36 21 22 42   Fax: (+81 3) 36 21 22 33
Web: www.keisei.co.jp

Interurban rail

Key personnel
President: Tsutomu Hanada
    Staff: 1,818

Passenger journeys: Not currently available

Current situation

Operates from Keisei Chiba Line from Tsudanuma station into Chiba-Chuo (42.6 km).

Rolling stock: 500 emu cars
Various builders   M432 T68

Keisei Bus Co Ltd

Tel: (+81 3) 36 21 24 18   Fax: (+81 3) 36 21 24 08
Web: www.keiseibus.co.jp

Key personnel

Managing Director: K Sato
    Staff: 2,200

Current situation

Keisei's bus division runs 980 buses, of which about 730 are operated on routes in Chiba city

and prefecture, including feeder services to monorail stations.

Developments

Volvo articulated buses have been introduced on routes serving Makuhari new town, Chiba.

Higashi Nihon Ryokaku Tetsudo – East Japan Railway Company (EJR) (JR East)

2-2-2 Yoyogi, Shibuya-ku, Tokyo 151-8578, Japan
Tel: (+81 3) 53 34 11 51
Fax: (+81 3) 53 34 11 10
Web: www.jreast.co.jp

Key personnel

Chair: Mutsutake Otsuka
President: Satoshi Seino
    Staff: 61,900 (whole company as at April 2008, includes 54,697 for rail operations)

Current situation

Chiba is the eastern terminus for cross-Tokyo Sobu Line local emus, which operate to Mitaka via Shinjuku. These are supplemented by frequent limited-stop rapid service emus between Kurihama, Yokohama, Tokyo and Chiba, continuing to Narita airport, and by Limited Expresses running between Tokyo, Chiba and Choshi. Chiba is also the terminus for regional local services on the Sobu, Narita, Uchibo and Sotobo lines.

In 1990, a second JR line was completed between Chiba and Tokyo, with five stations in Chiba city; the Keiyo Line serves major new development projects alongside Tokyo Bay including Disneyland, the Nippon Convention Centre and the commercial and residential development zone. Keiyo Line local and rapid service emus run between Tokyo and Soga (Chiba), supplemented by Uchibo and Sotobo Line Limited Expresses which call only at Soga.

For further information on JR East, please see other entries in *Jane's Urban Transport Systems* and *Jane's World Railways*.

Chiba Urban Monorail Company Ltd

199-1, HagiDaimachi, Inage-ku, Chiba-shi 263, Japan
Tel: (+81 43) 287 82 11
Fax: (+81 43) 252 72 34
Web: www.chiba-monorail.co.jp

Key personnel

President: Kunihiro Mikami

Type of operation: Townliner suspended monorail, opened 1988

Passenger journeys: Not currently available
Car-km: Not currently available

Route length: 15.2 km
Number of lines: 2
Number of stations: 19
Electrification: 1.5 kV DC

Current situation

Established in 1979, Chiba Urban Monorail is a third-sector company; shareholders include Chiba city and Chiba prefecture. The Chiba master plan envisages a 40 km monorail system to serve expanding commercial and residential development areas. The initial route, Line 2 linking Chiba and the new residential suburb of Chishirodai via the Sports Centre, was opened in 1988 and completed in 1991. The first section of Line 1 between Chiba and Chiba Port, with one intermediate station, opened in 1995, the service running through from Line 2.

A 0.7 km extension of Line 1 from Chiba to the Prefectural Government Office was opened in March 1999 following which separate services were introduced on the two lines.

Developments

A 2-km extension to Chiba University is being considered.

Chiba Urban Monorail plans to join the regional PASMO rechargeable contactless smartcard payment system in 2009.

There is a possibility that new Mitsubishi Urban Flyer O Type trains might be purchased in the future.

Monorail

Rolling stock: 20 two-car sets
Mitsubishi (1991/93)   M40

Service: Peak 5 min
First/last train: 05.30/00.10
Fare structure: Graduated; holiday, two day and lunchtime passes are available
One-person operation: All cars
Signalling: CTC

Fukuoka

Population: City 1.42 million (2007 estimate), Greater Fukuoka 2.5 million (2005 Census), Prefecture 5.06 million (2004 estimate)

Public transport

Bus services provided by private company also operating two separate commuter railways. Metro operated by municipal undertaking; suburban rail services provided by Japan Railways (JR); ferry services across Hakata Bay.

Nishi-Nippon Railroad Co Ltd 'Nishitetsu'

1-11-17 Tenjin, Chuo-ku, Fukuoka-shi 810-8570, Japan
Tel: (+81 92) 734 12 17
Fax: (+81 92) 781 25 83
Web: www.nishitetsu.co.jp

Key personnel

Representative President: Kazuyuki Yakeshima
    Staff: 27,851 (All operations (2008))

Current situation

Operates the local bus network, a 75 km interurban/commuter railway and a separate 11 km suburban railway.

Nishi-Nippon is the largest bus operator in Japan. Bus operations generate about 55 per cent of income and include urban networks in Fukuoka, Kitakyushu (see separate entry in), Kurume and Omuta as well as rural, interurban, express and sightseeing services. Of note is the network of frequent motorway express services linking Fukuoka, Fukuoka airport, Kitakyushu and other towns in northern Kyushu.

Developments

In early 2008, the nimoca smartcard ticketing system was introduced on some local bus lines in the city and on the Tenjin Omuta Line. There are plans to introduce the system on all local bus lines, some interurban lines and the Kaizuka Line in the future.

Bus

(Fukuoka operations)
Passenger journeys: Not currently available
Vehicle-km: Not currently available

Number of routes: 122 including seven express routes and an airport service

Fleet: Total 3,020 buses and 472 coaches. Approx 1,000 buses committed to Fukuoka local operations; types include Nishi Nippon Shatai-bodied Nissan Diesel, Hino, Isuzu and Mitsubishi. Recent deliveries include 'non-step' low-floor buses.

Fare structure: Flat fare zone covering central and inner Fukuoka with stage fares beyond. Some routes entirely flat fare. Prepurchase coupon tickets, season tickets, one-day city bus tickets (valid in flat fare zone)
Fare collection: Payment to farebox by driver on entry, or prepurchase; nimoca smartcard on some routes
One-person operation: All routes

Suburban railway

Staff: 900 (estimate)

Type of operation: Suburban/interurban railway

Passenger journeys: Not currently available
Train-km: Not currently available

Route length: 85.8 km (Fukuoka operations)

Number of lines: 2 (Fukuoka operations)
Number of stations: 58

Current situation
Nishi Nippon operates a four-line, 106-km rail network including the 75 km Fukuoka-Omuta main line (Tenjin Omuta Line) with branches, 1,435 mm gauge, electrified 1.5 kV DC, and the 11 km 1,067 mm gauge Kaizuka Line (previously known as the Miyajidake Line) from Kaizuka in the eastern suburbs of Fukuoka to Shingu.

Developments
The service on the Kaizuka Line between Shingu and Tsuyazaki stations was discontinued in early 2007.

In early 2008, the nimoca smartcard ticketing system was introduced on the Tenjin Omuta Line. There are plans to introduce the system on the Kaizuka Line in the future.

Rolling stock: 361 emu cars
| 1,435 mm gauge | M197 T129 |
| 1,067 mm gauge | M23 T12 |

Service: Local, Express and Limited Express; Rapid Express and Non-Stop morning peak period only

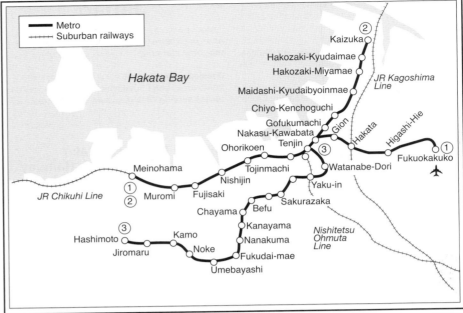

Fukuoka's metro and suburban rail lines

1298725

Fukuoka-shi Kotsu Kyoku (Fukuoka City Subway)
Fukuoka Municipal Transportation Bureau
2-5-31 Daimyo, Chuo-ku, Fukuoka 810-0041, Japan
Tel: (+81 92) 732 41 08
Fax: (+81 92) 721 07 54
e-mail: subway.fukuoka@md.neweb.ne.jp
Web: subway.city.fukuoka.jp

Key personnel
Superintendent, Transportation: K Nishi
  Staff: 650 (estimate)

Metro
Type of operation: Full metro, initial route opened 1981

Passenger journeys: Not currently available
Train-km: Not currently available

Route length: 40.2 km (trains also operate over 44.8 km of JR tracks)
  in tunnel: 29.4 km
Number of lines: three
Number of stations: 35 (trains also serve 16 JR Chikuhi line stations)

Gauge: 1,067 mm
  1,435 mm (Nanakuma Line)
Electrification: 1.5 kV DC, overhead

Current situation
Line 1 – Kuko Line connects with JR Chikuhi line at Meinohama and a through service is operated between Fukuoka-kuko (airport) and Nishi-karatsu (57.9 km) using metro and JR rolling stock. Interchange between Line 2 – Hakozaki Line and Nishitetsu Miyajidake line at Kaizuka.

Developments
Line 3 – Nanakuma Line, between Tenjin in central Fukuoka and Hashimoto in the western suburbs (12.7 km, 16 stations), opened in 2005. The 1,435 mm gauge line is operated by six-car linear-motor-powered trains. An extension from Tenjin to Hakata Waterfront and a branch from Watanabe-dori to Hakata JR station, totalling 4 km, are also planned but not yet authorised for construction.

The Hayakaken smartcard is due to be introduced in early 2009.

Rolling stock: 144 cars formed into six-car sets
Kinki Sharyo, Toshiba, Hitachi and Mitsubishi
Series 1000	M60 T30
Series 1000N	M12 T6
Series 2000	M24 T12
Series 3000 four-car sets	Not currently available

Service: Peak 3–4 min, 4–9 min off-peak; Line 1 trains operate through to JR Chikuhi line destinations every 15–30 min
First/last train: 05.30/00.25
Fare structure: Five section distance-related scale; one-day and one-, three- and six month passes; prepaid 'F-Card', Yoka-Net and Wai Wai Cards; reduced fares for children and disabled passengers
Fare collection: Full AFC
Arrangements for elderly/disabled: Free travel for over 70s and severely disabled
One-person operation: All trains
Signalling: Full ATO, ATC
Operating costs financed by: Fares 38.8 per cent, other commercial sources 3.2 per cent, subsidy/grants 30.6 per cent

Kyushu Railway Company (JR Kyushu)
Head Office
3-25-21, Hakataekimae, Hakata-ku, Fukuoka 812-8566, Japan
Tel: (+81 92) 474 25 01
Fax: (+81 92) 474 97 45
e-mail: service@jrkyushu.co.jp
Web: www.jrkuyshu.co.jp

Key personnel
Chairman of the Board: Koji Tanaka
President: Susumu Ishihara
Senior Managing Directors: Shuihi Honda
  Toshirou Kameyama
Managing Directors: Sojiro Kai
  Tsutomu Saito
  Staff: 9,700 (Group estimate)

Type of operation: Suburban/interurban heavy rail

Passenger journeys: Not currently available
Train-km: Not currently available

Current situation
JR Kyushu operates frequent 'Town Shuttle' emus between Fukuoka, Kokura and Moji, with some trains running through from Kurume, Omuta and Kumamoto. Emu services run to Nogata (41 km), with some trains continuing to Kurosaki in Kitakyushu. Also diesel railcar service on the 25 km Kashii Line in Fukuoka's eastern suburbs. A fleet of six-car Series 103 and 303 emus operates the through service between the Chikuhi Line and Line 1 of the metro.

For further information on this company, please see entry in *Jane's World Railways*.

Kyushu Railway Company (JR Kyushu) 303 commuter train

0572934

Nishi Nihon Ryokaku Tetsudo – West Japan Railway Co (JR West)

4-24, Shibata 2-chome, Kita-ku, Osaka 530-8341, Japan
Tel: (+81 6) 63 75 87 08
Fax: (+81 6) 63 75 87 09
e-mail: ia@westjr.co.jp
Web: www.westjr.co.jp

Key personnel
Chairman: Shojiro Nan-ya
President: Takeshi Kakiuchi
Executive Vice-President: Masao Yamazaki
Senior Managing Directors: Yasutada Ikeda, Kazuaki Maruo
Directors: Noboru Koide, Takashi Kondo, Satoru Sone, Akio Nomura, Yoshio Tateishi

Type of operation: Suburban/interurban heavy rail

Passenger journeys: Not currently available

Background
The railway runs passenger transport and related activities in the Hokuriku region and western Honshu, an area of 43 million inhabitants – 34 per cent of Japan's population. The network totals 51 lines, with 289 Shinkansen and 7,988 conventional trains operated daily in 2001.
JR West was totally privatised in March 2004.

Current situation
JR West operates a unique local passenger service using shinkansen trains running on the 8.5 km 1,435 mm gauge line between the Sanyo shinkansen terminus at Hakata and the shinkansen depot at Hakata Minami; runs about hourly with no intermediate stops.
For further information on JR West, please see *Jane's World Railways.*

Fukuoka City Ferries
Port & Harbour Bureau, Fukuoka City
13-1, Chikko Honmachi, Hakata-ku, Fukuoka 812-0021, Japan
Tel: (+81 92) 291 10 85
e-mail: shinko.PHB@city.fukuoka.jp
Web: www.port-of-hakata.or.jp

Current situation
Fukuoka municipality operates passenger ferry services across Hakata Bay.

Hakodate
Population: 289,500 (2008 estimate)

Public transport
Tramway services operated by municipal undertaking. Privately operated buses serve Hakodate and surrounding areas.

Hakodate Bus Corporation
10-1 Takamuri-cho, Hakodate-shi, Hokkaido 040-0024, Japan
Tel: (+81 138) 51 31 37
Fax: (+81 138) 51 39 60
e-mail: hakobus@hotweb.or.jp
Web: www.hotweb.or.jp/hakobus

Key personnel
President: Isao Terasaka
  Staff: 322

Bus
Data predates transfer to Hakodate Bus

Passenger journeys: (Annual) 16 million (estimate)

Fleet: 284 buses, 13 coaches

Current situation
Established in 1944, Hakodate Bus Corporation is a subsidiary of the Tokyu Corporation, which has extensive bus and rail interests in the Tokyo area. The company provides bus services over an area of some 5,868 km².

Developments
From 2001, Hakodate Bus began the process of taking over the bus operations from the Hakodate

Transportion Bureau. The transfer of operations was completed in April 2003.
In 2001, the company introduced low-floor, non-step buses.

Hakodate-shi Kotsu Kyoku
Hakodate Transportation Bureau
4-13 Shinome-cho, Hakodate-shi, Hokkaido 040, Japan
Tel: (+81 138) 32 17 30
Fax: (+81 138) 32 17 35
e-mail: koutsu@city.hakodate.hokkaido.jp
Web: www.city.hakodate.hokkaido.jp/transport

Key personnel
Contact: Koji Hirose
e-mail: ht-eigyou@city.hakodate.hokkaido.jp

Developments
To counter mounting debts, the municipal bus operation has been transferred to privately owned Hakodate Bus. The undertaking will continue to operate the tramway though its longer term future is under review.

Tramway
Staff: 121

Type of operation: Conventional tramway

Passenger journeys: Not currently available
Tram-km: Not currently available

Route length: 10.9 km
Number of routes: 2
Number of stops: 26
Gauge: 1,372 mm
Electrification: 600 V DC, overhead

Hakodate 'retro' car 39　　　1134986

Service: Peak 5 min, off-peak 10–20 min
First/last car: 06.18/23.05
Fare collection: Farebox
Fare structure: Zonal (JPY200-JPY250)
One-person operation: All cars

Rolling stock: 39 cars

Nippon Sharyo Type 500 (1948–50)	M1
Nippon Sharyo Type 1000 (ex-Tokyo, 1955)	M1
Niigata Type 710 (1959–61)	M10
Niigata Type 800 (1963–66)	M3
Niigata Type 8000 (rebodied 1990–97)	M8
Niigata Type 8000 (rebodied 2002)	M1
Alna Koki Type 2000 (1993/94)	M2
Alna Koki Type 3000 (1993/94/96)	M4
Alna Sharyo Type 9600 (2007)	M1
Historical car (1993)	M1
Special cars	
Hana car	M3
Sasara car	M2
Karaok car	M1

In peak service: 18 cars

Hiroshima
Population: City 1.2 million, prefecture 1.6 million (2005 estimates)

Public transport
Bus, light rail and tramway services provided by private company. Three main private bus operators and 18 other private operators. Commuter rail services run by JR West. Astram automated guideway.

Hiroshima Dentetsu Kabushiki-gaisha – Hiroshima Electric Railway Co Ltd – 'Hiroden'
2-9-29 Higashisenda-machi, Naka-ku, Hiroshima 730-8610, Japan
Tel: (+81 82) 242 35 25
Fax: (+81 82) 242 35 92
Web: www.hiroden.co.jp

Key personnel
President: Tetsuya Ota
Managing Director: Hitoshi Sato
  Staff: 1,377

Current situation
Founded in 1910, Hiroden is responsible for a substantial proportion of the Hiroshima area public transport. Tramways serve the inner city; a through service is operated across the city centre over tramway tracks to the main railway station from Hiroden's Miyajima light rail line. Bus services are provided by Hiroden and five other companies.
Other commercial activities, including the New Hiroden Hotel, retail stores and housing development, assist the public transport operation to remain generally subsidy-free apart from support to maintain bus services to outlying areas. Bus services account for 54.7 per cent of income, trams and light rail 30.5 per cent, and other activities 14.8 per cent.

Bus
Staff: 990

Passenger journeys: Not currently available
Vehicle-km: Not currently available

Number of routes: 51 (plus airport services)
Route length: Not currently available
On priority right-of-way: 128.3 km

Fleet: 490 buses (estimate)
Fleet breakdown is not currently available

Most intensive service: 2–3 min
One-person operation: All routes
Fare collection: Payment to farebox by driver on alighting, or prepurchase
Fare structure: Stage; 1-, 3- and 6-month passes; prepurchase coupons and stored fare 'Prepaid Card' valid for all six bus operators, tramway, light rail and Astram
Fare evasion control: Penalty payment

Integration with other modes: Bus operations fully integrated with light rail and Astram
Average distance between stops: 300–400 m
Average peak-hour speed: In mixed traffic, 12–13 km/h; in bus lanes, 20 km/h
Operational control: Computerised bus location and passenger information system on city routes

Bus priority: Bus lanes. Onboard traffic light control to give priority as bus approaches. A 'Centre Line Transfer System' was introduced on National Road Route 54, which connects the northwest area with the city centre, with one bus every 30 s in peak hours and one every 2 min at other times. One lane of a four-lane 5.7 km section of road is exclusively available to buses in peak hours.
New vehicles financed by: Internal funds. New low-floor buses part-subsidised by city and prefecture.

Current situation
Operations include a network of numbered city routes and a number of outer suburban and rural routes, mainly serving the western half of Hiroshima prefecture.

Light rail
Staff: (Light rail and tramway) 584

Type of operation: Light rail transit (Miyajima line)

Passenger journeys: Not currently available

Route length: 16.1 km
Number of lines: 1
Number of stops: 20
Gauge: 1,435 mm
Electrification: 600 V DC, overhead

Rolling stock: 48 articulated trams, 4 two-car sets and a single car; fleet includes 2 Duewag cars ex-Dortmund

Service: Peak 3 min, off-peak 6–7 min
First/last train: 05.50/23.33
One-person operation: None
Fare structure: Graduated; day tickets (city tramway and light rail); 1-, 3- and 6-month passes, 'Prepaid Card' valid for all six bus operators, tramway, light rail and Astram
Fare collection: Payment to farebox on alighting; at Hiroshima station pavement conductors collect fares with mobile fareboxes

Tramway
Type of operation: Conventional tramway

Passenger journeys: Not currently available
Car-km: Not currently available

Route length: 19.0 km
Number of lines: 6
Number of stops: 61
Gauge: 1,435 mm
Electrification: 600 V DC, overhead

Rolling stock: 77 bogie cars and 3 two-axle historical cars used on city routes; includes many second-hand cars from other Japanese systems

Kinami Sharyo (1940/42)	M7
Fuji Car (1950)	M3
Naniwa Koki (1953/55/57/58)	M26
Kawasaki Rolling Stock (1956/60)	M3
Kisha Seizo Kaisha (1958)	M1
Osaka Sharyo Kogyo (1957/60)	M12
Alna Koki (1982/83/85/87/89/90/92/97)	M25
Osaka Sharyo (1984) (historical car)	M1
Class 150 (1987) (historical car)	M1
Class 200 ex-Hannover	M1

Service: Peak 5–10 min; off-peak 5–11½ min
First/last tram: 06.00/23.03
Fare structure: Flat; day tickets (city tramway only and city tramway/light rail), 1-, 3- and 6-month passes, 'Prepaid Card' valid for all six bus operators, tramway, light rail and Astram
Fare collection: As light rail
One-person operation: All routes

Current situation
The city tramway system has a centralised control system. The location of cars is shown on an indicator board in the control centre and instructions to drivers are given by means of light signals at some stops. At some stops passenger information about the route of the next car is shown by light signals.

Hiroshima Kosoku Kotsu Kabushiki-gaisha – Hiroshima Rapid Transit Co Ltd
2-12-1, Choraku-ji, Asa minami-ku, Hiroshima-shi 731-0413, Japan
Tel: (+81 82) 830 31 11   Fax: (+81 82) 830 31 14
Web:www.astramline.co.jp

Key personnel
President: Mr Nakamura
  Staff: 221 (estimate)

Type of operation: Rubber-tyred guideway system Astram

Passenger journeys: (Annual) 18 million (estimate)
Car-km: Not currently available

Route length: 18.4 km
Number of lines: 1
Number of stations: 21
Track: Elevated with side guidance
Electrification: 750 V DC

Current situation
The Astram Line opened in 1994 linking central Hiroshima and the Asian Games stadium in the northern suburbs. Feeder bus routes link residential areas with several Astram stations and there are connecting rail services with Hiroshima Electric Railway and JR West.

Rolling stock: 24 six-car trains

Niigata/Mitsubishi Series 6000 (1994/98)	M138
Series 1000 (1999)	M6
In peak service: 114 cars	

Service: 2½–20 min
First/last train: 05.45/00.33
One-person operation: All trains
Fare structure: Graduated distance-related; commuter and student passes; bus/Astram transfer tickets; stored fare 'Astram Card'
Fare collection: AFC

Hiroshima Kotsu 'Hiroko'
14-17 Misasa-machi 3-chome, Nishi-ku, Hiroshima 733-8513, Japan
Tel: (+81 82) 238 77 55
Web:www.hiroko-group.co.jp

Key personnel
Representative President: Mr Yasuhiro
General Manager: Katsuhiko Hiraoka
  Staff: 292

Bus
Passenger journeys: (Annual) 26 million (estimate)

Number of routes: 21
Route length: 406.3 km

Fleet: 212 vehicles, including Nissan Diesel and Mitsubishi Fuso

Operating costs financed by: Fares 100 per cent
Bus priority: Services use 'Centre Line Transfer System' on National Road Route 54 (see above)

Geiyo Bus Co Ltd
21-39 Saijo Nishimoto, Saijo, Higashi Hiroshima-shi 739-0043, Japan
Tel: (+81 82) 424 47 21   Fax: (+81 82) 424 47 24
e-mail: soumu@geiyo.co.jp
Web: www.geiyo.co.jp

Bus
Passenger journeys: (Annual) 15 million (estimate)

Route length: 693.85 km

Fleet: 112 vehicles
Fleet breakdown is not currently available

Current situation
This Hiroden subsidiary operates suburban and longer-distance routes to the east of Hiroshima.

Nishi Nihon Ryokaku Tetsudo – West Japan Railway Co (JR West)
4-24, Shibata 2-chome, Kita-ku, Osaka 530-8341, Japan
Tel: (+81 6) 63 75 87 08
Fax: (+81 6) 63 75 87 09
e-mail: ia@westjr.co.jp
Web: www.westjr.co.jp

Key personnel
Chairman: Shojiro Nan-ya
President: Takeshi Kakiuchi
Executive Vice-President: Masao Yamazaki
Senior Managing Directors: Yasutada Ikeda, Kazuaki Maruo
Directors: Noboru Koide, Takashi Kondo, Satoru Sone, Akio Nomura, Yoshio Tateishi

Type of operation: Suburban/interurban heavy rail

Background
The railway runs passenger transport and related activities in the Hokuriku region and western Honshu, an area of 43 million inhabitants – 34 per cent of Japan's population. The network totals 51 lines, with 289 Shinkansen and 7,988 conventional trains operated daily in 2001.
  JR West was totally privatised in March 2004.

Current situation
Frequent all-stations interurban/commuter emu services run on the Sanyo main line, Hiroshima-Iwakuni (41 km) with some trains continuing to Ogori (138 km) or Shimonoseki (206 km) and Hiroshima-Shiraichi (41 km) with some continuing to Okayama (162 km). A number of trains start/finish at Hiroshima whilst others run through, for example Iwakuni-Hiroshima-Okayama. Also emu service on Kure line, Hiroshima-Kure-Mihara (96 km), and the Kabe line, Hiroshima-Kabe (17 km). A dmu service runs on the Geibi line, Hiroshima-Miyoshi (69 km).
  For further information on JR West, please see *Jane's World Railways*.

Kagoshima
Population: 552,000 (2000 Census)

Public transport
Bus and tramway services provided by municipal undertaking. Additional private bus services; JR suburban rail and some bus services.

Kagoshima-shi Kotsu Kyoku – City Transport Bureau
43-41 Korai-cho, Kagoshima-shi, Kyushu 890-0051, Japan
Tel: (+81 99) 257 21 11
Fax: (+81 99) 258 67 41
Web: www.city.kagoshima.kagoshima.jp/koutuu.nsf

Key personnel
General Manager: T Nagata
  Staff: 351

Bus
Passenger journeys: (2003/04) 12.2 million

Number of routes: 33
Route length: 414.3 km
Fleet: 179 vehicles, including Isuzu, Hino, Nissan and Mitsubishi

One-person operation: All routes (except tours)
Fare collection: Payment to onboard farebox or multitickets and passes
Fare structure: Zonal; multitickets, monthly and 3-monthly passes, one-day tickets (bus/tram)
Arrangements for elderly/disabled: Half fare or free passes for eligible elderly and disabled passengers
Average peak-hour speed: 15 km/h

Tramway

Type of operation: Conventional tramway

Passenger journeys: (2003/04) 10.2 million
Car-km: (annual) 1.6 million

Route length: 13.1 km
 on reserved track: 4.0 km
Number of lines: 2
Number of stops: 35
Gauge: 1,435 mm
Electrification: 600 V DC, overhead

Developments
Three four-axle Alna Sharyo trams were delivered in February 2005.

Rolling stock: 54 cars

Toyo Koki Type 500 (1955/56)	M8
Hitachi Type 600 (1959)	M3
Naniwa Koki Type 600 (1960)	M2
Teikoku Sharyo Type 600 (1962/63)	M4
JR Kyushu Type 2100 (1989/91/92/94)	M11
Alna Koki Type 9500 (rebuilt 1995/96/97/98/99)	M15
Alna Koki Type 9700 (1998)	M2
Alna Koki Type 1000 (2001/04/05)	M9

First/last car: 06.00/23.00
Fare structure: Flat; multitickets, monthly and 3-monthly passes, one-day tickets (bus/tram)
Fare collection: Coin to onboard farebox or multitickets and passes
One-person operation: All cars

Kawasaki

Population: 1.3 million (2006 estimate)

Public transport
Situated between Tokyo and Yokohama, Kawasaki is served by JR suburban trains linking those two cities and by private railways, with direct links to the Tokyo metro system provided by through running from the private railways. Bus services provided by municipal undertaking, private railways, private bus operator and the Yokohama municipal operator.

Kawasaki-shi Kotsu Kyoku – Kawasaki City Bus
Kawasaki City Transport Bureau
6 Miyamoto-cho, Kawasaki-ku, Kawasaki-shi 210-0004, Kanagawa-ken, Japan
Tel: (+81 44) 200 32 31   Fax: (+81 44) 233 84 44
e-mail: yashita-y@city.kawasaki.jp

Key personnel
General Director: Hisao Sugawara
 Staff: 628 (2006)

Current situation
Kawasaki-shi Kotsu Kyoku and private operators' routes are numbered in a common system. Municipal and private operators also share a common flat fare with prepurchase ticket strips

Arrangements for elderly/disabled: Half fare or free passes for eligible elderly and disabled passengers

Kagoshima Kotsu Transport Co Ltd
12-12 Kamoike-shinmachi, Kagoshima-shi 890-0064, Japan
Tel: (+81 99) 259 28 88
Web: www.iwasaki-group.com
 Staff: 703

Current situation
Part of the Iwasaki Group, this operator runs part of the Kagoshima city bus services, as well as local intercity routes, rural routes, school services, sightseeing tours and travel services.

Bus
Passenger journeys: (annual) 16.6 million (including tours)
Vehicle-km: (annual) 18.8 million (including tours)

Number of routes: 258 (including 25 city routes)
Route length: (One way) 2,044 km

Fleet: 420 buses (including charter vehicles)

Operating costs financed by: Fares 91 per cent, other commercial sources 7.5 per cent, subsidy/grants 1.5 per cent
Subsidy from: Government and local authorities

Nangoku Kotsu Co Ltd
Nangoku Nissei Building, 11-5 Chuo-machi, Kagoshima-shi 890-0053, Japan
Tel: (+81 99) 255 21 41   Fax: (+81 99) 255 48 31
Web: www.nils.jp/~nkk101

Bus
Current situation
Operates some 200 vehicles with routes serving the Kagoshima area.

Hayashida Bus Co Ltd
12-12 Kamoike Shinmachi, Kagoshima City 890-0064, Japan
Tel: (+81 99) 258 45 68

valid on all routes within Kawasaki except that operated by Yokohama-shi Kotsu Kyoku.

Bus
Passenger journeys: (2006) 47 million
Vehicle-km: (2006) 12.5 million

Number of routes: 28
Route length: 243 km (2006)
On priority right-of-way: 22.1 km (2006)

Fleet: 326 vehicles (2006)

Isuzu	90
Mitsubishi	78
Hino	59
Nissan Diesel	99

 Fleet includes 23 low-emission vehicles (CNG or diesel-electric hybrid)
In peak service: 302
New vehicles required each year: 18 (2006)

Most intensive service: 1 min
One-person operation: All routes
Fare collection: Payment to farebox by driver or prepurchase ticket strips
Fare structure: Flat; prepurchase ticket strips; monthly and 3-monthly passes; one-day 'Ecology' pass
Integration with other modes: Services integrated with JR and other railways
Average distance between stops: 380 m

Key personnel
General Manager: Kouichi Kawaharazono
 Staff: 350

Current situation
Formerly known as Hayashida Sangyo Kotsu Co Ltd, this private operator runs part of the services in Kagoshima, plus substantial tourist-related operations.

Bus
Passenger journeys: (annual) 8.5 million
Vehicle-km: (annual) 8.5 million

Number of routes: 149

Fleet: 210 vehicles, including Isuzu, Mitsubishi and Hino

Kyushu Railway Company (JR Kyushu) & JR Kyushu Bus
Head Office
3-25-21, Hakataekimae, Hakata-ku, Fukuoka 812-8566, Japan
Tel: (+81 92) 474 25 01
Fax: (+81 92) 474 97 45
e-mail: service@jrkyushu.co.jp
Web: www.jrkyushu.co.jp

Key personnel
Chairman of the Board: Koji Tanaka
President: Susumu Ishihara

Type of operation: Bus/interurban/suburban railway

Current situation
Buses operate over nine routes totalling 1,011.8 km, with a fleet of approximately 190 buses.

 Local emu services operate from Nishi Kagoshima to Sendai and beyond on the Kagoshima main line. Local stations towards Hayato on the Nippo main line have a mixed emu/dmu service. A dmu service operates to Kiire, 29 km south of Kagoshima, with some trains continuing to Yamakare (55 km).

 For further information on JR Kyushu, please see *Jane's World Railways.*

Operating costs financed by: Fares 78 per cent, other commercial sources 9 per cent, subsidy/grants 13 per cent (2006)
New vehicles financed by: Public bonds, subsidy and internal funds

Developments
Premium fare late journeys introduced on eight 'Midnight Bus' routes.

Kawasaki Tsurumi Rinko Bus Co Ltd
15-2 Nishin-machi, Kawasaki-ku, Kawasaki-shi 210-0024, Japan
Tel: (+81 44) 233 65 02   Fax: (+81 44) 233 35 39
Web: www.rinkobus.co.jp

Current situation
This company, part of the Keikyu Group, operates in Kawasaki and Yokohama; 30 of the routes (including five express) serve Kawasaki, some jointly with Kawasaki City Bus.

Bus
Number of routes: 36
Route length: 162 km

Fleet: 360 vehicles (estimate)

For details of the latest updates to *Jane's Urban Transport Systems* online and to discover the additional information available exclusively to online subscribers please visit

juts.janes.com

Higashi Nihon Ryokaku Tetsudo – East Japan Railway Company (EJR) (JR East)

2-2-2, Yoyogi, Shibuya-ku, Tokyo 151-8578, Japan
Tel: (+81 3) 53 34 11 51 Fax: (+81 3) 53 34 11 10
Web: www.jreast.co.jp

Key personnel
Chair: Mutsutake Otsuka
President: Satoshi Seino
Staff: 61,900 (whole company as at April 2008, includes 54,697 for rail operations)

Type of operation: Inner and outer suburban heavy rail

Current situation
Kawasaki is linked to both Tokyo and Yokohama by frequent Keihin Tohoku Line inner suburban 'E-den' trains and by outer suburban services on the Tokaido main line. Outer suburban trains on the Yokosuka Line link Shin-Kawasaki with Tokyo and Yokohama. Shonan-Shinjuku Line trains also pass Shin-Kawasaki station, providing direct service to Shinjuku and beyond.

'E-den' trains on the 35.5 km Nambu Line serve 18 stations in Kawasaki providing a link between central Kawasaki and suburban areas to the northwest.

'E-den' service also on 4.1 km branch from Shitte to Hama-Kawasaki and on 7 km Tsurumi Line from Tsurumi to Ogimachi.

For further information on JR East, please see other entries in *Jane's Urban Transport Systems* and *Jane's World Railways.*

Keihin Kyuko Dentetsu 'Keikyu' – Keihin Electric Express Railway Co Ltd (Keikyu)

2-20-20 Takanawa, Minato-ku, Tokyo 108-8625, Japan
Tel: (+81 3) 32 80 91 23 Fax: (+81 3) 32 80 91 93

e-mail: koho4@keikyu.co.jp
Web: www.keikyu.co.jp

Key personnel
President and Representative Director:
Masaru Kotani
Managing Director, General Affairs Department:
Kiyoshi Ishikawa

Interurban railway
Staff: 1,892 (2004)

Passenger journeys: (2002) 1.14 million, daily (2003) 1.15 million, daily

Route length: 87 km (total)

Background
Formed in 1898, the Keihin Electric Express Railway Co Ltd is part of the Keikyu Group. It is one of the major private railways in Japan and provides services which link central Tokyo to Haneda Airport and the southern metropolitan area.

The group also includes bus and taxi companies.

Current situation
Keikyu-Kawasaki station on the main line between Tokyo and Yokohama serves central Kawasaki. Through services are operated to central Tokyo via the Toei Asakusa metro line and on to the Keisei Railway. The 4.5 km Daishi branch links Keikyu-Kawasaki with Kojima-Shinden (see main entry under Tokyo).

Kawasaki
Type of operation:
Suburban/interurban railways

Suburban/interurban railways
Current situation
These railways serve areas to the northwest of central Kawasaki which function largely as outer suburbs of Tokyo. All three railways operate through trains to the Tokyo metro system. The Tokyu Toyoko Line from Tokyo to Yokohama serves three stations in Kawasaki (through service to Hibiya, Nambou and Mita metro lines) and the Denentoshi Line serves seven stations (through service to Hanzomon metro line) (Website: www.tokyu.co.jp). The Odakyu Odawara Line serves seven Kawasaki stations (through service to Chiyoda metro line) with three other stations served by the Tama branch line (Website: www.odakyu-group.co.jp). Keio Teito has two stations in Kawasaki on the Sagamihara Line (through service to Shinjuku metro line) (Website: www.keio.co.jp).

See also main entries for these railways in under Tokyo.

Kawasaki City Transportation Bureau
Kawasaki Urban Rapid Transit Project
Tel: (+81 44) 200 24 04   Fax: (+81 44) 200 39 48
e-mail: 82kosoku@city.kawasaki.jp
Web: www.city.kawasaki.jp/82/82tetudo/home

Current situation
The authority had been granted permission for the construction of a new 15.4 km underground line from Shin-Yurigaoka (Odakyu Odawara line) to Moto-Sumiyoshi (Tokyo Tokyo line) with eight intermediate stations (10 stations in total). Completion of this initial section was originally scheduled for 2011 and a further extension to central Kawasaki was planned.

Developments
In 2003, the city announced that the start of construction would be delayed by approximately five years.

In 2005, a further plan was proposed for the line. The route would now be 16.7 km long, 1,067 mm gauge, with 11 stations. The latest proposed date for opening is 2018.

Kitakyushu
Population: City 1.01 million (2005)

Public transport
Bus services operated in part of area by municipal undertaking and more extensively by private company, also responsible for bus and rail services in other parts of region. Privately owned light rail line; monorail operated by third-sector company; JR suburban/interurban rail; ferry services.

Transportation Bureau, City of Kitakyushu

Administration Department
1-1 Otemachi, Kokurakita Ward, 803-8510, Japan
Tel: (+81 93) 582 37 00   Fax: (+81 93) 562 69 01
e-mail: ki-kouryu@city.kitakyushu.lg.jp
Web: www.city.kitakyushu.jp

Current situation
The towns of Moji, Kokura, Tobata, Yahata and Wakamatsu were merged in 1963 to become the city of Kitakyushu, with the municipal bus undertaking in Wakamatsu becoming Kitakyushu-shi Kotsu Kyoku. Although the former Wakamatsu route network has been extended, operations are still concentrated on what is now Wakamatsu Ward in the new city. Nishi Nippon is the predominant operator in the other six wards.

Bus
Passenger journeys: (Annual) 25 million (estimate)
Vehicle-km: (Annual) 10 million (estimate)

Fleet: 143, comprising 132 buses and 11 coaches, including Nissan Diesel, Hino and Mitsubishi with Nishi Nippon Shatai bodies; includes lift-equipped vehicles (estimate).

Nishi-Nippon Railroad Co Ltd 'Nishitetsu'

1-11-17 Tenjin, Chuo-ku, Fukuoka-shi 810-8570, Japan
Tel: (+81 92) 734 12 17   Fax: (+81 92) 781 25 83
Web: www.nishitetsu.co.jp

Key personnel
Representative President: Kazuyuki Yakeshima
Staff: 27,851 (All operations) (2008)

Current situation
Operates buses in Kitakyushu as well as in many parts of Fukuoka Prefecture, including the city of Fukuoka.

Nishi Nippon is the main bus operator in Kitakyushu with a comprehensive network of routes, except in Wakamatsu which is served by the municipal undertaking. Some local express bus routes are operated as part of the urban network and motorway express services provide direct links from various parts of Kitakyushu to Fukuoka and Fukuoka airport.

Bus
(Kitakyushu operations)

Passenger journeys: 100 million (annual)
Vehicle-km: 30 million (annual)

Number of routes: 113 local routes

Fleet: Approx 700 vehicles, including Hino, Mitsubishi and Isuzu with Nishi Nippon Shatai bodies

Fare collection: Payment to farebox by driver on alighting, or prepurchase
Fare structure: Stage; prepurchase coupon tickets, season tickets
Bus priority: Peak-hour bus lanes, 07.00–09.00 and 17.00–19.00; also a 4 km busway on the roadside

alignment of the former reserved-track Tobata Line tramway which closed in 1985. The busway has 11 stops and is served by 226 return journeys per day including express journeys

Chikuho Denki Tetsudo – Chikuho Electric Railroad Co Ltd

1-6 Nabeyamacho, Nakama-shi, Fukuoka-ken 809-0022, Japan
Tel: (+81 93) 243 55 25   Fax: (+81 93) 243 55 26
Web: www.chikutetu.com

Key personnel
Representative: Naomi Kawano
Staff: 148

Current situation
A subsidiary of Nishi Nippon Tetsudo 'Nishitetsu' – Nishi-Nippon Railroad Co Ltd (16.0 km) using former tramway tracks between Kurosaki and Kumanishi (0.7 km).

Light rail
Type of operation: High-speed light rail

Passenger journeys: (2005) 6.0 million (2006) 6.0 million
Car-km: (2005) 2.9 million (2006) 2.9 million

Route length: 16.0 km
Number of lines: 1
Gauge: 1,435 mm
Electrification: 600 V DC, overhead

Fare structure: Stage; 1-, 3- and 6-month season tickets
Operating costs financed by: Fares 100 per cent

Rolling stock: 16 articulated tramcars

Hitachi Type 2000 (1963/64) M5
Kyushu Sharyo Type 2000 (1967) M2
Alna Koki Type 3000 (1988/89/95/96) M9
In peak service: 22

Kitakyushu Kosoku Tetsudo – Kitakyushu Urban Monorail Co Ltd

13-1, Kikugaoka 2-chome, Kokura-minami-ku, Kitakyushu-shi 803-0981, Japan
Tel: (+81 93) 961 01 01 Fax: (+81 93) 961 05 55
Web: www.kitakyushu-monorail.co.jp

Key personnel
President: Kosaku Takata
Managing Director: Hiroki Haga
  Staff: 156

Monorail
Type of operation: Straddle monorail, opened 1985

Passenger journeys: (2007) 11.6 million (estimate)
Car-km: Not currently available

Route length: 8.8 km
Number of lines: 1

Number of stations: 13
Electrification: 1.5 kV DC

Current situation
The Kokura Line, opened in 1985, is owned by the city of Kitakyushu.
  In 1998, the line was extended 0.4 km to a terminus within the JR Kokura station building.

Rolling stock: 10 four-car trains
Hitachi/Kawasaki (1982/84/98) M40
Service: Peak 6 min, off-peak 10 min
First/last train: 05.45/23.35
Fare structure: Zonal; commuter and student passes (30 per cent) other ordinary (70 per cent); Silver Pass, at reduced rate, for those over 65 years
Operating costs financed by: Fares 91 per cent, other commercial sources 9 per cent
Signalling: ATO, CTC
One-person operation: All trains

Kyushu Railway Company (JR Kyushu)

3-25-21, Hakataekimae, Hakata-ku, Fukuoka 812-8566, Japan
Tel: (+81 92) 474 25 01 Fax: (+81 92) 474 97 45
e-mail: service@jrkyushu.co.jp
Web: www.jrkyushu.co.jp

Key personnel
Chairman of the Board: Koji Tanaka
President: Susumu Ishihara
Senior Managing Directors: Shuihi Honda
  Toshirou Kameyama
Managing Directors: Sojiro Kai
  Tsutomu Saito
  Staff: 9,700 (Group estimate)

Type of operation: Suburban/interurban heavy rail

Passenger journeys: Not currently available
Train-km: Not currently available

Current situation
Frequent local emu service links the Moji-ko, Kokura, Tobata and Yahata wards with Fukuoka. Local stations are served by the Nippo, Hitahikosan, Chikuho and Kagoshima Lines
  For further information on JR Kyushu, please see entry in *Jane's World Railways.*

Kitakyushu
Ferries
Current situation
Ferries operate across the Kanmon Straits between Nishiminato (Kokura) and Hikinoshima (Shimonoseki) (10 minute journey, runs every 10–20 minutes) and from Moji-ko to Shimonoseki.

Kobe
Population: 1.5 million (2005 estimate)

Public transport
Bus services provided by municipal undertaking also operating metro. Automated guideway systems; private railways; JR suburban services; funiculars.

Kobe Municipal Transportation Bureau

5-1, 6-chome, Kano-cho Chuo-ku, Kobe-shi 650, Japan
Tel: (+81 78) 831 81 81
e-mail: kotsu@office.city.kobe.jp
Web: www.city.kobe.jp

Bus
Staff: 1,350 (estimate)

Number of routes: 248 (estimate)
Route length: 539 km (estimate)
On priority right-of-way: 98 km (estimate)

Fleet: 645 buses, plus 15 coaches for sightseeing and charter operations
Mitsubishi 245
Hino 216
Isuzu 181
Nissan 3

One-person operation: All routes
Fare collection: Payment to farebox by driver on alighting, or prepurchase tickets or passes
Fare structure: Flat; prepurchase ticket strips, 1- and 3-monthly passes, 1- and 2-day tickets, combined bus/metro passes
Average speed: 13.5 km/h
Operational control: Computer-controlled 'bus operation improvement system'
Integration with other modes: Feeder bus routes link residential districts with purpose-built bus/metro interchanges within Seishin New Town

Developments
Tramcar-style buses have been introduced on a loop service around central Kobe. Recent deliveries include no-step low-floor buses.

Metro
Staff: 222 (estimate)

Type of operation: Full metro, first line opened 1977

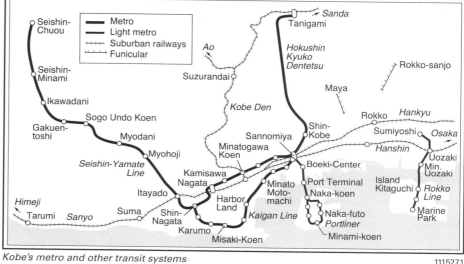

Kobe's metro and other transit systems

1115271

Passenger journeys: (2006) 121 million (estimate)

Route length: 30.7 km
  in tunnel: 23.5 km
Number of lines: 3
Number of stations: 25
Gauge: 1,435 mm
Track: 50 kg/m N long-welded rail on concrete sleepers with double elastic fastenings
Max gradient: 2.9%
Minimum curve radius: 300 m
Tunnel: Bored single-track (shield tunnelling method), bored double-track (mountain tunnelling method), and cut-and-cover
Electrification: 1.5 kV DC, overhead

Current situation
The Seishin and Yamate lines operate as a single route linking central Kobe with the large-scale Seishin New Town. It is operated jointly with the Hokushin-Kyuko Railway (see separate entry), which is designed for through running to the metro between Shin-Kobe and Tanigami. Interchange is available with the Portliner at Sannomiya and the Shin-kansen at Shin-Kobe.
  A small-profile linear-motor metro, the 8 km Kaigan line, opened in July 2001 between Shin-Nagata and Sannomiya via Wadamisaki. Four-car series 5000 stock serves this line.

Rolling stock: Seishan and Yamata line 168 cars, operated as six-car sets
Kawasaki 1000 M72 T36
Kawasaki 2000 M16 T8
Kawasaki 3000 (1993/94) M24 T12
Kaigan line, series 500 four car sets

Service: Peak 3–8 min, off-peak 7½–8 min
First/last train: 05.23/23.40
Fare structure: 8-section distance-related scale; 1- and 3-month passes, combined bus/metro passes; prepaid magnetic cards; commuter passes
Revenue control: Automatic entrance barriers, electronic reading devices at all stations; stored-value AFC
Operating costs financed by: Fares 19.3 per cent, other commercial sources 10.3 per cent, government grants 70.4 per cent
Signalling: Cab signalling, CTC and ATC
Surveillance: CCTV at each station

Hokushin Kyuko Railway Co Ltd – Hokushin Kyuko Electric Railway

27 Kami Aza Ohashi, Shimotani, Yamada-cho, Kita-ku Kobe-shi 651-12, Japan
Tel: (+81 78) 581 10 70 Fax: (+81 78) 583 52 69
Web: www.hokushinkyuko.co.jp
  Staff: 74 (estimate)

Type of operation: Suburban railway/metro

Passenger journeys: (2006) 10 million (estimate)

Current situation
Hokushin Kyuko Railway Co Ltd – Hokushin Kyuko Electric Railway is a private company. The tracks are owned by the Kobe Rapid Transit Railway Co Ltd and the stations are operated by Hokushin Kyuoko and the Kobe Municipal Subway.

The Hokushin Line is 7.5 km long, has two stations and extends the Kobe metro from Shin-Kobe through a tunnel under the Rokko mountains to Tanigami where there is interchange with Kobe Electric Railway's Sanda line. The line is 1,435 mm gauge with 1.5 kV DC overhead current collection for through running with the metro.

Rolling stock: 5 six-car emus
Kawasaki 7000   M15 T15

Kobe Shin Kotsu – Kobe New Transit Co Ltd
6-1 Minato-jima 6-chome, Chuo-ku, Kobe 650-0045, Japan
Tel: (+81 78) 302 25 00   Fax: (+81 78) 302 45 04
e-mail: message@knt-liner.co.jp
Web: www.knt-liner.co.jp
Staff: 190

Type of operation: Rubber-tyred automated transit systems; fully computerised unmanned operation controlled by ATO and ATC – Portliner (opened 1981) and Rokko Line (opened 1990)

Portliner:
Route length: 10.7 km
Number of lines: 1
Number of stations: 12

Rokko Line:
Route length: 4.5 km
Number of lines: 1
Number of stations: 6

Track: Double-track, elevated
Max gradient: 5.8%
Minimum curve radius: 60 m
Electrification: 3-phase 600 V AC

Passenger journeys: (Annual) Portliner 17.9 million, Rokko Line 10.5 million (estimates)
Vehicle-km: (Both services) (Annual) 5.4 million (estimate)

Current situation
Portliner, originally a 6.4 km link from Sannomiya station (Kobe) to Port Island, was the world's first unmanned metro. The guideway is entirely elevated and, having reached Port Island, 2.9 km from Sannomiya, formed a loop round the island. Flat fare; minimum service three minutes; electrified 600 V AC three-phase.

A second medium-capacity transit line, the Rokko Line, was opened in 1990, linking JR's Sumiyoshi station with Marine Park on Rokko Island, an artificial island constructed in Osaka Bay for industrial and residential development. The 4.5 km elevated line has six stations including interchange with the Hanshin Electric Railway at Uozaki. Flat fare; minimum service five minutes; electrified 600 V AC.

Kobe New Transit is a third-sector company, 55 per cent owned by Kobe City Council.

Developments
In February 2006, a 4.3 km extension to the Portliner, with three new stations, was opened to the new Kobe Airport, built on an artificial island. New Kawasaki Series 2000 trains have been purchased for the line. More of these vehicles may be manufactured in the future, to replace the existing Series 8000 trains.

Rolling stock: Portliner 15 six-car trains, Rokko Line 11 four-car trains
Kawasaki 8000 (Portliner)   M48 T24
Kawasaki 1000 (Rokko Line)   M22 T22
Kawasaki 2000 (Portliner) (2006)   M6 T6

Rokko Line (Kawasaki Heavy Industries Ltd)   0576006

Kawasaki 1000 series rubber-tyred vehicle for the Rokko Line (Kawasaki Heavy Industries Ltd)
0576007

Kawasaki 8000 series rubber-tyred vehicle for Portliner (Kawasaki Heavy Industries Ltd)   0576005

Kobe Kosoku Tetsudo – Kobe Rapid Transit Railway Co Ltd
3-3-9 Tamondori, Chuo-ku, Kobe-shi 650-0015, Japan
Tel: (+81 78) 351 00 81

Key personnel
President: Z Nakata

Type of operation: Underground railway, opened 1968

Current situation
The Kobe Rapid Railway does not operate its own trains but provides central area access for the four private interurban railways which serve Kobe. It is 50 per cent owned by Kobe City Council,

with the remainder held by the four railways. The 7.2 km east-west Tozai Line, with six intermediate stations, links the Sanyo Electric Railway west of Kobe, with the Hanshin and Hankyu railways to the east. Frequent cross-city trains run through from the Sanyo system to the Hanshin/Hankyu lines and vice versa, providing a metro-type service. A 0.4 km section of 1,067 mm gauge underground line brings Kobe Electric Railway trains to an interchange with the 1,435 mm gauge east-west line at Shin-Kaichi. Electrified 1.5 kV.

The 0.4 km Namboku Line is fully operated by Kobe Electric Railway and has only two stations. It connects the Kobe Electric Railway to an interchange with the 1,435 mm gauge east-west line at Shin-Kaichi, allowing Shintetsu passengers to transfer directly to Hankyu and Hanshin trains bound for Sannomiya and Umeda, and Sanyo line trains bound for Himeji. Narrow gauge and electrified 1.5 kV.

Kobe Rapid Transit Railway Co Ltd also owns the trackage of the Hokushin Line (see separate entry), but the stations are operated and administered by Hokushin Kyuoko and Kobe Municipal Subway.

Kobe Dentetsu – Kobe Electric Railway Co Ltd

8-1 Aza Akita, Tanigami, Yamada-cho, Kita-ku, Kobe-shi 651-1243, Japan
Tel: (+81 78) 576 86 51, 592 44 51
Fax: (+81 78) 577 24 67
Web: www.shintetsu.co.jp

Key personnel
President and Director: Kenji Harada

Type of operation: Suburban/interurban railway

Passenger journeys: Not currently available
Vehicle-km: Not currently available

Current situation
The company operates as a subsidiary of the Hankyu Corporation.

Operates four-line 69.6 km 1,067 mm gauge system, electrified 1.5 kV with 173 emu cars; Arima Line *Minatogawa-Arima Onsen), Sanda Line (Arimaguchi-Sanda), Koen-Toshi Line (Yokoyama-Woody Town Chuo) and Ao Line (Suzurandai-Ao).

Sanyo Denki Tetsudo – Sanyo Electric Railway Co Ltd

3-1-1, Oyashiki-dori, Nagata-ku, Kobe-shi 653-0843, Japan
Tel: (+81 78) 612 20 32   Fax: (+81 78) 612 20 77
Web: www.sanyo-railway.co.jp

Key personnel
President: M Nagayasu

Interurban rail
Current situation
Operates 63.3 km 1,435 mm gauge system, electrified 1.5 kV with 214 emu cars on route to Himeji. Trains run via Kobe Rapid Railway to Hankyu Sannomiya (in central Kobe) and via the

Hanshin system to Hanshin Umeda (in central Osaka).

Also operates fleet of 128 buses and 10 coaches. Services include suburban feeder routes which link with railway stations and the metro; total route length 48.3 km.

Nishi Nihon Ryokaku Tetsudo – West Japan Railway Co (JR West)/Hankyu Corporation/ Hanshin Electric Railway

Type of operation: Suburban/interurban railways

Current situation
JR West, Hankyu and Hanshin operate competing local rail services between Kobe and Osaka.

Local and rapid service 'Urban Network' trains, operated by JR West, cover 130 km between Himeji and Kyoto via Kobe and Osaka, with some trains extending further. Journeys on Kobe services amounted to 137 million in 1990/91.

Hankyu services from Osaka operate to Shin-kaichi on the Kobe Rapid Railway.

Hashin services operate to Sumaurakoen on the Sanyo Railway via the Kobe Rapid Railway (see main entry under Osaka).

For further information on these companies, please see *Jane's World Railways*.

Developments
In March 200, JR West introduced a new service, JR Kobe (Kobe-Osaka).

Kumamoto
Population: 1.85 million (2004 estimated)

Public transport
Bus and tram services operated by municipal undertaking with additional bus services provided by private operators, one of which also runs suburban railway. JR suburban/interurban rail.

Kumamoto-shi Kotsu Kyoku – Kumamoto City Transportation Bureau

5-1-40 Oe, Kumamoto-shi 862-0971, Japan
Tel: (+81 96) 361 52 11
Fax: (+81 96) 363 59 55
Web: www.kotsu-kumamoto.jp

Key personnel
Contact: Teruaki Miyazaki
  Staff: Bus 244; tramway 131

Operating costs financed by: Fares 62.1 per cent, other commercial sources 6.9 per cent, subsidy/ grants 31.0 per cent
Subsidy from: City and regional government

Bus
Number of routes: 28
Route length: 165.53 km

Fleet: 187 vehicles
Isuzu	44
Hino	62
Nissan Diesel	51
Mitsubishi	31

In peak service: 161
On order: 5 buses

Fare collection: Payment to farebox or prepurchase
Fare structure: Stage; 1- and 3-month season tickets, 1-day tickets (bus/tram); prepaid card
Operating costs financed by: Fares 57.9 per cent, other commercial sources 5.2 per cent, subsidy/ grants 36.9 per cent
Subsidy from: City and regional government

Bus priority: Peak-hour bus lanes, 07.00–09.00 and 17.00–19.00

Tramway
Passenger journeys: (2002) 10.2 million
(2003) 9.7 million
(2004) 9.2 million
(2005) 9.2 million

Route length: 12.1 km
Number of routes: 2
Gauge: 1,435 mm
Electrification: 600 V DC, overhead

Service: Peak 3–9 min, off-peak 4–11 min
First/last car: 06.00/24.09
Fare collection: Farebox
Fare structure: As bus
One-person operation: Almost all cars
Operating costs financed by: Fares 70.2 per cent, other commercial sources 10.2 per cent, subsidy/ grants 19.6 per cent
Subsidy from: City government

Rolling stock: 44 air conditioned cars
Hirose Sharyo (1951)	M1
Shin Kinami Sharyo (1954)	M1
Toyo Koki (1954/55/57/58/60)	M20
Kawasaki articulated (1957) ex-Nishitetsu	M3
Nippon Sharyo (1982)	M2
Alna Koki (1985/86/88/91/93/94)	M12
Niigata low-floor articulated (1997/2001)	M5

Developments
Plans for extensions into residential areas are under consideration.

Kyushu Sanko Bus Co Ltd

3-35 Sakura-machi, Kumamoto-shi 860-0805, Japan
Tel: (+81 96) 325 82 39
Fax: (+81 96) 327 00 62
e-mail: e-bus@kyusanko.co.jp
Web: www.kyusanko.co.jp

Bus
Passenger journeys: (Annual) 20 million (estimate)
Vehicle-km: Not currently available

Current situation
Many of the Sanko fleet of more than 600 buses are used on services in the Kumamoto area where a network of 75 urban/suburban routes is operated. Fleet includes lift-equipped vehicles. Services are also provided throughout Kumamoto Prefecture with some express routes serving cities such as Fukuoka and Nagasaki in adjoining prefectures.

Kumamoto Bus Ltd

Kumamoto 600, Kumamoto Prefecture, Kumamoto 862-0947, Japan
Tel: (+81 96) 370 81 81   Fax: (+81 96) 370 81 91
e-mail: kuma-bus@kuma.bus.co.jp
Web: www.kuma-bus.co.jp

Key personnel
President: Masato Kobori
  Staff: 212

Bus
Current situation
Runs a fleet of some 75 buses on services to the south of Kumamoto.

Kyushu Railway Company (JR Kyushu)

Head Office
3-25-21, Hakataekimae, Hakata-ku, Fukuoka 812-8566, Japan
Tel: (+81 92) 474 25 01   Fax: (+81 92) 474 97 45
e-mail: service@jrkyushu.co.jp
Web: www.jrkyushu.co.jp

Key personnel
Chairman of the Board: Koji Tanaka
President: Susumu Ishihara

Type of operation: Suburban/interurban heavy rail

Current situation
Local emu and occasional dmu services on Kagoshima main line; dmus serve suburban stations on the Hohi main line.

For further information on this company, please see entry in *Jane's World Railways*.

Kyoto

Population: 1.5 million (estimate)

Public transport

Bus and metro services provided by municipal undertaking. Private operators also provide bus services. Suburban services by JR West, private railways and bus company. The 'Surutto Kansai' stored-fare card system covers many rail and bus operators in the Kansai metropolitan region (Osaka, Kobe, Kyoto).

City of Kyoto

Municipal Transportation Bureau
Public Relations Department
488   Uehonnojimae-cho,   Teramachi-Oike, Nakagyo-ku, Kyoto-shi 604-8571, Japan
Tel: (+81 75) 222 31 11   Fax: (+81 75) 222 30 55
(Public Relations Department)
Tel: (+81 75) 822 91 04 (Transportation Bureau)
e-mail: kokusai@city.kyoto.jp
Web: www.city.kyoto.jp

Key personnel

Chair: T Tanabe
General Manager: S Miura
   Staff: 2,814

Operating costs financed by: Fares 82.4 per cent, other commercial sources 11.3 per cent, subsidy/grants 6.3 per cent
Subsidy from: City, prefecture and government

Bus

Staff: 2,113

Number of routes: 89
Route length: 469 km
On priority right-of-way: 94.9 km; 40 bus priority signals; staff patrol during peak hours to prevent illegal parking and ensure observance of lane discipline

Fleet: 928 vehicles, including Isuzu, Mitsubishi, Hino and Nissan, all air conditioned; tram replica buses operate on sightseeing services; recent deliveries include 'no-step' low-floor buses

One-person operation: All routes
Fare collection: Farebox on vehicle
Fare structure: Flat; coupon tickets, transfer tickets (bus/bus, bus/metro); 1-, 3- and 6-month passes, day passes (bus/metro)
Fares collected on board: 31.8 per cent
Fare evasion control: Driver inspection; penalty
Average distance between stops: 420 m
Average peak-hour speed: In bus lanes, 17 km/h; in mixed traffic, 14 km/h
Operational control: Inspectors; computerised bus location and passenger information systems installed on some routes
Arrangements for elderly/disabled: Fleet includes lift-equipped and 'no-step' low-floor buses; concessionary passes, based on income
Operating costs financed by: Fares 85.8 per cent, other commercial sources 8.2 per cent, subsidy/grants 6 per cent
Subsidy from: City and prefecture
New vehicles financed by: Debenture

Current situation

Bus services are provided by City Bus and a number of private operators.

Developments

In July 2006, the city started an experimental small bus and jumbo taxi service, in co-operation with private operators. Passenger numbers were sufficient for the experiment to be continued for a further year from April 2007.

In late 2006, the city promoted a Park-and-Ride scheme to try to reduce traffic congestion in the city during two peak weekends and a public holiday.

Metro

Staff: 713

Type of operation: Full metro, initial route opened 1981

Route length 28.8 km
Number of lines: 2
Number of stations: 29
Gauge: 1,435 mm
Track: 60 kg/m rail; sleepers on concrete with resilient pads, partly conventional sleepers on ballast
Max gradient: 3.2%
Minimum curve radius: 260 m
Tunnel: Bored plus some cut-and-cover
Electrification: 1.5 kV DC, overhead

Current situation

A through service is operated over Kinki Nippon Railway track from Takeda to Nara (16 km) using metro and Kintetsu stock.

Developments

The westward extension of the Tozai line, from Nijo to Nishoiji-Tenjin (2.4 km with two new stations), is currently under construction. Test running was scheduled for July 2007, with opening expected in January 2008.

In April 2007, the PiTaPa smartcard prepaid payment system was introduced on the metro system.

Rolling stock: 204 cars, in six-car sets

Hitachi/Kinki Sharyo Series 10	M80 T40
Kinki Sharyo Series 50	M56 T28

Service: Peak 4–5 min, off-peak 6–7½ min
First/last train: 05.21/23.28

Fare structure: Four-section fare scale; coupon tickets, single, 1- and 2-day tickets/passes, regional Surutto Kansai and local Traffica Kyoto prepaid contactless payment cards
Revenue control: AFC
Arrangements for elderly/disabled: As for bus
Operating costs financed by: Fares 75.4 per cent, other commercial sources 17.7 per cent, subsidy/grants 6.9 per cent
Signalling: CTC and ATC

Light rail (proposed)
Current situation

Kyoto City is considering the introduction of a light rail system. In January 2007, an experimental bus service commenced operations on Imadegawa Street, in order to examine how the proposed LRT system would work and to identify any problem areas.

Keihan Group

Head Office
1-7-31 Ohtemae, Chuo-ku, Osaka, Japan

Key personnel

Chairman & Chief Executive Officer: Shigetaka Sato
President & Chief Operating Officer: Seinosuke Ueda
   Staff: 1,775

Keihan Bus Company Ltd

5 Minami Ishida-cho, Higashi-Kujo, Minami-ku, Kyoto-shi 601-8033, Japan
Tel: (+81 75) 682 23 10   Fax: (+81 75) 682 23 27

Number of routes: 215
Route length: 627 km (estimate)

Fleet: 500 vehicles (estimate)
Full breakdown of fleet is not currently available

Current situation

Keihan Bus, a subsidiary of the Keihan Group, operates approximately 150 air conditioned buses on Kyoto area services. About 100 do double duty on sightseeing tours, especially at weekends. Most of the remainder operate in the Osaka area. Vehicles include Hino and Mitsubishi.

Developments

The company is continuing to introduce low-floor buses into the fleet. Since 2001, Keihan Bus has been contracted by the Kyoto Municipal Transportation Bureau to provide bus services, and currently handles more than 20 per cent of the Bureau's journeys.

In July 2005, the company acquired Kyoto Bus and expanded its operations to the western areas of Kyoto City.

Keihan Electric Railway Co Ltd

1-7-31 Ohtemae, Chuo-ku, Osaka 540-6591, Japan
Tel: (+81 6) 69 44 25 21   Fax: (+81 6) 69 44 25 01
Web: www.keihan.co.jp

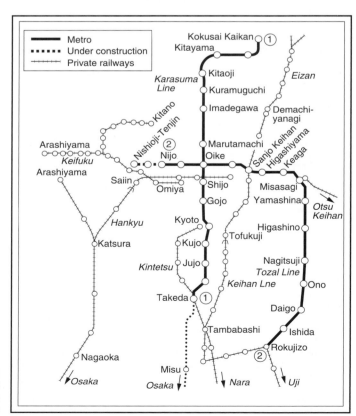

Kyoto metro and connecting rail lines
1124819

Key personnel
President: Shigetaka Sato

Passengers journeys: (All operations)
(2006) 294.1 million
(2007) 291.7 million
Vehicle-km: Not currently available

Interurban rail
Current situation
Subsidiary of the Keihan Group, providing frequent limited-express, express and local trains on Keihan main line compete with Hankyu and JR for Kyoto-Osaka traffic. Direct services run between Yodoyabashi (Osaka) and Demachi-yanagi in north Kyoto (for interchange with the Eizan Railway) via a 5.1 km underground link through central Kyoto. Also Kyoto-Uji local service (see Keihan entry under Osaka).

Light rail
Passenger journeys: Not currently available
Car-km: Not currently available

Route length: 21.6 km
Number of lines: 2
Number of stations: 27
Gauge: 1,435 mm
Electrification: 1.5 kV DC, overhead

Current situation
Keishin line runs 7.5 km from Misasagi to Hama-Otsu, with a through service to the Tozai line metro. The 14.1 km Ishiyama-Sakamoto line runs north-south through Otsu connecting at Hama-Otsu.

Rolling stock: 62 cars formed into 8 four-car and 15 two-car sets
Keihan Type 600 (rebuilt 1984/88)	M20
Keihan Type 700 (rebuilt 1992/93)	M10
Kawasaki Series 800 (1997)	M32

Fare structure: Zonal; prepurchase coupon tickets, season tickets; regional and local smart cards
One-person operation: None

Keifuku Electric Railroad Co Ltd
Address
3-20 Mibu-kayo-gosho-machi, Nakagyo-ku, Kyoto 604-8811, Japan
Tel: (+81 75) 841 93 81

Type of operation:
Light rail

Passenger journeys: Not currently available
Car-km: Not currently available

Route length: 11 km
Number of lines: 2
Number of stations: 20
Gauge: 1,435 mm
Electrification: 600 V DC, overhead

Current situation
This Keihan Group company operates two connecting lines in Kyoto's western suburbs – the 7.2 km Arashiyama main line and 3.8 km

Kitano line. Mostly reserved track but some street running on Arashiyama line. Also operates an interurban rail network and a 290-bus fleet in Fukui City, about 140 km from Kyoto.

Rolling stock: 28 cars
Mukogawa Sharyo (1971)	M2
Mukogawa Sharyo (1975/84/85-rebuilt)	M10
Mukogawa Sharyo (1990/92/93/95/96)	M14
Mukogawa Sharyo 'retro' historic cars (1994)	M2

Eizan Electric Railway Co Ltd (Eiden)
25-3, Tanaka-kamiyanagi-machi, Sakyo-ku, Kyoto-shi 606-8205, Japan
Tel: (+81 75) 702 81 10   Fax: (+81 75) 702 45 22
Web: www.keihannet.ne.jp/eiden

Type of operation: Interurban rail
Staff: 140 (estimate)

Passenger journeys: Not currently available
Car-km: Not currently available

Current situation
Eizan Electric Railway Co Ltd (Eiden), a subsidiary of the Keihan Group, operates a 1,435 mm gauge 600 V DC line north from Demachi-yanagi in Kyoto to Yaseyuen (5.6 km, 8 stations) with a branch to Kurama (8.8 km, 9 stations); fleet of 24 cars. Also Keifuku funicular (1.3 km) and cable car (aerial ropeway, 0.5 km) ascend Mt Hiei from the Eizan Yaseyuen terminus.

Fleet: 24 cars, in two-car sets
Type 900 panoramic two-car train 'Kirara' (1997/98)	12

Hankyu Corporation
Urban Transportation Business
16-1, Shibata 1-chome, Kita-ku, Osaka 530-8389, Japan
Tel: (+81 6) 63 73 50 85   Fax: (+81 6) 63 73 56 70
Web: www.hankyu.co.jp

Current situation
Frequent limited-express, express and local trains on Kyoto main line between Hankyu-Kawaramachi and Umeda (Osaka). Portion in central Kyoto runs underground with four stations. Connecting service on 4.1 km Hankyu-Arashiyama line in western suburbs (see main entry under Osaka).

Kinki Nippon Tetsudo 'Kintetsu' – Kinki Nippon Railway
6-1-55, Uehommachi, Tennoji-ku 6-chome, Osaka 543-8585, Japan
Tel: (+81 6) 67 75 34 44   Fax: (+81 6) 67 75 34 68
Web: www.kintetsu.co.jp

Key personnel
President: A Tsujii
Chairman: Wa Tashiro
General Manager, Rolling Stock Division: Shuji Okane
Staff: 8,835 (2003)

Interurban railway
Passenger journeys (all routes): (Daily) 1.8 million
Car-km: (2001/02) 311 million

Background
Founded in 1910 as the Osaka Electric Railway Co Ltd.

Current situation
Kinki Nippon's Kyoto line is served by frequent limited-express, express and local trains to Nara. Also longer-distance limited expresses to Kashikojima. A reciprocal through-service is operated between the Kyoto line and Kyoto's Karasuma Line metro via a connection at Takeda (see main entry in Osaka section).

Developments
Plans exist for a future link between Kintetsu's Nara Line at Ikoma and its Kyoto Line at Takanohara, to provide a through service between west Osaka and south Kyoto. The first 8.6 km section with three stations is scheduled to open in 2005.

Nishi Nihon Ryokaku Tetsudo – West Japan Railway Co (JR West)
4-24, Shibata 2-chome, Kita-ku, Osaka 530-8341, Japan
Tel: (+81 6) 63 75 87 08
Fax: (+81 6) 63 75 87 09
e-mail: ia@westjr.co.jp
Web: www.westjr.co.jp

Key personnel
Chairman: Shojiro Nan-ya
President: Takeshi Kakiuchi
Executive Vice-President: Masao Yamazaki
Senior Managing Directors: Yasutada Ikeda, Kazuaki Maruo
Directors: Noboru Koide, Takashi Kondo, Satoru Sone, Akio Nomura, Yoshio Tateishi

Type of operation: Suburban/interurban heavy rail

Background
The railway runs passenger transport and related activities in the Hokuriku region and western Honshu, an area of 43 million inhabitants – 34 per cent of Japan's population. The network totals 51 lines, with 289 Shinkansen and 7,988 conventional trains operated daily in 2001.
JR West was totally privatised in March 2004.

Current situation
Kyoto is a major hub on JR West's urban network; frequent local and rapid service emus operate on routes to Osaka, Kobe, Maibara, Nara and Sonobe.
For further information on JR West, please see *Jane's World Railways*.

Developments
A new service was introduced, JR Kyoto (Osaka-Kyoto).

Nagasaki
Population: City region 447,000 (2005 estimate)

Public transport
Bus services provided by municipal authority and private company. Privately owned tramway.

Nagasaki-Ken Kotsu Kyoku – Nagasaki Transportation Bureau
3-1 Yachiyo-machi, Nagasaki 850-0046, Kyushu, Japan
Tel: (+81 958) 22 51 41
Fax: (+81 958) 22 28 26
e-mail: s50200@pref.nagasaki.lg.jp

Key personnel
Director General: Kenichi Yasunaga
Director, Management Department: Haruo Hidako
Staff: 620

Bus
Current situation
Operates services over wide area of Nagasaki Prefecture (14 cities and 14 municipalities) including some urban routes in Nagasaki, though the predominant city operator is Nagasaki Bus.
The Nagasaki Smart Card, a contactless smartcard system, is used in the city, with six bus operators using the system. There is also a mobile phone payment service.

Passenger journeys: (annual) 16 million
Vehicle-km: (annual) 21.4 million

Number of routes: 608
Route length: 1,936 km
On priority right-of-way: 9.7 km

Fleet: 354 route buses and 64 long-distance coaches, including Mitsubishi Fuso, Hino, Isuzu and Nissan diesel

One-person operation: All routes (except overnight express routes)
Fare collection: Farebox; payment when leaving bus

Fare structure: City, segmentalised zonal; suburbs, distance-related. Cash, multi-tickets and monthly passes; half-price fare for young children
Operational control: Route inspectors; computerised monitoring
Arrangements for elderly/disabled: Designated seats; currently installing barrier-free buses; half-price discount card for disabled
Average distance between stops: 300 m
Average peak-hour speed: In mixed traffic, 10 km/h; in bus lanes, 18 km/h
Operating costs financed by: Fares 78.2 per cent, other commercial sources 7.6 per cent, subsidy/grants 14.2 per cent
Subsidy from: National, Prefecture and municipal governments
New vehicles financed by: Loans

Nagasaki Motor Bus Co Ltd

Head Office
3-17 Shinchi-Cho, Nagasaki-shi 850-8501, Japan
Tel: (+81 958) 26 11 11/2
Fax: (+81 958) 20 90 58, 22 70 04
Web: www.nagasaki-bus.co.jp
Staff: 1,203 (estimate)

Passenger journeys: (Annual) 74 million (estimate)
Vehicle-km: (Annual) 21 million (estimate)

Number of routes: 545 (15 in Nagasaki)
Route length: (One way) 526 km

Current situation
Operates the main network of urban routes as well as services throughout the western half of Nagasaki Prefecture. The head office in central Nagasaki includes a bus terminal, department store and hotel. Associated activities include sightseeing operations and housing developments.

Developments
Nagasaki Motor Bus Co Ltd is one of six bus operators that uses the Nagasaki Smart Card contactless payment system.

Fleet: 577 including Isuzu, Hino and Mitsubishi (includes sight-seeing vehicles)
Fare structure: Stage; pre-purchase coupon tickets, 1- and 3-monthly passes, Nagasaki City 1-day ticket
Fare collection: Payment to farebox by driver on alighting, or pre-purchase; Nagasaki Smart Card
Operating costs financed by: Fares 95 per cent, other commercial sources 5 per cent
Operational control: Bus location system

Other operators – bus

Current situation
There are five other bus operators in the Nagasaki area. These are: Nagasaki Prefectural Bus (www.keneibus.jp), Saihi Bus (www.bus.saihigroup.co.jp), Saikai Kotsu, Sasebo Municipal Bus and Shimatetsu Bus (www.shimatetsu.co.uk/bus).

Developments
All of these operators are part of the Nagasaki Smart Card contactless payment scheme.

Nagasaki Denki Kido – Nagasaki Electric Tramway Co Ltd

4-5 Ohashi Cho, Nagasaki 852-8134, Japan
Tel: (+81 958) 45 41 11
Fax: (+81 958) 43 26 09
Web: www.naga-den.com

Key personnel
President: R Sato
Staff: 200 (estimate)

Type of operation: Conventional tramway

Passenger journeys: (Annual) 20 million (estimate)
Car-km: (Annual) 2.5 million (estimate)

Route length: 11.5 km
Number of routes: 4
Number of stops: 39
Track: 40 kg/m N-rail (3.7 km), 37 kg/m A-rail (7.8 km); conventional sleepers on ballast (9 km), sleepers on concrete (2.4 km) and sleepers on concrete with resilient pads (0.1 km)
Gauge: 1,435 mm
Electrification: 600 V DC, overhead
One person operation: All cars

Developments
Series 3000 Alna Sharyo cars started to enter service in March 2004.

The company has announced its intention to begin accepting the Nagasaki Smart Card contactless payment card in early 2007, with the whole fleet having the necessary equipment installed by 2008.

Rolling stock: 76 cars
Breakdown of fleet is believed to be:

Hattori Seisakusho (1925) (ex-Odawara)	M1
Hitachi (1950/51/53/54)	M21
Nippon Sharyo (1950/61/62)	M19
Niigata (1952) (ex-Sendai)	M1
Shin Kinami Sharyo (1953) (ex-Kumamoto)	M1
Naniwa Koki (1955) (ex-Tokyo)	M1
(1966) (ex-Osaka)	M6
Alna Koki (1980-82/89/93/94/95/96/97/99/2000)	M23
Alna Sharyo low-floor, four-axle, three-car articulated Series 3000	M3

In peak service: Not currently available
Service: 4–10 min
First/last car: 06.15/23.25
Fare structure: Flat; transfer tickets, discount pre-purchase coupon tickets, 1- and 3-monthly passes, day tickets
Fare collection: Payment to farebox by driver on alighting or pre-purchase
Operating costs financed by: Fares 97 per cent, other commercial sources 3 per cent

Nagoya

Population: 2.24 million (2007 estimate)

Public transport
Bus and metro services operated by municipal undertaking, suburban/interurban rail services by private railways and JR Maglev.

Nagoya-shi Kotsu Kyoku – Nagoya City Transport Bureau

City Hall West Annex, 10th Floor, 1-1 Sannomaru 3-chome, Naka-ku, Nagoya 460-8508, Japan
Tel: (+81 52) 972 38 24   Fax: (+81 52) 972 39 38
Web: www.kotsu.city.nagoya.jp

Key personnel
General Manager: Nobuo Yoshii
Staff: 4,672

Current situation
Nagoya's municipally owned metro holds a share of about 11 per cent of daily travel in the city, with bus accounting for about four per cent. The private and JR rail services (see separate entry) are also important for commuting but much less so than in other comparable Japanese cities.

A network of eight metro lines is envisaged, and construction of new sections is under way to link existing lines with the commuter railways, including the metro, to provide easy interchange and a comprehensive network supplemented by upgraded trunk bus services on other corridors (see below).

The bus fleet includes 46 low-emission vehicles and 450 idling stop system buses, which automatically stop and start the engine as the buses stop and start.

The city authorities designate the 8th of every month as an Environment Preservation Day,

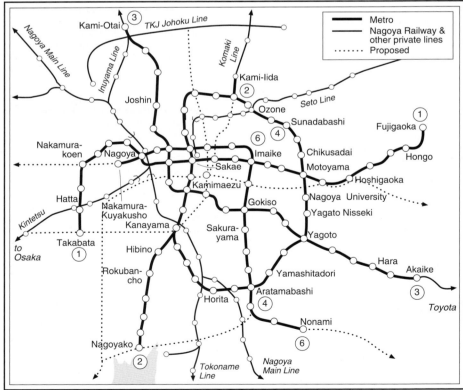

Nagoya metro and private railways   1115204

when car users are encouraged to switch to public transport.

Bus
Staff: 1,891

Passenger journeys:
(2000/2001) 160 million
(2001/2002) 159 million
(2002/2003) 157 million
(2003/2004) 154 million

Vehicle-km: (2000/2001) 44.1 million
(2001/2002) 43.5 million
(2002/2003) 40.9 million
(2003/2004) 38.9 million

Number of routes: 153
Number of stops: 1,257
Most intensive service: 1 min
Route length: (One way) 710 km
On priority right-of-way: 92 km

Fleet: 1,027 vehicles, including 'no-step' extra-low-floor buses
In peak service: 833

One-person operation: All routes
Fare collection: Payment to farebox or passes (multiride, period or 'Yurika' stored-fare); fareboxes have pass cancellation and change-giving facilities
Fare structure: Flat; single tickets, multiride passes (regular, off-peak 10.00-16.00 and holiday discount, bus/metro transfer, bus/key route bus transfer); 1-, 3- and 6-month passes (all routes, off-peak and holiday discount, commuter, student); day pass; day or monthly bus/metro pass; stored-fare 'Yurika' (bus/metro, off-peak discount); one-day 'Environment' pass (bus/metro) gives reduced rate travel on the 8th of every month
Operational control: Bus location system, with information display at stops in use on some routes
Average distance between stops: 455 m
Average speed: 13.8 km/h
Bus priority: Key route system (see below), and 30 bus lanes, total 92 km
Operating costs financed by: Fares 75.3 per cent, other commercial sources 6.2 per cent, subsidy/grants 18.2 per cent; deficit JPY2,380 million

Current situation
Low-pollution buses have been introduced since 1991.

Developments
The 'Loop Bus' service was introduced in May 1998 from Nagoya station and Sakae, with Mitsubishi MJ-series one-step midibuses.

Busway ('key route' system)
Current situation
The key route service features exclusive bus lanes, priority at traffic signals and stop spacing similar to that on the metro, raising scheduled running speed to 25 km/h.

On the first key route, between Sakae in the central area and Hoshizaki to the south (10.5 km), buses use nearside bus lanes in the morning rush hours. At ordinary bus stops, bus bays allow key route buses to pass ordinary buses easily.

On the Shindekimachi route, between Sakae and Hikiyama (10.4 km), buses run on yellow or red bus-only central lanes in the peak hours (during off-peak hours, the lanes are for buses' preferential use). Traffic signals are controlled for smooth bus operation and in the morning peak buses operate at 1–2 minute intervals, thus providing as frequent a service as the metro.

On the Shindekimachi route, both city buses and Meitetsu (private company) buses provide a co-ordinated service with tickets valid on either operator's vehicles. Meitetsu buses run to destinations beyond the key route itself.

Developments
The 'Guideway Bus' system comprises an elevated guideway and nine 'stations' constructed above existing roads. In March 2001 the 'Guideway Bus' system was introduced on the Shidami Line. Beyond the guideway there is a further 5.1 km section with extensive bus lane provision on the conventional road network. Services are operated by Nagoya-shi Kotsu Kyoku, Meitetsu, and JR Tokai using Mitsubishi GB-1000 and Hino GB-2000 vehicles in a common livery. Fares are collected on the buses.

Metro
Staff: 2,781

Type of operation: Full metro, first line opened 1957

Hitachi/Nippon Sharyo Class 6000 metro train on the Sakura-dori Line (Colin Brown) 0567221

Nagoya Meijo Line car at Nagoyako (Port) bound for Ozone (Colin Brown) 0554799

Passenger journeys: (2000/2001) 409 million
(2001/2002) 405 million
(2002/2003) 405 million
(2003/2004) 410 million
Car-km: (2000/2001) 68.8 million
(2001/2002) 68.8. million
(2002/2003) 68.6 million
(2003/2004) 65.8 million

Route length: 83.5 km (tunnel 80.4 km, elevated 3.1 km)
Number of lines: 6
Number of stations: 80
Gauge: 1,435 mm (Lines 1, 2 and 4); 1,067 mm (Lines 3, 6 and Kami iida)
Track: 50 kg/m rail
Tunnel: Cut-and-cover and bored
Electrification: 600 V DC, third rail (Lines 1, 2 and 4); 1.5 kV DC, overhead (Lines 3, 6 and Kami-iida)

Service: Peak 2–8 min, off-peak 4–15 min
First/last train: 05.30/00.28
One-person operation: On Line 6 only
Signalling: Automatic Train Control (ATC)
Revenue collection: Five-section fare scale, single tickets; multiride passes (regular); 1-, 3- and 6-month passes (all lines, bus/metro transfer, commuter, student); bus/metro passes (day or month); 'Yurika'

card (bus/metro, off-peak discount), 'Environment' pass (as bus)
Operating costs financed by: Fares 85.5 per cent, other commercial sources 6.2 per cent, subsidies 7.9 per cent; deficit JPY13,094 million

Rolling stock: 756 cars (all cars are air conditioned)
Hitachi/Nippon Sharyo

2000 Meijo Line (2) and Line 4 (1989 on)	M136 T68
3000 Tsurumai Line (3) (1977)	M92
3050 Tsurumai Line (3) (1993)	M29 T29
5000 Higashiyama Line (1) (1980 on)	M88 T44
5050 Higashiyama Line (1) (1992 on)	M108 T54
6000 Sakura-dori Line (6) (1989)	M60 T40
7000 Kami-iida Line (2003)	M4 T4

Current situation
Reciprocal through services operate between Line 3 and Meitetsu's Toyota Line and Inuyama Line, and between the Kami-iida Line and the Meitetsu's Komaki Line.

Developments
A network of eight metro lines is envisaged, totalling 130 km. The 5.1 km section between Nagoya University/Nagoya Daigaku and Aratama-bashi on Line 4 opened in October 2004.

Plans exist for further extensions to Line 6 and for construction of three other lines.

Nagoya Tetsudo 'Meitetsu' – Nagoya Railroad Company Ltd

1-2-4, Meieki, Nakamura-ku, Nagoya-shi 450-8501, Japan
Tel: (+81 52) 588 08 13   Fax: (+81 52) 588 08 15
Web: www.meitetsu.co.jp

Key personnel
Chair: Misao Kimura
President: Eiichiro Kinoshita
  Staff: 35,257 (all operations)

Current situation
Meitetsu operates interurban rail services in Nagoya and its hinterland.

Developments
In 2004, bus operations were divested and are now operated by Meitetsu Bus Co Ltd (www.metetsu-bus.co.jp).

Interurban railway
Staff: 5,182

Passenger journeys: (All modes)
(2003/04) 33.1 million
(2004/05) 33.3 million
(2006/07) 341 million
Car-km: (2003/04) 188 million
(2006/07) 194 million

Rolling stock: 1,130 cars

Current situation
Operates 21 lines in and around Nagoya, total 445.4 km, 1,067 mm gauge, electrified 1.5 kV DC. Main route is Toyohashi-Okazaki-Nagoya-Ichinomiya-Gifu, with frequent expresses and local trains. Fares cover 100 per cent of operating costs.

Meitetsu's main station is Meitetsu-Nagoya, built underground near JR's Nagoya station, and which handles more than 800 daily trains with only two tracks and three platforms. A connection opened in 1993 between the Inuyama Line and Line 3 of the metro at Kami-Otai, avoiding the Meitetsu-Nagoya bottleneck; reciprocal through running services operate between the Inuyama and Toyota lines and Line 3. The Seto Line runs to an underground terminal at Sakae in central Nagoya.

In 2005, the Airport Line opened. The Airport Limited Express train provides a direct service from Central Japan International Airport to the major cities of Gifu, Inuyama and Toyohashi. The Rapid Limited Express train 'μ-SKY' is the fastest and the most convenient access train to Meitetsu Nagoya station at a minimum travel time of 28 minutes.

Kinki Nippon Tetsudo 'Kintetsu' – Kinki Nippon Railway

6-1-55, Uehommachi, Tennoji-ku 6-chome, Osaka 543-8585, Japan
Tel: (+81 6) 67 75 34 44   Fax: (+81 6) 67 75 34 68
Web: www.kintetsu.co.jp

Key personnel
President: A Tsujii
Chairman: Wa Tashiro
General Manager, Rolling Stock Division: Shuji Okane
  Staff: 8,835 (2003)

Interurban railway
Passenger journeys (all routes): (Daily) 1.8 million
Car-km: (2001/02) 311 million

Background
Founded in 1910 as the Osaka Electric Railway Co Ltd.

Current situation
Kintetsu's main line runs from Nagoya to Kuwana, Nakagawa, Yamatoyagi and Osaka, with a branch to Toba and Kashikojima. Frequent express and local trains (see main entry in Osaka section).

Tokai Ryokaku Tetsudo (JR Tokai – JR Central – Central Japan Railway Company)

International Department, Corporate Planning Division
JR Central Towers, 1-1-4 Meieki, Nakamura-ku, Nagoya, Aichi 450-0003, Japan
Tel: (+81 52) 564 23 17   Fax: (+81 52) 587 13 00
Web: www.jr-central.co.jp

Key personnel
Chair: Yoshiyuki Kasai
President: Masayuki Matsumoto
Executive Director, Conventional Lines Operations: Koshi Akutsu
Directors Corporate Planning: Mitsuru Nakama
Marketing: Masayuki Kono

Other offices
The company has offices in Tokyo, Japan; Washington DC, USA; London, UK; and Sydney, Australia.

Interurban rail (Nagoya operations)
Staff: 8,040

Passenger journeys: (2006/07) 381 million (total for conventional lines)
Train-km: (2006/07) 206 million (total for conventional lines)

Rolling stock: 1,348 emu and dmu cars, plus 8 electric and 10 diesel locomotives and 26 passenger cars (total for conventional lines)

Operating costs financed by: Fares 100 per cent

Current situation
JR operations in Nagoya, which account for 17 per cent of daily travel within the city, are not on the same scale as the major networks in Tokyo and Osaka. Six 1,067 mm gauge lines are operated within the Nagoya region, of which three serve the city itself; local emu services (1.5 kV DC) run on the Chuo Line (Nagoya-Nakatsugawa, 79.9 km), the Tokaido Line (Toyohashi-Nagoya-Ogaki, 116.4 km), and the partly single-track Kansai Line (Nagoya-Kameyama, 59.9 km). Rapid service trains which omit some stations are operated on the Chuo and Tokaido lines.

Some 184,000 passengers per day use Nagoya station.

Developments
Developments include modernisation of stations, elevation of tracks to eliminate level crossings, installation of CTC, and introduction of high-quality reserved-seat 'Home Liner' commuter services on the Chuo and Tokaido lines.

The company is upgrading to double-track line with a side track at each station.

In November 2006, the TOICA Tokai IC Card pre-paid, contactless, smartcard ticketing system was introduced on conventional lines in the Nagoya area.

Tokai Kotsu Jigyo (TKJ) – Tokai Transport Service Company

8-1, Yasuji-cho, Nishi-ku, Nagoya-shi 452-0815, Japan
Tel: (+81 52) 504 30 02   Fax: (+81 52) 452 08 15
Web: www.tkj-i.co.jp

Suburban railway
Type of operation: Commuter heavy rail

Passenger journeys: Not currently available
Train-km: Not currently available

Route length: 11.2 km
Number of stations: 6
Gauge: 1,067 mm

Current situation
The Johoku Line provides an east-west suburban link between JR's Tokaido and Chuo lines. The largely elevated line was planned as part of a JNR loop connecting radial routes around Nagoya, but this project was abandoned and the line is run as a self-contained operation, with two or three trains per hour during peak periods and hourly trains off-peak on local service provided by four diesel railcars. It opened in 1991 and was extended by 1.9 km in 1993.

Trains are operated by the Tokai Transport Service Company (Tokai Kotsu Jigyo – TKJ), a wholly owned subsidiary of JR Central (also known as JR Tokai).

Aichi Kosoku Kotsu – Aichi Rapid Transit Co Ltd

Tel: (+81 56) 161 47 81   Fax: (+81 56) 161 62 21
e-mail: soumu@linimo.jp
Web: www.linimo.jp

Key personnel
HSST Systems International Inc: Yoichi Mera
Governor of Aichi Prefecture: Masaaki Kanda

Current situation
This third-sector company was established in 2000 to build and operate a new Maglev line, linking Fujigaoka (on metro Line 1) with Yakusa (on the Aichi Loop Line), adjacent to EXPO2005 in Nagakute Town. Shareholders include the city, prefecture and Meitetsu. Maglev linear motor technology provides a 6–15 minute service.

Developments
The 8.9 km line, 'Linimo', opened in March 2005.

'Limino' 3-car linear-powered magnetic levitation (Maglev) *emu*   1373688

Okayama

Population: 676,000 (2006 estimate)

Public transport

City bus services provided by private company which also operates the tramway. Additional suburban and longer-distance services provided by other private companies and JR West.

Okayama Denki Kido 'Okaden' – Okayama Electric Tramway Co Ltd

2-8-22 Tokuyoshicho, Okayama-shi 703-8291, Japan
Tel: (+81 86) 272 18 11
Fax: (+81 86) 272 12 88
e-mail: info@okayama-kido.co.jp
Web: www.okayama-kido.co.jp

Key personnel

President: Motoi Matsuda
   Staff: 289

Passenger journeys: (Both modes)
Not currently available

Operating costs financed by: Fares 96.3 per cent, other commercial sources 3.7 per cent

Current situation

Founded in 1910, Okaden is the main bus operator in central Okayama and also runs a tramway. It is part of the Ryobi Group.

Developments

In 2006, the company introduced the Hareca smartcard ticketing system.

Bus

1-14-41 Konancho, Okayama-shi 700-0866, Japan
Tel: (+81 862) 23 72 21

Key personnel

Director: Goro Okada
   Staff: 229

Passenger journeys: Not currently available

Number of routes: 72
Route length: (One way) 146 km
On priority right-of-way: Bus lanes 7.7 km

Fleet: 135 buses, 43 coaches, including Mitsubishi Fuso

Most intensive service: 5 min
One-person operation: All routes
Fare collection: Control tickets on entry from machine at centre doors, payment on exit to farebox at front door; Hareca smartcard; also PiTaPa and ICOCA payment systems
Fare structure: Flat/stage; 1-, 3- and 6-month passes
Fares collected on board: 76.4 per cent
Operational control: Route inspectors
Arrangements for elderly/disabled: Half fare
Average distance between stops: 400 m
Average peak-hour speed: Bus lanes 18 km/h; mixed traffic 14 km/h

Developments

Tram replica buses introduced on city sightseeing service in 1997.

Tramway

2-8-22 Tokuyoshicho, Okayama-shi 703-8291, Japan
Tel: (+81 86) 272 21 01
Fax: (+81 86) 272 12 88

Key personnel

President: Motoi Matsuda
Director: Goro Okada
   Staff: 69

Type of operation: Conventional tramway

Passenger journeys: Not currently available

Route length: 4.7 km
Number of lines: 2
Number of stops: 15
Gauge: 1,067 mm
Track: Conventional sleepers on ballast, sleepers on concrete, both types with resilient pads
Electrification: 600 V DC, overhead

Service: Peak 3 min, off-peak 5 min
First/last car: 06.00/21.50
Fare structure: Flat; pre-purchase coupon tickets and 1-, 3- or 6-month passes
Fare collection: Farebox or pre-purchase
Operating costs financed by: Fares 96.2 per cent, other commercial sources 3.8 per cent
One-person operation: All cars

Rolling stock: Not currently available
Fleet breakdown is not currently available, but includes:
Utsunomiya Sharyo (1953) (ex-Nikko)
Alna Koki air conditioned (1980-95)
Niigata ultra-low-floor 'MoMo'

Developments

The company has introduced ultra-low-floor vehicles to the fleet.

Nishi Nihon Ryokaku Tetsudo – West Japan Railway Company (JR West)

4-24, Shibata 2-chome, Kita-ku, Osaka 530-8341, Japan
Tel: (+81 6) 63 75 87 08
Fax: (+81 6) 63 75 87 09
e-mail: ia@westjr.co.jp
Web: www.westjr.co.jp

Key personnel

Chairman: Shojiro Nan-ya
President: Takeshi Kakiuchi
Executive Vice-President: Masao Yamazaki
Senior Managing Directors: Yasutada Ikeda
   Kazuaki Maruo
Directors: Noboru Koide, Takashi Kondo, Yoshio Tateishi, Akio Nomura, Satoru Sone

Background

The railway runs passenger transport and related activities in the Hokuriku region and western Honshu, an area of 43 million inhabitants – 34 per cent of Japan's population. The network totals 51 lines, with 289 Shinkansen and 7,988 conventional trains operated daily in 2001.
JR West was totally privatised in March 2004.

Suburban/interurban railway

Current situation
Operates local emu services Himeji-Okayama and Okayama-Hiroshima, also on routes to Uno, Niimi and Aioi. Dmu services operated on routes to Tsuyama and Kibi.
   For further information on JR West, please see *Jane's World Railways.*

Bus

Current situation
Local bus services provided by the Chugoku JR Bus Co.

Ryobi-Holdings Co

7-23 Nishikimachi, Okayama-shi 700-8518, Japan
Tel: (+81 86) 232 21 61
Fax: (+81 86) 232 22 12
e-mail: nomura.h@ryobi-bus.co.jp
Web: www.ryobi-bus.co.jp

Key personnel

Chairman: Takashi Matsuda
President: Mitsunobu Kojima
Corporate Planning Division: Hiroki Nomura
   Staff: 1,600

Bus

(whole company operations)
Passenger journeys: (2007) 10.7 million
Vehicle-km: (2007) 21.9 million

Number of routes: 196
Route length: 2,563 km

Fleet: 250 buses and 152 coaches, predominantly Mitsubishi Fuso
In peak service: 410

Operating costs financed by: Fares 98.0 per cent, other commercial sources 2.0 per cent
Fare collection: Control tickets on entry from machine at centre doors or rear doors, payment on exit to farebox at front door
Fare structure: Flat/stage; 1-, 3- and 6-month passes, bus cards, cash
Operational control: Route inspectors
Arrangements for disabled: Half fare
Average distance between stops: 200 m
Average peak-hour speed: (mixed traffic) 15 km/h

Current situation

Serves suburban areas of Okayama in the southern part of Okayama prefecture, as well as regions beyond.

Developments

In April 2007, Ryobi Bus Co merged with Ryobi-Unyo Co and Ryobi-Holdings Co was established.
   As well as bus/coach services, the company also operates taxi and ferry services.

Chutetsu Bus Co

2-8-50 Yamashita, Okyama City, Okayama-shi 700-0821, Japan
Tel: (+81 86) 222 66 01
Web: www.chutetsu-bus.co.jp

Key personnel

Chief Executive Officer: Masashi Fujita

Background

Established in 1896.

Current situation

Serves suburban areas of Okayama, in the northern part of Okayama Prefecture, with fleet of 130 buses.

Shimotsui Dentetsu Co Ltd 'Shimoden' – Shimotsui Electric Railway

3-61 Omoto-ekimae, Okayama-shi 700-0923, Japan
Tel: (+81 86) 233 88 11
Fax: (+81 86) 233 00 83
e-mail: info@shimoden.co.jp,
sdbus@shimoden.co.jp
Web: www.shimoden.co.jp

Key personnel

President/Representative: Nagayama Hisashi
   Staff: 210

Bus

Current situation
Runs bus services in suburban Okayama covering the southern part of Okayama Prefecture, with 124 buses and 90 coaches.

Osaka

Population: City: 2.64 million (2007 estimate), metropolitan area: 18.6 million (estimate)

Public transport

Bus, metro and elevated automated guided transport system operated by municipal authority. Several private commuter and interurban rail lines provide suburban services along with Japan Railways (JR), with through running to the metro. Some privately operated buses, monorail, tramway and ferry service on the Yodo river.

Osaka-shi Kotsu Kyoku – Osaka Municipal Transportation Bureau

Kujo Minami-1, Chome 12-62, Nishi-ku, Osaka 550-8552 Japan
Tel: (+81 6) 65 82 11 01   Fax: (+81 6) 65 85 61 27
Web: www.kotsu.city.osaka.jp/

Key personnel

General Manager: Yoshihide Kuzumoto
Staff: 6,900

Passenger journeys: (All modes)
(2007) 940.9 million

Current situation

The metro carries the vast majority of city travellers, being one of the most intensively used in the world, with 508,000 a day passing through the busiest station at Umeda.

On 1 July 2005, the operation of the 2.4 km section of Osaka Port Transport System Co Ltd's Nanko-Minato-ku line (former OTS Line) between Cosmosquare and Osakako was integrated into the metro network, with a view to enhancing passenger convenience. Line No.8 (Imazatosuji Line) between Itakano and Imazato opened on 24 December 2006. As a result, as of the end of FY2006, the metro network has eight lines over 129.9 km.

The integration of the former OTS Line into the metro network also expanded the route of the New Tram Service automated guideway transit system. With the addition of the 1.3 km section between Cosmosquqre and Nakafuto on the former OTS Line, the New Tram, as of the end of FY2006, covers 7.9 km and serves as a key means of transport in the Nanko District.

At present, the Municipal Transport Systems is a completed network, with the metro and New Tram as their core systems supplemented by the bus system. In response to a continued reduction in passenger volume on bus services, the Osaka Municipal Transport Bureau has reorganised its bus routes and service frequencies. As of the end of FY2006, 134 routes totalling 646.3 km were in service.

Developments

In partnership with the joint company Surutto-Kansai Co Ltd, shared by public and private railway/bus operators in the Kansai regional area, Osaka Municipal Transportation Bureau introduced the IC Fare Card (smartcard), named Osaka Pitapa, in February 2006. The card enables passengers to take all municipal transport by touching the card to the ticket gate or the bus farebox. For card users, reduced fare rates are applied in accordance with the monthly total of used fares. Payments are taken monthly directly from passengers' bank accounts. Other Pitapa IC cards issued by private railway companies and JR West's ICOCA card are also usable, and are fully compatible with each other's transport services.

Bus

Staff: 1,210

Passenger journeys: (2007) 78.4 million
Vehicle-km: (2007) 28.5 million

Number of routes: 134
Route length: (One way) 483 km (includes 163 km of minibus routes)
On priority right-of-way: 113 km

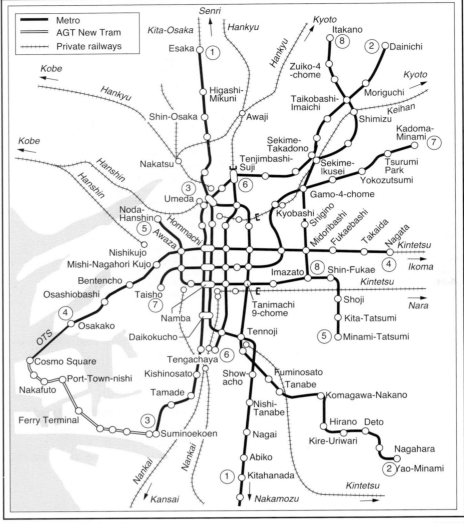

Osaka's urban rail network   1124816

Fleet: 845 vehicles, all air conditioned

Mitsubishi	160
Isuzu	221
Hino	211
Nissan Diesel	170
Minibus:	
Omni Nova	70
Mercedes-Benz	83

In peak service: 793

New vehicles required each year: 60

Most intensive service: 3 min
One-person operation: All routes
Fare collection: Payment on alighting to farebox, ticket or pass
Fare structure: Flat, with transfer between buses without charge within 90 minutes
Fare evasion control: None
Operational control: Computerised operational control with real-time bus location displays at 741 stops
Arrangements for elderly/disabled: Free passes and concessionary fares financed by city welfare bureau; 323 'non-step' low-floor buses (excluding minibuses) are in operation, together with 25 standard buses with wheelchair lifts. In total, 348 buses of these user-friendly designs serve 96 routes in Osaka.
Integration with other modes: Unified bus/rail fare scale; reduced fare bus/metro, New Tram transfer tickets
Average distance between stops: 434 m (minibus 335 m)
Average speed: In mixed traffic, 12.9 km/h
Bus priority: 82.3 km bus-only lanes; 7.9 km bus-only roads; 22.8 km bus priority lanes; 167 bus priority signals. Staff on duty during rush hours to ensure observance of lane discipline
Operating costs financed by: Fares 48.9 per cent, revenues from the City to finance fare arrangements (free passes and reduced fares) for the elderly

and the handicapped, 36.7 per cent, commercial sources 3.2 per cent, subsidy/grants 11.2 per cent
Subsidy from: City's general account (92.2 per cent), prefectural government (0.3 per cent) and national government (7.5 per cent)

Developments

New Urban Bus System concept adopted, involving bus priority measures, computerised operational control, bus shelters and real-time travel information displays. Diesel-electric hybrid and 'idling-stop' system buses are on trial.

Metro

Staff: 5,690 (including New Tram)

Type of operation: Full metro, initial route opened 1933

Passenger journeys: (2007) 834.9 million
Car-km: (2007) 110.9 million

Route length: 129.9 km
Number of lines: 8
Number of stations: 123
   in tunnel: 114
Gauge: 1,435 mm
Track: 50 kg/m flat-bottom rail
Max gradient: 5.0%
Minimum curve radius: 83 m
Electrification: 750 V DC, third rail; 1.5 kV DC, overhead (Line 6, 7 and 8)

Current situation

Reciprocal through running services operate between Line 1 and North Osaka Express Electric Railway, between Line 6 and the Hankyu Senri and Kyoto lines, and between Line 4 and Kintetsu Keihanna line. Line 7 and Line 8 are built to a small profile, with trains powered by linear motor.

Developments

Line 8, from Imazato to Itakano (12 km, 11 stations) opened in December 2006.

Rolling stock: 1,280 cars, Nippon, Hitachi, Kawasaki, Kinki, Tokyu and Alna Koki; all air conditioned

Series 10 Line 1	230
Series 20 Line 4	96
Series 20 Lines 1/2/3/4/5	572
Series 30 Lines 2/3	78
Series 66 Line 6	138
Series 70 Line 7	100
Series 80 Line 8	68

Service: Peak 2–5 min, off-peak 4–7.5 min
First/last train: 05.00/24.00
Fare structure: Five-section distance-based fare scale
Fare collection: Ticket machines and automatic barriers at all stations; with introduction of stored-value multiride tickets, almost all tickets are magnetically encoded for use in automatic barriers; monthly pass; IC Fare Card (smartcard), Osaka Pitapa
Arrangements for elderly/disabled: Free passes and concessionary fares as for bus. 212 trains have wheelchair space; lifts at 120 stations
Operating costs financed by: (including New Tram) Fares 86.1 per cent, other commercial sources 8.5 per cent; subsidy/grants 5.4 per cent
Subsidy from: City general account 88.4 per cent, national government 10.8 per cent, city 83.4 per cent, prefecture government 0.8 per cent (includes New Tram)
Integration with other modes: Free interchange with New Tram (see below) and reduced fare bus/ metro transfer tickets and passes; reduced fare single tickets for short-distance travel from/to reciprocal running sections of private railways
Signalling: ATC, CTC, and automatic block; cab signalling and ATC (Lines 5, 7 & 8)
Surveillance: CCTV on all platforms

ICTS

Type of operation: New Tram Intermediate Capacity Transit System (ICTS) opened 1981, fully automatic operation, rubber-tyred cars on concrete guideway

Passenger journeys: (2007) 27.6 million
Car-km: (2007) 5.0 million

Route length: 7.9 km
Number of stations: 10
Electrification: 600 V AC, third rail

Service: Peak 2½ min, off-peak 6 min
First/last train: 05.17/24.00
Fare structure: As metro
Operating costs financed by: (see metro)
Revenue control: Ticket machines and automatic barriers
Train control: Fully automated operation; no driver, but some trains have an attendant to provide customer information and deal with emergencies
Signalling: Fixed block (continuous transmission and receiving with check-in and check-out system); ATC, CTC
Surveillance: CCTV on all platforms

Rolling stock: 20 four-car trains, air conditioned
Niigata Iron Works Series 100   M80

Current situation
Under the same management as the metro, the elevated New Tram serves new residential and commercial development on land reclaimed from Osaka Bay.

Developments
Since July 2005, the Osaka Municipal Transportation Bureau has been operating the direct rail service between Cosmosquare and Suminoekoen (7.9 km), incorporating the Cosmosquare-Nakafuto section of the Osaka Port Transport System Line (the former OTS line) into the New Tram Nanko Port Town Line.

Hankyu Corporation
Urban Transportation Business
16-1, Shibata 1-chome, Kita-ku, Osaka 530-8389, Japan
Tel: (+81 6) 63 73 50 85
Fax: (+81 6) 63 73 56 70
Web: www.hankyu.co.jp

Nose Electric Railway, a subsidiary of Hankyu Dentetsu, train at Kawanishi Nose Guchi (Colin Brown)
0567220

Key personnel
Chairman: Taro Ohashi
President: Kazuo Sumi
Managing Director, Urban Transportation Headquarters: Kenji Harada
Public Relations Department: Tsunenori Kawashima
Staff: 4,576

Background
The Hankyu Corporation was established in 1907 and has 117 subsidiaries and 31 affiliates, of which nine are involved in railway operations, management and maintenance. Other subsidiaries operate bus services, taxi operations and freight transport.

Interurban railway
Passenger journeys (all lines/routes): (Daily) 1.8 million
Car-km: (1997/98) 168 million

Current situation
Operates five subsidiaries with nine lines and approximately 90 stations over 147 km of 1,435 mm gauge route, electrified 1.5 kV DC. Interurban routes run to Kobe, Kitasenri, Kyoto and Takarazuka, through running from Kitasenri and Kyoto Line stations to metro Line 6. A stored-fare card system was introduced in 1992 and its validity was extended in 1996 to other operators within the Surutto Kansai card network.

Developments
In August 2004, a monthly prepayment card was introduced at Hankyu Corporation and Nosé Electric Railway.

Rolling stock: 1,320 emu cars   M738 T582

Bus
Tel: (+81 6) 866 31 12   Fax: (+81 6) 866 31 42

Current situation
Hankyu Bus operates 733 buses on services linked to rail operations, including suburban bus routes in Osaka. A computer-controlled bus terminal/route information system is in operation between Osaka international airport and Hankyu Hotarugaike terminals.

Kita Osaka Kyuko Dentetsu (Kitakyu) – Kita-Osaka Kyuko Railway Co Ltd
2-4-1, Terauchi, Toyonaka-shi, Osaka 561-0872, Japan
Tel: (+81 6) 68 65 06 01   Fax: (+81 6) 68 66 02 54
Web: www.kita-kyu.co.jp

Key personnel
President: S Yamazawa
Staff: 162

Number of lines: 1
Route length: 5.9 km
Number of stations: 4
Electrification: 750 V DC, third rail

Background
Opened in 1970 to provide transport link to the Japanese International Exposition.

Current situation
This expressway median line extends from Esaka to Senri-Chuo serving residential development

Polestar Kita Osaka express trainset 8001 at Senri-Chue terminus (Colin Brown)
0126457

north of Osaka (Senri New Town). A reciprocal through-running service is operated to Line 1 of the metro; trains were lengthened from nine to 10 cars in 1995 to provide extra capacity on this intensively used line.

The company is part owned by the prefectural government and the Hankyu Electric Railway; operations are on a wholly commercial basis.

Surutto Kansai stored-fare card system introduced 1996.

Rolling stock: 70 emu cars in 10-car sets
8000 series Polestar Alna Koki
(1986–96)   M35 T35

Hanshin Denki Tetsudo – Hanshin Electric Railway Co Ltd

1-24, Ebie 1-chome, Fukushima-ku, Osaka 553-8553, Japan
Tel: (+81 6) 64 57 21 23
Fax: (+81 6) 64 57 21 41
Web: http://rail.hanshin.co.jp

Key personnel
President: M Tezuka
  Staff: 2,433

Interurban railway
Staff: 1,201

Passenger journeys: (1995/96) 191 million
(1998/99) 195 million

Background
Originally established in 1899 as the Settsu Electric Railway, the company was renamed in July of that year.

Current situation
Operates 40.1 km of 1,435 mm gauge route with 42 stations, comprising Osaka-Kobe main line and two branches, electrified 1.5 kV DC. Reciprocal through services operate on the Sanyo Railway via the underground Kobe Rapid Railway.

Developments
A 3.4 km extension of the Nishi-Osaka line is under construction from Nishi-kujo to Kintetsu Namba with three intermediate stations. Completion is scheduled for 2008.

Surutto Kansai stored-fare card system introduced 1996.

Rolling stock: 314 emu cars   M237 T77

Bus
Web: www.hanshin.co.jp/bus

Current situation
Operates 165 buses on 15 local routes extending to 153 km, consisting of Osaka-Kobe and Osaka-Takarazuka trunk routes, and feeder services to rail stations. Bus lanes and computer-aided bus location system introduced. Also operates sightseeing, long-distance express and airport services.

Keihan Denki Tetsudo – Keihan Electric Railway Co Ltd

OMM Building 7-31, Otemae 1-chome, Chuo-ku, Osaka 540-6591, Japan
Tel: (+81 6) 69 44 25 29
Fax: (+81 6) 69 44 25 84
Web: www.keihan.co.jp

Key personnel
President: Shigetaka Sato
  Staff: 1,785

Interurban railway
Passenger journeys: (Including Kyoto light rail)
(2005/06) 294 million
Car-km: (2005/06) 96.8 million

Current situation
Operates 66.1 km of 1,435 mm gauge route, electrified at 1.5 kV DC. Main line, 51.6 km with 42 stations, runs from underground terminal in Osaka (Yodoyabashi station) to Kyoto, with two branches. Frequent service of limited-express, express and local trains on main line, where all stations have automatic ticket barriers which accept multiple-ride cards.

Also operates 21.6 km light rail system in Kyoto and Otsu (see under Kyoto).

Developments
Authority has been granted for the construction of a 2.9 km underground link in central Osaka (Nakanoshima line) to serve the central business district. The line will have three intermediate stations. Completion is scheduled for FY2008.
Rolling stock: 730 cars, M418 T312, all air conditioned; limited-express trains have a car with television, and one double-deck car

Bus
Passenger journeys: (including Kyoto)
(2005/06) 52.7 million
Vehicle-km: (including Kyoto)
(2005/06) 22.7 million

Current situation
Keihan Bus, a railway subsidiary, operates approximately 384 of its 581 buses on services in Osaka Prefecture, including routes in Osaka's northeastern suburbs (see Kyoto entry).

Ferry
Current situation
Osaka Aqua-Bus ended a limited peak-hour commuting service in June 2006.

Kinki Nippon Tetsudo 'Kintetsu' – Kinki Nippon Railway

6-1-55, Uehommachi, Tennoji-ku 6-chome, Osaka 543-8585, Japan
Tel: (+81 6) 67 75 34 44   Fax: (+81 6) 67 75 34 68
Web: www.kintetsu.co.jp/

Key personnel
President: A Tsujii
Chairman: Wa Tashiro
General Manager, Rolling Stock Division: Shuji Okane
  Staff: 8,835 (2003)

Interurban railway
Passenger journeys (all routes): (Daily) 1.8 million
Car-km: (2001/02) 311 million

Background
Founded in 1910 as the Osaka Electric Railway Co Ltd.

Current situation
Operates express and local services over main line of 190 km from Osaka to Nagoya, and over several other routes totalling 574 km on 1,435, 1,067 and 762 mm gauges, electrified at 1.5 kV

DC and 750 V DC. A reciprocal through-running service operates between the Higashi-Osaka line and Line 4 of the Osaka metro. This is the largest private railway in Japan.

Developments
Plans exist for a future link between Kintetsu's Nara Line at Ikoma and its Kyoto Line at Takanohara, to provide a through service between west Osaka and south Kyoto. The first 8.6 km section with three stations is scheduled to open in 2005.

Rolling stock: 1,999 emu cars   M1,119 T880

Nishi Nihon Ryokaku Tetsudo – West Japan Railway Co (JR West)

4-24, Shibata 2-chome, Kita-ku, Osaka 530-8341, Japan
Tel: (+81 6) 63 75 87 08   Fax: (+81 6) 63 75 87 09
e-mail: ia@westjr.co.jp
Web: www.westjr.co.jp

Key personnel
Chairman: Shojiro Nan-ya
President and Executive Officer: Takeshi Kakiuchi
Executive Vice-President: Masao Yamazaki
Senior Managing Directors: Yasutada Ikeda
  Kazuaki Maruo
Directors: Noboru Koide, Takashi Kondo, Yoshio Tateishi, Akio Nomura, Satoru Sone

Type of operation: Interurban/suburban railway

Passenger journeys: (urban network only)
(2000/01) 1,812 million
(2001/02) 1,438 million
(2002/03) 1,409 million
(2003/04) 1,425 million
(2004/05) Data not yet available

Background
The railway runs passenger transport and related activities in the Hokuriku region and western Honshu, an area of 43 million inhabitants – 34 per cent of Japan's population. The network totals 51 lines, with 289 Shinkansen and 7,988 conventional trains operated daily in 2001.

JR West was totally privatised in March 2004.

Current situation
JR West's urban network comprises 14 lines serving Kobe, Osaka and Kyoto. Osaka is the hub of the network, with frequent local and rapid service emus colour-coded according to line of operation on eight routes including the 21.7 km Osaka loop around the central area.

JR West operates a rapid service from central Osaka to Kansai international airport using Series 223 emus, and an express service 'Haruka' from Kyoto and Shin-Osaka using purpose-built six-car Series 281 emus. Access to the airport is via a 11.1 km link from JR's Hanwa Line, 6.9 km of which is shared by competing Nankai airport services.

Series 21020 'Urban Liner Next' emu, operating on the non-stop service between Osaka and Nagoya
0595238

A new station on the JR Yumesaki line opened in March 2001 to serve Universal Studios' Japan theme park. A shuttle service is provided from central Osaka by four six-car Series 103 emus in dedicated USJ liveries.

For further information on JR West, please see *Jane's World Railways*.

Developments

Work is in progress for start-up of passenger service on JR's 18.6 km Joto freight line. An outer orbital service will be provided through Osaka's eastern suburbs linking Shin-Osaka, Shigino, Hanaten and Kyukoji. JR West, Osaka prefecture and Osaka city have set up a third-sector company to undertake the project, which includes double-tracking, electrification, new stations and new trains. The south section, between Hanaten and Kyuhoji, is scheduled to open in 2008.

The proposed Naniwasuji line would form a north-south route through the centre of Osaka, from Shin-Osaka via Umeda to the JR Namba station, providing improved access to Kansai international airport from northern Osaka to the Kyoto and Hyogo prefectures.

ATS-P (Automatic Train Stop-Pattern) train protection equipment has been installed on the Hanwa line, including the Kansai airport branch, the Osaka loop line and the Tozai line. Future planned installation will cover the Osaka-Maibara section of the Kyoto line and Osaka– Aboshi on the Kobe line.

Nankai Denki Tetsudo – Nankai Electric Railway Co Ltd

1-60 Namba 5-chome, Chuo-ku, Osaka 542-8503, Japan
Tel: (+81 6) 66 44 71 21   Fax: (+81 6) 66 44 71 23
Web: www.nankai.co.jp

Key personnel
Chairman: J Yoshida
President: M Yamanaka
Senior Managing Directors: H Yamano, H Uzawa
   Staff: 2,905 (plus bus staff)

Interurban railway
Passenger journeys: (1995/96) 302 million
(1998/99) 273 million

Current situation
Operates 163.5 km of 1,067 mm gauge lines of which 149.2 km electrified 1.5 kV DC and 14.3 km at 600 V DC.

Main routes Osaka-Wakayama (Nankai main line) and Osaka-Gokurakubashi (Koya line) served by frequent local and express services. Also through service using Nankai and Semboku cars from Namba to the Semboku Rapid Railway to serve suburban housing.

In 1994 new services were introduced between Nankai's Namba terminal in central Osaka and Kansai international airport, a distance of 43 km. The express 'Rapi:t' service, operated by distinctively styled purpose-built Series 50000 units, is supplemented by local services, both of which compete with JR services for airport traffic. Access to the airport is via an 8.8 km branch line from Izumi-Sano, part of which is shared with JR. To further compete with JR, Nankai proposes to lay mixed-gauge track along its existing 1,067 mm main line to enable airport services to operate through central Osaka via the 1,435 mm gauge Sakaisuji metro line and on to Kyoto and Nara via the Hankyu, Keihan and Kintetsu systems.

The company joined the Surutto Kansai stored-fare card network in 1999.

Rolling stock: 720 emu cars
M418 T302

Bus
Nankai Bus Co Ltd
Tel: (+81 72) 221 08 81   Fax: (+81 72) 221 10 37
Web: www.nankaibus.jp

Background
Wholly owned by Nankai Electric Railway Co Ltd; established in 2001 with some 600 staff.

Current situation
Approximately 535 vehicles run on routes related to rail services in the southern half of Osaka prefecture.

Semboku Kosoku Tetsudo (Semboku Rapid Railway)

Osaka Prefectural Urban Development Company Izumichuo Station Building, 5-1-1 Ibukino, Izumi City, Osaka 594-0041, Japan
Tel: (+81 7) 25 57 32 78   Fax: (+81 7) 25 57 31 36
Web: www.otk-group.co.jp
   www.semboku.jp

Key personnel
President: K Kichida

Suburban railway
Current situation
This 12.1 km line (1,067 mm gauge, electrified 1.5 kV DC), constructed and operated by Osaka Prefectural Urban Development Company, serves Semboku New Town (population 160,000) to the south of Osaka. A reciprocal through-running service is operated to central Osaka via the Nankai Railway.

Rolling stock: 126 emu cars   M69 T57

Hankai Denki Kido

3-14-72 Shimizugaoka, Sumiyoshi-ku, Osaka 558-0033, Japan
Tel: (+81 6) 66 71 30 80
Web: www.hankai.co.jp

Key personnel
President: Y Fukunaga
   Staff: 119

Current situation
This tramway,100 per cent owned by the Nankai Electric Railway, became a separate operation in 1980. It serves the southern part of Osaka and Sakai City from two terminals in Osaka.

Tramway
Number of lines: 2
Number of routes: 3
Route length: 18.7 km
Number of stops: 41
Gauge: 1,435 mm
Electrification: 600 V DC, overhead

Service: 2.5–12 min
First/last car: 05.15/23.35
Fare collection: Farebox or prepurchase
Fare structure: Stage; transfer tickets available between routes; prepurchase coupon tickets, 1-, 3- and 6-month passes, one-day free ticket
One-person operation: All cars

Rolling stock: 38 cars
Kawasaki Rolling Stock (1928)	M9
Tanaka Sharyo (1930)	M1
Teikoku Sharyo (1957/62/63)	M10
Tokyu Car (1987/88/89/90/91/92/93/94/95)	M11
Type 601 (rebuilt 1996/97/98)	M7

Osaka Kosoku Tetsudo – Osaka Monorail Co Ltd

Osaka Monorail
1-1-5, Higashi-machi, Shin-Senri, Toyonaka-shi, Osaka-fu 560-0082, Japan
Tel: (+81 6) 68 71 82 80
Fax: (+81 6) 68 71 82 84
Web: www.osaka-monorail.co.jp/
   Staff: 153

Type of operation: Straddle monorail, opened 1990

Current situation
This orbital monorail line round northeast Osaka links Osaka airport and Kadoma-shi providing interchange with the North Osaka Express Electric Railway, the Hankyu Senri, Kyoto and Takarazuka lines, and the Keihan main line.

Route length: 23.9 km
Number of lines: 1
Number of stations: 16
Electrification: 1.5 kV DC

Service: 5–12 min
One-person operation: All trains
Fare collection: Full AFC
Signalling: Cab signalling, ATP
Surveillance: CCTV
Operating costs financed by: Fares 100 per cent

Rolling stock: 13 four-car sets
Hitachi/Kawasaki Type 1000   M52

Developments
The initial 6.7 km line was extended by 3.5 km in 1994, and further extended from Shibahara to Osaka airport (3.1 km) and from Minami-Ibaraki to Kadoma-shi (7.9 km) in 1997. A 2.7 km northwards branch to Osaka University Hospital opened in 1998 and it is planned to extend this line a further 6.3 km to serve Kokusai Bunka garden city.

The line is designed for eventual operation by six-car trains running at three minute headways.

Osaka

Private bus
Current situation
A number of private bus operators, mainly private railway subsidiaries, provide suburban and commuter services.

Since the opening of the monorail, there have been reports that private bus and taxi ridership along the monorail route has declined.

Hankai tramway at Osaka Tennojieki-Mae on the Uemachi Line (Marcel Vleugels)   0109780

Sapporo

Population: 1.89 million (2007 estimate)

Public transport

Bus, metro, and tramway operated by municipal authority. Suburban services provided by private bus companies and JR.

Sapporo-shi Kotsu Kyoku – Sapporo Transportation Bureau

Higashi 2-4-1 Oyachi, Atsubetsu-ku, Sapporo, Hokkaido 004-0041, Japan
Tel: (+81 11) 896 27 08
Fax: (+81 11) 896 27 90
Web: www.city.sapporo.jp/st/

Key personnel

Managing Director: T Ikegami

Current situation

The three-line metro forms the nucleus of the city's transport system under the Long-Term Comprehensive Development Plan, with bus services seen increasingly as feeding the metro.

Bus

Staff: 1,447

Number of routes: 70
Route length: 409 km

Developments

Bus position indication system indicates time of arrival of next bus to passengers at stops. Hail-and-Ride introduced on one suburban route. 'Factory Line' service connects industrial zone with metro stations. Latest vehicles feature air conditioning and lower floors.

Some loss-making services have been transferred to Hokkaido Chuo Bus, JR Hokkaido and Jotetsu Bus.

Fleet: 555 vehicles, including Hino, Nissan, Mitsubishi-Fuso and Isuzu
Full breakdown of fleet is not currently available

In peak service: Not currently available
On order: Not currently available
One-person operation: All routes
Fare collection: Payment to farebox on exit, pass, stored-fare card
Fare structure: Zonal; metro transfer system; 'coupon tickets'; commuter passes; day tickets (metro/bus/tram); one-day Eco-Ticket gives reduced-rate travel on designated 'no car days' twice a month, when car drivers are encouraged to use public transport; stored-fare cards, 'With You Card' valid on metro/bus/tram, 'Common Card' valid on metro/tram/city bus/JR Bus/Chuo Bus
Fares collected on board: 62.9 per cent
Operational control: Radio
Arrangements for elderly/disabled: Pass for free travel covered by subsidy; wheelchair-accessible vehicles
Integration with other modes: Bus and metro systems closely integrated with many feeders and interchanges; transfer ticket system
Bus priority: 11 bus-only lanes (46.1 km); five bus priority lanes (13.2 km)
Operating costs financed by: Fares 80 per cent, other commercial sources 0.7 per cent, subsidy/grants 19.3 per cent
Subsidy from: City
New vehicles financed by: Internal resources

Metro

Staff: 1,225

Type of operation: Full metro, rubber-tyred system, initial route opened 1971

Route length: 48 km
  in tunnel: 43.3 km
Number of lines: 3
Number of stations: 46
Gauge: Rubber-tyred trains on concrete guideway, Line 1 spacing 2,180 mm; Line 2, 2,150 mm

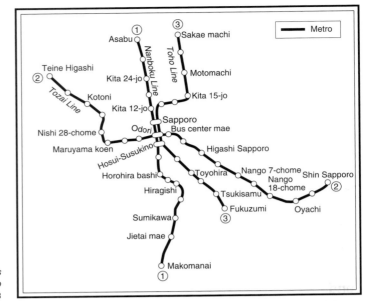

Map of Sapporo's metro
1124823

Track: Line 1 concrete slab track without sleepers, surface paved with epoxy-resin plastic; centre-guide steel I-beam. Line 2 similar but running track surface paved with steel plates; Line 3 track on concrete sleepers
Max gradient: 4.3%
Minimum curve radius: 200 m
Tunnel: Generally double-track, cut-and-cover; beneath the Toyohira river the section has been built by the caisson method. Elevated section has a circular aluminium shelter to prevent heavy snowfall affecting operations
Electrification: 750 V DC, third rail on Line 1; 1.5 kV DC, RS-AFB overhead conductor system on Lines 2 and 3

Rolling stock: 404 cars

Kawasaki 3000 Line 1	M40
Kawasaki 5000 Line 1	M51 T51
Kawasaki 6000 Line 2	M72 T72
Kawasaki 7000 Line 3	M40 T40
Kawasaki 8000 Line 2	M30 T8

In peak service: Not currently available

Service: Peak 3–5 min, off-peak 5–7 min
First/last train: 06.15/24.00
Fare structure: 6 sections; AFC handles interchange between metro and bus and provides 25 per cent discount on each fare; commuter passes; metro/bus/tram day tickets; one-day Eco-Tickets (see under bus); stored-fare 'With You Card' valid on metro/bus/tram, and 'Common Card', valid additionally on JR Bus and Chuo Bus services
Revenue control: Central processor, automatic ticket vending and fare adjusting machines, coin collecting unit and automatic gates with stored-fare card readers; automatic commuter pass vendor at main stations
Arrangements for elderly/disabled: Lifts at 24 stations
Operating costs financed by: Fares 92 per cent, other commercial sources 1 per cent, subsidy/grants 7 per cent
Signalling: Full ATC and CTC. Linked to the signalling is the Subway Total System, whose main subsystems comprise: optical total transmission line control; related operating control equipment; power control; automatic operations control; fire-control system; automatic inspection of rolling stock; ticket vending and inspection equipment; public address and surveillance. The system also allows automated driverless operation of empty trains over the 1.3 km link to Higashi depot

Tramway

Staff: 135

Type of operation: Conventional tramway
Number of routes: 1, retained as metro feeder
Route length: 8.4 km
Number of stops: 23
Gauge: 1,067 mm
Electrification: 600 V DC, overhead

Current situation

Audio/visual 'tram approaching' indicators installed at some stops. All passenger shelters are equipped with footway and roof heating to prevent snow accumulation.

Rolling stock: 30 cars

Sapporo Sogo Tekko Kumiai (1958/61)	M18
Hitachi (1958) (re-built by Alna Koki 1998/9, 2000)	M3
Nippon Sharyo (1961)	M1
Kawasaki (1985/87/88)	M6
Alna Koki (1998/99)	M2

In peak service: Not currently available

Service: 3-10 min
First/last car: 06.18/23.18
Fare collection: Farebox or prepurchase
Fare structure: Flat; tram/metro transfer tickets, day ticket (bus/metro/tram), one-day Eco-Ticket (see under bus); prepurchase coupon tickets, 1- and 3-monthly passes; stored-fare 'WithYou Card' valid on metro/bus/tram, and 'Common Card' valid additionally on JR Bus and Chuo Bus services

Hokkaido Chuo Bus Company

1-8-6 Ironai, Otaru-shi, Hokkaido 047-0031, Japan
Tel: (+81 134) 24 11 11
Web: www.chuo-bus.co.jp

Current situation

Provides suburban services in the Sapporo area, with transfer fare system to metro. Fleet of 965 buses and 161 coaches. Stored-fare 'Common Card' accepted on selected routes in Sapporo.

Jotetsu Bus Company

9-1-1 Toyahira-shijo, Toyohira-ku, Sapporo-shi 062-0904, Japan
Tel: (+81 11) 572 31 31, 588 33 21
Fax: (+81 11) 572 31 36, 588 33 25
Web: www.jotetsu.co.jp

Current situation

Provides suburban services in the Sapporo area with 60 buses and 25 coaches. Jotetsu is a subsidiary of theTokyu Corp, which has extensive bus and rail interests in the Tokyo area.

Hokkaido Railway Co – JR Hokkaido

Nishi 15-chome, Kita 11-jo, Chuo-ku, Sapporo 060-8644, Japan
Tel: (+81 11) 700 57 31   Fax: (+81 11) 700 57 19
e-mail: info@jrhokkaido.co.jp
Web: www.jrhokkaido.co.jp

Key personnel
Chair: Shin-ichi Sakamoto
President: Akio Koike

Suburban/interurban rail
Current situation
All-stations emu services operate Sapporo-Otaru (34 km) and Sapporo-Iwamizawa (40 km) on the Hakodate main line and Sapporo-Chitose airport (44 km) on the Chitose line. Some trains continue over longer distances. Local dmu service operates Sapporo-Daigaku-mae (30.5 km) on the Sassho line.

Developments
Suburban services in the Sapporo area have seen strong growth, particularly the routes to Teine and Ainosato-kyoikudai.

For further information on JR Hokkaido, please see *Jane's World Railways*.

Bus
Current situation
JR buses run 44 routes serving the northwest and southeast suburbs in association with rail services, and as feeders to the metro. Transfers available to metro. Stored-fare 'Common Card' accepted on all routes in Sapporo.

Sendai

Population: City 1.03 million (2008 estimate), metropolitan area 1.5 million (estimate)

Public transport
Bus services provided by municipality and private company; metro; suburban rail.

Sendai City Transportation Bureau

1-4-15 Kimachidouri, Aoba-ku, Sendai-shi, Miyagi-ken 980-0801, Japan
Tel: (+81 22) 224 51 11   Fax: (+81 22) 224 68 39
Web: www.kotsu.city.sendai.jp/e/

Bus
Staff: 1,096

Passenger journeys: (1997) 57.5 million
Vehicle-km: (1997) 22.9 million

Number of routes: 55
Route length: 633 km
Number of stops: 1,197
Most intensive service: 5 min

Fleet: 653 vehicles, including Hino, Isuzu, Nissan Diesel and Mitsubishi Fuso
In peak service: 600
On order: 30 buses
Average age of fleet: 6.5 years

Fare structure: Flat and distance-related, mixed system; multiride coupon tickets; wide range of passes including multimodal
Fare collection: Payment to farebox, prepurchase tickets and passes; prepaid card (bus, bus/metro)
Fares collected on board: 72.7 per cent
One-person operation: All routes
Arrangements for elderly/disabled: Some wheelchair-accessible vehicles
Operating costs financed by: Fares 72.3 per cent, other commercial sources 5 per cent, subsidy 22.7 per cent
Subsidy from: City
Average speed: peak hours 11.4 km
Bus priority: Bus lanes

Current situation
Metro feeder routes are organised around seven suburban bus/metro interchanges with through ticketing.

Tram replica buses introduced on city loop service in 1999.

Metro
Staff: 316

Type of operation: Full metro, initial route opened 1987

Passenger journeys: (1997/98) 61 million
Car-km: (1997/98) 6.8 million

Route length: 14.8 km
 in tunnel: 11.8 km
Number of lines: 1
Number of stations: 17
Gauge: 1,067 mm
Max gradient: 3.5%
Minimum curve radius: 160 m
Electrification: 1.5 kV DC, overhead

Service: Peak 3 min, off-peak 7 min
First/last train: 05:35/23:55
Fare structure: Graduated; multiride tickets, bus/metro transfer tickets and passes, day tickets, 1- and 3-month student passes; 1-, 3- and 6-month commuter passes; prepaid cards
Fare collection: Full AFC
One-person operation: All trains
Signalling: Full ATO, ATC
Operating costs financed by: Fares 53.6 per cent, other commercial sources 43.8 per cent, subsidy/grants 2.6 per cent
Subsidy from: National government 15 per cent, city 85 per cent

Rolling stock: 21 four-car trains
Kawasaki 1000 (1987 on)   M42 T42
In peak service: 18 trains

Current situation
Sendai's first metro route, the Nanboku line, links Izumi-Chuo in the north to Tomizawa in the south.

Developments
A second Line 2 is planned. It would run east-west with a length of 13.9 km and 13 stations.

Miyagi Kotsu Bus Co Ltd

3-13-20 Izumigaoka, Izumi-Ku, Sendai, MYG, Japan
Tel: (+81 22) 771 53 10

Key personnel
Staff 1,440

Vehicle-km: (Annual) 28 million (estimate)

Number of routes: 677
Route length: 5,278 km
Fleet: 624 buses including Isuzu, Mitsubishi, Hino and Nissan Diesel types; plus 149 coaches in charter division

Operating costs financed by: Fares 90 per cent, subsidy/grants 10 per cent
Subsidy from: National and local government

Current situation
Operates bus services throughout Miyagi Prefecture including Sendai city and suburbs. Miyagi Kotsu is part of the Meitetsu Group, which operates extensive bus and rail services in the Nagoya area.

Bus/metro transfer tickets available on feeder buses.

Higashi Nihon Ryokaku Tetsudo – East Japan Railway Company (EJR) (JR East)

2-2-2 Yoyogi, Shibuya-ku, Tokyo 151-8578, Japan
Tel: (+81 3) 53 34 11 51   Fax: (+81 3) 53 34 11 10
Web: www.jreast.co.jp

Key personnel
Chair: Mutsutake Otsuka
President: Satoshi Seino
 Staff: 61,900 (whole company as at April 2008, includes 54,697 for rail operations)

Type of operation: Inner and outer suburban heavy rail

Passenger journeys: (Sendai city)
(2004) 60.3 million
(2005) 87.0 million

Current situation
Commuter emu services run on the Senseki Line, Sendai (Aobadori)-Takagimachi-Ishinomaki (50.3 km), and on the Senzan Line, Sendai-Ayashi (15.2 km), with some trains continuing to Yamagata (62.8 km). Longer-distance all-stations local trains on Tohoku main line and Joban Line serve some suburban stations in Sendai. Also infrequent local service Sendai-Iwakiri-Rifu (12.2 km).

A 3.9 km underground section of the Senseki Line opened in March 2000 replacing the previous surface level alignment; a new underground terminus at Aobadori provides interchange with the Sendai metro.

For further information on JR East, please see other entries in *Jane's Urban Transport Systems* and *Jane's World Railways*.

Developments
The third sector Sendai Airport Access Railway has constructed a 7 km link between JR East's Tohoku main line and Sendai airport; the new line opened in March 2007.

Tokyo

Population: City (23 wards) 8.7 million, prefecture 12.8 million (2007 estimates), conurbation/metropolitan area in excess of 35 million (including Chiba, Kawasaki and Yokohama) (2005 estimate)

Public transport
Bus, tramway and metro services provided by municipal authority, with second metro system operated by the Tokyo Metro Co Ltd. Extensive suburban rail services operated by several private railways and JR, with through running to metro system from many lines; monorail and two automated guideway systems. Additional bus services by independent operators licensed by Transport Ministry. Majority of travel is by rail modes with approximately 80 per cent share of total passenger trips in the conurbation; suburban systems of JR and private railways account for about 32 per cent each, with the remainder by the metros.

Further major rail investment is planned under proposals put forward in 1985 by the Council for Transport Policy, affecting the metro, JR and private railways. Under the plans, some 530 km of the route would be constructed within 50 km of central Tokyo to serve expanding suburban areas and to disperse traffic and development from the congested central area to existing subcentres at Shibuya, Shinjuku and Ikebukuro and new ones at Ueno-Asakusa, Kinshicho-Kameido and Ohsaki.

The 'SF' stored-fare card system covers metro and private railway companies in the Kanto metropolitan region (Tokyo, Yokohama, Kawasaki).

Tokyo-to Kotsu Kyoku 'Toei'

Bureau of Transportation, Tokyo Metropolitan Government
2-8-1, Nishi-Shinjuku, Shinjuku-ku, Tokyo 163-8001, Japan
Tel: (+81 3) 53 20 60 26   Fax: (+81 3) 53 88 16 51
e-mail: koe@metro.tokyo.jp
Web: www.kotsu.metro.tokyo.jp

Key personnel

Director General: K Shimada
Staff: 6,445

Passenger journeys: (All modes)
(2004/05) 972 million
(2005/06) 991 million
(2006/07) 1,016 million

Current situation

Toei operates four of Tokyo's 13 metro lines, 138 bus routes, a tram route and a 0.3 km monorail (in Ueno Park).

Bus

Key personnel

Director, Service Division: S Saito
Staff: 2,566

Passenger journeys: (2004/05) 209 million
(2005/06) 209 million
(2006/07) 207 million
Vehicle-km: (2004/05) 49.5 million
(2005/06) 49.0 million
(2006/07) 49.1 million

Number of routes: 138
Route length: 781.7 km

Current situation

Within Tokyo's 23 urban wards buses account for a mere 5.4 per cent of the total number of public transport journeys of which Toei carries 38 per cent, with the remainder split between nine major private operators – Keihin Kyuko, Keio, Keisei, Odakyu, Seibu, Tobu, Tokyu, Kanto Bus and Kokusai Kogyo. Toei has a virtual monopoly in the central and inner areas while the majority of services in the outer wards are operated by the private companies with a few routes operated jointly with Toei.

Services in the outer metropolitan area are operated by the private railways and three other companies – Kanagawa Chuo Kotsu, Nishi Tokyo Bus and Tachikawa Bus.

Completion of the O-Edo metro line in December 2000 was accompanied by the rationalisation of parallel bus routes to reduce duplication and provide feeder services. New Urban Bus System concept adopted on eight routes, involving bus priority measures, computerised operational control and real-time travel information displays at bus stops.

Developments

1,136 low-floor buses have been introduced, including 10 lift-equipped buses. Buses using LPG-blend and CNG fuel, diesel-electric hybrids, and dust-particle-free buses have been tried out to assess their ability to reduce pollution. The fleet includes 162 CNG vehicles and 1,226 with the 'idling-stop' system. From 2003, vehicles over seven years old will require catalytic diesel particulate trap equipment thus requiring further changes to the bus fleet.

Fleet: 1,489 vehicles, all air conditioned, Isuzu, Hino, Nissan, Mitsubishi-Fuso.
Full breakdown of fleet is not currently available

In peak service: Not currently available
On order: Not currently available
Most intensive service: 2 min
One-person operation: All routes
Fare collection: Farebox at entrance or prepurchase
Fare structure: Flat; 1 and 3 month commuter passes, coupon tickets, Bus Common Card and day tickets (Toei bus, Toei metro/bus/tram and Toei metro/bus/tram/JR/Eidan); Bus Common Card valid

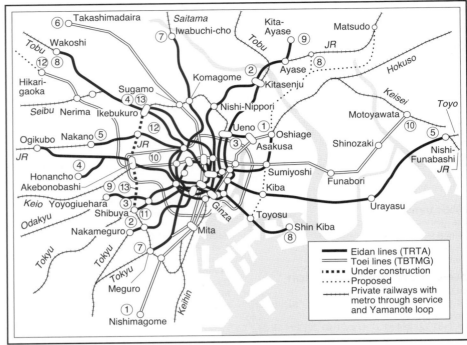

Tokyo's complex urban rail system   1124828

on Toei and private operators' buses within Tokyo and adjoining Kanagawa and Saitama prefectures
Operational control: Integrated Bus Control system
Arrangements for elderly/disabled: Fares concession compensated for by city; fleet includes wheelchair-accessible vehicles
Average distance between stops: 395 m
Average peak-hour speed: 11.3 km/h
Operating costs financed by: Fares 82.6 per cent, other commercial sources 7.9 per cent (including interest income and dividends received), subsidy/grants 9.5 per cent
Subsidy from: Metropolitan government
New vehicles financed by: Business bonds

Metro

Key personnel

Director, Subway and Streetcar Service Division: M Takane
Staff: 3,700

Type of operation: Full metro, initial line opened 1960

Passenger journeys: (2004/05) 742 million
(2005/06) 761 million
(2006/07) 788 million
Car-km: (2004/05) 113 million
(2005/06) 113 million
(2006/07) 115 million

Route length: 109.0 km
Number of lines: 4
Number of stations: 106
  in tunnel: 98
Gauge: Mita line 1,067 mm, Shinjuku line 1,372 mm, Asakusa line and O-Edo line 1,435 mm
Track: 50 kg/m N-rail; conventional sleepers on ballast, sleepers on concrete and slab track
Max gradient: 3.5%
Minimum curve radius: 161 m
Tunnel: Cut-and-cover, shield driven and concrete caisson
Electrification: 1.5 kV DC, overhead

Current situation

Through services operate between the Asakusa Line and the Keisei, Hokuso and Keihin Kyuko systems, between the Shinjuku Line and the Keio Railway and between the Mita Line and the Tokyu Toyoko Line.

The first 4.8 km section of small-profile O-Edo Line 12 between Nerima and Hikarigaoka opened 1991, and a further 9.1 km between Nerima and Shinjuku opened in 1997 to complete the radial section between the northwestern suburbs and central Tokyo. The 2.1 km section between

Shinjuku and Kokuritsu Kyogijo (International Stadium) opened in April 2000 and the remainder of the 29 km loop around central Tokyo and back to Shinjuku opened in December 2000. The line provides interchange with JR and private railways at 22 of its 38 stations.

A 1.6 km extension of the Mita Line from Mita to connect with Eidan's Namboku Line, allowing through running to Meguro and on to Tokyu tracks, opened in September 2000.

Developments

A 4 km westward extension of the O-Edo Line to Oizumi-Gakuen is at the planning stage, and a 9.7 km new transit system line, 'Nippori-toneri Liner', to serve Adachi ward (north Tokyo) is due to open in March 2008.

Rolling stock: 1,090 cars, all air conditioned
Breakdown of fleet is not currently available
Service: Peak 2–4 min, off-peak 5–8 min; some trains run through to other railways
First/last train: 05.00/00.30
Fare structure: Graduated, 1, 3 and 6 month commuter passes, day tickets (Toei metro/bus/tram and Toei metro/bus/tram/JR/Eidan)
Arrangements for elderly/disabled: 78 stations wheelchair accessible
Operating costs financed by: Fares 82.4 per cent, other commercial sources 6.6 per cent, subsidy/grants 11.0 per cent
Subsidy from: Metropolitan government
Signalling: Automatic block with three-aspect colourlight signalling and ATS, cab signalling and ATC
Surveillance: CCTV on platforms

Tramway

Staff: 136

Type of operation: Conventional tramway

Passenger journeys: (2004/05) 20.3 million
(2005/06) 19.9 million
(2006/07) 19.4 million
Car-km: (2006/07) 1.6 million

Route length: 12.2 km
Number of lines: 1
Number of stops: 30
Gauge: 1,372 mm
Track: 50 kg/m PS rail; conventional sleepers on ballast, and sleepers on concrete with resilient pads
Electrification: 600 V DC, overhead

Current situation

Toei's remaining tram line provides an orbital link through Tokyo's northwest suburbs from

Minowabashi to Waseda. The line is mostly on reserved track with high platforms.

Rolling stock: 42 cars
Breakdown of fleet is not currently available
In peak service: Not currently available

Service: Peak 3 min, off-peak 5 min
First/last car: 05.30/23.30
Fare structure: Flat; 1-, 3- and 6-month passes, day tickets (Toei metro/bus/tram and Toei metro/bus/tram/JR/Eidan)
Fare collection: Farebox or prepurchase
Operating costs financed by: Fares 92.7 per cent, other commercial sources 4.7 per cent, subsidy/grants from metropolitan government 2.6 per cent

Kanto Bus Co Ltd
Web: www.kanto-bus.co.jp
Further information has been removed at the company's request.

Kokusai Kogyo Co Ltd – Chukobus
2-10-3 Yaesu, Chuo-ku, Tokyo 104-8460, Japan
Tel: (+81 3) 32 73 40 41   Fax: (+81 3) 32 73 41 31
e-mail: chukobus@kokusaikogyo.co.jp
Web: www.chukobus.com
www.kokusaikogyo.co.jp

Key personnel
President: Osano Takamasa
Senior Vice-President, Bus: Teruaki Goto
Staff: 2,565 (total), 1,800 (Bus division)

Bus
Passenger journeys: Not currently available
Vehicle-km: Not currently available

Number of routes: 269
Route length: 2,491 km

Fleet: 779 buses
In peak service: 686

Current situation
Around 250 of the fleet are committed to Tokyo metropolitan area services. The operating area covers part of northwest Tokyo, with several routes terminating at Ikebukuro, and extends into outer suburban areas in adjoining Saitama prefecture. Fleet includes lift-equipped vehicles and the first production version of the Isuzu CNG non-step bus.

Nishi Tokyo Bus Co Ltd
3-1-7 Miyojin-cho, Hachioji-shi, Tokyo 192-0046, Japan
Tel: (+81 426) 48 65 22, 46 90 12
Fax: (+81 426) 45 12 23
e-mail: iken@nisitokyobus.co.jp
Web: www.nisitokyobus.co.jp

Bus
Current situation
Established in 1963, this company, a subsidiary of the Keio Group, provides regular, express and community bus services in the Tokyo metropolitan area. Tama Bus Co Ltd is a subsidiary.

Fleet: Not currently available
Full fleet details and breakdown are not currently available, but the fleet is believed to include Hino, Isuzu, Mitsubishi and Nissan Diesel vehicles.
On order: Not currently available
In peak service: Not currently available

Tachikawa Bus Co Ltd
2-27-27 Takamatsu-cho, Tachikawa-shi, Tokyo 190-0011, Japan
Tel: (+81 42) 524 31 11   Fax: (+81 42) 549 89 58
Web: www.tachikawabus.co.jp

Bus
Current situation
This Odakyu Group company operates 197 buses on services at Tachikawa City in the Tokyo metropolitan area, with a total route of length 186 km. Also operates coaches.

Odakyu Bus Co Ltd
2-19-5 Senkawa-cho, Chofu-shi, Tokyo 182-0002, Japan
Tel: (+81 3) 53 13 82 11
Web: www.odakyubus.co.jp

Key personnel
Staff: 1,137

Current situation
Subsidiary of the Odakyu Group.
A fleet of 396 buses and 65 coaches is operated by Odakyu Electric Railway's associate company Odakyu Bus, about 275 of them used on services in the Tokyo metropolitan area.

Developments
PASMO and Suica smartcards are now accepted on the network.

Tokyo Metro Co Ltd (Tokyo Metro)
3-19-6 Higashi-ueno, Taito-ku, Tokyo 110-8614, Japan
Tel: (+81 3) 38 37 70 46   Fax: (+81 3) 38 37 72 19
Web: www.tokyometro.jp

Key personnel
President: H Umezaki
Director of International Affairs: S Kawamura
Manager of International Affairs: N Kimura
Staff: 8,509

Type of operation: Full metro, initial line opened 1927

Current situation
Tokyo Metro is a transportation company whose network represents the core of the railway system for the Tokyo Metropolitan Area. Tokyo Metro lines account for 73.1 per cent of metro journeys.

With the opening of the Fukutoshin Line in June 2008, Tokyo Metro now operates a network of nine lines with a total length of 195.1 km. Seven of those lines, (Hibiya (2), Tozai (5), Namboku (7), Yurakucho (8), Chiyoda (9), Hanzomon (11) and Fukutoshin (13)), offer reciprocal through-service with lines operated by other railway companies.

As a transportation company carrying 6.22 million passengers every day, maintaining and enhancing transport safety is the number one priority. At the same time, Tokyo Metro is constantly striving to provide the best possible service with a customer focus. Also, by aggressively undertaking various affiliated businesses, support for passengers' daily lives is provided. Tokyo Metro is also aiming to achieve more efficient business management and accordingly is energetically pursuing initiatives to cut costs and raise productivity. Tokyo Metro aspires to be a corporate group that is highly regarded by society at large. To this end, diligent work on environmental protection and compliance management is being carried out, whilst at the same time maintaining close relationships with local communities.

Passenger journeys: (2003) 2,074 million
(2004) 2,075 million
(2005) 2,102 million
(2006) 2,153 million
(2007) 2,277 million
Car-km: (2003) 254 million
(2004) 254 million
(2005) 255 million
(2006) 258 million
(2007) 258 million

Route length: 195.1 km
in tunnel: 168.6 km
elevated: 26.5 km
Number of lines: 9
Number of stations: 179
Gauge: 1,435 mm (Ginza and Marunouchi lines), others 1,067 mm
Track: 50 and 60 kg/m rail; in tunnel, solid bed; at surface level, sleepers on ballast
Tunnel: Shield driven and cut-and-cover
Electrification: 600 V DC, third rail (Ginza and Marunouchi lines); others 1.5 kV DC, overhead

Service: Peak 1 min 50 s, off-peak 3-8 min; some trains on 6 lines run through to other private railways or JR lines
First/last train: 05.00/00.30
Fare structure: Graduated (kilometric-sectional); multitickets (Tokyo Metro/Toei metro, Tokyo Metro/JR East, Tokyo Metro/private rail), passes, day tickets (Tokyo Metro only and Tokyo Metro/JR/Toei

Platform at Meiji-jingumae station on the Fukutoshine Line   1368888

For details of the latest updates to *Jane's Urban Transport Systems* online and to discover the additional information available exclusively to online subscribers please visit
juts.janes.com

Series 10000 vehicle for the Yurakucho and Fukutoshin Lines   1368889

metro/bus/tram); stored-fare SF Metrocard (Tokyo Metro/Toei metro/private rail); PASMO contactless smartcard

Revenue control: AFC at all stations

Operating costs financed by: Fares 85.8 per cent, miscellaneous transportation revenue 10.4 per cent, track lease 0.7 per cent

One-person operation: Namboku Line, Chiyoda Line branch and Marunouchi Line branch

Signalling: CS-ATC (cab signalling) on all lines

Surveillance: CCTV on curved platforms

Rolling stock: 2,669 cars (as at July 2008)

01 Ginza Line 3 (1983 on)	M114 T114
02 Marunouchi Line 4 (1988 on)	M171 T165
03 Hibiya Line 2 (1988 on)	M168 T168
05 Tozai Line 5 (1988 on)	M199 T231
06 Chiyoda Line 9 (1993 on)	M4 T6
07 Yurakucho Line 8 and Fukutoshin Line 13 (1993 on)	M8 T12
07 Tozai Line 5 (1993 on)	M16 T24
08 Hanzomon Line 11 (2003 on)	M30 T30
5000 Tozai Line 5 and Chiyoda Line 9 (1964 on)	M4 T2
6000 Chiyoda Line 9 (1971 on)	M205 T148
7000 Yurakucho Line 8 and Fukutoshin Line 13(1974 on)	M173 T141
8000 Hanzomon Line 11 (1980 on)	M109 T81
9000 Namboku Line 7 (1991 on)	M84 T42
10000 Yurakucho Line 8 and Fukutoshin Line 13 (2006 on)	M110 T110

In peak service: 2,404

On order: Not currently available

Developments

The Fukutoshin Line (13) opened in June 2008. The Tokyo Metro network now totals 195.1 operating km with a total of 179 stations. The Fukutoshin line passes through three sub-centers of Tokyo. They are Ikebukuro, Shinjuku and Shibuya. Also, through-service is available with major private railway operators, namely Tobu Railway (on the Tojo line) and Seibu Railway Co Ltd. (on the Yurakucho and Ikebukuro lines). Through-service with Tokyu Corporation from Shibuya onto the Toyoko line will begin in 2012.

A new contactless smartcard, card called PASMO, was launched in March 2007. PASMO can be used throughout the Tokyo Metropolitan Area, greatly enhancing convenience for users. Currently, service is available on some 23 railway operators and 78 bus operators. Interoperability is also possible with Suica (JR East's IC card) affiliated operators. Response has been extremely positive, with over 8 million PASMO cards sold as of January 2008.

Higashi Nihon Ryokaku Tetsudo – East Japan Railway Company (EJR) (JR East)

2-2-2 Yoyogi, Shibuya-ku, Tokyo 151-8578, Japan
Tel: (+81 3) 53 34 11 51   Fax: (+81 3) 53 34 11 10
Web: www.jreast.co.jp

Key personnel

Chair: Mutsutake Otsuka

President and Chief Executive Officer: Satoshi Seino

Staff: 61,900 (whole company as at April 2008, includes 54,697 for rail operations)

Type of operation: Inner and outer suburban heavy rail

Passenger boardings: (Tokyo area)
(2003) 5,297 million
(2004) 5,339 million
(2005) 5,322 million
(2006) 5,373 million
(2007) 5,459 million

Train-km: Not available currently

Current situation

JR East's Tokyo metropolitan area network extends to 1,106.1 route-km, located within a radius of approximately 100 km from Tokyo station and including Chiba, Kawasaki and Yokohama, serving a population of some 34.8 million. All are 1,067 mm gauge, almost all are electrified, most are equipped with ATC or ATS-P (Automatic Train Stop-Pattern), and all trains are air conditioned. Trains on some JR lines run through to metro destinations and on to private lines. The 16 high-frequency inner-suburban services known as 'E-den' are operated by a large standardised fleet of emus, colour-coded according to line of operation. Headway on the Chuo Line (rapid service) is 2 min 10 sec and on the Yamanote and Keihin Tohoku lines 2¹/₂ min. ATS of an improved type is being introduced throughout the Tokyo area to reduce headways further. Automatic fare collection gates have been installed at most metropolitan area stations. The stored-fare magnetic-coded card system is supplemented by an IC card, *Suica*, and fare gates with both types of card have been installed at stations within a 100 km radius of Tokyo.

For further information on JR East, please see other entries in *Jane's Urban Transport Systems* and *Jane's World Railways*.

Developments

In 2008, the company prepared a new long-term plan – *JR East 2020 Vision-idomu-* (*idomu* meaning 'challenge' in Japanese). In this new plan, JR East states that it intends to strengthen the Tokyo metropolitan area network through collaboration with other railway operators. Limited express through-services based on co-operation with Tobu Railway Co Ltd began in March 2006 and preparations have started for the commencement of mutual through-services with Sagami Railway Co Ltd (known as Sotetsu), slated for FY2015. Another project would extend the services of the Utsunomiya Line, the Takasaki Line and the Joban Line to Tokyo Station by constructing the Tohoku Through Line. The resulting through-services would increase convenience, ease crowding and shorten journey times.

Also in the plan, JR East has announced its intentions to initiate work on the introduction of automatic platform gates on the Yamanote Line. Gates will be initially installed at Ebisu and Meguro stations in order to validate the full-scale introduction to all stations on the amanote Line. Currently, the company plans to commence the use of the automatic platform gates at Ebisu and Meguro stations in FY2010 and, after investigating technical issues and effects on train operations, intends to complete the installation of the gates at all stations on the Yamanote Line within 10 years of their initial introduction. The installation of the Train Automatic Stop Control system (TASC) is also planned.

Rolling stock: 9,670 cars and locomotives (Tokyo area)

Full breakdown of the fleet for the Tokyo area is not available currently, but it was understood to comprise:

Electric locomotives	56
Diesel locomotives	29
Emu cars	9,368
Dmu cars	83
Coaches	134

Keihin Kyuko Dentetsu 'Keikyu' – Keihin Electric Express Railway Co Ltd (Keikyu)

2-20-20 Takanawa, Minato-ku, Tokyo 108-8625, Japan
Tel: (+81 3) 32 80 91 23   Fax: (+81 3) 32 80 91 93
e-mail: koho4@keikyu.co.jp
Web: www.keikyu.co.jp

Key personnel

President and Representative Director: Masaru Kotani

Managing Director, General Affairs Department: Kiyoshi Ishikawa

Interurban rail

Staff: 1,892 (2004)

Passenger journeys: (2002) 1.14 million, daily
(2003) 1.15 million, daily

Route length: 87 km (total)

Background

Formed in 1898, the Keihin Electric Express Railway Co Ltd is part of the Keikyu Group. It is one of the major private railways in Japan and provides services which link central Tokyo to Haneda airport and the southern metropolitan area.

The group also includes bus and taxi companies.

Current situation

Trains link Shinagawa with Kawasaki, Yokohama, Yokosuka, Zushi and Miura on 1,435 mm gauge, electrified 1.5 kV DC.

In 1998 Keikyu opened a station at Tokyo International airport (Haneda airport), which established a link between that airport and Narita airport. More than 100 million passengers have used the new station since it opened.

Rolling stock: 758 emu cars   M606 T152

Keio Dentetsu – Keio Electric Railway Co Ltd

Keio Corporation
9-1, Sekido 1-chome, Tama City, Tokyo 206-8502, Japan
Tel: (+81 423) 37 31 06   Fax: (+81 423) 74 93 22
Web: www.keio.co.jp

Key personnel

President: Kan Kato

Staff: 6,812 (2008 – includes all transportation employees)

Background

Founded in 1910 as the Keio Denki Kido Co Ltd with operations commencing in 1913. There are nine transport companies within the Keio Group.

Interurban rail
Staff: 2,305

Passenger journeys: (2003) 599 million (railway operations)
Train-km: Not currently available

Route length: 84.7 km
Number of lines: 6
Number of stations: 69
Gauge: 1,372 mm, 1,067 mm (Inokashira Line)
Electrification: 1.5 kV DC
Operating costs financed by: Fares 88.7 per cent, other commercial sources 11.3 per cent

Current situation
Operates the main Keio Line out of an underground terminal below the Keio department store at Shinjuku, with four branches totalling 72 km, 1,372 mm gauge, electrified 1.5 kV DC.

The 3.6 km underground Keio new line links the main line with the Toei Shinjuku metro line, enabling trains to run through to central Tokyo (Iwamoto-cho). Also 12.8 km 1,067 mm gauge Inokashira Line, electrified 1.5 kV DC, runs from a terminal at Shibuya to Kichijoji.

Developments
Larger cars with five doors have been introduced to increase capacity; platforms have been lengthened to handle 10-car trains (Keio Line) or large five-car trains (Inokashira Line); track elevation is in progress to eliminate level crossings.

Trains have women-only cars during peak hours and late evening and priority seating is available for the elderly, disabled, people with infants and pregnant passengers.

Rolling stock: 848 emu cars   M505 T343

Keio Dentetsu Bus Co Ltd
Current situation
Keio Dentetsu Bus Co Ltd was established in 2002 and comprises four subsidiaries, which operate regular and express bus routes in the Tokyo area.

Fleet: Not currently available
Fleet breakdown is not currently available, but includes Hino, Isuzu, Mitsubishi Fuso and Nissan buses

Keisei Group
1-10-3 Oshiage, Sumida-ku, Tokyo 131-8555, Japan
Tel: (+81 3) 36 21 22 31
Fax: (+81 3) 36 21 22 33
Web: www.keisei.co.jp

Key personnel
President: H Otsuka
  Staff: 2,112

Bus
Keisei Bus Co Ltd
Address as for Keisei Group above.
Tel: (+81 3) 36 21 24 18
Fax: (+81 3) 36 21 24 08
Web: www.keiseibus.co.jp

Key personnel
Contact: Inada Ueda
  Staff: 2,005 (2008)

Current situation
Keisei's bus division runs 980 buses of which about 250 are operated on routes in Tokyo's northeastern wards and the rest in adjoining Chiba prefecture. The fleet comprises Isuzu, Hino and Mitsubishi types; 50 coaches are also operated. Bus services account for 28 per cent of revenue.

Keisei Electric Railway Co Ltd
Address as for Keisei Group above.
Tel:(+81 3) 36 21 22 42 (General Affairs Department)

Key personnel
President: Tsutomu Hanada
  Staff: 1,904 (2008)

Type of operation: Interurban rail

Passenger journeys: Not currently available
Train-km: Not currently available

Number of lines: 1 (four branches)
Route length: 102.4 km
Number of stations: 64
Gauge: 1,435 mm
Electrification: 1.5 kV DC

Current situation
Operates main line from Ueno station in Tokyo to Narita airport (Skyliner), and four branches. Through running to Toei Asakusa metro line, the Hokuso Railway and the Keihin Kyuko Railway.

Rolling stock: 546 emu cars
Breakdown of fleet is not currently available

Service: Limited airport express trains (Skyliner) run approximately every 40 minutes

Hokuso Kaihatsu Tetsudo – Hokuso Railway Co Ltd
c/o Keisei Group, 1-10-3, Oshiage, Sumida-ku, Tokyo 131-8555, Japan
Tel: (+81 3) 36 21 22 31   Fax: (+81 3) 36 21 22 33
Web: www.hokuso-railway.co.jp
  www.keisei.co.jp

Key personnel
President, Keisei Group: H Otsuka

Type of operation: Suburban/commuter rail

Passenger journeys: Not currently available
Train-km: Not currently available

Route length: 32.3 km
Number of lines: 2
Number of stations: 15
Gauge: 1,435 mm
Electrification: 1.5 kV DC

Current situation
This Keisei Group subsidiary operates the commuter Hokuso Line (19.8 km) and the Chiba New Town Railway (11.5 km), with local, express and limited express services.

Developments
An extension to provide a more direct route to Narita Airport is under construction and is expected to be completed in 2010.

Rolling stock: Not currently available

Odakyu Dentetsu – Odakyu Electric Railway Co Ltd
1-8-3 Nishi-Shinjuku, Shinjuku-ku, Tokyo 160-8309, Japan
Tel: (+81 3) 33 49 25 26   Fax: (+81 3) 33 49 24 47
e-mail: ir@odakyu-dentetsu.co.jp
Web: www.odakyu.jp

Key personnel
Executive President: Yorihiko Osuga
Executive Vice President: Toshimitsu Yamaki
  Staff: 3,450 (2005)

Type of operation: Interurban/commuter rail

Odakyu Romancecar Model 50000 'VSE'   1143558

Odakyu's commuter trains are running on the completed section of multiple double-track. This section is between Kyodo and Chitose-Funabashi, in Setagaya ward   1143557

Passenger journeys: (2004/05) 670 million
Car-km: (2004/05) 160 million

Current situation
Operates main line from Tokyo Shinjuku to Odawara, with two branches, totalling 120.5 km, 1,067 mm gauge, electrified 1.5 kV DC. Some trains run through to Tokyo metro Chiyoda Line and onward from Odawara over mixed-gauge track on 1,435 mm gauge Hakone Tozan Railway to Hakone-Yumoto (6.1 km), and from Matsuda to Nomazu over JR's Gotemba Line (50 km).

Developments
Odakyu Electric Railway is currently continuing with its plans for building multiple double-tracks in the Tokyo metropolitan area, increasing the number of tracks from two to four. This will allow an increase in the number of trains in operation, improving congestion and increasing the speed of travel. Doubling tracking is carried out at the same time as the Tokyo metropolitan government replaces railroad crossings with overpasses.

The double-tracking on the final 1.6 km section, between Higashi-Kitazawa and Setagaya-Daita, is currently under way and is scheduled for completion in 2013.

The number of women-only cars has been increased. Other improvements include centralised monitoring systems at a number of stations, reinforcement against earthquakes and new substations.

The new PASMO smartcard and the Suica card are now accepted on the network.

Odakyu Romancecar
The Odakyu Romancecar is a limited express train service, mainly connecting Shinjuku and Hakone. The service has been operating since 1948. In March 2005, new Odakyu Romancecar Model 50000s started operations.

Rolling stock: 1,065 cars
Full breakdown of fleet is not currently available, but is believed to comprise:

Commuter type	892
Limited Express type (Romancecar)	172
Inspection car	1

Fare structure: Distance-related
Fare collection: Single/one-way, return or connecting; limited express or commuter tickets from machines at stations; varies 2- and 3-month discounted passes; PASMO and Suica smartcards

Seibu Tetsudo – Seibu Railway Co Ltd

1-11-1 Kusunokidai, Tokorozawa-shi, Saitama 359-8520, Japan
Tel: (+81 42) 926 20 35   Fax: (+81 429) 26 22 37
Web: www.seibu-group.co.jp

Key personnel
President and Chief Executive Officer: Terumasa Koyanagi
   Staff: 3,644

Suburban rail

Passenger journeys: Not currently available
Car-km: Not currently available

Route length: 173.8 km
Number of lines: 2 (with 9 branch lines)
Gauge: 1,067 mm
Electrification: 1.5 kV DC

Current situation
Operates two busy suburban routes west from Ikebukuro and Shinjuku, with branches. These are particularly busy lines, with Ikebukuro terminal handling some 700 trains daily.

Developments
PASMO and Suica smartcards are accepted on the network.

Rolling stock: 1,223 emu cars
(all air-conditioned)   M779 T444

Fare structure: Distance-based

People mover (Leo Liner)
Type of operation: Intermediate capacity transit system, rubber-tyred guideway

Passenger journeys: Not currently available
Vehicle-km: Not currently available

Route length: 2.8 km
Number of lines: 1
Number of stations: 3
Electrification: 750 V DC

Current situation
The 2.8 km Yamaguchi Line (Leo Liner) single-track, rubber-tyred guideway, opened 1985, links two Seibu outer termini, Kyojomae and Yuenchi, about 25 km to the west of central Tokyo. Manual operation with driver on board.

Rolling stock: 12 cars in four-car sets
Niigata (1984/85)   M12

Seibu Bus Co Ltd
Web: www.seibu-group.co.jp/bus/mainpage.html

Passenger journeys: Not currently available
Vehicle-km: Not currently available

Number of routes: Not currently available
Route length: Not currently available

Current situation
Seibu's associated bus company owns a fleet of 709 buses and 98 coaches, about 400 of which are employed on services in the Tokyo metropolitan area, including Nissan/Fuji buses. The fleet includes lift-equipped vehicles.

Devlopments
As for the rail network, PASMO and Suica smartcards are accepted.

Tobu Tetsudo – Tobu Railway Co Ltd

1-1-2 Oshiage, Sumida-ku, Tokyo 131-8522, Japan
Tel: (+81 3) 36 21 50 61   Fax: (+81 3) 36 21 50 67
Web: www.tobu.co.jp
   www.tobu.co.jp/rail/

Key personnel
President: K Nezu
   Staff: 7,158

Interurban rail
Passenger journeys: (1996/97) 927 million
(1998/99) 890 million

Current situation
Tokyo's largest interurban railway operates 13 lines totalling 464 km, 202 stations, 1,067 mm gauge, electrified 1.5 kV DC. Main lines link Asakusa and Ikebukuro with Nikko and Yorii. Some trains on the Isesaki and Tojo lines run through to central Tokyo over metro lines.

Developments
Through running services to the extended Hanzomon metro line (11) are planned; the first of 14 Series 30000 emus for this service was delivered in 1997.

Rolling stock: 1,938 emu cars   M1,083 T855

Bus
Staff: 3,031

Current situation
Tobu Railway's bus operation has a fleet of 1,130 buses and 306 coaches, about 100 of which are used on Tokyo metropolitan area services. Recent deliveries include lift-equipped wheelchair-accessible vehicles. Bus services account for 13 per cent of revenue.

Tokyo Kyuko Dentetsu (Tokyu) – Tokyu Corporation – Tokyo Express Electric Railway

5-6, Nanpeidai-cho, Shibuya-ku, Tokyo 150-8511, Japan
Tel: (+81 3) 34 77 96 03   Fax: (+81 3) 54 59 70 61
Web: www.tokyu.co.jp/
   www.ir.tokyu.co.jp

Key personnel
Chairman: Kiyofumi Kamijo
President: Toshiaki Koshimura
Senior Managing Directors: Tadashi Igarashi, Takakumi Happo, Katsuhisa Suzuki, Tesuo Nakahara, Isao Adochi

Interurban rail
Staff: 2,319

Passenger journeys: (Including tramway)
(2003/04) 984 million
Passenger-km (total system): (2003/04) approx 9.469 million

Background
The Railway Headquarters of the Tokyu Corporation is responsible for the operations of the Tokyo Express Electric Railway. In addition to important Tokyo-based rail and bus operations (operated by the subsidiary Tokyu Bus Corporation), the Tokyu Group has interests in other railways, bus companies and rolling stock manufacture (Tokyu Car Corporation).

Current situation
Operates seven lines totalling 95.1 km, 1,067 mm gauge, electrified 1.5 kV DC. Principal route is from Shibuya (Tokyo) to Yokohama, with through trains over Tokyo Metro's Hibiya metro line from central Tokyo. Also underground metro-style route out of Shibuya to Futako-Tamagawaen and Chuo-Rinkan, with through trains from the Hanzomon metro line. A new line paralleling Tokyu's main line is planned in recommendations put forward by the Council for Transport Policy. The Tokyu also serves Yokohama commuters.

Developments
Fare revisions were introduced in March 2005. In the company's three year medium-term Management Plan (FY2005-FY2007), the completion of work on elevating the line and the quadrupling of the track from Musashi kosugi to Hiyoshi is planned for FY2007. Other projects planned for FY2007 are the expansion of the operating area of the Meguro Line to Hiyoshi and the start of operations on the municipal subway No 4 in Yokahama with a connection to Hiyoshi.

Rolling stock: 1,107 emu cars   M749 T358

Tramway
Staff: 68

Current situation
Tokyu also operates the 5 km reserved-track Setagaya tramway, 1,372 mm gauge, electrified 600 V DC, which feeds Tokyu's Shin-Tamagawa Line and Keio Railway's Keio Line.

The first Type 300 two-section articulated car, with VVVF control and wheelchair lifts, entered service July 1999.

Rolling stock: 10 Type 300 two-section articulated cars

Tokyu Bus Corporation
1-5-3 Ohashi, Meguro-ku, Tokyo 153-8518, Japan
Tel: (+81 3) 54 58 01 09
Fax: (+81 3) 54 58 20 21
Web: www.tokyubus.co.jp

Tokyu Bus service and regulators at Shibuya station (Colin Brown) 0079656

Key personnel
President: K Kamijo

Bus
Staff: 1,797

Current situation
Tokyu Bus Corp is an independent company in the Tokyu group. A fleet of 878 buses carries 372,000 passengers per day on 165 routes in southwest Tokyo, Kawasaki and Yokohama with a total route length of 2,028 km. A total of 467 vehicles are used on the routes operated in Tokyo. Services include five 'Tokyu Coach' demand-responsive routes, 'Midnight' routes which operate after last-train times, and upgraded urban routes featuring computerised bus location and passenger information systems. Fleet includes lift-equipped vehicles and no-step buses.

During 1998, a midibus service was introduced between Shibuya and Daikanyama under the 'Tokyu Transses' brand. Four Mitsubishi Fuso vehicles are used and, unusually for Japan, all drivers are women.

Tokyo Monorail Co Ltd
2-4-12, Hamamatsu-cho, Minato-ku, Tokyo 105-0013, Japan
Tel: (+81 3) 34 34 31 71
Fax: (+81 3) 34 33 43 13
Web: www.tokyo-monorail.co.jp

Key personnel
Representative Director and President: Masayuki Saito
Staff: 306 (as at April 2008)

Tokyo Monorail car 1144209

Type of operation: Monorail on the Alweg system, opened 1964

Passenger journeys: (2003/04) 46.8 million
(2004/05) 47.5 million
(2005/06) 46.5 million
(2006/07) 47.7 million
(2007/08) 48.8 million
Car-km: (2003/04) 18 million
(2004/05) 17.8 million
(2005/06) 18.1 million
(2006/07) 18.1 million
(2007/08) 19.3 million

Current situation
A 17.8 km straddle-monorail links Hamamatsu-cho station in Tokyo with Haneda Airport Terminal 2, formerly the main airport but now only handling domestic flights. Electrified 750 V DC; 10 stations; service every 3.3–5 minutes.

In 2002, Tokyo Monorail became a subsidiary company of East Japan Railway Company (JR East).

The company introduced ticket gates that accept smartcards in 2002. The smartcard system now applies to the JR East, JR West, JR Tokai (New Tokaido Line) and other private railway companies in Tokyo.

Developments
A further extension to the Haneda Airport Terminal 2 was opened in December 2004, with one new station.

There are plans to extend the system further to an international terminal, which is due to open at the end of October 2010.

In March 2007, an Airport Express service started, operating non-stop between Haneda

Tokyo Monorail car 1144206

Airport Terminal 1, Terminal 2 station and Hamamatsu-cho station.

Rolling stock: 20 six-car trains
Series 1000 (1989/94) M96
Series 2000 (1999/2001) M16 T8

Tokyo Tama Intercity Monorail Co Ltd – Tama Urban Monorail
1078-92 Izumicho, Tachikawa-shi, Tokyo 190-0015, Japan
Tel: (+81 42) 526 78 00   Fax: (+81 42) 526 78 57
e-mail: midori-fujimura@tama-monorail.co.jp
Web: www.tama-monorail.co.jp

Type of operation: Straddle monorail

Current situation
This third-sector company operates a 16 km north-south monorail line (straddle type, 1.5 kV DC) with 19 stations serving the Tama area in Tokyo's western suburbs. Shareholders comprise the metropolitan government (50.6 per cent), local government (8 per cent) and other undertakings, including the Seibu, Keio and Odakyu railways (21.9 per cent).

The line links Tama Center with Tachikawa and Kamikitadai, providing connections with several radial rail routes into central Tokyo. The first section, from Tachikawa to Kamikitadai (5.5 km, eight stations) opened in December 1998 with the remainder opening in January 2000.

Rolling stock: 15 four-car trains
Series 1000 (1998/99/2000) M60

Tokyo Waterfront New Transit – Yurikamome
Yurikamome Transport Division, Business Section Kotoku Ariake 3-22, Tokyo, Japan
Tel: (+81 3) 35 29 77 82   Fax: (+81 3) 35 29 77 70
Web: www.yurikamome.co.jp

Type of operation: Rubber-tyred guideway system 'Yurikamome' (Seagull)

Passenger journeys: (2004) 88,000 daily
(2005) 86,000 daily

Current situation
This third-sector company, 67 per cent owned by the Tokyo metropolitan government, opened the Yurikamome automated elevated rubber-tyred transit system (14.7 km, 16 stations) in 1995. It links central Tokyo with Tokyo Teleport Town, a commercial development area being built on land reclaimed from Tokyo Bay. The line runs from Shimbashi on the JR Yamanote Line to Ariake, crossing Tokyo Bay via the 918 m Rainbow Bridge, which also carries a road, and then on to Toyosu. Service is provided by a fleet of six-car trains with full ATO.

Developments
In March 2006, a 2.7 km extension, with four stations, from Ariake to Toyosu was opened.

Rolling stock: 26 six-car trains
Series 7000 (1995/97/98)	M108
Series 7200 (1999/2001/2005)	M48

Tokyo Rinkai Kosoku Tetsudo – Tokyo Waterfront Area Rapid Transit (TWART)
3-12-1 Tatsumi, Koto-ku, Tokyo 135-0053, Japan
Tel: (+81 3) 35 21 60 30
Fax: (+81 3) 35 21 61 40
Web: www.twr.co.jp/

Route length: 12.2 km
Number of stations: 8
Gauge: 1,067 mm
Electrification: 1,500 V DC

Type of operation: Urban rail

Current situation
This third-sector company, owned by the Tokyo metropolitan government (85.6 per cent) and JR East (5 per cent), is constructing the 12.2 km mainly underground Rinkai Fukutoshin Line to serve new development areas built on land reclaimed from Tokyo Bay. The first 4.9 km section from Shin-Kiba on JR East's Keiyo Line to Tokyo Teleport Town (four stations) opened in 1996. A further 2.9 km extension to Tennozu Isle opened in March 2001. Rolling stock currently comprises six four-car Series 70-000 sets based on JR East's Series 209 design.

Developments
The remaining 4.5 km section to Osaki opened in December 2002.

Kanagawa Chuo Kotsu Co Ltd
Transport Division
6-18 Yaezaki-cho, Hiratsuka-shi, Kanagawa-ken 254-0811, Japan
Tel: (+81 4) 63 22 88 00   Fax: (+81 4) 63 22 88 40
e-mail: info@kanachu.jp
Web: www.kanachu.co.jp

Key personnel
President, Representative Director: Miki Takahashi
    Staff: 3,250 (estimate)

Bus
Current situation
This Odakyu Group company operates a fleet of 1,784 buses in the region, providing services based on Machida City in Tokyo metropolitan area with about 150 buses. The company's main operating area is in adjoining Kanagawa prefecture including some routes in Yokohama. Also operates 31 coaches.

TWART six-car emu on the Rinkai Line at Tennozu Isle station (Colin Brown)   0567222

Yokohama
Population: 3.6 million (2007 estimate)

Public transport
Bus and metro services operated by divisions of Municipal Transport Bureau. Commuter rail services run by JR and private railway companies. Additional bus services provided by the private railways and private bus operators. Ferry service across Yokohama port. Automated guideway system.

Yokohama-shi Kotsu Kyoku – Yokohama Municipal Transportation Bureau
1-1 Minato-cho, Naka-ku, Yokohama 231-0017, Japan
Tel: (+81 45) 671 31 60
Fax: (+81 45) 664 32 66
e-mail: kt-somu@city.yokohama.jp
Web: www.city.yokohama.jp

Key personnel
Manager, General Affairs Division: Koichiro Obi

Current situation
Serves part of the Yokohama conurbation with a population of about 1 million.

Over half of Yokohama's bus routes are provided by this municipal operator with the remainder, serving mainly outer suburbs, run by seven private companies. All operators charge a common fare within the flat fare area which covers much of the city.

A computer-controlled bus location system, which relays information about approaching buses to bus stop panels, has been installed.

Late evening 'Midnight' services operate on 21 routes, and lift-equipped vehicles on four routes.

Yokohama's metro and private railway network
1168315

Bus
Staff: 2,322 (includes part-time employees)

Number of routes: 150
Route length: 566 km
On priority right-of-way: 68 km

Fleet: 1,023 vehicles, all air conditioned
Hino	313
Isuzu	192
Mitsubishi	259
Nissan Diesel	259

In peak service: 905

One-person operation: All vehicles
Fare collection: Farebox at entrance or prepurchase
Operational control: Inspectors; computerised 'bus operation improvement system' (see below)
Fare structure: Flat except for 9-stage fare routes which extend beyond flat fare zone; prepurchase coupon tickets, 1- and 3-month passes (bus, bus/metro), day tickets (bus, bus/metro). Prepurchase coupon tickets valid on buses of all 8 companies operating in Yokohama
Bus priority: Exclusive bus lanes (23 km), bus priority lanes (45 km), 2 bus priority traffic signal installations and one section of road with movable centre line allowing contraflow bus lane
Average peak hour speed: 15.3 km/h
Operating costs financed by: Fares 85.5 per cent, other commercial sources 1.5 per cent, subsidy/grants 13.0 per cent
Subsidy from: City 100 per cent

Developments
There are currently plans to re-organise 58 bus routes.

Metro
Staff: 788

Type of operation: Full metro, first line opened 1972

Route length: 53.5 km
  in tunnel: 43.4 km
Number of lines: 3 (2, operated as a single through route)
Number of stations: 42
Gauge: 1,435 mm
Max gradient: 3.5%
Minimum curve radius: 125 m
Tunnel: Box
Electrification: 750 V DC, third rail; Line 4 (Green) 1,500 V DC overhead

Service: Peak 4½ min, off-peak 8 min
First/last train: 05.19/00.33
Signalling: Full ATC with cab signalling and CTC
Operating costs financed by: Fares 61.1 per cent, other commercial sources 32.7 per cent, subsidy/grants 6.2 per cent
Subsidy from: National government 7.3 per cent, city 89.3 per cent, region 3.4 per cent

Rolling stock: 288 cars, 38 six-car sets, 15 four-car sets)

1000 series (1972/76/77/84)	M56 T28
2000 series (1986)	M36 T18
3000 series (1992/93)	M32 T16
3000 series (1999)	M28 T14
KHI 10000 series linear-motor, 4-car emus (2008)	M60

Developments
Line 4 (Green) opened in March 2008. It is the first part of a proposed loop line. The line is 13.1 km long with 10 stations. Interchange with the Blue Line is at Center Kita and Center Minami and connections with JR East's Yokohama Line at Nakayama and with Tokyu Railway's Toyoko Line at Hiyoshi.

Yokohama Shin Toshi Kotsu – Yokohama New Transit Co Ltd – Seaside Line
1-1 Sachiura 2-chome, Kanazawa-ku, Yokohama 236-0003, Japan
Tel: (+81 45) 787 70 02
Fax: (+81 45) 787 70 19
Web: www.seasideline.co.jp

Type of operation: Rubber-tyred automated guideway system 'Kanazawa Seaside Line'

Passenger journeys: Not currently available
Vehicle-km: Not currently available

Route length: 10.6 km
Number of lines: 1
Number of stations: 14
Track: Elevated with side guidance
Gauge: 2,900 mm between guide bars
Max gradient: 4%
Minimum curve radius: 50 m
Electrification: 750 V DC

Current situation
The Kanazawa Seaside Line, opened in 1989, serves new development areas built on land reclaimed from the sea and connects with JR's Negishi Line at Shin-Sugita and with Keihin Kyuko at Kanazawa-Hakkei. Yokohama New Transit is a third-sector company half-owned by Yokohama municipality.

Developments
A 0.2 km extension from the current provisional terminus at Kanazawa-Hakkei is planned to improve interchange with the Keihin-Kyuko Railway.

Rolling stock: 17 five-car trains

Service: Peak 5 min, off-peak 10 min
First/last train: 05.55/23.47

Fare structure: Flat; various tickets and passes available, discounts for children, elderly and disabled
Fare collection: Tickets from vending machines; PASMO rechargeable, contactless smartcard
Train operation: Driverless, ATO
Integration with other modes: Transfer to JR Negishi Line at one station and to the Keikyu Main Line and Keikyu Zushi Line at another

Sagami Tetsudo 'Sotetsu' – Sagami Railway Co Ltd
2-9-14 Kitasaiwai, Nishi-ku, Yokohama 220-0004, Japan
Tel: (+81 45) 319 20 57, 21 11
Fax: (+81 45) 319 21 91, 22 64
Web: www.sotetsu.co.jp

Key personnel
President and Chief Executive Officer: Makoto Torii
  Staff: 1,619 (2008)

Suburban railway
Passenger journeys: Not currently available
Train-km: Not currently available

Route length: 35.9 km
Number of lines: 1 (plus 1 branch)
Number of stations: 26
Gauge: 1,067 mm
Electrification: 1.5 kV DC

Current situation
Main line totalling 24.6 km runs from Yokohama to Ebina, with 11.3 km branch from Futamatagawa to Shonandai (Izumino Line).

Two services are offered on the Main Line, Rapid and Express. The Rapid service on the Izumino Line, however, stops at all stations.

Developments
A bypass, scheduled to be completed in 2015, is under construction to enable through-service to the Shonan Shinjuku Line. A further extension to Shin-Yokohama Station and the Tokyu Tokoyo Line is also under construction.

Women-only cars have been introduced at peak times.

18 stations are wheelchair accessible.

The PASMO rechargeable, contactless smartcard is accepted.

Rolling stock:
420 emu cars and 4 electric locomotives
Breakdown of fleet is not currently available

Bus
Bus Division
Tel: (+81 45) 319 23 45   Fax: (+81 45) 319 89 91
Web: www.sotetsu.co.jp/bus/

Key personnel
President: Hideo Itou
Executive Director: Masao Sugaya
  Staff: 154 (2008)

Current situation
Sagami Tetsudo operates 286 buses on Yokohama area services, totalling 243 route-km.

Keihin Kyuko Dentetsu 'Keikyu' – Keihin Electric Express Railway Co Ltd (Keikyu)
2-20-20 Takanawa, Minato-ku, Tokyo 108-8625, Japan
Tel: (+81 3) 32 80 91 23
Fax: (+81 3) 32 80 91 93
e-mail: koho4@keikyuco.jp
Web: www.keikyu.co.jp

Key personnel
President and Representative Director: Masaru Kotani
Managing Director, General Affairs Department: Kiyoshi Ishikawa

Interurban rail
Staff: 1,892 (2004)

Passenger journeys: (2002) 1.14 million, daily (2003) 1.15 million, daily

Route length: 87 km (total)

Background
Formed in 1898, the Keihin Electric Express Railway Co Ltd is part of the Keikyu Group. It is one of the major private railways in Japan and provides services which link central Tokyo to Haneda airport and the southern metropolitan area.

The group also includes bus and taxi companies.

Current situation
Trains link Shinagawa with Kawasaki, Yokohama, Yokosuka, Zushi and Miura on 1,435 mm gauge, electrified 1.5 kV DC.

See also entry for Tokyo.

Rolling stock: 758 emu cars   M606 T152

Tokyo Kyuko Dentetsu (Tokyu) – Tokyu Corporation – Tokyo Express Electric Railway
5-6, Nanpeidai-cho, Shibuya-ku, Tokyo 150-8511, Japan
Tel: (+81 3) 34 77 96 03
Fax: (+81 3) 54 59 70 61
Web: www.tokyu.co.jp
  www.ir.tokyu.cp.jp

Key personnel
Chairman: Kiyofumi Kamijo
President: Toshiaki Koshimura
Senior Managing Directors: Tadashi Igarashi, Takakumi Happo, Katsuhisa Suzuki, Tesuo Nakahara, Isao Adochi

Interurban rail
Passenger journeys (total system): (2003/04) 984 million
Passenger-km (total system): (2003/04) approx 9.469 million

Background
The Railway Headquarters of the Tokyu Corporation is responsible for the operations of the Tokyo Express Electric Railway. In addition to important Tokyo-based rail and bus operations (operated by the subsidiary Tokyu Bus Corporation), the Tokyu Group has interests in other railways, bus companies and rolling stock manufacture (Tokyu Car Corporation).

Current situation

Main Toyoko Line (24.2 km) links Tokyo (Shibuya) and Yokohama station, with through service from Hiyoshi, just within Yokohama, to central Tokyo via Tokyo Metro's Hibiya metro line. The Denentoshi Line provides a direct link from eight stations in Yokohama's northwest suburbs to central Tokyo via Tokyu's underground Shin-Tamagawa Line and the Eidan Hanzomon metro line.

Developments

Please see separate entry under Tokyo.

Rolling stock: 1,107 cars   M749 T358

Bus

Current situation

Tokyu Bus Corp (see separate entries) operates 41 Yokohama area routes including two 'Tokyu Coach' demand-responsive services.

Yokohama

Other bus operators

Current situation

Yokohama area services are also provided by Kanagawa Chuo Kotsu Co Ltd and Odakyu Bus Co Ltd (see Tokyo entry) and Kawasaki Tsurumi Rinko Bus Co Ltd (see Kawasaki entry).

Higashi Nihon Ryokaku Tetsudo – East Japan Railway Company (EJR) (JR East)

2-2-2 Yoyogi, Shibuya-ku, Tokyo 151-8578, Japan
Tel: (+81 3) 53 34 11 51   Fax: (+81 3) 53 34 11 10
Website: www.jreast.co.jp

Key personnel

Chair: Mutsutake Otsuka
President: Satoshi Seino
   Staff: 61,900 (whole company as at April 2008, includes 54,697 for rail operations)

Type of operation: Inner and outer suburban heavy rail

Current situation

Frequent trains between Tokyo and suburban areas to the south of Yokohama carry commuters to both cities. All-stations inner-suburban service is provided on the Keihin Tohoku Negishi Line (Ofuna-Isogo-Yokohama-Higashikanagawa-Kawasaki-Tokyo-Omiya, 81 km), and rapid service outer-suburban service on the Tokaido Line (Tokyo-Yokohama-Odawara) and Yokosuka Line (Tokyo-Yokohama-Kurihama).

In 2001, direct service was started between suburbs north of Omiya and southwest suburbs on the Tokaido and Yokosuka lines; these Shonan-Shinjuku Line trains run via Shinjuku and Yokohama stations.

Local suburban service on 43 km Yokohama Line from Hachioji to Higashi-Kanagawa via Shin-Yokohama with some trains continuing to Isogo and Ofuna on the Negishi Line. Also 7 km Tsurumi Line from Tsurumi to Ogimachi.

For further information on JR East, please see other entries in *Jane's Urban Transport Systems* and *Jane's World Railways*.

Yokohama Kosoku Tetsudo – Yokohama Minatomirai Railway Company

1-11 Motomachi, 2nd Floor, Naka-ku, Yokohama 231-0861, Japan

Tel: (+81 45) 664 16 21
Fax: (+81 45) 664 16 20
Web: www.mm21railway.co.jp

Type of operation: Metro, opened 2004

Passenger journeys: Not currently available
Train-km: Not currently available

Route length: 4.1 km
Number of lines: 1
Number of stations: 6
Gauge: 1,067 mm
Electrification: 1,500 V DC, overhead

Current situation

This joint venture company has built a 4.1 km underground line from Yokohama along the waterfront to Motomachi to serve the new Minato Mirai 21 commercial development area. Shareholders include Yokohama city, Kanagawa prefecture and the Tokyu Railway.

The line opened in February 2004.

The company also operates the 3.4 km former Tokyu Kodomo-no-kuni (Children's World) Line, which opened in March 2000 following closure for upgrading and the construction of an intermediate station.

Rolling stock: 8-car Tokyu Car Corporation Y500 series
Breakdown of fleet is not currently available

In peak service: Not currently available
Service: Peak 3 min, off-peak 3¾ min to 6 min 40 s/7½ min
Fare structure: Calculated by distance; half fare for childfen

---

Kazakhstan

Almaty

Population: 1.19 million (2004)

Public transport

Bus and trolleybus/tramway services overseen by separate government undertakings. Metro construction stalled. Extensive use is made of official taxis and unofficial taxis; whereby passengers hail private cars and small vans and negotiate fares with the driver.

City Board of Public Transport

42/44 Abai Avenue, Almaty, 050022, Kazakhstan
Tel: (+7 3272) 78 44 24, 92 43 99, 78 44 13
Fax: (+7 3272) 92 74 89

Current situation

Responsible for public transport in Almaty.

Bus

Staff: (1995) 4,390

Number of routes: (1995) 59

Fleet: (Feb 1996) 1,255 buses

LIAZ 677	389
LIAZ 5256	103
Ikarus 280	136
Ikarus 260, 263, 354, 256 & 250	135
LAZ 695, 699	316
Mercedes O325 and O305*	49
Karosa	3
Iveco**	1
RAF, KVZ, PAZ (minibuses)	123
MANAS SL232	200

In peak service: (1996) 1,045
*Some new Mercedes-Turk O325 and some ex-West Berlin Mercedes O305.
**By late 1996 a small number of Iveco midi buses had been added.

Almatyelectrotrans

64 Auezov Street, Almaty, 050008, Kazakhstan
Tel: (+7 3272) 42 08 89
Fax: (+7 3272) 43 63 57
e-mail: aet@aet.kz

Tramway

Type of operation: Conventional tramway

Current situation

Routes 4, 6 and 10 in operation serving about 80 per cent of the original network length, which remained intact in 1996. Fleet reduced from 196 cars in 1991 to 52 by 1996. All remaining KTM-5 and RVZ-6 trams received cosmetic treatment in summer 1996. In April 1998 the Tramway Manager claimed that a contract had been signed with ČKD Dopravni Systemy to rebuild the depot in 1999, and to deliver 60 new cars to replace the existing fleet and to enable most tram routes to be reopened.

Route length: Approx 40 km (non-duplicated) of which about 32 km is used by surviving routes
Number of routes: 3
Gauge: 1,524 mm

Rolling stock: (1996) 53 cars

Riga RVZ-6 (1984–86)	24
Ust-Katav KTM-5 (1989–91)	29

In peak service: (1996) 36

Trolleybus

Staff: (1995) 2,049

Current situation

By 1998, five routes had been closed but Route 6 was extended in 1996 to replace the outer end of closed tram routes 1 and 3. Several sections of wire have been abandoned in recent years, all in the central area. The future of Almaty's trolleybus

system does not appear to be defined in policy terms, although trolleybuses alone have retained their patronage at a reasonable level. Russian ZIU682 trolleybuses are imported as kits and assembled locally under the 'ElectroMash' brand, but a small number of Skoda vehicles acquired in 1998 was expected to be the start of a larger order.

Route length: (1996) approx 90 km (non-duplicated)
Number of routes: (1998) 13

Fleet: (1998) approx 270	
Uritsky ZIU9 (1983-92)	approx 250
ElectroMash ZIU682G-012EM (1996-98)	approx 10
Skoda 14Tr (1998)	10
In peak service: (1998) 220	

Almaty

Metro (under construction)

Current situation

Construction started in 1985 of the initial line of a proposed three-line metro. The project was being undertaken by the Turkish consortium Eko-Uzman. However, since the original 7.5 km of excavation, little progress has been made.

Monorail (proposed)

There have been reports of a proposal for a monorail in the city. The Almaty Metro Municipal Project would see a system with a total of approximately 40 km of track with 44 stations. Again, no recent progress appears to have been made on this project.

Korea, North

Pyongyang

Population: In excess of 2 million (estimated)

Public transport

Bus, trolleybus and tram services provided by People's Assembly of city under government supervision. Metro operated by government department.

Supreme People's Assembly

Transport Committee
Pyongyang, Democratic People's Republic of North Korea.

Bus and trolleybus

Passenger journeys: Approx 150 million (annual)
Number of routes: 50

Fleet: Approx 500 buses, including Ikarus 260 and 280 articulated; Karosa SM and B731

Fleet: There are about 1,000 locally built trolleybuses, both two-axle and articulated

One-person operation: None
Fare structure: Flat, prepaid tickets deposited in box at rear of vehicle
Fare collection: Conductors

Current situation

The trolleybus operation acts mainly as a feeder to the metro, though there are signs that the system is to be run down as the tramway develops. There are 10 routes.

Tramway

Current situation

In 1991 the first standard-gauge tram line 1 opened between Mangyongdae and Songsin with 20 route-km. Another two tram routes, 2 and 3, followed in 1992–94, bringing the total tram route-km to some 50.

Operation is provided by 45 Type KT8D5-K articulated trams and 129 Type T6B5-K trams, all built by CˇKD Tatra, Czech Republic. Another 60 four-axle trams are running, built by Shenfeng Works in China. They are based on CˇKD's Type KT4.

In 1995 a 1,000 mm tram line was built in the north-eastern suburb of the capital, stretching 3.5 km from Samhyng metro station to Kumsusan. The line is reported to be used exclusively for visitors to the Kim Ir Sen Mausoleum at Kumsusan. The fleet comprises 18 Type SWS/MFO trams purchased from Basle, Switzerland, and some four-axle trailers originally built by SIG, Switzerland.

Rolling stock: 234 cars

CKD Tatra KT8 articulated	M45
CKD Tatra T6B5	M129
Shenfeng Trolleybus Works KT4 articulated	M60

Pyongyang Metro

City Metro Unit, Railway Section, Transport & Communication Commission, Pyongyang,

Articulated LRV on shared tramway/cycleway, Pyongyang (Thomas Fischer)   0069658

Articulated trolleybus in Pyongyang city centre (Thomas Fischer)   0069657

Democratic People's Republic of North Korea

Type of operation: Full metro, initial route opened 1973

Route length: 22.5 km (estimated)
Number of routes: 2
Number of stations: 17
Gauge: 1,435 mm
Track: Concrete trackbed
Tunnel: Bored and blasted to maximum depth of 150 m; mostly single-bore
Electrification: 825 V DC, third rail

Service: Peak 2 min, off-peak 5–7 min
First/last train: 05.00/23.00
Fare structure: Flat
Fare collection: Automatic entry barriers, coin in slot, no tickets; manual surveillance
Signalling: Colourlights; CTC

Rolling stock: 168 cars

Kim Chong The works (1973)	M48
Ex-BVG Berlin	M120

Current situation

Line 1 opened 1973, Line 2 in 1978. The two lines are not connected but interchange is provided in the city centre between Chonu station on Line 1 and Chongsing station on Line 2.

Kwangmyong station is currently closed.

Developments

An east-west route through the city centre is planned in connection with a major residential development in the eastern suburbs, but progress has been hampered by shortage of funds.

Pressure on the rolling stock fleet was eased during 1997 by delivery of 120 cars of 1960s vintage second-hand from the Berlin U-Bahn.

Korea, South

Busan

Population: 3.66 million (2005)

Public transport

Transport planning, public transport and transport management are overseen by the Busan Metropolitan City's Transportation Bureau (http://english.busan.go.kr). Bus services provided by private companies. Busan Transportation Corporation operates metro; light rail under construction.

Busan

Private bus
Current situation

In 2005, there were 76,791 registered buses. There are three types of local buses, City Bus and City Express Bus, special local buses and express local buses. Frequencies and fares are set by a government agency. Fares may be paid by cash (coins), bus card, bus token or Mybi transport card.

Developments

A Bus Information System (BIS) is currently being trialled on some routes.

Busan Transportation Corporation

861-1 Beomcheon 1-dong, Busan Jin-gu, 614-021 Busan, South Korea
Tel: (+82 51) 640 70 00   Fax: (+82 51) 640 70 10
e-mail: admin@subway.busan.kr
Web: www.subway.busan.kr

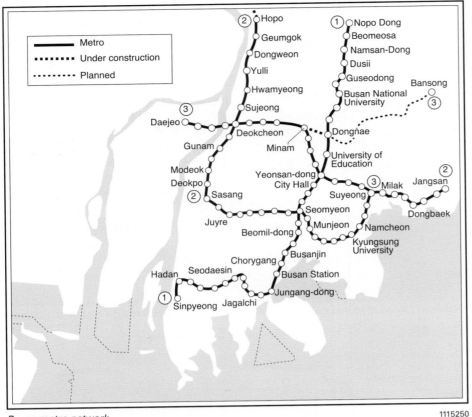

Busan metro network 1115250

Key personnel
President: Gu Hyun Kim
  Staff: 2,600

Type of operation: Full metro, opened 1985

Passenger journeys: (2005) 318 million (estimate)

Route length: 88.8 km
Number of lines: 3
Number of stations: 90
Gauge: 1,435 mm
Min curve radius: 180 m
Electrification: 1.5 kV DC, overhead

Current situation
Busan Transportation Corporation was established in January 2006. For historical information, please see entry for Busan Urban Transit Authority (BUTA) in previous editions of *Jane's Urban Transport Systems.*

Developments
Phase II of Line 2, from Suyeong to Jangsan (6.8 km), opened in 2002. A further extension to Line 2, from Hop'o to Bukjeong

(11.3 km with seven stations), is under construction, and is scheduled for completion in 2012.

The first phase of Line 3, from Daejeo Suyeong (18.3 km with 17 stations), opened in November 2005. The second phase, from Minam to Anpyeong (light rail, 12.7 km, with 14 stations), is due to open in 2008.

The network will total 112.4 km with 110 stations upon completion, scheduled for 2012.

Rolling stock: 776 cars formed into four-car, six-car eight-car or ten-car sets

DC trains
Line 1	M270 T90
Line 2	M168 T168
Line 3	M40 T40

Service: Peak 3½ min
First/last train: 05.20/23.53
Fare structure: 2 zones; single and return tickets with student discounts
Fare collection: Ticket from Automatic Vending Machine (AVM), stored-value Hanaro and Mybi cards (contactless smartcards); group discount

Signalling: ATO/ATC-equipped
Operating costs financed by: Fares 11 per cent
Arrangements for elderly/disabled: Free travel for the elderly, disabled veterans, disabled persons with relevant ID Card plus one companion for certain 'grades' of disability; wheelchair lifts and Braille facilities at all stations, ramps at 10 stations

Busan-Gimhae Light Rail Transit Co Ltd (BGL)
Busan-Gimhae Light Rail Transit Project
POSCO Engineering & Construction Co Ltd
(POSCO E&C)
128-9 Bowhang-Dong, Gimhae, Kyungsangnam-Do, 621-040, South Korea
Tel: (+82 55) 314 19 23
Fax: (+82 55) 314 19 22
Web: www.poscoenc.com

Key personnel
President and Chief Executive Officer, POSCO E&C:
  Han Soo-yang
Construction Manager: Suk Sang Kang

Type of operation: Light rail (under construction)

Background
The Busan-Gimhae/Kimhae Light Rail Transit Co Ltd (BGL) is a joint venture between POSCO E&C (49 per cent), Hyundai Development Company (49 per cent) and SYSTRA (2 per cent) to Build-Transfer-Operate (BTO) the Busan-Gimhae/Kimhae Light Rail Transit system. The project has an estimated escalated total construction cost of KRW9,738 billion.

The fully automated elevated system will be 23.455 km long and have 18 stations and is currently scheduled to open in April 2010. It will link Gimhae Airport with Lines 2 and 3 of the Busan Metro. Capacity will be 176,000 passengers per day.

The system will be transferred to local government as soon as construction is completed and will then be operated for a maximum of 30 years.

Developments
In February 2006, the Busan Gimhae Light Rail Transit Co Ltd (BGL) held the ground-breaking ceremony for the Busan-Gimhae Light Rail Transit.

Rotem will supply the rail vehicles, signalling, electrification and communications systems and stations and maintenance facilities, as a turnkey package.

The project was approximately 41.15 per cent completed as at the end of 2007.

Daegu
Population: 2.47 million (2005 Census)

Public transport
Bus services provided by private companies. Metro expansion under construction.

Daegu Metropolitan City
Transportation Bureau, Public Transportation Division
130 Gongpyeongno (1 Dongindong 1-ga), Jung-gu, Daegu 700-714, South Korea
Tel: (+82 53) 803 32 65, 32 94, 33 24
Fax: (+82 53) 803 36 09
e-mail: ewmaster@daegumail.net
Web: www.daegu.co.kr english.daegu.co.kr

Current situation
The Public Transportation Division is responsible for issuing permits to the city's public transit businesses and supervising bus and taxi

companies. The division is also responsible for constructing bus terminals for express buses and inter-city buses and for installing and maintaining bus and taxi stops and bus-only lanes. There is also a Bus Reform Division.

Bus
Current situation
Thirty-one companies run 1,719 buses on approximately 88 bus routes in Daegu.

There are three types of buses running in the city. The Iban bus is a basic city bus, the Jwaseok bus is a more comfortable and more expensive city express bus, and the Maeul bus is a shuttle bus service that runs on shorter distances to connect transitional points, including metro stations and bus stops. These buses are usually smaller and cheaper than normal buses.

Bus fares can be paid with cash, token or a Transportation Card on boarding. The Transportation Card is not available for the Maeul bus yet, and these fares have to be paid in cash.

Public Transport Reform
There are plans to introduce a semi-public bus management system and to restructure the public transport system, although details are not yet available.

Daegu Metropolitan Subway Corporation (DMSC)
307 Wolbae Street (1500 Sangin 1- dong), Dalseo-gu, Daegu City, South Korea
Tel: (+82 53) 640 23 61/7   Fax: (+82 53) 640 24 19
e-mail: webmaster@daegusubway.co.kr
Web: www.daegusubway.co.kr

Key personnel
President and Chief Executive Officer:
  Sang-min Bae
  Staff: 2,064

Metro
Type of operation: Full metro, first section opened in November 1997

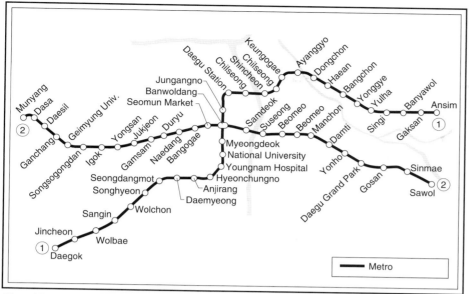

Map of Daegu metro system   1115149

Passenger journeys: (2000) 49.5 million
(2001) 50.3 million
(2002) 53.1 million
(2003) 26.2 million
(2004) 50.9 million
Route length: 53.9 km
Number of lines: 2

Number of stations: 56 (interchange at Banwoldang)
Gauge: 1,435 mm
Track: 60 kg/m heavy welded rail laid on concrete section
Tunnel: Box type 23.45 km, tunnel type 4.15 km
Electrification: 1,500 V DC, overhead

Current situation

An 11.4 km section of Line 1 between Wolbae and Daegu was opened in 1997, and it opened throughout in 1998.

Line 1 connects two major residential developments in the east and west with the city centre. Interchange facilities with KNR are provided at the main railway station, which is to the east of the business area.

The extension of Line 1 from Jincheon to Daegok opened in 2002.

Construction of Line 2 from Munyang to Sawol (29 km, 26 stations) was started in 1996 and finished in October 2005.

Developments

In Phase 1 of further improvements to the metro system, a 1.3 km extension of Line 1 from Ansim to Sabok is under construction.

Rolling stock: 64 six-car trains (Hanjin/Siemens)

Service: Peak 5 min, other times 7–12 min
First/last train: 05.30/23.58 (weekdays)

Fare collection: Stored-value tickets from Automatic Ticket Vending Machines (ATVM), with automatic fare-collection system at gates; Kookmin Pass Card, tokens; discunt for children
Operational control: Four control centres, ATC/ATO
Arrangements for elderly/disabled: Wheelchair lifts and Braille facilities at all stations
Security: CCTV in some places

Incheon

Population: 2.6 million (2005 estimate)

Public transport

Bus services provided by private companies; metro expanding, with link, via KORAIL, to Seoul.

Administrative guidance for public transport is provided by the Construction and Transportation Bureau of the Incheon City Government.

Incheon Metropolitan City

Construction and Transportation Bureau
1138 Guwol-dong, Namdong-gu, 405-750 Incheon, South Korea
Tel: (+82 32) 440 21 14   Fax: (+82 32) 440 30 09
e-mail: ec3072@incheon.go.kr
Web: www.incheon.go.kr

Incheon

Bus

Current situation

Twelve companies run 1,220 buses over a network of 67 routes.

There are three types of buses operating in Incheon: General (Iban) buses, operating urban routes; Express buses (Jwaseok – seat), which operate longer routes; and Maeul bus, a type of community shuttle bus which operates on shorter distances in urban areas. There are also specific routes which run to the Incheon International Airport.

Bus fares can be paid by cash or by prepaid Transportation Card, which can also be used on the metro.

Passenger journeys: (2004) 204,000 daily
(2005) 199,000 daily
(2006) 196,000 daily

Route length: 25.9 km
In tunnel: 22.8 km
Number of lines: 1
Number of stations: 23 (21 underground)
Gauge: 1,435 mm
Electrification: 1.5 kV DC, overhead

Background

The corporation was registered and established in 1998.

Developments

The Incheon metro Line 1 is connected with the Suwon-Incheon line at Bupyeong station. An extension from Gyulhyeon to Gyeyang opened in March 2007, which connects with the new Incheon Airport Railroad.

A further extension, southwards, will be 6.54 km long with six stations, and is currently due to open in 2009.

Two further lines are proposed.

Rolling stock: 25 eight-car sets from Daewoo/ALSTOM (1998)

Service: Peak 4.5 min, off-peak 8.5 min
Operating hours: 05.30-24.40
Fare structure: Zonal
Operational control: Control centre, ACS, ATP
Arrangements for elderly/disabled: Voice guide system for the blind; third and sixth car of each train has facilities for wheelchairs and baby carriages; all stations have Braille facilities, all stations have ramps and wheelchair lifts

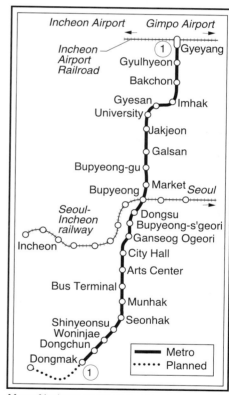

Map of Incheon metro and rail system   1124821

Incheon Rapid Transit Corporation (IRTC)

67-2 Ganseok 3-dong, Namdong-gu, Incheon, South Korea
Tel: (+82 32) 451 21 14-5   Fax: (+82 32) 451 21 60
e-mail: webmaster@irtc.co.kr
Web: www.irtc.co.kr

Key personnel

Manager, Public Relations Team: A K Cho
   Staff: 1,014

Type of operation: Full metro, opened 1999

Airport Rail Co Ltd (AREX)

8th Floor, Hyundai Annexe Building, 140-2 Gye-dong, Jongo-gu, Seoul, South Korea
Tel: (+82 32) 745 77 88   Fax: (+82 32) 745 88 99
Web: www.arex.or.kr

Type of operation: Heavy rail

Passenger journeys: n/a

Background

Incorporated in 2001, AREX has a 30-year concession, which will start from Phase 2 completion, to operate an express rail service that will link Seoul with its international and domestic airports at Incheon and Gimpo respectively, both of which are located west of the capital. The line will be Korea's first to be operated as a concession and will also carry commuter traffic.

IIARCO's main shareholders include: Hyundai Engineering and Construction Co Ltd (27 per cent); Daelim Industrial Co Ltd (17.5 per cent); Posco Engineering and Construction Co Ltd (11.9 per cent); the Ministry of Construction and Transportation (9.9 per cent); Dongbu Corporation (7.8 per cent); and KCC Corporation (7.6 per cent).

IIARCO has awarded a turnkey contract to the Incheon Korean French Consortium (IKFC) to undertake project management of the line's construction and to provide its power supply, train control and communications systems. IKFC comprises ALSTOM, Eukorail and Rotem.

Current situation

IIARCO foresees a half-hourly service frequency to the two airports, with a 45-minute journey time. A more intensive commuter service will be operated, serving intermediate stations and services will be operated under the 'AREX' brand name.

The project involves construction of a 61.7 km standard-gauge railway in two phases. The first phase (40.3 km with six stations), opened in March 2007, and provides a link between Incheon and Gimpo airports.

Construction on the second phase (20.7 km with four staions) started in January 2004 and is due to be completed in 2009–10. This phase will enable services to run into Seoul's main station. Around 60 per cent of the line is in tunnel.

The line is being electrified at 25 kV AC 60 Hz. Train control is being provided by ALSTOM, using its Urbalis 200 system.

Connections will be provided with both Incheon and Seoul metro systems and by serving Seoul's main station, a link will also be provided with KTX high-speed services south from the capital, as well as with conventional main line services.

Developments

Phase 1 opened in March 2007. Two services are available, commuter and express. An interchange at Gyeyang station provides a link to the Incheon metro Line 1 and onwards, via KORAIL, to Seoul.

Services run from 05.27 to 23.46, with minimum headway of three minutes.

Commuter fares are zonal. Stations have platform doors, lifts and escalators. LCD monitors at stations and on trains provide train information, news, airline information and other travel information.

Upon completion of Phase 2, airline check-in, baggage handling and immigration services for departing passengers will be available at the city airport terminal in Seoul Stations.

Fleet

IIARCO ordered 24 six-car aluminium-bodied 120 km/h emus from Rotem, to cover its requirements for both airport express and commuter services. Eighteen of these are intended for commuter services and feature four pairs of doors per side of each car plus high-density interiors; the remaining six trains for airport services have only two pairs of doors per car side and are provided with onboard luggage storage facilities.

Korean Railroad Corporation (KORAIL)

Daejeon Government Complex, 920, Dunsan-dong, Seo-Gu, Daejon, 302-701, South Korea
Tel: (+82 42) 15 44 77 88, 15 88 77 88
e-mail: cph-icd@mail.korail.go.kr
Web: www.korail.go.kr

Key personnel

President: Vacant
Vice-President: Park, Kwang-seok
  (Acting President)

Senior Executive Directors
  Planning & Co-operation: Choi, Han-ju
  Passenger Transport HQs: Kim, Cheon-hwan
  Metropolitan Transit HQs: Shin, Sung-ho
  Investment & Development HQs:
  Kim, Min-geun
  Engineering HQs: Park, Jae Keun
Director, International Co-operation Division:
  Yoo, Hee-bok

Current situation

Frequent electric train service operates between Incheon and Seoul (39 km).

For further information on KORAIL, please see Jane's World Railways.

Developments

In June 1998, KNR invited prequalification bids for a 30-year concession to build and operate a new 61.5 km electrified line from central Seoul to Gimpo Airport and to Incheon International Airport. A consortium led by Hyundai Engineering and Construction, the project operator, established the Airport Railroad Co Ltd (AREX) (www.arex.co.kr) in March 2001 to undertake the project, which is being constructed in two phases. The first phase is a 41 km route between Incheon International Airport and Gimpo Airport. The section between Incheon International Airport and Gimpo Airport was opened in early 2007, with the remaining section, Gimpo Airport-Seoul Station, due to be completed by 2010. Please see separate entry.

For further information, please see the entry for Seoul.

Seoul

Population: City 10.3 million (2005), metropolitan area 23 million (estimate)

Public transport

Bus services, including BRT, provided by private companies controlled by the government. Metro, with cross-city section shared with KORAIL suburban services. Rail link to Incheon under construction.

Seoul Metropolitan Government (SMG)

Transportation Bureau, Transport Planning Division
Euljiro 1, Jung-ju, Seoul 100–744, Republic of Korea
Tel: (+82 2) 37 07 97 11–2
Tel: (+82 2) 37 07 97 31–2 (Bus Operations Division)
e-mail: transp@seoul.gov.kr
  mass@seoul.go.kr (Public Transportation Division)
Web: www.english.seoul.go.kr

Passenger journeys: (2003/04) 1,752 million (estimate)
(2004/05) 1,862 million (estimate)

Number of routes: More than 415 (Blue Bus: 80, Green Bus: 292, Red Bus: 43) plus Yellow Line routes
Route length: Not currently available
BRT route length: 294 km (2004)

Background

Prior to 2004, bus services were operated by many private companies, with the government having control on fares but limited control of routes and schedules. Services were not co-ordinated with metro and other bus services and vehicles were old and poorly maintained.

In 2004, the government began a major reform of the city's bus services, including a complete redesign of the route network, the introduction a bus management system, improvements to the network of dedicated bus lanes to

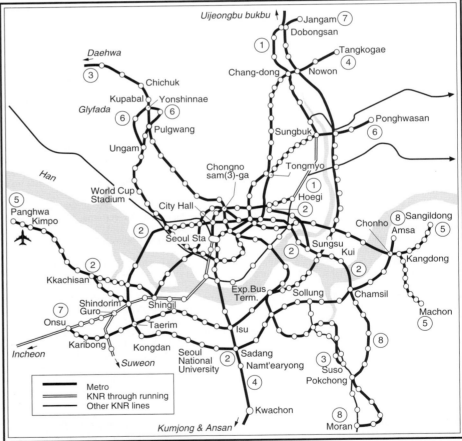

Map of Seoul metro and associated suburban lines   0580291

include a Bus Rapid Transit (BRT) system and co-ordination of bus services with the metro. The fare structure and ticketing system was also fully integrated.

Current situation

The Seoul Metropolitan Government (SMG) operates a semi-public operation system, which retains private bus companies to operate services

but in which the SMG has control over routes, scheduling and fares.

Bus services are now classified into four categories:

- **Blue Bus:** 80 arterial bus routes on dedicated bus lanes, operated by 726 buses, from downtown Seoul to suburban areas and satellite cities;
- **Green Bus:** 292 local bus routes, operated by 2,450 buses and private bus companies, on short

routes from residential areas for passengers transferring to Blue Line routes or the metro;

- **Red Bus:** 43 wide-area routes connecting satellite cities to downtown Seoul;
- **Yellow Bus:** Short routes in downtown areas of the city.

A Bus Management System (BMS) has been set up, using ITS and GPS technology to monitor and control all buses. This has greatly assisted in improving scheduling and therefore service, allowing communication with drivers and providing real-time information to passengers.

The network of dedicated bus lanes has been expanded and upgraded. The BRT network has been developed, with 36 km of BRT services by early 2005. An additional 62 km or BRT on seven corridors is expected to be operational by the end of 2006 and there are plans for further expansion.

There are also plans to purchase new buses, with more than 300 low-floor, mostly CNG, buses expected to be in service by the end of 2006. Some of these will be articulated vehicles. The longer-term plans are for all Blue and Red buses to be CNG and low-floor and all Red buses to be articulated.

There are a number of transfer centres under construction.

Developments
A fully computerised Transit Signal Priority (TSP) system has recently been inaugurated.

Bus
Fleet: More than 3,000 buses (Blue Bus: 726 buses, Green Bus: 2,450)

Fleet includes:

Daewoo BH115E, BH117E and 120H	Not currently available
Daewoo BS090 CNG city bus	Not currently available
Daewoo BS106 CNG city bus	Not currently available
Daewoo BS116 CNG city bus	Not currently available
Hyundai Super Aero city bus	Not currently available

On order: Not currently available

First/last bus: 05.00/02.00
One-person operation: City buses, none; seat buses, all services
Fare collection: Payment by tickets or T-money transportation smartcard. Discount for youths and school children.
Fare structure: Zonal (8 zones)
Integration with other modes:
Unified fare structure for bus and rail services
Average peak-hour speed: Not currently available
Operating costs financed by: Private companies are reimbursed by the SMG on the basis of vehicle/km of service

Light rail
Current situation
There are tentative plans for several new Light Rail Transit (LRT) lines. A proposed LRT line in northeastern Seoul is considered a cheaper option than previously planned metro extensions.

No progress has been made on these proposed lines, due mainly to a lack of financing.

Seoul Metropolitan Subway Corporation (SMSC)

447-7 Bangbae 2dong, Socho-gu, Seoul 133170, South Korea
Tel: (+82 2) 520 50 20-25   Fax: (+82 2) 520 50 39
e-mail: webadmin@seoulsubway.co.kr
Web: www.seoulsubway.co.kr

Key personnel
President: Kim Jung-Kook
Director of Operations: Lee Jae-back
Staff: 11,116

Type of operation: Full metro; first section opened 1974

Passenger journeys: (1999) 1,295 million
(2000) 1,420 million
(2001) 1,584 million
Approx 4 million per day

Route length: 135 km
Number of lines: 4
Number of stations: 115
Gauge: 1,435 mm
Track: 50 kg/m or 60 kg/m rail laid on timber sleepers and ballast; track rubber-padded for protection of city's historic East and South gates
Max gradient: 3.5%
Minimum curve radius: 400 m
Tunnel: Cut-and-cover; tunnels vibration-damped near East and South gates
Electrification: 1.5 kV DC, overhead (KNR suburban trains on Lines 1 and 4 dual-voltage, 25 kV 60 Hz and 1.5 kV DC)

Developments
In November 1999, the Dangsan railway bridge was reopened.

Service: Peak 2½ min, off-peak 4–10 min
Integration with other modes: Trains from KNR Incheon and Suweon suburban lines operate through metro Line 1 to reach Sungbuk, while Line 4 metro trains run through to KNR's Ansan and Kwacheon lines
Revenue collection: Full AFC system at all metro stations and 51 KNR stations

Rolling stock: 1,944 cars

Hitachi (1974)	M40 T20
Daewoo (1977)	M24 T12
Daewoo (1980)	M32
Hyundai (1982)	M24
Hyundai (1983)	M100 T2
GEC (1984)	M268 T134
Hyundai (1988)	M64 T68
Daewoo (1990)	M138
(1991)	M210
(1992)	M144
(1993)	M322
Others	342

Seoul Metropolitan Rapid Transit Corporation (SMRT)

223-3 Yongdap-dong, Songdong-gu, Seoul 133-170, South Korea
Tel: (+82 2) 62 11 22 00
Fax: (+82 2) 62 11 20 04
e-mail: webadmin@smrt.co.kr
Web: www.smrt.co.kr

Key personnel
President: Sung Jick Eum
Staff: 6,752

Type of operation: Full metro; first line opened 1994

Passenger journeys: (2006) 803 million

Route length: 152 km
Number of lines: 4
Number of stations: 148
Track: 60 kg/m rail laid on timber sleepers and ballast
Gauge: 1,435 mm
Electrification: 1.5 kV DC, overhead

Current situation
Established in 1994, the Seoul Metropolitan Rapid Transit Corporation (SMRT) operates subway lines 5, 6, 7 and 8. SMRT and the ASeoul Metropolitan Subway Co share 35.6 per cent of Seoul's public transport journeys.

Developments
There are plans to connect Line 7 to Incheon Subway Line 1, with nine stations to be added on the 9.8 km extension by 2010. The extension would run from Onsu Station of Line 7 to Pupyong-gu Office Station of Inchon Subway Line 1.

Rolling stock: 1,564 (in 6- and 8-car trains)

Airport Rail Co Ltd (AREX)

8th Floor, Hyundai Annexe Building, 140-2 Gye-dong, Jongo-gu, Seoul, South Korea
Tel: (+82 32) 745 77 88   Fax: (+82 32) 745 88 99
Web: www.arex.or.kr

Type of operation: Heavy rail

Passenger journeys: n/a
For further information, please see the entry for Incheon .

Korean Railroad Corporation (KORAIL)

Daejeon Government Complex, 920 Dunsan-dong, Seo-Gu, Daejon, 302-701, South Korea
Tel: (+82 42) 15 44 77 88, 15 88 77 88
e-mail: cph-icd@mail.korail.go.kr
Web: www.korail.go.kr

Key personnel
President: Vacant
  Vice-President: Park, Kwang-seok (Acting President)
Senior Executive Directors
  Planning & Co-operation: Choi, Han-ju
  Passenger Transport HQs: Kim, Cheon-hwan
  Metropolitan Transit HQs: Shin, Sung-ho
  Investment & Development HQs: Kim, Min-geun
  Engineering HQs: Park, Jae Keun
  Director, International Co-operation Division: Yoo, Hee-bok

Type of operation: Suburban heavy rail

Passenger journeys: (2002) 873.3 million
(2004) 810 million
(2006) 854 million
Car-km: (2004) 254 million

Gauge: 1,435 mm
Electrification: 25 kV/60 Hz
Route length: 288.4 km (total)
Number of lines: 8
Number of stations: 144

Current situation
KORAIL operates 259 emus on seven lines. Some of the lines operate within Seoul, linking Seoul station to major suburban cities, and the other KORAIL lines connect some satellite cities of Seoul to Seoul subway lines 1, 3, 4, 5, 6, 7 and 8.

Operating costs are covered entirely by fares.

For further information on KORAIL, please see *Jane's World Railways.*

Developments
In June 1998, KORAIL invited prequalification bids for a 30-year concession to build and operate a new 61.5 km electrified line from central Seoul to Gimpo Airport and to Incheon International Airport. A consortium led by Hyundai Engineering and Construction, the project operator, established the Airport Railroad Co Ltd (AREX) in March 2001 to undertake the project, which is being constructed in two phases. The first phase is a 41 km route between Incheon International Airport and Gimpo Airport, which opened in March 2007, with the remaining section, Gimpo Airport-Seoul Station, due to be completed by 2010.

A 55.6 km extension from Suwon to Cheonan, aimed at reducing traffic congestion in the Seoul metropolitan area, was started in 1996. The first 7.3 km section of this route, Suwon to Byungjeom, was opened for service in April 2003 and the remaining section from Byungjeom to Cheonan was opened for service in January 2005.

An 18 km route from Cheongnyangni to Deokso opened in December 2005.

Rolling stock: 2,086 cars (including locomotives)

Service: Peak: 2–12 min; off-peak: 3-15 min
First/last train: 05.00/01.00
Arrangements for elderly/disabled: Free passes for over 65s, disabled (including one escort) and national merit recipients; each station equipped with lifts or elevators
Average speed: 45 km/h
Average distance between stops: 2.2 km

Latvia

Riga

Population: 727,200 (2002 estimate)

Public transport
Bus, tram and trolleybus services provided by municipal enterprise; suburban rail services by subsidiary of public rail company (LDZ).

SIA Rīgas Satiksme – Rigatrans Ltd
Kleistu iela 28, LV-1067, Riga, Latvia
Tel: (+371 7) 06 54 00
Fax: (+371 7) 06 54 02
e-mail: info@rigassatiksme.lv
Web: www.rigassatiksme.lv

Key personnel
Board Chairman: Leons Bemhens
Board Members
  Finance Director: Tamāra Dāvidsone
  Infrastructure Director: Egils Dīriņš
  Administrative Director: Imants Rezebergs
  Development Director: Igors Volkinšteins
  Commercial Director: Igors Žagars
  Staff: 6,088

Background
SIA Rīgas Satiksme, an enterprise of Riga municipality, was established in February 2003. SIA Rīgas Satiksme is an enterprise of Riga municipality, established on February 20, 2003. The company ensures passenger transportation by public transport (buses, trolleybuses and trams), offers various means of transport for rent as well as provides parking services in Riga city.

The company holds ISO and OHSAS certification.

Current situation
In January 2005, four companies of Riga public transport, SIA Rīgas satiksme, SIA Tramvaju un trolejbusu pārvalde, SIA Rīgas autostāvvietas and SIA Rīgas domes autobāze, merged together.

The company is a member of the Latvian Association of Passenger Carriers, Latvian Quality Association and the Latvian Association of Motor Engineers.

SIA Rīga Satiksme trolleybus (SIA Rīga Satiksme) 1180237

Bus
Passenger journeys: (2005) 100.7 million
(2006) 107.9 million
Vehicle-km: (2005) 31.2 million
(2006) 30.6 million

Number of routes: 76
Route length: 2,770.6 km

Fleet: 488 buses	
Ikaruss-260	6
Ikaruss E-91	106
Solaris Urbino	167
MB-345	92
MB-530	117
In peak service: 359	

Operating costs financed by: Fares 32.7 per cent, subsidy 65.9 per cent, other income 2.1 per cent
Fare structure: Zonal; various season tickets available

Trolleybus
Passenger journeys: (2005) 96.7 million
(2006) 99.1 million
Vehicle-km: (2005) 17.3 million
(2006) 16.5 million

Number of routes: 20
Route length: 331.96 km

Fleet: 318 trolleybuses	
BKM-321	1
Skoda 14Tr	238
Skoda 15Tr articulated	33

SIA Rīga Satiksme buses (SIA Rīga Satiksme) 1180239

BKM-333 (Belkommunmash) articulated	10
GS-18 (Ganz-Solaris)	35
GM-103	1
In peak service: 268	

Operating costs financed by: Fares 57 per cent, subsidy 42 per cent, other income 1 per cent
Fare structure: Flat; various season tickets available

Tramway
Type of operation: Conventional tramway

Passenger journeys: (2005) 76.8 million
(2006) 80.3 million
Vehicle-km: (2005) 14.3 million
(2006) 14.1 million

Number of routes: 11
Route length: 267.6 km
Gauge: 1,524 mm
Electrification: 600 V DC, collection by trolley pole

Rolling stock: 252 cars	
ČKD Tatra T3 (1975/87)	M190
ČKD Tatra T3M (1988/90)	M62
In peak service: 186	

Operating costs financed by: Fares 55 per cent, subsidy 43 per cent, other income 2 per cent
Fare structure: Flat; various season tickets available

Developments
In late 2006, a contract was signed with Ganz Transelektro to upgrade the electrical equipment of 30 Tatra T-3M trams.

Joint Stock Company (JSC) Pasažieru Vilciens (PV)
Turgeņeva iela 14, Riga LV-1050, Latvia
Tel: (+371 67) 23 40 09
Fax: (+371 67) 23 30 49
e-mail: pv@pv.ldz.lv
Web: www.pv.lv

Key personnel
Chairman of the Board, PV: Reinholds Pelše
Finance Director, PV: Edgars Kreits
  Staff: Not currently available

Type of operations: Suburban heavy rail

Passenger journeys: (All routes)
(2003) 22.6 million
(2004) 23.5 million
(2005) 25.5 million
(2006) 27.0 million
(2007) 27.0 million
Train-km: Not currently available

Background
The joint stock company Pasažieru Vilciens (PV) was founded in November 2001 as part of the restructuring programme of the state stock company Latvijas Dzelzceļš (LDz). PV was established to combine the activities of the former Elektrovilciens (Electric Train) and

SIA Rīga Satiksme renovated Tatra 3M tram (SIA Rīga Satiksme) 1180238

Dīzeļvilciens (Diesel Train) divisions of LDz and became the first subsidiary of LDz.

Current situation
JSC Pasažieru Vilciens (PV) is responsible for domestic passenger services. It currently operates twelve routes, four of which are operated with electric trains (Riga – Aizkraukle; – Jelgava; – Skulte; – Tukums) and eight with diesel trains (Riga – Daugavpils; – Gulbene; – Krustpils; – Lugaži; Reņe; – Rēzekne-Zilupe; -Liepāja).

The main domestic lines link the capital Rīga with Daugavpils, 218 km away in the southeast of the country; Rēzekne, in the east (224 km), Jelgava, in the south (43 km) and Lugaži, in the northeast (168 km).

Suburban lines around Riga are operated by ER2 and ER2T 3 kV emus.

For further information on LDz, please see *Jane's World Railways*.

Developments
In March 2006, improved dmus started operating on the Rīga-Liepāja-Rīga line.

LDZ Class ER2 emu at Riga (Quintus Vosman)   0585034

Lithuania

Vilnius
Population: City: 553, 904 (2005)

Public transport
Bus and trolleybus services operated by municipally owned companies, with additional private bus/minibus/shared taxi operations.

UAB Vilniaus Autobusai (JSC Vilniaus Autobusai)
Verkių g 52, LT-09109 Vilnius, Lithuania
Tel: (+370 5) 273 86 02   Fax: (+370 5) 272 24 67
e-mail: autobusai@vap.lt
Web: www.vap.lt

Key personnel
General Manager: Gintaras Nakutis

Passenger journeys: (2005) 100 million (estimated)
(2006) 110 million (estimated)

Number of routes: 70 (+5 night routes)

Fleet: Approx 350 buses
Includes:
Volvo 7700 city bus (2004/06)   60
Volvo 7700 city bus, articulated (2004/06)   30

Current situation
Services run by this municipal company are supplemented by operations of an unknown number of private sector companies. Bus services operate from 03.30 to 01.00. On night routes, buses operate from 22.45 to 05.15. Fares are flat, with discounts for senior citizens and students. 1-, 3- and 10-day and monthly passes are available. There is a common tariff for bus and trolleybus services.

Developments
In June 2004, UAB Vilniaus Autobusai placed an order for 90 Volvo 7700 city buses. Of these, 60 will be standard vehicles and 30 articulated. The first 10 articulated buses and the first 20 standard buses had been delivered by the end of 2004. The remaining 60 buses were delivered in 2005 and 2006. The buses were produced at the Volvo factory in Wroclaw, Poland.

UAB Vilniaus troleibusai
Žolyno g 15, LT-10209 Vilnius, Lithuania
Tel: (+370 5) 239 47 00   Fax: (+370 5) 270 95 50
e-mail: vilnius@troleibusai.lt
Web: www.troleibusai.lt

UAB Vilniaus troleibusai Solaris Trollino 15M trolleybus   1181789

UAB Vilniaus troleibusai Skoda 14Tr trolleybus   1181786

Key personnel
Managing Director: Jonas Bagdonavicius
Technical Director: Jurijus Komarovas
    Staff: 1,317

Passenger journeys: (2005) 92.5 million
(2006) 88.7 million
(2007) 95.4 million
Car-km: (2007) 19.4 million (estimate)

Number of routes: 19
Route length: 445 km

Background
Operations started in 1956.

Fleet: 320 cars
Skoda 9Tr   1
Skoda 14Tr   270
Skoda 15Tr   4
Solaris Trollino 15M   45
In peak service: 259

First/last trolleybus: 04.00/01.00
Fare structure: Flat; 1-, 3- and 10-day and monthly
passes; discounts for senior citizens and students;
common tariff for bus and trolleybus services
Arrangements for elderly/disabled: The Solaris
Trollino low-floor vehicles operate on 11 routes

UAB Vilniaus troleibusai Skoda 9Tr trolleybus   1181790

Luxembourg

Luxembourg

Population: City 76,420 (2005), metropolitan area
103,970 (estimate)

Public transport
Bus services provided by municipal undertaking,
with some independent operators; rail services
and bus services, some provided jointly with
municipal undertaking, by Luxembourg Railways
(CFL).

Service des Transports en commun de la Ville de Luxembourg (VDL)
PO Box 914, L-2019, Luxembourg
Tel: (+352) 47 96 29 83
Fax: (+352) 29 68 08
e-mail: autobus@vdl.lu
Web: www.luxembourg-city.lu

Key personnel
Operating Manager: G Feltz
    Staff: 446

Bus
Passenger journeys: (2003) 26.8 million
(2004) 25.9 million
(2005) 25.3 million
(2006) 26.68 million
(2007) 27.79 million
Vehicle-km: (2003) 4.9 million
(2004) 5.2 million
(2005) 5.2 million
(2006) 5.2 million
(2007) 5.2 million

Number of routes: 31
Number of stops: 640
Route length: (One way) 147 km
On priority right-of-way: 23.2 km

Fleet: 149 buses (2007)
Mercedes VöV   7
Mercedes articulated   6
Mercedes low-floor   9
MAN low-floor articulated   35
MAN low-floor   16
Scania low-floor   30
    Irisbus (2006)   30
Steyr Puch minibus   1

VW midibus   5
Mercedes-Benz midibus   3
DAB midibus   7
On order: Not currently available
In peak service: 100
Average age of fleet: 9 years

Most intensive service: 3½ min
One-person operation: All routes
Fare collection: Single tickets issued on bus with
Almex system F, or prepurchase 10-ride ticket with
canceller on board
Fare structure: Flat; prepurchase multitickets;
monthly passes; common tariff and interavailability
of ticketing for all modes
Fares collected on board: 14 per cent
Fare evasion control: 14 controllers
Operational control: Route inspectors, with mobile
radio on buses; some CCTV cameras
Arrangements for elderly/disabled: Minibuses
equipped to carry disabled passengers
Integration with other modes: Several park-
and-ride sites served by 10 min frequency
Average distance between stops: 230 m
Average peak-hour speed: In mixed traffic, 18.7 km/h
Operating costs financed by: Fares 22.3 per cent,
other commercial sources 3 per cent, subsidy/
grants 16 per cent, deficit financed from profits on
other community services, such as gas, electricity
and water supply, and government support

Société Nationale des Chemins de Fer Luxembourgeois (CFL) – Luxembourg Railways
9 Place de la Gare, L-1616, Luxembourg
Tel: (+352) 499 00-1   Fax: (+352) 49 90 44 70
e-mail: info@cfl.lu
Web: www.cfl.lu

Key personnel
President of the Board: Jeannot Waringo
General Director: Alex Kremer
Directors: François Jaeger
    Nicolas Welsch
    Marc Wengler
Manager, Operations: Jean-Michel Flammang
Manager, Passenger Business: Monique Buschmann

Type of operation: Local rail

Passenger journeys: (2005) 14.05 million
(2006) 14.79 million
Train-km: Not currently available

Background
CFL is directed by a joint board of 15 which includes
members from the Luxembourg Government,
CFL, and one member each from the French and
Belgian Governments.

Current situation
CFL operates local services on five routes
radiating from the city centre, four of which
are electrified at 25 kV 50 Hz. The line to
Kleinbettingen (19 km) on the Belgian border is
electrified at 3 kV DC, but is now mostly diesel
operated.
   In 2002, the Luxembourg Government
launched the project 'mobiliteit.lu', aimed at
increasing public transport's market share
from 14 to 25 per cent by 2020. It is to finance
extensions to the rail network to achieve this.
A heavy rail branch to the airport and Kirchberg
off the Wasserbillig line is planned. A tram-train
project has been dropped in favour of a street
tramway from Howald CFL station, via a new
CFL station at Cessange and Luxembourg Ville
station to Kirchberg. These would open in 2012.
In addition, the Luxembourg-Sandweiler line will
be doubled.
   In 2006, CFL completed a major renewal of its
passenger stock, increasing capacity by over half
and bringing down the average age of stock from
around 30 years to five years. All new stock has
been financed by government.
   Commuter traffic from countries bordering
Luxembourg has grown very strongly in
recent years due to new season tickets and
additional services. In early 2004, CFL revealed
plans to extend several domestic services into
neighbouring countries to attract even more
cross-border commuters. In 2006, season ticket
sales from France increased by 13.5 per cent and
by 19 per cent from Belgium.
   CFL also runs a bus network, including school
routes, serving mainly rural areas where rail
lines have closed, but some urban routes run
jointly with VDL (see separate entry). Average of
538 daily journeys run by 54 buses.
   For further information on CFL, please see
Jane's World Railways.

Malaysia

Kuala Lumpur

Population: City 1.8 million, metropolitan area 6.9 million (estimates)

Public transport

Conventional bus services in metropolitan area provided by area-franchised private companies with many owner-operated route-licensed 'Bas Mini' fixed-route minibuses and metered taxis licensed by government board as well as special school and factory buses. Suburban rail; light rail; mini-metro; monorail.

Ministry of Transport Malaysia

Block D5, Complex D, Federal Government Administrative Centre, 62616 Putrajaya, Malaysia
Tel: (+60 3) 88 86 60 00
Fax: (+60 3) 88 89 15 69
e-mail: norbaya@mot.gov.my
Web: www.mot.gov.my

Key personnel

Minister of Transport: Datò Sri Chan Kong Choy
Deputy Ministers of Transport: Datuk Douglas Uggah Embas
  Tengku Dato' Seri Azlan Ibni Sultan Abu Bakar
Public Relations Officer: Norbaya Bt Jamaludin

Background

Responsible for the planning, formulation and implementation of transport policies, transport rules and regulations and development programmes. Also responsible for the agreements and franchises with operators, such as PUTRA, STAR, the monorail and ERL.

Bus (franchised operators)
Background

Franchised bus operators are regulated by the Road Transport Licensing Board.

Current situation

The two main operators are Park May Bhd and Intrakota Consolidated Bhd. Other operators include: Sri Jaya Kenderaan; Toon Fong; Foh Hup; Kuala Lumpur, Klang & Port Swettenham Bus; Selangor Bus; Len Bus; Len Seng; Len Chee. Each main bus operator is franchised to serve a specific sector of the city. Fleets range from 30 to 361 vehicles, with over 1,000 vehicles operated in total. Services run 06.00-24.00 on most routes at intervals varying from two minutes to hourly. There is considerable overlapping of routes.

Minibus (Bas Mini)
Background

Regulated by the Road Transport Licensing Board.

Current situation

Conventional services are largely duplicated by minibus routes, which have drawn business from buses and led the conventional operators into Bas Mini operation too. Minibuses were introduced in 1975; each is licensed for a particular route. A flat fare is set.

The largest bus operator, Sri Jaya Kenderaan, runs a fleet of Mercedes O309 minibuses on more lightly used routes.

Developments

The Board started franchising of minibus routes in 1994 as a direct replacement for Bas Mini operations, in an attempt to improve vehicle and passenger standards. The Optare Metrorider was selected as the fleet vehicle, and is equipped with air conditioning, tinted glazing, wide doors and low entry steps. The minibuses, known as Pekanriders, are imported in knocked-down form for local assembly by Diversified Resources Bhd (DRB), though there will be an increasing proportion of local content. A total

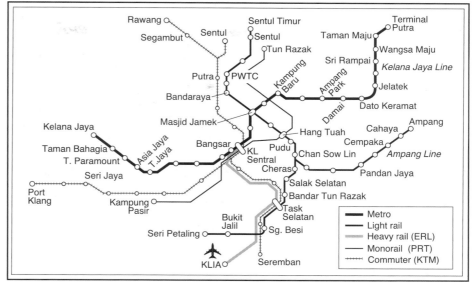

Map of Kuala Lumpur's rail systems   1293438

of 1,000 is being delivered over a five-year period starting in 1996, to replace 800 Bas Mini vehicles.

Eight cross-city routes have been franchised to Intrakota, which is a subsidiary of DRB.

Rangkaian Pengangkutan Integrasi Deras Sdn Bhd (RapidKL)

No 1, Jalan PJU 1A/46, Off Jalan Lapangan Terbang, Sultan Salahuddin Abdul Aziz Shah, 47301 Petaling Jaya, Selangor, Malaysia
Tel: (+60 3) 76 50 77 88
Fax: (+60 3) 76 25 66 67
e-mail: suggest@rapidkl.com.my
Web: www.rapidkl.com.my

Key personnel

Chief Executive Officer/Executive Director: Rein Westra
Chief Operating Officer (Rail)/Executive Director: En Nor Hassan Ismail
Chief Operating Officer (Bus)/Executive Director: En Mohd Ali Mohd Nor
Senior Manager, Corporate Communications Division: Katherine Chew
Staff: Not currently available

Passenger journeys: (All modes) (2006) 180 million (estimate)

Current situation

Rangkaian Pengangkutan Integrasi Deras Sdn Bhd (RapidKL) is a wholly owned government company, formed in 2004 to provide an integrated transport system in the Klang Valley, incorporating rail and bus services.

RapidKL operates the Ampang Line (formerly known as STAR), the Kelana Line (previously known as PUTRA) and the bus operations of the former Intrakota and Cityliner services.

All stations and trains are wheelchair accessible and underground platforms have screen door. Feeder bus services provide access to rail stations.

Developments

In April 2007, RapidKL launched an improved bus network. The Trunk Bus services have been extended to provide better access from residential areas to the city centre.

In early 2007, the government announced that RapidKL will also take over the management of the bus system in Penang.

Ampang Line (formerly known as STAR)
Staff: Not currently available

Type of operation: Light rail, initial section opened 1996

Passenger journeys: (2006) 49 million (estimate)
Vehicle-km: Not currently available

Route length: 27 km
  Elevated: 9.4 km
Number of lines: 2
Number of stations: 25
  Elevated: 8
Gauge: 1,435 mm
Electrification: 750 V DC, bottom contact third rail

Developments

In mid-2006, it was announced that the southern end of the Sri Petaling Line, which currently ends at Sri Petaling station, would be extended by some 10 km to the suburb of Puchong.

Rolling stock: 90 cars
Walkers/AEG (1995)   M34
Walkers/AEG (1996/97)   M56

Service interval: Peak 3-6 min
First/last car: 06.00/24.00
Fare structure: Distance-based; single and stored-value tickets
Fare collection: Ticket machines with automatic barriers at all stations
Signalling: Non-permissive automatic block, CTC and ATS with computer-based scheduling and headway regulation

Kelana Jaya Line (previously known as PUTRA)
Staff: Not currently available

Type of operation: Fully automated light rail, initial section opened 1998

Passenger journeys: (2006) 62 million (estimate)
Vehicle-km: Not currently available

Route length: 29 km
  In tunnel: 4.4 km
  Elevated: 24.6 km
Number of lines: 1
Number of stations: 23

Current situation

The Kelana Jaya Line services the route from the depot in Subang to the Terminal Putra in Gombak.

Developments

In late 2006, Bombardier Transportation and its local partner, Hartasuma Sdn Bhd, were awarded a contract for an initial 88 Advanced

Rapid Transit (ART) Mk II cars, to be operated as four-car sets, for the Kelana Jaya Line. The total contract value was some EUR167 million. There is an option for an additional 52 cars. Delivery of the initial batch of cars is scheduled for 2008–2010.

Fleet: 70 cars
ART Mk II two-car emus   35
In peak service: Not currently available
On order: 88 Bombardier ART MK II cars

Service interval: Peak 4 min
First/last car: 06.00/24.00 (Sunday 06.00/23.30)
Fare structure: Distance-based; single and stored-value tickets
Fare collection: Ticket machines with automatic barriers at all stations
Signalling: Non-permissive automatic block, CTC and ATS with computer-based scheduling and headway regulation

RapidKL bus
Staff: Not currently available

Passenger journeys: (2006) 70 million (estimate)
Vehicle-km: Not currently available

Route length: Not currently available
Number of routes: 165 (10 City Bus, 87 Local Bus, 65 Trunk Bus and 3 Express Bus)
Number of depots: 11

Fleet: In excess of 1,000 buses
Fleet breakdown is not currently available
In peak service: Not currently available
On order: Not currently available

Express Rail Link Sdn Bhd (ERL)
Level 2, City Air Terminal, KL Sentral Station, 50470 Kuala Lumpur, Malaysia
Tel: (+60 3) 22 67 80 88   Fax: (+60 3) 22 67 89 10
e-mail: air-rail@KLIAekspres.com
Web: www.kliaekspres.com

Key personnel
Executive Chairman: Mohamed Nadzmi Mohamed Salleh
Chief Executive Officer: Dr Aminuddin B Adnan
Senior Vice-President, Finance & Revenue Management: Jannis Boo
Vice-President, Marketing & Sales and Customer Service Management: Yeow Wei Wen

Type of operation: Express rail

Passenger journeys: (KLIA Ekspres)
(2003) 1.75 million
(KLIA Transit)
Not currently available
Train-km: Not currently available

Route length: 57 km
Gauge: 1,435 mm
Electrification: 25 kV AC 50 Hz

Express Rail Link (ERL)
Background
Shareholding in ERL, which was formally incorporated on 29 January 1996, is by YTL Corporation Bhd (50 per cent), Lembaga Tabung Haji Technologies (40 per cent) and Trisilco Equity Sdn Bhd (10 per cent).
In August 1997, Express Rail Link (ERL) was granted a 30-year government concession, with a 30-year extension option, to design, finance, construct, manage, operate and maintain an express rail system linking Kuala Lumpur Sentral at Brickfields and the city's then new international airport (KLIA) at Sepang, south of the capital.

Current situation
ERL operates two services: KLIA Ekspres, a non-stop service linking KL Sentral and KLIA, and

KLIA Transit, a commuter service linking the same two points but with additional stops at the three intermediate stations. Operations commenced in April and June 2002 respectively, with departing passengers on Malaysia Airlines, Cathay Pacific Airways and Royal Brunei Airlines having the option of using the city check-in service in Kuala Lumpur City Air Terminal (KL CAT). Effective December 2007, Emirates Airlines extended this facility to its out-bound passengers. In-town check-out facility in KL CAT for arriving passengers is expected to be operational by mid-2008.
KL Sentral is the city's transport hub housing the country's main interstate rail-lines, KTM and its intra-states' Komuter services, RapidKL's Light Rail Transit (LRT) system which plies between city centre and the outskirt townships, and the Monorail which serves within the city centre.
The KLIA Ekspres operates from 05.00 to 01.00 at a 15 minutes interval during peak and 20 minutes off-peak with a journey time of 28 minute, whilst the KLIA Transit operates at 30 min frequency with a 37-minute journey time.
For further information on ERL, please see *Jane's World Railways*.

Rolling stock
Services are operated using 12 four-car articulated emus supplied by Siemens Transportation Systems and based on the design of the Class ET 425 vehicles supplied to Deutsche Bahn AG and designated Type Desiro ET. Eight of the units are for KLIA Express services, and feature higher levels of comfort and seating for 156 passengers, as well as a stowage area for baggage containers; the remaining four units are high-density vehicles for KLIA Transit services, with seating for 144 and standing capacity for 396 passengers.
Siemens four-car Type Desiro ET emus   12

KL StarRail Sdn Bhd
Wisma Monorail, Jalan Tebing, Brickfields, 50470 Kuala Lumpur, Malaysia
Tel: (+60 3) 22 67 98 88
Fax: (+60 3) 22 67 99 99
e-mail: info@klstarrail.com.my
Web: www.klmonorail.com.my

Key personnel
Chief Executive Officer: Khairan Mohamed
Staff: Not available currently

Type of operation: Monorail, opened 2003

Passenger journeys: (2008) 13.1 million (estimate)
Train-km: Not currently available

Number of lines: 1
Route length: 8.6 km
Number of stations: 11

Background
A 40-year concession agreement has been signed between the government and KL Monorail System for the operation of the monorail. The troubled MYR2 billion (USD16 million) project was put on hold for more than two years because of financial problems, which resulted in KL Monorail needing a MYR300 million government loan to complete the project.
The service was planned to commence in 2002. KL Monorail has also been awarded a potentially lucrative riverside development project in Brickfields, Kuala Lumpur, and further equity injections and infrastructure loans, amounting to an additional MYR870 million, are planned to support the continued operations of the company.
The 8.6 km, 11-station KL Monorail opened in August 2003. There is provision for one further station. Five trains, manufactured by Monorail Malaysia Technology Sdn Bhd (MMT), initially

ran at 10 minute intervals. Hours of operation started at 07.00-20.00 hrs.

Current situation
The monorail system is protected by an Automatic Train Protection (ATP) system.
The second phase being complete, with the full fleet of 12 vehicles runs at three minute intervals during peak hours. The completed system is capable of carrying 5,000 passengers per hour, per direction.
Operating hours have been extended to 06.00–24.00.

Developments
In 2007, Syarikat Prasarana Negara Berhad (SPNB) signed a sale and purchase agreement with KL Monorail Systems Sdn Bhd (KLMS). The current operator for the KL Monorail system is KL StarRail Sdn Bhd, a wholly-owned subsidiary of SPNB.

Rolling stock:
MMT two-car trains   12

Service: Peak 3-5 min, off-peak 7-10 min
Operating hours: 06.00-24.00
One-person operation: All trains
Fare structure: Zonal; prepaid tickets and stored-value cards
Fare collection: Automatic fare collection system
Operational control: Automatic Train Protection (ATP), control centre
Average train speed: 30 km/h
Integration with other modes: STAR (two stations), PUTRA (two stations), ERL (one station), KTM (one station)

Keretapi Tanah Melayu Berhad (KTM Berhad) – Malaysian Railways
KTMB Corporate Headquarters
Jalan Sultan Hishamuddin, 50621 Kuala Lumpur, Malaysia
Tel: (+60 3) 22 63 11 11
Fax: (+60 3) 27 10 57 60
e-mail: corpcomm@ktmb.com.my
Web: www.ktmb.com.my

Key personnel
Chairman: Y Bhg Tan Sri Dato' Thong Yaw Hong
Managing Director: Y Bhg Datuk Mohd Salleh Abdullah
Senior Manager, Corporate Communications: Miss Azizah Ujang

Type of operation: Local/commuter railway (KTM Komuter)

Passenger journeys: 80,000 daily (average)

Current situation
Suburban KTM Komuter service, with two interconnecting routes: Seremban-Rawang and Sentul-Pelabuhan Klang. Track length 150 km, metre-gauge, double tracks, electrified 25 kV 50 Hz.
There are 247 services daily from Mondays to Fridays, 271 services on Saturdays and 228 services on Sundays. Train interval at peak time is 15 minutes and off-peak 20 minutes.
For further information, please see *Jane's World Railways*.

Developments
Ongoing project is the electrification of the Rawang-Ipoh section, due to be completed in 2007. The project will enable KTM Komuter services to be extended to Tanjung Malim, and a rapid train service to be introduced between Kuala Lumpur and Ipoh.

Rolling stock: 58 three-car emus

Mauritius

Mauritius

Population: 1.15 million (2005 estimate – main island), 1.19 million (including Rodrigues)

Public transport

Buses are run by the parastatal National Transport Corporation, four private companies, and by a number of independent operators; also privately run shared taxi operations. Public transport operations are currently under study by the Ministry of Public Infrastructure, Land Transport and Shipping, with a view to modernising services.

Ministry of Public Infrastructure, Land Transport and Shipping

Land Transport and Shipping Division
4th Floor, New Government Centre, Port Louis, Mauritius
Tel: (+230 201) 10 67   Fax: (+230 201) 33 87
Web: www.publicinfrastructure.gov.mu

Public Infrastructure Division
9th Floor, Moorgate House, Sir William Newton Street, Port Louis, Mauritius
Tel: (+230 208) 02 81   Fax: (+230 201) 33 87

Key personnel

The Senior Chief Executive: Vacant
The Permanent Secretary, Land Transport and Shipping Division: Mrs Nirmala Nababsing
The Permanent Secretary, Public Infrastructure Division: R Duva Pentiah

Bus

National Transport Authority (NTA)
MSI Building, Royal Road, Cassis, Mauritius.

Key personnel

Road Transport Commissioner: A R Nabheebaccus
Deputy Road Transport Commissioner: N A Khadun
Transport Planner: D Romooah
Transport Controllers: A A Peerboccus,
   A K Appajala

Current situation

Currently, there are 1,958 stage carrier buses registered in Mauritius.

Developments

Express bus services have been extended to the city centre during morning peak hours;
Extension of the contraflow traffic scheme along the motorway is being studied;
Rescheduling of bus timetables to ensure higher occupancy of buses and to reduce the number of buses entering the centre of Port Louis by retaining some buses at Coromandel;
Introduction of 32-seater buses on interurban services;
As from September 2005, a free transport scheme for all students and elderly or disabled passengers has been introduced. The government has taken the responsibility of compensating the bus operators for this scheme, according to an agreed rate of payment per month.

Institutional Measures:

The government has approved the setting up of the new Land Transport Authority (LTA). Several group discussions with all stakeholders have taken place and a consultancy company is currently being procured to assist the ministry in the design and implementation of the LTA.

Shared taxi

Current situation

Taxis are licenced by the National Transport Authority on the island, with the majority providing local trips to the inhabitants of the localities from which they operate.

Taxis can be recognised by white registration plates with black figures, their identification signs on the roof and their base of operation, affixed on the front doors.

Urban Transport Strategies

Type of project: The Urban Transport Package of Measures

A package of measures:

In September 2006, a new package of measures, which includes some 18 specific transport measures, were prepared in close co-operation with a wide range of public and private transportation stakeholders as well as economic and scientific partners. These measures will form the basis of modernisation of the sector.

Those measures which relate specifically to public transport were:

Public Transport Development

It was recommended that an open exclusive bus-way right-of-way be developed in the Curepipe-Port Louis Corridor. It was also proposed that a bus lane be developed on the motorway between Trianon and Port Louis. Both projects would provide necessary infrastructure to vastly improve the mobility of people by public transport. Reforms to bus route structures and fares are also proposed. A bus-only road in Port Louis was also proposed. All studies are under way and implementation of some of the schemes are expected shortly.

Other measures include congestion pricing, parking measures, road construction and management and taxi industry reform.

National Transport Corporation (NTC)

Bonne Terre, Vacoas, Mauritius
Tel: (+230) 427 50 00
Fax: (+230) 426 54 89
e-mail: cnt.bus@intnet.mu
Web: www.ntc.intnet.mu

Key personnel

Chairperson: C R Dookun
General Manager: D R Daliah
Deputy General Manager: P K Dash
Traffic Manager: Mrs D N Varshney
Chief Engineer: B Rajkoomar
Financial Controller: L Ramjatton
Secretary/Administrative Manager: A F Mallam Hassam
Human Resources Manager: B K Ramlaul
   Staff: 2,864 (2008)

Passenger journeys: Approx 210,000 per day

Background

The National Transport Corporation (NTC), a parastatal body, was formed in 1979 and commenced operations in March 1980.

Current situation

The company had 524 vehicles, including 51 air-conditioned buses, in its fleet as at September 2008, and operates 101 routes. It also has a fleet of 43 school/student buses.

NTC operates one park-and-ride facility.

Developments

The Corporation recently purchased a further 100 air-conditioned, Euro 2 buses (80 Tata and 20 Ashok Leyland).

A new depot is proposed at Rivière des Galets, Souillac and a corporate headquarters is under construction at Ebène, scheduled to be completed by April 2009.

The company will shortly be requesting bids for new two-door, low-floor buses and seven minibuses.

NTC has purchased 220 electronic ticket issuing machines with the aim of introducing smart card technology.

Rose Hill Transport Ltd (RHT)

14 Hugnin Road, Rose Hill, Mauritius
Tel: (+230) 464 12 21   Fax: (+230) 464 60 23
e-mail: rht@intnet.mu
Web: www.rht.mu

Key personnel

Chairperson: H Goburdhun
Vice-Chairperson: Mrs N Sharma
Managing Director: Sanjiv Goburdhun
Bus Hire: D Perbhoo
Coach Hire: Mrs C Francis Goburdhun
Confidential Secretary: Mrs D Chan
   Staff: 320

Background

Formed in 1952, originally as Route No 1 Bus Service, the company became a limited company with its present name in 1954. RHT was the first bus operator in Mauritius.

Current situation

RHT has a fleet of 88 buses which carry approximately 12 million passengers a year on 10 routes. Its 24- to 60-seater buses may also be privately hired.

United Bus Service Ltd (UBS)

Royal Road, Les Cassis, Port Louis, Mauritius
Tel: (+230) 212 20 26; 20 28; 80 85
Fax: (+230) 212 13 61
e-mail: acc-ubs@intnet.mu

Key personnel

Managing Director: Swaleh Ramjane
   Staff: 1,550

Current situation

United Bus Service Ltd (UBS) is the largest private transport company in Mauritius.

Developments

The company will be using an Electronic Ticketing Machine (ETM) until the planned introduction of a smartcard system is implemented.

Triolet Bus Service Ltd (TBS)

TBS Lane, Triolet, Mauritius
Tel: (+230) 261 65 16, 68 49
Fax: (+230) 261 51 86
e-mail: tbus@intnet.mu

Key personnel

Managing Director: Lekram Nundlall
   Staff: 790

Current situation

Provides school services and excursions.

For details of the latest updates to *Jane's Urban Transport Systems* online and to discover the additional information available exclusively to online subscribers please visit

juts.janes.com

Mexico

Guadalajara

Population: City 1.6 million, metropolitan area 4.1 million (estimates)

Public transport

Trolleybus and some bus services operated by state authority and state owned enterprise. Light rail service; most bus services provided by independent operators who are mostly members of a co-operative.

Sistema de Transporte Colectivo de la Zona Metropolitana (Sistecozome)

Antiguo Central Camionera, Avendida Dr R Michel No 275, Col Las Conchas, CP 44100 Guadalajara, Jalisco, Mexico
Tel: (+52 33) 36 19 08 20   Fax: (+52 33) 36 50 04 85
e-mail: sistecozome@jalisco.gob.mx
Web: www.sistecozome.jalisco.gob.mx

Key personnel

Director General: Lazaro Salas Ramirez
Director of Administration and Finance: Antonio de Jesús Martinez Mendoza
Staff: 450 (estimate)

Current situation

Sistecozome is a public corporation formed in 1974. It also supervises a network of Colectivos on 81 routes. Sistecozome owns all vehicles and leases them to individual drivers.

Developments

The trolleybus system has suffered from a lack of funds and the number of serviceable trolleybuses has declined sharply. Service on Route 600 has been suspended since 2006, leaving routes 200, 400 and 500 still in operation.

Bus and trolleybus (Guadalajara only)

Passenger journeys: (2001) 36 million; 12 million by trolleybus (estimates)
Vehicle-km: Approx 11 million (annual)

Number of routes: Bus 5, trolleybus 3
Route length (one-way): Bus 213.1 km, trolleybus 39 km
On priority right-of-way: 34 km

Fleet: 136 buses
In peak service: Not currently available

Fleet: Approx 115 trolleybuses, many unserviceable
Fleet breakdown is not currently available, but is believed to include:
MASA/Toshiba (1982/85), many unserviceable   97
MASA/Toshiba articulated (1985/87 ex-Mexico City), many or all unserviceable   18

Most intensive service: 5 min
Fare structure: Trolleybus: flat, cash or coins or discount card
Fare collection system: Payment to driver
Fare evasion control: Roving inspectors
Average distance between stops: 300 m
Average peak-hour speed: 18 km/h
Operating costs financed by: Fares 75 per cent, other commercial sources 5 per cent, subsidy/grants 20 per cent
Subsidy from: Government
New vehicles financed by: State and federal governments

Sistema de Tren Eléctrico Urbano (Siteur)

Av Federalismo Sur No 217, 44100 Guadalajara, Mexico
Tel: (+52 33) 38 27 00 00   Fax: (+52 33) 36 05 26 64
e-mail: siteur@jalisco.gob.mx
Web: http://siteur.jalisco.gob.mx

Map of Guadalajara light rail   0519189

Key personnel

Director General: Jorge Méndez Gallegos
Director of Administration: Rodolfo Pérez Mercado
Director of Transport: Francisco Castillo Iñiguez
Head of Operations: Gustavo Pérez Romero
Staff: 694

Current situation

Siteur operates the light rail network and a small network of feeder buses. Initial 8.5 km section of east-west Line 2 opened 1994, linking Benito Juarez and Tetlan. This line (including the proposed 4.3 km western extension to Minerva, if built) is entirely underground except for a large new maintenance depot just beyond Tetlán terminus.

Plans for additional lines appear to have stalled.

Light rail

Type of operation: Light rail, first line opened 1989

Passenger journeys: (2001) 50.8 million
(2006) 62.1 million
Vehicle-km: (2006) 5.4 million

Route length: 24 km
in tunnel: 15.1 km
Number of lines: 2
Number of stations: 29
Gauge: 1,435 mm
Track: 115RE 52 kg/m rail on concrete sleepers
Electrification: 750 V DC, overhead

Rolling stock: 48 cars
Concarril/Melmex TLG88 (1989)   M16
Bombardier/Siemens TEG90 (1993/94)   M32
In peak service: 40

Service: Peak 5 min, off-peak 10 min
First/last car: 05.00/22.57
Fare structure: Stage; transfer fee payable between Lines 1 and 2
Fare collection: Coin or token to turnstile; electronic cards
Integration with other modes: Bus feeders to each terminal
Operating costs financed by: Fares 60 per cent

Bus

Passenger journeys: Not currently available

Current situation

Seven routes extending to 29 km are operated as feeders to the light rail network, run under contract with 27 vehicles.

Servicios y Transportes OPD (SYT)

Avenida Juan Gil Preciado No 6735, Col Jardines de Nuevo Mexico, CP 44150, Zapopan, Jalisco, Mexico
Tel: (+52 33) 38 36 33 20
Fax: (+52 33) 38 36 33 43
e-mail: OpdSyt@jalisco.gob.mx
jnegrete@jalisco.gob.mx
Web: http://syt.jalisco.gob.mx

Key personnel

Director General: Raul Romero Mora
Director of Administration and Finance: Jose de Leon Carrillo Jimenz
Director of Operations and Traffic: Jose Venegas Jiminez

Type of operations: Private bus

Current situation

Servicios y Transportes (SYT), established in 1990, is a franchised private company with 99 per cent of shares now held by the state of Jalisco.

Servicios y Transportes runs a fleet of about 900 vehicles.

Passenger journeys: (All private bus operations) (Annual) 500 million (estimate)
Vehicle-km: (All private bus operations) (Annual) 130 million (estimate)

Number of routes: 31
Route length: Not currently available

One-person operation: All routes
Fare collection: Payment to driver, or pre-purchase
Fare structure: Flat, depending on route
Average speed: 15 km/h

Alianza de Camioneros de Jalisco AC

Circuito Jorge Alvarez del Castillo No 1078, Col Mezquitan Country, CP 44260, Guadalajara, Jalisco, Mexico
Tel: (+52 33) 38 48 52 00
e-mail: alianza-camioneros@hotmail.com
camioneros@megared.net.mx
Web: www.alianza-camioneros.com.mx

Type of operations: Private bus

Current situation

Alianza de Camioneros de Jalisco AC, an owners' co-operative formed in 1957, has 730 licence-holders who between them own 1,642 buses; the maximum number of buses that can be owned by any licence-holder is five. Operations are divided into seven sectors of 10-15 routes each. Alianza oversees operations with a small staff; all maintenance is contracted out. New vehicles are financed from a renewals fund supplied by 20 per cent of daily fares receipts.

Passenger journeys: (All private bus operations) 500 million (annual)
Vehicle-km: (All private bus operations) 130 million (annual)

Number of routes: 64
Route length: Not currently available

One-person operation: All routes
Fare collection: Payment to driver, or pre-purchase
Fare structure: Flat, depending on route
Average speed: 15 km/h

Mexico City

Population: 8.6 million federal district (2000 Census), 16.7 million metropolitan zone

Public transport

Trolleybus, light rail and metro and some bus services operated for urban area by separate public authorities, with many additional bus services run by concessionaires under overall control of co-ordinating body. Extensive private 'colectivo' shared taxi operation and privately run suburban bus services.

Secretaría de Transportes y Vialidad (STV – Setravi)

Avenida Álvaro Obregón 269, Piso 10, Colonia Roma, Mexico City DF 06700, Mexico
Tel: (+52 55) 33 30 30
e-mail: aquintero@df.gob.mx
Web: www.setravi.df.gob.mx

Key personnel

Secretary of Transport: Raúl Armando Quintero Martínez
Director of Information: Ricardo Quintero Magaña
Director General of Transport: Martín Mejía Zayas

Current situation

STV (Setravi) came into being at the beginning of 1995 as successor to the Coordinación General de Transporte. It is responsible for regulation of the city's public transport, and for control of roads, streets and parking. One of its first tasks was to cope with the shut-down of the state-owned city bus operator Ruta 100, which STV replaced in 2000 with a new state-owned bus operator, RTP.

Currently, some bus services are provided by RTP while other are operated by numerous private operators, under concessions which STV awarded during the five-year period between Ruta 100's bankruptcy and the creation of RTP.

Extensive shared taxi 'colectivo' operations continue, with about 60,000 vehicles, and suburban bus services remain in private hands.

Considerable problems are faced in catering for the massive demands of the world's fastest-growing urban area. A further complication is the pressure created by the high levels of atmospheric pollution. Transport provision, in particular the metro, has been expanded rapidly to handle some 30 million daily journeys in the city region. Government environmental regulations stipulate that the city's 2.8 million cars and commercial vehicles must not be used on one day each week, and taxis and 'colectivo' minibuses must be fitted with catalytic converters.

Amongst many proposals for public transport improvements have been schemes to expand trolleybus and light rail, and several extensions to the trolleybus system have been opened since 1995, some merely being reinstatements of services which were withdrawn in 1991–93. Several are, however, newly built trolleybus routes.

Shared taxis

Current situation

STV advises that there has been a considerable increase in the number of taxis in the city during the past 3–4 years, with the number of shared taxis standing at approximately 10,000 plus some 92,000 conventional taxis.

These services are estimated to carry between 8 and 10 million passengers daily.

Red de Transporte de Pasajeros del Distrito Federal (RTP)

Serapio Rendón 114, 4th Floor, Colonia San Rafael, Del Cuauhtémoc, CP 06470, Mexico City DF, Mexico
Tel: (+52 55) 57 05 55 95
Fax: (+52 55) 57 05 33 37
e-mail: publicidad@rtp.gob.mx
Web: www.rtp.gob.mx

Mexico City light rail and metro

1115209

Key personnel

Director General: Ariadna Montiel Reyes
Director of Operations: Oscar del Cueto García
Staff: Not currently available

Passenger journeys: (2002) 232.9 million
(2003) 217.6 million
(2004) 243.9 million
Vehicle-km: Approx 190,000 daily

Number of routes: 88 (2006)
Route length: 3,093.6 km

Background

RTP was established on 1 April 2000 as a new department of the federal district administration, to be the permanent successor to the former Ruta 100. The organisation is believed to be essentially the same as Ruta 100's, but the agency took five years to establish and is thought to be much smaller than Ruta 100.

After Ruta 100's bankruptcy, many bus routes were discontinued and passengers had no option but to use 'jitney' services, whilst suburban operators temporarily extended their services into the urban area. A temporary government agency, named Consejo de Incautación, managed operations of the remaining routes, with reduced service on many of those, and STV began offering concessions for all bus routes to private companies via competitive tendering.

During the next four years, the majority of the most profitable routes were given over to private operators, with Consejo de Incautación operating the other routes, until RTP was established.

Current situation

RTP currently provides bus services on a network of some 3,500 km. Travel on RTP services accounts for approximately four per cent of the total journeys in Mexico City.

Fleet: 1,300 buses

MASA/Somex S-502m (prior to 2000)	80
Prototype bus (prior to 2000)	175
Articulated U-18 (prior to 2000)	40
Ayco 3000 RE (2001)	237
Ayco Discap (2001)	26
Ayco 30030 RE (2001)	110
Ayco 30030 (2001)	100
Reco 4700 SFC (2001)	229
Reco Discap (2001)	25
Mercedes-Benz Torino (2002, 2004)	258
In peak service: 1,035	

First/last bus: 04.00/23.00
Fare structure: Flat
Arrangements for elderly/disabled: Senior citizens travel free of charge

Metrobús

Avenida Cuauhtémoc número 16, 5° piso, Colonia Doctores Delegación Cuauhtémoc, CP 06720, Mexico City DF, Mexico
Tel: (+52 55) 57 61 68 58, 57 61 68 60
e-mail: oip@metrous.df.gob.mx
Web: www.metrobus.df.gob.mx

Key personnel

Director General: Guillermo Calderón Aguilera
Manager, Public Information: Juan Manuel Gómez Rodríguez
Staff: Not currently available

Type of operation: Bus Rapid Transit (BRT)

Passenger journeys: (2007) 94.9 million (estimate)
Vehicle-km: Not currently available

Number of routes: 1
Route length: 20 km
Number of stops: 36

Current situation
In June 2005, the Metrobús Bus Rapid Transit (BRT) corridor was opened. The route is 20 km long and has 36 stops, operated by new articulated buses. The project was funded by a public-private partnership and cost an estimated USD50 million.

The STV created a separate body to operate Metrobús.

Developments
Construction of an 8.5 km extension of the first line, Ruta A (avenida Insurgentes), southwards to Monumento al Caminero began in mid-2007 and construction of a second line, Ruta B, along Eje 4, began in late 2007.

There are plans to build as many as nine further BRT lines.

Fleet: 98 buses
Scania articulated (2005)   98

Servicio de Transportes Eléctricos del Distrito Federal (STE)
Av Municipio Libre 402 Ote, Col San Andrés Tetepilco Del Iztapalapa, Mexico City 09440, DF, Mexico
Tel: (+52 55) 25 95 00 64, 25 95 00 00
Fax: (+52 55) 55 39 26 49
e-mail: infoste@df.gob.mx
   dt@ste.df.gob.mx
Web: www.ste.df.gob.mx

Key personnel
Director General: Rufino H León Tovar
Director, Transportation: Martín López Delgado
  Staff: 2,700

Current situation
STE is responsible for operation of trolleybus routes and a light rail line.

Developments
In 2003, the two-branched southern portion of Route F reverted to being operated as R1 and R2, bringing the total number of routes at that time back to 17.

Trolleybus routes K1 and T1 were extended by 2 km from San Lorenzo Tezonco in October 2004, to serve the newly opened university campus.

In September 2005, STE opened a new trolleybus route connecting the Politécnico metro station with the Instituto Politécnico Nacional (IPN).

In November 2006, routes R1 and R2 were extended northwards from Metro Escuadrón 201 to Metro Moctezuma.

In stages between October 2007 and January 2008, trolleybus Ñ was withdrawn, to clear the way for construction of its replacement, a new (but not electrified) Metrobús route.

Trolleybus
Passenger journeys: (2004) 68.8 million
(2005) 69.1 million
(2006) 67.0 million
(2007) 67.1 million
(2008) 31.0 million (to 30 June 2008)

Number of routes: 18
Route length: 445.5 km

Fleet: 405 trolleybuses
New Flyer Series 3200 (1875)	5
MASA/Toshiba Series 4200 (1981)	40
MASA/Toshiba Series 4300-4400 (1984/85)	115
MASA/Toshiba Series 4700 (1988)	30
MASA/Kiepe Series 7000 (1990)	15
MASA/Mitsubishi Series 9000 (1997-99)	200

In peak service: About 326
Trolleybus electrification: 600 V DC

Most intensive service: 7¾ min
One-person operation: All routes

Fare collection: Payment to driver
Fare structure: Flat, no transfers
Fare evasion control: Driver's check
Arrangements for elderly/disabled: By official decree, with effect from 27 December 2001 senior citizens travel free

Light rail (Tren Ligero)
Passenger journeys: (2004) 17.5 million
(2005) 18.3 million
(2006) 19.7 million
(2007) 21.0 million
(2008) 9.7 million (to 30 June 2008)

Route length: 12.76 km
Number of routes: 1
Number of stations: 16 (plus two termini)
Max gradient: 1%
Min curve radius: 30 m
Electrification: 750 V DC, overhead

Current situation
Links to metro Line 2 terminus at Tasqueña with Xochimilco.

Developments
The outer terminus of the line, Embarcadero, has been renamed Xochimilco and the penultimate station, which had been the terminus until 1995 and had been named Xochimilco, has been renamed Fco Goitia.

Work on a new terminal at Xochimilco started in November 2007.

Service: Peak 4 min, off-peak 6 min
First/last car: 05.00/23.00
Fare structure: Flat, single

Subway car for STC, Mexico (Bombardier Transportation)   0585133

CNCF FM86 trainset on STC's Line A at Pantitlán station   1112502

Fare collection: Ticket machines at all stations; magnetic ticket activates turnstile access
Arrangements for elderly/disabled: By official decree, with effect from 27 December 2001 senior citizens travel free

Rolling stock: 16 cars
Concarril/Siemens TE-90 articulated (1990/01)	M12
Bombardier/Siemens TE-95 (1995)	M4
In peak service: 15
On order: Four six-axle articulated LRVs from Bombardier for delivery in late 2009

Sistema de Transporte Colectivo (STC)
Sistema de Transporte Colectivo, Delicias 67, Colonia Centro, Delegación Cuahutémoc, CP 06070 DF, Mexico
Tel: (+52 55) 57 09 11 33   Fax: (+52 55) 57 09 07 44
Web: www.metro.df.gob.mx

Key personnel
Director General: Florencia Serrania Soto
Manager, Social Communication and Public
  Relations: Raúl Bretón Salinas
  Luis Moya 102, Planta Alta, Colonia Centro, Delegación Cuahutémoc, CP 06070 DF, Mexico
  e-mail: rbreton@metro.df.gob.mx

Type of operation: Full metro, first line opened 1969

Passenger journeys: (2001) 1,434 million
(2002) 1,396 million
(2003) 1,375 million

Car-km: (2001) 348 million
(2002) 344 million
(2003) 331 million

Route length: 201.4 km
   in tunnel: 113.3 km
   elevated: 18.5 km
Number of lines: 11
Number of stations: 175
Gauge: 1,436 mm (auxiliary guide rails, except Line A)
Track: Guideway for rubber tyres, security rail (39.6 kg/m); Line A is steel-wheel (56.9 kg/m rail)
Max gradient: 7%
Min curve radius: 105 m
Tunnel: Concrete caisson or bored tunnel with double-track
Electrification: 750 V DC, collected from two lateral guide bars; Line A, overhead

Service: Peak 1 min 55 s
First/last train: 05.00/24.00
Fare structure: Flat; single-trip
Revenue control: Turnstiles
Operating costs financed by: Fares 42.4 per cent, other commercial sources 4.6 per cent, Distrito Federal government 42.5 per cent, federal contributions (FIES) 10.5 per cent
Integration with other modes: 52 stations are connected with other lines, one with the STE and 44 with CETRAMS
One-person operation: All services
Signalling: Automatic block and interlocking; ATO; three control centres

Rolling stock: 3,139 cars (all rubber-tyred, except for steel-wheeled for line A – marked*)

Alsthom MP68 (1969/73)	M352 T176
CNCF NM73A-B-C (1975/79)	M231 T114
CNCF NM79 (1980/83)	M350 T177
Alsthom MP82 (1982/83)	M150 T177
Bombardier NC82 (1982/83)	M120 T60
CNCF NM83A (1984/85)	M184 T91
CNCF NM83B (1986/89)	M150 T74
CNCF FM86 (1990/92)*	M80 T86
CNCF FM95A (1998/99)*	M12 T6
CAF NE92 (1994/95)	M96 T48
Bombardier NM02 (2004/06)	M270 T135

On order: The Bombardier trainsets listed in the above table are being delivered from 2004 to 2006. The car shells and train design are being developed jointly with CAF.

Developments
East-west Line B (23.7 km, 21 stations) opened in stages, from Buenavista to Villa de Aragón in December 1989 and from Nezahualcóyotl to Ciudad Azteca in November 2000. This is the first rubber-tyred line to extend beyond the Distrito Federal boundary.

STC's master plan envisages expansion to 17 lines with 342 route-km.

Ferrocarriles Suburbanos SA de CV

Estación Terminal Buenavista, Avenida Insurgentes Norte, Esq Eje 1 Norte (Mosqueta), Col Buenavista, Deleg Cuauhtémoc, CP 06350, México DF, México
Tel: (+52 55) 19 46 07 90
Web: www.fsuburbanos.com

Key personnel
Director General: Maximiliano Zurita
   Staff: Not currently available

Type of operation: Suburban heavy rail

Passenger journeys: Not yet available
Train-km: Not yet available

Background
In August 2005, a 30-year concession to design, build and operate a 27 km suburban railway linking Buenavista, in Mexico City, with Cuautitlán, in Mexico state (Edomex), was awarded to the CAF-ICF consortium by the Secretariat of Communications and Transport (SCT).

About 50 per cent of the project's cost, estimated at USD500-600 million, is to be provided by the Mexican federal government, with the remainder coming from the consortium through internally generated funds and bank loans. Initial works associated with the project commenced in late 2005.

The CAF-ICF consortium, in which there is a Mexican shareholding of 20 per cent, is led by Spanish train-builder CAF; other participants include ADIF, Alcatel, Elecnor, Indra, Ineco and OHL.

Future development phases are expected to extend the initial system (Sistema 1) to 79 km, including a 22 km extension north to Huehuetoca and a 21 km branch to Xaltocán. In the longer term the initial Ferrocarriles Suburbanos system could form part of a 242 km three-line integrated network.

Developments
The initial 27 km standard-gauge electrified line is provided with seven stations, two of which are to provide connections with Mexico City's metro system. Construction was completed in 2007.

Services on a 22 km section between Buenavista and Lechería, serving five stations, commenced in April 2008; services on the remaining 5 km to Cuautitlán, serving two additional stations, are due to start in October 2008. At peak periods, trains run every six minutes in each direction; off-peak frequencies are six or four trains per hour. With a maximum journey time of 25 minutes, the line is expected to carry 282,000 passengers per day in the first year of the concession and 400,000 in the final year.

Rolling stock
CAF initially supplied 20 three-car emus, based on the design of RENFE's Class 447 units but configured to operate from a 25 kV AC power supply. The contract covers provision of a fourth car for each unit as demand for capacity grows. Test running with the first trains to be delivered commenced in late 2007.

Monterrey

Population: 1.1 million, Metropolitan area 3.8 million (2005 estimates)

Public transport
Bus services overseen by public authority; light rail/metro.

Sistema de Transporte Colectivo Metrorrey (STC Metrorrey)
Av Pino Suárez, 1123 Norte, CP-64000 Monterrey, Nuevo León, Mexico
Tel: (+52 81) 83 72 85 21
Fax: (+52 81) 83 74 08 80
e-mail: rolando.valle@nl.gob.mx,
   alfonso.reyes@nl.gob.mx
Web: www.nl.gob.mx/?P=metrorrey

Key personnel
Director General: Rolando Valle Favela
Director of Operations, Metro:
   Alfonso Reyes Santa Anna
Director of Operations, TransMetro and Metrobus:
   José Luis Cantú
Director, Administration and Finance: Manuel Chapa Gónzalez
Traffic Manager: Ernesto Picón Rubio

Light rail
Type of operation: Light rail, initial route (Line 1) opened 1991

Passenger journeys: (2000) 36.2 million
(2005) 57.2 million

Route length: 26.2 km
Number of lines: 2

Number of stations: 28
Gauge: 1,435 mm
Electrification: 1.5 kV DC, overhead

Current situation
Line 1 is an L-shaped elevated route running east-west and north-south, linking San Bernabé northwest with Exposición southeast. The initial section of Line 2 (4.8 km, six stations), opened in November 1994, runs north-south from General Anaya to Fundadores and west-east to Zaragoza and downtown Monterrey. Planned additional Lines 3, 4 and 5, plus extensions to existing lines, would bring network total to more than 90 km.

In June 2002, an extension to Line 1 from San Bernabé to Talleres was opened.

Developments
Construction on an 8.5 km extension to Line 2 (1.5 km in tunnel, 7 km elevated), started in August 2005, with completion scheduled for late 2007. It will run northwards from General Anaya station to a new terminus at Sendero and will have seven stations. The contact for the extension was awarded to a consortium consisting of Siemens Transportation Systems (TS), Bombardier Transportation Mexico and Constructora Garza Ponce. The total contract value is approximately USD244 million, with Bombardier's share standing at USD43 million.

Bombardier Transportation was awarded the contract to design and build 14 high-floor LRVs for the extension for some USD43 million. The vehicles were due for delivery in October 2007.

In October 2007, the first section of the northward extension of Line 2 was opened. It runs from General Anaya to Universidad (3.2 km, 3 stations). The remaining stretch, with a further

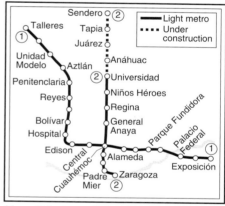

Map of Monterrey light rail/metro   1124827

four stations, is currently scheduled to open in early 2008.

Rolling stock: 70 articulated cars

Concarril (1990)	M25
Concarril (1993)	M23
CAF Line 2 (1994/95)	M22

On order: 14 Bombardier LRVs for Line 2 extension, for delivery in October 2007

Service: Peak 3½ min; off-peak: 8 min
First/last car: 05.00/24.00
Fare structure: Flat
Fare collection: Automatic system with reusable plastic tickets, multiple-trip tickets available
Operating costs financed by: Fares 100 per cent

Transmetro and Metrobus
Transmetro bus services operate with more than 30 buses on four routes. The service is operated

by a private operator, but overseen by Metrorrey, to improve public transport coverage. It provides a service at six minute intervals to a population of some 28,000 and operates from 05.30 to 22.30

daily. Metro tickets include a free transfer to Transmetro services.

Metrobus, a separate bus service, also links to Metrorrey stations, and operates with an

integrated fare system, which allows passengers to travel on Metrobus services plus the Metro. Metrobus ridership exceeds 37,000 passengers per day.

Namibia

Windhoek
Population: 223,364 (2001 Census)

Public transport
Bus services provided by municipal authority, with additional services by an independent operator.

City of Windhoek (WCC)
Bus Service Division
PO Box 59, 80 Independence Avenue, Windhoek, Namibia
Tel: (+264 61) 290 26 88/9
Fax: (+264 61) 290 25 46
e-mail: kaf@windhoekcc.org.na
Web: www.windhoekcc.org.na

Key personnel
Chief, Corporate Communications, Marketing and Customer Care: Ndangi Katoma
General Manager, Bus: Anton Muller
Staff: 86

Current situation
Bus service are provided by the Bus Service Division of the City of Windhoek. Services

are geared to peak-hour movement between townships and industrial areas, and there are no off-peak or leisure services.

Developments
Currently, the services run at a loss, which is recouped from property tax. There is some indication that the city council will investigate the possibility of outsourcing the services.

Bus
Route length: 575 km
Number of routes: 10 scheduled

Fleet: 60 buses

Mercedes OF16/17/Busaf B65F (1975/83)	16
Mercedes OF14/19/De Haan B65F (1985)	2
Mercedes OF14/19/Busaf B65F (1982)	2
Mercedes OF16/24/Busaf Sheerline (1992)	15
Nissan CB20N/Busaf B65F (1980)	7
Nissan CB20N/Busaf B70 (1991)	3
Mercedes OF16/24 (1992)	15

In peak service: 48
Average age of fleet: 10 years

Most intensive service: 30 min; most routes run commuting hours only, no evening service
One-person operation: All routes

Fare collection: Cash or prepurchase token to driver
Fare structure: Flat, 2 zones
Fare evasion control: Random inspectors
Arrangements for elderly/disabled: Reduced fare
Operating costs financed by: Fares 90 per cent, other commercial sources 10 per cent

Bailey's Transport (Pty) Ltd
PO Box 10330, Khomasdal, Windhoek, Namibia
Tel: (+264 61) 26 25 22, 37 57
Fax: (+264 61) 26 26 50

Street address
Bailey's Building, 3 Hansa Street, Northern Industrial Area, Lafrenz Township, Windhoek, Namibia.

Key personnel
Contact: C Jackson

Current situation
Runs services from Khomasdal township to Windhoek, and other routes on contract to employers, including minibus-operated off-peak services. Fleet of Mercedes/Busaf buses, plus some Japanese minibuses.

Nepal

Kathmandu
Population: 1.1 million (estimate)

Public transport
Bus and trolleybus services provided in populous area including neighbouring cities of Patan and Bhaktapur, with additional private buses and minibuses and extensive use of rickshaws, autorickshaws (based on motor scooters) and taxis.

Nepal Department of Transport and Management (DOTM)
Ministry of Works and Transport
1984 New Baneshwore, Kathmandu, Nepal
Tel: (+977 1) 483845, 483946, 483844

Key personnel
Director General: Chhabiraj Pant

Chief of Trolleybus Services:
Damodar Lama
Contact: Baija Nath Mallik
Staff: 250

Current situation
Established in 1966 to operate the country's two short railways. In 1974 inaugurated the trolleybus route from Kathmandu to Bhaktapur, a gift from the Chinese government. Bus operations started at the same time.

Trolleybus
Developments
The trolleybus system closed in 2001.

The system reopened in September 2003, after almost two years of suspension. The Nepal Transport Corporation was dissolved at the end of 2001, and the system is now run by a consortium of three municipalities – Kathmandu, Bhaktapur and Madhyapur. Only three vehicles, from the

six serviceable vehicles available, are currently running on a 5 km section of the 13 km route. There are believed to be a further 14 vehicles in need of repair.

Bus
Passenger journeys: 10 million (annual)
Vehicle-km: 1 million (annual)

Number of routes: 7
Route length: 80 km

Fleet: Approx 100 buses, all Isuzu

Most intensive service: Off-peak 12 min
One-person operation: None
Fare collection: By seated conductors on board at front of vehicle, or at roadside on boarding or alighting
Fare structure: Stage (4-stage) colour-coded tickets issued by conductors

Netherlands

Amsterdam
Population: City 744,736, urban area 1.0 million, Greater Amsterdam 1.5 million, metropolitan area Randstad 6.6 million (2006)

Public transport
Bus, metro, ferry, light rail and tram services operated by municipal transport department under national operating and financial framework. Suburban rail services provided by Netherlands Railways (NS) and buses by regional bus undertakings.

Gemeentevervoerbedrijf (GVB)
PO Box 2131, 1000 CC Amsterdam, Netherlands
Tel: (+31 20) 460 60 60   Fax: (+31 20) 460 60 66
Web: www.gvb.nl

Street address
Arlandaweg 100, 1048 HP Amsterdam, Netherlands

Key personnel
Chairman: J C M Hovers
Managing Director: J G Kroon

Technical Manager: M A G Weijenberg
Resources Manager: P F D Scotte
Transport Manager: A Bolier
Staff: Approximately 4,500

Passenger journeys (all modes): (2002) 250 million
(2003) 244 million
(2004) 242 million
(2005) 248 million
(2006) 253 million

Passenger-km (all modes): (2002) 971.7 million
(2003) 948 million
(2004) 941 million
(2005) 956.35 million
(2006) 986.95 million

Operating costs financed by: Not currently available
Subsidy from: Not currently available

Background

Officially founded in 1900, GVB serves a core area of the City of Amsterdam and the adjacent communities of Diemen and Amstelveen. Since 2002 it has been officially known by its initials GVB.

Current situation

GVB provides tram, metro/light rail, bus and ferry services.

Developments

City Cargo is negotiating with the city council for a fleet of 10–20 cargo trams to start service in 2008.

There are plans to purchase 150 new metro cars to replace the original cars and to operate on the new North/South line.

Bus

Number of routes: 66 (includes peak service, 'Movers' (school peak service), direct lines and 11 night bus routes)

Route length: (One way) 422 km
On priority right-of-way: 34.6 km

Fleet: 260 vehicles
Standard buses   Not currently available
Standard low-floor   Not currently available
Articulated
 low-floor buses   Not currently available
Articulated buses   Not currently available
Minibuses   Not currently available

Most intensive service: Not currently available
One-person operation: All routes
Fare collection: Prepurchase or payment to driver for strip tickets and day tickets, checked by driver.
Fare structure: Zonal; prepurchase weekly, monthly and annual passes, multiday tickets and national Strippenkaart scheme tickets, last also available on board and valid for transfers; 1 h ride-at-will ticket; services operate all night with higher flat fare.

Under the Strippenkaart system, the Netherlands is split into zones of 4.5 km each. National prepurchase season tickets, weekly, monthly and annual, can be bought for one zone or more and used on all buses, metro, tramways and urban railways of all companies in the zone(s) paid for. Single rides can be made with the national Strippenkaart, prepurchased in 15 and 45 strips, or from drivers in 2, 3 and 8 strips, cancelling one strip for each zone, plus one 'boarding fee'
Fare evasion control: Bus driver and roving inspectors; spot fines
Operational control: Centralised control through centre linked to buses by mobile radio and with CCTV installed at a number of key points for observation; all buses equipped with VETAG
Average distance between stops: 495 m (intended maximum 5 min walking distance)
Bus priority: 34.6 km of reserved bus lanes and traffic light priority
Average peak-hour speed: 16.5 km/h
Integration with other modes: Interchanges at main stations; fully integrated fares and ticket system

Developments

In March 2006, GVB started trials of three Mercedes-Benz Citaro prototype hybrid fuel cell buses on two routes, under the EU CUTE programme. The trials ended in January 2007.

Zuidtangent

Connexxion

Antwoordennummer 1860, 200, WC Haarlem, Netherlands
Tel: 0900 266 63 99   Fax: (+31 23) 542 84 18
e-mail: klantenservice@connexxion.nl
Web: www.connexxion.nl

GVB buses in front of Centraal Station (Peter Roelofs)   1327958

Mercedes-Benz Citaro fuel cell bus, on test with GVB during 2006 (René van den Burg)   1327955

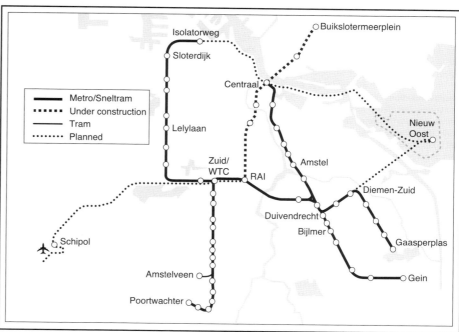

Map of Amsterdam's metro and sneltram   0567317

Current situation

The first section of this busway, which connects Schipol airport with Haarlem and Amsterdam Southeast, opened in January 2002. This initial section has a length of 24 km, with 16 stations and is almost all on an exclusive busway, except for short stretches at the airport and in Haarlem city centre. The whole system has a length of 40 km.

There are good intermodal connections along the route and some stations have parking facilities. The stations have electronic information boards and the system has priority signalling for the vehicles.

About 25,000 passengers use the system daily.

Developments

Two extensions to the system are planned. The first, to Nuew-vennep, southwest of Schipol, is under construction with a scheduled 2005 opening, and the second, at the Amsterdam end of the route, is proposed to run to the Ijmeer area.

Fleet: 33 Van Hool low-floor articulated buses

Metro/light rail (sneltram)

Type of operation: Full metro and hybrid metro/light rail (sneltram)

Route length: 81.2 km
  in tunnel: 5.5 km
  elevated: 24 km
Number of lines: 4
Number of stations: 49
  in tunnel: 5
  elevated: 30
Gauge: 1,435 mm
Track: 49 kg/m S 49 rail, concrete sleepers on ballast
Tunnel: Mainly concrete caisson
Electrification: 750 V DC, third rail/600 V DC, overhead

Service: Peak 3¾-7½ min, off-peak 5–15 min
First/last train: 05.37/00.25
Fare structure: Nationwide zonal system
Revenue control: Ticket and cancelling machines in all entrances, roving inspectors, inspection at entrances
One-person operation: All trains up to 3 coupled sets
Central control: All operations monitored from central control room; CCTV on all platforms

Rolling stock: 44 two-car sets, 37 dual-voltage LRVs, 25 (third rail) LRVs

Linke-Hofmann-Busch M2 (1976/77)	M66
Linke-Hofmann-Busch M3 (1980)	M14
BN dual-voltage Amstelveen line S1 (1990)	M13
BN dual-voltage S2 (1994)	M12
CAF dual-voltage S3 (1996)	M4
CAF single-voltage	M33
Other	M8

Current situation

Light rail line from Zuid-WTC to Amstelveen (Winkelcentrum) and Middenhoven opened 1990 (see below). The route is electrified at 600 V DC overhead, and is operated by cars with both third rail and overhead current collection to allow through running from the metro. Part of the route, between Amstelveen and Zuid-WTC (5 km), is also used by tram Route 5 (see below). A second new metro/sneltram opened in May 1997, the 11 km linking Isolatorweg with Zuid-WTC. This forms a ring route (Line 50) round the east, south and west sides of the city, with trains running through from Gein on the metro.

A further stage saw the ring extended from Isolatorweg to Centraal Station, with a later extension (the IJ line) along the banks of the IJ to the future Nieuw Oost residential area.

Developments

Smartcard use on the metro started in early 2006.

Developments
North/South Line (under construction)

Department of Infrastructure, Traffic and Transportation

Projectbureau North/South Line, Communication Department
Postbus 95089, NL-1090 HB Amsterdam, Netherlands
Tel: (+31 20) 556 54 26
e-mail: info.noordzuidlijn@ivv.amsterdam.nl
Web: www.northsouthline.com,
  www.ivv.amsterdam.nl/nzlijn

Information point

Quellijnsraat 83, Amsterdam
Tel: (+31 20) 470 40 70   Fax: (+31 20) 470 40 71

Construction on the first section of the planned North/South Line started in 2003. The 9.5 km line will run from Buikslotermeerplein in Amsterdam North, via Centraal Station and end at the Zuid/WTC station.

The initial work is being undertaken on the construction of the underground portion of the line, between Centraal Station and Ceintuurbaan station. There will be eight stations on this line, with the possibility of a further station at Sixhaven, and the construction/completion schedule is as follows:
Buikslotermeerplein and Jona Van Hasseltweg stations: construction commenced late 2004, completion 2009;
Centraal station: construction started 2003, completion 2009;
Rokin station: construction commenced January 2003, completion late 2008;
Vijzelgracht station: construction started April 2003, completion late 2008;
Ceintuurbaan station: construction started April 2003, completion late 2008;
Europaplein station: construction commenced late 2005, completion 2009;
Connection station at Zuid/WTC: construction commences 2005, completion 2010.

There are plans to further expand this line southwards, to Amsterdam Airport Schiphol and possibly to the suburb of Hoofddorp.

The line is expected to be completed in 2011, at a total cost of EUR1.5 billion, which is being financed by the City of Amsterdam (EUR346 million) and the Dutch Government.

A Siemens-built GVB Combino tram on an extension of the Amsterdam tram network: Line 19 has been extended into the redeveloped port area, east of the Central Station (Quintus Vosman)
1327858

GVB trams. Routes are shown by colour-coded 'flags' on the destination boards (Peter Roelofs)
1327959

Tramway
Staff: 1,564

Type of operation: Conventional tramway

Route length: 80.5 km
    reserved track: 66 km
Number of routes: 16
Number of stops: 762
Gauge: 1,435 mm
Track: Ri60 60 kg/m rail, timber sleepers on concrete or ballast
Electrification: 600 V DC, overhead

Service: Peak 5-9 min, off-peak 6-12 min, evening 10-15 min, weekends 5-15 min
First/last car: 05.41/00.33
Fare structure: As bus and metro; nationwide zonal system
Revenue control: Conductors, roving inspectors
One-person operation: Conductors reintroduced on all lines
Centralised control: Mobile radio contact between drivers and control room; automatic vehicle location and control on all lines, with countdown to departure information in cabs and real-time punctuality data displayed at stops. VETAG/VECOM detection system for traffic light priority, points control and vehicle identification

Rolling stock: 236 double-articulated tramcars

Ferry
Ferries Division
Aambeeldstraat 8, 1021 KB Amsterdam, Netherlands
Tel: (+31 20) 460 50 05

Current situation
GVB has been providing ferry services for more than 100 years. Currently, it provides four services:

Distelweg Ferry
Carries foot passengers, bicycles, mopeds, motor cycles, cars and lorries. It operates on weekdays only between 06.30 and 19.40. A fare is charged.

Buiksloterweg Ferry
Carries foot passengers, bicycles and mopeds 24 hours a day free of charge. It carries approximately 4.5 million passengers a year.

Adelaarsweg Ferry
Free of charge and carries foot passengers, bicycles and mopeds. Times of operation are 06.20–23.57. Total passenger journeys are approximately 2 million per year.

Waterbus
Carries foot passengers and bicycles. It is free of charge between Amsterdam Centraal station and Java-eiland and a fee of EUR1.10 per person is charged for the journey to Aambeldstraat or Boorstraat in Amsterdam Nord. The Waterbus operates from 06.15 to 21.25 and carries approximately 500,000 passengers a year.

Fleet: 8 vessels
Ro-Ro ferry (Distelweg Ferry)	2
30 Series IJ ferries (Adelaarsweg Ferry and other services)	3
3 IJ-veren 40 Series IJ ferries (Buiksloterweg Ferry)	3

Other ferries

Connexxion Fast Flying Ferries
Web: www.fastflyingferries.nl

Current situation
Connexxion operates the Fast Flying Ferries from Centraal Station to Velsen-Zuid (Pontplein). The service operate every half an hour Monday to Saturday and every hour on Sunday and holidays. The journey time is about 25 minutes.

Fleet: 3 HYD Voschod-2M hydrofoils

GVB ferry, leaving the south bank of the IJ, heading for Buiksloterweg (Peter Roelofs)   1327957

NS bi-level commuter train at Zaanstad station (Peter Roelofs)   1330089

NS-Groep NV – Nederlandse Spoorwegen (NS) – Netherlands Railways
PO Box 2025, NL-3500 HA Utrecht, Netherlands
Tel: (+31 30) 235 40 00
Fax: (+31 30) 235 61 93
Web: www.ns.nl

Street address
Laan van Puntenburg 100, NL-3511 ER, Utrecht, Netherlands

Key personnel
President: Aad Veenman
Commercial Director: Bert Meerstadt

Type of operation: Suburban heavy rail

Current situation
Suburban and interurban services, electrified at 1.5 kV DC, radiate from Amsterdam Centraal station on several routes and carry heavy traffic. Nine stations within city boundaries served by 3 to 31 trains hourly, with more at peak times.

Because of the dense pattern of NS operations, differentiation of 'suburban' services is hard; no distinction is made by NS, nor separate traffic figures kept. Stations within city boundaries are included in the Strippenkaart system, and trains are used as alternatives to bus and trams, particularly for interchange with other NS services. There is also much longer distance commuting.

Developments
The station at Amsterdam Zuid WTC is being developed to cope with extra demands imposed by high-speed services. A major new station is to be built at Amsterdam Zuid, with completion scheduled for 2015.

The Hague

Population: 457,726 (provisional data), service area 678,000

Public transport

Bus and tramway services (including interurban route to Delft) provided by company owned by the city, with additional suburban bus services operated by regional bus undertakings. Suburban rail services provided by Netherlands Railways (NS).

The regional body, responsible for the overall co-ordination of public transport, is:

Stadsgewest Haaglanden
PO Box 66, Grote Marktstraat 43, NL-2501 CB Den Haag, Netherlands
Tel: (+31 70) 750 15 00 Fax: (+31 70) 750 15 01
e-mail: informatie@haaglanden.nl
Web: www.haaglanden.nl

HTM Personenvervoer NV (HTM)

PO Box 28503, Fluwelen Burgwal 58, NL-2502 KM Den Haag, Netherlands
Tel: (+31 70) 374 90 00 Fax: (+31 70) 384 87 29
e-mail: info@htm.net
Web: www.htm.net

Key personnel
Director General: G A Kaper
Head of Communications: Frank Wetters
    Staff: 2,207 (2002 – excludes tour operator branch and City of Dordrecht)

Passenger boardings: (2000) 126.4 million
(2001) 125.7 million
(2002) 125.9 million

Operating costs financed by: Fares 36 per cent, subsidy 58 per cent, other income 6 per cent
Subsidy from: Government

Current situation

HTM is constituted as a private company, but all shares are owned by the city. From the start of 1996, the regional authority Stadsgewest Haaglanden became the overall co-ordinating body for public transport. It receives subsidy funding from the national government and transfers to HTM such subsidy as it is entitled to. Services extend beyond the city boundary to serve a total population of some 678,000, and there is close integration of routes and fares with regional bus services. The national standard tariff 'Strippenkaart' multiticket system applies (see the separate entry for Amsterdam for details).

From 2001, HTM took over the local bus company in the city of Dordrecht (population 120,000).

Developments

In 2001 the new tramway route 15 was taken into service to the new residential area Ypenburg. Two other tram routes are planned for 2006: Line 9 towards the new residential area Wateringse Veld and Line 19 from Delft to Leidschendam, partly using the aforementioned route of Line 15. Both extensions have not been decided yet, because they lack funding.

In October 2004 the construction of the tram tunnel was completed. The construction started in 1996 and had major setbacks because of leakage from groundwater during the construction period. The tunnel has a length of approximately 1,200 m and serves the inner city for the northwest tram lines, with two stations.

HTM is preparing for the operation of RandstadRail. The system consists of two lines from the southwest of The Hague to the city of Zoetermeer. Between the city of The Hague and Zoetermeer the services will be operated on a joined track (among others in the earlier mentioned tram tunnel) partly together with services to Rotterdam operated by RET (Rotterdam Electric Tram). The whole project converts the

HTM tram on the new Route 15 entering the new residential area of Ypenburg   1031939

HTM trams on the flyover from Centraal station   1031940

present heavy rail system into a light rail system. Between Zoetermeer and The Hague the system is fully segregated, in The Hague the vehicles will run mostly on free lanes with crossings for other traffic. About 4 km of new track and six new stations will be constructed. A tender for about 50 vehicles (37 m long and 2.65 m wide) was in preparation at the end of 2003.

In The Hague a complete renovation of the central station is planned for completion in 2006. The project is part of the further revitalisation of the inner city and facilitates the RandstadRail system and the new high-speed line between The Hague and Antwerp as part of the larger system between Paris and Amsterdam.

HTM is involved as a vehicle provider and as a partner for the safety design for the first experiment in Holland with light rail vehicles on the national railway system. Since early 2003, six vehicles (30 m long and 2.65 m wide) are operated between Alphen and Gouda, preliminary to a possible system between Gouda and Leiden, subject to funding.

HTA was the combined consultancy branch of RET (Rotterdam), GVB (Amsterdam) and HTM. From 2001 HTM took over all activities.

Bus

Passenger boardings: (2000) 38.4 million
(2001) 38.5 million
(2002) 37.7 million
Vehicle-km: (2002) 9.5 million

Number of routes: 17
Route length: 202.2 km
On priority right-of-way: 8.25 per cent

Fleet: 178 vehicles (of which 17 are articulated)
(Breakdown of makes/types and numbers of individual vehicles is not currently available.)
In peak service: 151
On order: 75 low-floor buses for use in The Hague and Dordrecht

Service: Peak 5–15 min, evening 15 min
One-person operation: All routes
Fare collection: Prepurchase pass or ticket with card validation on board by driver; Strippenkaart also available from driver
Fare structure: Zonal; prepurchase passes and national Strippenkaart multitickets valid on all modes
Fare evasion control: Check by driver on boarding; roving inspectors
Bus priority: Philips VECOM, also used for basic data for computer
Arrangements for elderly/disabled: Passengers aged 65 of over travel at a reduced price
Integration with other modes: Services co-ordinated with regional bus, tram services and

national railway (first and last trips); Strippenkaart gives ease of transfer (zonal system) and is standard for bus, tram and metro nationwide
Average speed: 19.1 km/h

Tramway

Type of operation: Conventional tramway

Passenger boardings: (2000) 88 million
(2001) 87.2 million
(2002) 88.2 million
Car-km: (2002) 9.0 million

Route length: 138.2 km
　reserved track: 86 per cent
Number of lines: 11
Gauge: 1,435 mm
Electrification: 600 V DC, overhead

Service: Peak 5-10 min, evening 15 min
One-person operation: All routes
Fare structure: As bus

Fare collection: Pass, prepurchase ticket card or payment to driver; boarding at other doors with cancelling machines for Strippenkaart
Fare evasion control: Roving inspectors
Tram priority: As bus, further use of tram warning lights on crossings and occasionally half-barriers
Average speed: 20 km/h

Rolling stock: 155 cars
BN GTL8 double-articulated cars
　(1981/84/92/93)　　　　　　　　　　　　M147
Duewag cars (from Hannover)　　　　　　M8
In peak service: 136

NS-Groep NV – Nederlandse Spoorwegen (NS) – Netherlands Railways

PO Box 2025, NL-3500 HA, Utrecht, Netherlands
Tel: (+31 30) 235 40 00　Fax: (+31 30) 235 61 93
Web: www.ns.nl

Street address
Laan van Puntenburg 100, NL-3511 ER, Utrecht, Netherlands

Key personnel
President: Aad Veenman
Commercial Director: Bert Meerstadt

Type of operation: Suburban heavy rail

Current situation
Services provided on five routes into Centraal station. There are seven stations within the city boundaries, served by 5 to 20 trains per hour, more at peak times.
　For further information on NS, please see *Jane's World Railways.*

Developments
An additional platform has been built at Centraal station, along with two four-tracking projects to raise capacity.

Rotterdam

Population: City 599,718 (2006 estimate), metropolitan area 1.1 million (estimate)

Public transport
Bus, tramway and metro/light rail (Sneltram) services provided by city transport authority effectively responsible to national government, with regional light rail (RandstadRail) under construction. Suburban bus services also provided by regional transport authorities and rail services by state railway, Netherlands Railways (NS). Ferry and watertaxi services.

RET NV
Postbus 112, NL-3000 AC Rotterdam, Netherlands
Tel: (+31 10) 447 69 11　Fax: (+31 10) 447 52 15
e-mail: info@ret.nl
Web: www.ret.nl

Street address
Vasteland 80, NL-3011 BN Rotterdam, Netherlands

Key personnel
Managing Director: Pedro G Peters
Director of Means (Finance, Assets, Development,
　Personnel and Organisation): Joop P M Bakker
Director of Exploitation: Ad H van Bavel
　Staff: 2,745 (2006)

Passenger journeys: (All modes)
(2002) 187 million
(2003) 176.0 million
(2004) 167 million
(2005) 160 million (estimate)
(2006) 159 million

Operating costs financed by: (All operations) Fares 31.8 per cent, subsidy/grants 68.2 per cent
Subsidy from: Regional council, drawing 100 per cent government contribution

Current situation
From 1 January 2007, RET became independently operated and was renamed RET NV. Two subsidiaries are responsible for operations, RET Infrastructuur BV and RET Materieel BV.

Developments
In August 2005, RET started using the OV-Chipkaart system in metro stations. Implementation on the bus and tram network was expected to take place starting in 2006. RET is a member of the Translink System, a joint venture of Dutch public transport companies (NS, RET, GVBA, HTM and Connexxion) set up in 2002 to introduce a nationwide contactless smartcard. This system is aimed at integrating public transport and reducing fare evasion.

June 2003 saw the start of the building of the tunnel traverse that will eventually link up the Hofpleinlijn to the metro system. When the building project is completed in 2008, the new light rail link called RandstadRail will directly link the city centres of Rotterdam and The Hague (see also the entry for The Hague).
　Upon completion and opening of the Rotterdam section of RandstadRail, there are plans for a partnership, named Hofbogen, to take over the operation of the redundant section of the Hofpleinlijn.
　RandstadRail: High-grade public transport between Rotterdam, The Hague and Zoetermeer.
　The Rotterdam city region is working hard on the improvement and expansion of the public transport system. Among other things, this is being done by the construction of the RandstadRail.
　RandstadRail is a fast and comfortable way of travelling, which lies between travelling by tram and travelling on the metro. It is an important contribution to the improvement of the public

transport between the cities of Rotterdam, The Hague and Zoetermeer.
　The RandstadRail section consists of a light rail connection between Rotterdam and The Hague (scheduled to be completed in 2008), a light rail connection between The Hague and Zoetermeer (due to be completed during 2007) and a high-grade bus connection between Zoetermeer and Rotterdam, the so-called ZoRo-bus.
　The Hague-Rotterdam section of RandstadRail will use part of the existing metro network (Erasmuslijn) and the Hofpleinlijn with Bombardier ***FLEXITY Swift*** high-floor, bi-directional vehicles. The 3 km Statenwegtunnel, currently under construction and with one new station, will link RandstadRail with the metro system in 2008.
　For more information on RandstadRail please see the website at www.randstadrail.nl.
　In July 2007, ALSTOM was selected by RET to supply a further 53 low-floor Citadis trams.
　In December 2007, the company awarded a contract to Bombardier Transportation for the

One of the new Mercedes-Benz Citaro buses, introduced into the RET fleet in 2006　　　1342691

design and build of 43 Bombardier FLEXITY Swift 3-car rail vehicles. The contract was valued at some EUR140 million, with an option for a further 21 vehicles. The new vehicles will be used on the Erasmus and Caland lines and delivery is scheduled to start in mid-2009.

Bus

Passenger journeys: (2002) 38.4 million
(2003) 35.2 million
(2004) 29.7 million
(2005) 26.2 million
(2006) 25 million
Vehicle-km: (2002) 12.1 million
(2004) 10.2 million
(2005) 8.8 million
(2006) 8.0 million

Number of routes: 23
Route length: 213.1 km

Fleet: 218 vehicles (2006)

Volvo (1993)	41
Mercedes-Benz (1994)	5
Den Oudsten (1996)	20
Peugeot (1996)	1
Den Oudsten (1997)	15
Mercedes-Benz (1999)	1
Den Oudsten (2001)	38
Den Oudsten (2002)	7
Mercedes-Benz Citaro (2006)	90

On order: Not currently available
In peak service: 218

Most intensive service: 4 min
One-person operation: All routes
Fare collection: Pre-purchase passes or multi- trip tickets, cancelled on board; also available from driver
Fare structure: National zonal scheme (12 zones locally); pre-purchase nationally available 'Strippenkaart' tickets, valid on all modes, also sold on vehicle (for details see under Amsterdam); day tickets; passes
Fare evasion control: Random inspection; penalty; all tickets must be shown to driver on boarding
Arrangements for elderly/disabled: Half-price 15-ticket Strippenkaarts sold under national scheme; Vervoer op Maat minibus service
Average peak-hour speed: In mixed traffic, 23.3 km/h
Bus priority: All buses equipped with VETAG onboard traffic light control
Integration with other modes: Services co-ordinated with those of Connexxion and NS

Developments

A new night bus service on Friday and Saturday, BOB-bus, and a new night bus service for weekdays, Nachtbus, started in 2006.

Metro/light rail (Sneltram)

Type of operation: Full metro/fast tramway, first line opened 1968

Passenger journeys: (2002) 84 million
(2003) 86.1 million
(2004) 84.0 million
(2005) 84.9 million
(2006) 85.0 million
Car-km: (2002) 13.7 million
(2004) 17.6 million
(2005) 16.5 million
(2006) 17.0 million

Route length: 173.9 km
  in tunnel: Not currently available
  elevated: Not currently available
Number of lines: 10
Number of stations: 48
  in tunnel: 15
Gauge: 1,435 mm
Track: RT 46 kg/m rail, direct fastening on concrete with resilient pads, in tunnel and on viaduct; concrete sleepers in ballast on embankment
Max gradient: 3%
Minimum curve radius: 60 m
Electrification: 750 V DC, third rail on metro and overhead on Sneltram sections

Bombardier Transportation FLEXITY Swift LRV, ordered in late December 2007 by RET NV (Bombardier Transportation)   1342692

Developments

In 2006, the Randstadrail branch was extended to the Hague, with power by overhead wire.

Rolling stock: 150 cars
Duewag/Holec (1981/85)   69
Bombardier (1999/2002)   81

Service: Peak 2½ min
First/last train: 05.30/24.00
Fare structure: Zonal (as bus)
Fare collection: Strip card, 1-, 2- and 3-day, weekly and monthly passes, OV-Chipcard contactless smartcard
Fare evasion control: Random checks, access gates
One-person operation: All trains
Signalling: Cab signalling with CTC
Surveillance: CCTV to platform superintendent
Integration with other modes: Bicycles carried free on weekdays after 19.00 and all day at weekends; park-and-ride at several stations, good bus interchange

Tramway

Type of operation: Conventional tramway

Passenger journeys: (2002) 60.6 million
(2003) 59 million
(2004) 53.4 million
(2005) 49.0 million
(2006) 49.0 million
Car-km: (2002) 6.2 million
(2004) 6.0 million
(2005) 5.9 million
(2006) 6.0 million

Route length: 113.6 km
Number of routes: 8
Reserved track: 75 per cent
Track: 46 kg/m RT rail

Rolling stock: 127 cars (2006)
Duewag/Holec ZGT 6 (1982/85)   50
Duewag/Holec ZGT 4-6 (1984/88)   17
ALSTOM Citadis (2003)   60
In peak service: 127

Service: Peak 5–8 min, off-peak 7–15 min
First/last car: 05.00/01.00
Fare structure: Zonal (as bus)
One-person operation: All trams

Developments

All stations on the Calandline and Erasmusline extension have been equipped with human and CCTV surveillance.

TramPlus

The RET, in co-operation with the city region of Rotterdam, is working on improvements to public transport and accessibility in the region of

Rotterdam. One of the projects which will enable this to happen is TramPlus. TramPlus is a high-grade tram connection where reliability, comfort and short travelling-time play important roles. The system uses mostly segregated tracks and right of way at crossroads with other traffic to provide a reliable timetable. Elevated platforms offer, in combination with the low step-in trams, complete ground floor access. Passengers are provided with information onboard and at tram stops.

Rotterdam

Regional bus
Current situation
Suburban and regional bus services are provided by Connexxion (www.connexxion.nl) and Arriva (www.arriva.nl). Some routes run straight into the centre of Rotterdam, while others act as feeders to the metro.

NS-Groep NV – Nederlandse Spoorwegen (NS) – Netherlands Railways

NS Reizigers
Head Office
PO Box 2025, NL-3500 HA Utrecht, Netherlands
Tel: (+31 30) 235 40 00
Fax: (+31 30) 235 61 93
Web: www.ns.nl

Street address
Laan van Puntenburg 100, NL-3511 ER, Utrecht, Netherlands

Key personnel
President: Aad Veenman
Commercial Director: Bert Meerstadt

Type of operation: Suburban heavy rail

Current situation
There are 12 city stations served by two to 25 trains per hour. About four trains per hour serve four routes out of Rotterdam Centraal, with an additional route from Hofpleinstation to The Hague. NS trains are better used for inner-city journeys than in other cities because there are fewer competing bus and tram routes.

For further information on NS, please see *Jane's World Railways.*

Developments
Rotterdam Centraal is being developed in order to receive increased passenger growth with the opening of high-speed services.

Utrecht

Population: 283,000 (2006 estimate)

Public transport

Most bus services provided by municipal undertaking with some additional suburban routes operated by private regional bus companies; separate company responsible for operation of light rail line. Suburban/interurban services by subsidiary of Netherlands Railways (NS).

GVU

PO Box 8222, NL-3503 RE Utrecht, Netherlands
Tel: (+31 30) 236 36 36
Fax: (+31 30) 231 65 40
e-mail: info@gvu.nl
Web: www.gvu.nl

Street address

Radboudkwartier 245, NL-3511 CK Utrecht, Netherlands

Key personnel

General Director: Ing Roos van Erp-Bruinsma
Staff: 717 (2006)

Background

Originally formed in 1904, the company changed its name from Gemeentelijk Vervoerbedrijf Utrecht to GVU in 2004.

Current situation

GVU operates most urban and some suburban bus services in and around Utrecht. Other operators run interurban services into the city.

In January 2007, GVU became owned by Connexxion.

Developments

After trials in 1997, a 13-station busway was opened in 2001. It connects the university area with the town centre. A fleet of 15 Van Hool bi-articulated vehicles provides frequent service on the route (15 buses per hour during peak periods). The busway has a vehicle priority system.

Two further busways are currently under construction; from the city centre to the university area, but on a more southerly route than the first busway, and from the city centre to a new residential area named Leidsche Rijn. Both are scheduled for completion in 2010.

Ridership on the current busway is estimated at 11,500 per day.

Bus

Passenger boardings: (2002) 34.0 million
(2003) 36.3 million
(2004) 37.4 million
(2005) 38.3 million
(2006) 39.0 million
Vehicle-km: (2002) 8.6 million
(2003) 10.2 million
(2004) 10.7 million
(2005) 10.5 million
(2006) Not yet available

Number of routes: 30
Route length: (One way) 223 km
On priority right-of-way: 25 km

Fleet: 199 vehicles

Standard bus	74
Articulated bus	94
Van Hool AGG 330 double-articulated bus (2004)	27
Midibus	4

In peak service: 152
On order: None.

Most intensive service: 2–3 min
One-person operation: All routes
Fare structure: Zonal; prepurchase nationally available 'Strippenkaart' tickets, also available on vehicle (see Amsterdam for details); passes; student ticket; Wenkelkaartje
Average distance between stops: 300–400 m

GVU Van Hool double-articulated bus (Quintus Vosman) 1198554

Average peak-hour speed: In mixed traffic, 16 km/h; in bus lanes, 25 km/h
Arrangements for elderly/disabled: Reduced fares (also for children)
Integration with other modes: Services co-ordinated with those of neighbouring regional public transport authority and NS. National 'Strippenkaart' gives standard tram, bus and metro fares throughout the Netherlands
Operating costs financed by: Fares 41 per cent, other commercial sources 4 per cent, subsidy/grants 55 per cent
Subsidy from: Regional council, drawing 100 per cent government contribution

Connexxion Openbaar Vervoer NV

Postbus 224, NL-1200 AE Hilversum, Netherlands
Tel: (+31 35) 625 16 00   Fax: (+31 35) 625 16 99
Web: www.connexxion.nl

Street address

Marathon 6, Hilversum, Netherlands

Key personnel

Chairman of the Executive Board: P J Kortenhorst
Vice-Chairman of the Executive Board: R van Holton
Chief Financial Officer: F Janssen
Director, Public Affairs and Secretary of the Executive Board: C W A Lely

Bus

Current situation

Connexxion operates suburban and regional bus routes in the provinces of Utrecht, Gelderland

Utrecht's Sneltram 0518337

and Flevoland, and urban routes in 10 medium-size cities.

Light rail (Sneltram)

Type of operation: Light rail, opened 1983

Current situation

The Sneltram light rail line was built by Netherlands Railways (NS) and is now operated by Connexxion.

Refurbished Connexxion LRV approaching the Utrecht terminus (Quintus Vosman) 0126548

A 2.5 km extension has been built to serve the Zenderpark housing development in Ijsselstein; it opened in May 2000.

Developments
Studies are being made to assess whether the Sneltram can play a part in the Randstad 2000 scheme for S-Bahn style train service throughout the region.

Passenger journeys: (1998) 36,000 daily
Car-km: (1998) 1.8 million

Route length: 21.5 km
Number of stops: 23
Number of lines: 1, with branches
Gauge: 1,435 mm
Track: 46 kg/m rail on concrete sleepers
Electrification: 750 V DC, overhead

Service: 5 min peak, 7½ min day, 10 min evening/weekend

Signalling: Only on 1.5 km section, otherwise ordinary street traffic lights

Rolling stock: 27 cars
SIG/Holec/BBC (1983)   M27

NS-Groep NV – Nederlandse Spoorwegen (NS) – Netherlands Railway

NS Reizigers
Head Office
PO Box 2025, NL-3500 HA Utrecht, Netherlands
Tel: (+31 30) 235 40 00   Fax: (+31 30) 235 61 93
Web: www.ns.nl

Street address
Laan van Puntenburg 100, NL-3511 ER, Utrecht, Netherlands

Key personnel
President: Aad W Veenman
Chief Commercial Director: Bert Meerstadt

Director, NS Reizigers: Pamela Boomeester
Director, Corporate Communications:
  Joost Ravoo
Staff: 26,116 (2005 Group total)

Type of operation: Suburban heavy rail

Current situation
Domestic passenger services are operated by the NS subsidiary NS Reizigers. Management of stations is carried out by NS Stations and the infrastructure is the responsibility of ProRail (please see entry in *Jane's World Railways* for further information on NS and ProRail).

Only Centraal and two suburban stations lie within the city boundaries, and are not heavily used for local trips, though there is much longer-distance commuting. Service of two to 34 trains per hour according to time of day.

Developments
Utrecht Centraal station is to be revamped.

New Zealand

Auckland

Population: City 419,800 (2006 Census – provisional), regional area 1.32 million (2006 Census – provisional)

Public transport
Bus, suburban rail and ferry services provided by commercial operators on contract to the Auckland Regional Council (ARC).

Auckland Regional Transport Authority (ARTA)

Private Bag 92 236, Auckland Mail Centre, Auckland, New Zealand
Tel: (+64 9) 379 44 22
e-mail: ARTAenquiry@arta.co.nz
Web:www.arta.co.nz, www.maxx.co.nz

Street address
Level 3, 21 Pitt Street, Auckland, New Zealand

Key personnel
Chair: Mark Ford
Chief Executive: Fergus Gammie
General Manager, Customer Services:
  Mark Lambert
General Manager, Project Delivery: Peter Spies
General Manager, Strategy & Planning: Peter Clark
General Manager, Corporate Services:
  Stephen Smith
  Staff: Not currently available

Passenger journeys: (All modes)
(2004) 52 million
(2005) 50.6 million
(2006) 51.1 million
(2007) 52.4 million
(2008) 54.4 million

Current situation
The Auckland Regional Transport Authority (ARTA) is Auckland's central transport agency and is responsible for the integrated planning, funding and implementation of transport (with the exception of State Highways and national rail) throughout the Auckland region.

The authority's objective is to plan, fund, develop and operate an integrated regional land transport system for the Auckland area.

ARTA was established as a statutory entry on 1 July 2004 by the Local Government (Auckland) Amendment Act (LGAAA) and officially began operations on 1 December 2004.

ARTA's key roles include:
• Integrating land transport planning for the Auckland region, and producing an Auckland Transport Plan to guide the detailed planning within ARTA and other transport agencies;

• Recommending projects to be funded through the Auckland Land Transport Programme;
• Specifying and planning for an electrified passenger rail network in Auckland, improving stations, trains and maintenance facilities and delivering ferry and intelligent transport system projects;
• Designing and operating bus, rail and ferry services in the Auckland region;
• Marketing passenger transport services and delivering travel plans in partnership with local councils and with schools, workplaces and communities.

Developments
Highlights for passenger transport services in 2007/08 are as follows:
• Trains in the Auckland regional carried a record 6.8 million passengers
• Passenger journeys by train reached 709,900 in August 2008, a new monthly record
• The Northern Busway, New Zealand's first dedicated bus infrastructure opened in February 2008
• Buses in the Auckland region carried 43 million passengers – an increase of 2.9 per cent over 2006/07
• Ferries in the Auckland region carried 4.38 million passengers
• Passenger journeys on the Northern Express bus service increased by 85 per cent in the period between February and June 2008 compared with the same period in 2007
• Patronage on school bus services is about 2.5 million per year.
Arrangements for elderly/disabled: The Total Mobility scheme provides half-price taxi fares for those who cannot use scheduled services

Bus, ferries and rail
Scheduled bus services in the Auckland region are operated by NZ Bus, Ritchies Transport, Howick and Eastern Buses Ltd, Birkenhead Transport, Urban Express, Waiheke Bus Company and Bayes Coachlines (school buses only). Ferries are operated by Fullers Group Ltd, Pine Harbour Ferries, Belaire Ferries, 360 discovery and SeaLink. Suburban rail is operated under contract by Veolia Transport Auckland Limited.

Transportation Auckland Corporation Limited – Stagecoach Auckland

Private Bag 47901, Ponsonby, Auckland, New Zealand
Tel: (+64 9) 373 91 18   Fax: (+64 9) 373 91 19
e-mail: info@stagecoach.co.nz
Web: www.stagecoach.co.nz/auckland

Office address
100 Halsey Street, Viaduct Harbour, Auckland, New Zealand

Key personnel
Managing Director, Stagecoach New Zealand:
  Bill Rae
Commercial Director, Stagecoach New Zealand:
  Ian Turner
Engineering Director, Stagecoach New Zealand:
  Allan Cannell
Finance Director, Stagecoach New Zealand: Treena Martin
Marketing Manager, Stagecoach New Zealand:
  Russell Turnbull
National Operations Director: Warren Fowler

Passenger boardings: (2002) 30 million
(2003) 30 million

Operating costs financed by: Fares 44 per cent, property taxes and central government funding 56 per cent on contracted services. Commercial services are 100 per cent funded by fares apart from concessionary fare reimbursement

Current situation
Owned by Stagecoach New Zealand, Stagecoach Auckland operates bus services, including those previously known as the Yellow Bus Company and Cityline Auckland, the Link bus service in Auckland city and a free City Circuit bus. Stagecoach also has a 96 per cent interest in ferry operator Fullers.

All buses now have electronic ticket machines capable of handling smartcards as a first step in the development of an integrated ticketing system.

Over the last four years, Stagecoach Auckland has taken delivery of more than 15 low-floor low-emission buses. This will substantially reduce the average age of buses in Auckland.

Four km of peak-period bus lanes were introduced on the congested Dominion Road corridor in March 1998, leading to significant reductions in bus times and increases in patronage. More fragmented bus lane sections in Mt Eden Road have had a lesser impact. Further priority measure for buses are programmed for other major arterials.

The inner-city Link service, launched in 1997, is now carrying around two million passengers a year.

Routes: 90+

Fleet: 630 vehicles +

Nissan Scorpion SLFx 1800 series	13
Nissan Scorpion SLF 1800 series	80
Nissan Scorpion LF 1200 series	40

MAN 16-230 'Remuera Rider'	4
MAN 243	50
MAN 11-190 SLF	60
MAN 12-220	60
MAN SG242 'Bendy Bus'	17
MAN SG220 'Bendy Bus'	15
MAN 20	40
MAN SL200	60
Mercedes-Benz 305	30
MAN 16-230	75
MAN 11-190 500 series LF (1994/95)	41
MAN SLF 600 series (1995/96)	17

MAXX train

1195203

Northern Busway Project Office

PO Box 1459, Auckland, New Zealand
Tel: (+64 9) 368 20 00
e-mail: northernbusway@transit.govt.nz
Web: www.busway.co.nz

Key personnel
Project Director: Mark Johnson

Type of operation: Busway, opened February 2008

Background
The partners in this project are: Transit New Zealand, the Auckland Regional Transport Authority, North Shore City Council, the Auckland Regional Council and the Auckland City Council.

Current situation
The Northern Busway Project, previously known as the North Shore Busway Project, is a 6 km dedicated two-way road for buses, running from Constellation Drive to Akoranga with five stations, two with park-and-ride facilities. It is the 'spine' of the planned North Shore City's Bus Rapid Transit (BRT) system. A further 2.5 km bus lane running south from Akoranga station to Harbour Bridge will be completed in early 2009.

In addition to this, there are two interchange upgrades, at Onewa Road and Esmonde Road.

The total estimated cost for the project is AUD266 million.

Developments
The Busway was opened in February 2008.

The Esmonde Road interchange upgrade was opened in May 2007 and the Onewa Interchange is due for completion in early 2009.

Veolia Transport Auckland Ltd

PO BO 105-355, Auckland, New Zealand
Tel: (+64 9) 969 77 77   Fax: (+64 9) 969 77 00
e-mail: info@veoliatransport.co.nz
Web: www.veoliatransport.co.nz

Street address
Level 7, Citibank Centre, 23 Customs St East, Auckland, New Zealand

Key personnel
Managing Director: Nick French
Marketing and Communications Manager: Silva Bassett
Staff: Not currently available

Type of operation: Suburban heavy rail

Passenger journeys: (2007) 6 million

Background
Veolia Transport Auckland runs suburban passenger trains in Auckland under a four-year

contract which took effect in August 2004 and has been extended for a further two years. The agreement is with Auckland Regional Council (ARC). The ARC is responsible for setting the strategy for land transport in the Auckland region and provides funding to the Auckland Regional Transport Authority (ARTA), which is responsible for co-ordinating the region's land transport and purchasing the provision of services from operators. The region's public transport is marketed as MAXX.

Current situation
Services over a three-line 40-station network totalling 94 route-km. The provision of additional locomotive-hauled trains has enabled frequency improvements to be made during peak hours. From December 2007, weekend and evening services have been enhanced, whilst a new timetable in July 2008 has seen increased choice for passengers with new and increased services. This includes 15-minute services on the Western line and a new trial service to Helensville as well as increased services to Pukekohe. Over six million passenger journeys were made in 2007 and patronage continues to increase. An objective of 16 million journeys has been set for 2014 and is believed achievable in the longer term.

Services are operated over the tracks of the national infrastructure owner, New Zealand Railways Corporation (Ontrack).

For further information on Veolia Transport Auckland Ltd, please see *Jane's World Railways*.

Developments
Previously known as Connex Auckland Limited, the company's current name was adopted in March 2006 following a corporate re-branding of the divisions of the company's French-based parent company, Veolia Environnement.

Further benefits will result from a planned NZD100 million programme funded by ARTA to upgrade 36 stations. The provision of a second track on the Western line between Henderson and Swanson has allowed the provision of 15-minute peak services from/to Swanson. Capacity enhancements will also be achieved by further doubling of sections of the Western line.

OnTrack has started work on the Onehunga branch line with a view to resuming passenger

service on that line, which last saw regular passenger service in 1973.

The rail fleet continues to be refurbished and expanded to accomodate increased passenger demand.

ARC and ARTA advocate electrification of the Auckland suburban network by 2013, which would necessitate a new fleet of emus.

Rolling stock: dmu cars (including 10 two-car

Goninan ex-Perth)	38
SX-type sets (ex-Brisbane)	1
SD Class driving trailer	17
DBR Class locomotive (leased)	2
DC Class locomotive (leased)	17
SA push-pull four-car sets (ex-British Rail)	68
RM-class rail car (leased, ex-TranzScenic)	3

Fullers Group Limited

PO Box 1346, Auckland, New Zealand
Tel: (+64 9) 367 91 11   Fax: (+64 9) 367 91 48
e-mail: Enquiries@fullers.co.nz
Web: www.fullers.co.nzStreet address
111 Quay Street, Auckland, New Zealand

Key personnel
Chairman: George Hudson
Chief Executive Officer: Douglas Hudson
General Manager: Michael Fitchett

Type of operation: Ferry

Background
The name Fullers Group Limited was adopted in 1994. In 1998 the majority of shares in Fullers Group were bought by Stagecoach Ltd, as that company's first venture into ferry operations.

Passenger journeys: (2002) 4.5 million
(2003) 4 million
(2004) 4 million
(2005) 4 million

Current situation
Nine ferry services operate in Waitemata Harbour and the Hauraki Gulf, linking central Auckland with Devonport, Stanley Bay, Birkenhead, Gulf Harbour, Bayswater, Half Moon Bay and Waiheke, with routes to other Hauraki Gulf islands mainly for recreational purposes.

Christchurch

Population: City 361,800 (2006 Census), Greater Christchurch in excess of 400,000

Public transport
Bus and ferry services are provided by private operators (three bus and one ferry) under contract to the regional council; tourist tramway.

Environment Canterbury (ECan)

PO Box 345, Christchurch, New Zealand
Tel: (+64 3) 365 38 28
Fax: (+64 3) 365 31 94
e-mail: wayne.holton-jeffreys@ecan.govt.nz
Web: www.ecan.govt.nz; www.metroinfo.org.nz

Key personnel
Manager, Passenger Services (ECan): Wayne Holton-Jeffreys

Current situation
Deregulation of public transport services was implemented in 1991. Of the 43 routes operating in Greater Christchurch, ECan contracts

and funds all but two, which are provided commercially.

Responsibility for transport is split between the Christchurch City Council (www.ccc.govt.nz) and Environment Canterbury (ECan). ECan is responsible for the registration of all passenger transport services in the Canterbury region, including bus, rail, taxi and ferry services. It contracts provision of bus and ferry services in Christchurch and other smaller centres in the Canterbury region where these would not otherwise be provided at a desired level on a commercial basis.

A 3 km tourist tram, built by the City Council and leased to operator Christchurch Tramway Ltd, runs in the city centre.

Five 20-seat Designline low-floor electric buses started running an inner city shuttle service in 1999 operated by Red Bus Ltd. They are funded by the City Council. The electric shuttle service continues to be a success, with peak patronage levels exceeding 3,000 passengers a day.

There is a total combined fleet of 349 vehicles, including urban and school services.

Environment Canterbury also contracts six bus services in Timaru City (population 43,800). In FY2006/07, these services carried 178,957 passengers.

Developments

Following deregulation of public transport in the early 1990s, patronage on public transport services fell dramatically. This led to the creation of a Passenger Transport Strategy, which set key goals aimed at doubling patronage by 2007/08. As part of this strategy, the following improvements have been introduced:

- introduction of the Orbiter and Metrostar cross-suburban services;
- a 40 per cent increase in frequency;
- 140 new low-floor buses;
- Metrocard – proximity debit card providing a fully integrated ticketing system;
- Creation of a unified system brand – 'metro';
- Central City Bus Exchange giving airport-type quality waiting and information areas;
- Real-time information has been developed including at-stop consoles as well as WAP cell phone capability.

These improvements have resulted in a 63 per cent increase in patronage since 1999/2000.

The high number of new low-floor vehicles has reduced the average age of the fleet to approximately 7.7 years. All inter-peak trips on contracted services are expected to run using low-floor vehicles.

Arrangements for elderly/disabled: The Total Mobility scheme provides a 50 per cent subsidy for taxi fares up to NZD20 for those who cannot use scheduled services; ECan also funds installation of wheelchair hoists in taxivans

Bus

Passenger boardings: (2001/02) 12.89 million
(2002/03) 14.73 million

(2003/04) 14.58 million
(2004/05) 15.21 million
(2005/06) 15.61 million
Vehicle-km: (2005/06) 18.19 million

Current situation

Services are provided by three contracted operators, the larger of which, Red Bus Ltd (www.redbus.co.nz), is a City Council-owned local authority trading enterprise. Red Bus Ltd also operates the electric hybrid shuttle under contract to the Christchurch City Council, which provides free travel within the central business district of Christchurch.

Leopard Citylines is the operator of the award-winning 'Orbiter' service, a cross-suburban route which was completed in 2001 and is the biggest route in the city. The company also runs several major services in the west and the east of the city as well as a service to the port of Lyttelton.

Christchurch Bus Services Ltd (CBS) is the newest of the contracted bus operators and runs several services across the city. This includes one new Northern Star services which connect towns in the Waimakariri District to Christchurch City. The four urban services in Timaru, South Canterbury, are also operated by Timaru Bus Services Ltd, a subsidiary of CBS.

Black Cat Group (www.blackcat.co.nz) operates the city's only ferry service between Lyttelton and Diamond Harbour.

Number of routes: 43
Fleet: 262 vehicles
Urban services fleet

SLF Dennis Dart	4
SLF MAN 11.220	50
MAN SL202	20
Electric hybrid shuttle	5
MAN 12.220	1
MAN 10.160	33
MAN 11.160	11
Volvo B10M ex-Wellington trolleybuses	1
Nissan Scorpion	1
Hino/Isuzu/others	3
Volvo B7	2
MAN 11.230	1
MAN 12.223	30
MAN 16.223	3
MAN 16.240	1
MAN 17.220	4
MAN 18.223	2
MAN 22.240	9
MAN DZ566 UH 205	20
Mercedes-Benz SLF	21
Optare	12
Zhong Tong	6
Black Diamond Ferry	1

Fare collection: Contactless smartcard ticketing system, Metrocard.
Fare structure: Flat NZD2.50 cash fare for any travel within Zone 1 (a 15 km radius from the central city exchange, Zone 2 is 15–20 km from the central city exchange and then concentric circles in 10 km

increments. If the Metrocard proximity card is used, all passengers receive a maximum 25 per cent discount on the equivalent cash fare. As of January 2007, 170,000 Metrocards had been issued, with approximately 80 per cent of all transactions being made with a Metrocard
Operating costs financed by: Fares 50 per cent, property taxes and central government funding 50 per cent

Main operators:

Red Bus Ltd
PO Box 10171, Christchurch, New Zealand
Tel: (+64 3) 379 42 60
Fax: (+64 3) 366 56 43
e-mail: redbus@redbus.co.nz
Web: www.redbus.co.nz

Street address
120 Ferry Road, Christchurch, New Zealand

Leopard Coachlines Ltd
Leopard Citylines
58 Laurence Street, Christchurch, New Zealand
Tel: (+64 3) 373 81 00
Fax: (+64 3) 381 13 99
e-mail: brent@leopard.co.nz

Christchurch Bus Services Ltd
PO Box 29327, Fendalton, Christchurch 8001, New Zealand
Tel: (+64 3) 359 00 83
Fax: (+64 3) 359 12 21
e-mail: info@christchurchbus.co.nz;
    clive@ christchurchbus.co.nz
Web: www.christchurchbus.co.nz

Tramway Operator:

Christchurch Tramway Ltd
7 Tramway Lane, PO Box 872, Christchurch, New Zealand
Tel: (+64 3) 366 78 30
Fax: (+64 3) 366 69 43
e-mail: enquiries@tram.co.nz
Web: www.tram.co.nz

Current situation
A 3 km city-centre loop was built by the city council; it opened in 1995 and is operated on concession by Christchurch Tramway Ltd. Five cars.

Passenger ferry Operator:

Black Cat Group
Lyttelton, New Zealand
Tel: (+64 3) 328 90 78
Fax: (+64 3) 328 86 99
e-mail: info@blackcat.co.nz
Web: www.blackcat.co.nz

Key personnel
Managing Director: Paul Bingham
General Manager: Vanetia Bingham

Current situation
A passenger ferry service connects the small community of Diamond Harbour with the port of Lyttelton.

Black Cat Group provides the ferry service on contract to Environment Canterbury.

The Orbiter, operated by Leopard Citylines, at Northlands Mall
0552499

Wellington
Population: 445,000 (2002 estimate)

Public transport
Bus, trolleybus and cable car services, urban/suburban bus services, rail and ferry operations provided by private companies.

Greater Wellington Regional Council
PO Box 11646, Wellington, New Zealand
Tel: (+64 4) 384 57 08   Fax: (+64 4) 385 69 60
Web: www.gw.govt.nz
    www.metlink.org.nz

Key personnel
Chief Executive: David Benham
Chief Financial Officer: Barry Turfrey
Divisional Manager, Corporate and Strategy:
  Jane Bradbury
Divisional Manager, Transport Infrastructure and Procurement: Wayne Hastie
Divisional Manager, Transport Policy and Strategy:
  Jane Davis

Current situation
Greater Wellington Regional Council is responsible for ensuring the delivery of a safe, fair, reliable and environmentally friendly transport system in the region at the minimum cost to the regional ratepayer. This is achieved by:
• Planning and monitoring the transport network;
• Funding bus and train services;
• Building the public transport infrastructure;
• Encouraging greater use of public transport, cycling and walking;
• Promoting reduced vehicle emissions and managing traffic growth;
• Supporting integrated land-use and transport planning;
• Supporting selective road improvements;
• Assisting people with disabilities.
The Council is responsible for purchasing and providing information on passenger transport services, including:
• Identifying operators that fulfil its quality standards and other criteria;
• Tendering service contracts;
• Contracting operators to provide specified services;
• Monitoring services provided under contract against quality criteria;
• Collecting service operational data;
• Providing information about Metlink – Greater Wellington's public transport network.
Greater Wellington provides Metlink information on buses, trains and harbour ferry services in the Greater Wellington region, publishing bus timetables, managing the Metlink website and operating the Metlink service centre.

Infratil Limited
NZ Bus
97 The Terrace, PO Box 320, Wellington,
New Zealand
Tel: (+64 4) 473 36 63
e-mail: admin@infratil.com
Web: www.infratil.com

Key personnel
Chairman, NZ Bus: Lib Petagna
Staff: Not currently available

Background
In November 2005, Infratil, New Zealand, purchased the entire Stagecoach New Zealand operation, including its stake in Fullers Auckland, from Stagecoach Group PLC, UK. Infratil was granted the rights to use the Stagecoach name for five years, from date of purchase.

Developments
An order was placed with Designline, NZ in early 2007 for the supply of 61 new low-floor three-axle rigid trolleybuses, for renewal of the fleet. Delivery of the vehicles began in December 2007.

Bus and trolleybus
Number of routes: 33 (Bus 25, trolleybus 8)
Route length: 223 km (Bus 170 km, trolleybus 53 km)

Fleet: 138 buses, plus Cityline Hutt Valley 70

Leyland Leopard	41
Renault S56	1
MAN SL202	30
MAN 16 200	11
Hino AC140 midibus	1
MAN/Designline 11.190 HOCL minibus	52
Mercedes 709D	2

In peak service: 113

Fleet: 61 trolleybuses

Volvo B58/BBC (1981/86)	56
Designline 2-axle prototypes (2003/05)	3
Designline 3-axle rigid (2007)	2

In peak service: 50

Most intensive service: Peak 5 min
One-person operation: All routes
Fare collection: Manual ticket issue by driver or prepurchase multitickets
Fare structure: Sections; 10-trip multitickets; monthly bus cards, day tripper tickets for an adult and two children
Fares collected on board: 53 per cent
Fare evasion control: Inspectors
Operational control: Route inspectors/mobile radio (fitted to 69 buses)
Arrangements for elderly/disabled: Reduced fares subsidised by local rates (property taxes)
Integration with other modes: Limited
Bus priority: Lambton Quay bus lane
Average distance between stops: 400 m
Average peak-hour speed: In mixed traffic, city section 10 km/h; suburban service, 19 km/h
Operating costs financed by: Fares 75 per cent, other commercial sources 0.4 per cent, subsidy/grants 25 per cent
Subsidy from: Contracted services financed by Regional Council using revenues from property and petrol taxes, plus limited central government support
New vehicles financed by: Accumulated profits

Cable car
Current situation
A cable car from Lambton Quay to Kelburn is used by both commuters and tourists, carrying about 800,000 passengers annually.

Mana Coach Services Limited
7 Commerce Crescent, Porirua 5024, Wellington, New Zealand
Tel: (+64 4) 235 88 19   Fax: (+64 4) 235 70 37
e-mail: info@manacoach.co.nz
Web: www.manacoach.co.nz

Key personnel
Operations Manager: Brian Gaskin

Type of operation: Urban/suburban bus

Passenger journeys: Not currently available

Current situation
Commuter services in Porirua, Whitby, Titahi Bay, Johnsonville, Tawa, Paraparaumu, Raumati and Waikanae. All services run to and from the suburbs and rail services and are timetabled to meet train arrivals and departures, through both peak and off-peak, seven days a week.

Fleet: Not currently available

Newlands Coach Services Limited
7 Commerce Crescent, Porirua, Wellington, New Zealand
Tel: (+64 4) 478 83 15   Fax: (+64 4) 478 23 06
e-mail: ncs@newlands.co.nz
Web: www.newlands.co.nz

Key personnel
Operations Manager: Brian Gaskin
  Staff: 55

Type of operation: Urban bus and charter services

Passenger journeys: Not currently available

Current situation
Urban bus services in Johnsonville, Johnsonville West, Broadmeadows, Newlands, Grenada Village, Churton Park and Wellington City.

Fleet: Not currently available

Tranz Metro Wellington
Private Bag, Wellington, New Zealand
Tel: (+64 4) 801 70 00 (Metlink)
Web: www.tranzmetro.co.nz

Passenger journeys: Removed at company's request

Background
Following deregulation of transport in the early 1990s the then New Zealand Railways divested itself of all urban bus services. All non-commercial urban services in Wellington went to tender with Tranz Metro Wellington successfully contracting to provide rail services. Tranz services were also extended and improved on all lines over this period. New Zealand Rail was sold to the private sector in 1993 and renamed Tranz Rail Ltd.
Tranz Metro is now owned by Toll NZ Consolidated Limited, which also operate Tranz Scenic long distance train services throughout New Zealand and Interislander ferries between the North and South Islands.

Current situation
The rail network consists of 261 route-km. The core network consists of four 1,067 mm gauge 1.6 kV DC electrified lines linking Wellington with Johnsonville, Paraparaumu, Melling and Upper Hutt. Outer urban services also run to Palmerston North and Masterton, provided by locomotive-hauled trains. All trains operate under CTC with single manning. Services are provided under contract to Wellington Regional Council. There are six routes, with a route length of 140 km and 55 stations. The fleet consists of 125 emu cars (as two-and three-car units) and 19 carriages.
Services operate seven days a week, usually between the hours of 05.30 and 24.00. Peak services run every seven to 19 minutes, whilst off-peak services run every 30 to 60 minutes.
Fare collection is on-train (manual) with a fare structure of singles, child, 10-trip, monthly, school pass, off-peak, day and rover tickets. Funding comes from fares (55 per cent), council grant (45 per cent) and major capital projects.
The majority of trains on the Paraparaumu and Upper Hutt lines and one train on the Johnsonville line are wheelchair accessible.

Developments
The past five years have seen major refurbishment programmes for the Ganz Mavag unit fleet and trainsets. Tranz Rail has also purchased former British Rail carriages to be refurbished and used on both suburban and long-distance rail services.

East by West Ferries
PO Box 5077, Wellington, New Zealand
Tel: (+64 4) 499 12 82   Fax: (+64 4) 499 12 88
e-mail: info@eastbywest.co.nz
Web: www.eastbywest.co.nz

Key personnel
Manager: Jeremy Ward

Type of operation: Ferry services

Passenger journeys: Not currently available

Current situation
Provides ferry services between Queens Wharf-Matiu Somes Island-Days Bay and, as of December 2005, a new daily service between Queens Wharf and Petone.
Ten-trip tickets and monthly passes are available.

Nigeria

Lagos

Population: Metropolitan area 15 million (2005 State Government estimate)

Public transport

Bus and ferry services provided by state transport corporations responsible to Ministry of Transportation. Many private operators of bus services, which are under review, with franchised operations due to be implemented in the near future. Commercial motorcycle operators regulated by Ministry of Transportation. Existing ferry services under review, with increased services proposed. Some peak-hour commuter trains run by Nigerian Railway Corporation (NRC). Light rail under study to ease serious traffic congestion problems. Bus Rapid Transit (BRT) under consideration.

Lagos Metropolitan Area Transport Authority (LAMATA)

Block C, 2nd Floor Motorways Centre, Motorways Avenue, Alausa, Ikeja, Lagos, Nigeria
Tel: (+234 1) 270 27 78-82
Fax: (+234 1) 270 27 83
e-mail: info@lamata-ng.com
Web: www.lamata-ng.com

Key personnel

Chairman: Yemi Sawyerr (part time)
Managing Director and Chief Executive Officer: Dayo Mobereola
Director of Finance: Iyiola Adegboye
Director of Corporate and Investment Planning: Olutayo Orekoya
Technical Advisor, Public Transport and Traffic Management: Gbenga Dairo
Corporate and Legal Secretary: Ajibike Oshodi

Background

LAMATA was established in 2002. It is governed by a 13-member board, which was inaugurated in December 2003.

Current situation

Lagos Metropolitan Area Transport Authority (LAMATA) provides corporate and strategic policy direction for the transport system of metropolitan Lagos. It aims to improve and maintain cost-effective transport services.

LAMATA works closely with the Ministry of Works (MOW), the Ministry of Transportation, the Lagos State Government and the World Bank.

The Lagos Metropolitan Area continues to experience severe traffic congestion, with an estimated population of between 12.5 and 15 million and a population growth of some six per cent per year. The metropolitan area is expanding into neighbouring Ogun State, with commuter trips growing in both length and number.

Developments

Lagos Urban Transport Project (LUTP)
LAMATA is overseeing and executing the Lagos Urban Transport Project (LUTP). LUTP consist of five major components:

- *Institutional Strengthening and Capacity Building:* Strengthening of traffic management units in the 50 local government areas within the Lagos metropolitan area; strengthening the capacity of existing transport sector agencies;
- *Urban Road Network Efficiency Improvement:* Maximisation of the existing road space; reduction in vehicle operating costs; promotion of road safety; introduction of traffic systems measures; improvement of main road network and drainage system;
- *Bus Services Enhancement:* Establishment of an effective bus regulator framework; establishment of bus pilot scheme; encouragement of bus re-fleeting by the private sector; implementation of Bus Rapid Transit (BRT) system;

- *Water & Non Motorised Transport Promotion:* Privatisation of existing state-owned ferries; encouragement of non-motorised transport e.g. provision of facilities for bicycles and pedestrians; encouragement of private sector participation; rehabilitation and judicious addition to existing terminal facilities;
- *Rail Mass Rapid Transit:* The development of rapid rail mass transit along the East-West Corridor (Orile-Iganmu to Agbara) and North-South Corridor (Algbado to Lekki).

Bus schemes

There are an estimated 75,000 buses in Lagos, owned almost exclusively by private individuals. LAMATA intends to reform bus services. This may include operating large-capacity buses and a Bus Rapid Transit (BRT) system. Also, scheduled to start in 2007, LAMATA will instigate a Pilot Bus Route Franchising scheme. This would involve establishing definite routes which would then be franchised to licensed corporate operators on a competitive tender basis. LAMATA will be the franchise regulator and there will be a total of no more than 100 operators. The scheme is to be piloted on the 10 km Iyana-Ipaja-Ikotun corridor. Route planning, fellet requirements and finance strategy are expected to be completed in the first half of 2006. Construction of infrastructure and tendering for operations are due to take place during late 2006 and mid 2007, with the scheme expected to start in June 2007.

There are also plans to integrate the bus system with improved ferry services.

Light rail

A light rail system has been proposed, and a contract signed with Lamna International for initial work on this project. Please see separate entry.

Ferry services

LAMATA is working to improve ferry services and integrate these with other transport modes. There will be encouragement for private sector participation in the provision of commuter ferry services, specifically the existing service between Mile 2, Apapa and Marina and new services to and from the Lekki area. LAMATA will also investigate the possibility of new services from the Ikorodu area.

Nigerian Railway Corporation (NRC)

Headquarters
PMB 1037, Ebute-Metta, Lagos, Nigeria
Tel: (+234 1) 774 73 20, 545 74 60
Fax: (+234 1) 583 13 67
e-mail: info.nrc@nrc-ng.org
Web: www.nrc-ng.org

Key personnel

Managing Director and Chief Executive: J C Nwankwo
Secretary: F Mba-Jonas
Directors
  Administration: V Nyamkyume
  Civil Engineering: E I Oradiegwu
  Operations: S I O Elechi
  Mechanical/Electrical: F E Okhiria
  Internal Audit: Felix Njoku
  Finance: A A Adamu
Managers
  Signalling and Telecommunications: I D Nasamu
  Materials Management: A G Mofikoya
  Legal Services: P I Onyeabo
  Corporate Planning: K Zayyana
  Staff: 6,427 (as at September 2007)

Other offices

Abuja office

Plot 739 Cadastral, Zone A6, Off Ibrahim Babangida Way, Maitama District, Abuja, Nigeria
Tel: (+234 9) 413 19 12   Fax: (+234 9) 413 19 13

London office

Suite C, First Floor (North), Astra House, 23/25 Arklow Road, London SE14 6EB, UK
Tel: (+44 208) 691 87 55
Fax: (+44 208) 692 44 71
e-mail: panchenlarge@hotmail.com

Key personnel

Contact: P G Large

NRC also has offices in Enugu, Ibadan, Zaria, Bauchi, Kafanchan and Minna.

Type of operation: Suburban heavy rail

Passenger journeys: 8,000 daily (estimate)

Current situation

Nigerian Railway Corporation (NRC) is organised as seven operational regional districts. As much as 80 per cent of the NCR track is reported to be in need of overhaul.

Currently, passenger services are as follows: One express passenger train from Iddo to Kanao (Friday), 12 intra-city trains per day, two tourist trains from Iddo to Abeokuta (weekends) and one mixed passenger/freight train from Iddo to Idogo (and back) every Sunday.

For further information on NRC, please see *Jane's World Railways*.

Developments

Recent improvements include the automation of level crossings, upgrading of the signalling system and the installation of a microwave technology telecommunications system.

New lines are being constructed, such as the 19 km Port Harcourt-Onne narrow-gauge line (1,067 mm), the 277 km Ajaokuta-Warri standard-gauge line and a contract has been awarded to construct a new standard-gauge line from Lagos to Kano.

In April 2005, the Nigerian Government's Bureau of Public Enterprise invited expressions of interest from potential advisers with regard to the concession for operation of the state-owned network. Privatisation is viewed as the only viable option for the system, which has been in decline despite some government funding in recent years. The successful bidder for the network would most likely be awarded a 25-year concession, with the new operator and the government working together on the rehabilitation of the system for the first five years.

Lagos State Government of Nigeria

Ministry of Transportation
Web: www.lagosstate.gov.ng

Key personnel

Commissioner: Adeyemi Banire
Permanent Secretary: Kamaldeen Abiodun Junaid
Director, Transportation Policy and Co-ordination Setonji Awoleke Ayeni
Director, Transport Operations: Aderemi O Thomas
Director, Transportation Engineering: Shakiru O Agbaje
Assistant Director, Transportation Policy and Co-ordination: Rotimi Toyin Abdul

Current situation

The Ministry of Transportation (MOT) works closely with Lagos Metropolitan Area Transport Authority (LAMATA) with regard to strategic policy direction for public transport service in the Lagos metropolitan area. For information on private bus operators and other transport modes, please see the separate entry for LAMATA.

Competition for regular bus service has come from a trend for motorcycle/scooter riders to offer paid lifts.

Developments

The state government has started to address the problem of unlicensed bus and taxi operators in the metropolitan area. It has put into place a hackney permit and reduced the time required to process applications for this, and reports that service has improved.

In March 2003, the MOT regulated the commercial motorcycle operations to improve the safety of passengers.

Lagos State Ferry Services Corporation

Current situation
The Corporation's ferry services run over four routes: Marina-Apapa, Elegbata-Oyingbo, Mile 2-Marina and the recently opened Elegbata-Apapa route.

Five ferries have been refurbished and brought into service to be added to the only two ferries previously operational.

Developments

The state government is encouraging private-sector participation in the operation of inland waterways and privatisation of the ferry service is under consideration. A hydrographic survey was completed from Badore to Egbin and it is hoped that the route will become operational shortly.

Lemna International

2445 Park Avenue, Minneapolis, MN 55404-3790, US
Tel: (+1 612) 253 20 00   Fax: (+1 612) 253 20 03
e-mail: intlsales@lemna.com
Web: www.lemna.com

Key personnel
President and CEO: Viet Ngo
Assistant Marketing Director: Mandy McMahon

Type of operation: Light rail (proposed)

Current situation

A 20 km light rail scheme has been proposed for Lagos. The system, which is expected to cost in the region of USD300 million, would be mainly funded and managed by private-sector investment.

Developments

In 2005, a contract was signed by the Lagos State Government with Lemna International, US, for the first-stage study, design and construction of the Build-Operate-Transfer (BOT) project.

Lemna is currently preparing a detailed feasibility study. After the engineering and design stage, Lemna International's subsidiary, Lemna Nigeria Limited, will construct, operate and maintain the system.

Studies are scheduled to be completed by the end of 2006 and construction of the first segment of the system will then commence in 2007.

Norway

Bergen

Population: 247,746 (2008)

Public transport

Bus and trolleybus services in inner city provided by municipal undertaking working with private bus companies serving suburban areas; local trains run Bergen-Arna; light rail under construction with extension planned.

Tide ASA

Møllendalsveien 1a, PO Box 6300, N-5893 Bergen, Norway
Tel: (+47) 55 23 87 00   Fax: (+47) 55 23 87 01
e-mail: post@tide.no
Web: www.tide.no

Key personnel
General Manager: Dagfinn Neteland
Director, Economics and Finance:
  Atle Harald Sandtorv
Director, Strategy and Business Development:
  Bjørn Ove Børnes
Director, Communications and Branding:
  Arild Sondre Sekse
Project Director: Gunnar Buvik
Corporate Director: Geir Olav Mandt
Director, Tide Sjø AS: Geir E Aga
Director, Tide Buss AS: Idar Sylta
Director, Tide Reiser AS: Rita Brokstad
  Staff: 3,000 (2007 estimate)

Current situation

In November 2006, HSD ASA and Gaia Trafikk AS merged to form the Tide group (Tide ASA). In June 2007, Stavangerske AS also merged into Tide.

Tide Buss AS

Type of operation: Bus and trolleybus

Passenger journeys: 25 million (estimate for Bergen operations)
Vehicle-km: Not currently available

Current situation

Tide Buss AS, with some 2,000 employees, operates public transport services in Hordaland and Nord-Rogaland. Tide Buss AS owns approximately 1,000 buses, and is the second largest bus company in Norway. The company operates from nine locations in Hordaland and one in Rogaland.

Subsidiaries of Tide Buss AS are Tide Verksted (heavy vehicle maintenance) and Tide Buss Haugesund (operates a bus service operation in the Haugesund area).

Another group company, Tide Reiser SA, co-operates with other bus companies to operate express bus routes.

Number of routes: 17 (bus 16, trolleybus 1)
Route length: (One way) 220 km (trolleybus 4.1 km)

Fleet: 1,000 buses (approximate)
Breakdown of fleet is not currently available
In peak service: Not currently available
On order: Not currently available

Fleet: 6 trolleybuses (Plus two dual-mode buses)
Mercedes/ABB articulated duobus (1992/94)   2
MAN/Neoplan/Kiepe 4-door 18 m trolleybus   6
In peak service: Not currently available

Most intensive service: 7 min and 30 seconds
One-person operation: All routes
Fare collection: All types of ticket and card, except school pass, available from driver; onboard card reader
Fare structure: Zonal; common for all operators throughout county area; single or multijourney tickets, 30-day season, value card, off-peak card; one free transfer (1 h); higher fare for night services on Friday and Saturday
Fares collected on board: 93.3 per cent
Fare evasion control: Inspectors
Operational control: Central control with travelling inspectors in radio contact
Arrangements for elderly/disabled: Prebooked van services using 25 Mercedes minibuses with wheelchair access, paid for by grants from county council
Average distance between stops: 400 m
Average peak-hour speed: In bus lanes, 25 km/h; in mixed traffic, 16 km/h
Bus priority: 30 km of bus lanes with priority at traffic lights at some intersections
Operating costs financed by: Fares 92 per cent, other commercial sources 6.5 per cent, subsidy/grants 1.5 per cent
Subsidy from: Regional government
New vehicles financed by: Loans

City of Bergen

Bybanen: Bergen Light Rail
PO Box 7700, N-5020 Bergen, Norway
Tel: (+47) 55 56 92 98   Fax: (+47) 55 56 95 75
e-mail: info@bybanen.no
Web: www.bybanen.no

Street address
Øvre Dreggsallmenningen 6, N-5003 Bergen, Norway

Key personnel
Project Director: Rune Haugsdal
Chief Engineer: Thomas J Potter
Director of Construction: Jostein Fjærestad
Director of Operations: Knut Serigstad
Director of Safety: Øyvind Knapskog
Director of Planning: Håkon Rasmussen

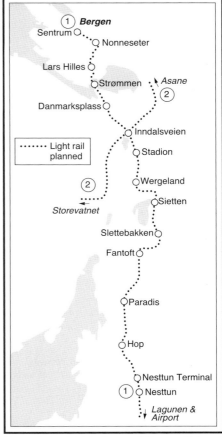

Map of the initial phase of Bergen light rail system, showing interchange with planned future Line 2
1115253

Type of operation: Light rail (under construction)

Background

The City of Bergen is responsible for the planning, design, construction, approval and operation of a new light rail system. The city has established a light rail project office (Bybanekontoret) to oversee activities. A light rail system of 40 km, based on two lines of equal distance, is planned and will serve the northern, western and southern areas of the city, including the airport.

Current situation

The construction of the light rail system is now under way and is being financed through a combination of toll funds, from the toll ring around Bergen (established in 1986), and national highway funds.

The bus system will be reorganised to support the light rail system with co-ordinated bus services. This will include the extension and integration of the existing trolleybus line, which saw the introduction of six new MAN-Neoplan-Kiepe 18 m trolleybuses in 2003.

Developments

The first section of the system will require twelve 32 m vehicles, in order to provide five minute service during peak periods. Ridership is projected at approximately 26,000 passengers per day by 2015.

Construction of road improvements and utility relocation began in 2006 and civil works, workshop construction and technical installations started in 2007.

The project, on behalf of the County of Hordaland, signed a contract with Stadler Pankow GmbH for the supply of twelve 32 m long Variobahn light rail vehicles. These vehicles are 2.65 m wide, 100 per cent low floor, with a level boarding height of 300 mm, bi-directional with seating for 80 and standing room for 140 passengers. The vehicles will be equipped with air conditioning, wireless internet and LED lighting. The first vehicle is expected to be delivered in December 2009. Stadler is also responsible for the maintenance of the vehicles for eight years, with an option for an additional period of eight years.

Stadler Variobahn light rail vehicle for the City of Bergen – showing final design and livery   1369084

Test operations are expected to start during the first half of 2010 and the opening of the system is tentatively scheduled for mid-2010.

Planning permission has now been granted for a 3 km extension of the first line from Nesttun to the major shopping centre at Rådal. Construction of the extension will begin in

2010 and operations are planned to start in 2012.

Strategic plans and environmental impact studies are expected to commence shortly for Line 2, connecting the northern and western suburbs with the city centre, the regional hospital and a new university area.

Oslo

Population: City: 544,073, metropolitan area: 825,105 (2006)

Public transport

Bus, metro, light rail and tramway services operated by authority governed by nominated board (including employee representatives) under overall control of city council. It also contracts private ferry and bus lines, provides support for common overall fare structure within city area, extending to local rail journeys on State Railway (NSB BA). Service to the airport is provided by a separate state-owned company, Flytoget AS. Agreements with Stor Oslo Lokaltrafikk A/S (responsible for public transport within the county surrounding Oslo and services into Oslo) give an integrated fare structure and transfer system for the whole region. Road pricing in force.

AS Oslo Sporveier

Postboks 2857 Tøyen, N-0608 Oslo, Norway
Tel: (+47) 81 54 44 11
Fax: (+47) 22 08 40 30
e-mail: firmapost@sporveien.no
Web: www.sporveien.no

Street address
Dronningens gate 40, Tøyen, Oslo, Norway

Key personnel
Chairman: Bernt Stilluf Karlsen
Managing Director: Kjell Knarbakk
Director, Planning: Tore Kåss
Manager, Contracts: Carl Sandstad
Head, Commercial Affairs Division:
   Rune Pedersen
Director, Communications:
   Merete Agerbak-Jensen
Director, Marketing: Kirsti Nøst
   Staff: (2002) 1,587 (excluding employees of subsidiary companies)

Passenger boardings: (All modes, including contracted operations)
(2002) 162 million
(2004) 160 million

Operating costs financed by: Fares 63 per cent, other commercial sources 7 per cent, subsidy/ grants and special agreements 30 per cent

Subsidy from: City of Oslo 95 per cent (financed by municipal income and property taxes), special agreements (Akershus/Baerum counties) five per cent; concessions to pensioners financed by operator
New vehicles financed by: Loans through Municipality of Oslo

Current situation
OS, popularly named Sporveier, has overall responsibility for public transport provision in the Oslo area and contracts with its own and three private bus operators, boat services and about 100 km of State Railway lines. For these, Sporveier collects all the revenue and pays the contractors a set rate, assuming responsibility for any deficits except those of the State Railway.

All bus service is now contracted out, following establishment of Sporveier's bus operations as a subsidiary company, AS Sporveisbussene, in 1997, competing on equal terms with private operators.

As of 1 July 2003, the metro and tram operations have been run by two new wholly owned subsidiaries: Oslo T-banedrift AS operates the metro (T-bane) and Oslo Sporvognsdrift AS operates the trams. AS Sproveisbusse operates the bus services.

In 2004, public transport accounted for 22 per cent of all journeys made by Oslo's population, of which AS Oslo Sporveier's metro, trams and buses conveyed 85 per cent.

Bus

AS Sporveisbussene

Key personnel
Staff: 725 (2002)

Passenger boardings*: (2001) 54.1 million
(2002) 54.9 million
(2004) 62.9 million
Vehicle-km: Not currently available

*Includes buses operated for Sporveier by Nettbuss AS, Norgesbuss AS, Ing M O Schøyens Bilcentraler and AS Spoorveisbussene.

Number of routes: 52 (+16 night routes)
Number of stops: Not currently available
Route length: (One way) 1,367 km

Fleet: 289 buses (total fleet operated by all of the contractors), (326 including reserve buses)
Articulated bus (of which,

low-floor)	121 (95)
Standard bus (of which, low-floor)	172 (112)
15 m buses, low-floor	20
Midibus, low-floor	5
Service bus, low-floor	8

One-person operation: All routes
Fare collection: Coupon cards cancelled on board; driver sells single tickets and various types of card, but not season tickets or passes

AS Sporveisbussene MAN bus (Bill Luke)   0583211

Fare structure: Flat, single zone covers the whole city; single ticket and eight-ticket Flexicard permit free transfer on all modes within 1 hour, other seasons/ passes unrestricted; 24-hour, seven-day, monthly and three-monthly passes; children, elderly and those on municipal pensions travel free; student card

Operational control: Mobile radio; two-way radio on all vehicles

Arrangements for elderly/disabled: Five routes operated by low-entry midibuses with wheelchair lifts link residential areas with local bus stations; door-to-door service for mobility impaired transferred in 1997 to the city's Department of Transport & Communications. 74 per cent of the fleet is low-floor.

Average peak-hour speed: 16 km/h

Bus priority: Buses and trams equipped to gain priority at some 120 signal-controlled intersections under plan for general adoption of system

Integration with other modes: Full integration between modes with free transfers (see above)

Developments
Sixteen new articulated buses and 20 new 15 m buses have been recently acquired.

Metro

Oslo T-banedrift AS (T-bane)
Key personnel
Head, Communications: Bjørn Rydmark
   Staff: 917 (2002)

Type of operation: Full metro, initial route opened 1966; suburban rail upgraded to metro standards

Passenger boardings: (2001) 67.1 million
(2002) 68.4 million
(2004) 59.4 million

Car-km: Not currently available

Route length: 118.7 km
   in tunnel: 16.5 km
Number of lines: 6
Number of stations: 106
   in tunnel: 16
Gauge: 1,435 mm
Max gradient: 5%
Minimum curve radius: 200 m
Electrification: 750 V DC, third rail; Frognerseteren line 750 V DC overhead, Kolsås line 680 V DC overhead

Service: 15 min all day on branches; peak 1¾ min, off-peak 3¾ min in central area
Fare structure: Flat, as bus
Integration with other modes: Full fare integration with all other modes within the city boundaries
Signalling: Cab signalling

Rolling stock: 207 cars
Strømmens Vaerksted
Series 1-1 (1966)   M60
Series 1-2 (1966)   M30
Series 2 (1970)   M15
Series 3 (1972)   M30
Series 4 (1976, 78)   M11
Series 5 (1978)   M18
Series 6 (1980/81)   M15
Series 7 (1986/87)   M10
Series 8 (1989)   M6
T-1000 (1993)   M12

On order: In 2003, 99 Siemens metro carriages (30 three-car trains). In September 2005, a further 30 trains. Delivery commenced in late 2005.

Developments
Trial operations of new Metro cars started in late 2005.
   The Metro Ring was completed in August 2006.
   The line between Montebello and Kolsås was closed in mid-2006 for upgrading.

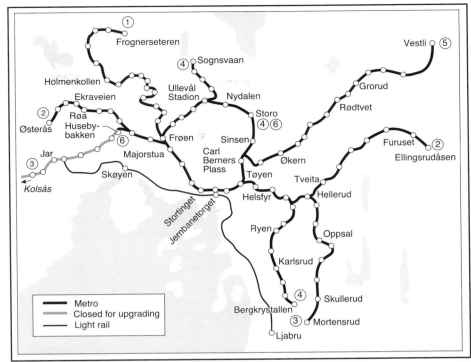

Map of Oslo's metro and light rail   1115288

Oslo T-banedrift AS metro train at Majorstieen station (Bill Luke)   0583210

Oslo Sporvognsdrift AS SL 95 tram (Bill Luke)   0583212

A new electronic ticketing system, in collaboration with SL and NSB, has been implemented in 2006.

Tramway/light rail (trikken)

Oslo Sporvognsdrift AS

Key personnel
Head, Communications: Cato Asperud
   Staff: 499 (2002)

Type of operation: Conventional tramway and light rail

Passenger journeys: (2001) 32.9 million
(2002) 33.6 million
(2004) 30.4 million
Car-km: Not currently available

Route length: 145.5 km
Number of lines: 12
Number of stops: 106
Electrification: 600 V DC, overhead

Service interval: Peak 15 min
One-person operation: All cars

Rolling stock: 40 cars plus 32 LRVs
Duewag, six-axle articulated SL 79
   (1982/89)   M40
Ansaldo SL 95 (1996/2004)   M32

Ferry
Current situation
Operated under contract by Skibs A/S Bygdøfergene from Rådhusplassen to Bygdø and by Oslo Fergene A/S to islands in the Oslofjord. The four routes (22 km) carry about 0.8 million passengers annually.

Stor-Oslo Lokaltrafikk AS (SL)

Postboks 9246, Grønland, N-0134 Oslo, Norway
Tel: (+47) 23 00 23 00
Fax: (+47) 23 00 23 99
e-mail: post@sl-lokaltrafikk.no
Web: www.slnett.no

Street address
Schweigaardsgt 10, N-0134 Oslo, Norway

Passenger journeys (all modes): (2004) 56 million (estimate)

Current situation
SL is responsible for the planning, co-ordination and marketing of public transport in the counties surrounding Oslo and provides services to Oslo. The company has agreements with AS Oslo Sporveier and Norges Statsbaner (NSB) to give an integrated fare structure and transfer system for the whole region.

Nettbuss AS

Corporate Headquarters
Skippergaten 31, Konsernstaben, N-0048 Oslo, Norway
Tel: (+47) 22 17 69 44   Fax: (+47) 22 17 69 44
e-mail: konsern@nettbuss.no
Web: www.nettbuss.no

Key personnel
Managing Director: Arne Veggeland
Staff: 5,000 (whole group estimate)

Stor-Oslo Lokaltrafikk AS (SL) Mercedes-Benz bus (Bill Luke)   0583213

Background
Established in 1925.

Current situation
Fully owned by Norges Statsbaner AS (NSB AS), the company provides local bus services in the Oslo area and express bus and travel services throughout Scandinavia.
   The company's annual turnover is approximately NOK2,800 million.

Fleet: Approx 2,300 buses (whole group)
Breakdown of fleet not currently available

Norges Statsbaner AS (NSB AS) – Norwegian State Railways

Prinsens gate 7-9, N-0048 Oslo, Norway
Tel: (+47) 23 15 00 00   Fax: (+47) 23 15 31 46
Web: www.nsb.no

Key personnel
Chairman: Ingeborg Borgerud
President and Chief Executive:
Einar Enger
Executive Director, Communications:
   Arne Wam
Managing Director, Passenger Business:
   Rolf Roverud
Directors:
   Planning: Tom Ingulstad
   Marketing: Marianne Einarsen
   Sales: Karen K Hancke
   Operation: Øysten Risan
   Strategy: Arne Fosen
   Economics: Irene Katrin Thunselle
   Staff: 10,648 (2005 Group total)

Type of operation: Suburban heavy rail

Passenger journeys: (2003) 45 million
(2004) 46 million
(2005) 47.3 million

Background
NSB BA, originally established in 1996, became a private limited company in July 2002. The company is owned by the Norwegian Ministry of Transport and Communications.

Current situation
NSB's suburban lines link Oslo Central with Moss, Mysen, Kongsvinger, Jaren, Eidsvoll, Kongsberg and Spikkestad, totalling 568 km, electrified 15 kV

16⅔ Hz. Trains run hourly or half-hourly. Services within the city boundaries extend to about 100 km.
   The line to the new airport at Gardermoen opened in October 1998 and is operated by a separate state-owned company, Flytoget AS (see separate entry).
   A subsidiary, Nettbuss AS, provides bus services in Oslo (see separate entry).
   For further information on NSB AS, please see *Jane's World Railways*.

Developments
In 2005, NSB AS acquired a shareholding of 34 per cent in Svenska Tågkompaniet AB, a Swedish passenger train operator.

Rolling stock: 182 emu cars

Flytoget AS

PO Box 19 Sentrum, N-0101 Oslo, Norway
Tel: (+47) 23 15 90 00   Fax: (+47) 23 15 90 01
e-mail: flytoget@flytoget.no
Web: www.flytoget.no

Key personnel
Chief Executive Officer: Thomas Havegjerde
Commercial Director: Sverre Hoeven
   Staff: 260 (2002)

Type of operation: Suburban heavy rail

Passenger journeys: (2005) 4.5 million
Passenger-km: (2005) 218 million

Background
Flytoget AS was originally established as a division of Norwegian State Railways (NSB AS) to operate dedicated services to Oslo's Gardermoen Airport, which opened in October 1998. Trains initially ran over mostly classic lines until a new 48 km direct link from Oslo was commissioned in August 1999.
   In 2003, Flytoget was separated from NSB AS, forming a separate state-owned company reporting to the Ministry of Industry and Trade.

Current situation
The core weekday service provides six services between Oslo and the airport every hour in each direction, half of these additionally calling at Lillestrøm and running west of Oslo to Asker.

Rolling stock: 16 three-car Adtranz emus

Pakistan

Karachi
Population: In excess of 14 million (estimate)

Public transport
Bus and minibus services provided by private companies; scooter rickshaws. Limited suburban rail services; light rail/BRT proposed.

Pakistan Railways (PR)
31 Sheikh Abdul Hameed Bin Badees, Lahore, Pakistan
Tel: (+92 42) 920 17 71
Fax: (+92 42) 920 17 60
Web: www.pakrail.com

Key personnel
General Manager, Operations:
   Tariq Yaseen
Director, Marketing:
   Rizwan Ahmed Bhatti
Deputy Director, Marketing/South:
   Syed Imran Hassain Gilani

Divisional Superintendent, Karachi:
  Mir Muhammad Khaskheli
  Staff: 86,564 (Total for all operations) (2006/07)

Passenger journeys: (Total operations)
(2004/05) 78.2 million
(2005/06) 81.4 million
(2006/07) 83.9 million
Train-km: (Total passenger operations)
(2004/05) 31.1 million
(2005/06) 31.5 million
(2006/07) 33.7 million

Current situation
Operates diesel suburban service on four routes, including a circular route (Karachi Circular Railway (KCR), totalling 98 km with 39 stations, irregular service, graduated fares.
  For further information on PR, please see *Jane's World Railways.*

Developments
The KCR is partly in operation, with plans to fully revitalise the system being pursued. The project has been approved in principle and would be overseen by a new company, the Karachi Urban Transport Corporation (KUTC), the board of which includes representatives from the provincial and city governments and Pakistan Railways. The cost of the project would be assisted by a Japanese loan.
  Computerised ticketing has been introduced at Karachi City and Karachi Cantt stations.

City District Government Karachi (CDGK)
EDO Transport & Communication
City Complex, Civic Center, Hasan Square, Gulshan-e-Iqbal, Gulshan Town, Karachi, Pakistan
Tel: (+92 21) 923 06 55, 13 04
Fax: (+92 21) 921 33 64
e-mail: edotc@karachicity.gov.pk
Web: www.karachicity.gov.pk

Key personnel
Executive District Officer, Transport & Communication: Muhammed Athar Hussain

Director General, KMTP:
  Malik Zaheerul Islam

Karachi Mass Transit Programme (KMTP)
Current situation
The Karachi Mass Transit Programme (KMTP) has been under study for several decades – please see previous editions of *Jane's Urban Transport Systems* for history.

Developments
Currently, pans are being investigate for the upgrade of the Karachi Circular Railway (KCR), and new Light Rail Transit (LRT) and Bus Rapid Transit (BRT) networks.
  The Asian Development Bank (ADB) has issued an invitation for submissions of Expression of Interest (EOI) for consultancy services to review the proposals for a Mass Transit System in the City. The closing date for EOIs was February 2007.

Peru

Lima
Population: City 7.8 million (2006 estimate), metropolitan area Lima/Callao 8.5 million (2007 estimate)

Public transport
Bus services, including busway, and metro currently operated in Lima and adjacent Callao by independent operators, with additional minibus, midibus and taxi services, supervised by government and municipal agencies. Further busways and extension/s to the metro network are planned.

Instituto Metropolitano Protransporte de Lima (Protransporte)
Municipality of Metropolitan Lima (MML)
Pasaje Acuña 127, 4° Piso Cercado, Lima, Lima, Peru
Tel: (+51 1) 428 33 33
Fax: (+51 1) 428 22 15
Web: www.protransporte.org.pe

Key personnel
President: Angel Perez Rodas
Executive Director:
  Ramon Arevalo Hernandez
General Manager:
  Mario Portocarrero Carpio
e-mail: mportocarrero@protransporte.gob.pe
Manager, Works & Maintenance:
  Walter Paredes Rojas
Manager, Studies & Projects:
  Fanny Eto Chero
Head of Administration and Finance:
  Orestes Cáceras Zapata

Background
Government agency responsible for establishing a mass rapid transit system for Metropolitan Lima (Lima/Callao). It is also responsible for monitoring and co-ordinating all project activities.

Since the end of the 1980s, services have been provided almost entirely by small private operators, often owner-drivers or one-route companies. There are networks of conventional, mini and midi buses and taxis, which together cater for more than 7.2 million journeys a day.

Bus
Developments
There is a busway, known as Corredor Segregado de Alta Capacidad (COSAC), which runs north-south in the city. There are plans for further segregated busways operated with CNG buses and the agency is planning to make the transport system accessible.

Fleet
Not currently available
Public transport vehicles (including buses, combis (12-passenger buses), coasters (approximately 35-passengers) and micros
Taxis (formal and informal)

Autoridad Autónoma del Proyecto Especial – Sistema Eléctrico de Transporte Masivo de Lima y Callao (AATE)
Authority of the Lima and Callao Electric Mass Transit Special Project
Jr Solidaridad Cuadra 8 (s/n), Parque Industrial de Villa El Salvador, Lima, Peru
Tel: (+51 1) 287 36 83
Web: www.trenurbano.gob.pe

Key personnel
Executive President:
  Victor Dario Pacahuala Velásquez
General Manager:
  Javier Enrique Cornejo Arana
Manager, Administration and Finance:
  Vladimir Américo Garcia Valverde

Manager, Operations:
  Walter Héctor Arboleda Gordon
  Staff: Not currently available

Type of operation: Metro, initial section opened for regular service 2003

Passenger journeys: Not currently available
Train-km: Not currently available

Route length: 9.8 km
Number of lines: 1
Number of stations: 7
Gauge: 1,435
Electrification: 1,500 V DC, overhead

Current situation
The municipality of Lima has called for an international tender for the concession of the urban train line. The current 9.8 km section runs from Villa El Salvador to Atocongo Bridge with seven stations and a workshop-yard. The double-track alignment, 1,435 mm gauge, is electrified at 1.5 kV DC overhead, and has centralised traffic control. The systems and the 32-car fleet were supplied by the Italian consortium Tralima (Intermetro, Ansaldo Trasporti, Breda).

Developments
Initial bids have been received for the operation of the existing section and for an extension to Line 1 on a 33-year contract, three years of which will be for the construction of the extension. This extension would run from Atocongo Bridge to Av Grau/Hospital 2 de Mayo in downtown Lima, 11.7 km, elevated with nine stations.
  There are long-term plans for a further six lines.

Rolling stock: 32 cars (includes 2 reserve cars)

Service: 10 min
First/last train: 06.00/18.00
Fare structure: Flat
Integration with other modes: Bus transfer

For details of the latest updates to *Jane's Urban Transport Systems* online and to discover the additional information available exclusively to online subscribers please visit
juts.janes.com

Philippines

Manila

Population: City 1.66 million, Metro Manila/National Capital Region (NCR) 11.55 million (2007 Census)

Public transport

Bus services for conurbation of 13 municipalities (including city of Manila, Quezon city and three others) provided in part by government-owned undertaking with additional bus, minibus and extensive shared taxi 'Jeepney' services provided by independent companies and owner-operators. Light rail lines operated under franchise from government. Suburban rail services by Philippine National Railways.

Metro Manila Transit Corporation (MMTC)

North Avenue, Quezon City, Philippines
Tel: (+63 2) 96 78 98; 95 12 34; 95 13 74
Staff: 2,055

Current situation

Government-owned MMTC is the largest single bus operator, but handles only a small proportion of total trips – around 20 million- compared with other bus and minibus operators and Jeepneys. Its fleet is thought to be no more than 100 vehicles, mainly Hino. Despite the beneficial effect of the light rail route (see separate entry in *Jane's Urban Transport Systems*), congestion remains severe and capacity badly strained.

Developments

In 2004, as part of the government's Natural Gas Vehicle Program for Public Transport (NGVPPT), Cummins Westport Inc was awarded a contract for 100 B-Series Compressed Natural Gas-fuelled (CNG) engines for buses in Metro Manila. These will be the first low-emissions CNG buses to be used in the country. Metro Manila plans to have 900 CNG buses in operation by the end of 2005. The buses will be supplied by the Chinese companies Anhui Ankai Automobiles and Zhengzhou Yutong Company.

The Department of Transport and Communications (DOTC) is proposing to build two new bus terminals, at Monumento in Caloocan and Alabang, Muntinlupa city, to improve intermodal transportation connections. The terminal at Monumento would be linked with the LRT system. The DOTC is considering a private-public partnership on a build-operate-transfer scheme for these terminals.

Private bus/minibus

Current situation

Some 5,500 private buses and minibuses, all single-deck, and many truck-derived, range in size from minibuses to full-size vehicles with capacity for more than 60 seated. Many are owner-operated or jointly operated by small groups, but busy commuter routes are operated by around 20 larger companies. Together with Metro Manila Transit, these operators offer a network of mostly full-size buses branded Metro-Bus. In addition, there are at least 65 smaller companies, and many owner-operators and small co-operatives. Peak-hour operation is fiercely competitive, most buses having a tout to encourage as many people as possible to board. There are no route numbers, but vehicles carry destination boards.

Vehicles used range from second-hand Japanese city buses, through locally built full-size and midi types on Hino, Nissan, Fuso and Mitsubishi chassis, to old American truck chassis with school bus bodies.

Buses account for about 750 million trips annually, amounting to about 25 per cent of total trips in Manila, the majority being made by Jeepneys, with which buses are in direct competition.

One-person operation: Buses, none; minibuses, some

Fare collection: To driver or conductor
Fare structure: Zonal, premium for air conditioned services
Fares collected on board: 100 per cent
Average peak-hour speed: 12 km/h

Light Rail Transit Authority (LRTA)

LRT Line 1 – Yellow Line

Pasay Depot
Administration Building, LRTA Compound, Aurora Boulevard, Pasay City, Metro Manila, Philippines
Tel: (+63 2) 853 00 41-60   Fax: (+63 2) 831 64 49
e-mail: lrtamain@lrta.gov.ph
Web: www.lrta.gov.ph

MRT Line 2 – Purple Line

Santolan Depot
LRTA Compound, Marcos Highway, Pasig City, Metro Manila, Philippines
Tel: (+63 2) 647 34 79-91

Key personnel

DOTC Secretary and LRTA Chairman of the Board: Leandro R Mendoza
Administrator: Melquiades A Robles
Deputy Administrator: Cesar B Chavez
Manager, Administrative Department: Elmo Stephen P Triste

Manager, Finance Department: Ms Marilou B Liscano
OIC, Planning Department: Ms Eleanore T Domingo
OIC, Line 1 Operations and Engineering Department: Federico J Canar
Manager, Line 2 Operations and Maintenance Department: Ms Annabelle C Ganancial
Project Manager, LRT Line 1 Capacity Expansion Project (Phase II): Federico J Canar
Project Manager, LRT Line 1 South Extension Project (now Cavite Extension Project): Danilo S Tolentino
OIC Project Manager, LRT Line 1 North Extension Project: Federico J Canar
Project Manager, LRT Line 1 Modernisation Phase II Project: Rodrigo P Bulario
Staff: 2,403 (42 permanent/regular, 1,504 contractual) (as at 31 January 2008)

Operated by: Metro Inc

Type of operation: Line 1: Light rail, opened 1984
Line 2: Metro, partially opened April 2003, full operation October 2004

Passenger journeys: Line 1: (2004) 96.86 million
(2007) 119.12 million
Line 2: (2004) 20.67 million
(2007) 52.93 million

Route length: Line 1: 15 km, elevated
Line 2: 13.8 km, elevated (except one underground station)
Number of lines: 2

LRTA vehicle on Line 2 – Purple   1142693

LRTA Line 1 three-car vehicle   1142692

Number of stations: Line 1: 18
Line 2: 11
Gauge: 1,435 mm
Track: Line 1: 50 kg/m EB50T rail, ballasted track on concrete trackbed
Line 2: IUC 54 kg/m
Max gradient: Line 1: 0.4%
Line 2: 5%
Min curve radius: Line 1: 250 m
Line 2: 175 m
Electrification: Line 1: 750 V DC, overhead
Line 2: 1,500 V DC, overhead

Background
The Light Rail Transit Authority (LRTA) is a wholly owned government corporation created in 1980. The Authority is primarily responsible for the construction, operation, maintenance and/or lease of light rail transit systems in the Philippines.

The LRTA is attached to the Department of Transportation and Communications (DOTC) and is governed by a nine-man board of directors.

Current situation
In September 2001, the Authority's new Automated Fare Collection System (AFCS) became operational. The system uses plastic magnetic cards and replaced the token system, which greatly reduced the incidence of fraud.

Also in 2001, the rolling stock for LRT Line 1 was refurbished.

In April 2002, the LRT Line 1 track maintenance and ballast renewal project was completed.

Developments
On 5 April 2003, the MRT Line 2 project began its partial operation with the completion of the first phase (Santolan-Cubao) of the project. On the same day the following year, Phase IIa (Cubao-Legarda) became operational, with only one station left to open (Recto), and was completed in October 2004.

Installation of air conditioning units on all the first-generation trains was completed in July 2004 under the LRT Line 1 Capacity Expansion Project (Phase II) Package B.

Presently continuing is the LRT Line 1 Capacity Expansion Project (Phase II) which aims to increase the current capacity of 27,000 passengers per peak hour per direction (pphpd) to 40,000 pphpd. It involves the acquisition of 12 additional air conditioned four-car trains, upgrading of equipment for signalling, telecommunications, traction power supply and distribution, track work and automated fare collection system, as well as additional civil works for some stations and the depot to accommodate the new trains and the enhanced headway.

Work on a southward extension to LRT 1 commenced in 2005. The extension will be approximately 12 km long, with 10 stations, two of which will be built at a later date when there is sufficient demand, and will serve the cities of Parañaque and Las Piñas and the adjoining municipality of Bacoor and, later, a further 11 km to Imus and 11 km to Dasmariñas. The new system will be compatible with and will connect with LRT 1 to allow through-running of trains between the two systems.

In 2003 and 2005, passenger transfer facilities were constructed to permit smooth transfer of passengers between the existing light rail systems. LRT 1, 2 and 3 are now physically connected via these newly constructed passenger concourses.

An extension to the new MRT Line 2 is awaiting approval. The extension would be a 4 km line running eastward from Santolan station to Masinag junction with two additional stations.

The Authority is also planning to introduce a unified ticketing system using a contactless smartcard system as an upgrade to its existing fare collection system in co-ordination with the Department of Transportation and Communications (DOTC)/MRT-3.

Rolling stock: 163 cars
Line 1
BN/ACEC articulated first-generation 3-car trains (1984)   21

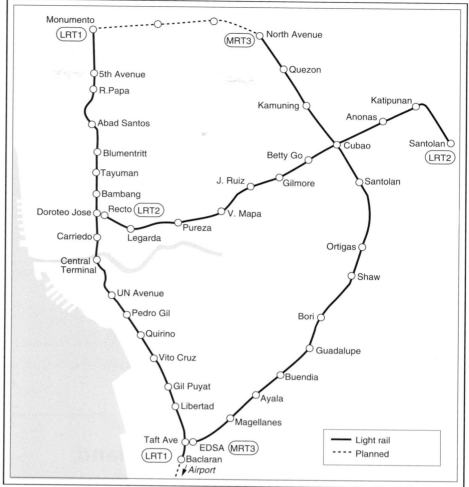

Manila light rail network

1115202

Second-generation 4-car trains   7
Line 2
Marubeni 4-car trains (1998)   18

Service: Peak 2.5 min, off-peak 3–5 min
First/last car: 04.00/23.00
Fare structure: Flat PHP12.00 for the first four stations and an additional PHP1.00 for every three stations. Maximum fare PHP15.00
Revenue control: Turnstiles at all stations, plastic magnetic ticket acceptors, automatic ticket vending machines (Line 2) and security guards
Signalling: Automatic train stop and speed control (Line 1), automatic train operation (Line 2)
One-person operation: All trains
Operating costs financed by: Fares 157 per cent

DOTC-MRT3 (Metrostar Express)

Department of Transportation and Communications
MRT3 Depot, North Avenue Corner EDSA, North Triangle Area, Quezon City, 1104, Philippines
Tel: (+63 2) 929 53 47
e-mail: cac@dotcmrt3.gov.ph
Web: www.dotcmrt3.gov.ph

Type of operation: Light rail, rapid transit system, first phase opened fully June 2000

Passenger journeys: (2001) 90.3 million
(2002) 102.6 million
(2003) 108.1 million
(2004) 122.5 million

Route length: 16.9 km (elevated)
Number of lines: 1
Number of stations: 13

Background
Built by Metro Rail Transit Corporation (MRTC) under a 25-year build-lease-transfer deal with the government.

Current situation
The first phase of Line 3 (DOTC-MRT3 – Blue Line), known as Metrostar Express, was completed in June 2000.

In September 2001, a new Automated Fare Collection System (AFCS) became operational. The system uses plastic magnetic cards and replaced the previous token system.

Developments
Phase 2 of the system, a 5.5 km mostly elevated northward extension with a further three stations, is under way.

Service: Peak: 3–7 min; off-peak: 5–7 min
First/last train:
05.30/22.30
Fare structure:
Zonal, cash (single ticket), stored value cards, reduced fare for senior citizens

Philippine National Railways (PNR)

PNR Management Centre, Torres Bugallon Street, Sangandaan, Caloocan City 1408, Philippines
Tel: (+63 2) 365 47 16, 287 30 62
Fax: (+63 2) 285 03 79
e-mail: info@pnr.gov.ph
Web: www.pnr.gov.ph

Key personnel
Chairman: Jose L Cortes
Vice-Chairman & General Manager: Jose M I Sarasola
Assistant General Manager, Administration and Finance & Manager, Corporate Planning and Management Services Department: Rafael F Mosura
Assistant General Manager, Operations and Maintenance: Edgardo R Remonte
Manager, Public Affairs/Development and Training: Ernesto B Capuz

Acting Manager, Area III – Manila Division: Gilbert Patulot
Manager, Marketing Department: Edward O Manapol
Staff: 1,300

Type of operation: Commuter rail

Passenger journeys: Not currently available

Number of routes: 7
Route length: 56 km
Number of stations: 34

Current situation
PNR operates diesel suburban service from Manila Paco northwards to Meycauayan (15 km) and south to Mamatid and Carmona (40 km), 1,067 mm gauge. Biggest flow is from Carmona, where extensive population resettlement was carried out in the 1970s and continues to expand. Trains comprise diesel multiple-unit cars (with power units defunct) and coaches, both locomotive-hauled.

Developments
Northrail-Southrail Linkage Project
The Northrail-Southrail Linkage Project was officially launched in December 2005. The project, a joint undertaking of the Governments of the Philippines and Korea, will be completed in two phases and aims to provide a mass transport service that will link the north of Manila from Caloocan to the south as far as Calamba, Laguna:

Phase I – Caloocan to Alabang, Muntinlupa
This phase will be 32 km long from Caloocan to Alabang, with 16 stations along the route. Average travel time from end to end will be 30–35 minutes, while twenty-one new diesel railcars are expected to accommodate 187,000 passengers daily.
    This phase includes:
• Improvement and upgrading of existing PNR facilities such as railroad tracks, stations, flagstops, level crossings and depot and maintenance facilities;
• Repair and reconstruction of existing bridges in Pandacan and Alabang;
• Installation of signalling and communication facilities.
    Phase 1 is estimated to cost USD50.42 million, 70 per cent (or USD35 million) of which will be funded through a loan from the Economic Development Cooperation Fund (EDCF) of Korea. The balance will be in the form of export credit from the Korean Export-Import Bank (KOEXIM).

Phase 2 – Alabang to Calamba
This phase will include:
• Double tracking of more than 27 km;
• Rehabilitation of existing stations;
• Construction of new stations at Pacita and Sta Rosa;
• Repair and reconstruction of five bridges in the Laguna area;

• Supply of railcars;
• Provision for signalling and communications;
• Road crossing improvements and control.
Rolling stock: 60 cars
Fare structures: Zonal, distance-based
Fare evasion control: Inspectors; installation of passenger control measures at stations

Land Transport Office (LTO)
National Capital Region Office (NCR)
NCR Building, Capitol Compound, Pasig City, Metro Manila, Philippines
Tel: (+63 2) 631 41 65, 633 48 98
e-mail: ltombox@lto.gov.ph
Web: www.lto.gov.ph

Key personnel
Head of NCR Office: Ricardo L Tan

Type of operation: Shared taxi 'Jeepney'

Passenger journeys: (Annual) Not currently available

Current situation
Public Utility Jeepneys (PUJs) are licensed by the Land Transport Office (LTO). These are shared taxi vehicles, mostly based on extended Jeep chassis, which travel fixed routes with a maximum capacity of 17.
    In 2006, there were 51,811 jeepneys registered in Metro Manila.

Poland

Gdansk
Population: Gdansk 480,000, Tri-City (with Gdynia, Sopot and several smaller urbanised areas) 800,000 (estimates)

Public transport
Bus and tramway services provided by local authority agency; suburban rail services.

Zaklad Komunikacji Miejskiej spolka zoo (ZKM Ltd) – Gdansk Public Transport Company
ul Jaskowa Dolina 2, PL-80-252 Gdansk, Poland
Tel: (+48 58) 341 00 21   Fax: (+48 58) 341 80 80

Key personnel
Managing Director: Jerzy Zgliczynski
Staff: 3,200

Current situation
The Gdansk Public Transport Company is a limited liability company, fully owned by the city. It operates some 77 bus lines and 10 tram lines in Gdansk and the surrounding areas and serves approximately 175 million passengers per year.

Developments
In late 2004, the European Bank for Reconstruction and Development (EBRD) agreed to fund the Gdansk Transport Company with up to €6.2 million to finance the purchase of up to 35 new buses and to co-finance an EU Structural Fund project with the City of Gdansk for the upgrading and extension of the tram tracks.
    Other future improvements may include the introduction of an electronic ticketing system and the construction of an intermodal facility.

Bus
Number of routes: 77
Route length: (One way) 618 km

Fleet: 322 vehicles	
Ikarus 280 articulated	172
Ikarus 260	59

Car 1230 on Route 8 at the main railway station (D Trevor Rowe)   0585154

Jelcz M11	74
Jelcz PR110	2
Mercedes O405N low-floor	15

Most intensive service: 10 min
Fare collection: Prepurchase tickets with validation/cancellation machines on board
Fare structure: Flat

Tramway
Type of operation: Conventional tramway

Number of lines: 10
Route length: 50 km
Number of stops: 368

Rolling stock: 250 cars	
Konstal 105N	M125
Konstal 105A	M125

PKP Przewozy Regionalne spółka zoo – PKP Regional Service Ltd
ul Grójecka 17, PL-02-021 Warsaw, Poland
Tel: (+48 22) 524 14 05; 524 47 44; 524 41 05; 524 46 50; 659 33 54   Fax: (+48 22) 524 16 01
e-mail: infodc@pkp.com.pl
    kzr@pkp.com.pl
Web: www.pr.pkp.pl
    www.pkp.com.pl

Key personnel
Chairman of the Management Board and Chief Executive Officer: Jan Tereszczuk

Type of operation: Suburban heavy rail

Passenger journeys: Not currently available

Current situation
At least five trains per hour run in the electrified Gdansk-Gdynia urban corridor (27 km), some extended to Wejherowo (44 km). Also Gdansk to

Tczew (32 km) about hourly, Gdansk to Gdansk Nowy Port two or three trains per hour, and from Gdynia southwards to Koscierzyna every 2 hours.

For further information on this company, please see *Jane's World Railways.*

Krakow

Population: City: 757,500, metropolitan area: 1.4 million (estimates)

Public transport
Bus and tramway services provided by municipal undertaking; suburban rail services by subsidiary of the Polish State Railways (PKP) – PKP Regional Service Ltd; some bus services by State Motor Transport – Panstwowa Komunikacja Samochodowa (PKS) – (www.pks.pl.)

Miejskie Przedsiębiorstwo Komunikacyjne ŚA w Krakówie (MPK SA) – Krakow Public Transport Company
ul Jana Brożka 3, PL-30-347 Kraków, Poland
Tel: (+48 12) 254 10 00   Fax: (+48 12) 254 10 13
e-mail: komunikaty@mpk.krakow.pl
Web: www.mpk.krakow.pl

Key personnel
Director General and Managing Director: Julian Pilszczek
Finance Director: Zbigniew Palenica
Director for Transportation: Mariusz Szałkowski
   Staff: 2,496 (2006)

Passenger journeys: (All modes)
(2003) 314 million
(2004) 302 million
(2005) 298 million
(2006) 302 million (estimate)

Operating costs financed by: Payment per vehicle-km based on public service contract with the City of Krakow
Subsidy from: None

Current situation
Miejskie Przedsiębiorstwo Komunikacyjne SA w Krakówie (MPK) is a joint stock company, fully owned by the city and providing bus and tram services in Krakow.

Currently, 80 per cent of the bus fleet is low-floor vehicles.

Developments
In 2005, MPK SA signed a contract connected with the EU project 'Integrated Project for Public Transport in Krakow Agglomeration – phase I', which comprises: Modernization of two sections of existing network (5-6 km of track); construction of a new bus interchange station and the purchase of 24 new low-floor trams. Total value amount was for more than EUR55 million.

The order for trams was placed with Bombardier for 24 26 m *FLEXITY Classic* low-floor trams in mid-2006. Electrical equipment will be provided by Vossloh-Kiepe and some logistics work will be carried out by Solaris. Delivery is scheduled to start in late 2007.

MPK SA is also currying out a project to introduce an electronic ticketing system for public transport, that includes installation of 60 stationary multi-functional ticketing machines, 300,000 e-ticket cards and 60 validation devices.

Since August 2006, MPK SA has operated public transport services through a contract, which is based on payment per vehicle km.

MPK SA has also taken part in two research projects, CIVITASII/CARAVEL and SPUTNIC, within the Sixth European Framework Programme for Research and Technological Development.

The organisation has been increasing the number of vehicles that meet European requirements for environment protection.

Bus
Number of routes: 126 (42 zonal)
Route length: 1,624.5 km (excluding night lines)

Fleet: 495 vehicles	
Ikarus 260	34
Jelcz 120 M	31
Jelcz 121 M	8
Jelcz 121 MB	77
Jelcz 181/182 MB	65
Scania 113 CLL	69
Scania 113 ALB	30
Scania OmniCity 6×2	17
Scania OmniCity 4×2	14
Scania Urbino 12	50
MAN NG 313	10
Autosan H 6	21
Solaris Urbino 18	26
Jelcz M 081MB 3	32
MAN SG 242	1
Neoplan N 4020	5
Jelcz 121 M/4 CNG	5
In peak service: 439	

Most intensive service: 6 min
One-person operation: All services
Fare collection: Pre-purchase with validation/cancellation equipment on board, or payment to driver
Fare structure: Urban, flat; suburban, zonal
Fare evasion control: Roving inspectors
Operational control: Traffic regulators and route inspectors; control by mini-computer to be introduced

MPK SA Scania OmniCity articulated bus   1323806

MPK SA Solaris bus   1323808

Bombardier Flexity *Classic/NGT6 tram*   1323805

Arrangements for elderly/disabled: Disabled soldiers, pensioners, students, scholars half fare; over 75's and blind people with escorts, free; installation of new display tables (with better contrast), stop-buttons adjusted to needs of disabled people, level of platforms the same as pavements, rough covering of platforms' surface for blind people to be implemented.
Average distance between stops: 690 m
Average peak-hour speed: 18 km/h

Rolling stock: 428	
Konstal 105N	M283
MAN/Siemens T4/B4 ex-Nuremberg	M8
GT6	M42
Bombardier *Flexity* Classic/NGT6	
(1999–2001)	M26
E1 (ex-Vienna)	33
C3 (ex-Vienna)	31
Konstal 111N	2
N8S (ex-Nuremberg)	3

In peak service: Not currently available
Fare structure: As bus
One-person operation: All routes

New vehicles financed by: Own resources, EU structural funds

Tramway
Type of operation: Conventional tramway/light rail

Number of lines: 25
Route length: 83.2 km
Gauge: 1,435 mm

PKP Przewozy Regionalne spółka zoo – PKP Regional Service Ltd

ul Grójecka 17, PL-02-021 Warsaw, Poland
Tel: (+48 22) 524 14 05; 524 47 44; 524 41 05;
   524 46 50; 659 33 54
Fax: (+48 22) 524 16 01
e-mail: infodc@pkp.com.pl; kzr@pkp.com.pl
Web: www.pr.pkp.pl; www.pkp.com.pl

Key personnel
Chairman of the Management Board and Chief Executive Officer: Jan Tereszczuk

Type of operation: Suburban heavy rail

Current situation
Trains run about hourly to Skawina (21 km), and to Wieliczka/Niepolomice. Also irregular services on several other routes.
   For further information on this company, please see *Jane's World Railways.*

Łódź

Population: City 764,168, province (Voivodship) 2.57 million (2006 estimates)

Public transport
Bus and urban tramway services operated by municipal undertaking, with suburban tram routes operated by separate companies; suburban rail services operated by Polish State Railways (PKP).

Miejskie Przedsiębiorstwo Komunikacyjne-Łódź Spólka z o o (MPK)

Skr Pocztowa 28, PL-90-950 Łódź, Poland
Tel: (+48 42) 672 11 11
Fax: (+48 42) 672 12 09
e-mail: mpk@mpk.lodz.pl
Web: www.mpk.lodz.pl

Key personnel
President and General Director: Krzysztof Wąsowicz
Managing Director: Jarosław Marec

Operating costs financed by: Company

Background
The company was established in 1992. It is wholly owned by Łódź Commune. The company is responsible for transport services within the administrative area of the City of Łódź.

Current situation
In April 2002, the company was licensed to provide the city with transport services, including specialised services for disabled persons, for a 50-year term.
   Repairs to and modernisation of buses and trams are carried out by the company's Technical Division (ZT). This division also carries out renovations of historical tram cars, 805N cars, assembly of Bombardier Cityrunners and authorised assembly of Ikarus 280.

The company also has a Rails And Power Network division, which carries out work such as laying tram rails, renovation and conservation of power networks and high voltage substations, and the production of rail and power network elements.

Developments
In August 2006, video and surveillance systems were installed in 60 buses and trams.
   Also that month, an agreement was signed with the Łódź Voivodship for co-financing of the Łódź Regional Tram Project. This project would require EU funding. Plans for this project include:
Modernisation of the 15 km of track and supply network (about 30 km of the single track);
Building and modernisation of 31 tram stops;
Purchase of 10 modern, lower deck trams;
Building a modern system for traffic control and supervision in the centre of Łódź.
Longer-term plans include:
The creation of an integrated transport tariff for the entire agglomeration, with the use of an electronic metropolitan area card;
The creation of an integrated passenger information system, covering the public transport services network in the entire agglomeration.

Bus
Passenger journeys: (2002) 111 million
Vehicle-km: (2002) 28.3 million

Number of routes: 66 (58 day and 8 night routes)
Route length: (One way) 614 km (158 km night routes)

Current situation
Some bus lines are operated by other companies: MKT Company, TP Company, MUK Company and KORO (a private company).

Fleet: 392 vehicles	
Volvo B10L low-floor (1998–99)	34
Volvo B10LA articulated low-floor (1999)	25
Volvo 7000 low-floor (2000/01)	40
Volvo 7000A low-floor (2001)	16
Mercedes-Benz 405N (1994/97)	34
Mercedes-Benz 405GN articulated, low-floor (1997)	1
Mercedes-Benz O 530 Citaro low-floor (2000)	25
Jelcz M181MB articulated, low-floor (1996/97)	39
Jelcz 120MM (1992)	4
Jelcz 121MB low-floor (1997)	4
Ikarus 280 articulated (1982/95)	82
Jelcz M121MB3 low-floor (2005)	34
Mercedes-Benz O 530 G Citaro low-floor (2006)	7
Mercedes-Benz O 345 G Conecto articulated (2006)	30
Jelcz M081 MB3 Vero low-floor midibus (2006)	17

In peak service: Not currently available

On order: 19 Jelcz 121MB buses
Most intensive service: 7 min
One-person operation: All routes
Fare collection: Prepurchase single timed tickets, one- and three-day, 14-day, 30-day, monthly, four- and five-month (student) or annual passes with validation machines on board
Fare structure: Flat
Fares collected on board: None
Fare evasion control: Roving inspectors
Operational control: Roving inspectors
Arrangements for elderly/disabled: Disabled servicemen, blind persons and their escorts, and over-70s, free; other retired or pensioners, half fare; paratransit services are provided with nine Volkswagen T4 and 5 Fiat Ducato cars adapted specially for transporting people in wheelchairs; the cars are fitted with special wheelchair lifts. Some 60,000 passenger journeys are undertaken every year
Average peak-hour speed: 18.2 km/h

Tramway
Type of operation: Conventional tramway

Passenger journeys: (2002) 116 million
Car-km: (2002) 29.5 million

Route length: 208 km
Number of lines: 15 (plus trambus line A)
Gauge: 1,000 mm
Max gradient: 2.5%
Minimum curve radius: 21 m
Electrification: 600 V DC, overhead

Development
During 2005/06, four further 805Na cars were modernised.
Rolling stock: 468 cars

Konstal 805Na	M453
(85 modernised)	
Bombardier Cityrunner (2001)	M15

In peak service: Not currently available
First/last car: 03.16/24.17

Fare structure/collection: As bus
One-person operation: All cars

Suburban/interurban tramways
Current situation
In 1994, interurban tramways were taken over by two new companies. Tramway Podmieskie operates two routes with 15 cars, and MKT runs four routes with 40 cars.

PKP Przewozy Regionalne spółka zoo – PKP Regional Service Ltd
ul Grójecka 17, PL-02-021 Warsaw, Poland
Tel: (+48 22) 524 14 05; 524 47 44; 524 41 05; 524 46 50; 659 33 54   Fax: (+48 22) 524 16 01

e-mail: infodc@pkp.com.pl; kzr@pkp.com.pl
Web: www.pr.pkp.pl; www.pkp.com.pl

Key personnel
Chairman of the Management Board and Chief Executive Officer: Jan Tereszczuk

Type of operation: Suburban heavy rail

Current situation
Trains run at least half-hourly to Koluszki (27 km), and about hourly to Tomaszow Mazowiecki and Zdunskawola. Also irregular services provided on several other routes.
For further information on this company, please see *Jane's World Railways.*

Poznan
Population: City 566,546, province (Voivodship) 3.4 million (2006 estimates)

Public transport
Bus and tramway services provided by municipal authority, with some contracted bus operations. Suburban rail services by State Railway (PKP).

Miejskie Przedsiębiorstwo Komunikacyjne w Poznaniu Spółka zoo (MPK)
ul Glogowska 131/133, PL-60-244 Poznan, Poland
Tel: (+48 61) 869 93 61   Fax: (+48 61) 866 37 08
Web: www.mpk.poznan.pl

Key personnel
General Director: Wojciech Tulibacki
Financial Manager: Lidia Bartosiak
Tramway Manager: Jan Firlik
Bus Manager: Krzysztof Ksiazyk
  Staff: 3,000 (estimate)

Passenger journeys: (All modes)
Not currently available

Operating costs financed by: Fares 48.9 per cent, subsidy/grants 51.1 per cent
Subsidy from: Municipal budget

Developments
In 2003, an electronic payment card, KOMKarta, was introduced.

Bus
Passenger journeys: Not currently available
Vehicle-km: Not currently available

Number of routes: 57 (plus 21 night routes)
Route length: (One way) 465 km

Fleet: 294 vehicles

Ikarus 260 (1985)	18
Jelcz M11 (1984/90)	36
Den Oudsten (1982)	14
Jelcz M121M low-floor (1985)	1
MAN NL202 low-floor (1996)	40
Neoplan N4016 low-floor (1996/97)	31
Neoplan N4009 low-floor (1996/97)	22
Ikarus 280 articulated (1983/94)	88
Ikarus (Yu) IK160P articulated (1992)	14
Ikarus 435 articulated (1994)	1
MAN NG272 low-floor articulated (1996)	10
Neoplan N4020 Megatrans low-floor articulated (1996/97)	19

In peak service: 230

One-person operation: All routes
Fare collection: Prepurchase day passes, carnets or single tickets; validation/cancelling machines on board; KOMKarta electronic payment system
Fare structure: Timed tickets, 10, 30, 60 min, 24 h, 7 days; free transfer
Fares collected on board: Nil; 47 per cent of passengers hold prepurchase tickets, 53 per cent passes
Fare evasion control: Inspectors
Operational control: Route inspectors
Arrangements for elderly/disabled: Invalids and over-75s travel free, pensioners pay reduced fare; seats allocated for disabled
Average distance between stops: 603 m
Average peak-hour speed: 19.2 km/h
New vehicles financed by: City Council

Tramway
Type of operation: Conventional tramway

Passenger boardings: Not currently available
Car-km: Not currently available

Route length: 150 km
Number of lines: 20 (plus 1 night route)
Number of stops: 237
Gauge: 1,435 mm
Max gradient: 5.6
Min curve radius: 25 m
Electrification: 600 V DC, overhead

Service: 15 min, evenings 20 min
First/last car: 04.49/22.49
Fare structure: As bus
One-person operation: All routes

Rolling stock: 330 cars (estimate)

LHB 1G ex-Amsterdam (1956–59)	M14
Duewag GT6 ex-Düsseldorf (1956/57)	M10
Duewag GT8 ex-Düsseldorf (1956/59)	M12
Konstal 105N (1970–90)	M240
Konstal 102N articulated (1975–90)	M29
HCP Cegielski 105N/2 low-floor articulated (1995)	M1
ČKD Tatra RT6N low-floor articulated (1997/98)	M10
Siemens Combino (2003/04)	M14

In peak service: Not currently available

PKP Przewozy Regionalne spółka zoo – PKP Regional Service Ltd
ul Grójecka 17, PL-02-021 Warsaw, Poland
Tel: (+48 22) 524 14 05; 524 47 44; 524 41 05; 524 46 50; 659 33 54
Fax: (+48 22) 524 16 01
e-mail: infodc@pkp.com.pl; kzr@pkp.com.pl
Web: www.pr.pkp.pl; www.pkp.com.pl

Key personnel
Chairman of the Management Board and Chief Executive Officer: Jan Tereszczuk

Type of operation: Suburban heavy rail

Current situation
Services operate irregularly (about every two hours, more frequently at commuting times) over nine routes into Poznan's main and inner suburban stations.
For further information on this company, please see *Jane's World Railways.*

Szczecin
Population: City 408,99, province (Voivodship) 1.69 million (2006 estimates)

Public transport
Bus and tramway services provided by municipal authority. Suburban rail services by State Railway (PKP).

Miejskie Zakłady Komunikacyjne Spółka z o o (MZK)
ul Inowroclawska 11, 85-153 Bydgoszsz, Szczecin, Poland
Tel: (+48 91) 324 94 10, 94 50
Fax: (+48 91) 324 94 51
e-mail: zarz@mzk.bydgoszcz.pl

bip@mzk.bydgoszsz.pl
Web: www.mzk.bydgoszcz.pl

Key personnel
Director: Witold Dębicki
Manager, Bus: Roman Obarek
Manager, Tramway: Jan Ciechomski
Manager, Public Relations: Agnieszka Konieczna
  Staff: 4,264

Operating costs financed by: Fares 37 per cent, subsidy from city 73 per cent

Current situation
In 1991, the former operating authority WPKM, which had provided public transport services in the cities of Szczecin, Stargard Szczecinski and Swinoujscie, was split into three organisations.

The Szczecin operation came under the control of the local authority and took a new name. An annual grant towards operating costs comes from central government, allocated by the Administrator of the province of Szczecin.

Bus
Number of routes: 66
Route length: 719 km

Fleet: 440 vehicles
Ikarus 280,70B & 280 articulated
Jelcz LO90M
Jelcz M121MB articulated
Jelcz M181MB articulated
Jelcz M181MB M/1 articulated
MAN NG313 articulated
MAN NL223

Volvo 7000A articulated
Volvo B10BLE
Volvo B10L
Volvo B10LA articulated
Volvo B10MA articulated
In peak service: 278

One-person operation: All routes
Fare collection: Prepurchase ticket or pass with validation and cancelling machines on board
Fare structure: Flat
Fare evasion control: Random inspectors
Average peak-hour speed: 19.6 km/h

Tramway
Type of operation: Conventional tramway with sections upgraded to light rail

Route length: 110 km
Number of lines: 12
Gauge: 1,435 mm

Service: Peak 5 min; 24 h service
Fare structure: As bus
Average peak-hour speed: 14.6 km/h

Rolling stock: 353 cars

Konstal Chorzow	
N (1952–62)	M93
102N (1971/72)	M24
105N (1975/79)	M94
105Na (1981–90)	M49
ND	T93

In peak service: 239

PKP Przewozy Regionalne spółka zoo – PKP Regional Service Ltd

ul Grójecka 17, PL-02-021 Warsaw, Poland
Tel: (+48 22) 524 14 05; 524 47 44;
524 41 05; 524 46 50; 659 33 54

Fax: (+48 22) 524 16 01
e-mail: infodc@pkp.com.pl; kzr@pkp.com.pl
Web: www.pr.pkp.pl; www.pkp.com.pl

Key personnel
Chairman of the Management Board and Chief Executive Officer: Jan Tereszczuk

Type of operation: Suburban heavy rail

Current situation
Services on several lines in Szczecin urban area and on routes to Trzebiez Szczecinski (37 km), Kostrzyn (104 km) and Choszczno (75 km); irregular, but about hourly.

For further information on this company, please see *Jane's World Railways*.

Warsaw

Population: City 1.7 million, metropolitan area 2.9 million (2006 estimates)

Public transport
Bus, tramway, light rail, metro and commuter and rapid commuter rail services provided by city-owned and private operators overseen by transport authority. Regional rail services operated by PKP Regional Services Ltd.

Zarząd Transportu Miejskiego (ZTM) – Warsaw Transport Authority

ul Senatorska 37, PO Box 988, PL-00-099 Warsaw 1, Poland
Tel: (+48 22) 826 82 11
Fax: (+48 22) 827 25 52
e-mail: ztm@ztm.waw.pl
Web: www.ztm.waw.pl

Key personnel
Director: Leszek Ruta
  Staff: 440

Current situation
The transport authority ZTM was established at the end of 1992 to oversee all urban transport planning and operations, ticket sales and marketing. Warsaw Transport Authority currently contracts with nine private operators to provide services, within the city and suburban lines in the metropolitan area, where each municipality contracts ZTM to provide operations and contributes towards costs.

Warsaw's public transport network is based on numerous bus and tram routes, which enable direct connection between the most frequented places in the city. There is one metro line, and a second one will be built in the next few years. In 2005, a local railway line was established, operating on regional railway tracks. Since 2006, passengers may use the regional trains with ZTM's tickets.

An extension of the local railway system and the ticket cooperation with the regional railways is planned.

Warsaw's aim is to develop a public transport system based on rail (both heavy and light), with a complementary bus routes. Plans exist for the creation of several more bus lanes to speed peak-hour journeys.

Developments
A second metro line is planned, which will run east-west and on which construction is scheduled to start in 2009. The line will run between the largest housing estates in eastern and western Warsaw and the city centre.

New tram lines and modernisation of existing ones are planned. New tram routes will be

built to districts without any rail connections. The main lines in the city centre will be modernised. Every tram project includes the purchase of new rolling stock. The investment costs will be partly covered by EU funds.

There are plans to install a new passenger information system on metro stations and along the modernised tram lines. An integrated, web information system on ZTM's website is also planned and is scheduled to be implemented in the next few years.

ZTM's goal is to improve the public transport integration organised by ZTM and by other authorities/operators. Today, there is a tariff integration between ZTM and regional railways (organised by the regional authority) inside of the borders of the City of Warsaw. ZTM wants to enlarge the co-operation to the whole metropolitan area, in order to improve the overall number of public transport passengers. There is a large number of regional and suburb bus companies (some 250), that provide bus services between agglomeration communities and Warsaw based on their own fare system. An integration of these services into the ZTM network and fare system is one of the challenges to be faced over the coming years.

Development of the Park-and-Ride (P+R) car park network: ZTM also plans to have 10 P+R car parks by the end of 2012. In the 1st phase, four car parks are planned. The aim of the P+R system is to offer an alternative mode for travelling to the city centre by leaving cars near the City border and then travelling by public transport.

During the next few years, there are plans for bus/tram lanes and intelligent traffic light systems to be installed. These works will be co-ordinated through an Integrated Public Transport Management System.

In mid-2006, a contract was awarded to ASEC SA, Poland , a subsidiary of On Track Innovations Ltd (OTI), for public transport contactless ticketing. The tickets will apply to bus, tramway or metro travel.
Fare collection: Prepurchase at kiosk with validation at cancelling machines on board
Fare structure: A new fare system was accepted in March, 2008, valid from 2 June 2008. It contains single tickets for one trip with transfer valid for 20, 40 or 60 minutes. There are also single tickets for one trip without transfer and passes for 1, 3, 7, 30 and 90 days. The ZTM network is divided in 2 fare Zones. Zone 1 contains the City of Warsaw, Zone 2 the suburbs. Tickets for Zone 2 are more expensive, but they are also valid for Zone 1. The ticketing system is a fully electronic system, delivered by Ascom Monetel during 2000/01. It consists of paper-based tickets with a magnetic strip (tickets up to 7-day ticket) in EDMONDSON standard and intelligent plastic cards in Mifare standard, which also enables parking payment. The system gives an opportunity to measure demand on tickets. Ticket controlling barriers are established at every metro station.

Arrangements for elderly/disabled: Half-price single tickets and monthly passes for pensioners and retired persons. Elderly pass for those over 65 (low-price flat fare for a whole year). Free travel for those over 70, war and army invalids, blind persons and their guides, disabled school children. Financed from budgeted subsidies
Operating costs financed by: (All modes) Fares 40 per cent, subsidy/grants from city 60 per cent

Miejskie Zakłady Autobusowe Sp zoo (MZA)

ul Senatorska 37, PL-00-099 Warsaw 1, Poland
Tel: (+48 22) 826 82 11
Fax: (+48 22) 827 46 78
Web: www.mza.waw.pl
Further information has been removed at the organisation's request.

Tramwaje Warszawskie Sp zoo – Warsaw Tramways Ltd

Biuro Zarządzania Zasobami Ludzkimi, ul Siedmiogrodzka 20, PL-01-232 Warsaw, Poland
Tel: (+48 22) 632 20 33
Fax: (+48 22) 827 05 43
e-mail: praca@tw.waw.pl
Web: www.tw.waw.pl

Key personnel
Head of Marketing: Ms Teresa Kotwica
  Staff: 3,200 (estimate)

Tramway
Type of operation: Conventional tramway

Passenger journeys: Not currently available
Car-km: (2003) 48.6 million

Route length: 121 km
  reserved track: 96 km
Number of routes: 31
Number of stops: 520
Average distance between stops: 457 m
Gauge: 1,435 mm
Electrification: 600 V DC, overhead

Rolling stock: 876 (March 2008)
Full breakdown of fleet is not currently available, but is believed to include:
Konstal 13N (1961 on)
  105N (1975 on)
  105Na
  105N2k
  112N
  116N
  123N
In peak service: 750

First/last service: 04.00/00.20, weekend night route (four cars): 23.25–04.41 (Friday to Monday)
Average speed: 18.3 km/h

Developments
A number of projects are due to be implemented or have recently been completed to upgrade existing tram routes. Some of these projects are part-funded by the EU.

One of these projects was the renewal of the tram tracks in Al Jerozolimske.

Metro Warszawskie Sp zoo – Warsaw Metro
Ul Wilczy Dół 5, PL-02-798 Warsaw, Poland
Tel: (+48 22) 655 40 00, 643 63 79, 643 93 69
Fax: (+48 22) 643 39 97
e-mail: info@metro.waw.pl
Web: www.metro.waw.pl

Key personnel
Managing President and General Director: Jerzy Lejk
Management Board Members: Ms Dorota Popińska, Grzegorz Ledzion, Radosław Żołnierzak
Staff: 1,440

Type of operation: Full metro; opened 1995

Passenger journeys: (2003) 75.9 million
(2004) 80.9 million
(2005) 93.4 million
(2006) 105.8 million
(2007) 113.5 million

Route length: 22.6 km
Number of lines: 1
Number of stations: 21
Gauge: 1,435 mm
Track: Concrete slab
Max gradient: 3.1%
Minimum curve radius: 300 m
Signalling: Automatic speed control with cab signalling
Surveillance: Automatic fire-control system; CCTV at stations
Electrification: 750 V DC, third rail

Current situation
The tender for the construction of Line II, the central section, was announced in October 2007.

Developments
Tunnel B20 and Słodowiec station (A20) opened in April 2008.

The Bielany subway is part of Line I and is co-financed with European funds.

Works in 2008 included:
- Construction of B21 tunnel (continuation);
- Construction of A21 Stare Bielany station (continuation);
- Construction of B22 tunnel (continuation);
- Construction of A22 Wawrzyszew station (continuation);
- Construction of B23 tunnel (continuation);
- Construction of A23 Młociny station (continuation);
- Construction of Młociny Junction (continuation).

These final three stations on Line I opened in 2008.

There are long-term plans for a third line.

Rolling stock: 198 cars
Metrovagonmash '81' type	90
Metropolis type	108

On order: 30 Metrovagonmash Type 81-714 cars
First/last train: 05.00/24.00

Service: Peak 2 min 50 secs
Fare structure: Flat (peak and off-peak tickets), time-based tickets; magnetic tickets (single, time-based, 24-hour, three-day and weekly tickets); contactless smartcards as monthly and three-monthly passes; free transfer to other modes; smartcards are valid on metro, trams, buses, WKD, SKM and KM trains within the city limits.

Warsaw metro Pl Wilsona Station 1322859

Warsaw metro Marymont Station 1322860

Słodowiec station, opened in April 2008 1344737

PKP Warszawska Kolej Dojazdowa Sp zoo (WKD)

ul Batorego 23, PL-05-825 Grodzisk Mazowiecki, Poland
Tel: (+48 22) 755 55 64
Fax: (+48 22) 755 20 95
e-mail: wkd@wkd.com.pl; marketing@wkd.com.pl
Web: www.wkd.com.pl

Key personnel
Representative, Mazovia Voivodship: Piotr
   Szprenałowicz

Type of operation: Light rail

Passenger journeys: (2004) 6.2 million (estimate)
(2005) 6.4 million (estimate)

Route length: 35 km (mostly double-track)
No of lines: 1 (with 2 branch)
No of stations: 28
Electrification: 600 V DC, overhead

Current situation
In September 2005, WKD was sold by PKP
to a consortium of local governments for an
estimated PLN3 million. Mazovia Voivodship and
the City of Warsaw each acquired 33 per cent of
the shares, with the remaining 34 per cent being
purchased by six communities which are located
along the WKD lines.

Developments
There are plans to order a further 12 new trains,
to modernise the existing route, to double-track
the section between Podkowa Leśna and Grodzisk
Mazowiecki and to build park-and-ride facilities.

Fleet: 53 emus
EN94 six-axle emu   40
EN95 ten-axle emu   13
On order: The 13 EN95 emus are currently being
delivered.

Service: 15 min (peak), 30 min (off-peak)
First/last train: 05.00/24.00

Szybka Kolej Miejska Sp zoo (SKM) – Rapid Commuter Railway Ltd

ul Mińska 25, lok 618, PL-03-808 Warsaw, Poland
Tel: (+48 22) 336 64 00
Fax: (+48 22) 336 64 10
e-mail: biuro@skm.warszawa.pl
Web: www.skm.warszawa.pl

Key personnel
Management, Chairman: Leszek Walczak
Management Board Member: Jerzy Obrębski
   Staff: 766 (estimate)

Type of operation: Suburban rail

Passenger journeys: (2007) 7 million
Train-km: Not currently available

Current situation
Szybka Kolej Miejska Sp zoo (SKM) is a joint
venture of Warsaw tram authority, Tramwaje
Waszawskie Sp zoo, and Metro Warszawskie
Sp zoo (Warsaw Metro Ltd), set up to create
rapid city-rail services over PKP PLK lines
within the greater Warsaw area. In June 2005,
SKM was granted a licence for the transport of
passengers and for leasing (or hiring) of traction
vehicles.
   The company provides a rail link from Warsaw's
southwest to eastern suburbs via the city centre;
Pruszkow-Sulejowek.

Developments
Warsaw services started in late 2006. Currently,
the service is operated with eight 14WE and
two EN57 emus, leased from PKP Przewozy
Regionale.

Further services, due to commence in 2010,
include: airport lines Warsaw Frideric Chopin
Airport-City-Centre-Legionowo/Sulejowek   and
Line S1 Proszkow-Otwock.

Service: Approximately every 30 minutes.

PKP Przewozy Regionalne spółka zoo – PKP Regional Service Ltd

ul Grójecka 17, PL-02-021 Warsaw, Poland
Tel: (+48 22) 524 14 05; 524 47 44; 524 41 05;
524 46 50; 659 33 54
Fax: (+48 22) 524 16 01
e-mail: infodc@pkp.com.pl; kzr@pkp.com.pl
Web: www.pr.pkp.pl; www.pkp.com.pl

Key personnel
*Chairman of the Management Board and Chief
   Executive Officer:* Jan Tereszczuk

Type of operation: Suburban heavy rail

Current situation
Operates extensive suburban services (some
electrified) on routes to Skierniewice (71 km, at
least every hour), Czachowek (42 km, hourly),
Lowicz (87 km, hourly), Nasielsk (56 km, at
least hourly), Tiuszcz (34 km, half-hourly),
Minsk Mazowiecki (45 km, half-hourly), Otwock
(32 km, half-hourly) and Milanowek/Grodzisk
(32 km, half-hourly to each). Frequent cross-
city service provided by these and other trains
between   Warsaw   Wlochy/Zachodnia   and
Wschodnia stations, about nine trains per
hour. Also at less regular intervals on other
routes.
   For further information on this company,
please see *Jane's World Railways.*

Wroclaw

Population: City 635,200 (2006)

Public transport
Bus and tramway services provided by municipal
authority, rail services provided by PKP Regional
Services Ltd.

Miejskie Przedsiebiorstwo Komunikacyjne Sp zoo (MPK)

Ul B Prusa 75-79, PL-50-316 Wroclaw, Poland
Tel: (+48 71) 325 08 88
Fax: (+48 71) 325 08 02
e-mail: biuro@mpk.wroc.pl
Web: www.mpk.wroc.pl

Key personnel
General Manager: Czeslaw Palczak
Bus Director: Halina Bolek
Tramway Director: J Wos
Financial Director: Alicja Zrobek
   Staff: 3,000

Passenger journeys: (Both modes)
Not currently available

Operating costs financed by: Fares 34.6 per cent,
subsidy/grants 65.4 per cent

Bus

Passenger journeys: Not currently available
Vehicle-km: Not currently available

Number of routes: Not currently available
Route length: 390 km (estimate)

Fleet: 395 vehicles
*Breakdown of fleet is not currently available, but is
believed to include:*
Jelcz M 11
Jelcz PR110
Jelcz 120MM/1
Jelcz M121M/MB
Jelcz 180MB articulated
Ikarus 280 articulated
Volvo
Asia Motors minibus
In peak service: 294

One-person operation: All routes
Fare collection: Prepurchase with validation and
cancelling machines on board
Fare structure: Flat; single and a range of tickets
from one-day to 90-day; reduced fare for students,
reduced or free travel for disabled passengers
Fare evasion control: Random inspectors
Average peak-hour speed: 19.9 km/h

Tramway

Type of operation: Conventional tramway

Route length: 85 km
Number of lines: 21
Gauge: 1,435 mm

Developments
In early 2007, the first of 17 Skoda 16T low-floor
trams and the first PROTRAM Type 205 WrAs
eight-axle tram with low-floor centre section
were delivered.
   There are plans for a further 13 km of new lines
and modernisation of some existing routes for the
UEFA Cup in 2012. There are also plans for a new
tram line to link the city centre with the airport.

Rolling stock: Not currently available
Full breakdown of fleet is not currently available
Type 102N
Type 105N
Type T2N
PROTRAM Type 204 WrAs
PROTRAM Type 205 WrAs
Skoda 16T, low-floor
In peak service: Not currently available
Fare structure: As bus

PKP Przewozy Regionalne spółka zoo – PKP Regional Service Ltd

ul Grójecka 17, PL-02-021 Warsaw, Poland
Tel: (+48 22) 524 14 05; 524 47 44; 524 41 05;
524 46 50; 659 33 54
Fax: (+48 22) 524 16 01
e-mail: infodc@pkp.com.pl; kzr@pkp.com.pl
Web: www.pr.pkp.pl; www.pkp.com.pl

Key personnel
*Chairman of the Management Board and Chief
   Executive Officer:* Jan Tereszczuk

Type of operation: Suburban heavy rail

Current situation
Irregular services (about every two hours) on
seven routes.
   For further information on this company,
please see *Jane's World Railways.*

Portugal

Lisbon

Population: City 564,477 (2001 Census), region 2.7 million (2005 estimate)

Public transport

Bus and tramway services provided in city area by public company also responsible for three funiculars and a public elevator. Metro operated by separate public undertaking, suburban rail lines by Portuguese Railways (CP), cross-river ferries by CP and Transtejo, and suburban bus services by municipally owned bus company and private operators. Fares are integrated. Rail infrastructure planning and construction is undertaken by a quasi-autonomous transport ministry department. Other arrangements apply in the south Tagus conurbation (see separate entries).

Companhia Carris de Ferro de Lisboa SA (Carris)

Rua Primeiro de Maio Numero 101-103, P-1300-472 Lisbon, Portugal
Tel: (+351 21) 361 30 00   Fax: (+351 21) 361 30 69
e-mail: linha.aberta@carris.pt (General Information),
  provedor.cliente@carris.pt (Customer Ombudsman)
Web: www.carris.pt

Executive office

Alameda António Sérgio Nr 62, Complexo de Miraflores, P-2795-221 Linda-a-Velha, Portugal

Key personnel

President: Dr José Manuel Silva Rodrigues
General Secretariat: Dr Luis M Vale do Couto
Finance Director: Dr Carlos Sousa Bentes
Commercial and Marketing Director: Eng Maria João Branco
Operational Control and Network Planning Unit Director: Eng José Manuel G Maia
Buses Business Unit Director: Eng Vitor Gonçalves
Trams Business Unit Director: Eng Élio J M Serra
Human Resources Director: Eng Pedro Martins Pereira
International Relations Director: Dr Arnaldo Pimentel
Logistics Director: Eng Carlos Figueiredo
Public Relations: Dra Maria Gabriela Pereira
Customer Ombudsman: Eng António Quaresma
  Staff: 2,778 (as at December 2007)

Passenger boardings: (All modes)
(2003) 276.7 million
(2004) 256.6 million
(2005) 240.8 million
(2006) 234.9 million
(2007) 236.4 million

Operating costs (2007) financed by: Fares 52.6 per cent, government subsidy 32.3 per cent

Current situation

Carris operates as exclusive concessionnaire for provision of surface transport in Lisbon.

Since January 2008, maintenance operations have been outsourced to a Carris subsidiary enterprise – CarrisBus.

Certification
Quality Management System

Having implemented a Quality Management System, Carris was certified to ISO 9001:2000 in January 2006.

Certification of Carris' lines

Along with the enterprise certification, three bus lines and one tramway line were certified to NP EN 13816:2003 standard in February 2006.

In June 2007, 18 more bus lines were certified followed by a further 18 lines in August 2008.

The certification of lines is based on the quality of the following characteristics:

• operating period
• line reliability

Carris Volvo B10L CNG bus 1342786

Carris Mereceds-Benz Sprinter minibus 1342783

- duration of trip
- regularity
- punctuality
- client information
- vehicles and sales offices cleaning
- client support.

Carris is now waiting for the certification of 12 more bus lines during late 2008/early 2009.

Environmental Certification

Carris is concerned about environmental issues and is developing a Management System, according the NP EN ISO 14001:2004, which will aim to control and minimise the impact of the Carris' services on the local environment, by adopting an effective management of the environmental aspects.

Developments

In 2008, the company acquired 20 medium and 20 articulated buses.

Integrated Systems developments and programmes include:

GERTRUDE: Priority for public transport, better fluidity

SAEIP: Automatic Vehicle Location system, based on GPS, monitored and controlled by a central control room; better network management; real-time information system for customers at bus stops; improved safety and security. This system has been installed throughout the fleet and at bus stops, and is now fully operational

Electronic Contactless Ticketing: The '7 Colinas' card can be charged for tickets and the 'Lisboa Viva' card is for passes – modal choice and ease of use on the transport system, information for better management resources. This system began in March 2004.

Video vigilance: For the safety of passengers and staff the whole fleet of buses and trams is now equipped with video vigilance cameras.

Electronic panels (real-time information): 348 bus/tram stops now have real-time arrival information panels.

SIP: An application is being developed to provide information via mobile phone, giving the exact timing of vehicle arrival at each stop.

New bus lanes are being introduced to improve service. Patrol cars were introduced in 2004 to prevent illegal parking in bus lanes. This latter project is supported by the Municipal Police.

Network restructuring: Work began in late 2006 and is foreseen to last until 2010. Restructuring will involve network segmentation, creating less overlap and better co-ordination with the subway network (Metropolitano de Lisboa). The circular and transverse connections will be reinforced. Fewer lines will operate but with better frequency during all periods of the day and year, and with an increase to the commercial speed.

Environmental issues: New buses have been brought into the fleet during the past eight years and this has led to significant reductions in the impact on the environment and energy use, in particular with regard to pollutant gases, along with reduced fuel consumption, increases in safety, comfort and operability and reduction of maintenance costs. All of the new vehicles comply with the Community Directive on exhaust emissions (Euro 3), with far lower levels than the vehicles being taken out of service. During the last five years, the company has been experiencing a reduction of 48 per cent on NOx, 74 per cent on HC, 67 per cent on CO and 80 per cent on PT, and also a reduction on the level of outside noise according to NP708.

Currently, all of Carris' buses (with the exception of those working with natural gas) are working with B3 (fuel with three per cent bio-diesel), with a resultant reduction of CO_2 emissions. However, the company is continuing to experiment with other alternative fuels:

- **Bio-diesel:** 18 are in experimental operation for one year with B15 (15 per cent bio-diesel) and B30 (30 per cent bio-diesel)
- **Natural Gas:** Carris has 40 vehicles operating with natural gas.

Carris has also been participating with the European Community in projects for the development of fuel cell buses.

Carris MAN HOCL 18.280 bus   1374002

Rebuilt tramway   1374011

During 2009, Carris is forecasting the acquisition of a further 20 CNG buses.

Other environmental and energy developments are:

- Special areas for the selective storage of waste
- Selective gathering of industrial waste, organic and hospital (medical office) solids, by certified enterprises

- Equipment for the separation of oil and fats (improve the quality of effluent liquids)
- Groundwater-holes and wells for irrigation and washing of cars (40 per cent of total consumption)
- Plan for rationalisation of energy
- Recovery of braking energy of trams.

Safety concerns: At the beginning of 2007, Carris signed the European Road Safety Charter, a forum and a platform for the signatories to exchange experiences and new ideas – across national borders – in their efforts towards greater safety on European roads. It is a manifestation of the responsibility that all stakeholders assume in order to achieve the common goal: halving the number of traffic fatalities by 2010.

Bus

Passenger boardings: (2003) 257.2 million
(2004) 238.5 million
(2005) 222.8 million
(2006) 216.2 million
(2007) 217.9 million
Vehicle-km: (2003) 42.5 million
(2004) 40.3 million
(2005) 38.2 million
(2006) 37.8 million
(2007) 38.7 million

Number of routes: 86
Route length: (One way) 662 km
On priority right-of-way: 69.1 km

Fleet: 744 vehicles (as at September 2008)
Standard
Volvo B10R	55
Volvo B7L	35
Volvo B7R	33
Volvo B10L	37
Mercedes-Benz O405 N2	110
Mercedes-Benz O530 Citaro	29
Mercedes-Benz 412 D (paratransit services)	4
Mercedes-Benz OC500	67
MAN HOCL 18.310	148
MAN HOCL 18.280	100

Articulated
Volvo B10M articulated	90

Minibuses
Mercedes-Benz Sprinter	36

In peak service: 637

Most intensive service: 9–10 min
One-person operation: All routes
Fare collection: Payment to conductor or driver, prepurchase electronic contactless fares (tickets and passes)
Fare structure: Passes 68 per cent of revenue, paper tickets 15.7 per cent, and electronic tickets 16.3 per cent. Passes are exclusive or intermodal monthly or 30 days passes, charged in an electronic contactless card 'Lisboa Viva'. Electronic Tickets charged in '7 Colinas' contactless card valid in Carris, (1 and 2 zones) and in Carris and Metro (Single Urban, Single Network, 1 Day Network).
Paper ticket valid in Carris: flat fare tickets
Fares collected on board (2007): 15.7 per cent of revenue
Fare evasion control: Roving inspectors
Arrangements for elderly/disabled: four Mercedes-Benz 412 D vehicles specially adapted for disabled; aiming to progressively improve the accessibility of persons with reduced mobility, since late 2006 the company has four lines fully adapted for wheelchair access.
Integration with other modes: Passes valid on all services in Lisbon area in different zone combinations; two airport lines
Average distance between stops: 350 m
Average peak-hour speed (2007): In mixed traffic, 14.6 km/h
Operating costs (2007) financed by: Fares 44.8 per cent
New vehicles financed by: Leasing

Tramway

Type of operation: Conventional tramway, plus one light rail line

Passenger boardings: (2003) 17.1 million
(2004) 16.0 million
(2005) 15.7 million
(2006) 16.5 million
(2007) 16.4 million
Car-km: (2003) 2 million
(2004) 1.8 million
(2005) 1.8 million

Carris Siemens three-section LRV 1342785

The Santa Justa Elevator 1342792

(2006) 1.8 million
(2007) 1.8 million

Number of lines: 5
Route length: 48 km
On priority right-of-way: 13.7 km
Number of stops: 89
Gauge: 900 mm
Track: 15 per cent conventional sleepers on ballast, 85 per cent on concrete with resilient pads
Max gradient: 14%
Minimum curve radius: 12 m
Electrification: 580 V DC, overhead

Service: (Line 15) Peak 9 min, off-peak 11–13 min
First/last car: (Line 28) 05.40/(Line 15) 01.10
Fare structure: Passes 39.2 per cent of revenue, paper tickets 31.4 per cent, and electronic tickets 29.4 per cent. Passes are exclusive or intermodal monthly or 30 days passes, charged in a electronic card 'Lisboa Viva'. Electronic Tickets charged in '7 Colinas' card valid for Carris,(1 and 2 zones) and for Carris and Metro (Single Urban, Single Network and 1 Day Network). Paper ticket valid in Carris: flat fare.
Fares collected on board (2007): 26.7 per cent of revenue
One-person operation: All routes
Operating costs (2007) financed by: Fares 1.4 per cent

Average peak-hour speed (2007): In mixed traffic, 10.5 km/h

Rolling stock: 67 cars (including tourist tramcars)
KIEP NF 51 (rebuilt)   M39
DB1K33 (reserve fleet)   M8
Siemens Duewag LRV three-section,
   single-ended, 70 per cent low-floor (1995)   M10
Tourist tramcars
KIEPP NF 51   6
DB1K33   2
K10   2
In peak service: 36

Current situation
In total, 45 heritage cars have been rebuilt with modern electrical and mechanical equipment, while retaining their original exterior appearance. Currently, only 39 are in regular service.

The four hill routes have been developed as a tourist attraction while continuing their traditional public-transport role in the narrow, steeply graded streets of the old city. Some streets are barely wide enough for a single track, and the section between São Tomé and Graça (Route 28) has interlaced track on sharp curves.

Developments
Waterfront Route 15 has been upgraded to near light-rail standards, including the creation of 4.2 km of reserved track and the introduction of 10 three-section, single-ended, articulated cars (70 per cent low-floor), for which upgraded depot facilities have been provided at Santo Amaro. These are currently operating between Praça Figueira and Algés.

Route 18 shares part of its alignment with Route 15. Also, Line 12 has been extended to form a circular route round Castelo de São Jorge.

Carris would also like to open three lines, under study: one exterior line from Algés to Loures (first phase – Algés to Praça Figueira) and two interior lines, one from Praça Figueira to Santa Apolónia Station and the other from Alcântara to Aeroporto, which would both be built to light rail standards.

Funiculars/elevator
Passenger journeys: (2003) 2.4 million
(2004) 2.1 million
(2005) 2.3 million
(2006) 2.2 million
(2007) 21. million
Car-km: (2003) 0.1 million
(2004) 0.1 million
(2005) 0.1 million
(2006) 0.1 million
(2007) 0.1 million

The Bica Funicular   1342780

The Gloria Funicular   1342788

The Lavra Funicular   1342789

Current situation
Carris operates three funicular (double cable tram) routes and one vertical public elevator with two cabins.

Metropolitano de Lisboa (ML)

Executive Headquarters
Avenida Barbosa du Bocage N° 5, P-1049-039 Lisbon, Portugal
Tel: (+351 21) 798 06 00; 350 01 00
Fax: (+351 21) 798 06 05
e-mail: relacoes.publicas@metrolisboa.pt
Web: www.metrolisboa.pt

Public Relations office
Tel: (+351 21) 213 50 01 15

Key personnel
President: Joaquim José de Oliveira Reis
Heads of Departments:
Commercial Operations: Pedro Machado Vazão de Almeida
Infrastructure Management: João Afonso Monteiro
Industrial Operations: José Osvaldo Bagarrão
Security and Safety: Armando Silva Neves
Economy and Finance: José Maria Ferreira de Melo
Secretary General and Communications: António José Pinto Mendes Mourão
Studies, Planning, Budget and Management Control: Luís Filipe Periera Melo de Almeida
Information Systems and Technology: Carlos José Duarte Rocha
Staff: 1,648 (2007)

Type of operation: Full metro, opened 1959

Passenger journeys: Not currently available
Car-km: Not currently available

Background
The company was founded on 26 January 1948, and the authorisation for the installation and development of public services was granted on 1 July 1949.

Route length: 35.6 km
Number of lines: 4
Number of stations: 44
Gauge: 1,435 mm
Track: Vignole (FB) 50 kg/m U50 profile rail on timber sleepers, normally on ballast, with resilient pads; new lines twin-block Stedef sleepers; on concrete at stations
Max gradient: 4%
Minimum curve radius: 150 m (some 100 m)
Tunnel: Cut-and-cover except 1 km bored
Electrification: 750 V DC, third rail

Rolling stock: 338 cars, in maximum of six-car sets

Sorefame ML90 (1993/96)	M38 T19
Adtranz ML95 (1997/98)	M76 T38
ML 97 (1999)	M36 T18
ML99 (2000/02)	M75 T38

Service: Peak 3 min 30 secs–4 min 40 secs
First/last train: 06.30/01.00
Fare structure: Zonal; tickets on Viva Viagem cards, metro 30-day passes charged on Lisboa Viva card
Fare collection: Contactless ticketing
Fare-evasion control: Spot checks at stations or on trains
Integration with other modes: Fares integrated with suburban bus, ferry and rail services through monthly and 30-working day zonal passes
Surveillance: CCTV on all platforms and in trains
Operating costs financed by: Fares 27 per cent, other commercial sources 11 per cent, government subsidy/grants 62 per cent

Developments
The extension of the Blue Line from Baixa/Chiado to Santa Apolónia opened in December 2007.
The following expansions are under way:
Pontinha to Reboleira, **Blue Line**;

Alameda to São Sebastião, **Red Line**;
Oriente to Aeroporto, **Red Line**.
When these extensions are complete, Lisbon will have four independent lines, with a total length of about 44 km and 56 stations.
Apart from the projects under construction, the following extensions are presently being studied:
Yellow Line: Extension from Rato to Alcântara, with a length of about 3 km and three new stations; this extension would provide a new interface with the Lisbon-Cascais suburban railway line, enabling a faster and easier connection with the northward zone of Lisbon;
Green Line: Extension from Telheiras to Pontinha, with a length of about 3 km and three stations; this extension would serve a fast-expanding area and would enable access to the Blue Line and to the 'Pontinha' Depot (PMO III);
Red Line: Extension westwards from San Sebastião in the direction of Campo de Ourique, with a length of about 3 km and three new stations. One of two branches on an extension at the north end from Oriente station is under construction. This branch will bend westwards and proceed in the direction of Lisbon International Airport, with a length of about 3 km and three new stations. The other branch, under consideration, would proceed northwards in the direction of Sacavém, with a length of about 2 km and two new stations.
Green Line Stations improvements are under way to improve accessibility and lengthen platforms for six-car trains. The total cost of the project is estimated at EUR53.7 million. One station has been completed with work under way on a second, and the other station improvements are at design and public tender stage.
Work is also being carried out on the Cais do Sodré multimodal complex and the Terreiro do Paço station.

Rede Ferroviária Nacional (REFER)

Portuguese National Rail Administration
Estação Santa Apolónia, P-1100-105 Lisbon, Portugal
Tel: (+351 21) 102 20 00
Fax: (+351 21) 102 24 39
e-mail: comercial@mail.refer.pt
Web: www.refer.pt

Key personnel
President: Dr Manuel Frasquilho

Background
REFER was established in 1997, when the operating and infrastructure areas of the Portuguese railways were separated into two companies (please also see separate entry for Caminhos de Ferros Portugueses (CP)). During the restructuring, REFER absorbed the public-sector authority Gabinete do Nó Ferroviaro de Lisboa (GNFL), the Lisbon Rail Development Board.

Current situation
REFER is responsible for rail infrastructure, including maintenance and development.
Construction of the cross-Tagus link, which is incorporated into the lower deck of the existing road bridge, was costed at Esc78 billion. Cross-Tagus rail service started in 1999, with trains running through from Azambuja on CP's northern line to Pinhal Novo and Setúbal on the south side via the ring line. Thirty four-car double-deck emus have been supplied by ALSTOM/CAF/Adtranz. Please see separate entry for Fertagus in *Jane's Urban Transport Systems* for more information.
Please see *Jane's World Railways* for further information on REFER.

Developments
In the Lisbon area, it is planned to introduce centralised traffic control, permitting 25 trains an hour in each direction on the 27 km

Lisbon–Sintra line. Four tracks in place of the present two will eventually be in service between Lisbon and Cacém (17.3 km). The route between Campolide and Benfica (3.1 km) has been expanded to four tracks, with trains operating at four minute headways at peak hours and serving a new station at Queluz-Massamá.
In addition to minor works to improve interchanges with the Lisbon metro, a modernisation programme costed at Esc60 billion has been proposed for the Lisbon–Cascais route.

Comboios de Portugal (CP) – Portuguese Railways

Calçada do Duque 20, P-1249-109 Lisbon, Portugal
Tel: (+351 21) 321 57 00
Fax: (+351 21) 347 30 93
Web: www.cp.pt

Business Unit
CP Lisboa (Unidade de Suburbanos da Grande Lisboa)
Largo da Estação de Campolide, P-1070-116 Lisbon, Portugal
Tel: (+351 21) 321 57 00
Fax: (+351 21) 347 30 93
e-mail: portavoz@mail.cp.pt

Suburban rail
Type of operation: Suburban heavy rail

Passenger journeys: (2003) 100 million

Current situation
The Unidade de Suburbanos da Grande Lisboa (USGL) manages four routes in the capital, serving Azambuja, Cascais, Sado and Sintra. All except the Sado line are electrically operated. Nearly 100 million passenger journeys were made in 2003, just over half of these on the Sintra line.
For further information on CP, please see *Jane's World Railways*.

Developments
In 2005, Caminhos de Ferro Portugueses changed its name to Comboios de Portugal (CP).
CP's main recent rolling stock procurement for the Lisbon suburban network has been 12 five-car sets for the Cascais line, equipped for dual-voltage operation.

Rolling stock: 104 emus, 7 dmus
Breakdown of fleet is not currently available.

Sociedade Fluvial de Transportes SA – Soflusa

Rua da Cintura do Porto de Lisboa, Terminal Fluvial do Cais do Sodré, P-1249-249 Lisbon, Portugal
Tel: (+351 210) 42 24 00, (+351 210) 42 24 33 (Sales and Marketing)
Fax: (+351 210) 42 24 99
Web: www.transtejo.pt

Key personnel
Finance Director: Pedro Rolo
Sales and Marketing Managing Director: Teresa Gato

Type of operation: Ferry

Current situation
Soflusa provides the Barreiro-Lisbon-Barreiro commuter ferry services for residents on Tejo's south bank and carries an estimated 30,000 passengers daily.
The fleet consists of nine vessels.
Soflusa is an associated company of the Transtejo Group, which provides all of the ferry services for the Lisbon metropolitan area.

South Tagus
Lisbon
South Tagus
Population: Setubal District: 714,222 (2001 Census)

Public transport
The south-bank Setubal District includes nine municipalities. CP ferry services provide a link with Lisbon, while also operating suburban rail services from its Barreiro station. Bus services are provided by a number of operators, notably Transportes Colectivos do Barreiro and Fertagus. A light rail network is under construction.

Transportes Colectivos do Barreiro (TCB)
Serviços Municipalizados de Transportes Colectivos do Barreiro (SMTCB)
Av Dos Resistentes Antifascistas, P-2830-523 Lavradio, Barreiro, Portugal
Tel: (+351 212) 06 48 00
Web: www.cm-barreiro.pt

Key personnel
General Manager: Pedro Alberta Correira de Andrade Canário
Staff: 234

Passenger journeys: (Annual) 23 million (estimate)

Number of routes: 16
Route length: 149 km

Fleet: 79 (including tourist vehicles, urban and leased vehicles)

Current situation
A municipal bus service is provided in Barreiro on the south bank of the Tagus, connected to Lisbon by ferry.

Travessia do Tejo, SA – Fertagus
Estação do Pragal, Porta 23, P-2800 Almada, Portugal
Tel: (+351 21) 106 63 00   Fax: (+352 21) 106 63 99
e-mail: info@fertagus.pt
Web: www.fertagus.pt

Key personnel
Managing Director: Cristina Dourado
Commercial Director: Clara Esquível

Passenger journeys: (2002) 17.5 million
(2003) 17.8 million
(2004) 19.0 million
(2005) 20.6 million
(2006) 21.4 million

Gauge: 1,668 mm
Route length: 54 km

Background
In July 1999, bus operator Barraqueiro commenced a 30-year concession to run Fertagus

suburban rail services linking central Lisbon with Fogueteiro, south of the River Tagus, via the lower deck of the 25 April bridge. Services are operated over infrastructure owned by the Portuguese Rail Infrastructure Authority (REFER).

Current situation
Fertagus serves a 14-station line linking Roma/Areeiro, in central Lisbon, with Setúbal, to which services were extended in October 2004. At Sete Rios and Entrecampos stations, connections are made with CP suburban and Lisbon metro services. At five stations in Almada, connections are provided with SulFertagus bus services. Peak-hour services run every 10 minutes (Lisbon-Coina) and every 30 minutes (Lisbon-Setúbal). Some 80,000 passengers are carried daily.

Fleet: The Fertagus fleet comprises 18 four-car double-deck air conditioned 25 kV AC emus, supplied by a consortium led by ALSTOM and including Bombardier Transportation (formerly Adtranz) and CAF.

Metro Transportes do Sul SA (MTS)
Av 25 de Abril, No 203, Amora, 2845-547 Seixal, Portugal
Tel: (+351 211) 12 70 00
Fax: (+351 211) 12 70 99
e-mail: geral@mts.pt
Web: www.mts.pt

Key personnel
President: José Luís Brandão

Type of operation: Light rail, first sections opened 2007

Passenger journeys: Not yet available
Vehicle-km: Not yet available

Route length: Not currently available
Number of lines: 3
Number of stations: 13
Gauge: 1,435 mm
Electrification: 750 V DC, overhead

Background
In 2002, the Portuguese Government awarded a 27-year concession to Metro Transportes do Sul (MTS) to build, operate and maintain a new light rail system on the south bank of the River Tagus. The estimated cost at the time was EUR820 million. The network will serve the towns of Almada and Seixa.

MTS is a PPP and is owned by Barraqueiro (34 per cent), civil engineering companies (33 per cent), Siemens (21.33 per cent) and MECI (11.67 per cent).

Siemens Transportation Systems received a contract for 24 low-floor, four-section Combino-type LRVs for the system and the communications system, overhead contact lines, the equipment for the LRV maintenance and repair facility and the building technologies, valued at some EUR136 million.

Current situation
The initial phase of the project will be three routes totalling 19.2 km with 19 stations. The first section of Line 1, opened in April 2007, runs from Corroios to Cova da Piedade. The remaining route of Line 1 will run from Cova da Piedade to Cacilhas. Line 2 runs from Corroios to Pragal and the first section of Line 3 from Ramalha to Universidade. The second phase of Line 3 will run from Ramalha to Cacilhas. The network has links with Fertagus at Corroios and Pragal stations and will be linked to ferry services in due course.

There will be a CCTV surveillance system and a communications system via the automated ticket vending machines.

Developments
Extensions to the system are already being planned.

Rolling stock: 24 vehicles
Siemens four-section, low-floor, bi-directional LRV (2005)   24
In peak service: Not currently available

Service: Peak 5–10 min, off-peak 10–30 min
First/last train: 06.27/23.02
Fare structure: Flat; multi-trip tickets, monthly passes; reduced fare for youths, elderly and those on reduced/minimum income

Comboios de Portugal (CP) – Portuguese Railways
Calçada do Duque 20, P-1249-109 Lisbon, Portugal
Tel: (+351 21) 321 57 00
Fax: (+351 21) 347 30 93
Web: www.cp.pt

Business Unit
Largo da Estação de Campolide, P-1070-116 Lisbon, Portugal
Tel: (+351 21) 321 57 00
Fax: (+351 21) 347 30 93
e-mail: portavoz@mail.cp.pt
Web: www.cp.pt

Type of operation: Suburban heavy rail

Passenger journeys: (2003) 100 million (for the whole of the Lisbon area)

Current situation
About hourly (peak half-hourly) service provided from 05.00 to 02.05 between Barreiro, where there is connection with the cross-Tagus ferries, and Setúbal (29 km).

For further information on CP, please see *Jane's World Railways*.

Developments
The Cross-Tagus rail link has improved access to central Lisbon. Improvements on the south bank include a new line to the bridge with six stations, an 8,000-space park-and-ride at Penalva, and electrification and upgrading between Pinhal Novo and Setúbal.

Oporto (Porto)
Population: 233,400 (2005 estimate), metropolitan area 1.6 million (2006 estimate)

Public transport
Bus and tram services operated in Porto and surrounding municipalities of Gaia, Matosinhos, Maia, Valongo and Gondomar by public company controlled by board responsible for central government, and contracting some bus services from private operators. Suburban and commuter bus services provided by private operators; rail services provided by Portuguese Railways (CP).

Sociedade de Transportes Colectivos do Porto, SA (STCP)
Avenida Fernão de Magalhães 1862, 13°, P-4350-158 Porto, Portugal
Tel: (+351 22) 507 10 00
Fax: (+351 22) 507 11 50
e-mail: geral@stcp.pt
Web: www.stcp.pt

Key personnel
Chairman: Fernanda Meneses
Operations Manager:
  João Marrana
  Staff: 1,623 (December 2007)

Passenger journeys: (All modes)
(2003) 222 million
(2004) 219 million
(2005) 209 million
(2006) 190 million
(2007) 109 million

Current situation
STCP provides services to the Greater Oporto area, including six of the nine councils in the Oporto Metropolitan Area (AMP), totalling 52 communities and approximately 1.6 million inhabitants.

There are 83 bus routes, currently operating using diesel and CNG buses.

STCP MAN CNG bus

1328496

Developments

The once extensive tram network has been reduced to three lines, with a total length of 9 km and performing mainly tourist services (three routes). There are 94 routes currently operated using diesel and CNG buses.

Since the end of 2002, the metro has been in operation. This has prompted a change to the STCP bus network in order to achieve complementary services between the two modes. The multimodal contactless ticket 'Andante' has gradually been introduced to bus routes and since November 2006, has been in general use on the whole network.

Operating costs financed by: Fares 57 per cent, other commercial sources 3.5 per cent, operating subsidies 21 per cent, remainder as deficit 18.5 per cent

Bus

Number of routes: 83
Route length: 532 km

Fleet: 493 buses

Mercedes-Benz O405 (1991–95)	50
Mercedes-Benz O405 N2 (1999)	90
Mercedes-Benz Citaro (2000–01)	75
MAN NL (1999)	5
MAN NL CNG (2000)	75
MAN 310 CNG (2002, 2007)	150
MAN 310 CNG articulated (2007)	30
Mercedes-Benz Citaro (2004)	3
Mercedes-Benz Sprinter minibus	5

Average age of fleet: 6.7 years

Most intensive service: 7½ min
One-person operation: All routes
Fare collection: To driver or prepurchase
Fare structure: Within the city there is a flat fare for prepurchased tickets, either one-mode, two- or 10-trip tickets or intermodal Andante tickets; monthly passes either one-mode two- or 10-trip tickets or intermodal Andante tickets; daily passes
Fares collected on board: 13 per cent (2007)
Fare evasion control: Subcontracted service/route inspectors
Integration between modes: Intermodal tariff (Andante), valid for the three main operators (rail, light rail and bus) available for the whole network; a few common passes with private bus operators as well as with CP (suburban rail)
Operational control: Central operation support system; inspectors, both at the dispatch centre and on the network
Arrangements for elderly/disabled: Reduced rate passes, 266 buses ramp-equipped, 434 low-floor buses

Average peak-hour speed: 16.0 km/h
Bus priority: Some bus access to pedestrianised areas; 23.4 km of bus lanes
New vehicles financed by: Bank loans

Tramway

Passenger journeys: (2003) 232,000
(2004) 84,000
(2005) 79,000
(2006) 80,000
(2007) 268,000

Current situation

Only Routes 18 and 1 and 22 remain in operation, extending to 9.0 km and operated by eight Brill cars.

Developments

The tram network in old downtown is being rebuilt (3.3 km). In 2005, a segment was completed which enabled Line 18 to return to its original track.

In 2007, a new line (22) was built, serving the city centre.

Bus (contracted operations)
Current situation
Several city routes are operated under contract to STCP by a number of private companies, including Valpi Bus, Empresa de Transportes Gondomarense and Auto Viação Pacense.

Metro do Porto SA

Avenida Fernão de Magalhães, 1862, 7°,
P-4350-158, Oporto, Portugal
Tel: (+351 22) 508 10 00;
Fax: (+351 22) 508 10 01
e-mail: metro@metro-porto.pt
Web: www.metrodoporto.pt

Key personnel
Chairman, Board of Directors:
  Valentim dos Santos Loureiro
Chairman, Executive Committee:
  Manuel de Oliveira Marques
Communications Department: Nuno Ortigão

Light rail

Type of operation: Light rail, first line (Line A – Blue) inaugurated December 2002; commercial operations commenced 1 January 2003

Route length: 59.3 km
  in tunnel: 7 km
Number of lines: 4
Number of stations: 66
  in tunnel: 15
Gauge: 1,435 mm

Background

Metro do Porto SA was set up in January 1993 to implement proposals to build a light rail network. Its share capital is held by Área Metropolitana do Porto 80 per cent, CP 15 per cent and Metropolitano de Lisboa (Lisbon Metro) five per cent.

Current situation

Oporto Metropolitan Authority owns 60 per cent of Metro do Porto SA, STCP owns 25 per cent, Estado Portugues owns 10 per cent, CP has a five per cent shareholding and each of the main Oporto metropolitan area municipalities has one share.

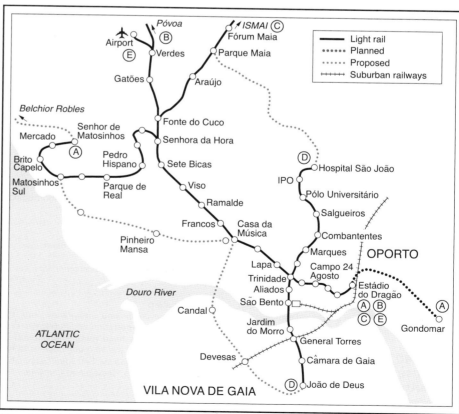

Map of Oporto's light rail system

1124801

The Oporto Light Rail Transit System project idea is seen as desirable for the Oporto metropolitan area, constituted by nine municipalities with more than 1.2 million inhabitants.

The first Bombardier Eurotram was received in May 2001.

The first section of Line A – Blue, which runs from Senhor de Matosinhos to Trindade, became operational on 1 January 2003. The remaining section of this line, from Trindade to Estádio do Dragão, was completed in mid-2004.

The network, with four lines, currently has a route length of 59.3 km and 67 stations.

The system's Eurotrams have been produced by Bombardier and are a variation of the company's *Flexity* Outlook series. The capacity of each LRV is 216 passengers (80 seated), and the fleet comprises 72 vehicles, with 100 per cent low floor, air conditioning and modularity. EIB, the Portuguese state, EU funds and the financial market have financed the project.

Developments
In 2005, the following sections were opened: March 2005: Line B – Red, Senhora da Hora-Pedras Rubras (6.8 km); July 2005: Line C – Green, Fonte do Cuco-Fórum Maia; September 2005: Line D –Yellow, Pólo Universitário-Câmara Gaia (5.7 km).

In May 2006, Line E – Purple (1.6 km), a branch line off Line D to the airport, opened. Line E services then commenced through-running to Estádio de Gragão on Line A. This development completed Phase 1 of Oporto's plans for light rail. 2006 had also seen the completion of Line D, extended northwards to Hospital São João (5.9 km) and south to terminate at João de Deus and Line B – Red from Pedras Rubras to Vila do Conde and Póvoa de Varzim (17.2 km). Line C was extended northwards to ISMAI (4.5 km), although a proposed extension to Trofa has been held back.

Phase 2 will see the start of the Gondomar extension to Line A, for which approval from the government is expected soon. Metro do Porto and STCP are looking at conversion to light rail of the abandoned Boavista to Matosinhos tram route. This revitalised 7 km route would be branded Line F, with 12 stations. An interchange station near Casa Da Música will be required.

Proposals for a 10-station Line G from Casa Da Música southwards across the Douro river to Quinta do Cedro in the Vila Nova de Gaia district are under consideration. A western extension to Line A from Matosinhos to Belchior Robles, as Line F, is also under study as well as a northern extension of Line D from Hospital São João to link up with Line C at Parque Maia.

In mid-2006, Bombardier Transportation, as part of a consortium, was awarded a contract to provide 30 bi-directional *Flexity Swift* low-floor LRVs. The contract also includes maintenance for

Bombardier Eurotram running on Oporto's new light rail system   1033683

these vehicles for five years. The total contract was valued at some EUR115 million, with Bombardier's share amounting to approximately EUR89 million. Delivery of the vehicles is due to take place between 2008 and 2009.

Fleet: 72 vehicles
Bombardier *Flexity* Outlook series Eurotram   72
On order: 30 Bombardier bi-directional *Flexity Swift* low-floor LRVs

Service: 4–15 min
First/last train: 06.00–01.00 daily
Fare structure: Zonal; one-trip, 10-trip, one-day and monthly season tickets
Integration with other modes: Fares integrated with STCP buses, CP trains and private operators' buses through Andante fare system
Surveillance: CCTV is to monitor all stations

Comboios de Portugal (CP) – Portuguese Railways
Calçada do Duque 20, P-1249-109 Lisbon, Portugal
Tel: (+351 21) 102 30 00   Fax: (+351 21) 347 30 93
Web: www.cp.pt

Business Unit
CP Porto (Unidade de Suburbanos do Grande Porto)
Estação de S Bento (Ala direita), Praça Almeida Garrett, P-4000-069 Porto, Portugal
Tel: (+351 21) 223 39 40 40

Fax: (+351 21) 223 39 40 79
e-mail: usgp@mail.cp.pt
    Staff: 300 (estimate)

Type of operation: Suburban heavy rail

Passenger journeys: (2003) 14.4 million

Current situation
Commuter services operate into three city-centre terminals. From São Bento, trains run to São Romao (19 km) and Braga (57 km); from Trindade, a frequent diesel service operates to Vilar do Pinheiro (17 km) and Póvoa (30 km), carrying about 6.5 million passengers a year, while hourly trains run to Guimaraes (62 km); lastly, from São Bento and Campanha stations, there is a combined suburban/regional service to Aveiro (67 km).

For further information on CP, please see *Jane's World Railways*.

Developments
Some stations have been equipped with new automatic ticket vending machines.

A major modernisation programme to improve services on this network was carried out in 2004, including the introduction of new rolling stock – Class 3400 emus.

Previously know as Caminhos de Ferro Portugueses, EP (CP), the company changed its name in 2005.

Fleet: 33 vehicles
Breakdown of fleet is not currently available.

Puerto Rico

San Juan
Population: City 426,618 (2006 estimate); Metropolitan area (including San Juan and the municipalities of Bayamón, Guaynabo, Cataño, Canóvanas, Caguas, Toa Alta, Toa Baja, Carolina and Trujillo Alto) 2 million (estimate)

Public transport
Bus services provided by private company under contract from the Department of Transportation; feeder, express and shuttle services operated by state bus authority, with private shared taxi 'publico' minibuses and Metrobus services; metro; ferry.

Autoridad Metropolitana de Autobuses (AMA) – Metropolitan Bus Authority (MBA)
Departamento de Transportación y Obras Públicas (DTOP)
PO Box 42007, San Juan, Puerto Rico 00940-2007

Tel: (+1 787) 792 71 10, 76 26   Fax: (+1 787) 727 54 56
Web: www.dtop.gobierno.pr/ama/amahompg.htm

Key personnel
President: Alexis Morales Frese
Executive Director: Evans González Baker
General Manager: Hector Rivera
Operations Manager: Cesar Cintron
    Staff: 1,198

Current situation
Established in 1959 and integrated into the Department of Transportation and Public Works in 1973, AMA provides fixed route and paratransit bus services in six of the 13 municiplaities in the San Juan metropolitan area: San Juan, Guaynabo, Bayamon, Trujillo Alto, Cataño and Carolina.

Developments
Some hybrid diesel-electric buses have been added to the fleet in recent years.

Bus
Passenger journeys: (2006) 40.8 million (estimate)
Vehicle-km: Not currently available

Number of routes: 30 (including two express services, plus a further first class Metrobus II service)
Route length: Not currently available
On priority right-of-way: 27.4 km exclusive bus lane

Fleet: 277 buses (plus 35 paratransit vehicles)
Full breakdown of fleet is not currently available, but includes:

Flxible (1995)	47
RTS Methanol	36
Ford E-350, diesel (1992)	9
Other (paratransit) (1996)	6

In peak service: 188

One-person operation: All routes
Fare collection: Exact fare to farebox on entry

Fare structure: Flat; premium for travel on air conditioned vehicles
Fares collected on board: 100 per cent
Arrangements for elderly/disabled: 138 buses wheelchair lift-equipped; paratransit services carried 32,000 passengers in 1994
Average peak-hour speed: 16 km/h
Operating costs financed by: Fares 14 per cent, subsidy/grants 86 per cent
Subsidy from: State 74 per cent, US FTA 26 per cent

Private bus
Current situation
Privately owned bus companies are authorised to operate in specific sectors within the metropolitan area. 'Publico' shared-taxi minibus (mostly vans) carry about 11,000 passengers daily, while the Metrobus network using contraflow bus lanes caters for some 20,000 journeys.

Departamento de Transportación y Obras Públicas (DTOP) – Department of Transportation & Public Works
Highway and Transportation Authority, Integrated Transport Alternative (ATI)
PO Box 42007, San Juan, PR-00940-2007, Puerto Rico
Tel: (+1 787) 721 87 87 Ex 1024
Fax: (+1 787) 727 54 56
Web: www.dtop.gov.pr

Street address
Office of the Executive Director
  South Building 10th Floor, Roberto Sánchez Vilella Government Center, José De Diego Avenue, Santurce, San Juan, Puerto Rico

Key personnel
Secretary of Transportation and Public Works: Carlos J González Miranda
Executive Director of PR Highway and Transportation Authority: Luis M Trinidad Garay
Deputy Executive Director for Transit (ATI Director): Marco A Quiñones Oquendo

Autoridad de Carreteras y Transportación de Puerto Rico (ACT) – Tren Urbano (TU)
Tel: (+1 787) 765 09 27 Fax: (+1 787) 765 38 85
Web: www.ati.gobierno.pr

Key personnel
Executive Director: Fernando Vargas Arroyo

Type of operation: Metro, opened in 2005

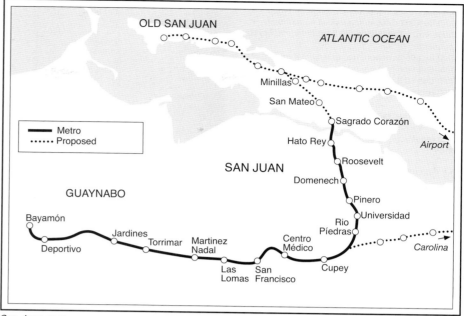
San Juan metro   1298724

Passenger journeys: (2005/06) 7.5 million
(2006/07) 7.5 million
Vehicle-km: (2005/06) 5.2 million
(2006/07) 5.2 million

Route length: 17.2 km
Number of lines: 1
Number of stations: 16
  in tunnel: 2
  elevated: 10
Gauge: 1,435 mm
Electrification: 750 V DC, third rail

Current situation
The first line of the system, which had been under construction since 1997, opened in June 2005, between Bayamón and Sagrado Corazón.

Developments
There are plans for extensions to the municipalities of Carolina and Caguas and to the district of Santurce. Also, proposed extensions to Old San Juan and the Luis Muñoz Marín International Airport.

Fleet: 37 two-car trains
Siemens stainless steel cars (2000/03)   M84

First/last train: 05.30/23.30
Control systems: Microprocessor-based Automatic Train Control (ATC)

Signalling: Transmission-based signalling for train detection and control
Fares structure: Flat, reduced if transfer from AMA buses; reduced fares for students and those aged 60–74; free travel for elderly (over 75), children under six years and unemployed persons; passes; pre-paid multi-use farecard
Integration with other modes: Transfers to/from AMA bus and minibus services
Arrangements for elderly/disabled: Free travel for passengers aged over 75

Acuaexpreso
PO Box 362829, San Juan, Puerto Rico 00936-2829
Tel: (+1 787) 729 86 49   Fax: (+1 787) 724 66 44

Key personnel
Director of Operations: Luis Sanchez
  Staff: 100 (estimate)

Ferry
Passenger journeys: (Annual) 1.1 million (estimate)

Current situation
Under the ownership of the Autoridad de Transporte Marítimo (ATM), Acuaexpreso operates a single commuter/tourist route across San Juan Bay from San Juan to Hato Rey, with bus connections in Hato Rey. Services run from 05.00 to 22.00.

Romania

Bucharest
Population: City 1.9 million, urban area 2.1 million, metropolitan area 2.6 million (2006 estimates)

Public transport
Bus, trolleybus and tramway services provided by state management company responsible to municipal council, with a Ministry of Transport enterprise operating the metro.

Regia Autonomă de Transport Bucureşti (RATB)
1 Bd Dinicu Golescu, Sector 1, R-79913, Bucharest, Romania
Tel: (+40 21) 315 10 10
Fax: (+40 21) 315 10 10, 311 05 95, 311 26 55
e-mail: info@ratb.ro
Web: www.ratb.ro

Key personnel
General Manager: Gheorghe Aron
  Staff: 11,912 (2007)

Passenger journeys: (All modes)
(2003) 896.2 million
(2004) 945 million
(2005) 969 million
(2006) 874 million
(2007) 829 million

Operating costs financed by: (All modes) Fares 37 per cent, government subsidy 63 per cent

Current situation
RATB was created in 1991 as successor to the former operator ITB. It is a state-owned autonomous enterprise responsible for surface public transport by bus, tramway and trolleybus.
  Since 1990 new routes have been introduced every year and additions to the fleet have helped to reduce overcrowding.

Developments
In 2007, 35.97 km (one-way) of track was modernised.
  An Automated Fare Collection system has also been implemented.
  500 Mercedes-Benz Citaro solo buses have recently been purchased.
  The Mercedes-Benz and Irisbus vehicles in the fleet, some 600 buses, are equipped with a data collection module that monitors activities such as departure/arrival times, average speed per one-way trip, average duration of a one-way trip at different times and energy and fuel consumption.

Bus and trolleybus
Staff: Bus: 2,708, trolleybus: 644 drivers

Passenger journeys: (2003) Bus 403.3 million, trolleybus 89.6 million
(2004) Bus 425 million, trolleybus 95 million
(2005) Bus 436 million, trolleybus 97 million

(2006) Bus 401 million, trolleybus 86 million
(2007) Bus 382 million, trolleybus 81 million
Vehicle-km: (2003) Bus 66.8 million, trolleybus 12.5 million
(2004) Bus 66.8 million, trolleybus 12.8 million
(2005) Bus 60.5 million, trolleybus 12.5 million
(2006) Bus 59.5 million, trolleybus 12.2 million
(2007) Bus 62.4 million, trolleybus 11.2 million

Number of routes: Urban bus 69 (PeriUrban bus 50*), trolleybus 19
Route length: (One way) bus 2,962 km, trolleybus 304 km

*The PeriUrban bus lines were re-opened in March 2006

Fleet: 1,290 buses
Mercedes-Benz/EvoBus Citaro solo (2006/07)   500
DAC 112 UDM   26
Ikarus 260   143
DAF SB 220   241
Rocar UL 70   5
Rocar U 412   334
Iveco   40
Renault   1
In peak service: 1,227 (2007)
On order: 500 EvoBus Citaro solo buses, to be delivered in mid-2009

Fleet: 296 trolleybuses
Rocar 512   9
Rocar 412 EA   2
Ikarus/Astra 415T (1999/2002)   200
Irisbus/Astra low-floor (2006/07)   84
Others   1
In peak service: 261 (2007)
On order: Not currently available

Most intensive service: Bus 2–30 min, trolleybus 2–20 min
Fare structure: Flat; express routes at higher fare by magnetic cards valid for two–10 journeys; prepurchase two-journey, multitickets, monthly passes for whole system or one or two lines
Fare collection: Tickets purchased from approved vendors, cancelling machines on board
Fare evasion control: Inspectors
Fares collected on board: None
Arrangements for retired, students, pupils and ex-servicemen: Free or 50 per cent reduced fare
Operational control: Route inspectors, mobile radio and 59 routes equipped with Automatic Vehicle Location (AVL) system
Average distance between stops: Bus 730 m, trolleybus 666 m
Average peak-hour speed: Bus 14 km/h, trolleybus 11 km/h

Tramway
Staff: 943 drivers (2007)

Type of operation: Conventional tramway

Passenger journeys: (2003) 403.3 million
(2004) 425 million
(2005) 436 million
(2006) 387 million
(2007) 366 million
Car-km: (2003) 26.1 million
(2004) 24.3 million
(2005) 24.1 million
(2006) 23.4 million
(2007) 21.6 million

Route length: 486 km
Number of lines: 23
Gauge: 1,435 mm
Track: Rail in prefabricated concrete panels on straight sections, in cobbles or tarmac on curves
Electrification: 750 V DC, overhead

Rolling stock: 512 (2007)
RATB Works V3ACHPPC 8-axle (1973 on)   M17
Electroputere – Holec V3A 93H (1993)   M3
Electroputere V3A 93M   M8
Faur V3A 93M   M44
RATB Works V3A 93M (modernised
  1995–2005)   M260

RATB buses during peak period in Bucharest (Peter Roelofs)   1178313

RATB Mercedes-Benz Citaro bus   1279605

RATB Irisbus Astra trolleybus in the city centre   1367276

RATB Works V2A 6-axle (1982)	M37
RATB Works V2ST 6-axle; two driver-cabs (1999–2003)	M2
ČKD Tatra T4R 4-axle (1971 on)	M116
Rathgeber M4 (ex-Munich) and Duewag 4-axle (ex-Frankfurt) (withdrawn)	M10 T6
RATB Works V2AT 6-axle	M9

In peak service: 432 (2007)

Service: 2–30 min
First/last car: 04.00/00.48
Fare structure/collection: As bus
One-person operation: All routes
Average distance between stops: 495 m
Average peak-hour speed: 13 km/h

SC Metrorex SA (Societatea Comercială de Transport cu Metroul Bucureşti)

38 Dinicu Golescu Avenue, RO-010873 Bucharest, Romania
Tel: (+40 21) 319 36 70
Fax: (+40 21) 312 51 49
e-mail: contact@metrorex.ro
Web: www.metrorex.ro

Key personnel
General Director: Gabriel Daniel Mocanu
Operation Director: Gabriel Sburlan
Infrastructure Director: Constantin Ionescu
Financial Director: Nicolae Grigore
Technical and Investment Director: Ştefan Rotaru
IT & Communications Director: Mariana Petre
   Staff: 4,254

Type of operation: Full metro; first line opened 1979

Current situation
The metro is undergoing comprehensive upgrading, with new vehicles and signalling for Metro Line 2. The 18 new trains (108 metro cars), manufactured and supplied by Bombardier Transportation, have been fully operational since 2004, each with a capacity of 1,200 passengers.

The extension from Gara de Nord to 1 Mai (3.3 km with four stations) was opened in March 2000, the extensions from 1 Mai to Zarea (3 km with two stations) and from Nicolae Grigorescu to Linia de Centura (4.57 km with four stations) are under construction, with completion due for 2008.

Further extensions are planned:
Metro Line 5, Drumul Taberei – Pantelimon: First section: Drumul Taberei – Universitate (9 km with 13 stations), scheduled for completion in 2014; Second section: Universitate – Pantelimon (8 km with 13 stations), scheduled for completion in 2018.

Developments
In December 2004, Metrorex awarded a contract to Bombardier Transportation for the supply of 20 new metro trains (120 metro cars) destined for use on Lines 1 and 3. Delivery began in September 2006 and were completed in 2007. A further order for six new trains (36 metro cars) was placed with Bombardier in 2007 and all of these trains are now in operation.

Bombardier was also involved in the renewal of the Central Traffic Control and Interlocking System on Line 2, which was completed in 2005. Similar work has started on Lines 1 and 3 and were scheduled for commissioning in 2008.

Passenger journeys: (2007) 164 million

Route length: 62.2 km
Number of lines: 4
Number of stations: 45

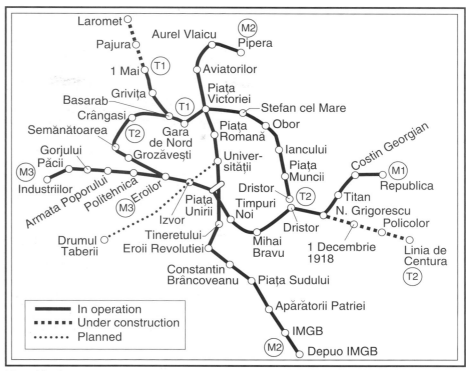

Map of Bucharest metro   1115233

Metro train approaching Universitate station on Line 2 (Peter Roelofs)   1178272

Number of depots: 3
Track: UIC 49/60 rail on timber sleepers; twin-block concrete sleepers in tunnel
Minimum curve radius: 150 m
Tunnel: Open-cut rectangular box section or separate bores for each track
Electrification: 750 V DC, third rail

Service: Peak 3 min, off-peak 8–10 min
Fare structure: Flat; two- and 10-trip tickets; daily/monthly passes
Fare collection: Magnetic tickets and contactless cards
Fare-evasion control: Roving inspectors
Integration with other modes: Interchange with surface transport

Operating costs financed by: Fares 37.9 per cent, other commercial sources 3.7 per cent, state subsidy 50.7 per cent
Signalling: Automatic block line and interlocking

Rolling stock: 398 cars

Type IVA (with ATP/ATO Dimetronic) (in 4-car trains)	M20
Type IVA (with ATP/ATO/INDUSI) (in 6-car trains)	M30
Type IVA (in 6-car trains)	M120
Bombardier MOVIA BM 2 (2002/04) (in 6-car trains)	M108
Bombardier BM 21 (2006/07) (in 6-car trains)	M120

In peak service: Not currently available
On order: None

For details of the latest updates to *Jane's Urban Transport Systems* online and to discover the additional information available exclusively to online subscribers please visit

juts.janes.com

Timişoara

Population: City 307,300 (2007 estimate), metropolitan area 359,000 (estimate)

Public transport

Bus, trolleybus, tramway and some taxi services operated by municipal undertaking. Suburban rail services provided by CFR Călători SA.

Regie Autonomă de Transport Timişoara (RATT)

B-dul Take Ionescu Nr 56,300074, Timişoara, Romania
Tel: (+40 56) 43 32 15   Fax: (+40 56) 43 33 54
e-mail: relatii@ratt.ro
Web: www.ratt.ro

Key personnel
Director General: Ioan Goia
Director, Marketing: Florian Zanfir
    Staff: 1,470

Passenger journeys: (All modes)
(2007) 86.2 million

Operating costs financed by: Fares 48.9 per cent, other commercial sources six per cent, subsidy/grants 45.1 per cent

Background

RATT was formed in 1990 and is responsible to the city hall of Timişoara. The organisation operates and maintains the bus, tram and trolleybus services, vehicles and infrastructure.

Current situation

Major works have continued to repair worn out and damaged tram tracks, with reconstruction on four busy streets. Trolleybus routes 15 and 16 were extended to Lidia Street. Proximity to the Banat (Timisç) tramcar works has ensured good maintenance of the tram fleet, and both tram and trolleybus networks are in better condition than in most other Romanian cities.

Developments

Recent major works has resulted in the repair of over 40 km of tram tracks, including the reconstruction of the streets along which the tracks run. Also, the fleet has been considerably modernised, with the introduction of 55 new Mercedes-Benz buses and 50 Skoda trolleybuses, which have entered service in the last two years (the buses in May 2005, the trolleybuses in May 2008).

Ex-Düsseldorf tram 2502, a 1956 Düwag, entered service in Timişoara in 2007 and wears RATT's new fleet livery. It is pictured crossing the Decebal Bridge (Steve Morgan)   1375714

Bus and trolleybus

Number of routes: Bus 16, trolleybus six
Route length: Bus 201.8 km, trolleybus 55.86 km

Fleet: 92 buses

Mercedes-Benz (2005)	55
Ikarus	29
Rocar	eight

In peak service: 50

Fleet: 89 trolleybuses

Skoda 24Tr (2008)	50
Various other types, all withdrawn	39

In peak service: 43

Most intensive service: 10 min
Fare collection: Prepurchase, with validation/cancellation on board
Fare structure: Flat. A day ticket is available.

Tramway

Passenger journeys: (2007) 43.4 million
Car-km: (2007) 3.9 million

Number of routes: 11
Route length: 134.3 km
Gauge: 1,435 mm

Rolling stock: 85 cars, 62 trailers
Breakdown of fleet is not currently available.
In peak service: 50

CFR Călători SA

B-dul Dinicu Golescu Nr 38, Sector 1, 010863, Bucharest, Romania
Tel: (+40 1) 222 25 18
Fax: (+40 1) 411 20 54
e-mail: RelPublic.Calatori@cfr.ro
Web: www.cfr.ro

Key personnel
Chairman and Director General: Valentin Bota
Deputy Director General: Vanghele Nacu
    Staff: 19,000 (whole company estimate)

Type of operation: Suburban rail

Current situation

The passenger rail operator CFR Călători SA runs suburban service over several routes.

For further information on CFR Călători SA, please see *Jane's World Railways.*

Russian Federation

Chelyabinsk

Population: 1.07 million (2002 Census)

Public transport

Bus and trolleybus/tramway services provided by municipal undertaking; metro under construction.

ChelGorTrans

Ulitsa Truda 66, 454091000 Chelyabinsk, Russian Federation
Tel: (+7 351) 263 77 52
e-mail: chelgortrans@inbox.ru
Web: www.chelgortrans.ru

Current situation
Bus, tram and trolleybus operations.

Bus

Number of routes: 63
Fleet: Not currently available

Trolleybus

Number of routes: 21
Fleet: Not currently available

Tramway

Number of routes: 18
Track length: 155 km

Rolling stock: About 370 cars

KTM5 (1982–92)	M320
KTM8 (1990–96)	M50

ChelMetro

Ul Kurchatova 19, 454092 Chelyabinsk, Russian Federation
Tel: (+7 351) 778 02 63
Fax: (+7 351) 778 06 76
e-mail: metro@incompany.ru
Web: www.chelmetro.ru

Type of operation: Metro (under construction)

Background

Construction of the initial phase of the first of three planned lines commenced in 1992.

Current situation

Work is under way on a 8.25-km section with 5 stations.

Developments

There are plans for extensions eastward and westwards to this initial section and a further two lines. However, there have been significant delays and funding has been a problem. No firm date has been given for the opening of the initial section, although this may take place in 2010 if funding is available.

Kazan

Population: 1.11 million (estimate)

Public transport

Bus and trolleybus/tramway services provided by separate municipal undertakings; substantial private minibus operations (*marshrutka*); metro.

Metroelektrotrans (Kazan Electric Transport)

Kazan Metropoliten (Kazan Metro)
Esperanto st 8, p/b 100, Kazan 420049, Republic of Tatarstan, Russian Federation
Tel: (+7 843) 533 70 02, 277 10 50, 277 27 93
e-mail: kazanmetro@mail.ru
Web: www.kazantransport.by.ru

Key personnel

Director General: Asfan G Galyavov
Chief Engineer: Elmir Zakirov

Bus

Passenger journeys: Not currently available
Vehicle-km: Not currently available

Route length: Not currently available
No of routes: 96

Fleet

The fleet total and breakdown are not currently available, but vehicles include Mercedes-Benz, Ikarus, Ford, Iveco, Hyundai and Karosa buses and minibuses.

Trolleybus

Passenger journeys: Not currently available
Vehicle-km: Not currently available

Route length: Not currently available
No of routes: 12

Fleet

The fleet total and breakdown are not currently available, but vehicles include Jelcz/Nordtroll.

Tramway

Passenger journeys: Not currently available
Vehicle-km: Not currently available

Route length: Not currently available
No of routes: 20 (with 5 further routes planned)

Fleet

The fleet total and breakdown are not currently available, but vehicles include KTM-5M3, KTM-8, KTM-8M, KTM-19, KTM-19M and KTM-19T.

Metro

Type of operation: Metro, opened 2005

Passenger journeys: Not yet available
Vehicle-km: Not yet available

Route length: 7.7 km
No of lines: 1
No of stations: 5

Background

Kazan Metropoliten was established in 2004, and in 2006 it was re-established as the Department of Metropoliten of the municipal enterprise Metroelektrotrans (Kazan Electric Transport).

Construction on the metro started in August 1997.

Current situation

The Metro was opened in August 2005, as part of the 1,000th anniversary celebrations of the city.

Service is provided by five four-car trains, for which Skoda supplied the traction and braking equipment and Vagonmash provided the mechanical part.

The line has a TErrestrial Trunked RAdio (TETRA) digital radio system, supplied by Optima, MS Spets Telecom and a certified distributor of Motorola's, RCI.

Developments

There are plans to extend the system to a three-line network with a total length of some 46 km. The existing line would be extended at both ends with two new lines being constructed.

Fleet: 20 cars (in four-car trains)
Vagonmash/Skoda series 81-553, 81-554, 81-555   20

Service: 4–5 minutes (peak), 7–8 minutes (off-peak)
First/last train: 05.00/24.00
Fare structure: Flat
Fare collection: Contactless smartcard

Moscow

Population: 10.4 million (2002 Census)

Public transport

Bus, trolleybus and tramway services provided state-owned undertaking. Metro, responsibility of government ministry, being extended. Bus transport in Moscow oblast also provided by state-owned company, Mostransavto (www.mostransavto.ru). Suburban rail services. Tourist monorail.

Mosgortrans

Raushskaya Naberezhnaya 22/21, Building 1, Moscow 115035, Russian Federation
Tel: (+7 495) 951 66 53 Fax: (+7 495) 951 38 27
e-mail: mail@mosgortrans.com
Web: www.mosgortrans.com

Key personnel

Director General: Peter I Ivanov
Deputy Director Generals: A A Vardanyan
  Boris I Tkachuk
  Viktor Baklanov
  Viktor Halzov
  Noospheric Georgievich
  Ardak H Koschugulov
  Ms Marina Y Trusenkova
Staff: 40,000 (approximate)

Current situation

Approximately 47 per cent of the city's total public transport journeys are carried out by Mosgortrans. Some 4.2 billion passengers are carried annually on all modes.

Operating costs financed by: Fares 11 per cent, subsidy/grants 89 per cent

Bus

Passenger journeys: (2006) 1,460 million (estimate)

Route length: 4,965 km
Number of routes: 487

Developments

Mosgortrans is actively pursuing the reduction of bus emissions and is introducing CNG buses.

There are some 420 accessible buses in the fleet. The company's aim is to have 40 per cent of the fleet accessible by the end of 2009.

Moscow metro, light rail and monorail network   1168260

Fleet: 5,095 buses
Full breakdown of fleet is not currently available, but is believed to include Ikarus 280 articulated, Ikarus 435, LIAZ 677 and Mercedes-Benz Türk 0325 vehicles.
In peak service: Not currently available

Trolleybus

Passenger journeys: Not currently available

Route length: 927 km
Number of routes: 87

Fleet: Approx 1,600 trolleybuses
Full breakdown of fleet is not currently available,
but is believed to include:
Uritsky ZIU9
Uritsky ZIU10
Ikarus 280 articulated
In peak service: 1,300 (estimate)

Tramway

Type of operation: Conventional tramway

Passenger journeys: Not currently available

Route length: 425 km
Number of routes: 41

Gauge: 1,524 mm
Electrification: 600 V DC, overhead

Developments
The prototype Ust-Kastav low-floor tram has
been tested in winter conditions.
   New LM-99 and KTM-19 cars have been
delivered.

Rolling stock: 687 cars
Full breakdown of fleet is not currently available,
but is believed to include:
CKD Tatra T3/T3M (1980–87)
CKD Tatra T7 (1990/93)
Kirov KTM8 (1990–96)
Kirov KTM8M
Kirov CTM16
PTMZ LM-99
Ust-Katav KTM-19
In peak service: Not currently available

Operational control: Despatchers based at route
terminals
Service: Frequent
One-person operation: All routes
Fare collection: Prepurchase with cancelling
machines on board
Fare structure: Flat. Monthly seasons for surface
network or plus metro
Fare evasion control: Random inspection by
controllers
Arrangements for elderly/disabled: War and
industrial invalids and elderly travel free
Average peak-hour speed: Bus 18.2 km/h, trolleybus
16.1 km/h

Moskovski Metropoliten – Moscow Metro
41 Prospekt Mira, Bld 2, Moscow 129100,
Russian Federation
Tel: (+7 495) 688 02 93
Fax: (+7 495) 631 37 55
e-mail: protocol@mosmetro.ru
Web: www.mosmetro.ru

Key personnel
Head: Dmitry Gaev

Type of operation: Full metro, first line opened 1935

Passenger journeys: (2007) 3,287.3 million (estimate)
Car-km: (2007) 688.5 million

Route length: 280.8 km
Number of lines: 11 (plus 1 'light metro')
Number of stations: 174
Gauge: 1,524 mm

Moscow Monorail   1115230

Max gradient: 4%
Min curve radius: 196 m
Electrification: 825 V DC, third rail

Service: Peak: 1 min 30 s, off-peak: 2–4 min, after
midnight: 10 min
First/last train: 06.00/01.00
Fare structure: Flat, daily, monthly and early
'ultralight' cards, multi-journey 'ultralight' cards,
smartcard
Revenue control: Turnstiles, electronically activated
barriers
Signalling: Central control; radio-telephone
communication with all trains, cab signalling with
automatic train speed control and driver-only
operation on 8 lines

Rolling stock: 4,476 cars, all motored, built by
Metrovagonmash Mytischi (Moscow)

Current situation
The metro is the city's principal mode of
transport, accounting for more than half of all
journeys. Installation of ATC on some lines has
reduced headway to 90 seconds.

Developments
In 2006, a new station, Mezhdunarodnaya, was
opened. In 2007, the Line 3 extension from Park
Pobedy to Strogino (11.5 km) opened, with new
stations at Kuntsevskaya and Strogino.
   There are currently three projects under
construction: a new intermediate station at
Slavyanskiy Bul'var (due to open in 2008), a
2.93 km extension to Line 10, with two stations)
and a 4.2 km extension to Line 3, with two new
stations (the latter two due to open in 2009).

Moscow Monorail
Moscow Monorail Roads
10 Beryozovaya alleya, Moscow 127273,
Russian Federation
Tel: (+7 095) 974 34 34, 31 70
Fax: (+7 095) 974 34 70
e-mail: office@monorail.ru
Web: www.monorail.ru

Key personnel
Vice President: Alexey Barkhatov

Type of operation: Monorail, opened 2005

Passenger journeys: Not yet available

Current situation
The elevated Moscow Monorail, Line M1, is now
in operation. Having opened in January 2005,
the system is 4.7 km long with six stations and is
operated with six-car trains.
   The system is based on Intamin technology
and incorporates heating equipment to combat
the harsh weather.

JSC Rossiiskoe Zheleznie Dorogi (RZD) – Joint Stock Company 'Russian Railways' (JSCo 'RZD')
2 Novoya Basmannaya Street, Moscow 107174,
Russian Federation
Tel: (+7 095) 262 99 01
e-mail: info@rzd.ru
Web: www.rzd.ru

Type of operation: Suburban heavy rail

Background
Fully state-owned, open joint-stock corporation
created by decree issued by the government of the
Russian Federation in September 2003, the board of
which was appointed in October 2003. The company
incorporates 987 enterprises and 165 subsidiaries,
with a total of some 1.2 million employees.

Current situation
As well as suburban services sharing main line
tracks there are lines serving commuter areas
and a rail link to Domodedovo airport. Total of
10 routes or groups of routes, 1,524 mm gauge.
Most of the system is electrified.
   For further information on RZD, please see
Jane's World Railways.

Rolling stock: Mostly Class ER911 trains

Nizhny Novgorod
Population: In excess of 1.3 million (estimate)

City Administration
Department for Transport and Communication
7a Revolution Square, Nizhny Novgorod, 603082,
Russian Federation
Tel: (+7 831) 246 82 80, 82 81
e-mail: deptrans@admgor.nnov.ru
Web: www.admgor.nnov.ru

Key personnel
Head of Department for Transport and
*   Communication:* Vladimir Grigorievich Gribov

Developments
In 2006, an order was placed for GPS
equipment to enable planning of transport
operations including timetables, vehicle
tracking, scheduling and for fleet maintenance
purposes.

Public transport
Bus and trolleybus/tramway services operated
by municipal undertakings; metro.

Bus
Current situation
There are 114 routes operated by state/municipal
enterprises and a further 87 routes operated by
private companies. Exact annual passenger journey
figures are not currently available, but are estimated

at some 119 million. The fleet of buses is believed to include Ikarus, LIAZ, LAZ and MAN vehicles.

Tram and trolleybus
Nizhegorodelektrotrans
GSP-182, ul Yaroslanskaya 25, Nizhny Novgorod, Nizhny Novgorod Region 603950, Russian Federation
Tel: (+7 8312) 33 23 20

Current situation
Currently, there are 20 tram and 20 trolleybus routes, operated by a state/municipal enterprise. Confirmed annual passenger journeys are not currently available, but are believed to be in the region of 175 million for both modes.

Developments
In mid-2007, ex-Moskva T3 trams, rebuilt as type T3R, started to enter service from Depot 2.

Tramway
Fleet:
Breakdown of fleet is not currently available, but includes:
CKD Tatra T3
CKD Tatra T3m
Kirov KTM5
Riga RVZ6
KTM8/KTM8M
KTM-19
T3R

Metro – Nizhny Novgorod Metro
Type of operation: Full metro, initial route opened 1985

Passenger journeys: (Annual) 16 million (estimate)

Route length: 16 km (estimate)
Number of lines: 2

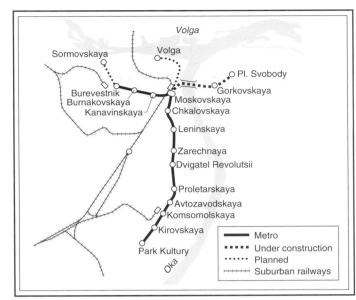

Map of Nizhny Novgorod metro
1040981

Number of stations: 13
  In tunnel: 12
Gauge: 1,524 mm
Electrification: 825 V DC, third rail

Current situation
There are plans to extend the Sormovska Line at both the northern and western ends, although progress has been slow. Also, on the Avtozavodskaya Line, a metro/road bridge into the city is under construction, and a tentative date of 2010 for the completion of this line has been forecast.

Developments
Federal funding for Nizhny Novgorod has been increased from RUR77.1 million in 2005 to RUR158.8 million in 2006. Some RUR100 million was destined for the metro/road bridge construction.

Rolling stock: 80 cars, in four-car units
Metrovagonmash 81-717/714   M80

Service: 3 min peak, 7–15 min off-peak
First/last train: 05.30/24.00
Fare structure: Flat; monthly pass
Fare collection: Token to turnstile

Novosibirsk
Population: 1.4 million (2002 Census)

Public transport
Bus and trolleybus/tramway services provided by separate municipal undertakings. Metro; suburban rail.

Novosibirsk Metropolitena Municipal Enterprise (Novosibirsk Metro)
Ul Serebrennikovskaya 34, 630099 Novosibirsk-99, Russian Federation
Tel: (+7 3832) 90 81 10   Fax: (+7 3832) 46 56 82
e-mail: nsk@metro.snt.ru
Web: www.metro-nsk.ru

Key personnel
Head of Metro: Vladimir M Koshkin
  Staff: 1,610

Type of operation: Full metro, initial route opened 1985

Passenger journeys: (Annual) 120 million (estimated)

Route length: 14.3 km
Number of lines: 2
Number of stations: 12

Gauge: 1,520 mm
Electrification: 825 V DC, third rail

Service: 4–5 min
Fare structure: Flat; single tickets, multi-trip tickets
Signalling: ATC, ALC signalling and train control equipment with track circuits

Rolling stock: 80 cars

Current situation
Initial section of the Leninskaya Line opened to passenger traffic in 1986. Two further extensions to this line opened in 1991 and 1992. The second Dzerzhinskaya Line opened in 1997. In December 2000 a new station, Marshall Pokryshkina, was opened.

Developments
In June 2005, a three-station extension opened from Marshala Pokryshkina to Beryozovaya Roshca on the Dzerzhinskaya Line. This line will continue to the east, with the current station-opening schedule: Zolotaya Niva in 2008, Gusinobrodskaya in 2011 and finally Volochaevskaya in 2014. Longer-term plans would see the line also extended westwards across the Ob river.
There are also plans to extend the Leninskaya Line, both to the southeast and to the north. The former would see a station at Ploshchad

Novosibirsk metro   1124826

Stanislavskogo opened in 2009, with the line then extended on to Permskaya and Yuzhnaya. At the northern end, three stations are planned for opening after 2015: Botanicheskiy Sad, Severnaya and Aviatsionnaya. Also a new surface-level station is planned, Sportivnaya, situated between Rechnoi Vokzal and Studencheskaya stations.

Omsk
Population: 1.1 million (2002 Census)

Public transport
Bus, tram and trolleybus. Metro under construction.
  Privately operated buses are currently the major mode of transport in the city. During the last few years, the city administration has started the process of regulating private operators. Some new vehicles have been brought into service.

Mostovik Engineering Company Limited
OmskTransProject Design Institute
5 Mira Avenue, Bldg 5, Omsk 644080, Russian Federation
Tel: (+7 3812) 65 97 55, 65 22 29, 65 97 19
Fax: (+7 3812) 69 66 86
e-mail: office@mostovik.ru
Web: www.mostovik.ru

Key personnel
Director: Oleg V Shishov
Chief Engineer: Viacheslav V Dvorakovski
Vice-Director, Manufacturing: Nikolai S Bondarenko
Vice-Director, Construction Projects: Sergei A Ksenzhenko
Manager, Public Relations: Lyudmila V Aleshkova

Type of operation: Metro (under construction)

Background
Since 1996 the Mostovik Engineering Company Limited has been working on the construction of Omsk metro and in 1997 it became the main contractor on the project.

Current situation
Construction started mid-1993 of the first line of a then-proposed three-line metro.

The latest indications are that four of the six stations on the first 6 km section are proposed for opening at the end of 2008.

Rostov-on-Don
Population: 1 million (2002 Census)

Public transport
Bus, and trolleybus/tramway services provided by municipal undertaking, with privately operated express buses and taxibuses.

Municipal Transportation Company 'Rostovpassazhirtrans'
63 Kirkovsky Prospekt, Rostov-on-Don 344010, Russian Federation
Tel: (+7 8632) 65 10 60
Fax: (+7 8632) 65 44 85
e-mail: rptrans@donpac.ru

Key personnel
General Director: Robert Sanamov

Passenger journeys: (2000) 246 million (estimate)

Background
Municipal enterprise established in 1997 by merger of previous municipal transport enterprises.

Current situation
The company provides bus, tram and trolleybus services within the city. Suburban and intercity services are also operated.

The company also maintains and repairs vehicles and assembles trolleybuses. In 2002, 14 ZIU-9 trolleybuses were assembled.

Municipal Transportation Company 'Rostovpassazhirtrans' sets tariffs and a formula has been established to reimburse concessionary travel.

Developments
In late 2005, two new KTM-19 trams entered service on route 4, with the possibility of 10 more vehicles to be delivered if funds are available.

Bus
Route length: 640.4 km (2002)

Fleet: Not currently available

One-person operation: All routes
Fare collection: Payment to driver on exit, conductors sometimes carried
Fare structure: Flat

Tram
Route length: 79.6 km (2002)

Fleet: 73 vehicles
KTM-5	39
KTM-8	14
KTM-19	2
Tatra T-6	18

Trolleybus
Route length: 200.5 km (2002)

Fleet: Not currently available

Samara
Population: City: 1.2 million, Metropolitan area: 3.3 million (estimate)

Public transport
Tramway/trolleybus, metro, bus and riverboat services provided by public enterprises under overall auspices of the city administration.

Samara Region Administration
Transport Division
Molodogvardeyskaya Street 210, 443006 Samara, Russian Federation
Tel: (+7 8462) 32 22 68   Fax: (+7 8462) 32 13 40
Web: www.adm.samara.ru

Bus
Passenger journeys: 26 million (annual estimate)

Number of routes: 60 (estimate)
Route length: Not currently available

Fleet: Includes LIAZ 677, Ikarus 260/280, Autosan and about 200 Mercedes Türk O345/O345G (financed by the World Bank)

Trolleybus
Passenger journeys: 260 million (annual estimate)

Number of routes: 17
Route length: 92 km (estimate)

Fleet: 260 (estimate)	
ZIU9, some in double-traction	250 (estimate)
ZIU10	5 (estimate)
SZTM Works using ZIU9 parts	5 (estimate)

Tramway
Passenger journeys: 261 million (annual estimate)

Number of routes: 19*
Route length: 76 km*
Gauge: 1,524 mm

*Estimated figures

Rolling stock: 428 cars*	
CKD Tatra TS3U	M340*
CKD Tatra T3SU ex-Moskva	M40*
CKD Tatra T3M	M48*

*Estimated figures

Samara Metro
Kommunisticheskaya ul 8, 443030, Samara, Russian Federation
Tel: (+7 8462) 27 25 31

Type of operation: Full metro, first line opened 1987

Route length: 10 km
Number of lines: 1
Number of stations: 8
Gauge: 1,524 mm
Electrification: 825 V DC, third rail

Passenger journeys: (1999) 24.9 million (estimate)

Fleet: 46 cars

Current situation
Extensions are under construction at both ends of the line. The eastward extension (one station) has been under way for some years, with a latest estimate for completion of 2008–9.

Developments
One further line is planned.

St Petersburg
Population: 5 million (estimated)

Public transport
Bus, and trolleybus/tramway services operated by separate municipal undertakings, private operators also provide bus services; metro; suburban rail and taxi services.

Public transport in St Petersburg is managed by the Committee for Transport of the St Petersburg Administration.

St Petersburg Administration
Committee for Transport
196084, Moskovsky District, Moscow Prospect, 83, Russian Federation
Tel: (+7 812) 316 48 28
Fax: (+7 812) 388 55 31
e-mail: transport@gov.spb.ru
Web: www.gov.spb.ru; petersburgcity.com

Key personnel
Chairman: Datsyuk Alexander Makarovich

Passajiravtotrans (PassengerAutotrans)
Ispolkomovskaya Street 16, 191024 St Petersburg, Russian Federation
Tel: (+7 812) 326 30 00
Fax: (+7 812) 271 76 08
e-mail: info@avtobus.spb.ru
Web: www.avtobus.spb.ru

Bus
Passenger journeys: Approx 470 million (annual)
Vehicle-km: Approx 60 million (annual)

Number of routes: 376
Route length: 1,100 km

Current situation
Most of the money available from the city government for public transport improvements is earmarked for renewal of the bus fleet. During 1997 a further 500 or so new buses were delivered, mainly of old models such as Ikarus 280 and LIAZ 677, but it is hoped that modern designs can be built locally at lower cost. Breda, Iveco, Volvo, Ikarus and Hyundai were bidders

in a competition for establishment of a local production facility.

The company currently has seven bus depots in St Petersburg.

Developments
In 2002, the city administration financed the purchase of 290 buses.

Fleet: Approx 2,000 vehicles, comprising LAZ 699R, LIAZ 677, Ikarus 280 articulated, Ikarus 250 and a few Ikarus 260. The LAZ 699R and Ikarus 250s operate limited-stop express routes

One-person operation: All services
Fare collection: Payment to driver/conductor
Fare structure: Flat, higher on express routes
Fare evasion control: Random inspection
Operating costs financed by: Fares 52 per cent, remainder subsidised by municipality

Gorelectrotrans
Zodchego Rossi Street 1/3, St Petersburg 191011, Russian Federation

Tel: (+7 812) 117 32 20, 05 29
Fax: (+7 812) 315 50 28; 110 46 92

Current situation
Currently, the company operates 11 depots: 5 tram depots, 5 trolleybus depots and 1 combined tram/trolleybus depot.

Trolleybus
Passenger journeys: Approx 330 million (annual) (tram + trolleybus)
Vehicle-km: 65 million (annual)

Number of routes: 46
Route length: 550 km

Developments
In 2002, the city administration financed the purchase of 20 trolleybuses.

Fleet: Approx 700 vehicles
Uritsky ZIU9
Uritsky ZIU10
Fare collection: Conductors
Fare structure: Flat; monthly seasons
Fare-evasion control: Random inspection
Average peak-hour speed: 16 km/h
Operating costs financed by: Fares 40 per cent, remainder subsidised by municipality

Tramway
Type of operation: Conventional tramway

Route length: 630 km
Number of lines: 48
Number of stops: 1,215
Gauge: 1,524 mm

Current situation
With the majority of city transport funding going towards renewal of the bus fleet, the tramway is in a steep decline. There are numerous temporary closures of tracks including reconstruction of the Liteyny bridge and street using expensive Western technology. Movement in the city centre is severely restricted by traffic congestion. Renewal of the fleet has ceased (22 new LVS97 cars in 1996, only five in 1997) and series production of the three-section LVS93 has not started as planned. A new two-section articulated variant of the LVS97 was produced in 1997 but with no real improvement over the LM68M of 1973 vintage.

Developments
Track has been removed from some streets in the city centre, and further restriction of tram routes in the centre is planned, initially on the Kirov bridge. A major new depot is under construction to house 300 trams, and there are plans for new central maintenance works to replace various sites around the city.

In 2002, the city administration financed the purchase of 28 tram coaches.

Rolling stock: About 1,000 cars
LM68M (1975/88)
KTM5 (1982/85)
LVS86 articulated (1987/97)

Fare structure: Flat
Fare collection: Conductors
Operating costs financed by: Fares 40 per cent, remainder subsidised by municipality

Petersburg Metropoliten

Moskovskii Prospect No 28, St Petersburg 190013, Russian Federation
Tel: (+7 812) 251 66 68   Fax: (+7 812) 316 14 41
Web: www.metro.spb.ru

Key personnel
Chief Executive: Vladimir A Garuigin
First Deputy of Chief Executive: Vladamir D Lysenkov
Chief Engineer: Vladimir D Ocheret
   Staff: 12,521

Type of operation: Full metro; first line opened 1955

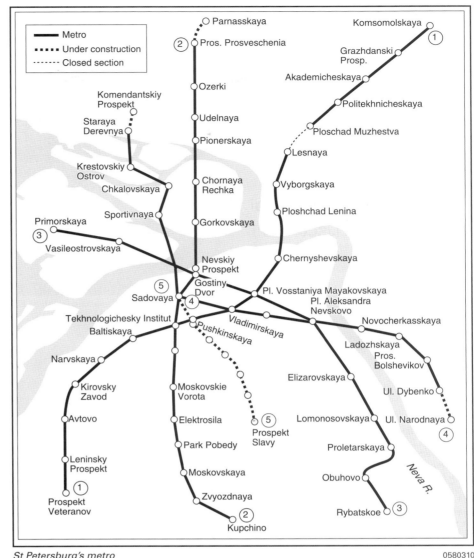

St Petersburg's metro   0580310

Trolleybus on Route 42 in St Petersburg (Heather Bennie)   0126482

Passenger journeys: (2002) 820.9 million

Route length: 96.8 km
Number of lines: 4
Number of stations: 58
Gauge: 1,520 mm
Max gradient: 6 per cent
Minimum curve radius: 300 m
Electrification: 825 V DC, third rail

Service: Peak 1 min 35 s, off-peak 4 min
First/last train: 05.40/01.00
Fare structure: Flat/flexible (tokens/stored-value ticketing based on magnetic or contactless smartcards)

Revenue control: Mechanical and photoelectric cell control
Stations: At many stations 'platforms' replaced by open halls with doors at either side, opened automatically to correspond with the train doors when the train has stopped. Platform doors close again before the train leaves.
Signalling: Automatic train stop; radio-telephone communication with trains; ATO

Rolling stock: 1,377 cars, formed into six-car and seven-car sets
Mytischy D/E/EJ   M1,377

Current situation

Further 14 km under construction, including northwest Line 4 extension with six stations, the initial portion of which from Pl Mira to Chkalovskaya opened in 1997.

In 1999 two new stations on the extension of Line 4 were opened.

Developments

A number of projects have been proposed for the expansion of the metro system, but owing largely to difficult conditions, both financial and geographical, there are no firm details or completion dates for these.

JSC Rossiiskie Zhelezni Dorogi (RZD) – Joint Stock Company 'Russian Railways' (JSCo 'RZD')

2 Novaya Basmannaya Street, Moscow, 107174, Russian Federation
Tel: (+7 95) 262 99 01
e-mail: info@rzd.ru
Web: www.rzd.ru

Key personnel

Chairman: Viktor B Khristenko
President: Gennady M Fadeev
Vice-Presidents: Hasyan S Zyabirov
   Vladimir I Yakunin

Type of operation: Suburban heavy rail

Background

Fully state-owned, open joint-stock corporation created by decree issued by the government of the Russian Federation in September 2003, the board of which was appointed in October 2003. The company incorporates 987 enterprises and 165 subsidiaries, with a total of some 1.2 million employees.

Current situation

Electrified (3 kV DC) commuter services operate on routes extending from the city's five terminals.

For further information on RZD, please see *Jane's World Railways.*

Tram on Route 34 in St Petersburg (Heather Bennie)　　0126481

Local emu at St Petersburg Finlandski station (Norman Griffiths)
0079643

Yekaterinburg

Population: 1.3 million (2006 estimate)

Public transport

Bus and trolleybus/tramway services. Metro. Suburban rail. Route taxis.

Yekaterinburg City Administration

Lenin Street 24a- 313a, 620014, Yekaterinburg City, Russian Federation
Tel: (+7 343) 371 72 99, 371 72 97
Fax: (+7 343) 371 72 97
e-mail: press@adm-ekburg.ru
Web: www.ekburg.ru

Bus

Developments

There are plans to purchase approximately 100 new NEFAZ buses, although the contract has not yet been signed. Buses are scheduled to be delivered at a rate of 10-15 vehicles per month. The vehicles will initially replace older buses, with later deliveries supplying buses on suburban routes which currently have insufficient capacity.

Trolleybus

Passenger journeys: Not currently available
Vehicle-km: Not currently available

Number of routes: 18
Route length: 65 km (estimate)

Fleet: 260 trolleybuses (estimate)
Fleet is believed to comprise:
Uritsky ZIU9　　　　　　　　　　　239
Uritsky ZIU10　　　　　　　　　　　21
In peak service: Not currently available

Tram

Passenger journeys: Not currently available
Car-km: Not currently available

Number of routes: 28
Route length: 180 km (estimate)
Gauge: 1,524 mm
Fleet: 471 cars
Fleet is believed to comprise:
CKD Tatra T3　　　　　　　　　　　M404
CKD Tatra T3M　　　　　　　　　　M21
In peak service: Not currently available

Taxis

Current situation

Privately owned taxis and Route Taxis provide many services in the city. The latter are small minibuses, seating up to 13 passengers, some of which follow the bus routes. Although fares are fixed by the operators, the city administration is currently meeting with representatives of those operators with a view to agreeing a base flat rate.

Metro

Type of operation: Metro, first section opened 1991

Passenger journeys: (2007) 42 million (estimate)
Train-km: Not currently available

Number of lines: 1
Route length: 8.6 km (all in tunnel)
Number of stations: 7
Gauge: 1,524 mm
Electrification: 824 V DC

Current situation

The metro is estimated to carry some 6 per cent of all public transport passengers in the city.

A southward extension is under construction, with three stations. Two of these stations are currently scheduled to open in 2010 at the earliest.

There are long-term plans for a further two lines.

Fleet: 54 cars (in four-car trains)
Fleet breakdown is not currently available
In peak service: Not currently available
Service: 3–10 mins
First/last train: 06.00/24.00
Fare structure: Flat
Fare collection: Token

Serbia

Belgrade

Population: 1.58 million (2002 Census)

Public transport

Bus, trolleybus and tramway services operated by municipal undertaking and bus/minibus services by other private companies; suburban rail. Light rail planned.

City Public Transport Company 'Beograd' (GSP 'Beograd')

Kneginje Ljubice 29, 11000 Belgrade, Serbia
Tel: (+381 11) 262 48 53   Fax: (+381 11) 263 17 60
e-mail: office@gspbeograd.com
Web: www.gsp.co.yu

Key personnel

President, Management Board: Slaven Tica
President, Supervisory Board: Sima Vučković
Acting Managing Director: Radoslav Nikolić
Deputy Managing Director: Slobodan Stević
Technical Managers: Branislav Pirković
  Siniša Lazarević
Transportation Manager: Mirjana Jovanović
Financial and Investment Manager: Marko Perović
General Logistics Manager: Gordana Garić
  Staff: Not currently available

Passenger journeys: (2006) 475.7 million
(2007) 475.8 million

Operating costs financed by: Fares: 50 per cent, other commercial sources: 15 per cent, subsidy/grants: 35 per cent

Current situation

GSP 'Beograd' has six organisation units and operates from six depots – tram, trolleybus and four bus depots. The company has a 75 per cent share of the city's public transport journeys.

The company also provides school transportation and paratransit services.

Bus and trolleybus

Passenger journeys: (2006) 326.0 million
(2007) Bus 324.7 million, trolleybus 55.3 million
Vehicle-km: (2006) Bus 61.7 million, trolleybus 5.5 million
(2007) Bus 63.1 million, trolleybus 5.59 million

Number of routes: Bus 125, trolleybus 8 (2007)
Route length: (One way) Bus 1,720.8 km, trolleybus 58.1 km (2007)
On priority right-of-way: 34.5 km
Trolleybus electrification: 600 V DC

Fleet: 852 buses (2008)

Ikarus standard buses (-101, -102, -103, -103 4V, -106, -111, -111 B, 112.30, -112N)	245
Karosa B 932 E	10
Mercedes-Benz (0405 N, 0345)	65
Sanos 115.2	1
MAN (SU-220, NL-202, SL-283)	23
FAP 537	40
Iveco U-Effueno	1
Ikarus articulated (IK-161, -166, -201, -201 L, -202, -203, -218N)	389
MAN SG 313 articulated	75
Mercedes-Benz 0405 GN articulated	3
In peak service: 692	

Fleet: 135 trolleybuses (2007)

ZIU-682 (B, B1, G)	67
ZIU-682 G1	2
ZIU-682 G-016	15
Gräf & Steyer OE 112 M11	2
Belkommunmas 201 01	10
Vologda VMZ-5298 (375)	1
Belkommunmas 321	10
Trolza 5275-05	1
Trolza 62-05-01 articulated	12
Belkommunmas 333 articulated	12
Gräf & Steyer OE 112 M16 articulated	3
In peak service: 97	

First/last bus/trolleybus: 04.00/24.00
One-person operation: All vehicles
Fare structure: Zonal. Single tickets may be purchased on the vehicles from the driver and in tobacconists. Monthly and fortnightly passes. Privileged monthly passes for certain categories of passengers (pupils, students, retired people, etc). Travel is free for children under the age of seven, citizens of Belgrade older than 70 and some other specific categories of passengers.
Fare collection: On vehicle from driver and pre-purchase in tobacconists
Fares collected on board: 0.98 per cent (2006)
Fare evasion control: 189 ticket inspectors/controllers
Arrangements for elderly/disabled: Bus, minibus and van paratransit services; free travel for those older than 70 and some disabled passengers
Integration with other modes: Full integration with tram service and other operators, including an integrated tariff system
Average distance between stops: Central area 300–350 m, suburban area 550–600 m
Bus priority: Bus lanes on most main roads

Developments

Delivery of 100 new low-floor, air-conditioned trolleybuses was completed in June 2008 (45 Ikarus -112N standard, 55 Ikarus -218N articulated).

Tramway

Staff: 835

Type of operation: Conventional tramway

Passenger journeys: (2006) 94.3 million
(2007) 95.7 million
Car-km: (2006) 9.9 million
(2007) 8.47 million

Route length: 127.3 km (2006)
Number of lines: 12
Gauge: 1,000 mm
Track: 60 kg/m Fenix rail, 'floating' track
Max gradient: 7.8%
Minimum curve radius: 20 m
Electrification: 600 V DC, overhead

Rolling stock: 203 articulated trams, 3 standard trams, 25 trailers (2007)

CKD Tatra KT-4 YUB	M158
CKD Tatra KT-4 M YUB	M20
CKD Tatra T-4	M1
Duewag BE 4/4	M1
Duewag BE 4/6	M25
Djuro Djakovic	M1
Duewag trailers	T25
In peak service: 150	
On order: None	

Service: Peak 6–7 min, off-peak 10 min
First/last car: 04.00/24.00
Fare structure: As bus
Integration with other modes: As bus
One-person operation: All vehicles

SP Lasta

Niški put 4, 11050 Belgrade, Srbija i Crna Gora, Serbia
Tel: (+381 11) 288 27 60, 27 40, 27 41
Fax: (+381 11) 289 23 92, 56 45
e-mail: splasta@verat.net
Web: www.lasta.co.yu

Key personnel

General Manager: Velibor Sovrovic
Deputy General Manager: Marinko Ljumovic
Assistant to General Manager, Suburban Transport: Snezana Provic

Type of operation: Suburban and local bus

Passenger journeys: Not currently available
Vehicle-km: Not currently available

Current situation

SP Lasta provides suburban and local bus services for the city of Belgrade and to the outlying suburban municipalities, where local services then provide further services.

SP Lasta's services are fully integrated with other public transport modes, including a tariff system.

Belgrade Land Development Public Agency

Project Implementation Unit (PIU)
84 Njegoševa Street, 11000 Belgrade, Serbia
Tel: (+381 11) 204 13 40-2
Fax: (+381 11) 204 13 45
e-mail: piu@beoland.com
Web: www.beoland.com

Key personnel

General Manager: Boris Ranković
Assistants and Advisors to the Director:
  Milan Mirosavljević
  Maja Vasić
  Brankica Popović
Projects Executive Director: Zoran Rubinjoni
LRT Project Director: Vladimir Depolo

Type of operation: Light rail (planned)

Current situation

Plans for a light rail system in the city have been under consideration for several decades. Current long-term plans foresee a three-line network.

Developments

Line 1 would be 12.5 km long, with 22/25 station (10/14 in tunnel) and will be integrated with the existing tram system and the Beovoz suburban rail network. The assessment of the investment required is between EUR349.6 million and EUR452.1 million, depending upon the tunnel length.

The pre-feasibility study was undertaken in 2003/04 by INECO, Madrid and sub-consultants JUGINUS, Belgrade. The consultancy service for project management was concluded with INECO and sub-consultants JUGINUS, CEP, Belgrade and Duo-Dec, Belgrade at the end of 2006. An Annex to the study was completed in June 2008 by the same consultants.

The tender for the preliminary design of Line 1 began in April 2007. Ten companies/consortia were listed and their tenders were delivered on 1 April 2008. The expected date of the completion of the preliminary design is June 2009.

SNC Lavalin is carrying out a parallel study for PPP financing. Completion date for this activity was November 2008.

The start of construction, previously planned for Q3 2009, is now scheduled for 2010/11.

Železničko Transportno Preduzeće 'Beograd' (ZTP Beograd) – Railway Transport Enterprise 'Beograd' (Beovoz)

Nemanjina 6, YU-11000 Belgrade, Serbia
Tel: (+381 11) 361 67 22; 48 11
Fax: (+381 11) 361 68 02
e-mail: medijacentar@yurail.co.yu
Web: www.serbianrailways.com

Key personnel

Director General: Milanko Sarancic
  Tel: (+381 11) 361 84 59
  Fax: (+381 11) 361 84 71
Deputy Director, Passenger Service Department: Vukasović Vesna
Head of Communications Department: Rade Vojvodić

Type of operation: Suburban heavy rail

Passenger journeys: (2006) 6.2 million
(2007) 7.1 million (projected)

Current situation
City railway, know as Beovoz, services run on six suburban routes with 41 stations (two underground), electrified 25 kV, utilising 13 km of tunnel in the city centre.

A new central railway station, to be named Beograd Center, has been under construction since 1977.

Developments
There are plans for a new light rail system to be built in the city, starting in 2008. When completed, this will link to the Beovoz at Vukov Spomenik station.

Singapore

Singapore
Population: 4.35 million (2006, whole island)

Public transport
Bus services provided by privately owned companies working in consultation with the Land Transport Authority which issues licences. All low-occupancy private vehicles entering the central business district during the day are required to display a special licence disc for which an additional fee is charged. Public buses are exempt. Included in the scheme is the provision of cheap car parks at the periphery of the licensed area to encourage motorists to use buses or trains. Metro; local ferries; cable car; light rapid transit feeder line opened 1999, others under construction.

Land Transport Authority (LTA)
1 Hampshire Road, Singapore 219428, Singapore
Tel: 1800 225 55 82 (1800-CALL LTA)
Fax: (+65) 63 96 15 95
Web: www.lta.gov.sg

Key personnel
Chairman: Michael Lim Choo San
Chief Executive: BG (NS) Yam Ah Mee

Current situation
The Land Transport Authority (LTA) is a statutory board under the Ministry of Transport. It leads land transport developments in Singapore.

Managing the limited land space in Singapore is an ongoing challenge for LTA, as the demand for mobility increases over the years. Hence, providing an attractive public transport system is the cornerstone of LTA's land transport strategy. This includes the provision of a comprehensive road and rail network, with emphasis on the rapid transit system as the backbone of the public transport system.

Developments
In January 2008, a speech given by Raymond Lim, the Minister for Transport and Second Minister for Foreign Affairs, outlined five major initiatives to enhance the 'hub and spoke' public transport system. These initiatives are:
- LTA to undertake Centralised Bus Planning
- Distance-based through-fares to facilitate transfers, which will eliminate the existing transfer fare penalty
- Further bus priority measures to increase bus speeds
- More integrated public transport hubs
- Enhanced integrated, real-time public transport service information, including the development of an integrated multi-modal travel information system.

There are also plans to gradually open up the basic bus sector to more competition and to expand the range of niche bus services.

The LTA will also launch a Community Outreach Programme.

North East Mass Rapid Transit (MRT) System
The North East Line (NEL) (20 km, 16 stations) from HarbourFront to Punggol opened in June 2003. In 2005, ridership had risen approximately 20 per cent since operations commenced.

The line is operated by SBS Transit Ltd (see separate entry).

Map of Singapore's metro and light rail system   1124802

Sengkang and Punggol Light Rapid Transit (LRT) Systems
To complement the MRT system and provide local feeder services from residential developments to metro stations, three automated light rapid transit networks have been approved. The first, the Bukit Panjang LRT, linking Bukit Panjang New Town with Choa Chu Kang metro station (approximately 8 km, 13 stations, 19 cars), opened in 1999.

The second system, the Sengkang LRT (East Loop), opened for service in 2003 whilst the SKLRT (West Loop) opened in January 2005. The SKLRT serves as a feeder for the North East Line for residents in this new town in the northeastern sector of Singapore. The system is approximately 11 km in length and has 14 stations.

The Punggol LRT (West Loop) opened in 2003 and the Punggol LRT (East Loop) opened in January 2005, after four years of construction. This line also serves as a feeder to the North East Line. The PGLRT system has 15 stations (including Punggol station), with five on the East Loop and four on the West Loop open for service. The remaining two stations on the East Loop and three stations along the West Loop will open at a later stage, when the areas surrounding them are more developed.

The BPLRT is operated by Singapore MRT Ltd, and the SKLRT and PGLRT are operated by SBS Transit Ltd (see separate entry).

Circle Line (CCL)
The Circle Line (CCL), costing some SGD6.7 billion, will be a fully underground orbital line linking all radial lines to the city. The line will interchange with the North-South Line, the East-West Line and the North-East Line. The CCL will be 33.3 km in length, with 29 stations. The entire Circle Line is targeted to be completed in 2010. The exact opening date for the stations will be announced later, when the operator is ready to start operations.

The project will be implemented in five stages and is scheduled to be fully completed in 2010, linking all of the existing MRT lines to the city:

Stage 1: The first stage of the CCL will run along the Bras Basah, Marina Centre and Stadium Boulevard. Work has started on the 5.4 km line.

Stage 2: Construction of Stage 2, from Stadium Boulevard to Upper Paya Lebar Road/Bartley Road, started in Q3 2002. It will be approximately 5.6 km in length, with six stations. Upon completion, it will connect to the East-West Line at Paya Lebar Station.

Stage 3: Construction started in Q3 2003 and is targeted for completion in mid-2009. The approximately 5.7 km long line includes five stations and extends from Upper Paya Lebar Road/Bartley Road and links to Serangoon station on the NEL. There will be a connection to the North-South Line at Bishan station.

Stages 4 and 5: These two stages, with a combined length of approximately 17 km and 13 stations, will terminate at HarbourFront Centre.

Boon Lay Extension
The Boon Lay Extension project started in the July 2005. It will be an approximately 3.8 km extension, with two stations, to the current East-West MRT line and will serve residents and commuters in the western part of Singapore, in particular to Jurong West Town and the Jurong and Tuas Industrial Estates.

The project is scheduled to be completed in 2009.

Kallang and Paya Lebar Expressway (KPE)
The 12 km Kallang and Paya Lebar Expressway (KPE), 9 km of which is underground, opened to traffic in September 2008. It links the East Coast Parkway (ECP) to the Tampines Expressway (TPE) and is expected to ease the traffic load on the Central Expressway (CTE).

Downtown Extension (DTL)
The Downtown Line (DTL) will be built in three stages, with Stage 1 due to be completed in 2013, Stage 2 to be completed in 2015 and Stage 3 in 2016. When fully completed, the DTL will enhance the connectivity of the Rapid Transit System

network and facilitates direct travel from the northwestern and eastern areas of the island to the Central Business District and the Marina Bay. The DTL is projected to see a daily ridership of more than half a million when in full operation.

Construction started in February 2008. The line will be 4.3 km long, all underground, with six stations.

Future lines

The Singapore Government has announced plans to build two new lines, the Thomson Line (TL) and the Eastern Region Line (ERL). Together, these two new lines will add 48 km to the rail network. The government has given the go-ahead for the TSL to be built by 2018 and the ERL by 2020.

There are also plans for extensions to the East-West and North-South lines by around 2015. The 14 km Tuas extension will bring the East-West line right into the heart of Tuas. The North-South line, that currently ends at the Marina Bay station, will be extended 1 km southwards to serve the developments in the southern Marina Bay area, such as the new cruise terminal in Marina South. These four additions, together with the lines now being built, will extend the rail network from the current 138 km of track to 278 km in 2020.

Eastern Region Line (ERL)

The Eastern Region Line (ERL) will serve the residential estates of Tanjong Rhu, Marine Parade, Siglap, Bedok South and Upper East Coast and link them to Changi in the east.

Thomson Line (TL)

A new MRT line, the Thomson Line (TL), will run from Marina Bay northwards, through the Central Business District and up through Ang Mo Kio to Woodlands, connecting estates such as Sin Ming, Kebun Baru, Thomson and Kim Seng, which currently do not have a direct MRT link.

SMRT Corporation Ltd (SMRT)

251 North Bridge Road, 179102 Singapore, Singapore
Tel: (+65) 63 31 10 00 (Headquarters)
Freephone: (1 800) 336 89 00
Fax: (+65) 63 34 04 27
Web: www.smrt.com.sg

Key personnel

Chairman: Choo Chiau Beng
President and Chief Executive Officer: Ms Saw Phaik Hwa
Executive Vice-President, Corporate Services: Yeo Meng Hin
Executive Vice-President, Finance: Patrick Lau
Senior Vice-President, Finance: Catherine Kuan
Vice-President, Rail Operations: Vincent Tan
Vice-President, Engineering: Harry Tan
Vice-President, SMRT Buses and SMRT Automotive Services: Lee Seng Kee
Vice-President, SMRT Taxis: Lo Chee Wen
Vice-President, Commercial: Teo Chew Hoon
Vice-President, Circle Line: Khoo Hean Siang
Vice-President, Corporate Marketing and Communications: Goh Chee Kong
Staff: 5,445 (as at 31 December 2005)

Current situation

SMRT, a holding company with transportation as its core business, was listed on the Singapore Exchange in July 2000.

Today, SMRT is Singapore's main multi-modal public transport provider, and offers train, bus and taxi services. In addition, it provides maintenance consultancy and project management expertise in railway systems in Singapore and overseas.

Developments

SMRT is an integrated transport service provider, offering a complete range of public transport services to facilitate seamless travel.

The company regularly introduces customer-focused promotions to reward passengers for travelling with SMRT's fleet of buses, trains and taxis. This includes turning stations into

SMRT LRT vehicle   0595075

SMRT Mercedes-Benz O405 low-floor bus   1109862

commuters' destination points by transforming stations into retail and lifestyle hubs, integrating travelling with shopping.

SMRT Trains Ltd (SMRT Trains)

Passenger journeys: (FY2004) 391 million (FY2005) 403 million

Route length: 89.4 km
  in tunnel: 23.3 km
Number of lines: 2
Number of stations: 51
  underground: 16 (all with platform screen doors)
  elevated: 34
  at grade: 1
Gauge: 1,435 mm
Track: About 75 per cent timber sleepers in ballast; concrete slab in tunnels; floating slab with rubber bearing pads near sensitive buildings
Electrification: 750 V DC, bottom-contact third rail

Current situation

Incorporated in 1987, SMRT Trains Ltd operates the first Mass Rapid Transit (MRT) system in Singapore, serving major high-density travel corridors. The 89.4 km SMRT system, which consists of the North-South and East-West lines stretching over 51 stations, serves more than a million commuters daily.

Developments

Future plans for the MRT system include the Circle Line (CCL), a fully underground orbital line linking all radial lines leading to the city. The CCL, which will be 33.3 km long with 29 stations planned for passenger service, will intersect with the North-South Line, East-West Line and North East Line.

SMRT embarked on a mid-life refurbishment programme to upgrade and renew its first generation trains in 2005. These trains have been in

operation since 1987 and the mid-life refurbishment programme comprises enhancements to both the interior saloon and the exterior body of the trains. The interior overhaul incorporates more comfortable, accessible and aesthetic customer-friendly features for safer and more comfortable travel. In addition, all the first generation trains will be equipped with an intelligent monitoring circuit system.

Rolling stock: 106 trains – 636 cars in six-car sets

Service: Peak 2–6 min, off-peak 7 min
First/last train: 05.11/00.56
Fare structure: Graduated
Revenue control: Booking office and self-service ticket machines, automatic entry/exit barriers, all controlled by central computer; system uses contactless smartcard
Signalling: Full ATO, ATP and line supervision
Average speed: 45 km/h

SMRT Light Rail Pte Ltd (SMRT Light Rail)

Passenger journeys: (FY2004) 14 million (FY2005) 14 million

Route length: 7.8 km
Number of lines: 3 loop services
Number of stations: 14
Gauge: 1,435 mm
Track: Concrete surface guideway; rubber-tyre operation
Electrification: 600 V AC 3-Phase system

Current situation

SMRT Light Rail Pte Ltd was set up in 1997 and operates Singapore's first fully automated Light Rapid Transit (LRT) system – the Bukit Panjang LRT system . The LRT system includes approximately 7.8 km of elevated guideways stretching over 14 stations.

Rolling stock: 19 trains

Service: Peak 2½–5 min, off-peak average 6 min
First/last train: 05.00/00.45
Fare structure: Graduated
Average speed: 25 km/h

SMRT Buses Ltd (SMRT Buses)
Passenger journeys: (2004) 265 million
(2005) 269 million
Vehicle-km: (2004) 79 million
(2005) 78 million

Number of routes: 74
Route length: 2,523.7 km (two-way)
Number of stops: 2,275
Number of bus interchanges: 6

Current situation
SMRT Buses Ltd operates a fleet of more than 800 buses from six interchanges. Its trunk, feeder and night bus services attract a daily ridership of some 746,000 passengers.

Developments
The Integrated Bus Operating System (IBOS) was introduced to all services in 2005 and 2006. With IBOS, bus operations on the road can be monitored in real time via the Global Positioning System (GPS), at a centralised Bus Operations Control Centre. Passengers can also enjoy enhanced service, as the system can better monitor bus arrivals and departments, and could facilitate timely activation of operating contingencies.

Fleet: 838 buses

DAF-WA SB220 low-floor	46
Hino HS3KRK	12
Mercedes-Benz O405 low-floor	323
Mercedes-Benz O405G articulated	313
Nissan U31RCN	25
Scania WA L113 low-floor	49
Scania ELBO L113 no-step stepless-aisle	15
Dennis Lance	55

In peak service: 788

One-person operation: All routes
Operation hours: 05.30–00.50 (day services), 23.30–04.30 (night services)
Most intensive service: 4 min
Fare structure: Graduated (0.8 km stages); premium for express services; concessionary passes available to schoolchildren, students and full-time national servicemen
Fare collection: Cash payment to farebox and stored-value ez-link cards (contactless smartcard) for non-cash payments (buses and MRT), validation and fare amount calculated on board
Arrangements for elderly/disabled: Concessionary travel for senior citizens during off-peak hours
Fares collected on board: 100 per cent
Integration with other modes: MRT and light rail
Average peak-hour speed: 18 km/h
Bus priority: Bus lanes, B-signal, exclusive right turn, contraflow lanes
New vehicles financed by: Commercial loans and internal funds

Bus-Plus Services Pte Ltd (Bus-Plus)
Passenger journeys: (FY2004) 3.6 million
(FY2005) 3 million

SMRT taxi 1109866

SMRT LRT vehicle 1179107

SMRT train 1177863

Vehicle-km: (FY2004) 3 million
(FY2005) 2.5 million

Number of routes: Three peak-hour scheduled services, two chartered express services and one off-peak service
Route length: 82 km
Number of stops: 43

Current situation
Bus-Plus was incorporated in 1994 and operates a luxury bus service, designed to bridge the gap between public bus services, the MRT system, the LRT system, taxis and private cars. Bus-Plus currently operates out of two depots with a fleet of air conditioned buses fitted with comfortable, Vogel aircraft-type seats, and is primarily focused on the charter business.

Fleet: 46 Toyota Coaster and Mitsubishi Rosa minibuses (7 scheduled and chartered express and 46 chartered)
Vehicles required for peak level of service: 46
Average age of fleet: 9 years

Most intensive service: 5 mins
One-person operation: All routes
Fare structure: Flat fares; cash payment to farebox and use of stored-value card on the validator which can also be used on the MRT; passengers can also purchase monthly reservation tickets
Fare collection on board: 100 per cent
Integration with other modes: Ticketing with MRT

Average peak-hour speed: 35 km/h
New vehicles financed by: Commercial loans

SMRT Taxis Pte Ltd (SMRT Taxis)
Fleet: 2,692

Toyota	1,035
Nissan	1,355
Mercedes-Benz	256
London taxis	46

Current situation
SMRT Taxis Pte Ltd is one of the major taxi operators in Singapore, with a fleet of over 2,000 taxis, including Mercedes-Benz and London taxis.

Developments
SMRT places importance in taking care of its taxi hirers. In June 2005, SMRT Taxis launched the 'SMRT Taxis Hirers' Care (Hi-Care) Programme' and three innovative, driver-friendly schemes – the Flexi-Benefits Scheme, Compassionate Leave and Courtesy Taxi Scheme to enhance welfare, boost income and lower operating costs for its hirers. The Hi-Care Programme was enhanced with monthly diesel and rental rebates, as well as daily loyalty discounts in March 2006.

To promote excellence in customer service, SMRT introduced the 'SMRT Taxis Service Promise and Money-Back Guarantee' and 'Tip-the-Drivers Initiative' in December 2005. Drivers are encouraged to deliver the 'service promise' and customers are urged to show appreciation of good service through tipping. To reward customers travelling with SMRT taxis, a three-month long 'Lowest Book Fee' promotion, featuring discounted booking fees and partial waiver of midnight surcharge, was launched.

Supporting the move towards more environmentally friendly vehicles, SMRT Taxis introduced 200 CDI Mercedes-Benz taxis that conform to the new Euro-4 standards. From 1 December 2005, only ultra-low Sulphur diesel was made available for sale to drivers at all SMRT diesel pumps.

SMRT Engineering Pte Ltd (SMRTE)
Current situation
SMRTE was set up in August 1999. Using its expertise in land transport, it offers operations and maintenance services, engineering consultancy and project management services, as well as providing communication infrastructure through the leasing of fibre-optic cables and related services.

Developments
A significant milestone during 2005 was SMRTE's participation as a founding member of the Singapore Land Transport Consortium. Facilitated and supported by International Enterprise (IE) Singapore, the Consortium was formed in October 2005 to utilise collective capabilities in regional business opportunities related to land transport systems.

SBS Transit Ltd

205 Braddell Road, Singapore 579701, Singapore
Tel: (+65) 62 84 88 66
Freephone: 1 800 287 27 27 (Customer Services Hotline)
Fax: (+65) 62 87 03 11
e-mail: crc@sbstransit.com.sg
Web: www.sbstransit.com.sg

Key personnel
Chairman: Lim Jit Poh
Deputy Chairman: Kua Hong Pak
Chief Operating Officer: Gan Juay Kiat
Executive Vice-President, Operations: Woon Chio Chong
Executive Vice-President, Engineering and Quality Assurance: Lim Gim Hong
Senior Vice-President (Rail): Wong Wai Keong
Director, Corporate Communications: Ms Tammy Tan
Staff: 7,312 (as at 31 December 2006)

Background
SBS Transit Ltd was formed in 1973, through the merger of three private bus companies. In 1978 Singapore Bus Service (1978) Limited was listed on the Stock Exchange of Singapore, and the company changed its name to SBS Transit Ltd in November 2001.

The company is a member of ComfortDelGro Corporation Limited.

Current situation
Currently, the company is the largest bus operator and one of the two train operators in Singapore.

The company has been awarded a number of ISO 9001 and 9002 certificates.

SBS Transit Ltd also operates the North East Line (NEL) MRT system, the Sengkang LRT system and the Punggol LRT system. In 2006, daily rail ridership was more than 260,000.

The automated NEL system is 20 km long and has a total of 16 underground stations. It runs from Punggol to HarbourFront and has interchange stations to the North-South and East-West lines at Dhoby Ghaut station and Outram Park station respectively.

The Sengkang LRT is 11 km long with a total of 13 stations on two loops – the East and West loops – with a total of 14 stations. The system connects residents of the Sengkang estate to the Sengkang MRT station.

The Punggol LRT system connects residents of the Punggol estate to the Punggol MRT station. It stretches 9.6 km over two loops – the East and

SBS Transit Ltd ALSTOM Metropolis train operating on the North East Line (NEL) 1146930

SBS Transit Dennis Trident bus 1146929

West loops – comprising 15 stations including the Punggol Town Centre.

Developments
In addition to 150 new units purchased in 2005, SBS Transit has purchased 50 air-conditioned, low-floor, double-deck buses. Total investment was SGD100 million. The company has also introduced five Wheelchair-Accessible Bus (WAB) routes for those passengers who have physical disabilities. The WAB services, Singapore's first, have been well-received by passengers and some 1,000 trips have been made on the services since they were launched in June 2006.

To manage the fleet efficiently, SBS Transit has invested in a SGD40 million Automatic Vehicle Management System (AVMS). The system uses satellite technology to locate buses and allows easier communication between the vehicles and the Operations Control Centre (OCC).

Following the introduction of the AVMS, the company now provides real-time bus arrival information.

Bus
Passenger journeys: (2002) 833 million
(2003) 764.2 million
(2004) 756.7 million
(2006) 763.2 million
Vehicle-km: (2002) 213.1 million (scheduled daily revenue-km)
(2003) 206.8 million (scheduled daily revenue-km)
(2004) 199.2 million (scheduled daily revenue-km)
(2006) 205.0 million (scheduled daily revenue-km)

Number of routes: 223 (2006)
Route length: 6,552 km
On priority right-of-way: 112 km bus lanes

Fleet: 2,794 vehicles, of which 92 per cent are air conditioned

Volvo B10M-61 Mk II (1988/89)	195
Volvo B10M-61 Mk III (1992/93)	300
Volvo B10M-60 Intercooled (1995–2000)	474
Volvo B10M-70 14.5 m (1995)	1
Volvo B10BLE (1998)	1
Volvo B10BLE CNG (2002)	12
Volvo Olympian 2-axle double-deck (1994/95)	98
Volvo Olympian 3-axle double-deck (1994–2000)	471
Volvo B10TL 3-axle double-deck (1999)	52
Leyland Olympian 3-axle double-deck (1993/94)	199
Leyland Lynx (1989)	1
Mercedes O405 (1990/92)	697
Scania N113CRB (1989/90)	195
Scania L94UB4X2 (1999)	1
Dennis Dart (1994)	10
Dennis Trident 3-axle double-deck (2001)	20
MAN 16.240HOCL (1990)	1
Volvo B9TL DD air-conditioned	200

In peak service: 2,529
Average age of fleet: 12 years
On order: None

Most intensive service: 2 min
One-person operation: All services
Fare structure: Governed by Public Transport Council; flat and graduated fares; concessionary

fares available to schoolchildren, servicemen, students and shareholders

Fare collection: Flat and graduated fare services: fareboxes and contactless smartcard ticketing upon entering and leaving vehicle; rebates for transfers between bus services and between bus services and trains

Fares collected on board: 93.2 per cent

Fare evasion control: Roving inspectors

Arrangements for elderly/disabled: Concession fare for over-60s; designated seats

Average distance between stops: 400 m

Average peak-hour speed: In mixed traffic, 20 km/h

Bus priority: Bus lanes operational 07.30–09.30 and 17.00–20.00 weekdays and Saturdays

Integration with other modes: Fare system (including concessions) standardised between SBS and Tibs; transfer ticketing system with metro (see above)

Operating costs financed by: Fares 100 per cent

New vehicles financed by: Commercial loans and internal funds

PSA Corporation Ltd (PSA)

Singapore Terminals
460 Alexandria Road, PSA Building, SE 119963, Singapore
Tel: (+65) 62 79 55 04   Fax: (+65) 62 79 54 63
e-mail: mikef@psa.com.sg
Web: www.internationalpsa.com
   www.singaporepsa.com

Key personnel

Senior Commercial Manager: Mike Formoso

Senior Manager, Multi-Purpose Terminal: Phua Chan Seng

Type of operation: Ferry

Current situation

A number of operators provide cross-harbour services to the Indonesian islands. In addition, local ferry operators, including the PSA, run ferries to several offshore islands for both industrial and leisure purposes. Some PSA ferries are also used for cross-harbour cruises. PSA ferry terminals handled some 4 million regional and domestic passengers in 1993. A PSA subsidiary also runs a cable car.

Slovakia

Bratislava

Population: City 426,000 (2006 estimate), urban area 500,000, metropolitan area 600,000 (estimates)

Public transport

Bus, trolleybus and tramway services provided by municipal department.

Dopravný podnik Bratislava as (DPB)

Olejkárska 1, SK-81452 Bratislava, Slovakia
Tel: (+421 2) 59 50 14 11
Fax: (+421 2) 59 50 14 00
e-mail: sekretariat.gr@dpb.sk; inf@dpb.sk
Web: www.dpb.sk

Key personnel

General Manager: Róbert Kadnár
Financial Director: Martin Přibáň

Passenger journeys: (All modes)
(2003) 254 million
(2004) 245 million
(2005) 250 million
(2006) 253 million
(2007) 257 million

Current situation

DPB was reorganised in 1992 and again in 1994. It provides public transport throughout the city.

Developments

Proposals for conversion of tramways to standard gauge are reported to have been shelved, despite 70 per cent of existing alignment having been rebuilt to facilitate the change. Nevertheless, plans for development of the network on the lines of Germany's Stadtbahn are still under consideration.

Fare structure: 24 h, 48 h, 7 day, 1, 3, 6 and 12 month tickets for 2 zones, (three timed tickets of 10, 30 and 60 mins) with free transfer

Fare collection: Prepurchase, cancelling machines

Fare evasion control: Roving inspectors

One-person operation: All routes

Bus

Passenger journeys: (2003) 146.4 million
(2004) 141.0 million
(2005) 142.5 million
(2006) 143.2 million
(2007) 145.0 million
Vehicle-km: (2003) 25.9 million
(2004) 26.3 million
(2005) 26.0 million
(2006) 25.8 million
(2007) 25.5 million

Number of routes: 91 (2007)
Route length: 1,787.3 km

Solaris Urbano 18 CNG bus (Michal Dekánek)   1344003

TAM 272 A 116 M and Skoda 14Tr in the Kramáre quarter (Michal Dekánek)   1344009

Fleet: 504 buses (2007)
Karosa B731/B732:

Diesel	52
CNG	64

Karosa B741/C744 articulated:

Diesel	30
CNG	75
TAM 232	11
TAM 260/TAM 272 articulated	31
Ikarus 415, Ikarus 415	47
Ikarus 280, Ikarus 283	23
Ikarus 435 articulated	96
SOR B 9.5	33
SOR BN 9.5 low-floor	18
Solaris Urbino 15 CNG	22
Mercedes-Benz Sprinter 416	2

In peak service: 354

Tramway

Type of operation: Conventional tramway

Passenger journeys: (2003) 79.3 million
(2004) 78.3 million
(2005) 80.0 million
(2006) 81.1 million
(2007) 82.0 million
Car-km: (2003) 11.1 million
(2004) 11.4 million
(2005) 11.4 million
(2006) 11.2 million
(2007) 11.3 million

Number of routes: 13 (2007)
Route length: 268.1 km
Gauge: 1,000 mm
Electrification: 600 V DC, overhead

Service interval: 12 min

Rolling stock: 229 cars

ČKD Tatra T3	136
ČKD Tatra T6A5	58
ČKD Tatra K2 articulated	35

In peak service: 178

Trolleybus

Passenger journeys: (2003) 28.0 million
(2004) 26.1 million
(2005) 27.5 million
(2006) 28.6 million
(2007) 30.0 million
Vehicle-km: (2003) 5.3 million
(2004) 5.2 million
(2005) 5.4 million
(2006) 5.4 million
(2007) 5.6 million

Number of routes: 17 (2007)
Route length: 232.1 km
Electrification: 600 V DC

Fleet: 128 trolleybuses

Skoda 14Tr	84
Skoda 15Tr articulated	37
Skoda 21Tr low-floor (2004)	1
Skoda 25Tr articulated low-floor (2006)	6

In peak service: 90

Developments
In 2001, Route 203 reverted to serve Koliba to Búdkova and Route 207 reverted to link Ružova dolina and Valašská.

METRO Bratislava as
Muchovo námestie č.1 851 01, Bratislava, Slovakia
Tel: (+421 2) 67 20 11 11 – 13
Fax: (+421 2) 62 41 21 41
e-mail: info@metroba.sk
Web: www.metroba.sk

Key personnel
Chairman and General Director: Ladislav Csáder
Vice-Chairperson and Deputy General Director: Marta Čarnogurská

Background
In November 1997, METRO Bratislava as, a joint stock company, was set up to prepare

Rebuilt ČKD Tatra K2 – Type K2S (Michal Dekánek)   1344002

ČKD Tatra T6A5 in Krasňany (Michal Dekánek)   1344006

Skoda 14TrM in the Kramáre quarter (Michal Dekánek)   1344010

*Skoda 21Tr next to Bratislava Castle
(Michal Dekánek)
1344011*

the 'Backbone of Public Transport Network in Bratislava'. The company was initially wholly owned by the Bratislava Municipality, but in 2001 the Ministry of Transport, Port and Telecommunications became a shareholder, with a 34 per cent holding.

Current situation
The first project which the company is undertaking is the construction of the Košická bridge. The bridge crosses the Danube, linking a relatively undeveloped area on the left bank with the Petržalka side. It is seen as being significant in the future improvements in transport for the city. Construction commenced in 2003.

Earlier plans for a VAL-type metro (please see previous editions of *Jane's Urban Transport Systems*) have been discontinued, mainly due to lack of financing. Current plans envisage an express tram crossing the Danube on the older Starý bridge.

South Africa

Cape Town
Population: 2.89 million (2001 Census)

Public transport
Scheduled bus services throughout metropolitan area provided by privately owned group; commuter/suburban rail service are currently being restructured. Substantial numbers of 'Kombi-taxi' minibus services, many of which are illegal.

Department of Transport and Public Works
Public Transport
Private Bag X9185, Cape Town, South Africa
Tel: (+27 21) 483 28 31 (Public Transport),
(+27 21) 483 21 32 (Department of Transport and Public Works)
Fax: (+27 21) 483 25 93 (Public Transport),
(+27 21) 483 50 68 (Department of Transport and Public Works)
e-mail: nmuller@pgwc.gov.za (Public Transport),
cwprins@pgwc.gov.za (Department of Transport and Public Works)
Web: www.capegateway.gov.za

Street address
9 Dorp Street, Cape Town 8000, South Africa

Key personnel
Executive Manager, Public Transport: Neil Muller
Contact, Department of Transport and Public Works: Chris Prins

Bus Rapid Transit (BRT) (proposed)
The provincial government has developed a mobility strategy to revitalise the public transport system and address some of the problems created by the existing infrastructure. The first phase of this extensive project will be the introduction of a Rapid Bus Transit (RBT) system along the Klipfontein corridor. This will entail a dedicated bus route from Khayalitsha to Mowbray, along with improved cycling and pedestrian paths. It is expected that the development of Klipfontein Road into a transport corridor will result in many advantages for businesses, communities and public transport operators.

The project is a joint initiative between the Department of Transport and Public Works and the City of Cape Town.

Taxis/shared taxis
Background
Estimates put the total number of Kombi-taxi operators at about 6,000 with some 7,500 vehicles. They run variable routes and schedules outside the normal bus licensing system. Their growth has had a major effect on the patronage of licensed bus operators. The Kombis were legalised under a government transport policy review in 1987, though some still operate illegally.

In 1997, the provincial government implemented a new regulatory regime for the Kombis, designed to control their numbers. Taxis can only obtain route permits if they belong to a registered association. At the cut-off date, some 92 associations and 2,450 operators with 3,800 vehicles had registered.

Current situation
The Provincial Government Department of Transport and Public Works is responsible for regulating the mini-bus taxi industry in the province. The regulating body is the provincial taxi office, which can be contacted on:
Tel: (+27 21) 592 4721   Fax: (+27 21) 591 6290

Development
The taxi recapitalisation programme was approved in September 1999 to reduce the number of old vehicles on the road and introduce an electronic management system to shift the taxi industry from a cash-based to a non-cash-based system. Government has undertaken to pay a 'scrapping allowance' to operators for replacing aging and unsafe minibus taxis with new 18- and 35-seater vehicles. The payment would be calculated as a percentage of the total cost of the new taxi.

In 2001, The National Minister of Transport, Provincial MECs for Transport and representatives of the minibus taxi industry organised in the South African Taxi Council (Sataco) stated in their Memorandum of Understanding on the future of the minibus taxi industry that the recapitalisation programme was an important economic issue requiring attention and resolution. The first taxi permits, which will allow taxi operators to qualify for the government's recapitalisation programme, were issued in May 2003.

The second key aspect of the recapitalisation scheme is the Electronic Management System (EMS). This is a smartcard system that will track the number of passengers using the new taxis, the route the taxi is following, and the fees paid.

Commuter rail
Developments
The state-owned transport organisation Metrorail, formerly a business unit of Transnet, was transferred to the Department of Transport in May 2006. The company operates commuter rail services under contract to the South African Rail Commuter Corporation (SARCC). The transfer of Metrorail to direct government control was seen as a first step in a restructuring process that would also see SARCC and the Shosoloza Meyl long-distance passenger rail business combined under the auspices of the Department of Transport.

Golden Arrow Bus Services (Pty) Ltd
PO Box 1795, Cape Town 8000, South Africa
Tel: (+27 21) 507 88 00   Fax: (+27 21) 534 88 18
e-mail: information@gabs.co.za
Web: www.gabs.co.za

Key personnel
Chair: V E Mphande
Vice-Chairman: M J A Golding
Chief Executive Officer: N S Cronjé
  Staff: 2,599

Background
The history of the company started in 1861, when the original Cape Town and Green Point Tramway Company was established. Thereafter, a succession of companies formed links in an unbroken chain of mergers and acquisitions that has lasted for more than 145 years.

Golden Arrow, in its current form, was established in 1992 when all the bus operations in the Western Cape controlled by the Tollgate Holdings subsidiary, Tramway Holdings, were taken over by a consortium of investors led by the Tramway Holdings management.

Current situation
The company serves an area of approximately 2,487 km² embracing the entire Cape Town municipality. Services are provided from six depots.

Golden Arrow's operating depots are responsible for maintaining the bus fleet. The company also has an engineering division, Multimech, which overhauls engines, gearboxes and other subassemblies and which carries out body repairs and refurbishing.

Developments

For the past few years Golden Arrow has been looking to improve the Black Economic Empowerment (BEE) profile of the company. In September 2001, a joint venture between Golden Arrow Bus Services (Pty) Ltd and two BEE companies, Abahlobo Transport Services and Siyakhula Bus Services, was established. The joint venture is called Sibanye and operates the Atlantis corridor on the west coast. Early in 2004, Hoskens Consolidated Investments Ltd acquired the entire shareholding of Golden Arrow Bus Services.

A number of factors have delayed completion of the statutorily required planning to implement the new transport legislation that provides for regulation of public transport modes on an integrated basis. In addition, no finality has yet been reached on the government's intention to replace the current passenger subsidy system with an open tender system. A considerable amount of complex technical work, much of it required by law, has to be done at both national and provincial levels before tenders can be invited for tendered or negotiated bus contracts.

The South African Bus Operators Association (SABOA), of which Golden Arrow is a member, is of the view that negotiated contracts, provided for in the legislation, would create the most conducive environment for restructuring public transport to comply with government policy to encourage smaller black-owned businesses to participate in the industry.

Passenger journeys: (2006) 53.6 million per year (estimate)
Vehicle-km: (2006) 55.8 million per year

Routes: 900 operated in most parts of the Cape Town municipality
Average journey length: 25.4 km
Passengers carried: More than 200,000 passengers per working day

Fleet: 1,012 vehicles
In peak service: 945

Most intensive service: 5–10 minutes
One-person operation: All routes
Fare collection: Setright ticketing machines used on all buses, except on the Atlantis services which have electronic Wayfarer ticketing machines, issuing cash tickets
Fare structure: Distance related, weekly 10-ride clipcards and 48-ride monthly clipcards, discounted cash fares apply during off-peak periods on some routes
Fare evasion control: Random inspectors
Operational control: Multichannel selective calling two-way radio with 150 field staff under centralised operations control centre with computerised database. Major termini controlled by regulators with bus time sheets
Integration with other modes: Complex network of routes interlinking at suburban rail stations
Ticket integration: None
Average distance between stops: 750 m
Operating costs: Financed by fares 94 per cent, other commercial sources 6 per cent
Passenger subsidy: Recoverable discount system on clipcards, operated in collaboration with National Department of Transport
New vehicles: Financed by own resources

iKapa Tours & Travel (Pty) Ltd

PO Box 102, Observatory, 7935, South Africa
Tel: (+27 21) 510 86 66
Freephone: 0800 60 08 95
Fax: (+27 21) 510 31 31
e-mail: info@ikapa.co.za
Web: www.ikapa.co.za

Street address
iKapa Place, 94 Voortrekker Road, Salt River 7925, South Africa

Key personnel
Managing Director: Kobus van Heerden

A Golden Arrow MAN bus pulling out of the Claremont terminus 1174426

A Golden Arrow bus on the road along the Atlantic Ocean on the west coast of Cape Town 1174423

Type of operation: Dial-a-Ride

Current situation
The Dial-a-Ride Service is a project funded by the City of Cape Town, the Provincial Administration of the Western Cape and the National Department of Transport. It is operated by iKapa Tours & Travel (Pty) Ltd for all eligible residents in the entire municipal area of the City of Cape Town.

The service operates from Monday to Friday between 06.00 and 19.00. Vehicles are equipped with lifts or ramps. Fares are based on a zonal system.

Developments
In early 2007, The Western Cape Department of Transport agreed to expand the dial-a-ride services and to extend the current contract with iKapa until the service goes out on a competitive tender.

South African Rail Commuter Corporation Metrorail (SARCC-Metrorail)

Private Bag X2, Sunninghill 2157, South Africa
Tel: (+27 11) 804 29 00   Fax: (+27 11) 804 38 52/3
e-mail: info@sarcc.co.za
Web: www.sarcc.co.za

Street address
Block B – Lincoln Wood, Office Park, Woodlands Drive, Woodmead East, South Africa

Key personnel
Chief Executive Officer: Lucky Montana
Chief Operations Officer: Andre Harrison
Chief Financial Officer: David Kekana
Acting Chief Information Officer: Mark Ganten Bein
Group Executives:
 Rolling Stock: Brian Jacobs
 Strategy, Network & Planning: Tando Mbikwana
 Compliance, Operational Safety & Security: Enos Ngutshane
 Business Engineering: Lauriette Modipane
 Human Resources: Grace Mabumbulu
 Infrastructure: Kevin Moonsamy
Regions:
 Durban: Sisa Mtwa
 Eastern Cape: Ms Claudia Williams
 Tshwane: Fufu Shoba
 Western Cape: Stephen Ngobeni
 Wits: Salani Sithole

Passenger journeys: (All areas)
(2003/04) 482 million
(2004/05) 491.9 million
(2005/06) 511.9 million
(Cape region)
(2004/05) 169.9 million
(2005/06) 174.7 million

Background
South African Rail Commuter Corporation Metrorail (SARCC-Metrorail) is the agency of the National Department of Transport and is responsible for the provision of commuter rail services in South Africa.

For more details, please see entry in *Jane's World Railways*.

Current situation
Over two million people use commuter services daily in the major metropolitan areas of Wits (Johannesburg), Tshwane (Pretoria), Ethekwini (Durban), Cape Town, Port Elizabeth and East London. SARCC has contracted Metrorail (a division of Transnet) to provide services on its behalf (see separate entry).

Its wholly owned subsidiary, Intersite Property Management Services (IPMS), manages its property portfolio, which consists of more than 470 stations countrywide.

Developments
In February 2005, the government announced that a due-diligence was being carried out on the three entities responsible for passenger rail, with

a view to consolidating the functions of these entities in a new entity – PAXCo, due to be in place by the end of 2005.

Metrorail

PO Box 5446, Cape Town 8000, South Africa
Tel: (+27 21) 449 61 81
Fax: (+27 21) 449 63 51
e-mail: infocpt@metrorail.co.za
Web: www.metrorail.co.za

Street address

Pail Sauer Building, 1 Adderley Street, Cape Town 8001, South Africa

Head office

PO Box 52238, Braamfontein, Johannesburg 2017, South Africa
Tel: (+27 11) 773 70 91; 92   Fax: (+27 11) 773 71 25
e-mail: infohq@metrorail.co.za

Key personnel

Regional Manager, Western Cape: André Harrison
Operations Manager: Stephen Ngobeni
Train Operations Manager: Saaliegah Mateus
Rolling Stock Manager: Ingwa Sichula

Infrastructure Manager: Louis Beukes
Marketing and Communications Manager: Riana Jacobs
Finance Manager: Mapule Moagi
  Staff: 2,900 (2003)

Type of operation: Suburban heavy rail

Passenger journeys (all regions): See above

Background

Metrorail operates commuter rail services under contract to the South African Rail Commuter Corporation (SARCC). The contract is intended to pave the way for the eventual concessioning of urban commuter rail operations.

Metrorail operates trains owned by SARCC over tracks owned either by SARCC or by Spoornet, the national rail system operator.

The company's headquarters are in Johannesburg, with regional offices in Cape Town, Durban, Eastern Cape, Pretoria and Wits.

Current situation

Frequent suburban service on 12 routes in the Western Cape area, serving 118 stations on the Cape Peninsula, total 305 km, 1,065 mm gauge, electrified 3 kV DC. Up to 35 trains per hour in the peak, off-peak services every 30 minutes. Fares cover 38 per cent of operating costs.

Developments

Two routes totalling 15 km – the Blue Downs line and the Khayelitsha extension – are proposed in Metrorail's 10-year capital development programme.

In February 2005, the government announced that a due-diligence was being carried out on the three entities responsible for passenger rail (Metrorail, Shosoloza Meyl and SARCC), with a view to consolidating the functions of these entities in a new entity – PAXCO (under the auspices of the National Department of Transport).

In October 2005, Sentry Technology Corporation shipped SentryVision® SmartTrack CCTV systems for installation on Metrorail's Cape Town intermodal terminals. The systems will monitor passenger platforms to improve security.

In May 2006, Metrorail was transferred to the Department of Transport and Public Works.

Rolling stock: 280 trains (all areas)

Durban

Population: Thekwini Municipal Area (EMA) 3.2 million (2006 estimate)

Public transport

Bus services privatised in 2003. Other operators running minibuses and legal and illegal combitaxis. Commuter/suburban rail services are currently being restructured. Light rail planned.

Remant/Alton Land Transport (Pty) Ltd

PO Box 1755, Durban 4000, South Africa
Tel: (+27 31) 309 41 26
Fax: (+27 31) 309 51 08 (Administration)
e-mail: daimo@mweb.co.za

Street address

102 Alice Street, Durban 4001, South Africa

Key personnel

Contact: Dan Cloete
  Staff: 1,192

Background

The e-Thekwini Municipality, formerly the Durban Metropolitan Unicity Council, completed the privatisation of its public transport operation, Durban Transport, in November 2003.

Current situation

Remant/Alton Land Transport (Pty) Ltd took over the e-Thekwini Municipality's bus operations on 1 June 2003. The company provides commuter bus services to the greater Durban metropolitan region, with a fleet of 563 standard buses and 69 midibuses.

Developments

e-Thekwini will introduce a new service called The People Mover, aimed primarily at the tourist market. The service will be operated by Remant and will run along the popular beach front route between the Casino and the U'Shaka Marine World, a distance of approximately 5 km. There will be 10 air-conditioned buses, all with wheelchair facilities.

South African Rail Commuter Corporation Metrorail (SARCC-Metrorail)

Private Bag X2, Sunninghill 2157, South Africa
Tel: (+27 11) 804 29 00   Fax: (+27 11) 804 38 52/3
e-mail: info@sarcc.co.za
Web: www.sarcc.co.za

Street address

Block B – Lincoln Wood, Office Park, Woodlands Drive, Woodmead East, South Africa

Key personnel

Chief Executive Officer: Lucky Montana
Chief Operations Officer: Andre Harrison
Chief Financial Officer: David Kekana
Acting Chief Information Officer: Mark Ganten Bein
Group Executives:
  Rolling Stock: Brian Jacobs
  Strategy, Network & Planning: Tando Mbikwana
  Compliance, Operational Safety & Security: Enos Ngutshane
  Business Engineering: Lauriette Modipane
  Human Resources: Grace Mabumbulu
  Infrastructure: Kevin Moonsamy
Regions:
  Durban: Sisa Mtwa
  Eastern Cape: Ms Claudia Williams
  Tshwane: Fufu Shoba
  Western Cape: Stephen Ngobeni
  Wits: Salani Sithole

Passenger journeys: (All areas)
(2003/04) 482 million
(2004/05) 491.9 million
(2005/06) 511.9 million
(Durban region)
(2004/05) 53.9 million
(2005/06) 60.1 million

Background

South African Rail Commuter Corporation Metrorail (SARCC-Metrorail) is the agency of the National Department of Transport and is responsible for the provision of commuter rail services in South Africa.

For more details, please see entry in *Jane's World Railways*.

Current situation

Over two million people use commuter services daily in the major metropolitan areas of Wits (Johannesburg), Tshwane (Pretoria), Ethekwini (Durban), Cape Town, Port Elizabeth and East London. SARCC has contracted Metrorail (a division of Transnet) to provide services on its behalf.

Its wholly owned subsidiary, Intersite Property Management Services (IPMS), manages its property portfolio, which consists of more than 470 stations countrywide.

Developments

In February 2005, the government announced that a due-diligence was being carried out on the three entities responsible for passenger rail, with a view to consolidating the functions of these entities in a new entity – PAXCO.

During FY2006, SARCC-Metrorail contributed ZAR160.4 million to establish a Rail Police Unit and for the construction of operations centres. Also during that year, a real-time CCTV system has been piloted.

Metrorail

PO Box 47452, Greyville 4023, South Africa
Tel: (+27 31) 361 79 73
Fax: (+27 31) 361 73 15
e-mail: infodbn@metrorail.co.za
Web: www.metrorail.co.za

Street address

Durban Station Building, NMR Avenue, Durban, South Africa

Key personnel

Regional Manager, Durban: Sisa Mtwa
Acting Marketing and Communications Manager: Isabel v d Westhuizen

Head office

PO Box 52238, Braamfontein, Johannesburg 2017, South Africa
Tel: (+27 11) 773 70 91; 92   Fax: (+27 11) 773 71 25
e-mail: infohq@metrorail.co.za

Type of operation: Suburban/commuter heavy rail

Passenger journeys: See above

Background

Metrorail operates commuter rail services under contract to the South African Rail Commuter Corporation (SARCC). The contract is intended to pave the way for the eventual concessioning of urban commuter rail operations.

Metrorail operates trains owned by SARCC over tracks owned by SARCC or by Spoornet (see entry in *Jane's World Railways*), the national rail system operator.

The company's headquarters are in Johannesburg, with regional offices in Cape Town, Durban, Eastern Cape, Pretoria and Wits.

Current situation

Frequent suburban services in the Natal metropolitan area on nine routes totalling 273 km, 1,067 mm gauge, electrified 3 kV DC, 100 stations; up to 22 trains per hour at peak times, every 30 minutes off-peak. Fares cover 22.8 per cent of operating costs.

Developments

A 3 km Inanda extension is proposed under Metrorail's 10-year capital investment programme.

In February 2005, the government announced that a due-diligence was being carried out on the three entities responsible for passenger rail, with a view to consolidating the functions of these entities in a new entity – PAXCO.

In May 2006, Metrorail was transferred to the Department of Transport and Public Works.

Rolling stock: 280 trains (all areas)

Johannesburg

Population: 3.23 million (2001 Census)

Public transport

Bus services provided for part of the city by municipal undertaking, with a network of suburban commuter routes by private companies and shared 'Kombi-taxis'. Commuter/suburban rail services are currently being restructured. A rapid rail link to the airport is planned.

Johannesburg Metropolitan Bus Service (Pty) Limited (Metrobus)

Transportation House, No 1 Raikes Road, PO Box 1787, Braamfontein, Johannesburg 2000, South Africa
Tel: (+27 11) 403 43 00   Fax: (+27 11) 403 16 13
e-mail: Beverley@mbus.co.za
Web: www.mbus.co.za

Key personnel

Chairperson: Operations, Technical and Marketing Subcommittee: Ms Mususumeli Mutshutshu
Committee
Chairperson, Metrobus Board of Directors: Thabo Seopa
Chairperson: Human Resources Committee: Ms Kokodi Morobe
Non-Executive Directors: Sindile Kwapuna, Ms Jennifer Gray
Managing Director: Bheki Shongwe
Executive Marketing and Business Development Officer: Ayanda Vilakazi
Executive Officer, Operations (Acting): Themba Ngcobo
Executive Officer, Technical (Acting): David Gregory
Executive Officer, Human Resources: Dave Hodgkinson
Executive Officer, Finance: Vinod Naidoo
Staff: 969

Background

Metrobus was incorporated in July 2000 as a result of the amalgamation of the Johannesburg Transport Department and the Roodepoort Bus Service in line with the 'iGoli 2002' Plan. It is 100 per cent owned by the City of Johannesburg.

Current situation

The company's head office is in Braamfontein and it has three main depots and three satellite depots.

Metrobus has five divisions: Technical, Operations, Finance, Human Resources, Marketing and Business Development.

Some 60 per cent of fares are paid using the company's BusTag prepaid contactless smartcard system.

Developments

Metrobus has invested ZAR 7 million in a Global Positioning System (GPS) vehicle tracking system.

A new customer service department, call centre and information centres have been established.

Passenger boardings: Approx 20 million per annum
Vehicle-km: Approx 14 million per annum

Number of routes: Approx 96
Route length: (One way) 630 km

Fleet: 511 buses

Mercedes O305 double-deck	122
Mercedes O305 single-deck	17
MAN	9
Volvo B10M	97
Volvo B7R single-deck	50
Volvo B7T double-deck	150
ERF	66

In peak service: 437
On order: None

Most intensive service: 10 min
One-person operation: All services
Fare collection: Cash and 'Tag' smartcard system (recorded by Wayfarer machines)

Fare structure: Zonal (8 zones); monthly tickets (peak or off-peak); 10-trip coupons
Operational control: Mobile inspectors with radio communication and computerised online monitoring
Arrangements for elderly/disabled: Low flat fare for pensioners. Cost of concessions included in city council's compensation for the undertaking's deficit; some buses with ramps and wheelchair access have been introduced
Average peak-hour speed: 17 km/h
Bus priority: With flow and contraflow bus lanes
Operating costs financed by: Fares 42 per cent, other commercial sources 3 per cent, subsidy/grants 55 per cent
Subsidy from: Johannesburg ratepayers 48 per cent, other local authorities 4 per cent, Central Witwatersrand regional services council 3 per cent
New vehicles financed by: Loans

South African Rail Commuter Corporation Metrorail (SARCC-Metrorail)

Private Bag X2, Sunninghill 2157, South Africa
Tel: (+27 11) 804 29 00
Fax: (+27 11) 804 38 52/3
e-mail: info@sarcc.co.za
Web: www.sarcc.co.za

Street address

Block B – Lincoln Wood, Office Park, Woodlands Drive, Woodmead East, South Africa

Key personnel

Chief Executive Officer: Lucky Montana
Chief Operations Officer: Andre Harrison
Chief Financial Officer: David Kekana
Acting Chief Information Officer: Mark Ganten Bein
Group Executives:
Rolling Stock: Brian Jacobs
Strategy, Network & Planning: Tando Mbikwana
Compliance, Operational Safety & Security: Enos Ngutshane
Business Engineering: Lauriette Modipane
Human Resources: Grace Mabumbulu
Infrastructure: Kevin Moonsamy
Regions:
Durban: Sisa Mtwa
Eastern Cape: Ms Claudia Williams
Tshwane: Fufu Shoba
Western Cape: Stephen Ngobeni
Wits: Salani Sithole

Passenger journeys: (All areas)
(2003/04) 482 million
(2004/05) 491.9 million
(2005/06) 511.9 million
(Wits region)
(2004/05) 184.6 million
(2005/06) 190.5 million

Background

South African Rail Commuter Corporation Metrorail (SARCC-Metrorail) is the agency of the National Department of Transport and is responsible for the provision of commuter rail services in South Africa.

For more details, please see entry in *Jane's World Railways*.

Current situation

Over two million people use commuter services daily in the major metropolitan areas of Wits (Johannesburg), Tshwane (Pretoria), Ethekwini (Durban), Cape Town, Port Elizabeth and East London. SARCC has contracted Metrorail (a division of Transnet) to provide services on its behalf.

Its wholly owned subsidiary, Intersite Property Management Services (IPMS), manages its property portfolio, which consists of more than 470 stations countrywide.

Developments

In February 2005, the government announced that a due-diligence was being carried out on the three entities responsible for passenger rail, with a view to consolidating the functions of these entities in a new entity – PAXC.

Metrorail

Wits Regional Office
PO Box 11579, Johannesburg 2000, South Africa
Tel: (+27 11) 774 47 01   Fax: (+27 11) 773 45 63
e-mail: infowits@metrorail.co.za
Web: www.metrorail.co.za

Street address

Corner Leyds and Loveday Street, Johannesburg 2000, South Africa

Key personnel

Regional Manager: Salani Sithole
Customer Operations Manager: Sifiso Lukhele
Technical Operations Manager: Senny van den Oever
Infrastructure Manager: David van der Merwe
Acting Marketing Manager: Brenda Motau
Finance Manager: Eugene Fourie
Staff: 2,900 (2003)

Head Office

PO Box 52238, Braamfontein 2017, South Africa
Tel: (+27 11) 773 70 91; 92   Fax: (+27 11) 773 71 25
e-mail: InfoHO@metrorail.co.za
Web: www.metrorail.co.za

Street address

222 Smit Street, Corner of Smit and Rissik Streets, Johannesburg, South Africa

Type of operation: Suburban heavy rail

Passenger journeys: See above

Background

A business unit of Transnet, the state-owned transport organisation, Metrorail operates commuter rail services under contract to the South African Rail Commuter Corporation (SARCC) (see separate entry). The contract is intended to pave the way for the eventual concessioning of urban commuter rail operations.

Metrorail operates trains owned by SARCC over tracks owned either by SARCC or by Spoornet, the national rail system operator.

The company's headquarters are in Johannesburg, with regional offices in Cape Town, Durban, Eastern Cape, Pretoria and Wits.

Current situation

Extensive network of 1,065 mm gauge suburban trains on 14 routes serving the whole southern Transvaal (Witwatersrand-Vereeniging area, population 5.5 million), totalling 456 km with 162 stations, electrified at 3 kV DC. Links with northern Transvaal area services (see under Pretoria). Up to 35 trains per hour run at peak times on the busiest sections, while off-peak the normal frequency is hourly. Fares cover 20.3 per cent of operating costs.

Developments

As well as proposals for two new lines totalling 16 km in northern Johannesburg, the corporation is also planning a route to serve the Baralink commercial and residential development in the southwest of the city. Comprising a loop and branch, the 20 km alignment would be built with private sector finance.

A start has been made with fleet renewal; bids were sought in mid-1998 for five 12-car trains intended for service on the Johannesburg-Soweto line.

In February 2005, the government announced that a due-diligence was being carried out on the three entities responsible for passenger rail (Metrorail, Shosoloza Meyl and SARCC), with a view to consolidating the functions of these entities in a new entity – PAXC (under the auspices of the National Department of Transport).

In May 2006, Metrorail was transferred to the Department of Transport and Public Works.

Rolling stock: 280 trains (all areas)

PUTCO Ltd

Private Bag 3, Wendywood 2144, Gauteng, South Africa
Tel: (+27 11) 945 10 43 (Nancefield)

Tel: (+27 11) 493 56 40 (Selby)
e-mail: info@putco.co.za
Web: www.putco.co.za

Key personnel
Managing Director: F G Pisapia
Financial Director: S R Pisapia
Corporate Director: M H Heyns
Business Development Director: A Sefala
    Staff: Not currently available

Passenger journeys: (All operations)
(2006/07) 91 million
Vehicle-km: Not currently available

Current situation
PUTCO operates a bus passenger service, principally in the Gauteng and Northwest/Mpumalanga areas. The company also operates scheduled long-distance services from Gauteng to the Limpopo Province. Separate eastern and western networks have a combined fleet of 1,731 buses (as at June 2007), carrying about 91 million passengers a year.

Developments
The company was delisted from the JSE Securities Exchange in 2005 and has introduced Broad Based Black Economic Empowerment (BBBEE), in line with the government's Black Economic Empowerment (BEE) objectives.

Fleet: 1,731 buses (all operations)
Breakdown of fleet is not currently available.

Gautrain Rapid Rail Link
Gautrain Project Office
Ten Sixty Six, 12th Floor, 35 Pritchard Street, Corner Loveday and Harrison Streets, Johannesburg, South Africa

Tel: (+27 11) 298 49 00
Fax: (+27 11) 298 49 16
Web: corporate.gautrain.co.za

Key personnel
Project Team Chairman: Jack van der Merwe

Type of operation: Suburban rail (planned)

Background
The Gautrain Rapid Rail Link is a public-private partnership project developed by the Gauteng provincial government to establish an 80 km fast electrified passenger rail system linking Tshwane (Pretoria) and Johannesburg International Airport (JIA) and Sandton. The scheme aims to improve transport links in South Africa's main economic region, reduce road congestion and stimulate development. Its estimated cost is ZAR7 billion.

The Gautrain Rapid Rail Link provides for an 80 km standard-gauge electrified network comprising a north-south line from Hatfield, north of Pretoria, to a southern terminus at Johannesburg Park. From Marlboro, northwest of Sandton, a line will run east to serve JIA. With 10 stations, the network will double as a commuter system and an airport rail link. Interchange with South African Rail Commuter Corporation (SARCC) Metrorail services will be available at Hatfield, Johannesburg Park and Pretoria; improved interchanges are planned at other locations.

A dedicated service is planned between Sandton (Johannesburg) and JIA, with in-town check-in provided at the former and a journey time of 15 minutes.

The network will employ continuously welded rail on concrete sleepers, with slab track in tunnel sections. It is expected that cab signalling will be used.

The project is expected to be built in two phases:
Phase 1: Sandton to Hatfield and Sandton to Johannesburg International Airport (JIA). Scheduled for completion by the end of 2008.
Phase 2: Sandton to Johannesburg Park station. Scheduled for completion in the first half of 2010.

Current situation
Initial planning and prefeasibility/feasibility studies were undertaken in the late 1990s and early 2000s. A Reference Route was published in 2002, leading to an environmental impact assessment and public consultation.

Management of the Gautrain Rapid Rail Link project is led by a provincial political steering committee, which acts as the main decision-making body. Executive responsibility rests with the Gautrain project team, with a project review committee providing specialist advice and guidance.

Developments
In early 2005, two shortlisted consortia had submitted their initial bids for a Design, Build and Operate (DBO) concession. A contract award and commencement of construction were both expected to take place in mid-2005. Commissioning of the Sandton-JIA section is expected by the end of 2008 and the remainder of the system by 2010.

Fleet: It is estimated that around 20 three- or four-car trainsets will be required for the commencement of services. These will employ either 3 kV DC or 25 kV AC power supply systems and will be capable of operating at up to 160 or 180 km/h.

Port Elizabeth
Population: 1 million (2001 Census)

Public transport
Bus services are provided by many small bus operators throughout the Eastern Cape area, but there are government plans to amalgamate all of these under a new single entity. Commuter/suburban rail services are currently being restructured. Shared taxi 'Kombi' minibuses are also available.

Algoa Bus Company (Pty) Ltd (ABC)
PO Box 225, Port Elizabeth 6000, South Africa
Tel: (+27 41) 404 12 00
Freephone: 080 142 14 44
Fax: (+27 41) 453 74 37

Street address
Perl Road, Korsten, Port Elizabeth, South Africa

Key personnel
Chief Executive Officer: Sicelo Duze
Managing Director: Gerald Botha
Financial Director: Douglas Govender
    Staff: 648

Background
Algoa Bus was formed in 1991 to take over the assets of the former operating company PE Tramways, and was later incorporated as a non-profit utility company.

Current situation
The company currently has an interim contract from the Department of Transport of the province of the Eastern Cape to provide bus services in the Nelson Mandela metro area. The company is subsidised by the National Department of Transport by an amount of approximately ZAR76 million and carried some 16.3 million passengers in 2004.

Developments
In May 2005, a meeting was scheduled to take place at which the Department of Transport for the province of the Eastern Cape consulted with the many bus operators, including Algoa Bus Company, which provide services in the region. The aim of this meeting was to explain the single legal entity, a proposal which would see these operators providing co-ordinated services as a group.

Bus
Passenger boardings: (2004) 16.3 million
Vehicle-km: Not currently available

Number of routes: 70
Route length: 900 km

Fleet: 274 vehicles	
AEC Regent	1
Leyland 680	10
ERF Super Trailblazer	30
Leyland Victory Mk II	154
Guy Big J Mk I	40
ERF Trailblazer single-deck	56
Mercedes 811/Busaf Speedliner midibus (1992/94)	8
Mercedes 812	1
AAD 320D minibus (1996)	5
In peak service: 248	
On order: none	

Most intensive service: 1 min
Fare collection: Wayfarer Mk III ETMs with integral smart-card readers; mobile ticket offices at major loading points; shops acting as agents for prepurchase multijourney coupons, exchanged for tickets on board
Fare structure: Flat and zonal, discount coupons
Fare evasion control: On-bus inspection
Bus priority: On certain main arterials, extreme left lane demarcated 'no stopping, except buses' in direction of peak flow for duration of peak period. New bus lanes in long-range planning stage by Metropolitan Transport Advisory Board
Average distance between stops: 400 m

Average peak-hour speed: In mixed traffic, 20 km/h
Operating costs financed by: Fares 45 per cent, other commercial sources 20 per cent, subsidy/grants 51 per cent
Subsidy from: National government 100 per cent

South African Rail Commuter Corporation Metrorail (SARCC-Metrorail)
Private Bag X2, Sunninghill 2157, South Africa
Tel: (+27 11) 804 29 00
Fax: (+27 11) 804 38 52/3
e-mail: info@sarcc.co.za
Web: www.sarcc.co.za

Street address
Block B – Lincoln Wood, Office Park, Woodlands Drive, Woodmead East, South Africa

Key personnel
Chief Executive Officer: Lucky Montana
Chief Operations Officer: Andre Harrison
Chief Financial Officer: David Kekana
Acting Chief Information Officer: Mark Ganten Bein
Group Executives:
    Rolling Stock: Brian Jacobs
    Strategy, Network & Planning: Tando Mbikwana
    Compliance, Operational Safety & Security: Enos Ngutshane
    Business Engineering: Lauriette Modipane
    Human Resources: Grace Mabumbulu
    Infrastructure: Kevin Moonsamy
Regions:
    Durban: Sisa Mtwa
    Eastern Cape: Ms Claudia Williams
    Tshwane: Fufu Shoba
    Western Cape: Stephen Ngobeni
    Wits: Salani Sithole

Passenger journeys: (All areas)
(2003/04) 482 million
(2004/05) 491.9 million
(2005/06) 511.9 million

(Port Elizabeth region)
(2004/05) 1.7 million
(2005/06) 1.8 million

Background
South African Rail Commuter Corporation Metrorail (SARCC-Metrorail) is the agency of the National Department of Transport and is responsible for the provision of commuter rail services in South Africa.

For more details, please see entry in *Jane's World Railways*.

Current situation
Over 2 million people use commuter services daily in the major metropolitan areas of Wits (Johannesburg), Tshwane (Pretoria), Ethekwini (Durban), Cape Town, Port Elizabeth and East London. SARCC has contracted Metrorail (a division of Transnet) to provide services on its behalf.

Its wholly owned subsidiary, Intersite Property Management Services (IPMS), manages its property portfolio, which consists of more than 470 stations countrywide.

Developments
In February 2005, the government announced that a due-diligence was being carried out on the three entities responsible for passenger rail, with a view to consolidating the functions of these entities in a new entity – PAXCO.

Metrorail
Eastern Cape Office
PO Box 266, East London 5200, South Africa
Tel (+27 11) 700 20 39   Fax: (+27 11) 700 20 38
e-mail: infoEL@metrorail.co.za
Web: www.metrorail.co.za

Street address
Station Building, Station Street, East London 5200, South Africa

Head office
PO Box 52238, Braamfontein 2017, South Africa
Tel: (+27 11) 773 70 91; 92
Fax: (+27 11) 773 71 25
e-mail: InfoHO@metrorail.co.za
Web: www.metrorail.co.za

Key personnel
Regional Manager: Mrs Claudia Williams
Finance Manager: Mrs Gcobisa Mtingane
Marketing and Communications Manager:
  Ms Alice King

Type of operation: Suburban heavy rail

Passenger journeys: See above

Background
Metrorail operates commuter rail services under contract to the South African Rail Commuter

Corporation (SARCC). The contract is intended to pave the way for the eventual concessioning of urban commuter rail operations.

Metrorail operates trains owned by SARCC over tracks owned either by SARCC or by Spoornet, the national rail system operator.

The company's headquarters are in Johannesburg, with regional offices in Cape Town, Durban, Eastern Cape, Pretoria and Wits.

Current situation
Operates 18 return weekday journeys between Port Elizabeth and Uitenhage (32 km), serving 11 stations, with a fleet of 51 diesel-hauled cars. Fares cover 19 per cent of operating costs.

Extension to Motherwell proposed using existing trackage plus a new short branch.

Developments
In February 2005, the government announced that a due-diligence was being carried out on the three entities responsible for passenger rail (Metrorail, Shosoloza Meyl and SARCC), with a view to consolidating the functions of these entities in a new entity – PAXCO (under the auspices of the National Department of Transport).

In May 2006, Metrorail was transferred to the Department of Transport and Public Works.

Rolling stock: 280 trains (all areas)

Pretoria

Population: City 1 million, metropolitan area 1.99 million (2001 census)

Public transport
City bus services provided by transport department of the city council. Extensive longer-distance commuter bus services operated by private companies. Commuter/suburban rail services are currently being restructured. Rapid rail link under construction.

Pretoria City Transport
City Council of Pretoria
PO Box 6338, Pretoria 0001, South Africa
Tel: (+27 12) 337 42 81
Fax: (+27 12) 337 43 42

Key personnel
Acting General Manager, Transport: Hubert Joynt
  Staff: 437

Current situation
Public transport policy is being revised and competitive tendering was expected to be introduced in 1998 covering all operators, with the aim of reducing costs and improving service quality.

Bus
Passenger journeys: (1995/96) 13.8 million
(1996/97) 13 million
Vehicle-km: (1995/96) 11.3 million
(1996/97) 11 million

Number of routes: 245, including school and contract routes
Route length: (One way) timetabled routes 685 km

Fleet: 300 vehicles

MAN City Bus	20
MAN semi-luxury	15
MAN double-deck	20
Mercedes O305 city bus	87
Mercedes O305 semi-luxury coach	50
Mercedes O305 double-deck	108

In peak service: 267

Most intensive service: 5 min
One-person operation: All services
Fare collection: Cash to driver or prepurchase
Fare structure: Stage; multiticket books (coupons); trip tickets valid 1 month for 1, 2, 3 or 4 stages allowing 4 trips per day, 2 on any route within the municipal boundary and 2 within the central area.

Monthly tickets allowing 6 trips per day on any routes within the municipal boundary
Fares collected on board: 26.7 per cent; 9.9 million passengers took prepurchase tickets in 1994/95
Fare evasion control: Ticket inspectors
Operational control: Route inspectors
Arrangements for elderly/disabled: Disabled and over-68s free; low-price senior citizens' monthly pass for unlimited off-peak travel
Average peak-hour speed: In bus lanes, 23.5 km/h; in mixed traffic, 20.5 km/h
Bus priority: 7.5 km of bus lanes
Operating costs financed by: Fares 49 per cent, other commercial sources 1 per cent, subsidy/grants 50 per cent
Subsidy from: City tax funds
New vehicles financed by: Loans/tax fund

South African Rail Commuter Corporation Metrorail (SARCC-Metrorail)
Private Bag X2, Sunninghill 2157, South Africa
Tel: (+27 11) 804 29 00   Fax: (+27 11) 804 38 52/3
e-mail: info@sarcc.co.za
Web: www.sarcc.co.za

Street address
Block B – Lincoln Wood, Office Park, Woodlands Drive, Woodmead East, South Africa

Key personnel
Chief Executive Officer: Lucky Montana
Chief Operations Officer: Andre Harrison
Chief Financial Officer: David Kekana
Acting Chief Information Officer: Mark Ganten
  Bein
Group Executives:
  Rolling Stock: Brian Jacobs
  Strategy, Network & Planning: Tando Mbikwana
  Compliance, Operational Safety & Security: Enos Ngutshane
  Business Engineering: Lauriette Modipane
  Human Resources: Grace Mabumbulu
  Infrastructure: Kevin Moonsamy
Regions:
  Durban: Sisa Mtwa
  Eastern Cape: Ms Claudia Williams
  Tshwane: Fufu Shoba
  Western Cape: Stephen Ngobeni
  Wits: Salani Sithole

Passenger journeys: (All areas)
(2003/04) 482 million
(2004/05) 491.9 million
(2005/06) 511.9 million

(Pretoria region)
(2004/05) 75.4 million
(2005/06) 77.6 million

Background
South African Rail Commuter Corporation Metrorail (SARCC-Metrorail) is the agency of the National Department of Transport and is responsible for provision of commuter rail services in South Africa.

For more details, please see entry in *Jane's World Railways*.

Current situation
Over 2 million people use commuter services daily in the major metropolitan areas of Wits (Johannesburg), Tshwane (Pretoria), Ethekwini (Durban), Cape Town, Port Elizabeth and East London. SARCC has contracted Metrorail (a division of Transnet) to provide services on its behalf.

Its wholly owned subsidiary, Intersite Property Management Services (IPMS), manages its property portfolio, which consists of more than 470 stations countrywide.

Developments
In February 2005, the government announced that a due-diligence was being carried out on the three entities responsible for passenger rail, with a view to consolidating the functions of these entities in a new entity – PAXCO.

Metrorail
Tshwane Regional Office
PO Box 12244, Tramshed 0126, South Africa
Tel: (+27 12) 315 32 83
Fax: (+27 12) 315 31 12
e-mail: infoPTA@metrorail.co.za
Web: www.metrorail.co.za

Street address
Pretoria Station Building, Corner of Scheiding & Paul Kruger, Pretoria 0001, South Africa

Key personnel
Regional Manager: Fufu Shoba
Operations Manager:
  Norman Magidigidi
Train Operations Manager: Moses Sefole
Rolling Stock Manager: Tino Gabryk
Infrastructure Manager:
  Francois De Jager
Marketing and Communications Manager:
  Thokozani Zitha
Acting Finance Manager: Riema Botha

Head office
PO Box 52238, Braamfontein, Johannesburg 2017, South Africa
Tel: (+27 11) 773 70 91; 92   Fax: (+27 11) 773 71 25
e-mail: InfoHO@metrorail.co.za
   Staff: 2,900 (2003)

Type of operation: Suburban heavy rail

Passenger journeys: See above

Background
Metrorail operates commuter rail services under contract to the South African Rail Commuter Corporation (SARCC) (see separate entry). The contract is intended to pave the way for the eventual concessioning of urban commuter rail operations.

Metrorail operates trains owned by SARCC over tracks owned either by SARCC or by Spoornet, the national rail system operator.

The company's headquarters are in Johannesburg, with regional offices in Cape Town, Durban, Eastern Cape, Pretoria and Wits.

Current situation
Suburban rail serving the whole of Pretoria (Northern Transvaal area, population 1.5 million);

seven routes totalling 146 km with 64 stations, 1,065 mm gauge, electrified 3 kV DC; links with Johannesburg area services. Peak service 10 trains per hour, off-peak every 20 minutes. Fares cover 30 per cent of operating costs.

Developments
An 18 km extension is proposed in Metrorail's 10-year capital development programme.

In February 2005, the government announced that a due-diligence was being carried out on the three entities responsible for passenger rail (Metrorail, Shosoloza Meyl and SARCC), with a view to consolidating the functions of these entities in a new entity – PAXCO (under the auspices of the National Department of Transport).

In May 2006, Metrorail was transferred to the Department of Transport and Public Works.

In November 2006, new 10M5 refurbished coaches were added to the fleet. Some ZAR40 million was spent on refurbishing the first 12 coaches, with a further 1,600 due to be refurbished over the next three years, at a cost of some ZAR 1 billion.

Rolling stock: 280 trains (all areas)

Gautrain Rapid Rail Link
Gautrain Project Office
Ten Sixty Six, 12th Floor, 35 Pritchard Street, Corner Loveday and Harrison Streets, Johannesburg, South Africa
Tel: (+27 11) 298 49 00
Fax: (+27 11) 298 49 16
Web: corporate.gautrain.co.za

Key personnel
Project Team Chairman: Jack van der Merwe

Type of operation: Suburban rail (planned)

Current situation
The Gautrain Rapid Rail Link is a public-private partnership project developed by the Gauteng provincial government to establish an 80 km fast electrified passenger rail system linking Tshwane (Pretoria) and Johannesburg International Airport (JIA) and Sandton. The scheme aims to improve transport links in South Africa's main economic region, reduce road congestion and stimulate development. Its estimated cost is ZA R7 billion.

For further information, please see entry under Johannnesburg.

Spain

Barcelona
Population: City 1.59 million, metropolitan area 4.69 million, province 5.2 million (2005 estimates)

Public transport
Bus, metro, leisure tramway, cable lift and funicular services operated by city-controlled authorities under common municipal directorate. Suburban railway run by regionally owned public company FGC, and other services operated by National Railways (RENFE). Private buses; Tram/light rail.

Entitat Metropolitana del Transport (EMT)
Area Metropolitana de Barcelona
Carrer 62, núm 16-18, Sector A, Zona Franca de Barcelona, Barcelona E-08040, Spain
Tel: (+34 93) 223 51 51   Fax: (+34 93) 223 44 43
e-mail: info@emt-amb.com
Web: www.emt-amb.com

Key personnel
Operations Manager: Eduard Unzeta

Passenger journeys: (2002) 236.98 million
Vehicle-km: (2002) 57.86 million

Fleet: 1,304 buses (all companie)

Current situation
In 1991, shares of both the metro and municipal bus companies were transferred to EMT, which now acts as the controlling body for public transport in the Barcelona conurbation and co-ordinates tariffs. A subsidiary is responsible for licensing taxis.

Nine companies, all but one privately owned, operate a total of 159 bus routes under EMT control. EMT is hiving off badly loss-making routes to private contractors, which generally operate them with lower levels of subsidy. Private operator Transports Ciutat Comptal was also awarded the airport shuttle service and the luxury Tomb Bus shuttle in the city centre.

ATM, Metropolitan Transport Authority, is a consortium of the local government of Catalunya, the city council of Barcelona and the Metropolitan Transport Entity (EMT). This consortium is developing a main infrastructure plan with action on railway infrastructure for the metropolitan area of Barcelona for the period 2001–2010. ATM is also co-ordinating introduction of common ticketing across all public transport, approved at the end of 2000.

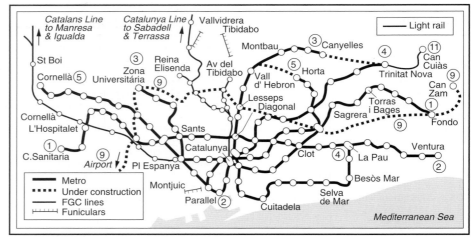

Barcelona's metro and associated suburban lines   0580290

The Vision 2010 programme envisages accommodation of the decade's entire traffic growth (21 per cent) by public transport, with private car use stabilised at its current level. Most of the growth will be absorbed by improved rail services, including metro extensions and a new cross-city Line 9, together adding 38 km and 50 stations to the network.

Developments
In December 2003 Line 11 (light rail) opened, from Trinitat Nova to Can Cuiàs.

Work on Metro Line 9 has commenced, and work on a new light rail line has also begun, with the first section scheduled to open in April 2004.

Ferrocarrils de la Generalitat de Catalunya (FGC)
4 Cardenal Sentmenat St, E-08017 Barcelona, Spain
Tel: (+34 93) 366 30 00   Fax: (+34 93) 366 33 50
e-mail: rrpp@fgc.cat
Web: www.fgc.cat

Key personnel
President: Joan Torres Carol
Corporate Directors
   Development & Planning: Albert Tortajada Flores
   Finance: Lluís Huguet Viñallonga
   Communication: Francesc Xavier Balagué Gea
   Personnel: Armand Aixut Freixanet
   Corporate ICT: Enric González Margarit
Railway Business Unit
   Director: Ramón Borrell Daniel

Projects: Pere Mateu Soler
Maintenance: Marc Serra Arnau
Technology: Josep Lluís Arques Patón
Operations: Oriol Juncadella Fortuny
Tourism and Mountain Unit
   Director: Albert Solà Marti
Commercial Director: Josep Mª Sabando Franch
   Staff: 1,416 (1,256 on railway network) (2008)

Type of operation: Urban/suburban/regional rail

Passenger journeys: (2003) 73.1 million
(2004) 75.8 million
(2005) 75.0 million
(2006) 77.9 million
(2007) 78.9 million
Train-km: Not available currently
Operating costs financed by: Fares 69 per cent, other commercial sources seven per cent, subsidy/grants 24 per cent
Subsidy from: ATM (Metropolitan Transport Authority of Barcelona)

Current situation
FGC operates two groups of lines providing suburban and regional services, totalling 143 km with 71 stations. The Barcelona-Vallès Line (previously known as the Catalunya & Sarria Line) comprises several routes feeding into a 7 km city-centre tunnel section which provides metro-style service. These lines run northwards from metro interchanges at the Plaça de Catalunya terminus and Provença station, with two main extensions to Terrassa (29.8 km) and Sabadell (26.8 km) from St Cugat junction,

totalling 45 km, 1,435 mm gauge, electrified 1.5 kV DC overhead.

The Llobregat-Anoia Line (previously known as the Catalans Line) runs west from Plaça d'Espanya, with suburban service as far as Martorell junction (30 km) and regional services to Manresa (60 km) and Igualada (60 km), totalling 98 km, metre gauge, electrified 1.5 kV DC overhead.

The ATM (Metropolitan Transport Authority of Barcelona) provides subsidy, with fares (69 per cent) and other commercial sources bringing in the remainder. Flat fare on urban sections, graduated elsewhere according to ATM integrated fare system; multijourney tickets and passes available.

For further information on FGC, please see *Jane's World Railways*.

Developments

Barcelona-Vallès Line
A new extension to the centre of Terrassa (3.9 km) is under construction and another extension to the city centre of Sabadell is planned.

Llobregat-Anoia Line
The extension of double track to Martorell and Olesa de Montserrat are already in service and new crossing stations are in service at Capellades and Vilanova del Camí to improve the headway on regional services.

A new timetable with 20 min headways during peak hours was introduced in February 2008 on long-distance regional lines from Barcelona to Manresa and Igualada.

An extension from the terminus at Plaça d'Espanya to the centre of the city is planned.

Rolling stock: 274 cars
MTM/Macosa/Alsthom (1981/95)	M50 T37
CAF/ABB/Meinfesa (1995/2003/2006)	M132 T55

In peak service: 195
On order: Total of 27 cars for suburban and regional services (six delivered for service as at the end of 2008)

Red Nacional de los Ferrocarriles Españoles (RENFE) – Spanish National Railways

Corporate Communications and External Relations Department
Avenida Pio XII nº 110, Edif Caracola 16, E-28036 Madrid, Spain
Tel: (+34 91) 300 66 00   Fax: (+34 91) 300 73 36
e-mail: comunicacion@renfe.es
cercanias@renfe.es
Web: www.renfe.com

Key personnel
Director, Barcelona: Josep Manau Fuster
    Staff: 1,084 (Barcelona area only)

Other offices

Barcelona office
Plaça Països Catalans s/n, Estación de Sants, E08014 Barcelona, Spain
Tel: (+34 93) 490 02 02
e-mail: cerbarna@cosme.renfe.es

Head office
Avenida Ciudad de Barcelona 8, E-28007 Madrid, Spain
Tel: (+34 91) 506 61 27
Fax: (+34 91) 506 69 39

Type of operation: Suburban heavy rail

FGC emu on commuter line to Barcelona at Monistrol de Montserrat (Tony Pattison)   1115218

Alstom Citadis LRVs at Barcelona city terminus (Tony Pattison)   1115251

Passenger journeys: (Total for Suburban Business Unit)
(2002) 439.6 million
(2003) 446 million

Current situation
A metro-style service is operated on three cross-city routes, with trains every 6–7 minutes during peak periods: Maçanet Massanes-Sant Vicenç de Calders, Maçanet Massanes-Hospitalet/El Prat airport, and Manresa-San Vicenç de Calders. Also less frequent service between Vic and Hospitalet. Four lines totalling 451 km with 112 stations, 1,668 mm gauge, electrified 3 kV DC; zonal fares with multijourney tickets and passes.

For further information on this company, please see *Jane's World Railways*.

Rolling stock: 507 emu cars
Class 440	M45 T90
Class 470	M18 T36
Class 447	M172 T86
Class 450 bilevel	M8 T16
Class 451 bilevel	M12 T24

Trambaix UTE – Trambesòse UTE

Ulises 18, E-28043 Madrid, Spain
Tel: (+34 90) 219 32 75
e-mail: info@trambcn.com
Web: www.trambcn.com

Background
Tramvia Metropolità SA (Trammet), a consortium of companies, including FCC Construcción SA, COMSA, Connex, Acciona, ALSTOM, Sarbus, Soler & Sauret, BancSabadell and Société Générale, was formed to build and operate two new tramways in Barcelona. The first was the Trambaix, 16.8 km long with 35 stops, which runs from the Diagonal at Francesc Macia northwest to San Joan Despi.

The second new tramway, the Trambesòs, would be approximately 15 km long. It would run from Estacio del Nord (also on Diagonal) to the eastern suburb of Sant Adria de Besos.

The rolling stock, 37 Citadis-type low-floor articulated trams, is being supplied by ALSTOM; 19 vehicles will be used on the Trambaix and 18 on the Trambesòs.

Current situation
In early 2003, ALSTOM was awarded the contract for the maintenance of the rolling stock and infrastructure of both the Trambaix and the Trambesòs tramways, valued at some EUR170 million. The maintenance of the platforms will be carried out by Comsa, Spain.

Ridership for the Trambaix is estimated to be approximately 19 million per year.

Trambaix
The Trambaix system consists of three lines with a total length of 14 km. All lines run along common track from Francesc Macià to Montesa, where line T3 branches off.

Trambesòs
The Trambesòs has current length of 6.5 km, with a further 7 km under construction.

Developments

The Trambaix was inaugurated in April 2004 and the Trambesòs in May 2004.

A 2.2 km extension of the Trambaix line T3 from Sant Martí de l'Erm to Consell Comarcl opened in January 2006.

Rolling stock: 37 LRVs

Alstom Citadis low-floor articulated bi-directional vehicles   37

Transports Metropolitans de Barcelona (TMB)

Ferrocarril Metropolità de Barcelona SA & Transportes de Barcelona SA
Carrer 60 No 21-23, Sector A, Pol. Ind. Zona Franca, E-08040 Barcelona, Spain
Tel: (+34 93) 298 70 00   Fax: (+34 93) 298 71 21
e-mail: gabpremsa@tmb.net
Web: www.tmb.net

Key personnel

Chief Executive Officer: Constantí Serrallonga Tintoré
Director, International and Business Management: Albert Busquets Blay
Director, Organisation and Information Systems: Lluís Garcia i Torrent
Director, Development and Network Planning: Jacinto Soler Trillo
Director, External Relations and Spokesman: José Antonio Patiño Saco
Director, Research and Co-ordination: Manuel Villante Llauradó
Commercial Director: Jorge Carles-Tolrà Hjorth-Andersen
General Manager, Bus: Josep M Satorres i Lapeña
General Manager, Metro: Agustín del Castillo i Jiménez
General Manager, Administration and Finance: Francesc Bellver i Creus
General Manager, Personnel and Quality Control: Luis Forniés Villagrasa
Staff: 6,036

Passenger journeys: (1998) 479.7 million
(2003) 536 million

Background

TMB is the management unit of the Ferrocarril Metropolità de Barcelona SA and Transportes de Barcelona SA.

Current situation

The municipality, which assumed control of the metro in 1959, also became responsible for urban bus operations in the 1960s. In 1980 bus and metro operations were brought under common management, though operationally the two companies remain separate entities.

Developments

Free transfer between metro and FGC services for multi-ride ticket holders, introduced in 1997, was extended to RENFE suburban trains in the central area.

Bus
Staff: 3,332

Background

Operating company: Transports de Barcelona SA.

Passenger journeys: (1996) 207.6 million
(1997) 207.5 million
(1998) 201.8 million
Vehicle-km: (1996) 36.4 million
(1997) 36.5 million

Current situation

The bus network provides services in Barcelona and other municipalities within the metropolitan area.

Of the current fleet, all are air conditioned and 672 are low-floor. The service is monitored using satellite technology and an Operation Assistance System (OAS).

Developments

A magnetic ticketing system has been introduced. Automatic vehicle monitoring has been extended to 300 vehicles. Electronic screens display news inside some buses, while others are equipped to show videos.

It was expected that 100 new buses, of which 70 will be standard vehicles and 30 will be articulated, would be delivered at the start of 2002. This was expected to increase passenger numbers, increase the frequency of buses and create 350 new positions within the company.

Number of routes: 104
Route length: More than 800 km
On priority right-of-way: 66.3 km

Fleet: 1,010 vehicles (breakdown of vehicle types and date brought into service are not currently known)
Pegaso 6038 (1980/83)
Pegaso 6420
Mercedes O405
Mercedes O405G articulated
Mercedes articulated low-floor
Mercedes low-floor
MAN low-floor
Iveco low-floor
Midibuses
Minibuses
In peak service: 717
Average age of fleet: 6 years

Most intensive service: 4–6 min
One-person operation: 100 per cent
Fare collection: By driver or prepurchase with cancelling machines on board
Fare structure: Flat; common bus/metro multiride tickets and passes
Fare evasion control: Inspectors
Fares collected on board: 13 per cent
Integration with other modes: Combined bus/metro/FGC tickets; bus multiride tickets also valid on metro; monthly passes also valid on RENFE trains in urban zone
Operational control: Route inspectors; automatic vehicle monitoring on 158 vehicles operating 10 routes
Arrangements for elderly/disabled: Reduced rate or free travel for over-65s according to pension level; 301 low-floor buses in service
Average distance between stops: 350 m
Average peak-hour speed: Bus lanes 12.8 km/h; mixed traffic: urban 11.3 km/h, interurban 15.5 km/h
Operating costs financed by: Fares 62.4 per cent, other commercial sources 2.8 per cent, subsidy/grants 34.8 per cent
Subsidy from: Local, central and regional government
New vehicles financed by: Credit and leasing

Metro
Staff: 2,715

Background

Operating company: Ferrocarril Metropolità de Barcelona SA.

Type of operation: Full metro, first line opened 1924

Passenger journeys: (1997) 259.2 million
(1998) 277.9 million
(1999) 280 million
Car-km: (1997) 53.2 million

Current situation

Of the current stations, 29 interconnect, 14 have links to other services, nine link to RENFE rail services, four link to the Generalitat de Catalunya railway and one links to the Montjuïc funicular.

An extension of Line 3 from Montbau to Canyelles (three stations) opened in 2001.

Developments

A major modernisation programme is in progress, including stations, fixed installations and depots.

In August 2003, the El Mareseme/Forum station was added to Line 4.

There are currently two extensions under construction: Line 5 from Horta to Vall d'Hebron, to provide a link with the northern end of Line 3, and an extension of Line 3 from Canyelles to Trinitat Nova, to link with Line 11 (see below).

Route length: 86.6 km
  in tunnel: 79.9 km
Number of lines: 5
Number of stations: 123
  in tunnel: 109
Gauge: Line 1, 1,674 mm; others, 1,435 mm
Track: 54 kg/m UIC 54 rail; new lines, sleepers on concrete; other lines, sleepers on ballast
Electrification: Line 1, 1.5 kV DC, steel third rail; others, 1.2 kV DC; Line 5, rigid catenary; Line 2, rigid catenary; Lines 3 and 4, aluminium third rail

Service: Peak 3–4$\frac{1}{2}$ min
First/last train: 05.00/23.00/02.00 (Friday/Saturday)/24.00 (Sunday)
Fare structure: Flat; multijourney tickets and passes
Revenue collection: AFC
Operating costs financed by: Fares 79.6 per cent, commercial and other sources 4.7 per cent, local, regional and central government subsidy 15.7 per cent
Integration with other modes: Combined metro/bus tickets; integrated metro/FGC tickets; monthly passes also valid on RENFE trains in urban zone
Arrangements for elderly/disabled: Reduced rate or free travel for over 65s according to pension levels; Line 2 fully accessible by street to platform lifts
Automatic control: ATP on Line 4, ATO/ATP on Line 2; automatic traffic regulation

Rolling stock: 488 cars

MTM/Macosa 1000 1 (1970/76)	M100
MTM/Macosa 1000 2 (1974/79)	M108
MTM/Macosa R1300 1 (1982/83)	T25
CAF R1400 2 (1984/86)	T27
CAF/MTM/Macosa 3000 (1986/88)	M72 T18
CAF/MTM/Macosa 4000 (1987)	M96 T24
CAF 2000 (1992)	M12 T6

Line 9 Project (under construction)

Gestió d'Infrastructures SA (GISA)

Carrer Josep Tarradellas 20-30, 1a planta, E-08029, Barcelona, Spain
Tel: (+34 93) 444 44 44
Fax: (+34 93) 419 54 17
e-mail: correu@gisa.es
Web: www.gisa.es

Background

Barcelona's Line 9 will be a fully automated system, 41.4 km long, with 43 stations, and will connect with RENFE and FGC services. The estimate for the total cost of the project is in the region of EUR1,700 million.

GISA is the consortium responsible for the project construction. The new line has been under construction since 2002 and passenger operations are scheduled to start in 2005, as stages are completed. The complete line is due to be completed by 2008.

Current situation

Siemens Transportation Systems (TS) has been contracted to supply the train protection and operational control system. The contract is valued at EUR72.5 million.

ALSTOM is supplying 250 metro cars for the new line.

Metro/light rail (Line 11)
Current situation

In December 2003, the new light rail Line 11, running from Trinitat Nova to Can Cuiàs, opened. It is 2.1 km long with five stations.

Funicular/cable lift/other services
Current situation

The Montjuïc funicular is 759 m in length (480 m in tunnel) and was rebuilt in 1992. It has a capacity of 8,000 passengers/h per direction. The Tramvia Blau is a 1.4 km route, operating with a fleet of seven vehicles, which provides service to the foot of the funicular.

The Montjuïc cable car (Teleferico de Montjuïc), which is mainly a tourist service linking to the funicular, is 836 m in length and has a capacity of 1,200 passengers/h per direction. It carries some 0.4 million passengers a year. Both operate summer only, and at weekends and public holidays.

TMB also manages a tourist bus service over two routes, using open-top double-deck buses.

Bilbao

Population: City: 354,000, metropolitan area: 947,000 (estimates)

Public transport

Most bus services provided by urban transport company, while separate company operates metro. Suburban rail lines operated by local government-controlled authority (Euskotren), state railways RENFE (broad-gauge) and FEVE (narrow-gauge).

Consorcio de Transportes de Bizkaia (CTB) – Biscay Transport Consortium

Ugasko, 5 bis, 1ª planta, E-48014 Bilbao, Spain
Tel: (+34 94) 476 61 50   Fax: (+34 94) 475 00 21
e-mail: partzuergoa@cotrabi.com
Web: www.cotrabi.com

Key personnel

Managing Director: Juan Cruz Nieves

Current situation

In 1975 the Bizkaia regional government founded the Consorcio de Transportes de Bizkaia (CTB) to supervise and implement the construction of the metro in Bilbao, including the infrastructure, equipment and rolling stock, and to manage the operation of the metro, via Metro Bilbao SA, a public limited company.

The consortium comprises representatives from the Basque government, the Biscay provincial government, the Bilbao city council, and other city councils that control areas through which the Bilbao Metropolitan Railway runs.

Line 1 of the Metro opened in 1995, Line 2 in 2002 and the final phase of Line 2 is currently under construction.

The consortium is currently carrying out the following functions: it co-ordinates the adoption of measures regarding the gradual restructuring of public transport in Biscay with the various institutions and carriers, such as uniform ticketing, Creditrans, common zoning and various fare policy measures; it is responsible for the design and co-ordination of the uniform ticketing, Creditrans, and is charged with issuing and managing it; it carries out research studies and analyses such as the annual reports on Public Passenger Transport and the studies on monitoring transportation in Biscay.

Transportes Colectivos sa (TC)

Francisco Macía 4, 2°, E-48014 Bilbao, Spain
Tel: (+34 94) 448 40 70, 80   Fax: (+34 94) 448 40 77
e-mail: tcsa@tcbilbao.com
Web: www.tcbilbao.com

Passenger journeys: (2006) 43.3 million (Bilbobus 27.3 million, Bizkaibus 16.0 million)
Vehicle-km: (2006) 14.6 million (Bilbobus 6.2 million, Bizkaibus 8.4 million)

Current situation

TC operates the Bilbobus (urban) (www.bilbao.net) and Bizkaibus (suburban) bus (www.bizkaia.net) networks.

Bus

Number of routes: 40 (Bilbobus), 37 (Bizkaibus)
Route length: Not currently available

Fleet: 274 vehicles
Full breakdown of fleet is not currently available, but comprises:
Urban fleet (Bilbobus)   144
Suburban fleet (Bizkaibus)   130

Fare collection: Creditrans pre-paid card; Public Transport Cards discount cards (red for those over 65 and/or some disabled passengers and grey for unemployed, retired passengers under 65, basic income earners and some disabled passengers), due to be replaced by the Gizatrans card
Arrangements for elderly/disabled: See above

Eusko Trenbideak – Ferrocarriles Vascos SA (Euskotren) (ET/FV)

Calle Atxuri 6, E-48006 Bilbao, Spain
Tel: (+34 94) 401 99 00   Fax: (+34 94) 401 99 01
e-mail: attcliente@euskotren.es
Web: www.euskotren.es

Key personnel

President: Nuria López Guereñu
Managing Director: Julián Eraso
Directors:
   Operations: Augustín Menoyo Barcena
   Infrastructure: José Antonio Gorostiza Emparanza
   Corporate: Silvia Gómez Santos
   Commercial: Rubén C Hidalgo González
   Communications and Innovation: Irune Elorriaga Urkijo
   Staff: 989 (2006) (All operations)

Passenger journeys: (All modes)
(2005) 25.6 million

Background

Operation of the electrified 1,000 mm gauge railway system in the Basque provinces of Bizkaia (Vizcaya) and Gipuzkoa (Guipúzcoa) was devolved from FEVE to the Basque autonomous community in 1979. ET/FV was created in 1982 and adopted the EuskoTren brand in 1996. EuskoTren remains in public ownership, controlled by the Department for Transport and Public Works of the Basque government, and operates several modes of public transport, along with freight services, branded EuskoKargo, in collaboration with FEVE. A separate public company, Euskal Trenbide Sarea, oversees construction and maintenance of transport infrastructure in the autonomous community.

A strategic plan, EuskoTren XXI, was launched in 2001. Its principal aims were to increase the number of annual passenger journeys to 39 million by 2012. To implement the plan, a new organisational structure was created in October 2002. An operations business unit responsible for all passenger services, freight, logistics and maintenance, sits alongside separate divisions for infrastructure, corporate services (including personnel, IT, marketing and purchasing), commercial services, and communications and innovation. At the beginning of 2006 EuskoTren employed 989 people.

Current situation

EuskoTren operates rail services over the following lines: Bilbao Atxuri to Bermeo; Bilbao Atxuri to Donostia (San Sebastián) Amara. An hourly through service operates from 06.00 with a typical journey time of 2 hours 39 minutes. A limited-stop service (fastest journey time 2 hours 10 minutes) runs twice daily in each direction calling at Bolueta, Durango, Eibar and Zarautz; Deusto (Duesto) to Lezama; and between Lasarte Oria and Hendaia (Hendaya) via Amara and Irún.

EuskoTren also operates the Larreineta-Escontrilla funicular railway and 12 local bus services in Bizkaia and 10 in Gipuzkoa.

For further information on rail operations, please see *Jane's World Railways.*

EuskoTran

Web: www.euskotren.es/euskotran/flash.html

Type of operation: Tramway, opened 2002

Passenger journeys: (2003) 1.14 million
(2004) 2.19 million
(2005) 2.82 million
(2006) 2.94 million

Number of lines: 1
Route length: 5 km
Number of stops: 12
Gauge: 1,000 mm

Current situation

EuskoTran operates 168 tram services daily in Bilbao over the 5 km between Atxuri and Basurto, running at 10 minute intervals (12 minute on Sundays and holidays). An extension from San Mamés to Basurto opened in July 2004. Two further stops were provided and an eighth tram introduced.

Developments

A further extension to EuskoTran in Bilbao from Basurto to La Plaza Rekalde will provide three new stops. The EUR7.5 million cost of the project will be shared by the local administration in Bilbao (35 per cent) and the Basque government (65 per cent).

Plans include the investment of EUR172 million in the development of tramway/light rail in seven urban areas, including a 7.6 km tramway built at a cost of EUR66 million to be operated by EuskoTran for Vitoria-Gasteiz. Other projects include reinstatement of the tramway between Irún and Hondarríbia (Fuenterrabia), the site of Donostia airport, and others at Leioa and Deba.

Fleet: 8 trams
CAF low-floor 5-car LRVs   8

First/last tram: 06.33/23.45 (weekdays), 07.33/23.45 (Saturday, Sunday and Holidays)
Fare structure: Flat; cash or Creditrans pre-paid card; Single, Bono 10 Reduced, DayTicket, Weekend Ticket, Combined tickets with EuskoTren; children under 5 travel free
Fare collection: Automated Ticket Machines (ATMs) at stops; cancellation prior to boarding
Arrangements for elderly/disabled: Access at platform level
Integration with other modes: Connections to Metro, RENFE, EuskoTren, FEVE and bus services
Surveillance: CCTV on all vehicles

Rail

Type of operation: Suburban rail

Passenger journeys: (2005) 17.8 million
Train-km: Not currently available

Fleet: 4 electric and 2 diesel locomotives, 53 electric multiple-units
On order: Some EUR36 million has been earmarked for a fleet of up to 12 diesel-electric locomotives for delivery in stages over a 10-year period

Metro Bilbao SA

Navarra 2, E-48001 Bilbao, Spain
Tel: (+34 94) 425 40 00
Fax: (+34 94) 425 40 39
e-mail: info@metrobilbao.net
Web: www.metrobilbao.com

Key personnel

Managing Director: Rafael Sarria
Operating Manager: José Miguel Ortega
   Staff: 641 (2007)

Type of operation: Full metro; opened 1995

Passenger journeys: (2003) 72.6 million
(2004) 73.1 million
(2005) 77.8 million
(2006) 79.78 million
(2007) 85.86 million

Route length: 74.42 km (35.51 km double-track, 3.40 km single-track)
Number of lines: 2
Number of stations: 36
Gauge: 1,000 mm
Electrification: 1.5 kV DC, overhead

Rolling stock: 148 cars

CAF/ABB Series 500 (1995)	M48 T48
CAF/Bombardier Series 550 (2002)	M26 T26

Service interval: Peak 2.5 min
First/last train: 06.00/23.00 (Saturday – 24-hour service; Friday until 02.00)
Fare structure: Zonal; Creditrans tickets and passes
Integration with other modes: Part of integrated transport authority in Bizkaia
Signalling: ATO/ATP

Current situation
Bilbao's first metro line, linking Plentzia and Casco Viejo, was opened in 1995 following transfer of the 20.5 km Plentzia line from ET/FV. This has been linked to a new 5 km city-centre tunnel to create metro Line 1.

The first stage of Line 2, between San Inazio and Urbinaga, was opened in April 2002.

Developments
The second stage of Line 2, between Urbinaga and Sestao, and the Line 1 extension between Bolueta and Etxebarri were opened in January 2005.

The third stage of Line 2, a 1.9 km extension with two stations, between Sestao and Portugalete was opened in January 2007.

There is a further extension to Line 2 underway – 3.5 km with three stations, from Portugalete to Kabiezes.

Line 1 extension Etxebarri to Basauri is now due to open in 2010; Line 2 Portugalete to Santurtzi in 2008 and Santurtzi to Kabiezes in 2009.

Ferrocarriles de Vía Estrecha (FEVE) – Spanish Narrow Gauge Railways

General Rodrigo 6, E-28003 Madrid, Spain
Tel: (+34 91) 453 38 00   Fax: (+34 91) 453 38 25
e-mail: info@feve.es
Web: www.feve.es

Key personnel
Manager, Press Relations: Miguel Ángel Ramos

Current situation
An hourly/half-hourly suburban service operates between Bilbao Concordia and Balmaseda (32 km, 18 stations), electrified 1.5 kV.

Red Nacional de los Ferrocarriles Españoles (RENFE) – Spanish National Railways

Corporate Communications and External Relations Department
Avenida Pio XII n° 110, Edif Caracola 16, E-28036 Madrid, Spain
Tel: (+34 91) 300 66 00
Fax: (+34 91) 300 73 36
e-mail: comunicacion@renfe.es
cercanias@renfe.es
Web: www.renfe.com

Key personnel
Director, Bilbao: Angel Ibañez García
  Staff: 310 (Bilbao area only)

Other offices

Bilbao Office
Plaza Circular, 2-3er piso, E-48008 Bilbao, Spain
Tel: (+34 94) 423 86 23
e-mail: clienetebilbao@renfe.es

Head Office
Avendia Ciudad de Barcelona 8, E-28007 Madrid, Spain
Tel: (+34 91) 506 61 27
Fax: (+34 91) 506 69 39

Type of operation: Suburban heavy rail

Passenger journeys: (Total for Suburban Business Unit)
(2002) 439.6 million
(2003) 446 million

Current situation
RENFE operates suburban trains from Abando station to Santurzi and San Julian de Musques. Bilbao is RENFE's third busiest suburban network. Total 67 km, 1,668 mm gauge, on three routes with 43 stations; electrified 3 kV DC.

For further information on this company, please see *Jane's World Railways*.

Developments
The Musques and Santurzi services were rerouted over a freight line (the Southern Variant) into Abando station.

Rolling stock: 22 three-car emus

Class 446	M44 T22

Madrid
Population: Municipality 3.2 million (2005 estimate)

Public transport
The Consorcio Regional de Transportes de Madrid (CRTM) has overall responsibility for public transport in the autonomous region of Madrid, which includes the city and surrounding conurbation. Main bus services provided by a municipal undertaking, while the metro is jointly owned by the municipality and the region and operated under a concession from CR TM. Suburban rail services run by Spanish National Railways (RENFE); some private suburban bus operations.

Consorcio Regional de Transportes de Madrid (CRTM)

Plaza Descubridor Diego de Ordás 3, E-28003 Madrid, Spain
Tel: (+34 91) 580 45 31   Fax: (+34 91) 580 46 34
e-mail: carlos.cristobal@ctm-comadrid.com
Web: www.ctm-madrid.es

Key personnel
General Manager: José Manuel Pradillo
Studies and Planning: Carlos Cristóbal
Intermodality and Concessions: Javier Aldecoa Dionisio González
Technical Innovations and I&D: Antonio Rubio
Fare Policy: Ms Carmen Sanz
  Staff: Not currently available

Passenger journeys: 1,623.0 million (2006, all modes under CRTM)

Background
Since its creation in 1985, Consorcio Regional de Transportes de Madrid (CRTM), the Public Transport Authority (PTA) for the Madrid Greater region (Comunidad de Madrid), has considered the integration of the different modes of public transport to be a high-priority objective in its functions:

- Planning of infrastructures and services;
- Pricing framework and multi-trip tickets;
- The image of the public transport system and information relating to it.

CRTM's Board includes representatives from central, regional and local Government authorities, trades unions, bus operators and users' associations.

Current situation
Transport modes, as at May 2007, in the Madrid Region include:
- Metro: 12 lines, plus a shuttle line, 282 network-km, 231 network-stations;
- Urban buses in Madrid city: 209 lines, 3,445 line-km, 10,430 line-stops;
- Suburban buses: 328 lines, 19,285 line-km, 16,056 line-stops;
- Urban buses in other municipalities: 120 lines, 1,690 line-km, 3,864 line-stops;
- Suburban railways: 9 lines, 339 network-km, 97 network-stations;
- Light rail: 4 lines, 36 network-km, 47 network-stations.

CRTM, as PTA, maintains contractual agreements with public/private operators. This may take the form of own-risk operation, contracted price or management contract.

Monthly or annual travel cards, used by 64 per cent of public transport passengers, are issued, along with other heavily discounted fares for students and the elderly.

Developments
The Regional Government of Madrid continues to develop the regional public transport system. Between 2003 and 2007 more than 80 km of new lines have been built, including conventional underground metro and light rail systems, with the following priorities:
- Extension of the metro network to peripheral areas of Madrid that are poorly served by existing services, such as La Elipa, Villaverde, Carabanchel, Alameda de Osuna, Manoteras and Pinar de Chamartín;

- Connection with municipalities adjoining Madrid that are important residential and employment areas, such as Alcobendas, San Sebastián de los Reyes, Coslada and San Fernando de Henares;
- Construction of three new light-rail lines, some 28 km in length, for the western municipalities of Pozuelo de Alarcón and Boadilla del Monte and the new residential areas of Sanchinarro and Las Tablas in the north of Madrid city. All the lines link up with different stations of the metro network or suburban railway.
- Parla municipality and the CRTM have opened the first section of an 8 km tramway.

In addition, CRTM is constructing various peripheral interchanges, located at the intersection between the border of the city centre and its seven main radial corridors. In 2004 CRTM drafted the specifications for public tender regarding the construction works, maintenance and operation of four new large transport interchanges. Two of these, Plaza Elíptica and Príncipe Pío, are already in service and the others, Moncloa and Plaza de Castilla, will open shortly. All are included within the 2004–2007 Interchanges Plan.

The total budget for these four intermodal centres is around EUR300 million, with quality and safety requirements regulated through the Operation and Maintenance Programme, suitably incorporated into the concession contracts.

In order to fulfil the Operation and Maintenance Programme's objective of providing a high-quality service to the end user (interchange building and access management, facilities and equipment supervision and control, traffic management, safety and security issues), CRTM is implementing a common Integrated Management System to monitor in real time all the new interchanges.

The next Plan 2007–2011 of the Regional Government includes the following actions:
- Extension of the metro network to residential neighbourhoods in the north of Madrid called Mirasierra (Line 9), in the east part to Las Rosas (Line 2), in the southwest to another municipality, Leganés, called La Fortuna (Line 11), and to El Casar in Getafe (Line 3) to connect with the

commuter railway and MetroSur network. The total length of all the extensions is 13 km;

- Two new lines of light rail (14 km total length), one of them in the northwest of the region, from Puerta de Hierro Hospital to Majadahonda and Las Rozas, and the other one will be an urban line in Valdemoro to link the railway station with the new hospital in that municipality;
- A major action to implement five BRT systems in the metropolitan context with more than 38 km total length, consisting of new bus-only platforms that are called Metrobús;
- A new commuter railway line (14.5 km), from Móstoles to Navalcarnero under a concession system.

Empresa Municipal de Transportes de Madrid SA (EMT de Madrid SA)

C/Cerro de la Plata 4, E-28007 Madrid, Spain
Tel: (+34 91) 406 88 00   Fax: (+34 91) 406 88 01
e-mail: secretaria@emtmadrid.es
Web: www.emtmadrid.es

Key personnel
President: Pedro Calvo Poch
Director Gerente: Javier Conde Londoño
Director Adjunto: Francisco Félix González García
Director, Economics/Financial: José Ángel Rivero Menéndez
Director, Marketing: José Luis de Bustos Miguel
Director, Human Resources: Juan Antonio Garrido Ramiro
Director, Rolling Stock and Infrastructure: Juan Ángel Terrón Alonso
Director, Technology and Quality: Arturo Manuel Martínez Ginestal
Director, Sustainability and Corporate Responsibility: José Luis Molinero Calvo
Sub-Director, Operations: Luis María Álvarez Vázquez
Sub-Director, Projects and Installations: Félix Cabezón López
Staff: 7,634 (December 2007)

Current situation
EMT was formed in 1971 as a limited liability company (Sociedad Anónima), to take over service provision from the former private operator. The company operates urban buses in the Madrid municipality and is also responsible for parking administration in central Madrid.

Bus
Passenger boardings: (2004) 476 million
(2005) 474 million
(2006) 491 million
(2007) 455 million
Vehicle-km: (2004) 96.8 million
(2005) 97.5 million
(2006) 99.9 million
(2007) 97.1 million

Number of routes: 208
Route length: (One way) 1,864.8 km
On priority right-of-way: 94 km

Fleet: 2,033 vehicles
Diesel
Iveco CityClass low-floor (1998, 2000/07)	392
MAN 14220 HOCL low-floor (1998/99)	66
MAN NG/313-F articulated low-floor (2001, 2002, 2004)	26
MAN NL low-floor (1997/98)	7
MAN NL/273-F low-floor (2006)	1
Mercedes-Benz O/405N-N2 low-floor (1995/96/97/98)	107
Mercedes-Benz O/530 Citaro low-floor (2000/03, 2006)	1
Scania N-94/UB Omnicity low-floor (2001/06)	185
Scania N-95/UA articulated low-floor (2006)	1
Volvo B9L low-floor (2007)	1

Biodiesel
Iveco CityClass low-floor (1998, 2000/07)	258
MAN 14220 HOCL low-floor (1998/99)	57
MAN NL low-floor (1997/98)	41
MAN NL/263-F low-floor (2001/05)	182
MAN NL/313-F Airport low-floor (2001)	6
MAN NG/313-F articulated low-floor (2001/02, 2004)	55

Tecnobus Gulliver low-floor electric minibus 1344144

Mercedes-Benz O/530 Cit-CNG low-floor bus 1344141

Mercedes-Benz O/530 Citaro low-floor (2000/03, 2006)	117
Renault City Line low-floor (2000/01)	106
Renault Citybus low-floor (1998)	40

Diesel-electric
Mercedes-Benz O/520 Cito low-floor (2000/01)	20

CNG
Iveco CityClass CNG-powered low-floor (1998, 2002/07)	236
MAN NL/233-F CNG-powered low-floor (2001)	20
MAN NL/313-F CNG-powered low-floor (2002/03, 2007)	60
Mercedes-Benz O/530 Cit-CNG low-floor (2007)	35

Electric
Tecnobus Gulliver low-floor (2007)	8

Ethanol
Scania L-094/UB ethanol low-floor (2006)	5
In peak service: 1,832	

Average age of fleet: 5.7 years

On order: Iveco CityClass CNG-powered low-floor: 30
Iveco CityClass low-floor: 52
MAN NL/273-F low-floor: 36
MAN NG/313-F articulated low-floor: 4
Scania N270 UB4: 52
Mercedes-Benz O/530 Citaro low-floor: 27
Tecnobus Gulliver low-floor: 12

Most intensive service: Peak 2–6 min, off-peak 4–12 min
One-person operation: All routes
Fare collection: Prepurchase 10-journey tickets validated on board or pass, or payment to driver
Fare structure: Flat; pre-purchase 'Metrobús' 10-journey tickets, monthly and annual CRTM passes cover urban/suburban buses and rail

Fares collected on board: 6.26 per cent (65.72 per cent use CRTM travelcards, 34.10 per cent EMT passes and 10-trip tickets)
Fare evasion control: Roving inspectors; minimal fraud attributed to widespread use of discounted travelcards
Operational control: Inspectors/14 mobile radio cars/NT SAE
Arrangements for elderly/disabled: 100 per cent of buses are low-floor (90 per cent of these buses include ramps to facilitate boarding and travel for disabled people)
Average peak-hour speed: 13.95 km/h
Bus priority: Extensive system of central area bus lanes totalling 18.16 km solely for buses, 75.66 km also available for taxis (39 km with physical separator)
Operating costs financed by: Fares 63.6 per cent, subsidy/grants 30.8 per cent, other commercial sources 5.6 per cent

Developments
Alternative energies
EMT has introduced five bio-ethanol vehicles (Madrid is one of the cities participating in the BEST Project) and eight electric minibuses to its fleet. The number of bio-diesel buses in the fleet has been increased to 882 vehicles at the end of 2007.

Accessibility
EMT's fleet of buses is 100 per cent low-floor. In order to improve bus accessibility systems, EMT has developed the Sistema Embarcado de Información Acústica (SIENA) Project to offer audio service information on-board buses and at bus stops.

Metro de Madrid SA

Cavanilles 58, E-28007 Madrid, Spain
Tel: (+34 91) 379 88 00
Fax: (+34 91) 379 89 97
Web: www.metromadrid.es

Key personnel
Chairman: Manuel Melis Maynar
Delegated Advisor: Ramón Aguirre
General Manager: Ildefonso de Matías Jiménez
Assistant Director, External Relations: Miguel
  Otamendi Pineda
Technical Co-ordinator of Operations: Emiliano
  Durán Sánchez
  Staff: 5,691

Type of operation: Full metro, first line opened 1919

Passenger journeys: (2002) 564 million
(2003) 601 million
(2004) 615.5 million
(2005) 644 million
Car-km: (2003) 148.6 million
(2004) 154.9 million
(2005) 154.4 million

Route length: 287.6 km
  in tunnel: Not currently available
Number of lines: 13 (1 light rail)*
Number of stations: 288
Gauge: 1,445 mm
Track: 45 kg/m rail (4%), 54 kg/m rail (96%)
Max gradient: 5%
Min curve radius: 90 m
Tunnel: Mostly bored
Electrification: 600 V DC, overhead, 1,500 V DC –
Lines 8, 10 and 12
*The part of Line 9, some 19 km in length, which is
outside the municipality of Madrid, is operated by
the concession Transportes Ferroviarios de Madrid
(TFM).

Developments
Other metro expansions currently planned for
2007–2011 include:
Line 2: La Ecipa-La Fortuna;
Line 3: Villaverde Alto-El Casar (2.8 km);
Line 7: Henares-San Fernando (Hospital de
Coslada) (one station) (2007);
(early 2007);
Line 9 TFM: New station Rivas Futura (December
2007) and Herrera Oria-Mirasierra (2 km);
Line 11: La Pesta-la Fortuna (one station, under
construction);
    The consortium of CAF/Bombardier/Siemens
will manufacture 432 Series 3000 (narrow gauge)
and 14 Series 8000 cars and Ansaldobreda will
produce 252 Series 9000 cars. All of the new
stock will be dual-voltage.
    Bombardier Transportation received an order
for its *Mitrac™* propulsion system for 90 new
metro trainsets (432 metro cars in total) and
14 intermediate cars. The order is valued at
approximately GBP37 million (EUR56 million).
Deliveries are due to take place between November
2005 and August 2007. The new trainsets are
36 Series S3000, sub-series 1, and 54 S3000, sub-
series 3. The first of these trains will be used on
Line 3. The intermediate motor cars are for the
existing S8000 series.
    In late 2006/early 2007, the following extensions
were opened: Line 1: Plaza Castilla to Pinar de
Chamartin (3.1 km, three stations) and Line 1:
Congosto to Valdecarros (3 km, three stations);
Line 2: Ventas to La Elipa (1.2 km, one station);
Line 3: Legazpi to Villaverde Alto (7.5 km, seven
stations); Line 4: Parque Santa Maria to Pinar
de Chamartin (2.3 km, three stations); Line 5:
Canillejas to Alameda de Osuna (2 km, two
stations); Line 6: New station at Planetario; Line 7:
Las Musas-Henares (seven stations); Line 8:
Barajas-Aeropuerto T-4 (2.2 km, one station) and
new station Pinar del Rey; Line 10: Fuencarral-
Tres Olivos-Alcobendas-San Sebastián de los
Reyes (Hospital del Norte) (15.7 km, eleven
stations); Line 10: New station Aviación Española;
Line 11: Pan Bendito to La Peseta (3.1 km, three
stations).

In May 2007, the light rail line ML1, Pinar de
Chamartin-Las Tablas (5.4 km, nine stations),
opened. This line is operated by Metros Ligeros
de Madrid SA (www.melimadrid.es), a subsidiary
of Metro de Madrid SA. The line is operated with
Citadis trams.

Service: Peak 2–3 min, off-peak 4–6 min, after 24.00
15 min
First/last train: 06.00/01.30
Fare structure: Single and 10-journey tickets
(Metro-bus), day and 2-day passes; CRTM monthly
and annual travelcards integrated with urban and
suburban buses, and suburban railways
One-person operation: All lines
Signalling: ATP on all lines, ATO on all lines
Surveillance: CCTV at all stations, being introduced
on trains
Operating costs financed by: Fares 45 per cent,
CRTM grants 41.3 per cent and other commercial
sources 13.7 per cent

Rolling stock: 1,556 cars

CAF 5000 (1974/94)	352
CAF 2000 (1984/94)	718
CAF/Alstom/Siemens/Adtranz 6000 (1998/99)	123
Series 7000	222
Series 8000	141

On order: 432 Series 3000 (narrow gauge) and
14 Series 8000 CAF/Bombardier/Siemens cars,
252 Series 9000 Ansaldobreda cars

Metroeste Ligero SA

Cocheras Metro Ligero, Ciudad de la Imagen, E-
28223 Pozuelo de Alarcón, Madrid, Spain
Tel: (+34 902) 28 26 56
Web: www.metroligero-oeste.es

Developments
In May 2007, lines ML2 and ML3 opened. Line ML2
Estación de Aravaca-Colonia Jardín is 8.7 km
long with 13 stations (three in tunnel) and line
ML3 Puerta de Boadilla-Colonia Jardín is 13.7 km
long with 15 stataions (one in tunnel).
    These lines are operated by Metro Ligero
Oeste SA (www.metroligero-oeste.es) with new
Citadis trams. All stations are accessible.
    There are plans for a new line Puerta de Hierro-
Majadahonda-Las Rozas (10 km).

Red Nacional de los
Ferrocarriles Españoles (RENFE) –
Spanish National Railways

Corporate Communications and External
Relations Department
Avenida Pio XII n° 110, Edif Caracola 16, E-28036
Madrid, Spain
Tel: (+34 91) 300 66 00   Fax: (+34 91) 300 73 36
e-mail: comunicacion@renfe.es
    cercanias@renfe.es
Web: www.renfe.com

Key personnel
Director, Madrid: Cecilio Gömez Comino
    Staff: 1,349

Other offices
Madrid office
Avenida Ciudad de Barcelona 8 3a, Planta,
E-28007 Madrid, Spain
Tel: (+34 91) 328 90 20; 506 69 69
Fax: (+34 91) 506 63 67

Head office
Avenida Ciudad de Barcelona 8, E-28007 Madrid,
Spain
Tel: (+34 91) 506 61 27   Fax: (+34 91) 506 69 39

Type of operation: Suburban heavy rail

Passenger journeys: (Total for Suburban Business
Unit)
(2002) 439.6 million
(2003) 446 million

Current situation
Suburban services are operated on 10 routes
or groups of routes totalling 278 km with

118 stations, from terminals at Príncipe Pío,
Atocha and Chamartin, the last two linked by a
cross-city tunnel; 1,668 mm gauge, electrified
3 kV DC overhead (except for one line, 19 km,
metre-gauge, electrified 1.5 kV DC overhead).
Most trains run half-hourly off-peak, but average
10 minutes in the peak, when some inner-
suburban sections have metro-style service.
    For further information on this company,
please see *Jane's World Railways.*

Developments
In mid-2003, work began on a project to build
a new tunnel in Madrid for suburban services
between Atocha and Charmartin. The project will
be carried out in three stages and new stations
will be built at Puerta del Sol-Gran Via and Alonso
Martinez.

Rolling stock: 696 emu cars

Class 440 three-car emu	M21 T42
Class 446 three-car emu	M286 T143
Class 470 three-car emu	M24 T48
Class 450 six-car bilevel emu	M40 T80
Class 442 two-car emu metre-gauge	M6 T6

Madrid
Private bus
Passenger journeys: (2002) 277.8 million

Current situation
A total of 33 private operators provide monopoly
services, either urban routes in the outer
municipalities or interurban within the conurbation.
All services are co-ordinated by CRTM.
    The management bodies for suburban buses
are:

Federación Nacional
Empresarial de Transporte en
Autobús (Fenebús)

Orense 20, E-28007 Madrid, Spain
Tel: (+34 91) 555 20 93/94
Fax: (+34 91) 555 20 95
e-mail: info@fenebus.es
Web: www.fenebus.es

Key personnel
Managing Director: J Luis Pertierra

Federación Española
Empresarial de Transportes de
Viajeros (Asintra)

Hermosilla 30, 5° Izda, E-28001 Madrid, Spain
Tel: (+34 91) 431 98 64
Fax: (+34 91) 431 24 17
e-mail: f.asintra@asintra.org
Web: www.asintra.org

Key personnel
Managing Director: Lorenzo Chácon

Number of routes: 186 suburban, 7 night and 45
urban (in municipalities other than Madrid)
Route length: (One way) 14,436 km

Fleet: 958 vehicles

Pegaso	447
Scania	263
Setra	16
Volvo	209
Others	23

Average age of fleet: 5.6 years

Most intensive service: 3 min
One-person operation: All routes
Fare structure: Zonal or distance-based, according
to route; CRTM monthly and annual travelcards
integrated with urban and suburban buses, and
suburban rail
Fare collection: Driver sells single tickets;
prepurchase 10-journey tickets, CRTM travelcards
Bus priority: 12.5 km exclusive bus and HOV
double lanes in northwest corridor, also 4 km bus-
only lane
Operating costs financed by: Fares 100 per cent

Malaga

Population: 535,686 (2002 estimate)

Public transport

Local bus and midibus services provided by municipal company, with longer-distance services to neighbouring resorts in the hands of private operators; local rail service; first two lines of light rail network approved.

Empresa Malagueña de Transportes SAM (EMT) – Malaga Transport Company

Camino de San Rafael 97, E-29006 Malaga, Spain
Tel: (+34 952) 36 72 00 Fax: (+34 952) 36 72 07
e-mail: info@emtsam.net
Web: www.emtsam.es

Key personnel
President: Javier Berlanga Fernández
Vice-President: Juan Ramón Casero Dominguez
Managing Director: Miguel Ruiz Montañez
Director of Operations: Manual Fernandez Andrade
 Staff: 605

Background
Owned by Malaga City Council, Empresa Malagueña de Transportes SAM (EMT) is responsible for the management of urban transport in the city.

Developments
The company has introduced contactless smartcards.

Bus
Passenger journeys: (1996) 34.7 million
Vehicle-km: (1996) 8.5 million

Number of routes: 35
Route length: 238 km

Fleet: 201 buses (as at July 2002)	
Pegaso 6424 (1991/93)	31
Pegaso 5317 midibus (1990/91/92)	20
Iveco City Class articulated	2
Iveco 623E2 (1996)	21
Iveco 490	1
Iveco 59.12 microbus	4
Renault City Bus articulated	15
Renault Citybus	62
Volvo B10M articulated (1997/98)	10
Mercedes O405N62 articulated	25
Others	10

Average age of fleet: 6.3 years

Most intensive service: 10 min
Fare structure: Flat
Fare collection: Single, multitravel (10 trips), monthly and student passes
Fares collected on board: 31.1 per cent
Arrangements for elderly/disabled: Pensioners travel free; Special Route 48 operated for disabled; some 50 per cent of the fleet is ramp-equipped
Operating costs financed by: Fares 64.6 per cent, other commercial sources 1.6 per cent, subsidy/grants 33.8 per cent

Pegaso of EMT on Route 24 to Prados at Arroyo del Cuarto (Bill Luke)

0045310

Red Nacional de los Ferrocarriles Españoles (RENFE) – Spanish National Railways

Corporate Communications and External Relations Department
Avenida Pio XII nº 110, Edif Caracola 16, E-28036 Madrid, Spain
Tel: (+34 91) 300 66 00   Fax: (+34 91) 300 73 36

Key personnel
Director, Malaga: Rafael Rodríguez Rebollo
 Staff: 122 (Malaga area)

Other officess
Malaga office
Estación de Málaga, E-29002 Malaga, Spain
Tel: (+34 91) 952 36 02 02; 12 80 70

Head office
Avenida Ciudad de Barcelona 8, E-28007 Madrid, Spain
Tel: (+34 91) 506 61 27   Fax: (+34 91) 506 69 39

Type of operation: Local railway

Passenger journeys: (1996) 7 million

Current situation
Electric trains (3 kV DC) run half-hourly from Malaga Centro-Alameda to Fuengirola and Alora, two routes totalling 68 km with 24 stations. A 30 minute service runs to the airport on the Fuengirola Line, which carries heavy tourist traffic.

Developments
A rolling programme of investment in stations is in progress, including provision of ticket machines and barriers to reduce fraud.

Rolling stock: 6 three-car emus

Junta de Andalucía

Consejería de Obras Públicas y Transportes
Calle Maese Rodrigo 1, E-41071 Seville, Spain
Tel: (+34 955) 05 74 20
Fax: (+34 955) 05 74 65
e-mail: comunica@metrodemalaga.info
Web: www.metrodemalaga.info,
 www.juntadeandalucia.es

Key personnel
Director General, Transport: Rafael Candau Ramila
Assistant Director, Transport: Amparo Solís Sarmiento

Type of operation: Light rail (proposed)

Current situation
In June 2002, the Andalucian government approved the draft design for Line 1 and 2 of the Malaga light rail system. Line 1 will be 7.2 km in length and Line 2 will be 6.4 km long. The cost of the works is estimated at EUR400 million. Some 70 per cent and 16 stations of the two lines will be underground.

 The system, when finished, is due to have five lines with 45 stations and a total length of some 45 km.

Developments
In mid-2004, the 35-year contract for the construction and operation of Lines 1 and 2 was awarded to a consortium led by Fomento de Constructiones y Contratas SA (FCC) and including Azvi, Comsa, Sando, Vera and Cajamar. Work is scheduled to commence in 2005 and the project is due to be completed in 2009.

Seville

Population: City 704,154, metropolitan area 1.3 million (2005 estimates)

Public transport
Bus services provided by municipal authority with some suburban services by private firms; suburban trains run by state railway; light rail (metro) under construction.

Transportes Urbanos de Sevilla SAM (TUSSAM)

Polígono Industrial Carretera Amarilla, Avenida de Andalucía 11, E-41007 Seville, Spain
Tel: (+34 95) 455 72 00; 902 45 99 54
e-mail: clientes@tussam.es
Web: www.tussam.es

TUSSAM Renault Citybus

1135735

Key personnel

President: Alfredo Sánchez Monteseirín
General Director: Carlos Arizaga de Pablo-Blanco
   Staff: 1,519 (as at December 2007)

Current situation

Since September 2002, TUSSAM has been integrated into the Transport Consortium of the Metropolitan Area of Seville, with zonal fare integration.

In December 2002, the company achieved ISO 9001:2000 certification.

Developments

A CNG fuelling station has been installed for up to 200 CNG-powered buses.

Solar panels have been installed at the bus park area.

Bus

Passenger boardings: (2003) 90.1 million
(2004) 89.1 million
(2005) 88.9 million
(2006) 87.4 million
(2007) 85.9 million
Vehicle-km: (2003) 17.2 million
(2004) 17.3 million
(2005) 17.2 million
(2006) 16.9 million
(2007) 17.2 million

Number of routes: 42
Route length: 531.05 km
On priority right-of-way: 12.8 km

Fleet: 399 vehicles

Renault PR100-2 (1990/92)	22
Renault PR112 (1996)	10
Volvo B10L (1996/97)	24
Renault Citybus (1998/99/2001/02)	71
Iveco CityClass (1998/99/2000/04/05)	64
Mercedes-Benz (Micro) (2000)	3
Dennis Dart (2001)	8
Renault Citybus articulated 18 m (2003/04)	32
Iveco Cityclass articulated 18 m (2005)	1
Scania N94 (2005/06)	15
Scania N27 (2006)	1
Irisbus CityClass articulated 18 m (2006/07)	43
Irisbus CityClass CNG (2006/07)	48
Iveco CityClass CNG (2007)	18
Iveco CityClass Euro 4 (2007)	1
MAN NG 363F articulated 18 m (2007)	11
MAN NG 313F/CNG (2007)	20
Gulliver electric vehicle (2007)	2

In peak service: 329
On order: Not currently available
Average age of fleet: 4.69 years

Most intensive service: 4 min
One-person operation: All routes
Fare collection: Onboard ticket machines and magnetic validators; contactless technology being introduced
Fare structure: Flat; pre-purchase 'bono-bus' multi-journey magnetic tickets; magnetic monthly passes
Fares collected on board: 12.4 per cent
Fare evasion control: Inspectors
Operational control: Central radio communication to all vehicles; automatic vehicle location – GPS technology
Arrangements for elderly/disabled: Free annual passes
Average distance between stops: 300 m
Average peak-hour speed: In mixed traffic, 11.56 km/h
Operating costs financed by: Fares 50 per cent, subsidy/grants 50 per cent
Subsidy from: Municipal budget
New vehicles financed by: Leasing

Private bus

Passenger journeys: (2003) 6.2 million
(2004) 6.1 million
(2005) 5.9 million
(2006) 5.7 million
(2007) 4.5 million

Current situation

TUSSAM Renault articulated Citybus   1121525

TUSSAM Irisbus CityClass CNG bus   1324574

TUSSAM Gulliver electric vehicle   1346137

Three suburban routes are run by private firms, controlled by the municipal authority and with the same fare system as TUSSAM.

Light rail (Tranvía – Metro-Centro)

Type of operation: Light rail, first surface section opened 2007

Passenger journeys: n/a
Vehicle-km: n/a

Number of routes: 1
Route length: 1.4 km
   in tunnel: None
Number of stops: 4
Gauge: 1,435 mm
Electrification: 750 V DC, overhead

TUSSAM CAF Tranvía LRV   1346138

Current situation

The first underground line (19 km, 23 stops) is currently under construction, scheduled to commence operations by the end of 2008.

There are longer-term plans for a further three lines in the Tranvía network.

Developments

The first section of surface light rail/tramway has been in operation since November 2007, operated by TUSSAM, on the main avenue in the old centre of the city.

Fleet: 5 LRVs
CAF Tranvía LRV (2007)   5
In peak service: Not currently available
On order: A total of 17 CAF LRVs has been ordered for the Tranvía network

Service: 6 min peak, 10 min off-peak
First/last tram: 06.10/01.45

Red Nacional de los Ferrocarriles Españoles (RENFE) – Spanish National Railways

Corporate Communications and External Relations Department
Avenida Pio XII n° 110, Edif Caracola 16, E-28036 Madrid, Spain
Tel: (+34 91) 300 66 00   Fax: (+34 91) 300 73 36
e-mail: comunicacion@renfe.es
 cercanias@renfe.es
Web: www.renfe.com

Key personnel

Director, Seville: Rafael Rodriguez Rebollo
 Staff: 141 (Seville area)

Other offices

Seville office
Avenida Kansas City, s/n, Estación Santa Justa, E-41007 Valencia, Spain
Tel: (+34 96) 353 71 77

Head office
Avenida Ciudad de Barcelona 8, E-28007 Madrid, Spain
Tel: (+34 91) 506 61 27   Fax: (+34 91) 506 69 39

Type of operation: Suburban heavy rail

Passenger journeys: (Total for Suburban Business Unit)
(2002) 439.6 million
(2003) 446 million

Current situation
Services operate on three routes extending to 134 km with 20 stations.
 For further information on this company, please see *Jane's World Railways*.

Rolling stock: 17 Class 470 three-car emus

Metro de Sevilla

C/ Luis de Morales 32, Edificio Fórum, Local 2-1A, Seville, Spain
Tel: (+34 902) 36 49 85
Web: www.metrodesevilla.net

Type of operation: Light rail (under construction)

Background
Originally, construction began in the 1970s of a three-line metro, but work was halted following the establishment of regional autonomy pending a thorough economic analysis. Some 5 km of tunnel had been completed, linking P Nueva in the city centre with La Plata in the southeast, as well as three unconnected station shells.

Current situation
Metro de Sevilla was formed in 1999 to oversee the development of the Seville Metro, a four-line light rail system with some routes in tunnel.
 Construction on Line 1 (19 km, 23 station) started in 2003, and is scheduled for completion in October 2008.

Valencia (Spain)

Population: City 807,400 (2006 estimate), urban area 1 million, metropolitan area 1.8 million, province 2.3 million (estimates)

Public transport

Urban bus services provided by municipal transport company; suburban services by Consorcio Municipal de Transportes and other private companies. Suburban rail, light rail and bus services operated by FGV regional railway upgraded with cross-city link. Other suburban services by State Railway.

Empresa Municipal de Transportes de Valencia SA (EMT Valencia)

Plaza Correo Viejo No 5, E-46001 Valencia, Spain
Tel: (+34 96) 315 85 00   Fax: (+34 96) 392 49 98
e-mail: emt@emtvalencia.es
Web: www.emtvalencia.es

Key personnel

Director General: Jesús Herrero
Head of Quality: José A Moncho
Head of Press/Communications: Julia López
Technical Director: José Luis Martínez
Operations Director: José M Mainez
Finance Director: Diego Navarrete
Commercial Director: Marcos Pérez
Human Resources Director: Andrés Bernabé
 Staff: 1,627 (2007)

Current situation

In 1986, EMT replaced the former municipal operator SALTUV, becoming the licensee for city bus operations. EMT serves the municipalities of

Alboraia, Burjassot, Mislata, Tavernes Blanques, Vinalesa and Xirivella.

Developments

One of the objectives of the company is that the fleet of buses works with alternative energies. Currently, the fleet incorporates biofuel, natural gas and electric buses. EMT is also taking part in European projects Life Medio Ambiente (Ecobus and Urbanbat), which pioneer techniques and methods in development and implementation related to the environment and sustainable development.

Bus

Passenger journeys: (2003) 103.2 million
(2004) 101 million
(2005) 102.8 million
(2006) 103.6 million
(2007) 102.6 million
Vehicle-km: (2003) 22 million
(2004) 21.5 million
(2005) 21.5 million
(2006) 21.3 million
(2007) 20.8 million

EMT bus   1097459

EMT bus   1097457

Number of routes: 58 (including 9 night routes, 4 special routes and paratransit services)
Number of stops: 1,111
Route length: 874.9 km

Developments
The fleet total has remained the same for years, with vehicles being replaced by more modern and environmentally friendly vehicles to reduce the average age of the fleet from 7.12 years in 2006 to 6.33 years in 2007.

Fleet: 480 vehicles

Renault R312	41
Renault Citybus	180
Mercedes-Benz O-405-N2	56
Mercedes-Benz Citaro	22
Scania	81
Iveco Cityclass CNG	45
Irisbus/Iveco	15
Van Hool AG 300 articulated	8
MAN 11190	1
Irisbus Európolis	3
Dennis Dart SLF	4
MAN NL 243 F/CNG	25

In peak service: 402
On order: 40 a year
Average age of fleet: 6.33 years

Most intensive service: 4 min
One-person operation: All routes
Fare collection: Payment to driver or pre-purchase
Fares collected on board: 16 per cent (approximate)
Fare structure: Flat; single ticket, bonobus, pre-purchase and B10 10-journey tickets; monthly passes
Arrangements for elderly/disabled: Discounted annual passes for unlimited travel; special door-to-door service at normal fares
Operating costs financed by: Fares 46.9 per cent, other commercial sources 4.4 per cent, subsidy/grants 48.7 per cent
Subsidy from: Municipal government

Ferrocarrils de la Generalitat Valenciana (FGV) – Valencia Railways

Partida de Xirivelleta, B de S Isidro, E-46014 Valencia, Spain
Tel: (+34 96) 397 65 65   Fax: (+34 96) 397 65 80
Web: www.fgv.es

Key personnel
President: Mario Flores Lanuza
Managing Director: Marisa Gracia Giménez
Manager Assistants:
  Technical & Strategy Manager: Vicente Contreras Bórnez
  Operations: Dionisio García Gómez
  Management Area: Noé Gutierrez
Directors
  Quality & Participation: Carlos Guillem Miralles
  Analysis & Audit Operating Control: Juan José Gimeno
  Communication, Image & External Relations: Juan Carlos Murillo
  Customer Service: J Fernando Álvaro Errazu

Finance: Jesús Cerverón Esteban
Transport: Manuel Sansano Muñoz
Organisation and Systems: Antonio Orduña Galán
Technical: Francisco García Sigüenza
Personnel: J Anotnio González Redondo
Alicante Representative: José Pascual Rubio
  Staff: 1,699 (2007)

Passenger journeys (including Alicante operations):
(2003) 53.51 million
(2004) 59.9 million
(2005) 64 million
(2006) 67 million
(2007) 70.4 million

Current situation
FGV is a public company set up by Valencia Community Government (Generalitat Valenciana) to operate the Valencia Community 1,000 mm gauge railways. In the Valencia metropolitan area, operating under the name Metrovalencia, it integrates Lines 1, 3 and 5 (linking suburban surface lines and underground urban services) and the Line 4 and Line 6 tramway. FGV also operates the non-electrified Alicante-Denia line and the Alicante tramway.

Developments
In 2007, FGV invested more than EUR41 million and EUR50 million in Metrovalencia and Alicante's tram infrastructure respectively.

Metrovalencia
Web: www.metrovalencia.com

Passenger journeys: (2003) 51 million
(2004) 57.61 million
(2005) 61.5 million
(2006) 64.6 million
(2007) 67.7 million

Number of lines: 5
Route length: 146.8 km
  in tunnel: 24.2 km
Number of station: 132
  in tunnel: 30

Current situation
Metrovalencia provides transport service to the Valencia metropolitan area with three rail lines (Line 1, 3 and 5) and modern tram lines. T4 and T6 tramway lines runs east-west across the north of the city.

Developments
Expansion projects
Metrovalencia, supported by Department of Infraestructures and Transport of the Generalitat Valenciana, is currently carrying out the Network Expansion Plan, which began in 1998 with the extension of Line 3 on the Alameda-Mislata and Colón-Jesús sections. Later on, it included the extension of the tram line from Empalme to Feria Valencia, the Parque Ayora-Alameda section of the metro's new Line 5 (port-airport), a new underground branch and station at Torrent and

the extension of the tram line T4 to La Coma and Terramelar.
Metrovalencia's latest expansion has been the Line T6, which connects Torrefiel-Orriols districts with downtown centre, both university campuses of Naranjos and Politécnica and the urban seafront.

Line 5 port-airport connection
Line 5 now provides a direct link between Valencia's seafront and Manises airport, connecting the metro network with the towns of Quart de Poblet and Manises. These two extensions, east and west, opened in April 2007. The new line represents a major arterial connection between the port, the airport and RENFE central railway station, integrating them with the urban and metropolitan transport network.
There is a planned further extension of Line 5 further to the west, to Riba-Roja.

L6 tram line
The first phase of L6 Tram Line covers the route between Tossal del Rei and Marítim-Serrería Stations. It is 2.4 km in length with five stop stations and the budget for this phase was EUR26.8 million.
This line provides transport service to more than 50,000 people from Torrefiel-Orriols districts. It operates with eight new 100 per cent low-floor trams built by Bombardier.
There are future plans for L6 to connect peripheral districts with Valencia downtown.

Incorporation of the T-2 line
The T-2 tram line will connect the northern zone of the city, the historical centre of Valencia, the central RENFE station, the City of Arts and Sciences and the Nazaret neighbourhood. The first phase of the project will connect Valencia north with the city centre. Construction on this phase has commenced. In a second phase, the line will cross from the north to the south of the city, and it is planned to have three stations within the old city historical centre.
On completion of these projects, Valencia will have an additional 52 km of metro and tram lines and 40 new stations, bringing the network services to more than half a million people.

Alicante TRAM Metropolitano
Avenida Villajoyosa 2, E-03016 Alicante, Spain
Web: www.fgvalicante.com

Passenger journeys: (2003) 1.7 million
(2004) 2.29 million
(2005) 2.5 million
(2006) 2.45 million
(2007) 2.73 million

Route length: 99.3 km
  in tunnel: 6.5 km
Number of stations: 51

Current situation
The Alicante-Denia line runs for 93 km along the northern coast of the province of Alicante and has 47 stations and halts. It is served by 10 diesel trains which operate on the regular line between Alicante and Denia.
The Alicante TRAM entered service in April 2003, between Puerta del Mar (Alicante) and El Campello.

Developments
In January 2005, Bombardier received an order from FGV for 30 bidirectional *FLEXITY Outlook* low-floor trams for service on the Valencia and Alicante networks. The contract was valued at some EUR81 million. The contract includes an option for a further 10 trams of the same type.

Fleet: 112 units
Line 1:

Babcock & Wilcox three-car units (1981)	10
CAF/ABB Class 3700 first series two-car units (1987)	30
CAF/ABB Class 3700 second series two-car units (1990)	10

Vossloh four-car 43012-10 emus
(see Lines 3 & 5 below)
Lines 3 & 5:
GEC/Alsthom Class 3900 three-car units 18
Vossloh four-car 43012-10 emus, used on
Lines 1, 3 and 5 (2006) 9
Line 4:
Siemens/Duewag 3800 Series
three-car trams 20
El Campello-Denia (Alicante):
Diesel 2300 Series train 10
Tramway Alicante-El Campello:
Siemens/Duewag 3800 Series
three-car trams 5
On order: 30 bidirectional Bombardier *FLEXITY Outlook* trams, with an option for a further 10 trams of the same type
40 Vossloh Class 3900, delivery due 2007–08.

Red Nacional de los Ferrocarriles Españoles (RENFE) – Spanish National Railways

Corporate Communications and External Relations Department
Avenida Pio XII n° 110, Edif Caracola 16, E-28036 Madrid, Spain
Tel: (+34 91) 300 66 00
Fax: (+34 91) 300 73 36
e-mail: comunicacion@renfe.es
cercanias@renfe.es
Web: www.renfe.com

Key personnel
Director, Valencia: Juan José Cholvi Puig
Staff: 414 (Valencia area)

Other offices
Valencia office
C/Xátiva 24, E-46007 Valencia, Spain
Tel: (+34 96) 353 71 77

Valencia tram at Dr Lluch (Alex Dasi-Sutton) 1115282

Head office
Avenida Ciudad de Barcelona 8, E-28007 Madrid, Spain
Tel: (+34 91) 506 61 27 Fax: (+34 91) 506 69 39

Type of operation: Suburban heavy rail

Passenger journeys: (Total for Suburban Business Unit)
(2002) 439.6 million
(2003) 446 million

Current situation
An intensive service is operated out of Norte station on six routes totalling 372 km, with 68 stations. Trains run to Gandia, Xàtiva and Castellón every 15 minutes during the peak, to Utiel and Riba-Roja every 30 minutes, and to Caudiel every hour. Four lines electrified, the others diesel-worked.

For further information on this company, please see *Jane's World Railways.*

Rolling stock: 117 emu cars and 39 dmu cars

Class 440 emu	M2 T1
Class 470 emu	M20 T10
Class 447 emu	M56 T28
Class 592 dmu	39

Sweden

Gothenburg

Population: 484,942 (December 2005), metropolitan area 880,000 (estimate)

Public transport
Bus and tramway/light rail and ferry services to the southern archipelago and in the port co-ordinated by city planning authority Trafikkontoret, a department of the Traffic and Public Transport Authority. Operations managed by Västtrafik AB. Styrsöbolaget (Connex) is the ferry contractor. Regional buses of several operators, and commuter rail services (operated by Swedish State Railways).

City of Göteburg

Traffic & Public Transport Authority – Trafikkontoret
PO Box 2403, SE-403 16 Gothenburg, Sweden
Tel: (+46 31) 61 37 00 Fax: (+46 31) 711 98 33
e-mail: trafikkontoret@trafikkontoret.goteborg.se
Web: www.trafikkontoret.goteborg.se

Street address
Köpmansgatan 20, Hållplats Brunnsparken, Gothenburg, Sweden

Key personnel
Chairman: Leif Blomqvist
Vice-Chairman: Roland Rydin
Traffic Director: Jonas Johansson
Staff: Approximately 100

Current situation
A department of the Traffic and Public Transport Authority, the Traffic & Public Transport Committee (Trafikkontoret) is formed of a Board of nine politically appointed members and six deputies and is responsible for the co-ordination of all traffic issues in Gothenburg.

Stadstrafiken is responsible for network planning, service standards, finance and fares policy, and acts as purchaser of services.

Västtrafik AB

Box 123, SE-541 23 Skövde, Sweden
Tel: (+46 500) 46 44 00 Fax: (+45 500) 48 91 48
e-mail: vasttrafik@vasttrafik.se
Web: www.vasttrafik.se

Street address
Stationsgatan 7, Skövde, Sweden

Key personnel
Managing Director: Leif Blomqvist
Operations: Mårten Ignell
Information: Gunilla Wicktor

Background
From January 1999 a new county authority took over responsibility for public transport in the city as well as three former counties in western Sweden. The name of this authority is Västtrafik AB. The Västra Götaland region owns 50 per cent of the company and 50 per cent is owned by the 49 municipalities of Västra Götaland.

Current situation
Västtrafik co-ordinates all public transport services in the whole of the Västra Götaland region. The authority is responsible for how public transport services should operate – when, where and with what changeovers etc. It proposes the cost of travel, the payment system and ticket types and the standard of vehicles used in public transport services. It also draws up timetables and develops information systems with the aim of improving the attractiveness of public transport services.

The authority procures transport from competing operators with the aim of appointing transport operators for the buses, ferries, trams and trains.

Developments
The company has recently introduced new smartcard tickets and machines.

Passenger journeys: (Bus and tram/light rail)
Not currently available

Fare structure: Within the city, there is a flat fare, but the fare system is integrated with the regional fare structure valid in Gothenburg and the 12 other municipalities administered by GLAB; magnetic tickets and monthly passes
Fare collection: Magnetic tickets at reduced rate; monthly smartcard passes; drivers sell magnetic tickets for single journeys; ticket machines on trams
Fares collected on board: Less than 15 per cent
Fare evasion control: Roving inspectors; spot penalty
Operating costs financed by: Fares 54 per cent, city council subsidy 46 per cent
Arrangements for elderly/disabled: Responsibility of a separate organisation; fare structure decided by Trafikkontoret. A fleet of 90 vehicles is run by five operators, along with 175 contract taxis; they carry 5,000 passengers a day. A computer-based system is used to arrange ride-sharing. A 'Service Line' with

low-floor buses operates on a regular route in areas where many senior citizens live, connecting with day centres and hospitals. This route is operated by GS as part of the regular bus system and regular passes are valid.

Bus

Passenger journeys: Not currently available
Vehicle-km: (2006) 17.3 million

Number of routes: 100
Route length: 1,080 km

Fleet: 133 buses (estimate)	
Scania CN112 (1987)	3
Scania CN113 (1990)	2
Scania CN113 (1991)	24
Volvo B10M (1988)	17
Volvo B10M CNG (1993)	19
Ontario II (1989)	6
Ontario II (1990)	1
Volvo B10MA (1991/95/96/97)	42
Volvo B10BLE CNG (1994/96/97)	19
In peak service: 115 (estimated)	

Most intensive service: 3 min
Bus priority: Traffic management system for central Gothenburg divides the area into five sections to which access for private traffic is only possible for internal movement, thereby preventing through traffic, though buses and trams can move freely

Light rail/tramway
Type of operation: Light rail/tramway

Passenger journeys: Not currently available
Car-km: (2006) 14.5 million

Route length: 162 km
    reserved track: 90%
Number of lines: 12, plus one peak-hours only
Gauge: 1,435 mm
Max gradient: 6%
Minimum curve radius: 17 m
Electrification: 750 V DC, overhead

Developments
In late 2005, route 10 was extended from Ekaträdatan to Boskopsgarden during peak periods.

Rolling stock: 219 cars	
Hägglunds M29 (1969/72)	58
ASEA/ASJ M28 (1965/67)	66
ASEA/ABB M21 articulated (1984/91)	80
AnsaldoBreda M32	15
In peak service: 168 (estimate)	

On order: 40 M32 cars are on order, with two entering service each month. An option for a further 20 vehicles has been exercised, with delivery scheduled to start after the first 40 vehicles have entered service in 2008.

Service: Peak 8–10 min, off-peak 12–20 min

Styrsöbolaget
PO Box 5085, SE-42605 Västra Frölunda, Sweden
Tel: (+46 31) 69 64 00
Fax: (+46 31) 69 42 85
e-mail: marieborg@styrsobolaget.se
Web: www.styrsobolaget.com

Street address
Talattagatan 18, Långedrag, \SE-426 76 Västra Frölunda, Sweden

Key personnel
General Manager: Magnus Arnström
Operations Manager: Gunnar Söderberg
    Staff: 64

Ferry
Passenger journeys: (2002) 3.3 million
(2003) 2.9 million
(2006) 2.8 million
(2007) 2.9 million

Den Ousten Alliance articulated low-floor bus on Route 49 service in Kungsportsavenyn (Ken Harris)
1181723

Type M21 tram with rebuilt low-floor centre section on Route 4 service at Kungsportsbron (Ken Harris)
1181724

Current situation
Ferry services on the River Göta between Lilla Bommen and Klippan and from Saltholmen to the southern archipelago operated under contract to Västtrafik by the Veolia Transportation-owned shareholding company Styrsöbolaget with nine vessels; four routes total 43 km. All ferries are integrated into the fares system, and there is no transfer fee. Fares cover 35 per cent of operating costs.

Swebus AB
Solna strandväg 78, SE-171 54 Solna, Sweden
Tel: (+46 8) 54 63 00 00
Fax: (+46 8) 54 63 00 30
e-mail: adm@swebus.se
Web: www.swebus.se

Key personnel
Managing Director: Jan Bosaeus
Deputy Managing Director and Marketing Director:
    Henrik Dangäs
Economic Director: Håkan Nilsson
    Staff: Not currently available

Background
Swebus is owned by Concordia Bus AB.

Current situation
Since June 1997, Swebus, a subsidiary of Concord Bus AB, operates a number of routes

for Stadstrafiken. It also operates regional routes for the regional authority.

Fleet: 55 buses	
Neoplan NE7 (1990)	2
Neoplan 8012 (1995)	1
Scania CN2 (1989)	2
Scania CN3 (1990/92)	3
Volvo B10R (1987)	1
Volvo B10M (1988-1996)	17
Volvo B10L (1997)	17
Volvo B10LA (1997)	12
In peak service: Not currently available	
On order: Not currently available	

SJ AB
Head Office, SE-105 50 Stockholm, Sweden
Tel: (+46 10) 751 60 00
e-mail: info@sj.se
Web: www.sj.se

Street address
Centralplan 19, Stockholm, Sweden

Key personnel
Chairman: Ulf Adelson
President and Chief Executive Officer: Jan Forsberg
Area Manager, Gothenburg: L-A Antonsson
Public Relations Manager: Kajsa Moström
    Staff: 4,053 (2007 average) (All operations)

Type of operation: Suburban heavy rail

Passenger journeys: (All operations)
(2003) 35.2 million
(2004) 34.7 million
(2005) 34.9 million
(2006) 37.4 million
(2007) 38.4 million
Train-km: Not currently available

Background
Formed from the passenger traffic unit of the former Swedish State Railways (SJ) in late 2000, the company took the name SJ AB. The company is wholly owned by the Swedish state and is overseen by the Ministry of Enterprise, Energy and Communications.

Current situation
Services operated on several routes under contract, electrified 15 kV 16⅔ Hz.
For further information on SJ AB, please see *Jane's World Railways*.

Malmö

Population: City 282,904, urban area 258,000, metropolitan area 605,000 (2008 estimates)

Public transport
Bus services in the city and the surrounding region are provided under contract by private companies, including Veolia, overseen by the regional transport authority Skånetrafiken. The latter operates train services on several lines in the area with other suburban rail services operated by state railway (SJ); Citytunnel mainline project under construction.

Skånetrafiken
281 83 Hässleholm, Sweden
Tel: (+46 451) 38 86 00
Fax: (+46 451) 38 86 99
Web: www.skanetrafiken.se

Street address
Andar Avenyen 7, Hässleholm, Sweden

Key personnel
Managing Director: Gösta Ahlberg
Staff: Not currently available

Type of operation: Suburban heavy rail

Passenger journeys: (2006) 113.4 million (estimate)
(2007) 121.9 million (estimate)

Current situation
Founded in 199, Skånetrafiken is part of the regional public body Region Skåne. It oversees public transport operations for 10 major cities, contracted regional bus services and operates train services on several lines in the area.
Skånetrafike is funded by the Region Skåne (35 per cent) and by revenues from ticket sales (65 per cent).

Developments
New trains are due to begin service in 2009.
Also in 2009, Skånetrafiken plans to implement a new integrated smartcard system.

SJ AB
Head Office, SE-105 50 Stockholm, Sweden
Tel: (+46 10) 751 60 00
e-mail: info@sj.se
Web: www.sj.se

Street address
Centralplan 19, Stockholm, Sweden

Key personnel
Chairman: Ulf Adelson
President and Chief Executive Officer: Jan Forsberg
Staff: 4,053 (2007 average) (All operations)

Type of operation: Suburban heavy rail

Passenger journeys: (All operations)
(2003) 35.2 million
(2004) 34.7 million
(2005) 34.9 million
(2006) 37.4 million
(2007) 38.4 million
Train-km: Not currently available

Background
Formed from the passenger traffic unit of the former Swedish State Railways (SJ) in late 2000, the company took the name SJ AB. The company is wholly owned by the Swedish state and is overseen by the Ministry of Enterprise, Energy and Communications.

Current situation
SJ operates suburban services over three routes totalling 130 km, from Malmö to Höör, Landskrona and Helsingborg, electrified 15 kV 16⅔ Hz. About hourly off-peak, half-hourly Malmö to Lund (17 km). Zonal and monthly travelcards available for half or all system; monthly cards accepted on buses. Fares contribute 47 per cent of income, local subsidy 53 per cent.
For further information on SJ AB, please see *Jane's World Railways*.

Rolling stock: 18 two-car emus
ASEA X10 (1983/85/88)   M18 T18

Citytunneln
The Citytunnel Project, PO Box 4012, SE-203 11 Malmö, Sweden
Tel: (+46 40) 32 14 00   Fax: (+46 40) 32 15 04 (Public Relations Department)
e-mail: upphandling@citytunneln.com
Web: www.citytunneln.se

Street address
Lilla Nygatan 7, SE-203 11 Malmö, Sweden

Key personnel
Head of Public Relations: Anders Mellberg
Staff: Not currently available

Type of operation: Suburban heavy rail

Passenger journeys: n/a
Train-km: n/a

Current situation
In 1997, a parliamentary decision was made to construct the Citytunnel, 17 km of main line rail line, to increase capacity for rail transport through Malmö. The project is being implemented by the National Rail Administration (Banverket). Funding comes from the National Rail Administration (Banverket), the City of Malmö, Region Skåne and the EU. The cost of the project, estimated at 2001 prices, is SEK9.45 billion.
The project comprises a 6 km tunnel under central Malmö, 5 km of at-grade line from the southern end of the tunnel to the Öresund Line and 6 km of at-grade line towards Ystad and Trelleborg. There will be three news stations on the line: Malmö C Nedre, Triangeln and Hyllie. Hyllie Station will be at-grade.
The contract to construct the tunnels between Malmö Central Railway Station (Malmö C) and Holma, including the excavation for Triangeln station and construction of the new, underground station at Malmö C was awarded in late 2004.
Construction on the project started in March 2005.

Developments
The project was originally scheduled to be completed in 2011. The latest schedule projects that the Citytunnel will now open in December 2010 and that the project is currently within budget.

Stockholm

Population: City 802,622, urban area 1.25 million, metropolitan area 1.95 million (2008 estimates)

Public transport
Bus, suburban rail, local rail, tramway and metro services provided under contract to company owned by Stockholm County Council and controlled by nominated board, with subsidiaries and private contractors operating metro, local rail, suburban rail and bus services; county-owned ferries.

AB Storstockholms Lokaltrafik (SL)
SE-120 80 Stockholm, Sweden
Tel: (+46 8) 686 16 00   Fax: (+46 8) 686 15 03
Web: www.sl.se

Street address
Arenavägen 27, SE-120 80 Stockholm, Sweden

Key personnel
President and Chief Executive Officer: Ingemar Ziegler
Staff (SL Group of Companies): 699 (2008)

Passenger boardings: (All modes)
(2007) 2,434 million
Operating costs financed by: Fares 46.9 per cent, other commercial sources 2 per cent, subsidy/grants 53.1 per cent (2007)
Subsidy from: County council

Background
Stockholm was one of the first West European cities to establish a fully integrated public transport system. The arrangements, agreed in 1964, brought together bus, metro and tramway services operated in the 26 county municipalities by AB Stockholms Spårvägar (SS) (based on former tramway companies), Swedish State Railways (SJ), two municipal bus companies and 10 private operators. As a result of the agreement, SS was reorganised as AB Storstockholms Lokaltrafik (SL) which began operations in 1967.
Following reorganisation in 1991, operations were progressively contracted-out, and on completion of the process in 1999, SL assumed the role of regional transport authority.

Current situation
Bus service is contracted mainly from two companies, Busslink and Swebus.

In 2006, the suburban rail routes operated by Swedish State Railways (SJ) were awarded to Stockholmståg. The metro and tramway networks are contracted to Veolia Transport (previously known as Connex), with one exception, Roslagsbanan, which is contracted to Roslagståg AB (www.roslagstag.se).
After less than one year in operation, the flat-fare system was discontinued and a new zone-fare system was introduced. Experience from the former zone system was reused and resulted in a more logical zone division. The new system is based on three zones, with the entire underground system contained within one zone. The pre-paid ticket strip was reintroduced for customers who travel infrequently with SL.
Period tickets are available for frequent travellers, and they are not confined to use by one person. About 70 per cent use some sort of period ticket for their journeys. Following a decision by the Swedish Work Environment Authority, all cash handling on SL's buses ceased as of 31 March 2007. In 2007, the range of tickets was revised in preparation for SL's new payment system, SL Access (smart card system).

There are also 51 biogas buses in the SL fleet, which will be increased to 120 buses in the near future. All of SL's rail traffic is powered with electricity from renewable sources. When purchasing new rolling stock, at least 95 per cent of the material in the vehicles must be recyclable. To facilitate systematic and structured environmental efforts, SL works according to the international ISO 14001 standard.

Developments

Several large projects are due to begin soon and need to be handled in a new way, not least with regard to financing. Refurbishment of the Slussen transport interchange is due soon and approval has been granted for the City Line commuter rail tunnel and its two new stations. An extension of the underground will also require construction of a new station. SL's rail-bound traffic includes more than 20 of Sweden's most heavily trafficked stations. These stations are essentially waiting areas in central locations around the Stockholm region that could easily be transformed to more attractive meeting places containing a range of everyday services. Aside from creating a more attractive and secure environment, the amount of commercial space will be increased by 50 per cent.

Bus

Passenger boardings: (2007) 975,000 per weekday
Vehicle-km: (2007) 1,295 million

Number of routes: 450
Route length: (One way) 9,451 km

Fleet: 1,897 vehicles, of which, 1,252 low floor buses and 441 powered by renewable fuels (2008)

One-person operation: All routes, except some local trains
Fare collection: Prepurchase multitickets (coupons) or passes, or single coupons bought from driver
Fare structure: Zonal (3 zones), pre-paid ticket strip; period tickets available; smartcard payment system (SL Access) due to be introduced
Fares collected on board: None
Operational control: Route inspectors/mobile radio with centralised radio control
Average distance between stops: City area, 350 m; outer zones, 700 m
Average peak-hour speed: In city; 15 km/h; in mixed traffic, 20 km/h; in bus lanes, 30 km/h
Bus priority: System for bus priority by means of on-board traffic light control. These buses are also equipped with a system to announce the destination/next stop; bus lanes provided and continuing programme for extensions; major traffic light priority scheme in city centre
Integration with other modes: All services and ticketing fully integrated; special bus services connect with Arlanda airport and ferries to Gotland and Finland
New vehicles financed by: Not currently available

Metro

Type of operation: Full metro (T-Banan)

Passenger boardings: (2003) 279 million
(2004) 278 million
(2005) 276 million
(2006) Not currently available
(2007) 1.09 million per weekday

Route length: 110 km
  in tunnel: 64 km
Number of lines: 3 with branches
Number of stations: 100
  in tunnel: 55
Gauge: 1,435 mm
Track: Flat-bottom 50 kg/m rail
Max gradient: 4.8%
Minimum curve radius: 200 m
Tunnel: Concrete, rock and steel
Electrification: 650–750 V DC, third rail

Service: Peak 2–5 min, off-peak 3–15 min
First/last train: 05.00/01.00 (ending at 03.00 at the weekend)

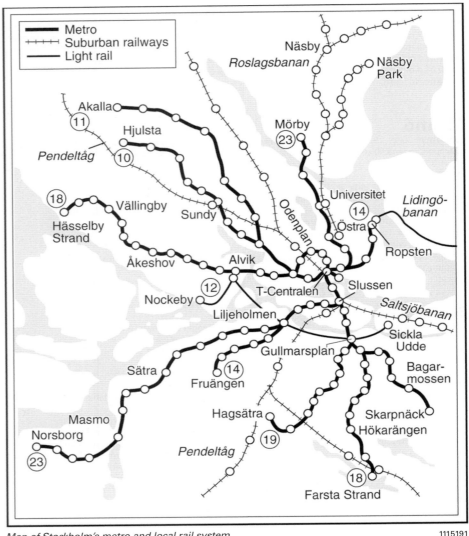

Map of Stockholm's metro and local rail system   1115191

SL Scania articulated bus (Bill Luke)   1115150

Fare structure: As bus
Revenue control: Barriers in all ticket halls, automatic gates for monthly passes in most stations; spot checks
One-person operation: All trains
Signalling: Cab signalling with fixed lineside signals installed only at junctions; central control office linked to all trains by radio
Surveillance: CCTV at 31 stations for passenger/train control

Rolling stock: 264 older cars, 271 new cars (2007) Full breakdown of fleet is not currently available.
In peak service: Not currently available
On order: Not currently available

Developments

The signalling system on the Red Line is nearing the end of its service life and must be replaced. A specification of requirements for a modern radio-based system was prepared during the year for procurement in 2008.

Security cameras were installed at all stations.

An extension of the Blue Line to the new university hospital Karolinska in Solna from Station Odenplan has been planned.

Tramway

Passenger boardings: Not currently available

Current situation

One former tram route remains, the Djurgårdslinjen, in the city centre, operated by a tramway society.

Light rail

Passenger journeys: Not currently available

Current situation

The light rail network provides connection between the western and southern peripheries of the city and is also co-ordinated with both the underground and commuter trains. Veolia Transport are currently operating the light railway lines.

Developments

In 2007, it was decided that new rail connections were to be made in the east and in the north. Light Rail East will be a 3.6 km long extension through Sickla and Hammarby Sjöstad to Slussen. It will also be linked to the Saltsjö suburban railway. Construction is scheduled to begin in 2010. The Light Rail North will be a 6.5 km long extension from Alvik via Ulvsunda and central Sundbyberg to Solna and the new national arena. Construction is scheduled to begin 2010. A further extension from Ulvsunda via Solvalla to Kista is also in the planning stage.

Rolling stock: 37 cars
Bombardier *FLEXITY* Swift (1999)   M22
Bombardier *FLEXITY* Swift low-floor (2008)   M9
On order: None

Local railway

Passenger boardings: Not currently available

Current situation

Veolia Transport currently operates Saltsjöbanan (19 km, 1,435 mm gauge, electrified 750 kV DC, 28 cars, 18 stations) and the Lidingöbanan (9 km, 1,435 mm gauge, electrified 700 V DC, 20 cars). The third local railway, the Roslagsbanan, (65 km, 891 mm gauge, electrified 1.5 kV DC, 101 cars, 39 stations) is operated under contract by Roslagståg.

The Saltsjöbanan links Stockholm Slussen with Saltsjöbaden, with a branch to Solsidan. The Lidingöbanan serves the island of Lidingö, with a bridge link to the metro at Ropsten, and the Roslagsbanan runs northwards from Stockholm Östra station to Kårsta with branches to Näsby Park and Österskär. Modern cars replaced the entire rolling stock starting in 1995.

In August 2003, SL decided that Roslagståg AB, owned by Danske Statsbaner (DSB) – Danish State Railways and Svenska Tågkompaniet AB, should operate the local railway, Roslagsbanan, in the northeastern part of Stockholm. This was the first time DSB had won a tender abroad. Roslagståg took over the operations of the railway on 7 January 2003.

Developments

A decision has been made to convert the entire Roslagen suburban railway to double-track. The city of Stockholm and Municipality of Nacka are planning the construction of new housing and work places at Hammarby Sjöstad, Danvikstull, Lugnet, Henriksdal, Kvarnholmen and the Port of Nacka, which will increase the need for public transport. SL has therefore started preparing for conversion of the Saltsjö suburban railway into a modern, fast-track railway of the same standard as the light rail system, to which it will also be inter-connected. Construction is currently scheduled to begin at the end 2009.

Suburban railway

Type of operation: Suburban heavy rail

Passenger journeys: (2007) 242,000 per weekday

Current situation

Services on three routes totalling 204 km with 51 stations; 1,435 mm gauge; electrified 15 kV

SL metro train at Slussen (Bill Luke)   1115151

SL light rail vehicle (Bill Luke)   1115152

Arlanda Express/A-Train emus (Sven Tideman)   1179159

16.6 Hz. Trains run every 15 minutes, with extras during peak hours.

Under an agreement between the former operator Swedish State Railways (SJ), the government and Stockholm county council, SL and the county council made a major financial commitment to raising capacity and improving standards on the lines into Stockholm Central station.

It is currently operated by Stockholmståg.

Developments

In 2007, the Swedish Government made a formal decision to build the City Line (an approximately 6 km long railway tunnel for commuter train

traffic) which will increase capacity by 100 per cent in commuter train traffic, that currently suffers from major restrictions in capacity.

Rolling stock: 117 older cars, 58 new cars (2007)
Full breakdown of fleet is not currently available.
In peak service: Not currently available
On order: Not currently available

Arlanda Express/A-Train AB

PO Box 130, SE-101 22 Stockholm, Sweden
Tel: (+46 8) 58 88 90 00; 20 22 22 24
e-mail: info@atrain.se
Web: www.arlandaexpress.com

Street address
Vasagatan 11, Stockholm, Sweden

Key personnel
Managing Director and Chief Executive Officer:
  Per Thorstenson
Marketing Director: Camilla Laaksonen
Traffic Director and Chief Financial Officer:
  Oscar Leopoldson
Business Director: Per Öster
Safety Director: Öystein Rönne-Petersén
Director, Infrastructure: Örjan Eriksson
Sales: Kimiko Sörensen
  Staff: 160

Passenger boardings: (2003) 2.2 million
(2005) 2.6 million

Background
Originally owned and operated by a consortium comprising NCC (40 per cent), Vattenfall (20 per cent), ALSTOM (29 per cent) and Mowlem (7 per cent). In October 2003 it was announced that the owner/operator consortium had agreed to the sale of A-Train AB to the Australian bank Macquarie Bank for some SEK400 million (USD52.5 million).
  A-Train AB will operate the system under concession until 2040.

Current situation
The Arlanda Link consortium opened its line serving Arlanda International airport at the end of November 1999. A-Trains' Arlanda Express is a 22 km loop off the Stockholm-Uppsala main line, running from Stockholm Central station to Stockholm Arlanda airport. It has three stations and is served by six trains an hour in peak periods and every 15 minutes off-peak.

Arrangements for elderly/disabled: All of the stations are accessible and one of the middle carriages of each four-car train has special spaces for wheelchairs

Rolling stock: Seven four-car trains
ALSTOM Transport (UK) (1998/99)   M14 T14

Arlanda Express/A-Train emu (Svren Tideman)   1179158

Waxholms Ångfartygs AB (Waxholmsbolaget) (WÅ)
PO Box 7422, 10391 Stockholm, Sweden
Tel: (+46 8) 614 64 50   Fax: (+46 8) 611 84 07
e-mail: info@waxholmsbolaget.sll.se
Web: www.waxholmsbolaget.se

Key personnel
Managing Director: Ewa Stenberg
  Staff: 21

Type of operation: Ferry

Passenger journeys: (2003) 4.2 million
(2004) 4.2 million
(2005) 4.1 million
(2006) 4.0 million
(2007) 3.8 million

Operating costs financed by: Fares 38 per cent, county council subsidy 62 per cent

Current situation
The 24 ships of WÅ, directly owned by Stockholm county council, form an integral part of the passenger services in the greater Stockholm area. There are 20 vessels operating in the sea inlets and to the islands of the archipelago, and four operating in Stockholm and Slussen-Djurgården, at frequent intervals.

Switzerland

Basle
Population: City 166,500 (2004 estimate), area of tariff agreement 560,000

Public transport
Bus, trolleybus and tramway services operated by a board elected by city council. Also local railways/tramways extending into the suburbs and into Baselland canton operated by separate undertaking. Tarifverbund Nordwestschweiz sets uniform fares structure for all modes.

Tarifverbund Nordwestschweiz (TNW)
Grenzweg 1, CH-4104 Oberwil, Switzerland
Tel: (+41 61) 406 11 11
Fax: (+41 61) 406 11 22
e-mail: info@tnw.ch
Web: www.tnw.ch

Key personnel
Director: A Büttiker
Head of Marketing: P Gschwind

Current situation
TNW, which is operated as a subsidiary of BLT Baselland Transport AG, organises and administers the uniform fare structure for trams, buses, post buses and SBB trains in the greater Basle area, comprising of five cantons with a total population of 560,000. It also co-ordinates marketing, promotional and advertising activities.

Basler Verkehrs-Betriebe (BVB)
Claragraben 55, CH-4005 Basle, Switzerland
Tel: (+41 61) 685 12 12
Fax: (+41 61) 685 12 48
e-mail: info@bvb.ch
Web: www.bvb.ch

Key personnel
Chair: C Brückner
General Manager: U Hanselmann
Operating Manager: R Messmer
  Staff: 997 (2006)

Passenger journeys: (All modes)
(2002) 117.3 million
(2003) 117.9 million
(2006) 120.3 million
Vehicle-km: (All modes)
(2002) 16.4 million
(2003) 16.4 million
(2006) 16.17 million

Fare collection: Ticket machines at all stops; no onboard sales

Fare structure: Zonal; day tickets; reduced-price monthly or annual Umwelt-Abonnement (U-Abo)
Fare evasion control: Penalty
Operating costs financed by: Fares 59.8 per cent, other commercial sources 11.6 per cent, subsidy/grants 28.6 per cent (2003)
Subsidy from: Canton, city and communities

Developments
In January 2006, BVB became an independent public organisation.

Bus and trolleybus
Passenger journeys: (2002) 29 million
(2003) 29.8 million
(2006) 31.8 million
Vehicle-km: (2002) 4.4 million
(2003) 5.3 million
(2006) 4.5 million

Number of routes: Bus 12, trolleybus 1
Route length: Bus 96.1 km, trolleybus 4.9 km
Trolleybus electrification: 600 V DC
Fleet: 70 buses

MAN articulated (2000)	38
Mercedes-Benz articulated (2005)	4
MAN standard (2000)	8
Merceedes-Benz/Evobus (CNG) (1996)	12
Minibuses (2000)	7
Oldtimer	1

Fleet: 7 trolleybuses
Neoplan low-floor articulated (1995)   7

Most intensive service: 7.5 min
One-person operation: All routes
Integration with other modes: Full integration with tramway service
Subsidy from: City of Basle

Tramway
Type of operation: Conventional tramway

Passenger journeys: (2002) 88.2 million
(2003) 88.1 million
(2006) 88.5 million
Vehicle-km: (2002) 11.1 million
(2003) 11.1 million
(2006) 10.7 million

Route length: 62.5 km
Number of lines: 8
Gauge: 1,000 mm
Electrification: 600 V DC, overhead

Rolling stock: 112 cars, 89 trailers

SWP Be 4/4 (1967/68)	M20
Schindler Be 4/4 (1986/87)	M26
Schindler Be 4/6 S/Siemens Be 4/6 (1990/91)	M28
Siemens/Duewag Be 6/8 Combino	M28
Trailers (various builders)	T79
Oldtimer	M10 T10

Service: Daytime 7.5 min, evenings (20.00–24.00) 15 min
First/last car: 05.30/00.30
Fare structure: Zonal
Revenue control: Automatic ticket machines
Integration with other modes: Fully integrated with bus and trolleybus and BLT services, and bus services into Germany
One-person operation: All routes

BLT Baselland Transport AG
Granzweg 1, CH-4104 Oberwil, Switzerland
Tel: (+41 61) 406 11 11   Fax: (+41 61) 406 11 22
e-mail: info@blt.ch
Web: www.blt.ch

Key personnel
Managing Director: Andreas Büttiker
Administrative and Financial Director: Robert Stöckli
Operating and Technical Director: Alfred Schödler
  Staff: 263 (2008)

Passenger journeys: (2004) 56.5 million
(2005) 58.2 million
(2006) 59.2 million
(2007) 59.0 million

Tramway
Current situation
The two original tramways are Route 11 to Aesch and Route 14 to Pratteln (worked by BVB cars). A third, Route 10 serving Dornach, was extended in 1986 from its former terminus at Heuwaage into the city centre over BVB tracks and linked with Route 17 to Rodersdorf. This route passes through French territory and terminates in Solothurn canton. At 25.6 km it is the longest tram route in Switzerland. Total network 65 km of 1,000 mm gauge, electrified 600 V DC.

Route length: 51.5 km
Number of stations/stops: 105
Gauge: 1,000 mm
Track: Conventional sleepers on ballast and sleepers on concrete with resilient pads
Max gradient: 5%
Min curve radius: 12 m

Rolling stock: 100 tramcars

Duewag (1967), ex-BVB (in 2001/02)	M7
Adtranz (Schindler) 1971–76 (with low-floor centre sections added 2001–02)	M15
Adtranz (Schindler) (1978–81)	M16
Adtranz (Schindler) (1978–81) (with low-floor centre sections added 1987–95)	M50

BVB MAN NG13 articulated bus on Route 34 (Ken Harris)   0554936

BVB Siemens Combino trams in Clarastrasse (Ken Harris)   0554935

BVB Combino tram No 327 (Marcel Vleugels)   0585178

Various (1947–64) ex-BVB	
	Not currently available
Adtranz (Schindler) (1973) ex-Zurich (in 1999)	
	Not currently available

On order:
40 Stadler Tango low-floor vehicles, delivery scheduled for 2008–2010.

Service: Peak 3.75 min, off-peak 7.5/15 min
First/last tram: 04.30/01.00

Bus
Passenger journeys: (2004) 6.2 million
(2005) 7.0 million
(2006) 7.4 million
(2007) 7.5 million

Vehicle-km: (2005) 2.8 million
(2006) 2.9 million
(2007) 3.0 million

Number of routes: 16
Route length: 126 km

Fleet: 52 vehicles
Full fleet breakdown is not currently available, but
includes:
Mercedes-Benz (1993/1998/2000/2001/
2003/2006)   48

Most intensive service: 7.5 min
Fare structure: Zonal
Operational control: Radio

Schweizerische Bundesbahnen AG (SBB AG) – Swiss Federal Railways

Communications Department
Hochschulstrasse 6, CH-3000 Bern 65,
Switzerland
Tel: (+41 51) 220 25 81
Fax: (+41 51) 220 44 33

BLT Adtranz Be4/8 LRVs (1978-81), with low-floor section added (1987–95), on Line 11 to Aesch
(Milan Sramek)   0585166

e-mail: railinfo@sbb.ch
Web: www.sbb.ch

Type of operation: Suburban heavy rail
Further information has been removed at the
company's request.

Bern

Population: City 122,178 (2005), metropolitan area
189,000 (estimate)

Public transport
Bus, trolleybus and tramway services operated
by undertaking responsible to city council.
Separate regional company RBS operates light
rail and bus services; BLS Lötschbergbahn
(BLS) operates part of the S-Bahn system and
PostBus provides some rural bus services.

Städtische Verkehrsbetriebe Bern – BERNMOBIL

Eigerplatz 3, PO Box 311, CH-3000, Bern 14,
Switzerland
Tel: (+41 31) 321 88 88   Fax: (+41 31) 321 88 66
e-mail: info@bernmobil.ch
Web: www.bernmobil.ch

Key personnel
Managing Director: René Schmied
Finance Director: Martin Stucki
Marketing Director: Roman Gattlen
Technical Director: Markus Anderegg
Operations Director: Christian Wohlwend
    Staff: 714

Passenger boardings: (All modes)
(2005) 84.4 million
(2006) 84.2 million

Fare collection: Self-service with Autelca ticket
issuing and validating equipment
Fare structure: Zonal, with ticket books and weekly,
monthly and annual passes
Fare evasion control: Roving inspectors; penalty fare
Operating costs financed by: (All modes) Fares 60
per cent, other commercial sources 10 per cent,
subsidy/grants 30 per cent
Subsidy from: Kanton Bern

Background
Previously known as Städtische Verkehrsbetriebe
Bern (SVB).

Bus and trolleybus
Passenger journeys: (2005) Bus 48.7 million,
trolleybus 56.7 million
(2006) Bus 65.9 million, trolleybus 47.3 million
Vehicle-km: (2005) Bus 4.2 million, trolleybus
2.7 million
(2006) Bus 4.2 million, trolleybus 2.7 million

Number of routes: Bus 13, trolleybus 5
Route length: (One way) bus 63.7 km, trolleybus
21.7 km
On priority right-of-way: Bus 1.3 km

BERNMOBIL Van Hool low-floor articulated bus (Bill Luke)   1115273

BERNMOBIL biogas bus   1194975

Number of stops: 160

Fleet: 142 buses

Volvo	9
MAN low-floor articulated	37
HESS/Volvo low-floor articulated	22
Van Hool low-floor articulated	9
Volvo CNG low-floor articulated	32
MAN midibus	11

On order: None

In peak service: Not currently available
Fleet: 25 trolleybuses, all articulated
In peak service: Not currently available
Trolleybus electrification: 600 V DC

Most intensive service: 3 min
One-person operation: All routes
Operational control: Computer-controlled
operations system
Average distance between stops: 390 m

Average peak-hour speed: 17 km/h
New vehicles financed by: BERNMOBIL

Tramway

Type of operation: Conventional tramway

Passenger journeys: (2005) 48.7 million
(2006) 48.0 million
Car-km: (2005) 1.9 million
(2006) 1.9 million

Route length: 17.4 km
  reserved track: 1.7 km
Number of lines: 3
Number of stops: 52
Gauge: 1,000 mm
Max gradient: 6%
Minimum curve radius: 15.5 m
Track: 60 kg/m Ri60 rail
Electrification: 600 V DC, overhead

Service: Peak 5 min, off-peak 6–12 min
First/last car: 05.40/23.45
Integration with other modes: Fully integrated with
urban bus and regional transport systems
One-person operation: All routes

Rolling stock: 45 cars

SWS/BBC Be 8/8 (1973)	M11
Vevey Be 4/8 low-floor (1989/90)	M12
Siemens Combino Be 4/6 low-floor	M15
B4	T7

In peak service: 29 motor cars
On order: 21 new Siemens 42 m Combino trams
have been ordered. Delivery is scheduled to
commence in mid-2009 and be completed by the
end of 2010.

Developments

Trolleybus routes 13 and 14 – SBB station to
Bümpliz and Gäbelbach – will be converted to
tramway operation in 2010.

Line 9 to Guisanplatz will be extended to the
S-Bahn Wankdorf Station (1.1 km) by the end of
2011.

Diesel buses are continuously being replaced
with gas buses from 2006–2010. The first 32 Volvo
7700 buses are fuelled by biogas.

BLS AG

Genfergasse 11, CH-3001 Bern, Switzerland
Tel: (+41 31) 327 27 27   Fax: (+41 31) 327 29 10
e-mail: personenverkehr@bls.ch (Passenger traffic)
  media@bls.ch
Web: www.bls.ch, www.s-bahn-bern.ch

Key personnel
Management:
Director: Bernard Guillelmon
Infrastructure: Kees van Hoek
Passenger Traffic: Anna Barbara Remund
Divisions:
  Safety: Eduard Wymann
  Installations: Jean-Pierre Kipfer
  Operations: Walter Flühmann
  Infrastructure Development: Ulrich Schaeffeler
  Electricity and Signalling: Daniel Pixley
  Regional Rail Passenger Traffic: Thomas Stupp
  Passenger Traffic Development: Andreas Scherrer
  Passenger Traffic Distribution: Beat Theiler
  Marketing: Damian Pfister
  Corporate Communications: Hans-Peter Ernst
  Media Relations: Hans Martin Schaer
    Staff: 2,650 (December 2007)

Type of operation: S-Bahn

Passenger journeys: Not currently available
Train-km: Not currently available
Number of lines: 10

BERNMOBIL FBW articulated trolleybus (Bill Luke)   1115274

BERNMOBIL Siemens Combino low-floor tram   1194974

Route length: Not currently available
Number of stations: Not currently available

Current situation
BLS AG now operates all former SBB suburban
services in the Bern area. Along with local railway
Regionalverkehr Mittelland and RBS, these have
been integrated and augmented to run as cross-
city routes providing S-Bahn style service.

For further information on BLS AG, please see
Jane's World Railways.

Developments
Planned improvements include higher platforms
for easier train access, an electronic information
system and improved station lighting. Some of
this work is already under way.

Rolling stock: 36 three-car emus
RABe 525 NINA (Niederflur-Nahverkehr)   36

Regionalverkehr Bern-Solothurn (RBS)

PO Box 119, CH-3048 Worblaufen, Switzerland
Tel: (+41 31) 925 55 55   Fax: (+41 31) 925 55 66
e-mail: info@rbs.ch
Web: www.rbs.ch

Key personnel
General Manager: Hans Amacker
Deputy Director: Hans-Jakob Stricker
Vice-Director: Ursula Gasser
  Staff: 400

Current situation
Two light railways, which had been under
common management since 1965, were merged
in 1984. They link Bern with Unterzollikofen,
Jegenstorf, Solothurn and Worb. The undertaking
also operates 18 feeder bus routes.

Developments
In December 2007, RBS started to provide a
7.5-min synchronised timetable on the
S7 line.

Light railway
Staff: 320

Type of operation: Suburban light rail

Passenger journeys: (Both modes)
(2003) 19.3 million
(2004) 19.5 million
(2005) 20.0 million
(2006) 23.5 million
(2007) 24.5 million

Route length: 57 km
Number of routes: 5
Number of stations: 45
Gauge: 1,000 mm
Electrification: 1.25 kV DC (47 km), 600 V DC (19 km),
overhead

Developments
New double-track lines near Bern were opened
in 2007.

For details of the latest updates to *Jane's Urban Transport Systems* online and to discover the
additional information available exclusively to online subscribers please visit
juts.janes.com

There are long-term plans for a new station in Bern, which would be constructed in partnership with SBB, the City of Bern and the Canton of Bern.

In March 2007, six new air-conditioned low-floor cars were ordered from Stadler. The vehicles are due for delivery in 2009, and the contract was valued at CHF53.4 million. When brought into service, they will provide a 15 min service between Bern and Solothurn.

Rolling stock: In 2007, RBS operated three electric and five diesel locomotives; 33 emu (consisting of 95 cars) and nine light rail units. Some historic passenger vehicles are retained for special traffic.

On order: Six 120 km/h, low-floor Stadler cars, scheduled for delivery in 2009.

Service: Peak 7.5–30 min, off-peak 15–30 min
Fare structure: Zonal
Integration with other modes: Fare integration with 14 companies in the region
Fare evasion control: Roving inspectors, penalty fare
Arrangements for elderly/disabled:
All trains have a section with a low-floor entrance
Signalling: ATC; all trains single-manned

Bus
Staff: 80

Passenger journeys: (2003) 4.4 million
(2004) 4.7 million
(2005) Not available
(2006) Not available
(2007) Not available

Current situation
Buses provide feeder services on 18 routes totalling 60 km serving a number of rail stations. Fleet of 32 buses, midibuses and rail service vehicles.

Geneva
Population: City 176,000; metropolitan area 414,300 (2001)

Public transport
Bus, trolleybus and tramway services operated by municipal authority. Swiss Federal Railways services on local lines; also French National Railways local route to Geneva Eaux-Vives. Two ferry companies provide some commuter services, although mostly providing tourist services.

A new overall transport tariff authority covering the Geneva canton, UNIRESO, was introduced in 2001, with overall responsibility for TPG (buses, trams and trolleybuses), SMGN shuttle boats on Lac Léman (Lake Geneva) in city area, and SBB (railways) in Swiss Geneva, but not in any of the French operation. It is no longer possible to buy tickets on any bus or tram and ticket vending machines have been installed at major stops.

TPG 'Megabus' 1146841

Transports Publics Genevois (TPG)
Route de la Chapelle 1, PO Box 950, CH-1212 Grand-Lancy 1, Switzerland
Tel: (+41 22) 308 33 11   Fax: (+41 22) 308 34 00
Web: www.tpg.ch

Key personnel
President: Michel Jacquet
General Manager: Stéphainie Fontugne
   Staff: 1,436

Operating costs financed by: (All modes) Fares 37 per cent, other commercial sources 1 per cent, subsidy/grants 57 per cent
Subsidy from: Canton, plus 2 per cent from government for country routes

Current situation
In 2002, the state/canton adopted a masterplan which aimed to increase public transport services by 20 per cent. The plan included extending services to areas outside the state/canton borders.

Bus and trolleybus
Number of routes: Bus 46, trolleybus 6
Route length: Bus 34.4 km, trolleybus 328.4 km

Fleet: 232

Mercedes O405 (1998)	40
Mercedes O405G articulated (1988)	48
Renault R312 (1991)	25
Mercedes O405GN articulated (1993, 1996)	24
Volvo 7000A articulated (2000, 2002)	90
Van Hool AGG 300 New (2004)	5
In peak service: 190	

Fleet: 93 trolleybuses

Saurer/Hess/BBC-Sécheron articulated (1982/83)	12
NAW/Hess/BBC-Sécheron articulated (1988)	20
NAW/Hess/Siemens articulated (1992)	12
NAW/Hess/Siemens double-articulated (prototype) (2004)	1
Hess/Kiepe articulated (2004/05)	38
Hess/Kiepe double-articulated (2005/06)	10
In peak service: 56	

Trolleybus electrification: 600 V DC

TPG articulated trolleybus No 746 1146842

TPG Bombardier Cityrunner FLEXITY tram 1146840

Most intensive service: 6 min

One-person operation: All routes

Fare collection: Self-service, from machines at stops; no fares payable on board

Fare structure;

Zonal: city centre fare and regional fare throughout Geneva and the frontier zones or area of Coppet; 48- and 72-hour passes; one-day and evening passes; multitickets of both types; monthly and annual passes, monthly passes also valid on all public transport in Canton of Geneva; P+R pass

Fares collected on board: None

Fare evasion control: Roving inspectors

Average distance between stops: 300 m

Average peak-hour speed: In mixed traffic, 15–20 km/h

Developments

In January 2004, the first 'mega-trolleybus' was put into service on Line 10. This vehicle is a double-articulated prototype and is 24 m in length and has a capacity of up to 140 passengers. There is a possible future requirement for a further 10 of these vehicles.

In December 2004, the first of 38 vehicles were delivered. These new vehicles will replace the 16 vehicles from 1975 and 12 from 1982/83. The trolleybus fleet will increase from 73 to 93 units.

Line 7 will be extended from Rive to Hospital by the end of 2006.

Tramway

Type of operation: Conventional tramway

Route length: 12.6 km

Number of lines: 4

Number of stops: 46

Gauge: 1,000 mm

Electrification: 600 V DC, overhead

Service: Peak 8 min, off-peak 10 min

First/last car: 05.30/00.30 (02.00 Saturday and Sunday)

Fare structure: As bus

One-person operation: All trams

Rolling stock: 67 cars

Vevey/Duewag Be4/6 (1987/89)	M24
Vevey/Duewag Be4/8 (1995/98)	M22
Bombardier Cityrunner FLEXITY (2004)	21

Developments

During 2006, work will start between the railway station and Meyrin, with completion expected between 2008 and 2010.

Other plans include new branches to Onex and Grand-Saconnex, near to the International Organisations.

Future project for extensions towards France, Annemasse, St-Gernis and Ferney are being studied.

Schweizerische Bundesbahnen AG (SBB AG) – Swiss Federal Railways

Communications Department

Hochschulstrasse 6, CH-3000 Bern 65, Switzerland

Tel: (+41 51) 220 25 81

Fax: (+41 51) 220 44 33

e-mail: railinfo@sbb.ch

Web: www.sbb.ch

Type of operation: Suburban heavy rail

Further information has been removed at the company's request.

Société Nationale des Chemins de Fer Français (SNCF) – French National Railways

Direction du Transport Public, Division Information et Relation Client

209/211 rue de Bercy, F- 75585, Paris Cedex 12, France

Web: www.sncf.fr

Key personnel

Business Director, Public Transport: Bernard Sinou

Director of Communications: Bernard Emsellem

Type of operation: Local railway

Current situation

The electrified line from Annemasse extends across the Swiss border to serve Geneva at Eaux-Vives in the southeast of the city. Trains run about hourly.

Société des Mouettes Genevoises Navigation SA (SMGN) – Swissboat

4, 8 Quai du Mont Blanc, CH-1201 Geneva, Switzerland

Tel: (+41 22) 732 29 44, 47 47

Fax: (+41 22) 738 79 88

e-mail: info@swissboat.com

Web: www.swissboat.com

Type of operation: Ferry

Current situation

Société des Mouettes Genevoises Navigation SA (SMGN) – Swissboat operates 'Mouette' ferry services on Lake Geneva. Two shuttle ferry routes operate every 10 minutes from 07.20 to 19.30 and two routes every 30 minutes from 07.20 to 19.20.

Transfer from bus to 'Mouette' is free.

Lausanne

Population: 128,432 (2006 estimate)

Public transport

Bus, trolleybus and light rail services provided by publicly owned undertaking, controlled by representative board. 'Metro' rubber-tyred route under construction (part of which is being converted from previous rack line); rail services by Swiss Federal Railways; local railway and lake steamers.

Transports Publics de la Région Lausannoise SA (TL)

Centre de Perrelet Transports publics de la région lausannoise sa

Chemin du Closel 15, CH-1020 Renens 1, Lausanne, Switzerland

Tel: (+41 21) 621 01 11

Fax: (+41 21) 625 01 22

e-mail: infoline@t-l.ch

Web: www.t-l.ch

Key personnel

Chair: Anne-Marie Depoisier

General Manager: M Joye

Staff: 927 (2007)

Passenger journeys: (2006) 71.6 million (2007) 74 million

Route length: 227.8 km (all modes)

Current situation

TL is owned by the canton of Vaud (26 per cent), local communities (67 per cent), the Vaud Cantonal Bank (4 per cent) and private individuals (3 per cent). It operates buses and trolleybuses, owns the vehicles and operates the light rail route built by TSOL (see below), and also embraces the LO rack line. Though separately constituted, the three undertakings are operated under a single administration.

TL provides services to a population of more than 260,000 in 12 communities.

The LEB line (now S1) was extended 1.1 km to Lausanne Flon in 2000. TSOL (Metro Ouést) has become Line M1 and Métro Gare and Métro Ouchy have been rebranded M2.

Bus and trolleybus

Number of routes: Bus 24, trolleybus 10

Route length: Bus 161.1 km, trolleybus 53.6 km

On priority right-of-way: 9.4 km

Fleet: 100 buses	
Standard buses	32
Articulated buses	55
Double-deck buses	6
Midsize	7

Average age of fleet: Buses 6 years

Fleet: 82 trolleybuses (plus 54 trailers)	
Standard	72
Articulated	10
Trailers	54

Average age of fleet: Trolleybuses 24 years, trailers 14 years

Trolleybus electrification: 600 V DC

Most intensive service: 5.5 min

One-person operation: All routes

Fare collection: Prepurchase tickets, passes, electronic purse; IEM prepurchase equipment at stops and (suburban) on board

Fare structure: Zonal system covers suburban and interurban operators and SBB trains; monthly passes, 24 h ticket

Fare evasion control: Roving inspectors; penalty

Operational control: Route inspectors/mobile radio

Arrangements for elderly/disabled: Reduced rate monthly passes

Average peak-hour speed: 15 km/h

Operating costs financed by: Fares 36.4 per cent (2007)

Subsidy from: State and city councils

New vehicles financed by: Loans

Light rail – Tramway du Sud Ouest Lausanne sa (TSOL)

Key personnel

President: Anne-Marie Depoisier

Type of operation: Light rail, opened 1991

Route length: 7.8 km

in tunnel: 0.7 km

Number of routes: 1

Number of stops: 15

Gauge: 1,435 mm

Electrification: 750 V DC, overhead

Current situation

Runs from the city centre at Flon westwards to the Institute of Technology and the suburb of Renens (SBB/CFF station). Single-track route with 12 passing loops mostly at grade and segregated; interchange with SBB trains at Renens and with the LEB local railway at Flon.

Rolling stock: 17 cars

VeVey (1990/91)	M17

Service: 10 min, evening 15 min; morning peak hour 5 min

First/last car: 05.16/00.35

Fare structure: As TL, through passes to LO and SBB/CFF services

Société du Métro Lausanne-Ouchy sa (Metro LO)

Key personnel

President: Daniel Brélaz

Type of operation: Rack railway

Current situation

1.5 km former funicular (recently rack-operated) with 10 cars links the lakeside at Ouchy with the centre of Lausanne, known locally as the 'Metro', ceased operations in January 2006.

Developments
A 4.6 km extension northeast to Croisettes (Epalinges) is under construction as a rubber-tyred light metro. The existing line is to be converted to provide a through service. ALSTOM will supply the rolling stock for this project, 15 two-car trainsets. The choice of rubber tyres over steel wheels was made because of the line gradients (12 per cent).

The first of the rubber-tyred metro sets was delivered in January 2006.

Schweizerische Bundesbahnen AG (SBB AG) – Swiss Federal Railways

Communications Department
Hochschulstrasse 6, CH-3000 Bern 65, Switzerland
Tel: (+41 51) 220 25 81
Fax: (+41 51) 220 44 33
e-mail: inforail@sbb.ch
Web: www.sbb.ch

Type of operation: Suburban heavy rail

Further information has been removed at the company's request.

Le Chemin de Fer Lausanne-Echallens-Bercher (LEB) – Lausanne-Echallens-Bercher Railway

Place de la Gare 9, Case postale 196, CH-1040 Echallens, Switzerland
Tel: (+41 21) 886 20 00   Fax: (+41 21) 886 20 19
e-mail: admin.leb@leb.ch
Web: www.leb.ch

Key personnel
Manager: U Gachet
  Staff: 52

Type of operation: Local railway

Passenger journeys: (2004) 2.2 million
(2006) 2.4 million
(2007) 2.5 million

Route length: 24 km
No of station: 9 stations, 12 halts
Gauge: 1,000 mm
Electrification: 1.5 KV DC

Current situation
Electric trains run half-hourly commuter services from Lausanne – Flon – Echallens – Bercher. A 1.1 km tunnel construction from Chauderon to Flon to link with the m1 and m2 lines was opened in 2000.

In Lausanne-Flon there is a connection to the m1 line and a link to the m2 line was opened in October 2008.

For further information on LEB, please see *Jane's World Railways*.

Rolling stock: 11 emu cars, 8 trailers

Zurich

Population: City 366,000, urban area 1.1 million, metropolitan area 1.3 million (estimates)

Public transport
Bus, trolleybus, tramway, funicular, rack and local railway services provided by municipal undertaking also running a privately owned rack railway for its owners and responsible for regional bus services. S-Bahn, including airport link, run by Swiss Federal Railways (SBB). Also two private railways. Lake ferries. Zürcher Verkehrsverbund (ZVV) co-ordinates these and other operations.

Zürcher Verkehrsverbund (ZVV)

Hofwiesenstrasse 370, CH-8090 Zürich, Switzerland
Tel: (+41 43) 288 48 48   Fax: (+41 43) 288 48 40
e-mail: contact@zvv.ch
Web: www.zvv.ch

Key personnel
Managing Director: Franz Kagerbauer
Head of Public Relations: Beatrice Henes

Current situation
ZVV was established in 1990 to co-ordinate and promote all forms of public transport in the canton of Zürich, with a total population of 1.3 million. Services are provided by 44 operators over a network extending to some 3,500 km. With approximately 900,000 daily journeys in the urban area, Zürich claims to have the highest use of public transport per head of population in the western world. Only 498 out of 1,000 citizens own a car in the canton (410 in the city of Zürich) and, in the city, public transport has a market share of more than 80 per cent of all commuter trips. There is a fully integrated ticketing system based on nine fare stages (45 zones).

All fares income is remitted to ZVV, which compensates individual operators in proportion to their costs and service quality.

Developments
The construction work for a new light rail system, called the Glattalbahn, started in September 2004. The Glattalbahn will link several areas to the north and east of Zürich and will also serve Zürich airport. Opening of the first phase took place in December 2006, with the final phases ready for operation between 2008 and 2010.

The area around Zurich main station and the section from Zurich to Winterthur have reached their capacity limits or have already exceeded it. There is a similar situation on many of the other S-Bahn lines. This may result in passengers switching to using their cars and subsequent major congestion of the road system. The planned fourth round of partial extensions to the

S-Bahn network is therefore considered to be an economic necessity.

The precondition for these capacity improvements is the construction of a second underground railway line linking Altstetten and Oerlikon, including a new station. This will give Zurich's central interchange a new fast through-line for the important west-east axis, which would relieve not only the S-Bahn network but also the national transport system. The new railway line is planned to be opened in 2013/2015.

There are also a number of proposals for extensions to the existing tram network, starting with a line from Escher-Wyss-Platz to the Altstetten train station. Construction is due to start in 2008, with completion in 2011.

Verkehrsbetriebe Zürich (VBZ)

Luggsewegstrasse 65, CH-8048 Zürich, Switzerland
Tel: (+41 44) 434 41 11
Fax: (+41 44) 434 47 49
e-mail: info@vbz.ch
Web: www.vbz.ch

Key personnel
Director: Hans-Peter Schär
Divisional Head, Corporate Staff: Andreas Uhl
Divisional Head, Technology: Ueli Frick
Divisional Head, Operations: Anton Westreicher
Divisional Head, Marketing: Jacques Baumann
Divisional Head, Personnel: Heinz Vögeli
Divisional Head, Finance: Beat Cagienard
Divisional Head, Infrastructure: Christoph Brändli
  Staff: 2,356 (2006)

Background
VBZ is the local public transport operator in the city of Zurich.

Passenger journeys: (All modes)
(2002) 298.4 million
(2003) 299.7 million
(2004) 308.3 million
(2005) 293.4 million
(2006) 296.7 million
Vehicle-km: Not currently available

Current situation
As the leading member of ZVV, VBZ has achieved spectacular success in promoting its services to non-users, in particular by sales of annual tickets through major employers. It also encourages walking and greater use of cycles. Also Mobility car rental (short term – by the hour).

Developments
Extensions to the tramway are being evaluated, in West-Zürich (Langstrasse), west of the Hardbrücke and to the Zollikerberg. Each would serve large residential or commercial developments, and would complement S-Bahn services.

In December 2006, the first phase of the Glattalbahn system opened.

Fare collection: pre-purchase of single tickets from 864 vending/validation machines
Fare structure: Zonal (2 city, 3 suburban), covers VBZ and 6 other operators in the Zürich region; daily, monthly and annual passes
Fares collected on board: Nil
Fare evasion control: Random inspection; penalty fare of CHF80/120/150
Operational control: Computerised online monitoring
Arrangements for elderly/disabled: Reduced-rate monthly and annual passes
Operating costs financed by: Fares sold by ZVV 88 per cent, other commercial sources 12 per cent

Bus and trolleybus
Passenger journeys: (2003) 103.6 million
(2005) 107.9 million
Vehicle-km: (2002) 33.133 million
(2003) 33.3 million
(2004) 33.953 million
(2006) 32.7 million
Number of routes: Bus 58 (27 intercity buses, 31 regional buses), trolleybus 6
Route length: (One way) bus 120.6 km, trolleybus 54 km

Fleet: 164 buses

Standard (Mercedes-Benz O405 and Neoplan Centroliner N45)	96
Articulated (Mercedes-Benz Gelenkbus O405 G and Neoplan Centroliner N45)	43
15-seat minibus	25

Fleet: 85 trolleybuses

Mercedes-Benz O405 GTZ Series 1 (1989)	23
Mercedes-Benz O405 GTZ Series 2 (1994)	43
Hess low-floor articulated (2006/07)	18
Hess low-floor double-articulated (2007)	1

On order: 16 double-articulated trolleybuses from Hess

Most intensive service: 5 min
One-person operation: All routes
Average peak-hour speed: Bus 16.5 km/h, trolleybus 15.5 km/h
Bus priority: Extensive system of bus lanes, including traffic light controlled dual-direction lane in narrow Langstrasse used by trolleybuses

Tramway
Type of operation: Conventional tramway

Passenger journeys:
(2003) 196.1 million
(2005) 185.4 million
Car-km: (2002) 18.9 million
(2003) 18.9 million
(2004) 19.2 million

Route length: 109.3 km
Number of lines: 13
Number of stops: 173

Gauge: 1,000 mm
Electrification: 600 V DC, overhead

Developments
In April 2006, the first of the new Cobra low-floor trams entered service.

In December 2007, VBZ exercised an option to order an additional 14 Bombardier 'Cobra' low-floor trams, bringing to 88 the total number of Cobra trams in the order (included ones now delivered). By December, 45 cars had been delivered.

A new tramway link between Bhf Oerlikon Ost and Letschenbach is believed to be under construction.

Rolling stock: 346 cars

Be 4/4 'Karpfen' (1959/60)	M15 T16
Be 4/6 'Mirage' (1966–68)	M90
Be 4/6 'Blinde Kuh' (1968/69)	M36
Anhänger B4 (1962/63)	T12
Be 4/6 Series 1 'Tram 2000' (1976–87)	M45
Anhänger Be 4/6 'Tram 2000' (1978)	M15
Be 4/6 Series 2 'Tram 2000' (1985–87)	M53
Anhänger Be 4/6 'Pony' (1985–87)	M20
Be 4/6 Series 3 'Tram 2000' (1992/93)	M23
Anhänger Be 4/6 'Pony' (1992/93)	M15
Bombardier/ALSTOM Be 5/6 'Cobra' (2001/06)	M6

On order: In 2003, a further 68 Bombardier/ALSTOM Cobra five-section low-floor trams were ordered for delivery from mid-2005. In December 2007, VBZ exercised an option to order an additional 14 Bombardier 'Cobra' low-floor trams, bringing to 88 the total number of Cobra trams in the order (included ones now delivered). By December, 45 cars had been delivered.

Service: Peak 5 min, off-peak 6, 7, 10 and 12 min
First/last car: 05.00/00.30

Local railway (Forchbahn)
e-mail: contact@zvv.ch
Web: www.forchbahn.ch

Current situation
This 16.4 km metre-gauge line links Zürich (Stadelhofen) and Esslingen, electrified 1.2 kV DC;

VBZ Cobra tram 3004 on route 4 service (John C Baker)   1124813

it carries about 4.3 million passengers annually.

Developments
13 new six-axle articulated cars built by Stadler were delivered in 2003/04, replacing older stock.

Rolling stock: 31 cars

SWS/SWP/SIG/BBC Be8/8×4 (1976/1988)	M6
SWS/SWP/BBC B+4×4 (1981)	T4
SWS/SIG/ABB Be4/4×4 (1994)	M8
Stadler Be 4/6 (2003/04)	M13

Funicular/rack railway
Current situation
A privately owned funicular railway, the UBS Polybahn, is operated by VBZ on behalf of the owner with sponsorship from a local bank.

Schweizerische Bundesbahnen AG (SBB AG) – Swiss Federal Railways

Communications Department
Hochschulstrasse 6, CH-3000 Bern 65, Switzerland
Tel: (+41 51) 220 25 81
Fax: (+41 51) 220 44 33
e-mail: railinfo@sbb.ch
Web: www.sbb.ch

Type of operation: Regional metro (S-Bahn)

Further information has been removed at the company's request.

Taiwan

Kaohsiung
Population: City 1.5 million, metropolitan area 3 million (2006 estimates)

Public transport
Bus services within city limits provided by city bus administration, with limited picking-up and setting-down rights accorded to private company which is sole provider of service in metropolitan and country areas of Kaohsiung County. Metro under construction. Light rail planned.

Kaohsiung Transportation Co Ltd
92 Fung Yan Road, Fengshan City, Kaohsiung, Taiwan
Tel: (+886 7) 746 21 41-5 Fax: (+886 7) 748 05 51
e-mail: kbus@ms26.hinet.net
Web: www.ksbus.com.tw

Current situation
Provides bus services to Kaohsiung City, neighbouring Tainan county and Pingtung county.

Developments
Bus passenger numbers have decreased with the increase in the number of travellers using private vehicles and scooters. However, the company intends to improve services with the addition of new routes and the purchase of new air-conditioned buses.

Bus
Number of routes: 60 (estimate)

Fleet: Not currently available
Fleet is believed to include: Hino (1988/95)
Mercedes (1979/83)
In peak service: Not currently available
Fare structure: Flat; 10 per cent discount on 10-trip ticket
Average peak-hour speed: 15.4 km/h
Operating costs financed by: Fares 75 per cent

Chungnan Bus Co
No 3, Yianhai Rd, Shiaugang District, Kaohsiung, Taiwan
Tel: (+886 7) 236 13 61

Current situation
Operations within the city on the following routes: Train Station-International Airport-Fangliao-Cherchen-Henchuan-Kenting-Universe Harbor-Sailboat Stone-Eluanbi. Service runs every 10 to 15 minutes, 24 hours a day.

Kaohsiung Mass Rapid Transit Bureau (KMRT)
10th Floor, 2 Ssu Wei 3rd Road, Kaohsiung, Taiwan
Tel: (+886 7) 337 37 15
Fax: (+886 7) 336 40 48

e-mail: mtbu@kcg.gov.tw
Web: mtbu.kcg.gov.tw

Key personnel
Director General: C P Lee
Deputy Director Generals: W S Jong
  D L Chou
Chief Engineer: L R Jong
Secretary General: C I Cheng

Concessionaire:

Kaohsiung Rapid Transit Corporation (KRTC)
1 Jung-An Road, Kaohsiung 806, Taiwan
Tel: (+886 7) 793 96 66
e-mail: krtc@krtco.com.tw
Web: www.krtco.com.tw

Key personnel
President: Y C Chiang
General Manager: C B Fan
Deputy General Manager: Y H Hsu

Type of operation: Metro (under construction)

Current situation
The Kaohsiung Mass Rapid Transit project, including a two-line 42.7 km network with 37 stations and three depots, is being built with public-private participation.

The concessionaire (Kaohsiung Rapid Transit Corporation, a consortium led by China Steel

Company, Taiwan) is responsible for the design, construction and operation of the project during the concession period (a total of 36 years).

The Kaohsiung Mass Rapid Transit network consists of the Red Line and the Orange lines. The civil works commenced in October 2001.

The Red Line, 28.3 km long with 23 stations, will run north-south and the Orange Line, 14.4 km with 14 stations, will run east-west.

Developments
There are long-term plans for further lines.

There are also plans for a Light Rail Transit System. This will be a circle line, 19.6 km in length with 32 stops. In 2004, the Kaohsiung City Government, with Siemens AG, built a two-station circular demonstration light rail system in Central Park.

Taipei

Population: City 2.63 million, urban area 6.8 million, metropolitan area 9.6 million (2007 Census)

Public transport
Integrated bus services for designated urban area provided by City Bus Administration and private groups and companies regulated by Taipei city government; suburban rail provided by Taiwan Railway Administration; metro/mass rapid transit.

Department of Transportation, Taipei City Government
6F, No 1 Shih Fu Road, Taipei 110, Taiwan
Tel: (+886 2) 27 20 88 89   Fax: (+886 2) 27 22 58 74
Web: www.dot.taipei.gov.tw/newch
english.taipei.gov.tw/dot

Key personnel
Commissioner for Transport: Shiaw-shyan Luo

Current situation
The Department of Transportation regulates private buses, minibuses, paratransit services and ferry operations.

Bus
Passenger journeys: Not currently available
Vehicle-km: (2006) 255.8 million (estimate)
Number of routes: 287 (January 2007)
Route length: Not currently available

Current situation
Fifteen companies operated bus services at the start of 2007, eight of which are city bus operators. The total bus fleet at that time was 2,809 vehicles.

Bus fares may be paid with the EasyCard pre-paid smartcard.

One-person operation: All routes
Fare collection: Cash and EasyCard pre-paid smartcard
Fare structure: 3 zones
Average peak-hour speed: 17 km/h
Operating costs financed by: Fares 100 per cent
Subsidy from: Taipei city government (if received)

Ferry
Blue Highway Project, No 1 Shih Fu Road, Taipei 110, Taiwan
Tel: (+ 886 2) 27 25 68 95

Current situation
The Blue Highway project, to improve the docks and ferry services along the Tamshui and Keelung rivers, was launched in early 2004. Intended to provide services for both tourists and commuters, there are now six lines along the two rivers, the Tamshui River Line and the Keelung River Line, totalling 44 km in length. Shuttle buses have also been put in place to integrate with the ferry routes.

Developments
There are plans to extend the existing routes.

Taipei Rapid Transit Corporation (TRTC)
7, Lane 48, Section 2, Zhongshan North Road, Taipei, Taiwan
Tel: (+886 2) 25 36 30 01   Fax: (+886 2) 25 11 50 03
e-mail: email@mail.trtc.com.tw
Web: www.trtc.com.tw

Key personnel
President: Huel-Sheng Tsay

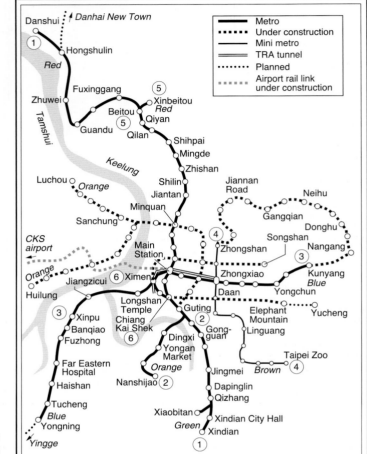

Map of Taipei's rail transit system
1115285

Route	Length (km)	No of stations	Date opened
Medium Capacity Transit System			
Muzha Line (Brown)	10.5	12 (elevated)	1996
Mass Rapid Transit System			
Danshui Line (Red)	23.5	22 (11 elevated, 5 at grade, 6 underground)	1997
Zhonghe Line (Orange)	5.4	4 (underground)	1998
Xindian Line (Green)	11.2	10 (underground)	1998/1999/2004
Nangang Line (Blue)	9.5	11 (underground)	1999/2000
Banqiao Line (Blue)	7.2	5 (underground)	1999/2000/2006
Xsiaonanmen Branch Line (Green)	1.6	1 (underground)	2000
Tuncheng Line (Blue)	5.5	4 (underground)	2006
Total	**74.4**	**69 (7 overlap)**	

Passenger journeys: (All lines)
(2003) 316.2 million
(2004) 350.1 million
(2005) 360.7 million
(2006) 383.9 million
(2007) 416.2 million
Passenger journeys: (Medium Capacity Transit System)
(2003) 30.2 million
(2004) 31.7 million
(2005) 31.4 million
(2006) 31.5 million
(2007) 33.8 million
Passenger journeys: (Mass Rapid Transit System)
(2003) 286.0 million
(2004) 318.4 million
(2005) 329.3 million
(2006) 352.4 million
(2007) 382.4 million

Background
TRTC was established in July 1994 to operate the Taipei Metro system.

In 1996, the first line, the Muzha Line, which is a Medium Capacity Transit system, was opened. This was followed by the Danshui Line of the Mass Rapid Transit System in 1997 and by the Zhonghe Line and the north section of the Xindian Line in 1998. In 1999, the remaining section of the Xindian Line was inaugurated, linking the northern and southern Taipei metropolitan area. Also in that year, the inaugurations of the Banqiao Line (Longshan Temple-Ximen) and the Nangang Line (Ximen-Taipei City Hall) took place, linking the area from east to west.

In 2000, the extension of the Panchiao Line to Hsinpu station was completed and the inauguration of the entire Nangang Line took place.

Current situation
All construction is in the hands of the Department Of Rapid Transit Systems (DORTS) (see separate entry).

The TRTC currently operates eight lines: Muzha Line (Brown), Danshui Line (Red), Zhonghe Line

(Orange), Xindian Line and Xsiaonanmen Branch Line (Green), Nangang Line, Banqiao Lines and Tuncheng Line (Blue). Details of the lines are shown in the table below.

Developments
Currently, projects for the system (overseen by DORTS) comprise:
Neihu Line: 14.8 km in length, projected to commence revenue service by December 2008;
Luzhou Line: 6.4 km in length, projected to commence revenue service by the end of 2009;
Xinzhuang Line: 19.7 km in length, projected to commence revenue service by the end of 2010;
Nangang Eastern Extension: 2.5 km in length, projected to commence revenue service by the end of 2010;
Xinyi Line: 6.4 km in length, projected to commence revenue service by the end of 2011;
Songshan Line: 8.5 km in length, projected to commence revenue service by the end of 2012.

In 2004, the Xiaobitan branch was opened as a branch of the Xindian Line

In 2006, Banqiao Line's Phase II and Tuncheng Line from Xinpu Station to Yongning Station were completed.

In July 2007, The Maokong Gondola, Taipei's first gondola system, was commissioned by the Taipei City Government and operated by the TRTC. With the addition of this new service, TRTC has entered into a new era of operations that combines metro and gondola service. The gondola system is 4.03 km long and has four passenger stations and two ancillary stations where the gondola changes direction.

Rolling Stock
Taipei Metro has two types of rolling stocks. The driverless medium capacity transit system introduced on the Muzha line has 25.5 trains in service. The mass rapid transit system on the other lines (eg: Danshui, Zhonghe, Xindian, Nangang, Banchiao, Xsiaonanmen and Tuncheng Lines) has 79 trains in service. Relevant data are shown in the following table.

Rolling stock/ System	Medium Capacity Transit Systems	Mass Rapid Transit Systems
Number of trains	25.5	79
Carriages per train	4	6
Seats per train	80	352
Maximum design speed	80	90

Department of Rapid Transit Systems (DORTS)

Taipei City Government
No 7, Lane 48, Zhongshan N Road Sec 2, Taipei 10448, Taiwan
Tel: (+886 2) 25 21 55 50
Fax: (+886 2) 25 11 53 35
e-mail: serv@trts.dorts.gov.tw
Web: www.dorts.gov.tw

Key personnel
Commissioner: Chang Chi-te
Chief Engineer: Kao Chung-cheng
Director, Public Relations Office: Tsai Bau-jen
  Staff: 640

Other offices
North District Project Office
3F, No. 86, Lane 527, Daye Rd, Taipei 11268, Taiwan
Tel: (+886 2) 28 96 96 33
e-mail: ndpo@trts.dorts.gov.tw

East District Project Office
3F, No. 300, Songde Road, Taipei, 11086 Taiwan
Tel: (+866 2) 23 46 23 58
e-mail: edpo@trts.dorts.gov.tw

South District Project Office
6F, No. 92, Roosevelt Road Sec 4, Taipei 10091, Taiwan
Tel: (+866 2) 23 65 78 11
e-mail: sdpo@trts.dorts.gov.tw

Central District Project Office
9F, No. 108, Zhongxiao East Road Sec 1, Taipei 10050, Taiwan
Tel: (+866 2) 23 94 68 39
e-mail: cdpo@trts.dorts.gov.tw

Systemwide Electrical and Mechanical Project Office
5F, No. 92, Roosevelt Road Sec 4, Taipei 10091, Taiwan
Tel: (+866 2) 23 67 18 18
e-mail: sempo@trts.dorts.gov.tw

Type of operation: Mass Rapid Transit (MRT) (planning, design and construction)

Background
Established in February 1987 under the jurisdiction of the Taipei City Government, DORTS oversees the planning, design and construction of the mass rapid transit system for the Taipei metropolitan area.

The department includes six divisions responsible for planning, design and engineering divisions, eight administrative offices, and a system-wide electrical and mechanical project office, along with four district project offices – East, North, South and Central.

Current situation
There are currently eight lines in operation, the Muzha, Danshui, Zhonghe, Xindian (including Xiaobitan branch line), Banqiao, Xiaonanmen and Nangang and Tucheng lines, spanning 76.6 km with 69 stations.

Joint development
Joint development combines characteristics of the public and private sectors to make the best use of real estate in areas adjacent to MRT stations and depots. It creates a situation in which landowners benefit from land development, investors profit from their investment, and the government may use the land required to complete its public construction projects. A total of 72 joint development projects are being implemented along the Taipei MRT network, amongst which 27 have been completed, 22 are under construction, 13 are being designed and 10 are currently soliciting investment or are making preparations to do so.

Developments

Noteworthy Construction

Sanchong to Taipei Station of Taiwan Taoyuan International Airport Access MRT System
The construction of the Taipei City section of Taiwan Taoyuan International Airport Access MRT System began on 25 April 2007. It features mostly underground construction with the first-ever adoption in Taiwan of the DOT (Double-O-Tube) method, highlighting the biggest challenge of the shield-tunnel section. It is believed that the construction can be taken as an indicator that more advanced shield tunnelling technology has entered domestic engineering in Taiwan. When the line is completed in 2013, it will take only 35 minutes to travel from Taipei Main Station to Taiwan Taoyuan International Airport. By that time, passengers can complete baggage check-in and boarding pass issuance at Taipei Main Station (A1). Taipei will be the world's third city to own this type of multi-function MRT station.

Hydro-pressure Anchor Caisson Construction of the Luzhou Line's Cross Passage
In the Luzhou line's Section Contract CL700A, because the construction site, featuring a vertically erected work shaft, is extremely narrow and located in a densely populated area, a hydro-pressure anchor caisson method is being used in the construction of the underground cross

passage. This construction method prevents damage to adjacent buildings and stabilises underground structures. The caisson application in the Luzhou line's cross passage is recognized as the first successful caisson construction in domestic engineering.

Construction Traversing Beneath the Existing TRS and THSR
The shield-tunnel section of Songshan MRT line ends at Tacheng Street section and meets with the up- and down-tracks of the shield-tunnel beneath Tacheng Street. The Songshan MRT line crosses Taiwan Railway System (TRS) and Taiwan High Speed Rail (THSR) at an angle of 60 degrees with one diaphragm wall and two Soil Mix Walls (SMW), which have already been installed. With the two operational systems directly alongside the construction site, the construction of this section, which entails first performing grouting treatments for earth improvement, removal of the diaphragm and retaining walls before launching the shield-tunnel boring machine, is a tough engineering challenge.

Neihu line
With the completion of track work, electrical and mechanical systems installation and power distribution, there have been trial runs on its entire route of the Neihu line since 4 August 2008. Commercial service is scheduled to start in 2009.

First stage (MRT routes completed):
Constructed over the past 21 years, the routes currently in operation are the Muzha, Danshui, Xindian, Zhonghe, Nangang, Banqiao, Xiaonanmen and Tucheng lines. They have a combined 76.6 km in length with 69 stations. Some 1.22 million people are carried on the network every day.

Second stage (MRT routes approved):
The second stage of MRT construction is well under way. Over the next seven years, the MRT network will be extended by 79.7 km, adding a further 66 stations. The additional lines are the Neihu line, Nangang eastern extension, Xinzhuang line, Luzhou line, Xinyi line, Songshan line, the Sanchong-to-Taipei section of the Taiwan Taoyuan International Airport Access MRT System, Circular line Phase I and the Tucheng extenion to Dingpu. Average daily passenger volume is expected to reach 2.3 million when these lines become fully operational in 2015.

Third stage (planned routes)
A planned 121.5 km long network comprising the North-South Line, the Minsheng-Xinzhi line, the Xinyi eastern extension, Ankeng line, Sanying line, Wanda-Zhonghe-Shulin line, Shezi, Shilin and Beitou Light Rail lines, and the North and South sections of the Circular line, is expected to extend the Taipei MRT network to more than 270 km and have an average of 3.6 million passenger trips per day.

Tentative Schedule of Implementation
For the second stage of MRT construction, the Nangang eastern extension will be completed and partially open for commercial service in 2008 and the Neihu line will be completed in June 2009. At the end of 2010, the entire Nangang eastern extension will be completed. The Luzhou and Xinzhuang lines will begin commercial service in 2010, 2011 and 2013, section by section. The Xinyi line is scheduled for completion in 2012. The Songshan line, Taiwan Taoyuan International Airport Access MRT System (Sanchong-to-Taipei section) and Tucheng extension to Dingpu will be completed in 2013, and the Circular line Phase I will be completed in 2015.

Taiwan Railway Administration (TRA)
3 Beiping West Road, Jhongjheng District, Taipei City 100, Taiwan
Tel: (+886 2) 23 81 52 26   Fax: (+886 2) 23 83 13 67
e-mail: railway@railway.gov.tw
Web: www.railway.gov.tw

Key personnel

Director General: Frank Fan
Deputy Directors General: C T Lin, Y N Sheu,
   C L Shu
Director, Transportation: Y Y Hong
Director, Rolling Stock: J S Siao
Director, General Affairs: C C Lai

Suburban rail

Type of operation: Suburban heavy rail

Passenger journeys: (Whole company operations)
(2002) 175.3 million
(2003) 161.4 million
(2004) 168.5 million
Passenger-km: (2002) 9,665.7 million
(2003) 8,726.4 million
(2004) 9,358.9 million

Current situation

TRA operates frequent local trains from Keelung through Taipei to Taoyuan and Hsinchu (electrified 25 kV AC), using the city-centre tunnel opened in 1990, plus other suburban services.

In 2004, a major project was underway which includes the extension of the Taipei cross-city line tunnel still further eastwards to beyond Nankang. The project also includes the construction of a considerable length of elevated guideway between Hsichih and Wutu. The new construction will eliminate a large number of level crossings, easing traffic congestion in these built-up areas and improving safety for both rail and road users.

A Daewoo two-set emu of TRA on a Taipei-Keelung local service (Bruce Evans)   0585157

In 2004, TRA launched a luxury circular train service for tourists, which travels around the island and is called the 'Star of Formosa'.

For further information on TRA, please see *Jane's World Railways.*

Developments

In January 2006, the Ministry of Transport and Communications awarded a contract valued at TWD25.49 billion to a Japanese consortium comprising Marubeni Corporation, Kawasaki Heavy Industries and Hitachi to construct and equip a 51.2-km rail link from Taipei to Chiang Kai-Shek International airport, southwest of the capital. As well as providing a connection to the airport, the line will serve commuters and will include 21 stations. Commissioning of the line is scheduled for 2013.

Rolling stock: Not currently available

Thailand

Bangkok

Population: 7 million (estimate)

Public transport

Most bus services operated by or on behalf of government Bangkok Mass Transit Authority (BMTA), supervised by Ministry of Transport. Private bus services supplement this network. Large fleet of taxis (both metered and unmetered) and three-wheel 'tuk-tuk' taxis; ferry services; limited suburban rail services; light rail; metro, expanding.

Bangkok Mass Transit System Public Company Limited – BTS SkyTrain (BTSC – BTS)

BTS Building, 1000 Phahonyothin Road, Chomphon, Chatuchak, Bangkok 10900, Thailand
Tel: (+66 2) 617 73 00
Fax: (+66 2) 617 71 33; 71 55
e-mail: patchaneeyap@bts.co.th
Web: www.bts.co.th

Key personnel

Chairman: Dr Paul Tong Yuk Lun
Executive Chairman and Chief Executive Officer: Keeree Kanjanapas
Corporate Communication Manager: Ms Patchaneeya Pootme

Heavy metro

Type of operation: Heavy metro, opened December 1999

Passenger boardings: 412,000 passenger trips per day (Jan–Nov 2007)

Route length: 23.5 km
Number of lines: 2
Number of stations: 23
Gauge: 1,435 mm
Electrification: 750 V DC, third rail

Background

Bangkok Transit System Corporation took control of the metro from the manufacturer consortium

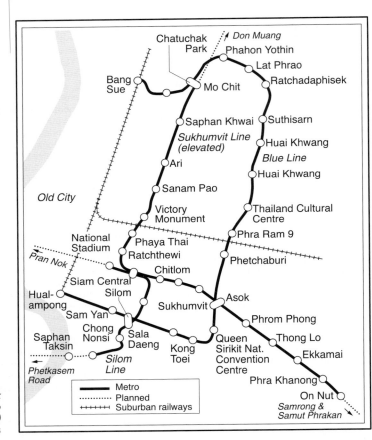

Map of Bangkok metro (whole system)
1115156

in December 1999. The order, worth a total of approximately USD1.3 billion, for turnkey construction of an elevated metro system was awarded to the consortium in July 1994.

The electrical and mechanical work share amounted to about USD650 million and that of the civil work around USD670 million. BTSC will operate the system on the Build-Operate-Transfer (BOT) principle for 30 years from completion. The infrastructure was handed over to the Bangkok Metropolitan Administration when operation began in December 1999. It becomes the owner of the electrical and mechanical equipment after 30 years.

The system is maintained by Siemens Transportation Systems (TS), which had its contract extended (contract value approximately EUR54 million) by 10 years in 2005.

Current situation

The rail network of the system is elevated and consists of two lines. The 16.8 km Sukhumvit

Line has a total of 17 stations. At a service interval of 153 seconds, 20,259 passengers can be conveyed in each direction every hour. The Silom Line is 6.3 km long with six stations, plus provision for an additional station, and carries 15,421 passengers in each direction per hour with a service interval of 210 seconds.

Ridership in the first year of operation was around 160,000 passengers a day.

The track gauge is 1,435 mm and current collection from protected aluminium-faced third rail at 750 V DC, with underneath contact. There are 12 traction substations and two 25 kV feeder substations.

Centralised Train Control (CTC) and Automatic Train Operation (ATO) are in operation on the system, with automatic route setting, train regulation, traction, door opening and reversal at terminal stations.

At Central Station (Siam Station), where the lines meet, passengers can change lines directly. The current three-car trains will be extended to six cars if necessary, to increase capacity to a maximum of 60,000 passengers per direction and hour. The service interval, currently 2.33 minutes at peak periods, will then be 2 minutes. The hours of operation are from 06.00 to midnight.

Distance-related fares have had to be introduced to cover costs and these are between THB15 and THB40. The total percentage of people using public transport in the Bangkok area is 40 per cent, though this falls to around 5 per cent in the city area.

Developments

The first stage of extensions will be: on the Silom Line, 2.2 km from Saphan Taksin station to Taksin Road and on the Sukhumvit Line, 5.25 km elevated with five stations, from On Nut station to Soi Baring. The contract for the latter was awarded in mid-2006, with construction scheduled to be completed in 2011.

The second stage of extensions will include: on the Silom Line, 6.8 km from National Stadium station to Pran Nok and and extending first extension from Taksin Road to Petkasem Road of approximately 4.5 km; and on the Sukhumvit Line, 1.7 km from Soi Baring to Samrong and 5.1 km from Mo Chit station to Kasetsart University.

BTS has co-operated in providing seamless transit between BTS and MRT systems. Direct linkage between the two systems is achieved by a system of escalators linking the BTS Asoke station with MRT's Sukhumvit station and a walkway and escalator system between BTS Sala Daeng station and the MRT's Lumpini station. These links were fully opened in 2005.

BTS is implementing a Smartcard ticketing system which will be compatible with the MRT's ticketing system and the Smartcard was launched officially on 1 April 2007.

In March 2008, the company is scheduled to add a further 108 CCTV cameras, which will bring the total number of cameras to 749 and which will ensure coverage of all areas in BTS stations. At Siam Station, the company has expanded the Tourist Information Center and installed a new Security Control Center, equipped with a modern surveillance technology system linked to the network of the Royal Thai Police.

BTS is also preparing for the future application of an additional safety standard system, OHSAS 18001.

The company has commenced the re-signalling of the system, which is due to be implemented by 2010.

A Passenger Information System has recently been installed and the radio system is to be upgraded from analog to digital.

An order for 12 4-car trains has been placed with Changchun Railway Vehicles Co Ltd (CRC) in a contract valued at some USD70 million. The trains will be equipped with Bombardier Transportation's **MITRAC** propulsion and control system and delivery is scheduled to start in 2009.

Rolling stock: 35 three-car Siemens Transportation Systems units

In peak service: Not currently available

BTS SkyTrain
1341032

BTS SkyTrain
1341026

On order: 12 4-car CRC trains, delivery scheduled to start in 2009
First/last train: 06.00/24.00
Fare structure: Single journey and stored value cards
Revenue control: Automatic Fare Collection (AFC) system
Surveillance: CCTV at all stations

Bangkok Mass Transit Authority (BMTA)

Head Office, 131 Thiemruam-mitre Road, Huaykwang, Bangkok 10320, Thailand
Tel: (+66 2) 247 21 89   Fax: (+66 2) 247 21 89
Web: www.bmta.co.th

Key personnel
Chairman: Athikhom Tanloet
Vice-Chairman: Predee Juljerm
    Kumropluk Suraswadi
Director and Secretary: Phinet Phaupattanakul
Director: Pinate Puapatankul
Deputy Director, Administration: Mrs Pranee
    Sugrasorn
Deputy Director, Private Joint Operation: Chattao
    Photonguak
Deputy Director, Bus Operation: Virat Chokkatiwat
    Staff: 18,394 (as at December 2006)

Current situation
The Bangkok Mass Transit Authority (BMTA) was established in 1976.

Currently, there are 20 agencies responsible for public transport in Bangkok. The Bangkok Mass Transit Authority (BMTA) is the principal government organisation providing bus transportation in Bangkok and the surrounding areas. The BMTA is under the supervision of the Ministry of Transport, through the Central Land Transport Control Board.

The local government organisation the Bangkok Metropolitan Administration (www.bma.go.th), is responsible for bus stops and mass transit, and although it is not currently engaged in bus transit it is planning and constructing the first pilot Bus Rapid Transit (BRT) line, the Silom Line, Ratchpruak.

BMTA bus operations are currently divided into eight zones, although these have extensive areas of overlap.

Developments
The BMTA has embarked upon a number of programmes to improve cost efficiency and service and has obtained ISO 9000 certification on all of its bus routes.

Although the BMTA operates some standard buses, these are increasingly being replaced by air-conditioned vehicles.

Bus
Passenger journeys: Not currently available

Number of routes: 442, of which 110 are BMTA buses, 85 are joint-service buses, 49 are minibuses, 103 are small buses (which ply the same routes as BMTA and joint-service buses) and 95 are van buses
Route length: About 4,000 km
On priority right-of-way: 250 km

Fleet: 3,623 buses (plus 13,229 under joint service arrangements)
The full breakdown of the fleet is not currently available, but includes:
BMTA-operated fleet:
Euro 2 air-conditioned buses (Cream/Orange)
Air-conditioned buses (White/Blue)
18 m articulated air-conditioned buses (White/Green)
Natural Gas Vehicle (NGV) buses
Standard buses (White/Blue)
Standard buses (Cream/Red)
BMTA joint-operated or non-BMTA fleet:
Private operators under sub-licence to BMTA
Bankok Metro buses (White/Green/Pink), under licence from the Department of Land Transport
Green minibuses (typically one-man operated)

Most intensive service: Peak 1–2 min
One-person operation: None
Fare collection: Roving conductors
Fare structure: Ordinary buses, flat, with higher flat fare for newer vehicles, supplements for limited-stop, Expressway and night services; same structure for private services. Air conditioned buses, graduated. Microbuses, premium flat (seated only)
Fares collected on board: 99 per cent
Fare evasion control: Frequent roving inspectors
Operational control: Route inspectors/mobile radio
Bus priority: 25 km of bus lanes, often contraflow
Average peak-hour speed: In mixed traffic, 8 km/h
Operating costs financed by: Fares 85.7 per cent, other commercial sources 1.7 per cent, subsidy/grants 12.5 per cent
Subsidy from: Government; bus fares had been held at low levels as a social measure, with BMTA permitted to cover its losses by bank loans, paying only the interest. Since 1991 fare increases have been permitted

State Railway of Thailand (SRT)

Rong Muang Road, Pathumwan, 10330 Bangkok, Thailand
Tel: (+66 2) 220 42 60; 220 42 66-7
Fax: (+66 2) 225 38 01
e-mail: srt_foreign@yahoo.com
Web: www.railway.co.th

Key personnel
Governor: Youdtana Tupcharoen
Deputy Governors: Bancha Yongnakorn
    Thavil Samnakorn
    Nakorn Chantasorn
    Prasert Attanandana
    Ithipon Paphavasit
    Prachack Manotham
    Wacharin Teevakul
Chief Financial Officer: Arak Ratboriharn
Traffic Manager: Sommai Tubwej
Marketing Manager: Viroj Treamphongpun
Chief Mechanical Engineer: Prachak Manotham
Chief Civil Engineer: Kamol Tangkijcharoenchai
Chief Special Project and Construction Engineer:
    Suprapas Senivongse Na Ayudhya
Chief, Policy, Planning, service Research and
    Development Bureau: Chumpol Sucharoen
Chief, Governor Bureau: Wimolrat Tupnoi
Chief, Public Relations and Tourism Service Center:
    Pairat Rojarearnngam
    Staff: Not currently available

Type of operation: Suburban heavy rail

Passenger journeys: (All operations)
(2004) 50.9 million
(2005) 49.7 million
(2006) 48.9 million
(2007) 45.1 million
Train-km: Not currently available

The SA-Express (red train), for services from Bangkok City Air Terminal to Suvarnabhumi International Airport, and the SA-City Line (blue train), for services from Phayathia Station to Suvarnabhumi International Airport   1368921

Bangkok City Air Terminal – due to open in late 2009   1368922

Current situation

SRT is state-owned: the Thai Government has a policy to rehabilitate SRT's organisation, which the Ministry of Finance and Ministry of Transport are pursuing.

The government has allocated funds to enable SRT to develop infrastructure, such as double-tracking, commuter train projects and the airport rail link project.

For further information, please see *Jane's World Railways*.

Developments

Airport Rail Link Project

In preparation for the commissioning in 2006 of the Second Bangkok International Airport (SBIA), also known as the 'Suwannabhumi' airport, SRT was assigned to construct a 28.8 km electrified standard gauge rail link to it from a new station in Bangkok, Bangkok City Air Terminal (BCAT). Following feasibility studies and an environmental impact assessment report, a EUR518 million turnkey contract to construct and equip the line was awarded in January 2005 to a consortium led by B Grimm International Ltd and B Grimm Hong Kong Ltd and also including Sino Thai Engineering and Construction plc (Stecon) and Siemens Transportation Systems. Siemens and B Grimm are to be responsible for design, supply, installation and project management of the entire electrical and mechanical systems. By June 2008, some 87.5 per cent of the rail link was complete. Currently, construction is scheduled to be completed in Q1 2009, with the line opening for service by Q4 2009.

Designed for use by both non-stop airport services and stopping commuter trains, the line is mostly elevated, although a 3.2 km section runs underground beyond the City Air Terminal station to provide a connection with the Skytrain metro system at Phaya Thai. There are eight stations. Check-in facilities are to be provided at City Air Terminal.

Rolling stock to be supplied by Siemens Transportation Systems for the Second Bangkok International Airport (SBIA) will comprise of five three-car and four four-car emus based on the company's Desiro UK design. The four-car sets are intended for non-stop airport services ('Express') and feature secure baggage storage facilities, while the three-car units are for 'City Line' commuter services over the airport link and feature high-density interior accommodation. The first train was unveiled at Siemens' Uerdingen (Germany) plant in March 2007. All nine were due to be delivered to Thailand by December 2007, but whether this has been completed is unknown.

Bangkok Red Line (MRT)

In May 2007, the Thai Government authorised the SRT to invite tenders for the construction of the first phase of an electrified, mostly elevated suburban railway, known as the Red Line, to serve the northeast of Bangkok. Construction of the 15 km section from Bang Sue to Taling Chan, with three stations, is expected to start in late 2008 for completion by 2011.

The Bang Sue to Rangsit section will be 26 km long with eight stations. Currently, construction is expected to commence at the start of 2011 and be completed in 2015.

Mass Rapid Transit Authority of Thailand (MRTA)

175 Rama IX Road, Huai Khwang, Bangkok 10320, Thailand
Tel: (+66 2) 612 24 44
Fax: (+66 2) 612 24 36
e-mail: pr@mrta.co.th
Web: www.mrta.co.th

MRTA Siemens three-car train
1328469

Metro

Type of operation: Full metro, inaugurated July 2004 (Blue Line – Chaloem Ratchamongkhon Line)

Passenger journeys: (2005) 57.19 million (estimate) (2006) 57.81 million (estimate) (2007) 59.68 million (estimate)
Train-km: Not currently available

Route length: 20 km
Number of lines: 1
Number of stations: 18

Operator:

Bangkok Metro Public Company Ltd (BMCL)

Administration Building, 189 Rama IX Road, Huai khwang, Bangkok 10310, Thailand
Tel: (+66 2) 354 20 00   Fax: (+66 2) 354 20 20
Tel: (+66 2) 624 52 00 (Customer Relations Center)
e-mail: crc@bangkokmetro.co.th
Web: www.bangkokmetro.co.th

Key personnel

Chairman of the Board of Directors: Plew Trivisvavet
Managing Director, Acting Marketing & Development Director: Sombat Kitjalaksana
Development Director: Witoon Hatairatana

Current situation

The Mass Rapid Transit Authority of Thailand (MRTA), a state enterprise under the supervision of the Transport Ministry, is tasked with the implementation of mass rapid transit lines throughout Thailand. The MRTA is currently in charge of the first underground railway system from Hua Lamphong Station to Bang Sue Railway station (20 km), the Chaloem Ratchamongkhon Line (Initial Blue Line), being operated by the Bangkok Metro Public Company Limited (BMCL) under concession for a period of 25 years, until 1 July 2029.

The network of the MRT Chaloem Ratchamongkhon Line includes 18 stations with a total length of 20 km. The route starts from Bangkok Railway Station (Hua Lamphong) along Rama 4 road, Ratchadaphisek Road, Lat Phrao road, Phahon Yothin road, Kamphaeng Phet Road and finally ends at Bang Sue Railway Station. The total of 18 underground stations are located approximately every 1 km. All stations are equipped with facilities such as lifts, escalators, kiosks, public telephones and air-conditioning system in the stations and the trains. For the blind/visually impaired, there are notices in the lifts and warning sings on the stair landings in Braille. In addition, parking facilities are also available. There are two park & ride buildings and seven ground-level parking facilities.

According to the Cabinet's resolution on 18 March 2008, MRTA was assigned to extend the existing mass rapid transit infrastructure by constructing three MRT lines/extensions with a total length of 75 km.

Developments

The three new lines/extensions include:

Purple Line

* *Bang Yai-Bang Sue Section:* Total length of 23 km, comprising an elevated line with 16 stations, will be the first project implementation. At present, this project is being tendered for civil works and the construction is scheduled to start in January 2009, with opening planned for April 2013.

Blue Line

Blue Line extensions are as follows:
* *Bang Sue-Tha Phra Section:* An elevated line running 13 km from Bang Sue to Tha Phra with 10 stations.
* *Hua Lamphong-Bang Khae Section:* This has a total length of 14 km, comprising 5 km of underground line and 9 km of elevated line. Of the 11 stations, four are underground and seven are elevated.

At present, this project has been approved by the Cabinet. The line will be implemented with construction scheduled to start in October 2009 and it will be opened for service in March 2015.

Green Line

* *Mor Chit-Phahonyothin-Sapan Mai Section:* Total length of 12 km, from Mor Chit to Sapan Mai, with 12 stations.
* *Baring-Samut Prakan Section:* An elevated line with a total length of 13 km, from Baring to Samut Prakan, with 10 stations.

At present, the design of the project is complete, and will be submitted to the Cabinet soon. Construction on the project is scheduled to start in July 2009 and it will be opened for service in February 2014.

Fleet: 19 three-car trains
Siemens (2004)   M38 T19

First/last train: 06.00/24.00
Security: CCTV at strategic points; K9 units for explosives detection; walk-through metal detectors at entrances (due to be in place by the end of 2008)

Trinidad and Tobago

Port of Spain
Population: 49,000 (2000 Census)

Public transport
Bus services in Port of Spain and other areas of Trinidad operated by state corporation which also operates busway; extensive private shared taxi operations. Rapid rail system planned.

Public Transport Service Corporation (PTSC)
Railway Building, South Quay, PO Box 391, Port of Spain, Trinidad and Tobago
Tel: (+1 868) 623 46 34
Fax: (+1 868) 625 65 02
e-mail: ceoptsc@tstt.net.tt
Web: www.ptsc.co.tt

Key personnel
Chief Executive Officer: Vincent Lynch
    Staff: 800

Background
Longstanding government subsidies were phased out in 1994, and PTSC embarked on a restructuring programme, which resulted in reduced operating costs. PTSC's market share has remained constant at about 10 per cent over the period 1996 to 2005, whilst its private hire and tour business has been increasing.

Market share is currently at an estimated 15 per cent.

Current situation
The Corporation is in the process of acquiring an additional 150 buses and is currently restructuring its operations towards achieving substantially higher levels of effectiveness in its delivery of services. The current emphasis is on the reintroduction of service schedules and higher levels of customer service.

New services are being investigated and a programme to improve vehicle maintenance is also under way.

Developments
Studies in relation to the introduction of light rail are in progress.

Bus
Number of routes: 45
On priority right-of-way: 24.8 km

Fleet: 130 vehicles (including 12 Volvo articulated buses (2005))

Most intensive service: Priority busway 30–45 min, other heavily used routes 15–30 min
One-person operation: All routes
Fare collection: Prepurchase tickets; cash on some routes
Fare structure: Graduated (telescopic)

Fare evasion control: Inspectors and fareboxes
Operational control: Inspection and audit
Arrangements for elderly/disabled: Pensioners and persons receiving public assistance carried free; accessible buses available for passengers with disabilities at reduced cost. Costs covered by financial support from the state.
Average peak-hour speed: On Priority Bus Route 30 km/h; in mixed traffic 15–20 km/h
Bus priority: 24.8 km busway links Port of Spain with Arima (see below), also used by a limited number of maxi-taxis to which a controlled number of passes are issued for a fee
Operating costs financed by: Fares 70 per cent, other commercial sources 30 per cent

Busway
Current situation
The Port of Spain to Arima busway (Priority Bus Route) is a two-lane, 7.3 m wide, single-carriageway reserved route using former railway trackbed with four major 'stations' and 27 stops. The route is shared with 700 privately owned minibuses (maxi-taxis), approximately 600 private cars with special passes, and emergency vehicles.

Taxis
Large numbers of taxis and shared maxi-taxis (minibuses) operate on fixed routes. Official taxis are recognisable by an 'H' licence plate.

Tunisia

Tunis
Population: City 990,000 (2007 estimate), metropolitan area 2.0 million (estimated)

Public transport
Bus services in Tunis and suburbs provided by central government corporation and some private operators. Light rail system run by another similar corporation, also responsible for suburban rail service. Both corporations directly responsible to Ministry of Transport. Other suburban rail services provided by national railway (SNCFT).

Société des Transports de Tunis (STT) – Tunis Transport Society – Transtu
PO Box 660, 1 Avenue Habib Bourguiba, Tunis 1001, Tunisia
Tel: (+216 71) 25 94 21
Fax: (+216 71) 34 27 27
e-mail: contact@snt.com.tn
Web: www.snt.com.tn

Key personnel
President/Director General: M Chedh el Hajn
Operating Manager: Ridha Essefi
Information and Publicity Manager: H Houa
    Staff: 5,193

Current situation
State-owned Société des Transports de Tunis (STT) (previously SNT) provides bus services in Tunis and its suburbs, the light rail system and the suburban rail line.

Bus
Number of routes: 163
Route length: (One way) 2,597 km
On priority right-of-way: 10 km

Fleet: 855 vehicles

Fiat 418	505
Volvo B10M	74
Volvo articulated	3
Fiat 418 articulated	94
Ikarus IK280 articulated	36
Iveco AP160	45
STIA AP160 (1994/95)	44
Others	54
In peak service: 678	

Most intensive service: 5 min
One-person operation: None
Fare collection: Season tickets, and onboard sales by seated conductor; some prepurchase, being extended
Fare structure: Stage; weekly and annual passes and season tickets; through ticketing to SMLT

Tunis light rail network   1168317

Fares collected on board: 41 per cent
Fare evasion control: Penalty payment
Average peak-hour speed: 10 km/h
Operating costs financed by: Fares 65.6 per cent, other commercial sources 3.1 per cent, subsidy/compensation 21.5 per cent, deficit 9.8 per cent
Subsidy from: Government; payments made to preserve financial equilibrium

Société du Metro Leger de Tunis (SMLT)
Type of operation: Light rail, initial route opened 1985

Passenger journeys: Not currently available
Car-km: Not currently available

Route length: 32 km
Number of lines: 5
Number of stations: 47
Gauge: 1,435 mm
Electrification: 750 V DC, overhead

Developments
There are currently plans for extensions to Line 4, to the Universtité de la Manouba, and southwards from Line 1 (6.5 km) to El Mourouj. The latter is under construction.

The first two of 30 Alstom Citadis LRVs have been delivered. An order for a further nine vehicles was placed in late 2007.

Rolling stock: 153
Siemens/Duewag (1984/85)	M77
(1991/92)	M43
(1997)	M14
Alstom Citadis LRVs (2007)	M19

In peak service: 108 cars
On order: A total of 39 Alstom Citadis LRVs, 19 of which had been delivered in late 2007

Service: Peak 4 min, off-peak 12 min
Fare structure: 2 zones per route, through-fares to buses

Tunis-Goulette-Marsa (TGM)
Type of operation: Suburban railway

Passenger journeys: Not currently available
Train-km: Not currently available

Route length: 19.5 km
Number of stations: 18
Gauge: 1,440 mm
Electrification: 750 V DC

Current situation
Suburban railway linking Tunis, La Goulette and La Marsa.

Rolling stock:
Full breakdown of fleet is not currently available, but includes:
Duewag/Man/Siemens (1977)	M18 T18

On order: Not currently available

Société Nationale des Chemins de Fer Tunisiens (SNCFT)

Gare de Tunis, Ville Place Barcelona, Tunis 1001, Tunisia
Tel: (+216 71) 34 51 88, 34 55 11
Fax: (+216 71) 34 85 40
e-mail: sncft@sncft.com.tn
Web: www.sncft.com.tn

Key personnel
President Director General: Abdelaziz Chaabane
Director, Communications and External Relations: Jalila Houssein
Manager, Communications Division: Latifa Jardak
Staff: 5,554

Type of operation: Suburban heavy rail

Passenger journeys: (Total system) (2003) 35.7 million (estimate)
Train-km: Not currently available.

Current situation
SNCFT operates suburban services on four routes totalling 142 km.

For further information, please see *Jane's World Railways*.

Developments
In early 2008, SNCFT awarded a contract, valued at some EUR54 million, to a consortium which includes Alstom and Ansaldo STS, to upgrade, electrify and re-signal the 23 km Tunis Ville-Borj Cedria line. The upgrade includes the extension of the automatic command and control system.

This upgrade is part of a project to develop an 85 km commuter rail network in Tunis, which is scheduled to be completed in 2010.

A contract was also awarded to Sumitomo, Japan and Hyundai Rotem for 76 dmu cars, for service on the line.

Rolling stock: Diesel-hauled push-pull trainsets and dmus
Breakdown of vehicles used on the Tunis network is not currently available
On order: 76 Sumitomo/Hyundai Rotem dmu cars, for service on the Tunis Ville-Borj Cedria line

Turkey

Ankara

Population: 4.3 million (2005 estimate)

Public transport
Municipally owned authority operates bus, metro and light metro services. Suburban rail services operated by State Railway. Also private operation of 'Minibus-Dolmus' services and conventional buses.

Elektrik, Gaz ve Otobüs Isletmesi Genel Müdürlügü (EGO)

General Directorate of Electricity, Gas & Bus Management
Toros Sokak No 12, TR-06042 Sihhiye, Ankara, Turkey
Tel: (+90 312) 231 71 80
Fax: (+90 312) 229 65 97
e-mail: bilgi@ego.gov.tr
Web: www.ego.gov.tr

Key personnel
General Director: Ihsan Fincanı
Staff: Not currently available

Current situation
The Electricity, Gas & Bus General Directorate (EGO) operates the Ankara Metro, the Ankaray light metro line and EGO Otobüs services.

Bus – EGO Otobüs
Tel: (+90 312) 384 03 60
Fax: (+90 312) 231 91 33; 230 81 09
Passenger journeys: Not currently available
Vehicle-km: Not currently available

Number of routes: 329 (regular 229, express 41)
Route length: (One way) 7,000 km

Fleet: 1,190 buses
Mercedes	353
MAN	5
MAN SL	76
Ikarus	327
Ikarus articulated	260

Ankara's metro, light and suburban rail network

1124834

MAN articulated	50
Mercedes articulated	70
BMC	49

In peak service: 921
New vehicles required each year: 285

Most intensive service: 4 min
One-person operation: All routes
Fare collection: Prepurchase magnetic tickets with ticket box on vehicles
Fare structure: Flat; prepurchase full fare tickets, reduced-rate student tickets
Fares collected on board: None
Fare evasion control: By driver; 10 × standard fare surcharge
Operational control: At terminal and dispatching points and by route inspectors
Average peak-hour speed: In mixed traffic, 12–15 km/h; express services, 30 km/h
Operating costs financed by: Fares 76 per cent, subsidy/grants 24 per cent
Subsidy from: Municipality of Greater Ankara
New vehicles financed by: Municipality and General Directorate of EGO

Light metro – Ankaray
Anakaray Yönetim Merkezi, TR-06520 Sögütözü, Anakara, Turkey
Tel: (+90 312) 224 11 70
Fax: (+90 312) 224 11 82
e-mail: info@ankaray.com.tr
Web: www.ankaray.com.tr

Type of operation: Light metro, opened 1996

Passenger journeys: (2006) 63.9 million (estimate)

Route length: 8.5 km
Number of lines: 1
Number of stations: 11
Gauge: 1,435 mm
Electrification: 750 V DC third rail

Current situation
This light metro, built as part of the main metro project (see below), opened in 1996. It runs on fully segregated (mostly underground) alignment along the main east-west highway linking Dikimevi with Bohcelievler and the ASOT

bus terminal. There is interchange with the heavy metro at Kizilay in the city centre.

Developments
There are planned extensions from Maltepe to Etlik (5.7 km), from Kurtulus to Haslöy (4 km) and from Dikimevi to Dogukent (7.7 km)

Rolling stock: 33 cars
Breda/Siemens (1994/95)   M33
In peak service: 27
Service: 3–5 min
First/last train: 06.15/24.00

Metro
İşletme ve Bakim Merkezi, TR-06370 Yenimahalle, Ankara, Turkey
Tel: (+90 312) 354 59 33   Fax: (+90 312) 354 59 32
e-mail: bilgi@ankarametrosu.com.tr
Web: www.ankarametrosu.com.tr

Type of operation: Full metro, opened 1997

Passenger journeys: (2006) 49.5 million (estimate)
Vehicle-km: Not currently available

Route length: 14.6 km
  in tunnel: 6.5 km
  elevated: 3.2 km
Number of lines: 1
Number of stations: 12
Gauge: 1,435 mm
Track: UIC54 rail on concrete sleepers, ballasted
Electrification: 750 V DC third rail

Current situation
Fully automated Line 1 links Kizilay in the city centre with new residential areas at Batikent in the west, running along the congested Atatürk Boulevard. It is fully segregated and capable of handling 31,500 passengers/h in each direction on opening, rising to 103,042/h in peak times by 2015.

Average distances between stations is 1.2 km with vehicles running at an average commercial speed of 38 km/h. From Batikent to Kizilay takes 22 minutes and a round trip Batikent-Kizilay-Batikent takes 48 minutes.

Developments
Three extensions are under construction; Kizilay to Çayyolu (18 km, 16 stations), Ulus to Keçiören (7.9 km, six stations) and Batikent to Sincan (18 km, 11 stations). An extension from TBMM to Dikmen (4.8 km, five stations) is planned.

Rolling stock: 108 cars, formed in six-car sets
Bombardier (1995/97)   M108

Service: 3–5 min peak, 8–9 min off-peak
First/last train: 06.00/24.00
Fare structure: Flat; 1- and 10-trip tickets
Fare collection: Magnetic tickets; ticket barriers

Türkiye Cumhuriyeti Devlet Demiryollari (TCDD) – Turkish State Railways
Genel Müdürlüğü
General Directorate of Turkish State Railways
Talatpaşa Bulvarı, TR-06330 Gar, Ankara, Turkey
Tel: (+90 312) 309 05 15, 312 32 14
Fax: (+90 312) 312 32 15, 324 40 61
e-mail: byhim@tcdd.gov.tr
Web: www.tcdd.gov.tr

Key personnel
General Manager and Head of Board of Directors:
  Süleyman Karaman
Vice General Manager and Member of Board of Directors: Veysi Kurt
Vice General Manager and Member of Board of Directors: Isa Apaydın
Vice General Manager: Şinasi Kazancıoğlu
Vice General Manager: Erol Inal
Vice General Manager: Mustafa Çavuşoğlu
Press and Public Relations Counsellor: Mehmet Aycı
Department Chiefs:
Operations: Ibrahim Çelik
Supplies: Ismet Duman
Research, Planning and Co-ordination Department (Deputy): Ismet Duman

External Affairs: Ibrahim Halil Çevik
Marketing: Emin Tekbaş

Suburban railway
Type of operation: Suburban heavy rail

Passenger-km: (2004) 378 million

Current situation
Suburban operations extend over a 37 km route from Sincan through central Ankara to Kayaş with 28 stations, electrified 25 kV 50 Hz, using E14000 emus. Flat-fare system.

For further information on TCDD, please see *Jane's World Railways.*

Developments
In 2006, a Japanese-Korean consortium of Mitsui and Rotem won a contract for 96 commuter rail cars to be used on the suburban lines around Ankara.

Rolling stock: 26 emu trains

Ankara

Private buses
Passenger journeys: (1996) 60 million

Current situation
Bus routes are operated by private companies, with Halk Otobüsü being the largest of these. Some double-deck vehicles. Fares are cash only. The numbers and routes are regulated by the city's Transportation Co-ordination Centre (UKOME). Other local operators also run services into Ankara from the surrounding area.

Minibus/shared taxi
Current situation
'Dolmus' (collective taxi) vehicles are operated by private owners providing services on fixed routes mainly in outer suburbs, with numbers and routes subject to restriction by UKOME. Fares are distance-related.

Istanbul
Population: Metropolitan area 10.3 million (2007 estimate)

Public transport
Conventional bus services and underground funicular railways and heritage tram services provided by municipal undertaking. Private bus services supervised by IETT. Private 'Dolmus' shared taxi and minibus operations. Suburban rail, and public and private boat services. Light rail and tramway; metro opened 2000.

Istanbul Elektrik Tramvay ve Tünel İşletmeleri Genel Müdürlüğü (IETT) – Greater Municipality of Istanbul Electricity, Tramway and Tunnel General Directorate
Istanbul Metropolitan Municipality Presidency
Directorate General of IETT Enterprises
Erkan-ı Harp Sokak No. 4 Tünel, 80050 Beyoólu, Istanbul, Turkey
Tel: (+90 212) 245 07 20
Fax: (+90 212) 243 08 83
e-mail: mozturk@iett.gov.tr
Web: www.iett.gov.tr/en/

Key personnel
General Manager: Mehmet Öztürk
  Staff: 8,828 (2007)

Operating costs financed by: Fares 85 per cent, other sources 15 per cent

Mercedes-Benz low-floor Citaro bus   1176399

Background
IETT has been in existence for 138 years and provides and administers predominantly the public bus services in and around Istanbul.

Current situation
The IETT administrative and service area covers 5,343 km² in and around Istanbul. IETT services account for approximately 15 per cent of general transportation and 65 per cent of all public transportation in Istanbul.

Developments
The new ticketing system, AKBİL, is now installed in all of the organisation's buses, rail and sea/ferry services. Transfers are reduced for five operators within 2 hours. Monthly AKBİL has been installed on IETT's services and private buses. Full integration, to include services and fares, is being developed.

50 high-capacity buses and 500 low-floor standard buses all with air conditioning, minimum Euro-3 standard, were purchased in 2007.

IETT Berkhof low-floor bus 1139586

IETT Tunel funicular 1139587

IETT tourist tramway 1139593

The purchase of 50 rubber-tyred trams and 200 high-capacity buses was planned for 2008.

The installation of an intelligent passenger information system, AK-YOL-BIL, project is scheduled to be completed by the end of 2009.

IETT has been overseeing the construction of metro and light rail extensions – please see separate entry for Istanbul Ulaşim Transportation Co.

Bus

Passenger journeys: (2004) 473 million
(2005) 477 million
(2006) 481 million
(2007) 519.5 million
Vehicle-km: (2004) 162 million
(2005) 178 million
(2006) 191 million
(2007) 195 million

Number of routes: 531
Number of stops: With shelters 5,708, open 3,545
Route length: 9,647 km

Fleet: 2,827 (average fleet in service, 2,337)

MAN	212
MAN articulated	173
Ikarus	1,136
Ikarus articulated	138
Mercedes-Benz (Euro 2: 523, Euro 3: 350)	873
Mercedes-Benz articulated (Euro 2: 85, Euro 3: 100.Euro 4: 31)	216
Berkhof	3
DAF/Optare	26
DAF/VDL double-deck (Euro 3: 14, Euro 4: 36)	50

In peak service: 2,500
New vehicles required each year: 250–300

Most intensive service: 2 min
One-person operation: All services
Fare collection: Prepurchase tickets, AKBİL and monthly AKBİL
Fare structure: Flat, reduced (students, over-60s and teachers); express routes double; Akbil and monthly Akbil tickets

Fare evasion control: Inspectors and drivers; penalty fare
Integration with other modes: With ferry, light rail, metro, tramway and private bus
Average distance between stops: 300–500 m
Average peak-hour speed: In mixed traffic, 10–17 km/h; express lines, 25 km/h

Contracted bus services
IETT is responsible for 2,078 private buses.

Funicular/tramway
Current situation
IETT operates a 573 m underground funicular railway, between Tünel and Karaköy. The two vehicles carry about 10,800 passengers daily. Fare collection is by token and AKBİL, through turnstiles.

A 1.6 km tourist tramway opened in 1991 betwen Tünel (funicular station) and Taksim (metro terminus); it carries about 1,550 passengers daily.

Developments
Services are now integrated and included in the AKBİL and Monthly AKBİL ticketing system.

IETT is investigating a series of rail projects for new systems. Areas targeted are Kadıköy-Kartal, Otogar-İkitelli and Edirnekapı-Sultançiftliği, Edirnekapı-Topkapı.

A rubber-tyred tram system is being considered for the MetroBus route.

Istanbul Deniz Otobusleri Sanayii ve Ticaret AS (IDO)
Istanbul Fast Ferry Co Inc
Kennedy Cad., Yenikap, Istanbul TR-34480, Turkey
Tel: (+90 212) 517 92 94; 96 96
Fax: (+90 212) 517 38 00
e-mail: info@ido.com.tr
Web: www.ido.com.tr

Key personnel
General Manager:
Dr Ahmet Paksoy
Marketing: Mustafa Ozturk
Staff: 3,150

Passenger journeys: (2005) 67.5 million (plus 4.5 million vehicles)

Fleet: 87 (2005)

Seabuses	20
Fast ferries	4
Ferry cats	2
Conventional passenger ferries	32
Auto passenger ferries	15
Passenger ship and ferryboats	2
Other	12

Current situation
The Istanbul Fast Ferries Company (IDO) was founded in 1987 by the Istanbul Metropolitan Municipality to provide alternative commuting services for the city.

Developments
In February 2005, City Line Administration amalgamated with IDO to become the sole waterborne transportation authority for Istanbul and the Sea of Marmara.

IDO has signed a shipbuilding contract with Damen Shipyards Group for construction and delivery of two fast car ferries of the Damen Fast RoPax (DFR) 8521 design. The ferries will operate on the existing line between terminals at Pendik and Yalova. The double-ended DFR 8521 is an aluminium catamaran, designed to transport up to 112 cars and 600 passengers at a service speed of 22 knots.

The first of two high-speed auto passenger ferries was launched in Australia. Built by Austal ships, the new ferries are designated to operate on a 39 nautical mile reciprocal service across the Marmara Sea between Yenikapi (Istanbul) and a new port development in Guzelyali servicing the city of Bursa. The ferries have the capacity to carry 1,200 passengers and 225 cars and will be capable of an operational speed of 36 knots when loaded.

IDO is also expanding its fleet with five new Seabus ferries, built by Damen Shipyards Group, Singapore. The catamaran ferries have a capacity of 449 passengers on two decks and 30 knots/h operational speed.

Istanbul Ulaşim Sanayii ve Ticaret AS – İstanbul Ulaşim Transportation Co
Ferhatpaşa Metro Tesisleri, İstanbul Cad, TR-34220 Esenler, Turkey
Tel: (+90 212) 568 99 70
Fax: (+90 212) 568 89 00
e-mail: info@istanbul-ulasim.com.tr
Web: www.istanbul-ulasim.com.tr

Key personnel
General Manager: Suleyman Pektas
Operations Manager: Kaan Yıldızgöz
Staff: 800

Passenger journeys: (All modes)
(2006) 205 million

Current situation
İstanbul Ulaşım was established in 1988 in order to undertake the operation and maintenance of the completed railway systems. Founded as a subsidiary of the Istanbul Metropolitan Municipality, İstanbul Ulaşım has been serving to the public for 19 years.

As the operator of metro, light rail, tramway, funicular and cable car in the city, İstanbul Ulaşım serves a population of more than 700,000 thousand, co-ordinated centrally from its headquarters in Esenler. With a 52 km long urban rail system, İstanbul Ulaşım serves more than 200 million passengers a year.

İstanbul Ulaşım has demonstrated its commitment to sustainable development by signing the UITP Sustainable Development Charter in 2005.

Developments

In 2006, the new Kabatas-Taksim funicular opened providing a connection between the tram line and the metro system. This funicular carries some 20,000 passengers daily.

Projects under way or under consideration includes:

- Marmaray Bosphorus Tube Crossing (please see separate entry under TCDD);
- 4th Levent-Ayazağa metro line (3.6 km);
- Central Bus Station-Bağcılar light rail line (20 km);
- Taksim-Yenikapı metro line (5.2 km);
- Aksaray-Yenikapı light rail extension (0.7 km);
- Edirnekapı-Sultançiftliği light rail line;
- Kadıköy-Kartal light rail line (22 km).

Maintenance and repair of the rolling stocks as well as rail system projects and research and development works are being carried out by İstanbul Ulaşım.

Light rail/tramway

Type of operation: Light rail/tramway, first line opened 1989

Passenger journeys: (Annual) 87.5 million (estimate)
Passenger-km: Not currently available

Route length: Light rail 20 km, tramway 14 km
Number of stations/stops: Light rail 18, tramway 24
Gauge: 1,435 mm
Electrification: 750 V DC, overhead

Current situation

İstanbul Ulaşım also operates the Kadıköy-Moda nostalgic tramway, Maçka-Taşkışla cable car and the Eyüp-Piyer Loti cable car systems.

Developments

The tram line was extended to Bağcılar in 2006. The line connects with the light rail system at Zeytinburnu and Aksaray stations. Also in 2006, the new Kabatas-Taksim funicular opened providing a connection between the tram line and the metro system. The funicular carries some 20,000 passengers daily.

Rolling stock: 55 vehicles
ABB (1988/89)   M55
In peak service: Not currently available
On order: Not currently available

Service: 5 min
First/last car: 06.00/24.00
Fare structure: Flat; passes
Fare collection: Reusable magnetic or touch-memory ticket opens platform access gate on light rail; tramway uses prepurchase paper tickets inspected manually

Metro

Passenger journeys: (2006) 65.7 million (estimate)
Car-km: Not currently available

Route length: 8 km
Number of lines: 1
Number of stations: 6
Gauge: 1,435 mm

Current situation
Rolling stock: 8 four-car trains
GEC/ALSTOM   M32

Service: Peak 4 min.off-peak 6–15 min
Fare collection: Tokens or Akbil smartcard

Istanbul funicular   1327920

Istanbul cable car   1327921

Istanbul light rail
1327919

Türkiye Denizcilik İşletmeleri Aş (TDI) – Turkish Maritime Organization Inc

Rihtim Caddesi Merkez Han No 4, (34425), Karaköy/Istanbul, Turkey
Tel: (+90 212) 251 50 00   Fax: (+90 212) 249 53 91
e-mail: tdi@tdi.com.tr
Web: www.tdi.gov.tr

Key personnel
General Manager: Burhan Külünk

Background
Subsidiary of TDI Group operating local services in the Istanbul, Bosphorus, Sea of Marmara, Dardanelles area and Izmir Bay.

Current situation
Extensive ferry services in the Dardanelles area.

Türkiye Cumhuriyeti Devlet Demiryollari (TCDD) – Turkish State Railways

Genel Müdürlüğü
General Directorate of Turkish State Railways
Talatpaşa Bulvarı, TR-06330 Gar, Ankara, Turkey
Tel: (+90 312) 309 05 15, 312 32 14
Fax: (+90 312) 312 32 15, 324 40 61
e-mail: byhim@tcdd.gov.tr
Web: www.tcdd.gov.tr

Key personnel
General Manager and Head of Board of Directors: Süleyman Karaman
Vice General Manager and Member of Board of Directors: Veysi Kurt
Vice General Manager and Member of Board of Directors: Isa Apaydın
Vice General Manager: Şinasi Kazancıoğlu
Vice General Manager: Erol Inal
Vice General Manager: Mustafa Çavuşoğlu
Press and Public Relations Counsellor: Mehmet Aycı
Department Chiefs: Operations: Ibrahim Çelik
Supplies: Ismet Duman
Research, Planning and Co-ordination Department (Deputy): Ismet Duman
External Affairs: Ibrahim Halil Çevik
Marketing: Emin Tekbaş

Type of operation: Suburban heavy rail

Passenger journeys: Not currently available
Passenger-km: (2004) 345 million

Current situation
TCDD operates suburban services over two routes totalling 72 km with 45 stations, electrified 25 kV 50 Hz, Haydarpasa to Gebze and Sirkeci to Halkali, carrying less than 10 per cent of Istanbul's commuters, using E14000 emus.

Developments
After a series of planning and preliminary engineering studies, which started in 1984, a rail tunnel project running under the Bosphorous strait, known as the Marmaray project, has started.

The second phase of the project will upgrade the Gebze-Haydarpaşa and Sirkeci-Halkalı suburban rail lines (increasing the number of routes from two to three), provide state-of-the-art technology, and connect the routes through the tunnel. The existing hourly passenger capacity of commuter rail will be increased and travel time from the Anatolian side to the European side will be reduced. This phase is scheduled to be completed in 2009.

Rolling stock: 75 emu trains

Istanbul Metro station   1327918

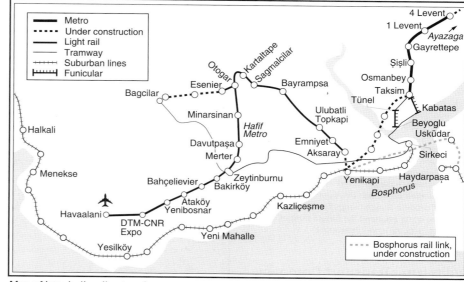
Map of Istanbul's rail network   1168066

TDI operates passenger ferry operations in the Dardannelles area
1181764

Izmir

Population: City 3.1 million, metropolitan area 3.8 million (2007 estimates)

Public transport
Public transport in the Izmir metropolitan area is overseen by the Greater Izmir Municipality (GIM).

Bus services provided by two municipal undertakings; municipal ferry operations; metro/light rail (opened in August 2000); commuter rail services provided by national railways; paratransit and shared taxi 'dolmus' operated by private owners on fixed-fare, fixed-route basis; private bus and minibus operations for industry employees and businesses; school services.

Greater Izmir Municipality (GIM)
Cumhuriyet Bulvari No 1 Konak, Izmir, Turkey
Tel: (+90 232) 293 12 00
Fax: (+90 232) 446 48 18
e-mail: him@izmir.bel.tr
Web: www.izmir.bel.tr

Elektrik Su Havagazi Otobüs Troleybüs (ESHOT)
ESHOT Genel Müdürlüğü
222 Sokak No 500, Gediz, Buca, Izmir, Turkey
Tel: (+90 232) 276 15 43
Fax: (+90 232) 275 01 07
e-mail: eshgn@superonline.com
Web: www.eshot.gov.tr

Key personnel
General Director: Ersu Hizir (ESHOT-İzulaş)
Operations Director: Veli Türkeli
Staff: 4,181

Background
ESHOT has supplied bus services since 1943 and operated the trolleybus services until those ceased in 1993.

Current situation
Bus services in the Izmir metropolitan area are operated by ESHOT, the main bus operator, in co-ordination with İzulaş (see separate entry in section), another municipal company. The routes, schedules and tarrifs are planned and operated as a single bus network, with integrated ferry and metro services.

ESHOT has a fleet of 1,120 buses. The table below shows the combined fleet of ESHOT and İzulaş.

Developments
The combined fleet of ESHOT and İzulaş was expanded and the average fleet age reduced by the purchase of 105 Mercedes-Benz articulated buses, 122 BMC standard buses and 50 Isuzu midibuses.

ESHOT will also complete the purchase of 50 single and 50 articulated buses and a further 100 single and 100 articulated buses. İzulaş will purchase 50 midibuses.

Bus
Number of routes: 295

Fleet (ESHOT and İzulaş combined): 1,539

Mercedes-Benz 302	39
Mercedes-Benz 302 T	66
Mercedes-Benz O345	134
BMC standard – Belde	194
Ikarus standard	65
MAN standard	135
Sanos standard	299
BMC standard	120
Volvo standard	20
Mercedes-Benz O345 articulated	105
Ikarus articulated	97
Sanos articulated	150
Volvo articulated	45
Isuzu midibus	50
DAF double-deck	5

On order: See above

Most intensive service: 5 min
One-person operation: All routes
Fare collection: Prepurchase smartcard (Kentkart)
Fare structure: Distance-based (5 zones)
Fares collected on board: Drivers may collect cash and then provide access using their own smartcard
Operating costs financed by: Single budget covers gas, water and transport operations

İzulaş İzmir Transport Company (İzulaş Inc)
222 Sokak No 500, Gediz, Bucar, İzmir, Turkey
Tel: (+90 232) 276 14 86
Fax: (+90 232) 276 24 98
Web: www.izmir-bld.gov.tr

Key personnel
General Director: Ersu Hizir (ESHOT-İzulaş)
Deputy General Director: Kenan Gülay

Current situation
Bus services in the İzmir metropolitan area are operated by İzulaş in co-ordination with ESHOT, the main bus operator (see separate entry), another municipal company. The routes, schedules and tariffs are planned and operated as a single bus network, with integrated ferry and metro services.

İzulaş has a fleet of 418 buses. Please see the entry for ESHOT for the combined fleet of İzulaş and ESHOT.

Developments
The combined fleet of İzulaş and ESHOT was expanded and the average fleet age reduced by the purchase of 105 Mercedes-Benz articulated, 52 BMC standard buses and 50 Isuzu midibuses between 2000 and 2004.

İzulaş will purchase a total of 50 midibuses between 2006 and 2007.

İzmir

Minibus/shared taxi
Current situation
There are currently 1,118 owner-operated private minibuses and 357 shared taxis (dolmus) operating in İzmir. Numbers and routes have officially been limited for years. Minibuses

Izmir Metro LRV on elevated section   1097464

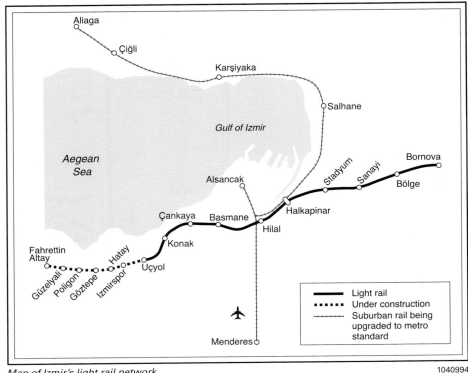
Map of Izmir's light rail network   1040994

are not allowed to operate in the central area. Minibus and shared taxis (dolmus) stops are differentiated from bus stops, where the private vehicles are not allowed to pick up passengers.

Izmir Metro SA
Greater Izmir Municipality
2844 Sokak No 5, Halkapinar, TR-35110-01 Mersinli, Izmir, Turkey
Tel: (+90 232) 461 54 45
Fax: (+90 232) 461 47 69
e-mail: info@izmirmetro.com.tr
Web: www.izmirmetro.com.tr

Key personnel
General Manager: Sönmez Alev
Public Relations: Mrs Mehlika Gökmen
e-mail: mgokmen@izmirmetro.com.tr
Staff: 264

Type of operation: Light rail, first line opened August 2000

Background
Izmir Metro SA is responsible for the operation of the Izmir metro.

Passenger boardings: (Annual) 30 million (estimate)

Route length: 11.6 km
  in tunnel: 4.5 km
  elevated: 2.5 km

Number of lines: 1
Number of stations: 10
Gauge: 1,435 mm
Track: 49 kg/m rail welded, on concrete sleepers
Electrification: 750 V DC, third-rail

Current situation
The 11.6 km LRT line opened in August 2000.

The line runs from Üçyol in the south to Bornova in the northeast, with 10 stations. Some 5.2 km in the city centre is in tunnel and a further 2.5 km is elevated. The route from Üçyol through the city centre to Halkapina forms the core of the proposed network.

Substantial ridership is expected; initially three-car trains provided capacity of 18,000 passengers/h. Later, five-car sets began running, raising capacity to 37,000 passengers/h. Within three months of opening, 80,000 passengers were being carried daily, double the expected figure. This figure is now 100,000 passengers per day.

Developments
Civil works on the second stage (Stage 2) of the existing system, running north to south of the city, have started. The new line will be a 5.5 km tunnel section, from Üçyol to Fahrettin Altay, with six stations. This section passes through a densely populated and commercial area, reaching a main bus terminal at the west end of the city centre at Fahrettin Altay.

First/last train: 06.00/24.00
Service: Peak 4–5 min, off-peak 7–15 min
One-person operation: 100 per cent
Fare structure: Flat (1.25 TRL); Kentkart (smartcard) all modes ticket valid and tokens
Integration with other modes: Kenkart is also valid on buses and ferries
Arrangements for elderly/disabled: Reduced cost annual pass for those over 60; disabled (and postmen and police officers) travel free

Rolling stock: 45 articulated cars, in three-, four- and five-car trains
Adtranz (1998/99) M45

Izmir Buyuksehir Belediyesi Deniz Isletmesi AS (IZDENIZ Inc)
Greater Izmir Municipality, Konak 35250, Izmir, Turkey
Tel: (+90 232) 445 20 34
Fax: (+90 232) 489 93 26
e-mail: izdeniz1@superonline
Web: www.izmir-bld.gov.tr

Key personnel
General Director: Ahmet Secer
Staff: 192

Type of operation: Ferry

Fleet: 8 passenger ferries, 3 car ferries and 14 hired passenger ferries

Current situation
Greater Izmir Municipality bought ferries and franchised rights of all ferry piers and bay operations from Turkish Maritime Lines in March 2000. IZDENIZ (Municipal Ferry Company) currently operates cross-bay ferry services.

There are several passenger services from Konak and Alsancak across the bay to residential sections at Karsiyaka, Bostanli and Guzelyali. Vehicle ferries also serve between Uckuyular and Bostanli piers, reducing journey times considerably compared to alternative highway routes crossing the city centre.

Türkiye Cumhuriyeti Devlet Demiroyollari (TCDD) – Turkish State Railways
Genel Müdürlügü
General Directorate of Turkish State Railways
Talatpaşa Bulvarı, TR-06330 Gar, Ankara, Turkey
Tel: (+90 312) 309 05 15, 312 32 14
Fax: (+90 312) 312 32 15, 324 40 61
e-mail: byhim@tcdd.gov.tr
Web: www.tcdd.gov.tr

Izmir Metro train in tunnel section between Konak and Cankaya 1097463

Key personnel
General Manager and Head of Board of Directors: Süleyman Karaman
Vice General Manager and Member of Board of Directors: Veysi Kurt
Vice General Manager and Member of Board of Directors: Isa Apaydın
Vice General Manager: Şinasi Kazancıoğlu
Vice General Manager: Erol Inal
Vice General Manager: Mustafa Çavuşoğlu
Press and Public Relations Counsellor: Mehmet Aycı
Department Chiefs:
    Operations: Ibrahim Çelik
    Supplies: Ismet Duman
    Research, Planning and Co-ordination Department (Deputy): Ismet Duman
External Affairs: Ibrahim Halil Çevic
Marketing: Emin Tekbaş

Type of operation: Suburban heavy rail

Passenger journeys: (2002) 0.275 million
(2003) 0.227 million
(2004) 0.187 million

Current situation
Turkish State Railways (TCDD) operates commuter rail services on suburban sections of two main railway lines reaching to Izmir city centre. TCDD runs commuter services between Çi'li and Basmane (from the north to the city centre) and Adnan Menderes to Alsancak (from the international airport in the southwest to the centre). These are operated by diesel railbuses and total 45 km with 24 stations.

Developments
TCDD is continuing studies to provide suburban train services to the suburbs of the city and the industrial centre of Aliağa.

Greater Izmir Municipality (GIM) has prepared a track-sharing project in co-ordination with TCDD to operate commuter rail services on TCDD tracks. The Izmir Commuter Railway Development Project is a comprehensive scheme for rehabilitation and upgrading of 79 km of existing rail system currently owned and operated by the Turkish State Railways. The eventual goal of this project is to transfer commuter rail operation from the TCDD to GIM. This project also includes the implementation of an electronic fare/fee collection system for 30 new passenger stations that must be compatible with common electronic fare collection systems for all public transportation systems in the Municipality of Izmir.

A protocol has been signed between GIM and TCDD for co-ordinating the operating of the suburban service. TCDD will own and manage the track and main line passenger and freight services. GIM will operate the commuter stations and purchase its own rolling stock. GIM will pay track access charges to TCDD to operate the suburban services. Each party will receive the ticket revenue from their respective services. This is the first project of this kind in Turkey. The project includes the purchase of new rolling stock and construction of new and refurbished stations and replacement or closure of 47 existing level crossings.

Ukraine

Dnipropetrovsk
Population: City 1.04 million (2007 estimate), metropolitan area 1.8 million (estimate)

Public transport
Bus and trolleybus/tramway services provided by municipal undertaking. Metro.

Dnipro MiskElectroTrans
Karla Marxa Prospekt 119-A, Dnipropetrovsk 49038, Ukraine
Tel: (+380 56) 242 65 24

Key personnel
Director: V T Karpenko

Current situation
Provides bus and trolleybus/tram services.

Bus
Number of routes: 150+
Route length: Not currently available

Fleet: Not currently available, but includes Ikarus and Liaz 677

First/last bus: 05.30/24.00
Fare collection: Conductors
Average speed: 19 km/h

Trolleybus
Number of routes: 20
Route length: 131 km

Fleet: 285 vehicles
ZIU9 (1980/93)   189
ZIU10 (1991/92)   17

YuMZ-T1 (1992/95)   55
YuMZ-T2 (1994/96)   24

First/last trolleybus: 05.30/23.00
One-person operation: All routes
Fare structure: Flat
Fare collection: Conductors
Fare evasion control: Roving inspectors check tickets as passengers exit
Average speed: 19 km/h

Tramway
Type of operation: Conventional tramway

Route length: 153 km
Number of lines: 16
Number of stops: 338
Gauge: 1,524 mm

First/last tram 05.30/23.00
Fare structure: Flat
Fare collection: As trolleybus
One-person operation: All routes

Rolling stock: 362 cars

CKD Tatra T3	M212
KTM5	M113
KTM8	M7
KTM8M (1996/97)	M24
Tatra T3Yug (1996/97)	M6

Funicular

A funicular runs from Central Hill to Monastryrski island and is operational from 09.00–19.00 in the summer months.

Dnipropetrovskogo Metropolitenu (Dnipropetrovsk Metro)

Metropolitan Main Office
vul Kurchatova 8, Dnipropetrovsk 49000, Ukraine
Tel: (+38 56) 249 93 44
Web: http://gorod.dp.ua/metro/eng

Key personnel
Head of Metro: Oleg N Kotlyarov

Type of operation: Opened 1995

Passenger journeys: (Annual) 15 million (estimate)
Vehicle km: Not currently available

Route length: 7.8 km
Number of lines: 1
Number of stations: 6

Current situation
The line is currently operated with 3-car trains at headways of 7–17 minutes. Hours of operation are 05.30–23.00. Fares are flat, one-way.

Developments
Three more stations are under construction to the city centre. The total length of the completed line will be 11.8 km.

There are plans for a second line which will cross the river Dnieper.

Long-term plans envisage a three-line network with a total length of some 80 km.

Kharkov

Population: 1.5 million (estimate)

Public transport
Bus and trolleybus/tramway services; private and hired minibus operations (*marshrutkas*); metro.

Gortransport Kharkov

UI Molodoy Gvardii 5, Kharkov 310006, Ukraine
Tel: (+380 57) 227 56 58
e-mail: info@gortransport.kharkov.ua
Web: www.gortransport.kharkov.ua

Current situation
Provides bus, trolleybus and tram transport services.

Buses carry an estimated 12 million passengers per year. Trolleybus/tram passenger journey figures are not currently available.

The trolleybus fleet is some 242 vehicles and the tram fleet stands at 298 cars. An estimated 40 per cent of daily public transport passengers use these two modes.

Fares are flat and most services are crew-operated.

Bus

Passenger journeys: 12 million (annual)
Vehicle-km: Not currently available

Route length: Not currently available
Number of routes: Not currently available

Fleet: Not currently available
In peak operation: Not currently available
On order: Not currently available

Fare collection: Conductors
Fare structure: Flat

Trolleybus

Passenger journeys: Not currently available
Vehicle-km: Not currently available

Route length: Not currently available
Number of routes: 28 (estimate)

Fleet: 242 vehicles
Fleet breakdown is not currently available.
On order: Not currently available

Fare collection: Conductors
Fare structure: Flat

Tramway
Type of operation: Conventional tramway

Route length: Not currently available
Number of lines: 20 (estimate)
Number of stops: Not currently available.
Gauge: 1,524 mm

Rolling stock: 298 cars
Fleet breakdown is not currently available
On order: Not currently available

Fare collection: Conductors
Fare structure: Flat

Kharkov Metro

Kharkiv Regional State Administration
64 Sums'ka Street, Kharkov 61002, Ukraine
Tel: (+380 572) 43 21 05   Fax: (+380) 572 43 22 01
e-mail: obladm@kharkivoda.gov.ua
Web: www.metro.kharkov.ua

Key personnel
Head of Kharkov Metro: Sergey Z Museev
   Staff: Not currently available

Type of operation: Full metro, initial line opened 1984

Passenger journeys: (Annual) 360 million (estimate)
Train-km: Not currently available

Route length: 35.3 km
Number of lines: 3
Number of stations: 28
Gauge: 1,524 mm
Max gradient: 4%
Minimum curve radius: 300 m
Electrification: 750 V DC, third rail

Current situation
The metro is under the supervision of the Ministry of Transport of Ukraine, although there have been proposals to transfer the system to the City Administration.

Developments
Extensions, north and south, to the Green Line are under construction.

Rolling stock: 287 cars in five-car sets

EJ-79	M287

Service: Peak 2^1/$_2$ min (Red and Blue Lines), 3 min (Green Line); off-peak 3–4 min
First/last train: 05.30/00.30
Fare structure: Flat, monthly season card
Revenue control: Prepurchase token or magnetic-strip season ticket activate access gates
One-person operation: None
Signalling: Automatic train stop; cab signalling, with automatic speed control; no signals; radio communication between control and trains

---

Kiev (Kyiv)

Population: 2.7 million (2005 estimate)

Public transport
Bus and trolleybus/tramway and funicular services provided by city-owned company; publicly-owned Metro; suburban rail services; river ferries; private-sector minibuses regulated by city government.

An EBRD Loan for a total of EUR100 million was provided in August 2007. This comprises two separate loans, the first of EUR60 million to Kyivpastrans and the other of EUR40 million to Kyivsky Metropolitien (Kiev Metro), both of which are for new rolling stock/vehicles and spare parts.

Kyivpastrans

2 Naberezhne Shosse Street, Kiev 04070, Ukraine
Tel: (+380 44) 287 02 50, 230 57 57

Fax: (+380 44) 230 57 58
Web: www.kpt.kiev.ua

Key personnel
Director: Mykola Lambutskyi
   Staff: Not currently available

Current situation
Bus, trolleybus, tram and one funicular operations are operated by municipally owned Kyivpastrans.

There are also privately owned minibuses (marshrutkas), which are regulated by the city.

Developments
In 2006, new LAZ 40-ft low-floor city buses were taken into service.

In August 2007, the European Bank for Reconstruction and Development (EBRD) provided a loan of EUR60 million to Kyivpastrans for the purchase of up to 225 new trolleybuses and 125 diesel buses.

Kyivpastrans is also in the process of installing an automated public transport control system.

Operating costs financed by: Fares 32.6 per cent, other commercial sources 3.3 per cent, subsidy/grants 51.5 per cent (estimate)

Trolleybus
Passenger journeys: Not currently available

Number of routes: Not currently available
Route length: Not currently available

Fleet: Not currently available
In peak service: Not currently available

Fare structure: Zonal; reduced rates for students; free travel for senior citizens; monthly passes

Tramway
Type of operation: Conventional tramway/light rail

Passenger journeys: Not currently available

Number of lines: Not currently available
Route length: Not currently available
Gauge: 1,524 mm

Rolling stock: Not currently available
In peak service: Not currently available

Kyivsky Metropoliten (Kiev Metro)

35 Prospect Peremogy, UA-03055 Kiev, Ukraine
Tel: (+380 44) 238 44 21   Fax: (+380 44) 229 18 57
Web: www.metro.kiev.ua

Key personnel
Director: Petro Miroshnikov
Staff: Not currently available

Type of operation: Full metro, first line constructed in 1960

Passenger journeys: (2005) 600.0 million (estimate)

Route length: 58.8 km
in tunnel: 50.6 km

Number of lines: 3
Number of stations: 45
Gauge: 1,520 mm
Max gradient: 42%
Maximum curve radius: 300 m in general, 200 m Svyatoshinsko-Brovarskoy line
Electrification: 825 V DC, third rail

Current situation
Kyivsky Metropoliten (Kiev Metro) is a municipally owned company.

Developments
Two extension to the Syrets'ko-Pechers'ka Line – Green, with two new stations, Syrets to the north-west and Boryspilska to the east, opened in 2005. In early 2006, Vyrlytsia station was added to the line. Construction is continuing at the eastward end of the line.

A new section of Line 2 (Kurenivs'ko-Chervonoarmiys'ka Line – Blue Line) is under construction and will extend the line southwards to Vystavkovyy Tsentr station. This section will be 6 km long with four new stations.

Two other lines are planned, the Podilsko-Vygurivska Line (Line 4) and the Livoberezhna Line (Line 5).

In August 2007, the EBRD agreed a loan of EUR40 million for the purchase of new rolling stock. Up to 15 new metro trains will operate on the Syrets'ko-Pechers'ka Line.

Rolling stock: 617 cars. Stock includes Mytischy E, ЕЖ, 81-501, 81-502, 81-714, 81-714.5M, 81-717, 81-717.5M, 81-553, 81-554 and 81-555.

In peak service: Not currently available
Service: Peak 50 sec–3 min, off-peak 3–7 min, after 21.00 9–18 min
First/last train: 06.00/00.00
Fare structure: Fixed flat, monthly pass season card, reduced fares for students and others
Revenue control: Prepurchase token or magnetic-strip season ticket activate access gates
Integration with other modes: With tram and/or trolleybus and/or bus
One-person operation: All lines
Signalling: Automatic train stop; radio communication between trains and control centre; CTC; CCTV at all stations; central traffic, power and environmental systems control

---

United Arab Emirates

Dubai
Population: City 1.2 million (estimate), emirate 1.4 million (Census 2006)

Public transport
Government operator provides bus services in city and environs. Other modes include foot ferry (abra) routes which provide additional links across Dubai creek. Metro under construction. Monorails under private development/construction and funding.

Roads & Transport Authority (RTA)
PO Box 118899, Dubai, United Arab Emirates
Tel: (+971 4) 284 44 44
Fax: (+971 4) 206 55 55
e-mail: info@rta.ae
Web: www.rta.ae

Bus
Public Transport Agency
Address as for RTA above.

Key personnel
Chief Executive Officer, Public Transport Agency: Mohammed Obaid Al Mulla
Marketing Manager: Adnan Al Bahar
Staff: 1,263 (Drivers); approx 100 (Maintenance) (estimates)

Passenger journeys: (2006) 90 million (estimate)
Vehicle-km: (2006) 61.3 million (estimate)

Number of routes: 62
Number of stops: More than 1,600

Current situation
The public bus system in Dubai is run by the Roads & Transport Authority's (RTA's) Public Transport Agency.

The bus fleet comprises custom-built buses equipped with individual seats, air conditioning, electronically operated destination display system and computerised fare equipment. Most of the buses have a carrying capacity of 51 seating and 10 standing passengers. Some smaller capacity buses are run to service inner CBD routes as also a few low-density corridors.

The bus fleet is maintained at two bus depots at Al Qusais and Al Awir.

The bus transport infrastructure includes nine bus stations, more than 1,600 bus stops, 153 wayside passenger shelters and point timetables at 500 bus stops.

The RTA also oversees taxi operations and provides driver training.

Night services are provided on Nightliner Routes, from 23.30 to 06.00.

Developments
In August 2007, the Public Transport Agency launched a new bus service shuttling between Dubai International Airport (Terminal 1) and Satwa Bus Station, Bur Dubai.

The RTA is currently in the process of installing some 500 air conditioned bus shelters. Other projects under development include purchasing new buses, building new bus stations and adding new facilities to existing bus shelters, such as bus arrival announcement systems and air-conditioning.

In April 2007, the RTA awarded a contract to Solaris Bus & Coach SA, in co-operation with its Dubai-based joint venture company Al Ghurair and Solaris Middle East Trading LLC, for the supply of 225 buses, 150 Solaris Urbino 18 articulated vehicles and 75 Solaris Urbino 12 units. The buses will be powered by DAF diesel engines. The contract was valued at more than EUR112 million. The contact includes servicing of the buses for a period of five years. A special feature of the buses will be a 'female and family' section at the front of each bus. The LCD passenger information system messages will be displayed in both Arabic and English.

There has also been an order placed with NEOPLAN for 395 buses, comprising 170 Centroliner DD double-deck buses, 150 Centroliner GL artilculated buses and 75 Centroliner single-deck buses.

The RTA plans to purchase a total of 620 new buses by the end of 2008.

In August 2007, Affiliated Computer Services Inc, announced that it will provide a contactless ticketing system for the public buses and water buses in Dubai. The two contracts were valued at some USD21 million and were awarded by Energy International, Dubai.

The RTA intends to launch several new bus routes.

Fleet: 504 buses
Breakdown of fleet is not currently available.
In peak service: Not currently available
On order: 225 Solaris buses; 400 NEOPLAN buses, delivery mainly due for 2008

Fare collection: Driver on board, electronic ticket machine
Fare structure: Cash on board; prepaid monthly passes and smartcards; student passes

Dubai Metro (under construction)
Rail Agency
Address as for RTA above.

Key personnel
Director of Planning and Design, Rail Agency: Abdulredha Abu Al Hassan
Director of Construction, Rail Agency: Adnan Al Hammadi

Background
The Rail Agency was created to provide all modes of rail transportation including the Metro, high-speed rail and trams, to help ease the congestion within Dubai.

Initial studies for developing a metro system started in 1997 with a feasibility study known as R7100. The study was completed during 1997–2000.

Between 2000 and 2002, a follow-up planning study was commissioned under the title PS002 – Dubai Transit Options Study, wherein the initial R700 findings were refined and an initial design concept for a main rail corridor and a Central Business District (CBD) circular were developed, with basic design drawings and routes defined.

During the period 2002 to 2004, a more detailed planning study known as PS007 was commissioned, in which the Dubai Metro team prepared the preliminary engineering design concepts, technical specifications and tender documentation for a design and build contract, based on FIDIC framework, and the work was tendered in October 2004.

In July 2005, a design and build contract was awarded to a consortium, known as Dubai Rail Link (DURL), comprising Japanese companies, including Mitsubishi Heavy Industries, Mitsubishi Corporation, Obayashi Corporation and Kajima Corporation, and Yapi Markezi of Turkey.

Current situation

Two automated lines are currently under construction, the Phase 1 Red Line (52.1 km, with 28 stations, 24 elevated, a at-grade and 4 underground) and the Phase 2 Green Line (23 km-15 km elevated, 8 km in tunnel), with 22 stations (including the two transfer stations). The two interchange stations will be at Burjuman and Union Square. The lines will run underground in the city centre (18 km in tunnel) and at elevation elsewhere.

The Red Line is currently scheduled to be in revenue service in September 2009 and the Green Line in March 2010. Once completed, there will be a fleet of some 100 KinkiSharyo 5-car trains (3M + 2T) operating on the network. There will be separate areas for women and children and a 'gold class' car.

Operational hours will be 05.00 to 00.30.

The Red Line will have park-and-ride facilities at Rashidiya and Jumeirah Islands.

The metro will be fully integrated with other public transport services. Bus routes and stops will be organised around the metro network and taxi stations and park-and-ride facilities will be included at key metro stations. Fares and fare collection systems will be common to all public transport services.

Developments

Features of the Metro system will include lifts/elevators at all stations, tactile guide paths, wide fare gates and an automatic fare collection system, platform screen doors, air-conditioning of all elevated stations concourses and platforms, Internet access and CCTV. Public announcements will be made both audibly and visually.

Construction of the rolling stock for the metro has commenced, with the first train being ready in late 2007.

In July 2007, the RTA announced that some 60 per cent of the USD4.22 billion project was complete.

There are plans for future Purple and Blue Lines and an extension of the Red Line to the Abu Dhabi border.

The 47 km Blue Line will run between Dubai International Airport and a new airport at Jebel Ali.

Ferry
Abra

Abra water transport, by rowing boat or motorised dhow, is available across the creek linking Deira and Bur Dubai. The RTA is responsible for safe and orderly operation of the 149 abras and four abra 'stations'.

Water Bus

Type of operation: Ferry, first route opened August 2007

Passenger journeys: (2006) 25 million (estimate)

Developments

In August 2007, the first of four planned Water Bus routes was opened. The route, between Al Sabkha and Bur Dubai, will be operated by two vessels. When all four routes are in operation there will be a total fleet of 10 vessels. Fares are paid by pre-paid card.

The Maritime Projects Department's objectives are to implement and operate a new water transport system which will integrate with the other transport systems in Dubai.

United Kingdom

Aberdeen

Population: 202,370 (2005)

Public transport

Bus services provided mainly by two private companies; local rail service.

Aberdeen City Council is the local tendering authority for bus and rail services. Aberdeenshire Council also provides public transport services.

Local tendering authorities:
Aberdeen City Council (Environment & Infrastructure Services)

St Nicholas House, Broad Street, Aberdeen AB10 1WL, UK
Tel: (+44 1224) 52 37 62
Fax: (+44 1224) 52 37 64
Web: www.aberdeencity.gov.uk

Aberdeenshire Council

Woodhill House, Westburn Road, Aberdeen AB16 5GB, UK
Tel: (+44 1224) 66 45 85
Web: www.aberdeenshire.gov.uk

Developments

The City Council funds Aberdeen Dial-a-Bus which is now run on behalf of the council by Stagecoach Bluebird. They operate the bus service and the call centre through which bookings for the demand-responsive service are made. The drivers recruited by Stagecoach Bluebird have gone through Midas training (UK-recognised minibus drivers' awareness scheme).

The service was set up to help people with limited access to transport to travel to shopping, health and leisure facilities and connect them to mainstream transport services. The two Aleros run seven days a week and bookings can be made up to one week in advance of the date of travel. Dial-a-Bus was funded until the end of March 2008 by the Scottish Executive. Aberdeen City Council now funds the service.

First in Aberdeen

395 King Street, Aberdeen AB24 5RP, UK
Tel: (+44 1224) 65 00 00
Fax: (+44 1224) 65 00 99
Web: www.firstgroup.com

Key personnel

Managing Director: George Mair
Staff: 500

Current situation

Formerly the regional council's transport undertaking, the company was sold to its workforce in 1989. It became a listed company four years later, and formed the embryo of FirstGroup, which is now the UK's largest bus operator.

Bus

Passenger journeys: (1999/2000) 20 million
Vehicle-km: (1999/2000) 10.1 million

Number of routes: 36
Route length: 190 km
On priority right-of-way: 800 m

Fleet: 171 vehicles	
Leyland Olympian/Alexander double-deck	28
Leyland Atlantean/Alexander open-top double-deck	1
Volvo B7TL/Alexander low-floor double-deck	6
Blue Bird American RE single-deck school bus	2
Volvo B10BLE/Wright low-floor single-deck	107
Mercedes-Benz O405G/Alexander articulated single-deck	1
Volvo B7LA/Wright articulated low-floor single-deck	6
Mercedes-Benz 709D/Alexander minibus	5
Volvo B58/Duple coach	1
Toyota Coaster/Caetano coach	1
Dennis Javelin/Plaxton coach	1
Volvo B10M/Jonckheere coach	4
Volvo B10M/Plaxton coach	4
Volvo B10M/Van Hool coach	1
Scania K113/Irizar coach	2
Scania K124/Irizar coach	1
In peak service: 140	

Most intensive service: 5 min
One-person operation: All routes
Fare collection: Pay-as-you-enter; electronic Wayfarer ticket issue and data collection equipment; stored value magnetic pass card
Fare structure: Stage; weekly/monthly/3-monthly passes
Fares collected on board: 76 per cent
Fare evasion control: Inspectors
Operational control: Route inspectors, mobile radio
Arrangements for elderly/disabled: Low maximum fare
Average distance between stops: 180 m
Average peak-hour speed: In mixed traffic, 16.5 km/h
Operating costs financed by: Fares 97 per cent, subsidy/grants 3 per cent
Subsidy from: Local council for non-commercial routes put out to tender, plus concessionary fare reimbursement

Stagecoach Bluebird

Bus Station, Guild Street, Aberdeen AB11 6GR, UK
Tel: (+44 1224) 59 13 81
Fax: (+44 1224) 58 42 02
e-mail: bluebird.enquiries@stagecoachbus.com
Web: www.stagecoachbus.com/bluebird

Key personnel

Regional Director (Scotland): Robert Andrew
Managing Director (Bluebird): Charlie Mullen
Operations Director (Bluebird): Bob Hall
Engineering Director (Bluebird): John MacPherson

Current situation

Formerly part of the state-owned Scottish Bus Group, the company was purchased in 1991 by Stagecoach. It operates the majority of commuter services into the city and routes throughout the Aberdeenshire, Highland, Moray and Perth & Kinross council areas, including frequent urban services between Aberdeen and Inverness, Peterhead, Fraserburgh and Elgin.

67 per cent of the fleet now meets Euro 2, 3 and 4 emission standards. All buses run on ultra-low sulphur biodiesel with a fuel additive to improve consumption.

Developments

A GBP5.5 million investment in 39 new accessible low-floor buses and coaches was made in 2008.

Fleet: 373 vehicles

Single-deck	58
Double-deck	53
Coaches	111
Midibuses	76
Minibuses	68
Taxi	7

First ScotRail Limited

Atrium Court, 500 Waterloo Street, Glasgow G2 6HQ, UK
Tel: (+44 8700) 00 51 51   Fax: (+44 141) 335 43 45
e-mail: scotrail.enquiries@firstgroup.com
Web: www.firstscotrail.com

Key personnel

Managing Director: Mary Grant
Commercial Director: Peter Williams
Finance Director: Kenny McPhail
Operations Director and Deputy Managing Director: Steve Montogomery

Engineering: Kenny Scott
New Trains Director: Nick Horten
Head of Hospitality: Garry Clark
Human Resources Director: Fiona Irvine
Divisional Operations Manager (Network Services): Jacqui Dey
Head of Public Relations: Iain Wilson
Acting Head of Marketing: Marc Sangster
Public Affairs Manager: Lally Cowell
    Staff: Not available currently

Type of operation: Heavy, interurban rail

Passenger journeys: (2007) 81 million (estimate)
Train-km: Not available currently

Current situation

The First ScotRail franchise is now funded and managed by Transport Scotland, a division of the Scottish Executive. In 2005/6 the company operated 2,347 million passenger-km and 39.3 million train-km. It now operates 341 stations.

One railway route passes through Aberdeen, and long-distance trains to and from the south call hourly (or more frequently) at Stonehaven where there is a park-and-ride facility. A limited peak-hour service is provided at Portlethen. Dyce station, near Aberdeen airport, has an hourly service to Aberdeen. Help Points and 24 hour CCTV, centrally monitored from First ScotRail's customer services centre, have been provided at Stonehaven, Dyce and Inverurie.

For further information on First ScotRail, please see *Jane's World Railways.*

Developments

In 2008, Transport Scotland rolled out a new identity for stations and trains, which brought together the previously separate First ScotRail and Strathclyde brands. It announced the December 2008 timetable which will see the biggest improvements since 1999, with the paths across the Forth Bridge released by coal trains that now run via Alloa to be used by a new hourly Edinburgh-Dundee service that, by allowing stops to be taken out of Edinburgh-Aberdeen trains, will reduce overcrowding and accelerate journey-times by up to 10 minutes. Edinburgh-Perth via Fife services will increase from two-hourly to hourly, Aberdeen-Inverurie will see an extra six trains a day, an additional train each way will link Aberdeen and Inverness and there will be a fourth train daily from Inverness to Wick, with four trains all year to and from Kyle of Lochalsh. The timetable will make provision for the reopening of Laurencekirk Station due later in 2009.

Also in 2008, First ScotRail was named Public Transport Operator of the Year for the third year in a row. Delays caused by First ScotRail have fallen by 15 per cent over the past year and are down 50 per cent since the franchise began. There has been 20 per cent passenger growth and, despite record numbers of journeys – now more than 81 million a year, overall crime on the railways is reported to have fallen.

Belfast

Population: City 276,450, metropolitan area 579,550 (estimates)

Public transport

Bus and suburban rail services provided by state-owned company, which also operates rural bus services.

Translink

Central Station, East Bridge Street, Belfast BT1 3PB, UK
Tel: (+44 2890) 89 94 00
    (+44 2890) 66 66 30 (Call Centre)
e-mail: feedback@translink.co.uk
Web: www.translink.co.uk

Key personnel

Chief Executive: Catherine Mason
    Staff: 3,755 (all operations)

Current situation

Translink, the brand name for Citybus, Northern Ireland Railways and Ulsterbus, employs more than 3,700 staff across Northern Ireland. Translink operates all bus and rail services in Northern Ireland, with the subsidiary, Flexibus, operating minibus services. Co-ordination of bus and rail services covers timetables, passenger information, integrated ticketing, feeder buses to railway stations, integrated travel facilities and a call centre, which handles approximately 100,000 calls a month.

Developments

Translink has taken delivery of 45 new-concept Wrightbus single-deck buses for the Ulsterbus rural services. The Wrightbus Solar Rural vehicles are specifically designed to make travelling by public transport more accessible. Built on a modified Scania K230 chassis, Wrightbus and Translink have worked together to design the new vehicles.

The Wrightbus Solar Rural design is a 12-m long, low-entry vehicle incorporating an elevated floor area to the rear. The seating configuration chosen by Translink comprises two-plus-two seating at the front of the vehicle and

Translink Alexander-bodied double-deck bus on Metro rapid transit service on busway in Belfast city centre (Tony Pattison) 1209465

two-plus-three seating at the rear. All seats are either forward or rear facing and are fitted with three-point integral seatbelts.

Plans were announced by the UK Government in April 2008 for a Bus Rapid Transit (BRT) system which would link Belfast city centre to Belfast City Airport through Titanic Quarter, with an extension of the scheme to serve a new retail development in the Harbour Estate. An extension of the core route to Queens University has also been considered. A range of technology options have been investigated, which includes non-guided buses which run on-street and guided buses (for the section of the route through Titanic Quarter). Services are due to start in 2011.

Bus (Belfast city operations)
Staff: 646

Passenger journeys: (2002/03) 19.9 million
(2003/04) 19.5 million
Vehicle-km: (2002/03) 11.3 million
(2003/04) 11.3 million

Number of routes: 72
Route length: 190 km
On priority right-of-way: 19.9 km

Fleet: 239 vehicles

Leyland Atlantean double-deck	1
Volvo B7TL/Alexander low-floor double-deck	40
Leyland Tiger/Alexander single-deck	71
Volvo B10L/Alexander low-floor single-deck	48
Volvo B10BLE/Wright low-floor single-deck	44
Volvo B10M/Plaxton	2
Mercedes-Benz O405N low-floor single-deck	6

Mercedes-Benz O405GN articulated low-floor single-deck	4
Dennis Dart/Wright midibus	3
Dennis Dart SLF/Wright low-floor midibus	3
DAF SBR2300/Van Hool double-deck coach	1
MAN/Ayats double-deck coach	16

In peak service: 199

Most intensive service: 7.5 min
One-person operation: All routes
Fare structure: Zone; Smartlink cards sold in shops
Fare collection: Onboard cancellation of prepurchased Smartlink cards, or payment of higher cash fare to driver
Fares collected on board: 70%
Fare evasion control: Inspectors; penalty fare
Integration with other modes: Centrelink distributor links all main bus and rail stations with principal shopping areas; free to rail and most bus passengers
Operational control: Route inspectors/mobile radio
Arrangements for elderly/disabled: Blind persons carried free and over-65s all free
Bus priority: 19.9 km of bus lanes and vehicle-activated traffic signals
Average peak-hour speed: In mixed traffic 14.5 km/h
Operating cost financed by: Fares 95%, grants 5%
Subsidy from: Government
New vehicles financed by: Department for Regional Development, bus companies and EU, Peace & Reconciliation Grant.

Suburban rail
Type of operation: Suburban heavy rail

Passenger journeys: (2002/03) 6.3 million
(2003/04) 6.9 million

Translink has taken delivery of 45 new-concept Wrightbus single-deck buses for the Ulsterbus rural services
1374319

Current situation
Trains run every 10-15 minutes inner suburban, 20-30 minutes outer suburban (peak hours), 30 minutes inner and 60 minutes outer (off-peak) over three routes extending to 460 km, 1,600 mm gauge, now fully integrated following opening of the cross-harbour link in 1994. Fare structure is graduated.

Rolling stock:

BREL Class 80 demu (1974/77)	M17 T32
BREL Class 450 demu (1985/86/87)	M9 T18
CAF Class 3000 dmu (2004/05)	23
Dietrich coaches	14

Birmingham (UK)
Population: City 1 million, West Midlands conurbation 2.6 million

Public transport
Bus services are operated by a major private company and over 20 other independent companies. As well as running commercial services, some operators are contracted for provision of supported services by the West Midlands Passenger Transport Executive (Centro), which also contracts for provision of local rail services. West Midlands area covers surrounding urban areas of Coventry, Wolverhampton, Walsall, Dudley, Solihull, West Bromwich. Light rail line in operation between Birmingham and Wolverhampton.

Birmingham

Other commercial operators
Current situation
Among those providing commercial services in the area are Arriva Midlands, Bharat/Red Arrow Express of Handsworth, Claribels of Tile Cross, First, Flights Hallmark of Handsworth, Hanson of Dudley, Johnson Coach Travel, North Birmingham Busways of Erdington, Pattersons of Selly Oak, Thandi Travel of Smethwick and Stagecoach Warwickshire.

Silverline Landflight park-and-ride Optare Solo shuttle service in Solihull.

Centro (West Midlands Passenger Transport Executive)
16 Summer Lane, Birmingham B19 3SD, UK
Tel: (+44 121) 200 27 87   Fax: (+44 121) 214 70 10
Web: www.centro.org.uk

Key personnel
Chief Executive: Geoff Inskip
Projects Director: Tom Magrath
Services Director: Robert Smith
Resources Director: Trevor Robinson
Head of Communications: Conrad Jones
    Staff: 360

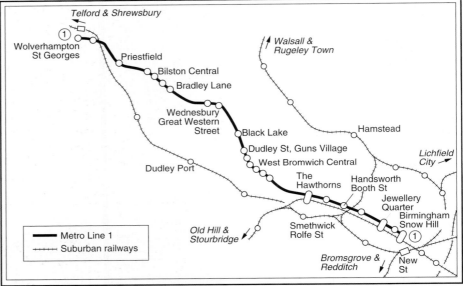

Map of Birmingham's metro and suburban railways
0045352

Passenger journeys: (All modes)
(2005/06) 344.6 million (estimate)

Current situation
Centro is the corporate identity of the West Midlands Passenger Transport Executive, the body that advises the WM Passenger Transport Authority (a political body) and carries out its policies. The PTA is a joint authority of the seven metropolitan councils of the West Midlands area – Birmingham City, Coventry City, and the metropolitan boroughs of Dudley, Sandwell, Solihull, Walsall and Wolverhampton. The PTA sets policies and budgets for public transport responsibilities in the area, and levies the councils for funds to carry out its work. The seven authorities and Centro submit a joint bid each year for central government funding of transport schemes.

The local rail service is operated by NEG for Centro, which subsidises the local rail network. Centro operates and funds the concessionary fares scheme, primarily one whereby senior citizens travel at off-peak times, free of charge. Centro provides public transport infrastructure, 5,000 bus shelters, 12 bus stations and local rail stations. It finances socially necessary bus services, those withdrawn by private operators on commercial grounds but which it is deemed are essential to provide accessibility to all social groups. These services are awarded to private operators on a contract/tender basis. Centro funds the operation of the Ring and Ride door-to-door services for people with disabilities, operated by West Midlands Special Needs Transport Ltd, a registered charity.

In partnership with the local councils and the private sector, Centro has promoted the Midland Metro light rail project, which opened in 1999.

Centro is also responsible for the rapid transit link between Birmingham International railway station and Birmingham International airport. It re-opened in 2003, using DCC-Doppelmeyer technology.

Developments

The branding 'Network West Midlands' was introduced in 2007 to cover bus, train and Metro services in the West Midlands metropolitan area. Signage is being introduced at bus stops, Metro stops and stations during 2007, together with improved maps and journey information. All bus stops are now SMS enabled, where mobile phone users are able to request a text message with scheduled and, at many stops, actual time of arrival of the next bus.

A GBP26 million package of improvements aimed at reducing congestion and improving bus journeys in the West Midlands was given the go-ahead by the UK Government in 2008. Improvements to traffic control systems will help improve bus journeys by giving priority to buses at key junctions. Variable message signs will also provide drivers with more accurate and reliable information on congestion, incidents and parking availability is expected that work will be completed by 2013.

The UK Government is investing almost GBP400 million to upgrade Birmingham New Street station. The government has provided all the funding grants sought by Birmingham City Council, Advantage West Midlands and Network Rail. The station redevelopment focuses on relieving the congested conditions, making it easier for the 17 million passengers who use the station each year to reach platform level. This investment will also help accommodate the increase in passenger levels, forecast to increase by around 30 per cent in the next 10 years. The scheme will double the size of the station concourse and all platforms will be served by escalators, which increase from five to 31, making it more accessible for disabled people, passengers with heavy luggage and parents. There will also three new entrances to the station from the city centre and new public square.

Contracted bus services

Passenger journeys: (2004/05) 314.5 million (2005/06) 308.5 million
Vehicle-km: (2005/06) 135.2 million (estimate)

Current situation

There are more than 50 operators providing services within the West Midlands area.

Subsidised bus cost: GBP7.3 million. The percentage share of subsidised bus service km is 7.2 per cent (some 187,790 km weekly). (2005/06)

Contracted rail services

Operated for Centro by:

London Midland

3rd Floor, 41-54 Grey Street, Newcastle-upon-Tyne, NE1 6EE, UK
Tel: (+44 121) 654 12 00   Fax: (+44 121) 654 12 34
e-mail: comms@londonmidland.com
Web: www.londonmidland.com

Key personnel

Managing Director: Stephen Banaghan
Operations Director: Andy Thomas
  Staff: Not currently available

Type of operation: Suburban heavy rail
Passenger journeys: (2004/05) 29.3 million (2005/06) 30.9 million

Current situation

Services operated with London Midland support on nine routes with 71 stations totalling 177 km. Five routes are electrified at 25 kV 50 Hz and four are diesel-worked. Seven radial routes to Birmingham city centre form three cross-city services.

The Central Trains (former operator) franchise ended in November 2007. Three franchises – East Midlands, West Midlands and Cross Country – replace the former four franchises operated by Central Trains, Silverlink, Virgin Cross Country and Midland Mainline.

The East Midlands franchise, operated by Stagecoach, operates services to and from London St Pancras, together with regional and local services in the East Midlands.

London Midland Class 323 emu at Wolverhampton station in the Centro operating area (Tony Pattison)
1374320

Midland Metro tram near Birmingham Snow Hill station
1374321

Doppelmeyer cable car running between Birmingham International airport and Birmingham International station (Tony Pattison)
0567142

The West Midlands franchise operates the West Coast Main Line outer suburban services to and from London Euston (formerly operated by Silverlink County) together with regional and local services in the West Midlands. It is operated by Govia and runs under the name London Midland.

Light rail

Type of operation: Conventional light rail

Passenger journeys: (2002/03) 4.9 million
(2004/05) 5.0 million
(2005/06) 5.2 million

Route length: 20.4 km
On reserved track: 18.4 km
Number of stops: 23
Gauge: 1,435 mm
Electrification: 750 V DC, overhead

Rolling stock: 16 cars
Ansaldo (1998)   M16

Current situation
Midland Metro Line 1 opened in 1999. Line 1 links Birmingham and Wolverhampton using former railway alignment and with a 2 km on-street running section in Wolverhampton town centre. A 23-year design/build/operate and maintain contract was awarded to the Altram consortium comprising Ansaldo Trasporti and civil engineering firm John Laing. Travel West Midlands joined the consortium later, and its subsidiary company Travel Midland Metro operates the system.

Choice Travel

Planetary Road, Willenhall, Wolverhampton, WV13 3SQ, UK
Tel: (+44 1902) 30 51 81
Fax: (+44 1902) 30 74 54
e-mail: info@choicetravelservices.co.uk
Web: www.choicetravelservices.co.uk

Key personnel
Managing Director: David Rees

Current situation
Established in 1992, the company operates in Wolverhampton, Walsall, Bloxwich and Lichfield. Operates tendered routes in the West Midlands, Shropshire, Staffordshire and Worcestershire.

Fleet: 38 vehicles
Optare Excel low-floor single-deck   7
Mercedes-Benz minibus   11
Mercedes-Benz 811D/Wright minibus   3
Optare Solo low-floor minibus   7
Dennis Dart bus   10

Diamond Bus Company Ltd

Cross Quays Business Park, Hallbridge Way, Tipton Road, Tividale, Oldbury B69 3HW, UK
Tel: (+44 121) 557 73 37
Fax: (+44 121) 520 49 99
Web: www.diamondbuses.com

Key personnel
Managing Director: Scott Dunn
Directors: Robert Anthony Dunn,
  Simon Dunn,
  Antony Goozee,
  Kim Taylor,
  Geoff Flight,
  John Gunn
  Staff: 361

Passenger journeys: (2007) 11 million (approximate)

Current situation
The former Go West Midlands Ltd was purchased by Rotala Plc on 29 February 2008.
Local bus services are provided under the company name of Diamond Bus Company Ltd.

The operations of People's Express (Pete's Travel) were bought in 2006.

Bus
Number of routes: 65

Fleet: 142 vehicles
DAF   14
Dennis   95
Volvo   26
LDV   3
MAN   6
In peak service: Not available currently

National Express West Midlands Ltd

PO Box 9854, Birmingham B16 8XN, UK
Tel: (+44 121) 254 72 00
Fax: (+44 121) 233 72 77
Web: www.travelwm.co.uk

Key personnel
Acting Chief Executive: Neil Barker
Financial Director: Peter Coates
Engineering Director: Jack Henry
  Staff: 4,500

Current situation
TWM was created from the bus operating interests of the PTE and was sold by the Passenger Transport Authority to its workforce in 1991. Acquired by the National Express Group in 1995, it remains the dominant bus operator in the area. Its operations include local bus services, school contracts and private hire. TWM subsidiary company Travel Merry Hill operates in the area.

TWM is a member of the Altram consortium which built the Midland Metro. This opened in mid-1999 and is also the operator of the system. National Express Group also owns Travel Dundee and Travel London.

The Coventry-based operations of the company were spun-off as a separate subsidiary in December 2002.

Developments
National Express unveiled a new livery and brand name towards the end of 2007. Buses now carry the National Express branding and TWM has become National Express West Midlands. The livery is similar to that used on the east coast main line National Express operation.

Bus
Passenger journeys: Not currently available
Vehicle-km: Not currently available

Number of routes: 600
Route length: 7,524 km
On priority right-of-way: 7 km

Fleet: 1,687 vehicles (including Travel Merry Hill)
Double-deck bus   978
Articulated bus   31
Single-deck bus   613
Minibus   65
Chassis
DAF   21
Dennis   360
Leyland   13
MCW   283
Mercedes-Benz   288
Optare   91
Plaxton   102
Volvo   620
Scania   11
Bodies
Alexander   412
Leyland   13
MCW   283
Mercedes-Benz   288
Optare   112
Plaxton   102
Wright   466
Scania   11
In peak service: 1,729

Most intensive service: 2–3 min
One-person operation: All services
Fare collection: Autofare farebox with Wayfarer driver-operated ticket-issuing machine
Fare structure: Graduated stage fares with maximum off-peak fare; prepurchase travelcards for varying areas and time periods, including annual and off-peak only; direct-debit Faresaver
Fares collected on board: 36 per cent; travelcards advance sales 36 per cent; concessionary travel passes 23 per cent
Fare evasion control: Spot checks by revenue control inspectors
Operational control: Route inspectors/mobile radio
Arrangements for elderly/disabled: Passes for free bus travel, at all times, issued by Metropolitan District Councils to all blind persons and, at discretion, to disabled persons. Councils pay TWM to accept these for travel on bus and local rail services outside the morning peak period and up to 23.29 daily. Passes for free off-peak bus travel issued to the elderly by PTE (Centro)
Average distance between stops: 300 m
Integration with other modes: One-day 'Centrocard' and 'Daytripper' passes sold on buses, valid for all operators' buses and trains, and on the metro system; rail travellers into West Midlands area can buy bus add-on tickets for all modes travel. Many timed interchanges between bus and rail
Operating costs financed by: Fares 99 per cent, tendered service support 1 per cent.

Developments
TWM has taken delivery of 60 Wrightbus Eclipse Gemini double-deck buses mainly for use on Line 33, the bus rapid transit route from Coventry to Pheasey.

National Express West Midlands Alexander Dennis ALX400 double-deck bus near to the National Express coach station in Birmingham (Tony Pattison)   1374322

Bristol

Population: City 410,500, metropolitan area 551,000 (2006 estimates)

Public transport

Most bus services in city and surrounding areas operated by First. Local trains operated by First Great Western; ferry services operated by private company.

Bristol City Council

Public Transport & Park & Ride Group
Brunel House, St George's Road, Bristol BS1 5UY, UK
Tel: (+44 117) 922 44 54
Fax: (+44 117) 922 38 86
e-mail: public.transport@bristol.gov.uk
Web: www.bristol.gov.uk

Developments

The Greater Bristol bus network, which delivers improvements in ten corridors at a cost of just under GBP70 million, has now been approved. This complements two existing Showcase bus routes. The Showcase routes aim to improve many aspects of bus travel by providing travellers with a more reliable, fast and efficient service.

Since Bristol's first Showcase scheme connecting Henbury, Southmead and Hartcliffe was launched, passenger figures have increased by 12 per cent and an estimated 1,200 fewer cars are travelling along the A38 each week. The number of trips being made by bicycle has also increased by 11 per cent.

In partnership with First, Bristol City Council has upgraded the quality of the bus service and the environment along the A420/A431 route from Bristol city centre to Kingswood and Hanham, launched in December 2007. First introduced 42 new, low-floor, advanced, double-deck buses with improved seating and wheelchair/buggy provision, Euro 4 engines, CCTV and satellite tracking to activate the real-time bus stop displays.

The Showcase improvements include bus lanes, traffic signals that change to green if a bus is running late and restrictions for parking and loading in bus lanes at peak travelling times.

The bus stop facilities include raised kerbs, new, larger bus shelters with seats, real-time information displays with an audio function, paving to clearly identify the bus stop waiting area and CCTV cameras.

First Bristol

Enterprise House, Easton Road, Lawrence Hill, Bristol BS5 0DZ, Avon, UK
Tel: (+44 117) 955 82 11
Fax: (+44 117) 955 12 48
Web: www.firstgroup.com

Key personnel

Managing Director: Justin Davies
Area Operations Director: Jenny McLeod
Engineering Director: David Porter
Finance Director: Mike Gahan

Current situation

First operates throughout the Bristol area. Services run within Bristol, Cribbs Causeway, Westbury, Avonmouth, Hartcliffe, Stockwood, Longwell Green, Kingswood, Frenchay and Bradley Stoke.

To serve the fast-growing Bristol international airport, a dedicated coach service, called Bristol International Flyer, runs between Bristol bus station and Bristol Temple Meads railway station and the airport every 20 minutes with a return fare of GBP6. Real-time bus information is provided at some of the bus stops.

The central bus and coach station at Broadmead was rebuilt in 2005, providing interchange with rural buses and a coach station as well as serving local buses and the airport express service (Airport Flyer). This service runs every 20 minutes and serves the city's main railway station, city centre and airport.

First Bristol Wrightbus-bodied double-deck bus on service 41 to Avonmouth in Bristol city centre (Tony Pattison)
1374323

Wessex Connect Ulink Wrightbus-bodied Volvo B7RLE single-deck bus on service to University of West England near Bristol (Tony Pattison)
1374324

Developments

In partnership with First, Bristol City Council has upgraded the quality of the bus service and the environment along the A420/A431 route from Bristol city centre to Kingswood and Hanham. It was launched at the end of 2007. First introduced 42 new low-floor, advanced double-deck buses with improved seating and wheelchair/buggy provision, Euro 4 engines, CCTV and satellite tracking to activate the real-time bus stop displays.

The Showcase improvements include bus lanes, traffic signals that change to green if a bus is running late and restrictions for parking and loading in bus lanes at peak travelling times.

The bus stop facilities include raised kerbs, new, larger bus shelters with seats, real-time information displays with an audio function, paving to clearly identify the bus stop waiting area and CCTV cameras.

Bristol is introducing Showcase bus routes that provide high-quality services similar to those enjoyed by users of Bus Rapid Transit (BRT) and light rail operations. First, which operates most services in Bristol, already markets some of its services as 'Overground', a generic name adopted by First for frequent services in UK cities.

Since Bristol's first showcase scheme connecting Henbury, Southmead and Hartcliffe

was launched, passenger figures have increased by 12 per cent and an estimated 1,200 fewer cars are travelling along the A38 each week. The number of trips being made by bicycle has also increased by 11 per cent.

Bus

Number of routes: 38

Fleet: 214 vehicles	
Double-deck bus	33
Single-deck buses	44
Midibus	124
Minibus	13

Most intensive service: 6 min
One-person operation: All routes
Fare collection: Stored-value prepurchase cards or payment on board with Wayfarer electronic ticket machines linked to magnetic card validators
Fare structure: Zones, off-peak reductions; prepurchased magnetic tickets
Fares collected on board: 80 per cent
Operational control: Route inspectors/mobile radio
Arrangements for elderly/disabled: Fares at two-thirds normal rate funded by city council; new buses equipped to DPTAC standards
Average peak-hour speed: 16.1 km/h
Operating costs financed by: Fares 92 per cent

Bristol

Other operators
Current situation
A small number of operators run some commercial and subsidised routes into the city, including Abus, Buglers of Brislington, Cotswold Edge Bus Company, Crown Coaches of St Phillips, Eurotaxi, Fatesaver Flights Hallmark, Severnside Transport, South Gloucestershire Bus and Coach, Stagecoach South Wales and Turners Coachways of St Phillips.

Flights Hallmark runs buses in the Bristol area under the Wessex Connect brand, operating services for students and staff into the University of West England under the Ulink banner. Flights also operates seven vehicles at the Long Ashton park-and-ride service.

First Great Western (FGW)
Milford House, 1 Milford Street, Swindon, SN1 1HL, UK
Tel: (+44 1793) 49 94 00
Fax: (+44 1793) 49 94 51
Web: www.firstgreatwestern.co.uk

Key personnel
Chief Operating Officer: Andrew Haines
Staff: Not available currently

Current situation
First Great Western operates an integrated network of services from London to the South Midlands, South Wales and the West of England between Bristol and the English Channel. First Group now operates most of the long-distance services serving Bristol.

First Great Western (FGW) provides regional and local rail services across Avon, Cornwall, Devon, Gloucestershire, Hampshire, Somerset and Wiltshire.

For further information on FGW, please see *Jane's World Railways.*

Developments
In May 2007, FGW restructured and simplified fares on the Severn Beach line (which runs from Bristol temple Meads to Severn Beach).

Bristol Ferry Boat Company (BFBCo)
M B Tempora, Welsh Back, Bristol, BS1 4SP, UK
Tel: (+44 117) 927 34 16
Fax: (+44 117) 929 40 77
e-mail: enquiries@bristolferry.co.uk
Web: www.bristolferry.co.uk

Passenger journeys (commuter): Not currently available

Current situation
Bristol Ferry Boat Company operate a timetabled ferry service daily all year round, incorporating a subsidised commuter service.

Bristol Ferry Boat Company ferry near The Great Britain ship built by Victorian British engineer, I K Brunel, Bristol Docks 1325559

Ultra Light Rail vehicle in Bristol 1325451

Bristol Electric Railbus Limited (BER)
Heron House, Chiswick Mall, London W4 2PR, UK
Tel: (+44 20) 89 95 30 00   Fax: (+44 20) 89 94 60 60
e-mail: james@jskinner.demon.co.uk
Web: www.ultralightrail.com
www.passenger-transit-systems.co.uk

Key personnel
Contact: James Skinner

Ultra Light Rail (proposed)
Background
BER has operated an Ultra Light Rail (ULR) service between the city and Great Eastern steamship in the Bristol dockside area, using a Parry People Mover flywheel-powered LRV (Bristol No 238).

Developments
BER is actively engaged in preparing a plan for the development of a new ULR route in Bristol and a new business case is being prepared together with a group of leading Bristolians to assist the Bristol City Council to implement the project for a ULR link between Ashton Gate and the City Centre. This project has been in the Local Transport Plan for some years without obtaining funding from the City or from the DfT, but is now expected to progress in the not-too-distant future.

BER has formed a UK technical consortium, Sustraco Ltd, to promote other projects outside Bristol (please see separate entry). Sustraco has calculated that stage one of the Ashton Link would reduce CO_2 emissions by some 250 tonnes per annum.

In 2007, BER/Sustraco joined the UITP as part of its ongoing commitment to the delivery of sustainable urban public transport.

Cardiff
Population: 305,353 (2001 Census)

Public transport
Bus services provided by privately owned companies; local rail services.

Cardiff Bus/Bws Caerdydd
Leckwith Depot, Sloper Road, Cardiff CF11 8TB, UK
Tel: (+44 2920) 78 77 00
Fax: (+44 2920) 78 77 42
e-mail: headoffice@cardiffbus.com
Web: www.cardiffbus.com

Key personnel
Managing Director: David Brown
Engineering Director: Andrew Hoseason
Staff: 750

Current situation
CCTS was established as a private company in 1986. Its sole shareholder is Cardiff county council. Fleet composition has been changed from mainly double-deck to a mix of double-deck, articulated, single-deck and midibuses.

Developments
The network is now a high-frequency corridor-based operations with simplified fare structures and colour-coded marketing.

Bus
Passenger journeys: (2003/04) 25.8 million
(2004/05) 26.1 million
(2005/06) 26.3 million
(2006/07) 26.7 million
(2007/08) 28.0 million
Vehicle-km: (2003/04) 13.2 million
(2004/05) 13.4 million
(2005/06) 13.4 million
(2006/07) 13.1 million
(2007/08) 13.0 million

Number of routes: 28
Route length: 1,451 km
On priority right-of-way: 3.05 km

Fleet: 217 vehicles

Scania Darwen low-floor double-deck	13
Alexander Dennis Enviro 300 low-floor single-deck	12
Scania tri-axle articulated OmniCity	19
Dennis Dart SPD/Plaxton low-floor single-deck	43
Dennis Dart SPD/Transbus low-floor single-deck	31
Dennis Dart/Alexander midibus	1
Dennis Dart SLF/Plaxton low-floor midibus	39
Dennis Dart SLF/Transbus low-floor midibus	44
Scania OmniCity low-floor single-deck	15

In peak service: 196

Most intensive service: 5 min

One-person operation: All routes

Fare collection: Driver-operated ticket issue by Wayfarer TGX150 electronic machine; three different multi-journey tickets (weekly, monthly) sold on bus and at travel shops in city centre; 'day to go' day-out ticket covers Cardiff, Penarth and part of the Vale of Glamorgan; day to go plus' day-out ticket covers whole of company's operating area; 'Network Rider' covers all routes in South East Wales in conjunction with other operators.

Fare structure: Zonal (four zones)

Operational control: Route inspectors; all vehicles have mobile radio contact with central control; real-time passenger information and vehicle location system implemented

Arrangements for elderly/disabled: Welsh Assembly Government free Old Age Pensioner (OAP) and disabled scheme

Average peak-hour speed: 13 km/h

Bus priority: Bus lanes on some services in short sections in city centre; recently introduced lanes have distinctive green finish; more are planned

Subsidy from: County council for specific services secured by tender

Cardiff

Other commercial operators
Current situation
First Cymru Buses Ltd, Stagecoach in South Wales, Newport Transport Ltd, Bebb Travel plc, Shamrock of Pontipridd, and Islwyn Borough Transport Ltd operate into the city from outlying areas.

Gwent operator Harris Coaches (Pengam) Limited operates Solo low-floor buses on a shared 20-minute frequency service between Bargoed and Caerphilly.

Shamrock Travel operates stage carriage services throughout the South Wales valleys and the Cardiff area and operates out of ten major bus interchanges.

Arriva Trains Wales (ATW)/ Trenau Arriva Cymru
St Mary's House, 47 Penarth Road, Cardiff CF10 5DJ, UK
Tel: (+44 845) 606 16 60
Web: www.arrivatrainswales.co.uk

Key personnel
Managing Director: Bob Holland
Staff: 1,975

Type of operation: Local rail

Passenger journeys: (2004/05) 21.9 million

Current situation
As one of the 26 rail companies within the UK, Arriva Trains Wales has a fleet of 116 trains covering a route of over 1,614 km (1,009 miles), supported by 1,860 employees. ATW operates 788 services a day on weekdays, resulting in its trains travelling 21.9 million miles each year.

Cardiff Bus is operating 19 Scania OmniCity 53-seat articulated buses on high-quality services. One is between the city centre and Cardiff Bay waterfront. The service, called Baycar, is in a dedicated blue livery. The other vehicles are branded Capital City Red. Each bus has BBC News 24 television
1194486

Cardiff Bus Scania double-deck bus in orange and blue livery promoting Cardiff & Co, the city of Cardiff marketing organisation
1340802

Cardiff Bus Scania double-deck bus in orange and blue livery promoting Cardiff & Co, the city of Cardiff marketing organisation
1369093

On average ATW services handle around 60,000 passenger journeys a day, with the ability to carry over 12,000 customers at any one time. It operates 238 stations throughout Wales of which 48 are currently staffed.

The 15 year rail franchise for Wales and the border counties was awarded to Arriva in December 2003.

Developments

The restored passenger service from Cardiff Central to Ebbw Vale started running in 2008. The route from Cardiff is 46 km long, and 29 km of track along the branch itself has been upgraded. The line closed to passengers in 1962, although it stayed in use for freight. Cross Keys and Llanhilleth, two stations on the line, were expected to open at the end of 2008.

Blaenau Gwent County Borough Council is seeking funding for a second phase in which the line would be doubled between Cross Keys and Llanhilleth, thus permitting a second hourly service. This could run through to Newport and there would also be additional capacity for future freight services. Second platforms would also be built at Newbridge and Llanhilleth.

Up to four more stations are also proposed, two of them on the present route at Cwm and Pye Corner. A third station is proposed nearer Ebbw Vale town centre, which would mean a short extension of the line from the terminus at Ebbw Vale Parkway and remove the need for the present feeder bus into the town.

There are also plans for a spur to Abertillery, which would provide a second terminus on the route and require the relaying of the track from Aberbeeg.

Rolling stock: 116 trains

Edinburgh

Population: 457,830 (2005 estimate)
Web: www.edinburgh.gov.uk

Public transport

Most bus services provided by company owned by local councils, with some by private operators. Local rail services. Light rail under construction.

A cross-Forth hovercraft solution has been proposed by Stagecoach, using a 150-passenger craft that would run from Kirkcaldy to Leith, with services starting from late 2007.

Airlink Scania N94UD Omnicity bus on route 100 city centre-Edinburgh Airport shuttle (operated by Lothian Buses) at Waverley station (Ken Harris)   1369068

Lothian Buses

Annandale Street, Edinburgh EH7 4AZ, UK
Tel: (+44 131) 554 44 94
Fax: (+44 131) 554 39 42
e-mail: mail@lothianbuses.co.uk
Web: www.lothianbuses.com

Key personnel

Chief Executive: Neil J Renilson
Managing Director: Ian Craig
Operations Director: William Campbell
Finance Director: Norman J Strachan
Engineering Director: Bill Devlin
Marketing Director: Iain Coupar
   Staff: 2,000

Current situation

The company operates commercial services and submits competitive tenders for any contracted operations. A comprehensive route network serves the city of Edinburgh and into East Lothian and Midlothian. Special services include Airlink between the city centre and Edinburgh airport, Night Buses Network and City Sightseeing Edinburgh, Edinburgh Tours, Mac Tour and Majestic Tour Sightseeing Tours.

Developments

Lothian Buses has put six Solo SR low-floor midibuses into service on its three MacTour branded routes. These are the first Solo SRs to enter service in Scotland and are being used on MacTour routes 60, 61 and 69, which provide high frequency circular services in the city suburbs on a hail-and-ride basis along some parts of the routes. Five of the Solos are in Lothian Buses harlequin livery. The sixth is finished in the colours of UK insurance company Standard Life as it is dedicated to a shuttle bus service that links three of their offices around Edinburgh. Internal finish is in Lothian Buses corporate style with the Lazzarini seats trimmed in durable, tartan moquette. There are 28 fixed seats and two tip-up seats in the wheelchair/buggy bay and with room for up to 19 standees the buses are able to cope comfortably with higher passenger numbers at peak times.

In 2008, Lothian Buses took delivery of another 60 Wrightbus-bodied vehicles. The order comprises 50 Wrightbus Eclipse Gemini double-deck buses and 10 Wrightbus Eclipse single-deck buses. All are on Euro 5-compliant Volvo chassis. The orders form part of Edinburgh-based Lothian Buses' ongoing fleet renewal process, aimed at improving the city's public transport services and making it completely low-floor by 2010. The 10 Wrightbus Eclipse single deck buses are built on the Volvo B7RLE chassis. All 10 are adapted for

Lothian Buses Volvo B7TL/Plaxton bus on route 45 passing the Royal Scottish Academy (Ken Harris)
1369072

compatibility with Edinburgh's guided busway system and have been specified with 38 Lazzerini Practico seats; facility for a wheelchair including an electronic ramp; and a seven-camera LOOK CCTV system. Lothian's order for 50 Eclipse Gemini double deck buses is identical in body specification to those previously delivered. All feature the Volvo B9TL chassis specified with their Euro 5 compliant 9.4 litre engine, rated at 260 bhp, coupled to a Voith gearbox. At 11.3 m, the low-floor, easy-access buses have Lazzerini Practico seating with 48 seats on the upper deck and 32 on the lower. Disabled access is by means of a power ramp and passengers have the benefit of the latest electronic destination equipment and a 12-camera CCTV system. An internal door can be deployed to restrict access to the top floor for added security.

Bus

Passenger journeys: (2002) 95 million
(2003) 99 million
(2004) 102 million
(2005) 103 million
(2006) 108 million
Vehicle-km: (2001) 33.9 million
(2002) 35.4 million
(2003) 36.0 million
(2004) 36.8 million

Number of routes: 58 (plus 4 open-top routes)
Route length: 1,288 km
On priority right-of-way: 46 km

Fleet: 667 vehicles
Lothian Buses

Leyland Olympian/Alexander RH double-deck	102
Volvo Olympian/Alexander RH double-deck	63
Dennis Trident II/Alexander ALX400 low-floor double-deck	2
Dennis Trident II/Plaxton President low-floor double-deck	188
Scania N94/East Lancs low-floor double-deck	1
Volvo B7L/Plaxton President low-floor double-deck	7
Volvo B7TL/Wrightbus Eclipse Gemini low-floor double-deck	175
Dennis Super Pointer Dart/Plaxton low-floor single-deck	90
Scania N94 OmniCity low-floor double-deck	5
Volvo B7RLE/Wrightbus Eclipse Urban low-floor single-deck	45

Edinburgh Tours

Solo SR low-floor midibus	6
Mercedes-Benz 709D minibus	1
In peak service: 515	

Most intensive service: 4 min (2–3 min on combined routes)

One-person operation: All routes

Fare collection: Wayfarer electronic machines with farebox on board; passes and smartcard season tickets

Fare structure: Stage; weekly, monthly and annual 'RidaCards'; flat fare on Night Buses, one-day tickets

Fares collected on board: 40 per cent

Fare evasion control: Route Managers

Operational control: Patrol inspectors in vans/ mobile radio

Average peak-hour speed: In mixed traffic, 15.4 km/h

Operating costs financed by: Fares 99 per cent, other commercial sources 1 per cent

Subsidy from: Specific support from councils' rate fund for any contracted services won by tender.

First Edinburgh

Carmuirs House, Stirling Road, Larbert, Falkirk FK5 3NJ, UK

Tel: (+44 1324) 60 22 00   Fax: (+44 1324) 61 12 87

Web: www.firstedinburgh.co.uk
   www.firstgroup.com

Key personnel

Managing Director: Brian Juffs

Finance Director: David Stewart

Current situation

Eastern Scottish based in Edinburgh was purchased from the Scottish Bus Group in 1990 by its workforce and became a subsidiary of FirstGroup in 1995. It operated a substantial proportion of the bus services in the Lothian area, including Edinburgh. There is a network of services to surrounding towns including commuter express workings.

First Edinburgh was formed during 1999 as an amalgam of the Midland Bluebird, Lowland and SMT fleets. Over 420 vehicles are operated in total, but this includes operations in the central lowlands, borders and southern uplands. Around 180 vehicles are operated in the Lothian area from Edinburgh, Musselburgh, Livingston and Dalkeith depots.

Bus (operations in Lothian area only)

Fleet: Not currently available

Edinburgh

Other operators

Current situation

The long-established Scottish coach operator Prentice Westwood moved into local bus operation in 2007, using an Optare Solo. The West Calder-based company won a contract to run an hourly service seven days a week connecting Livingston Hospital with Edinburgh and the local communities along the route. The service is subsidised jointly by Edinburgh City Council, West Lothian Council and the National Health Service.

Waverley Travel of Turnhouse operates some supported services in the city and Fife Scottish operates some services from towns across the Forth bridge.

First ScotRail Limited

Atrium Court, 50 Waterloo Street, Glasgow G2 6HQ, UK

Tel: (+44 8700) 00 51 51   Fax: (+44 141) 335 42 06

e-mail: scotrail.enquiries@firstgroup.com

Web: www.firstscotrail.com

First Edinburgh Volvo B7TL/Wrightbus Eclipse Gemini bus on Route 43 service in Princes Street (Ken Harris)
1369069

Prentice Westwood Optare Solo on local bus service connecting Livingston Hospital with Edinburgh and the local communities along the route (Optare Group Ltd)
1330180

First ScotRail Class 322 emu at Edinburgh Waverley station, prior to forming a service to North Berwick (Ken Harris)
1369070

Key personnel
Managing Director: Mary Dickson
Commercial Director: Peter Williams
Finance Director: Kenny McPhail
Deputy Managing Director/Operations Director:
 Steve Montgomery
Engineering Director: Kenny Scott
New Trains Director: Nick Horton
Human Resources Director: Fiona Irvine
Divisional Operations Manager (Network Services):
 Jacqui Dey
Head of Marketing: Ellie Murphy
Press and Communications Executive: Lally Cowell
Head of Public Relations: Iain Wilson
Head of Train Planning: Andrew Lightowler

Type of operation: Local rail

Current situation
The First ScotRail franchise is now funded and managed by Transport Scotland, a division of the Scottish Executive. In 2005/6 the company operated 2,347 million passenger-kilometres and 39.3 million train-km. It now operates 341 stations.

Frequent services are provided on several routes, operated mainly with dmus. Also electric trains to Berwick (36 km).

For further information on First ScotRail, please see *Jane's World Railways*.

Developments
Work was completed in 2007 on the upgrading of Edinburgh Waverley station, which provides four additional platforms.

While legislation was passed in 2007 to build a rail link to Glasgow Airport, Edinburgh Airport will now be served by an interchange with the new tram line at Gogar.

The Stirling-Alloa-Kincardine reopening is due to be completed in 2008. It will enable the Glasgow-Stirling service to be extended to a new station at Alloa and it will free up capacity for additional passenger trains across the Forth Bridge.

In 2008, First ScotRail became the first train operator in the UK to offer free travel for children aged 5 to 15, seven days a week. More than 200,000 children in the eligible age group travelled free in 2007. By extending the offer to seven days a week, First ScotRail expects to see a significant increase in the number of children travelling on these trains.

City of Edinburgh Council (CEC)
City Development Department
Waverley Court, 4 East Market Street, Edinburgh
EH8 8BG, UK
Tel: (+44 131) 469 36 31
Fax: (+44 131) 469 36 35
Web: www.edinburgh.gov.uk

Key personnel
Director of City Development: Dave Anderson

Park-and-Ride
The City of Edinburgh Council (CEC) has park-and-ride operations in the city, including facilities at Hermiston, Ingliston and Straiton. The centres have substantial infrastructure and high-quality bus services every 15 minutes (10 minutes during peak hours).

Bustracker Real-Time Passenger Information
Real-Time Passenger Information (RTPI) operates at more than 220 bus stops within Edinburgh, and is also available for all bus stops served by equipped Lothian Buses via the internet.

The provision and operation of on-street signs and the internet are the responsibility of CEC, whilst Lothian Buses procures and maintains the on-bus apparatus. Lothian Buses have now equipped over 90 per cent of their fleet with GPS and the necessary technology and, as well as giving the Council the ability to display RTPI, they have a comprehensive fleet management system.

Lothian Buses will soon have all of their fleet equipped and CEC continues to expand the provision of on-street signs. There are more than 300 signs on-street and some have been installed in Midlothian and East Lothian in order to cover the areas of the Lothian Buses network which lie outside Edinburgh.

Edinburgh Airport Rail Link (EARL)
Current situation
Work was suspended in June 2007, pending the outcome of a Scottish Government review.

In September 2007, the Government indicated that it would proceed with a different scheme comprising a tram station near the Airport, with a subsequent connecting route to/from the west. Edinburgh Tram is to run between the new station at Gogar and the Airport.

Light rail (under construction)
Tramtime
Freepost NATN466, Edinburgh EH1 0BR, UK
e-mail: info@tramsforedinburgh.com
Web: www.tt.tiedinburgh.co.uk,
 www.tramsforedinburgh.com

Current situation
Transport Scotland and the City of Edinburgh Council gave the go-ahead for construction of the tramway in 2007, bringing light rail to the streets of the city for the first time since 1955.

The City of Edinburgh's arms-length company, Transport Initiatives Edinburgh Ltd (TIE), was tasked with the provision of an initial network of tram routes in Edinburgh. Currently under construction is a tram network consisting of a route through Leith and Granton via the city centre to West Edinburgh, including Edinburgh Park and Edinburgh airport. There is the possibility of an additional route running from the Haymarket interchange to Granton.

Work on diverting utility cables and wires from beneath the road surfaces is under way, and track laying is expected to begin early in 2009. The new tram routes will include a significant proportion of reserved track.

The tramway is to be built in phases, with the first to be the 16-km line between Edinburgh Airport and Leith Waterfront via Haymarket and Princes Street.

Light rail vehicle manufacturer, CAF, is the preferred bidder for supply of the 27-tram fleet.

Developments
Construction started in 2008.

West Edinburgh Guided Busway (WEBS)
The West Edinburgh Guided Busway (WEBS) started operation at the end of 2004 between the city centre and Edinburgh Park. Called Fastlink, the 1.5 km guideway is part of an eight km rapid transit route serving the office complex at Edinburgh Park and has four stations on the guideway section.

It is operated by 30 Wright-bodied Volvo B7BLRE single-deck buses and 20 Dennis Trident double-deck buses, all having guidewheels for operation on the guided section.

The guided busway will be incorporated into the tram network during the tram track construction work in 2009 and 2010.

Glasgow
Population: City 609,000, metropolitan area 1.6 million (estimated)

Public transport
Principal bus services in Glasgow and surrounding areas operated by private company, with small private operators mostly serving suburban/commuter routes. The Passenger Transport Executive was replaced by the Strathclyde Partnership for Transport (SPT) in 2006. This is the Regional Transport Partnership (RTP) for the West of Scotland. It is one of seven RTPs established under the Transport (Scotland) Act 2005 covering the country. The Strathclyde Partnership for Transport takes over the roles and functions of the Strathclyde Passenger Transport Authority and Executive. The SPT brand name and brand identity is being kept to minimise change over costs and to capitalise on the goodwill and recognition generated by SPT's 30 years of service delivery and promotional activities.

Whilst SPT continues to invest in the local rail network a new body, Transport Scotland, specifies the routes, timetables, fares and quality standards for every train service and station within Strathclyde and on certain routes beyond the area. SPT continues to play a major role in developing strategic rail projects.

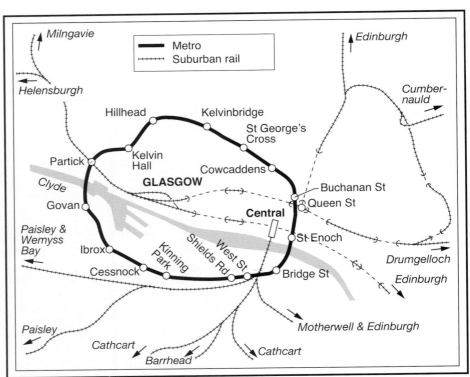

Glasgow's metro and suburban rail network

1168316

Strathclyde Partnership for Transport (SPT)

Consort House, 12 West George Street, Glasgow
G2 1HN, UK
Tel: (+44 141) 332 68 11
Fax: (+44 141) 332 30 76
e-mail: webfeedback@spt.co.uk
Web: www.spt.co.uk

Key personnel
Chief Executive: Ron Culley
Staff: 709

Total rail passengers journeys: (suburban in Strathclyde)
(2003/04) 45.0 million
(2004/05) 45.5 million
(2005/06) 49.9 million

Current situation

Strathclyde Partnership for Transport (SPT) is the regional transport authority for West Scotland, replacing the former Strathclyde Passenger Transport executive. Responsibility for rail services has passed to Transport Scotland, a division of the Scottish Executive. SPT runs the Subway underground metro service, ferries, specifies bus service provision and provides Dial-a-Bus wheelchair-accessible bus services.

Developments

Preparatory work on a section of the Glasgow Airport Rail Link (GARL) started in July 2007. The project involves upgrading 9 km of existing track between Shields Junction and Paisley Gilmour Street station, and laying 2 km of new track between Paisley, St James station and Glasgow airport. The expected opening date is 2011.

Subway (metro)

Tel: (+44 141) 332 31 59
Fax: (+44 141) 425 10 23

Key personnel
Director of Subway Operations: David Wallace
Commercial and Operations Manager: Liz Parkes
Maintenance Manager: W R Taggart
Staff: 333

Type of operation: Small-profile metro, opened 1896

Passenger journeys: (2005/06) 13.2 million

Route length: 10.4 km
Number of stations: 15
Gauge: 1,220 mm
Track: 38 kg/m BS80A rail laid on concrete blocks with resilient rubber inserts, fixed to concrete bed
Tunnel: Some bored, some cut-and-cover
Electrification: 600 V DC, third rail

Rolling stock: 41 cars
Metro-Cammell (1979)   M33
Hunslet TPL (1992)   T8
In peak service: 36

Service: Peak 4 min, off-peak 6–8 min
First/last train: 06.30/23.30; Sunday 10.00/17.50
Fare structure: Flat
Revenue control: AFC
Fare evasion control: Inward barrier check; on-train spot checks
Integration with other modes: Park-and-ride at four stations with 826 spaces; interchange with First ScotRail at two stations
One-person operation: All trains; ATO
Centralised control: Centralised control system from Broomloan depot; CCTV platform and concourse surveillance
Operating costs financed by: Fares 78.6 per cent, other commercial sources 2 per cent, subsidy from PTA 19.4 per cent

Dial-a-Bus

Tel: (+44 845) 128 40 25

Key personnel
Manager: Chris Carberry

Current situation

Door-to-door wheelchair-accessible bus service provided throughout SPT's area, serving about 200,000 mobility-impaired people. Also operates Ring 'n' Ride on-demand service for rural areas. Together, they carried 368,110 passengers in 2005/06.

Suburban rail

Operated by First ScotRail Ltd (please see separate entry).

Ferries

Renfrew-Yoker Ferry and Gourock/Kilcreggan Ferry
Tel: (+44 141) 333 37 08

Current situation

The Renfrew-Yoker ferry is operated by SPT. The Gourock-Kilcreggan ferry is subsidised by SPT and is operated by Clyde Marine. Both ferries carry approximately 200,000 passenger per year.

First Glasgow

197 Victoria Road, Glasgow G42 7AD, UK
Tel: (+44 141) 423 66 00
Fax: (+44 141) 636 32 28
Web: www.firstgroup.com

Key personnel
Managing Director: Mark Savelli
Public Relations Manager:
  Denise Robertson
Marketing Manager: Hazel McGuire
Marketing Co-ordinator: Emma Latimer
Staff: 2,700

Current situation

Established in 1986, the company originated from the PTE's former bus operations which were placed on a fully commercial footing. The company was purchased by its workforce in 1993, and was acquired by FirstGroup in 1996. It has adopted the marketing name First Glasgow.

Developments

In 2007, First Glasgow paid GBP6 million for a new depot in Blantyre, replacing the Motherwell depot.

Also in 2007, the company bought the bus business of Hutchinsons of Overtown and merged the operation into an improved network for Motherwell.

A Route Development Plan was started in 2007, focusing on the development of new and existing routes.

Bus

Passenger journeys: Not currently available
Vehicle-km: Not currently available

Number of routes: 117
Route length: Not currently available

Fleet: 994 vehicles
BMC 1100FE single-deck bus	3
Dennis Dart/Plaxton Pointer single-deck bus	54
Dennis Dart/UVG Urbanstar single-deck bus	15
Dennis Dart/Caetano single-deck bus	1
Dennis Dart/Marshall SLF single-deck bus	29
Dennis Dart/Alexander single-deck bus	4
Dennis Trident double-deck bus	36
Dennis Dart/Northern Counties single-deck	4
Leyland Olympian/Alexander RL double-deck bus	33
Optare Solo M850 single-deck bus	7
Optare Solo M920 single-deck bus	17
Optare Solo M950	3
Scania L113CRL/Wrights Axcess Ultraflow single-deck bus	32
Scania L94/Wrights Axcess Floline single-deck bus	87
Volvo B10BLE/Wrights Renown single-deck bus	41
Volvo B10M/Alexander PS single-deck bus	172
Volvo B10LA/Wright Fusion articulated bus	10
Volvo B7RLE/Wright Eclipse single-deck	117

First Glasgow bus in service in the city centre
1136156

First Glasgow buses in service in Hamden Park
1136157

Volvo B6LE/Alexander ALX200 single-deck bus	24
Volvo B7L/Wrights Eclipse double-deck bus	47
Volvo B7L tri-axle/East Lancs double-deck bus	10
Volvo B7LA/Wrights Fusion single-deck articulated bus	21
Volvo B7TL/Wrights Eclipse Gemini double-deck bus	104
Volvo D10M/Alexander RV single-deck bus	17
Volvo Olympian/Alexander Royale double-deck bus	48
Volvo Olympian/Alexander RL double-deck bus	18
Volvo Olympian/Northern Counties Palatine 2 double-deck bus	16

In peak service: Not currently available

Most intensive service: three min
One-person operation: All routes
Fare collection: Sealed vault farebox linked to Wayfarer ticket machine by driver
Fare structure: Stage; passes, season tickets and zone cards
Fare evasion control: Uniformed and plain clothes inspectors
Arrangements for elderly/disabled: Dial-a-bus network and additional new buses offering super-low-floor access, free concessionary travel funded by the Scottish Executive
Integration with other modes: Interchange bus stations with Glasgow Subway at Govan and Partick (also with First ScotRail at Hamilton and Partick). Zone card interavailable with the Glasgow subway, First ScotRail and other local operators; interstation service operating, Central station, Buchanan Street station and Queen Street station; PlusBus tickets available from points within the SPT area; Firstcard family of all-modes season tickets
Average distance between stops: 321 m
Average peak-hour speed: 19.2 km/h
Operating costs financed by: Fares 83 per cent, other commercial sources 0.3 per cent, subsidy/grants 16.7 per cent
Subsidy from: SPT for less than two per cent of the total mileage operated by First Glasgow

Arriva Scotland West Ltd

Inchinnan, Paisley PA3, UK
Web: www.arrivabus.co.uk

Key personnel

Director and General Manager: Ian Craig
Operations Manager: Murray Rogers
Staff: 500

Current situation

Clydeside Buses was sold to its workforce in the Scottish Bus Group privatisation, with a 25 per cent stake held by Luton & District. The company was sold to British Bus in 1994, and transferred to Arriva in 1996. Smaller operators acquired in 1997 were Argyll Group of Greenock (88 vehicles) and McGills Bus Service of Barrhead (28 vehicles).

Bus

Number of routes: 55
Route length: 478 km

Fleet: 158 vehicles	
Volvo B10M/Alexander double-deck	1
Volvo B10M/East Lancs double-deck	6
Volvo B10M/East Lancs single-deck	10
Leyland Leopard/Plaxton single-deck	2
Scania N113/East Lancs single-deck	6
Dennis Dart/Plaxton single-deck	4
Dennis Dart/Wright single-deck	5
Dennis Dart/Carlyle single-deck	2
Scania L113/East Lancs low-floor single-deck	8
Scania L113/Alexander low-floor single-deck	3
Volvo B10BLE/Wright low-floor single-deck	7
Dennis Dart SLF/Plaxton low-floor single-deck	28
Dennis Dart SLF/Alexander low-floor single-deck	25
Dennis Dart/Plaxton midibus	15
Dennis Dart/Northern Counties midibus	4
Dennis Dart SLF/Plaxton low-floor midibus	5
Optare Metrorider minibus	24

In peak service: 161

Most intensive service: 6 min
One-person operation: All routes
Fare collection: Wayfarer 3 equipment with change-giving
Fare structure: Stages
Fares collected on board: 80 per cent
Fare evasion control: Inspectors
Operational control: Inspectors
Average peak hour speed: 24 km/h

Stagecoach West Scotland

Sandgate, Ayr, KA7 1DD, UK
Tel: (+44 1292) 61 37 00 Fax: (+44 1563) 61 35 01
e-mail: west.scotland@stagecoachbus.com
Web: www.stagecoachbus.com

Key personnel

Managing Director: Sam Greer
Operations Director: Sarah Longair
Engineering Director: John Harper
Staff: 100

Current situation

Stagecoach West Scotland has a fleet of 25 buses and coaches operating in the Glasgow area and daily patronage is reported at 10,000.
The total fleet in the Stagecoach West Scotland fleet is 485.

Bus

Passenger journeys: Not currently available
Vehicle-km: Not currently available

Number of routes: 8
Route length: 160 km

Fleet: 25 vehicles (485 for all of Stagecoach West Scotland)
Volvo B10M/Alexander single-deck
    Breakdown of fleet not currently available
Volvo B6BLE/Alexander low-floor single-deck
    Breakdown of fleet not currently available
Volvo B10M/Plaxton interurban coach
    Breakdown of fleet not currently available

Most intensive service: 3 min
One-person operation: All routes
Fare collection: Wayfarer 3 electronic machines; passes and season tickets
Fare structure: Coarse zones; nominal fare for concessionary passengers

Glasgow

Other operators

Current situation

Smaller companies providing both commercial and subsidised services include; Allander Coaches, Canavan of Kilsyth, Henry Crawford

of Nielston, Doig's of Glasgow, Gibson Direct, Gillens Coaches of Port Glasgow, Glasgow Citybus Limited, Hutchison Coaches (Overtown) Ltd, Irvine's of Law, John Morrow Coaches, Stagecoach West Scotland, William Stokes of Carstairs, Stonehouse Coaches, Stuart's of Carluke and Whitelaw's Coaches of Stonehouse.

Six more Optare Solos have gone into service with Renfrew operator Gibson Direct, as part of a major renewal programme of the company's bus fleet. The Solos are operating on Gibson Direct's commercial route 68, which runs to a seven minute frequency between Paisley and the new Braehead shopping and leisure complex. As well as local bus operations, the company runs a Glasgow-wide 'Dial a Bus' service.

First ScotRail Limited

Atrium Court, 50 Waterloo Street, Glasgow G1 3TA, UK
Tel: (+44 8700) 00 51 51 Fax: (+44 141) 335 42 06
e-mail: scotrail.enquiries@firstgroup.com
Web: www.firstscotrail.com

Key personnel

Managing Director: Mary Grant
Commercial Director: Peter Williams
Finance Director: Kenny McPhail
Operations Director and Deputy Managing Director: Steve Montgomery
Engineering: Kenny Scott
New Trains Director: Nick Horten
Human Resources Director: Fiona Irvine
Divisional Operations Manager (Network Services): Jacqui Dey
Head of Hospitality: Garry Clark
Head of Public Relations: Iain Wilson
Acting Head of Marketing: Marc Sangster
Public Affairs Manager: Lally Cowell
Staff: Not available currently

Type of operation: Suburban heavy rail

Passenger journeys: (2007/08) 81 million
Train-km: Not available currently

Current situation

Electric and some diesel services operate on 14 routes on the north and south sides of the Clyde, and two cross-city lines – routes/services total 486 km, mostly electrified at 25 kV AC (346 km), with 177 stations.
The First ScotRail franchise is now funded and managed by Transport Scotland, a division of the Scottish Executive. In 2005/6, the company operated 2,347 million passenger-kilometres and 39.3 million train-km. It now operates 341 stations. The group also operates Hull Trains and First GB Railfreight.
For further information on First ScotRail, please see *Jane's World Railways.*

One of six more Optare Solos which have gone into service with Renfrew operator Gibson Direct on local bus services (Optare)
1375471

Developments

In 2008, Transport Scotland rolled out a new identity for stations and trains, which brought together the previously separate First ScotRail and Strathclyde brands. It announced the December 2008 timetable which will see the biggest improvements since 1999. The paths across the Forth Bridge (released by coal trains that now run via Alloa) will be used by a new hourly Edinburgh-Dundee service that, by allowing stops to be taken out of Edinburgh-Aberdeen trains, will reduce overcrowding and accelerate journey-times by up to 10 minutes. Edinburgh-Perth via Fife services will increase from two-hourly to hourly; Aberdeen-Inverurie will see an extra six trains a day; an additional train each way will link Aberdeen and Inverness and there will be a fourth train daily from Inverness to Wick, with four trains all year to and from Kyle of Lochalsh. The timetable will make provision for the reopening of Laurencekirk Station due later in 2009.

Also in 2008, First ScotRail was named Public Transport Operator of the Year for the third running. Delays caused by First ScotRail have fallen by 15 per cent over the past year and are down 50 per cent since the franchise began. There has been 20 per cent passenger growth and despite record numbers of journeys, now more than 81 million a year, overall crime on the railways is reported to have fallen.

Rolling stock: 99 three-car emus, 28 two-car dmus, three two-car dmus

CalMac Ferries Limited

The Ferry Terminal, Gourock PA19 1QP, UK
Tel: (+44 1475) 65 01 00
Fax: (+44 1475) 63 76 07
e-mail: info@calmac.co.uk
Web: www.calmac.co.uk

Key personnel

Chairman: Harold Mills
Managing Director: W Lawrie Sinclair
Finance Director: Alexander M Lynch
Technical Director: John Kerr
Operations Director: Philip Preston
Head of Communication and Customer Care: Hugh Dan MacLennan

Type of operation: Ferry

Passenger journeys: (2007/08) 5 million

Background

Formed in 1851 as a steamer company, the company became wholly owned by the Scottish Executive (formerly the Secretary of State for Scotland) in 1990.

In 2006, CalMac Ferries was incorporated and is a wholly-owned subsidiary of David MacBrayne Ltd. Caledonian MacBrayne became Caledonian Maritime Assets Ltd (CMAL) and this company owns the vessels and piers required for operation of the Clyde and Hebrides ferry services.

Current situation

CalMac Ferries provides ferry services on 26 routes to 22 islands and four peninsulas on the west of Scotland with a fleet of 29 vessels, leased from CMAL. Two other vessels are retained on separate charters.

More than five million passengers and one million cars have been carried on CalMac Ferries services every year for the past three years.

Hull

Population: 249,100 (2005 estimate)
Web: www.hullcc.gov.uk

Public transport

Most bus services provided by two private companies and co-ordinated by Hull City Council. Hull CC also supplies the infrastructure to support and improve public transport, by building bus lanes, priority signals and other installations. It also promotes the use of public transport to residents and businesses and supports essential bus services that are not viable. Hull CC also provides community transport services and provides school transport.

A ten-year programme of transport improvements to tackle congestion, improve safety and invest in public transport was announced for the Yorkshire and the Humber region in 2006. The programme includes an integrated transport scheme that includes a new relief road and a Park & Ride scheme in Beverley, Hull district.

The scheme involves the construction of a new southern relief road to the south of Beverley and a Park & Ride facility to link the relief road directly to the railway station and town centre via a high quality, frequent and affordable bus link. The scheme will alleviate traffic congestion in the town centre, improve access within Beverley, allow improvements to be made to the town centre environment and contribute to the economy of the town. Complementary measures will include improvements to the management of car parking in the town centre.

Stagecoach in Hull

Foster Street, Hull HU8 8BT, UK
Tel: (+44 1482) 22 23 33   Fax: (+44 1482) 21 76 23
Web: www.stagecoachbus.com

Key personnel

Managing Director: Gary Nolan
Operations Director: Richard Kay
Commercial Director: David Skepper
Engineering Director: John Taylor
  Staff: 350

Current situation

Formerly owned by the city council, Kingston upon Hull City Transport (KHCT) was sold to Cleveland Transit of Stockton in 1993, with employees holding 49 per cent of shares. KHCT and its parent company were bought by Stagecoach in 1994. Responsibilities for Hull passed to Stagecoach East Midlands in the 2001 consolidation of Stagecoach Group subsidiaries.

The current routes include 20 all-day routes, 17 Hull and East Riding school contracts, nine Earlybird services, six late-night services (00.00, 01.00, 02.00 Fridays/Saturdays), North Sea Ferries terminal daily service and express service to Leeds.

Developments

The old bus station, built in 1935, closed in 2004 and all services ran from a temporary on-street station along Albion Street and Bond Street. In September 2007 new interchange opened on the site of the old bus station adjacent to the railway station.

Bus

Passenger journeys: (2006/07) 17 million
(2007/08) 17 million
Vehicle-km: Not currently available

Number of routes: 54
Route length: 416 km

Fleet: 128 vehicles and 2 driver-training vehicles

Volvo Olympian/Northern Counties double-deck	23
Volvo Olympian/Alexander	22
Dennis Trident/Alexander	53
Volvo B10M/Northern Counties single-deck	3
Dennis Dart/Plaxton single-deck	6
Dennis Dart SLF/Alexander low-floor minibus	23
Volvo B10M/Plaxton coach (plus 2 training vehicles)	2
In peak service: 118	

Most intensive service: 7–8 min (10 minutes most other)
One-person operation: All services
Fare collection: Wayfarer: 3 equipment with card readers
Fare structure: Zonal; daily, weekly, monthly and 10-journey cards
Fares collected on board: 68 per cent (32 per cent of journeys by card holders)
Fare evasion control: Four inspectors
Operational control: Inspectors; mobile radios
Arrangements for elderly/disabled: Low-floor accessible buses operate some services and run on all night services
Bus priority: Bus lanes on Beverley Road, Anlaby Road, Holderness Road, Clarence Street, Alfred Gelder Street; buses-only streets in most of city centre
Operating costs financed by: Fares 95 per cent, other commercial sources 5 per cent, subsidy/grants (for specific services/concessions) 14 per cent
Subsidy from: City and county council grants and East Riding County Council.

Stagecoach in Hull low-floor Dennis Dart bus outside Kingston-upon-Hull stadium   1146932

East Yorkshire Motor Services Ltd (EYMS)

252 Anlaby Road, Hull HU3 2RS, UK
Tel: (+44 1482) 32 71 42
Fax: (+44 1482) 21 20 40
e-mail: enquiries@eyms.co.uk
Web: www.eyms.co.uk

Key personnel

Chairman and Chief Executive: Peter Shipp
Finance Director: Peter Harrison
   Staff: 940

Passenger journeys: (2003) 17.3 million
(2004) 16.9 million
(2005) 17.1 million
(2006) 17.8 million
(2007) 18.0 million
Vehicle-km: (2003) 16 million
(2004) 15.5 million
(2005) 15.3 million
(2006) 15 million
(2007) 14.7 million

Route length: 1,658 km (one way)

Background

The company, which celebrated its 80th anniversary in 2006, was a subsidiary of the National Bus Company until 1987, when it was sold to EYMS Group Ltd, a management consortium, which has grown into a sole shareholder major holding company.

Since 1987, EYMS Group has acquired several local bus and coach operators in its own traditional area and Finglands Coachways of Manchester in 1992, and Whittles Coaches of Kidderminster in 2004. The Group total fleet is now 425 and 940 staff are employed.

Coach operations were consolidated into a new leisure travel company, National Holidays, which was demerged from EYMS Group in 1997. East Yorkshire Coaches continues to cater for the local coach and short-break tour business. Low-floor single-deck and double-deck buses have been introduced on a number of specific routes in Hull and Beverley. In 2000, Scarborough became only the second town in the UK to have its whole town service network operated by wheelchair-accessible buses. Limited night services were introduced in Hull during 1998 and recently some radial routes in Hull have been linked to provide frequent cross-city routes.

Current situation

The company had long been the main operator of services throughout the East Riding of Yorkshire, and this is still the position, but the company has also developed its routes within the city boundary over the last 15 years. EYMS also provides a local bus network in and around Scarborough in North Yorkshire (using the Scarborough and District trading name) and runs longer-distance and interurban routes from Hull to York, Scunthorpe and Scarborough.

Developments

The company has recently won the contract for two new Park & Ride routes in Scarborough and has received six Volvo/Plaxton Centro buses to run the services, which had been delayed due to site preparation problems but were due to start in December 2008. Several buses are being fitted with real-time passenger information equipment for use in Scarborough and on routes into York.

Fleet: 319 vehicles

East Yorkshire Motor Services Volvo B9TL/Wright Eclipse Gemini low-floor double-deck bus 1343275

East Yorkshire Motor Services ADL Enviro 200 low-floor single-deck bus   1343274

AEC Routemaster/Park Royal open-top double-deck	1
AEC Regent/Willowbrook double-deck	1
Leyland PD2/East Lancs open-top double-deck	1
Bristol VR/ECW open-top double-deck	1
Leyland Olympian/Northern Counties double-deck	22
Leyland Olympian/Alexander double-deck	1
Volvo Olympian/Alexander double-deck	7
Volvo Olympian/Northern Counties double-deck	36
Volvo B7L/Plaxton low-floor double-deck	30
Volvo B6/Northern Counties single-deck	1
Volvo B10M/Alexander single-deck	4
Volvo B10M Citybus/Northern Counties open-top	5
Volvo B7TL/Wright low-floor double-deck	18
Volvo B9TL/Wright low-floor double-deck	28
Mercedes-Benz O405/Optare single-deck	15
ADL Enviro 400 low-floor double-deck	5
Dennis Dart SLF/Plaxton low-floor single-deck	11
Dennis Dart SLF/Caetano low-floor single-deck	2
Optare Excel low-floor single-deck	13
Volvo B10BLE/Alexander low-floor single-deck	10
MAN 18.220/Alexander low-floor single-deck	11
Volvo B7RLE/Wright low-floor single-deck	11
Dennis Dart SLF/Plaxton low-floor midibus	34
Mercedes-Benz 711D/Plaxton minibus	1
Mercedes-Benz O814/Plaxton minibus	2
Bedford OB/Duple coach	1
Leyland Tiger/Plaxton coach	1
Volvo B10M/Plaxton coach	2
Volvo B10M/Berkhof coach	5
Volvo B12M/Plaxton coach	1
Volvo B7R/Plaxton coach	1
Mercedes-Benz O405N2 integral single-deck	2
Volvo B12M/Berkhof coach	2
Volvo B12B/Plaxton coach	6
Plaxton Primo low-floor midibus	6
Volvo B12B/Caetano coach	8
Volvo B7RLE/Plaxton low-floor single-deck	6

In peak service: Not available currently

Most intensive service: 10 min
One-person operation: All services
Fare collection: Wayfarer TGX equipment with change given; smartcard stored-value tickets, prepaid passes
Operating costs financed by: Fares 67 per cent, subsidy/grants for specific services 10 per cent, concessionary fares 23 per cent
Fare evasion control: Ticket inspectors, mystery travellers, CCTV
Operation control: Inspectors, private two-way radio, GPS information via ticket machines (retrospective), in-house survey staff

Hull

Other commercial operators

Current situation

Services also provided by Alpha Coach, which is based in Hull and part of Dunn Line Holdings, which is itself a part of the Veolia group of companies.

Leeds-Bradford

Population: Leeds 726,000, Bradford 464,000, conurbation 2 million (estimated)

Public transport

Bus services in the West Yorkshire area including Leeds and Bradford and surrounding towns such as Huddersfield, Halifax and Wakefield, are provided by more than 40 operators, the largest of which is FirstGroup. Other major group operators include Arriva and Blazefield. The West Yorkshire Passenger Transport Executive (Metro) is responsible for contracting non-commercial bus services by competitive tender, local rail services, passenger facilities, information and policy development in partnership with district councils.

A ten-year programme of transport improvements to tackle congestion, improve safety and invest in public transport was announced for the Yorkshire and the Humber region in 2006. The programme includes implementation of the A65 Kirkstall Road Quality Bus Corridor. The scheme will consist of 24-hour bus lanes along a 3.5 km stretch of the A65 stretching from Kirkstall Bridge to the Leeds Inner Ring Roads, including road widening, junction improvements and Urban Traffic Control measures to give greater priority for buses, improving journey times and reliability.

First Leeds

Hunslet Park, Donisthorpe Street, Leeds LS10 1PL, UK
Tel: (+44 113) 381 55 50
Fax: (+44 113) 381 50 90
Web: www.firstgroup.com

Key personnel

Managing Director: Stephen Graham
Commercial Director: Richard Harris
  Staff: Not available currently

Current situation

Operates local bus services in Leeds in the West Yorkshire area, which includes Halifax, Huddersfield, Leeds and Bradford.

Developments

First, completed introduction of its fleet of 17 rapid-transit vehicles in Leeds in 2007. They operate on the 22 km service 4 linking Pudsey, the city centre and Whinmoor. First brands all its rapid transit services 'ftr' and they are operated with articulated Volvos with Wrightbus Streetcar bodywork. The ftr transport scheme was shortlisted in 2008 for the UK National Public Transport Operator of the Year in 2008. It has seen a 15 per cent passenger growth on service 4.

First opened its new garage and office complex in Donisthorpe Street in 2008. It gives First the opportunity to accommodate an extra 30 buses. The Kirkstall Road depot closed in 2008.

A pair of 24-seater Optare Solo low-floor buses have entered service with First as part of a strategy aimed at making local bus services in Todmorden more accessible to mobility-impaired passengers. They form part of the MetroConnect services across West Yorkshire, run by West Yorkshire PTE under the Metro brand name. In 2003, Metro was awarded funding from the Department for Transport for a project to enhance Todmorden's bus services. As a result, several new services have been introduced and frequency improved on some of the more heavily used services.

Guided busway

The first phase of the North Leeds guided busway was launched in 1995 on the A61 Scott Hall Road. The second phase opened in late 1996, with the third in 1997. Further extensions, including a park-and-ride, opened in 1998 and 1999. Low-floor single-deck and double-deck buses are equipped with guidewheels (to enable navigation through the busway) on their front axles.

Further guided bus projects have been developed in partnership with FirstGroup and Arriva, which received government approval because of substantial private-sector contributions towards costs. The East Leeds Quality Partnership ('Elite') corridor involved FirstGroup contributing GBP3.7 million, Arriva GBP1.3 million and the government GBP5 million towards the GBP10 million infrastructure and highway costs. Both bus operators have also introduced GBP6 million worth of new double-deck buses to complete the partnership, with Metro providing new bus shelters and street furniture along the corridor. The Elite corridor opened for service in November 2001, and comprises 2.5 km of new segregated guided busway, 2.8 km of additional bus priority lanes, and a further 1 km of upgraded bus lanes.

A smaller scheme along the Manchester Road corridor in Bradford opened at the end of January 2002. The Bradford scheme cost GBP7 million in total, for road works and infrastructure developments, including new bus shelters. GBP6 million had been allocated by central government with FirstGroup making a further GBP1 million contribution towards the infrastructure costs. The 3.5 km scheme includes 2 km of new guided busway. First Bradford had already upgraded its fleet substantially, as part of an ongoing investment, and expects to improve frequencies along the corridor. Proposals for a park-and-ride scheme from the redeveloped Odsal stadium are being pursued as part of an overall package of transport improvements for South Bradford. A fourth priority corridor has been opened on Kirkstall Road in Leeds.

Bus

Passenger journeys: Not available currently
Vehicle-km: Not available currently

Number of routes: 204

Fleet: 421 vehicles

Volvo Olympian/Alexander double-deck	40
MCW Metrobus double-deck	33
Scania N113/Alexander double-deck	37
Scania N113/Northern Counties double-deck	5
Dennis Arrow/Northern Counties double-deck	10
Volvo B7TL/Alexander low-floor double-deck	69
Scania N113/Alexander single-deck	55
Scania N113/East Lancs single-deck	1
Scania L113/Alexander single-deck	5
Dennis Lance/ Plaxton single-deck	23
Scania L113/Wright low-floor single-deck	22
Scania L94/Wright low-floor single-deck	28
Volvo B10BLA/Wright articulated low-floor single-deck	15
Dennis Dart/Alexander midibus	24
Dennis Dart/Plaxton midibus	26
Dennis Dart SLF/Plaxton low-floor midibus	1

Mercedes-Benz 709D/Plaxton minibus	3
Mercedes-Benz 711D/Leicester Carriage minibus	2
Mercedes-Benz 810D/Leicester Carriage minibus	2
Mercedes-Benz 711D/Keillor minibus	1
Optare Solo low-floor midibus	14

In peak service: Not available currently

Most intensive service: 3 min
One-person operation: All routes
Fare collection: By driver with Wayfarer; smartcard in Bradford, prepaid sales through 300 outlets
Fare structure: Stage, with off-peak maximum fare; weekly, monthly, quarterly and annual 'Metro Cards', District Rider cards, County Rider card; various Day Rovers
Fares collected on board: 70 per cent of passengers pay cash
Fare evasion control: Roving inspectorate staff
Integration with other modes: Prepurchase tickets/passes interavailable between bus and rail
Operational control: Route inspectors/mobile radio; radio communication between drivers and inspectors based at four district control rooms; all vehicles radio-equipped
Arrangements for elderly/disabled: Concessionary fares financed by PTE (half adult fare in peak hours, nominal interpeak)
Operating costs financed by: Fares 76 per cent, concessionary fares reimbursement 12.5 per cent, contracted services 11.6 per cent, other income 1.4 per cent
Subsidy from: PTA levy for contracted services

Arriva Yorkshire Ltd

24 Barnsley Road, Wakefield WF1 5JX, UK
Tel: (+44 1924) 23 13 00   Fax: (+44 1924) 20 01 06
Web: www.arrivabus.co.uk

Key personnel

Managing Director: Phil Stone
Financial Director: David Cocker
Commercial Director: Phil Booker
Engineering Director: Phil Cummings
  Staff: 1,200

Background

Formerly the Yorkshire Bus Group, the company's buses are branded Arriva Yorkshire.

Current situation

There is a network of services to the south and west of the two cities, serving the Five Towns area, and to the east of Leeds, based around Selby, North Yorkshire.

Guidewheel-fitted easy-access double-deck buses operate on the Elite corridor in Leeds – a project which the company part-funded.

Refurbished Class 321 emu at Leeds station   1198799

The 110, 201-3 and X33 services feature the Announce audio/visual bus stop identification system. Real-time service information will be available for all Arriva Yorkshire services from 2005 as part of a WYPTE/South Yorks PTE project.

Developments

Arriva Yorkshire has opted for 13 Wrightbus Eclipse single deck buses to be delivered during 2009. Built on the Volvo B7RLE chassis, the 45 seater buses will go into service on the company's Cleckheaton to Leeds route.

Bus

Number of routes: 140

Fleet: 383 vehicles

Leyland Lynx single-deck	9
Volvo Olympian/Northern Counties double-deck	6
Volvo Olympian/East Lancs double-deck	11
Volvo B10B/Alexander single-deck	35
Volvo B7RLE/Wrightbus Eclipse single-deck	13
Volvo B10B/WrightBus single-deck	4
Dennis Arrow/East Lancs double-deck	10
DAF DB250/Optare Spectra double-deck	18
Volvo B7TL/Alexander low-floor double-deck	20
Volvo B7TL/Plaxton low-floor double-deck	20
DAF DB250/Optare Spectra low-floor double-deck	24
Volvo B10M double-deck	3
Dennis Lance/Alexander single-deck	30
DAF SB220/Optare single-deck	3
VDL SB200 single-deck	5
Mercedes-Benz 709D	1
DAF SB220/Ikarus single-deck	24
DAF SB220/Alexander low-floor single-deck	51
Volvo B10BLE/Wright low-floor single-deck	7
Dennis Dart SLF/Alexander low-floor single-deck	3
Dennis Dart/Plaxton midibus	8
Dennis Dart/Carlyle midibus	1
Dennis Dart/Northern Counties midibus	15
Dennis Dart SLF/Alexander low-floor midibus	29
Dennis Dart SLF/UVG low-floor midibus	1
Optare Metrorider minibus	4
Dennis Dart SLF/Plaxton low-floor minibus	28

In peak service: Not available currently

Most intensive service: 7–8 min
One-person operation: 100 per cent
Fare structure: Adult fares between 30 pence and GBP 1.80. Senior citizens off-peak standard fare 30 pence. Return fares available in the North Yorkshire area. A range of unlimited-use day tickets are available across the network, as well as weekly and 4-weekly tickets on bus or through PayPoint in the West Yorkshire area.

Leeds-Bradford
Other commercial operators
Current situation
Blazefield Holdings subsidiaries Keighley & District, Harrogate & District, and Yorkshire Coastliner, operate in the area.

A number of smaller operators also run commercial or tendered services: Independent Coachways, J J Longstaff, A Lyles, Paul's Travel and Tetley's Motor Services Ltd.

Metro (West Yorkshire Passenger Transport Executive)
Wellington House, 40-50 Wellington Street, Leeds LS1 2DE, UK
Tel: (+44 113) 251 72 72
Fax: (+44 113) 251 73 33
e-mail: feedback@wypte.gov.uk
Web: www.wymetro.com

Key personnel
Director General: Kieran Preston
Director, Passenger Services: John Henkel
Director, Corporate Services: Sheena Pickersgill

Northern Rail Class 333 emu at Skipton on local service to Leeds (Tony Pattison)　1330181

Passenger journeys: (Bus and rail)
(2003/04) 226.1 million

Background
Metro is the operating name used by the West Yorkshire Passenger Transport Executive and is the public transport co-ordinating body which implements the policies set down by the West Yorkshire Passenger Transport Authority (WYPTA).

Current situation
Metro's activities, which are funded by the WYPTA, include securing subsidised bus services to complement the commercial network, specifying and financing the local rail network, administration of all concessionary travel and prepaid ticketing schemes. Metro operates 23 bus stations as well as providing and maintaining all bus stops and most shelters across the county. Metro also produces timetable and promotional information and provides accurate, up-to-date information on all public transport services within West Yorkshire through its website at www.wymetro.com and its 7-day-a-week 07.00–22.00 MetroLine call centre on (+44) 113 245 7676. The organisation also leads major transport developments such as guided bus schemes, bus station redevelopments and new rail stations and works with the district councils' planning and highway teams to promote increased use of public transport.

AccessBus, which provides wheelchair-accessible, dial-a-ride, door-to-door services free of charge to those who are unable to use conventional buses and trains, is also co-ordinated by Metro. The fleet of 33 AccessBus vehicles carries approximately 500,000 passengers each year.

Developments
Tram-train operation is to be trialled for the first time in the UK. Five new tram-trains, which can run on both railway tracks and tram lines, will replace conventional trains currently used on the 37-mile Penistone Line between Huddersfield, Barnsley and Sheffield. Tram-trains are lighter and 'greener' than conventional trains. They use less fuel and weigh less, which reduces wear and tear on tracks therefore decreasing the need for disruptive maintenance works. Tram-trains have faster acceleration and deceleration rates so they can also offer passengers better journey times.

The trial, which starts in 2010 and will last for two years, will look at the environmental benefits, operating costs and technical suitability of the tram-trains as well as testing how popular the vehicles are with passengers on the route. There is also an option for a second phase, which would test the vehicles on the Sheffield Supertram system to identify what additional benefits the

vehicles could deliver when extended onto city centre tram lines.

The project is a partnership between the UK Department for Transport (DfT), the train operator Northern Rail and rail infrastructure owner Network Rail, and seeks to establish whether tram-trains similar to those operating successfully in Europe are suitable for Britain's railway network.

Northern Rail, which is owned by Serco-Ned Railways, will run a competition for manufacturers to build the tram-trains, which Northern will lease, and Network Rail will spend GBP15 million on track improvements and alterations to stations as part of the trial, significant funding in the route. The DfT will contribute GBP9 million to fund the operation of the trial and Northern will bring experience from Europe through Ned Railways, which operates tram-trains in The Netherlands.

In 2007, the UK Government announced a capacity increase of 53 per cent for peak hour commuter trains serving Leeds to meet the expected demand for rail travel.

Additional capacity will be provided by lengthening trains on key routes operated by Trans-Pennine Express, with a 30 per cent increase in capacity on the northern section. Extra carriages will be available on Leeds and Sheffield suburban services. The enhancements are planned from 2009, with all the extra capacity in place by 2014.

Contracted bus services
Current situation
Changes in the market and better appreciation by operators of the commercial basis of their operations cause constant change in the bus network, and Metro is required to secure socially necessary services when commercial operators withdraw. Partnership working with bus operators has seen the start of the introduction of a core high-frequency network, which has contributed significantly to the increase in passenger journeys.

Developments
'Yournextbus' is Metro's new bus departure times service, using GPS satellite technology to track the location of buses in West and South Yorkshire. By texting the 8-digit bus stop number to short-code 63876 (which spells 'Metro'), passengers can find out the scheduled or real time for any bus, at any stop, in the two counties. The service is also available through Metro's web site at www.wymetro.com, and a telephone-based service was launched in 2007. Some 3,000 text messages are sent on average every working day.

First introduced ftr rapid transit vehicles, built by Wrightbus, on the Pudsey-Leeds-Whinmoor route (service 4) in 2007.

Contracted rail

Northern

Local rail services in Yorkshire, Manchester and the north of England.

Northern Rail Ltd

PO Box 208, Leeds, LS1 2BU, UK
Tel: (+44 845) 000 01 25 (Customer Relations)
Tel: (+44 845) 600 80 08 (Disabled person's helpline)
e-mail: customer.relations@northernrail.org
Web: www.northernrail.org

Key personnel

Managing Director: Heidi Mottram

Passenger journeys: (2007) 78.3 million

Current situation

Local rail services are operated to Metro's specifications on 19 routes totalling 349 km with 67 stations.

Developments

Tram-train operation is to be trialled on the Penistone line.

Glasshoughton station opened in 2005. Detailed design work has been carried out for a new station at Low Moor and feasibility studies have been undertaken for more new stations at Apperley Bridge, Kirkstall and Horsforth Woodside. Progress on these stations is dependent upon acquiring extra fleet for the network.

Rolling stock: 110 dmu cars, 19 emu car sets

First Keolis TransPennine Express

ADMAIL 3878, Manchester, M1 9YB, UK
Tel: (+44 845) 600 16 71 (Customer relations)
Tel: (+44 845) 600 16 74 (Disabled person's helpline)
e-mail: tpecustomer.relations@firstgroup.com
Web: www.firstgroup.com/tpexpress/

Current situation

Local rail services are operated to Metro's specifications on the Manchester-Huddersfield-Leeds-Hull/York-Newcastle route, supported jointly with Greater Manchester PTE and operated by First Keolis.

Rapid Transit Network (proposed)

Current situation

The Leeds Supertram scheme was cancelled by the Department for Transport (DfT) in 2005. Metro subsequently engaged with the DfT on discussions regarding Rapid Bus Transit for the three former Supertram routes, plus three other routes in West Yorkshire, as part of a long-term vision for the Leeds City Region.

In 2007, the Yorkshire & Humber Assembly's regional transport board backed WYPTE's proposal to introduce a 20 km trolleybus network which will run on part of the route proposed for the Supertram network.

Guided bus

Current situation

The first four phases of guided busway along Scott Hall Road were completed in July 1998

and included a 160-space park-and-ride site. A second more extensive project along the A64 York Road costing GBP10 million, was given the government go-ahead in December 1998 and was opened in November 2001.

In the first partnership of its kind, bus operators FirstGroup and Arriva contributed GBP5 million towards infrastructure costs, which was matched equally by a contribution from the government.

The new 2 km guideway in York Road is the backbone of the elite scheme, taking up to 10 minutes off a journey into town. Passengers travel on new low-floor double-deck buses which use a combination of guided busways and dedicated bus lanes. Sensors and traffic lights enable buses to transfer from guided sections to bus lanes easily.

A bid for the construction of a guided busway on the A641 Manchester Road, Bradford was granted in late 1999. Also financed in part by a contribution from First, its construction started in 2000, and it was opened in January 2002.

Metro is leading the Yorkshire Bus Initiative, which aims to effect a big improvement in the quality of bus services and to generate significant patronage growth including attracting passengers who were former car users. The joint project between Metro, South Yorkshire PTE and bus operators will build upon successes to date in Yorkshire, such as the guided busways in Leeds and Bradford.

Leicester

Population: City 292,600, urban area 441,213 (2007 estimates)

Public transport

Most bus services are provided by former municipally owned companies, local private companies and local rail services, supported by Leicester County Council.
Web: www.leics.gov.uk

First in Leicester

Abbey Lane, Leicester LE4 0DA, UK
Tel: (+44 116) 268 91 50   Fax: (+44 116) 268 91 98
Web: www.firstgroup.com

Key personnel

Managing Director: Maurice Bulmer
Staff: 377

Current situation

Operates bus services in Leicester and the surrounding area. In 2006, additional government funding was provided for new and improved bus services, which include the Leicester General Hospital bus link, providing a direct bus link specifically between St Margaret's bus station and the railway station to/from the General Hospital.

Bus

Number of routes: 20
Route length: 800 km
On private right-of-way: 3.6 km

Fleet: 124 vehicles

Volvo B7TL/Alexander low-floor double-deck	47
Volvo B7TL/Wright Eclipse Gemini low-floor double-deck	20
Volvo B7/Wright low-floor single-deck	23
Volvo B7RLE Wright low-floor single-deck	26
Dennis Lance/Plaxton coach	7

Most intensive service: 10 min
One-person operation: All services
Fare collection: Driver with Wayfarer equipment
Fare structure: Stage; single, day, weekly and monthly tickets

Operational control: All buses have two-way radio; 12 locations monitored by CCTV
Operating costs financed by: Fares 86 per cent, other commercial sources 12 per cent, tenders 2 per cent
Subsidy from: County Council for pensioners' concession fares and specific contracted routes

Arriva Midlands

PO Box 613, Leicester LE4 8ZN, UK
Tel: (+44 116) 264 04 00   Fax: (+44 116) 260 56 05
Web: www.arriva.co.uk

Key personnel

Managing Director: Bob Hind
Operations Director: Alf Lloyd
Finance Director: John Barlow
Engineering Director: Matthew Evans
Communications Manager: Keith Myatt
Staff: 1,900

Current situation

Local bus services cover Leicester and surrounding towns, while conventional buses run interurban services and a number of longer-distance out-of-town routes. It is a subsidiary of the Arriva Group and also has responsibility for city operations in Derby, and across Shropshire, Telford & Wrekin, Staffordshire, Warwickshire and parts of West Midlands.

Developments

In 2007 Arriva Midlands acquired Chase Bus Services, Birmingham.

Wrightbus are supplying 132 new buses to Arriva in 2008/2009. In a series of orders worth approximately GBP9.5 million, a variety of vehicles are being delivered to Arriva in the Midlands, North West and Wales, Yorkshire and Southern Counties.

In 2008, Arriva Midlands took delivery of eight Wrightbus Eclipse Gemini double-deck buses on Volvo B9TL chassis for use on Tamworth route 110, a 20 minute frequency service to Sutton Coldfield, Erdington and Birmingham.

All of the vehicles are single-door, feature CCTV systems (12 cameras on the double-decks and nine on the single-decks) and have Hanover destination equipment.

Bus (whole company operations)

Number of routes: 180
Route length: Not currently available

Fleet: 754

DAF DB250 low-floor double-deck	51
DAF SB200/Wright single-deck	27
DAF SB120/Wright Cadet single-deck	40
Daimler Fleetline/Northern Counties double-deck	1
Dennis MPD/Pointer single-deck	63
Dennis SLF single-deck	101
Dennis Dart single-deck	100
Dennis Super Pointer Dart single-deck	5
Leyland Lynx MkI single-deck	1
Leyland Olympian double-deck	7
Mercedes-Benz 709D single-deck	14
Mercedes-Benz 811D single-deck	2
Mercedes-Benz 810 single-deck	2
Mercedes-Benz 814D single-deck	25
Optare Excel single-deck	2
Optare Solo M850 single-deck	13
Optare Solo M920 single-deck	3
Optare Versa single-deck	1
Scania CN23 single-deck	2
Scania L113CRL single-deck	33
Scania N113DRB double-deck	33
VDL DB250LF double-deck	27
VDL SB200 single-deck	15
Volvo B10M city bus double-deck	34
Volvo B10B double-deck	5
Volvo B10BLE double-deck	12
Volvo B10M double-deck	10
Volvo B7TL double-deck	17
Volvo B6BLE single-deck	30
Volvo B6 single-deck	133
Volvo Olympian double-deck	56

In peak service: Not currently available

One-person operation: All services
Fare collection: Payment to driver with Wayfarer ticket machine; magnetic card system introduced 1997 in Leicester; stored-value ticketing in Telford from July 2007
Fare structure: Single, day return, season and area tickets
Fares collected on board: 74 per cent

Leicester
Other operators
Current situation
Other operators provide services in greater Leicester, including Confidence Bus/Coach Hire, Kinchbus and Hylton & Dawson.

East Midlands Trains Limited
8th Floor, Friars Bridge Court, 41-45 Blackfriars Road, London, SE1 8NZ, UK
Tel: (+44 1332) 26 20 40   Fax: (+44 1332) 26 25 61
e-mail: getintouch@eastmidlandstrains.co.uk
Web: www.eastmidlandstrains.co.uk

Key personnel
Project Manager: Chris Elliott
   Staff: Not available currently

Current situation
East Midlands Trains, operated by Stagecoach, runs high-speed long distance services from London St Pancras to Sheffield, Derby and Nottingham and regional services between Nottingham and Derby – Lincoln – Cleethorpes – Skegness, and between Derby and Crewe – Matlock and Norwich and Liverpool.

The franchise started on 11 November 2007 and will run until 31 March 2015, the last year and four months of which will be conditional upon achieving pre-set performance targets.

Developments
A refurbishment of East Midlands Trains' Class 158 trains was started in 2008. The work was be carried out in Derby by Delta Rail. The full refurbishment programme will see all 25 of the company's Class 158 trains going through a complete overhaul. It is expected to be completed by 2010.

The work includes: repainting in the new East Midlands Trains livery; internal refurbishment of every train, which includes improvements to seating design and capacity. In addition, a new toilet area will be included as part of the refurbishment programme; modification to various systems on the train to bring improved reliability; improved air conditioning units fitted to the majority of these trains to improve the reliability and efficiency; introduction of CCTV on every train; installation of a passenger counting device that allows passenger flows to be monitored.

Liverpool
Population: City 436,100 (2005 estimate), urban area 816,900 (2006 estimate), Merseyside county area 1.37 million (estimate)

Public transport
Main bus services provided by private firms. Passenger Transport Executive, under direction of a joint board of local districts and trading as Merseytravel, has direct responsibility for ferry operation, the Mersey road tunnels, subsidising contracted non-commercial bus services, rail services within Merseyside county area, including central area metro loop line, operated under contract, service promotion, and provision of bus station facilities; light rail (Merseytram) planned.

Arriva North West and Wales
73 Ormskirk Road, Aintree, Liverpool L9 5AE, UK
Tel: (+44 151) 522 28 00   Fax: (+44 151) 525 95 56
Web: www.arriva.co.uk

Key personnel
Managing Director: Phil Stone
Finance Director: Simon Mills
Marketing Manager: Nick Gordon
Engineering Director: Malcolm Gilkerson

Current situation
This is a Merseyside-based company providing an extensive network of services in Greater Manchester, Merseyside, Cheshire and North and West Wales.

Total fleet size is approximately 1,300 vehicles.

Developments
In 2007, Arriva's Airlink 700 service to Liverpool John Lennon Airport and Manchester was re-directed to serve Widnes.

Most intensive service: 3 min
One-person operation: All routes
Fare collection: Pre-purchase season tickets/passes, or payment to driver for single tickets
Fare structure: Zonal for season tickets, stage for single fares
Fare evasion control: Inspectors and other measures
Average distance between stops: 400 m
Average peak-hour speed: In mixed traffic, 20 km/h
Operating costs financed by: Fares 87 per cent, other commercial sources 5 per cent, contracted operations/subsidies 8 per cent.

First Chester & Wirral
659 New Chester Road, Rock Ferry CH42 1PZ, UK
Tel: (+44 151) 645 86 61
Web: www.firstgroup.com

Key personnel
Area Operations Manager: Peter Walch
   Staff: Not currently available

Current situation
First covers North West Cheshire and Wirral, serving places including Ellesmere Port, Birkenhead and Liverpool and Chester. The company operates about 100 buses from depots at Birkenhead, Ellesmere Port and Chester.

Stagecoach Merseyside
Gilmoss Garage, East Lancashire Road, Liverpool L11 0BB, UK
Tel: (+44 151) 330 62 04
e-mail: enquiries.merseyside@stagecoachbus.com
Web: www.stagecoachbus.com

Current situation
Glenvale Transport Limited (GTL) became part of Stagecoach in 2005 and was renamed Stagecoach Merseyside in 2006.

Developments
Since July 2005, 75 new low-floor buses have been added to the fleet to upgrade services.

Bus
Fleet: 186 vehicles

Volvo B10L double-deck	35
Volvo B10L single-deck	10
Volvo B10BLE single-deck	18
Volvo B6/Plaxton midibus	5
Dennis Dart SLF/Wrightbus midibus	12
Optare MetroRider minibus	2
Dennis Dart SLF/East Lancslow-floor minibus	8

Liverpool
Other commercial operators
Current situation
A number of smaller operators run commercial and contracted services in the area. These include AIA Travel of Birkenhead, A2B Travel of Prenton, Avon Buses of Prenton, Halton Transport, Happy Als of Birkenhead, Liverpool City Coaches, Selwyns Coaches of Runcorn and Supertravel Omnibus Ltd of Speke.

To cope with expansion of its network of commercial bus services on the Wirral peninsula, Avon Buses of Prenton has taken delivery of three new Plaxton Primos. The buses are operating on a newly-introduced route between Moreton and Clatterbridge Hospital.

Merseytravel
Merseyside Passenger Transport Executive (PTE)
24 Hatton Garden, Liverpool L3 2AN, UK
Tel: (+44 151) 227 51 81
Fax: (+44 151) 236 24 57
Web: www.merseytravel.gov.uk

Key personnel
Director General: Neil Scales OBE
Director of Resources: Jim Barclay
Director of Operations: Alan Stilwell

Background
Following the enactment of the Local Transport Act 2008, the Merseyside Passenger Transport Authority became the Merseyside Integrated Transport Authority.

Merseytravel is the operating name of the Merseyside Passenger Transport Executive (PTE) and the Merseyside Integrated Transport Authority (ITA). The ITA is a joint authority comprising, at present, 18 Councillors from the five metropolitan areas of Merseyside, being Liverpool, Sefton, Wirral, Knowsley and St Helens. The ITA raises finances mainly via levies on local councils. The ITA is responsible for setting budgets and policies, which are

Single-deck Arriva North West and Wales bus picks up in Liverpool city centre (Arriva plc)   1330248

Plaxton Primo bus of Avon Buses on service to Clatterbridge (Plaxton Limited) 1209463

then implemented by the PTE. As part of the developing Liverpool City Region, the ITA may well be extended to include the borough of Halton.

Current situation

Merseytravel monitors the commercial bus network to identify unmet demand and then plans, funds and manages a wide range of socially necessary bus services. It also manages the Merseyrail network, using refurbished trains by Northern Rail Ltd, and owns and operates Mersey Ferries and the two Mersey Tunnels. It also owns The Beatles Story, a central Liverpool visitor attraction, and works with partners Livesmart Ltd to develop smartcards and other leisure and tourism tickets. It operates Merseylink, a door-to-door bus service for people with mobility difficulties, and funds free travel for elderly and mobility-impaired people. Merseytravel, in partnership with the European Union, funds and manages various projects to develop new technology and also to encourage socially disadvantaged people to use the public transport system, so improving their quality of life. It also promotes public transport by providing bus stations and infrastructure, and comprehensive travel information.

Developments

Merseytravel's latest and largest construction project in the last 30 years – Liverpool South Parkway – was completed in June 2006. This is a major gateway scheme, delivered under the first Local Transport Plan, involved the amalgamation of two existing rail stations, Allerton on the City Line and Garston on the Northern Line. The interchange has transformed public transport into South Liverpool providing fast and efficient links to Liverpool John Lennon Airport, a major industrial park and growing retail park, for passengers from across the North of England and the Midlands as well as access to up to 11,000 jobs planned for the area. The eco-friendly futuristic facility incorporates sustainable elements, an eye-catching design, the use of building techniques and supports local regeneration. Liverpool South Parkway was a catalyst for the commencement of a 24-hour bus service to the airport, and over seven trains per hour into the multi-modal interchange.

There are now nine trains per hour to Liverpool, two trains per hour to Birmingham, three trains per hour to Manchester, including one that goes to Sheffield, Nottingham and East Anglia, and four trains per hour to Hunts Cross. Passenger usage of the facility has doubled over the first two years of operation and the interchange was recognised in the 2007 National UK Station of the Year competition. Enhanced bus operator facilities have now been developed to encourage further use of the state-of-the-art interchange.

In addition to Liverpool South Parkway, Merseytravel funded the major GBP6 million revitalisation of St Helens Central Rail Station.

Merseytravel has also completed the regeneration of Bootle Oriel Road Station including a new ticket office, booking hall, passenger waiting facilities, footbridge and lifts to provide step-free access throughout the station.

The GBP 8.3 million Olive Mount Chord project opened in December 2008. The project, led by Merseytravel in conjunction with its LTP partners, the North West Development Agency and Network Rail, provides improved rail access to the Port of Liverpool and supports the shift of freight from road to rail.

The new multi-million pound Paradise Street Bus Interchange opened in November 2005 and is a key gateway to the GBP920 million Paradise Project (Liverpool One). The Interchange will give up to 10 million people every year direct access to jobs, leisure and shopping facilities in and around the giant development in the heart of the city. Also undertaken was the expansion of Birkenhead Bus Station, as it was at capacity before the enhanced facility opened in June 2007.

Merseytravel submitted its second Local Transport Plan (LTP) to the Department for Transport in March 2006. This plan, which also includes complementary bus and rail strategies, is produced in partnership with the five district councils of Merseyside and sets out a transport strategy and delivery programme for the area for the period 2006-2011. The plan was awarded a 'double-excellence' rating (the highest standard) by the Department for Transport, excellent for delivery of the first LTP and excellent for the quality of LTP2.

Merseytravel successfully achieved Beacon Status in March 2008, for work undertaken in the delivery of transport projects which improve the quality of life of local residents and reduce social exclusion and transport barriers to jobs, education and training opportunities.

Merseytravel has an education programme, which engages with children and young people, offering curriculum packs for UK school Key stages 1–7. Key stage 4 includes 'Here to There' which, via the use of bus cards, is targeted at young children, people with learning difficulties and other sectors of the community for whom English is not the first language. Merseytravel launched an education pack, which focuses on business and leisure to compliment and support the role of the organisation within the education curriculum.

Merseytravel continues to be a key partner in TravelSafe, a cross-industry initiative addressing crime and the fear of crime on public transport. Working with police and operators, the partnership has delivered significant reductions in incidents and promoted reassurance amongst passengers.

Merseytravel co-ordinates the 'Your Choice' conferences, focusing on young people and the consequences of anti-social behaviours.

Merseytravel, in conjunction with strategic partners, is currently undertaking a review of Real Time Information technology. The main aim for 2009 is to develop a revised strategy prior to developing a web-based system within the medium term.

Merseytravel has trialled electric and hybrid buses in Birkenhead, Liverpool City Centre and St Helens. The trial of electric buses in St Helens is continuing.

Merseyrail Electrics 2002 Ltd

Rail House, Lord Nelson Street, Liverpool L1 1JF, UK
Tel: (+44 151) 227 51 81   Fax: (+44 151) 236 24 57
Web: www.merseytravel.gov.uk

Type of operation: Multi-operator suburban rail network

Passenger journeys: (Annual) 34 million (estimate) (excludes City Line)

Current situation

Services are provided on two groups of lines totalling 121 km, electrified at 750 V DC. Services (on the Northern and Wirral lines) feed into the city-centre loop and cross-city link lines. Total of 66 stations; 1,435 mm gauge; basic 15 minute daytime service.

Merseytravel Class 508 emu on underground section of Merseyrail network in Liverpool city centre
1141384

Merseytravel ferry across the Mersey, linking Liverpool with Birkenhead and Seacombe   1141383

Rail services are operated on behalf of Merseytravel by Merseyrail Electrics 2002 Ltd (a Serco/NedRailways company) under a locally managed concession for 25 years.

Fully integrated fare structure, with day and period tickets valid on all public transport in the Merseyside area.

Developments
All electric units operating on the Northern and Wirral Lines have now been refurbished.

On the Merseyrail Electrics network, 100 per cent of stations have now been granted Secure Station Status. A total of 75 per cent of Merseytravel supported stations on the City Line have also achieved this status. 95 per cent of stations on the Merseyrail Electrics network have been accredited with the Safer Parking (Park Mark).

Merseytravel's biggest project – the GBP32 million Liverpool South Parkway (LSP) Interchange, which opened in 2006, provides links to Liverpool John Lennon Airport as well as access to up to 11,000 jobs planned for the area.

Rolling stock: 177 emu cars, also dmus
Including: Class 507 three-car emu (1978/80)
Class 508 three-car emu (1979/80)

Mersey Ferries
Victoria Place, Seacombe, Wallasey CH44 6QY, UK
Tel: (+44 151) 639 06 09
Fax: (+44 151) 639 05 78

e-mail: info@merseyferries.co.uk
Web: www.merseyferries.co.uk

Current situation
Cross-Mersey ferry services are provided between Liverpool Pier Head, Seacombe and Woodside (Birkenhead). The service is split into peak-period commuter operations and daytime leisure cruises, including Manchester Ship Canal Cruises, with three vessels. In addition, there are special cruises, including those on the Manchester Ship Canal, and corporate hire of the vessels.

Developments
All three vessels in the fleet have been re-engined and refurbished and terminals improved. The GBP10 million space-themed visitor attraction, 'Spaceport', operated by Mersey ferries, opened at Seacombe ferry terminal in 2005. Further investment in terminals has since taken place including a new café, karting track and space-themed play area at Seacombe to support the Spaceport attraction. Spaceport holds major exhibitions and has significant schools educational markets.

A new GBP10 million ferry terminal is being constructed at the Pier Head and is expected to be opened in early 2009. The new terminal will feature enhanced passenger facilities, a Beatles-themed exhibition, café and restaurant. At the third terminal at Woodside, a new attraction

featuring a U534 U-boat and associated memorabilia will open in February 2009.

Mersey Tunnels
Georges Dock Building, Georges Dock Way, Pier Head Liverpool L3 1DD, UK
Tel: (+44 151) 255 06 10
e-mail: enquiries@merseytunnels.co.uk
Web: www.merseytunnels.co.uk

Current situation
The principal aim of Mersey Tunnels is to contribute to the social and economic development of the Merseyside region by safely and efficiently operating a round-the-clock environmentally responsible cross-river facility. The 2004 Tunnels Act also took a major step in providing stable toll levels, which are in line with inflation, and take account of the local economy.

Developments
Major investment in recent years has seen significant safety upgrades in both tunnels. This included the building of emergency cross passages in Kingsway Tunnel and escape refuges in Queensway Tunnel. According the EuroTAP inspection programme, Queensway is now recognised as the safest in Europe for its age and both Tunnels are recognised independently as the safest road tunnels in the UK. Such improvements, along with a dedicated police force and a team of control room engineers, helps to ensure that user safety is seen as the number one priority. Further investment is planned in the future to enhance safety provisions within both tunnels.

Light rail (Merseytram) (planned)
Type of operation: Tram

Current situation
A three-line light rail network is proposed. Line 1 would run to Kirkby via Croxteth. Originally, it was hoped this would be completed in late 2007, in time for the European Capital of Culture celebrations in 2008.

In late 2005, the UK government withdrew its funding for Line 1. However, Merseytravel remains committed to safeguarding the legal powers to construct Line 1, but in the short term to develop high quality bus facilities along the route as a compensatory measure.

London
Population: Greater London: 7.7 million (2007 estimate), Greater London Urban Area: 8.28 million (2001 Census), metropolitan area 12 million (estimate)

Public transport
Bus, tram and metro services are the responsibility of the Greater London Assembly, which is headed by London's elected Mayor. Transport for London (TfL), an organisation chaired by the Mayor, assumes overall responsibility for all public transport in London.

Bus services, both in the city and metropolitan area, are run mainly by private companies under contract, in a unique franchise situation for the UK, where the remainder of national bus services are deregulated and operated commercially.

Extensive network of suburban rail services run by mainly private operating companies. Light rail system serves Docklands area, operated under franchise and also suburban light rail network in Croydon.

Transport for London (TfL)
Windsor House, 42–50 Victoria Street, London SW1H 0TL, UK
Tel: (+44 20) 72 22 56 00
Fax: (+44 20) 72 22 60 16
e-mail: enquire@tfl.gov.uk
Web: www.tfl.gov.uk

Key personnel
Chairman: Vacant
Commissioner, TfL: Peter Hendy
Managing Director, LU: Tim O'Toole
Managing Director, Surface Transport: David Brown
Managing Director, Finance: Steve Allen
Managing Directors, Planning:
  Malcolm Murray-Clark
  Michele Dix
Managing Director, Communications and Marketing:
  Vernon Everitt
Managing Director, London Rail: Ian Brown
General Counsel: Howard Carter
  Staff: Not currently available

Passenger journeys: (Bus and metro)

Current situation
Transport for London (TfL) was created in 2000 as the integrated body responsible for London's transport system. The primary role of TfL, which is a functional body of the Greater London Authority, is to implement the Mayor of London's Transport Strategy and manage transport services across the city.

TfL is responsible for London's buses, the Underground, the Docklands Light Railway (DLR) and the management of Croydon Tramlink and London River Services. TfL also runs Victoria Coach Station and London's Transport Museum. In November 2007, TfL took over Silverlink franchise routes in London and commenced London Overground services.

TfL is responsible for a 580-km network of main roads and all of London's 4,600 traffic lights. In addition, TfL manage the central London Congestion Charging scheme and regulate the city's taxis and private hire trade. TfL also promote a range of walking and cycling initiatives across the Capital.

To ensure greater accessibility for travellers, TfL co-ordinates schemes for transport users with impaired mobility, as well as running the Dial-a-Ride scheme, which became free from January 2008.

The organisation is made up of a number of different companies:
- London Underground Ltd;
- London Buses Limited;
- London Bus Services Limited;
- Victoria Coach Station Limited;
- London River Services Limited;
- Docklands Light Railway Limited;
- TfL Trustee Company Limited;
- Transport Trading Limited;
- London Transport Insurance (Guernsey) Limited;
- Dial-a-RIDE Limited;
- UKTRAM Limited;
- Cross London Rail Links Limited;
- Rail for London Limited.

Developments
TfL is investing GBP10 billion to improve and expand London's transport network, over half of which is being spent on the Tube (metro).

Crossrail

Crossrail will be a new high-frequency railway across Central London, directly linking the key economic centres of Heathrow, the West End, City of London and Canary Wharf. The UK Prime Minister gave the go-ahead for the project in October 2007. Royal Assent was granted to the Crossrail Bill in July 2008, which gives the powers to build the line.

Crossrail will be Europe's largest civil engineering project, providing a state-of-the art modern, quick and reliable railway passing through Central London. The Crossrail route will travel from Heathrow and Maidenhead in the west to Paddington, through the West End, the City of London and Canary Wharf and on to East London, with the route splitting into two branches at Whitechapel. One branch will travel on to Shenfield in Essex and the second branch will run to Abbey Wood in Kent. The line will be built to high regional rail standards and provide direct interchange with other rail, underground and local transport services in London. It is estimated that it will increase rail capacity by 40 per cent and overall public transport capacity by 10 per cent.

It is a joint venture between TfL and the Department for Transport (DfT). With the main construction set to begin in 2010, Crossrail services are programmed to come into operation over the course of twelve months from 2017. The line will be integrated into TfL's existing zonal system, all existing ticketing options such as Oyster will apply.

Please also see separate entry for Crossrail.

Further information may be found at www.crossrail.co.uk.

London Overground

Represented by an orange roundel, London Overground began operation in November 2007 and involved TfL taking over four railway routes in the capital.

Services run on the North London line (Richmond to Stratford), Euston to Watford Junction local line, the West London line (Willesden Junction to Clapham Junction) and the Gospel Oak to Barking line. There are staff at every station and passengers can use Oyster to pay-as-you-go. In addition, services will operate on the extended East London line when it re-opens in 2010, following a GBP1 billion extension.

By 2011, in time for the Olympics, the extended East London line will connect to the North London line. This will create the beginning of an orbital railway around the Capital, with London Overground services running from Stratford in east London, to Richmond in the southwest and West Croydon in the south. Phase two, currently unfunded, would provide a further link between Surrey Quays and Clapham Junction, completing the orbital rail network.

London Overground announced in 2008 that it has taken up an option to order seven more trains from manufacturer Bombardier for its rail network. The dual-voltage Class 378s, each made up of four carriages, will cost GBP23 million. They will be delivered during the last quarter of 2009 and the first quarter of 2010, directly following an order for 44 trains, which are currently being assembled at Derby. The new trains will allow London Overground to increase the frequency of trains to eight per hour on the core route between Camden Road and Stratford, as required by London's Olympic and Paralympics Games Transport Plan and for future growth. The trains will have six passenger information displays inside and air conditioning. They will have the look and feel of Tube trains and will be walk-through, without doors between carriages.

London Overground emu (TfL)

1347143

Vauxhall Cross bus station, adjacent to the Underground and suburban rail stations, is partly solar-powered (Charlotte Gilhooly)

1115169

Trains for the new London Overground network will be leased from QW Rail Leasing Ltd, a joint venture between National Australia Bank and Sumitomo Mitsui Banking Corporation.

Further information on London Overground can be found at www.tfl.gov.uk/overground.

Heathrow Airport Terminal 5

The London Underground Limited Piccadilly line was extended to Heathrow Terminal 5 in March 2008. The new T5 station, which was delivered on time and on budget according to TfL, is also used by Heathrow Express services.

Five new bus routes started serving Terminal 5 from 27 March 2008, serving Hayes and Harlington Station, Stockley Park, West Drayton, Harmondsworth, Hounslow, Southall, Hatton Cross, Terminal 4, Richmond, Twickenham and Feltham Station. Route N9, a night bus, is also serving Terminal 5 and Heathrow (Terminals 1,2 & 3) providing a link every 20 minutes during the night to and from Central London.

Olympics

As part of London's bid to host the 2012 Olympic Games, TfL offered a choice of 10 rail routes serving the Olympic Park, Stratford, with a train every 15 seconds. It is also increasing capacity by 45 per cent on the Jubilee Line and, by 2012, the high-speed line from Europe to London will serve Stratford.

Low Emission Zone (LEZ)

The Low Emission Zone (LEZ), which aims to improve air quality in London, commenced on 4 February 2008. It is the first scheme of its type in the UK and the largest Low Emission Zone in the world, according to TfL. The zone aims to cut harmful emissions from the most polluting lorries, coaches and buses. It operates 24 hours a day, seven days a week, every day of the year and covers most of Greater London.

Cars and motorcycles are not affected by the scheme. The capital has the worst air pollution in the UK and among the worst in Europe.

Operators of vehicles that do not meet the required Euro 3 emissions standards for particulate matter will need to take action to comply with the scheme, for example by fitting pollution abatement equipment, or pay a GBP200 daily charge to drive within Greater

London. If this charge is not paid and the vehicle does not meet the required standards, owners risk a penalty charge of GBP1,000. To check whether a vehicle meets the Low Emission Zone emissions standards operators can log on to www.tfl.gov.uk/lezlondon or call 0845 607 0009.

The LEZ does not include the M25 motorway, even when it passes within the boundary of the zone. The M25 can be used by drivers as a diversionary route, should they wish to avoid the zone. However, some other motorways within Greater London are included in the scheme.

Non-GB registered vehicles that meet the Low Emission Zone emissions standards will need to be registered with TfL in order to avoid a penalty charge.

From February 2008, diesel-engined lorries over 12 tonnes have had to meet the Euro 3 standard for particulate matter. This includes heavy diesel-engined vehicles exceeding 12 tonnes Gross Vehicle Weight (GVW), including goods vehicles, motor caravans, motorised horseboxes and other specialist vehicles.

From 7 July 2008, the Euro 3 for particulate matter emissions standards were extended to all diesel-engined vehicles between 3.5 and 12 tonnes GVW, including goods vehicles, motor caravans, motorised horseboxes and other specialist vehicles. The emissions standard will also apply to buses and coaches, defined as: diesel-engined passenger vehicles with nine or more seats, exceeding five tonnes GVW.

From October 2010, the Euro 3 for particulate matter standard will be extended to diesel-engined vehicles between 1.205 tonnes unladen and 3.5 tonnes GVW and motor caravans between 2.5 tonnes and 3.5 tonnes GVW. In addition, minibuses, defined as diesel-engined passenger vehicles with more than eight seats, plus the driver's seat, below five tonnes GVW, will be affected.

From January 2012, all diesel-engined lorries, buses and coaches will be required to meet an emissions standard of Euro 4 for particulate matter in order to drive within the Low Emission Zone at no charge.

Congestion Charging
In 2007, the Mayor of London extended the congestion charging area to include the rest of Westminster and Kensington, doubling the original area.

In July 2008, the new Mayor, Boris Johnson, announced that a five-week public consultation on the future of the Western Extension would begin in September 2008.

Docklands Light Rail (DLR) extensions
The Docklands Light Rail (DLR) London City Airport extension (running between Canning Town and King George V) opened in December 2005. Further construction to extend the line under the River Thames to Woolwich Arsenal will see King George V station connected with Woolwich town centre by 2009. Along with upgrades and capacity increases, the extension of the DLR will continue to play a major role in the development of the Thames Gateway as well as providing essential cross-river connections for the 2012 Olympics.

See separate entry.

Fares
TfL's fare structure (which is determined annually by the Mayor) is designed to encourage the use of Oyster cards to increase the number and percentage of journeys made by bus and Underground using Oyster, thereby speeding up journeys and improving the efficiency of the transport network. Oyster is the cheapest way to travel around London.

Information on current fares and tickets can be viewed at www.tfl.gov.uk/tickets/faresandtickets/2930.aspx.

Oyster expansion
Launched in summer 2003, the Oyster card is now acknowledged as Europe's most advanced and widely used travel smartcard, according to TfL. The card has automatic top-up and

This major public transport interchange at Stratford, east London, brings together a recently-opened bus station and modernised station facilities. It will play a key role during the London Olympic games in 2012. The interchange is served by National Express East Anglia (previously One Railway) and Silverlink Metro suburban/main line rail services, LUL's Central and Jubilee Lines and Docklands Light Railway. From late 2007, the adjacent Stratford International station sees trains running on the Channel Tunnel Rail Link (Ken Harris) 1183523

pay-as-you-go options and has helped to cut queues, journey times and travel costs, and has simplified fare options. It is now proposed to extend the system to cover National Rail journeys in London progressively from 2008.

Cash fares on the Tube/Underground network dropped to 3.4 per cent in October 2007 – down from 5.7 per cent in one year.

Further information on Oystercard can be found at www.oystercard.com.

Arrangements for older and disabled passengers
As well as working to improve accessibility of all public transport, there is a network of lift-equipped Mobility Bus routes, while fully accessible low-floor buses are operating on conventional routes.

Dial-a-Ride is a multi occupancy, door-to-door transport service run by London Buses (part of TfL) for older or disabled people who cannot easily use public transport in the capital. It is available in all London boroughs, and uses specially adapted vehicles to take people on pre-booked, mainly local journeys. Free fares were introduced on Dial-a-Ride from 1 January 2008. There are currently around 50,000 users of the service making 1.2 million journeys per year.

In September 2008, the Mayor of London, Boris Johnson, announced 61 custom-built Dial-a-Ride minibuses to be introduced across London in 2008. The new vehicle from Bluebird is a purpose-built, small bus with a totally flat low floor and dual access at the side and rear of the vehicle. Tip and fold seats allow wheelchair users to manoeuvre around the vehicle more easily; they also provide greater flexibility for accommodating individual passengers' needs.

The new bus also offers an improved interior, including high levels of interior lighting, tinted windows and air conditioning, plus onboard CCTV for added safety and security. Older Dial-a-Ride vehicles will be phased out as the new vehicles go into service. The vehicles are the first of the new, custom-built buses to join the Dial-a-Ride fleet, and TfL plans to purchase more of these in the coming years. It is based on Bluebird's Tucana model, using a Volkswagen T5 chassis and is compliant with the Low Emission Zone environmental standards in London. TfL has already begun replacing the ageing Dial-a-Ride fleet, having bought 120 Mercedes Vito people carriers between 2004 and 2007.

Buses
Mini security cameras in buses have proved successful in helping police apprehend offenders

and the scheme has been extended by TfL to all of the fleet.

Alternative-Fuel Buses
The Mayor of London announced at the end of 2007 that ten new hydrogen-powered buses will join London's bus fleet by 2010. When operational on London's streets, the hydrogen fuel cell-powered vehicles will produce no pollution or carbon dioxide. Transport for London (TfL) has signed a contract with ISE – an American company with a record of delivering hydrogen buses – for five hydrogen fuel cell buses and five hydrogen internal combustion engine buses. This is one of the world's first commercial contracts for hydrogen buses. The vehicles will be operated by First on behalf of TfL.

The hydrogen buses will incorporate hybrid technology to ensure they make the most efficient use of hydrogen. It also allows hydrogen buses to match their diesel counterparts in terms of range and operating hours. Hydrogen fuel cell buses produce no exhaust emissions other than water vapour. Emissions from the buses with hydrogen internal combustion engines will also be much lower than from conventional diesel buses.

Siemens iBus satellite-based system, installed in Wrightbus/VDL diesel-electric hybrid double-deck bus (Peter Roelofs) 1310363

The 10 new hydrogen buses are part of the Mayor's plan to have up to 70 hydrogen vehicles in operation in London by 2010.

Six hybrid Electrocity Wright-bodied buses are now in operation in west London. Each bus is powered by electric batteries driving through a 120 kW motor, coupled with a 1.9 ltr diesel engine that charges the batteries. They are running on route 360.

Real-Time Information

TfL has completed trials of, and is now rolling out, the iBus system, one of the largest initiatives of its type in the world. Through a combination of technologies – including satellite tracking and General Packet Radio Service (GPRS) data transfer – iBus will assist in ensuring reliability and providing passengers with improved arrival information. Features include visual and audio next-stop announcements that benefit people with sight and hearing disabilities. By providing more accessible, reliable and timely travel information, it is believed that iBus will attract more passengers.

Further information on iBus can be found at www.tfl.gov.uk/iBus

Heritage Bus Routes

Two Routemaster heritage bus services started operation in 2005, keeping the Routemaster tradition alive following the demise of the vehicle in normal bus operation in December 2005. Routemaster bus operation has mainly been replaced by articulated Mercedes Citaro buses. The heritage Routemasters run as part of existing Route 15, linking Trafalgar Square, Fleet Street and Tower Hill. It is operated by Stagecoach. Heritage Routemasters are also operating as part of existing Route 9, serving the Royal Albert Hall, Knightsbridge, Piccadilly, Trafalgar Square and Aldwych. It is operated by First Group. A total of 16 Routemaster buses are needed to operate both routes.

Arriva London

Includes Arriva London North, Arriva London North East and Arriva South.
16 Watsons Road, Wood Green, London N22 7TZ, UK
Tel: (+44 20) 82 71 01 01   Fax: (+44 20) 82 71 01 20
Web: www.arriva.co.uk

Key personnel

Managing Director: Mark Yexley
Staff: 4,600

Passenger journeys: (Annual) 77.5 million

Number of routes: 69 (plus school routes)

Current situation

Operates in north, northeast and south London.

Arriva Kent Thameside

Invicta House, Armstrong Road, Maidstone, Kent ME15 6TX, UK
Tel: (+44 1622) 69 70 00   Fax: (+44 1622) 69 70 01
Web: www.arriva.co.uk

Key personnel

Managing Director: Heath Williams

Type of operation: Bus

Passenger journeys: Not currently available
Vehicle-km: Not currently available

Current situation

The company operates an extensive commercial network in the Kent Thameside area as well as LT contracted services in southeast London, from depots in Dartford and Northfleet.

Developments

A fleet of 14 high-specification Wright Eclipse on Volvo B7RLE chassis buses for the Kent

Arriva London bus with Wrightbus bodywork on route 141, to London Bridge railway station (Ken Harris)
1178655

Arriva Wright-bodied Volvo B7RLE single-deck bus on Fastrack rapid transit bus route near Dartford, east London (Ken Harris)
1195931

One of 13 new Volvo B7TLs recently placed into service with East Thames Buses
0589907

Thameside Fastrack service went into operation in 2006, with a further 12 vehicles in June 2007. Fastrack, the first section of which was opened in 2006, will link Dartford, Bluewater, Greenhithe and Gravesend using a mix of busway and on-road priority.

Kent County Council's Fastrack service took delivery of its second consignment of Volvo buses in 2007. The 12 B7RLE buses, with Wrightbus Eclipse Urban bodies, have joined 14 others and are being used on the second phase of the BRT service, which was originally started in June 2007.

Fleet: 170 vehicles

Volvo B10M/East Lancs double-deck	19
Dennis Dart/Northern Counties single-deck	5
Volvo B6/Northern Counties single-deck	2
Dennis Dart SLF/Plaxton low-floor single-deck	65
Volvo B7BLE/Wrightbus	26
Scania L113/Wright low-floor single-deck	10
DAF SB220/Plaxton low-floor single-deck	1
DAF SB120/Wrightbus single-deck	15
Volvo B7RLE/Wrightbus Eclipse Urban single-deck	26

In peak service: Not available currently

East Thames Buses (ETB)

Ash Grove Depot, Hackney, London E8 4RH, UK
Tel: (+44 20) 72 41 72 20   Fax: (+44 20) 72 41 72 39

Key personnel
Managing Director: Jeff Chamberlain
Finance Director: David Bowen
Engineering Director: Gary Philby

Current situation
East Thames Buses is the only public sector operator in London, set up when TfL's London Buses Ltd stepped in to ensure services on some routes in East London could continue, following difficulties with an operator. It has two garages, Ash Grove in Hackney and Belvedere in southeast London.

Fleet: 69 vehicles

DAF DB250/Northern Counties double-deck	6
Volvo Olympian/East Lancs double-deck	35
DAF SB220/Ikarus single-deck	2
Optare Excel low-floor single-deck	24
Mercedes-Benz 709D/Alexander minibus	2

First London

B Block, 3rd Floor, Macmillan House, Paddington Station, London W2 1TY, UK
Tel: (+44 20) 72 98 73 00   Fax: (+44 20) 77 06 87 89
Web: www.firstgroup.com/ukbus/london.co.uk

Key personnel
Managing Director: Adrian Jones
Finance Director: Jim Dow
Engineering Director: Russell Hargrave
Deputy Engineering Director: Alan Coney
   Staff: 4,342

Type of operation: Bus

Passenger journeys: Not available currently
Vehicle-km: Not available currently

Current situation
Operates local bus services in and around London, including commercial services and franchised LT contracts for both conventional and mobility services.

Fleet: 1,100 vehicles
Fleet breakdown is not currently available, but includes:
AEC-Park Royal Routemaster double-deck
Leyland Olympian/Northern Counties double-deck
Olympian/Northern Counties double-deck
Volvo Olympian/Alexander double-deck
Dennis Trident/Plaxton low-floor double-deck
Dennis Trident/Alexander low-floor double-deck
Volvo B7LT/East Lancs low-floor double-deck

London General Enviro 400 double-deck bus on busway in central Sutton (Tony Pattison)   1368786

Volvo B7LT/Plaxton low-floor double-deck
Volvo B7TL/Alexander double-deck
AEC Regal 4/Metro Cammell single-deck
Dennis Lance/Alexander single-deck
Dennis Dart/Plaxton midibus
Dennis Dart SLF/Marshall low-floor midibus
Volvo B7TL/Eclipse Gemini
Optare Solo midibus
Mercedes-Benz O530 Citaro low-floor midibus
LDV 400/Crystals minibus
Bluebird schoolbus
Scania L113/Wright single-deck bus
Scania L94/Wright single-deck bus
Dennis Dart/Alexander SLF single-deck bus
Dennis Dart/Caetano SLF single-deck bus
Dennis Javelin/Plaxton Expressliner single-deck coach
Scania K113/Berkhof single-deck coach
Scania Irizar coach
Evobus Citaro articulated

Evobus Citaro fuel cell	3

In peak service: Not available currently
On order: Not available currently

London Central Bus Company Limited

18 Merton High Street, London SW19 1DN, UK
Tel: (+44 20) 85 45 61 00   Fax: (+44 20) 85 45 61 01
e-mail: enquiries@go-ahead-london.com
Web: www.go-ahead-london.com

Key personnel
Managing Director: John Trayner
Operations Director: David Cutts
Finance Director: Paul Reeves
Engineering Director: Phil Margrave
   Staff: 4,000 (London General and London Central)

Current situation
This subsidiary of the Go-Ahead Group operates 40 routes in southeast London from four depots.

Six Wright Electrocity buses are being operated by London Central. They were delivered in 2005. They are diesel-electric hybrids, which reduce CO_2 emissions by around 30 per cent below current Euro-3 conventional bus levels, and provide a significant reduction in other emissions, including NO_x. The Electrocity vehicles operate on the 360 route linking Elephant & Castle and the Royal Albert Hall. The route was selected as being one of the few single-deck services operating in central London. The project has been sponsored by Transport for London (TfL), and marks a three-way partnership between TfL, London Central and the bus manufacturer Wrightbus.

The Wright Electrocity is powered by a heavy-duty 120 kW electric drive train coupled to a 1.9 litre Euro 4 common-rail diesel engine.

Regenerative braking harnesses additional energy which would otherwise be lost, and the vehicle has the latest generation lead acid batteries. The London vehicles carry upwards of 50 passengers.

Developments
A total of 62 low-floor, fully accessible Volvo double deck buses were delivered in 2006/07. The Volvo B7TLs with Wrightbus Gemini bodywork are operating on three new routes, under contract to Transport for London (TfL). The low-floor body and the kneeling function of the chassis facilitate boarding and alighting for those with limited mobility and the new vehicles are also fully wheelchair accessible. New safety features include a GPS system which can remotely monitor the vehicle speed, its braking and its use of indicators, a broadband roaming buzzer which gives pedestrians in the near vicinity a more directly targeted audible warning and a matt crackle finish to grab poles, providing better grip as passengers move along the vehicle.

Fleet: 624 vehicles

AEC Routemaster double-deck	3
Dennis Trident/Alexander double-deck	45
Dennis Dart midibus	20
Dennis Dart SLF low-floor midibus	98
Mercedes-Benz Citaro articulated	64
Volvo B7TL low-floor double-deck	46
Volvo B7TL/Plaxton low-floor double-dec	267
Volvo Eclipse Gemini low-floor double-deck	64
Volvo Olympian/Northern Counties double-deck	10
Wright Electrocity single-deck (2005)	7

In peak service: Not currently available

London General Transport Services Limited

18 Merton High Street, London, SW19 1DN, UK
Tel: (+44 20) 85 45 61 00
Fax: (+44 20) 85 45 61 01
e-mail: enquiries@go-ahead-london.com
Web: www.go-ahead-london.com

Key personnel
Managing Director: John Trayner
Operations Director: David Cutts
Finance Director: Paul Reeves
Engineering Director: Phil Margrave
   Staff: 4,000 (London General and London Central)

Current situation
Operates 50 routes in central and south London from seven depots. It is part of the Go-Ahead Group. Includes six Docklands routes and 14 Blue Triangle routes (five of which are operated for Essex County Council).

Developments

In 2006, Docklands Minibuses (now Docklands Buses) was acquired and in June 2007, Blue Triangle was acquired.

Fleet: 748 vehicles

Volvo Olympian/Northern Counties double-deck	25
Volvo B7/Plaxton low-floor double-deck	403
Dennis Trident II double-deck	48
Dennis Dart SLF/Plaxton low-floor midibus	141
Mercedes-Benz Citaro articulated	56
AEC Routemaster	4
Enviro 200, single-deck	17
Enviro 400, double-deck	54

In peak service: Not currently available

London United Busways Ltd

Busways House, Wellington Road, Twickenham, TW2 5NX, UK
Tel: (+44 20) 84 00 66 65
Fax: (+44 20) 89 43 26 88
Web: www.lonutd.co.uk

Key personnel

Chairman: Charlie Beaumont
Managing Director: Nigel Stevens
Finance Director: Richard Casling
Operations Director: Paul Matthews
Engineering Director: Les Birchley
   Staff: 2,000

Passenger journeys: (2005/06) 150 million
Vehicle-km: (2005/06) 40.8 million

Current situation

This subsidiary of the French Transdev Group (incorporating London United and London Sovereign) operates 73 routes in southwest London from six depots.

Fleet: 783 vehicles

Volvo B7L/Alexander low-floor double-deck	64
Dennis Trident/Alexander double-deck	156
Volvo Plaxton double-deck	53
Volvo Olympian/Wright double-deck	3
Volvo/East Lancs double-deck	55
Scania/East Lancs Myllenium	64
Scania/East Lancs Olympus	9
Scania Omnidecker Polish	37
Dennis/Plaxton Pointer	342

Metrobus Ltd

Wheatstone Close, Crawley, West Sussex, RH10 9UA, UK
Tel: (+44 01293) 44 91 92
Web: www.metrobus.co.uk

Key personnel

Managing Director: Alan Eatwell

Background

Formerly an independent operator which grew up developing services in the suburban belt around south London. Started contract operations in London in 1987, and has grown to become a major contractor in south London. Also operates in Kent, Surrey and Sussex and was acquired by the Go-Ahead group in 1999.

Current situation

Metrobus is the operator of the Fastway guided bus system in the Crawley/Gatwick area. The route links the airport with Crawley and is run as a bus rapid transit service, with guided sections, raised-platform loading, real-time information on the bus and at stops, priority at traffic lights and bus-only roads. The service has since been expanded to Horley (see entry for Suburban Bus, London) and to Redhill in 2008.

Developments

In 2005, Metrobus acquired the Tellings Golden Millar bus operation based in Dartford.

In December 2007, the Orpington operation of First London was taken over.

The Fastway guided bus network was expanded in 2007 to link Gatwick Airport with Horley, in addition to Crawley. Fastway was opened in 2003. It is operated by Metrobus with support from West Sussex County Council, Surrey County Council, British Airports Authority Gatwick, British Airways and Crawley Borough Council.

Fleet: 390 vehicles

Dennis Trident/East Lancs low-floor double-deck	2
Scania Omnidekka low-floor double-deck	116
Volvo Olympian/Northern Counties double-deck	11
Volvo Olympian/East Lancs double-deck	15
Dennis Dart SLF low-floor single-deck	156
Dennis Lance single-deck	2
Optare Solo low-floor single-deck	2
Scania Omnicity low-floor single-deck	81
MAN low-floor single-deck	5

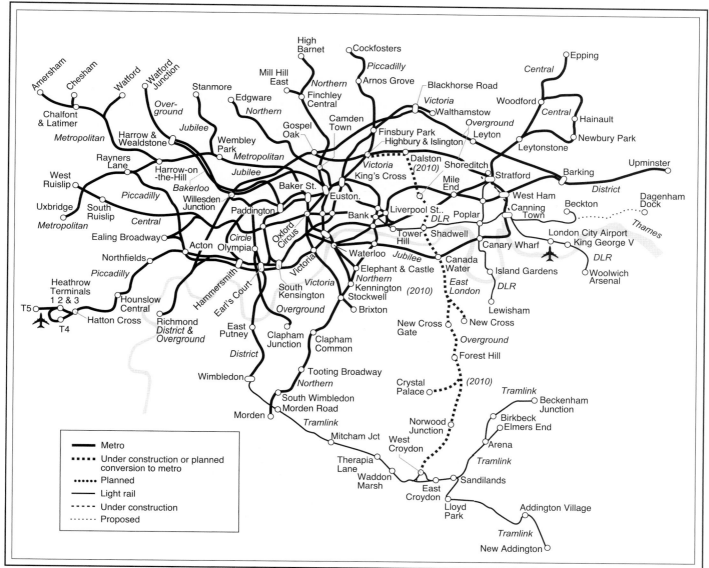

London's metro and light rail network

1168390

Metroline Plc

Hygeia House, 66 College Road, Harrow HA1 1BE, UK
Tel: (+44 20) 82 18 88 88
Fax: (+44 20) 82 18 88 40
Web: www.metroline.co.uk

Key personnel

Chief Executive Officer: Jaspal Singh
Chief Operating Officer: Sean O'Shea

Current situation

Owned by ComfortDelGro, Metroline operates 96 bus routes in North West London from 11 garages. All routes are operated under contract to Transport for London (TfL).

Developments

Metroline signed an order in 2005 for 28 new Alexander Dennis double deck Enviro 400s to go into service on Route 24 in London. The new investment is part of an ongoing modernisation programme following the sale of the fleet of Routemasters in 2004. The Enviro 400 double deck bus was chosen for a number of factors as well as the provision of up to nine more seats in the lower deck than any comparable bus. The Enviro 400 is a modern super-low-floor double decker that meets the requirements of forthcoming EU bus legislation, offers better passenger access and lower operating costs and lower emissions.

The Enviro 400 buses will be allocated to Metroline's Holloway Garage.

Fleet: 1,163 vehicles

Volvo Olympian/Alexander RH	17
Volvo Olympian/Alexander Belfast	16
Dennis Dart SLF/Alexander	13
Dennis Dart SLF/Plaxton Pointer	315
Dennis Dart/Marshall Capital	80
Dennis Trident/Alexander ALX400	90
Dennis Lance SLF/Wright Pathfinder	10
Optare Solo	7
Dennis Trident/Alexander Dennis	22
Dennis Trident/Alexander Dennis Enviro 400	8
Dennis Trident/Plaxton President	263
Volvo Olympian/Northern Counties Palatine	16
Volvo B7TL/Plaxton President	61
Volvo B7TL/Transbus International President	111
Volvo B7L/Plaxton President	134

East London Bus Group (ELBG)

2 Clements Road, Ilford IG1 1BA, UK
Tel: (+44 20) 85 53 34 20
Fax: (+44 20) 84 77 72 00
Web: www.elbg.com

Key personnel

Chief Executive Officer: Nigel Barrett
Engineering Director: Peter Sumner
  Staff: 4,600

Current situation

The East London Bus Group comprises of operating companies; East London Bus & Coach Company, South East London and Kent Bus Company (Selkent).

Developments

In 2008, ELBG announced that it had another 10 Enviro 400 double deck buses working at its Bromley garage. It also has another 24 Enviro 200 single deck midibuses, which have been introduced at the Bromley and Plumstead garages. ELBG is accepting a number of Optare hybrid buses starting in 2008, for trial and as a result of contract wins, has ordered 96 Scania Omnicity double-deck buses, 28 Enviro 200 single-deck vehicles and 14 Optare Versa single-deck vehicles.

In late 2007, two of ELBG's garages were relocated to allow development of the Olympic Park. Its Waterden Road garage moved to Rainham and the Stratford garage was relocated to West Ham, where a new purpose built garage is being constructed for operation in 2009/10.

Metroline Dennis Enviro 400 low-emission double-deck bus 1174977

Metrobus single-deck Scania OmniCity low-floor bus on Fastway guided section near London Gatwick airport (Bill Luke) 1115170

East London Bus Group newly delivered Scania Omnicity 1374306

Travel London Wrightbus Eclipse Gemini bus on route 188 to North Greenwich (Wrightbus) 1178779

National Express coach on commuter service to Milton Keynes picks up at Canary Wharf, London
(Tony Pattison) 1328035

Fleet: 1,281 vehicles

Double-deck	945
Single-deck	22
Midibus	265

In peak service: Not available currently
On order: Not available currently

Travel London Ltd
301 Camberwell New Road, London, SE5 0TF, UK
Tel: (+44 207) 805 35 35
Fax: (+44 207) 805 35 02
Web: www.travellondonbus.co.uk

Key personnel
Managing Director: Paul McGowan
Staff: Not available currently

Current situation
The company operates an extensive network in London. It is a subsidiary of National Express Group. The company was formed in March 2004 when National Express Group took over the former Connex business in the capital.

Developments
In 2007, the Travel Surrey brand was introduced for buses operating in the UK county of Surrey.

Fleet	433
Double-deck bus	198
Single-deck bus	223
Midibus	12

Chassis:
Dennis, Optare, Mercedes-Benz, Volvo
Bodies:
Alexander, Wrightbus, East Lancs, Plaxton, Caetano
In peak service: Not available currently
On order: Not available currently

London

Suburban bus
Current situation
Bus services in suburban areas around London are provided by six main companies and several smaller operators. Unlike London itself, bus operations in these areas were deregulated in 1986.

Between them the companies provide an extensive network of local bus services, including many routes feeding stations on the rail network, but in some circumstances competing with it, in London's outer suburban centres such as Watford, Croydon, Bromley, Uxbridge, Enfield and Romford, and towns further afield.

The guided bus system, linking London-Gatwick airport and Crawley, was completed during 2007. The rapid-transit-style service is operated by Go-Ahead company Metrobus, with Scania OmniCity dual-door vehicles. The route has 650 m of guideway, modern bus shelters, traffic light priority, real-time information and extensive priority. It runs every 10 minutes during the day, dropping down to 20 minutes during early mornings and evenings. The complete Fastway scheme is 24 km in length, with 8.8 km of bus lanes, 2.5 km of guideway and 23 vehicles. Funding has come from the private sector (GBP18 million) and from the government (GBP13 million). The Fastway consortium consists of West Sussex and Surrey county councils, Crawley and Banstead borough councils, British Airports Authority (Gatwick), British Airways and the Go-Ahead Group.

In July 2007, the second phase Kent County Council's Fastrack Bus Rapid Transit (BRT) service started with delivery of 12 Volvo B7RLE single-deck buses. It originally opened in 2006 and will ultimately link Dartford, Bluewater, Greenhithe and Gravesend using a mix of busway and on-road priority. It has a dedicated website, www.go-fastrack.co.uk.

Developments
UK express coach operator National Express introduced a new service specifically for

commuters in July 2007, from Milton Keynes to Canary Wharf, via tube stations in central London. The scheme provides commuters with a new way of travelling to the heart of London's business district five days a week. To encourage people to leave their cars behind, the service calls at two car parks at Atterbury, Childs Way and Kingston District Centre as well as Milton Keynes Coachway off J14 of the M1. In London, the coach serves six key locations including Angel Station in Islington as well as Archway Station on the Holloway Road.

A minibus service between Stansted Airport and London Baker Street was started in March 2007 by Easyjet subsidiary, Easybus. The buses are in the company's orange and white house colours.

A further 15 Optare minicoaches were ordered in 2008 by EasyBus to support expansion of its high-frequency London express airport transfer service to include Gatwick as well as Stansted and Luton airports. This second order doubles the EasyBus Soroco fleet to 30.

A busway, much of it guided, was given the go-ahead by the UK Government in 2008. It will run between London-Luton Airport, Luton and the nearby town of Dunstable. It will operate in part over the trackbed of a former railway line linking the two towns.

London Underground Ltd

55 Broadway, London SW1H 0BD, UK
Tel: (+44 20) 72 22 56 00
Web: www.tfl.gov.uk/tube/

Key personnel
General Manager: Tim O'Toole
  Staff: 12,300

Type of operation: Full metro, first line opened 1863

Passenger journeys: (2006/07) 1 billion
Train-km: (2004/05) 97.6 million

Route length: 408 km
  in tunnel: 181 km
Number of lines: 12
Number of stations: 275 (served), 253 (owned)
Gauge: 1,435 mm
Track: Running rail, 47 kg/m BH and 54 kg/m FB; conductor rail (open and subsurface), 74 kg/m FB and 53 kg/m FB; conductor rail (tube tunnel), 64 kg/m rectangular; conventional sleepers on ballast (concreted in tube tunnels)
Tunnel: Bored single-track (tube) and cut-and-cover double-track; 5 lines cut-and-cover, remainder bored tunnel
Electrification: 630 V DC, third and fourth rail

Background
London Underground Limited was formed in 1985.

As part of the PPP (Private Partnership Plan) for London Underground, one private company, Tube Lines, is responsible for maintenance. Tube Lines maintains and upgrades the infrastructure on the Jubilee, Northern and Piccadilly lines. The Tube Lines consortium consists of Amey, Bechtel and Jarvis.

Transport for London (TfL) (previously Metronet) is responsible for maintenance and upgrading of the infrastructure for the deep-level Bakerloo, Victoria, Central and Waterloo & City lines. TfL has also taken over responsibility for the maintenance and upgrading of the infrastructure of the subsurface Circle, District, Metropolitan, Hammersmith & City and East London lines.

Developments
Alcohol ban
TfL announced in June 2008 that alcohol is banned from the Tube, buses, Docklands Light Railway (DLR), tram services and stations across the capital.

Crime
Crime on the Underground and Docklands Light Railway (DLR) has gone down by 11 per cent

London Underground refurbished D78 emu at Barking with a west-bound service on the District Line (Roger Carvell)   1124805

London Underground Alstom-built emu on suface station of LUL network (TfL)   1357146

London Underground station at Westminster, serving Jubilee tube line and District/Circle sub-surface line (TfL)   1357148

in 2008, with robberies on the network cut by more than 50 per cent, TfL has reported. Continued investment in safety and security on the Tube network have helped to deliver the cut in recorded crime, shown by statistics released by the British Transport Police (BTP). There have also been reductions in pick-pocketing, criminal damage, violent crime and public disorder offences in the past year (2007/08).

East London Line (ELL) extension

Work is proceeding on the northern extension of the London Underground East London Line (ELL) which will see new stations at Shoreditch, Hoxton, Haggerston and Dalston Junction. The southern extension takes the line to West Croydon, serving New Cross Gate, Brockley, Honor Oak Park, Forest Hill, Sydenham, Penge West, Anerley and Norwood Junction, with a branch to Crystal Palace. Services are due to start in 2010. Further plans for extension of the ELL have been announced with extensions northwards to Highbury & Islington and westwards to Clapham Junction.

The bigger ELR will not be part of London Underground. It is moving to TfL's new division – London Rail (LR). TfL LR launched when it started running the four routes that currently form Silverlink Metro from November 2007 and substantial improvements are promised. The ELR and North London Railway – the ex-Silverlink lines – will form part of a wider network and there will be some through running.

Heathrow Airport Terminal 5

The London Underground Limited Piccadilly line was extended to Heathrow Terminal in March 2008. The Piccadilly line, which serves all of the airport's terminals, now also caters for passengers seeking to travel to and from Terminal 5. The new T5 station, which was delivered on time and on budget according to TfL, is also used by Heathrow Express services. This is the first extension to the Tube network since the Jubilee line was extended to Stratford in 1999. The new Tube service to T5 precedes a major upgrade of the Piccadilly line by Tube Lines, which is due to be delivered in 2014. The upgrade will provide new trains, a new signal control centre and a new line control centre.

The extension to Terminal 5 was wholly funded by Heathrow Airport Ltd, a subsidiary of BAA. The Terminal 5 station will be operated by BAA via the Heathrow Express Operating Company.

Metronet

Metronet Rail transferred to TfL in 2008. Over the next financial year, TfL's investment in trains, signalling and stations on the eight Tube lines that were formerly the responsibility of Metronet is forecast to be around GBP1.4 billion. The first new trains and signalling systems to be delivered on these lines will be as part of the GBP900 million Victoria Line upgrade. The new trains are currently being tested and are due to enter passenger service for the first time in 2009. They will have CCTV, wheelchair access, better ventilation and improved audio-visual customer information systems. The full upgrade is contractually due to be delivered by 2013, but with the Olympic and Paralympic Games in 2012, the upgrade is currently on course to deliver this major transport boost by late 2011. Continuing improvements at stations continues, with 39 stations already completed and work currently underway at a further 22.

Rolling stock: 4,149 cars
Tube stock (small profile)
Metro-Cammell
  (1972) Mk I/II Bakerloo/Northern
  Lines   M238 T175
  (1967/72) Victoria Line (ATO fitted)   M172 T172
  (1973) Piccadilly Line   M349 T174
ABB Transportation (1992)
  Central/W&C Lines   M700
GEC Alsthom (1996/97) Jubilee Line   M354
GEC Alsthom (1997/98) Northern Line   M636
Surface stock (normal profile)
Cravens A60/62 Metropolitan/E
  London Lines   M226 T227
Metro-Cammell
  C69/C77 (1969/77)
District/Circle/Hammersmith Lines   M138 T138
D78 (1978) District Line   M300 T150

Service: Peak in central area, two min
Revenue control: Fully automated system with self-service machines at nearly all stations; automatic

checking on entry and exit at all central area and some suburban stations; random on-train inspection; penalty fare
One-person operation: All lines except Northern; Victoria Line has full automatic train control ATO/ATP
Surveillance: CCTV at almost all stations
Operational control: Two-way radio on all lines
Operating costs financed by: Fares 125 per cent (before depreciation and renewals)

London

Suburban rail

Type of operation: Suburban heavy rail

Current situation

Suburban services run on all routes out of London to a distance of over 100 km, with an extensive network of inner-suburban routes serving east and northeast London, and the area south of the River Thames which is poorly served by metro. Much of the network is electrified south of the Thames at 660/750 V DC, the remainder mostly at 25 kV 50 Hz. Operations are franchised to private-sector companies. They run over track owned by the not-for-profit infrastructure company Network Rail, with trains leased from the privatised rolling stock leasing companies.

Trains run generally from about 05.00 to 24.00. Off-peak, the service interval is 10–30 minutes, stepped up in the peak hours to every few minutes at some stations. Fares are graduated, though zonal all-modes passes are available within Greater London. Most stations have self-service ticket machines; inspection is largely manual, though some of the franchisees are installing automatic barriers at busy stations to help reduce fraud.

The area served by the train operating companies created in 1994, and now franchised, extends far beyond the London commuting area, and separate data for London suburban operations is not available. Figures given in the individual entries cover the companies' entire operations. Southern runs the Gatwick Express dedicated service linking Victoria station in central London with Gatwick airport (43 km). Service to Heathrow airport (Heathrow Express, see separate entry) from Paddington station, operated by the airports authority BAA, was inaugurated in 1998.

Developments

Transport for London (TfL) is introducing new branding for its surface rail services. Called London Overground, it will be applied in the first instance to the former suburban North London Line.

It will also include the East London Line. Shoreditch station closed in 2006 to allow work

to be carried out on the northern extension of the line. A new station, Shoreditch High Street, is to open in 2010. It will also be extended to West Croydon. Cubic Transportation Systems Limited received a contract in 2006 to supply, install and maintain its FasTIS and Oyster ticket issuing system at 25 rail stations where London Underground and the privately-owned train operating companies share stations and ticketing systems.

A new simple fares structure for London train travel was introduced in 2007, to coincide with the Oyster ticket issuing equipment. From January 2007, the pricing for single and return rail tickets within London is based on the same zones already used for Underground and Travelcard tickets.

The new structure is to help pave the way for Oyster pay-as-you-go smart ticketing to be rolled out across national rail services in London over the next few years. It simplifies the former complex system of individually-priced station-to-station fares. There are over 330 rail stations within the Travelcard zones, and at present each of 97,300 different station-to-station combinations has its own set of fares. These have been replaced by 21 zone-to-zone combinations, with a single, return and cheap day return set for each.

c2c Rail

National Express Group, London Lines
207 Old Street, London EC1V 9NR, UK
Tel: (+44 20) 73 24 80 44
Web: www.c2c-online.co.uk

Key personnel
Managing Director: Mark Hopwood

Passenger journeys: (2004/05) 28.1 million

Current situation

Formerly called LTS Rail, c2c runs commuter trains between London Fenchurch Street, Southend and Shoeburyness, Basildon, Grays, Upminster and Barking. c2c is part of the National Express Group.

In 2003 the last of 74 four-car Electrostar 25 kV AC emus entered service. Built by Bombardier Transportation (formerly Adtranz), they are leased from Angel Trains and Porterbrook. Maintenance is undertaken by Bombardier at c2c's East Ham depot.

Developments

c2c has been transformed since the introduction of the new C357 fleet. Most stations have been completely refurbished (including the installation of new ticket machines, ticket gates and modern passenger information systems).

Rolling stock: 296 Class 357 emu cars

c2c class 357 emu at Southend on service from London (Tony Pattison)   1209457

Chiltern Railway Company Ltd – Chiltern Railways

Western House, 14 Rickfords Hill, Aylesbury HP20 2RX, UK
Tel: (+44 1296) 33 21 00
Fax: (+44 1296) 33 21 26
Web: www.chilternrailways.co.uk

Key personnel

Chairman/Acting Managing Director: Adrian Shooter
Staff: 729

Passenger journeys: (2007) 16.5 million

Current situation

Since winning the franchise in 1996, Chiltern Railways has run scheduled passenger services along the M40 corridor between London Marylebone and Birmingham Snow Hill and London Marylebone to Aylesbury via Amersham along the London underground Metropolitan line. In 2002, the company extended its operations as far as Kidderminster and in 2004, took over services between Stratford-upon-Avon and London.

Developments

In 2007, refurbishment of the Clubman dmus was carried out. The work included tables designed for lap-top computer use, computer power points, new interior colour scheme and a new trolley service offering filter coffee.

Also in 2007 a mobile phone ticket was introduced, costing from GBP5, available until 18.00 the day before travel.

In January 2008, the German rail operator Deutsche Bahn AG (DB) announced the acquisition of Laing Rail, owners of Chiltern Railways and joint owners of London Overground Rail Operations Ltd and the Wrexham, Shropshire and Marylebone Railway Ltd. Chiltern Railways becomes part of DB Regio AG, the division of Deutsche Bahn responsible for operating regional and local services.

In 2008, UK train leasing company, Angel Trains, placed an order for Class 172 cars from Bombardier Transportation. These are the next-generation 'GreenTrains' for London Overground Rail Operations Limited (LOROL) and Chiltern Railways. The contract, worth approximately GBP33 million, is for eight 2-car dmus for use on the London Overground network and four 2-car units for Chiltern Railways.

This vehicle is claimed to be one of the lightest and greenest modern dmus available, meeting the latest legislation in emissions. Production of the new Class 172s will take place in Bombardier's Derby factory. The units for LOROL will be delivered in 2009, with the delivery of units for Chiltern Railways in 2010.

Rolling stock: Operates 3 types of passenger train: Class 165 (Turbo), Class 168 (Clubman) and Class 121 (Bubble Car) – all of which are diesel-powered. Usually operate: 28 × 2-car sets and 11 × 3-car sets of the Class 165, 10 × 4-car sets and 9 × 3-car sets of the Class 168 and 1 × 1-car of the Class 121.

Gatwick Express Ltd

52 Grosvenor Gardens, London SW1W 0AU, UK
Tel: (+44 20) 79 73 50 00
Fax: (+44 20) 79 73 50 48
Web: www.gatwickexpress.co.uk

Key personnel

Managing Director: Mark Hopwood
Operations Director: James Adeshiyan
Route Director: Andrew Conroy

Passenger journeys: (2002/03) 4.2 million
(2003/04) 4.5 million
(2004/05) 5.0 million
Train-km: (2002/03) 2.1 million
(2003/04) 2.55 million
(2004/05) 2.36 million

Chiltern Railways Clubman dmu at London Marylebone station (Tony Pattison)   1330247

Current situation

Dedicated 23-hour express service between London Victoria and London Gatwick Airport. The company is owned by National Express Group plc. Heathrow Express, Gatwick Express and Heathrow Connect are marketed jointly under the Airport Express Alliance banner.

The rolling stock comprises eight Class 460 750 V DC ALSTOM Juniper eight-car emus.

For further information, please see *Jane's World Railways*.

Heathrow Express

3rd Floor, 50 Eastbourne Terrace, Paddington, London W2 6LE, UK
Tel: (+44 20) 750 66 00
Fax: (+44 20) 750 66 15
Web: www.heathrowexpress.com
    www.airportexpressalliance.com

Passenger journeys: (2006) 5.5 million (estimate)
Train-km: Not available currently

Key Personnel

Managing Director: Brian Raven
Head of Service Proposition: Steve Chambers
    Staff: Not available currently

Current situation

Dedicated express service between London Paddington and London-Heathrow airport. The company is owned by BAA plc. The line is electrified at 25 kV AC and a 15 minute headway is in operation.

Heathrow Express runs direct from London-Heathrow Airport Terminal 5 to central London (Paddington station) with connections for Terminals 1, 2 and 3.

The rolling stock comprises 14 Siemens Class 332 four-car and five-car units.

A semi-fast service was introduced in 2005, in partnership with FirstGroup. It is called Heathrow Connect, calling at Ealing Broadway, West Ealing, Hanwell, Southall and Hayes. The service is mainly for people living west of Paddington railway station and for Heathrow Airport staff. A fleet of four four-car Siemens Class 360/2 Desiro emus operates the service.

Heathrow Connect runs direct to Terminal 4 with an interchange between Connect and Express services at Heathrow Terminals 1, 2 and 3.

Developments

Heathrow Express, Heathrow Connect and Gatwick Express are now part of the Airport Express Alliance which operates from the address above.

National Express East Anglia

1st Floor, Oliver's Yard, 55 City Road, London, EC1Y 1HQ, UK
Tel: (+44 845) 600 72 45
Fax: (+44 1603) 21 45 17 (Customer service)
Tel: (+44 207) 549 59 66 (Press office)
e-mail: nxea.customerrelations@
    nationalexpress.com
Web: www.nationalexpresseastanglia.com

Key personnel

Managing Director: Andrew Chivers
Finance Director: Adam Golton

Current situation

National Express East Anglia (formerly 'One' Railway) is a subsidiary of the National Express Group. It started operations in 2004 as part of the

National Express East Anglia Class 315 emu on London suburban service   1330102

new Greater Anglia franchise. National Express East Anglia serves stations running north from London to Hertford East, Peterborough, Cambridge and King's Lynn, extending to 415 km; mostly electrified at 25 kV DC. It also operates the Stansted Express high-frequency service between London Liverpool Street and London Stansted airport, mainline intercity services between London and Norwich and connecting rural services in East Anglia.

Developments
Towards the end of 2007, National Express took over the east coast main line, re-branding it National Express East Coast.

Rolling stock: Includes 21 four-car Class 360 Siemens Desiro emus, 43 Class 315 and 77 Class 321 four-car emus, 18 Class 315 four-car emus and nine refurbished Class 317/7 units for the Stansted Express services.

London Midland

3rd Floor, 41–54 Grey Street, Newcastle-upon-Tyne NE1 6EE, UK
Tel: (+44 191) 232 31 23
e-mail: comments@londonmidland.com
Web: www.londonmidland.com

Key personnel
Managing Director: Stephen Banaghan

Passenger journeys: Not currently available

Current situation
The Silverlink (former operator) franchise ended in November 2007. Three franchises – East Midlands, West Midlands and Cross Country – replace the former four franchises operated by Central Trains, Silverlink, Virgin Cross Country and Midland Mainline.
The East Midlands franchise, operated by Stagecoach, operates services to and from London St. Pancras together with regional and local services in the East Midlands.
The West Midlands franchise operates the West Coast Main Line outer suburban services to and from London Euston (formerly operated by Silverlink County) together with regional and local services in the West Midlands. It is operated by Govia and runs under the name London Midland.
Services between Richmond, Willesden and Stratford passed to London Overground, part of Transport for London (TfL), in 2007.

Rolling stock: Not currently available

Southern Railway Limited – t/a Southern

Go-Ahead House, 26–28 Addiscombe Road, Croydon CR9 5GA, UK
Tel: (+44 20) 89 29 86 00   Fax: (+44 20) 89 29 86 87
Web: www.southernrailway.com

Key personnel
Managing Director: Chris Burchell
Acting Commercial Director: John Oliver
   Staff: Not currently available

Passenger journeys: (2003/04) 127.9 million
(2005/06) 134.8 million

Current situation
Southern (formerly called South Central) is the trading name for Southern Railway Limited, which is a wholly owned subsidiary of GoVia Ltd, which also operates the South Eastern and London Midland franchises and which took over the business in 2001, and is part of the Go-Ahead Group Rail Division.
Southern runs services on a 666-km network mostly of 750 V DC electrified lines out of London's Victoria and London Bridge termini to London Gatwick airport, Brighton and other towns on the south coast of England.

Southern Class 455 inner suburban emus at Sutton station (Roger Carvell)   1115292

Southern runs over 265 four-car and two-car electric multiple-units and 14 diesel-electric multiple-units (for the non-electrified Uckfield and Hastings-Ashford lines). Southern replaced the demus on this line with nine two-car and six four-car Bombardier Turbostar Class 170 dmus during 2004. The inner-suburban services are run by sliding-door units.
As part of the franchise contract which commenced in 2003, GoVia carried out a rolling refurbishment programme, in 2006, for its fleet of 184 Class 455 emu cars used on south London suburban services.
In 2005, slam-door trains were withdrawn and delivery was completed of 700 new Electrostar electric multiple-units and 42 diesel multiple-units. A broadband Wi-Fi service was launched on the express route between London and Brighton in 2005. Brighton station has also been wired for Wi-Fi. Penalty fares were raised in 2005 from GBP10 to GBP20.
Installation of 184 touch-screen ticket machines was completed in 2005. They allow for collection of pre-ordered tickets and also for purchase of tickets the following day. The machines accept cash or credit/debit cards.

Developments
In 2008, the company's Class 458 fleet underwent a refreshment programme.

Southeastern

Friar's Bridge Court, 41-45 Blackfriars Road, London, SE1 8PG, UK
Tel: (+44 870) 000 22 22
Fax: (+44 870) 603 05 05, (+ 44 845) 678 69 76)
Web: www.southeasternrailway.co.uk

Key personnel
Managing Director: Charles Horton

Type of operation: Suburban rail/commuter rail

Passenger journeys/boardings: (2003/04) 132.2 million
(2004/05) 140.93 million
(2005/06) 145 million

Current situation
Routes serve southeastern London, Kent, Surrey and part of East Sussex.

Developments
Southeastern Railway is part of the Go-Ahead group of companies which was awarded the Integrated Kent Franchise from April 2006.
In December 2009, high-speed services will be introduced into London St Pancras using 29 Class 395 Hitachi-built trains.

Route length: 1,066 km
Number of lines: 39
Number of stations: 182
Electrification: 750 V DC (25 kV AC high-speed lines and Willesden to Rugby section)

Fare evasion control: Penalty fares system over parts of network
Integration with other modes: Integrated fares with local bus operators and cycle hire at Tonbridge and Canterbury West
One-person operation: All services

Rolling stock: 1,362 cars
Southeastern   M592 T770
including 450 Class 375 cars (Bombardier)

South West Trains Limited

Friars Bridge Court, 41-45 Blackfriars Road, London SE1 8NZ, UK
Tel: (+44 870) 000 51 51
Tel: (+44 20) 84 56 00 06 50 (Customer Service Centre)
   (+44 8457) 48 49 50 (Passenger Services)
Web: www.southwesttrains.co.uk

Key personnel
Managing Director: Stewart Palmer
Commercial Director: Rufus Boyd
Operations Director: James Burt
Engineering Director: Mac Mackintosh
   Staff: 5,202

Passenger journeys: (2001/02) 138.4 million
(2002/03) 141.1 million
(2003/04) 143 million
(2004/05) 162 million
(2005/06) 160.6 million

Current situation
Delivery of 665 Desiro cars from Siemens Transportation was completed in 2005. The trains replace all slam-door stock with the exception of two refurbished units for the Lymington branch line near Southampton and one retained for special duties.
The fleet of 91 Class 455 emus is being refurbished.

Rolling stock: 328 units

Class	
158 2-car dmu	2
159 3-car dmu	30
421 slam-door 3-car emu	2
423 slam-door 4-car emu	1
444 Desiro main line 5-car emu	45
450 4-car emu	127
455 4-car emu	91
458 Juniper 4-car emu	30

On order: 444 Desiro main line 5-car emus (26)

First Capital Connect (FCC)

Hertford House, 1 Cranwood Street, London
EC1V 9QS, UK
Tel: (+44 20) 77 13 21 01
e-mail: customer.relations.fcc@firstgroup.com
Web: www.firstcapitalconnect.co.uk

Key personnel

Managing Director: Elaine Holt
Head of Communications: Rakesh Vasishtha
Human Resources Director: Michelle Smart
   Staff: Not currently available

Type of operation: Suburban heavy rail

Passenger journeys: (2005) 52.7 million
(2006/07) 47.6 million (Thameslink)
(2006/07) 37.1 million (Great Northern)
(2007/08) 50.7 million (Thameslink)
(2007/08) 41.5 million (Great Northern)

Current situation

In April 2006, FirstGroup plc launched its two new
rail franchises – First Capital Connect (FCC) and
First Great Western. First Capital Connect brings
together the Great Northern and Thameslink
franchises for six years with a possible extension
of up to three years. Awarded to FirstGroup in
December 2005 by the Department for Transport,
the new First Capital Connect franchise began
operation on 1 April 2006, and includes the
networks previously covered by the former
Thameslink and Great Northern franchises.

Developments

Network Rail is taking forward a major upgrade
of the Thameslink lines in a project known as
The Thameslink Programme. The government
announced the GBP5.5 billion funding for this in
July 2007. This will see upgrading of the power
supply and signalling through the central London
tunnels and improvements in track layouts to
increase capacity in south London. It is expected
that Peterborough, King's Lynn and Letchworth
to the north of London, along with Littlehampton,
Eastbourne, Horsham, Dartford and Ashford to
the south of London, will be new destinations.

   In December 2007, Kings Cross Thameslink
station was closed and First Capital Connect's
services transferred to St Pancras International
station.

Fleet: 140 emus
Class 365/5 three-car dual-voltage emu	40
Class 313 four-car emu 25 kV AC/750 v DV	41
Class 317 four-car emu 25 kV AC	12
Class 319/3 four-car dual-voltage emu	47

In peak service: Not currently available
On order: Not currently available

First Capital Connect Class 319 dual-voltage emu at London Blackfriars station   1327987

and Windsor. First Great Western Link also serves
the North Downs Line between Reading and Gatwick
airport via Guildford.

   First Great Western has a fleet of 494 high-
speed carriages and 282 carriages for commuter/
local use. The company has 960 staff and
manages 71 of the 104 stations that it serves.
Each weekday over 78,000 passengers use the
830 daily services operated.

   For further information on FGW, please see
Jane's World Railways.

Developments

The commuter fleet was refurbished in
2007/08 with improved interiors and other
enhancements.

Docklands Light Railway Ltd (DLR)

PO Box 154, London E14 0DX, UK
Tel: (+44 20) 73 63 98 98
Fax: (+44 20) 73 63 97 08
Web: www.dlr.co.uk

Key personnel

Director: Jonathan Fox
Head of Development and Planning: Robert Niven
Public Relations Manager: David Sanders
   Staff: Not available currently

Type of operation: Automated light metro, opened
1987

Background

Docklands Light Railway (DLR), part of Transport
for London (TfL), opened in 1987 as a modest
GBP77 million railway to serve the earliest
development sites in the Docklands area,
operating 11 vehicles via 15 stations.

Current situation

DLR is now a GBP1 billion, 31-km railway that
operates 94 vehicles and serves 39 stations. It has
expanded to serve Bank (1991), Beckton (1994),
Lewisham (1999) and London City Airport (2005)
and has played a key role in the regeneration of
London's Docklands.

   The DLR is stated to be the most technically
complex light rail network in Europe. It operates
using a driverless, computer-controlled system.
It is also stated to be the most reliable railway
in mainland UK, with punctuality levels at over
97 per cent.

   A series of forthcoming extensions and
enhancements will enable DLR to maintain its
contribution to sustainable local growth and the
London 2012 Olympic and Paralympic Games'
transport infrastructure. The developments will
also help meet booming passenger demand:
numbers are projected to rise from current levels
of over 60 million to 80 million by 2009.

First Great Western (FGW)

Milford House, 1 Milford Street, Swindon SN1
1HL, UK
Tel: (+44 1793) 49 94 00
Fax: (+44 1793) 49 94 51
Web: www.firstgreatwestern.co.uk

Key personnel

Chief Operating Officer: Andrew Haines
   Staff: 960 (estimate)

Passenger journeys: (Entire network)
(2005/06) 75.8 million
Train-km: Not available currently

Current situation

First Great Western operates an integrated
network of services from London to the South
Midlands, South Wales and the West of England,
between Bristol and the English Channel. First
Group now operates most of the long-distance
services serving Bristol.

   First Great Western (FGW) operates a network
of frequent services along the Thames Valley from
London Paddington. Main stations served include:
Slough, Maidenhead, Reading and Oxford. Branch
lines serve Basingstoke, Henley-on-Thames, Marlow

*Docklands Light Railway (DLR) service calling at Poplar station with an eastbound service for
Beckton (Ken Harris)*   1183520

Developments

Construction is under way to extend the London City Airport extension to Woolwich Arsenal. The 2.5-km Woolwich Arsenal extension, funded as part of TfL's five-year GBP10 billion Investment Programme, will run under the River Thames from DLR King George V station and connect with Woolwich town centre.

Due to open in February 2009, the route will connect Woolwich to London City Airport in five minutes, Canary Wharf in 19 minutes and Bank in 27 minutes. Local residents will benefit from improved access to employment and education opportunities, and Woolwich and the southern Royal Docks will see the creation of new jobs, homes, shops and leisure facilities.

During the Olympic Games, the extension will provide access to the Royal Artillery Barracks in Woolwich, which will hold the shooting events, and to the Olympic Park and other competition venues.

Construction is also under way on a further DLR extension, to Stratford International, which is projected to open in 2010. Similarly funded by TfL's Investment Programme, the route will be established by converting the North London Line between Canning Town and Stratford to DLR operation. It will encompass existing stations at Royal Victoria, Canning Town, West Ham and Stratford, and new stations at Star Lane, Abbey Road, Stratford High Street and Stratford International, the latter serving the Channel Tunnel Rail Link. The extension will provide capacity and flexibility for future growth along the Lower Lea Valley, and offer a more frequent and reliable service to that currently in place.

The route will play a particularly significant role during the 2012 Games as it will link to the Olympic Park and run up to 27 trains per hour, providing an hourly capacity of approximately 13,500 in each direction.

Construction has started on works that will enable DLR to lengthen its trains from two-car to three-car on its busiest route, Bank/Tower Gateway to Lewisham. The extended trains are due to start running by mid-2009. By 2010, an extra car will be added to train services across the rest of the DLR network.

Capacity is being further increased until 2010 by the addition of 55 new rail cars to the DLR fleet.

In the longer term, DLR is working towards an application for powers to extend the railway to Dagenham Dock, again assisting with the delivery of sustainable growth and redevelopment. The extension will consist of five new stations – Beckton Riverside, Creekmouth, Barking Riverside, Goresbrook and Dagenham Dock – which will serve extensive planned and approved riverside developments. If the relevant permissions are gained and funding sourced, the extension is planned to open in 2015.

Passenger journeys: (2003/04) 48.5 million
(2004/05) 50.1 million
(2005/06) 53.0 million
(2006/07) 61.3 million
(2007/08) 66.6 million
Train-km: (2007/08) 4.4 million

Route length: 31 km
Number of lines: five
Number of stations: 39
Gauge: 1,435 mm
Track: Running rail, 40 kg/m FB and 56 kg/m FB; conductor rail three kg/m shrouded steel/aluminium composite; mixture of concrete sleepers on ballast and concrete slab track
Electrification: 750 V DC shrouded third rail, underside contact

Service: Peak two min on city routes
First/last train: 05.30/00.43
Fare structure: As LT zonal system
Revenue control: Self-service machines at all mostly staffed stations with on-train checks (Bank, Island Gardens, Cutty Sark for Maritime Greenwich and London City Airport are staffed)

Docklands Light Railway (DLR) service calling at London City Airport station   1195890

Docklands Light Railway (DLR) service serving Canary Wharf station   1195891

Train control: ATO, ATP and ATS; there are no lineside signals or driving cabs, but each vehicle has emergency driving positions at the car ends; Seltrac moving block system
Surveillance: CCTV monitoring of trains and unstaffed stations from control centre with video recording of incidents; passenger alarms on platforms
Arrangements for elderly/disabled: Fully accessible to wheelchairs via ramps or lifts

Rolling stock: 94 articulated cars
Bombardier B92 (2003)   M94
On order: A further 55 cars.

Tramlink

Windsor House, 42–50 Victoria Street, London SW1H 0TL, UK
Tel: (+44 20) 86 62 98 00   Fax: (+44 20) 86 62 98 10
Web: www.tfl.gov.uk/trams

Key personnel

Managing Director, Tram Operations Ltd: Phil Hewitt
   Staff: 150 (estimate)

Type of operation: Light rail, opened 2000

Passenger journeys: (2006) 18 million (estimate)
(2007) 25 million
Vehicle-km: Not currently available

Route length: 38 km
Number of lines: 3
Number of stops: 39
Gauge: 1,435 mm
Electrification: 750 V DC, overhead

Current situation

Tramlink is a 28 km light rail system with three lines, providing a connection to and through a number of areas in south London, including Croydon and Wimbledon. It became fully operational on 30 May 2000, re-introducing street-running light rail to London after an absence of almost 50 years.

Tramlink is operated by Firts Tram Operations Ltd on behalf of Transport for London (TfL).

Development

TfL took direct control of Tramlink services in 2008. TfL acquired Tramtrack Croydon Ltd, the Private Finance Initiative (PFI) Concession holder which ran Tramlink.

Tramlink is now managed by TfL's London Rail directorate, allowing TfL to develop Tramlink as a key part of the capital's integrated public transport network.

Plans to extend Tramlink from Harrington Road to Anerley and Crystal Palace, however, will not be taken forward. Although TfL has progressed the scheme, there is no government funding to implement it. TfL is carrying out a wider study, working closely with Croydon Council and other key stakeholders, to assess how Tramlink can deliver the improvements outer London needs. TfL says that it is committed to including new proposals for extensions to the tram as part of a future bid to government.

In 2008, the livery was changed from the traditional red and white to green, blue and white.

Fleet: Bombardier Flexity Swift LRV   24

Service: Seven-Ten minutes peak

Fare structure: Flat; cash for ticket, oystercard and some other pre-paid cards for reduced fare; free travel for some children, students and for senior citizens and disabled users holding a freedom pass.

Integration with other modes: Connects with main line rail at seven stations, London Underground at one station and to bus feeder services at two stations; bus passes and some travelcards are valid on the system.

Arrangements for elderly/disabled: Two wheelchair positions in each tram; free travel for senior citizens and disabled users holding a Freedom Pass.

Cross London Rail Links Limited – Crossrail

Portland House, Bressendon Place, London, SW1H 0PT, UK
Tel: (+44 20) 30 23 91 00   Fax: (+44 20) 79 41 77 03
e-mail: ianrathbone@crossrail.co.uk
Web: www.crossrail.co.uk

Key Personnel
Operations Director: Keith Berryman
Media Manager: Ian Rathbone

Current situation
Cross London Rail Links, a 50/50 partnership between the Department for Transport and Transport for London, will link east and west London through the Crossrail project. Crossrail supports the continued development, economic growth and regeneration of London and at the same time tackle the congestion and lack of capacity on the existing network.

Crossrail is a proposed high-frequency and accessible west-east railway from Maidenhead in Berkshire to Shenfield in Essex and Abbey Wood in the Thames Gateway that will travel through central London linking up Heathrow, the West End, the City of London and Canary Wharf.

Developments
The Crossrail Bill received Royal Assent in July 2008. Following the UK Prime Minister's announcement last October that a GBP16 billion funding package had been secured for the construction of Crossrail, Parliamentary approval of the Bill means that the project is on track to be operational for passengers in 2017. The line will run from Maidenhead and Heathrow Airport in the west through tunnels under central London – with new stations at Paddington, Bond Street, Tottenham Court Road, Farringdon, Liverpool Street, Whitechapel, Isle of Dogs (Canary Wharf) – then out to Shenfield and Abbey Wood in the east.

The Crossrail Act grants powers to acquire land and for Crossrail to be built and maintained. Enabling works will take place next year, with main construction works set to begin in 2010.

Thames Clippers (Collins River Enterprises Ltd)

Nelson House, 265 Rotherhithe Street, London SE16 5HW, UK
Tel: (+44 870) 781 50 49   Fax: (+44 20) 72 37 40 19
e-mail: web@thamesclippers.com
Web: www.thamesclippers.com

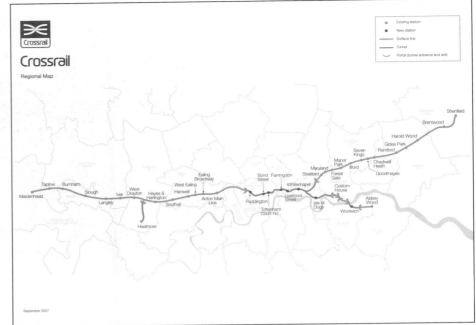

Crossrail
Regional Map

Crossrail regional map with section in tunnel between Paddington, Woolwich and Stratford, and a further section in tunnel to Heathrow Airport   1293465

Thames Clippers' fast catamaran Cyclone arriving at QEII Pier (O₂) (Peter Roelofs)   1375508

Key personnel
Chairman: Alan Woods
Managing Director: Sean Collins
PR and Marketing Manager: Rorie Delahooke

Type of operation: Ferry service

Passenger journeys: Not available currently
Vehicle-km: Not available currently

Current situation
Fast catamaran service linking Savoy Pier (Westminster) with London Bridge, Tower Bridge, Canary Wharf (London Docklands) and Isle of Dogs (Mast House Terrace). An hourly service is provided seven days a week with a higher frequency at weekday peak hours.

Thames Clippers also operates the Tate Boat and River Roamer. The Tate Boat cruises between Tate Modern and Tate Britain. The Tate Boat also calls at the London Eye. The Tate service runs from 09.55 to 17.13 weekdays and 09.52 to 17.36 on weekends.

Developments
One of the company's larger catamarans (the Hurricane, Sun or Moon Clipper) is operating weekday evening services from August 2006 until further notice, to cater for increased demand.

Fleet: 12 high-speed catamarans

Manchester

Population: City: 437,000, Greater Manchester Urban Area: 2.23 million (estimates)

Public transport
Bus services in Greater Manchester metropolitan area are provided by private companies operating about 800 vehicles, alongside the two former GM Buses companies which are now subsidiaries of large UK bus groups. The PTE invites tenders for supply of loss-making and socially desirable bus services which are not provided by commercial operators. An expanding light rail network and local rail systems provide intensive services in the Greater Manchester area.

First in Manchester
Wallshaw Street, Oldham OL1 3TR, UK
Tel: (+44 161) 627 29 29
Fax: (+44 161) 627 58 45
Web: www.firstgroup.com

Key personnel
Managing Director: Andy Scholey
  Staff: 2,400

Type of operation: Bus

Passenger journeys: (2008) 100 million (estimate)
Vehicle-km: Not available currently

Current situation
First in Manchester carries approximately 100 million passengers a year in all 10 local

authority areas of Greater Manchester. Commercial services account for 88 per cent, with 12 per cent on tendered or contracted services.

The company also operates in the Merseyside area, serving St Helens, Sefton and Liverpool.

There are 33 bus routes forming the Overground network, operating on a 'turn-up-and-go' frequency during the daytime Monday to Saturday. This is designed to simplify bus travel for the non-user and First reports that the majority of its customers use these services. There is also a night bus network.

First in Manchester has seven depots in Greater Manchester and one in Merseyside.

First in Manchester was a founding partner in the Greater Manchester Integrate Project, which brings together all involved in transport infrastructure, planning and provision for the Greater Manchester area.

Number of routes: 390

Fleet: 900 vehicles
Full breakdown of fleet is not available currently, but comprises:
Double-deck buses 126
Single-deck buses 520
Articulated buses 34
Midibuses 220
In peak service: Not available currently

Most intensive service: Five mins
One-person operation: 100 per cent
Fare collection: Payment on bus with ticket issue by driver
Fare structure: Stage, multijourney ticket; range of prepurchase weekly passes including add-on to rail season tickets and all modes
Fares collected on board: 89 per cent
Fare evasion control: Revenue inspectors charging higher fares
Arrangements for elderly/disabled: On ordinary services low flat fare charged; some single-decks have wheelchair ramps; all new buses are low-floor types
Average peak-hour speed: In bus lanes, 24 km/h; in mixed traffic, 18 km/h
Bus priority: Eight km of bus lanes; turning ban lifted at certain traffic lights; bus-only use of several main streets in city and surrounding town centres, generally during shopping hours
Integration with other modes: Co-ordination with supported rail services and light rail at major interchanges, and smaller feeder schemes. Integrated ticketing with other bus, train and tram operators. Combined operator telephone enquiry service
Operating costs financed by: Fares 72 per cent, concessionary fares support 16 per cent, other commercial sources 12 per cent

Stagecoach Manchester

Hyde Road, Manchester, M12 6JS, UK
Tel: (+44 161) 276 25 77
Fax: (+44 161) 276 25 94
e-mail: manchester.enquiries@stagecoachbus.com
Web: www.stagecoachbus.com

Key personnel
Managing Director: Mark Threapleton
Operations Director: Elisabeth Tasker
Commercial Director: Ray Cossins
Engineering Director: Darren Roe
Staff: 1,750

Current situation
The company operates in south and central Manchester, Stockport, Trafford and Tameside.

Bus
Passenger journeys: (2004/05) 82 million
(2006/07) 86.0 million
(2007/08) 89.7 million
Vehicle-km: (2004/05) 35.8 million
(2006/07) 36.4 million
(2007/08) 37.0 million

First in Manchester Optare Solo bus on Metroshuttle service in the city centre 1172761

Number of routes: 150
Fleet: 704 vehicles
Full breakdown of fleet is not currently available, but comprises:
Double-deck bus 444
Single-deck bus 200
Midibus 45
Minibus 15
Chassis
Iveco 4
Dennis 347
Leyland 13
MAN 127
Mercedes-Benz 14
Scania 56
Volvo 143
Bodies
Alexander 539
Duple 20
East Lancs 18
Northern Counties 69
Plaxton 46
Scolabus Vehixle 4
Marshall 8
In peak service: 549

Most intensive service: 2 min
One-person operation: 100 per cent
Fare collection: Payment on bus with ticket issue by driver
Fare structure: Stage, multi-journey ticket; range of pre-purchase weekly passes including add-on to rail season tickets and all modes
Fares collected on board: 92 per cent
Fare evasion control: Revenue inspectors charging higher fares
Arrangements for elderly/disabled: Free travel after 09.30 Mon-Fri, all day Sat, Sun and Holidays, low flat fare at other times; all new buses are low-floor with fully accessible low-floor space
Average peak-hour speed: In bus lanes, 24 km/h; in mixed traffic, 18 km/h
Bus priority: 27.5 km of bus lanes; turning ban lifted at certain traffic lights; bus-only use of several main streets in city and surrounding town centres, generally during shopping hours
Integration with other modes: Co-ordination with supported rail services and light rail at major interchanges, and smaller feeder schemes. Integrated ticketing with other bus, train and tram operators. Combined operator telephone enquiry service.

Operating costs financed by: Fares 72 per cent, concessionary fares support 20 per cent, service subsidy 6 per cent, other commercial sources 2 per cent

Arriva North West and Wales
73 Ormskirk Road, Aintree, Liverpool L9 5AE, UK
Tel: (+44 151) 522 28 80
Fax: (+44 151) 525 95 56
Web: www.arriva.co.uk

Key personnel
Managing Director: Bob Hind
Finance Director: Phil Stone
Marketing Manager: Nick Gordon
Engineering Director: Malcolm Gilkerson

Current situation
Merseyside-based company took over operations of Bee Line in Manchester, Blue Bus and Star Line of Knutsford. Extensive network of services is operated in Wigan, Leigh and south Manchester from depots in central Manchester, Wythenshawe and Haydock.

Also provides services in Merseyside, Cheshire and Wales. Networks of night buses are run in Liverpool and Manchester.

Total fleet size is approximately 1,300 vehicles.

Bullocks Coaches
Commercial Garage, Stockport Road, Cheadle, SK8 2AG, UK
Tel: (+44 161) 428 52 65   Fax: (+44 161) 428 90 74
Web: www.bullockscoaches.co.uk

Current situation
Family firm developed bus services after deregulation in 1986 and now runs commercial and tendered routes in South Manchester and Stockport. It was the first independent operator to introduce low-floor, single-deck buses in South Manchester on service to Stockport.

Developments
Several bus operations of Bullocks Coaches of Cheadle were sold to Stagecoach in 2008. The Oxford Road Link bus service and coach side of the business continues.

Fleet: 63 vehicles

Dennis Dominator/East Lancs double-deck	1
Leyland Olympian/East Lancs double-deck	4
Leyland Olympian/Northern Counties double-deck	2
Leyland Olympian/Alexander double-deck	9
Volvo Olympian/East Lancs double-deck	3
Volvo Olympian/Northern Counties double-deck	8
Scania N113/East Lancs double-deck	4
DAF DB250/Optare Spectra double-deck	2
Dennis Trident/East Lancashire low-floor double-deck	5
Leyland National single-deck	1
Bristol LH/ECW single-deck	1
Leyland Tiger/Duple single-deck	1
Scania L113/Wright low-floor single-deck	1
Leyland Tiger/Plaxton coach	3
Dennis Dorchester/Plaxton coach	1
Dennis Javelin/Berghof coach	1
Scania N112/Van Hool coach	1
Toyota Coaster/Caetano coach	1
Volvo B10M/Van Hool coach	2
Volvo B10M/Caetano coach	9
Volvo B12M/Caetano coach	1
Mercedes-Benz 709D/MtoM minibus	1
Ford Transit/Dormobile minibus	1

Bullocks East Lancs-bodied Scania on Service 42 to Piccadilly (Ken Harris)   1115175

Finglands Coachways Ltd

261 Wilmslow Road, Rusholme, Manchester M14 5JL, UK
Tel: (+44 161) 224 33 41
Fax: (+44 161) 257 31 54
e-mail: enquiry@finglands.co.uk
Web: www.finglands.co.uk

Key personnel
Chairman and Chief Executive Officer: P J S Shipp
Director: D J Shurden
Fleet Engineer: Tim Jenkins
 Staff: 130

Current situation
Acquired in 1992 by the EYMS Group of Hull, the company operates a high-profile CoachMarque-accredited coach company with 10 coaches. The bus fleet of 57 buses has recently been upgraded to all double-deck vehicles. Runs commercial and tendered bus services, mainly in south Manchester.

Fleet: 57 vehicles

Volvo Olympian/Alexander double-deck	17
Volvo Olympian/Northern Counties double-deck	15
Dennis Trident/Alexander low-floor double-deck	4
Volvo B7L/Plaxton low-floor double-deck	6
Alexander Dennis Enviro 300 single-deck	5
Volvo B10M/Plaxton coach	5
Volvo B12B 9700 coach	1
Volvo B12B/Plaxton coach	4

Manchester
Other operators
Current situation
Smaller private companies with stage services include Ashall's Coaches, Bluebird Bus & Coach, Bu-Val, Hayton's Executive Travel, Jones Executive Coaches, Selwyns Travel Services, Smiths Coaches (Marple) Ltd, South Lancs Travel and Vales Coaches (Manchester) Ltd.

Greater Manchester Passenger Transport Executive (GMPTE)

9 Portland Street, Manchester M60 1HX, UK
Tel: (+44 161) 242 60 00
e-mail: publicity@gmpte.com
Web: www.gmpte.com

Key personnel
Interim Director General: David Leather
Strategy Director: Keith Howcroft
Organisational Development Director: Urvashi Bramwell

Interim Finance Director: James Aspinal
Interim Projects Director: Paul Griffiths
Interim Service Delivery Director: Michael Renshaw

Current situation
GMPTE is responsible to the Greater Manchester Passenger Transport Authority. The PTE is responsible for contracting socially necessary bus services and supporting the local rail service. It also owns the Metrolink light rail system on behalf of the Authority and is responsible for planning for the future of the Metrolink network. GMPTE and the Authority are also committed to developing accessible transport, funding Ring and Ride, a fully accessible door to door transport service for people with mobility difficulties.

The PTE administers the concessionary fares scheme, which allows participants (pensioners, children and people with disabilities) either free or reduced rate travel. GMPTE owns and is responsible for the upkeep of bus stations and on-street infrastructure. It also provides information about public transport through telephone information lines, timetables, general publicity and Travelshops.

Developments
In June 2008, the UK Government announced that Greater Manchester was set to benefit from a GBP2.8 billion funding package to deliver major public transport improvements and tackle road congestion. Greater Manchester has been given authority to proceed with its bid to the government's Transport Innovation Fund (TIF).

The funding package includes plans for up to 35 km (22 miles) of extension to the Metrolink tram, transformed bus services across Manchester, including new, direct buses running from the north to the south of the city, and 120 extra yellow school buses. There will also be improvements to the rail network, including more carriages and seats, the upgrade of 41 train stations and the doubling of park and ride provision on the rail and Metrolink networks.

Information displays will be installed at all major bus and train stations giving passengers up-to-date information on when their bus or train will arrive. There will also be improved roadside information for drivers, warning them of accidents and delays. Integrated ticketing arrangements will be introduced, including smartcards.

The majority of these improvements are planned to be delivered before the introduction of the local congestion charge in 2013. The charging scheme will operate only at peak times, when congestion is at its worst.

The GBP2.8 billion package consists of GBP1.5 billion from the Department for Transport, GBP1.2 billion from local contributions, GBP0.1 billion local third-party contribution. This is over and above existing funding for Greater Manchester.

Greater Manchester's proposed congestion charge is designed around a 'twin cordon' system, which will operate at peak times only. Vehicles will be charged according to their crossing of cordons. The scheme will use tag and beacon technology supported by Automatic Number Plate Recognition (ANPR). The scheme is proposed to go live in mid-2013.

Light rail – Metrolink
Operated under franchise by:

Stagecoach Metrolink

Metrolink House, Queens Road, Manchester M8 0RY, UK
Tel: (+44 161) 205 86 65
Fax: (+44 161) 205 86 99
Web: www.metrolink.co.uk

Key personnel
Metrolink Director: Philip Purdy
 Staff: 340

Current situation
Metrolink is owned by GMPTE, which developed it with Greater Manchester Passenger Transport Authority. The first phase of Metrolink opened in 1992, linking Bury in the north of the conurbation to Altrincham in the south via Manchester city centre. The 31 km route was built under a DBOM contract by Greater Manchester Metrolink Ltd. The system was refranchised in 1997 to the Altram Consortium, comprising Laing, Ansaldo and the Serco Group. The extension opened to Salford Quays in late 1999 and Eccles in July 2000.

Stagecoach took over from Serco in July 2007, and will run the tram system until 2017. It is responsible for all lines, including the new lines to Oldham, Rochdale, Droylsden and Chorlton. A contract has been announced with Bombardier for the supply of eight Flexity Swift trams for delivery in 2009. Each LRV is 28.4 m long and carries 200 passengers.

Greater Manchester's Metrolink network is cited as one of the most successful light rail systems in the UK, carrying nearly 20 million passengers every year.

When the Bury and Altrincham lines (Phase 1) opened in 1992, Metrolink became the first modern light rail system in the UK to run along the street. Metrolink now covers 37 km (23 miles) following the completion of the Salford Quays/Eccles line (Phase 2) in 2000.

Developments
In 2008, Bombardier Transportation, together with consortium partner Vossloh Kiepe, signed an option to supply an additional 28 light rail vehicles. The option was from a contract signed in April 2007, for an initial eight vehicles, with another four ordered since. The additional

contract is valued at approximately EUR78 million (GBP62 million) with Bombardier's share amounting to approximately EUR58 million (GBP46 million). There are options in the contract to provide more vehicles in the future if the Metrolink network expands further.

The first new light rail vehicles are scheduled to be delivered during 2009. As consortium leader, Bombardier is designing and manufacturing the vehicles at its sites in Bautzen, Germany and Vienna, Austria. Bombardier's Siegen plant is responsible for delivering the bogies and consortium partner, Vossloh Kiepe is providing the electrical equipment.

The new Manchester vehicles are based on the Bombardier Flexity Swift family of light rail vehicles. The 28.4 m long light rail vehicles are 2.65 m wide and have the capacity for 200 passengers.

Also in 2008, the UK Government announced that it had pledged GBP244 million towards the GBP382 million total cost of enlarging the Metrolink network to serve Oldham, Rochdale and Chorlton, with upgrades to the existing network that will enable faster and more frequent services.

GMPTE is also constructing a further extension to the Metrolink network, funded separately, to Droylsden in the east of the city.

The extension to Oldham and Rochdale, which plans to open in 2012, will be about 23 km long. Work will include a conversion of Oldham's existing Loop rail line to Metrolink operation, allowing direct access to Manchester City Centre and Piccadilly rail station.

The section to Chorlton in South Manchester will be 4 km long and is expected to open in 2011. The disused railway line between Trafford Bar and Chorlton would be converted to Metrolink use as far as St Werburgh's Road. The extension provides improved access from the densely populated areas of Firswood and Chorlton to Manchester City Centre and will link them directly to growing job opportunities on the Oldham-Rochdale corridor and, with one interchange, Salford Quays.

Further extensions to Metrolink are included within Greater Manchester's Transport Innovation Fund bid, which is currently being considered by the Department.

Type of operation: Light rail

Bury to Altrincham: Suburban heavy lines converted to light rail operation with on-street city-centre running. Opened in 1992

Route length: 31 km

City centre to Eccles
Segregated track and on-street running. Opened to Salford Quays in December 1999, and to Eccles in July 2000

Route length: 6.4 km

Passenger journeys: (2007) 20 million

Number of lines: 2
Number of stations: 37
Gauge: 1,435 mm
Electrification: 750 kV DC overhead

Service: Bury to Altrincham every 6 min (peak), 12–15 min (off-peak); Eccles every 12 min (peak), 12–15 min (off-peak)
First/last car: 06.00/24.00 Monday-Saturday, 07.00/24.00 Sunday
Fare structure: Zonal
Fare collection: Self-service single and return tickets; prepurchase passes available from franchises
Fare evasion control: Roving inspectors and on-the-spot fines
Arrangements for elderly/disabled: Fully accessible to wheelchairs by ramps to raised platforms; GMPTE concessionary fare scheme applies
Integration with other modes: Bus feeders at several stations; some park-and-ride facilities

Rolling stock: 32 cars
GEC ALSTOM-Firema   M32
In peak service: 28

Northern Rail Ltd
Northern House, Rougier Street, York, YO1 6HZ, UK
e-mail: customer.relations@northernrail.org
Web: www.northernrail.org

Key personnel
Managing Director: Heidi Mottram
  Staff: 4,500

Type of operation: Suburban heavy rail

Passenger journeys (whole network): (2007) 78.3 million

Current situation
Local rail services are operated to the PTE's specifications on several routes in the Greater Manchester area, including the Manchester-Huddersfield-Wakefield route (69 km).

Northern Rail Ltd is a joint-venture company, set up in 2004, and brings together the management operations from parent organisations Serco Group and NedRailways. Serco is a global public service company and is expanding its partnering of contracts on behalf of government. NedRailways is a wholly owned subsidiary of Dutch Railways (NS). Besides fleet maintenance and operational planning and timetabling, NS develops and operates station hubs and retail facilities. NS also has a leading role in developing integrated transport solutions.

For further information on Northern Rail Ltd, please see *Jane's World Railways*.

Developments
Siemens delivered 56 three-car Desiro dmus which entered service in 2006.

Rolling stock: (Whole network)
245 dmus/railcars and three small batches of emus: Class 321/9 for the Leeds-Doncaster route; Class 323 for Manchester-based services; and Class 333 for the Leeds-Skipton line.

Middlesbrough-Teesside
Population: City 146,778 (estimate)

Public transport
Most bus services in the Middlesbrough urban area provided by two operators, both subsidiaries of large UK bus groups. Local rail services.

The local authority, Middlesbrough Borough Council (www.middlesbrough.gov.uk), operates the Middlesbrough Transporter Bridge, which carries passengers and vehicle across the River Tees. It is an elevated railway, 259 m long, from which is suspended the passenger/vehicle-carrying gondola and runs every day. The rails are 49 m high.

Stagecoach Transit Ltd
Church Road, Stockton, TS18 2HW, UK
Tel: (+44 1642) 60 21 12
Fax: (+44 1642) 61 77 33
Web: www.stagecoachbus.com

Key personnel
Managing Director: John Conroy
Operations Director: Nigel Winter
Engineering Director: David Kirsopp
Commercial Director: Robin Knight
  Staff: 465

Background
Cleveland Transit was purchased by its employees in 1991 from a consortium of local authorities. It purchased Kingston upon Hull City Transport in 1993, and was itself sold to Stagecoach in 1994.

Current situation
As part of the 2001 Stagecoach Group reorganisation the company relinquished control of Hull operations and senior management

Light rail with a difference – the Middlesbrough Transporter bridge carries passengers and small vehicles over the River Tees with a gondola suspended below an elevated railway (Tony Pattison)
1341038

merged with that of Stagecoach Busways to form a new Stagecoach North East company.

Bus
Passenger journeys: (2003/04) 22 million
(2004/05) 22 million
(2005/06) 22 million

Vehicle-km: (2003/04) 11.8 million
(2004/05) 11.9 million
(2005/06) 11.4 million

Number of routes: 41
Route length: 450 km (one way)

Fleet: 159 vehicles

Leyland Olympian/Alexander double-deck	2
Volvo Olympian double-deck	4
Volvo B10M/Northern Counties single-deck	38
Dennis Dart/Alexander single-deck	29
Dennis Dart SLF/Alexander low-floor midibus	27
MAN/Alexander low-floor single-deck	25
Volvo B10B/Plaxton coach	9
Volvo B10BLE	15

In peak service: 140

Most intensive service: 7/8 min
One-person operation: 100 per cent
Fare collection: Wayfarer machine with change-giving
Fare structure: Stage, monthly passes
Fares collected on board: 86 per cent (14 per cent of journeys by card holders)
Fare evasion control: Ticket Inspectors
Operational control: Inspectors; mobile radios
Arrangements for elderly/disabled: Reduced fares financed by council; low-floor vehicles operate in Stockton and Hartlepool
Average distance between stops: 400 m
Average peak-hour speed: In bus lanes, 22.5 km/h; in mixed traffic, 21 km/h
Subsidy from: Borough councils for tendered routes

Arriva North East

Admiral Way, Doxford International Business Park, Sunderland, SR3 3XP, UK
Tel: (+44 191) 520 42 00
Fax: (+44 191) 420 42 22
Web: www.arrivabus.co.uk

Key personnel
Managing Director: Jonathan May
Engineering Director: John Greaves

Operations Director: I McInroy
Finance Director: S Richardson
Commercial Director: L Esnouf

Subsidiaries
Arriva Durham County Ltd
Arriva Tees & District
Arriva Teesside
Arriva Northumbria

Current situation
Both Arriva Tees and District and Arriva Teesside operate local and interurban services across Teesside and Cleveland. Arriva Durham County operates in Durham City (to the south of Newcastle) and the east of the county. Other services are operated on a regional basis.

Most Arriva Northumbria routes run into Newcastle from outside the city, but a sizeable network has been developed in the northern suburbs and new developing areas.

The companies, as subsidiaries, became part of the Arriva group in 1996 and are managed as part of the Arriva North East Division.

Fleet: 640 vehicles

Leyland/Volvo Olympian double-deck bus	44
Volvo B7TL double-deck bus	2
DAF SDB250 double-deck bus	21
Dennis Trident ALX 400 double-deck bus	19
MCW Metrobus double-deck bus	5
Scania N113 double-deck bus	22
MAN Optare Vecta single-deck bus	44
Dennis Dart SLF Plaxton single-deck bus	59
Mercedes-Benz Optare Prisma single-deck bus	26
Volvo B10M/B10BLE single-deck bus	30
DAF SB120 single-deck bus	21
DAF SB220 single-deck bus	83
DAF SB200 single-deck bus	3

DAF SB3000 Plaxton single-deck coach	14
Scania L113 single-deck bus	18
Dennis MPD single-deck bus	87
Mercedes-Benz 814D single-deck midibus	27
Optare Metrorider single-deck midibus	96
Scania Omnicity	19

Middlesbrough-Teesside
Other operators
Current situation
Go-Ahead Northern, Go North East and Stagecoach run services into Teesside. Other independents include Jayline of Horden and Procters of Leeming.

Northern Rail Ltd
Station Rise, York YO1 6HT, UK
Tel: (+44 870) 000 51 51
Web: www.northernrail.org

Key personnel
Managing Director: Heidi Mottram

Type of operation: Local railway

Current situation
Local diesel trains run hourly/half-hourly on four routes radiating from Middlesbrough.

Developments
In 2006, Northern Rail Ltd replaced its previous APTIS system with a new ticketing system from Cubic Transportation Systems Ltd, known as FasTIS. Northern Rail installed and integrated 216 new FasTIS units at its 152 staffed stations over its operating area, as well as at its two training academies.

Newcastle Upon Tyne
Population: Newcastle 259,000, Tyne & Wear metropolitan area 1.1 million (estimates)

Public transport
Main city services and longer distance routes operated by private companies. Metro and ferry services operated by Passenger Transport Executive (Nexus), which also subsidises one of the three local rail services. The PTE area covers surrounding urban areas of Tyne & Wear (including Gateshead and Sunderland) as well as Newcastle itself.

Eight tram routes and a guided bus route have been proposed for the Newcastle area, serving Cramlington, Walbottle, Team Valley, Bensham, Washington, Sunderland, South Shields, Shiremoor and Percy Main are being progressed.

The UK Department for Transport announced in 2006 the funding of improvements to Eldon Square Bus Station.

Stagecoach North East
Wheatsheaf, Sunderland SR5 1AQ, UK
Tel: (+44 191) 567 52 51
Fax: (+44 191) 566 02 02
e-mail: info.northeast@stagecoachbus.com
Web: www.stagecoachbus.com

Key personnel
Managing Director: John Conroy
Operations Director: Nigel Winter
Engineering Director: David Kirsopp
Commercial Director: Robin Knight
  Staff: 1,600

Current situation
Stagecoach North East is formed of two limited companies, Busways Travel Services and Cleveland Transit. Both companies are former local authority municipally run operations, Busways Travel Services being the former Tyne &

Stagecoach Busways Alexander Enviro400 on route 63 in Newcastle Upon Tyne (Stephen Morris)
1198743

Wear PTE bus operation and Cleveland Transit being formed from former local authority-owned bus companies in the Tees Valley. Stagecoach North East is one of 19 operating units which form the Stagecoach UK Bus Division and is a subsidiary of Stagecoach Group PLC, Perth Scotland.

Stagecoach North East provides mainly urban local bus services in Tyne & Wear and the Tees Valley, serving a population of over 1 million.

Developments
A total of 50 Alexander Dennis Trident ENVIRO 400 double deck buses entered service in 2007 operating on Superoutes 62/63 and 39/40 in Newcastle.

Bus
Passenger journeys: (Local services)
(2005/06) 83 million
(2006/07) 85 million
Vehicle-km: (2005/06) 40.5 million
(2006/07) 40.2 million

Number of routes: 146
Route length: 2,050 km (buses)
Average route length: 14 km
On priority right-of-way: 7 km

Fleet: 528 vehicles
Double-deck	75
Single-deck	283
Midibus	161

Minibus	9
Bodies:	
Alexander	439
Jonckheere	1
Northern Counties	48
Plaxton	30
Designline	10

Most intensive service: 5 min

One-person operation: 100 per cent

Fare collection: ERGsystem4000 and Wayfarer machines for pre-purchase or on-bus purchase of own account MegaRider tickets and inter-operator Travelcards

Fare structure: Graduated for first 5 km then zonal. Limited through-ticketing with suburban rail and metro. Some bus-to-bus through-ticketing within the company. Travelcards for groups of zones and MegaRiders for geographic areas.

Operational Control: Radio/mobile inspectors

Integration with other modes: Partial integration with metro

Average peak-hour speed: In mixed traffic, 19.8 km/h

Operating costs financed by: Fares 95.8 per cent, contract service subsidy 4.2 per cent

Subsidy from: Tyne and Wear PTE and other local authorities for contracted services

New vehicles financed by: Leasing or direct purchase

Go North East

117 Queen Street, Gateshead, Tyne & Wear NE8 2UA, UK
Tel: (+44 191) 420 50 50   Fax: (+44 191) 420 02 25
Web: www.simplygo.com

Key personnel

Managing Director: Peter Huntley
   Staff: 1,962

Current situation

Operates services in Tyne & Wear, County Durham and parts of Cleveland and Northumberland. Also operates a network of limited-stop, regional and commuter services and local minibus networks.

Developments

Under new Managing Director Peter Huntley, Go North East has, since early 2006, undertaken a comprehensive network review.

As a result, the company launched a variety of new services and introduced individual branding on several routes. Services such as the 'Fab 56', the 10/11 'Blaydon Racers', the 26/36 'Black Cats' and the 309 'Cobalt Clipper' all use modern, high-specification, low-floor buses decorated in dedicated liveries, making them easily recognisable for passengers. The company has also taken delivery of nine high-specification, single-deck Mercedes-Benz Citaro buses in early 2007. These are route branded for the X2 'Red Arrows' service linking Sunderland to Newcastle via Washington and Gateshead.

Bus

Passenger journeys: (2003/04) 73.1 million
(2004/05) 73.2 million
(2005/06) 69.1 million
(2006/07) 69.3 million
(2007/08) 70.1 million
Vehicle-km: (2003/04) 60.3 million
(2004/05) 60 million
(2005/06) 57 million
(2006/07) 54.3 million
(2007/08) 55.2 million

Fleet: 668 vehicles

Double-deck bus	131
Single-deck bus	384
Coach	18

Go North East Wrightbus-bodies single-deck buses in dedicated liveries   1326983

Articulated bus	4
Minibus	131
Chassis	
DAF	64
Dennis	204
Leyland	21
Mercedes-Benz	53
Optare	14
Scania	137
Transbus	29
Volvo	146
Bodies	
Alexander	18
East Lancs	30
Marshall	17
Mercedes-Benz	53
Northern Counties	92
Optare	17
Plaxton	121
Scania	41
Transbus	70
Wright	187
Caetano	22

In peak service: 562

One-person operation: 100 per cent

Fare collection: Payment to driver or pre-purchased from bus shops, pay point, by telephone or website. Wayfarer 3 system with magnetic card reader capability; stored-value magnetic tickets

Operational control: All vehicles are radio fitted. AVL satellite tracking implemented in Gateshead and County Durham.

Integration with other modes: Extensive integration continues with Metro and Shields ferry

Operating costs financed by: Fares 93 per cent, subsidy/grants seven per cent

New vehicles financed by: Internal resources and Kick Start funding

Arriva North East

Arriva North East
Admiral Way, Doxford International Business Park, Sunderland, Tyne and Wear SR3 3XP, UK
Tel: (+44 191) 520 42 00   Fax: (+44 191) 420 42 22
Web: www.arrivabus.co.uk

Key personnel

Managing Director: Jonathan May
Engineering Director: John Greaves
Director of Service Delivery: Iain McInroy
Finance Director: Dave Barry
Commercial Director: Liz Esnouf
   Staff: Not available currently

Subsidiaries

Arriva Durham County
Arriva Tees and District
Arriva Teesside
Arriva Northumbria

Current situation

Most Arriva Northumbria routes run into Newcastle from outside the city, but a sizable network has been developed in the northern suburbs and new developing areas.

Both Arriva Tees, District and Arriva Teesside operate local and interurban services across Teesside and Cleveland. Arriva Durham County operates in Durham City (to the south of Newcastle) and the east of the county. Other services are operated on a regional basis.

The companies, as subsidiaries, became part of the Arriva group in 1996 and are managed as part of the Arriva North East Division.

Fleet: 569 vehicles

Leyland/Volvo Olympian double-deck bus	27
Volvo B7TL double-deck bus	2
DAF SDB250 double-deck bus	19
Dennis Trident ALX 400 double-deck bus	20
Scania N113 double-deck bus	22
MAN Optare Vecta single-deck bus	34
Dennis Dart SLF Plaxton single-deck bus	60
Mercedes-Benz Optare Prisma single-deck bus	23
Volvo B10M/B10BLE single-deck bus	30
DAF SB120 single-deck bus	21
DAF SB220 single-deck bus	65
DAF SB200 single-deck bus	3
DAF SB3000 Plaxton single-deck coach	14
Scania L113 single-deck bus	18
ADL MPD single-deck bus	87
Mercedes-Benz 814D single-deck midibus	26
Optare Metrorider single-deck midibus	28
Optare Solo single-deck midibus	51

In peak service: Not available currently
On order: Not available currently

Newcastle Upon Tyne

Other operators
Current situation

A few smaller companies operate both commercial and secured routes in Newcastle and the surrounding Tyne and Wear County. These include A-Line Coaches, Derwent Coaches and Redby of Sunderland.

Nexus

Nexus House, Saint James's Boulevard, Newcastle
upon Tyne NE1 4AX, UK
Tel: (+44 191) 203 33 33
Fax: (+44 191) 203 31 80
Web: www.tyneandwearmetro.co.uk,
   www.nexus.org.uk

Key personnel

Director General: Bernard Garner
Director of Rail & Infrastructure: Ken Mackay
Communications Director: Andrew H Bairstow
Human Resources Director: David Bartlett

Current situation

Nexus is the Tyne and Wear Passenger Transport
Executive and administers funds on behalf
of the Tyne and Wear Passenger Transport
Authority (PTA). It carries out the policies of
the PTA, and provides policy advice to the PTA
and the district councils on transport matters.
It also operates Metro and the Shields Ferry
service and manages bus stations in Tyne and
Wear.

Since deregulation, the former policy of
integration between bus and metro has had to be
promoted on a commercial basis with additional
metro feeder services secured by Nexus. There
remains a high level of bus/metro interchange,
with 23 per cent of passengers arriving at
stations by bus; 30 per cent of passengers use
Travelcards.

Although Nexus no longer operates buses, it
secures socially necessary services not provided
by commercial operators, and is involved in
management of some bus stations on behalf of
the local authorities which own them.

Quaylink is a Nexus-supported electric bus
service linking the Quayside area and the city
centres of Newcastle and Gateshead. It was
launched in 2005, using 10 diesel-electric hybrid
buses. The Designline Olymbus buses, built in
New Zealand, provide a 7-day frequent service
from 07.00 to 24.00. Funding was provided by the
UK Government Department for Transport and
Newcastle and Gateshead councils.

In Tyne and Wear, 75 per cent of pensioners
own a Concessionary Travel (CT) pass, against a
national average of 49 per cent. CT pass holders
made 36.2 million journeys in 2005/6 and this
is expected to rise now travel is free. Tyne and
Wear Passenger Transport Authority and Nexus
provide travel concessions for Tyne and Wear
residents aged 60 years and over and people
with certain types of disability.

Nexus TaxiLink is a specialised service for
residents of Tyne and Wear who are elderly or
disabled. It was launched in July 2006 to replace
the previous Care Service network.

Developments

Nexus has secured a GBP350 million
commitment from the UK Government to invest
in the next phase of renewal and modernisation
for the Tyne and Wear Metro over the next
10 years. It has also made a commitment to
underwrite the operating costs of Metro up to
2019.

Nexus's Metro Re-Invigoration plans are split
into three phases. Phase 1, already under way,
comprises more than GBP50 million investment,
including: new ticket machines and barriers; a
new station at Simonside (opened March 2008),
rebuilding of Haymarket and refurbishment of
Sunderland stations, and the overhaul of some
bridges and tunnels.

Phase 2 will start in April 2010 and last
nine years. It will include the modernisation
of stations, new communications system to
manage train movements, modernisation of
overhead power lines, plus other infrastructure
and technology, the overhaul of many bridges
and tunnels up to 160 years old, and the
complete refurbishment of the 90 Metrocars
that make up the train fleet.

Phase 3 will start in 2019, following further
negotiations with the UK Government. It will
see up to a further GBP300 million invested,
principally in a new fleet of Metrocars and

*There are two QuayLink routes, serving Haymarket, Monument, Quayside, Central Station,
Monument, The Sage Gateshead, BALTIC and Gateshead Interchange. They are operated with these
Designline hybrid diesel/battery single deck buses*   1229520

*Northumberland Park, a new Metro station at Backworth near Whitley Bay has 60-space park-&-ride
facility and serves around 1,500 nearby homes*   1341041

a new signalling system to manage them.
There will be further investment in ticket
machines, track, overhead lines, structures and
stations.

The GBP20 million redevelopment of
Haymarket Metro station is continuing and is
scheduled to be completed in July 2009. A four-
storey glass and steel building will rise above
the existing station, providing a new gateway to
the Northumberland Street shopping area and
university quarter for six million passengers
every year. The new building will feature shops,
a bar-restaurant and offices. GBP 5 million of
the total cost will go towards building a new
improved station area for Metro passengers,
including new escalators. Both of the station's
platforms are being refurbished, with new
floors, walls and ceilings to enhance the waiting
area.

Metro's 60th station, costing GBP3.2 million,
opened at Simonside in South Tyneside in March
2008. The station serves a large residential area
offering five trains in each direction per hour
during the day direct to South Shields town
centre, Gateshead and Newcastle. Metro is
expected to greatly improve public transport

links within Simonside, which is designed as a
wayside halt station.

Nexus has now secured GBP13 million of
government funding to replace its 249 ticket
machines with more modern machines that
accept bank notes and credit and debit card
payments. The money will also be used to
install electronic barriers, similar to those on
the London Underground, at 13 key stations –
Airport, Central, Gateshead, Haymarket, Heworth,
Jesmond, Manors, Monument, North Shields,
South Gosforth, South Shields, St James and
Wallsend. The project is expected to be completed
in early 2010.

Building work started on a new 400-space
multistorey car park for Northumberland Park
Metro station. The new car park marks the final
phase of development work at the station,
which has been used by more than a million
passengers since it opened in December 2005.
It will meet current and future demand for park-
and-ride at the station, close to the junction
of the A19 and A186 Earsdon Road in North
Tyneside.

Work has started on a GBP6.9 million 'facelift'
for Sunderland station platforms, funded

entirely by Nexus. The two-year project will see an escalator installed from the concourse above for the first time, new floors, ceilings, walls and waiting areas with a new lighting scheme to improve the ambience.

Nexus is hoping to make around 200,000 more taxi journeys available for people with mobility problems, while making it easier for passengers to book at short notice when they want to travel. The change, planned for September 2008, will see members of the existing TaxiLink scheme able to book journeys directly with a large number of taxi operators. Nexus would then pay for up to GBP2.50 of every journey from a new smart 'TaxiCard' – members and their travel companions would pay the first GBP1.50 plus any amount over a total of GBP4.00. Nexus predict the change will mean the number of mobility taxi journeys made in Tyne and Wear will rise from 125,000 to 320,000 each year. Nexus is also introducing a Carers Card – for scheme members initially – allowing a companion to travel with them free on conventional public transport.

Metro

Type of operation: Full metro, first line opened 1980

Passenger journeys: (2005/06) 35.8 million
(2006/07) 37.9 million
(2007/08) 39.8 million

Route length: 77.5 km
    in tunnel: 7.1 km
Number of lines: 2
Number of stations: 60
Gauge: 1,435 mm
Track: BS113A rail laid on tied concrete sleepers in tunnels; on concrete and timber sleepers with ballast on surface; PACT slab track on Byker Viaduct
Max gradient: 3.3%
Minimum curve radius: 210 m
Electrification: 1.5 kV DC, overhead

Current situation
Operates LRVs on reserved track in tunnel in central area and serving north, east and southern area of city. It runs partly on former heavy suburban rail alignments.

Rolling stock: 90 cars
Metro-Cammell (1979/80)   M90

Service: 7/8–10–15 min
First/last train: 05.22/00.14
Fare structure: Zonal
Integration with other modes: High level of integration; county-wide Travelticket, plus substantial multimodal single through-ticket network (Metrolink Transfares); through-ticketing to airport from rail stations nationwide
Fare collection: Crouzet automatic ticket vending machines; roving inspectors
Signalling: Two-aspect lineside signals with repeaters; inductive train stop equipment to prevent over-running signals; CSEE Automatic Route Setting
Operating costs financed by: Fares 84 per cent, grants from central and local government, and European Social Fund 16 per cent

Ferry

Passenger journeys: (2005/06) 449,500 (estimate)
(2006/07) 463,000
(2007/08) 474,000

Current situation
Cross-Tyne ferry operations by Nexus between North and South Shields. There is a half-hourly service; journey time is 7 minutes; two vessels.

Northern Rail Ltd

Northern House, 9 Rougier Street, York YO1 6HZ, UK
e-mail: customer.relations@northernrail.org
Web: www.northernrail.org

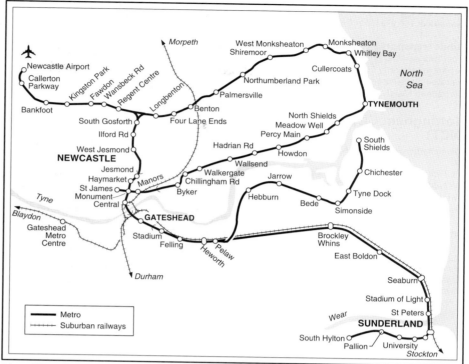
Map of Tyne & Wear rail network   1040982

Ferry service between North Shields and South Shields operated by Nexus   1341040

Key personnel
Managing Director: Heidi Mottram
    Staff: 4,500

Type of operation: Local railway

Passenger journeys (whole network): (2007) 78.3 million

Current situation
Northern Rail Ltd is a joint-venture company set up in 2004, and brings together the management operations from parent organisations Serco Group and NedRailways. Serco is a global public service company and is expanding its partnering of contracts on behalf of government. NedRailways is a wholly owned subsidiary of Dutch Railways (NS). Besides fleet maintenance and operational planning and timetabling, NS develops and operates station hubs and retail facilities. NS also has a leading role in developing integrated transport solutions.

Diesel service operated on three routes totalling 82 km. Newcastle-Sunderland line (every 15 minutes) receives Section 20 grant payments from Nexus, carrying 2.1 million passengers in 1997. Services also run to Gateshead Metro Centre (every 15 minutes), and to Hexham on the line to Carlisle (about half-hourly), and to Morpeth (irregular).

For further information on Northern Rail Ltd, please see *Jane's World Railways.*

Developments
The UK Department for Transport announced in 2007 that more carriages would be provided for Newcastle suburban services. The announcement is part of the government's plans to ensure that the national rail network can carry at least 180 million more passengers a year.

Nottingham

Population: 266,995 (2001 Census)

Public transport

Most bus services in city and suburbs provided by part-municipally owned company, with others operated by private firms. Local rail service; light rail opened March 2004.

Nottingham City Transport (NCT)

Lower Parliament Street, Nottingham NG1 1GG, UK

Tel: (+44 115) 950 57 45   Fax: (+44 115) 950 44 25
Tel: (+44 115) 950 60 70 (NCT Travel Centre)
e-mail: travelcentre@nctx.co.uk
Web: www.nctx.co.uk

Key personnel

Managing Director: Mark Fowles
Engineering Director: Barry Baxter
Finance Director: Rob Hicklin
Human Resources Director: Mick Leafe
Marketing and Communications Director:
  Nicola Tidy
  Staff: 1,200

Current situation

The city established its bus undertaking as a separate company in 1986. The fleet of South Notts of Gotham was acquired and integrated in 1991. Pathfinder of Newark was acquired in 1997, which opened up long-distance mini-coach operations for the company.

In October 2001, the city transport network was altered, with cross-city links replaced to improve punctuality and performance. A new 'Go2' network guarantees a low-floor bus every ten minutes or better on the 15 key corridors into Nottingham. A colour-coded livery was introduced across the network and has been applied to the Go2 and Nottingham Network services.

Nottingham City Transport (NCT) is a member of the Arrow Light Rail consortium, which was awarded the design/build/operate contract for Nottingham Express Transit (NET). In order to raise the equity the company needed to put into the consortium. In early 2000 it sold an 18 per cent stake to Transdev, the French conglomerate, which is another of the consortium partners. NET opened in March 2004. All NCT services have been planned to feed and integrate with the NET tram timetable.

Developments

NCT took delivery of 36 buses – 16 double-deck and 20 Optare Versa single-deck – in 2008. The Pathfinder 100 was the first route to receive the Optare Versa, following successful trials in 2007, which received favourable passenger feedback. The new buses were specified for the Pathfinder 100 route and include leather seats, air conditioning, CCTV, real-time tracking equipment, a bay for wheelchairs and pushchairs and a greater seating capacity to accommodate additional passengers.

The new buses have been introduced on Pathfinder 100 following the opening of the A612 Gedling bus-only Bus Plug, which has significantly reduced journey times into Nottingham and generated ten per cent patronage growth on the route in the past year.

To compliment the new bus investment, Nottinghamshire County Council, through the Greater Nottingham Transport Plan, committed GBP250,000 in 2008/09 to improve passenger infrastructure along the A612 corridor. This included new bus shelters and improved timetable information. It was expected that real-time bus information would be installed at key stops in 2009.

Go2 Night, Nottingham City Transport's late night weekend buses, celebrated their first birthday in December 2008 with a 104 per cent increase in passenger numbers compared to NCT's old night bus services. Launched in December 2007, the eight Go2 Night routes leave the City Centre at 01:15, 02:15 and 03:15

trentbarton have used high specification café style interiors featuring leather seats, air conditioning and wood effect floors to attract new business
1345338

every Friday and Saturday night, and carried 45,000 passengers in their first year.

In 2008, NCT improved bus services to the University of Nottingham. Branded Unilink, the new Unilink 34 was reported as one of NCT's top ten growth routes, carrying nearly 100,000 more passengers in the last financial year (2007/08), an increase of nearly 46 per cent compared to the previous year.

Bus

Number of routes: 100
Route length: (One way) 284 km

Fleet: 328 vehicles

Dennis Dart/Northern Counties single-deck	1
Dennis Trident/East Lancs low-floor double-deck	54
Optare Excel low-floor single-deck	23
Optare Solo low-floor	87
Scania L113/Northern Counties single-deck	1
Scania L94 Omnicity low-floor single-deck	44
Scania L94/Wright low-floor articulated single-deck	5
Scania L94 OmniDekka low-floor double-deck	75
Scania L94 OmniTown low-floor single-deck	7
Scania N113/Alexander single-deck	1
Volvo B10B/Plaxton single-deck	2
Volvo Olympian/East Lancs double-deck	27
Volvo B10M/Northern Counties	1

Most intensive service: 2½–5 min
One-person operation: 100 per cent
Fare collection: Farebox, Eurofare and smartcard
Fare structure: Stage; one, two and four-week, three and six month, annual network passes; day tickets, non-consecutive-day travelcards
Fare evasion control: Uniformed inspectors, customer service auditors
Operational control: Route inspectors/mobile radio
Arrangements for elderly/disabled: Half-fare travel before 09.30, then free travel on all services to close of normal operations
Average distance between stops: 200–250 m
Average peak-hour speed: 15 km/h
Bus priority: City-centre access priority by sections of bus-only road; 24-hour and part-time bus lanes

trentbarton

Mansfield Road, Heanor, Derbyshire, DE75 7BG, UK

Tel: (+44 1773) 71 22 65 (customer services)
(+44 1773) 53 63 36 (office)
Fax: (+44 1773) 53 63 33
e-mail: enquiries@trentbarton.co.uk
Web: www.trentbarton.co.uk

Fresh from refurbishment, despite being less than five years old, this coach operates on the company's flagship red arrow route non stop between Nottingham and Derby
1345339

Key personnel

Managing Director: Brian King
Commercial Director: Ian Morgan
Financial Director: Graham Sutton
Director of Service Delivery: Jeff Counsel
Commercial Manager: Mark Greasley
Head of Development: Keith Shayshutt
  Staff: 922

Current situation

trentbarton operates rural and interurban bus routes from bases in Nottingham and surrounding towns.

trentbarton has won the UK Bus Operator of the Year three times and was twice runner-up. The average age of the fleet is less than 5 years, making it one of the youngest bus fleets in the UK. Patronage on all main routes continues to grow.

Fleet: 280 vehicles

Optare Excel low-floor single-deck	52
Dennis Dart SLF/Plaxton low-floor single-deck	38
Optare Solo low-floor minibus	64
Volvo B10M/Plaxton coach	8
Optare Tempo single-deck	18
Scania L94UB/Wrightbus Solar low-floor single-deck	92
Scania/Irizar coach	8

Nottingham

Other operators

Current situation

Dunn Line Holdings of Basford, runs tendered local services, while Stagecoach runs long-distance services into the city. Paul James Coaches, Coalville operates a stage carriage service between Nottingham and Corby.

Nottingham Community Transport operates accessible services from its Sherwood base in Nottingham. Nottingham City Council operates a fleet of small buses, Optare Solo low-floor buses, for users attending day-centres and other venues within the city.

East Midlands Trains Limited

8th Floor, Friars Bridge Court, 41-45 Blackfriars Road, London SE1 8NZ, UK
Tel: (+44 207) 983 61 99
Web: www.eastmidlandstrains.co.uk

Key personnel

Project Manager: Chris Elliott
   Staff: Not available currently

Type of operation: Local railway

Current situation

East Midlands Trains, operated by Stagecoach, runs high-speed long distance services from St Pancras London to Sheffield, Derby and Nottingham and regional services between Nottingham and Derby – Lincoln – Cleethorpes – Skegness, and between Derby and Crewe – Matlock and Norwich and Liverpool.

The franchise started on 11 November 2007 and will run until 31 March 2015, the last year and four months of which will be conditional upon achieving pre-set performance targets.

Developments

A refurbishment of East Midlands Trains' Class 158 trains was started in 2008. The work was be carried out in Derby by Delta Rail. The full refurbishment programme will see all 25 of the company's Class 158 trains going through a complete overhaul. It is expected to be completed by 2010.

The work includes: repainting in the new East Midlands Trains livery; internal refurbishment of every train, which includes improvements to seating design and capacity. In addition, a new toilet area will be included as part of the refurbishment programme; modification to various systems on the train to bring improved reliability; improved air conditioning units fitted to the majority of these trains to improve the reliability and efficiency; introduction of CCTV on every train; installation of a passenger counting device that allows passenger flows to be monitored.

A new timetable was introduced in 2008 with faster journey times to London and Sunday services on the Robin Hood Line, Nottingham, for the first time since the 1960s. This offers a direct link between Mansfield, Nottingham and Worksop and is a result of a partnership with local authorities, including Nottinghamshire County Council, who have long campaigned for this new service.

A new Derby/Nottingham – Matlock service will see an increase in the number of trains between the two cities.

Nottingham Express Transit (NET)

Nottingham Express Transit (NET) Project Team Lawrence House, Talbot Street, Nottingham NG1 5NT, UK
Tel: (+44 115) 915 66 00   Fax: (+44 115) 915 60 92
Web: www.nottinghamexpresstransit.com;   www.thetram.net

Key personnel

Project Leader: Pat Armstrong

Type of operation: Light rail, opened March 2004

Passenger journeys: (2004/05) 8.4 million (2005/06) 9.7 million (2006/07) 10.1 million

Number of lines: 1
Number of stations: 23 (including six with park-and-ride facilities)

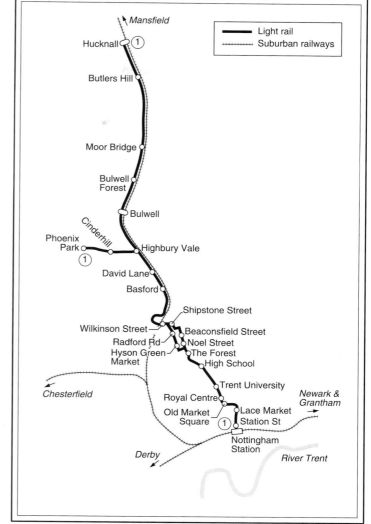

Map of Nottingham's light rail and suburban lines
0567840

NET LRV to Hucknall runs alongside the Robin Hood railway near Bulwell (Roger Carvell)   0585196

Gauge: 1,467 mm
Electrification: 600 V overhead

Background

In 1995 a private-sector consortium, consisting of manufacturer Adtranz (now Bombardier Transportation), civil contractor Tarmac (now Carillion) and operators Transdev and Nottingham City Transport, joined the promoters to develop the project. Now known as the Arrow Consortium, this group was awarded a 30.5-year concession to design, build, operate and maintain the line in 1997.

Transdev is also a shareholding partner with the local authority in Nottingham City Transport and the bus operation has been tailored to integrate with the trams. The operator of NET Line One is the Nottingham Tram Consortium.

Current situation

NET Line One runs from Hucknall, through Bulwell, Basford and Hyson Green before reaching the city centre and terminating at Nottingham railway station. There is also a spur to a park-and-ride site just off the M1 (Junction 26) at Phoenix Park.

Each tram carries 200 passengers and has a top speed of 80 km/h.

Fare collection is with conductors, who also assist passengers. The driver retains control of the doors as the cab is fitted with CCTV enabling the side of each vehicle to be viewed.

Tram passenger figures continued to rise during 2004/2005 and, as a result, trams were retimed at the beginning of 2005 to run every 5 minutes. The new services run between 07.15 and 09.30 in the morning and between

15.00 and 18.30 in the evening, to cater for the exceptional patronage seen at these times. This requires the use of 13 trams, up from the current 11 in service. NET has 15 trams, one of which is used as a spare and one other is usually in maintenance.

In October 2005, weekend frequencies were improved with services operating every 7–8 minutes between 10.30 and 18.00.

The second annual survey carried out by the Consortium showed that 98 per cent of those questioned would recommend the tram to friends and family and 80 per cent would like to see NET extend to further routes.

Over 30 per cent of passengers use Park & Ride.

Developments

The NET development team are currently working on proposals for extensions to Clifton via Wilford, and to Chilwell via Beeston and the QMC. These are collectively known as NET Phase Two. The UK Government has confirmed its intention to financially support the NET Phase Two tram project by approving the entry of the project into the Department for Transport's (DfT) Local Authority Major Schemes Programme.

A Transport and Works Act Order (TWAO) application into the NET Phase Two proposals was submitted to the Department for Transport on 26 April 2007. A Public Inquiry was held in November and December 2007 and the Secretary of State for Transport is likely to make a decision on the TWAO at the beginning of 2009.

Subject to the Secretary of State's decision, a competitive tendering process would commence during which private companies would bid for the work of building and running the expanded NET system. Following that, construction works could begin in early 2010 with the new extensions up and running in early 2013.

Fleet: 15 Bombardier Incentro five-section articulated tramcars

Revenue control: Roving conductors
Arrangements for elderly/disabled:
All stops are accessible

Sheffield
Population: City 516,100 (2004 estimate)

Public transport
Bus services operated by private companies. Light rail system owned by Passenger Transport Executive with operation franchised to a private company. The PTE, whose authority covers the surrounding urban areas of Doncaster, Rotherham, Barnsley and others, also contracts for provision of rail services. A new station for Robin Hood Doncaster-Sheffield airport at Finningley is to be built on the Doncaster-Lincoln line. This was announced in 2006.

A ten-year programme of transport improvements, which aims to tackle congestion, improve safety and invest in public transport, was announced for the Yorkshire and the Humber region in 2006. The programme includes the go-ahead for the Yorcard smartcard pilot in South Yorkshire, which will mean that smartcards on bus and rail journeys will be enjoyed by travellers on selected routes in South Yorkshire from 2007.

Developments
A GBP15 million quality bus corridor in Doncaster is being constructed. The UK Department for Transport gave the go-ahead for the scheme in 2006. It consists of new bus lanes on the A638 northern and southern approaches to Doncaster, including a stretch of dedicated busway and two new park-and-ride car parks which will be served by existing bus services. It is due to be completed by March 2008. The scheme is promoted jointly by Doncaster Metropolitan Borough Council and the South Yorkshire Passenger Transport Executive.

First South Yorkshire
Midland Road Depot, Midland Road, Rotherham S61 1TF, UK
Tel: (+44 1709) 56 60 00
Fax: (+44 1709) 56 60 63
Web: www.firstgroup.com

Key personnel
Managing Director: Gary Nolan
Operations Director: D Hajdukiowicz
Commercial Director: Brandon Jones
Engineering Director: John Clayton
Finance Director: Martin Wilson
Regional Divisional Engineering Director: Mark Hagreaves
Regional Divisional Commercial Director: Barbara Bedford
Staff: 2,019

Current situation
Operates local bus services in the Sheffield area, including Sheffield Overground high-frequency network offering regular frequencies of 10 minutes or better on 13 cross-city corridor routes.

Developments
A guided bus scheme is proposed for two major roads, and trials have taken place on a short test track at the Rotherham garage.

Bus
Passenger journeys: (1997/98) 93 million
Vehicle-km: (1997/98) 57 million

Number of routes: 300
Route length: 1,000 km
On priority right-of-way: 3 km

Fleet: 629 vehicles	
Volvo Olympian/Northern Counties	12
Volvo Olympian/Alexander	3
Dennis Dominator/Alexander double-deck	80
Dennis Dominator/Northern Counties double-deck	1
Dennis Dominator/East Lancs double-deck	1
Volvo B7TL/Alexander low-floor double-deck	31
Volvo B7TL/Wright low-floor double-deck	18
Volvo B10M/Alexander single-deck	160
Volvo B6/Alexander single-deck	2
Dennis Dart SLF/Plaxton low-floor single-deck	31
Volvo B10BLE/Wright low-floor single-deck	84
Volvo B7L/Wright low-floor single-deck	63
Dennis Dart/Plaxton midibus	17
Volvo B6/Plaxton midibus	31
Volvo B6BLE/Wright low-floor midibus	16
Mercedes-Benz 709D/Plaxton minibus	14
Mercedes-Benz 709D/Reeves Burgess minibus	10
Mercedes-Benz 811D/Plaxton minibus	2
Mercedes-Benz 811D/Carlyle minibus	7
Mercedes-Benz O814/Plaxton minibus	16
Optare Solo low-floor minibus	10
Scania/Wright single-deck	12
Dennis Dart/Wright Handybus single-deck	8
In peak service: 563	

Most intensive service: 5 min
One-person operation: 100 per cent
Fare collection: Wayfarer equipment; passes
Fare structure: Stage; all system and area passes
Fare evasion control: Inspectors
Arrangements for elderly/disabled: SYPTE concessionary flat fare; services for the disabled in Sheffield and Doncaster with specially adapted vehicles
Average distance between stops: 250 m
Average peak-hour speed: 16 km/h

Stagecoach Sheffield
Green Lane Depot, Ecclesfield, Sheffield S35 9WY, UK
Tel: (+44 114) 246 55 55   Fax: (+44 114) 257 03 43
Web: www.stagecoachbus.com

Key personnel
Managing Director: Paul Lynch
General Manager: Paul Payne
Engineering Manager: Steve Jowitt
Operations Manager: Ray Taylor
Staff: 250

Background
Established in 1986, Andrews (Sheffield) was bought by Yorkshire Traction in 1992. Sheffield Omnibus was acquired by YT in 1995, as was South Riding (a third independent), and operations were combined, trading as Andrews Sheffield Omnibus. In January 1998 Yorkshire Terrier was merged with Andrews, and the enlarged company traded as Yorkshire Terrier.

Current situation
The company operated as a subsidiary of the Yorkshire Traction Group until it, along with Yorkshire Traction, was absorbed by the Stagecoach Group in 2006 and now trades as Stagecoach Sheffield.

Developments
An integrated bus-tram network has been launched in Sheffield, following the acquisition of Traction Group by Stagecoach, supplementing the tram services with buses and interavailability of the Dayrider and weekly Megarider tickets to include former bus and tram.

Bus
Number of routes: 14 (plus school bus routes)

Fleet: 109 vehicles	
MCW Metrobus double-deck	12
Volvo B6/Alexander single-deck	24
Volvo B6LE/Plaxton low-floor single-deck	1
Dennis Dart SLF/East Lancs low-floor single-deck	28
DAF SB220/East Lancs low-floor single-deck	11
Optare Solo low-floor minibus	9
MCW midibus	1
In peak service: 90	

Sheffield
Other operators
Current situation
Local bus services are provided by Mass Leon, Finningley. Ladyline of Rawmarsh and John Powell Travel of Rotherham also provide local bus services.

South Yorkshire Passenger Transport Executive (SYPTE)
PO Box 801, Exchange Street, Sheffield S2 5YT, UK
Tel: (+44 114) 276 75 75,   Fax: (+44 114) 275 99 08
e-mail: comments@sypte.co.uk
Web: www.sypte.co.uk

Key personnel
Director General: David Brown
Staff: 360

Current situation
Financial resources are raised by a levy on local authorities of Barnsley, Doncaster, Rotherham and Sheffield, which also receive some government revenue support grant for transport. The Passenger Transport Authority (PTA), which is a joint undertaking comprising 12 local authority representatives, is responsible for collecting the levy and determining policy. The PTE is the managing agency.

Concessionary fares for children, elderly and disabled people are funded by the PTE, which is also the administrative and marketing agency for a wide range of countywide prepaid daily, weekly, monthly and annual travelcards and carnets on behalf of local bus and rail operators.

The PTE owns most of the bus infrastructure, and a major investment programme has provided multimodal interchanges in Doncaster, Sheffield, Meadowhall and Barnsley. It also contracts with Northern Rail to provide local rail services (see below). Travel information and a chain of travel information centres is also provided. The PTE also owns the Supertram light rail system which was completed in 1995.

Developments

Studies into Bus Rapid Transit are being pursued, following Government rejection of plans to extend the Supertram network. The Penistone to Sheffield Rail line has now been identified for a tram-train pilot commencing in 2010.

Following the 2007/08 Business Plan, SYPTE reports signs of continued growth across the county's transport network. Sheffield's new Free-Bee bus service is carrying 9,000 people a week, well in excess of its target of 5,000. In Barnsley the new Interchange provides a gateway to the town and a focus for the Remaking Barnsley programme. SYPTE is working with the regeneration teams in Rotherham to integrate improved transport infrastructure as part of the town's renaissance and delivering modern, attractive infrastructure across the South Yorkshire centres. The rail station in Doncaster is complete providing links to the Transport Interchange, Frenchgate Centre and Town Centre.

Contracted rail
Operated by:

Northern Rail Ltd

Northern House, 9 Rougier Street, York YO1 6HZ, UK
e-mail: customer.relations@northernrail.org
Web: www.northernrail.org

Key personnel
Managing Director: Heidi Mottram

Type of operation: Local rail

Current situation
Operates several suburban/interurban services in the PTE area, of which several routes from Sheffield are financially supported by the PTE. These are:
- Sheffield-Barnsley-Darton (en-route to Leeds);
- Sheffield-Barnsley-Penistone (en-route to Huddersfield);
- Sheffield-Doncaster-Thorne North (en-route to Hull);
- Sheffield-Kiveton Park (en-route to Worksop/Lincoln);
- Sheffield-Rotherham-Thurnscoe (en-route to Leeds);
- Sheffield-Doncaster-Thorne South (en-route to Scunthorpe);
- Sheffield-Dore (en-route to Manchester);
- Doncaster-Adwick (en-route to Leeds).

These total 215 km and serve 29 stations. Since 1992, the PTE has also made a financial contribution to maintain an hourly service between Doncaster and Scunthorpe. The PTE specifies service levels on these routes and some fares.

Contracted bus
Current situation
Several bus operators competing in the Sheffield area in a free market. The PTE finances those socially valuable services not provided by this market.

Stagecoach Supertram

Nunnery Depot, Woodburn Road, Sheffield S9 3LS, UK
Tel: (+44 114) 275 98 88   Fax: (+44 114) 279 81 20
e-mail: enquiries@supertram.com
Web: www.supertram.com

Key personnel
Managing Director: A Morris
Staff: 250

Type of operation: Light rail, opened 1994

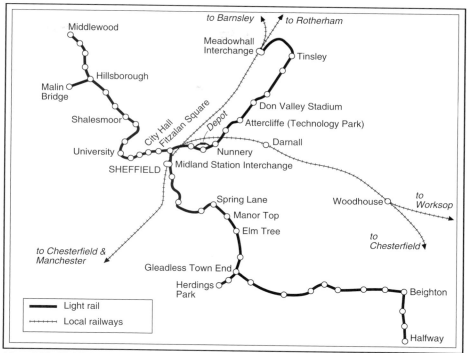

Map of Sheffield's light rail routes

0519183

Stagecoach Supertram LRV in Stagecoach livery

1179380

Stagecoach Supertram LRV at Sheffield railway station (Roger Carvell)

1168285

Passenger journeys: (2003/04) 12.3 million
(2004/05) 12.8 million
(2005/06) 13.1 million
(2006/07) 14.0 million
(2007/08) 14.8 million

Route length: 29 km
Number of lines: 3
Number of stops: 48
Gauge: 1,435 mm

Track: Part conventional ballasted, concrete slab on street sections
Max gradient: 10%
Minimum curve radius: 25 m
Electrification: 750 V DC, overhead

Current situation
The company operates a 28-km light rail network incorporating three routes in the city of Sheffield.

The operations franchise was sold to Stagecoach Holdings in 1997 for GBP1.1 million, giving it a 26-year operating franchise. Assets are owned by South Yorkshire Passenger Transport Executive (SYPTE).

Rolling stock: 25 cars
Siemens-Duewag articulated (1993)   M25
In peak service: 22

Service: Peak 10 min, off-peak 20 min
First/last car: 06.00/24.00
Fare structure: Stages, daily and weekly tickets – intermodal ticketing with buses
Fare collection: Cash to conductor
Fare evasion control: Inspectors; penalty fare
Arrangements for elderly/disabled: Low-floor cars
Signalling: Priority at road junctions

East Midlands Trains Limited

8th Floor, Friars Bridge Court, 41-45 Blackfriars Road, London SE1 8NZ, UK

Tel: (+44 207) 983 61 99
Web: www.eastmidlandstrains.co.uk

Key personnel
Project Manager: Chris Elliott
    Staff: Not available currently

Type of operation: Local rail

Current situation
East Midlands Trains, operated by Stagecoach, runs high-speed, long distance services from St Pancras London to Sheffield, Derby and Nottingham. In addition, there are regional services between Nottingham and Derby, which includes Lincoln, Cleethorpes and Skegness. There are also services between Derby and Crewe, which includes Matlock, Norwich and Liverpool. The franchise started on 11 November 2007 and will run until 31 March 2015, the last year and four months of which will be conditional upon achieving pre-set performance targets.

Services provided about two-hourly to Stafford and peak-hours only to Manchester (both 25 kV AC),

also to Crewe and Derby (diesel), serving local stations.

Developments
A refurbishment of East Midlands Trains' Class 158 trains was started in 2008. The work was be carried out in Derby by Delta Rail. The full refurbishment programme will see all 25 of the company's Class 158 trains going through a complete overhaul. It is expected to be completed by 2010.

The work includes: repainting in the new East Midlands Trains livery; internal refurbishment of every train, which includes improvements to seating design and capacity. In addition, a new toilet area will be included as part of the refurbishment programme; modification to various systems on the train to bring improved reliability; improved air conditioning units fitted to the majority of these trains to improve the reliability and efficiency; introduction of CCTV on every train; installation of a passenger counting device that allows passenger flows to be monitored.

Southampton
Population: 222,000 (estimate)

Public transport
Most city bus services provided by three main companies; cross-river ferry; local rail services.

Southampton City Council and Hampshire County Council promote public transport facilities in the city through Solent Transport, a partnership between transport authorities and operators, and a computer-based transport management system (ROMANSE). Southampton City Council's transport responsibilities also include traffic signals, street infrastructure and bus shelters (www.southampton.gov.uk).

First Hampshire & Dorset Ltd

226 Portswood Road, Southampton SO17 2BE, UK
Tel: (+44 23) 80 58 43 21
Fax: (+44 23) 80 67 14 48
Web: www.firstgroup.com

Key personnel
Managing Director: Richard Soper
    Staff: 300

Southampton
Type of operation: Bus

Current situation
Operates local bus services in the Southampton area with several high-frequency routes. Most of the routes are colour-coded, carrying easily identifiable route and frequency information. A complimentary colour map is available either from the city council or is contained within the timetable booklet.

Passenger journeys: (2006/07) 10.6 million
(2007/08) 11.9 million
Vehicle-km: (2007/08) 5.88 million

Number of routes: 25 (11 key high-frequency routes with 10 less frequent services including schools)
Route length: 488 km
On private right-of-way: 2 km

Fleet: 123 vehicles
Double-deck bus   42
Single-deck bus   21
Midibus   53
Minibus   7

Most intensive service: 10 min
One-person operation: 100 per cent
Fare collection: Cash payment to driver, prepurchase pass or ticket
Fare structure: Stage, with some zonal; tokens, monthly passes; day runabout tickets

First Hampshire & Dorset single- and double-deck buses in Southampton city centre (Tony Pattison)
1198732

Fares collected on board: 66 per cent
Fare evasion control: Mobile inspectors; excess fares charged
Operational control: Route inspectors/mobile radio
Arrangements for elderly/disabled: Off-peak passes for pensioners, funded by city council; accessible network using specially equipped buses
Average peak-hour speed: In bus lanes, 25 km/h; in mixed traffic, 15 km/h
Bus priority: 24 individual schemes; 2 km of bus lanes and area co-ordinated traffic management favouring buses on one corridor
Integration with other modes: Services co-ordinated with local trains and ferries
Operating costs financed by: Fares 64 per cent

Portsmouth
Current situation
Operates local bus services in the Portsmouth area with several high-frequency routes. Most of the routes are colour-coded, carrying easily identifiable route and frequency information. A complimentary colour map is available either from the city council or is contained within the timetable booklet.

Passenger journeys: (2006/07) 7.7 million
(2007/08) 8.8 million
Vehicle-km: (2007/08) 5.3 million

Number of routes: 26 (12 key high frequency routes with 14 less frequent service including schools)
Route length: Not currently available
On private right-of-way: 7 km

Fleet: 93 vehicles
Single-deck bus   38
Midibus   28
Minibus   27

Most intensive service: 10 min
One-person operation: 100 per cent
Fare collection: Cash payment to driver, prepurchase pass or ticket
Fare structure: Stage, with some zonal; tokens, monthly passes; day runabout tickets
Fares collected on board: 60 per cent
Fare evasion control: Mobile inspectors; excess fares charged
Operational control: Route inspectors/mobile radio
Arrangements for elderly/disabled: Off-peak passes for pensioners, funded by city council; accessible network using specially equipped buses
Average peak-hour speed: In bus lanes, 25 km/h; in mixed traffic, 15 km/h
Bus priority: 7 km of bus lanes and area co-ordinated traffic management favouring buses
Integration with other modes: Services co-ordinated with local trains and ferries
Operating costs financed by: Fares 60 per cent

Hythe-Southampton Ferry

White Horse Ferries
Stanley House, 65 Victoria Road, Swindon, Wiltshire, SN1 3BB, UK
Tel: (+44 1793) 61 85 66   Fax: (+44 1793) 48 84 28

e-mail: post@whitehorseferries.co.uk,
post@whitehorse.co.uk
Web: www.hytheferry.com,
www.whitehorse.co.uk

Key personnel
Director, White Horse Ferries: Peter Lay

Current situation
A ferry (also leisure cruises) connects Southampton with Hythe, carrying about 650,000 passengers annually. A free bus service is provided linking West Quay shopping centre with Town Quay. A further service, operated by Gosport Ferry Ltd (also leisure cruises), links Portsmouth with Gosport. It operates every 15 minutes daily.

Developments
White Horse Ferries purchased the route in 1994 after the previous operator went into liquidation. An operating subsidy is being paid by Hampshire county council for a five-year period.

Solent Blue Line
Barton Park, Eastleigh, Hampshire SO50 6RR, UK
Tel: (+44 23) 80 61 44 59   Fax: (+44 23) 80 61 42 34
e-mail: enquiries@solentblueline.com
Web: www.solentblueline.com

Key personnel
Managing Director: Alex Carter
Area Director: Phil Stockley
Engineering Director: Geoff Parsons
   Staff: 224

Current situation
Solent Blue Line was established in 1987, initially as a venture to compete in Southampton by Southern Vectis, the Isle of Wight-based transport operator. Following the acquisition later that year of the Southampton area operations of Stagecoach subsidiary Hampshire Bus and Eastleigh routes from Hants & Sussex, the company now runs a network of bus services in southern Hampshire together with local services in Southampton and Eastleigh. Since July 2005, Solent Blue Line has been part of the Go-Ahead Group.

Bluestar is the brand name for Solent Blue Line's key interurban and commuter routes into Southampton from the Winchester, Eastleigh, Romsey, Hedge End and Waterside areas, with frequent, simple and reliable services that follow the same pattern throughout the day and 'Nightstar' buses home from Southampton city centre until around 03.00 on Friday and Saturday nights. Bluestar services are run with specially branded vehicles bearing a contemporary star logo and supported by an innovative website (www.bluestarbus.info) featuring stop-by-stop timetables.

Cross-Southampton city services 18 and 19, together with a number of more rural routes, are operated under franchise by Marchwood Motorways of Totton and Brijan Tours of Bishops Waltham, bringing the total number of vehicles operating in Solent Blue Line colours to over 100.

Local bus services form the core part of the business, although the company also undertakes private hire, including organising transport for the recent Trafalgar 200 celebrations and rail-replacement bus services.

Developments
Solent Blue Line took over Uni-link services in 2008.

Bus
Passenger journeys: (2003/04) 3.95 million
(2004/05) 3.85 million
(2005/06) 4.04 million
Vehicle-km: (2003/04) 4.55 million
(2004/05) 4.9 million
(2005/06) 5.2 million

Number of routes: 44
Route length: 700 km

East Lancs-bodied Scania Uni-Link double-deck bus near Southampton city centre on U1C route serving the railway station and university (Tony Pattison)   1322753

Fleet: 82 vehicles, plus 27 operating on franchised services

BristolVR/ECW open-top double-deck	1
Bristol VR/Alexander open-top double-deck	1
Leyland Olympian/ECW double-deck	1
Leyland Olympian/Leyland double-deck	13
Volvo Olympian/East Lancs double-deck	2
Volvo Olympian/Northern Counties double-deck	3
Dennis Dart/Plaxton Pointer midibus	2
Dennis Dart/Alexander midibus	2
DennisTrident/East Lancs low-floor double-deck	8
Volvo B7TL/East Lancs low-floor double-deck	8
Volvo B10B/Alexander single-deck	3
Iveco 59-12/Marshall minibus	5
Iveco 59-12/Mellor minibus	1
Transbus Midi Pointer Dart low-floor midibus	12
Volvo B10B/Northern Counties single-deck	10
Mercedes-Benz Citaro low-floor single-deck	10

In peak service: 65

Most intensive service: 10 min
One-person operation: 100 per cent
Fare collection: Cash payment to driver, prepurchase pass or ticket; smartcard-based ticketing system introduced mid-2006
Fare structure: Zonal; day rover tickets, weekly, monthly and longer period network tickets; Solent Travelcard multi-operator ticket accepted by all operators within Travelcard area (south Hampshire)
Fares collected on board: 78 per cent
Fare evasion control: Mobile inspectors
Operational control: Control points; mobile inspectors with mobile phones; real-time information and base-vehicle communication
Arrangements for elderly/disabled: Off-peak passes for over 60s/disabled in Southampton; also Hampshire county-wide; Farepass half-fare scheme in most other districts
Average peak-hour speed: 18 km/h, better in sections with bus lanes
Bus priority: Bus lanes in Southampton, priority at junctions in locations, Southampton and Eastleigh
Integration with other modes: With rail at several local stations, at Hythe with ferry and air at Southampton international airport
Operating costs financed by: Fares 65 per cent, concessionary fares 10 per cent, other commercial sources 25 per cent

Southampton

Other operators

Current situation
Minerva Accord of Chichester operates a comprehensive city network contracted by Southampton University. The Uni-Link service is focused on the city campus and around 10 buses are operated. Stagecoach Hampshire Bus and Wilts & Dorset run longer-distance routes into the city.

South West Trains Limited
(See main entry under London)

Current situation
Local electric trains, at least hourly, operate on two routes through the city, serving local stations and providing a link to Southampton airport at Eastleigh (7 km).

A cross-city Totton-Southampton-Romsey service, introduced in 2003, runs with a half-hourly frequency.

Developments
733 Desiro cars have been delivered from Siemens Transportation. The trains replace all slam-door stock with the exception of two refurbished units for the Lymington branch line near Southampton and one retained for special duties.

Carr West Ltd (VLRS/Carr West)
95 Woodbridge Road, Guildford, GU1 4PY, UK
Tel: (+44 1483) 30 38 31
e-mail: vlrs@carrwest.force9.co.uk

Key personnel
Ambersham Group Chief Executive: Richard Savin
Ambersham Project Consultant: John Ayres
   Satff: Not available currently

Type of operation: Portsmouth Monorail (proposed) – Variable Level Rail System (VLRS)

Background
The project is being promoted, constructed and operated by, VLRS (Portsmouth) Ltd (VLRSP), a subsidiary of Ambersham Holdings Limited.

Carr West Limited was incorporated in January 1997 for the purpose of promoting the Intamin VLRS (see separate entry in New Technology/Innovative Transit Systems section) as a solution to urban transport needs. The company benefits from a range of skills in transport, banking, marketing and civil engineering, brought together through its board of directors.

Current situation
An elevated light rail system has been proposed to link a park-and-ride site at Port Solent with the ferry port, Portsmouth & Southsea station, Queen Alexander Hospital and The Hard (for ferries to the Isle of Wight).

Developments
The project has proceeded to planning level. An application under theTransport & Works Act 1992 (TWA) is expected to be made by 2010.

Stoke-on-Trent

Population: City: 239,000, conurbation: 360,000 (estimates)

Public transport

Bus services in 'Potteries' six-town city and conurbation mainly provided by private company. Local routes also operated by some private companies; local rail services.

The 2006 Delivery Report for the Stoke-on-Trent Local Transport Plan (LTP) states that bus trips rose from 9.9 million in 2003/2004 to 12.4 million in 2005/06. The LTP, produced by Stoke-on-Trent City Council, also reports that traffic levels in the city grew at less than half the national rate and less than half the projected increase.

First Potteries

Adderley Green Garage, Dividy Road, Stoke-on-Trent ST3 5YY, Staffordshire, UK
Tel: (+44 1782) 59 25 00
Fax: (+44 1782) 59 25 41
Web: www.firstgroup.com

Key personnel

Managing Director: Ken Poole
Commercial Director: Paul De Santis
Engineering Director: Michael Branigan
Operations Director: Peter Walch
Finance Director: Simon Davies
    Staff: Not available currently

Current situation

Until 1986, PMT (Potteries Motor Traction) was a subsidiary of state-owned National Bus. However, as part of the break-up and sale of the group, it was sold to its senior management. It is now a subsidiary of FirstGroup.

Bus

Number of routes: 60
Route length: 907 km

Fleet: 374 vehicles

Leyland Olympian/ECW double-deck	12
Leyland Olympian/Leyland double-deck	8
Volvo Olympian/Alexander double-deck	22
Scania N113/Northern Counties double-deck	1
Scania N113/Alexander double-deck	6
Scania L113/Wright low-floor single-deck	83
Scania L94/Wright low-floor single-deck	51
Scania Omnicity single-deck	17
Scania L94/Wrightbus Solar single-deck	18
DAF SB220/Optare single-deck	4
DAF SB220/Ikarus single-deck	3
Dennis Dart/Plaxton midibus	17
Mercedes-Benz O810/Plaxton minibus	20
Blue Bird American RE single-deck school bus	11
Dennis Dart SLF/Plaxton low-floor midibus	23
Dennis Dart SLF/Alexander low-floor midibus	17
Dennis Dart SLF/Marshall low-floor minibus	21
Optare Solo low-floor minibus	35
BMC Falcon single-deck	8

One-person operation: All routes
Fare collection: Payment to driver or passes
Fare structure: Flat; passes
Average peak-hour speed: 18.7 km/h

Stoke-on-Trent

Other commercial operators

Current situation

Arriva Midlands of Cannock, Baker's of Biddulph, Moorland Buses of Weston Coyney, Wardle Transport and Procters of Fenton operate bus services in the area.

Developments

An Optare Versa acquired by Stoke City Council started operating, running between the Potteries towns of Hanley and Burslem, in 2008. Local operator Wardle Transport is operating the bus on the part-subsidised 62/62A service, which runs half-hourly, six days a week. The hour-long

Scania Omnicity single-deck bus in service with First Potteries   1326869

Wardle Transport Optare Versa on local service in Stoke-on-Trent between Hanley and Burslem (Optare Group Ltd)   1374305

route takes in a hospital, a retail park, a sheltered accommodation unit and other employment, leisure and educational facilities. The growing popularity of the service, fuelled in part by the local and now national over-60s concessionary fare scheme, led the council to increase capacity by introducing the 38-seat Versa.

East Midlands Trains Limited

8th Floor, Friars Bridge Court, 41-45 Blackfriars Road, London SE1 8NZ, UK
Tel: (+44 207) 983 61 99
Web: www.eastmidlandstrains.co.uk

Key personnel

Project Manager: Chris Elliott
    Staff: Not available currently

Type of operation: Local rail

Current situation

East Midlands Trains, operated by Stagecoach, runs high-speed long distance services from London St Pancras to Sheffield, Derby and Nottingham and regional services between Nottingham and Derby – Lincoln – Cleethorpes – Skegness, and between Derby and Crewe – Matlock and Norwich and Liverpool. The franchise

started on 11 November 2007 and will run until 31 March 2015, the last year and four months of which will be conditional upon achieving pre-set performance targets.

Services provided about two-hourly to Stafford and peak-hours only to Manchester (both 25 kV AC), also to Crewe and Derby (diesel), serving local stations.

Developments

A refurbishment of East Midlands Trains' Class 158 trains was started in 2008. The work was being carried out in Derby by Delta Rail. The full refurbishment programme will see all 25 of the company's Class 158 trains going through a complete overhaul. It is expected to be completed by 2010.

The work includes: repainting in the new East Midlands Trains livery; internal refurbishment of every train, which includes improvements to seating design and capacity. In addition, a new toilet area will be included as part of the refurbishment programme; modification to various systems on the train to bring improved reliability; improved air conditioning units fitted to the majority of these trains to improve the reliability and efficiency; introduction of CCTV on every train; installation of a passenger counting device that allows passenger flows to be monitored.

United States

Anchorage

Population: Municipal area 278,700, metropolitan area 359,180 (2006 estimates)

Public transport
Fixed-route bus services and paratransit provided by municipal agency.

Anchorage People Mover
Anchorage Public Transportation, Municipality of Anchorage
PO Box 196650, 3600 Dr Martin Luther King Jr Ave, Anchorage, Alaska 99507-1222, US
Tel: (+1 907) 343 65 43 (Customer services)
Fax: (+1 907) 343 40 42
e-mail: wwtd@ci.anchorage.ak.us
Web: www.peoplemover.org
    www.muni.org/transit1

Key personnel
Director of Transit: Jody Karcz
Superintendent, Operating and Maintenance: Gary Taylor
Staff: 169

Current situation
The Municipality of Anchorage Transit System is known as People Mover. Services provided are People Mover fixed-route service, Share-A-Ride carpool and vanpool services, Anchor RIDES Paratransit service for people with disabilities and senior citizens, and free one-on-one travel training.

Developments
In July 2004, People Mover fixed-route service implemented the third phase of a route restructuring plan. These improvements include more efficient on-time performance, introduction of new services and provision of quicker and more direct services for passengers.

Bus
Passenger boardings: (2003) 3.3 million
(2004) 3.53 million
(2005) 3.97 million
(2006) 3.95 million
(2007) 3.99 million
Vehicle-km: (2003) 3.54 million
(2004) 3.73 million
(2005) 3.89 million
(2006) 3.91 million
(2007) 3.98 million

Number of routes: 17
Route length: (One way) 661 km

Fleet: 155 buses, including:
Fixed-route

GMC T6H 5307N (1984)	5
New Flyer D40 low-floor (1995)	18
New Flyer D40 low-floor (1998)	32
DCCB SLF229 low-floor (2003)	5

Paratransit service Owned by Municipality of Anchorage

Ford/Phoenix (2001)	3
Ford/Phoenix (2002)	3
Ford/Phoenix (2005)	10
Ford/Phoenix (2006)	10
Ford/Phoenix (2007)	10
Chevy Amerivan (2007)	5

Leased Revenue vehicles for co-ordination efforts from AK Community Services

Ford ElDorado (2007)	2

Vanpool service

Ford F350 van (2002)	10
Ford F350 van (2005)	9
Ford F350 van (2006)	32

In peak service (fixed route): 46

Most intensive service: 30 min
One-person operation: All routes
Fare collection: Payment to farebox
Fare structure: Flat USD1.75 adult, USD1.0 youth, 50 cents seniors and disabled; day pass – USD4.00 adult and youth, USD1.25 seniors and disabled; pre-purchase tokens and monthly passes
Fare evasion control: Driver supervision
Operational control: Shift supervisors
Arrangements for elderly/disabled: Services provided to ADA standards; fixed-route fares: 50 cents with ID card
Integration with other modes: Rideshare programme promotes carpools by providing matchlists with employer's help; funding from Federal Highway Administration grant; 181 carpools, with 365 members; 42 vanpools with 548 members; two park-and-ride lots served by Express buses to downtown
Operating costs financed by: Fares 17 per cent, other commercial sources three per cent, subsidy/grants 18 per cent, tax levy 62 per cent
Subsidy from: FTA and state grants, municipal property tax
New vehicles financed by: FTA and state grants

Atlanta
Population: City: 470,688 (2005 estimate), metropolitan area: 5.2 million (2006 estimate)

Public transport
Bus and metro services provided in Fulton and De Kalb counties and city of Atlanta by Transit Authority governed by 18-member representative board. Bus services in adjacent Cobb County link with Transit Authority services; tram and commuter rail proposed.

Metropolitan Atlanta Rapid Transit Authority (MARTA)
2424 Piedmont Road NE, Atlanta, Georgia 30324-3311, US
Tel: (+1 404) 848 50 00
Fax: (+1 404) 848 53 20
Web: www.itsmarta.com

Key personnel
Chairman: Edmund J Wall
Vice-Chair: Walter L Kimbrough
General Manager and Chief Executive Officer: Richard J McCrillis
Staff: 4,428 (2006)

Passenger journeys (all modes): (2006) 138.4 million
Vehicle-km (all modes): (2006) 110.95 million

Current situation
Created in 1965, MARTA provides bus, including paratransit, and metro services to a population of some 1.5 million.
    As each metro line opens, MARTA has integrated bus and rail, with bus routes diverted to feed rail lines. The result has been a significant reduction in bus traffic in the central business district.

Developments
In 2006, MARTA completed the installation of the Breeze fare collection system. The transition to a solely smartcard fare collection system is expected to be completed in the near future.

Expansion studies and projects include:
    West Line Corridor Study: Proposal for multi-modal services in the western part of Fulton Corridor. Preferred alternatives for this are an extension of heavy rail and Bus Rapid Transit (BRT).
    I-20 East Corridor Study: To reduce congestion in south-eastern DeKalb County, a BRT, in dedicated busway, has been proposed. The Draft Environmental Impact Statement is yet to be completed.
    North Line Transit Oriented Development Study: Study to identify areas suitable for possible future public transit centres.
    Beltline Corridor Study: Proposed 35-km (22-mile) transit route around the central city area.
    C-Loop Corridor Study: Investigation into the need for high-capacity transit connections in certain parts of the city and the surrounding areas.
    Memorial Drive Bus Rapid Transit (BRT) Project: BRT, with priority traffic signals, including an express service.
    In 2006, the Metropolitan Atlanta Rapid Transit Authority Police Department (MPD) received a USD3.2 million grant from the US Department of Homeland Security, a further USD2 million award for heavy rail security and USD600,000 for bus initiatives. The K-9 Unit obtained and trained three more Explosive Detection Canine teams.
Operating costs financed by: Fares 20 per cent, other commercial sources, subsidy/grants 13t, sales tax 67 per cent
Subsidy from: FTA
New vehicles financed by: FTA grants (80 per cent) with local matching funds

Bus
Passenger journeys: (2006) 69.2 million
Vehicle-km: (2006) 35.8 million (22.2 million miles) (plus 5.95 million (3.7 million miles) for paratransit services)

Number of routes: 120
Route length: 2,526 km

Fleet: 554 vehicles (plus 140 vans for paratransit services)

Full breakdown of fleet is not available, but is currently 395 CNG and 159 clean-diesel vehicles
In peak service: Not currently available

Most intensive service: 6 min
One-person operation: All routes
Fare collection: Cash, token or Breeze smartcard system (the latter currently for some passengers only)
Fare structure: Flat, with free transfer within service area and to metro; transfer charge on 3 routes into Clayton and Gwinnett counties. Isolated higher fares outside regular service area. Weekly and monthly passes; tokens
Fare evasion control: Driver surveillance, electronic fareboxes
Operational control: Route inspectors/mobile radio; all buses radio-equipped; AVL on 250 buses
Arrangements for elderly/disabled: E-Bus is special door-to-door service for elderly; L-Van for disabled; half fare on regular routes at all times; wheelchair lift-equipped vans and conventional buses with kneeling capability used on request; 82 per cent of buses wheelchair accessible. In 2006, paratransit passenger journeys stood at 289,258.
Integration with other modes: Unified bus/metro fare system with free transfers. All bus routes feed at least one metro station; 9 park-and-ride lots with 2,386 spaces
Security: Metropolitan Atlanta Rapid Transit Authority Police Department (MPD)
Average distance between stops: 152 m
Average peak-hour speed: Mixed traffic, 15.3 km/h

Developments
In 2006, MARTA was awarded the National Natural Gas Vehicle (NGV) Achievement Award. In the same year, it added 15 new 14-seater shuttle buses to its fleet to expand its Small Bus programme.
    Also in 2006, one existing bus route was modified and two new ones were added to improve connectivity in the city.

Metro
Type of operation: Full metro, first line opened 1979

Passenger journeys: (2006) 69.2 million
Train-km: (2006) 33.9 million (21.1 million miles)

Route length: 77.2 km (48 miles)
Number of lines: 3
Number of stations: 38
Gauge: 1,435 mm
Track: 52.1 kg/m 119RE continuously welded rail on concrete sleepers; elastomer springing under track in residential areas to reduce vibration; screens on surface and elevated sections to reduce noise
Max gradient: 3%
Minimum curve radius: 230 m
Electrification: 750 V DC, third rail

Service: 8 min
First/last train: 05.00/01.00 (Monday-Friday); 05.00/00.30 (weekends and holidays)
Fare structure: As bus
Revenue control: Automatic turnstiles accept coins, tokens, magnetic transfer tickets, smartcards and weekly and monthly passes; CCTV at all stations, which are unstaffed
Integration with other modes: Bus feeder services to all stations; 24 park-and-ride stations with 20,000 spaces
Arrangements for elderly/disabled: All stations wheelchair accessible
Signalling: ATP, ATO and automatic line supervision

Rolling stock: 338 cars
Franco-Belge 77A (1978/79) Not currently available
Hitachi/Itoh 82 (1985/86)   Not currently available
Breda   Not currently available
In peak service: 160 (estimate)

Developments
MARTA is currently in the process of rebuilding 218 of its older rail cars. In 2006, 24 cars were delivered and 12 were taken into service.

Work is also being undertaken to rebuild and upgrade the track.

Cobb Community Transit (CCT)
Transit Division
463 Commerce Park Drive, Marietta, Georgia 30060, USA
Tel: (+1 770) 528 16 10
Fax: (+1 770) 528 43 60
e-mail: RGutowsky@cobbcounty.org
Web: www.cobbdot.org
Web: http://dot.cobbcountyga.gov/cct.htm

Key personnel
Transit Division Manager: Rebecca Gutowsky
    Staff: 100 (estimate)

Passenger journeys: (2002) 2.7 million
Vehicle-km: Not currently available

Number of routes: 18 (includes 5 express routes and 2 peak-hour only services)

Route length: Not currently available
Operating costs: Fares cover approximately 35 per cent of operating costs

Background
Set up in 1989 to provide service in outer Atlanta suburbs in Cobb County. It is managed by the Cobb County Department of Transportation.

In 1994 CCT commenced a Paratransit service, which has a fleet of 15 midibuses.

Current situation
Thirteen local and two express routes, with several routes accessing MARTA stations with through ticketing. Four park-and-ride facilities. All buses are wheelchair accessible and have bicycle racks. There is no Sunday service.

Developments
Fleet: 55 vehicles
Flxible Metro 10.6 m (1989)   18
Flxible Metro 12 m (1989)   18
RTS-06 Suburban   19
In peak service: 43

Average age of fleet: 10 years
Fare structure: Flat; single, 10- and 20-ride tickets, round-trip ticket (express) and monthly pass; senior citizens, disabled and youths (under 18) at reduced fare; those under 42″ free; free local transfer
Fare collection: Cash to farebox
Arrangements for elderly/disabled: Fleet is 100 per cent wheelchair accessible; paratransit services
Integration with other modes: Accepts MARTA Breeze smartcard

Peachtree Corridor Task Force
600 West Peachtree Street, Suite 400, Atlanta, GA 30308, US
Tel: (+1 404) 817 04 11
Web: www.peachtreecorridor.com

Key personnel
Executive Director: Elli Kaplan
Co-Chairman: Tom Bell
Co-Chairman: Egbert Perry

Type of operation: Tram/LRV/streetcar (planned)

Current situation
The Peachtree Corridor Task Force was established to oversee the development of the 23.3 km (14.5 mile) corridor that runs through the centre of Atlanta. Plans include an initial 22.9 km tram (streetcar) line, cost estimated at some USD445 million in 2006, with several possible extensions.

Georgia Rail Passenger Program (GRPP)
Georgia Department of Transportation (GDOT)
Office of Intermodal Programs
West Annex, 276 Memorial Drive, SW, Atlanta, Georgia 30303, USA
Tel: (+1 404) 651 92 00
Fax: (+1 404) 657 42 21
e-mail: georgiatrains@garail.com
Web: www.garail.com

Key personnel
Rail Program Manager, GDOT: Gerald Ross
Projects Manager, Athens Corridor: Bill McCombs
Project Manager, Macon Corridor: Chris Kingsbury
Project Manager, Multi-Modal Passenger Terminal: Barry Hodges
Administrator, Intermodal Programs: Hal Wilson
Rail Manager, GRPA: Doug Alexander
Rail Program Manager, GDOT: Steve Yost
System data

Type of operation: Commuter rail (planned)

Current situation
Georgia Rail Passenger Program (GEORGIA RAIL) is the rail passenger programme for Georgia, US. The Georgia Department of Transportation (GDOT), the Georgia Rail Passenger Authority (GRPA) and the Georgia Regional Transportation Authority (GRTA) have joined forces to complete the planning and implement a system of commuter and intercity rail passenger service in Georgia.

Developments
Two routes, Athens-Atlanta and Macon-Atlanta, are the first phase of the programme.

Macon Corridor: Proposed commuter rail, served by four trains daily, over an initial 41.8 km (26 mile) route from Lovejoy to Atlanta, with later phases to extend to Macon. An Environmental Assessment has been completed on the Macon to Atlanta corridor with a Finding of No Significant Impact (FONSI). Implementation of commuter rail service in the corridor can progress as funds permit. Daily passenger journeys are forecast at 3,080 by 2009.

Athens Corridor: An Environmental Assessment has been completed on the Athens to Atlanta corridor with a Finding of No Significant Impact (FONSI). Implementation of commuter rail service in the corridor can progress as funds permit.

Atlanta MMPT (Multi-Modal Passenger Terminal): The Multi-Modal Passenger Terminal in downtown Atlanta will serve commuter rail and intercity bus passengers. A Finding of No Significant Impact (FONSI) was issued in 1995 and updated in December 2000. State and Federal funds are available to begin schematic design and necessary land preparation work. Initial bus and rail service could begin within two years of funding.

There are plans for a total of seven commuter lines, serving 45 stations, in the Atlanta metropolitan area and seven intercity lines.

Baltimore
Population: City 635,815, metropolitan area 2.66 million (2005 estimates)

Public transport
Bus, metro and light rail services operated by Maryland Transit Administration (MTA), an agency of the Maryland Department of Transportation (MDoT). Bus and rail services operated under contract.

Maryland Transit Administration (MTA)
6 Saint Paul Street, Baltimore, Maryland 21202-1614, US
Tel: (+1 410) 539 50 00
Tel: (+1 410) 767 39 36 (Communications)
Fax: (+1 410) 333 32 79
Fax: (+1 410) 333 08 93 (Communications)
Web: www.mtamaryland.com

Key personnel
Administrator: Paul J Wiederfeld
Deputy Administrator: Henry Kay
    Staff: 301 (Administrative)

Passenger boardings: (All modes)
(2004) 96.8 million
(2005) 91 6 million
(2006) 93.3 million
(2007) 96.6 million

Operating costs financed by: Fares 29.8 per cent, other commercial sources 1.6 per cent, subsidy/grants 68.6 per cent
Subsidy from: Consolidated Transportation Trust Fund and FTA

Current situation
MTA's service area has a population of some 2 million. The metro and light rail lines are fully integrated with the bus system, having the same flat fare. Integration has enhanced use of public transport, following a period of declining bus ridership which is now increasing.

MTA operates regular, Commuter Bus and Metro Connection circulator routes. Commuter Bus routes originate at park-and-ride lots and operate via expressways direct to downtown Baltimore. Metro Connection is a feeder bus service to Owings Mills, Old Court and Milford Mill metro stations from surrounding areas. In the Washington DC area, MTA contracts with private carriers to operate 14 commuter bus routes.

The MTA is required under a state law to recover 40 per cent of its operating costs from fares. In an unsuccessful attempt to achieve this goal in 1996, while avoiding the drop in ridership that usually accompanies a fares rise, the system of five zones and transfers was eliminated in favour of a new flat fare slightly higher than the former base rate. Instead of transfers, an all-day pass was introduced. As a result, bus ridership remained stable, metro travel (formerly four zones) rose by about 8 per cent, and light rail by 4 per cent. Fares for long-distance commuter buses, not part of the former zonal system, were also raised.

A five-year rehabilitation of the metro started was completed in 2006. Stations were improved and equipped with new public address systems and information displays, while the rolling stock was upgraded by Railworks Corp.

Developments

A number of projects are currently under way, including the Light Rail Double Track Project, details of which are given below. Other recommendations for future projects include extensions to the Red Line from Woodlawn to Fells Point, the Green Line from the Johns Hopkins Hospital station to the future Morgan State University station, and to the Bi-County Transit Way.

In early 2006, three new TSA-certified canine explosive detection teams joined the MTA Police.

In November 2006, the MTA announced the purchase of a new state-of-the-art security surveillance system. Using some USD12.7 million of state funds and federal grants, the MTA has begun the installation of the new system that will eventually enhance security at Metro, MARC and Light Rail stations.

Bus
Staff: 1,100 drivers, 716 others

Passenger journeys: (FY2004) 67.6 million
(FY2007) 64.3 million
Vehicle-km: (FY2004) 38.2 million
(FY2007) 40.2 million

Number of routes: 50
Route length: 2,200 km

Fleet: 671 vehicles	
30 ft buses	3
40 ft buses	639
60 ft buses	29

In peak service: Not currently available
On order: Approx 60 to 100 per year

Most intensive service: 3–5 min
One-person operation: All routes
Fare collection: Farebox beside driver
Fare structure: Flat; express bus services premiums; transfer by day pass which covers all modes
Arrangements for elderly/disabled: 606 buses lift-equipped, all routes accessible on Sundays; Mobility Bus service operated by lift-equipped vans operates on demand to routes otherwise unserved; demand-response services carried 653,414 passengers in FY 2006.
Average distance between stops: 1 city block
Average peak-hour speed: 20.8 km
Integration between modes: Bus/metro/light rail transfer tickets; 9 routes feed metro stations
New vehicles financed by: FTA grant 80 per cent, state funds 20 per cent

Developments

In late 2006, the MTA announced that the Next Vehicle Arrival technology (NVA) passenger information system would be installed at bus stops in the Baltimore region.

Metro
Staff: 389

Type of operation: Full metro, first line opened 1983

Passenger boardings: (FY 2006) 12.9 million

Route length: 23.7 km
  in tunnel: 7.2 km
Number of lines: 1
Number of stations: 14
Gauge: 1,435 mm
Max gradient: 4%
Track: 57.5 kg/m RE continuous welded rail
Electrification: 700 V DC, third rail

Service: Peak 8 min, off-peak 10–15 min, 7 days a week

First/last train: 05.00/24.00
Fare structure: Flat
Revenue control: Automatic access gates and ticket vending machines, stations manned
Integration with other modes: As above
Signalling: ATO, all trains single-manned
Operating costs financed by: Fares 32 per cent

Rolling stock: 100 cars	
Transit America (1983)	M72
Transit America (1986)	M28

Light rail
Staff: 241

Type of operation: Light rail, first line opened 1992

Passenger journeys: (FY 2006) 5.4 million
Route length: 40.5 km
Number of lines: 1
Number of stations: 33
Gauge: 1,435 mm
Electrification: 750 V DC, overhead

Service: 15 min
First/last car: 05.00/24.00
Fare structure: Flat fare
Fare collection: Vending machines at all stops
Fare evasion control: Roving transport police and fare inspectors
Arrangements for elderly/disabled: Full wheelchair accessibility
Integration with other modes: City-centre interchange with buses on Howard Street

Rolling stock: 53 cars	
Adtranz	M17
Adtranz MT 44 (1997/98/99)	M18
Other	M18

Current situation
A new depot for LRVs has been built at Cromwell. An extension from Cromwell to Glen Burnie (3 km) is under study, with the alignment yet to be chosen from three proposals.

Light Rail Double Track Project
Community Planning, Maryland Transit Administration,
6 Saint Paul Street, 9th Floor, Baltimore, Maryland 21202-1614, USA
Tel: (+1 410) 539 50 00
Freephone: (+1 866) 743 36 82
Web: www.mtamaryland.com

Legend	
━━	Metro
──	Light rail

Hunt Valley
Pepper Road
McCormick Road
Blue Line
Gilroy Road
Warren Road
Owings Mills
Timonium
Timonium Business Park
Lutherville
Old Court
Falls Road
Milford Mill
Mt Washington
Reisterstown Plaza
Cold Spring
Woodberry
West Cold Spring
North Ave
North Sta (YL)
Penn Sta (YL)
Penn-North
Johns Hopkins Hospital
Upton
Lexington Market
Charles Center
Camden Yds
Hamburg St
Cherry Hill
Westport
Patapsco
Baltimore Highlands
North Linthicum
Nursery Road
Blue Line
BWI Business District
Linthicum
Ferndale
Yellow Line
BWI Airport
Cromwell Sta/ Glen Burnie

Map of Baltimore's metro and light rail   1127074

Project overview
The Light Rail Double Track Project includes the design and construction necessary to double the track on almost all of the existing LRT system. Funding is provided by the US government and the state of Maryland, the cost of the project being estimated at USD150 million.

The project was completed in February 2006, putting double track on 15 km (9.4 miles) of the system. Four new platforms were also built at stations which currently only had one.

Veolia Transportation Inc
Mid Atlantic & North East Regional Office
2100 Huntingdon Avenue, Baltimore, MD 21211, US
Tel: (+1 410) 727 73 00   Fax: (+1 410) 783 24 48
e-mail: info@veoliatransportation.com
Web: www.veoliatransportation.com

Key personnel
Regional Vice-President: Steve Shaw
  Staff: 1,500 (estimate)

Passenger journeys: (Annual) 7 million (estimate)

Background
The company provides commuter, transit, paratransit, and school transportation services.

Current situation
Veolia Transportation Inc acquired Yellow Transportation in 2001.

Fleet: Not currently available

Maryland Transit Administration (MTA)
Maryland Commuter Rail (MARC)
6 St Paul Street, Baltimore, Maryland 21202-1614, US
Tel: (+1 410) 539 50 00
Tel: (+1 410) 767 39 96 (Communications)
Fax: (+1 410) 333 32 79
Fax: (+1 410) 333 08 93 (Communications)
Web: www.mtamaryland.com

Key personnel
Administrator: Paul J Wiederfeld
Deputy Administrator: Henry Kay
  Staff: 301 (Administrative)

Type of operation: Suburban heavy rail

Passenger journeys: (Total operations)
(2003) 6.4 million
(2004) 6.7 million

Operating costs: Financed by fares (56.8 per cent) and subsidy/grants (43.2 per cent)

Background
In 1992, the former State Railroad Administration was merged with the Mass Transit Administration, which now oversees the operation of the MARC Train Service.

Current situation
Service operated under contract by Amtrak and CSXT on three routes; the two serving Baltimore are from Baltimore (Camden) to Washington and Perryville-Baltimore (Penn)-Washington (see also Washington entry). There are 42 stations. An extension from Point of Rocks to Frederick, Maryland, opened in 2001. Frequency at peak hours is 20 to 30 minutes, hourly on the Washington to Baltimore Penn line.

Developments
In mid-2007, the MTA awarded Bombardier Transportation a contract, valued at USD14 million, for the refurbishment and overhaul of 34 MARC IIB push-pull commuter rails cars. The cars are due to return to service by 2010.

Rolling stock: 25 diesel and 10 electric locomotives plus 122 coaches/cars (all three routes)
AEM7 electric locomotive   4

HHP electric locomotive	6
GP40WH-2 diesel locomotives	19
GP39-2 diesel locomotive	6
Kawasaki and Sumitomo coaches	110
Gallery cars (ex-Matra)	12

Baltimore-Washington Maglev Project

Office of Planning, Maryland Transit Administration
6 Saint Paul Street, Baltimore, Maryland 21202-1614, USA
Tel: (+1 410) 767 37 88
e-mail: bwmaglev@mtamaryland.com
Web: www.bwmaglev.com

Key personnel
Project Manager: Suhair Alkhatib

Project overview
The project is being undertaken as part of the Federal Railroad Administration's

(FRA's) Magnetic Levitation (Maglev) Transportation Technology Deployment Program and was selected to proceed by the US Secretary of Transportation in January 2001.

The 64 km (40 mile) long Maglev would provide a connection between the downtown area of Baltimore and Union Station, Washington, DC, with a stop at Baltimore-Washington International Airport (BWI). There may also be a stop at the Capital Beltway. Ridership was projected to be 12.9 million in the first year of operation, rising to 13.9 million after the first 10 years of service.

The Project Team comprises the Maryland Department of Transport (MDoT), the District of Columbia, Baltimore City, Baltimore County and the Maryland Transit Administration.

Developments
The Draft Environmental Impact Statement (DEIS) has been completed.

Funding for the project is now uncertain.

The Water Taxi

Harbor Boating Inc, 1732 Thames Street, Baltimore, Maryland 21231, US
Tel: (+1 410) 563 39 01
Freephone: (+1 800) 658 89 47
e-mail: edkaneswatertaxi@comcast.net
Web: www.thewatertaxi.com

Key personnel
President and Chief Executive Officer: Cammie Kane

Type of operation: Ferry

Passenger journeys: (Annual) Not currently available

Current situation
Runs a continual daily waterbus-type service at 15 to 20 minute intervals, with boat capacities from 26 to 84 passengers, weather permitting. 12-month Frequent Floater Pass available. Early-morning commuter service runs from April to October.

Birmingham

Population: City 229,424 (2006 estimate), metropolitan area: 1.11 million (2007 estimate)

Public transport
Fixed-route and specialised bus services provided under contract by Transit Authority, controlled by a Board of Directors.

Birmingham-Jefferson County Transit Authority – Metro Area Express (MAX)

PO Box 10212, Birmingham, Alabama 35202-0212, USA
Tel: (+1 205) 521 01 61   Fax: (+1 205) 252 76 33
e-mail: info@bjcta.org
Web: www.bjcta.org

Street address
1735 Morris Avenue, Birmingham, Alabama 35203, USA

Key personnel
Chairman: Brian Hamilton
Vice-Chairman: Ms Johnnye P Lassiter
Executive Director: David C Hill
Secretary/Treasurer: Rev Patrick Sellers
Planning Manager: Sylvia Jankins
  Staff: 311

Passenger journeys: (2006) 3.7 million (estimate)
Vehicle-km: (2006) 5.5 million (3.4 million miles) (estimate)

Current situation
BJCTA is the principal transit operator, using the name Metro Area Express (MAX). The authority includes seven member municipalities and the unincorporated areas of Jefferson County with a service area of more than 518 km² (200 sq m) and a population of some 400,000.

In 1982 the Alabama state legislature approved a Levelised Beer Tax which guaranteed the authority a minimum USD2 million per year in local funding. Subsequently, the hours of service and patronage have steadily increased. Routes have been reorganised for more efficient scheduling, bringing additional services without an increase in the workforce.

Maxpool co-ordinates and arranges carpools through a free computerised matching system. Private employer support is encouraged for the vanpool programme by purchase of a 7–15 seat van which is then maintained by MAX. Maxpool is also responsible for operation of park-and-ride lots throughout the service area.

Developments
MAX has recently completed a programme to install wheelchair-accessible shelters and route signs.

The radio system has been upgraded to a digital system.

Bus
Number of routes: 40
Route length: 2,703 km

Fleet: 109 vehicles	
Orion CNG (2000)	43
Blue Bird CS (1995)	20
TMC	5
Vintage CNG Trolleys	10
Shuttles	7
Demand response	24
In peak service: 67	
First/last bus: 05.00/22.00	

Most intensive service: 30 min, no late evening service
One-person operation: All routes
Fare collection: Exact fare, registering farebox on board; Maxpass 7-day and monthly tickets
Fare structure: Flat, supplement for transfer; reduced fares for seniors and children, under-4's ride free
Operational control: Route inspectors/mobile radio
Arrangements for elderly/disabled: Accessible buses and door-to-door operation known as VIP Service
Integration with other modes: Maxpool encourages ride-sharing; extensive park-and-ride
Operating costs financed by: Fares 30.6 per cent, FTA subsidy/grants 22.5 per cent, state and local funds 44.9 per cent (Ad valorem and beer tax)
New vehicles financed by: 80 per cent FTA, 20 per cent local funding

---

Boston

Population: 559,0034, metropolitan area 4.41 million (2005 estimates)

Public transport
Bus, trolleybus, metro and light rail services operated by transport authority serving wide area with population of some 4.1 million, with some contracted services in outlying areas. Suburban rail services and ferries operated under contract.

Massachusetts Bay Transportation Authority (MBTA)

10 Park Plaza, Boston, Massachusetts 02116, US
Tel: (+1 617) 222 31 06
Fax: (+1 617) 222 61 80
Web: www.mbta.com

Key personnel
Secretary of Transportation and MBTA Chairman: Bernard Cohen
General Manager: Daniel A Grabauskas

Deputy General Manager: Philip Puccia
Chief of Staff: Mikel Oglesby
Chief Operating Officer: Michael Mulhern
Deputy Chief Operating Officer: Anne Herzenberg
Director of Subway Operations: Michael Francis
  Staff: 6,500

Passenger journeys: (All modes)
(Annual) Approx 300 million
Operating costs financed by: (All modes) Fares 30.2 per cent, other commercial sources 2.6 per cent, subsidy/grants 67.2 per cent
Subsidy from: Federal 1.8 per cent, Commonwealth of Massachusetts 47.5 per cent, local funding 17.9 per cent

Current situation
MBTA was created in 1964 as the forerunner of many regional transport planning and operating agencies. The MBTA area covers a total of 78 cities and towns in the greater Boston and eastern Massachusetts area. In addition, MBTA provides service to 52 communities outside the district, some provided under contract by 14 operators.

The metro network has its origins in an extensive system of street tramways. Today's light rail operation (the Green Line) comprises four branches feeding into a city-centre tunnel with good interchange to metro and commuter trains.

Developments
MBTA is in the process of implementing a new automated fare collection system. The plastic 'Charlie Card' is scheduled to be introduced in stages.

Bus Rapid Transit (Silver Line)
Current situation
The Silver Line BRT currently exists in two isolated sections, SL-Waterfront network (three duobus routes), opened in 2004/5, and the SL-Washington Street all-surface busway, which uses CNG buses.

Service on the line runs 7 days a week from 05.00 to 24.00. Peak headway (electrified portion) is approximately 3 minutes. Route SL1 to the airport runs every 10 minutes until 20.00 (Mon-Fri) and every 15 minutes after that and all day at weekends.

Of the 32 dual-mode buses, eight are owned by Massport, the owner-operator of the airport, and have an interior configuration specifically for use on the airport route, with fewer seats and large luggage areas.

Bus and trolleybus
Number of routes: Bus 155, trolleybus 4
Route length: Bus 1,100 km, trolleybus 25 km

Fleet: 1,071 buses
GMC RTS T80-604 (1985, rebuilt 1992/93)	80
GMC RTS T80-606 (1986/87)	90
TMC RTS T80-606 40 ft (1989)	119
TMC RTS T70-606 35 ft (1989)	23
TMC RTS (1994)	137
Nova Bus RTS T80-206 (1995)	260
Orion VI hybrid (1999) (stored)	2
New Flyer low-floor 40 ft CNG (1999/2001)	17
NABI 40 ft low-floor CNG (2003/04)	299
Neoplan 60 ft low-floor articulated CNG (2003)	44

In peak service: 753
On order: 175 Neoplan low-floor diesel buses, comprising 140 40 ft and 35 35 ft, delivery scheduled for 2004/05

Developments
In mid-2007, the MBTA awarded a USD1.4 million contract to install surveillance cameras on 155 of its buses.

Fleet: 65 trolleybuses
Flyer E800 40 ft (1976) (reserve use only)	5
Neoplan, USA/Skoda 40 ft low-floor (2004)	28
Neoplan USA/Skoda 60 ft articulated low-floor dual-mode (2003/05)	32

In peak service: 24 trolleybuses on the Cambridge-area network; 13 dual-mode vehicles and two trolleybuses (temporary) on the Piers Transitway
On order: None

Most intensive service: 15 min
One-person operation: All routes
Fare collection: Coin to farebox; 1-, 3- and 7-day passes
Fare structure: Flat, some zone fares
Average peak-hour speed: Bus 18.3 km/h, trolleybus 19.5 km/h
Arrangements for elderly/disabled: 32 routes operated by lift-equipped buses. Call-A-Lift service will provide lift-equipped buses on any other route on request

Developments
Trolleybus operation had been planned for Washington Street, to replace the relocated Orange Line metro service but those plans were eventually dropped, mostly to reduce costs, and a busway was built on Washington Street without trolleybus wiring and operated with CNG buses.

Construction began in 1995 of a 1.3 km underground trolleybus 'transitway' to link the South Boston piers area with South station, which opened in December 2004. This has been renamed Silver Line Waterfront.

Metro/light rail
Type of operation: Full metro and light rail

Route length: 125 km, comprising:
Orange Line (full metro) 17.5 km
Blue Line (full metro) 9.5 km
Red Line (full metro) 47.5 km
Green Line (light rail) 50 km
  in tunnel: 24 km
Number of stations: 84
  in tunnel: 28
  elevated: 3
Gauge: 1,435 mm
Track: 38.6 kg/m ASCE; 45.4 kg/m ARA-B; 68 kg/m RE rail on combination of conventional sleepers on ballast, wooden sleepers on steel and concrete sleepers with resilient pads. All new track continuous-welded on resilient pads
Tunnel: Cut-and-cover single-bored and caisson
Electrification: All 600 V DC. Collection: Red Line, third rail, Ashmont-Mattapan light rail extension, catenary; Orange Line, third rail; Blue Line, third rail and catenary; Green Line, catenary

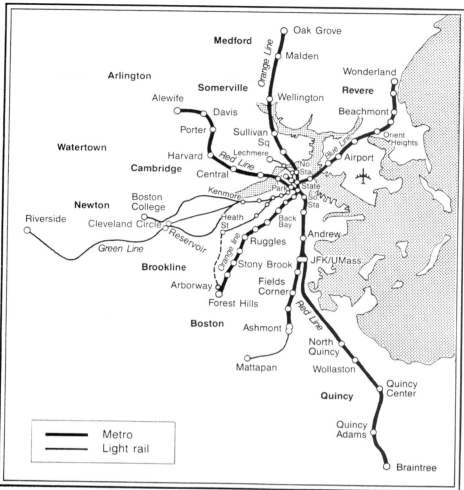

Map of Boston's metro and light rail system

0518327

New Neoplan USA low-floor trolleybus of MBTA near Harvard University. A distinctive feature of these vehicles is an off-side door for use at southbound stations in the Harvard Square bus subway (Steve Morgan)

0585135

Developments
The light rail line connecting Mattapan with Ashmont reopened in December 2007. The line's dedicated fleet of PCC vehicles, rehabilitated in 1999–2004, are again providing all of the service.

The last of the Boeing-Vertol LRVs were withdrawn in March 2007.
Service: Peak 4½ min, off-peak 8 min
First/last train: 05.00/00.30
Fare structure: Flat on Orange and Blue lines; zonal on Green and Red lines; no free transfers to bus
Revenue control: Mechanical turnstiles accept tokens and electronically coded passes at all stations
One-person operation: Red Line, 24 Series 1500 cars can be one-man operated, but there are no

plans to run these cars as singles. Green Line, one-man runs with LRV cars as single and multiple units, each added car with conductor
Automatic control: Red Line, automatic speed control on approx 69 per cent of present route. Station stops and starts under driver's control; ATO being installed on Orange Line
Surveillance: One end-of-line station (Braintree, Red Line) equipped with CCTV monitored by local police

Rolling stock: 621 cars (metro 408, Green Line (light rail) 213)
Pullman Standard 3000/3200 PCC (1945/46) (rehabilitated 1978/83 and again 1999/2004)

M10

Pullman Standard 01500/01600 Red Line (1969/70, rebuilt 1985/88)	M74
Hawker Siddeley 0600 Blue Line (1978/80)	M70
Hawker Siddeley 01200 Orange Line (1979/81)	M120
Kinki Sharyo 3600 Type 7 LRV (1986/87)	M95
Kinki Sharyo 3700 Type 7 LRV (1997)	M20
UTDC 01700 Red Line (1987/89)	M58
Bombardier 01800 Red Line (1993/94)	M86
Breda 3800 Type 8 LRV (1999/2007)	M88

On order: A further 7 Breda LRVs and 94 Siemens metro cars (Blue Line) for delivery 2007/09

Commuter rail

Type of operation: Suburban heavy rail

Passenger journeys: Not currently available

Current situation

Service provided under contract to MBTA by Amtrak over 13 routes totalling 528 km with 116 stations. Five routes serve Boston's North station, eight run to South station; irregular service outside peak hours.

Developments

In early 2006, MBTA announced that it would be replacing four single-deck cars with new double-deck cars on the Worcester/Framingham, Needham and Franklin commuter lines.

The Greenbush Line was opened in late 2007 (29 km (18 miles), seven stations, 3,100 park-and-ride spaces). The line runs between Boston and the South Shore.

Rolling stock: 80 diesel locomotives and 375 coaches

Buffalo

Population: City 276,059 (2006 estimate), Buffalo-Niagara Falls Metropolitan Area 1.13 million (2007 estimate), service area 1.2 million (2007)

Public transport

Bus and light rail services provided through operating subsidiary of Niagara Frontier Transportation Authority (NFTA), a New York State public benefit corporation governed by a Board of Commissioners.

Niagara Frontier Transportation Authority (NFT Metro)

181 Ellicott Street, PO Box 5008, Buffalo, New York 14203, US
Tel: (+1 716) 855 73 00   Fax: (+1 716) 855 66 79
e-mail: info@nfta.com
Web: www.nfta.com

Key personnel

Executive Director: Lawrence M Meckler
Director, Surface Transportation: Walter D Zmuda
Director, Public Affairs: C Douglas Hartmayer
General Manager, Engineering: Michael Bykowski
Staff: 1,540 (NFTA Metro: 1,119)

Passenger journeys: (All modes)
(2005) 23.7 million
(2006) 23.7 million
(2007) 25.6 million (estimate)

Operating costs financed by: Fares 30.5 per cent, subsidy/grants 69.5 per cent
Subsidy from: FTA 15 per cent, state (general revenues and petrol tax) 30 per cent, and local (general revenues, sales and mortgage transfer tax) 55 per cent

Current situation

NFT Metro was created in 1973 as a wholly owned subsidiary of NFTA to provide public transport services in Erie and Niagara counties after acquisition of six independent companies. It is the major area operator, serving an area of 4,080 km² (1,575 sq miles) and a population of approximately 1.2 million.

NFT Metro provides bus, light rail, paratransit and MetroLink services, plus a four-vehicle vintage-style trolleybus system.

The light rail line runs along Main Street in a traffic-free area at the heart of the city's central business district, and service is fare-free over this section. The line is unusual as it runs on the surface in the city centre and in tunnel elsewhere.

In 1990 NFTA obtained a dedicated source of revenue to fund its operating deficit. This consists of a percentage of a sales tax and a mortgage transfer tax. Nevertheless, NFTA remains short of its full requirement for capital expenditure.

Developments

In 2007, Metro added Erie Community College's 3,000 City Campus students to its College/University Unlimited Access programme.

Bus

Passenger km: (2005) 101.6 million
Car-km: (2005) 16.3 million
Number of routes: 80
Route length: 1,980 km

Developments

A new USD6.4 million state-of-the-art transportation centre opened in Niagara County, NY in December 2007.

Fleet: 332 buses (plus 60 vans and 5 trolleys)

Trolley replicas	5
NABI 416	65
Gillig 40 ft (2001/05)	98
New Flyer D40 40 ft (1993)	45
Gillig hybrid (2006/07)	43
Nova Bus Classic and low-floor	60
Gillig 30 ft buses (2004)	22

In peak service: 278
Average age of fleet: 7.94 years

Most intensive service: 10 min
One-person operation: All routes

Fleet control: FleetLynx GPS system
Fare collection: Registering farebox
Fare structure: 4 zones, monthly Metro Pass, day pass and rolling 30-day pass
Arrangements for elderly/disabled: All buses wheelchair-accessible; reduced fares. The Paratransit Access Line (PAL) carried some 75,000 passengers in FY2005. PAL Pass has been developed.
Average distance between stops: 488 m
Integration between modes: Bus services integrated with light rail; rail fare same as city bus with free transfer; 7 park-and-ride sites

Light rail
Staff: 157

Type of operation: Light rail, initial route opened 1985

Passenger boardings: (FY2005) 5.37 million
(FY2006) 5.63 million
(FY2007) 5.83 million
Passenger-km: (2005) 21.2 million
(2007) 23.1 million
Car-km: (2005) 1.9 million
(2007) 1.9 million

Map of Buffalo's light rail line   1115249

Route length: 10 km
 in tunnel: 7.7 km
Number of routes: 1
Number of stations: 14
 in tunnel: 8
Gauge: 1,435 mm
Electrification: 650 V DC, overhead

Current situation

Three extension proposals are included in the region's long-range transportation plan. The rolling stock will undergo half-life overhaul over the next 5 years.

Developments

The 27 operational railcars are due for overhaul. NFTA Metro intends to carry this out over a 5-year period and at a cost of approximately USD33 million.

NFTA Gillig hybrid bus   1344549

AnsaldoBreda Inc was awarded the contract for the overhaul of the LRVs. The contract was valued at some USD32.8 million. The work started in late 2006, with the first two vehicles expected to return to the NFTA in September 2008 for six weeks of trial commissioning.

Rolling stock: 27 cars
Tokyu Car LRV (1984/85)   M27
In peak service: 18
Average age of fleet: 24 years

Service: Peak 7 min, off-peak 10–15–20 min
Integration with other modes: Full integration with bus system
Revenue control: Fare-free on city-centre surface section; AFC, no barriers on underground portion
Arrangements for elderly/disabled: Ramps and snow-melting equipment on surface section; lifts to underground platforms
Signalling: Centrally controlled cab signalling

NFT Metro bus

1178276

Charlotte

Population: City 630,478, metropolitan area 1.6 million (2006 estimates)

Public transport
Bus services provided by the municipal organisation; private trolley; light rail.

State of North Carolina Department of Transportation (NCDOT)

1500 Mail Service Center, Raleigh, North Carolina 27699-1500, USA
Tel: (+1 919) 733 25 20   Fax: (+1 919) 733 91 50
e-mail: tdenning@dot.state.nc.us
Web: www.ncdot.org

Street address
1 South Wilmington Street, Raleigh, North Carolina 27611, USA

Key personnel
Secretary, Board of Transportation:
   Tammy B Denning

Background
Originally established in 1915 as the State Highway Commission, the current name was finally adopted in 1979.

Current situation
North Carolina Department of Transportation (NCDOT) provides an integrated transportation system for the state. Its responsibilities are to direct, plan, construct, maintain and operate the state-maintained transportation system, including aviation, ferry, public transportation, rail and highway systems. It also licenses and regulates the citizens and motor vehicles that utilise these transportation systems.

NCDOT employs over 14,000 people and is organised into 11 main divisions with 14 local division offices. The 14 local division offices are responsible for construction, maintenance, roadside environmental programmes, traffic services and fiscal and facility operations.

Charlotte Area Transit System (CATS)

600 East Fourth Street, Charlotte, North Carolina 28202-2858, USA
Tel: (+1 704) 336 79 02   Fax: (+1 704) 336 40 58
Web: www.charmeck.org/Departments/CATS/
   Home.htm

Key personnel
*Director of Public Transit for the City of Charlotte
   and Chief Executive Officer of the Charlotte Area
   Transit System:* Ronald Tober

Chief Operations Officer: James Zingale
*Deputy Director for Development and Chief
   Development Officer:* John Muth
Administration Manager: Dee Pereira
Marketing and Communications Manager: Olaf
   Kinard
   Staff: 360

Background
Managed by the Public Transit Department of the City of Charlotte, North Carolina, Charlotte Area Transit System (CATS) provides public transportation services throughout Mecklenburg and the surrounding counties.

In November 1998, the residents of Mecklenburg County approved, by a margin of 58 to 42 per cent, a $\frac{1}{2}$ cent increase in the local sales tax to fund new transit operations throughout the County.

Current situation
CATS currently operates local and express buses, neighbourhood shuttles, vanpools and carpools, and specialised transportation services for special needs customers. Bus passengers on the four express routes, mainly commuters whose services run only in peak times, have 'Guaranteed Ride Home' facility for urgent journeys between the peaks.

Developments
In November 2006, the Metropolitan Transit Commission (MTC) adopted the 2030 Transit Corridor System Plan. This consists of multiple rapid transit improvements in five corridors, a series of Center City improvements and bus service and facility improvements throughout the region. The implementation plan for the 2030 Transit Corridor System Plan includes the North and Northeast corridors, followed by the light rail/streetcar project. Once complete, the 2030 Transit Corridor System Plan will consist of 40 km (25 miles) of commuter rail, 33.8 km (21 miles) of light rail, 25.7 km (16 miles) of light rail/streetcar, 22.5 km (14 miles) of Bus Rapid Transit (BRT) and an expanded network of buses and other transit services. Also included in long-term plans are new park-and-ride facilities, the Charlotte Gateway Station intermodal facility and new community transit centres.

Bus
Passenger journeys: (2002) 14.7 million
(2003) 15.5 million
Vehicle-km: Not currently available

Number of routes: 43
Route length: Not currently available

Developments
From November 2007, 14 new bus routes where introduced and changes were made to some

existing routes to integrate with the new LYNX Blue Line light rail line.

Fleet: 161 buses

Flxible ADB (1982)	42
Flxible (1991)	40
MAN (1987)	39
RTS TMC (1990)	10
Goshen (1996)	6
Gillig (1997)	20
AVS electric bus (1995)	4

In peak service: 133

Most intensive service: 10 min
One-person operation: All routes
Fare collection: Farebox, no change given
Fare structure: Flat, surcharge for express routes; free transfers; weekly and monthly passes
Arrangements for elderly/disabled: Reduced off-peak fares; passes at reduced rates; most buses have kneeling capability; wheelchair lifts on 50 buses; demand-responsive service for those who cannot use fixed-route bus/mobile radio
Average distance between stops: 700 m
Average peak-hour speed: In mixed traffic, 15 km/h
Operating costs financed by: Fares 31.4 per cent, other commercial sources 3.3 per cent, subsidy/grants 65.3 per cent

LYNX Blue Line (light rail)
Current situation
The LYNX Blue Line (previously known as the South Corridor Light Rail Project (SCLRP)) was approved in late 2002. The system is 15.4 km (9.6 miles) long, with 15 stations, running from Uptown Charlotte to Interstate 485 on separate tracks on the existing rail alignment. Stations in the South End and Uptown areas connect with the Charlotte Trolley system. Seven of the new stations have connections to local and express bus services and have park-and-ride facilities. All stations are served by CAT feeder bus services.

Developments
The LYNX Blue Line was opened for free travel on 24–25 November 2007 and for revenue service on 26 November 2007.

Service runs seven days a week, with headways of 7.5 minutes peak and 15 minutes off-peak on weekdays and 20 to 30 minutes at weekends. Operating hours are 05.00 to 01.00.

Fares are flat, with pass holders riding for free. A free transfer from bus to light rail is available within a time limit.

Fleet: 16 vehicles
Siemens S70 LRVs   16

LYNX Blue Line Extension Northeast Corridor (proposed)
The 17.7-km (11-mile) Blue Line Extension, with 14 stations, would extend from 9th Street in Center City through the North Davidson (NoDa)

and University areas to I-485 north of UNC Charlotte. The service will operate generally within the existing railroad right of way from Center City to NoDa and then remain within the North Tryon Street (US 29) right of way from Sugar Creek north to I-485.

Trains will operate seven days a week from 05.00 to 01.00 and the fare will be the same as the cost of local bus fare. Headway will be 7.5 minutes during peak hours and every 15 minutes during non-peak hours. The line is currently scheduled to open in 2013. The Blue Line Extension is projected to cost USD740.5 million, with anticipated daily ridership of 17,500 in 2030.

Center City (streetcar/light rail – proposed)
The Center City Streetcar project alignment would serve the Central Business District (CBD) and provide connectivity to surrounding communities and institutions. The proposed light rail/streetcar line, with 36 stops, would run (16.1 km) 10 miles along Beatties Ford Road near I-85 through Center City (CBD) along Trade Street, along Elizabeth Avenue by Central Piedmont Community College (CPCC) and out to Central Avenue at Eastland Mall.

Southeast Corridor (Bus Rapid Transit (BRT) – proposed)
The Southeast Corridor would extend approximately 21.7 km (13.5 miles) from Charlotte's Center City to the border of Mecklenburg and Union Counties, terminating at Central Piedmont Community College's Levine Campus.

Two modes of transportation were evaluated for the Southeast Corridor – Bus Rapid Transit (BRT) and Light Rail Transit (LRT). In September 2006, the Metropolitan Transit Commission (MTC) reviewed study results from the DEIS and adopted the following motion that BRT be selected as the Locally Preferred Alternative in the SE Corridor. However, the MTC aslo adopted the motion that implementation of BRT be delayed for at least five years to allow for the future reconsideration of LRT in the Southeast Corridor, and that CATS' staff is directed to take the necessary steps in design and engineering with NCDOT on the Highway Project (Independence Boulevard) so that light rail could be considered in the future.

Sixteen stations have been identified, including eight with park-and-ride facilities, with a total of 3,350 spaces. The BRT would operate at three-minute headways in the peak period, and 10-minute headways in the off-peak times and weekends in order to provide the capacity required to meet projected demand. Thirty-three BRT vehicles would be required to operate this service.

West Corridor Rapid Transit Project (light rail/streetcar – proposed)
The proposed West Corridor project is a 10.3 km (6.4 mile) alignment that would operate from Trade Street to Cedar Street to West Morehead Street, then along Wilkinson Boulevard to Harlee Avenue, terminating at the airport employee parking lot on Harlee Ave.

The light rail/streetcar vehicles would travel in mixed traffic in the curb lanes. Ten stops have been identified. No park and ride lots have been included. The service would operate at 10-minute headways in the peak period and 15-minute headways in the off-peak times and weekends. Nine vehicles will be required to operate this service.

North Corridor (commuter rail – proposed)
The proposed North Corridor Commuter Rail Project would operate along 48.3 km (30 miles) of the existing Norfolk Southern rail line (the 'O' line) from Center City Charlotte to Mooresville in southern Iredell County. The alignment parallels Graham Street in the south and Old Statesville Road (NC-115) in the north.

The North Corridor commuter rail project is being planned in two phases and is projected to have more than 4,500 riders daily in the first phase. Initial service focuses on the rush-hour commuter with 16 daily commuter trains operating in one direction (rush direction) at a time. Project costs are estimated to be around USD260 million, plus the costs of the Charlotte Gateway Station. A combination of local, state and private funds are proposed to fund the project.

Charlotte Trolley Inc
2104 South Boulevard, Charlotte, North Carolina 28203, US
Tel: (+1 704) 375 08 50   Fax: (+1 704) 375 05 53
e-mail: info@charlottetrolley.org
Web: www.charlottetrolley.org

Key personnel
President: Terry Shook
Executive Director: Lisa Gray

Passenger journeys: 3,871 (2001)

Background
Originally formed in 1891 as the Charlotte Street Railway Company, the company was organised under its current name in 1988. It is a private, non-profit organisation.

Current situation
In 1988, the Charlotte city council voted to allocate USD16.7 million in city funds for the infrastructure to create a 2 mile transit corridor that would accommodate both vintage streetcar and light rail vehicles. The City of Charlotte was responsible for restoring Stonewall Street Bridge, laying track through the Convention Center, and restoring the 2-mile corridor from South End through Center City to 9th Street. Charlotte Trolley provides daily streetcar service and an expanded education and museum programme.

Developments
Recently, the company began negotiations with Charlotte Area Transit System (CATS) (see separate entry) for the latter to lease streetcars from Charlotte Trolley and provide the operations.

In late 2003, new catenary poles and wires were installed for the system, and testing of the overhead power system began in December 2003.

Regular service on the 3.4 km line was inaugurated in June 2004, operating seven days a week. About 100,000 passengers were carried in the first year of operation.

Fleet: 7 trolley cars (trams)

Various historic trolley cars/trams	M4
Gomaco 4-axle Birney replica (2004)	M3

North Carolina Railroad Company (NCRR)
Suite 100, 2809 Highwoods Boulevard, Raleigh, North Carolina 27604-1000, USA
Tel: (+1 919) 954 76 01   Fax: (+1 919) 954 70 99
www.ncrr.com

Key personnel
President: Scott M Saylor
Public Affairs Director: Kat Christian

Type of operation: Commuter rail

Passenger journeys: (2006) 300,000 (estimate)

Current situation
The NCRR carries an Amtrak-operated passenger service that runs from Charlotte to Selma under a contract with the North Carolina Department of Transportation.

NCRR owns no locomotives or rolling stock.

For further information on NCRR, please see *Jane's World Railways.*

Chicago
Population: City 2.83 million (2006 estimate), metropolitan area 9.5 million (2007 estimate)

Public transport
Bus, metro and commuter rail services in a 6,000 km² area encompassing the city of Chicago and suburban Cook County, and the surrounding counties of Will, McHenry, DuPage, Kane and Lake, controlled by Regional Transportation Authority through three service boards. City operations are undertaken through Chicago Transit Authority (CTA) under local representative board; regional metro and suburban rail services operated by Metra and independent railway companies; other RTA-controlled bus services run by suburban bus board (Pace) through independently administered mass transit districts in certain suburbs, based on previously independent operations.

Regional Transportation Authority (RTA)
RTA Administrative Offices
175 W Jackson Blvd, Suite 1550, Chicago, Illinois 60604, US
Tel: (+1 312) 913 32 00   Fax: (+1 312) 917 13 44

e-mail: communications@rtachicago.org
Web: www.rtachicago.com

Key personnel
Chair: Jim Reilly
Executive Director: Stephen E Schlickman
Directors: James Buchanan, Jan Carlson, William R Coulson, Rev L Tyrone Crider, Patrick J Durante, Armando Gomez, Al Jourdan, Dwight A Magalis, Patrick V Riley, Michael Rosenberg, J D Ross, Judy Baar Topinka, Douglas M Troiani, Phil Fuentes, Michael Scott

Passenger journeys: 2 million per weekday (estimate) (All modes)

Current situation
The RTA, established in 1974, exercises overall planning and financial control of public transport in the Greater Chicago area, provision of which is in the hands of three service boards. Operations in Chicago itself are run by CTA, regional and commuter rail services through Metra, and suburban bus operations by Pace, the Suburban Bus Division, serving parts of Chicago and suburbs including Oak Park, Waukegan, Harvey and Oak Lawn. Some local private bus operators are also supported.

Developments
In January 2008, the Regional Transportation Authority (RTA) Board of Directors approved a sales tax increase for the region that will provide critical operating funds to the CTA, Metra and Pace. The board action follows approval of transit funding and reform legislation adopted by the Illinois General Assembly on January 17 2008 and enacted into law the following day with Governor Blagojevich's approval.

The RTA board action enacts a 0.25 per cent sales tax increase in each of the six counties of northeastern Illinois, which will produce USD280 million in new operating funds. An additional 0.25 per cent sales tax increase will also be collected in the counties of DuPage, Kane, Lake, McHenry and Will and will produce approximately USD121 million for suburban transportation and public safety projects. Those sales tax increases began in April 2008.

The State of Illinois will continue its traditional paratransit funding of USD55 million annually, and when the legislation is fully implemented in 2009, the state will also annually match 25 per cent of the regional sales and real estate transfer tax funds raised. The state match will produce approximately USD70 million annually.

Pace Suburban Bus Service

550 West Algonquin Road, Arlington Heights,
Chicago, Illinois 60005-4412, USA
Tel: (+1 847) 364 72 23   Fax: (+1 847) 228 23 29
e-mail: passenger.services@pacebus.com
Web: www.pacebus.com

Key personnel

Chair: Richard A Kwasneski
Executive Director: T J Ross
Deputy Executive Directors:
 Finance & Administration: Terrance Brannon
 Operations: Melinda Metzger
 Planning: Michael Bolton
 Government Affairs: Rocky Donahue
 Media Contact: Patrick Wilmot
 Tel: (+1 847) 228 42 25
 Staff: 1,490

Passenger journeys: (2003) 34.9 million
(2006) 38.1 million
(2007) 39.2 million

Number of routes: 240 (fixed bus routes, all accessible)

Current situation

Pace was established in 1984 to assume operational responsibility for the RTA-funded suburban bus direct operations and contracted services, together covering the 5,500 km², 5.5 million population, six-county suburban region of Chicago.

In 2006, the RTA Act was further amended giving Pace operational responsibilities for the ADA paratransit services provided by the CTA. This expanded Pace's ADA paratransit service coverage area to include the 2.7 million residents of the City of Chicago.

Pace provides funding for 240 bus routes serving some 210 communities. It owns and operates nine suburban carriers, subsidises three municipal carriers and contracts with four private operators, primarily running express routes serving suburban employment centres and feeders to 133 CTA metro and Metra rail stations. A uniform fare structure exists for Pace services.

Some 80.6 per cent of passengers are carried by Pace-owned operations, 5.1 per cent by private contract carriers, 2.6 per cent by municipal services, 7.2 per cent by paratransit and 4.5 per cent by vanpools.

Paratransit services to all parts of the six-county area have seen increasing patronage. They are operated mainly by dial-a-ride and fixed-route deviation types of service. There are 66 local dial-a-ride projects along with 11 ADA-compliant paratransit services; Pace-owned lift-equipped vehicles and contractors vehicles are used. All Pace services are wheelchair accessible.

ADA paratransit services to the City of Chicago are provided via three contracts with private operators utilising 546 contractor-owned vehicles. Pace also operates approximately 760 vanpools, one of the largest vanpool programs in the USA.

Developments

Pace's capital programme includes funding for the replacement of fleet vehicles, bus overhaul/maintenance expenses as well as improvements to Pace's nine fixed facility garages. Additionally, the programme contains funds for the purchase of various traffic signal priority projects and the replacement of a system-wide radio system. Lastly, the programme contains funding for the purchase of computer systems and a new bus safety system.

The vanpool programme continues to grow and Pace estimates to have 855 vehicles in service by year end 2008, carrying 2.2 million riders. At such time, it will be the largest public vanpool program in the USA.

In late 2007, Pace retained MV Transportation Inc as the provider of ADA paratransit services in South Cook County and awarded the company a new USD33 million, five-year contract to operate ADA services in the northern area of Chicago.

There are plans for a single fare card and integrated fare system for Pace, Metra and CTA.

Fleet: 705 buses; 358 paratransit vehicles; 767 vanpool vans (minibuses)

NABI (1999/2005)	293
Orion I (1988–1993)	104
Orion VI (2000–2004)	159
Ikarus USA (1992)	13
Nova (1996)	22
ElDorado (2006/7)	99
Chance American Heritage Trolley (2000)	7
MCI (2002)	8
ElDorado cutaway paratransit bus/van	358
Other various vans (1998/2007)	767

In peak service: 607 buses, including contractors' vehicles
Average age: 6 years (fixed route)

Most intensive service: 5 min
Fare structure: Primarily flat
Fare collection: Registering farebox with ticket processing unit collects cash, CTA tokens, stored value card receipts and smart cards
Arrangements for elderly/disabled: Paratransit operations serve 210 municipalities
Integration with other modes: Full integration with CTA; bus and rail passes co-ordinated with CTA and Metra rail, 11 park-and-ride facilities
Average peak hour speed: 22.4 km/h
Bus priority: Slip ramp from Tollway is used to access CTA station; signal priority in demonstration phase
Operating costs financed by: Fares 38.5 per cent, subsidy/grants 61.5 per cent
Subsidy from: RTA provides support drawn from sales tax, federal capital/formula assistance and state subsidy via the public transportation fund

Chicago Transit Authority (CTA)

567 West Lake Street, Chicago, Illinois 60661, US
Tel: (+1 312) 664 72 00
Fax: (+1 312) 681 28 25 (Media Relations)
Web: www.transitchicago.com

Key personnel

Chair: Carole Brown
President: Ron Huberman
Chief Operations Officer: William Mooney
Executive Vice-President, Operations Support: Dorval R Carter
Vice-President, Transit Operations: Jack Hruby
Vice-President, Facilities Maintenance: Pat Taylor
 Staff: More than 11,000

Passenger boardings: (All modes)
(2003) 441 million
(2004) 444.5 million
(2005) 492.4 million
(2006) not currently available
(2007) 499.5 million

Operating costs financed by: Fares, other commercial sources and subsidy/grants

Current situation

The Chicago Transit Authority (CTA) is a regional transit system that serves the City of Chicago and 40 suburbs.

Developments

The CTA continues to identify and implement service enhancements and capital improvements to enhance service and bring its system to a state of good repair (see bus and rail developments).

In early 2008, the CTA began installing new express farecard vending machines at more than 45 rail stations.

Bus

Passenger journeys: (2003) 291.8 million
(2004) 294 million
(2005) 303.2 million
(2006) Not currently available
(2007) 309.3 million
Vehicle-km (per vehicle per day): (2007) 106.9–225.3 km (100–140 miles) per day

Number of routes: 154
Route length: More than 4,069 km (2,529 miles)

Developments

CTA is continuing to replace the older buses in its fleet with 40 ft and slightly smaller 30 ft vehicles from New Flyer and Optima Bus Corporation, respectively. CTA also successfully tested ten 40 ft hybrid buses and based on that success plans to obtain 150 60 ft hybrid buses from King County Metro, Seattle's public transit agency.

Fleet: 2,143 vehicles (as at 3 March 2007)

TMC lift-equipped AC(1991)	274
Flxible lift-equipped AC(1991)	101
Flxible lift-equipped AC(1995)	324
New Flyer low-floor AC (1995)	61
Nova Bus low-floor AC 6400 (2000/01)	480
NABI articulated lift-equipped AC (2003/04)	221
Optima 30-ft low-floor AC (2006)	45
New Flyer low-floor AC (2006/07)	637

In peak service: 1,839 (as at 31 January 2008)

Average age of fleet: 8.0 years (as at 31 January 2008)
On order: Approximately 650 vehicles (includes order for 150 low-floor articulated vehicles to be delivered in 2008–2009)

Most intensive service: Peak 1 min, off-peak 3 min
One-person operation: All routes
Fare collection: Cash (accepted on buses only; exact fare in coins and bills); Chicago Card/Chicago Card Plus (smart cards); Transit Card (deducts fares and transfers); Passes (offer unlimited rides for select number of days); Visitor Passes (offer unlimited rides for select number of days); U-Pass

CTA Nova Bus at Cicero station (Bill Luke)

1115284

(allows full-time students at participating colleges and universities to use U-Pass for unlimited rides on CTA buses and trains during the school term). Transfers are allowed with use of Chicago Card, Chicago Card Plus and Transit Cards. A USD2 bonus is applied to Chicago Cards for every USD20 purchase or added value.

Fare structure: Fares are determined by the type of payment: Cash: Full fare is USD2; reduced fare is USD1 (buses only); Chicago Card/Chicago Card Plus: Full Fare is USD1.75 on bus and rail; Passes: Unlimited ride full fare passes offered for USD5 (1-day); USD20 (7-day) and USD75 (30-day). Unlimited ride reduced fare pass offered for USD35 (30-day).

Visitor Passes: Unlimited ride full fare passes offered for USD5 (1-day); USD9 (2-day); USD12 (3-day) and USD18 (5-day); U-Pass: Unlimited ride reduced fare pass offered to participating colleges and universities at a rate of USD0.70 cents per student.

Operational control: Route supervisors/mobile radio; on-line monitoring for emergencies

Arrangements for elderly/disabled: CTA's bus fleet is 100 per cent accessible; every 'L' train has cars that are accessible; more than half (80 out of 144) rail stations are now accessible. CTA provided 2.4 million paratransit rides in 2005.

CTA transferred its paratransit services to Pace suburban bus system on 1 July 2006.

Integration with other modes: CTA bus service connects with 126 of 144 CTA rail stations, all of Metra (suburban commuter rail) and Amtrak downtown stations, and with many Pace (suburban) routes.

Average weekday speed: 10.6 km/h (approximate)
New vehicles financed by: Federal and local grants

Metro

Type of operation: Full metro

Passenger journeys: (2003) 150.3 million (unlinked trips)
(2004) 148.3 million
(2005) 186.7 million
(2006) Not currently available
(2007) 190.2 million
Car-km (per day): (2003) 328,265 (203,980 miles)
(2005) 352,881 (219,317 miles)
(2006) Not currently available
(2007) 337,407 (209,700 miles)

Route length: 358.2 km (222.6 miles)
in tunnel: 18.3 km (11.4 miles)
elevated: 339.8 km (211.2 miles)
Number of lines: 8
Number of stations: 144
in tunnel: 22
elevated: 122
Gauge: 1,435 mm
Track: Flat-bottom rail; timber sleepers on ballast; sleepers on concrete trackbed with resilient pads; timber sleepers on iron/steel elevated structure
Tunnel: 5.4 m diameter tube and cut-and-cover
Electrification: 600 V DC, third rail

Service: Peak 3–8 min, off-peak 7–20 min (approximate)
First/last train: Red: operates 24 hours (weekdays); Blue: 24 hours (between O'Hare Airport and Forest Park); Orange: 21 hours (weekdays), 20 hours (weekends); Pink: 21 hours (weekdays and weekends); Green: 20.5 hours (weekdays), 19.5 hours (weekends); Brown: 20 hours (weekdays and weekends); Purple: 20 hours (weekdays and weekends); Yellow: 17 hours (weekdays only).
Fare structure: As for bus
Revenue control: Magnetically coded fare cards sold at all stations; Chicago Cards/Chicago Card Plus (smartcards)
Arrangements for elderly/disabled: More than half (80 of 144) of CTA rail stations are accessible to customers with disabilities; every 'L' train has cars that are accessible.
Signalling: The CTA rail system is fully equipped with cab signals that provide train protection and civil speed limits via signal indications in the operator's cab. Wayside fixed signals are limited to junctions, crossovers and other interlocked locations. The interlocking signals are equipped

Map of Chicago's metro
1115296

with trip stops that will automatically stop a train that passes a stop signal.
One-person operation: All routes

Rolling stock: 1,190 cars

Budd 2200 (1969/70)	142
Boeing 2400 (1976/78)	194
Budd/Transit America 2600 (1981/87)	596
Morrison Knudsen 3200 (1992/93)	258
In peak service: 1,000 (2007)	

Developments
CTA continues to upgrade its rail fleet and will replace some of the older rail cars, some of which are more than 30 years old, such as the 2200-series Budd cars that were purchased in 1969-70, as well as the 2400-series Boeing-Vertol cars purchased in 1976–78 , with new rail cars.

The CTA plans to incorporate a variety of technology enhancements such as wireless connectivity and cellular modems to improve some of the previously planned features of the rail cars.

Adding wireless connectivity to the electronic systems will mean:

- Train operators will be able to view live video from any railcar when the passenger intercom unit is activated. This will ensure operators are better able to immediately provide information to first responders.
- In the future, suitably equipped emergency vehicles could also access rail car video through the wireless connection;
- Diagnostic information will be available in real-time to maintenance personnel, enabling them to quickly identify problems and develop repair strategies. This new diagnostic system will help reduce breakdowns and ensure that when problems occur, technical troubleshooting will begin in real-time, reducing the impact on customers.

Adding cellular modems to railcars will allow the CTA's Control Center to communicate directly with customers in real-time via audio and text messages using speakers and six visual displays in each car.

Other enhancements such as security cameras and aisle-facing seating are included in the specifications, as well as Alternating Current (AC) traction motor propulsion.

The project calls for a base order of 406 new rail cars with additional options that could bring the total purchase to 706 cars. CTA selected Bombardier Transit Corporation to manufacture the rail cars through a competitive proposal process.

CTA expects the delivery of 10 new rail car prototypes in 2009. These prototypes will undergo nine to 12 months of testing, including a complete winter and summer season, to evaluate all aspects of the car design and operation. Once the prototype cars pass this test period, the delivery of the remaining cars will begin.

Brown Line Capacity Expansion Project
CTA's ongoing USD530 million Brown Line Capacity Expansion Project will provide fully accessible stations capable of supporting eight-car trains to increase the capacity of one of CTA's fastest growing rail lines.

Northeast Illinois Regional Commuter Railroad Corporation – Metra

Metra Passenger Services
547 W Jackson Boulevard, 14th Floor, Chicago, Illinois 60661-5717, US
Tel: (+1 312) 322 67 77
Fax: (+1 312) 322 69 65
Web: www.metrarail.com

Key personnel
Chair: Carole R Doris
Executive Director: Philip A Pagano

Deputy Executive Director: G Richard Tidwell
Chief Operating Officer: William Tupper
Senior Director, Corporate Services:
   Patrick McAtee
Director of Media Relations: Frank Malone
   Staff: 2,600

Type of operation: Suburban heavy rail

Passenger journeys: (2007) 83.3 million
(2008) 87.8 million (projected)
(2009) 88.3 million (forecast)

Current situation
Metra evolved from the Northeast Illinois Railroad Corporation to operate the commuter lines of the former Rock Island Railroad (79 route-km) and later those of the Milwaukee Road (135 km), which had been purchased and leased respectively by the RTA. NIRC also had purchase of service agreements for other commuter services provided by the Illinois Central (125 km), Burlington Northern (59 km), Chicago & North Western (249 km), Norfolk Southern (39 km) and Chicago, South Shore & South Bend (from Chicago across the Illinois/Indiana border to South Bend, now the South Shore Line) railroads.

In 1984, the Commuter Rail Service Board took over, adopting the service name Metra.

Today NIRC (Metra) owns and operates (through NIRC) the former Rock Island, Milwaukee, IC (Metra Electric) and Norfolk Southern (taken over in 1993) lines. Trains on other lines operate under purchase of service agreements. Metra is responsible for setting fare and service levels, and provides for capital improvements, planning and marketing for all lines.

Operations extend to 796.5 route-km (495 miles) of 1,435 mm gauge on 11 routes and four branches serving 228 stations, of which 66 km (two routes) are electrified at 1.5 kV DC overhead. Other routes are worked by diesel push-pull trainsets. Trains run every 5–20 minutes at peak times, and every 1, 1½ or 2 hours off-peak; limited service evenings and weekends. Zonal fare structure, with monthly tickets giving an opportunity to purchase monthly bus pass (Link-up Passport) at a reduced rate. 10-ride tickets and an unlimited ride ticket Weekend Pass are also available and there are different fare programmes for senior citizens, those with disabilities, families, students and children. Fares account for 55 per cent of operating costs.

All of Metra's lines and most stations are fully accessible.

In addition, the South Shore Line has 117 km of 1,435 mm gauge route electrified at 1.5 kV DC overhead and operates interurban service from Chicago to South Bend in Indiana, serving Hammond, East Chicago, Gary, Miller, Ogden Dunes, Chesterton (Dune Park) and Michigan City. This route is subsidised 22 per cent by Metra and 78 per cent by the Northern Indiana Commuter Transportation District (NICTD) (www.nictd.com), which purchased the line in 1991.

For further information on Metra and NICTD, please see *Jane's World Railways.*

Developments
In January 2006, Metra implemented new or expanded services on three New Start projects. These projects doubled the amount of service offered on the North Central Service (NCS) Line, expanded service further into Kane County on the Union Pacific West (UP-W) Line and increased and expanded service on the South West Service (SWS) Line.

Two new lines have also been proposed, and preliminary planning studies are under way on a 53-km (33-mile) SouthEast Service (SES) Line to Crete and an initial segment of the 88.5-km (55-mile) Suburban Transit Access Route, or STAR Line. Estimated costs for these projects are USD524.5 milion and USD1.1 billion respectively.

A new station in New Lennox, at Laraway Road, on the SWS Line opened in 2006.

Rolling stock: 144 locomotives, 800 bi-level coaches, 165 Highliner cars

---

Cincinnati

Population: City: 308,728, metropolitan area: 2.0 million (2005 estimates)

Public transport
Bus services in city and environs provided by operating arm of Southwest Ohio Regional Transit Authority (SORTA), governed by representative Board of Trustees. Services also run into the city from Covington and Newport across the Ohio river in Kentucky, operated by similar undertaking. New rail, BRT, streetcar/trolley and tram systems are all under study.

Southwest Ohio Regional Transit Authority (SORTA) – Metro

1014 Vine Street, Cincinnati, Ohio 45202-1116, US
Tel: (+1 513) 621 94 50   Fax: (+1 513) 621 52 91
e-mail: info@go-metro.com
Web: www.go-metro.com

Key personnel
Chief Executive Officer and General Manager: Michael H Setzer
Chief Financial Officer: H Theodore 'Ted' Bergh
Chief Operations Officer: Marilyn Shazor
Chief Communications Officer: Sallie Hilvers
Transit Development Director: Tim Reynolds
Procurement Manager: Jerry Roetting
   Staff: 1,000

Current situation
Metro, SORTA's bus-operating subsidiary, was established in 1973 when voters approved a tax increase to fund purchase of the Cincinnati Transit bus system. It serves a total population of 867,000; 34 per cent of riders live outside the city of Cincinnati in other parts of Hamilton and Clermont counties and are served by 18 per cent of vehicle-km operated.

Bus

Passenger journeys: (2001) 23.7 million
(2002) 22.7 million
(2003) 22.4 million
(2004) 21.8 million
(2005) 12.9 million
Vehicle-km: (2000) 13.7 million
(2003) 13.6 million
(2004) 13.3 million

Number of routes: 54
Route length: (One way) 1,993 km

Fleet: 393 vehicles	
Neoplan (1989/90)	17
Gillig Phantom (1995/96/97)	147
Gillig (1998/99/2000/01/02/04)	189
Gillig (2006)	40
In peak service: 328	

Average age of fleet: 7.084 years

Most intensive service: 8 min
One-person operation: All routes
Fare collection: GFI fareboxes, 81 per cent collected on board
Fare structure: Flat, city; zonal, suburbs; prepurchase tickets, monthly passes; 25 cent transfers, 50 cent to TANK services; peak surcharge on express services
Arrangements for elderly/disabled: Access is a shared-ride public transit service of Metro, providing kerb-to-kerb transportation in Greater Cincinnati for people with disabilities. Access is a non-profit service of SORTA. A private company under contract with SORTA operates Access service.
Average distance between stops: 161 m
Average peak-hour speed: 20.5 km/h
Integration with other modes: 23 suburban park-and-ride sites
Operating costs financed by: Fares 27.9 per cent, city transit fund 50.8 per cent, federal 15.3 per cent, state 1.5 per cent, Access fares 0.7 per cent, other 3.8 per cent

Demand response fleet: 53 vehicles	
Ford van, 15-passenger (1994)	1
GMC van, 10-passenger (1996)	6
ElDorado Aerotech (1997/2000/2002)	46

Transit Authority of Northern Kentucky (TANK)

3375 Madison Pike, Fort Wright, Kentucky 41017, US
Tel: (+1 859) 331 82 35   Fax: (+1 859) 578 69 52
e-mail: info@tankbus.org
Web: www.tankbus.org

Key personnel
General Manager: David Malone
Director of Operations: Terri Pierce
Assistant Director of Operations: Gary Berkley
Director of Communications and Development: Gina Douthat
Director of Finance and Administration: Allison Ledford
Director of Maintenance: Don Neltner
   Staff: 208

Passenger journeys: (2004) 3.6 million
Vehicle-km: (2004) 4 million

Number of routes: 27

Background
The Transit Authority of Northern Kentucky (TANK) has provided transit services since 1973. TANK is governed by a nine-member Board of Directors.

Current situation
Provides transit services to the counties of Boone, Campbell, Kenton and downtown Cincinnati. TANK offers a 'Downtown Connection' service, with fast 'reverse commute'. Express bus travel on the expressway provide access to Downtown Cincinnati Central Business District plus Express service to Cincinnati/Northern Kentucky airport. Also provides Regional Area Mobility Program (RAMP) paratransit service. Fares cover approximately 25 per cent of operating costs.

Fleet (fixed route): 101 buses	
Fixed-route vehicles	
Gillig	32
Flxible	13
Low-floor Gillig (40 ft)	43
Low-floor Gillig (29 ft)	8
Orion	5
Demand-response vehicles	
Supremes	10
Goshen	9
E350 Ford van	6

Integration with other modes: 19 Park-&-Ride locations
Fare structure: Flat fixed route fare USD1.25, 10-ride ticket book, Monthly Pass, monthly Metro/Tank Pass, 12-ride Student Ticket Book, 10-ride RAMP Ticket Book, TANK RAMP Monthly Pass, discounts for seniors/disabled

Cleveland

Population: City 444,313, metropolitan area 2.1 million (2006 estimates)

Public transport

Bus, metro and light rail services provided for Cleveland, 65 towns in Cuyahoga County and some small outside areas by Regional Transit Authority under the control of representative Board of Trustees. Paratransit system, Community Responsive Transit, provided for elderly/disabled. All public transport agencies within the county were consolidated in 2005.

Greater Cleveland Regional Transit Authority (GCRTA)

1240 West Sixth Street, Cleveland, Ohio 44113, US

Tel: (+1 216) 566 51 01   Fax: (+1 216) 781 40 43
e-mail: myork@gcrta.org
Web: www.riderta.com

Key personnel

President, Board of Trustees: George F Dixon III
General Manager and Chief Executive Officer:
   Joseph A Calabrese
Deputy General Managers
   Operations: Michael York
   Legal: Sheryl King Benford
   Finance and Administration: Loretta Kirk
   Engineering and Project Management: Michael Schipper
   Human Resources: Bruce Hampton
Staff: 2,653

Passenger boardings: (All modes)
(2003) 59.7 million
(2004) 55.5 million
(2005) 57.1 million
(2006) 57.2 million
(2007) 57.3 million

Operating costs financed by: (All modes) fares 17 per cent, other commercial sources 3 per cent, subsidy/grants 80 per cent
Subsidy from: Dedicated 1 per cent sales tax 67 per cent

Current situation

The Greater Cleveland Regional Transit Authority (GCRTA) operates both bus and rapid transit service, providing approximately 57 million unlinked trips annually. Using the Red Line (heavy rail) rapid transit, customers can travel east from Cleveland Hopkins International Airport, located on Cleveland's far west side, to the Tower City Center, the east-west rail service hub and downtown Cleveland's premier shopping, entertainment and office facility, or as far east as the Louis Stokes Station at Windermere in the City of East Cleveland, Ohio. Altogether there are 18 stops along the Red Line's 32 km (20 mile) east-west corridor. GCRTA's Blue and Green Lines (light rail) serve Cleveland's eastern suburbs including Shaker Heights, Beachwood and Warrensville Heights. Starting with the Waterfront Line, the Blue and Green Lines are interlined and travel south and east to Tower City where the service connects with the Red Line service. All rail service is interlined from Tower City east to the East 55th/Central Rail stop after which the Red Line travels northeast and the interlined Blue/Green service travels east. The Blue/Green Line service remains interlined eastward to Shaker Square. From Shaker Square, the Green Line continues 6.4 km (4 miles) east to the city of Shaker Heights and the Blue Line travels 5.6 km (3.5 miles) southeast toward the cities of Beachwood and Warrensville Heights. Each line offers 12 stops after the Shaker Square split.

The Waterfront Line, GCRTA's newest light rail segment, opened in 1996. The Waterfront Line serves the Warehouse District, the Flats and other attractions along the city's north coast, including the Cleveland Browns Stadium, Rock-n-Roll Hall of Fame and Museum, Great Lakes Science Center and Burke Lakefront Airport. The Waterfront Line extended the Blue and Green Line rapid transit service for 3.5 km (2.2 miles) west from Tower City, then north along the Flats East Bank, east to stations serving the football stadium and the Rock-n-Roll Hall of Fame, terminating at the South Harbor Station.

GCRTA offers special loop bus services throughout the downtown area. In early 2006, new buses with 'historic trolley' features began serving these routes.

Community Circulator service is available in many central city and suburban communities. Circulators provide access to nearby supermarkets, retail stores, medical offices and other popular destinations. Customers may board at any regular GCRTA bus stop, or they may flag the Circulator to stop anywhere along the route.

The 8,500 parking spaces along the Red Line include spaces at Brookpark, Puritas, Triskett, West Park and Windermere. The major park-and-ride lots along the Blue and Green Lines are at Warrensville and Green Road.

GCRTA also operates four major bus park-and-ride facilities: Westlake, Euclid, Strongsville and North Olmsted. These are served by special coaches and a fare premium is charged. GCRTA provides service to a number of other park-and-ride lots throughout Greater Cleveland.

Special transit services are available for senior citizens born in 1931 or earlier and for persons with disabilities who qualify under the Americans with Disabilities Act and GCRTA's Complementary Paratransit Plan.

Developments

An alternatives analysis published in 1990 examined possible metro (heavy rail)/light rail system extensions and bus service improvements. These proposals were refined into a USD800 million 25-year development plan – the GCRTA's first long-term plan – known as Transit 2010.

The main provisions of the plan affect the bus services used by some 78 per cent of GCRTA riders. A major restructuring of the network will cater for changed travel patterns, especially suburb-to-suburb and reverse-flow commuting. Community circulator routes have been implemented as feeders both to local activity nodes, such as shopping centres and hospitals, and to interchanges with main bus and rail routes. Timed transfers are being offered at many hubs where two or more services intersect. Studies were completed for the Waterfront extension of the Red and Blue Lines, but plans for these expansions are on hold.

Greater Cleveland Regional Transit Authority has begun to rebuild an 8 km (5 mile) section of Euclid Avenue to provide for Bus Rapid Transit service on exclusive bus lanes. This project is now known as the Euclid Corridor Transportation Project (ECTP). Further details can be found below.

Provision of commuter service on several rail rights-of-way has been studied by the Northeast Ohio Areawide Co-ordinating Agency with GCRTA's support. One of the most promising, but highly unlikely to be implemented, is the 100 km (62 mile) Cleveland-Akron-Canton corridor, where disused freight trackage has been purchased by local authorities in Summit and Stark Counties with possible expansion to downtown Cleveland.

In 2005, GCRTA completed the process that had begun in 1975: the consolidation of all public transport agencies in Cuyahoga County, to improve efficiency. The cities of Maple Heights and North Olmsted transferred their municipal bus systems to the GCRTA in March 2005.

Bus

Passenger journeys: (2003) 45.8 million
(2004) 47.2 million
(2005) 48.37 million
(2006) 48.34 million
(2007) 47.66 million
Vehicle-km: (2003) 40.97 million

(2004) 40.6 million
(2005) 41.5 million
(2006) 38.4 million
(2007) 34.9 million

Number of routes: 99
Route length: Not currently available
Number of bus stops: Approx 8,500

Fleet: 601 buses, including Community Circulators on 12 routes

Most intensive service: 6 min
One-person operation: All services except light rail
Fare collection: Farebox adjacent to driver
Fare structure: USD1.75 bus and rail; USD2.00 park-and-ride; USD1.0 fare on downtown loop, trolley and circulators; daily, weekly and monthly passes
Fares collected on board: Not currently available
Integration with other modes: Total; extensive park-and-ride facilities with 8,500 spaces; more planned
Operational control: Route inspectors (stationary and mobile)/mobile radio
Arrangements for elderly/disabled: Fleet of 77 lift-equipped wheelchair-accessible paratransit buses plus 22 lift-equipped wheelchair-accessible buses under contract service; discount fares on conventional services
Average peak-hour speed: In mixed traffic, 18.5 km/h
New vehicles financed by: FTA grants (up to 80 per cent), state, local sales tax revenue and bonds

Metro (heavy rail)

Type of operation: Full metro (Red Line), initial route opened 1955

Passenger boardings: (2003) 7.4 million
(2004) 5.04 million
(2005) 5.45 million
(2006) 5.48 million
(2007) 5.9 million
Car-km: (2003) 2.2 million
(2004) 2.8 million
(2005) 3.88 million
(2006) 3.18 million
(2007) 2.74 million

Route length: 61.3 km (38 miles)
   in tunnel: 0.96 km (0.6 miles)
   on surface/at grade: 60.4 km (37.5 miles)
Number of lines: 1
Number of stations: 18
   in tunnel: 2
Gauge: 1,435 mm
Track: 45 kg/m AAR-EE continuously welded rail; sleepers on ballast
Tunnel: Cut-and-cover, or within structure
Electrification: 600 V DC, overhead

Rolling stock: 60 cars
Tokyu Car (1985/86)   M60
In peak service: 22 (more for special events)

Service: Peak 7½ min, off-peak 15 min
First/last train: 03.15/00.51
Fare structure: USD1.75, monthly, weekly and daily passes
Revenue control: One-way turnstiles
Integration with other modes: Park-and-ride places at many of the metro and light rail stations
One-person operation: All services
Signalling: GRS three-aspect lights with automatic stop; cab signalling

Light rail

Type of operation: Light rail (Blue and Green Lines), first line opened 1920 (includes Waterfront Line)

Passenger boardings: (2004) 2.73 million
(2005) 2.77 million
(2006) 2.91 million
(2007) 3.19 million
Car-km: (2004) 1.46 million
(2005) 1.64 million
(2006) 1.42 million
(2007) 1.30 million

Route length: 28 km (17.4 miles)
Number of lines: 2
Number of stops: 34
Electrification: 600 V DC, overhead

Developments

Shiftwatch/A4S Security has a USD1.3 million contract to install wireless surveillance cameras and recorders in 40 Breda LRV cars. Current plans call for completion during 2008.

Bombardier Transportation has a USD31.0 million contract to perform a mid-life rehabilitation on a maximum of 34 Breda LRV cars. Current plans call for delivery of all cars by Q1 2008.

Rolling stock: 48 cars
Breda LRV (1983)   M48
In peak service: 17 (more for special events)

Service: Peak 5 min, off-peak 15 min
First/last car: 04.05/00.11

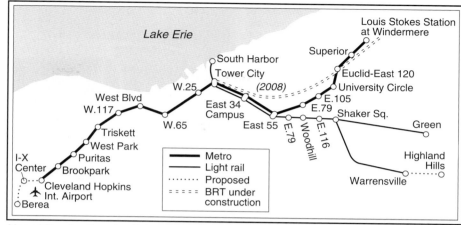

Map of Cleveland's metro, light rail and BRT system   1115297

Bus Rapid Transit (proposed) – Euclid Corridor Transportation project (ECTP) (Silver Line)

Address as for GCRTA above
Tel: (+1 216) 771 41 44   Fax: (+1 216) 771 41 45
e-mail: dwillis@gcrta.org
Web: www.euclidtransit.org

Key personnel

Deputy General Manager, Engineering and Project Development: Michael Schipper
Project Manager: Gary Thayer
Project Officer: Danielle Willis
Project Controls Manager: Bryan Moore
Media Enquiries: Chad Self
Tel: (+1 216) 566 52 11
e-mail: cself@gcrta.org

Background

The Euclid Corridor Transportation Project (ECTP) consists of an 11.4 km (7.1 mile) Bus Rapid Transit line operating from Public Square in Downtown Cleveland to the Stokes/ Windermere Red Line Rapid Transit station in East Cleveland, and a 3.9 km (2.4 mile) Transit Zone, which includes the parallel arterials of St Clair and Superior Avenues in Downtown Cleveland. Using an exclusive centre median busway, the Bus Rapid Transit Silver Line will connect the central business district (the region's largest employment centre) with the University Circle area (the second largest employment centre) and major cultural, medical and educational districts. From there, the transit vehicles will transition to the curb and continue

into neighbouring East Cleveland to serve one of GCRTA's most highly used facilities, the Stokes Rapid Transit Station at Windermere. The project will include related transit and roadway improvements along Euclid Avenue.

The East Side Transit Center is no longer in the ECTP programme and is proceeding as a stand-alone project. The Environmental Document has been revised and a Finding of No Significant Impact (FONSI) was issued. This centre, located east of Downtown Cleveland at the southeast corner of East 21st and Prospect near Cleveland State University (CSU), will serve CSU, the Convocation Center and other important destinations in the area. The project complements ECTP by providing interface between GCRTA's bus network and ECTP's Bus Rapid Transit (BRT) line. GCRTA is also pursuing parties interested in constructing joint development projects above the transit centre.

FTA New Starts funding represents 48.8 per cent of the total USD168.4 million project cost, with the remaining 51.2 per cent coming from the State of Ohio TRAC funds and local contributions from the City of Cleveland, Northeast Ohio Areawide Coordinating Agency (NOACA) and GCRTA.

Developments

The BRT project has completed the Preliminary Engineering phase of design, and a Finding Of No Significant Impact (FONSI) was issued in February 2002. The first phase of Value Engineering, completed in June 2002, resulted in USD8.8 million of project cost savings. Additional Value Engineering in 2003 and restructuring of the project has reduced costs by another USD40

million. In July 2002, GCRTA received formal approval by the FTA to enter into the Final Design phase of engineering. Procurement on the Hybrid Diesel-Electric Euclid Corridor Vehicle (ECV) has been completed.

In October 2004, GCRTA and the FTA executed a Full Funding Grant Agreement (FFGA) for the project, the first BRT project to receive a FFGA.

For FY2005, GCRTA received a USD25 million New Starts funding earmark to be used to begin land acquisition, construction management services and initial construction.

The New Starts Financial Plan acknowledges that all local commitments are in place. These local dollars from the City of Cleveland, the Ohio Department of Transportation, NOACA and the GCRTA are already being expended on continuing design activities.

In November 2005, construction of the 3.9 km (2.4 mile) transit zone roadway rehabilitation project was completed.

In August 2006, construction of the USD1.85 million modifications to the Hayden Bus Facility, which will house the BRT vehicles, was completed.

From January 2006 to June 2006, the GCRTA Board of Trustees approved five major contracts totalling USD92.2 million for all remaining work on Euclid Avenue. Work on these contracts started in March 2006 and will last for 30 months. Construction is currently 65 per cent complete.

In February 2006, New Flyer presented the first of the five-door, articulated BRT vehicles to the GCRTA. This Advanced Style pilot vehicle will be used for testing and training.

The Silver Line is scheduled to be fully operational in October 2008.

Columbus

Population: City 733,203, Metropolitan area 1.73 million (2006 estimates)

Public transport

Bus services provided for residents of Franklin County in central Ohio by Regional Transit Authority under control of representative Board of Trustees. Service area includes small portions of Delaware, Fairfield and Licking counties, whose boundaries adjoin Franklin County.

Central Ohio Transit Authority (COTA)

1600 McKinley Avenue, Columbus, Ohio 43222-1093, US
Tel: (+1 614) 275 58 00
Fax: (+1 614) 275 59 33
Web: www.cota.com

Key personnel

Chair: William G Porter
Vice-Chair: Linda Mauger
President and Chief Executive Officer: W J Lhota
   Staff: 616

Background

Formed in 1971, the Central Ohio Transit Authority (COTA) began providing service in Franklin County in January 1974. COTA's service area includes Franklin and small portions of Delaware, Fairfield and Licking Counties.

A 13-member board of trustees oversees the transit system and appoints the president/CEO to manage the day to day operations of the authority. In November 1999, Franklin County voters approved a 0.25 per cent permanent sales tax for COTA.

In August 2006, COTA placed on the 7 November 2006 ballot a 10-year renewable 0.25 per cent sales and use tax levy (Issue 7). Issue 7 passed, and will be combined with COTA's permanent 0.25 per cent local sales tax approved by voters in 1999.

Current situation

COTA operates fixed route bus and paratransit service (Project Mainstream), in a service area of 1,455.6 km² (562 sq miles).

Developments

Realising that COTA was not fully meeting the region's existing public transit needs, in late 2005, COTA began soliciting public and community

stakeholder input in order to develop the Long-Range Transit Plan (LRTP).

During this time period, the North Corridor Transit Project (NCTP) had been considering light rail and Bus Rapid Transit (BRT) as two options for new transit service. Both of these options will now not be pursued, after federal funding was not approved in mid-2006. Instead, COTA will focus on expanding it's bus system. However, COTA will continue to explore strategic investments, such as BRT, as potential new transit options. The LRTP estimates that there will be a requirement for a fleet of 440 vehicles by 2030.

In 2004, COTA implemented the more flexible Sedan Voucher programme. The Sedan Voucher Service program will be expanded to provide better service at a lower cost to persons with special transit needs in the community. This service is available 24 hours a day, seven days a week. For 2008, it is projected that COTA will provide approximately 170,000 total trips for persons with disabilities. By 2011, COTA's mobility service's budget is estimated to increase 29 per cent from 2006 mobility services expenditures.

Buses on Freeway Shoulder Program: Effective November 2006, buses travelling on I-70 east began merging onto the freeway shoulder to avoid congestion delays. Upon successful completion of this one-year pilot, the programme will be expanded to other key freeways (I-71 north and south, I-670 east and west, I-70 west and State Route 315).

Bus

Passenger boardings: (2005) 14.6 million
(2006) 14.84 million
Vehicle-km: (2006) 89 million

Number of routes: 56
Route length: (One way) 1,807 km (1,123 miles)

Fleet: 234 vehicles (including New Flyer, NovaBus and Gillig buses)
Full breakdown of fleet is not currently available
In peak service: 187
Average age of fleet: 8.88 yrs

Most intensive service: 6 min
One-person operation: All routes
Fare collection: Cash to electronic counting farebox with dollar bill facility
Fare structure: Flat, no change; monthly passes for Local and Express routes; free transfers, premium for Express services; college U-Pass programmes

Fare evasion control: Driver monitors payment
Operational control: Two-way radio
Arrangements for elderly/disabled: Reduced fares; all fixed routes accessible to wheelchairs. Project Mainstream provides transport for those who cannot use fixed-route services – Subscription

COTA NovaBus LFS on S High Street (Bill Luke) 1115263

riders make the same journey at least once a week, whilst Reservation riders request trips as required. Service is currently provided by First Transit, however, all Mainstream vehicles (51) are owned by COTA. Project Mainstream serves an average of 530 trips per weekday
Integration with other modes: 26 park-and-ride lots have a total of 2,131 spaces, and there are two parking loops with 12 spaces each. Development of five additional lots planned, mostly around the I-270 orbital highway; guaranteed ride home scheme reimburses participants 90 per cent of fare of four taxi rides per year at times when regular buses do not run

Average peak-hour speed: 22.3 km/h
Bus priority: Peak-hour priority lane in central business district
Operating costs financed by: Fares 18 per cent, other commercial sources 2 per cent, subsidy/grants 20 per cent, tax levy 61 per cent
Subsidy from: FTA 4.5 per cent, state 7.3 per cent, local 86.2 per cent, other 2 per cent
New vehicles financed by: FTA (80 per cent), state grants and sales tax (20 per cent). Following passage of Issue 7 in November 2006, some expansion vehicles will also be funded 100 per cent from local sales tax receipts

Dallas

Population: City: 1.24 million, metropolitan area (Dallas-Fort Worth-Arlington): 6.15 million (2007 estimates)

Public transport

Fixed-route bus, paratransit van, light and commuter rail services, and HOV lanes provided by regional transit authority controlled by representative board. Suburban bus and some paratransit services provided under contract; short heritage tramway.

Dallas Area Rapid Transit (DART)

1401 Pacific Avenue, Dallas, Texas 75266-7240, US
Tel: (+1 214) 749 32 78   Fax: (+1 214) 749 36 53
Web: www.dart.org

Key personnel
President and Executive Director: Gary Thomas
Executive Vice-President, Operations:
  Victor H Burke
Executive Vice-President, Administration:
  Ben Gomez
Senior Vice-President, Rail Program Development:
  Timothy McKay
Chief Financial Officer: Vacant
Vice-President, Economic Opportunity and Government Relations: Jerry Franklin
Vice-President, Commuter Rail and Railroad Management: Wayne Friesner
Vice-President, Paratransit: Doug Douglas
Vice-President, Transportation: Frank Jennings
Vice-President, Maintenance: Michael Hubbell
Vice-President, Marketing and Communications:
  Sue Bauman
Vice-President, Finance: Sharon Leary
Vice-President, Procurement: John Adler
Vice-President, Human Resources: Lynda Jackson
Chief of DART Police: James Spiller
Director, Media Relations: Morgan Lyons
  Staff: 3,286

Passenger journeys: (All modes, including HOV lane trips)
(2003) 94.4 million
(2004) 93 million
(2005) 98.1 million

(2006) 102.9 million
(2007) 103.8 million

Background
DART was created in 1983 following passage of a referendum to fund a regional transit agency through a 1 per cent sales tax. The DART service area covers more than 1,110 km², 13 cities and a population of 2.1 million. The 15-member board of directors is appointed by the member city councils, with representation based on population.

Bus
Number of routes: 130 (approximate)
Route length: 2,283 km
On priority right-of-way: 13.6 km

Current situation
DART Paratransit Services has modernised its fleet with 186 new vans.

HOV lanes have been developed in a joint project between DART and the Texas Department of Transportation; they are reserved for DART buses and vehicles carrying two or more passengers. DART currently operates 92 km of HOV lanes.

Developments
To further reduce bus emissions, DART has retrofitted the diesel engines of 360 buses for operation with Ultra-Low-Sulphur Diesel (ULSD) fuel. The programme was completed in early 2004.
DART has also made recent improvements to its bus shelters, including installation of shelters featuring lighting and infra-red heaters.

Fleet: 742 vehicles (675 active, 67 in reserve)

NABI	80
Nova Bus (diesel) (1998/99/2000)	403
Nova Bus (LNG) (1998/99)	183

High Occupancy Vehicle (HOV) lane on I-35E (South R L Thornton) (DART) 1325215

Champion Motor Coach (diesel) (1999)
76 (9 active, 67 in reserve)
MetroTran vans   100
In peak service: 672 (excluding paratransit)
Fixed route peak: 558
On order: None

Most intensive service: 5 min
One-person operation: All routes
Fare collection: Data-collecting electronic registering fareboxes accepting coins and dollar bills
Fare structure: Two flat fares based on local bus and rail services and premium express bus services between downtown Dallas and free park-and-ride facilities in Addison, Carrollton, Dallas, Farmers Branch, Garland, Glenn Heights, Irving, Plano and Rowlett; monthly pass; annual pass for local employers for rail and bus services
Fares collected on board: 60 per cent
Operational control: Route inspectors/mobile radio; satellite navigational system tracks all vehicles
Arrangements for elderly/disabled: Bus fleet is 100 per cent wheelchair accessible; kerb-to-kerb/curb-to-curb service for passengers who are unable to use DART buses or trains; free travel for certified paratransit customers with disabilities on fixed-route and rail services

Average peak-hour speed: 29 km/h
Bus priority: HOV lanes on six major roads; plans for lanes on a further four roads
Integration with other modes: Park-and-ride facilities; local bus networks feed light and commuter rail stations
Operating costs financed by: Fares, sales tax revenues, federal funds and debt issuances
New vehicles financed by: FTA 80 per cent, DART 20 per cent

Light rail

Type of operation: Light rail, first line opened 1996

Passenger boardings: (2003) 17 million
(2004) 16.5 million
(2005) 17.5 million
(2006) 18.6 million
(2007) 17.89 million

Route length: 72 km
  in tunnel: 5.6 km
Number of lines: 2
Number of stations: 35
Gauge: 1,435 mm
Electrification: 750 V DC, overhead

Current situation

DART's initial light rail route opened in three stages between June 1996 and May 1997, linking Park Lane in the north with central Dallas and branching in the south to serve West Oak Cliff (Red Line) and South Oak Cliff (Blue Line). One further station, Cityplace on the underground section running beneath the North central expressway, opened in 2000.

DART currently operates a 72 km light rail system which includes 35 stations.

In July 2002, DART opened a new extension, incorporating seven new stations, four in North Dallas and three in Richardson. This extended the Red Line by more than 14 km. The new stations in Dallas are at Park Lane, Walnut Hill, Forest Lane and LBJ/Central. Those in Richardson are located at Spring Valley, Arapaho Center and Galatyn Park.

A Blue Line expansion, completed in November 2002, added Forest/Jupiter and Downtown Garland stations, and the Red Line expansion, completed in December 2002, extended the service to the new Bush Turnpike in Richardson and Downtown Plano and Park Road in Plano.

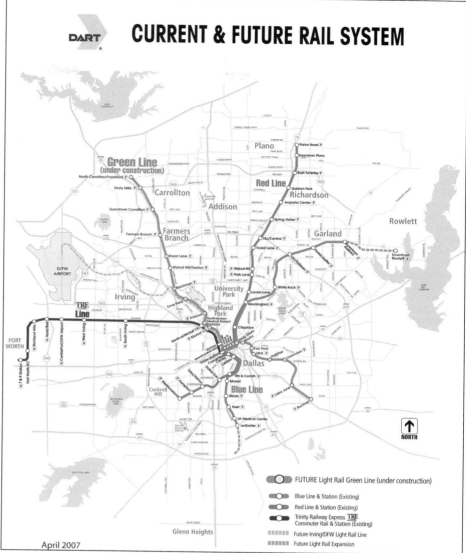

Map of Dallas light rail and Trinity Railway Express commuter rail systems (DART)   1325216

DART NABI bus (DART)   1136215

Developments

DART opened Victory station in downtown Dallas in late 2004. This is the first 2.4 km of the Northwest Corridor light rail expansion. Victory station will support both DART Rail and Trinity Railway Express commuter rail.

In August 2006, DART began construction on the Northwest/Southeast Corridor expansion (Green Line). The line will be 34 km long and run from Farmers Branch to Pleasant Green and is scheduled for completion in 2010, with the first phase from Victory Station to Fair Park due to open in September 2009. There are plans to extend this line further to Carrollton.

There are also plans for a new Orange Line, which will serve Las Colinas Urban Center and Dallas Fort Worth International Airport and for an extension of the Blue Line from Garland to Rowlett.

When complete in 2013, the rail system will be 144.8 km in length.

DART also intends to overhaul components of its LRV fleet and to rebuild ticket vending machines.

In October 2008, the first of the modified KinkiSharyo Super Light Rail Vehicles (SLRV) entered service on the Blue Line. The modified vehicles have a new low-floor 9.4 m centre section, which adds 25 seats to capacity. The modification programme is currently scheduled to be completed by the end of 2010.

Rolling stock: 115 cars

Kinkisharyo (1995)	M40
Kinkisharyo (1999)	M55
Kinkisharyo (2005)	M20
In peak service: 85	

Service: Peak 5–10 min, off-peak 20 min
First/last car: 05.30–00.10
Fare structure: As bus
Fare collection: Ticket machines at stations
Fare evasion control: Spot checks by inspectors; uniformed and plain clothes transit police
Arrangements for elderly/disabled: Stations and cars are wheelchair accessible

Trinity Railway Express (TRE)

4801 Rock Island Road, Irving, Texas 75061, US
Tel: (+1 214) 979 11 11 (Information Centre, DART)
Tel: (+1 817) 215 86 00 (Customer Relations, the T)
e-mail: tweb@the-t.com (the T)
　CustInfo@DART.org (DART)
Web: www.trinityrailwayexpress.org

Key personnel

Vice-President, Commuter Rail: Wayne Friesner
Chief Operating Officer, TRE: Bill Farquhar
Assistant Vice-President, Commuter Rail:
　Ms Norma De La Garza-Navarro
Chief Mechanical Officer: Salvatore J DeAngelo
Chief Engineering Officer: Daniel A Carrizales
　Staff: Not currently available

Type of operation: Commuter rail

Passenger journeys: (FY2003) 2.29 million
(FY2004) 2.16 million
(FY2005) 2.15 million
(FY2006) 2.4 million
(FY2007) 2.5 million (estimate)

Background

Operated jointly by DART and the Fort Worth Transportation Authority (The T), the Trinity Railway Express commuter rail line links downtown Dallas and downtown Fort Worth.

The first stage, the 16 km from Dallas Union station to South Irving, opened in 1996, and in December 2002 the line was completed to Fort Worth from Dallas.

Current situation

The service operates six days a week along the former Rock Island Railroad, now named TRE and forming the 54.7 km TRE/DFW subdivision,

Completed DART Super Light Rail Vehicle (SLRV), showing new low-floor middle section (DART)
1374677

DART Paratransit van loading (DART)　　　　0585186

TRE at Union Station (Peter Roelofs)　　　　1194987

with eight intermediate stations between Dallas and Fort Worth.

Services are provided under contract by Herzog Transit Services, Inc and right-of-way maintenance is provided under contract by Herzog Contracting Corporation.

In Dallas, the Union Station terminal offers connections to DART's light rail and bus services and to Amtrak. Fort Worth's Intermodal Transportation Center (ITC) provides interchange with Amtrak's long-distance services and The T's local bus services.

The Dallas/Fort Worth International Airport provides free shuttle bus services between

the CentrePort station and the Remote South Parking facility, where free shuttles to the airline terminals are available.

Developments

In March 2007, TRE awarded a contract to 4G Metro for the provision of wireless broadband services along the entire length of the railway.

Rolling stock: 13 diesel railcars, 6 locomotives, 11 bilevel coaches, 10 bilevel control/cab cars

Budd (ex-VIA Rail Canada)	M13
TRE F-59 PH (ex-Go Transit) (2000)	M4
TRE F-59 PHI (2001)	M2

Bilevel cab (Hawker-Siddeley, ex-Go Transit) (rebuilt 2000/01)	2
Bilevel coach (Hawker-Siddeley, ex-Go Transit) (rebuilt 2000/01)	10
Bilevel cab cars (Bombardier) (2000)	2
Bilevel cab cars (Bombardier) (2003)	3
Bilevel coach (Bombardier) (2007)	1
Bilevel cab car (Bombardier) (2007)	3

First/last train: Weekdays: From Ft. Worth: 05:36/20:45 (to Dallas) and 22:31 (to CentrePort) From Dallas: 06:16/20:15 From CentrePort: 05:29 (to Dallas) and 06:04 (to Ft. Worth)/21:19 (to Dallas) and 22:45 (to Ft. Worth). Saturdays: From Ft. Worth: 08:25/21:55 From Dallas: 08:22/22:26 (to Ft. Worth) and 23:15 (to CentrePort) From CentrePort: 07:33 to Dallas and 08:53 to Ft. Worth/22:33 to Dallas and 22:57 to Ft. Worth. Sundays and major holidays: No service.

Fare structure: Two zones; round-trip day pass, monthly pass

Arrangements for elderly/disabled: Reduced travel for certified paratransit customers with disabilities on fixed-route and rail services; all trains and stations are wheelchair accessible

Newest TRE locomotive at ITC Station (Trinity Railway Express)   1194988

McKinney Avenue Transit Authority (MATA)

3153 Oak Grove Avenue, Dallas, Texas 75204, US
Tel: (+1 214) 855 00 06   Fax: (+1 214) 855 52 50
e-mail: jvlate@yahoo.com (Chief Operating Officer)
Web: www.mata.org

Key personnel

Chairman: Phil Cobb
Chief Operating Officer: John Landrum
Business Director: Nancy Bannister
Secretary: Ed Landrum

Background

The McKinney Avenue Trolley, which began operations in July 1989, is a private, non-profit company operating under a City of Dallas, Texas, franchise.

Current situation

MATA operates 6.76 km (4.2 miles) of track, using a combination of paid employees and volunteers. Service is from the Downtown Dallas Arts District to the Uptown area of Dallas and operates 7 days a week. Hours of operation are 07.00-22.00 (Monday-Friday) and 10.00–22.00 (Saturday and Sunday).

In 2007, 250,924 people rode the McKinney Avenue Trolley and the cars travelled more than 120,245 km (74,717 miles).

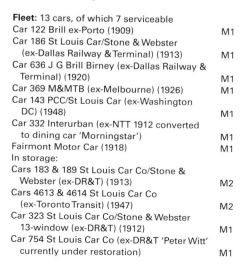

Passengers boarding Car 636 on McKinney Avenue (Peter Roelofs)   1115219

Developments

Current expansion plans will extend the line along Olive Street to a terminal near the DART Pearl Street light rail station. MATA is planning to start construction in 2009.

Plans to extend the line north to the Knox/Henderson area are being studied.

A grant has been received for the installation of air-conditioning in the cars.

Fleet: 13 cars, of which 7 serviceable

Car 122 Brill ex-Porto (1909)	M1
Car 186 St Louis Car/Stone & Webster (ex-Dallas Railway & Terminal) (1913)	M1
Car 636 J G Brill Birney (ex-Dallas Railway & Terminal) (1920)	M1
Car 369 M&MTB (ex-Melbourne) (1926)	M1
Car 143 PCC/St Louis Car (ex-Washington DC) (1948)	M1
Car 332 Interurban (ex-NTT 1912 converted to dining car 'Morningstar')	M1
Fairmont Motor Car (1918)	M1
In storage:	
Cars 183 & 189 St Louis Car Co/Stone & Webster (ex-DR&T) (1913)	M2
Cars 4613 & 4614 St Louis Car Co (ex-Toronto Transit) (1947)	M2
Car 323 St Louis Car Co/Stone & Webster 13-window (ex-DR&T) (1912)	M1
Car 754 St Louis Car Co (ex-DR&T 'Peter Witt' currently under restoration)	M1

Car 143 approaching the terminus on St Paul Street (Peter Roelofs)   1115221

Dayton

Population: Dayton/Springfield metropolitan area 918,689 (2002 estimate), Montgomery County 550,063

Public transport

Bus and trolleybus services operated by Regional Transit Authority, controlled by representative board of trustees.

Greater Dayton Regional Transit Authority (GDRTA)

PO Box 1301, 600 Longworth Street, Dayton, Ohio 45401-1301, USA
Tel: (+1 937) 425 84 00
Fax: (+1 937) 425 86 82
e-mail: info@greaterdaytonrta.org
Web: www.greaterdaytonrta.org

Key personnel

President, Board of Trustees: Brian Bucklew
Executive Director: Mark Donaghy
Director of Administrative Services:
    Judith Pepper
Interim Director of Planning: Frank Ecklar
Director of Community and Government Relations:
    Anthony Whitmore
Director of Transit Services: Jim Napier
Chief Maintenance Officer: John Thomas
Chief Financial Officer: Mary Stanforth
Director of Paratransit Services: Allison Ledford
    Staff: 669

Background

In early 2002, the Miami Valley RTA changed its name to Greater Dayton RTA (GDRTA).

Current situation

Greater Dayton RTA serves the Montgomery County area which has a total population of 550,063.

GDRTA has reorganised its bus services on a multihub system, which is based on a major hub located in downtown Dayton, and four regional hubs. This is making better use of existing resources while providing new suburb-to-suburb journey opportunities for commuters. Hubs are equipped with waiting areas, toilets/restrooms, cycle racks and information displays, as well as park-and-ride facilities and security.

The company has completely rebuilt the trolleybus network to restore it to its former position at the heart of the city's transit system.

Construction of a 5 km trolleybus extension over the western part of diesel bus Route 3 to Townview was completed in 2000 and several other trolleybus route extensions were also completed in 2000. Also, GDRTA added a service for the New Dayton Dragons baseball team.

Bus and trolleybus

Passenger boardings: (2001) Bus 14.5 million; trolleybus 0.3 million
(2002) Bus 10.3 million; trolleybus 3.2 million
(2003) Bus 9.0 million; trolleybus 4.6 million
(2004) Bus 8.5 million; trolleybus 4.3 million
Vehicle-km: (2001) Bus 13.9 million; trolleybus 0.2 million
(2002) Bus 10.8 million; trolleybus 2.2 million
(2003) Bus 10.1 million; trolleybus 2.7 million
(2004) Bus 13.1 million; trolleybus 2.6 million

Number of routes: Bus 28; trolleybus 7
Route length: (One way) Bus 1,526 km, trolleybus 199 km

Fleet: 153 buses (all diesel)
New Flyer 30 ft low-floor (2001)	22
New Flyer 35 ft low-floor (2001)	13
New Flyer 40 ft low-floor (2001,03)	34
Nova Bus RTS T70 606 (1997)	60
Flxible Metro 4102-6T (1992)	20
Chance Streetcars VS-24 (1992)	4
In peak service: 114 diesel buses	

Greater Dayton Regional Transit Authority Škoda trolleybuses on Main Street, Dayton   1173127

Greater Dayton Regional Transit Authority Nova Bus RTS diesel bus   1173125

Greater Dayton Regional Transit Authority New Flyer bus on Third Street, Dayton   1173123

Fleet: 57 trolleybuses
ETI/Škoda 14TrE (1996)	3
ETI/Škoda 14TrE2 (1998)	54
In peak service: 41	

Most intensive service: 10 min
One-person operation: All routes (except baseball trams)
Fare collection: Exact fare or token to farebox; magnetic strip passes and onboard electronic readers
Fare structure: Flat; prepurchase tokens, weekly, monthly passes, free tram fees
Fares collected on board: 47.5 per cent
Operational control: Route inspectors/mobile radio

Arrangements for elderly/disabled: Lift-equipped vehicles on all routes; paratransit service operates door-to-door facility; reduced rate passes; TDD information and reservation service; two senior routes and dial-a-ride. Demand-responsive services carried 230,434 passengers in 2004
Average peak-hour speed: Bus 24.6 km/h, trolleybus 17.5 km/h
Operating costs financed by: Fares 11.7 per cent, other commercial sources 3.7 per cent, subsidy/grants 21.2 per cent, Sales Tax levy 63.4 per cent
Subsidy from: State operating assistance 1.3 per cent, FTA operating assistance 98.7 per cent
New vehicles financed by: FTA, Ohio Department of Transportation and local matching funds

Denver

Population: City: 566,974, Metropolitan area: 2.4 million (2006 estimates)

Public transport

Bus and light rail services for 6,032 km² six-county area provided by Regional Transportation District, set up in 1969 by a State Act and operational from 1973 with the acquisition of six local bus systems, and governed by 15-member directly elected board.

Denver Regional Transportation District (RTD)

1600 Blake Street, Denver, Colorado 80202, US
Tel: (+1 303) 628 90 00
Fax: (+1 303) 299 23 61
Web: www.rtd-denver.com

Key personnel

Chairman: Christopher Martinez
First Vice-Chair: William M Christopher
Second Vice-Chair: O'Neill P Quinlan
Treasurer: Lee Kemp
Secretary: Barbara J Brohl
General Manager: Clarence Marsella
   Staff: 2,520

Passenger journeys: (All modes)
(2005/06) 86.4 million
(2006/07) 87 million
Vehicle-km: (All modes)
(2005/06) 79 million (49.1 million miles)
(2006/07) 81.4 million (50.6 million miles) (estimate)

Background

Created in 1969 to develop, operate and maintain the mass transportation system in the Regional Transportation District (RTD).

The RTD is governed by a 15-member Board.

Current situation

The RTD covers an area of 6,032 km² (2,329 sq miles) and a population of 2.6 million. This includes 37 municipalities in six counties plus city/county jurisdictions.

Services include bus (local/limited, express, regional and access-a-Ride paratransit), light rail, SeniorRide, skyRide (service to Denver International Airport) and call-n-Ride.

Developments

In late 2006, The Department of Homeland Security (DHS) awarded a grant of USD1.15 million to the RTD for video surveillance equipment at existing light rail stations.

Bus

Passenger journeys: (2005/06) 75.8 million
Vehicle-km: Not currently available

Number of routes: 166
Number of stops: 10,596
Route length: Not currently available

Developments

In May 2007, the RTD awarded a contract to UQM Technologies Inc to retrofit 18 hybrid-electric mall shuttle buses. When this work has been completede, all of the RTD's hybrid-electric buses will have been retrofitted.

Fleet: 1,056 (all wheelchair lift equipped), 412 operated by contractors
Breakdown of fleet is not currently available

In peak service: 851
Average age of fleet: 6.0 years

Most intensive service: Not currently available
One-person operation: All routes
Fare structure: Flat for each type of service; half fares on local services off-peak
Fare collection: Exact fare or prepurchase tokens/tickets to farebox; monthly pass; discounted 10-trip coupons for local, express and regional service;

Denver RTD Gillig bus (Bill Luke)   1115275

EcoPass available for employer-purchase; student passes; local, express and regional 5-day passes; day passes, Neighborhood pass; ValuPass
Integration with other modes: 79 park-and-ride sites, 20 transit centres and transfer stations, 37 leased and 4 jointly owned park-and-ride sites
Bus priority: Total 32.8 km and bus/HOV lanes in five segments; 24 hr operation on one segment, part time on others
Operational control: 15 service monitors and 35 street supervisors; mobile radio on all buses; Automatic Vehicle Location (AVL)
Arrangements for elderly/disabled: All buses have wheelchair lifts. Discounted fares and monthly passes; door-to-door subscription and demand-response service for disabled, SeniorRide programme
Operating costs financed by: Fares 20.7 per cent, other commercial sources 9.1 per cent, subsidy/grants 3.9 per cent, sales and use tax 66.3 per cent
New vehicles financed by: FTA grants, Certificates of Participation and sales/use tax

Light rail

Type of operation: Light rail, opened 1994

Passenger boardings: (2005/06) 10.4 million
(2006/07) 10.7 million

Route length: 56.3 km (35 miles)
Number of lines: 6
Number of stations: 36
Gauge: 1,435 mm
Track: Concrete sleepers set in concrete on-street, in ballast elsewhere
Electrification: 750 V DC, overhead

Service: Peak 5 min, off-peak 10 min, evening and weekend 15 min
First/last car: 03.30/02.15
Fare structure: Zonal; cash, monthly passes; discounted fares for students
Fare collection: Vending machines at each stop; proof-of-payment
Fare evasion control: Roving inspectors
Arrangements for elderly/disabled: Ramps at all stations; retractable platforms at cab end of each car; discounted fares for seniors and disabled passengers
Signalling: Automatic block outside city centre

Rolling stock: 87 cars
Fleet breakdown not currently available
On order: 30 Siemens cars (delivery 2007–2008)

Developments

The Regional Transportation District's (RTD's) FasTracks Program

FasTracks Overview

The RTD FasTracks Program is a USD6-billion, 12-year program to build 196.3 km (122 miles) of new commuter rail and light rail, 29 km (18 miles) of bus rapid transit, 21,000 new parking spaces at rail and bus stations, turn Denver Union Station into a multi-modal transportation hub and provide expanded bus service throughout the eight-county district. The program consists of six new rapid transit corridors and three extensions of existing corridors.

For further information on the FasTracks programme, please see www.rtd-fastracks.com

West Corridor

- 19.47 km (12.1 miles) of light rail;
- Connects downtown Denver, Jefferson County, Lakewood and Golden;
- 12 proposed stations;
- Scheduled completion date 2012;
- Projected ridership in 2025: 31,200–36,500.

East Corridor

- 38 km (23.6 miles) of commuter rail – Electric Multiple Unit (EMU);
- Connects downtown Denver to Denver International Airport;
- 5 proposed stations;
- Construction scheduled to begin in 2010;
- Scheduled completion date 2014;
- Projected ridership in 2025: 30,400–35,600.

Northwest Rail Corridor (formerly Longmont Diagonal Rail Project)

- (66 km (41 miles) of commuter rail–Diesel Multiple Unit (DMU);
- Connects downtown Denver, Westminster, Broomfield, Superior, Louisville, Boulder and Longmont;
- 7 proposed stations;
- Construction scheduled to begin 2010;
- Scheduled completion date 2015;
- Projected ridership in 2025: 8,600–10,100.

Gold Line

- 18 km (11.2 miles) of commuter rail–Electric Multiple Unit (EMU);
- Connects downtown Denver, Arvada and Wheat Ridge;

- 7 proposed stations;
- Construction scheduled to begin in 2011;
- Scheduled completion date 2015;
- Projected ridership in 2025: 16,300–19,100.

North Metro Corridor
- 29 km (18 miles) of commuter rail–Diesel Multiple Unit (DMU);
- Connects downtown Denver, Commerce City, Northglenn and Thornton;
- 8 proposed stations;
- Construction scheduled to begin in 2011;
- Scheduled completion date 2015;
- Projected ridership in 2025: 10,200–11,900.

I-225 Corridor
- 16.9 km (10.5 miles) of light rail;
- Connects the Southeast Corridor to the East Corridor through Aurora;
- 7 proposed stations;
- Construction scheduled to begin in 2011;
- Scheduled completion date 2015;
- Projected ridership in 2025: 15,200–17,800.

US 36 Corridor
- 29 km (18 miles) Bus Rapid Transit (BRT);
- Connects downtown Denver, Westminster, Broomfield, Superior, Louisville and Boulder;
- 6 proposed stations;
- Construction of BRT (stations and HOV lanes) scheduled to begin in 2009, pending identification of funds for related highway improvements;
- Scheduled completion date 2016;
- Projected ridership in 2025: 16,900.

Central Corridor
- 1.3-km (0.8-mile) light rail extension;
- Connects Central and East Corridors;
- 2 proposed stations;
- Scheduled completion date 2015;
- Projected ridership in 2025: 31,800–37,200.

Southeast Corridor
This light rail line, 30.7 km (19.1 miles) long with 13 stations running from Broadway to Parker Road, opened in November 2006 – ahead of schedule and under budget. All but one of the stations has park-and-ride facilities.

The line is operated by 34 new Siemens light rail vehicles and has a new communications and control system.

A bus feeder system has been provided.

An 3.7-km (2.3-mile) extension, with three stations, has been proposed. Construction is scheduled to begin in 2013, with completion in 2016.

Projected average weekday ridership by 2025 is 51,100 to 59,800.

Southwest Corridor
14 km (8.7 miles) of existing light rail opened in 2000
- 4-km (2.5-mile) light rail extension;
- Connects the Mineral Station in Littleton to Highlands Ranch;
- 2 proposed stations;
- Construction scheduled to begin in 2013;
- Scheduled completion date 2016;
- Projected ridership in 2025: 20,200–23,600.

Detroit

Population: City 871,121, metropolitan area 4.5 million (2006 estimates)

Public transport

Fixed-route and paratransit services in Detroit metropolitan area (city and six surrounding counties) provided by two operating authorities supervised by a Regional Transit Co-ordinating Council. Operations include a central area people mover.

Suburban Mobility Authority for Regional Transportation (SMART)

660 Woodward Avenue, Suite 900, Detroit, Michigan 48226, USA
Tel: (+1 313) 223 21 00 (General enquiries)
    (+1 313) 223 21 12 (Public Relations enquiries)
Fax: (+1 313) 223 21 35
e-mail: postmaster@smartbus.org (General enquiries)
    pr@smartbus.org (Public Relations enquiries)
Web: www.smartbus.org

Key personnel
General Manager: Dan G Dirks
Assistant General Manager: Paul Majka
    Staff: 990

Background
Originally established in 1967 as the Southeastern Michigan Transportation Authority (SEMTA), the authority was renamed Suburban Mobility Authority for Regional Transportation (SMART) in 1989.

Current situation
SMART no longer acts as grant recipient agency for DDOT (the City of Detroit Department of Transportation), but receives grants from the Regional Transit Co-ordinating Council on an equal basis with DDOT. The board comprises two members each from Macomb, Monroe, Oakland and Wayne counties.

SMART operates fixed-route and paratransit (Connector) services in Macombe county and portions of Oakland and Wayne counties, independently of those provided in the city centre and some suburbs by DDOT.

Developments
All of the SMART fleet vehicles are wheelchair accessible.

Bus

Passenger journey: 10.4 million (annual, approximate)

Number of routes: 54
Route length: (One way) 2,582 km

Fleet: 583 vehicles (including 62 vehicles owned by SMART but operated by local communities)

GMC RTS (1991)	65
Gillig Phantom (1992/93)	49
TMC RTS (1993/94/95)	124
Goshen van (1989)	18
Chance Challenger (1993/94/95)	145
Other	182

In peak service: 202 buses

Most intensive service: 15 min
One-person operation: All routes
Arrangements for elderly/disabled: Extensive Connector paratransit services; fleet 100 per cent wheelchair accessible
Operating costs financed by: Fares 21 per cent, other commercial sources 0.5 per cent, subsidy/grants 78.5 per cent
Subsidy from: State 77 per cent, FTA 23 per cent

Department of Transportation, City of Detroit (DDOT)

1301 East Warren Avenue, Detroit, Michigan 48207-1099, USA
Tel: (+1 313) 933 13 00
Fax: (+1 313) 833 55 23
Web: www.ci.detroit.mi.us/ddot/

Key personnel
Director: Norman L White
Deputy Director, Administration: Sandra B Parker
Director of Operations: Elliot C Jones
    Staff: 1,700 (Approximate)

Background
DDOT was created in 1974 to take over all Detroit municipal transport-related functions.

Current situation
DDOT is the major bus carrier in Michigan, serving the city of Detroit and more than 20 suburban communities over a service area of 453 km² (175 sq miles), and carries about 82 per cent of the area's bus passengers.

In 1999 DDOT discontinued the sale and acceptance of all DDOT tickets (adult, student and transfers) as fare payment. It continues to accept SMART bus tickets for fare payment. DDOT has introduced a new weekly prepaid fare pass for USD12.00. It now offers five prepaid passes as a cost-saving way to pay bus fares.

In November 2005, the ground breaking ceremony took place for the new Rosa Parks Transit Center.

Passenger journeys: (all modes) 35 million (annual estimate)
Passenger-km: (all modes) 186 million (annual estimate)

Bus

Number of routes: 42 (including eight 24-hour routes)
Route length: 1,196 km

Fleet: 520 vehicles
GMC (1980)
GML TC40102N (1986)
MCI Classic (1989)
Neoplan AN460 articulated (1989)
New Flyer D40 (1993)
Nova Bus RTS T80 (1995/96)

Most intensive service: 30 min
Fare collection: Coin to farebox
Fare structure: Flat, with some reduced fare zones; monthly passes, reduced rate carnets; small charge for transfers
Average peak-hour speed: 21.3 km/h
Arrangements for elderly/disabled: All routes wheelchair accessible; reduced fare for eligible passengers, free for elderly and blind; paratransit service with a fleet of 47 lift-equipped vehicles provides more than 328,500 trips annually
Integration with other modes: Transfers available to SMART services
Operating costs financed by: Fares 25 per cent, subsidy/grants 75 per cent
Subsidy from: FTA 13 per cent, state petrol tax 47 per cent, local 40 per cent

Tramway

Current situation
The tourist/heritage tramway was closed in mid-2003, and the trams put up for sale.

Detroit Transportation Corporation (DTC) – Detroit People Mover (DPM)

Julian Madison Building, 1420 Washington Boulevard, Third Floor, Detroit, Michigan 48226, US
Tel: (+1 313) 224 21 60
Fax: (+1 313) 224 21 34
Web: www.thepeoplemover.com

Key personnel
Chair: Albert Fields
General Manager: Barbara Hansen
Marketing Manager: Dennis R Green
    Staff: 85

Type of operation: Automated people mover, opened 1987

Passenger journeys: (2006) 3 million (estimate)
(2007) 3.2 million
Route length: 4.67 km (2.9 miles)
Number of stations: 13

Background
The Detroit People Mover (DPM) is owned
and operated by the Detroit Transportation
Corporation (DTC).

Current situation
Linear motor-powered fully automated people
mover loop (4.67 km, 13 stations), serving the
downtown Detroit Central Business District
(journey time approximately 13.5 minutes)
with capacity for 5,000 passengers per hour,
was originally intended as a distributor for the
planned LRT system.

Revenues cover approximately 9 per cent of
operating costs.

Rolling stock: 12 cars

Service: 3–4 mins
First/last car: 06.30/24.00 (Mon-Thur), 06.30–02.00
(Fri), 09.00–02.00 (Sat), 12.00–24.00 (Sun); The
People Mover may extend its hours for special
events, as needed
Fares structure: flat; monthly, six-monthly, annual
and convention/special event passes
Fare collection: Cash, pass or token
Arrangements for elderly/disabled: All stops are
accessible (except Grand Circus Park station, which
is accessible by stairway only); half fare for elderly,
disabled and Medicare cardholders

Detroit People Mover (DPM)
1342626

Fort Worth
Population: City 624,067, metropolitan area
5.82 million (Dallas-Fort Worth-Arlington) (2005
estimates)

Public transport
Bus services managed under contract for
Regional Transit Authority. Privately operated
light rail line, commuter rail link to Dallas (please
see entry in for Trinity Railway Express (TRE)
under Dallas). Light rail proposed.

Fort Worth Transportation Authority (The T)
1600 East Lancaster Avenue, Fort Worth, Texas
76102, USA
Tel: (+1 817) 215 86 00
Fax: (+1 817) 215 87 65
e-mail: tweb@the-t.com
Web: www.the-t.com

Key personnel
Chair: Robert L Jameson
Vice-Chair: Eduardo Cañas
President and Executive Director: Dick Ruddell
Director of Communications: Joan Hunter
Staff: 377

Passenger boardings: (All modes)
(Annual) 7 million (estimate)
Vehicle-km: Not currently available

Background
Managed by McDonald Transit Associates Inc.

Current situation
Bus and Mobility Impaired Transportation
Service (MITS) paratransit services, plus vanpool
operations.

A five-year plan approved in 1996 emphasised
the importance of commuter rail service between
Fort Worth and Dallas, a project jointly managed
by the two cities. See entry for Trinity Railway
Express (TRE) under Dallas in *Jane's Urban
Transport Systems* for details.

Developments
In October 2006, The T announced that regional
rail is the most suitable transportation alternative
for the southwest to northeast Tarrant County
corridor. Three alternatives had been identified
as possible solutions to improve transportation
in the corridor area, Bus Rapid Transit (BRT) and
two regional rail options. The draft preliminary
recommendation is for regional rail, using the
Fort Worth and Western Railroad (FWWR) tracks,

Union Pacific (UP) tracks and Cotton Belt tracks.
The corridor will be some 64.4 km (40 miles) long
running from southwest Fort Worth to north of
Dallas/Fort Worth International Airport and into
the airport.

In 2007, The T will conduct an environmental
review and submit an Environmental Impact
Statement (EIS) document to the Federal Transit
Administration, allowing The T to qualify for
possible federal funding assistance.

Bus
Passenger boardings: Not currently available
Vehicle-km: Not currently available

Number of routes: 37
Route length: 570 km

Fleet: 184 vehicles	
Flxible Metro (1986)	35
Flxible Metro (1987)	33
Flxible Metro (1990)	7
Flxible Metro (1991)	9
Flxible Metro (1992)	32
Flxible Metro (1995)	13
MCI coach (1984)	3
MCI coach (1990)	2
Vans/minibuses (disabled service)	33

Champion Route (1994)   12
ElDorado Route (1996)   5
In peak service: 116

Most intensive service: 15 min
One-person operation: All services
Fare collection: Registering farebox on vehicle, tokens or passes
Fare structure: Exact flat fare; monthly passes, tokens; free transfers; free central area travel;

reduced fares for children, students and senior citizens
Fare evasion control: Driver supervision
Operational control: Route inspectors/mobile radio
Arrangements for elderly/disabled: On-demand minibus service with 32 vehicles carried 269,000 passengers in 1995
Average peak-hour speed: 13 km/h
Bus priority: Peak-hour bus lanes on some inner radial routes

Integration with other modes: 21 park-and-ride sites, 13 served by special express routes; ridesharing/vanpools promoted; special service to airport with vans
Operating costs financed by: Fares and other commercial sources 14.8 per cent, FTA subsidy/grants 16 per cent, state and local sales tax 69.3 per cent
New vehicles financed by: FTA 80 per cent, 20 per cent FWTA funds (sales tax)

Hartford

Population: City 124,397, County 877,393 (2005 estimates), metropolitan area 1.185 million (2004 estimate)

Public transport

Bus services provided by publicly owned statewide transit company managed under contract. Separate Transit District regulates private bus operators and is instrumental in operation of separate dial-a-ride, suburban and commuter express services. Commuter rail proposed.

Greater Hartford Transit District (GHTD)

1 Union Place, Hartford, Connecticut 06103, USA
Tel: (+1 860) 247 53 29   Fax: (+1 860) 549 38 79
e-mail: mail@hartfordtransit.org
Web: www.hartfordtransit.org

Key personnel

Chair: William D Chiodo
Vice-Chair: Stephen Mitchell
Executive Director: Vicki L Shotland
Director of Fiscal and Administrative Services: Kimberley A Dunham
Director of Paratransit: Patricia M Williams
Fleet Co-ordinator: Samuel Wilson
ADA Paratransit Services Co-ordinator: Valerie K Ellis
Operations Administrator: D J Gonzalez

Current situation

Formed in 1971, the Transit District is a federally funded quasi-governmental organisation comprising 16 towns including Hartford. Its areas of responsibility include:

Demand Responsive Transportation Activities: The District plays two roles with respect to the area's demand response service. In the first role, the District acts as a Federal Transit Administration (FTA) grantee for public and private organisations that provide capital assistance for the demand-response services that the organisations' own employees or their contractors provide. In the second role, the District, under contract to the Connecticut Department of Transportation (CTDoT), provides complementary paratransit service required by the Americans with Disabilities Act of 1990 (ADA). The District contracts with a private operator, Laidlaw Transit Services, for the provision of its consolidated service. More than 90 lift-equipped vehicles are assigned to the consolidated service programme. District-wide programs employ more than 70 vehicles with ridership exceeding 480,000 passenger trips per year.

Commuter Express Services: The District leases 33 suburban coaches to four privately owned bus companies for use in State-supported commuter express service. The District owns the buses procured with grants from the FTA.

Union Station Transportation Center Operation: The restoration of the Union Station Transportation Center represents significant transit rehabilitation in the region and a major renewal effort in the downtown neighbourhood. The building was dedicated in 1987, and is now fully functional as a complete transportation hub with rail, bus and taxi services, and commuter support services.

Union Station Transportation Center (Spruce Street) Parking Facility: The Spruce Street Parking

Lot continues to serve passenger needs for Union Station. In addition, it provides an alternative parking resource for downtown special events and for the neighbourhood. Its lighting, fencing and 24 hour staffing make it a popular place to park.

Connecticut Statewide Transit District Insurance Consortium: On behalf of the State of Connecticut Department of Transportation, the District serves as Administrator of the Insurance Consortium which procures general automobile, property damage and excess automobile liability insurance on behalf of eleven transit districts in the state.

Connecticut Statewide FTA Drug and Alcohol Testing Consortium: More than seventy member locations across Connecticut are served under the auspice of the Consortium, which is co-ordinated by the District. Members secure testing and programme support services as well as a variety of resources and training to assist in the effective operation of drug and alcohol testing programs under CFR Parts 40 and 655 as dictated by the Federal Transit Administration.

Developments

The District has introduced the Star Shuttle bus service. The free shuttle follows a 14-stop continuous loop throughout Hartford every 12 minutes and allows easy access to hotels, restaurants, entertainment venues, shopping, the Riverfront and the Connecticut Convention Center. The Star Shuttle service is a result of the combined efforts of the Connecticut Department of Transportation, Capitol Region Council of Governments, CTTransit, Connecticut Convention and Visitors Bureau, Federal Transit Administration and the Greater Hartford Transit District (GHTD).

Connecticut Transit (CT Transit)

PO Box 66, 100 Leibert Road, Hartford, Connecticut 06141-0066, US
Tel: (+1 860) 522 81 01
Fax: (+1 860) 247 18 10
Web: www.cttransit.com

Key personnel

General Manager: David A Lee
Assistant General Managers:
  Maintenance: Stephen Warren
  Transportation: James Bradford
  Planning and Marketing: Phil Fry
  Administration: Kimberlee Morton
  Staff: 896

Current situation

Connecticut DoT acquired Connecticut Transit in 1976. There are three systems, based in Hartford, New Haven and Stamford, with a total fleet of 398 buses and 90 routes, including commuter express routes. Hartford serves as the corporate headquarters, whilst the operational functions of transportation and maintenance are conducted at the New Haven and Stamford Divisions.

Connecticut DoT contracts separately for operations in other areas: CT Transit Waterbury–fixed-route services operated under contract by the Northeast Transportation Company; CT Transit New Britain & Bristol – nine routes operated under contract by the New Britain Transportation Company and DATTCO; CTTransit Meriden & Wallingford – fixed-route services, with four local routes, operated under contract by the Northeast Transportation Company.

The Hartford, New Haven and Stamford operation carried 24 million passengers in

CTTransit New Flyer 40 ft bus   1327784

FY2006, of which 8.3 million were in New Haven and 2.9 million in Stamford.

Developments
In April 2007, CTTransit began operating its first hydrogen fuel-cell-powered bus. The fuel cell is provided by United technologies' Power Systems on a Van Hool platform. It is currently one of only four hydrogen fuel-cell-powered buses in North America and the only one to operate outside California. The bus will initially operate on the Star Shuttle route in downtown Hartford and will then be assigned to other routes throughout the system for valuation purposes.

Bus
Hartford Division
Address as above.
Staff: 512

Passenger journeys: (2005) 12.4 million
(2006) 13.0 million
Vehicle-km: (2005) 6.9 million
(2006) 7.1 million

Number of routes: 47
Route length: 1,456 km

Fleet: 237 buses
New Flyer (1993)	15
New Flyer (1994)	53
Nova Bus Classic (1996)	11
New Flyer low-floor (2002)	40
New Flyer low-floor (2003)	56
New Flyer low-floor (2005)	48
ElDorado 30 ft (1999)	6
MCI Commuter	7
Van Hool hydrogen fuel-cell (2007)	1

In peak service: 188
Average age of fleet: 5.8 years

Most intensive service: 5 min
Fare structure: Local base fare USD1.25; commuter, three zones at higher fares; tokens; 10-ride ticket, 1-, 7- and 31-day passes
Fare collection: Exact fare or magnetic pass to electronic farebox which also issues transfers
Arrangements for elderly/disabled: All buses have wheelchair lifts or ramps; reduced-rate 10-ride ticket; half-fare in effect at all times
Integration with other modes: Park-and-ride lots throughout the service areas; transfer arrangements with adjacent bus operations
Operating costs financed by: (For whole system) fares 28 per cent, subsidy/grants 72 per cent

New Haven Division
470 James Street, PO Box 1430, New Haven, Connecticut 06506-1430, US
Staff: 274

Passenger journeys: (2005) 7.8 million
(2006) 8.3 million
Vehicle-km: (2005) 3.3 million
(2006) 3.3 million

Number of routes: 24
Route length: 869 km

Fleet: 108 buses
Nova Bus Classic (1996)	24
New Flyer low-floor	84

In peak service: 85
Average age of fleet: 4.5 years

Most intensive service: 5 min
Fare structure: Local base fare USD1.25; tokens; 10-ride ticket, 1-, 7- and 31-day passes
Fare collection: Exact fare or magnetic pass to electronic farebox which also issues transfers
Arrangements for elderly/disabled: All buses have wheelchair lifts or ramps; reduced-rate 10-ride ticket; half-fare in effect at all times
Integration with other modes: Bus/rail Uniticket with Metro-North Railroad; transfer arrangements with adjacent bus operations
Operating costs financed by: (For whole system) fares 28 per cent, subsidy/grants 72 per cent

CTTransit MCI Commuter bus on Hartford Express service   1327783

CTTransit Van Hool hyrdogen fuel-cell bus   1327781

Stamford Division
26 Elm Court, Stamford, Connecticut 06902, US
Staff: 110

Passenger journeys: (2005) 2.9 million
(2006) 2.9 million
Vehicle-km: (2005) 1.3 million
(2006) 1.2 million

Number of routes: 18
Route length: 208 km

Fleet: 54 buses
Nova Bus Classic (1996)	12
New Flyer low-floor (2001)	32
ElDorado (1999)	8
New flyer hybrid	2

In peak service: 39
Average age of fleet: 6.3 years

Most intensive service: 15 min
Fare structure: Local base fare USD1.25; 10-ride ticket, 1-, 7- and 31-day passes
Fare collection: Exact fare or magnetic pass to electronic farebox which also issues transfers
Arrangements for elderly/disabled: All buses have wheelchair lifts or ramps; reduced-rate 10-ride ticket; half-fare in effect at all times
Integration with other modes: Bus/rail Uniticket with Metro-North Railroad; transfer arrangements with adjacent bus operations
Operating costs financed by: (For whole system) fares 28 per cent, subsidy/grants 72 per cent

Connecticut Department of Transportation
Bureau of Policy and Planning
2800 BerlinTurnpike, PO Box 317546, Newington, Connecticut 06131, US
Tel: (+1 860) 594 21 42
Fax: (+1 203) 594 30 28
e-mail: keith.hall@po.state.ct.us
Web: www.nhhsrail.com

Key personnel
Project Director: Leonard Lapsis

Type of operation: Commuter rail (proposed)

Current situation
New Haven-Hartford-Springfield Commuter Rail Implementation Project
The study area for the project is from New Haven through Hartford, ending in Springfield, Massachusetts. The Phase I Final Report, issued in June 2005, developed a recommended implementation plan for initial (start-up) and potential (future enhanced) commuter rail service. An Environmental Assessment and documentation will be prepared (this includes further refinement and analysis of the recommended implementation plan, and preliminary engineering for stations, parking and rail infrastructure).

Honolulu

Population: City: 377,379, Metropolitan area: 905,266 (2005 estimates)

Public transport

Bus and paratransit services provided by private non-profit undertaking under contract to public transit authority which co-ordinates bus and paratransit services.

The City and County of Honolulu Transportation Services

650 South King Street, Honolulu, Hawaii 96813, US
Tel: (+1 808) 523 41 25
Fax: (+1 808) 523 47 30
e-mail: csd@co.honolulu.hi.us
Web: www.honolulu.gov/dts

Key personnel

Director: Melvin N Kaku
Deputy Director: Richard Torres
Chief, Public Transit Division: James Burke
  Staff: Not currently available

Current situation

The Department of Transportation Services of the City and County of Honolulu oversees the city's bus and paratransit systems. Day-to-day operations are managed by Oahu Transit Services, a private non-profit corporation, under a transit management services contract.

Developments

TheBoat, an Intra-Island Passenger Ferry Demonstration Project, was initiated in September 2007. The ferry service offers three morning and afternoon peak hour round trips from West Oahu to downtown Honolulu. Connecting bus transportation to and from the ferry locations is provided by TheBus.

The City began work on the Draft Environmental Impact Statement (DEIS) for the Honolulu High-Capacity Transit Corridor Project.

Bus (TheBus) and paratransit (TheHandi-Van) (Contracted)

TheBus

Oahu Transit Services Inc, Customer Services, 811 Middle Street, Honolulu, Hawaii 96819, US
Tel: (+1 808) 848 45 00; 848 55 55
e-mail: custserv@thebus.org
Web: www.thebus.org

Passenger boardings: (2002/03) 69.1 million
(2003/04) 61.3 million*
(2004/05) 66 million
(2006/07) 71 million (estimate)
Vehicle-km: (2002/03) 29.5 million
(2003/04) 26.6 million*
(2004/05) 26.6 million
Note: * 34-day bus strike

Number of routes: 94
Route length: (One way) 2,400 km
Number of stops: Approx 4,000
Priority right-of-way: 'Zipper Lane' bus, vanpool and carpool HOV lane operating weekday mornings between 05.30 and 09.00 on the H-1 Freeway

Fleet: 525 vehicles (2006)	
Gillig low-floor 40 ft (2004)	55
New Flyer hybrid low-floor 60 ft (2004)	10
TMC RTS-08 35 ft (1993)	12
TMC 40 ft (1993)	31

City and County of Honolulu TheBus New Flyer 40 ft hybrid-electric bus   1322764

City and County of Honolulu TheBus New Flyer 60 ft articulated bus   1322763

Gillig 40 ft (1994/98)	219
Gillig 40 ft low-floor (1998)	3
Gillig 30 ft (1998)	10
New Flyer 60 ft low-floor (2000)	30
Gillig 40 ft (2000/02)	53
Chance 30 ft low-floor (2002)	15
New Flyer 60 ft low-floor (2002)	16
Gillig 40 ft (2003)	15
New Flyer 40 ft low-floor hybrid	40
New Flyer 60 ft low-floor (2003)	16
Other	26
In peak service: 424	

Most intensive service: 5 min
One-person operation: All routes
Fare collection: Exact fare, farebox on bus
Fares collected on board: 25 per cent cash
Fare structure: Flat or prepaid monthly adult, senior, youth, disabled and 4-day bus passes
Fare evasion control: By driver
Operational control: Radio and inspectors
Arrangements for elderly/disabled: All buses have wheelchair lifts
Average distance between stops: In high-density areas, 160 m; in rural areas, 305 m
Average peak-hour speed: In mixed traffic, 22.5 km/h; in bus lanes/HOV, 32–40 km/h

Operating costs financed by: Fares 28 per cent, subsidy/grants 72 per cent
Subsidy from: City government 81 per cent, FTA 19 per cent
New vehicles financed by: FTA grants (80 per cent) and city government (20 per cent)

TheHandi-Van

OTS Paratransit, 811 Middle Street, Honolulu, Hawaii 96819, US
Tel: (+1 808) 454 50 00
Web: www.thebus.org

Current situation

TheHandi-Van is the complementary paratransit services under the Americans with Disabilities Act (ADA) for the City and County of Honolulu. TheHandi-Van provides a curb-to-curb service for eligible persons, using specially equipped vans and sometimes taxis.

There are about 125 vans in the fleet providing services to 10,000 eligible customers. More than 760,000 trips are provided annually.

The service must be prearranged and operates during the same hours as fixed-route services. There is a flat, cash, exact fare of USD2 per person one way.

Houston

Population: City 2.15 million (2006 estimate), metropolitan area 5.63 million (2007 estimate)

Public transport

Bus, including BRT – existing with extensions planned, and light rail services provided by Metropolitan Transit Authority of Harris County (METRO), controlled by representative board. Commuter rail planned.

Metropolitan Transit Authority of Harris County – METRO

1900 Main, PO Box 61429, Houston, Texas 77208-1429, US

Tel: (+1 713) 739 40 00 (Main switchboard)
Fax: (+1 713) 759 95 37
e-mail: rro2@ridemetro.org
Web: www.ridemetro.org

Key personnel

Chair: David S Wolff
Vice-Chair: Gerald B Smith

President and Chief Executive Officer:
Frank J Wilson
Executive Vice-President: John M Sedlak
Senior Vice-President, Operations: David F Feeley
Vice-President and Chief Financial Officer:
Louise Richman
Vice-President, Communications and Marketing:
George F Smalley
Vice-President, Procurement and Materials:
Paul L Como
Vice-President, Human Resources & Diversity:
M Helen Cavazos
Senior Vice-President and Chief of Police:
Thomas C Lambert
Vice-President, Chief Information Officer:
Eric Oistad
Vice-President, Audit: Arthur Smiley
*Vice-President, Planning, Engineering and
Construction:* Bryan Pennington
General Council: Paula Alexander
Senior Director, Media Relations: Raquel Roberts
Staff: 3,429 (including part-time)

Background
Created in 1978, METRO has a service area of
some 3,398 km² (1,311 sq miles).

Current situation
Voters in Harris County approved creation of the
MTA in 1978, allowing the state to collect a 1 per
cent sales tax to partially fund the Authority. After
the 1983 rejection of a bond issue to finance an
initial rail line, voters approved in 1988 a USD2.6
billion 13-year programme of public transport
improvements known as the Phase 2 Mobility
Plan. As a result, by 1998, 20 transit centres,
27 park-and-ride sites, over 1,200 bus shelters
and 115 km of high-occupancy transitways had
been commissioned. Also approved in 1988 was
a measure to set aside at least 25 per cent of sales
tax revenue for general mobility projects such as
road, bridge and pavement construction.

Developments
Following the outline of the METRO Solutions
programme, approved by voters in 2003, the
Phase 2 Implementation Plan identifies almost
48.3 km (30 miles) of light rail transit and
more than 40.2 km (25 miles) of commuter rail,
plus 64.4 km (40 miles) of Signature Express/
Suburban Bus Rapid Transit (BRT). The net result
is almost 156 km (97 miles) of new rapid transit,
to be completed by 2012.

The nearly 48.3 km (30 miles) of light rail transit
will include rail and track infrastructure identical
to those currently on the METRORail line.

In late 2006, METRO began the installation of
security cameras at park-and-ride facilities and at
the Hillcroft Transit Center.

In May 2007, METRO was awarded a grant of
USD1.5 million for improvements to rail security
by the Transportation Security Administration
(TSA). METRO has also received bullet- and stab-
proof vests for the dogs in its K-9 unit.

In January 2008, METRO started the transition
to its new fare system and completed its
fare restructuring program by March 2008. It
eliminated the use of all magnetic fare tickets
by switching to a smart card called the Q Card.
This card contains a computer chip that stores
the cash balance directly onto the card. Fares are
automatically deducted from the card. Passengers
now pay their fares by tapping their Q Cards or
in cash.

Bus
Passenger boardings: (2003) 116.4 million
(2004) 119.6 million
(2005) 116.2 million
(2006) 125.3 million
(2007) 126.2 million
Vehicle-km: Not currently available

Number of routes: 122 (park-and-ride routes: 31)
Route length: 7,910 km (4,916 miles)

Fleet: 1,339 vehicles (includes paratransit and
METRO-owned buses operated by private
contractors under contract)

METRO bus with bike rack fitted

1330068

METRORail Avanto S70 LRV

1143760

Neoplan transit 60 ft	77
Neoplan suburban 60 ft	67
MCI 45 ft	164
Neoplan 45 ft	52
New Flyer 45 ft	101
New Flyer 40 ft	629
New Flyer 40 ft low-floor hybrid (2007)	30
New Flyer 40 ft low-floor hybrid (retro-fitted)	4
New Flyer 29 ft transit	87
Goshen METROLift vans	10
Champion METROLift vans	118
In peak service: 1,011	
On order: Not currently available	

Most intensive service: 3 min
One-person operation: All routes
Fare collection: Cash or Q Card
Fare structure: Local and express, flat; commuter,
zonal
Average peak-hour speed: 26.82 km/h
Integration with other modes: 27 park-and-ride sites
have 32,691 spaces; buses, carpools and vanpools
(2.4 million riders in 2007) use the transitways
Arrangements for elderly/disabled: METROLift
demand-responsive service operated under

contract carried 1.4 million passengers in 2007
using 118 lift-equipped vans on prebooked journeys,
supplemented by subscription taxi service and
subsidised on-demand service of commercial
taxis; all regular routes accessible; reduced fares
on regular routes
Bus priority: Barrier-separated transitways on
five freeways available to buses, high-occupancy
vehicles and carpools; reversible HOV lanes extend
to over 115 km
Operating costs financed by: Fares 17.9 per cent,
tax levy 82.1 per cent

Developments
In early 2007, METRO launched its Bikes on Buses
Program. Installation of the racks was completed in
September 2007, three months ahead of schedule.
All local METRO routes have bike racks.

In May 2007, METRO received 40 new hybrid
buses. Thirty are currently in service and ten are
being upgraded for Signature Service.

In late 2007, METRO opened two new park-
and-ride facilities.

Also in late 2007, METRO placed an order for 52
diesel-electric hybrid coaches for long-distance

commuter services. There is an option for a further 90 buses. Forty-eight transit diesel-electric hybrid buses were also procured.

Busway
Current situation
Transitways are barrier-separated one-direction single carriageways for use inbound from 05.00 to 11.00 and outbound from 14.00 to 20.00. They provide direct links with most park-and-ride lots and are open to all high-occupancy vehicles.

The current network is approximately 160.9 km (100 miles) in length.

Developments
In mid-2008, METRO was due to undergo procurement to convert the busways into High Occupancy/Toll (HOT) lanes to allow single-occupant vehicles the choice of entering the busway for a fee/toll whenever there is space available.

Light rail (METRORail Red Line)

Type of operation: Light rail, opened in January 2004

Route length: 12 km (7.5 miles)
Number of stops: 16

Current situation
The 12 km system, known as the Red Line, started operations in January 2004 and runs from Fannin South to a northern terminus at the University of Houston-Downtown.

The fleet vehicles, manufactured by Siemens Transportation, have a top speed of 105 km/h and a capacity of 200 (with 72 seated) and conform to ADA requirements. Siemens was also responsible for the project management and system integration, signalling and communications systems, power supply, overhead contact line and track construction.

Daily ridership has reached in excess of 40,000.

Developments
Under the MetroSolutions Plan, five new light rail lines will be built: the North, Southeast, Uptown, University and East End Lines. Construction of these lines was scheduled to begin in 2008, with service starting by the end of 2012.

Rolling stock: 18 three-section double-ended low-floor Siemens Avanto S70 vehicles

Most intensive service: 6 min
First/last car: 04.24/00.42 (Monday-Thursday), 04.24/02.47 (Friday & Saturday), 05.27/01.17 (Sunday)
Fare collection: Ticket Vending Machines (TVMs) at each station
Fare structure: Fixed fare per journey

Indianapolis
Population: City 755,112, metropolitan area 1.62 million (2002 estimates)

Public transport
Bus services provided by public transport corporation based on independent company acquired in 1975, and now controlled by representative appointed board.

Indianapolis Public Transportation Corporation – IndyGo
1501 West Washington Street, Indianapolis, Indiana 46222, USA
Tel: (+1 317) 635 21 00
Fax: (+1 317) 634 65 85
e-mail: info@indygo.net
Web: www.indygo.net

Key personnel
Chair: Curtis Wiley
Vice-Chair: Ms Tommie Jones
President/Chief Executive Officer: Gilbert L Holmes
Director, Business Development: Michael Terry
Director, Communications: Ronnetta Slaughter
Controller: Fred Armstrong
Staff: 400

Current situation
Provides fixed-route, paratransit (Open Door) and dial-a-ride (Indy *Flex*) services. There is also a late night service for commuters, operating between 23.00 hrs and 06.00 hrs.

Developments
IndyGo is currently involved in the DiRecTionS Rapid Transit Study to Improve Regional Mobility, which began in December 2002. Recommendations could include commuter or light rail services, express bus and expanded fixed-route operations.

IndyGo Gillig Phantom bus in Indianapolis (William A Luke)   0131645

The company has installed video monitors on one of its hybrid-electric buses, giving passengers access to IndyGo news. There are plans to install monitors on all hybrid buses and four additional buses.

In February 2005, IndyGo introduced two new hybrid-electric/diesel Gillig 40 ft low-floor buses to its fleet.

Bus
Passenger boardings: Approx 11.2 million per year
Vehicle-km: Approx 17.7 million (11 million miles) per year

Number of routes: 37 (2003)
Route length: (One way) 1,377 km
On priority right-of-way: 4.6 km

Fleet: 146 vehicles (plus 82 vans for Open Door and 8 vans for Flexible Service (Indy *Flex*))

Gillig low-floor	101
Gillig Phantom (1997/98)	40
Ford Supreme	82
Other	13

In peak service: 120

Most intensive service: 15 min
Fare collection: Prepurchase passes or exact fare to electronic-registering fareboxes
Fare structure: Base fare USD1.25, day pass USD3; 7-, 11- and 31-day passes available
Arrangements for elderly/disabled: Open Door kerb-to-kerb service with lift-equipped vehicles for disabled; half fare for elderly/disabled on regular services; carried 309,421 passengers in 2003
Average peak-hour speed: 25.3 km/h
Average distance between stops: 1 block, approx 160 m
Operating costs financed by: Fares 28 per cent, state/grants 37 per cent, tax levy 35 per cent
New vehicles financed by: General Obligation Bonds 20 per cent, FTA grants 80 per cent

---

Jacksonville
Population: City: 745,439, metropolitan area: 1.1 million (2002 estimates)

Public transport
Bus and Skyway monorail services and road construction projects provided by transit authority governed by appointed board. Bus Rapid Transit (BRT) under consideration.

Jacksonville Transportation Authority (JTA)
PO Drawer 'O', Jacksonville, Florida 32203, USA
Tel: (+1 904) 630 31 81   Fax: (+1 904) 630 31 66
Web: www.jtafla.com

Street address
100 N Myrtle Avenue, Jacksonville, Florida 32204, USA

Key personnel
Chairman: Cleve E Warren
Vice-Chairman: A J Johns
Treasurer: Donna L Harper
Secretary: Ava L Parker
Executive Director and Chief Executive Officer: Michael J Blaylock
Director of Mass Transit: Tom Jury
Director of External Affairs: Mike Miller
Director of Strategic Planning & Research: Steve Arrington
Chief of Staff: Jacquie Gibbs

Chief Financial Officer: Margo Smith
Chief Engineer: John Davis
Staff: 608 full-time, 57 part-time

Background
JTA, formed in 1971, provides regional transit services and road infrastructure connecting northeast Florida. Dedicated funding for transit services was assured from 1988, when a half-cent sales tax was instituted. Unlike the former bridge and highway tolls, the sales tax can be used for both road construction and support of public transport.

Jacksonville voters approved an additional half-cent sales tax in September 2000 to fund The Better Jacksonville Plan – a USD2.2 billion infrastructure and quality-of-life improvement initiative.

Current situation

The Jacksonville Transportation Authority (JTA), an independent state agency serving Duval County, has multimodal responsibilities. JTA designs and constructs bridges and highways and provides varied mass transit services. These include express and regular bus service, a downtown Skyway monorail, the Trolley service, the Stadium Shuttle for various sporting events at ALLTEL Stadium, JTA Connexion for the disabled and elderly, and ChoiceRide that connects employers and employees to job access through customised transportation options.

Flyers and express bus services provide minimal or non-stop service and serve popular areas like the Beaches, Arlington, Blanding, Orange Park, Mandarin, shopping areas, employment centres and downtown.

Interliner service combines two routes, providing one-seat transportation between two quadrants of town, eliminating the need to transfer or pay two fares. Nine Interliner routes currently serve Jacksonville residents.

Three Trolley lines – Sunflower, Magnolia and Azalea – carry commuters from peripheral parking lots to downtown employment centres and move workers and visitors around downtown. The Sunflower Line operates 06.30–19.00 on weekdays. The Magnolia and Azalea lines operate 05.30–19.00 on weekdays and 08.00–18.00 on Saturdays. There is a connection to the Skyway at Central station.

Developments

In October 2005, the JTA approved a long-term Rapid Transit System (RTS) plan that will include two main corridors, running east/southwest and north/southeast, with dedicated bus lanes and timed traffic signals. New buses for the RTS will be purchased over the next five years.

The north/southeast corridor study, examining alternative routes extending from the Dunn Avenue area in north Jacksonville to The Avenues Mall in the southeast, is nearing completion. The second corridor study, to examine east/southwest

routes from Orange Park to the Beaches, is under way.

In early 2006, the JTA awarded Digital Recorders a contract, valued at some USD1 million, to equip the authority's paratransit fleet with an automatic vehicles location system and its Talking Bus voice announcement system.

Bus

Passenger boardings: (2001) 8.0 million
(2002) 8.0 million
(2003) 8.5 million
(2004) 8.9 million
(2005) 9.8 million
Vehicle-km: (Annual) 8.5 million (estimate)

Number of routes: 56
Route length: (One way) 924 km (574 miles)

Fleet: 174 buses	
Neoplan (1991)	4
Flxible Metro (1992/93)	23
Flxible Metro (1995)	20
MCI Coach (1995)	3
Nova (1997)	31
Nova (1999)	15
Nova (2001)	24
Cable car trolley (2001)	5
Supreme trolley (2003)	3
Gillig 35 ft (2004)	25
Gillig 40 ft (2004)	21
In peak service: 143	

Most intensive service: 10 min
One-person operation: All routes
Integration with other modes: Skyway connects to three park-and-ride lots; Ride Request van shuttle service connects with three bus lines and Intercounty shuttle service connects with four bus lines
Fare structure: Flat, surcharge for special services; reduced rate multiride ticket books; weekly and monthly passes
Fare collection: Automatic farebox, exact change only
Arrangements for elderly/disabled: Entire fleet is lift-equipped and provides fixed-route services; 91 minibuses and other vehicles operate a contracted-out community transportation service; people over 60 travel free

Operating costs financed by: Fares and parking revenues 23.8 per cent

Skyway Monorail

Passenger journeys: (2001) 701,353
(2002) 732,029
(2003) 722,242
(2004) 690,666
(2005) 734,510

Current situation

Construction on the original 'starter line' of the Skyway was completed in 1989. In 1994, Bombardier replaced the former MATRA system with its UM-III monorail technology and completed construction of the 4 km (2.5 mile) system. The final extensions opened in 2000.

The Skyway is a fully automated monorail transit system operating on an elevated and electrified dual guideway. Nine two-car trains serve eight stations in the 'downtown' area on both sides of the St Johns River. The Kings Avenue parking garage and surface parking at Convention Center station offer 3,500 spaces for monthly park-and-ride customers.

The Skyway operates 06.00–23.00 (Monday-Friday), 10.00–23.00 (Saturday), with no service on Sunday. The fare, for non-monthly commuters, is USD0.35.

Transportation Alternatives Study
Current situation

JTA has completed two comprehensive Rapid Transit System (RTS) studies. Two main corridors were identified in each sector – north/southeast and east/southwest. Both main corridors would easily connect with one another in Jacksonville's downtown, and to the Skyway/trolley system, providing fast, convenient service to all parts of Jacksonville.

Also under consideration, High Occupancy Vehicle (HOV) lanes, a provision of dedicated lanes for rapid transit vehicles, light rail or others.

With RTS in place, Jacksonville transit will continue to evolve towards competitiveness with car travel in terms of speed, reliability and convenience.

Kansas City

Population: City 447,306 (2006 estimate), metropolitan area 1.98 million (2007 estimate)

Public transport

Fixed-route and paratransit services operated by a two-state transit authority supervised by governing board; light rail planned.

Kansas City Area Transportation Authority (KCATA) – The Metro

1200 East 18th Street, Kansas City, Missouri 64108, USA
Tel: (+1 816) 346 02 00
Fax: (+1 816) 346 03 05
e-mail: metro@kcata.org
Web: www.kcata.org

Key personnel

Chairman: Irene Caudillo
Vice-Chairman: Gary Mallory
General Manager: Mark Huffer
Staff: Not currently available

Current situation

Serves four Missouri counties and three Kansas counties as a corporate body and political subdivision of the states of Missouri and Kansas. The Authority was established in 1965 and commenced operations in 1969.

The Authority receives local subsidies under contracts with five local government areas in greater Kansas City, but principally from a sales

TMC RTS bus of KCATA on 12th Street, Kansas City (Bill Luke)

0554290

tax of the City of Kansas City, Missouri. The local subsidy must maintain at least a 50 per cent contribution towards the total subsidy.

The Metro provides fixed route bus, paratransit MetroFlex demand-response and one Bus Rapid Transit (BRT) services, the latter known as MAX

and which serves River Market, downtown, Crown Center, midtown and the Plaza.

Developments

Plans are under consideration for a new MAX BRT service in Kansas City, from downtown along Troost Avenue to Bannister Road and then on to the Three Trails Redevelopment area.

Bus
Passenger boardings: Not currently available

Vehicle-km: Not currently available
Number of routes: 70
Route length: 1,419 km

Developments
In June 2004, KCATA announced that it hoped to replace the #56-Country Club route with a new bus rapid transit line, known as MAX (Metro Area Express). The route will connect River Market, Downtown, Crown Center and the Plaza area with fast, frequent and easy-to-use all-day service. It is being developed in partnership with the City of Kansas City, Missouri.

Fleet: 290 vehicles	
GMC RTS-06 (1987)	20
TMC RTS-06 (1989/93/94)	145
Gillig 30 ft (1995/98)	16
Gillig 40 ft (1996)	39
Transmark National (1989)	20
Transmark National (1997)	32
Chance 30 ft (1995)	1
Ford vans	17

In peak service: 200
On order: Not currently available

Most intensive service: 10 min
One-person operation: All routes
Fare structure: Flat, with supplement for some intercommunity journeys and Express services; reduced fares for senior citizens (65 and older), youths (12–18 years) and disabled passengers; employers' Transit Riders' Incentive Plan (TRIP)

Gillig bus of KCATA on 11th Street, Kansas City (Bill Luke)   0554291

Fare collection: Exact cash fare to farebox; monthly, day and visitor passes
Arrangements for elderly/disabled: Share-a-Fare contracted door-to-door service for trips within city limits; trips booked in advance by phone. Fares are distance-based or limited to twice the comparable bus fare; KCATA pays the balance to the contractor. Buses with lifts serve 30 fixed routes; demand-responsive services carried 223,000 passengers in 1996
Operating costs financed by: Fares 19.3 per cent, other commercial sources 1.5 per cent, subsidy/ grants 79.2 per cent
Subsidy from: FTA 9.5 per cent, local sales tax in Kansas City Missouri plus some support from general revenues in other areas 81.9 per cent, State of Missouri 8.6 per cent

Light rail
Type of operation: Light rail, planned
Tel: (+1 816) 346 02 09
Web: www.kansascitylightrail.org

Current situation
In November 2006, voters approved a proposal for a light rail service. KCATA and the City of Kansas City, Mo (KCMO) have launched an Alternatives Analysis (AA), the findings of which will enable KCATA and KCMO to provide a recommended plan.

Las Vegas
Population: City: 545,147 (2005 estimate), metropolitan area: 1.8 million (2006 estimate)

Public transport
Bus services in city and surrounding area of Clark County operated under contract to Regional Transportation Commission. Leisure monorail. New monorail opened 2004, and further expansion under way. Pilot optical guidance transit (BRT) operated under contract to RTC. Regional Fixed Guideway (RFG) proposed. Maglev and electric-diesel train services under study.

Regional Transportation Commission of Southern Nevada (RTC)
600 South Grand Central Parkway, Suite 350, Las Vegas, Nevada 89106-4512, USA
Tel: (+1 702) 676 15 00
Fax: (+1 702) 676 15 18
Web: www.rtcsouthernnevada.com

Key personnel
Chairman, RTC: Bruce L Woodbury
Vice-Chairman, RTC: Chip Maxfield
General Manager: Jacob L Snow
Veolia Transportation General Manager: Barrick Neill
Veolia Transportation Public Information Officer: Valerie Michael
Staff: 1,200

Current situation
The Regional Transportation Commission of Southern Nevada (RTC) was set up in 1965 and is governed by an eight-member board.

The RTC is both the transit authority and the transportation planning agency for Southern Nevada. The RTC's vision is to provide a safe, convenient and effective regional transportation system that enhances mobility and air quality for citizens and visitors. The RTC encourages

residents and visitors to use alternate commute modes to help reduce traffic congestion and improve the air quality in Southern Nevada.

CAT ADA Paratransit Services are operated under separate contract by Laidlaw until 2010. The company also operates the Silver Star service.

Developments
In October 2005, the RTC launched its new Double Decker bus service (The Deuce) on the Las Vegas Strip. Currently, the route carries more than 30,000 riders daily. The RTC has also deployed the Deuce vehicles on several residential routes in Southern Nevada.

In May 2007, the RTC added new diesel-electric hybrid vehicles to its fleet. The RTC also has 35 CNG vehicles on order.

Bus
Operated under contract by:

Veolia Transportation Las Vegas
Las Vegas Support
3210 Citizen Avenue, North Las Vegas, NV 89032, US

Key personnel
Planning Manager: Thomas G Otten
Staff: 1,268

Irisbus Civis hybrid diesel-electric 18.5 m articulated bus used on the MAX BRT route (Bill Luke)
1124818

Passenger journeys: (2002) 45.3 million
(2006) 60.9 million
(2007) 63.8 million
Vehicle-km: (2006) 32.8 million

Number of routes: 37
Route length: Not currently available

Current situation
Veolia Transportation North America's Las Vegas Division is contracted to operate fixed route, MAX Bus Rapid Transit (BRT) and Deuce services in an area of some 1,409 km² (544 sq miles). The contract was renewed in January 2008 for two years.

Fleet: 626 vehicles
A full breakdown of the fleet is not currently available, but comprises:

Fixed route buses	372
BRT buses	10
Specialised service vehicles	254
Double-deck buses	130
Diesel-electric hybrid buses	60

Most intensive service: 7 min; 10 routes operate 24 h to serve the resort corridor
One-person operation: All routes
Fare collection: Coin to farebox; ticket vending machines
Fare structure: Flat, reduced off-peak; monthly passes
Arrangements for elderly/disabled: All buses lift-equipped
Operating costs financed by: Fares 46 per cent, federal subsidies 54 per cent

MAX
In June 2004, the RTC launched Southern Nevada's Metropolitan Area Express (MAX), a bus rapid transit project. Operating with Irisbus Civis hybrid diesel-electric 18.5 m articulated buses, the initial route runs along Las Vegas Boulevard North between the Downtown Transportation Center and Nellis Air Force Base.

The system uses an optical guidance system with lines painted onto the street surface.

ACE Rapid Transit (under construction)
In response to increasing demand for faster service along the Las Vegas Valley's busiest roads, the RTC is currently working on building a rapid transit system, ACE, that will connect downtown Las Vegas, the Las Vegas Convention Center, the Strip, Henderson and North Las Vegas.

The vehicles will travel in dedicated lanes where possible, with less frequent stops than fixed-route transit, enabling the service to change routes based on traffic patterns and move passengers longer distances in a shorter time period than fixed-route bus service. The ACE rapid transit system will be a seamless network of links throughout the Valley to various connection points of other transportation lines with more frequent stops, and will have many rail-like features such as level platform boarding and multiple doors for easy loading. Riders will wait at new, comfortable, and modern shelters. To help reduce wait times, commuters will be able to pay for the bus fare off of the vehicle. Also, all of the ACE vehicles will be equipped with wireless Internet access so that riders can bring a laptop and work while travelling to their destination. The ACE rapid transit system will have the appearance and feel of a light rail transit network at a considerably lower cost.

The first phase of the system is the construction of the ACE Downtown Connector. This new system will provide a convenient option for both residents and tourists between the resort corridor and downtown Las Vegas, whilst also providing service to the Fremont Street Experience, World Market Center, Clark County Government Center and the Las Vegas Premium Outlet Mall.

The City of Las Vegas in partnership with the RTC have begun work on the project, which includes roadway and station platform improvements along Grand Central Parkway, Casino Center Boulevard, 3rd Street, and Paradise Road.

Bombardier fully automated monorail system for Las Vegas (Bombardier)   0583262

Las Vegas fully automated monorail   1176873

Las Vegas
Other operators
The City of Las Vegas' Transportation Services Division operates the City Ride bus service on two routes (www.lasvegasnevada.gov). Fares are flat and paid on board, with reduced fares for senior citizens (over 62 years), youths (5 to 17 years) and passengers with disabilities. Children under 5 travel free.

A replica trolley service operates between hotels along the strip every 20–30 minutes for a flat fare (www.striptrolley.com).

Private operators provide shuttle buses between resort hotels and airports.

Las Vegas Monorail Company
3720 Howard Hughes Parkway, Suite 200, Las Vegas, Nevada 89109-0937, US
Tel: (+1 702) 699 82 00
Fax: (+1 702) 731 32 72
e-mail: contact@lvnvmonorail.com
Web: www.lvmonorail.com

Key personnel
Chairman: John Haycock
Vice-Chairman: Robert D Faiss
General Counsel: Michael C Niarchos
Secretary: Teresa Murphy
Treasurer: Pat Shalmy
Assistant Treasurer: Alex Hossack
President: Curtis L Myles
Vice-President, Operations: Lloyd Welch
Vice-President, Chief Financial Officer: Ross Johnson
Vice-President, Corporate Communications: Ingrid Reisman

Background
The monorail system is owned and operated by the Las Vegas Monorail Company, a non-profit corporation whose board is appointed by the Governor of Nevada.

Bombardier Transportation signed a contract with the Las Vegas Monorail Company in September 2000 to design and build a driverless urban monorail transportation system east of the Las Vegas Boulevard in the heart of the resort corridor. Bombardier will operate the system for an initial 5 years with an option for an additional 10 years. The 5 year contract covers operations and maintenance and it carries a value in excess of USD55 million.

It is a design-build-equip project and hence calls for Bombardier and its consortium partner Granite Construction Company to be responsible for the turnkey design, construction and assumed responsibility for civil works. The total capital project cost was valued at USD650 million.

Current situation
The Las Vegas Monorail connects eight major resorts, including the convention centre. The 6.8 km (4.2 mile) route has seven stations and runs along the Las Vegas resort corridor at a tope speed of 50 mph. Up to nine trains, each consisting of four cars, run on a single rail that is elevated to a height of 20 feet in most areas, with the highest point being at 70 feet at the Las Vegas Convention Center.

Developments
The first phase of the monorail, a 6.8 km (4.2 mile) segment with five new and two renovated stations, was opened in July 2004. Service is currently 07.00–02.00 Monday-Thursday and 07.00–03:00 Friday-Sunday. 1-ride, 1-day

(24-hour unlimited), 10-day and 3-day tickets/ passes are available.

An extension is currently under consideration, with plans that include routes to serve McCarran International Airport and the west side of the Las Vegas Strip.

Rolling stock: 9 four-car trains

Las Vegas

Other Monorail
Current situation
The Mandalay Bay Tram provides a link between the Excalibur, Luxor and Mandalay Bay Resort hotels. It operates 24 hours a day at 3–4 minute intervals. It consists of an 838 m elevated guideway and two independent shuttle systems running side by side. The guideway alignment passes above street level at a height of between 5 and 8 m. Each system is comprised of a train of five vehicles.

There is also a small monorail system running between the Mirage and Treasure Island hotels.

Los Angeles
Population: 3.84 million; 9.94 million in Los Angeles County; metropolitan area 12.93 million (2005 estimates)

Public transport
Bus services throughout most of Southern California, light rail and metro, operated by Metropolitan Transportation Authority, also responsible for administration, planning and rail construction. Separate authority operates commuter rail network. Municipal or sub-regional operators provide services in Los Angeles County, while many of 88 incorporated cities in LA County have contracted local circulator routes. Some bus routes contracted out to private operators. Separate transit authorities operate in Orange, Riverside, San Bernardino and Ventura counties.

Los Angeles County Metropolitan Transportation Authority (MTA)
One Gateway Plaza, Los Angeles, California 90012-2952, USA
Tel: (+1 213) 922 20 00 Fax: (+1 213) 244 60 13
e-mail: customerrelations@mta.net
Web: www.mta.net

Key personnel
Chair: Larry Zarian
Chief Executive Officer: Julian Burke
Media contacts: Dave Sotero, Marc Littman
   Staff: 8,320

Passenger boardings: (All modes)
(1996) 377.2 million

Current situation
The MTA was created in 1993 by merger of the Southern California Rapid Transit District and Los Angeles County Transportation Commission. MTA's divisions have responsibility for operating the bus and metro/light rail networks, for constructing the metro and light rail network, for overall planning of the region's public transport needs, and for administration of the entire network.

Serving a 5,928 km² area, the MTA runs the third largest bus system in the USA, two light rail lines, and the metro.

By the end of 1998, the MTA had expanded its previous capital programme to purchase 2,095 new buses between fiscal years 1998 and 2004, having added 800 additional vehicles to its commitment. Most of the buses will be powered by Compressed Natural Gas (CNG), and many will be low-floor. In October 1998, the MTA ordered 215 low-floor CNG buses from North American Bus Industries for delivery between December 1999 and June 2000, and the company exercised an option with Neoplan for 100 more high-floor CNG buses. In 1999, an option with New Flyer was exercised for 223 CNG low-floor buses.

Developments
The MTA introduced the Metro Rapid Bus Demonstration Programme in 2000 to complement the metro. Passengers board at special stops 1.5 km apart. In early 2003 MTA awarded a contract to Cubic Transportation Systems Inc to provide off-vehicle smartcard ticketing.

The final 10.1 km segment of the Metro Red Line, from Hollywood & Vine to North Hollywood, was opened in June 2000.

Los Angeles Green Line LRV (Julian Wolinsky)   0069436

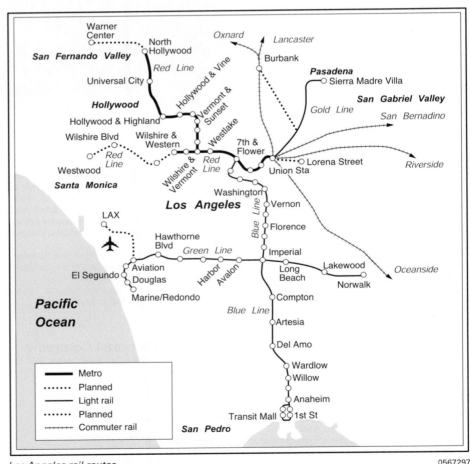
Los Angeles rail routes   0567297

There are plans to extend service from the Metro Red Line North Hollywood station to Warner Center in Woodland Hills with a 22.5 km (14 mile) transitway for the exclusive use of high-capacity Metro Rapid buses by 2005. Plans also include the use of CNG buses and priority traffic signal systems on a further 23 lines before 2008.

Phase I of the Metro Gold Line opened in July 2003. MTA has made more than 20 service improvements in the San Gabriel Valley to connect local bus lines with the Metro Gold Line. MTA has also added or consolidated bus service on many routes in anticipation of increased connections between its Metro Buses and the Metro Gold Line.

MTA Operating Division
Staff: 7,186

Bus

Passenger boardings: (1995) 335 million
(1996) 342.9 million
Vehicle-km: (1995) 139.7 million

Route length: (One way) 5,205 km
Number of routes: 200

Fleet: 2,570 vehicles

GMC RTS-II (1980/81/82)	587
Neoplan AN440A (1983/84/90)	411
TMC RTS-II (1989/90)	373
Flxible Metro (1989/90/91)	325
TMC RTS-II ethanol-powered (1989/92)	329
Neoplan AN440A CNG-powered (1995/96/97)	330
NABI low-floor CNG-powered (2000)	215

In peak service: 1,638

New vehicles required each year: Vehicles replaced after 12 years
On order: 223 New Flyer CNG-powered; also 125 ethanol-powered buses out of service because of engine problems are to be converted to diesel operation.

Most intensive service: 2–5 min
One-person operation: All routes
Fare collection: Prepurchase pass fares; discount pass fares, tokens or cash to Cubic Western electronic fareboxes
Fare structure: Flat on local routes, zonal on express lines; monthly passes for different services/users; 1 h transfers at nominal charge; joint passes with other operators; free trip if service is more than 15 min late
Fares collected on board: 25 per cent of revenue from pass sales
Fare-evasion control: Driver monitors cash fare, and passes have counterfeit-resistant holograms
Arrangements for elderly/disabled: All buses wheelchair accessible and many equipped for kneeling; seniors and disabled travel at reduced fare
Integration with other modes: Many routes feed light rail and Metrolink stations
Average peak-hour speed: In mixed traffic, 19–23 km/h
Bus priority: Express busway (also carrying car and vanpool traffic) from El Monte to Los Angeles caters for 25 per cent of all commuter trips from western San Gabriel Valley to central Los Angeles. Daily used by more than 22,000 passengers; journey time 15–20 min quicker than by car. Contraflow bus lane on Spring Street serves downtown area.
Operational control: Radio is being installed on buses to provide near real-time vehicle location information.
Operating costs financed by: Fares 32.6 per cent

Developments
Plans include bus signal priority systems, for which a pilot project is under way, an extension of the system from the Metro Red Line's North Hollywood station to Warner Center in Woodland Hills, via a 22.5 km (14 mile) transitway, and the use of CNG buses on a further 23 lines.

Metro Red Line
Staff: 199

Type of operation: Full metro, initial route opened 1993

Passenger boardings: (1995) 7.7 million
(1996) 11.6 million
(1998) 12 million

Route length: 28 km
Number of lines: 1
Number of stations: 16
Gauge: 1,435 mm
Electrification: 750 V DC, third rail

Service: Peak 5 min, off-peak 10 min
First/last train: 04.43/23.32
Fare structure: Flat, lower than standard fare
Fare collection: Honour system; tickets purchased from station machines
Fare-evasion control: By transit police on roving patrol
One-person operation: All trains
Operational control: From central control room
Arrangements for elderly/disabled: All stations have high platforms and lifts
Operating costs financed by: Fares 4.6 per cent

Rolling stock: 60 cars

Breda (1991/92)	M30
Breda (1998)	M30

In peak service: 16 cars
On order: A further 74 cars from Breda, under the option attached to the original order; the new cars will have AC inverter propulsion; 30 were delivered in 1998.

Current situation
The final section of metro, from Hollywood & Vine to North Hollywood, opened in June 2000, and it has been reported that ridership has doubled since this extension was completed.

Light rail (Blue, Green and Gold Lines)
Staff: 309

Type of operation: Light rail, initial route opened 1990

Passenger boardings: (1995) 18.8 million
(1996) 22.7 million
(1998) 22.3 million

Route length: 88.4 km
Number of routes: 3
Number of stops: 51
Gauge: 1,435 mm
Electrification: 750 V DC, overhead

Service: Peak 6 min, off-peak 10–15 min
First/last car: 04.03/23.42
Fare structure: Flat, 25 cent transfer; monthly passes
Fare collection: Prepurchase from ticket machines
Fare-evasion control: Random inspection by MTA police
Integration with other modes: All stations have bus feeders, six have park-and-ride lots
Arrangements for elderly/disabled: Stations and trains fully accessible with high platforms throughout
Operating costs financed by: Fares 26.8 per cent

Rolling stock: 173 cars

Sumitomo/Nippon Sharyo (1988/89)	M54
Sumitomo (1994)	M15
Siemens/Duewag (1997/98)	M52
Siemens SD40	52

In peak service: 46

Current situation
The first of 52 Siemens SD460 Light Rail Vehicles (LRVs) arrived at the Green Line depot in January 1999. Two of the LRVs will be used to fully prove out the aborted Automatic Train Control (ATC) system. These test vehicles will not carry passengers and, once the trials are completed, the automation equipment will be removed and the cars placed in normal service. Originally, ATC was to be fitted to the entire fleet, but the MTA ended that programme on financial grounds. However, all 52 cars will have provision for future installation of automation modules, and all will be equipped for ATC. The 15 Sumitomo cars purchased for Green Line service will be transferred to the Blue Line.

Los Angeles Blue Line LRV in new livery
(Julian Wolinsky)   0069434

In October 1998, the California state legislature passed a bill establishing a new autonomous transit authority to assume control of the stalled 22 km Pasadena Blue Line. Under terms of the legislation, the Pasadena Metro Blue Line Construction Authority (now called Metro Gold Line – see below) was authorised to spend all funds now allocated to the project, about USD359 million, and to take over the right-of-way and the civil works already completed, about 12 per cent of the total.

The authority produced a revised estimate of the cost of completing the line – USD683.7 million. In June 1999, the MTA released USD68.7 million in local funding. This was followed by an injection of USD277 million provided by the California Transport Commission.

Developments
Phase I of the Metro Gold Line, from Los Angeles to Pasadena, opened to the public on the 26 July 2003. Phase I is 22 km (13.7 miles) in length and runs from Union Station to Pasadena, with six new stations in Los Angeles, one in South Pasadena and six in Pasadena. MTA has taken over the operations of the Metro Gold Line from the Los Angeles to Pasadena Metro Construction Authority.

For information on Phase II, please see below.

Metro Gold Line (Phase II) (under study)

Los Angeles to Pasadena Metro Construction Authority
Project Headquarters, 625 Fair Oaks Avenue, Suite 200, South Pasadena, California 91030, USA
Tel: (+1 626) 799 0080   Fax: (+1 626) 799 8599
e-mail: publicaffairs@metrogoldline.org
Web: www.metrogoldline.org

Key personnel
Chief Executive Officer: Richard Thorpe

Background
Work on the project is being undertaken by a Joint Powers Authority – the Los Angeles to Pasadena Metro Construction Authority. There are two proposed phases to this new line, which will provide a light rail service using existing rail right-of-way.

Current situation
Phase I opened on 26 July 2003. Operation of Phase I of the Metro Gold Line was passed to the MTA.

Developments

Phase II is proposed to extend the system from Pasadena to Montclair, serving the cities of Pasadena, Arcadia, Monrovia, Duarte, Irwindale, Azusa, Glendora, San Dimas, La Verne, Pomona and Claremont. The Authority, in conjunction with the cities along the alignment, is due to prepare a draft Environmental Impact Statement for Phase II during 2004.

The City of Los Angeles Department of Transportation (LADOT)

100 S Main Street, Los Angeles, California 90012, US
Tel: (+1 213) 972 84 70
Fax: (+1 213) 580 11 88
e-mail: ladot@dot.lacity.org
Web: www.ci.la.ca.us/LADOT/index.htm,
    www.ladottransit.com

Key personnel

President: Howard Coleman
Interim General Manager: Frances T Banerjee
Assistant General Manager, Transportation Programs: James M Okazaki
Assistant General Manager, Transportation Operations: John E Fisher
Assistant General Manager, Finance and Administration: Wayne Moore

Current situation

LADOT operates a fleet of nearly 400 vehicles serving approximately 30 million passengers per year.

DASH

Current situation

Originally an acronym for Downtown Area Short Hop, it is now the name for seven separate shuttle or neighbourhood circulators operating throughout the city. There are four downtown routes, plus three local routes introduced in 1993. In addition there are two part-time routes – a weekend parking lot shuttle through the Westwood shopping/cinema district and a summer parking lot shuttle at Venice Beach. All routes use small buses with up to 30 seats, some CNG-powered. There are also two Community Connection lines, in Hollywood and San Pedro, using full-size buses.

Commuter Express

Current situation

Started in 1985 with one route from the San Fernando Valley taken over from RTD, it now consists of nine routes from the valley and western Los Angeles to downtown LA, all contracted to Laidlaw Transit. The routes are operated by Neoplan AN340 coaches equipped with particulate traps. The eight original routes run Gillig Phantoms.

Private bus

Current situation

Bus operations in and around the city have been opened up to private operators, and a large number of services are now contracted out.

Southern California Regional Rail Authority (SCRRA) – Metrolink

700 South Flower Street, Suite 2600, Los Angeles, California 90017-4606, US
Tel: (+1 213) 452 02 00   Fax: (+1 213) 452 04 25
Web: www.metrolinktrains.com

Key personnel

Chief Executive Officer: David R Solow
Assistant Executive Officers:
Operating Services: Harold Watson
    Finance and Administration: Steve Wylie
Directors
    Development and Communications: Stephen H Lantz

Metrolink diesel locomotive with Bombardier bilevel cars   1140508

Operations: Ed Quicksall
Equipment: William Lydon
Construction and Engineering: Darrell Maxey
Finance: Pat Katuara
Staff: 200

Passenger journeys: (2001) 7.4 million
(2002) 7.9 million
(2003) 9.1 million
(2004) 9.6 million (estimate)
(2005) 10.3 million (estimate)

Route length: 824 km
Number of stations: 54
Gauge: 1,435 mm

Background

In June 1990, the California Legislature enacted Senate Bill 1402, Chapter four of Division 12 of the Public Utilities Code. The bill required the transportation commissions of the counties of Los Angeles, Orange, Riverside and San Bernardino to develop jointly a plan for regional transit services within the multicounty region.

In August 1991, the Southern California Regional Rail Authority (SCRRA), a Joint Powers Agency (JPA), was formed. The purpose of the newly formed SCRRA was to plan, design, construct and administer the operation of regional passenger rail lines serving the counties of Los Angeles, Orange, Riverside, San Bernardino and Ventura. The SCRRA named the regional commuter rail system 'Metrolink'.

From 1990 to 1992 SCRRA's member agencies purchased right-of-way and operating rights from the Southern Pacific Railroad, the Union Pacific and the Santa Fe Railway Company.

Service on the first three lines of the present seven-line, 54-station network commenced in 1992.

Current situation

Commuter rail services run on seven routes: Antelope Valley (Lancaster-Los Angeles, 123.3 km); Inland Empire-Orange County (San Bernardino-Oceanside, 161.1 km); Orange County (Oceanside-Los Angeles, 140.3 km); Riverside (Riverside-Los Angeles, 94.5 km); San Bernardino (San Bernardino-Los Angeles, 90.4 km); Ventura County (Montalvo-Los Angeles, 114.1 km) and the 91 Line (Riverside-Fullerton-Los Angeles, 99.1 km).

Free transfer to MTA and other services. Amtrak is the designated operator. Revenues cover 54.9 per cent of operating costs.

In November 2002 SCRRA acquired four 'retired' GM-EMD F40PH diesel locomotives from Amtrak.

As of October 2002, SCRRA assumed the responsibility for dispatching Metrolink trains, with Amtrak still responsible for operating the trains, pending a tendering process for a new train-operating contract. This resulted in a 5-year operating contract being awarded in late 2004 to Connex North America, the US subsidiary of the global Connex group. Worth EUR77 million, the contract took effect in July 2005.

Developments

In February 2003, as the result of a competitive process, Bombardier was awarded the contract (7-year base, with one 3-year option) to continue providing equipment maintenance services to SCRRA. The contract term began in July 2003 and, if the option is exercised, will expire in June 2013. The contract is valued at USD90 million for the 7-year term.

In 2005, Metrolink operated 144 weekday trains.

In late 2004, an additional 12 Bombardier bilevel coaches and two GM-EMD F59PHI locomotives were leased from Sound Transit, Seattle, Washington.

In February 2006, the SCRRA Board authorised the award of a contract for 87 multi-level coaches to Rotem (54 trailer cars and 33 lead-position cab cars), valued at some USD177 million, and in October 2006 an option for 20 coaches valued at USD35.6 million was exercised, with deliveries anticipated from late 2008. There are three options to the contract, one for an additional 20 cab cars (estimated cost USD35.6 million), one for 6 cab cars and 4 trailers (estimated cost USD17.4 million) and one for 20 trailers (estimated cost USD35.2 million).

In March 2006, a further authorisation was made to purchase up to 11 MP36 P2R type locomotives from Motive Power Inc and Wabtec Co. A contract for these was signed in June 2006. In December 2006, an option for an additional 4 locomotives valued at USD12 million was exercised.

That same month, the Board approved a 5.5 per cent increase in all fares, effective from 1 July 2006. Metrolink has faced significant increase in the price of diesel fuel during that past 12 months.

In April 2006, Palmdale Station opened.

Rolling stock: 43 locomotives plus 155 passengers cars

GM-EMD F59PH & F59PHI low-emission diesel locomotives	39 (1 leased)
GM-EMD F40PH diesel locomotives (ex-Amtrak) (2002)	4
Bombardier multi-level cars	155 (16 leased)

Los Angeles

Other area operators
Current situation

There are many smaller operators providing services in the areas surrounding the Greater Los Angeles area. For further information, a suggested source is the American Passenger Transportation Association (APTA).

Long Beach Transit (LBT)

Long Beach Transit Administration Building
1963 East Anaheim Street, Long Beach, California 90813, US
Tel: (+1 562) 591 87 53
Fax: (+1 562) 218 19 94
Web: www.lbtransit.com

Key personnel
President and Chief Executive Officer: Laurence W Jackson

Executive Vice-President and Chief Operating Officer: Guy Heston

Executive Director and Vice-President, Operations and System Security: Robyn Gordon

Executive Director and Vice-President, Maintenance and Facilities: Rolando Cruz

Chief Financial Officer and Senior Vice-President, Financial and Information Systems: Deborah Ellis

Executive Director and Vice-President, Information Systems and Technology: Patrick Pham

Executive Director and Vice-President, Communications and Customer Services: Brynn Kernaghan

Staff: 760

Passenger journeys: (2007) 27 million (all modes)

Background
Municipally owned operator formed in 1963 and governed by a board of directors.

Current situation
Long Beach Transit's fixed-route system serves the residents of the communities of Long Beach, Lakewood and Signal Hill as well as portions of Artesia, Bellflower, Carson, Cerritos, Compton, Hawaiian Gardens, Norwalk, Paramount and Seal Beach, with connections to MTA, OCTA and other regional operators.

In addition to fixed-route services, Long Beach Transit offers free mobility between downtown attractions via the Passport shuttle service. Customers can also use Long Beach Transit's water taxi services: the AquaLink and AquaBus. Dial-A-Lift service is available to customers physically unable to use fixed-route services.

Developments
All LBT buses have been equipped with bike racks. Bus stops are currently being improved and some stops are being fitted with TranSmart, an electronic information system that provides real-time bus arrival times.

Buses are equipped with GPS for tracking, information and security, and passenger amenities such as real-time bus arrival information, automatic voice announcements and scrolling-screen stop announcements. Security cameras have been being installed on buses. Hybrid electric/petrol (gas) buses are the replacement vehicles of choice, producing less emissions than CNG/LNG and reducing fuel consumption by as much as 50 per cent.

In June 2005, the first 15 New Flyer 'E-Power' hybrid electric-petrol (gas) buses were introduced. A total of 62 of these were in operation as at September 2007. There is an option for 20 additional vehicles in each of the next 3 years.

Long Beach Transit will receive 25 new low-floor hybrid petrol (gasoline)-electric vehicles in December 2008, which will have a 'European' design.

In early 2008, LBT started construction of a new Transit and Visitor Information Center. The cost of the new facility is estimated at USD3.9 million and construction is scheduled to be completed by the end of 2008.

Bus
Passenger journeys: (2005) 27 million (2007) 27 million
Vehicle-km: (2007) 11.3 million

Number of routes: 38
Route length: 307 km

Fleet: 228 vehicles (plus 16 paratransit vans for Dial-A-Lift services)

Opus 27-passenger	30
New Flyer 39-passenger	185
New Flyer 59-passenger	13

In peak service (fixed route): 188

Long Beach Transit New Flyer articulated bus (Bill Luke)   1115117

Most intensive service: 6 min
Integration with other modes: Links to Metro Blue Line rail and Metro, OCTA, LADOT and Torrance Transit bus lines
Fare structure: Flat; USD0.50 to other operators (as of 12 June 2008)
Fare collection: Cash to farebox, 10-ride coupons, day pass, monthly passes, transfers
Arrangements for elderly/disabled: All routes are wheelchair accessible; reduced fares for elderly and disabled person, free for those with no sight, wheelchair users
Operating costs financed by: Fares 25 per cent, other commercial sources 2 per cent, subsidy/grants 73 per cent

Water taxis
Long Beach Transit operates two water taxis, the AquaBus, which commenced operations in 1998, and the AquaLink, which started service in 2001.

There are two 40-passenger AquaBus vessels (wheelchair accessible) that travel through the Long Beach Harbor between waterfront attractions such as the *Queen Mary*, the Aquarium of the Pacific, Pine Avenue Circle, and Shoreline Village.

The Aqualink is a 70-seat, high-speed catamaran that operates along the length of the Long Beach coast, from the Long Beach Harbor to Alamitos Bay Landing.

Santa Monica's Big Blue Bus
City of Santa Monica Transportation Department
1660 Seventh Street, Santa Monica, CA 90401, US
Tel: (+1 310) 451 54 44   Fax: (+1 310) 451 31 63
e-mail: dan.dawson@smgov.net
Web: www.bigbluebus.com

Customer service office
223 Broadway, Santa Monica, CA 90401, US

Key personnel
Director of Transit Services: Stephanie Negriff
Assistant Director of Transit Operations: Joe Stitcher
Marketing and Public Information: Dan Dawson
Staff: 370

Background
Originally established in 1928 as Santa Monica Municipal Bus Lines, the name was changed to the current Santa Monica's Big Blue Bus in 1999. Big Blue Bus serves an area of approximately 133.1 km2 (51.4 sq miles) and a population of 458,506.

Current situation
Operates 13 routes in the city of Santa Monica and western Los Angeles plus two commuter routes, UCLA Commuter and VA Commuter. The fare on local routes is 75 cents and 25 cents for

senior citizens. The fare on the express route is USD1.75 and 60 cents for seniors.

It also operates a loop service by the beach named The Tide. This service operates every 15 minutes, seven days a week from 12.00 hrs to 20.00 hrs. On The Tide there is a flat fare of 25 cents, with the fare being reduced to 10 cents for senior citizens (over 62), disabled and Medicare passengers.

The agency does not receive general funds from the city budget and is funded entirely through farebox revenues and a variety of county, state and federal subsidies.

More than 40 per cent of the fleet is fuelled by Liquified Natural Gas (LNG).

Bus
Passenger journeys: (Fixed-route) (2005) 20.54 million
Vehicle-km: (Fixed-route) (2005) 7.97 million (4.95 million miles)

Route length: 457 km

Fleet: 201 buses

NovaBus TC40102A (1995)	21
New Flyer low-floor D40LF (1997)	67
Thomas SLF200 (2000)	10
NABI low-floor 40LFW (2002)	37
New Flyer LNG (2005)	52
MCI 102DL3 (Charter buses)	4
New Flyer LNG (2006)	10

In peak service: 134
Average age of fleet: 3.3 years

Most intensive service: 5 min
Fare collection: Coin to farebox; prepaid debit card
Fare structure: Flat for local and express journeys
Integration with other modes: Transfers to light rail
Operating costs financed by: Fares 31.5 per cent, other commercial sources 11.2 per cent, subsidy/grants 57.3 per cent. Local sales tax covers the operating subsidy/grants.
Subsidy from: State funds 8 per cent, local 92 per cent

Montebello Bus Lines (MBL)
400 South Taylor Avenue, Montebello, California 90640, US
Tel: (+1 323) 887 46 00   Fax: (+1 323) 887 46 43
e-mail: businfo@cityofmontebello.com
Web: www.cityofmontebello.com

Key personnel
Director of Transportation: Allan Pollock
Vehicle Maintenance Manager: Tom Barrio
Operations Manager: Mannie Thomas
Transit Administration Manager: Paula Faust
Manager of Strategic Planning and Intergovernmental Relations: Laura Cornejo
Staff: 232

Passenger journeys: (2000) 7.8 million
(2001) 7.3 million
(2002) 7.3 million
(2004) 10.9 million
(2005) 9.6 million
Vehicle-km: (2002) 4.2 million (2.6 million miles)
(2004) 4.7 million (2.9 million miles)
(2005) 4.7 million (2.9 million miles)

Background
The City of Montebello began official bus services in 1922.

Current situation
A fleet of 86 fixed-route vehicles serves the communities of Alhambra, Bell Gardens, Boyle Heights, Commerce, Downtown Los Angeles, East Los Angeles, La Mirada, Montebello, Monterey Park, Pico Rivera, Rosemead, San Marino, South Gate, South San Gabriel and Whittier.

Services on fixed routes fall into three basic categories: major local services, which run at high frequency (15 minutes) over a long service day; minor local services, which run less frequently (30–60 minutes); peak express services, which operate peak-hour services, weekdays only, at a frequency of 30 minutes on two routes between downtown Los Angeles and Montebello, with a third route extending to Whittier.

The company also operates a dial-a-ride service, with a fleet of three minibuses and two vans, and a circulatory feed to the Montebello/Commerce Metrolink commuter train station. The DAR service carried nearly 22,000 passengers in 2002.

Developments
Montebello recently undertook a mechanical rehabilitation programme, which added new clean diesel engine packages to 39 of its ageing fleet. These enhancements will ensure that the fleet meets the strict air emission standards of Southern California, and the programme aims to extend the useful life of these vehicles by as much as six years.

In 2002, MBL partnered with MTA to accept MTA transit passes on all of its routes. This agreement expired in early 2004.

The company has also joined with 16 other municipal operators in the first regional pass system, EZ Transit Pass. MBL is also working with other operators to implement the Universal Fare System, a smartcard-based system.

Number of routes: 13
Number of stops: 777

Fleet: 91 vehicles
Standard buses	81
Minibuses	5
Dial-A-Ride (DAR)	
Minibuses	3
Vans	2

In peak service: 60
Average age of fleet: 12.3 years (bus fleet)

Fare structure: Cash, daily pass, Metrocard (prepayment card), EZ transit pass
Arrangements for elderly/disabled: Reduced fare, 100 per cent of the fleet is accessible

Gardena Municipal Bus Lines (GMBL)

City of Gardena, Transportation Department
15350 South Van Ness Avenue, Gardena, California 90249-4100, USA
Tel: (+1 310) 324 14 75   Fax: (+1 310) 538 19 89
e-mail: gmbl.web@ci.gardena.ca.us
Web: www.ci.gardena.ca.us/government/
Transportation/default.asp

Key personnel
Director: Whittman Ballenger

Background
The Gardena Municipal Bus Lines operates as an enterprise fund separate from the City of Gardena's General Fund operations.

Current situation
Serves the South Bay city of Gardena with four routes, including one to downtown Los Angeles, plus supplementary commuter 'Neighborhood Circulator' services; fleet of 50 buses, with 40 in peak service. Ridership is approximately 18,000 on an average weekday. Services connect with the Blue Line rail system, the Metropolitan Transportation Authority (MTA) and other area municipal bus services.

GMBL also provides the Gardena Special Transit door-to-door demand responsive service with a fleet of 10 vehicles.

Culver City Municipal Bus Lines (Culver CityBus)

4343 Duquesne Avenue, Jefferson Boulevard, Culver City, California 90232, USA
Tel: (+1 310) 253 65 00
Fax: (+1 310) 253 65 13
Web: www.culvercity.org

Key personnel
Director: Art Ida
Transit Operations Manager: Samantha Blackshire
Fleet Equipment & Maintenance Manager: Paul Condran

Passenger journeys: (2003) 5.3 million
(2007) 5.8 million (estimate)
Vehicle-km: Not currently available

No of routes: 7
Route length: 167.3 km (104 miles) (two-way)

Fleet: 46 buses (all CNG)
Breakdown of fleet is not currently available

Fare structure: Flat; premium fare for express services; reduced fares for students, seniors and disabled; free fare for the blind; free local transfer; EZ monthly transit pass
Fare collection: Exact cash fare to farebox, MTA tokens, EZ pass

Background
Established in 1928 as a result of a dispute between the City of Culver City and the Pacific Electric Railway over rising passenger fares, Culver CityBus provides public transportation services for the City of Culver City and surrounding communities.

Current situation
Serves Culver City, and the communities of Century City, Marina del Rey, Mar Vista, Palms, Rancho Park, Venice, West Los Angeles, Westchester and Westwood. The service area is approximately 66 k^{m}2 (25.5 sq miles) with a population of just under 300,000.

A high priority is placed on maintaining current service levels. When necessary and feasible, service is modified in response to public demand and changing travel and land use patterns. It is the city's policy to provide passengers with a reasonably priced and reliable alternative to the automobile and serve as an integral component of the regional transit system in Los Angeles County.

Vehicles facilities and equipment
Culver CityBus's operations (administration, operations, maintenance and dispatching) are based at the Culver City Transportation Department Facility, which includes the City Yard, located at 4343 Duquesne Avenue in the City of Culver City. The Department includes administrative offices, conference rooms, break areas, a maintenance garage with eight service bays (four are reserved for buses), a fuel island, several CNG pump stations, a welding shop, a vacuum station (for debris removal from buses), a warehouse, an automatic bus washer, and a split-level parking garage.

The transmitting equipment for Culver CityBus's two-way radio system is located at the City's Transportation Facility. The equipment enables supervision of drivers and increases the security of the operator.

Culver CityBus neither owns nor operates any park-and-ride facilities, nor does it operate a demand-responsive service. However, Culver CityBus recently completed its seventh year of providing Hollywood Bowl service for the LA Philharmonic through a contract with the County of Los Angeles. Bowl patrons are picked up at the Watseka Parking Structure in downtown Culver City.

Developments
Line 3 started running at weekends from January 2007.

Torrance Transit System

20500 Madrona Avenue, Torrance, California 90503, US
Tel: (+1 310) 781 69 30   Fax: (+1 310) 618 62 29
e-mail: kturner@torrnet.com
Web: www.torrnet.com/city/dept/transit/

Key personnel
Transit Director: Kim Turner
e-mail: kturner@torrnet.com
Administration Manager: Jim Mills
e-mail: jmills@torrnet.com
Maintenance Manager: Vacant
Operations Manager: Derick Mahome
e-mail: dmahome@torrnet.com
Staff: 141

Passenger journeys (all modes): (2006/07) 4.8 million
Vehicle-km: Not currently available

Current situation
Serves Torrance, Redondo Beach, Lomita, Long Beach, Carson, and portions of Gardena, the city of Los Angeles and the County of Los Angeles. The eight lines include two to downtown Los Angeles (including a portion of express service), one line to the Los Angeles International Airport (LAX), one to the Long Beach Transit Mall and service to the Green Line and Blue Line light rail service of the Los Angeles County MTA.

Torrance Transit System also serves as the lead for the Municipal Area Express, a commuter bus service connecting the South Bay area with the El Segundo employment centre. This service is provided with 14 buses on three routes, including one express line.

Fleet: 51 buses (plus 14 for commuter bus service)
Fleet breakdown is not currently available

Foothill Transit

100 South Vincent Avenue, Suite 200, West Covina, California 91790, USA
Tel: (+1 626) 967 31 47
Fax: (+1 626) 967 46 08
e-mail: info@foothilltransit.org
Web: www.foothilltransit.org

Key personnel
President: Paula Lantz
Vice-President: Peggy Delach
Treasurer and Auditor/Controller: Lola Stroing
Executive Board Members: John Fasana, Michael De la Torre
Executive Director: Doran J Barnes
Director, Procurement: Gary Wehls

Background
Foothill Transit was created in 1988. In an effort to provide better bus service to the San Gabriel and Pomona Valleys while reducing costs and improving local control, the Los Angeles County Transportation Commission (LACTC) approved Foothill Transit's joint powers authority application to assume operation of 14 lines which were operated by RTD.

Service began in December 1988. The remaining 12 lines were transferred over during the next five years. Foothill Transit also assumed administration of the Bus Service Continuation Project and began providing service on six additional former RTD lines. Foothill Transit improved service by modifying some existing lines, increasing weekday services, introducing weekend services and creating new services.

Passenger journeys: (Annual) 15 million (estimate)
Number of routes: 36 (local and express)

Current situation
Foothill Transit provides bus service to the San Gabriel and Pomona Valleys. It is governed by a five-person Executive Board: four members are elected by the general zone membership, and the fifth member is appointed by the Los Angeles County Board of Supervisors. General membership includes one city council member from each of 21 cities in the Foothill Transit Zone and three appointed representatives from the County of Los Angeles.

Foothill Transit's unique feature is that it has no employees – both management and operations are provided under contract. The five-member Executive Board, representing 21 cities and some unincorporated portions of Los Angeles County, directs policy.

The members are: Arcadia, Azusa, Baldwin Park, Bradbury, Claremont, Covina, Diamond Bar, Duarte, El Monte, Glendora, Industry, Irwindale, La Puente, La Verne, Los Angeles County, Monrovia, Pomona, San Dimas, South El Monte, Temple City, Walnut and West Covina. Foothill Transit is one of the largest transit privatisation efforts in the United States, serving an area of 847 km² (327 m²).

Management is by Veolia Transportation and operations are by First Transit Inc and MV Transportation.

Developments
In 2006, Foothill Transit added Wi-Fi facilities to selected buses.

In March 2007, a Bus Rapid Transit (BRT) line, named Silver Streak, began operations. The service is operated by NABI 60-ft buses.

Fleet: 314 (FY2009)

Gillig 30 ft low-floor diesel (2000)	7
Gillig 40 ft low-floor diesel (2000)	75
Orion V 40 ft CNG (2002/03)	117
NABI 40 ft low-floor CNG (2004/05/06)	85
NABI 60 ft low-floor articulated CNG (2006)	30

On order: None

Fare structure: Base cash fare: USD1.00; express cash fare: USD2.50 or USD4.40, depending on distance; transfer USD0.50; various passes available

Arrangements for elderly/disabled: Fleet 100 per cent accessible

Operating costs financed by: Farebox 25 per cent, remainder from Los Angeles County Proposition A and C funds, California State Transportation Development Act and State Transit Assistance funds

Foothill Transit NABI 40-LFW transit bus (NABI)   1115114

Norwalk Transit System (NTS)
Transit Offices
12650 East Imperial Highway, Norwalk, California 90650, US
Tel: (+1 562) 929 55 50
Fax: (+1 562) 929 55 72
e-mail: transit@ci.norwalk.ca.us
Web: www.ci.norwalk.ca.us/transit.asp

Key personnel
Director: Jim Parker

Passenger journeys: (2005) 2.5 million

Background
NTS has been in operation since 1974.

Current situation
NTS provides nine fixed routes which serve an area which includes the City of Norwalk and portions of Artesia, Bellflower, Cerritos, La Habra, La Mirada, Santa Fe Springs and Whittier. Norwalk Transit's paratransit dial-a-ride service operates within the jurisdictional boundary of the City of Norwalk and offers taxi vouchers to pre-approved medical facilities outside the city area.

NTS provides connector shuttle bus service between the Norwalk/Santa Fe Springs Transportation Center and the Green Line Studebaker station in Norwalk. Currently, Metrolink provides weekday train service to the Norwalk/Santa Fe Springs Transportation Center. This rail feeder service implemented by NTS provides direct interconnectivity between rail stations (Metrolink commuter rail and Green Line light rail).

Developments
In July 2003, NTS took over the operation of the dial-a-ride service within the city of La Mirada.

Fleet: 36 vehicles (2008)

RTS Nova Bus (1997)	9
Gillig low-floor (1998)	20
New Flyer hybrid vehicles	3
ElDorado Escort	4

Santa Clarita Transit (SCT)
City of Santa Clarita
Administrative Service Division – Transit
23920 Valencuia Boulevard, Suite 300, Santa Clarita, CA 91355, US
Tel: (+1 661) 294 12 87, 295 63 00
Fax: (+1 661) 294 25 17
Web: www.santa-clarita,com/cityhall/admin/transit/

Key personnel
Transit Manager: Jeff O'Keefe
Staff: Not currently available

Passenger journeys: (2004/05) 3.5 million

Current situation
Local operator started services 1991 with 74 routes, including 28 regional express routes, running to downtown Los Angeles, San Fernando Valley, Antelope Valley and Century City, with a fleet of 78 buses. SCT also provides Dial-A-Ride (DAR) services. Fares cover 25 per cent of operating costs. Eight park-and-ride facilities.

Developments
In 2006, a new Transit Maintenance Facility was opened.

Louisville
Population: City: 699,827, metropolitan area: 1.2 million (2005)

Public transport
The Transit Authority of River City (TARC) is the major public transportation provider in the Louisville metropolitan area with service in Jefferson, Oldham and Bullitt counties in Kentucky and Clark and Floyd counties in Southern Indiana. The bus and paratransit service is operated by TARC and is led by a representative board responsible to metropolitan area government.

The Transit Authority of River City's mission is to explore and implement transportation opportunities that enhance the social, economic and environmental wellbeing of the greater Louisville community.

Transit Authority of River City (TARC)
1000 West Broadway, Louisville, Kentucky 40203, USA
Tel: (+1 502) 561 51 02   Fax: (+1 502) 213 32 44
e-mail: info@ridetarc.org
Web: www.ridetarc.org

Key personnel
Chair, Board of Directors: Brad Baumert
Executive Director: J Barry Barker
Staff: 690

Passenger journeys: (Annual) 15.8 million
Revenue km (miles):
(FY2006) 12.2 million (19.6 million)

Background
TARC took over operations of the Louisville Transit Co in 1974. In 1975 a 0.2 per cent occupational tax was established in Louisville and Jefferson County to provide operating and capital matching funds for TARC. Funds are deposited in the Mass Transit Trust Fund (MTTF), which provides the largest source of subsidy for TARC operations. Before budget strains caused fares to increase in 2004, fares have been raised only three times: in 1980, 1993 and 1995.

State funding assistance was cut by 95 per cent in 1989, and declining subsidies from the federal government have put an increasing burden on the MTTF, which stands at USD10.6 million.

Current situation
TARC operates five types of fixed-route service:
• Express, providing direct service with limited stops;
• Radial, routes linking outlying areas with the central business district;

- Crosstown, routes linking areas without passing through the city centre;
- Feeder, routes providing access from low-density areas to Radial, Express and Crosstown services;
- Circulator, short close-headway shuttles serving the business district and immediate surrounding areas.

The downtown free 'Toonerville II' shuttles on Main Street and Fourth Street use replica tramcars.

Average weekday ridership is approximately 57,500.

Developments

In 2004, fares were increased to ease budget strains. New fares simplify fare structure with basic cash fare at USD1.00, USD0.50 and USD0.25 levels. Discounted off-peak fares were eliminated; trolleys and downtown circulator fares increased to USD0.25 and price of tickets and monthly passes increased.

In 2004, TARC added five hybrid-electric 40 ft low-floor Gillig vehicles to the fleet.

Bus

Route length: Not currently available
Number of routes: 53

Fleet: 255 vehicles
Flxible Metro (1989)	13
Flxible Metro (1994)	38
Chance Alamo replica tramcar (1987)	9
Chance Alamo replica tramcar (1997)	5
Gillig low-floor (1998)	27
Gillig low-floor (1999)	64
Gillig low-floor (2000)	12
Gillig low-floor (2001)	10
Gillig low-floor (2003)	20
Gillig low-floor 30 ft (2000)	8
Gillig low-floor 30 ft (2002)	17
Orion II w/ramps (1995)	6
Gillig hybrid-electric low-floor (2004)	5
Gillig low-floor (2005)	16
Optima replica tramcar (2005)	5

In peak service: 190
Average age of fleet: 8.4 years

Most intensive service: 10 min (am/pm peak)
One-person operation: All routes
Fare collection: Exact fare to farebox, cash or prepurchase, monthly pass
Fare structure: Flat; prepurchase discount strip tickets; free transfer; monthly pass; summer youth pass
Arrangements for elderly/disabled: TARC Lift provides special service for elderly/disabled, with two types of service for regular and occasional patrons. Currently, MV Transportation provides TARC 3 service, a door-to-door demand-responsive service. All buses are wheelchair accessible; TDD phone service and large-print timetables available
Average distance between stops: 1 block (approx 160 m)
Average peak-hour speed: In mixed traffic, 13.6 km/h
Integration with other modes: Park-and-ride sites provided; partner in local Vanpool programme
Operating costs financed by: Fares 12 per cent, federal grants 28 per cent, MTTF (local tax) 56 per cent, other commercial sources 4 per cent
Subsidy from: Not currently available
New vehicles financed by: FTA grants 95 per cent, local payroll tax/state capital assistance 5 per cent

Developments

In 2004, TARC added five hybrid-electric 40-ft low-floor Gilligs to the fleet. TARC's entire fleet was also converted to use cleaner ultra low-sulphur diesel fuel.

TARC was selected by the Federal Transit Administration, along with ten other US transit authorities, to take part in Environmental Management System training. This is a set of management processes and procedures that allow an organisation to investigate, control and reduce the environmental impact of its activities, products and services and operate with greater efficiency and control.

All TARC buses are bike-rack equipped.

TARC Hybrid bus (Erin Back)   1321958

TARC bus on 2nd Street Bridge, with Lousville skyline in the background (Ted Wathen)   1321957

TARC trolley in front of Louisville Slugger Field (Erin Back)   1321956

TARC is implementing trip-planning software on its website in 2007.

TARC has been selected as one of eight US cities to receive funds through the Federal Transit Administration for a demonstration project to plan and design a Travel Management Coordination Center (TMCC), utilising Intelligent Transportation Systems (ITS).

Memphis

Population: City 672,277, Metropolitan area 1.26 million (2005 estimates)

Public transport
Bus and tramway services operated by publicly owned transit operator, governed by representative board; regional rail projects under study.

Memphis Area Transit Authority (MATA)
1370 Levee Road, Memphis, Tennessee 38108, US
Tel: (+1 901) 722 71 00   Fax: (+1 901) 722 71 23
e-mail: webmail@matatransit.com
Web: www.matatransit.com

Key personnel
Chairman, MATA Board of Commissioners:
   Ray Holt
President and General Manager:
   William Hudson Jr
Planning & Capital Projects/Assistant General Manager: Tom Fox
Assistant General Manager of Operations:
   Alvin Pearson
Director of Transportation: Lawson Albritton
Director of Rail Operations: Dorothy Harris
Director of Marketing/Customer Service: Alison
   Burton
Director of Bus Maintenance: Glen Lockhart
Director of Rail Maintenance: Eli Williams
   Staff: 602 (plus four part-time) (as at end of
   FY2005)

Current situation
MATA was established as a publicly owned transit system in 1960, providing fixed-route and demand-responsive service in the Memphis urbanised area. The historic tramway route opened on Main Street in 1993, intended as the nucleus of a future light rail network.

Bus
Number of routes: 38
Route length: 2,997 km

Fleet: 249 vehicles

Neoplan articulated (2003)	7
TMC (1994)16 (10 active)	
Nova Bus LFS low-floor (1998/2000/2002)	129
Blue Bird (2001–03)	51
Champion (1999, 2003)	14
Gillig (2003)	20
Optima (2005)	12

In peak service: 144
On order: 4 vehicles (unspecified)

Most intensive service: 15 min
Fare collection: Electronic farebox
Fare structure: Zonal
Arrangements for elderly/disabled: MATAPlus paratransit service carries 883 passengers daily; reduced fare on fixed-route services
Integration with other modes: Park-and-ride on many routes
Operating costs financed by: Fares 19 per cent, other commercial sources 2 per cent, subsidy/grants 79 per cent
Subsidy from: FTA 24 per cent, state 24 per cent, City of Memphis 52 per cent

Tramway
Type of operation: Conventional tramway

Passenger boardings: (2000/01) 912,048
(2001/02) 925,336
(2002/03) 778,442
(2003/04) 982,467
(2004/05) 1.02 million

Route length: 9 km
Number of routes: 3
Number of stops: 34
Gauge: 1,435 mm
Track: RI59 and 115 lb/yd T rail; sleepers set in concrete
Max gradient: 5%
Minumum curve radius: 8.5 m
Electrification: 600 V DC, overhead

Service: Peak 8 min, off-peak 13 min
First/last car: 06.20/01.00
Fare structure: Flat (USD1.00), reduced rate (USD0.50), 'Lunch Fare' (USD0.50)
Revenue collection equipment: Electronic fareboxes onboard
Integration with other modes: Transfer to bus: USD1.50 (USD1.40 plus USD0.10)

Current situation
Initial 3 km section of tramway along Main Street in the Mid-America Mall redevelopment area opened 1993, designed as a downtown distributor and intended to become the core route of a future light rail network.
   A 4 km loop to and along the riverfront area opened in 1997. This makes use of little-used rail track running north-south and parallel to the existing tramway, with which it has been connected by new east-west links to form a loop. Four ex-Melbourne W2 cars were restored to operate the service.

Developments
A 3.5 km eastern extension to the Medical Center was completed in March 2004. Four trolleys were added to the fleet: three refurbished ex-Melbourne vehicles and one Birney (2003 model) from Gomaco.

Rolling stock: 19 cars

Gomaco replica 2-axle (1993)	M1
Ex-Rio de Janeiro	M1
Brill-type 2-axle ex-Oporto (1931–1940)	M6
Ex-Melbourne W2 (1924/29)	M10
Gomaco Birney	1

In peak service: 14 cars

Regional Rail Program (MATATRAC)
Background
MATA completed a Regional Transit Plan in June 1997 that includes rail projects in three major corridors. The Memphis Metropolitan Planning Organization (MPO) has adopted the Regional Transit Plan as the Transit Element of the Long-Range Transportation Plan.
   A Regional Rail Steering Committee was established in late 1999 for the purpose of assisting MATA in moving the rail program forward. The Steering Committee consists of approximately 35 individuals representing a broad range of community interests, including elected officials, private businesses, public agencies, and neighbourhoods.
   The three corridors in the Regional Transit Plan are:
* **North:** Serving Downtown, North Memphis, Frayser, and Millington;
* **Southeast:** Serving Downtown, Midtown, East Memphis, Germantown, and Collierville;
* **South:** Serving Downtown, South Memphis, Whitehaven, Southaven, and Horn Lake.
A connection to the airport from either the South Corridor or Southeast Corridor was also identified in the plan.
   Early in 2001, the Southeast Corridor, with a connection to the airport, was adopted as the top priority for preparation of detailed studies and environmental analysis. The Downtown-airport segment was chosen as the first phase of analysis for the Southeast Corridor.

Current situation
There are currently two alternatives for the alignments. A detailed study of these alternatives has been drafted. At the present time, the study is undergoing review by the Federal Transit Administration (FTA). Upon authorisation by FTA, it will be released to the public for review and comment.

Miami

Population: City 386,417 (2005 estimate), metropolitan area 5.5 million (2006 estimate)

Public transport
Bus, metro, downtown people mover, paratransit and commuter rail services provided by department of county authority, responsible to board of county commissioners; extensive unlicensed jitney operations.

Miami-Dade Transit Department (MDT)
Stephen P Clark Center, 111 NW 1st Street, 9th Floor, Suite 910, Miami, Florida 33128-1999, US
Tel: (+1 305) 770 31 31 (Main switchboard)
Tel: (+1 305) 375 25 46   Fax: (+1 305) 372 60 93
Web: www.miamidade.gov/transit

Key personnel
Director: Roosevelt Bradley
Assistant to the Director: Clinton Forbes
Transit Administration Co-ordinator:
   Armorel Guishard
Chief, Safety and Security: Bonnie Todd

Deputy Director of Operations: Harpal Kapoor
Deputy Director of Engineering, Planning and Development: Albert Hernandez
Deputy Director of Administration:
   Mayra Bustamante
Assistant Director of Customer Service: Ruby Hemingway-Adams
Chief Financial Officer (Acting): Charles Parkinson
Assistant Director of Rail Services (Acting): Richard Snedden

Background
Originally formed in 1960 as the Metropolitan Transit Authority, the current Miami-Dade Transit Department, known as Miami-DadeTransit (MDT), provides Metrobus, Metrorail, Metromover and Special Transportation Services (STS) paratransit service and is a department of the Miami-Dade county government.

Current situation
In November 2002, the public vote revealed an overwhelming approval of a 0.5 per cent sales surtax for transportation improvements. Known as the People's Transportation Plan, this called for major bus service improvements and an expansion of the Metrorail system.

Bus (Metrobus)
3300 NW 32nd Avenue, Miami, Florida 33142, US
Tel: (+1 305) 637 38 09

Key personnel
Assistant Director, Bus Operations and Maintenance: Patricia Emard
   Staff: 2,544

Passenger boardings: (2004) 72.1 million
(2005) 76.8 million
Vehicle-km: (2005/06) 61.2 million

Number of routes: 109
Route length (Directional route km/miles): 3,010.4 km (1,870.6 miles)

Fleet: 1,031 directly operated buses, plus 301 STS contracted vehicles (breakdown figures are not currently available, but the fleet includes:)
GMC RTS-II (1980)
Flxible (1987/88/90)
Flxible alternative fuel (1992)
FRD (1992/93)
MCI (1981/82)
DTD vans (1992)
FRD (1996/97)

Tri-Rail commuter train passengers transfer to Metrorail for the final leg of the trip to downtown Miami (Van Wilkins)   0069419

Metromover over the Miami River   1177067

Flxible (1993/94)
Ikarus articulated (1994/95)
NABI (1997)
Others
In peak service: 821

Most intensive service: 5 min
One-person operation: All routes
Fare collection: Exact fare to farebox or prepurchase pass/token
Fare structure: Flat; drivers issue USD0.50 transfer; monthly passes
Arrangements for elderly/disabled: Special Transportation Services (STS) (USD2.50 fare) carried around 1.4 million passengers in FY2005; reduced ordinary fares and discount passes on fixed routes to those eligible
Operating costs financed by: Fares 20 per cent, other revenue 2 per cent, subsidy/grants 78 per cent
Subsidy from: Local government 76 per cent, state government 7 per cent, FTA 17 per cent
New vehicles financed by: Depending on year, mostly funded by local (PTP) sources

Developments
An 8 km extension to the original 13.7 km South Dade Busway opened in April 2005, continuing the Florida Department of Transportation (FDOT) Bus Rapid Transit Project to SW 264th street. Segment 2, 10.43 km (6.48 miles), will reach SW 344 street.

Construction plans include another 12 bus stations and a continuation of the South Florida Greenway; a bike path spanning the southern end of the state.

The total investment for construction of this transportation project is estimated at USD43 million. MDT has full responsibility for Busway Phase II, including engineering and construction for the extension.

In May 2005, MDT exercised an option to purchase an additional 115 NABI Model 40LFW transit buses to be delivered in three phases. This commenced in late 2005.

Metro (Metrorail)
Key personnel
Operations Director, Rail: Richard Snedden
  Staff: 571

Type of operation: Full metro, initial section opened 1984

Passenger journeys: (2002) 13.8 million
(2003) 14.3 million

Route length: 36 km (22.4 miles), mostly elevated
  at surface level: 1 km
Number of lines: 1
Number of stations: 22
Gauge: 1,435 mm

MDT bus on the South Dade Busway, parallel to US-1   1177066

Track: Direct fixation fasteners with resilient pads
Electrification: 700 V DC, third rail

Service: Peak 6 min, 8–10 min weekday midday, 15–30 min after 18.00; 15 min weekends until 20.00 then at 30 min
First/last train: 05.00–24.00
Fare structure: Flat
Fare collection: Exact fare to turnstile; prepurchase pass/token
Arrangements for elderly/disabled: Reduced fare and discount passes; Special Transportation Service (STS) available for flat fee with an average daily boarding of 2,900 passengers
Integration with other modes: Transfers to bus at extra fare, free transfer to people mover; monthly pass; interchange with commuter rail; park-and-ride at some stations
One-person operation: All trains
Automatic control: Partial, with full operator override
Surveillance: CCTV for passenger/train control
Operating costs financed by: Fares 23 per cent, subsidy/grants 77 per cent

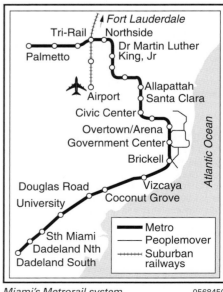

Miami's Metrorail system   0568450

Rolling stock: 136 cars
Transit America (Budd) (1983/84)   M136
In peak service: 104

Developments

A 2.3 km extension from Okeechobee to Palmetto opened in May 2003.

Plans to expand Metrorail by 35.4 km (22 miles) through to 2014, are moving forward.

A 3.9 km (2.4 mile) extension is planned, from Earlington Heights station to the Miami Intermodal Center (MIC) (adjacent to Miami International Airport (MIA). The project is being completed without federal funds. Final design commenced in May 2005. The definition of the station configuration within the MIC Core, collocating Metrorail with Tri-Rail and the MIA people mover, has been developed with the MIC steering committee. Approval of the finalised alignment will be sought through the Metropolitan Planning Organization and property acquisition within the alignment is in progress. The final design is scheduled to be completed in 2009.

A 15.3 km (9.5 mile) North Corridor to Broward County has received a favourable recommendation from the Federal Transit Administration and a 25 per cent funding commitment from the state. In June 2006, a Final Environmental Impact Statement (FEIS) will be submitted. It is anticipated that in October 2006, FTA will issue a record of decision. This will permit MDT to begin right-of-way acquisitions. The estimated completion date of the North Corridor project is 2012.

A 16.3 km (10.1 mile) east-west corridor extension to west Miami-Dade County along the County's main east-west expressway is also planned, with a projected completion of 2014. This is reliant on federal matching funds being obtained. A Supplemental Draft Environmental Impact Statement (SDEIS) is in progress.

People mover (Metromover)
Staff: 77

Passenger journeys: (2002) 4.77 million (2003) 6.8 million

Route length: 3.05 km (1.9 miles) (elevated double loop)
Number of stations/stops: 9

Current situation

Metromover, a downtown people mover, opened in 1986 and extended in 1994, links with metro and bus services for central area passenger distribution; 7.1 km, 21 stations. Unmanned cars carrying up to 120 passengers run at 90 second intervals (peak) on mostly elevated guideway using right-of-way integrated into a number of commercial developments.

Fleet: 29 cars
In peak service: 15

Service: 90 sec peak, 3 min off-peak
Fare structure: Free
First/last train: 05.00/24.00 every day

South Florida Regional Transportation Authority (SFRTA)

800 North West 33rd Street, Suite 100, Pompano Beach, Florida 33064, US
Tel: (+1 954) 942 72 45
Fax: (+1 954) 788 78 78

e-mail: marketingresponse@sfrta.fl.gov
Web: www.sfrta.fl.gov
www.tri-rail.com

Key personnel
Chair: Josephus Eggelletion
Vice-Chair: Jeff Koons
Executive Director: Joseph Giulietti
Deputy Director: Jack L Stephens

Suburban/commuter rail
Passenger journeys: (FY2004) 2.8 million
(FY2005) 2.8 million
(FY2006) 2.7 million
(FY2007) 3.4 million
(FY2008) 3.8 million

Current situation

On 1 July 2003, legislation passed by the Florida Senate and House of Representatives and signed by Governor Jeb Bush transformed the Tri-County Commuter Rail Authority (Tri-Rail) into the South Florida Regional Transportation Authority (SFRTA). The Authority was created with a vision to provide greater mobility in South Florida, thereby improving the economic viability and quality of life of the community, region and state. The Authority's mission is to co-ordinate, develop and implement a viable regional transportation system in South Florida that endeavours to meet the desires and needs for the movement of people, goods and services.

SFRTA began commuter rail service on 9 January 1989 and currently operates along the 116 km (72 mile) South Florida Rail Corridor (SFRC) extending northward from Miami Airport station in Miami-Dade County, throughout Broward County and into the northern terminus at Mangonia Park station in Palm Beach County. SFRTA unifies the three counties that comprise its service area (Miami-Dade, Broward and Palm Beach Counties), and provides mobility within the region for employees, shoppers, tourists, students and more. SFRTA is an effective and affordable alternative to the existing road/highway system, and permits those without access to an automobile to commute throughout the entire region.

During calendar year 2006, SFRTA set an all-time high for ridership, carrying 3.2 million passengers. Connecting bus services are available from all 18 stations. Passengers can connect to heavy rail at the Metrorail transfer station in Miami. All trains and stations are wheelchair accessible in accordance with the Americans with Disabilities Act (ADA) guidelines. The trains are currently operated by the SFRTA contract operator, Veolia Transportation Services Inc. SFRTA's fare system comprises six zones and weekday ticket prices are determined by the number of zones through which a passenger travels. Discounted flat fares are offered for weekend and holiday travel.

In June 2007, SFRTA/Tri-Rail began operating 50 trains per day on weekdays. 20- and 30-minute headways are now provided during the morning and evening peak periods, with hourly service provided throughout the rest of the day. SFRTA/Tri-Rail also operates 16 trains per day on weekends and major holidays, with service provided at two-hour intervals.

Developments
Segment 5 Double Track Corridor Improvement Program
The Double Track Corridor Improvement Program consisted of reconstruction along the 116 km

(72 mile) South Florida Rail Corridor (SFRC) and the addition of a second main line track parallel to the existing track. The Segment 5 Project was the final phase of the Double Tracking Program and opened for revenue service upon completion in March 2006. The project has allowed SFRTA/Tri-Rail to expand weekday service, increase the level of service during peak periods and improve on-time performance.

New River Bridge

In April 2007, a new high-level bridge over the New River in Fort Lauderdale was completed and opened for revenue service. This double tracked bridge is 55 feet above the river so that it is not impacted by boating traffic. The bridge's completion added capacity to the South Florida Rail Corridor and allowed SFRTA/Tri-Rail to implement a 50-train schedule in June 2007.

Universal Automated Fare Collection System (Smartcard)

SFRTA is leading the way to implement a multipurpose payment smartcard. The goal of the project is to provide a Universal Automated Fare Collection (UAFC) system that will support a regionwide magnetic and smartcard system for seamless fare payment among the multiple transit agencies that service the South Florida region.

Currently the UAFC is in a prolonged procurement process. The UAFC Request for Proposal (RFP) includes a complete fare collection system, including ticket vending machines, fare boxes, fare gates, smartcard readers, parking system, computer systems and other related equipment required to implement the system.

Transit Oriented Development

Transit oriented development projects are in the planning stages at 11 of the 18 SFRTA/Tri-Rail stations. The region's cities, counties, regional planning councils (RPC's) and the Florida Department of Transportation (FDOT) have all been partners in these efforts.

South Florida East Coast Corridor (SFECC) Transit Analysis Study

Since late 2005, the Florida Department of Transportation (FDOT) District 4 has been leading a regional partnership conducting the South Florida East Coast Corridor (SFECC) Transit Analysis Study. The scope of the transit analysis study is to develop and analyse alternatives that potentially integrate passenger and freight transport along the SFECC, which is centred along the existing FEC Railway. The study is considering various alignments and transit technologies. Right-of-way on streets and areas parallel to the SFECC, as well as stretches of waterways, are being evaluated for the alternative transit routes. The different technologies being considered include bus, waterway transit, light-rail, commuter-rail and heavy-rail. All of the alternatives under consideration connect with existing SFRTA/Tri-Rail service, and some would be extensions of the SFRTA/Tri-Rail system.

The study's Tier I was completed in December 2006, with a Draft Programmatic Environmental Impact Statement (DPEIS) submitted to the Federal Transit Administration (FTA). The study's Tier II is currently taking place.

Rolling stock: 16 diesel locomotives, 11 cab cars, 15 coaches, 3 dmu cars, 2 dmu coaches

---

Milwaukee
Population: City 573,358, metropolitan area 1.51 million (2006 estimates)

Public transport
Bus services provided throughout Milwaukee County by undertaking responsible to board of supervisors, managed under contract.

Milwaukee County Transit System (MCTS)
1942 N 17th Street, Milwaukee, Wisconsin 53205, US
Tel: (+1 414) 344 45 50
Fax: (+1 414) 931 83 42
Web: www.ridemcts.com

Key personnel
Managing Director: Anita Gulotta-Connelly
Marketing Director: Jacqueline Janz
Staff: 1,226 (including 792 drivers)

Background
Operated by: Milwaukee Transport Services Inc (MTS)

Current situation

County operation of public transport began in 1975, MCTS being the main provider in Milwaukee County. The system is directed by the Transportation, Public Works & Mass Transit Committee of the County Board of Supervisors, along with the County Executive. Milwaukee Transport Services Inc, a locally owned not-for-profit firm, has been the successful bidder for the operating contract since 1975.

Service is provided on a grid system including local, express, feeder and park-and-ride flyer routes, designed so that passengers should need change no more than once to reach the central business district or most other destinations. On weekdays, feeder shuttles serve industrial and business parks, as well as retail developments.

An innovation on the revenue side has been development of the U-PASS scheme in which students at five Milwaukee area universities must pay USD41 per term for an unlimited travel pass. For the 2007/08 academic year some 46,000 passes were taken up. MCTS also offers transit fare benefit programmes called Commuter Value Pass, which is an unlimited travel pass, and Commuter Value Certificate, which is a voucher equivalent in price to the system's weekly pass. Some 3,747 employees receive the CVP per month, and employers are sponsoring at least 50 per cent of the cost per passholder. In 2007, MCTS sold approximately 52,680 Commuter Value Certificates.

Developments

MCTS, Milwaukee County, the City of Milwaukee, the Metropolitan Milwaukee Chamber of Commerce and the Wisconsin Center District, which operates the City's convention centre, are collaborating on a study regarding improved transportation in Milwaukee's central business district and adjacent neighbourhoods. This Milwaukee Connector Study has examined a range of alternatives, which include expanded bus routes, bus rapid transit technology and light rail. It appears that the study will focus on bus rapid transit technology in its concluding phase. Two primary route schemes are emerging, one 12 km (7.5 miles) long and the other 20 km (12.5 miles) long. A final and preferred alternative for routes and technology is yet to be proposed.

Bus

Passenger journeys: (2003) 55.7 million (approx)
(2004) 46.5 million
(2005) 47.4 million
(2006) 46.6 million
(2007) 42.5 million
Vehicle-km: (2003) 19.7 million
(2004) 19.3 million
(2005) 19.2 million
(2006) 18.9 million
(2007) 18.4 million

Number of routes: More than 55

Fleet: 472 vehicles

New Flyer DL40LF (1996)	144
New Flyer D30LF low-floor (2000)	89
New Flyer D30LF low-floor (2001)	69
New Flyer D30LF low-floor (2002)	60
New Flyer (2003)	51
Gilligs (operated for Ozaukee County) (2002)	5
New Flyer (2004)	30
New Flyer (2005)	15
New Flyer (2006)	9

In peak service: 373 (am), 410 (pm)

Most intensive service: 4–8 min
One-person operation: All routes
Fare collection: Exact fare to electronic farebox, prepurchase tickets or passes
Fare structure: Flat, according to type of service; free 1 hr transfer; weekly passes; prepurchase 10-ride tickets; student passes
Fares collected on board: 36 per cent (49 per cent of passengers hold passes, 15 per cent prepurchase tickets)
Fare evasion control: Check by driver; electronic fareboxes
Operational control: Satellite-based vehicle management system
Arrangements for elderly/disabled: Half fare for disabled and those over 65; user subsidy for van and taxi service; all buses have kneeling facility or ramps
Integration with other modes: 10 Flyer routes serve 15 outlying parking lots, of which 12 are fully developed park-and-ride sites; reverse-flow Flyer service provided
Average distance between stops: Central business district 3 blocks in route group patterns, other areas 2 blocks
Average peak-hour speed: 20 km/h (approximately 12 mph)
Operating costs financed by: Fares 33.7 per cent, subsidy/grants 66.3 per cent
Subsidy from: State funds 41.6 per cent, FTA funds 12.8 per cent, local funds 11.5 per cent, grants 0.4 per cent
New vehicles financed by: FTA grants with local share

Minneapolis/St Paul

Population: Minneapolis 372,833, St Paul 273,535, metropolitan area 3.2 million (2006 estimates)

Public transport

Bus services provided by municipally owned operators and private operators, under overall control of Metropolitan Council responsible for transport planning, policy and day-to-day operations. Services for suburban areas are increasingly being provided independently by local communities. Ride-sharing and car- and vanpooling schemes encouraged. Light rail. Commuter rail planned.

Metropolitan Council

390 North Robert Street, St Paul, Minnesota 55101, US
Tel: (+1 651) 602 10 00; 11 40 (Data Center)
Fax: (+1 651) 602 14 64 (Data Center)
e-mail: data.center@metc.state.mn.us
Web: www.metrocouncil.org

Key personnel

Chair: Peter Bell
Director, Metropolitan Transportation Services: Arlene McCarthy
Director, Public Affairs: Steven Dornfeld
General Manager, Metro Transit: Brian Lamb
Contact, Transportation: David Vessel
Media Contact: Bonnie Kollodge

Passenger boardings: (2005) 69.7 million
(2006) 73.8 million
(2007) 77.0 million

Regional Transit operating costs financed by: Fares 26 per cent, motor vehicle excise taxes and state appropriation 62 per cent, federal and other sources 12 per cent

Current situation

The 17-member Metropolitan Council is responsible for public transport planning and policy-making, and for the day-to-day operations of the largest transport operator, Metro Transit.

Southwest Metro Transit Commission Gillig bus (Bill Luke)   0572935

A Hiawatha Line train, operated by Metro Transit, travelling southbound on a bridge over highways 55 and 62 towards the international airport and the Mall of America retail complex   1140384

In addition, the council contracts with private operators or communities to provide fixed-route and paratransit services throughout the Twin Cities area.

Twelve suburban cities are served by 'opt-out' transport systems. Ride-sharing and travel demand management programmes are managed by Metro Commuter Services.

The Metropolitan Council also contracts with operators to provide the Metro Mobility demand-response door-to-door paratransit service, which carries about 1 million passengers a year. All regional buses are fully accessible.

Developments
The Metropolitan Council has adopted a long-range Transportation Policy Plan which calls for construction of five new transitways. The plan proposes:
- A commuter rail line in the Northstar corridor between Minneapolis and Big Lake (see separate entry);
- Bus rapid transit on I-35W between Lakeville and downtown Minneapolis;
- Bus rapid transit or light rail transit on County Road 81 from Minneapolis to Osseo, Dayton and Rogers;
- Bus rapid transit on Cedar Avenue from Lakeville to the Mall of America;
- Light rail in the Central Corridor on University Avenue between downtown St Paul and downtown Minneapolis.

Light rail
Developments
Full light rail services from downtown Minneapolis to the airport and Mall of America started in December 2005. The 19.3 km (12 mile) Hiawatha Line has 17 stations with two major park-and-ride facilities. In its first full year of operation, ridership on the line was 7.8 million, 58 per cent higher than pre-construction estimates. In 2007, the line provided an average of 28,000 rides per day, exceeding pre-construction estimates for the year 2020.

In 2007, the Metropolitan Council began preliminary engineering on an LRT line in the Central Corridor, between downtown Minneapolis and downtown St Paul. The 17.7-km (11-mile) line will have 15 stations, plus five shared with the existing Hiawatha line. Construction is due to start in 2010, with operations starting in 2014.

In 2007, the Council began construction on a 64-km (40-mile) commuter rail line in the Northstar Corridor, with operations starting in 2009.

For more information, please see the separate entry for Metro Transit.

Other operators
Current situation
There are five opt-out programmes under which communities operate their own services: Maple Grove Transit System (peak period express service), Minnesota Valley Transit Authority (peak period express service), City of Plymouth (commuter express, reverse commute and dial-a-ride), City of Shakopee (dial-a-ride and vanpool/ride-share), and Southwest Metro Transit Commission (commuter express, reverse commute and dial-a-ride).

Metro Transit
560 Sixth Avenue North, Minneapolis, Minnesota 55411-4398, US
Tel: (+1 612) 349 74 00
Fax: (+1 612) 349 76 12
Web: www.metrotransit.org,
www.metrocouncil.org/transit/

Key personnel
General Manager: Brian Lamb
Director of Bus Transportation: Sam Jacobs
Director of Service Department: John Levin
Director of Bus Maintenance: Jan Hornan
Director of Rail Systems Maintenance:
Andy Lukaszewicz
Director of Rail Vehicle Maintenance:
Edward Toorney

Plymouth Metrolink Blue Bird bus (Bill Luke)
0572937

Minnesota Valley Transit Authority New Flyer articulated bus (Bill Luke)
0572938

Director of Finance: Edwin Petrie
Director of Customer Services and Public Relations:
Robert Gibbons
Director of Marketing: Bruce Howard
Director of Engineering and Construction:
Tom Thorstenson
Deputy General Manager: Mark Fuhrmann
Director of Purchasing Chris Gran
Chief Operating Officer, Bus and Rail Operations:
Vince Pellegrin
Assistant General Manager, Administration:
Julie Johanson
Assistant General Manager, Transit Systems Development: Rich Rovang
Deputy Chief Operating Officer, Bus Operations:
Bill Porter
Deputy Chief Operating Officer, Rail Operations:
Sheri Gingerich
Staff: 2,389

Current situation
Metro Transit is an operating division of the Metropolitan Council. It operates more than 90 per cent of regular routes in the region. Its service area covers Minneapolis, St Paul (the Twin Cities) and the majority of surrounding inner suburbs.

Developments
The Metropolitan Council has adopted a long-range Transportation Policy Plan which calls for construction of five new transitways (see separate entry).

Phase One of the Northwest Metro Transit Restructuring Plan was implemented in 2007.

This aims to improve service in the area west of the Mississippi River and north of Highway 55.

Over the next five years, under the 'Go Greener' initiative, Metro Transit intends to replace 314 buses with 150 next-generation hybrid electric buses. The other 164 new buses will incorporate the latest engine technology that will burn diesel fuel more efficiently, reduce emissions and improve fuel economy. In August 2007, Metro Transit doubled the biodiesel content of its fuel supply from 5 per cent to 10 per cent and operates in the summer months with a 20 per cent blend.

Bus
Passenger journeys: (2003) 67.2 million
(2004) 54.0 million (46-day transit strike)
(2005) 69.5 million
(2006) 73.4 million
(2007) 78.0 million
Vehicle-km: (2006) 46.8 million (29.1 million miles)
(2007) 47.9 million (29.8 million miles)

Number of routes: 118 (66 local, 52 express)
Route length: (One way) 2,260 km
On priority right-of-way: 447 km (278 miles)

Fleet: 880 vehicles
40 ft vehicles 734
60 ft articulated vehicles 146
In peak service: 758 (including LRVs)

Most intensive service: 5 min
One-person operation: All routes

Fare collection: Registering farebox, generally pay-as-you-enter; pre-purchase magnetic-strip passes; smartcard fully implemented; ticket vending machines on light rail platforms

Fare structure: Local and Express flat fares with peak surcharge; free transfer within 2½ h

Integration with other modes: Service to international airport and intercity bus terminal; van and car-pools encouraged, over 5,000 registered; park-and-ride schemes, connection with light rail services at 14 stations

Arrangements for elderly/disabled: Metro Mobility special bus services operated under contract; 14 county paratransit operations and 13 local community schemes; all buses are accessible

Security: 125 Metropolitan Transit Police officers

Bus priority: City-centre transit mall in Minneapolis provides exclusive bus access for most routes; 447 km (278 miles) of bus-only lanes on freeways

Average distance between stops: 400 m

Average peak-hour speed: In mixed traffic, 21 km/h; in bus lanes (central business area), 13 km/h

Operating costs financed by: Fares 35 per cent, state appropriations and motor vehicle sales taxes 60 per cent, federal and other sources 5 per cent

Subsidy from: n/a

Light rail (Hiawatha Line)

Passenger journeys: (2005) 7.9 million
(2006) 9.0 million
(2007) 9.1 million

Car-km: Not currently available

Route length: 19.3 km (12 miles)
in tunnel: 4.4 km (7 miles) (2 parallel tunnels of 2.2 km)

Number of lines: 1

Number of stations: 17

Electrification: Overhead

Current situation

The Hiawatha Line opened for partial service (12.9 km (8 miles), 12 stations), in June 2004. The full line opened in December 2004, to a total of 19.3 km (12 miles) and 17 stations.

Opening was 27 days ahead of schedule and within the USD715.3 million budget.

Developments

Ridership for the first full year of operation was 7.8 million, 58 per cent higher than pre-construction estimates. In 2007, ridership averaged 26,762 on weekdays, exceeding its ridership expectations for 2020.

Rolling stock: 27 Bombardier *Flexity*™ Light Rail Vehicles (LRVx)

Service: Peak: 7½ min, daytime: 10 min, early evening: 15 min, late evening/early morning: 30 min

First/last car: 04.00/01.00

Fare structure: As for bus, transfer valid for 150 min

Fare collection: Self-service tickets at stations

Integration with other modes: Connection with bus services at 14 stations

Arrangements for elderly/disabled: All stations are ADA compliant; four wheelchair positions per vehicle; ramps and tactile edges at all stations; lifts at stations on bridges

Northstar Corridor Development Authority (NCDA)

Northstar Project Office
155 Fifth Avenue South, Suite 755, Minneapolis, Minnesota 55401, USA
Tel: (+1 612) 215 82 00   Fax: (+1 612) 215 82 10
e-mail: info@mn-getonboard.com
Web: www.northstartrain.org
www.mn-getonboard.com

Key personnel

Northstar Corridor Project Director: Tim Yantos
Tel: (+1 763) 323 56 92
Fax: (+1 763) 323 56 82
e-mail: tim.yantos@co.anoka.mn.us
Administrative Assistant: Susan Youngs
Tel: (+1 763) 323 58 13

Passengers boarding a Haiwatha Line LRV at the Cedar-Riverside station near the University of Minnesota in Minneapolis   1140383

Franklin Avenue station on the Hiawatha Line. Each station has unique architecture and public art to reflect the character of its neighbourhood.   1140382

Metro Transit New Flyer articulated bus at Nicollet Mall (Bill Luke)   1115222

Commuter rail (proposed)

Background

Phase One of the Northstar Corridor is a proposed 64.5 km (40.1 mile) line with six stations running between Big Lake and downtown Minneapolis, where it will link with the Hiawatha light rail system and connect to existing bus services. The service is anticipated to be eight morning and evening trains plus one midday round-trip and would use existing track. Daily ridership has been estimated at 5,600 per day.

Project costs are estimated to be in the region of USD 265 million and the proposal states that this would be funded by local government (17 per cent) and the state (33 per cent), with the remainder from the federal government.

The NCDA is a joint powers board representing 30 counties, cities, townships and regional railroad authorities along the corridor.

Phase Two would continue the line from Big Lake to St Cloud/Rice.

Current situation
Local governments have already committed their share of USD44.2 million and in 2005, Minnesota Legislature committed USD37.5 million in low-interest state bonding to advance the project towards final funding. In July of the same year, US Congress approved an USD80 million authorisation for Northstar Commuter Rail.

The NCDA will be continuing to work with the FTA on final design and to obtain a 'Recommended' rating for the project.

Bus
Northstar Commuter Coach
Tel: (+1 888) 528 88 80
e-mail: commutercoach@commutercoach.org
Web: www.commutercoach.org

Background
In July 2003, the NCDA voted to fund the Northstar Commuter Coach bus service. This service would have been discontinued by the Minnesota Department of Transportation (MnDOT) after September 2003.

Current situation
The service provides eight morning and eight evening commuter bus trips daily, between Elk River and Minneapolis, and is mainly funded by fares, local government and federal grants.

Developments
Ridership has exceeded initial expectations. The Northstar Commuter Coach provides about 700 rides every day on the route from Elk River to downtown Minneapolis. Approximately 265 daily commuters board the bus at Elk River and another 90 board at Coon Rapids.

Monterey/Salinas
Population: 392,837 (2002 estimate)

Public transport
Fixed-route transit serving the six cities on the Monterey peninsula, and Salinas, Watsonville and several rural areas in the 280 km² area of Monterey County on the California coast. Extensive services provided in Monterey, Salinas and Carmel, with intercity routes linking Salinas with Monterey and Watsonville. Reinstatement of rail service proposed.

Monterey-Salinas Transit (MST)
One Ryan Ranch Road, Monterey, California 93940-5703, US
Tel: (+1 831) 899 25 55; 424 76 95, (+1 800) MST BUS1 (toll free)
Fax: (+1 831) 899 39 54
e-mail: customerservice@mst.org
Web: www.mst.org

Key personnel
General Manager and Chief Executive Officer:
  Carl Sedoryk
Director of Maintenance and Transportation:
  Michael Hernandez
  Staff: 214

Current situation
MST was formed in 1981 by the merger of Monterey Peninsula Transit and Salinas Transit System. MST serves an area of 712 km² (275 sq miles) and a population of approximately 352,000.

Developments
In September 2004, the company introduced the first of 46 new 40 ft low-floor 'smart buses'. The technology in this new bus, built by Gillig, includes passenger announcements in both English and Spanish, automated vehicle location and onboard surveillance, and the vehicle is powered by a clean-diesel engine.

In 2004, MST also took delivery of the remaining new Gillig CNG buses, completing the 46-unit upgrade which included 35 ft, 40 ft and trolley-style vehicles. The six trolleybuses were introduced on MST's seasonal Waterfront Area Visitor Express (WAVE) route. Ridership on this summer-only route exceeded previous levels by some 67 per cent. In July 2004, a second trolley line was introduced between Monterey Bay Aquarium and Pacific Grove.

An express service is in operation to Carmel and a further express route between South Monterey County and the Monterey peninsula began in September 2004.

MST is continuing to enhance its services, with a new holiday service being offered for the first time on Thanksgiving, Christmas and New Year's Day. Also for the first time, the MST Trolley operated during autumn, winter and spring holiday periods.

MST has recently completed a comprehensive operational analysis of its Salinas service area.

MST trolleybus   1140405

MST Gillig bus   1140403

Bus
Passenger boardings: (Includes paratransit)
(2000/01) 4.75 million
(2001/02) 4.8 million
(2002/03) 4.7 million
(2003/04) 4.7 million
(2004/05) 4.8 million
Vehicle-km: (2000/01) 4.4 million (2.75 million miles)
(2003/04) 5.2 million (3.2 million miles)
(2004/05) 5.8 million (3.6 million miles)

Number of routes: 33
Route length: 577.6 km (359 miles)
No of stops: 1,244

Fleet: 124 buses (plus 1 contingency and 2 historical buses)

Flxible 800-Series CNG (1995)	8
Orion 1000-Series CNG (1996)	9
Gillig 1100-Series (2000, 2003)	29
Gillig 1700-Series low-floor (2002, 2003)	24
Gillig 1800-Series suburban (2002, 2003)	8
Optima 1900-Series trolley (2003)	6
Ford Minibus 5000-Series (1998/99, 2001/05)	11
Chevrolet Minibus 5000-Series (1999, 2001, 2003)	10
Ford Minibus 900-Series (1999, 2002)	15
Chevrolet Minivan 5000-Series (2002, 2004)	4
Contingency fleet	
Ford Minibus 5000-Series (1997)	1
Historical fleet	
Fageol twin coach (1948)	1
GMC (1957)	1

In peak service: 109
Average age of fleet: 4.3 years

Most intensive service: 15 min peak service on Fremont Street and East Alisal Street Corridors; 30 min interurban routes
One-person operation: All routes

Fare collection: Pay-as-you-enter, exact fare

Fare structure: 5 zones, flat fare in each; free transfers for one-way journeys; monthly zonal and system passes; GoldPass for anyone over 65

Farebox recovery: 25 per cent

Operational control: Central dispatching; radio in all buses

Arrangements for elderly/disabled: All vehicles have wheelchair lifts; reduced fares

Integration with other modes: Connecting service is provided to Amtrak, Greyhound, Santa Cruz Metropolitan Transit District, Santa Clara Valley Transit Authority and Caltrain

Operating costs financed by: Fares 25 per cent, other commercial sources 1 per cent, subsidy/grants 74 per cent

Subsidy from: FTA 28 per cent, local 46 per cent

New vehicles financed by: Local and federal funding

Transportation Agency for Monterey County (TAMC)

55-B Plaza Circle, Salinas, California 93901-2902, US

Tel: (+1 831) 775 09 03   Fax: (+1 831) 775 08 97

e-mail: info@tamcmonterey.org

Web: www.tamcmonterey.org

Key personnel

Chair: Ralph Rubio

Vice-Chair: Mike Cunningham

1st Vice-Chair: Butch Lindley

2nd Vice-Chair: John P Huerta

TAMC Rail Programme Contact: Karen Clysdale

Current situation

The Transportation Agency for Monterey County (TAMC) is working to reinstate rail service between San Francisco and the Monterey Peninsula. Initially service would be one train a day Friday to Monday. Expansion to daily service and two trains a day is a future objective. TAMC supports the extension of the two state-funded trains 'Capitols' and 'San Diegans' south and north respectively to provide more train service through Salinas. TAMC is working with neighbouring counties to promote extension of the San Francisco-San Jose-Gilroy 'Caltrain' commuter service to Salinas.

TAMC received USD450,000 from the State of California to complete environmental review and preliminary engineering for the train service on the Monterey branch.

Nashville

Population: 552,120 (2006 estimate), metropolitan area 1.52 million (2007 estimate)

Public transport

Bus and commuter rail services provided by transit authority responsible to city council through transit board and managed under contract.

Nashville Metropolitan Transit Authority (MTA)

130 Nestor Street, Nashville, Tennessee 37210-2124, US

Tel: (+1 615) 862 59 69

Fax: (+1 615) 862 62 08

e-mail: mtacommunications@nashville.gov

Web: www.nashvillemta.org

Key personnel

Chair: Gail Carr Williams

Vice-Chair: Bill Barnes

Chief Executive Officer: Paul J Ballard

Chief Operating Officer: Robert Baulsir

Chief Financial Officer: Edward W Oliphant

Director of Communications: Patricia Harris-Morehead

Director of Planning: Jim McAteer

Director of Administration: Timothy Sanderson

Director of Customer Care: Lora Baulsir

AccessRide Manager: Cynthia Whitehead

Contract Manager: Lee Jackson

Maintenance Manager: Tim Williamson

Safety Manager: Earl Rhodes

Security Manager: Roger Farley

Operations Manager: Dawn Distler

   Staff: 486

Passenger journeys: (2005/06) 7 million (estimate)

(2006/07) 8.5 million

(2007/08) 9.4 million (estimate)

Vehicle-km: Not currently available

Current situation

The Metropolitan Transit Authority provides public transportation bus services (local and express routes) within the Metropolitan Nashville area. Customers may access more than 40 different routes in Metro Nashville. The agency also has contracts with the Regional Transportation Authority to run bus service to La Vergne, Smyrna, Murfreesboro, Lebanon and Hendersonville. Another key service that the MTA provides is the AccessRide door-to-door paratransit services for people with disabilities and those who are unable to ride the local and express buses.

The MTA promotes Easy Ride commuter benefits for area employers and employees and parking shuttle services.

A board of directors, whose five-member panel is appointed by the mayor, governs the MTA. A management team, headed by a chief executive officer, oversees the day-to-day operations.

MTA Gillig bus in downtown Nashville   1328303

Developments

Recently, the MTA placed an order for several articulated hybrid buses, to be delivered in late 2008.

A new Music City Central transit centre hub is under construction and is scheduled to open in late 2008.

Credit cards are now accepted at the fare box on all MTA buses and vans. The Nashville MTA is currently the only transit system in the US to implement this new technology on its entire fleet. Customers now can use their credit and debit Visa and Master Cards on the buses and vans to pay fares.

The Music City Star, Tennessee's first commuter rail, began service on 18 September 2006, and ridership continues to increase.

Bus (Fixed Route/Demand Response)

Number of routes: 41

Route length: 1,293 km

Fleet: 201 vehicles

Neoplan/300 series 40 ft (1997)	10
Goshen 24 ft (1998)	2
RTS 40 ft (1999, 2000)	15
Neoplan/150 series 60 ft (2000)	12
Startrans 24 ft (2001/03, 2005/07)	61
ElDorado 24 ft (2003)	1
Gillig/800 series Suburban 40 ft (2004)	86
Gillig/600 series Suburban 40 ft (2004/05)	4
Gillig/650 series 35 ft (2005)	10
In peak service: 116 buses, 48 AccessRide vehicles	

On order: NABI 60 ft hybrid articulated, number unspecified, delivery scheduled for late 2008

Most intensive service: 4 min

One-person operation: All routes

Fare collection: GFI farebox by driver

Fare structure: Flat, 20-ride tickets; all-day pass, 7- and 31-day passes

Fares collected on board: 25 per cent

Fare evasion control: Driver monitors fare payment; cameras on buses

Integration with other modes: System of peripheral park-and-ride areas; ride-sharing promoted

Arrangements for elderly/disabled: USD0.65 fare at all times on regular services, reduced rate monthly pass; AccessRide van service for mobility-impaired (USD2.70); all buses lift-equipped

Average distance between stops: 200 m

Average peak-hour speed: In mixed traffic, 13.5 km/h

Bus priority: On central business district transit mall, I-65 south HOV lane and I-24 east HOV lane

Operating costs financed by: Fares and other commercial sources 25 per cent, subsidy/grants 75 per cent

Subsidy from: Federal 15 per cent, state 12 per cent and local 48 per cent (FY 2007/08)

New vehicles financed by: Local 100 per cent

Commuter rail

Music City Star Commuter Service

The Music City Star, a 51 km (32 mile) East Corridor line, began service in September 2006, with Lebanon as the origination point. Other stops are in Martha, Mt Juliet, Hermitage and Donelson and Riverfront in downtown Nashville. MTA buses meet the train and provide feeder services.

Eleven bi-level gallery railcars for the new Music City Star Commuter Rail System were acquired by the Regional Transportation Authority from Chicago Metra.

Newark/New Jersey

Population: City 281,402, metropolitan area 2.15 million (2006 estimates)

Public transport

Bus, light rail and commuter rail services provided in Newark and other parts of New Jersey by divisions of state-owned New Jersey Transit Corporation and private bus companies supported and co-ordinated through NJ Transit. Operations extend across the state but particularly serve commuter needs of Newark, New York City and Philadelphia with substantial suburban and commuter bus, as well as rail provision, by both NJ Transit and private operators. Bi-state regional metro operation by Port Authority of New York and New Jersey (see also under New York) and other complementary services by Amtrak, New York MTA, PATCO and SEPTA.

New Jersey Transit (NJ Transit)

Headquarters
One Penn Plaza East, Newark, New Jersey 07105-2246, USA
Tel: (+1 973) 491 70 00
(+1 973) 491 94 00 (Customer service)
Fax: (+1 973) 491 82 18
Web: www.njtransit.com

Key personnel

Chairman: Kris Kolluri
Vice-Chairman: Myron P Shevell
Executive Director: Richard R Sarles
Chief, NJ Transit Police: Joseph C Bober
Assistant Executive Director, Corporate Communications and External Affairs: Lynn M Bowersox
Vice-President and General Manager, Rail Operations: William B Duggan
Acting Vice-President and General Manager, Bus Operations: James J Gigantino
Staff: 11,303 (2006)

Passenger boardings: (All modes, own operations) (FY2006) 241.1 million

Operating costs financed by: Fares 49 per cent, other commercial sources 9 per cent, subsidy/grants 28 per cent

Current situation

NJ Transit was created in 1979 as a state-wide corporation charged with overseeing public transit by operating, contracting for or subsidising services.

The Corporation operates through three subsidiaries, NJ Transit Bus Operations, NJ Transit Rail Operations Inc and NJ Transit Mercer Inc and covers an area of 5,325 sq miles.

NJ Transit provides bus, light rail, suburban rail, paratransit and rural services. The Access Link ADA Paratransit Program carried out 595,324 passenger trips in FY2006.

Developments

Trans-Hudson Express Tunnel (THE Tunnel Project)
This project would see two new single-track rail tunnels and an expanded Penn Station New York (PSNY) under 34th Street, aimed at increasing trans-Hudson rail capacity.

In mid-2007, Parsons, Tishman Construction Corp and Arup (THE Partnership) were awarded a contract to provide engineering services on Phase 1 of the project. THE Partnership has also been awarded the contract for preliminary design.

Monmouth-Ocean-Middlesex
NJ Transit is preparing a Draft Environmental Impact Statement (DEIS) for rail alternatives for this three county region.

West Trenton Line
The project involves restoring commuter rail service for 43.4 km (27 miles) on the West Trenton Line between the existing Southeastern Pennsylvania Transportation Authority (SEPTA) West Trenton Station in Ewing, Mercer County and Bridgewater Station in Bridgewater, Somerset County, where the line would connect with the existing Raritan Valley Line providing service into Newark Penn Station.

Work would include re-installation of previously removed track and installation of 20.6 km (12.8 miles) of new track within the existing rail right of way, signal improvements, restoration of the at-grade crossing of the Lehigh Line at Port Reading Junction, four new stations and parking facilities, a train storage yard and acquisition of additional rail rolling stock.

Lackawanna Cutoff
The project would reinstate passenger rail service on the abandoned rail right of way of the Lackawanna Cutoff and over existing freight right of way in Pennsylvania. The re-instituted rail line would provide service from Scranton to Hoboken, or to New York Penn Station via transfer to MidTown Direct service, by connecting to the existing NJ Transit Montclair-Boonton and Morris & Essex Lines.

Work would include complete reconstruction of the line including track and signal improvements to approximately 141.6 km (88 miles) of right-of-way, new stations, parking facilities, a train storage yard and additional rail rolling stock. It is assumed that NJ Transit would operate the new service. Proposed stations would serve Blairstown and Andover in New Jersey and Scranton, Tobyhanna, Pocono Mountain, Analomink, East Stroudsburg, and Delaware Water Gap in Pennsylvania.

Bus

Passenger journeys: (FY2006) 156.89 million
Vehicle-km: (FY2006) 107.8 million (67 million miles)

Number of routes: 240
Route length: 5,693 km (3,538 miles)

Developments

NJ Transit is purchasing new suburban and transit buses. All will be equipped with CCTV cameras. The company also continued a three-year trial of hybrid transit and cruiser buses.

Central New Jersey Route 1 Bus Rapid Transit Alternatives Analysis
The alternatives analysis is being managed by NJ Transit in close collaboration with its funding partners; New Jersey Department of Transportation (NJDOT), Delaware Valley Regional Planning Commission (DVRPC) and North Jersey Transportation Planning Authority (NJTPA).

The study will evaluate route alternatives, including use of existing roads with improvements and new alignments, station locations, ridership, potential for coordination with private sector development, municipal plans and cost effectiveness.

Fleet: 3,075 vehicles (including 966 vehicles owned by NJ Transit and leased to 17 private operators) (plus a fleet of 799 vehicles for local and community services)
Full breakdown of fleet is not currently available, but comprises:

Cruisers (commuter) (including 76 CNG vehicles)	1,542
Suburban	335
Articulated	85
Transit	1,072
Minibuses/WHEELS	41

In peak service: Not currently available

Most intensive service: 10 min
One-person operation: All routes
Fare collection: Farebox, or passes
Fare structure: Zonal, with passes
Operational control: All buses have radio
Arrangements for elderly/disabled: New buses are kneeling or lift-equipped and others are being retrofitted; almost all routes accessible; 50 accessible minibuses
Bus priority: Bus lanes introduced to central business district, operating 06.30-09.30 and 16.00-18.30
Average peak-hour speed: 22 km/h

Light rail

Type of operation: Light rail

Passenger boardings: (FY2006) 15.39 million
Car-km: (FY2006) 4.3 million (2.7 million miles)

Route length: 172 km (107 miles)
Number of lines: 3
Number of stations: 55
  in tunnel:
Gauge: 1,435 mm
Track: 50 kg/m TEE rail ARA type B on timber in ballast; in tunnel stations wood stub sleepers set in concrete
Max gradient: 6%
Minimum curve radius: 12 m
Tunnel: Cut-and-cover, double-track
Electrification: 600 V DC, overhead

Service: Peak 2 min, off-peak 6 min
First/last car: 05.00/01.00
Fare structure: Zonal, with transfer to certain bus lines
Fare collection: Proof-of-payment to be instituted during 1999
Integration with other modes: 38 bus routes serve the 11 stations, which are much used for transfer
Operating costs financed by: Included in bus data
One-person operation: All cars
Signalling: Simple track circuit block
Surveillance: CCTV

Rolling stock: 93 cars (including 72 cars owned by NJT and operated under contract)

In peak service: Not currently available

Newark City Subway

Passenger boardings: (2005/06) 5.2 million

Current situation

Construction started on the line in 1929, with the first section opening in late 1934. The line is currently 15.9 km (9.9 miles) long, with 17 stations.

21 Kinki-Sharyo LRVs operate on the line, with 5 PCCs in store.

Developments

In July 2006, a new 1.6 km segment opened from Newark-Penn Station to Newark-Broad Street Station. It runs partly in tunnel and has four stations. There are plans for an extension to Newark-Liberty International Airport.

Hudson-Bergen Light Rail

Web: www.mylightrail.com

Current situation

This system connects residential Bayonne and western Jersey City with Jersey City's Exchange Place and Newport Center, and Hoboken Terminal business and shopping centres with easy connections to New York City via PATH and NY Waterway.

The system is 43.8 km (27.2 miles) long with 23 stations.

52 Kinki-Sharyo LRVs operate on this line.

Developments

The final segment, running from Hoboken Terminal to Tonnelle Avenue Park-N-Ride in North Bergen and also extending to 22nd St. in Bayonne, was completed in February 2006.

River LINE

Web: www.riverline.com

Current situation

The River LINE is a 54.7 km (34 mile) light rail line, which links Trenton with Camden. It has 20 stations, serving communities along the Delaware River's Route 130 corridor, and connects to the transportation networks of NJ Transit, Amtrak, PATCO and SEPTA.

Suburban rail

Type of operation: Suburban heavy rail

Passenger boardings: (FY2005) 64.9 million
(FY2006) 68.81 million
Train-km: (FY2006) 90.3 million (56.1 million miles)

Route length: 1,604 km (997 miles)
Number of routes: 11
Number of stations: 163

Current situation
NJ Transit operates 11 routes. Routes run from the north and west into Hoboken, with connections via PATH metro to and from New York. Three routes (Pascack Valley, Main/Bergen, and Boonton, 178 km total) are diesel-operated, and three (the Morris and Essex lines – Morristown, Gladstone and Montclair, 108 km total) are electrified at 25 kV 60 Hz. The New York State portions of two of the diesel routes, the Main and Pascack Valley lines (113 km, 11 stations), are operated under contract with the New York MTA. The Morristown line now has through service to New York Penn station.

Three routes run from the south and west into Newark Penn station, with electrified services continuing direct to New York Penn station. PATH also connects this station with New York. NJ Transit operates between New York and Trenton, 94 km, on the Northeast Corridor line, which is electrified at 12 kV 25 Hz and is owned by Amtrak.

New Jersey stations on the Northeast Corridor have been taken over by NJ Transit. Some of these stations are served both by Amtrak intercity trains and NJ Transit suburban trains. Local trains on the Lindenwold-Atlantic City line, reopened in 1989, are also operated by NJ Transit. These were extended from suburban Lindenwold to Philadelphia's Amtrak 30th Street station in 1993 (see Philadelphia entry).

Rolling stock: 170 locomotives (including 11 owned by Metro-North and operated by NJ Transit), 230 emu units and 677 push-pull rail cars (including 67 owned by Metro-North and operated by NJ Transit)

Developments
NJ Transit has recently purchased 33 new PL-42 diesel locomotives. These have replaced older GP40PH and GP40FH locomotives. In addition, the company is purchasing more than 230 new bilevel rail cars. The most recent order was placed with Bombardier Transportation for 131 vehicles in late 2005. The contract value for this was approximately EUR171 million.

There are plans to build a new station, accessed by new tracks linked to the Pascack Valley line, at Meadowlands.

Private bus/commuter coach
Supported by New Jersey Transit

Current situation
About 40 per cent of New Jersey bus and commuter coach service is provided by 122 private operators, some of them grouped into associations of various kinds for co-ordination of timetables on shared routes, and in some cases pooling revenues. Some 1,500 vehicles ply on 177 routes, carrying about 78 million passengers a year.

Five carriers receiving subsidy from and four operating under contract to NJT carry about 8.5 per cent of the state's total ridership. The 122 private firms carry about 40 per cent of the state's ridership without operating support, but 13 receive substantial capital assistance in the form of 222 state-owned buses leased to them at a nominal rate.

Many of the private operators provide commuter services into New York, using the 4 km exclusive peak-only busway on the I-495 highway through the Lincoln tunnel under the Hudson river and into the Port Authority of New York and New Jersey bus terminal. Peak flows on this corridor carry up to 35,000 passengers/h.

Port Authority Trans-Hudson Corporation (PATH)
1 Path Plaza, Jersey City, New Jersey 07306-2944, USA
Tel: (+1 201) 216 62 47
Freephone: (+1 800) 234 72 84
Fax: (+1 201) 216 62 66
Web: www.pathrail.com
www.panynj.gov/path/

Key personnel
Chairman: Anthony R Coscia
Vice-Chairman: Charles A Cargano
President: Kenneth R Ringler
Director and General Manager: Michael P DePallo

Metro
Current situation
Services between New York and New Jersey (Hoboken, Journal Square and Newark Penn) are operated by PATH, a subsidiary of the Port Authority of New York and New Jersey, on four lines.

The Port Authority also operates the New York bus terminal at 42nd Street, into which many commuter operations run.

PATH serves as a ferry transportation 'clearinghouse' for the New York-New Jersey metropolitan area.

For full details of PATH's operations, please see the entry for New York.

New Orleans
Population: City 456,155, metropolitan area 1.3 million (2002 estimates)

Public transport
Regional Transit Authority controls and operates bus services and tramway. Authority also supervises other bus operations including routes contracted out to private sector. River ferries operated by Bridge Authority.

New Orleans Regional Transit Authority (NORTA)

6700 Plaza Drive, New Orleans, Louisiana 70127, USA
Tel: (+1 504) 827 83 00
Fax: (+1 504) 248 36 37
e-mail: marketingpublicrelations@norta.com
Web: www.norta.com

Key personnel
Chair: Cesar Burgos
General Manager: Mark Major
Staff: Not currently available

Background
Formed in 1983.

Passenger boardings: Not currently available

Operating costs financed by: Fares 45 per cent, other commercial sources 4 per cent, subsidy/grants 10 per cent, tax levy 41 per cent
Subsidy from: FTA 19.7 per cent, local sales tax 80 per cent

Current situation
The RTA, controlled by a board appointed by the City of New Orleans and Jefferson Parish Council, was created in 1979 and took over transit operations in 1983. In 1985 the RTA took over transit operations in the neighbouring

Car on the Riverfront service, New Orleans (Marcus Enoch)   0104730

city of Kenner. Contracted operations ended in 1989, when a local management team, Transit Management of Southeast Louisiana, took over.

An increase in the sales tax allocated to the RTA from ½ cent to 1 cent was approved in 1985 and is used to fund capital improvements (25 per cent) and operations (75 per cent). The RTA demands that 45 per cent of operating costs be covered from fares.

The tramway plays a modest part in the city's transit. Several proposals exist for modern light rail routes, in particular in the former tram right-of-way in the median of busy Canal Street from the Waterfront to City Park Avenue (6.4 km), on which construction is expected to start in late 1999, to link the airport with downtown (21 km) using mostly existing rail right-of-way, and several extensions. A new fleet of 35 cars would be required (see below).

The 1988-built Riverfront Line has been converted to 1,586 mm gauge to standardise the rolling stock fleet.

Bus

Passenger boardings: Not currently available
Vehicle-km: Not currently available

Number of routes: 28
Route length: Not currently available
On priority right-of-way: Not currently available

Fleet: Not currently available
In peak service: Not currently available

Most intensive service: 2–3 min
One-person operation: All routes
Fare collection: Cash or token to GFI electronic farebox; monthly or visitor pass
Fare structure: Flat base ordinary and express fares; prepurchase tokens; 10 cent coupon for multitransfers; monthly pass (not valid in Kenner); 1-and 3-day visitor passes
Operational control: Route inspectors; on-bus radio
Integration between modes: Park-and-ride
Arrangements for elderly/disabled: 'The Lift' special door-to-door lift service operated under contract carried 214,000 passengers in 1994; some fixed-route buses lift-equipped; dial-a-ride; reduced fare
Average peak-hour speed: 16.9 km/h

Tramway

Type of operation: Conventional tramway, opened 1835

Passenger boardings: Not currently available
Car-km: Not currently available

Route length: 31.7 km
Number of lines: 3
Gauge: 1,586 mm
Electrification: 600 V DC, overhead

Service: Peak 4–5 min, off-peak 7 min; 24 h service on St Charles route
Fare structure: Flat (as bus)
One-person operation: All cars

Rolling stock: 78 cars
Perley Thomas Car Co (1923)	M37
W2 (ex-Melbourne)	M2
PCC (ex-SEPTA Philadelphia)	M12
Replica Perley Thomas (2004)	M24
Others	M3

Current situation
The St Charles route runs along a median strip in St Charles Avenue and is the last remaining US tram line to run pre-PCC cars. It is designated a national monument. A three-year refurbishment was completed in 1990. Unconnected Riverfront route opened 1988 and extended in 1990.

Refurbishment of 1923-vintage cars was completed in 1995, and the Riverfront line was converted from 1,435 mm to 1,586 mm gauge in 1997. Further extensions planned (see above).

RTA has bought 12 PCC tramcars from SEPTA Philadelphia. Three are to be rebuilt with Perley Thomas replica bodies and wheelchair access for use on the Riverfront Line.

Developments

Canal Streetcar Line
In April 2004, the Canal Streetcar began service again. The new line runs for 5.7 km (3.5 miles)

from the Mississippi River to City Park Avenue, with a spur along North Carrollton Avenue. The 24 new cars in the fleet, which were constructed in NORTA's workshops, are designed to resemble the Perley Thomas vehicles used on the original line.

It is estimated ridership will be in excess of 31,000 daily by 2015.

Jefferson Transit- (JeT)

Department of Transit Administration
21 Westbank Expressway, Gretna, Louisiana 70053, US
Tel: (+1 504) 364 34 50
Fax: (+1 504) 364 34 53
e-mail: JPTransit@jeffparish.net
Web: www.jeffersontransit.org/

Key personnel
Director of Transit: Al Robichaux

Current situation
Services in Jefferson Parish are provided by Jefferson Transit. There are six routes on the east bank and 11 routes and five special routes on the west bank. All of the vehicles in the fleet are lift-equipped and have a Talking Bus system which announces stops and transfer points.

Jefferson Transit also provides a Mobility Impaired Transit System (MITS), which is kerb-to-kerb and demand-responsive, with a fleet of 18 vehicles. There were approximately 79,000 trips made using this service in 2002.

New York

Population: City 8.27 million, metropolitan area 18.82 million (2007 estimates)

Public transport

Bus, metro (subway) and suburban rail networks operated by various subsidiaries of the Metropolitan Transportation Authority (MTA). MTA, also responsible for bridges and tunnels, is governed by a board representing the city and suburban communities served. A regional metro (PATH) is operated between New York and New Jersey by the Port Authority. Private bus lines provide additional suburban and commuter services from and within New York under the City Department of Transportation, and other commuter bus services operate from New Jersey (see also Newark/New Jersey). There are also some private door-to-door minibus pick-up services and express routes to Manhattan. Commuter ferry services are provided by the City-operated Staten Island ferry and private operators, which run primarily between New Jersey and Manhattan. Recreational ferries serve New York Harbor and the Hudson River Corridor. Light rail and Bus Rapid Transit (BRT) proposed.

Metropolitan Transportation Authority (MTA)

347 Madison Avenue, New York, New York 10017-3706, US
Tel: (+1 212) 878 70 00
Web: www.mta.info

Key personnel
Chair: H Dale Hemmerdinger
Vice-Chairs: David S Mack
    Andrew M Saul
Executive Director and Chief Operating Officer: Elliot G Sander
Chief Operating Officer: Susan Kupferman
Chief of Staff: Myrna I Ramon
Deputy Executive Director/Corporate Affairs and Communications: Christopher P Boylan

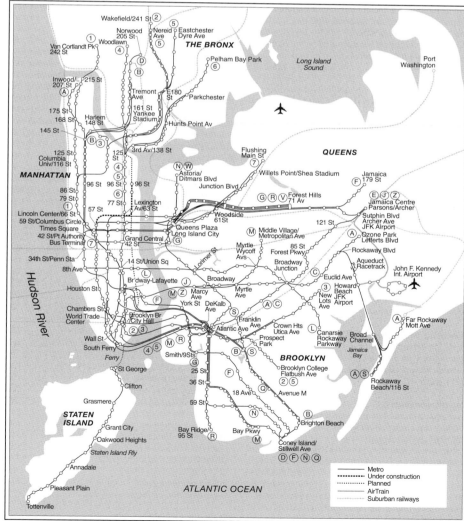

New York's metro network and suburban rail lines

1168387

Chief Financial Officer: Gary J Dellaverson
Deputy Executive Director of Administration: Linda G Kleinbaum
Headquarters staff: 683
Total staff: 69,117 (2007)

Passenger journeys: (All modes)
Approximately 2,600 million per year

Operating costs covered by: Fares 32 per cent, toll income 10 per cent, other commercial sources 3 per cent, subsidy/grants 49 per cent, other non-operating sources 6 per cent

Current situation
Created in 1965 by New York State as the Metropolitan Commuter Transportation Authority, it was initially given responsibility for purchase and rehabilitation of the Long Island Rail Road. In 1968 it was renamed MTA, and its powers were expanded to include additional agencies. These include the MTA Long Island Rail Road, MTA New York City Transit, MTA Metro-North Railroad, MTA Bridges & Tunnels, MTA Staten Island Railway, MTA Card Company, MTA Long Island Bus, MTA Bus Company and MTA Capital Construction. Some 14.8 million people in 14 counties and an area of 13,000 km² (5,000 sq miles) are served.

Over 300 million vehicles annually use the seven bridges and two tunnels operated by MTA Bridges & Tunnels. Surplus revenue from bridge and tunnel tolls helps support the other MTA operations, amounting to USD735 million in 2007.

Developments
In December 2006, MTA awarded Cubic Corporation a USD8.3 million contract to extend the MetroCard® fare payment system to all 390 buses operated by the Westchester County Department of Transportation (WCDOT). Installation of equipment was completed in 2007.

In 2007, major construction work began on the first phase of Second Avenue Subway, the first new subway line in New York City for 60 years. Phase I is scheduled for completion in 2015 and will cost USD4,347 million.

MTA New York City Transit

370 Jay Street, Brooklyn, New York 11201, US
Tel: (+1 718) 330 30 00
Fax: (+1 718) 243 45 66
Web: www.mta.info/nyct/index.html

Key personnel
President: Howard H Roberts
Executive Vice-President: Michael P Chubak
Senior Vice-Presidents
  Subways: Steve A Feil
  Buses: Joseph J Smith
  Capital Program Management: Connie Crawford
  Customer Services: Paul Fleuranges
  Staff: 48,910 (2007)

Passenger journeys: (Bus and metro, paratransit and MTA Staten Island Railway)
(2007) 7.4 million per day

Operating costs financed by: Fares 47.5 per cent, other commercial sources 6 per cent, subsidy/grants/taxes 46.5 per cent
Subsidy from: Federal, state and local government, and bridge subsidy

Current situation
Some 80 per cent of surface public transport in the five boroughs of New York City is provided by the MTA and its subsidiaries.

Free bus/metro transfers for MetroCard customers introduced 1997, currently offering a seven per cent discount on MetroCard purchase over USD7. Seven-day and monthly passes for unlimited travel on both modes introduced in 1998. A 14-day pass was introduced in 2008. These measures appear to have reversed the long-term decline in bus ridership in particular.

MTA Orion V bus (Bill Luke)   1115246

Developments
In 2007, MTA Transit services were carrying more than 7.4 million passengers daily.

MTA New York City Transit – Bus Operations
Staff: 14,736 (2007)

Passenger journeys: (Annual) 738 million
Vehicle-km: Not currently available

Number of routes: 243 (207 local, 36 express)
Route length: (One way) 3,209 km

Developments
The MTA has begun using articulated buses on high-volume routes and is putting hybrid-electric buses into service to lower greenhouse-gas emissions. It has retrofitted the diesel fleet to burn ultra-low-sulfer fuel.

A pilot Bus Rapid Transit (BRT) programme has begun along one route. Known as the Select Bus Service, vehicles make limited stops, customers pre-pay fares before boarding and buses are able to exert some control over traffic signals along the route. Additional routes are planned for the future.

Fleet: 4,576 vehicles, all air conditioned (2007)

TMC RTS 06 (1990)	36
TMC RTS 06 (1993)	157
Orion V (1993)	143
Orion V CNG (1993/94)	31
Orion V (1994)	192
TMC RTS 06 (1994)	104
Nova RTS 06 (1996)	597
BIA Orion V (1996)	50
New Flyer D60HF articulated (1997)	70
Nova RTS 06 (1998)	349
MCI 102DL3-D4501 (1998)	164
New Flyer D60HF articulated (1998)	40
Orion V (1999)	350
Nova RTS 06 (1999)	350
New Flyer C40LF CNG (1999)	189
MCI 102DL3-D4501 (1999)	99
New Flyer Viking	3
New Flyer D60HF articulated (2000)	254
MCI 102DL3-D4501 (2000)	100
MCI 102DL3-D4501 (2001)	70
MCI 102DL3-D4501 (2002)	120
Orion VII CNG (2003)	125
New Flyer D60HF aarticulated (2003)	260
Orion VII CNG (2004)	135
Orion VII hybrid-electric (2004)	245
Orion VII hybrid-electric (2005)	199
MCI 102DL3-D4501 (2005)	18
Orion VII hybrid-electric (2006)	100
Orion VII hybrid-electric (2007)	116
MCI 102DL3-D4501 (2007)	30
In peak service: 2,932	
On order: Not currently available	

Most intensive service: 1½ min
One-person operation: All routes

Fare collection: Electronic fare card (MetroCard) or cash to farebox (exact fare in coins); MetroCards sold at metro stations and retail outlets
Fare structure: Flat, higher for express routes; pay-per-ride MetroCard with 15 per cent bonus on cards value USD7 or more; one free transfer to any NYCT bus, MTA bus, LI bus or metro with MetroCard; 1-, 7-, 14 or 30-day unlimited-ride MetroCard (higher charge for express)
Operational control: Mobile radio link to central dispatch
Arrangements for elderly/disabled: A half-fare pass is offered in co-operation with the NY City Department for the Aging, the NY City DoT and MTA; seniors' fare concessions partially financed by reimbursement from the City of New York; bus fleet entirely lift-equipped; Access-A-Ride contracted demand-response service provides door-to-door transport for ADA eligible persons at standard bus fares, carried 5.8 million passengers in 2007; this is provided by 14 private contractors using 1,782 vehicles
Operating costs financed by: Fares 51 per cent, other commercial sources 7.1 per cent, subsidy/grants 13.1 per cent, tax levy 28.7 per cent
Source of subsidy: City and State of New York, FTA grants, MTA Bridges & Tunnel Authority surplus
New vehicles financed by: Capital programme funds

MTA Bus Company
Key personnel
President: Joseph J Smith
  Staff: 3,301 (2007)

Background
The MTA Bus Company was created in September 2004 to assume the operations of seven bus companies that operated under franchises granted by the New York City Department of Transportation. The merging of companies into the MTA Bus, began in January 2005 and was completed in February 2006.

Current situation
MTA Bus is responsible for both the local and express bus operations of the seven companies, consolidating their operations, maintaining current buses, purchasing new buses to replace the aging fleet currently in service, and adjusting schedules and route paths to better match travel demand. The seven companies operate 46 local bus routes in the Bronx, Brooklyn, and Queens and 35 express bus routes between Manhattan and the Bronx, Brooklyn, or Queens. Together the seven companies have 1,228 buses, which makes MTA Bus the 11th largest bus fleet in the United States and Canada, serving 400,000 riders daily.

Fares on the former franchise bus routes are now the same as those for MTA New York City Transit and MTA Long Island Bus: USD2 for local buses at all times and USD5 for express buses. Fares include a free transfer within a two-hour window to any subway or local bus, or to an express bus with payment of a fare differential. The Reduced-Fare Program for senior citizens and people with disabilities also continues.

Local bus fares are payable in coins or with either Pay-Per-Ride MetroCard or a 7-Day or 30-Day Unlimited Ride MetroCard or 1-Day Fun Pass. Express bus fares are also payable in coins, with a Pay-Per-Ride MetroCard or with a 7-Day Express Bus Plus MetroCard.

Developments

MTA Bus Company merged the routes of Triboro Coach Corporation into its operations in February 2006. The move completes the consolidation of operations of the seven private bus lines that operated under franchises for the City of New York into MTA Bus, which began with the merger of Liberty Lines Express in January 2005. It proceeded with the merger of the services operated by Queens Surface Corporation in February 2005, New York Bus Service in July 2005, Command Bus in December 2005, Jamaica Bus in January 2006 and Green Bus Line also in January 2006.

MTA Bus purchased 317 new express buses in 2005, of which more than 200 have already been received and placed into service; the remaining buses on this order will be received and placed into service later in 2006. In addition, MTA Bus has purchased 284 new local buses.

Fleet: 1,463 vehicles (2007)

Nova RTS 06 (1990/93)	219
Orion V (1993/99)	327
Orion V CNG (1997/99)	152
MCI 102DL3-D4501 (1998/2007)	480
Orion VII hybrid-electric (2006/07)	285

In peak service: Not currently available
On order: Not currently available

Most intensive service: 1½ min
One-person operation: All routes
Fare collection: Electronic fare card (MetroCard) or cash to farebox (exact fare in coins); MetroCards sold at metro stations and retail outlets
Fare structure: Flat, higher for express routes; pay-per-ride MetroCard with 15 per cent bonus on cards value USD7 or more; one free transfer to any NYCT bus, MTA bus, LI bus or metro with MetroCard; 1-, 7-, 14 or 30-day unlimited-ride MetroCard (higher charge for express)
Operational control: Mobile radio link to central dispatch
Arrangements for elderly/disabled: A half-fare pass is offered in co-operation with the NY City Department for the Aging, the NY City DoT and MTA; seniors' fare concessions partially financed by reimbursement from the City of New York; bus fleet entirely lift-equipped
Operating costs financed by: Fares 34 per cent, other commercial sources 5 per cent, subsidy/grants/taxes 60 per cent
Source of subsidy: City of New York, FTA grants, MTA Bridges & Tunnel Authority surplus
New vehicles financed by: Capital programme funds

MTA Long Island Bus (LI Bus)

700 Commercial Avenue, Garden City, New York 11530-6434, US
Tel: (+1 516) 542 01 00
Fax: (+1 516) 542 14 28
Web: www.libus.org

Key personnel

Chair: Joseph J Smith
Staff: 1,103 (2007)

Current situation

MTA Long Island Bus, formed in 1974, operates services for an area with about 1.3 million population in Nassau County, western Suffolk County and eastern Queens, serving five metro stations at Flushing, Jamaica and Far Rockaway, New York, and 47 LIRR stations. It also operates curb-to-curb bus services for people with disabilities.

NYCT hybrid-electric bus   1368508

MTA TMC RTS bus on Broadway near Times Square (Bill Luke)   1115247

All of the fixed-route buses operated by LI Bus use CNG.

Fleet: 416 vehicles (2007)

Orion V CNG-powered (1995/2004)	324
Navistar 3400 (1999)	1
MCI 102DL3-D4501 (2001)	3
Ford E450	2
Paratransit fleet	86

In peak service: 264
On order: Not currently available

Most intensive service: 8 min
Fare collection: Electronic fare card (MetroCard) or cash to farebox (exact fare in coins); MetroCard sold at metro stations and retail outlets
Fare structure: Flat, with additional charge for transfer; bus/rail through 'Unitickets' with LIRR (see below); pay-per-ride MetroCard with 15 per cent bonus on cards value USD7 or more; one free transfer to any NYCT bus, MTA Bus, LI Bus or metro with MetroCard; 1-, 7-, 14- or 30-day unlimited-ride MetroCard
Fares collected on board: 100 per cent
Operational control: Route dispatchers/radio-based control centre
Arrangements for elderly/disabled: Half-fare at all times; all buses lift-equipped
Integration with other modes: Routes serve 47 LIRR and 5 subway stations; joint weekly/monthly tickets
Operating costs financed by: Fares 32 per cent, other commercial sources 2 per cent, subsidy/grants 66 per cent
Subsidy from: County of Nassau 10.0 per cent, State of New York 37.4 per cent, Metropolitan Transportation Authority 7.1 per cent

MTA New York City Transit – Subway Operations
Staff: 25,078

Type of operation: Full metro, initial underground route opened 1904

Passenger journeys: (Annual) 1.6 billion (estimate)
Car-km: (2004) 566.7 million (352,232 million miles)

Route length: Approximately 1,061.9 km (660 miles)
in tunnel: 223 km
Number of lines: 26
Number of stations: 468
in tunnel: 277
elevated: 153
Gauge: 1,435 mm
Track: Timber sleepers on ballast or embedded in concrete, or concrete with resilient pads
Tunnel: Cut-and-cover, under-river bored tunnel, cast-iron with concrete liners, some concrete horse-shoe
Electrification: 625 V DC, third rail

Background

In 2002, Kawasaki and Alstom Transportation Inc formed a New York Limited Liability Company to supply a base order for 660 R160 subway cars to NYC Transit. Kawasaki will manufacture 260 cars out of the total 660 cars. Kawasaki is also serving as the engineering leader for the R160 contract, providing technical assistance that utilises the experience it gained with the R143 car which has been in revenue service in the NYC Transit since 2002. Kawasaki will supply bogies for all of the R160 cars including Alstom's portion. The contract includes two options for additional orders of 620 cars and 380 – 420 cars. The cars in the first optional agreement (620 cars) are scheduled for delivery before 2009, and those in the second optional agreement (380 – 420 cars), between 2009 and 2010.

Developments

In early 2006, the MTA Board voted to approve a contract with DMJM+Harris and Arup for the final design of the first segment of the Second Avenue subway. The initial segment will be 3.54 km long, with four stations and includes a connection to the BMT Broadway subway. The contract is valued at USD150.4 million.

A further USD17.1 million contract was approved for underwater subway tunnel reinforcement and another for USD80 million for additional surveillance cameras and motion sensors.

In November 2006, Kawasaki Heavy Industries Ltd delivered and received conditional acceptance of the first ten-car R160 subway trains.

Rolling stock: Approximately 6,494 (2007)

51 ft cars

Kawasaki R62 (1984/85)	315
Bombardier R62A (1985/87)	824
Kawasaki R110A (1992)	10
Bombardier R142 (1999/2003)	1,030
Kawasaki R142A (1999/2004)	600

75 ft cars

St Louis Car R44 (1972/74)	272
Pullman Standard R46 (1975/77)	252
Westinghouse-AmRail R68 (1986/88)	425
Kawasaki R68A (1988/89)	200
Bombardier R110B (67 ft) (1992)	9

60 ft 6 in cars

Budd R32 (1964/65)	594
St Louis Car R38 (1965/67)	196
St Louis Car R40S (1968/69)	292
St Louis Car R40M (1968/69)	99
St Louis Car R42 (1969/70)	391
Kawasaki R143 (2001/02)	212
Alstom R160A (2005/07)	114
Kawasaki R160B (2005/07)	150
In peak service: 5,284	

Service: Peak 2–10 min, off-peak 5–15 min, late night 20 min; 24 h service at most stations

Fare structure: Flat; MetroCard availability as bus, pay-per-ride MetroCard with 15 per cent bonus on cards value USD7 or more and with one free transfer to Staten island metro or any local bus of NYCT.MTA Bus or LI bus; 1-, 7-, 14- or 30-day unlimited-ride MetroCard

Fare collection: Automatic turnstiles accessed by electronic fare card (MetroCard)

Arrangements for elderly/disabled:
A half-fare pass is offered in co-operation with the NY City Department for the Aging, the NY City DoT and MTA; seniors' fare concessions partially financed by reimbursement from the City of New York; 63 stations are wheelchair accessible

Operating costs financed by: Fares 85.4 per cent, other commercial sources 2.1 per cent, FTA, state and local government subsidies 3.9 per cent, tax levy 8.5 per cent

One-person operation: On four shuttles and Line G only; may be extended to other routes at night and weekends during 1999

Signalling: Wayside signals/train control

MTA Staten Island Railway (SIR)

Staten Island Rapid Transit Operating Authority, 60 Bay Street, Staten Island, New York 10301, US
Tel: (+1 718) 876 82 39 Fax: (+1 718) 876 82 58
Web: www.mta.info/nyct/sir/

Key personnel
Chief Officer: John H McCabe
General Superintendent, Operations:
Owen P Swords
General Superintendent, Maintenance: Vacant
Staff: 310

Type of operation: Full metro

Passenger journeys: (2007) 4.1 million
Car-km: Not currently available

Route length: 23 km
Number of lines: 1
Number of stations: 22
Gauge: 1,435 mm
Track: 50 kg/m ARA-B rail on timber sleepers in rock and/or cinder ballast
Electrification: 600 V DC, third rail

Current situation
Though part of NYCT, this isolated line on Staten Island is separately operated.
MTA Staten Island Railway (SIR) service runs 24 hours daily between the St. George and Tottenville stations. At the St. George station, customers can make connections with Staten Island Ferry service.

Kawasaki's R160 subway car for MTA New York City Transit (Kawasaki Heavy Industries Ltd) 1209126

MTA train at Queensboro Plaza (Marcel Vleugels)   1115248

Fare collection for trips not passing St George (the only turnstile-equipped station) was abolished in July 1997. These journeys are no longer counted, leading to a drop in ridership as recorded below.

Rolling stock: 64 cars

St Louis Car R44 (1971/73)	M64
In peak service: 46	

Service: Peak 5 min, off-peak 30-60 min; 24 h service

Fare structure: Flat, as above

Fare collection: Automatic turnstiles at St. George terminal and Tompkinsville, accepting MetroCard; no fares collected for journeys that do not include St George or Tompkinsville

Arrangements for elderly/disabled: A half-fare pass is offered in co-operation with the NY City Department for the Aging, the NY City DoT and MTA; seniors' fare concessions partially financed by reimbursement from the City of New York. The St. George, Dongan Hills, Great Kills, and Tottenville stations are wheelchair-accessible.

Operating costs financed by: Fares 30.7 per cent, other commercial sources 2.2 per cent, subsidy/grants 58.1 per cent, tax levy 9 per cent

One-person operation: None

Signalling: Colour-position-approach light signals; double rail track circuit

MTA Long Island Rail Road (LIRR)

93-02 Sutphin Boulevard, Jamaica Station, Jamaica, New York 11435, US
Tel: (+1 718) 558 74 00 Fax: (+1 718) 558 82 12
Web:www.mta.info/lirr/

Key personnel
President: Helena E Williams
Executive Vice-President: Albert C Cosenza
Senior Vice-President, Operations:
Raymond P Kenny
Vice-President, Market Development and Public Affairs: Joseph Calderone
Chief Transportation Officer: Joseph Antonucci
Chief Mechanical Officer: Michael Gelorimo
Staff: 6,471 (2007)

Type of operation: Suburban heavy rail

Passenger journeys: (2007) 86.1 million

Number of lines: 11
Route length: 513.4 km (319 miles)
Number of stations: 124
Gauge: 1,435 mm
Electrification: 750 v DC third rail

Operating costs financed by: Fares 48 per cent, other commercial sources 3 per cent, subsidy/grants/taxes 49 per cent

Background

Long Island Rail Road (LIRR) is a wholly owned subsidiary of the Metropolitan Transportation Authority (MTA).

Current situation

Operates with 11 lines, 513.4 km (319 miles) of track, serving 124 stations, radiating from terminals in Manhattan (Pennsylvania station, shared with Amtrak and New Jersey Transit), Brooklyn (Atlantic Terminal-Flatbush Avenue) and Queens (Hunterspoint Avenue), 1,435 mm gauge, 220 km electrified at 750 V DC third rail. Zonal ticket system, with some higher price 'Unitickets' valid on local buses; most commuters use joint monthly LIRR tickets and NYCT MetroCard, purchased through Mail & Ride home delivery service. Operating subsidy from MTA accounts for about half of operating costs; the rest comes from fares revenue.

Electric trains provide service on virtually all lines in New York City and Nassau County, and from most major Suffolk County destinations. Remaining services are diesel-hauled (mostly push-pull).

Developments

By the end of 2006, MTA had placed further M-7 emus in service.

Rolling stock: Approximately 1,000 passenger vehicles

Metropolitan M-3 emu (1984–86)	M170
Mitsui/Kawasaki bilevel (1998/99)	T134
GM DE30AC dual-mode locomotives	M45
Metropolitan M-7 Bombardier emus (2002/07)	M836

On order: None

MTA Metro-North Railroad Co (MNR)

347 Madison Avenue, New York, New York 10017, US
Tel: (+1 212) 340 30 00   Fax: (+1 212) 340 20 58
Web: www.mta.info/mnr/

Key personnel

President: Howard R Permut
Senior Vice-Presidents:
  Operations: George F Walker
  Planning: Robert C MacLagger (Acting)
Vice-Presidents:
  Finance and Info Systems: Kim Porcelian
  General Council: Richard K Bernard
  Human Resources and Diversity:
  Gregory Bradley
Staff: 5,877 (2007)

Type of operation: Suburban heavy rail

Passenger boardings: (2006) 76.8 million (all lines)
Train-km: Not currently available

Number of lines: 6
Route length: 616.4 km (383 miles)
Number of stations: 120
Gauge: 1,435 mm
Electrification: Hudson and Harlem lines (139 km), 600 V DC third rail; New Haven line (116 km), 11 kV 60 Hz AC overhead

Operating costs financed by: Fares 38 per cent, other commercial sources 3 per cent, subsidy/grants/taxes 59 per cent

Background

An operating division of the MTA, the Metro-North Railroad Co was founded in 1983.

Current situation

Metro-North's three main lines that run north out of New York City and east of the Hudson river are the Hudson, Harlem and New Haven lines. These three routes operate out of New York's Grand Central Terminal and serve 120 stations.

Metro-North also provides services west of the Hudson in the New York state counties of Orange

LIRR locomotive with bi-level cars   1368506

MNR Genesis locomotive and coach cars   1368507

and Rockland on the Port Jervis and Pascack Valley lines (202 km); trains on these lines run out of the Hoboken terminal on the New Jersey shore of the Hudson. These services are operated by New Jersey Transit (NJT), under contract from Metro-North, which assigns part of its rolling stock fleet to NJT. In early 2003, Metro-North took a 49-year lease on the 105-km Port Jervis line from owner Norfolk Southern. This has allowed Metro-North to carry out track improvements to raise reliability of the passenger service.

Service on the 158 km, 29-station New Haven line, and its New Canaan, Danbury and Waterbury branches totalling 96 km and 17 stations, is provided by Metro-North under a contract between the Connecticut Department of Transportation (ConnDoT) and MTA/Metro-North. Stamford is the busiest station, boarding more than 11,000 passengers per weekday. At New Haven, connection is made with ConnDoT's Shore Line East service, which runs during commuter hours to Old Saybrook and New London. Capital improvements in Connecticut are funded by ConnDoT, which owns the infrastructure and part of the rolling stock fleet.

Developments

2004 saw completion of the Mid-Harlem upgrading project, comprising 5 km of three-track route, new signalling and communications cabling, and bridgeworks. Commissioning of the third track allowed introduction of direct commuting-hour trains from Westchester to Bronx stations.

In 2006, Metro-North and CDOT awarded a contract for a base order of 210 new M-8 emus, with an option for a further 90 emus, to replace the ageing M-2 fleet on the Newhaven Line. Options remain for 80 more cars. Delivery will begin in late 2008.

Non-electrified lines are worked by locomotive-hauled trains, using a variety of diesel traction including Genesis II locomotives equipped with third-rail pick-up shoes for operating into Grand Central Terminal.

Rolling stock:

Metropolitan M-1 emu (1971/73)	30
Metropolitan M-2 emu (1973/76)	235
Metropolitan M-3 emu (1983/85)	140
Metropolitan M-4 emu (1987)	54
Metropolitan M-6 emu (1994/95)	48
Metropolitan M-7 emu Bombardier (2003/05)	336
FL9 locomotive (1957/60)	8
F-10 (1949; rebuilt 1979)	3
P32 locomotive (1995/2001)	31
P40 locomotive (2005)	6
Switchers (various)	10
Phoebe Snow coaches – inspection only (1941/49)	3
Bombardier end doors (1985/87)	61
Bombardier (1991)	22
Bombardier centre doors (1996/2000)	99
Bombardier (2002)	10
Alstom Comet V coaches (2004)	65
General Motors GP40 locomotives (1966/81; 7 built in 1966/69 rebuilt 2006/08)	15

On order: 300 Kawasaki M-8 emus

New York City Department of Transportation (NYCDOT)

Passenger Transport Division, 59 Maiden Lane, 35th Floor, New York, New York 10038, USA
Tel: (+1 212) 487 83 31   Fax: (+1 212) 487 83 05
e-mail: nbower@dot.nyc.gov
Web: www.dot.nyc.gov

Key personnel

DOT Commissioner: Iris Wienshall
Deputy Commissioner for Passenger Transport: Robert Grotell
Director of Intermodal Co-ordination: Nancy Bower Bachana

Current situation

The Passenger Transport Division directly operates the Staten Island ferry and licenses the operation of other ferry routes by private companies. It also manages the franchised operation of express and local buses, primarily in the borough of Queens, with limited service to Brooklyn, Manhattan and the Bronx. Express commuter buses link Queens, Brooklyn and the Bronx with Manhattan's business districts.

Staten Island Ferry

Fleet: 7 ships

Kennedy Class (1965)	3
Barberi Class (1981–2)	2
Austen Class (1986)	2

Current situation

Approximately 65,000 passengers are carried daily on the 8.4 km (5.2 mile) route between the St George Terminal in Staten Island and the Whitehall Terminal in lower Manhattan. Since 1997 there has been no fare charged to foot passengers. Ferries operate 24 hours a day, from 15 minute headway at peak times to one-hour headway overnight. NYVDOT owns and operates the two ferry terminals and the boats.

Developments

Both the Staten Island and the Manhattan ferry terminals are undergoing major reconstruction. The total cost for both terminals for this work is estimated at some USD350 million, funded by a combination of federal, state and local contributions.

Three new Kennedy Class ferries are also under construction at a cost of USD120 million.

Because of the disruption of traffic in lower Manhattan since 11 September 2001, vehicles have not been allowed on the ferries, and this will continue until further notice.

Privately operated ferries

Current situation

The NYCDOT oversees the operations of five private ferry companies over 17 commuter routes in New York Harbour. The agency is responsible for issuing operating permits and landing slot licences to operators as well as for overall planning and policy development for the City's private ferry programme. NYCDOT shares jurisdiction and management over several ferry landing sites with the Economic Development Corp (EDC), maintained with fees collected from operators.

Developments

Prior to the events of 11 September 2001, five companies transported more than 30,000 passengers daily on approximately 15 ferry routes, and ridership had increased every year since 1986. Since September 2001, significant disruption to mass transit, coupled with the flexibility of private ferries, has seen ridership grow to 65,000 daily.

The City is building a USD50 million West Midtown Intermodal Ferry Terminal and five other landings are at the design stage for the East River from 90th Street south to the Battery.

Franchised bus

Current situation

NYCDOT's bus system carries more than 114 million passengers per year, through a mix of local and express bus services provided by

NYCDOT Staten Island ferry   0544567

At New York City, Command Bus Lines advertises its new compressed natural gas fleet (Van Wilkins)
0038911

seven private, franchised bus companies. Routes are operated in Queens, Brooklyn, the Bronx and Manhattan.

The City owns most of the buses, subsidises the cost of operations and covers the general financial risk of providing bus transportation. The City also owns two of the eight depots.

As part of the NYCDOT's Alternative Fuels Program, 356 buses (some 28 per cent of the fleet) are powered by CNG.

DOT buses accept the MTA New York City Transit MetroCard, which allows transfer between the two systems.

The City began subsidising capital purchases for the private bus companies in 1974. In 1986 the Department of Transportation created a Surface Transit office to monitor the quality of the franchised bus services and to manage the City, State and Federal subsidies. In 2001 the subsidies totalled nearly USD160 million, while fare revenue was just under USD110 million.

In 1997 the two-fare zone was abolished.

Developments

Negotiations are currently under way between the City of New York and the Metropolitan Transportation Authority (MTA) to have the Authority take over the privately operated routes.

Number of routes: 82 (local and express)

Fleet: 1,127 buses

Command Bus Company Inc	140
Green Bus Lines Inc	188
Jamaica Buses Inc	96
Queens Surface Corp	109
Liberty Lines Express Inc	113
New York Bus Service	273
Triboro Coach Corp	208

Port Authority Trans-Hudson Corporation (PATH)

1 Path Plaza, Jersey City, New Jersey 07306-2944, USA
Tel: (+1 201) 216 62 47
Fax: (+1 201) 216 62 66
Web: www.pathrail.com
    www.panynj.gov/path/

Key personnel

Chairman: Anthony R Coscia
Vice-Chairman: Charles A Cargano

President: Kenneth R Ringler
Director and General Manager: Michael DePallo

Current situation

The Port Authority Trans-Hudson Corporation (PATH) was established in 1962 as a subsidiary of The Port Authority of New York and New Jersey (PANYNJ). The heavy rail rapid transit system serves as the primary transit link between New York and New Jersey (Hoboken, Journal Square and Newark Penn) urban communities and suburban commuter railway lines.

PATH's temporary World Trade Center station opened in November 2003 and its Exchange Place station at the waterfront of Jersey City opened in June 2003.

All four of PATH's lines (Newark-WTC, Journal Square-33rd Street, Hoboken-WTC and Hoboken-33rd Street) are fully operational.

The Port Authority also operates the New York Bus terminal at 42nd Street into which many commuter operations run.

PATH serves as a ferry transportation 'clearinghouse' for the New York-New Jersey metropolitan area.

Metro

Staff: 1,163, including police

Type of operation: Full metro, initial route opened 1908, PATH created 1962

Passenger journeys: (2003) 47.92 million
(2004) 57.77 million

Route length: 22.2 km
    in tunnel: 11.9 km
Number of lines: 4
Number of stations: 13 (7 in NJ, 6 in NY)
    in tunnel: 10
Gauge: 1,435 mm
Track: Conventional sleepers on ballast; some sections on concrete trackbed with resilient pads, with 60 kg/m rail
Max gradient: 4.8%
Min curve radius: 27.4 m
Tunnel: Single track, mainly cast-iron or concrete construction
Electrification: 650 V DC, third rail

Service: 24 h, peak: 4–6 min
Fare structure: Flat; multijourney tickets; through-ticketing with other operators

Revenue control: Exact change, automatic turnstiles

Surveillance: Police monitoring; CCTV; surveillance of turnstiles by CCTV

Operating costs financed by: Fares 35 per cent, other commercial sources 1.6 per cent; deficit financed from revenues of the parent Port Authority, which is self-supporting

Signalling: Block signal system with automatic tripper

Rolling stock: 342 cars

St Louis Car PA1 (1965)	M157
St Louis Car PA2 (1967)	M44
Hawker Siddeley Canada PA3 (1972)	M46
Kawasaki PA4 (1986)	M95

Developments

After the 11 September attack in 2001, services were fully restored in 2003. Ridership grew significantly in 2004, the first full year of restored services to Lower Manhattan, with a 20.5 per cent increase over ridership for 2003.

In 2004, feasibility studies were authorised for a possible direct rail connection from Lower Manhattan to Kennedy airport and for an extension to the PATH network to Newark Liberty international airport.

In September 2005, Henry Bros Inc was awarded a USD1.1 million contract to upgrade PATH's existing CCTV system. The upgrade includes: new servers, which will be capable of controlling more than 600 cameras on PATH's network; high-speed data transmission equipment; and upgrade to a fully digital recording platform.

There is currently a plan to replace PATH's entire fleet of cars. The first of the new vehicles is expected to be delivered in late 2008. The modernisation plan also includes car maintenance equipment and preliminary work on a new signalling system. The programme costs are estimated at some USD809 million.

In late 2005, 340 new rapid transit cars were ordered from Kawasaki for USD499 million. Deliveries are scheduled to start in mid-2008 and finish in 2011.

Long-term plans, under a planning effort know as Access to the Region's Core (ARC), would see two additional PATH tracks between Secaucus Junction in the New Jersey Meadowlands and New York's Pennsylvania station, including a new tunnel under the Hudson River.

PATH is in the process of installing the final part of a fare collection system that will accept both PATH QuickCards and pay-per-ride MetroCards. QuickCard ticket vending machines will gradually be replace by the new vending machines.

In early 2006, the Phoenix Consortium was awarded a contract for engineering and construction work on the new World Trade Center PATH terminal and transport hub. The contract was valued at some USD1.1 billion. The project is scheduled for completion in 2009 and the hub will link PATH services with the metro/subway network and the World Financial Center ferry terminal. The total cost of the project is estimated at USD2.2 billion.

Commuter bus and coach terminal
Current situation

Extensive commuting by bus and coach into New York takes place, much of it across the Hudson river from New Jersey. Some 1,700 buses daily use the exclusive bus lane into the Port Authority Bus Terminal (PABT) in Manhattan. The 4 km bus lane operates in the eastbound direction along the westbound median lane of highway I-495 between the New Jersey Turnpike and the Lincoln Tunnel. Ramps link the tunnel directly to the bus terminal, facilitating commuter bus operations and helping to reduce traffic congestion in Manhattan streets. Interchange is provided with several metro lines.

The Port Authority Bus Terminal handles more than 200,000 passengers daily. A direct service to approximately 1,000 communities is provided by 22 bus carriers. In addition they provide a service to local airports and connecting services to most destinations throughout the United States.

George Washington Bridge bus station

Located in the Washington Heights area of Upper Manhattan. The main concourse is on the second level, with buses on the lower and upper levels. In 2002, on a typical weekday, almost 15,000 passengers on more than 700 buses used the GWB bus station.

Ferry

Passenger journeys: (2000) 2.4 million (2002) 5.6 million

Background

Ferry operations started in 1989 between Hoboken in New Jersey and Battery Park City (BPC), Lower Manhattan.

There are five service providers of ferry services in the metropolitan area. These are:
- NY Waterway (www.nywaterway.com)
- BillyBey
- Seastreak (www.seastreak.com)
- New York Water Taxi (www.nywatertaxi.com)
- NYC DOT (Public) (www.nyc.gov)

Weekday Services:
Ferries between Manhattan and New Jersey – 18 routes;
Ferries between Manhattan and Brooklyn: 1 route;
Ferries between Manhattan and Queens: 1 route;
Ferries between Manhattan and Staten Island: 1 route;
Ferries between Rockland and Westchester Counties: 1 route.
Weekend Services: 4 routes.
Seasonal services: 4 routes.

The Port Authority of New York and New Jersey

Public Affairs Department
225 Park Avenue South, 18th Floor, New York, New York 10003, USA
Tel: (+1 212) 435 70 00
Web: www.panynj.gov

AirTrain JFK – John F Kennedy International Airport
Web: www.jfkairtrain.com

Current situation

Automated 12.8 km (8 mile) light rail system circulating on-airport among nine terminal buildings in the Central Terminal Area, connecting to airport rental car, long-term and employee parking areas, and extending off-airport to regional mass transit hubs which provide service to Long Island, Brooklyn and Manhattan's central business districts. The system opened in December 2003. AirTrain allows JFK air passengers and employees direct access to New York's international gateway.

AirTrain Newark – Newark International Airport
Web: www.panynj.gov/airtrainnewark

Current situation

Fully automated computer-controlled monorail operating on a 7.7 km (4.8 mile) dual-lane bidirectional guideway. The airport circulator was completed in May 1996, providing transport between Newark International Airport's three terminals, public parking lots and car rental facilities. In June 1996, a project was authorised to extend the airport circulator to the Amtrak and New Jersey Transit rail system networks, providing a mass transit link to the region. The project was completed in 2001.

New York
Light rail (planned)
Background

Amongst several proposals, one for a 3.5 km (2.2 mile) light rail line with seven stations along 42nd Street in Manhattan was approved by the New York City Council in 1994. The promoters, the New York City DoT and the 42nd Street Development Corporation, received expressions of interest from 13 groups in 1992. A planning grant of USD0.9 million was made by the FTA in 1993 to maintain the project's impetus. A fleet of 17 cars would be required to handle traffic estimated at 9 million passengers annually. However, the plans never came to fruition.

Current situation

Although no plans have since been approved, there is still interest in a project for a 3.2 km (2 mile) light rail line on 42nd Street. The vision42 proposal was launched in July 1999 and more information on this proposed project can be found at the website www.vision42.org.

Developments

In early 2005, vision42 presented the results of three technical studies on the feasibility and benefits of constructing a light rail and pedestrian-only mall in Midtown.

In January 2006, a further round of technical studies was launched.

Norfolk

Population: City 229,112 (2006 estimate), metropolitan area 1.66 million (2007 estimate)

Public transport

Bus, paratransit, trolleybus and ferry services provided by public authority controlled by representative board; light rail under construction.

Hampton Roads Transit (HRT)

Headquarters
3400 Victoria Boulevard, Hampton, VA 23661, US
Tel: (+1 757) 222 60 00
Web: www.gohrt.com

Passenger journeys: (All modes)
(2006) 15.5 million
(2007) 18 million

Costs financed by: Fares and other revenue 23 per cent, federal funding 31 per cent, state funding 16 per cent, local funding 30 per cent

Key personnel
President/Chief Executive Officer:
  Michael S Townes
Senior Vice-President for Transit Operations:
  Homer Carter

For details of the latest updates to *Jane's Urban Transport Systems* online and to discover the additional information available exclusively to online subscribers please visit

juts.janes.com

Senior Vice-President for Development:
Jayne Whitney
Senior Vice-President for IT & Planning:
David Sullivan
Senior Vice-President for Finance & Administration:
Larry Davenport
Vice-President for Bus Operations: Michael Perry
Vice-President for Administration: Karen Burnette
Vice-President for Service Development & Planning
Vincent Jackson
Vice-President for Public Affairs & Communications:
James Toscano
Staff: 880

Background
Hampton Roads Transit (HRT) was formed in 1999 as a result of a merger between Pentran and Tidewater Regional Transportation (TRT).

Current situation
HRT serves an area population of 1.3 million in the Hampton Roads cities of Chesapeake, Hampton, Newport News, Norfolk, Portsmouth, Suffolk and Virginia Beach. Services include fixed-route bus operations, ADA paratransit, ferry and hybrid-electric shuttle buses. HRT has a total fleet of 509.

HRT also provides (TRAFFIX), a service that offers alternatives to the one-car/one-person commute (www.traffixonline.org).

Developments
Navigator (Advanced Communications System)
The Navigator, HRT's Advanced Communications System, is a USD8 million investment that will transform the communications and operations of transit service in Hampton Roads. Utilising Global Positioning System (GPS) technology, HRT can easily locate buses along their routes. Benefits of the new system include improved reliability and safety to HRT's operations, increased on-time performance and improved service connections.

Next Bus Stop Signs
As part of The Navigator, digital bus stop signs will be installed along major service areas and transfer centres that will allow customers waiting at a bus stop to know when the next bus will arrive.

Bus
Passenger boardings: (Including ferry)
(2006) 14.7 million (estimate)
(2007) 18 million
Vehicle-km: Not currently available

Number of routes: 47
Route length: Not currently available

Current situation
Fixed-route bus services on 47 routes serving the cities of Chesapeake, Hampton, Newport News, Norfolk, Portsmouth, Suffolk and Virginia Beach.

Shuttle services
Norfolk Electric Transit – free service through downtown Norfolk;
VB Wave – serves the Virginia Beach resort area;
The Loop – service through Downtown Portsmouth, connecting the downtown park & ride to the Paddlewheel Ferry.

Developments
Universal Shuttle
Beginning in early 2008, HRT rolled out its new line of hybrid diesel-electric buses. The shuttles will replace the existing fleet of trolleys at the Oceanfront in Virginia Beach as well as the electric buses in Downtown Norfolk. The buses will also operate Portsmouth's new downtown shuttle service, The Loop.

The new 29-ft hybrid diesel-electric buses play a major role in HRT's commitment to the environment. The shuttles also bear a modern universal identity, whilst maintaining the unique brand for each separate service. They are wheelchair accessible and carry bike racks.

Fleet: 509 vehicles
Breakdown of fleet is not currently available
In peak service: Not currently available
On order: Not currently available

Most intensive service: 15 min
One-person operation: All services
Fare collection: Payment to driver or prepurchase ticket or pass
Fare structure: Flat; reduced fare for those under 18 and senior citizens
Arrangements for elderly/disabled: Fleet of Handi-Ride vans and minibuses, 60 lift-equipped; network of accessible fixed-route services
Integration with other modes: Carpools, lease of vans to vanpool participants; park-and-ride
Operating costs financed by: Fares 39 per cent, subsidy/grants 61 per cent
Subsidy from: FTA 12 per cent, state 24 per cent, local 25 per cent

ADA Paratransit (Handi-Ride)
Current situation
Specialised services for persons with disabilities.

Ferry
Current situation
Service across the Elizabeth river between Norfolk and Portsmouth is aimed at both residents and visitors. The three paddle-wheel vessels, one of which is the world's first natural gas-powered pedestrian ferry, operate at 30 minute intervals (15 minutes during peak periods) and carry about 0.5 million passengers annually. The vessels are wheelchair accessible.

Commuters can purchase monthly discount passes.

Light Rail Transit (LRT) – The Tide (under construction)
Current situation
Currently under construction, The Tide will extend 12 km (7.4 miles) from the Eastern Virginia Medical Center through downtown Norfolk to Newtown Road, with eleven stops. HRT anticipates ridership of between 6,000 and 12,000 per day. An enhanced feeder bus system will provide strong bus connections to the rail system. The system will cost an estimated USD232.1 million and will require nine LRT vehicles.

Currently, opening is planned for 2010.

Oklahoma City
Population: City 537,734 (2006 estimate), metropolitan area 1.19 million (2007 estimate)

Public transport
Bus and trolleybus services provided by independent trust, controlled by transit/parking authority.

METRO Transit
Central Oklahoma Transportation & Parking Authority (COTPA)
300 SW 7th Street, Oklahoma City, Oklahoma 73109, US
Tel: (+1 405) 297 24 84
Fax: (+1 405) 297 21 11
Web: www.gometro.org

Key personnel
Chair, Transit Board: Chris Kauffman
Administrator: Rick Cain
Staff: 219

Current situation
Bus, paratransit and trolleybus services for Oklahoma City, and the suburban cities of Edmond, Norman and Midwest City are provided by the Central Oklahoma Transportation & Parking Authority (COTPA), by a division known under the marketing name METRO Transit. Figures below refer to the METRO operation only. In the suburban city of Norman, the marketing name is CART (Cleveland Area Rapid Transit), operating six local routes and contributing to the Express Commuter service to downtown Oklahoma City. CART also runs a demand-responsive van service for elderly and disabled people.

The city of Edmond contracts with COTPA for Express and local service, while Midwest City contracts for local service only.

Developments
The new Downtown Transit Center at NW 5th and Hudson opened in August 2004, complete with detailed information displays, climate-controlled waiting area and other facilities. The building is funded 80 per cent by federal grants and 20 per cent by city funds.

METRO Transit is working with community leaders from across the region to conduct the Fixed Guideway Study for the Oklahoma City Metropolitan Area. The Study aims to identify future guideway transportation systems like bus rapid transit, light rail transit, highway high occupancy vehicle (HOV) lanes, and other potential transportation solutions that would improve connections among greater Oklahoma City's growth centres, help encourage economic development opportunities, improve mobility, expand transportation options and improve air quality.

Bus
Passenger boardings: (2005) 3 million (approx)

Route length: 16,159 km (10,043 miles)
Number of routes: 34 (30 local, 2 commuter, 2 subscription)

Fleet: 94 vehicles	
Nova Bus RTS 35 ft (1997)	13
Nova Bus RTS CNG-powered (1997)	2
Gillig (1998)	11
Orion (2001)	10
New Flyer (2003)	15
Opus (2001/02)	10
Chance Trolley (1999/2000/02)	9
Eddy Trolley (2004)	3
Paratransit	18
Vans	3
In peak service: 52	

Most intensive service: Peak 20 min (10 min in Norman)
Fare structure: Flat on local routes, free transfers; express and subscription routes, variable
Fare collection: Exact fare to driver; 30-day passes
Arrangements for elderly/disabled: All vehicles lift-equipped; reduced fares; on-demand taxi and van service (METRO-Lift) free or at reduced cost, also STEP van service linking certain areas with shopping malls and medical facilities
Integration with other modes: 15 park-and-ride lots; carpool assistance
Operating costs financed by: Fares 12.3 per cent, other commercial sources 0.4 per cent, FTA grants 31.2 per cent, Oklahoma City 43.5 per cent, other cities and agencies 0.8 per cent
New vehicles financed by: FTA 80 per cent, local 20 per cent

Trolleybus
Current situation
The Oklahoma Spirit trolley service, one of the MAPS projects, runs shuttle services Monday to Saturday. Fares are flat, with reductions for disabled and senior citizens. Passengers using COPTA parking facilities ride free. All trolleys are wheelchair accessible.

Ferry/Oklahoma River Cruises
Type of operation: Ferry/cruises

Current situation
Oklahoma River Cruises is a division of Central Oklahoma Transportation and Parking

Authority (COTPA). Oklahoma River Cruises consists of three Cruisers; Devon Discovery, Devon Explorer and Devon Pioneer. The Cruisers travel a seven-mile stretch of the Oklahoma River between Meridian Landing at SW 15th & Meridian and Regatta Park Landing at SW 7th & Lincoln.

Proposed stops to be added during the second phase include Stockyards City, Oklahoma State Fairgrounds and Dell. Finally, in the third phase, service should extend to the American Indian Cultural Center and include stops at the Farmers Public Market, Wheeler Park,

Wiley Post Park, Riverfest Place and Walnut Grove.

The Oklahoma River Cruisers link directly with Oklahoma Spirit Trolley lines, making the Cruisers an integral part of the regional transit system.

Omaha

Population: City 409,416, metropolitan area 803,801 (2004 estimates)

Public transport
Bus services provided in Omaha, Council Bluffs and environs by autonomous governmental subdivision controlled by representative board.

Metro Area Transit (MAT)
Transit Authority of the City of Omaha
2222 Cuming Street, Omaha, Nebraska 68102, US
Tel: (+1 402) 341 75 60; 341 80 00
Fax: (+1 402) 342 09 49
e-mail: customerservice@metroareatransit.com
Web: www.metroareatransit.com

Key personnel
Chair: John Hilgert
Executive Director: Curt Simon
Senior Operations Director: Kelly Shadden
Staff: 290

Background
Created in 1972 from two private undertakings, MAT, an autonomous governmental subdivision

with a dedicated taxing authority within the Omaha city limits, serves Omaha and the metropolitan area, which includes surrounding Nebraska cities and Council Buffs, Iowa.

Current situation
Transit services outside Omaha city limits are provided by contractual agreement between MAT and the relevant agencies. Currently, there are three such contracts, for Council Bluffs, Iowa; Bellevue, Nebraska; and Tri-Communities (Ralston, LaVista and Papillion), Nebraska.

MAT is participating in a project with the city of Omaha to provide seven transit stations.

Bus
Number of routes: 38 (4 in Council Bluffs)
Route length: 491 km

Fleet: 151 vehicles	
GMC Retro Rebuild (1948, 1955)	5
Gillig (1998, 2000/2001)	67
Flxible Metro (1990, 1992/1994)	64
Ford Econo van (1998, 2005)	15
In peak service: 115	

Most intensive service: 15 to 30 min
One-person operation: All routes

Fare collection: Exact fare; cash or prepurchase paper tickets and magnetic cards
Fare structure: Flat; prepurchase multitickets available in Nebraska and Iowa; transfers are USD0.05; Nebraska fares apply in Iowa, including the transfer fee
Fares collected on board: 62 per cent
Operational control: Route supervisors/mobile radio/GPS
Arrangements for elderly/disabled: MOBY complementary paratransit curb-to-curb ADA service, disabled certification eligibility required; ½-fare flat fare on conventional services for elderly/disabled/medicare card holders, financed from general operating funds; demand-response passenger miles were 448,189 (721,136 km) in 2005
Average peak-hour speed: 20.5 km/h
Operating costs financed by: Fares 30 per cent, other commercial sources 4 per cent, subsidy/grants 65 per cent
Subsidy from: Local tax 69 per cent, FTA 27 per cent, state 4 per cent
New vehicles financed by: FTA 83 per cent, local funds 18 per cent

Orlando

Population: City 213,223 (2005 estimate), metropolitan area 1.98 million (2006 estimate)

Public transport
Fixed-route bus, demand-responsive services and commuter assistance programmes provided by authority governed by nine-member board; extensive private operations. Commuter rail planned.

Central Florida Regional Transportation Authority – LYNX
455 N Garland Avenue, Orlando, Florida 32801, USA
Tel: (+1 407) 841 22 79
Fax: (+1 407) 841 23 60
Web: www.golynx.com

Key personnel
Chairman: Carlton Henley
Vice-Chairman: Mildred Fernandez
Chief Executive Officer: Linda S Watson
Chief Operating Officer: Lisa Darnall
Chief Financial Officer: Bert Francis
Chief Marketing Officer: Peggy Gies
Chief of Staff: Edward Johnson
Deputy Chief of Planning & Technology: Jennifer Stults
Manager of Paratransit: Bill Hearndon
Manager of Media Relations: Matthew Friedman
Staff: 730 (estimate)

Current situation
The former Orange-Seminole-Osceola Transportation Authority was formed by inter-local agreement in 1972 to serve Orange, Seminole and Osceola counties. It adopted the trading name LYNX in 1992, and was merged with the Central Florida RTA in 1994 to create the Central Florida Regional Transportation Authority.

Fixed-route bus service is provided in Orange, Seminole and Osceola Counties, over an area of

some 6,475 km² (2,500 sq miles) with a population of more than 1.8 million. The 'Lymmo' fixed-route downtown circulator provides a fares-free link with parking, employment and entertainment centres. LYNX also operates a mobility assistance programme that co-ordinates van- and carpools and a ride-matching service throughout central Florida.

LYNX has no dedicated funding source and hopes to gain voter approval for a local sales, property or petrol tax.

A Rack 'n' Roll programme has equipped all buses with bike racks. The bike racks are being upgraded with the installation of 'Trilogy' bike racks allowing a third bike to be carried at the front of each bus.

Developments
In April 2007, LYNX started a new local service within Apopka (Link 405 Apopka Circulator) and between the UCF Super Stop and Waterford Lakes (Link 414).

In May 2007, Osceola County approved a USD1 million increase in the fiscal budget for LYNX. Orange County has proposed an increase of 40 per cent for LYNX. These funds will allow LYNX to order a planned 21 new buses.

Bus
Passenger journeys: (2003/04) 23.4 million
Vehicle-km: (Annual) 16 million (estimate)

Number of routes: 64
Route length: (One way) 1,142 km

Fleet: 238 vehicles	
Gillig Phantom 40 ft	158
Gillig Phantom 40 ft suburban	10
Orion V 31 ft	20
Orion V 31 ft CNG-powered	6
Orion V 40 ft	19
Orion V 40 ft suburban	4
Gillig Phantom 35 ft	11
New Flyer low-floor CNG-powered	10
In peak service: 191	

First/last bus: 04.30/00.15

Most intensive service: 15 min
One-person operation: All routes
Fare structure: Flat; weekly and monthly passes; discount for scholars and seniors
Fare collection: Automatic farebox, exact change only
Arrangements for elderly/disabled: Demand-responsive door-to-door service for those who cannot use fixed routes; reduced fare on fixed-route services for others
Operating costs financed by: Fares 31.8 per cent, other commercial sources 4.1 per cent, subsidy/grants 64.1 per cent
Subsidy from: Orange County, Seminole County, City of Orlando, Osceola County/City of Kissimmee, City of Altamonte Springs, City of St Cloud, total 63 per cent, state 16 per cent, FTA 21 per cent
New vehicles financed by: Local 10 per cent, state 10 per cent, FTA 80 per cent

Florida Department of Transportation (FDOT)
District 5
605 Suwannee Street, Tallahassee, Florida 32399-0450, US
Tel: (+1 850) 414 41 00
Web: www.cfrail.com
www.dot.state.fl.us

Key personnel
Public Information Director, District 5, FDOT: Steve Homan
Public Liaison, CFRail: Marianne Gurnee
Tel: (+1 407) 492 08 36
e-mail: mgurnee@cfl.rr.com

Type of operation: Commuter rail (planned)

Current situation
The proposed Central Florida Commuter Rail (CFRail) project would see a commuter rail service on 99 km (61.5 miles) of track currently owned by CSXT. The initial phase, 49.9 km (31 miles) long with 10 stations, would run from the Amtrak station at Orlando Regional Medical

Center to DeBary. Currently, this initial service is scheduled to be operational by 2010. A second phase, extending the service to the Poinciana area, is expected to start in 2013.

Funding for the project will be split 50:25:25, between federal funds, state funds and money from counties and cities respectively.

There are also plans for a third phase, with an extension north from DeBary to DeLand.

Service is planned with headways of 30 minutes at peak hours and at two hours at other times using double-deck trains of up to three cars.

Included in the plans are enhanced bus and other transportation services at station stops, 11 park-and-ride facilities in outlying areas and two intermodal centres at Lynx Central Station in downtown Orlando and in the Sand Lake Road area.

Developments
In May 2007, the FDOT received approval to acquire the right-of-way.

Other projects
Central Florida Light Rail project
The proposed Central Florida Light Rail Transit study/project would use traditional LRT technology and link Altamonte Springs and south Orange County with 35 km (22 miles) of track. An initial operating segment of 14–19 km (9–12 miles) would likely be developed first, with additional segments constructed as funding becomes available.

I-Drive Circulator
The I-Drive circulator would follow an 13 km (8 mile) route in and around the International Drive corridor. Located on the system would also be one of Orlando's proposed Intermodal Centers (Canadian Court Intermodal Center), where passengers could connect to the proposed OIA Connector and North/South Light Rail Transit (LRT) Systems.

The I-Drive Circulator Alternative/Technology Assessment Study began in December 2003 and was completed in August 2005. The purpose of the study was to determine the type of technology and proposed alignment most suitable for the I-Drive area.

Funding for the project has not yet been identified.

OIA Connector Light Rail
The proposed OIA Connector Light Rail Transit would be a 22 km (14 mile) long light rail system, connecting the Orlando International Airport with International Drive. The system is being planned as an extension of the North/South LRT project. Public and private ground transportation would also connect to the system.

The Alternative Analysis (AA) began in December 2003 and was completed in August 2005. Eight initial LRT alternatives were identified for evaluation. These alternatives were refined and amended based on comments received as part of the initial alternatives evaluation. Ultimately, the Sand Lake Road corridor was

selected as the recommended Locally Preferred Alternative (LPA).

Funding for the project has not yet been identified.

Rail Relocation Feasibility Study
The Rail Relocation Feasibility Study was initiated to determine the benefit of rerouting train movements from the existing CSXT 'A' Line from Deland in Volusia County to Poinciana in Osceola County. The project examines ways to relieve traffic conflicts that long, slow moving trains create, utilise the existing rail system for increased passenger use and to address safety concerns at crossings.

The Rail Relocation Feasibility Study was completed in March 2005.

Orlando International Airport (OIA) Intermodal Center
The Orlando International Airport (OIA) Intermodal Center is a transfer centre for passengers using the airport, commuter trains, rapid transit and local buses. Two stations are being proposed, at the North and South Terminals.

The Project Development and Environment (PD&E) Study was completed in December 2005. Preliminary engineering and design of the North Terminal Intermodal Center is currently under way.

Philadelphia
Population: City 1.45 million, metropolitan area 5.83 million (2007 estimates)

Public transport
Bus, trolleybus, metro, tramway and suburban rail services provided by divisions of transportation authority controlled by representative board appointed by state and local government jurisdictions, and based on acquired undertakings. Additional metro route to Lindenwold, New Jersey, run by Port Authority, with connecting NJ Transit local trains running Philadelphia-Lindenwold-Atlantic City.

Southeastern Pennsylvania Transportation Authority (SEPTA)
1234 Market Street, Philadelphia, Pennysylvania 19107-3780, US
Web: www.septa.org
Further information has been removed at SEPTA's request.

Port Authority Transit Corporation (PATCO)
PO Box 4262, Lindenwold, New Jersey 08021-0218, US
Tel: (+1 856) 772 69 00 (Main number)
(+1 856) 968 22 43 (Corporate communications)
Fax: (+1 215) 218 37 50 ext. 2226
(Corporate Communications)
Web: www.drpa.org/patco/

Key personnel
President: John J Matheussen
General Manager: Robert A Box
    Staff: 325

Type of operation: Full metro, opened 1969

Passenger boardings: (1995) 10.9 million
(1996) 10.7 million
Car-km: (1995) 7.2 million
(1996) 6.9 million

Route length: 23.3 km
    in tunnel: 4.1 km
    elevated: 3.7 km

SEPTA renewed its small trolleybus fleet in 2008 and reinstated trolleybus service, on three routes, after a five-year suspension. Pictured is one of 38 low-floor trolleybuses, supplied by New Flyer, arriving at Bells Corner terminus of route 59 (Charles Greene)   1375673

Number of lines: 1
Number of stations: 13
    in tunnel: 6
Gauge: 1,435 mm
Track: 66 kg/m continuous welded rail; in tunnel, sleepers encased in concrete; at grade, timber sleepers on ballast; on viaduct, track anchored to concrete deck

Max gradient: 5%
Minimum curve radius: 61 m
Tunnel: Cut-and-cover
Electrification: 685 V DC, third rail

Current situation
PATCO was the first of the new generation of highly automated transit lines in North America. Rebuilt from an existing (1935) line operated by the PTC (SEPTA's predecessor) connecting downtown tunnels in Philadelphia and Camden via the Ben Franklin Bridge, it was extended into the New Jersey suburbs over moribund rail right-of-way. It is owned by the Delaware River Port Authority, which subsidises PATCO from its toll bridge and river port operations.

Developments
In March 2005, PATCO awarded a USD11.3 million contract to Cubic Transportation Systems Inc for the design and integration of a new multi-modal,

contactless smartcard-based fare collection system which will link rail and parking services.

Service: Peak 3–4 min, off-peak 7–12 min; 24 h service
Fare structure: Zonal fares in 5 zones; 2-ride and 10-ride tickets
Revenue control: All stations unstaffed and equipped with change machines, automatic ticket vendors and bi-directional gates
Fare evasion control: CCTV in all fare areas, monitored at control and enforced by PATCO police
Arrangements for elderly/disabled: Reduced fare
Integration with other modes: Intersystem transfer arrangements with New Jersey Transit feeder buses and with SEPTA; also with NJT trains to and from Atlantic City; 7 stations have parking for over 12,000 cars
Operating costs financed by: Fares 56.4 per cent, deficit financed by loans from Delaware River Port Authority
One-person operation: All trains
Signalling: Cab signals, with wayside signals at all interlockings; full automation except doors and PA announcements
Surveillance: In 4 tunnel stations

Rolling stock: 121 cars

Budd (1968–69) single cars	M25
Budd (1968)	M50
Vickers Canada (1980–81)	M46
In peak service: 96	

Phoenix

Population: City 1.55 million, Metropolitan area 4.17 million (2007 estimate)

Public transport

Bus services for city and suburban area with total population of 3 million managed by the Public Transit Departments of Phoenix, Tempe, Scottsdale and the Regional Public Transportation Authority under the name Valley Metro, operated through contracts with private providers. The Regional Public Transportation Authority or local cities themselves either fund or operate other services in the region. Cross-county commuter bus service, MaricopaXpress, commenced 2008 from the City of Maricopa to Phoenix and Tempe (www.maricopa-az.gov). LRT under construction.

Valley Metro, Regional Public Transportation Authority (RPTA)

302 North First Avenue, Suite 700, Phoenix, Arizona 85003, US
Tel: (+1 602) 262 74 33
Fax: (+1 602) 495 04 11
Web: www.valleymetro.org

Key personnel

Chair: Mayor Elaine M Scruggs, City of Glendale
Vice-Chair: Wayne Ecton, City of Scottsdale
Executive Director: David A Boggs
Chief of Staff: Bryan Jungwirth
Chief Marketing Officer, RPTA: Mario Diaz
Deputy Executive Director of Finance, RPTA: Chris Curcio
Deputy Executive Director of Planning, RPTA: Carol Ketcherside
Deputy Executive Director of Operations, RPTA: Vacant
Senior Manager, Human Resources and Administration, RPTA: Penny Lynch
Staff: Not currently available

Background

In 1985, voters in Maricopa County (in which the city of Phoenix is situated) approved a 0.5 per cent sales tax to fund road construction and provide USD5 million (inflated annually) for public transport expansion. Valley Metro/RPTA

has been charged with developing a regional transportation plan, finding a dedicated funding source for public transportation and developing a network that included a regional rail system. Subsequent attempts were made in 1989 and 1994 to pass an additional 0.5 per cent sales tax to fund regional transportation, but both propositions were defeated.

In addition to the county sales tax, there have been several local funding initiatives targeting public transportation. In 1996, voters in the city of Tempe passed a 0.5 per cent sales tax to support transit improvements. In 1998, the same amount of sales tax was passed by voters in Mesa, but only a small portion was 'earmarked' for transit improvements.

Further evidence of local support for transit improvements was demonstrated in 2000 and 2001, when the cities of Phoenix and Glendale passed local sales tax initiatives for transit. In 2000, the city of Phoenix passed a 0.4 per cent sales tax to fund improvements in transit and an LRT initial operating segment. In 2001, the city of Glendale passed a 0.5 per cent sales tax to fund a mix of transportation investments. This was followed by passage of a 3/10 cent sales tax initiative by the City of Peoria in 2005.

In 2003, after an extensive outreach program, the Regional Transportation Plan was approved. This was followed in 2004 by Proposition 400. The citizens of Maricopa County passed a 0.5 per cent sales tax to fund improvements. Proposition 400, was a continuation of the 0.5 per cent sales tax originally approved in 1985.

Current situation

Working in partnership with Valley Metro/RPTA, three cities manage fixed-route transit services throughout the region. Funding for fixed-route transit services is provided by Avondale, Chandler, Gilbert, Glendale, Good Year, Litchfield Park, Mesa, Phoenix, Scottsdale, Surprise, Tempe, Tolleson and Valley Metro/RPTA. Fixed-route operations are contracted to six private operators and one municipal operator: Veolia/Phoenix, Veolia/RPTA, Veolia/Tempe, MV/Phoenix, Arnett and the city of Glendale. Shuttle/Circular service is operated by Veolia/Tempe, MV Transportation and the cities of Glendale and Scottsdale. Private contractors provide dial-a-ride services in Chandler, Gilbert, Mesa,

Paradise Valley, Phoenix, Scottsdale and Tempe. The cities of El Mirage, Glendale, Peoria, Surprise and the Sun Cities retirement communities operate their own dial-a-ride services.

Developments

As a result of the growing transportation needs in the Phoenix metropolitan area, the Maricopa Association of Governments has developed a Regional Transportation Plan (RTP), which is a comprehensive performance-based, multimodal and co-ordinated regional plan covering the period to FY2026. The RTP includes revenue from the 0.5 per cent sales tax extension, as well as other state, local and federal transportation funds. The RTP calls for 0.5 per cent sales tax to be split among public transit, freeways and arterial streets. Specifically, the RTP calls for operating and capital funding for regional transit services, capital funding for a 93 km (58 mile) LRT system which includes the 32 km (20 mile) Central Phoenix/East Valley Segment, operating and capital funding for two rural routes, capital funding for commuter vanpools, and capital and operating funding for paratransit transportation. The plan also includes funding for 13 park-and-ride, 13 transit centres and eight vehicle (fixed, rural, and paratransit) maintenance facilities, dedicated BRT ROW, arterial BRT ROW improvements, bus stop improvements and ITS/vehicle management system.

Bus

Passenger boardings (unlinked): (2002/03) 52.48 million
(2003/04) 56.4 million
(2004/05) 59.1 million
(2005/06) 61.1 million
(2006/07) 70.4 million
Vehicle-km: (2002/03) 59.83 million
(2003/04) 61.9 million
(2004/05) 61.5 million
(2005/06) 64.5 million
(2006/07) 71.5 million

Number of routes: 106
Route length: (One way) 3,725.5 km

Fleet: 1,184 buses (regional fixed route, shuttle/circulator and paratransit)

New Flyer 60 ft bio-diesel (2004)	20
North American Bus Industries (NABI) 45 ft LNG (2003–04)	64
TMC 40 ft diesel (1988–90)	29
New Flyer 40 ft diesel (1994–96)	54
North American Bus Industries (NABI) 40 ft LNG (1998–99/2001–02)	323
North American Bus Industries (NABI) 40 ft CNG (2001)	20
NOVA 40 ft diesel (1998)	20
New Flyer 40 ft CNG (2006)	52
New Flyer 40 ft bio-diesel (2007)	73
NABI 60 ft CNG (2006)	10
North American Bus Industries (NABI) 35 ft LNG (1999)	36
TMC 35 ft diesel (1989)	27
ElDorado (Ford) 30 ft diesel (2003/07)	4 2
Dodge Wide One 30 ft petrol/gasoline (1994)	1
Aerotech (Ford) 30 ft propane (1995–96)	3
Supreme 30 ft diesel (2002/06)	105
Dodge Wide One 30 ft CNG (1997–98)	2
ElDorado MST II 30 ft diesel (2006)	2
ElDorado MST 30 ft propane (2000)	1
ElDorado/National 30 ft LNG (1998–2002)	68
Aerotech (Ford) 30 ft diesel (2006/07)	12
Aerotech 30 ft unleaded (1998/99)	3
Braun 30 ft unleaded (1999–2001, 2004/06)	149
Supreme (Ford) 30 ft unleaded (2000–05)	15
Supreme (Ford) 30 ft CNG (2000–05)	11
Crusader (GM) 30 ft unleaded (2001–02)	9
Supreme 21 ft unleaded (2006/07)	39
Freightliner 30 ft bio-diesel (2003)	2
Supreme (Ford) 21 ft diesel (2002/04)	8
Chevrolet 30 ft diesel (2007)	1
Sprinter 30 ft diesel (2004)	5
Freightliner Trolley 30 ft diesel (2004/06)	16

On order: 61 vehicles (makes and models not currently available)
In peak service: 648

Valley Transit New Flyer articulated bus (Bill Luke)   1115138

NABI Compobus on Valley Transit RAPID service (Bill Luke)   1115137

A photo of the Metro light rail train in Phoenix (Photo courtesy of Valley Metro Rail. Circa 2008)
1367970

Valley Metro/RPTA New Flyer bus   1323647

Most intensive service: 5 min

One-person operation: All routes

Fare collection: Duncan recording fareboxes rebuilt to include magnetic card capability until 8/07; Tempe/some Mesa buses use GFI fareboxes until 9/07; New Scheidt & Bachmann validating fareboxes (includes magnetic-stripe passes, magnetic-stripe all day passes, and future smart card capability) for the entire region

Fare structure: Flat for local routes, premium for express/BRT routes, paratransit varies by service area and distance travelled; pre-purchased monthly magnetic-strip passes; magnetic-strip passes for direct billing of service

Fares collected on board: 28.8 per cent (based on FY2006/07) (This information has changed with the new fare policy implemented at the beginning of December 2007, but is not yet available)

Integration with other modes: All local routes have common fare structure; free transfers (except between local and express service) not accepted after 12/1/07; park-and-ride; all buses have cycle racks

Operational control: Route inspectors/mobile radio

Arrangements for elderly/disabled: All routes are fully accessible; paratransit operated mostly by local dial-a-ride when and where fixed-route buses run within 1.2 km; demand-response services carried 922,700 passengers in FY2006/2007

Bus priority: HOV lanes on Interstate 10 through downtown Phoenix, Interstate 17, State Route 51 and Red Mountain Freeway; priority bus and carpool entrance ramps at five freeway locations; reserved lanes on two downtown Phoenix approach streets

Average distance between stops: 400 m

Average speed: 24 km/h

Operating costs financed by: Fares 24.24 per cent, subsidy/grants 75.76 per cent

Operating revenue sources: Farebox: 24.24 per cent; dedicated sales tax: 43.4 per cent; federal: 6.8 per cent; other local: 31.4 per cent

New vehicles financed by: FTA grants 80 per cent, RPTA and member cities general fund revenues 20 per cent

Light rail (METRO)

Passenger journeys: n/a
Vehicle-km: n/a

Number of lines: 1
Route length: 32 km
Number of stations: 28

Developments

The 32-km (20-mile) METRO light rail starter line opened in December 2008. The at-grade light rail system has 28 stations, eight park-and-ride facilities and 50 vehicles. Ridership in the first year is projected at 26,000 boardings per day.

METRO exercised an option to purchase 14 vehicles in addition to the 36 originally purchased, bring the fleet total to 50, in order to support growth in the area and the large number of special events that will take place along the alignment.

The Regional Transportation Plan (RTP), adopted by the Maricopa Association of Governments (MAG) and financed under the one-half cent sales tax extension, identifies a further 59.5 km (37 miles) of major light rail/high capacity transit corridors to be implemented by 2025. Currently, these are:

- **Northwest Extension:** Length 8 km (5 miles), running north on 19th Avenue toward Rose Mofford Park. This light rail extension will be built in two phases, with the first phase of 5.15 km (3.2 miles) terminating at Dunlap Avenue. Planned to open in 2012;

- **Tempe South:** Length 3.2 km (2 miles), running south to near Southern Avenue in Tempe. Planned to open in 2015. Transit mode and route to be determined;

- **Central Mesa:** Length 4.3 km (2.7 miles) eastward to the downtown area. Planned to open in 2015. Transit mode and route to be determined;

- **Glendale:** Alignment and transit mode to be determined. Planned to open in 2017. Funded through Glendale and Phoenix city taxes;

- **I-10 West:** Length 17.7 km (11 miles), running near the freeway ending at 79th Ave. Planned to open in 2019. Transit mode and route to be determined;

- **Northeast Phoenix:** Length 19.3 km (12 miles), running northeast toward Paradise Valley Mall. Planned to open in 2025. Transit mode and route to be determined.

Valley Metro Rail Inc (METRO) is the agency charged with planning, designing, building and operating the Light Rail Transit (LRT) system in the area.

METRO initiated Alternatives Analysis studies for three of its corridors identified in the RTP, namely Central Mesa, I-10 West and Tempe South. The purpose of the studies are to evaluate potential High Capacity Transit (HCT) improvements such as LRT or Bus Rapid Transit (BRT) within the corridors. In March 2007, the Phoenix City Council approved the implementation of a phased Northwest extension project with the initial construction of a 5.2-km (3.2-mile) segment along 19th Ave from Montebello Ave to Dunlap Ave to be funded locally. This phase is scheduled for completion in 2012. Phase 2 of the project that will extend 2.3-km (1.4-mile) to 25th Ave and Mountain View Rd is scheduled for completion by 2017. The phase I of the LRT Operations Configuration Study was completed in 2007.

Pittsburgh

Population: City: 279,936, metropolitan area: 2.3 million (2002 estimates)

Public transport

Bus, reserved busway, tramway/light rail and funicular services provided by transport authority serving county area controlled by representative board. Maglev under study.

Port Authority of Allegheny County

345 Sixth Avenue, 3rd Floor, Pittsburgh, Pennsylvania 15222-2527, US

Tel: (+1 412) 566 55 00   Fax: (+1 412) 566 51 11
Web: www.portauthority.org

Key personnel
Chief Executive Officer: Stephen G Bland
Chairman: John A Brooks
Vice-Chairman: Guy Mattola

Director, Transit Operations: Winston Simmonds
Director, Media Relations: Bob Grove
    Staff: 2,700

Passenger boardings: (All modes)
(FY2003) 67.8 million
(FY2004) 67.8 million
(FY2005) 69.3 million
(FY2006) 70.0 million
(FY2007) 69.8 million

Operating costs financed by: Fares 38.2 per cent, other commercial sources 7.3 per cent, subsidy/grants 44 per cent, tax levy 10.5 per cent

Background
The Port Authority of Allegheny County was created by legislation and began operations in March 1964.

Current situation
The Port Authority's service area covers Allegheny County and portions of Armstrong, Beaver, Washington, Butler and Westmoreland counties, an area of some 1,956 km² (755 sq miles).

Pittsburgh's high level of transit usage, its extensive system of exclusive rights-of-way and the survival of its tramway are all due to its extreme topography, located in hilly terrain where the Allegheny and Monongahela rivers join to form the Ohio.

Partial upgrading of the tramway has been carried out, with new alignments and conversion to light rail standards of the 17 km route to South Hills. There are three busways (total length 29.6 km (18.4 miles)), three contraflow bus lanes (total length 6 km (3.7 miles)), and a High-Occupancy Vehicle (HOV) lane of 6.6 km (4.1 miles).

Developments
The Port Authority is currently involved in several projects for development of the transportation systems in its service area. These include:
The Parkway West Multimodal Corridor Study (completed);
The Eastern Corridor Transit Study (completed);
Strategic Regional Transit Visioning Study (completed).

In August 2005, the Port Authority, along with the Southwestern Pennsylvania Commission and the Three Rivers Workforce Investment Board, became involved in the Access-To-Work Interagency Cooperative, which aims to expand the work of the Access-To-Work Task Force. This will co-ordinate the efforts of the three organisations with regard to work related transportation across the region.

In September 2005, the Port Authority unveiled a new trip planner service on its website.

In October 2006, the US Department of Homeland Security announced that a transit security grant of USD898,530 had been awarded to the Port Authority. This will be used to deploy rail emergency carts and perimeter security, bus CCTV and security systems.

Bus
Passenger boardings: (FY2003) 58.4 million
(FY2004) 58.4 million
(FY2005) 59.5 million
(FY2006) 60.1 million
(FY2007) 60.3 million
Vehicle-km: Approx 25.6 million per year

Number of routes: 187
Route length: 3,996 km
On priority right-of-way: 42.2 km (26.2 miles)

Fleet: 880 vehicles
Neoplan (1999/2005)   249
Nova Bus Classic (1996)   171
Gillig (2003/05)   381
Navistar minibus   49
In peak service: 600
On order: Not currently available

Most intensive service: 3 min
One-person operation: All routes

Port Authority's Rail Center yard   1033422

Neoplan bus on the East Busway (Bill Luke)   1115232

Fare collection: Exact fare to electronic fareboxes; fare collected on entry for in-bound trips, on leaving for out-bound; passes
Fare structure: Zonal (central area plus 2 zones); 10-trip tickets; annual, weekly and monthly passes from 200 outlets
Average speed: 22.2 km/h (13.8 mph)
Bus priority: 6.9 km (4.3 mile) two-lane purpose-built exclusive busway (South Busway), 14.6 km (9.1 mile) Martin Luther King Jr East Busway, 8 km (5 mile) West Busway all on own right-of-way, with sheltered passenger stations (see below); exclusive right-of-way on three contraflow bus lanes in downtown Pittsburgh and Oakland; also 8 km of HOV lanes on I-279 expressway, used by 8 routes at peak hours
Integration with other modes: Tramway shares portion of South Busway track and connects with Martin Luther King Jr East Busway; park-and-ride extensively developed with 63 locations and 14,800 spaces
Arrangements for elderly/disabled: ACCESS door-to-door service with lift-equipped vehicles provided by 10 contractors carried 1.7 million passengers in FY2007. Senior citizens free on all regular services off-peak, funded by Pennsylvania lottery proceeds
New vehicles financed by: County, state and federal sources

Busway
Current situation
The South Busway, opened in 1977, carries some 11 bus routes with 470 movements and more than 9,000 riders on an average weekday. Certain portions share a pre-existing tramway alignment and the route is available for emergency police, ambulance or fire service use. A second exclusive busway, Martin Luther King Jr East

Busway, from Swissvale to the edge of the city centre at Penn Park station, opened in 1983, is 14.6 km (9.1 miles) long and has nine stations for walk-on riders. With buses originating from numerous suburban communities it is served by 32 Express and Flyer routes as well as an end-to-end shuttle. Approximately 24,000 riders per day are carried. The 8 km (5 mile) West Busway, opened in 2000, carries 8,700 weekday riders on eight routes operating between the city and the borough of Carnegie. Some 63 park-and-ride facilities with 14,800 spaces are provided on bus and tram routes, including those serving the busway.

Developments
Extension of the East Busway opened in June 2003.

Tramway/light rail (the T)
Type of operation: Conventional tramway partially reconstructed to light rail standards

Passenger boardings: (FY2003) 6.8 million
(FY2004) 6.8 million
(FY2005) 7.3 million
(FY2006) 7.4 million
(FY2007) 7.1 million
Car-km: (2003) 2.7 million

Route length: 40.5 km (25.2 miles)
    in tunnel: 3.9 km (2.4 miles)
Number of lines: 4
Gauge: 1,588 mm
Track: 57.5 kg/m RE standard rail; ballasted track at grade, ballasted track bridges, open deck bridges, direct fixation subway, direct fixation bridges
Electrification: 650 V AC, overhead

Rolling stock: 83 cars
Siemens-Duewag SD400 LRV (1984/85)
some remanufactured (2005)   M55*
CAF (2005)   M28
In peak service: 63 cars
On order: 55 of these vehicles are scheduled to be remanufactured by CAF. The first 44 have already been delivered. The remaining 11 vehicles will also be remanufactured.

Service: Peak 3 min, off-peak minimum 15 min
Integration with other modes: Connections with local bus routes at 12 stations
Fare collection: Fareboxes on vehicles, peak-hour platform collection at 12 stations
Average speed: 24.8 km/h (15.4 mph)

Developments
The Stage II Light Rail Transit Project was completed in June 2004, consisting of the reconstruction of the 8.4 km (5.2 mile) Overbrook Line, the purchase of 28 new vehicles and the remanufacture of 40 of the existing 55 light rail vehicles, the construction of 10 new stations, and the expansion and modernisation of the Operations Control Center. The remaining 15 original cars are also being remanufactured.

There is also a project to further extend the T to connect to the city's North Shore. This would pave the way for a further extension to the airport and to communities in the north and the west of the city. The North Shore Connector construction began in 2006 and is scheduled for completion in 2011.

Twenty-eight new CAF vehicles were delivered in early 2005.

In May 2006, a contract was awarded to CAF for the remanufacture of the last 15 of the 55 Siemens vehicles.

Funicular
Current situation
The 200 m 71 per cent incline Monongahela Incline funicular was reopened in 1983 after rehabilitation which coincided with its integration into the Port Authority system and

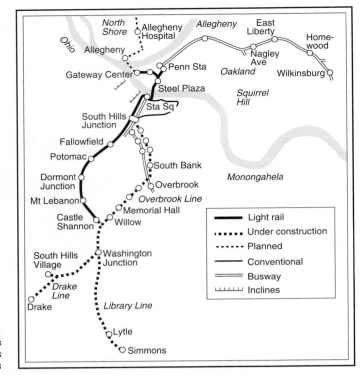

Map of Pittsburgh's light rail and busways
0576698

the Station Square commercial redevelopment project adjacent to the lower station. Built in 1870, it is the oldest inclined plane in the US. It carries about 700,000 passengers a year in two cars.

The neighbouring Duquesne Incline carries around 500,000 passengers a year in two cars. It is owned by the Port Authority, but operated by a non-profit-making historic society.

Maglev project
The Pennsylvania High-Speed Maglev Project would be a 54 mile Maglev line connecting Pittsburgh international airport, downtown Pittsburgh and Monroeville and Greensburg. There would be multimodal stations at the locations. The project is the initiative of Maglev Inc, the FRA and PENNDOT.

The Port Authority has completed a Final Environmental Impact Statement (FEIS) study in co-operation with the Pennsylvania Department of Transportation (PENNDOT) and the Federal Railroad Administration (FRA).

Portland
Population: City 533,427, metropolitan area 2.1 million (2005 estimates)

Public transport
Bus and light rail services provided by TriMet, a public agency responsible to the state and governed by a local volunteer representative board of directors appointed by the state governor. Service area is the 950 km² TriMet District in Oregon and Clark County, Washington, the latter served by a separate transit authority that integrates fares and co-ordinates services with TriMet. Central area tramway owned and managed by the city government and operated by TriMet under contract. Aerial tramway.

Tri-County Metropolitan Transportation District of Oregon (TriMet)
4012 SE 17th Avenue, Portland, Oregon 97202-3993, US
Tel: (+1 503) 962 49 10   Fax: (+1 503) 962 64 51
e-mail: customerservice@trimet.org,
   pr@trimet.org
Web: www.trimet.org

Key personnel
Board President: George Passadore
General Manager: Fred Hansen
Interim Executive Director of Operations: Tim Garling
Finance and Administration Executive Director/ Chief Financial Officer: Beth deHamel
Director, Bus Maintenance: Anton A 'Tony' Bryant
Acting Manager of Field Operations: Peggy Hanson
Acting Director, Systems Security and Safety: Shelly Lomax

Director, Rail Maintenance: Bruce Miller
Manager, Rail Maintenance-of-Way: Roland Henson
Manager, Rail Equipment Maintenance: Mark Grove
Director of Communications: Mary Fetsch
Public Information Officers: Peggy LaPoint
   Staff: 2,500

Passenger journeys: (All modes)
(2003/04) 71.3 million
(2004/05) 75.0 million
(2005/06) 75 million
(2006/07) 75.9 million
(2007/08) 99.1 million

Operating costs financed by: Fares (22 per cent), local employer payroll and other taxes (62 per cent), federal sources (14 per cent) and miscellaneous (two per cent) (FY2006).
New vehicles financed by: FTA grants (0–80 per cent), with local match from TriMet funds.

Current situation
TriMet was established in 1969 to serve the Portland metropolitan area, replacing private operations.

TriMet operates fixed-route bus services, MAX light rail and commuter rail services, park-and-ride facilities and RideWise and LIFT paratransit services.

TriMet operates 16 Frequent Service bus lines, which run at a frequency of 15 minutes or less every day. The service has distinctive bus stop signs. These services carry 57 per cent of all bus trips. Off-peak and weekend ridership on these lines has shown large gains.

All of TriMet's vehicles are accessible to both less-abled passengers and those with bikes.

Developments
In October 2006, the US Department of Homeland Security announced a USD800,000 grant to TriMet

to improve rail security. The funds will be used to install cameras at the downtown Portland Mall bus stops and along the I-205 MAX route.

Also in that month, the Transportation Security Administration's (TSA) three K-9 teams were announced for TriMet.

In September 2008, TriMet, with the support of the Transportation Security Administration (TSA) announced further expansion of the agency's security measures, including hiring more police officers, increasing fare inspection and adding more cameras to MAX stations. A USD1 million grant for TriMet was awarded by the TSA to add more security cameras to MAX platforms, as well as tools to work with first responders to better respond to a transit-related attack or emergency. When these cameras are installed, every Gresham station will have CCTV. Nowadays 41 of the 64 MAX stations have CCTV cameras, many funded with TSA grants.

Bus
Vehicle-km: (2002/03) 44 million
(2003/04) 44 million
(2005/06) 42 million
(2006/07) n/a
(2007/08) 63.9 million

Number of routes: 93 (including 16 Frequent Service lines)
Route length: 1,445 km (898 directional US route miles as reported to FTA – one way)
Number of stops: 7,280

Developments
The downtown Transit Mall, the bus-only sections of 5th Avenue (southbound) and 6th Avenue (northbound) in the city centre, closed in January 2007 to permit its heavy reconstruction, adding light rail tracks, and will not reopen until 2009.

TriMet have set up a website giving details of the project at www.portlandmall.org.

Rebuilding will be much more extensive than just the addition of light rail, with replacement of all passenger shelters and other amenities at the bus stops as well as at the new LRT stops.

Buses are to begin moving back onto the Transit Mall in early 2009, but in the meantime every bus route serving downtown Portland will be diverted, for two years, onto other streets, without any separation from other traffic.

Almost all of the new, temporary bus stops being created in downtown, for use into 2009, are equipped with shelters.

In October 2006, TriMet started to use biodiesel in its entire bus fleet. The biodiesel is blended in a B5 (five per cent biodiesel) mix with petroleum-based diesel. TriMet is also using Ultra-Low Sulfur Diesel (ULSD) and the combined biodiesel/ULSD blend should reduce particulate emissions from buses by up to 30 per cent.

In mid-2008, TriMet ordered 40 40-ft New Flyer diesel buses, with options for an 160 additional vehicles.

Fleet: 642 vehicles

Gillig Phantom 30 ft (1990/91)	43
Gillig Phantom 40 ft (1990)	53
Flxible Metro 40 ft (1992)	108
Flxible Metro 30 ft (1992)	10
Flxible Metro 40 ft (1994)	35
Gillig Phantom 40 ft (1997)	65
Flyer 40 ft low-floor (1997/2003, 2005)	319
Collins WT 300 26 ft (1998)	four
New Flyer 40 ft low-floor diesel-electric hybrid (2002)	two
138 Econoline van	three

In peak service: 533
On order: 40 40-ft New Flyer diesel buses

Most intensive service: Peak 5–20 min, off-peak 15–60 min

Fare collection: Cash or paper ticket to farebox, day, monthly and annual passes

Fare structure: Zonal (three radial zones); one hour free transfer; free travel in 'Fareless Square' area covering the entire city centre and a narrow section of the Lloyd district; discount fares for youth, elderly and disabled; 10-ride multitickets; six hour, one day ticket available

Fare evasion control: Driver monitoring and occasional random inspection

Arrangements for elderly/disabled: Door-to-door LIFT van service (220 vans) provide 1.0 million trips annually; fixed routes 100 per cent accessible; elderly and disabled travel at discounted fare at all times

Bus priority: 36-block city-centre transit mall; two adjacent one-way bus-priority streets offer improved passenger waiting facilities, information kiosks, and TV monitors with real-time information; intersection queue and signal priority at several locations

Integration with other modes: 56 park-and-ride lots, totalling 9,992 spaces, 22 purpose-built, the rest shared-use, mainly church parking areas. Connections with light rail at 31 stations outside the city centre, including 11 transit centres where buses and rail meet; carpooling encouraged and assistance provided; all buses have front-mounted racks for bicycles

Light rail (MAX)

Type of operation: Light rail, initial route opened 1986

Passenger boardings: (2003/04) 27.4 million
(2004/05) 31.9 million
(2005/06) 32.6 million
(2006/07) 34.0 million
(2007/08) 35.2 million
Car-km: (2003/04) 9.6 million
(2004/05) 10.8 million
(2005/06) 10.6 million
(2006/07) n/a
(2007/08) Not yet available

Route length: 71.3 km (44.3 miles)
Number of lines: four

A pair of 2003-built Siemens low-floor LRVs of TriMet, northbound on the MAX system's newest route, the 2004-opened Yellow Line. The line runs primarily in a newly created median in Interstate Avenue (Steve Morgan)
1115199

Number of stations: 64 (eight are unidirectional)
Gauge: 1,435 mm
Track: Continuously welded rail on timber or concrete sleepers in ballast
Max gradient: seven per cent
Electrification: 750 V DC, overhead

Service: Peak 5–7 min, off-peak and Saturdays 10 min, evenings and Sundays 15 min
First/last car: 03.33/00.32 (01.32 Fri/Sat nights)
Fare structure: Zonal, same fares as bus
Fare collection: Honour system with random inspectors. Change-giving ticket vending machines and prepaid ticket cancellers at all stations; free transfer to and from bus
Integration with other modes: Bus connections at 31 stations, including timed transfers at seven transit centres; 18 park-and-ride lots on the light rail line, providing 7,438 spaces, and 23 kiss-and-ride; cycle racks on all buses holding two cycles and storage lockers at 36 LRT stations; up to 12 cycles allowed on two-car trains
Arrangements for elderly/disabled: 100 per cent accessible with at least one low-floor car in every train
Signalling: Traffic-light priority on all in-street sections (employing bar signals for LRV operators); automatic block on all other sections

Rolling stock: 105 cars

Bombardier/BBC (1983/86)	M26
Gomaco Brill replica cars (1991/92)	M2
Siemens SD660 low-floor (1996/2004)	M77

In peak service: 83

Developments

In May 2006, TriMet placed an order with Siemens for 21 model S70 Avanto light-rail cars. Portland's LRVs will be single-ended, but with doors on both sides, and will be semi-permanently coupled back-to-back so as to be operated in the form of double-ended two-car trains. Delivery was scheduled to begin in mid-2008.

I-205/Portland Mall MAX Light Rail Project: Construction started in February 2007, on this 13.4-km (8.3-mile) light rail line that will connect Clackamas County with Portland State University (PSU) and possible future extensions to Milwaukie, Vancouver and to the southwest. Ridership estimates for the new line have been given as some 46,500 daily boardings by 2025. Headway is proposed to be 15 minutes. The line is currently scheduled to open in September 2009.

Construction on the 10.5-km (6.5-mile) I-205 segment of the line began in March 2007. It will have eight news stations and five park-and-ride facilities (with more than 2,300 parking spaces) and every station will be served by bus services, including 10 bus lines at Clackamas Town Center.

Portland-Milwaukie Light Rail Project: A further 11.7-km (7.3-mile) extension to the light rail extension is planned from PSU to SE Portland and Milwaukie. FTA funding is pending.

Vintage Trolley
Current situation

A fares-free vintage tram service operated by TriMet along the light-rail tracks between the city centre and Lloyd Center, on Sundays only, from March through December. Service was inaugurated in late 1991, funded primarily from private sources (mainly local businesses), and from 1994 to 1999 it operated daily for much of the year. From 2000, the service was reduced to Sundays only and TriMet took over financial responsibility for its operation from a not-for-profit group called Vintage Trolley Inc. Contrary to previously published reports, the four Gomaco-built replica trams were always owned by TriMet, not by VTI.

In January 2001, TriMet transferred ownership of two of the four Gomaco cars to the City of Portland, so that they could be used on the new Portland Streetcar line. The two cars remaining with TriMet continue to operate the same service as previously – half-hourly with two cars, Sundays only, but there are now no spares for that service. VTI continues to provide conductors for the two-man-operated replica vintage trams, but is now reimbursed by TriMet and the City, respectively, for wages due for Vintage Trolley conductor duties on MAX and the Portland Streetcar. (The conductors control the rear door, through which all boarding on these cars takes place, and provide tourist and historical commentary, but do not collect any fares).

Westside Area Express (WES) (commuter rail – under construction)
Current situation

In November 2006, construction started on the Westside Area Express (WES). The 23.6-km (14.7-mile) line will serve four cities: Beaverton, Tigard, Tualatin and Wilsonville, and will share freight train tracks with the Portland & Western Railroad (P&W) in eastern Washington County. WCCR will operate every 30 minutes during morning and evening peak hours on weekdays. Under an agreement between TriMet and P&W, the drivers of the trains will be P&W employees and the railroad will perform dispatching duties and right-of-way maintenance, but TriMet will oversee the service and provide all other staff. TriMet is building a maintenance facility for this operation in Wilsonville. Service will be provided by four dmus, which TriMet is working with Colorado Railcar to design and build.

The line's northern terminus will be at the Beaverton Transit Center, which is served by TriMet's Red and Blue light rail lines and 11 bus routes. There will be five stations in total: the two termini (Beaverton and Wilsonville) and three intermediate stations. All except Beaverton will have park-and-ride lots, providing almost 700 spaces. Almost the entire line follows previously-existing P&W right-of-way, on newly re-laid track. However, at the northern end, TriMet has built a new single-track spur, about 150 m in length, along Lombard Avenue to connect the P&W alignment with the Beaverton Transit Center.

The total cost of the project is estimated at USD117.3 million project, which will be funded by: USD58.65 million in federal funding, USD35.34 million from state lottery bond proceeds, USD15.56 million from TriMet and GARVEE bonds and USD7.75 million from local cities and Washington County. TriMet and Washington County will contribute a total of USD4.1 million toward annual operating costs.

The four Colorado Railcar dmus (three powered, one trailer) were delivered in 2008.

The line is scheduled to open in February 2009 and average daily ridership is projected to be between 3,000 and 4,000 trips by 2020.

Clark County Public Transportation Benefit Area Authority (C-TRAN)

PO Box 2529, Vancouver, Washington 98668-2529, US
Tel: (+1 360) 696 44 94
Fax: (+1 360) 906 73 45
e-mail: ctran@c-tran.com
Web: www.c-tran.com

Street address
2425 NE 65th Avenue, Vancouver, Washington 98661, US

Key personnel
Executive Director and Chief Executive Officer:
  Jeff Hamm
Chair: Betty Sue Morris
*Vice-Chair:*Tim Leavitt
Director of Operations: Lynn Halsey
Chief Information Officer/Director of Public Affairs:
  Scott Peterson
Manager, Marketing Services: Allison Shultz
  Staff: 364

Current situation
C-TRAN operations began in 1981 after voter endorsement of a plan to develop services for the fast-growing Clark County area with a total population of around 360,000, and including the city of Vancouver. Based on a private operation run by Vancouver city since 1969, C-TRAN is now a Public Transportation Benefit Area Authority under a representative board. C-TRAN and TriMet co-operate to provide a regional network for the Portland/Vancouver metropolitan area, including express commuter routes between the towns and integration of the two fare systems. Four per cent of the service is operated under contract to TriMet. Vanpool service inaugurated 1988 carpools in 1995 and in 1999 carried nearly 70,000 passengers.

In 2004, C-TRAN had a total ridership of more than 7 million.

Developments
In September 2005, Clark County voters approved a 0.2 per cent sale tax increase dedicated to mass transit. The new tax was projected to provide approximately USD9.4 million annually to C-Tran, making up for much of the revenue lost within the county by the passage of 1999's state-wide initiative 695 and has ended a period of cost-cutting which, among other measures, had threatened to end all Sunday service.

In addition to service reductions, other changes implemented by C-Tran during that period to reduce costs, included extensive fare-system revisions, mainly in 2005. Transfers were eliminated, and each passenger must now pay every time he/she boards, but the price of an all-day ticket was reduced as partial compensation. The nearly 30-year-old agreement with TriMet had to be modified: Although monthly passes and all-day tickets from TriMet or C-Tran are still valid on the other's system, no transfers or other tickets are accepted any longer, and C-Tran also stopped accepting all non-standard types

C-TRAN Gillig bus with bike rack (Bill Luke) 0576368

of TriMet passes, such as employer-sponsored annual passes, which have become increasingly popular with large employers in the TriMet district.

In December 2005, C-TRAN began the installation of a series of solar-powered bus stops (i-STOPs). A total of 90 i-STOPS were acquired with funds provided by a federal grant. The i-STOPS will use a flashing light to signal to approaching buses and some also light an area for waiting passengers.

In January 2006, a new route commenced, Route #19 Salmon Creek Shuttle.

In late 2006, C-TRAN was awarded more than USD605,000 in grant monies from the Washington State Department of Ecology to retrofit its entire bus fleet and eliminate up to 90 per cent of its harmful emissions caused by the use of diesel fuel.

Bus
Passenger journeys: (2001) 6.1 million
(2002) 6.4 million
Vehicle-km: Not currently available

Number of routes: 27 (9 commuter routes to Portland, 18 local routes in Clark County)
Route length: about 900 km

Fleet: 104 vehicles
GM RTS-II 40 ft (1982)	33
Gillig Phantom (1991/95)	60
Gillig 40 ft low-floor (1998)	2
ElDorado 25 ft (1996)	9

In peak service: 94

Fare structure: Zonal
Fare collection: Cash, monthly pass, annual pass
Arrangements for elderly/disabled: C-VAN paratransit service with 25 lift-equipped vehicles carried 180,867 passengers in 2002
Integration with other modes: 7 park-and-ride facilities, 3 transit centres
Operating costs financed by: A $\frac{1}{5}$ per cent sales tax 58 per cent, fares 19 per cent, grants 16 per cent, miscellaneous 7 per cent (2002)

Portland Streetcar Inc (PSI)

City of Portland, Office of Transportation
1120 Southwest 5th Avenue, Suite 800, Portland, Oregon 97204, US
Tel: (+1 503) 823 71 37   Fax: (+1 503) 823 73 71
e-mail: information@portlandstreetcar.org
Web: www.portlandstreetcar.org

Key personnel
Transportation Commissioner: Sam Adams
*General Manager:*Vicky L Diede
  Staff: 36

Type of operation: Conventional street tramway, opened July 2001

Passenger boardings: (2004/5) 2.1 million
(2005/06) 2.5 million
(2006/07) 3.0 million

One of Portland Streetcar's double-ended Skoda/Inekon 'Astra' 10T low-floor trams 1034536

Current situation

Under discussion since 1988, the Portland Streetcar (named Central City Streetcar until 2000) has been developed independently of TriMet by the City of Portland.

In 1995, the city invited proposals/tenders to design, build and possibly operate the then-proposed system, and a contract was signed with the only respondent: Portland Streetcar Inc (PSI), a unique non-profit body that had been newly formed specifically for the purpose. It is governed by a board of directors composed of representatives of the business community, major property owners and major public institutions along the route, and the city's Commissioner of Transportation, the city's Chief Financial Officer and TriMet's General Manager; its size has varied between nine and 19 board members. The city contracts with PSI for professional services for various aspects of work on the tramway.

PSI does not directly employ anyone, but rather it has contracted with existing professional companies to design and build the line and provide certain other services. Major decisions were subject to city council approval, and a citizens' advisory committee also provided regular input.

For operations and maintenance, PSI's subcontractor, local consultancy firm Shiels Obletz Johnsen (SOJ) is providing the tramway's Chief Operating Officer (part-time) and Community Relations Manager (part-time), and handling advertising/sponsorship and certain general administrative duties.

The initial 3.8 km circulator route connects Portland State University in the southern part of the city centre with Good Samaritan Hospital in the Northwest Portland district, the city's most densely populated neighbourhood. En route, it passes through some areas of relative low density, including surface car park lots, an abandoned railway freight yard and old industrial development. A major impetus of the tramway project was the desire by the city and by regional planning authority Metro to gradually replace these land uses with new high-density (multistorey) transit-friendly housing. A tramway was viewed as the best way to attract both developers and the future passengers and residents. Between 1997 and 2008, development activity within two blocks of the route totals more than USD3.5 billion and has provided 10,212 units of multifamily housing plus over 5.5 million sq ft of commercial space for ground-floor retail, office and classroom use.

Construction began early in 1999, and a short extension approved in 2000 (to 4th Ave) was added to the project in time to open concurrently with the original phase, in July 2001. The city decided to contract with TriMet for them to provide operators, superintendents and mechanics to

Two of Portland Streecar's Škoda-Inekon trams at RiverPlace, the terminus of an extension opened in March 2005 (Steve Morgan)
1115198

work for PSI. There are six city employees: General Manager (part-time), Manager of Maintenance, Assistant Manager of Maintenance, Manager of Operations and Safety, Assistant Manager of Operations and Safety and two utility workers to clean the tram vehicles. PSI is under contract to supply the Chief Operating Officer, Community Relations Manager and someone to provide other administrative duties (see above).

Service is provided by a fleet of 10 low-floor, articulated trams built in the Czech republic, the first seven by Skoda/Inekon and the last three by Inekon Trams (formerly DOP-Inekon).

Maintenance is carried out at a small depot built at NW 15th Avenue and Northrup Street. A single curve at the intersection of SW 10th Avenue and Morrison Street connects the Portland Streetcar system with the TriMet light rail system (MAX); although this will permit the Skoda low-floor cars to be taken to TriMet's large depots for major maintenance, this has proven not to be necessary.

The Portland Streetcar system was extended by 1 km from PSU to the banks of the Willamette River at RiverPlace in March 2005.

Developments

Three additional double-ended, partially low-floor cars were delivered in January 2007 and entered service in May/June. These were built by Inekon Trams (formerly DPO-Inekon) rather than by Skoda-Inekon, but are operationally nearly identical to the first seven cars.

Planning continues on a proposed second Portland Streetcar route, a 5.3 km extension to the east side via the Broadway Bridge and south

to the Oregon Museum of Science and Industry, which has an estimated overall cost of USD147 million. The city council approved the project in September 2007, committing USD27 million of city funding to it and submitting an application to the Federal Transit Administration for USD75 million in funds from the FTA's new Small Starts programme.

Originally, two 'Vintage Trolleys', Gomaco-built replicas of 1904 Brill trams, were transferred to the PSI fleet from TriMet and were operated on PSI at weekends (one car). However, this service became intermittent after 2004 and ceased altogether in December 2005. It is not expected to resume and the two trams are now being stored by TriMet, with various options for their future use under consideration.

The line was extended southwards from RiverPlace to Gibbs Street, at what is currently the northern end of the new South Waterfront district, in October 2006. This extension is two-way single track and, unlike almost the entire remainder of the line, is in private right-of-way, using sleepers-in-ballast track. The track was laid in an existing rail right-of-way, saving cost, a factor which was made more important by the fact that major redevelopment of this area is expected within the next few years, and when that takes place this initial alignment is likely to be replaced by a new alignment along newly-built streets.

In August 2007, the line was extended farther south, further into the South Waterfront district, to a new terminus at Lowell Street. As with the original portion of the route, this extension is a one-way loop along parallel streets, mostly without separation from other traffic. Its length is about 750 m each way, and its opening raised the peak vehicle requirement to seven. The Gibbs St stop is located directly across from the lower terminus of the new Portland Aerial Tram (aerial cableway), and in the northbound direction the 2007 extension of the PSI line opened a new stop located even closer to the cableway terminus.

To support the opening of these two extensions, three additional double-ended, partially low-floor cars were ordered in 2005 from Inekon Trams. These three cars were delivered in January 2007 and entered service in May/June 2007.

As part of an effort by Federal officials to establish a domestic manufacturer of modern trams, Portland was given a special Federal grant of USD4 million for the purpose of holding a competitive bidding and, in turn, awarding a contract, for the construction of one such car – to a design that would be fully compatible with Portland Streetcar's existing fleet and stop-design. Proposals were received in autumn 2006, and the successful bidder was Oregon Iron Works Inc, using Skoda's model-10T design under license. OIW is located in the Clackamas area of Portland's southeast suburbs. A new subsidiary of OIW was formed, named United Streetcar LLC, and in early 2007 the city of Portland awarded a USD3.2 million contract

One of Portland Streetcar's new Inekon Trio trams passes the lower terminus of the new aerial cableway, the Portland Aerial Tram, on the track that opened as an extension of the PSI line in August 2007 (Steve Morgan)
1341675

to OIW/United Streetcar for one streetcar. The traction motors, and possibly certain other components of the propulsion equipment, will be supplied by Skoda, but in almost all other respects this modern tram will be US-built. Delivery is projected for early 2009.

Portland Streetcar will evaluate this tram and add it to its fleet, but the hope is that, should this venture prove successful, additional orders will be generated from some of the many other US cities considering building modern 'streetcar' lines (conventional street tramways), avoiding the need for going overseas to obtain such equipment.

Route length: 6.4 km (4.0 miles)
Number of lines: 1
Number of stops: 46 (41 of which are unidirectional)
Gauge: 1,435 mm
Max gradient: 8.75%
Min curve radius: 25 m
Electrification: 750 V DC, overhead

Most intensive service: 12 min
First/last car: 05.30/23.30 (Monday-Thursday), 05.30/01.00 (Friday), 07.30/01.00 (Saturday), 07.30/22.30 (Sunday)
Fare structure: As TriMet, with all tickets and passes issued by one system valid on the other and vice versa (by formal agreement between TriMet and the City); the PS route lies entirely within one fare zone but since PS and TriMet are fully integrated with regard to fares, multizone tickets are available from the TVMs on board the PS trams; annual streetcar-only pass; tickets purchased on board the streetcars are now valid for the entire day on PS, but remain valid for only two hours on TriMet
Fare collection: Most of the present route is within TriMet's city centre fares-free zone; elsewhere it is an honour system with random inspections. Ticket machines and validators (for prepurchased TriMet tickets) on board all cars ; all fare tickets issued by TriMet are accepted)
Arrangements for elderly/disabled: All service is provided by low-floor cars and is fully wheelchair

accessible; elderly and disabled travel at discounted fare (as per TriMet)

Rolling stock: 10 cars
Skoda/Inekon 'Astra' 10T low-floor (2001/02)   M7
Inekon 12-Trio low-floor (2006)   M3

On order: One Skoda-design 10T car, to be built under license by Oregon Iron Works (United Streetcar LLC), for early 2009 delivery.

Portland Aerial Tram
City of Portland, Office of Transportation
1120 Southwest 5th Avenue, Suite 800, Portland, Oregon 97204, US
Tel: (+1 503) 823 51 85   Fax: (+1 503) 823 73 71
e-mail: info@portlandtram.org
Web: www.portlandtram.org

Key personnel
Transportation Commissioner: Sam Adams
Transportation Operations Manager: Mike Brooks

Type of operation: Aerial cableway (Opened 2007)

Route length: 1 km

Background
The City or Portland set up a private, non-profit board (with 12 members) called Portland Aerial Transportation Inc (PATI) to oversee the design of this aerial cableway project. In 2007, it was replaced by an Executive Management Committee, whose seven members include three city representatives, three OHSU representatives and one independent third-party representative jointly selected by the city and OHSU. The committee provides oversight and policy guidance. The tram was designed by agps architecture and Doppelmayr-CTEC.

Current situation
Test runs of the aerial cableway began in November 2006, and the line opened to Oregon

Health & Science University (OHSU) employees in late 2006. Operation of the line is managed by OHSU. Service operates year-round, six days/week. OHSU employees ride for free.

The 1-km line connects the hilltop campus of OHSU, located just south of Portland's city centre, with the new South Waterfront district, along the banks of the Willamette River southeast of the city centre. In exchange for the city's assistance in financing the cableway's construction and operation, OSHU agreed to invest heavily in the new district, which the city is transforming from light industrial uses and vacant land into a high-density neighbourhood of apartments and office buildings. OHSU opened a new 15-storey research centre and clinic next to the lower terminus of the cableway in December 2006 and has plans for additional buildings. OHSU is the largest employer in the city of Portland proper, with over 10,000 employees.

Under an agreement finalised in July 2006 between the City and OHSU, the latter will pay 85 per cent of the operating cost for five years and the city the remaining 15 per cent, based on pre-opening estimates that indicated approximately 85 per cent of the cableway's riders will be OHSU employees. OHSU paid USD38 million of the line's USD57 million construction cost.

The Portland line is considered to be one of only two aerial cableways in the USA that function as regular public transport rather than primarily or exclusively as tourist facilities, the other being the Roosevelt Island Tramway in New York City, which opened in 1976.

Developments
The cableway opened in January 2007. Fares for the public are USD4.00 (return) with children six years and under travelling free. An annual pass at USD100 will be available in the future. Hours of operation are: 06.00–22.00 (Monday-Friday) and 09.00–17.00 (Saturday). Cars depart every five minutes.

The line carried one million passengers during its first ten months of operation (starting from December 2006).

Providence
Population: City 175,255, County 635,596, metropolitan area (includes New Bedford and Fall River) 1.6 million (2006 estimates)

Public transport
Bus, paratransit, trolleybus and ferry services in Providence and in 38 of the other 39 communities in the state of Rhode Island provided by public transit authority controlled by representative board; commuter rail service to Boston.

Rhode Island Public Transit Authority (RIPTA)
265 Melrose Street, Providence, Rhode Island 02907, US
Tel: (+1 401) 784 95 00   Fax: (+1 401) 784 95 95
Web: www.ripta.com

Key personnel
Chair: Robert Batting
Vice-Chair: John Rupp
General Manager: Alfred J Moscola
Assistant General Manager for Planning:
   Mark Therrien
Director of Transportation: James Dean
Director of Maintenance: Bernie Harwood
Director of Marketing and Communications:
   Karen D Mensel
Director of Specialised Transportation: Ed Scott
   Staff: 839

Passenger journeys (all modes):
(2002) 20.5 million
(2003/04) 20.3 million
(2004/05) 21.976 million
(2005/06) 24.5 million
(2006/07) 26 million

Background
Established in 1966 to take over residual private bus operations. Governed by a seven-member appointed board, RIPTA provides statewide public transportation.

Current situation
RIPTA serves 38 of the 39 Rhode Island communities. Services provided include fixed-route bus and trolleybus, paratransit RIde service, a demand-response service provided to six suburban communities, and Providence/Newport ferry service.

Developments
In mid-2007, RIPTA awarded a contract, valued at more than USD1.5 million, to RouteMatch Software Inc to provide an intelligent

transportation system, including GIS-based paratransit scheduling software.

Bus
Number of routes: 58
Route length: 580 km

Fleet: 393 vehicles (including 241 fixed-route buses (including 20 CNG trolleys), 17 Flex vehicles and 135 paratransit vehicles
Bus fleet
TMC (1992)	24
GMC (refurbished) (1992)	2
Nova (1998-2000)	83
Ford Turtle Top (1999)	2
Orion (2001, 2004)	51
New Flyer CNG (2002)	5
Gillig low-floor	36

The catamaran Ocean State, *introduced in 2003, docked at Newport*   1109538

CNG trolleybus fleet
Chance Coach (1999, 2001)   19
Optima (2004)   1
Flex Service fleet
Ford Turtle Top (1999-2004)   17
In peak service: 195

Most intensive service: 20 min (Providence Trolley System)
One-person operation: All routes
Fare collection: Electronic fareboxes
Fare structure: One rate (USD1.50 one way) for entire state; USD0.10 transfers; 10-ticket books (USD15.00); monthly passes (USD45); USD5 for all-day statewide pass on buses and trolleybuses
Fares collected on board: 85 per cent
Operational control: Street Supervisors; radio
Arrangements for elderly/disabled: All vehicles equipped with wheelchair lifts, some are low-floor vehicles, ferry is wheelchair accessible; bus pass programme for seniors and people with disabilities provides discounted passes; free passes for eligible passengers
Bus priority: Buses use 300 m former tram tunnel under College Hill in central Providence
Integration with other modes: 26 park-and-ride sites, connections with Peter Pan and Greyhound bus lines, MBTA and Amtrak trains in Providence and Kingston, TF Green airport in Warwick and ferry service to Block Island and Martha's Vineyard
Average peak-hour speed: 16 km/h
Operating costs financed by: Fares 28 per cent, subsidy/grants 42 per cent, miscellaneous revenue 40 per cent
Subsidy from: FTA 16 per cent, state 43 per cent, other 41 per cent
New vehicles financed by: Voter-approved bonding and federal grants

Trolley
Current situation
Trackless CNG-fuelled vehicles on two routes, the Green Line and the Gold Line, in Providence and on one route in Newport. Fares are flat at USD1.50, with passes available. Disabled and senior citizens may use their discounted or no-fare passes. The service runs at 20 minute intervals.

Ferry
New England Fast Ferry Co
200 Seaport Boulevard, Suite 75, Boston, Massachusetts 02210, US
Tel: (+1 401) 453 68 00

RIPTA TMC/RTS bus (Bill Luke)   1115243

e-mail: info@nefastferry.com
Web: www.nefastferry.com

Current situation
RIPTA operates the Providence-Newport Ferry, a seasonal service that runs daily from 16 May to 16 October. The trolley and bus services integrate with the ferry service at the Providence and Newport docks.
The Federal Congestion Mitigation Air Quality Improvement grant that made the ferry service possible, permanently expired in 2008.

Developments
A new high-speed catamaran, the *Ocean State*, was introduced in 2003 to provide the ferry service. It replaced an older mono-hull vessel.

Massachusetts Bay Transportation Authority (MBTA)
10 Park Plaza, Boston, Massachusetts 02116, US
Tel: (+1 617) 222 31 06
Fax: (+1 617) 222 61 80
Web: www.mbta.com

Commuter Rail
45 High Street, 9th Floor, Boston, Massachusetts 02110, US
Tel: (+1 617) 222 58 79

Key personnel
Secretary of Transportation and MBTA Chairman: Bernard Cohen
MBTA General Manager: Daniel A Grabauskas
MBTA Commuter Rail Chief: Bob Stoetzel

Type of operation: Suburban heavy rail

Passenger journeys: Not currently available

Current situation
More than 25 Amtrak trains link Providence with Boston (69 km, 43 miles), plus 12 weekday services (plus nine Saturday and seven Sunday services) operated by MBTA Boston.
Electrification of the route, as part of Amtrak's Boston-New Haven upgrading, was completed in 1999.
For further information on MBTA, please see main entry in *Jane's Urban Transport Systems* under Boston.

Rochester
Population: Metropolitan area 1.1 million (2002 estimate)

Public transport
Bus services provided in Rochester and surrounding areas by operating agency of regional transport authority controlled by representative board.

Rochester-Genesee Regional Transportation Authority (RGRTA) – Regional Transit Service (RTS)
1372 East Main Street, Rochester, New York 14609, USA
Tel: (+1 585) 288 17 00   Fax: (+1 716) 654 02 93
e-mail: info@rgrta.com
Web: www.rgrta.org

Key personnel
Chairman: William Nojay
Vice-Chairman: William E Bishop
Chief Executive Officer: Mark Aesch
Director of Special Services: Robert Finke

Director of Urban Service: Ellen Cicero
  Staff: 500

Current situation
As well as a fixed-route urban network in Rochester and surrounding areas of Monroe County, supplemented by peak-hour express routes, RTS operates rural bus services in Livingston County (LATS), the city of Batavia (B-Line) in Genesee County, Wayne County (WATS) and Wyoming County (WYTS) – all operated by small buses, some on dial-a-bus basis. It also operates Lift Line Inc, a fully accessible paratransit service. Figures below cover all operations; rural services carried some 350,000 passengers in 1994/95.

Developments
In November 2001, RTS introduced five luxury coaches for service on the new Batavia and other park-and-ride routes.

Bus
Number of routes: 31
Route length: (One way) 960 km

Fleet: 342 vehicles
GMC RTS (1982/83)	75
Flxible Metro (1986)	17
Gillig Phantom (1988/91)	33
MAN SG310 articulated (1984)	10
Orion V (1990/93)	48
Orion V CNG-powered (1992)	5
Thomas/BIA/other midi/minibus	80
NovaBus Classic (1995/96)	69
Coaches	5

In peak service: 244

Most intensive service: 15 min
Fare structure: Flat; prepurchase 10-ride tickets and monthly pass; transfers 10 cents; free service 11.00–14.00 in downtown Rochester; Lift Line passengers travel free on regular services
Fare collection: Coin to farebox
Arrangements for elderly/disabled: 100 lift-equipped buses; Lift Line is demand-responsive accessible service provided throughout RTS area using 21 low-floor buses; carried 132,000 passengers in 1994/95.
Integration with other modes: Peak-hour express buses serve 31 suburban park-and-ride sites; Park-and-Ride Plus express routes provide suburb-to-suburb commuter service
Operating costs financed by: Fares 39 per cent, other commercial sources 6 per cent, subsidy/grants 45 per cent, tax levy 10 per cent
Subsidy from: FTA, state and county funds

Sacramento

Population: City 453,781, metropolitan area 2.07 million (2006 estimates)

Public transport

Bus and light rail services in city and regional area provided by transit authority controlled by appointed board, with paratransit services contracted out. Some commuter services and contracted bus operations in Yolo County and cities of Roseville and Folsom provided by private operator.

Sacramento Regional Transit District (RT)

PO Box 2110, Sacramento, California 95812-2110, US
Tel: (+1 916) 321 28 00   Fax: (+1 916) 444 21 56
Web: www.sacrt.com

Street address
1400 29th Street, Sacramento, California 95816, US

Key personnel
Chair: Roberta MacGlashan
Interim General Manager/Chief Executive Officer: Michael R Wiley
Chief Administrative Officer: Z Wayne Johnson
Chief Operating Officer: Mark Lonergan
Assistant General Manager of Planning and Transit System Development: Rosemary Covington
Chief of Facilities and Business Support Services Division: Michael A Mattos
Assistant General Manager of Engineering and Construction: Diane Nakano
Acting Chief Financial Officer: Dee Brookshire
Light Rail Manager: Mark Lonergan
Bus Transportation Manager: Al Schweim
   Staff: 1,236 (January 2007)

Passenger boardings: (All modes)
(2000) 26.4 million
(2002) 27.8 million
(2003) 27.8 million
(2005) 30.4 million
(2006) 31 million (estimate)
Passenger-km: (All modes)
(2002) 200 million (124 million miles)

Operating costs: (2002) USD89.5 million
Operating costs financed by: State sales taxes 41 per cent, fares 24 per cent, local sales taxes 18 per cent, federal assistance 7 per cent, other sources 10 per cent

Background
RT came into operation in 1973 with the acquisition of the Sacramento Transit Authority. Later that year RT completed a new maintenance facility and purchased 103 new buses.

Current situation
RT covers a service area of 673 km² (418 sq miles) and a population of some 2.08 million in the metropolitan area. It is governed by an 11-member board of directors.

RT's paratransit services, operated through a contract with Paratransit, Inc with 98 vehicles, had a ridership figure of 309,044 in FY2006.

RT also operates a Community Bus programme, using smaller circulatory 'Neighborhood Ride' buses to six neighbourhoods in Sacramento County.

Bus

Passenger boardings: (2002) 18.1 million
(2003) 18.1 million
(2005) 19.4 million
(2006) 16.8 million
Vehicle-km: (2003) 14.9 million (9.2 million miles)
(2005) 16.4 million (10.2 million miles)
(2006) 14.74 million (9.16 million miles)

Route length (weekday): (One way) 1,340 km (833 miles)
Number of routes: 97
Number of stops: 3,674

CAF light rail vehicle operated by Sacramento Regional Transit (RT) waits at Broadway station
0594972

Fleet: 272 vehicles (January 2007)
40 ft CNG total: 233
Orion 40 ft, Cummins L10G/280
   CNG-powered (2000)   Not currently available
Orion 40 ft, Cummins L10G/280
   CNG-powered (1996)   Not currently available
Orion 40 ft, Cummins L10G/240
   CNG-powered (1994)   Not currently available
Orion 40 ft, Cummins L10G/240
   CNG-powered (1993)   Not currently available
31 ft CNG total: 15
Orion 31 ft, Cummins L10G/280
   CNG-powered (1996)   Not currently available
Replica streetcar CNG total: 8
Chance replica streetcar, Cummins
   C5.9L CNG-powered (2000)   4
Other   4
Shuttle vans (9 diesel, 7 petrol)   16
In peak service: Not currently available
Average age of fleet: 5.9 years
On order: 106 low-floor Orion, Cummins 8.3 litre CNG-powered buses, for delivery starting April 2003 and to be completed by June 2004

Most intensive service: 15 min
First/last bus: 05.00/23.30
One-person operation: All routes
Fare collection: GFI electronic fareboxes; exact fare only
Fare structure: Flat, with free one-way intermodal transfer, low fare in city centre; prepurchase tickets, daily and monthly passes
Fares collected on board: 49 per cent
Fare evasion control: Driver supervision and police/sheriff inspection
Operational control: Road supervisors, all buses equipped with mobile radio
Arrangements for elderly/disabled: Lifts fitted to all vehicles, all services accessible; half fare and reduced rate passes for persons over 62 or disabled; free life-time pass for over-80s. Paratransit service with 125 minibuses for those unable to use fixed routes
Average distance between stops: 270 m
Average peak-hour speed: In mixed traffic, 23.2 km/h
Integration with other modes: Park-and-ride sites; 56 bus routes serve light rail stations; cycle lockers at some stations; 1 bus route serves Amtrak station
New vehicles financed by: FTA and local sales tax funds

Light rail

Staff: 168

Type of operation: Light rail, initial route opened 1987

Passenger boardings: (2000) 8.7 million
(2002) 8.5 million
(2003) 8.5 million
(2005) 11 million
(2006) 14.5 million
Car-km: (2005) 2 million (1.27 million miles)
(2006) 6.3 million (3.9 million miles)

Route length: 60.2 km (37.4 miles)
Number of routes: 2
Number of stops: 47
Transfer centres: 26
Gauge: 1,435 mm
Electrification: 750 V DC, overhead

Developments
In 2004/05, 21 UTDC-built LRVs were acquired second-hand from San Jose, but these will require modifications before they can enter service in Sacramento.

In December 2006, RT completed the final 1.1-km (0.7-mile) light rail section of the Amtrak/Folsom Corridor to Sacramento Valley Station.

There are plans for a further South Line phase 2 extension, by 6.8 km (4.2 miles) with four stations, from the existing terminus at Meadowview Road to Consumnes River College. RT has completed preliminary engineering and evaluation of the impact associated with the construction and operation of the proposed extension.

There are also plans for a Downtown Natomas Airport (DNA) light rail corridor. This would be 20.9-km (13 miles) in length with 14 stations and run from downtown to Sacramento International Airport. A revised Draft Environmental Impact Statement/Report (DEIS/R) was submitted to the Fedarl Transit Administration (FTA) in July 2007. For further information, please see www.dnart.org.

A Video Control Center (VCC) has been opened, to allow video surveillance of the light rail system. Funding was provide by a grant of USD606,250 from the Department of Homeland Security.

Rolling stock: 97 cars

Siemens SD100 single-articulated bidirectional (1987, 1991)	M36
CAF low-floor single-articulated bidirectional (2002–03)	M40
UTDC (1987) (ex-San Jose, in store) (2004/05)	M21

In peak service: Not currently available
On order: None

Service: 15 min daytime, 30 min evening
First/last car: 04.30/19.00 (Gold Line), 01.00 (Blue Line)

Fare structure: Flat, as bus

Fare collection: Vending machines at all stations; prepurchase tickets, monthly passes

Fare evasion control: Proof-of-payment enforced by RT fare inspection staff and police/sheriff officers

One-person operation: All trains

Arrangements for elderly/disabled: All but one station have ramps or lifts

Integration with other modes: 18 park-and-ride facilities with a total of 7,482 spaces, 26 bus transfer centres

End-to-end run time (entire system): 55 minutes

Sacramento
Other operators
Current situation
Contracted 'YOLOBUS' services give access to Sacramento (see separate entry). Unitrans

(www.unitrans.ucdavid.edu) operates in Davis only with a fleet of 40 vehicles over 15 routes, carrying more than 3 million passengers each year.

Other local services are provided in Carmichael, Davis, Folsom, Yuba City and El Dorado County.

Yolo County Transportation District (YCTD) – YOLOBUS
Industrial Way, Woodland, California 95776, US
Tel: (+1 530) 666 28 77
Fax: (+1 530) 661 17 32
e-mail: info@yolobus.com
Web: www.yolobus.com

Key personnel
Executive Director: Terry Bassett
Deputy Director: Troy Holt

Current situation
The Yolo County Transportation District (YCTD) administers YOLOBUS, which operates local and intercity bus service in Yolo County and neighbouring areas. YOLOBUS serves Davis, West Sacramento, Winters, Woodland, downtown Sacramento, Sacramento international airport, Cache Creek Casino, Esparto, Madison, Knights Landing and Dunnigan. Services are provided on 21 routes in Yolo County, 15 of which give access to Sacramento.

YOLOBUS has connections with other local public transportation systems – Unitrans and Citylink in Davis, and Regional Transit and Light Rail in Sacramento.

Developments
In early 2003, the Yolo County Transportation District purchased 13 new Compressed Natural Gas Orion VII buses.

Fleet: 37 CNG buses

Salt Lake City
Population: City: 178,605, metropolitan area: 1.02 million (2004 estimates), service area: 1.67 million

Public transport
Bus and light rail services provided by regional transit authority for city and surrounding areas of Salt Lake, Utah, Davis, Weber, Tooele and Box Elder counties; commuter rail proposed.

Utah Transit Authority (UTA)
3600 South 700 West, PO Box 30810, Salt Lake City, Utah 84130-0810, US
Tel: (+1 801) 262 56 26
Fax: (+1 801) 287 46 14; 46 22
Web: www.rideuta.com

Key personnel
Board President: Orrin T Colby
General Manager: John M Inglish
General Counsel: Bruce Jones
Chief Capital Development Officer: Michael Allegra
Chief Performance Officer: Jerry Benson
Chief Communications Officer: Andrea Packer
Rail Service General Manager: Paul O'Brien
Salt Lake Regional General Manager: David Huber
Mt Ogden Regional General Manager: Art Bowen
Timpanagos Regional General Manager:
  Hugh Johnson
Support Services General Manager:
  Kenneth D Montague
  Staff: 1,700

Passenger boardings (all modes): (2000) 28.3 million
(2003) 32.6 million
(2004) 34.5 million

Background
Following state legislative approval in the Utah Public Transit District Act of 1969, UTA was incorporated and began operations in Salt Lake County in 1970, whilst Davis and Weber counties annexed into the Transit District by voter approval in 1973. All of the private transit operations in the three-county area were incorporated into UTA by 1975.

In 1974, voters in Salt Lake and Weber counties approved a 0.25 per cent sales tax to provide a dedicated funding source for public transport, and Davis County followed suit a year later. In 1985, UTA expanded service into the cities of Provo and Orem in Utah County. In 1989, four cities in northern Utah County, American Fork, Lehi, Lindon and Pleasant Grove, agreed to join the transit district and impose the ¼ per cent tax. The following year, elections brought one more Utah County city, Springville, plus Tooele and Grantsville in Tooele County, into the district. Operations were extended to the cities of Alpine, Cedar Hills and Highland in 1994, and

to Mapleton, Payson, Salem, Spanish Fork and Sundance in 1995. The cities of Brigham City, Perry and Willard in Box Elder County joined the transit district in 1996.

UTA operates 129 fixed bus routes plus, during the winter months, five busy routes to five nearby skiing areas, four in Salt Lake City and one in Utah County.

Heavily discounted passes (Eco-Pass) introduced for large employers and the University of Utah have proved successful in reducing parking demands and costs, as well as increasing ridership. This popular programme has been extended to Brigham Young University, Utah Valley State College, Weber State University, and other educational institutions within the district. In 2005, UTA had 82 Eco Pass Contracts with a total of 171,104 participants, with educational institutions accounting for 151,076.

In 1992, Salt Lake County voters rejected imposition of an additional 0.25 per cent sales tax to fund the local share of a transit expansion programme. Three-quarters of the money raised would have been used to finance a greatly expanded bus system and an initial 24 km light rail line between Salt Lake City and Sandy. Despite the election result, UTA continued to pursue the federal process for implementation of the light rail system, and the Sandy Line was opened in 1999.

Current situation
UTA provides fixed-route bus, light rail, paratransit, and vanpool services to an area

covering over 1,400 square miles in six Wasatch Front counties: Salt Lake, Utah, Davis, Weber, Tooele, and Box Elder Counties, encompassing over 65 cities and towns, and unincorporated areas. The transit district serves over 80 per cent of the population of Utah, some 2.2 million people, and is governed by a 16-member board appointed by city and county governments within the district.

Developments
After community-wide consultation, a comprehensive transit plan has been developed for the coming 30 years. Planned improvements include the initiation of Commuter Rail from Brigham City to Payson, with the first phase from Pleasant View to Salt Lake expected in 2008. Furthermore, additional light rail lines, new bus rapid transit lines, and a doubling of the existing bus service are planned by 2030.

In 2007, a 0.25 cent sales tax was approved by voters to assist with the funding for commuter rail, TRAX and road projects by 2015 instead of 2030.

Bus
Passenger journeys: (2000) 21.6 million
(2003) 21.3 million
Vehicle-km: (2000) 27.8 million
(2003) 28 million

Number of routes: 129, plus 5 seasonal ski routes
Number of stops: 8,028

MCI commuter bus on Main Street in downtown Salt Lake City   1036706

Current situation

While the UTA service district covers all of three counties (Weber, Davis, and Salt Lake), and parts of three counties (Utah, Tooele, and Box Elder), bus service delivery is divided into three service areas. The Mt Ogden service area is comprised of Box Elder, Weber, and north Davis Counties; the Timpanogos service area covers Utah County; and the Salt Lake service area serves Salt Lake, Tooele, and south Davis County.

Developments

In April 2006, the UTA purchased an additional 10 Opus low-floor uses.

Fleet: 485 vehicles, plus 42 inactive

MCI 40 ft (1990)	27
MCI 40 ft Commuter (1990)	14
Orion 35 ft Ski (1991)	3
Orion V 40 ft (1992)	76
Orion V 40 ft CNG (1992)	5
Orion V 40 ft (1993)	47
Gillig 40 ft (1995)	61
Gillig 40 ft (1996)	15
ElDorado 32 ft (1996)	6
Gillig 35 ft Ski (1996)	15
Gillig 40 ft (1997)	11
Gillig 35 ft Ski (1997)	20
New Flyer 60 ft Artic (1998)	12
Gillig 35 ft low-floor (1999)	28
Gillig 40 ft low-floor (1999)	67
Gillig 35 ft low-floor (2001)	11
Gillig 40 ft low-floor (2001)	51
MCI 45 ft Commuter (2002)	13
New Flyer 40 ft low-floor hybrid-electric (2002)	3

In peak service: 371, plus 31 for seasonal ski service
Average age of fleet: 8 years

Most intensive service: 10 min
One-person operation: All routes
Fare collection: Manual drop fareboxes; tokens, day pass, monthly pass, Eco-Pass
Fare structure: Flat, free in Salt Lake City centre and state capitol zone; Premium Inter-City Express and ski bus services have higher fare; discount passes for large employers, students, faculty and staff
Fares collected on board: 50 per cent
Fare evasion control: Periodic observation of operators by UTA Transit Public Safety Officers
Integration with other modes: Unified bus/light rail fare system with free two-hour transfer. With the opening of each light rail line and the medical centre extension, UTA has planned for bus-rail integration, with bus routes realigned to serve rail stations. This has allowed for a more cost-effective reallocation of bus service, as well as resulting in a reduction in the total number of buses operating in downtown Salt Lake City, particularly in peak hours. Nearly all routes in Salt Lake County serve at least one rail station.

A total of 110 park-and-ride lots are served by bus routes: 70 of these through an agreement with the Church of Jesus Christ of Latter Day Saints for joint use of chapel lots, 12 lots are served by the light rail system, eight lots are utilised by ski service routes.

Exclusive-use lots	25
Light rail lots	12
Intermodal facility lots	1
LDS chapel lots	70
Mall lots	2
Total	110

UTA Rideshare regional ride-sharing programme facilitates carpools and co-ordinates vanpools, with 199 vanpools operating in 2003 providing 707,000 passenger trips. Each fixed-route bus equipped with front-mounted racks for 2 bicycles.

Bus priority: Total of 25.7 km of bidirectional bus/HOV lanes on one interstate segment in Salt Lake County
Operational control: Route supervisors with mobile radios, all buses radio-equipped, supported by a centralised radio control centre.
Arrangements for elderly/disabled: Reduced fares; 100 per cent lift-equipped accessible fixed-route service; Flextrans demand-responsive paratransit service in Salt Lake County; separate contracted

Gillig Ski Service bus in Little Cottonwood Canyon   1036707

demand-responsive paratransit service in other counties; customer services for persons with disabilities, eg Braille timetables
Operating costs financed by: Fares 12.8 per cent, other commercial sources 2.9 per cent, FTA subsidy 15.5 per cent, sales tax 68.8 per cent

Light rail

Type of operation: Light rail, initial route opened 1999

Passenger boardings: (2000) 6.1 million
(2003) 10.1 million
Vehicle-km: (2000) 2.4 million
(2003) 3.7 million

Route length: 32.2 km
Number of lines: 2
Number of stations: 23
Gauge: 1,435 mm
Electrification: 750 V DC, overhead

Current situation

The TRAX light rail line linking the centre of Salt Lake City with Sandy City at 10,000 South Street opened in 1999. This forms the initial stage of a regional rail system.

In 1995, following the selection of Salt Lake City to host the 2002 Winter Olympics, federal funding amounting to USD241 million was approved, and was supplemented by USD70 million raised locally. A fleet of 23 cars was supplied by Siemens Transportation.

The line has taken over a single-track Union Pacific Railroad route purchased by UTA in 1993, and over which freight trains are run by a short line operator between midnight and 5 am. With the exception of one bridge, the entire line has been double tracked.

Following the introduction of light rail to the region in December 1999, UTA has constructed two extensions to the original 24 km Sandy Line. The 5.3 km University Line opened in December 2001, prior to the Winter Olympic Games in February 2002. Construction began on the Medical Center extension of the University Line following the games. This project added 2.5 km to the University Line, opening in September 2003.

Additional light rail extensions to the Salt Lake international airport, Mid-Jordan, West Valley City, and Draper are at various stages in the planning process. The Airport line will add 10.6 km to the existing system with eight new stations between downtown Salt Lake City and the international airport. The line will primarily operate in city streets. The 16.7 km Mid-Jordan Line, serving Midvale, West Jordan and South Jordan, will be constructed in an existing UTA-owned railroad right-of-way, with full signal pre-emption at grade

crossings. This extension will add nine stations to the light rail system. The West Valley Line will have four stations on a 7.8 km alignment that will be constructed primarily at grade on tracks laid in existing local streets and new rights-of-way, with signal priority over the traffic system. The Draper extension of the original Sandy Line will add five stations on a 13.6 km alignment utilising UTA-owned railroad right-of-way. Ultimately, the implementation schedule for these extensions to the light rail system will be dependent on the timing of federal and local funding sources.

Developments

UTA has acquired 29 used 1987 UTDC LRVs from the Santa Clara Valley Transportation Authority, San Jose, CA. These vehicles will be utilised to address capacity constraints on the Sandy and University LRT Lines, facilitate planned frequency increases, and allow for a more effective preventive maintenance programme for the existing LRV fleet of 40 vehicles. These vehicles are expected to enter revenue service incrementally as they undergo a programme of rehabilitation and retrofit to ensure compatibility with the existing light rail system design characteristics. As these vehicles are already 20 years old, UTA awarded a contract to Bombardier in early 2007 to undertake a mid-life overhaul of all 29 UTDC cars.

Rolling stock: 69 cars

Siemens Transportation (1999)	M23
Siemens Transportation (2001)	M10
Siemens Transportation (2003)	M7
UTDC (1987) (ex-San Jose)	M29

Service: 15 min weekdays and Saturdays, 20 min Sundays and holidays
First/last car: 05.01/23.32 Monday to Thursday, 05.01/01.02 Friday and Saturday, 09.15/21.02 Sunday and holidays
One-person operation: All trains
Fare structure: Flat, as bus, free between the five Salt Lake City centre stations
Fare collection: Vending machines at all stations, monthly pass, day pass, Eco-pass, free two-hour transfers from bus
Fare evasion control: Proof of payment enforced by UTA Transit Public Safety Officers
Integration with other modes: Unified bus/light rail fare system with free two-hour transfer; park-and-ride facilities at 12 of the 23 stations, totalling 3,879 spaces; 11 stations with designated off-street bus staging areas, 12 with on-street bus transfers. Bicycles allowed on all vehicles
Arrangements for elderly/disabled: Reduced fares; 100 per cent accessible with ramps at all stations and retractable platform at cab end of each car

Commuter Rail (Proposed) – FrontRunner

Current situation

In 2002, UTA acquired over 282 km of railroad rights-of-way, facilities and usage agreements between Brigham City in Box Elder County and Payson in Utah County, which culminated in a USD185 million transaction. This deal secures rights-of-way for existing planned rail projects and preserves valuable railroad corridors for public transportation projects that may be decades in the making. This historic purchase will prove to be an integral component in the implementation of the Wasatch Front Regional Council's 30-year long-range transportation plan.

The first phase of a regional commuter rail system, to be known as FrontRunner, is currently in the environmental and preliminary engineering phases. The opening of the initial phase of the line will use diesel locomotives hauling bilevel coaches. This initial north segment will utilise approximately 71 km of right-of-way: 59.6 km of exclusive UTA right-of-way between Salt Lake City and Ogden, purchased in 2002, and 11.4 km between Ogden and Pleasant View operated on a shared-use section of Union Pacific railroad right-of-way. The line will travel north from the intermodal transportation centre, currently under construction, on the west end of Salt Lake City's central business district to the city of Pleasant View in Weber County, utilising the recently completed Ogden Intermodal Transit Center. Eight stations with park-and-ride facilities are planned for the north segment serving communities in Weber, Davis, and Salt Lake Counties. The line will be capable of supporting 20-minute peak operation headways in either direction and operate up to 127 kph on the alignment.

Siemens LRV at the 400/500 South 'S Curve' on the University Line   1036705

In 2004 UTA acquired 30 gallery cars at minimal cost from Metra, Chicago. These are to be refurbished. In 2005, UTA placed an order with Bombardier Transportation for 12 bi-level cab cars in a joint procurement with Albuquerque's Rail Runner Express. The contract includes an option of up to 23 additional coaches. Traction will take the form of 11 remanufactured 2,685 kW diesel locomotives, manufactured by Motive Power, Boise, Idaho, US. Train formations are to comprise two trailers and one cab car, with eight such sets in service at peak periods.

Developments

The UTA has prepared a Draft Environmental Study Report (Draft ESR) for the commuter rail project.

San Antonio

Population: City: 1.29 million, metropolitan area: 1.94 million (2006 estimates)

Public transport

Bus services provided by metropolitan transit authority, controlled by representative board.

VIA Metropolitan Transit Authority

800 West Myrtle Street, PO Box 12489, San Antonio, Texas 78212, US
Tel: (+1 210) 362 20 00   Fax: (+1 210) 362 25 70
Web: www.viainfo.net

Key personnel

Managing Director: John M Milam
Finance Director: Steve Lange
Operations Director: Keith Hom
Public Relations Director: Priscilla Ingle
Purchasing Manager: Terry Dudley
Community Relations Co-ordinator: Sylvia Mendiola
Tel: (+1 210) 362 23 70
Staff: 1,924, including part-time (as at July 2008)

Background

A confirmation election was held in the majority of Bexar County on 8 November 1977, and voters approved the creation and funding of VIA Metropolitan Transit through a one-half cent sales tax to be levied in San Antonio and seven other incorporated municipalities. In March 1978, VIA purchased transit system assets from the City of San Antonio and began operations.

Created in 1978, VIA is a political subdivision of the state of Texas with a board of trustees appointed by the city of San Antonio, Bexar County and 14 other incorporated cities in the county.

Current situation

VIA has a service area of some 3,175 km² (1,226 sq miles).

In November 2004, voters in San Antonio approved the formation of the Advanced Transportation District, or ATD. This district uses a quarter-cent sales tax to fund transportation improvement projects carried out by VIA Metropolitan Transit, the City of San Antonio, and the Texas Department of Transportation, or TxDOT. VIA receives half of the ATD revenues to enhance local public transportation services, and the other half is split between the city and TxDOT for improving streets, highways, and related transportation infrastructure.

Currently, VIA operates five park-and-ride facilities throughout its service area as well as four transfer centre facilities.

Developments

VIA is working to establish a Bus Rapid Transit (BRT) pilot line along Fredericksburg Road to connect the downtown area with the South Texas Medical Center. Service should begin in 2012.

Bus

Passenger journeys: (2002/03) 36.6 million (2006/07) 42.3 million
Vehicle-km: (2006/07) 50.5 million (31.4 million miles)

Number of routes: 91
Route length: (One way) 3,162 km (1,965 miles)
On priority right-of-way: (Contraflow) 820 m

Fleet: 435 vehicles	
GMC/TMC RTS II	23
North American Bus Industries	217
Chance/Optima/NABI American Heritage streetcar	19
New Flyer	176

In peak service: 375
On order: Not currently available

Most intensive service: 3–5 min
One-person operation: All routes

VIA Metropolitan Transit buses, such as this New Flyer vehicle, run on B5 biodiesel   1368948

Fare collection: Cash to farebox or pre-purchase multitickets or monthly passes

Fare structure: Flat, double-fare for express service; half-fare for selected individuals; monthly passes and employer-purchase pass scheme

Integration with other modes: 5 park-and-ride terminals in outlying areas offer free parking; local bus service available at intercity bus terminals

Arrangements for elderly/disabled: VIAtrans paratransit service carried 1,093,099 passengers in 2006/07; all 105 vans lift-equipped; all new North American Bus Industries and New Flyer buses equipped with low floors and ramps; RTS buses equipped with lifts.

Average distance between stops: 357 m

Operational control: Automatic vehicle location system installed on all buses and vans

Average peak-hour speed: 23.2 km/h

Operating costs financed by: Operating revenues 13.7 per cent; investment 1.8 per cent; grants 8.2 per cent; advertising and other revenue 0.4 per cent; local sales tax 75.9 per cent

New vehicles financed by: FTA grants 80 per cent, local funds and revenue 20 per cent

San Diego

Population: City 1.27 million; metropolitan area 2.98 million (2007 estimates)

Public transport

Bus and light rail services provided by operating subsidiaries of Metropolitan Transit System in southern part of San Diego County, and bus services, light rail and commuter rail by North County Transit District in the north. MTS also contracts and co-ordinates taxi and jitney services. Ferry service by private operator.

San Diego Association of Governments (SANDAG)

401 B Street, Suite 800, San Diego, California 92101, USA

Tel: (+1 619) 699 19 00   Fax: (+1 619) 699 19 05
e-mail: pio@sandag.org
Web: www.sandag.org

Key personnel

Chair: Mary T Sessom
First Vice-Chair: Lori H Pfeiler
Second Vice-Chair: Jerome Stocks
Executive Director: Gary L Gallegos
Director of Transportation and Land Use Planning:
  Bob Leiter
TransNet Programme Manager: Muggs Stoll
Transportation Committee:
  Chair: Jim Madaffer
  Vice-Chair: Jack Dale
  Staff: Not currently available

Background

In 1966, local governments create the Comprehensive Planning Organisation (CPO) as a long-range planning department within the San Diego County government under a state-authorised joint powers agreement. In 1980, the CPO was renamed as the San Diego Association of Governments (SANDAG).

In 1987, San Diego region voters approved Proposition A which initiated the *TransNet* programme – a half-cent sales tax to fund a variety of important transportation projects throughout the region. This 20-year USD3.3 billion transportation programme expires in 2008.

Current situation

SANDAG is San Diego's regional planning authority, including transportation development. It is governed by a board of directors comprising mayors, council members and a county supervisor from each of the region's 19 local governments.

The Transportation Committee advises the SANDAG board on major policy matters related to transportation. It assists with the preparation of the regional Transportation Plan and other regional transportation planning efforts and programmes.

Currently, public transit services are provided by nine scheduled bus operations, 12 demand-responsive systems, the Coaster express rail service and the San Diego Trolley. The region's transit systems provide about 33 million miles of annual transit service, carrying over 70 million total annual passengers. SANDAG provides funding administration and planning for public transit in the San Diego region. It shares public transit planning and decision-making responsibilities with several agencies: the California Department of Transportation,

the Metropolitan Transit System, the North County Transit District (NCTD) and other transit operators.

Current projects include:

- Trolley to SDSU and beyond: construction is finished on this 10 km (6 mile) extension from Qualcomm stadium in Mission Valley to San Diego State University and on to La Mesa;
- Unmet transit needs: San Diego region residents are asked to comment on transit needs to assist in the preparation of key transportation funding plans;
- Escondido Rapid Bus Transit Priority Concept Study: creating a rapid bus connection between the Escondido Transit Center, downtown and south Escondido, and Westfield Shoppingtown Escondido;
- Mid-Coast Trolley: this 18 km (11 mile) rail project will extend the San Diego Trolley from the Old Town Transit Center to UCSD and University City;
- Transit First: the Transit First strategy outlines a programme for increasing transit service and facilities in the region;
- Transportation Development Act Administration: Transportation Development Act Administration funds are allocated to programmes that improve the effectiveness, efficiency and economy of local transit systems;
- Los Angeles-San Diego-San Luis Obispo Rail Corridor: the coastal rail corridor is the focus of efforts by the coastal rail and planning agencies, Caltrans, and the Los Angeles-San Diego-San Luis Obispo Rail Corridor Agency, all of which seek to increase corridor ridership, revenue, capacity, reliability and safety;
- Assistance To Transit Operations and Planning: SANDAG conducts research and provides technical support to the region's transit operators to help them provide better, more reliable service;
- Downtown Comprehensive Transit Study: the Downtown Comprehensive Transit Study (DCTS) is one of several subregional studies under way to implement the Transit First strategy which encourages people to choose transit for their daily travel needs;
- Intelligent Transportation Systems: the cornerstone of the region's ITS strategy is the development of a network that connects the region's local transportation management centres. This enables local agencies to co-operatively manage the overall performance of both the local and regional transportation systems
- High-Speed Rail Plan: planning for commuter, intercity and high-speed rail efforts for the San Diego region;
- Short-Range Transit Plan: the Short-Range Transit Plan (SRTP) proposes how the region should balance the short-term needs of maintaining and optimising existing transit services, while beginning to implement the long-term transit vision identified in *Mobility 2030*;
- Regional Transit Vision: a strategy for improving San Diegans' quality of life by integrating transportation and local communities;
- Transportation Planning for Persons with Disabilities: SANDAG co-ordinates a number of programmes to assists transit and paratransit operators in implementing the Americans With Disabilities Act (ADA);
- Mid-City Rapid Bus Project: A 10.7-km (10-mile) high-speed bus service, connecting San Diego State University to Downtown San Diego. Planned to open in 2011.

SANDAG operates several commuter service programmes in addition to providing database and interactive applications used by area agencies to better inform and serve the commuting public.

Current projects include:

- Transportation Demand Management Programme: traffic congestion during rush hours can be reduced if more people carpool, ride the bus, train, or trolley, bike, or walk to their destinations;
- RideLink: SANDAG manages the regional RideLink programme, which offers ridematching, transportation information, and assistance to employers;
- Flexcar: SANDAG has teamed with Flexcar to provide car sharing services to commuters who live and work in the San Diego area;
- Co-ordinated Transportation Service Agency: the Co-ordinated Transportation Service Agency works to expand the availability and use of specialised transportation services.

TransNet

Progress continues on transportation projects in the San Diego region thanks to *TransNet*, the county's half-cent sales tax for transportation improvements. A new report highlights expanded freeways, more light rail lines and local street and road improvements. In 2004, voters countywide approved Proposition A, the 40-year extension of TransNet. The proposition is critical to help reduce the area's growing traffic congestion. The local sales tax extension, which garnered approval from 67 per cent of the voting public, will generate USD14 billion for transportation improvement projects. *TransNet* funding is combined with state and federal funding to improve the region's transportation network. The funding is distributed in thirds among highway, transit and local road projects. In addition, USD1 million is earmarked annually for bicycle paths and facilities. *TransNet* will support a robust public transportation system, including new Bus Rapid Transit services utilising new carpool/managed lanes along many of the major roads.

Developments

Oceanside-Escondido Rail Line (SPRINTER): this 39 km (24 mile) rail project links the downtown areas of four rapidly growing North County cities: Oceanside, Vista, San Marcos and Escondido. Sprinter service commenced in March 2008.

Metropolitan Transit System (MTS)

1255 Imperial Avenue, Suite 1000, San Diego, California 92101-7490, USA

Tel: (+1 619) 231 14 66   Fax: (+1 619) 234 34 07
Web: www.sdcommute.com

Key personnel

Chief Executive Officer: Paul C Jablonski
Director of Planning & Scheduling:
  Conan Cheung
Chief Operating Officer (Transit Services):
  Claire Spielberg
President & General Manager (Rail):
  Peter Tereschuck

Current situation

MTS, formerly the Metropolitan Transit Development Board (MTDB), was created in 1985 to provide a unified transit system.

The MTS is a federation of fixed-route and paratransit operators, comprising the cities of San Diego, Chula Vista, Coronado, El Cajon, Imperial Beach, La Mesa, Lemon Grove, National City, Poway, Santee and portions of the unincorporated area of southern San Diego County. MTS's jurisdiction covers about 76 per cent of the county with a service area of 8,357 km² and a population of 2.19 million.

Operation of the light rail transit network is delegated to the MTS Trolley (formerly known as the San Diego Trolley Inc), with three separate routes – the Blue, Orange and Green Lines. MTS Bus operates 110 bus routes throughout the San Diego region, directly, through private contractors and through public operator, Chula Vista Transit.

Planning and engineering for further expansion of the light rail network continues. This has transitioned to the San Diego Association of Governments (SANDAG). SANDAG is also working with CALTRANS to build a Bus Rapid Transit (BRT) route in the Interstate 15 corridor, which is projected to open by 2012.

MTS licenses and regulates taxis, jitneys and other for-hire vehicles for the City of San Diego and other suburban cities.

In November 2004, 67 per cent of San Diego voters approved continuation of the local 0.5 cent tax to support public transit, highways and local road improvements in the county.

Payment for single-occupancy usage of HOV lanes is currently practiced in one corridor.

Passenger journeys: (All modes)
(2002/03) 75.9 million
(2003/04) 75.4 million
(2004/05) 76.9 million
(2005/06) 82.6 million
Vehicle-km: (2002/03) 43.2 million
(2003/04) 51.3 million
(2004/05) 51.1 million
(2005/06) 58.5 million

Operating costs financed by: Fares 35.3 per cent, subsidy/grants 64.7 per cent
Subsidy from: Local Transportation Development Act (TDA) funds, State Transit Assistance (STA), Federal Transit Administration (FTA) grants and local ¹/₂ cent sales tax called TransNet

MTS Bus (previously San Diego Transit Corporation (SDTC))

PO Box 2511, San Diego, California 92112-2511, USA
Tel: (+1 619) 238 01 00   Fax: (+1 619) 696 81 59
Web: www.sdcommute.com/agencies/MTS/ SDTC/index.asp

Key personnel
Chief Operating Officer (Transit Services):
Claire Spielberg
Staff: 772

Passenger boardings: (2005/06) 48.8 million
Vehicle-km: (2005/06) 45.1 million

Number of routes: 110
Route length: (One way) 1,610/5 km

Background
Formed in 1886 and previously known as San Diego Transit Corporation (SDTC), MTS Bus is a wholly owned subsidiary of the Metropolitan Transit System (MTS), which also includes the MTS Trolley system.

Current situation
The company serves more than 2 million people and covers the cities of San Diego, Chula Vista,

MTS bus   1146511

Coronado, El Cajon, Imperial Beach, La Mesa, Lemon Grove, National City, Poway and Santee and other portions of San Diego County.

MTS Bus serves 45 park-and-ride facilities.

Fleet: 717 vehicles
Over-the-Road buses (OTRB)
MCI (1992/2005)   25
Van Hool (1998)   1
Articulated
New Flyer (1993, 2001)   41
Standard
New Flyer (1994/2005)   389
Gillig (1991/95)   43
Orion (1991)   2
Midibus
ElDorado National (1999/2005)   46
Blue Bird (1998)   7
Minibus
ElDorado National (1999/2006)   148
Goshen Coach (2003/04)   4
Vans
GMC (2000)   11
In peak service: 529

Most intensive service: 5 min
One-person operation: All routes
Fare collection: GFI dollar bill validating farebox
Fare structure: Flat; free transfers; month and half-month passes; multiride tickets; tokens
Fare evasion control: Driver supervision
Arrangements for elderly/disabled: All buses are wheelchair lift-equipped and kneel; 241 vehicles are low-floor
Average distance between stops: 2–3 blocks
Average peak-hour speed: 21.6 km/h

Integration with other modes: Timed interchange and co-operative transfer arrangements with light rail system and other bus operators, and through booking on dial-a-ride feeder services
Operating costs financed by: Fares 27.9 per cent, other commercial sources 1.3 per cent, subsidy/grants 70.8 per cent
Subsidy from: FTA 26.8 per cent, state of California 19.7 per cent, local 53.5 per cent
New vehicles financed by: FTA grants 80 per cent, local funds 20 per cent

MTS Trolley (previously San Diego Trolley Inc)

1255 Imperial Avenue, Suite 900, San Diego, California 92101-7492, USA
Tel: (+1 619) 595 49 49   Fax: (+1 619) 238 41 8
Web: www.sdcommute.com/Agencies/MTS/ SDTI/Index.asp

Key personnel
President & General Manager (Rail):
Peter Tereschuck
Staff: 461

Type of operation: Light rail, initial route opened 1981

Passenger journeys: (2005/06) 33.8 million
Car-km: (2005/06) 13.4 million

Route length: 86.9 km (54 miles)
Number of lines: 3

New Siemens S70 LRV for the MTS Trolley Green Route   1146510

Number of stations: 53
Gauge: 1,435 mm
Electrification: 600 V DC, overhead

Background
Created in 1980 and previously known as the San Diego Trolley Inc, MTS Trolley is a wholly owned subsidiary of the Metropolitan Transit System (MTS).

Current situation
Three routes are currently operated – the Blue, Orange and Green Lines.

Developments
Security measures include canine explosive detection teams and, in January 2007, a contract was awarded to the Cernium Corporation and Electro Speciality Systems for the installation of Perceptrak real-time video analysis system. The latter examines behaviours and alerts if unique conditions occur.

Fleet: 134 (LRV)
Siemens/Duewag U2 (1980/90)	M71
Siemens/Duewag SD100 (1993/95)	M52
Siemens S70 70 per cent low-floor (2004)	M11
In peak service: 93

Service: Peak 7½ min, off-peak 15 min, evenings 30 min
First/last car: 04.04/02.11
Fare structure: Floating zone, monthly and multiride passes
Revenue collection: Vending machines at all stations
Fare evasion control: Spot checks by roving inspectors
Integration with other modes: Monthly pass valid on buses; free and upgrade transfers to bus; bus connection from San Ysidro to downtown Tijuana, Mexico (see Tijuana entry); 5,803 parking spaces at 23 stations
Operating costs financed by: Fares 59.3 per cent, subsidy/grants 40.7 per cent

Coaster commuter train at Oceanside on the San Diego-Oceanside line, San Diego (Julian Wolinsky)   0126894

North San Diego County Transit Development Board – North County Transit District (NCTD)

810 Mission Avenue, Oceanside, California 92054, US
Tel: (+1 760) 967 28 27
Fax: (+1 760) 772 09 40
e-mail: lfernandes@nctd.org
Web: www.gonctd.com

Key personnel
Executive Director: Karen King
Director, Rail Services: Thomas Lichterman
Manager, Commuter Rail Services:
   Lane Fernandes
Manager, Maintenance-of-Way: Richard Walker
Manager, Light Rail Services: Walt Stringer
Rail Safety Officer: Wayne Penn
Manager, Bus Services: Kim Stone
   Staff: 600

Passenger boardings: (2002) 11.9 million
(2003) 11.7 million
(2004) 11.8 million

Current situation
Established in 1976, NCTD operates fixed-route bus services, paratransit and demand-response services in northern San Diego County, including routes into downtown San Diego.

It also operates the Coaster commuter rail service inaugurated in 1995 over the Amtrak route between Oceanside and San Diego, for which NCTD purchased the right-of-way. Coaster monthly tickets are valid on NCTD buses as well as connecting San Diego buses and Trolley.

Passengers alighting from North County Transit District buses in San Diego (Julian Wolinsky)   0126893

Construction of a 35 km (22 mile) rail line (SPRINTER) linking Oceanside and Escondido, using existing right-of-way started in 2004. The route will be operated by 12 Siemens Desiro two-car diesel-powered vehicles.

Bus
Number of routes: 53 (including 3 routes which connect to the Coaster commuter rail service)

Fleet: 174 vehicles
Flxible ADB	72
New Flyer (1997)	16
New Flyer (2000)	53
New Flyer (2003)	10
Thomas (2003)	13
Vans	10
In peak service: 149

Commuter rail
Route length: 67.2 km
Number of stations: 8

Passenger journeys: (2002) 1.3 million
(2003) 1.35 million
(2004) 1.43 million

Background
NCTD began its Coaster commuter rail operations in 1995.

Current situation
The service is operated under the name of San Diego Northern Railway. Runs 22 one-way weekday journeys and eight on Sundays, between Oceanside and San Diego. Operation and maintenance is contracted to Amtrak.

For further information, please see *Jane's World Railways*.

Developments
In July 2004, NCTD awarded West Rail Constructors a contract for the construction of the SPRINTER rail system. The line is 35 km (22 miles) in length, with 15 stations. The route is operated by 12 Siemens Desiro two-car dmus.

Rolling stock: 7 diesel locomotives, 28 Bombardier bilevel push-pull trailer coaches or cab-control coaches
Integration with other modes: All stations have bus connections

---

San Francisco Bay Area

Population: Metropolitan area: 6.9 million (2006 estimate)

Public transport

The San Francisco Bay region embraces nine counties – Alameda, Contra Costa, Marin, Napa, San Francisco, San Mateo, Santa Clara, Solano and Sonoma, and nearly 100 cities and towns, including San Francisco, San José and Oakland. There are 11 primary public transport systems and many other local operators providing services. In addition there are numerous special services for elderly and disabled people. Planning, performance monitoring and administration of certain funds is the responsibility of the Metropolitan Transportation Commission.

Information for the entire Bay Area may be found at http://transit.511.org.

Metropolitan Transport Commission (MTC)

101 Eighth Street, Oakland, California 94607-4700, USA
Tel: (+1 510) 817 57 00 Fax: (+1 510) 817 58 48
e-mail: info@mtc.ca.gov
Web: www.mtc.ca.gov

Key personnel

Chair: Bill Dodd
Vice-Chair: Scott Haggerty
Executive Director: Steve Heminger
Deputy Executive Director, Operations:
  Ann Flemer
Deputy Executive Director, Policy:
  Therese McMillan
Deputy Executive Director, Bay Area Toll Authority:
  Andrew Fremier

Chief Financial Officer: Brian Mayhew
Director, Legislation and Public Affairs:
  Randy Rentschler
Director, Planning: Doug Kimsey
  Staff: 170 (approximate)

Passenger journeys: (Bay Area – all operators)
(2002/03) 474.0 million
(2003/04) 472.7 million
(2004/05) 474.5 million
(2005/06) 480.8 million
(2006/07) 486.5 million

Current situation

The MTC was created in 1970 to provide transport planning for the nine-county region known as the Bay Area, which encompasses more than 100 municipalities and serves a population of some 7 million. It has been assigned responsibility for administering several sources of transit funding, including monies from the Transportation Development Act and FTA. In addition, the Commission has become responsible for overseeing the efficiency and effectiveness of transit operators in the region. MTC monitors their budgets, conducts performance audits and sets capital investment priorities for both public transport and highways in the Bay Area.

MTC's role has expanded beyond regional planning, programming and monitoring to include technical assistance and technology applications designed to make the Bay Area transportation system operate more efficiently. MTC addresses the problems of growth, traffic congestion and air pollution. Guidelines produced by MTC are helping counties to prepare congestion-management programmes that evaluate the impact of new land development on the transport network.

MTC is co-ordinating development of the TransLink stored-fare ticket intended as an area-wide all-modes pass. TransLink is now available for use on all AC Transit, Golden Gate Transit and Ferry and Dumbarton routes. BART, San Francisco MUNI and Caltrain were scheduled to begin accepting TransLink in 2008, SamTrans, Santa Clara VTA and 19 other Bay Area transit agencies by 2010. MTC has also inaugurated a commuter journey subsidy programme in which employers buy vouchers for their staff to use in part payment for transit passes.

The MTC is given policy direction by a 19-member panel, 14 of whom are appointed directly by local elected officials. Two members represent regional agencies: the Association of Bay Area Governments and the Bay Conservation & Development Commission. In addition, three non-voting members have been appointed to represent federal and state transport agencies and the federal housing department.

Developments

In February 2005, MTC adopted the Transportation 2030 long-term transportation plan.

Grant programmes for transportation in the Bay Area include the Transportation for Livable Communities (TLC) Program, which provides planning and capital grants for small-scale transportation projects that enhance community vitality and promote walking, bicycling and public transit use, the Low Income Flexible Transportation (LIFT) Program, which funds new or expanded services for getting low-income residents to and from work, school and other essential destinations and the State Transportation Improvement Program (STIP).

Expanded information for the area may be found on a county-by-county basis in the Systems section of *Jane's Urban Transport Systems*.

San Francisco

Population: City: 739,426 (2005 estimate)

Public transport

Bus, trolleybus, cable car and tramway/light rail services provided for city area by municipal undertaking; regional metro service by Bay Area Rapid Transit District (BART) within and between San Francisco, San Mateo, Alameda and Contra Costa counties. Suburban rail service links San Jose and San Francisco serving Santa Clara and San Mateo counties. Ferry and bus services offered on several cross-bay routes by various operators.

San Francisco Municipal Railway (Muni)

Public Relation/Communications Department, 1 South Van Ness Avenue, Floor 3, San Francisco, California 94103-1267, US
Tel: (+1 415) 934 39 00
Tel: (+1 415) 701 42 00 (Public Relations/ Communications)
Fax: (+1 415) 934 39 05
Fax: (+1 415) 701 43 91 (Public Relations/ Communications)
Web: www.sfmuni.com

Key personnel

Executive Director/Chief Executive Officer:
  Nathaniel P Ford
Chief of Staff/Director of Administration:
  Debra A Johnson
Chief Financial Officer/Director of Finance and Information Technology: Sonali Bose
Chief Operating Officer/Director of Muni Operations:
  Kenneth McDonald
Senior Director of Transportation Planning & Development: Carter R Rohan
Community and Media Relations Officer: Maggie Lynch
Staff: 3,441

Other offices
Services Departments, 949 Presidio Avenue, San Francisco, California 94115, US

Passenger boardings: (All modes)
(FY2003) 215.6 million
(FY2004) 215.7 million

Current situation

Muni bacame a department of the San Francisco Municipal Transportation Agency (SFMTA) in March 2000. It operates bus, trolleybus and cable car services, the Muni Metro tramway/light rail network, and the F-Market historic tramway.

Muni's service area covers some 122 km² (47 sq miles) and a population in excess of 745,000.

Developments

The ground breaking ceremony for the new Third Street light rail line took place in May 2002. The project will extend the Muni Metro service from the Caltrain Depot at Fourth and King Streets, linking Bayshore Street Boulevard and the Mission Bay development, south of Market, Downtown, Union Square and Chinatown.

Phase two, the Central Subway Project, will continue the new T-Line service from Fourth and King Street to Chinatown. In June 2005,

One of Muni's ETI 14TrSF trolleybuses descending a very steep section (approximately 20 per cent) on Castro Street, southbound on Route 24 (Steve Morgan)
0585134

the San Francisco Municipal Transportation Agency (SFMTA) adopted a 2.7-km (1.7-mile) Fourth/Stockton alignment with three underground stations as the Locally Preferred Alternative (LPA). Subsequently, in February 2008, the SFMTA adopted a modified LPA option that adds a surface station at Fourth and Brannan Streets, and extends the tunnels to North Beach. Construction is currently expected to start in 2010 and operation is expected to start in 2016.

In mid-2008, the SFMTA was awarded more than USD7 million to improve security and public safety on the Muni system.

In september 2008, the Muni Metro East (MME) facility was opened.

Operating costs financed by: Fares 32.6 per cent, other commercial sources 1.1 per cent, subsidy/grants 66.3 per cent

Subsidy from: City General Fund 12.7 per cent, city parking revenues 27.4 per cent, other city revenue transfers 4.3 per cent, federal/state/regional revenues 19.6 per cent, state and local paratransit revenues 2.3 per cent

Bus and trolleybus
Staff: Bus 1,269, trolleybus 736

Passenger journeys: (FY2003) Bus 90.9 million, trolleybus 74.4 million
(FY2004) Bus 87.5 million, trolleybus 75.2 million
Vehicle-km: Not currently available

Number of routes: Bus 52, trolleybus 17
Route length: Bus 625 km, trolleybus 158 km

Fleet: 538

New Flyer (1988/89)	106
Orion 30 ft (1990)	44
New Flyer D60 articulated (1991)	12
NABI 40 ft (1999)	45
Neoplan AN440 (2000/03)	206
Neoplan AN460 articulated (2001/03)	125

On order: 86 Orion VII diesel-electric hybrid buses, delivery from late 2006
In peak service: 356

Fleet: 333 trolleybuses

New Flyer articulated (1992/94) (many stored)	60
ETI (Skoda/AAI) 14TrSF 40 ft (2001/3)	240
ETI (Skoda/AAI) 15TrSF 60 ft articulated (2003)	33

On order: None
In peak service: Approximately 240

Trolleybus electrification: 600 V DC

One-person operation: All routes
Fare collection: Coin or note to farebox on board. Prepurchase monthly passes sold by over 200 vendors
Fare structure: Flat, monthly passes. Free 1½ hour transfers valid for two uses in any direction

Current situation
In 1997, an order was placed with Electric Transit Inc (a Skoda/AAI partnership) for 220 two-axle and 30 articulated trolleybuses, of standard floor height and with wheelchair lifts, and in 1999 Muni exercised contract options to add a further 20 two-axle and three articulated vehicles to the order.

Two 12.2 m (40 ft) prototypes arrived in 1999 for evaluation, and the first production two-axle vehicles entered service in mid-2001.

A study of several existing bus routes for possible conversion to trolleybus was undertaken in 2002.

Developments
In September 2004, the Municipal Transportation Agency (MTA) Board of Directors approved a Request for Proposals (RFP) from bus manufacturers for the acquisition of a fleet of diesel-electric hybrid buses for the Municipal Railway (Muni). Muni will be the first California transit agency to buy buses with the latest hybrid bus technology. Muni's Zero Emissions 2020 Plan, presented to the MTA board earlier in 2004, calls for Muni to establish an all-electric drive fleet that includes hybrid buses,

Muni ETI/Škoda trolleybus (Bill Luke)   1115116

battery buses and fuel-cell buses by 2020. The acquisition of the diesel-electric hybrid buses is in accordance with the plan, and will allow the removal of the oldest diesel buses from Muni's fleet.

The RFP will be for 56, 40 ft hybrid buses with an option for 56 more. In addition, an option for 40, 30 ft hybrid buses may be included, depending upon the results of investigations of the latest advances in hybrid-bus technology. The vehicles will be low-floor buses and will meet all of the accessibility specifications under the Americans with Disabilities Act (ADA) of 1990. The new buses are intended to replace the 1988 and 1989 New Flyer 40 ft buses and the 1990 Orion 30 ft buses that are now in Muni's fleet. The prototype vehicle began operating in 2006, with actual vehicle delivery from the second half of 2006 through early 2007.

In late 2006, Muni exercised options to purchase a further 30 Orion VII 30-ft hybrid buses, bringing the total to 86 units.

Muni has retrofitted 424 diesel buses with diesel exhaust filters.

As part of the ongoing refurbishment of the trolley Overhead Contact System (OCS), work is under way to replace existing poles and overhead wires on Lines 6 and 7.

After nearly 32 years of service, the last of the 1976/77 Flyer E800 trolleybuses were withdrawn in 2007. They were non-wheelchair-accessible, and their withdrawal means that, with the exception of the historic cable-car fleet and a few historic trams used only on a limited basis, Muni's fleet is now fully accessible.

Upon opening in April 2007, new light rail line T replaced bus route 15. New trolleybus route 20 (Columbus) was introduced in July 2007, using existing wiring.

Tramway/light rail ('Metro')
Staff: 627

Type of operation: Conventional tramway upgraded to light rail standards, 10 km city-centre tunnel with high-platform stations

Passenger journeys: (FY2003) 42.9 million
(FY2004) 45.2 million
Car-km: Not currently available

Route length: 50.2 km
Number of lines: seven
Gauge: 1,435 mm
Electrification: 600 V DC, overhead

Service: 6-10 min
First/last car: 05.00/00.30
Fare structure: Flat, monthly passes, Muni 'Passport'
Fare collection: In tunnel section, fares collected in stations with barrier access to platforms; on surface sections, coin or note to farebox, also two proof-of-payment surface stations
Signalling: Seltrac moving block in Market Street tunnel

Rolling stock: 192 cars

Various historic cars (1895/1952)	M23
Boeing-Vertol SLRV (1979) – preserved/historic, not in service	M1
St Louis Car PCC ex-Philadelphia (1948)	M14
St Louis Car PCC double-ended 1948, rebuilt 1994)	M3
Breda (1996/2003)	M151

In peak service: n/a

Developments
Powered test runs on new route T-Line (Third Street) began in spring 2006. Limited, introductory service on the new route was scheduled to be launched in mid-January 2007, running at weekends only (and daytime only), while the start of full service started in April 2007.

Cable cars
Staff: 272

Type of operation: Cable-and-grip tramway, opened 1873

Passenger journeys: (FY2003) 7.4 million
(FY2004) 7.9 million

Current situation
Three-route, 1,067 mm gauge network totalling 8.5 km.

Rolling stock: 40 cars

Powell single-end	M28
California double-end	M12

Golden Gate Bridge, Highway and Transportation District (GGBHTD) (Golden Gate Transit and Ferry)
Headquarters, Box 9000, Presidio Station, San Francisco, California 94129-0601, US
Tel: (+1 415) 921 58 58   Fax: (+1 415) 923 23 67
Web: www.goldengate.org

Key personnel
President, Board of Directors: John J Moylan
General Manager: Celia Kupersmith
Public Affairs Director: Mary C Currie
Tel: (+1 415) 923 22 22
Fax: (+1 415) 771 57 43
e-mail: mcurrie@goldengate.org
Staff: 836 (2008)

Passenger boardings: (Bus and ferry)
(2003/04) 9.6 million
(2004/05) 9.3 million
(2005/06) 9.3 million
(2006/07) 9.23 million
(2007/08) 9.35 million

Current situation
The Golden Gate Bridge, Highway and Transportation District (GGBHTD) provides

services for a population of 1.4 million in San Francisco, Marin and Sonoma counties, through Bus, Ferry and Bridge operating divisions. A 19-member board of directors is appointed by six constituent counties.

Surplus bridge tolls are used to subsidise public bus and ferry services between San Francisco and North Bay counties, but the GGBHTD is prohibited from using any toll revenues to subsidise local routes within Marin (see below). Commuter carpools of three or more people are encouraged with toll-free passage of the Golden Gate Bridge during peak hours on weekdays.

Bus
Golden Gate Bridge, Highway and Transportation District – Bus Transit Division

1011 Andersen Drive, San Rafael, California 94901-5381, US
Tel: (+1 415) 457 31 10   Fax: (+1 415) 257 44 11
Web: www.goldengate.org

Key personnel
Deputy General Manager, Bus Division:
  Teri Wheeldon Mantony
  Staff: 393

Passenger boardings: (2003/04) 7.94 million
(2004/05) 7.55 million
(2005/06) 7.43 million
(2006/07) 7.21 million
(2007/08) 7.37 million
Vehicle-km: (2003/04) 11.1 million
(2004/05) 9.55 million
(2005/06) 9.44 million
(2006/07) 9.54 million
(2007/08) 9.50 million

Number of routes: 52
Route length: (One way) 747 km

Fleet: 239 vehicles (40 not active)
Complete breakdown is not currently available, but includes:

TMC RTS T80 (1989/91)	27
MCI commuter bus (1996/ 97/ 99/2003)	52
Nova Bus (1997)	10
Nova Bus (2000)	14
Nova Bus (2001)	4
Orion (2003)	80
New Flyer articulated (1990)	8

In peak service: Not currently available

Most intensive service: 6 min
One-person operation: All routes
Fare collection: GFI farebox on bus; TransLink smartcard
Fare structure: Zonal
Fare evasion control: Zone identification checks by driver
Integration with other modes: Buses link with many BART/Muni services; 28 park-and-ride lots with 3,823 spaces; cycle racks at 45 stops; direct service to intercity rail (Amtrak)
Average distance between stops: 400 m
Average peak-hour speed: 32–40 km/h; on freeways, up to 88 km/h
Arrangements for elderly/disabled: All buses wheelchair-accessible
Bus priority: 46 km bus/carpool with-flow lane in peak periods
Operating costs financed by: Fares 29 per cent, bridge tolls 41 per cent, subsidy/grants 30 per cent, other 3 per cent
Subsidy from: State and local Transportation Development Act funds
New vehicles financed by: FTA grants 80 per cent, local 20 per cent

Current situation
Basic services operate all day every day, with express commute service operated on weekdays in the peak direction only, and some local bus routes run under contract in Marin County. Private operators under contract operate six subscription-type 'Club Buses' during commuting periods to serve markets not catered for by scheduled buses.

Computerised scheduling for fixed-route bus services was introduced 1997/98 and was fully functional during 1998/99. All buses have bike racks that can carry at least two bicycles.

Ferry
Golden Gate Bridge, Highway and Transportation District – Ferry Division

101 East Sir Francis Drake Boulevard, Larkspur, California 94939-1899, US
Tel: (+1 415) 925 55 70   Fax: (+1 415) 925 55 10

Key personnel
Deputy General Manager, Ferry Division:
  James Swindler
  Staff: 78

Passenger boardings: (2003/04) 1.66 million
(2004/05) 1.75 million
(2005/06) 1.87 million
(2006/07) 2.02 million
(2007/08) 1.98 million

Current situation
Operates two high-speed ferries (30 minute crossing) and three 715-passenger Spaulding vessels (45 minute crossing) for service between San Francisco and Larkspur, and one Spaulding vessel for the 30 minute journey between San Francisco and Sausalito; total route 27 km.

For further information, please see *Jane's High-Speed Marine Transportation*.

San Francisco Bay Area Rapid Transit District (BART)

PO Box 12688, 300 Lakeside Drive, Oakland, California 94612, US
Tel: (+1 510) 464 60 00   Fax: (+1 510) 464 71 03
Web: www.bart.gov

Key personnel
Board President: Gail Murray
General Manager: Dorothy W Dugger
Deputy General Manager: Vacant
Deputy General Manager, Operations:
  Paul Overseir
Executive Manager, External Affairs:
  Ms Katherine Strehl
Department Manager, Media and Public Affairs:
  Linton Johnson
  Staff: 3,200

Type of operation: Full metro, first line opened 1972

Passenger journeys: (2003/04) 91 million
(2004/05) 92.75 million

Route length: 167 km
in tunnel: 42 km
elevated: 38.4 km
Number of lines: 5
Number of stations: 43
Gauge: 1,676 mm
Track: Concrete sleepers on resilient pads
Max gradient: 4%
Minimum curve radius: 120 m
Tunnel: Transbay tube: twin-section submerged caisson of steel and concrete designed for high resistance to seismic disturbances
Electrification: 1 kV DC, third rail

Developments
In mid-2006, it was announced that BART would receive USD2.9 million in federal security funding. A newly graduated canine explosives detection team was allocated to BART.

Earthquake Safety Project
Tel: (+1 510) 464 75 95

Developments
Bay Area Rapid Transit (BART) has begun a USD1.3 billion Earthquake Safety Program to strengthen stations, elevated tracks and the Transbay Tube. The environmental analysis of the Transbay Tube and related work has been completed, design of the retrofits is in progress

and numerous design and construction-related contracts have been awarded. Construction is expected to last until 2017.

Oakland Airport Connector Project
Key personnel
Contact: Jean E Hamilton
Tel: (+1 510) 464 64 41

Current situation
In March 2002 the BART board of directors approved the BART link to Oakland international airport. The link will be 5 km (3.2 miles) long, running from the BART Coliseum station to the airport, with a new station at the airport and two stations along the elevated Automated Guideway Transit (AGT) system.

Warm Springs Extension (WSX)
Tel: (+1 510) 476 39 00

Current situation
BART is currently in the preliminary engineering phase for construction of a 8.7 km (5.4 mile) planned extension from Fremont station to Warm Springs.

In mid-2003, the Supplemental Environmental Impact Report (SEIR) was completed and in October of that year the BART board approved WSX for construction.

Developments
The Record of Decision for the extension was issued in October 2006, certifying that the project has satisfied all requirements for National Environmental Protection Act (NEPA) and is eligible for Federal funding. BART is proceeding with advance right-of-way acquisition, technical site surveys and pre-construction utility co-ordination and permitting in preparation for the project.

West Dublin/Pleasanton Infill Station Project
Developments
BART has broken ground on the West Dublin/Pleasanton infill station project. This mixed-use development between Castro Valley and Dublin/Pleasanton Stations is projected to open in 2009–2010.

Rolling stock: 669 cars

Rohr A cab (1970–72)	M166
Rohr B (1970–72)	M273
Alsthom C (1988/90)	M150
Amerail C2 (1994/95)	M80

On order: None

Service: Peak 2½–5 min, off-peak 5–15–20 min
First/last train: 04.00/00.34
Fare structure: Graduated; BART-Plus passes include unlimited travel on other modes
Integration with other modes: Feeder buses co-ordinated with other Bay Area public transport operators
Operating costs financed by: Fares 62 per cent
Revenue collection: All fare vending machines and gates systemwide have been replaced with Cubic Corp equipment. Entry gate records time, date and station and returns ticket. Exit gate computes required fare, accepts exact-fare ticket, instructs if additional payment is needed, or deducts proper amount from multiride ticket. Credit-card-size tickets, magnetically encoded with up to USD48 of fares
One-person operation: All trains

San Francisco International Airport

Marketing & Communications
PO Box 8097, San Francisco, CA-94128, US
Tel: (+1 650) 821 51 52
Web: www.flysfo.com

Key personnel
Director, Bureau of Community Affairs:
  Michael C McCarron

AirTrain

Type of system: Automated People Mover (APM)
Operation and maintenance: Bombardier Transportation

Passenger journeys: Not currently available
Train-km: Not currently available

Number of lines: 2
Number of stations: 9
Route length: 10 km (all elevated)

Current situation

A new CX-100 people mover system was launched at San Francisco International Airport in March 2003, which connects the new international terminal with the existing terminals, parking garages and rental car centre and to the Bay Area Rapid Transit (BART) station. The automated system was the first to feature Flexiblok communications-based automatic train control technology, now known as *CITYFLO 650*. The automated system serves nine passenger stations at the airport with a fleet of 38 CX-100 vehicles operating on 10 km of elevated guideway. The fleet is fully accessible and currently operates as two-car trains on the Red Line and as three-car trains on the Blue Line.

The company is responsible for operating and maintaining the system for three years, with three additional one-year options.

Fleet: 19 two-car trains, in two- and three-car trains
Bombardier CX-100   38

Service: 2$^{1}/_{2}$ minutes, 24-hours a day
Fare structure: Free
Arrangements for elderly/disabled: Fleet is fully accessible
Integration with other modes: Transfer to Bay Area Rapid Transit at Airport BART Station, transfer to CalTrain at Millbrae Station via BART

San Mateo

San Francisco Bay Area – San Mateo

Public transport

Main bus operations by SamTrans, which also administers the Caltrain commuter rail service operated under contract, supplemented by bus, metro and light rail services of Muni, BART, Santa Clara Valley Transportation Authority and Dumbarton Express.

San Mateo County Transit District (SamTrans)

PO Box 3006 San Carlos, CA 94070-1306, US
Tel: (+1 650) 508 62 00   Fax: (+1 650) 508 79 19
Web: www.samtrans.com

Street address
1250 San Carlos Avenue, PO Box 3006, San Carlos, California 94070-1306, US

Key personnel
Chair: Adrienne Tissier
General Manager and Chief Executive Officer:
  Michael J Scanlon
  Staff: 756

Current situation

SamTrans, which is a special transit district, serves San Mateo County, including the southern suburban areas of San Francisco and neighbouring areas, with a service population of 578,688 (2000 Census) over an area of 1,155.14 km² (446 sq miles). Some of the corridor service between Palo Alto and San Francisco city centre is operated under contract by MV Transportation Inc. The 'Redi-Wheels' door-to-door service for people with disabilities is also run under contract by MV Transportation Inc, with most vehicles supplied

by SamTrans. Other services which are contracted out are the Coastside Paratransit service, one Coastside fixed route and the employer shuttles to/from BART and Caltrain stations.

Developments

In 2007, service was extended on Coastside Routes 14 and 110, as part of a grant-funded pilot programme.

Existing fareboxes are being replaced with new computerised fareboxes which will allow the issue of day passes. In partnership with an advertising company (CBS Outdoor), shelters are also being upgraded, which will include installation of solar lighting. The advertising company is responsible for all costs. SamTrans plans to replace more than 100 buses in the next 18 months.

Bus

Passenger boardings: (2003/04) 15.2 million
(2006/07) 15.2 million
(2007/08) Not yet available
Vehicle-km: (2003/04) 16.8 million
(2006/07) 10.2 million
(2007/08) Not yet available

Number of routes: 54
Route length: (One-way) 1,708 km (estimate)
Number of stops: 2,526 (2007/08)

Fleet: 330 vehicles (plus 84 paratransit vehicles)
Full breakdown of fleet is not currently available, but comsprises:
Standard buses   212
Low-floor buses   60
Articulated buses   55
Cutaway buses   3
In peak service: 260
Average age of fleet: 8.4 years (2006/07)

Most intensive service: Peak 10 min
One-person operation: All routes
Fare collection: Prepurchase monthly pass, tokens or exact fare to cashbox
Fare structure: Flat; distance-based express supplement
Fares collected on board: 75 per cent
Fare evasion control: Driver supervision
Operational control: Fleet management control dispatchers using automated vehicle location systems (GPS-based) and schedule performance monitoring; route inspectors/mobile radio, with route checks
Arrangements for elderly/disabled: Door-to-door (kerb-to-kerb on request) Redi-Wheels service, operated under contract by MV Transportation Inc with 84 vehicles provided by SamTrans, carried 317,359 passengers in 2006/07; lifeline fare assistance programme; all fixed routes use lift-equipped or ramp-equipped buses; reduced fare for senior/disabled/Medicare Cardholder passengers.
Integration with other modes: Services and passes integrated with other operators including BART, Caltrain, Santa Clara Valley Transportation Authority, Dumbarton Express, Golden Gate Transit and San Francisco Muni
Operating costs financed by: Fares 18.1 per cent, other commercial sources 7.8 per cent, local/state/federal subsidy/grants 37.0 per cent, sales tax 37.1 per cent
New vehicles financed by: Local matching of FTA grants

Caltrain

PO Box 3006 San Carlos, CA 94070-1306, US
Tel: (+1 650) 508 62 00
Fax: (+1 650) 508 79 19
Web: www.caltrain.com

Street address
1250 San Carlos Avenue, PO Box 3006, San Carlos, California 94070-1306, US

Key personnel
Executive Director: Michael J Scanlon
Deputy Director, Rail Transportation:
  Michelle Bouchard

Manager of Equipment: Steve Coleman
Director of Maintenance: David Olmeda
  Staff: Not currently available

Type of operation: Suburban heavy rail

Passenger journeys: (2004/05) 9.45 million
(2005/06) 10.15 million
(2006/07) 10.98 million
(2007/08) 11.9 million
Train-km: Not currently available

Route length: 123.9 km (77 miles) (mainline 78.8 km (49 miles), entire line, which includes extended commuter-hour service 123.9 km (77 miles)
Number of stations: 31 (plus one stations, Stanford, for sports stadium services only)
Operating costs financed by: Fares 30.4 per cent, other commercial sources 8.4 per cent, subsidy/grants 61.2 per cent

Current situation

Service provided over 123 km route with 31 stations from Gilroy and San Jose to San Francisco. The Peninsula Corridor Joint Powers Board of San Mateo, San Francisco and Santa Clara counties took over the line in 1992, and operations have been contracted to Amtrak since that time. The current three-year contract with Amtrak, which includes two one-year options, runs until June 2009.

Weekday service comprises 98 San Francisco–San Jose return trains, including 22 'Baby Bullet' express services. Three trains in each direction are extended to serve Gilroy beyond San Jose. Under a 10-year plan, service levels are to rise to over 100 trains a day on the main line.

Local bus routes serve most stations, including 32 shuttle routes operated under contract, that connect stations to local businesses and downtown city areas.

For further information on Caltrain, please see *Jane's World Railways*.

Developments

In June 2003, a new intermodal station was opened in Millbrae to connect Caltrain rail services, BART rail services, SamTrans buses and shuttle bus service. The Millbrae Intermodal Station provides the opportunity for riders coming from the farthest reaches of the BART system to access Caltrain – and vice versa – through an easy cross-platform transfer.

Work to improve the track and signalling system at the north terminal (San Francisco) was completed by the end of 2007. The Burlingame station was recently upgraded to improve safety and accessibility, as well as aesthetics. The Palo Alto and California Avenue stations are currently being renovated, with construction scheduled to be completed by early 2009. Soon after, renovation work will begin on the Santa Clara and South San Francisco stations.

The new USD140 million Centralized Equipment Maintenance and Operations Facility (CEMOF) opened in September 2007 in San Jose.

Rolling stock

The fleet comprises 20 3,200 hp (2,385 kW) F40PH-2CAT locomotives from GM-EMD, three F40PH-2C locomotives from Boise Locomotive and six MP36PH-3C machines from the latter's successor, MotivePower. The last-mentioned were acquired in 2003 to provide power for 'Baby Bullet' limited stop services. Coaching stock consists of 73 double-deck gallery coaches from Nippon Sharyo, 20 from Sumitomo and 17 from Bombardier. A mid-life overhaul programme of the original coaches has been carried out by ALSTOM Transport Canada. ALSTOM also has a contract covering routine overhaul of the passenger coach fleet.

Rolling stock: 110 bilevel cars, 29 diesel locomotives
Locomotives
Sumitomo/GMC (1985) (rebuilt 199/2000)   20
Boise (1998)   3
Motive Power (2003)   6

Bilevel cars

Nippon Sharyo	73
Sumitomo cab (2000)	20
Bombardier (2002)	17

On order: 8 new Bombardier coaches, including two cab cars, delivery scheduled to commence in August 2008

Fare collection: Tickets must be purchased before boarding train
Fare structure: Zonal; Single and ten-ride tickets, day and monthly passes, zone upgrade tickets valid for four hours (one-way); reduced fare for those 17 years and younger; some free fares for children four years and younger
Fare evasion control: Random inspection
Arrangements for elderly/disabled: 25 stations are accessible; discounted fares for seniors, those with disabilities and Medicare cardholders

Alameda/Contra Costa County

San Francisco Bay Area
Public transport
Bus services operated for Oakland and 12 other cities (and adjacent unincorporated areas) in Alameda and Contra Costa counties by transit authority governed by publicly elected board, and by other local operators. Alameda city and area also served by BART metro. Contra Costa County is served by local operators and routes of AC Transit, BART and BART Express.

Alameda-Contra Costa Transit District (AC Transit)
1600 Franklin Street, Oakland, California 94612, USA
Tel: (+1 510) 891 47 77
Fax: (+1 510) 891 71 57
e-mail: customerservice@actransit.org
Web: www.actransit.org

Key personnel
General Manager: Richard C Fernandez
Deputy General Manager: Jim Gleich
Chief Financial Officer: Frank Haywood (Acting)
Deputy General Manager, Planning and Service Development: Nancy Skowbo
Chief Technology Officer: Blake Pelletier
Chief Maintenance Officer: Joe DeProspero
Chief Transportation Officer: Kathleen Kelly
Director of Human Resources: Kurt DeStigter
Assistant General Manager, Communications and External Affairs: Mary King
Media Affairs Manager: Clarence Johnson
General Council: Ken Scheidig
    Staff: 2,272 (includes bus operators)

Current situation
AC Transit was established in 1955 and began operations in 1960 as California's first public transit district. AC Transit provides fixed route and paratransit services to an area of 943 km² (364 sq m) and a population of some 1.5 million. Today, nearly 10 per cent of AC Transit riders use Transbay routes connecting the East Bay neighbourhoods with San Francisco via the Bay Bridge. Some 90 per cent use local routes covering the entire East Bay area, providing connections with BART metro, Amtrak and the ferry services reintroduced on San Francisco Bay following the 1989 earthquake.

Developments
AC Transit's first Rapid Bus (Bus Rapid Transit (BRT)) programme started in 2003, running along San Pablo Avenue. Ridership increased by 66 per cent above the level of the previous 'skip-stop' service. The system uses low-floor European-style coaches (manufactured by Van Hool) and high-tech operational and traffic management systems. Vehicles and bus stops are specially painted, so as to be easily identifiable.

A second Rapid Bus service has been implemented along a 27 km (17 mile) corridor connecting Berkeley to downtown San Leandro.

AC Transit has installed exhaust after-treatment traps to its fleet of nearly 700 buses, to reduce emissions and particulates. AC Transit is also working with Chevron and Cummins to develop standards for refining bio-diesel and gas to liquid.

Development is under way for a further BRT, to link the cities of Berkeley, Oakland and San Leandro. The 30.5 km (19 mile) 'Rapid' route is designed to serve 40,000 to 50,000 passengers daily, and is scheduled to commence in 2010.

In 2006, three zero-emission fuel cell buses were added to the fleet, as part of AC Transit's HyRoad Hydrogen Fuel Cell Program. Other projects under development are: construction of a prototype petrol/electric hybrid bus; design and construction of two additional hydrogen energy stations, one of which will be solar powered; participation in a regional zero-emission programme of up to 12 fuel cell buses and installation of solar power generators at two of its operating divisions.

The TransLink smartcard system has been implemented.

Bus
Passenger boardings: (2006/07) 67 million
Vehicle-km: Not currently available

Number of routes: 105
Route length: (One way) 2,096 km
Number of stops: 6,500 (approximate)

Fleet: 674 vehicles	
60 ft (18.3 m) articulated bus	112
45 ft (13.7 m) commuter coaches	78
40 ft (12.9 m) standard buses	342
30 ft (9.1 m) feeder buses	101
Paratransit vehicles	41

Average age of fleet: 5 years
In peak service: 579

Most intensive service: 4–12 min
One-person operation: All routes
Fare collection: Pre-purchase passes, tickets and cash to electronic fareboxes
Fare structure: Flat local, 25 cent transfer; higher fare for Transbay service with free transfer to local; 31-day passes and 10-coupon ticket books; supplementary stamp available for transfer to Muni services; special fares available to employee groups, schools and residential complexes
Integration with other modes: Extensive co-ordination with BART metro, and co-operation with eight other public and private bus systems; routes serve 21 BART stations, 6 Amtrak stations and 3 ferry terminals
Bus priority: High-occupancy vehicle lane on Freeway I-80 from West Contra Costa to Bay Bridge to San Francisco, on Freeway I-880 in Southern Alameda County and at Bay Bridge approaches
Operational control: Route inspectors/mobile voice and digital radio
Arrangements for elderly/disabled: All routes served by fully accessible buses with kneeling capability; reduced fare; paratransit services carried some 656,000 passengers in 2005/06.
Average distance between stops: 400–800 m
Average peak-hour speed: In mixed traffic, 22 km/h; on freeway, 66 km/h
Operating costs financed by: Fares 16 per cent, other revenue 17 per cent (interest and service contracts), subsidy/grants 4 per cent, tax levy 63 per cent (Fiscal year 2008/09).

Livermore Amador Valley Transit Authority (LAVTA) – Wheels
1362 Rutan Court, Suite 100, Livermore, California 94551, US
Tel: (+1 925) 455 75 55
Fax: (+1 925) 443 13 75
e-mail: info@lavta.org
Web: www.wheelsbus.com

Key personnel
Chair: Steve Brozosky
Vice-Chair: Janet Lockhart
General Manager: Barbara Duffy
Director of Marketing and Public Affairs: Rosemary Booth

Passenger boardings: (2004/05) 1.94 million
Vehicle-km: (2004/05) 2.9 million (1.8 million miles)

Number of routes: 2 (estimate)
Route length: 147 km (estimate)

Background
Joint Powers government agency formed in 1986.

Current situation
Provides fixed-route service in and to the cities of Dublin, connecting with BART Express and Central Contra Costa Transit. Also DART/paratransit demand-responsive service for seniors and disabled in Dublin and Livermore. Operated under contract by ATC/Vancom.

New route network introduced in 1997, bringing more frequent service with better connections at BART metro stations. DART demand-response service has replaced timetabled services at mid-day off-peak times on 11 routes Monday to Friday, and all routes but one on Saturdays.

Reduced fares for seniors and disabled, 10-ride tickets, SuperSaver and Monthly Passes.

Developments
In April 2004, Wheels launched a new Automated vehicle Location (AVL) System.

LAVTA is in the process of investigating the implementation of a Bus Rapid Transit route.

Fleet: 94 vehicles (76 fixed-route, 18 paratransit)	
Gillig Phantom 35 ft	8
Gillig Phantom 40 ft	17
Gillig low-floor 40 ft (2003)	38
New Flyer D40LF low-floor 40 ft	12
GMC coach 35 ft	1
DART/Paratransit	
Ford/ElDorado coach 27 ft	18

Union City Transit
34009 Alvarado-Niles Road, Union City, California 94587, USA
Tel: (+1 510) 471 32 32   Fax: (+1 510) 475 73 18
e-mail: transit@ci.union-city.ca.us
Web: www.ci.union-city.ca.us/transit/uctransit.htm

Key personnel
Transit Manager: Wilson Lee
    Staff: 27

Passenger journeys: Not currently available

Current situation
City-owned system runs five routes connecting with BART's Union City station, operated under contract by MV Transportation. Fleet of 15 buses. Fares cover 15 per cent of operating costs.

Fare structure: Flat; monthly passes; transfer fees: 50 cents BART-to-Bus, 25 cents AC Transit/Dumbarton Express; discounts for senior citizens and those with certified disabilities
Arrangements for elderly/disabled: All Union City Transit buses are wheelchair accessible; however, some stops are not suitable for lift deployment
Integration with other modes: Routes are co-ordinated with BART trains, AC Transit and the Dumbarton Express to areas outside the city; main transfer points are at the Union City BART station and the Union Landing transit facility

Paratransit
Union City Paratransit 476-1500: Union City Paratransit is a service of Union City Transit and the City of Union City and provides services required under the Americans with Disabilities Act (ADA)

within the city limits. Services are partially funded by the Measure B sales tax of Alameda County.

Paratransit Plus: offers limited service to southern Hayward, and northern Fremont and Newark.

For rides outside of Union City, *East Bay Paratransit (EBP)*, sponsored by AC Transit and BART, is available.

Central Contra Costa Transit Authority (CCCTA) – County Connection

2477 Arnold Industrial Way, Concord, California 94520-5335, USA
Tel: (+1 925) 676 19 76   Fax: (+1 925) 687 73 06
e-mail: customerservice@cccta.org
Web: www.cccta.org

Key personnel
Chair: Rob Schroder
General Manager: Rick Ramacier
    Staff: 286

Transportation Center
220 Ygnacio Valley Road, Walnut Creek, California 94596, USA
Tel: (+1 925) 676 75 00

Passenger boardings: (2007) 4.5 million
Vehicle-km: Not currently available

Background
Established in 1980, CCCTA took over existing operations in Walnut Creek and Concord and has subsequently expanded throughout Contra Costa. The County Connection serves Clayton, Concord, Danville, Lafayette, Martinez, Morago, Orinda, Pleasant Hill, San Ramon, Walnut Creek and other areas of the central county. It serves an area of approximately 520 km² (200 sq miles) and a population of about 491,700.

CCCTA is overseen by a board of directors with 11 members.

Current situation
Many connections with other operators, and there is through-ticketing (TransLink) to BART trains.

There are free shuttles between BART's Walnut Creek station and downtown and between the central county park-and-ride facilities and the Pleasanton ACE train station.

County LINK, operated by Laidlaw Transit Services Inc, provides door-to-door service for elderly and disabled people. The current contract expires in January 2011.

The bus fleet is fully accessible.

Developments
In 2007, three vehicles began service for the Monument Community.

Bus
Number of routes: 27 (including 5 express commuter routes)

Route length: Not currently available

Fleet: 131 buses
Full breakdown of fleet is not currently available, but comprises:
30 ft, low-floor buses	25
35 ft, low-floor buses	13
40 ft, low-floor buses	34
40 ft suburban buses	59

In peak service: Not currently available

First/last bus: 05.00/23.00 (Mon-Fri); 06.00/19.00 (Sat-Sun)
Most intensive service: 10 min (peak); 40 min (off-peak)
Fare structure: Flat; 12-ride, commuter and monthly passes, reduced cost youth pass; express service single ticket; bus transfers free
Fare collection: Cash to driver
Arrangements for elderly/disabled: Reduced fare and 20-ride pass; free rides at certain times;

paratransit single ticket. Paratransit ridership 135,213 (2007)
Operational control: Radio; inspectors
Integration with other modes: 28 routes provide feeder services to one or more Contra Costa BART stations
Operating costs financed by: Fares 16.5 per cent, various subsidies/grants 83.5 per cent

San Francisco bay area
Alameda/Contra Costa County
Other operators
Alameda
Other operators in the county area include:
* West Berkeley Shuttle (formerly Berkeley Electric Shuttle Transit (BEST)) www. westberkeleyshuttle.com: Connections to BART. All shuttles are powered using Compressed Natural Gas (CNG).
* WestCAT (www.westcat.org) (Western Contra Costa Transit Authority, WCCTA): Local (11 routes), express (four routes) and regional service (one route) to the cities of Pinole and Hercules and the unincorporated communities of Montalvin Manor, Tara Hills, Bayview, Rodeo, Crockett, and Port Costa. In addition, WestCAT operates regional service between Martinez and the El Cerrito del Norte BART station and between the Hercules Transit Center and Contra Costa College. Also, in September 2005 WestCAT began offering transbay service between the Hercules Transit Center and the San Francisco Transbay Terminal. Passenger journeys of 1.26 million (2005/06), vehicle-km 3.1 million (1.9 million miles). Fleet of 50 vehicles provides services to a population of approximately 62,000 inhabitants.
* Altamont Commuter Express (ACE) (www. acerail.com): Please see entry under Santa Clara.
* Alameda Harbor Bay Ferry (www.harborbayferry. com): Ferry connections to San Francisco, with connections to other transit modes. Monthly passes and free transfers to AC Transit and MUNI.
* Alameda/Oakland Ferry (www.eastbayferry.com): Ferry services to San Francisco. Connections with AC Transit, MUNI, BART and Amtrak.

Contra Costa County
Other operators within the county area include: , Tri Delta Transit (www.trideltatransit.com) (Eastern Contra Costa Transit Authority, ECCTA): Local buses (14 routes Monday-Friday, two routes at the weekends), express commuter and paratransit services, covering the cities of Brentwood, Antioch, Oakley, Pittsburg and Bay Point. Connections with BART. Fleet of 56 fixed-route buses, 20 dial-a-ride buses (all buses are wheelchair accessible), 10 commuter buses, three trolley replicas. Ridership is approximately 2.5 million per year to a population of some 230,000 residents. Laidlaw Transit Inc operates the buses under contract.
County Connection (www.ccta.org) (Central Contra Costa Transit Authority, CCCTA): Fixed-route (22 routes plus five express commuter routes) and paratransit LINK services, 131 fixed-route buses (all equipped with wheelchair ramps or lifts). Provides service to the cities of Clayton, Concord, Lafayette, Martinez, Orinda, Pleasant Hill, San Ramon, Walnut Creek; the towns of Danville and Moraga; and the unincorporated areas of central Contra Costa County. Connections with BART and rail stations. Ridership is approximately 4.5 million per year to a population of some 491,000 residents.

Santa Clara

San Francisco Bay Area
Public transport
Bus services provided in San Jose-Santa Clara County urban areas by transit agency, with transit policy controlled by board comprising representatives from local cities. Light rail system; suburban rail service to San Francisco; bus routes of other local and county operators.

Santa Clara Valley Transportation Authority (VTA)
3331 North First Street, San Jose, California 95134-1927, USA
Tel: (+1 408) 321 55 55   Fax: (+1 408) 321 75 37
Web: www.vta.org

Key personnel
Chairperson: Liz Kniss
Vice-Chairperson: Dolly Sandoval
General Manager: Michael T Burns
Acting Chief Financial Officer: Joseph Smith
Chief Silicon Valley Rapid Transit Program Officer:
    Carolyn Gonot

Passenger boardings: (All modes)
(2006) 39.2 million

Current situation
Created in 1972, the Authority oversees and operates the county's bus, light rail and paratransit networks, congestion management, specific highway improvements and countywide transportation planning.

As well as providing fixed-route services, the VTA provides light rail and paratransit services, and is a partner in the Highway 17 Express bus, Caltrain, Altamont Commuter Express (ACE), Capitol Corridor, Dumbarton Express bus, Monterey-San Jose Express and shuttle services.

The VTA is overseen by a 12-member board.

Paratransit services are contracted out to Outreach and Escort Inc.

Developments
Tasman East/Capitol Light Rail Project
A 13.2-km (8.2-mile) extension of VTA Light Rail transit into Milpitas and East San Jose with 11 new stations opened in June 2004.

Downtown East Valley Project
Proposed transportation improvements in the Downtown East Valley area, including:
* *Capitol Expressway Corridor:* Light Rail Transit (LRT) from the existing Alum Rock Light Rail Station (near Capitol Avenue) to Nieman Boulevard;
* *Santa Clara/Alum Rock Corridor:* Bus Rapid Transit (BRT) bus service or single-car light rail transit from the San Jose Diridon Station to the Alum Rock Light Rail Station;
* *Monterey Highway Corridor:* Bus Rapid Transit (BRT) from the San Jose Diridon Station to the Santa Teresa Station on the Guadalupe LRT Line.

VTA Rapid 522 Line 22 Corridor Service Improvements
Rapid 522 was implemented in July 2005, providing faster and more frequent service between Eastridge in San Jose and the Palo Alto Transit Center. The project included bus priority signalling at 55 intersections, 15-minute headways, specially 'wrapped' buses and queue-jump lanes. Ridership in the corridor has increased more than 2 per cent since the service was introduced.

Bus
Passenger boardings: (2004) 32.9 million
(2005) 30.3 million
(2006) 30.94 million
(2007) 31.6 million
(2008) 33.1 million
Vehicle-km: (2004) 30.1 million (18.7 million miles)
(2005) 29.4 million (18.3 million)
(2006) 29.8 million (18.5 million miles)
(2007) 30.1 million (18.7 million miles)
(2008) 30.3 million (18.8 million miles)

Number of routes: 75 (55 local, 15 Express (Limited), 22 community bus) (2006)
Route length: 2,217 km (1,378 miles) (round trip)

Fleet: 456 vehicles (active)
35-ft bus	22
40-ft bus	341
Articulated bus	40

Community bus	50
Zero-emission bus	3

In peak service: 333
Average Age of Fleet: 7.6 years

Most intensive service: 10 min
One-person operation: All routes
Fare collection: Exact fare or prepurchase; GFI registering farebox, locked vault
Fare structure: Flat; express premium; annual pass, monthly passes, multitickets; day passes (at three-times single fare); group passes; annual Eco Pass for local employers
Fares collected on board: 80 per cent (20 per cent from tickets and passes)
Operational control: Operations Control centre, field supervision
Arrangements for elderly/disabled: Low flat fare and reduced rate passes; all vehicles either lift-equipped or low-floor with ramps and all routes accessible; county-wide paratransit service
Average peak-hour speed: 24 km/h
Bus priority: Use of HOV lanes; signal pre-emption equipment; queue-jump lanes
Integration with other modes: Integration with rail systems: Caltrain and at Fremont BART, SamTrans at Palo Alto, and AC Transit at Milpitas, Fremont and San Jose; Altamont Commuter Express (ACE); Dumbarton Express Service; Highway 17 Express; Monterey-San Jose Express; Capitol Corridor trains; many routes serve the downtown shared transit mall with LRT for easy interchange. Park-and-ride at 21 light rail stations and 30 other locations (including 8 bus), total 12,008 spaces. Bicycles carried on light rail and buses
Operating costs financed by: Fares 14.0 per cent, subsidy/grants 22.0 per cent, other commercial sources 0.8 per cent, tax levy 63.0 per cent
Subsidy from: 1/2 cent sales tax; federal and state grants
New vehicles financed by: FTA grants and local funds from sales tax and state

Dumbarton Express Service

A regional weekday bus service that operates between Stanford Research Park in Palo Alto and the Union City BART station.

Highway 17 Express

Regional express bus service operating between Santa Cruz and San Jose every day.

Monterey – San Jose Express

Regional express service operating between Monterey and San Jose every day.

Light rail

Santa Clara Valley Transportation Authority (VTA) – Light rail operations

101 West Younger Avenue, San Jose, California 95110, USA
Tel: (+1 408) 299 86 00   Fax: (+1 408) 288 57 01

Type of operation: Light rail, initial route opened 1987

Passenger journeys: (2004) 5.5 million
(2005) 6.8 million
(2006) 8.3 million
(2007) 10.3 million
(2008) 10.4 million
Vehicle-km: (2004) 2.4 million (1.5 million miles)
(2005) 2.9 million (1.8 million miles)
(2006) 3.4 million (2.1 million miles)
(2007) 3.5 million (2.2 million miles)
(2008) 3.5 million (2.2 million miles)

Route length: 67.9 km (42.2 miles)
Number of routes: 2, plus branch
Number of stops: 62
Gauge: 1,435 mm
Electrification: 750 V DC overhead

Current situation

VTA currently operates two light rail lines, the Mountain View-Winchester Line and the Santa Teresa-Alum Rock Line, including the Almaden shuttle.

Developments

In 2005, two extensions were opened, from Convention Center to San Jose Diridon and from San Jose Diridon to Winchester.

Rolling stock: 100 cars (plus historic trolleys)	
Kinki Sharyo low-floor LRV (2002/03)	M100
Historic trolley	M3

In peak service: 53

Service: Peak 15 min (7 1/2 on section where 2 lines overlap (First Street corridor), mid-day 15–30 min, off-peak 15–60 min
First/last car: 04.30/01.30
Fare structure: As bus
Fare collection: Ticket machines at all stations; proof-of-payment, inspectors
Integration with other modes: Interchange with bus encouraged in transit mall; Caltrain at Tamien, Mt-View and SJ Diridon; park-and-ride at 10 stations, total 6,298 spaces; see also bus
Arrangements for elderly/disabled: Level boarding platforms at all stations; instructions in braille on all ticket machines; each LRV has space for four wheelchairs
Operating costs financed by: Fares 14 per cent

Other services
Caltrain

The Authority provides funding for a portion of the operating and capital costs of the Caltrain commuter rail services. This service is provided by the peninsula Corridor Joint Powers Board (the PCJPB), which is composed of three member agencies: the Authority, the San Mateo County Transit District (SamTrans) and the City and County of San Francisco.

Ninety-eight trains (including 22 Baby Bullet Express trains) operate between San Jose Diridon Station and San Francisco each week day, with 48 of these trains extended to the Tamien Station in San Jose, where connection can be made to the LRT system. Connection to the LRT system can also be made at the Mountain View Caltrain station. Six peak-hour trains extend south of Tamien station to Gilroy. Hourly weekend service (32 Saturday trains and 28 Sunday trains) is operated between San Jose Diridon Station and San Francisco.

Funding of operating costs is apportioned to each member agency of the PCJPB and is based on morning peak period boardings in each county, currently approximately 41 per cent for the Authority.

For further information on Caltrain, please see the entry for San Mateo County Transit District (SamTrans) in *Jane's Urban Transport Systems* and in *Jane's World Railways*.

Capitol Corridor Joint Powers Authority (Capitol Corridor JPA)

The Authority is also a member of the Capitol Corridor Joint Powers Authority (Capitol Corridor JPA), that provides the Capitol Corridor Intercity Rail Service, which runs 32 weekday trains between Oakland and Sacramento, with 14 of those continuing to San Jose. Stops are located at stations in Auburn, Rocklin, Roseville, Sacramento, Davis, Suisan/Fairfield, Martinez, Richmond, Berkeley, Emeryville, Oakland (2), Hayward, Fremont, Santa Clara and San Jose.

The Capitol Corridor JPA comprises the Authority, the Sacramento Regional Transit District, the Placer County Transportaion Planning Agency, the congestion management agencies of Solano and Yolo Counties and the San Francisco Bay Area Rapid Transit District (BART).

Under contract with the Capitol Corridor JPA, BART manages the service and Amtrak operates the service on tracks owned by Union Pacific Railroad.

Funding is provided by the State of California.

Altamont Commuter Express (ACE)

949 East Channel Street, Stockton, California 95202, US
Tel: (+1 209) 944 62 20
Fax: (+1 209) 944 62 25
Tel: (+1 800) 411 72 45 (Freephone/Toll free)
e-mail: info@acerail.com
Web: www.acerail.com

Type of operation: Commuter rail

Passenger journeys: 500,000 (estimate)
Train-km: Not currently available

Key personnel

Executive Director: Stacey Mortensen
Director of Operations: Gregg Baxter
Director of Fiscal Services and Administration: Nila Cordova
Director of Planning and Programming: Brian Schmidt
Manager of Customer Services and Marketing: Hubert Hanrahan
Manager of Fiscal Services and Administration: Leila Menor
Strategic Development and Communication Co-ordinator: Thomas W Reeves

Current situation

The Altamont Commuter Express (ACE) is administered under a co-operative agreement between the Authority, Alameda County Congestion Management Agency and the San Joaquin Regional Rail Commission (SJRRC). ACE rail service provides peak-hour and midday weekday commuter rail services from the central Valley to Santa Clara County. The rail line includes stops located in Stockton, Lathrop, Tracy, Livermore (2), Pleasanton, Fremont, Great America and San Jose Diridon Station.

Pursuant to the ACE agreement, funding of operating costs is based on FY2003 contributions, escalated annually by the Consumer Price Index (CPI). SJRRC, Caltrans and the San Joaquin/Amtrak Intercity Rail Service providing funding for the midday service.

The Authority provides 8 free shuttles to transport ACE passengers from the Great America Station to major employment sites. These shuttles are funded by a grant from the Transportation Fund for Clean Air through the Bay Area Quality Management District and SJRRC.

For further information on ACE, please see *Jane's World Railways*.

Developments

A midday train began operation in August 2006.

In mid-2006 consultants commenced two critically important studies. The first, the ACE Corridor Analysis study, is to examine the rail corridor over which the current ACE Stockton to San Jose commuter rail service is operated and to determine ways to improve this service, do a better job of serving the existing ridership, and attract more ridership.

The purpose of the ACE Service Expansion Study is to examine in detail the prospects for ACE service expansion to Sacramento, Modesto, Merced, Oakland and other points in the Central Valley.

Rolling stock

Services are operated with six F40PHM-3C Boise locomotives.

In 2007, the procurement of four additional Bombardier Bi-Level cars was initiated. In addition to new seat cushion material for increased comfort for the passengers, a new seating arrangement that allows for additional legroom will be implemented. The Agreement with Bombardier was signed in May and the cars have been delivered. The addition of the cars will bring the total agency fleet to 28 cars, which will provide needed capacity on peak trains and also allow the Joaquin Regional Rail Commission (SJRRC) to pursue new services.

Dumbarton Express

The Dumbarton Express is a transbay express bus route, operating between the Union City BART station and Stanford Research Park in Palo Alto. A consortium comprised of representatives from the Alameda-Contra Costa Transit District (AC Transit), BART, the City of Union City, SamTrans and the Authority fund the net operating costs of the service. Each member of the consortium has a share of the operating expenses, based on the origin and destination of the passengers, as determined by the ridership survey – currently approximately 41 per cent for the Authority. AC Transit manages and operates the service.

Highway 17 Express

The Highway 17 Express, operating between Sanata Cruz, Scotts Valley and downtown San Jose, is an inter-county bus service operated through a co-operative arrangement between the Authority, the Santa Cruz Metropolitan Transit District (Santa Cruz Metro), the Capitol Corridor JPA and the California Department of Transportation (CalTrans).

The Authority and the Santa Cruz Metropolitan Transit District share the majority of weekday net operating costs equally. The Capitol Corridor JPA and CalTrans provide funding for weekend and holiday service and costs associated with weekday trips not paid by the Authority and Santa Cruz Metro.

Paratransit

The Authority implemented a paratransit brokerage system in 1993, which operates throughout the Authority's service area. As an operator of bus and light rail services, the Authority is required under thee Americans with Disabilities Act (ADA) to ensure that paratransit service is provided to eligible individuals with disabilities. The level of service provided must be comparable, in terms of hours of service and area served, to the service provided by the bus and light rail systems.

The Authority does not directly provide paratransit service, but contracts with Outreach and Escort Inc (Outreach), a paratransit broker service. Outreach determines and certifies qualified individuals for paratransit eligibility, receives and schedules trip requests, builds vehicle manifests and contracts for services with taxi, sedan and accessible van service providers.

Rail Shuttle Program

Under the Authority's Rail Shuttle Program, the Authority offers financial support to shuttle bus services that operate between rail stations and neraby employment/activity centres. This service is operated by the Authority or through employers using a private contractor. Currently, DASH, River Oaks, Great America and IBM shuttles are included in this programme.

Funding to operate the programme is provided by the employers, the Authority and grants from the Transportation Fund for Clean Air Act through the Bay Area Air Quality Management District.

Airport Flyer

The Authority, in partnership with the City of San Jose, provides free Airport Flyer bus services connecting the Norman Y Mineta San Jose International Airport terminals with the Authority's Metro/Airport Light Rail Station and the Santa Clara Caltrain Station.

The City of San Jose contributes approximately 30 per cent to the net operating costs for this service, with the Authority funding the remainder.

Line 55 Monterey-San Jose Express

Effective from August 2006, the Authority, Moterey-Salinas Transit (MST) and the Capitol Corridor JPA entered into a three year memorandum of Understanding (MoU) to provide express bus service operating from Monterey to San Jose, funded by a federal Jobs Access Reverse Commute grant, the Capitol JPA and the Authority. The Authority's portion of the cost for the three years is USD90,000 for the first year

and USD35,000 for each of the following two years. The Line 55 Monterey-San Jose Express is managed and operated by MST and provides daily service with three round trips, covering commute times in the morning, midday and evening.

The service provides passengers with transfers to and from Capitol Corridor trains that operate between San Jose-Oakland-Sacramento, Caltrain (including Baby Bullet express trips) and the Authority's bus and light rail services. The service originates in downtown Monterey, with other stops in Monterey County before stopping at the Gilroy Caltarin Station, Morgan Hill Caltrain Station, San Jose State University, downtown San Jose and the San Jose Diridon Station.

Marin

San Francisco bay area
Marin County
Public transport

As well as the following local operators, the county (population 248,742 (2006 estimate)) is served by extensive bus and ferry routes of Golden Gate Bridge, Highway and Transportation District (see separate entry).

Local operators
Current situation

Local bus services are overseen by the recently re-named Marin Transit (previously Marin County Transit District (MCTD)) (www.marintransit.org). Principal bus services are provided by Golden Gate Bridge, Highway and Transportation District (www.goldengate.org), which provides local bus routes; the West Marin Stagecoach (www.marin-stagecoach.org); and Whistlestop Wheels paratransit, operated by the Marin Senior Coordinating Council (www.rideo.org/paratransit/whistle.html).

Ferry links to San Francisco are operated by Blue and Gold Fleet (www.blueandgoldfleet.com).

Commuter rail (proposed)
Current situation

Proposed commuter rail line, 112.6 km (70 miles) long with 14 stations, running from Cloverdale, through Sonoma and Marin counties, to a ferry terminal connecting with San Francisco. Please see entry for Sonoma-Marin Area Rail Transit (SMART) District under Sonoma County.

Napa

San Francisco bay area
NAPA
Napa County Transportation Planning Agency (NCTPA)

Valley Intercity Neighborhood Express (VINE) 707 Randolph, Suite 100, Napa, California 94559-2912, USA
Tel: (+1 707) 259 86 31; 251 28 00
Fax: (+1 707) 259 86 36
Web: www.nctpa.net/vine.cfm

Passenger boardings: (1995/96) 0.8 million
(1996/97) 0.8 million

Current situation

The VINE provides fixed-route, shuttle and paratransit services in the Napa region on more than 10 routes to the communities of American Canyon, Calistoga, Napa, St Helena, Vallejo and Yountville. There are links with Amtrak services and timed connections with Vallejo Transit Bartlink to El Cerrito del Norte metro station and Vallejo Ferry.

Fixed-route services run from 05.20 to 21.21 on weekdays, 06.00 to 20.10 on Saturdays and 08.15 to 18.00 on Sundays. Multiride tickets and monthly passes are available.

Solano

San Francisco bay area
Solano County
Public transport

Bus services provided by local operators, overseen by county transportation authority.

Solano Transportation Authority (STA)

One Harbor Center, Suite 130, Suisun City, CA 94585, US
Tel: (+1 707) 424 60 75   Fax: (+1 707) 424 60 74
e-mail: staplan@sta-snci.com
Web: www.sta.dst.ca.us

Key personnel

Chair: Len Augustine
Vice-Chair: Anthony Intintoli
Executive Director: Daryl K Halls
Assistant Executive Director/Director of Planning: Dan Christians
Director of Projects: Janet Adams
Director of Transit and Rideshare Services: Elizabeth Richards
Marketing and Legislative Programme Manager: Jayne Bauer
Staff: 17 (full time)

Current situation

The Solano Transportation Authority (STA) was created in 1990 through a Joint Powers Agreement between the cities of Benicia, Dixon, Fairfield, Rio Vista, Suisun City, Vacaville, Vallejo and the County of Solano, to serve as the Congestion Management Agency for Solano. As the Congestion Management Agency (CMA) for the Solano area, the STA partners with various transportation and planning agencies, such as the Metropolitan Transportation Commission (MTC) and Caltrans District 4.

The STA is responsible for countywide transportation planning, programming transportation funds, managing and providing transportation programmes and services, delivering transportation projects and setting transportation priorities.

Developments

Under the Solano Comprehensive Transportation Plan (CTP), adopted in June 2005, the STA proposes to double the number of daily transit trips, from 6,000 to 12,000, by 2030, funding allowing. Key elements of the plan include 15 minute frequency peak hour ferry services to San Francisco, 60 minute Capitol Corridor passenger rail services and 30 minute peak period commuter services with more Solano County stations, in order to improve access and increase intercity bus services threefold. In addition, new Sunday service is proposed on at least three key intercity bus routes. Improvements to the intercity transit services will be co-ordinated with improvements to local bus, pedestrian, bicycle and park-and-ride facilities.

The five components of the CTP are:
• Intercity Bus;
• Intercity Passenger Rail;
• Ferry Services;
• Intercity Transit Service for senior and disabled passengers (Paratransit);
• Support Systems.

Intercity transit services enhance travel mobility to/from and within Solano County as well as providing increased transportation capacity.

Further information on plans, studies, projects and construction may be obtained from the Authority's website, given above.

Vallejo Transit

Transportation Division
Vallejo City Hall, 555 Santa Clara Street, Vallejo, CA 94590, US
Tel: (+1 707) 648 46 66
Web: www.vallejotransit.com

Street address
1850 Broadway, Vallejo, CA 94589, US

Key personnel
Transportation Manager: Pamela J Belchamber
    Staff: 130 (including contracted)

Passenger journeys: Not currently available

Bus
Current situation
Operates 14 routes on a 30 min frequency with timed connections at three transit centres, with limited connections to ferries (see below). Connections to BART run from Vallejo on three routes. There is one Baylink ferry feeder route. Fleet of 52 buses; fares cover 44 per cent of operating costs. Some routes link with services provided by Benicia Transit (BT), Fairfield Suisan Transit (FST) and Napa County's VINE.
    RunAbout paratransit curb-to-curb transportation service for disabled travellers.

Fleet: Not currently available

Ferry (Baylink Ferry)
Tel: (+1 877) 643 37 79
e-mail: info@baylinkferry.com
Web: www.baylinkferry.com

Passenger journeys: (2003/04) 633,137

Background
Two fast ferries were delivered in 1997 – M/V *Mare Island* and M/V *Intintoli*.

Current situation
Operates 11 weekday, nine weekend summer and six weekend winter round trips between Vallejo, downtown San Francisco and the Fisherman's Wharf tourist area.

Fare structure: Bus: Zonal; single ticket, local monthly and 10-ride tickets; other monthly and 10-ride tickets; reduced fares for youths
    Ferry: Single ticket, DayPasses (bus/ferry), round trip, 10-ride and monthly passes
Fare evasion control: Ferry: Inspectors pre-boarding
Arrangements for elderly/disabled: Some reduced fares for seniors and disabled/medicare passengers; RunAbout paratransit service
Integration with other modes: Bus: Links with BART, BT, FST and VINE.
    Ferry: SF Muni Sticker for transfers to and from local transit in San Francisco
Operating costs financed by: Fares 59.3 per cent, subsidies from bridge tolls 40.7 per cent (2003/04)

Other operators
Current situation
Benicia Breeze (previously Benicia Transit) (www.ci.benicia.ca.us/transit.php), Fairfield/ Suisun Transit System (FSTS) (www.ci.fairfield. ca.us/busroutes.htm) and Vacaville City Coach (www.cityofvacaville.com/departments/ citycoach/) provide fixed-route and some demand-responsive services in their local areas, some under contract. Some operators link with BART stations and/or BART express buses.

Sonoma

San Francisco Bay Area
Sonoma County
Public transport
Bus services provided by local operators.

Santa Rosa Transit – CityBus

Transit and Parking Administration and Customer Services
City Hall, 100 Santa Rosa Avenue, Room 6, Santa Rosa, CA 95404, US
Tel: (+1 707) 543 33 25
Fax: (+1 707) 543 33 26
Web: http://ci.santa-rosa.ca.us

Key personnel
    Staff: 73 (full and part-time)

Passenger journeys: (2003/04) 2.66 million
Vehicle-km: (2003/04) 1.63 million (1.01 million miles)

Number of routes: 18 (two weekend-only)

Background
In 1958, the City of Santa Rosa took over the transit system from a private operator and in 1975 it assumed full operational responsibility for the system.

Current situation
The City of Santa Rosa's Transit and Parking Department provides CityBus fixed-route transit and paratransit services, primarily within the City of Santa Rosa, to a population of approximately 150,779 people.
    The City contracts with MV Transportation to provide curb-to-curb dial-a-ride services for elderly and disabled travellers with 11 vehicles in operation. In 2003/04, paratransit services ridership was in excess of 44,400 passengers.
    CityBus services connect with those operated by Sonoma County, Golden Gate Transit and Mendocino Transit Authority.

Developments
Two new paratransit buses were added to the fleet recently and a further four buses were delivered in early 2006. In 2007, five of the older vehicles were to be replaced with new federally-funded vehicles.
    There has also been a recent retrofit to some of the fixed route buses, which aims to reduce emissions levels.
    CityBus intends to participate in the Translink transit co-ordination programme at the earliest opportunity.

Fleet: 41 vehicles (includes contracted paratransit vehicles)

Gillig 40 ft low-floor diesel (2002)	5
Gillig 30 ft low-floor diesel (2002)	1
Thomas SLF diesel (2000)	2
ElDorado low-floor CNG (2000)	1
New Flyer 20 ft low-floor diesel (2000)	6
New Flyer 40 ft low-floor diesel (1998)	13
Gillig 35 ft low-floor diesel (refurbished 2005)	2
Ford diesel van (2006)	4
Ford diesel van (2005)	2
Ford diesel van (1998)	5

In peak service: 22 vehicles (fixed route)

First/last bus: 06.00/20.25 (Mon-Fri), 06.00/20.15 (Sat), 10.00/17.15 (Sun) (fixed route)
Most intensive service: 30 min
Fare structure: Flat, single and multi-ride ticket books, monthly passes, youth passes, free transfers within the CityBus system within 2 hrs of issue
Costs recovered by fares: 18.7 per cent (2003/04)
Arrangements for elderly/disabled: All routes are wheelchair accessible, paratransit services, Regional Transit Discount Card
Integration with other modes/operators: Connections with Sonoma County, Golden Gate Transit and Mendocino Transit Authority services

Sonoma County Transit
355 West Robles Avenue, Santa Rosa, CA 95407, US
Tel: (+1 707) 585 75 16
Fax: (+1 707) 585 77 13
e-mail: comments@sctransit.com
Web: www.sctransit.com

Key personnel
General Manager: Bryan Albee
    Staff: 95 (includes 85 contracted employees)

Passenger journeys: (2000/01) 1.51 million
Number of routes: 24

Current situation
Provides countywide service from Santa Rosa to nine incorporated cities and many small towns; 24 routes; 58 buses, seven minibuses/vans. It is operated under contract by ATC/Vancom and services co-ordinated with Golden Gate Transit routes to San Francisco and other local operators. Fares cover approximately 22 per cent of operating costs.
    Also provides paratransit services operated by Volunteer Wheels.

Fare structure: Zonal plus 'local'; Local and Countywide FastPASS, monthly, 31-day and 20-ride FastPASS passes; reduced fare for students
Arrangements for elderly/disabled: All vehicles are equipped with wheelchair lifts and kneeling vehicles. They also have reduced fares and passes
Integration with other modes/operators: Connections to local transit services provided by Cloverdale Transit, Healdsburg Transit, Santa Rosa CityBus, and Petaluma Transit. Links are also provided to Mendocino Transit Authority (MTA) for service to the Sonoma/Mendocino Coast and Golden Gate Transit for regional service to Marin and San Francisco counties; 20 park-and-ride sites with a total of 2,060 parking spaces

Other operators
Current situation
Local services operated by Cloverdale Transit, Healdsburg In-City Transit and Petaluma Transit. Round-trip commuter services are provided by Valley of the Moon Commute Club. Further information on these operators can be found at www.transitinfo.org/providers/index.asp.

Sonoma Marin Area Rail Transit (SMART)
SMART District Office
750 Lindaro Street, Suite 200, San Rafael, CA 94901, US
Tel: (+1 415) 226 08 80
Fax: (+1 415) 226 08 81
e-mail: info@sonomamarintrain.org
Web: www.sonomamarintrain.org

Key personnel
Chair: Charles McGlashan
Vice-Chair: Debora Fudge
Project Director/General Manager: Lillian Hames
Property Manager: Lucrecia Milla
Rail Planning Manager: John Nemeth
Community Outreach & Education Manager:
    Chris Coursey
    Staff: 5

Type of operation: Commuter rail (proposed)

Current situation
The Sonoma-Marin Area Rail Transit (SMART) District was established in 2003 to oversee the development and implementation of a proposed passenger rail service over publicly-owned railroad right-of-way in Sonoma and Marin counties.
    SMART is governed by a 12 member board and is charged with planning, engineering, evaluating and implementing passenger train services and corridor maintenance from Cloverdale to a Ferry terminal that connects with San Francisco.
    In 2000, SMART released the Sonoma Marin Rail Implementation Plan, following an 18 month process of consultant analysis and public meetings. The plan addressed the feasibility of implementing a commuter rail operating system, including recommendations for key station sites along the route; service intervals and funding options.
    In 2001, the project plan was further refined to include a 112.6 km (70 mile) corridor extending from Cloverdale in Sonoma County through Marin County to a San Francisco-bound ferry terminal, with 14 station sites along the

corridor, nine in Sonoma County and five in Marin County.

In September 2004, the SMART Board of Directors adopted an Expenditure Plan linked to the November 2006 quarter-cent ballot measure.

The plan was structured to provide funding for passenger rail services from Cloverdale to Larkspur using a mix of local, state and federal funding.

Developments
In November 2006, the vote fell just short of the required two thirds majority required to enact the quarter-cent sales tax. A revised plan was to be presented to voters in 2008.

Santa Ana/orange county

Population: City 371,837 (2002 estimate), county 2.8 million (2000 Census)

Public transport
Bus services in Santa Ana and 28 other cities in Orange County, including Anaheim, Garden Grove and Irvine, provided by County Transit Authority controlled by representative board, in co-operation with other public agencies and some employers with own operations. Demand-responsive dial-a-ride minibus scheme with operation contracted serves local neighbourhoods. Light rail proposed. Commuter rail.

Orange County Transport Authority (OCTA)

PO Box 14184, Orange, California 92863-1584, USA
Tel: (+1 714) 560 62 82
Fax: (+1 714) 560 57 95
Web: www.octa.net

Street address
550 South Main Street, Orange, California, USA

Key personnel
Chair: Gregory T Winterbottom
Chief Executive Officer: Arthur T Leahy
Assistant Chief Executive Officer:
  Ruchard Bacigalupo
Executive Director of Operations: Bill Foster
Director of Strategic Planning: Kia Mortazavi
Director of Transit Systems Development:
  Stan Phernambucq
Director of Finance and Administration:
  Jim Kenan
Director of Public Communications and Marketing:
  Manny Hernandez
Staff: 1,500 (includes dial-a-ride)

Current situation
The former Orange County Transit District (fixed-route operator), the Transportation Commission, the Consolidated Transportation Service Agency (provider of demand-responsive service) and other transit-related agencies were merged in 1991 to form the OCTA, with an 11-member governing board.

Suburban and interurban services are operated, as well as city routes and a demand-responsive (dial-a-ride) scheme. A ride-sharing brokerage is promoted for car- and vanpools by the Commute Management Services department, and overall services are co-ordinated under co-operative agreements with MTA Los Angeles, Long Beach Transit and other local transit agencies.

Development of a rapid transit system has long been proposed and a 0.5 cent tax was approved by voters in 1990 (Measure M), but progress with this and other projects was halted after the bankruptcy of Orange County in 1994. In 1997, approval was granted for studies of a 45 km light rail line from Fullerton to Disneyland, Santa Ana, South Coast Plaza and the new international airport.

Staged development continues of barrier-separated bus/carpool median transitways on freeway rights-of-way as busways which could ultimately be connected to the core rail system.

Some 70 per cent of services, mainly small-bus and paratransit routes in and around Irvine, were

Fullerton Transit Center, with OCTA bus on Route 43 to Costa Mesa departing 0126473

contracted to Laidlaw Transit services in late 1999 for a five year period.

Developments
In February 2003, the CenterLine light rail project received a 'recommended' rating from the Federal Transit Administration.

Bus
Passenger journeys: (2003) 65.1 million

Number of routes: Approx 80
Route length: 2,878 km

Fleet: 493 vehicles

GMC T8H (1980)	124
Gillig Phantom (1983/88/89)	241
New Flyer (1991)	53
Superbus	12
New Flyer D40LF low-floor (1995)	50
Others	13

On order: 38 CNG-powered low-floor buses from ElDorado; refurbishment completed of 75 Gillig Phantoms, 132 low-floor CNG-powered buses from North American Bus Industries.

One-person operation: All routes
Fare collection: Payment to driver or pass
Fare structure: Flat; 5 cent transfers; prepurchase 40-ticket books and monthly passes
Arrangements for elderly/disabled: Fully accessible; dial-a-ride scheme (zonal fares) also serves needs of elderly and disabled (see below), uses vans with wheelchair lifts; all full-size buses lift-equipped; reduced fare peak travel
Integration between modes: Ride-sharing/carpooling promoted; 33 park-and-ride/ride-sharing sites; many interconnection agreements with neighbouring operators; 17 operators use Santa Ana downtown transit terminal
Operating costs financed by: Fares 27 per cent, other commercial sources 7 per cent, subsidy/grants 59 per cent, tax levy 6 per cent
Subsidy from: Local transportation fund (from sales tax) 91.6 per cent, FTA 8.2 per cent, state 0.2 per cent

Minibus/dial-a-ride (contracted)
Current situation
Countywide dial-a-ride service, using District-owned vehicles operated by private companies under contract, is provided for short trips

within 30 zones covering local communities. The operations, on-demand with no fixed stops, provide both a facility for local trips within the zones (at a flat fare), and transfers to main conventional routes and to adjacent dial-a-rides.

In addition, dial-a-ride vans provide express and local commuter service to major work centres over routes which will be upgraded to full-size buses as ridership develops. These routes have been developed in response to Transportation Management Associations- a joint promotion between OCTA and employers to provide tailormade alternatives to private car commuting.

Light rail – CenterLine (proposed)
Background
The CenterLine light rail project is a 15 km (9.3 mile) route with 16 stations, proposed to provide service to John Wayne Airport, the South Coast Plaza shopping centre and Orange County Performing Arts Center, Mater Dei High School, the Santa Ana Civic Center, the County Government Center and courthouse, the Santa Ana Artists' Village and the depot at Santa Ana, where it will connect with Amtrak and Metrolink commuter trains as well as many OCTA bus services. It is the starter segment of a light rail system being developed by OCTA.

Projected costs for the CenterLine are estimated at between USD900 million and USD1 billion. Funding will come from a combination of federal and other state grants, Measure M funds and state rail bonds.

Initially, the system will operate with two-car trains running at 7.5 minute frequency at peak periods and at 15–20 minutes off-peak.

Current situation
In February 2003, the CenterLine light rail project received a 'recommended' rating from the Federal Transit Administration.

Projected daily ridership by 2025 is estimated to be more than 22,600.

Commuter rail
Current situation
Metrolink services link Oceanside, Santa Ana and Los Angeles (see Los Angeles Metrolink entry). At Oceanside the trains connect with those to San Diego run by the North County Transit District (see San Diego entry).

Seattle

Population: City 582,454, King County area 1.83 million, metropolitan area (Seattle-Tacoma-Bellevue) 3.26 million (2006 estimates)

Public transport

Bus, trolleybus, waterfront vintage tramway and commuter rail provided in metropolitan Seattle and King County by public agencies responsible to county government. City operates monorail; state ferries. Other operators provide bus service in adjacent Snohomish and Pierce counties, which have joined with King County in forming a regional transit authority. Light rail.

Central Puget Sound Regional Transit Authority – Sound Transit

401 South Jackson Street, Seattle, Washington 9804-2826, US
Tel: (+1 206) 398 50 00
Fax: (+1 206) 689 33 60
Freephone: (+1 800) 201 49 00
e-mail: main@soundtransit.org
Web: www.soundtransit.org

Key personnel

Chair: Greg Nickels
Vice-Chairs: Aaron Reardon, Claudia Thomas
Chief Executive Officer: Joni Earl
Chief Communications Officer: Ric Ilgenfritz
Capital Projects Director: Agnes Govern
Rail Operations Manager: Martin Young

Current situation

Sound Transit is a public agency created in 1993 to plan and provide a regional transport system for the urban areas of King, Pierce and Snohomish counties. It covers an area with a population of about 3 million, with another 1.2 million expected to be added by 2020. ST is governed by an 18-member board, of whom 17 are local city and county elected, appointed by the County Executive of each county; the eighteenth member is the State Transport Department Secretary. Three standing board committees assist in policy-making and programme oversight, and an independent Citizen Oversight Panel monitors ST's performance in meeting its public commitments.

The three-county area is also served by four local public transport agencies – King County Metro, Pierce Transit, Community Transit and Everett Transit.

In May 1996 Sound Transit adopted a proposal to build the first phase of a high-capacity transit system to provide the region with alternatives for its travel needs: Sound Move – the Ten-Year Regional Transit System Plan. Later that year, citizens within Sound Transit's district (the urban areas of Snohomish, Pierce and King counties), approved a 0.4 per cent local sales tax and a 0.3 per cent motor vehicle excise tax to provide the funding necessary to bring regional express buses, commuter trains and electric light rail to the area. Federal funds have also been made available.

Developments

Currently, the majority of the projects and services approved by voters in 1996 are either in service or under construction, carrying more than 10 million commuters a year. A proposed investment package for Sound Transit 2, an expansion of the regional transit system, was included in a Roads & Transit ballot measure rejected by voters in November 2007. Subsequent public research found that voters want a smaller package that can be delivered within a shorter timeframe. They also emphasised the importance of accountability guarantees for

using taxpayer resources and even greater focus on environmental sustainability.

The Sound Transit Board is taking a renewed look at which transit service expansions would make the biggest and quickest improvements for commuters for the least cost.

In early 2008, ST's environmental management system was certified to ISO 14001 standards.

ST Express (Regional bus service)

Passenger boardings: (2005) 8.8 million
(2006) 8.9 million (approximate)
(2007) 10.1 million (approximate)

Number of routes: 19

Current situation

The first routes of a planned network of 19 regional bus routes, known as ST Express, began operation in September 1999. Sound Transit contracts with the region's local public transit agencies (specifically King County Metro, Pierce Transit and Community Transit) to operate ST Express bus routes and maintain the vehicles in their respective areas. Sound Transit owns all of its vehicles.

ST Express includes construction of HOV freeway ramps to improve transit speed and reliability and other facilities such as park-and-ride and transit centres.

Developments

In February 2008, the new Redmond Transit Center opened.

Fleet: 228

Orion V CNG (1994/95)	27
Gillig Phantom 40 ft (1999/2001)	90
Gillig Phantom 40 ft (2005)	2
New Flyer low-floor articulated (1999/2000)	37
New Flyer low-floor articulated (2004)	16
New Flyer low-floor two-axle CNG (2001)	20
New Flyer low-floor 40 ft diesel-electric (2003)	1
New Flyer low-floor articulated diesel-electric hybrids (2004)	22
MCI interurban-type (2005)	13

On order: 39 vehicles, the first tranche of ST Express fleet replacements

Sounder commuter rail

Type of operation: Commuter rail, service began in 2000

Passenger journeys: (2005) 1.2 million
(2006) 1.7 million
(2007) 1.7 million (approximate)

Current situation

Commuter rail service connecting downtown Seattle with Tacoma (the south line), using

Burlington Northern Santa Fe (BNSF) Railway tracks, with five intermediate stations (and a total of seven stations), started in September 2000. Operation is in peak hours only, and was initially limited to two trips in the morning peak period and two in the afternoon. A third trip in each period was added in September 2002. A fourth round-trip was added in September 2005. In 2007, two more round-trips were added, including the first reverse commute, running from Seattle south to Tacoma and back.

In May 2003, an agreement was signed with BNSF to extend Sounder service north to Everett and south to Lakewood.

Service on the north line from Seattle to Everett, with one intermediate station (for a total of three stations) began in December 2003. A second round-trip was added in June 2005 and a third in 2007.

There are currently six trips in each peak-hour period on the south line, and three round-trips on the north line. Sounder also provides special event service to select weekend professional sporting events and concerts.

Developments

Plans to increase service on the north line would begin serving a second intermediate station and add a fourth round-trip. On the south line, up to three new round-trips are planned, bringing the number of daily round-trips on the south line to nine.

A southern extension from Tacoma to Lakewood (13 km), including two new stations currently under construction in South Tacoma and Lakewood, is in the design and planning stage.

Fleet:

GM-EMD F59PH Locomotive (2000)	11 (2 leased)
Bombardier Cab Car (2000)	18 (6 leased)
Bombardier Coach (2000)	40 (12 leased)

Tacoma LINK light rail

Type of operation: Electric light rail, opened August 2003

Passenger journeys: (2007) 0.9 million (approximate)

Route length: 2.6 km
Number of lines: 1
Number of stops: 5

Gauge: 1,435 mm
Electrification: 750 V DC, overhead

Current situation

The ground-breaking for this 2.6 km city-centre circulator took place in 2000. It is reserved-track

ST Express bus
1197903

street running throughout and is single-track for a little under half its length.

Three Inekon/Skoda Astra low-floor trams, ordered as an add-on to Portland's order, were delivered in September 2002. Construction of a three-track maintenance facility was completed in 2002 near the southeastern end of the L-shaped line.

Sound Transit directly employs the Tacoma Link operators and maintenance personnel.

Developments
Operations on the line commenced in August 2003. The service has carried more than 2 million passengers since opening.

Rolling stock: 3 trams
Skoda/Inekon Astra 10T low-floor (2002)   M3

Service: 10 min (Monday-Saturday & Sunday between 11.30 and 18.30), 20 min (Sunday 10.00–11.30 and 18.30–20.00)
First/last train: 06.00/20.00 (Monday-Friday), 08.00/22.00 (Saturday), 10.00/20.00 (Sunday)
Fare structure: Free

Central Link light rail (under construction)
Type of operation: Light rail (under construction)

Passenger journeys: n/a

Route length: 25.11 km
Number of lines: 1
Number of stops: 13

Background
In November 2003, Sound Transit broke ground on the initial segment of the Central Link light rail. Construction is more than 80 per cent complete on this 22.5 km (14 mile) segment with 12 stations from downtown Seattle to Tukwila. Testing of the light rail vehicles is currently under way on the line. Service is due to begin in 2009, running every six minutes during peak hours and every 10 to 15 minutes off-peak.

Current situation
In December 2004, Sound Transit and the Port of Seattle reached an agreement to extend Link light rail another 2.6 km (1.7 miles) to a new station at Seattle-Tacoma International Airport. The project broke ground in September 2006, and will open for service just a few months after the initial segment, in late 2009. In the months between the opening of the initial segment and the opening of the airport extension, a free shuttle bus will meet each train at Tukwila to carry passengers directly to the airport, just minutes away.

By 2020, it is projected that the 25.11 km (15.6 mile) line from downtown Seattle to Sea-Tac Airport will carry more than 45,000 people every day.

Developments
Planning is also underway for further extensions northward.

North Link will connect four urban centres – downtown Seattle, Capitol Hill, the University District and Northgate – with a light rail line through the region's highest ridership corridor. In April 2006, the Sound Transit Board approved the North Link project, including final route and station locations, and selected University Link as the first segment to be built.

University Link is a planned 5.07 km (3.15 mile) northward extension from downtown Seattle to the University of Washington, with stations at Capitol Hill and on the university campus. In November 2005, the Federal Transit Administration gave University Link a 'High' ranking, the best possible rating and a positive indication that University Link will be very competitive as it seeks a proposed USD700 million federal grant.

Final design of University Link is under way to bring the station and route design from 30 per cent to 100 per cent completion. Construction of University Link is expected to begin in

Central Link light rail vehicles (in testing)   1197902

late 2008 or early 2009, with service running in 2016.

Fleet (planned for 2009):
Kinki Sharyo/Mitsui 95-ft LR   35

King County Metro (KCM)
King Street Center, MS KSC-TR-0415, 201 South Jackson Street, Seattle, Washington 98104-3856, US
Tel: (+1 206) 296 01 00   Fax: (+1 206) 684 17 78
Web: www.metrokc.gov

Key personnel
County Executive: Ron Sims
Director, Department of Transportation: Harold S Taniguchi
General Manager, Transit: Kevin Desmond
Manager, Operations: Jim O'Rourke
     Staff: (2003) 3,692 (of which 2,700 drivers)

Passenger boardings: (All modes)
(2006) 106.5 million

Operating costs financed by: Fares 14 per cent, other operational revenue 2 per cent, sales tax 61 per cent, capital grants 12 per cent, Sound Transit 5 per cent, interest income 2 per cent, miscellaneous 4 per cent (2003)
Subsidy from: 51.5 per cent from 0.6 per cent local sales tax, 36.6 per cent from 1 per cent motor vehicle excise tax

Background
In 1973 public transport for Seattle and King County was brought under the control of the Municipality of Metropolitan Seattle (Metro), a public agency created in 1957 for water pollution control. A dedicated 0.3 per cent sales tax was increased to 0.6 per cent in 1982. One-half of the 1 per cent Washington State motor vehicle excise tax collected in Metro's service area is allocated to public transit.

In 1994, Metro was merged with the existing government of King County and ceased to exist as an independent government. Mass transit was taken over by the county's Department of Transportation. However, the name 'Metro' was retained for marketing and other references, and the department is commonly known as King County Metro.

A 2 km tunnel in the city centre opened in 1990 for use by dual-mode buses; it is designed for light rail use and will carry LRVs when Seattle's spine route opens (see above). There are three underground stations, and a combined station and bus staging area at each end. The tunnel is served by 27 routes carrying about 35,000 passengers a day.

Recent rapid expansion of population and employment growth in areas outside central Seattle has required new approaches to meet changed public transport demand. A transit development plan inaugurated in 1996 has added over 400,000 service-hours and reoriented the network towards a hub-and-spoke system, connecting new centres of population and employment in King County as well as maintaining links to downtown Seattle.

After a demonstration, the seven public transport authorities in central Puget Sound have completed the planning phase for a common area-wide fare collection system using smartcard technology. Proposals were sought from suppliers at the beginning of 1999. Region-wide PugetPass introduced 1999, valid with all five area operators.

Washington State's Commute Trip Reduction Law requires employers with 100 or more staff arriving during peak hours to implement schemes that promote the use of high-occupancy transport modes, as well as walking, cycling and telecommuting. The intention is to improve air quality, reduce traffic congestion and cut fuel consumption. With state grant funding, Metro assists employers to develop alternative commute plans as incentives for their employees.

Current situation

Metro Transit currently provides public transport services to a population of some 1.7 million in an area of 5,527 km² (2,134 sq miles). Services include bus, trolleybus, tram and paratransit. There is also a vanpool programme in operation with 660 vans carrying out 2.6 million passenger trips per year.

Developments

The fleet of diesel buses is currently using Ultra-Low Sulphur Diesel (ULSD) and Metro is intending to have its entire fleet of diesel buses powered by biodiesel.

A joint 'smart bus technology' project with Sound Transit was carried out in 2001/02. King County Metro is currently in the process of selecting a contractor to install this technology, onboard electronics and data systems, which will improve the mechanical and schedule reliability of the bus fleet.

In January 2005, the last of the Breda 5000 series dual-mode vehicles was withdrawn from service. These have been replaced by hybrid diesel-electric buses.

In September 2005, the Downtown Seattle Transit Tunnel (DSTT) was closed in preparation for Sound Transit's light rail project, which will link SeaTac and downtown Seattle. The tunnel will be closed for up to two years for upgrading, so that it may be used for both buses and light rail, and buses that used the tunnel will use surface streets until completion.

Metro will operate the Central Link light rail systems and the South Lake Union Streetcar line.

The Downtown Seattle Transit Tunnel's reopened in September 2007. The tunnel retrofit included lowering the roadbed in the stations to accommodate level boarding for passengers using either trains or buses, and installing new electrical, communications, and safety systems. For example, inside the tunnel passengers will benefit from better lighting and signage, more security cameras, and a new public announcement system. The DSTT retrofit also included excavating a new 550-ft extension to the tunnel under Pine Street. This new 'stub' tunnel will be the launching point for the 5 km (3 mile) University Link project, which will dig twin light rail tunnels to stations at Capitol Hill and the University of Washington.

Trolleybus routes 14 and 36 are due to be extended to the sites of the future Mount Baker and Othello St stations of the Link light-rail line. Route 7 may be extended also.

Bus and trolleybus

Passenger journeys: Not currently available
Vehicle-km: (2007) 69.5 million (estimate)
(2007) 9.1 million (Sound Transit routes operated by Metro)

Number of routes: Bus 216, trolleybus 17
Route length: (One way) 6,081 km
Trolleybus overhead: 199 km

Fleet: 1,156 buses plus paratransit and vanpool vehicles

Gillig 40 ft diesel (1996/1999)	395
Gillig 35 ft diesel (1997)	15
New Flyer 60 ft articulated (1998/2000)	272
Gillig 30 ft (1999/2000)	95
New Flyer 40 ft low-floor (2003)	100
New Flyer D60LF 60 ft low-floor articulated diesel (2004)	30
New Flyer DE60LF 60 ft low-floor articulated hybrid diesel-electric (2004)	214
Champion Transit van (2002)	28
ACCESS paratransit vans	280
Vanpool vans	700

On order: An additional 22 New Flyer DE60LFR articulated hybrid, for 2008 delivery

Fleet: 159 trolleybuses

Breda 60 ft articulated ex-dual-mode (1990/01 converted 2004–07) (plus 10 in storage)	59
Gillig/Alstom 40 ft (2002)	100

Most intensive service: 6 min

Seattle monorail   1367331

One-person operation: All routes
Fare collection: Payment to farebox; prepurchase tickets and 1- and 3-month/annual passes
Fare structure: Zonal (2 zones, covering Seattle and rest of area, with free central area travel); peak surcharge. Prepurchase monthly, quarterly and annual passes; multiticket books; free transfers, all-day passes at weekends. Subsidised employer-purchased pass scheme
Fares collected on board: 23 per cent
Operational control: Route inspectors/mobile radio; computerised radio communication; vehicle location system
Arrangements for elderly/disabled: 94 per cent of vehicles and 212 routes (91 per cent) accessible, average 480 daily passengers; reduced fares and passes; half-price subscription taxi scheme; paratransit and vanpool services carried 3.2 million passengers in 2006
Average peak-hour speed: Bus 23.8 km/h, trolleybus 10.8 km/h
Bus priority: 217 km of HOV lanes, with 2-km bus subway in city centre, to be shared with light rail from mid-2009
Integration with other modes: Cycle racks offered for free cycle carriage all routes; 122 park-and-ride lots with space for almost 20,000 cars; 10 transit centres
New vehicles financed by: Sales tax and motor vehicle tax with FTA grants

Tramway

Type of operation: Conventional tramway, mainly as tourist attraction, serving waterfront area

Length of route: 2.6 km (1.6 miles)

Passenger journeys: Not currently available

Developments
The service was suspended in November 2005 and the five vintage vehicles have been placed in storage.

Seattle Monorail Services

370 Thomas Street, Suite 200, Seattle, Washington 98109, US
Tel: (+1 206) 905 26 00   Fax: (+1 206) 905 22 06
e-mail: thomd@seattlemonorail.com (General Manager)
Web: www.seattlemonorail.com

Key personnel
General Manager: Thomas Ditty
Maintenance Manager: Russell Note
Office Manager: Joan Ogazi

Type of operation: Elevated monorail, opened 1962

Current situation
A 1.5 km two-track route, built in 1962 to serve the World's Fair site, links Westlake Center in the downtown area with the Seattle Center cultural and pleasure facility. It carries about 1.5 million passengers a year. Two cars provide a 10 minute service (09.00–23.00 seven days a week) at speeds of up to 65 km/h. Conductors are carried. The monorail is owned by the City of Seattle and operated under contract by Seattle Monorail Services.

There are two park-and-ride facilities for the monorail, with several pass options available.

Washington State Department of Transportation

Washington State Ferries (WSF)
2901 Third Avenue, Suite 500, Seattle, Washington 98121-3014, USA
Tel: (+1 206) 515 34 00
e-mail: wsfinfo @wsdot.wa.gov
Web: www.wsdot.wa.gov/ferries/

Key personnel
Assistant Secretary, Ferries Division:
    David Moseley
    Staff: 1,800+

Type of operation: Ferry

Passenger journeys: (2006) 24 million (estimate)
Vessel-km: Not currently available

Current situation
Puget Sound ferry services are provided by Washington State as an integral part of the highway system. A fleet of 28 vessels carries about 24 million passengers and 11 million vehicles annually, on 10 routes and to 20 terminals.

Security on ferry services is enhanced by the operation of K9 teams.

Developments
Washington State Ferries (WSF) is introducing a new electronic fare system – Wave2Go.

There are plans for improvements to a number of terminals.

The Steel Electric Class vessels have been removed from service since November 2007, for the replacement of hull plating.

Fleet: 24 vessels

Community Transit (CT)

Snohomish County Public Transit Benefit Area Corporation
7100 Hardeson Road, Everett, Washington 98203-5834, USA
Tel: (+1 425) 348 71 00
Fax: (+1 425) 438 61 41
e-mail: riders@commtrans.org
Web: www.commtrans.org

Key personnel

Chair: Dennis Kendall
Chief Executive Officer: Joyce Eleanor
Public Information Officer: Martin Munguia
Public Information Specialist: Tom Pearce
    Staff: 918 (including contracted staff)

Background

CT was created in 1975 to provide public transport in Snohomish County, immediately north of Seattle. The County Public Transportation Benefit Area Corp was the first such authority in Washington state. Voters initially approved a 0.3 per cent sales tax; in 1990 an additional 0.3 per cent was approved to fund service expansion, bringing the tax to the legal maximum of 0.6 per cent.

In 2001, voters approved an additional 0.3 per cent, bringing the tax to its legal maximum of 0.9 per cent. Other operational costs are covered by state and federal grants and fares.

Current situation

CT provides services to a rapidly growing area, with a population of over 469,650 (2006), and to 19 cities with an area of more than 3,365 km² (1,300 sq miles). Express commuter services run to downtown Seattle (contracted to First Transit), to the University of Washington, and to the growing employment centres of Bellevue and Overlake east of Seattle.

CT also operates DART paratransit services and a vanpool programme and links with the Sounder commuter rail service.

Developments

The new Mountlake Terrace Transit Center is under construction, with completion currently scheduled for early 2009.

CT is also in the process of developing new park-and-ride facilities, and expects to open at least one by 2010.

CT is currently trialling an ADL Enviro 500 double-deck bus, known as the Double Tall.

A new Bus Rapid Transit (BRT) route – branded 'Swift' – is under consideration. CT has started the environmental review for the 26.9-km (16.7-mile) service, which will run along Highway 99. The proposal includes 10 minute headways for 20 hours per day with some 15 stops. The route is due to be operational in 2009.

There are also plans to increase transit services by 16 per cent increase in the next six years. As well as BRT, plans for Advanced Public Transportation Systems (APTS), a smartcard system and new park-and-ride facilities are already under way.

Bus

Passenger journeys: (2004) 7.7 million
(2006) 9.9 million
(2007) 10.8 million
Vehicle-km: (2006) 4.8 million (13.9 million miles)

Number of routes: 64 (33 local, 31 commuter)

Fleet: 275 buses, plus 358 vanpool vans, plus 59 paratransit vehicles
Breakdown of fleet is not currently available
In peak service: 221 buses
Average age of fleet: 7.5 years

Most intensive service: 15 min
Fare structure: Flat USD1.25 fare for intra-county journeys; USD3 for university and commuter services
Fare collection: Exact fare to farebox; monthly and annual passes, ticket books
Fares collected on board: 17 per cent
Arrangements for elderly/disabled: DART demand-responsive service operated under contract by Senior Services of Snohomish County
Bus priority: HOV lanes and by-pass lanes
Integration with other modes:
20 Park-and-Ride facilities with a total of 6,137 spaces
Average peak-hour speed: 32 km/h
Operating costs financed by: Fares 17 per cent, other commercial sources 1 per cent, subsidy/grants 5 per cent, tax levy 77 per cent

Pierce County Public Transportation Benefit Area Corporation (Pierce Transit)

3701 96th Street Southwest, PO Box 99070, Lakewood, Washington 98499-0070, USA
Tel: (+1 253) 581 80 00
Fax: (+1 253) 581 80 75
e-mail: ptweb@piercetransit.org
Web: www.piercetransit.org

Key personnel

Chairman: Dave Enslow
Chief Executive Officer: Lynne M Griffith
Vice-President, Transportation Services Department:
    Sam Desue
Vice-President, Policy, Planning & Public Affairs Department: Louise Bray
Vice-President, Finance, Audit & Administration Department: Wayne Fanshier
    Staff: 1,008

Passenger boardings: (2003) 13.3 million
(2005) 15.0 million (estimate)
(2007) 16.1 million (estimate)
(2008) 16.3 million (projected)
Vehicle-km: (2007) 24.9 million (15.5 million miles) (estimate)

Number of routes: 52 (local)
Route length: 1,857 km
On priority right-of-way: High-occupancy vehicle (HOV) lanes 67.0 km, bus lanes 4.6 km
Number of stops: 3,300 (estimate)

Current situation

Pierce Transit serves a population of some 767,000 over an area of 1,072.2 km² (414 sq miles) in Pierce County immediately to the south of Seattle. It operates local bus routes, SHUTTLE service (paratransit), ridematching/vanpooling and inter-county express services to Seattle, Sea-Tac Airport and Plympia, provided in co-operation with Sound Transit (see separate entry) and Intercity Transit. The fleet is 100 per cent wheelchair-accessible and nearly all vehicles run on CNG.

The agency is governed by a Board of Commissioners, comprising of nine elected officials.

Developments

In 2004, Pierce Transit purchased 20 30 ft buses to better serve routes with lighter ridership. They are currently used on routes that operate in the more rural parts of the community where smaller and more manoeuvrable buses are a better fit than larger buses. These buses are also more cost effective to purchase and operate, and their design includes convenient low-floor wheelchair access.

Fleet: 223 vehicles (2003)

Twin Coach 41-S (1948)	(historical)	one
GMC (1973)	(historical)	one
Orion I (1991/92)		49
Orion I (2003)		68
New Flyer low-floor (1999/2000/2002/2003)		104

Fleet (Sound Transit Buses): 77 (2003)

Orion V (1994)	27
Gillig (1999)	21
New Flyer articulated (1999)	nine
New Flyer low-floor (2001)	20
In peak service (total): 199	

Most intensive service: four min
Fare structure: Flat, with premium fares for express and special event services; passes available; discounted passes for those under 18 years of age
Fares collected on board: 20 per cent
Arrangements for elderly/disabled: The fleet is 100 per cent wheelchair-accessible; SHUTTLE paratransit services made 435,000 trips in 2005.
Operating costs financed by: Sales tax 62 per cent, Sound Transit revenues 16 per cent, fares and advertising 11 per cent, federal and state revenues 10 per cent, interest income/other one per cent

Seattle Streetcar

Seattle Department of Transportation
Seattle Municipal Tower, 700 Fifth Avenue, Suite 3900, PO Box 34996, Seattle, WA 98124-4996, US
Tel: (+1 206) 684 31 36
Fax: (+1 206) 684 32 38
Web: www.seattlestreetcar.org

Key personnel

Operations Chief (KCM): Marwan Al-Mukhtar
Project Manager: Ethan Malone
Community Liaison: Josh Stepherson
Communications Manager: Richard Sheridan
    Staff: Not currently available

Type of operation: Street tramway, opened December 2007

Passenger journeys: Not available currently
Vehicle-km: Not available currently

Route length: 2.1 km
Number of stops: 11 (seven stops served per one-way trip; eight stops (four in each direction) are unidirectional)
Gauge: 1,435 mm
Electrification: 750 V DC (overhead)

New Flyer DE40LF hybrid buses of Pierce Transit, wearing a new livery, and a Skoda-Inekon 10T tram of Sound Transit's Tacoma Link, on Commerce Street in Downtown Tacoma (S J Morgan)
1375704

Current situation

This new 2.1 km (1.3 mile) street tramway/streetcar South Lake Union line was built by the city of Seattle. The city owns the system, now known as the Seattle Streetcar, but has contracted the operation and maintenance to King County Metro (KCM). The system runs between the Central Business District, just north of Westlake Center, and the South Lake Union neighbourhood, terminating on Fairview Avenue near the Fred Hutchinson Cancer Research Center. The system runs seven days a week, 15 hours per day, with service every 15 minutes. Projected early ridership is 330,000 to 380,000 per year, and is expected to grow to over one million as the Lake Union area develops.

The new system connects with Metro buses, Sound Transit buses, trains and light rail, the monorail and Washington State Ferries.

The line is served by modern, low-floor streetcars, based on the examples in Portland, operating on the same roadway as other traffic.

Global Position System (GPS) technology alerts passengers by Next Bus to streetcar arrival times at the 11 stops and is also available on-line.

Developments

Construction of the South Lake Union Streetcar line began in July 2006, and the line opened in December 2007.

There are long-term plans for a much extended network. Currently, the Seattle Department of Transportation has been authorised by the City Council to evaluate a network comprising three new lines and a branch/extension to the existing South Lake Union line.

One of Seattle Streetcar's Inekon Trio cars lays over at the outer terminus of the new street tramway, in Fairview Avenue, as a New Flyer hybrid bus of King County Metro passes (S J Morgan)   1375674

Most intensive service: 15 min
Hours of operation: Mon-Thur: 06.00–21.00, Fri-Sat: 06.00–23.00, Sun: 10.00–19.00
Fare structure: Flat, with two hour free transfer; no passes sold, but PugetPass, Metro passes, and Metro transfers are accepted
Fare collection: Honour system, with random inspections; payment to ticket vending machines on board each streetcar/tram

Arrangements for elderly/disabled: All service is provided by low-floor cars and is fully wheelchair-accessible; discounted fare
Integration with other modes: Connects with Metro buses, Sound Transit buses, trains and light rail, the monorail and Washington State Ferries

Fleet: three cars
Inekon Trio 12T low-floor (2007)   M3

St Louis

Population: City 347,181 (2006 estimate), metropolitan area 2.8 million (2007 estimate)

Public transport

Bus, light rail and paratransit service provided by regional authority serving St Louis and surrounding parts of Missouri and Illinois, controlled by representative board. Car and van-pool schemes.

Metro (DBA Bi-State Development Agency)

707 North First Street, St Louis, Missouri 63102-2595, US
Tel: (+1 314) 982 14 00   Fax: (+1 314) 923 30 34
e-mail: transitinformation@metrostlouis.org
Web: www.metrostlouis.org

Key personnel

Chairman, Board of Commissioners:
  Jeffrey Watson
President and Chief Executive Officer: Robert Baer
Vice-President, Government & Community Affairs:
  Adella Jones
General Counsel (Interim): Katie Forster
Senior Vice-President and Chief Financial Officer:
  John Noce
Vice-President and Chief Information Technology Officer: Debbie Erickson
Senior Vice-President, Business Enterprises:
  Jennifer Nixon
Senior Vice-President, Transit Operations:
  Ray Friem
Acting Senior Vice-President, Engineering and New Systems Development: Scott Grott
Executive Vice-President, Administration:
  Thomas Sehr
Vice-President, Human Resources: Melva Pete
Vice-President, Marketing: Patrick McLean
  Staff: More than 2,300

Background

Established in 1949 through an agreement between Missouri and Illinois that was ratified by the US Congress, Metro's remit enables it to cross local, county and state boundaries in

Map of St Louis light rail system   1115276

building and operating services and facilities for the region's citizens. The service area covers St Louis and surrounding parts of Missouri and Illinois.

Previously known as the Bi-State Development Agency, and under which it continues to do business, the new name 'Metro' was adopted in February 2003.

Current situation

Metro owns and operates the St Louis metropolitan region's public transportation systems including MetroBus, MetroLink (light rail) and Metro Call-A-Ride paratransit van system. The agency also owns and operates the Gateway Arch Tram System, Ticketing and Reservation Center, the Arch Parking Garage, Gateway Arch Riverboats, St Louis Downtown Airport and the adjoining industrial business park in Cahokia/Sauget, Illinois.

Developments

In October 2006, the US Department of Homeland Security (DHS) awarded a grant to Metro of

USD1.1 million to improve rail and intercity bus security.

Bus (MetroBus)

Type of operation: Fixed-route bus system

Passenger boardings: (2002/03) 30.6 million
(2003/04) 30.5 million
(2004/05) 30.2 million
(2005/06) 32.5 million
(2006/07) 31.5 million
Vehicle-km: (2002/03) 40.3 million
(2003/04) 40.6 million
(2004/05) 40.3 million
(2005/06) 31.1 million
(2006/07) 30.9 million

Number of routes: 79
Route length: (One-way) 3,631 km
On priority right-of-way: 6.4 km

Current situation

Metro has adopted a strategic service plan that expands MetroLink in key corridors and restructures MetroBus routes as a 'hub and spoke' network around key MetroLink stations, as well as multiple regional transit centres. Metro operates 75 MetroBus routes in the St Louis region, of which 20 are operated in St Clair County, Illinois. The remaining 55 routes are operated in the St Louis metropolitan area. Eight express and 12 local routes serve downtown St Louis and the central business district.

Metro also operates three flex-route van routes in St Louis County, in which the street configuration does not permit the use of regular transit vehicles.

Developments

The MetroBus system consists of 24 MetroBus transit centres with one funded transit centre: Delmar Transit Plaza. The new Central West End Transit Centre is located at the Central West End MetroLink Station (adjacent to the Barnes-Jewish Hospital – Washington University's School of Medicine Complex). The new Riverview-Hall Street Centre is located at the edge of North St. Louis and St. Louis County.

This service model, based upon city and suburban transfer centres, offers co-ordinated timed transfers and multi-direction access between numerous MetroBus routes and MetroLink, in addition to offering better customer information, security, and shelter.

Transit centres will also be the remote connection points for Metro's suburban Metro Call-A-Ride and the 'connector' flex-van routes serving low-density employment parks not accessible with traditional bus transit. The transit centres will also be promoted for linkage to the core accessible transit system by private institutions operating employee and school shuttles, car or vanpool arrangements.

Fleet: 412 vehicles

Gillig Phantom 40 ft (2000)	61
Gillig Phantom 40 ft (2001)	111
Gillig Phantom 40 ft (2002)	44
Gillig Phantom 40 ft (2004)	15
Gillig Phantom 35 ft (1995)	34
Gillig Phantom 35 ft (1996)	24
Neoplan AN440 articulated CNG-powered (1997)	36
Gillig Phantom 30 ft (2000)	59
Gillig Phantom 30 ft (2001)	23
Gillig Phantom ramp (2001)	2
Gillig Phantom ramp (2002)	3

In peak service: 345
On order: Not currently available

Most intensive service: 10–15 min
One-person operation: All routes
Fare collection: Exact fare to farebox
Fare structure: Flat fare plus unlimited 2-hour transfer and various passes (daily, weekly, monthly) rate premium fare
Fares collected on board: Approximately 50 per cent on board cash, 50 per cent pre-paid
Fare evasion control: Undercover police surveillance system, plus bus and video surveillance system
Operational control: Route inspectors/mobile radio (CAD/AVL on 64 buses and GIS-based APC system for on-time performance monitoring and passenger counts)
Arrangements for elderly/disabled: Reduced fares and lift-equipped buses, kneeling vehicles and announcement system
Integration with other modes: Fixed route bus system supplemented by MetroLink (light rail) and Metro Call-A-Ride (paratransit van) systems
Average distance between stops: Approximately 8 stops per mile in urban settings and 3 stops per mile in suburban areas
Average peak-hour speed: In mixed traffic, 8.3 km/h (13.6 mph)
Operating costs financed by: Fares 19.2 per cent, other commercial sources 2.8 per cent, subsidy/grants 78.0 per cent
Subsidy from: Annual appropriation of transport sales taxes in St Louis City, St Louis County and multi-year contracts with St Clair County Transit District for the Illinois Department of Transportation

Fund and St Clair County Transportation Sales Taxes
New vehicles financed by: FTA Capital Grants, local matching funds and the Illinois Department of Transportation Grants

MetroLink

Type of operation: Light rail, initial route opened July 1993

Passenger boardings: (2002/03) 14.8 million
(2003/04) 14.5 million
(2004/05) 15.6 million
(2005/06) 16.6 million
(2006/07) 21.8 million

Route length: 73 km
  in tunnel: 4.71 km
Number of lines: 2
Number of stations: 37
Gauge: 1,435 mm
Track: 45.7 km 57-kg/m RE rail on timber sleepers, 27.35 km 65-kg/m RE rail on wood sleepers, concrete slab in tunnels
Electrification: 860 V DC, overhead

Current situation

In May 2001, Metro opened the St Clair County extension of MetroLink, which added nearly 29 km (18 miles) to the original 27.4 km (17 mile) alignment. The St Clair MetroLink alignment added light rail service from the 5th & Missouri station in East St Louis to the campus of Southwestern Illinois College, in Belleville. MetroBus routes in St Clair County were fully integrated with the MetroLink System, allowing co-ordinated transfers between bus and train. The St Clair County extension was funded through a St Clair County 0.5 cent sales tax and federal New Starts Funds. The total cost of this project was USD339 million.

An additional 5.6-km (3.5-mile) segment of light rail in St Clair County opened in June 2003. Construction of the Shiloh-Scott extension began in early 2001, with a USD60 million grant from the Illinois First (Fund for Infrastructure, Roads, Schools, and Transit) Program and a local match by the St Clair County Transit District. The cost for this segment of the MetroLink extension was USD75 million. This segment completed the connection from Lambert St Louis International Airport in northwest St. Louis County, to Scott

Air Force Base and the rapidly developing communities of O'Fallon and Shiloh, Illinois.

Developments

Engineering and design of the next planned segment, 8.5 km (5.3 miles) from Shiloh-Scott station to Mid-America Airport has been completed. Construction funding is being sought at this time.

In August 2006, Metro opened the Cross County MetroLink extension, a 12.9-km (8-mile), 9 station branch that begins at the Forest Park – DeBaliviere MetroLink Station. The Cross County branch extends west to the edge of downtown Clayton, the region's second business district, and turns south toward Interstate 44 near Lansdowne Avenue. The Cross County alignment connects the communities of St Louis City, University City, Clayton, Richmond Heights, Brentwood, Maplewood and Shrewsbury.

The project was designed and constructed using 100 per cent local funding and cost USD676 million. Construction started in April 2003 and revenue service began on 28 August 2006.

Rolling stock: 87 cars

Siemens-Duewag SD400 (1992/93) – LRV1	M31	
Siemens-Duewag SD460 (1999/2000) – LRV2	M10	
Siemens-Duewag SD460 (2000/01) – LRV3	M24	
Siemens-Duewag SD460 (2004/05) – LRV4	M22	

In peak service: 56 cars
On order: None

Service: Peak 10 minutes, Off-peak 15 minutes on branches, Peak 5 minutes, Off-peak 7.5 minutes in trunk
First/last car: 05.00/01.00
One-person operation: All cars; cars are bidirectional
Fare structure: Flat
Fare collection: Prepurchase; proof-of-payment system
Integration with other modes: Park-and-ride at 19 stations; MetroBus feeders have timed transfers
Arrangements for elderly/disabled: All stations and trains are ADA accessible
Security arrangements: CCTV at all stations; police patrols; on-board two-way Passenger Assistance Telephones (PATS); Code Blue telephones in park-and-ride facilities with direct communication with MetroLink Central Control

St Louis MetroLink Siemen-Duewag LRV (Bill Luke)   0554286

Operating costs financed by: Fares 32.1 per cent, other commercial sources 4.6 per cent, subsidy/grants 63.3 per cent

Subsidy from: Federal Vehicle Maintenance and Illinois Department of Transportation; dedicated transport sales tax in St Louis City, St Louis County, Madison County and St Clair County

New vehicles financed by: FTA Capital Grants and local matching funds

Metro Call-A-Ride

Type of operation: Demand-response paratransit van system

Passenger boardings: (2003) 575,344
(2004) 682,097
(2005) 676,011
(2006) 668,122
(2007) 663,869

Route area: St Louis City and St Louis County

Current situation

Demand-response system serving the residents of the City of St Louis and St Louis County. All services are provided in-house – no services are subcontracted.

Developments

The ADA (Americans with Disabilities Act) Department Process was established in 2001, when Metro began to move toward full compliance with the ADA. As a part of Metro's ongoing commitment to attain full ADA compliance, the Transit Access Programme began in January 2004. This programme improved Metro's Call-A-Ride certification process, which had not been in compliance with the ADA.

The programme requires completion of the following: 1) a paper application with professional verification of disability; 2) an interview; 3) a physical or cognitive functional assessment of the applicant's transit-related abilities. There are different types of eligibility granted based the individual's ability to use available MetroBus and MetroLink services.

Eligibility assessments take place at the Transit Access Centre, a 4,200 ft² facility equipped with a partial bus, sidewalk, ticket vending machine, stoplight and other features to simulate the transit environment. All customers must complete the certification process. The Transit Access Program, which is based on the best nationwide practices, supports the use of Metro's fully accessible MetroBus and MetroLink System by all who have the ability to use the system, and ensures Metro Call-A-Ride service is available for those who truly need it. Additionally, in 2006, a Travel Training programme was added to teach people with disabilities to use MetroBus and MetroLink services independently. More than 450 customers have received travel training services on an individual or group basis.

Metro Call-A-Ride migrated from the PASS DOS routing and scheduling system to the Trapeze 4 software in April 2007. This software had an immediate impact on the phone intake, and the wait times in the call centre queues dropped dramatically. In January 2007, the average wait time in the queue was over nine minutes. By comparison, in June 2007 the average wait time was just under one minute. This has continued to diminish, with the average wait time for March 2008 at 25 seconds. The average talk time per call has also dropped to approximately two minutes 30 seconds.

In the current fiscal year (FY2008), Metro Call-A-Ride will work in consort with the ADA Department in the implementation of the Certification Module in the Trapeze 4 software. This system will merge the ADA Department and Metro Call-A-Ride client databases and help streamline the ADA certification process. Also, Metro Call-A-Ride will implement the ADA polygons which will delineate the 1.2-km (³/₄-mile) boundary around all existing bus routes, light rail stations and the light rail alignment. These polygons will help Call-A-Ride to immediately identify those trips that are ADA eligible both by

MetroBus Gillig Phantom   0559755

Metro Call-A-Ride Ford Aerotech E450 paratransit van   0559753

the trip origin and destination, and the time of day the passengers travel.

Also, in the current fiscal year (FY2008), Metro Call-A-Ride will upgrade to Trapeze 7, which will provide greater flexibility in scheduling van-to-van transfers eventually leading to the multimodal transfers for ADA passenger trips. This version of the software will give the operations staff more powerful tools to route and schedule and more powerful algorithms to schedule the more complex long distance transfer trips. In addition, Metro Call-A-Ride will be upgrading the entire Mobile Data Terminal system by installing new Mentor Range MDC's, which will have GPS capabilities. This will greatly enhance the ability to route and schedule in dispatch on the day of service in absolute real time. This should increase the on-time performance of 97 per cent.

In the last fiscal year, Metro Call-A-Ride continued its ambitious programme of Van Operator and Line Instructor Refresher Training. This involved two days of intensive training both in the classroom and on a practice track. The Metro Call-A-Ride practice track is based on the National Rodeo course employed by the Community Transit Association. This programme, in conjunction with a comprehensive and active operator incentive programme, has continued

to have an extremely positive effect on the daily operations.

Fleet: 123 vans

Ford Aerotech E450 Van (2001)	21
Ford Aerotech E450 Van (2002)	18
Ford Aerotech E450 Van (2003)	38
Ford Aerotech E450 Van (2004)	21
Ford Aerotech E450 Van (2005)	5
Ford Aerotech E456 Van (2006)	20

In peak service: Not currently available
On order: Not currently available

Most intensive service: Between the hours of 05.00 and 09.00 and 14.00 and 17.30
One-person operation: All routes
Fare structure: Operator collects fare and deposits fare in on-board lock box
Fares collected on board: Some fares collected monthly through contractual agreement and work
Operational control: Transit Service Manager (TSM) observation and incident follow-up and on-board mobile data terminal in every vehicle; spotter programme in place since July 2006
Fare evasion control: Internal auditing process
Arrangements for elderly/disabled: Reduced fares are available and all vans are lift-equipped and ADA accessible; trips begin-end within ³/₄ of a mile of a fixed-route bus or light rail station

Integration with other modes: Supplemented by MetroLink (light rail) and MetroBus fixed-route systems
Average trip distance: 12.1 km (7.55 mile) per trip FY2007
Average speed: 16.97 mph (FY2007)

Operating costs financed by: Fares 4.9 per cent, other commercial sources 27.7 per cent (contracts with the department of mental health and Medicaid as well as miscellaneous others), and subsidy/grants 67.4 per cent

Subsidy from: Federal vehicle maintenance and Illinois Department of Transportation, dedicated transport sales tax in St Louis City, St Louis County, Madison County and St Clair County
New vehicles financed by: FTA Capital Grants and local matching funds

---

Tampa

Population: City 332,888 (2006 estimate), county area 1.17 million (2007 estimate), metropolitan area 2.72 million (2007 estimates)

Public transport
Bus and paratransit services provided by Regional Transit Authority controlled by representative board. Light rail proposed. Historic streetcar.

Hillsborough Area Regional Transit Authority (HART)
1210 East 7th Avenue, Tampa, Florida 33605, US
Tel: (+1 813) 223 68 31   Fax: (+1 813) 224 05 21
e-mail: shavalierm@gohart.org
Web: www.gohart.org

Key personnel
Chair: Ron Goving
Executive Director: David Armijo
Director of Planning: Mary Shavalier
General Manager, Operations: Carlos Tobar
   Staff: 650

Current situation
HART was established in 1980 with funding provided by an *ad valorem* tax. It now operates in Hillsborough County and connects with Pinellas County across the bay. Vanpools operate nine transit centres within its service area, incuding staffed sites in downtown Tampa and the University of South Florida areas.
   In October 2002 HART began operation of a streetcar system.

Developments
In 2008, HART opened three new transfer centres; West Tampa Transit Center, Netpark Transit Center and Northwest Transit Center. All transfer centres

include passenger amenities such as restrooms, shelters and benches, automatic ticket vending machines and beverage/snack vending.
   Also in 2008, HART began implementation of its Intelligent Transportation Project that includes upgraded radio, AVL/GPS, automatic passenger counters and passenger information displays.

Bus
(Including contracted services)

Passenger boardings: (including contracted services)
(2004) 8.9 million
(2005) 10.0 million
(2006) 10.7 million
(2007) 11.1 million
(2008) 12.0 million
Vehicle-km: (2004) 11.5 million (7.2 million miles)
(2005) 12.0 million (7.5 million miles)
(2006) 12.3 million (7.6 million miles)
(2007) 13.4 million (8.3 million miles)
(2008) 13.0 million (8.1 million miles)

Route length: (One way) 1,300 km
Number of routes: 47

Fleet: 199 vehicles
Gillig	183
Champion	16
In peak service: 154

Fare collection: Payment to driver or prepurchase pass; exact fare only
Fare structure: Flat; higher rate for Express services; local passes; monthly passes
Arrangements for elderly/disabled: All buses kneeling with ramps or lift-equipped working regular schedules; half fare
Bus priority: Marion Street downtown transitway extends 9 blocks

Integration with other modes: 23 park-and-ride lots in Hillsborough County, 1 in Pinellas County; cycle racks on all buses
Operating costs financed by: Fares 22 per cent, other commercial sources 0.1 per cent, subsidy/grants: local 64 per cent (from *ad valorem* tax), FTA six per cent, State seven per cent, City 0.5 per cent

Rapid transit (proposed)
Current situation
Light rail is included in the Hillsborough County Metropolitan Planning Organization's long-range plans. A Final Environmental Impact Statement was filed and Record of Decision received in March 2003. Funding for Right of Way is not yet in place.

TECO Historic Streetcar Line
Tel: (+1 813) 254 42 78
e-mail: info@tecolinestreetcar.org
Web: www.tecolinestreetcar.org

Background
The streetcar system is managed by Tampa Historic Streetcar Inc, a non-profit corporation, and HART operates and maintains it.
   The fleet consists of 11 cars.

Current situation
In 2008, the total boardings was 440,738.

Developments
Phase 1, a 3.7 km (2.3 mile) section, opened in October 2002 running from Ybor City to Downtown Tampa.
   The next phase will be an extension of just over 0.5 km (0.3 miles) running north on Franklin Street to Whiting Street and the Fort Brooke parking garage. All environmental assessments on this project have been completed. The extension is expected to be completed in 2010.

Washington

Population: City 550,521, metropolitan area 5.2 million (2005 estimates)

Public transport
Bus and metro services in the city of Washington, DC and in parts of suburban Maryland and Virginia are provided by Area Transit Authority governed by representative board. Separate local bus services feeding metro provided by county agencies for Montgomery County suburban area, city of Alexandria and Fairfax and Prince George's counties. MARC commuter rail service supported by Maryland state; Virginia commuter rail service supported by local transportation commissions; commuter buses run by private companies; proposed maglev line (see entry for Baltimore).

Washington Metropolitan Area Transit Authority (WMATA) – Metro
600 Fifth Street Northwest, Washington, DC 20001, US
Tel: (+1 202) 962 12 34
Fax: (+1 202) 962 28 97
e-mail: csvc@wmata.com
Web: www.wmata.com

Key personnel
Chair: Dana Kauffman
Vice-Chair: Gladys W Mack

WMATA Orion bus on K Street (Bill Luke)   0558428

Second Vice-Chair: Charles Deegan
Chief Executive Officer/General Manager:
   Richard A White
*Deputy General Manager of Finance/Chief Financial
   Officer:* H Charles Woodruff
Assistant General Manager, Operations:
   James T Gallagher
Chief Operating Officer, Metrorail: Steven Feil
Red Line Manager: Belynda Jones

Blue/Orange Line Manager: Charles Dziduch
Green/Yellow Line Manager: Currently vacant
Chief Operating Officer, Metrobus: Jack Requa
   Staff: 10,018

Passenger journeys: (Both modes)
(FY2002) 328.7 million
(FY2004) 336 million
(FY2005) 344 million

Operating costs financed by: Fares and other revenue 51.5 per cent, state and local government 48.5 per cent

Background

The Authority was formed in 1967. Metrorail and Metrobus serve a population of 3.5 million within a 4,000 km² (1,500 sq mile) area. The transit zone covers the District of Columbia, the suburban Maryland counties of Montgomery and Prince George's and the Northern Virginia counties of Alexandria, Fairfax and Loudon and the cities of Alexandria, Fairfax and Falls Church.

Current situation

A major programme of metro construction and bus fleet renewal and service development has taken place since WMATA was created in 1967. The metro plan adopted called for a 166 km 83-station network, which was completed in January 2001.

LS Transit Systems Inc (LSTS) is supplying Rail Operations Simulation System software to WMATA. LSTS is serving as a subcontractor to Alstom Signalling Inc (formerly General Railway Signal Corporation) as part of Alstom's contract to provide a train control system for the Green Line extension.

With opening of the 10.5 km Green Line extension from Anacostia to Branch Avenue in Prince George's County, Maryland, in January 2001, WMATA completed the network approved in 1997. Now a goal has been set to double public transport use by 2025, based on the Transit Service Expansion Plan adopted in 1999. This outlined a number of rail projects that could extend the network by up to 240 km, including metro extensions and new light rail schemes. The next construction project will be the first phase of a line to serve Dulles international airport.

Cubic Transportation Systems (CTS) is installing smartcard systems and will retrofit smartcard readers to existing gates as the project proceeds. However, implementation will start with the installation of electric paddle gates at those stations which are not already gated.

Developments

In September 2005, it was announced that members of the Metro Transit Police Department (MTPD) will participate in the Transportation Security Administration's (TSA) National Explosives Detection Canine Team Program.

Metrobus

Passenger boardings: (2002) 147.7 million (2004) 146 million
Vehicle-km: (2002) 60 million (approx) (2004) 48 million (estimate)

Number of routes: 350 on 182 lines
Route length: (One way) 2,118 km
On priority right-of-way: 79.3 km

Fleet: 1,402 vehicles

Neoplan articulated 60 ft	21
Ikarus 436 articulated 60 ft (1995)	43
New Flyer CNG 40 ft	164
ADB Flxible Metro 40 ft (with lift)	452
ADB Flxible Metro 40 ft	74
Orion 40 ft	502
Orion 30 ft	51
Orion II low-floor 26 ft	42
ADB Flxible Metro Minibuses 30 ft	35
ADB Flxible Metro Minibuses 35 ft	18

In peak service: 1,155
On order: New Flyer CNG: 450 buses with delivery due to commence in early 2005; 50 New Flyer/GM hybrid diesel-electric buses, delivery scheduled to start by the end of 2005

Most intensive service: 5–6 min
One-person operation: All routes
Fare collection: Exact fare; GFI registering fareboxes
Fare structure: Zonal, 10 cent transfer; area monthly/2-weekly pass, monthly bus/rail pass; off-peak pass

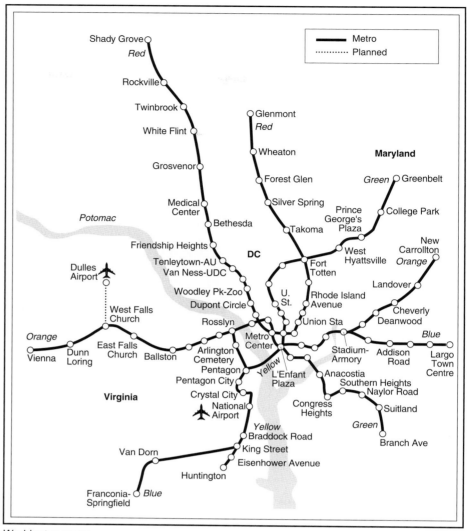

Washington metro   1127082

WMATA Blue Line train at Washington national airport (William A Luke)   0109556

Fare evasion control: Non-uniformed police officers; registering fareboxes
Integration with other modes: Buses feed metro stations; transfer from metro for journeys continued by bus
Operational control: Street supervisors/central radio
Surveillance: CCTV installed on some vehicles
Arrangements for elderly/disabled: Half fare, subsidised from local budgets; on call bus service; fleet of 35 vans; MetroAccess paratransit service
Average peak-hour speed: In mixed traffic, 11 km/h; in bus lanes, 25–27 km/h
Bus priority: I-66 road from Beltway into Washington open to buses and carpools only during peak hours in peak direction; I-395 has reversible-flow HOV lanes

Operating costs financed by: Fares 31.1 per cent, other commercial sources 2.8 per cent, subsidy/grants 66.1 per cent
New vehicles financed by: FTA grants 80 per cent, local funds 20 per cent

Current situation

MetroAccess complements Metrorail, Metrobus and local bus services for those with disabilities and is available seven days a week 05.30-24.00 on weekdays and 05.30-03.00 at weekends. Ridership was some 1.2 million passengers in FY2005.

Developments

Automatic Vehicle Locator (AVL) system installed in each vehicle.

In September 2005, the Metro board approved a four year USD210 million contract with MV Transportation for the management of the MetroAccess service. There are options for a further two year extensions to the contract.

As well as the current bus orders for new CNG and hybrid diesel-electric buses, improvements proposed over the next five years in the Metrobus Capital Improvements Programme include: an annual mid-life overhaul to 100 buses; further bus purchases, totalling approximately 420 vehicles; improvements to bus stops and shelters; real-time information accessed by telephone, from the internet, and displays at some locations; and improvements to the maintenance facilties.

Metrorail

Type of operation: Full metro, initial route opened 1976

Passenger boardings: (1996) 194 million
(2002) 181 million
(2004) 190 million
Car-km: (1996) 69.7 million

Route length: 169.6 km (106.1 miles)
  in tunnel: 81.2 km (50.5 miles)
  elevated: 14.84 km (9.22 miles)
Number of lines: 5
Number of stations: 86
  in tunnel: 47
  elevated: 6
Gauge: 1,435 mm
Track: 52.16 kg/m rail
Max gradient: 4%
Minimum curve radius: 213 m
Electrification: 750 V DC, third rail

Service: Peak 5–6 min, off-peak 12–20 min
First/last train: weekdays: 05.00, weekends: 07.00/ Sunday-Thursday: 24.00, Friday and Saturday: 03.00
Fare structure: Graduated; stored-value tickets; day, 2-week and monthly pass; bus/rail pass
Revenue control: AFC at all stations; staffed kiosk at all faregates, roving police patrols; electronic farecard verifier
Integration with other modes: 2 hour discount transfer to bus issued for metro ticket holders; 2-week bus pass includes limited metro travel
One-person operation: All trains
Signalling: Wayside and cab signals; ATS, ATO and ATP; trains can run in automatic, manual with ATP or manual without ATP modes
Surveillance: CCTV on all platforms, elevators and car parks; chemical sensors are installed at some underground stations; automated electronic fire protection system in stations and tunnels

Rolling stock: 904 cars, operated as 4- to 6-car sets
Rohr (1976/77/78)	M290
Breda Series 2000 and 3000	M428
CAF/AAI Series 5000	M186

In peak service: 564
On order: ALSTOM Series 6000: 62 cars on order with delivery starting in November 2004, option for a further 120 cars

Developments

ALSTOM is refurbishing 364 Breda Series 2000 and 3000 cars.

An extension of the Blue Line, from Addison Road to Largo Town, with an intermediate station at Morgan Boulevard, was opened in December 2004. The 5 km (3 mile) extension has two stations.

There is also a new station open on the Red Line. The New York Avenue station is midway between Union station and Rhode Island Avenue station.

In October 2005, a new parking facility was opened at White Flint Metrorail station.

Dulles Corridor Metrorail Project

The Virginia Department of Rail and Public Transportation (DRPT) and the WMATA are studying ways to implement public transportation improvements in the Dulles Corridor in Fairfax and Loudoun Counties. The 37.8 km (23.5 mile)

Washington DC Metro Centre (Van Wilkins)   0104815

system would serve as a link between the existing Metrorail system and service through Tysons Corner to Washington Dulles International Airport and Loudoun County.

Currently, the Final Environmental Impact Statement (Final EIS) has been completed and the Preliminary Engineering (PE) has started.

Anacostia Corridor Demonstration Project

Web: www.dctransitfuture.com/demos/anacostia/
WMATA and the District Department of Transportation are investigating a new transit line to southeast Washington. The Anacostia Corridor Demonstration Project, as originally conceived, was a six-stop, modern light rail/ streetcar service designed to travel along a 4.3 km (2.7 mile), unused CSX right-of-way adjacent to the neighbourhoods of Fairlawn, Anacostia and Barry Farm.

However, difficulties negotiating a satisfactory agreement for the purchase and/or use of the CSX Shepard Industrial Spur Right-of-Way have prompted consideration of an alignment that uses city streets. The newly proposed street-running alignment would serve the same communities as the original plan, and would provides an opportunity to identify additional stop locations along the proposed route.

The proposed route would start at the intersection of Pennsylvania and Minnesota Avenues SE and proceed southwest on Minnesota Avenue to Good Hope Road SE. Travelling west on Good Hope Road, vehicles would then proceed south onto Martin Luther King Jr Avenue to Howard Road. They would then travel northwest to Firth Sterling Avenue and proceed southwest, ending at South Capitol Street in the vicinity of Bolling Air Force Base.

In November 2004, a ground breaking ceremony was held for the demonstration project. Expected ridership is 3,000 per day.

Three trams have been ordered for the project from DPO Inekon, Czech Republic, a joint venture between Inekon and the transit authority of Ostrava.

Montgomery County Department of Public Works and Transportation (PW&T) – RIDE ON

Division of Transit Services
101 Monroe Street, 5th Floor, Rockville, Maryland 20850, US
Tel: (+1 240) 777 74 33
Fax: (+1 240) 777 58 01
e-mail: transit.dpwt@montgomerycountymd.gov
Web: www.montgomerycountymd.gov

Key personnel
Director, PW&T: Arthur Holmes
Chief, Division of Transit Services:
  Carolyn G Biggins
Chief, Operations Section: Steven Wells
Chief, Management Services Section:
  William Selby
Chief, Customer & Operations Support Section:
  Howard Benn
Chief, Commuter Services Section: Sandra Brecher

Passenger boardings: (2005/06) 27 million
Vehicle-km: Not currently available

Bus
Current situation

The county-owned Ride On operation provides feeder connections to the metro and intra-county bus services, totalling 80 routes (plus three Metrobus routes, which RIDE ON operates at weekends). Operations are focused on 11 Montgomery County metro stations, particularly those at Silver Spring, Wheaton, Rockville, Shady Grove and Bethesda. Some operations on lightly used routes are contracted out. Bus services cover most of Montgomery County's 810,000 population, with over 1,028 km of route. Peak fares are charged; bus-to-bus transfers are free on Ride On or local WMATA Metrobus services. A reciprocal arrangement applies.

As well as fixed route services, RIDE ON provides Call n Ride Special Transportation services for senior citizens with low incomes and those with disabilities.

The Division also provides carpool and vanpool services.

Developments

Security measures have been heightened, including the increased use of canine teams.

Fleet: 275 buses (plus 93 contracted)
Orion 30 ft diesel	20
Orion 35 ft diesel	69
Orion 40 ft diesel	20
Gillig 35 ft diesel	62
Orion 35 ft CNG	61
Orion 40 ft CNG	19
Flxible 40 ft diesel	4
New Flyer 40 ft CNG	15
Gillig 40 ft diesel-electric hybrid	5
Contracted	
ElDorado 27 ft diesel	81
Supreme 24 ft	12

In peak service: 297, including contracted vehicles
Average age of fleet: 6.9 years

Fare structure: Flat peak and off-peak; free transfers; bi-weekly passes; 20-trip tickets; all-day transfers and regional day pass

Arrangements for elderly/disabled: Free off-peak (09.30–15.00)

Operating costs financed by: Fares 17.2 per cent, other commercial sources 0.0 per cent, subsidy/grants 28.4 per cent, Montgomery County property tax levy 54.4 per cent

Integration with other modes:
The Division's services are co-ordinated with other transportation providers, including the WMATA's Metrobus and Metrorail and the Maryland Mass Transit Administration's MARC commuter rail and bus services.

Average peak hour speed: 20.9 km/h

Alexandria Transit Company – DASH

116 South Quaker Lane, Alexandria, Virginia 22314, US
Tel: (+1 703) 370 32 74   Fax: (+1 703) 370 34 04
e-mail: dashbus@alexandriava.gov
Web: www.dashbus.com

Key personnel
Chair: Paul Abramson
General Manager: Sandy Modell
Assistant General Manager: Brad Putzier
Director of Planning & Development: Al Himes
  Staff: 130

Background
Managed by First Transit Inc

Bus
Passenger boardings: (2004) 3.1 million
(2005) 3.3 million
(2006) 3.6 million
(2007) 3.7 million
(2008) 3.98 million
Vehicle-km: (2004) 2.18 million (1.36 million miles)
(2005) 2.25 million (1.4 million miles)
(2006) 2.25 million (1.4 million miles)
(2007) 2.35 million (1.46 million miles)
(2008) 2.41 million (1.5 million miles)

Fleet: 64 buses
Gillig 10.7 m (1996/98/99/2007)	23
Orion 10.7 m (2000/02/05/07)	41

On order: None

Current situation
Operates eight routes extending to 140 km for the 135,000 population city across the Potomac River from Washington DC. The publicly owned operation provides service within the city and feeders to five Metrorail stations. DASH is part of the National Capital Regional Fare Initiative – common bus transfers and bus day passes are used and accepted by all of the regional bus systems. DASH also accepts WMATA's Metrorail-to-bus transfer, Flashpass and tokens. Fares cover 28 per cent of operating costs.

Developments
Alexandria Transit Company is in the process of building a new bus maintenance facility, which is expected to open in early 2010 and which will make room for significant expansion of transit service in the city. The expansion of the fleet to 130 buses will also be eventually possible. DASH plans to increase frequencies on current routes, in addition to adding new cross-town routes to provide direct connections between new employment and retail centres with the rest of the city.

Maryland Transit Administration (MTA)

Maryland Commuter Rail (MARC)
6 Saint Paul Street, Baltimore, Maryland 21202-1614, US
Tel: (+1 410) 539 50 00
(+1 410) 767 39 96 (Communications)
Fax: (+1 410) 333 32 79
(+1 410) 333 08 93 (Communications)
Web: www.mtamaryland.com

Key personnel
Administrator: Paul J Wiederfeld
Deputy Administrator: Henry Kay
  Staff: 301 (Administrative)

Type of operation: Suburban rail

Passenger journeys: (Total operations)
(2003) 6.4 million
(2004) 6.7 million

Operating costs financed by: Fares 53 per cent, subsidy/grants 47 per cent

Current situation
Three routes in total are operated, with the Perryville-Baltimore-Washington DC service operating over Amtrak's Northeast Corridor route and Baltimore-Washington DC services over CSXT track. A Frederick/Martinsburg-Washington DC service is provided over CCSXT track. Total route 323 km with 42 stations.

In 2001, the network was extended by 21.6 km to Frederick.

Developments
In mid-2007, the MTA awarded Bombardier Transportation a contract, valued ate USD14 million, for the refurbishment and overhaul of 34 MARC IIB push-pull commuter rails

cars. The cars are due to return to service by 2010.

Rolling stock: 25 diesel and 10 electric locomotives, 122 coaches

Virginia Railway Express (VRE)

1500 King Street, Suite 202, Alexandria, Virginia 22314, USA
Tel: (+1 703) 684 10 01   Fax: (+1 703) 684 13 13
e-mail: gotrains@vre.org
Web: www.vre.org

Key personnel
Chief Executive Officer: Dale Zehner
Deputy Chief Executive Officer: Jennifer Straub
Counsel: Stephen A MacIsaac
Director, Finance: Donna Boxer
Director, Construction and Facilities:
  Sirel Mouchantaf
Director of Rail Equipment and Services:
  Dennis E Larson
Manager of Customer Communications:
  April Maguigad
Manager, Public Affairs: Mark Roeber
Manager of Marketing: Ann King
Manager, Transportation Services, Safety and Security: Sharmila Samarasinghe
  Staff: Not currently available

Virginia Railway Express G-4 Gallery car

1368935

Virginia Railway Express Sumitomo Gallery IV bilevel cab car

1368936

Passenger journeys: (2001/02) 3.3 million
(2002/03) 3.3 million
(2003/04) 3.5 million
(2004/05) 3.76 million
(2005/06) 3.64 million

Route length: 143.2 km (89 miles)
Number of lines: 2
Number of stations: 18
Gauge: 1422.4 mm (4 ft 8 in)

Background

In 1992, Virginia Railway Express (VRE), a partnership of the Northern Virginia Transportation Commission (NVTC) and the Potomac and Rappahannock Transportation Commissions, began commuter rail operations.

Current situation

VRE operates on two railroad lines: Fredericksburg (87 km, owned by CSXT) and Manassas (53 km, owned by NS). VRE currently serves 18 stations in northern and central Virginia and terminates service in Washington, DC, at Union station.

Operating aspects of VRE are overseen by the VRE Operations Board, which consists of seven members (three each from NVTC and PRTC and the Director of the Virginia Department of Rail and Public Transportation).

In 2006, VRE operated 29 trains per day. Services operate morning and evening peak on Monday to Friday only.

VRE's farebox recovery ratio is about 66 per cent. This allows VRE to provide services such as free parking, a guaranteed ride home outside train times, a 'Security Blanket' daycare programme to cover extra costs when trains are late, and free ride certificates for late-running services.

Developments

The VRE Operations Board has awarded a USD28 million contract to Abernathy Construction Corp to build a new double-track bridge across Quantico Creek, eliminating a single-track bottleneck on the Fredericksburg line. The project is part of a USD66 million capital improvement programme on the CSX-owned tracks used by VRE that will permit operation of more trains.

Virginia Railway Express GP-40 locomotive   1368937

In May 2005, 11 new Sumitomo Corp/Nippon Sharyo Ltd bi-level gallery cab cars were ordered. There was an option to purchase a further 50 cars, which was exercised in July 2006.

During FY2006, projects completed included the overhaul of gallery trucks and rebuilding of locomotives, renovation of the Washington Union terminal, Manassas Park platform extension and additional parking at Manassas Park and Broad Run.

More parking, 1,290 spaces, is under construction at the Burke Center. This project has an estimated cost of USD28.8 million

Rolling stock: 21 diesel locomotives, 97 cabs/trailers/coaches

Locomotives

GP 39 (remanufactured)	10
GP 40 (remanufactured)	5
F40 (owned)	3
F40 (leased)	3

Coaches

Kawasaki bilevel cab	4
Kawasaki bi-level trailer	13
TTA Gallery I, II and III trailers	30
Gallery IV cab cars	20
Gallery IV coaches	30

On order: 5 gallery cab cars, 10 gallery V cab cars

First/last train: 05.05/20.25
Service: Peak: 30 mins
Fare structure: Zonal; single-ride and 10-trip tickets, 5-day and monthly passes, discounted fares for youths aged 7 to 21, disabled passengers and senior citizens (aged 65 and over) and groups of more than 15 passengers; children 6 and under ride free
Arrangements for elderly/disabled: All stations are wheelchair accessible, with platform ramps and motorised lifts on trains.
Security: 130 non-uniformed, armed law enforcement officers
Integration with other modes: Step-Up Ticket programme for transfer to some Amtrak services

Uzbekistan

Tashkent

Population: 1.97 million (2006 estimate)

Public transport

Bus and trolleybus/tramway services provided by joint stock company, currently undergoing restructuring. Metro, with extensions under construction. Rail services provided by Uzbekistan Railway (UTY).

Toshshahartranshizmat JSC

Ul Shirokaya 6, 700000 Tashkent, Uzbekistan
Tel: (+998 71) 134 90 25, 133 03 23, 133 52 63
e-mail: tgpt@tgpt.uz
Web: www.tgpt.uz

Developments

In early 2006, the existing public transport company, Toshshaharyolovchitrans, was replaced by Toshshahartranshizmat JSC, an association for passenger transport. The intention is that the new association will unite the existing stakeholders, develop the transport infrastructure and co-ordinate tariffs.

There are plans to privatise the bus fleets, to restructure the public transport system to bring it back into profitability and to improve vehicles. Toshshahartranshizmat and the Asaka Bank have created a new 50:50 leasing company, Asaka-Trans-Leasing, which will lease buses to legal operators in the city.

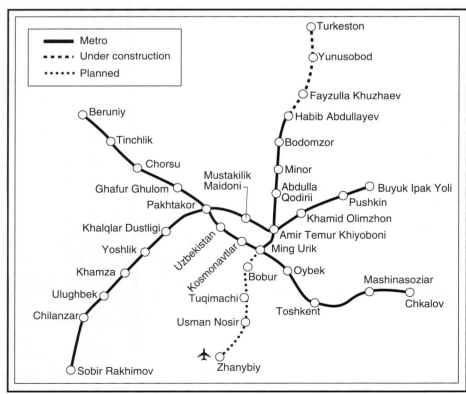

Tashkent metro   0547655

Also in 2006, it was announced that the association plans to purchase more than 60 Uraltransmach Spektr 71-402 trams in a contract valued at some USD17.2 million. Two of these vehicles have already been delivered for trials.

Bus
Number of routes: Not currently available
Route length: Not currently available

Fleet: Not currently available

One-person operation: All routes
Fare collection: Payment to roving conductor or prepurchase pass
Fare structure: Flat
Average peak-hour speed: Not currently available

Trolleybus
Number of routes: Not currently available
Route length: Not currently available

Fleet: Not currently available

One-person operation: All routes
Fare collection: As bus
Fare structure: Flat
Average peak-hour speed: Not currently available

Tramway
Type of operation: Conventional tramway

Route length: Not currently available
Number of lines: Not currently available
Gauge: 1,524 mm

Fare structure: Flat
Fare collection: As bus
One-person operation: All routes

Rolling stock: Not currently available

Tashkent Metro
Uzbekistan P rospekt 92A, Tashkent 600015, Uzbekistan
Tel: (+998 71) 32 38 52

Key personnel
Chief Executive: Shainoyat Rakhimovich Shaabdurakhimov
Chief Engineer: Khakim Gafurovich Gafurov

Type of operation: Full metro, first line opened 1977

Passenger journeys: (Annual) 126.7 million (estimate)

Route length: 39.1 km
Number of lines: 3
Number of stations: 29
Gauge: 1,524 mm
Max gradient: 4%
Minimum curve radius: 400 m
Electrification: 825 V DC, third rail

Current situation
The initial 7.6 km section of Line 3 opened in August 2001.

Developments
An extension to Line 3, northwards to Turkeston, is under construction.
A southern extension is planned, as is a fourth 8-km line, the Sirgali Line.

Rolling stock: 146 cars, in four-car sets
Mytischy EJ-T   M146

Service: Peak 2 min
First/last train: 06.00/01.00
Fare structure: Flat
Fare collection: Prepurchase plastic token to turnstile

Uzbekistan Temir Yullari (UTY) – Uzbekistan Railway
7 Shevchenko Street, 700060 Tashkent, Uzbekistan
Tel: (+998 71) 138 80 00
Fax: (+998 71) 138 84 23
Web: www.uzrailway.uz

Suburban rail
Current situation
UTY runs suburban trains on several routes into Tashkent Voksal, electrified 3 kV DC.
For further information on UTY, please see *Jane's World Railways.*

Venezuela

Caracas
Population: 3.2 million, metropolitan area 5 million (estimates)

Public transport
Metro and some bus services provided by Ministry of Infrastructure company. Many private bus operators; 'Por Puesto' minibus services with 18 to 32 seats; jeep transport with up to 12 seats on steep mountain slopes surrounding the city; commuter railway planned.

Compania Anonima Metro de Caracas (Caracas Metro)
Public Relations Office
Av Francisco de Miranda, Multicentro Empresarial del Este, núcleo Miranda, Torre B, Piso 7, Caracas, Venezuela
Tel: (+58 212) 206 77 41
Fax: (+58 212) 266 33 46
e-mail: multimedia@metrodecaracas.com.ve
Web: www.metrodecaracas.com.ve

Key personnel
President: Vicente Tortoriello V
Staff: 4,725

Current situation
As well as running the metro, the company operates a network of feeder bus routes.

Metro
Type of operation: Full metro, initial route opened 1983

Passenger journeys: 408.9 million (annual estimate)

Route length: 4.5.6 km
Number of lines: 3
Number of stations: 40

Gauge: 1,435 mm
Track: 54 kg/m continuously welded rail, on Stedef twin-block sleepers laid on concrete (tunnels) or ballast (surface)
Tunnel: Cut-and-cover and bored
Electrification: 750 V DC, third rail
First/last train: 05.30/23.00

Service: Peak 1½ min
Fare structure: Zonal; magnetically encoded single, 2-trip and 10-trip tickets
Revenue control: Entrance and exit turnstiles, ticket-issuing machines, validation on board
Signalling: Full ATC

Operating costs financed by: Fares 58 per cent, other commercial sources 5.8 per cent, subsidy/grants 36.2 per cent

Rolling stock: 456 cars
CIMT Type A (cab)	M110
CIMT Type B	M268
GEC Alsthom Type C (cab) (1995)	M34
GEC Alsthom Type D (1995)	M22
GEC Alsthom Type R (1995)	T22

In peak service: 345
On order: Six four-car trains for the extension from Las Adjuntas to Los Teques

Current situation
Line 3 extension from El Valle to Mercado, and then onwards to La Rinconada, is due to open in late 2006.

Caracas metro   0021697

For details of the latest updates to *Jane's Urban Transport Systems* online and to discover the additional information available exclusively to online subscribers please visit
juts.janes.com

Line 4 from Capuchinos to Plaza Venezuela (5.5 km with four stations) also under construction, to relieve the busiest central section of Line 1. This line will also extend eastwards, taking the total length of Line 4 to 12 km in due course.

There will be a suburban extension (9.5 km, no intermediate stations) of Line 2 from Las Adjuntas to Los Teques. The FRAMECO Consortium won the contract for this line, valued at some EUR204 million. The contract includes the delivery of six four-car trains, electrification and signalling.

There is also a long-term plan for a route to the southeast suburbs.

Bus
Staff: 1,018 (included above)

Passenger journeys: (1991) 26.5 million
(1994) 30.2 million
(1995) 34 million

Number of routes: 20 urban, 4 suburban

Current situation
MetroBus feeder buses connecting with the Metro were introduced in 1987 on a single route and the network has expanded each year.

There is integrated ticketing with the Metro.

Fleet: 274 buses

Leyland National Mk1	22
Renault PR100-2	99
Pegaso 6424	99
Renault Unicar Fanabus	54

In peak service: 160

Ferrocar – Venezuelan State Railways
Instituto Autónomo Ferrocarriles del Estado Torre
Avenida José Felix Sosa, Torre Británica de Seguros, Piso 7/8, Caracas 1062-A, Venezuela
Tel: (+58 212) 201 87 00, 88 97
Fax: (+58 212) 201 89 02
Web: www.iafe.gov.ve

Key personnel
President: Angel Gárcia Ontiveros
Vice-President: Frank Morales
Vice-President, Legal Affairs: Ana Puerta
Manager, Administration and Finance:
    Erika Palacios
Manager, Human Resource: Anelkis Avila
Manager, Construction: Wilfredo Salinas
Manager, Property: Edgar Patinis
Manager, Planning and Budgets: Anna Muro
Manager, Marketing and Commercial:
    Oswaldo Franco
Manager, Public Relations: Rubi Guadelis
Manager, Security: Roberto Anselmetti
Manager, Internal Accounting: Arlecia Araque

Type of operation: Commuter rail (under construction)

Commuter rail (planned)
Current situation
The major Ferrocar enterprise now under way is the long-planned east-west Central Region system, also known as the Central Trunk. This will extend from Caracas to Puerto Cabello via Cúa, Maracay and Valencia, and will link the capital and the central region of the country with the Central Western trunk at Puerto Cabello. It has been designated as a project of national importance. Patronage is expected to be very heavy, with some 600,000 daily journeys forecast within a year of opening.

After a call for tenders in 1989, an Italian-Japanese-Venezuelan consortium, Contuy Medio, led by Cogefar-Impresit SpA of Milan, won in 1991 the competition to build the first 41 km from Caracas to Cúa, serving the expanding new town of Tuy Medio. A revised contract valued at USD800 million was eventually signed with the Venezuelan government in 1996, whereby the consortium agreed to meet 50 per cent of the construction cost. Ferrocar's 1996 investment budget made provision for a VEB12.493 billion advance payment for civil works on the Caracas-Cúa route. Substantial delays were encountered during construction of the line through very hilly country.

This first stage traverses difficult terrain, with a difference of 623 m in level between its extremities, requiring a ruling gradient of 2.3 per cent and 10.6 km of tunnelling, including one bore of 6.8 km. The line is at 25 kV 60 Hz AC, and laid with a single track later to be doubled.

Maximum speed of 120 km/h will be exploited by 13 four-car emus from Nippon Sharyo, consisting of two motor cars enclosing two trailers, with a capacity for 448 passengers. CTC is located in Caracas and there are two intermediate stations. In Caracas the line's terminus is at La Rinconada on the extension of metro Line 3, which is planned to open on the same day.

The second stage of the Central Region system is the 176 km double-track line from Cúa to a point on the Puerto Cabello route close to Morón, costed at VEB52.7 billion for civil works and VEB12.6 billion for rolling stock. This route is being engineered in part for 180 km/h passenger operation, but is also expected to carry heavy freight traffic once Venezuela's national network emerges.

Ferrocar expects to handle 40,000 passengers and 31,000 tonnes of freight daily between Caracas and Puerto Cabello when the line opens in 2010. Construction has been concentrated on the 108 km section between the existing Puerto Cabello line and La Encrucijada, south of Cúa, traversing heavy terrain where 14 tunnels totalling 33 km are required. A further 23.8 km is on viaduct. This work is also being carried out by the Contuy consortium, while E&M work is being handled by the Ferrocentro. Operation will require a further eight emus immediately and another 17 later, as well as 14 electric locomotives and 425 wagons.

For further information on Ferrocar, please see *Jane's World Railways*.

Valencia (Venezuela)
Population: City 740,000, metropolitan area 1.5 million (estimates)

Public transport
Bus services provided by private operators. Light rail/metro, with extensions under construction and planned.

CA Metro de Valencia – Valmetro
Av Navas Espínolas, c/c Av Farriar No 97-25, Valencia, Estado Carabobo, Venezuela
Tel: (+58 241) 858 59 70, 857 71 66, 858 61 91
Fax: (+58 241) 858 24 84
e-mail: dominio@metrovalencia.gob.ve
Web: www.metrovalencia.gob.ve

Key personnel
General Manager, Transport:
    Leonardo Chumatschko
Commercial Manager: Edgar Patinis
Manager, Administration and Finance:
    Alejandro Sanchez
Manager, Planning and Budget: Mercedes Macedo
Manager, Information: Gilberto Guedez
Staff: Not currently available

Type of operation: Metro, first phase opened November 2007

Passenger journeys: n/a
Car-km: n/a

Route length: 6.2 km
Number of stations: 7

Background
CA Metro de Valencia – Valmetro was formed in 1991. The company has two shareholders: the Mayorship of Valencia with 98 per cent of participation and FUNVAL with 2 per cent.

Current situation
Construction started in mid-1997 on the initial section of a new metro line. Siemens Transportation is supplying electrical and mechanical equipment, as well as a fleet of 12 model SD 460 railcars.

A northern extension to Guaparo (4.5 km, six stations), is planned.

A second west-east line is also planned.

Developments
The first phase of the system opened in November 2007.

Fleet: 12 cars (currently operating in two-car sets)

Siemens SD 460	12

Service: 4 min
Hours of operation: 06.00–22.00
Fare structure: Flat; reduced fare for students; reduced fare for the elderly, disabled and children planned
Fare collection: Tickets issued manually; vending machines planned
Fare evasion: Automated ticket barriers

Vietnam

Hanoi
Population: 3.1 million (2005 estimate)

Public transport
Bus services provided by state organisation. Private minibus operations. Light rail/tram project under study. Urban rail line proposed.

Hanoi Bus Company
c/o Hanoi Transport Corporation (Transerco)
32 Nguyen Cong Tru Street, Hai Ba Trung District, Hanoi, Vietnam
Tel: (+84 4) 825 45 90, 971 27 95, 971 58 91
Web: www.hanoibus.com.vn

Key personnel
Chairman: Bui Xuan Dung

Passenger journeys: (2006) 365 million (estimate)

Number of routes: 40 (2003 estimate)

Bus
Current situation
The state-owned Hanoi Bus Company, formed by the amalgamation of three previous bus companies, provides standard-size bus

operations within the city and to Noi Bai International Airport.

The total Transerco bus fleet as at 2004 was estimated at 691 vehicles, with an average fleet age of some 3.4 years in 2003.

Developments

There have been recent proposals to privatise bus services. Currently, responsibility for public transport lies with the Transport and Public Works Service (TUPWS), which has set up a division, the Transport Management and Operations Centre (TRAMOC), that has specific responsibilities for management and operation of public transport. Transerco has overall control over all the routes, while TRAMOC is responsible for planning routes, issuing tickets, monitoring Transerco's performance and determining the amount of subsidy to be paid. TRAMOC liaises directly with Transerco which in turn liaises with the operating enterprises.

Six routes were put out for tender in 2004 and the evaluation was completed in early 2005. Two companies share the six routes. There are plans to tender out more bus routes.

Transerco has recently started five new routes in the city. There are plans to introduce express/BRT bus routes.

A contactless ticketing system is currently being implemented.

Ho Chi Minh City

Population: Municipality 6.2 million (mid-2005 estimate), metropolitan area 9 million (estimate)

Public transport

Bus services provided by state-owned company (Saigon Bus), one private joint-venture company (Saigon Star Bus Company) and other private operators, mostly in organised groups. Extensive use of shared taxis, 'Xiclos' (pedicabs) and 'Selam' (scooter taxis). Tram (Translohr) and metro planned. Monorail under study.

Department of Transport and Urban Public Works

63 Ly Tu Trong Street, District 1, Ho Chi Minh City, Vietnam
Tel: (+84 8) 29 52 95   Fax: (+84 8) 29 04 58
Web: www.eng.hochiminhcity.gov.vn

Key personnel
Director: Tran Quang Phuong

Monorail

In March 2007, Berjaya Corporation Bhd (BCB), Malaysia (www.berjaya.com.my) announced that it had signed a Memorandum of Understanding with the City's Department of Transport and Urban Public Works for a six-month study for a 32.5-km monorail system.

Metro

A city-wide metro network is planned for Ho Chi Minh. Construction of the initial 19.5-km line will link Ben Thanh Market to Suoi Tien. The line will be partly underground and partly at grade. The line is currently planned to open in 2012.

In late 2006, the Asian Development Bank's Japan Special Fund agreed to a Technical Assistance (TA) grant of USD1.7 million for preparation of a Master Plan for two further lines.

There are long-term proposals for a fourth north-south line, and for six lines in total.

MANUFACTURERS AND SERVICES

Rail vehicles
Electric traction equipment
Rail and bus components and subassemblies
Electrification contractors and equipment suppliers
New technology/innovative transit systems
Buses — chassis, integrals and bodies
Road vehicle chassis components
Signalling, communications and traffic control equipment
Passenger information systems
Revenue collection systems and station equipment
Vehicle maintenance equipment and services
Permanent way components, equipment and services
Turnkey systems contractors
Information technology systems
Consultancy services

RAIL VEHICLES

Company listing by country

AUSTRALIA
Downer EDI Rail
United Group Rail

BELGIUM
Cockerill Maintenance & Ingenierie SA (CMI)

BRAZIL
Gevisa SA

CANADA
Bombardier Transportation

CHINA
China Northern Locomotive and Rolling Stock Industry (Group) Corporation (CNR)
China South Locomotive and Rolling Stock Industry (Group) Corporation (CSR)
CNR Changchun Railway Vehicles Co Ltd

CROATIA
Djuro Djaković Holding dd
Končar – Electric Vehicles Inc

CZECH REPUBLIC
Inekon Group as
Škoda Transportation sro
Škoda Vagonka as

EGYPT
SEMAF

FINLAND
Transtech Oy

FRANCE
ALSTOM Transport

GERMANY
FTD Fahrzeugtechnik Dessau AG
G Zwiehoff GmbH
Leoliner Fahrzeugbau Leipzig GmbH (FBL)
Siemens AG
Vossloh Locomotives GmbH

INDIA
BEML Limited
Bharat Heavy Electricals Limited (BHEL)
RCF – Rail Coach Factory
The Integral Coach Factory (ICF)

INDONESIA
INKA

ITALY
Ansaldobreda SpA
CostaRail Srl
FIREMA Trasporti SpA

JAPAN
Alna Yusoki-Yohin Co Ltd
Hitachi Ltd
Kawasaki Heavy Industries Ltd
Kinki Sharyo Co Ltd
Niigata Transys Co Ltd
Nippon Sharyo Ltd
Tokyu Car Corporation

KOREA, SOUTH
Hyundai Rotem Company

LATVIA
RVR

POLAND
H Cegielski – Fabryka Pojazdów Szynowch Sp zoo
Modertrans Poznan Sp Zoo

Newag Spólka Akcyjna
PESA Bydoszcz SA
RMT Protram Wroclaw Sp zoo

ROMANIA
Astra Vagoane Călători SA/Arad

RUSSIAN FEDERATION
Metrowagonmash (MWM)
Mytischi
Power Machines Group
Ust-Katav Tramway Works

SLOVAKIA
ŽOS Vrútky Jsc

SOUTH AFRICA
The UCWPartnership

SPAIN
CAF – Construcciones y Auxiliar de Ferrocarriles SA
Vossloh Transportation Systems

SWITZERLAND
Alcan Extruded Products
Stadler Rail Group

TURKEY
Tüvasaş

UNITED KINGDOM
Brush Traction
TRAM Power Ltd
Wabtec Rail Ltd

UNITED STATES
Colorado Railcar Manufacturing LLC
Kawasaki Rail Car Inc
MotivePower Inc
United Streetcar LLC

Alcan Extruded Products

Alcan Aluminium Valais SA
LP Rail & Bus
PO Box 1812, Max Högger-Strasse 6, CH-8048
Zurich, Switzerland
Tel: (+41 43) 497 44 22   Fax: (+41 43) 497 44 06
Web: www.alcan-masstransportation.com

Key personnel
Director Large Profiles: *Hubert Zimmermann*
Segment Manager Rail & Bus: *Giorgio Destefani*
Deputy Segment Manager Rail & Bus: *Vito Melina*
Product Manager Components: *Olindo Bacciarini*
Product Manager Power Rail: *Patrick Küchler*

Background
Alcan Aluminium Valais SA LP Rail&Bus is a
member of the Engineered Products Division of
Rio Tinto Alcan. LP Rail&Bus is the specialised
segment dedicated to the mass transportation
business worldwide.

Products
Supply of types of aluminium extrusions,
sheets and plates, structural components
and sub-assemblies (such as finished floor
elements, side walls and crash modules) as
well as 2D composite components produced
by the different Alcan plants and partner
companies.

Contracts
Alcan Aluminium Valais SA LP Rail&Bus has
entered into co-operation and supply agreements
with more than 30 rolling stock manufacturers.

Recent projects include low-floor regional
train sets for Algerian, Austrian, Finnish, French,
Hungarian, Italian, Polish, Slovakian, Spanish,
Swiss and US railways; metro and suburban
train sets for Barcelona, Brussels, Helsinki,
Madrid, Melbourne, Paris and Rome; double-
deck coaches for Czech, Finnish, French and
Italian railways; tilting trains for Czech, German,
Italian, Spanish, Swiss and UK railways; high-
speed trains for French, German, Italian and
Spanish railways.

New generation of metro for Brussels, built by CAF in Spain, with body shell using large aluminium extrusion technology and crash modules from Alcan (CAF)   1373714

New regional 'FLIRT' train built by Stadler in Switzerland for different lines across Europe. The body shell is using large aluminium extrusion technology from Alcan (Stadler)   1373711

High-speed 'Velaro' train built by Siemens Transportation in Germany for Spanish railways. The body shell utilises large aluminium extrusion technology from Alcan (Siemens)   1373713

Double-deck regional emu built by Skoda Vagonka in the Czech Republic for the Czech and Lithuanian railways. The body shell utilises large aluminium extrusion technology from Alcan (Skoda)   1373709

New generation of Zurich 'Cobra' tramways built by Bombardier Transportation, with design and global material and component delivery from Alcan (VBZ)
1373710

Alna Yusoki-Yohin Co Ltd

4-5 Higashi Naniwa-cho 1-chome, Amagasaki
660-8572, Japan
Tel: (+81 6) 401 72 83

Fax: (+81 6) 401 61 68
Web: www.alna.co.jp

Key personnel
President: *N Yamazawa*

Products
Aluminium, mild steel and stainless-steel
electric railcars, passenger coaches and light rail
vehicles.

ALSTOM Transport

Worldwide Headquarters of Transport Sector:
48 rue Albert Dhalenne, F-93482 Saint-Ouen
Cedex France
Tel: (+33 1) 41 66 90 00   Fax: (+33 1) 41 66 96 66
Web: www.transport.alstom.com

Key personnel

President, Transport Sector: *Philippe Mellier*
Regional Senior Vice-Presidents:
   Finance: *Jean-Jacques Morin*
North Europe: *Roland Kientz*
South Europe: *Charles Carlier*
Asia Pacific: *Marc Chatelard*
NAFTA: *Roelof van Ark*
Iberian-Americas: *Antonio Oporto*
Senior Vice-President Human Resources: *Bruno
   Guillemet*
Senior Vice-President Legal: *Fred Einbinder*
Senior Vice-President Technical: *François Lacôte*
Senior Vice-President Communications: *Patrick
   Bessy*
Senior Vice-President Public Affairs: *Maurice
   Benassayag*
Senior Vice-President Business Excellence:
   Jean-Michel Geffriaud
Senior Vice-President of Operations Rolling Stock
   and Components: *Thierry Best*
Senior Vice-President of Operations Signalling,
   Maintenance and Services and Integrated &
   Global Transport Solutions: *Emilio Gallocchio*
Senior Vice-President Project Management:
   Alberto Pedrosa
Senior Vice-President Rolling Stock Engineering:
   Marc van Damme
Senior Vice-President Rolling Stock
   Manufacturing: *Frank Lecoq*
Senior Vice-President Train Life Services:
   Antonio Moreno
Senior Vice-President Infrastructure: *Alain Goga*
Senior Vice-President Transport Information
   Solutions: *Michel Marien*
Senior Vice-President Components: *Roberto
   Sestini*
Senior Vice-President Systems: *Yannic Bourbin*

Background

ALSTOM is represented in 70 countries
worldwide. The Group's power business
comprises the power turbo-systems/power
environment sector and the power service
sector. The group is also a leading player in the
marine sector.

The Transport Sector of ALSTOM employs
approximately 25,000 people. It has more than
100 production and maintenance facilities and a
commercial presence in over 50 countries.

Commercially, the company organises
itself into five regions – NAFTA (Canada, US
and Mexico), Asia Pacific, Iberian-American,
Southern Europe and Northern Europe and
these centres are supported by one operations
group. The five regional centres and operations
group are assisted by nine support functions,
which cover different activities and five product
lines including: rolling stock, information
solutions, train life services, infrastructure and
systems.

In December 2007 ALSTOM signed an agreement
with Russian company, Transmashholding, one
of the largest companies in the Russian rolling
stock market. The co-operation will take the form
of joint companies for the production of railway
components up to complete rolling stock.

Between 1 April 2007 and 31 March 2008,
ALSTOM's order intake increased by 23 per cent
and it recorded a net profit of EUR852 million for
2007–08, an increase of 56 per cent compared to
EUR547 million in 2006–07.

Products

ALSTOM designs, manufactures, tests and
commissions rolling stock for commuter, metro
and light rail applications; as well as single- or
double-deck, electric or diesel-electric trainsets
for suburban, regional high-speed and very-
high-speed use. ALSTOM also produces
locomotives and freight wagons and markets

ALSTOM's Class X60 Coradia Lirex emu for SL, Sweden   1122876

ALSTOM's Metropolis trainset for the Dominican Republic's Santo Domingo metro line   1341748

Citadis low-floor tram for Lyons, France   0585252

traction and electromechanical subsystems to
third-party wagon and carriage builders.

In addition, the company designs, configures,
integrates, tests and commissions rail transport
network signalling systems for urban and main
line rail infrastructure authorities. These include
traffic management, traffic control, maintenance
diagnostics and planning solutions, passenger

information facilities and automatic driving
systems.

These products and systems are also marketed
by ALSTOM within a range of rail transport
system solution packages and may include:
project management, project financing, civil
works, life-time maintenance, and initial or long-
term transport service operation. All this offering

is backed up by a worldwide service organisation offering customers a range of service packages from basic warranty and parts to 'lifetime support'.

Locomotives

ALSTOM has developed a family of locomotives, named Prima. These locomotives can be equipped with each of the relevant train control systems to enable them to run on all electrified lines in Europe and are available in both diesel and multivoltage electric versions. The design is claimed to cut traction costs by up to 30 per cent, through its ONIX technology. It is offered as the world's first locomotive to use an IGBT traction system. A 4,200 kW 140 km/h multivoltage demonstrator has been produced.

Passenger vehicles

ALSTOM has developed six comprehensive families of passenger rolling stock to address the rail transport market, from LRVs and metros through commuter, regional and intercity trains, to high-speed and very-high-speed trains. Optionic Design© is the name given to ALSTOM's product design process, which integrates from the very beginning a wide range of configurations, based on international customers' evolving needs around the world.

The six families are: Citadis™ (light rail vehicles for city operation), Metropolis™ (metro cars for city operation), X'trapolis™ (commuter trainsets), Coradia™ (regional and intercity trainsets), Pendolino™ (high-speed trainsets) and TGV (very-high-speed trainsets).

All these families use service-proven equipment, bogies and subassemblies such as ONIX™ Drive and Agate train control, produced by the many ALSTOM units around the world. These factors contribute to lower LCC and higher reliability and availability.

Citadis features include:
- modularity, with a choice of car dimensions, high or low floor
- improved vision and comfort, with 35 per cent more glass surfaces compared to a traditional tramway
- high safety levels for drivers and passengers, with reinforced cab structure and bodyshell structure easy maintenance thanks to centralised spare parts supply, with plug-in, pull-out layout of equipment interfaces
- quick repairability with easy-to-exchange windows and panelling.

Metropolis is the modular mass transit solution and addresses the different needs of customers worldwide, from the most traditional metro to the most sophisticated driverless version. Choices of train dimensions, train configurations, multiple-unit operation, train-monitoring architecture and manned or unmanned operation mean that customers are able to select design parameters to create the right metro for their network. ALSTOM also offers tailor-made metro solutions for networks with specific design requirements, such as those of Paris, London and New York.

X'trapolis is a high-capacity commuter train. Like the Citadis and Metropolis families, it offers flexibility in train dimensions and configurations. Other features include: electrical multiple-units and passenger coaches, single- and double-decks, easy maintenance and upgrading to deal with different passenger flow requirements.

X'trapolis is designed to meet all track gauge, vehicle gauge and voltage requirements.

Coradia addresses the increasing trends of urban and outer-city development. Coradia regional and intercity trains are modular flexible products, designed to provide high standards of comfort, safety and performance. The Coradia family holds the record for the fastest dmu and double-deck emu (200 and 220 km/h respectively).

The Coradia Duplex double-deck train concept with distributed power has a new bodyshell based on a system of laser-cut interlocking pieces. In this way, the structure is flexible and can adapt to any specific gauge dimensions or body shapes for technical or aesthetic purposes.

ALSTOM's Citadis™ tramway, Nice Cote-d'Azur (CANCA)   1341764

Cityway low-floor tram for Rome   0585250

Citadis low-floor tram for Montpellier, France   1194410

It can operate at up to 220 km/h in dmu, emu or locomotive-operated push-pull version.

The Pendolino family operates at maximum speeds in the 200–270 km/h range. Most of this family are tilting trains but a non-tilting version has also been developed to suit high-speed shuttle-type operations.

The TGV family of very-high-speed trains includes single-deck, double-deck and the new AGV (Automotrice à Grande Vitesse). They are all based on the articulated trainset concept, which provides high security for passengers and drivers alike. The TGV Duplex features an aluminium bodyshell, high capacity and speeds of up to 320 km/h. The AGV can travel up to 350 km/h and has the advantage of distributed power throughout the trainset. A tilting TGV is also possible.

The Pendolino and TGV product families can all be built as tilting trains, using ALSTOM's field-proven, third-generation Tiltronix technology. For the TGV, Tiltronix would be applied to optimise performance if the train were required to leave dedicated high-speed routes and operate on traditional lines. ALSTOM's industrial unit in Savigliano, Italy, is the company's centre for Tiltronix technology.

TGV is an SNCF trademark.

ALSTOM's Metropolis trainset for the Shanghai metro   1194409

Systems solutions, systems integration and project financing

Project management, systems integration and supply packages. These packages are custom-designed from a set of modules which start with the rolling stock and signalling system and extend to embrace the remaining electrical and mechanical systems, the civil works, project finance, lifetime maintenance and even initial or long-term transport service operation.

ALSTOM Transport Systems
48 rue Albert Dhalenne, F-93482 Saint-Ouen Cedex
Tel: (+33 1) 41 66 90 00   Fax: (+33 1) 41 66 96 66
Senior Vice-President International Systems Operations: *Laurent Troger*

ALSTOM Transport Systems Infrastructure Business Unit
33 rue des Bateliers, F-93404 Saint Ouen Cedex, France
Tel: (+33 1) 40 10 62 62   Fax: (+33 1) 40 10 60 60
Senior Vice-President, International Systems Infrastructure: *Alain Goga*

Traction equipment and subsystems

ALSTOM supplies fully integrated propulsion system packages, traction equipment and support services for modern railway and urban transportation vehicles. It offers a range of products, services and expertise in transport electronics, and in electrical and mechanical engineering, and establishes partnerships with its customers to support them throughout the life cycle of their equipment.

Contact points

Traction equipment, power modules and switchgear:
ALSTOM Transport SA
50 rue du Dr Guimier, PO Box 4, F-65600 Semeac, Tarbes
Tel: (+33 5) 62 53 41 21

Onboard electronic equipment:
ALSTOM Transport SA
11-13 avenue de Bel Air, F-69627 Villeurbanne Cedex
Tel: (+33 4) 72 81 52 00

Motors:
ALSTOM Transport
7 av de Lattre de Tassigny, BP 49, F-25290 Ornans Cedex
Tel: (+33 3) 81 62 44 00

Bogies and dampers:
ALSTOM Transport
1 rue Baptiste Marcet, PO Box 42, F-71202 Le Creusot Cedex
Tel: (+33 3) 85 77 60 00

ALSTOM's Coradia Duplex (TER 2N NG) double-deck regional emu for SNCF, France   1194406

Transport services:
ALSTOM Train Services

Maintenance, equipment and services section

Maintenance, renovation and spare parts:
ALSTOM Transport Train Life Services
48 rue Albert Dhalenne, F-93482 Saint-Ouen, Cedex, France
Tel: (+33 1) 41 66 90 00
Fax: (+33 1) 41 66 96 66
Senior Vice-President Train Life Services: *Dominique Pouliquen*

Signalling systems:
ALSTOM Transport Information Solutions
48 rue Albert Dhalenne, F-93482 Saint-Ouen, Cedex, France
Tel: (+33 1) 41 66 90 00   Fax: (+33 1) 41 66 96 66
Senior Vice-President Transport Information Solutions: *Michel Marien*
See main entry in Signalling, communications and traffic control equipment.

Contracts

Argentina: In July 2007, following the inauguration of the experimental East tramway line in Buenos Aires, two ALSTOM Citadis tramway trainsets are in operation. The Argentinian Government awarded ALSTOM an order for the supply of 16 metro cars for the Buenos Aires City subway. This order corresponds to an option included in a contract for the delivery of 80 cars which was signed in 1999 and reactivated in December 2004.

The delivery of the last car was scheduled for the end of 2007.

ALSTOM received an order from Métrovias SA for the supply of 16 Metropolis trainsets for Line A of the Buenos Aires metro system. The order calls for the manufacture of 80 stainless steel metro cars, to be equipped with ONIX traction systems and built in ALSTOM's Brazil unit.

Australia: In February 2008 ALSTOM was awarded a contract to supply the State of Victoria with 18 X'Trapolis six-car trainsets for the City of Melbourne's metropolitan network. Deliveries are scheduled from late 2009.

Brazil: In February 2006 Companhia Paulista de Trens Metropolitanos (CPTM) awarded an ALSTOM-led consortium a contract for the supply of 48 Metropolis cars for Sao Paulo's metro. This order is an option included in a contract signed in 1994.

Companhia Paulista de Trens Metropolitanos (CPTM), the public sector organisation responsible for suburban railway transport in São Paulo State, selected the Sistrem Consortium, led by ALSTOM, to build its new 9 km line from Capão Redondo to Largo Treze. The Sistrem Consortium was formed to undertake the project on a turnkey basis. Within it, ALSTOM is responsible for the overall technical management of the project, systems integration, provision from its factories in Brazil and France of eight six-car Metropolis trainsets, the signalling system, operations control centre and various items of electrical and mechanical equipment for the stations. Other members of the consortium are Bombardier Transportation, CAF and Siemens TSO.

The new line is the first phase of a project which is planned to extend as far as Chacara Klabin station (Vila Mariana region) in the future. ALSTOM supplied 48 Metropolis metro cars to CPTM, the public transport operator in São Paulo. The metros were manufactured in Brazil. These 48 Metropolis cars are part of an ALSTOM turnkey project and are destined for the Line 5 extension of the São Paulo network which was inaugurated in October 2002.

Belgium: In December 2008 ALSTOM, in consortium with Bombardier Transportation, signed a contract for 72 M6 double-deck passenger coaches for Belgian National Railways (SNCB).

China: In May 2007 ALSTOM, together with its Chinese partner CSR Nanjing Puzhen Rolling Stock Works, was awarded a contract to supply 144 metro coaches to Nanjing's Metro Line 2. The consortium also includes SATEE, the ALSTOM joint-venture located in Shanghai that specialises in traction equipment. 120 Metropolis cars have already been supplied for the Line 1 and in January 2008 the consortium was awarded a further contract by Nanjing Metro Company (NMC) for the supply of 126 metro cars. In total, 246 ALSTOM metro cars will equip Nanjing metro Line 1 after the delivery of this last order.

In April 2006, as part of a consortium, ALSTOM was awarded a contract by Shanghai Shentong Holdings Group, the operator and owner of Shanghai's metro network, for the delivery of 12 eight-car Metropolis trainsets for the extension of Shanghai's Mass Transit Line 2. The contract comprises an option for 72 additional Metropolis cars.

In October 2004 the Shanghai Shetong Holdings Group chose the ALSTOM consortium for the supply of Metropolis trains for the extension of Shanghai's metro line 1. The consortium, comprising SATCO (a joint venture of ALSTOM Transport and Shanghai Electric Corporation) and CSR Nanjing Puzhen Rolling Stock Works, was selected for the supply of 16 trainsets of eight cars each.

Also in October 2004 the Ministry of Railways of the People's Republic of China chose ALSTOM for the supply of regional trains and locomotives. The contract specifies that 60 regional trains are to be supplied and built in China by ALSTOM working in partnership with the Changchun Railway Company. ALSTOM will supply three complete trainsets, six trainsets in kits, and equipment for the remaining 51 trainsets from its sites in Savigliano, Italy and La Rochelle in France.

ALSTOM has been awarded a contract by the Shanghai Mass Transit Pearl Line Development Co Ltd for the supply of 28 six-car Metropolis trainsets, worth some EUR203 million, for Line 3 of the city's metro. The new line links the southeast to the north of the city. The trains' lightweight aluminium cars will be equipped with ALSTOM's ONIX 1500 drive propulsion system based on IGBT technology. A significant portion of work relating to the contract will be carried out in China by several factories, including the Shanghai ALSTOM Transport Electrical Equipment Company Ltd and Nanjing Puzhen Rolling Stock Works.

A contract for the new Shanghai tramway, the Xinmin line, covers the supply of 152 Metropolis cars, with an option for a further 148. This contract was between JIUSHI, a company representing the Municipality of Shanghai, and SATCO, a joint venture between ALSTOM (with a 40 per cent stake) and Shanghai Electric Corporation (SEC) (60 per cent).

Dominican Republic: In May 2006 ALSTOM was awarded a contract to supply 19 Metropolis trainsets comprising three cars for OPRET, the government authority in charge of public transport in the Dominican Republic. The metro line was to be put into service on 29 January 2009.

France: In January 2009 SNCF and Chemins de Fer Luxembourgeois placed a supplementary order with the consortium comprising ALSTOM

MF 2000 metro trainset for RATP, Paris   1194408

ALSTOM's interior of MF 2000 metro trainset   1194407

ALSTOM's Minuetto emu for Trenitalia, Italy   1194411

and Bombardier Transportation for 14 new-generation double-deck TER trains (TER 2N NG). The two companies are exercising an option written into a contract signed in 2000. The first of the new trains are due to be delivered from June 2010.

In June 2007 SYTRAL, the body responsible for organising public transport in the Rhône region and the Greater Lyon metropolitan area in France, ordered 13 additional Citadis tramsets for its new T4 line. Delivery is scheduled to take place between September 2008 and April 2009.

In June 2007 SNCF ordered 80 double-deck very high-speed trains from ALSTOM with an option for 40 additional train sets. First deliveries are scheduled in 2009.

In October 2006, the first Citadis tramset, as part of the second phase of deliveries, was delivered to the Urban Community of Bordeaux (CUB).

In July 2006 SNCF ordered 21 new Coradia Duplex™ trainsets from ALSTOM; seven of these are four-car and 14 others are three-car trainsets. This order is part of a long-term investment programme for the renewal of the regional express trains fleet.

In May 2006, a consortium comprising ALSTOM Transport, Bombardier Transportation and AREVA TA announced that it will deliver 45 MF2000 metro trainsets to RATP for use on Line 2 of the Paris metro, starting in July 2007. A pre-production trainset commenced operations in January 2007.

In June 2005 SNCF notified ALSTOM of an order for six double-deck trainsets for use in it's TER regional express fleet. This is a follow-on order that corresponds to an option in a contract signed in November 2000 and follows on from an order for 66 cars announced on 21 June 2005.

In March 2005 ALSTOM was awarded a contract by SNCF for the upgrade of 48 existing Corail regional cars. In addition, there are options for the transformation of up to 30 further regional cars. The first Series Corail 200 was delivered to SNCF in September 2006.

In January 2005, as part of the opening of the LEA line, ALSTOM was awarded a contract for the supply of 10 tramsets, identical to the 47 low-floor tramsets already delivered by ALSTOM since December 2000 for Lyon's tram lines 1 and 2.

In September 2004 Communauté de l'Agglomération de Nice Côte d'Azur (CANCA) ordered 20 Citadis trams for its new tramway in Nice which opened in 2007.

Germany: In December 2008 German rail operator LNVG placed an order with ALSTOM for 10 new Coradia Lint regional trains. Deliveries are scheduled for June 2010.

In July 2008 private operator BeNEX, a subsidiary of Hamburger Hochbahn AG, placed an order with ALSTOM for 26 Coradia Continental regional trains. The contract includes 26 electric propulsion trams, including 21 three-car trains and five four-car trains. These will be put into service in the Regensburg-Donauthalbahn regional network in late 2010.

In November 2007 DB Regio AG placed an order with ALSTOM for 25 Coradia LINT model regional trains. Delivery is scheduled to commence during 2009.

In July 2007 DB Regio AG placed two orders with ALSTOM for 39 Coradia Lirex regional trains.

In December 2006 Hamburger Hochbahn AG awarded a contract to ALSTOM, as part of a consortium with Bombardier Transportation, for the delivery of a new generation of underground trains Type DT5. The contract includes the delivery of 27 trains from 2009 to 2013 as well as an option of a minimum of 40 additional vehicles.

In January 2006, in consortium with Bombardier, ALSTOM was commissioned by DB Regio NRW GmbH to supply 78 four-section suburban multiple units of the 422 series. The vehicles are scheduled to be supplied between March 2008 and October 2010.

In September 2005 ALSTOM won a regional train contract from FAHMA, the leasing company of the regional trains running in the Frankfurt area, for the delivery of 10 Coradia LINT 41 trains.

Also in 2005 ALSTOM was awarded lead consortiums tram contracts by the cities of Braunschweig, Darmstadt and Gera. HEAG mobilio GmbH, the transport operatior in Darmstadt, has chosen an ALSTOM-led consortium for the delivery of 18 low-floor trams. Braunschweiger Verkehrs-AG has chosen an ALSTOM/Bombardier consortium for the delivery of 12 low-floor trams and Geraer Verkehrsbetrieb

ALSTOM's Regio Citadis tram-train for Regionalbahn Kassel, Germany   1194413

ALSTOM's six-car Metropolis trainset, Nanjing Metro Line 1, China   1344929

GmbH has awarded ALSTOM a contract for the delivery of six low-floor trams with an option for an additional six.

Hungary: In May 2006 BKV, the Budapest public transport operator, awarded the ALSTOM-led Budapest Metropolis Consortium, a contract for the supply of 170 Metropolis metro cars. The agreement includes additional provision for the maintenance of these vehicles for a three-year period as well an option for a further 28 cars.

International: In September 2007 ALSTOM was awarded a contract to supply four high-speed Pendolino trains for the Helsinki to St Petersburg rail link. The contract includes an option for two further trains. The customer, Karelian Trains, is a joint venture between Russian Railways (RZD) and Finnish Railways (VR). The trains are scheduled for delivery in early 2009 to be ready for service in 2010.

Italy: In January 2008 Nuovo Trasporto Viaggiatori (NTV) ordered 25 very high-speed AGV trains in a contract which includes the maintenance of the trains for a 30-year period and the potential for an option for a further 10 trains.

Netherlands: In September 2008 ALSTOM received an order from the private Dutch operator Rotterdam Rail Feeding (RRF) for three renovated freight Class 203 diesel-hydraulic locomotives. The locomotives will be renovated at the ALSTOM site in Stendal, Germany, which specialises in locomotive renovation.

In July 2007 ALSTOM was selected to supply 53 Citadis tramway train sets for RET, the public transport operator of Rotterdam. Delivery is scheduled for mid-2009 and will proceed at a rate of four train sets per month.

Poland: In 2005 ALSTOM completed delivery of 18 Metropolis six-car trainsets for Warsaw metro. Initial vehicles were supplied from the company's plant in Spain, with remaining production following from the ALSTOM facility at Chorzow, Poland.

Warsaw Metro chose ALSTOM for the delivery of the new rolling stock for the extended line which is part of the extension programme carried out by the Polish capital. Metro Warszawskie, the operator of the Polish metro, has now put into service the last six-car trainset of a total contract of 18 new Metropolis trainsets from ALSTOM.

ALSTOM won an order to upgrade the Bytom to Katowice tramway for the Tramway Communication Company of Katowice in Silesia. As well as provision of new vehicles, the turnkey order includes the refurbishment of the rail infrastructure and stations on the existing 20 km Line 6/41. The trams, which will be supplied by the company's Polish subsidiary ALSTOM Konstal, will be fitted with ONIX traction drives.

Russian Federation: In September 2007 ALSTOM was awarded a contract with Karelian Railways (a joint venture between RZD and VR of Finland) to supply Pendolino high-speed tilting trains, which will operate between Saint Petersburg and Helsinki.

Singapore: ALSTOM won an order to supply the Singapore Land Transport Authority (LTA) with 25 six-car Metropolis trainsets for its new North East Line. This was the largest electromechanical contract awarded within the current LTA development programme. It covers the design, implementation, production, and on-site testing of the trainsets. The driverless signalling and control system will also be supplied by ALSTOM.

South Korea: ALSTOM won a contract for the development of a new 400 km high-speed rail link between Seoul and Pusan. This project involves a substantial amount of local input and ALSTOM is managing the technology transfer and co-production needed to meet these objectives. In 1994, 46 TGV trainsets were ordered to serve this line, with production split between ALSTOM and its Korean partners. Commercial service began in April 2004.

Sweden: In March 2008 ALSTOM received an order from Östgötatrafiken for the supply of five Coradia Nordic regional trains with delivery scheduled for the second half of 2009. The contract includes an option for 10 trains.

In December 2006 ALSTOM received an order from Skånetrafiken for the supply of 49 Coradia Lirex regional trains. Delivery is scheduled for the second half of 2009.

In May 2006 ALSTOM received an order from Storstockholms Lokaltrafik (SL) for 16 additional Coradia Lirex (X60) regional emus. This order corresponds to an option included in the initial contract for 55 commuter trains signed in 2002.

Switzerland: In November 2006, BLS AG placed an order with ALSTOM in consortium with Bombardier, to supply 13 four-coach, low-floor NINA trainsets. The order includes an option for a further 20 trainsets.

In March 2004 Cisalpino, a joint venture between Swiss Federal Railways and the Italian national operator Trenitalia, ordered 14 seven-car Pendolino three voltage tilting trainsets.

As part of a turnkey contract awarded in 2002 by the Administration of Switzerland's Vaud canton, ALSTOM was contracted to supply 15 two-car driverless rubber-tyred metro trainsets for a new 6 km metro line linking Ouchy with the district of Epalinges, Lausanne; the new line entered commercial service in October 2008.

ALSTOM has supplied the URBALIS signalling system, the on-board video surveillance and passenger information system, as well as the electrification of the line.

Turkey: In October 2009 ALSTOM delivered the first of 20 Metropolis trainsets as part of a turnkey contract awarded by the Municipality of Istanbul (IBB). The second trainset, which has also already been completed and is undergoing the validation testing process, will be delivered once the tests are finished. In 2009 the deliveries of the 18 remaining trainsets will follow at the rate of 10 cars per month; the last trainset will be delivered in October 2009.

UK: In May 2008 the UK Department for Transport reached an agreement with ALSTOM for the supply and the maintenance of Pendolino high-speed tilting trains for use on the West Coast Main Line between London and Glasgow. This notice to proceed is intended to be followed by a firm contract for trains and maintenance.

ALSTOM delivered the last of 53 tilting Pendolino trains to Virgin Trains in 2004 for the West Coast Main Line route. They are built and tested for 225 km/h, but will run at a lower speed until the deferred infrastructure enhancement envisaged in Phase II of the West Coast upgrade is implemented.

US: In July 2007 the Metropolitan Transportation Authority Board of Directors voted to award an option for 620 new heavy rail subway cars to ALSTOM and Kawasaki. ALSTOM will supply 360 cars. The option is part of an original contract awarded in July 2002, which covers the design and manufacture of new R160 cars, spare parts and special tools.

Uzbekistan: 15 Prima 1,520 mm 25 kV gauge 4,200 kW electric locomotives have been delivered.

Venezuela: ALSTOM, as part of the FRAMECA consortium, was awarded a turnkey order from the Caracas metro authority, CAMC, for the 5.5 km Line 4 of the city's metro system. In addition to supplying 44 metro cars and the signalling system, ALSTOM will have carried out electrification of the line and provided a complete fire protection system.

Ansaldobreda SpA

Via Argine 425, I-80147 Naples, Italy
Tel: (+39 081) 243 11 11
Fax: (+39 081) 243 26 98; 99
Web: www.ansaldobreda.it

Key personnel
Chief Executive Officer: *Roberto Assereto*
Managing Director: *S Bianconi*
Commercial: *D Zanchi*
Engineering: *E Trombetta*
Public Relations: *G Gallini*

Background
Ansaldobreda is the Finmeccanica Transportation Sector company responsible for designing and manufacturing railway and mass transit vehicles. The company is a merger of the Ansaldo Trasporti unit, which produces electronic drives and vehicle-borne equipment, with Breda Costruzione Ferroviarie, a leading rail vehicle manufacturer.

Products
Ansaldobreda supplies railway and mass transit vehicles, applying three different construction technologies: aluminium, stainless steel and carbon steel. The range of its products varies from high-speed trains, electric and diesel locomotives, diesel multiple-units, all types of passenger coaches, single- and double-deck, freight wagons, bogies, metro cars, low-floor light rail vehicles.

Contracts
In 2004–2006 Ansaldobreda won a contract for 19 high-speed trains that will connect the Netherlands and Belgium.

Forty Sirio LRVs for Gothenburg. Each LRV is 29 m long and is single-ended, seating 83 with standing room for 96. Delivery was scheduled by 2005 through to 2007; 35 trams for the Greek city of Athens in operation during the Olympic Games in 2004. The company is building more than 150 similar trams for the cities of Milan, Naples, Fizenze, Sassari, Bergamo and Kaygeri (Turkey). The rolling stock fleet of 19 driverless vehicles with IGBT inverter control was supplied for a 15 km automated LRT system in Copenhagen

Ansaldobreda Sirio LRV for Sassari, Sardinia in operation   1325583

Ansaldobreda Sirio LRV for Athens   0567429

Sirio LRV for Naples   1325586

Ansaldobreda emu for North Milan Railways (FNM)   1325581

with 15 stops, linking Norreport in the centre with Orestaden and Lergravsparken. Similar vehicles are being supplied in Blescia and Thessolonika (Greece).

In 2003 Moroccan Railways (ONCFM) ordered 18 four-car double-deck emus, with an option on six more, based on the design of the TAF emus supplied to FS Trenitalia and North Milan Railway. First units went into operation in 2007.

Oslo Sporveier has taken delivery of 32 articulated LRVs with IGBT inverter drive. They have low floors and seat 96 with 122 standing. Each car is mounted on four bogies, each having two asynchronous traction motors; top speed is 80 km/h and floor height 350 mm. The cars are of the same type as those supplied for Line 1 of the Midland Metro.

Z1-type coaches for Italian Railways (FS); amenity coaches for Eurotunnel; panoramic coaches for BVZ, FO and MOB, Switzerland; trailer vehicles for ETR 500 high-speed trainsets for FS; and double-deck emu trailer cars for FS and North Milan Railway.

Traction equipment for 73 E652 chopper-controlled locomotives for Italian Railways (FS) has been supplied, also 60 ETR 500 high-speed trainsets for FS (supplied by the Trevi Consortium, of which Ansaldo Trasporti is a member); and 144 E402 electric locomotives with inverter drives and asynchronous traction motors for FS, with 80 equipped for operation at 3 kV DC and 25 kV 50 Hz AC, 24 Type E403 are multivoltage.

Astra Vagoane Călători SA/Arad

1-3 Petru Rareş, RO-310210 Arad, Romania
Tel: (+40 257) 23 36 51
Fax: (+40 257) 25 81 68
e-mail: astra@astra-passengers.ro
Web: www.astra-passengers.ro

Key personnel
General Manager: *Alexandru Truta*

Deputy General Manager:
   Dan Micalacian
Production Director:
   Gheorghe Vărşăndan
Commercial Director:
   Camelia Milcomete
Financial Director: *Gheorghe Sirbu*
International Relations Director:
   Romulus Nosner
International Relations Adviser:
   Ovidiu Bologea

Background
The company was formed in 1998 by splitting it from freight wagon and passenger coaches manufacturer Astra Vagaone Arad SA.

Products
Certified ISO 9001 for the design, manufacture and refurbishment of passenger coaches and urban rail passenger vehicles. Passenger coaches for international and domestic traffic, metro cars, dmus, emus, light rail vehicles. Refurbishment is also undertaken and the company has renovated coaches for Romanian Railways, alone and in co-operation with ALSTOM. Tailored solutions for manufacturing and maintenance facilities.

Astra built with Siemens, the dmu Desiro for Romanian Railways. ASTRA builds AVA 200 Zarand, AVA200 Express and AVA200 Express CB 200 km/h coaches.

Z1 UIC 200 km/h passenger coach AVA 200 – Corail licence
0142356

BEML Limited

BEML Soudha, 23/1 4th Main, SR Nagar, Bangalore 560 027, India
Tel: (+91 080) 22 22 41 41
Fax: (+91 080) 22 96 32 75
e-mail: office@pr.beml.co.in
Web: www.bemlindia.com

Key personnel
Chairman and Managing Director: *Shri V RS Natarajan*
Director, Metro & Railways: *Shri Sreenivasan N K*
Chief General Manager: *Shri Dwaraknath P*
General Manager R&D: *Shri Bayya Reddy*
Assistant General Manager (Public Relations):
   Shri B Sridhar

Background
BEML was formed in 1964 with the railway equipment division at Bangalore; the first rail coach factory in the Indian subcontinent. This unit has consolidated its status as a major supplier of integral rail coaches, meeting approximately 25 per cent of the country's demand. It has a production capacity of over 600 coaches per annum.

Two-axle 1,676 mm-gauge diesel railbus for Indian Railways   0527275

25 kV AC emu for Indian Railways
0527276

Products
Stainless steel metro cars for DMRC (metro coaches); passenger coaches – second class sleeper; DC emus; AC emus; overhead equipment inspection cars; broad gauge rail bus; treasury vans; spoil disposal vans; track laying equipment; Sky Bus; military coaches; utility track vehicle; all types of wagons.

Contracts
BEML has supplied 220 metro cars to Delhi Metro Rail Corporation (DMRC) phase I, and additionally to supply 156 metro cars. As a result of this order and the increased demand for metro cars, BEML is upgrading its metro coach manufacturing facility at its Bangalore works exclusively for metro car manufacture.

Recent contracts for Indian Railways include the supply of a lightweight, two-axle, 1,676 mm gauge diesel railbus and electric multiple-units with 25 kV AC traction equipment.

Lightweight passenger coaches of integral welded steel construction of all types including sleeper coaches, day travel coaches, treasury vans, postal vans, brake and luggage vans and motor-cum-parcel vans. The division has supplied over 12,000 coaches of different types for Indian Railways. Coaches have also been exported to Bangladesh and Sri Lanka.

Bharat Heavy Electricals Limited (BHEL)

Transportation Business Department
Integrated Office Complex
Lodhi Road, New Delhi 110003, India
Tel: (+91 11) 24 36 93 77; 41 79 33 64
Fax: (+91 11) 24 36 94 23
e-mail: vpandhi@bhelindustry.com
Web: www.bhel.com

Registered office
House, Siri Fort, New Delhi, 110049, India.
Tel: (+91 11) 26 00 10 10   Fax : (+91 11) 26 49 30 21

Key personnel
General Manager: *V Pandi*

Products
Complete rolling stock including a variety of AC and DC drive propulsion system, for example: traction machines, traction controls, traction

transformers and locomotive components for diesel locomotives, 25 kV AC locomotives, AC/DC locomotives, demus, AC emus, DC emus and AC/DC emus (three-phased drives). Complete AC and AC/DC locomotives, battery powered road locomotives and OHE test cars. Diesel shunting locomotives range from 261–1,939 kW (350–2,600 hp) and special purpose vehicles including diesel electric tower cars, rail-cum-road vehicles, dynamic track stabilisers, ballast cleaning machines.

Bombardier Transportation

Headquarters
Schöneberger Ufer 1, D-10785 Berlin, Germany
Tel: (+49 30) 98 60 70
Fax: (+49 30) 986 07 20 00
Web: www.transportation.bombardier.com

Key personnel
President and Chief Operating Officer: *André Navarri*
Vice-President, Sales and Business Development: *Chris Antonopoulos*
Vice-President, Communications and Public Affairs: *Sharon Christians*
Vice-President and Chief Procurement Officer: *Pierre Attendu*

Bombardier Transportation
North America
1101 Parent Street, Saint-Bruno, Québec J3V 6E6, Canada
Tel: (+1 450) 441 20 20
Fax: (+1 450) 441 15 15
President, North America: *Raymond Bachant*

Passengers
Am Rathenaupark, D-16761 Hennigsdorf, Germany
Tel: (+49 33) 028 90
Fax: (+49 33) 02 89 20 88

President, Passengers: *Stéphane Rambaud-Measson*

Locomotives and Equipment
Schöneberger Ufer 1, D-10785 Berlin, Germany
Tel: (+49 30) 98 60 70   Fax: (+49 30) 986 07 20-0
President, Locomotives and Equipment: *Åke Wennberg*

Systems
Schöneberger Ufer 1, D-10785 Berlin, Germany
Tel: (+49 30) 98 60 70   Fax: (+49 30) 986 07 20-0
President, Systems: *Eran Gartner*

Rail Control Solutions
Arstaangsvagen 29, PO Box 425 05, 126 16 Stockholm, Sweden
Tel: (+46 8) 681 50 00   Fax: (+46 8) 681 51 00
President, Rail Control Solutions: *Anders Lindberg*

Services
Schöneberger Ufer 1, D-10785 Berlin, Germany
Tel: (+49 30) 98 60 70   Fax: (+49 30) 986 07 20-0
President, Services: *Laurent Troger*

Background
Bombardier Transportation has its global headquarters in Berlin, Germany and operations in over 60 countries. It has an installed base of over a million vehicles worldwide.

The Group offers the broadest product portfolio and is recognised as one of the leaders in the global rail sector. Bombardier Transportation is a unit of Bombardier Inc, with headquarters in Canada and one of the world-leading manufacturers of transport solutions; from regional aircraft and business jets to rail transportation equipment, systems and services. Its revenues for the fiscal year ended 31 January 2008 were USD17.5 billion and its shares are traded on the Toronto Stock Exchange (BBD).

Products
Bombardier Transportation offers a full range of rail vehicles for urban and mainline operation as well as modernisation of rolling stock and operations and maintenance services. Products include: metro cars, light rail vehicles/trams, single and double-deck electric multiple units (emus), diesel multiple units (dmus) and coaches; tilting trains and high-speed trains. Bombardier Transportation also supplies complete transportation systems, from high-capacity urban transit systems to automated people movers. Moreover, Bombardier Transportation offers electric and diesel locomotives; propulsion and controls; rail control solutions and bogies.

Flexity, BiLevel, Electrostar, Turbostar, Regina, Talent, Spacium, Zefiro and *Traxx*, are trademarks of Bombardier Inc or its subsidiaries.

SkyTrain is a trademark of BC Transit Corp.

Contracts

Country	City/ Metro politan Area	Operator	Order by Month	Order by Year	Delivery Year	Class	Model	Vehicle Type	No of Examples	Options	Cars Per Unit/ Section per Vehicle	Order Value
Australia	–	Western Australia PTA	December	2006	2009– 2011	–	BEA/ BEB/BET	EMU	15	–	3	USD123 million (bombardier USD61 million)

Notes: Joint venture with Downer EDI Rail.

Australia	Queensland	QR	December	2006	2009– 2010	–	IMU/ SMU	EMU	20	–	3	USD138 million (bombardier USD63 million)

Notes: Joint venture with Downer EDI Rail. 6 IMU for interurban services; 14 SMU for suburban operations.

Australia	Adelaide	Trans Adelaide	September	2005	2007	–	Flexity Classic	LRV	2	–	3 (30 m)	–
Australia	Adelaide	Trans Adelaide	October	2004	2005	–	FLEXITY Classic	LRV	9	–	3 (30 m)	–
Australia	Queensland	QR	November	2004	2008	IMU/ SMU	–	EMU	24		3	USD158 million (Bombardier USD74 million)

Notes: Joint venture with Downer EDI Rail. 16 IMU for Gold Coast and other interurban services, remaining 8 SMU for increased suburban operations.

Australia			–	–	–	–	–	–	31			–

Notes: Joint venture with Downer EDI Rail. Includes maintenance for a 15-year period.

Australia	Perth	Western Australia PTA	May	2002	2004–2006	BEA/ BEB/BET	–	DMU	31		3	AUD437 million (Bombardier AUD218 million)

Austria	Vienna	Wiener Linien	December	2007	2009–2011	–	–	metro	15	–	6	EUR135 million (Bombardier EUR26 million)

Notes: In consortium with Siemens and ELIN EBG Traction.

Austria	–	Austrian Federal Railways (ÖBB)	October	2007	2008–2009	–	Talent	EMU	17	–	4	EUR76 million (Bombardier EUR56 million)
Austria	–	Austrian Federal Railways (ÖBB)	May	2005	2007–2008	–	Talent	EMU	60	–	4	EUR237 million (Bombardier EUR180 million)

Notes: In consortium with ELIN EBG Traction.

Austria	Innsbruck	Innsbrucker Verkehrsbetriebe GmbH (IVB)	October	2005	–	–	Flexity Outlook	low–floor tram	22	10	5 (27.6 m)	EUR51 million (Bombardier EUR 42 million)

Notes: Traction equipment by ELIN EBG Traction.

Austria	Linz	Linz Linien GmbH	August	2005	2008	–	Flexity Outlook	low–floor tram	12	6	7 (40 m)	–

Notes: Traction equipment by ELIN EBG Traction. This follows an order for 21 low–floor trams awarded by Linz Linien in 1999.

Austria	Vienna	Wiener Linien	December	2004	2006–2008	Type T	–	low–floor LRV	38	42		EUR91 million (Bombardier EUR69 million)

Notes: Traction equipment by Vossloh Kiepe.

Austria	Vienna	Wiener Lokalbahn AG	July	2004	2006	–	TW400	LRV	4	–	3	EUR12 million

Notes: Execution of an option from a previous contract for 6 vehicles which have been in operation since 2000.

Austria	–	Austrian Federal Railways (ÖBB)	November	2003	2005–2006	4024/ 4124	Talent	EMU	60	–	4	EUR215 million (Bombardier EUR160 million)

Notes: Follows a 2001 order for 40 4–car and 11 3–car EMUs from Bombardier and ELIN EBG Traction.

Belgium	–	Belgian National Railways (SNCB)	December	2008	2010–2011	M6	–	passenger coach (double-deck)	72	–	–	EUR128 million (Bombardier EUR64 million)

Notes: In consortium with ALSTOM. This is the fourth follow–on order.

Country	City/ Metro politan Area	Operator	Order by Month	Order by Year	Delivery Year	Class	Model	Vehicle Type	No of Examples	Options	Cars Per Unit/ Section per Vehicle	Order Value
Belgium	–	Brussels Transport Authority (STIB)	January	2008	2009–2012	–	Flexity Outlook	low-floor tram (bi-directional)	87	–	–	EUR195 million

Notes: The contract is part of the five-year framework agreement concluded with STIB in October 2003.

Country	City/ Metro politan Area	Operator	Order by Month	Order by Year	Delivery Year	Class	Model	Vehicle Type	No of Examples	Options	Cars Per Unit/ Section per Vehicle	Order Value
Belgium	–	Belgian National Railways (SNCB)	December	2005	2008–2009	M6	–	passenger coach (double-deck)	90	–	–	EUR166 million (Bombardier EUR90 million)

Notes: In consortium with ALSTOM.

Country	City/ Metro politan Area	Operator	Order by Month	Order by Year	Delivery Year	Class	Model	Vehicle Type	No of Examples	Options	Cars Per Unit/ Section per Vehicle	Order Value
Belgium	Brussels	Brussels Transport Authority (STIB)	September	2005	2007–2008	–	Flexity Outlook	low-floor tram	22		(note)	EUR52 million
Belgium	Brussels	Brussels Transport Authority (STIB)	September	2003	2005–2007	–	Flexity Outlook	low-floor tram	46	–	(note)	EUR125 million

Notes: STIB orders are for 19 × 7-section (43 m) and 49 5-section (32 m) vehicles; contracts include maintenance for a 15-year period.

Country	City/ Metro politan Area	Operator	Order by Month	Order by Year	Delivery Year	Class	Model	Vehicle Type	No of Examples	Options	Cars Per Unit/ Section per Vehicle	Order Value
Belgium	–	Belgian National Railways (SNCB)	October	2004	2006–2008	M6	–	passenger coach (double-deck)	70	–	–	EUR179 million (Bombardier EUR111 million)

Notes: Follows order in 1999 for 210 passenger coaches (double-deck) in consortium with ALSTOM.

Country	City/ Metro politan Area	Operator	Order by Month	Order by Year	Delivery Year	Class	Model	Vehicle Type	No of Examples	Options	Cars Per Unit/ Section per Vehicle	Order Value
Canada	Quebec	Agence Metropolitane de Transport (AMT)	December	2007	2009	–	Multilevel	passenger coach	160	130	–	EURO264 million
Canada	Toronto	–	December	2006	2009–2011	–	–	metro	39	–	6	EUR330 million
Canada	Toronto	GO Transit	December	2005	2007	–	BiLevel	passenger coach (double-deck)	20	–		–
Canada	Toronto	GO Transit	March	2005	2005–2006	–	BiLevel	passenger coach (double-deck)	10		–	USD21 million
Canada	Toronto	Go Transit	December	2004	2005–2006	–	BiLevel	passenger coach (double-deck)	10			USD22 million
Canada	Montreal	Agence Metropolitane de Transport (AMT)	September	2003	2005	–	BiLevel	passenger coach (double-deck)	22	–		USD44 million

Country	City/ Metro politan Area	Operator	Order by Month	Order by Year	Delivery Year	Class	Model	Vehicle Type	No of Examples	Options	Cars Per Unit/ Section per Vehicle	Order Value
China	–	Ministry of Railways (MOR)	October	2007	2009–2010	–	–	high–speed trainset	40	–	16	EUR413 million (Bombardier's share)

Notes: Joint venture partners, Power Corporation of Canada and China South Locomotive and Rolling Stock Industry (Group) Corporation, through their joint venture Bombardier Sifang Power (Qingdao) Transportation Ltd (BSP).

Country	City/ Metro politan Area	Operator	Order by Month	Order by Year	Delivery Year	Class	Model	Vehicle Type	No of Examples	Options	Cars Per Unit/ Section per Vehicle	Order Value
China	–	Shanghai Mass Transit Line 7	May	2007	2008–2009	–	MOVIA	metro	192		6	EUR51 million
China	–	Shanghai Shensong Line Mass Transit Co Ltd	November	2006	2008–2009	–	MOVIA	metro	51		6	EUR257 million

Notes: Joint venture partners, Power Corporation of Canada and China South Locomotive and Rolling Stock Industry (Group) Corporation, through their joint venture Bombardier Sifang Power (Qingdao) Transportation Ltd (BSP), along with consortium partner Sifang Locomotive and Rolling Stock Co Ltd.

Country	City/ Metro politan Area	Operator	Order by Month	Order by Year	Delivery Year	Class	Model	Vehicle Type	No of Examples	Options	Cars Per Unit/ Section per Vehicle	Order Value
China	Beijing	Beijing Dongzhimen Airport Express Rail Co Ltd	March	2006	2007–2008	–	ART MK II	people mover	40			EUR36 million (Bombardier share)

Notes: Joint venture partners, Power Corporation of Canada and China South Locomotive and Rolling Stock Industry (Group) Corporation, through their joint venture Bombardier Sifang Power (Qingdao) Transportation Ltd (BSP), along with consortium partner Sifang Locomotive and Rolling Stock Co Ltd.

Country	City/ Metro politan Area	Operator	Order by Month	Order by Year	Delivery Year	Class	Model	Vehicle Type	No of Examples	Options	Cars Per Unit/ Section per Vehicle	Order Value
China	–	Ministry of Railways (MOR)	May	2005	2006–2007	–	–	high–speed trainset	20		8	USD276 million (Bombardier USD119 million)

Notes: Joint venture partners, Power Corporation of Canada and China South Locomotive and Rolling Stock Industry (Group) Corporation, through their joint venture Bombardier Sifang Power (Qingdao) Transportation Ltd (BSP).

Country	City/Metropolitan Area	Operator	Order by Month	Order by Year	Delivery Year	Class	Model	Vehicle Type	No of Examples	Options	Cars Per Unit/Section per Vehicle	Order Value
China	–	Ministry of Railways (MOR)	February	2005	2005–2006	–	–	passenger coach	361			–

Notes: Joint venture partners, Power Corporation of Canada and China South Locomotive and Rolling Stock Industry (Group) Corporation, through their joint venture Bombardier Sifang Power (Qingdao) Transportation Ltd (BSP), along with consortium partner Sifang Locomotive and Rolling Stock Co Ltd.

Country	City/Metropolitan Area	Operator	Order by Month	Order by Year	Delivery Year	Class	Model	Vehicle Type	No of Examples	Options	Cars Per Unit/Section per Vehicle	Order Value
China	–	Ministry of Railways (MOR)	October	2004	2006–2007	–	–	high-speed trainset	20		8	USD424 million (Bombardier USD263 million)

Notes: Joint venture partners, Bombardier Sifang Power (Qingdao) Transportation Ltd (BSP) joint venture (Bombardier Transportation, Power Corporation of Canada, China South Locomotive and Rolling Stock Industry (Group) Corporation.

| China | Guangzhou | Guangzhou Metro Operation Company | October | 2004 | 2006 | – | Movia | metro | 8 | | 6 | EUR56 million (Bombardier EUR16 million) |

Notes: Joint venture partners, Power Corporation of Canada and China South Locomotive and Rolling Stock Industry (Group) Corporation, through their joint venture Bombardier Sifang Power (Qingdao) Transportation Ltd (BSP), along with consortium partner Sifang Locomotive and Rolling Stock Co Ltd. Follow on order from August 2000 order for 26 six-car Movia trainsets.

| China | Shenzen | Shenzen Metro Corporation | February | 2003 | 2004–2005 | – | Movia | metro | 3 | | 6 | – |

Notes: Joint venture between Bombardier Transportation and Changchun Car Company, Changchun Bombardier Railway Vehicle Ltd (CBRC). This follows an order from Shenzhen Metro Corporation for 114 similar metro cars (19 six-car trains).

| China | Shanghai | Shanghai Metro Operation Company | December | 2002 | 2004–2005 | – | Metro | – | 10 | | 6 | EUR76 million (Bombardier EUR49 million) |

Notes: Order received by CBRC consortium of Bombardier and Changchun Car Co.

| Denmark | – | Danish State Railways (DSB) | October | 2008 | 2009 | – | – | passenger coach (double-deck) | 45 | – | – | EUR75 million |

Notes: Order placed by Railpool.

| Denmark | – | Danish State Railways (DSB) | September | 2008 | 2009 | – | Contessa | EMU | 10 | 30 | 3 | EUR82 million |

Notes: 20 intermediate trailers and five driving cars. Order placed by Porterbrook Leasing Company Ltd.

| France | – | SNCF | December | 2008 | 2010 | – | Traxx F140 | diesel electric locomotive | 80 | – | – | EUR160 million |

Notes: Initial firm order of 45 locomotives.

| France | – | SNCF | July | 2007 | 2009 | | AGC | DMU/EMU | 19 | – | – | – |
| France | Haute Normandie | SNCF | March | 2007 | 2008–2010 | – | TER 2N NG | EMU | 16 | | 5 | EUR37 million |

Notes: Consortium of Bombardier Transportation and ALSTOM.

France	–	SNCF	April	2007	2009		AGC	DMU/EMU	67	–	–	–
France	–	SNCF	November	2006	2007	–	AGC	DMU/EMU	112	–	–	EUR467 million
France	Greater Paris	SNCF	October	2006	2009–2015	–	–	EMU	372	–	–	EUR2.7 billion
France	–	SNCF	January	2006	2007–2010	(note)	AGC	DMU/EMU	73		(note)	EUR290 million

Notes: The July and April orders represent a follow-on from the original framework contract. January 2006 order represents final batch against a September 2001 framework contract for 500 AGC vehicles. AGC produced in diesel (Class X76500), electric (Z27500) and dual-mode (B81500) versions and in three- and four-car configurations.

France	–	SNCF		2005		–	AGC	DMU/EMU	48		(note)	EUR186 million
France	–	SNCF	January	2005	2007–2009	(note)	AGC	DMU/EMU	100		(note)	EUR350 million
France	Marseille	Communauté Urbaine Provence Métropole (CUMPM)	December	2004	2006–2007	–	Flexity Outlook	low-floor tram	26		5 (32.5 m)	EUR61 million
France	–	SNCF	January	2003	2006	–	TER2N NG	EMU	25	302	3	

Notes: Consortium of Bombardier Transportation and ALSTOM. Order also includes 11 intermediate cars to be added to two-car trainsets already ordered for Rhone-Alpes region. Bombardier is responsible for the manufacture of 25 vehicles and 86 motor bogies.

| France | – | SNCF | December | 2001 | 2004–2005 | – | TGV Duplex | high-speed trainsets | 18 | | 3* | EUR63 million (*Bombardier's share) |

Notes: These represent part-confirmation of an option on 60 vehicles included in the contract placed in 2000. Bombardier's share of the contract also covers the manufacture of six carrying bogies for each 10-car trainset.

Country	City/ Metro politan Area	Operator	Order by Month	Order by Year	Delivery Year	Class	Model	Vehicle Type	No of Examples	Options	Cars Per Unit/ Section per Vehicle	Order Value
France	Paris	Paris Transport Authority (RATP)		2001	2003–2014	–	Type MF-2000	metro	161		5	EUR695 million (Bombardier EUR230 million)

Notes: In consortium with ALSTOM Transport and Technicatome.

Germany	–	Deutsche Bahn AG (DB)	January	2009	–	–	–	EMU (double-deck)/ passenger coach (double-deck)	800	–		EUR1.5 billion

Notes: Framework agreement.

| Germany | Schleswig-Holstein | Deutsche Bahn AG (DB) | December | 2007 | 2008–2009 | – | – | passenger coach (double-deck) | 64 | – | | EUR90 million |

Notes: The order is an option from the 2003 framework agreement.

| Germany | Rhine-Neckar region | Rhein-Neckar-Verkehr (RNV) GmbH | October | 2007 | 2009–2010 | – | – | low-floor tram | 19 | – | | EUR52 million |

Notes: The order is a further option from a contract signed in 1998 for 36 trams. The first option for 16 units was taken up in 2004.

| Germany | Dresden | Deutsche Bahn AG (DB) | April | 2007 | – | – | – | EMU (double-deck) | 53 | – | | EURO72 million |

Notes: The order is an option from the 2003 framework agreement.

| Germany | – | Deutsche Bahn AG (DB) | February | 2007 | 2009 | | *Talent* 2 | EMU | 321 | – | | EUR1.2 billion (estimated) |

Notes: By October 2008 the total number of trains ordered under this framework agreement contract was 76.

| Germany | Hamburg | Hochbahn | December | 2006 | 2009–2013 | – | DT5 | metro | 27 | 40 | – | EUR240 million (Bombardier EUR117 million) |

Notes: In consortium with ALSTOM Transport.

| Germany | – | Deutsche Bahn AG (DB) | October | 2006 | 2008 | – | – | passenger coach (double-deck) | 42 | – | – | EUR57 million |

Notes: Part of July 2003 option for 300 vehicles.

| Germany | Hanover | DB Regio AG | May | 2006 | 2008 | 425.2 | – | EMU | 13 | | 4 | EUR63 million (Bombardier EUR39 million) |

Notes: In consortium with Siemens.

Germany	Frankfurt	Verkehrsgesellschaft Frankfurt am Main, (VGF)	March	2006	2008–2015	–	Flexity Swift	high-floor LRV	146	24	2 (25 m)	EUR300 million
Germany	–	Deutsche Bahn AG (DB)	–	2005	2008	–	–	passenger coach (double-deck)	49	–	–	–
Germany	Nordrhein-Westfalen	DB Regio NRW	December	2005	2008–2010	422	–	EMU	78		4	EUR343 million (Bombardier EUR 224 million)
Germany	Dortmund	Dortmunder Stadtwerke AG	December	2005	2007–2010	–	Flexity Classic	high-floor tram	47	5	3 (30 m)	EUR70 million
Germany	Lower Saxony	Local Transport Authority of Lower Saxony (LNVG)	May	2005	2006–2007	–	–	passenger coach (double-deck)	78	–	–	EUR137 million

Notes: Contract brings to 184 the total of coaches ordered by LNVG since 2001.

| Germany | Lower Saxony | Local Transport Authority of Lower Saxony (LNVG) | May | 2005 | 2006–2007 | 146.1 | *Traxx* P160 AC | electric locomotive | 9 | – | – | Included above |

Notes: Contract brings to 27 the total of locomotives ordered by LNVG since 2001.

| Germany | Rhine-Neckar region | MVV OEG AG and MVV Verkehr AG | January | 2005 | 2006–2007 | – | – | low-floor tram | 16 | 9 | 5 (30 m) and 7 (42 m) | – |

Notes: This order is an option to a former order placed by four transport operators in the Rhine-Neckar region in 1999 for a total of 36 trams. 10 will be for MVV OEG AG and six for MVV Verkehr AG.

Country	City/Metropolitan Area	Operator	Order by Month	Order by Year	Delivery Year	Class	Model	Vehicle Type	No of Examples	Options	Cars Per Unit/Section per Vehicle	Order Value
Germany	Dresden	Dresden Transport Authority (DVB)	September	2004	2006–2007	–	Flexity Classic	low-floor tram	20		3 (30 m)	EUR43 million
Germany	Marschbahn Line	Connex (now Veolia)	July	2004	2005	–	Talent	DMU	9		3	–

Notes: Follow-on contract bringing to 40 the number of these vehicles ordered by this operator.

Country	City/Metropolitan Area	Operator	Order by Month	Order by Year	Delivery Year	Class	Model	Vehicle Type	No of Examples	Options	Cars Per Unit/Section per Vehicle	Order Value
Germany	Berlin	Berliner Verkehrsbetriebe (BVG)	May	2004	2006–2007	HK	–	metro	20	–	4	–

Notes: This followed the supply of four pre-production trainsets supplied to BVG in 2001.

Country	City/Metropolitan Area	Operator	Order by Month	Order by Year	Delivery Year	Class	Model	Vehicle Type	No of Examples	Options	Cars Per Unit/Section per Vehicle	Order Value
Germany	–	ATI	October	2004	–		Talent	DMU	3	–	3	–
Germany	–	Deutsche Bahn AG (DB)	–	2004	–	423	–	EMU	6			
Germany	–	Nordwestbahn	–	2004	–	–	Talent	DMU	3		3	–
Germany	Odenwaldbahn	Rhein-Main transport group (RMV)	November	2003	2005	–	Itino	DMU	22	–	2	EUR70 million
Germany	Marschbahn Line	Connex (now Veolia)	November	2003	2005	–	–	passenger coach (single-deck)	90	–	–	EUR120 million (including locomotives detailed below) (see above)
Germany	Marschbahn Line	Connex (now Veolia)	November	2003	2005	146.1	Traxx	electric locomotive	4	–	–	
Germany	Hamburg	S-Bahn Hamburg GmbH	November	2003	2006–2007	474	–	EMU	9	–	3	EUR90 million (Bombardier EUR45 million)

Notes: Consortium of Bombardier Transportation and ALSTOM LHB. Contract also includes retrofitting 33 emus of the same type for dual–voltage operation.

Country	City/Metropolitan Area	Operator	Order by Month	Order by Year	Delivery Year	Class	Model	Vehicle Type	No of Examples	Options	Cars Per Unit/Section per Vehicle	Order Value
Germany	Leipzig	LVB	October	2003	2005–2006	–	Flexity Classic	low-floor tram	12	12	5 (45 m)	EUR40 million
Germany	Dresden	Dresden Transport Authority (DVB)	October	2003	2005–2006	–	Flexity Classic	low-floor tram	12	–	5 (45 m)	EUR40 million
Germany	–	PEG Westmunsterland/ATI	–	2003	–	–	Talent	DMU	6	–	3	–
Germany	–	Deutsche Bahn AG (DB)	July	2003	2004–2006	–	–	passenger coach (double-deck)	298	300	–	EUR411 million

Notes: The order is for 78 driving trailers and 220 conventional trailers.

Country	City/Metropolitan Area	Operator	Order by Month	Order by Year	Delivery Year	Class	Model	Vehicle Type	No of Examples	Options	Cars Per Unit/Section per Vehicle	Order Value
Germany	Munich	Munich Transport Authority (MVG)	February	2003	2005–2006	Type C	–	metro	8	–	6	–

Notes: Consortium of Bombardier Transportation and Siemens Transportation Systems. This followed an earlier contract in 1997 for 10 trainsets of the same type. Siemens is the general contractor and is responsible for all electrical equipment.

Country	City/Metropolitan Area	Operator	Order by Month	Order by Year	Delivery Year	Class	Model	Vehicle Type	No of Examples	Options	Cars Per Unit/Section per Vehicle	Order Value
Germany	–	Local Transport Authority of Lower Saxony (LNVG)	January	2003	2005	146.1	Traxx P160 AC	electric locomotive	8	–	–	EUR130 million (including locomotives details below) (see above)
Germany	–	Local Transport Authority of Lower Saxony (LNVG)	January	2003	2005	–	–	passenger coach (double-deck)	40	–	–	
Germany	–	Bremer Strassenbahn AG	December	2002	September 2005-April 2007	–	Flexity Classic	low-floor tram	20			–

Notes: Traction equipment supplied by Kiepe-Elektrik (Now Vossloh Kiepe GmbH).

Country	City/Metropolitan Area	Operator	Order by Month	Order by Year	Delivery Year	Class	Model	Vehicle Type	No of Examples	Options	Cars Per Unit/Section per Vehicle	Order Value
Germany	Hamburg	Hamburger Hochbahn AG	December	2002	2004–2005	–	DT4.6	metro	15	–	4	EUR60 million (Bombardier EUR 29 million)

Notes: Consortium of Bombardier Transportation and ALSTOM LHB.

For details of the latest updates to *Jane's Urban Transport Systems* online and to discover the additional information available exclusively to online subscribers please visit
juts.janes.com

Country	City/ Metro politan Area	Operator	Order by Month	Order by Year	Delivery Year	Class	Model	Vehicle Type	No of Examples	Options	Cars Per Unit/ Section per Vehicle	Order Value
Germany	Frankfurt/Main	Frankfurt Transport Authority (VGF)	June	2002	2004–2007	–	LF2000	low-floor tram	60	11	3 (30 m)	EUR109 million
Germany	–	Deutsche Bahn AG (DB)	May	2002	2004–2006	411	ICE T	high-speed tilting trainset	28	–	7	EUR420 million (Bombardier EUR101 million)

Notes: Consortium of Bombardier Transportation, ALSTOM and Siemens.

Country	City/ Metro politan Area	Operator	Order by Month	Order by Year	Delivery Year	Class	Model	Vehicle Type	No of Examples	Options	Cars Per Unit/ Section per Vehicle	Order Value
Germany	Halle	Hallesche Verkehrs AG	November	2001	2003–2005	–	Flexity Classic	low-floor tram	30		2 (20.5 m)	EUR46 million
Germany	–	Deutsch Bahn Ag (DB)	–	2001		146	–	locomotives	31			–
Hungary	–	Hungarian National Railways (MÁV)	March	2006	2006	–	*Talent*	EMU	10	–	4	EUR45 million (Bombardier EUR33 million)
India	Delhi	Delhi Metro Rail Corporation Ltd (DMRC)	July	2007	2010	–	MOVIA	metro	424	–	4/6	EUR87 million

Notes: includes additional order received in March 2008 for 84 metro cars. Deliveries of the latest order to commence upon completion of original deliveries.

Country	City/ Metro politan Area	Operator	Order by Month	Order by Year	Delivery Year	Class	Model	Vehicle Type	No of Examples	Options	Cars Per Unit/ Section per Vehicle	Order Value
International	–	–	September	2007	–	–	*Traxx*	locomotives	60	–	–	EUR225 million

Notes: order from pan-European leasing company, Angel Trains.

Country	City/ Metro politan Area	Operator	Order by Month	Order by Year	Delivery Year	Class	Model	Vehicle Type	No of Examples	Options	Cars Per Unit/ Section per Vehicle	Order Value
Israel	–	Israel Railways (IR)	June	2004	2005–2006	–	–	passenger coach (double-deck)	54	–	–	EUR78 million

Notes: order brings to 147 the number of vehicles of this type ordered by IR.

Country	City/ Metro politan Area	Operator	Order by Month	Order by Year	Delivery Year	Class	Model	Vehicle Type	No of Examples	Options	Cars Per Unit/ Section per Vehicle	Order Value
Italy	–	Trenitalia	April	2005	2005–2007	E464	*Traxx*	electric locomotive	100	–	–	EUR250 million

Notes: This follows an initial order for 50 units placed in 1996 followed by three additional options for 90, 100 and 48 units received in 1999, 2001 and 2003 respectively.

Country	City/ Metro politan Area	Operator	Order by Month	Order by Year	Delivery Year	Class	Model	Vehicle Type	No of Examples	Options	Cars Per Unit/ Section per Vehicle	Order Value
Italy	–	Ferrovia Emilia Romagna (FER)	June	2003	2005	E464	Traxx	electric locomotive	3	3	–	
Italy	–	Trenitalia	May	2002	–	E405	EU11	electric locomotive	42	–	–	CAD188 million
Luxembourg	–	Luxembourg Railways (CFL)	February	2003	2004–2005	–	–	passenger coach (double-deck)	85	–	–	EUR121 million

Notes: 67 trailers and 18 driving trailers.

Country	City/ Metro politan Area	Operator	Order by Month	Order by Year	Delivery Year	Class	Model	Vehicle Type	No of Examples	Options	Cars Per Unit/ Section per Vehicle	Order Value
Luxembourg	–	Luxembourg Railways (CFL)	September	2001	2004–2006	2200	TER2N NG	EMU (double-deck)	12	–	3	EUR70 million (Bombardier EUR15 million)
Malaysia	Kuala Lumpur	Syarikat Prasarana Negara Berhad (SPNB)	October	2006	2008–2010	–	ART MK II	people mover	88	–	–	EUR117 million
Mexico	Monterrey	Metrorrey	August	2005	2007	–	–	high-floor LRV	14	–	–	USD244 million (Bombardier USD43 million)

Notes: Consortium partners Siemens and Grupo Gaza Ponce, SA de CV.

Country	City/ Metro politan Area	Operator	Order by Month	Order by Year	Delivery Year	Class	Model	Vehicle Type	No of Examples	Options	Cars Per Unit/ Section per Vehicle	Order Value
Mexico	Mexico City	Sistema de Transporte Colectivo Metro (STC)	October	2002	2004–2006	–	–	metro	45	–	9	USD478 million (Bombardier USD319 million)

Country	City/ Metro politan Area	Operator	Order by Month	Order by Year	Delivery Year	Class	Model	Vehicle Type	No of Examples	Options	Cars Per Unit/ Section per Vehicle	Order Value
Netherlands	Rotterdam	RET	December	2007	2009–2011	–	Flexity Swfit	high-floor LRV	43	21	3	EUR140 million
Netherlands	–	Netherlands Railways (NS)	September	2007	2009–2010	–	–	EMU	32/32	–	(4/6)	EUR399 million (Bombardier 162 million)

Notes: As part of the Sprinter consortium with Siemens, this order covers the first two options of the initial contract signed in 2005.

Netherlands	–	Netherlands Railways (NS)	December	2006	2008	–	VIRM	EMU (double-deck)	50	–	4	EUR433 million
Netherlands	Rotterdam	RET	June	2005	2008	–	Flexity Swift	high-floor LRV	21	21	3	EUR83 million
Poland	Mazovia	Koleje Mazowieckie	July	2007	2008	–	–	passenger coach (double-deck)	37	–	–	EUR55 million
Portugal	–	Metro do Porto	May	2006	2008–2009	–	Flexity Swift	low-floor LRV	30	–	3 (37 m)	EUR115 million (Bombardier EUR89 million)

Notes: In consortium with Vossloh-Kiepe.

Romania	Bucharest	Metrorex RA	January	2007	2008	–	Movia	metro	36	–	6	EUR143 million

Notes: This is an additional order following the 2002 order for 108 Movia vehicles. Deliveries of these commenced in 2002.

Spain	–	RENFE	November	2006	2008–2010	–	*Traxx F140 DC*	locomotive	100	–	–	EUR419 million
Spain	Valencia and Alicante	Ferrocarrils de la Generalitat Valenciana (FGV)	January	2005	2006–2007	–	Flexity Outlook	low-floor tram	30	10	5 (32.5 m)	EUR81 million
Spain	–	Spanish National Railways (RENFE Operadora)	December	2005	2008–2010	–	AVES-102	high-speed trainsets	30	–	14	EUR655 million (Bombardier EUR243 million)

Notes: Consortium comprising Bombardier and Patentes Talgo.

Spain	–	Spanish National Railways (RENFE Operadora)	October	2005	2007–2009	–	–	high-speed trainsets	18	–	11	EUR338 million (Bombardier EUR122 million) (including power cars detailed below)

Notes: Consortium comprising Bombardier and Patentes Talgo.

Spain	–	Spanish National Railways (RENFE Operadora)	October	2005	2007–2009	–	–	variable gauge power cars	10	–	–	(see above)

Notes: Consortium comprising Bombardier and Patentes Talgo.

Spain	–	Spanish National Railways (RENFE Operadora)	April	2004	2006–2008	–	–	variable gauge power cars	44	–	–	EUR188 million (Bombardier EUR100 million)

Notes: For 22 nine-car trainsets. Consortium comprising Bombardier and Patentes Talgo.

Sweden	–	SJ AB	May	2008	2010	–	*Regina*	EMU	20	20	4	EUR221 million
Sweden	–	LKAB/MTAB	August	2007	–	–	IORE	electric locomotive	8	–	–	EUR52 million
Sweden	Norrköping	Norrköping transport authority	March	2005	2006	–	Flexity	low-floor tram	5			–
Sweden	–	Region Skåne	March	2005	–	–	–	EMU	8		3	–

Notes: Region Skåne previously ordered 32 similar Oeresund trains.

Sweden	–	Västtrafik	–	2004	–	–	Itino	DMU	2		2	–
Sweden	–	Vämlandstrafik	–	2004	–	–	Itino	DMU			2	–

Country	City/Metropolitan Area	Operator	Order by Month	Order by Year	Delivery Year	Class	Model	Vehicle Type	No of Examples	Options	Cars Per Unit/Section per Vehicle	Order Value
Sweden	–	Skånetrafiken	November	2003	2005	–	Contessa	EMU	11	19	3	CAD121 million
Sweden	–	Västtrafik	March	2003	–	–	Regina	EMU	3		3	

Notes: Consortium comprising Bombardier and Siemens Transportation Systems. 113 coaches will be delivered to SBB and 8 to Sihltal Zurich Uetliberg Bahn (SZU).

Country	City/Metropolitan Area	Operator	Order by Month	Order by Year	Delivery Year	Class	Model	Vehicle Type	No of Examples	Options	Cars Per Unit/Section per Vehicle	Order Value
Switzerland	Zurich	SBB/SZU	September	2008	2010–2016	–	–	passenger coaches (double-deck)	121	40	–	EUR189 million (Bombardier EUR67 million)
Switzerland	–	BLS AG	November	2006	–	RABe 525	–	EMU	13	20	4	EUR38 million

Notes: Consortium comprising Bombardier and ALSTOM Transport.

Country	City/Metropolitan Area	Operator	Order by Month	Order by Year	Delivery Year	Class	Model	Vehicle Type	No of Examples	Options	Cars Per Unit/Section per Vehicle	Order Value
Switzerland	–	Swiss Federal Railways	January	2007	2008–2012			passenger coaches (low-floor)	140	48	–	EUR138
Switzerland	–	SBB Cargo	May	2003	2004–2005	484	Traxx	electric locomotive	18	–	–	CAD103 million

Notes: This was a follow-on order to a contract placed in September 2002 for 40 similar locomotives for delivery from December 2002.

Country	City/Metropolitan Area	Operator	Order by Month	Order by Year	Delivery Year	Class	Model	Vehicle Type	No of Examples	Options	Cars Per Unit/Section per Vehicle	Order Value
Switzerland	Zurich	Zurich Transport Authority (VBZ)	–	2003	2005	–	Cobra	low-floor tram	68		5 (37 m)	CAD239 million (Bombardier CAD194 million)

Notes: consortium comprising Bombardier and ALSTOM Transport.

Country	City/Metropolitan Area	Operator	Order by Month	Order by Year	Delivery Year	Class	Model	Vehicle Type	No of Examples	Options	Cars Per Unit/Section per Vehicle	Order Value
Switzerland	Geneva	Geneva @ Transport Authority (TPG)	November	2002	2004–2005	–	Cityrunner	low-floor tram	21	17	(42 m)	EUR57 million
Switzerland	–	SBB Cargo	September	2002	2002–2005	482	Traxx	electric locomotive	40	–	–	EUR111 million

Country	City/Metropolitan Area	Operator	Order by Month	Order by Year	Delivery Year	Class	Model	Vehicle Type	No of Examples	Options	Cars Per Unit/Section per Vehicle	Order Value
Taiwan	Taipei	KSECO	June	2003	2007–2008	–	–	rapid transit cars	202	–	–	CAD729 million

Country	City/Metropolitan Area	Operator	Order by Month	Order by Year	Delivery Year	Class	Model	Vehicle Type	No of Examples	Options	Cars Per Unit/Section per Vehicle	Order Value
UK	–	Southern	March	2008	2009	377	Electrostar	EMU	11	–	4	EUR70 million
UK	–	Southern	May	2007	2009	376	Electrostar	EMU	48	–	–	EUR85 million
UK	Manchester/Metrolink	Greater manchester Passenger Transport Executive (GMPTE)	June	2008	2009	–	Flexity Swift	LRV	28	–	–	EUR78 million (Bombardier EUR58 million)
UK	Manchester/Metrolink	Greater manchester Passenger Transport Executive (GMPTE)	April	2007	2009	–	Flexity Swift	LRV	12	28	–	EUR29 million

Notes: A consortium of Bombardier Transportation and Vossloh Kiepe.

Country	City/Metropolitan Area	Operator	Order by Month	Order by Year	Delivery Year	Class	Model	Vehicle Type	No of Examples	Options	Cars Per Unit/Section per Vehicle	Order Value
UK	London	Transport for London	August	2006	2008–2009	376	Electrostar	EMU	152	196	–	EUR331 million
UK	London	Docklands Light Railway	June	2006	2008–2009	–	–	light rail cars 31 (automatically guided)				EUR50 million
UK	–	CB Rail	February	2006	2007–2008	–		Traxx	diesel/electric locomotive	25/10	70		EUR130 million

Notes: For lease to operators in mainland Europe.

Country	City/Metropolitan Area	Operator	Order by Month	Order by Year	Delivery Year	Class	Model	Vehicle Type	No of Examples	Options	Cars Per Unit/Section per Vehicle	Order Value
UK	–	Chiltern Railways	–	2005	–	–	Turbostar	DMU	6	–	–	–
UK	London	Docklands Light Railway	May	2005	2007–2008	–	–	light rail cars (automatically guided)	24	9	–	EUR73 million
UK	–	Angel Trains	March	2005	2006–2007	–	Traxx	electric locomotives	36	64	–	EUR150 million

Notes: for lease to operators in mainland Europe.

Country	City/Metropolitan Area	Operator	Order by Month	Order by Year	Delivery Year	Class	Model	Vehicle Type	No of Examples	Options	Cars Per Unit/Section per Vehicle	Order Value
UK	Nottingham	Nottingham Express Transit (NET)	March	2004	–	–	–	low-floor LRV	15		5	–

Notes: As a member of the Arrow Light Rail Ltd concession.

Country	City/Metropolitan Area	Operator	Order by Month	Order by Year	Delivery Year	Class	Model	Vehicle Type	No of Examples	Options	Cars Per Unit/Section per Vehicle	Order Value
UK	London	London Underground	April	2003	2008–2015	–	–	metro	1,738	–	–	–

Notes: Awarded by Metronet consortium, of which Bombardier is a member.

Country	City/Metropolitan Area	Operator	Order by Month	Order by Year	Delivery Year	Class	Model	Vehicle Type	No of Examples	Options	Cars Per Unit/Section per Vehicle	Order Value
UK	–	GB Railway Group plc (Hull Trains) (now First Group)	September	2002	2005	222	–	DMU	4	–	4	–

Country	City/Metro politan Area	Operator	Order by Month	Order by Year	Delivery Year	Class	Model	Vehicle Type	No of Examples	Options	Cars Per Unit/Section per Vehicle	Order Value
UK	–	Midland Mainline	February	2002	2004–2005	–	Meridian	DMU	127	–	–	CAD512 million (includes 4-year maintenance)
UK	–	Govia	March	2002		377	*Electrostar*	EMU	460	–	–	CAD848 million
US	New Jersey	NJ Transit	February	2008	2009	ALP-46A	–	electric locomotive	27	33	–	EUR155 million
US	New Jersey	NJ Transit	September	2005	2007–2008	–	–	passenger coach (multi-level)		131		EUR171 million

Notes: exercised option, following an original contract in November 2002 for 100 cars. Options remain on a further 45 cars.

Country	City/Metro politan Area	Operator	Order by Month	Order by Year	Delivery Year	Class	Model	Vehicle Type	No of Examples	Options	Cars Per Unit/Section per Vehicle	Order Value
US	Salt Lake City	Utah Transit Authority	August	2005	June–October 2006	–	*BiLevel*	passenger coach (multi-level)	12	23	–	USD29 million
US	New York	Metropolitan Transportation Authority/Long Island Rail Road (MTA/LIRR) and Metropolitan Transportation Authority/Metro-North Railroad (MTA/MNR)	July	2005	–	–	M-7	EMU	158 (MTA/LIRR) and 36 (MTA/MNR)	–	–	USD425 million
US	New Mexico	Mid-Region Council of Governments and the New Mexico Department of Transportation	October	2004	2005	–	*BiLevel*	passenger coach (multi-level)	10	–	–	USD22 million
US	New York	Metropolitan Transportation Authority/Metro-North Railroad (MTA/MNR)	April	2004	–	–	M7	EMU	120	–	–	USD206 million
US	New Jersey	NJ Transit	December	2002	2005–2006	–	–	passenger coach (multi-level)	100	176	–	USD243 million

Developments

Bombardier Transportation has moved beyond the supply of basic equipment to deliver specialised solutions tailored to customer's specific needs, with examples such as the agreement with national rail operator Deutsche Bahn for its next-generation *Talent* 2 commuter trains; a flexible vehicle platform featuring great adaptability, enabling the customer to reconfigure and redeploy vehicles in parallel with the national network's evolving needs.

In France, Bombardier rolled out the world's first bi-modal, bi-electric train. AGC 'bi-bi' technology can enable seamless rail transport across France's diverse rail infrastructure. In addition to its order for hybrid AGC trains, SNCF made multiple firm orders for Bombardier's standard AGC trains.

In Montreal, a deal for Bombardier multilevel commuter coaches, specially designed to operate within tight infrastructure constraints common to older lines, will help Agence métropolitane de transport expand capacity on its network.

For the Russian market, Bombardier established new joint ventures in engineering and production of propulsion technology with rail equipment supplier Transmashholding, augmenting a long-standing signalling joint venture with another Russian partner.

In China and India, Bombardier's long-term focus on market development is yielding results. Along with its Chinese local joint venture partners, Bombardier was awarded prominent contracts across a number of product lines, including a landmark deal for high-speed trains. In India there have been breakthrough orders for Movia metro cars and a Cityflo 350 signalling system.

In April 2008 Bombardier Transportation and AnsaldoBreda, Finmeccanica's subsidiary for the railway sector announced their signature of an agreement to jointly develop, bid and manufacture a new high-speed train capable of travelling at more than 300 km/h.

BiLevel commuter cars for US and Canada   1194839

Electric multiple unit for Australia   1194841

M-7 emu for New York, US   1194837

Flexity Swift LRV type K4500 for Cologne   1129865

Flexity *Outlook low-floor tram for Brussels, Belgium*   1129864

Flexity *Swift high-floor tram for VGF, Frankfurt* (Ken Harris)   1375609

Flexity Classic tram for BSAG, Bremen   1289675

Flexity LRV for Minneapolis/St Paul   0585207

Bombardier Metro, Mexico City, Mexico   1289677

Talent 2 regional train, Germany   1375701

Bombardier R142 subway car for New York, US   1289674

Bombardier Metro, Berlin, Germany   1289676

Double-deck train for Germany   1368945

Low-floor single-deck train for Germany   1368942

Bombardier Flexity Classic tram, Dresden, Germany   1289678

Flexity Classic tram, Adelaide, Australia   1289680

Flexity Outlook, Valencia, Spain   1375702

Movia metro, Singapore   1375703

Flexity *Berlin tram, Germany*   1375700

'Rocket' *subway, Toronto, Canada*   1375699

Movia *metro, Delhi, India*   1375698

AGC bi-mode unit (dmu/emu) for SNCF, France (Class B 82500)
(Ken Harris)   1375608

Computer-generated image of Spacium *commuter train for Paris, France*   1368943

Brush Traction

PO Box 17, Loughborough LE11 1HS, UK
Tel: (+44 1509) 61 70 00   Fax: (+44 1509) 61 70 01
e-mail: sales@brushtraction.com
Web: www.brushtraction.com

Key personnel
Managing Director: *J M G Bidewell*
Sales Manager: *P L Needham*
Engineering Manager: *A Haworth*
Operations Director: *I G Hall*
Purchasing Manager: *M McDaniel*

Subsidiary
Hunslet-Barclay Ltd
Caledonia Works, West Langlands Street,
Kilmarnock KA1 2QD, UK
Tel: (+44 1563) 52 35 73   Fax: (+44 1563) 54 10 76

Background
Brush Electrical Engineering was founded in 1889. Today the company is a major supplier of electric propulsion equipment and locomotives and is able to undertake refurbishment and re-engineering of complete vehicles or components. The company is a member of the FKI Group.

In November 2007 FKI acquired, on behalf of Brush Traction, the business and assets of Hunslet-Barclay Ltd.

Products
Diesel electric and electric locomotives for mainline and shunting applications, also battery-electric service locomotives for metro systems; complete AC and DC propulsion packages, including traction motors and control equipment; locomotive servicing, refurbishment and upgrade.

Brush Traction is able to offer complete design and installation packages to include locomotive repowering, new cooler groups and new electronics.

Contracts
Channel Tunnel Shuttle locomotives for Eurotunnel, Class 92 electric locomotives for Railfreight distribution and dual-mode battery-electric locomotives for Hong Kong MTRC. Brush Traction has also undertaken a number of major locomotive mid-life overhaul and repowering projects, examples including contracts with Porterbrook Leasing for the repower and re-engineering of Class 47 locomotives, creating Class 57 type. The Class 57 locomotives have 500 kW electric train supply facility and are used for rescue and diversionary working of passenger trains.

The mid-life overhaul and upgrading to 7.0 MW of 39 Eurotunnel Shuttle locomotives is also being undertaken at the Brush Traction works, over a seven-year period.

More recently Brush Traction has undertaken a number of life extension modifications to high-speed train power cars. The most extensive modification has been the installation of two trial engines for performance enhancement. Other fleetwide fitments include new cooler groups, electronics, driver's desks and headlight units.

CAF – Construcciones y Auxiliar de Ferrocarriles SA

Padilla 17 – 6°, E-28006 Madrid, Spain
Tel: (+34 91) 435 25 00
Fax: (+34 91) 436 03 96
e-mail: export.caf@caf.es
Web: www.caf.es

Key personnel
President: *J M Baztarrica*
Chief Executive Officer: *A Arizcorreta*
Managing Director: *A Legarda*

Works
Beasain
J M Iturrioz 26, E-20200 Beasain, Spain
Tel: (+34 943) 88 01 00
Fax: (+34 943) 88 14 20

Irún
Calle Anaca 13, E-20301 Irún, Spain
Tel: (+34 943) 61 33 42
Fax: (+34 943) 61 81 55

Zaragoza
Av de Cataluña 299, E-50014 Zaragoza, Spain
Tel: (+34 976) 76 51 00
Fax: (+34 976) 57 26 48
Elmira NY USA
300 East Eighteenth Street, NY 14903-1333, US

Trenasa
Polígono Industrial Castejón, Parcela P1, E-31590 Castejón, Navarra

Linares
Construcciones Ferroviarias CAF-Santana SA
Avda Primero de Mayo s/n 23700 Linares (Jaén), Spain

Offices
Argentina
CAF Argentina SA
e-mail: cafadministracion@cafarg.com.ar

Brazil
CAF Brasil Industria e Comercio
e-mail: cafsaopaulo@cafbrasil.com.br

Mexico
CAF Mexico SA de CV
e-mail: cafmex@prodigy.net.mx

Computer-generated Trainset for Madrid metro   1374172

Design concept for tram for Edinburgh
1374173

US
CAF USA Inc
e-mail: cafusa@cafusa.com

Products

High-speed trains, electric and diesel regional trains; electric, diesel-electric and diesel-hydraulic locomotives; multiple-units and hauled coaches; metro cars; light rail vehicles/trams.

Contracts

Algeria: In January 2006, as a member of a consortium with Siemens Transportation Systems and Vinci Construction Grand Projects, CAF was awarded a contract by Entreprise Métro d'Alger (EMA) to supply 14 six-car trainsets for the Algiers metro. The contract included an option covering the provision of maintenance services for 10 years.

Brazil: CAF has signed two contracts for the delivery of train units to Sao Paulo. These include the supply of 40 eight-car units (320 cars) for Compañia Paulista de Trenes Metropolitanos (CPTM) and for the supply of 17 units for the Sao Paulo Metro, six cars each, which are scheduled for commissioning on lines 1 and 3 of the city metropolitan network.

Chile: In September 2007 CAF was awarded a contract to supply 144 cars for Santiago de Chile Metro. In February 2008 CAF was awarded an extension to this contract to supply a further 36 cars, whereby the total fleet to be supplied by CAF will increase to 180 cars, a total of 20 trains, each with nine cars. The contract includes the maintenance of the units.

Italy: In December 2002, CAF was awarded a EUR230 million contract to supply 33 trains to the Rome Metro. This was extended by six new trains with final delivery of the units in 2007. The order includes maintenance work on rolling stock supplied. CAF is creating a subsidiary in Rome to perform the task.

In February 2008 CAF was awarded an extension for the supply of trains for Line A of the Rome Metro, to include eight additional train units, each with six cars. The contract includes the maintenance of the units.

Mexico: In December 2007 CAF was awarded a contract to supply nine trains for Line A of the Mexico City Metro.

In August 2005 CAF was awarded a 30-year contract for the supply of 20 electric trains for the suburban rail system in Mexico City.

Saudi Arabia: In July 2008 CAF signed a contract with the Saudi Railways Organisation for the supply of eight train units, each comprising one electric-diesel locomotive, which powers five cars with austenitic steel bodyshells. The contract also includes the maintenance of the units for an initial period of four years.

Spain: In September 2008 CAF was awarded a contract by Metro Madrid for the supply of 60 trains (302) cars under a 17 year purchase lease operation which includes maintenance. The first units are scheduled to be incorporated into the network by mid 2010.

In March 2007 CAF was awarded a contract by the executive committee of the Municipal Transport Company of Seville (Tussam) to supply rolling stock for Metrocentro Sevilla.

In July 2006 Spanish National Railways (RENFE) placed an order with CAF for the supply of 107 regional trains (435 cars) to be delivered between 2008 and 2011. The contract covers 50 three-car dmus and 57 five-car emus. All the dmus and 34 of the emus are to be pre-equipped for the later installation of variable gauge running gear.

In February 2006 CAF received a contract to supply 14 five-section articulated vehicles for the Malaga Light Metro. An option exists covering the supply of a fifteenth vehicle.

Six-car metro trainset for STIB Brussels

1374170

Class 449 emu for RENFE's Media Distancia services

1374171

LRV for Metrocentro, Seville
1374174

In January 2006 RENFE awarded CAF a follow-on order for 40 Civia commuter emus (200 cars) for delivery from May 2006 until early 2010. The contract includes the provision of maintenance services for six years.

Turkey: In July 2008 CAF was awarded a contract for the supply of 33 suburban emus for the city of Izmir. The contract is between CAF and Izban, which is 50 per cent owned by TCDD

(Turkish Railway Organisation) and 50 per cent by the Izmir Metropolitan Municipality. The first deliveries are scheduled for early 2010.

In June 2007 CAF was awarded a contract by Natalia Metropolitan Municipality, in conjunction with the builder Alarco, for the development and commissioning of a network of trams for the city of Antalya. CAF is to supply 14 35 m low-floor trams. The contract also includes the

construction of 16 stations, a depot for rolling stock maintenance, electrification at 750 V and line signalling.

US: Recent contracts include: the supply of 192 metro cars for WMATA, Washington; supply of 40 LRVs to Sacramento Regional Transit District; and the supply of 28 new trams and the refurbishment of 55 existing vehicles for PATCO, Pittsburgh.

CNR Changchun Railway Vehicles Co Ltd

5 Qingyin Road, Changchun 130062, Jilin, China
Tel: (+86 431) 790 23 01   Fax: (+86 431) 293 87 40
Web: www.cccar.com

Key personnel
Director of Factory: *Ma Shukun*

Background
Changchun Railway Vehicle Co Ltd was founded in March 2002. Initiated by China's Northern

Locomotive and Rolling Stock Industry (group) Corporation and based upon the major business and the capital of the former Changchun Car Company, it was established as a new joint-stock company.

Products
Development, design, production, sales, installation, refurbishment, maintenance and aftersales service for metro cars; electric multiple-units for main line applications; sleeping cars, dining cars, mail vans, generator vans and passenger coaches.

Metro cars include DK20 and the DK9 with chopper voltage control. All cars are motored (4 × 86 kW) and designed to operate in multiples of two, four or six.

China Northern Locomotive and Rolling Stock Industry (Group) Corporation (CNR)

Corporate headquarters
No 11 Yangfangdian Road, Haidian District, Beijing 100038, China
Tel: (+86 10) 51 86 23 70   Fax: (+86 10) 51 86 23 74
e-mail: loriciec@cnrgc.com.cn
Web: www.cnrgc.com

Key personnel
President: *Cui Dianguo*
Vice-President: *Zhao Guangxing*
Chairman of Board of LORIC Import & Export Corporation Ltd: *Cao Guobing*
President of LORIC Import & Export Corporation Ltd: *Chen Dayong*
Senior Engineer of LORIC Import & Export Corporation Ltd: *Yang Xiangjing*

Subsidiaries
The corporation comprises 18 production plants, three research institutes and one trade company.

Production plants
CNR Changchun Railway Vehicle Co Ltd
425 Qingyin Road, Changchun 130062, Jilin, China
Tel: (+86 431) 790 23 01   Fax: (+86 431) 293 87 40
Legal Representative: *Dong Xiaofeng*

CNR Tangshan Railway Vehicle Co Ltd
3 Changqian Road, Fengrun District, Tangshan 063035, Hebei, China
Tel: (+86 315) 308 90 23   Fax: (+86 315) 324 16 12
Legal Representative: *Yu Weiping*

CNR Dalian Locomotive & Rolling Stock Work
51 Zhongchang Street, Shahekou District, Dalian 116022, Liaoning, China
Tel: (+86 411) 84 60 20 43
Fax: (+86 411) 465 42 45
Legal Representative: *Sun Xiyun*

CNR Qiqihar Railway Rolling Stock (Group) Co Ltd
10 Zhinghua East Road, Qiqihar 161002, Heilongjiang, China
Tel: (+86 452) 293 83 34
Fax: (+86 452) 251 44 64
Legal Representative: *Wei Yan*

CNR Datong Electric Locomotive Co Ltd
1 Qianjin Street, Datong 037038, Shanxi, China
Tel: (+86 352) 716 38 88
Fax: (+86 352) 509 09 84
Legal Representative: *Shi Xiaoding*

CNR DKZ2 metro train-set for Tehran Urban & Suburban Railway Co, Iran   1342596

CNR AC metro car for Beijing Line 10   1342598

CNR Shenyang Locomotive & Rolling Stock Co Ltd
75 Kunshan West Road, Huanggu District,
Shenyang 110035, China
Tel: (+86 24) 62 05 64 58
Fax: (+86 24) 86 40 87 30
Legal Representative: *Miao Huangsheng*

CNR Xi'an Rolling Stock Works
Jianzhang Road, Sanqiao Town, Xi'an 710086,
Shannxi, China
Tel: (+86 29) 82 36 91 26   Fax: (+86 29) 82 36 88 88
Legal Representative: *Liu Yingguo*

CNR Jinan Locomotive & Rolling Stock Works
73 Huaichun Street, Huaiyin District, Jinan
250022, Shandong, China
Tel: (+86 531) 88 30 56 90
Fax: (+86 531) 87 95 75 48
Legal Representative: *Jia Shirui*

CNR Yongji Electric Machine Factory
18 Dianji Street, Yongji 044502, Shanxi, China
Tel: (+86 359) 807 51 62
Fax: (+86 359) 807 52 90
Legal Representative: *Dong Yu*

CNR rapid transit vehicle with linear motor for Beijing Airport line 1342597

CNR electric locomotives

Type	Wheel arrangement	Line voltage	Output (kW) continuous	Speed (km/h)	Weight (t)	First built	Builders
HXD2	2 (Bo-Bo)	25 kV/50 Hz	9,600	120	2 × 138	2007	Datong
HXD3	Co-Co	25 kV/50 Hz	7,200	120	138	2006	Dalian
SS4G	2(Bo-Bo)	25 kV/50 Hz	6,400	100	184	1994	Datong, Dalian
SS7E	Co-Co	25 kV/50 Hz	4,800	170	126	2001	Datong
SSJ3	Co-Co	25 kV/50 Hz	7,200	120	150	2004	Dalian

CNR electric multiple-units

Class	Cars per unit	Line voltage	Motor cars per unit	Wheel arrangement	Output (kW) per motor	Speed (km/h)	Weight (t) per car	No in service	First built	Builders
CRH5	8	25 kV/50 Hz	5	Bo-Bo	550	200	M55/T56	480	2007	Changchun
China Star	11	25 kV/50 Hz	2	Bo-Bo	1,225	270	M78 T44/48	11	2002	Datong Changchun
Changbaishan	9	25 kV/50 Hz	6	Bo-Bo	265	210	M52.5 T53	9	2003	Changchun

CNR metro cars

Class	Cars Per Unit	Line voltage	Motor cars per unit	Wheel arrangement	Output (kW) per motor	Speed (km/h)	Weight (t) per car	No in service	First built	Builders
Beijing Line 5	6	750 V DC	3	Bo-Bo	180	80	M',M:35 Tc30 T29	192	2006	Changchun
Beijing Line 10	6	750 V DC	3	Bo-Bo	180	80	M',M:35 Tc30 T29	204	2007	Changchun
Iran	7	750 V DC	7	Bo-Bo	180	80	M, Mc37.5 T32.5	224	2005	Changchun
Guangzhou	6	1,500 V DC	4	Bo-Bo	220	100	A35 B/C38	156	2003	Changchun
Shanghai	6	1,000–1500 V DC	4	Bo-Bo	220	80	M38.3 T35.5	60	2004	Changchun
Tianjin	4	1,500 V DC	2	Bo-Bo	180	80	Mcp35.5 T31.0	100	2005	Changchun

CNR mass transit vehicles

Class	Cars Per Unit	Line voltage	Motor cars per unit	Wheel arrangement	Output (kW) per motor	Speed (km/h)	Weight (t) per car	No in service	First built	Builders
Beijing Airport	4	750 V DC	4	B-B	200	110	M, Mc25	40	2007	Changchun
DK32/34	4	750 V DC	2	Bo-Bo	180	80	M37, T29	136	2002	Changchun
Tianjin	4	1,500 V DC	2	Bo-Bo	200	100	Mcp39.4, T33.4	114	2003	Changchun
Wuhan	4	750 V DC	2	Bo-Bo	180	100	M35.5, Tc31.5	48	2003	Changchun
Changchun	3	750 V DC	2	Bo-2-Bo	120	70	45.0	40	2006	Changchun
DL6W	1	750 V DC	1	Bo-Bo	170	100	M36, T32	40	2002	Dalian Institute
FG	4	1,500 V DC	2	Bo-Bo	170	100	Mcp35.5	100	2005	Dalian Institute
Tianjin	4	1,500 V DC	2	Bo-Bo	180	80	Mcp35.5 T31.0	100	2005	Changchun

CNR diesel railcars and multiple-units

Class	Cars per unit	Motor cars per unit	Motored axles per motor car	Transmission	Rated power (kW) per motor	Speed (km/h)	Weight (t) per car	First built	Builders
SYZ25	4	2	4	AC/DC	91	120	Mc72, T68	1998	Tangshan
NZJ2	12	2	Co-Co	AC/DC	600	180	M135, T53.8	2000	Dalian
Harbin	7	2	B-2	Hydraulic	–	140	M84, T43	2000	Changchun
Putian		1	A1A-A1A	AC/DC	600	160	M111	2002	Dalian
160 km/h	5	4	1A-2, 2-2, 2-A1	Hydraulic	–	160	M64.3, T53	2003	Tangshan

CNR diesel locomotives								
Type	Wheel arrangement	Transmission	Power (kW)	Speed (km/h)	Weight (t)	First built	Diesel engine	Builders
DF4D	Co-Co	AC/DC	2,940	170/100	138	1996	16V240ZJD	Dalian
DF7G	Co-Co	AC/DC	1,840	100	138	2004	12V240ZJ6F	Feb 7th
DF101	Co-Co	AC/DC	1,840	140	120	2004	12V240ZJD-2	Dalian
GK1E31	B-B	Hydraulic	1,000	80/40	92	1999	EQ6240ZJ	Feb 7th
GKD1	Bo-Bo	AC/DC	990	80	84	1990	6240ZJ	Dalian
CK1E	C-C	Hydraulic	970	50		2003	CAT3508B	Feb 7th
CK6E	Co-Co	AC/DC	1,678	80	99	2006	CAT3516B	Feb 7th
CK6E1	Co-Co	AC/DC	1,500	90		2006	CAT3512B	Feb 7th
CKD7	Bo-Bo-Bo	AC/DC	1,250	90		1993	CAT3516	Dalian
CKD8A	Co-Co	AC/DC	1,985	100		1996	12V240ZJD	Dalian
CKD8B	Co-Co	AC/DC	2,200	100		1997	12V240ZJD	Dalian
CKD8C	Co-Co	AC/DC	1,840	180		2001	12V240ZJD-2	Dalian
CKD8E	Co-Co	AC/AC	2,508	120		2005	16RK215T	Dalian
CKD9	Co-Co	AC/DC	1,678	80		2003	16V240ZJD1	Dalian

CNR Taiyuan Locomotive & Rolling Stock Works
10 Jiefang North Road, Taiyuan 030009, Shanxi, China
Tel: (+86 351) 264 94 50   Fax: (+86 351) 304 95 63
Legal Representative: *Zhang Yili*

CNR Changchun Car Company
435 Qingyin Road, Changchun 130062, Jilin, China
Tel: (+86 431) 790 11 14
Fax: (+86 431) 790 31 49
Legal Representative: *Lou Yanjun*

CNR Harbin Railway Rolling Stock Co Ltd
82 Tongjiang Street, Daoli District, Harbin 150018, Heilongjiang, China
Tel: (+86 451) 86 46 71 00
Fax: (+86 451) 86 46 70 60
Legal Representative: *Fang Zhijian*

CNR Beijing February 7th Locomotives Works
1 Yanggingzhuang, Changxindian, Fengtai District, Beijing 100072, China
Tel: (+86 10) 83 30 60 01   Fax: (+86 10) 83 30 37 36
Legal Representative: *Wang Dongming*

CNR Lanzhou Locomotive Works
49 Wuwei Road, Qilihe District, Lanzhou 730050, Gansu, China
Tel: (+86 931) 298 54 61   Fax: (+86 931) 286 72 79
Legal Representative: *Chen Beiqun*

CNR Tianjin Locomotive & Rolling Stock Machinery Works
1 Nankou East Road, Hebei District, Tianjin 300232, China
Tel: (+86 22) 26 27 02 68
Fax: (+86 22) 26 27 12 34
Legal Representative: *Zong Baoquan*

CNR Beijing Nankou Locomotive & Rolling Stock Machunery Works
Daobei, Nankou Town, Changping District, Beijing 102202, China
Tel: (+86 10) 51 01 33 61   Fax: (+86 10) 69 77 18 09
Legal Representative: *Song Zhigui*

CNR Mudanjiang Locomotive and Rolling Stock Works
55 Locomotive Road, Yangming District, Mudanjiang 157013, Heilongjiang, China
Tel: (+86 453) 896 82 30
Fax: (+86 453) 633 10 08
Legal Representative: *Zhang Xiuchen*

Research institutes
CNR Dalian Locomotive Research Institute
49 Zhongchang Street, Shahekou District, Dalian 116021, Liaoning, China
Tel: (+86 411) 460 10 10   Fax: (+86 411) 460 16 17
Legal Representative: *Zhang Yan*

CNR Sifang Rolling Stock Research Institute
231 Ruichang Road, Sifang District, Qingdao 266031, Shandong, China
Tel: (+86 532) 86 08 31 06
Fax: (+86 532) 84 99 29 61
Legal Representative: *Ren Yujun*

CNR Electric Traction Technology Research and Development Center

CNR battery-powered tunnelling locomotive for India 1342600

CNR aluminium-bodied metro car for Tianjin 1198291

51 Zhongchang Street, Shahekou District, Dalian 116022, Liaoning, China
Tel: (+86 411) 84 19 95 54
Fax: (+86 411) 84 61 23 57
Legal Representative: *Xie Buming*

Trade company
LORIC Import & Export Corporation Ltd
No 11 Yangfangdian Road, Haidian District, Beijing 100038, China
Tel: (+86 10) 51 86 23 70
Fax: (+86 10) 51 86 23 74
Legal Representative: *Cao Guobing*

Background
CNR was established in September 2000 as a result of the division into two regional groups of the former China National Railway Locomotive and Rolling Stock Industry Corporation (LORIC). It is one of the world's leading suppliers of a complete range of systems, components and services for locomotive and rolling stock covering design, manufacture, refurbishment, maintenance and leasing. CNR has a presence in over 40 countries and regions and employs 100,000 people.

The annual output is 370 electric locomotives, 460 diesel locomotives, 2,300 passenger coaches and multiple-unit trainsets, 1,100 urban railway vehicles, 26,000 freight wagons and 150 railway cranes. Its locomotive, coach and wagon manufacturing plants are among the largest in the world.

Products
CNR undertakes the design, manufacture, testing, commissioning and maintenance of locomotives and rolling stock, including: electric locomotives, diesel-electric and diesel-hydraulic locomotives from 280 to 9,600 kW for main line and shunting duties; dmus and emus for urban, suburban and regional transport; tilting and high-speed trains; trams and light rail vehicles; metro cars; and passenger coaches as well as a full line of freight wagons.

Electric locomotives
The HX series is a new AC drive electric locomotive for freight traffic. In co-operation with ALSTOM

and Toshiba, the 7,200 kW locomotive features high tractive power capability for drawing over 5,000 tons with a single locomotive. The HXD2 9,600 kW electric locomotives showed good performance in hauling a 20,000 ton coal train on the Datong-Qinhaungdao line in January 2008.

The SS range of electric locomotives features microprocessor control and anti-slip braking. The SS4G and SS3B eight-axle double units are suitable for heavy haul freight service. The SS7 series is used for high-speed passenger service. The SS7E is the modular mass transit solution which addresses the need for higher speeds. Type DJ3 is a high-power AC propulsion electric locomotive to be used to boost main line freight services in China.

Diesel locomotives
DF family
The DF range of diesel-electric locomotives, with a four-stroke turbocharged diesel engine and AC/DC transmission, are the main types of main line locomotive for both passenger and freight traffic. They run on three-axle bogies with roller bearings. The traction motors are fully suspended with hollow shaft quill drive.

Types DF4D, DF8B are designed for heavy-duty freight trains, Types DF4D, DF10F and DF11 for high-speed passenger service and Types DF5 and DF7 for shunting work. Type DF4DJ is equipped with AC traction equipment and IGBT converters.

GK family
The GK range of diesel locomotives are intended for shunting and industrial applications. Many have hydraulic transmission and have a B-B configuration to suit tight curves.

CK family
The CK series diesel locomotives are designed for markets other than China and feature a lower axle load; examples are in operation on the narrow-gauge or broad-gauge railways of Angola, Congo, Malaysia, Myanmar, Nigeria, Pakistan, Tanzania and Vietnam.

Passenger coaches
All types of passenger coaches including single- or double-deck seating coaches, sleeping cars and restaurant cars, as well as mail vans, luggage vans and generator vans, with air-conditioning or normal ventilation. They were delivered to Bangladesh, Kazakhstan, Iran, Malaysia, Mongolia, Myanmar, North Korea, Pakistan, Sri Lanka and Turkmenistan. The 25T family is a new product range used in Chinese Railways' fifth speed acceleration. Capable of operating at up to 160 km/h, it is the latest in a series of designs first built in 1992.

Metro trainsets, multiple-units and trams/ LRVs
CNR products address increasing trends of urban and suburban development. Its regional and intercity trains are flexible products, designed to provide high standards of comfort, safety and performance. The 'China Star' holds the Chinese speed record for an emu of 321.5 km/h.

Travelling cranes
CNR produces an extensive range of travelling cranes, with lifting capacities from eight to 160 tonnes and capable of hauled speeds of up to 120 km/h. As well as supplying the domestic Chinese market, CNR has also delivered cranes to Myanmar, Pakistan and Tanzania.

CNR railway crane
MODEL, LIFT CAPACITY (T), FACTORY NAME
N151 (15t), China, Qiqihar
N603 (60t), Burma, Qiqihar
N1002 (100t), China, Lanzhou
N1004 (100t), China, Lanzhou
N1005 (100t), Tanzania, Lanzhou
N1601 (160t), China, Qiqihar
NS1252 (125t), China, Qiqihar
NS1601 (160t), China, Qiqihar
BT8.3 (8t), Pakistan, Lanzhou

CNR Type CKD8E AC drive diesel-electric train for Malaysia   1198290

CNR Type DF7G-C diesel-hydraulic locomotive for Cuba   1198297

CNR double-deck coach for Iran   1198294

Contracts
China: From 2000 to 2007, CNR supplied 1,373 electric locomotives, 2,371 diesel locomotives, 9,845 passenger coaches, 1,626 urban railway vehicles and 129,541 freight wagons. Most of them were used by the Ministry of Railways (MOR).

In 2007, CNR delivered 244 electric locomotives, 212 diesel locomotives, 916 passenger coaches, 379 urban railway vehicles and 18,749 freight wagons.

During 2007, CNR delivered hundreds of CRH5 200 km/h emu trains, 7,200 kW HXD3 electric locomotives and 9,600 kW HXD2 electric locomotives to the MOR, which fully supports the sixth speed acceleration of Chinese rail and plays a very important role for improving existing conventional lines to high speed.

In December 2007 CNR received a contract for the supply of 168 Type C aluminium-bodied metro cars for Line 9 of the Shanghai Subway following on from the contract at the beginning of 2007 for the supply of 306 metro cars for Line 9 and 192 metro cars for Line 7.

In November 2007, CNR received a contract for the supply of 112 cars for Line 13 of the Beijing Metro. In September 2007 the first of 40 rapid transit vehicles for Beijing Airport were rolled out.

In July 2007 an order for 36 stainless steel LRVs was awarded to CNR for operation on the Tianjin shore line.

In February 2007, CNR signed a contract with MOR to supply 500 9,600 kW electric locomotives in co-operation with Bombardier. In March 2007,

CNR Type HXD3 7,200 kW AC freight electric locomotive   1325324

CNR Type HXD2 9,600 kW AC freight electric locomotive   1325325

a contract was signed for a further 500 sets in co-operation with ALSTOM.

In January 2007, 40, 70 per cent low-floor LRVs were put into operation in Changchun for the 6th Asian Winter Games.

In December 2006, CNR was awarded a contract to supply 24 Type A aluminium-bodied metros for Shenzhen and was contracted by the Shenyang Subway for the supply of 138 metro cars for the first subway. In January 2008 CNR was awarded a contract to supply 60 Type A metro cars for Shenzhen.

In December 2006 CNR was contracted by the Shenyang Subway to supply 138 metro cars for the first subway line. Deliveries are scheduled to commence in November 2008.

In January 2007, 40, 70 per cent low-floor LRVs commenced operation in Changchun for the 6th Asian Winter Games.

In May 2006, Beijing purchased 84 new metro trains from CNR and updated 60 old vehicles for Line 2. In November 2005 CNR was awarded a contract to supply 34 sets of 204 stainless steel-bodied metro cars for Line 10 of the Beijing subway. In December 2004, CNR received a contract from Beijing Metro to supply 192 metros for Line 5.

In November 2005, CNR was awarded a contract with MOR to supply 60 300 km/h high-speed trains in co-operation with Siemens.

In September 2005, CNR signed a contract with MOR to supply 300 high-power diesel locomotives in co-operation with EMD.

Angola: In October 2007, 15 1,678 kW locomotives were delivered. In September 2005, CNR signed a contract for the supply of six diesel locomotives which included four 1,500 kW locomotives and two 1,678 kW locomotives. In January 2006, a further contract for two 1,500 kW locomotives was awarded. The eight locomotives were delivered to Angola in mid-2006.

Australia: In December 2006, CNR and EDI Rail signed a subcontract for the provision of 626 double-deck passenger coaches with stainless steel car-bodies for the Public-Private Project of New South Wales State of Australia. Deliveries were scheduled to commence in October 2008 and continue to September 2013.

Bangladesh: In 2005, CNR was awarded a contract for 80 metro coaches.

Burma: In May 2007 CNR was awarded a contract for the supply of 20 diesel locomotives, with the addition of a diesel crane.

Congo: In July 2005 CNR delivered a CK6E diesel locomotive to Congo. An order for two locomotives was received in September 2006 and a further one in October 2007.

Cuba: In January 2006, 12 Type DF7G-C diesel locomotives were delivered. In 2007 a further 40 diesel locomotives were delivered.

Ghana: In 2007 a contract for two dmus was signed.

India: In October 2007 four battery-powered tunnelling locomotives were delivered, the first batch of nine locomotives for the New Delhi subway.

Iran: In February 2007 CNR was awarded a contract to supply 60 70 per cent low-floor LRVs for Iran Mashhad mass Transit Company. In

CNR Type CRH5 200 km/h AC propulsion emu with distributed power   1325326

CNR Type CK6E1 1,500 kW diesel locomotive for Angola   1325328

December 2005, CNR was awarded a contract for the supply of 160 metro cars and 29 double-deck coaches for Tehran Urban & Suburban Railways. In April 2006, 50 double-deck coaches were ordered.

Iraq: In April 2002, 50 model DF10FI 1,840 kW diesel-electric locomotives were delivered to Iraq under a tender contract approved by the United Nations.

Kazakhstan: In 2006 CNR was awarded a contract for 152 coaches.

Malaysia: In November 2001, two Type CKD8C 1,840 kW diesel-electric locomotives were delivered to Malayan Railway (KTM). CNR was awarded a further order by Malayan Railways for 20 three-phase propulsion diesel-electric locomotives in November 2003. They are to be metre gauge Co-Co machines with a 20 tonne axleload. Twenty had been delivered to Malaysia by the end of 2005.

Mongolia: In January 2008 16 passenger coaches were tested for use between Ulaanbaatar and

Beijing. The coaches include sleeping, diner and luggage cars and a power van.

North Korea: Two model GKD4A 2,940 kW Co-Co diesel-electric locomotives were delivered to North Korea in July 2002. The diesel engine type is 16V240ZJD.

Pakistan: A first batch of eight 2,450 kW diesel-electric locomotives were delivered in June 2003 to Pakistan Railways (PR), followed by a second batch formed of seven 1,840 kW diesel-electric locomotives in July of the same year. Delivery of these 15 locomotives were to be followed by the local construction of 54 further machines supplied by CNR in CKD or SKD under a technology transfer contract awarded in November 2002. This covered the supply of 44 2,450 kW diesel locomotives and 25 1,840 kW 1,676 mm gauge locomotives. They are equipped with VVVF/CVCF transmission.

Sri Lanka: In February 2006, a contract was signed for the supply of 100 coaches. Deliveries were scheduled to be completed by 2007.

Thailand: In June 2007 a contract was signed for the supply of 48 metro cars.

Turkey: In October 2005, Turkey Steel Company awarded CNR a contract for the supply of 10 diesel-electric locomotives. Four locomotives were delivered in October 2006.

Turkmenistan: In mid-2005, 54 CNR coaches were delivered.

Vietnam: Vietnamese coal mining and phosphor mining companies selected CNR to supply 14 metre gauge diesel-hydraulic locomotives. Six were delivered from 2003 to 2004, two were delivered in 2005, two in 2006 and four in 2007.

China South Locomotive and Rolling Stock Industry (Group) Corporation (CSR)

11 Yangfangdian Road, Haidian District, Beijing, China
Tel: (+86 10) 63 98 47 70   Fax: (+86 10) 63 98 47 66
e-mail: csrft@csrgc.com.cn
Web: www.csrgc.com.cn

Key personnel
General Manager: *Zhao Xiaogang*

Background
CSR was established in 2000 as a result of the division into two regional groups of the former China National Railway Locomotive and Rolling Stock Industry Corporation (LORIC). The corporation comprises 25 state-owned enterprises employing around 112,000 staff. Some facilities are listed as part of CSR and of its northern China counterpart, China North Locomotive and Rolling Stock Industry (Group) Corporation (CNR).

In November 2007 NTN Corporation signed a joint venture with CSR Nanjing Puzhen Rolling Stock Works in which CSR will hold a 60 per cent stake and NTN the remainder. The train bearing operation is expected to be set up CSR's factory in Nanjing.

Subsidiaries
CSR comprises 16 manufacturing plants and eight holding companies. There are also three mutual shareholding subsidiaries.

Works
CSR Beijing Feb 7th Rolling Stock Works
Zhangguozhuang Fengtai District, Beijing 100072, China
Web: www.eqc.com.cn

CSR Beijing Locomotive & Rolling Stock Machinery Works
West Changping Railway Station, Beijing 102249, China
Web: www.cpgc.com

CSR Chengdu Locomotive & Rolling Stock Works
Erxian Bridge, North Road, Chengdu 610057, Sichuan, China
Web: www.cdjcc.com

CSR Guiyang Rolling Stock Works
Baiyun District, Guiyang 550017, Guizhou, China
Web: www.southhuiton.com

CSR Luoyang Locomotive Works
Qiming East Road, Luoyang 471002, Henan, China
Web: www.lylw.co.cn

CSR Meishan Rolling Stock Works
Dongpo, Meishan 620032, Sichuan, China
Web: www.msrsco.com

CSR Nanjing Puzhen Rolling Stock Works
Puzhen, Nanjing 210032, Jiangsu, China
Web: www.njpzclc.com

CSR Qishuyan Locomotive & Rolling Stock Works
Qishuyan, Changzhou 213011, Jiangsu, China
Web: www.qscn.com

CSR Shijiazhuang Rolling Stock Works
Front Street of Rolling Stock Works, Shijiazhuang 050000, Hebei, China
Web: www.sjzclc.com

CSR Tongling Rolling Stock Works
Phoenix Mountain Avenue, Tongling 244142, Anhui, China
Web: www.tlclc.com

CSR Wuchang Rolling Stock Works
Peace Avenue, Wuchang, Wuhan 430062, Hubei, China
Web: www.chinacool168.com

CSR Wuhan Jiang'an Rolling Stock Works
Jiang'an District, Wuhan 430012, Hubei, China
Web: www.csrgc-ja.com

CSR Xiangfan Diesel Locomotive Works
Xiangyang District, Xiangfan 441105, Hubei, China
Web: www.csr-xfjc.com

CSR Zhuzhou Electric Locomotive Works
Tianxin, Zhuzhou 412001, Hunan, China
Web: www.gofront.com
(see Zhuzhou Electric Locomotive Works entry in *Locomotives and powered/non-powered passenger vehicles* section)

CSR Zhuzhou Rolling Stock Works
Hetang District, Zhuzhou 412003, Hunan, China
Web: www.csr-zrsw.com

CSR Ziyang Locomotive Works
Ziyang 641301, Sichuan, China
Web: www.zyloco.com

Holding companies
Beijing Railway Industry Trade Co
11 Yangfandian Road, Haidan District, Beijing 100038, China

CSR Marketing & Leasing Corp
11 Yangfandian Road, Haidan District, Beijing 100038, China

CSR Qishuyan Locomotive & Rolling Stock Technology Research Institute

Qishuyan, Changzhou 441047, Jiangsu, China
Web: www.jcqys.com

CSR Sifang Locomotive & Rolling Stock Co Ltd
Laoshan District, Qingdao 266101, Shandong, China
Web: www.cqsf.com

CSR Xiangfan Traction Motor Co Ltd
Changhong North Road, Xiangfan 441047, Hubei, China
Web: www.xqdj.com

CSR Zhuzhou Electric Locomotive Research Institute
Shifeng District, Zhuzhou 412001, Hunan, China
Web: www.zelri.com

Sifang Locomotive & Rolling Stock Co Ltd
Sifang District, Qingdao 266031, Shandong, China
Web: www.csrsf.com

South Huitong Co Ltd
Baiyun District, Guiyang 550017, Guizhou, China
Web: www.southhuiton.com

Mutual shareholding subsidiaries
CNR Dalian Locomotive Research Institute
CNR Sifang Rolling Stock Research Institute
LORIC Import & Export Corp Ltd

Products
Diesel and electric locomotives, high-speed trainsets, dmus and emus, metro trainsets and passenger coaches, including:

High-speed trainsets
China Star 25 kV AC 50 Hz power cars: 4,800 kW, 78 tonnes, maximum speed 270 km/h.

Diesel locomotives
DF8B Co-Co diesel-electric freight locomotive: 3,100 kW, 138 or 150 tones, maximum speed 100 km/h. A variant of this design for high-altitude operation has been developed for service in Tibet.

Electric locomotives
DJ2 25 kV AC 50 Hz Bo-Bo electric passenger locomotive: 4,800 kW, 84 tonnes, maximum speed 200 km/h.
SS8 25 kV AC 50 Hz Bo-Bo electric passenger locomotive: 3,600 kW, 88 tonnes, maximum speed 240 km/h.

Emus
25 kV AC 50 Hz 160 km/h 3,200 emu with AC propulsion.

Contracts
Export contracts include the supply of high-powered 25 kV AC 50 Hz electric locomotives to Uzbekistan.

Cockerill Maintenance & Ingenierie SA (CMI)

Avenue Greiner 1, B-4100 Seraing, Belgium
Tel: (+32 4) 330 24 33   Fax: (+32 4) 330 25 45
e-mail: locos.diesel@cmigroupe.com
Web: www.cmigroupe.com

Key personnel
President: *B Serin*
General Manager, Locomotives and Diesel Engines: *P Lempereur*
Sales Manager, Locomotives and Diesel Engines: *M Metz*

Products
A range of two, three and four-axle shunting locomotives with hydrostatic transmission from 260 to 560 kW (350 to 750 hp), 30 to 100 tonnes, for sale or lease. Modernisation and refurbishment of all types of locomotives. Maintenance contracts, services and spare parts.

Colorado Railcar Manufacturing LLC

1011 14th Street, Fort Lupton, Colorado 80621, US
Tel: (+1 303) 857 10 66   Fax: (+1 303) 857 42 09
e-mail: sales@coloradorailcar.com
Web: www.coloradorailcar.com

Key personnel
President: *Tom Rader*
Vice-President, Sales: *Tom Janaky*
Director of Sales: *Arthur Rader*

Products
Passenger rail vehicles. The company has developed and built one of the world's largest double-deck commuter passenger dmus that is fully compliant with Federal Railroad Administration and APTA structural safety requirements. Each steel-bodied power car is equipped with two Detroit Diesel Series 60 440 kW engines with Voith T212 hydrodynamic transmission and Voith KE553 final drive. A 130 kW Deutz water-cooled diesel engine provides power for auxiliaries such as heating and air-conditioning. Vehicle configuration proposals provide for up to three intermediate trailer cars, for streamlined and non-streamlined power cars and for double-deck power cars and trailers.

Colorado Railcar also manufactures passenger coaches and has specialised in low-volume

Colorado Railcar single-deck prototype dmu demonstrator, subsequently ordered by SFRTA 0585219

contracts for operators of tourist services, supplying single-level and bi-level dome cars to customers that include Rocky Mountaineer Railtours, Canada, the Alaska Railroad and Princess Cruises and Tours.

Recent developments have included a new double-deck dmu which raises the seating capacity from 90 to 188 passengers. The bilevel passenger car has 200 seats in a low-floor, ADA accessible configuration.

CostaRail Srl

Viale IV Novembre, I-23845 Costa Masnaga (LC), Italy
Tel: (+39 031) 86 94 11   Fax: (+39 031) 85 53 30
e-mail: hkastner@costarail.it

Key personnel
Commercial Manager: *Heinz Kastner*

Background
Formerly Costaferroviaria, the company went into temporary receivership and was taken over by Rail Services International Group, for which RSI Italia SpA is the operative leader. In October 2004, CostaRail Srl was established, re-launching all existing Costaferroviaria activities, including orders, trademarks, patents and projects.

Products
Electric multiple-units, passenger coaches, freight wagons and bogies.

Contracts
CostaRail has restarted the construction of three battery powered locomotives for a tourist train in Aosta Valley, Italy, following the interruption during the takeover of Costaferroviaria by RSI.

As part of a consortium, CostaRail has been awarded a contract by Italian State Railway, Trenitalia, for the construction of 39 double-deck passenger coaches.

Repair of a fire damaged electric locomotive for Skoda of Ferrovie Nord Milano.

Djuro Djaković Holding dd

Vehicle and Machines Business Unit
Dr Mile Budaka 1, 35000, Slavonski Brod, Croatia
Tel: (+385 035) 44 59 96   Fax: (+385 035) 44 41 08
e-mail: uprava@duro-dakovic.com
Web: www.duro-dakovic.com

Key personnel
President: *Nadzorni Odbor*

Products
Diesel multiple-units and railcars; light rail vehicles and trams including eight-axle double-articulated LRV, with low-floor option.

Downer EDI Rail

2B Factory Street, Granville, New South Wales 2142, Australia
Tel: (+61 2) 96 37 82 88   Fax: (+61 2) 96 37 67 83
e-mail: sales@edirail.com.au
Web: www.downeredirail.com.au

Key personnel
Chief Executive Officer: *Guy Wannop*
Executive General Manager, Freight: *Danny Broad*
Executive General Manager, Passenger: *Michael Bourke*

Background
A division of Downer EDI Ltd, Downer EDI Rail is the result of a merger of Clyde Engineering and the rail activities of Walkers Ltd, changing its name to Downer EDI Rail as part of the company re-branding in July 2007.

Works
Downer EDI Rail has manufacturing, maintenance and design facilities in: Bathurst, Granville, Kooragang Island, Clyde, Cootamundra, Enfield, Eveleigh, Port Kembla and Cardiff, New South Wales; Berrimah, Northern Territory; Kewdale, Port Hedland and Nowergup, Western Australia;

Millennium double-deck emu by Downer EDI Rail for SRA's CityRail suburban services in Sydney
0594642

Rockhampton, Gladstone, Maryborough, Callemondah, Townsville and Brisbane, Queensland; Newport, West Melbourne and Geelong, Victoria; Port Augusta, Dry Creek, Whyalla, Port Lincoln, South Australia.

Products

Downer EDI Rail's business includes the design, manufacture, refurbishment, overhaul and maintenance of freight and passenger rolling stock, including: diesel-electric locomotives, electric locomotives, electric and diesel multiple-units, rail wagons, traction motors and rolling stock generally.

Contracts

In December 2006, as a member of the Reliance Rail Public Private Partnership (PPP) consortium, Downer EDI Rail was awarded a contract by Railcorp to supply 626 double-deck 1.5 kV DC emu cars for Sydney's CityRail suburban network. The vehicles are to be formed as 78 eight-car sets, with two spare cars. Downer EDI Rail is to undertake design and assembly of the vehicles at its Cardiff facility. Manufacture of bodyshells is to be sub-contracted to CNR Changchun Railway Vehicle Co in China; electrical equipment is supplied by Hitachi. Deliveries are due from 2010 to 2013. Downer EDI Rail is also to maintain the trains for 30 years.

Also in December 2006, in a joint venture with Bombardier, Downer EDI Rail was awarded a contract by the Western Australian Government to build 15 three-car electric commuter trains (B-Series) for delivery during 2009 and 2010.

Downer EDI Rail, again in a joint venture with Bombardier, was awarded an order by the Queensland Government for 20 three-car emus for delivery during 2009 and 2010.

In late 2005, Downer EDI Rail was awarded a contract by SCT Logistics (SCT) to design and supply 11 mainline standard gauge AC traction diesel-electric locomotives and provide maintenance services over a 10-year period. The locomotives are currently being delivered.

In 2005 Downer EDI Rail was awarded a contract to design, build and supply SCT Victoria 11 4300 hp AC standard-gauge locomotives. The award includes a 10-year maintenance contract.

Downer EDI Rail has supplied BHP Billiton Iron Ore Pty Ltd (PHPBIO) 23 EMD SD70ACe locomotives for their operations in Port Headland, Western Australia.

A further 20 EMD SD70ACe locomotives will be delivered in 2008/09.

Downer EDI Rail has built and supplied Pacific National four 90 Class locomotives for their coal operations within New South Wales in 2005.

Also for Pacific National Downer EDI Rail built 10 off-tilt bed wagons, with delivery completed in December 2005.

4000 Class diesel-electric locomotive supplied by Downer EDI Rail to QR (Brian Webber)   0099111

Type SD70ACe/lc diesel-electric heavy-haul locomotive built by EMD and supplied by Downer EDI Rail to BHP Billiton Iron Ore Pty Ltd   1174741

Downer EDI Rail completed the build and supply of 58 new generation narrow gauge bottom dump iron ore wagons, with higher capacity and increased operating speed for OneSteel in mid-2006, with a further 20 due for delivery in 2008.

In 2005 Downer EDI Rail delivered to Pacific national 13 PN Class locomotives. The PN Class is a 2,424 kW AC traction narrow gauge diesel-electric locomotive of a similar design to that of QR's 4,100 Class. In early 2006 it was announced that Downer EDI Rail was awarded the contract for the supply of 15 more 4,100 Class AC traction narrow gauge diesel-electric locomotives. This will bring the

total number of 4,000/4,100 Class locomotives for Queensland Rail to 64.

In November 2004 Queensland Rail ordered 24 three-car emu's from the Downer EDI-Bombardier joint venture. These are the latest in a series of emu's delivered to QR by the joint venture and extend the size of the QR fleet to 164 emus.

In 2004 Downer EDI Rail completed the delivery of locomotives and wagons for Asia Pacific Transport for operation on the Alice Springs to Darwin standard gauge rail link. The four FQ Class diesel-electric locomotives are powered with EMD 16 cylinder 710G3B 3,095 kW engines combined with Downer EDI Rail's radial steering bogies.

FTD Fahrzeugtechnik Dessau AG

Am Waggonbau 11, D-06844 Dessau, Germany
Tel: (+49 340) 253 70   Fax: (+49 340) 253 71 05
e-mail: zentrale@fahrzeugtechnik-dessau.de
Web: www.fahrzeugtechnik-dessau.com

Key personnel

Chairman of the Supervisory Board: *Pavel V Ulimenko*
Board of Directors: *Dr Ing Joachim Pfannmüller, Eberhard Mann, Walter Schulz, Audrey I Vashchenko*
Sales: *Frank Schäfer, Thomas Winkler*
Public Relations: *Birgid Hartmann*

Subsidiaries

Fahrzeug-Outfit GmbH
FTD Metall- und Komponentenbau GmbH Dessau

Background

Fahrzeugtechnik Dessau AG was acquired by CJCS Transmashholding in June 2006.

Products

Car bodies and subassemblies for rail vehicles; prototypes and small series of complete vehicles; driver's cab modules; rail vehicle doors; rail vehicle drive systems; repair, welding, supplier auditing, construction supervision and testing, production rig development and construction and technical calculation services; and anti-corrosion, blasting and painting and external finishing services for rail vehicles (via the Fahrzeug-Outfit subsidiary).

Contracts

In 2006 Fahrzeugtechnik Dessau announced a contract to supply the first examples of its PROTOS regional rail vehicle design to the Dutch operator Connexxion. The PROTOS is an electrically or diesel-electrically powered low-floor regional train. The design is flexible with regard to the type of power unit and internal fittings. Five two-car 1.5 kV emu versions of the type were to be supplied in 2007. It was the company's first commercial 'own account' passenger design and the vehicles can be produced in one-,

two- or three-car versions as dmus or emus. Top speed is 160 km/h.

Other rail vehicle contracts: Dortmund 2 vehicles (H-Bahngesellschaft); Type Rimms 660 wagons (DB Cargo AG); sliding wall wagons (Bombardier/ Greenbrier); Metropolitan intercity trainsets (DB AG); Type Falns128 wagons (Bombardier); prototype and pre-series Class 670 double-deck railbus (Bombardier/DB AG). Underframe modules for: Combino LRVs (Siemens); cars for Karlsruhe trams (Siemens); subassemblies for GT6 trams for Jena (Bombardier); roof sections for Class 101, 145, 152 and 185 electric locomotives (Bombardier and Siemens); LIREX dmu (ALSTOM); aluminium assemblies for ICE 3, VT 605 and VT 605 trainsets; trams for Magdeburg (ALSTOM); various cab modules, including Guangzhou metro (Bombardier); drive systems for Talent dmus for NSB, Norway (Bombardier), DB Class VT 612 dmus (Cummins/Adtranz), DB Class VT 642 dmus (MTU/Siemens).

FIREMA Trasporti SpA

Headquarters
Via Provinciale Appia, Località Ponteselice, I-81100 Caserta, Italy
Tel: (+39 0823) 09 71 11   Fax: (+39 0823) 46 68 12
e-mail: info@firema.it
Web: www.firema.it

Key personnel
Chairman and Chief Executive Officer:
Gianfranco Fiore

Commercial Manager: *Sergio d'Arminio*
Marketing Manager: *Agostino Astori*

Products
Electric locomotives, high-speed trainsets, electric multiple-units, railcars, advanced guided transit systems, metro rolling stock and light rail vehicles.

Developments
Bombardier Transportation and FIREMA Trasporti have signed an agreement to develop and manufacture Bombardier railway products in their respective Italian plants. The products have been customised together with FIREMA to meet the needs of the Italian market and they include the Bombardier Zefiro high-speed train and the Bombardier Talent emus to be used on commuter services. Under the terms of the agreement the two companies will put in bids for contracts in Italy and for specific projects in other countries.

Gevisa SA

Praça Papa João XXIII 28, Cicade Industrial, CEP 32210-100 Contagem, Brazil
Tel: (+55 31) 369 33 33
Fax: (+55 31) 369 33 34
e-mail: faleconosco.getrans@trans.ge.com
Web: www.getransportation.com.br

Key personnel
Director, South American Operations: *M Mosci*

Products
Electric traction motors, auxiliary power and control equipment for metro cars, emus and light rail vehicles; motor generator sets for emus; rehabilitation of control equipment and traction motors.

Rolling stock: diesel-powered locomotives; refurbishment and repair; remanufacture/reconstruction; maintenance; painting/livery and spare parts. Traction/control: (diesel) complete traction package, engines, components, traction motors, generators, mechanical equipment, gears/shafts/couplings and turbochargers.

H Cegielski – Fabryka Pojazdów Szynowch Sp zoo

28 Czerwca 1956R, 223/229, PL-60-965, Poznan, Poland
Fax: (+48 61) 831 20 07   Tel: (+48 61) 831 10 41
e-mail: fpstx4@hcp.com.pl
Web: www.hcp.com.pl/fps

Key personnel
President/General Director: *Piotr Szafran*
Vice-President: *Sławomir Raniszewski*

Products
Passenger coaches; railbuses; trams. The company also undertakes refurbishment and modernisation of passenger rail vehicles.

Contracts
In 2007 30 high-floor trams were supplied to Warsaw Tramways.

Developments
The Type 118N Puma three-section was introduced in 2007. The 2.4 m wide vehicle is part low-floor (67 per cent) and is equipped with asynchronous traction motors.

Prototype of the Type 118N Puma part low-floor tram exhibited at InnoTrans 2008 (Ken Harris)
1373683

Hitachi Ltd

Transportation Systems Division
18-13, Soto-Kanda 1-chome, Chiyudo-ku, Tokyo, 101-8608, Japan
Tel: (+81 3) 258 11 11   Fax: (+81 3) 45 64 62 52
Web: www.hitachi-rail.com

Key personnel
Chief Operating Officer of Transportation Systems: *Toshihide Uchimura*

Main works
Kasado Works, Mito Works, Hitachi Works

Subsidiaries
Hitachi Europe Ltd
Old Change House, 128 Queen Victoria Street, London EC4V 4BJ, UK
Tel: (+44 20) 79 70 27 11   Fax: (+44 20) 79 70 27 99
e-mail: hirofumi.ojima@hitachi-eu.com
Web: www.hitachi-eu.com

Background
Founded in 1910, Hitachi is one of the world's leading global electrical engineering companies generating one per cent of Japan's GDP. Hitachi manufactures and markets a wide range of products, including computers, semiconductors,

Series 683 for JR West Railway Company
0134966

consumer products, rolling stock and power and industrial equipment. Hitachi's share of the Japanese rolling stock market is approximately 40 per cent and it has delivered vehicles into all market sectors, including Shinkansen, 'Limited Express', commuter emu and metro trains.

Hitachi Europe is a wholly owned subsidiary of Hitachi Ltd with operations in 15 countries across Europe, Asia and Africa.

Products

Hitachi is a main supplier for Shinkansen, Monorail System, Linear Metro System, Maglev System, tilting train, signalling and sub-station systems. They include emus and dmus for city, urban and regional networks, monorail cars, linear induction motor powered metro trains for small-bore tunnels; lightweight alluminium and stainless steel and steel body shells; AC propulsion system using IGBT inverter; auxiliary power supply; air-conditioning; ATC, ATO and automatic train diagnostics systems. Hitachi has developed an aluminium car body train with friction stir welding and module construction.

Developments

In collaboration with Tokyu Car Corporation and East Japan Railway Co, Hitachi has developed the NE Train; an environmentally friendly test vehicle equipped with innovative propulsion technology. This employs a low-emission diesel engine and induction generator that feeds a hybrid system using roof-mounted lithium ion batteries, as well as optionally powering conventional traction motors. These last-mentioned also charge the batteries when in braking mode. Battery power can be used on its own or combined with power from the diesel engine. The system allows the diesel engine to be closed down during stations stops, reducing noise and pollution, with battery power used to restart the vehicle. The control system employs a converter and a VVF inverter.

Contracts

Monorail systems: Sentosa Express for Sentosa Development Corporation, Singapore; Okinawa Monorail, Japan; Series 2000 for Tokyo Monorail, Japan; Series 1000 for Tokyo Tama Inter City Monorail, Japan; Monorail cars for Chongqing, China IGBT propulsion systems; IGBT inverters for Beijing Urban Railway Construction Project.

High-speed trains: rolling stock, control system for Taiwan High Speed Rail Corporation.

Limited Express: Tsukuba Express for Metropolitan Intercity Railway Company, Japan; Series 257 Limited Express for JR East, Japan; Series 683 Limited Express for JR West, Japan; Series 885 Limited Express for JR Kyushu, Japan.

Commuter emu: KL3-97 stainless steel emu for Jabotabek suburban network in Jakarta, Indonesia; transit vehicle for Metropolitan Atlanta Rapid Transit Authority (MARTA) in US;

Series 257 for JR East   0134968

Hitachi monorail   0098273

Series 20000 for Seibu Railway Company, Japan; Series 815 for JR Kyushu, Japan.

Metro emu: Series 12000 linear motor propulsion emu for Transportation Bureau of Monorail System; Series 2000 for Tokyo Monorail, Tokyo Metropolitan Government; Series 1000 for Tokyo Tama InterCity Monorail, Japan.

Current customers include: Beijing, Taiwan Railway Administration, Sentosa Development Railway Corporation, Chongqing Rail Transit General Corporation, MPS, Hokkaido Railway

Company, East Japan Railway Company, Central Japan Railway Company, West Japan Railway Company, Kyushu Railway Company, Teito Rapid Transit Authority, Transportation Bureau of Tokyo Metropolitan Government, Seibu Railway, Tokyo Corporation, Tobu Railway, Kinki Nippon Railway, Japan, UK, supply of 29 high-speed 'A' trains to operate domestic services on the Channel Tunnel Rail Link (CTRL) and local lines in Kent as part of the new integrated Kent franchise. The trains are expected to come into service in 2009.

Hitachi's Series 815 emu for Kyushu Railway Company, Japan   0098048

Series 12000 linear motor drive emu from Hitachi for the Transportation Bureau of Tokyo Metropolitan Government, Japan   0098047

Hyundai Rotem Company

Headquarters
231, Yangjae-dong, Seocho-gu, Seoul, 137-938,
South Korea
Tel: (+82 2) 34 64 11 14
Fax: (+82 2) 34 64 75 86
Web: www.hyundai-rotem.co.kr

Key personnel

Executive Vice-Chairman and Chief Executive
Officer: *Yeo-Sung Lee*
President and Chief Executive Officer: *Yong-Hoon
Lee*
Senior Executive Vice-President and Chief
Operating Officer: *Sang-Kil Lee*
Vice-President: *Jae-Hong Kim (R&D centre)*

Works

Changwon plant
85, Daewon-dong, Changwon, Gyeongsangnam-
do 641-808, Korea
Tel: (+82 55) 273 13 41
Fax: (+82 55) 273 17 41
Fax: (+82 55) 273 17 41

Uiwang central research and development centre
462-18, Sam-dong, Uiwang-city, Kyunggi-do,
Korea
Tel: (+82 31) 460 11 14
Fax: (+82 31) 460 17 81

Background

Established in 1964 when Daewoo Heavy Industry
started manufacturing rolling stock, followed by
Hyundai Precision & Industry and Hanjin Heavy
Industry a few years later. In 1999, the three
companies were consolidated into KOROS by
the Korean Government. Hyundai Motor Group
acquired the share of Daewoo Heavy Industry
in October 2001 and KOROS became Rotem
Company in January 2002. As of November
2007, Rotem Company changed its company
name and CI to Hyundai Rotem Company. An
affiliate of Hyundai Motor Group, Hyundai Rotem
Company has its headquarters in Seoul and two
facilities, the central research and development
centre in Uiwang and the manufacturing plant
in Changwon. The Changwon plant has the
capability to manufacture 1,000 emus per
year and electrical equipment such as traction
motors, SIV inverters. Certifications such as the
ISO 9001:2000/KS A 9001:2001 for quality, ISO
14001:2004/KS A 14001:2004 for environment
and OHSAS 18001:1999 for occupational health
and safety management have been acquired at
all three sites.
In October 2007 Hyundai Rotem took up a 20-
year lease on premises in southern Philadelphia
which it is to use to manufacture vehicles for the
US market.

Products

Hyundai Rotem manufactures the full range of
rail products, for example emus, dmus, light
rail vehicles, high-speed trains, magnetically
levitated vehicles (Maglev), diesel-electric

Hyundai Rotem's Irish dmus 1340485

locomotives, electric locomotives, passenger
coaches, electrical equipment and also provide
turnkey systems as a total rail systems
supplier.

Electric multiple units

Hyundai Rotem produces a wide variety of
emus for suburban and inter-city transportation
services. Hyundai Rotem's emus have adopted
the VVVF inverter controls and the car body
structure is made of not only stainless steel,
but also aluminum materials, which have been
successfully proven over time by the domestic
commercial services. Hyundai Rotem's emus
focus on safe and comfortable transportation by
using special materials for interior facilities, which
have excellent fire resistance qualities equivalent
to the materials used on aircraft. Hyundai Rotem
produces emus through the design verification
process using updated technology and skills for
the analysis of car body and bogie strength and
digital mock-up verification steps before mass
production.

Diesel-multiple units

Hyundai Rotem has been developing and
supplying several types of dmus such as demus
and dhmus (diesel hydraulic multiple units).
The push-pull type dmus of Korea Railroad
Corporation (KORAIL), delivered in 1988 to 2000,
with a 2,954 kW (3,960 hp) engine operates at
the speed of 150 km/h for commercial service. In
2007, 150 Irish dmus were delivered to Dublin and
put into revenue service running at a maximum
speed of 160 km/h. Hyundai Rotem can design
and manufacture other types of dmus according
to various clients needs, providing flexibility to
the basic formation and power distribution and/
or changing the location of power units (under
frame or upper frame).

High-speed trains

Hyundai Rotem and Korea Rail Research Institute
(KRRI) successfully co-developed the new
high-speed train (G7) system which can reach
the maximum speed of 350 km/h. Currently,
Hyundai Rotem is building the new Korean high-
speed trains, KTX-II with 350 km/h high-speed
rail technology. KTX-II will be put into revenue
service on the Honam line from 2010. In the
second phase, it will run through the Jeolla line,
Kyeongieon line and Kyungbu line.

Diesel-electric locomotives

Hyundai Rotem's diesel-electric locomotives
have been manufactured under license from
(General Motors) GM/EMD in the US since the
mid-1970s. The traction power ranges from
746 kW (1,000 hp) to 2,760 kW (3,700 hp) and the
most popular model, the GT26CW-2 is equipped
with GM's 645 16-cylinder turbo-charged diesel
engine. Over 260 Hyundai Rotem locomotive
units are presently operating on Korea's national
railroads and 35 units have been exported to the
Middle East, Africa and Asia since 1984. Hyundai
Rotem can design various types of locomotives
for operation in any conditions.

Electric locomotives

Hyundai Rotem's electric locomotives have been
manufactured for several years since 1998 for Korea
Railroad Corporation (KORAIL) on AC25 kV/60Hz
electrified sections, coupled with passenger
coaches of 700 tons with a maximum running
speed of 150 km/h. The propulsion equipment
uses a three-phase AC motor that is controlled by
a VVVF inverter, higher traction power per axle.

Contracts

India: Hyundai Rotem was awarded the supply
of 240 emus to DMRC in 2001. Hyundai Rotem

Computer-generated Hyundai Rotem's LRV, Istanbul, Turkey 1340474

Hyundai Rotem's Attiko Metro emus, Athens, Greece 1340484

was assigned to design, produce and supply 60 complete emus in Korea and supply of the remaining 180 emus in India. In 2007 Hyundai rotem concluded a contract with DMRC to supply 156 emus with an option for a further 36.

Iran: Hyundai Rotem will provide 120 dmus and transfer technology to the Iran Khodro Rail Transport Industries Co (IRICO). 24 units will be delivered to IRICO and the remainder will be produced in Iran, with the help of Hyundai Rotem's technology.

Ireland: Hyundai Rotem was awarded a contract for the supply of 150 dmus to Ireland in 2005. The trains will be operated on 1,947 km of wide gauge track owned by IE and will be manufactured according to European safety standards.

Korea: In 2005, a consortium led by Hyundai Rotem and several engineering and civil construction companies, won a tender for the construction of Seoul metro line 9 (due to be open in 2009). Through the Seoul metro 9 project,

Hyundai Rotem, in addition to being a vehicle supplier, is aiming to be a global rail system turn-key supplier.

Seoul Metro ordered 280 metro trains for the replacement line 2 trains in 2006. In addition Hyundai Rotem has received refurbishment orders from domestic and overseas customers totalling approximately 1,200 units and these outdated train sets will be upgraded and well equipped to allow safe and comfortable passenger service.

Hyundai Rotem received the order for 190 cars of Korean high-speed train, KTX-II from KORAIL in 2006.

Turkey: In November 2008 Hyundai Rotem won a contract for the supply of 440 emus to Turkey's General Directorate of Railways, Harbors and Airport Construction as part of the Marmaray Projects, providing an upgrade to the commuter rail system in Ankara. Delivery is scheduled between 2012 and 2014 in three deliveries.

The contract also covered personnel training, pre-hiring training, spare parts and operating maintenance for five years.

US: In April 2008 Hyundai Rotem was awarded a contract to deliver passenger trains to the city of Boston in an order which requires the delivery of 75 rail vehicles by 2012. In April 2007 Southeastern Pennsylvania Transportation Authority (SEPTA) ordered 16 additional SilverlineV regional rail cars from Hyundai Rotem. An option for the purchase of the additional cars was included in the original contract with United Transit Systems, LLC (a consortium of Sojitz Corporation of America and Hyundai Rotem Company), originally approved in 2006. Approval of the option increases the order to 120.

In 2006 Hyundai Rotem was awarded bi-level passenger coaches contracts by Southern California Regional Rail Authority (Metrolink) for 87 vehicles.

Inekon Group as

Address
U Průhonu 773/12, CZ-17000 Prague 7, Czech Republic
Tel: (+420 234) 12 21 11   Fax: (+420 234) 12 21 22
e-mail: inekon@ms.anet.cz
Web: www.inekon.cz

Works
Inekon Trams as
Martinovská 42/3244, CZ-72300 Ostrava-Martinov, Czech Republic

Tel: (+420 597) 40 22 33
Fax: (+420 234) 12 23 43
e-mail: dpoinekon@inekon.cz

Products
Light rail vehicles. The company has developed the TRIO model, a 20 metre, three-section 1,435 mm gauge design equipped with two bogies (both motored) and featuring a low (350 mm) floor height for more than 50 per cent of the vehicle length. Traction equipment includes IGBT inverters and air-cooled three-phase traction motors.

Contracts
The company has supplied its 01-Trio model tram to the Czech cities of Ostrava and Olomouc. It also received contracts for its 12-Trio model tram from three US cities. Those for Portland and Seattle (three-cars each) were all delivered in 2007, while three for Washington DC's planned Anacostia line were completed in 2007 and are currently stored in Ostrava awaiting construction of a depot for this new line.

INKA

Indonesian Railway Industry
Jl Yos Sudarso No 71, Madiun 63122 East Java, Indonesia
e-mail: support@inka.web.id
Web: www.inka.web.id

Key personnel
President: *Ir Roos Diatmoko*
Commercial Director: *Ir Gunesti Wahyu Handiko*
General Manager, Railway Rolling Stock Division: *Suryanto*

Administration and Finance Director: *Ir Bambang Soenjaswono*
Government Project Marketing Manager: *Drs Nazuar*
Export and Private Company Marketing Director: *Ir I Gede Agus P*
Design and Engineering Manager: *Ir Yunendar Aryo H*

Background
PT INKA was originally established in 1981 as a state owned company, transforming from

Indonesian State Railway's steam locomotive maintenance shop.

Products
Assembly and renovation of freight wagons (300 units a year), passenger coaches (120 units a year), diesel and electric railcars (40 units a year), bogies (200 units a year).

Locomotives (in collaboration with GE Transportation, 15 units a year). Various special vehicles, including track motor and inspection cars and amusement park trains.

The Integral Coach Factory (ICF)

Ministry of Railways, Chennai 600 038, Tamil Nadu, India
Tel: (+91 44) 26 26 30 91   Fax: (+91 44) 26 26 31 11
e-mail: coachnet@vsnl.com
Web: www.icf.gov.in

Key personnel
General Manager: *Dr P Raja Goundan*
Financial Advisor and Chief Accounts Officer: *S Ram Mohan*
Secretary to General Manager: *P Uday Kumar Reddy*
Public Relations: *G Subramanian*

Background
ICF was established in 1955 in collaboration with the Swiss Car & Elevator Manufacturing Co. The agreement ended in 1961, and the company is now controlled by the Ministry of Railways. With a staff of 13,000, ICF is capable of producing over 1,000 coaches a year and was able to turn out 1,291 coaches of various designs during production year 2007-2008. Since inception ICF has produced more than 35,000 coaches of nearly 200 types.

ICF is ISO-9001 accredited for Quality Management System and ISO 14001 for 'Environmental Management System'.

Products
ICF produces many different types of electric multiple units, metro cars and diesel railcars

ICF AC/DC emu for MRVC, Mumbai 1344710

and luxury tourist cars (Palace-on-Wheels). The company offers in-house design and development facilities and can manufacture and supply any type of coach.

Golden Chariot manufactured by ICF for the Karnataka State Tourism Train and contain classic styled interiors to reflect the heritage of the

Karnataka State, including modern facilities such as onboard internet communication, a gym, car and conference car.

Life Line Express a hospital on wheels manufactured by ICF for an NGO M/s Impact India Foundation to provide medical facilities for the Indian communities in rural areas.

ICF has produced the first of its kind /DC dual voltage emu, capable of being operated in both AC and DC tractions, these trains will enable smooth change over of Mumbai Suburban Transit System from its 1,400 V DC traction to 25 kV AC traction without distruption.

Contracts

As part of the order received from Angolan Railways for the export of 56 coaches, ICF has successfully exported dmu rakes to the company during 2007–08, completing the order.

AC/DC emus for Mumbai Railway Vikas Corporation (MRVC).

ICF Life Line Express hospital on wheels

1344711

Kawasaki Heavy Industries Ltd

Rolling Stock Company, Rolling Stock Division
World Trade Center Building, 4-1 Hamamatsu-cho
2-chome, Minato-ku, Tokyo 105-6116, Japan
Tel: (+81 3) 34 35 25 72   Fax: (+81 3) 34 35 21 57
Web: www.khi.co.jp

Works

Hyogo Works
1-18 Wadayama-dori 2-chome, Hyogo-ku, Kobe
652-0884, Japan

Kawasaki Rail Car, Inc
Yonkers Plant
29 Wells Avenue, Building #4, Yonkers, New York
10701, US

Kawasaki Motors Manufacturing Corp, US
Lincoln Plant
6600 Northwest 27th Street, Lincoln, Nebraska
68524, US

Key personnel

Senior Vice-President, Kawasaki Heavy Industries Ltd, President, Rolling Stock Company: *Masashi Segawa*
Managing Executive Officer, Kawasaki Heavy Industries Ltd, Vice-President, Rolling Stock Company: *Kyohei Matsuoka*
General Manager, Rolling Stock Division, Rolling Stock Company: *Yoshinori Kanehana*
General Manager, Marketing and Sales Centre, Rolling Stock Division, Rolling Stock Company: *Ryoshi Hirano*
Senior Manager, Overseas Marketing Department, Marketing and Sales Centre, Rolling Stock Division, Rolling Stock Company: *Hiroshi Murao*

Background

Established in 1906, including other business segments such as aerospace, shipbuilding and consumer products, Kawasaki continues to contribute to the development and modernisation of railway transportation and rolling stocks. Kawasaki established its subsidiary company, Kawasaki Rail Car, Inc, in 1986 for the manufacture of rolling stock in the US. The newest Lincoln plant, established in 2002, is equipped with

Kawasaki's R160 subway car for MTA New York City Transit

1209126

state-of-the-art manufacturing facilities and is the only rolling stock manufacturing plant in North America for mass production of rapid transit and passenger cars covering the full process from fabrication of carbody to final assembly.

Kawasaki is expanding its overseas rolling stock operations to keep pace with the growing demands worldwide.

Products

High-speed trainsets; electric and diesel railcars; MRT vehicles; monorail vehicles; automated guideway transit systems; passenger coaches; electric, diesel-electric, diesel-hydraulic locomotives; freight cars; complete bogie sets; platform screen doors.

Contracts

Current or recent contracts include: as a member of Taiwan Shinkansen Corporation, 360 high-speed trainset cars to Taiwan High Speed Rail Corporation (THSRC) (2004–2005); 321 rapid trainset emus to Taipei's Department of Rapid Transit Systems (DORTS) in Taiwan (2003 and ongoing); 100 towing locomotives to Panama Canal Authority (ACP, formerly Panama Canal Commission) (1999–2006).

Most recent overseas contracts include ongoing projects to supply, as a member of the consortium with ALSTOM Transportation, 660 R160B subway cars to NYCT (New York City Transit), 340 PA-5 cars to Port Authority Trans-Hudson (PATH) system of Port Authority of New York and New Jersey (in association with CSR Sifang Locomotive and Rolling Stock Co Ltd); emus for Guangzhou Line No 4 and No 5; 123 emus to Bureau of High Speed Rail in Taiwan; 300 AC/DC M-8 electric passenger cars to MTA Metro-North Railroad; 138 subway cars to DORTS in Taiwan.

Kawasaki Rail Car Inc

29 Wells Avenue, Building 4, Yonkers, New York
10701, US
Tel: (+1 914) 376 47 00
Fax : (+1 914) 376 47 79
e-mail: KawasakirailCar@KawasakiRailCar.com
Web: www.kawasakirailcar.com

Key personnel

President: *Akira Hattori*
Executive Vice-President: *Hiroji Iwasaki*

Products

Electric multiple-units, rapid transit cars, passenger coaches, light rail vehicles.

Contracts

In November 2006 KRC received conditional acceptance of the first ten of the 660 R160 subway trains to MTA New York City Transit after successful commissioning and type testing since July 2005. In August 2007 NYCT executed the first option of 620 cars and second option for 382 cars in November 2008 to the ALSTOM-Kawasaki joint venture. KRC designs and provides all trucks for the R160 program and also builds approximately 40 per cent of the complete R160 subway cars.

In August 2006 KRC signed a contract to provide 300 M-8 multiple-unit rail cars with an option for 80 additional rail cars jointly procured by the State of Connecticut and MTA Metro-North Railroad.

In May 2005 KRC was awarded a contract by the Port Authority Trans-Hudson Corporation to build 340 new PA-5 rapid transit cars, which when delivered will replace the entire PATH fleet.

Kinki Sharyo Co Ltd

The Kinki Sharyo Co Ltd
2-6-41 Inada-Uemachi, Higashi-Osaka City, Osaka
577-8511, Japan
Tel: (+81 6) 67 46 52 40   Fax: (+81 6) 67 45 51 35
e-mail: sharyo@kinkisharyo.co.jp
Web: www.kinkisharyo.co.jp

Key personnel
President: *Koichi Sakurai*
Executive Vice-President: *Toshitake Iida*
Senior Managing Director, Chief Operating
  Officer: *Akio Yammamoto*
Director, International Business Center: *Yoshitaka
  Sugimoto*

Subsidiaries
Kinkisharyo (US) Inc/Kinkisharyo International,
LLC
55 Shawmut Road, Canton, Massachusetts
02021, US
Tel: (+1 617) 949 24 40
Fax: (+1 781) 828 80 25

Cosmo Kinki Co Ltd
3-2-11, Nishi-Shinjuku, Shinjuku-ku, Tokyo 160-
0023, Japan
Tel: (+81 3) 53 39 20 80

Background
Kinki Sharyo Co Ltd is a subsidiary of the Kinki
Nippon Railway.

Products
Electric multiple-units for main line, commuter,
rapid transit, metro and light rail vehicles,
double-deck passenger coaches.

Contracts
Recent orders include: emu for Cairo Metro Line 3;
Series N700 Shinkansen for JR West; low-floor
centre section LRV for Dallas, US; emu for
Hanshin Railway; 3000 Series subway for Osaka
City; Limited Express Electric train for Kinki
Nippon Railway and emu for Dubai, UAE.

Kinki Sharyo low-floor LRV for Phoenix Valley Metro Rail   1198283

Kinki Sharyo low-floor LRV for Seattle Sound Transit   1198282

Končar – Electric Vehicles Inc

Velimira Škorpika 7, HR-10090 Zagreb, Croatia
Tel: (+385 1) 349 69 59, 349 69 50
Fax: (+385 1) 349 69 60
e-mail: sales@koncar-kev.hr, info@koncar-kev.hr
Web: www.koncar-kev.hr

Key personnel
President: *Ivan Bahun*
Director of Development and Sales: *Jusuf Crnalić*
Head of Marketing and Sales: *Zvonimir Cvijin*

Background
Founded in Zagreb in 1970 and a member of
Končar Group, Končar – Electric Vehicles Inc
designs, manufactures, repairs, rebuilds and
refurbishes electric rail vehicles and vehicle
equipment.
  In January 2008 the company received ISO
14001:2004 certification for its Environmental
Protection Management System.

Products
Electric locomotives for AC and DC traction;
electric multiple-units; trams; shunting
locomotives; light rail vehicles; parts, components
and systems for electric traction.
  In 2005 Končar rolled out the first of 70 Type
TMK 2200 low-floor trams for ZET Zagreb. The
five-section articulated metre-gauge vehicles
employ asynchronous traction motors and IGBT
convertors. Body construction is of steel, with
some GRP elements.

Type TMK 2200 low-floor tram for ZET Zagreb (Toma Bacic)   1129938

*25 kV Class 444
Bo-Bo electric locomotive
for Serbian Railways (ŽS)*
1176859

Contracts

In December 2007, Končar – Electric Vehicles Inc and its partner TŽV Gredelj (both members of the CROTRAM Consortium) delivered the first tram from its second series of low floor TMK 2200 trams to the City Of Zagreb. The first series of 70 low floor trams was delivered to the City Of Zagreb between May 2005 and May 2007.

25 kV Class E52
Bo-Bo electric locomotive for
Turkish State Railways
1176860

25 kV Class 461
Co-Co electric locomotive for
Serbian Railways (ŽS)
1176861

Leoliner Fahrzeugbau Leipzig GmbH (FBL)

Teslastrasse 2, D-04347 Leipzig, Germany
Tel: (+49 341) 492 16 66
Fax: (+49 341) 492 15 02
e-mail: lbinfo@lfb.de
Web: www.lfb.de

Background

Established in 2000 initially as Leipziger Fahrzeugservice-Betriebe GmbH (LFB), FBL is a subsidiary of Leipzig's public transport undertaking, Leipziger Verkehrsbetriebe GmbH (LVB).

Products

Low-cost low-floor trams. The Leoliner range of articulated steel-bodied vehicles has been developed as a low-cost alternative to established manufacturers' products. The first version to be built is the NGTW6, a 22 m two-section tram with 60 per cent of its interior low-floor. Other versions offered are the NGTW8 (30 m three-section) and NGTW12 (45 m five-section). Vehicles can be supplied for 1,000, 1,435 or 1,458 mm track gauge. Traction equipment is by Vossloh Electrical Systems and includes IGBT inverters and air-cooled three-phase traction motors.

FBL Leoliner Type NGTW6 part-low-floor tram (Ken Harris) 0585022

Metrowagonmash (MWM)

Mytishchi, the Moscow region, Russian Federation
54 Ozerkovskaya Emb, Building 1, Moscow 115054, Russian Federation
Tel: (+7 495) 744 70 93   Fax: (+7 495) 744 70 94
e-mail: info@tmholding.ru
Web: www.tmholding.ru

Key personnel
General Director of MWM: *Andrey Andreev*

Background
Established in 1897, Metrowagonmash (MWM) is part of CJSC Transmashholding, manufacturing metro cars for underground systems within Russia, CIS countries and other European countries.

Products
MWM specialises in developing, designing and manufacturing metro cars and dmu, spare parts for the manufactured rolling stock, and is also active in overhaul and service maintenance. In addition, the plant produces automotive vehicles and special-purpose tracked chassis.

Modertrans Poznan Sp Zoo

Poznań Branch ul Gajowa 1a, PL-60 815 Poznań, Poland
Tel: (+48 61) 866 90 15
Fax: (+48 61) 843 44 35
e-mail LRV@modertrans.poznan.pl
Web: www.modertrans.poznan.pl

Key personnel
Director: *Jaroslaw Bakinowski*

Background
Modertrans Poznan is based in the workshops of Poznan's urban transport operator MPKP and is 25 per cent-owned by the authority, with the remaining stake held by Zakładu Napraw Autobusów, a bus repair company. As well as modernising existing trams, it has developed its own new models.

Products
The tram product range includes: the Moderus Alfa, a single car high-floor design offered with either AC or DC traction motors; the Moderus Beta, created by rebuilding existing Duewag high-floor vehicles and adding a new low-floor centre section; and the Moderus Gamma, a planned new all low-floor design offered in three- or four-section versions.

Contracts
Small numbers of the Moderus Alfa vehicle have been supplied to or ordered by operators in Katowice and Poznan. The company also received an order for 46 Moderus Beta vehicles for Gdansk.

MotivePower Inc

4600 Apple Street, Boise, Idaho 83716, US
Tel: (+1 208) 947 48 00
Fax: (+1 208) 947 48 20
e-mail: motivepowerinc@wabtec.com
Web: www.motivepower-wabtec.com

Key personnel
Vice-President and General Manager: *Mark S Warner*

Background
MotivePower Inc is a subsidiary company of Wabtec Corporation, the latter created in 1999 as a result of the 1999 merger of Westinghouse Air Brake Co and MotivePower Industries Inc.

Products
New and remanufactured passenger diesel locomotives, switching locomotives, liquefied natural gas locomotives, remanufactured locomotives.

Contracts
Contracts for new-build locomotives include the following:
Canada: In October 2005, the Government of Ontario awarded the company a contract to supply 27 Type MP40PH-3C MPXpress® new diesel locomotives for its 'Go Transit' commuter rail service. They will be designed to allow a single locomotive to power a train consisting of 12 bi-level cars at speeds up to 93 mph/150 kph. Delivery is scheduled for 2008–09. The contract included an option on an additional 26 locomotives of the same type.
US: In April 2008 an order was received for 26 MPXpress® commuter locomotives from the Maryland Transit Administration for its MARC commuter rail service. The locomotives, to be built in Boise, Idaho, are scheduled for delivery in 2008–09.

In February 2008 an order was received for 10 MPXpress® commuter locomotives from the Utah Transit Authority (UTA). In addition, UTA awarded MotivePower a four-year contract to maintain 11 other MPXpress® locomotives, which have already been delivered.

In June 2007 orders were received for 12 MPXpress® commuter locomotives from transit agencies in California, Minnesota and New Mexico. The locomotives, to be manufactured in Boise, Idaho, are expected to be delivered in 2008-09.

In July 2006 the company was awarded a contract by New Jersey Transit Corporation to supply five "clean-diesel" switcher locomotives operating at the Environmental Protection Agency's Tier 2 emissions levels. The locomotives, remanufactured at MotivePower's Boise, Idaho facility, met new environmental emissions standards and were equipped with an automatic start/stop system to improve fuel efficiency and extend component life on idling units. The locomotives were delivered in 2007.

In May 2006 Pacific Harbor Line, Inc (PHL) awarded MotivePower a contract to supply 16 'clean-diesel' locomotives in 2007 for use at the California ports of Los Angeles and Long Beach.

In the first quarter of 2006 the Utah Transit Authority (UTA), Salt Lake City, Utah, awarded the company a contract to supply 11 Type MP36PH-3C MPXpress® remanufactured diesel locomotives to enhance their commuter rail service. Delivery commenced in 2007. In the last quarter of 2005 MotivePower was awarded a contract by the New York City Transit Authority, New York, to supply 28 Type MP8AC new diesel locomotives to enhance their subway system work trains.

Developments
In 2008 MotivePower introduced a new, ultra low emissions switcher locomotive with a multi-engine design. Known as the MPEx, the locomotive is expected to begin revenue service testing with Class I railroads in the first quarter of 2008.

Mytischi

Metrowagonmash Joint Stock Company
4 Kolontsov Str, Mytischi 141009, Moscow Region, Russian Federation
Tel: (+7 495) 581 12 56   Fax: (+7 495) 581 12 56
Web: www.metrowagonmash.ru

Key personnel
President & General Director: *A Andreev*
Vice President and Technical Director: *V Vorobiev*

Products
Metro cars, dmus.

Contracts
Mytischi has built cars for all metro systems in the former USSR, and for the Prague, Sofia, Budapest and Warsaw metros. Standard designs are the 81–717 driving and 81-714 intermediate car, built for both 1,520 mm and 1,435 mm gauges.

The N5 trainset was developed by the Avtovaz Institute for Moscow metro Line 9 with 750 V third-rail current collection and power equipment from the Dynamo works (qv, Trolleybus Traction Equipment section). The cars have stainless steel bodyshells, double-glazed windows, fold-down emergency door at the front, microprocessor traction control and disc brakes.

An air conditioned railcar prototype for low-density secondary routes has been developed with a Cummins underfloor diesel engine and Voith transmission, seating 64 with 160 standing.

Newag Spólka Akcyjna

Ul Wyspiańskiego 3, PL-33-300 Nowy Sącz, Poland
Tel: (+48 18) 449 63 60   Fax: (+48 18) 449 63 66
e-mail: newag@newag.pl
Web: www.newag.pl

Key personnel
President: *Zbigniew Konieczek*
Vice-President and Director of Production and Technology: *Wieslaw Piwowar*

*Prototype Type 19WE
regional emu (Ken Harris)*
1374688

Background

Formerly the state-owned rail vehicle repair company ZNTK Nowy Sacz SA, Newag passed into private ownership in 2003 and adopted its present name in 2005.

Products

New-build emus; modernisation and refurbishment of diesel locomotives, emus and passenger coaches. Recently built emus include the Type 14WE three-car unit for local and suburban services, examples of which have been supplied to PKP SKM, and the Type 19WE asynchronous-motored regional emu. Modernisation of Class EN57 emus has also been undertaken. Diesel locomotive modernisation programmes include the 2,133 kW Type 311D, a rebuild of the Soviet-built M62 with a GE Transportation 7FDL 12 EF145 V12 power unit and updated control equipment. In 2007 Newag also produced a prototype of its 652 kW Type 6Dg diesel-electric locomotive, rebuilt from an SM42 machine with a Caterpillar C27 power unit.

Type 311D diesel-electric locomotive for Heavy Haul Power International, rebuilt from a Soviet-built M62 machine (Ken Harris)   1373633

Niigata Transys Co Ltd

F 9-7, Yaesu 2-chome, Chuo-ku, Tokyo
Tel: (+81 3) 62 14 28 77
Fax: (+81 3) 62 14 28 71
Web: www.niigata-transys.com

Background

Niigata Transys Co Ltd was formed in 2003 by Ishikawajima-Harima Industries Co Ltd (IHI) following the insolvency of Niigata Engineering Co Ltd.

Key personnel

President: *H Otsubo*

Products

Manufacture and sale of dmus, emus and LRVs and design manufacture and construction of guided railway systems.

Niigata Series HOT7000 tilting dmu for Chizu Express Railway   1180176

Nippon Sharyo Ltd

Head office

1-1 Sanbonmatsu-cho, Atsuta-ku, Nagoya 456-8691, Japan
Tel: (+81 3) 36 68 33 30   Fax: (+81 3) 36 69 02 38
Web: www.n-sharyo.co.jp

Overseas contact

Marunouchi Central Building, 1-9-1 Marunouchi, Chiyoda-ku, Tokyo 100-0005, Japan
Tel: (+81 3) 66 88 67 94   Fax: (+81 3) 66 88 68 10

Key personnel

President and Chief Executive Officer: *Katsuyuki Ikushima*
Director and General Manager, Rolling Stock Division: *Hiroshi Nagata*
Business Contact Director and General Manager, International Sales Dept: *Masataka Nakajima*

Subsidiaries

Nippon Sharyo USA Inc
2340 S Arlington Heights Road, Suite 605, Arlington Heights, Illinois 60005, US
Tel: (+1 847) 228 27 00   Fax: (+1 847) 228 55 30

Background

Established in September 1896, the company employs 1,851 staff and is ISO9001 accredited.
In August 2008 JR Tokai (Central Japan Railway Co) made a tender offer to increase its

Nippon Sharyo N700 Series Shinkansen emu for JR Central and JR West, Japan   1344762

Nippon Sharyo 50000 Series express emu for Odakyu Electric Railway, Japan
1344761

shareholding in Nippon Sharyo from 1.8 per cent to a controlling interest of 50.1 per cent.

Products

Electric and diesel multiple-unit cars, LRVs, automated guideway transit cars, monorail cars, bogies for urban and suburban trainsets, high-speed trains.

Contracts

In co-operation with Sumitomo Corporation, Nippon Sharyo is completing the deliveries of 61 bi-level push-pull cars for Virginia Railway Express and 14 bi-level emus for Northern Indiana Commuter Transportation District.

In Taiwan, Nippon Sharyo collaborated with Taiwan Rolling Stock Company to deliver 160 commuter emus for Taiwan Railway Administration.

N700 series Shinkansen emus are being manufactured and delivered to Central Japan Railway and West Japan Railway. The deliveries commenced in 2007 and will continue for a few years. In addition, Nippon Sharyo is delivering express, suburban and commuter emus for various customers, including Keio Corporation, Nagoya Railroad, Odakyu Electric Railway, Tokyo Metro and others.

Nippon Sharyo stainless steel gallery emu for Metra, Chicago, US   1143110

PESA Bydoszcz SA

Zygmunta Augusta 11 Street, PL-85-082 Bydgoszcz
Tel: (+48 52) 339 11 04
Fax: (+48 52) 339 11 14
e-mail: pesa@pesa.pl
Web: www.pesa.pl

Key personnel

President and General Director: *Tomasz Zaboklicki*
Directors
  Production and Technology: *Zenon Duszynski*
  Marketing and Development: *Zygfryd Zurawski*
  Financial: *Robert Swiechowicz*
  Director of Marketing and Development: *Jerzy Berg*

Background

PESA Bydoszcz SA formerly traded as ZNTK Bydoszcz SA. PESA's holding company is Pojazdy Szynowe PESA Bydgoszcz Spólka Akcyjna Holding.

Products

Lightweight diesel railcars; electric railcars and emus, trams, air-conditioned open and compartment coaches; sleeping cars. The company also undertakes refurbishment and modernisation of locomotives, passenger coaches and trams.

The Type 214M 'Partner' diesel-hydraulic railcar was introduced in 2001 to provide a low-cost vehicle for regional lines. Built on a former coach underframe with new bogies, the part-low-floor (30 per cent) single-car unit is powered by a 500 kW power pack. Maximum speed is 120 km/h, axleload 14 t.

In 2005 PESA rolled out a prototype Type 308B single-car electric railbus designated Class EN81 and featuring IGBT traction equipment.

Open and compartment passenger coaches are built under licence to Ukrainian designs.

Contracts

Italy: In 2006 PESA was awarded a contract by Ferrovie Sud Est to supply ATR 220 three-car dmus. The deliveries commenced in July 2008 when PESA started to supply the 23 vehicles.
Poland: In 2004 a prototype Class EN95 four-car articulated emu was delivered to PKP Warsaw Suburban Railway Ltd.

In 2005 PESA received a contract from Dolnoslaskie Koleje Regionalne for one single-car and one two-car Partner railbuses.

Type 122N all low-floor five-section tram (Ken Harris)   1374672

Class ED-74 four-car articulated emu for PKP Regional Services (Ken Harris)   1374673

Also in 2005 the northern Polish town of Elblag ordered six three-section low-floor trams.

In 2006 PESA delivered a four-car Class ED74 articulated emu to Lódz regional authority for local services between the city and Skierniewice. A batch of 11 similar vehicles was also ordered by PKP Regional Services for operation between Warsaw and Lódz.

In 2006 the company received a contract from Warsaw Tramways to supply 15 31.8 m five-section low-floor trams.

Partner diesel railbuses have also been supplied to regional authorities in Lubelskie (four single-car and one two-car), Podlasie (four single-car), Podkarpackie (two single-car) and Zachodnopomorskie (three single-car). Electric railbuses (see *Products* above) have been supplied to authorities in Malopolskie and Swietokrzyskie (two each).

In July 2008 PESA signed a contract for the supply of two 218Md two-car dmus for the Wielkopolska region.

Earlier in July 2008, PESA signed a contract with the Management Board of Opole Voivodeship for the delivery of five 218Md two-car dmus, designed for regional passenger

Class ATR 220 three-car articulated dmu for Ferrovia del Sud-Est, Italy (Ken Harris) 1374674

traffic on unelectrified lines. The first vehicle was scheduled to be delivered to Opole in 2008, a further two in 2009, and the last two in 2010.

Ukraine: In 2004 the Ukrainian National Railway Transport Administration (UZ) ordered 70 diesel railcars. The contract is for 64 vehicles to be used for passenger services and six to be used as inspection cars.

Power Machines Group

(Energomachexport + LMZ + Electrosila + ZTL + KTZ)
25A Protopopovsky per, 129090 Moscow, Russian Federation
Tel: (+7 095) 725 27 63
Fax: (+7 095) 688 79 90
e-mail: mail@power-m.ru
Web: www.power-m.ru

Key personnel
Chairman: *Sergei Batekhin*
Chief Executive Officer: *Igor Kostin*
Managing Director: *Alexander Chuvaev*
Technical Director: *Yuri Petrenya*
Sales Director: *Sergey Kuzmin*

Background
Power Machines unites the leading Russian power equipment enterprises and supplies railway and

transport equipment produced by Kalugaputmash, Luganskteplovoz, Muromteplovoz, Railway Repair-Mechanical Plant of Sverdlovsk, Kolomensky Zavod, Metrowagonmash, Vyksa Steel Works.

Products
Shunting and main line locomotives.

RCF – Rail Coach Factory

Kapurthala 144602, Punjab, India
Tel: (+91 181) 245 83 56
Fax: (+91 181) 245 70 91
e-mail: rcfcple@yahoo.co.in
Web: www.rcfkapurthala.com

Key personnel
General Manager: *S K Suri*
Chief Mechanical Engineer:
  Charanjit Singh
Chief Electrical Engineer: *Jagdev Kalia*
Controller of Stores: *Rajendra Singh*

Financial Adviser and Chief Accounts Officer:
  Maga Ram Choudhari
Chief Planning Engineer: *Dinesh Kumar*
Chief Design Engineer: *R N Misra*

Background
Established in 1986, RCF is a coach manufacturing unit of Indian Railways. It has manufactured more than 18,000 passenger coaches including self-propelled passenger vehicles. RCF produces approximately 1,300 coaches per year including both broad gauge and metre gauge with approximately 30 per cent air-conditioned coaches. It is an ISO-9001 and ISO-14001 certified unit.

Products
Stainless steel coaches incorporating disc brakes, flexi-coil secondary suspension, centre buffer couplers with sound an thermal insulation. These coaches have been successfully tested up to 180 km/h. Carbon steel bodied coaches (air-conditioned and non-air-conditioned); power generation cars; parcel vans. Diesel-electric multiple-units; electric multiple-units ; self-propelled accident relief trains. Also designed and manufactured special purpose vehicles such as refrigerated vans for transportation of perishables and double-deck coaches.

RMT Protram Wroclaw Sp zoo

54-206 Wroclaw, ul Legnicka 54, Poland
Tel: (+48 71) 350 06 37   Fax: (+48 71) 350 06 35
e-mail: protram@protram.com.pl
Web: www.protram.com.pl

Background
RMT Protram Wroclaw Sp zoo was formed in 1999 following the restructuring of the Tramways

Reparation Company of MPK Wroclaw (Public Transport Company of Wroclaw). The company employs 120 staff.

Products
Production of the three-module Type 205 WrAs tram and Type 204 WrAs tram. Modernisation of Type 105 N tram.

The company also carries out maintenance and overhaul.

Contracts
Customers include MPK Wroclaw, MPK Gdansk and MPK Poznan.

RVR

AS Rígas Vagonbúves Rúpníca
JSC Riga Carriage Building Works
201 Brivibas Gatve, Riga LV-1039, Latvia
Tel: (+371 7) 67 55 31 80

Fax: (+371 7) 67 55 23 40
e-mail: office@rvr.lv
Web: www.rvr.lv

Key personnel
Chairman: *Vladimirs Chamans*

Financial Manager: *Armands Svikis*
Production Manager: *Ziedonis Jorens*

Products
Diesel and electrical (AC/DC) multip-units for city and suburban passenger transportation.

SEMAF

Société Générale Egyptienne de Matériel des Chemins de Fer
Ein Helwan, Cairo, Egypt
Tel: (+20 2) 556 21 77; 555 00 37
Fax: (+20 2) 556 40 96; 555 00 37
e-mail: semaf_rw1@yahoo.com
  semaf_rw2@yahoo.com

Key personnel
Chairman: *Eng Talaat Housny*
Project and Research Manager: *Eng Ramadan Abdel Rahman*
Commercial Manager: *Erfan Abdel Hameed*
Financial Manager: *Mamdouh Abdel Maksoud*
Production Manager: *Eng Hosny El Mahdy*
Marketing General Manager: *Mohamed Said Dawoud*

Background
SEMAF was established in 1955. Its services cover the demand of Egyptian National Railways (ENR) for freight wagons, passenger coaches, metro and tram cars.

Products
Freight wagons, passenger coaches and metro cars.

Contracts

Current projects for Egyptian National Railways (ENR) include 100, 40 tonnes freight wagons, 200 A/C 2nd Class passenger coaches and two 18-car underground trains.

SEMAF has produced 18 cars for Line 1 of the Cairo metro, under a contract awarded jointly with Mitsubishi. It has also produced 200 suburban coaches, 100 cargo cars (40 tonnes) 200 Ganz high-speed bogies and 12 Heliopolis metro bogies.

Future projects include contract negotiations for the production of 150 petroleum tank wagons for Syria. The subcontract of rolling stock to the winner of the third phase underground metro for greater Cairo.

Siemens AG

Mobility

Corporate Headquarters
Siemens AG
Industry Sector – Mobility
PO Box 3240, D-91050 Erlangen, Germany
Tel: (+49 9131) 7-0
e-mail: contact.mobility@siemens.com
Web: www.siemens.com/mobility

Key personnel

Division Chief Executive Officer: *Dr Hans-Jörg Grundmann*
Head of Business Administration: *Michael Schulz-Drost*

Works

Austria

Siemens Transportation Systems GmbH & Co KG
Leberstrasse 34, A-1110 Vienna
Tel: (+43 51) 70 70   Fax: (+43 51) 70 75 15 95

Siemens Transportation Systems GmbH & Co KG
Eggenberger Strasse 31, A-8021 Graz
Tel: (+43 51) 70 70   Fax: (+43 51) 70 75 35 08

Czech Republic

Siemens sro
Transportation Systems
Evropska 33a, CZ-160 00 Prague 6
Tel: (+420 233) 03 33 03
Fax: (+420 233) 03 11 12

Germany

Siemens AG
Transportation Systems
Duisburger Strasse 145, D-47829 Krefeld
Tel: (+49 2151) 45 00
Fax: (+49 2151) 450 12 14

Siemens AG
Transportation Systems
Krauss-Maffei-Strasse 2, D-80997 Munich
Tel: (+49 89) 889 90
Fax: (+49 211) 88 99 33 36

US

Siemens Transportation Inc
7464 French Road, Sacramento, California 95828
Tel: (+1 916) 681 30 00
Fax: (+1 916) 681 30 06
Test centre

Siemens AG

Transportation Systems
Friedrich-List-Allee 1, D-41844 Wegberg-Wildenrath, Germany
Tel: (+49 2432) 97 00
Fax: (+49 2432) 97 02 00

Organisation

Following a reorganisation of its operations in January 2008, Siemens AG has restructured its 'Industry Sector' bringing together six divisions: Building Technologies, Industry Automation, Industry Solutions, Mobility, Drive Technologies and Osram. The Siemens 'Mobility Division', based in Erlangen Germany, provides transportation and logistics solutions and now combines railways and traffic control systems for roadways together with solutions for airport logistics, postal automation, traction power supplies and rolling stock for mass transit, regional and mainline services.

Project management and forward-looking service concepts complement the portfolio.

Metro trainset for Oslo (Ken Harris)   1374693

Desiro ML emu for German regional operator trans regio (Ken Harris)   1374684

Desiro ML emu for German regional operator trans regio undergoing trials at Siemens' Wildenrath test track (David Haydock)   1368500

Business activities

Rail automation (see entry in *Signalling and communications systems* **section):** signalling and control systems; interlockings; automatic train control systems; signalling systems and components; telecommunications systems; and communications systems for mass transit and main line systems.

Electrification (see entry in *Electrification contractors and equipment suppliers* **section):** products and systems for main line and mass transit contact lines; and products and systems for main line and mass transit traction power supplies.

Locomotives: electric locomotives; diesel-electric locomotives; special purpose locomotives; and refurbishment.

Trains: high-speed and intercity trains; commuter and regional trains; passenger coaches.

Mass transit: metro vehicles; suburban trains; trams; light rail vehicles; components.

Integrated services (see entry in *Vehicle maintenance equipment and services* **section):** maintenance; spare parts; training; documentation; diagnostic services; and consultancy.

Turnkey systems (see entry in *Turnkey systems contractors* **section):** turnkey systems for mass transit and main line systems.

Subsidiaries

Siemens Transportation Systems SAS (France) (100 per cent*)
Siemens Transportation Systems Inc (US) (100 per cent)

Mass Transit; Locomotives, Trains
Siemens Transportation Systems GmbH & Co KG, Austria (100 per cent*)
ELIN EBG Traction GmbH, Austria (100 per cent*)
Technisches Gemeinschaftsbüro GmbH (TGB), Germany (100 per cent)
Siemens kolejová vozidla sro (SKV), Czech Republic (67.05 per cent)
Siemens Traction Equipment Ltd (STEZ), China (51 per cent*)

Rail Automation
messMa GmbH, Germany (100 per cent)
Transmitton Ltd, UK (100 per cent*)
Siemens Signalling Ltd, Xi'an (SSCX), China (70 per cent*)
ESTEL Rail Automation SPA, Algeria (51 per cent)

Electrification/Turnkey Systems
Transrapid International GmbH & Co kg (TRI), Germany (50 per cent)
Saitong Railway Electrification (Nanjing) Co Ltd, China (50 per cent)

Integrated Services
Siemens Rail Services Pty Ltd (SRSBS), Australia (100 per cent)
Siemens Rail Services Pty Swanston Ltd (SRSSW), Australia (100 per cent)
Dienstleistungensgesellschaft für Kommunikation des Stadt – und Regionalverkehrs mbH (DKS), (Germany (51 per cent)
NERTUS Mantienimiento Feroviario SA, (Spain (51 per cent)
IFTEC GmbH & Co KG, Germany (50 per cent)

Bogies
Siemens Transportation Systems doo, Slovenia (100 per cent)*
*Shareholding held by Siemens AG parent company in each country

Background

In 2006, Siemens divested its Siemens Dispolok GmbH locomotive leasing business to Mitsui & Co Ltd.

In July 2008, Siemens Mobility Division announced its intention to reorganise its manufacturing activities in Europe. Approximately 1,800 jobs are to be cut in engineering and manufacturing worldwide. Siemens intends to close its production facility

Ultra-low-floor tram for Wiener Linien, Vienna 1129902

AGT trainset for Nuremburg's Rubin driverless metro project 1129901

Type S70 LRV for Houston 1129900

in Prague by the end of 2009 at the latest, whilst the German and Austrian locations of the Division are to be retained. In Krefeld-Uerdingen, Germany, Siemens proposes to cut 220 jobs after all the repair services for the Combino come to an end there. Further planned job reductions will primarily affect the Mobility locations in Braunschweig, Nuremberg, Erlangen, Berlin, Offenbach, Constance, Düsseldorf, Vienna and Graz.

Products

Design, development and manufacture of main line electric locomotives; diesel-electric locomotives; high-speed trainsets; diesel and electric tilting and non-tilting trainsets; emus; dmus with electric, hydraulic or mechanical transmission; passenger coaches; lightweight diesel or electric railcars; suburban and metro cars; light rail vehicles and trams, fully automated steel-wheeled metro systems (AGT); fully automated rubber-tyred metro systems (Val); Ultra Low Floor trams (ULF); locomotive and rail vehicle refurbishment. The current product portfolio includes:

Eurosprinter

Designed as a universal high-performance three-phase electric locomotive primarily for European networks, the Eurosprinter can be supplied with a continuous rating of 4,200–6,400 kW and top speeds of up to 230 km/h. Siemens has received orders for the type both from national railway companies and from open access operators.

Eurorunner

The Eurorunner is a multi-purpose main line diesel-electric locomotive aimed primarily at European markets and is designed to be supplied in power outputs ranging from 1,500 kW to 4,200 kW. The first order for the type was for a 2,000 kW 140 km/h version from Austrian Federal Railways.

Velaro

This latest development in the family of high-speed trains initially designed for the German Rail network as ICE features distributed power rather than the power car and trailers concept of earlier ICE units. As well as supplying examples of the type to DB AG, Siemens has won high-speed train orders from NS, Netherlands, RENFE, Spain, where it is designated Velaro E by Siemens and China, where it is designated CH3 by the MoR (Ministry of Railways).

ICE T

Tilting version of the ICE high-speed train, supplied to DB AG.

Venturio

The Venturio family has been developed for intercity and inter-regional applications where operations in the 160 km/h to 250 km/h speed range are required. A modular platform enables trains to be supplied in tilting or non-tilting, electric or diesel-electric versions in formations from three to nine cars.

Desiro

This modular family of articulated dmu and emu vehicles is intended for suburban, commuter and regional traffic. Diesel versions can be supplied in diesel-electric or-mechanical versions. Customers include: DB AG (dmu Class VT 642 and emu Classes 424–426); SŽ, Slovenia; Express Rail Link, Malaysia; ÖBB, Austria; MÁV, Hungary; and CFR, Romania. A non-articulated version has been developed for the UK market and has attracted orders from several operators, including a diesel version for TransPennine Express.

Avanto/S70

The Avanto/S70 is a hybrid design of low-floor light rail vehicle intended to operate both on city centre tram routes and over outlying main line suburban networks. The vehicle concept is configured to allow multi- voltage operation and provision is made to incorporate a diesel engine

Type DT8.10 LRV for Stuttgart   1129899

Class 350 Desiro UK initially operated by Silverlink and subsequently by the London Midland franchise (Ken Harris)   1327982

to permit operations on non- electrified routes. The first order for the type was received from SNCF, France, in July 2002.

AGT

AGT is a fully automated steel-wheeled metro system. The system has been ordered by VAG Nuremberg for its Rubin metro project.

Val

The Val rubber-tyred fully automated metro system is already proven in several cities worldwide. Recent contracts are for systems in Rennes, Roissy-Charles de Gaulle and Toulouse, France, and Turin, Italy.

ULF

The ULF ultra-low floor modular tramcar features the lowest entrance height in the world. Low-floor throughout, the entrance height is 197 mm. The Vienna transit operator Wiener Linien placed the first order for 150 ULFs in 1997 and a second one for another 150 in 2004.

Transrapid

With ThyssenKrupp and Transrapid International, Siemens is a joint partner in the development and supply of the Transrapid magnetic levitation high-speed transit system. Siemens supplies traction technology, power supply, operations control and communications systems for Transrapid projects.

A key element of Siemens' product strategy is the company's Wildenrath Test Center in northwest Germany. Commissioned in January 1997, this facility includes five test tracks, the longest 6.083 km and four of them dual-gauge (standard/metre), together with a capability to energise the overhead power supply systems at various voltages. These features enable the company to undertake exhaustive test running and mileage accumulation of all types of vehicle.

Contracts

Recent contracts include:

Australia: In October 2007, Siemens was awarded a contract by Queensland Rail (QR) in Australia to supply 25 Class 3800 heavy haul electric locomotives. The 25 Class 3800 heavy haul electric locomotives will be delivered over a period of 12 months commencing at the end of 2009.

Austria: In December 2007 a consortium of Siemens, Bombardier and Elin EBG Traction, received an order from Wiener Linien for 15 metro trains. Delivery is scheduled for between May 2009 and May 2011.

In October 2007, Siemens Systems received an order for 44 Railjet trains from Austrian Federal Railways. The additional 44 Railjets mean that Austrian Federal Railways will have a fleet of 67 Railjet trainsets. The first of these trains will be used in international service from 2010 onwards.

In June 2004 a consortium of Siemens and Elin EBG was awarded a contract by the Vienna urban operator Wiener Linien to supply 150 additional Ultra-Low-Floor (ULF) trams, with an option for 150 more. Siemens' share of the contract is about 70 per cent by value. Delivery of the vehicles, which will join 150 similar trams in service in Vienna, is taking place from Siemens' plant in the city from 2006 to 2012.

Belgium: In May 2008, Siemens received an order from the Belgian rail operator SNCB to deliver 305 multiple-unit trains, to be used in Belgium's regional rail service. The Desiro ML type trains are due to be delivered between 2011 and 2016.

In January 2007, Siemens received an order from the SNCB for 60 Eurosprinter (Class 18) Type ES60U3 electric locomotives. Deliveries are scheduled between January 2009 and June 2010.

Bulgaria: In January 2005, Siemens and Bulgarian State Railways (BDZ) signed a contract for the delivery of 25 diesel-powered regional multiple units and their subsequent maintenance for the period of seven years. The contract also includes an option for the delivery of 25 electrically powered trains.

Canada: Siemens was awarded an order from Edmonton in Canada, for 26 Class SD 160 light rail vehicles in October 2005.

China: In November 2005, in collaboration with its Chinese partner Tangshan Locomotive & Rolling Stock Works, Siemens signed a contract with the Chinese Ministry of Railways to build 60 high-speed trains for China. Three of the Velaro trains, designated CH3 by the MoR (Ministry of Railways), have been built in Krefeld in Germany and are now in operation between the two Olympic sports venues, while the other 57 units are being built at Tangshan.

Also, together with its local partner Zhuzhou Electric Locomotive Company Ltd (ZELC), Siemens is delivering 72 new cars for the expansion of Shanghai Metro Line 1 and also adapting 24 existing cars for the same line. The cars will be manufactured by consortium leader ZELC in Zhuzhou, Hunan Province.

In December 2007, the same consortium was awarded a contract for two further metro projects including the supply of control systems and rolling stock for the expansion of Metro Line II in Shanghai. In Guangzhou, the consortium will expand Metro Lines 2 and 8 with trains and control systems.

France: Siemens is to convert five ICE 3 units for service in France in co-operation with Bombardier Transportation. The Siemens-led consortium and German Railways reached an agreement in October 2005 on a corresponding project. The conversion work will be carried out at Bombardier and at the Siemens rolling stock test centre in Wegberg-Wildenrath. The ICE 3 trainsets were due to go into service from 2007 in the German-French railway network on a direct Paris-Eastern France-Frankfurt line.

In February 2004, a consortium of Siemens and ALSTOM won a contract from French National Railways (SNCF) to supply 400 84 tonne 1,600 kW diesel-electric freight locomotives. Delivery was scheduled from 2006 to 2015. Siemens is supplying propulsion and control systems and manufacturing 130 bodyshells at its Munich plant. ALSTOM is to manufacture mechanical equipment and assemble the locomotives at its Belfort facility in France.

In May 2001, Siemens subsidiary Matra Transport International (now Siemens Transportation Systems SAS) was awarded a turnkey contract by SMTC, Toulouse, to supply and equip the city's second fully automated metro line, the 16 km Line B. The contract included the supply of VAL 208 driverless metro vehicles. The line opened in 2007 and Siemens supplied a total of 56 new vehicles.

Germany: In December 2008, Siemens received an order from Deutsche Bahn AG for 15 high-speed Velaro ICE-3 trains. The first vehicles are scheduled to go into operation in December 2011 and the first trains will be available for in-depth testing in mid-2011. All 15 multiple units are to be delivered by 2012.

Four-car standard-gauge emu supplied to the State Railway of Thailand for the Bangkok Airport Rail Link 1326696

Siemen's VAL – fully automated driverless metro system, Turin Italy 1341824

In September 2007 Siemens Systems received an order from Benex GmbH, a subsidiary of Hamburger Hochbahn AG, for six Desiro Classic trains.

In January 2007, through a contract with Angel Trains, Siemens is supplying trans regio Deutsche Regionalbahn GmbH with Desiro ML emus. The first 16 trains have been ordered and will be leased to trans Deutsche Regionalbahn GmbH by Angel Trains for a 15-year period commencing in December 2008.

In November 2001 Siemens announced an order from Verkehrs AG (VAG), Nuremburg, to equip the new U3 automated metro line in the city and to retrofit the existing VAG U2 metro lines for automatic operation. The contract includes the supply of 30 Type DT 3 driverless trainsets, 16 for service on Line U3 and 14 for Line U2.

India: In May 2005 Siemens received a notification of award of a contract for the Mumbai Railway Vikas Corporation (MRVc) for propulsion system and electrical equipment for emu rolling stock to be built at the Integral Coach Factory, Chennai. The emus will be in operation on both of Mumbai's suburban arterial networks, the Central and Western Railway.

Italy: In October 2007 a new 2.1 km section of Line 1 of the Turin metro system was opened for which Siemens supplied both the automation systems and the rolling stock.

Lithuania: In October 2008 Lithuanian Railways (LG) ordered a further 10 Class ER20 CF freight

locomotives from Siemens following the 2005 order for the supply of 34 Class DE 20 six-axle diesel-electric locomotives which included an option for the delivery of 10 further locomotives. A total of 20 of the of the overall 34 units have been delivered.

Malaysia: In April 2002 the Express Rail Link system connecting Kuala Lumpur with its new international airport was commissioned. The line was built by a Siemens-led consortium and is served by 12 four-car Desiro articulated 25 kV AC emus. Eight of these are used for KLIA Express airport services, while the remaining four are assigned to high-density suburban services on the new line.

Norway: In July 2003 Oslo's urban transport operator, AS Oslo Sporveier, placed an order with Siemens for 33 three-car metro trainsets. Delivery ran from the end of 2005 and continued through to 2008. In September 2008 Oslo Vognselskap, the public transport rolling stock company of the Norwegian capital, ordered a further 20 metro trains from Siemens. Delivery is scheduled to be completed by 2010. This order marks a further option exercised under the terms of the 2003 order that was originally placed for the 33 three-car metro trainsets. In September 2005 an option was taken up for a second batch of 30 metro trains.

Romania: In January 2008 OTL, the urban transit operator in Oradea, placed an initial order with Siemens for 10 ultra-low-floor trams. The order, which includes vehicle maintenance for a period of four years, is scheduled to be delivered between May 2008 and June 2009.

Russian Federation: In May 2006 Siemens was awarded a contract to supply eight Velaro high-speed trains to Russian Railways (RZD). This followed the award to Siemens in April 2005 of a contract for the development of high-speed trains for the Russian Federation. RZD intends to place orders for 60 of these trains following an agreement reached in December 2004. In November 2008, the first of the eight high-speed trains was shipped.

Slovenia: In July 2004 Siemens was awarded a contract by Slovenian Railways to supply 20 Class 541 three-system Eurosprinter electric locomotives which were delivered in the period from June 2006 and May 2007. In January 2008 Slovenian Railways exercised an option from its 2004 supply contract and placed an order for a further 12 Eurosprinter SZ Class 541 locomotives.

Spain: In March 2001 Siemens announced that it had won a contract to supply Spanish National Railways (RENFE) with 16 trainsets, based on the ICE 3 operated by DB, for service on the Madrid-Barcelona high-speed line. Designated the Velaro E model by Siemens and AVE S 103 by RENFE, delivery commenced in 2004. In March 2004, RENFE placed a further order for 10 additional trains of this type.

Switzerland: In September 2008, in consortium with Bombardier Transportation, a contract was received from SBB for the supply of 121 low-floor double-deck passenger coaches. A total of 113 will be delivered to SBB and eight to Sihltal Zurich Uetliberg Bahn (SZU). These are scheduled to be delivered between October 2010 and March 2016.

In November 2007 Siemens received an order from Bernmobil, the transit authority in Bern, for 21 Combino trams. The new trams will be delivered by the end of 2010.

Combino trams have been supplied to BVB, Basel (28 seven-section single-ended metre-gauge), and SVB, Berne (15 five-section single-ended metre-gauge).

Taiwan: In August 2001, Siemens announced that it had secured a contract from Kaohsiung Rapid Transit Corporation to equip two metro lines in the city, including the supply of 42 three-car trainsets.

Thailand: As part of a turnkey contact awarded to Siemens in January 2002 to construct, equip and maintain the 20 km Bangkok Blue Line for Bangkok Metro Co Ltd, the company is supplying 19 three-car trainsets. The first vehicle was rolled out in Vienna in July 2003.

UK: In July 2008 Siemens received an order from First ScotRail and Transport Scotland for the supply of 38 Desiro UK type electric multiple units. The trains are scheduled to enter service at the end of 2010.

In August 2007, the UK rail leasing company Porterbrook placed an order with Siemens for 37 Class 350 Desiro electric multiple units. Siemens delivered the first of the 37 ordered trains in October 2008. Porterbrook will lease the four-unit trains to London Midland, the operator which holds the concession for the West Coast Main Line between London and Birmingham.

Siemen's 'Combino Classic' tram for Bern transit authority, Switzerland   1341825

Siemen's six-car metro train for Shanghai Shentong Metro Group, China   1341765

In March 2007 Angel Trains, a UK-based rolling stock leasing company, signed an agreement with Siemens for the purchase of Desiro ML emus. The first 16 trains have been ordered and will be leased to trans regio Deutsche Regionalbahn GmbH. The agreement between Siemens and Angel Trains includes an option for a further 84 trains to meet the needs of its portfolio and its clients.

In March 2006, Siemens announced a contract for an additional 17 four-car Class 450 Desiro emus to be used by South West Trains and the operator of the Southern Western franchise.

In 2002 deliveries commenced of an original order for 785 Desiro UK emu cars for South West Trains, with finance provided by Angel Trains. The trains were to be configured as 45 five-car sets for express services (Class 444), and 100 four-car and 32 five-car sets for suburban services (both Class 450). Deliveries were due to be completed by 2004. Subsequent changes to the contract led to the Class 450 order being amended to 110 four-car trains, with 24 further four-car trains built

as Class 350/1 AC-only units for services on the UK's West Coast Main Line currently operated by Central Trains and Silverlink. The SWT contract included an option on 321 additional cars to be delivered by 2009.

US: In May 2008, Siemens received notice to proceed from Salt Lake City's Utah Transit Authority (UTA) to deliver 77 S70 LRVs. The contract includes an option for up to an additional 180 cars. All the vehicles are scheduled to be ready for service by 2012.

In February 2008 the Regional Transportation District (RTD) of Denver, Colardo, placed an order for a further 55 Type SD160 LRVs, following on from a previous order of 34 cars (still in process), seven of which are already in operation. The new vehicles are due to be delivered between 2009 and 2012.

In May 2006, Siemens received an order from Tri-County Metropolitan Transportation District of Oregon (TriMet) for 21 S70 low-floor LRVs. The order includes an option for three further S70 LRVs.

Škoda Transportation sro

Tylova 1/57, CZ-31600 Plzeň, Czech Republic
Tel: (+420 37) 818 66 66
Fax: (+420 37) 813 90 59
e-mail: transportation@skoda.cz
Web: www.skoda.cz/transportation

Key personnel

Chief Executive Officer: *Tomas Krsek*
Chief Operating Officer: *Michal Korecky*
Commercial Director: *Jaromir Jelinek*

Finance Director : *Pavel Cibulka*
Manufacturing Director: *Ales Jedlicka*
Technical Director: *Vladimir Maly*
Purchasing Director: *Renata Nyvltova*

Background

Škoda Transportation sro is part of Škoda Holding as Transportation group (together with Škoda Electric, Škoda Vagonka, Ganz-Škoda, Vúkv and in joint enterprise with the Dedal group in the Russian Federation, Sibelektroprivod).

Together with the other companies in the Škoda Holding as Transportation group, its focus is to become a leader in the central European market and to achieve more success in the commercial territories in which it has been successful in the past (particularly the Russian Federation and the countries of Eastern Europe).

The company acquired Pars nova in Šumperk in March 2008 and in July purchased a 50 per cent share in the assets of POLL sro, an important Czech manufacturer of electronic systems for application in performance electronics and other

Škoda's Type 10 T1 LRV for Sound Transit, Tacoma, Washington, US (Milan Srámek)
1330146

Škoda's Type 14 T tramcar for Prague, Czech Republic (Rudolf Pischek)
1330147

areas of heavy current electrical engineering. Pilsen-based MOVO spol sro has also become part of the Transportation Group.

Products

Škoda Transportation sro is among the most significant central European manufacturers of rail vehicles with regard to its product range. In addition to locomotives it also manufactures trams and metro trains and participates in the modernisation of previously supplied locomotives. It uses electrical drives from its sister company, Škoda Electric, for all its vehicles.

The company continuously invests in research and development of new products, information systems and strengthening of additional competence such as construction. This will result in new types of low-floor trams, locomotives and metro trains. The company has also invested in the construction of a new manufacturing hall.

Contracts

Current examples of some of the most significant contracts include deliveries of low-floor trams for Prague; three-system locomotives for Czech railways and long-term deliveries of modernised metro units for Prague. Other major contracts include low-floor trams for Wroclaw (Poland) and Cagliari (Italy) and participation in the modernisation of locomotives in the Ukraine and Bulgaria. Together with its Russian partner, Vagonmash, St Petersburg, Škoda Transportation sro also participates in deliveries of new metro trains for the Russian Federation. The company has also acquired valuable references on the North American market by manufacturing 10 low-floor trams for the US cities of Portland (seven) and Tacoma (three).

Developments

In September 2008, Škoda Transportation introduced the prototype for its new 'Škoda ForCity' trams for Prague (model ŠKODA 15T). Škoda Transportation will supply Prague's public transportation company with a total of 250 three-car low-floor 'Škoda ForCity' trams by 2017.

Škoda Vagonka as

1 máje 3176/102, CZ-703 00, Czech Republic
Tel: (+420 59) 747 71 11
Fax: (+420 59) 747 71 90
e-mail: vagonka@skoda.cz
Web: www.skoda.cz
www.vagonka.cz

Key personnel

Chairman of the Board of Directors: *Tomáš Krsek*
Company Director and Member of the Board: *Jiří Paruza*
Commercial Director: *Jaromír Jelínek*
Financial Director: *Pavel Cibulka*
Manufacturing Director: *Zdeněk Holaň*

Background

Originally founded in January 2000 as ČKD Vagonka, the company name changed to Škoda Vagonka in March 2008. The company is a direct successor of the traditional railway passenger vehicles production plant which was established at Studénka in 1900, and has key capabilities in development, design, technology and production of railway passenger vehicles.

Since January 2005, the company has been part of the Transportation Group of Škoda Holdingas.

Products

The main operation is the development, design and manufacture of double-deck electric multiple-units using aluminium bodyshells; diesel-electric and diesel-hydraulic railcars and multiple-units; light regional vehicles; railcars; trailers and coaches.

A supplementary operation consists of repairs and modernisation of vehicles, delivery of spare parts and manufacturing co-operation with foreign partners.

Contracts

In 2006, the company received an order from Lithuanian Railways for two Type E J 575 25 kV AC double-deck emus for delivery in 2008. In 2008, the company signed another contract for a further two of this type for delivery in 2009.

Škoda Vagonka double-deck Class 471 emu for Czech Railways
1325123

Škoda Vagonka Dm 12 diesel railcar for VR-Group, Finland
1325121

Other recent contracts include the supply of 60 (three-car unit) double-deck Class 471 emus for Czech Railways, designed for rapid suburban traffic using three kV DC nominal voltage. The contract for 16 component pieces for four-axle railcars for Finnish Railways (VR Ltd) intended for traffic on secondary non-electrified tracks was completed in March 2006. Electric multiple-units for suburban transport on electrified tracks with three kV DC nominal voltage and 25 kV AC 50 Hz, optionally for regional transport. Repairs and modernisation of passenger cars. Aluminium alloy constructions of sub-assembly parts for passenger vehicles.

Stadler Rail Group

Stadler Rail AG
Bahnhofplatz, CH-9565 Bussnang, Switzerland
Tel: (+41 71) 626 21 20   Fax: (+41 71) 626 21 28
e-mail: stadler.rail@stadlerrail.ch

Stadler Bussnang AG
Industriestrasse 4, CH-9565 Bussnang, Switzerland
Tel: (+41 71) 626 20 20
Fax: (+41 71) 626 20 21
e-mail: stadler.bussnang@stadlerrail.ch

Stadler Altenrhein AG
Park Altenrhein für Industrie und Gewerbe,
CH-9423 Altenrhein, Switzerland
Tel: (+41 71) 858 41 41   Fax: (+41 71) 858 41 42
e-mail: stadler.altenrhein@stadlerrail.ch

Stadler Winterthur AG
Zürcherstrasse 41, CH-8400 Winterthur, Swtizerland
Tel: (+41 52) 262 11 77   Fax: (+41 52) 262 03 03
e-mail: stadler.winterthur@stadlerrail.ch

Stadler Pankow GmbH
Lessingstrasse 102, D-13158 Berlin, Germany
Tel: (+49 30) 91 91 16 16
Fax: (+49 30) 91 91 21 50
e-mail: stadler.pankow@stadlerrail.de

Stadler Trains Hungary Ltd
Köztársaság tér 27, HU-1086 Budapest, Hungary
Tel: (+36 1) 887 52 50   Fax: (+36 1) 887 52 51
e-mail: stadler.budapest@stadlerrail.hu

Stadler Polska Sp zoo
ul Targowa 50, PL-08-110 Siedlce, Poland
Tel: (+48 25) 643 30 06
e-mail: stadler.siedlce@stadlerrail.pl

Media Relations Stadler Rail Group
Frau Vincenza Trivigno
Tel: (+41 71) 626 20 34
e-mail: vincenza.trivigno@stadlerrail.ch
Web: www.stadlerrail.com

Key personnel

President and Chief Executive Officer, Stadler
    Rail Group: *Peter Spuhler*
Deputy Chief Executive Officer, Stadler Rail
    Group: *Michael Daum*
Managing Director, Stadler Bussnang: *Markus
    Bernsteiner*
Managing Director, Stadler Altenrhein: *Hans
    Kubat*
Managing Director, Stadler Winterthur: *Jürg
    Gygax*
Managing Director, Stadler Pankow: *Michael
    Daum*
Managing Director, Stadler Trains Hungary Ltd:
    Zoltán Dunai
Managing Director, Stadler Polska Sp. zoo:
    Christian Spichiger
Sales and Marketing Group: *Peter Jenelten*
Sales, Switzerland: *Christian König*
Service and Retrofit, Switzerland: *Jürg Gygax*
Sales and Service, Germany: *Michael Daum*

Stadler FLIRT three-car emu for Cantus, Germany (David Haydock)   1164048

Stadler type GTW 2/6 and 2/8 articulated electric railcar built for Thurbo AG, Switzerland   1329660

Artist impression of Stadler's low-floor street car (one-directional) *Baselland Transport AG and
Basler Verkehrsbetriebe,* (BLT and BVB), *Switzerland*   1310375

Stadler's low-floor multiple unit FLIRT for MÁV ZRt, Budapest, Hungary
1329656

Stadler's low-floor multiple unit FLIRT for Zug, Switzerland   1329655

Stadler's low-floor streetcar (one-directional) Stadt Nurnber (VAG), Germany 1329914

Stadler's low-floor streetcar for Bochum-Gelsenkirchener Strassenbahn AG, Bogestra, Germany 1329912

Stadler's rack-railway-adhesion-double, Bayerische Zugspitzbahn Bergbahn AG (BZB), Germany 1310377

Stadler's rack-railway, Gornergrat Bahn GGB, Switzerland 1329659

Stadler's articulated GTW dmu, Arriva, Netherlands 1310374

Stadler's Type Regio Shuttle RS1 low-floor railcar dmu, Deutsche Bahn (DB), Germany 1310372

Background

The Stadler Rail Group includes, in addition to Stadler Bussnang AG, Stadler Altenrhein AG and Stadler Winterthur AG in Switzerland, Stadler Pankow GmbH and Stadler Weiden GmbH in Germany, Stadler Trains Hungary Kft, in Hungary and Stadler Polska Sp. zoo in Poland. Over 2,300 co-workers are employed within the group. Stadler Rail Group's most well-known vehicle family, in addition to the GTW articulated railcar (429 trains sold), is the FLIRT (4634 trains sold) together with the Regio Shuttle RS1 (364 trains sold).

Products

The Stadler Rail Group focuses on the segments of regional and suburban transport, urban light railway transport, trams and rack railways as well as diesel-electric locomotives. The product portfolio ranges from individual and special vehicles through small and medium production runs, modernisations and repairs of rail vehicles. The best known models of the Stadler range are the GTW low-floor articulated railcar, the RS1 Regio-Shuttle as well as the FLIRT. Stadler offers URL vehicles and trams in the form of the Variobahn and the Tango.

The Stadler Rail Group operations are carried out under one roof, from body and bogie production through to final assembly providing complete vehicle concepts.

Tokyu Car Corporation

Head Office

Overseas Project Department, Railway Division:
3-1 Ohkawa, Kanazawa-ward, Yokohama-city 236-0043, Japan
Tel: (+81 45) 785 30 09
Fax: (+81 45) 785 65 50

Sales Department

Kokuryu Shiba-Kouen building
2-6-15 Shiba-Kouen Minato-City, Tokyo, 105-0011, Japan
Tel: (+81 3) 34 36 12 60
Fax: (+81 3) 34 36 12 71
Web: www.tokyu-car.co.jp

Key personnel

President: *Kazuo Ochiai*
Executive Vice-Presidents: *Kanji Tajino*

Works

Yokohama Plant (Railway rolling stock and heavy duty trailer)
3-1 Ohkawa, Kanazawa-ward, Yokohama-city 236-0043, Japan
Wakayama Plant (Railway track turnout, container and logistics equipment)
770-8 Kitaseida, Kinokawa-city Wakayama-prefecture 649-6402, Japan

Background

Tokyu Car Corporation, previously called Tokyu Car Manufacturing Co Ltd, was jointly established by Keihin Electric Express Railway,

Double-deck, first and ordinary class 5000 Series emu for Marine Liner, Shikoku Railway 1180932

Recent Tokyu electric multiple-unit

Class (Railway's own designation)	Cars per unit	Line voltage	Motor cars per unit	Motored axles per motor car	Rated output per motor (kW)	Max speed (km/h)	Weight (t) per car	Total seating capacity	Length per car (mm)	No in service	Rate of acceleration (km/h /s)	Year first built	Builders Mechanical parts	Electrical parts
Yokohama Minato-Mirai emu Y 500	8	DC 1,500 V	4	4	190	120	26.0 (cab car) 32.0–33.0 (motorcar) 24.5	48 (total 141) (cab car) 51 or 54 (total 152) (middle car)	20,200 (cab car) 20,000 (middle car)	48	3.3	2003	Tokyu Car	Hitachi
Shikoku Railway 5000 emu	1	DC 1,500 V	1		Trailer	130	41	First class: 36, ordinary class: 36	20,860	6		2003	Tokyu Car	
East Japan Railway E231 emu (suburban use)	10 or 15	DC 1,500 V	4 or 6		Trailer (first class)	120	34.5 to 35.4	First class: 90	20,500	Before		2004 debut	Tokyu Car	
East Japan Railway E231 emu (suburban use)	10 or 15	DC 1,500 V	4 or 6	95	95	120	26.8 to 27.9 (cab car), 28.8 to 29.9 (motor car) 23.0 to 23.5 (trailer car)	36 to 43 (total of 138 to 143) (cab car), 54 to 60 (total 162) (middle car)	20,000,		2.5	2000	Tokyu Car Kawasaki Heavy Industries, East Japan Railways	Hitachi, Mitsubishi Electric, Toshiba, Toyo Denki
8520 (Irish Rail) emu	4	DC 1,500 V	2	4	140	110	34.2, 34.5 (cab car) 39.7 (motorcar)		20,130 (cab car) 20,000 (motorcar)	40	3.3	2004	Tokyu Car	Toshiba
Bureau of Transportation, Tokyo Metropolitan Government, 10-300 Series emu	8	DC 1,500 V	5	4		120	27.1, 27.2 (cab car) 28.1–30.2 (motorcar) 23.8 (trailer car)		20,200 (cab car) 20,000 (middle car)					

Odakyu Electric Railway and Keio Corporation in 1948. Tokyu Car Corporation and the rolling stock builder, Teikoku Car and Manufacturing Co Ltd, merged into one company on an equal basis in 1968. Today, Tokyu Car Corporation is a subsidiary of Tokyu Corporation (Tokyo Express Electric Railway).

Products

Electric and diesel railcars, passenger coaches and light rail vehicles. Recent products include:

Yokohama Minato-Mirai Y 500 series for subway and commuter use

Yokohama Minato-Mirai line is a new subway approximately 4.1 km from Yokohama to Motomachi-Chuukagai (China-town) via Minato-Mirai 21 area of Yokohama harbor new town. The new line's train has run to Shibuya terminal on Tokyu's Touyoko line since 1 February 2004. Tokyu will finally manufacture 150 vehicles of it's emu 5000 Series and Y500 Series. The Y500 Series is based on Tokyu Corporation's emu 5000 commuter Series resulting in lower costs due to the common design of car body construction, interior and electrical equipment.

East Japan Railway's E 231 Series for commuter and suburban use

In 2000, Tokyu Car and East Japan Railway developed JR East's E231 series as a standard suburban and commuter vehicle and manufactured 450 vehicles. In 2004 Tokyu Car manufactured a double-deck first class vehicle for the E231 which will be used in the metropolitan area.

Double-deck first and ordinary Class 5000 Series emu for 'Marine Line'

Tokyu Car has built up to six double-deck vehicles for the rapid service train 'Marine Liner' which was released in October 2003. These vehicles are based on JR East's double-deck first class E217 Series. The train conventionally runs for 58 minutes per 71.7 km between Okayama and Takamatsu with maximum velocity of 130 km/h.

10-300 Series emu for underground, Bureau of Transportation, Tokyo Metropolitan Government
1180934

Y500 Series emu for Yokohama Minato-Mirai Railway
1180936

Double-deck, first class E231 Series emu for East Japan Railways 1180935

Class 8520 emu for Irish Rail 1180933

Irish Rail Class 8520 Series emu

Irish Rail Class 8520 Series emu is based on the Class 8510 emu which was delivered to Irish Rail in 2001. An air-conditioning system has been added to the vehicle. The new Series (Class 8520) is built with maximum priority on vehicle safety as well as accessibility for mobility impaired or disabled passengers. The car body has been constructed to comply with British fire safety standard BS 6853 cat. Ib. Closed Circuit Television (CCTV) has also been installed and there is arrangement for wheelchair space.

Contracts

East Japan Railways and other private companies have ordered various vehicles for super express and commuter trains.

Typical orders include: East Japan Railways – 130 E233 series emu for commuter and subway use; 21 E3-2000 series emu for Shinkansen; Tokyu Corporation – 18 5080 series emu for commuter and subway use; Keihin Electric Express Railway – 24 1000 series emu for commuter and subway use.

TRAM Power Ltd

Unit 4 Carraway Road, Gillmoss Industrial Estate, Liverpool L11 0EE, UK
Tel: (+44 151) 547 14 25   Fax: (+44 151) 546 60 66
e-mail: marketing@trampower.co.uk
Web: www.trampower.co.uk

Key personnel

Managing Director: *Vaughan Smart*
Technical Director: *Prof Lewis Lesley*

Background

TRAM Power Ltd is a privately owned company, established to develop and promote light rail technology that is safe, efficient, reliable and affordable. As well as the vehicle concept mentioned below, rail and overhead line systems have been developed.

In 2005 an accord was signed with East Lancashire Coachbuilders to negotiate a partnership to build production vehicles.

Products

Low-cost low-floor modular trams. A 29 m 22 tonne prototype of the City Class tram was produced in 2005 as a three-section vehicle with an integral body of rustless steel. Propulsion is via body-mounted three-phase AC traction motors powering the outer bogies via a modified heavy goods

City Class tram prototype on the Birkenhead tramway, Merseyside, UK (TRAM Power Ltd) 1129933

vehicle prop shaft and axle combination. In the prototype a two-wheeled central module provides articulation. All wheels rotate independently, eliminating curve squeal. Extensive use is made of off-the-shelf components.

The design of the City Class tram provides for vehicles of between 16 and 38 m in length, in widths of 2.4 or 3.5 m and in full low- or high-floor versions.

Transtech Oy

Elektroniikkatie 2, FIN-90570 Oulu, Finland
Tel: (+358 8) 870 69 00
Fax: (+358 8) 870 69 70
e-mail: sales@transtech.fi
www.transtech.fi

Key personnel

Chairman: *Curt Lindbom*
Managing Director: *Markku Blomberg*

Background

Previously called Talgo Oy, the company has reverted to its former name Transtech Oy, following its sale by Patentes Talgo to Primaca Partners, an investment group.

Products

Passenger coaches.

Tüvasaş

Türkiye Vagon Sanayii AS
Turkish Wagon Industry Corporation
Milli Egemenlik Caddesi 123, Adapazari, Turkey
Tel: (+90 264) 275 16 60
Fax: (+90 264) 275 16 79
e-mail: info@tuvasas.com.tr
Web: www.tuvasas.com.tr

Background

An affiliate company of Turkish State Railways (TCDD), Tüvasas was originally a passenger coach repair facility. It commenced vehicle manufacturing in 1975.

Products

Passenger coaches, dmus, emus and LRVs. Coaching stock production centres on the TVS 2000 family of vehicles, which has been produced in open, compartment, restaurant car, sleeping car and couchette versions for TCDD. The company has also produced the Sakarya single-unit railcar, which is powered by a Cummins 410 kW engine with Voith transmission, participated in the manufacture of LRVs for Bursa (in co-operation with Siemens TS) and has developed concepts for a 160 km/h three-car dmu.

The UCWPartnership

Marievale Road, Nigel, South Africa
Tel: (+27 11) 814 44 11   Fax: (+27 11) 814 51 56
e-mail: info@ucw.co.za
Web: www.ucw.co.za

Key personnel
Chief Executive: *L Taljaard*
Financial Manager: *G Blewitt*
Contracts Manager: *D Ward*

Engineering Manager: *P Watts*
Manufacturing and Media: *E Wills*

Background
The UCW Partnership was formed in 2003 and is a joint initiative between the Murray & Roberts subsidiary, Union Carriage & Wagon Co. (Pty) Ltd, and a consortium led by the J & J Group.

With over 13,000 locomotives, coaches and special vehicles successfully delivered, The UCW Partnership is a significant manufacturer of rolling stock.

Products
Electric, diesel-electric, diesel-hydraulic and diesel-mechanical locomotives from 50 to 180 t; railcars; electric and diesel-electric multiple-units; main line passenger coaching stock; specialised freight vehicles.

United Group Rail

Head Office
PO Box 525, 3 Bridge Street, Plymble New South Wales 2073, Australia
Tel: (+61 2) 44 88 48 88   Fax: (+61 2) 94 88 49 55
Web: www.unitedgroupltd.com

Key personnel
Chief Operating Officer: *John McLuckie*

Background
United Group Rail was formed as part of a Group restructure in 2005 and is the amalgamation of United Goninan and Alstom Transport – Australia and New Zealand.

Products
Diesel-electric locomotives. United Goninan is a licensee of GE Transportation Systems, USA. Diesel locomotive refurbishment.

Powered single- and double-deck vehicles, light rail vehicles.

Passenger coaches and passenger coach refurbishment.

Contracts
In November 2006 the first of seven 'Hunter' two-car dmus ordered in 2004 by RailCorp entered service on CityRail Hunter Valley services in New South Wales.

In October 2006, in cooperation with GE Transportation, the company was awarded a contract by Pilbara Iron for 10 GE Dash 9 Evolution diesel locomotives.

In September 2006 an AUD127 million contract was received from The Pilbara Infrastructure (TPI) for 15 GE Dash 9 Evolution diesel locomotives to be supplied in partnership with GE Transportation and 480 heavy-duty 'Gondola' Golynx iron ore wagons.

In March 2006 United Group Rail won an order from QR National to supply three 5000 Class

Prospector dmu designed by United Goninan for Western Australian Government Railways 1037002

diesel locomotives for Hunter Valley coal traffic in New South Wales.

Also in March 2006 a contract was awarded by Pilbara iron to supply new GE power units to be fitted to existing Dash 9 locomotives to operate in Western Australia.

In April 2005 a follow-up contract was placed to bring to 122 the number of Oscar (H-Set)

double-deck emu cars ordered by RailCorp in New South Wales for its CityRail suburban services in Sydney. First examples entered service in December 2006. The trains are configured as 30 four-car units. The orders cover two spare driving trailers.

United Streetcar LLC

9700 SE Lawnfield Road, Clackamas, Oregon 97015, US
Tel: (+1 503) 653 63 00
Fax: (+1 503) 653 58 70
e-mail: cbrown@unitedstreetcar.com
Web: www.unitedstreetcar.com

Key personnel
President: *Chandra Brown*
Marketing and Business Development: *Marion Olsen*
Program Manager: *Leon Kaunitz*

Background
United Streetcar, LLC is a newly formed subsidiary of Oregon Iron Works (OIW) and is currently located at its parent company's facility. Additional manufacturing facilities are located in Vancouver, WA.

In February 2006 OIW signed a technology transfer agreement with Skoda which gave United Streetcar, LLC the latest European technology in rail vehicle design and electric traction equipment and products for the US.

Products
In conjunction with Skoda, the production of the 10 T3 streetcar, which has four axles,

double-ended, three sections, low-floor, two motorised trucks.

Developments
United Streetcar's latest vehicle design is a three body, articulated, low-floor streetcar which is being manufactured in the US.

The new streetcar uses design and technology from the existing Skoda vehicle and will be equipped with the Skoda electric traction system and some components produced in the Czech Republic by Skoda Electric. The vehicle prototype project is scheduled to be at a six month testing stage by the end of 2008.

Ust-Katav Tramway Works

456040 Ust-Katav, Russia
Tel: (+7 351) 672 65 41   Fax: (+7 351) 672 55 48

Key personnel
General Director: *Yuri Kirilitchev*
Deputy Chief of Marketing Department: *V N Mikheev*

Background
Ust-Katav was formerly the S m Kirov Works.

Products
Tramcars and light rail vehicles.

Contracts
Has supplied tramcars to the systems in many cities in Russia and neighbouring countries.

Range
Includes the 71–616 tram, developed jointly with Siemens, is now in operation. It has up to four doors, the two centre ones being double-width, and is 15.25 m long and 2.5 m wide. It seats 32 with 110 standing.

Vossloh Locomotives GmbH

PO Box 9293, D-24152 Kiel
Falckensteiner Strasse 2, D-24159 Kiel, Germany
Tel: (+49 431) 39 99 34 37
Fax: (+49 431) 39 99 22 74
e-mail: vertrieb.kiel@vl.vossloh.com
Web: www.vossloh-locomotives.com

Works
Service-Zentrum Moers, Baerler Strasse 100,
D-47441 Moers, Germany
Tel: (+49 2841) 14 04 10
Fax: (+49 2841) 14 04 50

Key personnel
Managing Directors: *Andreas Hopmann, Olaf Pölderl*
Director Service Centre: *Hosrt Hackenthal*

Subsidiaries
Vossloh Locomotives has a 100 per cent shareholding in Locomotion Service GmbH to maintain locomotives in service on certain routes.

Background
The Kiel works started production in 1920 of the benzene-driven railcar and in 1925 the first diesel locomotives. In 1947 the Deutsche Bundesbahn DB placed its first order for diesel locomotives with 31 units. In 1971 the Kiel works celebrated the delivery of 1,000 units for DB. In 1998 Siemens Schienenfahrzeugtechnik GmbH, formerly Krupp MaK Maschinenbau, was acquired by Vossloh AG and renamed Vossloh Schienenfahrzeugtechnik GmbH, since then it has become a member of the Vossloh Group.

In April 2003, the entire Vossloh Group adopted a uniform corporate design and VSFT became Vossloh Locomotives GmbH. Current annual production is 60 to 80 locomotives.

Products
Diesel-hydraulic locomotives ranging from 390 to 2,700 kW for all duties, gauges, speeds for both main line and industrial service. Rail vehicle components including bogies and cooling systems. Maintenance, rehabilitation and repowering of locomotives (in Moers).

Vossloh Locomotives has delivered its vehicles in recent years to state and private railways as well as to leasing companies like Angel Trains Cargo and Mitsui Rail Capital, within Europe: G 400 B (MK 600, 390 kW) to DSB (Denmark) and NS Reizigers (NS 700, 390 kW), HLD 77/78 (1,150 kW) to SNCB (Belgium), Rh 2070 (738 kW) to ÖBB (Austria), Am 843 (1,500 kW) to SBB (Switzerland), G 1206 (BB 61000, 1,500 kW) to SNCF (France). G 1206 locomotives are already in operation on private railways in the Netherlands, Germany, Italy, Luxembourg, Switzerland and France; many of them in frontier crossing services. The G 2000 BB (2,240 and 2,700 kW) locomotives are also in operation on private railways in the Netherlands, Germany, Italy, France, as country combination in Germany/Netherlands and Germany/Belgium/ Netherlands and Germany/Sweden. Full certification is in preparation for Poland and country combinations such as Sweden/Norway and France/Belgium/Netherlands.

In 2002 Vossloh Locomotives completed its range with the models G 1000 BB (1,100 kW), certificated in Germany, Switzerland, Italy and France and the G 1700 BB (1,700 kW), certificated in Germany, Austria, Slovenia, Slovakia and Hungary.

The new, main line G 2000-4 BB and G 2000-5 BB, the latter for services in cold climates (–40°C) with diesel engine outputs upgraded to 2,700 kW, makes these two of the world's most most powerful, four-axle, single-engine, diesel-powered locomotives.

They can be delivered with a soot filter like all locomotives of Vossloh Locomotives, installed already in series in the Class AM843 (79 units) for Switzerland and in a few G 1206.

Developments
Responding to the increased demand for shunting locomotives in freight transportation, Vossloh

Vossloh Locomotives G 2000 BB 5th Series for Sweden/Germany and Sweden/Norway 1323229

Vossloh Locomotives G 1206for France, Germany, France/Germany, Germany/Netherlands and Switzerland. 1323230

Vossloh Locomotives Class AM843 (Type G 1700-2 BB) for SBB Cargo in Switzerland/Germany, BLS and SERSA Switzerland, Aceralia Spain 1036757

Locomotives has developed the three-axle G 6 as the first model of a new-look family, with traction effort up to 220 kN. Based on innovative new modules combined with approved components, this development resulted in a sustainable locomotive that complies with all German and international regulations regarding exhaust emission, noise control, software and fire protection – whilst also being prepared for adaptation to future norms and standards such as the EU stage 3A and 3B exhaust emission parameters.

Vossloh Transportation Systems

Pol Ind Del Mediterraneo, C/Mitxera N°6, E-46550
Albuixec, Valencia, Spain
Tel: (+34 96) 141 50 00
Fax: (+34 96) 141 50 07
e-mail: juan-jose.sanchis@ve.vossloh.com
Web: www.vossloh-transportation-systems.com

Key personnel

Managing Director: *Iñigo Parra*
Head of Commercial Affairs: *Jose Daniel Mesa*
Head of Marketing and Communications: *Juan Jose Sanchis*

Background

Originating in 1891 as Talleres Devis, in 1929 the plant became Construcciones Devis and then merged in 1947 with the Catalonian company, Material para ferrocarrilly Construcciones which then became MACOSA (Material y Construcciones SA). In 1989 ALSTOM took over the company and it moved to the Albuixech plant in 1997. On 31 March 2005, Vossloh AG completed its purchase of the engineering and production unit and it was then renamed Vossloh Transportation Systems.

In December 2006 the Vossloh Group together with Spanish National Railways, RENFE, set up a joint venture (ERION) for the purpose of maintaining and repairing locomotives. Vossloh holds a 51 per cent majority stake in the venture, the remaining 49 per cent is owned by RENFE.

Products

Main line diesel electric locomotives: Euro-4000 (passenger and freight). In 2007 Vossloh Transportation Systems will launch the Euro-4000, a Co-Co diesel-electric locomotive powered by a 3.178 kW engine supplied by EMD and compliant with all existing EU regulations. It has a top operating speed of 120 km/h for freight operations and 160 km/h for passenger operation. A fuel tank capacity of 7,000 litres and a range of 2,000 km.

Euro-3000 Bo-Bo diesel-electric locomotive powered by a 2,390 kW engine supplied by EMD. Compliant with all existing EU regulations, prepared for freight application with a maximum speed of 120 km/h and for passenger application up to 200 km/h.

Shunting locomotives: Euro-1000, manufactured for SNCF (France), a diesel-electric, single cab, with three-phase and asynchronous electric drive system with two bogies with two drive axles each. This locomotive can be used for hauling freight trains as well as being suited to shunting operations in inter-modal platforms and in sorting yards.

Passenger rolling stock: Metro (ordered by FGV, Valencia, Spain).

Train-tram, a light articulated vehicle that functions as a suburban train in the metropolitan area and as a tram in the urban context. This is a bi-directional electric train unit, capable of surface and underground travel.

Contracts

Vossloh Transportation Systems exports to a number of countries including: Brazil, France, US, UK and Yugoslavia.

In 2004 28 units of the Class 334 diesel-electric locomotive were produced for RENFE (Spain). 160 shunting locomotives for SNCF (France) and in 2005, as a follow on to the initial 18 metro units supplied in 1994, FGV (Spain) ordered a further 20 and a further 20 in 2006.

In 2006, 30 locomotives were produced for Angel Trains (UK), two for Comsa (Spain) and six Class ST428W locomotives for Israel Railways (IR) in 2006.

Three-car articulated Train-Tram LRV for FGV, Spain   1129897

Vossloh Euro 4000 prototype diesel-electric locomotive   1322902

Vossloh Class 333 diesel-electric locomotives modernised by Vossloh for Spanish open access operator Continental Rail
1129894

Vossloh Class BB 60000 (Type Euro-1000) *diesel-electric locomotive for SNCF Fret, France* 1322903

Vossloh Class 334 diesel-electric locomotive for RENFE, Spain 1322905

Class 333: in 2004, two locomotives for Continental Rail (Spain), in 2005 two locomotives were ordered by Acciona (Spain) and in 2006 two locomotives for Azvi (Spain) and two for FCC (Spain).

Developments
As part of an initiative integrated into the EU's strategic projects for eliminating fossil fuel dependency, a feasibility study is being carried out in collaboration with universities, research centres and Spanish foreign companies.

Vossloh Metro trainset for FGV, Valencia, Spain 1322904

Wabtec Rail Ltd

PO Box 400, Doncaster Works, Hexthorpe Road, Doncaster DN1 1SL, UK
Tel: (+44 1302) 34 07 00
Fax: (+44 1302) 32 13 49
Web: www.wabtecrail.co.uk

Key personnel
Managing Director: *John Meehan*
Engineering Director: *Mike Roe*
Finance Director: *Robert Johnson*
Operations Director: *David Haynes*

Commercial Manager: *Paul Robinson*
Commercial Director: *Chris Weatherall*

Background
Wabtec Rail is a railway rolling stock engineering that undertakes the overhaul of: passenger rolling stock, mainline locomotives, bogies, wheelsets, air brake equipment, hydraulic dampers and buffer design, along with the manufacture of shunting locomotives and freight wagons.

As part of the Wabtec Corporation, Wabtec Rail also supplies to the UK rolling stock owners and maintainers, composite brake blocks and pads, Wabtec Railway Electronics train data recorders and electronic equipment, Cardwell TMX braking systems and Wabtec air brake equipment.

Products
Passenger rolling stock heavy maintenance, interior refurbishments and conversions. The design and construction of new freight wagons and the conversion, refurbishment and maintenance of existing wagons. The refurbishment and modification of main line and industrial shunting locomotives. The overhaul of locomotive, passenger rolling stock, diesel and electric multiple-unit bogies.

ŽOS Vrútky Jsc

Dielenska Kružná, SK-038 61 Vrútky, Slovakia
Tel: (+421 842) 420 51 01
Fax: (+421 842) 428 15 95
e-mail: zos-vrutky@zos-vrutky.sk
Web: www.zos-vrutky.sk

Key personnel
Director for Business and Production: *Ladislav Bonda*

Background
Formerly the Vrútky workshops of the Czechoslovak and subsequently Slovakian Republic Railways

(ŽSR), ŽOS Vrútky became a joint stock company in 1994.

The company is ISO 9001-2000, ISO 14001:2004 and TransQ accredited.

Products
Emus and dmus for 1,000 and 1,435 mm gauge. In a consortium with EMU GTW – High Tatras, consisting also of Stadler Fahrzeuge of Switzerland and Bombardier Transportation, the company produced 14 1.5 kV DC Class 425.95 metre-gauge emus for ŽSR's High Tatras network. The vehicles are based on Stadler's GTW 2/6 design. The company is currently modernising Class 350 electric locomotives which are able to

operate on international corridors in both 3 kV DC and 25 kV 50 Hz AC, at speeds of up to 160 km/h.

Contracts
In 2006, production included new Type Bmpeer air-conditioned coaches for Slovakian Railways and 760 mm gauge low-floor driving cars and intermediate trailers for the Zillertalbahn and Austrian Federal Railways.

G Zwiehoff GmbH

Tegernseestrasse 15, D-83022 Rosenheim, Germany
Tel: (+49 8031) 2328 50
Fax: (+49 8031) 232 85 19
e-mail: info@zwiehoff.com
Web: www.zwiehoff.com

Key personnel
Managing Director: *Gerd Zwiehoff*
Office Manager: *Anne Kinshofer*

Products
Road/rail vehicles with a shunting capacity of up to 3,000 tonnes or equipped as multipurpose

vehicles; self-propelled Mini Shunter with a shunting capacity of up to 150 tonnes; self-propelled Maxi Shunter with a shunting capacity of up to 200 tonnes; forklift truck-propelled wagon shunter with a shunting capacity of up to 300 tonnes.

ALSTOM Transport

48 rue Albert Dhalenne, F-93482 Saint-Ouen
Cedex, France
Tel: (+33 1) 41 66 90 00   Fax: (+33 1) 41 66 96 66
Web: www.transport.alstom.com

Contact points
Traction drives, power modules, switchgear
ALSTOM Transport
50 rue du Dr Guimier, BP 4, F-65600 Semeac,
Tarbes, France
Tel: (+33 5) 62 53 41 21   Fax: (+33 5) 62 53 40 01
Contact: Eric Lenoir

Traction drives, auxiliary converters
ALSTOM Transport
11-13 avenue du Bel Air, F-69627 Villeurbanne
Cedex, France
Tel: (+33 4) 72 81 52 00   Fax: (+33 4) 72 81 52 87
Contact: Eric Lenoir

Motors
On-board electronic systems
ALSTOM Transport
7 av de Lattre de Tassigny, BP 49, F-25290 Ornans
Cedex
Tel: (+33 3) 81 62 44 00
Fax: (+33 3) 81 62 44 01
Contact: Eric Lenoir

Motors
ALSTOM Transport
50/52 rue Cambier Dupret 6001, Charleroi, Belgium
Tel: (+32 71) 44 54 11   Fax: (+32 71) 44 57 82
Contact: Jacques Toppet
ALSTOM Transport Netherlands BV
PO Box 3021, NL-2980 DA, Ridderkerk, Netherlands
Tel: (+31 180) 45 28 57   Fax: (+31 180) 45 28 60
Contact: Mathilde De Winter
ALSTOM Transportation Inc
1 Transit Drive, Hornell, New York 14843
Tel: (+1 607) 324 45 95
Fax: (+1 607) 324 23 68
Contact: Jennifer Luo

Manhattan office
ALSTOM Transportation Inc
353 Lexington Avenue, Suite 1100, New York,
New York 10016, US
Tel: (+1 201) 692 53 20

**Traction drives, auxiliary converters, switchgear,
motors, transformers**
ALSTOM Transport Ltd
F – 4, East of Kailash, New Delhi 110 065, India
Tel: (+91 11) 628 77 16; 77 47; 77 48
Fax: (+91 11) 628 77 15
Contact: Sudha Gupta

Traction drives, auxiliary converters, switchgear
Shanghai ALSTOM Transport Electrical
Equipment Co Ltd
Room 915, Electric Power Building, 430 Xu Jia
Hui Road, 200025 Shanghai, China

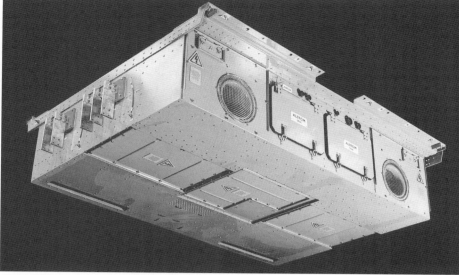

ONIX 800 propulsion set for Virgin Trains Pendolino tilting trainset   0114492

Tel: (+86 21) 64 72 51 57
Fax: (+86 21) 64 72 96 62
Contact: Lu Yin

Products
The company's strategy for traction equipment
centres on its IGBT propulsion system known as
ONIX (Onduleur à Integration exceptionnelle).
The know-how in advanced IGBT power
modules, Agate control electronic systems and
ONIX asynchronous traction motors provides a
compact, lightweight, integrated traction system,
which is in reliable service around the world. ONIX
is suitable for all line voltages (including the latest
3,000 V). In the ONIX range is the 350, for electric
and trolleybuses (up to a line voltage of 400 V),
800 for metros and LRVs (up to a line voltage of
900 V), 1,500 for metros, emus, locomotives and
high-speed trains (up to a line voltage of 2,000 V)
and 3,000 V for emus, locomotives and high-
speed trains (up to a line voltage of 3,000 V).
ONIX's modularity enables quick and easy
maintenance and its flexibility allows a choice
of cooling system to suit the local operating
environment.

ALSTOM's electric and electronic sub-systems
include: electronic systems featuring the AGATE
integrated family of traction control (AGATE
Control), auxiliary control (AGATE Aux), Train
Control Management Systems (AGATE Link),
passenger information systems (AGATE Media,
see Passenger Information Systems section), as
well as depot monitoring systems.

A modular range of asynchronous, synchronous
and DC motors, which are lightweight, compact
and can be readily adapted to specific needs.

Auxiliary converters based on the modular
CARA auxiliary power conversion and distribution
packages.

A range of AC and DC switchgear, circuit
breakers and cab equipment.

Contracts
Brazil: ALSTOM has won a turnkey order from
Metrofor for a metro system in Fortaleza, north
eastern Brazil. The order covers 10 four-car
trainsets, which incorporate the new ONIX 3000
drive system supplied by ALSTOM's plant in
Tarbes, France.

For the Rio de Janeiro and Salvador metros,
ALSTOM will respectively supply 20 TU ONIX
3 kV and 20 TU ONIX 152 HP modules.

Mexico: In December 2006 the Mexico City
authority, STC (Sistema de Transporte Colectivo),
announced its intent to award ALSTOM a contract
for the refurbishment of 25 trainsets for its Line
8 fleet with new propulsion technology.

ALSTOM received an order from Bombardier
Concarril and CAF for 13 six-car trainsets for Line
A of the Mexico City metro. This was ALSTOM's
first complete order for its new-generation ONIX
traction system with Agate electronic power
control.

South Africa: ALSTOM was selected by Spoornet
to supply and install its Agate control electronics
in 99 locomotives as part of its locomotive
refurbishment programme.

UK: ALSTOM Transport has supplied Bombardier
Transportation with ONIX traction drive systems
(352 ONIX IGBT inverter drives including
ALSTOM's standard AGATE microprocessor
system) and auxiliary equipment for the fleet of
352 Class 220/221 demu cars operated by Virgin
CrossCountry. Under the terms of the contract
ALSTOM is responsible for providing all spares
for the trains until the end of the franchise
in 2012.

Ansaldobreda SpA

425 Via Argine, I-80147 Naples, Italy
Tel: (+39 081) 243 11 11   Fax: (+39 081) 243 26 98
Web: www.ansaldobreda.it

Key personnel
Chief Executive Officer: *Roberto Assereto*

Managing Director: *S Bianconi*
Commercial: *D Zanchi*
Engineering: *E Trombetta*
Public Relations: *G Gallini*

Products
Electric propulsion equipment for mainline,
urban and suburban railway vehicles with AC

and DC traction motors; electronic converters
and controls; auxiliary equipment; planning,
design and management methodologies for
public transport; sales, assembly, start-up
servicing.

APS electronic AG

Neumatt 4, CH-4626 Niederbuchsiten,
Switzerland
Tel: (+41 62) 389 88 88
Fax: (+41 62) 389 88 80
e-mail: aps@apsag.com
Web: www.apsag.com

Key personnel
Managing Director: *Urs Christen*
Head of Marketing and Sales: *Ralph Disteli*

Products
APS electronic AG is experienced in the field
of power electronics as well as monitoring
electronic technology. It offers a complete

family of pure convection cooled auxiliary
converters and battery chargers designed
for railway applications, tramways and
trolleybuses. The modular concept builds the
base of the auxiliary converter system which
enables the customisation of the system to
meet customers' specific weight and space
requirements.

BAE Systems

Electronics and Integrated Solutions
600 Main Street, Johnson City, New York 13790, US
Tel: (+1 607) 770 41 88   Fax: (+1 607) 770 35 24
e-mail: platformsolutions@baesystems.com
Web: www.hybridrive.com

Key personnel

President: *Sean Bond*
Director of Transport Systems, UK and Europe: *Rob Lindsey*

Products

Hybrid propulsion system for buses and medium to large trucks. Combines traditional vehicle power sources (currently diesel engines) with electric drive motors to reduce emissions and fuel consumption. A diesel engine turns a generator that produces electricity to run the drive motor and charge a battery pack.

Hybrid vehicles also eliminate transmission maintenance, as there is no transmission, and they reduce brake wear by employing a regenerative braking system that uses the drive motor to slow the vehicle and generate additional electricity during deceleration.

The vehicles also accelerate faster and run more quietly. Hybrids currently in service use diesel engines, but technology is also compatible with other fuel types, such as compressed natural gas and emerging technologies including fuel cells.

Developments

An Enviro400 London bus with a BAE Systems hybrid electric drive train was delivered at the end of 2008 to Transport for London and Metrobus, one of the city's principal bus operators. The bus, a double-deck model built by Alexander Dennis Limited (ADL), is among 17 hybrid units built by ADL and BAE Systems that are being evaluated in passenger service. The diesel-electric drive system, is already in use on more than 1,500 buses in North American cities. The bus delivered to the London fleet uses a lithium-ion energy storage system. BAE Systems, Isuzu and ITOCHU

Alexander Dennis Limited (ADL) double-deck bus with BAE Systems hybrid-electric drive train, delivered to Transport for London (TfL) and Metrobus for evaluation in passenger service, starting in late 2008 (BAE Systems)   1374311

Corp are introducing low-emission hybrid buses in Japan in 2009. BAE Systems' HybriDrive™ propulsion system will be demonstrated and tested on 30-foot ISUZU ERGA buses. Isuzu will install the HybriDrive™ system on two buses, evaluating their performance at Isuzu's proving grounds and in passenger service. The system consists of a generator, an electric motor, and an energy storage system managed by computerised controls. A diesel engine that powers the generator operates independent of the electric drive motor, running at a nearly consistent speed. BAE Systems' HybriDrive™ system have been fitted in more than 1,500 buses in cities such as New York, San Francisco, Toronto and, in the near future, London. In 2008 BAE Systems introduced an improved version of its hybrid propulsion system that can be used on multiple

bus platforms, is mechanically simpler, reduces maintenance costs, and makes possible the use of electric accessories. The new system, based on the company's series diesel-electric hybrid technology already in use by transit agencies across North America, can be configured with the diesel engine and generator arranged inline or transversely to make it adaptable to a wider range of bus models. It also can generate power for electrically operated systems such as air conditioning, power steering, engine cooling, and lighting, serving these electrical loads without belt-driven alternators. Buses equipped with the new hybrid system also will use a lithium-ion energy storage system that increases battery life and reduces vehicle weight, improving fuel economy and reducing emissions. The battery system is self-monitoring and easy to service for further savings in maintenance costs.

Behr Industry GmbH & Co, KG

Heilbronner Strasse 380, D-70469 Stuttgart, Germany
Tel: (+49 711) 896 20 11
Fax: (+49 711) 896 30 75
e-mail: behrindustry@behrgroup.com
Web: www.behrindustry.behrgroup.com

Key personnel

Sales Director: *Ruediger Wanner*
Sales Manager: *Alexander Prokopp*

Products

Cooling for electrically driven vehicles: converter cooling (oil/water), transformer cooling (oil), cooling of driving E-motors (water) for

locomotives and multiple units. Installation: underfloor, on the roof or inside the vehicle. Components or complete systems. Solutions for new vehicles, refurbishment, overhaul of existing systems. Electronic cooling: watercooled cooling plates for semiconductors in converters, air/air heat exchangers for electronic racks and cabinets.

Bombardier Transportation

Locomotives and Equipment
Schöneberger Ufer 1, D-10785 Berlin, Germany
Tel (+49 30) 98 60 70   Fax: (+49 30) 986 07 20-0
Web: www.transportation.bombardier.com

Key personnel

President, Locomotives and Equipment: *Åke Wennberg*

Products

Bombardier Transportation is the leading supplier for complete propulsion, train control and management system and related services, both to internal railcar manufacturing divisions, as well as to other railcar manufacturers. Being a single-source supplier for the entire scope of propulsion and control, Bombardier Transportation ensures full integration of the functionality and turnkey solutions. *MITRAC* propulsion systems include converters, traction motors, gears and auxiliary power systems supplies for all types of railway applications. *MITRAC* train control and management systems (TCMS) are used

Introduced in 2007, the MITRAC DCU 2   1328059

Bombardier MITRAC Energy Saver   0585211

for automation, communication and diagnosis including train network, data communication onboard the train and from train to ground as well as train functionality (including processor units and driver's display units).

MITRAC is a trademark of Bombardier Inc or its subsidiaries.

Developments

Bombardier's developments help guarantee higher levels of performance, increased safety and reliability, improved life cycle cost and reduced energy consumption. Bombardier's *MITRAC* Energy Saver, for example, is an onboard solution which allows energy savings of up to 30 per cent and catenary free operation in section up to 1,000 m. Bombardier's train adapted, Internet Protocol-based MITRAC Train Control and Management Systems is based on an open and standardised information protocol. Data transference will be possible on a much larger scale, data access will be easier and faster and information exchange with other infrastructures will be quicker. This new technology will enable applications for better fleet and service management as well as better service for passengers. Between its launch in late 2006 until mid-2007, nine customers had

selected the product for applications ranging from regional trains to locomotives in France, Germany, the Netherlands, the UK and the US.

Projects

Belgium: Brussels T3000 1, 46 trams; Angel Trains Cargo, 26 multi-system freight locomotives, Angel Trains Cargo 10 3 kV DC freight locomotives.

China: Dalian Locomotive & Rolling Stock Co Ltd, 500 heavy-haul electric freight locomotives; Beijing Metro, 33 metro B trains; Ministry of Railways, 40 high-speed trains; Shenzen Metro Corporation, Line 1, 26 metro A trains; Shanghai Metro Operation Company, 93 metro A trains; Guangzhou Metro, metro A trains; Qishuyan Locomotive and Rolling Stock, 76 diesel-electric locomotives.

France: Marseilles, 80 trams; SNCF, additional 67 AGC vehicles (total of 679 AGC trains); Eurotunnel, 37 Type ESL V locomotives.

Germany: Gera/Darmstadt/Braunschweig, 34 trams; Frankfurt/ Berlin/Augsburg 160 Flexity trams DB AG, 261 Class ET 422/ET 423 emus; DB AG, 250 two-system Class BR185 electric locomotives; DB Regio, 24 BR146 locomotives; LNVG: new 11 TRAXX P160 DE diesel-electric locomotives for a total of 184 double-deck coaches, 27 TRAXX P160 AC electric and 11 TRAXX P160 DE diesel-electric

locomotives; Frankfurt, 60 Flexity Classic trams; Halle, 30 Flexity Classic trams; Rhein Neckar, 36 Variobahn vehicles; converter units for Stuttgart, 27 trams Class sdt 8,10 114; Dresden, 20 Flexity Classic trams.

India: Supply of propulsion components for locomotives.

Iran: Tehran/North Ext Line 1, 15 Metro trains.

Israel: Israel Railways, 54 double deck coaches.

Italy: Palermo, 17 Flexity trams; Metro Rome, 270 metro cars; Trenitalia Cargo/Trenitalia, 42 Class EU11 locomotives and 250 Class E464 locomotives.

Luxembourg: CFL, 85 multi-voltage system cars.

Netherlands: Rotterdam, 21 trans.

Russian Federation: Novocherkassk Locomotive Works, nine Class EP10 dual-voltage electric passenger locomotives.

South Africa: Gauteng Provincial Government, 100 regional emu cars.

Spain: Renfe Mercancias, 100 TRAXX F140 DC 2E electric locomotives; Valencia/Alicante, 30 trams; Metro Madrid, in total more than 700 metro cars; Renfe, AVE S/102 high-speed power heads; Renfe, 44 HSP 250 high-speed multi-system power head with variable gauge; FGC, 13 emu cars/Series 213 extension.

Sweden: 160 Regina emu cars for various operators in Sweden; some 250 OTU emu cars for SJ, DSB and various operators in Sweden; Stockholm Public Transport Authority, Class C20/C21 metro trains and A32 Tvärbanan light rail vehicles.

Switzerland: SBB Cargo, 18 multi-system freight locomotives RE484, Zurich, 69 Cobra trams.

Turkey: Eskisehir, 18 Flexity Outlook trams.

United Kingdom: Docklands Light Railway, 18 light rail vehicles; London Underground sub-surface-lines and the Victoria Line, 1,738 metro cars, c2c, South Eastern trains and GoVia Southern (formerly South Central), 1,614 Electrostar trains since 1997; during 2007 for Transport for London's East London Line and North London Railway, Porterbrook ordered in total 200 Electrostar emu cars. In total 1,600 Electrostar cars have been placed in service.

United States: Atlanta, 118 metro cars, New York City Authority, 80 metro carsets (Kawasaki R142 and R143 series); Dallas-Fort Worth Airport, 64 Innovia Class 20 people movers; San Francisco Bay Area Rapid Transit, 439 car sets; Washington DC Metro, 165 metro cars; Pittsburgh, 166 LRV cars, Chicago, 406 metro cars; Toronto, 234 metro cars.

Venezuela: In May 2006 Bombardier was awarded an order from Neoman Bus Group for the design and manufacture of its *MITRAC 500* propulsion system to power 80 trolleybuses for Barquisimeto.

Brecknell Willis & Co Ltd

Member of the Fandstan Electric Group
PO Box 10, Tapstone Road, Chard TA20 2DE, UK
Tel: (+44 1460) 649 41
Fax: (+44 1460) 661 22
e-mail: enquiries@brecknellwillis.com
Web: www.brecknell-willis.com

Key personnel

Managing Director: *Tony White*
Sales Manager, Trainborne Equipment: *Andrew Hales*
Third Rail, Commercial Operations Manager: *David Bailey*
Overhead Systems, Chief Engineer: *David Hartland*

Overseas office

Brecknell Willis, Taiwan
Brecknell Willis, France
Brecknell Willis (Tianjin) Electrification Systems Ltd, China

Products

Current collection and power distribution equipment for the transport sector. This includes

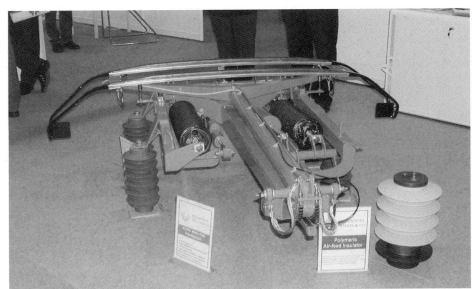

Brecknell Willis emu pantograph for KCRC, Hong Kong   0077582

the design, manufacture, supply and installation of complete systems and after-sales service.

The product groups are pantographs and third rail current collectors; conductor rail systems; light rail overhead systems and automatic gas tensioning equipment for overhead systems.

Contracts

Conductor rail systems for the East London Railway, Jubilee Line Extension Project and the Northern Line Upgrade (London Underground Ltd), Algiers, Ankara, Beijing, Brescia, Copenhagen, Dubai, Oslo and Taipei Metro systems. Overhead contact systems for the Dublin Luas, Midland Metro LRT system, Vancouver, Manchester Metro and refurbishment of Blackpool Tramway. Aluminium composite rail for DB, Berlin and Merseyrail UK.

Current collector systems for all new UK emu vehicles, West Coast Main Line Pendolino and current collection equipment for Shanghai Maglev; current collectors for the new vehicles for Hong Kong, Delhi Metro, KL-Monorail.

Supplied Eurostar and Channel Tunnel Shuttle trainborne current collectors as well as all standard high-speed pantographs for 25 kV electrified line operation in the UK. Light rail pantographs were supplied for the Strasbourg, Manchester, Birmingham, Sheffield and Tyne & Wear trams and shoegear for Glasgow, Amsterdam and Taipei Metros.

Dockland Light Railways Shoegear, Brecknell Willis
1135121

Brush Traction

PO Box 17, Loughborough LE11 1HS, UK
Tel: (+44 1509) 61 70 00   Fax: (+44 1509) 61 70 01
e-mail: sales@brushtraction.com
Web: www.brushtraction.com

Key personnel
Managing Director: *J M G Bidewell*
Sales Manager: *P L Needham*

Background
Brush Electrical Engineering was founded in 1889 and today the company is a major supplier and refurbisher of electric propulsion equipment. The company is a member of the FKI Group.

In June 2005 Brush Traction entered into a licence agreement with RailPower Technologies Corp, Vancouver, Canada, to be the exclusive Green Goat® Series locomotive manufacturer for the UK and Ireland rail markets. Brush Traction will also have the exclusive rights for service and maintenance of the hybrid locomotives in these countries.

Products
Electrical propulsion equipment including control equipment, traction motors, transformers and electrical auxiliaries for electric multiple-units, metro cars and light rail vehicles utilising both DC and AC traction motors.

China Northern Locomotive and Rolling Stock Industry (Group) Corporation (CNR)

No 11 Yangfangdian Road, Haidian District, Beijing 100038, China
Tel: (+86 10) 51 86 23 70
Fax: (+86 10) 51 86 23 74
e-mail: loriciec@cnrgc.com.cn
Web: www.cnrgc.com

Key personnel
President: *Cui Dianguo*
Vice-President: *Zhao Guangxing*
Chairman of Board of LORIC Import & Export Corporation Ltd: *Cao Guobing*
President of LORIC Import & Export Corporation Ltd: *Chen Dayong*
Senior Engineer of LORIC Import & Export Corporation Ltd: *Yang Xiangjing*

Products
Development, design, engineering, production, sales, installation, refurbishment, maintenance and after sales service for all types of electric propulsion equipment (traction motors, drive gears, flexible couplings, chopper controllers, main transformers, rectifiers, main alternators); auxiliary electrical equipment (converters, inverters, motor-alternators); train control equipment.

Traction motors are powered with outputs from 32 to 1,200 kW and alternators from 400 to 5,000 kVA.

CNR high power rectifier diodes and thysistors
1135822

Contracts
CNR traction and electrical equipment has been sold to customers in Canada, Egypt, Iran, Malaysia, Switzerland and the US.

Crompton Greaves Ltd

6th floor, CG House, Dr Annie Besant Road, Worli, Mumbai 400 030, India
Tel: (+91 22) 24 23 77 77
Fax: (+91 22) 24 23 77 88
Web: www.cglonline.com

Rail Transportation Systems Division
Vandhna 11, Tolstoy Marg, New Delhi 110 001, India
Tel: (+91 11) 30 41 63 00
Fax: (+91 11) 23 32 43 60, 23 35 21 34
e-mail: salil.kumar@cgl.co.in

Key personnel
Managing Director: *S M Trehan*
Vice-President Rail Transportation Systems Division: *A K Raina*
Senior Manager Rail Transportation Systems Division: *Salil Kumar*

Products
AC and DC traction motors; traction alternators; AC and DC auxiliary motors; brushless alternators; locomotive transformers; surge arrestors; rotary converters; static inverters. Complete electrics for demus and Diesel-Electric Tower Cars (DETC).

Developments
Three-phase electric equipment for emus is under development.

Contracts
A four-wheel powered tower wagon has been supplied to the Indian Railway Board.

DBB Fuel Cell Engines

3900 North Fraser Way, Burnaby, British Columbia
V5J 5G1, Canada
Tel: (+1 604) 432 92 00
Fax: (+1 604) 419 63 50
Web: www.ballard.com

Key personnel
President: *Dr Ferdinand Panik*

Background
DBB is a joint venture with Ballard Power Systems, DaimlerChrysler and Ford.

Developments
Ballard has introduced its new generation 205 kW (275 hp) zero emission Phase 4 fuel cell engine with fuel cell stacks from Ballard Power Systems, which is a major supplier of proton exchange membrane (PEM) fuel cells. The Phase 4 engine is 2,000 kg lighter and is less complex than the Phase 3 engine tested in Chicago and Vancouver. The engine is being tested in California as part of the California Fuel Cell Partnership – Driving for the Future, and is expected to be tested on 25 buses. The bus is powered by hydrogen but methanol is an option being worked on. DBB's parent company DBB Fuel Cell Engines GmbH, is responsible for development and manufacture of fuel cell engines for cars, buses and lorries.

EFACEC Sistemas de Electrónica, SA Ing

Av Eng Ulrich, PO Box 31, P-4470 Maia, Portugal
Tel: (+351 2) 941 36 66   Fax: (+351 2) 948 54 28

e-mail: se@efacec.pt
Web: www.efacec.pt

Key personnel
Chairman: *Francisco de La Fuente Sánchez*

Vice-Chairman: *Alberto Joaquim Milheiro Barbosa*
Market Relations: *Maria Elisa Oliveira*

Products
DC and AC traction motors, transformers.

ELIN EBG Traction GmbH

Cumberlandstrasse 32-34, A-1140 Vienna, Austria
Tel: (+43) 51 70 73 03 58   Fax: (+43) 51 70 75 13 83
e-mail: karl.haselboeck@siemens.com
Web: www.elinebgtraction.at

Key personnel
Chair: *Gerhard Skorepa*
Sales and Marketing Manager: *Natascha Ostermann*

Background
ELIN EBG Traction GmbH is a subsidiary of Siemens.

Products
Systems supplier of electric traction equipment for main line locomotives, railcars, light rail vehicles, trams and metros. ELIN EBG Traction delivers custom designed three phase traction equipment such as IGBT traction inverters (yype ETRIS), three phase asynchronous traction motors, microprocessor control systems (ELTAS).

Contracts
Vehicles for which ELIN has supplied equipment include: Talent emus and dmus in Austria, Hungary, Germany and Canada; LRVs and trams for Vienna, Portland, Phoenix, Seattle, Lodz, Linz, Innsbruck, Seville and Antalya; metros for Brussels and Vienna.

---

e-Traction

Parent company
e-Traction Worldwide SCA
Great Hill Farm Road, Bedford, New York 10506, US
Tel: (+1 914) 764 02 95   Fax: (+1 914) 764 02 92
e-mail: info@e-Traction.com
Web: www.e-Traction.com

Key personnel
Chief Executive officer: *Peter le Comte*

Subsidiaries
e-Traction Europe BV
Vissenstraat 36, NL-7324 AL Apeldoorn, Netherlands
Tel: (+31 55) 521 11 11
Fax: (+31 55) 522 23 66

e-Traction North America, LLC
Great Hill Farm Road, Bedford, New York 10506, US
Tel: (+1 914) 764 02 95   Fax: (+1 914) 764 02 92
Chief Technology Officer: *Ing Arjan Heinen*

Background
e-Traction has been involved in electric mobility since 1980. In April 2003 a substantial change in ownership occurred which resulted in a change to the current name and the creation of additional operating entities. In addition to the Dutch subsidiary e-Traction Europe BV, e-Traction North America, LLC was created to service the rapidly developing business opportunities in that region. These two operating companies are wholly owned by e-Traction Worldwide SCA, a Luxembourg registered company. In January 2005 two additional subsidiaries, e-Traction Manufacturing BV and e-Traction Finance BV, were created to act as manufacturing contractor and provider of financing/leasing services respectively.

'the Whisper' demonstrator bus equipped with e-Traction's battery-powered hub motor propulsion system (Ken Harris)
0585244

Products/Services
e-Traction has developed a propulsion system that lends itself particularly well to buses which operate on battery power and a patented design of hub motor, TheWheel™, together with associated control and mechanical systems.

In the design of TheWheel, the exterior of the motor, on which permanent magnets are mounted, forms the rotor and the stationary interior, which contains the electro-magnets, forms the stator. The tyre is mounted directly on the motor exterior. Axle and suspension systems have been developed to accommodate TheWheel. The direct propulsion system eliminates energy loss through gears and drivelines, with benefits in fuel efficiency. Vehicles equipped are also virtually silent in operation and require reduced maintenance.

The primary energy source for e-Traction-equipped buses are lithium-ion batteries supplied by Valence Technologies. These are recharged by a fuel-efficient onboard auxiliary power unit, which while diesel-powered in demonstrator versions, could also be CNG-powered. On downhill runs, the braking resistance of the hub motors generates electrical energy which is used to recharge the batteries.

Traction control is via the e-Traction® Energy Management System, which employs a Programmable Logic Computer (PLC) supplied by CANopen to manage the entire propulsion system. This includes provision for accommodating the mechanical differential needed during turning by a vehicle equipped with TheWheel motors.

By late 2005, three bus conversions as demonstrators for the e-Traction system had been carried out, including a vehicle known as 'the Whisper™', originally built by Fokker as a monocoque design for service in Rotterdam.

EVPÚ as

Elektrotechnický Vyskumný a Projectový Ústav
Trencianska 19 SK-018 51 Nová Dubnica, Slovakia
Tel: (+421 42) 440 91 02   Fax: (+421 42) 443 42 52
e-mail: buday@evpu.sk
Web: www.evpu.sk

Key personnel
Chairman: *Igor Gerek*
General Manager: *Jozef Buday*
Business Director: *Ivan Lokšeninec*
Production Manager: *Ondrej Bočák*
Technical Director: *Ivan Buday*

Products
Electric traction control equipment for locomotives, including three-phase systems; electric traction control equipment for trams, trolleybuses and metro cars; transformers; electrical components for rail vehicles and trolleybuses; battery charging equipment.

Faiveley Transport SA

143 boulevard Anatole France, Carrefour Pleyel,
F-93285 Saint-Denis Cedex, France
Tel: (+33 1) 48 13 65 00
Fax: (+33 1) 48 13 65 75
Web: www.faiveley.com

Key personnel

Chairman and Chief Executive Officer: *Robert Joyeux*
Financial Director: *Etienne Haumont*
General Manager: *Pierre Sainfort*
Communications Manager: *K Dougall*

Background

Faivelely Transport is a leading supplier of onboard railway systems. It completed the acquisition of SAB WABCO in November 2004 and Neu Systèmes Ferroviaire in 2006.

In 2008 the Faivelely acquired 75 per cent shares in NOWE Streugeräte, a sanding systems company based in Hannover, Germany.

The remaining 25 per cent will be retained by the Co-Managing Director of NOWE.

In December 2007, Faiveley Transport completed the acquisition of 50 per cent of Shi Jia Zhuang Jia Xiang Precision Machinery Co Ltd, based in the Hebei Province.

Also in December 2007, Faiveley completed the acquisition of the railway assets of the Australian company Integrian Pty Ltd, this will enable Faiveley to complement its range of existing products in the field of video surveillance, event recorders (black box), driver vigilance devices and driver aid equipment.

In August 2008 Faiveley completed the acquisition of 100 per cent of Ellcon-National equity shares, a US based railway brake specialist.

Products

Pantographs, high-voltage switching, auxiliary converters, master controllers.

Recent developments include the CX family of pneumatically cushioned pantographs, comprising the AX and CX designs. The AX can operate where other pantographs are extended at speeds up to 220 km/h; it has been fitted to SNCF Class BB22200 locomotives. The AX is fitted with a regulator that ensures a constant pressure is maintained against the contact wire, at all speeds, using aerodynamic devices.

The CX operates at speeds up to 320 km/h. The CX is controlled by a microprocessor which varies the contact force (via a servo-valve in the pantograph's pneumatic system) in line with the train's speed and direction of travel, the position of the pantograph and the type of catenary overhead. The CX also features an automatic drop device, a low-friction spring box suspension and a collection head with independent wear strips.

With the most recent development of its Pegase concept, Faiveley Transport is capable of supplying a fully integrated high voltage roof system which provides a significant reduction in weight and space.

In 2008 Faiveley won a contract from PTMX, a Russian tramway car builder from St. Petersburg, to supply 36 pantographs.

Ferraz Shawmut

1, Chaussée de la Comtesse, F-77160 Provins, France
Tel: (+33 1) 60 58 56 20
Fax : (+33 1) 64 08 88 34
Web: www.ferrazshawmut.com

Background

Ferraz Shawmut is a division of Carbone Lorraine.

Products

Earth return current units and associated resistors to prevent current flowing through bearing of axleboxes and associated resistors; fuses with very high breaking capacity for DC/AC converter protection and for heating circuits protection.

FIREMA Trasporti SpA

Headquarters
Via Provinciale Appia, Località Ponteselice,
I-81100 Caserta, Italy
Tel: (+39 0823) 09 71 11
Fax: (+39 0823) 46 68 12
e-mail: info@firema.it
Web: www.firema.it

Key personnel

Chairman and Chief Executive Officer: *Gianfranco Fiore*

Commercial Manager: *Sergio d'Arminio*
Marketing Manager: *Agostino Astori*

Products

Electromechanical and electronic (chopper and inverter) traction equipment for mainline and suburban, metro and light rail applications. Traction motors for AC and DC equipment, main generators for diesel-electric locomotives.

Contracts

Contracts include electrical equipment for E652 and E402 locomotives for Italian Railways (FS); electrical equipment, including traction motors, for double-deck emus for FS/North Milan Railway; auxiliary static converters for ETR 500 high-speed trainsets for FS; and traction equipment for emus for Circumetnea Railway and remote control for Type Z1 coaches.

Fuji Electric Systems Co, Ltd

Gate City Ohsaki, East Tower 11-2, Osaki 1-chome,
Shinagawa-ku, Tokyo 141-0032, Japan
Tel: (+81 3) 54 35 70 46
Fax: (+81 3) 54 35 74 22
e-mail: info@fesys.co.jp
Web: www.fesys.co.jp

Key personnel

President and Director: *Mitsunori Shirakura*
Assistant Manager, Transportation Systems Sales Department: *Tomoaki Yokoyama*

Background

The Transportation Systems Sales Department of what was previously Fuji Electric Co Ltd, is part of the newly divided Fuji Electric Systems Co, Ltd.

Products

Traction motors with VVVF control, static auxiliary power supply (SIV) systems, linear motor-drive door systems for rail vehicles, power supply equipment; computer-based supervisory remote-control equipment; water-cooled silicon rectifiers. GIS (Gas Insulated Switchgear) and mini high-speed circuit breakers; moulded transformers; control systems incorporating electric power management, station office apparatus control, data management and disaster prevention management.

Singapore MRT train using Fuji Electric inverter control systems   0098044

Ganz Škoda Traction Electrics Ltd

Budafoki str 59, H-1111 Budapest, Hungary
Tel: (+36 1) 880 95 00   Fax: (+36 1) 880 95 10
e-mail: info@ganz-skoda.hu
Web: www.skoda.cz/ganz-skoda

Key personnel

Technical Director: *Tamás Ruzsányi*
Director of Production: *András Csikvári*
Chief Financial Officer: *Zsolt Nagy*
Project Management & After Sales: *József Kovács*

Background

Formerly a state enterprise, the company was privatised in 1991 as Ganz Ansaldo Electric Ltd, with the Italian company initially taking a shareholding of 51 per cent but increasing this to 99.99 per cent in 1998. In 1999 Ansaldo divested its interest, leading to the establishment of the present private sector company in 2000.

Škoda Holding took over the necessary assets and activities of Ganz Transelektro Traction Electrics Ltd and established with Hungarian Resonator Kft, a new company Ganz Škoda Traction Electrics Ltd in August 2006.

Products

Electric traction equipment for heavy rail vehicles, trams and trolleybuses, including control equipment, IGBT-based DC choppers for trolleybuses, IGBT-based auxiliary converters and IGBT-based inverters for mass transit and heavy rail vehicles, pantographs, braking resistors.

Contracts

Recently the company has supplied electric traction equipment for tram refurbishment projects in Budapest, Miskolc and Riga (Latvia), as well as for new vehicles for Debrecen, Hungary. Equipment has also been supplied for Ganz-Solaris trolleybuses operating in Riga, Rome and Tallinn and for Astra-Ikarus vehicles for Bucharest.

Hall Industries Inc

514 Mecklem Lane, Ellwood City, Pennsylvania 16117, USA
Tel: (+1 724) 752 20 00   Fax: (+1 724) 758 15 58
e-mail: service@hallindustries.com
Web: www.hallind.com

Key personnel

Contact: *Scott Kennedy*

Products

Pantographs for light rail vehicles, emus and locomotives for 750 V DC and 3,000 V DC and 25 kV AC power supply systems, master controllers, traction control equipment.

Hitachi Ltd

Transportation Systems Division
18-13, Soto-Kanda 1-chome, Chiyudo-ku, Tokyo, 101-8608, Japan
Tel: (+81 3) 258 11 11   Fax: (+81 3) 45 64 62 52
Web: www.hitachi-rail.com

Key personnel

Chief Operating Officer of Transportation Systems: *Toshihide Uchimura*

Products

Propulsion systems, auxiliary power supply, and since the first manufacture of the IGBT inverter in 1991, Hitachi has delivered more than 1,500 IGBT traction systems.

In view of the increasing use of asynchronous motor propulsion systems, Hitachi has been developing VVVF inverters for trainsets with low noise levels, greater compactness and higher efficiency. Direct digital control provides accuracy in constant speed control, slip-skid correction control and start control on up-gradients. The signalling systems is protected from noise and electromagnetic interference by extensive shielding and optimised wiring layout.

Contracts

In December 2006 Hitachi was awarded a contract by RailCorporation, New South Wales (Australia) as part of the Reliance Rail consortium to deliver VVVF propulsion system for 626 rail vehicles.

Hyundai Heavy Industries Co Ltd

Hyundai Building Main 15F, 140-2, Gye-dong, Jongno-gu, 110793 Seoul, South Korea
Tel: (+82 2) 746 75 31   Fax: (+82 2) 746 76 48
e-mail: railway@hhi.co.kr
Web: www.hyundai-elec.co.kr

Key personnel

Contact: *Myoung-yong Shim*

Products

Traction and control: diesel traction motors and generators. Electric: traction motors, power converters and auxiliary converters. Emu traction motors, VVVF inverters, SIV and TCMS. Control: train information management systems, AC traction motors. Static inverters, train control management systems and traction transformers. Electrification: substations, GIS, transformers, switch gears, rectifiers. Power supply and distribution, SCADA.

Hyundai Rotem Company

Headquarters
231, Yangjae-dong, Seocho-gu, Seoul, 137-938, Republic of Korea
Tel: (+82 2) 34 64 11 14   Fax: (+82 2) 34 64 75 86
Web: www.hyundai-rotem.co.kr

Key personnel

Executive Vice-Chairman and Chief Executive Officer: *Yeo-Sung Lee*
President and Chief Executive Officer: *Yong-Hoon Lee*
Senior Executive Vice-President and Chief Operating Officer: *Sang-Kil Lee*
Vice-President: *Jae-Hong Kim (R&D centre)*

Works

Changwon Plant,
85 Daewon-dong, Changwon, Gyeongsangnam-do 641-808, Korea
Tel: (+82 55) 273 13 41
Fax: (+82 55) 273 17 41; (+82 55) 273 17 41
Uiwang Central Research and Development Center
#462-18, Sam-Dong, Uiwang-city, Kyunggi-do, Korea
Tel: (+82 31) 460 11 14   Fax: (+82 31) 460 17 81

Background

Established in 1964 when Daewoo Heavy Industry started manufacturing rolling stock, followed by Hyundai Precision & Industry and Hanjin Heavy Industry a few years later. In 1999, the three companies were consolidated into KOROS by the Korean Government. Hyundai Motor Group acquired the share of Daewoo Heavy Industry in October 2001 and KOROS became Rotem Company in January 2002. As of November 2007, Rotem Company changed its company name and CI to Hyundai Rotem Company. An affiliate of Hyundai Motor Group, Hyundai Rotem Company has its headquarters in Seoul and two facilities, the central research & development centre in Uiwang and the manufacturing plant in Changwon. The Changwon plant has the capability to manufacture 1,000 emus per year and also has the capability to manufacture electrical equipment such as traction motors, SIV inverters etc. Certifications such as the ISO 9001:2000/KS A 9001:2001 for quality, ISO 14001:2004 / KS A 14001:2004 for environment and OHSAS 18001:1999 for occupational health and safety management have been acquired at all three sites.

Products

Hyundai Rotem supplies fully integrated propulsion system packages, traction equipment, auxiliary power supply systems, support services for modern railway and urban transport vehicles. It manufactures electrical equipment for emus, electric locomotives and light rail vehicles, including PWM converter control, VVVF inverter control, chopper control equipment using power semiconductor device such as IGBT, IPM and GTO technology, AC and DC traction motors, main transformer and auxiliary power supply, train control and monitoring systems and onboard signalling systems. Recently Hyundai Rotem has developed integrated propulsion system packages, traction equipment and train control systems for the Korean high-speed trains.

Contracts

GTO VVVF inverter AC drive systems have been supplied for Seoul metro line 7 and 8 and also more than 200 sets of chopper control system for Seoul metro line 3 and 4. Recently the VVVF inverter system using IGBT or IPM devices have been supplied to local authorities such as Daegu, Busan, Seoul metro and Airport Railroad Co Ltd (AREX).

Hyundai Rotem has been manufacturing various traction motors for electric locomotives and cars as well as high-speed trains. Hyundai Rotem supplied more than 7,800 sets of AC/DC traction motors for Korea Railroad Corporation (KORAIL), and local authorities such as Gwangju, Daegu, Busan, Daejeon, Seoul metro, AREX etc.

Hyundai Rotem supplied more than 2,300 sets of static inverters using IGBT, GTO and power transistors for the lines of Seoul metro authorities, KORAILand overseas railway authorities in Taiwan, Philippines and Greece.

Recent orders include 180 kVA IGBT static inverters for Attiko Metro II in Greece and 190 kVA IGBT static inverters for AREX.

Hyundai Rotem supplied more than 830 sets of train control and monitoring system (TCMS) or train monitoring system (TMS) to several domestic and overseas authorities. Currently Hyundai Rotem is designing more than 670 of these sets for Seoul metro line 9, Incheon metro, Brazil Salvador emus, Iran dmus, Ireland dmus, Turkey emus and Korean high-speed trains (KTX-II).

Končar – Electric Vehicles Inc

Velimira Škorpika 7, HR-10090 Zagreb, Croatia
Tel: (+385 1) 349 69 59
Fax: (+385 1) 349 69 60
e-mail: uprava@knovar-kev.hr, info@koncar-kev.hr
Web: www.koncar-kev.hr

Key personnel
President: *Ivan Bahun*
Director of Development and Sales:
  Jusuf Crnalić
Head of Marketing and Sales: *Tomica Kolman*

Background
Founded in 1970 and a member of Koncar Group, Koncar – Electric Vehicles Inc designs, manufactures, repairs, rebuilds and refurbishes electric rail vehicles and vehicle equipment.

Products
Light rail vehicles; parts, components and systems for electric traction.

Contracts
In June 2008 a contract was signed by Končar and the Railways of the Federation of Bosnia and Herzegovina to manufacture and deliver a prototype of a low floor electric multiple unit to serve Bosnia and Herzegovina's regional rail. The project is due for completion within 12 months, and will be financed by long term loans funded by Croatian banks.

Lekov as

Jirotova 375, CZ-336 01 Blovice, Czech Republic
Tel: (+420 379) 20 71 11; 20 71 62
Fax: (+420 379) 20 72 01; 20 72 02
e-mail: lekov@lekov.cz
Web: www.lekov.cz

Key personnel
Chief Executive Officer: *Michal Ovsjannikov*
Accounting Manager: *Alena Zoubková*
Sales Manager: *Jan Ovsjannikov*
Technical Manager: *Tomáš Lorenc*
Production Manager: *Stanislav Zoubek*
Quality Manager: *Lucie Skrivanová*

Background
Faively Transport purchased a 75 per cent shareholding in Lekov in December 2002.

Products
Components for trolleybuses, trams, metros and railways. These include high-speed circuit breakers, electromagnetic and electropneumatic contactors, master controllers, protection relays, reversers, disconnecting switches, earthing switches, pantographs, resistors and magnetic valves, trolleybus current collectors, lock systems.

Contracts
Contracts include delivery of electrical equipment to Škoda for Prague trams, Cagliari, Warsaw and Prague metro. Supply of: electrical units to Czech Railways; switches to GE Rail (US); electrical devices to the cities of Ostrava, Pilsen, Liberec, Brno, Bratislava; electrical devices for Fret and diesel Fret locomotives for ALSTOM Transport, (France); supply of sets of reversers for locomotives ÖBB 1116 manufactured by Siemens AG, (Germany); trolleybus current collectors for Vilnius, Ostrava ; electrical equipment for AGC, Bombardier (France); switches for Mitsubishi, (Japan); electrical equipment for the new Pendolino, ALSTOM Ferroviaria, (Italy); spare parts for Russian Railways; pantographs for trams for Sankt-Petersburg, (Russia); trolleybus current collectors for Venezuela; controllers for London Underground, for Bombardier (UK).

Mitsubishi Electric Corporation

Global headquarters
Tokyo Building, 2-7-3, Marunouchi, Chiyoda-ku, Tokyo 100-8310, Japan
Tel: (+81 3) 32 18 21 11
Web: www.mitsubishielectric.com

Key personnel
President and Chief Executive Officer: *Setsuhiro Shimomura*
Executive Vice-President: *Fumitada Shimana*
Senior Vice-President: *Yukihiro Sato*

Products
Electric propulsion equipment (traction motors, VVVF inverters, chopper controllers, main transformers, rectifiers, drive gears, flexible couplings), brake systems, auxiliary electrical equipment (static inverters). Air conditioning systems, train control equipment (ATC, ATO, ATS). Integral control systems, communication systems, substation systems (DC and AC) and equipment, station depot and inspection equipment, magnetic and super conduction magnets.

Morio Denki Co Ltd

34-1 Tateishi 4-chome, Katsushika-ku, Tokyo 124-0012, Japan
Tel: (+81 3) 36 91 31 81
Fax: (+81 3) 36 92 13 33
Web: www.morio.co.jp

Main works
2 Natooka, Ryugasaki City, Ibaragi Pref 301-0845, Japan

Key personnel
Chairman: *S Yamagata*
President: *K Miura*
Senior Managing Director: *T Yagishita*

Subsidiaries
Shanghai Morio Denki Co, Ltd (China)

Products
Control equipment, including master controllers, switch boxes, distribution boards, junction boxes and conductor switches. Digital speedometers.

Riga Electric Machine Building Works

31 Ganibu dambis, LV-1005 Riga, Latvia
Tel: (+371 7) 38 13 50   Fax: (+371 7) 733 41 33

Products
Electric control sets for 3 kV DC and 25 kV AC trainsets; electrical control sets for passenger vehicle lighting and power supply; 100 to 280 kW DC traction motors for 3 kV DC emus; repair and refurbishment of DC motors; low voltage DC motors up to 20 kW for forklifts.

Saminco Inc

10030 Amberwood Road, Fort Myers, Florida 33913, USA
Tel: (+1 941) 561 15 61
Fax: (+1 941) 561 15 02
e-mail: saminco@samincoinc.com
Web: www.samincoinc.com

Key personnel
Chief Executive Officer: *Bonne W Posma*

Background
Saminco is a privately owned company specialising in the design and manufacturing of high power AC and DC motor control products.

Products
Electric traction drive systems for high-power AC and DC applications. These include traction inverters and converters for drive systems in diesel-electric and fuel cell vehicles.

Contracts
Saminco has worked closely with Ballard, a Vancouver-based company developing fuel cell technology, in the development of drive systems buses, including the XCELLSiS P5 model. The company has also supplied its A300 electric drive system for 23 vintage-style streetcars built for New Orleans Regional Transit Authority's Canal Street Line.

Schunk Bahntechnik GmbH

Aupoint 23, A-5101 Bergheim bei Salzburg, Austria
Tel: (+43 662) 45 92 00   Fax: (+43 662) 459 20 01

e-mail: office@schunk-group.at
Web: www.schunk-group.com

Key personnel
Director: *F Rabacher*

Products
Electric traction equipment, pantographs for locomotives, high-speed trains, LRVs and trams, earthing contacts and ground switches.

Schunk Kohlenstofftechnik GmbH

Rodheimer Strasse 59, D-35452 Heuchelheim, Germany
Tel: (+49 641) 60 80   Fax: (+49 641) 608 17 48
e-mail: infobox@schunk-group.com
Web: www.schunk-group.com

Key personnel
Marketing Coordinator: *Wencke Seewald*

Products
Carbon sliding strips for main line and urban rail vehicle pantographs, third and fourth rail current collector shoes, trolleybus and trolley pole systems, carbon brushes, brush holders, pantographs (high-speed and urban rail vehicles), earthing contacts, contactor sets, cam gear switchers, third rail pantographs, foil connectors.

Sécheron SA

Rue Pré-Bouvier 25 – Zimeysa, CH-1217 Meyrin, Geneva, Switzerland
Tel: (+41 22) 739 41 11   Fax: (+41 22) 739 48 11
e-mail: info@secheron.com
Web: www.secheron.com

Key personnel
Chief Executive Officer and PBU Substations Director: *Martin Balters*
Marketing: *Roch-Henri de Peretti*

Subsidiaries
Sécheron Tchéquie sro, Prague, Czech Republic

Background
Sécheron SA is a member of Sécheron Hasler AG Group.

Products
Switching and protection devices: DC High-Speed Circuit Breakers HSCB; AC and DC power and auxiliary contactors, AC vacuum circuit-breakers, disconnectors, roof swtiches, changeover switches, earthing switches master controllers, wheel flange lubricators.

Sécheron MACS earth switch and LA   1323672

Sécheron roofswitch   1323673

Siemens AG

Mobility
Trains
Duisburger Strasse 145, D-47820 Krefeld, Germany
Tel: (+49 2151) 450-0
Fax: (+49 2151) 450-12 14
e-mail: trains@siemens.com
Web: www.siemens.com/mobility

Corporate headquarters
Siemens AG
Industry Sector – Mobility
PO Box 3240, D-91050 Erlangen, Germany
Tel: (+49 9131) 7-0
e-mail: contact.mobility@siemens.com
Web: www.siemens.com/mobility

Key personnel
Mobility
Division Chief Executive Officer:
  Dr Hans-Jörg Grundmann
Head of Business Administration:
  Michael Schulz-Drost

Products
Major products include: traction power supply systems and equipment and auxiliary power supply systems for diesel and electric locomotives and passenger rail vehicles of all types; microprocessor controllers; equipment cabinets; test and diagnostic equipment.

Contracts
Recent or current contracts include:
India: In May 2005 Siemens received a notification of award of a contract from the Mumbai Railway Vikas Corporation (MRVc) for propulsion system and electrical equipment for emu rolling stock to be built at the Integral Coach Factory, Chennai. The emus will be in operation on both of Mumbai's suburban arterial networks, the Central and Western Railway.

In January 2004 Siemens was awarded a contract by the Indian Railway Board to supply complete electrical equipment for 70 three-car dual-voltage (1.5 kV DC/25 kV AC 50 Hz) emus to be used on Central Railway and Western Railway services in the greater Mumbai area. The scope of supply covers pantographs, transformers, traction converters and auxiliary power converters, traction motors, train control equipment and passenger information systems, all to be produced locally. Mechanical assembly of the vehicles will be undertaken by Integral Coach Factory (ICF) in Chennai.

Spain: In June 2002 Siemens received an order from Spanish National Railways (RENFE) for electrical equipment for 40 Civia regional emus, comprising 31 five-car and nine three-car trains. The contract includes the supply of the first 3 kV DC IGBT converter to be supplied to the rail market. Deliveries of the trains, to be built in Spain by CAF, are scheduled to take place between 2004 and 2009. Siemens also supplied electrical equipment for the first 14 Civia emus, the first of which entered service in 2003.

Ukraine: In February 2000 Siemens announced a contract to supply three-phase AC traction and control equipment for a prototype Class DS 3 4.8 MW electric locomotive to be built by GP NPK Electrovozostroeniya for the Ukrainian national railway company (Ukrzaliznizija). Following successful testing of this prototype, equipment was ordered in April 2004 for 100 additional machines to be supplied between 2004 and 2009.

Škoda Electric sro

Tylova 1/57, Plzeň, CZ-316 00, Plzeň, Czech Republic
Tel: (+420 378) 181 11 46   Fax: (+420 378) 18 13 68
e-mail: electric@skoda.cz
Web: www.skoda.cz/electric

Key personnel

General Director and Company Executive: *Jaromir Silhanek*
Development Director and Company Executive: *Dr Ladislav Sobotka*
Director of BU Traction Motors: *Martin Sobotka*
Director of BU Trolleybuses: *Karel Majer*
Finance Director: *Petr Šunk*

Background

Škoda Electric sro is a subsidiary of Škoda Holding as and is an important European manufacturer of traction vehicles. Škoda Electric sro is organised into three business units covering traction motors, traction control systems and trolleybus propulsion systems with customers in Europe, North America and Asia.

Products

The production range for the traction motors business units includes: AC and DC traction motors to power electric locomotives, public transport vehicles (trolleybuses, tramcars, electrocars), mining trucks, other traction vehicles, auxiliary motors (fans, compressors); DC traction motors up to 1,000 kW, AC traction motors up to 1,600 kW and class of insulation B, F, H, 200; major overhauls of traction motors, manufacture of spare parts for electric motors, reconstruction and modernisation of old motors and electrical components of linear motors for operation under high temperatures.

The production range for the traction control systems unit includes: complete electric equipment for public transportation vehicles including trolleybuses, streetcars, metro coaches, emus, electric and diesel-electric locomotives and similar vehicles. Main AC and DC propulsion converters for 600 V and 750 V trolley line; main AC propulsion converters for railway applications (3,000 V DC, 25 kV 50 Hz); propulsion control units (HW and SW); superior vehicle control systems; EPU NiCd batteries and EPU battery chargers; on-board diagnostics; field-portable diagnostic software and equipment; bench test units and back shop diagnostics with training and on-site support.

The production range for the trolleybus propulsion systems unit includes: complete trolleybuses; installation of electrical equipment into car body; complete traction electric equipment deliveries; spare parts for trolleybuses; trolleybus service and maintenance.

Contracts

Škoda Electric sro has provided AC traction motors for trolleybuses in Bologna, Parma, Milan, Modena, Cagliari, Lecce, Verona and Genua (Italy); trolleybuses in Bern, Biel, Fribourg, Lucerne and Geneva (Switzerland); trolleybuses in Minsk (Belarus) Riga (Latvia); metro in Kiev (Ukraine); tram cars and metro in Kazan (Russian Federation); trolleybuses in Budapest and Szeged (Hungary); trolleybuses in Lyon and metro in Paris (France); trolleybuses in Salzburg, Linz and Graz (Austria); trolleybuses in Bergen (Norway); trolleybuses in Bucharest (Romania); trolleybuses in Athens (Greece); low-floor trams, low-floor trolleybus in Plzeň and metro in Prague, three-system locomotives and trolleybuses in Plzn, Zlin, Jihlava, Marianske Lazne, Bratislava, České Budějovice, and trams in Prague (Czech Republic); low-floor trams in Kassel, Schwerin, Cologne, Bonn, Solingen, Esslingen (Germany); low-floor trams (Taiwan); low-floor trams for Krakow and trams for Wroclav (Poland); trolleybuses for Vancouver (Canada); mining truck and tramcars for Changchun (China); metro for Monterrey (Mexico); mining truck for Portland, Tacoma and metro cars for New York (blower motors); streetcars for Philadelphia and trolleybus for Boston (US).

Škoda has provided traction and auxiliary drives for trolleybuses, tramcars, metro cars, emus, streetcars and locomotives in the Czech Republic; streetcars in Italy, trolleybuses and tramcars in the US and metro cars in the Ukraine and the Russian Federation.

To date Škoda has delivered over 13,000 trolleybuses to 27 countries.

Stemmann-Technik GmbH

Quendorfer Strasse 34, D-48465 Schüttorf, Germany
Tel: (+49 5923) 810
Fax: (+49 5923) 811 00
e-mail: info@stemmann.de
Web: www.stemmann.de

Background

Stemmann-Technik is a member of the Fandstand Electric Group.

Key personnel

Director (Roof-Mounted Pantographs): *Werner Ütrecht*
Director (Ground Contacts/Third-Rail Pantographs): *Thomas Wilmes*
Director (Service Centre Railway Technology): *Timo van den Hooven*

Products

Standard pantographs for light rail vehicles, underground tramways and suburban transit systems per German DIN specification 43,187, and modified versions to suit customer requirements; heavy-duty pantographs for trunk railroads for all catenary voltages (up to 25 kV) in conventional (diamond) and contemporary single-arm style; pantographs for industrial locomotives, custom-designed to suit any catenary arrangement. Frost earthing contacts for railway vehicles. Third rail shoegear for metro vehicles. Stinger system overhead conduction rail current collection for depot installations.

Third rail current collection equipment; Stinger roof-mounted conductor rail systems for installation in depots and workshops.

Contracts

DSA 380 pantographs for Talgo 350 high-speed trainsets for the line linking Madrid, Barcelona and the French border; DSA pantographs for the French AGV prototype high-speed trainset; Fb 215 third rail shoegear and AB 433A ground contacts for Series M1 Prague metro trainsets; Stinger roof-mounted catenary for Athens metro depot.

Stesalit Limited

71 Park Street, North Block, 7th Floor Calcutta 700 016, India
e-mail: office@stesalitltd.com
Web: www.stesalitltd.com

Background

Stesalit Limited has alliances with ABB and Spring AG, Switzerland; TELEMA SpA, Italy; Jacques Galland, France.

The company is ISO 9001:2000 accredited, with in excess of 60,000 square feet of manufacturing facilities.

Products

Developing and manufacturing high-end electronic and engineering products for locomotives, coaches, emus, rail signalling and industry, to global quality standards. Products include: transformers, contactors, reactors, motors and alternator regulators.

Toyo Denki Seizo KK

Toyo Electric Manufacturing Co Ltd
No.1 Nurihiko Building, 9-2 Kyobashi 2-chome, Chuo-ku, Tokyo 104-0031, Japan
Tel: (+81 3) 35 35 06 41   Fax: (+81 3) 35 35 06 50

Key personnel

President: *Teruyuki Osawa*
Vice President: *Keisuke Tanaka*
Managing Director: *Kenzo Terashima*

Works

Yokohama: 3-8 Fukuura 3-chome, Kanazawa-ku, Yokohama 236, Japan

Products

Electrical equipment for electric multiple-units, electric and diesel-electric locomotives, light rail vehicles, rubber-tyred vehicles and maglev systems. Propulsion equipment, including AC traction motors, drive gear units, VVVF inverter control systems, master controllers, high-speed circuit breakers, unit switches and monitoring systems and microprocessor-controlled electronic devices. Auxiliary power supply equipment, including static inverters and converters and brushless motor-alternators. Current collection devices, door actuators, train information control systems and speedometers.

Traktionssysteme Austria GmbH

Brown Boveri Strasse 1, A-2351 Wiener Neudorf, Austria
Tel: (+43 2236) 81 18-203
Fax: (+43 2236) 81 18-237
e-mail: office@traktionssysteme.at
Web: www.traktionssysteme.at

Key personnel

Executive Directors: *Dr Günter Eichhübl, Mag Robert Tencl*

Background

Formery ABB Antriebssysteme GmbH, in 2002 the company acquired a majority shareholding in Elin EBG Motoeren GmbH.

Products

Liquid-cooled and air-cooled AC traction motors in a power range from 45 to 1,600 kW. Synchronised and asynchronous traction generators with a power of approximately 400 kVA up to approximately 4,000 kVA.

TransTech of SC Inc

709 Augusta Arbor Way, Piedmont, South
Carolina 29673, US
Tel: (+1 864) 299 38 70
Fax: (+1 864) 277 71 00
Web: www.transtech-sc.com

Key personnel
Vice President: *Ian Paradis*

Commercial Director: *Brad Porter*
Technical Director: *Douglas Robertson*

Background
TransTech of SC has been part of the Fandstan
Group since 1995.

Products
Traction motor components, brush holders,
connectors, control components; licensee for

Stemmann (Germany) and Brecknell Willis (UK)
pantographs and components; slip springs,
festoon systems, electrical distributors;
Ringsdorff carbon collector shoes. Pantograph
refurbishment; current collectors, ground brush
assemblies, conductor rail. Composite stainless
steel/aluminium conductor rail. Industrial crane
collection systems.

Uzina de Masini Electrice Bucuresti SA (UMEB-SA)

6A, Timisoara Blvd, 061328, Bucharest, District 6,
Romania
Tel: (+40 21) 440 25 20 (main number)
Fax: (+40 21) 440 02 99

e-mail: office@umeb.ro
Web: www.umeb.ro

Key personnel
General Manager: *Giurgiu Constantin*
Marketing Manager: *Constantinoiu Nicolae*
Head of Sales Department: *Doru Horghidan*
Deputy General Manager: *Mihai Popescu*

Products
Trolleybus, tramway and metro electrical
equipment – motors and auxiliary equipment.

Vossloh Kiepe GmbH

Kiepe-Platz 1, D-40599 Düsseldorf, Germany
PO Box 16 02 51, D-40555 Düsseldorf, Germany
Tel: (+49 211) 749 7-0
Fax: (+49 211) 749 7-3 00
e-mail: info@vkd.vossloh.com
Web: www.vossloh-kiepe.com

Subsidiaries
Vossloh Kiepe Ges mbH, Vienna, Austria
Vossloh Kiepe Srl, Italy
Vossloh Kiepe Corporation, Ottawa, Canada

Key personnel
General Managers: *Thomas Weber, Volker Schenk*
Key Account Manager, Marketing Director and
Public Relations: *Martin Schmitz*

Background
In Europe Vossloh Kiepe GmbH is one of the
leading manufacturers of electrical equipment
for hybrid buses, trolleybuses, light rail vehicles,
tramways, subways, commuter trains and their
modernisations.
Kiepe was established in 1906 as a family
business. It has been a subsidiary of the
following companies: ACEC (1972), ALSTOM
(1998), AEG Rail Systems (1993) and Schaltbau
Group (1996). In 2002 it became a member of the
Vossloh Group.

Products
Complete electrical equipment for trolley, hybrid
and mega-e-buses, light rail vehicles, tramways,
subways rated DC 600/750/1,500 V and commuter
trains.

Range
Includes latest technology in three-phase IGBT
AC (direct pulse inverter) and DC chopper
power electronics controlled by microprocessor
technology, with regenerative braking, built-
in diagnosis interface, and roll-back inhibitors.
Some recent modernisation orders even
involved historic contactor banks or rotating
pedal controllers.

Contracts
The latest contract was from Manchester
for a further 32 low-floor trams fitted with
electrical equipment. Together with Bombardier
Transportation, Vossloh Kiepe forms a consortium
for the supply of these triple-section, low-floor
trams.
Electrical equipment for 55 low-floor
trolleybuses with Kiepe double-axle-drive for
Lausanne and Neuchâtel, 33 for Zurich, 188 low-
floor and 40 articulated low-floor trolleybuses for
Vancouver, the modernisation of 18 PCC tramcars
with Kiepe IGBT direct pulse inverter traction
equipment for Philadelphia, USA, and of 28
articulated low-floor units for Philadelphia; also
three-phase inverter drives, databus and on-board

diagnostic systems. The same equipment was
delivered for 15 high-floor LRVs for Bonn. 69 sets
of equipment for a new low-floor LRV will be
delivered for Cologne up to 2007.
Recent contracts also include sets of equipment
for a further 20 low-floor trams for Bremen, 15
for Düsseldorf, 28 for Schwerin, 50 for Kraków in
Poland, 18 for Graz in Austria and prototypes for
Taiwan and Istanbul.
28 dual-voltage LRVs (tram-trains) are being
supplied for Saarbrücken; these can operate
on 750 V DC in the city and on 15 kV interurban
lines.
Kiepe supplies components and subassemblies
for most metro and LRV systems in Germany, and
undertakes installation and wiring of electrical
equipment in manufacturers' works.
Supply of 30 sets of electric traction equipment
for the first low-floor 24 m double-articulated
trolleybuses with a passenger capacity of 200
and the first 24 m double-articulated Hybridbus.
Recently and currently supplying three-phase
equipment for electric trolleybuses in: Arnhem,
Avelino, Bologna, Genoa, Lecce, Parma, Milan and
Modena, Italy; Bern, Biel, Montreux, Lausanne,
Lucerne and Fribourg, Zurich, Lucerne, St Gallen,
Switzerland; Lyon, France; Innsbruck, Salzburg
and Linz, Austria; Quito, Ecuador; Athens,
Greece; Budapest, Hungary; Minsk, Belarus; Riga,
Latvia; Merida, Venezuela; Vancouver, Canada;
Philadelphia, US; Solingen, Eberswalde and
Esslingen, Germany; and Bergen in Norway.

RAIL AND BUS COMPONENTS AND SUBASSEMBLIES

Company listing by country

AUSTRALIA
Fischer Industries Pty Ltd
iQR
SIGMA Coachair Group

AUSTRIA
Knorr-Bremse GmbH

BELGIUM
Cockerill Forges & Ringmill SA
Consolis
WABCO

BRAZIL
MWL Brasil Rodas & Eixos Ltda

CANADA
International Nameplate Supplies Ltd
Mobile Climate Control Industries Inc
Vapor Bus International

CZECH REPUBLIC
Bonatrans Group AS
ČKD Kutná Hora AS
Pars Komponenty sro
Thermo King Corporation
UniControls AS

DENMARK
Anpartsselskabet BG Teknik Århus
Dansk Dekor-Laminat A/S
egetæpper A/S
Ferro International A/S
Fiberline Composites A/S
Gabriel A/S
Glova GmbH
San Electro Heat A/S
Semvac A/S

FINLAND
EC-Engineering Oy
EKE-Electronics Ltd
Lumikko Oy
Oy Tamware AB
Polarteknik PMC Oy AB
Teknoware Oy

FRANCE
ADES Technologies
Auteroche Industrie
Brot Technologies SA
Compin Group
Ederena Concept
Faiveley Transport
Fels SA
Ferraz Shawmut
Gerflor SA
Jarret SAS
Le Réservoir SA
Martec
Métal Déployé Resistor
MS Relais
Neu Systèmes Ferroviaires
SAFT

GERMANY
Bochumer Verein Verkehrstechnik GmbH
Bremskerl Reibbelagwerke Emerling & Co KG
Captron Electronic GmbH
Carrier Sütrak Zweigniederlassung der Carrier
   Deutschland GmbH & Co KG Cleff
ContiTech Luftfedersysteme GmbH
Deuta-Werke GmbH
DKS Dienstleistungsgesellschaft für
   Kommunikationsanlagen des Stadt- und
   Regionalverkehrs mbH
EVAC GmbH
Freudenberg Schwab GmbH
Gardner Denver Wittig GmbH

Gebrüder Bode GmbH & Co KG
GEZE GmbH
Grammer AG
Gummi-Metall-Technik GmbH (GMT)
Gutehoffnungshütte Radsatz GmbH
Hanning & Kahl GmbH & Co KG
Hekatron Vertriebs GmbH
Hübner GmbH
IBG Monforts GmbH & Co KG
INIT Innovative Informatikanwendungen in
   Transport-, Verkehrs- und Leitsystemen
   GmbH
Knorr-Bremse AG
Konvekta AG
Mayser GmbH & Co KG
Pintsch Bamag Antriebs-und Verkehrstechnik
   GmbH
REBS Zentralschmiertechnik GmbH
Robert Wagner
SBF Spezialleuchten Wurzen GmbH
Schaeffler KG
Trevira GmbH
Vogelsitze GmbH
Voith Turbo GmbH & Co KG
Voith Turbo Scharfenberg GmbH & Co KG
Webasto AG
Weidmüller
Weserland Sitzsysteme GmbH
ZF Friedrichshafen AG

INDIA
Escorts Ltd
Greysham and Co
Stesalit Limited
Westinghouse Saxby Farmer Ltd

ISRAEL
Paltechnica

ITALY
Ameli SpA
Autoclima SpA
Bertone Glass
Corifer
Ellamp Interiors SpA
Eurotech SpA
Ferrero Turbo Service SpA (FTS SpA)
FIREMA Trasporti SpA
FISA Srl
Frensistemi Srl
ISAF Bus Components Srl
Isoclima SpA
Klimat-Fer SpA
Lucchini Sidermeccanica
Metalnastri srl
Microelettrica Scientifica SpA
MSA Mediterr Shock-Absorbers SpA
Poli Costruzione Materiali Trazione SpA
Rail Interiors SpA
RICA
Roberto Nuti SpA
Ruspa Officine SpA
Sess Klein SpA

JAPAN
Alna Yusoki-Yohin Co Ltd
Fuji Electric Systems Co Ltd
Morio Denki Co Ltd
Nabtesco Corporation
Narita Manufacturing Ltd
Sumitomo Metal Industries Ltd
Toshiba Corporation
Yutaka Manufacturing Co Ltd

MACEDONIA, FORMER YUGOSLAV REPUBLIC OF
MZT HEPOS AD

NETHERLANDS
Avery Dennison
Etrometa BV
Koni BV
Mors Smitt
Pallas BV

NORWAY
Norsk Hydro ASA
Ring Mekanikk AS

POLAND
Astromal Sp zoo

PORTUGAL
EFACEC Sistemas de Electrónica, SA

SOUTH AFRICA
Pretoria Transit Interiors, Inc
Widney Transport Components (Pty) Ltd

SPAIN
Albatros Corporation
CMC
Diaz
FAINSA – Fabricación Asientos Vehículos
   Industriales SA
Hispacold
Merak Sistemas Integrados de Climatización SA
SEPSA
Técnicas Modulares e Industriales SA
   (Temoinsa)

SWEDEN
Dellner Couplers AB
Pascal International AB
SKF AB
UWE Verken AB

SWITZERLAND
Alcan Composite Structures
EAO AG
Mäder Lacke AG
PIXY AG
Power-One AG
RailTronic AG
Rex Articoli Tecnici SA (REX)
Schlegel AG
Selectron Systems AG
Seratec Verkehrstechnik
Seratec Verkehrstechnik

TURKEY
Silindir ve MotorElemanlari san ve Tic, AS
   (SILSAN)
SILSAN

UKRAINE
Nizhnedneprovsky

UNITED KINGDOM
Airscrew Ltd
Albright International
Altro Limited
Bonar Floors Ltd
Bowmonk Limited
Clayton
Compak Ramps Ltd
Craig and Derricott Ltd
Deans Systems Ltd
Denco Lubrication Ltd
Dewhurst plc
Disc-Lock Europe Ltd
Dynex Semiconductor
Eberspacher (UK) Ltd
Eminox Ltd
European Friction Industries
Federal-Mogul (FERODO) Ltd
Ferranti Technologies Ltd

Company listing by country–*continued*

UNITED KINGDOM–*continued*

Ferro
Fuchs Lubricants (UK) plc
GAI-Tronics
GKN Aerospace Transparency Systems Kings Norton
Halo Rail
Hepworth Rail International
Hodgson and Hodgson Group Ltd
Holdsworth Fabrics Ltd
Icon Polymer Ltd
Icore International Ltd
Invertec Ltd
John Holdsworth & Co Ltd
Kay-Metzeler Ltd
Kleeneze Sealtech Ltd
Knorr-Bremse Rail Systems (UK) Limited
Leigh's Paints
LPA Niphan Systems
Marl International Ltd
Multipart Universal
NMB – Minebea UK Ltd
Oleo International Ltd
People Seating Ltd
Percy Lane Products
Petards Joyce-Loebl Ltd
Pickersgill-Kaye Ltd

Polymer Engineering Ltd
Portaramp
Powernetics International Ltd
Powertron Converters Ltd
Railko Ltd
Rohm and Haas (UK) Ltd
Sabre Rail Services Ltd
Slingsby Advanced Composites Ltd
Supersine Duramark Limited
TBA Textiles Ltd
Technical Resin Bonders
Tiflex Ltd
Time 24 Ltd
Timken Rail Services
TMD Friction UK Ltd
Translec Limited
Trelleborg Industrial AVS
Trelleborg Woodville Rail
Twiflex Ltd
Tyco Electronics UK Ltd
Vapor Stone UK

UNITED STATES
American Seating Company
BODE Corporation

Carrier Transicold
Cattco USA, Inc
Deutsch Relays Inc
Eaton Corporation
Electric Fan Engineering Inc (EFE)
Firestone Industrial Products Company, LLC
Freedman Seating Company
H O Bostrom Co Inc
Integrian, Inc
ITT Veam, LLC
J T Nelson Company LLC
Lift-U
Microphor
Post Glover Resistors Inc
Q'Straint International
Ricon
Rosco, Inc
Safety Vision
Simclar Corporation
Specialty Bulb Co Inc
Sportworks Northwest, Inc
Transmatic Inc
Twin Disc Incorporated
Ultimate Transportation Equipment
Vapor Bus International

ADES Technologies

13 rue Edouard Martel, ZI de la Chauvetière, F-42100 St Etienne, France
Tel: (+33 4) 77 59 59 37   Fax: (+33 4) 77 80 95 64
e-mail: business@ades-technologies.com
Web: www.ades-technologies.com

Key personnel
Managing Director: *Jean-Louis Modrin*
Commercial Director: *Jean-Michel Pagnerre*

Products
Design, manufacture and maintenance of hydraulic and pneumatic systems, including: Auxim cock and isolating valves for compressed air applications; Raflex fittings for metal tubing to SNCF STM 820 A Norm and UIC 803 35 OR standards; and Auxim internal safety devices for tank wagons. The company's Someplan department provides its Systemier concept for the design and assembly of modules and panels from preformed tubes or manifold blocks.

Contracts
ADES Technologies is supplying ALSTOM, Bombardier, Siemens and SNCF.

Airscrew Ltd

111 Windmill Road, Sunbury-on-Thames TW16 7EF, UK
Tel: (+44 1932) 76 58 22   Fax: (+44 1932) 76 10 98
e-mail: mail@airscrew.co.uk
Web: www.airscrew.co.uk

Key personnel
Sales Manager, Rail Products: *Peter Heapy*
Marketing Director: *Bryan Hiscock*

Associate company
Aircontrol Technologies Limited

Products
Cooling fans and systems for locomotives, dmus and emus. Applications include transformer cooling units, converter cooling modules, traction motor blowers and brake compressor cooling fans.
Heating and ventilation units for rail vehicle cabs and saloons.

Contracts
Contracts include supply of traction motor blowers for UK Class 92 locomotives, Eurostar common block cooling, networker brake resistor cooling and equipment cask cooling for West Coast Main Line, UK.

Albatros Corporation

C/ Ruiz de Alarcón, 13, 3°, E-28014 Madrid, Spain
Tel: (+34 91) 532 41 81   Fax: (+34 91) 522 76 97
e-mail: albatros@albatros-sl.es
Web: www.albatros-sl.es

Works
Sistemas Electrónicos de potencia, SA
Polígono Ind 'La Estación', C/Albatros 7 & 9, E-28320 Pinto, Madrid, Spain
Tel: (+34 91) 495 70 00
CMC
Pl Can Roca, C/Mar del Japón, parc 13, Santa Perpètua de la Mogoda, E-08130, Barcelona, Spain
Tel: (+34 93) 544 66 66   Fax: (+34 93) 544 82 19
Commercial offices:
Albatros UK; Albatros US; Albatros Brazil

Key personnel
President and Chief Executive Officer: *Nicolás Fúster*
Marketing Director: *Alejandro Fúster*
Commercial Director: *Enrique Galavis*

Background
Albatros is formed by various units of engineers and manufacturers in Spain and other countries. It has a team of over 900 employees with over 22,000 static converters, 20,000 passenger information systems and a variety of designs for the exterior and interior of trains, metros and tramways worldwide.

Products
Albatros Corporation is specialised in the design, manufacture, commercialisation and maintenance of equipment for the railway industry. Products include: power electronics – static converters and battery chargers; onboard security – black box and auxiliary control system; comfort – video entertainment, information passenger system and WC and interior design; communications – wide band, GSM-GPRS, route manager; protection – video surveillance system; brake systems – electric, pneumatic, hydraulic and electromagnetic; locomotive simulators, test bend, automatic coupling, open and closing of doors, vacuum toilets.

Albright International

125 Red Lion Road, Tolworth, Surbiton KT6 7QS, UK
Tel: (+44 20) 83 90 53 57
Fax: (+44 20) 83 90 19 27
e-mail: sales@albright.co.uk,
   technical@albright.co.uk
Web: www.albright.co.uk

Also at
Evingar Trading Estate, Whitchurch RG28 7BB
Tel: (+44 125) 689 30 60

Key personnel
Joint Managing Directors: *N Bedggood, A Catt*
Sales, Home and Export: *R Pickworth*
Quality Assurance & Technical Manager:
   P Digance

Products
DC solenoid switches, contactors and battery disconnecting switches. Albright contactors are used to switch the following equipment: cab and corridor lighting, windscreen demister, auxiliary compressor, pantograph heater, saloon half lighting, toilet trace heating, battery isolation.
The contactors are manufactured in five basic ranges, extending from 80 A to 600 A continuous rating and are available in normally open, normally closed and changeover configurations.
Magnetic blowouts can be fitted to most of the range to allow safe operation at voltages in excess of 48 V.
Operating coils can be wound to suit voltages from 6 to 240 for continuous or intermittent operation.
Emergency battery disconnect switches are made in single-pole and double-pole variants with current ratings of 100 A to 250 A. These switches are capable of rupturing full-load battery currents in an emergency.

Alcan Composite Structures

Alcan Airex AG Park, Altenrhein CH-9423 Altenrhein, Switzerland
Tel: (+41 71) 858 48 48
Fax: (+41 71) 858 48 44
e-mail: acs.info@alcan.com
Web: www.alcancompositestructures.com

Key personnel
Managing Director: *Dr Ing Nikos Ilias*
Manager Research & Developement:
   Dr Ing Dirk Wilde

Background
Alcan Composite Structures is part of Alcom Inc.

Products
Roof-, side-, floor panels and front cabins for railway vehicles and buses.

Alna Yusoki-Yohin Co Ltd

A subsidiary of the Hankyu Corp
No 665-2, Sawada, Yoro-Cho, Yoro-Gun, Gifu, 503-1241, Japan
Tel: (+81 5) 84 32 32 82
Fax: (+81 5) 32 29 34
e-mail: info@alna.co.jp
Web: www.alna.co.jp

Key personnel
President: *N Yamazawa*
Senior Director, Engineering: *T Kaihara*
Managing Director, Sales and Production: *K Torao*

Products
Window frames and doors for rail vehicles and buses.

Altro Limited

Works Road, Letchworth SG6 1NW, Hertfordshire, UK
Tel: (+44 1462) 48 04 80   Fax: (+44 1462) 48 00 10
e-mail: info@altro.co.uk
Web: www.altro.co.uk

Other offices
Australia
Australian Safety Flooring Pty Ltd, Transit Division
Tel: (+61 3) 97 64 56 66

Canada
Altro – Transit Division
Tel: (+1 800) 565 46 58

Germany
Altro GmbH, Transit Abteilung
Tel: (+49 40) 51 94 90

Sweden
Altro Nordic AB, Transit Abteilung
Tel: (+46 40) 31 22 00

UK
Altro Limited, Transit Division
Tel: (+44 1462) 48 04 80

US
Altro – Transit Division
Tel: (+1 800) 382 03 33

Key personnel
Contact: *Stephane Lévêque*

Background
Altro Limited is an independent, privately owned UK company, with subsidiaries in Australia, Canada, Denmark, Germany, Sweden and the US, and distributors in more than 50 countries throughout the world.

Products
Altro Transflor supplies a range of safety floorings, Meta and Chroma. They are durable and retain lifetime slip resistance, complying with international standards for fire resistance and toxicity. The floor material is manufactured from pure PVC and contains abrasive grains and coloured quartz aggregates. The flooring is lightweight and completely impervious, normally installed with hot welded joints.

Contracts
Flooring has been supplied to Duewag, Neoplan, Van Hool, MAN, Aabenraa, Kässbohrer, LHB, Scania, Säffle and DAB Silkeborg.

Ameli SpA

Via Guido Rossa, 10, Loc. Cascine del Riccio
I-50023 Impruneta, Firenze, Italy
Tel: (+39 055) 20 92 59   Fax: (+39 055) 23 49 11
e-mail: info@amelispa.com
Web: www.amelispa.com

Products
Bus and LRV video surveillance systems.

American Seating Company

Transportation Products Group
401 American Seating Center, Grand Rapids,
Michigan 49504, US
Tel: (+1 616) 732 64 06   Fax: (+1 616) 732 64 91
e-mail: kelly.bagnall@amseco.com
Web: www.americanseating.com

Key personnel
Vice President, Transportation Products: *Dave
McLaughlin*
National Sales Manager: *Michael Hoffman*

Products
Passenger seating for bus, metro, rapid
transit and trams; aftermarket service; parts
on all American Seating models; seating and
securement systems for special service vehicles.

Developments
Lightweight modular seating has been introduced
with interchangeable parts.
   Insight™, the newest product line, which
offers the largest personal sitting area through
increased leg-room and back height.

Anpartsselskabet BG Teknik Århus

Grenåvej 148, PO Box 2116, DK-8240 Risskov,
Denmark
Tel: (+45) 87 41 80 10   Fax: (+45) 86 17 44 44
e-mail: info@bgteknik.dk
Web: www.bgteknik.dk

Key personnel
Project Manager: *Gert Rasmussen*
Sales/Logistics Manager: *Allan Nørgaard*

Products
Vehicle front and tail light systems; LED interior
lighting systems; windscreen wiper and washer
systems; power supply systems for lighting and
wiper systems.

Astromal Sp zoo

Graniczna 7, Wilkowice, PL-64 115, Swieciechowa,
Poland
Tel: (+64 65) 529 91 91   Fax: (+48 65) 529 78 88
e-mail: info@astromal.pl
Web: www.astromal.pl

Products
Design and production of polyester-glass
laminated products for buses, coaches, trams,
rail buses, metro cars, and passenger coaches.

Auteroche Industrie

3/5 rue de la Cotonnière, ZI du Chemin Vert,
F-14000 Caen, France
Tel: (+33 2) 31 74 73 13   Fax: (+33 2) 31 74 75 98
e-mail: auteroche@auteroche.com
Web: www.auteroche.com

Subsidiaries
ABL Lights
660 Golf Club Boulevard, Mosinee, Wisconsin
45455, United States
Tel: (+1 715) 693 15 30   Fax: (+1 715) 693 15 34
e-mail: sales@abllights.com
Web: www.abllights.com

Products
Exterior lighting systems and indicators for rail
vehicles.

Autoclima SpA

Via Cavalieri di Vittorio Veneto 15, I-10020
Cambiano, Italy
Tel: (+39 011) 944 32 10   Fax: (+39 011) 944 32 60
e-mail:autoclima@autoclima.com
Web: www.autoclima.com

Key personnel
Export Sales Manager: *Luigi Lanfranco*
Special Customers Manager: *Mirella Serra*

Products
Air conditioning equipment, roof-mounted or
in-vehicle.
   Autoclima is ISO 9001-certified.

Avery Dennison

Graphics Division
Rijndijk 86, PO Box 118, NL-2394 ZG Hazerswoude,
The Netherlands
Tel: (+31 71) 342 15 00   Fax: (+31 71) 342 15 38
Web: www.averygraphics.com

Products
Anti-graffiti film for rail vehicles; glass protection
film; adhesive colour vinyl film for livery
applications and vandal and graffiti resistant.

Bertone Glass

Strada Vecchia Orbassano 94, I-10040 Volvera,
Italy
Tel: (+39 011) 990 06 11   Fax: (+39 011) 990 06 93
e-mail: info@bertoneglass.it
Web: www.bertone.it

Key personnel
Chief Executive Officer: *Peter Kaminsky*

Background
Part of the Bertone Group and previously called
Socar ICS SpA, the company name changed to
Bertone Glass in 2004.

Products
Glazing, including laminated windscreens.

Bochumer Verein Verkehrstechnik GmbH

PO Box 101466, D-44714 Bochum, Germany
Tel: (+49 234) 689 10   Fax: (+49 234) 689 15 80
e-mail: info@bochumer-verein.de
Web: www.bochumer-verein.de

Key personnel
Head of Sales and Marketing: *Andreas Dal
Canton*
Head of Design and Calculation: *Dipl Ing Franz
Murawa*
Head of Quality Management: *Dipl Ing Michael
Ditzler*

Products
Rolling stock components, wheels/wheelsets
and axles. The production programme also
includes rubber cushioned wheels for urban
traffic, low-floor axles with independent wheels
for low-floor cars, stress balanced wheels with
noise absorbers for high-speed trains and other
passenger cars.

BODE Corporation

PO Box 4399 Spartanburg, SC 29305, US
Tel: (+1 864) 578 96 83   Fax: (+1 864) 578 88 02
e-mail: bodecorp@aol.com
Web: www.bodecorpusa.com

Key personnel
Chief Executive Officer: *Alexander Bode*
Project Manager: *Kevin Belue*

Products
Door systems for buses.

Bonar Floors Ltd

High Holborn Road, Ripley DE5 3NT, UK
Tel: (+44 1773) 74 41 21   Fax: (+44 1773) 74 41 42
e-mail: customerservice@bonarfloors.com
Web: www.bonarfloors.com

Key personnel
Sales and Marketing Director: *Mark Warner*
Divisional Managing Director: *Mark Sefton*

Products
Floorcoverings for rail vehicles, including Flotex
Transport, which is fully waterproof and has been
designed to trap dust mites and other allergens.

Bonatrans Group AS

Revolucni 1234 , CZ-735 94 Bohumín, Czech
Republic
Tel: (+420) 597 08 23 04   Fax: (+420) 597 08 28 05
e-mail: info@bonatrans.cz
Web: www.bonatrans.cz

Key personnel
Managing Director: *Pavel Lazar*
Commercial Director: *Jakub Weimann*
Marketing Director: *Vilem Balcarek*
Purchasing Director: *Jaroslav Sedlák*
Technical Director: *Radim Zima*
Production Director: *Jan Kusněř*
Financial Director: *Vaclav Paprok*
Logistics Director: *Marek Pieklo*

Background
In December 2006, Bonatrans AS merged with
Bonatrans Group AS, with the transfer of all
merged business activity to Bonatrans Group AS.

Products
Manufacture and delivery of wheelsets, solid
wheels, resilient wheels, axles, tyres and wheel
centres for passenger coaches, high-speed
trains, light rail and city vehicles, metro cars,
locomotives, and freight wagons.

H O Bostrom Co Inc

818 Progress Avenue, Waukesha, Wisconsin
53186, US
Tel: (+1 262) 542 02 22
Fax: (+1 262) 542 37 84
e-mail: sales@hobostrom.com
Web: www.hobostrom.com

Key personnel
Presidents: *John Bostrom, Kurt Bostrom*
Sales and Marketing: *Paul Bostrom*

Products
Driver seating systems

Bowmonk Limited

Diamond Road, St Faith's Industrial Estate, Norwich, Norfolk NR6 6AW, UK
Tel: (+44 1603) 48 51 53   Fax: (+44 1603) 41 81 50
e-mail: info@bowmonk.com
Web: www.bowmonk.com

Key personnel
General Manager: *Y Hatcher*
Managing Director: *Roy J Street*

Products
Portable mechanical and electronic vehicle brake testers and calibration.
   The Water Eliminator, produced by an associate company, absorbs water in fuel including petrol.
   Also, the Bowmonk VI, a portable electronic brake and acceleration tester.

Bremskerl Reibbelagwerke Emerling & Co KG

Production Plant and Headquarters
Brakenhof 7, D-31629 Estorf-Leeseringen, Germany
Tel: (+49 5025) 97 80   Fax: (+49 5025) 97 81 10
e-mail:info@bremskerl.de
Web: www.bremskerl.de

Key personnel
Managing Director: *Herr Gramatke*
Sales Director: *Herr Wolf*
Technical Director: *Herr Hering*

UK office
Bremskerl (UK) Ltd, Unit 2, Stable Yard, Windsor Bridge Road, Bath BA2 3AY, UK
Tel: (+44 1225) 44 28 95   Fax: (+44 1225) 44 28 96
e-mail: online@bremskerl.uk.com
General Manager: *Chris Prior*

North American office
PO Box 965, Arlington Heights, Chicago, Illinois 60006-0965, USA

Products
Asbestos-free organic and sintered metal disc brake pads and wheel tread brake blocks.

Contracts
Customers include: DB, SNCF, FS, ÖBB, SJ, VR, RATP, SBB and MTA Los Angeles.

Brot Technologies SA

4 rue de la Fauvette, F-95100 Argenteuil, France
Tel: (+33 1) 34 10 79 76   Fax: (+33 1) 34 10 79 79
e-mail: inforail@brot.fr
Web: www.brot.fr

Products
Windscreen wiper systems for rail vehicles. A recent addition to the product range is the Brot 4, an electro-pneumatic model which features electronic control.

Captron Electronic GmbH

Bodenseestrasse 129, D-81243 Munich, Germany
Tel: (+49 89) 889 69 50   Fax: (+49 89) 88 96 95 55

e-mail: info@captron.de
Web: www.captron.de

Key personnel
General Manager: *Reinhard Bellm, Petra Bellm*
Assistant to General Management: *Stefan Becker*
Purchasing: *Jörg Klein*

Products
CHT series wall- and glass-mounted pushbutton sensors for buses and rail vehicles; HWT series wall- and pole-mounted pushbutton stop request sensors; associated connector systems.

Carrier Sütrak Zweigniederlassung der Carrier Deutschland GmbH & Co KG

Heinkelstrasse 5, D-71272 Renningen, Germany
Tel: (+49 7159) 92 30
Fax: (+49 7159) 92 31 08
e-mail: info.suetrak@carrier.utc.com
Web: www.suetrak.com
   www.carrier.com

Key personnel
Marketing and Distribution: *Renzo Roli*

UK office
Carrier Sütrak UK
24-25 Saddleback Road, Westgate Industrial Estate, Northampton NN5 5HL
Tel: (+44 1604) 58 14 68   Fax: (+44 1604) 75 81 32
Sales Director: Peter Adams
e-mail: info.suetrak@carrier.utc.com

Background
Carrier Sütrak, a business unit of the Carrier Corporation, is a subcompany of the United Technologies Corporation. Sister companies are Otis Elevators, Pratt & Whitney Aircraft Engines, Sikorsky Helicopters and Hamilton Sundstrand Aerospace Systems.

Products
Carrier Sütrak designs, manufactures, sells and services over 50 different brands of residential, commercial and transport air conditioning, as well as commercial and transport refrigeration.

Carrier Transicold

Carrier Refrigeration Operations (Division of Carrier Corporation)
PO Box 4805, Carrier Parkway, Building TR20, Syracuse, New York 13221, US
Tel: (+1 315) 432 64 34   Fax: (+1 315) 432 72 18
e-mail: carrier.transicoldcarrier.utc.com
Web: www.carrier.transicold.com

Key personnel
President: *Mark Cywilko*
Vice-President: *David Roth*

Regional Sales Offices
North America:
Carrier Transicold-Transport A/C
50 Grumbacher Road, York, Pennsylvania 17402, US
Tel: (+1 717) 767 65 31   Fax: (+1 717) 764 04 01

Latin America:
Carrier Transicold-Mexico
Ejercito Nacional 418 Piso 4, Col. Chapultepec Morales, Mexico DF 11570
Tel: (+52 5) 591 26 03 00   Fax: (+52 5) 591 26 03 73

Europe/Middle East/Africa:
Carrier-Sütrak, Heinkelstrasse 5, D-71272 Renningen, Germany
Tel: (+49 7159) 92 31 00
Fax: (+49 7159) 92 31 08

Asia Pacific:
Carrier Transicold-APO
12 Gul Road, Singapore 629343
Tel: (+65) 68 62 00 98
Fax (+65) 68 62 32 86

Business units
Transport Air Conditioning Group
Transport Refrigeration and Air Conditioning

Products
Air conditioning and heating systems for rail and bus applications, roof-mounted, rear-mounted or in-vehicle; air conditioners for small vehicles; components including compressors, evaporators and heater coils, open drive and semi-hermetic compressors; and replacement components.

Cattco USA, Inc

7167 Route 353, Cattaraugus, New York 14719-9537, US
Tel: (+1 716) 373 62 04
Fax: (+1 716) 373 64 72
e-mail: wayne.johnston@cattcousa.com
Web: www.cattcousa.com

Background
Cattco USA, Inc was previously called TODCO Inc.
   In October 2007, Cattco USA acquired the DecoLite brand from Alcan Baltek.

Key personnel
Sales Manager: *Wayne Johnston*
General Manager: *Bud Stange*

Products
Doors, floors, walls, windscreens, ceilings, seating and other interior modules for rail vehicles and buses. Panels are produced without seals, glazing or furniture and in primed-only condition. Recent products include the Partner door, which is capable of being operated in sliding-plug configuration.

Clayton

Hunter Terrace, Fletchworth Gate, Burnsall Road, Coventry CV5 6SP, UK
Tel: (+44 24) 76 69 19 16
Fax: (+44 24) 76 69 19 69
e-mail: admin@claytoncc.co.uk

Products
Design, development and manufacture of demisting, air conditioning, heating, ventilator and convector systems; climate control systems for road and rail vehicles, service and maintenance of air conditioning.

Contracts
Major body builders are supplied in UK and other countries including North America and Hong Kong. UK agents for Hispacold.

Developments
Saloon air conditioning for buses with extensive service and maintenance contracts offered.

Cleff

Carl Wilhelm Cleff GmbH & Co KG
Postfach 260180, D-42243 Wuppertal, Germany
Tel: (+49 202) 64 79 90
Fax: (+49 202) 647 99 88
e-mail: scott@cleff-wpt.de
Web: www.cleff.biz

Key personnel
Contact: *Peter Scott*

Products

Ventilation and lighting systems for buses and coaches; windows for rail vehicles; interior doors; interior fittings.

CMC

Pol. Ind Can Roca, C/. Mar del Japon, n° 3, E-08130 Sta Perpetua de Mogoda, Barcelona, Spain
Tel: (+34 93) 544 66 66   Fax: (+34 93) 544 82 19
e-mail: cmc@cmc.albatros-sl.es

Key personnel

General Manager: *Antonio Lillo*
Sales Manager: *Miguel Aliseda*

Background

CMC is a member of the Albatros Group.

Products

Concept, design, fabrication and maintenance service of complete interiors, in particular, fully equipped toilet systems, for new and refurbished passenger rolling stock.

Cockerill Forges & Ringmill SA

PO Box 65, B-4100 Seraing 1, Belgium
Tel: (+32 4) 330 35 35   Fax: (+32 4) 337 79 02
e-mail: cfr@cfr.be

Works

Main Cockerill Site, Seraing, Belgium

Key personnel

Chief Executive Officer: *Marc Theunissen*
Marketing and Sales: *Raymond Rauw*

Products

Steel tyres for all types of railway, light rail, tramway and metro rolling stock.

Compak Ramps Ltd

VIP Trading Estate, Anchor & Hope Lane, Charlton, London SE7 7RY, UK
Tel: (+44 20) 88 58 37 81   Fax: (+44 20) 88 58 56 63
e-mail: admin@vipgroupltd.co.uk

Compak Ramps powered low-floor bus ramp
1180200

Compak Ramps manual low-floor bus ramp
1180201

Key personnel

Managing Director: *Lee Allen*
Operations Manager: *Gerald Laing*
Director of International Sales and Marketing: *Tony Rodwell*

Background

Compak Ramps Ltd is one of three manufacturing companies comprising the VIP Group of Companies, located on one of two five-acre industrial estates owned by the VIP Group of Companies in south east London.

Products/Services

Design, manufacture and in some instances installation of powered and manual access ramps for low-floor buses. It is a dominant supplier of products to the UK market and also includes several European bus builders in its customer portfolio.

Contracts

Contracts have recently been secured with customers in Singapore, South Africa and Australia. China is currently being investigated.

Compin Group

Head office

1, rue du Guesclin, ZI de Netreville, PO Box 1804, F-27018 Evreux, France
Tel: (+33 2) 32 33 92 21   Fax: (+33 2) 32 33 92 29
e-mail: commercial@compin.com
Web: www.compin.com

Key personnel

President: *Marc Granger*
Sales Manager: *Frédéric Danton*
Engineering Director: *Claude Martin*
Industrial Director: *Dominique Ummenhover*
Financial Director: *Esteban Fisher*

Background

In 2006 Compin took over Sofanor and Defi 22, to create Compin Group.

Products

Seating systems and accessories for urban, suburban, regional and high-speed trains. Maintenance, refurbishment and spare parts for seat ranges of public transport operators.

Contracts

Customers for seat design and manufacture include
Intercity: TGV 3G, TGV (Duplex, Korea), Eurostar, Thalys, TRD (Corail Teoz), Pendolino (Portugal), ICR (Holland), BSP (China), IC (Ireland). Refurbishments for SRO (Saudi Arabia), ÖBB IC (Austria), EW3 BLS (Switzerland), ICM (Netherlands).
Regional: TER 2N NG, AGC, CRD ÖBB, 2N ÖBB/Siemens, Connex and Govia vehicles (UK), Autorail Corse. Refurbishments for Z2N SNCF, Ansaldo Breda ONCF.
Refurbishments for SRO (Saudi Arabia), ÖBB IC (Austria), EW3 BLS (Switzerland), ICM (Netherlands).
Commuter: Eole refurbishment for Transilien and Z6400, Connex 8 and 9 (UK), Desiro UK (Siemens) and MS 61 (RATP).
Urban: MP89, Brussels Metro, Lisbon Metro, Lausanne Metro, Montpellier Tramway, Porto Metro.
Refurbishments for MF 77 (RATP), train-tram Avanto (Siemens), London Underground SSL, MP05 (ALSTOM). Buses for Irisbus, Evobus, Scania, Van Hool and Volvo.

Sofanor

Head office
94, Rue Valériani, F-59920 Quiévrechain, France
Tel: (+33 3) 27 22 76 00   Fax: (+33 3) 27 22 76 22

Products

Design and manufacture of interior systems and fitting for new vehicles and refurbishment

projects. These include: ceiling modules; air-conditioning ducting; luggage racks; lighting fittings; gangway doors; fire-break partitions; seats; vandal-resistant upholstery; and electrical cubicles.

Défi 22

Aytré, (near La Rochelle), France.

Products

Design and manufacture of modules made of composite materials for railway vehicles, particularly train cabins, front ends and driving panels.

Consolis

Head Office

IT Tower, Avenue Louise 480 BE-1050 Brussels Belgium
Tel: (+32 2) 290 36 00   Fax: (+32 2) 290 36 10
e-mail: info@consolis.com
Web: www.consolis.com

Key personnel

Chief Executive Officer and President: *Philippe Milliet*

Background

Consolis was formed through the merger of Consolis Oy Ab and French Bonna Sabla in November 2005. Consolis major shareholders are Industri Kapital and ABN Amro Capital (70 per cent) together with management (30 per cent).

In August 2006, Consolis sold Elematic Oy Ab to a private equity fund managed by Sentica Partners Oy, alongside Finnish Industry Investment Ltd, Etera Mutual Pension Insurance Company and the management of Elematic Group; Consolis will retain a minority stake in the business.

Products

Consolis produces a wide range of prefabricated concrete products including railway sleepers, with over 100 factories, operating in Finland, France, Great Britain, Spain, Sweden, Norway, the Netherlands, Germany, Latvia, Estonia, the Czech Republic, Poland, Lithuania, Russia, Tunisia, Morocco, Indonesia, Belgium, Switzerland and Portugal.

Corifer

Via Borgo Pieve 146, I-30133 Castelfranco Veneto (TV), Italy
Tel: (+39 0423) 42 05 36   Fax: (+39 0423) 72 96 29
e-mail: corifer@corifer.it
Web: www.corifer.it

Commercial office

Commercial office Via della Fortezza 6, I-50129 Florence, Italy
Tel: (+39 055) 49 97 36   Fax: (+39 055) 44 63 26 59
e-mail: marketing@corifer.it
Web: www.corifer.it

Consortium members

FERVET SpA
Via Borgo Pieve 146, I-31033 Castelfranco Veneto (TV), Italy
Tel: (+39 0423) 42 72   Fax: (+39 0423) 72 01 04
e-mail: segreteria@fervetspa.it

Magliola Antonio & Figli SpA Piazza I° Maggio 1, I-13048 Santhia' (VC), Italy
Tel: (+39 0161) 93 63 11   Fax: (+39 0161) 92 22 62
e-mail: magliola@magliola.it
Web: www.magliola.it
Officine Ferroviarie Veronesi SpA
Lungadige Galtarossa 21, I-37133 Verona, Italy
Tel: (+39 045) 806 41 11
Fax: (+39 045) 806 42 22
e-mail: segreteria@ofv.it
Web: www.ofvspa.it

RSI Italia SpA
Viale IV Novembre 2, I-23845 Costamasnaga (LC), Italy
Tel: (+39 031) 86 94 11   Fax: (+39 031) 85 53 30
Via U Partini 20, I-00159 Rome, Italy
Tel: (+39 06) 43 99 21   Fax: (+39 06) 438 56 91
e-mail: info@railsi.it
Web: www.railsi.com

Background
The Corifer consortium was formed in 2002 by Fervet SpA and Magliola Antonio & Figli SpA. In 2003 Rail Service International SpA and OFV SpA also became members. The mission of the consortium involves: offering higher-quality standards of maintenance, refurbishment and construction of rolling stock and related components; coordinating procurement; study and the promotion of common projects; and the development of project designs.

Products
Passenger rail vehicles; maintenance, overhaul and refurbishment of passenger vehicles and components.

ContiTech Luftfedersysteme GmbH

Vahrenwalder Strasse 9, D-30165 Hanover, Germany
Tel: (+49 511) 938 13 04
Fax: (+49 511) 938 938 13 05
e-mail: railway_suspension_part@ls.contitech.de
Web: www.contitech.de

US office
ContiTech North America Inc
136 Summit Avenue, Montvale, New Jersey 07645
Tel: (+1 201) 930 06 00 (ext. 101)
Fax: (+1 201) 930 00 50
e-mail: rkremmeicke@contitech-usa.com
Product Manager: *Rainer Kremmeicke*

Key personnel
Customer Management, Rolling Stock: *Manfred Hunze*

Background
ContiTech Profile GmbH is a member of the ContiTech Group, part of Continental AG.

Products
Door and window sealing profiles.

Craig and Derricott Ltd

Hall Lane, Walsall Wood, Walsall WS9 9DP, UK
Tel: (+44 1543) 37 55 41   Fax: (+44 1543) 45 26 10
(+44 1543) 36 16 19 (Direct Sales)
e-mail: info@craigandderricott.com
Web: www.craigandderricott.com

Key personnel
Managing Director: *Andy Dolman*
Sales Director: *Paul Cranshaw*

Background
Established in 1944 Craig and Derricott is owned by The Victory Group of India.

Products
Design, manufacture and supply of a range of switchgear and custom-designed control panels adapted to meet the control and safety requirements of the rail industry, control desks, uncouplers, control panels, equipment cases, switches, communication panels, safety-related equipment and wiring harnesses. Specifically including: shunting control panels; customised

Craig and Derricott's passenger talk-back unit   1136294

rotary switches and isolators; rotary switches featuring high-security key locks; and mushroom-headed push-buttons used as both emergency stops and passenger alarm switches. Also supplied is a range of limit and reed switches suitable for mounting in or around all rail equipment.

Low-profile push-button and LED indicator units, master drivers key switches, passenger alarm handles, drum switches and underframe starting switches.

Contracts
Supply of uncouplers and all the communication panels within the Virgin Pendolino trains, supply of switch panels into Virgin CrossCountry. Supply of uncouplers and earthing switches into Bombardier Electrostar Vehicles, supply of passenger communications handles for Hong Kong MRTC, supply of switches for drivers cabs into Bombardier, Siemens and London Underground, supply of passenger emergency handles into London Underground.

Dansk Dekor-Laminat A/S

Grønlandsveg 197, DK-7100 Vejle, Denmark
Tel: (+45 7642) 82 82   Fax: (+45 7582) 71 21
e-mail: dd@dandekor.dk
Web: www.dandekor.dk

Background
Dansk Dekor-Laminat A/S is a member of the Elektro-Isola company group.

Products
Etronit-M high-pressure and compact laminates, DanDekor real veneer laminates and Alunit lightweight construction material for rail vehicle interiors. Applications include wall and ceiling panels, tables, partitions and door panels.

Deans Systems Ltd

PO Box 8, Borwick Drive, Beverley HU17 0HQ, UK
Tel: (+44 1482) 86 81 11   Fax: (+44 1482) 88 18 90
e-mail: aharper@deanssystems.com
Web: www.deanssystems.com

Key personnel
Managing Director: *Malcolm Phillips*

Products
Powered doors, powered and manual access ramps, handrail and handrails and handrail fittings, microprocessor controllers and diagnostics for city buses, coaches and LRVs.

Range includes inward-opening glider doors: one conventionally glazed, the other featuring flush-bonded glazing. Both doors are driven by reliable, cost-effective pneumatic actuators. The flush-bonded door is fitted with Deans' positive seal, which lifts out of the way when the door is opened. The seal is effective up to the DDA (Disability Discrimination Act, UK) limit of 5°.

Deans' range also includes 'lift and lock' actuator and door systems for coach/minibus and specialist vehicle applications.

Denco Lubrication Ltd

Ramsden Court, Ramsden Road, Rotherwas Industrial Estate, Hereford, HR2 6LR, UK
Tel: (+44 1432) 36 50 00　Fax: (+44 1432) 36 50 01
e-mail: info@delimon.co.uk
Web: www.delimon.co.uk

Key personnel
Managing Director: *Steve Hayward*

Background
Denco Lubrication Ltd is a member of Bijur Delimon International

Products
Railjet wheel flange lubrication systems for high-speed main line, metro and light line rail vehicles.

Dellner Couplers AB

Vikavägen 144, SE-791 95 Falun, Sweden
Tel: (+46 23) 76 54 00　Fax: (+46 23) 76 54 10
e-mail: info@dellner.se
Web: www.dellner.com

Key personnel
Managing Director: *C Nicolin*
Technical Director: *D Ernst*
Marketing Director: *H Gustafsson*

Background
Dellner Couplers is part of Dellner Invest AB, including other companies such as Dellner Brakes (industrial brakes) and Texotan AB (extrusion products).

Products
Supply of automatic couplers, semi-permanent couplers, side buffers, semi-trailer joints, adapters, hatches, snow gaiters and other front-end parts for rail vehicles.

Deuta-Werke GmbH

Main Works
Paffrather Strasse 140, D- 51465 Bergisch Gladbach, Germany
Tel: (+49 2202) 95 80　Fax: (+49 2202) 95 81 45
e-mail: support@deuta.de
Web: www.deuta.com

Key personnel
Manager Marketing and Sales: *Wolfgang Fabek*

Deuta-Werke's modular driver desk　1170349

Deuta-Werke's MFT 1 terminal technology　1026868

Subsidiaries
Shanghai Deuta Electronic & Electrical Equipment Co Ltd

Products
Sensors: pickups, AC generators, electronic/electric pulse generators, opto-electronic generators, radar sensors.

Indicators: electric indicators, electric meters, eddy current tachometers, panel-mounted clocks, electric and mechanical counters, modular driver's cab indicators, multi-function displays with virtual instruments, digital indicators.

Control systems and boardcomputer: electric incident records, short-distance incident recorders, digital storage cassettes, evaluation software for data recorders.

System components: central distance and speed measuring units, electronic control units, multi-function modules.

Telematics and DMI systems: Speed, Distance Unit (SDU) for train navigation and protection, tracing and tracking information systems for passenger and freight, train information systems, network databank systems for fleet management and diagnostics.

Embedded systems: Deuta-embedded PC boards and components are suitable for use over a wide temperature range (–40° to +85°C) and in environments exposed to vibration and shock. All-in-one Geode EPC – compact single board computer with low-power processor, inboard graphics and environment controller, field bus functionality and an integrated power supply. Especially suitable for use in mobile applications for process visualisation and control terminal (MMI). DSP module, highly integrated DSP module with a programmable, eight-channel, 14/16 bit ADC, including data pre-processing and CAN bus controller. For universal usage in mobile and stationary industrial measuring and control systems. Combination of the DSP module with an EPC enables inexpensive implementation of an all-in-one solution with integrated MMI interfaces and industrial field bus functionality.

Driver desks: Deuta-Werke develops modular driver's desks as complete systems with latest technologies such as integrated CAN bus networks.

Deutsch Relays Inc

55 Engineers Road, Hauppauge, New York 11788, US
Tel: (+1 631) 342 17 00　Fax: (+1 631) 342 94 55
e-mail: info@deutschrelays.com
Web: www.deutschrelays.com

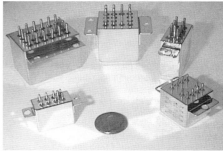

Deutsch Relays hermetically sealed relays in standard metal enclosure　0087707

Key personnel
President: *Tom Sadusky*
Account Manager, Railway Market: *Eugene Agresta*
Engineering Manager: *Keith Gaedje*
Purchasing Manager: *Warren Stricoff*

Products
Hermetically sealed relays, sockets and solid-state timers/time delay relays which are designed for reliable operation under severe environmental conditions. Relays, sockets and timers are available in a variety of terminations and mounting styles for the railway industry such as PC board, panel, track and wiring harness installations. Relays are designed for long life switching of low to medium current levels in 1, 2, 3, 4 and 6 pole form C and form Z configurations. All relays can be included with internal voltage suppression directly on the coil of the relay. Deutsch's design also features a single pivoting armature switching whereby all movable pole weld resistant contacts switch together and 'non-overlapping', 'back-check' or 'force-guided' principles can be capitalised on. Environment characteristics for the critical safety relays include a wide temperature range: –40°C to +125°C, vibration (any axis): 20 g 2,000 Hz and shock (any axis): 200 g 6MS. Applications include logic interface in automatic and manual train control systems, sensor and actuator interface, lighting, braking and other control and sensing systems.

New developments
Deutsch Relays has released a new micro contactor called the MCT 110. The MCT 110 series is a 1 cu in contactor that switches 10 amps resistive at 110 V DC for 100,000 cycles. Applications include emergency braking systems.

Deutsch Relays also offers DEST, a hermetically sealed voltage sensor. The DEST is able to detect voltage spikes according to specified voltage

Deutsch Relays railway sockets   0120204

Deutsch Relays railway sockets   1048812

thresholds. Applications include connecting the DEST up to a battery to avoid power loss.

Contracts

Contracts include relays, sockets and timers, designed for: MTA LIRR M-7 emu project – Bombardier Transportation; Minneapolis LRV project – Bombardier Transportation; Port Authority New York/New Jersey JFK Airport LRV 'AirTrain' – Bombardier Transportation; Amtrak Northeast Corridor (Acela) project – Bombardier/ALSTOM; Dallas Area Rapid Transit (DART) project – Kinki Sharyo; VTA LRV project – Kinki Sharyo; NJT Hudson Bergen LRV – Kinki Sharyo; Washington DC Metro (WMATA) project – ALSTOM.

Dewhurst plc

Inverness Road, Hounslow TW3 3LT, UK
Tel: (+44 20) 86 07 73 16   Fax: (+44 20) 86 07 73 09
e-mail: mleach@dewhurt.co.uk
Web: www.dewhurst.co.uk

Key personnel

Managing Director: *David Dewhurst*
Rail Sales Office: *Mike Leach*

Subsidiaries

Australian Lift Components, Australia
Dewhurst, Hungary
Dupar Controls, Canada
The Fixture Company, US
LiftMaterial, Australia
LiftStore, UK
Switching Components, UK
Traffic Management Products, UK

Products

Push-button controls and indicators to meet the requirements of retrofit and new rolling stock vehicles. Standard ranges of vandal-resistant push-buttons, keypads and push-button control panels for internal and external passenger doors, vestibule doors, emergency call panels, drivers' cab controls, guard stations and crew access.

Platform TR and RA signal boxes and signalling control panels.

Contracts

Contracts include LED bodyside status indicators on the new generation of Adtranz passenger vehicles.

Other contracts include passenger door push-buttons for Heathrow Express and Stockholm LRVs. Driver's cab controls for MTRC Lantau Airport extension, Hong Kong. Upgrade to LED illumination of passenger controls on the Mk IV intercity fleet and status indicators on London

Underground's Hammersmith, Bakerloo, Metropolitan, Central and Circle Lines. Connex header panels with illumination.

Diaz

Industrias E Diaz SA
Ctra. Castellón Km, 6,2 I-50720 La Cartuja Baja, Spain
Tel: (+34 976) 45 40 07   Fax: (+34 976) 45 40 13
Web: www.industias-diaz.com

Key personnel

Managing Director: *Emilio Diaz Gascón*
Associate Managing Director: *Emilio José Diaz Escanero*
Technical Supervisor: *Igor Gómez Ortiz*
Quality Supervisor: *Antonio Sarrablo*
Managing Administration: *Jesús Aragón*
Managing Export: *Ma Eugenia Díaz Escanero y Rosendo Roman*

Products

Window systems for rail vehicles and buses.

Contracts

Rail market customers include: ALSTOM Transport, Bombardier Transportation, CAF, RENFE, Siemens Transportation and SNCF. Bus clients include: Hispano Carrocera, Irizar, Mercedes-Benz, Merkavim and Van Hool.

Disc-Lock Europe Ltd

PO Box 134, Sittingbourne ME9 7TF, UK
Tel: (+44 1795) 84 43 32
Fax: (+44 1795) 84 39 86
e-mail: info@disc-lock.com
Web: www.disc-lock.com

Key personnel

Managing Director: *Bob Hope*
Sales Manager: *Jean Harvey*

Products

Disc-Lock Safety Wheel Nut: locking wheel nut for commercial vehicles including trucks, trailers and buses. Also in use on UK and US military vehicles. Disc-Lock Washer: heavy duty vibration proof locking washer for high stress applications. Disc-Lock Locking Nut: vibration and shock proof lock nut for use in high stress and safety critical applications.

DKS Dienstleistungsgesellschaft für Kommunikationsanlagen des Stadt- und Regionalverkehrs mbH

Robert-Perthel-Strasse 79, D-50739 Cologne, Germany
Tel: (+49 221) 954 44 20
Fax: (+49 221) 95 44 42 23
e-mail: info@dks-koeln.de
Web: www.dks-koeln.de

Key personnel

Chairman: *Rolf Bender*
Deputy Chairman: *Manfred Seibert*
Chief Executive Officer: *Christian Döring*
Chief Financial Officer: *Ralf Kochs*

Other office
Essen Branch
Kupferdreher Strasse 114, D-45257 Essen, Germany
Tel: (+49 201) 847 03 90
Fax: (+49 201) 847 03 99

Products

SIUS onboard monitoring and recording systems for rail vehicles, trams and LRVs and buses. The ruggedised systems can be equipped for video or digital recording and can be installed in both newbuild and retrofit applications. A driver's monitor can also be provided.

Dynex Semiconductor

Doddington Road, Lincoln LN6 3LF
Tel: (+44 1522) 50 05 00   Fax: (+44 1522) 50 00 20
e-mail: power_solutions@dynexsemi.com
Web: www.dynexsemi.com

Key personnel

President and Chief Executive Officer: *Dr Paul Taylor*
Chief Financial Officer: *Bob Lockwood*

Products

Power semiconductor devices: thyristors, diodes, transistors, IGBTs, gate turn-off thyristors, power modules, and air, oil, water and phase change cooling assemblies. These products may be used for onboard or track side applications.

Contracts

Contracts include Eurostar, TGV Nord, Sybic, Metro Interconnexion (RER), France; Hong Kong MTRC; London Underground Ltd's Jubilee Line, Class 325 emus for Royal Mail, Networker Class 465 in the UK; Seoul Metro, South Korea; and locomotives for Taiwan.

EAO AG

Tannwaldstrasse 88, CH-4601, Olten, Switzerland
Tel: (+41 622) 80 92 95
e-mail: info@eao.com
Web: www.eao.com

Key personnel

Contact: *Thomas Blatter*

Other offices
Austria
Tel:(+49 201) 858 70   Fax: (+49 201) 858 72 57
e-mail: sales.ede@eao.com

Belgium
Tel (+32 3) 777 82 36   Fax: (+32 3) 777 84 19
e-mail: sales.ebl@eaocom

China
Tel: (+852 27) 86 91 41
e-mail: sales.ehk@eao.com

France
Tel: (+33 1) 64 43 37 37   Fax: (+ 33 1) 64 43 37 48
e-mail: sales.ese@eao.com

Germany
Tel: (+49 201) 858 70   Fax: (+49 201) 858 72 57
e-mail: sales.ede@eao.com

Japan
Tel: (+81 3) 54 01 09 53   Fax: (+81 3) 54 01 09 68
e-mail: sales.esj@eao.com

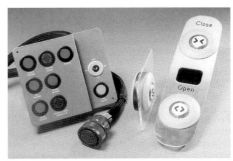

EAO's panel combination   0087708

Netherlands
Tel: (+31 78) 653 17 00   Fax: (+31 78) 653 17 99
e-mail: sales.enl@eao.com

Sweden
Tel: (+46 8) 683 86 60   Fax: (+46 8) 724 29 12
e-mail: sales.esw@eao.com

Switzerland
Tel: (+41 62) 388 95 00   Fax: (+41 62) 388 95 55
e-mail: sales.ech@eao.com

UK
Tel: (+44 1444) 23 60 00
Fax: (+44 1444) 23 66 41
e-mail: sales.euk@eao.com

USA
Tel: (+1 203) 877 45 77   Fax: (+1 203) 877 36 94
e-mail: sales.eus@eao.com

Background
EAO is a global manufacturer of high-quality human machine interface products and solutions, from switches, key pads and keyboards to complete custom built control panels.

Founded in 1947, EAO's range of target industries include: transportation; machinery; telecommunications; process control; lifting and moving and automative.

EAO has nine specialised sales and customer service centres around the world and a network of trained specialist agents and representatives in more than 50 countries. EAO is certified and managed according to international standards ISO9001:2000, ISO 14001 and VDA6.1.

Products
Driver's cab and door control switch components and customised HMI panels. Components include: push-buttons, rotary switches, emergency stop switches and crew and access switches. Passenger operated buttons include halo illuminated push buttons for door control and toilets.

Contracts
EAO supplies products to many train manufacturing companies on a global scale, including ALSTOM Transport, CAF, Firema, Hitachi, Kawasaki, Kinki Sharyo, Rotem, Siemens Transportation, Skoda, Stadler, Talgo and Vossloh. Typical examples of end user projects using EAO materials include: AGC & TER2NNG (SNCF); NINA (BLS); FLIRT (SBB); West Rail emu (KCRC); Desiro (ÖBB); Desiro (Angel Trains); X40 (SJ); IC4 (DSB); AM96 (SNCB); CL 471 (CD); BR 152 (DB); Electrostar (UK); Class 455 (UK); Class 465 (UK); Javelin CTRL (UK).

Eaton Corporation

Hydraulics Business
14615 Lone Oak Road, Eden Prairie, Minnesota 55344, US
Tel: (+1 952) 294 79 92
e-mail: lynnsoule@eaton.com
Web: www.eaton.com
Corporate Headquarters
Eaton Corporation
Eaton Center, 1111 Superior Avenue, Cleveland, Ohio 44114-2584
Tel: (+1 216) 523 50 00

Key personnel
Senior Product Manager: *Doris Showalter*

Background
Eaton Hydraulics Business is a segment of the Eaton Fluid Power Group.

Products
Design, manufacture and marketing of a comprehensive line of hydraulic systems and components for use in mobile and industrial applications.

Developments
In September 2008 Eaton introduced a new line of flexible rubber hose designed for use with biodiesel B2 to B100 in diesel engines, trucks, buses, agricultural vehicles and off-highway applications.

Eberspacher (UK) Ltd

Headlands Business Park, Salisbury Road, Ringwood BH24 3PB, UK
Tel: (+44 1425) 48 01 51   Fax: (+44 1425) 48 01 52
e-mail: enquiries@eberspacher.com
Web: www.eberspacher.com

Key personnel
General Manager: *Vince Lee*

Background
Eberspächer (UK) Ltd is a wholly owned subsidiary of J Eberspächer GmbH of Germany and was established in 1977.

Products
Air conditioning and heating systems for buses and coaches using state-of-the-art digital electronic controls to give separate manual or automatic settings in different parts of the vehicle. Toilet systems.

EC-Engineering Oy

Kangastie 2, FI-61330 Koskenkorva, Finland
Tel: (+358 6) 456 63 00   Fax: (+358 6) 456 63 01
e-mail: ec-engineering@ec-engineering.fi
Web: www.ec-engineering.fi

Key personnel
Managing Director: *Tapio Ollanketo*

German office
Infobüro EC-Engineering
Postfach 2029, D-32779 Lage, Germany
Tel: (+49 5232) 784 33   Fax: (+49 5232) 781 33
e-mail: ec-vs@t-online.de
Contact: Frhr Horst v Schleinitz

Background
EC-Engineering Oy is a member of the Finnish Transportation Expertise Network (Finten) association.

Products
Custom-designed sandwich panels and fibre-reinforced plastic components for passenger rail vehicles. Ready-to-install and complete modules for modern train interiors and exteriors, such as load-bearing wall-systems and stairs for double-deck coaches, panelling systems for windowed walls, floors, exterior roofs and front-ends for metros and trams.

Contracts
Front and rear mask for VAL metro (Siemens), interior side wall and roof panels for Rubin metro (Siemens), roof fairings for Pendolino trains (ALSTOM), exterior roof and wall panels for RegioShuttle dmu (Bombardier), floor panels for Class ET 423 emu (ALSTOM), interior wall, window and roof panels for ICS double-deck coaches (Talgo).

Ederena Concept

Avenue du Parc, F-40230 St Vincent de Tyrosse, France
Tel: (+33 5) 58 77 46 46
Fax: (+33 5) 58 77 46 45
e-mail: sales@ederena.com
Web: www.ederena.com

Products
Ederena designs and manufactures high-performance composite/mechanical sub-assemblies with sandwich bonding materials.

Applications include light flooring for passenger transport, separating walls, flooring and ceilings.

EFACEC Sistemas de Electrónica, SA

Av Eng Frederico Ulrich, PO Box 31, P-4470 Maia, Portugal
Tel: (+351 2) 941 36 66   Fax: (+351 2) 948 54 28
e-mail: se@efacec.pt
Web: www.efacec.pt

Key personnel
Chairman: *Francisco de La Fuente Sánchez*
Vice-Chairman: *Alberto Joaquim Milheiro Barbosa*
Market Relations: *Maria Elisa Oliveira*

Products
Static converters.

Contracts
Recent contracts include supply of static converters for Corail-type coaches for CP.

egetæpper A/S

Head Office
PO Box 190, Industrivej Nord 25, DK-7400 Herning, Denmark
Tel: (+45) 97 11 88 11
Fax: (+45) 97 11 95 80
e-mail: ege@ege.dk
Web: www.egecarpet.com

Products
ege range of flooring textiles for rail vehicles.

EKE-Electronics Ltd

Piispanportti 7, FIN-02240 Espoo, Finland
Tel: (+358 9) 61 30 33 08
Fax: (+358 9) 61 30 33 00
e-mail: electronics@eke.fi
Web: www.eke.com

Key personnel
Chief Executive Officer: *Pekka Kuusela*
Administration Manager: *Anna Karki*
RD Manager: *Jyrki Keurulainen*
Sales Manager: *Samuel Krueger*
Customer Support Manager: *Mika Linden*
Marketing Manager: *Hanna Ojala*

Products
EKE-Trainnet® TCN standard-based integrated train management systems. Products include a comprehensive set of modules, components and tools for complete train monitoring, diagnostics

EKE-Trainnet® event recorder   1325794

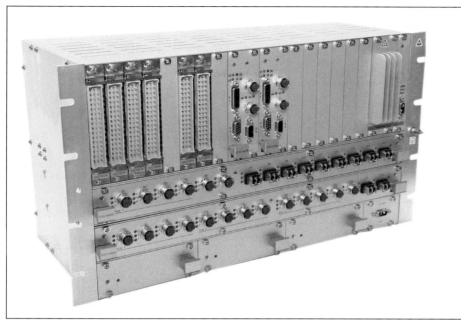

EKE-Trainet® rack   1343550

and control systems. System solutions include EKE-TMS train management systems and TCN gateways, EKE-TDR event recorders with protected memory and EKE-MMI user interface with display and keypad.

Contracts
Australia: IP-based train information system for Downer EDI Rail Pty Ltd for Sydney's suburban train project. First trains to be commissioned in 2010. Hunter Rail Car Project for United Goninan, 2004–2005.
China: Refurbishment of SS Series locomotives for Wuhan Z & Y Railway Electric Co Ltd, 2004; TCN gateway for Zhuzhou Electric Loco. Res. Institute (ZELRI, High-Speed Train project), 2002.
Finland: In 2007 EKE-Electronics provided new generation train data recorders for the new FLIRT commuter trains for Helsinki Metropolitan Area ordered by Finnish Railways.
France: AGC regional trains for Bombardier Transportation, 2002–2005.
Israel: In 2007, EKE-Electronics provided a complete control and diagnostic system for Siemens' low-floor coaches for Israel Railways. TMS, TCN gateway and remote control and user interface for Bombardier Transportation, TCN gateway and remote control and user interface for Bombardier Transportation (FAGA, Israel double-deck project) 2002–2003.
Korea: TDR Event Recorder for Korean Railroad Research Institute/Rotem (Korean G7 High-Speed Train), 2002.
Sweden: SL Stockholms local traffic commuter trains for ALSTOM Transport, 2004–2005.
UK: MML Hull Trains for Bombardier Transportation, 2002-2004; WTB Trainbus for Bombardier Transportation (Virgin CrossCountry demus, UK), 1999–2001.
US: N J Transit Diesel Locomotives for ALSTOM Transport, 2003–2004.

Electric Fan Engineering Inc (EFE)

8 Crown Plaza, Unit 105, Hazlet, New Jersey 07730, US
Tel: (+1 732) 203 03 20
Fax: (+1 732) 203 11 99
e-mail: roger@electricfanengineering.com
Web: www.electricfanengineering.com

Products
Turbine electric and hydraulic fans; heat transfer systems.

Ellamp Interiors SpA

Via Verdi 10, I-21020 Bodio Lomnago Varese, Italy
Tel: (+39 0332) 94 37 11   Fax: (+39 0332) 94 37 65
e-mail: info@elleampgroup.com
Web: www.ellampgroup.com

Background
Ellamp Interiors SpA is part of the Happich Ellamp Group (GHE) and has its headquarters in Milan, Italy.

Products
Design and manufacture of interior modules, components and fabrications for main line and urban rail vehicles, buses and coaches in aluminium alloy, composite materials, high-pressure laminate postforming and reinforced fibreglass. Products include air conditioning channels, handrails, interior panels, lighting systems and luggage racks.

Contracts
Projects undertaken recently include products for Pendolino-series tilting trainsets (ALSTOM Transport, Fiat Ferroviaria) and Talent dmus for Norway (Bombardier Transportation).

Eminox Ltd

North Warren Road, Gainsborough DN21 2TU, UK
Tel: (+44 1427) 81 00 88
Fax: (+44 1427) 81 00 61
e-mail: enquiry@eminox.com
Web: www.eminox.com

Key personnel
Key Account Manager, Non-road: *John Perry*

Products
Design and manufacture of stainless steel exhaust systems for use on diesel multiple-units and railcars, including emissions reduction technologies which significantly reduce Particulate Matter (PM), Hydrocarbons (HC) Carbon Monoxide (CO) and oxides of nitrogen (NOx).

Escorts Ltd

Railway Equipment Division
Plot No 115, Sector 24, Faridabad 121 005, India
Tel: (+91 129) 223 38 25

Fax: (+91 129) 223 21 48
e-mail: nsred@escortsred.com
Web: www.escortsgroup.com

Key personnel
Vice-President and Business Head: *Krishna Havaldar (Railway Equipment Div)*
Associate Vice President: *Naveen Sangari*
Head, Exports: *Sunil Jain*

Background
Certified to ISO 9001–2000, products conform to UIC and AAR specification with initial source of technology from companies such as Schaku and Knorr-Bremse (Germany), General and Railways Supplies and Vulcanite (Australia) and ICER (Spain).

Products
Compressed airbrake systems for freight wagons and coaches; brake accessories; slack adjusters for coaches and freight wagons; electro-pneumatic braking system for emus, dmus and metro coaches; heavy duty hydraulic shock absorbers/dampers for coaches, emus and locomotives; test equipment for brake systems and dampers; non-asbestos low and high friction composition brake blocks for coaches, wagons and locomotives; Schaku type automatic and semi-permanent centre buffer couplers; AAR 'H' type tight lock centre buffer couplers; side buffers, crash buffers and drawgear.

Etrometa BV

Kerkewal 49, NL-8401 CH, Gorredijk, Netherlands
Tel: (+31 513) 46 34 35
Fax: (+31 513) 46 31 12
e-mail: info@etrometa.nl

Products
Electronic automatic kneeling control systems for buses.

European Friction Industries

Enterprise House, 6/7 Bonville Road, Brislington, Bristol BS4 5NZ, UK
Tel: (+44 117) 971 48 37   Fax: (+44 117) 971 65 78
e-mail: rail@efiltd.co.uk
Web: www.europeanfriction.co.uk

Key personnel
Managing Director: *Andy Freeman*
Operations Manager: *Tony Prideaux*
General Sales Manager: *Alan Dickinson*
Engineering Manager: *Chris Mapperson*
IT and Marketing Manager: *James Hallett*
Research and Development: *Eddie Blackburn*

Products
Composite friction materials for braking for all types of rail vehicles, including tram, heavy freight, high-speed and mining applications; OE and replacement pads and blocks.

New developments
Asbestos-free materials including E308, organic-based material developed for applications with a maximum speed of 120 km/h, A349 developed for applications with a maximum speed of 140 km/h. It has found success on rapid transit, underground and metro systems demanding frequent braking, with high rates of retardation and high disc temperatures. E401 designed specifically for the braking of railway vehicles such as high-speed intercity passenger coaches, surburban multiple units and freight vehicles braking from speeds of 200 km/h, developed to meet the criteria specified in the UIC code 541-3. E500 developed as a tread brake block in railway braking, particularly recommended for use on main line and suburban passenger vehicles

operating to a maximum speed of 160 km/h. A501, a new friction material developed as a wheel tread brake block, designed to be interchangeable with that of cast iron.

Eurotech SpA

Via Solari, 3, I-33020 Amaro, Italy
Tel: (+39 0433) 48 54 11   Fax: (+39 0433) 48 54 99
e-mail: sales@eurotech.com
Web: www.eurotech.com

Background
With headquarters in Amaro, Italy, Eurotech also has offices in Kansas City and Salt Lake City, US; Cambridge, UK; Lyon, France; Helsinki, Finland; Caronno and Trento, Italy; Munich, Germany and Peking, China.

Key personnel
President and Chief Executive Officer: *Roberto Siagri*

Products
Video surveillance products include: the Alphabox DVR, an intelligent device for video surveillance applications specifically developed to be installed onboard rail transport networks. Also the Rugged Digital Video Recorder (DVR), a Eurotech modular platform that performs advanced video capture and compression and has the ability to acquire and store high-resolution video streams onto an integrated data storage module, and will allow the user to transmit the images through long distance wireless connections (GPRS, UMTS, WiFi 802.11.X or Bluetooth).

The Eurotech Passenger Counter features highly accurate stereoscopic cameras integrated within a robust and lightweight extruded aluminium enclosure. The device can be installed in the doorways of buses, trams and trains and can also be used over gateways, corridors or turnstiles.

EVAC GmbH

Hafenstrasse 32a, D-22880, Wedel, Germany
Tel: (+49 4103) 916 80   Fax: (+49 4103) 91 68 90
e-mail: mail@zodiac.com
Web: www.evac-train.de

Key personnel
Managing Directors: *Hans Wörmcke, Mike Rozenblatt*
Sales Director: *Nils Andersson*
Sales Managers: *Robert Gigengack*
  Jürgen Lindenlauf
  Stefan Klingler
  Dieter Stein

Background
EVAC GmbH is a member of the ZODIAC Corporation.

Products
Vacuum toilet systems and sewage handling systems.

FAINSA – Fabricación Asientos Vehículos Industriales SA

Calle Horta s/n, E-08107 Martorelles (Barcelona), Spain
Tel: (+34 93) 579 69 70   Fax: (+34 93) 570 18 38
e-mail: fainsa@fainsa.com
Web: www.fainsa.com

Key personnel
President: *Juan Singla*
Managing Director: *Rafaél Roldán*
Commercial Manager: *Francesc Puig*
Export Manager: *Marc Vidal*

Products
Passenger seating for railway vehicles, LRVs and metro cars, including beds for sleeping cars.

Recent developments include: introduction of a three-point safety belt system that features an automatic height adjustment system, allowing it to be used by children above three years old and adults.

Contracts
Recent contracts worldwide include: metro projects; light rail transit; first and second class seating; high-speed seating. FAINSA's main customers are: CAF, Talgo, ALSTOM, Renfe, Temoinsa, Feve, Siemens and Bombardier.

Faiveley Transport

Head Office, International Division
Carrefour Pleyel, 143 boulevard Anatole France, F-93285 Saint-Denis Cedex, France
Tel: (+33 1) 48 13 65 00   Fax: (+33 1) 48 13 65 75
Web: www.faiveley.com

Main works
Electromechanical Division
Les Yvaudières, 75 avenue Yves Farge, F-37705 Saint-Pierre-des-Corps, France
Tel: (+33 2) 47 32 55 55   Fax: (+33 2) 47 44 80 24

Production Centre, Electromechanics and Air-Conditioning Division
ZI, 1 rue des Grands Mortiers, F-37705 Saint-Pierre-des-Corps, France
Tel: (+33 2) 47 32 55 55   Fax: (+33 2) 47 63 19 31

Electronics Division
rue Amélia Earhart, ZI du Bois de Plante, PO Box 43, F-37700 La-Ville-aux-Dames, France
Tel: (+33 2) 47 32 55 55
Fax: (+33 2) 47 32 56 61

Background
Faivelely Transport is a leading supplier of onboard railway systems. It completed the acquisition of SAB WABCO in November 2004 and Neu Systèmes Ferroviaire in 2006.

In 2008 the Faivelely acquired 75 per cent shares in NOWE Streugeräte, a sanding systems company based in Hannover, Germany. The remaining 25 per cent will be retained by the Co-Managing Director of NOWE.

In December 2007, Faiveley Transport completed the acquisition of 50 per cent of Shi Jia Zhuang Jia Xiang Precision Machinery Co Ltd, based in the Hebei Province.

Also in December 2007, Faiveley completed the acquisition of the railway assets of the Australian company Integrian Pty Ltd, this will enable Faiveley to complement its range of existing products in the field of video surveillance, event recorders (black box), driver vigilance devices and driver aid equipment.

In August 2008 Faiveley completed the acquisition of 100 per cent of Ellcon-National equity shares, a US based railway brake specialist.

Key personnel
Chairman and Chief Executive Officer: *Robert Joyeux*
Financial Director: *Etienne Haumont*
General Manager: *Pierre Sainfort*
Communications Manager: *K Dougall*

Subsidiaries
Faiveley Transport Amiens
Faiveley Transport NSF
Faiveley Transport Ibérica SA & Transequipos
Faiveley Transport Italia SpA
Faiveley Transport Do Brasil S/A
Faiveley UK Ltd
Faiveley Transport Birkenhead
Faiveley Transport Leipzig GmbH & Co KG
Faiveley Transport Remscheid GmbH
Faiveley Transport Nordic AB
Faiveley Transport Australia Ltd
Faiveley Transport India Ltd
Faiveley Transport Korea Ltd
Shanghai Faiveley Railway Technology Co Ltd
Faiveley Far East Ltd
Faiveley Rail Inc
Lekov as
Faiveley Transport Tremošnice sro
Faiveley Transport Plzen sro
Faiveley Transport Polska Sp zoo
Faiveley Transport Iran Branch Office

Products
Air-conditioning, pantographs, intercirculation gangways, internal doors, access doors, platform screen doors, brakes, couplers, odometry/tachometry systems and event recorders, video surveillance systems, services (renovate, maintain, install, advise).

Federal-Mogul (FERODO) Ltd

Chapel-en-le-Frith, High Peak SK23 0JP, UK
Tel: (+44 1298) 81 15 98
Fax: (+44 1298) 81 15 80
e-mail: fpgrailenquiries@eu.fmo.com
Web: www.federal-mogul.com

Key personnel
Director of Operations: *T M Saxby*
Commercial Manager: *H Lavender*

Products
High-performance, cost-effective friction brake materials for all types of rail vehicles, including high-speed, passenger and light rail vehicles. Composite disc brake pad materials including Sinter Metal Pads. Low-friction 'L' and 'LL' blocks and high-friction 'K' blocks are supplied, covering a wide spectrum of braking requirements.

Fels SA

2 rue J M Jacquard, F-67400 Illkirch Graffenstaden, France
Tel: (+33 3) 88 67 10 60
Fax: (+33 3) 88 67 33 10
e-mail: fels@fels.fr
Web: www.fels.fr

Key personnel
Commercial Director: *Jean-Claude Fels*
Financial Director: *Danièle Russo*
Export Manager: *Hervé Demuth*
Purchasing Manager: *Geneviève Meoni-Berthet*

Products
Electrical contacts; special purpose-made connectors.

Ferranti Technologies Ltd

Cairo House, Waterhead, Oldham OL4 3JA, UK
Tel: (+44 161) 624 02 81
Fax: (+44 161) 624 52 44
e-mail: sales@ferranti-technologies.co.uk
Web: www.ferranti-technologies.co.uk

Key personnel
Managing Director: *T C Scuoler*
Finance Director: *F Brinksman*
Commercial Director: *K R Mills*
Operations Director: *R Gaskell*
Business Development Director: *S R Warren*

Products
Distance/Velocity Measurement Device (DVMD) utilising non-contact Doppler radar sensing and featuring integral processing electronics. Train-mounted applications include traction

Ferranti Technologies distance/velocity measurement device   0023846

control, slip/slide protection, odometry and speed measurement; track-located applications for sensing speed and length of passing rolling stock.

Design, development and production of control electronics to customer specifications; manufacture and repair of third-party electronic and electromechanical assemblies.

Range of power conversion equipment, including transformer rectifier units, inverters, power supplies and other equipment for low-power auxiliary functions.

UV laser cable marking and manufacture of cable looms; environmental testing (UKAS-approved).

Contracts

Contracts include a DVMD device selected by ALSTOM Transport Service UK for integration into the traction control package of an overseas refurbishment programme.

Production for Alstom Traction Ltd, following previous design and development contracts, of a family of key electronic subsystems for use on the Juniper generic train.

Ferraz Shawmut

1 rue Jean Novel, F-69100 Villeurbanne Cedex, France
Tel: (+33 4) 722 266 11
Fax: (+33 4) 722 267 13
Web: www.ferrazshawmut.com

Works

28 rue Saint Philippe, F-69003 Lyon, France
70 avenue de la Gare, PO Box 18, F-38290 La Verpilliere, France
rue Vaucanson, F-69720 St Bonnet de Mure, France

North American Headquarters

374 Merrimac Street, Newburyport, MA-01950, US
Tel: (+1 978) 462 66 62
Fax: (+1 978) 465 64 19

Key personnel

Marketing Manager: *M Renart*
Export Sales Manager: *H Behr*
Commercial Director: *J Brenet*

Subsidiaries

Fouilleret, Ferraz Corporation (US)
Nihon Ferraz (Japan)

Background

Ferraz Shawmut's parent company is Groupe Carbone Lorraine.

Products

Earth return current units; brush-holders for electric traction motors; current-collecting device on live rail; fuses with very high breaking capacity for protection of power semiconductors; shoe fuses; automatic earthing device with large short-circuit capability; resistors, disconnectors and switches.

Ferrero Turbo Service SpA (FTS SpA)

Corso Canale 4, I-12051 Alba (CN), Italy
Tel: (+39 0173) 36 51 11
Fax: (+39 0173) 36 22 24
e-mail: fts@fts.it
Web: www.fts.it

Other office

Cantù branch
Via Susa 15, I-22063, Cantù, Italy
Tel: (+39 031) 71 17 92
Fax: (+39 031) 709 26 84
Chairman: *Ferrero Ferdinando*
Managing Director: *Giorgio Moffa*
Head of Turbocharger Sales: *Mariangela Viglino*
Head of Thermal Sales: *Renato Currado*
Head of Cooling Sales: *Daniele Bronzetti*
Head of Export Department: *Daniela Bera*
Head of Purchasing Department: *Lorena Cauda*

Products

Repair and supply of turbochargers, steering boxes, fans, heaters, air conditioners and automatic transmissions.

Ferro

Burslem Ferro (Great Britain) Limited
Nile Street Burslem, Stoke-on-Trent, ST6 2BQ, UK
Tel: (+44 1782) 82 04 00   Fax: (+44 1782) 82 04 02
Web: www.ferro.com

Head office

Ferro Corporation
1000 Lakeside Avenue Cleveland, Ohio 44114-7000 US
Tel: (+1 216) 641 85 80

Key personnel

General Manager: *A J Pitchford*
UK Sales Manager: *M F Haines*
Export Director: *M Davies*
Transportation Market Manager: *A Phillips*

Products

Powder coatings for the rail industry for passenger vehicle interiors, station fittings and signage, cladding, trunking and switchgear assemblies.

Range includes: Bonalux AG 2000 anti-graffiti, 491 series polyesters, 4620 series epoxies, all fire resistant to BS 476 Pys 6 and 7 (Class 1) and smoke emission to BS 6853.

Ferro coatings have been supplied to London Underground Ltd's Central, Piccadilly, Northern and Jubilee lines and Hong Kong MTRC, Virgin Trains, First Great Western, Midland Mainline and specified by major rolling stock manufacturers.

Ferro International A/S

Tirsbækvej 15, DK-7120 Vejle Ø, Denmark
Tel: (+45 75) 89 56 11   Fax: (+45 75) 89 59 37
e-mail: info@ferro-int.dk
Web: www.ferro-int.dk

Key personnel

Managing Director: *Michael Sørensen*

Products

Complete powered and automated doors for trains and buses, sliding interior doors for passenger vehicles, including electric and pneumatic doors operated by push-buttons or automatically by sensors; curved electric sliding doors for toilet modules and compartments.

Contracts

Recent contracts include: interior doors and gangway doors for VR, Talgo-Transtech, Bombardier and EVAC AB, Sweden; the supply of interior sliding doors to Bombardier (M6); and curved automatic doors for EVAC.

Fiberline Composites A/S

Barmstedt Allé 5, DK-5500 Middelfart, Denmark
Tel: (+45) 70 13 77 13   Fax: (+45) 70 13 77 14
e-mail: fiberline@fiberline.com
Web: www.fiberline.com

Key personnel

Sales Manager: *Stig Krogh Pedersen*
Market Co-ordinators: *Susanne Engelbrecht Lauridsen, Juno Outzen*

Products

Lightweight corrosion-resistant GRP profiles for rail vehicles.

Contracts

Germany: Exterior panels for Talent dmus built by Bombardier Transportation for German Rail (DB AG).
Interior and exterior panels for the Citadis tram in Kassel, built by ALSTOM LHB.
Sweden: Panels for the Swedish Regina and Öresund trains produced by Bombardier Transportation AB.
US: Exterior panels for the Los Angeles tramway, produced by Ansaldobreda.

FIREMA Trasporti SpA

Headquarters

Via Provinciale Appia, Località Ponteselice, I-81100 Caserta, Italy
Tel: (+39 0823) 09 71 11   Fax: (+39 0823) 46 68 12
e-mail: info@firema.it
Web: www.firema.it

Key personnel

Chairman and Chief Executive Officer: *Gianfranco Fiore*
Commercial Manager: *Sergio d'Arminio*
Marketing Manager: *Agostino Astori*

Commercial and technical offices

Via Triboniano n 220, I-20156 Milan, Italy
Tel: (+39 02) 23 02 02 23   Fax: (+39 02) 23 02 03 00

Products

Motor and trailer bogies for high-speed trainsets and locomotives. including motor bogies for E402 locomotives and trailer and motor bogies for ETR 500 high-speed trains, all for Italian Railways.

Firestone Industrial Products Company, LLC

250 W 96th Street, Indianapolis, Indiana 46260, US
Tel: (+1 317) 818 86 00   Fax: (+1 317) 818 86 45
Web: www.firestoneindustrial.com

Corporate Headquarters

Bridgestone Americas Holding Inc
535 Marriott Drive, Nashville, TN-37214, US
Tel: (+1 615) 937 10 00
Fax: (+1 615) 937 36 21

Key personnel

President: *Mike Cerio*
Global Operations Director: *Nick Janicki*
Finance Director: *Phil Kincaid*
Marketing Director: *Arun Kumar*
Purchasing Manager: *Rob Hackman*
Technical Director: *Steve Lindsey*

Products

Airail and Airide air springs for rail and bus suspension applications. The Airail air spring is a highly engineered rubber and fabric flexible member which contains a column of compressed air. A variety of lateral as well as horizontal spring rates are available. Optional emergency springs that are contained within the air spring are also available in a variety of configurations.

Contracts

Include supply to Bombardier Transportation for NYCTA, Metro-North, TTC, SEPTA railcars and Indian Rail.

Developments

Include the use of engineered plastic components in air spring assemblies.

FISA Srl

Zona industriale Rivoli
I-33010 Osoppo, Udine, Italy
Tel: (+39 0432) 98 60 71
Fax: (+39 0432) 98 60 86
e-mail: fisa@fisaitaly.com; info@fisaitaly.com
Web: www.fisaitaly.com

Key personnel

Contact: *Clara De Simon*

Products

Passenger and driver seating for buses and rail vehicles including double-deck.

Fischer Industries Pty Ltd

13 Whiting Street, Atarmon, New South Wales 2064, Australia
Tel: (+61 2) 94 36 06 11
Fax: (+61 2) 94 38 24 35
e-mail: info@fischerind.com.au
Web: www.fischerind.com.au

Key personnel

Director: *Peter Fischer*
General Manager: *Warren Hocking*

Background

United Group Rail acquired Fischer Industries Pty Ltd in 2006.

Products

Events recorders/data loggers, vigilance systems, Train Management Systems (TMS), analogue and digital meters, door controllers, inverters/converters.

Freedman Seating Company

4545 West Augusta Blvd, Chicago, Illinois 60651, US
Tel: (+1 800) 443 45 40
Fax: (+1 773) 252 74 50
e-mail: sales@freedmanseat.com
Web: www.freedmanseating.com

Key personnel

Vice-President, Sales and Marketing: *Dan Cohen*
Director of Customer Services: *Christy Nunes*
Sales Manager: *John Mienik*

Products

Freedman Seating manufactures seats for small and mini coaches, paratransit vans and buses, public transit buses, private bus operators and the rail industry.

Frensistemi Srl

Via della Cupola, 112, I-50145 Florence, Italy
Tel (+39 055) 302 01
Fax: (+39 055) 302 03 33
e-mail: sales.frensistemi@knorr-bremse.com
Web: www.knorr-bremse.it

Background

Frensistemi is a subsidiary of Knorr-Bremse AG (see entry in *Brakes and drawgear* section).

Products

Supply, commissioning and servicing of complete toilet systems for passenger rail vehicles; onboard stand-alone and networked video surveillance systems.

Contracts

Vehicles equipped with Frensistemi toilet systems include ETR 500 high-speed trainsets and TAF emus (both Trenitalia), Class BM72 emus for NSB, Norway, and Type VB2N emus for SNCF, France.

Freudenberg Schwab GmbH

Postplatz 3, D-16761 Hennigsdorf, Germany
Tel: (+49 3302) 206 20   Fax: (+49 3302) 20 62 77
e-mail: info@freudenberg-schwab.de
Web: www.freudenberg-schwab.de

Key personnel

Chief Executive Officers: *Dr Detlef Cordts, Peter Kofmel, Henrik Egeter, Claus Möhlenkamp*
Quality Manager: *Leo S E Lang*
Marketing Director: *Bernd Werner*

Background

Freudenberg Schwab GmbH is jointly owned by Freudenberg & Co (51 per cent) and Schwab Holding AG (49 per cent). The company collaborates closely with Schwab Schwingungstechnik AG in Switzerland.

Product

Noise reduction and vibration control systems and components especially multi-layer springs, cone springs, axle type bushes, ultra bushes, spherical bearings, buffers, spring seats, elastic coupling elements, hydrobushings, active vibration absorbers.

The company has worked with: ALSTOM, Bombardier Transportation, ContiTech, Deutsche Bahn AG, A Friedr Flender AG, Phoenix AG, Scharfenbergkupplung, SAB WABCO BSI Verkehrstechnik Products, Siemens, Voith Turbo, Vossloh Schienenfahrzeugtechnik, WATTEEUW Power Transmission Co and ZF Bahntechnik.

Fuchs Lubricants (UK) plc

New Century Street, Hanley, Stoke-on-Trent ST1 5HU, UK
Tel: (+44 1782) 20 37 00
Fax: (+44 1782) 20 20 72
e-mail: contact-uk@fuchs-oil.com
Web: www.fuchslubricants.com

Key personnel

Managing Director: *R Halhead*
Executive Sales Manager: *David Atkin*
Sales Manager – Energy and Utilities: *Peter Baker*

Products

Manufacture and supply of a full range of lubricants for the railway industry including: diesel engine oils; transmission fluids; hydraulic oils, special greases for wheel-flange and switch-plate applications; biodegradable products for most applications, including engine oils, gear oils, hydraulic oils and grease. The company is also a supplier of industrial cleaning products, degreasing fluids, hygiene products and anti-freeze for engine cooling systems.

Fuji Electric Systems Co Ltd

Gate City Ohsaki, East Tower 11-2, Osaki 1-chome, Shinagawa-ku, Tokyo 141-0032, Japan
Tel: (+81 3) 54 35 70 46
Fax: (+81 3) 54 35 74 22
e-mail: info@fesys.co.jp
Web: www.fesys.co.jp

Key personnel

President and Director: *Mitsunori Shirakura*
Assistant Manager, Transportation Systems Sales
    Department: *Tomoaki Yokoyama*

Background

The Transportation Systems Sales Department of what was previously Fuji Electric Co Ltd, is part of the newly divided Fuji Electric Systems Co, Ltd.

Products

Traction motors with VVVF control; static auxiliary power supply systems; linear motor-drive door systems for rail vehicles; converter-inverter for Shinkansen.

Gabriel A/S

Hjulmagervej 55, PO Box 59, DK-9100 Aalborg, Denmark
Tel: (+45) 96 30 31 00
Fax: (+45) 98 13 25 44
e-mail: mail@gabriel.dk
Web: www.gabriel.dk

Key personnel

Managing Director: *Jørgen Kjaer Jacobsen*

Products

Textiles for rail vehicle interiors with high performance in flammability- and abrasion-resistance.

GAI-Tronics

A division of Hubbell Limited
Brunel Drive, Stretton Park, Burton-on-Trent DE13 0BZ, UK
Tel: (+44 1283) 50 05 00
Fax: (+44 1283) 50 04 00
e-mail: sales@gai-tronics.co.uk
Web: www.gai-tronics.co.uk

Key personnel

Business Unit General Manager: *Graham Lines*
Business Unit Controller: *Toby Balmer*
Engineering Manager, Applications:
    Richard Rumsby
Manufacturing Director: *Mark Bradford*
Commercial Manager: *Roger Goodall*
Marketing Manager: *Nicole Ireland*
Special Projects Manager: *Steve Smith*

Other offices

GAI-Tronics Corporation, US
Tel: (+1 610) 777 13 74   Fax: (+1 610) 775 65 40
Web: www.gai-tronics.com
GAI-Tronics Srl, Italy
Tel: (+39 02) 48 60 14 60   Fax: (+39 02) 458 56 25
GAI-Tronics Corporation, Malaysia
Tel: (+60 3) 89 45 40 35   Fax: (+60 3) 89 45 46 75
GAI-Tronics Australia (Austdac)
Tel: (+61 2) 96 34 70 55   Fax: (+61 2) 98 99 24 90

Background

Established in 1964, GAI-Tronics is a major provider of specialised telecommunications for both UK and worldwide railways, manufacturing weather- and vandal-resistant communication equipment.

Products

Onboard communications and information systems including passenger announcement system; crew communications; driver/control centre radio communications; emergency driver/passenger communications; disabled persons communications; on-train entertainment; audible warning and pre-recorded digitised special messages.

The products and systems are developed for use in hazardous or hostile areas and are vandal and weather resistant.

Gardner Denver Wittig GmbH

Roggenbachstrasse 58, D-79650 Schopfheim, Germany
Tel: (+49 7622) 39 20
Fax: (+49 7622) 39 23 00
e-mail: info.sch@de.gardnerdenver.com
Web: www.gdwittig.de

Key personnel

Marketing and Business Development:
Jonathan Marsh
Product Manager (Rail Applications):
Andrew Quirk

Other office

Gardner Denver Inc
Web: www.gardnerdenver.com

Products

Rotary vane compressors for road and rail vehicles, including LRVs, low-floor trams, metro cars and trolleybuses. Compressed air generators are used predominantly for the following vehicle systems: brakes, air suspension, door activating system, current collector, sander and flexible coupling units.

Gardner Denver Wittig rotary vane compressors can be installed either under the floor or on the roof of the vehicle. They are therefore suitable for installation in low-floor chassis/vehicles.

Range

Wittig ROL M: Suitable for trams, metro vehicles, high-speed rail vehicles, trolleybuses, emus, hybrid and fuel cell buses.

Gebrüder Bode GmbH & Co KG

Ochshäuserstrasse 14, D-34123 Kassel, Germany
Tel: (+49 561) 500 90
Fax: (+49 561) 559 56
e-mail: info@bode-kassel.com
Web: www.bode-kassel.com

Key personnel

Managing Directors: *Dr Andreas Schunke, Harald Gieren*
Sales Manager: *Harald Kilian (Division Rail), Jürgen Holz (Division Road)*

Background

Gebrüder Bode GmbH & Co kg is a wholly owned subsidiary of Schaltbau Holding AG and has subsidiaries and production sites in China, Germany, Poland and Turkey.

Products

Electric and pneumatic door systems for LRVs, regional metro trains and high-speed vehicles, outswing plug doors and inswing plug doors for city buses and travel coaches; pressure-sealed doors for high-speed trains; ramp systems; step systems; door controls.

Contracts

Contracts have included supply of door systems to Hong Kong MTRC airport link; Amtrak Northeast Corridor; ICE and ICT, Germany; Transrapid, Germany; ICN, Switzerland; Kuala Lumpur metro, Talent dmus and emus, LRVs for Amsterdam, Lisbon, Dortmund, Stuttgart, Dresden, Sheffield, Desiro trains Class 185, 350, 360, 444 and 450.

Gerflor SA

Transport Flooring Division
43 Boulevard Garibaldi, F-69170 Tarare, France
Tel: (+33 4) 74 05 40 00
Fax: (+33 4) 74 05 06 83
e-mail: gerflortransport@gerflor.com
Web: www.gerflor.com

Key personnel

Chairman and Chief Executive Officer: *Bertrand Chammas*

Products

Floor coverings for buses, coaches, trains, trams, light rail vehicles and aircraft.

Range

Vinyl floor coverings, including Tarabus, Traveller and Batiflex brands.

GEZE GmbH

PO Box 1363, D-71226 Leonberg, Germany
Tel: (+49 7152) 20 30
Fax: (+49 7152) 20 33 10
e-mail: marketing-services.de@geze.com
Web: www.geze.com

Key personnel

Management: *Brigitte Vöster-Alber (Chairman), Hermann Alber, Dirk Hallberg, Joachim Schulz*

UK subsidiary

GEZE UK Ltd
Bleinheim Way, Fradley Park, Lichfield, WS13 8SY
Tel: (+44 1543) 44 30 00
Fax: (+44 1543) 44 30 01
e-mail: info.uk@geze.com
Web: www.geze.co.uk
Sales Director: *Andy Howland*

Products

Window and door systems (single, double and telescopic); closing mechanisms, electromechanical or electropneumatic drives for single- and double-leaf doors; actuators; boarding and alighting equipment for buses trams and trains. RWA and safety technology glass systems.

GKN Aerospace Transparency Systems Kings Norton

Eckersall Road, Kings Norton, Birmingham B38 8SS, UK
Tel: (+44 121) 606 41 00   Fax: (+44 121) 606 41 91
e-mail: sales@gknaerospace.com
Web: www.gkntransparencysystems.com

Key personnel

General Manager: *R A Harper*

Background

GKN Aerospace Transparency Systems Kings Norton is a division of GKN Aerospace.

Products

Design and manufacture of heated/unheated, curved/flat, framed/unframed impact-resistant transparencies for railway and transit industries.

Glova GmbH

Elvej 3, DK-5260 Odense S, Denmark
Tel: (+45 66) 19 00 55   Fax: (+45 66) 19 02 55
e-mail: train@glova.com
Web: www.glova.com

Key personnel

Chairman: *Horst Kirchner*
General Manager, Train Toilets Division: *Lars Genild*

Background

Founded in 2002 to supply toilet systems to the bus market from its facility in Borkheide, Germany, Glova in 2004 established a train toilets division based in Odense, Denmark.

Products

Toilet systems for rail vehicles, compliant with current EU and UIC standards. The current model is the Cirrus, designed for both new-build and refurbishment projects.

Grammer AG

Köferinger Strasse 9-13, D-92245 Kümmersbruck, Germany
Tel: (+49 9621) 88 00   Fax: (+49 9621) 88 01 30
e-mail: info@grammer.com
Web: www.grammer.com

Key personnel

Chairman and Chief Executive Officer: *Heinz-J Otto*
Director, Seating Systems: *Peter Nagel*

Associate company

Lazzerini & Co Srl
Via Toscana, I-60030 Monsano (AN), Italy
Tel: (+39 0731) 602 61   Fax: (+39 0731) 604 49
e-mail: cml.lazzerini@fastnet.it

Works

Amber, Kummersbruck

Products

Suspension driver seats, passenger seats and other passenger coach equipment. Three-point seat belts, tables and interior fittings and the passenger seat range includes the Comfort reclining seat with arm rest and leather trim.

Recent developments include a new lightweight scratchproof seat called New Compact, designed to be installed in city buses and trams.

Also the new 'Linea' and 'Tourea' driver seats with active seat climate control.

Greysham and Co

7249 (1/1) Roop Nagar, Delhi 110 007, India
Tel: (+91 11) 23 84 37 46; 23 84 40 89; 23 84 53 68; 65 90 84 05
Fax: (+91 11) 23 84 08 92
e-mail: greysham@nda.vsnl.net.in
Web: www.greysham.in

Key personnel

Managing Director: *Mohan Singh*
Chief Executive Officer: *Subodh Singh*
Export Manager: *ST Ghosh*

Products

The company is ISO 9002 accredited and is a Grade A approved supplier for Indian Railways for air brake equipment.

Braking system – complete air brake systems for freight and passenger vehicles; compressed air control equipment for OHE (overhead inspection) cars, dmu (motor and trailer) cars, C3W distributor valves to SAB WABCO design; EST distributor valve; automatic load sensing device; empty/load change-over valves; bogie-mounted brake systems and brake cylinders; reservoirs and rubber hoses; slack adjusters for brake riggings for all types of rolling stock.

Vacuum brake equipment, including 'E' and 'F' type cylinders; Prestall cylinders; QSA valves; couplings; release valves; couplings and similar equipment.

Gummi-Metall-Technik GmbH (GMT)

5 Liechtersmatten, D-77815 Bühl, Germany
Tel: (+49 7223) 80 40   Fax: (+49 7223) 210 75
e-mail: info@gmt-gmbh.de
Web: www.gmt-gmbh.de

Key personnel
Manager: *S Engstler*
Sales Manager: *Robert Weber*

Sales offices
Austria
GMT Gummi-Metall-Technik Ges mbH
Teuflingen 4, A-4872 Neukirchen an der Vöckla, Austria
Tel: (+43 767) 46 49 48 44
Fax: (+43 767) 46 49 48 99
Contacts: Robert Weber, Joseph Fellinger

Belgium
GMT Belgium SA/NV
165 Chaussée de Louvain, B-5310 Eghezée
Tel: (+32 81) 81 14 40   Fax: (+32 81) 81 24 40
e-mail: info@gmt-belgium.be
Web: www.gmt-belgium.be
Contact: Jean De Corte

France
GMT France Sarl
ZI Ste Agathe, Rue Paul Langevin, BP 10049, F-57192 Florange
Tel: (+33 3) 82 59 33 90   Fax: (+33 3) 82 59 33 99
e-mail: info@gmt-france@fr
Web: www.gmt-france.fr
Contact: Didier Pouchèle

Ireland
GMT Ireland Ltd
Clifden, Co Galway
Tel: (+353 95) 213 82   Fax: (+353 95) 217 04
e-mail: gmtirl@iol.ie
Contact: Susanne Engstler

Italy
Pantecnica SpA
Via Magenta, 77/14 A, I-20017 Rho (MI)
Tel: (+39 02) 93 26 10 20
Fax: (+39 02) 93 26 10 90
e-mail: info@pantecnica.it
Contacts: Davide Fatigat, Flavia Fatigati

Malaysia
GMT Gummi-Metall-Technik (M) SDN BHD
Industrial Estate, PO Box 82, 33000 Kuala Kangsar/Perak
Tel: (+60 5) 776 17 42   Fax: (+60 5) 776 57 00
e-mail: info@gmt.com.my
Contact: Jurgen Werner Howing

Netherlands
GMT Benelux BV
Rudolf Dieselweg 14, PO 3298, NL-5928 RA Venlo
Tel: (+31 77) 387 25 56
Fax: (+31 77) 382 44 91
e-mail: info@gmt-benelux.nl
Contact: Mijnheer Jan Lagewaard

Switzerland
GMT Gumeta AG
Kautschuk-Werk, Buchrainstrasse 2, CH-6030 Ebikon
Tel: (+41 41)) 440 17 17
Fax: (+41 41) 41 50 60
Contact: Herr Hertzfeldt

UK
GMT Rubber Metal Technic Ltd
The Sidings, Station Road, Guiseley, Leeds LS20 8BX
Tel: (+44 1943) 87 06 70
Fax: (+44 1943) 87 06 31
e-mail: info@gmt.gb.com
Contact: Andrew Melville

US
GMT International Corp
PO Box 117 Villa Industrial, Villa Rica, Georgia 30180
Tel: (+1 770) 459 57 57   Fax: (+1 770) 459 09 57
e-mail: gmt@gmt-international.com
Web: www.gmt-international.com
Contact: Heiko Beutner

Products
Primary and secondary suspensions (cones, bolsters, axle springs, chevrons, side bearers, roller springs), bushes, reaction and traction rods, lateral buffers, centre pivot, all bogies applications. Floor suspensions, resilient wheels (all existing systems).

Contracts
ICE and ICE II high-speed trains, Germany; DWA (Bombardier) railbus project. Clients include ALSTOM, Bombardier (Adtranz), SNCF, SNCB, DB, Siemens.

Gutehoffnungshütte Radsatz GmbH

Postfach 110226, D-46122 Oberhausen, Germany
Tel: (+49 208) 740 0-0
Fax: (+49 208) 740 03 20
e-mail: info@ghh-valdunes.com
Web: www.ghh-radsatz.com

Key personnel
Contact: *Dieter Hoffmann*

Background
Ownership was divested by Faiveley in September 2005 following a management takeover.

Products
Driven and non-driven wheelsets for locomotives, dmus, emus, metro cars, light rail vehicles, passenger coaches and freight wagons; running gear components and systems for low-floor light rail vehicles; independent wheel axles; independent wheel units; EEF non-driven wheel pairs; solid wheels; tyred wheels; rubber-sprung wheels; wheelset axles; track wheels; sound absorbers and laser measuring technology. Wheelsets are also manufactured for special vehicles for the rail and steel industries.

Halo Rail

Stewart Signs Ltd
Trafalgar Close, Chandler's Ford Industrial Estate, Eastleigh, Hampshire SO53 4BW, UK
Tel: (+44 23) 80 24 07 77
e-mail: sales@stewartsigns.co.uk
Web: www.halographics.co.uk

Key personnel
Managing Director: *Paul McGlone*
Sales Director: *John Veasey*
Commercial Manager: *Adrien Box*

Products
Digital signs and graphics; vehicle livery production.

Contracts
Livery contracts with rail and bus operations across the UK, some examples include: the appointment by Transport for London (TfL) to fully wrap 24 of the Type CR-4000 trams in brand new corporate livery following TfL's acquisition of Tramtrack Croydon Limited in June 2008.

The recent completion by Bombardier Transportation and Halo Rail of the first new Class 378 Electrostar units for the London Overground network included longitudinal seating and hard wearing livery, designed to tackle the high passenger volumes on popular overground lines. A second batch of 23 Class 378 4-car units will be added to the fleet by 2010.

Hanning & Kahl GmbH & Co KG

Rudolf Diesel Strasse 6, D-33813 Oerlinghausen, Germany
PO Box 1342, D-33806 Oerlinghausen, Germany
Tel: (+49 5202) 70 76 00
Fax: (+49 5202) 70 76 29
e-mail: info@huk.hanning.com
Web: www.hanning-kahl.de

Key personnel
General Manager: *Wolfgang Helas*
Brake Division Manager: *Dietrich Radtke*
LRT Division Manager: *Christian Schmidt*
Service Division Manager: *Peter Spilker*
Sales Manager, Brakes: *Jürgen Stammeier*
Sales Manager, LRT: *Joachim Pütsch*
Sales Manager, Services/LRT: *Joachim Zehn*
Sales Manager, Services/Brakes: *Martin Epp*

Products
Brake Division: Electrohydraulic brake systems; spring-applied actuators, active callipers, hydraulic-power units, hydraulic emergency release units, electronic brake control systems with slide protection, track brakes, and filter and flushing units.

Service Division: Services and testing and measuring equipment for track brakes and hydraulic brake systems.

Contracts
Contracts include the supply of equipment to operators in Potsdam, Helsinki, Chemnitz, Bielefeld, Kassel, St Etienne, Bucharest and FVG Delijn.

Hekatron Vertriebs GmbH

Brühlmatten 9, D-79295 Sulzburg, Germany
Tel: (+49 7634) 50 02 64   Fax: (+49 7634) 50 03 23
e-mail: export@hekatron.de
Web: www.hekatron.com

Background
Hekatron Vetriebs GmbH is a member of the Swiss Securitas Group.

Products
Smoke switches for fire protection systems in passenger and freight rolling stock and locomotives.

Hepworth Rail International

B Hepworth & Co Ltd
2-4 Merse Road, North Moons Moat, Redditch B98 9HL, UK
e-mail: markjones@b-hepworth.com
Web: www.b-hepworth.com

Key personnel
Chief Executive Officer: *J P Eddy*
Rail Account Executive: *Mark Jones*

Subsidiary companies
Dudleys Screenwipers (address as above)
Window Wipers Technologies Inc
Hepworth Marine International
Wynn Performance Wiper Systems

Products
Windscreen wash/wipe systems for road and rail vehicles and marine applications.

Hispacold

Autovía Seville-Malaga, km 1,8, Avda. Hacienda San Antonio, 1, E-41016 Seville, Spain
Tel: (+34 954) 67 74 80   Fax: (+34 954) 99 97 28
e-mail: hispacold@hispacold.es
Web: www.hispacold.es

Key personnel
Area Manager: *Loli Miguela*

Products
Bus air-conditioning systems. Recent developments include the introduction, in conjunction with Tussam, of air curtains for buses in order to maintain interior temperatures during frequent stops. Also Ecomaster, which is a range of advanced electronic control for air-conditioning units.

Contracts
As well as having a share of approximately 60 per cent of the domestic Spanish market, Hispacold has also secured major contracts in Europe, Iran and Mexico.

Examples include the installation of 50 integrated air-conditioning systems for MTF's new double-deck bus fleet in Istanbul.

Hodgson and Hodgson Group Ltd

Crown Business Park, Old Dalby, Melton Mowbray LE14 3NQ, UK
Tel: (+44 1664) 82 18 10   Fax: (+44 1664) 82 18 20
e-mail: info@hodgsongroup.co.uk
Web: www.acoustic.co.uk

Key personnel
Chairman: *G Balshaw-Jones*
Managing Director: *J Roberts*
Technical Director: *N Grundy*
Sales Manager: *Terry Carney*
Commercial Director: *P Rollinson*
Export Sales Manager: *E Fitzpatrick*

Products
Thermal and acoustic component services for bus and railway traction units and rolling stock. Thermal and acoustic products for associated buildings. Design, manufacture and supply of finished products or components direct to site or the production line.

Contracts
Projects have included: Waterloo Eurostar Terminal (buildings), St Petersburg Rail Terminal (buildings), Barratt Housing Project (trackside development), Eurotram (complete vehicle), Europa Transrapid (complete vehicle), MTRC Hong Kong (complete vehicle), Arlanda, Stockholm (complete vehicle), Gatwick Express (complete vehicle), Juniper, Turbostar and Electrostar (complete vehicles), West Coast Main Line (complete vehicle), First Bus, Mellor Vancraft, Optare and Marshalls (exhaust jacketing, moulded engine compartment and interior panelling).

Hübner GmbH

Heinrich-Hertz-Strasse 2, D-34123 Kassel, Germany
Postfach 101920, D-34019 Kassel, Germany
Tel: (+49 561) 99 80   Fax: (+49 561) 998 15 15
e-mail: info@hubner-germany.com
Web: www.hubner-germany.com

Key personnel
General Managers: *Reinhard Hübner, Harald Ossendorff*
Director Train Passageway Design: *André Goebels*

Products
Gangway systems for metros and commuter trains, regional trains, passenger trains and super high-speed rail vehicles. Folding and corrugated bellows for articulated buses, railway vehicles, boarding bridges and special requirements; vehicle articulation systems; rail vehicle gangways; moulded rubber parts; rubber profiles.

Hübner has supplied gangways for Class 158, 165, 168, Turbostar, Electrostar DB class 643 emus, Juniper and Pendolino emus, ICE cars, Berlin metro, Strasbourg metro and metros in Cologne, Amsterdam and Rotterdam.

John Holdsworth & Co Ltd

Shaw Lodge Mills, Halifax HX3 9ET, UK
Tel: (+44 1422) 43 30 00   Fax: (+44 1422) 43 33 00
e-mail: info@holdsworth.co.uk
Web: www.holdsworth.co.uk

Key personnel
Executive Sales Director: *Michael Holdsworth*
Sales Director: *Neil Roberts*
Sales: *Peter Hobson, Mike Formby*
European Sales Director: *Richard Field*

Subsidiaries
Holdsworth North America Inc
Holdsworth Australasia Pty Ltd

Products

Manufacturers of transport seating fabrics for the rail, bus, coach, airport and ferry markets worldwide, incorporating a bespoke design and styling service. The 7,000 series of fabrics has been developed to meet BS6853:1999 railway specification.

Contracts

Supply of seat fabrics for Virgin CrossCountry and West Coast Main Line vehicles; the Desiro trains for South West Trains, all London Underground Lines plus other projects within the UK and worldwide. The company has reached a new market in South Korea by supplying fabrics for Korean National Railways and Incheon Metro.

Suppliers to all the major bus and coach manufacturers within Europe including Evobus, Neoman, Van Hool, Plaxtons and the VDL Group. Recent contracts include the exclusive supply of seating to Arriva Group throughout Europe, First Group, Stagecoach and Travel West Midlands bus group.

The company is to supply fabric to RATP Paris Metro for Line 1 and the TGV refurbishment programme for SNCF.

Holdsworth Fabrics Ltd

Hopton Mills, Mirfield, West Yorkshire WF14 8HE, UK
Tel: (+44 1924) 49 05 91   Fax: (+44 1924) 49 56 05
e-mail: info@camirafabrics.com
Web: www.holdsworthfabrics.com

Key personnel

Director of Business Development (Transport): *Terry Colbert*

Background

Following a management buy out in 2006, the company, previously called Interface Fabrics Ltd changed its name to Camira Fabrics Ltd.

In 2007, Camira and Holdsworth formed a strategic alliance and the new company is called Holdsworth Fabrics Ltd.

Products

Holdsworth Fabrics for the transportation sector are suitable for bus, coach and railway interiors, products cover traditional moquette upholstery fabrics as well as co-ordinating trims for wallsides, ceilings, curtains, headrests and interior panels.

IBG Monforts GmbH & Co KG

An der Waldesruh 23, D-41238 Mönchengladbach, Germany
Tel: (+49 2166) 86 82 40   Fax: (+49 2166) 86 82 44
e-mail: info@ibg-monforts.de
Web: www.ibg-monforts.de

Key personnel

Managing Director: *Klaus Sasserath*

Products

Slide bearing systems for applications such as bogie air springs.

Contracts

Contracts include the supply of bearing systems for ICE-2 high-speed trainsets, VT611 tilting dmus and double-deck coaches for DB AG as well as for ICT trainsets.

Icon Polymer Ltd

Thrumpton Road, Retford DN22 6HH, UK
Tel: (+44 1777) 71 43 00   Fax: (+44 1777) 70 97 39
e-mail: info@iconpolymer.com
Web: www.iconpolymer.com

Key personnel

Group Chief Executive: *R Gogerty*

Products

Gangway diaphragms, inter-car gap protection systems and other fabric-reinforced rubber products. Fire-resistant kick straps on ticket gates, inter-car protection mouldings. Carriage interior covings.

Contracts

Contracts include inter-car gap protection mouldings for ALSTOM rolling stock for London Underground Northern and Jubilee Lines; fire-resistant kick strips on WCL ticket gates for London Underground.

Icore International Ltd

220 Bedford Avenue, Slough SL1 4RY, UK
Tel: (+44 1753) 89 66 00   Fax: (+44 1753) 89 66 01
e-mail: information@icore.zodiac.com
Web: www.icoregroup.com

Key personnel

Business Unit Manager, Fluid Systems: *James Hart*
Business Unit Manager, Electrical Interconnect: *Christine Wickings*
European Sales Director: *Eric Martin*
Business Unit Manager-Power Contacts: *Martin Bieg*
Industrial Sales Manager: *Aidan Butler*

Products

Icore designs, manufactures and supplies wired interconnect systems, including lightweight and heavy duty zero halogen conduit systems, EMC protection for wired harnesses, specialised high power connectors and custom designed solutions. Typical applications include: intercarriage signal and power jumpers and carriage to bogie links; automatic coupling systems, sensors and braking systems.

INIT Innovative Informatikanwendungen in Transport-, Verkehrs- und Leitsystemen GmbH

Kaeppelestrasse 4-6, D-76131 Karlsruhe, Germany
Tel: (+49 721) 610 00   Fax: (+49 721) 610 03 99
e-mail: postmaster@init-ka.de
Web: www.init-ka.de

Subsidiaries

Australia
INIT Pty Ltd
Level 5, Toowong Tower, 9 Sherwood Road, Toowong Qld, 4066 Australia
Tel: (+61 7) 33 10 88 18   Fax: (+61 7) 33 10 88 00

US
Innovations in Transportation Inc
1420 Kristina Way, Suite 101, Chesapeake, Virginia 23320
Tel: (+1 757) 413 91 00   Fax: (+1 757) 413 50 19

Canada
INIT Innovations in Transportation (Eastern Canada) Inc/INIT Innovations en Transport (Canada Est) Inc
14 Place du Commerce, suite 360, Île-des-Soeurs, Montréal, Québec H3E 1T7 , Canada
Tel: (+1 514) 766 28 36
Fax: (+1 514) 766 15 78

INIT, Innovations in Transportation (Western Canada) Inc
949 West 41st Avenue, Vancouver, BC V5Z2N5, Canada
Tel: (+1 778) 995 04 93

United Arab Emirates
Init Innovation in Traffic Systems FZE
Dubai Airport Free Zone, Office 6EB 244, Dubai, UAE
Tel: (+971) 47 01 72 86

Key personnel

Chief Sales Officer: *Dr Jürgen Greschner*

Background

INIT GmbH was founded in 1983 by Dr Ing Gottfried Greschner and established a branch in the US in 1999.

Products

Mobile data terminals, onboard computers as the core unit and central database onboard vehicles. Automatic management of electronic onboard peripherals (information signs, fare management devices). Automatic passenger counters (infra-red sensor technology, suitable for all types of vehicles). Operational status displays. Next stop announcement and display.

Integrian, Inc

511 David Drive, Morrisville, North Carolina 27560, US
Tel: (+1 919) 472 50 09
Fax: (+1 919) 472 50 99
e-mail: info@integrian.com
Web: www.integrian.com

Key personnel

Board of Directors: *Ich-Kien Lao, Davie Barrett, Peter Durand, Olin Giles, John Glushik, Gregory G Johnson*

Background

Integrian Inc acquired Australian-based Innovonics Ltd in December 2005.

Products/Services

Integrian specialises in design, development, manufacture, project management and installation of transportation surveillance systems. The company has delivered over 2,000 transit and fleet computer systems over the past 10 years to transit authorities and companies around the world.

Contracts

Integrian is currently supplying CCTV systems to large mainline fleets in the UK and has won additional contracts onboard CCTV systems in Ireland, Spain and Australia.

Current projects in North America include installation of onboard digital video equipment with 90 days of onboard video storage and streaming data capability, plus back-end software applications.

Next Generation onboard CCTV systems supplied Integrian (Innovonics in Europe) for use on London Underground tube stock include cameras, driver's monitors and digital video recorders.

International Nameplate Supplies Ltd

1420 Crumlin Road North, London, Ontario N5V 1S1, Canada
Tel: (+1 800) 565 35 09   Fax: (+1 519) 455 44 09
e-mail: sales@inps.ca
Web: www.inps.on.ca

Key personnel

Director: *David Gibson*

Products

Dead-front graphics (panels which have a dull finish, and hidden lights; they are commonly found on cars for the indicating lights). The company has the technology to form small runs of plastic without incurring the enormous tooling required for injection moulding. It also engraves serial plates, wire and hydraulic markers, warning and informational signs; hot stamping of customer cards, wire markers, parking and expiration decals. Cutting of stencils and legends, corporate logos, painting patterns, vehicle identification, and numbering vehicles. Silk screen printing of warning and information nameplates, rate decals and corporate logos.

Stainless steel etching, aluminium anodising, screen printing and four-colour process and reverse screened polycarbonate.

Contracts

Supplied General Motors Coach and Motor Coach Industries. Currently INPS is the sole supplier of locomotive graphics services to General Motors EMD division, CSX Transportation and Amtrak. INPS also engineers, manufactures and supplies National Steel Car, Bombardier Transportation, ALSTOM, New Flyer, Nova Bus, Orion Bus, Thomas Built Bus and other companies. AdvancedThermo Dynamics Ltd (ATC) is affiliated to IRR and INPS through joint ownership. ATC is involved in both transit, transportation and military projects and products that involve heating and cooling (HVAC) and generator set manufacture and design.

Invertec Ltd

Whelford Road, Fairford GL7 4DT, UK
Tel: (+44 1285) 71 35 50
Fax: (+44 1285) 71 35 48
e-mail: sales@invertec.co.uk
Web: www.invertec.co.uk

Key personnel

Managing Director: *David Paulson*
Sales Director: *Ian King*

Subsidiaries

Invertec Technology (Asia) Sdn Bhd
No 3 Jalan Mutiara 5, Taman Perindustrian Plentong, 81750 Plentong, Johor Darul Takzim, Malaysia
Tel: (+60 7) 356 22 00
Fax: (+60 7) 355 62 00
e-mail: melong@invertec.com.my
Managing Director: *Roland Read*
Speciality Manufacturing Co, Invertec North America Inc
10200 Pineville Road, PO Box 790, Pineville, North Carolina 28134, US
Tel: (+1 704) 889 75 18
Fax: (+1 704) 889 27 60
e-mail: danassmmc@specmfg.com
Web: www.specmfg.com
Sales Director: *Douglas Campbell*

Background

Invertec is a family-owned company formed in 1980 and now exports 55 per cent of its production to Europe. Production facility is at Fairford, UK, employing 100 staff.
ISO 9000 accredited.

Products

Low-voltage DC lighting for the transport industry, including trains and buses.
Manufacturers of fluorescent lighting inverters, LED lighting and signs, individual luminaries, continuous lighting and interior ceiling systems.

Contracts

Preferred suppliers with the UK coach building industry and to many other European bus and coach manufacturers. Specified by large operators such as Stagecoach and FirstGroup and is supplying to: Alexander Dennis Ltd, Bova AB, Den Oudsten Bussen, East Lancs Coachbuilders, EvoBus (UK) Ltd, Marshall SPV, Optare Group, Plaxton Coach and Bus, Robert Wright & Son and Scania.

Rail lighting inverters are also supplied to the industry including Bombardier Transportation, BP Solar, Shell Solar Energy, Total Energie and Isofoton.

---

iQR

Railcentre 1, 305 Edward Street, Brisbane, Queensland, Australia 4000
GPO Box 1429, Brisbane, Queensland 4001
Tel: (+61 7) 32 32 33 90   Fax: (+61 7) 32 35 33 46
e-mail: sales@iqr.com.au
Web: www.iqr.com.au

Key personnel

General Manager: *Michael Walsh*
Marketing and Business Development Manager: *Peter Harris*
Sales Manager: *Youfa Chen*

Background

iQR was previously Queensland Rail Consultancy Services.

Products

iQR's Train Information and Entertainment System (TIES) is an audio-visual information and entertainment system. TIES is designed specifically for rail applications where the system is distributed throughout multiple passenger cars and can be tailored for client's specific requirements. The passenger video screens can be mounted overhead, on seat-backs or in seat armrests. The system supports Media File Server, DVD, satellite TV, driver's-view camera and computer generated information.

iQR's Train Information Entertainment Systems (TIES)   1140307

Contracts

QR's Cairns and Rockhampton tilt trains have train information and entertainment systems installed and operating.

ISAF Bus Components Srl

Via Stazione 43, I-21020 Mornago (Varese), Italy
Tel: (+39 0331) 90 35 40
Fax: (+39 0331) 90 32 09
e-mail: info@isaf-bus-components.com
Web: www.isaf-bus-components.com

Key personnel

Director: *Massimo Sessa*
Production Manager: *Gianni Turcatti*
Sales Manager: *Michela Pierobon*

Products

Swing plug doors (outside and inside); folding doors, sliding doors, driver doors, pneumatic and electric door operators; pneumatic kit for luggage compartment and headlining systems. Company certified to ISO9001 standard.

Isoclima SpA

Head office and factory
via A Volta, 14 I-35042, Este (PD), Italy
Tel: (+39 0429) 41 88
Fax: (+39 0429) 38 78
e-mail: info@agtgroup.it
Web: www.isoclima.net

Key personnel

General Manager: *Alberto Bertolini*

Products

Windscreens: flat, curved, heated, framed with antispall, high-impact-resistant for high-speed trains, locomotives, emus, dmus, LRVs, trams and buses; glass for light covers, interior glazing and partitions.

For details of the latest updates to *Jane's Urban Transport Systems* online and to discover the additional information available exclusively to online subscribers please visit
juts.janes.com

ITT Veam, LLC

100 New Wood Road, Watertown, Conneticut 06795, US
Tel: (+1 860) 274 96 81
Fax: (+1 860) 274 49 63
Web: www.ittcannon.com

Key personnel
General Manager: *Mike Hansen*

Background
ITT Veam is part of the ITT Industries group of companies.

Products
Electrical, optical and pneumatic connectors for trainline, brake systems, air conditioning, speed sensing, communications, lighting, automatic coupling and traction motor applications.

Jarret SAS

14-38, rue Alexandre, Bat E2, BP35 Gennevilliers, Cedex F-92234, France
Tel: (+33 1) 41 32 26 60
Fax: (+33 1) 40 86 12 82
e-mail: daniela.daloia@itt.com
Web: www.jarret.com

Key personnel
Managing Director: *Scott Taylor*
Office Manager: *Daniela d'Aloia*

Products
Shock-absorbers for protection within industry, rail and defence area.

Kay-Metzeler Ltd

Wellington Road, Bollington, Macclesfield SK10 5JJ, UK
e-mail: info@kay-metzeler.co.uk
Web: www.kay-metzeler.co.uk

Background
Kay-Metzeler Ltd is a subsidiary of British Vita plc.

Products
Transprotect™ foam for use in rail vehicle seating. The material conforms to leading European fire protection standards, with resistance to ignition, low heat release, low smoke and toxic gas emission, together with physical properties that offer wide-ranging design potential.

Developments
Kay-Metzeler has launched a new, advanced range of latex-like polyurethane foams under the trade name Laytech™.

ČKD Kutná Hora AS

Karlov č p 197, CZ-284 49 Kutná Hora, Czech Republic
Tel: (+420 327) 50 61 11
Fax: (+420 327) 50 65 87
e-mail: sales@ckdkh.cz
Web: www.ckdkh.cz

Background
Founded in 1967, the company was transformed from a state-owned enterprise to a joint stock company in 1995 as part of the Czech Republic's privatisation reforms.

Products
Y25, Y33 and TF25 bogies; bogies to special designs for main line and light rail vehicles; cast and welded bogie frames and components.

Kleeneze Sealtech Ltd

Ansteys Road, Hanham, Bristol BS15 3SS, UK
Tel: (+44 117) 958 24 50
Fax: (+44 117) 960 01 41
e-mail: enq@ksltd.com
Web: www.ksltd.com

Key personnel
Commercial Director: *David Love*
Export Manager: *David Eggleden*

Subsidiaries
Record Industrial Brushes (sister company)
Kullen GmbH (parent company)

Products
Carriage door brushstrip seals. Rodent brush, internal panel seals, pillar seals, cab door seals. Draft proofing and pest control sealing for buildings.

Klimat-Fer SpA

Via Cadore 3, I-20098 Sesto Ulteriano – San Giuliano Milanese (MI), Italy
Tel: (+39 02) 98 86 91
Fax: (+39 02) 98 28 12 34
e-mail: commerciale@klimat-fer.com
Web: www.klimat-fer.com

Works
Corso Stati Uniti 1/1, I-35127 Padova (PD), Italy
Tel: (+39 049) 698 84 02
Fax: (+39 049) 870 48 56

Background
Formed by a merger of Klimat SpA and Fer Elettromeccanica Srl, Klimat-Fer SpA entered the rail market in 2003.

Products
Air conditioning systems for rail vehicles; maintenance and cleansing services for air conditioning systems; supply of electronic equipment such as choppers, converters, battery chargers, inverters, and diode thyristor, IGBT and GTO modules.

Contracts
Clients include SNCF, SNCB, Ferrovie Nord Milano, Metropolitana di Roma as well as ALSTOM Transport, Bombardier Transportation, Ansaldobreda, Firema Trasporti and Corifer. Projects for which equipment has been supplied include: Minuetto; TAF; Class ETR 500, E402B, E 412, E 464 and D146 power cars/locomotives; various coach refurbishment projects; trams for Milan, Oslo, Rome, Strasburg and Turin; and the Rome and Athens metros.

Knorr-Bremse AG

Moosacher Strasse 80, D-80809 Munich, Germany
Tel: (+49 89) 354 70
Fax: (+49 89) 35 47 27 67
Web: www.knorr-bremse.com

Key personnel
Chairman: *Dr Raimund Klinker*

Knorr-Bremse compact brake calliper with aluminium brake disc 1326754

Executive Board: *Jens Theuerkorn, Dr Dieter Wilhelm, Dr Lorenz Zwingmann (Chief Financial Officer)*

Knorr-Bremse Systeme für Schienenfahrzeuge GmbH
(address as Knorr-Bremse AG)
Managing Directors: *Dr Frank Gropengiesser, Dr Wolfgang Schlosser, Dr Albrecht Köhler*

Works
Berlin and Munich.

Subsidiaries
Knorr-Bremse Australia Pty Ltd, Granville, Australia
Dr techn J Zelisko GmbH, Mödling, Austria
Knorr-Bremse GmbH Division IFE Automatic Door Systems, Waidhofen an de Ybbs, Austria
Knorr-Bremse GmbH, Mödling, Austria
Knorr-Bremse Sistemas para Veículos Ferroiários Ltda, São Paulo, Brazil
Knorr Brake Ltd, Kingston, Canada
Knorr-Bremse Systems for Rail Vehicles Co Ltd, Suzhou, China
Knorr-Bremse Asia Pacific (Holding), Hong Kong, China
Knorr-Bremse Systems for Rail Vehicles (Suzhou) Co Ltd, Beijing Office, Beijing, China
Knorr-Bremse CARS LD Vehicle Brake Disc Manufacturing (Beijing) Co Ltd, Beijing China
Knorr-Bremse/Nankou Air Supply Unit (Beijing) Co, Ltd, Beijing, China
IFE-Victall Railway Vehicle Door Systems (Qingdao) Co, Ltd, Qingdao, China
Westinghouse Platform Screen Doors (Guangzhou) Ltd, Guangzhou, China
Merak Railways Technologies Shanghai, Shanghai, China
Freinrail Systèmes Ferroviaires SA, Reims Cedex, France
Knorr-Bremse Vasúti Jármü Rendszerek Hungária Kft, Budapest, Hungary
Frensistemi Srl, Florence, Italy
Microelettrica Scientifica SpA, Rozzano, Italy
Knorr-Bremse India Private Ltd, Faridabad, India
Knorr-Bremse Rail Systems Japan, Tokyo, Japan
Kknorr-Bremse Rail Systems Korea Ltd, Seoul, Korea
Knorr-Bremse Systemy dla Kolejowych Srodków, Lokomicji PL Sp Zoo, Katowice, Poland
Knorr Bremse SA Pty Ltd, Kempton Park, South Africa
Sociedad Espanola de Frenos, Calefaccion y Señales SA, Pinto/Madrid, Pinto/Madrid, Pinto (Madrid), Spain
Merak Sistemas Integrados de Climatización, SA, Pinto (Madrid), Spain
Knorr-Bremse Nordic Rail Services AB, Lund, Sweden
Oerlikon-Knorr Eisenbahntechnik AG, Niederhasli, Switzerland
Knorr-Bremse Rail Systems(UK) Limited, Melksham, UK
IFE North America Inc, US
Merak North America Company, US
Knorr Brake Corporation, Westminster, US
New York Air Brake Corporation, Watertown, US

Background

In July 2008, Knorr-Bremse concluded a long-term agreement with Bombardier Transportation for Knorr-Bremse to become the preferred partner for Bombardier braking systems. It is the intention of both companies to implement common technical standard solutions.

Products

Knorr-Bremse Rail Vehicle Systems projects, develops, manufactures and supplies brake systems and on-board systems for all kinds of rail vehicles worldwide. This comprises brake systems and on-board systems for locomotives and freight cars with AAR-technology and locomotives, freight and passenger cars, multiple-units with UIC-technology. The product range also includes brake and on-board systems for tramways, metros, people movers and special vehicles. The product range of brake systems comprises air supply systems (piston- and screw compressors, oil-free compressors, air dryers, oil filters, condensate collectors, complete air-supply systems), brake control systems (carrier systems, control units, brake controller, valves, ESRA platform, sensor systems for wheel slide control, pressure management and load control), bogie equipment (brake discs and pads, brake callipers, block brake units, magnetic track brakes, eddy-current brakes) and hydraulic systems (hydraulic units, brake actuators, suspension systems). The product range of on-board systems comprises automatic door systems, platform screen doors, air-conditioning systems, power electrics, dampers, toilet systems, windscreen wipers, sanding equipment, passenger information systems. A comprehensive after-sales package is offered. The broad spectrum of different services from urban traffic enterprises up to national operating companies covers the entire life cycle of the products of Knorr-Bremse Rail Vehicle Systems.

Developments

Knorr-Bremse has developed the EP1001 wheel flat protection system for freight cars; a robust, self-powered system designed to cope with the harsh operating environment in the rail freight sector.

Contracts

Recent contracts include: brake equipment for Ile de France (France), Metronetn SSL (UK), JWR-West 223 (Japan), emus and locomotives (China), passenger coaches for IR (Israel), HVAC systems for Citadis trams (Algeria, Israel) and regional trains (Spain).

Knorr-Bremse GmbH

Division IFE Automatic Door Systems
Patertal 20, A-3340 Waidhofen/Ybbs, Austria
Tel: (+43 7442) 51 50   Fax: (+43 7442) 515 12
e-mail: doors_vk@ife-doors.com
Web: www.ife-doors.com

Key personnel

Managing Director: *Dr Stefan Haas*
Sales Director, Export and Marketing:
   Ing Wolfgang Steiner

Background

Previously called IFE Industrie-Einrichtungen Fertigungs AG, in 1997 Knorr-Bremse Systems for Rail Vehicles GmbH took a 49 per cent shareholding. The company fully merged into Knorr-Bremse in August 2002 and changed its name to Knorr-Bremse GmbH, Division IFE Automatic Door Systems.

Products

Sliding and sliding plug door systems for rail vehicles; external sliding doors, pocket sliding doors, inside swing doors; internal doors, cab and slam doors, connecting doors; access ramps, movable steps, gap bridges; detection systems,

door control equipment units, microprocessor control units.

The company equips trams and urban railroads, underground and express lines, RIC cars and high speed trains throughout the world.

Knorr-Bremse Rail Systems (UK) Limited

Westinghouse Way, Hampton Park East, Melksham SN12 6TL, UK
Tel: (+44 1225) 89 87 00   Fax: (+44 1225) 89 87 10
e-mail: wbl.sales@westbrake.com
Web: www.knorr-bremse.co.uk

Key personnel

Managing Director: *Paul R Johnson*
Executive Director: *Neil Wilkinson*
Engineering Director, UK Rail: *Jason Abbott*
Marketing Director: *Peter C Johnson*
PSD Director: *Richard Bew*
Operations Director: *Martyn T Perkins*
Finance Director: *Stephen Thomas*
Business Development Manager, Brakes : *Ian Palmer*

Background

Knorr-Bremse Rail Systems (UK) Limited is a member of Knorr-Bremse group. In March 2005, the company moved from Chippenham to a purpose-built factory in Melksham. At the same time the company changed its name from Westinghouse Brakes to Knorr-Bremse Rail Systems (UK) Ltd to reflect its enhanced sales and service role within the global Knorr-Bremse Group.

Products

Brake systems comprising air and vacuum brake equipment, electro-pneumatic brake systems with digital or analogue control for metro and commuter passenger trains. Equipment includes: rotary and reciprocating air compressors, air treatment equipment, drivers brake and brake/traction controllers, wheelslide protection equipment, sanding systems, warning equipment, air suspension control equipment, brake actuation equipment, tread and disc brake equipment and magnetic track brakes.

A comprehensive product support service is available providing equipment repair, overhaul and long-term maintenance and spare parts supply for the UK and Irish markets, which is for the complete Knorr-Bremse product range. In addition to braking systems and associated equipment, other products supported within the 'on-board systems' division include IFE train doors, Merak HVAC, Frensistemi toilet systems and passenger information systems, and Microelettrica power electrics components.

Contracts

The most recent contracts include brake systems for: London Underground Victoria Line upgrade, Metro Manila, Beijing Metro Line 10 and Guangzhou Metro Line 3, 4 and 5.

In September 2004, Westinghouse Brakes was awarded over GBP100 million of braking systems and maintenance business by Bombardier Transportation for its new London Underground trains. The initial contract is for the supply of the entire brake system for 376 new deep tube fleet metro cars being built by Bombardier Transportation for Metronet Rail use on the Victoria Line. The braking system incorporates the latest technology from Knorr-Bremse Sfs, including EP2002 Distributed Brake Control and the VV120T Oil-Free Compressor. The second stage of the contract includes the supply of braking systems to a further 1,362 Bombardier cars for Metronet's sub-surface lines, for example Circle, District, Hammersmith and City, and Metropolitan Lines. Westinghouse Brakes will also provide maintenance and service support for the brake control, bogie brake and air supply equipment.

Other recent contracts include: brake systems for Desiro, Electrostar, Juniper and Coradia multiple-unit vehicle platforms, Arriva Trains Northern trains, 'Voyager' CrossCountry and Midland Mainline 'Meridian' demus, Kuala Lumpur Airport Express trains, Docklands Light Railway, Shanghai Pearl Line and Shanghai Xin Min metro trains, Class 66 locomotives, and wheelslide equipment for the First Great Western high-speed trains.

Koni BV

Langeweg 1, PO Box 1014, NL-3260 AA Oud-Beijerland, Netherlands
Tel: (+31 186) 63 55 00
Fax: (+31 186) 63 56 05
e-mail: clagendyk@koni.nl
Web: www.koni.com

Background

In September 2007 International Motion Control, who owned Enidine Incorporated, was acquired by ITT Corporation, who in turn owns Koni. As a result of this transaction, Koni and Enidine have been merged and are now both part of ITT's Motion and Flow Control division.

Products

In-house research, development, engineering and manufacturing of dampers for buses, trailers, trains, metros, passenger coaches and freight wagons, locomotives, high-speed trains and pantographs; electrically controlled dampers.

Konvekta AG

Am Nordbahnhof 5, D-34613 Schwalmstadt, Germany
Tel: (+49 66 91) 760
Fax: (+49 66 91) 761 71
e-mail: info@konvekta.com
Web: www.konvekta.com

Key personnel

Chairman of the Supervisory Board: *Carl-H Schmitt*

Background

Konvekta was founded in 1957 and is a family owned company.

Products

Air-conditioning systems for buses and rail vehicles.

Leigh's Paints

Tower Works, Kestor Street, Bolton BL2 2AL, UK
Tel: (+44 1204) 52 17 71   Fax: (+44 1204) 38 21 15
e-mail: enquiries@wjleigh.co.uk
Web: www.wjleigh.co.uk

Key personnel

Chief Executive Officer: *Dick Frost*

Products

The company produces Transgard high-performance paints and coatings for the transport industry.

Contracts

92 cast-iron columns at Victoria Station and station refurbishment at Bournemouth, Darlington, Eastbourne, Manchester Metrolink, North Greenwich tube; Newark Dyke Bridge on the East Coast Main Line and steelwork near Leeds station.

Lift-U

Division of Hogan Mfg Inc
1520 First Street, Escalon, California 95320, US
Tel: (+1 209) 838 24 00
Fax: (+1 209) 838 86 48
e-mail: info@hoganmfg.com
Web: www.liftu.hoganmfg.com

Key personnel
Marketing: *John Fusco*
Sales: *Larry M Green*

Works
PO Box 398, Escalon, California 95320, USA

Background
Lift-U is a division of Hogan Mfg Inc.

Products
Wheelchair lifts and ramps for heavy-duty mass transit buses.

LPA Niphan Systems

PO Box 15, Tudor Works, Debden Road, Saffron Walden CB11 4AN, UK
Tel: (+44 1799) 51 28 00   Fax: (+44 1799) 51 28 28
e-mail: sales@lpa-niphan.com
Web: www.lpa-group.com

Key personnel
Chief Executive Officer: *Peter Pollock*
Sales and Marketing Director: *George Renshaw*
Exports Manager: *Derek Orley*
Chief Operating Officer: *Jim Henderson*

Background
LPA Niphan Systems is a member of LPA Group plc and is ISO 9001 and 9002 certified.

Products
Plugs, sockets and other electrical and electromechanical terminations and connectors.

Lucchini Sidermeccanica

Via Giorgio Paglia, 45 I-24065 Lovere (BG), Italy

Key personnel
President: *Giuseppe Lucchini*
Vice-President and Chief Executive Officer:
    Erder Mingoli
General Manager: *Augusto Mensi*
Commercial and Marketing Director:
    Roberto Forcella

Rolling stock components
Lucchini Sidermeccanica SpA
Via G. Paglia 45, I-24065 Lovere (BG), Italy
Tel: (+39 035) 96 35 66
Fax: (+39 035) 96 35 52
e-mail: rollingstock@lucchini.it

Subsidiaries
Lucchini UK
Ashburton Road West, Trafford Park, Manchester M17 1GU, UK
Tel: (+44 161) 872 04 92
Fax: (+44 161) 872 28 95
e-mail: salesuk@lucchini.co.uk
Chairman: *Erder Mingoli*
General Manager: *Ian Dolman*
Sales Manager: *Chris Fawdry*

Lucchini Sweden
Bruks Gatan, Box 210, SE-73523 Surahammar, Sweden
Tel: (+46 22) 03 47 00   Fax: (+46 22) 03 47 80
e-mail: info@lucchini.se
Chairman: *Erder Mingoli*
Managing Director and Sales Manager: *Lennart Nordhall*

Lucchini Poland

ul Palisadowa 20/22, PL-01-940 Warsaw, Poland
Tel: (+48 22) 569 93 00
Fax: (+48 22) 569 93 39
e-mail: info@lucchini.pl
Chairman: *Erder Mingoli*
General Manager: *Krzysztof Laskowski*
Sales Manager: *Albert Siekierka*

Products
Lucchini Sidermeccanica SpA, Lovere Works: design and manufacture of wheels, tyres, axles and assembly of wheelsets with axleboxes, brake discs and drive units.

Lucchini Sidermeccanica SpA, LMF Works: overhaul and full refurbishment of wheelsets including axleboxes, bearings, disc brakes and drive units. Production of axleboxes for railway and mass transit systems.

Lucchini UK – Wheel Systems Division, Manchester Works: production of all types of railway wheels and assembly of complete wheelsets for trucks, carriages and locomotives.

Lucchini Sweden, Surahammar Works: wheels, tyres, axles and wheelsets with axleboxes and drive units.

Lucchini Poland, Warsaw Works: wheels, axles and complete wheelsets with axleboxes and drive units.

Lumikko Oy

PO Box 304, FIN-60101 Seinäjoki, Finland
Tel: (+358 10) 835 54 00
Fax: (+358 6) 414 19 21
e-mail: lumikko@lumikko.com
Web: www.lumikko.com

Key personnel
Managing Director: *Kari Saikkonen*

Products
Lumikko® HVAC devices for locomotives, passenger coaches and other rail vehicles; systems are capable of operation in temperatures ranging from –40 to +40°C.

Contracts
Contracts include: the supply of over 500 cab air-conditioning units for locomotives, dmus and emus operated by Finnish Railways (VR-Group Ltd); air-conditioners for 12 VR-Group restaurant cars; refrigeration and freezing equipment for restaurant cars manufactured by Talgo Oy.

HVAC-systems for 20 double-decker sleeping cars for Talgo Oy, cars will be operated by Finnish Railways.

Mäder Lacke AG

Industriestrasse 1, CH-8956 Killwangen, Switzerland
Tel: (+41 56) 417 85 55
Fax: (+41 56) 401 64 44
e-mail: maeder_lacke@bluewin.ch
Web: www.maederlacke.ch

Key personnel
Head of Division, Synthetic Resins: *Dr Giacomo Siragna*

Products
Water-borne paints and coating systems for rail vehicles, graffiti-protection coatings.

Marl International Ltd

Marl Business Park, Ulverston LA12 9BN, UK
Tel: (+44 1229) 58 24 30   Fax: (+44 1229) 58 51 55
e-mail: sales@marl.co.uk
    gemma.birkett@@marl.co.uk (Rail Sector)
Web: www.marlrail.com; www.marl.co.uk

Key personnel
Marl Rail Sector: *Gemma Birkett*

Products
The company's current portfolio of products provides an LED light source for both illumination and indication applications on rail vehicles, along side its signalling products.

Emergency Lighting
Hi-light: high-integrity emergency lighting; Electronic Egress Lighting System EELS: low-location marking system.

Rolling stock products
A full range of filament bulb replacements including the 214 series: BA9s bulb replacements with built in transient protection; LED door pressels; LED illuminated gauge rings for applications such as rail vehicle speedometer and brake gauges; cab clipboard light; step lights; saloon lighting to replace fluorescent tube fixtures.

Martec

Martec Tekelec Systèmes
29 avenue de la Baltique, F-91953 Les Ulis Cedex, France
Tel: (+33 1) 69 82 20 00
Fax: (+33 1) 64 46 45 50
e-mail: contact.securitedestransport@martec.fr
Web: www.martec.fr

Key personnel
President and Managing Director:
    Béatrice Bacconnet

Background
Martec is a French-based group specialising in electronics and communications in aerospace, defence, environment, industrial and marine sectors, as well as in transport. The group employs 350 staff.

Products
Onboard video surveillance systems for urban and main-line public transport applications. Latest products include the Scene 3 digital recording system, which records up to 100 images per second, offers synchronised audio recording and can be linked to GPS mapping software to provide details of vehicle location.

Contracts
More than 3,500 digital recording systems have been deployed among public transport operators, in both France and Europe, in partnership with the main rolling stock and automotive manufacturers.

In 2005 Martec secured a contract to provide onboard video surveillance systems for nearly 500 buses operated by the TEC Group in the Walloon area of Belgium. Other customers include SNCF and bus operators in Dijon, Rennes and Rouen.

Mayser GmbH & Co KG

Örlinger Strasse 1-3, D-89072 Ulm, Germany
Tel: (+49 731) 206 10
Fax: (+49 731) 206 12 22
Web: www.mayser.de

Key personnel
Contact: *Peter Konradt*

Products
Specialising in the safety technology sector, the company's products range from tactile sensors such as safety mats, safety edges and safety bumpers, to non-contact safety equipment

One example of safe obstacle detection for public transport users from Mayser   1143619

Example of a Mayser door safety system   1344880

and industrial sensors. The systems are used in various areas of application, including the public transport sector (on buses and rail vehicles).

MSA Mediterr Shock-Absorbers SpA

Head Office
C da Cusatino sn, SP 154, I-93100 Caltanissetta, Italy
Tel: (+39 0934) 93 50 11   Fax: (+39 0934) 93 50 20
e-mail: info@gimonmsa.com
Web: www.gimonmsa.com
Plant
C so Alessandria 501, I-14100 Asti, Italy
Tel: (+39 0141) 29 57 00
Fax: (+39 0141) 47 74 43

Key personnel
Sales Director: *Elena Giulivi*

Products
Design and production of shock absorbers for road transport (bus, truck, trailer, axle) and railway applications such as primary and secondary suspension dampers, yaw dampers, inter-cars dampers, pantographs dampers as well as shock absorbers for special applications.

Merak Sistemas Integrados de Climatización SA

Parque Empresarial La Carpetania, Miuel Faraday, 1, E-28906 Getafe, Madrid, Spain
Tel: (+34 91) 495 90 00   Fax: (+34 91) 691 09 97
e-mail: merak@merak-sa-hvac.com
Web: www.merak-sa.com

Merak equipment for emu project, China   1198681

Merak equipment for Citadis platform   1198680

Key personnel
Chief Executive Officer: *Ignacio Fúster*
General Manager: *Henrik Thiele*
Sales and Systems Director: *Laselo Szigethi*

Background
Merak formerly traded as Stone Ibérica SA and since September 2005 has been a member of the Knorr-Bremse Group.

Products
Design, manufacture and maintenance of air-conditioning equipment, heating and ventilation equipment, electronic and microprocessor controls, inverter ballasts for fluorescent tubes, and static speed regulator for asynchronous motors.

Contracts
Projects include: Velaro Spain, China and Russia (2006, 2007 and 2008).

Métal Déployé Resistor

1 route de Semur, F-21500 Montbard, France
Tel: (+33 3) 80 89 58 75
Fax: (+33 3) 80 92 24 33
Web: www.mdresistor.com

Key personnel
Managing Director: *Yann Fouquet*
Sales Manager: *Jean-Louis Ragot*

Products
High-power resistors for starting, braking and shunt applications; snubbers; auxiliary resistors; snubber for high-speed trains, braking resistors for urban transport applications, static braking load banks.

Metalnastri srl

Via Magenta 1/c, I-20053 Muggio (MI), Italy
Tel: (+39 039) 214 47 33   Fax: (+39 039) 79 63 67
e-mail: info@metalnastri.it
Web: www.zinctape.it

Key personnel
General Manager: *Dr Cocucci Vincenzo*
Sales Director: *Sem Massimo*

Products
Design and manufacture of zinc, copper and aluminium anti-corrosive foil.

Microelettrica Scientifica SpA

Via Alberelle 56/58, I-20089 Rozzano (MI), Italy
Tel: (+39 02) 57 57 31
Fax: (+39 02) 57 51 09 40
e-mail: info@microelettrica.com
Web: www.microelettrica.com

Key personnel
Managing Director: *Dr Lorenzo Stendardi*

Products
Standard and custom-designed contactors, digital electronic protection relays and power resistors for braking and other rail applications.

Microphor

452 East Hill Road, Willits, California 95490, US
Tel: (+1 707) 459 55 63
Fax: (+1 707) 459 66 17
e-mail: info@microphor.com
Web: www.microphor.com

Key personnel
General Manager: *Janice Rivera*
Customer Service: *Brian Banzhaf*
Marketing and Sales Manager: *Walter Hess*

Background
Microphor is part of the Wabtec Corporation.

Products
Macerator and air-assisted flush toilets/waste retention and treatment systems (32 ounce, one quart and two quart per flush) for passenger vehicles and locomotives; thermoelectric refrigerators and ice boxes, low-temperature protection systems, air compressors, freeze dump valves, ditch lights and accessories for locomotives; custom-manufactured components in plastic and sheet metal for locomotives, passenger vehicles and freight wagons.
New developments include: vacuum toilets, toilet room modules for locomotives and passenger coaches and water jet flush toilets.

Contracts
Contracts include the supply of toilets and waste retention/treatment systems to Metro-North, Amtrak, MARC, New Jersey Transit, Amerail, GE Transportation Systems and Electro-Motive Division, General Motors Corporation.
Products are supplied to customers in Australia, Canada, China, Mexico, South Africa, Vietnam and the UK.

Mobile Climate Control Industries Inc

7540 Jane Street, Concord, Ontario L4K 0A6, Canada
Tel: (+1 416) 242 64 06   Fax: (+1 416) 242 64 06
e-mail: info-mccii@mccii.com
Web: www.mccii.com

Subsidiaries
UWE Verken AB
SE-601 04 Norrköping, Sweden
USA West
426 Winnebago Avenue, Fairmont, Minnesota 56031, US
Tel: (+ 1 507) 238 27 83   Fax: (+1 507) 238 41 51
MCC Europe
AB Baldersgatan 24, Box 96, S-761 21 Norrtälje, Sweden
Tel: (+46 176) 20 78 00   Fax: (+46 176) 20 78 10

Background
Mobile Climate Control Corporation (MCC) was originally formed in 1975 as Klimatsystems AB which was subsequently sold in 1982. In 1997, MCC repurchased Klimatsystems AB, which was

re-branded MCC Europe AB and relocated to Norrtälje, Sweden.
In 2004 MCC purchased Swedish company UWE Verken.

Products
Air conditioning in specialty vehicles and bus and mass transit, including HVAC systems, evaporators, condensers, heaters, electronics and controls, refrigerant lines, components including blowers and compressors, ramp system, plumbing and piping, regulation equipment.

Morio Denki Co Ltd

34-1 Tateishi 4-chome, Katsushika-ku, Tokyo 124-0012, Japan
Tel: (+81 3) 36 91 31 81
Fax: (+81 3) 36 92 13 33
Web: www.morio.co.jp

Key personnel
Chairman: *S Yamagata*
President: *K Miura*
Senior Managing Director: *T Yagishita*

Products
Fluorescent ceiling lights, headlights and tail-lights, destination display systems, heating systems, door-operating switches.

Mors Smitt

PO Box 7023, NL-3502 KA, Utrecht, Netherlands
Vrieslantlaan 6, NL-3526 AA, Utrecht, Netherlands
Tel: (+31 30) 288 13 11
Fax: (+31 30) 289 88 16
e-mail: sales@nieaf-smitt.nl
Web: www.morssmitt.com

Key personnel
Managing Director: *Arne J Wijnmaalen*
Area Sales Managers: *Igor Cubleac, Qi Guo, Hideki Ono, Christiaan Brouwers, Wing Iam*
Commercial Manager Rolling Stock: *Erwin K G Veldman*

Subsidiaries
Nieaf-Smitt BV
Web: www.morssmit.com

Products
Circuit protection components: hydraulic-magnetic circuit breakers, ground fault breakers and remotely operated circuit breakers; electrical control solutions: form, fit and function electrical control solutions for new built and retrofit/refurbishment applications; electronic time delay relays: delay on drop-out (instantaneous contacts), delay on pull-in (instantaneous contacts), delay on pull-in and/or drop-out (selectable by dip switch), delay on pull-in or drop-out pulse controlled, one shot on pull-in or drop-out, threshold with delay on drop-out and flashing; electronic timers: delay on drop-out, delay on pull-in, one shot on pull-in or drop-out, threshold with delay on drop-out and flashing; instantaneous relays: dry circuit, latching, miniature, PCB and safety-critical; measuring and monitoring relays: voltage monitoring, current monitoring and analogue value monitoring; panel indicators: analogue indicators for speed, voltage, power and current; protection relays: high voltage, frequency and current monitoring; track safety equipment: high voltage electrical monitoring and measuring equipment; accessories: relay sockets, retaining clips.

MS Relais

Tour Rosny 2, Avenue du Général de Gaulle, Rosny sous Bois, F-93118, France
Tel: (+33 1) 48 12 14 40   Fax: (+33 1) 48 55 90 01
e-mail: sales@morssmittrelais.com
Web: www.morssmittrelais.com

Key personnel
Sales Manager France: *M Fardo*
Sales Manager North and South America: *C Acard*
Area Sales Manager: *G Morgado*
Product Market Manager: *E Veldman*

Products
Railway relays, protection traction relays, panel indicators, relay panels, rehabilitation relay panels, circuit breakers.

Contracts
International contracts include: Bombardier, ALSTOM, Siemens, Rotem, Kinki Sharyo, Nippon Sharyo. Projects include: COMET 5, LIRR M7, Mexico subway, TGV, WMATA 6K. End users: AMTRAK, KCRC, LIRR, NJT, NYCTA, RATP, RENFE, Shanghai Metro, SNCF, STM, TTC, VIA Rail, WAMATA, NS, Virgin, London Underground.

Multipart Universal

8 Stevenson Way, Attercliffe, Sheffield S9 3WZ, UK
Tel: (+44 114) 261 11 88
Fax: (+44 114) 261 11 99
Web: www.ucukltd.com
Managing Director: *Brian Sneyd*
Sales Director: *Chris Chapman*

Products
Fleetwatch Model 392 electronic trip recorder, which fits on to the rear wheel hub. A data recorder via a radio link automatically transfers mileage information and vehicle number as the vehicle enters the depot.
Low-cost catalytic converter which does not rely on precious metals.

Developments
Multipart Universal launched Fleetserve, a new arm dedicated to boosting business among a growing number of major bus fleets who prefer to deal direct with a principal supplier. Offering services from straightforward supply to total control of inventory, Fleetserve offers a one-stop-shop for all-makes parts, the operator reaping the associated cost and efficiency benefits.

MWL Brasil Rodas & Eixos Ltda

Rodovia Vito Ardito, s/n km I – CP 189-CEP, 12280-000 Cacapava, São Paulo, Brazil
Tel: (+55 12) 32 21 24 00   Fax: (+55 12) 32 21 24 10
e-mail: mwlbrasil@mwlbrasil.com.br
Web: www.mwlbrasil.com.br

Key personnel
President: *Samuel Vieira Gambier Neto*
Industrial Director: *Sylvio Roberto Ferreira*
Technology and Development Director: *Domingos José Miniccuci*
Financial Director: *João Aquino Carvalho Junior*

Background
MWL Brasil Rodas & Exios purchased the technology and licence of Mafersa in November 1999 and manufactures its products under the MWL name.

Products
Forged railroad wheels, forged railroad axles, forged railroad wheelsets, forged steel gear rough pieces, forged crane wheels, forged steel sheaves, carbon steel ingots.

MZT HEPOS AD

Pero Nakov bb, 1000 Skopje, PO BOx 409, Republic of Macedonia
Tel: (+389 2) 254 97 80; 254 97 91
Fax: (+389 2) 254 98 51; 254 98 48
e-mail: mzthepos@mzthepos.com.mk
Web: www.hepos.com.mk

Key personnel

General Manager: *Vlado Atanasovski*
Sales and Project Director: *Stojče Smileski*
Head of Sales and Marketing Department:
Aleksandar Anevski

Background

MZT HEPOS was established in 1953 with the purchase of the licenses from Oerlikon (for various driver's brake valves, distributer type Est, electro-pneumatic valves). SAB (for DRV slack adjusters, weighing valves, changeover boxes), and STABEG (for brake cylinders). Although originally designed to produce components and devices for the former Yugoslav Railways and wagon and locomotive builders, the company has grown to be one of the biggest brake equipment producers in southern and eastern Europe. All products are manufactured to applicable International Railway Standards (UIC) under strict ISO 9001 quality conditions. MZT HEPOS has been part of the POLi Group (Italy) since September 2003.

Products

Complete pneumatic and brake systems for locomotives, passenger and freight vehicles; brake equipment (UIC approved) including pneumatic, electropneumatic, hydropneumatic systems and electronic components; driver's brake valves, distributors, disc brakes and tread brake actuators, brake cylinders, slack adjusters, load brake valves, auxiliary pneumatic equipment, end cocks, hoses and coupling heads, air dryers, brake panels, windscreen washers, wheelslide protection devices, diagnostic and test stands.

MZT HEPOS has developed and manufactured the new distributor valve MH3f HBG310, the main control unit for pneumatic systems of railway vehicles, that was approved by the UIC in 2003. All vehicles that run with the MH3f HBG300 unit also carry the brake system, MH, which is an acronym of MZT HEPOS.

New developments

Three new products were developed, manufactured and UIC approved in 2007: a derailment detector; a knick valve and a new relay valve.

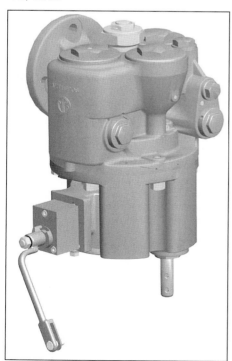

MZT-HEPOS distributor valve   1113740

Nabtesco Corporation

Railroad Products Company, 9-18 Kaigan 1-chome, Minato-ku, Tokyo 105-0022, Japan
Tel: (+81 3) 578 70 70   Fax: (+81 3) 35 78 72 37
e-mail: noriaki_kaneko@nabtesco.com
Web: www.nabtesco.com

Key personnel

President and Chief Executive Officer:
Kazuyuki Matsumoto
Senior Managing Director: *Ryuhei Koyama*
General Manager, Sales and Marketing:
Yukiyasu Fujimoto
General Manager, Overseas Marketing:
Takashi Koyama

Background

Nabtesco Corporation was previously called NABCO Ltd.

Products

Plug and sliding door systems; platform doors (manufactured and supplied by Nabtesco Corporation, NABCO Company); pressure-sealing systems for passenger coaches; windscreen wiper motors.

Contracts

Recent contracts include the supply of automatic sliding door systems to JR East for commuter trainsets; to Automated People Mover Systems in Singapore and Miami plus various other airports. Nabtesco supplied over 30,000 sets of automatic electric sliding door systems (including the products licensed by Faiveley) for various Japanese operators including JR East commuter trainsets.

Narita Manufacturing Ltd

20-12 Hanaomote-cho, Atsuta-ku, Nagoya 456-0033, Japan
Tel: (+81 52) 881 61 91   Fax: (+81 52) 881 67 48
e-mail: sinarita@narita.co.jp
Web: www.narita.co.jp

Key personnel

Chairman: *Masatoshi Narita*
President (Export Sales and Marketing):
Shuichi Narita
Executive Director, General Affairs and Quality Assurance: *Haruo Narita*

Products

Vestibule diaphragms, gangways, rubber bellows, inter-car barriers, door leaves, driving consoles, fuel and water tanks, interior panels, air ducts for railway vehicles and platform door leaves.

Contracts

Recent contracts include the supply of gangway systems for Singapore MRT C151 upgrade, for

Narita sound proof gangway for EMU of Melbourne Bayside on testing device   0533656

Taipei Metro CK371, for Series N700 Shinkansen (JR Central); door leaves for Series N700 Shinkansen; and emergency doors for Taipei Metro CK371 (JR Central).

JT Nelson Company LLC

1733 Research Drive, Louisville, Kentucky 40299, US
Tel: (+1 502) 493 01 05
Fax: (+1 502) 491 43 95
e-mail: info@jtnelson.com
Web: www.jtnelson.com

Key personnel

President: *Susan Mingus*
Production Manager: *Robert Thompson*

Products

Windows and glazing systems.

Neu Systèmes Ferroviaires

PO Box 2026, 70 rue du Collège, F-59700 Marcq en Baroeul, France
Tel: (+33 3) 20 45 65 46
Fax: (+33 3) 20 45 64 98
e-mail: mail@neu-nsf.com
Web: www.neu-nsf.com

Key personnel

Chief Executive Officer: *Guy Leblon*
Commercial Manager: *Franck Vinchon*
Export Assistant: *Caroline Dufour*

Subsidiaries

Atelier Neu Systems Ferroviaires
ZI Neuville en Ferrain, Voie Nouvelle, rue de Reckem, F-599960 Neuville en Ferrain

Conestra
Trupbacher Strasse 26a, D-57072 Siegen, Germany
Tel: (+49 271) 372 05 03; 372 05 05
Contact: Karl Heinz Brull

Neu SF Polska
ul Krucza 28, PL-00522 Warsaw, Poland
Tel: (+48 22) 622 84 71; 622 84 72

Background

Neu Systèmes Ferroviaires was founded in January 1991 and is a member of the NEU Group.

Products

Air-conditioning, heating and ventilation equipment, control systems for HVAC, exhaust fans, cooling fans, high-pressure fans for adjustment of pressure inside coach.

Contracts include heating and ventilation equipment for Rotterdam metro (168 units), Z2N driving cabs for SNCF (800 units), NINA cars for BLS Switzerland (Bombardier Transportation, 24 units).

Recent contracts: Rotterdam metro for Bombardier; Z2N driving cabs for SNCF; NINA/BLS; Metro VAL 208, Lille for Matra; TVR Nancy for Alstom de Dietrich; Warsaw metro for AISTOM Konstal; metro VAL 208 Rennes for Siemens and Citadis for ALSTOM.

Nizhnedneprovsky

Nizhnedneprovsky Tube Rolling Plant Dnepropetrovsk, 49081, Ukraine
Tel: (+380 56) 235 93 01
Fax: (+380 56) 234 90 99

Key personnel

Head of Communications: *Svetlana Chernikova*

Background
Nizhnedneprovsky Tube Rolling Plant has been manufacturing wheels and tyres for over 60 years.

Products
Manufacturer and supply of more than 50 sizes of wheels and tyres for emus, LRVs, metrocars, trainsets, locomotives and freight wagons. Steel for the wheels and tyres is produced in the company's open-hearth furnaces and is refined for resistance to fatigue and brittleness.

NMB – Minebea UK Ltd

Doddington Road, Lincoln LN6 3RA, UK
Tel: (+44 1522) 50 09 33
Fax: (+44 1522) 69 64 85
Web: www.nmb-minebea.co.uk

Key personnel
Managing Director: *Mark N Stansfield*
Engineering Manager: *S Essam*
Sales Manager: *A E Morton*

Background
NMB – Minebea UK Ltd was previously called Rose Bearings Ltd and is the creator of the original 'Rose Joint'.

Products
Rod end and spherical bearings to aerospace, railway, automotive and power generation industries. All types from military standard to customer bespoke. Specialist in coupling bearings for articulated PSV.

Norsk Hydro ASA

Hydro Aluminium
N-0240 Oslo, Norway
Tel: (+47 22) 53 81 00   Fax: (+47 22) 53 27 25
e-mail: corporate@hyrdo.com
Web: www.hydro.com

Street address
Drammensveien 264, N-0283 Oslo, Norway

Key personnel
President and Chief Executive Officer, Hydro: *Eivind Reiten*
Executive Vice-President and Chief Financial Officer: *John Ove Ottestad*
Executive Vice-President, Aluminium Metal: *Hilde Merete Aasheim*
Executive Vice-President, Aluminium Products: *Svein Richard Brabdtzæg*

Background
In January 2002, VAW aluminium AG was acquired by Norsk Hydro ASA. The company was transformed to a limited liability company and is now known as Hydro Aluminium Deutschland GmbH.

Products
Metal production and fabrication including rolling and converting of aluminium; aluminium engine castings; flexible packaging; extruded products.

Oleo International Ltd

PO Box 216, Grovelands Estate, Longford Road, Exhall, Coventry CV7 9NE, UK
Tel: (+44 2476) 64 55 55
Fax: (+44 2476) 36 42 87
e-mail: info@oleo.co.uk
Web: www.oleo.demon.co.uk

Key personnel
Managing Director: *A P Fulford*
Sales Manager: *R Hunt*

Products
Oleo produces a wide range of long-stroke hydraulic buffers suitable for mounting on fixed or sliding end-stops. Applications include freight yards, steelworks and passenger terminals.
On sliding friction end-stops the need for continual resetting of the friction elements is eliminated, and the hydraulic buffers absorb all of the impact energy at low speeds. Typically a 400 tonne train may be arrested by a pair of 800 mm stroke buffers at 6 km/h without causing the end-stop to slide. Initial and final jerk forces are also eliminated. These buffer units are available for all types of rail operation from LRVs to heavy freight.

Oy Tamware AB

Yrittäjänkulma 5, FIN-33710 Tampere, Finland
Tel: (+358 3) 283 11 11
Fax: (+358 3) 283 15 00
e-mail: info@tamware.fi
Web: www.tamware.fi

Key personnel
Managing Director: *Harri Salminen*
Financial Director: *Tommi Latva*
Sales Manager: *Jason Thomas*
Technical Director: *Kalervo Vainiomäki*

Products
Doors systems (pneumatic, electric and manual) for buses, coaches, trains, metros and trams; side hatches, engine hatches, indoor information signs, destination signs.

Pallas BV

Biesheuvelplein 10, NL-2064 WL Spaarndam, Netherlands
Tel: (+31 235) 49 26 99
Fax: (+31 235) 38 39 42
e-mail: info@pallasbv.com
Web: www.pallasbv.com

Products
Coloured coating and graffiti removers for use on public transport and public areas. Permanent coating for easy repeated cleaning without the need to renew treatment, available in many colours.

Paltechnica

Kibbutz Nitzanim M P Evtach IL-79290, Israel
Tel: (+972 8) 672 10 81
Fax: (+972 8) 672 79 91
e-mail: sec@paltechnica.co.il
Web: www.paltechnica.co.il

Key personnel
President and Chief Executive Officer: *Aki Marmur*
Transportation Division Manager: *Ricardo Schneir*

Background
Paltechnica is a limited liability company owned by Kibbutz Nitzanim, Israel.

Products
Seating for trains, buses and mini-buses.

Contracts
Paltechnica seating systems have been supplied for ALSTOM coaches, Bombardier Transportation IC3 dmus and double-deck coaches and new cars supplied to Siemens for Israel Railways.

Pars Komponenty sro

Butovická ul, (areál TVS), CZ-742 13 Studénka, Czech Republic
Tel: (+420 556) 45 50 00
Fax: (+420 556) 45 50 10
e-mail: info@parskomponenty.cz
Web: www.parskomponenty.cz

Key personnel
Director: *Vladimír Vyhlídal*
Technical Director: *Schreier Jirí*
Financial Director: *Martina Mazancová*
Production Director: *René Krístek*

Background
The company was originally founded in 1999 following the merger of Komponenty sro and Pars Holding sro Sumperk.
Pars Komponenty develops and manufactures parts for the mass transportation industry.

Products
Subsystems and components for passenger rail systems and buses, including: exterior and interior door systems; windows; luggage racks; interior walls; lifting platforms for passengers with limited mobility.

Pascal International AB

Box 33, SE-280 10 Sösdala, Sweden
Tel: (+46 451) 660 80   Fax: (+46 451) 603 70
e-mail: contact@pascal-system.com
Web: www.pascal-system.com

Products
DUX spring technology for passenger rail vehicle seating. The system comprises a self-contained spring unit consisting of multiple rows of springs mounted into channels of non-woven fabric.
Pascal FR meets fire resistance standards to BS 5852 – Crib 7, UIC 564-2, ISO 6941 and M1.

People Seating Ltd

Unit 9, Washington Street Industrial Estate, Netherton, Dudley DY2 9RE, UK
Tel: (+44 1384) 25 71 24   Fax: (+44 1384) 24 21 06
e-mail: info@peopleseating.com
Web: www.peopleseating.co.uk

Key personnel
Managing Director: *David J Poston*
Sales and Marketing Co-ordinator: *Kaye Blunt*

Products
Passenger and driver seating, interior trim components. Speciality seat refurbishment upgrade.

Percy Lane Products

Lichfield Road, Tamworth B79 7TL, UK
Tel: (+44 1827) 638 21   Fax: (+44 1827) 31 01 59
e-mail: main@percy-lane.co.uk
Web: www.percy-lane.co.uk

Key personnel
Executive Chairman: *G H Fowler*
Managing Director: *P S Wright*
Sales Director: *J W Whetton*
Business Development Director: *N Greenhalgh*
Commercial Manager: *D J Knight*

Products
Windows, sashes, impact-resistant windscreens, luggage racks, detrainment devices, Beclawat range of products; aluminium fabrications, including gangway frames, doors.

Contracts

Contracts include cabside windows for European high-speed trains; bodyside windows specifically for UK rolling stock and selected European; bodyend droplight windows and detrainment devices (train to track and train to train) for underground vehicles, both new and refurbished carriages; aluminium windscreen frames; gangway frames; Beclawat range of products for spares demand.

Developments

Cassette bodyside windows creating flush exterior glazed effect but with the benefits of simple maintenance, for example no adhesive bonding on the vehicle; detrainment steps for train to train and train to track applications; type testing of bodyside windows to improve passenger safety in crash conditions.

Petards Joyce-Loebl Ltd

390 Princesway, Team Valley Trading Estate, Gateshead NE11 0TU, UK
Tel: (+44 191) 420 30 00
Fax: (+44 191) 420 30 30
e-mail: sales@joyce-loebl.com
Web: www.petardsplc.com

Key personnel

Chief Executive: *Bill Conn*
Director, Transport Systems: *Mike Wade*
Finance Director: *Andy Wonnacott*

Background

Formerly Joyce-Loebl Ltd, the company adopted its current name in 2005 following its acquisition by Petards Group plc, a specialist in security and surveillance systems.

Products

Train-borne digital CCTV systems.

Pickersgill-Kaye Ltd

Pepper Road, Hunslet, Leeds LS10 2PP, UK
Tel: (+44 113) 277 55 31   Fax: (+44 113) 276 02 21
e-mail: sales@pkaye.co.uk
Web: www.pkaye.co.uk

Key personnel

Managing Director: *Peter Murphy*
Sales Manager: *Harry Griffiths*
Rail Product Sales: *Andrew Hewitt*

Products

Lock assemblies for internal and external applications; passenger emergency alarm handles and emergency talkback units; side skirt locks; LED indicators for door status, driver's desk; emergency hammer box units and emergency access break panels.

Pintsch Bamag Antriebs-und Verkehrstechnik GmbH

PO Box 100420, D-46524 Dinslaken, Germany
Tel: (+49 2064) 60 20
Fax: (+49 2064) 60 22 66
e-mail: info@pintschbamag.de
Web: www.pintschbamag.de

Key personnel

Managing Director: *Dr Rolf-Dieter Krächter (spokesperson), Hans Ulrich Reichling*
Strategic Concerns: *Ulrich Nagorski*
Head of Business Unit: *Alexsandar Lenhart*
Head of Sales: *Goetz Dittmar*
Export Manager: *Peter Bunzeck*
Manager, Quality Control: *Uwe Reske*

Background

Pintsch Bamag is a member of the Schaltbau Group.

Products

Railway vehicle equipment for high-speed, regional and local traffic. Door systems, door step systems, door control systems, door attachments, diagnosis systems, MVB bus system interfaces. All kinds of power supply systems (single- and multi-voltage), battery chargers. Current collection systems, lighting components (top and rear lights), heating devices.

PIXY AG

Schiffmühlestrasse 7, PO Box, CH-5300 Turgi, Switzerland
Tel: (+41 56) 200 03 10   Fax: (+41 56) 200 03 29
e-mail: franz.steuri@pixy.ch
Web: www.pixy.ch

Key personnel

Managing Director: *Mark Meier*
Chief Executive Officer and Sales and Marketing: *Franz Steuri*
Corporate Communications: *Fadri Casty*
Customer Service Centre: *Peter Zuercher*
Chief, Development: *Marc Michalewicz*
Chief, Production: *Markus Koller*
Quality Assurance: *Peter Zuercher*

Background

Founded in 1988, PIXY AG became independent of the Sécheron Group following a management takeover in 2002. The company is ISO 9001/14001 and OHSAS18001 certified and is currently applying for CMMI level 2.0 and IRIS certification. In 2006 PIXY opened its own facilities (sales/engineering and production) in Shanghai to serve the local market. In 2008 the company relocated to new premises in Turgi, Switzerland.

Products

Design and manufacture of a wide range of advanced HMI- / DMI- screenboards for ground-based or mobile (train) applications suitable for tough environments in terms of vibration, shock, EMC, temperature and humidity. PIXY also designs and manufactures screenboards and screen links to customer specification and provides solutions to specific interface needs (serial, MVB, CAN, LON etc). PIXY AG has experience in designing robust hardware such as PC-based motherboards, which involves the design of application software (Screensoft) as well as specific device driver software (MVB, Profibus, LON, CAN) to form complete display solutions. This equipment can be plugged in directly to the end user's application. PIXY offers enhanced training and after sales support backed-up by maintenance contracts.

Polarteknik PMC Oy AB

Klaavolantie 1, FIN-3270 Huittinen, Finland
Tel: (+358 2) 560 15 00   Fax: (+358 2) 56 85 01
e-mail: jouni.saarnia@polarteknik.com
Web: www.polarteknik.com

Head Office

Mestarintie 7, PO Box 24, FIN-01731 Vantaa, Finland
Tel: (+358 9) 87 80 80   Fax: (+358 9) 87 80 81 80
e-mail: info@polarteknik.com

Key personnel

Managing Director: *Inger Eriksson-Blom*
Divisional Director of Doorsystem: *Jouni Saarnia*

Background

Previously Berendsen PMC Oy Ab, Pimatic, the company is owned by Dacke PMC.

Products

Pimatic automatic interior door systems; pressure-sealed gangway doors; interior doors; fire barrier doors; electro-pneumatic and electric-powered door gear for rail vehicles; pneumatic bus actuators.

Contracts

Contracts include the supply of interior door systems for Bombardier Transportation projects, including Electrostar emus for the UK, and for double-deck intercity coaches supply to VR, Finland, by Talgo, ALSTOM Sweden, Talgo Spain high-speed trains, Rotem, Korea, and CAF, Spain.

Poli Costruzione Materiali Trazione SpA

Via Fontanella 11, I-26010 Camisano, Cremona, Italy
Tel: (+39 0373) 77 72 33
Fax: (+39 0373) 77 72 29
e-mail: info@polibrakes.com
Web: www.polibrakes.com

Key personnel

Chief Executive Officer: *Francesco Poli*
Technical Director: *Paolo Poli*
Technical Export Sales Manager: *Giuseppe Poli*
Finance Director: *Alessandro Poli*
Purchasing Manager: *Alberto Poli*

Subsidiaries

MZT HEPOS AD
Pero Nakov bb, 1000 Skopje, Macedonia

Products

Complete brake systems and their components for any kind of railway vehicle, high-speed train, passenger car, freight car, locomotive, track maintenance vehicle, tread brake units; axle-mounted and wheel-mounted brake discs by sectors; electro-magnetic track brakes; resilient wheels; wheelsets. All products comply with UNI EN ISO 9001:2000 quality system, with the new EC regulations. They comply with UIC standards.

Polymer Engineering Ltd

Quakers Coppice, Crewe Gates Farm Industrial Estate, Crewe, Cheshire, CW1 6FA, UK
Tel: (+44 1270) 58 37 23   Fax: (+44 1270) 58 08 46
e-mail: enquiries@polymer.co.uk
Web: www.polymer.co.uk

Key personnel

Managing Director: *Nick Coorke*
Sales Director: *E Hammond*

Products

Resin-moulded transfer technology components.

Contracts

Supply of composites components for Strasbourg Eurotram, including exterior panels, pantograph roof assembly, roof end panels, arc panels, line filter covers and all side exterior panels.

Portaramp

Trident House, Roudham Road, East Harling, Norfolk NR16 2QN, UK
Tel: (+44 1953) 714 599
Fax: (+44 1953) 714 598
e-mail: sales@portaramp.co.uk
Web: www.portaramp.co.uk

Key personnel

Sales & Marketing Director: *Mandy Lancaster*

Products

Portable wheelchair ramp, to provide access to rail vehicles for wheelchair users. Available in four standard lengths and fully DIPTAC (Disabled Persons Transport Advisory Committee) compliant; manufactured from lightweight, strong aluminium alloy; folds in half for compact easy storage.

Developments

Pneumatically powered integrated bus ramp developed in conjunction with Norgren pneumatics. The ramp has been designed to be DIPTAC compliant.

Post Glover Resistors Inc

4750 Olympic Blvd., Erlanger, Kentucky 41018, US
Tel: (+1 859) 283 07 78   Fax: (+1 859) 283 29 78
e-mail: sales@postglover.com
Web: www.postglover.com

Key personnel

President: *Richard Field*
Vice-President, Operations: *Dave Flynn*
Vice President Sales & Marketing: *Scott Fuller*
Director of Sales: *Stuart Gibbon*

Products

Power resistors for transport applications, including naturally cooled and forced cooled roof or under-car-mounted resistors, designed to meet the load requirements of each vehicle. Infra-red temperature monitoring and protection system offering remote indication and status.

Powernetics International Ltd

Jason Works, Clarence Street, Loughborough LE11 1DX, UK
Tel: (+44 1509) 21 41 53   Fax: (+44 1509) 26 24 60
e-mail: jag@powernetics.co.uk
Web: www.powernetics.co.uk

Key personnel

Managing Director: *Satish Chada*
Sales Director: *Kevin Pateman*
Engineering Director: *Nilesh Chouhan*
Operations Director: *Konrad Chada*
Sales Manager: *Jim Goddard*

Products

Independent private limited company with 35 years' experience in design, manufacture, test, installation, commissioning and maintenance of auxiliary, standby/emergency AC/DC power supply systems for the rail industry in trackside, tunnel, switchroom, REB and trainborne environments.

RailPower UPS systems for signalling, radio, telecoms and level crossing applications. Static inverters for trainborne HVAC and domestic catering applications. Heavy duty battery chargers to BR1875Std for lineside signalling. DC PSUs for NRN driver/train radio, secondary door locking and track circuit actuation applications.

Powernetics is a BS EN ISO9001 accredited company.

System design and integration of UPS and associated switchgear/power monitoring within REBs and switchrooms for SSI, FSP and PSP applications.

Contracts

Derby PSB/Life Extension Works – 5 × RailPower UPS 540 V 30–60 kVA for Network Rail Midlands Zone 2000/500 k Horsham area resignalling (HARSTL2K) – 6 × RailPower UPS/REBs 400 V 4–40 kVA for Network Rail Southern Zone 2001/500 k.

East Anglia signalling upgrade – 20 × RailPower 240/400 V HV UPS for Network Rail East Anglia Zone 2002/500 k NRS supply RailPower

BR1875Std battery chargers to IMCs throughout Network Rail 1994–2003 onwards 1,000–3,000 k.

Chiltern Lines – Project Evergreen – 2 × RailPower UPS/REBs 650 V 20 kVA for Network Rail Midlands Zone 2002–2003/250 k.

Cherwell Valley resignalling project, Leamington Spa retro-fit 30 kVA UPS and PEB for Network Rail Midlands Region 2002–2003/100 k.

Quintrell Downs resignalling project, 5 kVA RailPower UPS for Network Rail Great Western Regional 2003–2004/15 k.

Three Bridges and Eastleigh 4 × 5 kVA RailPower UPS for Network Rail Southern Region – 62 k – 2004 (UPS for TD's).

Sheerness PSB – 1 × 3 kVA RailPower UPS for Sherbourne Resignalling Project on Network Rail Southern Region – 15 k – 2004 (UPS for TDR). DC PSU – Tube Lines Heathrow Terminal 5.

25 Line side AC/DC UPS for Chicago Transport Authority (CTA) 2006/07.

Power-One AG

Ackerstrasse 56, CH-8610 Uster, Switzerland
Tel: (+41 1) 944 82 16   Fax: (+41 1) 944 80 11
e-mail: info@power-one.com
Web: www.power-one.com

Key personnel

President: *Hans Grüter*
Product Manager: *Claude Abächerli*

Background

Power-One products were formerly marketed under the Melcher name.

Products

DC-DC and AC-DC converters, inverters, battery chargers – 80 product families with output power in a range of 1 to 1,000 W. All Power-One power products are ISO 9001 certified. Miniature-size switching regulator.

Powertron Converters Ltd

Glebe Farm Technical Campus, Knapwell, Cambridge CB3 8GG, UK
Tel: (+44 1954) 26 77 26   Fax: (+44 1954) 26 76 26
e-mail: sales@powertron.co.uk
Web: www.powertron.co.uk

Key personnel

Chairman: *Miles Rackowe*
Managing Director: *Mike Carter*
Technical Director: *Andy Dickeson*

Background

Powertron Converters Ltd is an internationally trading company recently formed as a continuation of the activities of Powertron Ltd, which was founded in 1971.

In March 2007 Powertron Converters Ltd joined the Martek Power group of companies.

Products

High-reliability switch mode power supplies and DC-DC converters in the power range 5 W to 1 kW. A principal area of activity is DC-DC converters for use on railway rolling stock. Applications include lighting, communications, brake monitoring equipment, fire protection equipment and train management systems.

Pretoria Transit Interiors, Inc

1975 Joe B Jackson Parkway, Murfreesboro, TN 37127, South Africa
Tel: (+615) 687 85 15   Fax: (+615) 867 87 90
e-mail: j.stallworth@pretoriausa.com
Web: www.pretoriausa.com

Key personnel

Sales Manager: *John Stallworth*

Products

Lighting, ducting and luggage rack systems for bus manufacturing companies throughout the US and Canada.

Q'Straint International

5553 Ravenswood Road, Building 110, Ft. Lauderdale, Florida 33312, US
Tel: (+1 954) 986 66 65   Fax: (+1 954) 986 00 21
e-mail: qstraint@qstraint.com
Web: www.qstraint.com

Key personnel

President: *Jean Girardin*
Managing Director: *Mike Simmonds*
General Manager: *Jim Reaume*

Other offices

Australia
Tramanco Pty Ltd
21 Shoebury Street, Rocklea, Queensland 4106, Australia
Tel: (+61 7) 38 92 23 11   Fax: (+61 7) 38 92 65 29

Canada
100 Sheldon Drive, Unit 18, Cambridge, Ontario N1R 7S7, Canada
Tel: (+1 800) 987 99 87

UK (Europe)
Q'Straint Ltd
Unit 72-76 John Wilson Business Park, Whitstable, Kent CT5 3QT, UK
Tel: (+44 12 27) 77 30 35   Fax: (+44 12 27) 77 00 35
e-mail: aroth@www.QStraint.com
Sales Manager, Europe: *Alexander Roth*

Products

Wheelchair and occupant restraint systems for buses and rail rolling stock.

A low-profile high-efficiency floor fastening restrains the individual with a lap belt attached to the rear wheelchair fasteners and a shoulder belt that fastens to the vehicle side.

A variant of the wheelchair and occupant restraint system is available for operators who do not want to fit floor pockets. It allows installation on vehicles fitted with tracking.

Developments

In 2008 Q'Straint announced an automatic universal rearward facing wheelchair restraint system for city transport and rail applications. The new system known as the QTT-100 is able to secure virtually all wheelchairs and does not need any direct external assistance to operate. It uses pneumatic power arms (designed with an integrated air system) to engage the wheelchair. The wheelchair passenger is rearwards facing for travel, and the unit complies with USA ADA (Americans with Disabilities Act) directive EC2001/85. It also complies with the proposed ISO 10865-1 standard and other applicable regulations worldwide. The system is remotely

Q'Straint's automatic universal rearward facing wheelchair restraint system (Tony Patterson)
1374843

activated by the driver or train guard from his or her seat to ensure the safety of all passengers when not in use.

Rail Interiors SpA

Via Carrara, snc, I-04013 Tor Tre Ponti (Latina), Italy
Tel: (+39 0773) 44 41 (+39 0773) 44 47 44
e-mail: rail@railinteriors.com
Web: www.railinteriors.com

Background
Established in 1972, Rail Interiors is a division of Aviointeriors SpA.

In February 1999 Rail Interiors acquired Testori Interiors which specialised in the production of interior components for the Pendolino high-speed train. Most recently, Rail Interiors bought Pianfei Compositi, enabling it to provide turnkey solutions.

Products
Rail Interiors technologies include advanced composites, vacuum bags, hot presses, aluminium, wet painting, filming, anti-graffiti finishing, anti-corrosion finishing and sanding. Full train car interiors including integration of any bar, electrical, heating equipment. The core business includes the engineering and production of heating profiles, under window panels and window panels, baggage racks, ceiling panels, tables, end walls and connection kit for wheel chairs, seats (standard and disabled), toilets (standard and disabled), driver cabin operating desks, panels and ceiling panels. Flooring and external body components.

Contracts
Rail Interiors' current customers include ALSTOM Transport and The Chinese Ministry of Railways.

The company is currently producing interior parts for the new Pendolino trainsets for Trenitalia and Cisalpino and high-speed regional emus for China.

Railko Ltd

Ashburton Road West, Trafford Park M17 1RU, UK
Tel: (+44 161) 872 16 81
Fax: (+44 161) 872 75 96
e-mail: info@railko.co.uk
Web: www.railko.co.uk

Key personnel
Managing Director: *Tony Moore*
Sales : *Neil Firth*

Products
Low friction and long wear life composite bearings. Applications include centre pivot liners, side bearer liners, sliding pads, torsion bar bearings, friction dampers, brake gear bushes, door slides, gangway liners, and axle box guides.

Materials include Railko NF and Railko RG grades.

RailTronic AG

Postfach, Fabrikstrasse 10, CH-8370 Sirnach, Switzerland
Tel: (+41 71) 969 37 73
Fax: (+41 71) 969 37 74
e-mail: info@railtronic.com
Web: www.railtronic.com

Key personnel
Managing Director: *Ulrich Plathner*
General Manager Business Development and Marketing: *Pieter de Ruijter*
Sales: *Gerald Plathner*

Products
Electronic ballasts, timetable illuminators, high-voltage charging and power supply systems and complete interior lighting and ceiling systems for urban and main line rail vehicles.

REBS Zentralschmiertechnik GmbH

Duisburger Strasse 115, D-40885 Ratingen, Germany
Tel: (+49 2102) 930 60
Fax: (+49 2102) 93 06 40
e-mail: info@rebs.de
Web: www.rebs.de

Products
Wheel flange lubrication systems for trains, metro vehicles, trams and LRVs.

Le Réservoir SA

rue Eugène Sue, PO Box 1139, F-03103 Montluçon Cedex, France
Tel: (+33 4) 70 03 47 47   Fax: (+33 4) 70 03 77 03
e-mail: lereservoir@lereservoir.com
Web: www.fayat.com

Key personnel
Director: *Jean Claude Mardele*
Commercial Director: *Pierre Poncie*
Export Manager: *Clotilde Aufaure*

Background
Le Réservoir SA is part of the Fayat Group.

Products
Air vessels for brake and suspension systems for trains and buses.

Contracts
Le Réservoir's air vessels are mounted on the French TGV high-speed train, TGV double-deck TER new generation (regional train) and for export on the Eurostar TGV, KTGV in Korea and the metro trains in Mexico.

Rex Articoli Tecnici SA (REX)

Via Catenazzi 1, CH-6850 Mendrisio, Switzerland
Tel: (+41 91) 640 50 50   Fax: (+41 91) 640 50 55
e-mail: sales@rex.ch
Web: www.rex.ch

Key personnel
General Manager: *M Favini*

Products
Design and manufacture of rubber and elastic thermoplastic products for the rail industry.

RICA

Via Podgora 26, I-31029 Vittorio Veneto (TV), Italy
Tel: (+39 0438) 91 01
Fax: (+39 0438) 91 22 36; 91 22 72; 91 03 26
e-mail: rica@zoppas.com
Web: www.rica.it

Background
RICA is a member of the Zoppas Industries Group.

Products
Heating systems for rail vehicles, including: finned element duct heaters; air-conditioning duct heaters; insulator mounted heaters; horizontal upflow heater units; wall and floor heating elements; cab heater units; vertical convection heaters; toilet heater units and boilers; waste tank heaters; windscreen defrosting systems; flexible heater systems; coach entrance floor heating systems; locomotive anti-slip system heating systems; and pipe and exhaust tank heating systems.

Ricon

Corporate Headquarters
7900 Nelson Road, Panorama City, California CA 91402, US
Tel: (+1 818) 267 30 00   Fax: (+1 818) 267 30 01
Web: www.riconcorp.com

Other offices
Ricon UK
Littlemoss Business Park, Littlemoss Road, Droylsden, Manchester M43 7EF, UK
Web: www.riconuk.com

Key personnel
Vice-President and Managing Director, Ricon Europe: *Andreas Boch*
Vice-President of Sales and Marketing, Ricon Bus Products: *Keith Nippes*
Director of Product Assurance: *Jon Mitcham*

Background
Ricon was acquired by Wabtec in June 2007.

Products
Design, manufacture and installation of wheelchair lifts and ramps for commercial, paratransit, heavy transit and motorcoach vehicles.

Recent developments include Ricon's pneumatic bus door actuator systems, which are designed to be compatible on existing bus door systems.

Ring Mekanikk AS

Postboks 144, N-2391 Moelv, Norway
Tel: (+47 62) 33 00 00   Fax: (+47 62) 33 00 01
e-mail: mail@ringmek.com
Web: www.ringmek.com

Key personnel
Managing Director: *Trond Høgetveit*
Marketing Director: *Mai Riise*

Products
Seating for rail vehicles.

Roberto Nuti SpA

Via 1° Maggio, 7, ZI Poggio Piccolo, I-40023 Castel Guelfo, Italy
Tel: (+39 0542) 67 18 11
Fax: (+39 0542) 67 18 00
e-mail: mail@rnb.it
Web: www.rnb.it

Key personnel
Commercial Director: *Massimo Nuti*
Export Sales Manager: *Roberto Romanelli*

Background
The company is certified to ISO 9001:2000 standards.

Products
SABO shock-absorbers.

Robert Wagner

PO Box 1604, D-42477 Radevormwald, Germany
Tel: (+49 2195) 70 04; 70 05   Fax: (+49 2195) 10 19
e-mail: mail@robertwagner.de
Web: www.robertwagner.de

Key personnel
Managing Director: *Reinhold Wagner*

Products
Hinges for doors, window locks and mechanisms, water valves and associated equipment, interior fittings for rail vehicles.

Rohm and Haas (UK) Ltd

Powder Coatings Division
Herald Way, Coventry CV3 2RQ, UK
Tel: (+44 2476) 65 44 00   Fax: (+44 2476) 65 37 60
Web: www.rohmhaaspowdercoatings.com

Key personnel
Site Director: *Tony Pitchford*
European Product Manager: *Richard Norris*
Rail Industry Manager: *Alan Phillips*

Products
Powder coatings for the rail industry for use in passenger vehicle interiors, on station fittings and signage, and on electrical trunking and switchgear assemblies. The product range comprises: Bonalux AG 2000 anti-graffiti powder coatings; 491 Series polyester powder coatings; and 4620 Series epoxy powder coatings. All are fire-resistant to BS 476 Parts 6 and 7, smoke and toxic fume emission complying with BS 2583. Impress, a new range of innovative powder coatings for 'in-mould' application to plastic composite, for example: rolling stock seating.

Contracts
Powder coatings have been supplied to London Underground Ltd (Central, Jubilee, Piccadilly and Northern Lines), MTRC Hong Kong, First Great Western, Midland Mainline, Virgin Trains and to leading rolling stock manufacturers.

Rosco, Inc

90-21 144th Place, Jamaica, New York, New York 11435, US
Tel: (+1 718) 526 26 01   Fax: (+1 718) 297 03 23
e-mail: info@roscomirrors.com
Web: www.roscomirrors.com

Key personnel
Commercial Sales and Marketing: *Peter Plate*

Products
Rosco provides equipment to manufacturers in the school bus, transit and shuttle bus, motor coach, and other market vehicles.

Developments
Rosco's PerformaStyle system, an OEM-installed production system on new transit and coach buses which provides front-window viewing of the mirrors on both sides.

Ruspa Officine SpA

Via Cristoforo Colombo 2, I-10070 Robassomero, Italy
Tel: (+39 011) 923 41 11   Fax: (+39 011) 923 41 06
e-mail: info@ruspa.com
Web: www.ruspa.com

Key personnel
President: *R Ruspa*
General Manager: *L Ruspa*
Chief of Sales Department: *C Ruspa*

Products
Interior styling equipment, including magazine nets, ashtrays, handles, glass holders, food trays, lighting, and stainless steel wheel covers; seat systems for bus and rail applications; foot rests; arm rests.

Sabre Rail Services Ltd

Grindon Way, Heighington Lane Business Park, Newton Aycliffe DL5 6SH, UK
Tel: (+44 1325) 30 05 05   Fax: (+44 1325) 30 04 85
Web: www.sabre-rail.co.uk

Key personnel
Managing Director: *David A Thompson*
Sales Director: *Stephen Thompson*

Products
Re-manufacture of hydraulic dampers for rail rolling stock, also brake cylinders, slack adjusters, valves and current collection equipment.

Safety Vision

Headquarters
6100 W Sam Houston Parkway North, House, Texas 77041-5113, US
Tel: (+1 713) 896 66 00   Fax: (+1 713) 896 66 40
e-mail: email@safetyvision.com
Web: www.safetyvision.com

Key personnel
President and Chief Executive Officer: *Bruce Smith*
Chief Financial Officer: *Michael Ondruch*
Chief Technology Officer: *Chris Fritz*
Vice-President of Sales: *Rex Colorado*
Marketing Director: *Teresa Phillips*

Background
Founded in 1993, Safety Vision has 100 employees in six locations.
The company is a minority-owned SDB (Small Disadvantaged Business) and is an approved vendor for the Federal Government's GSA Supply Schedule, the 1122 program, and the Department of Homeland Security.

Products
Onboard surveillance and recording systems for public transport using mobile-rated digital video and audio tools.
Safety Vision has recently introduced the RouteRecorder® 4C, a mobile recorder which supports four cameras, providing transit, para-transit and light rail with quality video.

SAFT

Industrial Battery Group
12 rue Sadi Carnot, F-93170 Bagnolet, France
Tel: (+33 1) 49 93 17 69   Fax: (+33 1) 49 93 19 50
Web: www.saftbatteries.com

Key personnel
Chairman: *John Searle*
Chief Financial Officer: *Bruno Dathis*
General Manager, IBG: *Xavier Delacroix*
Communications Director and Investor Relations: *Jill Ledger*

Products
Ni-Cd batteries, pocket plates or sintered/plastic bonded electrode types for emergency supply and security purposes. All items are lightweight and compact and are available in stainless steel, flame-retardant or standard plastic containers.
SAFT offers an integrated battery assembly for onboard power for railway networks by combining advanced Ni-Cd batteries with custom-made containers, reducing weight and volume.

The Matrix (MRX) range of Ni-Cd batteries, sintered/PBE, improve weight and volume by 40 per cent. These batteries are built for trams, emus, electric locomotives and light rail.
The Nickel metal hydride, Ni-MH integrated battery systems, offer power storage, making the ideal solution for various hybrid applications, such as the source of traction power when overhead catenaries are not present.

Contracts
The company has supplied rail and bus companies in 56 countries and contracts include supply to the Pendolino tilting trainsets and passenger coaches for SNCB, RENFE, Taipei and Pakistan. Recent contracts include: supply of MRX batteries for Turin trams, SNCF's new AGC regional express trains, AVES 103 high-speed train in Spain built by Siemens, ALSTOM hybrid tramways for Nice city in France.

San Electro Heat A/S

Gillelejevej 30, Esbønderup, DK-3230 Graested, Denmark
Tel: (+45) 48 39 88 88   Fax: (+45) 48 39 88 98
e-mail: san@san-as.com
Web: www.san-as.com

Key personnel
Managing Director: *Michael H Laursen*
Sales Manager: *Stefan Novod*

Products
Driver's cab and passenger compartment heating systems for rail vehicles and buses.

SBF Spezialleuchten Wurzen GmbH

Badergraben 16, D-04808 Wurzen, Germany
Tel: (+49 3425) 905 15   Fax: (+49 3425) 90 51 62
e-mail: info@sbf-spezialleuchten.de
Web: www.sbf-spezialleuchten.de

Key personnel
Managing Director: *Hans D Sehn*
Sales Manager: *Fritz Strobelt*

Products
Light fittings for passenger car interiors and exteriors including: components of general lighting, ceiling spotlights and elements of individual seat lighting, reflectors and front-of-train lights, as well as signal and end-of-train lights.
Customers include Siemens Transportation Systems, Bombardier Transportation, ALSTOM LHB, Deutsche Bahn AG (German Railway Company) and other regional transportation companies.

Schaeffler KG

Product Line Railway
Georg-Schäfer-Strasse 30, D-97421 Schweinfurt, Germany
Tel: (+49 9721) 91 39 98   Fax: (+49 9721) 91 37 88
e-mail: rail_transport@schaeffler.com
Web: www.fag.com, www.ina.com

Key personnel
Division Manager: *Dr Raimund Abele*
International Sales: *Simone Purbs*
Application Engineering: *Reinhold Schmitt*

Background
FAG, the product brand, has been part of the Schaeffler Group since 2001 and has been active in all of the group's divisions – Aerospace, Automotive and Industrial. Together with INA's complementary product range, Schaeffler Group Industrial has one of the widest product portfolios in the rolling bearing industry, covering nearly

FAG axlebox for the Autorail Grande Capacité
1176420

INA slewing ring with integrated yaw dampers in VAL 208 trains   1176421

all applications in production machinery, power transmission and rail technology, heavy industry and consumer products.

Products and services

Schaeffler's products for rail vehicles equip locomotives, freight cars, passenger coaches, commuter train vehicles, subways, and tramways. The product brand FAG provides bearings for various types of wheelsets (also light alloy housings and wheelsets equipped with speed, temperature and vibration sensors); cartridge units TAROL, current-insulated traction motor bearings; gearbox bearings, test rigs for wheelsets with mounted bearings; specific Arcanol greases; mounting and dismounting devices. Additionally, FAG Industrial Services (FIS) offers the reconditioning of axlebox bearings.

INA, an additional Schaeffler product brand, provides, for example, yoke-type track roller units for tilting systems, plain bearings for automatic gauge adjustment mechanisms, slewing rings and spherical plain bearings for local traffic trains, spherical plain bearings for couplings and anti-rolling devices as well as bearings for train doors.

Schlegel AG

Blumenfeldstrasse 14, CH-9403 Goldach, Switzerland
Tel: (+41 71) 844 26 26   Fax: (+41 71) 844 26 27
e-mail: info@schlegel.ch
Web: www.schlegel.ch

Key personnel

Managing Director: *Daniel Niederer*
Business Development and Marketing:
   Roman Hächler

Products

Seats; interior fittings including luggage racks and wall-mounted tables; interior doors and door systems; self-contained submodules for all kinds of passenger coaches, walls, ceilings and other interior components and complete subsystems.

Selectron Systems AG

Bernstrasse 70 CH-3250 Lyss, Switzerland
Tel: (+41 32) 387 61 61   Fax: (+41 32) 387 61 00
e-mail: info@selectron.ch
Web: www.selectron.ch

Background

Selectron Systems is a member of the Schneider Electric Group.

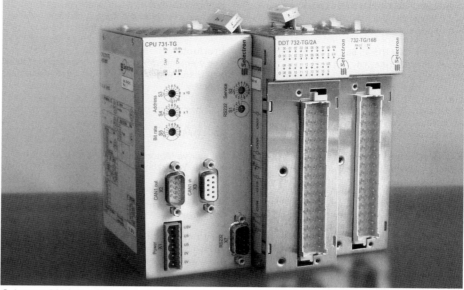

Selectron MAS 73x -T module   1310745

Products

Automation, control and network systems for rail vehicles, including TCMS (Train Control and Monitoring System) and MAS-Traffic open control and communication system. This integrates control units regarding traction and propulsion monitoring braking, vehicle speed control, power supply, lighting, heating, ventilation, air conditioning, toilets, doors and other functions.

Selectron Systems also supplies control components and undertakes hardware manufacturing and engineering for vehicle subsystems and for stationary applications.

Selectron Systems control technology is in service with operators in Austria, Poland, Germany, Netherlands, Switzerland, US, Canada, China and others.

Developments

The modules have a robus steel housing and comply with EN 50155 standards.

Selectron has developed the MAS (Multifunction Automation System) controller family, designed to achieve compact dimensions and a high number of I/O signal conditions. Some modules are in accordance with SIL2 standard.

Semvac A/S

Svendborgvej 226, DK-5260 Odense S, Denmark
Tel: (+45) 63 15 33 00   Fax: (+45) 63 15 33 01
e-mail: info@semvac.dk
Web: www.semvac.dk

Key personnel

Managing Director: *Bent Clausen*
Sales Manager: *Sørensen*

Background

Previously called Semco Vakuumeteknik A/S, the company changed its name to Semvac A/S in 2006.

Products

Vacuum toilet systems; complete toilet compartments; toilet system components, effluent tanks, water tanks, sensors and spares.

Contracts

Contracts include 210 toilet systems for Bombardier Transportation for M6 coaches for SNCB, 239 vacuum toilets for Bombardier Transportation for TER '2N'NG, 294 vacuum toilets for ALSTOM for A-TER and Z-TER, 249 toilet modules for Ansaldobreda for IC4, 505 toilet modules for Siemens AG, VT642 – Desiro and vacuum toilets for Australia, Korea, Russian Federation, US and many other countries.

SEPSA

Sistemas Electrónicos de Potencia SA
Polígono Ind La Estación, C/Albatros 7&9,
E-28320 Pinto, Madrid, Spain
Tel: (+34 91) 495 70 00
Fax: (+34 91) 495 70 60
e-mail: af@albatros-sl.es
Web: www.albatros-sl.es

Background

Established in 1981, SEPSA is a member of the Albatros Corporation.

Products

Static converters with large power range up to 400 kVA. DC and AC inputs and multivoltage outputs to feed auxiliary rail equipment such as air-conditioning, heating, compressors and lighting. Power electronic equipment for railway applications includes converters, inverters, choppers, rectifiers and battery chargers. Microprocessor control, high-switching frequency and IGBT technology.

Passenger information systems, public address, station announcers and displays (IRIS). Monitoring and Controlling System (PLC) to drive both auxiliary equipment and traction. CESIS crash event recording equipment.

Contracts

Customers include the NYCT (New York, US), LUL (London, UK), German Railways, RATP (Paris, France), SNCF (France), Via Rail (Canada), MTRC (Hong Kong) and also within Hungary, Mexico, Brazil and Taiwan.

Seratec Verkehrstechnik

Hühnerstrasse 66, CH-3123 Belp, Switzerland
Tel/Fax: (+41 31) 819 45 66
e-mail: info@seratec.ch
Web: www.seratec.ch

German office

Brückenstrasse 16, D-86153 Augsburg, Germany
Tel: (+49 821) 301 10
Fax: (+49 821) 333 80
e-mail: info@seratec.de

Products

Data recording systems for rail vehicles and buses. Products include journey data recording equipment, tachometers/speed recorders, speedometers, driver vigilance systems and journey data analysis systems.

Seratec Verkehrstechnik

Airport Business Center 66, CH-3123 Belp, Switzerland
Tel/Fax: (+41 31) 819 45 66
e-mail: info@seratec.ch
Web: www.seratec.ch

German office
Brückenstrasse 16, D-86153 Augsburg, Germany
Tel: (+49 821) 301 10   Fax: (+49 821) 333 80
e-mail: info@seratec.de

Key personnel
Managing Director: *Peter Streit*

Products
Data recording systems for rail vehicles and buses. Products include journey data recording equipment, tachometers/speed recorders, speedometers, driver vigilance systems and journey data analysis systems.

Sess Klein SpA

Via Cavour 8, I-21040 Castronno (VA), Italy
Tel: (+39 0332) 89 68 11   Fax: (+39 0332) 89 31 51
e-mail: info@sessaklein.com
Web: www.sessaklien.com

Key personnel
President and Chief Executive Officer: *Alfredo Novelli*
Chief Executive Officer and Sales and Marketing Director: *Federico Mazzuchi*
Technical Director: *Maurizio Preti*
Chief Operating Officer: *Matteo Massone*

Products
Window and glazing systems for locomotives and passenger rail vehicles of all types.

SIGMA Coachair Group

11 McIlwraith Street, Wetherill Park, New South Wales, Australia
Tel: (+61 2) 98 27 00 00   Fax: (+61 2) 97 56 28 66
e-mail: scg@sigmacoachair.com
Web: www.aitransit.com

Key personnel
Managing Director: *Mark Parow*
General Manager, Rail Business Unit: *Joe Schembri*

Background
SIGMA Coachair Group (SCG) is a global company in the development of transport and heavy duty HVAC systems for the rail, bus, mining, industrial and defence markets.

Products
Air conditioning and ventilation systems for rolling stock including saloon and locomotive cabs and buses. Unit configurations include integrated roof mounts, split systems, wall/side mounts. Auxiliary power supplies. System controls using programmable logic control or relay logic with diagnostic facilities.

Silindir ve MotorElemanlari san ve Tic, AS (SILSAN)

PO Box 127, TR-01322, Adana, Turkey
Tel: (+90 322) 441 00 12; 03 11; 03 12
Fax: (+90 322) 441 00 86
e-mail: info@silsan.com
Web: www.silsan.com

Street address
Mersin Yolu Uzeri 10, PK 127 Carsi, TR-01210 Adana, Turkey

Key personnel
Managing Director: *Mehmet Bacaksizlar*
Sales and Marketing: *Çaghan Bacaksizlar*

Products
The company manufactures reciprocating diesel and petrol engine components for rail and road vehicles.

SILSAN

Silindir ve MotorElemanlari san ve Tic, AS
Mersin Yolu Uzeri 10, PK 127 Carsi, TR-01210 Adana, Turkey
Tel: (+90 322) 441 00 12   Fax: (+90 322) 441 00 86
e-mail: info@silsan.com
Web: www.silsan.com

Key personnel
Managing Director: *Mehmet Bacaksizlar*
Sales and Marketing: *Çaghan Bacaksizlar*

Products
The company manufactures reciprocating diesel and petrol engine components for rail and road vehicles.

Simclar Corporation

9114 58th Place, Suite 500, Kenosha, Wisconsin 53144, US
Tel: (+1 262) 653 99 99
Fax: (+1 262) 653 95 09
e-mail: simclar@execpc.com
Web: www.simclar.com

Head office
Simclar International Ltd
Pitreavie Business Park, Dunfermline KT11 8UN, UK
Tel: (+44 1383) 73 51 61
Fax: (+44 1383) 73 99 86
e-mail: sales@simclar.com

Key personnel
Chairman: *Sam Russell*

Products
Cable harness assemblies for traction equipment, cabs, high-voltage and low-voltage applications, data communications systems and earthing equipment.

SKF AB

Hornsgatan 1, SE-415 50 Gothenburg, Sweden
Tel: (+46 31) 337 14 32   Fax: (+46 31) 337 17 77
e-mail: rutger.barrdahl@skf.com
Web: www.railways.skf.com

Key personnel
President and Chief Executive Officer: *Tom Johnstone*
Director, Railway Business Unit: *Rutger Barrdahl*

Background
SKF employs 39,900 employees across 100 production sites in 24 countries.
ISO 14001 certified.

Products
Axleboxes for all types of rolling stock; axlebridges for low-floor vehicles, sealed and greased, double row taper bearing units, speed and temperature sensors; bogie monitoring systems; traction motor and transmission bearings; motor support housings and roller bearings; self-lubricating plain bearings; electrically insulated bearings; maintenance, mounting/dismounting equipment; bearing refurbishment.
   Latest developments include integrated sensor solutions to detect speed, direction of rotation and vibration.

Contracts
High-speed locomotives and multiple-unit applications:
Australia: Explorer diesel railcars.
Austria: 1012, 1014, 1016, 1116 and 1822 electric locomotives.
Finland: Sr2 electric locomotives, Sun 3 Pendolino tilting trains.
France: TML. MI 2N, M10N, Z2 and X-TER trains.
Germany: 101, 145 and 152 electric locomotives, ICE1, ICE2 and ICE3.
   LVT 642 and 611 tilting trains, suburban electrical and diesel units.
Italy: E 402, E 412 and E 464 electric locomotives.
   TAF trains. ETR 450, ETR 460, ETR 470 Pendolino tilting trains, ETR 500.
Netherlands: DM 90 and IRM.
Norway: El 18 electric locomotives, FTP trains.
Spain: S 252 electric locomotives, Alaris tilting trains.
Sweden: X- 15 and Oeresund trains.
Switzerland: Lok 2000, Cisalpino and ICU tilting trains.
UK: Class 58, 60 and 67 locomotives, West Coast Main Line.
   Class 165, 315, 317, 318, 319, 320, 321, 322, 323, 357, 442, 456, 465 and 466.
US: Diesel electric locomotives manufactured by EMD.

Slingsby Advanced Composites Ltd

Kirkbymoorside, York YO62 6EZ, UK
Tel: (+44 1751) 43 24 74   Fax: (+44 1751) 43 11 73
e-mail: sales@slingsby.co.uk
Web: www.slingsby.co.uk

Key personnel
Sales Director: *Steven Boyd*

Products
Emergency detrainment doors in aluminium, steel and composites. Welding to DIN 6700 standard.

Specialty Bulb Co Inc

The Specialty Bulb Co Inc
80 Orville Drive, Bohemia, New York 11716-0231, US
Tel: (+1 631) 589 33 93
Fax: (+1 631) 563 30 89
e-mail: info@bulbspecialists.com
Web: www.bulbspecialists.com

Key personnel
President: *Judith Beja*
Vice-President, Technical: *Caden Zollo*
Vice-President, Sales and Marketing: *Edie Muldoon*

Products
Major supplier to rail and mass transit industry of US and European lamps for car, signal, headlights and other applications.

Sportworks Northwest, Inc

15540 Wood-Red Road NE, Bldg A-200, Woodinville, Washington 98072, US
Tel: (+1 425) 483 70 00
Fax: (+1 425) 488 90 01
e-mail: customerservice@sportworks.com
Web: www.sportworks.com

Key personnel
Vice-President Multi-Modal Products: *Derek Sanden*
Customer Service: *Hayley Crow*

Sportworks Northwest's 'VeloPorter 3' bike rack
1323607

Sportworks Northwest's 'VeloPorter 2' bike rack
1323606

Sportworks Northwest's 'Sportworks 10' bike rack   1323605

Products

Manufacturer of the industry standard Bike-Rack-for-Buses. Products include front-mounted cycle rack for buses, able to carry two to three cycles per vehicle.

Contracts

Sportworks bike racks are used in more than 500 undertakings, totalling tens of thousands of racks on buses. Supplied 2,000 racks to MTA Los Angeles and 1,450 to Washington DC and 1,300 NEW modular VeloPorter 3 racks to King Country Metro, Seattle. Usage of racks estimated at more than 12 million a year in North America.

Stesalit Limited

71, Park Street, North Block, 7th Floor Calcutta 700 016, India
e-mail: office@stesalitltd.com
Web: www.stesalitltd.com

Background

Stesalit Limited has alliances with ABB and Spring AG, Switzerland; TELEMA SpA, Italy; Skoda, Czech Republic; Jacques Galland, France; EVPU, Slovakia, and MWB, Germany.

The company is ISO 9001:2000 accredited, with in excess of 60,000 square feet of manufacturing facilities.

Products

Developing and manufacturing high-end electronic and engineering products for locomotives, coaches, emus, rail signalling and industry, to global quality standards. Products include: microprocessor-based event recorders; wheel slip and slide controls; cam shaft controllers; assembly line control systems and control panels.

Sumitomo Metal Industries Ltd

8-11 Harumi I-Chome, Chu-ku, Tokyo 104-6111, Japan
Tel: (+81 3) 44 16 61 11   Fax: (+81 3) 44 16 67 90
e-mail: skr@sumitomometals.co.jp
Web: www.sumitomometals.co.jp/e/index.html

Key personnel

President: *Hiroshi Tomono*
Directors: *Tsutomu Ando, Fumio Hombe, Yasuyuki Tozaki, Shozo Nishizawa, Syuichiro Kozuka, Yoshinari Ishizuka, Kouji Morita, Yasuo Imai*
Managing Executive Officer: *Mitsunori Okada*
General Manager: *Shiuji Morinobu*
Senior Manager: *Yukinari Akimoto*

Works

Osaka Steelworks, 5-1-109 Shimaya, Konohana-Ku, Osaka 554-0024

Products

Wheels, tyres, axles, wheelsets, bogies, air springs, gear units, brake discs, automatic couplers, draftgear.

Sumitomo has developed a bolsterless bogie with 40 per cent fewer components and weighing some 15 per cent less than conventional designs. Better running performance through curves is claimed. Also developed linear induction motors for the Osaka and Tokyo mini-metro systems.

Contracts

Numerous types of powered and trailing bogies have been supplied to Japanese private railways and metro systems. Sumitomo's market share of bogies for Japanese private railways and metros is put at over 70 per cent.

Supersine Duramark Limited

Freemantle Road, Lowestoft, Suffolk NR33 0EA, UK
Tel: (+44 0845) 052 52 41   Fax: (+44 0845) 052 52 42
e-mail: talk2me@ssdm.co.uk
Web: www.ssdm.co.uk

Products

Self-adhesive vinyls and laminates for use on trains as replacement paint, with anti-graffiti options; overground and underground applications; bespoke graphics for exterior and interior applications; promotional and corporate applications; anti-graffiti, glass protection and heat reduction/retention window films; floor graphics; film durability to suit operational and budget requirements; nationwide in-house application service, including full preparation of rolling stock; quick response graffiti removal service; full project management, quality assurance and product warranty.

TBA Textiles Ltd

PO Box 40, Rochdale OL12 7EQ, UK
Tel: (+44 1706) 64 74 22   Fax: (+44 1706) 35 42 95
e-mail: info@tbatextiles.co.uk
Web: www.tbatextiles.co.uk

Key personnel

Managing Director: *Dr A V Ruddy*

Products

Fireblocking and anti-vandal fabrics for passenger transport seating. Fire resisting/insulating liners for use within the bodywork. Moulded fire-resistant seat pans.

Technical Resin Bonders

12 Clifton Road, Huntingdon, Cambridgeshire PE29 7EN, UK
Tel: (+44 1480) 44 74 00 Fax: (+44 1480) 41 49 92
e-mail: sales@trbonders.co.uk
Web: www.technicalresinbonders.co.uk

Key personnel

Chief Executive: *Jonathan McQueen*
Sales Manager: *Robert Hodgson*

Background

Technical Resin Bonders was founded in the early 1950's and was one of the first companies in the UK to manufacture products based on Honeycomb Sandwich Panel Technology. The company has since diversified and expanded its technical products for the rail, aerospace, marine, defence and motorsports industries.

Products

Lightweight structural and decorative honeycomb panels for vehicle new build and refurbishment programmes, including: aluminium honeycomb floors; external doors; internal doors; partitions; draught screens; table tops; ceiling panels; lower body sides; tables for passengers with disabilities; toilet modules; catering modules; overhead lockers; train skirts; energy absorbers; driver protection panels and cladding panels.

Técnicas Modulares e Industriales SA (Temoinsa)

Polígono Industrial Congost, Avenida San Juliá 100, E-08403 Granollers, Barcelona, Spain
Tel: (+34 93) 860 92 00   Fax: (+34 93) 860 92 13
e-mail: tmi@temoinsa.com
Web: www.temoinsa.com

Key personnel

General Manager: *Miguel de Sagarra Romeo*
Engineering and Projects Manager: *Agustí Candela*
Finance Manager: *Joan García*

Organisation

Temoinsa Granollers (Spain) – headquarters
MYPE (Spain) – electrical equipment and installations
Tecnicas de Composites SL (Spain) – manufacture of composite materials
Alte Transportations SL (Spain) – HVAC and toilet modules and systems
Temoinsa (Malaysia) – commercial office
Temoinsa (Chile) – maintenance of rolling stock
Temoinsa do Brasil (Brazil) – HVAC manufacture and maintenance
Temoinsa Qingdao (China) – manufacture of composite materials and pre-assemblies
Temoinsa (France) – commercial office
Kineco Temoinsa Transporation Ltd – manufacture of composite materials and pre-assemblies

Products

Design, engineering, manufacture, supply and technical assistance for fitting out of complete passenger coach interiors with fully developed modular systems, including air conditioning (HVAC units), toilet modules and vacuum systems.

Turnkey projects for equipment of new vehicles and modernisation/upgrading of second-hand rolling stock.

Contracts

Contracts include: HVAC units for NSB Class 5 and Class 7 coaches (Norway), Sirio tram interiors

Temoinsa's 1st Class saloon coach interior for SNCF   1345580

for Ansaldobreda (Italy), disabled toilet module and technical walls in standard toilet modules for GNER (Great North Eastern Railway) by Wabtec Rail Limited, HVAC units for SNTF GLJ and GLN coaches (Algeria), different types of complete coaches for OSE (Greece), complete interiors for s/9000 Metro Madrid coaches for Ansaldobreda (Italy), toilet modules and vacuum systems for Civia Coaches for ALSTOM and CAF (Spain), interiors for s/4000 metro units for TMB (Spain), toilet modules and systems for saloon coaches for ONCF (Morocco), complete fitting out of passenger compartments in Tren Hotel s/7000 for Talgo (Spain).

Teknoware Oy

Ilmarisentie 8, FI-15200 Lahti, Finland
Tel: (+358 3) 88 30 20   Fax: (+358 3) 883 02 40
e-mail: sales@teknoware.fi
Web: www.teknoware.fi

Key personnel
Business Unit Director: *Esa Melkko*

Products
Interior lighting electronics and lighting systems for bus, coaches and rolling stock; inverters/ballasts and fluorescent lighting systems, halogen and LED spots, LED-based fibre optic solutions and emergency lighting solutions as well as diagnostics system indicating errors in interior lighting system.

Thermo King Corporation

314 West 90th Street, Minneapolis, Minnesota 55420, US
Tel: (+1 952) 887 22 00   Fax: (+1 952) 887 25 29
Web: www.thermoking.com

Key personnel
Contact: *Kim Thorsen*
Vice-President, North America: *P Smith*

Subsidiaries
Thermo King Asia Pacific
Hong Kong
Tel: (+852) 25 07 91 00   Fax: (+852) 28 27 51 59

Thermo King do Brasil
Campinas, Brazil
Tel: (+55 19) 745 64 00   Fax: (+55 19) 245 11 06

Thermo King Europe
Brussels, Belgium
Tel: (+32 2) 714 57 11   Fax: (+32 2) 714 57 12

Thermo King Europe
Kolin, Czech Republic
Tel: (+420 321) 75 71 11   Fax: (+420 321) 75 71 70

Background
Thermo King Corporation is part of the Ingersoll-Rand Company.

Products
Heating, Ventilation and Air Conditioning units (HVAC) for buses and light rail vehicles. Range includes roof-mounted and integral systems, front-mounted systems, heating convection systems and small bus air conditioning systems, backed up by global service network and electrical HVAC units designed for any type of bus, including electric, hybrid or diesel/gas engine driven.

Tiflex Ltd

Tiflex House, Liskeard, PL14 4NB, UK
Tel: (+44 1579) 32 08 08   Fax: (+44 1579) 32 08 02
e-mail: treadmaster@tiflex.co.uk
Web: www.tiflex.co.uk

Key personnel
Managing Director: *Nick Spearman*
Sales and Marketing Director: *Andy Tuffield*
Product Manager: *Trevor Smith*
Marketing Department: *Emmaline Bowker*

Products
Treadmaster smoke- and fire-resistant floor coverings, slip-resistant floor coverings, for rail and road vehicles and for buildings; specialist stair nosings.
Contracts include the supply of floorings for the Heathrow Express trainsets, Midland Metro LRVs and MoD naval vessels.

Time 24 Ltd

19 Victoria Gardens, Burgess Hill RH15 9NB, UK
Tel: (+44 1444) 25 76 55   Fax: (+44 1444) 25 90 00
e-mail: sales@time24.co.uk
Web: www.time24.co.uk

Key personnel
Managing Director: *David Shore*
Finance Director: *Mark Willifer*
Purchasing Manager: *Steve Vaughan*
Internal Sales Manager: *Barrie Dumbleton*

Background
Established in 1987, Time 24 employs 600 staff in sites within the UK and has partnerships in China, India and Eastern Europe.

Products
Traction and brake controllers; cable assemblies, harnesses and looms; cab desks; project management. Body end cubicles, drivers' cupboards, lighting systems and vestibules.

Timken Rail Services

Unit 5 io Centre, Barn Way, Lodge Farm Industrial Estate, Duston, Northampton NN5 7UW, UK
Tel: (+44 1604) 59 36 37   Fax: (+44 1604) 59 34 67
e-mail: gary.thornton@timken.com
Web: www.timken.com

Key personnel
Director, Rail: *Hans Landin (Canton, USA)*
Manager, Sales and Marketing – Rail OEM, Europe: *Kai Ethner (Haan, Germany)*
Manager, Aftermarket Sales and Operations – Rail, Europe: *David Burrows (Northampton)*
Market Manager Rail, Europe: *Gary Thornton (Northampton)*

Works
Manufacturing plants for rail bearings in Italy, India, South Africa and US.

Products and Services
Provider of tapered roller bearings; AP and SP tapered roller bearing cartridge units; and complete axleboxes and motor suspension units. Timken design, manufacture and supply tapered roller bearings and ancillary equipment covering transmissions, axleboxes, traction motor suspension units and other equipment, such as cooling fans and screw compressors. They also provide reconditioning and re-manufacturing of tapered roller bearings for rail applications.

Contracts
In January 2007 Timken was awarded a contract for the supply of 480 high-tech axle bearing assemblies to Bombardier Transportation for use in the locomotives of the next 30 trains that RENFE has ordered from Talgo in Spain.
In December 2006 The Timken Company announced that it is to supply an integrated system of bearings and housings to Vossloh Locomotives for its new EURO 4000 diesel-electric locomotive.
In August 2006 the company was awarded a contract to supply the journal bearing assembly

and housing for the new PROTOS train in Germany, built by FTD Fahrzeugtechnik Dessau AG.

TMD Friction UK Ltd

PO Box 18, Hunsworth Lane, Cleckheaton, BD19 3UJ, UK
Tel: (+44 1274) 85 40 00
Fax: (+44 1274) 85 40 01
e-mail: info@tmdfriction.co.uk
Web: www.tmdfriction.com

Key personnel
Managing Director: *Deri Doyle*

Products
Asbestos-free low- and high-friction composition brake blocks for passenger and freight applications. Asbestos-free disc pads for a variety of applications.

Contracts
Recent contracts include the supply of brake blocks for London Underground rolling stock for the Victoria Line.

Toshiba Corporation

Transportation Systems Division
Toshiba Building, 1-Shibaura 1-chome, Minato-ku, Tokyo 105-8001, Japan
Tel: (+81 3) 34 57 49 24
Fax: (+81 3) 54 44 92 63
e-mail: miki.ogata@toshiba.jp
Web: www.toshiba.co.jp

Key personnel
President and Chief Executive Officer: *Atsutoshi Nishida*
Vice-President, Transportation Systems Division: *Toshiyuki Onishi*
Senior Manager, Railway Projects Department: *Yoshiji Ito*
Group Manager, Overseas Business Planning Group: *Michihiko Ogata*

Products
Heating, ventilation and air conditioning equipment; AC and DC electrification equipment.

Translec Limited

Saddleworth Business Park, Huddersfield Road, Delph, Oldham OL3 5DF, UK
Tel: (+44 1457) 87 88 88
Fax: (+44 1457) 87 88 87
e-mail: mail@translec.co.uk
Web: www.translec.co.uk

Key personnel
Director: *Keith Parker*

Products
Exterior and interior lighting and electronic control systems for use on rail vehicles.
Exterior lighting product range: headlight (HID, halogen, LED light sources); signal, marker, tail and combined lights (LED), bodyside indicator lights (LED), door status indicator lights (LED), cab step lights (LED), driver's indicator (mimic) panel, control units incorporating power supplies, control and monitoring, headlight aperture covers. Interior lighting product range: main saloon and vestibule luminaires, fluorescent, LED and filament lamp drivers, step lights, reading lights, table lamps, decorative/ambience lighting.

Projects
Translec supplies lighting systems for new build and refurbishment projects. Recent major projects have been with: ALSTOM Transport, Bombardier Transportation, CAF and Siemens Transportation Systems.

Transmatic Inc

6145 Delfield Industrial Drive, Waterford, Michigan 48329, US
Tel: (+1 248) 623 25 00   Fax: (+1 248) 623 28 39
Web: www.transmaticgroup.com

Key personnel

President: *O K Dealey Jr*
Vice-President, Sales and Marketing: *M T Hoffman*
Vice-President, Environmental Systems: *D Scott McConnell*

UK subsidiary

Transmatic Europe Ltd
Unit 2, City Park Industrial Estate, Gelderd Road, Leeds LS12 6DR, UK
Tel: (+44 113) 279 99 89   Fax: (+44 113) 279 41 27
e-mail: sales@transmatic.co.uk
Managing Director: *Terry Calnon*

Products

Interior lighting and advertising coving for buses and urban transit vehicles, multipurpose lighting/air conditioning duct modules, surface-mounted fluorescent lighting, destination sign lighting, interior cleaning systems for buses and rail vehicles.

Trelleborg Industrial AVS

1 Hoods Close, Leicester LE4 2BN, UK
Tel: (+44 116) 267 03 00   Fax: (+44 116) 267 03 01
e-mail: industrialavs.uk@trelleborg.com
Web: www.trelleborg.com/industriaAVS

Key personnel

President: *Ron Smith*
Sales and Marketing Director: *Keith Croysdale*

Background

Trelleborg Industrial AVS is the amalgamation of Metalastik Limited and Novibra, Sweden.

Products

Design and manufacture of anti-vibration mounting for engine, instrument, cabin, machinery and couplings. Metalastik© suspension components; bearer springs; control links and suspension bushes; primary and secondary rail springs.

Contracts

Recent contracts include the supply of secondary suspension air-spring systems to Bombardier for the London Underground SSL project. To CAF for the London Heathrow Express and to Indian Railways for various major refurbishment projects.

Supply of rubber chevron springs to refurbish 109 of the Mafersa-built rolling stock fleet in use on the 47.1 km São Paulo metro, Brazil. The springs are rubber/metal laminated units fitted between the wheel axles and bogie frame, designed to absorb high levels of shock and vibration.

Trelleborg Woodville Rail

Hearthcote Road, Swadlincote, DE11 9DX, UK
Tel: (+44 1283) 22 11 22   Fax: (+44 1283) 21 97 68
e-mail: sam.redley@trelleborg.com
Web: www.trelleborg.com

Key personnel

Plant Manager: *John Blackham*
Technical Manager: *Nigel Bailey*
Operations Manager: *Allan Harper*
Quality Manager: *Alan Brotherhood*
Senior Account Manager: *Mike Stevens*

Background

Trelleborg Woodville Rail, formerly Woodville Polymer Engineering, is part of Trelleborg AB, within the Trelleborg Sealing Solutions division.

Products

Design, development and manufacture of gangways, flexible treadplates and rail accessories fabrication and industrial engineering services.

Contracts

Recent contracts have included: Virgin CrossCountry, UK; MTRC TKE Line, Hong Kong; Vancouver Sky Train, Canada; Juniper emus, UK; Øresund Link emus, Sweden/Denmark; Delhi Metro, India; Manila Metro, Philippines; Prospector Avon Link, Western Australia; Circle Line, Singapore; Shanghai Metro Pearl Line, China; Gwang Ju Metro, Korea; Attiko Metro, Greece; Hunter Valley, New South Wales, Australia; Daegu Line 2, South Korea; Seoul Metropolitan, South Korea; Daejeon Line 1, Korea; MTRC Tung Chung Line, Hong Kong; Brazil Metro, Rio; Busan Line 3, Korea; Incheon Airport (express and commuter vehicles), Korea; Channel Tunnel Rail Link, UK; DART 8100 refurbishment, Ireland; Irish Rail, Ireland; Canada Line Rapid Transit, Vancouver, Canada; AGV; Budapest Metro, Hungary.

Trevira GmbH

Philipp-Reis-Strasse 2, D-65795 Hattersheim, Germany
Fax: (+49 69) 305 163 42
e-mail: treviracs.info@trevira.com
Web: www.treviracs.com

Products

Flame-retardant fibres and filament yarns for interior textiles such as upholstery.

Twiflex Ltd

104 The Green, Twickenham TW2 5AQ, UK
Tel: (+44 20) 88 94 11 61
Fax: (+44 20) 88 94 60 56
e-mail: info@twiflex.com
Web: www.twiflex.com

Key personnel

Managing Director: *Peter Wood*
Sales and Marketing Director: *Jonathan P Cooksley*
Financial Director: *David Sewell*
Operations Director: *Ray Buttifant*

Background

Twiflex Limited was previously owned by Hay Hall Group and was then acquired by Altra Industrial Motion in February 2006.

Products

Advanced braking technology, industrial disc brakes, Layrub and Laylink flexible shafts and couplings; industrial and marine disc brakes and Flexi-clutch couplings.

Both Layrub and Laylink couplings incorporate compressed cylindrical rubber blocks. The Laylink coupling carries these blocks in links, while the Layrub coupling carries them in a carrying plate. The use of these couplings and flexible shafts allows large amounts of angular and axial misalignment to be accommodated; it also absorbs shock, controls vibrations and simplifies close coupling in confined spaces. The units need no servicing or lubrication and can cater for very high operating speeds and transmission of high power without loss.

Twin Disc Incorporated

1328 Racine Street, Racine, Wisconsin 53403-1758, US
Tel: (+1 262) 638 40 00
Fax: (+1 262) 638 44 82
Web: www.twindisc.com

Key personnel

Chairman, Chief Executive Officer: *M E Batten*
Corporate Controller: *J F Knutson*
Vice-President, Marine Marketing and Distribution: *H C Fabry*
Commercial Manager, Production Systems and Operations: *J H Batten*

Principal subsidiaries

Twin Disc International SA, Chaussée de Namur 54, B-1400 Nivelles, Belgium
Tel: (+32 67) 88 72 11   Fax: (+32 67) 88 73 33

Twin Disc (Pacific) Pty Ltd, PO Box 442, Virginia, Queensland 4014, Australia
Tel: (+61 7) 32 65 12 00   Fax: (+61 7) 38 65 13 71

Twin Disc (South Africa) Pty Ltd, PO Box 40542, Cleveland 2022, South Africa
Tel: (+27 11) 626 27 14   Fax: (+27 11) 626 27 17

Twin Disc (Far East) Ltd, PO Box 155, Jurong Town Post Office, Singapore 9161
Tel: (+65) 62 61 89 09   Fax: (+65) 62 64 20 80

Products

Universal joints; hydraulic torque converters, power shift transmissions and controls suitable for locomotives and railcars.

Tyco Electronics UK Ltd

Faraday Road, Dorcan, Swindon SN3 5HH, UK
Tel: (+44 1793) 52 81 71
Fax: (+44 1793) 57 25 16
Web: www.tycoelectronics.com

Main offices

Tyco Electronics Corporation, 300 Constitution Drive, Menlo Park, California 94025, US
Tel: (+1 650) 316 33 33   Fax: (+1 650) 316 21 13

Key personnel

Worldwide Marketing Manager for Rail: *Vito Provenzano*
Worldwide Marketing Communications Manager: *Ruth Amedelle*

Background

Previously traded as Agastat, AMP, Bowthorp, Critchley, CTT, HTS and Raychem Ltd.

Products

Products based on plastics, metals and chemicals including: low fire hazard wire and cable, heat-shrinkable zero-halogen tubing and moulded parts, wire marking systems, electrical interconnection devices, freeze protection of contact rails, points and crossings, brake and diesel fuel lines; temperature and condensation control; HV and LV cable accessories; electrical harness sealing products, electrical connector adapters; electrical connectors including rectangular and custom rail interconnect solutions; fully approved cable termination systems; electrical, electronic and electro-pneumatic relays and time delay relays; surge protection; high voltage cable assembly systems; vacuum circuit breakers and HV switches for rolling stock; computerised and manual cable marking systems; labelling systems; overhead line system.

Computerised marking with TMS System 90 equipment reduces time and effort spent on electrical installations for locomotives.

Ultimate Transportation Equipment

Head office
T&T International
1355 Murchison Drive, Millbrae, California 94030, US
Tel: (+1 650) 697 87 38
Fax: (+1 650) 697 37 11
Web: www.ultimate-eur.com

Subsidiaries

Ultimate Europe Transportation Equipment GmbH
Franz Kollmann Strasse 4, A-3300 Amstetten, Austria
Tel: (+43 7472) 65 51 01 11　Fax: (+43 7472) 655 10 20
e-mail: transport@ultimate-eur.com

T&T International Transportation Equipment (BJ) Co Ltd
Rm 301/302, Unit 2, Building 8A, Julong Garden, No. 68 Xinzhongjie, Dongcheng District, 100027 Beijing, China
Tel: (+86 10) 65 52 22 88　Fax: (+86 10) 65 52 50 71
e-mail: ttin@public.bta.net.cn

Qingdao Ultimate Transportation Equipment Co Ltd
No 178 Zhuzhou Road, Hi-Tech Zone, 266101 Qingdao, Shandong province, China
Tel: (+86 532) 870 43 33　Fax: (+86 532) 870 43 38
e-mail: utmrd@qdutm.com
Web: www.qdutm.com

Ultimate Australia Transportation Equipment Pty Ltd
Factory 1/75, Star Crescent, Hallam, Victoria 3803, Australia
Tel: (+61 3) 97 08 62 55　Fax: (+61 3) 97 08 65 99

Products

Hydraulically damped turntables (Hemscheidt) and bellows systems (Ultimate) for articulated buses; interconnection gangways for buses and rail vehicles; interior and exterior door systems; vehicle interior systems, including interior panelling and partitions, toilet modules, seats and exterior front masks. Materials used for interiors include Glass-fibre-Reinforced Plastic (GRP), thermoplastics and aluminium sandwich construction.

Contracts

Clients include ALSTOM Transport, Bombardier Transportation, CAF, EDI Rail, Koncar and Siemens Transportation Systems.

UniControls AS

Křenická ulice-2257, CZ-100 00 Prague 10, Czech Republic
Tel: (+420 2) 72 01 14 11　Fax: (+420 2) 72 01 14 88
e-mail: unic@unicontrols.cz
Web: www.unicontrols.cz

Key personnel

Chief Executive Officer: *Petr Stroner*
Marketing Manager: *Marian Belosovic*

Products

Communications and control systems for trains and rail vehicles, including: train communication network, wire-train-bus equipment; multivehicle communication equipment; vehicle communication devices; and driver's cab equipment and displays.

Contracts

Contracts include train communications and control systems for refurbished Russian-built Prague metro stock; train communications system for St Petersburg metro stock; train and vehicle communications system and driver's cab equipment for Czech Railways Class 471 emus; communication node UIC Gateway for Czech Railways Class 680 tilting trainsets; driver's cab equipment for refurbished Class 772 locomotive for Slovakian Railways (ZSSK).

　Class 575 emus for Lithuanian Railways are being tested during July and August 2008. These units are similar to the Class 471 operated by Czech Railways. UniControls supplied complete control and information systems and for the first time the units are equipped with UniControls camera surveillance system with recording unit. External cameras replace wing-mirrors and internal cameras monitor the interior of the vehicles.

UWE Verken AB

PO Box 262, SE-601 04 Norrköping, Sweden
Tel: (+46 11) 24 88 00
Fax: (+46 11) 12 47 04
e-mail: info@uwe.se
Web: www.uwe.se

Subsidiaries

The company has subsidiaries in Germany and Poland.

Products

A complete range of convectors, blowers and control systems for buses, coaches, boats and trains. Design service and total system supply available.

Vapor Bus International

10655 Henri-Bourassa West, Saint-Laurent, Quebec H4S 1A1, Canada
Tel: (+1 514) 335 42 00
Fax: (+1 514) 335 42 31
Web: www.wabtec.com

Key personnel

Vice-President and General Manager: *Robert S. Andress, Jr.*

Background

A member of the WABCO Transit Group, a Wabtec company.

Products

Design and manufacture of passenger door systems for buses, including actuators, door panels, controls, seals and accessory items. The company also manufactures heavy-duty relays and contactors for locomotives and passenger rail cars.

Vapor Bus International

1010 Johnson Drive, Buffalo Grove, Illinois 60089, US
Tel: (+1 847) 777 64 00
Fax: (+1 847) 84 75 20 22 22
e-mail: vaporbusinfo@wabtec.com
Web: www.vapordoors.com

Key personnel

Vice-President and General Manager: *Robert Andress*
Vice-President, Sales and Marketing: *Robert Gallant*
Engineering Manager: *Frank Golemis*

Background

Founded in 1903 as a supplier of steam heating equipment for railroad passenger cars, Vapor Bus International has evolved as a leader in door system equipment for buses. Vapor Bus is a subsidiary of Wabtec Corporation.

Products

Vapor designs and manufactures highly engineered passenger door systems for buses including pneumatic and electric actuators, mechanical linkages, controls, door panels, passenger actuation devices, emergency release devices and driver's door controller handles. The company has extensive experience in applications for slide-glide, swing, bi-fold and parallelogram plug door geometries. Vapor supplies door equipment to all of the North American transit bus manufacturers and many builders of medium- and light-duty buses. Also manufactures heavy-duty relays and contactors for use on passenger rail vehicles and locomotives.

　The company is certified to ISO9001:2000.

Vapor Stone UK

(Part of Wabtec Rail Limited)
PO Box 400, Doncaster Works, Hexthorpe Road DN1 ISL, UK
Tel: (+44 1302) 34 07 00　Fax: (+44 1302) 32 13 49
e-mail: wabtecrail@wabtec.com
Web: www.wabtecrail.co.uk

Key personnel

Commercial Manager: *Paul Robinson*

Background

Vapor Stone UK is part of Wabtec Rail Limited and undertakes the overhaul of passenger rolling stock, main line locomotives, bogies, wheelsets, air brake equipment, hydraulic dampers and buffers, along with the manufacture and overhaul of freight wagons, air conditioning units and door systems.

　As part of the Wabtec Corporation, Wabtec Rail also supplies to UK rolling stock owners and maintainers composite brake blocks and pads, Wabtec Railway Electronics train data recorders and electronic equipment, Cardwell TMX braking systems, Young Touchstone heat exchangers and radiators and Wabtec Westinghouse air brake equipment.

Products

Supply of air conditioning units and passenger door systems to railways around the world. Vapor Stone UK's engineers are able to design new air conditioning systems and undertake the upgrade and refurbishment of existing systems, and carry out air conditioning system health checks at its customer's train operating depots.

　Vapor Stone UK also has expertise in the overhaul and upgrade of passenger rolling stock door systems. Modern door actuators and control systems which can be fitted and existing actuators overhauled. Through Wabtec Rail's parts department, spares can be supplied for all Vapor, Stone and Westinghouse Temperature air conditioning systems and Stones, Peters and Deans door systems.

　As part of Wabtec Rail Ltd, air conditioning unit upgrades and passenger door system overhauls can be incorporated into a complete passenger vehicle refurbishment contract, with all work being carried out at its main Doncaster Works.

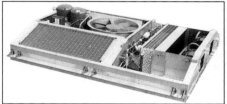

Vapor Stone UK roof mounted air conditioning unit　　　　1180376

Vogelsitze GmbH

Kleinsteinbacher Strasse 44, D-76228 Karlsruhe, Germany
Tel: (+49 721) 470 20　Fax: (+49 721) 470 21 70
e-mail: info@vogelsitze.de
Web: www.vogelsitze.de

Key personnel

Chief Operating Officer: *Dr Robert Kocsis*

Products

Seating.

Voith Turbo GmbH & Co KG

Alexanderstrasse 2, D-89522 Heidenheim, Germany
Tel: (+49 7321) 37 40 69　Fax: (+49 7321) 37 76 16
e-mail: rail-division@voith.com
Web: www.voithturbo.com

Key personnel
Chairman and Regular member of the Corporate Management Board of Voith AG: *Peter Edelmann*
Executive Vice-President of the Market Division Rail: *Dr Manfred Lerch*
General Manager Hydrodynamic Components and Systems for Railway Vehicles: *Heinz Tengler*
General Manager, Mechanical Drives: *Arno Hoepner*
General Manager Cooling Systems: *Thomas Bassmann*
Managing Director, Voith Turbo Scharfenberg: *Martin Wawra*
Managing Director, Voith Turbo Lokomotivtechnik: *Hinrich Krey*

Background
Voith Turbo offers high quality components, systems and services for the division industry, rail, road and marine to customer worldwide.

A supplier of systems and components for rail vehicles, low-floor trams, high-speed or tilting trains, as well as in locomotives or special vehicles.

Voith turbo has been building diesel-hydraulic locomotives since 2005.

Products
Hydrodynamic transmissions and retarders, torque converters and automatic hydromechanical transmissions. Final drive reduction gearboxes for mechanical or electrical drives in locomotives, metro cars and light rail vehicles. DIWA hydromechanical transmissions for light rail vehicles. Limited-slip differential device for metro cars and light rail vehicles. Voith Turbo provides drive solutions for rail vehicles. Customer-specific drive systems, extending from the technical design, configuration and construction to application and testing created using technology innovative systems solutions and services.

Voith automatic hydrodynamic transmissions are designed specifically for installation in rail vehicles. The basic components are drainable hydraulic torque converters and fluid couplings, which in combination provide tractive effort over a wide speed range in an efficient and cost-effective manner. The filling characteristics ensure wear-free, smooth shifting without interruption of tractive effort. Turbo-reversing transmissions used in shunting locomotives extend the principle to allow direction shifting in a similar manner. All non-reversing turbo transmissions can be fitted with a wear-free retarder.

Voith final drives are available in bevel and spur gear configurations, from axle-hung drives to bogie or body-suspended quill-shaft drives, with single or double reduction.

Scharfenberg® coupler has developed into one of the most important and successful coupling systems since its invention and introduction in 1903. Over the years, continuous technical refinements and up-to-date technology has made the 'Schaku' one of the most prominent railway coupler systems in use, from light rail vehicles up to high-speed trains. The company has also made its mark as a system supplier for complete front end solutions, including front nose assemblies with energy absorbing components and control modules.

Development
The LS 640 re V2 split turbo transmission with an output of 2,700 kW is in development.

Voith Turbo Scharfenberg GmbH & Co KG

Gottfried-Linke-Strasse 205 38239 Salzgitter, Germany
Tel: (+49 5341) 21 02
Fax: (+49 5341) 21 42 02
e-mail: info.schaku@voith.com
Web: www.voithturbo.de

Key personnel
General Manager: *M Wawra*
Sales Director: *H Costard*
Technical Director: *S Kobert*
Research Director: *R Krawse*

Principal licensees and subsidiary companies
Australia: Voith Turbo Scharfenberg Pty Ltd 503 Victoria Street, Wetherill Park, 2164, New South Wales,

France: Voith Turbo Scharfenberg GmbH & Co kg Succursale Couplematic, 21 rue de Clichy, F-93584 Saint Ouen Cedex,

Spain: Construcciones y Auxiliar de Ferrocarriles (CAF), SA Padilla 17 – 6°, E-28006 Madrid

Background
The company name changed from Scharfenbergkupplung GmbH & Co kg to Voith Turbo Scharfenberg GmbH & Co kg in September 2002.

Products
Automatic multifunction couplers, semi-permanent couplers and drawgear for light rail, rapid transit, trams, metros, powered and non-powered passenger vehicles, freight wagons, locomotives, automated guideway transit, mountain railways; special couplers for shunting vehicles, ladle cars, cranes; adaptor couplers, electric couplers; impact protection modules, complete front noses, articulations.

Contracts
Contracts have included automatic and semi-permanent couplers for high-speed trains including: Talgo 350 and 250 and Velaro E, Spain; TGV, France; ICE 3, Germany; Chinese metros such as Guangzhou, Shenzen, Nanjing and Shanghai, also Delhi Metro, India, Singapore Circle Line and North-East Line, Vienna subway, Austria; Oresund OTU trains, Sweden; Rubin Nürnberg, Germany; V'locity and PURD Perth, Australia; the AVE S 102 (Talgo 350, Spain) plus delivery of the complete front nose including driver's cabin.

WABCO

WABCO Europe BVBA
Head Office, Chaussée de Wavre 1789, Box 15, B-1160 Brussels, Belgium
Tel: (+32 2) 663 98 00   Fax: (+32 2) 675 43 42
Web: www.wabco-auto.com

Key personnel
Chief Executive Officer: *Jacques Esculier*
Chief Information Officer: *Peter Bal*
Vice-President Aftermarket: *Jena-Francois Barth*
Vice-President, Original Equipment (OE) Sales: *Harald Kaess*
Chief Financial Officer: *Ulrich Michel*
Vice-President, Strategy and Investor Relations: *Michael E Thompson*
Chief Technology Officer: *Dr Christian Wiehen*
Media Contact: *Tobias Mueller*
Staff: *7,700*

Other offices
The company has 34 production facilities and offices worldwide.

Background
Originally formed as Westinghouse Air Brake Company, WABCO was acquired by American Standard in 1968 and spun off in 2007.

Products
Brake systems comprising air and vacuum brake equipment, electropneumatic brake equipment with digital or analogue control for metro and commuter passenger trains. Equipment includes: rotary and reciprocating air compressors, air dryers, drivers' brake and traction controllers, wheelside control equipment, brake actuation equipment, tread and disc brake equipment and magnetic track brakes. Equipment repair, overhaul or long-term maintenance and spare parts provided.

Contracts
Recent contracts include: brake systems currently being supplied for the Desiro, Electrostar and Juniper multiple-unit vehicle platforms, Voyager CrossCountry multiple-units, Kuala Lumpur Airport Express trains, Singapore-Changi extension, wheelside equipment on Midland Mainline trains.

Brake and coupler equipment has been supplied for Los Angeles Green line cars; brake equipment has been supplied for Mexico Line A; brake, coupler and current collection equipment has been supplied for NYCTA R142 and R142A rolling stock; coupler equipment has been supplied for Portland LRVs.

Cab Aquasphere is a new system developed for use in city buses and designed for original equipment fitting. The system provides a full climate control system for the driver, which is fully integrated into the heater and demister system of the base vehicle using just one system for heating and cooling. It is operated by an engine-driven power pack, which is located within the engine compartment. It fits directly into the existing system and has a small refrigerant circuit. It is effective in use and easy to service. Cab Aquasphere has already been tested by Firstbus.

Developments
Include the E+A air dryer for improved drying capability; R-style magnet valves and a new-design actuator.

Webasto AG

Head office
Kraillinger Strasse 5, D-82131 Stockdorf, Germany
Tel: (+49 89) 85 79 40   Fax: (+49 89) 85 79 44 48
Web: www.webasto.com

Key personnel
Chairman: *Franz-Josef Kortüm*

UK office
Webasto Product UK Ltd
(Aftermarket Product Range)
Webasto House, White Rose Way, Doncaster Carr, DN4 5JH, UK
Tel: (+44 1302) 32 22 32
Fax: (+44 1302) 32 22 31
Web: www.webasto.co.uk
Managing Director: *Roger Edwards*
Webasto Roof Systems Ltd
(OE Roof Systems only)
Unit 7 Kingsbury Road, Minworth, Sutton Coldfield, B76 9DL, UK
Tel: (+44 121) 313 56 00
Fax: (+44 121) 351 49 05
Managing Director: *Matthew Webb*

Background
The company was founded in 1901 by Wilhelm Baier in Esslingen, Germany. In addition to its three production sites in Germany, Webasto has production plants in a number of European and other countries, including the UK, the Netherlands, Italy and Turkey, as well as the US.

Products
Convertible roof and body systems plus sunroofs for passenger cars. Combustion heaters for engine pre-heating and passenger saloon heating for rail, road vehicles and marine craft. Air conditioning systems for the defence vehicle industry, 'on' road and 'off' road vehicles and marine craft. Emergency escape and ventilation roof hatches for bus and coach applications.

Weidmüller

821 Southlake Boulevard
Richmond, Virginia 23236
US
Tel: (+1 804) 794 28 77
Fax (+1 804) 794 02 52
e-mail: info@weidmueller.com
Web: www.weidmuller.com

Key personnel
Owner: *W Schubel*

Subsidiaries
Australia, Austria, Bahrain, Belgium, Brazil, Bulgaria, Canada, China, Croatia, Czech Republic, Denmark, Finland, France, Germany, Greece, Hong Kong, Hungary, India, Israel, Italy, Japan, South Korea, Former Yugoslav Republic of Macedonia, Malaysia, Mexico, Netherlands, Norway, Pakistan, Poland, Portugal, Romania, Singapore, Slovakia, Slovenia, South Africa, Spain, Sweden, Switzerland, Taiwan, Thailand, Turkey, UK, Ukraine and US.

Products
Connectors and connection equipment including terminal blocks and terminal strips, HD connectors and terminal connectors for printed circuits.
Installation: wire, cables, terminals and instruments, enclosures, manual and automatic tools, ferrules and mounting trails.
Electronic interface modules, relay interface and PLC interfaces, power supply.
I/O components: decentralised I/O, field bus, SCADA and control software, industrial PC.
Customers include ALSTOM, Bombardier and Siemens.

Weserland Sitzsysteme GmbH

Immenweg 19-21, D-31582 Nienburg, Germany
Tel: (+49 5021) 960 99 15
Fax: (+49 5021) 960 99 18
e-mail: info@wesersitz.de
Web: www.wesersitz.de

Key personnel
Managing Director: *Walter Anklam*

Products
Design, development and manufacture of seating systems for main line and urban rail vehicles. The company also undertakes the refurbishment and cleaning of rail vehicle seating and interiors.

Westinghouse Saxby Farmer Ltd

17 Convent Road, Entally, Calcutta 700014, India
Tel: (+91 33) 22 44 71 61   Fax: (+91 33) 22 44 71 65
e-mail: wsfedp@cal2.vsnl.net.in

Key personnel
Managing Director: *A N Dutta*
Director, Finance : *D K De Sarker*

Products
Electropneumatic brake system including regenerative brake blending equipment for emu coaches; air and vacuum brake system for locomotives, passenger coaches, diesel rail cranes, special purpose railway vehicles and tramcars; semi-permanent and automatic centre buffer couplers for passenger coaches.

Contracts
Current contracts include the supply of 100 sets of electro-pneumatic brake equipment, 150 sets of semi-permanent centre buffer couplers and spares to Indian Railways.

Widney Transport Components (Pty) Ltd

Widney Transport Components (Pty) Ltd
PO Box 17291, Randhart, 1457, Gauteng, South Africa
Tel: (+27 11) 864 48 04
Fax: (+27 11) 908 18 56
Web: www.shatterprufe.co.za

Key personnel
Managing Director: *M Williamson*
Export Marketing Director: *K Luyt*
General Manager: *C Govender*
Sales and Marketing Manager: *J Labutte*

Products
Windows for passenger vehicles, including sliding, hopper and double-glazed types; doors for metro coaches, general carriage fittings, door windows for metro coaches and drop windows (MKIV).

Contracts
Contracts have included supply of bus sliding glass.

Yutaka Manufacturing Co Ltd

1-18-17 Kitakojiya Ota-ku, Tokyo 144-0032, Japan
Tel: (+81 3) 37 41 41 31
Fax: (+81 3) 57 05 70 65
e-mail: hideo.kamei@yutaka-ss.co.jp
Web: www.yutaka-ss.co.jp/

Key personnel
President and Chief Executive Officer: *Tishio Tanino*

Products
Jumper cable connectors; high- and low-voltage connectors; multi-contact connectors for power input and output.

ZF Friedrichshafen AG

ZF Friedrichshafen AG
D-88038 Friedrichshafen, Germany
Tel: (+49 7541) 770
Fax: (+49 7541) 77 90 80 00
e-mail: postoffice@zf.com
Web: www.zf.com

Key personnel
Supervisory Board:
Chairman: *Wolf Hartmut Prellwitz*
Vice-Chairman, Employee-elected representative: *Johann Kirchgässner*
Board of Management:
  Chief Executive Officer: *Siegfried Goll*
  Paul Ballmeier, Uwe Berner, Michael Paul, Wolfgang Vogel

Business Units
Car Driveline Technology, ZF Getriebe GmbH, Saarbrücken, Germany; car chassis technology, ZF Lemförder Fahrwerktechnik AG & Co KG, Lemförder, Germany; commercial vehicles and special driveline technology, ZF Friedrichshafen AG, Friedrichshafen, Germany; off-road driveline technology and axle systems, ZF Passau GmbH, Passau, Germany; powertrain and chassis components, ZF Sachs AG, Schweinfurt, Germany; steering technology, ZF Lenksysteme GmbH, a joint venture of ZF Friedrichshafen AG und Robert Boch GmbH, Schwäbisch Gmünd, Germany.

Background
Shareholders include Zeppelin Foundation, Friedrichshafen, Germany 93.8 per cent; Dr Jürgen Ulderup Foundation, Lemförder, Germany 6.2 per cent.

Products
Rail driveline technology, including transmissions for locomotives, driveline units for underground trains, city rail vehicles, and metro trains as well as input kits for regional trains (electric and diesel railcars). In collaboration with ZF Sachs AG, ZF Bahntechnik GmbH can supply diesel railcar engine manufacturers with complete systems, comprising clutches, transmissions and electronic control units. This is especially important when using transmissions in rail vehicles such as diesel railcars, where each car has its own driveline: in this case, a highly developed electronic control unit has to perfectly synchronise several transmissions in line with gear change operations to the millisecond.

The company is developing and producing new transmission systems in co-operation with suppliers of wheels, engines, axles and brakes. This ensures that all cost and delivery advantages can be offered by one supplier. For example, ZF Bahntechnik has supplied the new IC4 intercity train for Danish State Railways with the AS Rail Transmission, as well as the clutch, prop shaft, axle reversing transmission and torque support.

ZF also produces powertrain and suspension components for rail vehicles. The product range of dampers for rail vehicle applications includes primary and secondary dampers (vertical and horizontal), yaw dampers, dampers for engines, superstructures and articulated roof structures.

ZF Sachs has further developed Pneumatic Damping Control (PDC) dampers for use in freight wagons. Pneumatically controlled proportional damper valves progressively adapt the damping to the respective load condition via the brake pressure. This system is especially suitable as a horizontal damper system for major load differences. In their function as vertical dampers, PDC dampers also improve comfort in pneumatically damped rail vehicles. This allows for higher speeds at a lower driveload.

Complete rubber-metal modules and individual components for vibration damping in rail vehicles in close co-operation with the leading locomotives, tram and wagon manufacturers. ZF Boge Elastmetall plays an active part in future-oriented developments like monorail technology (Transrapid), tilting technology (Neitec), high-speed trains (ICE), and low-floor tram technology (Combino).

Complete heavy damping systems are developed in close co-operation with ZF Sachs. The bearings of these systems are suitable for any application. ZF Boge Elastmetall offers elaborate fully machined rubber-metal parts, components and ready-to-install modules from one source, due to the high vertical range of manufacture.

Special transmissions and high-quality gears for rail vehicles. The product range includes cylindrical and cone-shaped geometry. Supplies for all kinds of trains are provided, including high-speed trains, including the Italian ETR 500 and the French TGV, underground trains and trams.

ZF Padova is equipped for spare parts production to customer specifications and drawings. New components can be produced by reverse engineering based on a sample. A technical department, set up especially for these tasks, offers customer support and has the expertise to develop new transmissions according to requirements and technical conditions.

ELECTRIFICATION CONTRACTORS
AND EQUIPMENT SUPPLIERS

Company listing by country

AUSTRALIA
Ampcontrol Pty Ltd

AUSTRIA
Ing Karl und Albert Kruch GesmbH & Co KG (Kruch)

CROATIA
Končar – Power Plan and Electric Traction
 Engineering Inc

FRANCE
AMEC SPIE Rail
Carbone Lorraine Applications Electriques
Deutsch®
Ferraz Shawmut
Galland S.A.S.
Geismar
Lerc SA

GERMANY
Balfour Beatty Rail GmbH
Elpro BahnstromAnlagen GmbH
Siemens AG
Windhoff Bahn-und Anlagentechnik GmbH

INDIA
Crompton Greaves Ltd
HIM Polymers & Elastomers Private Limited

ITALY
FIREMA Trasporti SpA
Pfisterer Srl

JAPAN
Fuji ElectricSystems Co, Ltd
Hitachi Ltd
Toshiba Corporation

NETHERLANDS
voestalpine Railpro BV

PORTUGAL
EFACEC Sistemas de Electrónica SA

SPAIN
Cuadrelec SA

SWEDEN
Alcad Limited

SWITZERLAND
A Kaufmann AG
Flury
Furrer + Frey AG
Kummler & Matter AG
Pfisterer Sefag AG
Sécheron SA

UNITED KINGDOM
ALSTOM Transport
Brecknell Willis & Co Ltd
Elec-Track Installations Limited
FKI Switchgear
GrantRail Power Ltd
Matrix Power Ltd
Powernetics International Ltd
Transmitton – A Siemens Business
TrendRail Ltd
Ultra Electronics Ltd

UNITED STATES
Conductix Corporation
Delta Star Inc

For details of the latest updates to *Jane's Urban Transport Systems* online and to discover the
additional information available exclusively to online subscribers please visit
juts.janes.com

Alcad Limited

Norra Strandgatan 35, Box 504, S-572 25 Oskarshamn, Sweden
Tel: (+46 491) 681 00   Fax: (+46 491) 681 10
Web: www.alcad.com

Key personnel
Contact: Trevor Maddocks

Other offices
Sales Offices
1st Floor, Unit 5 Astra Centre, Edinburgh Way, Harlow CM20 2BN, UK
Tel: (+44 1279) 77 25 55   Fax: (+44 1279) 42 06 96
Alcad Batteries ME
PO Box 57180, 3313 Limassol, Cyprus
Tel: (+357 25) 87 18 16   Fax: (+357 25) 34 35 42
54, Genting Lane, #03-02 Ruby Land Complex Block II, Singapore 349562
Tel: (+65) 67 48 44 86   Fax: (+65) 67 48 46 39
Alcad Inc
3 Powdered Metals Drive, North Haven, Connecticut 06473, US
Tel: (+1 203) 985 25 00   Fax: (+1 203) 985 25 39

Products
Products include the Vantage and XHP battery ranges, to meet peak electricity demand or provide back-up power for essential services in rail infrastructure applications such as signalling, switching, points and barrier control/operations. Also suited to applications in substations, Alcad XHP batteries feature sintered positive electrode and a compact plastic bonded negative electrode (pbe) to offer a combination of low maintenance and high performance to provide reliable power back-up in rail infrastructure applications including UPS and switchgear.

ALSTOM Transport

48, rue Albert Dhalenne, F-93482 Saint Ouen, Cedex
Tel (+ 33 1) 41 66 90 00   Fax: (+ 33 1) 41 66 96 66
Web: www.transport.alstom.com

Key personnel
President, Transport Sector: *Philippe Mellier*
Chief Operating Officer: *Gérard Blanc*
Senior Vice-Presidents:
   Finance: Jean-Jacques Morin
   International Product Line Development: *Alain Goga*
   Asia Pacific: Marc Chatelard
   Southern Europe: Charles Carlier
   Americas: Francis Jelensperger
   Northern Europe: Roland Kientz
   Press Contact, Transport: *Cécile Dodat*

Electrification SpA
10 Via Lago dei Tartari, I-00012 Guidonia, Rome, Italy
Tel: (+39 06) 0774 37 74 85
Fax: (+39 06) 0774 35 34 30

ALSTOM Transport Service (PanChex)
48 rue Albert Dhalenne, F-93482 Saint-Ouen Cedex, France
Tel: (+33 1) 41 66 86 09   Fax: (+33 1) 41 66 92 70

Services
The Infrastructure Business unit of ALSTOM Transport Systems offers solutions at the system or subsystem level for power generation and distribution including: AC and DC traction substations; overhead facilities; contact lines or catenaries; third-rail or at-level integrated supply system; SCADA; auxiliary power supply; track laying; maintenance workshops; communications; signalling (tramways); electromechanical equipment in station; and electronic guidance systems for buses.

Its scope includes design, procurement, installation, commissioning, technical assistance, maintenance and training.

The electrification activities of ALSTOM cover power supply production, distribution and control of the traction current.

ALSTOM provides AC power distribution networks from high-voltage to medium-voltage conversion to feed traction substations and low-voltage station utilities.

Conversion is to AC single-phase current, primarily for main line railways:
- 25 kV 50 Hz for conventional railways
- 15 kV $16^2/_3$ Hz for Rail Link
- 2 × 25 kV 50 Hz for high-speed trains
Conversion to DC current in six-pulse or 12-pulse rectification:
- 3,000 V for conventional railways
- 1,500 V for suburban trains and urban mass transit systems with overhead catenary
- 750 V for mass rail transit metro systems through third rail
- 750 V for light rail transit systems and trolleybuses through overhead contact wire.
More than 1,100 rectifier units have been supplied by ALSTOM, supplying more than 3.3 million MW.

ALSTOM provides in-line traction current distribution:
- Third rail (or fourth rail) for mass transit systems, mainly 750 V.
- Overhead catenary for 25 kV AC high-speed trains, single-phase AC for conventional railways and for DC systems in 3,000, 1,500 and 750 V light rail transit systems.

ALSTOM provides innovative power electronics solutions, and control systems for local and remote traction substations. The company has developed a new concept for urban light transit systems (tramways and rubber-tyred vehicles with electric propulsion) to minimise the impact on the environment in the heart of a city and to provide traction power supply avoiding overhead contact wires.

ALISS (At Level Integrated Supply System) is a hidden, reliable, maintenance-free flexible system using static safety-redundant IGBT commutation, to provide vehicles with traction power, only on adequate sectors with dynamic identification under the vehicle assemblies. A diagnostic and monitoring management signalling system ensures communication with the centralised control centre. After successful reliability and performance laboratory tests, on-site demonstration with real loaded vehicles took place from mid-2000 on ALSTOM's Aytré plant's test tracks. PanChex overhead line protection system is a trackside asset protection system that monitors the interaction of each passing train with the overhead line system. PanChex is a licensed technology from AEA Technology Rail Ltd.

Contracts
25 kV: The Tunisian national rail company (SNCFT), TGV France (SNCF) and TGV Korea (KHRC)
25 kV: Algeria (SNTF), Portugal (CP), Costa Rica
$16^2/_3$ Hz: Arlanda Express airport rail link
3,000 V: Brazilian railways (Fepasa, CBTU), Morocco (ONCFM), Italy (FS)
1,500 V: Cairo metro line 1 (NAT), La Paz Pantitlan (Covitur, Mexico), Dublin (CIE) for Howth Bray line, Serpong and Tangerang for Indonesia (Jabotabek), Hong Kong Lantau airport rail link
750 V third-rail metros: Caracas lines 1 to 4 (CAMC), Athens lines 2 and 3, Mexico (STC and Covitur), Santiago de Chile (Metro SA), Cairo line 2 (NAT), Istanbul, Ankara, Lyon, Marseille
750 V overhead: tramways and trolleybuses (contact wire): Azteca Xochimilco (Mexico), Manchester Metrolink
Tramways in France: Rouen, Grenoble, Montpellier, Lyon, Nantes, Lille, Bobigny
Trolleybuses: Belo Horizonte, Lyon, Nancy, Grenoble, Marseille, Mexico
600–750 V: London Underground, Manchester, Hong Kong tramways, Mexico trolleybuses, New York, Chicago

Developments
Modular Traction Substations
To avoid the installation of unsightly metallic shelters in towns, ALSTOM has developed a modular traction substation, the use of which means that storage of materials on site and long construction periods are no longer necessary. Increasing worldwide demand for light metros or tramway systems, the growing trend towards standardisation of substations and the search for the most competitive overall price are all factors which prompted ALSTOM to develop the modular substation.

A complete substation is created, using production distribution and traction current control equipment. This consists of two concrete shelters easy to transport by road, each one comprising premises equipped with access doors for operational personnel as well as for possible handling of equipment. Once the concrete slab is constructed, installation is fast. All cable links are prepared for a quick assembly on site and only an easy connection to the electrical network is required. Tests carried out in factory conditions using reduced voltage, allow immediate commissioning.

AMEC SPIE Rail

Parc Saint-Christophe, Cergy-Pontoise Cedex, France
Tel: (+33 1) 34 22 50 00   Fax: (+33 1) 34 22 51 26
Web: www.amecspie.com

Key personnel
Chairman: *Pierre Fortuné*
Managing Director: *Jean-Pierre Bertrand*
Business Development Manager: *Riccardo Zampieri*

Background
Previously called Spie Enertrans, AMEC SPIE Rail is a subsidiary of AMEC.

In December 2006, AMEC plc reached an unconditional agreement to dispose of its 50 per cent interest in AMEC SPIE Rail Systems Ltd to the French infrastructure company, Colas SA.

Products
Design, construction and maintenance of railway infrastructure including: trackwork, catenary systems, power supplies, electromechanical, control and communications for rail systems including high-speed rail, metros, tramways and other transport systems.

Contracts
Recent contracts include:
UK: Channel Tunnel Rail Link; Wessex Power Upgrade; West Anglia.
France: LGV East; tramway of Bordeaux; tramway of Le Mans; tramway of Paris; tramway of Nice; tramway of Mulhouse.
Italy: catenary renewals south of Italy.
Romania: railway electrification for CFR; tramway of Bucharest.
Venezuela: Caracas metro.

Ampcontrol Pty Ltd

16 Old Punt Road, Tomago, New South Wales 2322, Australia
Tel: (+61 2) 49 61 90 00   Fax: (+61 2) 49 61 90 09
e-mail: corporate@ampcontrol.com.au
Web: www.ampcontrol.com.au

Key personnel
Chairman: *Robert Humpris*
Technical Director: *Peter Cockbain*
National Sales Manager: *Gary Hillier*
Business Development Manager: *Peter Hogg*

Products
Traction control switchgear; traction power control systems; traction substation switchrooms (AC and DC); specialised transformers and switchgear; rail communications.

Contracts

220 intelligent field telephones for the NSW Rail Infrastructure Corporation (RIC). Solar powered trackside wireless phones as well as electronic magneto and CB types supplied to the NSW Rail Infrastructure Corporation (RIC).

Balfour Beatty Rail GmbH

Power Systems
Garmischer Strasse 35, D-81373 Munich, Germany
Tel: (+49 89) 41 99 90 Fax: (+49 89) 41 99 92 70
e-mail: info.powersystems@bbrail.com
Web: www.bbrail.com

Key personnel

Managing Director: *Manfred Leger*

Background

In August 2005 Balfour Beatty acquired SBB, the specialist German signalling contractor.

Products and services

Railway electrification products and services, covering complete system design, supply, installation, construction management and commissioning for main line, mass transit and light rail systems.

Catenary system products and services include: main line catenary systems for speeds of up to 400 km/h; mass transit overhead contact line systems; mass transit conductor rail systems; catenary components and equipment; project management; commissioning; and customer support.

Power supply system products and services for AC systems include: $16\frac{2}{3}$ Hz and 50 Hz substations; static converters; boosters and auto-transformer stations; station control technology/ protection systems; outdoor cabling systems and indoor installation. For DC systems these include: substations; diode rectifiers; voltage-controlled rectifiers; and switchgear.

For both AC and DC systems Balfour Beatty Rail provides: network control and telecontrol systems; project management; commissioning; and customer support.

Contracts

Germany: In August 2007 Verkehrsgesellschaft Frankfurt am Main mbH commissioned Balfour Beatty Rail GmbH with the network calculation of the traction supply systems for U 5 vehicles. The network study includes simulations for normal operation and the malfunctioning of feed points during the use of the new generation of U 5 traction vehicles.

Brecknell Willis & Co Ltd

Member of the Fandstan Electric Group
PO Box 10, Tapstone Road, Chard TA20 2DE, UK
Tel: (+44 1460) 649 41 Fax: (+44 1460) 661 22
e-mail: enquiries@brecknellwillis.com
Web: www.brecknell-willis.com

Key personnel

Managing Director: *Tony White*
Sales Manager, Trainborne Equipment: *Andrew Hales*
Third Rail, Commercial Operations Manager: *David Bailey*
Overhead Systems, Chief Engineer: *David Hartland*

Products

Current collection and power distribution equipment for the transport sector. This includes design, manufacture, supply, installation, commissioning of complete systems and after sales service.

The product groups are pantographs and third rail current collectors; conductor rail systems;

Brecknell Willis Copenhagen conductor rail 1135120

Brecknell Willis, Dublin Luas – overhead lines 1135122

aluminium/stainless composite conductor rail and accessories, light rail overhead systems, automatic gas tensioning equipment, spring boxes and ground return units for railways, metro, light rail systems and tramways.

Contracts

Conductor rail systems for the East London Railway, Jubilee Line Extension Project and the Northern Line Upgrade (London Underground Ltd), Algiers, Ankara, Beijing, Brescia, Copenhagen, Dubai, Oslo and Taipei Metro systems. Overhead contact systems for the Dublin Luas, Midland Metro LRT system, Vancouver, Manchester Metro and refurbishment of Blackpool Tramway. Aluminium composite rail for DB, Berlin and Merseyrail UK.

Current collector systems for all new UK emu vehicles, West Coast Main Line Pendolino and current collection equipment for Shanghai Maglev; current collectors for the new vehicles for Hong Kong, Delhi Metro, KL-Monorail.

Supplied Eurostar and Channel Tunnel Shuttle trainborne current collectors as well as all standard high-speed pantographs for 25 kV electrified line operation in the UK. Light rail pantographs were supplied for the Strasbourg, Manchester, Birmingham, Sheffield and Tyne & Wear trams and shoegear for Glasgow, Amsterdam and Taipei Metros.

Carbone Lorraine Applications Electriques

10 rue Roger Dumoulin, F-80084 Amiens Cedex 02, France
Tel: (+33 3) 22 54 47 51 Fax: (+33 3) 22 54 47 72
e-mail: clae.be-infos@carbonelorraine.com
Web: www.elec.carbonelorraine.com

Key personnel

Marketing contact: *Erika Morvany Manquat*

Background

Carbone Lorraine Applications Electriques has expertise in power and signal transmission solutions and is part of the Carbone Lorraine group.

Products

Power and signal transmission solutions including pantograph strips, third rail collector shoes, trolley bus inserts, carbon brushes, brush-holders, slip rings and signal transfer systems.

Conductix Corporation

10102 F Street, Omaha, Nebraska 68127, US
Tel: (+1 402) 339 93 00 Fax: (+1 402) 339 96 27
e-mail: info@conductix.us
Web: www.conductix.us

Key personnel

President: *Lon Miller*
Division Manager: *Richard Prell*
Other offices in Australia, Canada, Manchester, Monterrey, Mexico and UK.

Background

Conductix is part of the Delachaux Group, Gennevilliers, France.

Products

Conductor rail systems up to 6,000 A. Specialises in conductor rail with stainless steel on aluminium extrusion which can be used for overhead cranes, and specialised rail for transit systems. Also manufactures cable reels, festoon systems, push button pendants and radio remote controls.

Supplier of overhead stinger systems for maintenance facilities.

Contracts

Vancouver/RAV project, Las Vegas Monorail, Lisbon Airport, Toronto Airport.

Developments

Contact rails with choice of amperage range to meet system demands, including welded aluminium-stainless conductor rail.

Crompton Greaves Ltd

6th floor, CG House, Dr Annie Besant Road, Worli, Mumbai 400 030, India
Tel: (+91 22) 24 23 77 77
Fax: (+91 22) 24 23 77 88
Web: www.cglonline.com

Rail Transportation Systems Division
5-E Vandhna 11, Tolstoy Marg, New Delhi 110 001, India
Tel: (+91 11) 30 41 63 00
Fax: (+91 11) 23 32 43 60, 23 35 21 34
e-mail: salil.kumar@cgl.co.in

Key personnel

Managing Director: *S M Trehan*
Vice-President Rail Transportation Systems Division: *A K Raina*
Senior Manager Rail Transportation Systems Division: *Salil Kumar*

Products

Traction transformers, SF6 gas interrupters/circuit breakers, lightning arrestors, turnkey electrification contracts.

Cuadrelec SA

C/ Bruselas, 18 Parc 25 y 26, E-28813 Torres de la Alameda, Madrid, Spain
Tel: (+34 91) 886 33 66   Fax: (+34 91) 886 33 62
e-mail: cuadrelec@sistelcom.com
Web: www.cuadrelec.com

Products

Traction rectifiers for 3.3 kV, 1.5 kV and 750 V DC power supply systems.

Delta Star Inc

Delta Star East
3550 Mayflower Drive, Lynchburg, Virginia 24501, US
Tel: (+1 804) 845 09 21
Fax: (+1 804) 845 70 89
Web: www.deltastar.com

Key personnel

International Contract Sales: *Robert Ratcliffe*

Products

Aluminium/steel composite conductor rail, insulators and other third-rail electrification equipment; catenary systems and components.

Deutsch®

Carrier Khéops Bac
8 Boulevard Pierre Lefaucheux, F-72027 Le Mans, Cedex 2, France
Tel: (+33 2) 43 61 45 45
Fax: (+33 2) 43 61 45 00
e-mail: ckb@deutsch.net
Web: www.deutsch.net

Key personnel

General Manager: *Denis Plantey*
Finance Director: *Emmanuelle Douvinet*
Railway Director: *Patrick Roseleur*
Railway Marketing Manager: *Jean-Paul Denovillers*
Railway Engineering Manager: *Patrice Pivetta*

Background

Deutsch previously traded as Compagnie Deutsch.

Products

Electrical connectors for signalling, power and control supply for metro, suburban rail, high-speed trains and LRT systems. Also fibre optic systems, coaxial connection systems.

Contracts

Equipment has been supplied for metro systems in Paris, Santiago, Mexico City and Caracas, for tramways in Grenoble, St Etienne Zurich, Boston and also emu/dmu (AGT, NAT) and high-speed trains (TGV, KTX).

Developments

EKO series, new concept for power connection. SRC series, reverse bayonet signal connection derived from MS5015. MCM series, new concept for rectangular signal connectors.

EFACEC Sistemas de Electrónica SA

Av Eng Frederico Ulrich, PO Box 31, P-4470 Maia, Portugal
Tel: (+351 2) 941 36 66
Fax: (+351 2) 948 54 28
e-mail: se@efacec.pt
Web: www.efacec.pt

Key personnel

Chairman: *Francisco de La Fuente Sánchez*
Vice-Chairman: *Alberto Joaquim Milheiro Barbosa*
Market Relations: *Maria Elisa Oliveira*

Products

Electrification equipment, including traction substations (1,500 V DC and 25 kV 50 Hz AC) and associated telecontrol systems, catenary systems.

Elec-Track Installations Limited

ETI Ltd
Unit 1, Pennypot Industrial Estate, Hythe, Kent CT21 6PE, UK
Tel: (+44 1303) 26 45 55
Fax: (+44 1303) 26 44 99
e-mail: info@elec-track.co.uk
Web: www.elec-track.co.uk

Key personnel

Chairman ETI Group: *David Jackson*
Managing Director: *Ian Bailey*
Engineering and Business Development Director: *John Fry*
Operations Director, OLE Division: *Brian Smith*

Background

ETI was founded in 1995 and is fully accredited to contract directly with Network Rail and holds ISO 9001 (2000) quality for accreditation and ISO 14001 environmental management system.

Products

Overhead line contact system electrification construction and maintenance. Isolation provision and isolation management for AC and DC systems. Possession management and provision of safety critical staff. Road rail plant hire and railway safety case. Overhead line contact system design and engineering.

Power supply and distribution for AC and DC systems including cabling installation and cable route works. Training and assessment for railway staff. Complimentary works including track-work, TPWS installation, de-vegetation, scrap rail recovery and level crossing (RRAP) installation.

Contracts

As well as serving Network Rail and its principal contractors, ETI has worked extensively on many tramway and metro projects, including the London Underground and also within Europe including Holland and France, with experience in installing European high-speed catenary systems as found on the TGV network in France.

Elpro BahnstromAnlagen GmbH

Marzahner Strasse 34, D-13053 Berlin, Germany
Tel: (+49 30) 98 61 22 53
Fax: (+49 30) 98 61 22 51
e-mail: elpro@elpro.de
Web: www.elpro.de

Key personnel

Contact: *Franz Peter Lung*

Products

Equipment for AC and DC electrification systems, including substations, switchgear, overhead lines, control and distribution systems.

Ferraz Shawmut

1, Chaussée de la Comtesse, F-77160 Provins, France
Tel: (+33 1) 60 58 56 20
Fax : (+33 1) 64 08 88 34
Web: www.ferrazshawmut.com

Background

Ferraz Shawmut is a division of Carbone Lorraine.

Products

AC protistor fuses for the internal protection of the AC/DC and/or AC/DC/AC substation converters, large power filters and auxiliary circuits; disconnectors to isolate substation converters; automatic fast-acting earthing device with large short-circuit capability, which can be either bi- or unidirectional.

FIREMA Trasporti SpA

Headquarters and main facilities
Via Provinciale Appia, Località Ponteselice, I-81100 Caserta, Italy
Tel: (+39 0823) 09 71 11
Fax: (+39 0823) 46 68 12
e-mail: info@firema.it
Web: www.firema.it

Key personnel

Chairman and Chief Executive Officer: *Gianfranco Fiore*
Commercial Manager: *Sergio d'Arminio*
Marketing Manager: *Agostino Astori*

Products

Substation equipment for AC and DC electrification; converting group and auxiliary transformers; solid-state rectifiers; high-/medium-voltage switchgear with high-speed circuit breakers, auxiliary and protection relays; minor parts and maintenance.

Work continues on development of diagnostics and automatic maintenance systems.

FKI Switchgear

e-mail: sales@fkiswitchgear.com
Web: www.fkiswitchgear.com
Street address
FKI Switchgear
Hawker Siddeley Switchgear Ltd
Newport Road, Blackwood, South Wales NP12
2XH, UK
Tel: (+44 1495) 22 30 01   Fax: (+44 1495) 22 56 74

Key personnel
Managing Director: *Brian Gardner*
Engineering Director: *Steve Lane*
Sales and Marketing Director: *Steve Dymond*
Tactical Marketing Executive: *Greig Jones*

Background
FKI Switchgear brings together Whipp & Bourne
and Hawker Siddley Switchgear Limited, two
successful UK switchgear companies. Whipp &
Bourne is a long-established major manufacturer
of heavy-duty electrical switchgear, the original
company being formed in 1903. The company has
large experience in the production of electrical
switchgear, specifically designed to meet the
system requirements of AC and DC electrification
for controlling the power supplies to both heavy
and light rail transit systems together with metro
systems.

Hawker Siddeley Switchgear Limited is an
international producer of switchgear, producing
a range of indoor and outdoor distribution
switchgear.

Products and services
A major national and international manufacturer
of a range of distribution switchgear, FKI
Switchgear offers both AC and DC switchgear
solutions to electrical distribution utilities
worldwide, and to other market sectors.

The Eclipse, 'fit & forget', ground mounting,
11 kV/25 kA max. Indoor metalclad, air insulated,
fixed pattern, magnetic actuator mechanism
vacuum circuit breakers with full internal arc
containment features and current ratings up to
2,000 A. The Eclipse is now also available as a
pre-engineered solution in ratings up to 25 kA,
2000 A. Alternatively it can be fully engineered to
meet exact customer requirements.

The Lightning incorporates the high-speed NDC
circuit breaker. It provides a new DC switchgear
solution for a variety of markets and demanding
applications. The Lightning (rated 900 VDC, 4000 –
8000 A; 1800 VDC, 4000 – 6000 A) has many dc
switchgear applications, including: transport:
traction (heavy and light railways/ mass rapid
transit and tram systems).

The Horizon is a round mounted 15 kV or 38 kV
application, Outdoor, SF6 insulated, magnetic
actuator mechanism vacuum circuit breaker
with current ratings up to 2000 A and BIL up to
200 kVp.

The Horizon Compact is the latest addition to
the Fit & Forget range of switchgear products.
It is a substation frame, stand or pole-mounted
vacuum circuit breaker with SF6 insulation in a
self-contained package. Designed for a 15 kV or
26 kV application, the Horizon Compact can be
used with other products from FKI Switchgear to
provide cost-effective and compact substations,
or can be used to replace old and obsolete
equipment in existing substations.

Flury

Arthur Flury AG
Fabrikstrasse 4, CH-4543 Deitingen, Switzerland
Tel: (+41 32) 613 33 66   Fax: (+41 32) 613 33 68
e-mail: info@flury.ch
Web: www.aflury.ch

Key personnel
President: *Adrian Flury*
Vice-President: *Daniel Bizegger*
Executive Sales Manager: *Kurt Kummer*

Products
Components for overhead electrification systems,
including section insulators and phase breaks;
messenger wire and contact wire insulators;
earthing equipment; terminals, suspension
clamps, connecting clamps and feeder clamps.

Fuji ElectricSystems Co, Ltd

Gate City Ohsaki, East Tower, 11-2, Osaki
1-chome,
Shimagawa-ku, Tokyo 141-0032, Japan
Tel: (+81 3) 54 35 70 46
Fax: (+81 3) 54 35 74 23
e-mail: info@ffesys.co.jp
Web: www.fesys.co.jp

Key personnel
Managing Director, Electrical Systems Company
Group: *G Yanai*
General Manager, Transportation Systems Sales
Department: *K Kimura*

Background
The Transportation Systems Sales Department of
what was previously Fuji Electric Co Ltd, is part of
the newly divided Fuji Electric Systems Co, Ltd.

Products
Power supply equipment: computer-based
remote supervisory control equipment; water
cooling silicon rectifiers; SF6 gas circuit
breakers and mini high-speed circuit breakers;
moulded transformers; total control systems
including electric power management, station
office apparatus control, data management and
disaster prevention management.

Furrer + Frey AG

PO Box 182, Thunstrasse 35, CH-3000 Berne 6,
Switzerland
Tel: (+41 31) 357 61 11   Fax: (+41 31) 357 61 00
e-mail: adm@furrerfrey.ch
Web: www.furrerfrey.ch

Key personnel
Chief Executive Officer, Export and Marketing:
  B Furrer
Executive Officer, Construction Department for
  Railway Electrification: *F Friedli*
Executive Officer, Electrification and Design
  Products: *R Marti*
Executive Officer, Export Department: *R D Brodbek*
Consulting Officer: *U Wili*

Works
PO Box, Eisenbahnstrasse 62-64, CH-3645 Gwatt

Subsidiary
UP AG, Berne

Products
Design, manufacture and installation of
overhead contact lines for railways, up to 25 kV
AC, tramways and light rail.

Specialist equipment includes overhead
contact lines for track railways, tram and
light rail systems; overhead conductor rail
system; movable conductor rail for depots and
maintenance facilities; railway safety control
systems for depots; software for electrification
projects; consultancy; measuring of existing OHL
in order to assess contact force, uplift, contact
wire height, stagger.

Contracts
1998–2004: electrification of Zimmerbergtunnel
on section Zurich-Thalwil for Swiss Federal
Railways within project Rail 2000, with a design
speed of 200 km/h.

1999–2008: fixed and moveable overhead
conductor rail installations in depots and
maintenance facilities in Switzerland, Germany,
Denmark, Sweden, Norway, Italy and Hong Kong.

Moveable conductor rail installations on five
swing and bascule bridges on the northeast
corridor section between Boston and Newhaven
for Amtrak.

2000–2007: upgrading in eight stages of
railway station Frutigen, 1.5 km, for the access to
the new Lötschberg tunnel.

2001–2005: supply of > 400 supports for narrow
tunnels to Norwegian Rail Administration (5 km).

2003–2004: overhead conductor rail installation
for speeds ≥ 200 km/h in Sittenbergtunnel (2 km),
Austria.

2005–2006: conductor rail installation in tunnel
and Lehrter railway station on the north-south
connection Berlin, (19.6 km, 15 kV AC).

2005–2007: MOB Montreaux-Oberland Railways:
several renewals for Golden Pass, such as the
equipment for seven small and narrow tunnels on
the Les Avants-Jor line, with overhead conductor
rail and conventional cantenary between the
tunnels (1.5 kV).

2006–2007: conductor rail for Lines 6, 8, 9 of
Shanghai Metro, (119 km).

2007–2008: Network Rail, Great Eastern upgrade.
Overhead contact line system design.

Galland S.A.S.

ZI de l'Ilot, F-33240 La Lande de Fronsac, France
Tel: (+33 5) 57 94 07 20
Fax: (+33 5) 57 94 07 11
e-mail: info@j-galland.com
Web: www.j-galland.com

Key personnel
Chairman: *Philippe d'Huy*
Technical Director: *Dominique Bec*
Export Manager: *Frèdèric Glemet*

Products
Catenary equipment including catenary from
750 V to 25 kV; normal, reinforced and flexible
gantries; lightweight section insulators from
tramway to high-speed train (tested at 270 km/h);
spring and pulley tensioning devices; isolating
and selector switches, with and without earth
(new European standard); tramway equipment –
catenary, anchorage, section insulators, Kevlar
terminations, delta suspension, tensioning
devices, isolator and selector switches.

Geismar

113 bis avenue Charles-de-Gaulle, F-92200
Neuilly sur Seine, France
Tel: (+33 1) 41 43 40 40
Fax: (+33 1) 46 40 71 70
e-mail: geismar@geismar.com
Web: www.geismar.com

Works
5 rue d'Altkirch, F-68006 Colmar Cedex, France
Tel: (+33 3) 89 80 22 11
Fax: (+33 3) 89 79 78 45
e-mail: colmar@geismar.com

Key personnel
Publicity: *Patrick Lambert*

Products
Geismar provides equipment to erect, maintain
and inspect AC and DC catenary lines; a large
variety of dedicated tools; a range of overhead
line components; overhead line unrolling/
renewal equipment: skids, wagons and trains;
access units and vehicles: elevators, road-
railers, maintenance and inspection motorcars;
electronic measuring/recording: hand-held
devices and onboard systems.

Geismar also provides tracklaying and
maintenance equipment.

GrantRail Power Ltd

Carolina Court, Lakeside, Doncaster DN4 5RA, UK
Tel: (+44 1302) 79 11 00
Fax: (+44 1302) 79 12 00
Web: www.grantrail.com

Key personnel
Chief Executive Officer: *Gren Edwards*
Managing Director: *Martin Hawley*
General Manager: *Tony Lyons*

Background
GrantRail Power is a subsidiary company of the GrantRail Group, part of VokerWessels Group of companies.

Services
Capabilities include: project planning and management; consultancy services; design, supply and installation construction works; new works commissioning; isolation planning and implementation services; design and data verification; design supply and installation of 25 kV AC overhead line equipment.
Through Matrix Power Ltd work undertaken includes: test, commissioning of switchgear, transformers, ancillary equipment and protection systems, provision of SAP's; installation of switchgear, transformers and ancillary equipment; cabling installation, cable jointing and civil works; high and low voltage works.

Contracts
Resignalling project, Coventry: major remodelling of the Coventry controlled signalling system to the West Midlands Signalling Centre; OLE installation works, Tottenham; Cambridge booster renewals; overhead line installation – remodelling works, Bescot Down Siding; Harpenden Span wire replacements on the Midland mainline.

Hitachi Ltd

Transportation Systems
18-13, Soto-Kanda 1-chome, Chiyudo-ku, Tokyo, 101-8608, Japan
Tel: (+81 3) 258 11 11   Fax: (+81 3) 45 64 62 52
Web: www.hitachi-rail.com

Key personnel
Chief Operating Officer of Transportation Systems: *Toshihide Uchimura*

Products
Traction substation equipment for AC and DC electrification projects; diode and thyristor rectifiers; power regenerative inverters; transformers; AC and DC switchgear; control and protection devices; computerised systems – substation supervisory remote-control systems (controlled by Supervisory Control and Data Acquisition, SCADA), automatic car diagnosis system, station management system, security system.

Contracts
Substation for Taiwan Taoyuan International Airport Access MRT, Taiwan; Palm island Monorail, UAE; Sentosa Monorail, Singapore.

HIM Polymers & Elastomers Private Limited

B1/J2, Mohan Co Operative Industrial Estate, Mathura Road, New Delhi 110 044, India
Tel: (+91 11) 41 68 25 00
Fax: (+91 11) 41 68 25 02
info@himpolymers.com
e-mail: him_polymers@yahoo.co.in
Web: www.himpolymers.com

Works
Plot no 63, Gondpur Industrial Area, Paonta Sahib 173025, India

Key personnel
Chairman: *Madhusudan Tantia*
Director: *Pradeep Gupta*

Background
An associate company of BESCO Limited (Wagon Division), a manufacturer and supplier of freight cars in India, Him Polymers & Elastomers Private Limited is ISO 9001:2000 certified.

Products
Manufacturer and supplier of rubber, rubber metal bonded, silicone rubber, polyurethane and other polymers for use on railway rolling stock, railway electrification and railway track maintenance.

Ing Karl und Albert Kruch GesmbH & Co kg (Kruch)

Pfarrgasse 87, A-1230 Vienna, Austria
Tel: (+43 1) 616 31 65
Fax: (+43 1) 616 31 68
e-mail: office@kruch.com
Web: www.kruch.com

Products
Suspension clamps and hanger clamps for bearer cables and overhead contact wires.

A Kaufmann AG

Pilatusstrasse 2, CH-6300 Zug, Switzerland
Tel: (+41 41) 711 67 00
Fax: (+41 41) 859 16 01
e-mail: info@kago.ch
Web: www.kago.com

Products
KAGO specialist engineering products for railways, including a complete range of non-screwed rail contact clamps, discs and strips for electrical rail connections (return current, signalling circuits, earthing), cable fastenings for rails and sleepers, special welding electrodes for copper welding; complete range of screwing, welding and grounding fittings; self-tapping sleeper screws for concrete, steel or wooden sleepers; sleeper spring clips; high-voltage insulations.
Recent development: KAGO axle counter box.

Services
Track returns and earthing wires; earthing poles; heavy-duty and special mountings and drillings; suspensions for radiating cables.

Končar – Power Plan and Electric Traction Engineering Inc

Fallerovo Šetalište 22, HR-10000 Zagreb, Croatia
Tel: (+385 1) 366 71 88, 366 71 95
Fax: (+385 1) 366 71 96
e-mail: info@koncar-ket.hr
Web: www.koncar-ket.hr

Key personnel
President: *Darinko Bago*
Members of Board: *Božidar Piller, Vladimir Plečko, Jozo Miloloža, Marina Kralj-Miliša*
Marketing and Sales Manager: *Renata Godek*

Background
Končar – Power Plan and Electric Traction Engineering Inc is a member of Končar Group.

Products
Electric traction substations 110/25 kV; reactive power compensation plants 25 kV; sectioning posts 25 kV; rectifier substations for electric traction; track circuits; point machine heating; level crossings.

Kummler & Matter AG

Hohlstrasse 176, CH-8026 Zürich, Switzerland
Tel: (+41 44) 247 47 66
Fax: (+41 44) 247 47 47
e-mail: kuma@kuma.ch
Web: www.kuma.ch

Key personnel
President and Chief Executive Officer: *Daniel Steiner*
Finance Director: *Rudolf Büschlen*
Manager, Overhead Contact Lines: *Reto Hügli*
Purchasing Manager: *H P Villringer*
Area Sales Managers: *Rodolfo Middelmann, Reto Hügli, Willy-Urs Brassel, André Eichhorn*

Products
Overhead contact line equipment for light rail, branch lines, suburban and main line railways, and trolleybuses. Engineering and feasibility studies. Installation and supervision of installation.

KAGO rail contact clamps (inset) and cable connection in progress   0006271

Lerc SA

Chemin des Hamaïdes, PO Box 119, F-59732 Saint Amand les Eaux Cedex, France
Tel: (+33 3) 27 22 85 50
Fax: (+33 3) 27 22 85 05
e-mail: commercial@lerc.fr
Web: www.lerc.fr

Key personnel
Managing Director: *J Mourey*
Technical Director: *Y Foissac*
Business Unit Manager: *Vincent Lernoud*

Subsidiaries
Janssen Engineering

Products
A range of insulators with silicon shed shells for railway, tram and metro lines; bushing and insulating systems; composite insulators for energy (transport and distribution). Production and refurbishment of composite bushings. Synthetic insulators for catenaries, insulated steady arms for urban transport, insulated consoles for urban transport, composite parts processed by pultrusion, moulding and winding.

Matrix Power Ltd

18 Ellerbeck Way, Stokesley Business Park, Stokesley TS9 5JZ, UK
Tel: (+44 1642) 71 77 55   Fax: (+44 1642) 71 42 70
e-mail: matrix@matrixpower.co.uk
Web: www.matrixpower.co.uk

Key personnel
Chief Executive: *Gren Edwards*
Managing Director: *Martin Hawley*
General Manager: *Neil Guest*

Background
Matrix Power was formed in early 1997. In September 2006 it was acquired by the GrantRail Group, which is part of the VokerWessels Group of companies.

Capabilities
Matrix Power is a specialist company providing all manner of support services to the electrical construction, power and rail sectors.

Work undertaken includes: test and commissioning of switchgear, transformers, ancillary equipment and protection systems; provision of SAPs (Senior Authorised Person); installation of switchgear, transformers and ancillary equipment up to 132 kV; cabling installations, cable jointing and termination up to 66 kV; civil works; maintenance and emergency callout; design and project management; low voltage works and rail E&P.

Pfisterer Srl

Articoli Elettrici Speciali
Via Sirtori 45d, I-20017 Passirana di Rho (MI), Italy
Tel: (+39 02) 931 58 11
Fax: (+39 02) 931 581 27
e-mail: pfisterer@pfisterer.it
Web: www.pfisterer.it

Key personnel
Managing Director: *Ing Luciano Femminis*
Export Manager: *Ing Lorenzo Mosna*

Other offices
Pfisterer
Kontaktsysteme GmbH & Co KG
Rosenstrasse 44, D-73650 Winterbach, Germany
Tel: (+49 7181) 70 05
Fax: (+49 711) 301 21 97
Web: www.pfisterer.it

Pfisterer GmbH
A-1091 Wien, Augasse 17, Austria
Tel: (+43 1) 31 76 53 10
Fax: (+43 1) 317 65 31 12

Sefag Export
CH-6102 Malters/Luzern, Werkstrasse 7, Switzerland
Tel: (+41 41) 499 72 72
Fax: (+41 41) 497 22 69

Upresa SA
E-08025 Barcelona, Calle Industria 90-92, Spain
Tel: (+34 93) 436 47 01
Fax: (+34 93) 436 77 01
Web: www.upresa.es

Upresa SA
Arroya Fontarròn 39, E-28030, Madrid, Spain
Tel: (+34 91) 430 51 51   Fax: (+34 91) 437 39 10
Web: www.upresa.es

Solikap Acessòrios Eléctricos SA
Rua da Rainha 340, Apartado 2075, 4407 S Felix da Marinha, Codex, Portugal
Tel: (+351 22) 762 47 14 64
Fax: (+351 22) 762 47 39
e-mail:solikap.ruiribeiro@netc.pt

Products
Silicon rubber composite insulators for railway, tram and metro lines; clamps and earthing devices; equi-potential reversible cable hanger for use on Italian Railways (FS) high-speed lines electrified at 25 kV 50 Hz AC; voltage detectors, tensioning system Tensorex®, a mechanical pull regulation system which can handle continuous tension on the contact wire specially designed for narrow spaces like tunnels.

PU+ clamp; Ambrosius, automatic controlling system for contact wire and catenary tensioning, designed for the automatic remote control of the tensioning performance; Phantom Tensorex, automatic tensioning device for tramway and railway contact lines, not visible, with low impact on the environment.

Pfisterer Sefag AG

Werkstrasse 7, CH-6102 Malters, Switzerland
Tel: (+41 41) 499 72 72
Fax: (+41 41) 497 22 69
e-mail: connect@sefag.ch
Web: www.pfisterer.com

Key personnel
Managing Director: *Samuel Ansorge*
Managing Director and Director Services: *Hans Wicki*
Director Local CoC Overhead Lines and Director Services: *Walter Fluri*
Director Local Sales Organisation: *Walter Bachmann*
Director Local CoC Components: *Jörg Fries*

Products
Silcosil composite insulators with silicon sheds as suspension, dead-end and post insulators, and as special insulators for tunnels and high-speed routes.

Contracts
Contracts include the supply of insulators to Swiss Federal Railways, Austrian Federal Railways, Bern-Lötschberg-Simplon Railway, and other railways in Switzerland and abroad.

Powernetics International Ltd

Jason Works, Clarence Street, Loughborough LE11 1DX, UK
Tel: (+44 1509) 21 41 53
Fax: (+44 1509) 26 24 60
e-mail: jag@powernetics.co.uk
Web: www.powernetics.co.uk

Key personnel
Managing Director: *Satish Chada*
Sales Director: *Kevin Pateman*
Engineering Director: *Nilesh Chouhan*
Operations Director: *Konrad Chada*
Sales Manager: *Jim Goddard*

Products
Independent private limited company with 35 years' experience in design, manufacture, test, installation, commissioning and maintenance of auxiliary, standby/emergency AC/DC power supply systems for the rail industry in trackside, tunnel, switchroom, REB and trainborne environments.

System design and integration of UPS and associated switchgear/power monitoring within REBs and switchrooms for SSI, FSP and PSP applications.

Sécheron SA

Rue Pré-Bouvier 25 – Zimeysa, CH-1217 Meyrin, Geneva, Switzerland
Tel: (+41 22) 739 41 11   Fax: (+41 22) 739 48 11
e-mail: info@secheron.com
Web: www.secheron.com

Key personnel
Chief Executive Officer and PBU Substations Director: *Martin Balters*
PBU Components Director: *Jo Murer*
Marketing: *Roch-Henri de Peretti*
PBU Substation Sales Manager: *Jimmy Cuche*
PBU Components Sales Manager: *Jean-François Bretton*

Subsidiaries
Sécheron Tchéquie, spol sro, Prague, Czech Republic.

Background
Sécheron SA is a member of Sécheron Hasler AG Group.

Products
DC traction power substations and ancillary equipment including system engineering and network computer simulation; solid-state rectifiers and inverters; harmonic filters; DC switchgear; DC high-speed circuit breakers, isolating and changeover switches; electronic protection relays; microprocessor-based remote-control and protection systems.

Sécheron disconnector for fixed installation
1323671

Siemens AG

Mobility
Infrastructure Networks – Electrification
PO Box 3240, D-91050 Erlangen, Germany
Tel: (+49 9131) 70   Fax: (+49 9131) 72 83 64
e-mail: railway.electrification@siemens.com
Web: www.siemens.com/mobility

Siemens trackside installations for 750 V DC traction power upgrade for Network Rail, UK   0585227

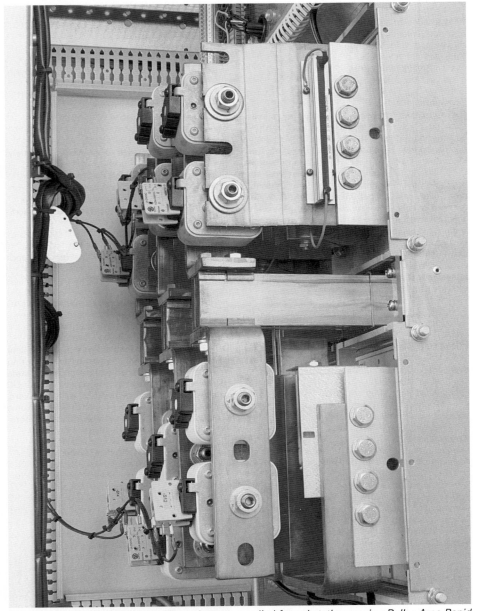

Siemens DC traction power supply equipment supplied for substation serving Dallas Area Rapid Transit   1327983

Corporate headquarters
Siemens AG
Industry Sector – Mobility
PO Box 3240, D-91050 Erlangen, Germany
Tel: (+49 9131) 7-0
e-mail: contact.mobility@siemens.com
Web: www.siemens.com/mobility

Key personnel
Mobility
Division Chief Executive Officer: *Dr Hans-Jörg Grundmann*
Head of Business Administration (BA): *Michael Schulz-Drost*

Products and services
Supply and installation of traction power supply systems for mass transit and main line railways; supply and installation of contact lines for mass transit and main line railways.

Contracts
Recent contracts include:
Thailand: In January 2005 Siemens, together with consortium partners B Grimm and Sino Thai Engineering and Construction plc (STECON) signed a contract with State Railway of Thailand for the construction of the 28 km Suvarnabhumi Airport Rail Link and the City Air Terminal.

Both Siemens and B Grimm are taking responsibility for the design, supply, installation and project management of the whole electrical and mechanical system.
UK: In April 2003 Siemens, in a joint venture with AMEC SPIE Rail Systems Ltd, signed a seven-year framework agreement to upgrade the traction power supply system in the Wessex area of southern England, covering 750 V DC lines from London to Bournemouth and Weymouth. Siemens' role in the project covers the design, manufacture and supply of new DC substations.

Other orders for electrification technology form part of turnkey contracts, detailed in the Siemens Mobility entry in the *Turnkey systems contractors* section.
US: In April 2008 Siemens approved the installation of a one megawatt solar energy system at its Sacramento light rail manufacturing facility.

Toshiba Corporation

Transportation Systems Division
Toshiba Building, 1-Shibaura 1-chome, Minato-ku, Tokyo 105-8001, Japan
Tel: (+81 3) 34 57 49 24   Fax: (+81 3) 54 44 92 63
e-mail: miki.ogata@toshiba.co.jp
Web: www.toshiba.co.jp

Key personnel
President and Chief Executive Officer: *Atsutoshi Nishida*
Vice-President, Transportation Systems Division: *Toshiyuki Onishi*
Senior Manager, Railway Projects Department: *Yoshiji Ito*
Group Manager, Overseas Business Planning Group: *Michihiko Ogata*

Products
SCADA (Supervisory Control and Data aquisitions) for power supply systems. AC and DC electrified systems, power transmission and distribution systems. SCADA for facilities.

Transmitton – A Siemens Business

Ashby Park, Ashby-de-la-Zouch LE65 1JD, UK
Tel: (+44 1530) 25 80 00   Fax: (+44 1530) 25 80 08
e-mail: sales@transmitton.co.uk
Web: www.transmitton.co.uk

Key personnel
Business Unit Director: *I Wright*
Head of Sales and Marketing: *E Turnock*
Finance and Commercial Manager: *G Lowndes*

Background
In August 2005 Transmitton Ltd was acquired by Siemens plc from the Alchemy backed ICS Group Ltd. Transmitton now forms part of Siemens in the UK reporting to Siemens Transportation Systems (STS).

The Transmitton team are now a vital element within the STS rail communications group, incorporating the 120 strong Transmitton team at Ashby and STS Poole based mobile communications, GSM-R cab radio business of around 80 employees.

Products
Transmitton provides a range of integrated control and asset management solutions to the rail industry. These include; integrated station management and network management systems, real-time passenger information systems, remote condition monitoring, intelligent asset management solutions, traction power SCADA, and Open Transport Network (OTN).

At the core of these solutions are Transmitton's cromos and fastflex technologies. The fastflex

Remote Terminal Unit (RTU) is modular in design and suits a wide range of applications for stand alone control, point-to-point and remote communications. Transmitton's cromos software offers real-time control and asset management technologies.

Transmitton holds a strong position in the global market place, having gained cross market and international experience by providing systems in America, Asia and the Far East, Africa, Australia, Eastern and Western Europe including the UK.

Transmitton has a fully documented quality system and is accredited to BS ISO 9001:2000 (TickIT), has a Network Rail Contractors Assurance Case Certificate, product approval certificates and is a qualified supplier on both Link-Up (UVDB) and FPAL databases.

Contracts

Transmitton's continuing project work for customers includes Balfour Beatty, Beijing Metro, Carillion Rail, Docklands Light Railway, EMCOR, Gleeson MCL, Metronet, Network Rail, Tubelines, AMEC, BP, Transco, GAS de Portugal, Interconnector, Shell and TotalFina.

TrendRail Ltd

Unit 8, Brindley Road, St Helens WA9 4HY, UK
Tel: (+44 1744) 85 11 00　Fax: (+44 1744) 85 11 22
e-mail: info@trendrail.com
Web: www.trendrail.com

Key personnel

Managing Director: *Jack Taylor*
Company Secretary: *Margaret Taylor*
General Manager: *Marion Smith*
Production Manager: *Gary Birchall*

Products

Railway engineering and electrification products/ catenary wire fittings; small parts steelwork including arcing horns, angles, fabrications, plates, links and balance weights and fasteners. ISO 9002 accredited, Investors in People and Link-up approved.

Ultra Electronics Ltd

PMES
Armitage Road, Rugeley, WS15 1DR, UK
Tel: (+44 1889) 50 33 00　Fax: (+44 1889) 57 29 29
e-mail: enquiries@ultra-pmes.com
Web: www.ultra-pmes.com

Key personnel

Managing Director: *A M Freer*
Marketing Director: *J S Greenhalgh*
Engineering Director: *J P Wardale*
Sales Manager, Transit Systems: *T W Boston*
Public Relations: *L M John*

Subsidiaries

PMES (Asia) Pte Ltd, Singapore

Background

Previously Foster Rectifiers, and THORN EMI Electronics, and with 40 years' experience of design and manufacture of transformer rectifier systems for traction applications, Ultra Electronics is an operating division of Ultra Electronics Holdings Ltd.

Products and services

Supplier of high-quality DC power systems. Equipment has been supplied to the Network Rail (UK), London Underground and overseas transit authorities.

Equipment can be supplied as 'stand alone' units, although contracts are often for turnkey projects including complete DC substations design and supply. Scope of supply may include system design, integration, co-ordination, project management, equipment supply, installation and commissioning. Scope of equipment supply includes modular buildings, transformers, rectifiers, AC, DC and LV switchboard, SCADA, auxiliary equipment, power cables and civil works.

Major projects

AMEC for Docklands Light Railway – London City Airport extension: turnkey project incuding provision of new modular substations.

Network Rail (UK) – Power supply upgrade project: contract for the provision of four new modular substations (within tight timescales) as part of the renewal of the Southern Zone DC power supply system.

Ansaldo Trasporti – Dublin Light Rail (Luas) project: design and supply of 15 900 V, 750 DC indoor air natural rectifiers complete with Open Circuit Arm Detectors.

Balfour Beatty Rail for Network Rail – Tyne & Wear Metro Sunderland Extension: complete project including provision of new modular substations.

Balfour Kilpatrick: London Underground Northern Line, 19 transformer rectifiers.

ABB for London Underground Ltd, Asset Renewal: design, supply and commissioning of 2,000 kW 630/750 DC air natural rectifiers with LNAN transformers complete with Open Circuit Arm Detectors.

Meiden Europe: Manila EDSA LRT Line 3, 10 rectifiers.

City of Edmonton Alberta Canada: power system upgrade, six transformers.

Illinois Gulf Central Railroad, Chicago: provision of DC substation, complete project including two transformer rectifiers AC and DC switchgear.

---

voestalpine Railpro BV

Nieuwe Crailoseweg 8, PO Box 888, NL-1222 AB Hilversum, Netherlands
Tel: (+31 35) 688 96 00
Fax: (+31 35) 688 96 66
e-mail: info.railpro@voestalpine.com
Web: www.voestalpine.com/railpro

Key personnel

Managing Director: *Franz Kainersdorfer (Interim)*
Financial Director: *Michaela Konrad (Interim)*
Director, Corporate Development: *Erno Chevallier*
Manager Marketing and Innovations: *Wouter Lampe*

Background

voestalpine Rail BV is a subsidiary of voestalpine Bahnsysteme GmbH & Co KG, part of the Austrian-based voestalpine AG steelmaking group.

Products

Suppliers of all materials required in railway infrastructure work, acting as a stockist for contractors. The company can arrange transport to the worksite by road, water or rail; it operates a fleet of 2,200 rail wagons.

Developments

As a result of the conversion of catenary voltage from 1.5 to 25 kV, there is a demand for new types of catenary systems. voestalpine Railpro entered an agreement with VD Leegte Metaal for the production of welded overhead support arms and enables the company to supply fully engineered and complete catenary systems, both for train, tram and metro systems, and for light rail.

Recently voestalpine Rail BV concluded an agreement with Strukton for the supply of catenary components for the Amsterdam-Utrecht project.

Windhoff Bahn-und Anlagentechnik GmbH

PO Box 1963, D-48409 Rheine, Germany
Tel: (+49 5971) 580
Fax: (+49 5971) 582 09
e-mail: info@windhoff.de
Web: www.windhoff.de

Key personnel

Board Members: *Herbert Liessem, Georg Vennemann, Manfred Schmitz*
Finance Director: *Helmut Gielians*
Sales Directors: *Dr Martin Hindersmann, Uwe Dolkemeyer,*
Technical Director: *Juergen Auschner*
Purchasing Manager: *Stefan Berkemeyer*

Products

Installation and maintenance of catenary systems: placing of foundations, mast mounting, installation of catenary wires, catenary maintenance, catenary measuring, complete catenary reconstruction.

NEW TECHNOLOGY/INNOVATIVE TRANSIT SYSTEMS

Company listing by country

AUSTRIA
DCC Doppelmayr Cable Car GmbH & Co
Doppelmayr/Garaventa Group

CANADA
Bombardier Transportation – APM System
Bombardier Transportation – ART
Bombardier Transportation – Monorail System

CHINA
Harbin Electric Inc

FRANCE
ALSTOM – AXONIS™
Lohr Group

GERMANY
Das Fraunhofer-Institut für Verkehrs- und Infrastruktursysteme (IVI) – Fraunhofer Institute for Transportation and Infrastructure Systems

ITALY
Ansaldo Trasporti Sistemi Ferroviai SpA (ATSF)
Leitner SpA
Pirelli & C Ambiente Eco Technology SpA

JAPAN
CHUBU HSST Development Corporation
Hitachi Ltd
Kawasaki Heavy Industries Ltd
Nippon Sharyo Ltd – Vehicles Of New Age (VONA)
Toyota Motor Corporation (TMC)

KOREA, SOUTH
Hyundai Rotem Company

LIECHTENSTEIN
Intamin Transportation Ltd

MALAYSIA
Monorail Malaysia Technology Sdn Bhd (MMT)
Scomi Engineering Bhd

NETHERLANDS
2getthere BV
Advanced Netherlands Transport (ANT)

UNITED KINGDOM
Advanced Transport Systems Ltd (ATS)
Axeon Holdings plc
Eminox Limited

Johnson Matthey PLC
Kleenair Systems International plc
Severn-Lamb UK Limited
Sustainable Transport Company Ltd (Sustraco)
Transport Design International Ltd (TDI)

UNITED STATES
Aerobus International Inc
Aeromovel USA Inc
Autokinetics Inc
Azure Dynamics Corporation (AZD)
Clean Diesel Technologies Inc
Cobasys LLC
Delphi Corporation
FUTREX Inc
Global Electric Motorcars LLC (GEM)
Hydrogen Engine Center Inc
Hythane Company LLC
ISE Corporation
Maxwell Technologies Inc
NextEnergy
UQM Technologies Inc
UTC Power
Valence Technology Inc

2getthere BV

Proostwetering 26, NL-3543 AE Utrecht, Netherlands
Tel: (+31 30) 238 72 03
Fax: (+31 30) 241 59 31
e-mail: info@2getthere.eu
Web: www.2getthere.eu

Key personnel
Chief Executive Officer: *Carel C Van Helsdingen*
Project Director: *Rein J C Kielstra*
Sales/Marketing Manager: *Robbert H C Lohmann*

Type of system
Automated People Mover Systems for personal and group transit.

Description
2getthere BV markets and develops Automated People Mover Systems for personal and group transportation, which provide efficient, high quality, tailored transport solutions. The company has a worldwide exclusive license for the application of FROG-technology in people mover applications and owns the rights to the products ParkShuttle (Group Rapid Transit (GRT)) and CyberCab (Personal Rapid Transit (PRT)).

2getthere builds on nearly 10 years of experience gathered through multiple projects, focusing on the market and its requirements. Application engineering, controls development and project management is performed in-house, adding to the existing knowledge regarding the requirements of automated people mover systems, applications and customers. 2getthere co-operates with development and (local) project partners to supply a customized application to the customer.

2getthere's PRT system features a number of automated taxi's (CyberCabs) and the supervisory control system TOMS (Transit Operations Monitoring and Supervision). The guideway can be constructed at grade, but also elevated, embedded in buildings or underground. The system in configurable as 'true' PRT – providing direct connections, on-demand operations and personal transportation – but alternatively 'ride sharing' (single origin, multiple destinations) and scheduled operations (to optimise capacity) can also be implemented.

2getthere's GRT system consists of a number of automated mini-buses (ParkShuttles) and the supervisory control system TOMS. The ParkShuttle vehicle can accommodate 20 (12 seats, 8 standees) to 25 passengers (8 seats, 17 standees) and allows for easy wheelchair access. The guideway is typically constructed at grade, allowing for at grade crossings or, when required, may be elevated or underground.

PRT demonstration project at the horticultural exhibition Floriade 2002 1368822

ParkShuttle vehicles at Rivium business park 1368821

Status/recent contracts
The 2nd Generation ParkShuttle (GRT) is in operation in the Netherlands at the business park Rivium in the city of Capelle aan den IJssel. The 2nd Generation CyberCab (PRT) is in production for a new application in the Middle East.

Advanced Netherlands Transport (ANT)

Waldorpstraat 17b, NL-2521 CA Den Haag, Netherlands
Tel: (+31 70) 330 10 33   Fax: (+31 70) 330 10 30
e-mail: info@ant-consultants.nl
Web: www.ant-consultants.nl

Key personnel
Directors: *O Pruis, N de Ronde Bresser*

Type of system
Park Shuttle electronically guided people mover.

Description
Rubber-tyred automatic vehicle, seating six with two standing and a maximum speed of 30 km/h. It is computer-controlled and guidance is by wires sunk into the roadway. There is no mechanical guidance. It can run on public roads, with laser beams detecting obstacles.

Development
Park Shuttle was developed on behalf of the Dutch government with the participation of bus

Park Shuttle car by ANT Netherlands 0518403

company ZWN OpenbaarVervoer as the operator, Frog Navigation Systems, which supplied the technology, and local authority Capelle a/d IJssel – Bedrijvenpark Rivium. The vehicle was built by Carosserie Akkermans. Test operation started in 1997 between Kralingse Zoom metro station, in the eastern suburbs of Rotterdam, and the Rivium Business Park 1.2 km away, with three vehicles.

Advanced Transport Systems Ltd (ATS)

Unit 5, Brunel Way, Thornbury, Bristol, BS35 3UR, United Kingdom
Tel: (+44 1454) 41 47 00
Fax: (+44 1454) 41 47 70
e-mail: office@atsltd.co.uk
Web: www.atsltd.co.uk

Key personnel
Directors
Chief Executive Officer: *Martin V Lowson*
Chief Operating Officer: *Chris V Cook*
Director, Business Development: *Richard Teychenné*
Non-Executive Directors: *Trevor Smallwood, Nigel Clarke*

Background
Advanced Transport Systems was formed in 1995 to develop the ULTra concept, which grew from work in the Advanced Transport Group at the University of Bristol. The work has been taken forward in conjunction with a number of partners, including Arup, AMEC, Altran and Corus.

The system has completed the first stage of prototype testing on a 1 km test track in Cardiff, UK, culminating in successful passenger trials for which clearance to carry passengers was granted by HM Rail Inspectorate.

Type of system
ULTra system of driverless, automatic taxis on own guideway.

Description
ULTra is an on-demand system of driverless automatic taxis travelling on their own guideway network, providing a personal travel service taking the passenger non-stop anywhere on the network. It offers journeys that are three times quicker than by bus, car or light rail and offers operating costs that are less than these methods as well as trains. The system is typically one-third the capital cost of equivalent light rail to install. It also uses one-third to one-quarter of the energy used by other public or private transport systems.

Each electrically powered vehicle is rated at 2 kW continuous, carries four persons (maximum) and has a gross weight of 800 kg. The maximum speed is 40 km/h (25 mph).

An ULTra guideway has the same capacity as a motorway lane (1,800 vehicles/hour) but costs one-tenth of the price and uses a quarter of the land.

Trip speeds in city centres are approximately 40 km/h, compared with a general traffic average of around 13 km/h. All stations are off-line, so that stopping vehicles do not impede other traffic.

Normally a vehicle will be waiting for a passenger at each station. Simulations confirm that 95 per cent of all ULTra passengers will wait less than 1 minute, even at peak times.

The ULTra guideway is designed to minimise visual intrusion with a depth of 450 mm, width of 2 m and collision-resistant columns 508 mm at 18 m spacing (typical). The guideway is at ground level where appropriate, for instance alongside roads and railways. With electric drive and rubber-tyred wheels, it is also quiet – the prototype is measured at 43 dB at 2.5 m. The ULTra vehicles can accommodate wheelchair users, bicycles or pushchairs and luggage. The system is intended to integrate with other forms of transport and can increase the effectiveness and attraction of trains and buses. It is also offered as an effective service for park-and-ride operations or for special applications such as airports.

Developments
NESTA (National Endowment for Science, Technology and the Arts) supports the project under an invention and innovation programme. The Altran Foundation has provided EUR1 million of technical support. The UK DTI (Department of Trade and Industry) is supporting the work with grants under their Foresight Vehicle Programme. The UK Department of Transport supported prototype manufacture and the testing of the ULTra system with a major contract under their Innovative Transport Programme.

Contracts
ATS has been selected as a partner in the recently launched EU research project CityMobil.

ULTra driverless automatic taxi 0137479

The project involves 28 partners from 10 countries, with an overall value of EUR40 million. CityMobil is co-funded by the European Union through the Sixth Framework Programme for Research & Development.

ATS is working with BAA to develop a pilot demonstration of the ULTra PRT system at Heathrow Airport. As part of the CityMobil project, ATS will evaluate the effectiveness of ULTra in an airport environment. In addition, ATS will develop new PRT simulation models for wider application by the user community and, with other partners, undertake research on communication based collision avoidance techniques.

The CityMobil project will also create two other demonstration sites, one at the new Rome exhibition centre and one at the Spanish town of Castellón. Each of these will evaluate one form of automated transport. The global objective of CityMobil is to achieve a more effective approach to urban transport.

ATS have started the work programme under contract to BAA, which will lead to the pilot operation at Heathrow. The planned route for the pilot is from the N3 passenger car park to the new Heathrow Terminal 5. The route requires 4.2 km of track, including station loops, and 18 vehicles. The guideway will connect into the multi-storey car park at T5 to provide a station at the entrance to the Terminal. The system is scheduled to open for carrying passengers following the opening of T5 in March 2008.

Aerobus International Inc

7700 San Felipe, Suite 330, Houston, Texas 77063, US
Tel: (+1 713) 222 66 55   Fax: (+1 713) 222 75 01
e-mail: dward@aerobus.com
Web: www.aerobus.com

Key personnel
President: *Dennis K Stallings*
Director, Aerobus China Inc: *Li Song*
Senior Vice-President: *Richard H Ward*
Project Manager: *Jerry W Pyles*

Type of system
Suspended cable guideway people mover.

Background
Originally developed in Switzerland and Canada, the patents and technology are owned by Aerobus International. The design was inspired by the SLRT (Suspended Light Railway Technology) competition in which Aerobus was one of the three finalists. Engineering and manufacturing expertise is assembled from both Switzerland and US.

Description
Electrically powered vehicles operate on suspended cable guideway on light, cable-supported tracks,

Concept drawing of Aerobus suspended cable guideway people mover 1323664

up to eight per cent gradients and with speeds of up to 80 km/h. Vehicle configuration is available from two to 12 passenger modules with a maximum vehicle capacity of 480 passengers. Spans of 200 to 300 m are normal, with a maximum span of more than 600 m possible for river crossings or to pass over major obstacles.

Contracts

In 2004, the city of Weihai, China selected Aerobus China Development Inc, a subsidiary of Aerobus International Inc to provide a transit system which will cross Weihai Bay and connect Liugong Island to the downtown section of Weihai in Shandong Province. The system consists of a dual guideway with three stations (one of which will be incorporated into a viewing tower/pylon) The system, built entirely over water, will be 4.2 km long. The system is currently at the design phase and the site construction work has commenced.

Concept drawing of multi-module Aerobus suspended cable guideway people mover   1323663

Aeromovel USA Inc

2637 Townsgate Road, Suite 300, Westlake Village, California 91361, US
Tel: (+1 805) 497 62 84   Fax: (+1 805) 496 24 14
e-mail: info@aeromovel.com
Web: www.aeromovel.com

Key personnel

Vice-President, Engineering and Construction: *Steve Ivins*
Vice-President, Finance and Administration: *Pauline Jackson*

Other offices

Aeromovel Middle East
Hidada Ltd, 4th Floor, Xenel Building, PO Box 11809, Jeddah 21463, Saudi Arabia
Tel: (+966 2) 643 28 08   Fax: (+966 2) 643 40 59
e-mail: aeromovel@zajil.net

Type of system

Air-propelled automated guideway transport system.

Description

A lightweight high-capacity car runs on steel wheels on steel rail track mounted on the top surface of an elevated hollow concrete box girder. It has no electric motor or magnet and uses air propulsion, much in the same way as a sailing ship. A pylon projects from the bottom of the car bogie into the hollow beam, where it

Aeromovel installation in Brazil   0518359

forms a flat plate entirely occupying the cross-section of the beam. Stationary centrifugal air blowers generate an air flow in the beam, causing the plate, and hence the vehicle, to be propelled.

A 1.1 km single-track demonstration track has been in operation in Porto Alegre, Brazil (see Systems section, Porto Alegre entry).

A 3.2 km route at the Taman Mini-Indonesia theme park in Jakarta, Indonesia, opened in 1989.

ALSTOM – AXONIS™

Systems Business
48 rue Albert Dhalenne, F-93482 Saint-Ouen Cedex, Paris, France
Tel: (+33 1) 41 66 90 00   Fax: (+33 1) 41 66 96 66
Web: www.transport.alstom.com

Description

Driverless metro system with modular automated capabilities from door operations, passenger information to train movements and maintenance. It is designed for transportation systems needs from 3,000 up to 80,000 pphpd.

The rolling stock's modular design process allows for the following configuration: rubber tyre (for small/medium capacity) or steel-wheel (for medium/large) version, third rail (for small/medium capacity) or overhead (for medium/large) version.

The range is: AXONIS 100 (3,000–12,000 pphpd), AXONIS 200 (10,000–40,000 pphpd) and AXONIS 300 (33,000–60,000 pphpd).

Development

Singapore's Land Transport Authority (LTA) has awarded the ALSTOM/ST Elec consortium an

Singapore's Northeast Line automated metro system   0585260

order worth EUR170 million, for the second phase of construction of its automatic Circular metro line. ALSTOM's share of this contract is valued at EUR123 million. ALSTOM will supply its AXONIS™ automatic metro system for this line.

This new order is an extension of the Circular Line Phase 1 project, awarded to ALSTOM on a turnkey basis in December 2000. The first stage covers 5.6 km and has six stations. This second section will extend the Marina Line by 5 km and add five new stations. Subsequent contracts placed with Alstom covered construction of the remainder of the line, which will eventually cover

34 km and circle the island of Singapore, making it the world's longest automatic metro line.

For this second phase, ALSTOM will supply seven three-car Metropolis™ trainsets, the signalling system and related infrastructure and will be responsible for the overall management of the project. The delivery of the first trainsets was scheduled for 2004, with commercial service commencing in 2006.

In addition to the Circle Line, ALSTOM also supplied and is supplying the Northeast Line with its AXONIS™ automatic metro system. The Northeast Line is also a turnkey contract for which ALSTOM supplied the rolling stock, signalling

and information solution, with expertise in structuring, financing, designing, constructing, testing and commissioning integrated rail systems. It is the largest fully automatic metro in the world and entered commercial service in 2003.

Alstom is also delivering a system, m2, to Lausanne.

APTIS

This is a complete systems package entirely managed by ALSTOM, and integrates a range of service subsystems: rolling stock, information systems, infrastructure and project management.

Ansaldo Trasporti Sistemi Ferroviai SpA (ATSF)

Systema di Trasporto Elettrico ad Attrazione Magnetica (STREAM)
Via Argine 425, I-80147 Naples, Italy
Tel: (+39 081) 24 31
Fax: (+39 081) 243 25 70
Web: www.atsf.it

Key personnel
Responsible for STREAM Business: *Sante Roberti*

Area Manager, International Projects: *Pierfranco Romano*
Fax: (+30 010) 655 20 28
e-mail: Pierfranco.Romano@atsf.it

Background
Ansaldo Trasporti Sistemi Ferroviai SpA (ATSF) is a Finmeccanica Company.

Type of system
Rubber-tyred guided bus, taking power from central roadway source.

Description
Traction power is taken by the vehicle at 380 V DC from a contact line in the centre of the roadway, insulated until the vehicle passes over it, when a magnetic contact activates the power supply. The electrically powered vehicle is based on bus technology and can be 12, 18 or 24 m in length, carrying up to 180 passengers. It can run in guided or unguided mode and has auxiliary batteries when not taking power from the central source.

Autokinetics Inc

1711 West Hamlin Road, Rochester Hills, MI 48309-3368, US
Tel: (+1 248) 852 44 50   Fax: (+1 248) 852 71 82
e-mail: jbemmons@autokinetic.com
Web: www.autokinetics.com

Key personnel
Contact: *Bruce Emmons*
    Staff: Currently unavailable

Current situation
Autokinetics Inc is an engineering design and prototype company.

Developments
The company is developing a new ultralight stainless steel transit bus in partnership with the DOE Office of FreedomCar and Vehicle Technologies, Oak Ridge National Laboratory, Argonne National Laboratory, AK Steel, UQM, D&N Bending, AristoCast and IBIS Associates.

The design features fully low-floor architecture, battery electric and hybrid drive propulsion systems, high-capacity seating, monocoque body structure and fully independent suspension.

Axeon Holdings plc

Nobel Court, Wester Gourdie, Dundee DD2 4UH, Scotland, UK
Tel: (+44 1382) 40 00 40
Fax: (+44 1382) 40 00 44
e-mail: info@axeon.com
Web: www.axeon.com

Key personnel
Chief Executive Officer: *Lawrence Berns*
Chief Financial Officer: *David Campbell*
Group Chief Operating Officer: *Jim Ferguson*
Group Technical Director: *Don Newton*
Group Marketing Manager: *Rebecca Trengrove*
    Staff: Not available currently

Background
Axeon Holdings plc is an independent supplier of lithium-ion battery solutions, manufacturing more than five million battery packs.

Axeon has been listed on the Alternative Investment Market (AIM) of the London

Stock Exchange (LSE:AXE) since 2005 and is headquartered in the UK, with operations in the UK, Switzerland, Germany and Poland. The company was founded in 1998.

The company is a certified ISO 9001:2000 supplier and is working towards ISO 14001 certification.

Products
Designer and manufacture of complete lithium-ion battery systems for electric and hybrid electric vehicles (EVs and HEVs).

This includes a Battery Management System (BMS). As well as monitoring state of charge, managing cell optimisation and ensuring safety, Axeon's BMS is designed to integrate and communicate with the vehicle Controller Area Network (CAN) for best vehicle performance over a warranted number of charge-discharge cycles.

Axeon designs and manufactures batteries and battery management systems for three main sectors: automotive (EV and HEV), power tools and mobile power systems.

Axeon offers batteries with a range of up to 120 miles on a single charge and with stored energy capacity from 5 kWh to 180 kWh.

The company also produces both off-board and on-board chargers for EVs and HEVs.

Contracts
By the end of 2008, there were more than 100 production EVs operating in Europe powered by Axeon lithium-ion battery systems. The main customer is Modec, which manufactures commercial electric vehicles.

Axeon has also supplied batteries to a fleet of city buses in Sorrento, Italy.

Developments
In mid-2008, Axeon announced an agreement with an Italian electric bus manufacturer to provide a prototype battery. The prototype battery was due to be delivered in late Q3 2008, and then be evaluated for six months. If successful, the evaluation may lead to a production programme in 2009.

Azure Dynamics Corporation (AZD)

3900 North Fraser Way, Burnaby, BC Canada, V5J 5H6
Tel: (+1 604) 224 24 21   Fax: (+1 604) 419 63 92
e-mail: info@azuredynamics.com
Web: www.azuredynamics.com

Key personnel
Chairman: *D Campbell Deacon*
Chief Executive Officer: *Scott T Harrison*
Chief Operating Officer: *Curt Anthony Huston*
Chief Technology Officer: *Ronald V Iacobelli*
Chief Financial Officer: *Ryan S Carr*

Vice-President, Operations: *Rajan Johal*
Vice-President, Engineering: *Ricardo Espinosa*
Vice-President, Marketing: *Michael L Elwood*
Vice-President, Business Development: *Dean Z McGrew*
    Staff: 100 (estimate)

Background
Azure Dynamics Corporation (AZD) develops and produces hybrid electric and electric components and powertrain systems for commercial vehicles, including shuttle bus applications.

Headquartered in Vancouver, the company also has offices in Detroit and Boston.

Products
Series Hybrid Electric and Parallel Hybrid Electric powertrains for paratransit and shuttle buses.

Citibus: The CitiBus uses the Senator HD bus body manufactured by StarTrans. The bus foundation is a Workhorse W42 16,000 lb GVW long-life chassis hybridised by AZD.

Developments
In November 2007, the company announced that it had successfully completed the US Government's bus certification durability test for its series hybrid electric shuttle bus.

Bombardier Transportation – APM System

Systems Division
Schöneberger Ufer 1, D-10785 Berlin, Germany
Tel: (+49 30) 98 60 70
Fax: (+49 30) 986 07 20 00
Web: www.transportation.bombardier.com

Key personnel
President, Systems: *Eran Gartner*

Type of system
*Bombardier * Innovia ** and *Bombardier * CX-100 ** Automated People Mover (APM) systems.

Description
The *Bombardier Innovia*[1] system features a rubber-tyred vehicle running on a flat guideway design employing road construction tolerances. The system uses *Bombardier* CITYFLO* 650 automatic train control technology, the first Communication-Based Train Control (CBTC) system in the world to use radio as a communication medium. Bombardier offers turnkey capability plus full operation and maintenance services.

Bombardier has over 20 APM systems in operation with three new systems and expansion projects under construction, including: Guangzhou Pearl River New City, China; George Bush Intercontinental Airport, McCarran International Airport and Scaramento International Airport, USA; London Gatwick Airport, UK and Kuala Lumpur International Airport, Malaysia. Recent APM system installations include London Heathrow International Airport, UK, and Beijing Capital International Airport in China.

Development

US – Las Vegas, Nevada
Bombardier's recent contracts at McCarran International Airport in Las Vegas, Nevada, include an APM underground system to connect the new Terminal 3 with the existing D-gate concourse and electrical and mechanical upgrades to the existing shuttles, legs C & D. The two contracts include a total of 16 *CX-100* vehicles to be delivered between 2008 and 2011.

US – Miami, Florida
Bombardier received a contract from Miami-Dade County to replace 12 of its ageing fleet of 29 Miami Metromover APM's. Entering service in 2008, the new *CX-100* APMs feature an aesthetic change to the carbody, wireless transmission of on-board CCTV, improved diagnostic and troubleshooting technology, enhanced corrosion resistance and improved air-conditioning.

US – Atlanta, Georgia
In Atlanta, Bombardier is extending the existing automated people mover system to the new Maynard H Jackson International Terminal at Atlanta International Airport. The contract includes the supply of all the electrical and mechanical equipment associated with the extension and 10 new *CX-100* vehicles, increasing the fleet to 59 vehicles. Hartsfield-Jackson is the busiest airport in the world in terms of passenger traffic, moving in excess of 80 million passengers per year. In 2005, Bombardier received a 10-year contract to operate and maintain the existing Bombardier-built *CX-100* APM.

US – San Francisco, California
In San Francisco, Bombardier has operated and maintained the Bombardier-supplied APM system, known as SFO AirTrain, since it opened to passenger service in 2003. Using Bombardier *CX-100* technology, the 2-line APM system operates 24 hours a day, consistently surpassing the contract availability of 99.5 per cent. The AirTrain fleet of 38 *CX-100* vehicles serves nine stations along 10 km of elevated guideway and connects all the airport's terminals, parking garages and the Bay Area Rapid Transit (BART) Station with the Rental Car Center. Bombardier received an 8-year operations and maintenance contract in November 2008.

Bombardier Innovia *at Dallas/Fort Worth Airport, Texas, US*   1310179

Bombardier CX-100 at Kuala Lumpur Airport   1375604

US – Dallas/Fort Worth, Texas

An 8-km *Innovia* rubber-tyred automated people mover system opened to passenger service at Dallas/Fort Worth International Airport in May 2005. *CITYFLO* 650 train control technology automatically guides the 64-car fleet, allowing a greater degree of flexibility at peak passenger periods. The system operates at two-minute intervals, with an average passenger ride time of 5 to 8 minutes. Bombardier's contract includes maintenance for five years.

US – Tampa, Florida

As complete turnkey supplier, Bombardier was responsible for re-constructing the APM system that serves the new airside C terminal. Currently, a mixed fleet of 16 *CX-100* and C-100 vehicles link the airport's landside terminal with four airside satellites. A total of 28 Bombardier-supplied vehicles have been delivered since its opening in 1971.

US – Seattle-Tacoma, Washington

The APM system at Seattle-Tacoma International Airport has been in operation since 1973. The replacement APM system entered service on both north and south and Shuttle lines in 2003. A new fleet of 21 *CX-100* vehicles replaced the original fleet of C-100 vehicles supplied by Bombardier. Because of the overlay capability of the *CITYFLO* automatic train control, full passenger service was maintained during the vehicle and system upgrade.

China

In 2007, Bombardier Transportation was awarded a contract for a 4-km *CX-100* APM system for Guangzhou Pearl River New City. Scheduled for completion in June 2010, the APM system is the first ever in China to be deployed in an urban environment. The dual-lane, underground system will serve the Zhujiang Xincheng Central District of Guangzhou City. Four of the system's nine stations will provide connections to Lines 1, 3 and 5 of the Guangzhou City metro network. Bombardier is responsible for the design and supply of 14 *CX-100* vehicles and the *CITYFLO 650* automatic train control system; as well as 18 guideway switches to be fabricated in China.

In February 2008, the Bombardier-supplied 2-km APM system for Beijing Capital International Airport, China, opened for passenger service. Bombardier was responsible for project management, systems engineering and integration, testing and commissioning, in addition to the design and supply of 11 *CX-100* vehicles, the *CITYFLO* 550 automated train control, communications systems, platform screen doors, switches, and equipping the maintenance facility. The APM system operates on dual-guideway between three stations, serving the new international terminal. Bombardier is operating and maintaining the APM and is currently supplying seven additional *CX-100* vehicles.

Kuala Lumpur, Malaysia

The Bombardier-supplied APM system at Kuala Lumpur International Airport began operations in 1998. In 2005, Bombardier supplied two new *CX-100* vehicles and electrical and mechanical system upgrades to the existing system, including the existing *CITYFLO* 550 automatic train control.

In 2008, Bombardier and its local partner Hartasuma Sdn Bhd were awarded a contract that includes a spur line extension to the new Operations, Maintenance and Storage Facility and three additional *CX-100* vehicles

Madrid, Spain

At the Barajas airport in Madrid, Bombardier supplied the first fully automated transit system in Spain, which opened in February 2006. The driverless system connects a new terminal and a new satellite terminal, located 3 km from existing airport facilities. Bombardier supplied 19 *CX-100* vehicles, along with all related electrical and mechanical systems for the 2.7-km

Bombardier Innovia *at London Heathrow International Airport, UK*   1310181

Bombardier CX-100 *in Miami, Florida*   1375605

Bombardier CX-100 *at Beijing Capital Airport*   1375606

line, including the *CITYFLO* 650 automatic train control and power distribution systems, station doors for two stations, switches and maintenance facilities.

London, UK
The *Innovia* APM system at London Heathrow International Airport connects the new landside building of the fifth terminal with a remote satellite. The 1.4-km shuttle features six *Innovia* vehicles operating as two three-car trains. Bombardier designed and supplied all of the

electrical and mechanical equipment, the *CITYFLO* 650 automatic train control as well as equipping the control centre. This is the first application of the *Innovia* system in Europe. The *Innovia* APM began operating in 2008.

Bombardier is replacing the existing inter-terminal transit system at London Gatwick Airport. The contract includes the supply of six *CX-100* vehicles and all of the electrical and mechanical equipment for the fully automated system. The 1.2-km dual-lane system is scheduled for completion in spring 2010.

US – Sacramento, California
As part of Sacramento Airport's terminal modernisation program, Bombardier is supplying all the system-wide electrical and mechanical elements for the *CX-100* shuttle system, including two *CX-100* vehicles and five years of operations and maintenance services.

Bombardier, *CITYFLOW*, *Innovia* and *CX-100* are Trademarks of Bombardier Inc or its subsidiaries.

Bombardier Transportation – ART

Systems Division
Schöneberger Ufer 1, D-10785 Berlin, Germany
Tel: (+49 30) 98 60 70
Fax: (+49 30) 986 07 20 00
Web: www.transportation.bombardier.com

Key personnel
President, Systems: *Rean Gartner*

Type of system
Advanced Rapid Transit (ART) System, also known as SkyTrain in Vancouver, Canada, the Kelana Jaya Line in Malaysia, AirTrain JFK at JFK international airport in New York, Beijing Airport Link in China and, soon to open, the Yongin EverLine in South Korea. ART powered by Linear Induction Motors (LIMs), has steerable-axle bogies and moving block ATC; traction power is at 600 to 750 V DC from side contact rail.

Description
The principal features of ART MK II technology include LIM propulsion combined with a unique steerable suspension, which together provide reliable performance and superior ride comfort, even on tight curves and steep grades. The moving block Automatic Train Control (ATC) system enhances system operational flexibility and expandability to meet sudden changes in passenger demand and greater long-term travel demands.

Development
Malaysia – Kuala Lumpur
Under contract to Syarikat Prasarana Negara Berhad (Prasarana), Bombardier Transportation and local partner Hartasuma Sdn Bhd are upgrading the wayside Electrical and Mechanical (E&M) systems on the 29-km Kelana Jaya Line in Kuala Lumpur, Malaysia. The work is to accommodate 140 new Bombardier Advanced Rapid Transit (ART) MK II vehicles currently in production. The new vehicle order was awarded under a separate contract to Bombardier and Hartsuma Sdn Bhd in October 2006. The system is expected to more than double its ridership capacity to about 370,000 passengers a day.

During 1998 to 1999, a Bombardier-led consortium supplied all the system-wide E&M equipment for the Kelana Jaya Line, including a fleet of 70 MK II vehicles. As the longest fully automated driverless transit system in Asia, the Kelana Jaya Line links the western and eastern suburbs with Kuala Lumpur's city core, on mostly elevated dual-line guideway that incorporates 24 stations.

US – New York/JFK
Bombardier, as part of the AirRail Transit Consortium, supplied a fully automated light rail system for the New York JFK Airport Access Programme. The system features Bombardier's Advanced Rapid Transit (ART) MK II linear induction motor technology and opened in December 2003.

Under contract to the Port Authority of New York and New Jersey, using a Design-Build-Operate-Maintain (DBOM) approach, the consortium was responsible for the turnkey design and construction of the driverless ART

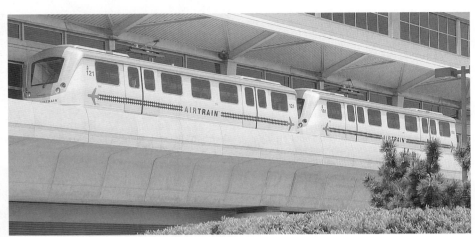
Bombardier ART for JFK airport, New York, US   0583062

Bombardier ART SkyTrain, Vancouver   1375610

system. Bombardier is operating and maintaining the AirTrain JFK system for a period of up to 15 years.

AirTrain JFK connects 10 fully enclosed stations using predominantly elevated dual-track guideway and features a 2.5-km loop, linking all terminals in JFK's central terminal area, with two branches that interface with New York's regional transit system.

The 32 LIM-powered vehicles, with steerable axle bogies, employ technology similar to the Bombardier-supplied vehicles for Kuala Lumpur, Malaysia.

Besides manufacture and supply of 32 LIM-powered ART vehicles, Bombardier's share of project work included systems engineering and integration, testing and commissioning, supply of onboard and wayside automatic train control communications systems, automatic fare collection system, the traction power system, platform doors for all 10 stations and workshop equipment. In addition, Bombardier also provided training, manuals and operations start-up services. The system opened in December 2003.

Canada – Vancouver
In November 2006, Bombardier received a contract from the Greater Vancouver Transportation Authority (TransLink) for 34 Bombardier ART MK II vehicles. In May 2008, an option was exercised for an additional 14 ART MK II vehicles. These new orders augment the existing 210 Bombardier-supplied ART vehicles now operating on the Vancouver SkyTrain Expo and Millennium Lines.

Bombardier designed and supplied all of the electrical and mechanical systems for the Millennium Line, a 21-km extension to the Bombardier-supplied 29-km Sky Train Expo Line. The Millennium Line, which links downtown Vancouver with neighbouring municipalities in Greater Vancouver, opened for revenue service in August 2002. At 49 km, the 2-line Sky Train is the longest fully automated driverless transit system in the world.

Bombardier's scope of work for the Millennium Line included: automatic train control and communications systems, power supply and distribution system, trackwork, power rail, platform and guideway intrusion detection systems, system engineering and integration, and testing and commissioning for 21 km of dual-track guideway. The Millennium Line uses Bombardier's LIM-powered technology, and is also employed on the Kelana Jaya Line in Kuala Lumpur, Malaysia, on the AirTrain JFK system at the JFK International Airport, New York, USA, the Beijing Airport Link in China and on the future Yongin Line, South Korea.

South Korea – Yongin
The Yongin LRT Consortium, of which Bombardier is the lead member, was awarded a 35-year Build-Transfer-Operate (BTO) concession contract for a fully automated 18.5-km ART system by the City of Yongin, Republic of Korea. Intended to serve 15 stations on mostly elevated double-track guideway, the new line will link the Seoul subway, via Yongin City, and will terminate in Everland, a popular theme park.

Bombardier is responsible for the design and supply of 30 driverless ART LIM-powered vehicles, the Bombardier *CITYFLO 650* automatic train control technology, communications systems, project management, systems engineering and integration, testing and commissioning, as well as up to 30 years of operations and maintenance services. Bombardier will lead the integration of the scope of work with Daelim Industrial Co., who will be the co-lead for the design-build portion of the contract.

The Yongin system is scheduled to enter revenue service in 2010.

China – Beijing
In 2006, Bombardier Transportation received an order for the supply of 40 ART MK II vehicles

Bombardier ART vehicle for Yongin, South Korea   1341853

from Changchun Railway Vehicles (CRC). It was part of a contract awarded to CRC by the Beijing Dongzhimen Airport Express Rail Co Ltd for the Beijing Airport Link.

Bombardier participated in project management and was responsible for vehicle systems engineering and integration, design and manufacture of the bogies, as well as the propulsion and braking systems. Changchun Railway Vehicles (CRC) manufactured the 40 ART MK II vehicles. The 28-km Beijing Airport Link opened in 2008, connecting Dongzhimen Station to the Beijing Capital International Airport. Featuring Bombardier's ART technology, the fleet serves four stations: Dongzhimen, Sanyuanqiao, Terminal 2 and Terminal 3.

Bombardier Transportation – Monorail System

Systems Division
Schöneberger Ufer 1, D-10785 Berlin, Germany
Tel: (+49 30) 98 60 70   Fax: (+49 30) 986 07 20 00
Web: www.transportation.bombardier.com

Key personnel
President, Systems: *Eran Gartner*

Type of system
Fully automated, straddle-type monorail.

Description
The semi-permanent four-car trains offer wider, outside sliding doors and increased interior. Pneumatic tyres at the car ends support and propel the AC motor-driven vehicle. Lateral guidance is provided by upper and lower side tyres.

Development
Bombardier Transportation, as the lead member of the Las Vegas Monorail Team, supplied its Monorail System in the heart of the resort corridor. Designed to urban transit safety standards, the 6.4 km system links eight major resort properties and the Las Vegas Convention Center. The 36 cars operate in nine four-car trains and represent the latest innovation in monorail technology. To date, the Monorail system has carried over 28 million passengers.

Entering revenue service in 2004, the system is carrying up to 8,000 passengers per hour per direction (pphpd) at an average line speed of 28 km/h. Featuring a fully elevated dual guideway, the maximum grade is 6.5 per cent.

The full turnkey system contract is completely financed through tax-exempt non-recourse bonds tied to the farebox and advertising revenues.

Bombardier monorail system, Las Vegas, US   1375612

Bombardier was responsible for providing all the electrical and mechanical elements of the system including design and supply of 36 monorail cars, overall project management, automatic train control, communications systems, power supply and distribution systems, automatic fare collection systems, guideway and guidance switching systems, system engineering and integration, platform doors for seven stations, testing and commissioning, training and manuals, and up to 15 years of operations and maintenance services.

In January 2009, Bombardier Transportation received the first 5-year option order from the Las Vegas Monorail Company (LVMC) to operate and maintain the Monorail system. The order was valued at approximately EUR44 million.

CHUBU HSST Development Corporation

3-14 Kafuku-cho, Minami-ku, 457-0837 Nagoya, Japan

Tel: (+81 52) 882 30 42   Fax: (+81 52) 882 30 42
Web: www.hsst.jp

Key personnel
Vehicle System Group Manager: *Minoru Morita*

Type of operation: Maglev, opened March 2005.

Passenger journeys: (2007) Not currently available
Train-km: (2007) Not currently available

Background

Chubu HSST Development Corporation was established in 1989, mainly by the Nagoya Railroad Co Group, Aichi Prefecture and HSST Corporation. The corporation was formed to develop and supply Maglev technology called HSST (High Speed Surface Transport).

Description

Tobu Kyuryo Line in Aichi Prefecture

Chubu HSST Development Corporation has been involved in the system design and the supervision of the construction of the Tobu Kyuryo Line as the first HSST commercial line since 2000. The 8.9 km line, with nine stations, runs from Fujigaoka metro station through Nagakute Town to Yakusa station on the Aichi Kanjo (Loop) Line in Yakusa-cho, Toyota City. The Aichi Rapid Transit Co Ltd was established to construct and operate the line (see separate entry under Nagoya).

Current situation

The commercial operation began in March 2005.

Clean Diesel Technologies Inc

300 Atlantic Street, Suite 702, Stamford, CT 06901, US
Tel: (+1 203) 327 70 50   Fax: (+1 203) 323 04 61
e-mail: info@cdti.com
Web: www.cdti.com

Key personnel

Non-Executive Chairman: *Derek R Gray*
Chief Executive Officer: *Bernhard Steiner*
Vice-President and Company Secretary: *Charles W Grinnell*

Other office

Clean Diesel International LLC
4 Whyteleafe Business Village Whyteleafe Hill
Whyteleafe Surrey CR3 OAT, UK
Tel: (+44 1883) 62 90 90   Fax: (+44 1883) 62 37 58

Current situation

Clean Diesel Technologies Inc provides a broad range of emission-control technology.

Products

Areas of activity include selective catalytic reduction, exhaust gas recirculation, diesel particulate filters and fuel-borne catalysts. Market areas include passenger car OEM and retrofit manufacturers, heavy- and light-duty OEM and retrofit manufacturers and stationary engines.

Range

Clean Diesel's global expertise provides a broad perspective on emissions reduction technologies. With a wide-ranging intellectual property portfolio of more than 250 issued and pending patents, the company has achieved extensive market coverage through licensing to strategic partners for worldwide manufacturing, distribution, sales and service, with partners who provide a range of products, including:
- Airless injection and Selective Catalytic Reduction (SCR) systems to dramatically reduce NOx;
- Patented combination of SCR and Exhaust Gas Recirculation (EGR) to maximize NOx reduction and optimise fuel efficiency;
- Hydrocarbon and other reagent injection for emissions control applications;
- Fuel-Borne Catalyst (FBC) formulations for fuel economy and after treatment device synergy;
- Wire Mesh Filter (WMF) particulate filter technologies;
- Filter systems for retrofits of on-road and off-road vehicles.

Cobasys LLC

3740 Lapeer Road South, Orion, Michigan 48359, USA
Tel: (+1 248) 620 57 00
Fax: (+1 248) 620 57 02
e-mail: info@cobasys.com
    sales@cobasys.com
Web: www.cobasys.com

Key personnel

President and Chief Executive Officer: *Tom Neslage*
Vice-President, Product Development: *Gary Absher*
Vice-President, Finance: *Joseph S Crocrnzi*
Vice-President, Manufacturing: *Jim Greiwe*
Vive-President of Systems Engineering and Chief Sales Officer: *Scott Lindholm*

Vice-President, Marketing and Communications: *Ray Wagner*
Acting Director, Human Resources: *Debi Davies-Martin*
General Manager, Planing and Business Strategy: *Ivan Lenjak*
General Manager, Sales: *Erik Hansen*

Manufacturing facility
50 Ovonic Way, Springboro, Ohio 45066, US
Tel: (+1 937) 743 10 01   Fax: (+1 937) 743 10 50

Background

Previously known as Texaco Ovonic Battery Systems LLC, Cobasys LLC is a joint venture between Chevron Technology Ventures LLC, a subsidiary unit of Chevron Corporation, and Energy Conversion Devices Inc.

Products

Advanced NiMH battery systems for transportation and other applications.

Range

NiMHax advanced battery systems solutions for Hybrid Electric Vehicles (HEV), Electric Vehicles (EV), Heavy Duty Vehicles (HDV) and vehicles with 42-volt electrical systems.

Developments

In June 2005, the company announced that it had received an order from Denver Regional Transportation District (RTD) to convert ten hybrid buses from lead acid batteries to their Nickel Metal Hydride (NiMH) battery system solution.

Das Fraunhofer-Institut für Verkehrs- und Infrastruktursysteme (IVI) – Fraunhofer Institute for Transportation and Infrastructure Systems

Zeunerstrasse 38, D-01069 Dresden, Germany
Tel: (+49 351) 464 08 01   Fax: (+49 351) 464 08 03
e-mail: info@ivi.fraunhofer.de
Web: www.ivi.fraunhofer.de

Key personnel

Director (Acting): *Matthias Klinger*
Head of Administration: *Kornelia Brüggert*
Press and Public Relations: *Konstantin Jonas*
    Staff: 60 (plus 40 students) (estimate)

Current situation

Founded in 1999, the Institute carries out applied research and development in the following fields:

Intermodal traffic information and transport management systems;
Transportation, energy and environment;
Vehicle and transport system engineering.
    Projects include:
Spatial and Intermodal Networked Information Systems; Passenger Information Systems; Personal Digital Assistant;
Components for Real-Time Schedule Information and Disposition; Live-Camera Systems for Acquisition of Traffic Data; Traffic Jam Detection and Forecast;
IT-based Disposition and Resource Management; System Development for Integrated Traffic and Disaster; Traffic Process Analysis – Evaluation and Optimisation;
Electronic Ticketing; Innovative Pay Scale Models and Pay Scale Simulation; Supply and Demand Management for Public Transport Systems (flexible suburban train);
Low/zero Emission Propulsion; Automatic Steering Control and Driver Assistance Systems;
Hybrid and Fuel Cell Vehicle for Public Traffic; Flexible Infrastructure; Cost-efficient Design; Traffic-Related Environmental Studies; Monitoring of Emissions;
Secure Software Design; Complex Development Environment for Design and Modelling of Vehicle Propulsion Controls and Transport Systems; Regulation and Control of Mechatronic Systems;
Vehicle and Roadside Energy Converter and Energy Storage Technology for Vehicle and Transport Systems; Design, Modelling and Simulation of Different Propulsion Systems (Fuel Cells, Batteries and Supercapacitors);
Mobile Transportation Systems for Municipal Applications; Intermediate Systems; Logistic Systems; Life Cycle Cost Analysis (LCC); Operational Planning; Time Schedules Optimisation.
    The Institute also provides consulting and analysis services.

DCC Doppelmayr Cable Car GmbH & Co

Holzriedstrasse 29, PO Box 6, A-6961 Wolfurt, Austria
Tel: (+43 5574) 604 12 30
Fax: (+43 5574) 604 12 31
e-mail: dcc@doppelmayr.com
Web: www.dcc.at

Key personnel

Marketing Manager: *Bo Birk Pedersen*

Subsidiary company

DCC North America LLC
160 Highway 6, First Bank Center Suite 205,
PO Box 2109, Silverthorne, Colorado 80498, USA
Tel: (+1 970) 262 15 69
Fax: (+1 970) 513 91 94
e-mail: bruce.butler@doppelmayr.com

Type of system

Cable-propelled people movers.

Description of products

Cable Liner
Automated people mover with individual vehicles drawn by a continuously moving cable loop (haul rope) integrated into a steel guideway. A detachable grip assembly integrated into the bogie of the vehicle forms the mechanical

connection between the vehicle and the haul rope. Spacing between vehicles is defined by the grips and cannot change once a vehicle has left the station.

The system is fully automated and can be operated from a central control room. Its modular design allows for great flexibility. Cable Liner offers continuous movement with a system capacity of up to 5,000 p/h/d (passengers per hour per direction – 5,500 expected in the near future) and station vehicle intervals of approximately 25 seconds. Vehicles can accommodate up to 33 passengers.

Development

The demonstration track in Wolfurt has completed more than 10,000 hours of problem-free operation.

A 1.7 km long system is currently projected in Vienna, Austria. This installation will connect the most important facilities (shopping, parking lots, public transport) of one of Europe's biggest shopping centres.

Cable Liner Shuttle

This was developed for short distances of approximately 300 m to 1.6 km and peak passenger flows of approximately 700 to 4,000 p/h/d. It is based on the standard modules of the Cable Liner system but features reversible instead of circulating movement. Like Cable Liner, the Shuttle runs on a guideway which is usually elevated or in tunnel. The individual vehicles or trains travel along a single or double track at system speeds of 6 m/s and 12 m/s. Vehicle capacity ranges from 30 to approximately 160 passengers. As a rule, a track

Doppelmayr system in Las Vegas   0089057

has two end stations and one to two intermediate stations.

Development

Two systems were taken into operation in Las Vegas in April 1999. They connect three major hotels on the Strip of Las Vegas and have been successful.

Applications

Both the Cable Liner and the Cable Liner Shuttle serve as feeders (for example, to link other existing transport systems or airport terminals),

as part of park and ride systems, as direct transfer between two points or as an additional attraction in tourist resorts.

Recent contracts

Contracts include a CABLE Liner Shuttle for Birmingham International Airport, UK, which connects the terminal building and the train station and a CABLE Liner Shuttle for Toronto Pearson International Airport, Canada, which connects terminal NTB1, terminal 3 and area 6. Recent contracts include a CABLE Liner Shuttle system for Mexico City Airport.

Delphi Corporation

5725 Delphi Drive, Troy, Michigan 48098-2815, US
Tel: (+1 248) 813 20 00   Fax: (+1 248) 813 26 70
Web: www.delphi.com

Other offices

The company also has offices in Brazil, France, Indiana, Japan and US.

Key personnel

Chairman and Chief Executive Officer: *Robert S Miller*
President and Chief Operating Officer: *Rodney O'Neal*
Executive Vice-President and Chief Financial Officer: *Robert J Dellinger*
Executive Vice-President, Global Business Services: *Mark R Weber*
Vice-President, Corporate Affairs, Marketing Communications and Facilities: *Karen L Healy*
Vice-President and Chief Information Officer: *Bette M Walker*
Staff: Approximately 177,000 (2005)

Background

Incorporated in 1998, conducted an initial public offering of its common stock in February 1999

and completed its spin-off from General Motors at the end of May 1999.

The company is active in the mobile electronics and transportation components and systems technology markets.

Delphi operates 161 wholly owned manufacturing sites, 39 joint ventures, 56 customer centres and sales offices and 32 technical centres in 38 countries.

On 8 October 2005, Delphi and certain of its US subsidiaries filed voluntary petitions for business reorganisation under Chapter 11 of the US Bankruptcy Code. The filing only involves Delphi's wholly owned US operating subsidiaries and should not materially affect the company's non-US subsidiaries.

Products

Delphi has been developing fuel cell technology for more than 10 years. The company is focusing on the development of Solid Oxide Fuel Cells (SOFC) that generate auxiliary electric power for passenger vehicles, including public transport and school buses, and other applications. The SOFC converts chemical energy in conventional fuels, such as diesel, gasoline or natural gas, directly into useful electrical power without combustion. It has very few moving parts

and, as a result creates only a low level of sound.

Developments

Delphi has been developing SOFC systems since 1999. After demonstrating its first generation SOFC power system in 2001, Delphi teamed with the Battelle Memorial Institute, US under the Solid State Energy Conversion Alliance (SECA) programme to improve the basic cell and stack technology, while Delphi developed the system integration, system packaging and assembly, heat exchanger, fuel reformer, and power conditioning and control electronics, along with other component technologies.

For commercial vehicles, Delphi's Solid Oxide Fuel Cell technology will be implemented as an Auxiliary Power Unit (APU) to provide an energy efficient, compact, quiet, low-emissions device for powering climate control and electrical accessories as an alternative to idling the main engine. In future variations, it is hoped that the Delphi SOFC APU will also be able to power current belt-driven vehicle loads such as the engine cooling fan and water pump, thus removing them from the primary engine and resulting in improved fuel economy.

Doppelmayr/Garaventa Group

Doppelmayr Seilbahnen GmbH
PO Box 20, Rickenbacherstrasse 8-10, A-6961 Wolfurt, Austria
Tel: (+43 5574) 604   Fax: (+43 5574) 755 90
e-mail: dm@doppelmayr.com
Web: www.doppelmayr.com

Key personnel

Doppelmayr/Garaventa Group Board: *Michael Doppelmayr*
   Hanno Ulmer
   Werner Inderbitzin

Subsidiary companies

The Doppelmayr/Garaventa Group has production facilities, sales and service locations in more than 30 countries worldwide, including Australia, Austria, Canada, China, France, Italy, Russian

Galzigbahn, Austria   1325401

Federation, Spain, Switzerland, UK and US. For further information please see the company's web sites.

Switzerland
Garaventa AG
Bergstrasse 9, CH-6410 Goldau, Switzerland
Tel: (+41 41) 859 11 11
Fax: (+41 41) 859 11 00
e-mail: contact@garaventa.com
Web: www.garaventa.com

US
Doppelmayr CTEC Inc
3160 West 500 South, Salt Lake City, Utah 84104, US
Tel: (+1 801) 973 79 77
Fax: (+1 801) 973 95 80
e-mail: info@doppelmayrctec.com
Web: www.doppelmayrctec.com
    See also separate entry for Doppelmayr Cable Car GmbH, which builds and operates Automated People Movers.

Background
Founded in 1892, Doppelmayr Holding AG merged with Garaventa AG in early 2002. All of the subsidiaries listed are part of the Ropeway Division.

Types of system
Reversible ropeways, gondola ropeways, bicable and tricable ropeways, pulsed-movement ropeways, funicular railways, detachable and fixed-grip chairlifts, surface lifts and material handling systems.

Description
Funitel
Funitel – advanced ropeway technology. Perfected by Doppelmayr/Garaventa, the Funitel system offers outstanding lateral stability for operation at wind speeds of 100 km/h and more. The use of two parallel haul ropes 3.2 m apart makes it possible to achieve extremely long spans.
    Pneumatic suspension ensures that the 24 passengers enjoy the ride in maximum comfort. Line speeds of up to 7 m/s generate transport capacities of 3,200 to 4,000 persons per hour.

Reversible ropeways
Reversible or jig-back ropeways operate with one or two carriers, comprising a carriage, a hanger and the actual car, which travel to and fro between the terminals. Traction is provided via a haul rope, with the carriage running on single or twin-track ropes. The cars can be built to carry anything between 20 and 200 persons at speeds of up to 12 m/s. Depending on the size of the car, line speed and line length, transport capacities vary between 500 and 2,000 persons per hour.

Gondola ropeways
Gondola ropeways offer a highly comfortable ride and are the system of choice for feeder services in ski areas, tourism resorts and the urban environment. The enclosed carriers provide full protection against the elements, and Doppelmayr's design engineers also focus on the special needs of families and older people.
    The gondolas are attached to the haul rope with detachable grips for safe and easy loading and unloading, with the carriers travelling through the terminals at creep speed before accelerating to a line speed of up to 6 m/s. Carrier capacity varies from four to 15 persons and system capacity can be as much as 3,600 persons per hour.

Bicable and tricable ropeways
Bicable and tricable ropeways combine features of both gondola and reversible systems. These detachable circulating ropeways operate with carrier capacities of up to 30 passengers for a maximum transport capacity of 6,000 persons per hour.

Steinplatte, Austria   1325398

'Malcesine', Italy   0595091

The advantages of bicable and tricable ropeways derive from their outstanding stability in wind, low power consumption and the use of very long spans. Maximum line speed is 7 m/s.

Pulsed-movement aerial ropeways

In terms of the ropeway engineering involved, pulsed-movement systems are a relatively uncomplicated solution, operating with fixed-gripped gondolas running in sets. Pulsed-movement aerial ropeways are suitable for both summer and winter facilities with relatively short line lengths, and passengers can be transported either seated or standing. Maximum line speed is 7 m/s.

Funicular

Funicular railways operate with one or two cars or train sets running on a dedicated guideway or track. Operation is normally in the to-and-fro mode, with a haul rope used to provide the traction. Maximum line speed is 14 m/s, and car or train capacity can be anything between 20 and 400 persons. Transport capacity can also vary between 500 and 3,000 persons per hour, depending on car capacity, line speed and line length. Funiculars offer maximum availability in windy conditions.

Contracts

Systems in operation include Roosevelt Island aerial tramway, New York; Singapore Cable Car; Haifa Carmelite underground funicular; Lyon St Just underground funicular: Yokohama Fair passenger gondola railway; Hakone Gora-Souzan funicular, Japan; Télécabine d'Oran, Algeria; Hong Kong Peak Tramway funicular; Expo 98 Lisboa gondola system and others.

Development

The new CABLE Liner Shuttle 'SkyRail' shuttle system at Birmingham International Airport UK was opened in March 2003. This links Birmingham International Airport with a new multimodal public transport interchange. The contract had a value of approximately EUR16 million.

Klaussee II, Italy 1325400

Skyline Skyrides, New Zealand 1325399

Eminox Limited

North Warren Road, Gainsborough, Lincolnshire, DN21 2TU, UK
Tel: (+44 1427) 81 00 88
Fax: (+44 1427) 81 00 61
e-mail: enquiry@eminox.com
Web: www.eminox.com

Key personnel

Director of Marketing: *Mike Galey*
  Staff: 200

Background

Eminox Limited is a privately-owned company, established in 1978.

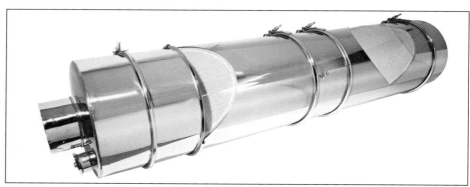

Eminox SCRT© System – Selective Catalytic Reduction + CRT© 1342224

Current situation

The company also has offices in Stoke-on-Trent, UK, France, Sweden and Denmark.

Eminox designs and manufactures high-performance stainless steel exhausts and emission control systems for commercial vehicles. Systems can be designed as original equipment or supplied as a retrofit.

The company is approved to ISO TS16949 (the global automotive standard) and the environment standard: BS EN ISO 14001.

Products and services

Eminox CRT® System – Continuously Regenerating Trap;

Eminox FBC System – Fuel Borne Catalyst;
Eminox SCRT® System – Selective Catalytic Reduction + CRT®;
Eminox Diesel Oxidation Catalyst;
Eminox Exhaust Stacks;
Eminox Spark Arrestors;
Eminox Electronic Service Indicator;
Eminox Filter Exchange Schemes.

Contracts

Bus manufacturers such as Mercedes, Iris Bus, Volvo, Scania, MAN and Alexander Dennis have selected Eminox systems for exhaust after-treatment technology. Eminox systems are also used by rail car manufacturers including

Bombardier Transportation and Alstom Transport.

In October 2007, public transport operator De Lijn, Belgium announced that it was to fit Eminox Limited's advanced SCRT© emissions technology to 165 buses in its fleet. This included city buses in Antwerp and Limburg, plus regional and inter-city buses. The system has been on trial at De Lijn since November 2006. The new systems will be installed in 2008.

Research and developments

Research and development necessary for the design of exhaust and emission control systems is undertaken in Gainsborough and at

---

the company's Gothenburg Technical Centre, Sweden, which is shared with its sister company, Swenox.

The company also has a partnership with Johnson Matthey, one of the world's leading chemical and catalyst technology companies, and the companies work in close co-operation in the development of new products and technologies. They are actively involved in the development of the next-generation exhaust systems, incorporating emission control technologies such as CRT® and SCRT®, enabling vehicles to meet Euro 4 and 5 emissions standards. Eminox is currently undertaking work aimed at meeting the forthcoming Euro 6 standard.

Eminox has also carried out SCRT© trials with Transport for London (Tfl), London, UK and Régie Autonome des Transports Parisiens (RATP), Paris, France.

De Lijn bus, fitted with Eminox Limited's SCRT© emissions system   1342190

FUTREX Inc

1445 McMillan Avenue, North Charleston, South Carolina 29405, US
Tel: (+1 843) 745 94 50
Fax: (+1 843) 745 94 67
e-mail: waldman@futrexinc.com
Web: www.futrexinc.com

Key personnel
President and Chief Executive Officer: *Byron E Waldman*
Vice-President, Engineering: *James M Tuten*

Type of system
Side-suspended monorail.

Background
FUTREX was chartered in 1986 as a privately held, Delaware C-corporation.

A Board of Directors helps to provide strategic direction and management for the company.

In *System 21*'s development to date, and in plans for full-scale development and commercialisation, FUTREX has adopted a consortium approach to attract the best and most capable expertise. Leading companies involved in the consortium have included Battelle Memorial Institute, DMJM+HARRIS, Gangloff AG and SYSTRA Consulting, Inc. The feasibility and soundness of the company's plan for developing the *System 21* technology has been validated by input from its consortium and by an independent, investment-grade engineering evaluation. Working with patent counsel, the company has also devised an international patent strategy and begun to catalogue potential inventions during full-scale development that might be candidates for protection. *System 21* is poised for Phase III full-scale development through either a planned, R & D prototype project, or during the construction and acceptance testing of an initial commercial installation.

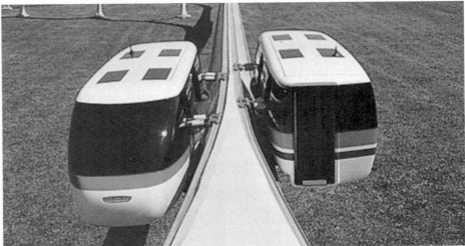

FUTREX's System 21 *monobeam system, showing two cars side-by-side*   1343883

FUTREX's System 21 *vehicles in-station*   1343887

Description
In *System 21*, cars travel in either direction on a monobeam, allowing two-way traffic. Features include lower-cost construction, slender, elevated guideway to minimize intrusion, modular construction, a unique switch design to permit broader operating flexibility and the potential for relocation to accommodate changing demand. It is suitable for use as a 'feeder' system, as extensions to existing transit systems or as automated people movers at airports, resorts and theme parks and large campuses or corporate settings.

Development
In Asia, FUTREX has worked with joint venture partners since 2000 to market System 21 in countries such as China, Indonesia, the Philippines and South Korea. The company has also received interest from a number of US cities.

Global Electric Motorcars LLC (GEM)

3601 7th Avenue Nw, Fargo, North Dakota 58102, US
Tel: (+1 701) 232 25 00   Fax: (+1 701) 232 06 00
e-mail: newgem@gemcar.com
Web: www.gemcar.com

Key personnel
President and Chief Operating Officer: *Rick Kasper*
    Staff: Approximately 80

Background
Global Electric Motors LLC (GEM) is a DaimlerChrysler company.

Products
Manufacturer of electric vehicles suitable for city centre, shuttle and other applications.

Range
e6 and *e6S*: Six-seater electric vehicle.

Harbin Electric Inc

No 9 Ha Ping Xi Lu, Ha Ping Lu Ji Zhong Qu, Harbin Kai Fa Qu, Harbin 150060, China
Tel: (+86 451) 86 11 67 57
Fax: (+86 451) 86 11 67 69
e-mail: mainlandIR@harbinelectric.com
Web: www.harbinelectric.com

Key personnel
Chairman and Chief Executive Officer: *Yang Tianfu*
Executive Vice-President, Finance and Corporate
Development: *Barry L Raeburn*
Vice-President: *Xu Suofei*
    Yang Tianli

Chief Financial Officer: *Xu Zedong*
Chief Technical Advisor: *Ye Yunyue*
    Staff: *223*

Current situation
Harbin Electric, Inc designs, develops and manufactures linear motors and special electric motors for a variety of applications, including mass transportation systems.

Developments
The company's subsidiary, Harbin Tech. Full Electric Co Ltd, hosted the China Linear Motor and Advanced Drive Science annual meeting in August 2006. The main purpose of this

meeting was to discuss application techniques and markets of the magnetic levitation rail transportation and urban rail transportation networks which are driven by linear motors.

Also in August 2006, the company's subsidiary Harbin Tech. Full Electric Co Ltd entered into a joint development agreement with the Electrical Engineering Institute of the Chinese Academy of Sciences (IEECAS) to build a train and track transportation system driven by high-powered linear motors. The initial development will be of the train and system, which will be tested at Beijing Airport railway line before the end of 2008.

Hitachi Ltd

Transportation Systems Division
18-13, Soto-Kanda 1-chome, Chiyudo-ku, Tokyo, 101-8608, Japan
Tel: (+81 3) 32 58 11 11   Fax: (+81 3) 45 64 62 52
Web: www.hitachi-rail.com

Key personnel
Chief Operating Officer of Transportation Systems:
    Toshihide Uchimura

Main works
Transportation Equipment
Kasado Works, Mito Works, Hitachi Works.

Type of system
Monorail system, including monorail cars, track switching, signalling and control systems and power systems.

Hitachi monorail system, based upon the 'Alweg' guideway straddle design, offers mass transit planners an alternative to other public transportation systems, with features such as

Hitachi monorail   0098273

minimal public impact, route flexibility and lower construction costs.

Contracts
Kita-Kyushu, Osaka, Tama and Okinawa Monorails, Japan; Sentosa Express for Sentosa Development

Corporation, Singapore; Chongqing Monorail, China; Palm Island Monorail, UAE.

Hydrogen Engine Center Inc

602 East Fair Street, Algona, IA-50511, US
Tel: (+1 515) 295 31 78
Fax: (+1 515) 295 24 53
e-mail: info@hydrogenenginecenter.com
Web: www.hydrogenenginecenter.com

Key personnel
President: *Ted Hollinger*

Vice-President of Research and Development:
    Tapan Bose
Vice-President of Operations: *Mike Schaltz*

Current situation
The Hydrogen Engine Center Inc designs, manufactures and distributes flex-fuel internal combustion engines. The engines can run on either regular-grade hydrogen, petrol/gasoline, propane, natural gas or ethanol interchangeably

or, with an additional fuel reformer, on biodiesel.

Products
Applications include engines for buses and long-term applications should include the hybrid bus market.
6.8L/7.5L Oxx Power™ Engine: The company has produced two 6.8L V10 engines which have been shipped to unspecified bus companies.

Hythane Company LLC

12420 N Dumont Way, Littleton, CO 80125, US
Tel: (+1 303) 468 17 05   Fax: (+1 303) 791 79 75
e-mail: info@hythane.com
Web: www.hythane.com

Key personnel
Chairman: *Gregory Solomon*
Chief Executive Officer: *Gregory Egan*
President: *Roger Marmaro*
Engineering Manager: *Justin Fullerton*
Press/Media Enquiries: *Luke Bruschuk*

Background
Hythane Company LLC operates as the technical division and wholly owned subsidiary of Brehon Energy plc.

Products
Produces Hythane®, a mixture of natural gas and hydrogen, for alternatively fuelled vehicles, including buses.

Developments
In December 2005, the company announced that it would begin demonstrating its low-

emissions vehicle fuel system to five cities in China.

In February 2006, the company stated that it would be partnering with consultants Gladstein, Neandross & Associates to examine ways in which heavy-duty trucks and buses might be equipped with Hythane® technology to help to reduce air pollution in California, US.

In April 2006, the City of Barstow, California, signed a Memorandum of Understanding (MoU) with the company stating its intention to explore the use of Hythane® for its fleet.

Hyundai Rotem Company

Headquarters
231 Yangjae-dong, Seocho-gu, Seoul, 137-938, South Korea
Tel: (+82 2) 34 64 11 14   Fax: (+82 2) 34 64 75 86
Web: www.hyundai-rotem.co.kr

Key personnel
Executive Vice-Chairman and Chief Executive
    Officer: *Yeo-Sung Lee*

President and Chief Executive Officer:
    Yong-Hoon Lee
Senior Executive Vice-President and Chief
    Operating Officer: *Sang-Kil Lee*
Vice-President, R&D Center: *Jae-Hong Kim*
    Staff: Not available currently

Works
Changwon plant
85 Daewon-Dong, Changwon, Gyeongsangnam-do, 641-808, South Korea

Tel: (+82 55) 273 13 41
Fax: (+82 55) 273 17 41

Uiwang R & D centre
462-18 Sam-Dong, Uiwang-city, Kyunggi-do, South Korea
Tel: (+82 31) 460 11 14   Fax: (+82 31) 460 17 81

Background
Established in 1964 when Daewoo Heavy Industry started manufacturing rolling stock, followed by

Hyundai Precision & Industry and Hanjin Heavy Industry a few years later. In 1999, the three companies were consolidated into KOROS by the Korean Government. Hyundai Motors Group acquired the share of Daewoo Heavy Industry in October 2001 and KOROS became Rotem Company in January 2002.

As of November 2007, Rotem Company has changed its company name to Hyundai Rotem Company.

An affiliate of Hyundai Motor Group, Hyundai Rotem Company has its headquarters in Seoul and two facilities, the central research and development centre in Uiwang and the manufacturing plant in Changwon.

The Changwon plant has the capability to manufacture 1,000 emus per year and also has the capability to manufacture electrical equipment such as traction motors, SIV inverters etc. Certificates such as the ISO 9001:2000/KS A 9001:2001 for quality, ISO 14001:2004/KS A 14001:2004 for environment and OHSAS 18001:1999 for occupational health and safety management have been acquired at all three sites.

Products

Lightweight aluminium vehicle, with a passenger capacity of 100 persons per car, is mounted on three magnetically levitated air-sprung bogies and runs on an elevated guideway. Levitation is achieved by means of attraction; electromagnets in the bogies attract steel rails mounted underneath the guideway. A fixed air gap between rails and bogies is maintained. A set of magnets arranged in a staggered formation within the bogies also provides guidance through attractive force. A single-sided linear induction motor provides propulsion with traction control by a VVVF inverter. Operation is controlled by a radio-based communication link from a central command.

See also other entries in *Jane's Urban Transport Systems* and *Jane's World Railways*.

Type of system

Magnetically levitated vehicles powered by linear induction motor glide on elevated guideway; current collected from side-mounted bars (third rail) at 1,500 V DC.

Description

The following vehicle specification will be enhanced to enter commercial production by the Urban Transit Maglev (UTM) Project Planning Corporation, established in January, 2007.

Magnetically Levitated Vehicles (MLV – Maglev)

Vehicle specification:

Train formation: 2 vehicles (Mc1-Mc2)

Vehicle dimensions (L × W × H):	12,000 × 2,700 × 3,450 mm
Passenger capacity:	Standard: 93 persons/car (5 persons/m²)
Power supply:	Voltage: 1,500 V DC
Train performance:	Maximum design speed: 110 km/h
	Maximum operating speed: 80–100 km/h
	Maximum acceleration: 4.0 km/h/s
	Maximum deceleration: 4.0 km/h/s in service, 4.5 km/h/s in emergency
	Noise level: maximum. 65 dB(A)
	Ride comfort: Below 2.0 in terms of UIC
	Maximum gradient: 70 %
	Minimum curve radius: 50 mR (Lateral)
Propulsion system:	Linear induction motor, VVVF inverter
Levitation system:	Electromagnets, providing combined levitation and guidance, 8 mm levitation gap
Brake system:	Blending of regenerative & mechanical brake
Signalling system:	ATP/ATO by CBTC

Intamin Transportation Ltd

Landstrasse 126, FL-9494 Schaan, Liechtenstein
Tel: (+423) 237 03 63
Fax: (+423) 237 03 60
e-mail: franz.zuercher@intamintransportation.com
info@intamintransportation.com
Web: www.intamintransportation.com

Key personnel

Vice-President: *P Spieldiener*
Product Manager and Sales: *Franz Zürcher*

Type of system

Straddle and suspended monorails, people movers, electric rubber-tyred vehicles; complete systems.

Description

Intamin monorail trains are designed for a typical capacity of up to approximately 10,000 passengers per h per direction and the trains run silently on a slim, lightweight guideway.

Development

A new monorail people mover system, based on the train type P30, has been installed in Moscow, Russia, for urban transport in the city. Each train has a capacity of 200 passengers. The first line of eight km double track is designed for a transport capacity of 6,000 passengers per hour in each direction.

Another new monorail train, P8, has been developed for urban operation. The complete trains offer space for around 72 passengers.

Monorail installations have been built at Rio de Janeiro, Brazil; Shenzen, China (10 trains); Gelsenkirchen, Germany (eight trains); Magdeburg, Germany (eight trains); Stuttgart, Germany (18 trains); Moscow, Russia (one train); Taejon, South Korea (three trains); Seoul, South Korea (20 trains); Manila, Philippines (two trains); Bangkok, Thailand (four trains); Tampa, Florida, USA (six trains), Moscow, Russia (eight trains). Other systems are at planning stage in various cities worldwide.

VLRS (Portsmouth) Ltd (VLRSP), a subsidiary of Ambersham Holdings Limited, is promoting the Portsmouth Monorail project. If successful, it will also construct and operate it. Carr West Limited (see VLRS entry in Southampton, UK Operators) was incorporated in January 1997 for the purpose of promoting the INTAMIN VLRS as a solution to urban transport needs.

ISE Corporation

12302 Kerran Street, Poway, CA 92064-6884, US
Tel: (+1 858) 413 17 20   Fax: (+1 858) 413 17 33
e-mail: marketing@isecorp.com
Web: www.isecorp.com

Key personnel

Chairman of the Board: *Stephen P Strait*
President & Chief Executive Officer: *David M Mazaika*
Chief Operating Officer: *Rick Sander*
Chief Financial Officer: *David Morash*
Chief Science Officer: *Paul B Scott*
Director of Quality and Service: *Gary Vaissiere*
Vice-President of Manufacturing: *Terry Sana*
Vice-President Business Development: *Gary Willms*
Manager of New Business: *Tom Bartley*
Manager Marketing Communications: *Cuong Huynh*
Staff: 60 (estimate)

Background

The privately owned company was incorporated in January 1995.

Products

ISE Corporation is a supplier of integrated hybrid-electric drive systems and control software for large buses and trucks.

ISE combines its control systems with electric motors, generators and other components purchased from various suppliers and partners, integrating all of the parts into complete *ThunderVolt®* hybrid-electric drive systems that it sells to bus and truck manufacturers. In addition to its principal business as a supplier of fully integrated drive systems to vehicle manufacturers, ISE installs its systems into buses, trucks and other vehicles on a smaller scale.

Range

ISE's product offering is supported by a key strategic agreement with Siemens, which supplies the electric motors, motor controllers and generators used in nearly all of ISE's *ThunderVolt®* hybrid drive systems. ISE is in the third year of a five-year agreement with Siemens that establishes ISE as the preferred distributor and integrator of Siemens' *ELFA®* components for the US transit bus market.

The company's product range includes petrol/gasoline hybrid drive systems, diesel hybrid drive systems, Hydrogen Hybrid Internal Combustion Engines (HHICEs) and it also integrates fuel cells and fuel cell-base drive systems into heavy-duty vehicles.

The company also offers all-electric drive systems, such as electric rubber-tyred 'trams'.

Contracts

In April 2007, ISE Corporation delivered a 40-foot hybrid-electric fuel cell-powered transit bus to Connecticut Transit (CTTRANSIT).

In May 2007, the Board of City of Montebello, CA authorised the purchase of 150 gasoline hybrid-electric 40-foot buses, to be supplied by the team of New Flyer and ISE Corporation.

In June 2007, ISE Corporation received orders for its *ThunderVolt®* diesel hybrid-electric drive systems for additional 30-foot Optima Opus buses. These are part of a contract awarded to Optima Bus LLC in 2006 by the Town of Avon, CO. The original award included a base order of up to five hybrid Opus buses with an option of an additional 10 buses. In addition to one hybrid Opus for the Town of Avon, an additional three were ordered by Lake Erie Transit Authority, Monroe, MI and two more by Hampton Roads Transit, Hampton Roads, VA.

In August 2007, a team of New Flyer Industries, ISE Corporation and Ballard Power Systems Inc was selected by BCTransit to supply 20 hydrogen hybrid fuel cell buses.

Developments

In May 2007, ISE Corporation and Altair Nanotechnologies Inc entered into an agreement to jointly develop and supply commercially Lithium rechargeable battery packs for use in hybrid electric and all-electric heavy-duty vehicles.

Johnson Matthey PLC

Environmental Catalysts and Technologies
Orchard Road, Royston, Hertfordshire SG8 5HE,
UK
Tel: (+44 176) 325 35 29
Fax: (44 176) 325 60 15
e-mail: hdde@matthey.com
Web: http://ect.jmcatalysts.com

Contact: Colin Maloney

Other offices
The company also has offices in Brazil, China
(and in Hong Kong), India, Japan, Korea,
Malaysia, South Africa, Taiwan and the US. There
are 10 manufacturing plants and six technology
centres worldwide.

Products
A range of catalytic exhaust systems for trucks
and buses, which are available on either ceramic
or metallic flow-through substrates.

CRT™ (Continuously Regenerating Trap) is a
combined catalyst and filter system being used
in buses and other public vehicles throughout
Europe. It has been designed to be used with
ultra low sulphur diesel.

Kawasaki Heavy Industries Ltd

Rolling Stock Company
Rolling Stock Division, Marketing & Sales Center,
Overseas Marketing Department
World Trade Center Building 4-1, Hamamatsu-cho
2-chome, Minato-ku, Tokyo 105-6116, Japan
Tel: (+81 3) 34 35 25 88   Fax: (+81 3) 34 35 21 57
e-mail: yashiro_y@khi.co.jp
Web: www.khi.co.jp

Key personnel
Senior Vice-President, Kawasaki Heavy Industries
    Ltd, President, Rolling Stock Company:
    Masashi Segawa
Managing Executive Officer, Kawasaki Heavy
    Industries Ltd, Vice-President, Rolling Stock
    Company: *Kyohei Matsuoka*
General Manager, Rolling Stock Division, Rolling
    Stock Company: *Akira Hattori*
General Manager, Marketing and Sales Center,
    Rolling Stock Division, Rolling Stock Company:
    Ryoshi Hirano
Senior Manager, Overseas Marketing Department,
    Marketing and Sales Center, Rolling Stock
    Division, Rolling Stock Company: *Hiroshi Murao*

Background
The company's Hyogo Works, which produces
rolling stock, was originally established as a
branch works of Kawasaki Dockyards in 1906.

Kawasaki Heavy Industries supplied the rolling
stock for the new transit systems Portliner and
Rokko Island systems, which are operated by
Kobe New Transit Co Ltd.

(see separate entry under Urban Transport
Systems and Operators, Kobe).

The company produces rolling stock for
monorails and has also developed a battery-
powered, low-floor light rail vehicle named
SWIMO.

Type of system
Portliner and Rokko Island systems:
Automated rubber-tyred light metro on steel/
concrete guideway, lateral guidance by wheels
bearing on guidebars, traction power at 600 V AC
three-phase.

Description
Two-axle rubber-tyred cars normally have all
axles driven by 90 kW DC motors. Maximum
gradient is 5 per cent and minimum curve radius

30 m. Full ATO and ATP systems are fitted for
driverless operation.

KCV (Kawasaki Computer-controlled Vehicle)
system, under development since 1970 and
tested on a 1.3 km track in 1974, was used for a
link to the reclaimed Port Island industrial area.
The now-extended 10.8 km Portliner route has
12 stations.

A second route of 4.5 km opened in 1989
to serve Rokko Island, a new residential and
industrial development.

SWIMO
Powered by Gigacell, Kawasaki's nickel metal-
hydride battery, SWIMO can be operated for
more than 10 km without charging. In electrified
sections, SWIMO uses electricity supplied from
overhead lines and charges the Gigacell from that
supply and from regenerative braking. In non-
electrified sections, SWIMO uses power from
the battery and recharges it from regenerative
braking. The vehicle will be suitable for use in
areas where preserving the 'cityscape' is of
importance.

Kawasaki SWIMO-X articulated vehicle (the prototype of SWIMO), which uses a 110 kWh Gigacell battery, enabling it to be operated without an electricity supply   1346007

Kawasaki Type 2000 Automated Guideway Transit (AGT) system rubber-tyred train for the Port Island Line (Portliner), Kobe, Japan   1328448

Kleenair Systems International plc

Unit D, Beaver Centre, Ashburton Industrial
Estate, Ross-on-Wye HR9 7BW, UK
Tel/Fax: (+44 1989) 56 69 02
e-mail: sharon.morris@kleenairsystems.co.uk
Web: www.kleenairsystems.co.uk

Key personnel
Chairman and Chief Executive: *Lionel Simons*
Managing Director: *Peter Newell*
Sales Director: *Alan Barnard*
Technical Director: *Karl Grimston*
Senior Technical Sales Engineer: *Mark Joyce*
Chief Financial Officer: *Katie MacDonald*
    Staff: Not currently available

Products
NOx reduction and emission control systems
technology for diesel engines, aimed at the
retrofitting market.

Range
Patented NOx abatement technology combined
with particulate reduction technologies. Products
for reducing emissions in buses and coaches
include:
Partial Flow Diesel Particulate Filter (DPF):
Partial Flow Filter (PFF), based upon a metallic
substrate with an alternating tapered network of
flow through channels consisting of corrugated
metals foils and a metal fiber fleece. The PFF is
particularly suited to vehicles that have low-load

duty cycles such as those operating in inner city
environments.
Full Flow Diesel Particulate Filter (DPF): The
substrate material is normally either a ceramic
that is applied with a catalyst coating for
passive regeneration, or an uncoated silicon
carbide substrate with a hydrocarbon catalyst
upstream that reacts with a fuel injection
system to actively regenerate the soot trapped
by the filter. This technology is capable of
taking a Euro-II engine to a Euro-IV emission
standard.
Active Regeneration: The active regeneration
system, used in conjunction with the full flow
DPF, actively regenerates the particulates trapped
within the filter.

Leitner SpA

Headquarters
Via Brennero 34, I-39049, Vipiteno (BZ), Italy
Tel: (+39 0472) 72 21 11
Fax: (+39 0472) 72 41 11
e-mail: info@leitner-lifts.com, sales.minimetro@
leitner-lifts.com
Web: www.leitner-lifts.com
PTS Department
Via Volta 17, I-39100, Bolzano, Italy

Key personnel
President and Managing Director: *Anton Seeber*
Technical Office Manager: *Giuseppe Conte*
Sales Manager: *Ermenegildo Zordan*
Research and Development Manager: *Andrea Durante*
Project Engineering Manager: *Alessandro Pivetta*
Staff: 700 (estimate)

Other offices
The company has offices and representatives in Austria, Brazil, Canada, China, Croatia, Dominican Republic, Finland, France, Germany, Greece, Iceland, Japan, Lebanon, Norway, Spain, Sweden, Switzerland, Turkey and the US.

Background
The company was originally established in 1988 by Gabriel Leitner.

Type of system
LEITNER MiniMetro® Automated People Mover (APM), funicular systems, gondola lifts, inclined lifts, rack railways, aerial tramways.

Description
The completion of the MiniMetro is the culmination of an intense research and development process by the international company based in Italy, Leitner Technologies. The innovative system is based on ropeway technology and can be used in medium-sized cities, for short- and medium-distance local public transport services. It has been designed for operations such as park-and-ride services or for linking shopping centres, universities and interchanges etc. Rope-hauled vehicles run on a fixed track, up to 4 km long. Longer systems use sections in sequence. The fixed-grip reversible system can carry up to 8,000 passengers/h in each direction and the detachable-grip circulating system up to 3,000 passengers/h in each direction, with a frequency in the stations of one minute, and an incline of up to 12 per cent. Capability for overhead guideways or underground sections.

MiniMetro cars at Cupa station, Perugia, Italy   1344590

Cortonese station, MiniMetro, Perugia, Italy   1344589

Range
LEITNER MiniMetro®
MiniMetro® fixed-grip reversible system: The cars are permanently fixed to the haul rope. The system can operate with a single car or car trains. Maximum line speed is 36–43 km/h.

MiniMetro® detachable-grip circulating system: Detachable cars travel spaced on the haul rope at short intervals. Allows for additional cars to be attached for peak-traffic service. Maximum line speed is 22–30 km/h.

Recent contracts
Construction has been completed in Perugia, Italy on a MiniMetro® system which is 3 km in length, 1.5 km of which have overhead guideway and with 700 m of tunnel. It is known locally as the 'Linea Rossa' (Red Line). There are seven stations and 25 cars, each with a capacity of 50 passengers, and is capable of a carrying a maximum of 3,000 passengers/h. The automated system links the suburb of Pian di Massiano with the town centre and opened in January 2008.

Lohr Group

Translohr Activities
PO Box 1 Hangenbieten, F-67838, Tanneries Cedex, France
Tel: (+33 3) 88 38 98 00   Fax: (+33 3) 88 96 06 36
e-mail: translohr@lohr.fr
Web: www.lohr.fr

Street address
29 rue du 14-Juillet, F-67980 Hangenbieten, France

Key personnel
Managing Director: *Philibert d'Hotelans*
Contact: *O Hauchard*

Other office
Industrial site
Duppigheim, F-67120, France

Background
Lohr Group, a French private group based in Alsace, is active in the sector of urban transport with Translohr (tramway on tires) and, in co-operation with Siemens, NEOVAL (automatic people mover).

The Group has five industrial subsidiaries worldwide and had a 2006 consolidated turnover

Translohr vehicles in Clermont-Ferrand, France   1310752

of EUR250 million. It has some 2,500 employees, of which 70 per cent are based in Alsace.

Type of system

Translohr: Range of rubber-tyred guided light rail vehicles.

Description

Translohr is the 'new generation' of tramways, with vehicles from 25 to 46 m in length. The system has the characteristics of a modern traditional tramway (fully guided, high transport capacity, bi-directional, modular, 100 per cent low-floor) but without the current drawbacks linked to the bogie (crunching, vibration, weak grip). The combination of the mechanical guiding and the rolling on tyres provide high technical performances (13 per cent gradient capacity, security, efficient braking, good insertion, 10.5 m turning length) and discretion (silence, fluidity, lightness).

Contracts

Almost 100 Translohr vehicles have been sold worldwide. In France, Clermont-Ferrand inaugurated its first line in November 2006. Systems are also in commercial operation in Padua, Italy and Tianjin, China. L' Aquila and Mestre-Venezia will follow. In Japan, a test line was implemented in 2005, in partnership with Japanese companies, led by the Mitsui Group.

Translohr vehicle, Padua, Italy   1310753

Maxwell Technologies Inc

9244 Balboa Avenue, San Diego, CA 92123, US
Tel: (+1 858) 503 33 00   Fax: (+1 858) 503 33 01
Web: www.maxwell.com

Key personnel

President and Chief Executive Officer: *David J Schramm*
Vice-President, Chief Financial Officer & Treasurer: *Tim T Hart*
Vice President, General Manager of Maxwell Technologies SA, Rossens, Switzerland: *Alain R Riedo*
Senior Vice-President, Operations: *George Kreigler*
Vice-President, Systems, Applications & Integration: *John M Miller*
President, Business Development, Sales & Marketing: *Michael J Liedtke*
Vice-President, Communications and Investor Relations: *Michael W Sund*
Vice-President, Chief technical Officer: *Michael A Everett*
Vice President, Quality & Process Engineering: *Everett E (Earl) Wiggins*
Staff: Not currently available

Current situation

Maxwell is a leading developer and manufacturer of innovative energy storage and power delivery solutions.

The company has offices in San Diego, US, Rossens, Switzerland and Shanghai, China.

Products

BOOSTCAP®: Ultracapacitor cells and multi-cell packs and modules provide power solutions for applications in consumer and industrial electronics, transportation and telecommunications.

CONDIS®: High-voltage grading and coupling capacitors help to ensure the safety and reliability of electric utility infrastructure and other applications involving transport, distribution and measurement of high-voltage electrical energy.

Contracts

In July 2008, the company announced that Golden Dragon Bus Co Ltd, a leading producers of medium- and heavy-duty buses, had selected Maxwell's BOOSTCAP® ultracapacitors for braking energy recuperation and torque assist in fuel-efficient, low-emission, diesel-electric hybrid buses that Golden Dragon is producing for the Public Transport Group Co Ltd, Hangzhou, China.

720 48-volt BMOD0165 P048 multi-cell ultracapacitor modules were delivered to Golden Dragon for installation in 45 hybrid buses.

Also in July 2008, Vossloh Kiepe GmbH selected Maxwell's 125-volt BOOSTCAP® ultracapacitor modules for braking energy recuperation and torque assist in emission-free electric buses it is producing in collaboration with Van Hool NV for the municipal transit system in Milan, Italy.

The Vossloh/Van Hool buses for Milan are low-floor articulated vehicles equipped with ultracapacitor-based energy storage systems that absorb and store energy from recuperative braking for reuse in powering zero-emission electric motors. The basic drive system can be augmented with energy supplied via overhead lines or a 100 kw diesel generator set that is certified in compliance with the Euro 5 emission standard. The city of Milan recently announced that it is taking delivery of the first 15 of a total of 70 vehicles it has ordered from Vossloh Kiepe and Van Hool.

Monorail Malaysia Technology Sdn Bhd (MMT)

Wisma Monorail, Jalan Tebing, Brickfields, 50470 Kuala Lumpur, Malaysia
Tel: (+60 3) 22 67 98 88
Fax: (+60 3) 22 67 99 99
e-mail: mmt@mmt.com.my
Web: www.monorail.com.my/mmt/about.htm

Manufacturing facility

Lot 795, Jalan Monorel, Sungai Choh, Rawang, 48000 Selangor, Malaysia

Tel: (+60 3) 60 92 38 88
Fax: (+60 3) 60 91 92 03

Background

A subsidiary of MTrans Holdings Sdn Bhd, Monorail Malaysia Technology Sdn Bhd (MMT) was incorporated in 1995.

Products

The main business of the company is the provision and supply of monorail-based systems for mass transit.

MMT designed, manufactured, installed and commissioned the 12 monorail trainsets and all related equipment for the KL Monorail system (see separate entry).

Developments

In 2004, the company signed an agreement with Gangam District, Seoul to establish a joint-venture company to develop a 6.7 km monorail system on a privatised basis. The system would cost an estimated USD175 million and the project is subject to the approval of relevant South Korean and Malaysian authorities.

NextEnergy

461 Burroughs, Detroit, Michigan 48202, US
Tel: (+1 313) 833 01 00   Fax: (+1 313) 833 01 01
Web: www.nextenergy.org

Key personnel

President/Chairman of the Board: *Chris Rizik*
Chief Executive Officer: *James A Croce*
Chief Financial Officer: *Kenneth Fiema*
Chief Operating Officer: *Dave McLean*

Director, Industry Services: *Dan Radomski*
Director, External Relations: *Mark Beyer*
Director, Business Development: *James Saber*
Staff: Not currently available

Current situation

Established in 2002 as a 501(c)(3) nonprofit organisation, NextEnergy carries out research and development on alternative and renewable energy for a number of market areas and manages research projects.

NextEnergy offers a variety of services, programmes and resources for the transportation industry, including:
- Technical & Research Services;
- Permitting Guide for Hydrogen Technologies;
- National Biofuels Energy Laboratory Projects;
- Hydraulic Hybrid Working Group;
- Advancing Hydrogen in Michigan Working Group;
- Detroit Area Clean Cities Coalition.

Nippon Sharyo Ltd – Vehicles Of New Age (VONA)

Engineering Department
JR Central Towers, Suite 2210, 22nd Floor, 1-1-4 Meieki, Nakamura-ku, Nagoya 450-6022, Japan
Tel: (+81 52) 589 81 31   Fax: (+81 52) 589 81 32
Web: www.n-sharyo.co.jp

Key personnel
Director and General Manager: *Tomiji Ogawa*

Type of system
Automated Guideway Transit (AGT) system and Guided Bus System.

Development
Following the Automated Guideway Transit system, called Vehicle Of New Age (VONA), inaugurated over 3.6 km in Yukarigaoka, near Tokyo, the company has also delivered the 'Peach Liner' system in Aichi and the Tokyo waterfront new transit system, Yurikamome, which opened in 1995.

In 2001 a specially designed Guided Bus system started revenue service in Nagoya City.

Research and development
The company is pursuing further technology for next-generation transit systems, such as a mini-sized railway and lightweight monorail.

Pirelli & C Ambiente Eco Technology SpA

Viale Luraghi snc, 20020 Arese (MI), Italy
Tel: (+39 02) 93 87 46 00   Fax: (+39 02) 93 87 46 64
Web: www.pirelliambiente.com

Products
Particulate filters.
Retrofit filter systems for buses and heavy vehicles are manufactured in the factory in Arese in the province of Milan. A new factory in Romania will also produce original equipment filters.

Range
Pirelli Diesel Particulate System Feelpure™ (Pirelli DPF), for the treatment of exhaust gases and decrease emissions in Euro 0 to Euro 4 diesel engines for commercial and transport use.

Recent contracts
In July 2008, Pirelli won a pilot project in Beijing to test particulate filter technology, initially on buses used by the local transport company.

In May 2008, the company signed an agreement for the supply of some 150 particulate filters to companies in the Arriva Italia Group. The aim of the initiative is to reduce the particulate emissions by more than 90 per cent in about 150 inter-city buses.

Scomi Engineering Bhd

Scomi Rail Bhd
5th Floor, Wisma Chase Perdana, Off Jalan Semantan, Damansara Heights, 50490 Kuala Lumpur, Malaysia
Tel: (+60 3) 20 80 62 22   Fax: (+60 3) 20 80 63 33
Web: www.scomiengineering.com.my

Background
In July 2006, Scomi Engineering Bhd completed the acquisition of MTrans Transportation Systems Sdn Bhd, making it a subsidiary of the company. Scomi Rail Bhd was formerly known as MTrans Technology Bhd. It is wholly owned by Scomi Transportation System Sdn Bdn, which in turn is wholly owned by Scomi Engineering Bhd.

Products
Scomi Rail Bhd is a provider of integrated monorail systems, offering design, fabrication and integration of monorail rolling stock and related electro-mechanical systems.

In November 2007, Scomi launched its next generation monorail Scomi Urban Transit Rail Application (SUTRA). SUTRA has improved features to provide better capacity, ergonomics and safety. Enhanced features include composite body and interior panel, new bogie system and structure, mass transit components drive train, improved propulsion and control system and regenerative and pneumatic brake system.

The SUTRA system is currently being trialled at the company's manufacturing plant at Rawang.

For further information on Scomi, please also see also under Buses – Chassis, Integrals and Bodies section.

Developments
Scomi has formed alliances to participate in bids and proposals for a number of projects in countries such as India, Saudi Arabia, Thailand, Vietnam, Bangladesh, Pakistan, Syria, Egypt and Korea.

Severn-Lamb UK Limited

Tything Road, Alcester,
B49 6ET, UK
Tel: (+44 1789) 40 01 40
Fax: (+44 1789) 40 02 40
e-mail: sales@severn-lambuk.com
Web: www.severn-lambuk.com

Other office
Severn-Lamb North America
2061 East Prescott Place, Chandler, Arizona 85249, US

Tel: (+1 480) 588 68 06
Fax: (+1 480) 325 09 00
e-mail: sales@severn-lambnorthamerica.com

Current situation
The company manufactures rail trains, road trains, monorails and customised vehicles.

Range
Rail trains ;
Road trains: A range of pneumatic-tyred road trains for car parking, shuttle and general people-moving solutions;

Monorails: A range of monorails, including the **SL Series**, the **Themed Series** and fully automated versions;
Custom vehicles: Including replicas of antique and vintage vehicles and themed all-terrain vehicles.

Developments
Severn-Lamb North America was established in May 2005 and represents the company in North, Central and South America.

In November 2005, the company was awarded ISO 9001:2000 certification.

Sustainable Transport Company Ltd (Sustraco)

Heron House, Chiswick Mall,
London W4 2PR, UK
Tel: (+44 20) 89 95 30 00
Fax: (+44 20) 89 94 60 60
e-mail: james@jskinner.demon.co.uk
Web: www.ultralightrail.com
    www.passenger-transit-systems.co.uk

Key personnel
Contact: James Skinner

Type of system: Ultra Light Rail vehicles and technology, running on steel rail, on-street or on private right-of-way.

Developments
Sustraco, through its associated company, Bristol Electric Railbus Limited (BER) (please see separate entry), is actively engaged in preparing a plan for the development of a new ULR route in Bristol and a business case is being prepared together with a group of leading Bristolians to assist the Bristol City Council to implement the project for a ULR link between Ashton Gate and the City Centre. This project has been in the Local Transport Plan for some years without obtaining funding from the City or from the DfT, but is now expected to progress in the not-too-distant future. Sustraco has calculated that stage one of the Ashton Link would reduce CO_2 emissions by some 250 tonnes per annum.

A project in Kalamata, Greece is currently held up by funding problems but other projects overseas in Mauritius and China are under discussion.

In 2007, BER/Sustraco joined the UITP as part of its ongoing commitment to the delivery of sustainable urban public transport.

Toyota Motor Corporation (TMC)

Corporate Communications Department, Public Affairs Division
4-18, Koraku 1-chome, Bunkyo-ku, Tokyo 112-8701, Japan
Tel: (+81 3) 38 17 91 50   Fax: (+81 3) 38 17 90 92
Web: www.toyota.co.jp

Key personnel
Chairman: *Fujui Cho*

President: *Katsuaki Watanabe*
Honorary Chairman: *Shoichiro Toyoda*
    Staff: 299,394 (March 2007 – worldwide consolidated total)

Type of system
Intelligent Multimode Transit System (IMTS)
IMTS is a next-generation transportation system. The vehicles are navigated and controlled by magnetic markers embedded in the middle of their dedicated roads. A thorough fail-safe system is adopted, featuring automatic speed regulation and braking functions assured by inter-vehicle communication, ground signals and other means.

Course-keeping function: Magnetic markers embedded in the middle of the dedicated roads ensure automatic navigation and control;

Platoon running function: Three electronically linked vehicles run in file formation at uniform speeds;

Toyota's Intelligent Multimode Transit System (IMTS), as trialled at the 2005 World Exposition in Aichi, Japan   1115231

Speed-keeping function: Stops at stations, departures and travelling speed are automatically regulated in line with the operation timetable;

Fixed-point stop function: Each vehicle in a platoon is controlled to stop exactly at set points along the station platform;

Anti-collision function: Inter-vehicle communication, ground signals and other means allow automatic brake control.

IMTS has the following features:

As the units in platoon operation (file formation at uniform speeds) are not mechanically linked,

it is easy to increase or decrease their number, depending on fluctuations in demand;

Vehicles running in platoons on dedicated roads achieve speed and punctuality suitable for an advanced transit system;

Dual mode operation (in a platoon on dedicated roads and as independent units on ordinary roads) allows smooth, limited-transfer travel;

The combined use of dedicated roads and ordinary roads can be flexibly arranged, and this, together with a far-smaller turning radius and the ability to ascend much sharper inclines than is possible with trains, allows flexibility in setting routes;

The absence of need for rails and power transformers (which are necessary in conventional rail-based systems), along with the system's compact control system and compact vehicle terminals, contributes to construction and maintenance cost efficiency. Unmanned operation on dedicated roads also reduces labour and related costs.

The IMTS system was successfully trialled at the 2005 World Exposition, Aichi, Japan with the co-operation and assistance of the Japan Association for the 2005 World Exposition.

For further information on Toyota Motor Corporation, please see separate entry in *Jane's Urban Transport Systems, Manufacturers – Buses – Chassis, Integrals and Bodies.*

Transport Design International Ltd (TDI)

Suite 3, Clifford Mill, Clifford Chambers, Stratford upon Avon, Warwickshire, CV37 8HW, UK
Tel: (+44 777) 093 12 74
e-mail: martin.p@tdi.uk.com
Web: www.tdi.uk.com

Key personnel
Chairman: *Roger Aylward*
Design Director: *Martin Pemberton*
Design Manager: *Paul Salkeld*

Background
Founded in 1987, TDI is the lead partner in the development of the electric 'Minitram' urban transit system (Minitram Systems Ltd). This low cost, environmentally friendly transport mode is available in both electronically guided and Ultra Light Rail (ULR) versions.

See also entry under Consultancy services.

Type of system
Rubber-tyred wire-guided mini-trams.

Description
Minitram Systems provides high-quality zero-emission ultra-light public transport vehicles and infrastructure delivering characteristics which are normally associated with light rail, but at less cost. The rubber-tyred vehicles are electronically guided using below-ground wire guidance technology and do not require overhead wires or electrified rails.

The vehicles are suitable for park-and-ride schemes and other intermodal shuttle applications within small cities and historic town centres.

They can use roadways with shared occupancy, dedicated alignments, through pedestrian areas and even indoors.

Variants, which can be bidirectional, include:
Type 1: single 45-passenger car 2.3 m wide and 8 m long
Type 2: twin-car articulated 90-passenger car 2.3 m wide and 16 m long
Type 3: single 30-passenger car 1.75 m wide and 8 m long
Type 4: twin-car articulated 90-passenger car 1.75 m wide and 16 m long.

In collaboration with industrial partners, Minitram Systems Ltd will design, procure, project manage and install complete Minitram systems on a turnkey basis. The fully installed capital cost per km of a complete Minitram system, inclusive of vehicles and infrastructure, is under GPB1 million.

UQM Technologies Inc

7501 Miller Drive, PO Box 439, Frederick, CO 80530, US
Tel: (+1 303) 278 20 02
Fax: (+1 303) 278 70 07
e-mail: sales@uqm.com
Web: www.uqm.com

Key personnel
President and Chief Executive Officer: *William G Rankin*
Secretary, Treasurer and Chief Financial Officer: *Donald A French*
Executive Vice-President of Operations: *Ron Burton*
Vice-President of Technology: *John Lutz*
Manufacturing Manager: *Jim McVeigh*

Current situation
The company develops products for the alternative energy technologies sector, including propulsion systems for electric, hybrid-electric and fuel cell electric vehicles, accessories, auxiliaries and distributed power generation applications.

Developments
UQM Technologies Inc has developed a new 150 kW propulsion system for electric, hybrid-electric and fuel cell-powered vehicles. The PowerPhase 150 uses the same external package as the 100 kW PowerPhase 100 system, but incorporates advancements in both motor magnetic properties and motor control strategies to produce 50 per cent more power from the same 200 lb machine.

Contracts
In July 2007, the company announced that Mobile Energy Solutions had selected its newly developed PowerPhase 150 system to power a fuel cell hybrid-electric bus which is being developed under the Federal Transit Administration's National Fuel Cell Bus Program.

UQM Technologies' PowerPhase® 150 traction system   1329346

UTC Power

195 Governor's Highway, South Windsor,
CT 06074, US
Tel: (+1 860) 727 22 00 (Main number)
(+1 866) 383 52 35 (Sales)
e-mail: info@utcpower.com
Web: www.utcpower.com

Key personnel

President: *Jan van Dokkum*
Vice-President, Business Development and
General Counsel: *Mike Brown*
Vice-President, Finance and Chief Financial
Officer: *Jim Van Hoof*
Vice-President, Engineering: *Frank Preli*
Vice-President, Sales: *Ken Stewart*

Background

UTC Power is part of United Technologies
Corporation (NYSE: UTX). The unit is based in
South Windsor, Connecticut, US. With nearly
50 years experience, UTC Power develops
and produces fuel cells for on-site power,
transportation, space and defence applications.

The company has been supplying fuel
cell bus powerplants since 1998 for transit
programmes in the US and Europe. UTC Power
also has a significant role on the US Federal
Transit Administration's National Fuel Cell Bus
Technology Development programme.

Current situation

Van Hool buses powered by the company's system
are in revenue service at AC Transit and SunLine

Transit Agency, California and with CTTRANSIT
in Hartford, Connecticut in the US. Over the next
four years, four more zero-emission UTC Power
fuel cell-powered hybrid buses will be built and
tested with CTTRANSIT.

Developments

UTC Power worked with Van Hool, Belgium,
to deliver a fuel cell-powered hybrid-electric
demonstration bus to the Belgian operator
DeLijn in 2007. The bus was due to operate in
Belgium for six months before being leased to
other European transit agencies.

Valence Technology Inc

12303 Technology Boulevard, Suite 950, Austin,
TX 78727, US
Tel: (+1 512) 527 29 00
Fax: (+1 512) 527 29 10
www.valence.com

Europe/Asia Pacific Sales

Mallusk, N Ireland – EMEA Sales Office
Valence Technology, Unit 63 Mallusk Enterprise
Park, Mallusk Drive, Mallusk, Newtownabbey,
Co Antrim, Northern Ireland BT36 4GN
Tel: (+44 28) 90 84 54 00
Fax: (+44 28) 90 83 89 12

Research & Development Center

Valence Technology, 1889 E Maule, Suite A,
Las Vegas, Nevada 89119, US
Tel: +1 702) 558 10 00   Fax: (+1 702) 558 10 01

Key personnel

President and Chief Executive Officer:
  Robert L Kanode
Chief Financial Officer: *Galen Fischer*
Director and Chairman of the Board: *Carl E Berg*
Vice-President, Worldwide Sales and Marketing:
  Alastair Johnston
Vice-President, Engineering and Product
  Development: *Joel E Sandahl*
  Staff: 490 (June 2008)

Current situation

Valence Technology Inc develops and
manufactures lithium phosphate energy storage
solutions and works with a number of bus and
coach builders, as well as system integrators, to
develop standard and customised solutions for
commercial and private bus applications.

Founded in 1989, the company has facilities in
Nevada, China and Northern Ireland.

Valence is traded on the NASDAQ Capital
Market under the ticker symbol VLNC.

The company is ISO 9001 certified and is
working towards TS 16949.

BUSES – CHASSIS, INTEGRALS AND BODIES

Company listing by country

AUSTRALIA
Custom Coaches (Sales) Pty Ltd
Volgren Australia Pty Ltd

AUSTRIA
Kutsenits Handels- und BuskonstruktionsgmbH
Österreichische Automobilfabrik ÖAF – Gräf & Stift AG (ÖAF)

BELARUS
Minsk Automobile Plant (MAZ)

BELGIUM
Van Hool NV
VDL Jonckheere Bus & Coach NV

BRAZIL
Agrale SA
Busscar Ônibus SA
Caio Induscar
Ciferal Indústria de Ônibus Ltda (Ciferal)
Comil Carrocerias e Ônibus Ltda (Comil)
Eletra Industrial Ltda
Marcopolo SA
Metalbus Ind Metalúrgica Ltda
San Marino Ônibus e Implementos Ltda (San Marino Neobus)
Volkswagen Caminhões e Ônibus Ltda

CANADA
Dupon Trolley Industries
Girardin Minibus Inc
New Flyer Industries
Nova Bus
Overland Custom Coach Inc
Prévost

CHINA
Changzhou Iveco Bus Co Ltd (CBC-Iveco Ltd)
Changzhou Changjiang Bus Group Co Ltd
Chongqing Hengtong Bus Co Ltd
Dongfeng Motor Co Ltd (DFL)
Guangzhou Denway Bus Co Ltd
Guangzhou Isuzu Bus Co Ltd
Guangzhou Junda Automobile Enterprise Group
Guangzhou Yangcheng Automobile Co Ltd
Jinhua Neoplan Vehicle Co Ltd
Shanghai Automotive Industry Corporation (Group) (SAIC)
Sunwin Bus Corporation
Xi'an Silver Bus Corporation
Xiamen Golden Dragon Bus Co Ltd
Zhongwei Passenger Car Co Ltd

CZECH REPUBLIC
Iveco Czech Republic as
SOR Libchavy spol sro – SOR Libchavy Ltd
Ekobus as
KH motor Centrum (KHMC)
TEDOM sro

EGYPT
Engineering Automotive Manufacturing Co (EAMCO)
Ghabbour Group

FINLAND
Kiitokori Oy
Lahden Autokori Oy

FRANCE
Durisotti SA
Gruau Group
Heuliez Bus

Irisbus Iveco
PVI
VehiXeL Trouillet Constructeur

GERMANY
Daimler AG
Auwärter Omnibusse-Fahrzeugbau GmbH (EA)
Contrac GmbH
EA Karosserie-und Fahrzeugbau Gera GmbH (EA KFB)
EvoBus GmbH – Setra Omnibusse
Göppel Bus GmbH
KOWEX Omnibusse und Fahrzeugtechnik GmbH (KOWEX)
MAN Nutzfahrzeuge Group
Viseon Bus GmbH

GHANA
NEOPLAN Ghana Limited

GREECE
Hellenic Vehicle Industry SA (EΛBO/ELBO)

HUNGARY
Alfa Busz Kft
Rába Automotive Holding Plc

INDIA
Ashok Leyland Limited
Eicher Motors Limited (EML)
JCBL Limited
Tata Motors Limited

IRAN
RunIran Co
Shahab Khodro Co

IRELAND
Euro Coach Builders

ISRAEL
Haargaz Ltd
Merkavim Transportation Technologies Ltd

ITALY
BredaMenarinibus SpA
Cacciamali Spa
Mauri & C SaS
Sitcar SpA
Tomassini Style srl

JAPAN
Hino Motors Ltd
Isuzu Motors Limited
Mazda Motor Corporation
Mitsubishi Fuso Truck and Bus Corporation (MFTBC)
Nishi-Nippon Coach Industry Co Ltd – NSK-Coach
Nissan Motor Co Ltd
Toyota Motor Corporation (TMC)

KENYA
Banbros Limited
Labh Singh Harnam Singh Ltd (LSHS)

KOREA, SOUTH
Daewoo Bus Corporation
Hyundai Motor Company

MACEDONIA, FORMER YUGOSLAV REPUBLIC OF
SANOS DOO Skopje (Bus & Coach Factory 'Sanos' Co Ltd)

MALAYSIA
Scomi Engineering Bhd

MEXICO
Consorcio G Grupo Dina SA de CV (Dina)

MOROCCO
Berliet Maroc SA

NETHERLANDS
VDL Bus and Coach Centre
Advanced Public Transport Systems BV (APTS)
BUSiness BV
Busland BV
Spijkstaal Elektro BV
VDL Berkhof Heerenveen BV
VDL Berkhof Valkenswaard BV
VDL BOVA BV
VDL Bus International BV
VDL Groep bv
VDL Kusters BV

PAKISTAN
Hinopak Motors Limited

POLAND
Autosan SA
Fabryka Autobusów Solbus Sp zoo (Solbus)
Jakłady Samochodowe Jelcz SA (Jelcz Automotive Works)
Kapena SA
Polskie Autobusy Sp zoo
Solaris Bus & Coach SA

PORTUGAL
CaetanoBus SA
Camo-Indústria de Autocarros SA (Camo)

RUSSIAN FEDERATION
AMO ZIL
JSC Pavlovo Bus (PAZ)
KAMAZ Incorporated
Trolza CC

SERBIA
FFB Komerc SA Beograd (FAP-FAMOS BEOGRAD)
Ikarbus AD

SLOVENIA
Tovarna Vozil Maribor doo (TVM)

SOUTH AFRICA
Busaf Bus Manufacturing
MAN Bus & Coach (Pty) Ltd

SPAIN
Andecar SA
Beulas SA
Carrocera Castrosua SA
Carrocerías Ayats SA (Ayats)
Carrocerias Ferqui SL (Ferqui)
Hispano Carrocera SA
INDCAR SA (Industrial Carrocera Arbuciense SA)
Irizar S Cooperativa
Nissan Motor España SA
Noge SL
Sunsundegui SA
Unidad de Véhiculos Industriales, SA (UNVI SA)

SWEDEN
Helmark Carosseri AB
Scania Bus and Coach
Volvo Bus Corporation
Volvo Bussar Säffle AB

SWITZERLAND
Carrosserie HESS AG (HESS)

Company listing by country —continued

TAIWAN
Tar-Fue Vehicle Body Co Ltd

TUNISIA
Société Tunisienne d'Industrie Automobile (STIA)

TURKEY
Anadolu Isuzu Otomotiv Sanayi ve Ticaret AŞ (Anadolu)
BMC Sanayi ve Ticaret AŞ
MAN Türkiye AŞ
Otokar Otobüs Karoseri Sanayi AŞ (Otokar)
Temsa Sanayi ve Ticaret AŞ

UKRAINE
Antonov Aeronautical Scientific & Technical Complex (Antonov ASTC)
Bogdan Industrial and Investment Holding
LAZ
Lvovskyi Automobusnyi Zavod (LAZ)

UNITED ARAB EMIRATES
Transcontinental Industries

UNITED KINGDOM
Advanced Vehicle Builders Ltd
Alexander Dennis Limited (ADL)
Darwen Group Limited
Darwen LPD
Ford Motor Company Limited
Jubilee Automotive Group
LDV Group Limited
Leicester Carriage Builders
Mellor Coachcraft
Optare plc
Piaggio Ltd
Plaxton Holdings Limited
SA Automobiles Citroën (Citroën)
The Vehicle Application Centre Limited (TVAC)
The Wright Group
Trailertech Services Ltd (t/a Bluebird Vehicles Ltd)
Vauxhall

UNITED STATES
Advanced Vehicle Systems Inc (AVS)
Blue Bird Corporation
Cable Car Classics Inc
Cable Car Concepts Inc
Champion Bus Inc

Coachmen Industries Inc
Diamond Coach Corporation
Double K Inc
ElDorado National
Fisher Coachworks LLC
Freightliner Custom Chassis Corporation (FCCC)
Gillig Corporation
Glaval Bus
Goshen Coach Inc
IC Corporation
International Truck and Engine Corporation
Krystal Enterprises
Motor Coach Industries International (MCI)
North American Bus Industries Inc (NABI Inc)
Optima Bus Corporation
Spartan Chassis, Inc
Starcraft Bus
Thomas Built Buses Inc
TMC Group Inc
Turtle Top Inc
Workhorse Custom Chassis LLC
World Trans Inc

VENEZUELA
Carrocerías Andinas CA

Advanced Public Transport Systems BV (APTS)

PO Box 1015, NL-5700 MC Helmond, Netherlands
Tel: (+31 492) 56 20 13   Fax: (+31 492) 56 23 38
e-mail: apts.info@pdeautomotive.com
Web: www.apts-phileas.com

Street address

Steenovenweg 1, NL-5708 HN Helmond, Netherlands

Key personnel

General Manager: *Ruud Bouwman*
   e-mail: rbouwman@pdeautomotive.com
Marketing and Project Management: *Jos C Jansen*
   e-mail: josjansen@pdeautomotive.com

Background

Advanced Public Transport Systems BV (APTS) is owned by the VDL Groep (70 per cent), SIMAC (18 per cent) and BOM (12 per cent) and is part of VDL Bus and Coach BV.

Products

APTS has developed Phileas; a modular concept, low-floor, public transport vehicle. It is equipped with an automatic guidance system, from Frog Navigation Systems, using small magnets embedded in the road surface every 4 m, providing electronic lane assistance and precision docking. The vehicles can be driven in automatic, semi-automatic or manual mode.

The first generation Phileas has series hybrid electric propulsion, the generator of which is driven by a lightweight LPG engine and nickel metal hydride batteries; all wheels, except for those at the front, are driven by electric motors.

The second generation Phileas has parallel hybrid propulsion, supplied by GM Allison, and only the wheels of the rear axle are driven. Just

APTS Phileas guided bus   1194949

as with the first generation vehicles, all axles are steerable.

The second generation of the Phileas vehicles will be also be available as a trolley version for the Italian market.

The vehicle is available in two lengths, single- or double-articulated: 18 or 24 m.

Developments

In November 2005, a license and technology transfer agreement was signed between APTSystems and the Korea Railroad Research Institute (KRRI). With the transfer agreement KRRI can engineer, develop, test and produce a Korean version of the Phileas.

Contracts

The first order for 12 vehicles (11 single-articulated, 18 m and one double-articulated, 24 m) was received from the SRE (co-operation of the region of Eindhoven), with delivery starting at the beginning of 2004. The vehicles entered service in July 2004.

A second contract was signed in July 2005, for the supply of 12 Phileas 18 m vehicles to the Syndicat Mixte des Transport du Douaisis, northern France. The guidance system of the Phileas will be homologated as a rail vehicle.

Advanced Vehicle Builders Ltd

Upper Mantle Close, Clay Cross, Chesterfield, Derbyshire S45 9NU, UK
Tel: (+44 1246) 25 00 22   Fax: (+44 1246) 25 00 16
e-mail: info@minibus.co.uk
Web: www.minibus.co.uk

Key personnel

Managing Director: *Chris Parkin*

Background

Advanced Vehicle Builders Ltd have been manufacturing minibuses since 1976.

Range

Minibuses are based on base vehicles: Citroën Relay, Fiat Ducato, Ford Transit, Mercedes-Benz Sprinter, Nissan Interstar and Primastar, Peugeot Boxer, Renault Master and Trafic, Vauxhall Movano and Vivaro and Volkswagen LT and Transporter.

Contracts

In early 2004, Citroën announced an expanded range to the Relay minibus series, including

The Citroën Relay Advanced Xcessible wheelchair accessible minibus   0573270

the Relay 1100 × 12 (12-seater), Relay 1900 × 17 (17-seater) and the wheelchair accessible Relay

1800 Xcessible. These vehicles were developed in conjunction with Advanced Vehicle Builders Ltd.

Advanced Vehicle Systems Inc (AVS)

7801 Lee Highway, Chattanooga, Tennessee 37421, USA
Tel: (+1 423) 821 31 46   Fax: (+1 423) 821 00 42
e-mail: media@avsbus.com
Web: www.avsbus.com

Key personnel

Chairman: *L Joe Ferguson*
Presidents: *Rick Hitchcock*

Products

AVS22 Hybrid Electric Bus: Medium-duty, low-floor shuttle bus, designed for all shuttle-type

services where top speed requirements are less than 45 mph and the average route speed is less than 18 mph. Up to 20 seated passengers, 11 standees and one wheelchair location. The vehicle has ranges in excess of 250 miles under normal conditions and will operate on CNG, standard or bio-diesel, LNG or LPG. The bus is ultra-low emission during hybrid operation and zero emission when operating in pure electric mode.

AVS22 Electric Bus: Designed for where top speeds do not exceed 40 mph and the average route speeds are between 8 and 15 mph. Accommodates up to 20 seated passengers, 11 standees and one wheelchair location. The vehicle is capable of 65+ miles of range on a

single charge under normal conditions, with air conditioning. The vehicle is most suited to flat, downtown shuttle operations. The bus may be equipped with an all-electric, climate control system. The AVS22 Electric is a zero-emission vehicle.

AVS32 and AVS38 Hybrid Electric Buses: Low-floor transit buses designed for heavy-duty operations with limited high-speed requirements. The vehicles are capable of 55+ mph speeds in standard configuration, for short periods of time and designed for average route speeds of less than 20 mph. Accommodate 31 and 39 seated passengers, with nine and 13 standees respectively. Both buses meet ADA specifications utilising a pneumatic kneeling system with telescoping wheelchair ramps. AVS bus emissions are rated ultra-low. AVS hybrid buses meet or exceed all current CARB emission requirements for heavy truck and buses.

Contracts
Chattanooga is running a fleet of 17 AVS buses and the hybrid electric is the most advanced in the fleet. CARTA uses them on its downtown

shuttle. Tempe, Arizona, has ordered 31 hybrids with Capstone MicroTurbines, joining an existing fleet of three.

Agrale SA

BR 116, km 145 No 15104, CEP 95059-520, Caxias do Sul – RS, Brazil
Tel: (+55 54) 238 80 00   Fax: (+55 54) 229 22 90
Web: www.agrale.com.br

Key personnel
President: *Francisco Stedile*
Director, Marketing: *Flávio Crosa*

Products
Front engine chassis.

Alexander Dennis Limited (ADL)

Dennis Way, Guildford, Surrey, GU1 1AF, UK
Tel: (+44 1483) 57 12 71   Fax: (+ 44 1483) 30 16 97
Web: www.alexander-dennis.com

Key personnel
Chief Executive Officer: *Colin Robertson*
Chief Operating Officer: *Brian Davidson*
Director of Corporate Affairs: *Bill Simpson*
    Staff: 1,400 (estimate)

Other offices/subsidiaries
Alexander Dennis Inc
31566 Railroad Canyon Road #342, Canyon Lake, CA 92587-9446, US
Tel: (+1 951) 244 94 29   Fax: (+1 951) 755 03 18

Alexander Dennis (Far East) Ltd
3rd Floor CAC Tower, 165 Hoi Bun Road, Kwun Tong, Kowloon Hong Kong
Tel: (+ 852) 27 57 80 57   Fax: (+ 852) 27 57 77 66

Background
Alexander Dennis Limited (ADL) was established in May 2004, when a consortium of business entrepreneurs, led by Noble Grossart (merchant bankers) and supported by the Bank of Scotland, acquired the major part of the bus manufacturing operations previously, held by TransBus International.

Current situation
The company's principal manufacturing centres are in Guildford, Surrey, UK (chassis production) and Falkirk, Stirlingshire, UK (body production). Alexander Dennis Limited is a market leader in the UK bus sector, with an installed fleet of around 70,000 vehicles. It supplies all of the UK's major bus operators and is the market leader in Hong Kong where it has an established sales and after-market operation.
    Plaxton Holdings is part of the ADL group (please see separate entry in *Jane's Urban Transport Systems*).

Products
Alexander Dennis produces bus chassis and body options, as well as integrated single and double deck vehicles for the UK, Far East and North America.

Range
Enviro400: 10.2 m or 10.9 m double-deck bus available as a fully integrated vehicle on an ADL chassis, or as a body solution for alternative chassis manufacturers. The engine is a 6.7 l Cummins ISB6.7E5 6 cylinder turbocharged and intercooled diesel engine certified to Euro 5 emission standards, driving through a choice of Voith D854.5E 4-speed or ZF 6HP1203B 6-speed automatic gearbox, both fitted with integral retarders and interlocks. Full air suspension is mounted within chassis frame floor contours eliminating component intrusion in passenger saloon areas. Fast kneel facility on front suspension, reduces height typically from 325 mm to 245 mm.
    The gross plated weight is 17,800 kg. The structure is jig-built from aluminium extrusions and stress panel. Dissimilar metals are treated with dielectric paint and the completed vehicle is

Alexander Dennis Ltd (ADL) Enviro400H hybrid double-deck bus   1375548

Alexander Dennis Ltd (ADL) Enviro400 double-deck bus promoting the London Olympics   1375549

undersealed upon build completion. Aluminium exterior panels are used, butt jointed and bonded to the frame. The side skirt panels are easily detachable for speedy replacement. The roof is aluminium sheet and bonded to the frame. The front and rear domes and glazing surrounds are GRP mouldings. The vehicle is available with bonded or gasket glazing with single piece windscreens. Hopper windows, tinted glass and heated windscreens are available.
    The entrance is fitted with a 1,200 mm wide twin leaf glider door with active seals to improve sealing. The two-door variant has a twin leaf sliding plug door providing a clear exit platform.
    The standard vehicle is supplied with blown air heating in both saloons with forced air ventilation from the front dash area in the upper saloon. Integrated driver's air conditioning

system supplies cool or warm air directly to the driver. Upper saloon air chill system can be fitted providing cool air via roof ducting over the full length of the saloon. The optional systems can be supplied independently or together as a fully integrated heating and ventilation system controlled to preset vehicle temperatures by the vehicle system.
Enviro400H: Hybrid double-deck bus with lithium ion batteries that do not need mains recharging during their extended life cycle. Available as 10.1 m (two door) with 37 seated on the upper deck and 26 or 24 plus one wheelchair on the lower deck. The 10.8 m (two door) version seats 30 or 28 plus one wheelchair on the lower deck and 41 on the upper deck. The 10.8 m version (single door) seats 32 plus one wheelchair on the lower deck and 41 on the upper deck.

The gross plated weight for both versions is 17,800 kg. As with the Enviro400 the structure is jig built from aluminium extrusions.

The engine is a 4.5 l Cummins ISBe4 4 cylinder turbocharged and intercooled, certified to Euro 4 emission levels. The BAE Systems HybriDrive hybrid driveline incorporates a 120 kW compact permanent magnet generator and 185 kW compact oil cooled motor. The storage system uses lithium Ion nano-phosphate technology.

Enviro 200: Low-floor midibus powered by Euro 5 Cummins ISBe intercooled diesel engine rated at 103 kW and certified to Euro 5 emission standards using Selective Catalytic Reduction (SCR). It drives through an Allison 2100 5-speed automatic transmission. It has a Telma F5750 electromagnetic retarder, axle mounted and all-round disc brakes, enhanced suspension system and multiplexed wiring.

Suspension is full air with two 250 mm air springs for front and rear axles. Location by trailing taper leaf springs and panhard rod. Two double acting dampers front and rear. Front kneel as standard. The frame is all welded construction of channel and box section, designed for direct flooring and full integration with the body. The floor forward of the rear axle is lowered to provide a single step entry.

The cooling system features improved access for maintenance through new design of a parallel cooling pack. The radiator and intercooler are mounted side by side at the rear right-hand side, allowing access from the side of the vehicle. The hydraulic driven fan is controlled by the engine management system to maintain maximum overall efficiency.

It is available is 8.9 m, 9.1 m, 9.3 m, 9.5 m, 10.2 m, 10.4 m, 10.7 m, 10.9 m and 11.3 m lengths with an overall width of 2,440 mm.

The body work is a jig-built structure in extruded aluminium section with steel structures to floor and tress beams in lower saloon and wheel arch areas. Steel structures are welded assemblies in Cr12. Aluminium structures are assembled with magnagrip and magnalock rivets to provide full structural integrity. Underseal treatment is given on completion. Aluminium panels are used with easily removed side skirts for speedy repair. The front/rear moulded panels are in sections for ease of repair and cost effectiveness.

Bonded or gasket glazing can be specified, plain or tinted glass, single or double glazed. Doors are air operated with active seals and complying with UK DDA disability requirements. The first step is 320 mm lowering to 240 mm with the kneel/squat facility. Two door vehicles are available with various middle door options.

Heating is provided by convector skirting heaters fitted to both sides of the body in the forward saloon area and on one side in the rear. A separate heavy-duty heater provides cab heating, windscreen demisting and additional heat in the entrance area. The body is insulated with fire-retardent polystyrene sheet. Full or partial air conditioning is available as an option.

Enviro 200H: This is an 8.9 m, 10.2 m or 10.7 m single- or two-door hybrid bus seating 29 or 26 plus one wheelchair. The hybrid technology reduces fuel consumption and greenhouse gas emissions by over 30 per cent. The advanced technology derives from a partnership between Alexander Dennis Limited and BAE Systems. The Enviro200H's lithium ion batteries do not need mains recharging during their extended life cycle. The engine is a Cummins ISBe 4 5.5 l cylinder turbocharged and intercooled diesel engine certified to Euro 5 emission levels. The TB200 hybrid driveline incorporates a 200 kW compact permanent magnet generator with integrated starter. The storage system uses lithium Ion nano-phosphate technology. The gross plated weight is 12,580 kg.

Enviro300: Low-floor city single-deck bus, 12 m to 12.5 m long. The 6.7 l engine is a Cummins ISBe 6 cylinder turbocharged and intercooled, certified to Euro 5 emission standards. It is rated at 166 kW and drives through a ZF 6HP504C 6-speed overdrive automatic gearbox. All fitted with integral retarders. Voith DIWA D854.5

Alexander Dennis Ltd (ADL) Enviro200H hybrid single-deck bus 1375546

Alexander Dennis Ltd (ADL) Enviro300 in Stagecoach livery 1375547

4-speed automatic and Allison T280 5-speed automatic are options.

Suspension is full air with two 254 mm air springs for front and rear axles. Front kneel as standard (70 mm).

The frame is all welded construction of channel and box section, designed for direct flooring and full integration with the body. The floor forward of the rear axle is lowered to provide a single step entry. Full air disc brakes.

The gross plated weight is 14,440 kg.

The body is jig-built in extruded aluminium section with steel structures to floor and tress beams in lower saloon and wheel arch areas. Aluminium exterior panels are used with easily removed side skirts for speedy repair. Gasket glazing is standard, with the option of bonded glass – plain or tinted, single or double glazed. All main glass apertures along the side of the bus are the same size, to simplify replacements. There is a stepless entry onto a sloping, low main floor with single step to raised seating area. Full length convector skirting heating is fitted.

Enviro500: low-floor high-capacity three-axle double-deck bus, 11.3 m or 12 m in length. The two door 11.3 m version for Hong Kong seats 51 on the upper deck and 26 plus one wheelchair on the lower deck. The 12.0 m single door version for Hong Kong seats 31 plus one wheelchair on the lower deck and 55 on the upper deck.

The 12.1 m single door version for the UK seats 31 or 29 plus one wheelchair on the lower deck with 53 on the upper deck. Alternative seating and staircase layouts available which affect seating capacity are available. Space for 27 standing passengers.

It has an 8.9 l Cummins ISL, 6 cylinder turbocharged intercooled diesel engine, rated at 246 kW and certified to Euro 4 emission standard. There is a choice of ZF 6HP 602 6-speed automatic or Voith D864.5 4-speed automatic, both fitted with integral retarders. Denso full air conditioning can be fitted in upper and lower decks. Body construction in 3CR12 (or equivalent) stainless steel underfame structure fully integrated with chassis frame. Extruded aluminium body frame with main exterior body panels in aluminium. Flush direct bonded glazing. Single step low floor entry with 322 mm (250 mm when knelt). Manual one-piece entry ramp. Straight forward ascending staircase with enhanced safety features. Gross plated weight 24,000 kg.

Production

ADL reports that its order book is in excess of GBP200 million for 2009. This follows a period in which the manufacturer has already increased year-on-year turnover from GBP200 million to GBP300 million and extended its manufacturing capacity by 50 per cent.

Developments

ADL is now building buses in China, working with WZL in Shenzhan, a move that protects its market position in Hong Kong. Similarly, ADL has entered into a collaboration deal in the US and will shortly be assembling buses in California. This will give it full 'Buy America' compliance and enable it to tender for significant federal-funded projects in North America.

In 2008, ADL unveiled four new-generation vehicles, including single and double deck hybrid buses (powered by a combination of diesel-electric) that reduce fuel consumption and greenhouse gas emissions by over 30 per cent.

The new technology was developed jointly by ADL and BAE Systems and 17 vehicles, collectively costing GBP5 million, were due go into operation in London in 2009 with Metroline, East Thames, London General and Transdev. ADL says that they deliver a 30 per cent fuel saving and reduce greenhouse gas emissions by a similar figure. The batteries in this system do not need mains recharging. The system is totally regenerative.

Alongside its hybrid vehicles, ADL introduced a new version of its double-deck Enviro400 in 2008. It will now be available with new technical features, including a new driveline, offside cooling pack and improved service access. It also introduces Euro 5 engine technology and a new-look multiplex binnacle that is set to become standard across all ADL bus products.

Contracts

17 hybrid buses, collectively costing GBP5 million, are due go into operation in London in 2009 with Metroline, East Thames, London General and Transdev. Further orders for more than 30 hybrid buses have been received for delivery in 2009 and early 2010.

Alfa Busz Kft

8000 Székesfehérvár, Repülőtér HRSZ 7609/4, Hungary
Tel: (+36 622) 54 66 10   Fax: (+36 622) 54 66 14
e-mail: alfabusz@alfabusz.hu
Web: www.alfabusz.hu

Key personnel
President: *Tibor Mogyorossy*
   Staff: Not currently available

Current situation
Manufacturer of urban and suburban/intercity buses and coaches.

The company's main partner is Volvo Bus Corporation, on whose chassis vehicles are built.

Range
Alfa Regio: Suburban/intercity bus.
Alfa Regio LE: Suburban/intercity bus.
Alfa Localo: Urban low-floor bus. Trolleybus version available.

Alfa Urbano: Suburban/intercity bus.
Alfa Inter Regio GT: Coach.

Recent contracts
Volvo Bus Corporation has received an order from Hungary, which includes 55 Volvo B12B/BLE chassis and 100 Volvo B9L chassis. The bodies for these chassis will be provided by Alfa Busz. Deliveries will be made in late 2008 and early 2009.

AMO ZIL

23 Avtozavodskaya Street, 115280 Moscow, Russian Federation
Tel: (+7 095) 277 95 00
Fax: (+7 095) 274 61 71
Web: www.amo-zil.ru

Key personnel
General Director of the Management Company:
   Konstantin Victorovich Laptev
Executive Director: *Igor Vjacheslavovich Printsev*
Chief Engineer: *Genadij Alekseevich Yarkov*
Head of International and Public Relations Department (Acting): *Uma Jakubovna Abulova*

Foreign trade firm
Director FTF 'ZIL Export': *Irina Igorevna Gorshkova*

Background
AMO ZIL is one of Russia's largest truck manufacturers, though it is perhaps best known in Western countries for its limousines. Buses on ZIL chassis are produced in Moscow.

The company is currently undergoing restructuring.

Products
Truck chassis suitable for bus bodywork.

Range
ZIL-325000: City bus, available in two versions – 19+1 and 21+1 seats.
ZIL-325010: City bus seating 15+1 with a capacity of 22 passengers.
ZIL-32500R 'De Luxe': City bus seating 13+1 passengers.

Other versions
The company also produces a range of special purpose vehicles and trucks.

AMO ZIL ZIL-32500R 'De Luxe' city bus. Air conditioning is available as an option   0585172

Anadolu Isuzu Otomotiv Sanayi ve Ticaret AŞ (Anadolu)

Yedipınarlar Mevkii Şekerpınar Köyü, Gebze TR-41400 Kocaeli, Turkey
Tel: (+90 262) 658 88 43; 44
Fax: (+90 262) 658 88 42
e-mail: efe.yazici@isuzu.com.tr
   info.pazarlama@isuzu.com.tr (Marketing)
Web: www.isuzu.com.tr

Key personnel
General Manager: *Omer Lutfu Ablay*

Background
Anadolu Isuzu has been manufacturing (and in the case of minibuses, designing) Isuzu vehicles since 1984. The company has authorised distributors in Algeria, Azerbaijan, Bosnia, Bulgaria, Croatia, Czech Republic, Estonia, France, Germany, Greece, Hungary, Italy, Latvia, Lithuania, Macedonia, Montenegro, Poland, Romania, Serbia, Slovakia and Slovenia.

Products
Midibuses and commercial vehicles, built under licence agreement with Isuzu Motors Ltd.

Range
Turquoise (190): 26-seat midibus, *Turquoise (175)* 31-seat midibus.

Roybus: 27-seat midibus.
Classic: 27-seat midibus suitable for shuttle service.

Urban: Municipal/urban buses. *Urban 50* – seats 20+1 with 30 standees, *Urban 27* – seats 27+1 with 10 standees and *Urban 22* – seats 22+1 with 21 standees.

Isuzu Turquoise 190 midibus/coach   1325356

Andecar SA

Poligono Industrial De Las Quemadas S/N,
Parcela 92, E-14014 Córdoba, Spain
Tel: (+34 957) 32 56 93
Fax: (+34 957) 32 56 91
e-mail: frandecar@infonegocio.com

Key personnel
President: *Baldomero Caceres Cubero*
Commercial Department: *José Maestre*

Products
Coach bodies.

Range
Viana: 12 m luxury coach available with
Iveco, MAN and Mercedes-Benz mechanical
components.

Production
Annual production is 85 vehicles.

Antonov Aeronautical Scientific & Technical Complex (Antonov ASTC)

Land Transit System Division
1 Tupolev Street, 03062 Kyiv, Ukraine
Tel: (+38 44) 454 31 49   Fax: (+38 44) 400 81 44
e-mail: info@antonov.com
Web: www.anatanov.com

Key personnel
Deputy Main Designer/Chief of Division:
    Alexander I Rabichev
Other key personnel: *Viktor A Matsak*
    Alexander I Onufrienko
    Kostyantyn K Borovskiy

Current situation
Antonov Aeronautical Scientific & Technical
Complex (Antonov ASTC) is a state-owned
company. The company has been engaged in the
production of trolleybuses since 1990, utilising
technologies acquired during the company's
aviation production.

Since 1990, four trolleybus models have been
designed, manufactured and certified: K12.01,
K12.03, K12.05 (articulated) and K12.04.

More than 100 trolleybuses with the 'Kyivskiy'
brand are operating in cities including Kyiv,
Cherkassy and Simferopol.

The Kyivskiy trolleybuses are manufactured
using corrosion-resistant aluminium alloys
and polymer composite materials. Electrical
equipment is made by Skoda and axles by Raba.

Trolleybuses are produced at the AVIANT Kyiv
Aviation Plant.

Antonov Type K12.04 trolleybus at the Taras Shevchenko National University, Kyiv   1330378

Antonov Type K12.01 trolleybus
1330379

Ashok Leyland Limited

Registered office
1 Sardar Patel Road, Guindy, Chennai 32, India
Tel: (+91 44) 22 20 60 00
Fax: (+91 44) 22 20 60 01
Web: www.ashokleyland.com

Key personnel
Chairman: *R J Shahaney*
Managing Director: *R Seshasayee*
Chief Operating Officer & Director: *Vinod
    K Dasari*
Chief Financial Officer: *K Sridharan*
Executive Director, Construction & Allied
    Businesses: *J N Amrolia*
Executive Director, HR: *Shekar Arora*
Executive Director, Project Co-ordination:
    S Balasubramanian
Executive Director, Strategic Sourcing: *Anup
    Bhat*
Executive Director, Project Planning: *A K Jain*
Executive Director, International Operations:
    Rajinder Malham
Executive Director, Product Development: *R R G
    Menon*
Executive Director, Marketing: *Rajive Saharia*

Executive Director, Manufacturing: *B M
    Udayashankar*
Chief Programme Mentor: *M Nataraj*
Special Director, Business Planning: *Sundaram
    Parthasarathi*
General Manager, Corporate Communications:
    Thomas T Abraham
    e-mail: tta@ashokleyland.com

Other offices
Marketing Office
As above.
Executive Director, Marketing: *Arun Pande*

Main works
Ennore
Ennore, Chennai 600 057, India
Tel: (+91 44) 25 75 10 01
Fax: (+91 44) 25 75 17 98
Plant Director: *M Murugappan*

Alwar
Plot No Spl. 298, Matsya Industrial Area, Alwar
301 030 (Rajasthan), India
Tel: (+91 144) 288 14 25
Fax: (+91 144) 288 13 55
General Manager: *A K Chopra*

Bhandara
Plot No 1, MIDC Industrial Area, Village Gadegaon,
Sakoli Taluk, Bhandara 441 904 (Maharashtra),
India
Tel: (+91 718) 27 44 33
Fax: (+91 718) 27 44 31
General Manager: *A K Chatterjee*

Hosur (Unit I)
175 Hosur Industrial Complex, Hosur 635 126,
India
Tel: (+91 43 44) 40 70 00
Fax: (+91 43 44) 27 60 67
Plant Director: *G Soundara Rajan*

Hosur (Unit II) and Cab Panel Press Shop
77 Electronic Complex, Perandapalli Village,
Hosur 635 109, India
Tel: (+91 43 44) 26 00 01
Fax: (+91 43 44) 26 00 48
Plant Director: *P Harihar*

Background
Ashok Motors was established in 1948 to
assemble Austin cars. In 1995, with equity
participation from Leyland Motors, it switched
to commercial vehicle production and became

Ashok Leyland. In 1987, majority shareholding was taken over by a Hinduja Group-Iveco joint venture.

ISO 9002 certification was awarded in 1993, with ISO 9001 in 1994, QS 9000 in 1998 and ISO 14001 for all vehicle manufacturing in 2002. In 2006, the company was awarded the TS 16949 Corporate Certification for all its manufacturing units.

The company's associate companies include IRIZAR-TVS (a joint venture between Ashok Leyland, TVS & Sons Ltd and IRIZAR for the manufacture of high-end luxury buses), AVIA Ashok Leyland Motors in Prague, Czech Republic, Automotive Coaches and Components Limited and Ashok Leyland Nissan (for the manufacture of Light Commercial Vehicles by 2010).

Products

The passenger vehicle range includes single-deck and articulated vehicles, with seating ranging from 18 to 80 passengers. Some of the premium models include the rear engine bus, models with air suspension, low-floor buses for city operations and the double-decker and vestibule buses, for which the company is the only source in India.

Range

LCV Range (7 ton)

Stag: 'H' series: 84 Kw, 4-cylinder in-line diesel engine conforming to EURO 2 and EURO 3 emission norms available in 3,600 mm, 3,900 mm and 4,200 mm wheelbase and overall length starting from 7 m to 8 m with a seating capacity of 30–36 passengers. Suitable for intra-city travel, for schools and transport of staff of institutions.

Stag CNG: 4,200 mm wheelbase powered by 'H' series 58 Kw 4-cylinder in-line engine conforming to EURO 3, having CNG cylinder capacity of 375 litres with an overall length up to 8 m with capacity of 30–36 seats.

ICV Range (11- 13 ton)

Lynx: Powered by the H-Series 84 Kw diesel engine conforming to EURO 2 and EURO 3 emission norms available in 3,900 mm and 4,200 mm wheelbase and overall length starting from 7 m to 8 m with seating capacity of 32–45 passengers.

Lynx CNG (13 ton): Powered by 'H' series 58 Kw H series 4-cylinder in-line engine conforming to EURO 3 in 4,900 mm wheelbase with an overall length of 9 m having a cylinder capacity of 545 litres with a seating capacity of 47.

MDV Range

Viking: 9 m length with seating capacity of up to 45; 10.5 m length with seating capacity of up to 57; 11 m length with seating capacity of up to 59.

Cheetah: 10 m length with seating capacity of up to 48; 10.5 m length with seating capacity of up to 57; 12 m length with seating capacity of up to 72.

12 m bus: With a seating capacity of up to 72 passengers.

Front engine – Semi Low Floor (SLF) bus (entry + 2 steps): Powered by 'H' series diesel 123 Kw in-line engine conforming to EURO 3 emission norms. Suitable for intra-city/institutions applications; rubber- end suspension at the front and air suspension at the rear with an option of engine-driven AC. Available in 11 m overall length with a seating capacity of 45 seats, depending upon the seating layout.

Rear engine – Semi Low Floor (SLF) (635 mm) bus (entry + 1 step): Overall length of 12 m with air suspension, it comes with an option of diesel- and CNG-powered engines conforming to EURO 3 emission norms. The Euro 2 version is powered by the 'H' series 122 Kw 6-cylinder diesel engine and conforms to EURO 3 norms; it is powered by 123 Kw 6-cylinder diesel engine. Suitable for intra-city application with seating capacity of 40–44 passengers. The CNG version is also available, conforming to EURO 3 norms powered by 145 Kw engine with engine-driven AC option, with seating capacity of 40–44 passengers.

Ultra Low Entry – 390 mm (stepless entry): Fully built bus with an overall length of 12 m with full air suspension, AC and Non AC, CNG-powered engine conforming to EURO 3 emission norms with a seating capacity of 45–52. The AC version is powered by the Cummins 260 hp engine, while the Non-AC version is powered by the 230 hp engine. Roof-mounted CNG cylinders have a capacity of 720 litres.

Luxura: This 12 m coach is powered by the J-Series 6-cylinder diesel 260 hp engine with direct drive AC conforming to EURO 2 norms, full air suspension, overdrive gear box with electromagnetic retarder. The coach has 45 reclining seats and is suitable for long distance inter-city operations.

Special Purpose Range

Vestibule Bus: Articulated bus with a front engine; powered by the 'H' Series 6-cylinder 123 Kw diesel engine conforming to EURO 3 norms, has unique turning circle advantage which is almost equivalent to that of a regular bus 12 m bus. The 16 m long bus

has a seating capacity of 80 passengers and 25 standees and is suitable for intra-city applications.

The CNG version of the Vestibule Bus – the *MEGA BUS* – is powered by 145 Kw Cummins engine conforming to EURO 3 norms, roof-mounted CNG cylinders having 880 litres capacity. The tractor portion of the bus has a floor height of 1,050 mm and the trailer portion has a floor height of 400 mm, with a retractable ramp for wheelchair roll in and roll out.

AVION – ULE: Fully built 11 m bus, fully air-conditioned, stepless low floor with a uniform floor of 340 mm. It has two entrances of 1,200 mm width on either side that enables quick clearance of passengers at arrival and departure terminals. The coach can accommodate 55-60 passengers. Powered by the 'H' series, 88 Kw diesel engine conforming to EURO 3 norms, mounted in front with an automatic transmission and air suspension.

Double Decker: 8 m long, suitable for intra-city operations. Seating capacity is 82 plus 25 standees with floor height of 865 mm. The bus is powered by the 'H'-Series 123 Kw 6-cylinder diesel engine conforming to EURO 3 norms.

Production

Current installed annual capacity is 84,000 vehicles, with projected production of 184,000 vehicles by 2011–2012.

Developments

The company is setting up an integrated, state-of-the-art manufacturing unit at a greenfield site in Uttarakhand (North-east India), scheduled to start production in Q1 2009. Overseas, an integrated chassis and bus assembly plant is being planned in the Middle East at Ras al Khaimah, which will start production of 2,000 buses annually.

The company now owns Prague- (Czech Republic) based AVIA Ashok Leyland Motors. Ashok Leyland has also acquired Defiance Testing & Engineering, Detroit, a testing partner for the American automotive industry for more than two decades.

Ashok Leyland is entering the high-growth Light Commercial Vehicle segment in partnership with Nissan Motor Company, with the first products scheduled to be launched by 2010.

A 50:50 Joint Venture, forged with Continental AG, is for the design, development and adaptation of 'infotronic' products and services for the transportation sector.

Autosan SA

ul Lipińskiego 109, 38-500 Sanok, Poland
Tel: (+48 13) 465 01 26 (Polish), 04 79 (English), 04 74 (German/English)
Fax: (+48 13) 465 04 00
e-mail: sekretariat@autosan.pl
Web: www.autosan.pl

Key personnel

Chairman: *Wieslaw Wyzycki*
Deputy Chairmen: *Dr Marek Zmarz*
Manufacturing and Procurement Manager: *Zygmunt Suski*
Finance Director: *Maciej Brygidyn*

Key personnel (Bus Sales)

Polskie Austobusy Sp zoo (see separate entry)
Chairman: *Dr Franciszek Gaik*
1st Deputy Chairman: Roman Majewski

Background

The Autosan SA factory was established in 1832 and previously known as Sanocka Fabryka Autobusów (SFA Autosan). Autosan is part of the Zasada Group.

Products

Buses and coaches for urban, suburban, intercity and tourist operations. Chassis and bodies for rail buses and electric trains.

Range

Complete vehicles (mainly CBU), Partly Knocked Down (PKD) and Semi Knocked Down (SKD) buses and bodies.

A12.13C 'Eurolider': 13.2 m high-deck long-distance bus, seating 53 with a wheelchair, 51 and a wheelchair or 49 and a wheelchair and a toilet or 59 seats only.

A1112T 'Ramzes': 12 m high-deck tourist coach, seating 47 + guide or 45 + guide + toilet.

A1012T 'Lider': 12 m intercity bus, seats 51.

A1012T 'Lider': 12 m suburban bus, seats 45 + platform, or 49.

A1012T RHD 'Eagle': 12 m school bus with 67 or 70 seats (3+2 layout) or 55 (2+2) seats for intercity operation (UK, Ireland & Malta markets).

A1010T 'Lider 2': 10.8 m suburban bus, seats 43 plus 31 standing, optional lower floor.

A1010T 'Lider 3': 10.8 m intercity bus, capacity 43 seated (+1) plus 13 standing or 39 seated (+1) plus 13 standing.

A0909L 'Tramp': 9.3 m intercity bus (capacity 39/17), suburban bus (capacity 25/45) and school bus *A0909L 'Smyk'.*

A0808T 'Gemini': 8.5 m intercity/tourist minibus, capacity 29 (+1), 33/10 or 33/5.

A0808M 'Sancity': 8.5 m city minibus, low-entry, capacity 20–22 seated plus space for a wheelchair.

H7-10 'Solina': 7.8 m intercity minibus, capacity 28/7.

A8V 'Wetlina': 7.8 m tourist/intercity minibus, capacity 26 (front engine).

H7-20 'Solina': 7.8 m city minibus, capacity 18 seated/32 standing. Optional low rear platform for a wheelchair, with collapsible seats.

The company also produces specialised vehicles based on trucks or pickups, trailers, also carries out repairs on older or damaged vehicles.

For images of buses, please see separate entry for *Polskie Autobusy Sp z.o.o.*

Production

Production in 2006 was 310 buses (of which, 78 for export) plus 4 rail buses.

Auwärter Omnibusse-Fahrzeugbau GmbH (EA)

Postfach 1214, D-71141, Steinenbronn b. Stuttgart, Germany
Tel: (+49 7157) 40 81
Fax: (+49 7157) 93 90
e-mail: info@auwaerter.de,
  marketing@auwaerter.de
Web: www.auwaerter.de

Street address
Industriegebiet Kringstrasse 2, D71144, Steinenbronn b. Stuttgart, Germany
Managing Directors: *Kurt Pucher, Harald Rath*
Sales Director: *Markus Nothelfer*
Purchasing Manager: *Harald Magerl*
Technical Director: *Jürgen Schöllhammer*

Products
Mini- and midibus bodies, also full-sized coach bodywork.

Range
Includes tourist coaches, city buses and minibuses and accessible vehicles from 10 to 38 seats.

Coaches
Clubstar Atego 1223/42: Touring bus on Mercedes-Benz chassis with Euro-3 engine seating 26–38.
Clubstar MAN 14.280: Touring coach on MAN 14.280 HOCL chassis with Euro-3 engine seating 33–38.

City bus
Teamstar 818/48 City: Low-floor city bus on Mercedes-Benz chassis with a Euro-4 engine and new Allison automatic gearbox, seating 24 with approximately 16 standing.

Minibuses
Super Sprinter MB 416D: Minibus on Mercedes-Benz chassis with Euro-4 engine and seating 16–19 passengers.
Super Sprinter MB 616: Minibus on Mercedes-benz chassis MB 616 CDI, Euro-3 engine and seating 19 to 21 +1 +1. Also available with rear low-floor platform, 13 seats plus 4 'flap' seats with electrical or hand-operated ramp for wheelchairs and baby carriages.
Economy MB 815 D: Minibus on Mercedes-Benz chassis with Euro-4 engine and seating 20–23 passengers.
Teamster 818 D 42: Minibus on Mercedes-Benz chassis, Euro-4 engine and seating 26–31 passengers.

Accessible buses
Super Sprinter Handicap: Low-floor minibuses available in three versions: ***Super Sprinter 416 CDI,*** with low-floor platform at the front, ***Sprinter Light Handicap 416*** and ***Super Sprinter MB 616 CDI*** with low-platform lift at rear.
Teamstar Handicap 818 D: City bus on Mercedes-Benz 818 chassis, accommodating a maximum of two wheelchairs.
Teamster City MB815/818: Coach accommodating 8 to 10 wheelchairs with combinations of 26 to 31 seats and electric lift to side.
Clubstar Handicap 1223/1228: Coach with combination of a maximum of nine wheelchairs with 26–38 seats and electric lift at side.

EA Teamstar City bus   1172305

EA Super Sprinter MB 616 CDI *with low-floor platform at rear*   1135712

EA Clubstar MAN coach   1172304

Developments
In February 2005, the company Ernst Auwärter went into insolvency. From 1 September 2005, the Austrian group Pucher, Linz took over the activities of the company. The company has been renamed Auwärter Omnibusse-Fahrzeugbau GmbH (EA).

In 2006, at the IAA exhibition, new vehicles were presented; the ***Teamstar MB 818/Euro-4***, in city and tourist versions, and the ***Sprinter 518 Euro-4***.

Production
Previously 210 vehicles annually. Current production figures are not yet known, as the new company only started in September 2005.

For details of the latest updates to *Jane's Urban Transport Systems* online and to discover the additional information available exclusively to online subscribers please visit
juts.janes.com

Banbros Limited

PO Box 76511-00508, Main Mombasa Road, Mavoko, Nairobi, Kenya
Tel: (+254 20) 82 19 93/4　Fax: (+254 20) 82 19 95
e-mail: banbros@banbros.co.ke

Key personnel
Managing Director: *M S Bansal*
General Manager: *C S Suri*

Products
Bus and coach bodywork, including city buses, express buses and coaches.

Banbros coach　　　　　　　1323737

Banbros coach　　　　　　　1342660

Banbros city midibus　　　　1342659

Banbros coach　　　　　　　1342662

Berliet Maroc SA

BP 2624, Rte de Rabat, Ain Sebaa, Casablanca, Morocco
Tel: (+212 22) 73 32 90　Fax: (+212 22) 73 10 42

Key personnel
Chairman, Managing Director and Chief Executive
　Officer: *Nabil Zniber*

Administrative and Financial Director: *Benoit Coudeville*
Staff: Not currently available

Background
Assembly operations for vehicles supplied to CKD. The company is part-owned by Volvo and partly by local private interests including investment and insurance companies.

Products
Bus chassis: ***FRH 340*** intercity coach.

Beulas SA

C. Riera Xica s/n, E-17401 Arbúcies (Girona), Spain
Tel: (+34 972) 86 01 00, 86 04 00
Fax: (+34 972) 86 12 86, 16 26 19
e-mail: info@beulas.net
　beulas@beulas.net
Web: www.beulas.net

Key personnel
Managing Director: *Joaquin Beulas Julia*
Administration Director: *T Pascual de Beulas*
Commercial Director: *R B Pascual*
Financial Director: *Dolors Beulas Pascual*
　Staff: 200

Background
This family company, which was established in 1934, builds a range of interurban and luxury coach models from 8.75 to 15 m long and in three overall heights.

Products
Mainly coaches on all brands of chassis.

Range
Aura: High-deck coach, available in lengths of 12, 13.7 and 15 m, width 2.55 m, height 3.625 m. Seat 55, 63 or 71 (+1+1) passengers.
Cygnus: High-deck coach, in 12, 12.72, 13.7 and 15 m versions, width 2.55 m, height 3.425 m. Seat 55, 59, 63 or 71 (+1+1) passengers.

Eurostar: High-deck coach available in three lengths: 12, 13.7 and 15 m, width 2.55 m, height 3.625 m. Seat 55, 63 or 71 (+1+1) passengers.
Stergo: High-deck coach available in 12, 12.72, 13.7 and 15 m versions, width 2.55 m, height 3.425 m. Seat 55, 59, 63 or 71 (+1+1) passengers.
Midi Star: High-deck midibus available in lengths of 8.75, 8.83, 9.57, 9.8 and 10.3 m lengths, width 2.55 m, height 3.225 m. Seat 35, 39, or 43 (+1+1) passengers.

Production
Annual production is approximately 250 vehicles.

Blue Bird Corporation

Bluebird Commercial Bus & Coach
402 Blue Bird Boulevard, PO Box 937, Fort Valley,
Georgia 31030, US
Tel: (+1 800) 486 71 22
Fax: (+1 478) 822 24 59
e-mail: info@blue-bird.com
Web: www.blue-bird.com,
www.bluebirdcoachworks.com

Key personnel
President and Chief Executive Officer: *Jeffry
D Bust*
Vice-President and General Manager, Commercial
Bus Division: *Barry Hines*
Vice-President and General Manager, Coach &
RV Division: *Wayne Joseph*
Vice-President of Quality and Business
Improvement: *Mike Beck*
Director of Sales and Marketing, Commercial
Bus Division: *Buddy Cox*
Staff: Approximately 3,000 worldwide

Works
Assembly operations in Monterrey (Mexico),
Venezuela and Saudi Arabia

Overseas associate
Canadian Blue Bird
Brantford, Ontario

Background
Originally founded in 1927, Blue Bird was a
subsidiary of Henlys Group plc. In October 2006,
the company announced that its acquisition
by Cerberus Capital Management LP had been
completed. Terms of the transaction were not
disclosed.

Products
Buses, minibuses and coaches; bus bodywork
(including kits for overseas assembly and mobile
homes).

Range
Ultra LF: Available in two lengths (under 30 ft and
35 ft) at an ultra wide width (102 in), for shuttle
and transit applications.

Blue Bird Ultra LF™ low-floor shuttle bus   0569836

Ultra LMB: Low floor shuttle bus. Length just
under 28 ft and fully ADA compliant, with 10 in
floor height in kneeled position.
XCEL 102: Transit and shuttle bus with two-step
entry and width of 102 in.
Wanderlodge range: M380 – 38 ft coach; LX – 40 ft
coach; LXi 43 ft coach.
School bus range: VISION, All American, Micro
Bird Type A (available in 12 versions, seating
from 10 to 30 passengers) and conventional
buses mounted on International chassis.
Express 4500: Multipurpose coach, 45 ft length
seating up to 55 passengers.

Contracts
In October 2005, three new 30 ft Blue Bird Ultra
LF low-floor buses were delivered to Macatawa
Area Express, Holland, US.

In January 2006, Toledo Area Regional Transit
Authority (TARTA) took delivery of 10, 35 ft Ultra
LF buses.

In June 2006, the company announced that
it will provide its All *American Type D* school
buses to Laidlaw Education Services, the largest
private contractor of student transportation
services in North America, through to 2009.

In addition, Blue Bird will supply Laidlaw
with its *Micro Bird Type A* buses. The delivery
of initial orders under the new agreement
began in early 2006, with the shipment of
more than 150 buses for Laidlaw's Alaskan
operations.

In mid-2006, the company was awarded a
sales contract with the US General Services
Administration (GSA) to supply buses to
agencies of the Federal Government. The
contract was for one year, with an additional
four-year option.

Developments
In September 2005, the company introduced
the Raven Series One low-floor trolley. The 24-
or 30-passenger trolley is built on a Blue Bird
Ultra low-floor chassis by Trolley Enterprises Inc
and is available in diesel, CNG or hybrid-electric
versions.

In July 2006, deliveries started of Satellite
Security Systems Inc's GlobalGuard System
to Blue Bird for incorporating into the product
line. This GPS-based system offers school
districts safety and security features as well as
monitoring, routing and scheduling processes.

BMC Sanayi ve Ticaret AŞ

Kemalpaşa Caddesi No 32, Pınarbaşı, TR-35060
İzmir, Turkey
Tel: (+90 232) 477 18 00 (Sales (Exports) &
Service)
Tel: (+90 232) 477 18 73 (Defence Industry and
Special Projects Unit)
Fax: (+90 232) 479 18 77 (Sales (Exports) & Service)
Fax: (+90 232) 477 18 75 (Defence Industry and
Special Projects Unit)
e-mail: savunma@bmc.com.tr,
exportsales@bmc.com.tr
Web: www.bmc.com.tr

Key personnel
Managing Director/Vice-Chairman:
Mehmet Demirpençe
Vice-President, Operations: *Muharrem Erkan*
Vice-President, Technical: *Hüsnü Ergenç*
Vice-President, Sales and Marketing:
Turgut Cankiliç
Manager, Defence Industry and Special Projects
Unit: *Nadi Postoğlu*
Staff: 3,500

Other offices
UK office
Havenfields, Aylesbury Road, Great Missenden,
Buckinghamshire, HP16 9LS, UK
Tel: (+44 14 94) 89 08 88   Fax: (+44 14 94) 89 08 84
e-mail: bmc.uk@btinternet.com

Background
BMC was established in 1964 to build light
and heavy commercial vehicles and buses

Belde 220 CB   1171391

under licence from the former British Motor
Corporation. It is now part of the Turkish
Çukurova Holding Group (turnover USD9.1
billion), and has a licence agreement with
Cummins Engines.

Products
Integral city buses, also chassis for developing
markets.

Range
Belde 220 SLF: City bus with Cummins Euro 3
engine; 33 seated, 67 standees +1.
Belde 260 CB: City bus with Cummins Euro 3
engine; 36 seated, 64 standees +1.
1100 FE: School bus with Cummins Euro 3 engine;
60 +1 seated.
1100 LF Falcon: City bus with Cummins Euro 3 engine;
39 seated (or 36 + wheelchair), 26 standees +1.

Probus 850 TB/TBX   1171394   *Probus 215 SCB*   1171393

Condor 220 SLF: City bus with Cummins Euro 4+ engine; 45 seated, 46 standees +1.
Probus 850 TBX: Midibus with Cummins Euro 3 engine; 34 seated +1 +1. The Probus 850 Club is available with manual or automatic gearbox.
Probus 215 SCB: Midibus with Cummins Euro 3 engine; 20 seated, 50 standees +1.
Hawk 900 LF: City bus with Cummins Euro 4+ engine; 27 seated, 33 standees +1.
750 Midilux L: Midibus with Cummins Euro 4+ engine; 27 seated +1 +1.
Karisma: Midibus with Cummins Euro 4+ engine; 35 seated +1 +1.

Production
BMC has a production capacity of 21,500 vehicles and 22,000 engines a year.

In 2007, some 850 buses were produced, of which some 550 were exported.

BMC (UK) limited launched its new 7.5 m luxury coach, the Nifty, at Bus and Coach in October 2007.

Developments
In early 2008, the company displayed a CNG-powered ProBus low-floor citybus prototype, fitted with a 5.88-litre Cummins BGe EEV/Euro 5 compliant 234 hp engine.

Also displayed was the 750 Midi-LUX left-hand drive vehicle for export to Europe.

Belde 260 SLF   1171392

Contracts
BMC exports its products to 72 countries, including Azerbaijan, Bulgaria, Germany, Ghana, Hungary, Italy, Kazakhstan, Malaysia, Nigeria, Romania, South Africa, Spain, Sudan, Taiwan and the UK.

Bogdan Industrial and Investment Holding

8 Pavla Usenko Street, Kiev (Kyiv) 02105, Ukraine
Tel: (+380 44) 536 07 71
Fax: (+380 44) 536 07 72
e-mail: sales@bogdan.com.ua
Web: http://bogdan.ua

Key personnel
Representative: *Oleg Svinarchuk*

Background
The bus production companies of Bogdan Industrial and Investment Holding are JSC Cherkasskiy Autobus and Autobus plant 'Bogdan'.

The origins of the company are from 1964, when the Cherkassy Autorepair Plant (ChARZ) was started, followed by the commencement of production in 1966. In 1994, the company was privatised and reorganised as the Open Joint Stock Company Cherkassy Autorepair Plant.

In 2002, ChARZ was renamed the Joint Stock Company Cherkassy Autobus.

In 2003, Bogdan Industrial and Investment Holding acquired additional production facilities for the Autobus plant 'Bogdan'.

The company has a representative office in Kazakhstan.

Products
Import, development, assembly and sales of buses.

Range
A-064 Bogdan: City minibus, with Isuzu MXA5R 5-speed gearbox, seating 14 plus 27 standing plus driver.
A-091 Bogdan: City minibus with Isuzu 4HG1 diesel engine and MXA5R 5-speed gearbox, available in three versions – City (seating 21), Intercity (seating 27) and Tourist (seating 24).
A-092 Bogdan: City minibus, launched in 2003, with Isuzu 4HE1-TC turbocharged Euro 3 engine and MBP6R 6-speed gearbox, seating 21 plus 25 standing plus driver.
A-092.2 Bogdan: Long-distance city minibus with Isuzu 4HE1-TC turbocharged Euro 3 engine and MBP6R 6-speed gearbox, seating 27.
A-144 Bogdan: Suburban bus, produced since 2003, available with Isuzu 6HH 1 Euro 1 or Cummins B180 Euro 2 diesel engines, Isuzu MLD 6Q or GMP21.17 gearboxes and seating 31 plus 49 standing plus driver.
A-144.2 Bogdan: Suburban bus, with Cummins B215.20 Euro 2 diesel engine and PRAGA 6PS90 6-speed gearbox, seating 31 plus 49 standing plus driver.
A-145 Bogdan: Suburban bus, available in shuttle and tourist versions, with Isuzu 6HH 1S Euro 1 diesel engine and Isuzu MLD 6Q 6-speed gearbox, with total capacity of 80 plus driver.
A-231 Bogdan: Triple-axle low-floor city bus, with Euro 2 engine and a total capacity of 164 passengers.

Production
In total, some 1,490 units per year.

Developments
In July 2005, the company announced it had signed an agreement with Isuzu Motors Limited and Sojitz Corporation to carry out a study for possible expansion of the truck and bus markets in Ukraine and possible future exports to Russia-CIS.

Contracts
In April 2004, 15 A-091 buses were purchased by the Aviatrans Company, Armenia.

In November 2004, 30 A-092 buses were exported to Georgia. Other recent contracts include vehicles sold to Kiev, Mariupol, Odessa and Zaporozhye.

BredaMenarinibus SpA

Via San Donato 190, I-40127 Bologna, Italy
Tel: (+39 051) 637 21 11   Fax: (+39 051) 50 18 30
e-mail: info@bredamenarinibus.it
Web: www.bredamenarinibus.it

Parent company

Finmeccanica SpA
Piazza Monte Grappa 4, I-00195 Rome, Italy
Tel: (+39 06) 32 47 31
Web: www.finmeccanica.it

Key personnel

President: *Roberto Ceraudo*
Vice-President: *Giuseppe Comes*
Chief Financial Officer: *Luca D'Aquila*
   Staff: 300

Background

BredaMenarinibus was set up in 1919 and is based in Bologna, Italy.

   The company specialises in buses for urban transport and intercity buses and has an annual turnover of some EUR100 million.

Products

City buses (diesel and CNG), intercity buses, electric minibuses and hybrid buses.

Range

Avancity+: Available in 10.8 m and 12 m lengths.

BredaMenarinibus **Avancity+ S** *articulated bus*   1370490

Vivacity+: Available in 8 m and 9.4 m lengths.
Avancity+ S: Articulated 18 m bus.
Lander: 12 m intercity bus.
Zeus: Low-floor electric battery-powered 6 m minibus.

Developments

During the last two years, the company has formed agreements for technical collaboration with other manufacturers, in Italy and abroad. The aim is to expand the range of products to compete in international transport markets.

Production

More than 500 per annum.

BredaMenarinibus **Avancity+** *bus*   1370491

BredaMenarinibus **Lander** *intercity bus*   1370492

BredaMenarinibus **Vivacity** *bus*   1370493

BredaMenarinibus **Zeus** *electric minibus*   1370494

Busaf Bus Manufacturing

PO Box 139, Boksburg 1460, Gauteng, South Africa
Tel: (+27 11) 914 14 14   Fax: (+27 11) 914 14 15
e-mail: gmbusaf@hixnet.co.za
   budaf@hixnet.co.za
Web: www.busaf-bus.co.za

Street address

Corner West/Bain Street, Boksburg East, Gauteng 1459, South Africa

Key personnel

General Manager: *Ian A Armitage*

Background

The company has been manufacturing buses since 1946. Busaf is part of Dorbyl Transport Products, a division of Dorbyl Limited.

Products

Busaf designs and manufactures bus and coach bodies and repairs buses.

Range

Panorama: coaches, commuter and bustrain articulated buses; semi-trailers.

   Midi-buses, with seating for 26 to 30 passengers;

   Semi-trailers.

BUSiness BV

PO Box 410, NL-5500 AK Veldhoven, Netherlands
Tel: (+31 40) 255 44 33   Fax: (+31 40) 255 44 11
e-mail: info@businessbv.nl
Web: www.businessbv.nl

Key personnel
Director: *O E P Veldhuizen*

Works
De Run 4425, NL-5503 LS Veldhoven, Netherlands

Background
The company was formed in 1995.

Products
12-seat minibus (13 standing) based on Peugeot Boxer chassis cowl. Also conversions on Mercedes, Volkswagen, Renault, Opel, Iveco, Citroën and Peugeot base vehicles.

The BUSiness 2002 body can be mounted on Citroën, Peugeot or Fiat chassis. It carries up to 25 and has a flat floor 320 mm above the road surface. The vehicle can kneel a further 50 mm.

Busland BV

Steenoven 17, NL-5626 DK Eindhoven, Netherlands
Tel: (+31 40) 262 86 00   Fax: (+31 40) 262 86 86
Web: www.busland.nl

Key personnel
Director: *Ton van Eijndhoven*

Background
A subsidiary of the Dutch VDL Groep and part of VDL Bus and Coach BV.

Services
Sales of bus and coaches.

Busscar Ônibus SA

Cx Postal 477, CEP 89219-201, Joinville, Santa Catarina, Brazil
Tel: (+55 47) 441 11 33   Fax: (+55 47) 441 11 03
e-mail: busscar@busscar.com.br
Web: www.busscar.com

Key personnel
President: *Rosita Nielson*
Executive Vice-President: *Edson Andrade*

Street address
Rua Augusto Bruno Nielson, 345 District Industrial, CEP 89219-201, Joinville, Santa Catarina, Brazil

Other offices
Busscar has 7 branch offices in Brazil and offices and representatives in Argentina, Bolivia, Chile, Costa Rica, Cuba, Dominican Republic, Ecuador, Paraguay, Peru, South Africa, Uruguay and Venezuela.

Manufacturing plants are located in Colombia, Cuba, Mexico, Norway and Venezuela.

Background
Founded in 1946 by Augusto Bruno and Eugenio Nielson, the company, then Carrocerias Nielson, started manufacture of wooden bus bodies and produced its first metal body in 1956.

The company is ISO 9001 certified.

Products
Bus and coach bodies.

Range
Panorâmico DD: Double deck bus, on the following chassis: Mercedes Benz O400RSD; Scania K113TLB, K124EB and IB; Volvo B12B and B12.
Jum Buss 400: Hi-deck bus on the following chassis: Mercedes Benz O400RSD; Scania K113TLB, K124 EB and IB; Volvo B12B and B12.
Jum Buss 380: Hi-deck bus on the following chassis: Mercedes Benz O400RSD; Scania K113TLB, K124 EB and IB; Volvo B12B and B12.
Jum Buss 360: Hi-deck bus on the following chassis: Mercedes Benz O400RSE and O400RSD; Scania K113CLB, K113TLB, K124 EB and IB; Volvo B10M, B12B and B12.
El Buss 340: Hi-deck bus on the following chassis: Mercedes Benz OF1318, OF1417, OF1721, OH1420, OH1421L, OH1621LE, OH1628L and O400RSE; Scania K113CLB, K113TLB, L113, L94, F113 and F94; Volvo B10M, B12B and B7R; Ford B1618 and B1621; Volkswagen 16210CO.
El Buss 320: Hi-deck bus on the following chassis: Mercedes Benz OF1318, OF1417, OF1721, OH1420, OH1421L and OH1621LE; Ford B1618 and B1621; Volkswagen 16210CO.
Vissta Buss LO and Vissta Bus HI: Hi-deck buses.
Micruss, Mini Micruss and Micro Buss: Microbuses.
Urbanuss and Urbanuss Pluss: Can be specified with three doors for city operation, seating 45 with up to 55 standing. For city use, it is mounted on Mercedes-Benz, Volvo, Scania, Volkswagen and Ford chassis. Framework, external panelling and flooring is in heavy-duty aluminium alloy. The latter is articulated.

Production
The Joinville plant has an average daily production of approximately 25 units. Exports now account for some 28 per cent of total production.

Contracts
The company has formed a joint venture with Norwegian Vest to operate in Scandinavian countries.

Cable Car Classics Inc

3239 Rio Lindo Avenue, Healdsburg, California 95448, USA
Tel: (+1 707) 433 68 10
Freephone: (800) 348 18 73
Fax: (+1 707) 433 58 28
e-mail: rick@cablecarclassics.com
Web: www.cablecarclassics.com

Key personnel
President: *Matthew Etchell*
Vice-President: *Bryant Goodwin*
Sales & Marketing Director: *Rick Ward*
Operations Manager: *John Eder*

Products
Trolleybuses.

Range
Trolleybuses are available in many configurations and models and to many floor plans, according to customers' specifications. Fuel options include diesel, CNG, LNG, LPG, petrol and hybrid electric.
California Trolley: A smaller trolley with capacity of 31 seated and eight standing passengers. Two side-facing wheelchair positions.
San Francisco Trolley: Passenger capacity of 42 seated and 18 standing passengers. Two forward-facing wheelchair positions.

San Francisco model open-air trolleybus for 42 passengers 0572147

Golden Gate Trolley: Larger trolleybus, with capacity of 35 seated and 20 standing passengers. Two side-facing wheelchair positions.

Contracts
The company worked with Hino Motors, a division of Toyota Japan, on the design and integration of a Hino bus chassis and a Cable Car Classics, Inc., Golden Gate body. The right-hand drive trolleys were delivered to Japan in late 1998/early 1999. The vehicles are powered by Hino 215 hp diesel engines.

The company has also supplied trolleybuses to the Whatcom Transit Authority, based in Bellingham, Washington.

Other contracts include Sonoma County, California; Chico, California; North Lake Tahoe, Nevada; South Lake Tahoe, California; Trans Hawaiian Services, Hawaii; and Roberts Hawaii, Hawaii.

Cable Car Concepts Inc

821 Shunpike Road, Cape May, New Jersey 08204, US
Tel: (+1 609) 884 52 30   Fax: (+1 609) 884 59 80
Freephone: (+1 800) 422 83 66
e-mail: info@trolley.com
Web: www.trolley.com

Key personnel
President: *R Adelizzi*

Other offices
Florida manufacturing facility
18052 US HWY 301 North, Strake, Florida 32091, US

Background
Originally formed in 1964 as Themed Trackless Trolleys, Cable Car Concepts became part of the Great American Trolley Co in 1997.

Products
The company produces trackless trolleys, trolley-trams, road trains, cable carts, trolley shelters and fareboxes.

Range
Trackless trolleys in three versions: mini (up to 16–18 adults seated); midi (23-35 seated) and maxi (25-50 seated).

Cable Car Concepts 23/27 passenger Midi   1194491

New to the Cable Car Concepts range, the 50+ passenger Trolley Coach®
1194493

Cacciamali Spa

Cacciamali Engineering Spa
Via IV Novembre 28, I-25030 Mairano (BS), Italy
Tel: (+39 030) 975 07 11   Fax: (+39 030) 975 08 03
e-mail: infocac@cacciamali.it
   estero@cacciamali.it
Web: http://www.cacciamali-engineering.it

Subsidiary
Cacciamali Engineering Spa

Background
Cacciamali owns 85 per cent of Kapena.

In 1990 the company created Cacciamali Engineering Spa to enable complete buses to be produced.

Products
Buses up to 10 m, on many Iveco chassis. Variants include school buses, private service and tourist buses, urban and suburban buses and intercity vehicles.

Range
For urban and suburban applications, the company is building bodywork on Iveco chassis and has developed a range of integral vehicles, including the ***TCC 635N, TCC 635L, TCM 920, TCN 105*** and ***760*** versions. All employ Iveco engines, of varying sizes, mounted in line in the offside rear corner.

In 2000, the ***Grifone***, a low-floor diesel- or battery-powered midibus was introduced.

CaetanoBus SA

Avenida de Vasco da Gama, 1410, P-4431-901 Vila Nova Gaia, Portugal
Tel: (+351 227) 86 70 00
Fax: (+351 227) 86 71 71
e-mail: caetanobus@caetanobus.pt
Web: www.caetanobus.pt

Key personnel
Chairman: *Salvador Caetano*
Vice-President: *José Reis da Silva Ramos*

Background
CaetanoBus SA, established in 2001, is a joint venture between the Salvador Caetano Group (74 per cent holding) and EvoBus (26 per cent).

Salvador Caetano is one of Portugal's leading companies, with a wide range of interests mainly connected with the motor industry. The roots of the company date back to 1946, when Salvador F Caetano started building wooden-framed coaches. The Caetano group of companies now employs over 2,200 people.

Other than coach building, activities include manufacture of a variety of automotive products, assembly of Toyota light commercial vehicles and distribution of Toyota, BMW and MAN products throughout Portugal.

For further background information, please see previous editions of *Jane's Urban Transport Systems*.

The company has subsidiaries and representatives in several countries (for more information, please see the above Web

site), including Salvador Caetano UK Ltd (www.caetano.co.uk), which is responsible for the commercial activities of bus products.

Products
Manufacture and marketing of bus and coach bodies.

Range
The range includes the ***Enigma*** coach, available on Dennis and Volvo chassis, the ***Midi Enigma***, available on the MAN 14.280 chassis, the ***Cutlass***, on the Dennis Javelin chassis, the ***Nimbus***, on a Dennis SLF Dart chassis, the ***Slimbus***, a 2.3 m wide bus based on the Nimbus, and the ***Optima***, supplied on a Toyota chassis. Disabled access is available as an option.

Caio Induscar

Commercial office
Avenida das Nações Unidas, 12901, 5o. andar, Torre Oeste – Centro Empresarial Nações Unidas CEP 04578-000 – Brooklin Paulista Novo São Paulo/SP, Brazil
Tel: (+55 11) 21 48 80 01
Fax: (+55 11) 21 48 80 00
e-mail: imprensa@caio.com.br
Web: www.caio.com.br

Factory
Rodovia Marechal Rondon, km 252.2, Distrito Industrial, Botucatu – SP, CEP 18607-810, Brazil
   Tel: (+55 14) 38 11 39 00

Key personnel
Marketing: *Patricia Coelho*
   Staff: 3,000

Background
Founded in 1946, Caio Induscar is a bus and coach body builder.

In January 2001, the Ruas Group of bus companies, through the Induscar company, took over the plant and the right to use and sell products under the CAIO label, including selling commercial vehicles, and using national and imported chassis for buses, trucks, and automobiles.

The company has representatives throughout Brazil and international representatives in Latin and North America, The Middle East, South Africa, Tahiti and Canada.

Range

Articulated and bi-articulated buses: Mondego LA, Mondego HA, Millennium, Apache VIP, Topbus.
Urban buses: Apache S22, Apache VIP and Millennium urban buses.

Coaches: Giro 3200, 3400 and 3600.
Midibus: FOZ Super, urban midibus.
Minibus: Atilis and Piccolino minibuses.
Micros: Range of FOZ microbuses.
The company will also produce bodies to customers' specifications.

Production

Some 40 bodies per day.

Contracts

No recent contract information is available currently.

Camo-Indústria de Autocarros SA (Camo)

1st Maio Street, 215, Ap 508, 4406-401 Canelas, Portugal
Tel: (+351 22) 715 13 90
Fax: (+351 22) 713 49 51
e-mail: info@camo.pt
Web: www.camo.pt

Key personnel

General Manager: *Manuel Leão e Seabra*
Commercial Department: *Verónica Pinho*

Background

Established in 1965. A subsidiary of Auto-Sueca set up with Volvo interests to mount bodies on Volvo chassis assembled locally.
The company is certified to ISO 9001:2000 standards.

Products

Manufacture and repair of bus and coach bodies.

Range

Urban
City-Tour: Double-deck bus, 12 m long, 3.97 m high and 2.55 m wide. Upper floor seats 49, lower floor capacity 10 + 1 wheelchair or 9 standees, plus driver. Volvo B7R LE, IVECO City Class, MAN 18.310 or Mercedes-Benz OC500 LE chassis.
Citadino: Urban bus, 12 m long, 3.08 to 3.24 m high, 2.55 m wide, capacity 33 + 55 standees + driver. Volvo B7L, N7r LE, MAN NL223/263 F, 18.230 Hocl, 18.240 Hocl, 18.22 Hocl, Mercedes-Benz OC500 LE and Scania L94 UB chassis.
Pollux Urban: Minibus, 7.379 m long, 3.170 m high, 2.4 m wide with capacity of 18 + 7 standees + 1 wheelchair + driver on Mercedes-Benz Sprinter 616 CDI chassis.

Intercity/tourist
Jupiter: Coach available in two versions: 12 m long, 3.76 m high, 2.55 m wide (capacity 51 seated +2) and 13 m long, 3.76 m high, 2.55 m wide (capacity 55 seated +2). Volvo B12B, MAN 18.310 Hocl, 18.410 Hocl, Mercedes-Benz OC500, Scania K114IB, K124IB or IVECO 391.12.35 chassis.
Olympus: Midibus, 8.6 or 9.28 m long, 3.25 m high, 2.4 m wide, capacity 33 seated + 2, on Mercedes-Benz Vario 0815D/48, MAN 10.225 Focl or IVECO C100E21/P chassis.
Minerva: Coach, 12 m long, 3.59 m high, 2.55 m wide, capacity 55 seated+, 20 standees + 2 on Volvo B12B, B10B, B7R, MAN 18.260 Hocl, 18.310 Hocl, 18.410 Hocl, Mercedes-Benz OC500, Scania L94IB, K114IB, K124IB or IVECO 391.12.35 chassis.
Pollux Tourism: Midibus, 7.379 m long, 3.170 m high, 2.4 m wide, capacity 22 seated + 2, on Mercedes-Benz Sprinter 616 CDI chassis.

Carrocera Castrosua SA

Carretera de A Coruña, km 59.5, E-15890, Santiago de Compostela, Spain
Tel: (+34 981) 55 24 60
Fax: (+34 981) 55 24 61
e-mail: info@castrosua.com
Web: www.castrosua.com

Key personnel

President: *José Castro Suárez*
Chairman: *Beatriz Castro Carcia*
Sales Manager: *José Ramón Porto Rivas*
Export Sales Manager: *Roberto Suárez Barcala*
Staff: 380

Products

Urban and suburban bus and coach bodies.

Range

City VERSUS: This urban bus body is available in lengths from 9 m to 18 m, depending upon the chassis used. Built on super-low-floor chassis, with diesel, Ethanol, CNG and LPG fuel systems from many European chassis manufacturers, including Scania, Volvo, MAN, Mercedes-Benz, Renault, DAF, Iveco and Dennis.
According to customer requirements, versions are available with up to four passenger doors, full matrix route indicators, climatised air conditioning units, powered wheelchair ramp and predisposition for GPS systems.

MAGNUS and MAGNUS-S: Intercity vehicles, for distances up to 150 km. The bus body can be built on a variety of standard, low-entry chassis. Available in lengths from 9 to 18 m and on chassis from many European manufacturers.

Production

Approximately 450 vehicles per year.

Contracts

Castrosua is a regular supplier of urban vehicles to many municipalities in Spain, as well as to private operators. The company has manufactured vehicles for the Czech Republic, France, Israel, Italy and Romania.

Carrocerías Andinas CA

Zona Industrial – Av Los Parceleros N° 17-41, Aguas Calientes, Ureña Estado Tachira, Venezuela
Tel: (+58 276) 787 27 45, 787 27 45, 787 16 81
Fax: (+58 276) 787 26 58
e-mail: pvelez@carroceriasandinas.com (Administration)
rvicini@carroceriasandinas.com (Sales)
Web: www.carroceriasandinas.com

Key personnel

Manager, Administration: *P Velez*
Manager, Manufacturing: *R Rodriguez*
Manager, Sales: *R Vicini*

Products

Mini- and midibuses, urban and intercity buses.

Range

Minibus Mercedes L0-712: Minibus on Mercedes-Benz chassis.

Periférico 4X4: Minibus on Ford chassis.
Periférico 40.10: Minibus on Iveco chassis.
Periférico Canter: Midibus on Mitsubishi chassis.
Minibús Nevado: Midibus available in Urbana and Turismo versions.
Autobús Novus Urbano: Urban bus, also available in an executive version.
Autobús Novus Intercity: Intercity bus.

Carrocerías Ayats SA (Ayats)

Paratge Can Call, km 1, E-1740l Arbúcies (Girona), Spain
Tel: (+34 972) 86 00 29
Fax: (+34 972) 86 11 14
e-mail: ventas@carroceriasayats.es
Web: www.carroceriasayats.es

Other offices

The company has plants in Tona, Barcelona, Spain and Tétouan, Morocco.

Products

Integral buses and coaches, in co-operation with MAN, DAF and Mercedes-Benz. Coach bodies on all chassis.

Range

Bravo I R: Interurban double-decker available in 12.45 m, 13.20 m, 13.95 m and 15.00 m versions, width 2.55 m, height 4.00 m.
Bravo City: Open top double-decker available in 12.00 m and up to 13.95 m versions, width 2.55 m, height 4.00 m.

Ayats **Bravo I R** *coach*

1373999

Ayats **Bravo City** *coach*   1373998

Ayats **Atlas 2** *coach*   1373997

Platinum: High-decker, available in 9.65 m, 10.30 m and 12.00 m versions, width 2.50 m, height 3.30 m.

Atlas 2: High-decker available in 12.25 m, 12.85 m and up to 15.00 m versions, width 2.55 m and height 3.67 m.

The company also builds vehicles to customers' specifications.

Carrocerias Ferqui SL (Ferqui)

Polígono Industrial La Barreda, Parcela 15, E-33180 Noreña, Prinicipado de Asturias, Spain
Tel: (+34 98) 574 04 20   Fax: (+34 98) 574 28 69
e-mail: ferqui@ferqui.com
Web: www.ferqui.com

Key personnel
Commercial Director: *José Faustina Quince Riestra*
Production Director: *José María Fernández*
    Staff: 70

Background
The company was established in 1969 and is certified to ISO 9002 standards.

Products
Midibus bodies.

Range
Transit17: High-deck midibus, built on Ford Transit chassis.
F3-iVD: High-deck midibus, built on Iveco CC 130 chassis.

F3-MND: High-deck midibus, built on MAN 10225 chassis.
Sunsett II/Soroco Plus: Midibus built on Sprinter 616 chassis. Available in two options, 19 seats (+1) and 22 seats (+1).
Solera SR: High-deck midibus built on the Atego 12.23 chassis, and available in versions ranging from 31 to 39 seats.

Production
118 bodies during 1998, of which 45 were exported.

Carrosserie HESS AG (HESS)

Bielstrasse 7, CH-4512 Bellach, Switzerland
Tel: (+41 32) 617 34 11
Fax: (+41 32) 617 34 00
e-mail: info@hess-ag.ch
Web: www.hess-ag.ch

Key personnel
General Manager and Sales and Marketing Manager: *Alex Naef*
Finance and Administration: *Ernst Basler*
Research and Development Manager: *Hans-Jörg Gisler*
Production: *Marco Brancato*
Sales Director: *Stefano Corona*
    Staff: Not currently available

Associated companies
Fahrzeug- und Maschinenbau AG, CH-3367, Thörigen
Carrosserie Tüscher AG, CH-8108, Dällikon-Zürich
Carrosserie Lauber SA, CH-1197, Prangins

Background
The company first started building buses in 1919. HESS has partners in Australia, Israel, Romania, Portugal, the UK and the US.

Products
Buses and trolleybuses, including articulated and bi-articulated. Van-to-minibus and specialist vehicle conversions. Engineering for urban road transit projects. Passenger trailer exchange kits.

Range
Bus, trolleybus and hybrid bus, including articulated and bi-articulated kits.

A specialist in aluminium body structure, Hess uses space-frame technology for its trolleybuses and buses.

The method of assembly is by Co-Bolt® bolting instead of welding. The bolting process is a combination of bolt and two-component

HESS passenger trailer for Wolfsburg, Germany   1136185

HESS **ligh**Tram® *Hybrid for ZVB, Zug, Switzerland*   1373707

HESS lighTram®^Trolley for VBZ, Zurich, Switzerland   1373708

HESS-Scania N UB (Euro 4) for Bamert, Wollerau, Switzerland   1194945

adhesive. The bolt cannot be vibrated or shaken loose, but can be readily undone when required even after years in service. A Co-Bolt-N system has been developed for construction of low-floor buses and trolleybuses.

Minibus conversions have been undertaken based on the Volkswagen LT series window van and the latest bodywork has double glazing and an air-chill system for warm weather use.

The range currently includes:
HESS Trolleybuses 12–25 m;
HESS Dieselbuses 9.5–13.5 m;
HESS passenger-trailers 13–23.5 m;
HESS Hybrid Bus 18–25 m.
HESS also produces airport buses.

Contracts
HESS trolleybuses have been supplied recently to Swiss operators in Lucerne, Fribourg, St Gallen,

Geneva and Zurich. City buses have been delivered to Swiss operators in Lucerne, St Gallen, Zug, Baden, Rheinthal, Wettingen and Schaffhausen and passenger trailers to Lucerne and Zug (Switzerland), Wolfsburg and Lehnin (Germany), Tyrol (Austria), and Luxembourg.

Developments
In 2007, HESS has built a hybrid version of its 25 m lighTram®^Trolley bus, called lighTram® ^Hybrid.

Changzhou Iveco Bus Co Ltd (CBC-Iveco Ltd)

No 138, Changxin Road, 213002 Nanjing City, Jiangsu Province, China
Tel: (+86 519) 676 04 04   Fax: (+86 519) 675 21 77
Web: www.cbc-iveco.com

Key personnel
Director, Sales and Marketing: *Sean Li*
    Staff: Approximately 3,000

Background
CBC-Iveco Ltd is a joint venture between Iveco Co, part of the Fiat Group, and Changzhou Changjiang Bus Group Co Ltd.

Products
Production of city buses, intercity coaches, minibuses and bus chassis and also offers parts and after-service support.

Range
The range includes low-floor and ultra-low-floor city buses, double-deck buses, vehicles for Bus Rapid Transit (BRT), intercity/touring coaches and chassis.

Production
In 2003, the company produced in excess of 4,000 buses and chassis.

Products are distributed to more than 350 cities in China, including Beijing, Shanghai, Tianjin and

Chongqing and buses are also exported to Saudi Arabia, the Russian Federation, Tanzania and others.

Developments
In 2005, the company announced that it would offer a low-entry, 18 m articulated bus.

Contracts
The company has recently won a contract to supply 50 low-floor articulated buses for the BRT system in Beijing.

Champion Bus Inc

331 Graham Road, PO Box 158, Imlay City, Michigan 48444, US
Tel: (+1 810) 724 64 74
Freephone: (800) 776 49 43
Fax: (+1 810) 724 18 44
e-mail: sales@championbus.com
Web: www.championbus.com

Key personnel
Vice-President and General Manager: *John Resnik*
Operations Manager: *Gerald Buck*
Controller: *Theresa Smith*

Background
Champion Bus Inc is part of the Thor Industries Commercial Bus Division.
The company is ISO 9001 certified.

Products
Manufacturer of small to medium-size buses, seating between eight and 45 passengers.

Range
Challenger: Seats up to 25.
Crusader: For short-run transit needs.
CTS-FE: Long-run vehicle for up to 45 passengers.
CTS-RE also available.
Defender: Medium-duty bus with various chassis manufacturers.

Changzhou Changjiang Bus Group Co Ltd

138 Changxin Rd. Changzhou, Jiangsu 213002, China
Tel: (+86 519) 675 00 20   Fax: (+86 519) 675 21 77
e-mail: changjc@mx.js.cei.gov.cn
Web: www.js.cei.gov.cn/
    JSfamous/0400053/echangjq.htm

Key personnel
President: *Mr. Yuanlin Sun*
Tel: (+86 519) 675 18 74   Fax: (+86 519) 675 21 77
Business Contact: *Mr Jianwei Tang*

Background
The Changzhou Changjiang Bus Group Co Ltd was formerly known as the Changzhou Bus Factory.

Capabilities
The company's plant covers an area of 261,600 m², with 124,000 m² of construction space. Facilities include a complete bus welding line, complete bus painting line, complete bus assembling line, casting line, front and rear axles assembly line, chassis assembly line, complete bus waterproof testing line and a complete bus performance testing line. The company is also capable of developing bus bodies and chassis.

Production
The annual production capacity has reached 3,000 complete buses and 5,000 bus chassis.

Contracts
The company's products have been sold all over China and exports have been made to Africa, Southeast Asia, South Asia and Russia.

Subsidiary
Changzhou Iveco Bus Co Ltd
Changzhou Iveco Bus Co Ltd is a joint venture of Fiat Group Iveco Company and Changzhou Changjiang Bus Group Co Ltd. The company offers various types of city buses, bus chassis, parts and after-sales services. This company is a city public traffic infrastructure innovation project and has the support of the state. It is the largest foreign investment programme in Changzhou.

The major products are low floor city bus, extra-low-floor city bus, twin fuel and double fuel city bus, conductor-free city bus, double deck city bus, expressway bus, tour bus and special chassis.

Changzhou Iveco Bus Co Ltd employs over 3,000 people, among whom more than 700 are technicians (including over 500 engineers with advanced or intermediate technical titles).

Chongqing Hengtong Bus Co Ltd

888 Xiangyu Road, North District, Chongqing, China
Tel: (+86 23) 67 18 92 00
Fax: (+86 23) 67 18 92 08
e-mail: bgs@hengtongbus.com
Web: www.hengtongbus.com

Key personnel
Staff: 1,800 (estimate)

Background
Established in 1939, Chongqing Hengtong Bus Co Ltd is a wholly owned subsidiary of Chongqing Bus General Manufactory.

The company is certified to ISO 9001: 2000 standards and is planning to qualify for ISO/TS 16949:2000 certification in the near future.

Products
Design and manufacture of CNG-fuelled minibus, midibuses, city buses and coaches.

Production
Annual output is in excess of 6,000 units, including city buses, tour and long-distance buses/coaches.

Developments
The company has a dedicated R&D centre and also co-operates with a number of companies for research.

In 2008, the company completed a new factory in Konggang Industrial Park in the northern district of Chongqing, with annual capacity rising correspondingly to 10,000 buses.

Ciferal Indústria de Ônibus Ltda (Ciferal)

Rua Pastor Manoel Avelino de Souza 2064 – Xerém, 25.250-000 Duque de Caixas, Rio de Janeiro, Brazil
Tel: (+55 21) 26 79 10 11   Fax: (+55 21) 26 79 15 21
Export Division, Tel: (+55 21) 26 79 17 24
e-mail: ciferal@ciferal.com.br
Web: www.ciferal.com.br

Key personnel
General Manager: *Oscar Barbieri*
Production: *Adelar Schmaedeke*
Finance Administration: *José Freitas*
Systems: *Cristiano de Carvlho*
Technical: *Hermano Vieira Lins*
Engineering: *José Antonio Latini Júnior*

Background
Originally formed in 1955, the company expanded in 1992 to a new 300,000 m² plant 50 km from its previous 40,000 m² location in Rio de Janeiro. It now employs 800.

In 2001, Ciferal became 100 per cent owned by Marcopolo (see separate entry).

Products
Bus bodies.

Range
Citmax: Urban bus built on the OF1417 and OF1721 Mercedes-Benz chassis or the 17-210 OD Volkswagen chassis.
Turquesa: Urban bus on Mercedes-Benz, Scania, Volvo, or Volkswagen chassis, seating up to 49 passengers.

Fratello: Available in four versions, Urban, Commuter, Executive and School Bus, and seating up to 30 passengers, built on Volkswagen or Iveco chassis.
Vicino: Built on Mercedes-Benz chassis and available in four versions, as for the Fratello, and seating up to 30 passengers.
Marcopolo Viale: Urban bus available in standard (front and rear engine), low-entry, articulated, bi-articulated and electric-hybrid bus versions and also as a trolleybus version.
Minimax: Minibus on Mercedes-Benz, Volkswagen or Agraleda chassis and seating up to 26 passengers.
Torino: Available in four versions, this urban bus can seat up to 36 passengers.

Production
Production capacity of 3,000 units per year.

SA Automobiles Citroën (Citroën)

Communications Division
Citroën UK Ltd
221 Bath Road, Slough, SL1 4BA, UK
Tel: (+44 870) 606 90 00
Web: www.citroen.co.uk
www.citroen.com

Key personnel
Head of Corporate Sales: *Ian Hughes*
Director of Communications: *Marc Raven*

Products
Minibuses and chassis.

Range
Jumper (named *Relay* in UK): Available in 2.9, 3.3 and 3.5 tonne gvw. As a minibus, this range is available with capacities ranging from 9 to 17 seats. The Jumper is also available as a chassis cab, which is suitable for conversion to three-axle format to suit high-capacity, low-loading specialist wheelchair-accessible minibus applications. Front-wheel drive, with a choice of 2.0 HDi 86 hp, 2.2 HDi 104 hp or 2.8 HDi 127 hp diesel engines.
Jumpy (named *Dispatch* in the UK): A smaller vehicle, available as a six-seat Combi. Front-wheel drive, with a choice of 1.9 D 71hp or 2.0 HDi 110 hp diesel engines.

Citroën Ready to Run *Advanced Vehicle Builders Relay minibus*   1124817

Developments
In 2007, Citroën launched a new, expanded *Ready to Run* vehicle programme. Included in this is a range of Advanced Vehicle Builders' 12-, 15- and 17-seat minibuses and wheelchair accessible minibuses. The latter two are Relay minibuses, available in a total of three options.

Coachmen Industries Inc

PO Box 30, Middlebury, IN 46540, US
Tel: (+1 574) 825 58 21
Fax: (+1 574) 825 81 41
e-mail: CRVinfo@coachmen.com
Web: www.coachmen.com

Street address
423 North Main Middlebury, IN 46540, US

Key personnel
President and Chief Executive Officer: *Richard M Lavers*

President of Coachmen Recreational Vehicles: *Michael R Terlep*
Chief Financial Officer: *Ms Colleen A Zuhl*
Director of Planning and Investor Relations: *Jeffery A Tryka*
Staff: 2,305 (2007)

Background
A publicly held company, with stock listed on the New York Stock Exchange (COA).

Current situation
Manufacturer of recreational vehicles, the company has recently started to produce accessible buses.

Developments
In March 2008, the company announced that it had entered into an agreement to produce ADA-compliant, low-floor, accessible buses for ARBOC Mobility LLC. ARBOC Mobility's *Spirit of Mobility* specialised transit and shuttle bus will be produced by Coachmen's Recreational Vehicle Group on a dedicated assembly line.

The vehicles will feature kneeling air suspension chassis and ramp system and will be available in four lengths and with petrol or diesel engines. Capacity will range from 12 to 25 passengers.

Comil Carrocerias e Ônibus Ltda (Comil)

Comil Bodies and Buses Ltd
Rua Alberto Parenti 1382, Distrito Industrial, CEP
99700-000 Erechim, RS, Brazil
Tel: (+55 54) 520 87 00
Fax: (+55 54) 321 33 14
e-mail: comercial@comilonibus.com.br
    marketing@comilonibus.com.br
Web: www.comilonibus.com.br

Key personnel
President: *Deoclécio Corradi*
Commercial Director: *Dairto Corradi*
Supplies Director:
    Diones Corradi Pagliosa
Financial Director: *Jussara Corradi*
International Commercial Director:
    Luiz Edgard Ferraz do Amaral
Industrial and Human Resources Director:
    Antônio Camilo Policastro
International Sales Managers: *Aderbal Marchi,
    Airton Dalla Corte*
Brazilian Sales Managers: *João Busatta,
    Luis Roberto Fonseca Ribeiro*
Marketing Co-ordinator: *Angela Valiera*

Background
Founded in 1985, the company began its activities
in January 1986.
    At the beginning of 2005, the company had in
excess of 1,900 employees. More than 35 per cent
of production is exported to 30 countries.

Products
Bus bodies.

Range
*Campione 4.05, Campione 3.85, Campione 3.65,
Campione 3.45, Campione 3.25:* Inter-urban/
intercity/long-distance buses.
Versátile: Inter-urban bus.
Svelto: Urban bus, also available in an articulated
version.
Micro Piá: Midibus, available in executive, tourism,
urban, school, jitney or special vehicle versions.
Bella Executive: Minibus available in tourism,
school with one or two doors, urban and
executive services versions.
Bello Urban: Minibus for urban applications.

Production
2,200 units were produced in 2004, an increase
of 8 per cent over the previous year.

Contracts
In 2003, Comil started the production of the
Doppio articulated vehicle for Transmilnio,
Columbia. Since then, 62 of these vehicles
have been produced for the Transmassivo
Company.
    In 2004, 273 buses were sold to the Saudi
Arabian company Taseco. The order comprised
200 units of the long-distance *Campione* model
and 73 *Svelto* urban vehicles.
    Between 2003 and 2004, contracts with Brazilian
companies included Real Expresso, Pluma,
Grupo Jacob Barata and Viação Progresso.
    In 2005, the company was awarded a contract
for 514 buses for Qatar. The order comprises 414
urban buses and 100 long-distance vehicles.

Developments
In 2003 the company produced its first natural
gas bus. The vehicle is a *Svelto* model with
Mercedes chassis. The project was undertaken
in association with Petrobrás and Mercedes-
Benz.
    In 2004, the company's second unit was
formed – Comil Bus de Maxico.

Consorcio G Grupo Dina SA de CV (Dina)

Tlacoquemécatl #41, Colonia del Valle, Delegación
Benito Juár, 03100 México, DF, Mexico
Tel: (+52 55) 54 20 39 00
Fax: (+52 55) 54 20 39 87

Key personnel
Chairman: *Rafael Gómez Flores*
Director, Finance: *Renato Mendez Islas*
Director, Marketing: *Jose Martin Melendez
    Romero*

Background
To alleviate some of its debts, the company sold
61 per cent of its subsidiary MCI.

Products
Buses and coaches.

Range
The company's products are sold under the Dina
name. The current models are: *F11, F12, F14* and
the *Suburbano*.

Contrac GmbH

Max-Planck-Ring 43, D-65205 Wiesbaden,
Germany
Tel: (+49 6122) 955 30   Fax: (+49 6122) 514 61
e-mail: info@contrac-cobus.de
Web: www.contrac-cobus.de

Key personnel
Managing Directors: *Jürgen Kamps, Lothar Elbel*
Sales Director: *Andreas Funk*

Subsidiary companies
Contrac International (GB) Ltd
63 Tarlington Road, Coventry CV6 1FY, UK
Tel: (+44 24) 76 33 32 46

Products
Low-floor airport buses.

Range
Cobus 2400-C, 2700-S, 2700 and 3000: Low-floor
airport buses.

Cobus 3000 low-floor airport bus   1341091

Developments
The Cobus is now available with a CNG-
powered engine option in order to fulfil the latest
environment emission requirements. A special
high capacity direct-drive air-conditioning
system is powered by the main engine of
the bus.
    The CNG-powered option is available on the
Cobus 3000/2700 and 2700-S as well as the 3000
Business Class bus.

Custom Coaches (Sales) Pty Ltd

PO Box 3, Guildford, New South Wales 2161,
Australia
Tel: (+61 2) 97 21 51 00   Fax: (+61 2) 96 32 74 48
e-mail: stevej@custom-coaches.com.au
Web: www.custom-coaches.com.au

Street address
New South Wales Office
Head Office, 31-39 Sturt Street, Smithfield, New
South Wales 2164, Australia

Key personnel
Chief Executive Officer: *Mark Burgess*
National Sales and Marketing Director: *Stephen
    Jackson*
New South Wales Sales Manager: *Norm Stott*
Victoria and Tasmania State Manager: *Geoff
    Ross*

Custom Coaches SB40   1367188

Queensland Sales and Service Manager: *Chris Jones*
New South Wales Service Manager: *Sam Trovato*
South Australia Sales Manager: *Geoff Ross*
South Australia Service Manager: *Paul Saxty*
Staff: *606 (2008)*

Other offices

Queensland office

32 Demand Avenue, Arundel, Queensland 4214/5, Australia
Tel: (+61 7) 55 71 66 55   Fax: (+61 7) 55 71 66 77
e-mail: chris@custom-coaches.com.au (Sales & Services)

South Australia office

7 Brandwood Street, Royal Park, SA 5014, Australia
Tel: (+61 8) 82 40 91 00
Fax: (+61 8) 82 40 91 92 (Sales & Enquiries)
Tel: (+61 8) 82 40 41 66
Fax: (+61 8) 82 40 91 92 (Service)
e-mail: grahamw@abmco.com.au (Service)
geoffr@abmco.com.au (Sales)

Manufacturing plants

Adelaide, South Australia; Arundel, Queensland and Smithfield, New South Wales.

Parts and Services

Custom Care: Service centre. Also for parts and accessories as well as repairs and refurbishments for any vehicle type.

Products

Bus and coach bodies.

Range

CB60 Evo II Low-Floor Citybus: This is a low-floor bus.
CB30 Low-Floor Midibus: This is a low-floor midibus body with wheelchair accessibility, seating 30 to 42 passengers.
Government Citybus: Government vehicles, such as the current New South Wales State

Custom Coaches CB60 Evo II 1367184

Custom Coaches Government Articulated CNG bus 1367185

Custom Coaches CB60 Hybrid 1367189

Custom Coaches SB400 1195835

Custom Coaches SB30 midi school bus 1367187

Custom Coaches CB30 1367186

Transit and Transport South Australia buses, Action Buses Canberra and Brisbane City Council buses.
SB30 Midi School Bus: Front-engined school bus with 43 school seats, including seat belts. Air conditioning, rear boot, disc brakes, ABS and air suspension, ECAS and front and rear sway bars are all standard.
SB400 and SB40 School/Charter Bus: School/charter buses. The SB400 is the prestige range of the SB40, with a coach-style exterior and superior features.
CB60 Hybrid: Low-floor citybus, also suitable for charter and school bus applications.

Daewoo Bus Corporation

Head Office
188-9 Jeonpo-Dong, Busanjin-Gu, Busan, Republic of Korea
Tel: (+82 51) 811 40 14
Fax: (+82 51) 811 40 44
e-mail: jangjc@daewoobus.co.kr
Web: www.daewoobus.com

Other offices
Korea
Dongrae Factory
75-11 Gumsa-Dong, Gumjeong-Gu, Busan, Republic of Korea
Tel: (+82 51) 520 50 03
Fax: (+82 51) 520 50 14

Onsan Factory
749 Hwasan-Ri, Onsan-Myon, Ulju-Gun, Ulsan, Republic of Korea
Tel: (+82 51) 239 83 66
Fax: (+82 51) 239 83 71

Delivery Yard
1058-1 Banyeo-1-Dong, Haeundae-Gu, Busan, Republic of Korea
Tel: (+82 51) 528 59 14   Fax: (+82 51) 523 63 69

Daewoo Bus Global Co Ltd (Overseas Business) and International Showroom
201-1 Ojung-Dong, Ojung-Gu, Buchon City, Kyunggi-Do, Republic of Korea
Tel: (+82 51) 680 66 26
Fax: (+82 51) 680 66 10/66 20

Subsidiaries
Daewoo Bus Global Co Ltd
201-1 Ojung-Dong, Ojung-Gu, Buchon City, Kyunggi-Do, Republic of Korea
Tel: (+82 51) 680 66 26   Fax: (+82 51) 680 66 10/66 20

Guilin Daewoo Bus Co Ltd
10 Jing Ping Road, Guilin, Guangxi, China
Tel: (+86 773) 360 07 00
Fax: (+86 773) 360 29 28

Daewoo Bus Costa Rica SA
2.5 km AL Oeste, Del Centro Comercial, Santa Ana 2000, Costa Rica
(Apartado: 12143-1000 San Jose, Costa Rica)
Tel: (+506) 282 93 22   Fax: (+506) 282 55 55

Master Transportation Bus Manufacturing Ltd
8F.4, No 151, Jung Jeng 4th Rd, Kaohsiung, Taiwan
Tel: (+886 8) 869 19 15   Fax: (+886 8) 869 07 65

Key personnel
President: *Young Jae Choi*
General Manager, Business Planning Team: *Myung Jun Kim*

Products
Coaches and buses.

Range
Buses and coaches with lengths between 9 m and 12 m, including CBU, KD, SDA and parts. The range comprises:
Luxury coaches: BH120HD, BX212H/S;
Inter-city buses: BH115E, BH116, BH117, BH119, BH120E/F;
City buses: BS090, BH090, BF106, BS106, BV120MA, BS120CN.
Models are also available as Natural Gas vehicles (NGV s).

Background
Joint venture company, founded in 1994, producing city buses and coaches.

Production
Manufacturing capacity in Korea is 7,000 units per year and the capacity of overseas subsidiaries is 3,000 units per year.

Daimler AG

Daimler Buses
70546 Stuttgart, Germany
Tel: (+49 711) 170   Fax: (+49 711) 172 22 44
Web: www.daimler.com

Key personnel
Chairman: *Dieter Zetsche*
Global Business Communications, Truck Group & Buses: *Julia Kroeber-Riel*

Background
Daimler AG (previously DaimlerChrysler) is the world's largest bus manufacturer, producing buses and coaches under the Mercedes-Benz, Setra (see separate entry) and Orion (www.orionbus.com) brands.
Besides its operations in Germany, the company maintains a variety of overseas subsidiaries or associates worldwide.

Current situation
The name change from DaimlerChrysler AG to Daimler AG became legally effective on a global basis as of the date of the entry into the German commercial register (Handelsregister) on 19 October 2007.

Products
Complete integral buses and coaches, chassis, including articulated chassis on integral and ladder frame basis, and articulated trolleybuses. The products are built in more than 200 versions.
In Europe Mercedes builds only low-emission vehicles (LEVs). The emission figures for LEV engines are reduced by one half and they meet current EU guidelines. LEV engines have a specification including quieter engine running and high tractive power-to-weight ratio. LEV engines meet Euro-2 regulations.

Range
CapaCity: Low-floor, high-capacity bus, which was presented as a prototype in 2005. Its four-axle, four-door articulated bus design (with only one articulation joint) opens up a new chapter in the development of high-capacity urban buses for regular service operations. The Capa-City,

Citaro city bus for Bucharest   1341739

Mercedes-Benz Sprinter Travel 65 minibus   1341740

which is 19.54 m long, is also equipped with a Euro 4 engine.

The Capa-City can transport up to 193 passengers, and its four double-width doors enable passengers to enter and exit the vehicle quickly.

Citaro: the Mercedes-Benz Citaro bus family includes a range of bus variants, covering local public transport requirements across the board on urban and rural regular-service routes. Drive systems meet the Euro 4 and Euro 5 emission standards as well as voluntary standards such as EEV (Enhanced Environmentally-friendly Vehicle). This urban bus also forms the basis for a test fleet of 36 fuel-cell buses and for the recently unveiled Mercedes-Benz Citaro G BlueTec Hybrid bus.

Conecto: Low-floor urban bus designed to open up a new segment for EvoBus GmbH in the markets of Eastern Europe. It is a robust, low-floor vehicle for urban use; it is not only very quiet and extremely manoeuvrable, even in busy city centres, but also available with environmentally-friendly Euro-3 and Euro-4-compliant engines.

Integro: Two-door bus, available in three lengths on two (*Integro* and *Integro M*) or three axles (*Integro L*) suitable for a range of operations from suburban services on short routes to long-distance rural services and is also suitable for shuttle services. Powered by engines which comply with the Euro 4 exhaust emissions standard and which feature BlueTec diesel technology based on the SCR principle. All models of the new Integro use the horizontally mounted Mercedes-Benz OM 457 hLA six-cylinder in-line unit with a displacement of 12 litres. In its standard form, it has an output of 220 kW (299 hp) and maximum torque of 1,250 Nm at the low engine speed of just 1,100 rpm. A 260-kW (354-hp) variant with 1,600 Nm of torque at 1,100 rpm is available as an option. This is the standard power plant for the 15-m long, three-axle Integro L. As an alternative, the longest Integro can be ordered with an output of 300 kW (408 hp) and 1,900 Nm of torque.

Intouro: High-floor vehicle which has been specially designed for rural-service applications such as rural regular-service use and regular school-bus services. It is manufactured by DaimlerChrysler's Turkish subsidiary Mercedes-Benz Türk AS at the advanced Hoşdere plant (near Istanbul) which underwent a major expansion in 2005. Launched at the beginning of 2007, the Mercedes-Benz Intouro replaces the successful rural-service variant of the Mercedes-Benz Conecto Ü which has been built for the Turkish and Eastern European markets since 1998.

Sprinter Transfer: Five basic variants in four lengths and with 12 to 22 passenger seats, the new Mercedes-Benz Sprinter Transfer minibus is suitable for inter-urban and shuttle service.

Orion VII Next Generation diesel-electric hybrid transit bus   1341738

It comes from the product range of Mercedes-Benz Minibus GmbH, a wholly-owned subsidiary of EvoBus GmbH, which handles the European bus and coach business of the DaimlerChrysler Group.

The standard equipment includes the OM 646 DE 22 LA four-cylinder diesel engines with outputs ranging from 65 kW (88 hp) and 80 kW (109 hp) to 110 kW (150 hp). All engines are low-pollutant in compliance with the Euro 4 emissions standard and feature a diesel particulate filter as standard. A six-speed manual transmission transfers power to the road wheels, or buyers can choose an optional five-speed automatic transmission.

Tourino: Midi touring coach, which is 9.35 m long and can seat up to 36 passengers. Powered by a rear-mounted OM 926 LA turbo-diesel engine with a displacement of 7.2 litres. However, the drive system now uses Blue-Tec diesel technology with an SCR catalytic converter, thereby enabling the coach to meet the Euro 4 emission limits. This adjustment has been accompanied by a noticeable increase in engine power, with maximum output now at 210 kW/286 hp at 2,200 rpm. Maximum torque has increased to 1120 Nm at the unchanged engine speed of 1200–1600 rpm.

Tourismo: Series of touring coaches. The range of models includes four high-deck touring coaches along with a new 13-m two-axle variant, all with extensive safety features including ESP.

Travego: Manufactured solely for the Turkish market, Mercedes-Benz Travego's line-up for the

export markets consists of the high-deck touring coach Travego (max. 15 rows of seats. 12.14 m long, two axles), the Travego M (max. 16 rows of seats, 12.96 m long, three axles) and the Travego L (max. 17 rows of seats, 13.99 m long, three axles). The overall height of all three variants is 3.71 m.

Chassis: A range of chassis is available, including the OC 500 RF (RF = Raised Floor) chassis which provides the foundation for the latest generation of touring coaches and rural-service buses.

Contracts

The Romanian bus operator Regia Autonoma de Transport Bucuresti (RATB) and the DaimlerChrysler subsidiary EvoBus GmbH signed a contract in mid-September 2007 for the delivery of a second batch of 500 urban buses for the city of Bucharest. The first 50 buses were scheduled for delivery in December 2007, and the remaining 450 are to be delivered by the end of 2009.

In December 2007, Daimler Buses North America has received orders totalling 1,052 Orion VII Next Generation diesel-electric hybrid transit buses from some of North America's largest transit authorities. MTA New York City Transit has ordered 850 and the City of Ottawa (OC Transpo) 202 Orion VII Next Generation diesel-electric hybrid transit buses. These buses will be powered by BAE Systems' HybriDrive® diesel-electric hybrid propulsion system and delivered into 2010.

Darwen Group Limited

Please now see under Optare plc.

Darwen LPD

Please now see under Optare plc.

Diamond Coach Corporation

PO Box 489, 2300 West Fourth Street, Oswego, Kansas 67356, USA
Tel: (+1 620) 795 21 91
Fax: (+1 620) 795 48 16
e-mail: diamond@diamondcoach.com
Web: www.diamondcoach.com

Key personnel
President: *Richard Seybolt*

Background
The company was formed in 1957 and began manufacturing buses in the late 1970s and early

1980s. In 1988 the company was purchased by Dick Seybolt and Wayne Lowe.

Products
Minibus bodies.

Range
VIP Series: Carries between 12 and 33 passengers on a dual rear axle chassis. Wheelchair lift can be fitted. The VIP body series is built to either 2.44 m or 2.59 m width, depending upon the length. Ford or GM chassis with petrol engines are used, though there is a diesel option. The Ford chassis is available in three lengths and the GM chassis in five lengths. Body structure

is a lightweight combination of glass fibre and honeycomb unibody structure. Many seating plans can be provided, with up to 10 wheelchair placements.

UFL Model: Ford chassis available in three body lengths.

Dongfeng Motor Co Ltd (DFL)

10 Dongfeng Road, Wuhan, Hubei 430056, China
Web: www.dfl.com.cn

Key personnel
Chairman: *Xu Ping*
President and Chief Executive Officer: *Katsumi Nakamura*
Staff: 70,000 (DFL total)

Background
Established in 2003, as a co-operation between Dong Feng Motor Corporation (DFM) and Nissan Motors Co.

Current situation
The company produces trucks, buses, commercial vehicles and passenger vehicles.

DFL has nine subsidiaries and operating units, some of which produce complete buses and chassis. Please see below for details.

Developments
DFL plans to establish an R&D centre for passenger vehicles.

Commercial Vehicle Company
Key personnel
General Manager: *Tong Dongcheng*
Vice-General Managers: *Zhou Qiang*
  Huang Gang
  Hu Jianguo
Staff: 34,000+

Background
The Commercial Vehicle Company was established in 2003, with the integration of Liuzhou Automobile Company, Hangzhou Automobile Company, Xinjiang Automobile Company, Hiuzhou Automobile Company and Shenzhen Automobile Company.

Current situation
The Commercial Vehicle Company has eight plants and 12 subsidiaries.

Products
The company produces heavy-, medium- and light-duty commercial vehicles and buses including the production and assembly of engine, cab, frame, bus chassis and blanks.

Range
Vossen DHZ6113HR: Bus/coach.

Production
Capacity for the production of 300,000 whole vehicles per year.

Dongfeng Bus Chassis Co Ltd
36# Bailang Middle Road, Bailang Economic Development Zone, Shiyan City, Hubei Province, China

Key personnel
General Manager: *Hu Jianguo*
  Staff: 860

Background
A subsidiary of DFL, Dongfeng Bus Chassis Co Ltd is a joint venture between DFL and Dongfeng Industrial Company.

The company holds ISO09001:2000 and ISO14000 certification.

Products
Bus chassis.

Range
More than 300 types of chassis from minibus to 12 m urban coaches, including bus chassis with super-low floor, double-fuel bus chassis, bus chassis with the engine separated from the transmission, off-road 4×4 bus chassis, bus chassis with post-positioned engine and bus chassis with central-positioned engine. Versions include: **EQ6900KT**, **EQ6920KS**, **EQ6100KR**, **EQ6890RC-104**, **EQ6781KR** and **EQ6890RC**.

Production
In 2003, the company produced 28,032 units.

Dong Feng Automobile Co Ltd (DFAC)
No 1 Dong Feng Road, Xiangfan, 441004, Hubei Province, China
Tel: (+86 710) 339 60 06   Fax: (+86 710) 339 68 09
Web: www.dfac.com

Key personnel
Chairman: *Xu Ping*
General Manager: *Zhu Fushou*

Current situation
The company comprises six subsidiaries. Of these, some produce bus-related products.

Dong Xiangfan Tourist Bus Co Ltd designs and produces more than 300 bus chassis models which have been used by more than 90 bus manufactures in China.

Products
Manufacture and sale of light commercial vehicles, engines and components.

Double K Inc

Hometown Trolley
701 North Railroad Avenue, Crandon, WI 54520, US
Tel: (+1 715) 478 50 90   Fax: (+1 715) 478 50 95
e-mail: kristina@newnorth.net
Web: www.hometowntrolley.com

Key personnel
President: *Kristina Pence-Dunow*

Background
Trolleybuses were first built in 1976, when the company was known as Lazy N Inc.

Products
Rear- and front-engine trolleybuses, with alternative fuel systems, such as CNG or propane, as options.

Range
Villager F2 Series: front-engine, rubber-tyred trolleybuses, width 95-102 in, height 126 in, with wheelchair lift and restraints, available in the following models:
FE158: Length 27 ft, capacity 20–24 passengers;
FE178: Length 29 ft, capacity 24–28 passengers;
FE190: Length 31 ft, capacity 28–32 passengers;
FE208: Length 32 ft, capacity 32–34 passengers;
FE228: Length 35 ft, capacity 38–40+ passengers.

Main Street R3 Series: Rear-engine, rubber-tyred trolleybuses, width 96-102 in, height 130 in, with wheelchair lift and restraints, available in the following models:
RE190: Length 31ft, capacity 28–32 passengers;
RE208: Length 35ft, capacity 32–34 passengers;
RE228: Length 39ft, capacity 38–40+ passengers.

Production
More than 400 trolleybuses have been produced since 1976.

Dupon Trolley Industries

240 3rd Rue, Quebec City, G1L 2S8, Canada
Tel: (+1 418) 529 06 19
Fax: (+1 418) 529 38 30
Freephone: (800) 267 06 16
e-mail: j.dupont@dupontrolley.com
Web: www.dupontrolley.com

Key personnel
President and General Manager: *Jean Dupont*
Vice-President & Production Director: *Joël Dupont*

Background
Originally formed as a family business, Dupont Motorcoach, in 1936.

Products
All vehicles are ADA compliant. The company also carries out urban bus refurbishment.
Champlain 1608: Tramcar replica bus with multiplex wiring and increased width of 2.59 m, allowing aisle width to be enlarged to 482 mm. A Ricon wheelchair lift can be fitted in the centre door. The chassis is by ThomasBuilt and a CNG engine can be specified. It is 10.4 m long and seats up to 41 with up to 20 standing.

Dupon Trolley Frontenac 1672 trolleybus
0547538

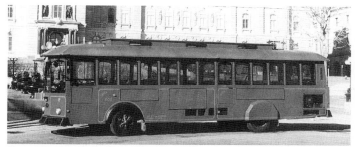

DuponTrolley Champlain 1608 trolley replica bus   0547536

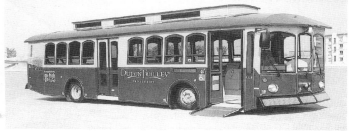

DuponTrolley Champlain Low Floor 1608 trolleybus   0547535

Frontenac 1672: Rubber-tyred urban transit bus, with a front-mounted diesel-fuel-powered unit, designed for heavy-duty transit service and for extremes in both temperature and humidity. The vehicle is capable of negotiating grades of 16 per cent or greater.

Champlain Low Floor 1608: Low-floor rubber-tyred urban transit bus with a rear-mounted diesel-fuel- or CNG-powered unit designed for heavy-duty transit service. The vehicle has front entrance and rear exit doors.

Durisotti SA

Avenue de la Fosse 13, PO Box 4, F-62430 Sallaumines, France
Tel: (+33 3) 21 69 24 24   Fax: (+33 3) 21 78 27 00
e-mail: durisotti@durisotti.com
Web: www.durisotti.fr,
   www.durisotti.com

Key personnel
President: *Jean-Pierre Durisotti*
General Manager: *Jean-François Durisotti*

Works Director: *Philippe Hauet*
Commercial Director: *François Loor*
Sales Director: *Yves Parquet*
Export Manager: *Nicolas Cornec*
Communications Assistant: *Delphine Kolaczyk*
   Staff: 550 (2008)

Background
The company has offices and production sites at Saullaumines, Lens (main site), Lille, Metz, Agen and Lyon. In 2007 the company had a turnover of some EUR65 million.

Durisotti is certified to ISO 9001 (2000) standards.

Products
Bus bodies, mini-buses for handicapped persons, mini-coaches seating up to 28 passengers, urban mini-buses and other vehicles.

EA Karosserie-und Fahrzeugbau Gera GmbH (EA KFB)

Siemensstrasse 37, D-07546 Gera, Germany
Tel: (+49 365) 43 76 90
Fax: (+49 365) 437 69 24
e-mail: info@eakfb.de
Web: www.eakfb.de

General Manager: *Peter Schilling*

Background
Associated with Ernst Auwärter of Steinenbronn.

Products
Bodywork for mini- and midibuses.

Range
CITY:
Sprinter Skate L – HNF
City Skate Shuttle
City Skate Max
Maxi Skate Shuttle
Midi Skate City

KOMBI:
Sprinter Skate

Sprinter Skate L
City Skate Shuttle
Kombi Skate
Midi Skate Kombi

TRAVEL:
Sprinter Skate
Sprinter Skate L
Sunny Skate
Travel Skate HD
Midi Skate Travel

Eicher Motors Limited (EML)

Plot 102 & 102A, Industrial Area No 1, Distt Dhar, Pithampur – 454 775, Madhya Pradesh, India
Tel: (+91 7292) 40 26 33   Fax: (+91 7292) 40 26 11
e-mail: reach@eicher.in
Web: www.eicherworld.com

Corporate office
Eicher Motors Limited
No 12, Commercial Complex, Greater Kaialsh-II, Masjid Moth, New Delhi 110048, India
Tel: (+91 11) 41 43 76 00   Fax: (+91 11) 41 43 77 00

Key personnel
Chairman & Director: *S Sandilya*
Managing Director & Chief Executive Officer: *Siddhartha Lal*

Chief Executive, Eicher Motors:
   A Ramasubramanian
Other Directors: *P N Vijay, Priya Brat, M J Subbaiah*
   Staff: Not currently available

Background
Eicher Motors Limited consists of the automotive businesses of the Eicher Group. Eicher Motors was founded in 1982 to manufacture a range of commercial vehicles.

Products
Medium-sized buses, chassis and other automotive products. Light commercial and heavy commercial bus versions range from 21 to 69 seats. The company also has a network of dealers for sale, service and maintenance network.

Range
Bus
Eicher Skyline Bus: Available in three wheelbase options.
Eicher Skyline CNG: Bus with engine designed for CNG and Euro 3 compliant. Available in three versions.
Eicher Cruiser: Available in three seating options. A CNG version is also available.
Eicher School Bus: Designed jointly with the Institute of Road Traffic Education (IRTE), featuring hazard warning lamps, auto-retractable footsteps and speed alarm.

Chassis
The company also offers bus chassis in a number of models and wheel-bases.

Ekobus as

Lumiérů 1025/34a, CZ-152 00 Prague 5, Czech Republic
Tel: (+420 2) 51 68 23 93   Fax: (+420 2) 51 68 23 64
e-mail: info@ekobus.cz
Web: www.ekobus.cz

Key personnel
Member of the Board of Directors: *Michal Jergl*

Background
The NORDlogistic company was renamed Ekobus as on March 2004.

Products
Production of EKOBUS Compressed Natural Gas (CNG) buses. Vehicles, available in three lengths (9.5, 10.5 and 12 m), are powered by Cumins Westport B5.9 or 8.3 engines. Range, dependent on the number of Ullit SA, France storage tanks installed, is from 450 to 700 km.

The company also provides service and repair work and trades in buses, spare parts, tyres, batteries and safety devices. It carries out refits of older buses to CNG-powered engines and can provide technical advice and service for vehicle users.

Range
EKOBUS City (90+1), **EKOBUS Intercity** (75 (81)+1), **EKOBUS Intercity LC** (45(46)+1), **EKOBUS City plus** (102+1) and **EKOBUS Intercity plus** (83+1).

Developments
There are currently more than 100 EKOBUSes in service.

In 2006, EKOBUS was the winner of a Gold Medal at the International Trade Fair in Plovdiv.

ElDorado National

9670 Galena Street, Riverside, California 92509, US
Tel: (+1 909) 591 95 57
Fax: (+1 909) 591 52 85
e-mail: info@eldorado-ca.com
Web: www.enconline.com

Other office
1655 Wall Street, Salina, Kansas 67401, US
Tel: (+1 785) 827 10 33
Freephone: (+1 800) 850 12 87
Fax: (+1 785) 827 09 65
e-mail: sales@enconline.com
Web: As above

Key personnel
Group President, Thor Industries, Commercial Bus Division: *Andrew Imanse*
President and General Manager, Kansas: *Sheldon Walle*
President and General Manager, California: *Tony Wayne*
Staff: 644

ElDorado National E-Z Rider II BRT 1374509

ElDorado National Passport 1374511

ElDorado National Aero Elite 1195970

ElDorado National Aerotech 1374507

ElDorado National Aerolite 1374506

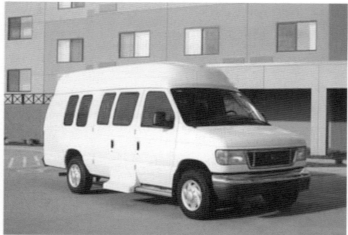

ElDorado National Express 1195978

ElDorado National Amerivan PT 1374508

Parent company

Thor Industries Inc.

Background

Thor Industries Inc entered the small to mid-size bus industry in 1988 by acquiring ElDorado Bus, which had been building buses since 1979. Thor expanded its participation in this industry in 1991 by acquiring National Coach Corporation, which was established in 1975. ElDorado National is the organisation which resulted from this combination.

The company's sales and service network covers the US, Canada, the Pacific Rim and the Caribbean.

The company is ISO 9001 certified to current standards.

Products

Mobility vans, mid-size and heavy-duty buses. Fuel systems available include petrol (gas), diesel, clean diesel, LPG, CNG, LNG and hybrid-electric. Over 600 standard floor plans are available, but the company will manufacture to customers' specific requirements.

All vehicles comply with ADA, FMVSS and CMVSS requirements.

Range

Axess: 40-ft, low-floor, 102 in wide, heavy-duty bus. Rear engine, with chassis designed by ElDorado National. Available with diesel or alternate fuel engines.

EZ-Rider II: Heavy-duty, low-floor transit bus. Rear engine, with chassis designed by ElDorado National. Available in 30 ft, 32 ft and 35 ft lengths and 8.5 ft wide. A variety of floor plans with diesel or alternative fuel engines are available. In 2008, a Bus Rapid Transit (BRT) option was introduced.

Passport: Medium-duty low-floor cutaway bus available in 29 ft or 34 ft lengths. Built on the Chevy 26,000 lb chassis with seating for up to 31 passengers. The Passport is built at the Riverside, California facility which is the same facility that builds the company's heavy-duty models. The Passport is manufactured with many of the processes used in our heavy-duty buses. Petrol, diesel and alternate fuels are available.

Transmark RE & XHF: Heavy-duty, rear engine, mid-size transit bus. Available in 29 ft, 32 ft or 35 ft lengths, with seating capacities of 29 to 41 passengers. The vehicle can be adapted for elderly or disabled accessibility. Diesel or alternate fuel engines are available.

Aerolite: Small steel reinforced composite cutaway bus, seating up to 14 passengers. Can be configured not to require a commercial driver's licence. Dual rear wheels. Available on Ford or Chevy chassis and lengths from 19 ft to 21 ft.

Aerotech: Mid-sized steel reinforced composite cutaway bus available on Ford or Chevy chassis, and in lengths from 20 ft to 25 ft, giving seating capacity of up to 25 passengers. Crash-tested in an automotive testing facility.

Aero Elite: Medium-duty steel reinforced composite cutaway bus, seating up to 37 passengers. Available on the International or Chevrolet chassis and lengths from 25 ft to 35 ft.

Transtech: Mid-sized integrated steel cutaway bus, seating up to 25 passengers. Available on Ford or Chevy chassis and lengths from 20 ft to 25 ft.

Trans Elite: 37-ft mid-sized integrated steel cutaway bus, seating up to 37 passengers. Available on the Chevy chassis.

Trans Elite XTRM: 37-ft mid-sized integrated steel cutaway bus, seating up to 37 passengers. Available on the Chevy chassis.

Amerivan PT: Lowered-floor accessible minivan with capacity for up to 6 passengers or 4 ambulatory and 2 wheelchair passengers. Crash-tested and meeting or exceeding all applicable US vehicle safety standards.

Express: Raised-top Ford van seating up to 9 passengers with rear luggage or 12 passengers without rear luggage. Suitable for shuttle applications.

ElDorado National Transtech 1374514

ElDorado National Trans Elite 1374512

ElDorado National XHF 1325377

ElDorado National Axess 1374510

VersaShuttle: Raised-top Ford van seating up to 10 passengers with rear or side lift. Suitable for on-demand transportation for the elderly or physically challenged.

Production
Average of 3,300 vehicles per year.

Developments
In its continuing effort to assure maximum levels of quality and durability of their products, ElDorado National has built on-site simulated FTA test tracks at both of its new manufacturing facilities in Riverside, California and Salina, Kansas. The design criterion is the same used for the durability track in Altoona, Pennsylvania. It includes multiple elements that are staged to provide an accurate simulation and reaction by the vehicle to various operating conditions.

Contracts
In November 2005, the company received a 5-year contract for up to 222 30 ft E-Z Rider II low-floor buses for PACE in Illinois.

In 2007, the company received an order from Dallas Area Transit (DART) for 209 25-ft Aero Elite buses on International 3200 chassis.

ElDorado National, California recently delivered 146 CNG- and diesel-powered rear-engine low-floor buses to the following airports: Los Angeles, O'Hare, Dallas/Ft. Worth, Denver, Reagan National, Phoenix, Kansas City, Indianapolis, Sacramento and Salt Lake City.

In 2008, ElDorado National, California received an order from the City of Santa Monica for the new E-Z Rider II BRT powered by gasoline hybrid electric.

ElDorado National Trans Elite XTRM   1374513

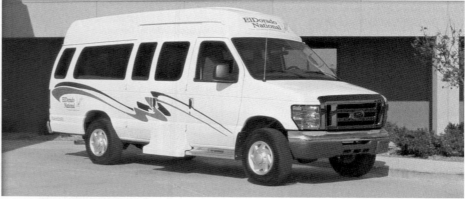

ElDorado National VersaShuttle   1374515

Eletra Industrial Ltda

Rua Monteiro Lobato 100, Montanhão 09791-253, São Bernardo do Campo, São Paulo, Brazil
Tel: (+55 11) 41 27 92 92   Fax: (+55 11) 43 39 63 09
e-mail: eletra@eletrabus.com
Web: www.eletrabus.com.br

Key personnel
Commercial Director: *Ieda Maria de Oliveira*
    Staff: Not currently available

Current situation
The company develops hybrid technology and produces a range of hybrid-electric vehicles, the first of which was launched in 2000.

Range
The company produces standard and articulated, including bi-articulated, low- and high-floor hybrid buses and trolleybuses.

Engineering Automotive Manufacturing Co (EAMCO)

Wadi Hof, Helwan, Cairo, Egypt
Tel: (+20 2) 371 22 73, 369 05 73
Fax: (+20 2) 370 14 67, 369 54 24
e-mail: it_eamco@egyfit.com.eg
Web: www.eamcoegypt.com

Key personnel
Chairman and Managing Director:
    Ahmed Barakat
Planning and Technical Affairs Director:
    Hasan AbdEl Latif Merza
Technical Director:
    ElSayed Mahrous
    Staff: 1,864

Background
Established in July 2000, when the El Nasr Automotive Manufacturing Co (originally formed in 1959) separated into two independent companies.

The company has three factories: Factory No. 1: Chassis assembly, truck and agricultural tractors; Factory No. 2: Machine assembly and testing of diesel engines; Factory No. 3: Bus body building.

Products
Buses, midibuses, minibuses, microbuses and coaches, including bodywork. The company works in cooperation with companies such as: Ashok-Leyland, Cummins, Daewoo, Deutz, IMR, Iveco, MAN, MWM, Renault and Scania.

Range
Long-distance, tourist and luxury buses: Eamco/Eurorider 35, Eamco/Daewoo BH 177.
Inter-city buses: Eamco/Cummins, Eamco/Daewoo BS 106L, Eamco/MAN 964, Eamco/MAN 982, Eamco/MWM 965/1, Eamxo 965.
City buses: Eamco/Eurorider 26, Eamco/MAN 976/1, Eamco midibus, Eamco minibus.
Midi- and minibuses.

Contracts
The company's main customers include the Cairo Transport Authority (CTA), the Alexandria Passenger Transport Authority (APTA) and the Greater Cairo Bus Company (GCBC). In 2002 EAMCO obtained a contract from the Greater Cairo bus company for 100 bus skeletons and 100 AC minibuses.

Euro Coach Builders

Gweedore Business Park, Derrybeg, Letterkenny, Co Donegal, Ireland
Tel: (+353 74) 953 15 28
Fax: (+353 74) 953 19 30
e-mail: info@eurocoachbuilders.ie
Web: www.eurocoachbuilders.ie

Key personnel
Managing Director:
    Paul Gribben
Business Development and Commercial
    Manager: *Chris Watts*
    Staff: 80

Products
Established in 1988. Mini- and midibuses.

Range
ARORA 200: Launched in 2008 on the Mercedes-Benz Vario 816D chassis, the coach carries up to 29 passengers with a flexible seating layout that can be quickly converted to 16 VIP extra-large seats. Length 8.52 m, width 2.35 m and up to 4.3 m³ of luggage space.
V29/33: Built on the Mercedes-Benz Vario 816D chassis, seating up to 29 (V29) and up to 33 (V33), length 8.24 m, width 2.37 m, height 2.835 m.
Sprinter: Mercedes-Benz bus, seating up to 18 (LWB) or 19 (EX-LWB), length 6.94 m (LWB) or 7.345 m (EX-LWB), width 1.993 m, height 2.82 m (excluding air-conditioning).
Crew Cab: Euro Coach can undertake all types of crew cab conversions and modifications.

Services
In 2008, Euro Coach entered an agreement with UK Carlyle Bus & Coach to manage its after-sales spare parts activity across Europe.

Euro Coach has also established a broader network of dealers across UK and Ireland, totalling 15. Euro Coach intends to announce five new dealers in Europe, with three in Germany, one Swiss and one Benelux.

EvoBus GmbH – Setra Omnibusse

PO Box 2660, D-89016 Ulm, Germany
Tel: (+49 731) 18 10
Fax: (+49 731) 181 24 91
Web: www.setra.de

Street address
Carl-Zeiss-Strasse 2, D-89237 Neu-Ulm, Germany

Key personnel
Chairman, EvoBus: *Hartmut Schick*
Setra Product Director: *Werner Staib*
Public Relations: *Udo Sürig*
  Staff: Not currently available

Subsidiary
Setra of North America Inc
6012-B High Point Road, Greensboro, North Carolina 27407, US
Tel: (+1 336) 878 54 11   Fax: (+1 336) 878 54 10
President: *Andreas Strecker*

Background

In July 1994, Mercedes-Benz agreed to buy Kässbohrer Setra. EvoBus was then established to run all of the bus and coach operations of Mercedes-Benz and Setra. EvoBus has retained the two marques but has now dropped Kässbohrer from the Setra name. There has been rationalisation of the production facilities and some components, including underframes, are shared.

Products

Integral buses and coaches, including articulated and double-deck.

Range

Setra models are grouped into three classes, TopClass, ComfortClass and MultiClass. The last includes all interurban models.

Multiclass 400:

The MultiClass 400 is suitable for regular-service passenger transport and excursions. Setra offers bus operators a choice of six different models in this product segment. Measuring 10.8 m, the **S 412 UL** is suitable for operation on regular-service routes in regions with challenging terrain, such as narrow or steep mountain passes. The rest of the MultiClass 400 range consists of the 12.2 m **S 415 UL**, the **S 417 UL**, measuring 14.05 m, and the **S 419 UL**, which measures 14.98 m in length.

Low-floor versions are the 12 m **S 415 NF** and the 13 m **S 416 NF**, with an entrance height of 360 mm and fitted with 11 R 22.5 tyres. These two models are ideal for regular-service operations with a high passenger flow and also for accommodating parents with young children or wheelchair users.

ComfortClass 400:

The ComfortClass 400 series is suitable for touring and rural operations. The series has been redesigned, with new vehicle lengths and a cockpit that has been completely redeveloped, plus technical innovations both inside and out for all of the models: the **S 415 GT**, **S 415 GT-HD**, **S 416 GT-HD** and **S 417 GT-HD**.

TopClass 400:

The TopClass 400 is a new coach concept from Setra. It has 2.1 m of standing height in the central aisle. The roof, with its broad lockers moved well towards the outer panels, creates more vertical space, and the large deep windows increase the feeling of space at the sides and create a bright interior. The seats, manufactured by Setra, each have a lap-type safety belt. Together

Setra ComfortClass 400 series S 419 GT-HD three-axle coach (EvoBus GmbH Setra Omnibusse)
1375344

Setra TopClass 400 series S 431 DT double-deck coach (EvoBus GmbH Setra Omnibusse)   1375342

Setra MultiClass 400 series S 415 NF low-floor bus (EvoBus GmbH Setra Omnibusse)   1375343

with the energy-absorbing backrest on the front seat, a high level of safety is assured. It has a completely new heating system called TopAir, where air is drawn in over the entire length of the vehicle. Air conditioning is powered by means of an environmentally friendly waterglycol circuit. The water is heated in a compact and, therefore, maintenance-friendly `energy station'.

Power is available with the Mercedes-Benz in-line, six-cylinder OM 501 LA engine or the OM 457 LA engine or the OM 502 LA V8. Power outputs range from 300 kW or 315 kW from the in-line engine to 350 kW or 370 kW from the V8. All engines comply with the Euro 4 emission limits

and are optimised for low fuel consumption. Two six-speed manual shift gearboxes with different specifications, the GO 190 or the GO 210, make up the driveline. Optional is the ZF 12-speed HP automatic transmission with integral retarder. Three final drive ratios from 2.846 to 3.583 are available. The new HO6 driven bus and coach axle is of pressed-steel construction, making it considerably lighter than cast or welded designs without affecting its rigidity.

The TopClass 400 range comprises the **S 411 HD** club bus, measuring 10.1 m in length, the 12 m long **S 415 HD**, the three-axle **S 415 HDH** super high-decker, the 12.99 m long **S 416 HDH**, also with three axles, plus the **S 417 HDH** super high-decker measuring 13.85 m. The premium model is the **S 431 DT** double-decker model, measuring 13.89 m. Setra purposely designed the **S 417** model for the North American market, adapting it to requirements in the US before unveiling it there in Spring 2003. The **S 415 HD** comes in a right-hand-drive version for countries such as the UK, the Republic of Ireland and Cyprus.

On all three-axle vehicles, the trailing axle is controlled by active Rear Axle Steering (RAS), which is standard equipment. The Setra TopClass 400 running gear and the body have an overall width of 2.55 m. An anti-roll bar is standard.

A standard feature of the new Setra TopClass 400 is an Electronically controlled Brake System (EBS). It transfers all signals electronically to compress air valves near the wheels, thus optimising the braking system's response and pressure build-up times. This more rapid and precise braking pressure input reduces total stopping distances more effectively.

The complete vehicle electrics are networked with the Flexible Programmed Control (FPC) system via a CAN databus. Two of its benefits are that far fewer cables, relays and small components have to be used, and the operating reliability of these networked electronics is noticeably higher than in earlier systems. FPC consists of several intelligent modules located decentrally on the vehicle wherever there is equipment to control.

Developments

In May 2006, the first production vehicle with Lane Assistant was presented. The Lane Assistant system provides crucial safety support by helping the driver to stay aware at all times. Using a video camera that permanently monitors the distance between the side of the vehicle and the marker lines at the edge of the lane. The Lane Assistant also detects any danger of the vehicle leaving its lane unintentionally. If there is a risk of the vehicle crossing the marker lines, the driver receives a warning in a fraction of a second in the form of vibrations in the seat. Passengers will not be aware of this warning. The vibration warning is issued in keeping with the direction in which the vehicle starts to take through one of two vibrating motors built into the driver's seat cushion at thigh level.

In 2008, the Setra S 415 NF low-floor bus was chosen as the Bus of the Year 2009.

Fabryka Autobusów Solbus Sp zoo (Solbus)

ul Powstańców 7, PL-86-050 Solec Kujawski, Poland
Tel: (+48 52) 387 95 30   Fax: (+48 52) 387 95 53
e-mail: solbus@solbus.com.pl
Web: www.solbus.ic.net.pl

Current situation

Formed in 2001, Solbus produces buses and minibuses based on licensed technology from SOR Libchavy sro.

Range

B 9.5: Medium-floor city bus, length 9.52 m, width 2.525 m, height 2.95 m, seating 24–26+1, total capacity 86+1.
SN 11: Low-entry city bus, length 10.73 m, width 2.52 m, height 3.0 m, seating 28–30+1, total capacity 92+1.
C 9.5: Intercity bus, length 9.52 m, width 2.52 m, height 2.95 m, seating 34–39+1, total capacity 67+1.
C 10.5: Intercity bus, length 10.73 m, width 2.525 m, height 2.95 m, seating 43–47+1, total capacity 77+1.

LH 9.5: Tourist bus, length 9.52 m, width 2.525 m, height 3.15 m, seating 36–39+1.
Mercedes-Benz Sprinter: Minibus, length 6.59 m, width 1.994 m, height 2.665 m, seating up to 19+1 (school version).

Developments

The company has announced that it intends to start production of a new bus, to its own design. The new **Solbus SN 11** is a low-floor city bus powered by an Iveco Euro-4 engine.

FFB Komerc SA Beograd (FAP-FAMOS BEOGRAD)

Francuska Street 61–65, 11001 Belgrade, Serbia
Tel: (+381 11) 63 01 91, 328 21 82
Fax: (+381 11) 63 69 61
e-mail: ffbkomerc@ptt.yu
Web: www.ffbkomerc.co.yu

Key personnel

General Manager: *Zoran Kijac*
Export Manager: *Nenad Kravic*
Sales Manager: *Rade Pavlica*

Factories

Bus chassis, chassis components and truck production: FAP, Priboj.
Engines under licence from Mercedes-Benz, gearboxes under licence from ZF; clutches: Famos, Sarajevo.
Buses and bus bodies: NEOBUS, Novi Sad and FAP, Priboj.

Background

FFB Komerc has had co-operation with Mercedes-Benz for more than 30 years with the majority of models being made under licence and with German technology. The main FFB bus and coach production plants are in Novi Sad (NEOBUS), and Priboj (FAP), Serbia, where integral vehicles are assembled.
NEOBUS bodies are built onto locally made and Volvo chassis.

Products

Suburban, city, intercity buses and coaches, including articulated buses. Bus and coach bodywork. CKD kits.

Fisher Coachworks LLC

1150 Stephenson Highway, Troy, Michigan 48083, US
Tel: (+1 313) 483 37 00
Fax: (+1 313) 483 37 01
e-mail: info@fishercoachworks.com
Web: www.fishercoachworks.com

Key personnel

Chief Executive Officer: *Greg Fisher*
Chief Technology Officer: *Bruce Emmons*
Chief Operating Officer: *Griffin Burgh*
Vice-President, Marketing: *John VanAlstyne*
Staff: Currently unavailable

Current situation

Fisher Coachworks LLC was formed in 2007 to manufacture advanced hybrid vehicles, using a patented ultra-lightweight stainless steel unibody structural system.

Developments

In 2008, the company began road-testing its first prototype vehicle, the low-floor GTB-40 PHEV Transit Bus, which was formally launched in September 2008. The propulsion system is a battery-diesel system, with the sodium nickel chloride batteries being charged by regenerative braking and by plugging into the mains during off-duty hours.

Fisher Coachworks are monitoring the development of battery technology and is currently evaluating lithium ion, lithium phosphate and titanium oxide technology.

The company intends to relocate to a larger manufacturing facility in order to prepare for production of vehicles in early 2009.

Ford Motor Company Limited

Registered Office
Eagle Way, Brentwood, Essex, CM13 3BW, UK
Tel: (+44 1277) 25 30 00
Fax: (+44 1277) 21 12 85
Web: www.ford.co.uk

Other offices

Information Services
PO Box 4430, Coventry, CV3 9BH, G2 4XF, UK
Tel: (+44 845) 841 11 11

Products

Minibuses.

Range

Transit minibus: The Transit van is available as a 'window-van' minibus production version with 9, 12, 15 or 17 seats or as a chassis cowl for subsequent conversion by specialist body builders. The design GVW is in the range 2,180 to 3,500 kg. Power options include an improved 2.5 litre direct injection diesel engine and a new five-speed gearbox. Automatic transmission is available on diesel-powered Transits. The engine complies with the latest emission and particulate standards. A catalytic converter is available, coupled to the 2 litre low-emission central fuel injection engine. Power-assisted steering is also available.

A number of builders produce built-up chassis cowls as panel vans for later conversion by other body builders into minibuses as well as welfare/ambulance applications.

The minibus features driver and passenger airbags as standard with three-point seatbelts fitted to passenger seats.

Assembly of Ford Transits was started in 1996 at a plant in Obchuk, near Minsk, Belarus.

The Ford Transit was revamped in 2000 with new styling, 2l Duratorq direct-injection engine, front-wheel drive options, three wheelbases and three roof heights. Initially it is being produced as a rear-wheel drive model with medium- or long-wheelbase and medium- or high-roof options.
Transit Tourneo: 8 (7+1) or 9 (8+1) seat versions available.

Freightliner Custom Chassis Corporation (FCCC)

552 Hyatt Street, Gaffney, South Carolina 29341, USA
Tel: (+1 864) 487 17 00   Fax: (+1 864) 487 64 00
e-mail: fcccquestions@freightliner.com
Web: www.freightlinerchassis.com

Key personnel
President: *Robert Harbin*
Director, Sales and Marketing: *Jonathan Randall*

Technical Sales Manager, Commercial Bus:
   Phillip Woolen
Staff: Approximately 750

Background
Freightliner is a subsidiary of Daimler Trucks North America LLC (formerly Freightliner LLC) and is a Daimler company.

Products
Bus and speciality chassis, school bus chassis.

Range
XB Series: Bus chassis powered by a rear-mounted Cummins ISB-02 diesel engine, driving through an Allison transmission.
MB Series: Recently redesigned series, which includes the MB-55 chassis, suitable for light- to medium-duty shuttle applications. Option Clean Air Series, for CNG and LPG.
S2 chassis: Suitable for public transport, shuttle and special transport needs.

Ghabbour Group

Alexandria Desert Road, km 28, Industrial Zone, Abo Rawash, Cairo, Egypt
Tel: (+20 2) 539 10 88   Fax: (+20 2) 539 00 44
Web: www.ghabbour.com

Key personnel
Group Chairman and Chief Executive Officer:
   Raouf Ghabbour

Products
Bus and coach bodywork.

Range
Ghabbour began bus building in 1985 with kits supplied from Duple (Metsec) UK for mounting on Scania underframes as semi-integral coaches. A factory with capacity for building 250 buses a year was established with Metsec assistance

for eventual production of a range of luxury coaches, intercity buses and city buses, all based on mechanical units supplied from Scania.

Contracts
Ghabbour is now mainly supplying Volvo chassis.

Gillig Corporation

PO Box 3008, Hayward, California 94545-3008, US
Tel: (+1 510) 785 15 00   Fax: (+1 510) 785 68 19
Fax: (+1 510) 887 09 81 (Parts Division)
Web: www.gillig.com

Street address
25800 Clawiter Road, Hayward, California 94545, US

Key personnel
Vice-President, Marketing: *Brian Macleod*
Director, National Sales: *Joseph Policarpio*
Sales Managers: *Jerry Anderson, Clark Ahrens, San Enochian*

Background
Founded in 1890, the company is part of the Herrick Corporation.

Products
Integral buses and specialist vehicles.

Range
Gillig Phantom: The Phantom is available in three lengths, 12.19 m (40 ft), 10.64 m (35 ft) and 9.14 m (30 ft), and in two widths, 2.44 m (96 in) or 2.59 m (102 in), with maximum seating of 45, 37 and 25 respectively (all including two wheelchair positions).

Gillig 8.8 m (29 ft) low-floor bus   0547539

Powered by a Cummins (ISL, ISM) or DDC (S-50) engine driving through an Allison B400R, Voith or ZF gearbox, they have Meritor axles.
The Phantom can also be configured as an airport shuttle or urban commuter vehicle.
Gillig Low Floor Bus: Available in three options:
12.19 m (40 ft) long × 2.59 m (102 in) wide, seating 40
10.64 m (35 ft) long × 2.59 m (102 in) wide, seating 32
8.84 m (29 ft) long × 2.59 m (102 in) wide, seating 28

All are powered by a Cummins ISL engine driving through an Allison, Voith or ZF gearbox. They have Meritor axles and lightweight bodies.

Development
The company is involved in research and development in the following areas:
   Hybrid electric projects, including a current project with GM's Allison Division;
   Fuel cells, including development work with Ballard.

Girardin Minibus Inc

Trans-Canada Highway, Drummondville, Quebec, J2B 6V4, Canada
Tel: (+1 819) 477 82 22   Fax: (+1 819) 475 96 33
e-mail: minibussales@girardin.com
Web: www.girardin.com

Key personnel
President: *Steve Girardin*
Executive Assistant: *Jennifer Loblaw*

Background
Since 1966 the company has produced small commercial minibuses and school buses. Girardin Minibus Inc is the last family-owned bus manufacturing company in North America.

Products
Manufacturer of small and mid-size school, commercial and Multifunction School Activity Buses (MFSAB) from nine to 30 passengers and

special needs (ADA), on Ford, GM and Chevrolet cutaway chassis from 4,350 kg (9,600 lb) to 11,800 kg (26,000 lb) GVWR. Overall length from 5.79 m (19 ft) to 7.62 m (25 ft). Width of 218 cm (86 in) or 244 cm (96 in). Various petrol or turbo diesel engines, driving through four-speed automatic gearbox with overdrive. Available in a variety of wheelbases according to customer requirements.

Glaval Bus

Division of Forest River Inc
014 CR 1, Elkhart, IN 46514, US
Tel: (+1 800) 445 28 25   Fax: (+1 574) 264 42 59
e-mail: info@glavalbuc.com
Web: www.glavalbus.com

Key personnel
General Manager: *Phil Hayes*
Director, Sales and Marketing: *Doug Wright*

Background
Glaval Bus is a Division of Forest River Inc.

Products
Manufacturers of transit and shuttle buses from 21 to 38 ft in length. ADA equipment is available as options on all models.

Range
Primetime™: Steel buses seating up to 15 passengers on Ford E350 RV chassis with petrol or diesel engines.
Titan II: Mid-size bus seating up to 21 passengers on GMC G-Cutaway chassis with petrol or diesel engines.

Universal: Mid-size bus seating up to 25 passengers on Fors E350/E450 SuperDuty chassis, with petrol or diesel engines.
Easy On™: Low-entry bus, with optional kneeling, built on LF72 Workhorse custom chassis, a Duramax 6.6 litre engine and seating up to 28 passengers.
Titan: Range of buses seating up to 45 passengers, with Duramax 6.6 litre diesel or 8.1 litre petrol engines.
Apollo: Shuttle and transit bus seating up to 40 passengers, built on Freightlines MB55 chassis with Cummins ISB-02 engine.

Göppel Bus GmbH

Augsburg subsidiary (Sales and Marketing)
Alter Postweg 94, D-86159 Augsburg, Germany
Tel: (+49 821) 24 17 90   Fax: (+49 821) 241 79 30
e-mail: info@goeppel-bus.de
Web: www.goeppel-bus.de

Registered office
Mittelweg 4, D-04603 Nobitz/OT, Ehrenhain, Germany
Tel: (+49 344) 948 60   Fax: (+49 344) 948 61 44

Key personnel
Managing Director: *Bernhard Schmidt*
Marketing: *Irene Gossner*
Sales: *Eugen Baumstark*
Construction/Development: *Stefan Wetzstein*

Products
Bus and coach bodywork on NEOPLAN/NEOMAN/MAN chassis. Mini-coaches on Mercedes-Benz Sprinter chassis. Special purpose vehicles, such as library buses, prisoner transportation buses etc. Service and maintenance for buses as well as accident repairs and vehicle conditioning. Exclusive sale of Marbus coaches in Germany. Upholstery for bus seats for all bus interiors.

Developments
In October 2006, the company changed its name to Göppel Bus GmbH. Effective from 1 October 2006, operational business was spun off to Göppel Bus GmbH, with its registered office in Nobitz, Ehrenhain.

Goshen Coach Inc

25161 Leer Drive, Elkhart, Indiana 46514, US
Tel: (+1 866) 522 54 24
Fax: (+1 574) 266 58 66
e-mail: sales@goshencoach.com
Web: www.goshencoach.com

Key personnel
President: *Troy Snyder*
General Manager: *Vacant*
Staff: *170*

Background
Thor Industries acquired Goshen Coach in May 2005. Goshen Coach Inc now operates out of a newly purchased location in Elkhart, Indiana.
    The company is ISO 9001:2000 certified.

Products
Small and medium-sized bus bodies. Numerous floor plans are available with the flexibility to accommodate specific requirements. All vehicles comply with ADA, FMVSS and CMVSS requirements.

Range
Pacer II: Narrow body cutaway, up to 13 passengers. Ideal for rural and paratransit services. Various floor plans available in both gas and diesel engines.
Pacer II Ltd: Narrow body cutaway with co-pilot seat. Ideal for rural and shuttle services. Various floor plans available in both gas and diesel engines.
GC II: Wide body cutaway, up to 24 passengers. Available on Ford or Chevy gas and diesel chassis.

GC II – 5500: Medium duty cutaway bus, up to 39 passengers. Available on Chevy 4500 and 5500 chassis. Ideal for tour, shuttle, paratransit services.
Sentinel: Medium duty cutaway bus, up to 33 passengers. Ideal for tour, shuttle and paratransit services, based on International chassis.

Production
Average of 1,600 vehicles per year.

Developments
Goshen Coach Inc continues to invest and maximize levels of quality and product improvement. The company is completely renovating the lamination department with new state-of-the-art equipment and process controls.

Gruau Group

Gruau Laval
9 Boulevard Marius et Rene Gruau, F-53942 St-Berthevin Cedex, France
Tel: (+33 2) 43 66 38 88   Fax: (+33 2) 43 02 87 84
e-mail: commercial@gruau.com
Web: www.gruau.com

Key personnel
Director General: *Yvon Peurou*
Export Department: *Géraldine David*
Contact: *Léandre Provost*
    Staff: 330

Products
Minibus and microbus bodies.

Range
Electric **Microbus**, for on-demand transport, seating up to 22 passengers.
Minibuses: Available in multipurpose, school and shuttle versions, seating from 9 to 16 passengers, built on various chassis.
Special vehicles: The company has a range of vehicles designed for the transport of disabled people, including:
STHANDY version: Rear access using a manual ramp.

HACCESS version: Rear access using a lifting tailgate.
HACCESS Plus version: Rear access with a pneumatic lowering system.
KANGOO TPMR: Lengthened vehicle available in two versions, with a lowered rear floor.
FAMILY: Rear access with a pneumatic ramp system and lowered rear floor.
COLLECTY: Minibus adapted for the transport of 5/6 passengers + 1 wheelchair or 5/6/8/9 passengers.

Guangzhou Denway Bus Co Ltd

No 451, Shi Sha Road, Shi Jin Town, Baiyun District, Guangzhou 510430, China
Tel: (+86 20) 36 41 43 30
Fax: (+86 20) 36 41 55 66

Products
Major products are Denway brand, Pearl River brand large and medium (7.912 m) series buses covering all areas of mass transportation, public transportation, tourism and long-range transportation.

Range
Denwaybus: GZ6107, GZ6950, GZ6108, GZ6106, GZ6116, GZ6890, GZ6820S, GZ6880S1/

GZ6880S2, GZ6112S2/S3/SC/SV1/SV3, GZ6112S1/SV/SV2, GZ6112S5/S6/S7/6113S, GZ6120S and GZ5100XGC.

Developments
Latest products include 6105 air-conditioned electrical trolleybus, 12 m low-entrance city bus, 6102VSI (LPG) sole-fuel, environmental-friendly air-conditioned city bus, 6116 and 6950 tourist bus.

Guangzhou Isuzu Bus Co Ltd

No 68, Yanling YuanGang Road, Guangzhou 510507, China
Tel: (+86 20) 38 07 22 88
Fax: (+86 20) 37 08 11 80
e-mail: gzisuzu@gzisuzu.com
Web: www.gzisuzu.com

Background
Established in 2000, Guangzhou Isuzu Bus Co Ltd is a joint venture between Guangzhou Automobile Group , Isuzu Motors Limited and Isuzu (China) Investments Co Ltd.

Products
Coaches.

Range
Gala: GLK6121D (SHD), GLK6121D4 (LHD), GLK6120D (HD), GLK6120D5 (EHD) and GLK6121DW (WHD).
V: GLK6940H (V9) and GLK6110H1(V11).

Production
Annual capacity is 1,200 units.

Guangzhou Junda Automobile Enterprise Group

DaDe Road 114#, Guangzhou, Guangdong, China
Tel: (+86 20) 81 85 26 91   Fax: (+86 20) 81 86 27 80

Key personnel
Contact: *Youde Xie*

Background
Until 1992 was called Guangzhou Automobile & Agricultural Machinery Co. Two of the three subsidiaries offer buses.

Guangzhou Automobile Plant
Products
Guangzhou Dongfeng GZ650 and GZ655 buses have been built since the 1970s. Current production includes the GZ6890 and GZ6921 buses.

Guangzhou Bus Plant
Products
Offers buses under the Guangzhou trade mark; the range includes the GZK6700 7 m, GZK6944 9.4 m, GZ6972 9.7 m, GZK6100 10 m and GZK 6120 12 m buses.

Guangzhou Yangcheng Automobile Co Ltd

No 333, Guang Yuan Zhing Road, Guangzhou 510405, China
Tel: (+86 20) 86 59 28 07   Fax: (+86 20) 86 57 12 01

Yangchen Automobile Co Ltd
Background
Joint venture (50:50) between Guangzhou Automobile Group Co Ltd and China Lounge Investments Co Ltd.

Products
Manufacturer of minibuses.

Guangzhou Yancheng Tourist Bus Automobile Co Ltd
Key personnel
Staff: 300

Background
Bus manufacturer invested by Guangzhou Yangcheng Automobile Group Co Ltd and Guangzhou Automobile Group Co Ltd.

Production
Annual production capacity is 2,000 units.

Range
Minibuses and midibuses, including YC6591C1/C2, YC6701C1, YC6591C6, YC6701C6, YC6590Q3, YC6700Q3 YC6790 and YC6840.

Haargaz Ltd

Haargaz Transportation
PO Box 9318, 94 Yigaal Alon Street, Tel Aviv, IL-61092, Israel
Tel: (+972 3) 568 58 58
Fax: (+972 3) 561 89 78
e-mail: sraz@haargaz.co.il
Web: www.haargaz.co.il

Key personnel
Chief Executive Officer and Marketing Manager: *Shlomo Raz*
Staff: 155

Background
Part of the Haargaz Group (1932). The company is ISO 9001-2000 certified.

Products
City and Intercity bus and coach bodies, including armour-plated buses, on Mercedes-Benz, Volvo, Scania, MAN and DAF chassis and renovation of older vehicles.

Range
'Barak' 21 Bus: length 12 m, width 2.55 m, height 3.6 m on DAF, Scania, Mercedes-Benz or MAN chassis. Armoured version available on MAN-HOCL chassis.

One of 20 new Hess/Scania low-floor buses manufactured by Haargaz Ltd for bus operator Affifi (Aharon Gazit) 1168251

Low Floor Urban Buses **MAN NL 263 & 313**, with entry ramps. Articulated version available on MAN NG-363 chassis.
'Saar' 21 Bus.
Municipal Authority Model bus.

Production
Approximately 200 buses annually.

Production follows R-66 roll-over standards and bus design follows Euro 4 standard.

Contracts
Buses have been supplied to Israeli bus operators EGGED, DAN, Connex Israel, municipal authorities and private companies.

Hellenic Vehicle Industry SA (EΛBO/ELBO)

Industrial Area of Thessaloniki, GR-570 22 Thessaloniki, Greece
Tel: (+30 2310) 71 71 00
Fax: (+30 2310) 79 84 26
e-mail: info@elvo.gr
Web: www.elvo.gr

Key personnel
Managing Director: *Evangelos Mytilineos*
Deputy Managing Director: *Dimitrios Gagalis*
Commercial Director: *Dr D Koutras*
Staff: 1,000 (estimate)

Other offices
Athens branch
Leoforos NATO, Industrial Area of Aspropyrgos, Athens, Greece
Tel: (+30 210) 559 44 30
Fax: (+30 210) 559 44 23

Background
Hellenic Vehicle Industry SA (EΛBO/ELBO) was founded in 1972 as Steyr Hellas SR to build trucks and tractors. In 1986 it became Hellenic Vehicle Industry. In 2000, the Greek government sold a 43 per cent shareholding in EΛBO (ELBO) to two Greek companies, METKA SA and MYTILINEOS Group, and in December 2001 that shareholding was increased to 47.5 per cent.

The company is qualified to ISO 9001:2000 standards.

Products
Buses, trucks, military and other commercial vehicles.

Range
The company manufactures low-floor urban buses, including an articulated version, trolleybuses, intercity buses and coaches.

Contracts
In March 2003, the company signed a contract with OASTH for 54 low-floor buses. ELBO is also providing 90 buses to ILPAP.

Helmark Carosseri AB

Hyltevägen 25, SE-285 32 Markaryd, Sweden
Tel: (+46 433) 712 30
Fax: (+46 433) 163 04
e-mail: info@helmark.se
Web: www.helmark.se

Keypersonnel
General Manager: *Christer Helgesson*

Products
Bus and coach bodies including double-deckers and special-purpose vehicles. All body structure and panels are made of stainless steel.

Range
Helmark 325 S: 40 to 65 passengers; 2.55 m wide, 3.25 m high, 10 to 15 m long; chassis Scania or Volvo.
Helmark 345 S: 40 to 65 passengers; 2.55 m wide, 3.45 m high, 10 to 15 m long; chassis Scania or Volvo.

Helmark 360 S: 40 to 65 passengers; 2.55 m wide, 3.6 m high, 12 to 15 m long; chassis Scania or Volvo.
Helmark 370 S: 40 to 65 passengers; 2.55 m wide, 3.7 m high, 12 to 15 m long; baggage 14 m³, chassis Scania or Volvo.
Helmark 420 S: 69 passengers, 2.55 m wide, 4.25 m high, 12 to 15 m long; chassis Scania.

Production
30 coaches a year.

Heuliez Bus

PO Box 27, F-79700 Rorthais, Poitou-Charentes, France
Tel: (+33 5) 49 81 07 07
Fax: (+33 5) 49 81 09 91
Web: www.heuliezbus.com

Key personnel
Chief Executive Officer: *Antoine Garnier*
Sales Manager: *Remy Foyer*
After-sales Manager: *Gerard Quenot*
Finance Manager: *Pascal Watine*
Production Manager: *Thierry Pinel*
Technical Manager: *Bruno Tessier*
Quality Manager: *Jean-Pierre Debes*
Staff: 435 (2006)

Background
Heuliez Bus has been building buses for 50 years.

Products
Integral buses, including articulated, bus and coach bodies and spare parts. Specialist developments. All of the vehicle engines are Euro 4, 5 and EEV compliant.

Range

ACCESS'BUS GX 127: Low-floor midibus.
ACCESS'BUS GX 127L: Low-floor midibus.
ACCESS'BUS GX 327: Low floor standard bus, available in two versions, including a 3-door version.

ACCESS'BUS GX 327 CNG: Low-floor standard bus with CNG engine.
ACCESS BUS GX 427: Articulated low-floor bus, 3- or 4-door versions available.

Production

The company produced 442 vehicles in 2006.

Developments

Heuliez is building the ***Civis*** and ***Cristalis*** advanced guided buses for Irisbus.

Hino Motors Ltd

1-1 Hinodai 3-chome, Hino, Tokyo 191-8660, Japan
Tel: (+81 3) 54 19 93 20
Fax: (+81 3) 54 19 93 63
Web: www.hino.co.jp

Key personnel

Chairman: *Tadaaki Jagawa*
President: *Shoji Kondo*
Deputy General Manager, Corporate
    Communications: *Toru Matsui*
    Staff: 9,030

Other offices

Tamachi Office (Overseas Operations), Corporate Communications Department
11-3 Shiba 4-chome, Minato-ku, Tokyo 108-0014, Japan
Tel/Fax: as above
   Hino has overseas affiliates and offices in Australia, Canada, China, Indonesia, Malaysia, Pakistan, the Philippines, Taiwan, Thailand, Vietnam and the US. Contact details are available on the company web site.

Works

The company has plants at Hino, Humura and Nitta, and proving grounds at Gozenyama, Hamura and Memuro.

Background

Hino Motors is the commercial vehicle specialist associate of the Toyota Group.

Products

Complete buses and bus bodies.

Range

SELEGA Series: Large touring coach.
Blue Ribbon City Series: Large low-floor city bus.

LIESSE Series: Small bus.
Hino and Isuzu are collaborating on bus manufacture.

Developments

In January 2005, the company released the ***Hino Blue Ribbon City Hybrid*** bus.

Hino Selega *coach*

1174305

Hino Blue Ribbon City Hybrid
low-floor city bus
1174306

Hinopak Motors Limited

Head Office
D-2, S.I.T.E., Manghopir Road, PO Box No 10714, Karachi, Pakistan
Tel: (+92 21) 256 39 33; 256 35 10-19
Fax: (+92 21) 256 45 17; 256 30 28
e-mail: info@hinopak.com
    marketing@hinopak.com
Web: www.hinopak.com

Area offices

Lahore Office
19 Km, Multan Road, Lahore, Pakistan
Tel: (+92 42) 751 20 03-6
Fax: (+92 42) 751 20 05
e-mail: hino-lahore@hinopak.com

Islamabad Office
1-D, Unit 14, Rehmat Plaza, 2nd Floor, Blue Area, Islamabad, Pakistan
Tel: (+92 51) 227 62 34-5
Fax: (+92 51) 227 22 68
e-mail: hino-islamabad@hinopak.com

Peshawar Office
Adnan Mansion, Near Metro Cinema, GT Road, Peshawar, Pakistan

Tel & Fax: (+92 91) 21 88 98
e-mail: hino-peshawar@hinopak.com

Faisalabad Office
Hino Faisalabad, Street No 6, Rashid Abad, Main Jhang Road, Faisalabad, Pakistan
Tel: (+92 41) 55 13 31; 32
Fax: (+92 41) 55 13 32
e-mail: hino-faisalabad@hinopak.com

Multan Office
Opp. Central Telephone Exchange Building, LMQ Road, Multan, Pakistan
Tel & Fax: (+92 61) 58 69 67
e-mail: hino-multan@hinopak.com

Quetta Office
Room No 3, Kasi Plaza No 1, Zarghoon Road, Quetta, Pakistan
Tel & Fax: (+92 81) 45 25 98
e-mail: hino-quetta@hinopak.com

Key personnel

Managing Director/Chief Executive Officer:
    Hideichiro Chikahiro
General Manager, Sales and Marketing:
    Mohammad Irfan Sheikh

Background

In 1985, Hino Motors Limited, Toyota Tsusho Corporation of Japan, Al-Futtaim Group of UAE and PACO Pakistan formed a joint venture – Hinopak Motors Limited. Hino Motors Ltd and Toyota Tshucho Corporation of Japan are the majority shareholders.

Products

Hinopak manufactures buses and trucks and provides after-sales services, including mobile workshops, spare parts and training. The latest range has CNG engines.
   The company is ISO 9001 and ISO 14001 certified.

Range

The range includes:
Hino Splendor;
Shangrila: Luxury bus;
Hino Senator: Air conditioned coach;
Rapidliner: Single-deck, deluxe coach.

Contracts

The company has supplied buses to operators in Lahore and Rawalpindi/Islamabad under the government's Urban Transport Scheme. It also exports vehicles.

Hispano Carrocera SA

Camino del Canal, s/n, E-50720 La Cartuja Baja,
Zaragoza, E-50720, Spain
Mail: PO Box 588, E-50080 Zaragoza, Spain
Tel: (+34 976) 72 05 00   Fax: (+34 976) 72 05 14
e-mail: info@hispano-net.com
Web: www.hispano-net.com

Key personnel

Chairman Hispano Carrocera SA and Executive
   Director, Tata Motors: *Ravi Kant*
Chief Executive Officer & Managing Directors:
   Andrés Múgica Jiménez de la Cuesta
   Gerardo Múgica Jiménez de la Cuesta
Sales Director: *Bruno Ribó Ruiz*
After Sales Director: *Pedro Cotera*
Operations Director: *Jose Luiz Ramirez*
International Business Development Director:
   Gustavo A Marqueta-Siibert Larrayad
   Staff: 450

Background

The company is a bus and coach body builder with
experience in bus manufacturing since the 1930s.
The company has production facilities in two
countries and has had commercial relationships
in more than 50 countries in its history.

In early 2005, Tata Motors, India acquired a 21
per cent holding in the company, with an option
to acquire a 100 per cent holding.

In early 2006, the company announced that
it had completed a new factory in Casablanca,
Morocco for the production of vehicles, the
Mosaic coach and the Orbit city bus, for the
North African market.

Products

Design, development and production of bodies
for buses, trolleybuses and coaches.

The company also provides technical training,
maintenance and repair services, consultancy
services and global spare parts shipment.

Range

Habit: City bus body in 10 m, 12 m and articulated
18 m versions on various European chassis,
including Mercedes-Benz, Volvo, Scania, MAN
and Irisbus, designed by Studi Pininfarina.

Within the last 3 years, more than 1,000 units
have been produced. The Habit urban bus,
designed by Pininfarina, was awarded the 2000
Spanish Bus of the Year and was runner-up for
the 2001 European Bus of the Year.
Orbit: Urban bus, manufactured in the company's
factory in Casablanca, Morocco.
DIVO GT/Tourist Coach: Touring coach 3.7 m high
on various European chassis including Irisbus,
Mercedes-Benz, Scania, Volvo and MAN.

The company has worked with research
organisations such as INSIA, the INTA, the
Higher Polytechnic Centre of the University of
Zaragoza and Pininfarina Ricerca e Sviluppo SpA
and with the main suppliers to the industry in
the development of this vehicle, to meet industry
standards.

Hispano Habit   0552296

Hispano Habit 18 m articulated low-floor   0552297

Key features include: design by Studi Pininfarina;
Aerodynamic Coefficient CX:0.349, which
reduces fuel rate and noise level; PVS finished
wheel-arch (zero-corrosion); enlarged crew
compartment; LED lighting; large luggage
rack (2m³).
DIVO Intercity: Intercity coach 3.3 m high, on
various European chassis including Irisbus,
Mercedes-Benz, Scania, Volvo and MAN.
Designed by Pininfarina.
MOSAIC: Touring coach 12 m long and 2.5 m
wide, available in three versions, Intercity (3.3 m
high), Touring (3.5 m high) and High-Decker
(3.7 m high).
Trolleybus: Dual system-powered articulated
18 m bus. Capacity range of 169 people, available
on Mercedes-Benz and Volvo chassis.

Production

The company has an overall production capacity
of some 4,000 units a year.

Contracts

Apart from the Spanish market, buses have
been delivered to operators in 50 countries,
the latest being Cyprus, France, Greece, Israel,
Italy, Libya, Pakistan, Singapore, UK and
Venezuela.

In mid-2005, the subsidiary company
Carrosseries Hispano Maghreb received an order
for 800 Habit 12 m city buses from M'Dina Bus
Consortium for Casablanca. The buses are being
delivered in batches of around 200 vehicles per
year from 2006.

Research and development

Hispano, along with the University of Zaragoza
and several automotive research institutes, has
developed the COMPOBUS project. The project
focuses on the development of design and
structure to improve safety in passenger road
transport vehicles.

Hyundai Motor Company

Head Office, 231 Yangjae-dong, Seocho-Gu,
Seoul 137-938, Republic of Korea
Tel: (+82 2) 34 64 11 14, 31 92
Fax: (+82 2) 34 64 35 13
e-mail: ihlim@hyundai-motor.com
Web: www.hyundai-motor.com

Key personnel

Chairman and Chief Executive Officer: *Mong-Koo
   Chung*
Vice-Chairman: *Dong-Jin Kim*
President, Commercial Vehicle Division: *Han-
   Young Choi*
   Staff: Not currently available

Other offices

Hyundai has plants and Research & Development
offices in Japan, and subsidiaries and offices in

Canada, China, Germany, India, Japan, Poland,
Turkey and the US. Full details may be found at
the company's Web site above.

Products

Buses and coaches and bare chassis.

Range

County: Midibus available in two lengths,
five engine variants and with varying seating
configurations.
Aero: Range of midi-buses, buses and coach
brands, including **Aero**, **Aero Town** and **Super
Aero City**.
Universe: Range of coaches, including **Universe
Space Luxury** and **Classic** (standard deck) and
Universe Express Noble (high deck). A CNG bus
is available.

Bare chassis are also available for some
models.

Developments

The company is developing mild-hybrid, full-
hybrid and fuel-cell powered vehicles.

Recent contracts

In March 2008, the company signed a 5-year
technical CKD agreement with Caparo India
plc to build Aero buses and enter the Indian
commercial vehicle market. Hyundai will provide
the parts and technology, whilst Caparo will build
a factory capable of producing 1,500 units per
year. The plant is scheduled to start production
by early 2009, with 350 units being manufactured
initially. Hyundai will receive USD4 million for
the technical transfer.

In June 2008, Hyundai signed an agreement
to supply city buses to the Seoul Metropolitan
Government. The contract calls for 7,748 hybrid
buses to be delivered by 2018.

IC Corporation

751 S Harkrider, Conway, AR 72032, US
Tel: (+1 501) 327 77 61
Web: www.ic-corp.com

Key personnel
Vice-President and General Manager, Bus Vehicle
Center: *Michael Cancilliere*
Vice-President, Bus Sales: *Tom Grogan*
Assistant General Manager, Bus: *Dennis
Huffmon*
Marketing Director, Bus: *David Hillman*
Marketing Managers, Bus: *Mark Brakeall*, Keith
Kladder, Randy Ray
Manager, Pricing: *Zoran Ilijevski*

Background
IC Corporation is a wholly owned subsidiary of
International Truck and Engine Corporation.

Products
IC Corporation produces school and commercial
buses.

Range
School buses
The range includes:
RE Series: RE 300 rear-engine bus;
FE Series: FE 300 front-engine bus;
CE Series: CE 200 and **CE 300** conventional
models;
BE Series: BE 200 small bus.

Commercial buses
The company's new range of commercial buses
will include a new low-floor bus (**LC Series**), built
specifically for easy accessibility, a new medium-
duty bus (**HC Series**), a new front-engine transit
bus (**FC Series**), a new rear-engine transit bus
(**RC Series**) and a new small bus (**BE Series**).

Developments
In June 2006, the company announced that it
was expanding into the commercial bus market.

Ikarbus AD

Autoput 24, YU-11080 Zemun, Serbia
Tel: (+38 11) 314 92 29; 33; 314 92 39; 43
Fax: (+38 11) 314 90 78
Telex: 11631
e-mail: ikarbus@eunet.yu
Web: www.ikarbus.co.yu

Key personnel
President: *Stanislav Glumac*
General Director: *Srećko Nijemćević*
Marketing Director: *Milenko Babić*
Technical Director: *Srećko Nijemćević*
Staff: 1,000

Background
Formerly Ikarus of Zemun (not related to the
Hungarian bus manufacturer Ikarus), Ikarbus
is now a joint stock company, part of the FAP-
Famos group.

Products
Urban and suburban buses, including articulated;
trolleybuses and intercity buses. Bus bodywork.

Range
IK-104CNG: Natural gas bus.
IK-103: City bus.
IK-104: Low-floor city bus.
IK-106: Low-floor city bus.

IK-201: Articulated city bus.
IK-202: Articulated city bus.
IK-203: Articulated city bus.
IK-103P: Suburban bus.
IK-104P: Suburban bus.
IK-301: Inter-urban bus.
IK-308: Inter-urban/city midibus.
IK-404: High-deck intercity coach.
IK-412: High-deck intercity coach.
IK-415: High-deck intercity coach.

INDCAR SA (Industrial Carrocera Arbuciense SA)

Polígono Industrial Torres Pujals 4, E-17401
Arbúcies (Girona), Spain
Tel: (+34 972) 86 01 65; 86 07 61
Fax: (+34 972) 86 00 54
e-mail: comercial@indcar.es
Web: www.indcar.es

Key personnel
Managing Director: *Gael Queralt*

Background
The company was established in 1978 and the
first Mago bus was produced in 1992. It is ISO
9001 certified.
    The company has dealers in Finland, France,
Hong Kong, Ireland, Italy, Spain, Sweden,
Switzerland and the UK.

Products
Bodywork for mini- and midibuses on Iveco,
Man, Mercedes-Benz and Renault chassis.

Range
Mago2 series: Built on Iveco, MAN or Mercedes-
Benz chassis, seating from 27 to 32 passengers.

A version adapted for disabled passengers is
available.
Wing series: Built on Iveco or Mercedes-
Benz Sprinter chassis, seating from 23 to
33 passengers. City bus and a version adapted
for disabled passengers are available.
Strada series: Built on Iveco chassis, seating from
16 to 19 passengers. The **Strada Plus** seats 19 to
22 passengers. Versions adapted for disabled
passengers are available.

Production
500 units per annum. Exports account for 60 per
cent of production.

International Truck and Engine Corporation

4201 Winfield Road, PO Box 1488, Warrenville,
Illinois 60555, USA
Tel: (+1 630) 753 57 00
Fax: (+1 630) 753 30 38 (Admin)
    (+1 630) 753 30 49 (Marketing)
Web: www.nav-international.com

Key personnel
President Chief Executive Officer: *Daniel C Ustian*
Chairman: *John R Horne*

Vice Chairman and Chief Financial Officer: *Robert
C Lannert*
Vice-President and General Manager, Bus Vehicle
Center: *Tom Cellitti*
Manager, School Bus Marketing: *John Fay*
Manager, Strategic Planning and Business
Development: *Suzann Lillig*
Marketing Manager: *Bob Neitzel*

Background
International Truck and Engine Corporation is
the operating company of Navistar International
Corporation.

Products
International Truck and Engine Corporation is a
producer of mid-range diesel engines, medium
trucks, school buses, heavy trucks, severe service
vehicles and parts and services sold under the
International® brand.
    It also manufactures chassis for the commercial
passenger industry in addition to participating in
the export market.

Irisbus Iveco

Headquarters
Parc Technologique de Lyon, BP 59, 9 Allée Irène
Joliot Curie, F-69802 Saint-Priest, France
Tel: (+33 4) 72 79 65 00
Fax: (+33 4) 72 79 66 70
Web: www.irisbus.com

Key personnel
Chief Executive Officer: *Jean Plénat*
Sales & Marketing Vice-President: *Danilo
Salvatore Martelli*
Communications & Press Manager:
    Lydie Le Corre
Tel: (+33 4) 72 79 66 74
e-mail: lydie.lecorre@irisbus.iveco.com

Irisbus Civis 18.5 m guided trolleybus (Bologna)   1343844

Other offices
Irisbus (UK) Limited
Iveco House, Station Road, Watford WD17 1SR, UK
Tel: (+44 19 23) 25 96 60
Fax: (+44 19 23) 25 96 23
e-mail: info@irisbus-sl.com
Web: www.irisbus.co.uk

Key personnel
UK Director: *Massimo Revetria*

Works
Irisbus operates five factories in Europe: Annonay and Rorthais (France), Valle Ufita (Italy), Barcelona (Spain) and Vysoke Myto (the Czech Republic).

Background
Irisbus was created in 1999 from the merger of the bus activities of Iveco and Renault, two of the biggest companies in this sector in Europe. Iveco became the sole owner of Irisbus in January 2003.

Irisbus has its headquarters in Lyon, France, and industrial, research and development facilities in France, Italy, Spain and the Czech Republic. The total workforce is 5,581.

The company develops and manufactures a comprehensive range of integral buses and coaches and chassis and markets the minibus version of the Iveco Daily.

Products
Complete buses and coaches, chassis, and CKD kits. Low-emission vehicles, zero-emission vehicles (electric). Environmentally-friendly solutions include particle filters, natural gas, electric and hybrid buses and trolleybuses.

Range
Citybus
Citelis: The Citelis range is the result of the product merge of the previous Agora and Cityclass ranges. Citelis is a built up city bus, but is also available as chassis. The Citelis range includes 10.46 m and 12 m long 2-axle vehicles, as well as articulated 18 m. The drive train is transverse at the rear overhang, which helps passenger flow. For the 12 m version it is possible to have a horizontal longitudinal engine (***Citelis Line***) in order to maximize seating capacity. Air suspension is provided at the front and the rear and there are discs all round. On the front axle, independent front suspension is mounted to improving the turning circle of the vehicle. The vehicles can be equipped with camera-based optical guidance system from Siemens. ABS anti-locking braking is also standard, with the option of ABS/ASR anti-lock and anti-slip systems.

The 7.8 litre Iveco Cursor Euro-4 engine is available with optional power ratings of 180 kW or 213 kW (245 or 290 bhp). For the 18 m version, 280 kW (380 bhp) is available. Also Euro-5 or EEV (with a particle filter). The technology used is SCR, with the additive of Adblue.

A CNG-powered version of the Citelis has the new 7.8 litre Iveco Cursor CNG engine, with higher output for 2009, with emissions lower than Euro-5 and EEV rated at 180 kW, 213 kW and 243 kW (only for articulated 18 m).
Citelis 12 m and 18 m are also available as Trolley versions, sold in East European countries and the Baltic States.

Civis and Cristalis
Advanced transportation system presented as an alternative to light rail schemes – cheaper and faster to build and easier to operate whilst providing the same level of service. The Civis and Cristalis are fully integral low-floor vehicles, with four sliding doors and four hub-mounted motors, providing large passenger areas. The Civis version features a Siemens Transportation Systems optical guidance system.

The articulated version is available in two configurations at the front end: 18 m with LHD drive and 18.5 m long with central drive.

To date, 159 units are in operation with an additional 60 units ordered. 12 m versions or

Irisbus Cristalis 18 m trolleybus (Lyon)   1343843

EuroRider *chassis*   1328868

Europolis *midibus*   1343845

Recreo *school bus*   1328870

articulated versions have been sold in equal proportions.

Vehicles are in operation in Lyon, Saint-Etienne and Limoges, France; Milan (with Bologna under construction), Italy; Las Vegas, US; and Castellon (Valencia), Spain. All of the vehicles have been sold as electric-powered trolleybuses, except the Las Vegas vehicles which are diesel-electric powered.

Rear engine chassis range
EuroRider: This is a multipurpose, heavy-duty chassis designed for bodies with lengths from 11.4 m up to 15 m and floor heights from 800 mm up to 1,600 mm. The engine is the Iveco Cursor 8 or Cursor 10, complying with Euro 4, Euro 5 or EEV standards. Eurorider is also available with Iveco Tector or Cursor 8 complying to Euro 3 for extra Europe markets. Gearboxes are mechanical,

automatic or mechanical robotised. It is available with air suspension and disc brakes. For some models, ABS/ASR braking is fitted.

MidiRider: Chassis designed for midsize school/intercity buses or coaches with body lengths from 9.5 m to 10.5 m and floor heights up to 1,100 mm. The engine is the Iveco Tector, complying with Euro 4 or EEV standards. Max GVW is 14,200 kg. Gearboxes are mechanical or automatic.

Midibus

Europolis is a range of midibuses, available as 7.4 m electric-powered, 8 m and 9.2 m diesel-powered and 9.4 m CNG-powered buses.

GX127: is a midibus produced by Heuliezbus, available as 2.33 m wide and 9.42 m long. It is powered by the Tector 6 engine providing 246 hp and 1,000 Nm.

Minibus

Daily: Range of minibuses, based on the Daily van. New body and interior features were launched in 2006. The minibus is powered with Diesel Particulate Filter or CNG engines.

The minibus seats from 14 to 28 and conforms with the European regulation 2001/85. The Daily minibus range offers a large range and level of personalisation in order to adapt vehicles to customer needs. In 2009, Irisbus will launch the new Euro 5 Daily minibus.

Proxys/Proway: Irisbus launched the new Proxys/Proway in 2008. Proxys is intended primarily for tourist excursions. Proway is designed for use as regular-service and interurban buses. This new minibus seats from 28 to 36 and is based on the Euromidi chassis.

Coach and Intercity range

Magelys: Grand tourism luxury coach available in HD (length 12.2 m and 12.8 m, width 2.55 m, height 3.62 m) versions. Both are powered by Iveco Cursor 10 engine complying with Euro 4, Euro 5 or EEV standards. Magelys has mechanical or robotised gearboxes.

Domino: Luxury tourist coach available in HD (length 12.41 m, width 2.55 m, height 3.68 m) and HDH (length 12.41 m, width 2.55 m, height 3.85 m) versions. Both are powered by Iveco Cursor 10 engine, complying with Euro 4, Euro 5 or EEV standards. Domino has mechanical or robotised gearboxes.

Evadys H/HD: Luxury tourist coach available in HD and H (length 12 m and 12.8 m, height 3.45 m and 3.75 m) versions. The engine is the Iveco Cursor 8 or Cursor 10 complying with Euro 4, Euro 5 or EEV standards. Gearbox can be mechanical, automatic or mechanical robotised.

Midys: Midsize tourist coach available in 9.95 m length powered by Iveco Tector engine (300 hp). The engine is the Iveco Tector 6 complying with Euro 4 or EEV standards. Gearbox can be mechanical or automatic.

Arway: Intercity coach, available in 10.6 m, 12 m, 12.8 m and 15 m lengths. Floor height is 860 mm. The engine is the Iveco Cursor 8 (330 hp or 380 hp) and Cursor 10 (380 hp or 450 hp) for 15 m. Both engines comply with Euro 4, Euro 5 or EEV standards. Gearbox can be mechanical, automatic or mechanical robotised.

Crossway: This intercity model is available in 10.6 m, 12 m and 12.8 m lengths. Floor height is 860 mm. The engine is the Iveco Tector (300 hp) or Iveco Cursor 8 (330 hp). Both engines comply with Euro 4, Euro 5 or EEV standards. Crossway is also available with the Iveco Cursor 8 engine complying with Euro 3 standards. Gearbox can be mechanical or automatic.

Crossway LE low-entry city & intercity version: Both models are available in 12 m and 12.8 m lengths. Floor height is 320 mm (low-entry vehicle part). The engine is the Iveco Tector (264 hp and 300 hp) or Iveco Cursor 8 (330 hp). Both engines comply with Euro 4, Euro 5 or EEV standards. Gearbox can be mechanical or automatic.

Récréo: This is a school bus model available in 10.6 m, 12 m and 12.8 m lengths. Floor height is 860 mm. The engine is the Iveco Tector (260 hp or 300 hp) or Iveco Cursor 8 (330 hp), complying

Magelys *luxury coach, presented in October 2007*   1328869

Irisbus Citelis Line *low-entry city bus*   1174757

Irisbus Arway *coach*   1174756

with Euro 4 or EEV standards. Gearbox can be mechanical or automatic.

Midway: Midsize intercity coach available in 9.95 m length powered by Iveco Tector engine (300 hp). The engine is the Iveco Tector 6 complying with Euro 4 or EEV standards. Gearbox can be mechanical or automatic.

Production

During 2007, Irisbus sold 10,077 vehicles and over 3.5 tonnes worldwide. This volume corresponds to 3.256 coaches, 2,384 buses and 3,319 minibuses and derivative vehicles on medium-weight truck

chassis as well as 1,118 chassis. Among European vehicle manufacturers, Irisbus is ranked second in the field of passenger-carrying vehicles over 3.5 tonnes.

Its market share in Europe's five leading markets, including Germany, Spain, France, Italy and the UK (which represents more than 75 per cent of the vehicles registered in the European Union) was 23.4 per cent in 2007.

Developments

In 2008, Irisbus introduced the new *Proxys/ Proway* vehicles (see above).

Irizar S Cooperativa

Zumarraga Bidea 8, E-20216 Ormaiztegi
Guipuzcoa, Spain
Tel: (+34 943) 80 91 00
Fax: (+34 943) 88 91 01
e-mail: irizar@irizar.com
Web: www.irizar.com

Key personnel
Managing Director: *Andoni Etxebarrieta*
Export Director: *Jose Manuel Orcasttas*
    Staff: 730 (Ormaiztegi) (3,000 worldwide) (2006)

UK distributor
Scania Bus & Coach UK Ltd
Claylands Avenue, Worksop S81 7DJ, UK
Tel: (+44 1909) 50 08 22   Fax: (+44 1909) 50 01 65
Managing Director: *Geoff Bell*

Other companies
Other companies in the Irizar Group are:

Irizar Brasil S/A
Rodovia Marechal Rondon, km 252.5, Botucatu,
Brazil

Irizar México SA de CV
Parque Industrial Bernardo Quintana, Parc 7 al 12,
Manzana 14, Municipo el Marqués, Queretaro,
Mexico

Irizar Magreb
0.3000 Km, Oulija, Sale, Marruecos, Morocco

Irizar TVS Ltd
Trichi Road, Viralimalai, Tamil Nadu, India

Irizar Tianjin Coach Manufacturing Co Ltd
218 Hong Qi Road, Nankai District, Tiajin, China

Background
Irizar was founded in 1889 and became a co-
operative in 1956. It is part of Mondragón
Corporación Cooperative (MCC) Group.

Products
Manufacture of bodywork for interurban buses
and coaches.

Irizar PB luxury coach   1020653

Range
Century: Range of coaches available in more than
400 options. Lengths vary from 9 m to 15 m.
InterCentury: Interurban coaches seating between
69 and 115 passengers (including standing).
Irizar PB: Launched in 2001 – luxury coach body
in lengths of 12 m, 13 m , 14 m and 15 m, 3.7 or
3.5 m high and seating 55 on the 12 m version.
It has a forward-mounted streamlined roof pod
with air conditioning and TV monitors mounted
inside the vehicle. The frame is high carbon steel
and the company says that this vehicle has a 30
per cent improvement in strength.

Production
More than 1,600 coach bodies per year in Europe.

Developments
In 1998, major extensions were made to bring
production into one factory. Further installations
during 1999 and 2000 raised capacity to 1,300
units a year. Irizar works exclusively with
Scania in Austria, Belgium, France, Germany,
Holland, Ireland, UK and the Nordic countries
and 600 bodies were produced during 2005.
It is supplying bodywork on several makes of
chassis to the Spanish market and is active in
over 70 markets. Joint ventures have been set
up in China and India and the company has
wholly owned subsidiaries in Rabat (Morocco),
Brazil and Mexico as well as being a majority
shareholder in Hispacold and Masats.

Contracts
Irizar provided 80 countries with buses and
coaches during 2006, with a total of 3,600 units
sold during that year.

Isuzu Motors Limited

Head Office
6-26-1 Minami-oi, Shinagawa-ku, Tokyo 140-
8722, Japan
Tel: (+81 3) 54 71 11 41   Fax: (+81 3) 54 71 10 42
Web: www.isuzu.co.jp/world

Key personnel
Chairman and Representative Director:
 Yoshinori Ida
President and Representative Director:
 Susumu Hosoi

Executive Vice-Presidents and Directors:
 Goro Shintani
 Yoshihiro Tadaki
 Naotoshi Tsutsumi

Background
Established in 1937. The company has worldwide
offices, production facilities and subsidiaries.
Details may be found on the company's
website.

Products
Buses, chassis and engines.

Range
Complete buses and chassis are offered in a
variety of configurations and lengths. Isuzu-built
diesel engines are fitted. The range includes:
Gala series heavy-duty buses; **Erga series** heavy-
duty bus.

Standard Isuzu buses have traditionally been
designed for rugged operating conditions with
a heavy-duty ladder-type frame, though more
sophisticated integral city buses are now in
production.

Isuzu also manufactures diesel engines for
passenger vehicles.

Iveco Czech Republic as

Dobrovskeho 74/II, CZ-566 03 Vysoké Mýto, Czech
Republic
Tel: (+420 465) 45 11 11   Fax: (+420 465) 42 03 86
e-mail: info.ez@irisbus.iveco.com
Web: www.irisbus.iveco.cz

Key personnel
Managing Director: *Daniel Patka*
Director, Industry and Technology: *Jan Rulec*
Director, Finance: *Jacques Averbuch*
Director, Organisation & IT: *Vladimir Holub*
Director, Commercial: *ALfredo D'Errico*
Director, Aftersales Services: *Radek Linhart*
Director, Quality Control: *Milan Radimersky*

Director, Purchasing: *Pavel Pachovsky*
Director, New Products: *Frantisek Seranek*
Director, Construction and Development:
 Jiri Vanek
 Staff: Approximately 2,000

Other office
Iveco Slovakia sro (SK)
Lamacska cesta 3, 841 04 Bratislava, Slovakia
Tel: (+421 259) 41 82 60
Fax: (+421 259) 41 82 61
e-mail: info.cz@irisbus.iveco.sk
Web: www.irisbus.iveco.sk

Key personnel
Company Director: *Ivan Solensky*

Background
Previously known as Karosa AS, Iveco Czech
Republic AS is 97.52 per cent owned by
Irisbus.

Iveco Slovakia sro (SK) was established in
1999 as a wholly owned subsidiary to sell Irisbus
products in Slovakia.

Products
Coaches, intercity buses, city buses and
minibuses.

Range
Coaches: Midys 9.7 m, Evadys H 12 m and
12.8 m, Evadys HD 12 m and 12.8 m, Domino HD
and Domino HDH.

Intercity buses: Midway 9.7 m, Arway 12 m and 12.8 m, Crossway 10.6 m and 12 m.
Citybuses: Citelis 12 m diesel, Citelis 18 m diesel, Citelis 12 m CNG, Citelis 18 m CNG.
Minibuses: Daily Tourys and Daily Way.
Please see separate entry for Irisbus for specifications of these vehicles.

Production
(2002) 1,554 buses
(2003) 1,522 buses
(2004) 1,703 buses
(2005) 1,883 buses
(2006) 2,438 buses

Developments
In addition to its responsibility for Irisbus activities in the Czech Republic and Slovakia, the company is responsible for activities in Bosnia-Herzegovina, Croatia, Estonia, Finland, Iceland, Latvia, Lithuania, Macedonia, Montenegro, Poland, Russia, Serbia, Slovenia, Bulgaria and Romania.

Jakłady Samochodowe Jelcz SA (Jelcz Automotive Works)

ul Inżynierska 3, PL-55-221 Jelcz-Laskowice, Wroclaw, Poland
Tel: (+48 71) 318 85 05
   (+48 71) 381 68 86 (Marketing)
Fax: (+48 71) 318 84 56
   (+48 71) 381 67 93 (Marketing)
e-mail: jelcz@jelcz.com.pl
Web: www.jelcz.com.pl

Key personnel
Export Manager: *Ryszard Wrzesinski*

Exports
ul Lucka 11, Warsaw, Poland
Tel: (+48 22) 66 56 32 89

Background
Buses are generally based on imported designs. Autosan and Jelcz are now part of the Zasada Group which holds an interest of 52 per cent in each, though each firm will continue to trade separately. Zasada is also the Mercedes-Benz importer for Poland and Mercedes-Benz engines are increasingly being used by both manufacturers.

Products
Buses, trolleybus bodies.

Range
Supero: Bus with Mielec-Autogas power unit derived from a former licence-built Leyland 680 engine.
M1011: Two-door low-floor 9.9 m midibus seating 26 with around 20 standing.

Gdynia, Poland, is operating 80 Jelcz trolleybuses on seven routes (Milan Šrámek)   0100218

M081MB: 7.7 m midibus on Mercedes-Benz OM904LA chassis, seating 20.
120, 120M/2, 120M/3: 11.9 m buses, each with three doors, single-step entrance and rear engine, carrying up to 110 passengers.

Production
Production in 1998 was 375.

Contracts
Buses and coaches have been supplied to city transport operators in Warsaw, Krakow and Lublin.

Developments
The company has restructured into three divisions, covering truck manufacturing, car parts manufacture and bus building.

JCBL Limited

Corporate Office
Plot No 75, Industrial Area – Phase-I, Chandigarh, 160002, India
Tel: (+91 172) 301 30 95/96
Fax: (91 172) 301 30 97
e-mail: contact@jcbl.com
Web: www.jcbl.com

Works
Ambala Chandigarh Road, Ialru 140501, District Mohali Punjab, India
Tel: (+91 1762) 30 82 00/01   Fax: (+91 1762) 30 82 36
e-mail: jcbl@jcbl.com

Key personnel
General Manager: *Capt M S Grewal*
Product Manager: *Manoj Kumar Das*
   Staff: 500+

Background
JCBL Limited (JCBL) was incorporated in 1989 and its commercial production commenced in 1991. The company was established to manufacture Japanese technology buses/ambulances and load carriers for Swaraj Mazda Limited (SML), a joint venture of Global Auto Major Mazda Motor Corporation of Japan and Punjab Tractors Limited (PTL). JCBL has now diversified into manufacturing luxury coaches and motor homes.
   The company is certified to ISO 9001 standards.
   JCBL had signed an agreement with King Long United Automotive Company Pvt Ltd to manufacture and market integral chassis in India.

Products
Bus, minibus and coach builder. Also bus components.

Production
Before expansion, the company had capacity to produce 600 minibuses/ambulances per annum. Recently installed facilities for the manufacture of luxury coaches have added capacity for a further 300 coaches per annum. JCBL has also increased its capacity to produce minibuses to 4,500 per annum. In 2005/06, the company produced 3,014 buses, ambulances and load-carriers.

Contracts
JCBL's customer list includes OEMs such as Swaraj Mazda, Eicher Motors, Ashok Leyland, Tata Motors, JCB India Ltd, Airports Authority of India, Indian Army, Indian Air Force, hotels, airlines, tour operators and schools.

Developments
The company has launched its JCBL Kinglong IC 6113 integral coach.

Jinhua Neoplan Vehicle Co Ltd

501 Bada Road, Jinhua, Zhejiang 321017, China
Tel: (+86 579) 225 61 60   Fax: (+86 579) 225 61 61
Web: www.neoplan.com.cn

Products
Luxury coaches and city buses produced under license to Neoplan/MAN.

Range
The product range includes:
Young MAN-City: 12 m city bus;
Young MAN-Metropolis: 18 m articulated bus;
Young MAN-Spaceliner: 13.7 m coach;
Young MAN-Euro Star: 12 m luxury coach;
Young MAN-Starliner: 13.7 m coach;
Young MAN-Euroliner: luxury coach;
Young MAN-City liner: inter-city coach.

Production
Production capacity is 2,000 vehicles per year.

Developments
In 2005, the company announced that it would enter the city bus market, with the Youngman-City line.

Jubilee Automotive Group

Woden Road South, Wednesbury WS10 0NQ, UK
Tel: (+44 121) 502 22 52   Fax: (+44 121) 502 22 58
e-mail: sales@jubileeauto.co.uk
Web: www.jubileeauto.co.uk

Key personnel
Director: *Michael Holland*

Products
Bus and coach bodies.

Range
Bus and coach bodies are built on Ford, LDV, Mercedes-Benz, Mazda and Volkswagen running units. They include the Service-Master, a local bus body on Mercedes 609 chassis, seating up to 24. It has a wide folding door.

Jubilee Automotive has introduced the EuroCab taxi range, based on the Mercedes-Benz Traveliner and V-Class MPV base vehicles. A full London-style taxi conversion or a seven-passenger upmarket minibus with wheelchair accessibility can be specified.

Jubilee Automotive's EuroCab Mercedes-Benz-based taxi range includes this minibus version, the driving position of which is shown here (Tony Pattison)   0100219

KAMAZ Incorporated

PO Box 423800, Musa Jalil pr 29, Naberezhnye Chelny, Tatarstan, Russian Federation
Web: www.kamaz.net

PR Department
Tel: (+7 8552) 37 19 08   Fax: (+7 8552) 37 19 08
e-mail: cso@kamaz.net

Export Department
Tel: (+7 8552) 37 18 16   Fax: (+7 8552) 53 24 04
e-mail: export@kamaztrade.ru

Key personnel
Director General: *Sergey A Kogoghin*

Background
Kamaz Inc, an open joint-stock company, was established in August 1990 by the privatisation of the KAMAZ Heavy-Duty Truck Production Complex.

Products
Bus builder.

Production
The company produces approximately 1,000 buses annually.

Developments
In early 2006, the company signed a Memorandum Of Understanding (MOU) with Tatra Vectra Motoros Ltd, India with the intention of manufacturing bus chassis for the Indian market.

Kapena SA

Ul Grunwaldzka 12, PL-76-200 Slupsk, Poland
Tel: (+48 59) 843 88 71   Fax: (+48 59) 843 84 16
e-mail: marketing@kapena.com.pl
Web: www.kapena.com.pl

Background
Kapena is 85 per cent owned by Cacciamali.
The company is ISO 9001:2000 certified.

Products
Mini- and midibuses, including low-floor three- and two-door citybus and express bus.

Range
Includes mini and midibuses, using Iveco power units and drivelines.

Irisbus 50C13 Daily City, Cacciamali 65C15 Urbanino, Irisbus Agora, Irisbus B951E, Irisbus B961E, Irisbus 50C13 Daily Intercity, Cacciamali 65C15 Thesi Intercity, Cacciamali 100E21 Tema, Irisbus C954, Irisbus C956 AXER, Irisbus Ares, Irisbus Midirider 395E

Developments
In early 2003, the company became a representative of Irisbus, and began construction of small Irisbus vehicles, starting with the 50C13 Daily minibus.

KH motor Centrum (KHMC)

Kamil Hrbáč, Palhanecká 16, Opava CZ-747 07, Czech Republic
Tel/Fax: (+420 5) 53 62 05 95
e-mail: khmc@volny.cz
Web: www.khmc.cz

Products
KHMC produces small buses and mini-buses based on light commercial vehicles, including the Mercedes-Benz Sprinter.

Developments
In 2004, the company, in co-operation with EA Karosserie- und Fahrzeugbau Gera GmbH, started building a range of three-axle small buses called the KHMC City. These are converted from Fiat, Citroen, Peugeot and Renault light commercial vehicles.

Kiitokori Oy

PO Box 22, Rautatienkatu 2, FI-47401 Kausala, Finland
Tel: (+358 1) 06 16 12 00
Fax: (+358 1) 06 16 12 22
e-mail: info@kiitokori.fi
Web: www.kiitokori.fi

Key personnel
Managing Director, Kiitokori Group: *Antero Sirkka*
Marketing Manager: *Tuomo Närekorpi*
   Tel: (+358 1) 06 16 12 12
   e-mail: tuomo.narekorpi@kiitokori.fi
Sales Engineer: *Olli Aarnio*
   Tel: (+358 1) 06 16 12 11
   e-mail: olli.aarnio@kiitokori.fi
Plant Manager: *Pentti Nikula*

Background
Kiitokori Oy is one of four companies which comprise the Kiitokori Group.

Kiitokori CityStar bus   1033928

Products

The company produces buses, shuttle buses and coaches on a variety of chassis and specialised vehicles.

Range

OmniStar

Available on all commercial heavy-duty chassis, from 12 to 24 tonnes.

CityStar

Available on all commercial heavy-duty, low-entry chassis, from 12 to 24 tonnes.

The company also provides maintenance services, repairs and spare parts.

KOWEX Omnibusse und Fahrzeugtechnik GmbH (KOWEX)

Seestrasse 48, D-74232 Abstatt, Germany
Tel: (+49 7062) 954 90
Fax: (+49 7062) 95 49 29

e-mail: service@kowex.de
Web: www.kowex.de

Key personnel

Managing Director: *Armin Maurer*

Products

Minibuses and midibuses.

Range

Sprinter 413/416 CDI: Minibus on Mercedes-Benz chassis, available in several variants seating from nine to 26 passengers.
Regio Vario 815 D: Midibus on Mercedes-Benz chassis, seating from 27 to 31 passengers.

Krystal Enterprises

Bus Sales
2701 E Imperial Hwy, Brea, CA 92821, US
Tel: (+1 714) 961 23 39
Fax: (+1 714) 986 12 46

e-mail: bussales@krystal.cc
Web: www.krystalkoach.com

Key personnel

President: *E Grech*
 Staff: 800

Current situation

Founded in 1983, the company produces mid-size luxury buses, including **Limo Bus**, **International Tour**, **Internationals Shuttle**, **Ford F550** and **Ford E450**.

Kutsenits Handels- und BuskonstruktionsgmbH

Siget 39 Industriegebiet II/4, A-7053 Hornstein, Austria
Tel: (+43 2689) 221 60
Fax: (+43 2689) 22 16 10
e-mail: kutsenits.bus@kutsenits.at
Web: www.kutsenits.at

Works

Kutsenits ddo
Lendavska 29, SI-9000 Murska Sobota, Slovenia

Products

City buses, midibuses, mini-midi coaches, and special vehicles for disabled persons.

Range

Mercedes-Benz
416 Sprinter: 20 seats.
416/616 Sprinter: Citybus.
616 Sprinter: 26-seater coach.
Vario: Coach.
Vario City V: coach.

VW

CITY I: Available in petrol, diesel and CNG versions, 10 seats + eight standees.
CITY II – Handicap: Seating 15, up to eight seats plus seven wheelchairs possible, available in petrol, diesel and CNG versions.
CITY III: Available in petrol, diesel and CNG versions, 20 seats and 12 standees.

Mercedes-bodied Citybus in service with Citybus Braunau supplied by Kutsenits   0098740

VW-bodied CNG-powered three-axle bus by Kutsenits   0098739

Labh Singh Harnam Singh Ltd (LSHS)

PO Box 45569, Nairobi, Kenya
Tel: (+254 20) 353 81 74, 75
Fax: (+254 20) 353 81 76
e-mail: lshs@lshs.co.ke
Web: www.lshs.co.ke

Street address

Mombasa Road, Mombasa-Nairobi Highway, Kenya

Key personnel

Managing Director: *Harjeet Singh Sokhi*
PR Manager: *Sheila Muthoka*

Background

Established in 1950, the company supplies vehicles to East Africa, Ethiopia, Rwanda, Burundi, Malawi, Zambia, Mozambique and Zimbabwe.

LSHS coach with fibreglass at front and rear   1323701

Products
Bus and coach bodywork. Specialised vehicles.

Range
Isuzu
MV123: Bus, available in standard, semi-luxury, upgraded semi-luxury and luxury versions.

NPR/66/Minibus: Available in standard, semi-luxury and luxury versions, seating 29.
NQR66P Minibus: Short wheelbase coach available in standard, semi-luxury and luxury versions, seating 33.

Developments
The company has recently introduced vehicles with fibreglass construction at the front and the rear.

Lahden Autokori Oy

Koritie 2, FIN-15540 Villähde, Finland
Tel: (+358 3) 88 71 00   Fax: (+358 3) 887 12 00
e-mail: info@lahdenautokori.fi
Web: www.lahdenautokori.fi

Key personnel
Managing Director: *Markku Ikonen*
   Staff: 200

Background
Founded in 1945. The company is certified to ISO 9001 standards. The company's main markets are Finland and other Nordic countries.

Products
Bodies for buses and coaches.

Range
Lightweight aluminium bodies – four different body types:
Eagle: Coach for long-distance and touring, length 10.2 to 15.0 m, height: 3.60 m, width 2.55 m, roof height 3.60 m.

Scala low-floor 13.5 m bus on Scania L94UB 4× 2 chassis; three-axle version also available   0533596

Falcon: Coach, length 10.2 to 15.0 m, height 3.40 m, width 2.55 m.
Flyer 520: Bus suitable for suburban and school uses, length 10.2 to 14.5 m, height 3.25 m, width 2.55 m.

Scala: Low-floor citybus also suitable for suburban and school applications, built on Scania L94UB chassis, length 11.4 to 14.8 m, height: 3.10 m, width 2.55 m.

LAZ

45 Stryiska, UA-79053 Lviv, Ukraine
Tel: (+38 322) 65 30 50   Fax: (+38 322) 65 98 50
e-mail: lazbus@mail.lviv.ua

Key personnel
Chairman: *Y Sorokin*

Background
Joint stock company.

Products
Bus manufacturer.

Developments
In 2004, the company exhibited two new models, the low-floor A-183 CityLAZ city bus and the AX-183 FlyLaz airport bus.

LDV Group Limited

Bromfield House, Drews Lane, Birmingham, B8 2QG, UK
Tel: (+44 121) 322 20 00,
   (+44 800) 400 407
Fax: (+44 121) 327 44 87
Web: www.ldv.com
   www.ldvmaxus.com

Key personnel
Chairman: *Martin Leach*
Chief Executive: Evgeniy Vereshchagin
Sales & Marketing Director: *Tony Lewis*
Export Director: *Robert Drewery*
Marketing Director: *Steve Miller*
   Staff: Approximately 850

Products
Light commercial vehicles.

Range
In 2005, LDV introduced the Maxus range of light commercial vehicles. The company designs, manufactures and distributes the Maxus range of vehicles – van, minibus, Kombi and bi-purpose. The range has two wheelbases and three roof heights, with 95 ps and 120 ps engines.

Developments
In August 2006, LDV was acquired by Gaz Group, Russian Federation. Gaz Group produces more than 140,000 commercial vehicles per year and has a sales turnover exceeding USD4.5 billion.

In early 2008, LDV Group launched its new MAXUS School Bus and the MAXUS luxury minibus.

The company is also involved in initiatives to develop a DC-DC regenerative braking converter for hybrid and electric vehicles and the development of an electric-powered version of the MAXUS.

Production
Approximately 10,000 light commercial vehicles per year.

Leicester Carriage Builders

Marlow Road, Leicester LE3 2BQ, UK
Tel: (+44 116) 282 42 70
Fax: (+44 116) 263 05 54
e-mail: rick.johnson@midlandsco-op.com
Web: www.leicestercarriagebuilders.co.uk

Key personnel
General Manager: *Rick Johnson*
Quality Manager: *Kim Connolly*
Production Manager: *Steve Stones*
Workshop Manager: *Rob Burford*
Design Engineer: *Peter Holt*
   Staff: Not currently available

Wheelchair-accessible conversion for Leicester City Council, UK
1344626

Background

The company has been accredited with the British Standards Approval Certificate ISO 9002.

Range

Minibuses, seating 8 to 29 on Mercedes-Benz, Iveco, Ford, Renault, Peugeot and Fiat chassis, including wheelchair accessible vehicles.

Coachbuilt wheelchair-accessible vehicle for The Learning Trust, UK
1344625

Lvovskyi Automobusnyi Zavod (LAZ)

Lviv Bus Works
Stryiska Str 45, Lvov 290618, Ukraine
Tel: (+380 322) 63 60 55
Fax: (+380 322) 63 60 75

Key personnel

President: *Stepan Davydiak*
Financial Director: *Vasyl Trach*
Accountant: *Nadiya Kolos*
Technical Director: *Yevstachi Kostiv*
Director, Foreign Trade: *Roman Popovych*

Products

Buses and trolleybuses.

Range

A joint venture between Usautotrans, Uzbekistan's state transport company, and LAZ has been set up to build between 700 and 1,000 buses annually. An 11.2 m city bus has been submitted for type approval in Germany.

Contracts

Seven LAZ-52522 trolleybuses have been supplied to Ukrainian systems.

MAN Bus & Coach (Pty) Ltd

PO Box 8717, 0046 Centurion, South Africa
Tel: (+27 11) 206 00 00
Fax: (+27 11) 206 00 27
e-mail: bussales@man-mn.co.za
Web: www.man-mn.co.za

Key personnel

General Manager: *Torsten Siemund*
National Sales and Marketing Manager: *Ray Karshagen*
Communications Manager, Group Marketing: *Marja Brunninger*
Tel: (+27 11) 928 68 41
Staff: 67

Head Office

MAN Truck & Bus (SA) (Pty) Ltd
Tel: (+27 11) 928 68 41   Fax: (+27 11) 974 32 41

Works

6 Hammer Road, Clayville Ext 8, Gauteng 1665, South Africa

Background

To tap the South African bus market still further, MAN Nutzfahrzeuge took over the Bus and Coach division of TFM in 2000.

Products

Range of MAN front- and rear-engined chassis and buses, assembled locally.

Range

Explorer: Bus for urban and intercity use, exclusively designed for MAN front-engined chassis, that have been adapted to suit arduous African operating coniditions.
Chassis: Full range of MAN front- and rear-engined chassis, assembled locally.

Production

In 2002, 414 units were produced.

Contracts

Contracts have been awarded by most of the major fleet operators in South Africa, resulting in the company having a 40 per cent market share in 2002.

MAN Nutzfahrzeuge Group

PO Box 50 06 20, D-80976 Munich, Germany
Tel: (+49 89) 15 80 01
Fax: (+49 89) 150 39 72
e-mail: info@man-mn.com
Web: www.man-mn.de

Key personnel

Chief Executive Officer: *Joachim Dürr*
Staff: 8,000

Works

Salzgitter, Pilsting, Plauen, Posen, Starachowice and Ankara.

UK MAN Truck & Bus UK Ltd

Frankland Road, Blagrove, Swindon SN5 8YU, UK
Tel: (44 1793) 44 81 76   Fax: (44 1793) 44 82 65
Managing Director, UK Bus and Coach Division: *Vince Welsh*
UK General Manager: *John Hill*
UK Coach Sales Executives: *Julie Hartley*
John Hill
Shaun Miller

Background

The MAN Nutzfahrzeuge Group develops, manufactures and markets buses with the brands MAN and Neoplan.

New MAN/Neoplan Starliner delivered to Ellisons, UK
1375663

Products

Integral low-floor buses, articulated airport buses, integral coaches, single-deck and double-deck, coach and bus bodywork.

All models indicated with an 'N' are Neoplan and the remainder are MAN vehicles.

Range

City buses – Centroliner
N4522: 18.7 m articulated low-floor.
N4516: 12 m low-floor bus, CNG/LPG versions and EEV engine available.

NEOPLAN – Trendliner
N3516/17/18 Ü/ÜC/ÜL: Interurban buses, 12.25 m, 13.01 m or 13.9 m long.

Coaches
All Neoplan coaches are built with engines from MAN. They are also available in 12 m, 13.7 m and 15 m lengths.
Cityliner N1216 HD, N1217 HDC: High-deck coaches.
Starliner N5217 SHD, N5218 SHD2: Luxury coaches.
Skyliner N1122/3 L, N1122/3 C: Double-deck, also available with a Cummins engine.
Tourliner N2216/3 SHDL: Super high-decker 13.8 m long, *N2216 SHD:* 12 m version, *SHDC:* 13.26 m long.

MAN vehicles
In mid-2004, all MAN buses and coaches were allocated their own product names. The generic/'family' name is **Lion's Family**.

The new MAN product names for the various types of vehicles in the range are:
Lion's City: For all low-floor buses;
Lion's Classic: For all standard scheduled-service buses;
Lion's Regio: For all intercity scheduled-service buses;
Lion's Coach: For all standard coaches;

In the future, variants designations will feature the product name/vehicle designation and a length abbreviation. The length abbreviation specifies the various models.

Variant descriptions
Midibus	M
Articulated bus	G
Double decker	DD
Intercity variant	Ü
13.8 m variant	L
15 m variant	LL
Low-entry	T (Twin = double use)

The full range is:

Low-floor bus family, Lion's City
NM 223/283.3 and NM 223.2	*Lion's City M*
NL 223/263/283/313 and	*Lion's City*
NL 243/283	
NO 263/283/313	*Lion's City Ü*
NG 263/313/363 and	*Lion's City G/GL*
NG 263/313/363-18.75 m	
ND 313/363	*Lion's City DD*
EL 223/283	*Lion's City T*
EL 223/283	*Lion's City TÜ*

MAN Wrightbus Meridian low-floor city bus in service with Whitelaw's Coaches of Stonehouse, UK   1375664

Standard bus family, Lion's Classic:
SL 223/283	*Lion's Classic*
SG 263/313	*Lion's Classic G*
SÜ 263/283/313/363	*Lion's Classic Ü*

Intercity bus family, Lion's Regio:
ÜL 314/364/414	*Lion's Regio*
ÜL 314/364/414-13.9 m	*Lion's Regio L*

Standard coach family, Lion's Coach:
RHC 414/464	*Lion's Coach*
	(+ Regio C – 13 m)
RHC 414/464-13.8 m	*Lion's Coach L*

Premium coach family, Lion's Star:
RHS 414/464	*Lion's Star*
RHS 414/464-13.8 m	*Lion's Star L*
13.26 m	*Lion's Coach C*

Developments
The first Euro 5 coach variants were due to be field tested in 2007, with series models expected to be available by the end of 2008.

The new Lion's City Hybrid diesel-electric 12 m bus is reportedly on trial.

MAN Truck & Bus UK Ltd unveiled, for the first time in the UK, its new Neoplan Starliner luxury tourer in 2008. The Starliner is an integral three-axle luxury touring coach. It is 13.99 m long and 3.97 m high. It is powered by MAN's D26 Euro 4 EGR engine driving through a fully automatic 12-speed MAN TipMatic gearbox and newly-developed 'Easy Start' moving-off aid.

Production
In FY 2006, the company sold 7,338 units (buses, chassis and CKD kits).

Contracts
The company has received an order for 395 Neoplan buses from the Roads and Transport Authority (RTA), Dubai. The order comprises 170 newly-developed Centroliner DD double-deck buses, 150 Centroliner GL articulated buses and 75 Centroliner single-deck buses.

Whitelaw's Coaches of Stonehouse, UK, the first bus operator in the UK to take the new MAN Wrightbus Meridian low-floor city bus, has added a further five vehicles to take its Meridian fleet to six. The Meridian fleet runs on local bus service operations throughout Lanarkshire. Based on the 12 m MAN A22 Euro 4 chassis and Wrightbus's patented Aluminique bodywork, the new product was launched in September 2007.

Stagecoach UK Bus, one of the largest operators in the UK with express and local bus services across the country, and a network of intercity operations, has taken its 1,000th MAN chassis. Stagecoach has been taking MAN chassis since 1997 and currently has MAN A66 14.240 midibus chassis and MAN A69 12m low-floor, full size city bus chassis across its inner city services fleet. A further fleet of some 50 NEOPLAN Skyliners are operating on the company's Oxford Tube and Megabus services.

MAN Türkiye AŞ

Esenboga Havalimanı Yolu 22 km, Akyurt TR-06750, Ankara, Turkey
Tel: (+90 312) 398 02 20   Fax: (+90 312) 398 01 69
Web: www.tr-man-mn.com
Staff: 2,950

Background
Previously known as MAN Kamyon ve Otobüs Sanayi AS (MANAS), the company is now known as MAN Türkiyw AŞand is 99.9 per cent owned by MAN Nutzfahrzeuge AG, Germany.

Products
NEOMAN articulated and rigid city buses, interurban, touring coaches and bus chassis with petrol and alternative fuel engines.

Production
Bus production capacity is 2,000 per year.

Marcopolo SA

Unidad Planalto, Avenue Marcopolo 280, Bairro Planalto, Caixa Postal 238, 95086-200 Caixas do Sul, RS, Brazil
Tel: (+55 54) 209 40 00   Fax: (+55 54) 209 41 21

e-mail: contato@marcopolo.com.br
Web: www.marcopolo.com.br

Key personnel
President: *Paulo P Bellini*
Vice-President: *José A F Martins*

Subsidiaries
MVC Componentes Plásticos Ltda
Rua Maria Isabel Zagonel, 205, Colônia Afonso Pena, 83045-430 São José dos Pinhais, PR, Brazil
Tel: (+55 41) 283 32 33   Fax: (+55 41) 282 00 92
e-mail: comercial@mvc-marcopolo.com.br

Ciferal Comércio, Indústria e Participações S/A
Rua Pastor Manoel Avelino de Souza, 2064 –
Xërem, 25250-000 Duque de Caxias, RJ, Brazil
Tel: (+55 21) 679 10 11   Fax: (+55 21) 679 10 32
e-mail: ciferal@ciferal.com.br

Marcopolo Indústria de Carroçarias S/A
Estrada de Eiras, Apartado 8043, P-3020 Coimbra,
Portugal
Tel: (+351 39) 43 18 56   Fax: (+351 39) 43 91 74
e-mail: marcopolo@mail.telepac.pt

Marcopolo Latinoamérica S/A
Rua Nacional 8, km 605, Província de Córdoba,
Cidade de Rio Cuarto, Argentina
Tel: (+54 358) 463 56 00   Fax (+54 358) 463 92 81
e-mail: mapla@ar.marcopolo.com.br

Polomex SA de CV
Carretera A Garcia, km 6.5, Zona Industrial,
O Bispo Garcia, Garcia – Nuevo Leon, NL, México
Tel: (+52 8) 130 23 00   Fax: (+52 8) 319 39 93
e-mail: ventas@polomex.com.mx

Marcopolo South Africa PTY Limited
Seshego, Pieterburgo, South Africa
Tel: (+27 15) 223 03 65   Fax: (+27 15) 223 04 16

Superpolo SA
Autopista Sur, 77-31, Santafé de Bogotá, DC,
Colômbia
Tel: (+571) 730 57 00   Fax: (+571) 730 57 62
e-mail: superpolo@superpolo.com.co

Background
Initially formed under the name Nicola & Cia
in 1949, the company's trade name became
Marcopolo SA in 1992. The company is certified
to ISO 9002 and 9001 standards.
   The Company owns Ciferal.

Products
Bus and coach bodies.

Range
City, interurban and touring coach designs.

Long-distance/intercity vehicles
Paradiso: Intercity and touring coach. It is a
high-deck coach on two or three axles. Build
on Mercedes-Benz, Scania or Volvo chassis.
A double-deck version is available.
Allegro/Viaggio/Andare: Designed for express
or intercity operation. Seats up to 55 passengers.
Built on Mercedes-Benz, Scania, Volkswagen or
Volvo chassis.
MP-120: Built on a Mercedes-Benz chassis, this
model seats up to 54 passengers.
Multego: Mercedes-Benz chassis, seating up to
54 passengers.

Urban/city vehicles
Torino/Viale: Series of urban bus designs,
suited to locally built Mercedes-Benz, Scania,
Volkswagen and Volvo chassis. Available in
articulated and hybrid versions.
Boxer: Mercedes-Benz chassis, seats up to 37.

Allegro Urbano: Up to 41 seats, on Iveco, Scania,
Volvo or DAF chassis.

Midibus
Senior: Designed for city, school and touring
use and seats up to 26 in its suburban version.
Built on Mercedes-Benz, Volkswagen or Agrale
chassis.
Minimax: Designed primarily for fleet operations
and seating up to 26.
Temple: Built in Colombia for city operations on
various chassis and seating up to 33.
Listo: Built in Colombia for city operations on
Chevrolet or Nissan chassis and seating up to 21.

Minibus
Fratello: Available in Executive, Commuter, Urban
and School Bus versions. Seat up to 27 on Iveco,
Mercedes-Benz, Volkswagen or Isuzu chassis.
Vicino: Suitable for commuter or school use and
seating up to 30 on Mercedes-Benz chassis.

Production
In 2003, the company produced 14,362 bus
bodies. Exports account for nearly 50 per cent of
net income.

Contracts
CKD and ready-built versions are exported to
South, Central and North America, Africa, Asia
and Europe. They are on Mercedes-Benz, Scania,
Volvo, Volkswagen and Dina chassis.

Mauri & C SaS

Via Togliatti 4, I-20033 Desio, Milan, Italy
Tel: (+39 02) 362 62 62 47   Fax: (+39 02) 362 62 91 89
info.mauri@mauri-bus.it
Web: www.mauri-bus.it

Key personnel
Co-directors: *Carlo Mauri, Umberto Mauri*

Background
The company started producing bus bodies in
1966, and also bodied trams for Milan in the early
1970s, and trolleybuses in the late 1970s.
   Mauri has collaborated with Neoplan since
1988, including fitting out Neoplan buses for

the Italian market and incorporating Neoplan
running units.
   In 1998, Mauir signed an agreement with Ayats,
Spain.

Products
Standard and articulated buses and trolleybuses;
bus bodywork.

Range
Kronos: Range of low-floor city and suburban
buses, 9.7, 10.6, 10.8, 11.7 and 12 m, stainless
steel, MAN engines with CANBUS multiplex
wiring. Range includes:
Interurbano 9KV26-I: 9.7 m citybus;
Suburbano 9KV26-S: 9.7 m citybus;

Urbano 9KV26-U: 9.7 m citybus;
Interurbano 10KV26-I: 10.6 m citybus;
Suburbano 10KV26-S 2p: 10.6 m citybus;
Suburbano 10KV26-S 3p: 10.8 m citynus;
Urbano 10KV26-U: 10.8 m citybus;
Interurbano 12KV26-I: 12 m citybus;
Suburbano 12KV26-S 2p: 12 m citybus;
Suburbano 12KV26-S 3p: 11.7 m citybus;
Suburbano 12KV26-U: 11.7 m citybus.

   Mauri pioneered the use of light alloy
body structures in Italy, for both buses and
trolleybuses. The standard trolleybus carries up
to 100 with 29 seated. Mauri has produced a bi-
mode trolleybus, with an auxiliary diesel engine.

Mazda Motor Corporation

3-1 Shinchi, Fuchu-cho, Aki-gun, Hiroshima, 730-
8670, Japan
Tel: (+81 82) 282 52 53
Fax: (+81 82) 287 52 25
Web: www.mazda.co.jp

Key personnel
Managing Executive Officer, Corporate
   Communications Division: *Yuji Harada*

Subsidiary
Mazda Motor Europe GmbH (MME)
Hitdorfer Strasse 73, D-51371 Leverkusen,
Germany
Tel: (+49 2173) 94 31 56
Fax: (+49 2173) 94 35 53
e-mail: mazda-press@mazdaeur.com

Key personnel
Vice-President, Public Relations: *Franz Danner*

Products
E-Series midi and minibuses.

Production
Mazda's commercial vehicles are exported to
markets in Europe, Asia, Central US, the Middle
East and Oceania.

Mellor Coachcraft

Miall Street, Rochdale, OL11 1HY, UK
Tel: (+44 1706) 86 06 10   Fax: (+44 1706) 86 04 02
e-mail: mcsales@woodall-nicholson.co.uk
Web: www.woodall-nicholson.co.uk

Key personnel
Managing Director: *Neil D Crowther*
Sales and Marketing Director: *Geoff K Hudson*
Finance Director: *P L F Thompson*

Background
Formerly a subsidiary of the Plaxton Group,
Mellor is now a division of Woodall Nicholson
Ltd.
   The company's quality control procedures and
manufacturing methods have been accredited to
ISO 9001:2000 standards.

Products
Minibus van conversions; coachbuilt buses.
Chassis used include: Iveco Daily 50C15, Iveco

Daily 65C18, Mercedes-Benz Sprinter, Mercedes-
Benz Vario, Volkswagen Crafter and Renault.

Developments
Mellor has recently remodelled the Mercedes-
Benz Sprinter and Volkswagen Crafter, with
updated and modernised designs and features.

Merkavim Transportation Technologies Ltd

22 Granit Street, PO Box 3050, Caesarea 38900, Israel
Tel: (+972 4) 617 60 60
Fax: (+972 4) 617 60 64
e-mail: marketing@merkavim.co.il
Web: www.merkavim.co.il

Key personnel

President: *Michael Maixner*
Chairman: *Shell Johanson*
Vice-President, Marketing: *Rami Tesler*
Vice-President, Finance (Chief Financial Officer): *Moshe Lazar*
Vice-President, Operations: *David Philosoph*
Vice-President, Engineering: *Eytan Markovetzky*
Vice-President, Procurement: *Ed Shtang*
Staff: 400

Background

Merkavim was established in 1946 and is the leading body builder in Israel. Ownership is by Mayers Cars & Trucks (73.5 per cent) and Volvo Bus Corporation (26.5 per cent).

Products

City, intercity bus bodies, coach bodies, minibuses and armoured buses.

Range

Armoured

Armoured bus – Mars 'Defender': Armoured bus on Volvo B12B 6X2 chassis. Seats 53.

City bus

'Mercury': Built on Volvo B7L chassis, suitable for public transport and shuttle operations. Disabled access.
MAN SL – low-floor city bus: An articulated version on the MAN NL 313, low-floor city bus

MAN R33 chassis seats 61 with 69 standing. It is 17 m long, and has three double doors.
LE: Built on Volvo B12B LE chassis for public transportation.
'Apollo': Luxury coach, built on Volvo B12B and MAN chassis.
'Mars': Intercity coach/bus, built on Volvo B12B, Man, DAF 4000 and Mercedes-Benz OC5000 chassis.
M20E: Low floor minibus, built on Fiat Ducato 3000 cc, 165 hp chassis.

Production

Approximately 500 buses per year.

Recent contracts

In April 2008, Volvo Buses received an order for 107 bus chassis from Mayers Cars & Trucks Ltd, Israel, the bodies for which will be produced by Merkavim.

Merkavim low-floor articulated city bus on MAN NL 313 chassis   1340455

Merkavim Appolo bus on Volvo B12B chassis   1330395

Merkavim M20E low-floor minibus on Fiat Ducato chassis   1340454

Merkavim Mars tri-axle intercity bus on Volvo B12B chassis   1330396

Merkavim low-floor city bus, showing disabled access   1340456

Merkavim Mercury partially low-floor bus on Volvo B7L chassis   1330397

Metalbus Ind Metalúrgica Ltda

Estrada das Oliveiras 161, PO Box 294, CEP 95270-000, Flores da Cunha, RS, Brazil
Tel: (+55 54) 32 92 82 00
Fax: Not currently available
e-mail: maxibus@maxibus.com.br
Web: www.maxibus.com.br

Background
Commenced operations in 1995.

Products
Bus bodies, manufactured under the brand name Maxibus.

Range
Dolphin: Urban bus.
Astor Urbano and Turismo: Microbuses, suitable for urban services, tourism and school services.
Lynx 3.45 and 3.65: Coach.

Minsk Automobile Plant (MAZ)

Bus Division (AMAZ)
2 Socialisticheskaya Street, Minsk 220021, Belarus
Tel: (+375 17) 246 96 68
Fax: (+375 17) 246 07 33
Web: www.maz.by

Background
MAZ has been producing motor vehicles since 1947. Its AMAZ bus division started production in 1992, under licence from Neoplan (now NeoMAN).
    The company is ISO 9001 certified.

Products
City and suburban buses and coaches. Trolleybuses have been manufactured since 2001.

Range
12 m, 15 m and 18 m buses and trolleybuses.

Buses
Single deck: MAZ 103, MAZ 103C, MAZ 104, MAZ 104C, MAZ 105 (articulated), MAZ 107

Midibus
MAZ-256: 28-seater midibus.

Trolleybus
MAZ 103T: 12 m long, seats 25, maximum capacity 100.

Coach
MAZ-251.

Production
Up to 600 buses per year. The company manufactured 481 units in 2003.

Developments
In mid-2004, the company started the manufacture of the MAZ-256 midibus, which seats 28 and is made of fibreglass.

Mitsubishi Fuso Truck and Bus Corporation (MFTBC)

2-16-4, Konan, Minato-ku, Tokyo 108-8285, Japan
Tel: (+81 3) 67 19 48 21
Fax: (+81 3) 67 19 01 11
e-mail: michael.behrens@mitsubishi-fuso.com
Web: www.mitsubishi-fuso.com

Key personnel
Chairman & Chief Business Ethics Officer: *Michio Hori*
President & Chief Executive Officer: *Wilfried Porth*
Senior Vice-President, Research & Development and Procurement Headquarters: *Joerg Zuern*
Senior Vice-President & Corporate General Manager of Domestic Sales & Service Office: *Masayuki Nagano*
Senior Vice-President & Corporate General Manager of International Sales & Service Office: *Bert van Dijk*
Senior Vice-President & Corporate General Manager of Production Office: *Tetsuo Fujii*
Senior Vice-President & Chief Financial Officer: *Dieter Buhl*
Senior Executive Officers:
    Corporate General Manager of Procurement & Supply Office: *Karl Deppen*
Corporate General Manager of Quality & Technical Affairs Office: *Hideyuki Shiozawa*
Executive Officers:
    Corporate General Manager of Corporate Office: *Michael Grahe, Helmut Schuett, Manfred Mayer, Nobuo Iijima, Yoshihiro Yoshida, Yasuo Sasaki*
PR Department: *Michael Behrens*

Bus production
Toyama (Mitsubishi Fuso Bus Manufacturing Co Ltd (MFBM))
    Nagoya (Oye plant) Tokyo (Kawasaki plant)

Manufacturing subsidiaries
Bangladesh, Egypt, Indonesia, Ivory Coast, Kenya, Morocco, Taiwan, Thailand, Turkey.

Mitsubishi's light bus Rosa   0585121

Bus assembly operations
Indonesia (by KRM)
Turkey (by TEMSA)

Background
Mitsubishi Fuso Truck and Bus Corporation was established in January 2003 as a spin-off from Mitsubishi Motors Corporation, with DaimlerChrysler AG and Mitsubishi Motors Corporation being the largest shareholders (65 and 20 per cent respectively). The company produces light buses at its Oye Bus Plant in Nagoya, medium and heavy buses are produced by Mitsubishi Fuso Bus Manufacturing Co Ltd (MFBM), also in Japan, and heavy buses are produced by TEMSA in Turkey.

Products
Buses, coaches and chassis, cars, trucks and engines.

Range
Bus and coach models for city bus, interurban and tourist operations.

Light bus
Rosa: Available in Custom and Standard versions. Also available in long and super-long variations and can be adapted as a wheelchair-accessible vehicle.
Medium buses
MK Series: Available in three models: general use (*MK215JG*) and delux (*MK215JD*) seating 37+1 passengers and a high-roof superior model (*MK215JH*) with a 33 + 1 capacity.
Large buses
MP Series: Available in two leaf-sprung models (*MP317MA* – capacity 49+1 and *MP317PA* – capacity 53+1) and two air-sprung models (*MP717MA* – capacity 49+1 and *MP717PA* – capacity 53+1).
MS Series: Available in two models (MS815SAH and MS815SGH), both seating 46 passengers.
    Mitsubishi's Hybrid Electric Vehicle (HEV) has a diesel engine driving a generator through lithium-ion batteries.
Chassis: Front engine (BM Bus Chassis) and rear engine (RK/RP Bus Chassis) are available.

Motor Coach Industries International (MCI)

1700 East Golf Road, Schaumburg, Illinois 60173, US
Tel: (+1 847) 285 20 00
Fax: (+1 847) 285 21 03
e-mail: corporate@mcicoach.net, marketing@mcicoach.net
Web: www.mcicoach.com

Key personnel
President and Chief Executive Officer: *Tom Sorrells*
Vice-President of Public Sector Accounts: *Michael P Melaniphy*
Vice-President of Coach Sales: *John Morrison*
Vice-President of Private Sector Accounts: *Gene Hall*
Vice-President of Corporate Marketing: *Patricia Ziska*

Manufacturing
1475 Clarence Avenue, Winnipeg, Manitoba RT3 1TS, Canada
Tel: (+1 204) 284 53 60   Fax: (+1 204) 478 32 05
Executive Vice-President and General Manager: *Mario Gonzales*

Background
MCI is no longer Dina-owned but Dina has an interest. Since 1999 Joseph Littlejohn-Levy,

a New York finance house, has had a 61 per cent share.

After-sales and service centre facilities are provided under the name MCI Fleet Support and MCI Fleet Support Service Parts, the latter being situated in Louisville, US.

Products

MCI motor coaches for intercity, suburban, charter and commuter routes.

Range

MCI E4500: Intercity coach with spiral entryway, tiered theatre-style seating and large baggage capacity. Overall length (with bumper): 13.89 m (45.58 ft), overall width: 2.59 m (102 in), overall height: 3.59 m (141.25 in). Optional extras include a wheelchair lift and a Caterpillar C-12 engine. Seats 56 passengers.

MCI J4500: Long-distance/intercity coach. Overall Length (with bumper): 13.89 m (45.58 ft), overall width: 2.59 m (102 in), overall height: 3.59 m (141.25 in). Optional extras include a wheelchair lift and a Caterpillar C-12 engine. Seats 56 passengers.

MCI D4500: Commuter coach, overall length: 13.84 m (45.42 ft), overall width: 2.59 m (102 in), overall height: 3.48 m (137 in). Seats 49 or 57 passengers. Optional extras include a wheelchair lift.

MCI D4500 commuter coach   1034695

Production

Up to seven coaches a day from the Winnipeg and Pembina plants.

Developments

In early 2005, MCI introduced two new D series coaches, the **D4505** (seating up to 55 passengers) and the **D4005** (seating up to 47 passengers).

It also introduced an LX version of the **E4500** coach.

Contracts

Recent contracts include orders from MTA Bus Company, New York and Straline Transportation, Seattle, US.

NEOPLAN Ghana Limited

PO Box 14699, Service Center Accra, Accra, Ghana
Tel: (+233 51) 270 79, (+233 21) 40 12 89
Fax: (+233 21) 40 02 83, (+233 51) 244 29
e-mail: neoplan@ghana.com
neoplank@africaonline.com.gh

Key personnel

Managing Director: *Helmut Clever*
Commercial Officer: *Maxwell Richards*

Background

Neoplan's Ghana operation was established in 1974 to offer a range of rugged 'Tropic' buses to the African market. Basic body-on-chassis, chassis-only and integral bus designs are offered.

Neoplan Ghana Limited is a joint venture between the Ghanaian Government and Neoman Bus GmbH.

Products

Buses, coaches and bus chassis for local and West African markets.

The company has integrated service centres in Kumasi and Accra.

Range

Includes simple front-engine designs with leaf springs and an air-suspension double-deck intercity bus.

Neoplan Ghana coach on DAF chassis   1328087

Contracts

100 new Tropicliner city buses have been delivered to Metro Mass Transit Limited (MMTL) in Accra and a further 150 vehicles are currently being built.

Ten luxury buses are being built for Transport Confort Voyageur (TCV), Burkina Faso.

New Flyer Industries

711 Kernaghan Avenue, Winnipeg, Manitoba R2C 3T4, Canada
Tel: (+1 204) 224 12 51   Fax: (+1 204) 224 42 14
e-mail: buses@newflyer.com
Web: www.newflyer.com

Other offices

Customer services, parts, publications, service and training
25 DeBaets Street, Winnipeg, Manitoba R2J 4GS, Canada
Tel: (+1 204) 982 84 00

Manufacturing facilities
711 Kernaghan Avenue, Winnipeg, Manitoba R2C 3T4, Canada
214 – 5th Avenue SW, Crookston, Minnesota 56716, US
6200 Glenn Carlson Drive, St Cloud, Minnesota 56301, US

New Flyer BRT DE60LFA (Eugene, US)   1328342

Key personnel

President and Chief Executive Officer: *John S Marinucci*

Executive Vice-President, Sales and Marketing: *Paul Smith*

Executive Vice-President, Parts and Services: *Hans Peper*

Chief Financial Officer: *Glenn Asham*

Background

In 2004, the company was acquired by Harvest Partners and Lightyear Capital, after having undergone significant growth. In 2005, the company successfully completed its Initial Public Offering.

New Flyer Industries and New Flyer Industries Canada ULC are public companies trading on the Toronto Stock Exchange.

Products

Heavy-duty low-floor transit buses and shuttles, parts, sales and services. Buses are available with optional restyled front mask and rear cap or with Bus Rapid Transit (BRT) design.

Range

Low-floor

D40LF

A 12.3 m, 2.6 m wide low-floor bus. The vehicles seat up to 39 seated passengers with wheelchair access by the front door flip-out ramp and kneeling features. The D40LF is powered by a Cummins 280 bhp engine with an Allison B400R automatic transmission and low-floor heavy-duty MAN axles.

D35LF

Seats 30 passengers and is 1.5 m shorter than the D40LF, but otherwise similar.

D30LF

Seats 25 passengers and is 3 m shorter but otherwise similar to the D40LF.

C40LF, C35LF, C30LF

These are fuelled by Compressed Natural Gas (CNG). Also available with Liquified Natural Gas (NLG) configuration.

DE40LF, DE60LF, GE40LF

These hybrid vehicles are available with parallel or series configurations providing reduced emissions, reduced maintenance costs and increased fuel economy.

D60LF

Articulated low-floor bus (18.3 m) seating up to 64 passengers.

Trolleybuses

E40LF, E60LF

New Flyer will provide information on demand. The company manufactures trolleybuses in 12.4 m and 18.5 m lengths, incorporating an AC solid state electronic system and AC traction motors located in the rear axle. A regenerative braking system puts power back into the power grid or into the Emergency Power Unit (EPU)

New Flyer BRT DE60LFA (Cleveland, US)   1344039

New Flyer 'Advanced-Style' DE40LFA BRT   1124808

New Flyer DE60LF low-floor articulated bus   1143011

New Flyer 'Restyled' DE40LFR diesel-electric hybrid transit bus   1124809

New Flyer 40 ft low-floor bus (Halifax, Canada)   1143013

when required. The EPU (or batteries) provide additional power during periods of acceleration and off-wire operation.

Service
Customer services
All customer support activities have been combined within one business unit. This unit comprises parts, publications, training and service departments and is primarily located in Winnipeg. Staff are located in various locations across North America.

Production
Approximately 2,200 buses in 2007.

Contracts
Key contracts include Seattle, Washington; Edmonton, Alberta; Victoria, British Columbia; Baltimore, Maryland; Chicago, Illinois; Philadelphia, Pennsylvania; Washington DC and San Diego, California.

In early 2005, the company created its 'Restyled' front mask and rear cap and its new 'Advanced-Style' BRT.

In 2007, New Flyer Industries received contracts from many US public transit authorities, with a total value, including options, of some USD1.9 billion. The vehicles on order include 40 ft and 60 ft vehicles with diesel, natural gas, hybrid and fuel cell propulsion systems.

Developments
New Flyer was named as the manufacturer of the world's first hydrogen fuel cell fleet of 20 buses for BC Transit in British Columbia Canada. These buses will be used during the 2010 Winter Olympics.

New Flyer was awarded a contract for up to 715 hybrid articulated buses for King County Metro in Seattle, Washington, US.

Montebello, CA, US has ordered 150 petrol (gasoline)-electric buses for California agencies.

A Californian agency placed a New Flyer hydrogen hybrid in active service. In February 2005, this bus was loaned to Winnipeg, Manitoba for in-service cold weather testing.

The company has re-entered electric trolleybus production with a contract for Translink (Greater Vancouver Transportation Authority). Delivery of the 18.3-m vehicles has begun. The company also won the contract for the Southeast Pennsylvania Transportation Authority (SEPTA) trolleybuses.

New Flyer has delivered Canada's first diesel-electric buses to BC Transit.

New Flyer was presented with the 2006 MARTA Effective Partnership in Quality Award and has received the 2006 CCME Pollution Prevention Award, Minnesota Safety Council's Governor's Safety Award to the Crookston manufacturing facility for excellence in workplace safety and health, the NSF-ISR, the WestStart-CALSTART 2004 Blue Sky award.

New Flyer has been named in Canada's Top 100 Companies in 2006 and 2007.

Record FY 2007 revenue of USD887.1 million and Adjusted Earnings Before Interest, Taxes, Depreciation and Amortization (EBITDA) of USD95.9 million increased by 46.0 per cent and 61.3 per cent, respectively compared to FY 2006.

New Flyer DE60LFR hybrid bus (Hamilton, Canada)   1344040

New Flyer GE40LF hybrid bus   1143012

New Flyer C40LF bus   1328345

New Flyer Trolley   1328344

New Flyer hydrogen hybrid bus   1143008

Ramp-up of bus manufacturing operations and continued growth of aftermarket operations resulted in highest quarterly and annual revenue and Adjusted EBITDA reported in the history of the company.

Continued growth of aftermarket operations resulted in FY 2007 revenue and Adjusted EBITDA increase of 22.7 per cent and 25.0 per cent, respectively, compared to FY 2006.

FY 2007 Distributable Cash of CAD66.1 million resulted in excess of CAD15.2 million over distributions declared in FY 2007.

Total order backlog of USD2.8 billion (representing 6,916 equivalent units) increased by 54.5 per cent compared to 31 December 2006 total order backlog of USD1.8 billion (representing 5,313 equivalent units).

The company signed an exclusive five-year agreement with Ballard Power Systems, an industry leader in fuel cell products, for use of fuel cell modules in shuttle buses that New Flyer plans to develop.

New Flyer's commercial relationship with Ballard began in 1993, when the two companies developed the world's first hydrogen fuel cell bus. In 2007, New Flyer was awarded a contract by BC Transit for the world's largest fleet of hydrogen fuel cell buses, and Ballard was named as the fuel cell technology provider.

Nishi-Nippon Coach Industry Co Ltd – NSK-Coach

c/o Nishi-Nippon Railroad Co Ltd
11-17 Tenjin 1-Chome, Chuo-Ku, Fukuoka 810-8570, Japan
Tel: (+81 92) 734 15 53
e-mail: www-admin@nnr.co.jp
Web: www.nnr.co.jp

Key personnel
President, Nishi-Nippon Railroad Co Ltd: *Tsuguo Nagao*

Background
Nishi-Nippon Coach Industry Co Ltd – NSK-Coach is an affiliate of Nishi-Nippon Railroad Co Ltd.

Products
Bus and coach bodies.

Range
One of Japan's two main independent body builders, NSK-Coach offers standard urban bus bodywork, touring coach bodies and express coach bodywork on Hino, Mitsubishi, Isuzu and Nissan chassis. Midibus bodywork is provided for Mazda, on behalf of the manufacturer.

A wheelchair lift can be fitted at the entrance door. The front structure can now be reinforced to protect the driver in the event of a collision.

Nissan Motor Co Ltd

17-1, Ginza 6-chome, Chuo-ku, Tokyo 104-8023, Japan
Tel: (+81 3) 55 65 21 41   Fax: (+81 3) 35 46 26 69
Web: www.nissan-global.com

Key personnel
President and Chief Executive Officer: *Carlos Ghosn*

Background
Nissan was the first Japanese automotive manufacturer to expand overseas and now has factories in Australia, Mexico, Spain, UK and US. The Vanette is made in Spain, and has spearheaded the success of Nissan's sales in the UK.

Nissan Motor, the car and light vehicle manufacturing company in the Nissan Group, builds under the Nissan marque. Extensive overseas manufacturing interests include the Motor Iberica operation in Spain producing 'Patrol' vehicles and Nissan-originated designs.

Since 1999, vehicles, including light commercial vehicles, have also been produced under the Renault-Nissan Alliance, which is managed by the jointly owned company Renault-Nissan bv.

Products
Mini and midibuses.

Nissan Motor España SA

Torre Nissan (Plaza Cerdá), General Almirante 4-10, E-08014 Barcelona, Spain
Tel: (+34 931) 902 1 80 85
Web: www.nissan.es

Key personnel
Executive Chairman: *J Echevarria*
Managing Director: *Rafael Boronat*
Communication Director: *Emelio Godes*

Background
A subsidiary of Nissan. Spain's largest manufacturer of commercial and 4 × 4 vehicles.

Motor Iberica designs have carried the Ebro badge, but this is increasingly also being used for locally assembled versions of Nissan vehicles.

Products
Small buses and truck-derived chassis suitable for bus bodywork, including off-road light and medium trucks, vans and multipurpose vehicles.

Noge SL

PO Box 55, Carretera St, Hilari, km 3, E-17401 Arbúcies, Girona, Spain
Tel: (+34 972) 86 01 03   Fax: (+34 972) 86 11 86
e-mail: info@noge-sl.com
Web: www.noge-sl.com

Key personnel
President: *m Genabat*
Director: *Mr Fajardo*
Export Manager: *Simon Vitalla*
   Staff: Not currently available

Background
Founded in 1964.
In 2001, NOGE Bus France was founded.
In 2008, NOGE Italy was founded.

Products
Bus and coach bodies.

Range
Cittour range:
Model 12: Low-floor urban transit bus, length 12 m, width 2.5 m, height 3.0 m, capacity 32 seated, 76 standing, chassis MAN NL 263F.

Model 10.5: Low-floor urban transit bus, length 10.5 m, width 2.5 m, height 3.0 m, capacity 25 seated, 52 standing, chassis MAN NL 263F.

Touring range:
STAR 15 m Model: 3.70/15: Coach, length 15 m, height 3.675 m, width 2.55 m, capacity 71 + WC + 1T + 1C.
STAR 13 m Models: 3.70/13.8 and 3.45/13: Coach, available in two lengths, 13.755 m (capacity 63 + WC + 1T + C) and 12.29 m (capacity 59 + WC + 1T + C), height 3.675 m and 3.445 m respectively, width 2.55 m.
STAR 12 m Models 3.70/12 and 3.45/12: Coach, available in two versions, length 12 m, width 2.55 m, height 3.675 m (Model 3.70/12) and 3.445 m (Model3.45/12), capacity 55 + WC + 1T + C and 53 + WC + 1T + C respectively.
STAR 10 m Model: 3.45 /10: Length 9.95 m, width 2.335 m, height 3.64 m, capacity 39 + 1T + 1C.
STAR 8 m Model: 3.00/8: Lenght 7.950 m, width 2.335 m, height 3.055 m, capacity: 30+1C.

Titanium range:
TITANIUM 15 m Model 3.70/15: Coach, length 15 m, height 3.675 m, width 2.55 m, maximum capacity 71+WC+1T+1C.

TITANIUM 13 m Models: 3.70/13.8 and 3.45/13: Coach, available in two lengths 12.92 m (capacity 57+WC+1T+1C) and 13.80 m (capacity 63+WC+1T+1C).
TITANIUM 12 m Models: 3.70/12 and 3.45/12: Coach, available in two versions: length 12.20 m, width 2.55 m, height 3.675 m (model 3.70/12) and 3.445 m (model 3.45/12), capacity 55+WC+1T+C and 53+WC+1T+C respectively.

Intercity range:
INTERCITY Models 3.30/12 and 3.30/13: City bus, available in two lengths; 12 m (capacity 53+1C+24) or 12.92 m (capacity 57+1C+19); height 3.475 m, width 2.55 m.

Production
Annual production is more than 600 vehicles.

Contracts
Include exports to Austria, Belgium, Croatia, Denmark, Former Yugoslav Republic of Macedonia, France, Germany, Hong Kong, Ireland, Israel, Italy, Netherlands, Portugal, and the UK.

North American Bus Industries Inc (NABI Inc)

106 National Drive, Anniston, Alabama 36207, US
Tel: (+1 256) 831 42 96
Fax: (+1 256) 831 42 99
e-mail: nabiusa@nabiusa.com
Web: www.nabiusa.com

Key personnel
President and Chief Executive Officer: *Robert M Shaughnessy*
Senior Vice-President and General Manager, Transportation and Coach Operations: *James 'Jim' Bernacchi*
Senior Vice-President, Transit Sales and Marketing: *Joseph 'Joe' Gibson*

Vice-President, Western Region Transit Sales: *Bill Coryell*
Director, Public Sector Sales: *Rich Himes*

Sales Office
3450 East Philadelphia Street, Ontario, CA-91761, US
Tel: (+1 909) 773 05 00   Fax: (+1 909) 923 82 63
e-mail: bussales@nabiusa.com

Bus shell manufacturing facility
Ujszasz u. 45, H-1165 Budapest, XVI, Hungary
Tel: (+36 1) 407 94 44
Fax: (+36 1) 407 29 31
e-mail: nabihq@nabi.hu
Web: www.nabi.hu
Director: *Katalin Patkos*

Aftermarket Parts Division
1275 South Houk Road, Delaware, Ohio 43015, US
Tel: (+1 740) 369 10 56
Fax: (+1 740) 363 58 97
e-mail: parts@nabiusa.com

Background
NABI is an ISO 9001 registered company.

Products
NABI designs and manufactures heavy-duty transit buses with diesel, CNG or LNG and diesel hybrid-electric propulsion in standard- or low-floor versions ranging from 35 to 60 ft in length. Structures are made of stainless or mild-steel. Bus shells are received from the manufacturing plant in Budapest, Hungary and final assembly is carried out in the US.

Range
Rear-engine bus models are offered in standard and low-floor configurations. Rigid buses are offered in 10.7 m and 12.3 m lengths and the articulated version is 18.4 m long.

Low-floor buses are available in 9.4 m, 10.7 m and 12.3 m lengths.

All standard models can be fitted with front door- or rear door-mounted wheelchair lifts and low-floor models have a wheelchair ramp at either door.

A choice of Cummins, Caterpillar or Deere engines is available (diesel or alternative fuel). Transmission options are Allison, Voith or ZF. Rear-mounted or roof-mounted air conditioning is available using either Thermo King, Carrier-Transicold or Sütrak systems.

The body structures of its low-floor, standard-floor and articulated buses are available in coated mild steel or stainless steel.

Contracts
In July 2006, the company received orders from Foothill Transit and the Regional Public Transportation Authority, Mesa. The former ordered 42 CNG 40-LFW transit buses and the latter 28 40-LFW CNG buses plus 10 60-BRT articulated buses.

In February 2006, an order was received for 96 additional CNG 60-BRT buses from Los Angeles County Metropolitan Transportation Authority (Metro) as an option to a previous order for 200 vehicles. The contract is valued at USD70 million and the vehicles were due to be delivered late 2006 and early 2007.

In March 2006, NABI received an order for 30 articulated CNG 60-BRT buses from Foothill Transit, US. The contract is valued at approximately USD22 million and the vehicles were delivered in late 2006, for inauguration into service in early 2007.

In July 2006, the company received an order for 35 40 ft low-floor CNG buses from Sun Metro Mass Transit department, El Paso, Texas in a contract valued at approximately USD14 million. Delivery was scheduled for March 2007.

In August 2006, NABI completed delivery of 12 60-ft 60-BRT CNG buses to Los Angeles World Airports.

In September 2006, Rockford Mass Transit District awarded NABI a contract for 20 35-ft low-floor model 35-LFW diesle buses. The contract was valued at approximately USD6 million,

NABI 60-BRT articulated bus 1115113

Foothill Transit NABI 40-LFW transit bus 1115114

NABI 60-ft 60-BRT articulated bus for Los Angeles World Airports 1322683

For details of the latest updates to *Jane's Urban Transport Systems* online and to discover the additional information available exclusively to online subscribers please visit
juts.janes.com

with the vehicles scheduled for delivery in early 2007.

In December 2006, NABI received an order for 21 35-ft low-floor CNG buses for Los Amgeles World Airports (LAWA). The contract was valued at USD7.3 million and the vehicles were due for delivery in July 2007.

Production
In 2005, NABI Inc delivered 489 buses, a large proportion of which were articulated buses.

Developments
In August 2005, NABI announced an agreement to sell its UK subsidiary, Optare Holdings Ltd. NABI has entered into an agreement to provide spare parts and technical services for the Optare 30-LFN buses which were supplied to customers in the US.

In February 2006, NABI was acquired by affiliates of Cerberus Capital Management LP, a US-based private equity fund manager.

In May 2006, the company unveiled its new, low-floor, heavy duty, model 42-BRT transit bus. This vehicle is in the same range as the 60-BRT articulated bus.

In August 2006, NABI acquired Optima Bus Corporation.

Nova Bus

1000 Industriel Boulevard, Saint-Eustache, Quebec J7R 5A5, Canada
Tel: (+1 450) 472 64 10
Fax: (+1 450) 974 30 01
e-mail: novabus.sales@volvo.com
Web: www.novabus.com

Key personnel
President and Chief Executive Officer: *Gilles Dion*
Vice-President, Business Development:
 Jean-Pierre Baracat
Director of Sales, North America: *Jean-Marc Landry*
Strategic Advisors: *Anthony Kouneski*
 Bob Irwin
Marketing Co-ordinator: *Hélène Lamouche*
Business Development Manager: *Nadine Bernard*
Regional Sales Managers: *Wayne Feagan, Lee Morris, Lou Quaglia*

Other offices
Parts Division
Quebec Parts Center
2955-A Watt Street, Sainte-Foy, Quebec G1X 3W1, Canada
Tel: (+1 418) 654 01 74 (Administration)
Freephone: (+1 800) 771 66 82 (transit parts)
 (+1 800) 463 88 76 (coach parts)
Fax: (+1 418) 658 17 23; (+1 800) 939 01 33
Web: www.prevostparts.com

The company also has offices in the US, in Illinois, New Jersey, California, Tennessee, Florida and Texas.

Background
Nova Bus is a wholly owned subsidiary of Volvo Bus Corporation. The company is a leading designer and manufacturer of city, suburban and shuttle buses in North America.

The company has company-wide ISO 9001 and ISO 14001 certification.

Nova Bus operates two plants, both located in the Province of Quebec. The Saint-Eustache plant is the assembly and finishing plant and the Saint-Francois-du-Lac plant produces structure, parts and components.

Products
Nova Bus manufactures the Nova LFS (transit, suburban and shuttle versions) and the LFS Artic (articulated model).

Nova LFS
The Nova LFS is a 40 ft low-floor bus, which features a stainless steel structure and high impact thermoplastic skirt panels and gel-coat finished fibreglass skin. It is one of the lightest vehicles in its category.

The LFS is available in three versions for urban, suburban and shuttle applications, with

Nova LFS bus   1344772

Nova LFS HEV hybrid bus (Volvo Bus Corporation)   1345137

seating capacity up to 49, depending on internal configuration. Other specifications include a Cummins engine up to 280 hp, ABS disk brakes and wide doors for easy passenger access.

In November 2006, Nova Bus launched the Nova LFS HEV, a diesel-electric Hybrid Electric Vehicle based on its proven LFS platform. The Nova LFS HEV features a standard stainless steel structure, a Cummins ISL 280 hp engine, Allison E^P 40 electric drive system, ABS disk brakes and a seating capacity of up to 41.

The vehicles meets ADA, FMVSS and CMVSS criteria.

Prevost Parts Division
Prevost Parts is the exclusive distributor of all Nova Bus certified parts and components.

Developments
In November 2007, Nova Bus unveiled the Nova LFS Artic, which shares its platform with the Nova LFS and integrates a number of innovations which focus on safety, reliability and productivity. As with all Nova Bus products, the needs of operators, drivers and passengers have been taken into consideration in designing the bus.

Contracts
In January 2008, Nova Bus announced the signing of an agreement with TransLink, the Greater Vancouver Area transit authority, for the purchase of 141 Nova LFS HEV hybrid electric buses for delivery beginning in mid-2009, with options totalling an additional 110 vehicles.

Optare plc

T/A Optare UK Limited
Whitebirk Industrial Estate, Lower Philips Road, Blackburn, BB1 5UD, UK
Tel: (+44 845) 838 99 01   Fax: (+44 845) 838 99 02
e-mail: bussales@optare.com
Web: www.optare.com

T/A Optare Group Limited
Manston Lane, Leeds LS15 8SU, UK
Tel: (+44 113) 264 51 82   Fax: (+44 113) 260 66 35
e-mail: As above
Web: As above

Key personnel
Non-Executive Chairman: *John Fickling*

Non-Executive Directors: *Roy Stanley*
 David Maughan
 David Stonehouse
Chief Executive Officer: *Andrew Brian*
Chief Financial Officer: *Mike Dunn*
Chief Operating Officer: *Chris Powell*
Commercial Director: *Glenn Saint*
Marketing Director: *Louise Yates*

Supply Chain Director: *Amanda McLaren*
Product Support Director: *Ritchie Bignell*
Group Production Director: *Colin Childs*
Sales Director: *John Horn*
Key Account Director: *Chris Wise*
Regional Sales Managers: *Steph Baker, Paul Beyer, David Cheeseman, Charles Waggott*
International Sales Manager: *Steve Johnson*
European Sales Manager: *Jos van der Putten*
    Staff: Not available currently

Subsidiary division
Optare Product Support
Product Support Director: *Ritchie Bignell*
General Manager, UK Service Centres: *Mark Wallis*

Background
The Board of Optare Holdings Ltd announced on 12 March 2008 that it had reached agreement to sell the entire issued share capital of the company to Jamesstan Investments Ltd. Shortly afterwards, in July 2008, Optare plc was formed following the reverse takeover by the AIM listed Darwen company, to create a new business employing 830 people and with a GBP90 million turnover.

The change of ownership continues Optare's independence whilst providing a platform for further business growth in the UK and European markets.

Products
Integral mini, midi and full-size single- and double-deck buses.

Range
Solo
Integral low-floor midibus range available in a choice of six lengths between 7.1 m and 10.2 m, with full-width body (2.5 m) and narrower slimline body (2.33 m). The vehicle is fitted with the a choice of Mercedes-Benz OM904LA or Cummins ISBe engines, with Selective Catalytic Reduction (SGR) or the MAN D083 engine with Exhaust Gas Recirculation (EGR). An Allison B2100 fully automatic gearbox is standard, along with a KLAM electro magnetic retarder and disc brakes all round. Full air suspension with front-end kneeling as standard makes the vehicle fully accessible for wheelchairs, buggies and semi-ambulant passengers. The normal ride height is 265 mm at the entrance platform, kneeling to 200 mm. Seating capacities up to 37 with up to 21 also standing.

Available in left- or right-hand drive, the Solo was named as a Millennium Products award by the UK Design Council in 2008 and also won a Queen's Awards for Enterprise 2000 (Innovation category). A range of equipment can be specified to accommodate various operational requirements.

Solo SE
This is a shorter version of the Solo, at 7.1 m or 7.8 m, with up to 23 seats and powered by the standard Mercedes 95 kW (127 bhp) SCR Euro 4 engine. It has been specified to ensure the lowest-possible entry price to the Solo range.

Solo SR
An extension to the Optare Solo range, the Solo SR was unveiled at the 2007 Coach and Bus Live exhibition. Combining all the attributes of the original Solo design but adding new styling inside and out, the Solo SR is an extension to the midibus range and is to be produced alongside the established models.

The SR model is initially available in body lengths of 8.9 m and 9.6 m with the standard body width of 2.5 m. Mechanical specifications are identical to the standard Solo.

Solo+
Introduced at EuroBus Expo 2008, the Solo+ features new contemporary styling both inside and out to follow a new family appearance unveiled on the flagship product the Optare Rapta double-deck citybus (see below). This evolutionary development maintains all the features of the original standard Solo and is available in a choice of lengths at 8.8 m and 9.5 m with the standard 2.5 m body width.

Solo EV
An alternative driveline variant of the Solo, providing zero emissions featuring the Enova EDU120 Panther traction motor. Accessories are electrically driven, whilst heating is provided by an Eberspacher vehicle water heater, which is fuel-fired.

Enova Systems offers Optare hybrid electric, plug-in hybrid electric and full electric drive systems that fit a range of vehicle platforms. Additional system options include integrated battery chargers and DC/DC converters. This flexibility allows Optare to create hybrid electric and full electric buses from a common architecture.

Rapta
Newly introduced at the UK EuroBus 2008 show, the Rapta from Optare has a target design weight of 10,700 kg for the diesel variant and is powered by a MAN EGR engine for Euro 5 compliance without additives.

A high mounted charge-air-cooler, together with low velocity offside separate radiator are featured to reduce dirt ingress and provide longer period between cleaning. Other features include:
- Independent front suspension for improved ride characteristics;
- Aluminium integral body with foam core aluminium composite roof and inter-deck for long life and durability;
- A forward mounted fuel tank beneath the driver's cab providing easy filling at a convenient level;
- LED saloon lighting;
- Integrated driver's area and protection screens for clean, modern design.

The Rapta is also available with an optional Enova Hybrid drive system – completely interchangeable with the diesel power-pack and utilising Lithium Ion battery technology.

Olympus
The Optare Olympus is available on a range of heavy-duty chassis, offering both SCR and EGR engines. The body structure is constructed using heavy-duty extruded aluminium alloy sections, bolted together for optimum strength and ease of repair.

The model is available in a range of body lengths to suit a choice of chassis – Volvo B9TL, Scania N230UD and ADL E400 – using heavy-duty mechanical components to meet operator requirements.

Optare Solo+, with new styling inside and out, introduced at EuroBus Expo 2008 (Optare plc)
1374733

New Optare Rapta double-deck bus, introduced at EuroBus Expo 2008, available with an optional Enova Hybrid drive system (Optare plc)
1374734

Optare Versa to Transport for London (TfL) specification (Optare plc)   1375345

Optare Soroco minicoach on the 515 CDi Mercedes-Benz Sprinter chassis. It has 16 Kiel reclining seats (Optare plc)   1375346

Versa

A single-deck bus, which targets the gap between Optare's Solo and Tempo vehicles. It is initially available in two lengths, 10.3 m and 11 m and is 2.5 m wide. It has a completely new look, although it has the design architecture of both the smaller and larger models.

The Versa has an additional seating capacity compared to the 10.2 m Solo, with 40 seats, but the major difference is that the forward control driving position gives a wheelbase of only 5.8 m, improving manoeuvrability.

Tempo

Low-floor, heavy-duty, single-deck bus available in four lengths: 10.6 m, 11.3 m, 12 m and 12.6 m, seating up to 46 plus 26 standees. Mercedes-Benz OM906LA engine with SCR or the MAN D0836 engine with EGR are available with Allison T310R or ZF6HP500 automatic gearbox, both with integral retarder. All-round disc braking and front-end kneeling.

Toro

This is a midicoach on the 816 Mercedes-Benz Vario chassis, 8.74 m long and 2.44 m wide, which uses SCR emission-control technology to bring it to meet current Euro 4 emissions legislation. Standard on the Toro are 28 + 1 Kiel seats with three-point belts, courier seat, double glazing and air conditioning and an R66 compliant structure. Mercedes-Benz 136 bhp turbocharged/intercooled engine with six-speed ZF synchromesh gearbox with an automatic option if required. Air-operated plug door and large luggage capacity. A range of optional equipment is available.

Optare Soroco

The Soroco was originally introduced in 1999 and has sold in large numbers. The 2008 Soroco features a redesigned body integrated with the Mercedes-Benz 515 CDi chassis cowl. A total of 19 seats is standard.

The interior has been restyled with new luggage racks and personal control units whilst retaining the Esteban seats. The 515 Sprinter chassis offers a blend of performance and economy using a 112 kW (150 bhp) EGR engine to meet current emissions legislation. A five-speed, fully automatic gearbox option is available.

Optare International, Export Division

Offering access to Optare services and products worldwide. Complete vehicles, left- or right-hand drive, CKD kits, technology transfer and manufacturing licences are available on Optare's range of integral products.

International activities include deliveries of Optare-built vehicles to Malaysia, Turkey, Hungary, Denmark, Netherlands, Germany and the US. The company has also developed left-hand drive variants of the Solo and Tempo for global markets.

Optare Product Support Division

Provides spare parts and service support for all Optare Group products, both domestic and overseas. Comprehensive technical documentation is available from the division, and accident damage repairs and vehicle maintenance are provided by strategically located service centres. In-service problem solving and product training facilities are also provided.

Parts ordering is now available online through the Expressway Internet portal. Operators are able to interrogate the comprehensive online parts catalogues, review stock levels, confirm availability, order and pay for spare parts from their offices 24 hours per day, seven days per week. A new 'Picomat' warehouse system has been introduced to give increased 'first time pick' levels.

Production

In 2008, more than 800 buses and coaches were delivered to UK operators across the combined group with significant volume increases projected for 2009 and beyond.

Contracts

In 2008, Optare continued to maintain strong relationships with major bus group operators Stagecoach, Arriva, First Group, Go Ahead and Veolia and local authorities with further significant orders for the Mistral Group for the smaller independents.

Following on from the success of 11 Optare Versas that recently entered service, Transdev Yellow Buses (TYB) of Bournemouth has confirmed an order for 11 Optare Tempo heavy-duty, integral single-deckers.

The 12 m, 43-seat Tempos will be delivered in March and April 2009. Internal specifications have yet to be determined but are expected to be of the same high standard as the Versas, which feature leather trimmed seats with padded head restraints and wood-effect flooring.

This will be the second time that TYB has taken Optare products into its fleet, which now numbers 107 buses. The Tempos will be powered by the Mercedes-Benz OM 906LA six-cylinder engine, which uses SCR technology to achieve Euro 5 emissions compliance.

London tour bus company Big Bus Tours has put ten Optare Visionaire open-top double-deckers into its fleet on sightseeing services in the capital. The 82-seater buses were delivered from Optare's Blackburn plant fully fitted out and painted and lettered in the distinctive burgundy and cream Big Bus livery ready to immediately enter service. Three are fully open-topped and seven have a covered area over the front two bays.

In November 2008, Optare was awarded a contract valued at more than GBP6 million for 53 buses to be delivered for Arriva's UK fleet. The Tempo (13 vehicles), Versa (10 vehicles) and Solo (30 vehicles) models will be delivered in a three-month period, starting in February 2009.

Developments

In 2008, Optare launched the Solo+ single-deck and Rapta double-deck bus ranges – see above.

Through the integral construction techniques employed in the manufacturing processes, further developments expected in 2009 include hybrid solutions across the entire bus range.

The first Tempo hybrid, using the Allison EP40 system, is complete and undergoing final testing with orders secured for a number of units. Versa and Solo hybrid development is at an advanced stage with super capacitor electrical energy storage.

The technology uses a Mercedes-Benz Euro 5 diesel engine with super capacitors to store energy, rather than batteries. It is expected to deliver a significant saving in fuel consumption and emissions, when compared with a conventionally powered Euro 4 vehicle of similar specification.

As with all Optare products, the mechanical package is mounted together as a removable power pack carrying the cooling system, exhaust and all ancillaries to aid major servicing. The power pack can be removed in less than one hour.

Optima Bus Corporation

PO Box 19140, Wichita, Kansas 67204-9140, US
Tel: (+1 316) 779 77 00
Fax: (+1 316) 779 77 27
e-mail: sales@optimabus.com
Web: www.optimabus.com

Key personnel

Chief Executive Officer: *Michael Monteferrante*
Chief Financial Officer: *Gene Johnson*
Vice-President, Operations: *Scott Brown*
Vice-President, Projects: *Doug Brehm*
Director of Purchasing and Materials:
  Roger Brickell
Marketing and Sales Manager:
  Diane Hawkins

Works

1601 East 77th Street North, Valley Center, Kansas 67219, US

Background

Originally formed in 1979 as the Chance Coach division of Chance Industries, the company's assets were purchased by the management group and American Capital Strategies in 1998 to become a privately-held corporation.

In 2003, the company adopted its current name and in 2004 it achieved ISO 9001:2000 certification.

Products

Complete heavy-duty small buses and articulated modular vehicles and rubber-tyred replica vintage trams (streetcars).

Range

Opus low-floor bus: Heavy-duty chassis with lightweight bolted aluminium body. Two versions are available, a 9.15 m (under 30 ft) model with a total capacity of 53 (27 seated, 23 with two wheelchair positions), which is available with either one or double doors, and a 10.66 m (under 35 ft) double-door model with a total capacity of 60 (31 seated, 27 with two wheelchair positions). ADA-compliant wheelchair accessibility is available for both models and both accommodate the hearing impaired with visual displays and the sight impaired with a public address system. Entry height for both is 254 mm (10 in). Turning circles are: 7.62 m (25 ft) (9.15 m/30 ft model) and 7.62 m (25 ft) (10.66 m/ 35 ft model). A removable cradle enables access to the engine and transmission.

Opus ISE series hybrid low-floor bus: Announced in March 2005, these buses use a conventional internal combustion engine only to generate electricity with ISE-Siemens ThunderVolt® hybrid technology and Siemens ELFA motors, generators and inverters.

American Heritage Streetcar: The *AH-28 Diesel*-powered car has a body in the style of a nineteenth century streetcar (tram), with brass fittings and mahogany woodwork. It seats up to 28. The transit chassis provides a 9.4 m turning circle for congested areas. A wheelchair lift can be provided and a high-capacity heating and air conditioning system is fitted, along with heavy-duty insulation. A natural-gas-powered version is available (*AH-28 Natural Gas*) and a propane-powered versions (*AH-28 Propane*).

Contracts

In February 2006, Optima delivered nine Opus buses to IndyGo.

In April 2006, Miami-Dade County awarded Optima a contract valued at USD178 million for 300 Opus 30-ft low-floor buses. Delivery was scheduled to begin in October 2006 and was due to be completed by the end of March 2007.

In May 2006, the company received its first order for its new Opus ISE series hybrid low-floor bus. A base order of five vehicles valued at approximately USD7.5 million, with an option for 10 additional vehicles, was received from the Town of Avon Transit, Avon, Colorado.

Developments

In February 2005, the company announced the development of a hybrid-electric powered version of its Opus low-floor bus. The new vehicle became available in mid-2005.

In August 2006, Optima Bus Corporation was acquired by North American Bus Industries Inc (NABI).

Österreichische Automobilfabrik ÖAF – Gräf & Stift AG (ÖAF)

Brunner Strasse 44-50, A-1231 Vienna, Austria
Tel: (+43 1) 86 32 58 59
Fax: (+43 1) 86 32 58 99
Web: www.man-nutzfahrzeuge.de
  www.man.at

Key personnel

Bus Manager: *Ing Barnerth*
Marketing Manager: *Helmut Haidmeier*
Managing and Operations Director: *Bruno Krainz*

Background

Österreichische Automobilfabrik (ÖAF)/Gräf & Stift AG buses are based on the designs of its parent company MAN, which took control of the joint company formed by the merger of Austrian commercial vehicle builders ÖAF and Gräf & Stift in 1971. The company is building trolleybuses for the group as a whole.

Products

Trolleybuses and bus floor assemblies.

Otokar Otobüs Karoseri Sanayi AŞ (Otokar)

Aydınevler Mah. Dumlupınar Cad. No 24, A Blok, TR-34550 Küçükyalı-İstanbul, Turkey
Tel: (+90 216) 489 29 50   Fax: (+90 216) 489 29 67
e-mail: kyl@otokar.com.tr
Web: www.otokar.com.tr

Manufacturing plant

Atatürk Cad No 9, PK 10, TR-54580 Arifiye-Sakarya, Turkey
Tel: (+90 264) 229 22 44   Fax: (+90 264) 229 22 42
e-mail: arf@otokar.com.tr

Key personnel

General Manager: *Serdar Görgüç*
Assistant General Manager: *H Basri Akgül*
Export Manager: *Sedef Vehbi*
  Staff: Not currently available

Background

Otokar was set up in 1963 to produce coaches under Magirus-Deutz licence. During the early 1970s, the company commenced the design and manufacture of its own range of coaches and city buses.

The 80 E5 series minibus, for example, was one of the Otokar products designed primarily for in-city transport. It still enjoys more than 90 per cent market share in the commuter transport segment in big cities, in Turkey. Now under the new brand name of M-2000.

Products

Midibuses and minibuses. The company also designs a range of special vehicles.

Range

M-2000: Heavy duty minibus, remodelled in 2002 and 2004. Length 5.6 m, width 2.04 m.
M-3000: Heavy duty minibus series, seating 14, 18 and 19 passengers; available with 125 hp engine options.

Otokar M-2000 heavy-duty minibus 1367277

Otokar Navigo midibus 1367279

Navigo: Range of midibuses available in intercity, citybus and shuttle bus versions. Seating 25, 27, 31 and 33 passengers, it is available with 125 hp, 145 hp, 160 hp and 185 hp engine options. **Sultan** is the brand name for Navigo in the Turkish market.

Vectio/Doruk: Range of 9 m buses available in intercity, citybus and urban bus versions. Seating versions depend on customer requirements; engine options: 190 hp, 200 hp, 215 hp and 240 hp. **Vectio** is the brand name for **Doruk** in the Turkish market.

Developments

In 2006, the company contracted Cummins to provide the Euro 4 engines for its Navigo range of midibuses.

In December 2007, the latest member of the Otokar minibus family, the M-3000, was introduced to the market throughout Turkey. This new minibus series was developed according to the requirements of local customers and several cities in Turkey.

Also in 2007, the company launched a 9-m bus series, Doruk. Two new models were available in 2008, the Doruk 190 LE and the Doruk 190S. The Doruk 160LE Hibra electric-diesel hybrid was launched in late 2007.

Otokar M-3000 heavy-duty minibus 1367278

Otokar Vectio 9-m bus 1367281

Otokar Vectio/Doruk 160LE Hibra diesel-electric hybrid 9-m bus 1367283

Overland Custom Coach Inc

R.R.2, 21051 Nissouri Road, Thorndale, Ontario, N0M 2P0, Canada
Tel: (+1 519) 461 11 40   Fax: (+1 519) 461 05 23
e-mail: contactus@overlandcustomcoach.com
Web: www.overlandcustomcoach.com

Other office

Overland Custom Coach US Inc
6880 Maple Valley Road Brown City, Michigan 48416, USA
Tel: (+1 810) 346 34 85   Fax: (+1 810) 346 20 24

Background

Overland Custom Coach Inc was established in 1981 to manufacture and distribute medium duty cutaway buses and specialty vehicles across Canada. In 1989, the company introduced the ELF (Economical Low Floor) Bus, which was first offered for sale in 1991.

Products

Overland Custom Coach, together with Starcraft Corporation, currently manufactures a range of ELF buses.

Range

The ELF is currently available in 22 ft, 25 ft and 28 ft models with petrol/gasoline, diesel and CNG powered drive trains.

ELF 122 HD: Heavy duty, low-floor transit/paratransit bus with fold-out ramp.
ELF 125 HD: Heavy duty, low-floor transit/paratransit bus with fold-out ramp.
ELF 128 HD: Heavy duty, low-floor transit/paratransit bus with fold-out ramp.

Alternative fuel versions
ELF Environmental: Low-floor, medium duty electric bus with fold-out ramp.

ELF CNG: Low-floor, medium duty CNG bus with fold-out ramp.

Developments

The company is working towards producing electric and hybrid-electric versions of the ELF vehicles.

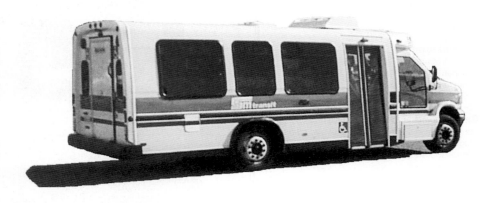

ELF 125 HD heavy duty bus 0585110

JSC Pavlovo Bus (PAZ)

Suvorov Str 1, Pavlovo, Nizhny Novgorod Region, 606108, Russian Federation
Tel: (+7 831) 716 09 97; 86 80; 30 71; 86 80
Fax: (+7 831) 716 88 75
e-mail: market@paz.nnov.ru
Web: www.paz.nnov.ru

Key personnel

Director General: *Sergey G Zanozin*
Marketing and Sales Director (Acting): *Vladimir V Berezhnoy*
Directors:
  Commerce: *Vladislav V Valiliev*
  Technical: *Vasily I Caplun*
  Production: *Stanislav V Chinenkov*

Background

PAZ is part of the Avtokron bus manufacturing group, Golizyno, Moscow, the country's largest bus manufacturer. Avtokron builds Mercedes vehicles under licence. Bus production started in 1952.

The company has representatives in Argentina, Bulgaria, Estonia, Greece, Khazakhstan, Latvia, Lithuania, Mongolia, Poland, Romania and Venezuela.

Products
Buses and chassis.

Range

Small buses:

PAZ 3205: Small bus, length 7 m, width 2.5 m, height 2.9 m, seating 28 passengers. Other versions available include: **PAZ 32053**, with pneumatically driven brake system, ABC, with petrol engine; **PAZ 32053-07** with pneumatically driven brake system, ABC, with diesel engine; **PAZ 3205-07** with diesel engine; **PAZ 320507-110** with petrol engine, tropic version; **PAZ 320507-07** with diesel engine, tropic version.

PAZ 32051: Small bus, length 7 m, width 2.5 m, height 2.9 m, seating 24 passengers. Other versions include: **PAZ-32054** with pneumatically driven brake system, ABC, with petrol engine; **PAZ-32054-07** with pneumatically driven brake system, ABC, with diesel engine; **PAZ 32051-07** diesel engine; **PAZ 320517-110** petrol engine in tropical version; **PAZ 320517-07** petrol engine in tropical version.

PAZ 3205-60: Small bus, length 7 m, width 2.5 m, height 2.9 m, seating 28 passengers. Other versions and modifications include: **PAZ-32053-60** with pneumatically driven brake system, ABC, petrol

engine; **PAZ-32053-67** with pneumatically driven brake system, ABC, diesel engine, full-gear (4 × 4) on PAZ 3206 base, double-doors on PAZ 32051 base, improved comfort on PAZ-3205-50 base.

PAZ 3205-50: Small bus, length 7 m, width 2.5 m, height 2.9 m, seating 22 passengers. Other versions include: **PAZ-32053-50** with pneumatically driven brake system, ABC, petrol engine; **PAZ-32053-57** with pneumatically driven brake system, ABC, petrol engine.

PAZ 320520: Small bus, length 7 m, width 2.5 m, height 2.9 m, seating 5, 11 or 12 passengers. Other versions include: **PAZ 3205-27** with diesel engine; **PAZ 3206-110-20** with petrol engine, full-driven; **PAZ 3206-27** with diesel engine, full-driven; **PAZ 3205-110-21** with petrol engine and isothermic cargo compartment; **PAZ 3205-110-21** with petrol engine and isothermic cargo compartment; **PAZ 3205-28** with petrol engine and isothermic cargo compartment; **PAZ 3205-29** with petrol engine and isothermic cargo compartment.

PAZ 3206: Small bus, length 7 m, width 2.5 m, height 3.1 m, seating 28 passengers.

Medium bus:

PAZ 4230: Intercity bus, length 8.3 m, width 2.5 m, height 2.9 m.

Large buses:

PAZ 4223: Intercity bus, length 10.5 m, width 2.5 m, height 3 m, seating 27 passengers, total passengers 90.

PAZ 4228: Intercity bus, length 10.5 m, width 2.5 m, height 3 m, seating 27 passengers, total passengers 90.

PAZ 5272: Urban bus, seating 33 passengers, total passengers 108.

PAZ 5271: Urban bus, length 12 m, width 2.5 m, height 3 m, seating 35, total passengers 110.

Other products:

PAZ-3205, improved comfort.
School bus PAZ-3205.
Chassis PAZ 3205-40.
Chassis PAZ 3206-40 (4 × 4).

Production
8,503 vehicles were produced in 1998.

Contracts
PAZ minibuses are extensively used throughout the former Soviet Union for both urban bus and other collective transport duties.

Piaggio Ltd

LTV Division
1 Boundary Row, London, SE1 8HP, UK
Tel: (+44 207) 401 43 00   Fax: (+44 207) 401 43 01
e-mail: markbrown@piaggio.co.uk
Web: www.uk.vtl.piaggio.com

Key personnel
Sales Manager: *Mark Brown*

Products
Light commercial vehicles. The Light Transportation Division was established in 2004.

Range
Porter: Light commercial vehicle, manufactured in co-operation with Daihatsu, for the transportation of disabled persons. Available as an electric version.

Plaxton Holdings Limited

Plaxton Park, Cayton Low Road, Eastfield, Scarborough YO11 3BY, UK
Tel: (+44 1723) 58 15 00
Fax: (+44 1723) 58 13 28
e-mail: enquiries@plaxtonlimited.co.uk
Web: www.plaxtonlimited.co.uk

Key personnel
Managing Director: *Bob Coombes*
Sales and Marketing Director: *Kevin Wood*
   Staff: 530 (estimate)

Background
Plaxton became part of the Alexander Dennis Group in 2007 and is a major builder of single-deck buses and coaches.

Products
Coach and bus bodies.

Range
Pronto: 6.5 m midicoach, 12 – 16 seats, accessible mobility coach. Mercedes-Benz Sprinter-based.
Beaver 2: 7.8 – 8.5 m, 24 – 33 seats, available as accessible and conventional bus and coach variants, mobility, local bus and local coach/dual purpose versions available. Based on the Mercedes-Benz Vario range of Euro 4 chassis.
Beaver 3: 7.8 – 8.5 m, 24 – 33 seats. A newly introduced and re-styled vehicle based on the Beaver 2. Mobility and local coach/dual purpose versions available. Based on the Mercedes-Benz Vario range of Euro 4 chassis.
Cheetah: 8.5 m, 25 – 33 seats. Plaxton reports this as the UK's best selling small coach. Available in various levels of trim to cater for touring or more local applications. Based on the Mercedes-Benz Vario range of Euro 4 chassis.

Plaxton Cheeta midibus   1375464

Plaxton Elite coach
1375465

Profile: 12 m coach, conventional height coach platform, available in variants suitable for touring, interurban and specialist high-capacity applications, where it can accommodate up to 70 seats. Both conventional and accessible versions are offered with two options of wheelchair access location. Available on Volvo B7R Euro 3 and Euro 4 chassis, as well as Dennis Javelin Euro 3.

Paragon: 12 – 12.8 m, Plaxton's entry level high-floor coach platform for touring, express and interurban duties. Both conventional and wheelchair friendly versions are offered with central access lifts. Available on Volvo, IrisBus and MAN platforms.

Panther: 12 – 15 m, Plaxton's high-floor touring or express coach. Both conventional and wheelchair friendly applications are offered including the front entry lift variant. Available on Volvo, Irisbus or MAN chassis.

Elite: 14 m (additional lengths are due to be added in 2009). New for 2009, this is Plaxton's flagship model, a high-floor coach for more specialist corporate applications. Both conventional and wheelchair friendly applications are offered. Available initially on Volvo or MAN chassis, other options to be considered for 2009/10.

Production

Plaxton expected to sell 250 coaches for the 2009 season. By the end of 2009, bus production will have reached 15 units a week.

Contracts

Country Lion of Northampton, UK has taken delivery of an Elite coach, with a further 10, for Logan's Coaches of Dunloy in Northern Ireland for its Corporate Coaching brand, which provides touring coaches for a number of leading international tour operators.

Stagecoach ordered 22 vehicles for 2009, a mix of Panther B9R and Profile B7R. Parks of Hamilton was due to take 14 high-capacity 15 m-long Panthers for express and touring operation.

Smaller operators who have confirmed orders for 2009 include: Country Lion of Northampton with a trio of Elite, Panther and Cheetah; Alfa Travel, Allans of Gorebridge, Andrews of Tideswell, Banstead Coaches and Woodstones Coaches of Kidderminster. The Plaxton Cheetah midicoach is expected to see sales of some around 100 units in 2009. Barton's Transport of Maynooth is one of the biggest Cheetah buyers, having taken 25 Cheetahs in 2008 with a similar number likely to be purchased for 2009.

Developments

In 2008, the company launched its new flagship model, the Elite (see above), following the introduction of the Volvo B9R Panther in the summer of 2008 (see Volvo entry). The B9R joins the Volvo B7R, B12M and B12B in Plaxton's range, alongside chassis from Dennis, MAN and Irisbus for full-size coaches, and the Mercedes-Benz Vario for the Cheetah midicoach.

Plaxton Panther coach   1375467

Plaxton Paragon coach   1375466

Plaxton Profile coach
1375469

Polskie Autobusy Sp zoo

27 Omulewska Street, PL-04-128 Warsaw, Poland
Tel: (+48 22) 611 69 37   Fax: (+48 22) 610 82 60
Web: www.polskieautobusy.com.pl

Representative Office, Sanok
109 Lipińskiego Street, PL-38-500 Sanok, Poland
Tel: (+48 13) 465 01 30   Fax: (+48 13) 465 04 30,
04 56 (English/German)
e-mail: j.winnik@polskieautobusy.com.pl
Web: www.polskieautobusy.com.pl

Key personnel
President: *Franciszek Gaik*
1st Deputy Chairman: *Roman Majewski*
Sanok Branch Office Representative Director:
  Sławomir Łopatowski
Jelcz Branch Office Representative Director:
  Marek Bartkowiak
Finance Director: *Arkadiusz Kazana*
  Staff: Not currently available

Background
Polskie Autobusy Sp zoo was established in 2002. This Polish trading company is privately

Jelcz M125M/M125i 'Vecto' bus (Polskie Autobusy Sp zoo)   1341634

Autosan A1010T 'Lider 2' suburban bus   1341300

Autosan A0909L 'Smyk' school bus (Polskie Autobusy Sp zoo)   1341262

Autosan A1112T 'Ramzes' high-deck tourist bus (Polskie Autobusy Sp zoo)
1341394

Autosan A1012T RHD 'Eagle' school bus (Polskie Autobusy Sp zoo)
1341425

Autosan A0909L 'Tramp' intercity bus (Polskie Autobusy Sp zoo)   1341127

Autosan A1012T 'Lider' intercity bus (Polskie Autobusy Sp zoo)   1341118

owned and is the exclusive trade representative of two Polish bus manufacturers – Autosan SA and Jelcz SA.

Autosan SA and Jelcz SA factories (established respectively in 1832 and 1952) have been major suppliers of city and inter-city buses in Poland for some 50 years. These two factories together have manufactured more than 171,700 buses (as at February 2007) for domestic and foreign markets; Russia, Ukraine, Kazakhstan, China, Mongolia, Egypt, Angola, Libya, Ghana, Bulgaria, Albania, Greece, Hungary, Romania, Slovakia, Lithuania, Latvia, Sweden, Norway and the UK.

Products

Buses for urban, suburban, regional and long-distance operations.

Specialised buses: Ambulance buses, school buses, buses for transportation of prisoners, pilgrim buses, rail buses, self-propelled chassis, bus bodies, bodies built onto Mercedes-Benz or MAN chassis, optional right-hand drive steering and vehicles adapted for the disabled.

The following forms of delivery are available: Complete vehicles (CBU), Partly Knocked Down (PKD) and Semi Knocked Down (SKD) buses and bodies; self-propelled chassis.

Range

Autosan models

A1112T 'Ramzes': 12 m high-deck tourist bus, seating 47 + guide (or 45 + guide + toilet).

A1012T 'Lider': 12 m intercity bus, maximum 51 seats or suburban bus, 45 seats + platform, or 49 seats.

A1012T RHD 'Eagle': 12 m schoolbus with 67 or 70 seats (3+2 layout) or 55 (2+2) seats for intercity operation (UK, Ireland & Malta market).

A1010T 'Lider 2': 10 m suburban bus, 43 seated plus 31 standees, optional lowered floor.

A1010T 'Lider 3': 10 m intercity bus, capacity 43 seated (+1) plus 13 standees or 39 seated (+ guide) plus 13 standing.

A0909L 'Tramp': 9 m intercity bus (capacity 39/17), suburban bus (capacity 25/45).

Jelcz M181I4 'Tantus' articulated bus (Polskie Autobusy Sp zoo)   1341630

Jelcz M083C 'Libero' city bus (Polskie Autobusy Sp zoo)   1341349

Autosan A8V 'Osprey' on Mercedes-Benz Vario chassis (Polskie Autobusy Sp zoo)   1341108

Jelcz M120M/4 'Supero' bus (Polskie Autobusy Sp zoo)   1341117

Autosan H7-20MB suburban minibus on Mercedes-Benz Vario chassis (Polskie Autobusy Sp zoo)   1341440

Jelcz M125M/4 'Vecto' CNG bus (Polskie Autobusy Sp zoo)   1341636

A0909L 'Smyk': 9 m school bus (several variants).
A0808T 'Gemini': 8 m intercity / tourist minibus, capacity 29 (+1), 33/10 or 33/5.
A8V 'Osprey': 7 m intercity minibus on Mercedes-Benz Vario chassis, capacity 26–28/7.
H7-10MB 'Solina': 7 m intercity minibus on Mercedes-Benz Vario chassis, capacity 28/7.
H7-20MB 'Solina': 7 m city minibus on Mercedes-Benz Vario chassis, capacity 18 seated/32 standing. Optional low rear platform for the wheelchair, with collapsible seats.

Jelcz models
M181I4 'Tantus': 18 m articulated city bus, low-entry (partially low-floor), 43 seated / 137 standees.
M125M / M125i 'Vecto': 12 m city bus, low-floor, capacity 28–35 seated / 73-65 standing.
M125M/4 (CNG) 'Vecto': 12 m city bus, low-floor, seats 28–35, standing 56-49.
M121i / M121MB 'Mastero': 12 m city bus, low-entry, 27–35 seated, total 106.
M120M/4 'Supero': 12 m city bus, seats 33–37, standing 55–59.

M101i 'Salus': 10 m city bus, low-entry, seated 22–26, standing 49–55.
M083C 'Libero': 8 m city minibus, low-entry, on chassis made by Autosan, capacity 16-17/44.

Sales
310 Autosan buses (of which, 78 exported) and 128 Jelcz buses (of which, 6 exported (2006).

Prévost

35 Gagnon Boulevard, Sainte-Claire, Québec G0R 2V0, Canada
Tel: (+1 418) 883 33 91   Fax: (+1 418) 883 40 50
Web: www.prevostcar.com

Key personnel
President and Chief Executive Officer: *Gaetan Bolduc*
Vice-President, Parts, Service: *Clay Flint*
Vice-President, Marketing & VIP Bus Shell Sales: *Vacant*
Vice-President, Finance: *Gilles Boutte*
Vice-President, Commercial Administration & IT: *Rene Begin*
Vice-President, Human Resources: *Robert Drouin*
Vice-President, Parts Sales & Business Development: *Jack R Forbes*
Vice President, Coach Sales: *Dann Wiltgen*

Background
Prevost was founded in 1924. Now a fully owned subsidiary of Volvo Bus Corporation, Prevost is a prominent North American manufacturer of intercity touring coaches and speciality conversion coach shells.

Products
Coaches and bus shells for conversion.
The company has its manufacturing facility in Sainte-Claire, Canada and a worldwide network of parts and service centres.

Range
Prevost H-Series: Prevost H3-Series premium touring coaches. The integral structure combines a stainless steel upper frame with high tensile low alloy steel subframe. The outer shell is made of composite material reinforced with carbon fibre. Removable Wheelchair Lift – lift cassette can serve many pre-equipped Prevost coaches.
Prevost X3-45: The Prevost X3-45 has a wheelbase of 334.5 in and features an underfloor surface area of 139 ft^2. The Prevost X3-45 has the a low overall height of 134 in, providing easy access. It is equipped with the Prevost Advanced Multiplex System.
The 45-ft Prevost XLII has a GVWR of 54,500 lbs and is suitable for corporate, VIP hospitality, showroom, mobile medical clinic or mobile command post conversions.

Prevost H-Series touring coach   1328179

Prevost X3-45 touring coach   1322810

Prevost H3-45 VIP Bus Shell   1322808

Prevost XLII ENTERTAINER   1322812

Prevost H3-45 VIP Bus Shell: The Prevost H3-45 VIP bus has a large underfloor storage capacity and a flat floor that provides flexibility to accommodate many conversion projects.

Prevost XLII ENTERTAINER: The 45-foot Prevost XLII ENTERTAINER bus shell is configured to suit the needs of travelling entertainers and their crew. It features Prevost's independent suspension system with integral structure and stainless steel outer shell (up to window level). Floor-to-ceiling height is 89 in and the underfloor cargo bays have a capacity of 433 ft^3.

Developments

In January 2008, Prévost launched new interior designs in the H-Series Collection range.

Also in that month, the company announced that the Volvo D13 engine will be available as an option.

Prevost XLII Bus Shell
1322809

PVI

Route de Maison-Rouge, BP 40091, F-77223 Tournan Cedex, France
Tel: (+33 1) 64 42 14 00   Fax: (+33 1) 64 42 14 60
e-mail: e.bois@gepebus.fr
Web: www.pvi.biz

Key personnel

Chassis Exports Manager: *Pierre Godbillon*
Sales Director: *Emmanuel Bois*

Background

Subsidiary of Société de Véhicules Electriques (SVE), Dassault Group, France and Financiere Centuria, France.

Products

Bus and truck chassis and electric vehicles. The PVI electric bus range is commercialised by the Gepebus Division.

Range

OREOS 22 Electric Minibus: Carries up to 22 passengers with up to 10 seated, equipped with lead exchangeable battery packs (range 55 km per pack).

Low-entry chassis: 12 m to 12.8 m for coach and intercity vehicles, GVW 18.5 tonnes and low-floor chassis for three-door city bus 12 m to 12.8 m.

Developments

OREOS 2X Electric Minibus: Due to be available in early 2009, this vehicle will have a capacity of 22 passengers with 13 seated and will be equipped with Lithium-Ion batteries. Range: 120 km per day.

OREOS 4X Electric Minibus: Due to be available in early 2009, this vehicle will have a capacity of 47 passengers with 29 seated and will be equipped with Lithium-Ion batteries and (optional) supercapacitors. Range: 120 km per day.

Rába Automotive Holding Plc

Rába Vehicle Ltd
PO Box 195, H-9002 Györ, Hungary
Tel: (+36 96) 62 26 00   Fax: (+36 96) 62 40 77
e-mail: jarmu@raba.hu
Web: www.raba.hu

Street address
Martin u 1, H-9027 Györ, Hungary

Key personnel

Managing Director, Rába Vehicle Ltd: *Torma János*
Staff: 182 (permanent employees)

Background

The company mainly manufactures drive axles for commercial and military vehicles (see separate entry in Road Vehicle Chassis Components section).

Rába Vehicle Ltd is certified to ISO 9001:2000 standards.

Products

Chassis for buses and coaches.

Production

The company has the capacity to produce metal sheet parts for 150 bus chassis units per annum.

RunIran Co

PO Box 1549948111, No 226, Mirdamad Boulevard, Between Modarres and Naft-e-Jounobi Street, Tehran, Iran
Tel: (+98 21) 22 27 83 24
Fax: (+98 21) 22 27 56 79
e-mail: info@runiran.com
Web: www.runiran.com

Key personnel

Managing Director: *Reza Tehrani*
Commercial Manager: *Mehdi Motalebzadeh*
Marketing Administrator: *Mrs M Najafi*

Factory address
Km 3rd of Isfahan Road, Saveh, Iran
Tel: (+98 255) 422 60 20; 422 60 30
Fax: (+98 225) 422 63 21

Background

Reza Tehrani and his brother Asgar established the 'Pars Lux' company back in 1952. Licence production of Magirus buses started in 1964. The company went bankrupt in 1971 and was taken over by the military.

The current company was founded by the Tehrani brothers in 1991.

RunIran/Volvo intercity bus
1115124

Products
Buses.

Range
Volvo B7R, B10 M, B12, B12 B (TX), B7R MKII and B7R MKIII, built under licence.

Production
Currently 4 buses daily.

Contracts
Until now the production has only been sold on the local market. Enquiries have been received from Kuwait, Saudi Arabia, Syria, west coast African countries and Dubai. Negotiations are taking place regarding exports to CIS countries, with the proviso that after-sales services are established in those countries.

In 2005, the company placed an order with Volvo for 521 bus chassis, for delivery in the same year. The B7R MKII intercity bus chassis were delivered as CKD kits, which were then assembled at RunIran's factory. The bodies are of RunIran's design, but based on a Volvo concept and both companies work closely with one another.

Research and Development
The company will start production of the B7R MKIII (Euro-3) in Q3 2006.

RunIran/Volvo B7R MKII-R8500 coach

1178317

RunIran is also intending to produce CNG city buses, to assist with environmental strategies, which aim to reduce air pollution in Tehran and other cities.

San Marino Ônibus e Implementos Ltda (San Marino Neobus)

Rua Irmão Gildo Schiavo, 110 – Bairro Ana Rech, CEP 95058-510, Caxias do Sul, RS, Brazil
Tel: (+55 54) 30 26 22 00   Fax: (+55 54) 30 26 22 99
e-mail: neobus@neobus.com.br
Web: www.neobus.com.br

Key personnel
President: *Edson Tomiello*
Commercial Director: *Jaime Pasini*
Engineering Director: *Adelir Boschetti*
Industrial Director: *Geferson Buzini*
Finance and Administrative Director: *Alexandre Pontalti*
Staff: 1,400 (2007)

Background
The company commenced bus bodybuilding operations in 1999, and has distributors throughout Brazil and in Chile, Uruguay and Costa Rica.

There is a manufacturing facility in Mexico.

Products
Bus bodywork on various chassis.

Range
Articulado: Articulated bus on Mercedes-Benz, Volvo or Scania chassis.
Mega: Transit bus on Mercedes-Benz or Volkswagen chassis.
Mega Low Entry: Transit bus on Mercedes-Benz, Volvo or Agrale chassis.
Thunder Way: Midibus for urban and school applications on Volkswagen, Agrale or Mercedes-Benz chassis.
Thunder Plus: Midicoach on Agrale or Volkswagen chassis.
Thunder +: Urbano and *Turismo* midibus/coach on Volkswagen, Mercedes-Benz or Agrale chassis.
Spectrum Road: Coach on Mercedes-Benz, Scania, Volkswagen or Agrale chassis.
Spectrum City: City bus on Volkswagen, Agrale, Mercedes-Benz or Scania chassis.

Production
Current production capacity is 20 units per day.

Neobus' main markets are in Chile, Equator, Angola, Costa Rica, Nigeria, Mexico, Algeria, Nicaragua, El Salvador, Venezuela, Jordan, Sierra Leone, Iran, Morocco, Uruguay, Argentina and the US.

Developments
In 2006, the Spectrum Road coach was launched.

In August 2007, Neobus delivered 56 Mega low-entry buses to Urban Redbus SA Co, part of the Veolia group, for services in Santiago.

SANOS DOO Skopje (Bus & Coach Factory 'Sanos' Co Ltd)

516 Street, No 10, Skopje 1000, Macedonia
Tel: (+389 2) 310 91 00
Fax: (+389 2) 311 30 00
e-mail: sanos@mt.net.mk
Web: www.sanos.com.mk

Key personnel
Chairman & Chief Executive Officer: *Slave Raspaskovski*
Director of Finance: *Mrs Violeta Terzioska*
Staff: 200

Background
Established in 2004.

Products
Bus and coach bodies and semi-finished chassis. The company also offers spare parts, service, refurbishment and repairs.

Range
Production of bus and coach bodywork, chassis and integral vehicles takes place under the Sanos name. Buses and coaches are manufactured with DAF Motors, Mercedes-Benz, Cummins Diesel Motors and Raba running units.
S-715: High-deck coach.
S-403: High-deck coach.
S-404: High-deck coach.
S-608: Minibus.
S-415: S-415.5P suburban and *S-415.5M* intercity buses.
S-213: Urban bus.

Developments
On the basis of the decision of the Assembly of creditors and the Board of creditors, Bankruptcy Trustee of FAS '11 Oktomvri' in bankruptcy, bids had been invited for the purchase of the Bus and Coach production facility. In 2004, under new ownership, production was restarted and the company was renamed.

Production
Maximum capacity is 1,500 vehicles per year, but currently some 250 vehicles are produced annually.

Developments
The S-715 prototype luxury coach is in production and the S-208 prototype urban/city bus is in development.

Scania Bus and Coach

Vingåkersvägen 71, SE-641 81 Katrineholm, Sweden
Tel: (+46 150) 585 00
Fax: (+46 150) 532 30
e-mail: gunnar.boman@scania.com
Web: www.scania.com

Key personnel
Senior Vice-President, Bus and Coach: *Robert Sobocki*
Managing Director, Scania Bus Europe: *Rolf Teljeby*
Senior Advisor, Corporate Relations: *Gunnar Boman*

Head office
Scania AB
Verkstadsvägen 11, SE-151 87 Södertälje, Sweden
Tel: (+46 8) 55 38 10 00   Fax: (+46 8) 55 38 10 37
e-mail: bo.jarnsjo@scania.com
Web: www.scania.com
President and Chief Executive Officer: *Leif Östling*
Group Vice-President, Corporate Development: *Kaj Lingren*
Group Vice-President, Sales and Marketing: *Gunnar Rustad*
Group Vice-President, Research and Development: *Hasse Johansson*
Senior Vice-President, Business Communications: *Magnus Hahn*

Other offices
Scania Sverige AB
Address and contact details as for Scania Group above

Scania (Great Britain) Ltd

Tongwell, Milton Keynes, MK15 8H, UK
Tel: (+44 1908) 32 92 70.32 93 84
Web: www.scania.co.uk
Bus, Coach and Engine Sales Director: *Mark Grant*

Background

Based in Sweden and with production facilities in Europe and Latin America, Scania employs a total of 35,096 people. The company's products are marketed in some 100 countries worldwide.

Scania is a major supplier to British industry. Additionally, the company provides a wide range of complementary and ancillary services in support of its products and customers through its network of more than 90 service centres in the UK. In 2007, according to the company, Scania's share of the UK heavy truck market was 17.8 per cent and its combined bus and coach market share amounted to 14.8 per cent.

Products

Rear-engined bus chassis made up of units designed either for use in integral construction or with chassis frames for conventional bodyworking, as single- or double-deck and articulated vehicles. Other products include conventional front-engined chassis, bodywork for integral models, kits, and engines.

Range

Scania Irizar i4: Luxury tourist coach with advanced bodywork based on the Scania K310 IB chassis, this vehicle features a nine litre, five-cylinder Scania DC9-18 Euro four engine with Scania EGR and a fully-automatic six-speed ZF 6HP604C gearbox. The Scania Irizar i4 can be specified with up to 59 seats in 12.9 m format.

Chassis modules

The chassis range is comprised of seven modules. A chassis module consists of a front and a rear section, including frame components and driver's station. Although the number of components is reduced, the system offers greater opportunities of customising the chassis to individual requirements while simplifying the body building operation.

With the Scania module-based approach, a tourist coach chassis shares up to 80 per cent of its chassis and powertrain components with the Scania truck range. Scania says that this promotes better and simpler access to parts and service.

Scania-Irizar: active partnership

Co-operation between Irizar and Scania has been underway since 1993. During that time, co-operation has developed into active partnership that has led to joint activities in about 15 countries.

Partnership has also been boosted in the important after-market sector. For example, Irizar components are supplied from Scania's central warehouse in Belgium, to importers in Scania's European organisation selling Scania Irizar products on their respective markets.

Buses

The Scania Omni range has a module-based design, and it can be adapted to suit local regulations and individual customer wishes and needs.

OmniLine: This is an intercity bus with an aluminium body powered by a nine litre engine. It has a high windscreen and 860 mm floor height. Since the launch of OmniLine in 2000, a new European version has been developed. The most important changes compared with the Nordic version are the lowering of the floor height to 860 mm, the high windscreen and the integration of the interior.

The Scania OmniLine is built on the Scania IL94IB intercity bus chassis, and it features vertical convector ventilation, separate air vents and lighting for each passenger seat and an optional climate unit.

The bus is available in a choice of 12 m and 13.5 m overall lengths, with between 47 and 55 seats and a floor height of 960 mm or 860 mm.

Scania Omnicity double-deck bus in service with East London Bus Group   1375350

Scania Omnicity double-deck bus in service with Blue Star, Southampton   1375351

Scania OmniExpress coach   1375352

The all-through luggage compartment with its capacity of 5.2 m³ to 7.2 m³ is accessed via large side hatches.

The OmniLine is powered by the Scania nine litre Euro-3 engine producing a choice of 172 kW, 194 kW or 224 kW. The engines are installed longitudinally and inclined 60° to permit a low floor at the rear of the bus, thus minimising the total vehicle height and weight.

All the engines are optionally available with a particle trap known as a CRT filter, which reduces emissions of particulates. The three engine options are combined with an automatic transmission from ZF or the Scania Comfort Shift with integral retarder.

The bus was successful when it took the European ECE R66 rollover test, which is developed for tourist coaches. The bus also has anti-lock disc brakes.

Like all the other buses in the Omni range, the OmniLine has a body made of aluminium.

OmniCity: City bus with all-through low floor available in both normal 12 m and three-axle articulated bus 18 m versions. The aluminium body is a monocoque construction, which means that the OmniCity does not have a separate chassis in the traditional manner. Instead, the chassis function is served by two chassis modules for the two-axle version and three main modules in articulated bus configuration.

The OmniCity is powered as standard by the Scania nine litre Euro-3 engine. It is installed transversely and inclined 60° to the rear to maximise passenger space. It is available in three versions, two with diesel power producing 172 kW and 194 kW respectively, and one powered by Ethanol that produces 172 kW.

OmniLink: City and suburban bus built on the Scania low-entry L94UB chassis and powered by a Scania nine litre Euro-3 engine, installed longitudinally and inclined 60°.

The Scania OmniLink has a low floor all the way to the end of the middle doors. This is followed by a single step, after which the floor slopes gently all the way to the seats at the very rear. All the seats at the rear of the bus face forwards.

The Scania OmniLink has large windows and sharp edges and corners have been eliminated for safety reasons.

Hybrid concept bus: Scania's hybrid concept vehicle is a full-size, low-floor city bus that cuts carbon dioxide emissions by up to 90 per cent when fuelled with ethanol and saves at least 25 per cent fuel, according to Scania. The emission levels meet the Euro 5 standards. This vehicle is currently undergoing trials in Scandinavia with the first examples due to enter service with Stockholm' bus operator, SL, in 2009.

Solar Fusion: Scania and Wrightbus introduced an articulated bus with Wrightbus body in 2001. It has a low floor, anti-lock disc brakes, nine litre Euro-3 engine and all-aluminium body with 59 passenger seating capacity.

The model – Solar Fusion – can carry up to 150 passengers, 50 per cent more than a double-decker. The articulated bus is based on Scania's L94UA 6x2/2 city bus chassis and is 18 m long. The model is powered by Scania's new environmentally optimised nine litre Euro-3 engine with a rating of 194 kW. Standard equipment includes a ZF four-speed Generation-2 automatic transmission. The engine is mounted longitudinally and is inclined at 60° to provide a low floor in the rear section of the bus.

Diesel engines and gearboxes
Range
Scania's range of engines for bus and coach operation includes the nine litre Omni Series, driving through an automatic gearbox. They come in the range of 164 kW to 231 kW (220 bhp to 310 bhp), with the option of an ethanol-powered version producing 172 kW (230 bhp).

The top power version is for intercity operation and articulated buses.

Scania Opticruise: Scania Opticruise is a computerised management system governing the vehicle's powertrain. It permits automatic gear changing, engine braking with down-changes and retarder application, but it can also be controlled manually in a variety of ways to suit the driver's needs and road conditions.

Contracts
In 2008, Dorset-based Go South Coast, UK, took delivery of 34 Scania OmniCity double-deck service buses. In addition, the company has a further 39 Scania double-deckers, comprising 27 OmniCitys and 12 Optare-bodied vehicles, on order for 2009 delivery, plus nine Scania

Scania OmniLink single-deck bus 1375401

Scania Hybrid single-deck bus 1375402

Scania Irizar i4 coach 1375403

OmniCity single-deckers scheduled for delivery in November 2008.

East London Bus Group, the Ilford-based operator serving north-east and south-east London, has ordered 96 Scania OmniCity double-deck buses. Being supplied by Scania (Great Britain) Limited's Purfleet branch, these vehicles are the first double-deckers to be purchased by the East London Bus Group since the company became an independent operator two years ago. Delivery was due to start in October 2008.

Developments

Launched at EuroBus Expo 2008 in the UK, the Scania OmniExpress is the latest addition to Scania's fully-built up Omni range of passenger carrying vehicles. Positioned broadly between the Scania Irizar i4 and the Scania Irizar Century, the Scania OmniExpress is a touring coach. A choice of three Scania OmniExpress models – 340 4 × 2 (3,400 mm high,12.8 m overall length), 360 4 × 2 (3,600 mm high, 12.8 m overall length) and 360 6 × 2*4 (3,600 mm

high, 14 m overall length with a steering rear-axle).

In 4 × 2 configuration, the 340 has 55 seats, plus driver and courier seats, a centre door and centre-mounted toilet, whilst the 360 seats 51, plus driver and courier, with a centre door and centre sunken toilet. The 6 × 2*4 format provides 63 seats, plus driver and courier seats, with centre door and centre sunken toilet.

Scania's Euro 4 Exhaust Gas Recirculation (EGR) technology is used across the range.

Scomi Engineering Bhd

MTrans Bus Sdn Bhd
Lot 795, Jalan Monorel, Sungai Choh, Rawang, 48000 Selangor Darul Ehsan, Malaysia
Tel: (+60 3) 60 92 38 88
Fax: (+60 3) 60 91 92 03
Web: www.scomiengineering.com.my

Background

In July 2006, Scomi Engineering Bhd completed the acquisition of MTrans Transportation Systems Sdn Bhd, making it a subsidiary of the company.

Products

Manufactures buses for urban, intercity and tourist services. Vehicles are manufactured for

local markets and exported to Europe, Hong Kong and China and the Middle East. Vehicles meet Euro-2 and Euro-3 standards.

MTrans Bus also supplies special purpose vehicles.

See also under New Technology/Innovative Transit Systems section.

Shahab Khodro Co

Km 8th of Karaj Makhsus Road, PO Box 13185-531, Tehran 13954, Iran
Tel: (+98 21) 45 04 70-3   Fax: (+98 21) 450 47 46
e-mail: info@shahabkhodro.com
    commerce@shahabkhodro.com
Web: www.shahabkhodro.com

Key personnel

Managing Director: *H Choopankareh*
Commercial Deputy to Managing Director: *S M Hejazi*

Head of Purchasing Department: *H A Sadeghi*
Sales Manager: *M Eslami*
    Staff: Not currently available

Background

This is Iran's oldest and second biggest bus builder, with a production capacity of 1,500 buses annually. A subisdiary of Astan Quds Razavi.

Products

Diesel city and intercity buses, CNG city buses and service vehicles.

Contracts

Export contracts with the Ministry of the Interior, Iran, municipalities and Syria and Turkmenistan.

Developments

In 2007, Shahab Khodro Co formed a new, jointly owned company named France Methods Kish (FMK), Iran with Ponticelli Vehicules Industriels (PVI), France.

Shanghai Automotive Industry Corporation (Group) (SAIC)

489 Wei Hai Road, Shanghai 200041, China
Tel: (+86 21) 64 33 68 92
Fax: (+86 21) 64 33 05 18

e-mail: xingy@didibaba.com
Web: www.saicgroup.com

Key personnel

Chairman: *Chen Xianglin*
Vice Chairman: *Zhang Guangsheng*
President: *Hu Maoyuan*

Background

The company produces buses and other vehicles.

Please see separate entry for Sunwin Bus Corporation.

Sitcar SpA

Via Copernico 41, I-41041 Casinalbo di Formigine, Modena, Italy
Tel: (+39 059) 577 09 11
Fax: (+39 059) 57 33 61, 55 89 77
e-mail: info@sitcar.it
Web: www.sitcar.com

Key personnel

General Director: *Zanasi Giuseppe*
Commercial Manager: *Fabio Pannoli*

Background

The company has dealers in Austria, Germany and the UK.

Associated Moseley Companies, UK, is distributing the Sitcar *Belluga Midicoach*. This is a luxury Italian-styled 27-seat coach.

Products

Bus bodywork and van conversions.

Range

Beluga: Chassis, Mercedes-Benz 0 815 S EU/3 VARIO, seats from 21 to 33 passengers.
Strike: Chassis, Mercedes-Benz 616 DT Sprinter, seating from 20 to 22 passengers.
Citytour: Chassis, Iveco 50C13, in two versions: Urbano (8/10+23+1 wheelchair), Suburbano (12/14 + 17 + 1 wheelchair).

Europa: Chassis, Mercedes-Benz 416 DT Sprinter, seating 13 or 16 passengers.
Joy: Chassis, Mercedes-Benz 416 DF Sprinter, seating 13 to 19 passengers and available as a school bus.
Eurojoy: Chassis, Mercedes-Benz 416 DF Sprinter, seating 16 or 18 passengers.
Beluga2: Chassis, Mercedes-Benz 0 818 D VARIO, seating 28 + 1.

Developments

In August 2004, the company announced the launch of a VIP version of the *Beluga2*.

Société Tunisienne d'Industrie Automobile (STIA)

Head office
Z I Sidi Abdelhamid, 4000 Sousse, Tunisia
Tel: (+216 73) 23 25 30
Fax: (+216 73) 23 32 78
e-mail: stia.marketing@gnet.tn
Web: www.stia.com.tn

Bus factory
Av Hédi Nouira, 4003 Sousse, Tunisia
Tel: (+216 73) 22 12 44
Fax: (+216 73) 22 94 60
e-mail: stia.dcef@gnet.tn

Tunis office
19 rue de Turkie, 1000 Tunis, Tunisia
Tel: (+216 71) 34 63 33   Fax: (+216 71) 25 40 57

Key personnel
General Manager: *Afif Khefacha*
Director, Purchasing: *Mohamed Frad*
    Staff: 750

Background
The company was formed in 1961. STIA undertakes bodybuilding and industrial vehicle assembly.

Products
City bus, intercity bus, minibus and coaches on full-frame chassis, from 7 to 18 m. Partners

include Ikarusbus, Irisbus, Iveco, Mercedes-Benz, Renault and Scania.

Range
Buses: Standard Irsibus 391.12.26 and articulated Ikarusbus 283.20. Iveco 35.10 minibus.
Coaches: Irisbus 391.12.29, Mercedes-benz tourist coach and articulated Ikarusbus 283.20.

Production
Capacity for minibus, bus and coach production is a maximum of 300 units per annum. Actual annual production is currently standing at approximately 220 units per annum.

Solaris Bus & Coach SA

Ul Obornicka 46, Bolechowo-Osiedle, PL-62-005
Owińska, Poland
Tel: (+48 61) 811 83 00   Fax: (+48 61) 811 83 10
e-mail: solarisbus@solarisbus.pl
Web: www.solarisbus.pl

Key personnel
Directors: *Krzysztof Olszewski*
   Solange Olszewski
Director, Coach Sales: *Adam Milewski*
Director, City Bus Sales: *Wiesław Cieśla*
   Staff: 836 (December 2004)

Background
Originally formed in 1994 under the name Neoplan Polska Sp zoo (Neoplan Poland Ltd), the company began manufacturing buses in 1996. It was renamed Solaris Bus & Coach Sp zoo (Solaris Bus & Coach Limited) in 2001.

In January 2005, the company was awarded ISO 14001:2004 certification.

In July 2005, the company became a joint-stock company and was renamed Solaris Bus & Coach SA. There are plans to float the company on the Warsaw Stock Exchange.

Export sales account for some 80 per cent of production. Solaris vehicles are in service in 17 European countries. Deliveries of 225 city buses to Dubai started in 2008.

Solaris hybrid buses are in service in Dresden, Leipzig and Bochum, Germany and in Lenzburg, Switzerland. Vehicles for the cities of Bremen, Munich and Hanover are in production.

Turnover in 2007 was PLN714 million.

Products
Low-floor buses, coach and trolleybus assembly.

Range
Vacanza: Coach available in two versions, 12 m and 13 m.

Urbino: City bus, available in four lengths, 10 m, 12 m, 15 m rigid and 18 m articulated and in a CNG 15 m length. Vehicles are powered by diesel or CNG engines. A partially low-floor version is available.

Also available is the **Solaris Alpino**, with a length of only 8.6 m and 2.4 m wide, it is especially suited to the narrow and winding lanes of towns in mountainous regions.

Solaris Urbino 18 Hybrid: Diesel-electric, low-floor hybrid bus.

Trollino: Trolleybus available in three versions, 12 m, 15 m rigid and 18 m articulated.

Special buses: The company also produces special buses, including a bus for the Regional Blood Centre in Katowice and the VIP-mobile bus for Okęcie Warsaw Airport.

Production
In 2007, the company produced 702 vehicles, with 400 of these being exported to 12 European countries.

Contracts
In January 2008, Münchner Verkehrsgesellschaft mbH (MVG), Germany ordered a Solaris Urbino 18 hybrid bus for delivery in mid-2008.

Solaris Urbino 18-m articulated bus, Berlin, Germany   1367344

Solaris Urbino 10 low-floor city bus   1115108

Solaris Urbino 18 Hybrid articulated bus   1367345

Solaris Urbino 15 m CNG bus   1113041

Solaris Vacanza 13 m coach   1113045

Solaris Trollino 15 m Trolleybus   1113040

In April 2008, Solaris was awarded a contract to supply a Solaris Urbino 18 Hybrid bus to MPK Poznan, Poland. The 18 m, low-floor, articulated bus is due to be delivered in late 2008.

In June 2006, the company received a contract from the Warsaw Municipal Bus Company for a total of 150 Solaris Urbino buses. The contract, valued at PLN160 million (EUR47.3 million), is for 70 Solaris Urbino 12 low-floor buses and 80 articulated Solaris Urbino 18 low-floor buses. The vehicles will all have air-conditioning and are due to be delivered to Warsaw by mid-January 2009.

Developments
In 2006, the first Solaris Urbino 18 Hybrid diesel-electric bus was displayed at the IAA Commercial vehicle exhibition.

The company is in the process of forming a new subsidiary, Solaris Ukraina, in the Ukraine.

SOR Libchavy spol sro – SOR Libchavy Ltd

Dolni Libchavy 48, CZ-561 16, Libchavy, Czech Republic
Tel: (+420 4) 65 51 94 11
Fax: (+420 4) 65 51 94 71
e-mail: sor@sor.cz
Web: www.sor.cz

Key personnel
Director: *Jaroslav Trnka*
Sales Director: *Vlastimil Mokrejš*
Sales Manager: *Jindřich Chudý*
Finance Director: *Jiří Svatoš*
Production Director: *Jiří Bezdíček*
Chief Designer: *Jan Černý*

Background
SOR Libchavy Ltd was established in 1991 by privatisation by direct sale. The development and manufacture of buses began in 1995.

Current situation
SOR Libchavy is engaged in the following activities:
- Manufacture of medium buses in versions: 7.5 m, 9.5 m, 10.5 m and 12 m, for city, intercity and tourist operations;
- Service, repairs and sale of spare parts for SOR buses;
- Service of IVECO Aifo engines for the Czech Republic;
- Sale of IVECO Aifo engines in the Czech Republic and Slovakia.

Range
Intercity bus SOR C 7.5;
Tourist bus SOR LC 7.5;
City bus SOR B 7.5;
Intercity bus SOR C 9.5;
Tourist bus SOR LC 9.5;
City bus SOR B 9.5;
Intercity bus SOR C 10.5;
Tourist bus SOR LH 10.5;
City bus SOR B 10.5;

Intercity bus C 12.

The company is also able to produce vehicles to customers' requirements.

The company's vehicles are produced under licence by Kravex Kereskedelmi Kft in Hungary.

Developments
The company is working to intensify the capacity for production to approximately 200 buses a year and improve the quality management system including ISO implementation. The bus range has been extended by the production of a 10.5 m version with city and tourist apllications, and included Euro 3 engines in all bus models.

Currently, the 7.5 m series is not in production.

Recent contracts
The company continues to produce and deliver vehicles for Beograd, Serbia and Montenegro, with 15 buses delivered in 2004. More than 50 buses have been delivered to Serbia and Montenegro since 2002.

Spartan Chassis, Inc

1000 Reynolds Road, Charlotte, Michigan 48813, US
Tel: (+1 517) 543 64 00
Fax: (+1 517) 543 77 28
e-mail: ejhendle@spartanmotors.com
   info@spartanmotors.com
Web: www.spartanchassis.com

Key personnel
President: *Richard Schalter*
Vice-President of Sales and Marketing: *Ed Dobbs*

Director of Sales, Military and Export: *Edward Hendler*

Products
Custom-designed and -built chassis for firefighting vehicles and appliances, coaches, motor homes, military vehicles and specialist applications.

Range
Front-, rear-, and mid-engined ladder-frame chassis in various formats. The chassis are available in various lengths with a range of GVWs, and feature air brakes, leaf spring or air suspension and diesel power; automatic transmissions.

Various configurations are available, including 4 × 4 and 6 × 6.

Spijkstaal Elektro BV

Postbus 9, NL-3200 Spijkenisse, Netherlands
Tel: (+31 181) 45 70 30   Fax: (+31 181) 62 39 58
e-mail: info@spijkstaal.nl
Web: www.spijkstaal.nl

Street address
Wattweg 10, NL-3208 KH Spijkenisse, Netherlands

Key personnel
Managing Director: *W Heijboer*
Sales: *Gerard C van Es*

Works
PO Box 9, NL-3200 AA Spijkenisse

Background
Spijkstaal Elektro BV is an independent company, has an annual turnover of GBP9 million and employs 75 people.

Products
Electric vehicles.

Range
M200E Zeus: Spijkstaal has developed, together with BredaMenarinibus of Bologna, Italy, the Ecobus Zeus M200. The Zeus M200 has space for 32 passengers with nine seated. This low-floor electric bus has an entrance height of 30 cm, air suspension and a pneumatic/hydraulic

The M 200E Zeus Ecobus by Spijkstaal Elektro was developed with BredaMenarinibus of Italy
0132803

brake system with ABS. The range is 80 km, top speed is 35 km/h and to recharge the batteries takes three minutes. Its weight when empty, but with 96 V 500 A/h battery, is 4,500 kg; overall length is 5.9 m, width 2.08 m, height 2.6 m. The Zeus was designed by Pininfarina.

Starcraft Bus

Division of Forest River Inc
2703 College Avenue, Goshen, IN 46528, US
Tel: (+1 574) 533 11 05
Fax: (+1 574) 533 68 50
Web: www.starcraftbus.com

Background
Formed in 1903, since 2001, Starcraft Bus has been a division of Forest River Inc.

Current situation
Manufacturers of transit and shuttle buses. Customers include government and other transit agencies and private transportation operators.

Range
- **STARQUEST:** low profile multi-option vehicles on cutaway chassis;
- **StarLite:** Narrow-body small buses on cutaway chassis;
- **AllStar:** Small buses built on cutaway chassis, seating up to 25+1.;
- **XLT:** Mid-size buses built on medium-duty chassis cabs;
- **ELF:** Low-floor front-wheel-drive transit buses.

Starcraft **StarLite** narrow-body bus
1115244

Starcraft **AllStar** small bus
1115245

Sunsundegui SA

Polígono Industrial Ibarrea s/n, E-31800 Alsasua (Navarra), Spain
Tel: (+34 948) 56 20 11
Fax: (+34 948) 56 32 02
e-mail: sunsundegui@sunsundegui.com
Web: www.sunsundegui.com

Key personnel
Export Sales Director: *Alejandro Irizar*
Export Area Manager: *Iñigo Garmendia*
    Staff: *310*

Background
Established in 1944, the company began building bus and coach bodywork in 1987.

Products
Bus and coach bodies. For the UK market, vehicles are manufactured on Volvo chassis and marketed by Volvo Buses Limited.

Range
Sideral 2000: Luxury coach, available in 12 m (up to 55 seats), 12.8 m (up to 55 seats), 13.7 m (up to 63 seats), 14.5 m (up to 67 seats) and 15 m (up to 71 seats) and in two heights, 3.3 m and 3.6 m.
Astral: Interurban/intercity coach, available in 12 m, 13 m and 15 m lengths. Available in an articulated, 18.75 m version, seating up to 65 passengers plus 56 standees. Also available in Low Entry and Intercity version.
Volvo B9R Elegance: The Volvo B9R is manufactured in co-operation with Volvo. The new Volvo B9R/Sunsundegui vehicle expands the Volvo coach range and offers the advantage that Volvo Bus or an authorised Volvo dealer can take responsibility for the entire product for service and repairs of chassis and body. The new Volvo B9R Elegance features the Sideral

Sunsundegui Sideral 2000 12 m coach
1178128

Sunsundegui Astral 18.75 m articulated vehicle
1178126

Sunsundegui Astral 12.5 m buses
1178124

2000 body, with design features such as a large windscreen and exclusive exterior mirrors. The standard body has a basic specification with a ride range of options, including air conditioning, Volvo's exclusive AV system Sound & Vision, WC, refrigerator, higher capacity heating system and hydraulically operated luggage compartment doors. The Volvo B9R Elegance will be offered in two different lengths; 12.2 m with room for up to 55 passengers and 12.9 m with room for up to 59 passengers.

Production
480 units (2006), 2/3 domestic market, 1/3 export markets.
   Target for 2007: 550 units.

Developments
In 2007, some external and internal changes to the **Sideral 2000** will be introduced, as part of the '2007 year-model' facelift, with improvements such as the wider entrance to the coach, new 19" front TFT screen and a new driver-friendly dashboard.

Sunsundegui/Volvo B9R Elegance
1311301

Sunwin Bus Corporation

18 Guang Zhong Road, Minhang District, Shanghai 201 108, China
Tel: (+86 21) 64 89 72 88
   (+86 21) 64 89 72 88
ext. 1103, 1105-6 (Sales and marketing)
Fax: (+86 21) 64 89 06 77
   (+86 21) 64 89 14 43 (Sales and marketing)
Web: www.sunwinbus.com
   Staff: 1,200

Background
Sunwin Bus Corporation was established in June 2000, by joint investment of SAIC Group,

Volvo Bus Corporation and Volvo (China) Investment Co Ltd. SAIC holds 50 per cent of the shares.

Products
The company develops, manufactures and assembles commuter buses, chassis, body parts, components and accessories. It also provides repair and aftersales services.
   The vehicles are based on those developed by Shanghai Coach Plant, with upgraded bodies jointly developed by Volvo and Sunwin to be built on Volvo chassis.
   Volvo products, built with stainless steel bodies, are also to be introduced.

Range
Low-floor City Buses
SWB6122
SWB61111
SWB6115HP2-3
SWB6105HP1-3
SWB6115CQ-3 Natural Gas Bus
SWB5115GP-3
SWB6120KHV-3

Recent developments/contracts
The company launched the Shenhao City Bus (SWB6120KHV-3), developed for an operator in Shanghai.

Tar-Fue Vehicle Body Co Ltd

No 29, Section 3 Liu Ying Road, Liu Ying Hsiang, Tainan Hsien, Taiwan
Tel: (+886 6) 622 12 12/13
Fax: (+886 6) 622 33 81
e-mail: tarfue@ms22.hinet.net
Web: www.tarfue.com.tw

Key personnel
Chairman and Technical Director: *Su, Ta Fu*
Import and Export Manager and General Manager: *Frank Sue (Su, When Shih)*
Plant Manager: *Hu, Sun Bin*

Subsidiaries
SAFEBUS International Co Ltd
   Manufacture and supply of components and equipment for buses and coaches.

Background
Founded in 1967 by Mr Su, Ta Fu, Tar-Fue is a leading independent manufacturer of buses and luxury coaches in Taiwan. In addition, Tar-Fue has been exporting since 1982 and builds many chassis including Volvo, Scania, Mercedes-Benz, Renault VI, MAN, DAF, Pegaso, Iveco, Fuso, Hino, Isuzu and Spartan (with Cummins engine).

Products
Bodywork for city/intercity/school buses and luxury coaches (high-deck, double-deck and articulated).

Range
City and intercity buses
TF Midi: Seats: 33–35; length: 11–11.3 m; width: 2.45 m; height: 3.35 m.
TF City: Seats: 45–49; length: 12–12.2 m; width: 2.50 m; height: 3.45-3.65 m; fitted with rear engine such as Hino LRM2KSL or Isuzu K-CPM580.
TF Inter: Seats: 45–49; length: 12–12.2 m; width: 2.50 m; height: 3.55–3.70 m; fitted with rear or mid-mounted engine such as Scania 1241B4X2, Volvo B10M or Hino LRM2KSL. Standard facilities: two televisions and one interior monitor with electric clock, toilet, refrigerator and audio system.
TF School: Same specification as TF City and mostly mounted on Isuzu chassis.

Tar-Fue high-deck luxury coach on Volvo chassis 0526556

Tar-Fue luxury coach on rear-engine chassis 0526558

Coaches

TF 210ST: The newest design of luxury coach and mostly built on Fuso U-MP618PL (320 hp and 350 hp), Volvo B12 (385 hp) and B7R (300 hp), Scania K124IB4X2 (360 hp), MAN (430 hp) with rear engines. Seats 45–49; length: 12.2 m; width: 2.50 m; height: 3.67–3.80 m. There is a **TF 210T** version.

TF 210SH: High-deck version. Same specifications as for the TF 210ST. Height: 3.50–3.65 m.

Production

Annual capacity is 120 units (60 per cent coaches and 40 per cent buses) with a target of 180–200 units.

Contracts/Projects

Tar-Fue has a long-term agreement with the Taiwan dealers of Volvo, Scania, Fuso, Hino and Renault VI for local and overseas markets. Export customers include China, Egypt, Hong Kong, Singapore and South Africa.

Tata Motors Limited

Bombay House 24, Homi Mody St, Fort, Mumbai 400 001, India
Tel: (+91 22) 56 65 82 82   Fax: (+91 22) 22 04 54 74
e-mail: debasis.ray@tatamotors.com
Web: www.tatamotors.com

Key personnel

Chairman: *Ratan N Tata*
Managing Director: *Ravi Kant*
Executive Director, Passenger Car Business Unit: *Currently vacant*
Vice-President, Corporate Communications: *V Krishnan*
Head, Corporate Communications: *Debasis Ray*

International Business

Block A, Shivsagar Estates, Dr Annie Besant Road, Worli, Mumbai 400 018
Tel: (+91 22) 24 93 85 66   Fax: (+91 22) 24 95 03 76

Works

Jamshedpur, Lucknow and Pune

Assembly operation

Bangladesh, Kenya, Korea, Malaysia, Russian Federation, South Africa and Ukraine.

Background

The Tata Group is one of India's largest industrial companies, with interests in iron and steel, engineering, chemicals, commercial vehicles and other areas. Tata Motors is the vehicle manufacturing unit of the group. Total sales of passenger cars and utility vehicles was 179,076 and sales of light, medium and heavy commercial vehicles and buses was 189,993 for FY2005.

Products

Cars, sports utility vehicles, pickups, light, medium and heavy commercial vehicles and buses.

Range

A variety of single-deck buses are produced in rugged designs suited to conditions in the Indian subcontinent and other developing countries. Vehicles are available in left- and right-hand drive form, full forward control, semi-forward control with front and rear engines.

The bus range includes 12-seater to 68-seater buses, CNG, diesel and low-floor fully monocoque buses for mass transportation.

Tata Motors has recently launched its **Globus** coach and **Starbus** range.

Globus: Range of luxury coaches available in 13-, 18-, 20- and 45-seat configurations.

Starbus: Available in a number of variants, seating 16 to 67 passengers.

Starbus Skool: School bus available in 17-, 32- and 52 seat configurations.

Starbus Standard: Available in 16-, 18-, 20-, 32-, 54- and 67-seat configurations.

Starbus Low Floor: Low-floor bus also available as an Ultra Low Floor City Bus.

Starbus Deluxe: Inter-city bus, available with 18, 20, 28 and 35 seats.

Developments

Tata Motors has set up joint ventures with a number of companies such as the Cummins Engines Company, US for the manufacture of high-performance, fuel-efficient and environmentally friendly diesel engines which conform to the strict Euro emissions standards.

Tata Motors Limited has acquired a 21 per cent equity stake in Hispano Carrocera SA. Tata Motors will have the license for technology and brand rights from Hispano Carrocera SA.

Tata Motors **Starbus** *bus*   1143806

Tata Motors **Starbus Ultra Low Floor CNG City Bus**   1143805

Tata Motors **Globus** *coach*   1143804

TEDOM sro

Bus Division
Hrotovická – průmyslová zóna 160, Střítež, 674 01
Třebíč, Czech Republic
Tel: (+420 568) 83 72 11   Fax: (+420 568) 83 72 15
e-mail: infobus@bus.tedom.cz
Web: www.tedom.eu

Key personnel
Director, Bus Division and General Manager:
  Josef Jeleček

Assistant to General Manager: *Petra
  Vaničková*
Marketing Manager: *Viado Murár*
Staff: Not currently available

Products
Manufacturer of engines and buses.

Range
TEDOM C12 G: Low-floor urban bus with
TEDOM TG 210 AV 04 natural gas engine (CNG)
Euro 4 engine. A diesel version, ***TEDOM C12 D,***

is also available. Capacity totals 88 to 100
(seated 29+4 seated, 55 to 67 standees).
TEDOM L12 G: Low-floor suburban bus.

Developments
In April 2006, construction started on a new bus
manufacturing plant. Production of vehicles
started in 2007.
  In April 2008, the last of an order of nine urban
CNG buses was delivered to Sofia, Bulgaria.
  The company has stated that it intends to
specialise in CNG buses.

Temsa Sanayi ve Ticaret AŞ

Mersin Yolu 10.km, PK 480, TR-01323 Adana, Turkey
Tel: (+90 322) 441 02 26   Fax: (+90 322) 441 01 05
e-mail: info@temsa.com
Web: www.temsa.com

Key personnel
Chief Executive Officer: *Mehmet Buldurgan*
Director, International Relations and Business
  Development: *Ömer Sözütek*
Director, Technology and Production: *Timucin
  Bayraktar*
Managing Director, Temsa Euorpe: *Wim Van Hool*
Export Manager: *Ali Murat Atlas*
Export Support Manager: *Acar Kocaer*
  Staff: 1,600 (approximate)

Temsa Europe NV
Dellingstraat 32, B-2800 Mechelen, Belgium
Tel: (+32 15) 44 00 00   Fax: (+32 15) 44 00 09
e-mail and Web: As above

Key personnel
Marketing Manager, Temsa Europe NV: *Sylvestre
  De Jaegher*

Background
Temsa is a subsidiary of the Turkish financial and
industrial conglomerate Sabanci Holding. Temsa
is one of the most prominent manufacturers of
coaches and midicoaches in Turkey, has a large
share of the local Turkish market and has a
sizeable export market. Temsa currently exports
75 per cent of its coach production, mainly to
European countries. Temsa is an independent
manufacturer that produces coaches based on
DAF, Mitsubishi, MAN, Volvo and Mercedes-Benz
power trains, whilst manufacturing the chassis
and bodies in its factory.

Products
Buses, coaches, midicoaches and midibuses for
tourism, intercity and city travel.

Range
Bus & Coach
Temsa Safari: Coach, 10.66 m, 12 m or 12.8 m long
and 2.5 m wide, seats up to 53+2 and is powered
by the MAN D2866 LOH 28 (Euro-3) powertrain,
driving through a six-speed manual or automatic
gearbox.
  Temsa Safari Intercity: Low-floor version of the
Safari, 12.2 m or 12.8 m long and 2.5 m wide, seats
up to 57+2 and is powered by the MAN D2866
LOH 28 (Euro-3) powertrain, driving through a
six-speed manual or automatic gearbox.

Temsa Avenue low-floor city bus in Arriva UK livery   1375408

  Temsa Safari HD: High-deck version of the
Safari, ideal for long-distance travel, 12.2 m
or 12.8 m long and 2.5 m wide, seats up to
55+2 and is powered by the DAF XE 315C or
PE 228C powertrain, driving through an eight-
speed manual (for 12.8 m version) or six-speed
manual or automatic gearbox (for the 12.2 m
version).
  Temsa Safari RD: Launched in 2007, this coach is
available with Euro 4 and Euro 5 engine options.
Also available in stainless steel.
  Temsa Diamond: The company's top-of-the-
line coach, 12.99 m or 13.975 m long and 2.55 m
wide, seats up to 59+2 and is powered by the
MAN D2876 LOH 02 (Euro-3) powertrain, driving
through and eight-speed manual or automatic
gearbox.
  Temsa Tourmalin: Coach, 12 m or 12.8 m
long and 2.55 m wide, seats up to 78+2 and is
powered by the DAF PE 228C (Euro-2, ECE R24-
03 ISO 1585) engine, driving through a six-speed
manual gearbox (automatic option available for
the 12 m version). An intercity *Temsa Tourmalin IC*
version is available.
  Temsa Safir: Coach, 12 m long and 2.5 m wide,
seats 46+2 and is powered by a Mitsubishi 6D24T
(Euro-2) powertrain, driving through a six-speed
manual gearbox.

Midicoach
Temsa Opalin 8/9: Temsa's medium sized bus,
7.6 m or 8.4 m long and 2.3 m wide, seats up
to 35+2 and is powered by the MAN DO836LFL

(Euro-3) or MAN DO834LFL (Euro-3) powertrain,
driving through a six-speed manual gearbox.
  Temsa Metropol: The company's first city bus,
9.66 m long and 2.4 m wide, seats up to 35 (+40
standing) and is powered by the MAN DO834
LOHO3 (Euro-3) powertrain, driving through a
six-speed manual gearbox. An intercity *Temsa
Metropol IC* version is available.

Midibus
Temsa Prestij: Midibus, 7 m long and 2.22 m
wide, in three versions – Deluxe, Sport and
City – seating up to 27+1. It is powered by the
Mitsubishi 4D34-2AT4 (Euro-2) turbocharged
engine, driving through a five-speed manual
transmission.

Developments
In 2008, Temsa announced the Avenue city bus,
available as a low-entry model and one with a
full-length low floor. It is also being constructed
in a right-hand drive configuration for the UK
market, in association with Arriva. The Avenue
is 12 m long, 2.55 m wide and 3.00 m high,
and can have two or three double doors.
It is powered by a DAF 9.2 litre engine (6.7 l
Cummins engine for the UK market) and meets
Euro 5 emission standards. It carries up to 97
passengers.
  Also in 2008, Temsa launched an updated
version of the Safari HD with stainless steel
construction and a Euro 5 engine.

Thomas Built Buses Inc

PO Box 2450, 1408 Courtesy Road, High Point,
North Carolina 27260, US
Tel: (+1 336) 889 48 71   Fax: (+1 336) 881 65 09
Web: www.thomasbus.com

Key personnel
President and Chief Executive Officer: *John
  O'Leary*
Interim Vice President, Domestic Sales: *Ken
  Hedgecock*

Manager, Marketing & Center for Education: *Mary
  Aufdemberg*
  Staff: Approximately 1,500

Background
Thomas Built Buses Inc is a wholly owned subsidiary
of Daimler Trucks North America (formerly
Freightliner LLC), which is a unit of Daimler AG.
  Originally founded in 1916, the company was
acquired by Daimler Trucks North America in 1998.
  The company has more than 50 dealers in
North America.

Products
Buses for school/activity transport and other
non-school applications.

Range
Commercial vehicles
School/activity buses
Type A Minotour Bus;
Type C Saf-T-Liner C2;
Type D Saf-T-Liner EF & HDX.
  The company also produces a variety of
speciality vehicles.

Production
Some 15,000 units annually.

Contracts
Buses are sold in Canada and the US.

Developments
A new 275,000 sq ft manufacturing facility in High Point, North Carolina, US opened in 2004 and is currently producing the Type C Saf-T-Liner C2.

Thomas Built school products, from left to right: Type C Saf-T-Liner C2, Type A Minotour, Type D Saf-T-Liner EF and Type D Saf-T-Liner HDX
1323838

TMC Group Inc

53387 Ada Drive, Elkhart, Indiana 46514, US
Tel: (+1 574) 262 89 35
Fax: (+1 574) 266 06 42
Web: www.tmcgroupinc.com

Products
Manufacture of small- and medium-sized buses.

Range
Ameritrans™ buses, built to customers' requirements.

Developments
In 2005, the company announced its Ameritrans™ Retro Style Touring Bus.

Tomassini Style srl

Via dell'Industria 1, I-06065 Passignano sul Trasimeno (PG), Italy
Tel: (+39 075) 82 92 45   Fax: (+39 075) 82 92 47
e-mail: segreteria@tomassinistyle.it
Web: www.tomassinistyle.it

Key personnel
President: *Renzo Agenore Tomassini*
Director, Administration: *Patrizia Tomassini*
Director, Production: *Fabrizio Cincini*
Manager, Administration: *Sembolini Valter*
Manager, Technical: *Alessio Mezzetti*

Background
The company was set up by Agenore Tomassini in 1964 and it moved to its present location in 1972.

Products
Urban buses and shuttle vehicles, including VIP minibus shuttles.

Tovarna Vozil Maribor doo (TVM)

Cesta k Tamu 33, SI-2000 Maribor, Slovenia
Tel: (+386 2) 460 11 00; 11 02   Fax: (+386 2) 460 11 18
e-mail: marketing@tvm.si
Web: www.tvm.si

Key personnel
General Manager and Chief Executive Officer: *Dušan Mežnar*
Economics Director: *Nedeljka Bazdulj*
Marketing Director: *Niko Bien*
Development Director: *Bojan Puklavec*
Procurement Director: *Damir Jelenc*
Executive Director for Production & Technology: *Janez Lipuž*
Staff: 250

Background
The company was formed in April 2001 by the merger of the two companies MPP Vozila doo (vehicle manufacturer) and MPP Razvoj doo (vehicle development), which had been operating as independent companies since they were established in 1996, though production at this location dates back to 1945 when the company Tovarna Avtomobilov in Motorjev Maribor (TAM Maribor) was founded.

In 2004, the company was sold to become part of the VIATOR & VEKTOR group of companies.

Products
Airport buses, mini- and midibuses and bus chassis.

The company also produces trucks and truck chassis, bodywork and components and carries out vehicle overhaul and reconstruction.

TVM MARBUS B4 080 Viveo minibus
1322684

Range
MARBUS B4 080 VIVEO: Minibus, 30+1+1 seats, water-cooled, turbo-diesel engine MAN D0834 LOH 51 (151 kW, 206 hp) Euro 4, length 9.8 m, width 2.4 m, height 2.9 m.

MARBUD B3 090 VIVETH: High-deck minibus, available in two seating configurations, 33+1+1 seats, MAN D0836 LOH 55 , Euro 4, length 9.8 m, width 2.4 m, height 3.5 m.

MARBUS B3 090 TL: Touring bus, manufactured in two versions: 33+1 and 39+1 seats, MAN D0836 LOH engine, length 9.5 m, width 2.4 m, height 3.2 m.

MARBUS B3 090 TLL: Inter-city bus manufactured in two versions: 43+1 and 47+1 seats, MAN D0836 LOH engine, length 11.1 m, width 2.4 m, height 3.2 m.

Production
Bus production capacity is estimated at being 100 vehicles per year, increasing to 350 per year.

Toyota Motor Corporation (TMC)

Corporate Communications Department, Public Affairs Division
4-18, Koraku 1-chome, Bunkyo-ku, Tokyo 112-8701, Japan
Tel: (+81 3) 38 17 91 50
Fax: (+81 3) 38 17 90 92
Web: www.toyota.co.jp

Key personnel
Chairman: *Fujio Cho*
President: *Katsuaki Watanabe*
Honorary Chairman: *Shoichiro Toyoda*
    Staff: 299,394 (March 2007 – worldwide consolidated total)

Head office
1 Toyota-cho, Toyota City, Aichi Pref 471-8571, Japan
Tel: (+81 565) 28 21 21

Nagoya office
4-7-1 Meieki, Nakamura-ku, Nagoya City, Aichi Prefecture 461-8711, Japan
Tel: (+81 52) 552 21 11

Main minibus production plant
Honsha – chassis only
Toyota Autobody Co Ltd (affiliated company plant)

Overseas minibus assembly operations
China

Background
Established in 1937, Toyota is a major car and light van builder and also produces purpose-designed minibus chassis and bodied vehicles. The company has 12 plants and a number of manufacturing subsidiaries and affiliates in Japan and 52 manufacturing companies in 26 other countries/regions.

Products
Mini- and midibuses, including:
Optimo V: Midibus with bodywork built by Salvador Caetano on the Toyota Coaster chassis. Available in five versions, seating 18+2, 21+2, 22+2, 24+2 or 26+2 passengers.

Contracts
Assembly operations for minibuses are currently situated in Japan (including exports) and China (for China). Toyota minibuses are widely used for paratransit operations in China (4,700 units), Middle East (3,700 units), Africa (2,400 units) and South America and the Caribbean (1,300 units). Figures given are for units sold in 2006.

Research and development
Toyota Motors is developing the Intelligent Multimode Transit System (IMTS), a next-generation transportation system. The vehicles are navigated and controlled by magnetic markers embedded in the middle of their allocated roads. A thorough fail-safe system is adopted, featuring automatic speed regulation and braking functions assured by inter-vehicle communication, ground signals and other means.

For further information on IMTS, please see separate entry in *Jane's Urban Transport Systems, New Technology/innovative transit systems*.

TMC demonstrated a fuel cell hybrid bus at EXPO 2005 Aichi, Japan. This is an improved version of the Fuel Cell Hybrid Vehicle – Bus (FCHV-BUS2), a large low-floor commuter bus that features a hybrid system powered by high-pressure hydrogen, that TMC and Hino Motors Ltd have been jointly developing since 2000.

The FCHV-BUS2, equipped with two units of TMC's high-performance Toyota FC Stack and incorporating the hybrid technologies found in the Toyota Prius hybrid passenger sedan and Hino's HIMR System, achieves high running efficiency by recovering energy during deceleration and delicately alternating between its fuel cells and secondary battery for power supply to the motor according to running conditions.

The FCHV-BUS2 was the first fuel cell-powered bus officially approved by Japan's Ministry of Land, Infrastructure and Transportation. Issued a licence plate in 2002, the vehicle, after carrying out trial runs on public roads, participated in a fuel-cell bus pilot project, promoted by the Tokyo Metropolitan Government in 2004. That project has now ended.

In July 2006, Toyota Motor Corporation and Hino Motors Ltd announced that its FCHV-BUS, which operated on public routes in mid-March around the Central Japan International Airport (Centrair) south of Nagoya, was to renew operations on 22 July, including expanded services to and within the airport. The effort is part of a fuel cell demonstration program of the Ministry of Economy, Trade and Industry's (METI's) Japan Hydrogen & Fuel Cell Demonstration Project (JHFC) and is intended to provide TMC and others with data necessary for the commercialisation of fuel cell hybrid buses. In addition, two units of the FCHV-BUS will be used by Chubu Sky Support Co Ltd (CSS) to shuttle passengers between Centrair's passenger terminal and aircraft. Further information may be found at www.toyota.co.jp/en/news/06/0718.html.

Trailertech Services Ltd (t/a Bluebird Vehicles Ltd)

Unit 7, Plaxton Park, Cayton Low Road, Scarborough, YO11 3BY, UK
Tel: (+44 1723) 86 08 00   Fax: (+44 1723) 58 52 35
e-mail: info@bluebirdvehicles.com
Web: www.bluebirdvehicles.com

Key personnel
Managing Director: *Rob Miller*
   Staff: Not currently available

Background
Trailertech Services Ltd was founded in 2003 and trades under the brand name Bluebird Vehicles Ltd.

Products
Accessible mini- and midibuses.

Range
Tucana: Volkswagen (VW) T5 platform, with double rear axle, carrying seven wheelchair users and up to 16 passengers with flexible seating layout. Low-floor single-step with double rear doors and foldout ramp. Kneeling air suspension. Length 7.42 m, width 2.20 m.
Auriga: on the VW T5 platform, carrying five wheelchair users and up to 15 passengers with flexible seating layout. Flat low-floor with double rear doors and foldout ramp. Kneeling air suspension. Length 6.83 m, width 2.08 m.
Compact: on the VW T5 platform carrying three wheelchair users and up to 11 passengers with flexible seating layout. Low-floor with stepless electric folding side door and fold-out ramp.

Low-floor Bluebird Tucana minibus entering service with Transport for London's (TfL) Dial-a-Ride minibus network (Tony Pattison)   1375555

Kneeling air suspension. Length 6.17 m, width 2.08 m.
The company also carried out van conversions.

Production
Production information is not available currently.

Contracts
About 60 Tucanas were ordered in 2008 by Transport for London (TfL) for its London Dial-a-Ride minibus services.

Transcontinental Industries

PO Box 46711, Abu Dhabi, United Arab Emirates

Factory
Plot 8E5-M41 Mussafah Industrial Area, Abu Dhabi, United Arab Emirates
Vectra Azad
36 Paradise Road, Richmond upon Thames, Surrey, TW9 1SE, UK
Tel: (+44 20) 89 48 29 90   Fax: (+44 20) 89 48 29 91

Background
Transcontinental Industries, established in 2003, is a joint venture between Vectra Azad and the Bin Jabr Group, Abu Dhabi.

Transcontinental Industries factory, in Abu Dhabi
1323872

Current situation

The factory has commenced production, supplying vehicles to customers in the domestic market and to other Gulf Cooperation Council (GCC) countries (Bahrain, Kuwait, Oman, Qatar, Saudi Arabia and the United Arab Emirates).

Range

The company produces coaches and minibuses, built on Ashok Leyland, Eicher and other manufacturers' chassis.

Trolza CC

Trolleybus plant
Engels, mincroraion-1, Saratov District, 413105, Russian Federation
Tel: (+7 8453) 79 10 01, 79 10 51
  (+7 8453) 79 11 52 (Export sales)
Fax: (+7 8453) 95 38 91, 56 29 45
  (+7 8453) 56 22 47 (Export sales)
e-mail: info@trolza.ru
Web: www.trolza.ru

Key personnel

Executive Director: *Michael P Petrichenko*
  Staff: Not available currently

Products

Buses and trolleybuses.

Range

Trolza 5265 Megapolis: Low-floor accessible trolleybus. Commercial production started in 2006. The vehicle is in operation in Moscow, Briansk, Kazan, Krasnodar, Murmansk and Iaroslavl.

Trolza 6206 Megapolis: Low-floor, articulated trolleybus, based on the **Trolza 5265 Megapolis** model. Production started in 2007. The trolleybus is in operation in Moscow.

Trolza 5250 Megapolis ECObus: Low-floor, hybrid bus with regenerative braking system. Production started in 2008.
Trolza 5275.05 Optima: Low-floor trolleybus. Production commenced in 2000.
ZiU 682G-016: High-capacity trolleybus. Production started in 2002.
Trolza 6205: Articulated trolleybus, with capacity of 158 passengers. Production started in 1995.

Production

Total annual capacity is more than 1,000 trolleybuses.

ZiU 682G-016 trolleybus   1375197

Trolza 6205 trolleybus   1375196

Trolza 6206 Megapolis articulated trolleybus   1375195

Trolza 5265 Megapolis trolleybus   1375194

Trolza 5250 Megapolis ECObus   1375193

Trolza 5275.05 Optima trolleybus   1375199

Turtle Top Inc

67819 State Road 15, New Paris, Indiana
46553, US
Tel: (+1 574) 831 43 40
Freephone: (+1 800) 296 21 05
Fax: (+1 574) 831 43 49
e-mail: ttsp@turtletop.com
Web: www.turtletop.com

Key personnel
Executive Vice-President and General Manager:
    Robert E Cripe Jr
Corporate Executive Vice-President: *Phil Tom Jr*

Background
Turtle Top has been producing vehicles since
1962.

Products
Mini- and midibus bodies, including the Van
Terra and Terra Transport, Terra Transit and
Odyssey, for up to 25 passengers, and the GM
Odyssey XL which seats up to 37.

Turtle Top Terra Transport van on GM 3500 chassis

1115119

A side wheelchair lift is available on some
models.

Developments
The Van Terra model was introduced in April
2005. It is available in various versions with up
to 15 passenger capacities.

Unidad de Véhiculos Industriales, SA (UNVI SA)

Polígono Industrial San Ciprián de Viñas, E-32901
Ourense, Spain
Tel: (+34 988) 98 06 00
Fax: (+34 988) 25 69 04
e-mail: comercial@unvi-sa.com
Web: www.unvi.es

Key personnel
President: *E P Nieto*
General Manager: *J G Pereira*
Commercial Director: *A Lecompte*

Background
Founded in November 1995, UNVI is part of the
Perez Rumbao Group. The company has two
production plants, one in Ourense, Spain and
CAMO Industria de Autocarros SA, Portugal.
    UNVI is ISO 9001 certified.

Products
Manufacturer of buses, mini and midibuses,
coaches, wheelchair accessible vehicles, luxury
vehicles and special vehicles.

Range
Interurban buses
COMPA Iveco Daily 65c18: from 22 to 33 seats.
COMPA Mercedes-Benz Vario 816/818: up to 33
seats. Available in 4 versions: Compa Standard,
Compa Wheelchair accessible, Compa Extra Boot
and Compa School bus.
COMPA MIXTO Iveco Daily 65c18: offers capacity
for 28 seaters and 2 standees, for both school
transport and suburban routing.
CIMO I XL Mercedes-Benz Atego 1024: up to 36
seats.
CIMO II MD Mercedes-Benz Atego 1524: up to 42
seats.
COMPA GT Mercedes-Benz Vario 816: New
model. This is an evolution from the COMPA
range of products. Available in 3 versions:
COMPA GT Standard: 29 seater, *COMPA GT Extra
Boot version:* up to 25 seats and *COMPA GT Vip
version:* up to 20 seats.

Urban buses
KERALA Mercedes-Benz Sprinter 515/518: Available
in three versions, one standard version with lowered
area for wheelchair, one version with full flat floor,
and one airport version adapted to carry luggage.

CIDADE I Iveco Daily 65c18/50c18: 33 seats or
20 seats.
COMPA CITY BUS Mercedes-Benz Vario 816: For
operation in either city areas (Class I) or in the
outskirts/in suburban areas (Class II).
URBIS 2.5 Volvo B9TL: full flat floor 10 m-long
vehicle with capacity for 26 seats, 1 wheelchair,
44 standees and tip-up seats.
COMPA CITY BUS IVECO DAILY 65C18 (4350):
city bus version of the COMPA midicoach. Built
on Iveco Daily 65c18 chassis with rear lowered
floor. The COMPA CITY BUS is also available
with flat floor. Seat capacity up to 20 seats,
11 standees and one wheelchair or two tip-up
seats.

Open-top vehicles
URBIS 2.5 DD Sightseeing: open-top double
decker, full flat floor, with up to 77 seats. It is
available as 10 m or 12 m.

Production
Together, UNVI and CAMO Industria de
Autocarros SA have a production capacity of 600
buses and coaches per year.

Van Hool NV

Bernard van Hoolstraat 58, B-2500 Lier-
Koningshooikt, Belgium
Tel: (+32 3) 420 20 20   Fax: (+32 3) 482 30 68
e-mail: info@vanhool.be
Web: www.vanhool.be

Key personnel
Managing Directors: *Jos Van Hool, Denis Van
Hool, Leopold Van Hool, Filip Van Hool, Jan
Van Hool*
Public Relations Manager: *Yves Goffin*

Background
Van Hool NV was founded in 1947 and is one
of the largest independent manufacturers of
integral buses and coaches in Western Europe.
Approximately 1,600 buses and coaches are
produced each year. Van Hool also builds semi-
trailers, trailers and tank containers.
    Van Hool won the 'Bus of the Year 2003' with
the new range of A330 citybuses.

Products
Integral city and intercity buses (standard, midi,
articulated, double-articulated (three-section)
and CNG/hybrid/fuel cell/trolleybuses). Integral
coaches (conventional, high-deck, articulated
and double-deck). Bus and coach bodies.

Range
100 per cent low-floor buses, with mid-mounted engine
Van Hool's 100 per cent low-floor concept,
launched in 1991, was based on a mid-mounted
engine fitted sideways and vertically between
the axles, ensuring a stepless low floor
throughout the entire vehicle length. This low
floor, combined with large platforms, double
doors and a boarding height of only 320 mm,
gives easy access at all doors. The concept is still
available in four versions:
A300: 12 m long with three double doors.
Maximum passenger capacity is 110 and various
interior arrangements are possible.
A308: Two doors and 9.4 m long and carrying up
to 63.
AG300: The articulated version of the low-floor
A300, with three or four double doors. It is
17.98 m long and carries up to 160.
AGG300: The AGG300 is a double-articulated
three-section bus 24.785 m long and works on
the puller principle with side-mounted engine
and driveline in the tractor part. It has five
double doors. Maximum passenger capacity
is 185.

100 per cent low-floor buses with rear engine
A309: The A309 midibus has an offside, underfloor
rear engine. The vehicle is 9.9 m long and 2.35 m

wide. It has two doors – one at the front and one
in the middle, giving a large area for standees
opposite the middle door.
A330: A 12 m, full-length, low-floor bus with the
engine positioned offside, vertically at the left
rear. The engine cooler is mounted on top of
the engine. There is a three-door version with
platforms at the second and third doors. The
A330 was voted 'Bus of the Year 2003'.
    This 100 per cent low-floor range is also
available with alternative fuels and drive
systems. The additional components such as gas
tanks, traction batteries and power electronics,
are integrated in the roof structure and do not
compromise the low-floor concept.
    Available are:
    The CNG-powered *A308 CNG* (midibus), *A300
CNG* (12 m), and *AG300 CNG* (articulated bus).
    The articulated trolleybus *AG300T*, available in
two versions: one with a diesel auxiliary group
and one dual-mode version. The 12 m trolleybus
A300T is the solo version.
    The hybrid midibus *A308 HYB*, powered by
either a set of batteries or a diesel generator,
powering the electric motor or batteries. In
this way, the bus can run without exhaust
emissions on batteries only, when in the city
centre. When outside, the diesel generator is
switched on.
Fuel cell bus: (See Developments on page 712).

Low-floor buses

A360: The A360 has been altered to allow the incorporation of a vertical, rear-mounted mid engine. It is a two-door bus with a low floor forward of the rear axle. The rear section is for seating and the vehicle is designed for urban and suburban transport.

Van Hool's new-generation bus range was unveiled at the 54th UITP World Congress and Mobility & City Transport Exhibition in May 2001.

The new range has a new external and interior design, as well as further improved technical features. More throat-width between smaller front wheel arches, enabled by a modified suspension, and an option for sliding doors at the second and subsequent exits, facilitate passenger flow.

The driveline is accessible from inside and outside the vehicle. This applies to all variants, ranging from midi-size, over rigid standard length – with mid or rear engine – to articulated and double-articulated buses.

Euro-4 engines (or Euro-5 and Enhanced Environmental(ly friendly) Vehicle (EEV) as options) and disc brakes are specified. The use of alternative fuels and future evolutions in this respect, are catered for in the bus concept.

The engine cooling unit on articulated buses is located on the front of the roof. This results in a smaller and ample sized engine compartment, giving more space in the passenger saloon.

Compared to classic roadside location, the radiator is less subject to dirt ingress and gets an enhanced air flow, requiring less frequent fan use.

The current range of low-floor buses with these new design features is:

A308: midibus

A309: midibus (see Developments below)

A300: mid-engined 12 m bus

A360: vertical-rear-engined 12 m bus

A330: vertical-rear-engined 12 m bus: combines low-floor over the total length of the vehicle with spacious platforms at the middle and rear door

AG300: articulated bus

AGG300: double-articulated bus.

Special attention is given to accessibility for people with reduced mobility and wheelchairs.

Coaches

Van Hool offers a range of coaches in different lengths and heights. The range consists of:

The Alicron (height 3.47 m):
T911 Alicron: length 10.50 m
T915 Alicron: length 12.20 m
T916 Alicron: length 13.05 m
The Acron (height 3.6 m):
T915 Acron: length 12.20 m
T916 Acron: length 13.20 m
T917 Acron: length 14.04 m
The Astron (height 3.73 m):
T916 Astron: length 13.20 m
T917 Astron: length 14.04 m
The Altano: (height 3.73 m):
T917 Altano: length 13.20 m
T918 Altano: 14.04 m
TD921 Altano: 14.40 m (see under Developments)
The Astromega (height 4 m):
TD925 Astromega: length 13.145 m
TD927 Astromega: length 14.1 m

Van Hool A309 midibus   1146786

Van Hool AG300 articulated low-floor bus   1035030

Van Hool AG300 double-articulated bus for Aachen   1146788

Van Hool A330 fuel cell bus   1367299

Van Hool TD921 Altano tri-axle coach   1367302

Intercity coaches

Van Hool offers the range of CL and TL vehicles for intercity transport and shorter journeys. These types are known as 'Car de Ligne' in France and 'Überlandbus' in Germany. They are offered in 12.20 m and 13.20 m lengths, both versions on two axles.

Bodywork

Van Hool bodywork, to the same design as its integral buses and coaches, has been built on Volvo, Mercedes-Benz, Scania, VDL-Bus and other chassis.

For markets in Africa and the Middle East, Van Hool has developed a range of rugged bus bodywork to the needs of each customer.

Contracts

Six additional low-floor AGG300 buses have been ordered by the public transport system of Aachen, Germany, as well as 15 further AGG300 double-articulated low-floor buses for delivery to Hamburg Hochbahn.

AC Transit of Oakland, California, US placed repeat orders for 10 + 5 AG300 low-floor articulated buses and an order for 25 A300K models (see Developments below). In addition, an order was placed for 25 A300L buses.

In co-operation with AC Transit, ISE Research and UTC Fuel Cells, five A330 40-ft vehicles were shipped to the US, where a hybrid hydrogen propulsion system was integrated. The first of these vehicles was shown at the APTA exhibition in Dallas, Texas, US in September 2005.

Together with Kiepe, Van Hool has won a tender for 12 A330T low-floor trolleybuses for Leece, Italy and 17 AG300T articulated trolleybuses for Genoa, Italy.

A more recent order was received for 11 A330T vehicles from Avelino, Italy. Van Hool has also received an order for 30 articulated trolleybuses for Milan and seven articulated trolleybuses for Rimini.

Orders have been received for nine of the new TD921 Altano coach.

VAN HOOL has been awarded a new order for eight new-generation fuel cell buses by AC Transit, with an option for another four units.

Van Hool A330T 12 m low-floor trolleybus for Lecce, Italy, at a presentation at Vossloh Kiepe for their 100th anniversary   1342173

The vehicles will have the UTC Power PureMotion® Model 120 fuel cell system with a power output of 120 kW. For the first time, these new buses will be completely integrated by VanHool.

Developments

For the US market, Van Hool has developed the A300K. This is a low-floor bus approximately 30 ft long and 102 in wide. The engine is located vertically at the left side between the axles. This gives a good weight distribution and a low floor up to the end of the vehicle. As in other Van Hool articulated buses, the cooling system is mounted on the roof. The bus has two doors, one at the front and one in the middle.

In March 2006, the company announced that it will work with UTC Power, part of the United Technologies Corporation, to deliver a hybrid fuel cell-powered bus to DeLijn, Belgium. The vehicle will operate in Belgium for six months, before being leased to other transit agencies in Europe. The hybrid fuel cell bus was in operation with De Lijn for some months, starting in July 2007. Since June 2008, the bus has been operating at the Zaragoza World Exhibition in Spain. It will run there for three months. Later in 2008, leasing is planned with Connexxion (Zuid Holland).

The new TD921 Altano tri-axle, Euro 5, wheelchair-accessible coach is now available.

Vauxhall

Head Office

Griffin House, Osborne Road, Luton, Bedfordshire, LU1 3YT, UK
Tel: (+44 1582) 72 11 22   Fax: (+44 1582) 42 74 00
Web: www.vauxhall.co.uk

Key personnel

Commercial Vehicle Brand Manager: *Steve Bryant*

Background

Founded in 1903, the company is part of the GM Group of companies. Vauxhall entered the minibus market in late 2004.

Products

Minibuses seating 6, 9, 12, 15, 16 and 17 passengers.

Range

Nine-seat Combi and 12-seat minibus, based on the Vivaro, with 2.0 CDTI (90PS or 115PS) common rail diesel engine.

Six and nine-seat Combi and 15, 16 and 17 seat minibuses based on the Movano with 2.5 CDTI 100PS, 120PS and 146PS common rail diesel engines.

Vauxhall minibuses
1329661

VDL Berkhof Heerenveen BV

PO Box 118, NL-8440 AC Heerenveen, Netherlands
Tel: (+31 513) 61 85 00
(+31 6) 21 89 12 42 (24 hour)
Fax: (+31 513) 61 50 24
e-mail: info@vdlberkhof.nl
Web: www.vdlberkhof.nl

Street address

Wetterwille 12, NL-8447 GC Heerenveen, Netherlands

Key personnel

Director: *Drs Marc L van Doorn*

Background

Founded in 1907 as Hainje Vehicle Builder by Mr Hainje. Since 1998, the company has been a subsidiary of the Dutch VDL Groep and is part of VDL Bus and Coach BV. VDL Berkhof Heerenveen BV is ISO 9001 certified.

Products

Buses for public transport (city/inter-city).

Range

Buses:
City and regional operations
Ambassador 200: A 12 m lightweight bus concept for city and regional transport. Since the introduction in 2001, more than 1,400 of these buses have sold, driven by the VDL Bus SB200 modular chassis with Cummins ISBe4

6.7 litre, 6-cylinder, vertical, rear-placed diesel engine. Special attention is given to items for easy accessibility for maintenance and use of high-grade materials to reduce maintenance costs.

Ambassador 180: A shorter version of the standard Ambassador lightweight bus concept. The length of 10.6 m, together with the low weight, make this an ideal vehicle for city centres, the countryside and platforms which are difficult to reach by the ordinary public transport buses.

Diplomat: Ultra low-floor city bus introduced in 2003. Initially developed for heavy-duty public transport situations in large cities like The Hague. Its three low-floor entry doors make boarding easier and reduce the boarding and exit times at bus stops. This city bus offers the advantages of the low-floor bus and the low fuel consumption and optimum torque of the DAF engine.

*VDL Berkhof **Ambassador 200** bus*   1179784

VDL Berkhof Valkenswaard BV

PO Box 585, NL-5550 AN Valkenswaard, Netherlands
Tel: (+31 40) 208 24 24   Fax: (+31 40) 208 24 25
e-mail: sales@vdlberkhof.com
Web: www.vdlberkhof.com

Street address
De Vest 55, NL-5555 XP Valkenswaard, Netherlands

Key personnel
Managing Director: *Hans Engels*
    Staff: Approximately 250

Background
Founded in 1970 by A Berkhof and his son H Berkhof. A subsidiary of the Dutch VDL Groep and part of VDL Bus and Coach BV.

The company has dealers in the following countries: Montenegro and Serbia (MTA), and UK (Scania and Volvo).

VDL Berkhof Valkenswaard Axial 50 coach   0568286

Products
Luxury coaches from 30 to 85 passengers, VIP coaches, intercity buses and double-deck buses.

Range
Axial 50: The Axial 50 is a luxury coach, 3.5 m high and available in lengths of 10.8, 12 or 12.9 on various chassis. It is also available as an Inter-City, VIP or Team bus.

Axial 70: The Axial 70 is a luxury coach, 3.7 m high and available in lengths of 12, 12.9, 13.2 or 14.1 m on various chassis. It is also available as an Inter-City, VIP or Team bus.

Axial 100 DD: A luxury, double-deck coach, 4 m high and available in lengths of 12, 13, 13.5 or 14.1 m on various chassis. It is also available as a Band or Team bus.

The company can also build coaches and design interiors to customers' specifications.

Production
200 coaches per year.

Contracts
VDL Berkhof Valkenswaard's coaches are sold in most European countries.

VDL Berkhof Valkenswaard Axial 70 coach   0568287

VDL Berkhof Valkenswaard Axial 100 DD double-deck coach
0568288

VDL BOVA BV

Background
VDL BOVA bv is a subsidiary of VDL Groep bv.

For further information, please see the entry for VDL Groep bv.

VDL Bus and Coach Centre

De Run 4232, NL-5503 LL Veldhoven, Netherlands
Tel: (+31 40) 295 46 53
Fax: (+31 40) 255 78 80
e-mail: info@kleyn-bova.nl
Web: www.kleyn.com

Key personnel
Director: *Silke Tödter*

Background
Formerly Kleyn-BOVA Buses BV, VDL Bus and Coach Centre is a subsidiary of the Dutch VDL Groep and part of VDL Bus and Coach BV.

Services
Purchase and sale of used buses and coaches of all makes and models.

VDL Bus International BV

Hoevenweg 1, NL-5652 AW Eindhoven, Netherlands
Tel: (+31 40) 250 05 00   Fax: (+31 40) 257 09 04
e-mail: info@vdlbus.nl
Web: www.vdlbus.nl

Key personnel
Managing Director: *Henri Koolen*
VDL Bus International products are sold in the UK through:

Arriva Bus & Coach
Lodge Garage, Whitehall Road West, Gomersal BD19 4BJ, UK
Tel: (+44 1274) 68 11 44   Fax: (+44 1274) 65 11 98

Background
Formerly known as DAF Bus International BV, the now renamed VDL Bus International was acquired in 1993 and is a subsidiary of the Dutch VDL Groep, as part of VDL Bus and Coach BV.

Products
Bus and coach underframes, including articulated. Sales and service of modules and CKD packs for city, regional and coach transport.

Range
SB 120: 8.5 to 10.8 m midibus category. Cummins ISBe 4-cylinder engine, Allison LCT 2000 automatic 5-speed overdrive gearbox, heavy-duty components (such as gearbox, drivehead and air compressor) and powder coating, combined with features such as multiplexed electrics, disc brakes all round, a stainless steel exhaust and fast-response kneeling.
SB 200: For 12 m buses. 44 seats and an overall capacity of 74, heavy-duty components

VDL Bus International SB4000   0568285

(such as the big gearbox and rear axle, two 80 A alternators, 200 Ah batteries and 460 cc compressor) and powder coating combined with features such as multiplexed electrics, disc brakes all round, a stainless steel exhaust and fast-response kneeling.
SB 250+: Full-length low-floor city bus.
SB 4000 and 4000+: Suitable for all coaching; from tour to express and inter-urban. Varying in length between 10.5 and 13 m, the range encompasses two engine ranges, four gearboxes, two retarders and a full options list, with modular underframe. DAF XF Euro 3, 12.6 litre engine has an electronic throttle and CAN driveline. Alternatively, the 9.2 litre DAF PF Euro 3 engine delivers up to 265 kW/360 hp and 1,450 Nm of torque and also features an electronic throttle and CAN driveline. ZF 5HP592 and 5HP602 automatic gearboxes or Voith GO-170 and 190 manual gearboxes with

integrated Voith R115 retarder, and a proven four air-bag rear suspension.
SBR 4000+: New addition to the VDL Bus range, with new front module and trailing axle.
DB 250 +: Low-floor, double decker. More than 1,000 units supplied. Available with the complete range of body options, most recently augmented with the Wrightbus Pulsar Gemini body exhibited at the recent Coach and Bus 2003 show in Birmingham.
TB 2175: Dedicated heavy-duty export model. Includes disc brakes all round.

Developments
Recent developments include:
New Front Module;
Enhanced Drivers Cockpit;
New Trailing Axle Module;
New steering module.

VDL Groep bv

Communications Department
PO Box 8811, NL-5605 LV Eindhoven, Netherlands
Tel: (+31 40) 292 50 00   Fax: (+31 40) 292 50 50
e-mail: info@vdlgroep.com
    info@vdlbuscoach.com
Web: www.vdlgroep.com, www.vdlbuscoach.com

Street address
Hoevenweg 1, NL-5652 AW Eindhoven, Netherlands

Key personnel
Chairman, President and Director:
    Wim van der Leegte

Directors: *Wim Maathuis, Jan Mooren, Lau Pas, Rini Vermeulen*
Deputy Directors: *Wim van Bakel, Jan Karssen, Theo Toussaint, Ted van der Put, Henri Koolen, Rémi Henkemans, Pieter van der Leegte*
Staff: 7,500

Background
The VDL Groep bv is an international company engaged in the development, production and sales of semi-finished and finished products, with 77 subsidiaries in 16 countries.
    VDL Bus & Coach bv is the bus and coach division of the VDL Groep bv. VDL Bus & Coach offers a complete range of buses: touring coaches, public transport buses, high-quality public

transport systems, mini- and midi buses, chassis modules and used coaches. Sales of VDL Bus & Coach products take place through a worldwide network, consisting of corporate-owned sales offices, importers and agents in more than 30 countries. Companies of VDL Bus & Coach which are operating under their own name on the market are:
Advanced Public Transport Systems BV (APTS);
VDL Coach & Bus Center;
VDL Busland bv;
VDL Parts bv;
    Please see individual entries for VDL companies in *Jane's Urban Transport Systems* for more information.

VDL Jonckheere Bus & Coach NV

Schoolstraat 50, B-8800 Roeselare, Belgium
Tel: (+32 51) 23 26 11
    (+32 59) 34 00 18 (24-hour service number)

Fax: (+32 51) 23 27 63
e-mail: info@vdljonckheere.be
Web: www.vdljonckheere.be

Key personnel
Managing Director: *Tony Buyck*

Background
A subsidiary of the Dutch VDL Groep and part of VDL Bus and Coach BV.

Products
Buses for public transport, school buses, double-deckers and minibuses, luxury and VIP coaches.

VDL Jonckheere 70 LHD coach
1322790

VDL Jonckheere Pacific heavy-duty bus
1322791

Range

Buses:

Transit 2000: Low-floor bus for city and inter-city transport, completely built of stainless steel. Easy access for disabled persons. Available in the following versions: VDL Bus SB230 – 310/360 bhp; Volvo B7RLE 275 bhp; Scania K UB 230/270/310 bhp. Lengths: 12 m. Options: low-floor or semi-low-floor, two- or three-door layout, stainless steel construction, roof heating and ventilation system, choice of seats and seat layouts, air-conditioning.

Pacific: Heavy-duty bus. Several hundred have been delivered to the African continent and the Caribbean. Available on various chassis.

Pro-City: Low-floor city bus, with a full flat floor, on the Volkswagen T5 chassis, Euro 4. Easy access for disabled persons. High manoeuvrability. Specifications: Wheel-base: 4,650 mm; Length: 7,835 mm; Width: 2,200 mm, Height: 2,450 mm, Passengers: up to 30+1 . Engine: diesel – turbo, Power output: 128 kW – 174 bhp, Gearbox: TIP6, Rear axle: air suspension, panoramic windows, entry width 1,200 mm, entry height 265 mm, stainless steel construction, optional wheelchair lift.

School bus: Lower frame is completely built of stainless steel. The bus offers 42 or 46 seats and with lengths of 9.5 and 10.2 m respectively. Chassis: DAF LF 45, completely flat floor.

Coaches:

Jonckheere 50: Stainless steel luxury coach built on VDL Bus platforms: SB(R)4000+ PR/ MX 360/410/460 bhp. Specifications: lengths: 12.2, 13.4 and 14 m (depending on platform), stainless steel, roll bar R66, climate control (Thermo King), Fainsa seats, optional wheelchair lift, LHD.

Stainless steel luxury coach built on Volvo platforms: Volvo B12B 420/460 bhp, Volvo B12M 420/460 bhp. Specifications: Lengths: 12.2 and 12.57 m (depending on platform), stainless steel, roll bar R66, climate control (Thermo King), Fainsa seats, optional wheelchair lift, RHD.

Luggage capacity up to 11 m³.

Jonckheere 70: Stainless steel luxury coach built on VDL Bus platforms: SB(R)4000+ MX 410/460/510 bhp. Specifications: lengths: 12.2, 13.4 and 14 m (depending on platform), stainless steel, roll bar R66, climate control (Thermo King), Fainsa seats, optional wheelchair lift, LHD.

Stainless steel luxury coach built on Volvo platforms: Volvo B12B 420/460 bhp. Specifications: lengths: 12.2, 13.4 and 14 m (depending on platform), stainless steel, roll bar R66, climate control (Thermo King), Fainsa seats, optional wheelchair lift, RHD, LHD.

Luggage capacity up to 14 m³.

Production

Up to 500 buses and coaches per year.

Contracts

VDL Jonckheere secured an order of 36 Euro 4 buses and 73 Euro 5 buses for the Flemisch

VDL Jonckheere school bus
1322747

VDL Jonckheere Pro-City bus
1322746

VDL Jonckheere 50 RHD coach
1322789

Public Transport Company 'De Lijn', to be built on the Volvo B7RLE-platform.

Also, 19 Pro-city buses are to be built for the same company. The Walloon Public Transport Company 'TEC' has ordered 44 Euro 5 buses on the Volvo B7RLE platform.

For Ghana, VDL Jonckheere is building 225 Pacific buses over three years. A first delivery of 75 buses has already been made. The buses are built on the VDL Bus TB 2175-plaform.

VDL Kusters BV

PO Box 38, NL-5900 AA Venlo, Netherlands
Tel: (+31 77) 351 70 45   Fax: (+31 77) 351 70 48
e-mail: info@vdlkusters.nl
Web: www.vdlkusters.nl

Street address
Huiskensstraat 49, NL-5916 PN Venlo, Veegtes industrial estate Venlo, No. 2894, Netherlands

Key personnel
Managing Director: *Huub Verdonck*

Background
Since 1998, VDL Kusters has been a subsidiary of the VDL Groep, Netherlands and is part of VDL Bus and Coach BV.

The company is ISO 9001 certified.

Products
Production of mini and midibuses.

Range
Mid-City II: Low-floor minibus. Boarding height is 30 cm from the road surface. Designed for urban, scheduled and shuttle transport. Seats up to 11 plus 14 standees.

Parade OV: Low-floor minibus, with space for 17 seated and 15 standing passengers.
Mercedes-Benz Vario: Midibus with a maximum capacity of 24 passengers.
Mid-Euro XL: Luxury midibus. Various seating configurations.

The company also offers taxi buses and touring buses (*Parade Tour* – 25 seats and Mercedes-Benz Vario – 22 seats), airport shuttle, police and fitting out of special transport vehicles and buses for carrying handicapped persons.

VDL Kusters Mid-Euro XL midibus   0568284

VDL Kusters Mid-City II low-floor minibus   0568282

VDL Kusters Parade OV low-floor minibus   0568283

The Vehicle Application Centre Limited (TVAC)

Passenger Transport Division
Enterprise Business Park, Centurion Way, Leyland, Lancashire, PR26 6TZ, UK
Tel: (+44 01772) 45 71 16
Fax: (+44 01772) 45 71 17
e-mail: info@tvac.co.uk
Web: www.tvac.co.uk

Key personnel
Managing Director: *G Smith*
PT Operations & Design Manager: *Ben Jardine*

Current situation
The Vehicle Application Centre Limited (TVAC), a private limited company, was formed in 1993.

Products
Minibus manufacture.

Range
Eclipse 6 × 2 Low Floor Wheelchair Accessible Mini Bus: Designed for local authority and community transport needs, this low-floor

TVAC Eclipse 16-seat minibus, showing plug side door   1323173

minibus is powered by a Renault Master Euro 4 150 bhp engine with a Renault 6-speed manual or Quick shift gearbox on TVAC's 6 × low line ladder chassis. The body is Glass Reinforced Plastic (GRP) composite. The vehicle is 7.5 m long, 2.345 m wide and 2.75 m high with 16 +1 seats. There is a portable fold-away rear loading ramp. Optional extras include an automatic gearbox, wheelchair restraints, electric side door and rear-access lift.

Developments

There are plans to launch a 'facelift' version of the vehicle in late 2008 and also a short wheelbase version.

TVAC Eclipse 16-seat minibus, showing fold-away ramp at rear
1323174

VehiXeL Trouillet Constructeur

Zone d'Activé, F-01340 Attignatt, France
Tel: (+33 4) 74 25 10 96
Fax: (+33 4) 74 25 11 12
e-mail: vehixel@vehixel.com
Web: www.vehixel.com

Key personnel

Contact: *Jean-Pierre Robinet*

Background

The company was formed in 1956 by Andre Trouillet. In 1962, it produced the first cash-in-transit vehicle in France. In 1982 it brought an insulated body manufacturer in Bourg-en-Bresse, which lies between Lyon and Geneva. Further expansion occurred in 1987 when the company brought a factory building coach and minicoach bodies from Chardon, the seat manufacturer. By this time, the group was producing coach and minicoach bodies, cash-in-transit vans, tipper bodywork, trailers and semi-trailers. By 1990, the group employed 1,200 people and had nine subsidiaries. The four sons of the founder were given responsibility for separate plants. In 1996, all production was consolidated in the factory at Attignat, near Bourg-en-Bresse. It has capacity for 1,000 bodies of various types per year. The factory has ISO 9001 accreditation.

Products

Bus and coach bodywork.

Production

Annual levels are approximately as follows: 120 large coach bodies, 120 midicoaches (30–40 seats), 300 small coaches, 100 cash-in-transit vans and 40 coaches for the French police. Turnover in 2004 was approximately EUR25 million.

Contracts

The bodywork on the Iveco EuroMidi 150 E24 ScolaBus is built in France by VehiXeL.

Viseon Bus GmbH

Gottlob – Auwärter Strasse 1, D-94431 Pilsting, Germany
Tel: (+49 99 53) 980 14 90
Fax: (+49 99 53) 980 14 91
e-mail: info@viseon-bus.com
Web: www.viseon-bus.com

Key personnel

Managing Director: *Joachim Reimuth*
PR Contact: *Andreas Lubitz*
Assistant to Management: *Martina Schott*
   Staff: 20 (current estimate)

Current situation

Viseon Bus GmbH was established in July 2008. The majority shareholder is the Managing Director, Joachim Reimuth. Ernö Bartha, due to join the management board in April 2009, will take a 29 per cent share in the company's capital. A third share, currently 19.9 per cent, is held by MAN Nutzfahrzeuge.

The company took over the trolleybus and airport apron bus business from NEOPLAN.

Range

NEOPLAN Electroliner: *Trolleybus*.
NEOPLAN Airliner: *Airport apron bus N91 series.* These vehicles will be manufactured by TVM's Maribor plant and offered under the brand name of NEOPLAN.

Developments

Viseon Bus GmbH plans to take over the former NEOPLAN plant in Pilsting, with some 200 employees, in mid-2009, subject to negotiations. It will produce MAN Nutzfahrzeuge city and touring buses and NEOPLAN series vehicles.

Long-term plans include the development and production of the NEOPLAN Skyliner double-decker, and coach and bus models under its own brand.

Production

Viseon Bus GmbH will manufacture in the former plant of NEOPLAN Bus GmbH in Pilsting, Germany.

Volgren Australia Pty Ltd

Locked Bag 1410, Dandenong South, Victoria 3164, Australia
Tel: (+61 3) 97 91 42 55
Fax: (+61 3) 97 94 03 36
e-mail: rshortt@volgren.com.au
   sales@volgren.com.au
Web: www.grenda.com.au/gw/volgren/
   index_vol.html

Street address

221-243 Hammond Road, Dandenong 3175, Victoria, Australia

Background

Volgren is part of the Grenda Corporation.

Products

Bus and coach bodies, including both articulated and 14.5 m units.

Bodies are made in aluminium under the Carosserie Hess AG system of construction. They can be mounted on Scania, Volvo, Mercedes, MAN, Hino and Isuzu chassis.

Range

CR221L: Route bus body, for low-floor chassis, such as the Volvo B10BLE, though it can be mounted on the Volvo B10M chassis.
SC221: School bus.

Volkswagen Caminhões e Ônibus Ltda

Volkswagen Trucks & Buses
Rua Engenheiro Alan da Costa Batista 100, Pedra Selada, Resende RJ, CEP-27511-970, Brazil

Tel: (+55 24) 33 81 10 63   Fax: (+55 24) 33 81 10 39
e-mail: larissa.rodrigues@volkswagen.com.br
Web: www.vwtbpress.com.br

Key personnel

President: *Antonio Roberto Cortes*

Director of Marketing: *José Ricardo Alouche*
Director of Exports: *Marcos Vinícius Forgioni*
Director, Aftersales: *Luiz Antonio Penteado De Luca*
Director, Governmental Affairs: *Marco Antonio Saltini*

Manager, National Sales: *Antonio Cammarosano Filho*
Manager, Marketing: *Ricardo Barion*
Head of Manufacturing: *João da Silva*
Communications, PR and Press Supervisor: *Marcos Brito*
 Staff: 5,000 (Factory)

Background
Parent company: Volkswagen AG, Germany
Operations launched: March 1981

Products
The company assembles light and heavy trucks and a range of buses at its plant in Resende, Brazil. This is in association with seven main suppliers in a Consórcio Modular (Modular Consortium) who are directly involved in the assembly line.

Modular Consortium
Volkswagen has selected seven partners to assemble kits: Maxion (chassis assembly), Arvin Meritor (axles and suspension), Remon (wheels and tires), Powertrain (engines), AKC (cabin structure), Carese (paintwork) and Continental (fabrics).

Volkswagen is responsible for quality assurance and product development. The Modular Consortium seeks to reduce the costs involved in production, investment, stocks and production time.

The partners do not participate in the end profit of the products: they remain suppliers, they assemble the parts that they sell. At the plant, they share the infrastructure with Volkswagen.

Chassis assembly uses mechanical conveyor belts, bridge cranes and lifting assemblies, which economise assembly efforts and increase productivity. The assembly line is the first one in Brazil to install a climate control system.

The company follows strict technical regulations when treating solid, liquid and gaseous effluents and recovering degraded areas. The assembly building does not have any pollutant sources. In the paintwork building, an effluent treatment station with tanks and filters guarantees that the water which returns to the river is cleaned. In the pre-treatment, E-Coat (electrodeposits painting) and Sealer areas, any gaseous effluent is burned off. Domestic residues are treated using a biological process, and only neutral pH water reaches the river.

Plants
Resende, Brazil
The plant certified to ISO TS and ISO 14001 standards. It received investments of USD250 million to produce the Modular Consortium, which brings the main vehicle assembly suppliers into the factory (see above). The current technical capacity is 57,600 vehicles per year.

The plant covers an area of 1 million m², with a workforce of 5,000, 92 per cent of who are from the surrounding region. Daily production is 220 vehicles, split between two shifts. Deployment of the second shift in October 2005 created an additional 400 jobs. With the third shift announced by the President, Roberto Cortes, there will be more 1,300 jobs in September 2008.

Puebla, México
Inaugurated in October 2004, the unit, the first built outside Brazil, is responsible for manufacturing four truck models and two bus chassis. Using the SKD (Semi-Knocked Down)

VW bus on 15.190 EOD chassis   1368609

VW bus on 17.230 EOD chassis   1368610

production system, the plant assembles over 100 vehicles per month.

Following the same successful formula as the Modular Consortium in Resende, the assembly line covers 11,000 m² and provides jobs for 60 Mexicans and Brazilians. After starting its Mexican operations, VW began supplying buses and trucks to the entire Latin American region.

Six Volkswagen Trucks and Buses dealerships have already opened in Mexico, providing distribution and technical services for the company's vehicles in the country's main regions.

Port Elizabeth, South Africa
The third Volkswagen Trucks and Buses plant began operating in August 2006. The unit is responsible for assembling three Volkswagen bus chassis models.

With 22 employees, all of them from South Africa, the plant aims to reach a target of 80 vehicles per month and up to 900 units produced annually, 200 of which will be buses.

The South African dealership network currently encompasses 10 outlets and the company is aiming for a 10 per cent share in the South African market within three years.

Range
Micro and minibuses, mid-range and Highway buses (8 models).
Minibus: Models: **VW 5.140 EOD**, **VW 8.120 OD** and **VW 8.150 EOD**.
Microbus: Model: **VW 9.150 EOD**.
Mid-range: Models: **VW 15.190 EOD**, **VW 17.230 EOD** and **VW 17.260 EOT**.
Highway: Model: **VW 18.320 EOT**.

Production
The company assembled 47,000 trucks and buses in 2007.

Contracts
In 2007, the company exported 10,801 vehicles to 30 countries, including Argentina, Chile, Uruguay, Bolivia, Colombia, Venezuela, Paraguay, the Dominican Republic, the Ivory Coast, Nigeria and Saudi Arabia.

Developments
Since 2003, Volkswagen Trucks and Buses has been investing in research into and testing of alternate fuels such as biodiesel, and has started tests on 'ecological fuel' and authorised its use in its products, mixed with conventional diesel.

Volvo Bus Corporation

405 08 Göteborg, Sweden
Tel: (+46 31) 66 80 00   Fax: (+46 31) 53 68 08
e-mail: info.bus@volvo.com
Web: www.volvo.com

Key personnel
President: *Håkan Karlsson*
Senior Vice-President, Corporate Communications: *Christina Fjellman*

Tel: (46 31) 322 42 80
Fax: (+46 31) 53 68 08

Senior Vice-Presidents, Business Regions
Europe: Stefan Nordström
 Tel: (+46 31) 66 74 00

North, Central and South America:
Tore Bäckström
 Tel: (+46 31) 66 72 00

International: Rune Lundberg
 Tel: (+46 31) 66 64 00

Area Managers, Business Areas, Europe
Area Nordic: Stefan Guttman
 Tel: (+46 31) 66 86 81
Area UK and Eire: Steve Dewhurst
 Tel: (+44 1926) 41 45 79
Area West: Erland Morelissen
 Tel: (+31 345) 68 85 30

Area East: Kjell Johansson
Tel: (+46 31) 322 22 35
Area South: Thierry Currit
Tel: (+41 31) 868 83 29

Body building subsidiaries/associates
Volvo Polska sp, Poland
Volvo Bus Finland Oy, Finland
Volvo Bus Säffle AB, Sweden
Xian Silver Bus Corporation, China
Sunwin Corp, China
Merkavim Metal Works Ltd, Israel

Major subsidiaries/associates
Volvo Bus Ltd, UK
Wedgnock Lane, Warwick, CV34 5YA, UK
Tel: (+44 1926) 40 74 07
Fax: (+44 1926) 40 17 77

Key personnel
Managing Director, Volvo Bus UK and Ireland:
Steve Dewhurst
UK Product Director: *Ian Downie*
Coach Sales Director: *Nick Page*
Volvo do Brasil Veículos Ltda
Prévost Car Inc, Canada, including Nova Bus
Corporation
Volvo Bussar Sverige AB, Sweden
Volvo Italia SpA, Italy
Volvo Bus Asia Pacific Ltd, Hong Kong
Volvo East Asia (Pte) Ltd, VEA Bus, Singapore
Volvo Coach Sales (Loughborough) Ltd
Volvo India PVT Ltd
Volvo Buses de Mexico, Mexico

Bus manufacturing plants
Wroclaw, Poland; Borås and Säffle, Sweden;
Curitiba, Brazil; St Claire and St Eustache, Canada;
Durban, South Africa; Tampere and Turku,
Finland; Caesarea, Israel; Xian and Shanghai,
China; Mexico City, Mexico; Bangalore, India.
Bus chassis assembly plants also in Malaysia,
Morocco and Taiwan.

Background

Volvo Bus Corporation is the world's second-
largest manufacturer of large buses and coaches.
The range comprises complete vehicles, chassis,
bus bodies, transport system solutions for
metropolitan traffic, leasing, financing and service
contract maintenance. Volvo Bus Corporation is
part of the Volvo Group, one of the world's leading
manufacturers of trucks, buses and construction
equipment, drive systems for marine and
industrial applications, aerospace components
and services. The Group also provides complete
solutions for financing and service.

Developments

In 2008, Volvo Bus announced the introduction
of a new factory-renovated engine scheme, an
engine emission upgrade offer for certain Volvo
buses (see below), further enhancements to
Volvo Action Service and Volvo's Driver CPC
training programme.

Volvo Bus launched its new hybrid bus
programme in autumn 2008 – the Volvo B5TL
double-deck in the UK and the Volvo 7700 hybrid
in mainland Europe. With a hybrid solution that
is largely based on standard products and with
fuel savings of up to 30 per cent, customers can
achieve payback on the incremental capital costs
far quicker than was previously the case, Volvo
reports. The technology also lowers the exhaust
emissions and noise levels.

SCR Technology: Volvo chose the Selective
Catalytic Reduction (SCR) technology route to
achieve the current Euro 4 emission standard.
When launching the Euro 4 compliant
drivelines, Volvo Bus anticipated a reduction
in fuel consumption of five to seven per
cent compared with Euro 3 engines. Data,
downloaded from vehicles during planned
servicing, shows that these figures are not only
being achieved, but on some models bettering
initial predictions. Euro 5 comes into force in
October 2009, requiring a further 40 per cent
reduction in NOx levels. Volvo's adoption of
SCR technology means that it can already

Volvo 9700, International Coach of the Year 2008, in special Volvo Ocean Race livery 1374432

Volvo B5LH hybrid double-deck bus with Wrightbus bodywork 1375409

Volvo 9700 Prestige Plus coach 1375412

offer products that meet Euro 5, Enhanced
Environmentally Friendly Vehicle (EEV) and
Euro 5 Incentive.

Euro 5 Emissions Upgrade: This is now available
on B9TL double-deck buses (subject to chassis
age), raising them from Euro 4 to Euro 5
compliance. As well as operators benefiting from

even cleaner engines with further reductions in
emissions, the upgrade will also ensure that
vehicles will qualify for a Reduced Pollution
Certificate. This means a potential saving of
GBP335 per vehicle each year for the duration
of the vehicle's lifetime, based on current
legislation.

Bus Rapid Transit (BRT): In 1975, Volvo Bus helped develop the world's first BRT system in Curitiba, Brazil. Today, Volvo BRT systems are operating in cities such as Bogotá (Colombia), Mexico City (Mexico), Göteborg (Sweden) and Santiago (Chile). Volvo has also worked closely with FirstGroup and Wrightbus on the ftr projects here in the UK. Worldwide, there are about 50 cities with various degrees of BRT implementation, and a further 100 cities planning for BRT.

Minimising environmental impact: Volvo Buses environmental efforts are based on a life cycle approach, considering the impact of the products from design right through to scrapping and recycling.

Since more than 90 per cent of the total environmental impact of a vehicle arises when it is in operation, the emphasis of Volvo's environmental work is focused on reducing fuel consumption, carbon dioxide emissions and other air pollutants, which may be harmful to human beings and the environment. However, Volvo is also continually looking at reducing energy and water consumption at their ISO14001 certified production plants. The overall aim is to reduce emissions of various pollutants such as solvents, nitrogen oxides and sulphur dioxide during the production process.

Ozone depleting compounds such as CFC and halons are rapidly being phased out. At most Volvo production facilities, production waste and packaging materials are all source separated for recycling, with material logistics also streamlined.

Volvo Dynafleet: This is now standard on 9700 and available throughout the coach range. Dynafleet is an integrated transport information system from Volvo increasingly used by both bus and coach operators to improve the efficiency and effectiveness of their fleets. Supplied as a complete package with all the necessary hardware and software, Volvo Dynafleet enables operators to see in real time the current location of any number of vehicles in a fleet and to monitor a wide variety of key information.

Products and services
Volvo manufactures city and intercity buses and coaches. Capacity varies from 24 to 300 passengers and the vehicles are in the weight class 12 tonnes and above.

Range
Intercity buses and coaches
B9R: this is the latest addition to the Volvo coach range and made its debut appearance in the UK in 2008. Powered by the nine litre Volvo D9B engine, rated at 380 hp and coupled with Volvo I-Shift (a ZF 6HP602 automatic gearbox can be specified with a 340 hp rated D9B engine), the B9R combines the driving qualities of the Volvo's B12B and B12M, with the full size, yet lightweight characteristics of the Volvo B7R.

Bodywork options are available from Sunsundegui and Plaxton. It is also available at a 10.3 m length, exclusively with the Sunsundegui body.

B7R Sideral 10: this coach can accommodate up to 43 passengers and is for applications where a full-sized coach is unnecessary, or when a luxury corporate vehicle is required and optimum luggage capacity is still essential.

B12B: although the mid engine layout of the B12M coach continues to be favoured by a number of operators, the rear engine Volvo B12B is now Volvo's best selling coach model in the British Isles.

Volvo 9700: this coach was named International Coach of the Year 2008. An example of this award winning coach was a central feature at this year's EuroBus Expo 2008 show at the NEC Birmingham, UK, exhibited in a special livery designed to celebrate the Volvo Ocean Race which is currently circumnavigating the globe.

The Volvo 9700 Prestige Plus specification is powered by the Euro 5 DH12E Volvo engine and coupled to a Volvo I-Shift gearbox. It seats 50 passengers. The specification of the Volvo 9700

Volvo B7RLE single-deck bus with ADL bodywork in Translink Ulsterbus livery   1375413

Volvo B9R coach with Sunsundegui bodywork   1375414

Volvo B12B coach with new Plaxton Elite bodywork   1375415

Prestige Plus has been further enhanced for the 2009 coach season with the addition of Volvo Dynafleet as standard.

Volvo 8500 city and intercity bus: Available in many versions: with a raised floor, as a low-entry bus and as an articulated bus. Common to all is Volvo Buses' lightweight, corrosion-resistant aluminium body. The level of safety has been further increased with the availability of ESP on certain models.

Volvo 8700 multipurpose buses: Available in a number of configurations for intercity, express and city traffic. The latest generation of the Volvo 8700 meets the Euro 4 standard and is also available in an Incentive configuration for Euro 5.

City buses
B5L Hybrid: this is a double-deck bus, due to enter series production in 2009 and deliveries of complete production double-deck vehicles will commence early in 2010. There will be some early production vehicles on the road in 2009. The chassis layout follows the same principles as the Volvo 7700 Hybrid, which was recently launched at the IAA in Hanover, with a rear offset driveline. The battery energy storage unit is installed under two of the seats in the lower saloon, just behind the front axle, to achieve the minimum intrusion into the gangway and to optimise the weight distribution.

The first vehicle produced has Gemini bodywork, from Wrightbus in Ballymena, Northern Ireland. With an overall length of 10.4 m, the vehicle offers 66 seats (45 upper saloon, 21 lower saloon) and space for up to 20 further passengers standing.

The key elements of the Volvo Hybrid are:

- D5E 4 cylinder 5 litre Volvo diesel engine to Euro 5 emissions level with SCR exhaust aftertreatment;
- Volvo ISAM integrated starter alternator motor electric machine to provide parallel operation of diesel and electric power;
- Volvo I-Shift 12 speed automatic transmission;
- Lithium-Ion battery energy storage system, rated at 600 Volts, water-cooled;
- Electrically-driven air compressor, hydraulic pumps and air conditioning/air chill compressor.

The chassis module is very similar to that of the existing Volvo B9TL double-deck bus.

The vehicle can be driven by both the diesel engine or the electric motor, or even any combination of the two.

This means that the diesel engine can be downsized from that of a conventional bus, and at the same time the electric motor can also be smaller, because it does not have to provide the maximum power level on its own. Combining the two sources provides the power needed to climb steeper hills or for maximum acceleration.

It is also possible to operate in purely electric mode, at bus stops for example, to minimise local air quality emissions in sensitive areas: the bus can pull away from the bus stop in quiet electric mode and engage diesel power as the system requires for maintaining battery charge. Normal braking can drive the ISAM unit in alternator mode to achieve regenerative braking/ energy recovery to charge the battery and this is another key step to reduce fuel consumption. The next step will be the in-service operation of six double-deck buses in London and a single-deck bus in Sweden. As well as defining the best control strategies for the vehicles to deliver the best results, this operation will also give operators, drivers and maintenance staff the practical experience needed ahead of volume introduction.

The Arriva London vehicles will be taken care of through the Volvo Truck and Bus Centre at Enfield, as the hybrid package and much of the chassis will be on a Contract Maintenance agreement. In addition, Transport for London are supporting the programme.

Volvo Buses will be following the introduction of the hybrid system in single and double-deck buses with an articulated vehicle in the future.

In the long term, a parallel hybrid has the potential to also deliver fuel savings on intercity and express routes, although savings may not be as significant as on a city bus, the longer distances travelled in express services still result in significant fuel savings. There is therefore considerable potential for greater sales volumes in the future.

Volvo 7700: Has a new, environmentally adapted nine litre engine, in both diesel and gas configurations, a modern driver's environment, high manoeuvrability and safety features. The bus is available both as a single bus and in an articulated version. The latest generation of the low-entry Volvo 7700 bus is built to provide efficient, comfortable and safe city traffic.

Volvo 7500: Complete city bus bus with a low floor throughout, to facilitate boarding and exiting. The fully electronic-controlled, nine litre engine is at the side of the bus, ahead of the second axle. This means that the engine pulls the vehicle rather than pushing it, which aids manoeuvrability. The bus is available in an 18 m articulated version but also a 24 m bi-articulated version with room for up to 200 passengers.

Chassis for local body building

The new **Volvo B9TL** double-deck bus was introduced in 2006. Building on the Volvo **B7TL** and the **Volvo Olympian** before it, the new **Volvo B9TL** is the latest generation of Volvo double deck chassis for Euro 4 onwards.

The new vehicle features the transversely mounted Volvo D9B 9.4 litre engine. As with all units in the Volvo European engine programme, it features SCR technology.

The **B9TL** continues to be bodied by three key bodybuilders for the UK and Irish market.

The **B9TL** is offered in two-axle form and a three-axle version for high capacity applications, both in the British Isles and other double deck markets, such as Hong Kong and Singapore.

The **B7RLE** bus chassis with D7E 290 hp engine, ZF 6HP554-N 6-speed gearbox with electronic control system. An option of Voith transmission is available with various UK bodybuilder.

The **B7R** coach chassis for the UK market now features the new 7.1 litre Volvo D7E rated at 213 kW (290 hp). It is equipped with SCR technology. The **B7R** continues to be available with both Plaxton Profile and Sunsundegui Sideral body styles with around 53 seats.

The **B12M** and **B12B** coach chassis features SCR technology on 2/3-axle variants.

All of the Volvo bus chassis are available for local body building.

Contracts

Orders totalling more than 200 vehicles were confirmed at the UK's Euro Bus Expo show in 2008. Six Volvo B5L Hybrid buses were due to enter service with Arriva London during the period December 2008 to January 2009 and are operating on Route 141, being based at Wood Green.

Transdev Blazefield, has ordered 19 Euro 5 compliant Volvo B7RLE Eclipse 2s for their Burnley & Pendle operation, whilst Warrington Borough Transport has ordered 12 similarly specified vehicles – its first of this combination – as part of its fleet upgrade programme, which are due to go into service on a variety of routes around the borough in June 2009.

In addition to the 27 Volvo B7RLE Eclipses delivered in the summer to trentbarton for their Rainbow 5 service between Derby and Nottingham, a further 14 of the new Eclipse 2 bodied B7RLEs will be delivered in the New Year for their Calverton Link service running from Nottingham. GHA in Wrexham have also taken three of the Ballymena-bodied Volvo single decks.

Rotala plc has purchased 33 Volvo B7RLE single decks for use on its Diamond Bus Network in the Midlands, 22 of which feature the Plaxton Centro bodies and have gone into service on a number of key routes in the Black Country under the 'Black Diamond' brand. The remaining eleven B7RLEs have Wrightbus Eclipse bodywork and are entering service in partnership with Worcestershire County Council under the 'Red Diamond' brand.

Kent County Council will be the first operator to put the new Volvo/Optare single deck combination into service with a total of six such vehicles. Whippet Coaches have three more due to enter service on the Cambridge busway in 2009 – a further 10 Volvo B7RLEs with Wrightbus Eclipse bodies, operated by Stagecoach and fuelled by bio-diesel are set to join them.

The Isle of Man will see its first ever new Volvo bus when 11 Wrightbus Gemini bodied Volvo B9TL Double Decks enter service on the island in early 2009. Also 10 B9TL Geminis are currently being delivered to Bus Eireann, whilst Dublin Bus is currently taking delivery of 50 Volvo B9TLs with ADL Enviro 400 bodywork, with a further 50 to follow.

London sighting tour operator Big Bus have recently taken delivery of 10 Volvo B9TL Double Decks with Optare Visionaire body work – three of which are open top, with the other seven 'half top'. The Euro 5 compliant vehicles are being deployed on all three of the companies 'hop-on hop-off' tour routes, which take in many of the capital's tourist sights. A further order for another 10 buses has been confirmed for delivery during 2009.

Volvo Bussar Säffle AB

PO Box 59, SE-661 22 Säffle, Sweden
Tel: (+46 533) 466 00
Fax: (+46 533) 466 90
Web: www.volvo.com

Key personnel

President: *Kjell Berg*
Purchasing Manager: *Bert Ove Larsson*
Production Manager: *Staffan Ljungdahl*
Business/International Manager: *Jerry Guttman*

Finance Manager: *Vacant*
Design Manager: *Jan Thorell*
Quality/Environment Manager: *Toivo Pentonen*

Background

Founded in 1913, the company is a wholly owned subsidiary of Volvo Bus Corporation, Sweden.

Products

Bus bodies, including articulated. The company also delivers buses in Partly Knocked Down (PKD) and/or Completely Knocked Down (CKD) form.

Range

Bodies are offered only on Volvo-built chassis: B12M, B12M Bogie, B12MA, B12BLE59, B12BLE70, B12BLE-Bogie, B7R, B7RLE, B10BLE CNG, B10BLE Bogie CNG, B10L CNG, B10LA CNG, B7L and B7LA, primarily for the Nordic market. Both structure and panelling are made of aluminium, with front and rear end in glass-reinforced plastic.

System 2000: Bus models, rigid and articulated, for urban and interurban use.

Workhorse Custom Chassis LLC

940 S State Route 32, Union City, In-47390, US
Tel: (+1 765) 964 40 00
(+1 866) 467 73 00 (Bus sales)
Web: www.workhorse.com

Key personnel

President: *Dave Olsen*
Staff: Approximately 500 (including parts business)

Background

Originally formed in 1998 and acquired in August 2005, Workhorse Custom Chassis LLC is a wholly owned subsidiary of International Truck and Engine Corporation.

Products

Chassis for buses and other vehicles.

Range

Workhorse Low-Floor LF72 Chassis: With Duramax™ diesel engine, for shuttlebus applications. Includes kneeling feature. Bodybuilders for this chassis are Glaval Bus and StarTrans Bus.

Production

In 2004, Workhorse produced more than 18,000 chassis for buses and other vehicles.

World Trans Inc

PO Box 2946, Hutchinson, Kansas 67504-2946, USA
Tel: (+1 620) 669 01 00
Web: www.wtrans.com

Street address
415 West 65th Avenue, Hutchinson, Kansas 67501, USA

Key personnel
President: *Phil Roberts*
National Sales Manager: *Jim Elliott*

Background
World Trans was formerly known as Collins.

Products
Mini- and midibus bodies and specialist conversions.

The Wright Group

Galgorm, Ballymena, Co Antrim, Northern Ireland, BT42 1PY, UK
Tel: (+44 28) 25 64 12 12   Fax: (+44 28) 25 64 97 03
e-mail: info@wright-bus.com
Web: www.wright-bus.com;
   www.wrightbus.com

Key personnel
Chairman: *Jeff Wright*
Group Managing Director: *Mark Nodder*
Finance Director: *James Nicholl*
Wrightbus Managing Director: *Lorraine Rock*
Managing Director, Hybrid Technology Partnership Programmes: *William Wright*
Hybrid Electric Vehicles Director: *Jonathan Poynton*
Customcare Director: *Geoff Potter*
Commercial Director: *Sam McLaren*
Product Development Director: *Damian McGarry*
   Staff: Not available currently

Background
The Wright Group is an independent, privately owned bus body builder, with more than 60 years' experience in passenger transit solutions. The group currently employs more than 1,000 people. The company supplies buses to both the home and global markets.

The Wright Group comprises four separate divisions: Wrightbus, Customcare, Expotech and Composites.

Wrightbus: Responsible for the design and production of bus bodywork within the UK. The company's plant at Ballymena produces between 20 and 25 buses per week, with a capacity for approximately 1,000 buses per year.

Customcare: Customcare is dedicated to the provision of aftermarket support for the Wrightbus and Expotech range, including spare parts, technical support, product training courses and specialised items such as cleaning materials and interior refurbishment kits. The division has a network of 25 aftersales locations in the UK.

Expotech: The range of Expotech products and services is as follows: Partial and completely knocked down kits for local assembly; transfer of technology and licensed build and industrial design and vehicle styling.

Products
Bus bodies.

Range
Currently, the Wright Group offers a range of product models, from 9 m to 18 m in length, on Volvo, Scania, MAN and VDL Bus chassis. The product range currently comprises:
Eclipse, Eclipse Gemini, School Run, Solar, Meridian, Pulsar, Pulsar Gemini, Gemini HEV (Hybrid-Electric Vehicle), **Electrocity, StreetCar** and **StreetCar RTV**.

Production
Wrightbus has an annual production capacity of some 1,000 vehicles.

Developments
Gemini 2 Hybrid: The first of a new generation of double-deck bus, the Gemini 2, that can be powered by both diesel and hybrid-electric drivelines was unveiled towards the end of 2008. The Gemini 2 HEV is the first of an order of five hybrid-electric powered double-deck buses which will enter service with Arriva in London, UK, in 2009, with five of nine Gemini 2 orders from FirstGroup also destined for hybrid-powered

Wrightbus Gemini 2 diesel-electric Hybrid Electric Vehicle (HEV) (Wrightbus Limited)   1374313

Wright Group StreetCar Rapid Transit Vehicle (RTV) (The Wright Group)   1374314

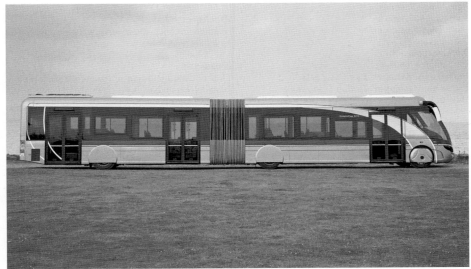
Wright Group StreetCar Rapid Transit Vehicle (RTV) (The Wright Group)   1374315

operation in the capital. The Wrightbus Gemini 2 has been developed as a modular concept, with the option of Euro 5/EEV Diesel (DL) and Hybrid Electric (HEV) power, whilst at the same time being fully compliant with both Transport for London (TfL) and provincial specifications.

Hybrid-powered buses are seen as an important way of further reducing emissions. With high oil prices now likely to be the norm, the potential fuel savings that can result from deployment of hybrid-powered vehicles means that the payback on the incremental capital cost is much quicker than was previously the case, making such vehicles a realistic economic proposition.

The HEV version of the Gemini 2 features Siemens ELFA® traction components, has energy provided by a Ford Puma 2.4 litre diesel engine. The diesel (DL) version of the Gemini 2 features a 6.7 litre Cummins engine, with both variants offering the choice of ZF or Voith automatic transmission driving through a Spicer rear axle. A key objective was to develop a weight-optimised vehicle to improve fuel economy. Wrightbus has also used its growing expertise and capability in Light Resin Transfer Moulding (LRTM) composite materials to extend the use of automotive quality panels on the new vehicle, enhancing fit and finish, as well as further reducing vehicle weight. Emission standards have been achieved without the need to fit a particulate trap, further reducing vehicle weight.

The resulting unladen weights of the new Gemini 2 are 12,271 kg and 12,075 kg respectively for the HEV and DL versions to TfL specification, with the provincial specification DL version having a tare weight of 11,200 kg (all weights stated are specification dependent).

Another major objective for the new bus has been to maximise seated passenger capacity, not just in the low-floor area (where the new vehicle has ten seats) but throughout the entire vehicle. Overall capacities are 87 (for HEV) and 91 (for DL) passengers in a two-door bus to the latest London specification and 96 for the Gemini 2 DL to provincial specification.

Integral to the development of a modular driveline approach has been a new flat radiator design which sits 1.5 m above ground, providing both improved engine cooling and quieter operation for passengers and other road users. The Wrightbus product development team has worked closely with chassis partner VDL on this and other aspects of chassis weight and layout optimisation.

Eclipse 2: The Eclipse 2 single-deck bus and the new Gemini 2 double-deck bus have been given a new look. The latest evolutionary design treatment retains the iconic Wrights windscreen shape, whilst incorporating styling revisions to the headlight/light cluster and bumper. The Eclipse 2 continues the partnership with the Volvo B7RLE chassis which now features the Euro 5/EEV compliant engine.

Alternative drivelines: As well as hybrid-electric technology, the Wright Group is also working as a key partner with San Diego-based ISE Corporation on a batch of ten vehicles due to be delivered to TfL by 2010, as part of the ongoing London Hydrogen Partnership. All ten of the new Wrightbus single-deck vehicles will be powered by an ISE hybrid-electric drive system, five of which will incorporate Ballard fuel cells, with the other five buses utilising a hydrogen internal combustion engine developed by Ford Power Products.

Hydrogen fuel cells produce energy by chemical reaction rather than combustion, oxidising hydrogen into water, with heat (electricity) and water vapour (steam) the only by-products of the process. The hydrogen is stored in pressurised cylinders in the roof of the vehicle. The power from the fuel cell or hydrogen engine is then delivered to the wheels by a series hybrid driveline. As there is no carbon in the fuel, hydrogen-powered vehicles produce no carbon monoxide, carbon dioxide or particulate emissions. They also have the additional benefit of being exceptionally quiet in operation.

Wrightbus Eclipse 2 single-deck vehicle with new styling (Wrightbus Limited)   1374316

Wrightbus Pulsar 2 single-deck bus (Wrightbus Limited)   1374318

Composites: Wright Composites, a wholly owned subsidiary of the Wright Group, was set up in 2005 as a specialist producer of fibre glass components, to secure the supply of vital components for the Wright Group. Continued growth in demand from both in-house and external customers has led to a further expansion of production capacity. It now has a 4,800 m² production facility, employing more than 125 people, in a building immediately adjacent to the Wrightbus factory at Galgorm.

Wright Composites is already supplying around 70 per cent of the production requirements at the Ballymena bus facility. As well as an immediate need to supply in-house production requirements, there is also a growing demand to supply OEM quality panels through the Wright Group's Customcare aftermarket organisation, for both Wrightbus and non-Wrightbus branded products.

Wright Composites is able to undertake the development of new fibreglass components, including the construction of moulds and tools for production. This was augmented in May 2008 by the introduction of LRTM (Light Resin Transfer Moulding) technology, which further improves surface finish quality and reduces wastage during the process.

Customcare

Customcare was established more than a decade ago to provide parts and service for Wrightbus products. It is today a major part of the Wright Group's operations. The division is responsible for all aspects of customer support, including front-line service in the field, technician training and technical advice, and specialised support for hybrid-electric vehicles. It also has a major accident repair facility to return damaged vehicles to an OEM-level of finish.

The division, which supports the growing number of Wright Group products in the UK, Ireland, Hong Kong, USA and the Netherlands, now boasts an extensive team. Customcare

can call upon 40 direct employees, including 14 mobile support engineers and four area service managers, as well as its integrated network of 25 Customcare Centres.

A number of national contracts for large bus groups are also in operation, not only for the supply of parts. Customcare signed a five-year contract maintenance agreement in 2008 with National Express for every aspect of the service and maintenance of five vehicles, with specially trained Customcare staff at the National Express depot in London, UK, checking every vehicle at four am (Monday to Friday) before they go out on daily operations.

StreetCar

A dedicated production line – the seventh line now in operation at the Ballymena production facility – is building the StreetCar. Eleven StreetCars went into service in York, UK, in May 2006.

Originally launched in 2005, it is a service designed to look like a tram, run on dedicated road space in congested areas but have the route flexibility of a bus.

Volvo has been a key partner in the process, developing bespoke chassis modules and components for StreetCar. Significant investments have been made, most notably in a new cooling pack, improved ride and suspension and a modified turntable.

StreetCar typically carries a maximum of 125 passengers, with the modular approach of the design allowing flexibility for operators to adapt seating layouts.

Two passenger entrances are standard, one behind the front wheels and one located in the rear section. The forward entrance, positioned behind the front axle, facilitates access for all passengers. A ramp for wheelchair users is available at the forward door, with the entrance layout designed so that priority seating and the wheelchair space are immediately accessible. Three- and four-door versions are also deliverable.

The fare system requires no driver involvement, greatly reducing dwell time at stops and significantly improving service times along the route. The advanced ticket vending equipment can be customised to manage a variety of fare transactions according to customer choice.

Once on board, StreetCar passengers have a range of options available to them with both conventional and perimeter seats, as well as a lounge-style area at the rear. A number of perches provide support throughout the length of the vehicle, whilst open standing areas can be utilised by people making short journeys.

LCD screens provide information to passengers throughout their journey and all the on-board telematics have been carefully developed to ensure that different systems such as CCTV, automatic vehicle location and passenger information can interact seamlessly.

The interior ambience is enhanced by concealed lighting, backed up by LED spotlights.

The driver is in a totally-enclosed full-width compartment, separated from passengers by a full-height partition with tinted glazing. The air-conditioned workstation is as spacious as that on a rail-bound vehicle, with the offset and elevated driving position giving a comprehensive field of vision.

Underneath the skin of the StreetCar is the Wright Group's patented Aluminique™ structure and a new design of cant rail extrusion allows the use of deep windows.

Contracts

A total of 50 StreetCar RTVs are being delivered during 2008/2009 to the Regional Transportation Commission (RTC) of Southern Nevada. The ACE Downtown Connector service will introduce a high-speed transit connection from downtown Las Vegas, through the resort corridor, serving both commuters and tourists who visit Las Vegas and the surrounding area. Each of the 18.7 m long StreetCar RTVs is powered by a hybrid-electric drive system developed in conjunction with the ISE Corporation and Siemens. With a modular driveline, the Siemens (ISE) Electric Hybrid Drive System includes a Cummins ISL engine, features water-cooled nickel metal hydride batteries, and also incorporates a Siemens permanent-magnet motor for the first time in transit buses.

Incorporating a Carrier Avantac all-electric, modular air conditioning system, Streetcar RTV features three double doors, a sealed driver's compartment, integrated telematics and Real Time Passenger Information (RTPI) and WiFi, as well as ambient lighting. Further innovations incorporated specifically for Las Vegas include two wheelchair positions, one of which is rearward facing in full compliance of US legislation, and three interior bike racks.

The safety and security of the StreetCar RTV's 104 passengers at maximum capacity (44 seated) is enhanced by a 'Panic' button, with live video feed from CCTV cameras capable of being relayed both back to its operational base as well as the local Police Department.

Wrightbus announced in 2008 that it had won a major order for a total of 268 vehicles from European transport operator Arriva. The order will see the vehicles delivered in 2009 to Arriva operations across the UK, with the bulk of the order being for Wrightbus Pulsar 2 single-deck buses, based on the VDL SB200 chassis. These vehicles, which will share the exterior Wrightbus product styling enhancements introduced recently, all feature Euro 5/EEV compliant engines and are specified with 44 seats.

New diesel-powered Euro 5/EEV compliant Wrightbus Gemini 2 (DL) double-deck buses are also included in the order, destined for service both with Arriva London, UK and also in its provincial operations.

Xiamen Golden Dragon Bus Co Ltd

No 69 Huli Street, Huli Area, Xiamen City 361006, People's Republic of China
Tel: (+86 592) 560 89 16   Fax: (+86 592) 560 89 79
e-mail: ied@xmjl.com
Web: www.goldendragonbus.com

Key personnel
General Manager: *Ye Hongting*
Hybrid Bus Programme Engineer: *George Dong*
Contact: *Ms Emily*
    Staff: 2,000 (estimate)

Current situation
Xiamen Golden Dragon Bus Co Ltd is a joint venture company established in 1992. The company develops, manufactures and sells medium- to large-sized buses under the trademark 'Golden Dragon'. Bus models are available from 5 to 12 m in length, with seating capacity from 5 to 65 seats.

Range
Light bus series
XML6601: Medium sized bus with CY4102BZLQ (Euro 2) diesel or JM495QF-E (Euro 2) petrol engine, length 5.99 m, width 2.050 m, height 2.680 m, seating 10 to 25.

XML6700: Medium sized bus with CY4102BZLQ (Euro 2) diesel, JM495QF-E (Euro 2) petrol or TD42T (Euro 2) diesel engine, length 6.970 m, width 2.050 m, height 2.680 m, seating 19 to 30.
XML6720: Medium sized bus with Cummins EQB125 20 engine, length 7.200 m, width 2.120 m, height 2.920 m, seating 23 to 27.

Commuter bus series
XML6101: YC6A240-20 (Euro 2) engine, length 1.0420 m, width 2.500 m, height 3.240 m, seating 24 to 57.
XML6121: Cummins ISBe250 30 (Euro 3), Cummins C220-20 (Euro 2) or YC6G300-20 (Euro 2) engine, length 11.985 m, width 2.540 m, height 3.292 m, seating 24 to 66.

City bus series
XML6840: Small to medium-sized buses, YC4G170-20 (Euro 2) MTM or Cummins ISBe180 30 (Euro 3), ATM engine, length 8.390 m, width 2.420 m, height 3.100 m, seating 10 to 29.
XML6112: YC6G240-20 (Euro 2), MTM or Cummins CKD C220-20 (Euro 2), MTM engine, length 11.480 m, width 2.480 m, height 3.100 m, seating 20 to 42.
XML6123: YC6G270-30 (Euro 2), ATM or ISBE 250 31, ATM engine, length 11.980 (12.000) m, width 2.500 m, height 3.250 m, seating 10 to 40.

Tourist coach series
The company produces a range of tourist coaches with lengths from 8 to 12 m.

Developments
Newly developed vehicles include the *XML6125* coach, seating 24 to 55, the *XML6115* bus, with a capacity of 80 passengers (incuding standees) and the *XML6745* bus, with a capacity of 30 passengers.

The company is developing right-hand drive vehicles for export.

In mid-2008, the company selected Maxwell Technologies Inc's BOOSTCAP® ultracapacitors for braking energy recuperation and torque assist for diesel-electric buses being produced for the Hangzhou Public Transport Group Co Ltd.

Also in mid-2008, the company signed a co-operation agreement with Korean Hyundai Motor Co for the supply of chassis and power systems.

Production
Production capacity is currently some 15,000 large and medium-sized buses per year.

Contracts
Golden Dragon exports to United Arab Emirates, Yemen, the Philippines, Saudi Arabia, Jordan, Ukraine, Russian Federation and Thailand.

Xi'an Silver Bus Corporation

Yanling Economic Development Zone, Xi-an, Shaanxi 710089, China
Tel: (+86 29) 87 44 56 78
Fax: (+86 29) 86 20 37 13
e-mail: qhb@xac.com.cn
Web: www.xac.com.cn

Key personnel
President: *Joost de Vries*

Background
Established in 1994, Xi'an Silver Bus Corporation is a joint venture between the Xi'an Aircraft Industry (Group) Company Limited and Volvo Bus Corporation.

Products
Volvo coaches, including the B10M and the Volvo 9300 commuter coach.

Developments
The company is carrying out redesign of certain vehicles and intends to introduce new product lines in the near future. Other developments include the introduction of service contracts, financial services and more workshops.

Contracts
Orders for some 150 Volvo 9300 commuter coaches have been received, including an order for 100 vehicles from Quick Deer.

Zhongwei Passenger Car Co Ltd

No 56 Tonhyu Zhing Road, Yancheng, Jiangsu, China
Tel: (+86 515) 833 38 88
Fax: (+86 515) 833 37 77
Web: www.zhongwei.net

Key personnel
Contact: *Xu Liankuan*
    Staff: Approximately 1,600

Background
Part of the Zhonda Group's Automotive Industry Department.

Current situation
Manufacturer of coaches and buses.

Range
Ten bus series, including high-deck coaches, with more than 30 variations. Seating capacities range from 16 to 49.

Production
Annual production capacity of the Zhonda Group is more than 5,000 vehicles.

ROAD VEHICLE CHASSIS COMPONENTS

Company listing by country

CANADA
Cummins Westport Inc (CWI)

CHINA
Weichai Power Co Ltd

GERMANY
Deutz AG
Voith Turbo GmbH & Co KG·
ZF Friedrichshafen AG

HUNGARY
Rába Automotive Holding Plc

ITALY
Fiat Powertrain Technologies (FPT)

JAPAN
Hino Motors Ltd
Isuzu Motors Limited

UNITED KINGDOM
Cummins Ltd (UK)
ThyssenKrupp Bilstein Woodhead Ltd

UNITED STATES
Allison Transmission
ArvinMeritor Inc
Caterpillar Inc
Cummins Inc
Dana Corporation
Detroit Diesel Corporation
Eaton Corporation

For details of the latest updates to *Jane's Urban Transport Systems* online and to discover the additional information available exclusively to online subscribers please visit
juts.janes.com

Allison Transmission

4700 West 100th Street, Indianapolis, Indiana
46222, US
Tel: (+1 317) 242 50 00   Fax: (+1 317) 242 36 26
Web: www.allisontransmission.com

Key personnel
President: *Lawrence E Dewey*
Director of Engineering: *Laurie Tuttle*
US Senior Marketing Manager: *Lou Gilbert*
US OEM Account Manager: *Tony Dinkel*
General Sales Director Worldwide: *Michael Headly*
Managing Director Allison Transmission Europe:
   Skip Clark

UK office
Allison Transmission
Allison House, 36 Duncan Close, Moulton Park,
Northampton, NN3 6WL, UK
Tel: (+44 1604) 49 54 96   Fax: (+44 1604) 49 51 10
Contact: *Claire Brack*
e-mail: claire.brack@europe.allison.gm.com

Background
Founded in 1915 and a part of GM since 1929,
Allison Transmission is a leading designer,
manufacturer and seller of medium- and heavy-
duty automatic transmissions for trucks, buses,
off-road and military vehicles.

Products
Automatic transmissions.

Range
Transmission models are available for bus and
coach applications. The range includes:

Allison B Series:
B Series transmission are designed to serve
a wide range of city and school bus and coach
applications. An integral output retarder can
be specified on certain models to assist vehicle
braking and extend brake life, especially when
operating on stop-go and hilly terrain routes.
   The Allison B Series is designed to match diesel
engines up to 367 kW input power and 2,067 Nm
input torque. The models are of six-speed design,
with the top two ratios as overdrives to optimise
fuel consumption. The combination of torque
converter and planetary gear design enables
vehicles to start without surging and provide
ratio shifting without power interruption.

Allison 2000 Series:
The Allison 2000 Series has been designed to
provide more torque capacity for higher-powered
diesels, within a lighter weight transmission. The
transmission's characteristics make it suitable for
city, shuttle and school bus applications.
   Gross torque of 630 Nm and gross power of
149 kW are available, for vehicles up to 12 tonnes.
Adaptive technology enables the transmission to
compensate for variations in driving conditions
such as passenger load, driver and traffic patterns.
Standard features on the 2000 Series include lock-
up operation in second to fifth range and helical
gearing for reduced transmission noise.

Allison hybrid electric transmission   0568311

Regeared Thamesdown Transport SLF Dart bus   0576727

Allison Transmission environmental policies
ensure that transmissions are over 98 per cent
recyclable.

Torqmatic®Series:
Fully automatic powershifting transmissions
suitable for bus and coach applications and for
engines up to 194 kW gross input power and up
to 895 Nm gross input torque.

Allison Electric Drives™ Eᴾ System™:
Hybrid electric drive system for buses and
coaches, giving reduced emissions and greater

fuel economy. Two models are available, the
Eᴾ 40, which is suitable for buses 11 to 12 m in
length, and the Eᴾ 50, which is appropriate for
18 m articulated buses.

Developments
In early 2006, the company won orders for a
total pf 3,435 fully automatic transmissions from
Beijing Public Transport Holdings Ltd.
   In mid-2006, Allison announced that Solaris
Bus & Coach and APTS will use its advanced
two-mode, diesel-electric GM Allison Hybrid
System.

ArvinMeritor Inc

2135 West Maple Road, Troy, Michigan 48084, USA
Tel: (+1 248) 435 10 00   Fax: (+1 248) 435 13 93
e-mail: contact.us@arvinmeritor.com
Web: www.arvinmeritor.com

Key personnel
Chairman and Chief Executive Officer: *Larry D
   Yost*
President and Chief Operating Officer: *Terry
   O'Rourke*
Senior Vice-President, Communications:
   Lin Cummins
Senior Director, Marketing Communications:
   Mike Pennington
Senior Vice-President and President, Light Vehicle
   Aftermarket: *Dan Daniel*

Senior Vice-President and President, Commercial
   Vehicle Systems: *Tom Gosnell*
Senior Vice-President and President, Light Vehicle
   Systems: *Craig Stinson*

Italy office
Strada Provinciale Cameri, Belin zago, Km5,
I-28060, Cameri, Novora, Italy

Works
In 56 international locations.

Background
ArvinMeritor Inc was created in July 2000 by
the merger of Meritor Automotive Inc and Arvin
Industries Inc.
   In July 2003 ArvinMeritor Inc announced
that it had commenced a tender offer for all

of the outstanding common shares of Dana
Corporation, but the bid was later dropped.

Products
Axles, brakes, automatic slack adjusters,
drivelines, clutches, anti-lock braking systems,
and air dryers.

Developments
In early 2003, the company opened a new
manufacturing facility in the Shanghai Free
Trade Zone, China to manufacture bus and coach
axles.
   In September 2004, the company announced
that it will make and supply driven and non-
driven axles for Volvo group's European truck
and bus products.

Caterpillar Inc

Power Systems Division
100 Northeast Adams Street, Peoria, Illinois
61629, US
Tel: (+1 309) 578 44 19   Fax: (+1 309) 578 72 76
e-mail: cat-power@cat.com
Web: www.cat.com, www.cattruckengines.com

Key personnel

Vice-President, Power Systems Marketing
Division: *James J Parker*
General Manager, Truck Engine Division: *James S McReynolds*
International Region Manager, On-Highway
Engines: *Michael Leyden*
Staff: 72,000

Works

Engine Products Division
PO Box 610, Mossville, Illinois 61552-6107, US

Principal subsidiary companies

Perkins Engine Company Ltd
MaK Motoren GmbH
F G Wilson (Engineering) Ltd
Solar Turbines Inc

Products

Diesel and natural gas engines.
   Diesel engines 3.7 to 15,000 kW (5 to 20,100 hp)
for traction, electric power generation and
maintenance-of-way equipment.
   Currently, parts are distributed through 26
Caterpillar distribution centres in 10 countries

and a worldwide network of 207 independent
dealers in 1,800 locations.
   In early 2003 the company announced new
on-highway truck and bus engines, equipped
with new ACERT™ technology. This technology
reduces emissions at the point of combustion.

Developments

In late 2004, the company announced that it
will off er a range of Euro 4 compliant engines
with ACERT™ technology for the European
on-highway truck and bus markets. The engines,
which include the C7, C9, C13 and C15 power
units, are in development.
   Caterpillar also plans to provide Euro 5
compliant engines in late 2008.

Cummins Inc

Corporate Headquarters
500 Jackson Street, Columbus, Indiana 47201, US
Tel: (+1 812) 377 50 00
Web: www.cummins.com

Key personnel

General Manager, Worldwide Bus Business:
Roe East
   Tel: (+1 812) 377 39 15
General Manager, Automotive Business,
   Europe/Central Area: *Neil Pattison*
   Tel: (+44 1325) 55 61 31

Europe/Central Area Operations

Cummins Engine Company Ltd
Yarm Road, Darlington, Co Durham, DL1 4PW,
UK
Tel: (+44 1325) 55 60 00
e-mail: cabo.customerassistance@cummins.com
Web: www.cummins.com

Global operations

Cummins manufactures automotive engines in
Brazil, China, India, North America and the UK.
Customer support is provided through a network
of 550 company-owned and independent
distributor facilities and more than 5,000 dealer
locations.

Products

Bus applications

Cummins is one of the world's largest suppliers
of diesel engines for urban transport vehicles,
with a power range extending from 130 to
450 hp (97 to 335 kW) covering Euro 2, Euro 3,
Euro 4 and EPA 2004 emission standards. Five
engine platforms are available, from a highly
compact 3.9 litre to a heavy-duty 11 litre offering
a complete range of installation options for
midibuses, transit buses, school buses, double-
deck buses and motor coaches.

Range

B Series 130 – 235 ps: 3.9 litre, four-cylinder and
5.9 litre, six-cylinder engines with mechanically
controlled fuel system for Euro 2 applications.
B Gas Plus 195 – 230 ps: 5.9 litre, six-cylinder
natural gas engine, designed for either
compressed (CNG) or liquefied (LNG) natural gas
vehicles and certified to Euro 3 standards.
ISB 185-275 hp: 5.9 litre, 24-valve electronically
controlled engine meeting EPA 2004 emission
standards with exhaust gas recirculation (EGR).
High pressure common rail contributes to very
low noise operation and high power density.
ISBe 135-170 ps: 3.9 litre, 16-valve and 5.9 litre,
24-valve engines for Euro 3 applications. Feature
high pressure common rail, rear gear drive
and full authority electronic controls with the
advantage of high power density.
ISBe Euro 4 140-185 hp: 4.5 litre, 16-valve engines
for Euro 4 applications. Feature new common
rail system, rear gear drive and new electronic
control module with the advantage of high
power density.

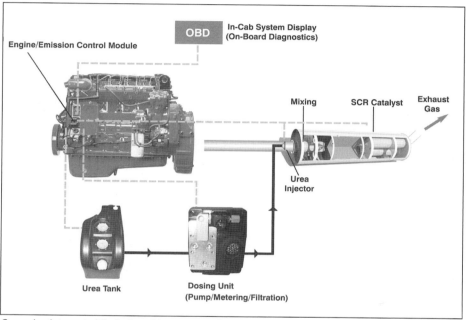

Cummins Integrated Emissions Management (IEM) system   1172721

Cummins ISBe Euro 4 4.5-litre, 140-185 ps diesel engine   1172720

ISBe Euro 4 205–300 hp: 6.7 litre, 24-valve engines for Euro 4 applications. Feature new common rail system, rear gear drive and new electronic control module with the advantage of high power density.

C Series 220–300 ps: 8.3 litre, six-cylinder, 12-valve with mechanically controlled fuel system for Euro 2 applications.

C Gas Plus 250–280 ps: 8.3 litre, six-cylinder Lean-Burn Spark-Ignited (LBSI) natural gas vehicle engine and certified with a catalyst to Euro 3 standards.

ISC 240–315 hp: 8.3 litre, 24-valve electronically controlled engine meeting EPA 2004 emission standards. Incorporates a new common rail fuel system providing high pressure injection regardless of engine speed across the rpm range.

ISL 250–330 hp: 9 litre, 24-valve electronically controlled engine meeting EPA 2004 emission standards. Features high pressure common rail, variable geometry turbocharging and heavy-duty articulated pistons for premium performance.

ISLe Plus 280-350 ps: 9 litre, 24-valve electronically controlled engine for Euro 3 applications. Latest common rail fuel system offers reduced

noise and highly refined power delivery. High strength components ensure long operational life.

ISLe Euro 4 280-380 hp: 8.9 litre. 24-valve electronically controlled engine for Euro 4 applications. Latest common rail fuel system offers reduced noise and highly refined power delivery. High strength components ensure long operational life.

ISM 280-450 hp: 11 litre, 24-valve electronically controlled engine meeting EPA 2004 emission standards with exhaust gas recirculation and variable geometry turbocharging. Provides heavy duty performance and durability.

ISMe 335-420 ps: 11 litre, 24-valve electronically controlled engine for Euro 2 and Euro 3 applications. Compact, lightweight design offers high levels of fuel-efficiency and high torque output across the rpm range.

Contracts

The Chicago Transit Authority (CTA) has placed an order for 265 ISM-powered New Flyer buses 2005. The Toronto Transit Commission (TTC) has placed an order for 180 ISL-powered Orion buses with ISB hybrid power.

Research and development

Cummins has recently launched a Euro 4 version of the ISBe engine with SCR (Selective Catalytic Reduction) after-treatment technology. Both power and torque are significantly increased, giving the latest six-cylinder 300 ps, 1100 Nm ISBe the highest power-to-weight ratio in its class. To meet EPA 2007 emission standards in North America, the product range will utilise EGR (exhaust gas recirculation), combined with a Cummins particulate filter after-treatment. Cummins capability to design and manufacture the engine and after-teatment as a fully integrated system, offers significant packaging and performance benefits.

Cummins Westport Inc is a leading supplier of natural gas engines for urban bus installations. The B Gas Plus, C Gas Plus and L Gas Plus platforms have proved an ideal solution in both North America and Europe. In the rapidly developing markets of China and India, Cummins Westport Inc powers the world's largest city fleets of natural gas buses. Looking ahead, the company is undertaking development work on Hydrogen Compressed Natural Gas (HCNG) engines.

Cummins Ltd (UK)

Yarm Road, Darlington, Co Durham, DL1 4PW, UK
Tel: (+44 13 25) 55 48 28
Fax: (+44 13 25) 35 93 80
e-mail: cabo.customerassistance@cummins.com
Web: www.everytime.cummins.com

Key personnel

Director, On Highway Engine Business
(EMEA + CIS): *Neil Pattison*

Production plants

Darlington, UK

Reconditioning plant

Diesel ReCon, Cumbernauld, Scotland

Background

A subsidiary of Cummins Engine Company Inc (US).

Products

Diesel and natural gas engines.

Range

100-600 hp engines.
Latest Euro 2, 3, 4 and 5 products:
ISBᵉ: 4.5 Specifications: Interact System 4.5 litre, 140-185 ps, 550–760 Nm.
ISBᵉ: 6.7 Specifications: Interact System 6.7 litre, 205-300 ps, 750–1100 Nm.
ISLᵉ: 8.9 Specifications: Interact System 8.9 litre, 280-400 ps, 1,060–1,700 Nm.
InSite™: Interactive diagnostics and servicing software, compatible with Windows™ operating

systems and available in two versions, *InSite Lite* and *InSite Pro*.
Other emissions products:
ISMᵉ: 11 litre heavy-duty engine re-engineered to meet Euro 2 and 3 requirements. Specifications: Interact System 11 litre, 305 – 420 ps, 1,410 – 2,010 Nm.
InSite™: Interactive diagnostics and servicing software, compatible with Windows™ operating systems and available in two versions, *InSite Lite* and *InSite Pro*.
QuickCheck™ 5100: Electronic datalink tool for Palm™ hand-held organisers for real-time viewing of engine, transmission and ABS data.
Other products:
EPA 99 – 07 versions of ISB, ISC, ISL, ISM, and ISX engines. Further details of these products can be found at the company's website (see above).

Cummins Westport Inc (CWI)

101-1750 West 75th Avenue, Vancouver, British Columbia, V6P 6G2, Canada
Tel: (+1 604) 718 81 00   Fax: (+1 604) 718 20 01
e-mail: info@cumminswestport.com
    sales@cumminswestport.com
Web: www.cumminswestport.com

Key personnel

President: *Guan Saw*

Background

Cummins Westport Inc is a 50:50 Joint Venture (JV) between Cummins Inc and Westport Innovations Inc. The company was formed in 2001 to develop and market low-emissions high-performance natural gas and propane-powered engines.

Products

CWI sells natural gas and liquid propane engines (5.9 litres and 8.9 litres), which are manufactured by Cummins Inc and sold via the Cummins distributor channel worldwide. The company produces economical natural gas engines to meet the growing demand for lower-emissions power worldwide. Key markets are transit, refuse and medium duty trucks.

Range

B Gas Plus: Natural gas engine range suitable for transit/school and shuttle bus applications.
C Gas Plus: Range of natural gas engines suitable for transit/school and shuttle buses.
B5.9G/LPG: Natural gas/liquid propane gas engine series, for medium-duty, transit/school and shuttle buses.

ISL G: An 8.9 litre engine suitable for transit, refuse, vocational truck & other medium and heavy duty applications.

Contracts

In April 2008, the company announced that the San Diego Metropolitan Transit System (San Diego MTS) had ordered 250 CWI ISL G engines, to be installed in New Flyer 40-ft, low-floor vehicles.

In September 2008, CWI received an order for more than 200 CWI natural gas engines to equip new buses for transit providers in Lima, Peru.

In October 2008, CWI and Cummins India Ltd (CIL) announced that the Delhi Transport Corporation (DTC) had ordered 3,125 natural gas buses equipped with B Gas Plus engines.

Dana Corporation

Corporate Communications
PO Box 1000, Toledo, Ohio 43697, US
Tel: (+1 419) 535 45 00   Fax: (+1 419) 535 46 43
Web: www.dana.com

Street address

4500 Dorr Street, Toledo, OH 43615, US

Key personnel

Chairman, President and Chief Executive Officer: *Mike J Burns*
President, Automotive Systems Group: *James M Laisure*
President, Technology Development and Diversified Products: *Charles F Heine*
Vice-President and Chief Financial Officer: *Robert C Richter*

Vice-President and Chief Information Officer: *Bruce C Carver*
Vice-President, Corporate Communications: *Gary Corrigan*
Tel: (+1 419) 535 48 13
e-mail: gary.corrigan@dana.com
Manager, Marketing Communications: *Jeff Cole*
Tel: (+1 419) 535 47 04
e-mail: jeff.cole@dana.com
Staff: More than 46,000 worldwide

Background

The Dana Corporation was formed in 1904. The company has facilities in 28 countries.

Products

The companies core products are: driveshafts and axles, vehicle architecture, brakes and

chassis, thermal and fluid management systems, bearings and seals.

Contracts

Major customers include: AGCO, BMW, Caterpillar, DaimlerChrysler, Ford, GM, International Truck and Engine, Manitou, PACCAR, PSA Peugeot Citroën, Renault-Nissan, Tamrock, Toyota, VW and the Volvo Group.

Developments

In early 2005, the corporation signed an agreement with the Dongfeng Motor Co Ltd to form a 50/50 joint-venture company to develop and produce commercial axles in China. The company will be named Dongfeng Dana Axle Co Ltd.

Detroit Diesel Corporation

13400 Outer Drive, West Detroit, Michigan 48239-4001, USA
Tel: (+1 313) 592 50 00; 59 90
Fax: (+1 313) 592 58 87
Web: www.detroitdiesel.com

Key personnel
Director of Marketing: *David Siler*
  Staff: 2,000 (approximate)

Background
Since 2000, Detroit Diesel has been a subsidiary of Daimler AG, and is the Daimler Truck Group and an affiliate of Freightliner LLC.

The company has a worldwide service network of more than 800 outlets in North America.

The company is certified to ISO 9001:2001 standards.

Products
Diesel and alternative fuel engines, for coach and bus.

Range
Detroit Diesel engines for coach and bus applications are available as standard or optional power. Detroit Diesel electronically controlled engines feature high performance, and superior fuel economy. Options include driver management programmes, electronic diagnostic analysis and engine performance data storage. School Bus Thomas Built buses use the MBE 900 engine Detroit Diesel engine.

Deutz AG

Deutz-Mülheimer Strasse, D-51063 Cologne, Germany
Tel: (+49 221) 82 20
  (+49 221) 822 24 91
  (Corporate Communications)
Fax: (+49 221) 822 35 25
  (+49 221) 822 21 16
  (Corporate Comunications)
e-mail: info@deutz.de
Web: www.deutz.de

Key personnel
Management Board:
  Chief Executive Officer: *Gordon Riske*
    Technology: Karl Huebser
  Finance and Human Resources: *Helmut Meyer*
  Corporate Communications and Marketing: *Georg Diderich*

Products
Range of air-cooled and water-cooled diesel engines, including the 2013 series of commercial vehicle engines.

Contracts
As a result of a co-operation agreement with Volvo, Deutz has become Volvo's main supplier of small and mid-sized diesel engines.

In 2003, Deutz obtained a contract from Otokar, Turkey, to supply engines for the latter's new range of midi-and minibuses.

Eaton Corporation

Truck Group
PO Box 4013, Kalamazoo, MI 49003, US
Tel: (+1 800) 826 43 57
Web: www.eaton.com

Corporate Headquarters
Eaton Centre, 1111 Superior Avenue, Cleveland, Ohio 44114-2584, US
Tel: (+1 216) 523 50 00
Web: www.eaton.com

Key personnel
Chairman, Chief Executive Officer and President: *Alexander M Cutler*
Executive Vice-President and Chief Financial and Planning Officer: *Richard H Fearon*
Chief Executive Officer, Truck Group: *James E Sweetnam*
  Staff: 79,000 (Corporate worldwide total)

Current situation
Manufacturer of hybrid powertrain systems suitable for buses.

Contracts
In April 2008, the company announced that it had reached an agreement with Guangzhou Armada Development Corporation and Guangzhou Yiqi Bus Co Ltd for the Purchase of 207 diesel-electric hybrid power systems to be installed in new buses for operation in the city of Guangzhou. The value of the contract was not disclosed.

Fiat Powertrain Technologies (FPT)

Headquarters
Strada Torino 50, I-10043 Orbassano (TO), Italy
Tel: (+39 011) 003 13 47   Fax: (+39 011) 003 86 55
e-mail: sales-pc@fptpowertrain.com
Web: www.fptpowertrain.com

Key personnel
Chief Executive Officer: *A Altavilla*
Manager, Sales & Marketing, Passenger and Commercial Vehicles: *G Bartoli*
Manager, Powertrain Research & Development: *R Rinolfi*

Background
Created in 2005, Fiat Powertrain Technologies (FPT) includes all of the powertrain activities of the Fiat Group, including Iveco Motors.

Products
Petrol/gasoline, diesel and alternative fuel engines and transmissions for passenger and commercial vehicles.

Production
FPT has an annual production of some 2.5 million engines and 2 million transmissions.

Contracts
In April 2006, FPT signed an agreement with Beijing Public Transport Company for the supply of 1,000 natural gas-powered engines. The engines will be used in buses manufactured in China.

Research and Development
Powertrain Research & Technology focuses on the development and application of innovative technologies for the improvement of the powertrain performance and for the reduction of engine and vehicle emissions and fuel consumption. The majority of these technologies are based on the integration of mechanical and/or electro-hydraulic actuation systems, with advanced electronics with aim to control the combustion process, the exhaust gas after-treatment system and the power transmission systems. With regard to the new emerging powertrain technologies, efforts are concentrated on the development of cost-effective hybrid propulsion systems using conventional fuels and tailored for urban transportation. Development is also focused on the Hydrogen Fuel Cell propulsion systems.

Hino Motors Ltd

1-1 Hinodai 3-chome, Hino, Tokyo 191-8660, Japan
Tel: (+81 3) 54 19 93 20   Fax: (+81 3) 54 19 93 63
Web: www.hino.co.jp

Key personnel
Chairman: *Tadaaki Jagawa*
President: *Shoji Kondo*
Deputy General Manager, Corporate Communications: *Toru Matsui*
  Staff: 9,030

Other offices
Tamachi Office (Overseas Operations), Corporate Communications Department
  11-3 Shiba 4-chome, Minato-ku, Tokyo 108-0014, Japan
  Tel/Fax: as above

Hino has overseas affiliates and offices in Australia, Canada, China, Indonesia, Malaysia, Pakistan, the Philippines, Taiwan, Thailand, Vietnam and the US. Contact details are available on the company web site.

Works
The company has plants at Hino, Humura and Nitta, and proving grounds at Gozenyama, Hamura and Memuro.

Background
Hino Motors is the commercial vehicle specialist associate of the Toyota Group.

Products
Diesel engines, 77–382 kW (105–520 bhp).

Isuzu Motors Limited

For information on Isuzu engines, please see main entry in the Buses – Chassis, Integrals and Bodies section.

Rába Automotive Holding Plc

Rába Axle Ltd
PO Box 141, H-9002 Győr, Budia u. 1, Hungary
Tel: (+36 96) 62 26 00
Fax: (+36 96) 62 49 09
e-mail: futomu@raba.hu
Web: www.raba.hu

Street address
Martin u 1, H-9027 Győr, Hungary

Key personnel
Chief Executive Officer and Managing Director,
Rába Axle Ltd: *István Pintér*
Director of Purchasing and Asset Management:
József Szabó

Chief Financial Officer and Director of Finance,
Rába Axle Ltd: *Béla Balog*

Products
Axles, suspension elements and steering systems
for bus and trolleybus.
Please also see the entry in Bus – Chassis,
Integrals and Bodies section.

ThyssenKrupp Bilstein Woodhead Ltd

177 Kirkstall Road, Leeds LS4 2AQ, UK
Tel: (+44 113) 244 12 02   Fax: (+44 113) 242 03 87
Web: www.thyssenkrupp-automotive.de

Key personnel
Managing Director: *J A Sandground*

Background
The company is a subsidiary of Thyssen Krupp
Automotive, Bochum, Germany.

Products
Vehicle suspension coil springs.

Range
Previously known as Krupp Hoesch Woodhead
Ltd, ThyssenKrupp Bilstein Woodhead Ltd
manufactures coil springs.

Voith Turbo GmbH & Co KG

Alexanderstrasse   2,   D-89522   Heidenheim,
Germany
Tel: (+49 7321) 37 28 62
Fax: (+49 7321) 37 71 10
e-mail: info-turbo@voith.com
Web: www.voith.com
    www.voithturbo.com

Key personnel
President and Chief Executive Officer: *Peter
Edelmann*
Marketing: *Marion Joos*
    Tel: (+49 7321) 37 28 32

Subsidiaries
Voith Turbo Ltd
6 Beddington Farm Road, Croydon, CR0 4XB, UK
Tel: (+44 20) 86 67 03 33
Fax: (+44 20) 86 67 04 03
e-mail: turbo.uk@voith.com
Web: www.uk.voithturbo.com
Managing Director: *R Jarvis*
Sales & Marketing Manager: *John Domigan*
After Sales Executive: *D Holdsworth*

Background
Voith has been in business since 1869, and
subsidiary company Voith Turbo Ltd (previously
Voith Engineering Ltd and renamed in
September 2002), has been established in the
UK since 1962.

Products
Automatic transmissions for urban and suburban
buses; torsional vibration dampers.
    DIWA: Since 1932, Voith has pioneered
hydrodynamic transmissions for vehicles and
stationary units. Automatic transmissions in
buses were first used in Berlin in 1953.

Range
DIWA: This has been improved without altering
the basic concept of hydrodynamics and
mechanics. The main improvements are:
1. A new control system that improves the gear
   shifting quality in such a way that makes gear
   changes almost undetectable.
2. Economic operation is possible by selecting
   special gear shifting programmes.
3. A gradient programme measures acceleration
   and load conditions of the vehicle and then
   selects the best gear shifting point.

4. A new control system memorises data and
   transmits it via an interface for diagnostic and
   other purposes.

Developments
The Voith PGS gearshifting system has been
introduced to allow low manual effort and precise
gear changes. It is cable-actuated, with either one
or two cables and is suited to high-floor vehicles
where rod linkages would be difficult to install.
    An electric drive system for buses, called ELVO
Drive, features Transverse Flux Machines (TFMs),
inverters, induction motors and electronic system
control. Two versions are available:
1. Central motor version: A TFM generator
   mounted on the diesel engine powers two
   traction motors via inverters. The motors are
   coupled together through a gearbox and drive
   a standard low-floor axle through a cardan
   shaft.
2. Electric drive axle system: A TFM generator
   powers two traction motors via inverters.
   The motors are fitted into electric low-floor
   axles. Each road wheel is driven by a separate
   motor, each linked electronically. With this
   set-up, independent suspension can be fitted.

Weichai Power Co Ltd

26 Minsheng Road, Weifang City, 261001,
Shandong Province, China
Tel: (+86 536) 819 77 77   Fax: (+86 536) 823 10 74
e-mail: weichai@weichai.com
Web: www.weichai.com

Key personnel
Chairman and Chief Executive Officer: *Tan
Xuguang*
Executive Director and General Manager,
Operations: *Xu Xinyu*
General Manager, Manufacturing: *Xu Hong*
General Manager and Deputy General Manager,
Marketing: *Zhong Geng Hui*

Deputy General Manager, Weichai Diesel Engine
Works: *Liu Huisheng*
Executive Director and General Manager,
Technology: *Sun Shaojun*
Deputy General Manager, Technology: *Tong
Dehui*
Director of Finance: *Wu Hongwei*
Director of Human Resources: *Ding Yingdong*
Director, Information Management: *Han Lisheng*
Executive Director and General Manager,
Marketing: *Zhang Quan*
Deputy General Manager, Marketing: *Feng Gang*
Chief Financial Officer and Company Secretary:
Zhang Yuanfu

Other office
Suite 2501-2, 25th Floor, One International
Finance centre, 1 Harbour View Street Central,
Hong Kong, China

Products
Manufacturer of diesel engines.

Range
Diesel engines for buses:
Landking WP10 series Euro-III diesel engine;
WD615 bus engine;
TBD226B bus engine;
WT615/226B series CNG/LPG bus engine.

ZF Friedrichshafen AG

Corporate Headquarters, D-88038 Friedrichshafen,
Germany
Tel: (+49 7541) 77 0
Fax: (+49 7541) 77 90 80 00
e-mail: postoffice@zf.com
Web: www.zf.com

Street address
Graf-von-Soden-Platz 1, D-88046 Friedrichshafen,
Germany

Key personnel
Chief Executive Officer: *Siegfried Goll*
Executive Vice-President, Finance, Controlling
and Information Technology: *Willi Berchtold*
Executive Vice-President, Human Resources and
Service Companies: *Uwe Berner*
Executive   Vice-President,   Car   Driveline
Technology Division: *Michael Paul*
Executive Vice-President, Commercial vehicle
and Special Driveline Technology Division:
Wolfgang Vogel

Board   Members: *Reinhard   Buhl,   Manfred
Schwab, Hans-Georg Härter*
Senior Sales Manager: *Herbert Demel*
Business Development and Marketing: *Christoph
Ehrendeich*
Technical Press Contact: *Klaus Hader*

Other companies
ZF Passau GmbH
D-94030 Passau, Germany
Tel: (+49 851) 494 22 04   Fax: (+49 851) 494 21 91
Marketing Manager: *J Weidemann*

ZF Bahntechnik GmbH
D-88046 Friedrichshafen, Germany
Tel: (+49 7541) 306 01
Fax: (+49 7541) 30 64 00
Sales Manager: *M C Cleobury*
ZF Great Britain Ltd
Abbeyfield Rd, Lenton, Nottingham NG7 2SX, UK
Tel: (+44 115) 986 92 11
Fax (+44 115) 986 92 61
Marketing Manager: *G A Buck*

Background

In 1995, ZF Hurth Bahntechnik was formed, combining the rail business of ZF AG and Hurth Antriebstechnik. The following year, ZF Friedrichshafen's commercial vehicle transmissions division was re-organised, a specialist Bus Group and Truck Group being established.

Shareholders include Zeppelin Foundation, Friedrichshafen, Germany (93.8 per cent); Dr Jürgen Ulderup Foundation, Lemförder, Germany (6.2 per cent).

Products

Gearboxes, axles, final drives, steering gear, and suspension components for city buses, tourist coaches, midi- and minibuses, trams, LRVs and metros.

For information on company activities in other areas, please see entries in *Jane's Urban Transport Systems* and *Jane's World Railways* and other Jane's titles.

Range

Manual: 5-, 6- and 8-speed synchromesh gearboxes with option of **ZF Intarder** (secondary retarder).

Automatic: 4-, 5-, and 6-speed **ZF Ecomat** torque convertor/epicyclic gearbox for buses, coaches, and rail applications. Available in in-line or angle drive variants, and with integral primary retarder. New variant **ZF Ecomat 2** suitable for vehicles with EDC and CANBUS electrical systems.

Ten-speed **ZF AS Tronic** automatic layshaft gearbox for bus and coach applications with engines with EDC (electronic diesel control).

Rear axles: Conventional and low-floor portal axles available with special low-noise gearing for bus and coach applications, and angled input options for transverse rear engine layouts.

Rail drives: Drive units for metro, tram and regional dmu/emu systems.

Steering gear: ZF Servocom power steering systems for buses with axle loads up to 10 tonnes. Electronically controlled rear axle steering systems (**ZF RAS-EC**) for three-axle city buses and coaches.

ZF introduced the **10AS 201 AS Tronic** in 1999. This 10-speed transmission has been specifically developed for the new generation of high-performance luxury coaches with engines producing up to 2,300 N m of torque.

ZF has developed its third generation of drop-centre axles for low-floor buses, the **AV 132**. An essential objective of ZF's development work for the AV 132 was to achieve a reduction in the variety of parts and noise levels in order to improve passenger comfort. The slim axle housing, with laterally offset axle drive (drive angle: 80°, 87° or 90°) and differential, is connected on its left and right side to a portal drive. The portal drives are designed as power-split spur gears and represent the dynamic core of the axle. As a result of the splitting, the high torques required can be transmitted in spite of the limited portal distance.

To enable a low floor to be achieved throughout the length of the bus, ZF can now provide modern low-floor components and systems for the front axle. Depending on the customer's wishes, independent suspensions or systems with rigid beam axles can be used. The **RL 85A** is a complete system for axle loads up to 8.5 tonnes. Its robustness is highlighted by ZF as well as ease of maintenance and its kinematics contribute to ride comfort. The RL 85A front axle also combines well with the ZF-RAS EC steering system to produce an actively steered third axle to aid tight manoeuvring.

The six-speed *Ecomat 6HP592* automatic transmission was introduced in 2001. This follows the successful introduction of ZF's four- and five-speed Ecomat transmissions. A new range of lightweight axle systems and chassis components for low-floor midibuses has been introduced, offering substantial weight savings.

SIGNALLING, COMMUNICATIONS AND TRAFFIC CONTROL EQUIPMENT

Company listing by country

AUSTRALIA
Trackside Intelligence Pty Ltd

AUSTRIA
Ing Karl und Albert Kruch GesmbH & Co kg (Kruch)
VAEE

BELGIUM
Zenitel NV

CANADA
International Road Dynamics Inc (IRD)
BelAir Networks
Infodev EDI Inc
VerifEye Technologies Inc

CZECH REPUBLIC
UniControls AS

FINLAND
Nokia

FRANCE
Alcatel-Lucent
ALSTOM Transport
AREVA TA
Balogh-Frid
Capsys SA
EBO Systems
Fels SA
Gorgy Timing SA
Hypertac
INEO Systrans
Lumiplan Technologies de Communication
SCLE SFE
STERIA Group
Thales Rail Signalling

GERMANY
EADS Telecom Deutschland GmbH
Pepperl + Fuchs GmbH
Atron Electronic GmbH
BBR Verkehrstechnik GmbH
Dambach-Werke GmbH
Hanning & Kahl GmbH & Co KG
Hypercom Corporation
INIT Innovative Informatikanwendungen in Transport-, Verkehrs- und Leitsystemen GmbH

Nortel Networks Germany GmbH & Co
Pintsch Bamag Antriebs- und Verkehrstechnik GmbH
Siemens AG

HUNGARY
Ganz Škoda Traction Electrics Ltd

INDIA
Crompton Greaves Ltd
Stesalit Limited
Westinghouse Saxby Farmer Limited

IRELAND
Data Display Co Ltd

ITALY
SELEX Communications-OTE SpA
Aesys SpA
Ansaldo STS
Eurotech SpA
Ingegneria dei Sistemi Elettronici srl (ISE)
Italtel SpA

JAPAN
Hitachi Kokusai Electric Inc
Hitachi Ltd
Kyosan Electric Mfg Co Ltd
Morio Denki Co Ltd
Nippon Signal Co Ltd

NETHERLANDS
Peek Traffic BV
Vialis NMA
Vialis Verkeer & Mobiliteit bv

PORTUGAL
EFACEC Sistemas de Electrónica SA

SPAIN
Telvent GITS SA (Telecom Ventures)
Dimetronic SA

SWEDEN
Alcad Limited
Bombardier Transportation
Mobitec AB
TagMaster AB

Thoreb AB
Trivector System AB

SWITZERLAND
Hasler Rail AG
Siemens Switzerland

UNITED KINGDOM
DaimlerChrysler Services FleetBoard UK Limited
Brand-Rex Ltd
Chloride Power Protection
Craig and Derricott Ltd
GAI-Tronics
GrantRail Projects
GrantRail Signalling Ltd
Howells Railway Products Limited
Marl International Ltd
Minorplanet Systems plc
Mirror Technology Ltd
  on365
Poletech Systems Ltd
Powernetics International Ltd
Regional Services Ltd (RSL)
Thales Telecom Services
Transmitton – A Siemens Business
Westinghouse Rail Systems Ltd

UNITED STATES
Quixote Transportation Technologies
Verint Systems Inc
3M Intelligent Transport Systems
ARINC Inc
Casey Systems Inc
DRI Corporation
Fleet Management Solutions Inc (FMS)
Global Traffic Technologies LLC
Globe Transportation Graphics
Integrian, Inc
Iteris
Optelecom-NFK, Inc
Orbital Sciences Corporation
Safetran Systems Corporation
Specialty Bulb Co Inc
Telephonics Corporation
TransCore
Tyco Electronics Wireless Systems
Vecom USA, LLC
Wabtec Railway Electronics

3M Intelligent Transport Systems

3M Center, Building 0225-05-S-08, St Paul, Minnesota 55144-1000, US
Tel: (+1 651) 575 55 32, 733 38 79
Fax: (+1 651) 733 25 74, 737 10 55
Web: www.3M.com/ITS

Key personnel
Executive Vice-President, Industrial and Transportation Business: *H C Shin*

Products
Bus guidance systems. 3M is developing a magnetic level indication system to help drivers with precise docking and manoeuvring situations as well as low- and high-speed guidance along dedicated rapid transit bus lanes.

The system under development consists of magnetic lateral warning and guidance tape installed on the road and an onboard sensor and display mounted in the vehicle. Once the sensor detects the magnetic tape, the lane location is displayed to the operator allowing the bus to be brought tight against the kerb. Future development will allow onboard mechanics to take over bus control to facilitate precision docking or to guide the bus along a dedicated rapid transit route.

It was first used for snowplough guidance in Minnesota.

Aesys SpA

Via Pastrengo 7c, I-24068 Seriate (BG), Italy
Tel: (+39 035) 292 40   Fax: (+39 035) 68 00 30
e-mail: info@aesys.it
Web: www.aesys.it

Key personnel
General Manager: *Dr Marcello Biava*
Assistant to General Manager: *Giuseppe Biava*
Export Sales: *Michele Ganz*

Products
Electronic LED bus destination signs; passenger information systems; information displays at bus stops; vehicle control systems; variable message signs.

Alcad Limited

Norra Strandgatan 35, Box 504, S-572 25 Oskarshamn, Sweden
Tel: (+46 491) 681 00   Fax: (+46 491) 681 10
Web: www.alcad.com

Key personnel
Contact: *Trevor Maddocks*

Other offices
Sales Offices
1st Floor, Unit 5 Astra Centre, Edinburgh Way, Harlow CM20 2BN, UK
Tel: (+44 1279) 77 25 55   Fax: (+44 1279) 42 06 96
Alcad Batteries ME
PO Box 57180, 3313 Limassol, Cyprus
Tel: (+357 25) 87 18 16   Fax: (+357 25) 34 35 42
54, Genting Lane, #03-02 Ruby Land Complex Block II, Singapore 349562
Tel: (+65) 67 48 44 86   Fax: (+65) 67 48 46 39
Alcad Inc
3 Powdered Metals Drive, North Haven, Connecticut 06473, US
Tel: (+1 203) 985 25 00   Fax: (+1 203) 985 25 39

Products
Products include the Vantage and XHP battery ranges, to meet peak electricity demand or provide back-up power for essential services in rail infrastructure applications such as signalling, switching, points and barrier control/operations.

Also suited to applications in substations, Alcad XHP batteries feature sintered positive electrode and a compact plastic bonded negative electrode (pbe) to offer a combination of low maintenance and high performance to provide reliable power back-up in rail infrastructure applications including UPS and switchgear.

Alcatel-Lucent

Alcatel Transport Automation Solutions
10 rue Latécoère, Vélizy F-78141, France
Tel: (+33 1) 30 77 17 30
Fax: (+33 1) 30 77 12 68
Web: www.alcatel-lucent.com/tas

Key personnel
President: *Jean-Pierre Forestier*
Vice-President, Business Development Main Lines: *Robert Mattenberger*
Vice-President, Business Development Urban Rail: *John D Mills*
Director, Communication: *Bénédicte Massin*

Subsidiaries
Alcatel TAS Austria
Scheydgasse 41, A-1210 Vienna
Tel: (+43 127) 722 57 79   Fax: (+43 127) 722 36 24
Managing Director: *Alfred Veider*
Communication Manager: *Christian Studnicka*

Alcatel TAS Canada
1235 Ormont Drive, Weston, Ontario, M9L 2W6
Tel: (+1 416) 742 39 00   Fax: (+1 416) 742 11 36
Managing Director: *Walter Friesen*
Communication Manager: *Roger Fradgley*

Alcatel TAS China
32F Times Square, 500 Zhangyang Road, Pu Dong 200122 Shanghai
Tel: (+ 86 21) 68 60 45 45 11 90
Fax: (+ 86 21) 58 36 83 00
Managing Director: *Guy Sellier*

Alcatel TAS France
1 rue Ampère, Massy, PO Box 56, F-91302, France
Tel: (+33 1) 69 76 90 02   Fax: (+33 1) 69 76 90 01
Managing Director: *Gérard Avice*

Alcatel TAS Germany
Holderaeckerstrasse 10, D-70499 Stuttgart
Tel: (+49 711) 82 14 65 00
Fax: (+49 711) 82 14 67 19
Managing Director: *Hans Leibbrand*
Communication Manager: *Hans-Jürgen Krehle*

Alcatel TAS Portugal
Estrada Malveira da Serra 955, P-2750-782 Cascais
Tel: (+351 21) 485 91 52   Fax: (+351 21) 485 91 12
Managing Director: *Joao Araujo*
Communication Manager: *Joao Salgueiro*

Alcatel TAS Spain
5 Ramirez de Prado, E-28045 Madrid
Tel: (+34 91) 330 95 70   Fax: (+34 91) 330 95 76
Managing Director: *Anastasio Gallego*
Communication Manager: *Ramon Mayorga*

Alcatel TAS Switzerland
Friesenbergstrasse 75, CH-8055 Zürich
Tel: (+41 1) 465 35 00   Fax: (+41 1) 465 23 19
Managing Director: *Franz Stampfli*

Alcatel TAS UK
2N140 Christchurch Way, Greenwich, London SE10 0AG
Tel: (+44 20) 84 65 12 11   Fax: (+44 20) 84 65 14 51
Managing Director: *John D Mills*

Alcatel TAS USA
5700 Corporate Drive, Suite 300, Pittsburgh, Pennsylvania 15237
Tel: (+1 412) 366 88 14   Fax: (+1 412) 366 88 17
Managing Director: *John Brohm*

Background
Alcatel Transport Automation Solutions (TAS) employs 2,750 people and has main offices in Austria, Canada, China, France, Germany, Portugal, Spain, Switzerland, UK and US.

In December 2006 Alcatel announced its new brand name as Alcatel-Lucent following its merger with the US company Lucent Technologies.

Products
Alcatel offers a host of proven main line railway and urban transit solutions to move people safely through the network in a comfortable, reliable and cost-effective way. Drawing on wide international experience in all aspects of transport automation, Alcatel is one of the leading suppliers of signalling and train control, train routing, control centres and integrated rail communications technologies.

For main line operators, Alcatel offers AlTrac (in compliance with ERTMS/ETCS specifications) for train control, NetTrac network management, LockTrack electronic interlocking system, and FieldTrac field equipment (axle counters, point machines, signals). For urban line operators, Alcatel offers proven SelTrac® communications-based train control, NetTrack MT network management, and LockTrac electronic interlocking system solutions.

Contracts
China: Alcatel has been selected to provide its SelTrac® communications-based train control (CBTC) system for Guangzhou Metro Line 3 with moving-block technology for system-wide safety, reliability and availability. The 36.3 km long Guangzhou Metro Line 3, links three suburbs and crosses the Zhujiang River. Guangzhou, the capital of Guangdong Province and the largest city in southern China, is implementing an aggressive plan to build new metro lines over the next decade.
Finland: Alcatel has been selected to equip the new section of the Finnish double-tracked line, Kerava-Lahti, with its innovative control, supervision and operation systems for interlocking zones.
France: Alcatel has been awarded a contract to provide a complete Radio Communications-Based Train Control (CBTC) solution to the Régie Autonome des Transports Parisiens (RATP) for metro-line 13 crossing Paris from Porte de Châtillon to Saint-Denis and Asnières. The contract is for four years.
Egypt: Alcatel, as a member of the Interinfra consortium, delivered the communications system for the extension of Cairo's metro line 2.
Hungary: Alcatel has been awarded two contracts by Hungarian Railways to equip the Budapest-Cegléd-Szolnok main line with modern electronic interlocking systems and to upgrade the line between Budapest and the Austrian border with the standardised European Train Control System (ETCS).
Romania: October 2004, Compania Nationala Caile Ferate Romane (CN CFR), awarded Alacatel a contract to equip railways in the southern region of Romania with its electronic interlocking solutions to replace the old relay-based interlocking systems. Alcatel will modernise 11 stations, mainly located in the Pan-European Transport Corridor IV, crossing the country in the south and linking the cities of Constanta and Lugoj.
Spain: Alcatel has been awarded three contracts by the Transport Ministry of Spain/GIF to deploy the European standard ETCS (European Train Control System) Level 1 and 2 for the three new sections of the Spanish high-speed lines, Lerida-Barcelona, Segovia-Valladolid and Madrid-Toledo. Alcatel will also equip the Lerida-Barcelona and Segovia-Valladolid sections with a fixed communications network.
Switzerland: Alcatel has been awarded a contract by BLS AlpTransit AG for the engineering, installation and delivery of railway security and signalling systems for the 34.6 km Lötschberg base tunnel, as well as for the Frutigen and Visp railway stations in Switzerland. The Lötschberg

tunnel is the core of the Lötschberg base line between Frutigen and St German which forms an important part of the Swiss rail corridor through the Alps from north to south.

Turkey: Alcatel has been awarded a contract to supply signalling and telecommunication systems to the Turkish State Railways (TCDD) for the first renovation phase of the Ankara-Istanbul Railway Line Rehabilitation Project. Alcatel's solutions, including an ETCS system, will ensure traffic control and safety along the 250 km double line section and bi-directional operations between the Inönü and Essenkent stations.

United Arab Emirates: Alcatel was awarded a contract by Mitsubishi Heavy Industries to supply, integrate and deploy its driverless train control and telecommunication systems for the Dubai Metro.

UK: Alcatel has been selected by Tube Lines to re-signal the London Underground Jubilee and Northern Lines with SelTrac®, its proven communications-based train control technology incorporating NetTrac MT central control. This contract is for a term of 7 years.

US: Alcatel has been selected to provide open-standards wireless Communications-Based Train Control to US's first fully automated, line-haul, urban monorail rapid transit system in Las Vegas.

(PTC) and Communications-based Train Control (CBTC). The system integrates track transponder transmission systems, mobile communication radios and onboard computers, speed sensors and aspect display units.

For mass transit operations, ALSTOM offers the URBALIS solution for heavy metro and suburban networks as well as for light rail systems.

These systems are modular and adaptable and can be designed to follow changes in railway design.

With the contract for provision of a fully integrated signalling system to the NEL metro, ALSTOM is offering to this first fully automatic heavy metro state-of-the-art technology for automatic train control, electronic interlocking, and automatic train supervision.

ALSTOM has developed five product categories:

- Smartway: conventional signalling products covering basic needs including train detection, points equipment, level crossing equipment, signals, relays and accessories.
- Smartlock: mainly electronic interlocking for railway stations.
- Advantik: ATC systems for main line operation.
- Mastria: ATC for mass transit operation including ATP, ATO and all attached facilities. The ATC system can be fully integrated with interlocking and train supervision functions.

- Iconis: Automatic Train Superversion (ATS) also called Integrated Electronic Control Center System, integrating all activities required for train control, train supervision or monitoring, management functions, SCADA requirements, maintenance or alarm centralisation and supervision.
- AGATE e-Media: passenger information systems for trains and stations.

Other contracts

Belgium: In September 2008 SNCB placed an order with ALSTOM for 956 sets of equipment for the introduction of the TBL1+ safety system on its locomotives and power cars, as a part of its Five Year Plan aimed at safety improvement. This was the second such order, as Alstom was previously chosen in 2007 to supply the SNCB with 866 hardware devices of this type.

Brazil: In July 2005 Companhia do Metropolitano de São Paulo awarded an ALSTOM-led consortium a contract for the supply, installation and testing of signalling and control equipment for the extension of São Paulo's metro line 2 (green line).

Chile: In December 2008 Santiago Metro awarded ALSTOM a contract to supply an automatic train control for Santiago metro's line 5 extension. The contract includes engineering, installation, tests and commissioning. The 14 km line will enter commercial service in December 2009.

ALSTOM Transport

Information Solutions
48 rue Albert Dhalenne, F-93482 Saint-Ouen Cedex, France
Tel: (+33 1) 41 66 90 00
Fax: (+33 1) 41 66 96 66
Web: www.transport.alstom.com

Key personnel
Senior Vice-President, International Product Line Management: *Michel Marien*

Background
In October 2007, ALSTOM and Balfour Beatty launched their newly formed 50/50 joint venture company, Signalling Solutions Limited.

With headquarters in Borehamwood in the UK, the company is led by Managing Director David Felton, with approximately 340 people from ALSTOM and Balfour Beatty. The company is focused on delivering signalling projects for Network Rail and other customers in the UK.

Products
Covers main line and mass transit. For main line, ALSTOM offers ATLAS for high-speed lines, intercity and regional lines as well as for low-density lines, freight-only lines and single-track operations. This new-generation signalling system applies the latest technologies for train detection, interlocking, route management and speed control. ATLAS implements the new European Rail Traffic Management System (ERTMS) which sets interoperability standards for train control throughout the continent.

The modular ATLAS system is available at three ERTMS levels, ATLAS 100, 200 and 300, while ATLAS 400 offers a low-cost solution for low- to medium-density lines.

ALSTOM's ATLAS-based Advanced Civil Speed Enforcement System (ACSES) has been successfully tested on the Transportation Test Center test track in Pueblo, US and is looked on favourably for installation on Amtrak's Northeast Corridor from Washington DC to Boston. ACSES is designed to control and enforce train movements at various speeds, enforce civil speed restrictions (including curves, bridges and poor track conditions), provide positive train stopping at interlockings and protect work crews with temporary speed restrictions. ACSES generates and enforces profiles for various train types as required by Positive Train Control

ERTMS Eurobalise installed by ALSTOM in Greece 1194412

Development monitoring console for ERTMS installation in Switzerland 1194414

In April 2005 ALSTOM was awarded a contract by Santiago Metro for signalling equipment and automatic train control as part of its extension programme for line 2 north Recoleta Avenue. URBALIS Automatic Train Control equipment features in a turnkey project secured by ALSTOM in July 2002 to equip the 32 km Line 4 of Santiago's metro network.

China: In April 2006 ALSTOM, as part of a consortium comprising CASCO, an ALSTOM Transport joint venture present in both Beijing and Shanghai, and EEB (Electrification Engineering Bureau) was awarded a contract by BMOC, Beijing's metro operator, for the supply of the communication-based Train Control systems (CBTC) as well as the renovation of the metro line 2 signalling system.

The Kowloon-Canton Railway Corporation (KCRC) of Hong Kong awarded ALSTOM a contract for supply of a signalling system for its East Rail line. The order has two aspects: a signalling system for the new 9 km two-station East Rail line extension; and a capacity upgrade of the entire East Rail line to allow up to 27 trains to operate on the line per hour. The East Rail line is already in operation with an ALSTOM signalling system. The upgrade will be made possible by integrating ALSTOM's AXONIS Automatic Train Control and Signalling system. This will increase line capacity and enhance line safety without requiring any major modification to rolling stock or infrastructure.

France: In July 2008 the RATP awarded ALSTOM a contract for the installation of a video surveillance system for 119 MI79 trainsets on Line B of the Réseau Ferré de France (RFF) in the Ile-de-France region. The contract covers an optional system for transmitting images to a control centre over a wi-fi connection.

In April 2006 ALSTOM signed a contract with RFF for the supply of new-generation computerised interlocking machines (PAI-NG) for major railway stations, in line with the RFF's policy to upgrade French national railway network facilities.

In January 2005 ALSTOM received a contract, as part of the opening of the LEA line, to supply (within a consortium led by Cegelec Centre Est) automation and signalling equipment for the 26 crossings on this line.

Germany: In April 2008 Deutsche Bahn signed a contract with ALSTOM to install the onboard ATLAS control system on 10 very high-speed ICE3 trains built by Siemens. The contract includes an option for equipping a further seven trains.

India: In June 2007 DMRC (Delhi Metro Rail Corporation) awarded the ALSTOM led consortium with the design, manufacture, supply, installation and commissioning of Train Control & Signalling System for its Metro Line 1 and 2 extensions, which are scheduled for completion in March 2010.

Italy: In December 2006 ALSTOM was awarded a contract by ATM, the Milanese urban transit operator, for the supply of a new signalling system for Milan's Metropolitana 1 red metro line. ALSTOM started the renewal work in early 2007.

Netherlands: In October 2003, in consortium with its partner Holland Railconsult, ALSTOM won a contract from ProRail to supply its ATLAS 200 train control and signalling system for the Betuwe dedicated freight line linking Rotterdam with the German border. The system is ALSTOM's implementation of ERTMS Level 2.

Spain: In February 2005 Mintra (Madrid Infraestructuras del Transporte), chose an ALSTOM-led consortium for the supply and maintenance of signalling equipment for Madrid's four new light rail lines.

Switzerland: In January 2009 ALSTOM was awarded a contract by the Chemins de Fer Fédéraux Suisses (SBB/CFF/FFS) for the supply and repair of level 2 ATLAS signalling equipment. The contract will run for a period of 10 years, commencing 14 January 2009.

ALSTOM has supplied the URBALIS signalling system as part of the turnkey contract awarded in 2002 by the Administration of Switzerland's Vaud canton for a new 6 km metro line linking Ouchy with the district of Epalinges, Lausanne; the new line entered commercial service in October 2008.

Ansaldo STS

Italy Headquarters
Via Paolo Mantovani, 3-5, I-16151 Genova, Italy
Tel: (+39 010) 655 20 68   Fax: (+39 010) 655 29 39
e-mail: info@ansaldo-sts.com
    investorelations@ansaldo-sts.com
Web: www.ansaldo-sts.com

Key personnel

Managing Director: *Sergio De Luca*
Chief Financial Officer: *Jean Paul Giani*
Head of Investor Relations: *Andrea Razeto*
Senior Vice-President Business Development:
    Emmanuel Viollet
General Counsel: *Mario Orlando*
Communications Manager (Contact): *Paco Cabeza-López*

Background

Ansaldo STS is a one of the leading technology companies listed on the Milan stock exchange and operating in the global railway and mass transit transportation systems business. It provides traffic management, planning, train control and signalling systems and services and acts as a lead contractor and turnkey provider on major projects worldwide.

Ansaldo STS brings together the technological expertise of companies like Ansaldo Signal, Ansaldo Trasporti Sistemi Ferroviari, Union Switch & Signal and CSEE Transport. The activities of Ansaldo STS are organised in two business units: signalling and transportation systems. The local companies are co-ordinated by four regional companies with full profit accountability

for both business units across several countries.

Ansaldo STS is headquartered in Genoa, Italy, and employs over 400 people in 26 different countries.

Subsidiaries

Ansaldo STS Italia
Ansaldo STS France
Union Switch & Signal Inc (US)
Ansaldo STS Australia
Ansaldo STS Deutschland
Ansaldo STS UK
Ansaldo STS Ireland
Ansaldo STS Spain
Ansaldo STS Sweden
Ansaldo STS Finland
Ansaldo STS Nederland
Ansaldo STS India
Ansaldo STS Malaysia

Products and services

High Speed Ansaldo STS has applied its signalling systems to over 56 per cent of all high-speed lines worldwide (excluding Japan, according to independent sources).

Main Lines Ansaldo STS provides full-service capabilities to large railway networks such as India, France, Italy and the US. It supplies systems for new lines being built in fast developing countries such as China and Australia. In Europe the company is central to upgrading towards ERTMS, leading to the interoperability of differing country networks.

Mass Transit Ansaldo STS built the first steel wheel driverless Cenelec compliant (automatic and unmanned) metro in Copenhagen. Rome, Milan, Thessalonika, Brescia and other cities have recently acquired similar systems from the company. A CBTC version of this system is also available.

Computer-based Interlocking Ansaldo STS provides traffic solutions to stations of all sizes. Their integration with Centralised Traffic Control (CTC) and with Automatic Train Protection (ATP) systems has also been proved in high-speed applications.

Supervision & Traffic Control Ansaldo STS has developed solutions to supervise and optimise the use of complex infrastructures including managing traffic in and out of the most demanding networks and stations such as Rome, Manchester or in the US.

Ansaldo's CTC Rome Termini Station   1325854

Ansaldo's Hamersley Iron control room   1325852

Ansaldo's Kuala Lumpur Monorail system   1325853

Ansaldo's ERTMS High Speed on-board equipment   1325855

Components Ansaldo STS supplies track circuits, switch machines, signals, Eurobalises®, relays, hot wheel detectors, highway crossing mechanisms, event recorders, the MicroLok®, end of train systems etc.

Operations and Maintenance Ansaldo STS provides complete maintenance on its transportation systems to ensure full service availability.

Projects
High Speed:
Entire French TGV network; Italian HS network; Paris-Brussels-London connection; Madrid-Lleida; Figueras- Perpignan (Spain, France); Seoul-Pusan (South Korea); Qinhuangdao-Shenyang (China)

Main Lines:
Applications in – Australia, Botswana, China, Finland, India, Italy, Turkey, UK, US.

Mass Transit:
Driverless: Brescia, Copenhagen, Milan, Rome and Thessalonika.

Conventional: Belo Horizonte, Boston, Caracas, China, Dublin, Hong Kong, Italy, Kuala Lumpur, Lisbon, Los Angeles, Madrid, Manchester, Mexico, New York, Paris, Philadelphia, Rio de Janeiro, Sao Paulo, Seoul, Shanghai, Washington.

Supervision and Traffic Control:
Six SCC in Italy, Hong Kong, Union Pacific and CSX (US), Lyon, Paris, Boden (Sweden), Boston, Pittsburgh, Caracas etc.

Operation and Maintenance:
Madrid-Lleida high-speed line (Spain); Copenhagen Driverless (Denmark); Paris and Lyon (France); Northwest and Perth TCS (Australia); Gaborone (Botswana); Kansas City (US); Caracas (Venezuela).

AREVA TA

Société Technique pour l'énergie atomique
BP 17, F-91192 Gif-sur-Yvette Cedex, France
Tel: (+33 1) 69 33 80 38
Fax: (+33 1) 69 33 80 12
e-mail: sales-transport@technicatome.com
Web: www.areva.com

Background
Originally established to serve France's nuclear industry and still active in that sector, previously called Technicatome, the company became a member of the Areva energy group in 2001 and changed its name to AREVA TA in 2006.

Products/Services
Signalling and automatic train control systems, including: onboard Communications-Based Train Control (CBTC) systems; ATO and ATP systems; and Solid State Interlocking (SSI) systems.

Onboard train control systems, including: door control systems; traction and braking management systems; occasional signal repetition with automatic stop; speedometers; driver supervision systems; event recorders; safety location devices; and safety display consoles.

Train-to-ground data communications systems, including links covering: onboard CCTV; event recorder data; maintenance data; remote control 'wake-up'; and passenger loading data.

Contracts
Clients to which AREVA TA has supplied signalling and automatic train control technology include: Eurotunnel; RATP, Paris; and STIB, Brussels.

Onboard train control systems have been supplied to RATP, Paris, and SNCF (TGV GPS location systems).

Train-to-ground data communications systems have been supplied to RATP, Paris.

ARINC Inc

2551 Riva Road, Annapolis, Maryland 21401-7465, US
Tel: (+1 410) 266 40 00
e-mail: corpcomm@arinc.com
Web: www.arinc.com

Key personnel
Senior Director, Brand Management and Communications: *Linda Hartwig*

Background
As well as serving the surface transport market, ARINC Inc provides communications, systems engineering and integration solutions for airports, aviation, defence and government.

Products
The ARINC Advanced Information Management (AIM®) platform uses virtually off-the-shelf hardware for integrated train control, Supervisory Control And Data Acquisition (SCADA), passenger information system and security command/control functions.

ARINC's integrated passenger information system provides up-to-date estimated times of arrival and departure for trains, buses and planes.

ARINC is a systems engineering contractor for Communications-Based Train Control (CBTC) which tracks train locations and speeds with great accuracy. CBTC also provides movement authorities to trains based on this precise information, and enforces speeds and limits of authority as necessary.

Contracts
ARINC designed and furnished the complete communications capability for nine new stations, as well as radio subsystems for new rail tunnels for the Saint Louis MetroLink extension. ARINC also upgraded MetroLink's fiber communications infrastructure, and furnished all devices and interfaces required for emergency telephones, public address equipment, passenger signs, and closed circuit television.

ARINC's AIM® technology was used to provide Metro with the ability to enhance its train control functions and expand control centre operations.

Atron Electronic GmbH

Am Ziegelstadel 12 + 14, D-85570 Markt Schwaben, Germany
Tel: (+49 8121) 934 20
Fax: (+49 8121) 93 42 77
e-mail: vertrieb@atron.de
Web: www.atron.de

Key personnel
Marketing: *Jörg Wolff*

Products
Automatic Vehicle Location and Control (AVLC) systems based on spontaneous data transmission that communicates deviations from the planned status to central control, optimising bandwidth use of systems such as GSM and Tetra/Tetrapol.

Balogh-Frid

189 rue d'Aubervilliers CP 97, FR-75886 Paris, Cedex 18, France
Tel: (+33 1) 44 65 65 00   Fax: (+33 1) 44 65 65 10
e-mail: contact@balogh-rfid.com
Web: www.balogh-rfid.com

Key personnel
Chief Executive Officer: *Etienne Balogh*
Vice-President Business Development: *Xavier Leblan*
Chief Technology Officer: *Philippe Gobrecht*

Products
Design and production of a wide range of long-range radio frequency identification (RFID).

BBR Verkehrstechnik GmbH

Pillaustrasse 1e, DE-38126 Braunschweig, Germany
Tel: (+49 531) 27 30 00   Fax: (+49 531) 27 30 09 99
e-mail: info@bbr-vt.de
Web: www.bbr-vt.de

Products
Signalling transmission and train control: onboard and trackside equipment, based on the principles of either magnetic or inductive signal transmission (IMU). Areas of application include: vehicle detection; data exchange between onboard and trackside equipment; and initialising train stops.

BelAir Networks

603 March Road Kanata, Ontario Canada K2K 2M5
Tel: (+1 613) 254 70 70   Fax: (+1 613) 254 71 71
e-mail: info@belairnetworks.com
Web: www.belairnetworks.com

Key personnel
President and Chief Executive Officer: *Bernard Herscovich*
Chief Technology Officer: *Stephen Rayment*
Vice-President of Engineering: *Marcel Chénier*
Vice-President of Finance and Chief Financial Officer: *Peter Rose*
Vice-President of Business Development: *Martin Suter*
Vice-President of Product Marketing: *David Park*
Vice-President of Marketing Communications: *Sheila Burpee Duncan*

Products
Rugged, high-performance broadband wireless gear deployed in trains, stations, railyards and trackside to support a variety of applications including video security, public Wi-Fi access, and train mechanical telematics and diagnostics.

Bombardier Transportation

Rail Control Solutions
Arstaangsvagen 29, PO Box 425 05, 126 16 Stockholm, Sweden
Tel: (+46 8) 681 50 00   Fax: (+46 8) 681 51 00
Web: www.transportation.bombardier.com

Key personnel
President, Rail Control Solutions: *Anders Lindberg*

Products
Development, design, engineering, production, sales, installation, maintenance, after-sales service of, and customer support for, rail control and signalling systems for main line, ERTMS and mass transit.

Bombardier Transportation EBI Lock   1310172

Bombardier INTERFLO* offers main line solutions individually tailored to customers' needs, encompassing integrated operations control systems and computer-based interlocking systems, as well as automatic train protection and wayside equipment. INTERFLO also provides ERTMS/ETCS (The European Rail Traffic Management System/European Train Control System) solutions for ERTMS Level 1 and ERTMS Level 2.

Bombardier CITYFLO* provides complete mass transit solutions for all types of mass transit such as trams, light rail vehicles and metros, to suit various operating modes and customers' needs. These include cab signalling, semi-automatic train operation and unattended train operation.

Bombardier's product portfolio encompasses a wide range of products available as stand-alone products, or as part of Bombardier INTERFLO and CITYFLO solutions, products include:

- EBI* Screen control rooms, traffic management systems for efficient and economic management of main line and mass transit networks
- EBI Lock computer-based interlockings, which supervise and control wayside objects such as signals, point machines and level crossings
- EBI Com radio block centre, compiles information from interlockings and trains in its control area and sends movement authorities and other information to individual trains, taking into account a safe distance to the train ahead
- EBI Link ATC (Automatic Train Control) wayside equipment, providing either fixed or variable data from track to train utilising balises
- EBI Track train detection, a range of equipment consisting of train location systems, jointless track circuits, coded jointless track circuits and axle counters, providing train detection and track-to-train communication
- EBI Switch point machines, a range of point machines that includes sleeper-integrated point machines, conventional end-of-sleeper machines and machines mounted in a recess between the rails
- EBI Light signals, a range of optical signals including colour light multi-aspect signals, fibre optic searchlight signals, fibre optic alpha numeric signals and tunnel signals
- EBI Gate level crossings, providing barriers and signals
- EBI Cab ATC onboard equipment, which supports the driver and continuously supervises the speed of the train. The EBI Cab onboard system warns the driver if the maximum permitted speed is exceeded and activates the brakes in the event of danger. The system guarantees the highest possible level of safety
- EBI Star SatNav onboard units, providing enhanced transport timeliness and improved utilisation of locomotives by reducing standstill and empty runs, offering punctuality, cost-effectiveness and environmental protection
- EBI Tool design and maintenance, which generates site data automatically allowing engineering to be achieved quickly and efficiently.
- In 1995 European railways unanimously selected Bombardier Transportation's magnetic transponder (Balise) technology for track-to-train communication proposed for the Euro-Balise.

*INTERFLO and CITYFLO are trademarks of Bombardier or its subsidiaries.

Contracts

China: In August 2007 Bombardier received a contract for rail signalling equipment in China from systems integrator China Railway Signalling and Communications Corp (CRSC). The contract involves the supply, installation, testing and commissioning of INTERFLO 450 ERTMS Level 2 onboard and wayside signalling equipment for CRSC and its customer the Chinese Ministry of Railways (MOR).

Denmark: The EBI Lock 950 computer-based interlocking system will be installed in Denmark, providing Lollandbanen with a modern interlocking system, almost 20 years ahead of the current installed base.

Finland: Bombardier Transportation developed a stationary-based passenger information system concept for travel centres. Today, 10 main line stations are equipped with systems controlling LCD-based concourse displays and arrival/departure displays.

Bombardier Transportation delivered the first section of the nationwide ATC system to the Kirkkonummi-Turku coast line. Today, 4,134 km of the Finnish rail network and the complete rolling stock fleet has been equipped with ATC.

Germany: In 2006 the first EBI Lock 950 computer-based interlocking system for Deutsche Bahn in Germany was commissioned at the Mannheim-Rheinau station in the south west of the country.

In 2005 Bombardier Transportation received an order to supply EBI Lock 500 computer-based interlocking (CBI) systems to Deutsche Bahn (DB Netz AG), commissioned on the Appenweier-Bad Griesbach line in July 2006. Today there are 90 interlocking systems in operation.

Greece: Bombardier Transportation has delivered to Hellenic Railways Organisation (OSE) a centralised traffic control and signalling system to increase capacity between Athens and Larissa. In addition, Bombardier Transportation has upgraded EBI Gate level crossing systems to the railway around Athens.

India: In October 2007 Bombardier received a contract for rail signalling equipment from the Delhi Metro Rail Corporation Ltd (DMRC). The contract includes the design, manufacture, supply, installation, testing and commissioning of Bombardier CITYFLO 350 train control and signalling systems for two new sections of lines, totalling 37 kms.

Iran: Tehran Metro Line 1 and 2 are managed using the CITYFLO 350 automatic train control (ATC) system. 31 trains run along 54 km of track between 44 stations. Higher speeds and shorter headways between trains are a benefit of the system's continuous distance-to-go speed supervision.

Italy: In July 2006 Bombardier Transportation received a contract to supply a traffic management system for the city of Palermol. The CITYFLO 150 traffic management solution will be designed for the city's new 15 km light rail transit system. Bombardier will also supply the 17 bi-directional FLEXITY Outlook trams and scope includes a

Bombardier Transportation EBI Lock Mannheim-Rheinau   1310173

four-year maintenance contract. Commissioning is expected in 2009–10.

Bombardier Transportation was awarded two contracts from Italferr, the engineering subsidiary of the Italian State Railways, to supply its EBI Lock 950 computer-based interlocking, an automatic block and telecommunications system for the Italian railway network. Italferr awarded Bombardier Transportation two contracts for the implementation of an INTERFLO 200 solution comprising railway traffic management and safety systems, EBI Lock computer-based interlockings, and automatic block on the Pozzuolo-Treviglio line. Under the contracts, Bombardier Transportation will supply, install, test and commission four EBI Lock computer-based interlockings. The new interlockings will control a total of 333 signals, 161 point machines and 169 track circuits.

Bombardier Transportation received a further contract from Italferr for the implementation of EBI Lock computer-based interlockings, on the Milan junction. This technology will be applied to Pioltello, Melzo Scalo and the double junction of Pozzuolo; the automatic block on the Pioltello – D.B. Pozzuolo section; telecommunication equipment on the rail stations and sections on the Milano-Treviglio line.

Bombardier Transportation has provided Rete Ferroviaria Italiana Eurobalise and LEUs covering the areas of Turin, Milan, Rome and Ancona. This is the first phase of a project that covers around 45 per cent of all the line to be equipped. Projects to cover phases B and C are in progress.

Latvia: Bombardier Transportation's first project in Latvia for Latvian Railways, includes the design, supply, installation, test and commissioning of EBI Lock computer-based interlockings for Latvia's major railway junction, Riga Passenger Station, and the supply of 140 EBI Switch point machines.

Lithuania: Bombardier Transportation was awarded a contract by Lithuanuan Railways for the design, installation and commissioning of a complete EBI Lock computer-based interlocking system with connection to an EBI Screen control room and installation of EBI Link ATC wayside equipment and telecommunication along the 120 km line from Vilnius-Kleipeda.

Netherlands: In June 2006 Bombardier Transportation signed a Memorandum of Understanding (MoU) with ALSTOM, NedTrain, Siemens and ProRail for the homologation of the ETCS equipment. This is used on locomotives suitable for the European Rail Traffic Management System (ERTMS) infrastructure on the Betweroute; the new freight railway being constructed from Rotterdam to Germany. As part of the Bev21 programme, Pro Rail awarded Bombardier Transportation a contract to develop the Bev21 System and gain Dutch national safety acceptance of both wayside and onboard systems that support the ERTMS/ETCS Standards at levels 1, 2 and STM and dual signalling, for both ERTMS equipped and conventionally equipped trains.

Pro Rail awarded Bombardier Transportation a further contract to design, supply, install, test and commission an ERTMS Level 2 dual signalling safety system for the Amsterdam – Utrecht track doubling project, thereby upgrading the line.

In 2005 Bombardier Transportation successfully completed cross exchange tests between its INTERFLO 450 ERTMS Level 2 and both ALSTOM and Siemens ERTMS equipment on the Bev 21 ERTMS lines in the Netherlands. In April 2005 Bombardier Transportation and NedTrain Consulting, an independent engineering and consulting office established by NedTrain, entered into an agreement for the development and distribution of ATB-AG Specific Transmission Modules (STMs) and ATB-EG Phase 5 stand alone systems. Used in conjunction with ETCS onboard equipment, these products make it possible for rolling stock to run not only on the new ERTMS equipped cross border lines, but also on the existing Dutch domestic railway network.

Bombardier Transportation TMS control centre Gothenburg   1310174

Bombardier Transportation was also awarded a contract by Railinfrabeheer for the delivery of 1,200 EBI Switch point machines.

Philippines: Bombardier Transportation designed, manufactured, tested and delivered a complete CITYFLO 250 solution for Line 3 of the LRT in Manila. This fully integrated system includes EBI Lock computer-based interlockings, EBI Screen control room and EBI Cab ATC onboard equipment, guaranteeing a low cost solid and reliable solution. Bombardier Transportation was also awarded a five year maintenance contact for Line 3, which includes training. Since then a three year extension has been awarded for the maintenance contract.

Poland: In 2007 Bombardier won a new contract from the Polish rail network company PKP Polskie Linie Kolejowe to install state-of-the-art rail control equipment on the Koluszki to Lodz Widzew section of the Warsaw Lodz main line. Bombardier will design, manufacture, deliver, install and put in to operation its INTERFLO 200 solution comprising of an EBI Screen control room, EBI Lock computer-based interlocking systems, an EBI Track train detection system and an EBI Gate level crossing system. This follows the 2006 contract for the INTERFLO 200 solution on the E30 main line between Wroclaw and Legnica.

Bombardier Transportation previously supplied PKP with 33 EBI lock computer-based interlockings for the E-20 and E-30 main lines (part of the transportation corridors linking Eastern and Western Europe), 220 EBI Gate level crossings, EBI light signals, EBI switch point machines and track circuits to the whole PKP network.

Portugal: Bombardier Transportation has delivered a full turnkey project for Metro do Porto, including the project management, in-house design, installation and commissioning of a CITYFLO 250 solution.

A traffic management system including automatic vehicle regulation (AVR), 17 EBI lock computer-based interlockings, EBI Cab ATC onboard equipment, EBI link ATC wayside equipment EBI light signals, EBI switch point machines, EBI gate level crossings and EBI track train detection were supplied. In total, Metro do Porto covers 70 km of track, 50 km of which is converted rail tracks with an additional 20 km of newly built tracks, stopping at 66 stations with 72 vehicles also supplied by Bombardier Transportation.

Romania: Bombardier Transportation delivered the Bucharest Metro Authorities, Metrorex, in-house design, installation, commissioning and supply of the state-of-the-art CITYFLO 350 mass transit signalling system for Line 2. The CITYFLO 350 solution includes EBI Lock computer-based interlockings, EBI Screen control room, EBI Switch point machines, EBI Cab ATC onboard equipment with jointless audio frequency coded track circuits and EBI Cruise ATO. Building on the success of the Line 2 contract Bombardier Transportation was awarded a further signalling contract from Metrorex to supply an additional CITYFLO 350 mass transit solution for Bucharest Metro Lines 1 and 3.

Russian Federation: Bombardier Transportation has supplied EBI Lock computer-based interlockings to Russian Railways. To date, 57 stations have been equipped with EBI Lock, with orders received to supply additional stations in the near future.

South Africa: As part of a DBOM concession for the Gautrain Rapid Rail Link, for which the Bombardier-led Bombela consortium was named preferred bidder in 2005, the company is to supply CITYFLO 250 train control technology and communications systems.

South Korea: The Yong-In project was awarded to Bombardier Transportation to supply a CITYFLO 650 solution. The driverless system which is planned to be in service in 2009, will cover 18.6 km of track across 15 stations with 30 trains.

Bombardier Transportation was awarded a contract by a consortium led by Taejung Electric Construction Co to supply INTERFLO 250 ERMTS Level 1 to the Korean National Railroad (KNR). The system consists of Bombardier EBI Cab ATC onboard equipment, EBI Link ATC wayside equipment consisting of lineside electronic units (LEUs) and balises for the lines from Seoul to Busan and from Daejon to Mokpo, totalling 760 km.

Bombardier Transportation supplied the Busan Urban Transport Authority (BUTA), through LGIS, a contract for the in-house design, installation and commissioning of CITYFLO 350 solution on Busan Line 2. EBI computer-based interlockings, EBI Switch point machines, EBI Cruise ATO and EBI Cab ATC onboard equipment with EBI Track train detection jointless audio frequency coded track circuits were included. A further contract has been awarded for an extension to Line 2.

Spain: Metro Madrid awarded a contract to Bombardier Transportation to supply its CITYFLO 450 solution for the renovation of Lines 1 and 6. The CITYFLO 450 solution is a state-of-the-art communication-based train control (CBTC) system featuring moving block (MB) operation with the driver using radio communication between train and wayside. Included in the contract are onboard equipment for 117 trains, EBI Lock computer based interlockings, EBI Screen control rooms, EBI Track jointless track circuits and EBI Switch point machines as well as LED (Light Emitting Diode) type signals. Madrid Metro Line 1 is 16.7 km long, has 27 stations and for this line 68 trains have to be equipped with ATP and ATO. Madrid Metro Line 6 is 23.5 km long and has 27 stations. For this line, 49 trains have to be equipped with ATP and ATO.

As a continuation of the ERTMS Level 1 line from Albacete-Villar de Chincilla, Bombardier was awarded a further contract by the Spanish Rail Infrastructure Administrator (ADIF) to install ERTMS Level 1 wayside equipment on the extension of this ERTMS Level 1 line, from Villar de Chincilla-La Encina, linking with the EBI Cab 900 area from the Mediterranean Corridor. With a 50 km extension of the double-track line it will be possible to drive under ATP for more than 500 km from Albacete to Barcelona via Valencia.

Barcelona Metro awarded Bombardier Transportation a contract for the in-house design, installation and commissioning of a CITYFLO 350 solution for Line1 and 3. The CITYFLO 350 solution supplied includes EBI Lock computer-based interlockings, EBI Cab ATC onboard equipment with EBI Track train detection jointless audio frequency coded track circuits and EBI Cruise ATO.

Bombardier Transportation onboard equipment in a Swiss ERTMS train   1310175

Bombardier Transportation ERTMS The Netherlands   1310178

The Bilbao Metro awarded Bombardier Transportation a contract for the in-house design, installation and commissioning of a CITYFLO 350 solution for Lines 1 and 2. The solution supplied includes EBI Lock computer-based interlockings, EBI Cab ATC onboard equipment with jointless audio frequency coded track circuits and EBI Cruise ATO. In service for more than a decade, the metro currently covers 36 km of track with 34 stations and 37 trains, with further extensions in progress.

Sweden: In April 2008 Bombardier Transportation was awarded a contract for the development of ERTMS onboard equipment, as part of the extensive ERTMS roll-out programme in Scandinavia. The initial total order includes equipping up to 220 vehicles with ERTMS systems. The order from the Swedish Rail Administration, Banverket (BV), together with the Norwegian National Rail Administration, Jernbaneverket (JBV), is part of a framework agreement for the specification and development of Bombardier EBI Cab 2000 ETCS onboard systems and the delivery of products and services on all new and retrofitted vehicles in Sweden and Norway.

In May 2007 following a 2005 contract win from Botniabanan AB to produce the ERTMS system specifications as the first phase in introducing the new system on the Bothnia Line, Bombardier Transportation completed the first successful ERTMS level 2 testing in Sweden on a 20 km test track between Arnäsvall and Husum on the Botnia Line. Bombardier is building the INTERFLO 450 main line signalling system, providing ERTMS/ETCS Level 2 functionality for the entire Bothnia Line, from Nyland to Gimonäs. Work on the 190 km line is scheduled to be complete in 2010. In February 2007, Bombardier Transportation was awarded a contract from Swedish rail operator, Banverket, to install a new ERTMS state of the art signalling system on the regional Västerdalsbanan line between Repbäcken and Malung. Bombardier Transportation has won orders to supply the Swedish Railway Administration, Banverket, with 160 EBI Lock computer-based interlockings and seven EBI Screen control rooms. Currently there are contracts to upgrade the EBI Screen control rooms. The Storstockholms Lokaltvafik, Stockholm, chose Bombardier Transportation for the provision of the CITYFLO 250 system on the Snabbspårvägen/Saltsjöbanan line. The 10 km of track has had 12 stations and 12 trains in operation since 2000.

Switzerland: Bombardier Transportation is the first supplier in the industry to have successfully proven in full commercial operation its INTERFLO 450 ERTMS Level 2 technology on its pilot line in Switzerland. The world's first commercial ERTMS/ETCS Level 2 system was accepted by Swiss Federal Railways, SBB, in November 2003.

Bombardier Transportation developed the trackside equipment and the train-borne equipment. 63 vehicles of five different types were equipped to run on the Olten-Lucerne line, a 35 km double track with nine stations and a line speed of 140 km/h, capable of running up to 57,000 trains per year and transporting more than 3,000,000 passengers and 240,000 tonnes of goods.

The INTERFLO 450 solution is proven to be reliable and safe, meeting the standards set

by SBB. The test results show outstanding performance levels of 99.6 per cent availability, reaching standards above conventional systems.
Taiwan: Bombardier Transportation was awarded a contract by the Department of Rapid Transit Systems (DORTS) for the provision of a CITYFLO 650 solution for the Neihu and Mucha lines. The 76 trains are fully automated four-car Innovia vehicles and will run across 14.8 km of track and 24 stations.

Bombardier Transportation was awarded a contract by the Taiwan Railway Administration for a complete INTERFLO 250 ERTMS Level 1 ATP system which included ATP computers for 768 locomotives, 14,000 balises, and 2,000 encoders. The order also included 13 simulators for driver training and systems for train data presentation including driver panels.

Thailand: In 2006, Bombardier Transportation supplied the State Railway of Thailand with an INTERFLO 200 signalling system, consisting of EBI Lock computer-based interlocking systems, EBI Link ATC wayside equipment and associated communications systems on all four new double-track routes into and out of Bangkok, covering 174 km of double- and triple- track and 33 stations.

Turkey: Bombardier Transportation has supplied its CITYFLO 250 solution to Turkey, including the Municipality of Istanbul with 17 km, 16 stations and 105 trains in operation; the Municipality of Izmir with 11 km of track, 10 stations and 30 trains in operation. The Municipality of Adana has also awarded Bombardier a contract to cover 13.5 km of track with 13 stations and 36 trains.

United Kingdom: In June 2006 Bombardier Transportation was awarded a signalling order from Balfour Beatty to supply its EBI Screen control room system for the Waterloo & City line on the London Underground. The EBI Screen system is part of the enhancement works being carried out on the Waterloo & City line for Metronet Rail, the company responsible for the maintenance and upgrade of two thirds of the city's underground system.

London Heathrow International Airport Terminal 5 awarded Bombardier Transportation a contract for the provision of a CITYFLO 650 Automatic Train Control (ATC) driverless system for its Airport People Mover.

Bombardier Transportation is a member of the Metronet Consortium, which is currently undertaking a major programme to modernise the London Underground network's signals. Additionally, Bombardier Transportation is currently delivering an upgraded control room solution for the East London line of the Underground. The first line of the network was commissioned in 2004.

Bombardier Transportation has also been awarded contracts from Strathclyde Passenger Transport to replace the Glasgow Subway's existing centralised control centre (CTC) and from both Nottingham Express Transit (NET) and Greater Manchester's Metrolink to provide a fully integrated light rail signalling and control solution, CITYFLO 150.

United States: The world's largest Airport People Mover in Dallas Fort Worth awarded Bombardier Transportation the contract to provide the CITYFLO 650 solution. The 64 trains are running with an Automatic Train Control (ATC) system between nine stations across 8 km of track.

San Francisco International Airport awarded Bombardier Transportation a contract to provide a CITYFLO 650 Automatic Train Control (ATC) system on its 4.8 km dual elevated guideway with nine stations and 38 trains.

The South Eastern Pennsylvania Transport Authorities (SEPTA) awarded Bombardier Transportation a contract for the in-house design, installation support and commissioning of a CITYFLO 450 solution for the loop under the city. The CITYFLO 450 solution supplied includes the EBI Com radio block centre, EBI Cab ATC onboard equipment and the EBI Screen control room. The CITYFLO 450 solution was chosen as the cab-signalling system can be adapted to

manually operated vehicles running in mixed traffic and in a transit tunnel.

The Bay Area Rapid Transit (BART) system in San Francisco, California commissioned its link to San Francisco Airport. Bombardier Transportation supplied the proven fixed block signalling system, CITYFLO 450. Bombardier Transportation has also commissioned the completely refurbished automatic people mover system at the Seattle Tacoma Airport in Seattle, Washington with its CITYFLO 650 solutions, utilising communication-based moving block technology.

Uzbekistan: In April 2007 Bombardier Transportation was awarded a landmark contract by the Japanese trading house Mitsui & Co Ltd to install the first modern signalling system in the Commonwealth of Independent States (CIS). The new signalling system will be installed on Uzbekistan's southern Tashguzar to Kumkurgan line, covering more than 200 km and serving 17 stations. Bombardier will provide its advanced EBI Lock 950 computer-based interlocking systems, object controllers and wayside equipment including point machines, LED signals, level crossings, axle counters and track circuits as well as supervising all design, engineering and installation.

Developments

In March 2008 Bombardier Transportation Rail Control Solutions launched the new Bombardier EBI Track 400 jointless coded track circuit. It forms the latest part of the existing range of EBI Track train detection equipment.

Brand-Rex Ltd

Viewfield Industrial Estate, Glenrothes, Fife KT6 2RS, UK
Tel: (+44 1592) 77 21 24   Fax: (+44 1592) 77 53 14
e-mail: jdonnel@brand-rex.com
Web: www.brand-rex.com

Other offices

Argentina, Australia, Brazil, Colombia, France, Germany, Hong Kong, Italy, Singapore, Spain, United Arab Emirates and US.

Key personnel

Chief Executive Officer: *Paul Lines*
Chief Financial Officer: *Haley Stewart*
Business and Marketing Director: *Ian Wilkie*
Technical and Operations Director: *Iain Ballingall*
Global Business Development Manager: *Isaac Garson*

Background

In February 2008 Murray Capital, the private equity arm of Murray International Holdings announced its acquisition of Brand-Rex Ltd in a transaction that allowed management to be director owners as well as operational directors.

Products

Brand-Rex is a specialist copper and fibre wiring systems manufacturer supplying power, control, data and communication cables, using irradiation cross-linking technology, to the rail mass transit industries. The company makes structured wiring systems for data networks and cabling solutions for military and other industries. All Brand-Rex optical fibre cables contain fibres manufactured by Corning Inc.

Capsys SA

Parc Technologies, 190 Chemin des Fontaines, F-38190 Bernin, France
Tel: (+33 4) 76 08 90 75
Fax: (+33 4) 76 08 89 85
e-mail: commercial@capsys.eu
Web: www.capsys.eu

Products

GPS-based priority systems including pedestrian detectors, loop detectors, data transmission, radar control and real-time urban transport priority.

Casey Systems Inc

209 Lafayette Drive, Syosset, New York, New York 11791, US
Tel: (+1 516) 433 47 00
Fax: (+1 516) 433 11 31
e-mail: sales@caseysystems.com
Web: www.caseysystems.com
www.synergxsystems.com

Key personnel

President: *Al Koenig*
Information Technology Manager: *Neal LoCurto*
Vice-President of Transportation Engineering: *Joseph M DeCarlo*
Sales Director: *Vincent Milanesi*

Background

Casey Systems is a subsidiary of Synergx Systems Inc, a Delaware-based organisation.

The Comco division of Casey manufactures, markets products, on-board information and communication systems with applications for municipal transit carriers, long-distance passenger trains and bus and train builders. Its products and systems are operating on transit systems across North America including New York, Boston, New Jersey, Washington-DC, Chicago, St. Louis, Salt Lake City and San Diego.

Since 1991, Casey Systems has concentrated on mass transit with an emphasis on the New York City Transit (NYCT) market.

Products

Public address systems, Closed Circuit Television (CCTV), intercom, security alarm systems, train dispatch, customer information signs, gate control, telephone, scanners, telephone terminal units and fire alarms.

Contracts

In February 2007, Casey Systems secured a new contract to provide low voltage communications solutions for a new New York City Transit Authority rail yard.

In November 2006, the Casey Systems Transit group began preparation for the supply of the next generation passenger identification and security system for the New York City Transit Authority's 231st Street station.

In November, the company completed a Siedle colour video intercom system and camera system for CB Richard Ellis at 3 East 48th Street.

In July 2006, the next in a line of the New York City Transit Authority security system upgrades was the Seventh Avenue Express – White Plains Road Line at the 233rd Street Station in the Bronx. The Casey Systems Transit Engineering Group provided the systems integration and engineering for the systems upgrade for this station. Casey delivered the fire alarms, communications for the recently reopened 233rd Street Station.

Chloride Power Protection

Chloride Group PLC Head office
Ebury Gate 23 Lower Belgrave Street, London SW1W 0NR, UK
Tel: (+44 207) 881 14 40
Fax: (+44 207) 730 50 85
e-mail: enquiries@chloridegroup.com
Web: www.chloridepower.com

Other offices

Australia, Brazil, France, Germany, Italy, Portugal, Singapore, Spain, Thailand, Turkey and the US.

Background

Chloride Power Protection is part of Chloride Group plc.

Products

Supply of electrical power supply protection systems.

Craig and Derricott Ltd

Hall Lane, Walsall Wood, Walsall WS9 9DP, UK
Tel: (+44 1543) 37 55 41   Fax: (+44 1543) 45 26 10
Fax: (+44 1543) 36 16 19 (Direct Sales)
e-mail: info@craigandderricott.com
Web: www.craigandderricott.com

Key personnel

Managing Director: *Andy Dolman*
Sales Director: *Paul Cranshaw*

Background

Established in 1944 Craig and Derricott is owned by The Victory Group of India.

Products

Design, manufacture and supply of a range of switchgear and custom-designed control panels adapted to meet the control and safety requirements of the rail industry, control desks, uncouplers, control panels, equipment cases, switches, communication panels, safety-related equipment and wiring harnesses. Specifically including: shunting control panels; customised rotary switches and isolators; rotary switches featuring high-security key locks; and mushroom-headed push-buttons used as both emergency stops and passenger alarm switches. Also supplied is a range of limit and reed switches suitable for mounting in or around all rail equipment.

Low-profile push-button and LED indicator units, master drivers key switches, passenger alarm handles, drum switches and underframe starting switches.

Crompton Greaves Ltd

6th floor, CG House, Dr Annie Besant Road, Worli, Mumbai 400 030, India
Tel: (+91 22) 24 23 77 77   Fax: (+91 22) 24 23 77 88
Web: www.cglonline.com

Rail Transportation Systems Division
5G, Vandhna, 11 Tolstoy Marg, 110 001 New Delhi, India
Tel: (+91 11) 30 41 63 00
Fax: (+91 11) 23 32 43 60, 23 35 21 34
e-mail: salil.kumar@cgl.co.in

Key personnel

Managing Director: *S M Trehan*
Vice-President Rail Transportation Systems Division: *A K Raina*
Senior Manager Rail Transportation Systems Division: *Salil Kumar*

Products

Signalling relays, point machines, axle counters, route relay interlocking systems, solid state signalling and data loggers.

Developments

AFTC and digital axle counters.

DaimlerChrysler Services FleetBoard UK Limited

18 Pebble Close Business Village, Tamworth, Staffordshire B77 4RD, UK
Tel: (+44 1827) 31 19 12   Fax: (+44 1872) 31 19 16

e-mail: enquiries@fleetboard.co.uk
Web: www.fleetboard.co.uk

Key personnel

Managing Director: *Richard Case*
Sales & Marketing Manager: *Ray Mullard*
Customer Services Manager: *David Wyton*
Finance & Administration Manager: *Ron Thompson*
Staff: 85

Background

Previously known as VeMIS Limited, the company is a subsidiary of DaimlerChryslerServices FleetBoard GmbH and was renamed DaimlerChrysler Services FleetBoard UK Limited in 2004. Since its 1994 launch, VeMIS had installed 10,000 systems, which were originally developed for heavy goods vehicles.

Products

Computerised driver training device/system for public service vehicles. The system aims to improve driving skills and provide fuel economy.

Contracts

Arriva the Shires and West has installed systems into vehicles at their training centres in Watford and Harlow.

Dambach-Werke GmbH

Main Administration and Works Office
D-76568 Gaggenau, Germany
Tel: (+49 7225) 64 01   Fax: (+49 7225) 643 00
e-mail: info@dw.dambach.de
Web: www.dambach.de

Products

Infra-red bus location system; clock systems.

Data Display Co Ltd

Deerpark Industrial Estate, Ennistymon, Co Clare, Ireland
Tel: (+353 65) 707 26 00
Fax: (+353 65) 707 13 11
e-mail: sales@data-display.com
Web: www.data-display.com

Key personnel

Managing Director: *Paul Neville*
Marketing Manager: *Ann Marie Neville*

Subsidiaries

Data Display UK Ltd
Tel: (+44 23) 92 24 75 00
e-mail: sales@datadisplayuk.com

Data Display US
Tel: (+1 631) 218 21 30
e-mail: salesinfo@ddusa.com

Data Display Netherlands
Tel: (+31 78) 684 05 04
e-mail: info@data-display.nl

Data Display Dublin
Tel: (+353 65) 707 26 00
e-mail: maryhowe@data-display.com

Data Display France
Tel: (+33 1) 43 03 75 00
e-mail: infos@datadisplayfrance.com

Data Display Portugal
Tel: (+351 21) 910 67 60
e-mail: datadisplayportugal@mail.telepac.pt

Poltech, Sweden
Tel: (+46 171) 41 45 90
e-mail: info@poltech.se

Data Display Australia
Tel: (+61 3) 95 87 85 77
e-mail: info@datadisplay.com.au

Products

Data Display designs and manufactures electronic passenger information displays for the railway market. It provides a comprehensive range of platform, concourse and on-train displays. Technologies include LED and LCD/TFT.

Contracts

Supply of LED passenger information displays to London Underground, Denver Light Rail (US), Mersey Rail, London Line, Heathrow Express, Denver Bus (US), Wales & Borders Trains (now Arriva Trains Wales), and VTA (US). Further railway projects include Thales (Hong Kong), DRIMS (Netherlands), Paris Metro (France), Lisbon Metro, Dublin Area Rapid Transit as well as London Underground Central and Jubilee Lines (UK).

Dimetronic SA

Avda de Castella 2, Parque Empresarial, E-28830 San Fernando de Henares, Madrid, Spain
Tel: (+34 91) 675 42 12
Fax: (+34 91) 756 21 15
e-mail: marketing.dimetronic@invensys.com
Web: www.dimetronic.es

Key personnel

Managing Director: *Carlos Manzano*
International Export Director: *Luis Garcia*

Subsidiaries

Dimetronic Portugal

Background

Dimetronic is part of Invensys Rail Group.

Products

Signalling systems; electronic interlockings, CTC, ATP, ATO, ATC, ERTMS, train describer, automatic route setting, cab signalling and traffic regulation equipment.

Contracts

Most of the projects are of a turnkey nature. Contracts include Westrace electronic Interlockings ERTMS and CTC systems for RENFE in Spain; ATP/ATO, CTC and Westrace for Madrid metro, Lisbon, Barcelona, Manila, Valencia and Bucharest metro; SSI and CTC for REFER (Portugal); and Westrace electronic interlocking for FGC Spain. ERTMS for high-speed lines in Spain. Signalling and communications for Ankara-Konya high-speed line, with Turkish civil contractor, Yepi Merkezi.

DRI Corporation

Headquarters
13760 Noel Road, Suite 830, Dallas, Texas 75240, USA
Tel: (+1 214) 378 89 92
Web: www.digrec.com

Key personnel

Chairman, President and Chief Executive Officer: *David L Turney*
Vice-President, Chief Financial Officer, Secretary and Treasurer: *Stephen P Stay*
Vice-President, Chief Technology Officer: *Lawrence A Hagemann*
Manager, Corporate Communications: *Veronica B Marks*
Executive Vice-President: *David Calusdian*

Background

Incorporated in 1983, DRI Corporation is traded on The NASDAQ® Capital Market.

Subsidiaries
Digital Recorders, Inc
TwinVision na, Inc
Robinson Turney International, Inc
Mobitec AB
Mobitec GmbH
Mobitec Australia Pty Ltd
Mobitec Brazil Ltda
Castmaster
Mobitec India Private Ltd

Products
TwinVision® and Mobitec® electronic destination sign systems
Talking Bus® voice announcement systems.
Digital Recorders® Internet-based passenger information and automatic vehicle location/monitoring systems.
VacTell™ video actionable intelligence systems.

EADS Telecom Deutschland GmbH

Wilhelm-Runge-Strasse 11, D-89081, Ulm, Germany
Tel: (+49 731) 505 02
Fax: (+49 731) 505 18 00
Web: www.eads-telecom.de, www.eads.com

Key personnel
Managing Director: *Matthias Bierling*
Finance and Administration Director: *Reiner Winkelbauer*
Sales Director: *Wolfgang Lingenhoel*
Communications and Public Relations Manager: *Susanne Hartwein*
Staff: 11 (2003)

Background
Previously AEG Mobile Communication GmbH, EADS Telecom Deutschland GmbH is a subsidiary of EADS European Aeronautics Defence and Space Company.

Products
Train radio systems for long distance, shunting and maintenance (trunking radio) and metro applications.

EBO Systems

Head Office
132, Boulevard d'Europe, BP 10, F-67211 Obernai Cedex, France
Tel: (+33 3) 88 49 50 51
Fax: (+33 3) 88 49 50 14
e-mail: info@ebo-systems.com
Web: www.ebo-systems.com

Other offices
The company has production facilities in France, Germany, Italy, Switzerland and the United Arab Emirates.

Products
Cable management systems; halogen-free cable trays and ground ducts in GRP; pultruded profiles for electric cabinets, ladders, grates and guard rails.

Contracts
Supplied equipment for DB rolling stock reconstruction, BVG Berlin, RER Paris and London Underground Ltd.

Developments
Include insulation systems for overhead lines, cable tray systems for suspension of heavy lighting units and non-conductive support systems.

EFACEC Sistemas de Electrónica SA

Signalling Systems Division, Av Eng Ulrich, PO Box 31, P-4470 Maia, Portugal
Tel: (+351 2) 941 36 66   Fax: (+351 2) 948 54 28
Web: www.efacec.pt

Key personnel
Chairman: *Francisco de La Fuente Sánchez*
Vice-Chairman: *Alberto Joaquim Milheiro Barbosa*
Market Relations: *Maria Elisa Oliveira*

Products
Signalling and telecommunications systems and components, including electronic interlocking, automatic train speed control, track circuits, level crossing equipment including barrier machines, and ATP panels, encoders, recording and evaluation units. Installation, repair and maintenance of signalling equipment.

Eurotech SpA

Via Solari, 3, I-33020 Amaro, Italy
Tel: (+39 0433) 48 54 11   Fax: (+39 0433) 48 54 99
e-mail: sales@eurotech.com
Web: www.eurotech.com

Background
With headquarters in Amaro, Italy, Eurotech also has offices in Kansas City and Salt Lake City, US; Cambridge, UK; Lyon, France; Helsinki, Finland; Caronno and Trento, Italy; Munich, Germany and Peking, China.

Key personnel
President and Chief Executive Officer: *Roberto Siagri*

Products
The AVL Light is a low power embedded hardware platform specifically designed for real time vehicle tracking applications for fleet management and real-time vehicle tracking. A new Linux® and WinCE® compatible system based on the Intel® Xscale® architecture, it incorporates enhanced communication interfaces.
The Eurotech Passenger Counter features highly accurate stereoscopic cameras integrated within a robust and lightweight extruded aluminium enclosure. The device can be installed in the doorways of buses, trams and trains and can also be used over gateways, corridors or turnstiles.

Fels SA

2 rue J M Jacquard, F-67400 Illkirch Graffenstaden, France
Tel: (+33 3) 88 67 10 60   Fax: (+33 3) 88 67 33 10
e-mail: fels@fels.fr
Web: www.fels.fr

Key personnel
Commercial Director: *Jean-Claude Fels*
Financial Director: *Danièle Russo*
Export Manager: *Hervé Demuth*
Purchasing Manager: *Geneviève Meoni-Berthet*

Products
Electrical contacts; special connectors.

Fleet Management Solutions Inc (FMS)

1150 Osos Street, Suite 110, San Luis Obispo, California 93401, US
Tel: (+1 805) 787 05 08   Fax: (+1 805) 787 05 09

e-mail: info@fmsgps.com
Web: www.fmsgps.com

Other office:
Fleet Management Solutions Canada Ltd
109-53016 Hwy 60, Acheson (Edmonton), Alberta, Canada T7X 5A7
Tel: (+1 780) 962 38 50
Fax: (+1 780) 962 38 05

Key personnel
President, Chief Executive Officer: *Cliff Henley*
Chief Financial Officer: *Sheila Henley-Roth*
Vice-President, Worldwide Sales: *Michael Prescott*
Vice-President Marketing: *Steve Marriner*
Director of International Business Development: *Brian Meek*
Director of Software Development: *Tahn Amuchastegui*

Products
Fleet Management Solutions Inc manufactures, distributes and supports all satellite-based mobile asset tracking, locating and reporting solutions. FMS solutions are comprised of hardware, firmware and software; including GPS, wireless, satellite and the latest in web-based asset tracking.
Range includes the MLT-300 Mobile Tracking System.

Contracts
FMS entered into an agreement with ABC Companies under which FMS will provide ABC's requirements for satellite-based coach tracking, locating and reporting systems. ABC will use the FMS MLT-300 all-satellite system for both their internal tracking requirements.

GAI-Tronics

A division of Hubbell Limited
Brunel Drive, Stretton Park, Burton-on-Trent DE13 0BZ, UK
Tel: (+44 1283) 50 05 00
Fax: (+44 1283) 50 04 00
e-mail: sales@gai-tronics.co.uk
Web: www.gai-tronics.co.uk

Key personnel
Business Unit General Manager: *Graham Lines*
Business Unit Controller: *Toby Balmer*
Engineering Manager: *Richard Rumsby*
Manufacturing Director: *Mark Bradford*
Commercial Manager: *Roger Goodall*
Marketing Manager: *Nicole Ireland*
Special Projects Manager: *Steve Smith*

Other offices
GAI-Tronics Corporation, US
Tel: (+1 610) 777 13 74   Fax: (+1 610) 775 65 40
Web: www.gai-tronics.com
GAI-Tronics Srl, Italy
Tel: (+39 02) 48 60 14 60   Fax: (+39 02) 458 56 25
Web: www.gai-tronics.co.uk
GAI-Tronics Corporation, Malaysia
Tel: (+60 3) 89 45 40 35   Fax: (+60 3) 89 45 46 75
Web: www.gai-tronics.co.uk
GAI-Tronics Australia (Austdac)
Tel: (+61 2) 96 34 70 55   Fax: (+61 2) 98 99 24 90

Background
Established in 1964, GAI-Tronics is a major provider of specialised telecommunications for both UK and worldwide railways, manufacturing weather- and vandal-resistant communication equipment.

Products
Metal-bodied weather-resilient telephones; SMART self-monitoring and reporting telephone systems. Network Rail certified telephones for trackside and level crossings. Illuminated crossing telephones.

Ganz Škoda Traction Electrics Ltd

Budafoki str 59, H-1111 Budapest, Hungary
Tel: (+36 1) 880 95 00   Fax: (+36 1) 880 95 10
e-mail: info@ganz-skoda.hu
Web: www.skoda.cz/ganz-skoda

Key personnel

Chief Executive Officer: *Zdenek Majer*
Technical Director: *Tamás Ruzsányi*
Director of Production: *András Csikvári*
Chief Financial Officer: *Zsolt Nagy*
Project Management & After Sales:
   József Kovács

Background

Formerly a state enterprise, the company was privatised in 1991 as Ganz Ansaldo Electric Ltd, with the Italian company initially taking a shareholding of 51 per cent but increasing this to 99.99 per cent in 1998. In 1999 Ansaldo divested its interest, leading to the establishment of the present private sector company in 2000.

Škoda Holding took over the necessary assets and activities of Ganz Transelektro Traction Electrics Ltd and established with Hungarian Resonator Kft, a new company Ganz Škoda Traction Electrics Ltd in August 2006.

Products

Centralised traffic control systems, signalling systems for stations, block interlocking equipment, track circuit equipment and axle-counters, level crossing systems, automatic train control equipment, control systems, panels and mimic boards, point machines.

Global Traffic Technologies LLC

7800 Third Street North St Paul, Minnesota 55128 5441, USA
Tel: (+1 651) 789 73 33   Fax: (+1 651) 789 73 34
e-mail: gttsales@gtt.com
Web: www.gtt.com

Background

Global Traffic Technologies LLC (GTT) is a privately held company that includes senior management ownership.

Products

GTT's Opticom™, GPS and infrared systems assist the movement of mass-transit and emergency vehicles through signal-controlled intersections to optimise on-schedule service. GTT's Canoga™ traffic sensing system provides real-time information on individual vehicles and traffic patterns.

Globe Transportation Graphics

2097 East Aurora Road, Twinsburg, Ohio 44087, USUS
Tel: (+1 410) 685 67 50   Fax: (+1 330) 425 93 71
e-mail: info@globegrafix.com
Web: www.globegrafix.com

Key personnel

Contact: Vicki Porter

Products

Globe Transportation Graphics interior and exterior durable TransGrafix® markings, decals and signage can be customised, are graffiti- and chemical-proof, weather- and vandal-resistant and available with raised letters and braille. Globe sub-surface prints on the most durable and impervious of surface materials and utilises adhesives of unprecedented strength and bond. TransGrafix® also features High Performance Photo-Luminescence (HPPL) to glow safely in a power failure.

Contracts

Globe has sold TransGrafix® to the passenger rail markets in Hong Kong, Australia, Turkey, France, Russian Federation, Switzerland, Singapore and Canada.

Gorgy Timing SA

8 Av Pierre de Coubertin, ZI Percevaliere 7402, F-38174 Seyssinet, France
Tel: (+33 4) 76 70 19 60   Fax: (+33 4) 76 49 06 21
e-mail: gorgy@gorgy-timing.fr
Web: www.gorgy-timing.fr

Key personnel

Sales Export Division: *Maryse Grondin*

Products

Radio-synchronised clocks, time centres, electronic message displays, NTP time server, GPS master clocks, desk/console clocks.

GrantRail Projects

1 Carolina Court, Lakeside, Doncaster DN4 5RA, UK
Tel: (+44 1302) 79 11 00   Fax: (+44 1302) 79 12 00
e-mail: marketing@grantrail.co.uk
Web: www.grantrail.co.uk
12 Fitzroy Place, Sauchiehall Street, Glasgow G3 7RW, UK
Tel: (+44 141) 248 49 22   Fax: (+44 141) 221 80 94
10 Finsbury Square, Moorgate, London EC2A 1AD, UK
Tel: (+44 207) 496 33 00   Fax: (+44 207) 496 33 01

Key personnel

Chief Executive: *Gren Edwards*
Managing Director: *David Moorland*
Regional Director, London and South East England:
   Andrew Richards
Regional Director, Central England: *Paul Jones*

Background

GrantRail Projects is a subsidiary of the GrantRail Group, part of the VolkerWessels Group.

Capabilities

GrantRail can undertake a wide variety of rail sector development and construction projects, ranging from the re-establishment of disused railways to the construction of urban mass transit systems. GrantRail Projects has a fully integrated project management solution for all rail sector projects which is supported by the multidisciplinary capability within the GrantRail Group of companies.

Contracts

Current projects include: Manchester Metrolink Phase 3a; Dublin Lias Line C extensions to the Point; Lea Valley On Network Works; Nuneaton Area remodelling – West Coast Mainline; Hull Docks branchline; Docklands Light Railway work packages 6 and 8 serving Stratford and the 2012 Olympic Games facilities; and Manchester Metrolink.

GrantRail Projects, as part of the MPact-Thales consortium, has been awarded the design, construction and main contract for the Manchester Metrolink extensions to Oldham and Rochdale, Droylsden and Chorlton. Greater Manchester Passenger Transport Executive (GMPTE) has appointed MPact-Thales as the main contractor for the new lines as part of the project. The new Metrolink lines will cover nearly 20 miles and include 26 stops.

Lea Valley On Network Works: as part of the improvements to transport links and capacity for the London 2012 Olympic Games, the project involves the extension of the Stratford Station platform, the remodelling of the existing signalling system, erection of 12 new OHLE stations and new permanent way layouts which are to be wired to suit bi-directional running.

Hull Docks Branchline enhancement: a nine month multi-discipline contract to increase the line speed of the track for Network Rail. Permanent way works consist of the installation of turnout and twin track and smooth lining of the realignment throughout.

GrantRail Signalling Ltd

1 Carolina Court, Lakeside, Doncaster DN4 5RA, UK
Tel: (+44 1302) 79 11 00   Fax: (+44 1302) 79 12 00
e-mail: marketing@grantrail.co.uk
Web: www.grantrail.co.uk
Queens House, Micklegate, York Y01 6JH, UK
Tel: (+44 1904) 68 64 68   Fax: (+44 1904) 68 64 69
Derwent House, RTC Business Park, London Road DE24 8UP, UK
Somerton House, Hazell Drive, Newport, South Wales NP10 8FY, UK
Fax: (+44 1633) 81 63 38

Key personnel

Chief Executive: *Gren Edwards*
Managing Director: *Martin Hawley*
Head of Engineering, Signalling: *Naomi Stone*
General Manager: *Steve Wright*
Professional Head of Signalling: *Rod Jewell*

Background

GrantRail Signalling is a subsidiary business within GrantRail Group Ltd, part of the VolkerWessels Group.

Capabilities

Capabilities include: modifications and renewals of signalling design; construction and installation and testing of new signalling; post commissioning support.

Contracts

Calder Valley, single cut, double cut; line side signalling renewal, Cottage Lane.

Hanning & Kahl GmbH & Co KG

Rudolf Diesel Strasse 6, D-33813 Oerlinghausen, Germany
PO Box 1342, D-33806 Oerlinghausen, Germany
Tel: (+49 5202) 70 76 00   Fax: (+49 5202) 70 76 29
e-mail: info@huk.hanning.com
Web: www.hanning-kahl.de

Key personnel

General Managers: *Wolfgang Helas*
Brake Division Manager: *Dietrich Radtke*
LRT Division Manager: *Christian Schmidt*
Service Division Manager: *Peter Spilker*
Sales Manager, Brakes: *Jürgen Stammeier*
Sales Manager, LRT: *Joachim Pütsch*
Sales Manager, Services/LRT: *Joachim Zehn*
Sales Manager, Services/Brakes: *Martin Epp*

Products
LRT Division
Point controls, signalling systems, level crossing safety devices, single-line track safety devices, track circuits, mass detectors, vehicle reporting system, radio control, electronic data recorder and accessories including insulated guard rail

tie bars, rail termination boxes and contact systems.

Point setting mechanisms
LRT Division: Point controls, signalling systems, level crossing safety devices, single-line track safety devices, track circuits, mass detectors, vehicle reporting systems, radio control, electronic data recorders and accessories including guard rail tie bars, rail boxes and contact systems. Point setting mechanisms for all gauges and types of rail, manual point mechanisms, electric point mechanisms with magnetic, motor, electrohydraulic or central control.

All point mechanisms can also be set manually and are available with a tongue detector and a mechanical double-interlocking device for tongues in open and closed positions.

Train to Wayside Communication Systems (TWC), LED signalling devices, passenger information systems, vehicle management systems, depot management systems, point management systems (WEDIS), route diagnosis systems (FADIS), point heaters, point heater controllers and electrical locally-set points.

Service Division: Services and testing and measuring equipment for point setting mechanisms and controllers, signalling installations, TWC systems.

Contracts
Recent contracts include projects in: Melbourne (Australia); Calgary (Canada); Milan, Rome and Turin (Italy); Birmingham, Croydon, Manchester and Sheffield (UK); Dallas, Salt Lake City, San Diego and San Jose (US); and cities in Austria, Belgium, Finland, Germany, Hong Kong, Netherlands, Norway, Sweden and Switzerland.

Hasler Rail AG

Untermattweg 8, CH-3027 Bern, Switzerland
Tel: (+41 31) 990 71 11   Fax: (+41 31) 990 72 22
e-mail: info@haslerrail.com
Web: www.haslerrail.com

Key personnel
Sales Manager: *Gilbert Lile*

Background
Hasler Rail AG is a member of Sécheron Hasler AG Group.

Products
Microprocessor-controlled Hasler TELOC® On-Train Monitoring and Recording (OTMR) systems, speed and distance measuring systems, Hasler optical pulse generators for axle or gearbox mounting, modular cab display systems for ATC and ATP applications.

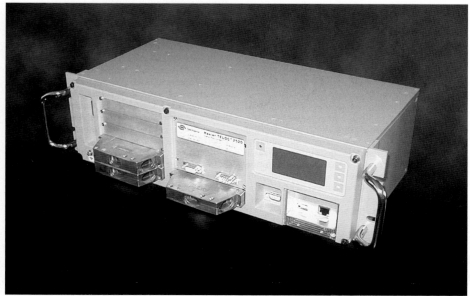

Hasler TELOC® 2500 system   1136192

Recent orders include the supply of Hasler TELOC® systems; ETCS SBB with ALSTOM; Attiko Greece with Melco; ETCS for Talgo 350 with Bombardier; ETCS for Korean National Railway.

Hitachi Ltd

Transportation Systems
18-13, Soto-Kanda 1-chome, Chiyudo-ku, Tokyo, 101-8608, Japan
Tel: (+81 3) 258 11 11
Fax: (+81 3) 45 64 62 52
Web: www.hitachi-rail.com

Key personnel
Chief Operating Officer of Transportation Systems: *Toshihide Uchimura*

Products
Total railway traffic management system including data acquisition and passenger information service, Automatic Train Control (ATC), Automatic Train Operation (ATO), Autonomous Train Integration (ATI) train communication networks, electronic interlocking devices.

Hitachi Kokusai Electric Inc

Head Office
Wireless Communications Systems Division, 4-14-1 Sotokanda, Chiyoda-ku, Tokyo 101-8980, Japan
Tel: (+81 3) 52 09 59 31 (Main)
(+81 3) 67 34 95 00 (Wireless Communications Division)
Fax: (+81 3) 52 09 61 19 (Main)
(+81 3) 52 09 59 84 (Wireless Communications Division)
e-mail: www.admin@h-kokusai.com
Web: www.h-kokusai.com

Key personnel
President and Chief Executive Officer: *Kunio Hasegawa*
Executive Vice-President and Executive Officer: *Ryoichi Tanaka*
Staff: 2,274

Subsidiaries
The company has subsidiaries in Canada, Germany, the UK and the US.

Background
In October 2000, Kokusai Electric Co Ltd, Hitachi Denshi Ltd and Yagi Antenna Co Ltd were merged to form Hitachi Kokusai Electric Inc.

Products
Train radio communication systems.

Howells Railway Products Limited

Longley Lane, Sharston Industrial Estate, Wythenshawe, Manchester M22 4SS, UK
Tel: (+44 161) 945 55 67
Fax: (+44 161) 945 55 97
e-mail: info@howells-railway.co.uk
Web: www.howells-railway.co.uk

Key personnel
Sales Engineer: *John Husles*

Products
AWS electroindicators; impedance bonds; lineside disconnection box; terminal blocks; signal passed at danger indicators.

Hypercom Corporation

Robert-Bosch-Strasse 25, D-63225 Langen, Germany
Tel: (+49 6103) 911 62 51
Fax: (+49 6103) 911 61 00
e-mail: bfontius@hypercom.com
Web: www.hypercom.com

Key personnel
Chairman: *Norma Stout*
Chief Executive Officer and President: *Philippe Tartavull*
Interim Chief Financial Officer: *Robert M Vreeland*
Senior Vice-President, Global Operations: *Henry Gaillard*
Staff: 550

Background
In 2008 Thales e-Transactions was purchased by Hypercom Corporation.

Products
Vehicle monitoring and passenger information systems allow public transport operators to manage their urban bus and tramway fleets more efficiently and improve onboard safety. These tools help vehicles respect schedules and intervals, assure interchanges and provide information for passengers on board and at stops. The company offers a global system integrating a number of useful functions enabling operators to operate their fleet more efficiently and safely (with intelligent radio communications systems, continuous vehicle positioning, management of priority at traffic lights, for example), to broadcast real-time information to users, to technically monitor vehicles, control fare collection equipment and acquire an in depth knowledge of their network.

The company also offers a range of services including deployment, operation and maintenance, electronic toll collection systems and urban traffic management systems.

Hypertac

31 rue Isidore Maille, F-76410 Saint Aubin lès Elbeuf, France
Tel: (+33 2) 32 96 91 76   Fax: (+33 2) 32 96 91 70
e-mail: info@hypertac.fr
Web: www.hypertac.com

Background
Hypertac is part of Smiths Interconnect, a division of Smiths Group. Hypertac designs and manufactures connectors for electrical and electronic applications.

The company also has offices in China, Germany, Italy, the UK and US.

Products

Design, development and manufacturing of electrical connection systems for the rail traction industry.

All Hypertac Interconnect solutions have machine-turned round pins in the male half and the special Hypertac hyperboloid socket contact in the female half. This socket has a number of spring wires, set at a small angle to the centre line giving the special hyperboloid contact. As the pin enters the socket, the spring wires are deflected within their elastic limit. There is a very smooth wiping action and as result, minimal wear.

Products include rectangular connectors lhs/lhf series including modular connectors, rack and panel connectors and amovable contacts, as approved by SNCF and RATP.

Circular couplers include three-pole connectors, power couplers, car-to-car connection.

The Hypertac group has provided interconnect products for more than 40 years for mass and rapid transit projects throughout the world, including TGV, Eurostar, Mass Transit Railway Hong Kong, London Underground and Seoul subway, using its engineering expertise to design connectors for applications such as signalling equipment, power supplies, AC/DC converters, lighting, communications such as ERTMS systems (RF/HF link) and auxiliary equipment.

Developments

Eurobalise Hypertac Transponder is the latest connector system technology for the Eurobalise system. The Hypertac transponder connector ensures correct data transmission and reliable signal integrity through the use of special alloys and conductive plating to ensure the connector resistance to harsh environment conditions. A bayonet locking system features easy maintenance and download/upload of new information into the Balise.

INEO Systrans

Avenue de Conflans – 2 allée Edouard Branly, F-78260, France
Tel: (+33 1) 39 22 57 00
Fax: (+33 1) 39 22 57 99
e-mail: systrans@ineo.com
Web: www.ineo-systrans.com

Background

INEO Systrans, part of the INEO group of companies, is a subsidiary of the Services and Energy division of the Suez Group.

Products/Services

Supply and installation of signalling, supervision, communications and information systems, including: railway and road traffic signalling; infrastructure management, SCADA, automatic fleet management and vehicle location systems; radio and multi-service networks, platform video surveillance and security communications systems; and real time passenger information and public address systems.

Contracts

INEO Systrans has equipped 50 light rail systems and bus networks in Belgium, France, Israel, Spain, Switzerland and the UK.

Infodev EDI Inc

PO Box 1222 HV, Quebec G1R 5A7, Canada
Tel: (+1 418) 681 35 39
Fax: (+1 418) 681 12 09
e-mail: info@infodev.ca
Web: www.infodev.ca

Products

Automatic Passenger Counting (APC) systems for buses and urban and main line passenger rail vehicles; BusStops-2 reporting software to provide trip, run, route and stops analysis; Traffic Light Priority Systems (TLPS) for public transport operations.

Infodev's APC systems collect data via multiple-sensor bars and directional counters, process the data using an onboard microprocessor and transmit information via radio links, using a GPS antenna to provide vehicle location details.

Ingegneria dei Sistemi Elettronici srl (ISE)

Via Nuova 128, I-56010 Migliarino Pisano, (Vecchiano), Pisa, Italy
Tel: (+39 050) 80 43 43
Fax: (+39 050) 80 47 27
e-mail: acremoncini@ise-srl.com
Web: www.ise-srl.com

Key personnel

Managing Director: *Daniele Bianchi*
Technical Director: *Marco Lazzarotti*
Marketing Manager: *Andrea Cremoncini*
Railway Systems: *Riccardo Bufalini*

Background

Certified to ISO 9001 quality standards, (certification to UNIFE IRIS Quality standard is also in progress), the company has experience in the fields of engineering, design and development of real-time systems in embedded applications, and is included in the list of official Research and Development Laboratories of the Italian Ministry of Scientific Research (MIUR).

Current capabilities include engineering, prototype development, series production, installation and lifetime support of onboard railway electronic systems and software.

Products

Monitoring, communication, supervision, fault investigation and control systems for light rail and transit vehicles. Bench Test Units (BTU) and Portable Test Equipment (PTE) and software for diagnostic field maintenance and for production tests on vehicle electronic units and sub-assemblies. Fail-safe systems and software engineering and manufacturing, including complete fire detection, alarm dispatching and extinguishing systems.

Contracts

Between 2004 and 2007 the company has completed the supply of onboard diagnostic, propulsion and vehicle logic control for CQ310-311 Atlanta transit authority (MARTA) on behalf of ALSTOM of Hornell (New York), as the prime contractor, and is now providing spare parts and repair support (both to ALSTOM and also directly to MARTA). ISE also supplies spare parts and services to the MBTA Transportation Authority in Boston (MA), as well as to several major rolling stock manufacturing and prime contractors. Between 2008 and 2012, the company will provide video surveillance systems, monitoring/diagnostic equipment and fire alert systems mass transit and rail vehicles, on behalf of AnsaldoBreda SpA (Italy).

Integrian, Inc

511 David Drive, Morrisville, North Carolina 27560, US
Tel: (+1 919) 472 50 09
Fax: (+1 919) 472 50 99
e-mail: info@integrian.com
Web: www.integrian.com

Key personnel

Board of Directors: *Ich-Kien Lao, Davie Barrett, Peter Durand, Olin Giles, John Glushik, Gregory G Johnson,*

Background

Integrian Inc acquired Australian-based Innovonics Ltd in December 2005.

Products/Services

Integrian specialises in design, development, manufacture, project management and installation of transportation surveillance systems. The company has delivered over 2,000 transit and fleet computer systems over the past 10 years to transit authorities and companies around the world.

INIT Innovative Informatikanwendungen in Transport-, Verkehrs- und Leitsystemen GmbH

Kaeppelestrasse 4-6, D-76131 Karlsruhe, Germany
Tel: (+49 721) 610 00   Fax: (+49 721) 610 03 99
e-mail: postmaster@init-ka.de
Web: www.init-ka.de

Subsidiaries

Australia
INIT Pty Ltd
Level 5, Toowong Tower, 9 Sherwood Road, Toowong Qld, 4066 Australia
Tel: (+61 7) 33 10 88 18   Fax: (+61 7) 33 10 88 00

US
INIT Innovations in Transportation Inc
1420 Kristina Way, Suite 101, Chesapeake, Virginia 23320
Tel: (+1 757) 413 91 00   Fax: (+1 757) 413 50 19

Canada
INIT Innovations in Transportation (Eastern Canada) Inc/INIT Innovations en Transport (Canada Est) Inc
14 Place du Commerce, suite 360, Île-des-Soeurs, Montréal, Québec H3E 1T7, Canada
Tel: (+1 514) 766 28 36   Fax: (+1 514) 766 15 78
INIT, Innovations in Transportation (Western Canada) Inc
949 West 41st Avenue, Vancouver, BC V5Z2N5, Canada
Tel: (+1 778) 995 04 93

United Arab Emirates
Init Innovation in Traffic Systems FZE
Dubai Airport Free Zone, Office 6EB 244, Dubai, UAE
Tel: (+971) 47 01 72 86

Key personnel

Chief Sales Officer: *Dr Jürgen Greschner*

Products

Computer Aided Dispatch (CAD) and Automated Vehicle Location (now called ITCS, Intermodal Transport Control System) (GPS/DGPS based).

Vehicle dispatch and service restoration.

Advanced voice and data radio communication (analogue and digital private systems and subscriber systems).

Traffic signal priority systems.

Terminal Management Systems.

International Road Dynamics Inc (IRD)

702 – 43rd Street East, Saskatoon, SK, S7K 3T9, Canada
Tel: (+1 306) 653 66 00
Fax: (+1 306) 242 55 99
e-mail: info@irdinc.com
Web: www.irdinc.com

Key personnel

Chairman: *Arthur Bergan*
President and Chief Executive Officer: *Terry Bergan*
Vice-President, Corporate Resources: *Sharon Parker*
Executive Vice-President and Chief Operating Officer: *Randy Hanson*
Vice-President, Finance: *Lorne Green*
Vice-President, Technical Sales and Domestic Business Strategy: *Brian Taylor*
Vice-President, Project Operations and Customer Service: *Basil Ciepliski*
Vice-President, Sales: *Rod Klashinsky*
Vice-President, International Business: *Greg Wallis*
Vice-President, Business Development, Special Projects and Risk Management: *Mel Karakochuk*

Products

Intelligent transport systems applications and technology for commercial vehicle operations, traffic data collection and toll road systems. IRD also offers fleet management and public transport computer software and systems through its IRD Teleride Division and Teleride (UK).

Driver management, scheduling, fleet maintenance, public information, onboard computer-aided dispatch and automated vehicle location software and computer systems.

Italtel SpA

I-20019 Settimo Milanese (Milan), Italy
Tel: (+39 02) 438 81   Fax: (+39 02) 43 88 72 00

Key personnel

Chairman: *Roberto Quarta*
Chief Executive Officer: *Mauro Righetti*
General Manager and Chief Financial Officer: *Rinaldo Tonsi*
General Manager, Chief Technology Officer and Head of Product Unit Mulitmedia Products and Solutions: *Antonino d'Angelo*
General Manager and Chief Strategic Officer: *Claudio Chiarenza*
Staff: Approximately 2,300

Products

Information technology systems for traffic and transport; urban traffic control systems; GPS and radio-based Automatic Vehicle Monitoring (AVM) systems; passenger information systems; communication networks for mass transport systems; security systems for rail stations.

Iteris

Corporate Headquarters
1700 Carnegie Avenue, Santa Ana, California 92705, USA
Tel: (+1 949) 270 94 00   Fax: (+1 949) 270 94 01
e-mail: pr@iteris.com
Web: www.iteris.com

Key personnel

President and Chief Executive Officer: *Abbas Mohaddes*
Senior Vice-President and General Manager, Transportation Systems: *Alan Clelland*
Vice President of Finance and Chief Financial Officer: *James S Miele*

Background

Iteris works with transport planning companies to improve systems' efficiency and safety. They design Intelligent Transport Systems (ITS) for a range of urban and rural transport systems using engineering consultancy services for traffic engineering and transportation planning. Solutions are developed with US clients to solve projected, future transport issues to design and implement technologically advanced systems.

Contracts

In August 2008 Iteris was awarded a contract from the Los Angeles County Metropolitan Transportation Authority (LA Metro) to implement bus signal priority systems for three Metro Rapid transit corridors. Under the terms of the contract, Iteris will be responsible for the design, acquisition, deployment and ongoing operation and maintenance of bus traffic signal priority systems. Deployment of the bus signal priority systems is scheduled to be completed within 30 months.

Ing Karl und Albert Kruch GesmbH & Co KG (Kruch)

Pfarrgasse 87, A-1230 Vienna, Austria
Tel: (+43 1) 616 31 65
Fax: (+43 1) 616 31 68
e-mail: office@kruch.com
Web: www.kruch.com

Products

Signal masts; signal lights; mast-mounted switch cabinets.

Kyosan Electric Mfg Co Ltd

4-2 Marunouchi 3-chome, Chiyoda-ku, Tokyo 100-0005, Japan
Tel: (+81 3) 32 14 81 36
Fax: (+81 3) 32 11 24 50
Web: www.kyosan.co.jp
Head office
29-1, Heian-cho, 2-chome, Tsurumi-ku, Yokohama, Japan
Tel: (+81 45) 503 81 00
Fax: (+81 45) 503 15 61

Key personnel

President: *T Nishikawa*
Director and Executive Officer, Export Sales: *Kazuo Hinata*
General Manager, Overseas Department: *Norihiro Ishii*

Subsidiary

Taiwan Kyosan Co Ltd, Taichung, Taiwan

Products

Centralised Traffic Control (CTC) system, Automatic Train Protection (ATP) system, Automatic Train Operation (ATO) system, Automatic Train Supervision (ATS) system, automatic block signal equipment, solid-state interlocking equipment, relay interlocking equipment, level crossing signal and gate equipment, information display system, half-height platform screen door, gap-filler.

Contracts

Contracts include supply of signalling system for the Automated People Mover for Hong Kong International Airport, Singapore Changi Airport and Incheon International Airport. Signalling systems for Singapore LRT Sengkang and Punggol line. Solid state interlocking system for Seoul Rolling Stock Depot. Signalling system for Caracas Suburban line, Venezuela. Signalling system for Busan subway Line 3, Korea.

Lumiplan Technologies de Communication

ZA du Moulin Neuf, Impasse Fresnel, PO Box 227, F-44815 Saint Herblain, Cedex, France
Tel: (+33 2) 40 92 15 43
Fax: (+33 2) 40 92 35 43
e-mail: lumiplan@lumiplan.com
Web: www.lumiplan.com

Key personnel

President: *Jacques Daniel*
Managers: *Jacques Cesbron, Arnaud Bailly*
Sales: *Alain Paumier, Charlotte Simon, Catherine Troufleau*

Products

Real-time information systems for public transport users including electronic display (at stop, on board, bus station and platform); interactive public access terminals.

Contracts

Systems have been installed in major cities for over 20 years, including: Brest, Arras, Grenoble, Nantes, Ile de France, Limoges, Nîmes, Bordeaux, Nancy, Douai, Lyon, Rouen, Reims, Toulouse, Le Havre, Orleans, La Rochelle, Valenciennes, Maubeuge, Angers, Geneva, Lausanne, Thionville, Valence.

Marl International Ltd

Marl Business Park, Ulverston LA12 9BN, UK
Tel: (+44 1229) 58 24 30
Fax: (+44 1229) 58 51 55
e-mail: sales@marl.co.uk
    gemma.birkett@marl.co.uk (Rail Sector)
Web: www.marlrail.com; www.marl.co.uk

Key personnel

Marl Rail Sector: *Gemma Birkett*

Products
Signalling

Lumarled: LED signal lamps as a direct replacement for existing filament lamps in tunnel signal heads; a full range of filament bulb replacements including 253 and 238 series; LED lamps for signal applications – both Network Rail approved; LED buffer stop light/barrow crossing indicators with Network Rail approval; a range of signalling products for use on London Underground.

Minorplanet Systems plc

Head Office
Greenwich House, 223 North Street, Leeds LS7 2AA, UK
Tel: (+44 113) 251 16 00   Fax: (+44 113) 251 16 85
e-mail: hq@minorplanet.com
Web: www.minorplanet.com

Key personnel

Chief Executive: *Terry Donovan*
Finance Director: *Richard Hopkin*
Operations Director: *Carolanne Hurley*

Other offices

The company also has offices in Bristol, Glasgow and Luton, UK and in Australia, Germany, Ireland, Italy, the Netherlands, New Zealand and Singapore.

Products

MVA provides real-time and historical information of a vehicle's movement, which is utilised by fleet managers to reduce their operating costs. Minorplanet's core business is Vehicle Management Information (VMI™), which comprises a comprehensive suite of software-based reports taken from the information collected by Minorplanet's own Data Collection Unit (DCU), a small GPS unit with the processing power of a laptop computer and its own built-in artificial intelligence, which is installed in each vehicle.

The DCU collects GPS data in either second or minute intervals while the vehicle is moving. The captured data is transmitted by the mobile phone network (GSM) and downloaded to a base station computer running the VMI™ software.

Information can also be downloaded automatically and free of cost by short-wave radio when the vehicle returns to the depot. Minorplanet also offers the ability to 'live-track' a vehicle, giving an almost instant pinpointed location, which can be saved and replayed on highly detailed digital maps.

Minorplanet has a customer base of approximately 8,000 businesses.

Mirror Technology Ltd

Unit 4, Redwood House, Orchard Industrial Estate, Toddington GL54 5EB, UK
Tel: (+44 1242) 62 15 34
Fax: (+44 1242) 62 15 29
e-mail: enquiries@mirrortechnology.co.uk
Web: www.mirrortechnology.co.uk

Key personnel
Sales Director: *Malcolm Robertson*
Production Director: *R M J Chambers*

Products
Platform mirrors for driver-only operation, surveillance and as an aid to safety by providing rearward visibility from the driver's cab; vandal-resistant polycarbonate pedestrian subway mirrors.

A variety of models are available in different sizes and designs to suit most station layouts. Special versions are also available for underground and light rail.

Contracts
UK train operating companies supplied include Chiltern Railways, South Central, Docklands Light Rail; Lisbon Metro, Manchester, Medellin Metro, Metrolink, Midland Metro, Sheffield Supertram, Thames Trains and West Anglia Great Northern and most main line operators.

Mobitec AB

Ölltorp Industrial Area, Box 97, SE-524 21, Sweden
Tel: (+46 513) 29 00
Fax: (+49 513) 229 22
e-mail: info@mobitec.eu
Web: www.mobitec.eu

Key personnel
Managing Director: *Oliver Wels*
Marketing Manager: *Katrin Sure*

Background
Mobitec AB is a Business Unit of Digital Recorders Inc.

Products
LED/Flipdot destination sign systems; LED-based interior route indicators with automatic next-stop indication; LED based interior next-stop indicators; digital voice announcers; sunlight-readable LED destination sign systems; multi-media interior TFT screen systems.

Morio Denki Co Ltd

34-1 Tateishi 4-chome, Katsushika-ku, Tokyo 124-0012, Japan
Tel: (+81 3) 36 91 31 81
Fax: (+81 3) 36 92 13 33
Web: www.morio.co.jp

Key personnel
Chairman: *S Yamagata*
President: *K Miura*
Senior Managing Director: *T Yagishita*

Products
Automatic Train Control and Automatic Train Stop units, station override prevention systems, event recorders, monitoring systems and alarm systems.

Nippon Signal Co Ltd

Head Office
1-5-1, Marunouchi, Chiyoda-ku, Tokyo 100-6513, Japan
Tel: (+81 3) 32 17 72 00   Fax: (+81 3) 32 17 73 00
e-mail: info@signal.co.jp
Web: www.signal.co.jp

Key personnel
President and Chief Executive Officer: *Yohei Furuhata*

Products
Integrated Traffic Control by Computer (ITC); Centralised Traffic Control System (CTC); Automatic Program Route Control System (PRC); Automatic Train Control System (ATC); Automatic Train Operation (ATO); Automatic Train Stop System (ATS); train detection equipment; transponder; maintenance management system; relay interlocking equipment; train information processing system; electronic interlocking equipment; electronic block system; railway crossing monitor system; Train Navigation System (TNS); other signal equipment; universal traffic management system; centralised area traffic control system; local controllers; traffic signal-integrated street lights; ultrasonic vehicle detector; vehicle-type classifying detector; image processing vehicle detector; road traffic information system; traffic information board; traffic flow data counter.

Nokia

Head office
Keilalahdentie 2-4, PO Box 226, FIN-00045 Nikia Group, Finland
Tel: (+358) 718 00 80 00
Web: www.nokia.com

Key personnel
Senior Vice-President: *Matti Peltola*
Vice-President Communications: *Arja Suominen*

Products
Digital radio technology such as TETRA networks and terminals which includes communication security, fast group calls, emergency call functionality, prioritised calls, advanced messaging and data communication services.

Contracts
Nokia was selected by the Nanjing Metro in Jiangsu province, China, to supply its digital TETRA professional mobile radio system. The system provides TETRA voice and data service to staff operating the urban rail system.

Nokia provided DXTip switching equipment, TETRA base stations, a Nokia dispatcher workstation and a large number of TETRA terminals.

Nortel Networks Germany GmbH & Co

Hahnstrasse 37-39, D-60528 Frankfurt am Main, Germany
Tel: (+49 69) 669 70
Fax: (+49 69) 97 11 11
e-mail: euroinfo@nortelnetworks.com
Web: www.nortelnetworks.com

Key personnel
Assistant Business Development GSM-R: *Leonie Geray*

Subsidiary companies
Offices in Canada, Europe, Asia-Pacific, Caribbean, Latin Amercia, Middle East, Africa and USA.

Products
Missioncritical telephony and IP-optimised networks supplied to customers in 150 countries; ASCI (Advanced Speech Call Items) for high-speed trains. GSM-R base transceiver station (BTS) for trackside coverage under adverse environmental conditions; specially-adapted radio algorithms to allow error-free voice and data communications at train speeds up to 500 km/h. Nortel is a member of the MORANE consortium (Mobile Radio for Railway Networks in Europe).

Projects
In November 2005, Nortel was selected by Thales UK to provide a digital wireless communications network and support services for the Channel Tunnel Rail Link between London and Folkestone.

on365

Weldon Road, Loughborough LE11 5RN, UK
Tel: (+44 1509) 26 11 00   Fax: (+44 1509) 26 11 48
e-mail: supporting technology@on365.co.uk
Web: www.on365.co.uk

Key personnel
Sales and Marketing Director: *Chris Smith*

Background
Founded in 1984, the company was previously called Universal Power Systems Ltd.

Products
Major turnkey supplier of complete data centre solutions including power, cooling racks, distribution, security, environmental monitoring, structured cabling, fire protection and management.

Support capabilities encompass installation, integrated system testing, network integration, on-site maintenance and audit/review services.

Optelecom-NFK, Inc

Headquarters Americas and Japan
12920 Cloverleaf Center Drive, Germantown, Maryland 20874, US
Tel: (+1 301) 444 22 00
Fax: (+1 301) 444 22 99
e-mail: sales.us@optelecom-nfk.com
Web: www.optelecom-nkf.com
Headquarters EMEA & Asia
Optelecom-NFK BV
Zuidelijk Halfrond 4, NL-2801 DD Gouda, Netherlands
Tel: (+31 182) 59 23 33   Fax: (+31 182) 59 21 23
e-mail: sales.nl@optelecom-nfk.com

Key personnel
Chairman and President: *Edmund Ludwig*
Chief Financial Officer: *James Armstrong*
Executive Vice-President and Chief Operating Officer: *Thomas Overwijn*
Vice-President of Sales and Marketing: *Roland Hooghiemstra*

Background
Founded in 1972, Optelecom-NKF Inc has offices in the US, the Netherlands, France, Spain, the UK and Singapore.

Products
A global supplier of network video equipment including video servers, Ethernet switches,

fiber optic systems, network video recorders, and video management software with complete solutions for traffic management and security surveillance.

New developments

The new Siqura® Camera Line is available in both IP and analog versions including box cameras, fixed dome cameras, and PTZ dome cameras for both indoor and outdoor applications.

Traficon and Optelecom-NKF have been working together through 2008 to develop the Siqura® TrafficServer™, an IP-based Automatic Incident Detection (AID) solution for the traffic monitoring market to be commercially released in the second quarter of 2009. The TrafficServer™ will detect major incidents within seconds, including stopped vehicles, smoke in tunnels, wrong-way drivers, fallen objects, and slow moving vehicles. TrafficServer™ displays incident verification data on-screen and provides real-time DVD-quality video content for accurate verification and recording at the Traffic Management Center.

Contracts

Optelecom-NFK provided the video surveillance and communication system serving Line 1 and Line 2 of the Beijing Metro System. The contract was in partnership with Keybridge Communications Co Ltd, a China-based system integrator.

Orbital Sciences Corporation

Transportation Management Systems (Orbital TMS)
21839 Atlantic Boulevard, Dulles, Virginia 20166, US
Tel: (+1 703) 406 50 00   Fax: (+1 703) 406 55 72
e-mail: yuhas.franny@orbital.com
Web: www.orbital.com, www.orbitaltms.com

Key personnel

Chairman and Chief Executive Officer: *David W Thompson*
Vice-Chairman, President and Chief Operating Officer: *James R Thompson*
Vice-Chairman and Chief Financial Officer: *Garrett F Pierce*
Senior Vice-President and General Manager, Transportation Management Systems: *David A Kachemov*
Staff: Approximately 2,800

Products

GPS-based asset management services for bus and commuter rail systems, including OrbCAD™, a GPS system that provides customer information, vehicle tracking, digital cellular communications and timekeeping information.

Contracts

In December 2005, Orbital TMS was awarded a contract by Foothill Transit, USA for a SmartBus™ System (SBS) to track and manage its fleet of vehicles. The SBS includes a Bus Signal Priority (BSP) capability and Orbitals; Advanced Traveler Information System (ATIS). The contract was valued at USD11.7 million.

In March 2006, Orbital TMS was awarded a contract, valued at USD8.2million, to provide a next-vehicle-arrival system for 200 bus stops and to upgrade the existing CAD/AVL capabilities for Maryland Transit Administration's fleet.

Peek Traffic BV

Basicweg 16, PO Box 2542, NL-3800 GB Amersfoort, Netherlands
Tel: (+31 33) 454 17 77   Fax: (+31 33) 454 17 40
e-mail: info@peektraffic.nl
Web: www.peektraffic.nl

Key personnel

Business Manager, Railway Products: *J R Opperman*
Export Manager: *A Koopmans*

Products

Train identification and information systems for metros and light rail systems.

Pepperl + Fuchs GmbH

Visolux
Kitzingstrasse 25-27, D-12277 Berlin, Germany
Tel: (+49 30) 61 67 20
Fax: (+49 30) 61 67 24 68
e-mail: info@pepperl-fuchs.com
Web: www.pepperl-fuchs.com

Products

Light-beam switches; proximity switches; ultrasonic sensors; data transmission sensors; distance measuring devices; onboard and stationary PIR detectors.

Pintsch Bamag Antriebs – und Verkehrstechnik GmbH

Hünxer Strasse 149 46537 Dinslaken Germany
Tel: (+49 2064) 60 20
Fax: (+49 2064) 60 22 66
e-mail: info@pintschbamag.de
Web: www.pintschbamag.de

Key personnel

Managing Director: *Dr Rolf-Dieter Krächter (spokesperson), Hans Ulrich Reichling*
Head of Business Unit: *Dieter Schiminski*
Strategic Concerns: *Ulrich Nagorski*
Head of Sales and Export Manager: *Ulrich Rink*
Manager, Quality Control: *Uwe Reske*

Background

Pintsch Bamag is a member of the Schaltbau Group.

Products

Level crossing protection systems and components, computer controlled level crossing protection (all types of supervision: main signal indication, locally and remote monitoring), train detection devices, trackside signals (bulbs and LED technology), roadside signals (flashing or static light), barriers (different types), audible alarm devices, radar obstacle detection (danger area warning system), four-quad protection; fibre-optic speed indicators.

Poletech Systems Ltd

Bowbridge Road, Newark NG24 4EQ, UK
Tel: (+44 1636) 61 14 26
Fax: (+44 1636) 61 21 21
e-mail: sales@poletech.co.uk
Web: www.poletech.co.uk
    www.passivelysafe.co.uk

Key personnel

Chairman: *James R Lee*
Managing Director: *Dr A John Lawrenson*
Sales Director: *Barrie H Burke*

Products

Poletech demountable pole-mounting system allowing quick replacement of pole without civil works, also suitable for LRT systems; MAC modular access chambers, covers and frames. HA approved 'break-away' wiring systems for lattix and other passively safe columns and sign posts. Retractable utility towers for water and electricity supplies to market squares.

Contracts

Responsibility for upgrading all of London's bus stations rests with London Bus Passenger Infrastructure. The Poletech system is being used to support all lighting columns, traffic signals, pedestrian rails and signs.

Poletech has supplied MAC modular access chambers to Balfour Beatty and other railway contractors and to most local authorities in the UK.

Powernetics International Ltd

Jason Works, Clarence Street, Loughborough LE11 1DX, UK
Tel: (+44 1509) 21 41 53
Fax: (+44 1509) 26 24 60
e-mail: jag@powernetics.co.uk
Web: www.powernetics.co.uk

Key personnel

Managing Director: *Satish Chada*
Sales Director: *Kevin Pateman*
Engineering Director: *Nilesh Chouhan*
Operations Director: *Konrad Chada*
Sales Manager: *Jim Goddard*

Products

Independent private limited company with 35 years' experience in design, manufacture, test, installation, commissioning and maintenance of auxiliary, standby/emergency AC/DC power supply systems for the rail industry in trackside, tunnel, switchroom, REB and trainborne environments.

System design and integration of UPS and associated switchgear/power monitoring within REBs and switchrooms for SSI, FSP and PSP applications.

Quixote Transportation Technologies

4021 Stirrup Creek Drive, Suite 100, Durham, North Carolina 27703, US
Tel: (+1 919) 361 24 79
Fax: (+1 919) 361 29 48
e-mail: QTT_International_Sales@quixotecorp.com
Web: www.nu-metrics.com

Key personnel

Sales and Marketing Manager: *John D Hunter*

Products

Distance measuring equipment the Nu-Metrics product line consists of permanent and portable traffic sensing and analysis systems, distance measuring and safety solutions.

Vehicle Magnetic Imaging (VMI):
VMI traffic counters, classifiers; wireless systems, communications software, data management software.

Regional Services Ltd (RSL)

3 Fullwood Close, Aldermans Green Industrial Estate, Coventry CV2 2SS, UK
Tel: (+44 2476) 61 81 89
Fax: (+44 2476) 62 22 46
e-mail: info@rslkiosks.co.uk
Web: www.rslkiosks.co.uk

Products

Public information interior and exterior display units, video screens, TV monitors, liquid crystal displays, LED units and plasma panels. Also installation and maintenance options available.

Safetran Systems Corporation

An Invensys company
2400 Nelson Miller Parkway, Louisville, Kentucky
40223, US
Tel: (+1 502) 618 88 00   Fax: (+1 502) 618 89 50
e-mail: safetran.sales@safetran.com
Web: www.safetran.com

Key personnel
General Manager, Marketing: *M L Dampier*
Product Line Manager (Crossings): *Pat Venneman*
Product Line Manager (Signals): *Omar Metel*

Products
Signalling, communications, and grade crossing
warning equipment for railway and mass transit
applications.

Products include: crossing warning products;
power supplies; wayside signal products; freight
yard products; communications services; transit
signal systems, housings and foundations and
design and engineering services.

SCLE SFE

25 Chemin de Paléficat, F-31204 Toulouse Cedex,
France
Tel: (+33 5) 61 61 74 89   Fax: (+33 5) 61 61 74 03
e-mail: brigitte.verite@scle.fr
Web: www.scle.fr

Key personnel
Sales Manager, France: *Benoît Renhas*
Sales Manager, International: *Marie-Line Segol*

Products
Signalling and detection systems and train
simulators.

SELEX Communications–OTE SpA

Via Eugenio Barsanti 8, I-50127 Florence, Italy
Tel: (+39 055) 438 11 11   Fax: (+39 055) 438 13 21
e-mail: marketing.tetra@selex-comms.com,
    mauro.paino@selex-comms.com (GSM-
    Railway products)
Web: www.otefinmeccanica.com

Key personnel
Chariman: *Gen Guido Bellini*
Chief Executive Officer: *Maurizio Tucci*
Chief Operating Officer: *Lorenzo Costagli*
Sales Director: *Luigi Papoff*
Marketing and Product Definition Director:
    Mauro De Lauri

Background
The Finmeccanica Company.

Products
Radio equipment for railway communications to
international standard EIRENE (GSM-Railways).

Siemens AG

Mobility
Rail Automation Division
PO Box 3327, D-38023 Braunschweig, Germany
Tel: (+49 531) 22 60   Fax: (+49 531) 226 64
e-mail: rail-automation@siemens.com
Web: www.siemens.com/mobility

Corporate headquarters
Siemens AG
Industry Sector – Mobility
PO Box 3240, D-91050 Erlangen, Germany
Tel: (+49 9131) 7-0

e-mail: contact.mobility@siemens.com
Web: www.siemens.com/moblity

Key personnel
Mobility
Division Chief Executive Officer: *Dr Hans-Jörg
    Grundmann*
Head of Business Administration: *Michael Schulz-
    Drost*

Products and services
Major product categories include:
Signalling: relay-based and electronic
interlockings; radio-based train control systems;
intermittent and continuous Automatic Train
Control (ATC) and Automatic Train Protection
(ATP) systems; hump yard systems; level
crossing systems; and signalling components.

Operations control systems: centralised train
control systems; train describer systems; control
centres; Man-Machine Interface (HMI) systems;
and marshalling yard equipment.

Rail communications: ACCS control centre
software; transmission technologies (OTN,
ATM, SDH, SONET, IP), CCTV surveillance;
public address and passenger information; clock
systems; help point and information systems;

PABX; SCADA; emergency and security systems;
GSM-R infrastructure; cab radio; analogue and
digital radio systems; systems integration;
project management; RAMS.

Passenger information systems: simulation of
railway operation; optimised operational planning
and control; training; project management;
life-cycle costing; systems integration; testing
before commissioning using the Braunschweig
Test Center; installation, commissioning and
maintenance; and financing.

Planning, control and monitoring of humping
operations in marshalling yards; Automatic
Vehicle Identification systems; electrically
operated points; freight management and
dispatching systems. Marshalling yard operation
and freight traffic solutions. Systems for
marshalling yard operation (flat type and gravity
type); freight management and dispatching
systems; identification systems; management and
consulting services for freight traffic. Marshalling
yard systems comprise a multicomputer
system in hot standby operation that can be
extended with locally controlled systems. The
marshalling yard system is designed for hump
yards (for example with variable hump speed
and computer-controlled retarder) and shunting

Sicas computer cabinet for the Cologne-Mülheim interlocking   0525407

Desiro railcar equipped as a demonstrator for Siemens' Trainguard ETCS family   0585295

areas. It reduces the time and costs for shunting operations and improves shunting quality. These systems offer high reliability and easy handling in combination with accurate slowing down even on curved tracks. Freight management and dispatching systems include client server systems with standard relational databases to administer train, wagon and freight data. It reduces the need for shunting manpower. Identification and location systems aid in net-wide optimisation for handling freight wagons and trains. Marshalling yard systems have been installed in Vienna and Villach (ÖBB), Bologna and Milan (FS), Munich (DB), Ludwigshafen (industry – BASF), Hamburg Harbour Railway, Antwerp (SNCB), Limmattal (SBB) and Kijfhoek (NS). Customers for freight management and dispatching systems include Vienna (ÖBB), Limmattal and Chiasso (SBB), Hamburg Maschen (DB) and Bologna (FS).

Contracts

Recent or current contracts include:

Belgium: In June 2007, Infrabel, the infrastructure operator for the Belgian railways, concluded a master agreement with Siemens in a consortium with ALSTOM, for the modernisation of its signalling equipment. Siemens is to supply the operations control system.

Canada: In December 2007, Siemens received an order from the Canadian transit authority Go Transit to upgrade the entire signalling and communication systems in and around Toronto's Union Station, as well as the traffic control centre.

China: In November 2002, a consortium of Siemens and the Nanjing Research Institute of Electronic Technology was awarded a contract to provide signalling and control equipment for Nanjing's first metro line. The 39 km, 16-station line is the first element of a planned six-line, 139 track-km metro and light rail network. Signalling equipment for the first line will feature Sicas electronic interlocking equipment and the LZB 700 m automatic train control system.

Dominican Republic: In a consortium with Thales, Siemens is to supply the electromechanical equipment for the first metro line in Santo Domingo. The contract was signed with the Dominican Republic's Oficina para la Reorganización del Transporte (OPRET). Siemens scope of supply involves the project management, signalling and safety systems, automatic train protection, operations control systems and the power supply.

France: In November 2005, Siemens received an order to equip Line 1 of the Paris Metro for fully automatic operation. A corresponding order was awarded to Siemens by the RATP (Régie Autonome des Transportes Parisiens). Driverless operation is scheduled to start by the end of 2010.

In February 2004, Siemens was awarded a contract by the Paris public transport authority, RATP, to supply train control and route protection systems for Paris Métro Lines 3, 5, 9, 10 and 12. This covers technology for transmitting data between trackside and trains for all five lines, onboard equipment for trains on Lines 3, 10 and 12 (112 Type MF67 metro cars) and trackside equipment for Lines 5 and 9 (34.2 km). Phased completion is to extend from 2007 to 2009.

In December 2003, an extension to the fully automated Paris Métro Line 14 between Bibliothèque François Mitterand and Gare Saint Lazare was commissioned, featuring train control, signalling and communications systems supplied by Siemens.

Germany: In December 2008, as part of its program to expand the Nuremberg-Fuerth line to four tracks, Deutsche Bahn AG has ordered an electronic interlocking from Siemens. Commissioning will take place in stages up to 2011.

Hungary: In January 2005, Siemens was awarded a contract by Budapest's transit authorities (BKV Rt) for the supply of a new control, signalling and safety system to the M2 metro line.

Control centre by Siemens for the Houston light rail system   0585223

Control centre by Siemens for Hanover's mass transit system   0585222

Netherlands: In 2002, a general agreement was signed with Railinfrabeheer covering the provision of its Simis W electronic interlocking technology to upgrade Elektronische Beveiliging Siemens (EBS) interlockings on the Netherlands rail network. A first phase of the project covers several interlockings on the Vleugel route, south of Utrecht, where work is due to be completed by 2011.

Portugal: As part of a turnkey contract signed in August 2002 to establish a 13 km light rail system between Almada and Seixal, south of Lisbon, Siemens is to supply signalling and operations control equipment.

Romania: In January 2005, Siemens received an order from Romanian National Railway, CFR, for the supply of type Simis W electronic interlockings. These interlockings are intended for seven stations to the northwest of Bucharest.

Russian Federation: In October 2007, following a one-year trial operation period, the Simis electronic interlocking developed by Siemens and its Russian partner Foratec AT has been certified for operation by the Russian railway operator RZD.

Spain: In March 2003 Siemens, in a consortium with Dimetronic SA, won a contract to equip Barcelona's automatic driverless Metro Line 9 (41.4 km) with a train protection and operations control system.

Venezuela: In October 2005, Siemens was awarded a contract to supply its Automation Train Control systems for the new metro line in Caracas, Venezuela. As part of an overall contract won by the FRAMECA consortium, Siemens will equip tracks and trains with its PA 135 automation system. The first track entered service in October 2006 and the second followed in 2008.

Siemens Switzerland

Siemens Switzerland Ltd, Transportation Systems
Hammerweg 1, CH-8304 Wallisellen, Switzerland
Tel: (+41 585) 58 01 11   Fax: (+41 585) 58 05 01
e-mail: ts@siemens.ch
Web: www.siemens.ch/ts

Key personnel

Managing Director: *Gerhard Greiter*
Manager, Export Department, South East Asia: *A Hefti*

Products

Electronic, hybrid and relay interlockings; intermittent and continuous ATP and ATC systems, including vehicle and trackside equipment; CTC and electronic remote-control systems; block and track vacancy proving equipment (axle counters, track circuits, last vehicle detection); point locking equipment including point machines and point locking system; signals and indicators; safety relays. IT solutions for the rail automation market.

Developments

Borderless control system: The Iltis operation control system from Siemens has been tried and tested over many years and has been extended to create a system of control system cells that can be flexibly networked. In co-operation with Swiss Federal Railways (SBB), the Iltis-N-system has been created. (The N is for Network). The system allows flexible monitoring and control of the SBB rail network independent of the location of the control system hardware and it is therefore possible to control the entire operating area from a few locations. The first cells of the Iltis-N-system were put into operation in January 2008.

Specialty Bulb Co Inc

The Specialty Bulb Co Inc
80 Orville Grove, Bohemia, New York 11716-0231, US
Tel: (+1 631) 589 33 93 Fax: (+1 631) 563 30 89
e-mail: info@bulbspecialists.com
Web: www.bulbspecialists.com

Key personnel

President: *Judith Beja*
Vice-President, Technical: *Caden Zollo*
Vice-President, Sales and Marketing: *Edie Muldoon*

Products

Lamps for signal applications.

STERIA Group

46 rue Camille Desmoulins, F-92782 Issy les Moulineaux, France
Tel: (+33 1) 34 38 60 00
Fax: (+33 1) 34 88 60 15
Web: www.steria.fr

Key personnel

President Director General: *François Enaud*
Transport and Public Sector Director: *Jean Charles Tarlier*
Transportation Sales Manager: *Jacques Lafay*
Transportation Communication Representative: *Isabelle Grangé*

Products

Traffic regulation and monitoring systems, road pricing and supervisory systems, railway supervisory and monitoring systems; passenger information systems, data processing, management control, training simulators and programmes, computer-aided diagnosis, traffic simulation; ticketing systems.

Contracts

Supervisory Control System/OCC for RATP: Metro lines 1, 2, 3, 5, 6, 7, 8, 9, 10, 11, 12, 13; Paris Rapid Mass Transit (RER A & B); Lyons Metro – Lines A,B,C; CFF/SBB Swiss Federal Railways. Railway equipment supervision for Lei T Fü Deutsche Bahn (Germany).

Stesalit Limited

71, Park Street, North Block, 7th Floor Calcutta 700 016, India
e-mail: office@stesalitltd.com
Web: www.stesalitltd.com

Background

Stesalit Limited has alliances with ABB and Spring AG, Switzerland; TELEMA SpA, Italy; Skoda, Czech Republic; Jacques Galland, France; EVPU, Slovakia and MWB, Germany.

The company is ISO 9001:2000 accredited, with in excess of 60,000 square feet of manufacturing facilities.

Products

Developing and manufacturing high-end electronic and engineering products for locomotives, coaches, emus, rail signalling and industry, to global quality standards. Products include data acquisition systems, control systems and digital axle counters.

TagMaster AB

Kronborgsgränd 1, Kista, Stockholm, Postal address SE-164 87 Kista, Sweden
Tel: (+46 8) 632 19 50 Fax: (+46 8) 750 53 62
e-mail: sales@tagmaster.se
Web: www.tagmaster.com

Key personnel

President: *Magnus Rehn*
Vice-Presidents
  Marketing and Sales: *Christian Nordberg*
  Information Solutions/Research and Development: *Mikael Willgert*
  Production: *Peter Beijar*
  Finance and Administration: *Marika Falk*
  International Sales Security: *Thore Wahlin*

Products

Long-range Radio Frequency Identification (RFID) systems for rail and public transport applications, providing position and identification data. System components comprise fixed ID programmable identification tags and the TagMaster Reader, which reads tag information and offers various interfaces for onward data transmission. Systems can be configured with either tags or readers on moving vehicles according to data requirements. Applications include maintenance and operational or quality control, high-precision event triggering and traffic and passenger information.

Contracts

Users include Netherlands Railways, measuring wheel quality and axleloads, London Underground, enabling an onboard radio system automatically to change talk-group when moving between different areas of coverage, and the Pearl Line light rail system, using TagMaster RFID technology for train identification for traffic and passenger information purposes.

Trackside Intelligence Pty Ltd

17-19 King William Street Kent Town, South Australia 5067, Australia
e-mail: info@teknis.net
Web: www.teknis.net

Other offices

US
Tel: (+1 336) 454 02 12
Scandinavia
Tel: (+47 67) 97 22 62 Fax: (+47 67) 97 22 64
Spain and Portugal
Tel: (+91 458) 25 45 Fax: (+91 630) 95 77 41

Key personnel

Managing Director: *K Bladon*
Business Manager: *K Searle*

Products

Electronic control systems, SCADA systems. DDU (Driver Display Unit), as in-cab train driver's display for signalling and train orders.

WCM (Wheel Condition Monitor) for analysing wheel condition and detecting wheel faults causing damage to track structure. In-motion train weighing at line speed. WMS (Wayside Monitoring System) integrating the WCM and other industry standard sensors and instrumentation into a single web-based data/communications system. Real-time remote site monitoring.

Telephonics Corporation

815 Broadhollow Road, Farmingdale, New York 11735, US
Tel: (+1 516) 549 60 62
Fax: (+1 516) 549 60 18
Web: www.telephonics.com

Key personnel

Vice-President, Business Development: *Philip Greco*
Manager, Business Development: *Norbert Trokki*
Senior Manager, Corporate Communications: *Carrie Petrocca*

Products

Communication, information and surveillance systems for mass transit: integrated car communication and passenger information systems; wayside communication and central control systems; closed circuit television systems for wayside, stations and vehicles; train line multiplexers; network controller and vehicle monitoring.

Contracts

Vehicle communication, train multiplexer, network controller for New York City Transit subway cars.

Vehicle communication, radios and door observation CCTV for South Eastern Pennsylvania Transit Authority.

Vehicle communication system for Massachusetts Bay Transit Authority light rail.

Vehicle communication, health monitoring and vehicle CCTV at Hudson Bergen light rail transit system.

Integrated wayside communication system for Newark APM.

Vehicle communication and passenger entertainment for Caltrans.

Developments

Train line multiplexer for transport of vehicle controls and digital audio using EI standards; car network controller is used to convert LON to propulsion/brake commands; public address and information systems based on internet technology.

Telvent GITS SA (Telecom Ventures)

Valgrande 6, E-28108 Alcobendas, Madrid, Spain
Tel: (+34 91) 714 70 00
Fax: (+34 91) 714 70 01
e-mail: info@telvent.com
Web: www.telvent.com

Key personnel

Director, Chairman and Chief Executive Officer: *Manuel Sánchez*
Vice-President Business and Corporate Development: *José Ignacio del Barrio*
Executive Vice President, Telvent North America: *Larry Stack*
Chief Financial Officer: *Ana María Plaza*
Chief Technology Officer: *Francisco Cáceres*
President and Chairman of Telvent North America: *Dave Jardine*
Vice-President, China: *Dai Yue*
Vice-President, México: *Luis Rancé*
Vice-President, Brazil: *Marcio Leonardo*

Vice-President, Traffic and Transport: *José Montoya*
Communications Manager: *Cristina Poole Quintana*
Staff: Approximately 2,600

Other offices
The company has offices in Australia, Brazil, Canada, China, Mexico, Turkey and the US.

Products
Bus
ValTick: Transport ticket sales and cancellation management and control systems;
ClearingTrans: Clearing systems for ticket sales and cancellation systems.

Rail
MobiFast: Management and control system of ticket sales and cancellation for travellers at railway stations;
CTC: Centralised rail Traffic Control system;
TR2000 – STA: Rail station facility control system.

Contracts
In March 2006, Telvent GIT SA was awarded a contract, valued at nearly EUR4 million, by Madrid Infraestructuras del Transporte (MINTRA) for the supply and installation of ticket vending and cancellation machines for the Colonia Jardin-Pozuelo and Colonia Jardin-Boadilla light metro lines.

In April 2006, Telvent GIT SA received a contract from the Spanish Railway Infrastructure Administrator for the installation and maintenance of energy control systems on two new AVE high-speed lines, the Madrid-Segovia line and the Valdestillas-Valladolid line.

Thales Rail Signalling

Head Office
4 rue Léon Jost F-75017, Paris, France
Tel: (+ 33 1) 57 77 80 00
Fax: (+ 33 1) 57 77 83 53
Web: www.thalesgroup.com

Key personnel
Executive Vice-President: *Olivier Houssin*

Products
Centralised control systems for metro, light and heavy rail applications, including traffic supervision, and regulation and public information display systems; SCADA systems; computer-aided operating systems for bus networks.

Contracts
In February 2007, Thales received the Notice to Proceed (NTP) with signalling and telecommunications work on Dubai Metro's Green Line from Mitsubishi Heavy Industries (MHI). Work on the Green Line project will take 44 months, with completion due in March 2010.

In January 2007, UK company, Tube Lines awarded a GBP160m extension to the contract it has with Thales's rail signalling solutions business (formerly of Alcatel) to provide a new signalling system on the Piccadilly line by 2014.

In November 2006, Alcatel was awarded a contract by the Spanish Ministry of Transport, through the Railways General Office, as part of a global Euro 69 million project to provide safety and communications solutions. This will be done with ERTMS/ETCS Level 1 and 2 for the new tunnel linking Atocha – the central high speed and commuter lines station – and Chamartin – the main north and northwest bound station – in Madrid, and to extend the ERTMS/ETCS level 1 system to the convergent sections of five commuter lines. In January 2007, this contract was transferred to Thales.

Thales Telecom Services

Phoenix House, Station Hill, Reading RG1 1NB, UK
Tel: (+44 118) 908 60 00
Fax: (+44 118) 908 63 85
Web: www.thales-ts.com

Key personnel
Chief Executive Officer: *Peter Batley*

Background
Thales Telecom Services was formed in April 2002 by the merger of its project and maintenance organisations, Thales Translink and Thales Fieldforce. The company is part of the Thales Group formed by the merger of Thomson-CSF and Racal. Formerly trading as Racal Telecom, the company's origins lie in its acquisition of the former BRT private telecommunications network during the privatisation of British Rail in the 1990s.

Products
The business of Thales Telecom Services principally consists of the provision of specialist operational and business telecommunications services to the UK railway industry. Its core network comprised 17,000 km of trunk cable, of which 4,000 route-km are made up of fibre-optic cable. During 1997 the former Racal upgraded the network by creating a resilient SDH backbone network, which includes a further 1,200 route-km of fibre-optic cable. Facilities provided include national fixed-line telecommunications systems in support of trackside telephony, signalling control systems, CCTV and mainframe computer connections. The company also provides facilities management for Network Rail's National Radio Network, which provides driver to shore communications.

Thales Telecom Services also installs and maintains telecommunications systems. The comprehensive service includes national cable and fibre networks, PABXs and call routing equipment, radio and VSAT systems, customer information systems, customer premises equipment, local and wide area networks, transmission systems and structured cabling. The company offers a nationwide service with support on call 24 hours a day, seven days a week. The company also has service partner status with Ericsson.

Contracts
Thales Telecom Services is the leading partner in CityLink Telecommunications Ltd, a company formed to operate, maintain and renew London Underground's operational radio and transmission systems. The 20-year contract has been let on a Private Finance Initiative (PFI) basis. Its contribution to the project includes; the design, installation, testing and commissioning of a new network-wide SDH transmission system with CCTV, and to manage the implementation of a new digital Tetra radio system. Also for London Underground, Thales Telecom Services developed in-cab CCTV, a system designed to enhance the safety of passengers on station platforms by enabling drivers to view the whole platform clearly before arrival, while the train berths and on departure, all from within the cab.

Thoreb AB

Gruvgatan 37, SE-421 30 Västra Frölunda, Sweden
Tel: (+46 31) 734 39 00   Fax: (+46 31) 734 39 10
e-mail: info@thoreb.se
Web: www.thoreb.se; www.true-realtime.com

Key personnel
Managing Director: *Michael Sigvardsson*
Marketing Directors: *Johan Kallvik; Esbjorn Lif*
Chief Financial Officer: *Thord Brynielsson*

Products
Automatic vehicle location, passenger counting, data communication, passenger information displays, communication systems for public transport vehicles and multiplex electrical systems for heavy vehicles. Real time passenger information systems.

TransCore

19111 Dallas Parkway, Suite 300, Dallas, Texas 75287-3106, US
Tel: (+1 972) 397 81 97   Fax: (+1 972) 733 64 86
Web: www.transcore.com

Key personnel
President and Chief Executive Officer: *John Worthington*
Chief Operating Officer: *John Simler*
Executive Vice-President, Marketing: *Dick Blackwell*
Executive Vice-President: *John Foote*
Executive Vice-President and Chief Technical Officer: *Kelly Gravelle*
Chief Scientist and Executive Vice-President: *Dr Jerry Landt*

Products
Rail and rail transit
Amtech® brand radio frequency technology for automatic train control. Automatic equipment identification; automatic equipment monitoring systems; automatic train positioning systems; automatic train location; automatic train separation. Activation of audio and visual annunciation.

Transmitton – A Siemens Business

Ashby Park, Ashby-de-la-Zouch LE65 1JD, UK
Tel: (+44 1530) 25 80 00   Fax: (+44 1530) 25 80 08
e-mail: sales@transmitton.co.uk
Web: www.transmitton.co.uk

Key personnel
Business Unit Director: *I Wright*
Head of Sales and Marketing: *E Turnock*
Finance and Commercial Manager: *G Lowndes*

Background
In August 2005 Transmitton Ltd was acquired by Siemens plc from the Alchemy backed ICS Group Ltd. Transmitton now forms part of Siemens in the UK reporting to Siemens Transportation Systems (STS).

The Transmitton team are now a vital element within the STS rail communications group, incorporating the 120 strong Transmitton team at Ashby and STS Poole based mobile communications, GSM-R cab radio business of around 80 employees.

Products
Transmitton provides a range of integrated control and asset management solutions to the rail industry. These include; integrated station management and network management systems, real-time passenger information systems, remote condition monitoring, intelligent asset management solutions, traction power SCADA, and Open Transport Network (OTN).

At the core of these solutions are Transmitton's cromos and fastflex technologies. The fastflex Remote Terminal Unit (RTU) is modular in design and suits a wide range of applications for stand alone control, point-to-point and remote communications. Transmitton's cromos software offers real-time control and asset management technologies.

Transmitton holds a strong position in the global market place, having gained cross market and international experience by providing systems in America, Asia and the Far East, Africa, Australia, Eastern and Western Europe including the UK.

Transmitton has a fully documented quality system and is accredited to BS ISO 9001:2000 (TickIT), has a Network Rail Contractors Assurance Case Certificate, product approval certificates and is a qualified supplier on both Link-Up (UVDB) and FPAL databases.

Contracts

Transmitton's continuing project work for customers includes Balfour Beatty, Beijing Metro, Carillion Rail, Docklands Light Railway, EMCOR, Gleeson MCL, Metronet, Network Rail, Tubelines, AMEC, BP, Transco, GAS de Portugal, Interconnector, Shell and TotalFina.

Trivector System AB

Åldermansgatan 13, SE-227 64 Lund, Sweden
Tel: (+46 42) 38 65 00
Fax: (+46 42) 38 65 25
e-mail: info@trivector.se
Web: www.trivector.se

Key personnel

Managing Director: *Klas Odelid*
Marketing Manager: *Ola Fogelberg*
Project Manager: *Anders Månsson*

Products

RASC (RAdio Signal Control) system for assigning priority to buses at crossings regulated by signals. This system consists of the software contained in Triveco 8 together with the component system IRU-SS, an intelligent receiver unit contained in the control apparatus. It has been installed at 40 intersections in Malmö, Sweden and is to be installed in the city of Karlstad in the future.

Tyco Electronics Wireless Systems

M/A-COM Inc
221 Jefferson Ridge Parkway, Lynchburg, Virginia 24501, US
Tel: (+1 434) 455 66 00 (+1 434) 455 66 85
Web: www.macom-wireless.com

Key personnel

President: *Chuck Dougherty*
Director for International Business Development: *Robert Jastram*

Background

Tyco Electronics' Wireless Systems business is a supplier of critical communications systems and equipment for public safety, utility, federal and select commercial markets such as transit.

Products

Secure critical voice and data communications on a single IP network. Tyco's Voice, Interoperability, Data and Access (VIDA) network solutions employ end-to-end digital packet-switched IP technology.

UniControls AS

Křenická ulice-2257, CZ-100 00 Prague 10, Czech Republic
Tel: (+420 2) 72 01 14 11
Fax: (+420 2) 74 81 44 75
e-mail: unic@unicontrols.cz
Web: www.unicontrols.cz

Key personnel

Marketing Manager: *Marian Belosovic*

Products

Communications and control systems for trains and rail vehicles, including: Train Communication Network-Wire Train Bus (TCN-WTB) equipment; multi-vehicle communications equipment; vehicle communications devices; and drivers cab equipment and displays.

Contracts

UniControls, together with Japanese partner ToyoDenki, won the tender for the supply of train control and management system and power part for 17 six-carriage sets for the metro in Chengdu, China.

Train communications and control systems for refurbished Russian-built Prague metro stock; train communications system for St Petersburg metro stock; train and vehicle communications system and drivers cab equipment for Czech Railways Class 471 emus; communication node UIC Gateway for Czech Railways Class 680 tilting trainsets; drivers cab equipment for refurbished Class 772 locomotive for Slovakian Railways (ZSSK).

VAEE

Alpinestrasse 1, A-8740 Zeltweg, Austria
Tel: (+43 50304) 291 20
Fax: (+43 50304) 681 29
e-mail: Marketing.VAE@vae.co.at
Web: www.voestalpine.com/vaee

Key personnel

General Managers: *D Fritz, G Neureiter*

Background

VAE GmbH is the shareholder of VAEE.

Products and services

Points control, hydraulic setting devices, electronic monitoring systems, hot box detectors.

Vecom USA, LLC

4803 George Road, Unit 300, Tampa, Florida 33634, US
Tel: (+1 813) 901 53 00
Fax: (+1 813) 433 24 58
e-mail: info@vecom-usa.com
Web: www.vecom-usa.com

Key personnel

President and Chief Executive Officer: *J J H M 'Koos' van Starrenburg*
Director of Marketing: *Sharon L Rice*

Products

Vecom USA manufactures and distributes communications and electronics equipment to the public transit industry. Its primary product is the Vetag-Vecom line of train to wayside control equipment. See Vecom USA in *Passenger Information Systems* section for further information.

VerifEye Technologies Inc

7100 Warden Avenue, Unit 3, Markham, Ontario, L3R 8B5, Canada
Tel: (+1 905) 948 00 15
e-mail: sales@verifeye.com
Web: www.verifeye.com

Key personnel

President and Chief Executive Officer: *Steven Holmes*
Sales and Marketing Director: *Kevin Holmes*

Other offices

Australia
9/11 Wises Road, PO Box 8259, Maroochydore, QLD 4558, Australia
e-mail: info@verifeye.com.au
Web: www.verifeye.com.au

United Kingdom
1 Branksome Business Centre, Cortry Close, Poole, Dorset, BH12 4BQ, UK
Tel: (+44 2380) 28 47 27
e-mail: sales@verifeye.co.uk
Web: www.verifeye.co.uk

Product

VerifEye family of digital video recorders for mobile applications.

Verint Systems Inc

330 South Service Road, Melville, NY 11747, US
Tel: (+1 631) 962 96 00
Fax: (+1 631) 962 93 00
e-mail: info@verint.com
Web: www.verint.com/video_solutions; www.verint.com

Key personnel

President, Chief Executive Officer and Director: *Dan Bodner*
Chief Financial Officer : *Doug Robinson*
Chief Legal Officer and Secretary: *Peter Fante*

Products

CCTV recording and storage system for buses and rail vehicles.

Vialis NMA

Vialis NMA Railsystems bv
PO Box 318, NL-3700 AH Zeist, Netherlands
Tel: (+31 30) 698 38 00   Fax: (+31 30) 698 38 09
e-mail: info@vialis.nl
Web: www.vialis.nl
Vialis NMA Railway Signalling bv
PO Box 70, NL-1723 ZH Noord-Scharwoude, Netherlands
Tel: (+31 226) 33 67 00   Fax: (+31 226) 33 67 10
e-mail: sales@nmarail.nl
Web: www.vialis.nl

Other offices

Kwekerijweg 6, NL-3709 JA Zeist, Netherlands

Background

NMA Railsystems bv and its sister company Vialis NMA Railway Signalling bv are subsidiaries of Vialis bv, part of the Koninklijke Volker Wessels Stevin nv (KVWS) group.

Products

Vialis NMA Railsystems bv develops, assembles and overhauls power systems and signalling components for level crossing, signalling and switch systems. It also develops and implements entire systems. Vialis NMA Railway Signalling manufactures electrical components for signalling systems, including signals, switch components and level crossing protection systems.

Recent product developments include: the application of LED technology to railway signals; the introduction of a maintenance-free, vandal-resistant level crossing barrier mechanism; a monitoring system to detect faults in level crossing half-barriers; an in-sleeper low-maintenance point switch system; and an integrated safety system incorporating axle-counters, automatic vehicle identification and other detection systems to enable trains of different types, including LRVs, to utilise the same sections of track.

Vialis Verkeer & Mobiliteit bv

Oudeweg 115, NL-2031 CC Harlem, Netherlands
PO Box 665, NL-2003 RR Haarlem, Netherlands
Tel: (+31 23) 518 91 91   Fax: (+31 23) 518 91 11
e-mail: info@nedhlm.nl
Web: www.vialis.nl

Key personnel
Managing Directors: *Rolf Van Groenewould, Henk Barentsen*
PR Contact: *Michel Vesseur*

Other offices
Kwekerijweg 6, NL-3709 JA Zeist, Netherlands
Postbus 318, NL-3700 AH Zeist, Netherlands
Tel: (+31 30) 698 38 00   Fax: (+31 30) 698 31 00
Stationsweg 15, NL-3972 KA Driebergen
Tel: (+31 30) 698 38 00   Fax: (+31 30) 698 31 00
(Public Transport); 698 31 50 (Infra Techniek)

Subsidiaries
Vialis Belgium
Kapelanielaan 14, B-9140 Temse, Belgium
Tel: (+32 3886) 59 15   Fax: (+32 3886) 99 31
e-mail: info@vialis.be
Web: www.vialis.be
Vialis Polska
ul Modrzewiowa 8a, PL-62-081 Prezezmierowo, Poland
Tel: (+ 48 61) 652 46 10   Fax: (+48 61) 652 46 11
e-mail: biuro@vialis.pl
Web: www.vialis.pl

Background
Vialis Verkeer & Mobiliteit bv is part of Vialis bv, a subsidiary of Royal Volker Wessels Stevin nv.

Products
Traffic control systems; lane indication systems; queue and speed detection; black ice warning systems; tunnel control; barriers and level crossing control systems.

TravelMan® information systems; illuminated signs; traffic signals; dot-matrix signs; lighting poles.

Wabtec Railway Electronics

21200 Dorsey Mill Road, Germantown, Maryland 20876, US
Tel: (+1 301) 515 20 00
Fax: (+1 301) 515 21 00
Web: www.wabtec.com

Key personnel
President: *Robert Haag*
Vice-President Marketing and Sales: *Mark T Kramer*

Background
Wabtec Railway Electronics formerly Pulse Electronics, is a division of Wabtec Corporation. WRE was founded in 1977 and its first product was the locomotive event recorder, Train Trax, which is currently installed worldwide and is a standard on many US railroads.

Products
Train Trax solid-state locomotive even recording system, a flexible, virtually maintenance-free, fully FRA-compliant recording system designed to improve operational safety and performance by monitoring and recording key channels from the locomotive; TrainLink II End of Train Telemetry System, which continuously monitors key conditions on the last car including brake pipe pressure, end of train motion, battery condition and marker light status and communicate the information to the lead locomotive while adding end of train emergency braking capability; locomotive speed indicators with both MPH and KPH models; Iso-Amp Speed Isolation Amplifier an alternative to the Axle Generator or passive sensors mounted on the locomotive drive gear; Train Sentry III Engineman Alertness Device, a solid-state system designed to enhance the safe operation of railway vehicles by monitoring the alertness of the engineman; FuelLink fuel measurement system, which incorporates solid-state electronics and advanced pneumatics for determining locomotive fuel levels accurate to +/– one per cent; Q-Tron's QEG 1000 Electronic autostart system, which reduces engine fuel consumption, resulting in significant fuel savings by safely shutting down and restarting the locomotive engine during appropriate idle periods; LocoTemp II cooling system controller, which reliably monitors and controls locomotive coolings systems temperature, providing 'New Locomotive' technology to a non-microprocessor fleet; Q-Tron QTRAC 1000 locomotive traction control system, a standalone unit that monitors and controls locomotive wheel slip by reducing excitation to the main AC (or DC) generator when wheel slip is detected; Wayside Device Monitor (WDM-450) vigilant highway crossing monitoring system, which provides continuous real-time monitoring and event recording of the status of grade crossing installations; electronically controlled pneumatic braking system.

New developments
In January 2007, the Federal Railroad Administration (FRA) approved the Product Safety Plan that will allow BNSF Railway company to begin implementing Wabtec's Electronic Train Management System™ (ETMS™) on portions of its network.

BNSF began an ETMS pilot program in 2004, after Wabtec installed ETMS equipment on 50 locomotives to be used in a 135-mile corridor between Beardstown and Centralia, Ill.

Westinghouse Rail Systems Ltd

PO Box 79, Pew Hill, Chippenham SN15 1JD, UK
Tel: (+44 1249) 44 14 41   Fax: (+44 1249) 44 14 42
e-mail: marketing@wrsl.com
Web: www.wrsl.com

Key personnel
Managing Director: *Alistair McPhee*
General Manager Mainline: *Mark Wild*
General Manager Mass Transit: *Charles Riley*
Operations Director: *Steve Barry*
Finance Director: *Andy Bryan*
Head of Human Resources: *Richard Drury*

Background
Westinghouse Rail Systems Ltd (WRSL), part of Invensys Rail Group, is one of the world leaders in advanced signalling and integrated control systems for mainline and mass transit railways.

The company has a comprehensive range of equipment, systems and services to meet railway needs from single lines to heavy-haul freight, suburban, inter-city and complex mass transit networks.

Other companies within the Invensys Rail Group include Safetran (US), Westinghouse Australia, Westinghouse India and Dimetronic in Spain. Many of the current products are the result of joint development work across the group, including WESTRACE and WESTLOCK interlockings, WESTeX level crossing systems; WESTCAD and SystemICS control and display systems, as well as Sirius and FUTUR ERTMS train control systems for mainline and metro railways.

Capabilities
Westinghouse Rail Systems specialises in all aspects of railway control and signalling, with an extensive range of products, systems and services in the following areas:

Wabtec Railway Electronics M6W Locomotive event recorder with wireless and memory card download port
0134169

Westinghouse Rail Systems WESTLOCK: new generation computer-based interlocking system
1341772

- control systems
- protection systems
- trackside equipment
- customer services: including training, support and maintenance
- signalling design software
- manufacturing

Key products include: solid state and relay interlocking; WESTRACE 4th generation computer based interlocking safety processor; WESTCAD control and display system; Automatic Train Control (ATC); train to signalbox radio; centralised traffic control; electronic management centres; train describers; transmission based signalling; colour light signals; position-light junction route indicators; fibre optic theatre and stencil route indicators; electric point machines; jointed and jointless track circuits; control panels; safety plug-in relays.

Contracts

Westinghouse has projects across the UK, Singapore, Hong Hong, China, Norway, Canada, Ireland, Germany, Portugal and Spain. The company is currently working on a range of contracts, including a number of major resignalling projects for Network Rail, the resignalling of the Victoria Line of London Underground as well as projects in Norway, Singapore, Canada (Vancouver), China, Taiwan and Ireland.

Westinghouse Saxby Farmer Limited

17 Convent Road, Entally, Calcutta 700014, India
Tel: (+91 33) 22 44 71 61   Fax: (+91 33) 22 44 71 65
e-mail: wsfedp@cal2.vsnl.net.in

Key personnel
Managing Director: *A N Dutta*
Director, Finance: *D K De Sarker*

Products
Signalling equipment including route relay and point interlocking systems and signalling relays of all types, semi-permanent coupler for emu coaches, AAR 'H' coupler.

Contracts
Current contracts include the supply of route relay and interlocking system for seven stations and 36,900 nos of different types of signalling relays to Indian railways.

Zenitel NV

Wireless solutions
Research Park Zellik, Pontbeek 63, B-1731 Zelik, Belgium
Tel: (+32 2) 370 53 11
Fax: (+32 2) 370 51 19
e-mail: info@zenitel.com
Web: www.zenitel.com

Key personnel
Managing Director and Chief Executive Officer: *Eugeen Beckers*
Chief Financial Officer: *Rika Coppens*

Products
Turnkey implementation of HF, VHF, UHF, SHF fixed and mobile telecommunication networks; communication and control systems for public transport, including use of radio in underground and other difficult environments.

PASSENGER INFORMATION SYSTEMS

Company listing by country

AUSTRIA
Infoscreen Austria Gesellschaft für Stadtinformationsanlagen GmbH
Mattig-Schauer GmbH

BELGIUM
Televic NV

CANADA
Interalia Inc
Mark IV Industries Inc

CZECH REPUBLIC
Metra Blansko AS
UniControls AS

DENMARK
FARA Denmark A/S
Focon Electronic Systems A/S
Pallas Informatik A/S
SA ViewCom A/S

FINLAND
Mitron Oy

FRANCE
ALSTOM Transport
INEO Systrans
JCDecaux Group
SLE
Socel Visioner

GERMANY
LAWO – Mark IV Industries GmbH
AEG MIS

Annax Anzeigesysteme GmbH
BBR Verkehrstechnik GmbH
Conrac GmbH
INIT Innovative Informatikanwendungen in Transport–, Verkehrs- und Leitsystemen GmbH
KJ GmbH Installationen
Lumino Licht Elektronik GmbH
Meister Electronic GmbH

IRELAND
Data Display Co Ltd

ITALY
Ameli SpA
FIREMA Trasporti SpA
Frensistemi Srl
Solari di Udine SpA
Sysco SpA

JAPAN
Morio Denki Co Ltd

POLAND
Emax SA

SPAIN
Albatros Corporation
Ikusi – Ángel Iglesias SA
SEPSA

SWEDEN
Mobitec AB
Trivector System AB
Volvo Bus Corporation

SWITZERLAND
Gorba AG
Moser-Baer SA
Omega Electronics SA
Precimation SA
Ruf Telematik AG

UNITED KINGDOM
Connexionz UK Ltd
Titan Bus UK Ltd
BT Group plc
Clear Channel UK
Ferrograph Ltd
GAI-Tronics
Hanover Displays Ltd
Hi-Force Limited
Infotec Limited
KeTech Group
Petards Joyce-Loebl
Postfield Systems
Procyon Ltd
Techspan Systems Ltd
TEW Engineering Limited
Trueform Engineering Limited
Voice Perfect Ltd
Vultron International Ltd

UNITED STATES
Emcom Systems
LogicTree
Oval Window Audio
Talking Signs Inc
Vecom USA, LLC

AEG MIS

AEG Gesellschaft für moderne Informationssysteme mbH
Söflinger Strasse 100, D-89077 Ulm, Germany
Tel: (+49 731) 933 15 61   Fax: (+49 731) 933 16 01
e-mail: info@aegmis.de
Web: www.aegmis.de

Key personnel
Managing Directors: *Dr Reiner Bayrle, Peter Mack*

Products
Planning, design, manufacture, installation and commissioning of LCD-based passenger information systems, including corresponding software systems. These are supplied for both fixed applications such as train destination boards, arrival/departure information systems and for vehicle onboard external and internal systems.

Albatros Corporation

C/ Ruiz de Alarcón, 13, 3°, E-28014 Madrid, Spain
Tel: (+34 91) 532 41 81   Fax: (+34 91) 522 76 97
e-mail: albatros@albatros-sl.es
Web: www.albatros-sl.es

Works
Sistemas Electrónicos de potencia, SA
Polígono Ind 'La Estación', C/Albatros 7 & 9,
E-28320 Pinto, Madrid, Spain
Tel: (+34 91) 495 70 00
CMC
Pl Can Roca, C/Mar del Japón, parc 13, Santa Perpètua de la Mogoda, E-08130, Barcelona, Spain
Tel: (+34 93) 544 66 66
Fax: (+34 93) 544 82 19

Commercial offices:
Albatros UK; Albatros US; Albatros Brazil

Key personnel
President and Chief Executive Officer:
  Nicolás Fúster
Marketing Director: *Alejandro Fúster*
Commercial Director: *Enrique Galavis*

Background
Albatros is formed by various units of engineers and manufacturers in Spain and other countries. It has a team of over 900 employees with over 22,000 static converters, 20,000 passenger information systems and a variety of designs for the exterior and interior of trains, metros and tramways worldwide.

Products
Albatros Corporation is specialised in the design, manufacture, commercialisation and maintenance of equipment for the railway industry. Products include: power electronics – static converters and battery chargers; onboard security – black box and auxiliary control system; comfort – video entertainment, information passenger system and WC and interior design; communications – wide band, GSM-GPRS, route manager; protection – video surveillance system; brake systems – electric, pneumatic, hydraulic and electromagnetic; locomotive simulators, test bend, automatic coupling, open and closing of doors, vacuum toilets.

ALSTOM Transport

Information Solutions
33, rue des Bâteliers – BP 165 Saint Ouen,
F-93404, France
(Tel: + 33 1) 40 10 62 62
Fax: (+ 33 1) 40 10 60 60
Web: www.transport.alstom.com

Key personnel
Managing Director: *Angelo Guercioni*

Products
Real-time onboard passenger information systems for rolling stock: AGATE e-Media passenger information systems for mass transit and railway stations.

ALSTOM acquired Telecite Inc in 1999. The Montréal-based Telecite becomes ALSTOM's worldwide centre of excellence in Advanced Traveller Information Systems (ATIS).

The company specialises in conceiving, deploying, maintaining and marketing real-time information and communication systems for public transportation and other applications. The continued pursuit of innovation, coupled with system engineering and integration, has allowed ALSTOM (formerly Telecite Inc) to refine and expand its offerings to include LCD passenger information displays, public address, CCTV surveillance, seat reservation system and at-seat audio and video on demand with full interactive Intranet/Internet HTML content as part of an integrated multi-modal system.

The acquisition of Telecite further strengthens ALSTOM's presence in North America. Recent acquisitions have expanded its rolling stock, traction equipment, signalling systems, field service and turn-key project management capabilities in the US and Canada, complementing its already strong presence in Mexico.

ALSTOM's co-operation with Telecite over the years leading to acquisition has brought orders from Europe, Latin America and Asia. For example, ALSTOM chose Telecite as its partner to supply real-time advanced traveller information systems to the Mass Transit Railway Corporation (MTRC) in Hong Kong.

Contracts
Switzerland: ALSTOM has supplied the on-board video surveillance and passenger information system as part of the turnkey contract awarded in 2002 by the Administration of Switzerland's Vaud canton for a new 6 km metro line linking Ouchy with the district of Epalinges, Lausanne. The new line entered commercial service in October 2008.

Other projects implemented include advanced transit systems such as MTRC in Hong Kong, STCUM in Montreal and NYCT in New York.

Ameli SpA

Via Guido Rossa, 10, Loc. Cascine del Riccio
I-50023 Impruneta, Firenze, Italy
Tel: (+39 055) 20 92 59   Fax: (+39 055) 23 49 11
e-mail: info@amelispa.com
Web: www.amelispa.com

Products
Onboard exterior and interior passenger information display systems using LCD, LED and RGB Iride technologies; acoustic passenger information systems.

Annax Anzeigesysteme GmbH

Wettersteinstrasse 18, D-82024 Taufkirchen, Germany
Tel: (+49 89) 614 43 60   Fax: (+49 89) 614 436 63
e-mail: vertrieb@annax.de
Web: www.annax.de

Sales office
Kurmainzer Ring 51, D-63834 Sulzbach/Main, Germany
Tel: (+49 89) 614 436 30   Fax: (+49 89) 614 436 81

Products
Information display systems for external and internal onboard vehicle applications and for stationary use at bus and tram stops and in stations. Annax offers displays emplying LCD, LED and BiLED technologies.

The stationary displays can be configured to operate with the Annax-DECT wireless transmission system which receives vehicles location and running information and supplies this as real time information at bus and tram stops.

BBR Verkehrstechnik GmbH

Pillaustrasse 1e, DE-38126 Braunschweig, Germany
Tel: (+49 531) 27 30 00   Fax: (+49 531) 27 30 09 99
e-mail: info@bbr-vt.de
Web: www.bbr-vt.de

Products
Modular passenger information systems for up-to-date information about arrival and departure times, disruptions and other events. Fast and secure wirebound or wireless data transmission via radio, GPRS or W-LAN.

BT Group plc

BT Centre, 81 Newgate Street, London EC1A 7AJ, UK
Tel: (+44 20) 73 56 50 00   Fax: (+44 20) 73 56 55 20
Web: www.btglobalservices.com

Products
Web ticketing and information system; contact centre management, monitoring and measurement system; communications infrastructure for operating companies which is designed to improve public safety with 24-hour coverage through CCTV, giving faster and better quality of travel information to passengers; voice and data network communications (in conjunction with Cisco AVVID); electronic route scheduling for bus companies; Multi Protocol Label Switching (MPLS) platform to provide customer information and manage security at stations; BTnet Equip provides data, video and internet services with the option of voice traffic.

Contracts
BT, in conjunction with Connectivity, has delivered Frame Backbone network and LAN scheduling system to the Data Centre, Manchester.

MPLS customer information system to 176 stations for train operating company.

Clear Channel UK

33 Golden Square, London W1F 9JT, UK
Tel: (+44 20) 74 78 22 00   Fax: (+44 20) 74 34 45 30
Web: www.clearchanneladshel.com

Key personnel
Global President: *Paul Meyer*
Group Sales Director, UK: *Rob Atkinson*
PR Manager: *Janet Guest*

Products
Street furniture including bus shelters, information points, electronic displays and a bicycle loan scheme.

The range includes the i-plus unit, which has been developed in conjunction with multimedia company Cityspace to provide free information on entertainment, jobs, transport services and local government services for local residents and tourists alike.

SmartBike is a bicycle loan scheme, which provides an environmentally friendly mode of transport for local residents at no cost to the municipality or local taxpayer. Entirely funded by advertising the scheme involves a number of bicycles and docking stations located at various points around a city. Users are invited to apply for and are issued with an electronic SmartCard, which acts as a key and allows individuals access to the bikes.

Contracts
Clear Channel operates over 6,000 contracts around the world, including recent street furniture agreements in Cheshire and West Yorkshire, UK and Rome, Italy.

Developments
The latest technology developed at the Clear Channel Development Centre is a broadcast software system that can be combined with Plasma (for indoor use) or LED (for outdoor use) screens in a network to provide an innovative e-communications package for advertisers.

Web-based digital advertising and non-commercial information, such as news, time and weather reports can be displayed in an animated format. Remotely managed, rapid copy and creative changes can be made to offer flexibility in advertising display. LED technology has recently been installed in the UK, France and Malaysia.

Connexionz UK Ltd

Suite F4, Worth Corner, Turners Hill Road, Pound Hill, Sussex RH10 7SL, UK
Tel: (+44 1293) 88 73 08   Fax: (+44 1293) 88 41 00

Key personnel
Managing Director: *Robert Burke*
Operations Director: *Russell Gard*
Technical Director: *Adrian Waters*
National Engineering Manager: *Mike Barlett*

Background
Connexionz was founded in 1998 and took over the assets of Infocell Telecom which went into liquidation in 2006.

Products
Public transport passenger real-time information systems; street furniture, and vehicles with advanced telemetry and screen information units.

Conrac GmbH

Lindenstrasse 8, D-97990 Weikersheim, Germany
Tel: (+49 7934) 10 10   Fax: (+49 7934) 10 11 01
e-mail: info@conrac.de
Web: www.conrac.de

Key personnel
General Managers: *Walter Hammel,*
  Ralf Zimmermann
Director, Product Marketing: *Ingo Richter*
Manager, Marketing Communications:
  Petra Ollhoff
Manager, Product Management Transport
  Solutions: *Klaus Schipper*
Manager, Conrac France: *Patrick Heurtaux*
Manager, Conrac Asia: *Kee Sek Huat*
Manager, Conrac MENA: *Binu Sharma*
Manager, Conrac LTDA Latin America: *Toni Lang*
Manager, Conrac South Africa: *Gary Human*
Manager, Sales Office Southern Europe:
  Bernhard Gemassmer
Manager, Sales Office Northern Europe:
  Elisabeth Brandel

Subsidiaries
Conrac France SARL
Conrac Asia Display Products Ltd
Conrac MENA FZE
Conrac LTDA Latin America
Conrac LTDA South Africa

Conrac LCD/TFT at Antwerpen Station, Belgium   1341802

Background
Conrac GmbH is part of the Data Modul group of companies and is ISO 9001:2000 accredited.

Products
Intelligent information display systems for railway applications (hardware and software). Special customised solutions, single- and double-sided displays, various configurations, front access facilities, climate control; large-screen colour LCD/TFT displays, LED and LCD boards on request. IP54 or IP65 protection for outdoor applications, IP20 protection for indoor applications. Different models for connection to standard PC systems or with integrated Graphic Engine Board (GEB) or industrial PC for control and monitoring of the key display functions from a central server in the network. The large screen LCD/TFT displays feature robust aluminium housings and laminated safety glass with high efficiency anti-glare treatment. Designed for reliable operation in landscape and portrait mode applications, the Public Display Series features a high quality direct digital interface and gamma correction circuitry.

Developments
New developments include an 82 in high-resolution colour LCD/TFT display in 16:9 format, an intelligent cooling system with touch option.

cCOOL, a new cooling system has been introduced which prolongs the lifetime of the displays and is also very energy efficient and maintenance free.

Data Display Co Ltd

Deerpark Industrial Estate, Ennistymon, Co Clare, Ireland
Tel: (+353 65) 707 26 00   Fax: (+353 65) 707 13 11
e-mail: sales@data-display.com
Web: www.data-display.com

Key personnel
Managing Director: *Kevin Neville*
Marketing Manager: *Paul Neville*

Subsidiary companies
Data Display UK Ltd
Tel: (+44 23) 92 24 75 00
e-mail: sales@datadisplayuk.com

Data Display US
Tel: (+1 631) 218 21 30
e-mail: salesinfo@ddusa.com

Data Display Netherlands
Tel: (+31 78) 684 05 04
e-mail: info@data-display.nl

Data Display Dublin
Tel: (+353 65) 707 26 00
e-mail: maryhowe@data-display.com

Data Display France
Tel: (+33 1) 43 03 75 00
e-mail: infos@datadisplayfrance.com

Data Display Portugal
Tel: (+351 21) 910 67 60
e-mail: datadisplayportugal@mail.telepac.pt

Poltech, Sweden
Tel: (+46 171) 41 45 90
e-mail: info@poltech.se

Data Display Australia
Tel: (+61 3) 95 87 85 77
e-mail: info@datadisplay.com.au

Products
Data Display designs and manufactures electronic passenger information displays for the railway market. It provides a comprehensive range of platform, concourse and on-train displays. Technologies include LED, LCD, electromechanical, TFT and monitors.

Contracts
Supply of LED passenger information displays to London Underground, Denver Light Rail (US), Mersey Rail, London Line, Heathrow Express, Denver Bus (US), Wales & Borders Trains (now Arriva Trains Wales) and VTA (US). Further railway projects include Thales (Hong Kong), DRIMS (Netherlands), Paris Metro (France), Lisbon Metro, Dublin Area Rapid Transit as well as London Underground Central and Jubilee Lines (UK).

Emax SA

Public Transport & Electronic Identification Systems Dept
ul Chmielna 63/64, PL-80-748, Gdansk, Poland
Tel: (+48 58) 300 20 60   Fax: (+48 58) 305 86 10
e-mail: tp@emax.pl
Web: www.emax.pl

Key personnel
Director: *Tadeusz Iwanowski*

Background

In late 2006 the merger of Emax SA and ComputerLand SA commenced with the formal merger to one company.

Products

GPS-based real time passenger information systems, including: destination signs; next stop information; voice announcements; bus stop information displays.

Emcom Systems

127 Route 206 South, Suite 27 Trenton, New Jersey 08610, US
Tel: (+1 609) 585 55 00   Fax: (+1 609) 585 77 23
e-mail: ronkeppel@emcomsys.com
Web: emcomsys.com

Key personnel

Contact: Jonathan O'L Zeier
e-mail: ZeierAssociates@aol.com

Products

Emcom Systems provides Voice over Internet Protocol (VoIP) communications systems and components for mass transit and security applications.

FARA Denmark A/S

Augustenborg Landevej 19, DK-6400 Sønderborg, Denmark
Tel: (+45) 82 24 80 00   Fax: (+45) 82 84 80 80
e-mail: info@fara.dk.com
Web: www.fara.dk

Key personnel

UK General Manager: *Jay Prothero*

Subsidiaries

FARA UK
Ash House, Fairfield Avenue, Staines TW18 4AB, UK
Tel: (+44 1784) 22 42 21   Fax: (+44 1784) 22 42 31
e-mail: info@fara.uk.com.com
Web: www.fara.uk.com

Background

The company was previously named TNC, but following a purchase by a Norwegian company, the company has changed its name to FARA Denmark A/S.

Products

FARA delivers intelligent transport solutions to public bus operators and local authorities. The solutions are all integrated systems, being a range of advanced real-time passenger information systems, automatic vehicle location, and traffic management solutions.

Ferrograph Ltd

New York Way, New York Industrial Park, Newcastle-upon-Tyne NE27 0QF, UK
Tel: (+44 191) 280 88 00
Fax: (+44 191) 280 88 10
e-mail: info@ferrograph.com
Web: www.ferrograph.com

Key personnel

Sales Director: *Carl Littlejohn*

Products

Digital display solutions for public transport. LED, LCD, TFT and projection displays.

FIREMA Trasporti SpA

Headquarters

Via Provinciale Appia, Località Ponteselice, I-81100 Caserta, Italy
Tel: (+39 0823) 09 71 11   Fax: (+39 0823) 46 68 12
e-mail: info@firema.it
Web: www.firema.it

Key personnel

Chairman and Chief Executive Officer:
  Gianfranco Fiore
Commercial Manager: *Sergio d'Arminio*
Marketing Manager: *Agostino Astori*

Products

Onboard computers; automatic voice announcement of next stop, public address for buses and trains.

Focon Electronic Systems A/S

Damvang, PO Box 269, DK-6400 Sønderborg, Denmark
Tel: (+45) 73 42 25 00   Fax: (+45) 73 42 25 01
e-mail: focon@focon.dk
Web: www.focon.com

Key personnel

Managing Director: *Niels-Henrik Hedegaard*
Vice-Director (In Charge of Project, IT & Logistics):
  Per Viggo Rasmussen
Senior Managers
  Sales and Business Development: Bent Olsen
  Finance: *Brian Christensen*
  R & D: *Lars Bo Kjoeng-Rasmussen*
Managers:
  Service/Quality Management: *Jan Østergaard Pedersen*
  Procurement & Customer Logistics:
  Jonna Rehhoff-Nør

Background

Focon is part of the Mark IV IDS Group.

Products

High performance passenger information systems including: audio-visual and communication systems for onboard applications, passenger entertainment systems, public address, alarm, crew communications and talk-back systems, automatic seat reservation systems. Video surveillance and full-colour graphic displays.

Contracts

Intercity trains: AVE S103 (Spain), Icx (Germany), IC4 (Denmark), CP2000 (Portugal), IR4/IC3 (Denmark, Sweden, Israel), Regina (Sweden), OTU (Denmark, Sweden), Pendoluso (Portugal), ICE (Germany), X2000 (Sweden). Metro: London Underground Victoria Line Upgrade (UK), D-stock (UK), London Underground Jubilee Line (UK), Bucharest Metro (Romania), C20/C21 (Sweden), S-Train Copenhagen (Denmark). Regional Trains: IC2 (Denmark), X60 (Sweden), SGM III (Denmark), Itino (Sweden, Germany). Light Rail: Satra (Brazil), Metro do Porto (Portugal), A32 (Sweden, Netherlands, Turkey), Strasbourg (France).

Frensistemi Srl

Via della Cupla, 112, I-50145 Florence, Italy
Tel (+39 055) 302 01   Fax: (+39 055) 302 03 33
e-mail: sales.frensistemi@knorr-bremse.com
Web: www.knorr-bremse.it

Background

Frensistemi is a subsidiary of Knorr-Bremse AG (see entry in *Brakes and drawgear* section).

Products

Integrated passenger information systems incorporating functions that include train tracking,

transmission of audio and video information, transmission of ground-to-train information, GSM-R communication and seat reservation. Equipment supplied includes: crew and passenger MMIs; GSM/GSM-R devices; interior and external displays; communication and train logic devices; and main electronic control and train audio communications systems.

Contracts

Customers include ALSTOM Ferroviaria, Ansaldobreda, Bombardier Transportation, CAF, Ferrovie Nord Milano, Firema Trasporti, MerMec, NSB, SNCF and Trenitalia.

GAI-Tronics

A division of Hubbell Limited
Brunel Drive, Stretton Park, Burton-on-Trent DE13 0BZ, UK
Tel: (+44 1283) 50 05 00   Fax: (+44 1283) 50 04 00
e-mail: sales@gai-tronics.co.uk
Web: www.gai-tronics.co.uk

Key personnel

Business Unit General Manager: *Graham Lines*
Business Unit Controller: *Toby Balmer*
Engineering Manager: *Richard Rumsby*
Manufacturing Director: *Mark Bradford*
Commercial Manager: *Roger Goodall*
Marketing Manager: *Nicole Ireland*
Special Projects Manager: *Steve Smith*

Other offices

GAI-Tronics Corporation, US
Tel: (+1 610) 777 13 74
Fax: (+1 610) 775 65 40
Web: www.gai-tronics.com
GAI-Tronics Srl, Italy
Tel: (+39 02) 48 60 14 60
Fax: (+39 02) 458 56 25
GAI-Tronics Corporation, Malaysia
Tel: (+60 3) 89 45 40 35
Fax: (+60 3) 89 45 46 75
GAI-Tronics Australia (Austdac)
Tel: (+61 2) 96 34 70 55
Fax: (+61 2) 98 99 24 90

Background

GAI-Tronics was established in 1964 to provide communications equipment to the mining industry. It has now expanded into the provision of specialised communications equipment for road and rail transportation industries.

Products

Help point telephone: hands-free use, weather- and vandal-resistant. Allows easy access to information or emergency assistance and there is an option for remote monitoring, programming and maintenance. Available as analogue or VoIP.

'Vision'; a vandal resistant, interactive touchscreen unit with bespoke housing and software to suit customers' environment and to comply with DDA regulations. Vision has the option of an integrated audio help point which can be accessed via soft keys or a push to call button. Connection can be made via H232, SIP or analogue depending upon customer requirements. An internal induction loop is included.

Monitoring capability: the units have SMART software technology which allows them to be remotely monitored by a central control station. This reduces customer maintenance costs and enables valuable marketing analysis for the customer.

Gorba AG

Sandackerstrasse, CH-9245 Oberbüren, Switzerland
Tel: (+41 71) 955 74 74   Fax: (+44 71) 951 96 74
e-mail: info@gorba.com
Web: www.gorba.com

Key personnel

President: *Daniel Fäh*
Sales: *Beat Jans, Reto Diem, Jürgen Geckens*
Administration: *Andrea Blatter*

Subsidiaries

Gorba GmbH
Osterbooksweg 69, D-22869 Schenefeld b.
Hamburg, Germany
Tel: (+49 40) 41 597 30
Fax: (+49 40) 41 45 97 33
e-mail: gerkens@gorba.com

Products

Audio and visual passenger information systems including Liquid Crystal Displays (LCD), Dot-/LED and LED. LCD and LED colour modules for exterior use are also available. The latest product 'TopBox' allows the control of all TFT systems with a large variety of technical functions.

Hanover Displays Ltd

Unit 24, Cliffe Industrial Estate, Lewes BN8 6JL, UK
Tel: (+44 1273) 47 75 28
Fax: (+44 1273) 40 77 66
e-mail: sales@hanoverdisplays.com
Web: www.hanoverdisplays.com

Key personnel

Managing Director: *Gavin Williams*
International Sales Manager: *Andrew Williams*
General Manager: *Steve Colquhoun*
Development Manager: *Phil Sturgeon*
Operations Manager: *Steve Alpin*
UK Sales Manager: *Alan Cressey*
Administration Manager: *Steve Holland*
Technical Engineer: *Anthony Gapper*
Advanced Projects Manager: *Mike Siverns*
Engineering and Quality Manager:
    Simon Braddick
Marketing Manager: *Nick Robertson*
IT Manager: *Ben Richardson*
Materials Manager: *Roger Smith*
Business Development Manager: *Jon Wood*

Products

Electronic information display systems using electromagnetic flip-dot and LED technologies for use in vehicles and fixed installations including bus stops and stations. The systems provide large memory capacity with simple reprogramming facilities for route network updating. An autonomous driver's controller is provided, but the signs can also be slaved to onboard electronic equipment such as ticket machines.

A curved display version of the company's flip-dot sign, specifically for new rail vehicles with steeply inclined curved screens, has been introduced. The sign bends to the shape of the screen and fixes against it without the need for a second window.

Hi-Force Limited

Bentley Way, Daventry NN11 8QH, UK
Tel: (+44 1327) 30 10 00
Fax: (+44 1327) 70 65 55
e-mail: sales@hi-force.com
Web: www.hi-force.com/hi-force

Key personnel

Group Managing Director: *Kevin Brown*
Directors: *John Taylor, Stephen Hudson*
Finance Director: *Lin Whaymand*
Worldwide Marketing Manager: *Mar Noordhoek*
UK Sales Manager: *Stefan Gunter*

Background

Previously called Hi-Force Hydraulics Limited, the name has changed to Hi-Force Limited.

Products

High-pressure hydraulic tools, including: pumps, cylinders, jacks, cutters, cable crimpers, nut splitters, manual and hydraulic torque wrenches, stud bolt tensioners and hydrotest pumps.

Ikusi – Ángel Iglesias SA

PO Box 1320, E-20080 San Sebastian, Spain
Tel: (+34 943) 44 88 00   Fax: (+34 943) 44 88 20
e-mail: sb@ikusi.com
Web: www.ikusi.com

Key personnel

Deputy Director, Public Information Systems:
    Imanol Saenz
Marketing Manager: *Nora Iglesias*

Products

Displays, monitors and automated public address, audio and video entertainment systems; video monitoring by CCTV of passenger coach interior and exterior, with integrated alarm systems; mobile phone coverage on trains and on stations.

Contracts

In December 2006, Ikusi was chosen to supply and integrate the communications system for the new Pamplona (Spain) bus station, currently under construction. It is a "turnkey" project that includes operating support systems for automatic dock assignation, public information system, access control, security, video surveillance and car parking systems.

In July 2006, two orders were received for Ikusi's remote control portfolio: the company is to supply TM70 range remote control units to the London Underground and to the Toyota plant in the French city of Lille. The 23 TM70 1.13 units equipped with displays are now operational in the maintenance shops of the London Underground.

INEO Systrans

Avenue de Conflans – 2 allée Edouard Branly, F-78260, France
Tel: (+33 1) 39 22 57 00   Fax: (+33 1) 39 22 57 99
e-mail: systrans@ineo.com
Web: www.ineo-systrans.com

Background

INEO Systrans, part of the INEO group of companies, is a subsidiary of the Services and Energy division of the Suez Group.

Products/Services

Supply and installation of real time passenger information and automatic vehicle location systems.

Contracts

INEO Systrans has equipped 50 light rail systems and bus networks in Belgium, France, Israel, Spain, Switzerland and the UK.

Most recently INEO Systrans was awarded a new contract linked to the extension of the three existing tram lines in Bordeaux. The contract includes equipping 36 new tram stations and 26 new tram rails.

Infoscreen Austria Gesellschaft für Stadtinformationsanlagen GmbH

Hainburgerstrasse 11, A-1030 Vienna, Austria
Tel: (+43 1) 71 05 20 00
Fax: (+43 1) 710 52 00 71
e-mail: doris.trummer@infoscreen.at
Web: www.infoscreen.at

Key personnel

Contact: Doris Trummer

Products

Information systems including TFT-LCD displays, loudspeaker systems and moving display units.

Infotec Limited

The Maltings, Tamworth Road, Ashby de la Zouch LE65 2PS, UK
Tel: (+44 1530) 56 65 01
Fax (+44 1530) 56 01 11
e-mail: sales@infotec.co.uk
Web: www.infotec.co.uk

Key personnel

Managing Director: *Jeff Court*
Sales Manager: *Anthony Thompson*

Background

Asbhy-based Infotec was established in 1992 as a designer and manufacturer of electronic displays. The company also provides display networking equipment, secondary steelwork and where required offers a full service of design, manufacture, supply, installation and maintenance.

Products

Infotec produces a range of IP 66 rated, IP addressable LED, TFT and LCD displays for all environments featuring full remote programming, self diagnostics, asset management and the ability to handle all industry standard protocols over WAN, LAN, Ethernet, Internet, wireless or serial communications.

Contracts

Historically, 80 per cent of Infotec's business has been within the UK rail market, but increasingly other sectors are opening up and it is active in the bus, road, underground, air, multimodal transport and urban areas.

Clients include Acis, Amey Infrastructure Services, Atos Origin, Bailey Rail, Bombardier Transportation, Marconi, Network Rail, Thales and other UK train operating companies. Contracts awarded include: the design, manufacture, supply and commissioning of a large number of bespoke LCD displays for the redeveloped St Pancras Station; the planning, design, production and project management of LED customer information systems to replace life-expired CRT displays at 13 GNER station and to supply all of the displays and project manage the installation of the customer information systems at Sheffield station. In addition to hardware, Infotec supplied an eight-way hub router and a maintenance PC connected to Midland Mainline/Sheffield network.

INIT Innovative Informatikanwendungen in Transport-, Verkehrs- und Leitsystemen GmbH

Kaeppelestrasse 4-6, D-76131 Karlsruhe, Germany
Tel: (+49 721) 610 00
Fax: (+49 721) 610 03 99
e-mail: postmaster@init-ka.de
Web: www.init-ka.de

Subsidiaries

Australia
INIT Pty Ltd
Level 5, Toowong Tower, 9 Sherwood Road, Toowong Qld, 4066 Australia
Tel: (+61 7) 33 10 88 18
Fax: (+61 7) 33 10 88 00

US
INIT Innovations in Transportation Inc
1420 Kristina Way, Suite 101, Chesapeake, Virginia 23320
Tel: (+1 757) 413 91 00   Fax: (+1 757) 413 50 19

Canada
INIT Innovations in Transportation (Eastern Canada) Inc/INIT Innovations en Transport (Canada Est) Inc
14 Place du Commerce, suite 360, Île-des-Soeurs, Montréal, Québec H3E 1T7, Canada
Tel: (+1 514) 766 28 36   Fax: (+1 514) 766 15 78
INIT, Innovations in Transportation (Western Canada) Inc
949 West 41st Avenue, Vancouver, BC V5Z2N5, Canada
Tel: (+1 778) 995 04 93

United Arab Emirates
Init Innovation in Traffic Systems FZE
Dubai Airport Free Zone, Office 6EB 244, Dubai, UAE
Tel: (+971) 47 01 72 86

Key personnel
Chief Sales Officer: *Dr Jürgen Greschner*

Products
Real-time passenger information (on-board, wayside, home including Internet and mobile devices).

Interalia Inc

4110 79th Street NW, Calgary, Alberta T3B 5C2, Canada
Tel: (+1 403) 288 27 06 (ext. 105)
Fax: (+1 403) 288 59 35
e-mail: rcormack@interalia.com
Web: www.interalia.com

Key personnel
President and Chief Financial Officer: *Garth Hunter*
Chief Operations Officer and Vice-President Business Development: *Robert Cormack*

Subsidiaries
Interalia Communications Inc, US
Interalia Communications Ltd, UK

Products
Passenger information systems including customer information systems, onboard and platform announcers:
- *DVA-Lite* – platform announcement systems for use in low passenger volume stations.
- *CIS-DVA* – a standalone customer information system that automatically plays train arrival, departure, platform and other messages based on the master train timetable supplied from Network Rail.
- *Trouncer* – onboard and platform announcer/sign controller
- *Trouncer DVA* – digital voice announcement systems with flat panel touch screen interface designed to provide high quality audio announcements and visual display messages (LED, LCD, electro-mechanical or other). It interfaces with common public address systems to provide both audio and visual messages for applications requiring less than eight zones. It is especially good for small train or bus platforms among other locations.
- *Live Announcement Bridge (LAB)* – a fully digital VOIP-based live announcement bridge, which allows an operator located at a central control centre to make live audio broadcast announcements to one, all, or any combination of stations where the Interalia systems are installed.
Passenger help point systems:
- *IBBISS* – provides passengers with a direct communication line to transportation staff in case of a fire, emergency, or a need for general information.

Engineering and technical support for services in the transportation sector:
Interalia now provides engineering expertise for the following: station surveys (pre-install and detail studies), station design (PA/CCTV/DVA/Help point systems), fault identification and rectification for most standard communication systems, project management for design, supply, and installation of communication systems, particularly with the London Underground and Network Rail.
Interalia has worked for various integrating companies supplying the rail networks and has a wide experience in the many different manufacturers equipment, including the latest digital versions of the older analogue systems.

Contracts
- *Commander* – 27 installations at the London Underground.
- *DVA-Lite* – currently being deployed on nine station operated by Tubelines as part of the station upgrade initiative.
- *CIS-DVA* – currently being deployed in eight stations operated by Virgin Trains on Network Rail stations in the UK and Scotland.
- *Trouncer* – installations through Geofocus at the Chicago Metra, Capital Corridor Oakland, Salt Lake City, and Ft Lauderdale. Also installations at Trak Com Wireless at Vancouver Skytrain, People Mover, Detroit, Calgary Transit, Edmonton Transit, Warrington, Poole and Manchester in the UK, Cologne Arena, Germany and stations in Korea and Kuala Lumpur.
- *Canada Line* – Interalia is providing complete station PA/VA systems for the new Canada Line system being constructed in Vancouver, British Columbia. It is also providing on-board messages on the vehicles being supplied by Rotem, as well as managing and controlling the visual displays supplied by Mitron.

JCDecaux Group

JCDecaux SA
Communications Department
17 rue Soyer, F-92523 Neuilly-sur-Seine Cedex, France
Tel: (+33 1) 30 79 79 79
Web: www.jcdecaux.com

Worldwide offices
The Group has offices in 48 countries worldwide.

Key personnel
Chairman, Supervisory Board: *Jean-Claude Decaux*
Vice-Chairman, Supervisory Board: *Jean-Pierre Decaux*
Executive Board
Chairman: *Jean-Charles Decaux*
Chief Executive: *Jean-François Decaux*
Chief Operating Officer: *Robert Caudron*
Chief Financial Officer: *Gérard Degonse*
Managing Director, Northern and Central European Operations: *Jeremy Male*
  Staff: 7,900 worldwide

Background
Since 2001, a public limited corporation governed by an Executive Board and a Supervisory Board.

Products
JCDecaux designs, manufactures, installs and maintains and cleans street furniture which is financed by advertising. Products include illuminated signs and illuminated bus shelters.

Contracts
In May 2006, the wholly owned subsidiary JCDecaux Texon, Hong Kong, announced that it had been awarded a five-year contract by Hong Kong Tramways Limited for full-body tram advertising on its fleet of 140 trams.

KeTech Group

KeTech Group Limited, Clifton House, 4a Goldington Road, Bedford, MK40 3NF, UK
Tel: (+44 1772) 70 63 30   Fax: (+44 1772) 70 22 71
e-mail: info@ketech.com
Web: www.ketech.com

Subsidiaries
KeTech Systems Ltd
Units 1-2, Eastway Business Village, Olivers Place, Fulwood, Preston PR2 9WT, UK
Tel: (+44 1772) 70 63 30   Fax: (+44 1772) 70 22 71
e-mail: info@ketech.com
Web: www.ketech.com
Other companies within the group include: KeTech Defence Ltd, KeTech Ditra, Ltd, Key Radio Systems Ltd, KeTech Security Ltd and 2As' Ltd.

Other offices
The Group also has offices in London, Nottingham, Preston, Aldermaston and Bristol in the UK.

Background
KeTech is a multi-disciplined group of companies specialising in communication, information and detection technologies.

Key personnel
Chief Executive: *John Kearney*
Managing Director (KeTech Systems and KeTech Defence): *Eddie Weir*
Managing Director (KeTech Ditra and Key Radio Systems Ltd): *Matt Cox*
Managing Director (2As' Ltd): *Paul Battersbee*
General Manager (KeTech Security Systems Ltd): *Ian Carling*

Products
Control and management systems; customer information systems; passenger information systems (on-vehicle); CCTV surveillance and security systems; platform to train systems; public address and voice alarm systems; driver operator multi-functional displays; digital transmission systems; help points; SCADA systems; access control and intruder detection systems; protocol and data conversion; roadside communications; equipment monitoring; PMR and trunked radio systems. Building Management Control Systems.
The technology is suitable for rail or bus applications.

Contracts
The growth of KeTech Systems began in 2000 when the company was awarded contracts to modify and extend the platform to train systems (PtT) on the Jubilee Line and new rolling stock. This participation in the Tubelines Seventh Car project, where six-car rolling stock was extended to seven cars, required modification of the PtT. This was to include platform side CCTV system reconfiguration at all the stations along the route. PtT provision continues with a contract for the complete system on the Victoria Line, completed in August 2008. KeTech Systems are currently undertaking a project to provide the communications systems for six new stations as part of the Docklands Light Railway Olympic extension programme.

KJ GmbH Installationen

Fechnerstrasse 29, D-01139 Dresden, Germany
Tel: (+49 351) 89 45 60   Fax: (+49 351) 894 561 00
e-mail: info@kj-gmbh.de
Web: www.kj-gmbh.de

Key personnel
Managing Directors: *Maik Juppe; Uwe Köhn*

Products
Stationary passenger information display systems using LCD technology and related control systems.

Contracts

In 2004, KJ installed a major new passenger information system at the DB station in Halle, Germany.

LAWO – Mark IV Industries GmbH

Stockfeldstrasse 1, D-76437 Rastatt, Germany
Tel: (+49 7222) 100 10   Fax: (+49 7222) 100 11 34
e-mail: vertrieb@lawo.info
Web: www.lawo.info

Key personnel

Managing Director: *Hans-Joachim Reich*
Controller/Financial Officer: *Michael Terlaak*
Sales Director: *Robert Gels*

Background

Established in 1985, the company became part of the holdings of Mark IV Industries Inc in 1989.

Products

Passenger information system.

LogicTree

4901 Telsa Drive, Suite F, Bowie, Maryland 20715, US
Tel: (+1 301) 352 10 50   Fax: (+1 301) 352 10 51
e-mail: brent@logictree.com
Web: www.logictree.com

Key personnel

National Director, ITS Solutions: *Brent Isenberg*

Background

LogicTree was established in 1997.

Products

LogicTree provides 24-hour transit information and 511 IVR (Interactive Voice Response) services with products: TransitSpeak™ and TravelerSpeak™.

In September 2008, the company launched its new TransitSpeak Express™ hosted transit IVR service.

Lumino Licht Elektronik GmbH

Europark Fichtenhain A8, D-47807 Krefeld, Germany
Tel: (+49 2151) 819 61 28
Fax: (+49 2151) 819 63 59
e-mail: info@lumino.de
Web: www.lumino.de

Key personnel

Export Manager: *Peter Mueller*
Engineers: *Karl Heinz Ronkholz, Rolf Aengenendt*
Business Economist: *Mario Fullert*
Sales: *Mario Fullert, Peter Bahr, Peter Müller*

Products

Passenger information systems for public transport, manufacturing LED displays for station platforms and bus or tramway stops. Displays can be configured to show text, graphics and logos. Commune LED colours include amber and red with automatic brightness control. Formats include single- or double-sided displays with a full matrix panel. Dynamic audio announcement and clock systems can be integrated in the systems, which are supplied with complete software and hardware.

Mark IV Industries Inc

PO Box 810, Amherst, NY 14226, US
Tel: (+1 716) 689 49 72
e-mail: information@mark-iv.com
Web: www.mark-iv.com

Key personnel

Chief Executive Officer and Director: *William P Montague*
Chief Executive Officer, Automotive OEM: *Giuliano Zucco*
Vice-President, Chief Financial Officer and Treasurer: *Mark G Barberio*
Vice-President and Chief Accounting Officer: *Richard L Grenolds*
President, Transportation Technologies: *Avi Zisman*

Other offices

The company has an office in Airasca, Italy and operations in 16 countries.

Products

Electronic display components and systems for outdoor applications; passenger information displays for public transport applications; variable message signs for highway applications.

Mattig-Schauer GmbH

Matznergasse 34, A-1140 Vienna, Austria
Tel: (+43 1) 78 97 98 90   Fax: (+43 1) 78 97 98 92 39
e-mail: time@mattig-schauer.at
Web: www.mattig-schauer.at

Key personnel

International Sales Manager: *Ing Ralf Larcher*
Key Account Manager: *Ing Karl Stöckner*
Key Account Manager, Export: *Erich Blaschka*

Products

Time display systems, clock systems; automatic announcement systems for stations and trains; voice logging systems for emergency calls.

Meister Electronic GmbH

Postfach 90 31 60, DE-51124 Cologne, Germany
Tel: (+49 2203) 17 01 20   Fax: (+49 2203) 17 01 30
e-mail: koeln@meister-electronic.com
Web: www.meister-electronic.de

Key personnel

Chief Executive Officer: *Fritz E Meister*
Chief Financial Officer: *René Stoffels*
Chief Operating Officer: *Frank Krüger*

Products

Onboard multimedia systems, electronic destination signs, digital announcement and intercom systems; video surveillance systems, refurbishment of onboard communication systems.

Metra Blansko AS

Pražská 7, č p 1602, CZ-678 49 Blansko, Czech Republic
Tel: (+420 506) 49 41 15   Fax: (+420 506) 49 41 45
e-mail: metra@metra.cz
Web: www.metra.cz

Key personnel

Chairman: *Roman Pilát*
Vice-Chairmen: *Ivo Pernica, Oldří Zouhar*
Commercial Director: *Ladislav Nečas*
Technical Director: *Jiří Zouhar*
Financial Director: *Oldřich Zlámal*

Background

Metra Blansko AS is part of the APOS Group of companies.

Products

On-train interior and exterior dot matrix and LED display systems.

Contracts

Include provision of information systems for Czech Railways Class 471 double-deck emu vehicles and for new metro cars for Prague.

Mitron Oy

PO Box 113, (Kutomonkuja 2 C 1), FIN-30101 Forssa, Finland
Tel: (+358 3) 424 04 00   Fax: (+358 3) 435 53 21
e-mail: feedback@mitron.fi
Web: www.mitron.fi

Key personnel

Business Unit Director, Mobile Systems: *Juha Siitonen*
Business Unit Director, Stationary Displays: *Kimmo Ylander*
Sales Mobile Systems: *Hannu Oksa, Jarkko Vehkala*
Sales Stationary Displays: *Abdessamad Essalim, Timo Ali-Lekkala, Juha Strandberg*

Background

Founded in 1988, Mitron is ISO 14011 and ISO 9001 accredited.

Products

Design and manufacture of public transport information systems for stations, platforms and stops and also information display, announcement, entertainment and security systems for trains, trams and subways.

Contracts

In June 2007, Mitron signed a regional agency agreement with Transport Data Management Ltd (TDM) in the UK, TDM will distribute and market all Mitron systems and products in the UK.

In April 2006, Mitron and DB Kommunikationstechnik AG signed a co-operation agreement relating to the installation and maintenance services for passenger information displays for German Railways.

Mobitec AB

Ölltorp Industrial Area, Box 97, SE-524 21, Herrljunga, Sweden
Tel: (+46 513) 229 00   Fax: (+46 513) 229 22
e-mail: info@mobitec.eu
Web: www.mobitec.eu

Key personnel

Managing Director: *Oliver Wels*

Background

Mobitec, a member of Degital Recorders Inc, designs and manufactures system technology for mobile passenger information on buses and rail-bounded vehicles and has products on buses and trams in over 30 countries around the world. Mobitec operates from three production facilities and is ISO 9001 and 14001 accredited.

Products

Passenger information systems for public transport vehicles applications. Including destination signs, internal next-stop signs, voice announcement, control units, GPS, wireless data transfer and software program for design of text and graphics.

For details of the latest updates to *Jane's Urban Transport Systems* online and to discover the additional information available exclusively to online subscribers please visit

juts.janes.com

Morio Denki Co Ltd

34-1 Tateishi 4-chome, Katsushika-ku, Tokyo 124-0012, Japan
Tel: (+81 3) 36 91 31 81
Fax: (+81 3) 36 92 13 33
Web: www.morio.co.jp

Key personnel
Chairman: *S Yamagata*
President: *K Miura*
Senior Managing Director: *T Yagishita*

Products
Information systems featuring LED, liquid crystal and plasma display. Train destination displays.

Contracts
Recent contracts include the supply of passenger information systems for Taiwan High Speed rail cars, China Railway and 700 Shinkansen high-speed trainsets.

Moser-Baer SA

Export Division
Ch du Champ-des-Filles 19 CH-1228 Plan-les-Ouates, Switzerland
Tel: (+41 22) 884 96 11   Fax: (+41 22) 884 96 90
e-mail: export@mobatime.com
Web: www.mobatime.com

Key personnel
Export Division Manager: *J C Zgraggen*
Export Sales Manager: *T Fric*

Products
Industrial timing equipment: modular master clock systems, time distribution to computers/networks (NTP server), mains frequency supervision, radio and satellite (GPS) time receivers, digital and analogue secondary clock systems, self-setting Mobaline digital and analogue secondary clock systems, façade clocks, tower and decorative clocks.

Omega Electronics SA

Mattenstrasse 149, CH-2503 Biel/Bienne, Switzerland
Tel: (+41 32) 343 37 11   Fax: (+41 32) 343 38 00
e-mail: info@omega-electronics.ch
Web: www.omega-electronics.ch

Key personnel
Managing Director: *H Kayal*

Products
Passenger information systems. Flap and LCD display with white characters on a blue background; also three-colour LED display for general use, CRT, Plasma and TFT monitors.

Contracts
Contracts have included supply of systems for Leipzig main station, Germany, Zurich airport main station, Fribourg bus station, several Swiss and German railway stations and many others.

Oval Window Audio

33 Wildflower Court, Nederland, Colorado 80466, US
Tel: (+1 303) 447 36 07   Fax: (+1 303) 447 36 07
e-mail: info@ovalwindowaudio.com
Web: www.ovalwindowaudio.com

Key personnel
Director of Research & Development: *Norman Lederman*

Products
Induction loop hearing assistance systems for buses, Mobiloop hearing assistance system for buses and rail vehicles.

Pallas Informatik A/S

Allerød Stationsvej 2D, DK-3450 Allerød, Denmark
Tel: (+45) 48 10 24 10   Fax: (+45) 48 10 24 01
e-mail: pallas@pallas.dk
Web: www.pallas.dk

Key personnel
Chairman of the Board: *Svend Vitting Andersen*
Managing Director: *Karsten Funder*

Products
Tele and Radio base Information systems for Trains (TRIT), comprising train running information displays on platforms, a central TRIT server, a TRIT computer on all trains and a communications system providing links with all other units in the system. The system is based on data supplied by the infrastructure operator, the train operator's timetable, the operational management disposition of equipment, current train running information and train layout, including seat availability.

Contracts
Since 1998 Pallas Informatik has worked with Danish State Railways to develop and install a TRIT system for the national rail network.

Petards Joyce-Loebl

390 Princesway, Team Valley Trading Estate, Gateshead NE11 0TU, UK
Tel: (+44 191) 420 30 00   Fax: (+44 191) 420 30 30
e-mail: sales@joyce-loebl.com
Web: www.petardsplc.com

Key personnel
Director, Transport Systems: *Mike Wade*

Background
Formerly Joyce-Loebl Ltd, the company adopted its current name in 2005 following its acquisition by Petards Group plc, a specialist in security and surveillance systems.

Products
Integrated electronic onboard passenger information systems including: seat reservation displays; front of train displays; side of train displays; audio systems; and digital CCTV security systems.

Petards also offers transmission of video from the trains using wireless data capacity; live video or logged events can be transferred without stopping the vehicle's normal operation.

Contracts
In June 2008, Petards was awarded a contract for the supply of the eyeTrain™ Digital CCTV System by Porterbrook Leasing Company for the class 153 fleet, operated by London Midland Trains, part of Govia (partnership between the Go-Ahead Group and Keolis).

Petards was awarded a contract by Bombardier Transportation to supply and install Petards eyeTrain™ on-board digital CCTV systems for Class 465 and 466 'Networker' trains.

Postfield Systems

53 Ullswater Crescent, Coulsdon CR5 2HR, UK
Tel: (+44 20) 86 55 60 60
Fax: (+44 20) 86 55 60 70
e-mail: sales@postfield.co.uk
Web: www.postfield.co.uk

Key personnel
Directors: *Phil Clayton, Bob Clayton, Chris Helden*
Sales Contact: *Wendy Coward*

Products
Manufacturer of hi-tech information software and visual display equipment, which specialises in both customer information and data display. The company supplies the rail industry and has experience in the design, development, fabrication, assembly, project management, commissioning and maintenance support for the following: Customer Information Systems (CIS), CCTV, Public Address (PA) Systems and environmental monitors.

Postfield Systems has a separate 'maintenance and support services' division, which offers around the clock support for CIS, CCTV and PA. The division has a repair centre, training suite and call centre.

Contracts
Survey, design, supply and testing of DOO mirrors and CCTV for the re-opened Larkhall branch line.

Manufacture ruggedised environmental monitors for the London Underground.

Precimation SA

Erlenstrasse 35A, CH-2555 Brügg BE, Switzerland
Tel: (+41 32) 366 69 99   Fax: (+41 32) 366 69 90
e-mail: welcome@precimation.ch
Web: www.precimation.ch; www.precimation.com

Key personnel
Chief Executive Officer: *Daniel Lenz*
Chief Operating Officer: *Stephan Brünig*
Director Sales and Marketing: *Ufuk Ebcinoglu*

Products
Connectors for industry, defence, aerospace and railways, electromechanical components, electronic displays and information systems, fibre optic products.

iqube: autonomous passenger information network with direct data transmission between bus stops and with buses. Intelligent cubes display actual departure times. Information centre allows real-time monitoring, offers download capabilities on the net.

Procyon Ltd

44 Oxford Street, Wellingborough, Northamptonshire NN8 4JH, UK
Tel: (+44 1933) 27 87 87   Fax: (+44 1933) 27 87 89
Web: www.procyon.ltd.uk

Key personnel
Managing Director: *Pat Taylor*

Background
Procyon has been providing media solutions since 1992.

Products
Digital information system linked with flat-screen technology for staff communication at

Procyon's digital information system for a Stagecoach depot   1289681

Procyon's digital information system onboard First's new ftr vehicle in York, UK   1289682

depots and onboard installations for passenger information.

Contracts
System installation on First's advanced 'ftr' (future) passenger vehicles in York.

Other companies that have implemented the system include Arriva, Metroline and Stagecoach.

Ruf Telematik AG

Rütistrasse 12, CH-8952 Schlieren, Switzerland
Tel: (+41 1) 733 84 00   Fax: (+41 1) 733 83 00
Web: www.ruf.ch

Key personnel
Marketing: *Rolf Hess*

Products
VisiWeb onboard dynamic passenger information systems; station departure/arrival displays; multimedia passenger interior displays and acoustic announcements.

Contracts
Ruf Telematik passenger information systems are installed on Swiss Federal Railways' FLIRT emus and ICN tilting trainsets, on trains operated by the Matterhorn Gotthard Bahn and on Basle Euro-Airport bus shuttle, providing dynamic details of flight departures.

SA ViewCom A/S

Gefionsweg 7 DK-3400 Hillerød, Denmark
Tel: (+45) 72 19 35 00   Fax: (+45) 72 19 35 01
e-mail: mail@saviewcom.com
Web: www.saviewcom.com

Key personnel
General Manager: *Henrik Beck-Bang*
Vice-President, Sales and Marketing: *Povl Moustgaard Knudsen*
Quality Assurance Manager: *Daniel Deschênes*

Background
A wholly owned subsidiary of Axion Technologies, Canada, SA ViewCom was founded in 1999 as a merger of Modulex ViewCom and ScanAcoustic. The company strategy is to concentrate on serving rolling stock in the rail market.

Products
Onboard train solutions including: visual passenger information systems; public address; onboard intercom; passenger alarm units; digital audio announcements; passenger entertainment; GPS or tacho positioning; seat reservation; GSM-GPRS- and Wi-Fi communications; integration of door signals; CCTV.

Contracts
SA ViewCom has supplied PILON equipment to: Express Rail Link (Malaysia) Desiro emus; NSB Class 73 Signatur and 73B Agenda emus (Norway); SL Class X10 emus (Sweden); and Angel Trains Class 350, One (First Great Eastern) 360, and South West Trains Class 444 and 450

Desiro emus (all UK) and Helsinki Metro (Finland). A number of refurbishment projects have been delivered or are in the process of delivery (UK market) as well as systems for new trains for CTRL (UK) and IE (Ireland).

Most recently SA Viewcom won an order from Bombardier Transportation for a passenger information system for operation on the London Underground rolling stock.

SEPSA

Sistemas Electrónicas de Potencia SA
Polígono Ind La Estación, C/Albatros 7&9,
E-28320 Pinto, Madrid, Spain
Tel: (+34 91) 495 70 00   Fax: (+34 91) 495 70 60
e-mail: albatros@albatros-sl.es
Web: www.albatros-sl.es

Background
Established in 1981, SEPSA is a member of the Albatros Corporation.

Products
Onboard passenger information systems comprising public address systems, automatic station announcement systems and internal (LED or dot matrix) and external (LED or electromagnetic) information display units.

SLE

SLE Mark IV - M Ian C Day
80 route des Lucioles, "Les espaces de Sophia",
Bâtiment E, F-06560 Valbonne, France
Tel: (+33 4) 97 24 59 00   Fax: (+33 4) 97 24 59 01
e-mail: sle@sle-fr.com
Web: www.sle-fr.com

Key personnel
Company Manager and Sales and Marketing Director: *Marcos Reichert*

Background
SLE is a subsidiary of the Mark IV Industries group.

Products and services
Real-time information and automatic vehicle location systems (real-time location and tracking of vehicles through GPS or microwave beacons); statistics tools for travel time of vehicles; real-time information systems; information and vocal announcements systems; onboard video surveillance systems; bus stop information signs; onboard display signs; external destination signs (LED or LCD); driver keyboards.

Contracts
Recent awards for Suffolk County Council, real-time information and automatic vehicle location systems; Hampshire County Council (UK): real-time information and automatic vehicle location systems (location and forecasting of estimated times of arrival at bus stops, WEB, WAP, SMS services); RATP (Paris, France) voice announcement systems for 3,500 buses; Marseille RTM, real-time passenger information and signs at stops, Meaux-Marne et Morin, France, automatic vehicle location and real time passenger information systems (GPS location), London (London Bus Systems) real-time information and automatic vehicle location systems (regulation, location and forecasting of estimated times of arrival at bus stops); Neuchâtel (Switzerland) real-time information and automatic vehicle location systems (regulation, GPS location); Lyon (SYTRAL, France) real-time information and automatic vehicle location systems with microwave beacon location for tramways; Avignon and Vitrolles (France) real-time information and automatic vehicle location systems with GPS location; Lansing and Cincinnati (US) onboard voice announcement system.

Socel Visioner

702 rue du Pont Rouge, BP 3, F-59236 Frelinghien, France
Tel: (+33 3) 20 48 81 78
Fax: (+33 3) 20 48 85 10
e-mail: visionor@visionor.fr
Web: www.visionor.fr

TFT bus stop information display by Socel Visioner   0585287

Products

Fixed and onboard passenger information systems and displays. Displays employ CRT, LCD, LED, Plasma, TFT and VFD technologies.

Solari di Udine SpA

Via Gino Pieri 29, I-33100 Udine, Italy
Tel: (+39 0432) 49 71
Fax: (+39 0432) 48 01 60
e-mail: info@solari.it
Web: www.solari.it

Key personnel
Chairman: *Massimo Paniccia*
Vice-President: *Arduino Paniccia*
Export Products Sales Director: *Dino Domeneghetti*
Systems Sales Director: *Alberto Vazzoler*
Products Sales Director: *Alberto Zuliani*
Technical Director: *Giorgio Segatto*

Products
Passenger and staff information display systems using monitors and display boards (flaps: LED; TA; LCD; plasma; 16/9 – 4/3 monitors); master and slave clocks; automatic announcement systems; time and attendance recording systems; advertising display systems; automatic information systems; access control systems. Provision of systems on a turnkey basis; staff training and organisation of maintenance.

Contracts
Recent contracts have included projects at 20 railway stations in Morocco, SNCF (France), NJT Secaucus (USA), Torino (Italy), Milan Airport FIDS (Italy).

Sysco SpA

Headquarters and works
Via Bruno Pontecorvo snc, I-00012 Guidonia Montecelio, Rome, Italy
e-mail: info@syscospa.it
Web: www.syscospa.it

Key personnel
President and Chief Executive Officer: *Vincenzo Manzini*
Marketing Manager: *Bruno Angius*
Technical Manager: *Romano Mariani*

Products
An ISO 9001 certified company, Sysco SpA supplies turnkey passenger information systems and peripheral equipment for railway stations, airports, bus and ferry terminals. Sysco designs and supplies LED and LCD/TFT peripheral panels for any specific passenger information application. The equipment is compliant with the advanced technological standards of Rete Ferroviaria Italiana (RFI), with high reliability, real-time diagnostic capability and fiber optic ethernet interace. The Sysco catalogue encompasses a wide range of peripheral equipment: large arrivals and departures boards, platform and underpass indicators and any kind of monitor displays, both with LED or TFT technology.
Sysco application software includes stand-alone and distributed multistation packages in Windows system environments, operating in fault tolerant server configuration.

Sysco's LED arrivals and departures board
1368467

Contracts
Sysco is currently a preferred supplier of the main Italian railways: Rete Ferroviaria Italiana and Ferrovie Nord. The company also provides all types of peripheral passenger indicators to other railways system integrators.

Talking Signs Inc

812 North Boulevard, Baton Rouge, Louisiana 70802, US
Tel: (+1 225) 344 28 12   Fax: (+1 225) 344 28 11
e-mail: ward@talkingsigns.com
Web: www.talkingsigns.com

Key personnel
President: *C Ward Bond*

Products
Talking Signs® technology is an infrared wireless communication system that provides a remote directional human voice message that aids the visually impaired and individuals with a reading disability. Installed in transit stations and airports, the infra-red remote audible signs technology is used to identify approaching buses transmitting destination information to the user's hand-held receiver from 100 ft away. Luminator, a Mark IV Industries company is making and marketing this system whilst for the Japanese market, Mitsubishi Precision Company of Kamakura, Japan, manufacturers these units for Talking Signs, Inc.

Developments
A new multi-lingual Talking Signs® system has been designed to work, initially in a closed environment, and will allow users to scan the environment and 'read' signs by hearing the recorded translation in their own language. The translations are carried onboard the hand-held receiver and the recorded message is triggered by the infrared transmitter at each location.

Techspan Systems Ltd

Griffin Lane, Aylesbury, HP19 8BP, UK
Tel: (+44 1296) 67 30 00
Fax: (+44 1296) 67 30 02
e-mail: enquiries@techspan.co.uk
Web: www.techspan.co.uk

Key personnel
General Manager: *Jim Smith*
Finance Director: *Louise Martin*
Business Development Manager: *Darren Smith*
Technical Director: *Jeremy Hinton*
Manufacturing Director: *John Stottor*

Background
Previously owned by Jarivs plc, Techspan has now become the technology division of Hill & Smith Infrastructure Products Group.

Products
Design, supply, installation and commission of Variable Message Signs (VMS). Also a product range including LED and electro-mechanical equipment used for highways applications, with plasma, CRT monitor displays and LED being used for Customer Information Systems (CIS). Intelligent controllers such as VDG's VMS drivers, signalling data loggers and telematic decoders. Techspan supplies complete control systems and bespoke software, or can integrate its products with existing IT networks. Techspan can manage and maintain the equipment 24 hours a day all year round providing a full support service.

Televic NV

Leo Bekaertlaan 1, B-8870 Izegem, Belgium
Tel: (+32 51) 30 30 45   Fax: (+32 51) 31 06 70
e-mail: sales@televic.com
Web: www.televic.com

Subsidiaries
Televic SA
Parc d'activité du Chat, 249 rue Marie Curie, F-59118 Wambrechies, France
Tel: (+33 3) 28 33 88 10
Fax: (+33 3) 28 33 88 11

Televic Bulgaria Ltd
1 Assenovradsko shosse strasse, P O Box 203, BU-4023 Plovdiv, Bulgaria
Tel: (+359 32) 94 94 96
Fax: (+359 32) 94 94 95

Televic UK Ltd
Trident One, Styal Road, Manchester, M22 5XB, UK
Tel: (+44 870) 774 42 76
Fax: (+44 870) 774 42 79

Products
Onboard passenger information systems incorporating public address and intercom facilities; passenger at-seat entertainment and 'infotainment' systems; control systems for onboard systems. Capabilities include research and development, project management, production and total quality management.

TEW Engineering Limited

Crocus Street, Nottingham NG2 3DR, UK
Tel: (+44 1159) 35 43 54   Fax: (+44 1159) 35 43 55
e-mail: sales@tew.co.uk
Web: www.tew.co.uk

Products
Passenger information systems including: Cathode Ray Tube (CRT), Plasma (PDP) Thin Film Transistor (TfT), rear projection and LED/LCD. TEW carries out an environmental audit to determine the most suitable display for its customers, providing mechanical design and the design of drive electronics for bespoke display requirements.

Titan Bus UK Ltd

Head Office
Adhouse, East Parade, Harrogate HG1 5LT, UK
Tel: (+44 1423) 52 62 53   Fax: (+44 1423) 50 25 22
e-mail: enquiries@titanbus.co.uk
Web: www.titanbus.co.uk

Other office
Decker House, Lowater Street, Carlton, Nottingham, NG4 1JJ, UK
Tel: (+44 115) 940 24 06   Fax: (+44 115) 940 24 07
e-mail: miketerry@adbus.co.uk

Background
Previously called Adbus Ltd, Titan Bus UK Ltd is part of Adgroup.

Products
Bus, airport and ferry advertising and roundabout sponsorship.

Trivector System AB

Åldermansgatan 13, SE-227 64 Lund, Sweden
Tel: (+46 42) 38 65 00   Fax: (+46 42) 38 65 25
e-mail: info@trivector.se
Web: www.trivector.se

Key personnel
Managing Director: *Klas Odelid*
Marketing Manager: *Ola Fogelberg*
Project Manager: *Anders Månsson*

Products
TriTrans, a module-based information system for public transport, which operates in real time and serves all parties involved such as planners, dispatchers, drivers and passengers. TriTrans is based on a network of onboard vehicle computers and a traffic control centre where information is stored and processed to provide the different user groups with the most reliable information. IVIS (In-Vehicle Information System) contains the complete set of information system components which include vehicle computer Triveco 8, speech modules, message displays and passenger counter. It is currently in use in the Skania region of southern Sweden; Karlstad, Sweden; and Oslo, Norway. IntraInfo, a system for real-time information at bus or train stops, which provides travellers with information in real time on train and bus departure and arrival times. The system contains the computer unit IRU-IS, together with whatever message displays and monitors the customer requires. It is in use in Karlstad and soon to be in use in Dalarna.

UniControls trial operation of infotainment system for Czech Railways Class 814 demu   1181746

Trueform Engineering Limited

Unit 4 Pasadena Trading Estate, Pasadena Close, Hayes UB3 3NQ, UK
Tel: (+44 20) 85 61 49 59   Fax: (+44 20) 88 48 13 97
e-mail: sales@trueformengineering.com
Web: www.trueformengineering.com

Key personnel
Marketing and Communications: *Verra Mawhinney*
Technical Director: *J Morley*

Other office
666 Fifth Avenue, #364, New York, New York 10103 US
Tel: (+1 866) 849 01 33
e-mail: sales@busstops.net
Web: www.busstops.net

Products
Transport infrastructure hardware, street signs, display systems, architectural metalwork, installation, cleaning and maintenance.

UniControls AS

Křenická ulice-2257, CZ-100 00 Prague 10, Czech Republic
Tel: (+420 2) 72 01 14 11   Fax: (+420 2) 74 81 44 75
e-mail: unic@unicontrols.cz
Web: www.unicontrols.cz

Key personnel
Marketing Manager: *Marian Belosovic*

Products
LED- and DOT-LED based passenger information systems; infotainment systems.

Contracts
Passenger information system for Czech Railways Class 471 emus, Czech Railways Class 814 (Regionova) demus, trial operation of infotainment system in metro Prague.

Vecom USA, LLC

4803 George Road, Unit 300, Tampa, Florida 33634, US
Tel: (+1 813) 901 53 00
Fax: (+1 813) 433 24 58
e-mail: info@vecom-usa.com
Web: www.vecom-usa.com

Key personnel
President and Chief Executive Officer: *J J H M 'Koos' van Starrenburg*
Director of Marketing: *Sharon L Rice*

Products
Vecom USA manufactures and distributes communications and electronics equipment to the public transit industry. Products include LED signs for LRVs, trains, platforms and stations; PA next-stop announcement systems; passenger information and entertainment systems; passenger counting; train/LRV monitoring diagnostic systems; surveillance Smart cameras.

Voice Perfect Ltd

(All departments and Registered Office) 103 Friern Barnet Road, London N11 3EU, UK
Tel: (+44 20) 82 11 32 11
Fax: (+44 20) 83 68 08 88
e-mail: barbara@voiceperfect.co.uk
Web: www.voiceperfect.co.uk

Key personnel
Managing Director: *Nick Hallett*
Commercial Director: *Barbara Laing*
Technical Director: *Nicola Spiers*

Products
Digital Voice Announcers (DVA): PC-scheduled customer announcing system (PC-SCAS), PC-SCAS-based long line broadcasting systems.
Voice transfer systems (VTU): Talk-2 with audio induction loops (AFILs).
Voice Perfect offers design, manufacture, supply, installation, user and management training, commissioning and administrative support, together with preventative and corrective maintenance of its products and is ISO 9002 accredited.
Over 150 PC-SCAS and variants are now installed on London Underground stations either as stand-alone or integrated with help point systems or passenger information displays or long-line messaging systems (with up to three separate control points). SCAS features a schedule of the user's own compiled announcements for 'fixed' or unchanging messages, users' own recordings and announcements compiled from fragments of variable announcements.
3-Factors software and repertoire structure is the engine for production of both seamless and believable variable announcements selected from a cascading series of icons by the user. Other languages can be accommodated as a pre-recorded human voice is used. PC-SCAS uses a scheduler as its compilation engine. 3-Factors still provides seamless variable messages, augmented by the capability to broadcast differing input from remote signalling sources, up to 12 destination zones. This can be linked to a CIS server to replicate and augment visual messages on platform train describers and electronic whiteboards; if required, SCAS can be

UniControls passenger information system for Czech Railways Class 471 emu   1181745

integrated into a single-screen GUI. Talk-2 in up to five different variants provides a customised solution to new or retrofit secure ticketing window situations. Around 500 units are installed in London Underground ticket offices. The new ticket offices, developed with Arup and Partners at Kings Cross, are fitted with Talk-2 D-Digital, which allows ultra-fine, stable tuning of both cashier and customer voice levels, with adjustment for background noise available to the cashier. All systems have inductive loops to comply with DDA requirements.

Contracts

Supply and installation of 30 DVA systems at SSL/BCV London Underground Stations. Six year maintenance contract for all DVAs and associated cabling on performance contract 24/7 with 48 hour fault clearance. Design, manufacture, installation of new digital VTU for new Kings Cross booking office windows.

Volvo Bus Corporation

405 08 Göteborg, Sweden
Tel: (+46 31) 66 80 00
Fax: (+46 31) 53 68 08
e-mail: info.bus@volvo.com
Web: www.volvo.com

Key personnel

President: *Håkan Karlsson*
Senior Vice-President, Corporate Communications:
   Christina Fjellman

Background

Volvo Bus Corporation is fully owned by AB Volvo, Gothenberg, Sweden. The Volvo Group of companies is one of the leading manufacturers in the world of trucks, buses and construction equipment, as well as drivelines for marine and industrial purposes and jet engines, propulsion systems and components for the aviation and space industries.

For main Volvo Bus Corporation entry see – Buses – Chassis, Integrals and Bogies section.

Products

ITS4mobility advanced technological platform, which supports operators' control of bus operations through real-time monitoring and text messaging between traffic controllers and drivers. For passengers, the system provides electronic information boards at bus stops giving real-time bus departure times and onboard automatic loudspeaker 'stop' announcements.

The systems can be used for all types of buses regardless of manufacture.

Contracts

In June 2008, Volvo Buses secured an order for the ITS4mobility telematics systems for installation on 1,400 buses in the city of Goiânia in Brazil.

Vultron International Ltd

Unit 2, Stadium Way, Elland Road, Leeds LS11 0EW, UK
Tel: (+44 113) 387 73 10   Fax: (+44 113) 387 73 17

e-mail: sales@vultron.co.uk
Web: www.vultron.co.uk

Key personnel

Managing Director: *John Moorhouse*
Project Manager: *Paul Kiley*
Purchasing Manager: *Rod Giles*

Products

Vultron International Ltd is a manufacturer and supplier of electronic information display systems. This includes: talking information systems that translate passenger information text into speech using a speech conversion software and enabling operators to address the needs of visually impaired passengers. Vultron's manufacturing facility is capable of producing information displays in LCD and LED technologies. The in-house design and manufacturing skills and range of technologies enable the company to offer customer-tailored products.

Contracts

Vultron's LCD clocks have been installed at Glasgow's Partick and Queen Street stations. Recently display boards, using the new LCDs, have been supplied to West Yorkshire PTE for eight of its largest bus stations.

Developments

Recent developments in products for the bus market have seen the introduction of a range of LCD products for use at bus stops and bus shelters. These displays, which utilise a graphic panel LCD, can be used to display scheduled and/ or real-time bus information.

REVENUE COLLECTION SYSTEMS AND STATION EQUIPMENT

Company listing by country

AUSTRALIA
Abberfield Technology Pty Ltd
ERG Transit Systems Ltd

BELGIUM
Automatic Systems SA

CANADA
Carmanah Technologies Inc

FRANCE
ASK
Gemplus International SA (Gemplus)
Parkeon SAS
Thales

GERMANY
Atron Electronic GmbH
Automaten Technik Baumann GmbH
Elgeba Gerätebau GmbH
Fleischhauer Datenträger GmbH (FD)
Giesecke & Devrient GmbH (G&D)
Höft & Wessel AG
ICA Traffic GmbH
INIT Innovative Informatikanwendungen in Transport-, Verkehrs-und Leitsystemen GmbH
Krauth
Scheidt & Bachmann GmbH

ISRAEL
On Track Innovations (OTI)
TransWay

ITALY
4P Mobile Data Processing
FIREMA Trasporti SpA
Gunnebo Entrance Control SpA
Saima Sicurezza SpA

JAPAN
LECIP Corporation
Nabtesco Corporation
Narita Manufacturing Ltd
Nippon Signal Co Ltd
Omron Corporation
Takamisawa Cybernetics Co Ltd
Toshiba Corporation
Toyo Denki Seizo KK

POLAND
Emax SA

SPAIN
Indra
Maexbic SA

SWEDEN
Cambist AB

SWITZERLAND
Ascom AG
Kaba Gilgen AG
Mars Electronics International (MEI)
Regazzi SA
Sadamel Ticketing Systems

TURKEY
BelBim AS
Kentkart Ltd

UNITED KINGDOM
Almex Information Systems
Bemrose Booth Ltd
Burall InfoSmart Ltd
Bus Shelters Ltd
Captrad Ltd
Craig and Derricott Ltd
Fujitsu Services
Macemain + Amstad Ltd
Magnadata International Ltd
Newbury Data Recording Ltd
Rail Waiting Structures
Scan Coin Ltd
Shere Limited
Time 24 Ltd
TranSys
Wayfarer Transit Systems Limited
Westinghouse Platform Screen Doors

UNITED STATES
Affiliated Computer Services, Inc
Cubic Transportation Systems
Denominator Company Inc
Diamond Manufacturing Inc
Gateway Ticketing Systems Inc
Globe Ticket and Label Company
Lacor Streetscape
Magnetic Autocontrol
Main Fare Box Co

4P Mobile Data Processing

Viale della Regione Veneto 26, I-35127 Padova, Italy
Tel: (+39 049) 806 98 11   Fax: (+39 049) 806 98 43
e-mail: webinfo@4p-online.com
Web: www.4p-online.com

Key personnel
Managing Director: *Silvano Mansutti*

US office
7400 Oxford Avenue, Philadelphia, Pennsylvania 19111-3095

Product
Hand-held computer with card reader for outdoor operations.

Abberfield Technology Pty Ltd

32 Cross Street, Brookvale, New South Wales 2100, Australia
Tel: (+61 2) 99 33 28 44   Fax: (+61 2) 99 38 34 62
e-mail: contact@abberfield.com.au
Web: www.abberfield.com.au

Key personnel
Managing Director: *John M Colyer*
Sales: *Ann Stokes*

Products
Ticket vending machines and ticket validators; design and manufacture of ticketing systems.

Affiliated Computer Services, Inc

ACS Corporate Headquarters
2828 North Haskell, Dallas, Texas 75205, US
Tel: (+1 214) 841 61 11
e-mail: info@acs-inc.com
Web: www.acs-inc.com

Key personnel
President and Chief Executive Officer: *Lynn Blodgett*
Executive Vice-President and Chief Operating Officer: *Tom Burlin*
Chief Information Officer: *Tasos Tsolakis*
Vice-President Corporate Communications: *Kevin Lightfoot*
Communications Directors: *Tom Clary, Andy Wilson*
Account Manager: *Jennille Logan*

Background
The company provides business process outsourcing and information technology solutions for commercial and government clients.

Products
Electronic toll collection for some of the world's largest electronic toll systems including the ARCOS™ contactless ticketing system.

Contracts
The Public Transport Agency and the Marine Agency of the Dubai Roads and Transport Authority (RTA) will be equipping their public buses and the piers for their waterbuses with the ACS ARCOS™ fare collection system, replacing the current paper-based system.
Major transport authorities such as the Austrian National Railways, The City of Vienna, Norwegian State Railways and the Berlin transport operator BVG, have implemented ACS' contactless system.

Almex Information Systems

Metric Group
Metric House, Westmead Industrial Estate, Westlea, Swindon, SN5 7AD, UK
Tel: (+44 1793) 64 78 00   Fax: (+44 1793) 64 78 02
e-mail: info@almex.demon.co.uk
Web: www.hoeft-wessel.com/en/almex

Key personnel
Managing Director: *Marcus Burton*
Sales Team: *Ashley Bailey*
   Alistair Aitken, Sophie Fitzpatrick, Claudia Johnston

Subsidiaries
Allwood Brighton Office Centre
2 Brighton Road, 3rd Floor, Clifton, New Jersey 07012, US
Tel: (+1 201) 777 59 69
General Manager: James Meany
Almex GmbH
Kuehnstrasse 71, D-22045 Hamburg, Germany
Tel: (+49 40) 66 99 22 20
Managing Director: Klaus Schiering

Background
Almex Information Systems is a member of the Hanover-based Höft & Wessel group.

Products
Ticketing and revenue collection systems for railway and light rail applications; ticket issuing machines, portable ticket issuing machines, magnetic ticket validators, automatic vending machines; contact and contactless smartcards.

Ascom AG

Belpstrasse 37, CH-3000 Bern 14, Switzerland
Tel: (+41 31) 999 11 11   Fax: (+41 31) 999 23 00
e-mail: ask-ascom@ascom.ch
Web: www.ascom.com

Key personnel
Head of Transport Revenue and Deputy Chief Executive Officer, Ascom Group: *Riet Cadonau*
Chief Financial Officer, Ascom Group: *Dr Martin Zwyssig*
General Secretary & Director of Communications, Ascom Holding AG: *Daniel Lack*
Marketing: *Daniel Burkhalter*

Background
Affiliated Computer Services, Inc (ACS), a US listed company, acquired the transport revenue division of Ascom in August 2005.

Products
Automatic revenue collection systems including stationary and onboard ticket vending machines, ticket office machines, driver consoles, access gates and validators for rail, metro, tramway and bus operators. Ascom's fare collection systems are designed for use with magnetic tickets (TFCO and TFC1 formats) or with contactless smartcards (memory type A and microprocessor type B).
Collection and processing of all relevant data, revenue collection in multi-operator transport networks and clearing of cash and cashless payments are covered by customised data management systems.

Contracts
Recent contracts include the supply of equipment to DB AG, SBB, ÖBB, NS, MTRC Hong Kong, rail operators in UK, New Jersey Transit, RATP Paris, Mexico City, Medellín (Colombia), Kuala Lumpur, Brasilia, Toulouse, Goiania (Brazil), Adelaide, Nice, Montpellier, Porto and Malaysia.

ASK

2405 route des Dolines, F-06560 Sophia Antipolis, France
Tel: (+33 4) 97 21 40 00   Fax: (+33 4) 92 38 93 21
e-mail: info@ask.fr
Web: www.ask.fr

Key personnel
Chief Executive Officer: *Bruno Moreau*
Vice-President Sales, Marketing and Research & Development: *Amand Cochet*
Chief Operations Officer: *François Monteil*

Products
Contactless smartcards and related equipment for public transport revenue collection. Products include contact and contactless smartcards, contactless memory cards, contactless paper tickets, contact and contactless smartcard readers and handheld readers. Support services include project and service management and the development and production of customised smartcards.

Contracts
More than 100 cites use contactless technology based on ASK products in France, Italy, Portugal, Germany, UK, the Netherlands, Luxemburg, and Belgium.
ASK products are also used in Taiwan, the Americas and Canada.
In 2008 OTLIS, the Lisbon transport operators have continued their contract by re-selecting C.ticket®, ASK contactless paper tickets for their automatic fare collection ticketing system. The order of 25 million tickets will be delivered over the next two years.
In June 2008 ASK announced that it had joined the UK-based Integrated Transport Smartcard Organization (ITSO) and successfully passed the ITSO certification. This certificate strengthens ASK's market presence in the UK.

Atron Electronic GmbH

Am Ziegelstadel 12 + 14, D-85570 Markt Schwaben, Germany
Tel: (+49 8121) 934 20   Fax: (+49 8121) 93 42 77
e-mail: vertrieb@atron.de
Web: www.atron.de

Key personnel
Marketing: *Jörg Wolff*

Products
Smartcard terminals; AFC systems; stationary and mobile ticket machines.

Automaten Technik Baumann GmbH

An der Bahn 11, D-92706 Luhe-Wildenau, Germany
Tel: (+49 9607) 922 20   Fax: (+49 9607) 922 22 35
e-mail: info@atb-online.eu
Web: www.atb-online.eu

Key personnel
Sales Director: *Reinhard Haas*

Background
ATB Automaten Technik Baumann ATB is an independent company within the Dr Baumann corporate group, employing over 500 people at eight locations in Germany.

Products
Parking 'pay and display' machines, stamp cancelling machines and ticket validators.

Automatic Systems SA

Avenue Mercator 5, B-1300 Wavre, Brussels, Belgium
Tel: (+32 10) 23 02 11   Fax: (+32 10) 23 02 02
e-mail: asmail@automatic-systems.com
Web: www.automatic-systems.com

Key personnel
Chairman of the Board: *Edmond Marchegay*
Chief Executive Officer: *Maxime Boulvain*
Commercial Director: *John De Winter*
Financial Director: *Roland Buggenhout*
Projects Director: *Wilfried Simon*

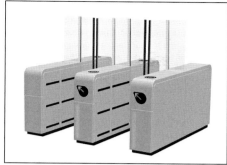

Automatic Systems TGH 800 high-security gate
1374233

Marketing Director: *Jean-Pierre Leleu*
Engineering Director: *Pierre Bruynseels*
Manufacturing Director: *Etienne Bertrand*
Quality Director: *Jean Bareel*
Communications Manager: *Dominique Gilbart*
Industrial Development Manager: *Philippe Dalcq*
Communication Manager: *Dominique Gilbart*

Background
Automatic Systems is a member of the IER; a subsidiary of the French group Bolloré.

Subsidiaries
Canada – Montreal
Automatic Systems America Inc
4005, Boulevard Matte Local D, Brossard, Québec J4Y 2P4
Tel: (+1 450) 659 07 37   Fax: (+1 450) 659 09 66
Toll free: (+1 800) 263 65 48
e-mail: sales@automatic-systems.ca
Web: www.automatic-systems.com

France
Automatic Systems SA
30 rue du Morvan, Silic BP 20518, F-94623 Rungis, Cedex, Paris
Tel: (+33 1) 56 70 07 07   Fax: (+33 1) 56 70 07 08
e-mail: asmail@automatic-systems.fr
Web: www.automatic-systems.com

Spain
Automatic Systems Española SA
C/Vallés, 52-54 E-08820, El Prat de Llobregat, Barcelona
Tel: (+34 93) 478 77 55   Fax: (+34 93) 478 67 02
e-mail: asemadrid@automatic-systems.net
Web: www.automatic-systems.com

UK
Automatic Systems Equipment UK Ltd
Unit G4, Middlesex Business Centre, Bridge Road, Southall UB2 4AB
Tel: (+44 2087) 44 76 69   Fax: (+44 2087) 44 76 70
e-mail: sales@automaticsystems.co.uk
Web: www.automaticsystems.com

US
Automatic Control Systems Inc
8 Haven Avenue, Suite 205, Port Washington, New York 11050
Tel: (+1 516) 944 94 98   Fax: (+1 516) 767 34 46
e-mail: info@automaticsystems.com
Web: www.automaticsystems.com

Products
Design and manufacture of access control and security equipment: TGH 800 high-security gates, TGH 810 wide high-security gates, TGL 870 high-security interlock doors, TFG 820 and TGF 880 flap gates, TGD 830 gates for people with reduced mobility and TFT 850 tripod turnstiles.

Automatic Systems is in a position to provide metro operators, major integrators and engineering companies with a specific range of products for specialised applications. This includes: public transport; high engineering content required to customise specific products; project feasibility specifications and analysis; specific detection control technology; and project management to provide services other than usual for installation and maintenance.

Contracts
Belgium: 2007 – Charleroi Brussels South Airport.
France: 2003-2008 – Paris Ile de France, SNCF.
Germany: Munich.
Italy: 2007-2008 – Milan Metro, Napoli Circumvesuviana, Perugia Metro, Torino Metro.
Spain: 2006-2008 – Barcelona Metro (several stations), Catalogna Regional rail network, RENFE National railways (Cercanias), Barcelona light rail Besos.
UK/Belgium/France: Eurostar, London (Ashford Station, Ebbsfleet, St Pancras), Paris (Lille), Brussels.
Sweden: Stockholm Metro.

Developments
Automatic Systems is introducing its new line of high-security gates for revenue collection systems, targeting passengers in metros and railways. This new access control equipment guarantees rapid and safe access to the station platforms, while enabling an efficient and fluid control of passengers.

BelBim AS

Atatürk Hava Limani KarŞisi, Istanbul Dünya Ticaret Merkezi IŞ A3/3 TR-34149 YeŞilköy, Istanbul, Turkey
e-mail: info@belbim.com.tr
Web: www.belbim.com.tr

Key personnel
General Manager: *Ahmet Kozokoğlu*
Project Co-ordinator: *Figen Kiliç*

Background
BelBim is affiliated to Istanbul Municipality and was established in 1987.

Products
Advice on design, development, production of electronic and computer automation projects, electronic fare collection equipment and other utility issues for both public and private institutions.

A smartcard electronic ticket named AKBIL-iButton technology was developed for Istanbul. The city has 14 million inhabitants and six million passengers a day, and has steamship, seabuses, motorboat, ferry, suburban railway, light rail transport, subway, trams, public and private buses. Until AKBIL was introduced, passengers used over 45 different tickets, tokens, passes and cards. AKBIL stands for Electronic Ticket and Fare Collection System for the Intermodal Public Transport System.

The system is based on touch-based technology and the electronic ticket is recharged at automatic refilling machines and ticket offices. Each ticket has a coloured plastic handle about 5 cm long with transponder. It has a minimum operational life of six years and is water resistant.

The fare collection system now comprises:
- 5,620 validators, bus type
- 24 validators, tram type.
- 1,600 turnstiles (seabus, steamships, subways, suburban railway system)
- 290 selling/refilling ticket offices for AKBIL
- 55 automatic refilling machines for AKBIL
- various station data collection computers
- transmission equipment
- database management software.

Developments
The fare collection system is now being upgraded to include contactless smartcards, credit cards and single trip electronic paper tickets as payment forms together with GPS, GPRS, WiFi and POS technologies in validators.

Bemrose Booth Ltd

Stockholm Road, Sutton Fields, Hull HU7 0XY, UK
Tel: (+44 1482) 82 63 43
Fax: (+44 1482) 37 13 88
Web: www.bemrosebooth.com

Key personnel
Managing Director: *David Murray*
Finance Director: *John Buist*
Operations Director: *Tim Dyer*
Commercial Director: *David Duncan*

Background
Bemrose Booth Ltd was formed by a management buyout in July 2000 from Bemrose Corporation plc. The company was acquired in December 2003 by Appleton, a US manufacturer of value-added paper products based in Appleton, Wisconsin.

Products
Printing of specialised secure tickets including related controlled stationery for transit auto parking applications.

Contracts
Recent contracts include a five-year deal to single source supply the UK rail network's requirements for tickets and controlled stationery.

Burall InfoSmart Ltd

Venture House, Venture Court, Boleness Road, Wisbech PE13 2XQ, UK
Tel: (+44 0845) 257 80 01   Fax: (+44 0845) 257 80 04
Web: www.burall-infosmart.com

Key personnel
Managing Director: *R J Duddin*
Divisional Manager: *J A Henson*
Business Development Director: *L S Faulkner*

Products
Low-coercivity and high-coercivity magnetic stripe cards, tickets and tokens, in plain and thermal paper, card, laminate and plastic; pre-encoding is a speciality. Contactless chip cards including high-frequency proximity cards to the Philips Mifare® and ISO 14443A/B standards. Full bureau service, software and systems for colourcard personalisation, numbering and programming.

Developments
Card personalisation products and services certified compatible with the emerging ITSO standard in the UK. Small-memory, disposable contactless tickets.

Newly launched, a two-part contactless smart travel ID card: iGo.

Bus Shelters Ltd

Unit 60, Dyffryn Business Park, Llantwit Major Road, Llandow, Cowbridge, South Glamorgan CF71 7PY
Tel: (+44 1446) 79 54 44
Fax: (+44 1446) 79 33 44
Web: www.shelters.co.uk

Background
Bus Shelters Ltd was the first company founded by BSW Group and has been trading for over 20 years manufacturing and installing street furniture. The business underwent rapid expansion in 1998 by introducing new products. BSW Group is the holding company for a number of companies, including Rail Waiting Structures, BSW Systems Ltd and Metal Box Manufacturing.

Products
The company offers a fully inclusive service providing its customers with the ability to purchase street furniture, including bus shelters that are designed, manufactured and installed as a complete package of works. Rail Waiting Structures, also part of BSW Group, designs and manufactures robust waiting facilities including a range of rail waiting rooms in conjunction with Network Rail.

Cambist AB

Stockholmsvägen 59, PO Box 204, SE-761 23 Norrtälje, Sweden
Tel: (+46 176) 172 45   Fax: (+46 176) 139 51
e-mail: info@cambist.se
Web: www.cambist.se

Key personnel
Managing Director: *Anders Nyström*

Background
Cambist AB has developed coin handling products for fare collection in public transport since 1969.

Products
Coin change dispensers, cash tables, conductors' bags, ticket punches.

Captrad Ltd

19 Hewitt Business Park, Winstanley Road, Orrell, Wigan WN5 7XB, UK
Tel: (+44 1695) 68 00 10   Fax: (+44 1695) 68 00 09
e-mail: sales@captrad.co.uk
Web: www.captrad.co.uk

Key personnel
Managing Director: *Phil Capstick*

Products
Bus/cycle/smoking shelters and bespoke custom designs. GRP/fibreglass products.

Carmanah Technologies Inc

Building 4, 203 Harbour Road, Victoria, British Columbia V9A 3S2, Canada
Tel: (+1 250) 380 00 52   Fax: (+1 250) 380 00 62
e-mail: info@carmanah.com
Web: www.carmanah.com
European representative: *Mark Harold*
Tel: (+44 7879) 64 81 57
e-mail: mharold@carmanah.com

Head office
Building 4, 203 Harbour Road Victoria, British Columbia Canada V9A 3S2
Tel: (+1 250) 380 00 52   Fax: (+1 250) 380 00 62
e-mail: info@carmanah.com

Key personnel
Chief Executive Officer: *Ted Lattimore*
Business Development Manager: *Jeff Peters*

Products
Bus stop and bus shelter systems employing solar-powered LED lighting.

The I-STOP bus stop system incorporates an on-demand signalling beacon to alert drivers of the presence of passengers, security downlighting and timetable illumination. No external wiring is required and the system requires servicing only at five-year intervals.

The I-Shelter is a solar-powered LED lighting kit for bus shelters and also requires no external wiring or power.

Contracts
In April 2007, Carmanah was awarded a follow-on contract to supply its solar LED-illuminated bus stops to California's Orange County Transportation Authority (OCTA). OCTA originally began a field trial of the STOP illuminated bus stops in May 2003 and proceeded to roll out 710 systems over a two-year period beginning in April 2005.

Carmanah was one of three participants in a three-year trial with Transport for London (Tfl) using solar power systems to illuminate 200 bus stops in the City of London. A total of 300 Carmanah solar-powered LED bus shelter lighting systems have been installed and are operating in the Greater London area.

Edinburgh is also using Carmanah's solar LED shelter lighting system, in co-operation with Commutaports, Edinburgh City's shelter supplier.

Craig and Derricott Ltd

Hall Lane, Walsall Wood, Walsall WS9 9DP, UK
Tel: (+44 1543) 37 55 41   Fax: (+44 1543) 45 26 10
Fax: (+44 1543) 36 16 19 (Direct Sales)
e-mail: info@craiganddderricott.com
Web: www.craiganddderricott.com

Key personnel
Managing Director: *Andy Dolman*
Sales Director: *Paul Cranshaw*

Background
Established in 1944 Craig and Derricott is owned by The Victory Group of India.

Products
Station equipment, depot equipment, safety systems and emergency controls.

Cubic Transportation Systems

Cubic Transportation Systems Inc
5650 Kearny Mesa Road, San Diego, California 92111, US
Tel: (+1 619) 268 31 00   Fax: (+1 619) 292 99 87
Web: www.cubic.com

Key personnel
Chairman: *Walter C Zable*
Senior Vice-President, Business Operations: *Raymond L deKozan*
Senior Vice-President Service and Production: *David M Lapczynski*
Senior Vice-President Technology and Marketing: *Walt Bonneau, Jr*
President of Cubic Transportation Systems Worldwide: *Stephen O Shewmaker*

Subsidiaries
Cubic Transportation Systems Limited, European Headquarters, UK
Cubic Nordic, branch of Cubic Transportation Systems Limited
Cubic Transportation Systems (Australia) Pty Limited, Australia
Cubic Transportation Systems (Deutschland) GmbH, Germany

Background
The company has major operating units in the UK; Australia; Denmark and San Diego, Tennessee, New York and Washington DC, US. Cubic Transportation Systems is one of two major business segments of Cubic Corporation. The company has expanded its customer services operations to include a full range of managed services in support of regional electronic fare payment systems.

Products
Design, manufacture, installation and maintenance of electronic ticketing and automatic fare collection systems, including magnetic and contactless smartcard systems for advanced fare collection applications. Cubic has developed Nextfare® Solution Suite, a fare collection enterprise management system incorporating industry standards, open platforms and commercial off-the-shelf applications.

Nextfare supplies the core smartcard transaction processing; financial operations including revenue clearing, settlement and reporting; a debit/credit account gateway for payments, customer service database support and a range of web-enabled convenience features designed to facilitate both operators' assisted and self-service requirements.

Range
Provision of turnkey systems for automatic fare collection for public transport including; bus, bus rapid transit, light rail, commuter rail, heavy rail, ferry and parking. Cubic solutions and services include; system design, central computer systems, equipment design and manufacturing, device-level software, integration, test, installation, warranty, maintenance, computer hosting services, call centre services, card management and distribution services, financial clearing and settlement, multi-application support and outsourcing services.

Developments
Cubic has developed technology to enable passengers, for the first time, to use a one ticket issuing facility for travel by their chosen route from Heathrow to anywhere within the London region. This new fare system integration for Heathrow Express and London Underground has been operational in Heathrow Airport's new Terminal 5 train station since March 2008.

Contracts
Active projects include: London; New York/New Jersey region; Washington DC/Baltimore/Virginia region; Los Angeles region; San Diego region; San Francisco; Minneapolis/St Paul; Chicago; Atlanta; Vancouver and Edmonton, Canada; Brisbane, Australia; Singapore; Bangkok, Thailand and Scandinavia (Skaane).

In 2007 Cubic joined with Barclays Bank to launch the OnePulse card, a travel and payment card
1342127

Denominator Company Inc

744 Main Street South, PO Box 5004, Woodbury, Connecticut 06798, US
Tel: (+1 203) 263 32 10
Fax: (+1 203) 263 53 51
Web: www.denominatorcompany.com

Key personnel
General Manager: *Thomas C Clark*

Products
Ridership classification counters.

Diamond Manufacturing Inc

2330 Burlington, North Kansas City, Missouri 64116, US
Tel: (+1 816) 421 83 63
Fax: (+1 816) 421 47 35
e-mail: todcull@aol.com
Web: www.diamondmfg.com

Key personnel
President: *Dick Cull*

Products
Fare collection equipment for mass transit.

Elgeba Gerätebau GmbH

Eudenbacher Strasse 10-12, D-53604 Bad Honnef, Germany
Tel: (+49 2224) 828 50
Fax: (+49 2224) 802 94
e-mail: info@elgeba.de
Web: www.elgeba.de

Key personnel
Managing Director: *Harold F Wolter*
Executive Assistant: *Petra Sommerfield*

Products
Chipcard terminals, portable hand-held ticket vendors, integrated ticket vendors and on-board computers. Also, euro exchange terminals, pre-sale ticket vendors, stationary ticket vendors and information terminals, background systems with accounting station, mobile ticket vendors for buses and undergrounds and oem products.

Emax SA

Public Transport & Electronic Identification Systems Dept
ul Chmielna 63/64, PL-80-748, Gdansk, Poland
Tel: (+48 58) 300 20 60
Fax: (+48 58) 305 86 10
e-mail: tp@emax.pl
Web: www.emax.pl

Key personnel
Director: *Tadeusz Iwanowski*

Background
In late 2006, the merger of Emax SA and ComputerLand SA commenced with the formal merger to one company.

Products
Integrated fare collection systems based on contactless smartcards, including: onboard equipment; back office systems; and point of sale equipment. Systems are part of a larger IT network that also covers timetable monitoring, communications between vehicle and control centre, traffic planning and timetabling and data processing for statistical, planning and financial purposes.

ERG Transit Systems Ltd

247 Balcatta Road, Balcatta Western Australia 6021, Australia
Tel: (+61 8) 92 73 11 00   Fax: (+61 8) 92 73 15 70
e-mail: info@au.ergtransit.com
Web: www.erggroup.com

Key personnel
Executive Director, Operations: *Steve Gallagher*
Executive Director, Finance: *James Carroll*
Business Development and Sales: *Bruce Were*

Subsidiaries
ERG Transit Systems (USA) Inc
Suite 900, 1800 Sutter Street, Concord, California 94520, US
Tel: (+1 925) 686 82 00   Fax: (+1 925) 686 82 20
e-mail: info@us.ergtransit.com
Business Development and Sales: Larry Weissbach

ERG Transit Systems (Fra) SA
Parc Temis, 17B, rue Alain Savary, F-25000, Besançon, France
Tel: (+33 3) 81 40 11 40   Fax: (+33 3) 81 53 73 84
e-mail: info@fr.ergtransit.com
Business Development and Sales:
  Norbert Schüwer

ERG Transit Systems (Eur) NV
Kleine Kloosterstraat 23, B-1932 Zaventum, Belgium
Tel: (+32 2) 722 89 11   Fax: (+32 2) 720 87 94
e-mail: info@be.ergtransit.com
Business Development and Sales:
  Norbert Schüwer

ERG Limited, Italy
Via Giuseppe Armellini 37, Rome 00143, Italy
Tel: (+39 06) 519 61 61   Fax: (+39 06) 593 51 30
e-mail: info@it.ergtransit.com
Business Development and Sales:
  Norbert Schüwer

ERG Transit Systems (UK) Ltd
Unit 1 Riverside, Waters Meeting Road, Bolton BL1 8TT, UK
Tel: (+44 1204) 38 47 09   Fax: (+44 1204) 38 48 06
Business Development and Sales: Peter Levy

ERG Transit Systems (Scand) AB
Arenavägen 29, S-121 77 Stockholm-Globen,
Tel: (+46 8) 659 08 00   Fax: (+46 8) 659 77 30
e-mail: info@se.ergtransit.com
Business Development and Sales: Ulf Wassdahl

ERG Transit Systems China
Suite 2205, 22/F Teng Da Bldg, No 168 Xi Zhi Men Wai Avenue, Hai Dian District, Beijing 100044, China
Tel: (+86 10) 88 57 62 00   Fax: (+86 10) 88 57 65 00
Business Development and Sales: Frank Havelka

ERG Transit Systems Asia Pacific
Level 21, 456 Kent Street, Sydney 2000, Australia
Tel: (+61 2) 93 90 55 00   Fax: (+61 2) 93 90 55 99
Business Development and Sales: Frank Havelka

ERG Transit Systems (HK) Ltd, Hong Kong
Unit A, 4/F, Chuan Hing Ind Bldg, 14 Wang Tai Road, Kowloon Bay, Kowloon, Hong Kong
Tel: (+85 2) 27 98 73 39   Fax: (+85 2) 27 53 87 98
e-mail: info@hk.ergtransit.com
Business Development and Sales:
  Mark Shoulder
50 Kallang Avenue, #07-03/05 Noel Corporate Building, Singapore 339505
Tel: (+65 6) 837 22 73   Fax: (+65 6) 837 22 98
e-mail: info@sg.ergtransit.com
Business Development and Sales: Wilson Kan

Background
ERG Transit Systems specialises in the design, development, supply and operation of integrated fare management and software systems for public transport. The company pioneered the use of contactless smartcards on public transport.

Products and Services
ERG Transit Systems provides fare collection products and systems for all modes of transport using all types of ticket technology including paper, magnetic stripe, contactless and dual interface smartcards.

Range includes: advanced on-board devices such as ticket issuing machines, validators, contactless smartcard readers, portable inspection and ticket issuing devices; on-station equipment such as platform validators, add value machines, gate control units; data communications equipment and software; back-office software for small, medium and large complex multi-modal transit systems; central clearing house software.

The company provides outsourced services to support, operate and maintain automated fare collection systems on behalf of transit operators.

Contracts
ERG Transit Systems has delivered automated fare collection systems to a large number of transit operators in cities around the world including Rome, Bordeaux, Melbourne, San Francisco, Seattle, Beijing, Stockholm, Gothenburg and Oslo. Other key examples include customers in Singapore, Hong Kong, UK, Washington, Boston, Spain, Portugal, Belgium, Norway, Canada, Israel, Dubai, Brazil, New Zealand and the Russian Federation.

FIREMA Trasporti SpA

Headquarters
Via Provinciale Appia, Località Ponteselice, I-81100 Caserta, Italy
Tel: (+39 0823) 09 71 11
Fax: (+39 0823) 46 68 12
e-mail: info@firema.it
Web: www.firema.it

Key personnel
Chairman and Chief Executive Officer: *Gianfranco Fiore*
Commercial Manager: *Sergio d'Arminio*
Marketing Manager: *Agostino Astori*

Products
Automatic fare collection systems employing magnetic or paper tickets and/or contactless smartcards; integrated ticketing and station automation.

Contracts
Previous contracts have included the supply of automatic fare collection systems for eight stations on Rome Metro Line A; 10 stations on the Rome Metro Line B and entry/exit gates for four stations on Milan's Passante Ferroviario.

Fleischhauer Datenträger GmbH (FD)

Forellstrasse 120, D-44653 Herne, Germany
Tel: (+49 2323) 98 77 90
Fax: (+49 2323) 98 77 94 99
e-mail: direct@fdas.de
Web: www.fdas.de

Key personnel
Managing Director: *Phillip Halbach*

Products
Magnetic stripe tickets, smartcards and contactless chip cards; prepaid value cards; tokens; barcode labels, RFID tickets and labels.

Fujitsu Services

22 Baker Street, London W1U 3BW, UK
Tel: (+44 870) 242 79 98
Fax: (+44 870) 242 44 45
e-mail: askfujitsu@services.fujitsu.com
Web: www.fujitsu.com; www.ukfujitsu.com

Key personnel
Press Contact: *Graham Goulden*

Products
Rail Journey Information Service (RJIS), an integrated solution for rail journey information providing timetable, fares, routeing guide and other supplementary information. RJIS has been accredited by the Association of Train Operating Companies (ATOC).

Station Terminals for Advanced Rail retailing (STAR), a new ticketing issuing system, accredited by the Rail Settlement Plan (RSP). STAR is fully integrated with RJIS and offers a comprehensive and integrated rail journey enquiry and ticket issuing system. It also streamlines the capture of warrant and voucher information for submission to the Travel Trade and Warrants Services (TTWS). STAR is also designed to be fully compatible with the new chip and PIN technologies, which are designed to make credit and debit card transactions more secure.

Gateway Ticketing Systems Inc

315 E Second Street, Boyertown, Philadelphia 19512, US
Tel: (+1 610) 987 40 00
Fax (+1 610) 987 40 01
e-mail: sales@gatewayticketing.com
Web: www.gatewayticketing.com

Key personnel
Vice-President: *Darryl Moser*

Products
Revenue management and admission control systems for bus companies.

Gemplus International SA (Gemplus)

Avenue du Pic de Bertagne, PO Box 100, F-13881 Gémenos Cedex, France
Tel: (+33 4) 42 36 50 00
Fax: (+33 4) 42 36 59 99
Web: www.gemplus.com

Key personnel
Chairman: *Dominique Vignon*
Chief Executive Officer: *Alex Mandl*
Executive Vice-President, Strategy: *Jean-François Schreiber*
Executive Vice-President and Chief Financial Officer: *Frans Spaargaren*
Executive Vice-President, Operations: *Emmanuel Unguran*
Executive Vice-President, Product and Marketing: *Philippe Vallée*
Senior Vice-President, Corporate Communications: *Rémi Calvet*
  e-mail: remi.calvet@gemplus.com

Background
Formed in 1988, the company has 58 sales and marketing offices, six research and development centres, 20 personalisation facilities and 11 manufacturing sites worldwide.

Products
GemFare new-generation ticketing software.

Giesecke & Devrient GmbH (G&D)

Headquarters
PO Box 80 07 29, D-81607 Munich, Germany
Tel: (+49 89) 411 90   Fax: (+49 89) 41 19 15 35
e-mail: info@gdai.com
Web: www.gdai.com

Street address
Prinzregentenstrasse 159, D-81677 Munich, Germany

Key personnel
Chairman, Management Board and Chief Executive Officer: *Karsten Ottenberg*
Head of Cards and Services Business Unit: *Michael Kuemmerie*
Chief Financial Officer: *Peter Zattler*
Director, Marketing Communications: *Heather Klein*
  e-mail: heather.klein@gdai.com
  Staff: 8,250 (worldwide)

Background
Giesecke & Devrient GmbH (G&D) provides smartcard based solutions in a number of areas including transportation and is dominant in the field of currency automation. Established in 1852, the company is headquartered in Munich, with subsidiaries and joint ventures around the world.

Products
Banknotes and banknote processing systems, plus smartcards and solutions.

Globe Ticket and Label Company

1800 Greenleaf Ave Elk Grove Village, Illinois 60007, US
Tel: (+1 847) 258 10 27   Fax: (+1 847) 258 10 06
e-mail: sales@globeticket.com
Web: www.globeticket.com

Key personnel
Executive Chairman: *Mike Whitaker*
President and Chief Executive Officer: *Robert Castillo*
Chief Financial Officer: *Joe Kania*
Vice-President Sales and Marketing: *Randy Nipper*

Background
Globe Ticket and Label Company is owned by Premier Card Solutions.

Products
Tickets, press or computer printed, ticket books, boarding passes; magnetic tickets.

Gunnebo Entrance Control SpA

Via A Volta 15, I-38015 Lavis (Trento), Italy
Tel: (+39 0461) 24 89 00
Fax: (+39 0461) 24 89 71
e-mail: metro@gunneboentrance.com
Web: www.gunneboentrance.com

Head Office
Gunnebo AB
PO Box 5181, SE-402 Göteborg, Sweden
President: *Lars Proos*
Market Communication Manager: *Johan Holmgvist*

Background
Gunnebo Entrance Control SpA, part of the Gunnebo Group is a fast-growing international security group with 6,800 employees.

Products
The Italdis product line offers a wide selection of standardised, functional entrance control solutions. This includes basic tripod turnstiles to more advanced speed gates, full height turnstiles and high performance anti-return gates and security manlocks.

Contracts
Recent contracts include: Transadelaide Light Rail, Australia; Montreal Metro, Montreal, Canada; Shanghai Metro, China; Shenzhen Metro, China; Transmilénio Mass Transit System, Bogotà, Colombia; Toulouse Metro, Toulouse, France; KCRC West Rail, Hong Kong; MTRC, Hong Kong; Tehran Metro, Iran; SBME Metro Milan, Italy; Genova Metro, Italy; Napoli Railways, Naples, Italy; TMB Barcelona Metro, Spain; SL Stockholm Metro, Sweden; Bursa Ray, Bursa, Turkey.

Höft & Wessel AG

Rotenburger Strasse 20, D-30659 Hannover, Germany
Tel: (+49 511) 610 20   Fax: (+49 511) 610 24 11
e-mail: IR@hoeft-wessel.com
Web: www.hoeft-wessel.com

Key personnel
Chairman: *Hansjoachim Oehmen*
Deputy Chairman, Marketing and Sales: *Peter Claussen*
Business Division Almex (Ticketing): *Thomas Wolf*

Subsidiaries
Metric Group Ltd
Metric House, Westmead Industrial Estate, Westlea, Swindon SN5 7AD, UK
Tel: (+44 1793) 64 78 00   Fax: (+44 1793) 64 78 02
e-mail: info@metricgroup.co.uk
Web: www.metricgroup.co.uk
Managing Director: *Hansjoachim Oehmen*

Background
Established in 1978, Höft & Wessel AG develops, manufactures and distributes hard- and software for the three business segments of Mobile Data Acquisition, e-Ticketing and Parking Systems, one of which – Almex Information Systems business unit – manages ticketing solutions for air, bus, rail and road toll.

Products
Development and production of ticketing systems, electronic payment, devices for mobile data acquisition, internet terminals, parking systems and telematics.

ICA Traffic GmbH

Walter Welp Strasse 27, D-44149 Dortmund, Germany
Tel: (+49 231) 917 04 40   Fax: (+49 231) 17 13 83
e-mail: info@ica-traffic.de
Web: www.ica-traffic.de

Key personnel
Sales Director: *Jörg Metzger*

Products
Complete system solutions for ticketing and the management of public transport fares. The DUALIS family comprises self-service ticket vending equipment for both stationary as well as for on-vehicle environments and a Central Management System (CMS). ICA Ticket Vending Machines can be administrated and comprehensive revenue administration and accounting can be managed.

Indra

Avda de Bruselas, 35 Arroyo de la Vega E-28108, Alcobendas, Madrid, Spain 34 91 480 50 00 FAX: 34 91 480 50 80 e-mail: indra@indra.es
Tel: (+34 91) 480 50 00   Fax: (+34 91) 480 50 80
e-mail: indra@indra.es
Web: www.indra.es

Indra's AVTM ticketing machines, Madrid 1174690

Indra's tram validator machine 1174688

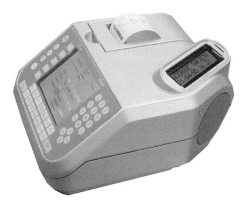

Indra's driver console 1174684

Key personnel
Chairman: *Javier Monzón*
Managing Director: *Regino Moranchel*

Products
Automatic fare collection and access control systems. Indra supplies tailor-made solutions that can be integrated with any client's internal systems, using a variety of ticket formats and technologies, for example, magnetic, stripe or smartcards.

Indra's hardware includes automatic ticket vending machines (ATVMs), driver consoles, portable inspection and sales terminals, smartcard readers/writers, magnetic strip ticket processors, access gates, booking office machines, smartcard management centres and automatic smartcard reloading machines.

Integrated railway control and management systems. The Da Vinci system controls the following in real time: passenger information, signalling (on track and onboard), electrical systems; communications and security systems; track sensors (objects' presence, impacts); and temperature, pressure and wind sensors.

INIT Innovative Informatikanwendungen in Transport-, Verkehrs-und Leitsystemen GmbH

Kaeppelestrasse 4-6, D-76131 Karlsruhe, Germany
Tel: (+49 721) 610 00   Fax: (+49 721) 610 03 99
e-mail: postmaster@init-ka.de
Web: www.init-ka.de

Subsidiaries
Australia
INIT Pty Ltd
Level 5, Toowong Tower, 9 Sherwood Road, Toowong Qld, 4066 Australia
Tel: (+61 7) 33 10 88 18   Fax: (+61 7) 33 10 88 00
US
INIT Innovations in Transportation Inc
1420 Kristina Way, Suite 101, Chesapeake, Virginia 23320
Tel: (+1 757) 413 91 00   Fax: (+1 757) 413 50 19
Canada
INIT Innovations in Transportation (Eastern Canada) Inc/INIT Innovations en Transport (Canada Est) Inc
14 Place du Commerce, suite 360, Île-des-Soeurs, Montréal, Québec H3E 1T7, Canada
Tel: (+1 514) 766 28 36   Fax: (+1 514) 766 15 78
INIT, Innovations in Transportation (Western Canada) Inc
949 West 41st Avenue, Vancouver, BC V5Z2N5, Canada
Tel: (+1 778) 995 04 93
United Arab Emirates
Init Innovation in Traffic Systems FZE
Dubai Airport Free Zone, Office 6EB 244, Dubai, UAE
Tel: (+971) 47 01 72 86

Key personnel
Chief Sales Officer: *Dr Jürgen Greschner*

Products
Fare collection/management including cashless payment and clearance.

Kaba Gilgen AG

Freiburgstrasse 34, CH-3150 Schwarzenburg, Switzerland
Tel: (+41 31) 734 41 11   Fax: (+41 31) 734 44 75
e-mail: info@kgs.kaba.com
Web: www.kaba-gilgen.ch

Key personnel
Sales Director: *Konrad Zweifel*
Director ADP, Automatic Doors for Public Transport: *Hans Krähenbühl*

Products
Platform screen door systems, platform gate door systems, access control systems, automatic pedestrian doors.

Kentkart Ltd

Osmanli Yokuşu Muhtar Kamil Sok Basmaci Han No 5/5, 34437 Taksim, Istanbul, Turkey
Tel: (+90 212) 249 67 20   Fax: (+90 212) 251 39 24
e-mail: info@kentkart.com
Web: www.kentkart.com

Key personnel
Marketing Manager: *Güner Faika Halici*

Products
Automatic fare collection systems based on contactless smartcard technology. Scope of supply includes: hardware, such as validators, rechargers and driver's panels; integration software and back-office systems; card management; and system operation and maintenance. An innovation launched in 2005 was a GPS-based vehicle tracking system that provides real time data on bus location via a GPS module located in the onboard card validator. This transfers data every two seconds.

Contracts
Kentcard smartcard revenue collection systems are used in Adana, Bandirma, Çanakkale, Denizli, Gebze, Izmir, Kocaeli and Manisa.

Krauth

Professor Alfred Krauth Apparatebau GmbH & Co KG
Ohrsbergweg 1 + 2, D-69412 Eberbach, PO Box 1334 Eberbach, Germany
Tel: (+49 6271) 80 50   Fax: (+49 6271) 805 39
e-mail: info@krauth-online.de
Web: www.krauth-online.de

Key personnel
Managing Directors: *Jürgen Hidding, Dr Bernd Teufel*
Sales Engineer: *Mr Kloss*

Products/Services
Mobile and stationary ticket vending machines, including cashless models; mobile ticket printers; reservation and ticketing systems; accounting and analysis software; return change systems; ticket printer systems, including thermotransfer, thermochromic and Edmonson; and left luggage locker systems.

Lacor Streetscape

8837 N. Central Avenue, Phoenix, Arizona 85020, US
Tel: (+1 602) 371 31 10   Fax: (+1 602) 371 37 21
e-mail: info@lacorss.com
Web: www.lacorss.com

Key personnel
Sales Manager: *Robin Stacy*

Products
Transit, urban and landscape site amenities including shelters and benches, display panels and lighting systems.

LECIP Corporation

1260-2 Kaminoho, Motosu City, Gifu 501-0401, Japan
Tel: (+81 58) 320 03 00   Fax: (+81 58) 320 03 02
e-mail: sysop@mb.lecip.co.jp
Web: www.lecip.co.jp

Background

Formerly traded as Sanyo Electric Works Ltd. The company's brand name also changed in January 2002 from S-light to LECIP.

Key personnel

President and Chief Executive Officer: *Makoto Sugimoto*

Products

Automatic vehicle management system, ticketing machines, data collection and revenue counting equipment.

Macemain + Amstad Ltd

Boyle Rd, Willowbrook Industrial Estate, Corby, Northamptonshire NN17 5XU, UK
Tel: (+44 1536) 40 13 31   Fax: (+44 1536) 40 12 98
e-mail: info@macemainamstad.com
Web: www.macemainamstad.com

Products

Walkways, canopies, shelters, trolley bays, kiosks, litter bins, fire bins, ticket bins, picnic units, tables, stools, cycle racks and bollards, metal and timber seating, information boards.

Maexbic SA

Ctra C 17, km 26.300, Centro Comercial Sant Jordi, E-08480 L'Ametlla de Vallés, Spain
Tel: (+34 938) 43 24 00   Fax: (+34 938) 43 21 02
e-mail: maexbic@maexbic.es
Web: www.maexbic.es

Key personnel

Director: *Camilo Vieira*

Products

Fixed automatic ticket vending machines capable of selling and recharging contactless smartcards, onboard electronic ticket vending machines with built-in smartcard readers, onboard smartcard readers/cancellers, fixed magnetic and smartcard validators, multi-journey card cancellers, management software for revenue and journey analysis.

Magnadata International Ltd

Horncastle Road, Boston PE21 9HZ, UK
Tel: (+44 1205) 31 00 31   Fax: (+44 1205) 31 26 12
e-mail: sales@magnadata.co.uk
Web: www.magnadata.co.uk

Key personnel

Managing Director: *Roy Colclough*
Group Sales Director: *Alan Laidlaw*
Smart iX Manager: *John Wise*

Overseas sales offices

Magnadata USA Inc
100 Route 70, Suite 9, Lakewood, New Jersey 08701, US
Tel: (+1 732) 901 93 99   Fax: (+1 732) 901 71 71
e-mail: jbonannomagusa@optonline.net
Magnadata Pty Ltd
Sydney, Australia
Tel: (+61 2) 96 23 74 00   Fax: (+61 2) 98 33 10 86
e-mail: gregg@magnadata.com.au

Products

Magnetic striped tickets and low cost limited use RF smart cards for automatic fare collection systems. These can be supplied in a number of formats (cut single, fan-folded, reel to dimensional requirement) on a variety of materials (paper, plastic, paper/plastic sandwich), including thermally coated materials. Both low- and high-coercivity magnetic striped tickets can be supplied along with chips conforming to both ISO 14443A and B.

Numerous security features can be incorporated into the ticket design, including anti-photocopying inks, UV inks and security backgrounds. Magnadata also manufactures ATB tickets, and can supply plastic thermal material for medium- and long-term magnetic transport tickets and also plastic smartcards.

Contracts

Magnadata has supplied some of the world's first projects with ticketing solutions. Supply of the first countrywide smart project in the Netherlands with low-cost smart tickets.

Magnadata was recently awarded one of the worlds largest RF ticket orders for Oslo transport, and in early 2006 the company secured the supply of Breeze tickets for MARTA in Atlanta.

In conjunction wtih Z-Card, Magnadata produced the first ticket to include an underground map to support the 2012 London Olympic bid.

Magnadata gained International Transport Smartcard Organisation (ITSO) approval for the Ik and 4K Mifare product.

Magnetic Autocontrol

Magnetic Automation Corporation
3160 Murrell Road, Rockledge, Florida 32955, US
Tel: (+1 321) 635 85 85   Fax: (+1 321) 635 94 49
e-mail: info@ac.magnetic-usa.com
Web: www.ac-magnetic.com

Key personnel

Chief Executive Officer: *Dieter Schwald*
Chief Financial Officer: *Hubert Giesbertz*

Products

Magnetic Autocontrol access control systems. Barriers can be connected to control systems which include light barriers and readers for code cards, coins, tickets and fingerprints. Barriers are produced in a variety of versions and all models can operate in 'open' mode.

Main Fare Box Co

div of Euclid Products Co Inc
3625 Lost Nation Road, Willoughby, Ohio 44094, US
Tel: (+1 440) 942 73 10   Fax: (+1 440) 942 41 84
e-mail: sales@epco-mfb.com
Web: www.epco-mfb.com

Key personnel

Contact: *Beth McCarty*

Products

Mechanical, non-registering fare boxes with removable vaults (self-locking or open) and donation boxes. Available in standard or antique styles.

Mars Electronics International (MEI)

Switzerland Office

Chemin du Port-Du-Centenaire 109, PO Box 2650, CH-1211 Geneva 2, Switzerland
Tel: (+41 22) 884 05 05   Fax: (+41 22) 884 05 04
Web: www.meiglobal.com

Head office

1301 Wilson Drive West Chester, Philadelphia 19380, US
Tel: (+ 1 610) 430 27 00   Fax: (+ 1 610) 430 26 94

Key personnel

Industry Manager: *Reinhard Banasch*
Marketing Manager: *Serge Guillod*
Business Development Manager: *F Maurice Reber*
Area Sales Manager: *Ruedi Lüthi*

Other offices

The company also has offices in Australia, Canada, Japan, Mexico, the UK and the US.

Products

Bank note validators produced under the trademark Sodeco® Cash Management Systems for incorporation into ticket vending machines.

Nabtesco Corporation

Railroad Products Company, 9-18 Kaigan 1-chome, Minato-ku, Tokyo 105-0022, Japan
Tel: (+81 3) 54 70 24 01
Fax: (+81 3) 54 70 24 24
e-mail: noriaki_kaneko@nabtesco.com
Web: www.nabtesco.com

Key personnel

Company President (Managing Director, Director of the Board): *Ryuhei Koyama*
General Manager of Planning (Executive Officer): *Kazunori Sakamoto*
General Manager, Overseas Marketing and Sales: *Jirokomei Yoshida*
Senior Manager, Overseas Marketing and Sales: *Takashi Koyama*

Background

Nabtesco Corporation was previously called NABCO Ltd.

Products

Various brake and door systems. Platform doors (manufactured and supplied by Nabtesco Corporation, NABCO Company).

Narita Manufacturing Ltd

20-12 Hanaomote-cho, Atsuta-ku, Nagoya 456-0033, Japan
Tel: (+81 52) 881 61 91
Fax: (+81 52) 881 67 48 (General Affairs)
e-mail: sinarita@narita.co.jp
Web: www.narita.co.jp

Key personnel

Chairman: *Masatoshi Narita*
President (Export Sales and Marketing): *Shuichi Narita*
Executive Director, General Affairs and Quality Assurance: *Haruo Narita*

Products

Platform door leaves.

Newbury Data Recording Ltd

Unit 2, Ion Path, Road 3, Winsford Industrial Estate, Winsford, CW7 3GE, UK
Tel: (+44 1606) 59 34 24
Fax: (+44 1606) 55 83 83
e-mail: ndsales@newburydata.co.uk
Web: www.newburydata.com

Key personnel

Managing Director: *Bill Johnson*
Director: *John Steadman*
Sales Director: *Jamie Tilley*

Products

Flexstore is a hand-held AB ticket reader, designed to read and display information held on magnetic stripe tickets and to download that data into a central computer for passenger and ticket analysis purposes. Currently supplied to European Passenger Services for the Eurostar trains.

Flexfare is a modular booking office ticketing system, comprising a terminal, receipt printer and ISO-sized card ticket issuer. Fully configurable to customer's requirements.

Nippon Signal Co Ltd

1-5-1, Marunouchi, Chiyoda-ku, Tokyo 100-6513, Japan
Tel: (+81 3) 32 17 72 00
Fax: (+81 3) 32 17 73 00
e-mail: info@signal.co.jp
Web: www.signal.co.jp

Key personnel
President: *Yohei Furuhata*

Products
Automatic gate; automatic ticket vending machine; automatic fare adjustment machine; data processing equipment; station controller; coupon vending machine; automatic coupon vending machine; automatic pre-paid card vending machine; centralised card encoder; ticket issuing machine for staff; centralised monitoring equipment.

Nippon Signal Co Ltd also makes systems for contactless IC rewritable card read/writers and the RFID item management system.

Omron Corporation

Omron Tokyo Building, 3-4-10 Toranomon, Minato-Ku, Tokyo 105-0001, Japan
Tel: (+81 3) 34 36 72 64
Fax: (+81 3) 34 36 71 27
Web: www.omron.co.jp

Key personnel
Manager, Social Systems Solutions Business Company: *Haruki Nomaru*

Products
Complete automatic fare collection systems for LRT, MRT, tram, monorail and others with contactless smartcard, token and magnetic striped ticket. Omron's system includes a central computer, station computer, encoder/sorter, ticket issuing machines, barrier equipment, validators and fare adjustment machines.

On Track Innovations (OTI)

ZHR Industrial Zone, PO Box 32, Rosh Pina, 12000, Israel
Tel: (+972 4) 686 80 00
Fax: (+972 4) 693 88 87
e-mail: info@otiglobal.com
Web: www.otiglobal.com

Key personnel
Chairman, President and Chief Executive Officer: *Oded Bashan*
Vice-President of Projects: *Ronnie Gilboa*
Chief Financial Officer: *Guy Shafran*

Subsidaries
ASEC SA
Tel: (+48 12) 293 02 00

Other offices
The company also has offices in the US, Africa and Poland.

Products
OTI designs, develops and markets secure contactless microprocessor-based smartcard solutions including smartcards, readers, application development software and communications technology.

Contracts
OTI was awarded a contract for the supply of Calypso (an electronic ticketing standard for mass transit marketing) compliant contactless smartcards for use on multiple transport operators such as buses, train and light rail.

Parkeon SAS

Le Barjac, 1 boulevard Victor, F-75015 Paris, France
1) 58 09 81 10
Fax: (+33 1) 58 09 81 26
e-mail: npoirier@parkeon.com
Web: www.parkeon.com

Key personnel
Contact: *Nicolas Poirier*

Other offices
Parkeon has offices in Belgium, France (headquarters), Germany, Italy, Spain, UK and North America

Background
Parkeon was created in November 2003 following the spin-off of the parking and ticketing division of Schlumberger formerly known as e-City.

Products
Transport ticketing solutions including contactless technology solutions. Range includes: Astreo™ and Galexio™ ticket vending terminals. Transfolio™ ticketing server, a fully centralised public transport ticketing systems management.

Contracts
Parkeon has developed and installed 5,000 ticket vending machines for local and inter city rail, underground and multi-modal transport operators particularly in France, Belgium, the United Kingdom, Sweden and Denmark.

Rail Waiting Structures

Unit 60, Dyffryn Business Park, Llantwit Major Road, Llandow, Cowbridge, South Glamorgan CF71 7PY, UK
Tel:(+44 1446) 79 54 44   Fax: (+44 1446) 79 33 44
e-mail: bus@shelters.co.uk
Web: www.shelters.co.uk

Key personnel
Sales Manager: *Lisa Black*

Background
Due to the increasing demand for rail passenger waiting facilities on platforms, Rail Waiting Structures was set up and acquired by BSW Group which is the holding company for a number of companies, including Bus Shelters Ltd, BSW Systems Ltd and Metal Box Manufacturing.

Products/Services
Design and manufacture of robust waiting facilities, tailored to the harsh usage of rail platforms. This includes a range of waiting rooms in conjunction with Network Rail.

Regazzi SA

Via alle Gerre
Zona Industriale, CH-6596 Gordola, Switzerland
Tel: (+41 91) 735 66 00
Fax: (+41 91) 735 66 99
e-mail: info@regazzi.ch
Web: www.regazzi.ch

Key personnel
Sales Manager: *Barry Gibson*

Products
Stainless steel seating and waste bins for stations.

Contracts
Regazzi has recently supplied seating and waste bins for 620 Swiss railway stations.

Sadamel Ticketing Systems

73 rue du Collège, CH-2300 La Chaux-de-Fonds, Switzerland
Tel: (+41 32) 968 07 70   Fax: (+41 32) 968 08 85
e-mail: info@sadamel.ch
Web: www.sadamel.ch

Key personnel
Chairman: *Roger Cattin*
Managing Director: *Jerôme Froidevaux*
Development Director: *Yvan Schwab*
Production Director: *Daniel Courtet*
Commercial and Marketing Manager: *Telma Gomes*

Products
Automatic ticket vending machines suitable for paper, magnetic and contactless tickets with payment by coins, banknotes and bank cards. Automatic fare collection management system including monitoring of networked ticket vending and validating equipment. Passenger-operated automatic vending machines. Onboard or counter-based automatic ticket vending machines, ticket cancelling units. Coins recycling unit.

Contracts
Contracts include Portuguese Railways (CP Lisbon and CP Porto) for a complete automatic fare collection system with 220 ticket vending machines and 320 magnetic card validators. All of the machines and validators are networked to a management system (Sadagest).

In 2004 a contract was received from SATU/Oeiras for a contactless system with access gates, in addition to ticket vending devices. Sadamel currently supplies the universal Coin Recycling Unit CRU04-06, operating LIFO and providing intelligent coin management for a large number of currencies and integrations.

Saima Sicurezza SpA

Indicatore 60/G, I-52020 Arezzo, Italy
Tel: (+39 05) 75 92 91
Fax: (+39 05) 75 98 70 97
e-mail: sicurezzaexport@saimanews.com
Web: www.saimasicurezza.com

Key personnel
President: *Paolo Moretti*
Marketing Manager: *Orietta Moretti*
Export Manager: *Alfredo Soderi*

Background
Saima Sicurezza is part of the Saima Group SpA.

Products
Access control systems for urban transport applications, including tripod turnstiles, motorised gates and rotating gates. Saima also supplies security access booths and archway metal detectors.

The company is UNI ISO 9001:2000 accredited.

Saima Sicurezza's access control system
1289807

Scan Coin Ltd

Dutch House, 110 Broadway, Salford Quays, Salford M50 2UW, UK
Tel: (+44 161) 873 05 00   Fax: (+44 161) 873 05 01
e-mail: sales@scancoin.co.uk
Web: www.scancoin.co.uk

Key personnel
Managing Director: *Jeffrey G Carr*
Sales Director: *Steve Fitton*
Service Manager: *Andy Kershaw*
Financial Controller, Company Secretary: *Ruth Pringle*

Products
Note changers, coin sachet packing systems, cash deposit points and coin sorters. The Super 7 note changer accepts up to eight international denominations and around 9,000 coins can be stored in the machine.

The Scan Coin 4,000 value sorter sorts up to 16 coin types at 4,000 coins a minute.

Scan Coin has introduced the CDP Euro which has a capability to handle up to 64 coin types in 17 sorting locations.

The Scan Coin CDP3 cash deposit system features fault logging facilities as standard.

The SC20 and SC22 coin sorting machines use electronic sensing technology. These microsorters are for sites that are processing lower volumes of coin.

Contracts
Scan Coin has been awarded a three-year contract by bus operator Stagecoach to supply and service cash handling systems throughout the company's network.

New developments
The CDP4 module, compatible with all existing Scan Coin CDP installations. Additional security enhancements include a magnetic card reader that can be fitted for driver and operator identification. The facility has been incorporated to allow for the future integration of a ticket module reader.

Scheidt & Bachmann GmbH

PO Box 201143, D-41211 Mönchengladbach, Germany
Tel: (+49 2166) 26 65 50   Fax: (+49 2166) 26 66 99
e-mail: farecollection@scheidt-bachmann.de
Web: www.scheidt-bachmann.com

Key personnel
Managing Director: *Matthias Augustyniak*
Director of Projects and Applications: *Manfred Feiter*
Director of Business Development: *Frithjof Struye*

Background
The company was founded in 1872 by Friedrich Scheidt and Carl Bachmann and remains privately owned in the fifth generation.

Products
Automatic fare collection and ticket vending machines for stationary and onboard applications; point of sales; central support system for accounting; data provision and technical administration of associated fare collection equipment. Complete smartcard solutions.

Recent products include the FAA-2000/C (cashless) and the FAA-2000/M (cards and coins) ticket vending machines incorporating the main features of the FAA 2000 family of machines. The FAA-2000/C and the FAA 2000/M can be used in onboard or stationary applications, will validate electronic tickets and can serve as an information point. The FAA-2000/M can also encode and distribute smart cards. The FAA 2000 machines can also be used as multimedia terminals, providing advertising and marketing potential, or as an information platform displaying

information on unique local events or common local data.

The TicketXpress TVM enables people with physical disabilities to access public transport which corresponds to the guideline of the SRA (Strategic Rail Authority). It is in over 1,000 installations in the UK.

The newly developed ticket 'esprit' is the future intelligent fare collection management. This medium, which is the size of a key ring, contains a processor, a storage medium and wireless communication.

Shere Limited

4 Bridge Park, Merrow Industrial Estate, Guildford, GU4 7BF, UK
Tel: (+44 1483) 55 74 00   Fax: (+44 1483) 55 74 01
e-mail: neil.briscoe@shere.com
Web: www.shere.com

Key personnel
Managing Director: *Iain Kingsley*
Sales Director: *Neil Briscoe*
Financial Director: *David Parson*

Products
Self-service transactional kiosk and web-based systems for travel and hospitality sectors combining ticket and receipt printers; chip and PIN and magnetic swipe card readers; card issuing devices; smart cards; PIN pads; touchscreens; scanners; signature capture devices; UPS, sensors and alarms.

Takamisawa Cybernetics Co Ltd

Nakano Heiwa Building, 48-5, 2-Chome Chuo, Nakano-ku, Tokyo 164-0011, Japan
Tel: (+81 3) 53 71 33 62   Fax: (+81 3) 53 71 33 64
e-mail: export_dept@tacy.co.jp
Web: www.tacy.co.jp

Key personnel
Manager of Trading Department: *J Tada*

Works
Nagano Factory No 1
525 Kitagawa, Saku-City, Nagano, 384-0304, Japan
Takamisawa Service Co Ltd
Takamisawa Mex Co Ltd

Products
Design and manufacture of automatic fare collection systems and equipment, including automatic ticket vending machines, automatic gates, fare adjustment machines and ticket printers; AFC-related currency and card handling unit.

Customers include all Japanese railway companies and operators in some Asian countries.

Thales

Transport & Energy activities
Centre du Bois des Bordes, PO Box 57, F-91229 Brétigny-sur-Orge Cedex, France
Tei: (+33 1) 69 88 52 00   Fax: (+33 1) 60 84 82 30
e-mail: info@thales-transportservices.com
Web: www.thalesgroup.com/transport

Key personnel
Chairman and Chief Executive Officer: *Jean-Louis Olié*
Vice-Chairman: *Tim Cavanagh*
Sales and Marketing Director: *Ian Woodroofe*

Background
Thales is an international electronics and systems group, serving defence, aerospace, services and security markets. The group employs 61,500

people worldwide and generated revenues of €10.6 billion in 2003.

Products and Services
Thales's Transport & Energy business line integrates secure systems for customers in the public transport and energy sectors. Its solutions span integrated ticketing and fare collection systems, train supervision and control, motorway toll collection, traffic and vehicle fleet management, public car park systems, telematics and geolocation. Thales has major contracts in Bangkok, France, Hong Kong, Mexico, Nanjing, the Netherlands, New Delhi, Oslo, Singapore, Taiwan and the United Kingdom.

Time 24 Ltd

19 Victoria Gardens, Burgess Hill RH15 9NB, UK
Tel: (+44 1444) 25 76 55
Fax: (+44 1444) 25 90 00
e-mail: sales@time24.co.uk
Web: www.time24.co.uk

Key personnel
Managing Director: *David Shore*
Finance Director: *Mark Willifer*
Purchasing Manager: *Steve Vaughan*
Internal Sales Manager: *Barrie Dumbleton*

Products
Ticketing systems, including technology for platform purchase of tickets and checking routes.

Toshiba Corporation

Transportation Systems Division
1-1 Shibaura, 1-chome, Minato-ku, Tokyo 105-8001, Japan
Tel: (+81 3) 34 57 49 24
Fax: (+81 3) 54 44 92 63
e-mail: miki.ogata@toshiba.co.jp
Web: www.toshiba.co.jp

Key personnel
President and Chief Executive Officer: *Atsutoshi Nishida*
Vice-President, Transportation Systems Division: *Toshiyuki Onishi*
Senior Manager, Railway Projects Department: *Yoshiji Ito*
Group Manager, Overseas Business Planning Group: *Michihiko Ogata*

Products
Automatic fare and toll collection systems based on customised units from a basic range.

Toyo Denki Seizo KK

Toyo Electric Manufacturing Co Ltd
No 1 Nurihiko Bldg, 9-2 Kyobashi, 2-chome, Chuo-ku, Tokyo 104-0031, Japan
Tel: (+81 3) 35 35 06 41
Fax: (+81 3) 35 35 06 50

Key personnel
President: *Teruyuki Osawa*
Vice-President: *Keisuke Tanaka*
Managing Director: *Kenzo Terashima*

Products
Ticket issuing systems for suburban and rapid transit railway systems; automatic ticket issuing machines and fare adjusting equipment.

Toyo Denki's ticket issuing system for suburban and rapid transit systems can issue magnetic tickets for automatic gates. It can also calculate fares for complex urban networks where different routeings are possible and there is much interline traffic between different operators.

TransWay

31 Lechi Street, PO Box 1461, Bnei-Brak IL-51114, Israel
Tel: (+972 3) 577 68 38
Fax: (+972 3) 616 14 17
e-mail: marketing@transway.co.il
Web: www.transway.co.il

Key personnel
Chairman: *Alex Milner*
General Manager: *Moshe Panijel*
Vice-President, Operations and Quality Assurance: *Baruch Vachterman*
Chief Finance Officer: *Lior Ben Simon*
Marketing Manager: *Dany Goldraij*

Background
TransWay is a subsidiary of O R Tech (Rapac Technologies Ltd), an Israeli company traded on the Tel-Aviv Stock Exchange and one of the leading companies in the local smart card and mobile transaction terminal fields.

Projects
TransWay's system is an integrated revenue management system that provides the public transport provider with the capabilities to sell transit tickets, collect money deposits and manage the overall ticketing database for various applications that are necessary for planning, operating and controlling of collected revenues. The system can handle a variety of transit tickets such as regular fixed-price tickets, specially discounted tickets (child, senior citizen, disabled, student), round-trip tickets, zone-based tickets. When exercising smartcard readers and validators, the system is also capable of handling periodical, season tickets, multiride and other sophisticated schemes of ticketing.

The onboard vehicle equipment records with great accuracy, the transaction details and transmits the collected data for further processing to the MIS. The system is based on an open system concept. Adding functionalities and interfacing with other equipment is possible, such as with a tachograph, fueling system, internal electronic displays, GPS, passenger-counting devices and other transport related equipment.

Contracts
In 1996 EGGED (the National Israeli Public Transport Company) nominated TransWay and IBM Israel (75/25) as the successful tenders for the implementation of its electronic fare collection system. The system has been successfully supplied and installed on 4,000 buses.

TranSys

1 Warwick Row, London SW1 5ER, UK
Tel: (+44 20) 78 08 71 08
Fax: (+44 20) 78 08 71 09
e-mail: tricia.edeam@eds.com
Web: www.transys.com

Key personnel
Chief Executive: *John Stout*

Products
Revenue collection and ticketing systems.

Contracts
TranSys is a consortium of companies led by EDS (Electronic Data Systems) and Cubic Transportation Systems (CTS). It is responsible for building, implementing, managing and marketing the integrated ticketing system as part of the GBP1.2 billion Prestige project in partnership with Transport for London (TfL). The main focus of the Prestige project has been the enhancement and replacement of the legacy revenue collection systems throughout London's complex transport network which serves 8.5 million passengers per day, spans almost 5,000 km and encompasses five modes of transport: bus, tube, national rail, Docklands Light Railway and Croydon Tramlink. TranSys has completely overhauled the system, installing the necessary infrastructure to deliver a multi-modal, smartcard-based ticketing system. The new system was installed alongside the existing one which was then decommissioned and removed, limiting distruption to travellers and revenue loss to TfL. The key element of the project has been the development of Oyster, London's travel smartcard, and the associated 16,000 card readers which have been fitted to ticketing equipment across the networks. There are 36 million journeys every week made using Oyster. Other features of the project include: the gating of over 300 underground and national rail stations, installing ticketing equipment on over 8,500 buses, updating all ticketing machines in ticket halls across the travel network and installing multifunctional machines to offer a variety of payment and language options. They also offer customers Internet and telephone ticket purchasing, and have established a new data centre providing data processing and back office systems.

Wayfarer Transit Systems Limited

10 Willis Way, Fleets Industrial Estate, Poole BH15 3SS, UK
Tel: (+44 1202) 33 93 39
Fax: (+44 1202) 33 93 69
e-mail: sales@poole.parkeon.com
Web: www.parkeon.com/wayfarer

Key personnel
Deputy Chairman: *Tony McNamara*
Director of Sales and Marketing: *Paul Moirano*
Head of Standard Projects Team: *Peter Gowan*

US office
1170 McLester Street, Unit 4, Elizabeth, New Jersey
Tel: (+1 908) 354 45 42
Fax: (+1 908) 354 46 65

Background
Acquired by Parkeon SAS in 2007, the Wayfarer Group Ltd will retain the Wayfarer name and its major centres in Poole, Croydon, Manchester and Glasgow. The companies Research and Development facilities will be combined while their service centres will be fully integrated.

Products
Automatic fare collection and associated peripheral systems and software for road and rail transport. The range includes automatic ticket issuing and fare collection systems including magnetic card validators, contact and contactless (proximity) smartcard processors, point-of-sale systems, passenger counting and vehicle location systems, on-vehicle terminals and portable ticket issuing systems, ticket verification systems, Ibis interface, ISO standard compatibility, data analysis and management information software.

Developments
e-bus has been developed by Wayfarer Transit Systems for on-vehicle systems integration for public transport operators.

Contracts
In the UK over 80 per cent of bus operators are cited by Wayfarer as using its equipment. Through local agents and distributors, Wayfarer has installed systems in Argentina, Australia, Ireland, Israel, Italy, the Lebanon, Malaysia, Netherlands, New Zealand, Norway, Portugal, South Africa, Spain, Sweden and the US.

The first Wayfarer contact smartcard system was installed in Auckland, New Zealand in 1991, with over 10,000 smartcards in daily use. Wayfarer also has several contactless smartcard systems in use, the largest being in Bradford, which is the largest commercial smartcard system in the UK.

Westinghouse Platform Screen Doors

Westinghouse Way, Hampton Park East, Melksham SN12 6TL, UK
Tel: (+44 1225) 89 88 35
Fax: (+44 1249) 89 87 15
e-mail: psd@westbrake.com
Web: www.platformscreendoors.com

Key personnel
Managing Director: *Paul R Johnson*
Marketing Director: *Peter C Johnson*
PSD Director: *Richard Bew*
Business Development Manager: *Colin Fullalove*

Background
Westinghouse Platform Screen Doors is a division of Knorr-Bremse Rail Systems (UK) Ltd which is part of the Knorr-Bremse Group.

In November 2008, Knorr-Bremse and Japanese signal equipment manufacturer Kyosan Electric Manufacturing Company Limited concluded a strategic co-operation agreement. The agreement initially provides for Knorr-Bremse to sell its Westinghouse Platform Screen Door (WPSD) systems through Kyosan in the Japanese market. In return, Knorr-Bremse will market and sell certain Kyosan rail products and systems under the WPSD brand to the global market outside Japan through the Knorr-Bremse sales network.

Products
Platform screen door systems, platform edge doors and platform safety gates.

Westinghouse Platform Screen Doors designs and installs railway-based automatic platform screen doors. Systems are tailored to suit individual customer specifications for new and retrofit applications, combining safety, reliability and architecturally pleasing designs. Asset management capabilities include comprehensive after-sales services, training and maintenance programmes.

Contracts
Projects worldwide include:
China: Beijing Line 5, Shanghai Line 1 retrofit, Guangzhou Metro Lines 2 and 4, Shenzhen Metro Lines 1 and 4, Hong Kong International Airport.
Denmark: Copenhagen Metro, Copenhagen Airport.
France: Toulouse Line B, Roissy Line 1 and 3.
Italy: Brescia Metrobus.
Malaysia: Kuala Lumpur LRT2.
Singapore: North South Line, East West Line, North East Line, Changi Airport Line, Circle Line, Bishan Station reftrofit.
United Arab Emirates: Dubai Metro Red and Green Lines.
UK: London Underground Jubilee Line Extension.

Westinghouse platform safety gates, Guangzhou Line 4, China 1322890

VEHICLE MAINTENANCE EQUIPMENT AND SERVICES

Company listing by country

AUSTRALIA
EDI Rail
iQR
United Group Rail

BELGIUM
Bombardier Transportation

BRAZIL
Gevisa SA

CROATIA
Končar – Electric Vehicles Inc

CZECH REPUBLIC
Pars nova as

FINLAND
Transtech Oy

FRANCE
ALSTOM Transport
NEU International Railways
SEFAC SA
Sogema Engineering

GERMANY
Fraunhofer Institute for Non-Destructive Testing
Hegenscheidt-MFD GmbH & Co KG
HYWEMA Lifting Systems
Alfred Kärcher GmbH & Co KG
Neuero Technology GmbH
Pfaff-silberblau Verkehrstechnik GmbH & Co KG
Siemens AG
Spedition Kübler GmbH (Kübler Spedition)

Üstra Hannoversche Verkhersbetriebe AG
Windhoff Bahn-und Anlagentechnik GmbH

INDONESIA
INKA

ITALY
Ceccato SpA
CESPA Manufacturing Srl
Consorzio Corifer
Emanuel srl
PESA Bydoszcz SA
Ravaglioli SpA
SAFOP SpA

KOREA, SOUTH
Hyundai Rotem Company

NETHERLANDS
NedTrain
Voith Railservices BV

SLOVAKIA
ŽOS Vrútky Jsc
ŽOS Zvolen as

SPAIN
CAF – Construcciones y Auxiliar de Ferrocarriles SA
Rocafort Ingenieros SL

SWEDEN
Kambre Consulting
Revatec Kambre AB
STT

SWITZERLAND
Nencki AG
Von Roll BETEC

UNITED KINGDOM
Clyde Materials Handling
Dawson
Lloyds Somers
Mechan Ltd
Metronet REW Ltd
Planet Platforms
Railway Projects Limited (RPL)
Smith Bros & Webb Ltd
System Chassijet Ltd
Ultrasonic Sciences Ltd
UpRight Powered Access
Wesurail Limited
Wilcomatic Ltd

UNITED STATES
CAM Innovation, Inc
Delaware Car Company
InterClean Equipment Inc
Marmac
MotivePower Inc
Proceco Ltd
Railquip Inc
Ross & White Company
Simmons
SSI North America Incorporated
Whiting Corporation

For details of the latest updates to *Jane's Urban Transport Systems* online and to discover the additional information available exclusively to online subscribers please visit
juts.janes.com

ALSTOM Transport

Service Business
48 rue Albert Dhalenne, F-93482 Saint-Ouen,
France
Tel: (+33 1) 41 66 90 00   Fax: (+33 1) 41 66 96 66
Web: www.transport.alstom.com

Key personnel

President, Transport Sector: *Philippe Mellier*
Chief Operating Officer: *Gérard Blanc*
Senior Vice-President Train Life Services: *Dominique Pouliquen*

Train Life Services
Total TrainLife Management©

Service Business of ALSTOM Transport has created distinct service-product ranges within its Total TrainLife Management concept. These can be provided individually or combined into comprehensive support packages. Principal service-products include:

Maintenance

This provides operators and owners with a maintenance service regardless of the original manufacturer. ALSTOM can take its people and expertise to the operators' premises and assume control and ownership of the facilities and manpower, or it can complement the operator's existing resources through a maintenance management function. ALSTOM also offers the option of maintaining rolling stock at existing ALSTOM depots, where the servicing of 'passing traffic' can be accommodated.

In addition, it provides technical support services where it identifies performance improvements to enhance a network's availability.

Renovation and modernisation

As well as routine, heavy overhaul and repair activities, ALSTOM's renovation service offers interior retrofits and technology upgrades which together deliver 'new vehicle' features, for both ALSTOM-built and other manufacturers' rolling stock.

Parts supply

ALSTOM offers a worldwide supply chain management service. This is designed to provide a flexible response to different customer needs. ALSTOM has the ability to source replacement parts for all makes of rolling stock, from the latest equipment to vehicles that have been in service for more than 30 years. ALSTOM can also provide turnkey warehousing, procurement and inventory management.

Contracts

Brazil: In December 2007, CPTM (Companhia Paulista de Trens Metropolitanos) awarded two new contracts for the maintenance of 78 of its trains to the COMAFER and Cobraman II consortia, in which ALSTOM is a partner.
France: In November 2007, RATP and SNCF selected ALSTOM to perform the interior refitting of 119 suburban trains that operate on line B of the Ile-de-France regional express (RER) network in the Paris area. Delivery of the 118 series kits will commence in the first part of 2010 and continue between 18 and 46 units per year.

In December 2006, the Urban Community of Lille and Transpole (operator of the public transport network for the greater Lille area) selected a consortium comprising of ALSTOM and Safra to modernise VAL, the city's driverless metro car. The contract includes the modernisation of 38 metro trainsets consisting of rolling stock designed and manufactured by ALSTOM in the early 1980s.

In February 2004, a consortium led by ALSTOM including Cannes La Bocca Industries (CLBI) was awarded a contract by SNCF to refurbish 71 Class Z2 emus by 2008. Refurbishment work was undertaken in CLBI and SNCF workshops with ALSTOM acting as project manager and supplying major equipment.

In August 2003, ALSTOM signed a three-year contract with French National Railways (SNCF) covering the maintenance of cooling units for power modules of the operator's fleet of TGV high-speed trainsets. An option would extend the contract for two years and bring to 4,000 the number of cooling units treated.
Hungary: In May 2006, BKV, the Budapest public transport operator, awarded the ALSTOM-led Budapest Metropolis Consortium, a contract for the supply of 170 Metropolis metro cars. The agreement includes additional provision for the maintenance of these vehicles for a three-year period as well an option for a further 28 cars.
Mexico: In December 2006 the Mexico City authority, STC (Sistema de Transporte Colectivo), announced its intent to award ALSTOM a contract for the refurbishment of 25 trainsets for its Line 8 fleet with new propulsion technology. ALSTOM has secured the maintenance for them over 10 years as part of the contract.
Russian Federation: In May 2006, as part of an order to supply eight Velaro high-speed trains to Russian Railways (RZD), Siemens will also assume responsibility for their maintenance for a period of 30-years.
Spain: A contract placed by RENFE in February 2004 with a consortium of ALSTOM and CAF for the supply of 30 high-speed shuttle trains and 45 variable-gauge high-speed trains includes the provision of comprehensive maintenance services for a period of 14 years from the introduction of the trains in 2006. In October 2002, ALSTOM was awarded a contract by Spanish National Railways to undertake the maintenance for 14 years of 24 trains in its high-speed fleet. The contract covers 18 AVE high-speed trainsets used on the Madrid-Seville line, six Euromed trainsets used on the Barcelona-Valencia-Alicante line and 21 Class 252 electric locomotives which power 200 km/h push-pull services on the Madrid-Seville and Madrid-Barcelona routes.
UK: In September 2006, ALSTOM was awarded a five-year-plus contract by Northern Rail, covering the maintenance of Northern Rail's fleet of 17 three-car Class 323 emus.
US: In March 2006, ALSTOM was awarded a multi-year contract by Amtrak to manage spare parts supply and provide technical assistance to Amtrak's Acela passenger fleet.

Bombardier Transportation

Services
Schöneberger Ufer 1, D-10785 Berlin, Germany
Tel: (+49 30) 98 60 70   Fax: (+49 30) 986 07 20-0

Key personnel
President, Services: *Laurent Troger*

Services

Bombardier Transportation's complete range of operations, maintenance and support services are designed to meet the rapidly changing needs of the rail industry worldwide. The company's portfolio includes; full train and fleet maintenance, materials and logistics solutions, both vehicle overhaul and modernisation and component re-engineering, as well as operations and maintenance of complete transportation systems. While working in partnership with operators, Bombardier Transportation develops long-term support packages to meet individual client requirements. This can include; customer-supported management information systems, supply and training of staff, consulting services, O&M planning services and system security enhancements. This comprehensive portfolio and experience offers customers a range of benefits, including increased availability for a given fleet through balanced maintenance, increased reliability through monitoring and upgrades, lower life cycle costs, full support parts management and, above all, safe trains.

Bombardier has a number of parts supply contracts around the world. These include, consignment stock agreements whereby stocks of Bombardier-owned parts are stored at the clients' premises awaiting drawdown: examples include BVG, the Berlin public transport authority, Öresund Trains (OTU) and the Gardermoen Airport Shuttle in Norway. In the UK Bombardier is supplying kits of parts to several train operators; these kits have been developed with the operator to provide the specific self-contained package of parts that are required for specific maintenance operations. For Gardermoen in Norway Bombardier provides a vendor-managed inventory of parts. These different arrangements are optimised to provide maximum availability of parts at minimal cost to the operator. The company is developing Internet parts ordering, which will further simplify and lower the costs of operators' ordering processes.

Bombardier operates and maintains automated people mover systems at a number of airports including: Atlanta, Beijing, Denver, Frankfurt, Madrid Barajas, Miami, Rome, San Francisco and the future APM in Sacramento. It provides maintenance and technical assistance at other international airports such as Dallas/Fort Worth, Heathrow, Kuala Lumpur, Las Vegas, Orlando, Pittsburgh and Tampa. On behalf of transportation authorities, Bombardier is operating and maintaining the fully automated Las Vegas Monorail, AirTrain JKF in New York City, AirTrain Newark in New Jersey and the future Yongin EverLine advanced rapid transit (ART) system upon its completion in 2010.

Bombardier's Refurbishment Centre at Derby, UK, with a Mark 3 coach and Class 315 emu undergoing modernisation, both for One Railway (now National Express East Anglia)   0585279

Other maintenance examples include locomotives in Italy and in Germany, where the LNVG operation is supported by Bombardier Transportation.

Bombardier has a range of facilities around the world, where it is modernising vehicles and re-engineering components.

Contracts

Australia: The contract from the Victoria State Government and V/Line to provide passenger rolling stock for regional services in Victoria, Australia, includes a 15-year maintenance agreement for a total of 38 V/locity two-car dmus.

Provision of maintenance for 15 years, including the construction of a maintenance and stabling facility, was a feature of a contract placed in 2002 with a joint venture of Bombardier Transportation and EDI-Rail to supply new emus for Perth area suburban services. From mid-2004 31 three-car B-Series emus were delivered to the Western Australian Government for the southern leg of the Perth Urban Rail Development project. In December 2006, 15 additional trains of this type were ordered.

Belgium: In April 2007, Belgian National Railways (SNCB) commissioned Bombardier Transportation to refurbish 130 type M5 double-deck coaches and to conduct the heavy maintenance of all bogies and brakes. The M5 vehicles will be refurbished from October 2008 until the end of 2011.

Canada: In Toronto, Bombardier maintains GO Transit's commuter rail fleet of 415 Bombardier BiLevel* cars and 45 locomotives. Full preventive maintenance services are provided. Bombardier began its services relationship with GO in 1996 with a six-year contract. GO exercised a three-year option in 2002, followed by two one-year extensions. Bombardier's maintenance operations at GO Transit are OHSAS 18001 and ISO 9001:2000 certified.

In December 2007, Bombardier won a further contract with GO Transit to provide fleet maintenance services for a commuter rail system serving Toronto and surrounding regions. The five-year contract includes options for up to 15 additional years of service.

In Ottawa, Bombardier designed, built, commissioned and now maintains a fleet of three light diesel multiple units for OC Transpo. A dedicated team has carried out maintenance services, maintenance management and technical support for the fleet since the system started revenue service in 2001. OC Transpo awarded Bombardier a two-year extension in 2005.

In November 2007, Bombardier announced that it had received a further five-year contract with GO which includes options for up to 15 additional years. Under the contract Bombardier will be responsible for train operations as well as management of train crews on six of GO Transit's seven commuter rail lines.

China: In September 2002, Bombardier Transportation was awarded a contract by Shanghai Metro Operation Corporation to undertake a 10 year overhaul on 96 metro cars between 2002 and 2005.

Germany: Locomotive re-engineering and modernisation contracts in Germany include: equipping 80 Class 298 diesel locomotives with radio remote control and MICAS-L control technology for DB Cargo; modernising 16 MaK diesel locomotives for HGK Cologne; modernising four Class V100.4 and two Class 60 diesel locomotives for various German operators. Additionally refurbishment of two Class 232, 2,460 kW diesel locomotives for Schauffele; and the supply of four Class 293 diesel locomotives for GSG, a rail infrastructure company.

Bombardier also has a 15 year contract with LNVG providing fleet maintenance for 18 locomotives, 88 double-deck coaches and 18 driving van trailers.

Hungary: Bombardier is the majority owner of Bombardier MAV Kft, the rail coach manufacturing plant located in Dunakeszi. Over the last decade more than 600 coaches have been modernised at this site.

Italy: In June 2005, Bombardier received an order from Trenitalia (Italian Railways) for the upgrade of 60 ETR 500 electric power-heads.

Netherlands: In April 2007, Bombardier Transportation was commissioned by Nederlandse Spoorwegen Reizigers, a subsidiary of the Dutch railway company, Nederlandse Spoorwegen (NS), to refurbish 30 two-car units of the SGM II vehicles.

Norway: In October 2007, Bombardier Transportation was commissioned by the Norwegian State Railway (NSB) to refurbish 56 Class 5 coaches. In June 2007, Bombardier had also been commissioned by NSB to refurbish 13 Class 69C train sets (39 vehicles). The refurbishment was scheduled to end with the last vehicle returning to service in May 2009.

South Africa: Bombardier won a contract for the modernisation and overhaul of 45 Class 11E electric locomotives for Spoornet: this includes upgrading the control technology with the MITRAC system. The locomotives are used to haul heavy coal trains between the Mpumalanga coalfields and Richards Bay.

In 2006 Bombardier, as a member of the Bombela Consortium, was awarded a contract to provide an 80 km rapid rail transit system that will connect Johannesburg, Tshwane (Pretoria) and the OR Tambo International Airport. Bombardier is responsible for the design and supply of the core electrical and mechanical systems, including a fleet of 96 Bombardier Electrostar vehicles, for which it will provide 15-years of maintenance services starting in 2010.

Spain: In July 2008, Bombardier Transportation, in consortium with Talgo, was awarded a 14-year contract with RENFE, the Spanish National Rail Operator, for the maintenance of 45 AVE S-130 high-speed trains.

Sweden: Bombardier has maintenance contracts for approximately 192 emu cars being operated in Sweden.

In January 2005, Bombardier received an order from Affarsverket Statens Jarnvagar (Swedish State Railways) for the heavy maintenance of 16 locomotives, nine emus and components including bogies, axles and traction motors.

In June 2007, Bombardier Transportation was awarded a major modernisation contract by the Swedish freight company Green Cargo. The order relates to the modernisation of 42 electric locomotives Type Rc2 and 62 diesel locomotives Type T33. The prototypes were scheduled to be delivered in 2008 and the remaining units over the next six years.

UK: In June 2006, Bombardier was awarded two contracts from First Great Western, part of FirstGroup plc. The first order is for the renovation of 405 High-Speed Train (HST) trailer cars to include an extensive interior refresh and an exterior repaint. The second contract is for HST bogie overhaul and technical development work, to be undertaken throughout the life of the new Great Western franchise, for up to 10 years.

In May 2006, Bombardier was awarded a contract by First ScotRail for fleet support of their Class 170 Bombardier-built Turbostar trains. Under the fleet agreement, Bombardier will provide, until 2011, technical support, remote monitoring and diagnostic systems and spare parts and maintenance materials for the 59 Turbostar trains that operates services in Scotland.

Bombardier Transportation has a 14-year contract with Virgin Trains to maintain 352 Class 220/221 demu cars. The fleet is maintained at a purpose-built facility at Central Rivers, near Burton upon Trent, UK and at other sites.

The 99-year Croydon Tramlink concession in the UK has been awarded to Tramtrack Croydon – a consortium with Bombardier as a key member. Bombardier was awarded the contract to manufacture the 24 trams and is now maintaining them.

Bombardier has built 296 emu cars for c2c, part of the National Express Group. Bombardier is maintaining these vehicles at the East Ham Depot.

As part of the Metronet consortium Bombardier will be refurbishing District Line vehicles. Bombardier has a rolling contract to supply 1,738 new cars for four of Metronet's six lines by the end of 2015. During 2007, the company was scheduled to take over all maintenance of the Victoria Line and sub surface line fleets to the end of the 30 year PPP contract, subject to periodic review.

US: In March 2007, Bombardier Transportation was awarded a seven-year contract by the South Florida Regional Transportation Authority (SFRTA) to provide maintenance services for SFRTA's fleet of commuter rail vehicles. The agreement includes one option for a three-year extension. The fleet includes 26 Bombardier BiLevel vehicles and some dmus that are part of a demonstration project.

Bombardier has established facilities in Kanona and Dansville, New York for the overhaul of passenger rail vehicles. Current contracts include the overhaul of major components for the MBTA's commuter rail fleet and for Metro-North Railroad, as well as a complete vehicle overhaul program for Cleveland's fleet of light rail vehicles. In San Diego, Bombardier has set up passenger rail vehicle painting and body shop operations in the North County Transit District's facilities.

*Trademarks of Bombardier

CAF – Construcciones y Auxiliar de Ferrocarriles SA

Padilla 17 – 6°, E-28006 Madrid, Spain
Tel: (+34 91) 435 25 00   Fax: (+34 91) 436 03 96
e-mail: export.caf@caf.es
Web: www.caf.es

Key personnel
President and Chief Executive Officer:
   J M Baztarrica
Chief Executive Officer: *A Arizcorreta*
Managing Director: *A Legarda*

Works
Beasain
J M Iturrioz 26 E-20200 Beasain, Spain
Tel: (+34 943) 88 01 00   Fax: (+34 943) 88 14 20

Irún
Calle Anaca 13, E-20301 Irún, Spain
Tel: (+34 943) 61 33 42   Fax: (+34 943) 61 81 55

Zaragoza
Av de Cataluña 299, E-50014 Zaragoza, Spain
Tel: (+34 976) 76 51 00   Fax: (+34 976) 57 26 48
Elmira NY USA
300 East Eighteenth Street, NY 14903-1333, US

TRENASA
Polígono Industrial Castejón, Parcela P1, E-31590 Castejón, Navarra

Linares
Construcciones Ferroviarias CAF-Santana SA
Avda Primero de Mayo s/n 23700 Linares (Jaén), Spain

Services
Maintenance of emus, dmus, metros, locomotives and other rail vehicles: scheduled and unscheduled maintenance, repairs, modifications and upgrades, supply of materials, operations support, staff training, technical assessments, computerised support.

Refurbishment and modernisation of rail vehicles.

Contracts
Contracts include: maintenance of vehicles for the Cercanías and Trenes Regionales divisions of

RENFE, Spain, for metro systems in Barcelona, Madrid, Mexico City, Rome and Sao Paulo, emus used by MTRC, Hong Kong, for its Airport Express and Tung Chung Line services.

As part of the contract to supply 144 cars for Santiago de Chile Metro, CAF will carry out train maintenance for 20 years from the successful delivery of the first train.

Refurbishment contracts include work on 3 kV DC emus for RENFE, Spain, dmus for FEVE and emus for ET/FV, both Spain, metro cars for STC, Mexico, and Metrovías, Argentina, suburban emus for Rio de Janeiro and tank wagons for Saltra.

CAM Innovation, Inc

215 Philadelphia Street, Hanover, Pennsylvania 17331, US
Tel: (+1 717) 637 59 88   Fax: (+1 717) 637 93 29
e-mail: sales@cam-innovation.com
Web: www.caminnovation.com; www.custom-taping-machines.com

Key personnel
President: *Charles A McGough III*

Products
Test equipment, varnish insulation, armature repair, cleaning and handling machinery. All machinery designed to improve the quality and reliability of the electric motors on locomotives.

Contracts
Russia, South Africa.

Ceccato SpA

Via Selva Maiolo, 5/7, I-36075, Alte Di Montecchio Maggiore (VI), Italy
Tel: (+39 0444) 70 84 11
Fax: (+39 0444) 69 55 44
e-mail: special@ceccato-carwash.it
Web: www.ceccato.it

Key personnel
Managing Director: *Piero Rizzon*
Technical Director: *Leopoldo Cosma*
Sales Director: *Riccardo Dolcetta*

Products
Complete plants for the external washing of surface trains, trams, underground trains and associated rolling stock. Units can be configurated with a high number of modular groups; each one designed to perform a specific washing function on different shapes and surfaces of the vehicles.

CESPA Manufacturing Srl

Via Luigi Volpicella 145, I-80147 Napoli, Italy
Tel: (+39 081) 752 48 63
Fax: (+39 081) 559 05 61
e-mail: info@cespaitaly.com
Web: www.cespaitaly.com

Key personnel
Managing Director and Technical Director: *Massimo Spavone*

Products
Workshop equipment; mobile lifting jacks for railway vehicles; provisory bogies for supporting coach bodies during assembly and maintenance; testing platforms for bogie rotation test; elevated platforms for bogie rotation testing; elevated platform for roof access; lifting and handling equipment on customer request.

Clyde Materials Handling

Carolina Court, Lakeside, Doncaster DN4 5RA, UK
Tel: (+44 1302) 32 13 13   Fax: (+44 1302) 55 44 00
e-mail: solutions@clydematerials.co.uk
Web: www.clydematerials.co.uk

Key personnel
Managing Director: *Richard Sims*

Other offices
The company also has offices in Brazil, China, South Africa and the US and has representatives in more than 30 countries worldwide.

Background
Clyde Materials Handling was established in 1974 and its parent company is Clyde Blowers Ltd, UK.

Products
Automated sand filling systems for locomotives and heavy and light rail vehicles.

Consorzio Corifer

Via Borgo Pieve 146, I-31033 Castelfranco Veneto (TV), Italy
Tel: (+39 0423) 42 05 36
Fax: (+39 0423) 72 96 29
e-mail: corifer@corifer.it

Commercial office
Commercial office Via della Fortezza 6, I-50129 Florence, Italy
Tel: (+39 055) 49 97 36
Fax: (+39 055) 44 63 26 59
e-mail: marketing@corifer.it
Web: www.corifer.it

Consortium members
FERVET SpA
Via Borgo Pieve 146, I-31033 Castelfranco Veneto (TV), Italy
Tel: (+39 0423) 42 72
Fax: (+39 0423) 72 01 04
e-mail: segreteria@fervetspa.it

Magliola Antonio & Figli SpA Piazza I° Maggio 1, I-13048 Santhia' (VC), Italy
Tel: (+39 0161) 93 63 11
Fax: (+39 0161) 92 22 62
e-mail: magliola@magliola.it
Web: www.magliola.it

Officine Ferroviarie Veronesi SpA
Lungadige Galtarossa 21, I-37133 Verona, Italy
Tel: (+39 045) 806 41 11   Fax: (+39 045) 806 42 22
e-mail: segreteria@ofv.it
Web: www.ofvspa.it

RSI Italia SpA
Viale IV Novembre 2, I-23845 Costamasnaga (LC), Italy
Tel: (+39 031) 86 94 11   Fax: (+39 031) 85 53 30
Via U Partini 20, I-00159 Rome, Italy
Tel: (+39 06) 43 99 21   Fax: (+39 06) 438 56 91
e-mail: info@railsi.it
Web: www.railsi.com

Background
The Corifer consortium was formed in 2002 by Fervet SpA and Magliola Antonio & Figli SpA. In 2003 Rail Service International SpA and OFV SpA also became members. The mission of the consortium is to: offer refurbishment and construction of rolling stock and related components; coordinate procurement; study and promote common projects; and develop project designs.

Services
Maintenance, overhaul and refurbishment of passenger vehicles and components.

Dawson

Unit 22, Victoria Spring Business Park, Wormald Street, Heckmondwike, West Yorkshire WF15 6RA, UK
Tel: (+44 1924) 41 46 00   Fax: (+44 1924) 41 46 01
e-mail: customerservice@dawson-uk.com
Web: www.dawsonspares.com

Key personnel
Managing Director: *Dennis Tallon*
Project Engineer: *K Dews/Ken Dews*

Background
Dawson is part of the IWKA Pacunion GmbH.

Products
Train washing plant for light rail, underground and main line stock, including brushing systems for sides, roofs, fronts, rears and skirts; water recycling, neutralisation and air knife blowers.

Delaware Car Company

200 North Lombard Street, Wilmington, Delaware 19899, US
Tel: (+1 302) 655 66 65   Fax: (+1 302) 655 71 26

Key personnel
President: *Harry E Hill*
Vice-President, General Manager: *T J Crowley*
Chief Engineer: *J L Winter*
Marketing and Special Projects Engineer: *S F Rogowski*
Mechanical Superintendent: *L J Reed*

Products
Refurbishment, repair and assembly of passenger rolling stock, including metro, suburban and commuter cars. Specialities include stainless steel parts fabrication and bogie repair and overhaul.

Contracts
Current contracts include: Amtrak – repairs to and painting of 40 Acela power cars. Caltrans – structural repair to one Surfliner commuter coach/cafe car. North Carolina DOT – refurbishment of one coach and modification and refurbishment of two lounge cars to lounge/baggage cars. Northern Indiana Commuter Transit District (NICTD) structural repairs to one suburban car.

EDI Rail

2B Factory Street, Granville, New South Wales 2142, Australia
Tel: (+61 2) 96 37 82 88   Fax: (+61 2) 96 37 67 83
e-mail: sales@edirail.com.au
Web: www.edirail.com.au

Key personnel
Chief Executive Officer: *Guy Wannop*
Executive General Manager, Freight: *Danny Broad*
Executive General Manager, Passenger: *David Williamson*

Background
A division of Downer EDI Ltd, EDI Rail is the result of a merger of Clyde Engineering and the rail activities of Walkers Ltd.

Works
EDI Rail has manufacturing, maintenance or design facilities in: Bathurst, Granville, Kooragang Island, Clyde, Cootamundra, Enfield, Eveleigh, Port Kembla and Cardiff, New South Wales; Berrimah, Northern Territory; Kewdale, Port Hedland and Nowergup, Western Australia; Rockhampton, Gladstone, Maryborough, Callemondah, Townsville and Brisbane, Queensland; Newport, West Melbourne and Geelong, Victoria; Port Augusta, Dry Creek, Whyalla, Port Lincoln, South Australia.

Services

EDI Rail's business includes the design, manufacture, refurbishment, overhaul and maintenance of freight and passenger rolling stock, including: diesel-electric locomotives, electric locomotives, electric and diesel multiple-units, rail wagons, traction motors and rolling stock generally.

Contracts

Recent contracts include:

Maintenance over a 10-year period of 11 of EDI Rail's newest locomotive design, the 4300 hp AC standard-gauge locomotive for SCT Victoria. Inclusion into an ongoing maintenance contract with Pacific Nation of an additional four 90 Class and 13 4000 Class locomotives. Inclusion into an ongoing maintenance contract with QR of an additional 11 4000 Class locomotives. Maintenance of FQ Class diesel locomotives and freight rolling stock for Asia Pacific Transport for a 10-year period from the end of 2003.

Maintenance for 15 years of SRA's Millennium emus used on CityRail suburban services in Sydney, with an option to extend the term of the contract to 35 years.

Refurbishment of some 300 Comeng-built emus for M>Train, Melbourne (now Connex Melbourne).

Emanuel srl

Via Marconi 3, I-40011 Anzola Emilia (BO), Italy
Tel: (+39 051) 73 26 52
Fax: (+39 051) 73 40 01
e-mail: info@emanuel1899.com
Web: www.emanuel1899.com

Products

Hydraulic and electro-mechanical lifting systems and equipment for heavy-rail and light-rail vehicles.

Fraunhofer Institute for Non-Destructive Testing

Fraunhofer Institute for Non-Destructive Testing
Fraunhofer Institut Zerstörungsfreie Prüfverfahren
Universität Gebäude 37, D-66123 Saarbrücken, Germany
Tel: (+49 681) 930 20
Fax: (+49 681) 93 02 59 01
e-mail: info@izfp.fhg.de
Web: www.izfp.fhg.de

Key personnel

Managing Director: *Prof Dr Michael Kröning*
Director, Applications Centre: *Dipl-Ing Bernd Rockstroh*
Public Relations: *Dr Eckhardt Schneider*

Products and services

Automated ultrasonic wheelset testing such as test and measurement technology, including specification, design, development and manufacturing and continuing through all service cycles, including operations and maintenance.

Policymakers and the Deutsche Bahn respond to the high density of German business transportation by implementing specific measures to enhance profitability, efficiency, availability and safety of railroad operations, including non-destructive testing of railroad wheels, complete wheelsets and rails.

Gevisa SA

Transit Area, Av Mofarrej, 592 CEP 05311-000, São Paulo SP, Brazil
Tel: (+55 11) 838 25 60; 858 25 03
Fax: (+55 11) 838 25 70; 25 00

Key personnel

Commercial Director: *Ronald H Moriyama*
Transit Division Manager: *Arnaldo Adoglio Júnior*
Marketing Manager: *Mário Calvani*
Director, South American Operations, GE Transportation Systems: *Marcelo Mosci*
Sales Manager: *Carlos E Teixeira*

Background

Gevisa SA is a subsidiary of General Electric.

Services

Rolling stock overhaul and workshop services, including: refurbishment; repair; re-manufacturing and reconstruction; maintenance; painting; supply of spares.

Gevisa SA assembled the General Electric C30 locomotives that were supplied to Sheltam Grindrod in South Africa.

Hegenscheidt-MFD GmbH & Co KG

PO Box 1652/1657, D-41806 Erkelenz, Germany
Tel: (+49 2431) 860   Fax: (+49 2431) 864 66
e-mail: hegenscheidt-mfd@nshgroup.com
Web: www.hegenscheidt-mfd.de

Key personnel

Managing Director: *Dr W Büdenbender*
Head of Sales and Service, Railway Division: *Dr Christian Becker*
Head of Marketing and Turnkey Solution: *Horst Herold*
Head of Sales and Service, Automotive Division: *Daniel Knipping*

Subsidiary

Hegenscheidt-MFD Corporation
6255 Center Drive, Sterling Heights, Michigan 48311-8004, US
Tel: (+1 526) 274 49 00   Fax: (+1 526) 274 49 16

Other offices

Hegenscheidt-MFD GmbH & Co kg also has offices in Australia, China, India, South Africa, The Russian Federation and UK.

Background

Hegenscheidt-MFD GmbH & Co kg is a member of the NSH Machine Tool Group.

Products

Underfloor wheel lathes for machining wheelsets *in situ* or dismantled; mobile wheel lathes; heavy-duty wheel lathes for machining dismantled wheelsets; in-track wheelset diagnostic systems; oil hydraulic rerailing equipment; wheelset mounting and demounting presses; axle lathes; plant and machinery for manufacture of wheels and wheelsets; flexible deep rolling and roll straightening machines for crankshaft machining; thrust face turning and roller burnishing machines for crankshaft machining.

Hyundai Rotem Company

Headquarters
231, Yangjae-dong, Seocho-gu, Seoul, 137-938, Republic of Korea
Tel: (+82 2) 34 64 11 14
Fax: (+82 2) 34 64 75 86
Web: www.hyundai-rotem.co.kr

Key personnel

Executive Vice-Chairman and Chief Executive Officer: *Yeo-Sung Lee*
President and Chief Executive Officer: *Yong-Hoon Lee*
Senior Executive Vice-President and Chief Operating Officer: *Sang-Kil Lee*
Vice-President: *Jae-Hong Kim (R&D centre)*

Background

Established in 1964 when Daewoo Heavy Industry started manufacturing rolling stock, followed by Hyundai Precision & Industry and Hanjin Heavy Industry a few years later. In 1999, the three companies were consolidated into KOROS by the Korean Government. Hyundai Motor Group acquired the share of Daewoo Heavy Industry in October 2001 and KOROS became Rotem Company in January 2002. As of November 2007,

Hyundai Rotem's Korean high-speed train KTX in Busan Depot   1340481

Rotem Company changed its company name and CI to Hyundai Rotem Company. An affiliate of Hyundai Motor Group, Hyundai Rotem Company has its headquarters in Seoul and two facilities, the central research and development centre in Uiwang and the manufacturing plant in Changwon. The Changwon plant has the capability to manufacture 1,000 emus per year and also has the capability to manufacture electrical equipment such as traction motors, SIV inverters etc. Certifications such as the ISO 9001:2000/KS A 9001:2001 for quality, ISO 14001:2004 / KS A 14001:2004 for environment and OHSAS 18001:1999 for occupational health and safety management have been acquired at all three sites.

Services

Logistics systems include the design and construction of turnkey maintenance and overhaul workshops with E&M facilities and computerised maintenance information systems. Hyundai Rotem provides full fleet maintenance services for new and existing rolling stock technology and experience in maintenance service. Hyundai Rotem has a high-level rolling stock availability and reliability for its customer to focus only on key task operations.

Contracts

Hyundai Rotem has completed the manufacture and delivery of Korean high-speed train, KTX (Korean Train Express) and provided maintenance services for KTX to Korea Railroad Corporation (KORAIL) in the Busan Depot.

Hyundai Rotem and Veolia Transport of France agreed to establish a joint venture company, South Link 9 for the maintenance and repair of Seoul Metro Line 9. The companies signed a shareholder's agreement on 2 November 2007.

In August 2008 Hyundai Rotem established a joint venture company Maintrans for performing the maintenance and repair of Seoul Metro Line 9 and others.

Hywema lift-jack model FL VN 16/SA for German Railways (DB) 1174400

HYWEMA Lifting Systems

Wuppertaler Strasse 134-148, D-42653 Solingen, Germany
Tel: (+49 212) 257 70
Fax: (+49 212) 257 71 00
Web: www.hywema.de

Key personnel

General Manager: *G Greupner*
Sales: *R Heidtmann*
Purchase: *G Greupner*

Products

HYWEMA mobile lift jacks for all types of railcars such as LRV's, tramway, subway, metro, wagons and locomotives.

Standard system with four lift jacks from 30 – 160 tonnes or individually for articulated trains with eight, 12, 16 and 32 lift jacks. Universal system model FL-VN for all types of railcars and model FL-N for individual solutions. Different accessories as support stands model AV, assembly work platform model MB and bogie turning device model DW/FL.

Hywema lift-jack in use at DVB-AG's Dresden tramway workshop
1174401

INKA

Address
Head office and factory
T (Persero) Industri Kereta Api (PT INKA)
Jalan Yos Sudarso No 71, Madiun 63122,
Indonesia
Tel: (+62 351) 45 22 71
Fax: (+62 351) 45 22 75
e-mail: sekretariat@inka.web.id
Web: www.inka.web.id

Representative office
Arthaloka building, 3rd Floor, Jalan Jend,
Sudirman Kav 2, Jakarta
Tel: (+62 21) 251 44 24   Fax: (+62 21) 251 44 23
e-mail: inkajkt@cbn.net.id

Key personnel
President: *Ir Roos Diatmoko*
General Manager, Railway Rolling Stock Division:
Suryanto
Finance and Administration Director: *Drs Udin
Supriatman*
General Manager of Technology: *Ir M Harsan
Badawi*
Engineering Manager: *Ir Gunesti Wahyu*
Design Manager: *Ir Indarto Wibisono*
Marketing Manager: *Ir M Dedi Tarmidi*
Business Development Manager: *Ir Muchlis
Budiman*
Procurement Manager: *Soedjito Taathadi*

Background
PT INKA was originally established in 1981 as
a state owned company, transforming from
Indonesian State Railway's steam locomotive
maintenance shop.

Products
Assembly and renovation of freight wagons,
passenger coaches, diesel and electric railcars,
and bogies.
   Locomotives (in collaboration with GE
Transportation). Various special vehicles,
including track motor and inspection cars and
amusement park trains.

InterClean Equipment Inc

3939 Bestech Drive, Ypsilanti, Michigan 48197,
US
Tel: (+1 734) 975 29 67
Fax: (+1 734) 975 16 46
e-mail: sales@interclean.com
Web: www.interclean.com

Key personnel
President: *Mia Lamminen*
Vice-President: *Pasi Kaipainen*

Products
Range of high-pressure automatic vehicle
washing systems; also touchless bus wash, rail
vehicle and locomotive cleaning systems.

---

iQR

Railcentre 1, 305 Edward Street, Brisbane,
Queensland, Australia 4000
GPO Box 1429, Brisbane, Queensland 4001
Tel: (+61 7) 32 32 33 90
Fax: (+61 7) 32 35 33 46
e-mail: sales@iqr.com.au
Web: www.iqr.com.au

Key personnel
General Manager: *Michael Walsh*
Marketing and Business Development Manager:
Peter Harris
Sales Manager: *Youfa Chen*

Maintenance on QR's tilt train   1140311

Background
iQR was previously Queensland Rail Consultancy
Services.

Services
iQR provides maintenance services for rolling
stock, including: locomotives, wagons, passenger
carriages, electric, suburban and interurban
multiple units. All workshops are Quality Certified
to ISO 9002.
   iQR also provides maintenance programmes
that suit specific rollingstock or total system
operations and can assist in the development of
maintenance facilities, including concept, design
and performance specifications.
   Locomotives: iQR can complete the overhaul,
component change out, maintenance and repair
as well as remanufacture back to OEM standards
for diesel electric locomotives. This includes:
de-wheeling and steam cleaning, repair or
replacement of wear surfaces, bushes, springs
and brake systems, complete re-assembly.
   Wagons: modification and maintenance of
all types of wagons, including coal, ore, and
refrigeration containers. Services include:
overhaul, complete component change out, such
as doors, door mechanisms, shedder shields,
couplers and draft gear. Repair of accident
damaged wagons, overhaul of bogies, testing of
airbrakes, state of the art equipment to ensure
component reliability to OEM standards, air
conditioning and refrigeration.

Contracts
Sistem Transit Aliran Ringan Sdn Bhd
(STAR), Malaysia: inspection, testing and
acceptance of 90 sets of light rail vehicles
manufactured at Walkers Ltd, Maryborough
for parts one & two of the Kuala Lumpur STAR
project.
   Westrail (New Metro Rail), Perth Western
Australia: inspection of five new emu two-car
sets of rail passenger vehicles during
manufacture at Walters Ltd, Maryborough.
Inspection of 31 new emu three-car sets, of rail
passenger vehicles during manufacture at EDI
Rail (formerly Walkers Ltd, Maryborough).

Kambre Consulting

Karl-Axel Kambre
Vidarstigen 5, SE-141 39 Huddinge, Sweden
e-mail: ka.kambre@kambre.se
Web: www.kambre.se

Key personnel
Chairman: *Otto Suensson*
Managing Director: *Karl-Axel Kambre*

Principal subsidiaries
Halltoap Gruppen AB

Products
Train washing machines, featuring brush and
brushless washing equipment; specialised
washing machines for cleaning the upper
and lower surfaces of raked train noses; train
interior cleaning systems. Bus maintenance
systems, including washing and interior cleaning
systems.

Alfred Kärcher GmbH & Co KG

Alfred-Kärcher-Strasse   28-40,   D-71364
Winnenden, Germany
Tel: (+49 7195) 140   Fax: (+49 7195) 14 22 12
e-mail: info@kaercher.com
Web: www.kaercher.com

Key personnel
Managing Directors: *Hartmut Jenner, George
Metz, Dr Bernhard Graf*

Subsidiaries
Karcher (UK) Ltd
Karcher House, Beaumont Road, Banbury, Oxon
OX16 1TB, UK
Tel: (+44 1295) 75 20 82   Fax: (+44 1295) 75 21 03
e-mail: enquiries@karcher.co.uk

Products
Kärcher manufactures high pressure cleaners
such as the CHH 8000 OptiWash. The product

Fully automated washing plant for DB AG ICE high-speed trainsets installed by Kärcher at Frankfurt/Höchst 0103637

range includes vacuum cleaners, steam cleaners, cleaning robots, sweepers, scrubber-driers, cleaning agents, brush-type vehicle washers and water treatment plants.

Services
Project planning, architecture, implementation and turnkey handover. Kärcher offers assistance with financing issues.

Končar – Electric Vehicles Inc

Velimira Škorpika 7, HR-10090 Zagreb, Croatia
Tel: (+385 1) 349 69 59, 349 69 50
Fax: (+385 1) 349 69 60
e-mail: uprava@koncar-kev.hr; info@koncar-kev.hr
Web: www.koncar-kev.hr

Key personnel
President: *Ivan Bahun*
Director of Development and Sales: *Jusuf Crnalić*
Head of Marketing and Sales: *Tomica Kolman*

Background
Founded in Zagreb in 1970 and a member of Končar Group, Končar – Electric Vehicles Inc designs, manufactures, repairs, rebuilds and refurbishes electric rail vehicles and vehicle equipment.

In January 2008, the company received ISO 14001:2004 certification for its Environmental Protection Management System.

Services
Manufacture, repair, reconstruction, refurbishment and modernisation of electric rail vehicles.

Contracts
In March 2008, Končar – Electric Vehicles Inc and Makedonski železnici Transport ad Skopje signed a contract for the repair and modernisation of

two MŽ 461 series locomotives. This follows on from previous projects to refurbish three MŽ 442 electric locomotives in 2001/2002.

Lloyds Somers

Atlas house, 4/6 Belwell Lane, Four Oaks, Sutton Coldfield, West Midlands B74 4AB, UK
Tel: (+44 121) 569 12 50
Fax: (+44 121) 569 12 52
e-mail: enquiries@somers-handling.co.uk
Web: www.lloydsbritish.com

Transit jacking bogie system supplied by Somers Railway Engineering to Alstom 0105893

Key personnel
Director: *Stephen Reece*
Sales Manager: *Alec Foley*

Background
Lloyds Somers is a division of Lloyds British Testing Ltd.

Products
Mobile and fixed rail vehicle lifting jacks; traversers; scissor lift tables; bogie rotators; bogie drop systems; bogie turntables; bogie turning systems; rail drop systems; all types of workshop equipment.

Marmac

The Marmac Company
PO Box 157, Xenia, Ohio 45385, US
Tel: (+1 937) 372 80 93   Fax: (+1 937) 372 71 01
Web: www.marmacco.com

Key personnel
Executive Vice President: *Sharon M Walthall*
President: *Gary D Walthall*

Products
Heavy-duty hydraulic lifting equipment.

Mechan Ltd

Thorncliffe Park, Chapeltown, Sheffield S35 2PH, UK
Tel: (+44 114) 257 05 63   Fax: (+44 114) 245 11 24
e-mail: info@mechan.co.uk
Web: www.mechan.co.uk

Key personnel
Managing Director: *Richard Carr*
Financial Director: *Zahir Altaf*
Sales Director: *Graham Cofield*
Technical Director: *Christian Fletcher*

Background
In August 2007, Mechan Ltd was subject to a management buyout.

The company will continue to operate from its current premises with a relocation scheduled in 2009.

Products
Depot maintenance equipment for the rail industry including bogie drop systems and wheel drop systems; rail vehicle lifting jacks with the following capacities: six- and 10-tonne jacks for trams, metro/light rail and underground trains, 15- and 20-tonne jacks for rail coaches and multiple-units and 25- and 35-tonne jacks for locomotives and on-track plant.

Contracts
During 2006, Mechan completed and commissioned a contract for Siemens at its new Northampton and Manchester Traincare facilities in the UK. This comprised of new intelligent low profile bogie drop/change units with the latest distributed control system and remote diagnostics, a depot personnel protection system linked to Mechan Depot Manager™, and an information retrieval system, which displays the depot status on a plasma screen in the supervisor's office.

Metronet REW Ltd

130 Bollo Lane, Acton, London W3 8BZ, UK
Tel: (+44 20) 79 18 55 25
Fax: (+44 20) 79 18 65 99
e-mail: ian.ferguson@metronetrail.com
Web: www.metronetrail.com

25 kV Class E52 Bo-Bo electric locomotive refurbished for Turkish State Railways 1176860

Background

A subsidiary of Metronet Rail SSL Ltd, REW has 75 years' experience in rolling stock and signal equipment maintenance.

In July 2007 the company announced that it is to enter voluntary administration.

Services

Repair and overhaul of railway compressors and control systems, traction motors including on- and off-site capability for all railway equipment, electronics, clocks and passenger seating, signalling equipment, wheelsets and gearboxes.

MotivePower Inc

4600 Apple Street, Boise, Idaho 83716, US
Tel: (+1 208) 947 48 00   Fax: (+1 208) 947 48 20
e-mail: motivepowerinc@wabtec.com
Web: www.motivepower-wabtec.com

Key personnel

Vice-President and General Manager: *Mark S Warner*

Background

MotivePower Inc is a subsidiary company of Wabtec Corporation, the latter created in 1999 as a result of the 1999 merger of Westinghouse Air Brake Co and MotivePower Industries Inc.

Services

Locomotive overhauls; fleet maintenance; frame and body fabrication and collision repairs; locomotive remanufacturing; electrical upgrades; locomotive testing.

NedTrain

PO Box 2167, KTT-9, NL-3500 GD Utrecht, Netherlands
Tel: (+31 30) 300 46 01   Fax: (+31 30) 300 46 48
e-mail: info@nedtrain.nl
Web: www.nedtrain.nl

Key personnel

Chief Executive Officer: *J P B Huberts*
Director Business and Development: *A J M Spaninks*
Financial Director: *G Taute*

Subsidiary companies

NedTrain Consulting
PO Box 2016-KTT 6, NL-3500 GA Utrecht, Netherlands
Tel: (+31 30) 300 47 00
Fax: (+31 30) 300 48 00

Ematech
PO Box 8093, NL-3503 RB Utrecht, Netherlands
Tel: (+31 30) 246 91 60
Fax: (+31 30) 246 91 76

Background

NedTrain supports operators and owners of rolling stock during the entire life cycle of their fleets, optimising performance.

Services

Service and maintenance, upgrading and overhauling, refurbishment, consulting, components and damage repair of railway rolling stock, both passenger and freight. Refurbishment, overhaul, modification and damage repair of rolling stock. Refurbishment and overhaul of rolling stock systems and components, including bogies, wheelsets, traction motors, brake components and automatic couplers.

Contracts

Contracts include the maintenance and service of NS Reizigers, NS International, Syntus and NoordNed passenger rolling stock and maintenance of Railion locomotives. Other contracts include major refurbishment and upgrading projects of NS Reizigers rolling stock, modification of GM (class 66) locomotives and maintenance and overhaul of freight wagons for DB Cargo, VTG, AAE, GE Capital, GATX.

Nencki AG

Anlagen und Fahrzeugbau, Gaswerkstrasse 27, CH-4901 Langenthal, Switzerland
Tel: (+41 62) 919 93 93   Fax: (+41 62) 919 93 90
e-mail: info@nencki.ch
Web: www.nencki.ch

Key personnel

Chief Executive Officer: *Rolf Loosli*
Sales Managers: *Andreas Gerber, Walter Kellenberger*

Products

Testing equipment including: bogie presses and test stands, spring test presses, wheel weighing facilities. Lifting systems consisting of: bogie and wheelset lifting and exchanging platforms for paint cabins. Machinery for rail welding plants and switch and crossing assemblies including: rail end brushing machines, stationary straightening presses with integrated laser measuring system, rail profile grinding machines, test presses for welded rail joints, mobile rail and switch tongue straightening presses.

Neuero Technology GmbH

Neuerostrasse 1, D-49324 Melle, Germany
Tel: (+49 5422) 60 70   Fax: (+49 5422) 60 72 10
e-mail: info@neuero-tec.de
Web: www.neuero-tec.de

Key personnel

Managing Director: *Dipl Ing Bernhard Uhlen*
Sales Directors: *Dipl Ing Kurt Holtgräfe, Dipl Ing Heinrich Wöstefeld, Dipl Ing Heiko Schäffer, Dipl Ing Hagen Thiel*

Products

Lifting jacks; underfloor lifting plants; bogie repair hoists; lifting platform trucks and lifting tables; dismantling devices for wheelsets and bogies; turntables; auxiliary bogies; lifting and turning devices; test- and measuring benches for bogies; stationary and movable working platforms; shunting vehicles; traversers; washing plants; storage systems.

Contracts

Recent contracts include: different lifting equipment for RAJA, Iran; different lifting equipment for Hyundi ROTEM, Korea; different lifting equipment for Dubai Municipality Green Line, Dubai; underfloor lifting equipment for Metro North, New York; elevated tracks and stationary roof working platforms for DB, Germany; liftable side- and roof working platforms for DB, Germany; movable side- and roof working platforms for DB Germany; complete equipment for High Speed Workshop St. Petersburg, Russia; bogies testing equipment for IRICO, Iran; lifting equipment for South Africa; different lifting equipment and turntables for KTMB, Malaysia; underfloor lifting equipment for Metro Shenyang, China.

NEU International Railways

70 rue du Collège, PO Box 4039, F-4039 Marcq en Baroeul, France
Tel: (+33 3) 20 45 65 09   Fax: (+33 3) 20 45 65 55
e-mail: railways@neu-railways.com
Web: www.neu-railways.com

Twin sand pump for Ferromex, Manzanillo, Mexico to fill high capacity sand boxes   1033688

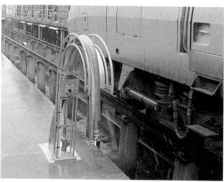

CET Installation for SNCF at Châtillon, France for TGV trains   1033690

NEU International Railway's train washing plant   1033687

Other offices

NEU Inc
PO Box 488, Paoli, Pennsylvania 19301-0488, US
Tel: (+1 610) 725 04 01   Fax: (+1 610) 725 04 02
e-mail: mail@neu-inc.com

Products

NEU International Railways develops specific solutions for safety, cleanliness and reliability of all types of railway networks and depots (train, tramway, metro).

Equipment for depots
Sand distribution systems for clean and automatic feeding of all types of train sandboxes, fixed sand pumps or mobile unit, platform or overhead installation. CET installation to empty chemical and/or retention toilet tanks, fixed installation or mobile unit. Train wash facility for all types of train including drvie through or gantry systems. Completely modular and expandable construction with total or partial water recycling.

NEU International Rail's Vaktrak cleaning train for the Munich metro   1033689

Track cleaning

Vaktrak for track cleaning in stations and tunnels, based on patented technology for the combined suck/blow system, specially designed for underground metro networks. The number, size and position of these modules are designed to match the required working configuration. The Vaktrak rail/road unit has been designed for light rail tracks, stations, tunnels or outside, on ballast, on concerete slab with grooved rail or on sleepers.

Pars nova as

Žerotíinova 1833/56, CZ-787 01 Šumperk, Czech Republic
Tel: (+420 583) 36 51 11
Fax: (+420 583) 36 54 10
e-mail: pars@parsnova.cz
Web: www.parsnova.cz

Key personnel
General Manager: *Ing Tomáš Ignačák*

Background
Formerly the State Railways workshops of the former Czechoslovak State Railways, Pars nova commenced commercial activities in 1993 as Pars DMN sro Sumperk, which at this time, remained state-owned. The current name was adopted in August 2000, when Pars nova became a joint-stock company.

Services
Modernisation, refurbishment, overhaul and crash repair of: diesel locomotives; electric locomotives; dmus; railcars; trams and light rail vehicles, passenger coaches and inspection and maintenance vehicles. Overhaul and repair of: diesel engines; electric traction equipment; wheelsets; batteries.

PESA Bydoszcz SA

Zygmunta Augusta 11 Street, PL-85-082 Bydgoszcz
Tel: (+48 52) 339 11 04
Fax: (+48 52) 339 11 14
e-mail: pesa@pesa.pl
Web: www.pesa.pl

Key personnel
President and General Director: *Tomasz Zaboklicki*
Directors:
   Production and Technical: Zenon Duszynski
   Marketing and Development: *Zygfryd Zurawski*
   Financial: *Robert Swiechowicz*
   Proxy Deputy Director and Head of Production:
      Andrzej Karwasz
   Head of Marketing, Passenger Coaches:
      Jerzy Berg
   Head of Development: *Andrzej Ciupa*

Background
PESA Bydoszcz SA formerly traded as ZNTK Bydoszcz SA.

Services
Modernisation, refurbishment and repair of diesel locomotives, passenger coaches, trams and freight wagons.

Pfaff-silberblau Verkehrstechnik GmbH & Co KG

Am Silberpark 2-8, D-86438 Kissing, Germany
Tel: (+49 8233) 21 21 45 00
Fax: (+49 8233) 21 21 45 55
e-mail: verkehrstechnik@pfaff-silberblau.de
Web: www.pfaff-silberblau.de

Key personnel
Managing Director: *Peter Zeller*
Chief Engineer: *Rudolf Eichner*

Background
Pfaff-silberblau has over 140 years experience in the industry and is recognised for its range of lifting equipment.
   Pfaff-silberblau Verkehrstechnik is the specialist within the group for executing turnkey projects for its clients within the railway industry.

Products
Lifting systems and jacks for rail vehicles. Lifting systems are available for rail vehicles (trams, metros, railways) built to the customer's specification and to the loading capacity required. The systems are fully lowerable to below ground level. The lifting of different types of vehicles of various lengths can be achieved by means of one lifting arrangement.
   Standard duty lifting jacks are produced with capacities from 5,000 to 10,000 kg. Heavy duty lifting jacks are produced with capacities from 10,000 to 50,000 kg. Direct drive to the spindle is by a worm gear reduction box with automatic lubrication system. These lifting jacks can be delivered stationary, mobile on concrete floor, or on a manually or electrically driven auxiliary rail system, with fixed or mobile load supports.
   Also supplied: lifting-turning devices, underfloor bogie- and wheelset lowering systems (drop tables), accommodation bogies, rescue bogies, bogie disassembly wagons, bogie handling systems, turntables, hydraulic lifting tables, working platforms and spinning posts.

Pfaff-silberblau Verkehrstechnik lifting system   1328193

Contracts
Lifting jacks and underfloor lifting installations have been installed in Algeria, Australia, Belgium, Canada, Chile, China, Denmark, France, Germany, Greece, Hong Kong, India, Ireland, Italy, Japan, Korea, Lithuania, Malaysia, Netherlands, Portugal, South Africa, Spain, Taiwan, Turkey, UK and the US.

Planet Platforms

Brunel Close, Century Park, Wakefield 41 Industrial Estate, Wakefield, WF2 0XG, UK
Tel: (+44 0800) 085 41 61
e-mail: info@planetplatforms.co.uk
Web: www.planetplatforms.co.uk

Key personnel
Marketing Manager: *Tim Mee*

Background
Established in 1977, Planet Platforms manufactures and distributes work place access solutions.

Products/Services
Aluminium towers, glass reinforced plastic towers, access machines, low-level access products and custom access solutions. The company provides a number of safety inspection and 'working at height' training programmes.

Contracts
Supply of access system to First Bus that is being used for the painting, maintenance and general upkeep of their buses.

Planet Platforms 'work at height' system, installed at the First Bus' Leeds depot   1373827

Proceco Ltd

Head office
7300 Tellier Street, Montreal QC H1N 3T7, Canada
Tel: (+1 514) 254 84 94   Fax: (+1 514) 254 81 84
e-mail: cleaning@proceco.com
Web: www.proceco.com

Proceco's automatic cleaning of locomotives, transit and passenger bogies   1322832

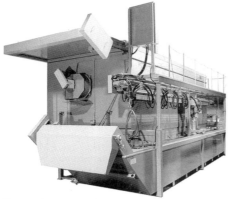

Proceco's automatic cleaning of locomotive engine blocks and bogies   1322831

Key personnel
Chief Marketing/Marketing Manager: *Chantal Rousseau*

Products
Water based parts washers, degreasers and cleaning machinery for items such as bogies, diesel engine components, wheelsets, bearings etc.

Locomotive traction motor and main generator (alternator) spray washing and vacuum drying system.

Railquip Inc

3731 Northcrest Road, Suite 6, Atlanta, Georgia 30340, US
Tel: (+1 770) 458 41 57; (+1 800) 325 02 96
Fax: (+1 770) 458 53 65
e-mail: sales@railquip.com
Web: www.railquip.com

Key personnel
President: *Helmut Schroeder*
Sales Director: *Paul Wojcik*
Sales Manager: *Denis Zulfic*
Treasurer and Office Manager: *Debbie Fox*

Products
Maintenance equipment for railcar and locomotive workshops; portable hydraulic rerailing equipment and containers; underfloor and above-ground car hoists; body stands; turntables; spinning posts; bogie assembly and test stands; emergency truck for locked axles; mobile train wash; power lift bags; compressed air stations; wheel presses and wheel lathes; mechanical wheel handlers; railcar movers; mobile and stationary waste removal systems; hydraulic track jacks; road/rail-equipped trailers; stationary roof and car access platforms; mobile roof and car access platforms; bogie hoists; transfer tables.

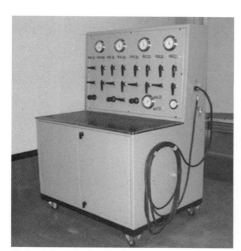

Railquip's airbrake test bench   1209421

Railquip's transit railcar mover   1209425

Contracts
Recent contracts include: maintenance equipment for Metro North Commuter Railroad Company, Harmon Yard Phase III Shop, six sets of car hoists and body stands, 11 turntable, New York. Maintenance equipment for Capital Metropolitan Transportation Authority, Austin, Texas – one set of eight electrically powered spindle jacks, movable on concrete floor, one fueling station, one stationary roof access platform. Dulles Automatic People Mover, Chantilly, Virginia: one 18,000 lb forklift truck, gantry cranes, bogie stands, bogie repair jigs and other maintenance equipment. Hartsfield-Jackson Atlanta Airport, Atlanta, Georgia: maintenance equipment for people mover. Washington Metropolitan Area Transit Authority, Washington DC: one set of 16 electrically powered spindle jacks, movable on concrete floor. Maintenance equipment for ALSTOM Transportation, Hornell, New York: two sets of 16 electrically powered spindle jacks. Utah Transit, Salt Lake City, Utah: one set of rerailing equipment, one fleetcleaner mobile train wash. Charlotte Area Transit System: one set of rerailing equipment. Canadian National Railroad: portable hydraulic rerailing equipment. Trinity Heads Inc: one Maxi railcar mover. Dulles Airport Facility. Maintenance equipment for Utah Transit. Valley Metro Rail, Phoenix, Arizona: one set of re-railing equipment. Exxon Mobile: one Maxi railcar mover. Utah Transit, Salt Lake City, Utah: two auxiliary trucks. TA San Diego, California: one set of re-railing equipment. Charlotte Area Transit System, Charlotte: one set of re-railing equipment. Canadian National Railroad: portable hydraulic re-railing equipment. Trinity Heads Inc: one Maxi railcar mover.

Railway Projects Limited (RPL)

Lisbon House, 5-7 St Mary's Gate, Derby DE1 3JA, UK
Tel: (+44 1332) 34 92 55   Fax: (+44 1332) 29 46 88
e-mail: sales@railwayprojects.co.uk
Web: www.railwayprojects.co.uk

Key personnel
Managing Director: *Ian Duffy*
Financial Director: *Sue Llanos*
Engineering Director: *Jim Thomson*
Production Director: *Jeremy Ward*
Sales and Marketing Director: *Kelvin Roberts*

Services
Railway Projects Limited is an engineering services company offering a turnkey approach for rolling stock maintenance, refurbishment, modification, overhaul and installation projects. RPL specialises in on-site working and is ISO 9002 certified and Link Up approved.

Ravaglioli SpA

Via I Maggio 3, I-40037 Sasso Marconi, Bologne, Italy
Tel: (+39 051) 678 15 11   Fax: (+39 051) 84 63 49
e-mail: rav@ravaglioli.com
Web: www.ravaglioli.com

Subsidiaries
Companies in France, Germany, Spain, UK and USA.

Products
Lifting equipment for rail and road vehicles, including mobile column lifts, scissor lifts, four-post lifts; tyre changers; wheel balancers; cranes; presses; brake testing equipment, underground piston lifts, wheel alignment systems.

Contracts
Include various equipment supplied to transport organisations in Paris, Singapore, Hong Kong, Taipei, Berlin, Calgary, Rome, Bordeaux, Milan and Strasbourg.

Revatec Kambre AB

Engelska Vägen 3B, SE-393 54 Kalmer, Sweden
Tel: (+46 480) 36 25 00   Fax: (+46 480) 49 05 90
e-mail: revatec@revatec.se
Web: www.revatec.se

Key personnel
Chairman: *Christer Nordström*
Managing Director: *Olof Nordstöm*

Background
Previously called Kambre AB, the business was sold and became Revatec AB.

Products
Train washing machines, featuring brush and brushless washing equipment; specialised washing machines for cleaning the upper and lower surfaces of raked train noses; train interior cleaning systems. Bus maintenance systems, including washing and interior cleaning systems.

Rocafort Ingenieros SL

C/Ciencia 25, Pol Ind El Regàs, E-08850 Gavà (Barcelona), Spain
Tel: (+34 93) 633 39 10   Fax: (+34 93) 662 94 50
e-mail: rocafort@rocafort.net
Web: http://rocafort.net

Key personnel
President, General Manager: *Gerardo Rocafort*
Deputy General Manager: *Gerardo Gállego*
Technical Manager: *Daniel Dedieu*
Export Manager: *José Cañelles*

Affiliated company
PMS SA, Avenida Esplugas 77, E-08034 Barcelona, Spain
Tel: (+34 93) 205 10 11   Fax: (+34 93) 203 41 00
e-mail: pms@pms.es

Services
Supply of equipment for railway vehicles: bogies, coupling and traction systems, brakes, electric and explosion motors, hydraulic transmissions, traction converters, static converters, gear regulators, air conditioning equipment, door mechanisms and vacuum WCs.

Projects for new layouts, renewal and signalling of the rail track, communications and supply of materials.

Ross & White Company

1090 Alexander Court, PO Box 970, Cary, Illinois 60013-0970, USA
Tel: (+1 847) 516 39 00
Fax: (+1 847) 516 39 89
e-mail: sales@rossandwhite.com
Web: www.rossandwhite.com

Ross & White Company pressure washing equipment   0125199

Key personnel
President: *Jeffery A Ross*
Vice-President: *Roy A Schuetz*

Products
Design, manufacture and installation of train washing and companion water reclamation systems; sand handling equipment; Buck Cyclone cleaners for passenger coach interiors; brush scrubbing and pressure washing equipment for passenger coach exteriors.

Contracts
Include the installation of a coach washing facility for Metra, USA; development and installation of a car progression train washing system for Chicago Transit Authority, USA; development and installation of a gantry-type moving washing system for Chicago Transit Authority; design, supply and installation of a three-lane train washing system for MBTA, USA; and design and installation of six-train washing systems for WMATA, USA.

SAFOP SpA

Corso L Zanussi 55, I-33080 Porcia (PN), Italy
Tel: (+39 0434) 59 77 11
Fax: (+39 0434) 92 25 83
e-mail: safop@safop.com
Web: www.safop.com

Products
Wheelset reprofiling systems, including: underfloor lathes; single and tandem lathes; portal and universal lathes.

SEFAC SA

1 rue André Compain, BP 101, F-08800 Monthermé, France
Tel: (+33 3) 24 53 01 82
Fax: (+33 3) 24 53 29 18
e-mail: commercial@sefac.fr
Web: www.sefac.fr

Key personnel
President: *Emmanuel de Rohan Chabot*
Engineering Manager: *Eric Letellier*
Sales Manager: *Vincent Jolliot*

Subsidiaries
SEFAC UK Ltd
Unit F 1D – NK2 Business Centre, Barton Road, Water Eaton, Bletchley MK2 3HU, UK
Tel: (+44 1908) 82 12 74   Fax: (+44 1908) 82 12 75
e-mail: info@sefac-lift.co.uk
Web: www.sefac-lift.co.uk
Manager: *F Lacoste*

SEFAC SA
Camino de Rejas, Nave 10, E-28820 Coslada, Spain
Tel: (+34 91) 672 36 12   Fax: (+34 91) 672 33 96
e-mail: commercial@sefac.es
Manager: *P Maigre*

Products
Electromechanical lifting systems with mobile columns, capacity per column from five to 30 tonnes. SEFAC lifting systems allow the lifting of power cars, Trams, LRVs, trainsets and wagons, as well as bus, coaches and heavy duty vehicles for maintenance work to be carried out.

Additionally, SEFAC can provide central vacuum cleaning services, Nettotram and Nettobus, for both tramways and buses.

Contracts
Contracts include the supply of lifting systems to railway operators including SNCF, SNTF, SNCB; metro operators in Paris, Rotterdam, Cairo, Tokyo, Toulouse, Rennes, Nice, Lyon, Marseille; and to rolling stock manufacturers including ALSTOM, Bombardier and Siemens.

Developments
SEFAC has developed a specific lifting system for trams.

Siemens AG

Mobility
Integrated Services Division
Sieboldstrasse 16, D-91052 Erlangen, Germany
Tel: (+49 9131) 72 38 12
Fax: (+49 9131) 72 11 63
e-mail: service.ts@siemens.com
Web: www.transportation.siemens.com

Corporate Headquarters
Siemens AG
Moiblity
PO Box 3240, D-91050 Erlangen, Germany
Tel: (+49 9131) 7-0

Key personnel
Chief Financial Officer, Industry: *Ralf P Thomas*
Chief Executive Officer, Mobility: *Michael Schulz-Drost*

Services
Integrated Services was established in December 1999, offering service and maintenance provision for: rolling stock; infrastructure; signalling and communications systems; and power supply systems.

Rolling stock service provision includes: routine vehicle maintenance; spare parts supply; and bogie overhaul. Infrastructure service provision includes: maintenance; spare parts supply; and diagnostic services. The Charter Rail service is based on using the customer's own staff, which are sub-contracted at a fixed price, with Siemens assuming responsibility for maintenance

SEFAC's vehicle lifting system   1345356

planning, spares provision and services with guaranteed costs and availability.

Integrated Services also offers consulting, training and documentation.

Contracts

Current contracts include:

Argentina: rolling stock maintenance for Metrovías, Buenos Aires, providing maintenance and refurbishment of 16 four-section vehicles.

Australia: Siemens received contracts from National Express Group Australia covering full service provision for 59 Combino five-and three-section Melbourne Swanston Combino LRVs from 2003 to 2019 and 62 three-car Melbourne Bayside metro trains from 2003 to 2021. The franchise has since been taken over by Connex Trains Melbourne.

Brazil: In December 2002, Siemens concluded an agreement with Companhia de Trens Metropolitanos (CPTM), São Paulo, to provide maintenance services for 10 Class S3000 emus for five years.

Czech Republic: In September 2004, Siemens signed a Memorandum of Understanding with the Prague transit authorities covering the maintenance of 48 Type M1 metro trains for a period of 14-years. The fleet includes six trains which were delivered by Siemens in 2005-06.

Denmark: From January 2003, Siemens took over complete maintenance of 13 Class EG 3100 25 kV/15 kV AC electric freight locomotives operated by Railion Denmark. The contract, which initially runs for five years with an option for a one-year extension, includes a 'Mobile Service' facility which provides for maintenance and service of the locomotives when they operate outside Denmark.

Egypt: Siemens is responsible for the maintenance of Egyptian National Railways' 350 km Cairo-Baharya freight line, covering track, signalling and communications systems.

Hungary: In conjunction with a contract to supply 40 Combino low-floor trams to the Budapest urban transport authority, BKV, Siemens concluded a two-year agreement to provide maintenance services following the vehicles' delivery in 2005-06.

India: In February 2003, Siemens took over the maintenance of traction converters and traction control units (Siemens' scope of supply) for 31 GT46 six-axle diesel-electric locomotives operated by Indian Railways.

Poland: In January 2003, Siemens announced a Charter Rail 12-year agreement to provide maintenance services for 14 Combino trams that it was to supply to MPK, Poznan, from November 2003. The contract includes a five-year extension option.

Russia: In April 2007, Siemens signed a contract with Russian Railways (RZD), to assume responsibility for the complete maintenance of the Velaro RUS high-speed trains for a period of 30-years.

Spain: Under a contract signed in July 2001 Siemens is to be responsible for the maintenance for 14 years of 16 new Velaro E high-speed trainsets which the company is to supply for RENFE's 625 km Madrid-Barcelona line.

Under a five-year agreement with Spanish National Railways, Siemens is responsible for substations serving the 471 km Madrid Seville high-speed line, and for maintenance of the power supply and telecommunications systems.

Thailand: Having supplied and equipped the 23.1 km BTS mass transit system in Bangkok, Siemens is responsible for maintenance, covering 35 metro vehicles, track, signalling, operations control systems, power supply, safety systems, stations and all technical equipment for the period 2000-10.

As part of a turnkey contract Siemens is to maintain for 10 years the Bangkok Blue Line of Bangkok Metro Co Ltd, which commenced operations in 2004.

UK: In August 2004, Siemens received a contract from National Express Group (NEG) (fleet since taken over by Govia) covering maintenance and spare parts supply for 20-years for 30 Class 350/1

Desiro emus employed on commuter services at the southern end of the West Coast Main Line. The contract also covers the creation of a new depot at Northampton. In May 2004, Siemens was awarded a contract by NEG to maintain 21 Desiro UK Class 360 emus for seven years with a possible extension for three more years. The trains are operated by NEG's National Express East Anglia franchise. Maintenance will be undertaken at Ilford, East London.

Siemens has secured rolling stock maintenance contracts for several other urban and main line operators in the UK. These include: Arriva Trains Northern, servicing Class 333 emus supplied by Siemens, using a depot in Leeds (now Northern Rail); Heathrow Express, for which Siemens constructed and operates a dedicated depot in West London to maintain the operator's fleet of Siemens-supplied Class 332 emus; South Yorkshire Supertram, maintaining 25 trams at a purpose-built depot in Sheffield. In addition, Siemens has a 20-year contract starting in 2003 covering the maintenance of a fleet of 665 Desiro Class 444 and 450 emu cars being supplied to South West Trains. This is being undertaken at a depot at Southampton commissioned in 2003.

In October 2004 Heathrow Express renewed its contract with Siemens to cover maintenance of its fleet until 2023.

Other orders for infrastructure and rolling stock maintenance services form part of turnkey contracts, detailed in the *Turnkey systems contractors* section.

Simmons

Simmons Machine Tool Corporation
1700 North Broadway, Albany, New York 12204, US
Tel: (+1 518) 462 54 31   Fax: (+1 518) 462 03 71
e-mail: smt@smtgroup.com
Web: www.smtgroup.com

Key personnel
Chairman and Chief Executive: *Hans J Naumann*
President: *John O Naumann*
Finance Director: *David A Simonian*

Subsidiaries
Simmons-Stanray Wheel Truing Machine Corporation
  (address as above)

Affiliated company
Niles-Simmons Industrieanlagen GmbH
Zwickauer Strasse 355, D-09117 Chemnitz, Germany

Background
Simmons Machine Tool Corporation was founded in 1910 and is a member of the NSH Group.

Products
Design and manufacture of equipment and machines for manual and automated railway and transit wheel workshops, including: underfloor wheel profiling machines; special machines for wheel, axle and wheelset maintenance; CNC grinding centres; CNC vertical turning and boring centres. Simmons also provides engineering design and layout services for complete wheel shops.

Smith Bros & Webb Ltd

Britannia Works, Arden Forest Industrial Estate, Alcester, Warwickshire B49 6EX, UK
Tel: (+44 1789) 40 00 96   Fax: (+44 1789) 40 02 31
e-mail: info@vehicle-washing-systems.co.uk
Web: www.vehicle-washing-systems.co.uk

Key personnel
Managing Director: *John P Bennett*

Technical Manager: *Antoni Sozanski*
Business Development Manager – Rail: *Mark Prockter*

Products
Britannia automatic washing systems for all rail applications; main line, light rail and tram systems. Options available include: a range of detergent/chemical application modules; front, rear, roof, eaves, valence and skirt washing; blow-drying; pure water final rinse; train speed indication; water recycling and effluent treatment. Worldwide after-sales support offered.

Recent contracts include train washing installations for Channel Tunnel Rail Link, Severn Valley Railway (preserved railway), Dubai Metro, Northern Rail, Gautrain South Africa, KTMB Malaysia and TTI Airport Access Taiwan.

Sogema Engineering

Zone Industrielle Roubaix Est, Rue de la Papinerie, BP 62, F-59452 Lys Lez Lannoy, Cedex, France
Tel: (+33 3) 20 66 10 70   Fax: (+33 3) 20 66 10 71
e-mail: contact@sogema-engineering.com
Web: www.sogema-engineering.com

Products
Bogie and wheelset maintenance equipment, including: bogie presses; wheel presses; test benches; bogie turning equipment; bearing removal tools; spring calibration presses; and wheelset measuring benches.

Spedition Kübler GmbH (Kübler Spedition)

Neubergstrasse 19, D-74523 Schwäbisch Hall, Germany
Tel: (+49 791) 93 00 00   Fax: (+49 791) 930 00 12
e-mail: info@kuebler-spedition.de
Web: www.kuebler-spedition.de

Services
Transport of rail vehicles with specialised fleet of road haulage vehicles.

SSI North America Incorporated

235 W Florence Ave, Inglewood, California 90301, US
Tel: (+1 866) 465 (toll free)   Fax: (+1 310) 673 02 76
e-mail: info@ssiwashsystems.com
Web: www.ssiwash.com

Key personnel
President: *Christian Bernert*

Products
Modular train bus and track washing systems; vehicle interior vacuum cleaning systems; dryers.

Üstra Hannoversche Verkhersbetriebe AG

Postfach 25 40, D-30025 Hannover, Germany
Tel: (+49 511) 166 80   Fax: (+49 511) 16 68 26 66
Web: www.uestra.de

Key personnel
Chairman: *André Neiss*

Background
Üstra is one of the operators of Hanover's public transport system. Its workshops offer services commercially to other urban and main line

rail operators and to vehicle and subsystems manufacturers.

Services
Rail vehicle inspection, maintenance, overhaul, refurbishment, subsystems assembly and overhaul.

Contracts
Transport operators featuring in Üstra's list of customers include: BVG, Berlin; Stadtwerke Bielefeld; VGF, Frankfurt am Main. Manufacturer clients include: Alstom LHB; Bombardier Transportation; Siemens; and ZF Hurth Bahntechnik.

STT

Swedish Train Technology
Gölgatan, SE-571 34 Nässjö, Sweden
Tel: (+46 380) 51 43 50   Fax: (+46 380) 51 43 67
e-mail: info@stt-train.se
Web: www.stt-train.se

Key personnel
Managing Director: *Magnus Enstroem*
Marketing Manager: *Leif Mattsson*

Background
Swedish Train Technology is a privately owned company which was originally founded in 1923 as BK Transport. It became STT, a workshop for railcars, in 1990 and STT Swedish Train Technology was founded in 2003 to further develop the rail business into an engineering company.

Services
Overhaul and maintenance of major rail vehicle components and subsystems, including engines, gearboxes and bogies. Operations are primarily based at a component centre workshop in Sävsjö.

System Chassijet Ltd

348 Spon Lane South, West Bromwich, West Midlands B70 6AZ, UK
Tel: (+44 08 45) 053 02 20   Fax: (+44 08 45) 053 02 21
e-mail: sales@systemchassijet.com
Web: www.systemchassijet.com

Key personnel
Managing Directors: *Martin Barker, Mark Read, Nigel Bache*

Products
Vehicle washing systems, and automated chassis cleaning equipment.

Transtech Oy

Elektroniikkatie 2, FIN-90570 Oulu, Finland
Tel: (+358 8) 870 69 00   Fax: (+358 8) 870 69 70
e-mail: sales@talgo.fi
Web: www.talgo.fi

Key personnel
Chairman: *Curt Lindborn*
Managing Director: *Markku Blomberg*
Sales Director: *Matti Haapakangas*
Sales Manager: *Matti Asikainen*

Services
Rail vehicle refurbishment.

Ultrasonic Sciences Ltd

Unit 4 Springlakes Industrial Estate, Deadbrook Lane, Aldershot, Hants, GU12 4UH, UK
Tel: (+44 1252) 35 05 50   Fax: (+44 1252) 35 04 45

e-mail: info@ultrasonic-sciences.co.uk
Web: www.ultrasonic-sciences.co.uk

Key personnel
Chairman: *J B Kennelly*
Sales Director: *C S Gartside*

Products
Automated and semi-automated ultrasonic testing systems for manufacturing plant and in-service inspection. Applications include testing of machined solid axles and forged or cast wheels, *in situ* inspection of hollow axles from the bore, and inspection of wheelsets in maintenance or services workshops.

Contracts
Systems have been supplied to Lucchini, SNCF, Bombardier Transportation, ALSTOM, Korean Railways and Indian Railways.

United Group Rail

Head Office
PO Box 525, 3 Bridge Street, Plymble New South Wales 2073, Australia
Tel: (+61 2) 44 88 48 88   Fax: (+61 2) 94 88 49 55
Web: www.unitedgroupltd.com

Key personnel
Chief Operating Officer: *John McLuckie*

Background
United Group Rail was formed as part of a Group restructure in 2005 and is the amalgamation of United Goninan and Alstom Transport – Australia and New Zealand.

Services
Rail vehicle maintenance; locomotive and passenger vehicle overhaul, upgrading and refurbishment.

Contracts
Maintenance and management of the Connex fleet (700 cars) performance in Melbourne. Asset maintenance of 830 km track, signalling, overhead wiring, communications systems and 208 stations of the Melbourne heavy rail 1,500 v dc network.

Emu fleet heavy maintenance for RailCorp of 1,450 cars at Auburn, Sydney. XPT fleet heavy maintenance for RailCorp at Chullora, Sydney. Endeavour/X'plorer fleet heavy maintenance for RailCorp at Chullora, Sydney. Citadis fleet maintenance for Yarra Trams, at Southbank, Melbourne. NR locomotive maintenance at Spotswood, Victoria.

Upgrade of 2600 Class, rebuild of 442 Class and refurbishment of 3700 Class locomotives; refurbishment of 158 Comeng emus; modernisation of metro emu; convertion of emu for Hong Kong Disneyland and refurbishment of ADK/ADL New Zealand.

UpRight Powered Access

Vigo Centre, Birtley Road, Washington, Tyne & Wear NE38 9DA, UK
Tel: (+44 845) 155 00 57   Fax: (+44 845) 155 77 56
e-mail: info@uprighteuro.com
Web: www.upright.com

Key personnel
Sales and Marketing Director: *Richard Tindale*

Other offices
Upright International also has offices in China, Ireland, Japan and the US.

Background
The Tanfield Group Plc, a UK-based company, acquired the aerial lift division of UpRight

International in June 2006 and the business was re-branded UpRight Powered Access.

Products
Range of access equipment such as aluminium towers and power platforms. Other products include scissors lifts, articulated booms, personnel lifts, Spandeck walkway and Instant Zip-up/Span 400 towers.

Developments

Voith Railservices BV

Koppelstraat 3, NL-7391 AK Twello, Netherlands
Tel: (+31 571) 27 96 00   Fax: (+31 571) 27 64 45
e-mail: voithnederland@voith.com
Web: www.voithturbo.com

Background
Voith Railservices BV is a subsidiary of Voith Turbo Niederlande BV, in turn part of Voith Turbo GmbH & Co KG.

Services
In 2005 Voith Railservices BV signed a 15-year contract with Arriva Openbaar Vervoer NV to undertake the maintenance of a fleet of 43 Stadler-built GTW railcars that will operate services in Friesland, Groningen and into Lower Saxony, Germany. Maintenance will be carried out at a depot at Leeuwarden, construction of which started in March 2006.

Von Roll BETEC

Edenstrasse 20, Post Box, CH-8045 Zurich, Switzerland
Tel: (+41 1) 204 31 11   Fax: (+41 1) 204 31 12
Web: www.vonroll.ch

Key personnel
Chief Executive Officer: *Walter T Vogel*
Chief Financial Officer: *Stephan Naef*

Products
DAMIVAL resin systems including potting compounds specially designed for public transportation. A selection of flexible, semi-flexible and rigid potting compounds used for different electrical insulation applications such as transformers, ballasts, capacitors, filters, sensors and coating of printed circuit boards.

Von Roll has specially developed a range of flame retardant and halogen free materials: DELMAT, PAMITHERM, VETRONITE – for application in metros, trams, tramways, buses, trolley-buses, trains, cable cars, etc. They are fire classified M0 F0 according to NF F 16 101 and meet the requirements of Italian railways LAPI (Laboratorio Prevenzione Incendi).

Wesurail Limited

21-22 Auster Road, Clifton Moor, York YO30 4XA, UK
Tel: (+44 1904) 69 25 44
Fax: (+44 1904) 69 25 66
e-mail: admin@wesurail.co.uk
Web: www.wesurail.com

Key personnel
Managing Director: *Brian Thomas*
Design Manager: *Graham Smith*
Engineering Manager: *Dave Perry*
Commercial Manager: *Bev Rackham*

Background
Wesurail was acquired by Blue Diamond in 2006.

Products

Automatic controlled emission toilet systems; mobile CET bowsers; automatic train wash systems.

Contracts

West Coast Traincare, five train wash systems, five CET systems, fuelling system; Israel Railways, automatic CET system; Delhi Metro, automatic train wash system; South West Trains, four CET systems; Siemens, four CET's, four train wash systems, one water recycling; Irish Rail, one trainwash; Network Rail, four train wash systems; Fiztpatrick, three train wash systems; First Great Western, one train wash.

Whiting Corporation

26000 Whiting Way, Monee, Illinois 60449-8060, US
Tel: (+1 800) 255 85 94
Fax: (+1 708) 587 20 01
e-mail: info@whitingcorp.com
Web: www.whitingcorp.com

Key personnel

President: *J L Kahn*
Vice-President, Sales and Marketing: *Alan J Burke*
Director of Marketing: *Stuart J Lipsteuer*
Manager, Transportation Sales: *Dave Cunningham*
Manager Heavy Rail Equipment Sales:
    Jim Thompson

Products

Custom designed and pre-engineered overhead travelling cranes for all types of critical applications. The maintenance cranes are long-life and low maintenance, built in capacities up to 800 t for a single hook and potentially cab, floor or remote controlled. Deep and shallow pit car hoists, body hoists/supports, bogie repair hoists, transfer tables, bogie/vehicle turntables, portable electric jacks, wagon/train progression systems, drop tables, overhead and gantry cranes, traction motor dollies, truck locomotive and wagon/car turntables, rip jacks, sanding cranes.

Developments

The company has introduced an electro-mechanical bus lift system, designed for customers, to replace existing hydraulic bus lift systems or install new.

Wilcomatic Ltd

Unit 5, Commerce Park, 19 Commerce Way, Croydon, Surrey, CR0 4YL
Tel: (+44 20) 86 49 57 60
Fax: (+44 20) 86 86 95 71
e-mail: sales@wilcomatic.co.uk
Web: www.wilcomatic.co.uk

Key personnel

Managing Director: *Kevin Pay*
Finance Director: *Selwyn Rodriques*
Service Director: *Brad Lawrence*
Business Development Director: *Paul Bruen*

Products

Vehicle washing equipment (three-brush fully automatic gantry machines, two- and four-brush drive-through machines); underchassis wash equipment; biological controlled water recycling equipment to suit site conditions; hot and cold pressure washing equipment; washing chemicals and a full vehicle washing and forecourt equipment; wash facility design, all civil works associated with a wash facility; wash screens; lighting and redesign and construction of wash halls. The company also provides a full seven day, 52 weeks a year service cover for both its own and third party machinery.

Windhoff Bahn-und Anlagentechnik GmbH

PO Box 1963, D-48409 Rheine, Germany
Tel: (+49 5971) 580
Fax: (+49 5971) 582 09
e-mail: info@windhoff.de
Web: www.windhoff.de

Key personnel

Board Members: *Manfred Schmitz, Georg Vennemann*
Finance Director: *Bernadett Frericks, Monika Schoppe*
Sales Directors: *Detlef Mueller*
Technical Director: *Juergen Auschner*
Purchasing Manager: *Stefan Berkemeyer*

Products

Rail systems: elevated tracks; train/rail car lifting system. Plants and equipment for handling, maintenance and repair of rail cars and dedicated assemblies: exchange of wheelsets and bogies, bogie measuring stand, mobile works platforms, roof access platforms, traverses, turntables, wheel scales, non-destructive testing equipment. Equipment for handling and transport of components: bogies transport and storage, wheelset transport and storage; ultrasonic equipment for non-destructive testing.

ŽOS Vrútky Jsc

Dielenska Kružná, SK-038 61 Vrútky, Slovakia
Tel: (+421 842) 420 51 01
Fax: (+421 842) 428 15 95
e-mail: zos-vrutky@zos-vrutky.sk
Web: www.zos-vrutky.sk

Background

Formerly the Vrútky workshops of the Czechoslovak and subsequently Slovakian Republic Railways (ŽSR), ŽOS Vrútky became a joint stock company in 1994.

The company is ISO 9001-2000, ISO 14001:2004 and TransQ accredited.

Services

ŽOS Vrútky carries out servicing and general overhaul of electric locomotives, emus, passenger coaches and special cars. The company also carries out repairs to components including bogies, wheelsets, traction and auxiliary motors, traction transformers and other electric and electronic rotating machinery, transformers of various types and designs.

The company also produces spare parts for railway track vehicles.

Most recently ŽOS Vrútky has bought the complete technology and equipment, including complete drawing, manufacturing and technological documentation and rights, to enable the manufacture of the following combustion engines: 6 S 310 DR, K6 S 310, DR, K6 S 230 DR, K 12 V230 DR and also the spare parts from their original manufacturer, ČKD Naftové motory, Praha, Smíchov.

Contracts

In 2006, refurbishment was in progress of Type Beer second class coaches and Type WRRmeer restaurant cars for Slovakian Railways. Previous refurbishment contracts for the same customer have covered Types Aeer, Apeer, Beer, Bpeer and BDsheer first and second class coaches and Types ARpeer and WRReer catering vehicles, as well as other special cars.

In 2004, the company was undertaking the modernisation of Class 350 dual-voltage electric locomotives.

ŽOS Zvolen as

Môtovská cesta 259/11, SK-960 03 Zvolen, Slovakia
Tel: (+421 45) 530 21 11
Fax: (+421 45) 532 05 26
e-mail: zoszv@zoszv.sk
Web: www.zoszv.sk

Background

Formerly the Zvolen workshops of the Czechoslovak and subsequently Slovakian Republic Railways (ŽSR), ŽOS Zvolen was privatised in 1995.

Services

Modernisation, refurbishment, overhaul and repair of diesel locomotives, railcars and passenger coaches.

PERMANENT WAY COMPONENTS, EQUIPMENT AND SERVICES

Company listing by country

AUSTRALIA
Delkor Rail Pty Limited
Harsco Track Technologies Pty Ltd

AUSTRIA
Getzner Werkstoffe GmbH
Plasser & Theurer
Semperit
VAE GmbH
voestalpine Bahnsysteme GmbH & Co KG

CANADA
H J Skelton (Canada) Ltd

FRANCE
ALSTOM Transport
Eliatis sarl
ETF-Eurovia Travaux Ferroviaires
Fassetta mécanique
Geismar
Interep SA
NEU International Railways
Sateba
SPIE Rail
Techni-Métal Systèmes
Vossloh Cogifer

GERMANY
Calenberg Ingenieure planmässig elastisch
  lagern GmbH
Elektro-Thermit GmbH and Co KG
GMB Gleisbaumechanik Brandenburg/H GmbH
Hanning & Kahl GmbH & Co KG
ORTEC Gesellschaft für Schienentechnische
  Systeme mbH
Phoenix AG
polyplan ® GmbH
Profilbeton GmbH
RAIL.ONE GmbH
A Rawie GmbH & Co KG
Robel
Schalker Eisenhütte Maschinenfabrik GmbH

Schreck-Mieves GmbH
Spezialfahrzeugaufbau und Kabeltechnik GmbH
  (SPEFAKA)
Spitzke AG
STRAIL Verkehrssysteme
ThyssenKrupp GfT Gleistechnik GmbH
Tiefenbach GmbH
TSTG Schienen Technik GmbH & Co KG
Vossloh Fastening Systems GmbH
Windhoff Bahn-und Anlagentechnik GmbH

ITALY
Cometi Mecnan SpA
Lucchini Group
RICA

NETHERLANDS
BAM Rail bv
edilon)(sedra GmbH
Kloos Oving bv
Pintsch Aben BV
voestalpine Railpro BV

SPAIN
ArcelorMittal
Comsa SA
JEZ Sistemas Ferroviarios
Travipos

SWITZERLAND
A Kaufmann AG
MATISA Matériel Industriel SA
Rex Articoli Tecnici (REX)
Schwihag AG Gleis- und Weichentechnik
Siemens Switzerland
Speno International SA

UNITED KINGDOM
Abloy UK
Abtus Ltd
ALH Rail Coatings Ltd
Atlas Copco Construction + Mining Ltd

Babcock Rail
Balfour Beatty Rail Ltd
British In-Situ Concrete Paving Association
Carillion Rail
Cembre Ltd
Cemex Rail Products
Corus Cogifer
Corus Rail Products
Cowans Sheldon
DaimlerChrysler UK Ltd
Denco Lubrication Ltd
Edmund Nuttall Ltd
Gamble Group
GrantPlant Ltd
GrantRail Group
H J Skelton & Co Ltd
Hall Rail
IAD Rail Systems
Jarvis Rail
Laser Rail Ltd
Lindapter International
Nomix Enviro
Pandrol Rail Fastenings
Polysafe Level Crossing Systems Ltd
R Bance & Co Ltd
Rotamag Track Equipment
Sika Ltd
Sonatest NDE Group
Tarmac Precast Concrete Ltd
Thermit Welding (GB) Ltd
Tiflex Ltd
Vortok International
Weedfree Limited

UNITED STATES
Century Group Inc
Holland Company LP
L B Foster
Loram Maintenance of Way, Inc
Railquip Inc
Western-Cullen-Hayes Inc

Abloy UK

Abloy House, Hatters Lane, Croxley Green Business Park, Watford WD18 8QY, UK
Tel: (+44 1923) 25 50 66   Fax: (+44 1923) 65 50 01
e-mail: tiffany.cook@abloy.co.uk
Web: www.abloy.co.uk

Key personnel
Marketing Manager: *Tiffany Cook*

Background
Abloy UK is a member of the Assa Abloy Group.

Products
A range of high security cylinder systems, mechanical and electric locks, padlocks, cam and furniture locks, panic exit hardware and standalone access control products to the UK and Ireland.

Abtus Ltd

Falconer Road, Haverhill CB9 7XU, UK
Tel: (+44 1440) 70 29 38   Fax: (+44 1440) 70 29 61
e-mail: info@abtus.com
Web: www.abtus.com

Key personnel
Managing Director: *Russell Owen*
Financial Director: *Peter Cladton*
Technical Manager: *Chris Down*
Rail Product Manager: *Chris Loveday*

Principal subsidiary
Tergor Electronics Ltd

Products
Sighting, void detection, track and overhead line measurement (digital and analogue), bond drilling and track slewing equipment; self-powered track maintenance vehicles; design, consultancy, full repair and recalibration; design and manufacture of railway surveying equipment.

Contracts
Recent contracts include the supply of standard and purpose-made equipment to Railtrack (now Network Rail), London Underground Ltd, Docklands Light Railway, British Rail Infrastructure Services, all major European railway systems and Hong Kong.

ALH Rail Coatings Ltd

Carolina Court, Lakeside, Doncaster DN4 5RA, UK
Tel: (+44 1302) 79 11 00   Fax: (+44 1302) 79 12 00
Web: www.alhrc.com

Works
Hebden Road, Scunthorpe DN15 8DT, UK
Tel: (+44 1724) 84 87 65
Fax: (+44 1724) 84 87 65

Key personnel
Director: *George Thompson*
Technical Manager: *Robin Wolfendale*

Background
ALH Rail Coatings is a joint venture between GrantRail and Dow Hyperlast.

Products
Using its expertise as a formulator and manufacturer of polyurethane and epoxy resin systems, ALH supplies a patented precoated rail system, offering high electrical insulation properties combined with reduced noise and vibration characteristics.

The system was chosen for street running sections of the Midland Metro project, Phase 2 extension of the Manchester Metrolink, Dublin Luas Phase 1 and Nottingham Express Tramway light rail systems.

ALSTOM Transport

Infrastructure Operations
48 rue Albert Dhalenne, F-93482 Saint-Ouen Cedex, France
Tel: (+33 1) 41 66 90 00
Fax: (+33 1) 41 66 96 66
Web: www.transport.alstom.com

Key personnel
President, Transport Sector: *Philippe Mellier*
Senior Vice-President Infrastructure: *Alain Goga*

Services
ALSTOM Transport Infrastructure product line covers the design, procurement and installation of electromechanical fixed infrastructure and its maintenance.

Products
Infrastructure Operations offers comprehensive solutions at the system or subsystem level for power generation and distribution including AC and DC traction substations; overhead facilities; contact lines or catenaries; third rail or at-level integrated supply system; auxiliary power supply; track laying; maintenance workshops; communications; signalling (installations); electrical and mechanical equipment in stations; and electronic guidance systems for buses.

ALSTOM has considerable experience relating to urban track for mass transit and light rail/tramway systems, both for ballasted and concrete-bed applications, and steel-wheeled or rubber-tyred vehicles.

Through its expertise in concrete, ALSTOM has developed a new concept in urban track laying. APPITRACK™ is a new automatic process for the construction of track on a concrete bed which avoids the use of sleepers. The method involves slip-form concreting derived from motorway and airport runway construction.

The track is automatically constructed directly on the project alignment using automatic plate and pin inserts. The process reduces erection time, costs and nuisance impact on the urban environment and allows higher noise and vibration requirements to be met. The APPITRACK™ process uses computerised monitoring aids for accuracy of execution and allows:
- speed of execution and limitation of disturbance (noise, vibrations);
- cost savings combined with a high performance level.

Contracts
Brazil: In May 2007, ALSTOM signed a contract to supply 96 new cars for Line 2 of São Paulo Metro. The project is a continuation of a contract originally signed for the supply of 132 cars, of which 66 were provided in the 1990s and which currently circulate on the Line 2.
Ireland: In February 2004, an ALSTOM-led consortium was awarded a five-year contract, with an extension option for a further five years, to maintain the infrastructure of Dublin's Luas tram network from later that year.
France: In July 2006, Reims Metropolitan authority selected the Mobilité Agglomération Rémoise (MARS) consortium, led by ALSTOM, to build the first line of the metropolitan authority's tram system. In May 2006, ALSTOM was awarded a contract by Toulouse's joint public transport authority (SMTC: Syndicat Mixte des Transports en Commun de l'Agglomération de Toulouse) for the city's tramway and will include a fixed portion for design studies and the production of a full-scale model as well as four other parts for the supply and maintenance of 27 tramway sets.

Also in July 2006 the French Angers Loire Metropolitan Authority selected ALSTOM for the supply of 17 Citadis™ trams equipped with the APS power supply system. The order includes a firm part of the design, a full scale tram model and the supply of the APS system. An optional part provides for the supply of the 17 trams.

In November 2004 SYTRAL, the transport union of the Lyon metropolitan area, chose ALSTOM for the supply and installation of tram infrastructure for LEA, the eastern line of the Lyon agglomeration. The contract covers the supply and installation of a 2,150 m double concrete track, a 13,300 m double ballast track and a 1,700 m single track in the depot.
Spain: ALSTOM Transport Infrastructure designed and installed the substations, electrical installations and control systems – 11 substations 2 × 25 kV/400 kV/2 × 60 MVA and 54 autotransformer post 2 × 15 MVA – for the Madrid-Barcelona high-speed line. A confidence in ALSTOM which has been renewed for the Madrid-Alicante and Cordoba-Malaga lines.
Thailand: For the Bangkok Blue Line, ALSTOM Infrastructure laid 54 km of metro lines within 18 months. The contract also covered the design and installation of the entire tunnel ventilation system, the environmental control system, fire protection/detection and drainage for three stations.
UK: In July 2007, ALSTOM completed the final track and overhead catenary system sections of the Paris-London line, High-Speed 1, linking Ebbsfleet (Kent) with St Pancras station in central London. The contract was originally awarded in 2002 to ACT, an integrated joint venture led by ALSTOM which also includes Carillion and TSO. ALSTOM's share of the contracts 40 per cent.

Additional contracts
ALSTOM has taken responsibility for the full electromechanical fixed infrastructure in metro projects including Caracas line 1, 2, 3 and 4, Cairo line 1 and 2, Athens 2 and 3, Santiago line 5 and Istanbul.

ALSTOM has also supplied electromechanical fixed equipment for the Paris and Toulouse VAL systems and the Saint-Etienne, Rouen, Orleans, Lyon, Bordeaux, Grenoble and Barcelona tramway systems.

ArcelorMittal

ArcelorMittal Rail Head office
Apartado 520 Edificio Energías 2aP, E-33200 Gijón, Asturias, Spain
Tel: (+34 985) 18 71 67
Fax: (+34 985) 18 75 43
e-mail: fernando.sainz-varona@arcelormittal.com
Web: www.arcelormittal.com

Key personnel
Rail Commercial Director: *Victor Ruíz Piñeiro*

Background
ArcelorMittal was created by the merger of two major international steel manufacturers, Arcelor and Mittal, the steel company.

Products
ArcelorMittal produces a wide range of sizes and steel grades in rails, especially for high-speed and heavy-haul lines including UIC 60, UIC 54, RN 45, TR 45, TR 57, TR 68, Vignole 46, 100A, 90A, 80A, 49E1, 54E1, 54E3, 5E1A1, 60E1, 60 E1A1, A69, A73, S49, S54, IRS52, China 50 and China 60, 85 ASCE, 100RE, 100ARA-B, 119RE, 132RE, 141RE, Ri60, Ri60N, Ri55NK, LK1.

Atlas Copco
Construction + Mining Ltd

PO Box 79, Swallowdale Lane, Hemel Hempstead HP2 7HA, UK
Tel: (+44 1442) 22 21 00
Fax: (+44 1442) 23 44 67
e-mail: ac.cmtuk@ukatlascopco.com
Web: www.atlascopco.co.uk

Key personnel
Marketing and Communications: *Jessica Hammond*

Products
Self-contained power tamper/drill and pneumatic equipment, hydraulic breakers.

Babcock Rail

Head office
Kintail House, 3 Lister Way, Hamilton International Park, Blantyre G72 0FT, UK
Tel: (+44 845) 000 30 05   Fax: (+44 845) 30 06
Web: www.babcock.co.uk

Key personnel
Chief Executive: *Andrew Pearson*
Commercial Director: *Bobby Forbes*
Key Account Director: *Meirion Thomas*

Background
Previously called First Engineering, the company is part of Babcock International Group plc. It has regional offices located in London, York, Birmingham, Manchester and Hamilton.

Services
Capabilities include feasibility, design, installation, construction, testing, commissioning, ongoing maintenance and repair of a wide range of infrastructure. Track renewals; signalling; telecommunications; control systems; permanent way; power systems, including overhead line electrification; mechanical and electrical engineering; property maintenance and management; consultancy services; civil engineering; structural engineering.

Balfour Beatty Rail Ltd

7 Mayday Road, Thornton Heath, CR7 7XA, UK
Tel: (+44 20) 86 84 69 22
e-mail: info@bbrail.com
Web: www.bbrail.com

Key personnel
Group Managing Director: *Jim Cohen*
Chief Operating Officer: *Andy Rose*
Marketing and Planning Manager: *Sean Pang*

Background
Balfour Beatty Rail is an international leader in rail engineering projects. Employing 7,000 staff, the company services the full range of rail infrastructure activities from high-speed rail to mass rapid transit, covering inter-city, rural and commuter routes, for both public and private railways. Balfour Beatty Rail also works in partnerships and alliances.

In August 2005, the company acquired the Pennine Group, the UK ground engineering specialists.

Capabilities
Balfour Beatty Rail can deliver large, complex, multi-disciplinary projects using its professional project management skills throughout the whole cycle. The company undertakes work from the initial planning phase, the identification of project requirements and interfaces through to construction, testing and commissioning and handover of the works.

Balfour Beatty Rail has the capability to supply all types of track systems; high-speed main line, heavy haul, urban mass transit and commuter systems, and light rail transits, working on new systems as well as re-modelling and renewals of existing lines. In addition to contracting skills, the company is an international designer and manufacturer of switches and crossing, special trackwork and associated products.

The company has experience in the design and construction of ballasted track, track on concrete including advanced techniques for noise and vibration problems and has developed its own patented embedded slab track system.

Balfour Beatty Rail provides a total power and electrification capability for all types of new railway projects as well as upgrading, renovating and converting existing systems. The company has a large, competent and diverse capability for power and electrification projects ranging from overhead lines, AC and DC power supply to conductor rail systems.

The company also has in-house capability to undertake turnkey signalling and rail telecommunications solutions including design, planning, application engineering, installation, commissioning and testing. It can support established technology, ranging over a wide variety of signalling systems from high-speed lines, low-speed freight lines, metro systems and level crossing and has an in-house design capability based through the UK. This now also includes Solid State Interlocking (SSI) suite based at Derby.

Balfour Beatty Rail can offer asset management including management systems, software and tools to facilitate data acquisition, perform inspection and monitoring and support decision making and planning. It can also support remedial activities through its own resources and wide range of equipment and plants. Balfour Beatty Rail specialises in the care of switches, rails, track systems, signalling systems, current collection systems and power supply systems.

Subsidiaries
Balfour Beatty Rail Infrastructure Ltd
7th Floor, Russell Square House, 10-12 Russell Square, London WC1B 5EH, UK
Tel: (+44 20) 70 79 47 00   Fax: (+44 20) 70 79 47 01
Web: www.bbrail.com

Key personnel
Managing Director: *Eric Prescott*
Marketing Manager: *Liz Murray-Leslie*

Services
Balfour Beatty Rail Infrastructure Services Ltd undertakes all types of infrastructure inspection, maintenance and renewal, covering track, signalling, and overhead and third rail power supply systems on main line and urban rail networks.

Balfour Beatty Rail Plant Ltd
PO Box 5065, Raynesway, Derby DE21 7ZQ, UK
Tel: (+44 1332) 66 14 91   Fax: (+44 1332) 28 82 22
Web: www.bbrail.com

Key personnel
Managing Director: *Keith Fidler*
Engineering and Safety Director: *Raymond Reed*
Finance Director: *Kate Busman*
Fleet Services Director: *Jeff Bussey*
Plant Services Director: *David Watson*
Business Development Manager: *Steve MacIver*
Head of Engineering, Health, Safety, Quality and Environment: *Dave Elias*
Quality and Environment Systems Manager: *Tim Russell*
Safety Advisor: *Peter Turner*
Business Development: *Lynne Sherlock*

Services
Balfour Beatty Rail Plant Ltd has three operating units: the Rail Plant Unit provides mechanised on-track equipment services, including tampers for plain line and for switches and crossings, trams, rail cranes, tracklayers, ballast regulators, ballast cleaners and gophers. The Raynesway Plant Unit provides road/rail equipment, general plant maintenance and hire services for portable tools, accommodation, safety equipment, communications and CCTV systems plus design and manufacture of specialised road/rail equipment. The Fleet Services Unit undertakes transport fleet maintenance and fleet management and maintains Balfour Beatty's 7,000-vehicle fleet.

Balfour Beatty Rail Power Systems GmbH
For further information refer to Balfour Beatty Rail GmbH entry in *Electrification contractors and equipment suppliers* section

Balfour Beatty Rail Projects Ltd.
For further information refer to Balfour Beatty Rail Projects Ltd entry in *Turnkey systems contractors*

Balfour Beatty Rail Technologies Ltd
For further information refer to Balfour Beatty Rail Technologies Ltd entry in *Consultancy* section

Balfour Beatty Rail Track Systems Ltd
Osmaston Street, Sandiacre, Nottingham NG10 5AN, UK
Tel: (+44 115) 921 82 18
Fax: (+44 115) 921 82 38
e-mail: phil.bean@bbrail.co.uk
Web: www.balfourbeatty.com

Key personnel
General Manager: *Keith Churm*
Business Development Manager: *Philip Bean*

US subsidiaries
Balfour Beatty Rail Systems Inc
1024 Route 519, Suite 300, Eighty Four, Pennsylvania 15330, US
Tel: (+1 724) 225 61 55
Fax: (+1 724) 228 81 13
Balfour Beatty Rail Maintenance, Inc
Marta Track Constructors Inc
Metroplex Corporation

BAM Rail bv

Stadionstraat 40, NL-4815 ng Breda, Netherlands
Tel: (+31 76) 573 43 00   Fax: (+31 76) 573 44 00
e-mail: info@bamrail.nl
Web: www.bamrail.nl

Background
BAM Rail bv is part of Royal Group nv.

Products
Operating throughout the Netherlands and neighbouring countries, BAM Rail's activities cover all rail disciplines from underground cables to the overhead catenary.

Projects
Metro Dublin and Edinburgh tramway.

British In-Situ Concrete Paving Association

Riverside House, 4 Meadows Business Park, Station Approach, Blackwater, Camberley, Surrey GU17 9AB, UK
Tel: (+44 1276) 331 60
Fax: (+44 1276) 331 70
e-mail: info@britpave.org.uk
Web: www.britpave.org.uk

Key personnel
Chairman: *David York*
Director and Company Secretary: *David P Jones*
Treasurer: *James F Troy*
Committee Chairman: *John Donegan*

Background
Formed in 1991, Britpave, the British In-situ Concrete Paving Association is active in all areas of transport infrastructure including roads, airfields, light and heavy rail, guided bus, safety barrier and drainage channels, soil stabilisation and recycling. It has a broad corporate membership base that includes contractors, consulting engineers and designers, suppliers of plant, equipment and materials, academics and clients, both in the UK and internationally.

Services
Britpave provides members and clients alike with opportunities and aims to develop technical excellence and best practice in key cement and concrete markets through its publications: Guided Busway – Construction Handbook and Guide Busway – Design Handbook, also through seminars and their website.

Calenberg Ingenieure planmässig elastisch lagern GmbH

Am Knübel 2-4, D-31020 Salzhemmendorf, Germany
Tel: (+49 5153) 940 00
Fax: (+49 5153) 94 00 49
e-mail: info@calenberg-ingenieure.de
Web: www.calenberg-ingenieure.de

Key personnel
Managing Director: *Peter Wisniewski*
Marketing Manager: *Marita Pirk*

Background
In 2001, Calenberg Ingenieure took over development, consulting and sales activities of ContiTech Clouth, a specialist in elastomeric matting and bearings for mass-spring systems used in track construction. At the end of 2005 ContiTech passed on this business segment completely to Calenberg Ingenieure.

Products
Sub-ballast mats for vibration control; elastomeric bearings for mass-spring systems; elastomeric bearings for vibration isolation used in railway tracks.

Carillion Rail

24 Birch Street, Wolverhampton WV1 4HY, UK
Tel: (+44 1902) 42 24 31
Fax: (+44 1902) 31 61 65
Web: www.carillionrail.com

Key personnel
Managing Director: *Adam Green*
Operations Director – Projects: *Steve Bramwell*
Operations Director – Major Projects: *Mark Robinson*

Subsidiaries
Carillion Rail Sverige AB
Box 50324, SE-202 14 Malmö, Sweden
Tel: (+46 40) 663 98 00
Fax: (+46 40) 663 98 29
e-mail: carillion@carillion.se
Web: www.carillion.se
Managing Director: *Lars Nihlén*

Background
Carillion Rail is a trading name of GT Railway Maintenance Ltd and is wholly owned by Carillion plc. Carillion Rail was formally launched in April 2002 as a new rail business combining the resources of GTRM, Centrac and Carillion Infrastructure, and has three business groups: Projects; Infrastructure Maintenance; and Rail Services. GTRM Ltd was previously owned by a joint venture between Alstom and Carillion plc (formerly Tarmac Construction Ltd). Formerly known as Central Infrastructure Maintenance Co, GTRM Ltd was one of the British Rail Infrastructure Service units, sold off to Alstom and Carillion in 1996 as part of the British Rail privatisation.

Carillion Rail took over Swedish Rail Systems Entreprenad (SRSE), the Swedish-based rail infrastructure maintenance specialist which also has interests in Norway, Denmark and Finland. SRSE became Carillion Rail Sverige AB and has major contracts in Sweden with Malmo City Tunnel and Inlandsbanen. It has new assets worth about SEK80 million.

In February 2006, Carillion plc completed its acquisition of Mowlem plc and then in March 2006 completed the sale of Edgar Allen, formerly part of Mowlem plc, to Balfour Beatty.

Services
The activities of Carillion Rail embrace the disciplines of permanent way, civil engineering, signalling, telecommunications, power supplies, OLE and plant and consultancy. All projects incorporate design, installation, testing and commissioning.

The Infrastructure Maintenance Group is responsible for maintenance and repair work on many major routes throughout the UK railway network. This includes the West Coast Main Line from London Euston to Scotland and much of the central band of England and Wales. The group offers expertise in permanent way maintenance and inspection; signalling maintenance and inspection; electrical distribution equipment maintenance and inspection; off-track maintenance and inspection, including vegetation management; rapid response and repair works; telecommunications maintenance and inspection; overhead line and third rail equipment maintenance and inspection, closed branch lines maintenance and inspection and station and platform regeneration and refurbishment.

The Rail Services Group, headed by the Rail Services Directors, contains the following units: Rail Plant; Eurailscout GB and Rail Testing. Rail Plant provides on-track machines, having a full range of machine maintenance plant, track renewals plant, electrification plant, wiring trains and an autoballaster. Eurailscout GB offers innovative solutions to track inspection and analysis, asset management. A joint venture between Carillion plc and Europool BV, Eurailscout offers services throughout the UK, including track recording and track analysis using software programmes such as IRIS. Rail Testing provides a comprehensive range of welding, testing and calibration services to deliver to both internal and external customers. The Calibration and Test Centre in Crewe provides an extensive calibration and repair service for instrumentation and tools used within the rail industry which require calibration in accordance with the current standards.

Contracts
In July 2007 Carillion, with its Joint Venture (JV) partners, ALSTOM and Travaux du Sud-Ouest, handed over the system-wide track and overhead catenary system works following completion of the design, installation, testing and commissioning of the new systems from Southfleet junction to the London tunnel portal on Section 2 of High Speed 1. The contract was originally awarded in 2002 to the ACT JV, an integrated joint venture led by ALSTOM, of which Carillion and Travaux du Sud-Ouest has a 30% share each and ALSTOM a 40 per cent share. Carillion has also separately handed over a further contract on Section 2 – which comprised the remodelling of track into the refurbished St Pancras station in order to accommodate high-speed services alongside the existing Midland Mainline service.

Cembre Ltd

Dunton Park, Kingsbury Road, Curdworth, Sutton Coldfield B76 9EB, UK
Tel: (+44 1675) 47 04 40   Fax: (+44 1675) 47 02 20
Web: www.cembre.com

Subsidiaries
Cembre SpA
Via Serenissima 9, I-25135 Brescia, Italy
Tel: (+39 030) 369 21   Fax: (+39 030) 336 57 66
e-mail: info@cembre.com
Web: www.cembre.com

Cembre Sarl
22 avenue Ferdinand de Lesseps, F-91420 Morangis, France
Tel: (+33 1) 60 49 11 90   Fax: (+33 1) 60 49 29 10
e-mail: info@cembre.es

Cembre España SL
Calle Llanos de Jerez, 2 Pol Ind de Coslada, E-28823 Coslada, Madrid, Spain
Tel: (+34 91) 485 25 80   Fax: (+34 91) 485 25 81
e-mail: info@cembre.com

Cembre AS
Fossnes Senter, N-3160 Stokke, Norway
Tel: (+47 33) 36 17 65
Fax: (+47 33) 36 17 66
e-mail: cembre@cembre.no

Rail mounted support trolley for Cembre sleeper drills　0567156

Pandrol clip machine　0567155

Cembre GmbH
Heidemannstrasse 166, D-80939 Munich, Germany
Tel: (+49 89) 358 06 76   Fax: (+49 89) 35 80 67 77
e-mail: info@cembre.com

Cembre Inc
Raritan Center Business Park,
181 Fieldcrest Avenue, Edison, New Jersey 08837, US
Tel: (+1 732) 225 74 15   Fax: (+1 732) 225 74 14
e-mail: salesus@cembre.com

Products
Drilling machines for rail web and wooden sleepers, Pandrol clip machines, nut runners; rail bonding kit; related accessories.

Cemex Rail Products

Aston Church Road, Saltley, Birmingham B8 1QF, UK
Tel: (+44 121) 327 08 44
Fax: (+44 121) 327 75 45
Andrew.Carey@cemex.com
Web: www.railway-technology.com

Key personnel
Business Manager: *Stuart Neil*
Sales Manager: *Andy Carey*
Quality Manager: *Paul Crowther*

Other offices
Birchwood Way, Cotes Park Industrial Estate, Somercotes, DE55 4PY, UK
Tel: (+44 1773) 60 41 43
Fax: (+44 1773) 60 79 12

Background
Following the acquisition of the RMC Group by Cemex in early 2005, RMC Rail Products was renamed Cemex Rail Products.

Products
Pretensioned concrete monobloc sleepers; reinforced concrete sleepers; crossing bearers.

Contracts
Over half of the annual requirement of concrete sleepers used by Network Rail and all of the sleepers used by London Underground are supplied by Cemex, which is also a large supplier of concrete crossing bearers to S & C manufacturers.

Century Group Inc

PO Box 228, Sulphur, Louisiana 70664-0228, US
Tel: (+1 800) 527 52 32 ext 118
Fax: (+1 800) 887 21 53
e-mail: railroad@centurygrp.com
Web: www.centurygrp.com

Century's concrete turnout grade crossing
1149686

Century's passenger railcar wash facility
1194487

Century's custom concrete grade crossing turnout
1149685

Key personnel
President/Chief Executive Officer, Railroad Products Division: *Rusty Vincent*
Vice-President, Sales and Marketing, Railroad Products Division: *Jerry McCombs*

Products
Full-depth concrete grade crossings in North America. Manufactured of high-strength reinforced concrete, the Century crossings are durable, safe, economical and simple to install. The versatile concrete grade crossings are manufactured to fit any size rail and are compatible with all major types of rail fastening systems. The crossings are manufactured for curves, turnouts, diamond crossings, devil strips and many other applications. All crossings come with an innovative elastomeric flangeway filler for the safety of pedestrians and vehicular traffic. This is also used to protect the track structure from contaminants.

The HDPE Enviropan system is a state-of-the-art railroad spill collection system to assist railroads, military facilities, light rail transit and industry to protect the environment. It is a high impact puncture- and tear-resistant closed drain system which minimises exposure at pan and cross drain connections. The Enviropan modular lightweight construction allows for fast installation, eliminating railroad track downtime.

Contracts
Recent contracts include: Railroad crossings and spill collection systems for Metropolitan Atlanta Rapid Transit (MARTA) (2007); Exxon Mobil (2007).

Cometi Mecnan SpA

Zona Industriale Fiumicello 19, I-52037 Sansepolcro (AR), Italy
Tel: (+39 0575) 74 42 11   Fax: (+39 0575) 74 42 24
e-mail: info@cometimecnan.com
Web: www.cometimecnan.com

Products
Transport and telecommunication: shelter for telecommunication; railway vehicles; metal structural work and collection booths. Painting: spray booth; prep 'n' spray; preparation area and mixing box.

Comsa SA

Edificio Numancia 1, Calle Viriato 47, E-08014 Barcelona, Spain
Tel: (+34 93) 430 15 152
Fax: (+34 93) 405 13 30
Web: www.comsa.com

Subsidiaries
Intraesa
(address as parent company)
Tel: (+34 93) 430 49 44
Fax: (+34 93) 439 17 69
Travipos SA
Pfleiderer Verkehrstechnik GmbH & Co KG
Calle Irlanda del Norte s/n, Poligono Industrial Constanti, Sector Norte, E-43120 Constanti, Tarragona, Spain
Tel: (+34 977) 29 65 53
Fax: (+34 977) 29 65 53

Services
Construction and maintenance of high-speed, conventional and mass transit railway infrastructure including metro and light rail; construction of railway installations such as traction and rolling stock maintenance depots and marshalling yards.

Comsa uses new automated methods such as the Track Renewal Train (TRT), which allows track renewal work at speeds of greater than 500 m an hour. Comsa also has equipment for assembling or renewing track with an intermittent system, suitable for new layouts or lines with greater intervals of time for carrying out the work.

Contracts
In January 2008 Comsa's Argentinean subsidiary was awarded the contract to move the Sarmiento line underground between the Caballito and Moreno stations.

MVM Rail, the Australian subsidiary of Comsa was awarded three new rail contracts in April 2008. The first of the projects consists of remodelling the Pring terminal and track renewal at the Abbot terminal in Queensland. The second contract involves track work as part of the extension of the facilities of BHP Billiton, the mining company in the Pilbara region in Western Australia. Finally, MVM has landed the contract to reconfigure track and overhead contact lines at Lawson station in the Sydney commuter trains network.

In August 2007 Comsa was awarded the contract to build the Las Cabezas de San Juan-Lebrija section of the Seville to Cadiz high-speed rail line. The project, operating in a joint venture with GEA 21, includes building the rail platform, laying double track, electrification and installing safety equipment. The completion deadline is 30 months.

In July 2007 Comsa received the contract to build the platform for the first section of the high-speed rail access to the city of Valencia. The project, called the Red Arterial Ferroviaria (RAF – Arterial Rail Network) Valencia – South Intersection, has a 26-month completion deadline.

Corus Cogifer

Hebden Road, Scunthorpe DN15 8XX, UK
Tel: (+44 1724) 86 21 31
Fax: (+44 1724) 29 52 43
e-mail: info@coruscogifer.com
Web: www.coruscogifer.com

Key personnel
Managing Director: *Ian Lindsay*
Commercial Manager: *Andrew Norris*

Capabilities
Corus Cogifer is one of the leaders in the supply of railway switches and crossings and related track components in the UK. The company is a 50/50 joint venture between Corus and Vossloh Cogifer. The business designs, manufactures and assembles switches, crossings and railway track layout systems for the railway maintenance and renewals market.

Contracts
Corus Cogifer are in the process of supplying the NR60 type switches and crossing required for the Rugby Station remodelling project on the West Coast route Modernisation scheme. The company is also working with Network Rail as part of an integrated team on the Modular Switch and Crossing development project.

Corus Rail Products

UK – Mill and Commercial
Rail Service Centre, PO Box 1, Brigg Road, Scunthorpe, DN16 1BP, UK
Tel: (+44 1724) 40 33 98
Fax: (+44 1724) 40 34 42
France – Commercial
2 avenue du President Kennedy, F-78100 Saint-Germain-en-Laye, France
Tel: (+33 1) 39 04 63 00   Fax: (+33 1) 39 04 63 44
France – Mill
164 rue du Marechal Foch, F-57705 Hayange Cedex, France
Tel: (+33 3) 82 57 45 04   Fax: (+33 3) 82 57 45 41
e-mail: rail@corusgroup.com
Web: www.muchmorethanrail.com

Key personnel
Managing Director: *Joe Guérin*
Commercial Director, International: *Hubert Dabas*
Commercial Director, UK and Ireland: *Geoff Suitor*
Technical Director, France: *Daniel Boulanger*

Background
Corus manufactures rail products at facilities in the UK and France. Supported by comprehensive quality and testing procedures and advanced logistical systems, the business supplies rail networks worldwide. Commercial and technical teams are supported by local representatives in over 85 countries with extensive experience in international trade. Its customers benefit from

expertise in high-speed lines, heavy haul, urban transport, logistics and establishing finance packages.

Products and services
The product portfolio includes: heavy rail (flat bottom, bullhead, conductor) in all grades, also head hardened, grooved, stainless steel clad, corrosion resistant, asymmetric, light bridge and crane rail, long welded rail strings up to 220 m and steel sleepers.

Corus is also able to offer a wide range of railway infrastructure services.

Developments
Corus has developed the innovative Silent Track™ noise reduction rail system, which significantly reduces noise generated by railway traffic.

Cowans Sheldon

The Clarke Chapman Group Ltd, PO Box 9, Saltmeadows Road, Gateshead NE8 1SW, UK
Tel: (+44 191) 477 22 71
Fax: (+44 191) 477 10 09
Web: www.cowanssheldon.co.uk

Key personnel
General Manager: *Les Richardson*
Business Sales Manager: *Martin Howell*

Products
Diesel-electric and diesel-hydraulic railway breakdown, general purpose and tracklaying cranes from 12 tonnes to 250 tonnes lifting capacity. Rail delivery and recovery systems and modular maintenance systems.

Refurbishment, life extension and upgrade of existing cranes as well as track maintenance machines.

DaimlerChrysler UK Ltd

Unimog Sales
Tongwell, Milton Keynes MK15 8BA, UK
Tel: (+44 1908) 24 57 61   Fax: (+44 1908) 24 51 07
Web: www.unimog.co.uk

Products
Models U300 and U400 high-stability multifunction road and rail vehicles have been developed by a partnership between the DaimlerChrysler organisation and leading international implement manufacturers.

The Unimog system is fitted with low-maintenance Euro-3 Mercedes-Benz engines giving 110 kW (150 hp) and 130 kW (177 hp) direct injection. It has three-valve technology, exhaust supercharger and intercooling, permanent four-wheel drive and ABS. The vehicle has a small turning circle and can pull low-bed trucks or two trailers and still be within 18 m in length. The engine and gearbox are rated for both heavy-duty and top-speed pulling operations.

For rail operations the Unimog can become a shunting locomotive. By lowering the rail guide it can provide wagon braking weights up to 1,000 t and speeds up to 50 km/h in both directions.

Delkor Rail Pty Limited

Street address: Unit R4, 391 Park Road, Regents Park, New South Wales 2143, Australia
PO Box 63, Regents Park, New South Wales 2143, Australia
Tel: (+61 2) 87 17 92 00   Fax: (+61 2) 96 44 92 22
e-mail: delkorrail@delkorrail.com
Web: www.delkorrail.com

Key personnel
Technical Director: *Peter Schonstein*
General Manager: *George Stamboulis*
Project Manager: *Jake Cherviakov*

Products
Elastomeric baseplates, Delkor Eggs and Alt 1, designed for noise and vibration reduction for tunnels, bridges and viaducts; ballast mats for ballasted and slab track; fixation items including screwspikes, washers, special studs and dowels.

Contracts
The supply of noise and vibration reducing baseplates for the Sydney Harbour Bridge, Australia; Tsing Ma Bridge Hong Kong Airport Rail Link, KCRC West Rail, Hong Kong; Chatswood to Epping Rail Link, Sydney, Australia.

Denco Lubrication Ltd

Ramsden Court, Ramsden Road, Rotherwas Industrial Estate, Hereford, HR2 6LR, UK
Tel: (+44 1432) 36 50 00   Fax: (+44 1432) 36 50 01
e-mail: info@delimon.co.uk
Web: www.delimon.co.uk

Key personnel
Managing Director: *Steve Hayward*

Background
Denco Lubrication Ltd is a member of Bijur Delimon International.

Products
Stationary track lubrication systems for all track types, including grooved rail and Vignoles.

edilon)(sedra GmbH

Joergstrasse 23, D-80689 Munich, Germany
Tel: (+49 89) 892 86 40   Fax: (+49 89) 89 28 64 20
e-mail: muenchen@edilonsedra.com
Web: www.edilon.com

Key personnel
Sales Directors: *Pam Schram, Jean-Pierre Frottier*
Contact: *P Rieger*

Background
Infundo GmbH was set up in 1999 as the joint subsidiary of contractors Leonhard Weiss GmbH & Co, Göppingen, and Edilon BV, Haarlem, Netherlands. LW sold its 50 per cent share to Edilon BV in 2001. As a result the name changed to Edilon GmbH. Following the merger of the Edilon group with Sedra GmbH, Wiesbaden in March 2007, the names for the whole group changed to edilon)(sedra.

Products
Embedded Rail Systems: slab track systems (ERS) for tunnels, bridge, light rail, heavy rail, industrial applications. Level crossing systems: Stelfundo level crossing, Stelundo switch crossings. Modular railway bridges: steel bridges, concrete bridges. Gantry crane track systems. Services: consulting services, project management.

The systems are designed to handle extreme axle loads for both rail bound and road vehicles, and feature low maintenance and economic life cycle costs with life spans of more than 30 years.

Edmund Nuttall Ltd

St James House, Knoll Road, Camberley GU15 3XW, UK
Tel: (+44 1276) 634 84
Fax: (+44 1276) 660 60
e-mail: headoffice@edmund-nuttall.co.uk
Web: www.edmund-nuttall.co.uk

Key personnel
Chief Executive: *Martin J Rogers*
Directors: *Robert Treadgold, David K Belsham, Steve C Fox*
Director, Business Development: *Mike Pipe*

Director of Finance and Company Secretary: *Geoff Renshaw*
Head of Public Relations: *Peter Bishop*

Services
Civil engineering contractors serving both private and public sectors for large- and small-scale projects in many sectors.

Contracts
Include: five-year alliance for infrastructure renewals with Network Rail Southern Zone; involvement in a slope stabilisation contract with Network Rail throughout its Scottish Zone; signalling installation for Network Rail and London Underground. Remediation/earthworks contract for Olympic Park, Guided Busway, Cambridge.

Elektro-Thermit GmbH and Co KG

Chemiestrasse 24, D-06132 Halle, Germany
Tel: (+49 345) 779 56 00
Fax: (+49 345) 779 57 70
e-mail: info@elektro-thermit.de
Web: www.elektro-thermit.de

Key personnel
Managing Director: *Dr Jörg Keichel*

Products
Thermit rail welding equipment and consumables, heating devices and accessories, hydraulic equipment, measuring devices, insulated and non-insulated fishplate joints.

Eliatis sarl

ZA La Pichatière, BP 71, F-38430 Moirans, France
Tel: (+33 4) 76 35 30 08
Fax: (+33 4) 76 35 60 51
e-mail: eliatis@eliatis.com
Web: www.eliatis.com

Key personnel
Managing Directors: *Jean Luc Perrin, Olivier Gallifet*

Products
Aspirail road-rail unit for vacuum cleaning roadway and tram rails, including leaf removal. Can be fitted on to existing vehicles. Speed of operation is 25 km/h. Optional Total Road-Rail system for use on all surfaces including asphalt, ballast, sand and grass.

ETF-Eurovia Travaux Ferroviaires

Lionel Péraud 267, chaussée Jules César, BP 62 F-95250, Beauchamp, France
Tel: (+33 1) 30 40 59 04
Fax: (+33 1) 30 40 59 20
e-mail: lionel.peraud@eurovia.com
Web: www.eurovia-travaux-ferroviaires.com

Key personnel
Chief Executive Officer: *Henri Dehe*

Background
In September 2008 VINCI's subsidiary Eurovia completed its aquisition of Vossloh Infrastructure Services. As a result the company name became ETF-Eurovia Travaux Ferroviaires.

Services
Track laying for railways, high-speed railways, metros, automatic metros (VAL), tramways (on rails and rubber tyre), industrial sidings, track renewal.
   Catenary design, studies, manufacturing, installation and commissioning.

Fassetta mécanique

36 boulevard de la Gare, F-13713 La Penne S/Huveaune, Cedex, France
Tel: (+33 4) 91 87 70 30   Fax: (+33 4) 91 87 70 39
e-mail: fasmec@fassetta.com
Web: www.fassetta.com

Key personnel
General and Export Manager: *Frederic Fassetta*

Products
Track construction and maintenance equipment including switch relaying equipment. Special machines designed and produced on request. Tamping machines, re-sleepering machines, track geometry, recording and inspection trolleys.

Gamble Group

Head Office
Gamble Rail
Meadow Road Industrial Estate, Dale Road, Worthing BN11 2RY, UK
Tel: (+44 1903) 23 47 27   Fax: (+44 1903) 82 03 11
e-mail: info@gamblegroup.co.uk
Web: www.gamblegroup.co.uk

Other offices
The group also has offices in Horsham, Ashford, Colchester, Uckfield, Newhaven, Heathrow and Guildford, UK.

Products
Road-rail equipment including ballast broom attachment for lines with third rail, crane with various attachments including dipper arms, tool hangers, notched bucket and concrete breaker; road-rail access platform.

Geismar

113 bis avenue Charles-de-Gaulle, F-92200 Neuilly sur Seine, France
Tel: (+33 1) 41 43 40 40
Fax: (+33 1) 46 40 71 70
e-mail: geismar@geismar.com
Web: www.geismar.com

Works
5 rue d'Altkirch, F-68006 Colmar Cedex, France
Tel: (+33 3) 89 80 22 11
Fax: (+33 3) 89 79 78 45
e-mail: colmar@geismar.com

Key personnel
Publicity: *Patrick Lambert*

Products and services
Tracklaying and maintenance equipment and services. Permanent way tools. Hand-held machinery, including rail drills, saws, disc cutters, grinders, benders, weld shears, tensors, pre-heaters, strikers, descalers, lifters, loaders; sleeper drills, benders, adzers, plug drivers; fastening machines, fishbolters, coachscrewers, impact wrenches, elastic clip and spike inserters and extractors.
   Heavy equipment, including gantries for laying and replacing track panels and switches, threaders, slewers, sleeper-changers, tampers and regulators.
   Transport and maintenance vehicles, including inspection and flying gang trolleys, heavy-duty track cars, shunters, trailers, and railway excavators.
   Turnkey plants and workshop machinery for rail welding, reprofiling or machining, timber sleeper machining and impregnation, steel sleeper reclamation.
   Measuring instrumentation, including manual gauges and devices, hand-pushed or self-propelled or onboard electronic systems.
   Geismar also supplies equipment to install, maintain and inspect AC and DC overhead catenary.

Getzner Werkstoffe GmbH

Head Office
Herrenau 5, A-6706 Bürs, Austria
Tel: (+43 5552) 20 10   Fax: (+43 5552) 20 18 99
e-mail: info.buers@getzner.com
Web: www.getzner.com

Key personnel
Managing Director and Sales Director: *Roland Pfefferkorn*
Advertising Manager: *Guntram Pollak*

Associated companies
Getzner Werkstoffe GmbH
Nördliche Münchner Strasse 27a, D-82031 Grünwald, Germany
Tel: (+49 89) 693 50 00
Fax: (+49 89) 69 35 00 11
e-mail: infogruenwald@getzner.com

Getzner Werkstoffe GmbH
Am Borsigturm 11, D-13507 Berlin, Germany
Tel: (+49 30) 40 50 34 00   Fax: (+49 30) 40 50 34 35
e-mail: info.berlin@getzner.com

Getzner Werkstoffe GmbH
Middle East Regional Office
Abdul-Hameed Sharaf Strasse, 114, Rimawi Center, Shmeisani, PO Box 961 303, Amman 11196, Jordan
Tel: (+96 26) 560 73 41   Fax: (+96 26) 569 73 52
e-mail: info@geme.jo

Nihon Getzner K K
Shinjuku Park Tower, 30th Floor, 3-7-1 Nishi-Shinjuku, Shinjuku-ku, Tokyo 163-1030, Japan
Tel: (+81 3) 53 26 30 30   Fax: (+81 3) 53 26 30 01
e-mail: sylomer@getzner.co.jp

Products
System solutions with elastic materials: Sylomer, Sylodyn and Sylodamp (all polyurethane materials), used for noise and vibration reduction in track and structure construction, sleeper pads, ballast mats for subways, light rail and main line track; elastic bearings for track slabs; resilient baseplate pads and resilient rail pads.
   Getzner Werkstoffe can also supply tailor-made orders to customer's requirements.

GMB Gleisbaumechanik Brandenburg/H GmbH

D-14774 Brandenburg-Kirchmoser, Germany
Tel: (+49 3381) 804 44 32   Fax: (+49 3381) 804 43 81
e-mail: gleisbaumechanik@t-online.de
Web: www.gleisbaumechanik.de

Series 711.1 self-propelled catenary inspection and maintenance vehicle in display at InnoTrans 2002 (Ken Harris)   0536546

Key personnel

Production: *Rainer Bardenberg*
(Tel: (+49 3381) 804 44 35
Marketing: *Lutz Wende*
(Tel: (+49 3381) 804 44 32

Products

Self-propelled rail, signalling and catenary inspection and maintenance vehicles. Train Control Testcar (TCT) for testing European Train Control Systems installations; Series 711.1 catenary inspection and maintenance vehicle for high-speed lines.

GrantPlant Ltd

Dawes Lane, Frodingham, Scunthorpe DN15 6UW, UK
Tel: (+44 1724) 87 83 00   Fax: (+44 1724) 87 83 01
e-mail: marketing@grantrail.co.uk
Web: www.grantrail.co.uk

Key personnel

Chief Executive Officer: *Gren Edwards*
Managing Director: *Martin Hawley*
General Manager: *Mark Jackson*

Background

GrantPlant Ltd is a subsidiary business within GrantRail Group Ltd, part of the VolkerWessels Group.

Capabilities

GrantPlant offers a range of equipment for track renewals, track maintenance, signalling and telecommunications work, overhead line equipment, REB installation and bridge replacements. GrantPlant's fleet of equipment includes: three Matisa B45 tampers and five Matisa B41 tampers (one fitted with PALAS), two Matisa R24S ballast regulators, all of which are engaged within Network Rail's on track plant contract. One Kirow 1200 crane with 125 t lifting capacity, one Kirow 810 crane with 100 t lifting capacity, two Kirow 250 cranes with 25 t lifting capacity, panel handling beams and a hydraulically operated loose sleeper lifting beam. One plasser twin jib tracklayer, four Colmar Road/Rail Vehicles (RRV's), two beavers inside a possession only tamping machine, mobile flash butt welders, a gauge corner restoration welding machine, a Mobile Elevated Working Platform (MEWP) and a comprehensive range of small plant and equipment.

Contracts

National tamping contract: switches and crossings and plain line tamping and ballast regulations on Network Rail infrastructure. GrantPlant is required to provide Network Rail with top of the range switches and crossing tamping to enable it to fulfil its contract obligations to its stakeholders for renewals and maintenance contracts.

Tamping contract – Nexus PTE: the contract utilises the VokerRail Beaver 90/ZW tamper, complete with crew, which was previously used in the UK for the Ashford and Ramsgate train care depot contracts.

GrantRail Group

1 Carolina Court, Lakeside, Doncaster DN4 5RA, UK
Tel: (+44 1302) 79 11 00   Fax: (+44 1302) 79 12 00
e-mail: marketing@grantrail.co.uk
Web: www.grantrail.co.uk

Key personnel

Group Chief Executive Officer: *Gren Edwards*
Group Finance Director: *Richard Taylor*
Group Business Development and
   Communications Director: *George Thompson*
Group Commercial Director: *Stephen Mitchell*
Group Safety and Compliance Director: *Chris Hext*
Group HR Director: *Bryan Webster*

Group Engineering Director: *David Philpott*
Managing Director, Specialist Businesses: *Martin Hawley*
Managing Director, Projects: *David Moreland*

Background

GrantRail Group is a UK-based group of multi-disciplinary railway infrastructure companies, formed in 1996 and part of VolkerWessels Group of companies.

Subsidiaries

GrantRail Power Limited
Matrix Power Limited
GrantRail Signalling Limited
GrantPlant Limited
GrantWeld Limited
Managing Director (for above subsidiaries): *Martin Hawley*

Associate companies

ALH Rail Coatings Ltd (50 per cent)
Directors: *George Thompson and Martin Hawley*

Capabilities

Through integrated resources from the wider group and partnerships, GrantRail can service areas of the railway infrastructure industry. This includes: construction of new railway systems and urban mass transit networks; re-establishment of former railways; construction of associated support infrastructure (including sidings and depots); renewal and refurbishment of existing rail infrastructure – plain line track renewals, switches and crossing renewals; signalling design, installation, testing and commissioning of new works and supporting track renewals; track welding – aluminothermic welding, mobile flash butt welding, superweld and gauge corner restoration welding; coated rail systems – liquid polymer for pour in situ, pre-coated rail, pre-moulded elastomer 'booted' rail; overhead line electrification and power supply; installation, testing and commissioning of switchgear, transformers, ancillary equipment and protection systems, cabling installations, HV/LV power distribution works; supply and operation of specialised plant and equipment; investment and development in new technologies and innovations.

Plant and equipment

Twin Job Tracklayer TRM; sleeper beam for TRM; two Kirow 250 (includes beams and wagons) with 25 t lifting capacity; Kirow 810 (includes beams and wagons) with 100 t lifting capacity; Kirow 1200 (includes beams and wagons) with 125 t lifting capacity; three Matisa B45 tampers; five Matisa B41 tampers; two Matisa R24 regulators; four Colmar RRV's; S&C Beaver tamper; mobile flash butt welding; comprehensive range of small plant and equipment.

Contracts

In 2008, GrantRail was awarded a contract for Manchester Metrolink. As part of the MPact-Thales consortium, GrantRail will design, construct and maintain the Oldham and Rochdale, Droylsden and Chorlton Metrolink extensions.

In May 2008, GrantRail was awarded a multi-disciplinary contract by Network Rail to undertake Lea Valley works. Also in May 2008, GrantRail, as part of the MPact Group (Laing O'Rourke and GrantRail), was awarded a contract by the Railway Procurement Agency in Dublin to construct the Dublin C1-400 Luas Line extension.

In 2007, GrantRail, in joint venture with Skanska UK, was awarded contracts for both Package six and Package eight for the Docklands Light Railways (DLR) extension to Stratford International Station. These works play a key role in the transport plans for the London 2012 Olympic Games.

In October 2007, GrantRail was awarded a contract by Network Rail to undertake the Hull Docks Branch enhancement. GrantRail also successfully completed the permanent way and Over Head Line Equipment (OHLE) elements of the Ashford Hitachi Train Care Depot project, working

with main contractor Fitzpatrick Contractors Limited for the client, HSBC Rail (UK).

Major key clients include: Docklands Light Railway, Network Rail, Sheffield Supertram, Manchester Metrolink, London Underground – Tube Lines, and Associated British Ports.

As well as fulfilling numerous industrial and freight facilities contracts, GrantRail Group has developed its own signalling, welding, plant and electrification companies which complete contracts for various clients and industries – such as Matrix Power, which recently completed contracts for McCain and Nestle, and GrantRail Projects which has completed work for Lafarge in Hope.

Hall Rail

Hetton Lyons Industrial Estate, Hetton-le-Hole DH5 0RF, UK
(+44 191) 526 21 14   Fax: (+44 191) 517 01 12
e-mail: enquiries@hallrail.co.uk, reg@hallrail.co.uk
Web: www.hallrail.com

Key personnel

Managing Director: *Reg Hall*
Technical Director: *Russell Tapping*
Track Engineer/Techical Advisor: *Mike Andrews*
Procurement and Safety Manager: *Graeme Kitto*
Sales/Technical Manager: *Trevor Canning*
Technical Support: *Ashley Hodgson*
Production Manager: *Steve Handie*

Products

Track products, including: switches and crossings for main line, urban, industrial and narrow gauge railways; buffer stops; components for switches and crossings; AWS magnets.

New developments

Manufacture of hollow cable sleepers to Tenconi Design for UK, Belgium, Estonia and Eire markets.

Contracts

Hall Rail has supplied rail operators and infrastructure maintenance companies in Australia, Ireland, Nigeria, Sudan and Thailand, as well as in the UK.

Hanning & Kahl GmbH & Co KG

Rudolf Diesel Strasse 6, D-33818 Oerlinghausen, Germany
PO Box 1342, D-33806 Oerlinghausen, Germany
Tel: (+49 5202) 70 76 00
Fax: (+49 5202) 70 76 29
e-mail: info@huk.hanning.com
Web: www.hanning-kahl.de

Key Personnel

General Managers: *Wolfgang Helas*
Brake Division Manager: *Dietrich Radtke*
LRT Division Manager: *Christian Schmidt*
Service Division Manager: *Peter Spilker*
Sales Manager, Brakes: *Jürgen Stammeier*
Sales Manager, LRT: *Joachim Pütsch*
Sales Manager, Services/LRT: *Joachim Zehn*
Sales Manager, Services/Brakes: *Martin Epp*

Products

LRT Division: points mechanisms for all gauges and types of rail with magnetic, motor or electrohydraulic drive; manual setting mechanisms. Point setting mechanisms are also available with a tongue detector and mechanical double-interlocking for tongues in open and closed positions and electrical locally-set point.

Point controllers, depot controllers, signalling systems for point controllers, level crossing safety devices, single-line track safety devices, mass detectors, vehicle reporting systems, radio control, electronic data recorders and accessories including guard rail tie bars, rail boxes and contact systems.

Service Division: Services and testing and measuring equipment for point setting mechanisms and controllers, signalling installations, TWC systems.

Contracts

Contracts include the supply of point-setting mechanisms to Calgary (Canada); Salt Lake City, Dallas, San Diego, San Jose (US); Manchester, Birmingham, Croydon and Sheffield (UK); Rome, Turin, Milan (Italy); Melbourne (Australia); Hong Kong; and cities in Germany, Switzerland, Austria, Belgium, the Netherlands, Norway, Sweden and Finland.

Harsco Track Technologies Pty Ltd

4 Strathwyn Street, PO Box 5287, Brendale, Queensland 4500, Australia
Tel: (+61 7) 32 05 65 00   Fax: (+61 7) 32 05 73 69
Web: www.harscotrack.com

Key personnel

Managing Director: *Kim Harley*
Sales Manager: *G A Twilley*
Service Manager: *P R Hibberson*

Other offices

Main office and plant
2401 Edmund Road, Box 20, Cayce-West Columbia, South Carolina 29171-0020, US
Tel: (+1 803) 822 91 60   Fax: (+1 803) 822 81 07
e-mail: dbenza@harscotrack.com
Web: www.harscotrack.com
Ludington Office and Plant
Harsco Track Technologies
200 South Jackson Road, Ludington, Michigan 49431, US
Tel: (+1 231) 843 34 31   Fax: (+1 231) 843 48 30
Fairmont Office and Plant
Harsco Track Technologies
415 N Main Street, PO Box 415, Fairmont, Minnesota 56031-0415, US
Tel: (+1 507) 235 33 61   Fax: (+1 507) 235 73 70
Harsco Track Technologies Ltd
Unit 1, Chewton Street, Eastwood, Nottingham NG16 3HB, UK
Tel: (+44 1773) 53 94 80   Fax: (+44 1773) 53 94 81
e-mail: httuk@harsco.com

Background

Since 1909 Harsco Track Technologies, Harsco Corporation, has been a major international supplier to the world's railways and transit systems of track construction and maintenance equipment.

Harsco track construction   1325313

Harsco mud mantis track and switch undercutter cleaner   1325315

Harsco PGM-48 production rail grinder for China   1198478

Harsco RMS-8 production rail grinder working on the Union Pacific Railroad   1198479

TRT-909 track renewal system working on Union Pacific Railroad   1198482

For details of the latest updates to *Jane's Urban Transport Systems* online and to discover the additional information available exclusively to online subscribers please visit
juts.janes.com

Harsco stone blower   1325314

HTT is a single source for over 140 types and models of work equipment for track and structure maintenance, track renewal and new track construction. All equipment is manufactured to ISO 9001:2000 certified facilities.

Products
Design and manufacture of an extensive line of equipment including: rail grinders, production and switch; tampers, production and switch; stoneblowers; new track construction machines; track renewal systems; track and turnout undercutting; tie replacement; rail renewal/tie pad change-out on concrete cross ties; specialised utility track vehicles; HY-Rail® guide wheel attachments; re-manufacturing services providing in-plant re-manufacturing and upgrading of customer machines and additional track maintenance machines.

Contracts
Harsco's railway track maintenance division has launched a new track ballast cleaning service. The first contract was signed with Florida East Coast Railway (FECR) and involves HTT's 'Mud Mantis'; a new-generation switch undercutting and ballast cleaning machine.

Indian Railways, track renewal trains; rail grinder, Mauritania; 2nd switch and crossing rail grinder, Germany; narrow-gauge tamping machine, US; three-year agreement to operate and maintain the HTT rail grinders previously sold to Network Rail in the UK. Rail grinders for Japan and Singapore, 40 new rail grinding machines for China, 96 stone rail grinder for Brazil, rail grinding for Israel.

H J Skelton (Canada) Ltd

165 Oxford Street E, London, Ontario N6A ITA, Canada
Tel: (+1 519) 679 91 80   Fax: (+1 519) 679 01 93
e-mail: skelton@skelton-metals.com
Web: www.skelton-metals.com

Key personnel
President: *Geoff Richey*
Director: *Peter Fraser*
General Manager: *Janet Heffernan*
Sales Manager: *Scott Wordtmann*

Products
Supplier of a wide variety of track components, special trackwork, sliding rail expansion joints, switch machines, sliding rail buffer stops. North American agent for Sika 'Icosit' polyurethane grout for undersealing grooved rail and injected pads for direct fixation. Specialises in LRT in-street applications, as well as railway rail (both T and grooved), crane rails and turnouts. Rawie sliding friction bumping posts to stop trains at up to 56 km/h as well as low-floor LRVs. Contec switch machines and track wiring systems. Range of rails, points, crossing and special trackwork. AREMA 115/132/136 joint bars, insulated and standard bonded joint bars for 115.132/136RE rail and UIC54, tie plates, screw spikes and fe6 double-spring washers.

Contracts
Supply contract for TTC Toronto, Boston MBTA, Cabo San Lucas, Mexico and San Antonio, Texas for all manganese frogs, crossings and points for tram tracks. Special trackwork for Calgary and Edmonton LRT systems including concrete ties. Polyurethane grout for Calgary and Vancouver's Canada Line. Direct fixation fasteners for Edmonton LRT and Canada Line by Transit Products as well as track fasteners including screw spikes and washers, for Canada Line and many North American railroads.

H J Skelton & Co Ltd

9 The Broadway, Thatcham RG19 3JA, UK
Tel: (+44 1635) 86 52 56
Fax: (+44 1635) 86 57 10
e-mail: info@hjskelton.com
Web: www.hjskelton.co.uk

Key personnel
Director: *J W G Smith*

Products
Agents for Rawie sliding friction buffer stops, fixed stops and wheel stops throughout the UK and Ireland. Suppliers of railway rails and crane rail to British, European and North American (BS, UIC and ASTM) standards. Specialist permanent way items as required in all track building projects.

Contracts
Recent contracts include the supply of Rawie friction element buffer stops for St Pancras International Station; Irish Rail; DLR; LUAS-Dublin and Kings Cross.

Holland Company LP

1000 Holland Drive, Crete, Illinois 60417-2120, US
Tel: (+1 708) 672 23 00   Fax: (+1 708) 672 01 19
e-mail: sales@hollandco.com
Web: www.hollandco.com

Key personnel
President: *Phil Moeller*
Vice-President Rail Mechanical Group: *Len O'Kray*
Vice President/General Manager Track Testing Services: *Robert Madderom*
General Manager Mobile Welding Operations: *Mark Rovnyak*
Controller: *Frank Francis*
General Manager Equipment Division: *Robert Norby*
General Manager, MOW Sales: *Kevin Flaherty*

Products
Sales and contracting of electric flash-butt welding personnel and equipment; rail and road mobile welders, portable on-site welding plants; track measurement services, including geometry, rail wear and track strength measurement. Products also include the Intelliweld® fully digitised flash-butt welding control system. Holland can supply all support equipment or provide a turnkey operation.

Supply of rail welding equipment, rail and Continuous Welded Rail (CWR) handling and processing equipment, track testing services equipment and railroad maintenance-of-way equipment. Products include Holland's mobilewelder in-track flash-butt welding machine, containerised welding units, railpullers, welding plant equipment, rail grinders and polishers, CWR unloader units, railtrains, pick-up units and TrackSTAR®.

IAD Rail Systems

63 + 64 Gazelle Road, Weston-super-Mare, BS24 9ES, UK
Tel: (+44 1934) 42 70 00
Fax: (+44 1934) 42 70 20
e-mail: enquiries@iadrailsystems.com
Web: www.iadrailsystems.com

Key personnel
Managing Director: *Mick Ledger*

Background
IAD Rail Systems is the division of Claverham Ltd supplying the needs of the rail industry. The company is a wholly owned subsidiary of Hamilton Standard Corporation, itself, part of the United Technologies Corporation.

Products
Switch and crossing actuation systems. The company developed its High Performance Switch Actuator (HPSA), which incorporates reliable actuation, locking and detection technologies in close co-operation with the UK rail industry. The expertise developed was extended to in-sleeper torsional back-drives to create the company's PowerLink backdrive, which when combined with HPSA provides a high reliability total system. Suitable for high line speeds and high axle weights, the system is claimed to be easy to install and to require no scheduled maintenance. Through-tamping and remote monitoring is also possible.

The first production installation of HPSA took place in the UK at a location in south London on Network Rail's Southern Zone late in 2000. Since then over 550 systems have been installed across the UK.

Interep SA

rue de l'Industrie, F-43110 Aurec/Loire, France
Tel: (+33 4) 77 35 20 21
Fax: (+33 4) 77 35 26 17
e-mail: sales@interep.fr
Web: www.interep.fr

Key personnel
Managing Director: *Dr Francis Joachim*
Sales and Marketing Manager: *Philippe Charbonnier*
Research and Development Manager: *Jean-Philippe Montagnon*
Financial Manager: *Patrice Cusin*
Technical Manager: *Laure Walter*

Products
Microcellular rubber foams to reduce vibrations, for use as a ballast mat or under the sleeper for conventional ballasted tracks (marketed under the name Caoutchouc Mousse); also pad under block or baseplate for non-ballasted tracks.

Contracts
Microcellular mats under floating slabs have been supplied for tram lines in Turin, Italy. Microcellular rubber pads for non-ballasted tracks have been supplied to Bilbao, Spain, RATP Paris (Eole and Météor) and Athens, Greece.

Developments
A microcellular rubber mat with advanced damping properties Type 43-45 is suitable for metro systems. An in-house dynamic test machine for controls and simulation has been developed.

Jarvis Rail

Head office
Jarvis House, Frenchgate Towers, St Sepulchre Gate, Doncaster DN1 1SW, UK
Tel: (+44 1302) 30 93 00
Fax: (+44 1302) 30 93 79
e-mail: enquiries@jarvis-uk.com
Web: www.jarvisplc.com

Key personnel
Managing Director: *Pat McHale*
Press: *Toni Jackson*
Operations Director, Track Renewals: *Rick Thompson*
Managing Director, Electrical Projects: *Stuart Birch*
Project Manager: *Andy Blakeley*

Services

Responsible for track renewals and maintenance, Jarvis is one of the largest railway engineering organisations in the UK with a workforce of over 5,000. It owns approximately 60 per cent of the UK's on-track plant. Regional offices across the UK are supported by a network of over 70 depots at key points on the infrastructure.

Contracts

Jarvis Rail secured the final stage contract for the Rugby Station Re-modelling Project. This extension to the contract, which originated in January 2007, commenced in June 2008. The works included plain line and switches and crossing renewals and all associated through alignment tamping.

In 2007 Jarvis Rail was selected by Network Rail as one of four primary contractors for its track renewals programme.

JEZ Sistemas Ferroviarios

Arantzar S/N, E-01400 Llodio Laudio, Spain
Tel: (+34 94) 672 12 00
Fax: (+34 94) 672 00 92
e-mail: uerrazti@jez.es
Web: www.voestalpine.com/jez

Key personnel

General Manager: *U Errazti*

Background

VAE GmbH is the shareholder of JEZ Sistemas Ferroviarios.

Products

Turnout systems, cast manganese crossings, switches and crossings, points/crossings, track components, track materials and equipment.

A Kaufmann AG

Pilatusstrasse 2, CH-6300 Zug, Switzerland
Tel: (+41 41) 711 67 00
Fax: (+41 41) 859 16 01
e-mail: info@kago.com
Web: www.kago.com

Products

KAGO specialist engineering products for railways, including a complete range of non-screwed rail contact clamps, discs and strips for electrical rail connections (return current, signalling circuits, earthing), cable fastenings for rails and sleepers, special welding electrodes for copper welding; complete range of screwing, welding and grounding fittings; self-tapping sleeper screws for concrete, steel or wooden sleepers; sleeper spring clips; high-voltage insulations.

Recent development: KAGO axle counter box.

Services

Track returns and earthing wires; earthing poles; heavy-duty and special mountings and drillings; suspensions for radiating cables.

KAGO easily mounted electrical rail contact with vibration-resistant cable fixing 0093216

Kloos Oving bv

West-Kinderdijk 24, NL-2953 XW Alblasserdam, Netherlands
PO Box 3, NL-2960 AA Kinderdijk, Netherlands
Tel: (+31 78) 691 40 00
Fax: (+31 78) 691 45 42
e-mail: info@kloos-oving.nl
Web: www.kloos-oving.nl

Key personnel

General Manager: *J van Houwelingen*

Background

In February 2008 Kloos Oving was acquired by French company, Vossloh Cogifer AG, an industrial subsidiary of the German based Vossloh Group.

Products

Design, development, construction and delivery of standard and custom-built track materials for main line, metro, light rail systems and heavy-duty systems including: turnouts, crossings, points, isolated rail joints and special constructions.

Contracts

Recent contracts include the supply of track materials to operators in Egypt, Germany, Indonesia, Iran and the Netherlands.

Laser Rail Ltd

Fitology House, Smedley Street East, Matlock DE4 3GH, UK
Tel: (+44 1629) 76 07 50
Fax: (+44 1629) 76 07 51
e-mail: info@laser-rail.co.uk
Web: www.laser-rail.co.uk

Key personnel

Chief Executive Officer: *David M Johnson*
Executive Director: *Alison B Stansfield*
Managing Director: *Steve Ingleton*
Non-Executive Director: *Hugh Fenwick*

Background

Laser Rail, established in 1989, is a technical consultancy supplying complete turnkey projects for rail infrastructure and metro networks. It combines experienced engineers with the latest high-technology laser-gauging systems and software to measure and analyse clients' infrastructure and provide new and innovative vehicle designs. Laser Rail is part of Balfour Beatty Rail Technologies, itself part of the Balfour

Laser Rail's LaserPeT, designed to measure metro networks 1310439

Beatty Rail group. The recent acquisition of Laser Rail has extended Balfour Beatty's technology base with expertise in gauging technologies, analysis and data management and a specialist team engaged in the area of track geometry measurement and evaluation. As part of Balfour Beatty, Laser Rail is now able to include design and implementation of schemes providing their clients with the possibility of turnkey solutions.

Products

Measuring systems: Laser Gauging Vehicle (LGV), a road-rail vehicle for measuring structure profiles accurately and at speed. Laser Profiling Trolley (LaserPeT), a portable version of the LGV used at walking speed and designed to measure metro infrastructure. LaserFleX™ structure profile measuring systems, LaserSweep™, a portable measuring device for measuring structure profiles in areas where larger systems are uneconomical to use. Product approval received from Network Rail and London Underground.

Software: ClearRoute™, Stress Route™, DesignRoute™ software for vehicles and infrastructure management, 3-Dimensional databases and advanced change detection software, which provides new tools for the catalogue and management of assets.

Services: Track geometry measurement and design, route assessment for existing and new rolling stock, interoperability, feasibility studies for existing and new routes, design of new rolling stock. Risk assessment.

Track technologies: XiTRACK, a process for treating track ballast to maintain or restore its performance by the application of designed polymers.

Laser Rail has a formal research and development group to develop core technologies associated with its activities. Projects being undertaken include infrastructure measurement, monitoring and analysis, vehicle/track interaction

Laser Rail's XiTrack process for treating track ballast 1344775

Laser Rail's LaserSweep™, portable measurement system   1344774

technology and intelligent video systems. Laser Rail also provides software training and certification to various levels of competency and this can be supplied as part of the overall support package. Laser Rail operates in the UK, Europe and Australasia.

L B Foster

2420 N Pioneer Lane, Spokane, Washington 99216, US
Tel: (+1 509) 924 63 00   Fax: (+1 509) 927 02 99
e-mail: info@cxtinc.com
Web: www.lbfoster.com

Key personnel
President and Chief Executive Officer: *Stan L Hasselbusch*
Senior Vice-President, CFO and Treasurer: *David J Russo*
Senior Vice-President, Rail Products: *Samuel K Fisher*
Vice-President, Rail Product Sales: *Gregory W Lippard*

Works
2420 N Pioneer Lane, Spokane, Washington 99216
15708 E Marietta, Spokane, Washington 99216
710 E US Highway 30, Grand Island, Nebraska 68801
Grand Island Tie Plant
710 E US Highway #20, PO Box 1808, Grand Island, Nebraska 68801
Tel: (+1 308) 382 54 00
Fax: (+1 308) 382 32 50

Background
In 1999, LB Foster acquired CXT Inc, a manufacturer of engineered concrete products for the railroad and transit industries. The acquisition better positioned L B Foster to serve rail and transit customers with a mix of products and services.

Products
Prestressed concrete sleepers for track and turnouts; prefabricated buildings and precast concrete grade crossing panels.
Geometric design capabilities for turnout layouts; for track, with a facility for gauge widening; for tangent sleeper development, and for standard track sleepers.

Contracts
In January 2005, the company was awarded a long-term contract (through 2012) for the supply of prestressed concrete railroad sleepers to the Union Pacific Railroad (UPRR).
Concrete sleepers supplied to the Calgary LRT, MTA Baltimore, Vancouver, Utah, Los Angeles, New Jersey, Denver, Portland and Southern California Regional Rail Authority, UP, BNSF and many other heavy-haul railways.
Standard and curved concrete level crossing panels supplied to the UPRR, Burlington Northern Santa Fe Railway and other mainline railroads through North America as well as light rail transit systems in California, Oregon, Utah and Washington State.

Lindapter International

Lindsay House, Brackenbeck Road, Bradford BD7 2NF, UK
Tel: (+44 1274) 52 14 44
Fax: (+44 1274) 52 11 30
e-mail: enquiries@lindapter.com
Web: www.lindapter.com

Key personnel
Technical Support Manager: *Michael Knight*

Other offices
Lindapter SA
Paris Nord II, 14 rue de la Perdix, F-95700 Roissy, France
Tel: (+33 1) 48 17 87 90
Fax: (+33 1) 48 17 87 99
Contact: Jaques Babault

Lindapter GmbH
Ernestinestr. 67, D-45141 Essen, Germany
Tel: (+49 201) 21 47 78   Fax: (+49 201) 29 06 14
Contact: Sabine Reimann

Background
Lindapter International was formed in 1934 by Henry Lindsay to market traditional hook bolt adapters.

Lindapter's rail clip   0092275

Products
Type HD adjustable rail clips; the Soft clip holds rails in precise alignment while the Hard clip prevents vertical rail movement. A Spring clip also caters for rail wave while holding the rail down. A Type BR clip suits flat bottom or bridge rails up to an 8° slope. The Temporary Support System supports and insulates running rails while essential repair work is being carried out.

Contracts
Manchester Piccadilly station reroofing. Greenwich station transport interchange (connections in roof structure), London Underground rerailing project. Other contracts include Rome metro, Channel Tunnel and the East Coast Main Line, UK.

Loram Maintenance of Way, Inc

3900 Arrowhead Drive, Hamel, Minnesota 55340, US
Tel: (+1 763) 478 60 14   Fax: (+1 763) 478 22 21
e-mail: sales@loram.com
Web: www.loram.com

Key personnel
Vice-President, Marketing & Sales: *D F DeJoseph*
Vice-President, OEM/Sales: *J M Carlin*
Manager, International: *T L Smith*

Products
Loram manufactures equipment and provides a full-service approach to railroad maintenance services for heavy haul, passenger/freight and transit railroads. Customers can opt either to purchase or lease, or contract one of Loram's leased equipment crews. Products include a full range of self-propelled rail grinders, self-propelled ditch cleaner; self-propelled shoulder ballast cleaners, L & J Series of self-propelled transit grinders, Raptor rail handling system, undercutters and rail-mounted vacuum excavators.

Lucchini Group

Lucchini SpA
Via Oberdan 1/a, I-25128 Brescia, Italy
Tel: (+39 030) 399 21   Fax: (+39 030) 30 06 69
Web: www.lucchini.com

Key personnel
President: *Giuseppe Lucchini*
Vice-Presidents: *Vadim Makhov, Giovanni Gillerio*
Chief Executive Officer: *Hervè Kerbrat*
Corporate Commercial and Marketing Director: *Rinaldo Baldi*
Rail Sales Manager: *Priamo Priami*
Rail Business Manager: *Paolo Fillini*

Works
Piombino Works (Lucchini SpA)
Largo Caduti sul Lavoro 21, I-57025 Piombino Livorno, Italy
Tel: (+39 0565) 641 11   Fax: (+39 0565) 641 33
Bari Fonderie Meridionali – BFM
Via Tommaso Columbo 7, I-70123 Bari, Italy
Tel: (+39 080) 582 71 11
Fax: (+39 080) 582 72 73
e-mail: i.mariani@lucchini.it
President and Managing Director: *Marchello Calcagni*
General Manager: *Igor Mariani*

Products
Lucchini Piombino: Rails from 27 kg/m to 70 kg/m in various steel grades. Maximum rail lengths: 108 m.
Bari Fonderie Meridionali (BFM) Bari Works: Manganese steel castings of monobloc frogs for railways switches and castings for various applications in the railway, petrolchemical, steel and energy production sectors.

MATISA Matériel Industriel SA

Case Postale, CH-1023 Crissier 1, Switzerland
Tel: (+41 21) 631 21 11   Fax: (+41 21) 631 21 68
e-mail: matisa@matisa.ch
Web: www.matisa.ch

Key personnel

Managing Director: *Rainer von Schack*
Technical Director: *Jörg Ganz*
Marketing Director: *Jörg Marbach*

Subsidiaries

France
MATISA SAS
Offices and workshop: 9 rue de l'Industrie, ZI Les
Sablons, F-89100 Sens
Tel: (+33 3) 86 95 83 35
Fax: (+33 3) 86 95 36 94
e-mail: matisa.@matisa.fr
Commercial Manager: *P Boetti*
General Manager: *E Fuchs*
   Sales of MATISA group products in Belgium,
France, Luxembourg, and French-speaking Africa.
After-sales service, spare parts and overhaul of
MATISA machines in France.

Germany
MATISA Maschinen GmbH
Kronenstrasse 2, D-78166 Donaueschingen
Tel: (+49 771) 15 80 63   Fax: (+49 771) 15 80 64
e-mail: matisa@matisa.de
General Manager: *F Wernick*
   Sales of MATISA group products in Germany,
after-sales service and spare parts of MATISA
machines operating in Germany.

Italy
MATISA SpA
Via Ardeatina km 21, I-00040 Pomezia/Santa
Palomba (Rome)
Tel: (+39 06) 91 82 91   Fax: (+39 06) 91 98 45 74
e-mail: matisa@matisa.it
General Manager: *Eng J Berga*
   Sales of MATISA group products and after-sales
service, spare parts and overhaul of MATISA
machines in Italy.

Japan
MATISA Japan Co Ltd
JR Hatchobori Bldg, 8F, 3-25-10 Hatchoboro,
Chuo-Ku, Tokyo 104-0032
Tel: (+81 3) 55 40 82 11   Fax: (+81 3) 55 40 82 20
e-mail: matisa@matisa.jp
General Manager: *André Zimmermann*
   Sales of MATISA group products and after-sales
service, spare parts and overhaul of MATISA
machines operating in Japan.

Spain
MATISA Matériel Industriel SA
Sucursal Española
C/Francia, 39 Polgono Industrial "La Estación",
ES-28971 Grinón, Madrid
Tel: (+34 91) 814 01 71   Fax: (+34 91) 814 11 94
e-mail: matisa@matisa.e.telefonica.net
Commercial Director: *E Puertas*
Technical Director: *S Gonzalez*
   Sales of MATISA group products in Spain;
after-sales service, spare parts and overhaul
of MATISAmachines operating in Spain and
Portugal.

UK
MATISA (UK) Ltd
PO Box 202, Scunthorpe DN15 6XR
Tel: (+44 1724) 87 70 00   Fax: (+44 1724) 87 70 01
e-mail: matisa@matisa.co.uk
General Manager: *R Grossniklaus*
   Sales of MATISA group products and after-sales
service, spare parts and overhaul of MATISA
machines operating in the UK.

Products

Manufacture and sale of track construction and
maintenance machinery, including tamper-leveller-
liners (continuous, conventional, combined for
points and crossings and plain track); regulators
with and without hoppers; tracklaying and track
renewal trains; ballast cleaners; track and catenary
measuring, recording and analysis vehicles; track
and catenary service vehicles.

NEU International Railways

70 rue du Collège, PO Box 4039, F-4039 Marcq en
Baroeul, France
Tel: (+33 3) 20 45 65 09   Fax: (+33 3) 20 45 65 99
e-mail: railways@neu-railways.com
Web: www.neu-railways.com

Other offices

NEU Inc
PO Box 488, Paoli, Pennsylvania 19301-0488, US
Tel: (+1 610) 725 04 01   Fax: (+1 610) 725 04 02
e-mail: mail@neu-inc.com

Products

NEU International Railways develops specific
solutions for safety, cleanliness and reliability of
all types of railway networks and depots (train,
tramway, metro).

Equipment for depots

Sand distribution systems for clean and
automatic feeding of all types of train sandboxes,
fixed sand pumps or mobile unit, platform or
overhead installation. CET installation to empty
chemical and/or retention toilet tanks, fixed
installation or mobile unit. Train wash facility for
all types of train including drive through or gantry
systems. Completely modular and expandable
construction with total or partial water recycling.

Track cleaning

Vaktrak for track cleaning in stations and tunnels,
based on patented technology for the combined
suck/blow system, specially designed for
underground metro networks. The number, size
and position of these modules are designed to
match the required working configuration. The
Vaktrak rail/road unit has been designed for light
rail tracks, stations, tunnels or outside, on ballast,
on concerete slab with grooved rail or on sleepers.

Nomix Enviro

The Grain Silos, Weyhill Road, Andover SP10
3NT, UK
Tel: (+44 1264) 38 80 50   Fax: (+44 1264) 33 76 42
e-mail: info@nomix.co.uk
Web: www.nomixenviro.co.uk

Key personnel

Managing Director: *Mark Phillips*
Finance Director: *Mark Long*
UK Sales Manager: *Ian Samms*
Commercial and Technical Support Executive:
   Amanda Evans

Products

On-track weed control, off-track scrub clearance,
lead-jetting, traction gel application, weed
chemicals and equipment; drain clearing.

ORTEC Gesellschaft für Schienentechnische Systeme mbH

Eigelstein 10-12, D-50668 Cologne, Germany
Tel: (+49 221) 120 69 60   Fax: (+49 221) 12 06 96 66
e-mail: info@ortec-gmbh.de
Web: www.ortec-gmbh.de

Key personnel

Managing Director: *Hermann Ortwein*

Products

Vibration-insulating rail fasteners, Whisper Rail
continuous elastic rail embedment material,
noise insulation material, ISOLast insulating
embedment material, Loadmaster for reduction
of ground and structure-borne vibrations.

Pandrol Rail Fastenings

63 Station Road, Addlestone, Weybridge KT15
2AR, UK
Tel: (+44 1932) 83 45 00   Fax: (+44 1932) 85 08 58
e-mail: info@pandrol.com
Web: www.pandrol.com

Key personnel

Chief Executive: *J Beal-Preston*
Group Marketing and Services Director: *B Forster*

Subsidiaries

Pandrol Asia Pacific Office, Perth, Australia
Pandrol Australia Pty Ltd, Blacktown, Australia
Pandrol Canada Ltd, Edmonton, Canada
PT Pandrol Indonesia, Jakarta, Indonesia
Pandrol Italia SpA, Teramo, Italy
Pandrol Korea Ltd, Seoul, Republic of Korea
Pandrol South Africa
Pandrol UK Ltd, Worksop, UK
Vortok International Ltd, Addlestone, Surrey, UK
Pandrol USA LP, Bridgeport, New Jersey, US

Products

Design and manufacture of rail fastening
systems and associated installation equipment;
resilient rail pads; resiliently supported direct
fixation (DF) systems; Vortok Coils for restoring
worn screwspike holes (see entry for Vortok
International).
   Pandrol continues its research into the dynamic
behaviour of track to increase understanding
of the relationship between forces in track and
component performance, and of the generation
of noise and vibration. Pandrol has developed

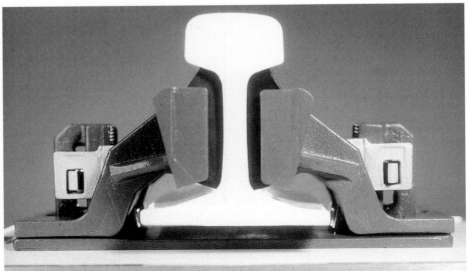

Pandrol VANGUARD system

0526814

a new range of fastening designs for specific applications, including the Pandrol Fastclip® system, which is designed for low-cost installation and maintenance, and the new track support systems designed for application in areas which are sensitive to noise and vibration, including Pandrol VIPA-SP, the latest product in the Pandrol VIPA range incorporating FASTCLIP® and VANGUARD.

Phoenix AG

Hannoversche Strasse 88, D-21079 Hamburg, Germany
Tel: (+49 40) 76 67 20 01   Fax: (+49 40) 76 67 22 11
e-mail: mailservice@contitech.de
Web: www.phoenix-ag.com

Key personnel
Chairman: *Manfred Wennemer*
Chief Engineer: *Bernd Pahl*
Sales Manager: *Thomas Barschke*

Background
Phoenix AG is part of ContiTech AG, a Continental subsidiary.

Products
Elastomer trackbed matting: CentriCon and Megiflex rail fasteners; rubber groove-sealing sections for safety of rails in workshops and other pedestrian areas; rubber boots with pads; continuous rail seating; and noise-absorbing material.

Pintsch Aben BV

Herenweg 24a, NL-3602 AP Maarssen, Netherlands
Tel: (+31 346) 58 39 58   Fax: (+31 346) 55 43 93
e-mail: info@pintschaben.com
Web: www.pintschaben.com

Key personnel
Managing Director and Branch Manager: *Arnd Konze*
Sales Manager: *Hans van Marlen*

Background
Pintsch Aben BV is a subsidiary of Pintsch Bamag, a member of the Schaltbau Group.

Products
Point heating systems (electric and propane gas), point heating components, solid-state snow detectors; local and regional control and communication technology (data transmission, supervision centres).

Plasser & Theurer

Johannesgasse 3, A-1010 Vienna, Austria
Tel: (+43 1) 51 57 20   Fax: (+43 1) 513 18 01
Web: www.showroom.creative.co.at

Main works
Pummererstrasse 5, A-4021 Linz/Donau, Austria

Subsidiaries
Worldwide including; Australia, Brazil, Canada, Denmark, France, Germany, Hong Kong, India, Italy, Japan, Mexico, Spain, South Africa, UK and US.

UK
Plasser (UK) Ltd
Manor Road, West Ealing, London W13 0PP, UK
Tel: (+44 20) 89 98 47 81   Fax: (+44 20) 89 97 82 06
e-mail: info@plasser.co.uk

Products
Tracklaying and maintenance machinery; levelling, lifting, lining and tamping machines; ballast distributing, profiling and cleaning machines; material conveyor and hopper units; track and

Self-loading Plassermatic 08-275 4 ZW levelling, lining and tamping machine working at the Vienna Metro   1375554

switch relaying machines; rail rectification machines, grinding and welding machines; vacuum scraper excavators; catenary maintenance and inspection cars; track geometry measuring cars; permanent way motor vehicles.

Several different models with special features have been built for urban rail systems and industrial railways. This includes the Metropolitan series for maintaining track with short radii, tight clearance gauges or narrow-gauge track or self-loading and rail/road-going machines.

polyplan ® GmbH

Mitterstrassweg 23, D-82064 Strasslach, Germany
Tel: (+49 81) 709 30 50   Fax: (+49 81) 706 17
e-mail: contact@polyplangmbh.de
Web: www.fluesterschiene.de

Key personnel
Directors: *Johann Resch, Jürgen Huber, Reinhard Giglmaier*

Products
polyplan ® produces a permanent coating for light rail called the *polyplan* ® SILENCE whisper rail, which reduces traffic noise and vibration and helps decrease material fatigue.

Polysafe Level Crossing Systems Ltd

King Street Industrial Estate, Langtoft, Peterborough PE6 9NF, UK
Tel: (+44 1778) 56 05 55
Fax: (+44 1778) 56 07 73
e-mail: sales@polysafe.co.uk
Web: www.polysafe.co.uk

Key personnel
Managing Director: *Michael Austin*

Products
Steel-framed polymer concrete level crossing systems for main line, urban and industrial railway applications.

Profilbeton GmbH

Waberner Strasse 40, D-34582 Borken/Hess, Germany
Tel: (+49 5682) 738 60   Fax: (+49 5682) 73 86 42
e-mail: info@profilbeton.de
Web: www.profilbeton.de

Key personnel
Director: *Wolfgang Hasch*

Profilbeton's Kassel Kerb installed in Germany   0114002

Sales Manager: *Hannes Stechmann*
Technical Support: *Carsten Hasch*

Products

The Kassel Kerb is a self-guiding kerbstone designed to reduce damage to tyres and provide improved conditions for passengers entering and leaving trams and buses. Driving on the concave surface reduces the horizontal and vertical distances between the vehicle and the stop to almost nothing. The kerbstone is available in 160, 180, 210 and 240 mm ramp height and various curves.

Contracts

The Kassel Kerb has been used for tram and bus stops in more than 700 towns and cities in Europe.

RAIL.ONE GmbH

Pfleiderer track systems
Ingolstaedter Strasse 51, D-92318 Neumarkt, Germany
Tel: (+49 9181) 28 0
Fax: (+49 9181) 28 83 44
e-mail: info@railone.com
Web: www.railone.com

Key personnel

Managing Directors: *Richard Ziegler (Chief Executive Officer)*

Background

Since 1954 RAIL.ONE, formerly Pfleiderer track systems, has produced concrete main-track and turnout sleepers for railways and urban traffic in Germany and around the world. As one of the market leaders in Germany, RAIL.ONE offers engineering, production, supply, logistics and quality management. RAIL.ONE has locations in Germany, Hungary, Korea, the Netherlands, China, Romania, Spain and Turkey and annually produces more than 2.5 million main-track sleepers, and over 500,000 linear metres of turnout sleepers. It offers all services from one source for product development, manufacturing and application.

Products

RAIL.ONE offers an extensive portfolio of innovative track systems for installation on ballast, asphalt and concrete for a great number and variety of applications.

The RHEDA CITY ballastless system is based on the same functional principles as are all systems in the RHEDA family. It was developed for urban transport and is especially effective in applications for trams and surface commuter train lines. With its tracks installed flush with the street surface, the RHEDA CITY ballastless system features modified bi-block sleepers that are embedded in a compact concrete slab with lattice girders. Depending on the track model being implemented, the final track will represent either a continuously elastically supported track, or a system with elastic supports on the sleepers. The top layer can be executed in multilayer courses of asphalt, concrete or paving blocks. These options enable the system to optimally match the street surface. Further benefits include the monolithic structure of the track-supporting layer (TSL), as well as the low structural height. With RHEDA CITY, turnouts can also be integrated in the same technological system. The newest model offered is RHEDA CITY GREEN, the grassed version of the RHEDA CITY system.

The ATD-G ballastless track system for urban traffic – the Green Track – is the rapid-transit variation of the ATD track system for main line application. The core of both systems is an asphalt track-supporting layer with a directly mounted track panel. The ATD-G model features installation of a cross-sleeper track panel, consisting of concrete bi-block sleepers and rails, directly onto an asphalt layer executed to precise elevation specifications. Examples

of line sections include straight and curved through-track sections, canted track curves, rail-station and stop sections, transitions to different rail profiles, crossings for pedestrians and vehicles.

RHEDA MRT was developed for applications with underground rail systems. The B355 U300-54M modified concrete bi-block sleeper with lattice girders represents the core of this system. Applications with this solution significantly reduce structural track height, and eliminate the need for longitudinal concrete upstands at the edges of the TSL. RHEDA MRT is effective for application in tunnels, including those with smaller radii; the smooth surface of the RHEDA MRT provides favourable conditions for rescue and emergency access. The system provides two different sleeper types: the normal-length models and extended sleepers to mount the power rail. RHEDA MRT is also available as light or heavy mass-spring systems. The RHEDA 2000® ballastless track for high-speed main lines.

RAIL.ONE's RHEDA MRT was especially developed for applications with underground rail systems 1340427

RAIL.ONE's ATD-G transition area form grooved rail to flat bottom rail 1340428

RAIL.ONE's ATD-G turnout and station 1340429

RAIL.ONE's ATD-G asphalt sub-layer (three layers) 1340431

This product was implemented for the first time on the line between Erfurt and Halle-Leipzig, in Germany. The GETRAC® ballastless track model features direct support of the track panel on an asphalt supporting layer. The wide sleepers that are part of the system reduce the extent of loads transmitted into the sub-grade.

Contracts

Since 1995 approximately 30,000 m of ATD-G Green Track have been installed in a number of cities and projects. Since 1998 more than 130 km of RHEDA CITY track have been installed in a number of German cities, e.g. Berlin,

RAIL.ONE's ATD-G fully assembled and aligned track section 1340432

RAIL.ONE's newest model, the grassed version of the RHEDA CITY system, RHEDA CITY GREEN 1340433

RAIL.ONE's Berlin North-South Link, approx 9 km track in RHEDA 2000®, bedded on a mass-spring-system 1340434

RAIL.ONE's Brandleite Tunnel: 6.3 km in GETRAC® A3 on asphalt layer 1340435

Dresden, Karlsruhe, Mannheim, and Nuremberg. Additional major national and international projects are now being planned or are shortly before execution. From August to October 2006, the Aaltje Noorderwierstraat tram line in The Hague, was equipped with ballastless track technology by RAIL.ONE. The system models RHEDA CITY and RHEDA CITY GREEN were installed over 2.6 km of tram line in the City of Peace and Justice. In addition to delivery of approximately 2,800 bi-block sleepers, RAIL.ONE was responsible in this track project for system supervision, quality assurance and surveying services. An additional contract has already been awarded for approximately 800 m of track along the Royal Library. RAIL.ONE has also been awarded the projects Iancu de Hunedoara Site and Sos Oltenitel, with delivery of TB/ZB sleepers. RAIL.ONE is delivering a total of around 20,000 m of track for these projects in Bucharest. The RHEDA CITY system is used for a length of 5,000 m, for the first time in Warsaw, Poland, on the Aleje Jerozolimskie line. In addition to delivery of the system itself, RAIL.ONE was also responsible for engineering and quality assurance for this project. An additional contract has already been awarded for approximately 300 metres. The North-South Commuter-Rail project in Cologne – according to the Cologne Rapid Transit Authority, the largest urban infrastructure project in Germany and almost the entire line, 4 km long, is underground – including a section 30 m under the Philharmonic Hall. For the first constriction stage, RAIL.ONE is delivering 650 m of RHEDA CITY track and, in collaboration with a partner, two turnouts with high-elastic support of the rails. System monitoring is an additional component of the project contract for RAIL ONE.

Railquip Inc

3731 Northcrest Road, Suite 6, Atlanta, Georgia 30340, US
Tel: (+1 770) 458 41 57; (+1 800) 325 02 96
Fax: (+1 770) 458 53 65
e-mail: sales@railquip.com
Web: www.railquip.com

Key personnel

President: *Helmut Schroeder*
Sales Director: *Paul Wojcik*
Sales Manager: *Denis Zulfic*
Treasurer and Office Manager: *Debbie Fox*

Products

Supply of: track maintenance equipment; hydraulic track jacks; CNC controlled rail bending machines; DH tracklaying pile driving/bridgework/rescue cranes with horizontally extendable boom up to 180 tons (capacity) road/rail equipped trailers; cable channels; laser track measuring device; tamper machine and rail grinding

Railquip's road/rail equipped trailer with rerailing containers, bogie assembly stand and maxi railcar mover   1143022

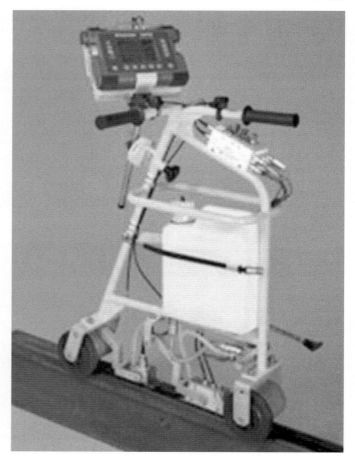

Railquip's ultrasonic rail flaw detector
1344899

Railquip's plastic cable channels   1344898

machines; track gauges, portable hydraulic rerailing equipment, portable car movers, digital switch gauge and cant measurement device, mobile switch inspection system, ultransonic rail flaw detector, fleetcleaner mobile train wash, automatic rail welding machine.

Contracts

Toronto Transit Commission, Toronto, Canada: plastic cable channels. Canadian National Railway, Toronto, Canada: plastic cable channels. Amtrak, Philadelphia, PA: track gauges. Valley Metro Rail, Phoenix, Arizona: auxiliary trucks for locked axles. North County Transit District, Oceanside, California: portable hydraulic rerailing equipment; Rail Transit District, Denver, Colorado: one set of portable hydraulic rerailing equipment. Capital Metro, Austin, Texas: portable hydraulic rerailing equipment, one road/rail equipped trailer, two rerailing equipment storage containers. Trinity Heads Inc, Navasota, Texas: one Maxi railcar mover. Canada Line Rapid Transit, Vancouver, BC: one Maxi railcar mover, one set of rerailing equipment, one rerailing equipment storage container. Utah Transit Authority, Salt Lake City, Utah: one fleetcleaner train wash unit, one road/rail equipped speed/swing car mover.

Bance Alumicart inspection/haulage vehicle   0536547

A Rawie GmbH & Co KG

Dornierstrasse 11, D-49090 Osnabrück, Germany
Tel: (+49 541) 91 20 70
Fax: (+49 541) 912 07 10
e-mail: info@rawie.de
Web: www.rawie.de

Key personnel

Managing Directors: *Jost Fründ, Renate Högermann,*
Head of Railway Technology Exports: *Torsten Riesopp*
Senior Design Engineer: *Christoph Dahm*
Export Manager: *Torsten Riesopp*

Products

Fixed and friction buffer stops; fixed and/or friction buffer stops with hydraulic or elastomeric cylinders; friction, fixed and folding wheel stops; specialist track endings to customer requirements, including folding buffer stops and buffer stops with integral loading ramps.

Contracts

Customers include: Delhi Metro Ph II; N E Line, Singapore; Dubai Metro Ph I and II; Metronet, UK; Metro Sevilla, Metro Barcelona; Rapid Kuala Lumpur, Malaysia; Airport Link, Bangkok.

R Bance & Co Ltd

Cockcrow Hill House, St Mary's Road, Surbiton KT6 5HE, UK
Tel: (+44 20) 83 98 71 41
Fax: (+44 20) 83 98 47 65
e-mail: admin@bance.com
Web: www.bance.com

Key personnel

Managing Director: *R Bance*
Sales Director: *G Smales*
Technical Director: *B Steel*

Products

Continuous rail flaw detection vehicles; rail moving vehicles for confined environments; emergency response vehicles; motorised trolleys; Alumicart inspection/haulage vehicles; trolleys and skates; tapered rail joint shims for maintaining jointed track; impact wrenches, sockets and augers; rail disc cutters 12 and 14 in; rail drills; tampers; hydraulic tools; track measurement gauges; platform measurement gauges; rechargeable lamps (worksite and emergency).

Bance 2 Diesel with two loaded trailers   0125198

Services

Ultrasonic rail flaw detection; continuous rail depth recording; continuous platform gauge recording.

Rex Articoli Tecnici (REX)

Via Catenazzi 1, CH-6850 Mendrisio, Switzerland
Tel: (+41 91) 640 50 50
Fax: (+41 91) 640 50 55
e-mail: sales@rex.ch
Web: www.rex.ch

Key personnel

General Manager: *M Favini*

Products

Swisscross modular rubber level crossing system suitable for various track gauges; rail pads; microcellular pads; rubber boots for concrete sleepers; heatable rubber elements for station platforms.

RICA

Via Podgora 26, I-31029 Vittorio Veneto (TV), Italy
Tel: (+39 0438) 91 01
Fax: (+39 0438) 91 22 36; 91 22 72; 91 03 26
e-mail: rica@zoppas.com
Web: www.rica.it

Background

RICA is a member of the Zoppas Industries Group.

Products

Switch-point and rail de-icing systems.

Robel

Robel Bahnbaumaschinen GmbH
Industriestrasse 31, D-83395 Freilassing, Germany
Tel: (+49 8654) 60 90
Fax: (+49 8654) 60 91 00
e-mail: info@robel.info
Web: www.robel.info

Key personnel

Managing Director: *Erwin Stocker*

Products

Heavy machinery: track vehicles, rail handling vehicles, track laying machines for panels, sleepers and switches, rail loading and transportation equipment, catenary maintenance systems, special wagons and trailers.

Small machinery: clipping machines, rail drills, rail cutters, rail grinders (profile, web and switch), rail lifting devices, rail clamps for temporary joints, rail benders, plain line and switch blade, power wrenches, carrying tongs for sleepers and rail, track jacks, mechanical and hydraulic, track lifting and slewing machines, material transport trolleys (1 and 12 tonnes) lightweight tamping units, site illumination systems, track measuring devices, full range of special railway hand tools.

ROBEL is ISO 9001 certified.

Rotamag Track Equipment

Level 3, 41 Catley Road, Darnall, Sheffield S9 5JF, UK
Tel: (+44 114) 291 10 20
Fax: (+44 114) 261 31 86
e-mail: bobsenior@bryar.co.uk
Web: www.rotamag.co.uk

Key personnel

Managing Directors: *Vic Archer*
Operations Director (Contact): *Bob Senior*

Background

Rotamag Rail is part of the Bryar Group.

Products

Rail drilling machines; rail broaching cutters; rail jacks; rail bonding equipment; permanent way hand tools; third rail shrouds; rail trolleys; weld shears; and track-handling equipment.

Contracts

Contracts include the supply of rail bonding equipment, drilling machines and pulling tools for London Underground Ltd, Glasgow Underground, SNCB and SJ.

Sateba

Tour Ariane
5 place de la Pyramide, F-92088 Paris La Défense, Cedex, France
Tel: (+33 1) 46 53 29 00
Fax: (+33 1) 46 53 29 01
e-mail: sateba.paris@sateba.com
Web: www.sateba.com

Key personnel

General Manager: *D Vallet*
Deputy General Manager: *J L Bourbon*

Works

Chalon sur Sâone, Tours La Riche, Charmes, France
Morocco, Portugal and UK.

Background

Sateba Système Vagneux is a public limited company and the main shareholder is Bonna Sabla which is owned by Consolis.

The company manufactures under licence in Egypt, Greece, Italy, Korea, Mexico, Morocco, UK and Venezuela.

Products

Design and manufacture of Vagneux system of concrete sleepers, prestressed concrete sleepers for turnouts and SAT S312 solution for slab track; design and commissioning of sleeper manufacturing plants. Also technical studies, assistance and staff training.

Contracts

Sateba has been a major supplier of concrete sleepers for the construction of TGV lines in France including: South East TGV; Paris-Lyon; North TGV; Paris-Lille; TAtlantic TGV Paris-Tours/Le Mans; Mediterranean TGV and imminently the East TGV line.

Other contracts include tramways at Strabourg, Grenoble, Rouen, St Etienne, Geneva, Montpellier and also the supply to Belgium, Brazil, Portugal, Switzerland and the US.

Schalker Eisenhütte Maschinenfabrik GmbH

Magdeburger Strasse 37, D-45881 Gelsenkirchen, Germany
Tel: (+49 209) 980 50
Fax: (+49 209) 980 51 03
e-mail: info@schalker-eisenhuette.de;
info@schalke.eu
Web: www.schalke.eu

Key personnel

General Managers: *Jochen Braksiek, Werner Ehrhardt*

Products

Design and construction of hybrid battery and overhead electric vehicles; rail grinding vehicles; diesel/electric hybrid rail maintenance vehicle.

Contracts

In September 2005, the company received an order for two wire locomotives for the Solvay Soda Company.

In October 2005, workshop testing was completed for a second shunting locomotive fro Bangkok.

Schreck-Mieves GmbH

Bünnerhelfstrasse 10, D-44379 Dortmund, Germany
Tel: (+49 231) 97 67-0
Fax: (+49 231) 976 71 11
e-mail: info@schreck-mieves.de
Web: www.schreck-mieves.de

Key personnel

Management: *Dipl Ökonom Dr Wolfgang Ropella, Dr Ing Ralf Brüning, Dipl Ökonom Herbert Grützmader*

Products and services

Planning, construction and maintenance of complete track systems; supply of turnouts and track materials; EKOS switch tongue roller systems for main line and light rail applications; EWOS lubrication-free switch locking systems; EMA mobile track inspection and electronic measurement equipment and services; switch inspection services; wheel-rail interface investigation and analysis; consultancy services on track and switch maintenance, and management of track systems.

Schwihag AG Gleis- und Weichentechnik

Lebernstrasse 3, CH-8274 Tägerwilen, Switzerland
Tel: (+41 71) 666 88 00
Fax: (+41 71) 666 88 01
e-mail: info@schwihag.com
Web: www.schwihag.com

Key personnel

Managing Director: *Dipl Betriebswirt Karl-Heinz Schwiede*
Sales Director: *Dr Ing Roland Buda*
Technical Director: *Frank Meyer*

Background

Schwihag AG Gleis- und Weichentechnik was founded in 1971 and has ISO 9001 certification.

Research and development, design, production and marketing of progressive components for railway switches and crossing assemblies.

Products

IBSR and IBRR rail anchoring systems for turnouts, including clips, baseplates and slide plates.

Roller slide plates for lubrication-free operation, available for full and shallow depth switch assemblies. Boltless check rail support for continuous check rails in curved track and opposite crossings. Modular sleepers with an integrated switch actuating system. Hollow steel sleepers for cable crossings.

Equipment has been supplied to the MTRC Lantau Airport Railway, KCRC Hong Kong, SMRT Singapore, TRC Taipei, Canadian National, TTC Toronto and Network Rail, UK as well as to many other major European national railway companies including DB, RENFE, RFI Italy, SNCB and SNCF.

Semperit

Semperit Technische Produkte Gesellschaft mbH.
Triester Bundesstrasse 26, A-2632 Wimpassing, Austria
Tel: (+43 2630) 31 05 46
Fax: (+43 2630) 31 05 38
Web: www.semperit.at

Key personnel

Divisional Manager: *Dr Günther Mai*
BU Rail Track Systems: *Dipl Ing Wolfgang Meyer*

Products

Rubber and plastic track items, including rail pads, elastic sleeper supports and plastic fastenings. Elastomer profiles, including track trough sealing sections.

Siemens Switzerland

Siemens Switzerland Ltd, Transportation Systems
Hammerweg 1, CH-8304 Wallisellen, Switzerland
Tel: (+41 585) 58 01 11   Fax: (+41 585) 58 05 01
e-mail: ts@siemens.ch
Web: www.siemens.ch/ts

Key personnel

Managing Director: *Gerhard Greiter*
Manager, Export Department, South East Asia: *A Hefti*

Products

Block and track vacancy proving equipment (axle counters, track circuits, last vehicle detection); point locking equipment including point machines and point locking system; signals and indicators; safety relays.

Sika Ltd

Watchmead, Welwyn Garden City AL7 1BQ, UK
Tel: (+44 1707) 39 44 44   Fax: (+44 1707) 32 91 29
e-mail: sales@uk.sika.com
Web: www.sika.co.uk

Key personnel

Managing Director: *D Bratt*
Projects Manager: *M Richardson*

Products

Sika Rail resilient rail-fixing systems are a combination of tough elastic, polyurethane reaction-curing binders and compressible fillers that absorb vibration and reduce noise. They are available in a variety of grades to ensure suitability with differing load-bearing requirements.

Sika also provides specialist construction products including high-specification concrete admixtures, jointing systems, mortars and grouts, adhesives and bonding agents, waterproofing, corrosion inhibitors, concrete repair and protective coatings, single-ply roofing membranes and high performance industrial and commercial flooring systems.

Contracts

Contracts within the UK include:
Base-plate bedding material for direct fixation system for LUL Northern Line; Heathrow Express (track fixation at Paddington station platforms and at Semi-Outside Double Slip (SODS) crossover, Heathrow Airport); Leeds Portal Link, Liverpool; Tyne and Wear Metro; Docklands Light Railway; The Channel Tunnel Rail Link, Clerkenwell.

Structural strengthening: Church Street Cast Iron Bridge, Telford; North Harrow Bridge; Worston Bridge; The Approach Bridge at Humber Sea Terminal; Ealing Road Bridge; LUL Edgeware Road Station, London; Birmingham Airport cable train, Hook-a-Gate Bridge and Gypsy Lane Flyover, A38 Bristol.

Rail fixing and grouting: Tate & Lyle Crane Rails, London; Rugby Maintenance Depot; Tyne and Wear Metro, Docklands Light Railway and Liverpool Portal Link Tunnel.

Roofing: Stockport railway station, Burnley bus station and Salisbury railway station.

Industrial flooring: Arriva Bus Depot, Birkenhead; Turner Powertrains; The Channel Tunnel Rail Link, Contracts 230 and 240; Northern Traincare Facility, Ealing Common Wash Depot and Bombardier Transportation in Kent.

Concrete repair and protection: Kirklees bus station car park.

Sonatest NDE Group

Dickens Road, Old Wolverton, Milton Keynes
MK12 5QQ, UK
Tel: (+44 1908) 31 63 45
Fax: (+44 1908) 32 13 23
e-mail: sales@sonatest.com
Web: www.sonatest.com

Key personnel
Managing Director: *W Woodhead*
UK Sales Director: *Kelvin Cook*
Commercial Manager: *Carol Stevenson*

Subsidiaries
Sonatest Inc
4734 Research Drive, San Antonio, Texas, US
Tel: (+1 210) 697 03 35   Fax: (+1 210) 697 07 67
e-mail: sonatest@sbcglobal.net
Vice-President: *R Sidney*

Products
Ultrasonic digital flaw detectors and thickness
gauges. This includes the special application
Railscan 125 ultra-sonic portable flaw detector
for rail testing; Powerscan 450P for axle testing;
ultrasonic transducers for testing rail, wheels and
axles, including special probes used in systems
for Thermit weld testing; rail tester trolleys and
equipment for the Bance rail cart. Sonatest also
supplies equipment for x-ray, phased array and
eddy current testing. Also available are systems
and robotic methods of NDT. Current research
and development projects are focused on dry
scanning systems and concrete testing.

Contracts
Equipment has been supplied to Applied
Inspection, Network Rail, Balfour Beatty Rail
Maintenance, SNCF, GTRM, London Underground
Ltd, MTR Corporation of Hong Kong and Serco
Ltd. Current research and development projects
are focused on dry scanning systems and
concrete testing.

Speno International SA

PO Box 16, 26 Parc Château-Banquet, CH-1211
Geneva 21, Switzerland
Tel: (+41 22) 906 46 00   Fax: (+41 22) 906 46 01
e-mail: info@speno.ch
Web: www.speno.ch

Key personnel
Managing Director: *J J Méroz*
Marketing Managers: *D Mor; R Koller*
Finance Manager: *G Chignol*
Technical Manager: *L Palmieri*
Purchasing Manager: *G Tochon*
Production Manager: *J Neumayer*
Maintenance Manager: *G Stranczl*
Manager External Affairs: *W Schöch*
Quality Assurance Manager: *G Ferioli*

Subsidiaries
Speno Rail Maintenance Australia Pty Ltd
168 Campbell Street, Belmont, Western Australia
6104, Australia
Tel: (+61 8) 94 79 14 99   Fax: (+61 8) 94 79 13 49
Nippon Speno KK
Resona Gotanda Building 5F, 1-23-9 Nishigotanda,
Shinagawa-Ku, Tokyo 141-0031, Japan
Tel: (+81 3) 34 95 71 61   Fax: (+81 3) 34 95 71 62

Products
Design, development and manufacture of
machines for in-track rail maintenance, including
rail rectification, rail measurement and internal
rail flaw detection.

There are almost 200 Speno machines in service
around the world, engaged on high-speed and
conventional lines, and also in the demanding
conditions of heavy-haul and metropolitan
traffic. Speno machines are operated by
railway authorities, intermediaries or by Speno
International itself on a service basis.

*Speno US 2 ultrasonic rail flaw detection
vehicle*   1290027

Speno RR 48 M-2 rail grinding train   1290028

Speno rail grinders are grouped in series,
depending on production requirements. There
are typically a series of machines with eight,
16, 24 or 48 units. Machines can be coupled
to produce intermediate numbers of units.
Specialised versions exist for operation on
plain track and in the complicated conditions
of switches and crossings. Optional equipment
permits underground working. The machines
have multiple applications. They can treat rail
deformation in both the longitudinal and the
transverse planes as well as damaged surface
condition. Speno rail grinders are suitable for
preventative and corrective rail maintenance
strategies.

Speno measurement equipment provides
continuous recording of longitudinal and
transverse rail profiles. There are two main
versions, distinguished by operating speed. The
high-speed equipment, fitted on independent
vehicles, supplies data for network-wide asset
monitoring and maintenance planning. The
second version is incorporated into rail grinders.
Its role is to facilitate machine operation by
computer assistance, and to check and record
work progress for management.

Speno rail flaw detection units include rail
vehicles that run non-stop while reporting
potential flaws for subsequent confirmation, and
rail/road vehicles that can stop for immediate
confirmation where local conditions permit.
The non-stop operating speeds of Speno rail
flaw detectors are exceptionally high. Detection
is assured by continuous automatic analysis of
flaw information combined with graphic display.
Location of potential flaws is facilitated by paint
marking of the track.

Speno International runs an extensive research
and development programme both in the design
and the use of its products.

Spezialfahrzeugaufbau und Kabeltechnik GmbH (SPEFAKA)

Verlängerte Apoldaer Strasse 18, D-06116 Halle,
Sachsen-Anhalt, Germany
Tel: (+49 345) 560 22 65; 22 65
Fax: (+49 345) 560 81 61

Key personnel
General Manager: *G Hofmann*

Products
Road-rail vehicles from 3 to 25 tonnes for
installation and maintenance of catenary
infrastructures for urban and interurban
railway; railcars (light, medium and heavy) with
hydrostatic drive, adjustable for varying track

gauges; hydraulic platforms; rail cleaners; high-
pressure cleaning apparatus; ballast cleaning;
rerailing equipment; road-rail trailers with cable
and wire drums/reels or as motive power.

SPIE Rail

SPIE Headquarters
Parc Saint Cristophe, 10 avenue de l'enterprise,
F-95863 Cergy Pontoise Cedex, France
Tel: (+33 1) 34 24 30 00   Fax: (+33 1) 34 22 51 26
e-mail: transport@spie.com
Web: www.spie.eu

Key personnel
Chief Executive Officer, SPIE: *Gauthier Louette*
Director, Railway Projects and Systems: *Jean-
Pierre Courel*
Communications Director: *Pascal Omnès*

Background
SPIE Rail, previously operating as AMEC SPIE,
has returned to independence after three years
as the Continental Europe division of the UK
group, AMEC.

SPIE's shareholder is PAI, a leading French
investment fund.

SPIE is a specialist in railway infrastructure,
from track laying and electrification to turnkey
integrated systems and works alongside its
clients and partners to deliver railway solutions
throughout Europe and also worldwide.

Products
Design, construction and maintenance of railway
infrastructure including: track work, catenary
systems, power supplies, electromechanical,
control and communications for rail systems
including high-speed rail, metros, tramways and
other transport systems.

Contracts
Recent contracts include: In April 2007, SPIE
Rail, acting as a member of a Franco-Egyptian
consortium, signed a contract with Egypt's
National Authority for Tunnels (NAT) for phase 1
of Line 3 of Cairo's underground railway system.

Also in April 2007 SPIE, in consortium with
ISAF SA, was awarded a contract to overhaul
the catenaries and electric power supply system
for the Campina-to-Predeal section of Trans-
European Corridor IV.

In January 2007 SPIE Rail, as leader of
the consortium comprising ALSTOM, Arab
Contractors, Orascom and Thales, was awarded
the contract for lot G3 for the first phase of line 3
of the Cairo metro.

Other contracts include: Channel Tunnel Rail
Link (UK), LGV East (France), Caracas Metro
(Venezuela), Bordeaux tramway (France); Le
Mans tramway (France), West Anglia (UK),
Paris tramway (France), Bucharest tramway
(Romania), Nice tramway (France), Mulhouse
tramway (France), railway electrification for CFR
(Romania), catenary renewals South of Italy
(Italy), Wessex Power Upgrade (UK).

Spitzke AG

Güterverkehrszentrum (GVZ) Berlin Süd,
Märkische Allee 39/41, D-14979 Grossbeeren,
Germany
Tel: (+49 33701) 901-0   Fax: (+49 30701) 90 11 10
Web: www.spitzke.de
Electrical engineering/contact lines division
Markgrafendamm 24/Haus 16, D-10245 Berlin,
Germany
Tel: (+49 30) 293 46 50   Fax: (+49 30) 29 34 65 99

Key personnel
Chairman of Board: *Waldemar Münich*
Corporate Communications: *Dr Christina
Meinhardt*

Subsidiaries

Spitzke Spoorbouw BV
Peppelkade 3, NL-3992 AL Amsterdam
Tel: (+31 30) 639 41 00   Fax: (+31 30) 639 41 10
e-mail: Tjark.deVries@spitzke.com
Managing Director: *de Vries Tjark*

Spitzke Scandinavia A/S
Industribuen 19 A, 2635 Ishøj, Denmark
Tel: (+45) 33 79 25 50   Fax: (+45) 33 79 25 29
e-mail: Ralf-Peter.Wagner@spitzke.com
Managing Director: *Ralf-Peter Wagner*

Spitzke Hoch-Und Ingenieurbau GmbH
as Spitzke AG
Tel: (+49 33701) 90 14 01
Fax: (+49 33701) 90 14 29
e-mail: Gesina.Wunnicke@spitzke-hochbau.de
Secretary: *Gerd Bartsch@spitzke.com*

SLG Spitzke Logistik GmbH
as Spitzke AG
Tel: (+49 33701) 90 13 55
Fax: (+49 33701) 90 13 99
e-mail: Ralf.Mackensen@spitzke.com
Managing Director: *Ralf Mackensen*

Spitzke-Schomburg Spezialtiefbau GmbH
Spezial Tiefbau GmbH
Kupferstrasse 4, D-26789 Leer, Germany
Tel: (+49 491) 979 85-0   Fax: (+49 491) 979 85 25
e-mail: Albert.Dej@spitzke.com
Managing Director: *Albert Dej*

Schienenfahrzeugbau Grossbeeren GmbH
as Spitzke AG
Tel: (+49 33701) 90 14 51
Fax: (+49 33701) 90 14 99
e-mail: Ronald.Stollen@spitzke.com
Managing Director: *Ronald Stollens*

Background

Spitzke AG is part of the Spitzke Group which has subsidiaries in the Netherlands, Denmark and Sweden.

Services

Planning, development, construction and maintenance of track facilities for main line, metro and light rail networks, including conductor rail installation and maintenance, cable installation and laying, electrical engineering and the installation and maintenance of overhead power supply lines, and civil engineering work such as the construction of new platforms. A logistics department oversees the planning and implementation of materials supply to track construction sites.

Spitzke equipment includes: tamping machines; rapid ballast levelling machines; a 45 tonne crane; ballast bed cleaning machines; V100 and two LDK 1250 locomotives; and various excavators, bulldozers and wheel loaders.

Spitzke latest investment is in the the UM-S 2001, which provides a system for fast and cost-efficient track renewal for classic superstructures.

STRAIL Verkehrssysteme

Gummiwerk Kraiburg Elastik GmbH
Göllstrasse 8, D-84529 Tittmoning, Germany
Tel: (+49 8683) 70 10
Fax: (+49 8683) 70 11 26
e-mail: info@strail.de
Web: www.strail.com

Key personnel

Managing Director: *Dr Andreas Starnecker*
Executive Director: *Andreas Herder*
Sales Managers: *Walter Gruber, Robert Kaser, Hubert Mayer*
Production Manager: *Andreas Mörtl*
Manager Logistics: *Walter Hauser*
Elastic Rail Profiles: *Thomas Wiescholek*
Marketing and Communication: *Luise Hafner*

Background

STRAIL is a brand of the Kraiburg group.

Products

Modular level crossing surfaces for main line railways, metros, light rail and industrial sidings. Products include: STRAIL, for heavy duty rail and road applications; innoSTRAIL often used for track access platforms at emergency points and construction sides, providing easy access for both road and rail vehicles; pedeSTRAIL for pedestrian crossing, for example – at railway stations, tram stops, in depots and other working areas; veloSTRAIL, the inner panel system without a flange groove to allow safe track crossing for cyclists, the physically impaired and wheelchair and baby buggy users; pontiSTRAIL is an extra strong outer panel system for maximum loads. STRAIL/Kraiburg also manufactures elastic rail profiles to enable the trackwork of urban railways to be harmonised with its environment.

Tarmac Precast Concrete Ltd

Tallington Factory, Tallington, Stamford PR9 4RL, UK
Tel: (+44 1778) 38 10 00
Fax: (+44 1778) 34 80 41
e-mail: tarmacprecastenquiries@tarmac.co.uk
Web: www.tarmacprecast.co.uk

Key personnel

Key Account Manager: *Howard Lloyd*
Standards Products Manager: *David Evans*
Technical Consultant: *Howard Taylor*
Administrator, Rail: *Natalie Twell*
Sales Administrator, RCC: *Tim O'Dell*

Subsidiaries

RCC
Charcon Tunnels

Products

Approved precast products for the rail industry. The product range includes sleepers, bearers and other bespoke products.

Techni-Métal Systèmes

Parc d'activités de Fiancey, F-26250 Livron, France
Tel: (+33 4) 75 85 85 30
Fax: (+33 4) 75 85 85 35
e-mail: techni.metal@wanadoo.fr
Web: www.techni-metal.fr

Key personnel

Chief Executive: *Christian Berger*
Technical Manager: *Olivier Bony*
Manager's Assistant: *Brigitte Campos*

Background

Techni-Métal Systèmes is a subsidiary of Techni-Métal Entreprise SA.

Products

Equipment for railway and tunnel construction, including rubber-tyred or rail-mounted self-propelled gantries for applications such as rail handling, road-rail multi-purpose vehicles, self-propelled cranes, handling equipment for track panels, sleepers and tunnel segments, equipment for slab track construction and hoists and access platforms.

Contracts

Equipment has been supplied to Cogifer and Sols Bétonnage for the Lyons metro, Ferreira for the Lisbon metro, Cogifer for the Turin metro, SNFC, France and to the Italian-Thai joint venture for railway construction in Thailand.

Thermit Welding (GB) Ltd

87 Ferry Lane, Rainham RM13 9YH, UK
Tel: (+44 1708) 52 26 26
Fax: (+44 1708) 55 38 06
e-mail: tcc@thermitwelding.demon.co.uk
Web: www.thermitwelding.demon.co.uk

Key personnel

Director, Operations: *T C Clifton*
Director, Technical Sales: *R S Johnson*

Subsidiaries

Thermitrex (Pty) Ltd, Boksburg, South Africa

Products

Aluminothermic rail welding products and rail welding, training and inspection; insulated rail joints; ballast stabilisation.

Contracts

Recent contracts have included Hong Kong Lantau Airport Railway; Heathrow Express; Jubilee Line Extension; Kuala Lumpur LRT and Midland Metro and Croydon Tramlink.

ThyssenKrupp GfT Gleistechnik GmbH

Altendorfer Strasse 120, D-45143 Essen, Germany
Tel: (+49 201) 188 37 64   Fax: (+49 201) 188 37 57
e-mail: gleistechnik@thyssenkrupp.com
Web: www.tkgftgleistechnik.de

Background

ThyssenKrupp GfT Gleistechnik GmbH is the railway division of ThyssenKrupp AG and is a successful manufacturer and single-source supplier in the international market for track materials and services.

Products/Capabilities

Rails (flat-bottom rails, grooved rails, crane rails, special rail sections); turnouts, crossings and complete track systems, manufactured by its special trackwork mill; rail fastening systems; rail mounting systems; sleepers (wooden, concrete, steel, Y-steel sleepers, slab track); logistics: stock keeping, spare parts supply, just-in-time delivery directly on site; technical consulting; planning and engineering of track and turnout systems; system responsibility and project management as a sub-system supplier; financing for delivery; maintenance of tracks, turnout and crossing.

Projects

Metro, LRT and MRT projects and also long-distance rail projects. The company has participated in major railway projects worldwide with many international customers including: transit organisations in Europe, North Africa, Asia (such as LRT Kuala Lumpur, Skytrain Bangkok) and the US (such as Monterrey/Mexico, Calgary, Edmonton, Vancouver). State railway authorities in most European countries (such as ICE high-speed line, Germany, Channel Tunnel Railway Link, UK) and Asian countries (such as high-speed line Taiwan). Private track operators, port authorities and contractors and turnkey companies worldwide.

Thyssen Krupp Y-steel sleeper system   0105890

Tiefenbach GmbH

PO Box 91 13 60, D-45538 Sprockhoevel, Germany
Tel: (+49 2324) 70 54   Fax: (+49 2324) 70 53 22
e-mail: info@tiefenbach.de
Web: www.tiefenbach.de

Key personnel
Managing Director: *Dr Martin Hüttermann*
Managing Director (Technical): *Dr Ulrich Samland*
General Sales Manager: *Axel Reitz*

Subsidiary company
Tiefenbach GmbH
Transportation Technology
810 Skyline Drive, Marion, Illinois 62959, US
Tel: (+1 618) 993 85 13   Fax: (+1 618) 993 84 03
Web: www.tiefenbach.com

Background
Tiefenbach is a member of the Hauhinco Group.

Products
Axle counting system, switch control system, level crossing system, depot signalling and yard control system, marshalling yard system.
  The axle counting system is the main component of all systems and is based on Tiefenbach's double wheel sensor.

Contracts
Complete systems design and supply of hump yards, including brake and route control for DB AG. Complete systems design and supply of marshalling yard control and signalling for DB AG and ÖBB Austria. Complete systems design and supply of axle counter systems for SOB-Sudostbahn, Switzerland (main line); AKN Eisenbahn AG suburban feeder service at Hamburg; VNR Vietnam, CSX, US; CN, Canada and BHP Australia. Grade crossing systems for Conrail, BNSF; Ford Motor Company, US; VNR Vietnam and SRT, Thailand.

Tiflex Ltd

Tiflex House, Liskeard, PL14 4NB, UK
Tel: (+44 1579) 32 08 08
Fax: (+44 1579) 32 08 02
e-mail: trackelast@tiflex.co.uk
Web: www.tiflex.co.uk

Key personnel
Managing Director: *Nick Spearman*
Sales and Marketing Director: *Andy Tuffield*
Product Specialist: *Barry Curtis*
Marketing Department: *Emmaline Bowker*

Products
Rail pads, baseplate pads, undersleeper pads, ballast mats, floating slab track bearings, anti-vibration track support materials.
  Contracts include the supply of trackform bearings for the Tsing Ma Bridge, Hong Kong, floating slab track bearings for the Jubilee Line Extension, London, undersleeper pads for the Sabadell tunnel in Spain and anti-vibration materials for the refurbishment of the Bucharest metro.

Travipos

Calle Irlanda s/n, Sector Norte Poligono, Industrial Constanti, E-43120 Constanti (Tarragona), Spain
Tel: (+34 977) 29 65 53   Fax: (+34 977) 29 65 35
e-mail: administracion@travipos.com
Web: www.travipos.com

Background
The company was founded in 1994 and is a limited company with shares split between two partners, the German company RAIL.ONE (51%) and the Spanish company, Coms (49%).

Products
Pre-stressed concrete sleepers for high-speed and main line railways and for sidings.

TSTG Schienen Technik GmbH & Co KG

Kaiser-Wilhelm-Strasse 100, D-47166 Duisburg, Germany
Tel: (+49 203) 522 46 93
Fax: (+49 203) 522 46 94
e-mail: info@tstg.de
Web: www.tstg.de

Key personnel
Chairman: *Peter Sokolowsky*
Board of Management: *Karl Ebner*
  Hans Pfeiler

Background
TSTG Schienen Technik GmbH is a wholly owned subsidiary of voestalpine Bahnsysteme GmbH & Co KG.

Products
Manufacturer of rail worldwide including: flat-bottom rail, grooved rails, crane rails, rails for switches and crossings, msc rails, steel-sleepers; up to 120 m without welding.

VAE GmbH

Rotenturmstrasse 5-9, A-1010 Vienna, Austria
Tel: (+43) 503 04/122 20   Fax: (+43) 503 04/522 22
e-mail: Marketing.VAE@voestalpine.com
Web: www.voestalpine.com/vae

Key personnel
Chief Executive Officer: *Mag Dr Marc Kaddoura*
Chief Operating Officer: *Dipl Ing Johannes Rainer Oswald*
Chief Financial Officer: *MagWerner Saringer*

Background
VAE GmbH is the railway systems division of voestalpine Bahnsysteme GmbH & Co kg (see entry in *Permanent way components, equipment and services* section).

Products
Turnout systems, switches and crossing, points/crossing, track components, track materials and equipment.
  See also VAE GmbH entry in *Signalling and communication equipment* section.

voestalpine Bahnsysteme GmbH & Co KG

Kerpelystrasse 199, A-8704 Leoben/Donawitz, Austria
Tel: (+43 38 42) 202 41 31
Fax: (+43 38 42) 202 49 81
e-mail: info.bahnsysteme@voestalpine.com
Web: www.voestalpine.com

Key personnel
Chairman: *Dipl Ing Josef Mülner*
Contact: Dr Martin Platzer

Background
The Railway Systems Division of the Austrian steel making group voestalpine AG, voestalpine Bahnsysteme GmbH & Co kg is a holding company for the following, which are wholly owned except where indicated:

voestalpine Stahl Donawitz GmbH & Co KG
Kerpelystrasse 199, A-8700 Leoben-Donawitz, Austria
Tel: (+43 3842) 20 10
Fax: (+43 3842) 201
e-mail: info.stahldonawitz@voestalpine.com
Web: www.voestalpine.com/stahldonawitz

voestalpine Schienen GmbH
Kerpelystrasse 199, A-8700 Leoben-Donawitz, Austria
Tel: (+43 3842) 20 20
Fax: (+43 3842) 202
e-mail: info.schienen@voestalpine.com
Web: www.voestalpine.com/schienen

voestalpine Klöckner Bahntechnik GmbH
Neudorfer Strasse 3-5, D-47057 Duisburg, Germany
Tel: (+49 203) 54 46 45 54
Fax: (+49 203) 54 46 44 76
e-mail: oliver.plattes@vak-bahntechnik.de
Web: www.vak-bahntechnik.de

TSTG Schienen Technik GmbH (see entry in *Permanent way components, equipment and services* section)

VAE GmbH (see entry in *Permanent way components, equipment and services* section)

voestalpine Railpro BV (70 per cent) (see entries in *Electrification contractors and equipment suppliers* and *Permanent way components, equipment and services* sections)

voestalpine Austria Draht GmbH
Bahnhofstrasse 2, A-8600 Bruck/Mur, Austria
Tel: (+43 3862) 89 30
Fax: (+43 3862) 893
e-mail: info.austriadraht@voestalpine.com
Web: www.voestalpine.com/austriadraht

voestalpine Tubulars GmbH (50 per cent)
Alpinestrasse 17, A-8652 Kindberg-Aumühl, Austria
Tel: (+43 3865) 221 50
Fax: (+43 3865) 221 50
e-mail: info@vatubulars.com
Web: www.vatubulars.com

voestalpine Railpro BV

Nieuwe Crailoseweg 8, PO Box 888, NL-1200 AW Hilversum, Netherlands
Tel: (+31 35) 688 96 00
Fax: (+31 35) 688 96 66
e-mail: railinfo@railpro.nl
Web: www.railpro.nl

Key personnel
Managing Director: *Jos Peters*
Manager Business Development: *Mark de Vries*

Background
voestalpine Railpro BV is a subsidiary of voestalpine Bahnsysteme GmbH & Co KG, part of the Austrian-based voestalpine AG steelmaking group.

Products
Suppliers of all materials required in railway infrastructure work, acting as a stockist for contractors. The company can arrange transport to the worksite by road, water or rail; it operates a fleet of 2,200 rail wagons.
  As a result of the conversion of catenary voltage from 1,500 to 25 kV there is a demand for new types of catenary systems. voestalpine Railpro entered an agreement with VD Leegte Metaal for the production of welded overhead support arms and enables the company to supply fully engineered and complete catenary systems, both for train, tram and metro systems, and for light rail.

Vortok International

6-8 Haxter Close, Belliver Industrial Estate, Roborough, Plymouth PL6 7DD, UK
Tel: (+44 1752) 70 06 01 (main sales and enquiries)
Fax: (+44 1752) 70 23 53
e-mail: sales@vortok.co.uk
Web: www.vortok.co.uk

Head office
Osprey House, 63 Station Road, Addlestone KT15 2AR, UK
Tel: (+44 1752) 70 06 01 (Main Sales and Enquiries)
Fax: (+44 1752) 70 23 53
e-mail: sales@vortok.co.uk
Web: www.vortok.demon.co.uk

Key personnel
Managing Director: *Peter Shrubsall*
Technical Director: *Richard Bointon*
Sales and Marketing Director: *Richard Robertson*

Principal subsidiary
Multiclip Company Ltd

Products
Permanent way maintenance equipment and components, including: the Vortok Coil, for the rehabilitation of loose screws in wood sleepers; temporary sign board supports for securely and safely placing signs near the rail without ballast penetration; clip-on insulators for the prevention of track circuit signal failure by items passing under both rails; insulated block joint trimmers, portable and self-powered grinders for deburring rail ends at block joints; VERSE, a non-destructive method of measuring stress-free rail temperature; adjustable block spacers, enabling worn check block to be moved without removal from the track; and rigid safety barriers, fitted to the foot of the adjacent open line to enable green zone working at higher train speeds; stressing rollers to improve efficiency and quality of rail stressing; Rotorrail – retrofit switch rollers.

Vortok is a supplier to most European railway companies.

Vossloh Cogifer

Headquarters
54 avenue Victor Hugo, BP 56606, F-92566 Rueil Malmaison, Cedex, France
Tel: (+33 1) 55 47 73 00   Fax: (+33 1) 55 47 73 92
e-mail: contact@vcsa.vossloh.com
Web: www.vossloh-cogifer.com

Key personnel
Chairman and Chief Executive Officer:
   Guy Delorme
Deputy General Manager: *Dirk Redda*
Managing Director Signalling Department:
   Jean-Louis Binder
Director Affiliated Companies:
   Baudouin Bachollet
Business Development Marketing and Sales Director: *Marc-Antoine de Dietrich*
Sales Manager: *Freddy Sudol*

Works
Reichshoffen – Points and Crossings Department
Rue des Forges, BP 1, F-67110 Reichshoffen, France
Tel: (+33 3) 88 80 86 80   Fax: (+33 3) 88 09 67 33
e-mail: contact@vcsa.vossloh.com

Reichshoffen – Signalling Products and Systems
4 rue d'Oberbronn, Reichshoffen BP 02, F-67891 Niederbronn Cedex, France
Tel: (+33 3) 88 80 85 00   Fax: (+33 3) 88 80 85 18/19
e-mail: contact@vcsa.vossloh.com

Fére en Tardenois – Points and Crossings Department
Zone Industrielle, F-02130 Fère en Tardenois, France
Tel: (+33 3) 23 82 58 88

Fax: (+33 3) 23 82 71 99
e-mail: contact@vcsa.vossloh.com

Subsidiaries
Vossloh Cogifer has two subsidiaries in France, and worldwide subsidiaries in Australia, Belgium, Denmark, Finland, Germany, India, Italy, Luxembourg, Netherlands, Poland, Portugal, Serbia, Spain, Sweden, Thailand, UK and US.
Jacquemard – AVR
389 rue des Frères Lumière, ZI de Molina la Chazotte, F-42650 Saint Jean Bonnefonds, France
Tel: (+33 4) 77 47 68 68
Fax: (+33 4) 77 47 68 69
e-mail: michel.cuminetti@vcsa.vossloh.com

Siema Application
35 rue Alfred Brinon, F-69100 Villeurbanne, France
Tel: (+33 4) 78 85 14 14   Fax: (+33 4) 78 68 98 44
e-mail: siema@siema.fr

Background
Vossloh Cogifer is part of the Vossloh Group, a global company in the rail infrastructure and rail technology markets. The group has organised its operations into two divisions – Rail Infrastructure and Motive Power & Components – and is made up of over 80 companies operating in some 30 countries.

Products
Design, manufacture and installation of switches and crossings for high-speed railways, metro systems, light rail systems and main line and suburban rail networks. Products include: moveable manganese frogs; countered switches and crossings; manganese frogs with welded legs; and special forgings for switch rails; switch mechanisms; clamp lock systems; traffic detectors; and the Paulvé, mechanically driven points detector. Support services include: diagnostic reports on points in service; inspection; use and maintenance training; technology transfer; and financial services.

Vossloh Fastening Systems GmbH

Vosslohstrasse 4, D-58791 Werdohl, Germany
Tel: (+49 2392) 520
Fax: (+49 2392) 523 75
e-mail: info@vfs.vossloh.com
Web: www.vossloh.com
   www.vossloh-fastening-systems.de

Key personnel
General Managers: *Dr Hans-Peter Mertens, James N Sanders*

Vossloh's Sk1 24, first tension clamp for ribbed-plate tracks, enabling the use of 'soft buffer bearings' in this section of the tracks (Vossloh)
0585289

Vice-President Sales: *Sascha Kelterborn*
Technical Sales: *Winfried Bösterling*
Overseas Business Office, Regional Sales
  Managers, Düsseldorf: *Joachim Spors;*
  Dirk Pfeiffer

Works
Vossloh Werdohl GmbH
Vosslohstrasse 4, D-58791, Werdohl
Overseas business office, Düsseldorf
Tel: (+49 2102) 490 90
Fax: (+49 2102) 490 94

Products
Rail fastening systems for both ballast-bed and slab substructures compatible with all climatic zones and load profiles ranging from heavy-load to high-speed lines. Logistic services for tracks and special trackworks, noise protection for railways, plastic cable duct systems, surface coating (according to the Dacromet process).
  Vossloh has developed the Sk1 24, which is the first clamping plate available for the ribbed-plate permanent way that permits the use of 'soft intermediate bearings' in this track segment.

Weedfree Limited

Holly Tree Farm, Park Lane, Balne, Goole, DN14 0EP, UK
Tel: (+44 1405) 86 00 22   Fax: (+44 1405) 86 22 83
e-mail: sales@weedfree.net
Web: www.weedfree.net

Key personnel
Rail Contracts Manager: *Richard Stow*

Huddersfield office
115 North Road, Kirkburton, Huddersfield HD8 0RL
Tel: (+44 1484) 60 83 61
Fax: (+44 1484) 60 83 40

Background
Weedfree Ltd was formed in 1967.

Products
Vegetation control including trees, on and off track weed control.
  Recent clients include Network Rail, Serco, Harsco, EWS and a wide range of rail operating and infrastructure maintenance companies.

Western-Cullen-Hayes Inc

2700 West 36th Place, Chicago, Illinois 60632-1682, US
Tel: (+1 773) 254 96 00
Fax: (+1 773) 254 11 10
e-mail: wch@wch.com
Web: www.wch.com

Key personnel
President: *Ronald L McDaniel*
Vice-President: *Barbara Gulick*
Sales Manager: *Carl J Pambianco*
Customer Service Manager: *Bill Crain*
Systems Application: *Rodney Yourist*

Subsidiaries
Hayes Plant Western-Cullen-Hayes Inc
120 North 3rd Street, Box 756, Richmond, Indiana 47374, US

Products
Railway safety track appliances; bumping posts, fixed, sliding and hydraulic; wheel stops and chocks; switch point guards; yard switch machines; WCHT-72 programmable and Solar Tech switch machines; track drills; rail benders; rail tongs; journal and hydraulic jacks; sliding, hinged and portable derails; derail operators; Eldo, DeLectric and solar-powered derail operators; blue flags; and other custom-designed equipment for railway and industrial applications.

Windhoff Bahn-und Anlagentechnik GmbH

PO Box 1963, D-48409 Rheine, Germany
Tel: (+49 5971) 580   Fax: (+49 5971) 582 09
e-mail: info@windhoff.de
Web: www.windhoff.de

Key personnel
Board Members: *Georg Vennemann, Manfred Schmitz*
Finance Director: *Bernadett Freicks*
Sales Directors: *Uwe Dolkemeyer, Detlef Mueller*
Technical Director: *Juergen Auschner*
Purchasing Manager: *Stefan Berkemeyer*

Products
Construction and maintenance of rail tracks: Multi-Purpose Vehicles (MPV), vehicles with crane or excavator, attachments (ballast broom, tamping unit), rail grinding and finished vehicles. Catenary vehicles, bridge/tunnel inspection vehicles, track welding vehicles, recovery vehicles, flexible vehicles, special vehicles, fire-fighting and rescue trains. Workshop equipment for railway depots.

TURNKEY SYSTEMS CONTRACTORS

Company listing by country

CANADA
Bombardier Transportation

FRANCE
ALSTOM Transport
Interinfra

GERMANY
Siemens AG

KOREA, SOUTH
Hyundai Rotem Company

UNITED KINGDOM
Balfour Beatty Rail Projects Ltd
Transys Projects Ltd

UNITED STATES
PB

For details of the latest updates to *Jane's Urban Transport Systems* online and to discover the additional information available exclusively to online subscribers please visit
juts.janes.com

ALSTOM Transport

Systems Business
48 rue Albert Dhalenne, F-93482 Saint-Ouen
Cedex, Paris, France
Tel: (+33 1) 41 66 90 00
Fax: (+33 1) 41 66 96 66
Web: www.transport.alstom.com

Key personnel

President, Transport Sector: *Philippe Mellier*
Chief Operating Officer: *Gérard Blanc*
Senior Vice-Presidents:
    Finance: *Jean-Jacques Morin*
North Europe: *Roland Kientz*
Systems Business, International Product Line
    Management: *Laurent Troger*
Regional Asia Pacific: *Marc Chatelard*
Southern Europe: *Charles Carlier*
Americas: *Francis Jelensperger*
Northern Europe: *Terence Watson*

Services

Systems Business of ALSTOM Transport offers global public transportation solutions including turnkey management, execution of infrastructure packages, interfaces with civil works and rolling stock.

The business addresses, urban transit systems, suburban lines and main lines can be involved in projects at the individual subsystem level, or at the full turnkey level.

Systems Business acts as main contractor for metro and light rail transit systems, airport rail links and fully automatic metros. It houses all the competencies necessary for the development of a project concept, its detailed design, and its delivery.

The Infrastructure Business unit of ALSTOM Transport Systems offers solutions at the system or subsystem level for including power generation and distribution. It includes AC and DC traction substations, overhead lines, surface contact third rail, at-level integrated supply system, SCADA, auxiliary power supply, track laying, maintenance workshops, communications, signalling (tramways), electrical and mechanical equipment in-station.

Its scope embraces design, development, installation, financing, managing, commissioning, technical assistance, maintenance and training.

Contracts

Algeria: In June 2006, as part of an international consortium, ALSTOM was awarded a contract by Entreprise du Métro d'Alger (EMA) to supply a turnkey system for the first tramway line of the Algerian capital. The contract covers the rolling stock, the tracks, the power supply systems, the traction electrification, signalling equipment, part of the civil works and a workshop. The first trainsets will enter into service 30 months after the contract takes effect.

Argentina: In January 2008 ALSTOM, as consortium leader, and its partners IECSA, Emepa, Isolux Corsan was awarded the first very high-speed link project between Buenos Aires, Rosario and Cordoba. The project will involve the construction of the infrastructure, including seven stations and 780 km of track, electrification, signalling (ERMTS level 2) and the supply of rolling stock and maintenance.

Chile: In December 2008, Santiago Metro awarded ALSTOM a contract to supply an automatic train control for Santiago metro's line 5 extension. The contract includes engineering, installation, tests and commissioning. The 14 km line will enter commercial service in December 2009.

Egypt: In January 2007, NAT awarded two packages to two consortia in which ALSTOM is a member as part of its complete tender for Cairo's metro system. The signalling and telecommunications package to the ALSTOM/Alcatel/Orascom consortium and the electromechanical equipment to the Spie/ALSTOM/Thales/Orsascom consortium. These packages relate to phase 1 (4.3 km) of metro line 3 (starting in 2022), and will link the district of Embaba to the city's airport.

Singapore's Northeast Line automated metro system   0585260

Italy: In February 2006, ALSTOM announced it is to participate in a consortium undertaking the construction of Milan's metro Line 5, the city's first automatic driverless metro line. ALSTOM will supply infrastructure, including the electric supply system, electrical substations, traction systems and the platform screen doors.

Poland: ALSTOM has also won an order to upgrade the Bytom to Katowice tramway for the Tramway Communication Company of Katowice in Silesia. As well as provision of new vehicles, the turnkey order includes the refurbishment of the rail infrastructure and stations on the existing 20 km Line 6/41. The trams, which will be supplied by the company's Polish subsidiary ALSTOM Konstal, will be fitted with ONIX traction drives.

Singapore: Singapore's Land Transport Authority (LTA) was awarded the ALSTOM/STE consortium an order worth EUR170 million, for the second phase of construction of its automatic Circle metro line. ALSTOM's share of this contract is valued at EUR123 million. ALSTOM will supply its AXONIS™ automatic metro system for this line.

This new order was an extension of the Circle Line Phase 1 project, awarded to ALSTOM on a turnkey basis in December 2000. The first stage covers 5.6 km and has six stations. This second section will extend the Marina line by 5 km and add five new stations. Subsequent contracts placed with ALSTOM covered construction of the remainder of the line, which will eventually cover 34 km and circle the island of Singapore, making it the world's longest automatic metro line.

Spain: The Trambesòs tramway new line entered commercial service in October 2006. ALSTOM was responsible for the system engineering, power supply, telecommunications, ticketing, railways signalling, road signalling, SCADA, AVLS and information systems.

As part of the TramMet consortium, ALSTOM was awarded contracts to build and equip Lines 1 and 2 of the Barcelona light rail system. As well as supplying 19 and 18 Citadis tramsets respectively for the new lines, ALSTOM is responsible for system engineering, traction power supply substations, telecommunications, ticketing, signalling, workshop equipment and project management of the electrical and mechanical package. ALSTOM holds a shareholding of 25 per cent in TramMet, which holds 15-year operating and maintenance concessions on the system. The first phase was commissioned in March 2004.

Switzerland: As part of a turnkey contract awarded in 2002 by the Administration of Switzerland's Vaud canton, ALSTOM was contracted to supply 15 two-car driverless rubber-tyred metro trainsets for a new 6 km metro line linking Ouchy with the district of Epalinges, Lausanne; the new line entered commercial service in October 2008. ALSTOM has supplied

the URBALIS signalling system, the on-board video surveillance and passenger information system, and the electrification of the line.

Trinidad and Tobago: In April 2008, the government of Trinidad and Tobago and the National Infrastructure Development Company Limited (NIDCO), chose the Trinitrain consortium which consists of Bouygues Construction, ALSTOM and RATP Développement, to design, build, operate and maintain an express train railway system on the island of Trinidad. The project includes the construction of two express train lines totalling 105 km (inc. approx. 20 km of viaducts) and around 10 stations. ALSTOM will manage the railway system and the supply of rolling stock over an estimated four-year period.

United Arab Emirates: In April 2008, Dubai's Roads and Transport Authority (RTA) awarded the ABS consortium, comprising ALSTOM, Besix and Serco, the phase 1 of the Al Safooh transit system tramway project, with an option for a phase 2. The project includes, for phase 1, 11 tramways, a 10 km track and 13 stations. Phase 2 includes 14 additional trainsets, as well as 4 km of tracks and six stations. The project is planned to enter into commercial service by 2011. ALSTOM will provide Citadis type 402 tramways, equipped with catenary-free APS technology, as well as the signalling and ticketing system.

Balfour Beatty Rail Projects Ltd

Head office

B203 Midland House, Nelson Street, Derby DE1 2SA
Tel: (+44 1332) 26 26 66   Fax: (+44 1332) 26 22 95
e-mail: info.bbrp@bbrail.com

Background

In October 2007 Balfour Beatty and ALSTOM launched their newly formed 50/50 joint venture company, Signalling Solutions Limited. With headquarters in Borehamwood in the UK, the company is led by Managing Director David Felton, with approximately 340 people from ALSTOM and Balfour Beatty. The company is focused on delivering signalling projects for Network Rail and other customers in the UK.

In August 2005 Balfour Beatty acquired Pennine Group, the UK ground engineering specialists.

Products

Design, supply, installation, testing and commissioning of railway infrastructure, including track, overhead line systems, traction power supplies and telecommunications for high-speed, mixed traffic, heavy haul, light rail and mass transit systems. The company provides multidisciplinary project implementation including project management design and construction.

Contracts

Current contracts include the design, supply and installation of multi-disciplinary rail infrastructure works for Heathrow Terminal 5 and Watford-Bletchley, UK; the design, supply and installation of overhead line and power supply on the West Coast Main Line, UK; supply, installation and commissioning of the entire section of new track including the power rail for the first steel-wheeled tram on the Santiago metro system, Chile.

Overseas, the company is currently constructing Lines 4 and 4A of the Santiago Metro in Chile, the first steel wheel and steel rail systems on the network, as well as constructing 110 km of track on the Botniabanan Line in Sweden.

Bombardier Transportation

Systems
Schöneberger Ufer 1, D-10785 Berlin, Germany
Tel: (+49 30) 98 60 70
Fax: (+49 30) 986 07 20-00
Web: www.transportation.bombardier.com

Key personnel
President, Systems: *Eran Gartner*

Products and Services

Working in partnership with major international, regional and local civil engineering and construction companies, as well as local suppliers, Bombardier Transportation develops, designs, integrates, installs and delivers the industry's broadest range of technologies – from large-scale commuter transportation systems to fully automated people movers.
- Automated people mover systems
- Automated monorail systems
- Automated Advanced Rapid Transit (ART)
- Light rail transit systems
- Automated Metros
- Commuter transportation systems
- Operations and maintenance services
- Bombardier Sekurflo transit security solutions
  Bombardier, Cityflo, Innovia, CX-100, Sekurflo are trademarks of Bombardier Inc or its subsidiaries.
  SkyTrain is a trademark of BC Transit Corp.

Contracts

Canada: The Millennium Line, an extension to Vancouver's fully automated SkyTrain system, opened in August 2002. Bombardier Transportation completed the design, supply and installation of the electrical and mechanical systems for the 20.5 km line. Bombardier's scope of work included automatic train control and communication systems, power supply and distribution system, trackwork, power rail, platform and guideway intrusion detection systems, system engineering and integration, and testing and commissioning for 20.5 km of dual-track guideway. In November 2006, Bombardier received an order for 34 new Advanced Rapid Transit (ART) MK II vehicles. In May 2008, an option was exercised for an additional 14 ART MK II vehicles. Under a previous contract, Bombardier supplied 60 ART MK II SkyTrain vehicles, employing Bombardier's LIM technology. Bombardier had previously supplied the original Vancouver Expo Line, as well as 150 ART MK I vehicles.

China: In May 2007, Bombardier received a contract for a fully automated people mover system for Guangzhou City. The 4 km dual-lane, underground system will serve the Zhujiang Xincheng Central District of Guangzhou City and is scheduled to open in 2010. Four of the system's nine stations will provide connections to Lines 1, 3 and 5 of the Guangzhou City metro network. Bombardier is responsible for the design and supply of 14 Bombardier CX-100 vehicles and the Bombardier Cityflo 650 automatic train control system. Bombardier will work in partnership with Guangzhou Metro Corporation who will supply the power systems, communications and platform screen doors.

In February 2008, the Bombardier-supplied 2 km APM system for Beijing Capital International Airport opened for passenger service. Bombardier was responsible for project management, systems engineering and integration, testing and commissioning, in addition to the design and supply of 11 CX-100 vehicles, the Cityflo 550 automated train control communications systems, platform screen doors, switches and equipping the maintenance facility. The APM system operates on dual-guideway between three stations, serving the new international terminal. Bombardier is operating and maintaining the APM and is currently supplying seven addition CX-100 vehicles.

Korea, South: The Young-In LRT consortium, of which Bombardier is the lead member, was awarded a 35 year Build-Transfer-Operate (BTO) concession contract for a fully automated 18.5 km ART system by the city of Yongin, Republic of Korea. Intended to serve 15 stations on mostly elevated double-track guideway, the new line will link the Seoul subway, via Yongin City, and will terminate in Everland, one of the world's most popular theme parks. Bombardier is responsible for the design and supply of 30 driverless ART LIM powered vehicles, the BombardierCityflo 650 automatic train control technology, communications systems, project management, systems engineering and integration, testing and commissioning, as well as up to 30 years of operation and maintenance services. Bombardier will lead the integration of the scope of work with Daelim Industrial Co, who will be the co-lead for the design-build portion of the contract. The Yongin system is scheduled to enter revenue service in 2010.

Malaysia: In August 2007, Bombardier and Hartasuma Sdn Bhd signed a contract with Syarikat Prasarana Negara Berhad (Prasarana) to upgrade wayside electrical and mechanical (E&M) systems on the Kelana Jaya Line in Kuala Lumpur. The work will upgrade the line to accommodate the 88 ART vehicles which were a new order for Bombardier in 2006. An option order was subsequently exercised for 52 additional ART vehicles, tripling the fleet. The Bombardier-led consortium delivered the 29 km Kelana Jaya advanced rapid transit system and fleet of 70 ART MK II vehicles in 1998–1999.

South Africa: In 2006 Bombardier, as part of the Bombela consortium, received Notice to Proceed for a concession to design, build, operate and maintain the Gautrain Rapid Rail Link under a Public Private Partnership approach. Planned for completion in 2010, the 80 km electrified standard-gauge system will link Johannesburg, Tshwane (Pretoria) and OR Tambo International Airport, serving 10 stations. Bombardier is responsible for the core electrical and mechanical systems, including a fleet of 96 Bombardier Electrostar emus, Cityflo 250 train control technology, the

Sekurflo transit security solution, power supply and distribution systems, communications systems, automatic fare collection, trackwork and maintenance equipment. Also provided by the company will be project management, systems engineering and integration, testing and commissioning and 15 years of maintenance services.

Spain: Bombardier Transportation supplied the first application of automated people mover technology in Spain at the Barajas International Airport in Madrid. The system connects a new mid-field terminal with a new satellite terminal. The project included the supply of 19 vehicles, 2.7 km of underground guideway running surface, and the Cityflo 550 automatic train control and power distribution systems. Bombardier is operating this system which began operations in February 2006.

Taiwan: Bombardier Transportation is supplying a 15 km rapid transit system in the city of Taipei. As prime subcontractor to Kung Sing Engineering Corporation (KSECO), a Taiwanese construction company, Bombardier is designing and supplying all of the system-wide electrical and mechanical elements for the new Neihu Line, an extension of the existing Muzha Line. The contract includes 202 rubber-tyred vehicles and the ATC retrofit of 102 existing vehicles, as well as upgrading the Muzha Line Control Centre. Following the deployment of BombardierCityflo 650 automatic train control technology, both the new fleet and the original fleet will be capable of operating interchangeably on both lines. Passenger service is scheduled to begin in 2009.

United Kingdom: At London-Heathrow International Airport, Bombardier introduced its Innovia system technology at the airport's new Terminal 5 which opened in March 2008. Bombardier supplied the core electrical and mechanical systems including six Innovia APM vehicles and Cityflo 650 automatic train control. The system is designed to carry over 6,500 passengers per hour per direction.

As a member of the Arrow Light Rail Ltd Concession Company, Bombardier Transportation was responsible for the landmark 30.5-year contract to design, build, operate and maintain the Nottingham Express Transit (NET) Line 1 light rail system. Bombardier's scope for the 14 km turnkey system included 15 low-floor light rail vehicles, project management, system engineering and integration, power supply and distribution system, signalling and system control, communications and security systems, ticketing equipment and depot maintenance equipment. The system opened in March 2004.

United States: In 2006, Bombardier signed two contracts at McCarran International Airport in Las Vegas. The first contract comprises the supply of six CX-100 vehicles and associated electrical and mechanical equipment for a 366-metre shuttle system, scheduled for completion in

Bombardier light rail system for Eskişehir, Turkey

0585265

January 2011. The second contract includes the supply of 10 CX-100 vehicles and upgrades to some of the electrical and mechanical equipment on two existing shuttles. The APM vehicles will be delivered between 2008 and 2009.

At Atlanta International Airport, Bombardier is extending the existing Bombardier-supplied automated people mover system to the new Maynard H Jackson International Terminal. The contract includes the supply of all the electrical and mechanical equipment associated with the extension and 10 new CX-100 vehicles, thus increasing the fleet to 59 vehicles. In 2005, Bombardier received a 10-year contract to operate and maintain the existing Bombardier-built CX-100 APM.

At Dallas/Fort Worth International Airport, Bombardier supplied the first application of its new Bombardier Innovia technology, with Cityflo 650 automatic train control technology. The system connects the airport's existing terminals with a new terminal and a new parking garage. The eight km dual-track guideway system includes 64 vehicles and a five-year system-wide maintenance contract. The system opened in May 2005.

Bombardier Transportation, as the lead member of the Las Vegas Monorail Team, supplied its Monorail System in the heart of the resort corridor. Designed according to urban transit safety standards, the system links eight major resort properties and the Las Vegas Convention Center. Bombardier was responsible for providing all the electrical and mechanical elements of the system including design and supply of 36 monorail cars, overall project management, automatic train control, communications systems, power supply and distribution systems, automatic fare collection systems, guideway and guidance switching systems, system engineering and integration, platform doors for seven stations, testing and commissioning, training and manuals, and up to 15 years of operations and maintenance services. The system entered revenue service in 2004 and has carried over 28 million passengers.

As part of the AirRail Transit Consortium, Bombardier Transportation supplied a fully automated rapid transit system for the JFK International Airport, New York, US. Under contract to the Port Authority of New York and New Jersey, using a design-build-operate and maintain approach, the consortium was responsible for the turnkey design and construction of the driverless light rail system, including 32 ART MK II LIM-powered vehicles, as well as operations and maintenance for a period of up to 15 years. The system opened in December 2003. In San Francisco, Bombardier has operated and maintained the Bombardier-supplied APM system, known as SFO AirTrain, since it opened to passenger service in 2003. Using Bombardier CX-100 technology, the two-line APM system operates 24 hours a day. The AirTrain fleet of 38 CX-100 vehicles serves nine stations along 10 km of elevated guideway and connects all the airport's terminals, parking garages and the Bay Area Rapid Transit (BART) Station with the rental car centre. Bombardier received an eight-year operations and maintenance contract in November 2008.

Hyundai Rotem Company

Headquarters
231, Yangjae-dong, Seocho-gu, Seoul, 137-938, Republic of Korea
Tel: (+82 2) 34 64 11 14
Fax: (+82 2) 34 64 75 86
Web: www.hyundai-rotem.co.kr

Key personnel
Executive Vice-Chairman and Chief Executive Officer: *Yeo-Sung Lee*
President and Chief Executive Officer: *Yong-Hoon Lee*

Busan-Gimhae LRV, Hyundai Rotem   1340478

Senior Executive Vice-President and Chief Operating Officer: *Sang-Kil Lee*
Vice-President: *Jae-Hong Kim (R&D centre)*

Works
Changwon plant
85, Daewon-dong, Changwon, Gyeongsangnam-do 641-808, Korea
Tel: (+82 55) 273 13 41   Fax: (+82 55) 273 17 41
Fax: (+82 55) 273 17 41
Uiwang central research and development centre
462-18, Sam-dong, Uiwang-city, Kyunggi-do, Korea
Tel: (+82 31) 460 11 14   Fax: (+82 31) 460 17 81

Background
Established in 1964 when Daewoo Heavy Industry started manufacturing rolling stock, followed by Hyundai Precision and Industry, and Hanjin Heavy Industry a few years later. In 1999, the three companies were consolidated into KOROS by the Korean Government. Hyundai Motor Group acquired the share of Daewoo Heavy Industry in October 2001 and KOROS became Rotem Company in January 2002. As of November 2007, Rotem Company changed its company name and CI to Hyundai Rotem Company. An affiliate of Hyundai Motor Group, Hyundai Rotem Company has its headquarters in Seoul and two facilities, the central research and development centre in Uiwang and the manufacturing plant in Changwon. The Changwon plant has the capability to manufacture 1,000 emus per year and also has the capability to manufacture electrical equipment such as traction motors, SIV inverters etc. Certifications such as the ISO 9001:2000/KS A 9001:2001 for quality, ISO 14001:2004 / KS A 14001:2004 for environment and OHSAS 18001:1999 for occupational health and safety management have been acquired at all three sites.

Projects
Currently Hyundai Rotem is engaged in metro rail system turnkey projects and light rail system turnkey projects in Korea and overseas countries. Hyundai Rotem's experience in the total rail system technology is based on over 40-years of rolling stock production and supply and rail systems interface experience between vehicles and wayside systems. Hyundai Rotem supplies electrical and mechanical (E&M) systems and holds full responsibility in project management and systems engineering/integration. Hyundai Rotem also provides operations and maintenance (O&M) services ranging from light rail to metro rail systems with efficient management and high maintenance technology. Hyundai Rotem also maintains good partnerships with major international and domestic civil construction companies and E&M subsystem suppliers.

Contracts
Seoul Metro Subway Line No 9: a first private capital investment project for Korea's urban railroad, participants include Hyundai Rotem, Hyundai E&C, POSCON, POSDATA, Daewoo Engineering, Ssangyong E&C, Ultra E&C and Sampyo E&C. The consortium was originally awarded the project in 2005. The construction on the line from Gimpo Airport to Gangnam Seoul is scheduled for completion by 2009. The construction includes the supply of 96 emus, design, electrical and mechanical system, signalling system, telecommunications system, track/depot/station facilities, operation and maintenance for 30-years.

Hyundai Rotem is participating in the Busan-Gimhae LRT project which was realised in 2006. The project is expected to start commercial service in 2011. Hyundai Rotem will provide detailed design, supply and installation of the E&M system including the supply of 50 cars (LRT), signalling systems, electric systems, telecommunication systems, AFC systems, platform screen doors, elevator and escalator maintenance facilities and systems engineering.

Interinfra

Parc Dhalenne, 2 rue Albert Dhalenne, F-93400 St Ouen Cedex, France
Tel: (+33 1) 41 66 84 15
Fax: (+33 1) 41 66 84 62

Key personnel
Chairman and Chief Executive Officer: *Charles Carlier*
Deputy Managing Director: *Henry Bussery*
General Secretary: *Bertrand Dupuy*

Projects
Turnkey contracts for the supply of railway and rapid transit systems outside France.

PB

Parsons Brinckerhoff Inc
Headquarters
One Penn Plaza, New York, New York 10119, USA
Tel: (+1 212) 465 50 00
Fax: (+1 212) 465 50 96
e-mail: pbinfo@pbworld.com
Web: www.pbworld.com

Key personnel
President: *Thomas J O'Neill*
Chairman: *Morris S Levy*
Controller: *Richard A Schrader*

Projects

In April 2007 the Delhi Metro Rail Corporation named a joint venture including PB as the general consultant for the Delhi Airport Rail Link, a four-station, 19 km express rail line that will connect Indira Gandhi International Airport and the city centre. The Airport Rail Link is being delivered as a public-private partnership (PPP) and is due to open in time for the 2010 Commonwealth Games.

PB is the lead member of the ongoing joint venture for the Metropolitan Atlanta Rapid Transit Authority (MARTA) Transit System, Georgia, US.

Siemens AG

Mobility

Turnkey Systems Division
PO Box 910220, D-12414 Berlin, Germany
Tel: (+49 30) 386 50
Fax: (+49 30) 386 514 31
e-mail: turnkey.transportation@siemens.com
Web: www.mobility.siemens.com

Corporate headquarters

Siemens AG, Mobility, PO Box 3240, 91050 Erlangen, Germany
Tel: (+49 9131) 7-0

Key personnel

Chief Financial Officer, Industry: *Ralf P Thomas*
Chief Executive Officer, Mobility: *Michael Schulz-Drost*

Services

Turnkey projects including: new construction or refurbishment of main line systems; intercity and high-speed systems; commuter and express rail links; mass transit systems; light rail systems; automated guided transit systems; and maglev systems. Capabilities include:

- development of technical concepts including operational concepts, line plans, specifications, RAMS and EMC studies;
- provision or procurement of: civil engineering; infrastructure; traction power supply and distribution; control systems; signalling and safety systems; telecommunications systems; rolling stock; automated fare collection systems; trackwork; building services including fire alarm and fire-fighting systems; lifts and escalators; signage; UPS; testing, commissioning and training services; and operation and maintenance;
- project management functions include project planning; project control; project supervision; and system integration and co-ordination.

Siemens also arranges financing of turnkey projects.

Projects

Recent or current projects include:
China: As an equal partner in the Transrapid International consortium, Siemens is participating in the fulfilment of a contract to build and equip a 30 km magnetic levitation line linking Shanghai's Pudong international airport with the city's Lujiazui financial district. The system was commissioned in December 2003, with maglev trains operating at speeds of up to 430 km/h to complete the journey in seven minutes.
Dominican Republic: In a consortium with Thales, Siemens is to supply the electromechanical equipment for the first metro line in Santo Domingo. The contract was signed with the Dominican Republic's Oficina para la Reorganización del Transporte (OPRET). Siemens scope of supply involves the project management, signalling and safety systems, automatic train protection, operations control systems and the power supply.
France: In June 2007, the second automated metro line, the 16 km 20-station Line B was inaugurated in Toulouse. The contract was awarded in May 2001 by SMTC, Toulouse, and included the

Shanghai maglev system installed by the Transrapid International consortium, of which Siemens is a member   0585297

supply of 56 new vehicles. The company worked with the Toulouse metro operator, SMAT, as system integrator on the project.
Germany: For the 204 km Cologne Rhein/Main high-speed line, which was commissioned in 2002, Siemens acted as consortium leader for the equipment technology group, which covered: project management; electronic interlocking; overhead contact line; telecommunications and remote monitoring systems; and the implementation of a tunnel rescue system.
Italy: In October 2007, a new 2.1 km section of Line 1 of the Turin metro system was opened for which Siemens supplied both the automation systems and the rolling stock.
Malaysia: In April 2002 the Express Rail Link system, connecting Kuala Lumpur with its new airport, was commissioned. As leader of the SYZ Consortium, Siemens was responsible to the line's concessionaire, ERL SB, for track, signalling and train control systems, traction power supply and overhead line equipment, telecommunications systems, E & M construction, SCADA equipment, depot and workshop facilities and rolling stock. The last-mentioned took the form of 12 articulated four-car Desiro ET emus. Siemens is also the majority partner in EMAS, which is responsible for maintenance of the entire system.
Mexico: In August 2005, a Siemens led consortium received an order from the Sistema de Transporte Colectivo Metrorrey, in Monterrey, Mexico, to extend metro line 2. Partners in the consortium are Bombardier Transportation Mexico and the Mexican construction company Constructora Garza Ponce.
Netherlands: In 2001, as a partner in the 'Infaspeed' concession, Siemens won a contract to supply the power supply and distribution system, the ETCS Level 2 signalling system, communications systems and ancillary equipment, as well as maintenance over a 25-year period, for the new high-speed line between Amsterdam and the Belgian border (HSL-Zuid). Siemens is also leading systems integration for the high-speed link.
Portugal: In August 2002 Siemens secured a turnkey contract to build and equip an initial 13 km phase of a light rail system for Metro Transportes do Sul (MTS) linking the communities of Almada and Seixal, south of Lisbon. MTS has a concession to establish the system and operate it for 27 years. Siemens' contract covers: the supply of 24 five-section Combino low-floor LRVs; complete signalling and operations control equipment; a communications system; traction power supply equipment and overhead contact lines; and the equipment for a vehicle maintenance and

repair facility. A 20 km extension to the system is projected.
Taiwan: In August 2001 Siemens won a contract from the Kaohsiung Rapid Transit Corporation (KRTC) to supply signalling equipment, traction power supply equipment and 42 three-car trainsets for the Red Line (28 km, including nine km elevated, 23 stations) and Orange Line (14 km, 14 stations) of the city's metro system. Siemens was also to be responsible for project management and systems integration of the electromechanical portion of the project.
Thailand: In January 2005 Siemens, together with consortium partners B Grimm and Sino Thai Engineering and Construction plc (STECON) signed a contract with State Railway of Thailand for the construction of the 28 km Suvarnabhumi Airport Rail Link and the City Air Terminal. Both Siemens and B Grimm are taking responsibility for the design, supply, installation and project management of the whole electrical and mechanical system including trackwork, rolling stock, signalling system, power supply, communication systems, automatic fare collection, tunnel equipment, depot and workshop equipment, check-in facilities as well as baggage handling system.

In January 2002 Siemens announced that it had signed an agreement with Bangkok Metro Corporation Ltd for the supply and maintenance of the Thai capital's first metro system, a 20 km line with 18 stations. The project entails supply of the line's complete infrastructure, including signalling, power supply, communications and depot equipment, as well as the manufacture of 19 three-car trainsets to serve the line. The contract also covers project management and maintenance of the line over a 10-year period. The line was commissioned in July 2004.
US: In March 2001 Siemens was awarded a contract by the Metropolitan Transit Authority of Harris County to construct Houston's first light rail system. Siemens was responsible for project management, planning, delivery, installation and commissioning of the 11 km line, which was commissioned in January 2004. This included the manufacture and supply of 18 S 70 LRVs, and of the line's signalling, control and traction power supply systems.
Venezuela: In January 2001 Siemens signed a turnkey contract to build the initial phase of the first light rail line in Maracaibo, including the supply of infrastructure equipment, signalling and communications systems, traction power supply equipment, ticketing systems and a maintenance depot for the 6.9 km line. Siemens delivered a total of seven three-unit metro trains in by December 2006.

Transys Projects Ltd

2 Priestley Wharf, Holt Street, Aston Science Park,
Birmingham B7 4BN, UK
Tel: (+44 121) 359 77 77   Fax: (+44 121) 359 18 11
e-mail: info@transysprojects.ltd.uk
Web: www.transysprojects.ltd.uk

Key personnel
Managing Director: *Kevin Lane*
Sales and Marketing Manager: *Andy Colver*
Engineering Director: *Karl J Barras*
Financial Director: *Emma Stamps*

Background
Transys Project Ltd is an independent company.

Capabilities
Multi-disciplined engineering consultancy and turnkey solutions provider, covering all aspects of passenger rail vehicles and their related support services. This covers mass transit vehicles, light rail vehicles and tramcars as well as main line diesel and electric multiple units and passenger coaches. Certified to BS EN ISO 9001 with 'link-up' accreditation in 26 relevant areas.

Specific capabilities include: complete turnkey service for traction and rolling stock; refurbishment and enhancements; modifications and reliability improvements; roll out of modifications and installations such as TPWS, OTMR, GSMR, ERTMS, New WSP and train sander equipment.

Projects
Turnkey installation of on-train monitor record for six UK fleets. Turnkey installation of over 700 sets of trainborne sanders to combat low adhesion in leaf-fall seasons. Turnkey installation of new public address and power outlets for computers. Installation of train protection warning systems. Complete control system rewire. Turnkey installation of new wheel-slide protection equipment. Numerous projects for reliability and passenger comfort enhancement.

INFORMATION TECHNOLOGY SYSTEMS

Company listing by country

AUSTRALIA
Austrics
ICG Transport Systems
Vigil Systems Pty Ltd

CANADA
InfodevEDI Inc
March Networks Corporation
Trapeze Software Group

DENMARK
Pallas Informatik A/S

FRANCE
Cityway SA

GERMANY
DILAX Intelcom GmbH
INIT Innovative Informatikanwendungen in
Transport-, Verkehrs-und Leitsystemen
GmbH

IVU Traffic Technologies AG
PC-Soft GmbH
PSI Transcom GmbH

IRELAND
Nexala

ISRAEL
NICE Systems Ltd

SPAIN
Goal Systems
Indra Sistemas SA

SWEDEN
Axis Communications AB
Trivector System AB
VIPS AB

SWITZERLAND
Inovex Digital Training

UNITED KINGDOM
Advanced Communications and Information
Systems (ACIS) Ltd
Excel Solutions
Freeway Fleet Systems
The IKI Group
Inovas Ltd
Laser Rail Ltd
Southern Vectis plc

UNITED STATES
Affiliated Computer Services, Inc
Bentley Systems Inc
Com-Net Software
Doron Precision Systems Inc
Hansen Information Technologies, Inc
Info Global Solutions
S&A Systems Inc
SYSTRA Consulting Inc
Verint Systems Inc

Advanced Communications and Information Systems (ACIS) Ltd

ACIS House, Knaves Beech Business Centre, Loudwater, Buckinghamshire HP10 9QR, UK
Tel: (+44 1628) 52 49 00
Fax: (+44 1628) 52 32 22
e-mail: enquiries@acis.uk.com
Web: www.acis.uk.com

Key personnel
Chief Executive Officer: *Dan Sandhu*
Chief Finance Officer: *Richard Smith*
Business Development Director: *Keith Allen*
Operations Director: *Craig Gulliford*

Products
BusNet information systems, a package of IT providing real-time information to the public, real-time fleet management information and historical performance data to bus operators, data and voice communications and intelligent variable traffic signal priority control and links to systems monitoring pollution and traffic flows.

Contracts
Recent contracts for Angus, West Sussex, Cambridgeshire, Bedfordshire & Peterborough, Newport and a trial system in Carlisle, UK.

Affiliated Computer Services, Inc

ACS Corporate Headquarters
2828 North Haskell, Dallas, Texas 75205, US
Tel: (+1 214) 841 61 11
e-mail: info@acs-inc.com
Web: www.acs-inc.com

Key personnel
President and Chief Executive Officer: *Lynn Blodgett*
Executive Vice-President and Chief Operating Officer: *Tom Burlin*
Chief Information Officer: *Tasos Tsolakis*
Vice-President Corporate Communications: *Kevin Lightfoot*
Communications Directors: *Tom Clary, Andy Wilson*
Account Manager: *Jennille Logan*

Background
The company provides business process outsourcing and information technology solutions for commercial and government clients.

Products
Fare collection, toll solutions, back-office processing, infrastructure installation – ACS provides systems and services to help solve intractable transportation problems.

Contracts
The City of Brampton, Canada, signed a contract with ACS to enable its transit authority to improve the effectiveness of its bus services as well as its future AcceleRide Bus Rapid Transit (BRT) services that are scheduled to be operational in 2010. ACS will supply Brampton Transit with an integrated suite of real-time analytical tools that will assist in overall operations management of its 250 vehicle fixed route fleet as well as its nine supervisory vehicles. Brampton Transit will utilize ACS' latest Computer Aided Dispatch (CAD) and Automatic Vehicle Location (AVL) system called OrbCAD XP.

Austrics

Level 2, 50 Pirie Street, Adelaide 5000, South Australia, Australia
Tel: (+61 8) 82 07 20 21
Fax: (+61 8) 82 31 48 21

e-mail: support@austrics.com.au
Web: www.austrics.com.au

Key personnel
Director, Business Development: *Dale Warren*

Products
Scheduling software for urban transport systems, covering: network planning and design; fleet management; driver scheduling and staff rostering; and depot mangement. Austrics also provides consultancy services and provides scheduling services for operators and authorities wishing to outsource this function.

Axis Communications AB

Corporate Headquarters
Emdalavägen 14, SE-223 69 Lund, Sweden
Tel: (+46 46) 272 18 00
Fax: (+46 46) 13 61 30
e-mail: pressoffice@axis.com
Web: www.axis.com

Key personnel
President and Chief Executive Officer: *Ray Mauritsson*
Vice-President and Chief Financial Officer: *Fredrik Sjöstrand*
Vice President, Product Management: *Johan Lembre*
Vice President, Operations: *Per Ädelroth*
Vice President, GlobalSales: *Bodil Sonesson*
Vice President, Engineering: *Kenneth Jonsson*
Chief Technology Officer: *Johan Paulsson*
Director, Chief Information Officer: *Jonas Hansson*
IR & Corporate Communications Manager: *Margareta Lantz*

Other offices
Axis Communications has other offices in Australia, Canada, China, France, Germany, Italy, Japan, Korea, Netherlands, Singapore, South Africa, Spain, Taiwan, the UK, the UAE and the US.

Background
Founded in 1984, Axis is a 'connectivity' company providing specialised hardware and software solutions that enable people with different operating systems to access all kinds of resources on a network. The company operates globally with offices in 17 countries.

Products/Services
Axis specialises in professional network video solutions for remote monitoring, security surveillance and broadcasting. The company's range of products includes network cameras, video servers, video decoders, video management software, and a full range of audio and video accessories.

Its TrainSafe system includes on-train cameras, platform video surveillance, emergency call buttons on trains and platforms, as well as improved lighting.

Network cameras suitable for transport surveillance and monitoring roles include the

AXIS Q1755 network camera   1375624

AXIS 225FD, AXIS 212PTZ and the recently developed AXIS 209FD-R.

Contracts
Axis Communications is one of the suppliers included in a major underground and commuter train security project being undertaken by the Greater Stockholm Public Transport Company Limited (SL) which has decided to install AXIS 225FD and AXIS 212PTZ network cameras. The current project covers 80 stations, including 12 commuter train stations. An additional order has also been received from SL for approximately 1,200 network cameras as part of SL's security initiative.

Axis new AXIS 209FD-R network cameras will be installed in 2,100 of Stockholm Transport's (SL's) buses. Axis' partner Visual Defence (VDI) has been awarded the contract for an integrated mobile solution for SL's fleet of buses.

Axis network video products are already integrated into Honeywell's Enterprise Building Integrator (EBI) and Digital Video Manager (DVM) security solutions. An order was received from Honeywell Ltd for the supply of 800 video servers as part of an integrated security system for Western Australia Transport Authority.

Developments
Axis has developed the AXIS Q1755 network camera which is connected to an HDTV monitor; a solution for securing areas where greater image detail is required. The camera has a built-in slot for an SD/SDHC memory card which makes it possible to store days of recording without any external equipment. It includes video intelligence such as enhanced video motion detection, audio detection and detection of camera tampering such as blocking or spray-painting. In addition, it includes a 'gatekeeper' functionality which automatically zooms in when there is activity in the scene, and then zooms out after a preset time interval.

Bentley Systems Inc

685 Stockton Drive, Exton, Pennsylvania 19341-0678, US
Tel: (+1 610) 458 50 00
Fax: (+1 610) 458 10 60
Web: www.bentley.com

Key personnel
Chief Executive Officer: *Greg Bentley*
Chief Marketing Officer: *Ed Mueller*
International headquarters:
Bentley Systems Europe BV
Wegalaan 2, NL-2132 JC Hoofddorp, Netherlands
Tel: (+31 23) 556 05 60   Fax: (+31 23) 556 05 65

Axis Communication AB's AXIS 209FD-R Network Camera, due to be installed in SL's bus fleet during 2007   1310167

Products

Software solutions for architecture, engineering and construction. Rail-specific software includes InRail, part of Bentley's InRoads suite, which provides track design and layout functions applicable to high-speed, conventional heavy rail or light rail systems. Functionality includes: regression points; curvature diagrams; horizontal regression analysis; vertical regression analysis; slew diagrams; a horizontal connection editor; layout of turnouts; cant; interactive geometry; alignment by elements; coordinate geometry; and feature-based digital terrain model generation.

Bentley's portfolio also includes: EED (Elementary Electrical Diagrams) Software, from which was developed EED Signal Relay, which is used to support the maintenance of existing signalling systems and in the design of new signalling schemes; and MicroStation V8, which allows users to create 3-D models of permanent assets.

Projects in which Bentley software solutions have been used include the Madrid-Seville high-speed line in Spain, the Alameda Corridor project linking Los Angeles with Long Beach, California, and London Underground's Jubilee Line Extension.

Cityway SA

Parc du Golf, Bâtiment 7, F-13856 Aix en Provence Cedex 03, France
Tel: (+33 4) 42 37 18 40
Fax: (+33 4) 42 39 45 15
e-mail: info@cityway.fr
Web: www.cityway.fr

Key personnel
Managing Director: *Laurent Briant*
Customer Relations Manager: *Olivier Joyeux*
Sales Assistant: *Chloé Spano*

Background
A majority shareholding in Cityway is held by 'Veolia Transport (formerly Connex), the transport subsidiary of Veolia Environnement'.

Products
Transport information management tools, including: Go@T, a multimodal trip planner search engine; Transinfo, a website design tool for public transport operators; Know Now, providing real-time traffic disruption management; Contakt, a call centre management tool; Rapido, a management tool for timetable and stop-points mapping; and Guid'Edit, for editing bus guides and timetables.

Com-Net Software

3728 Benner Road, Miamisburg, OH 45342, US
Tel: (+1 937) 859 63 23
Fax: (+1 937) 859 75 11
e-mail: contact@comnetsoftware.com
Web: www.comnet-fids.com,
   www.comnetsoftware.com

Key personnel
Chief Executive Officer, Signature Technologies Inc: *Elie Geva*
President and Chief Financial Officer: *Dave Michaels*
Vice-President, Business Development: *Bob Roalef*
Vice-President, Product Development: *Chad Timms*
Vice-President, Operations: *Stephen Rohrig*
Vice-President, Sales and Marketing: *Chance Fultz*

Background
Com-Net Software is a division of Signature Technologies Inc.

Products
ECLIPSX® Transit: Real-time Passenger Information Display Solution (PIDS).

Info Global Solutions

Head office
13560 Morris Road Suite 4100 Alpharetta, GA 30004, US
Tel: (+1 678) 319 80 00
Fax: (+1 678) 393 50 01
Web: www.infor.com
   www.datastream.net

Key personnel
Chairman and Chief Executive Officer: *Jim Schaper*
Chief Operating Officer: *Robin Pederson*

Background
In 2006 Info acquired Datastream Systems Inc, an asset performance management software and services provider.

Products
Asset management system, Info 7i, for rail applications, covering both infrastructure and rolling stock.

DILAX Intelcom GmbH

Headquarters
Alt-Moabit 96b, D-10559 Berlin, Germany
Tel: (+49 30) 77 30 92 40
Fax: (+49 30) 77 30 92 50
e-mail: info@dilax.com
Web: www.dilax.com

Subsidiaries
DILAX has subsidiaries and other offices in Italy, France, Spain, Swizterland, the UK and Canada.

Key personnel
President and Chief Executive Officer: *Uwe Hinrichsen*
General Manager: *Jan Karsch*

Background
DILAX has been active in the Automatic People Counting (APC) industry since its inception in 1988.

Products
Design manufacture and supply of automatic passenger/people counting systems; trip analysis systems; data transmission systems (GPRS/WLAN); web-based data management systems; customised solutions.

DILAX also markets an advanced 'people counting technology' specifically designed for stationary applications such as metro stations, shopping malls and airports etc.

Contracts
DILAX has equipped several thousand vehicles (buses, trains and trams) with its system throughout Europe, the US and Canada.

Doron Precision Systems Inc

PO Box 400, Binghamton, New York 13902-0400, US
Tel: (+1 607) 772 16 10
Fax: (+1 607) 772 67 60
e-mail: sales@doronprecision.com
Web: www.doronprecision.com

Key personnel
President: *Donald E Wenzinger*
Director of International Sales: *David Kong*

Products
Complete driving simulation systems – car, truck, bus, fire, law enforcement.

Excel Solutions

1 Abbey Street, Eynsham, Oxfordshire OX29 4TB, UK
Tel: (+44 870) 242 62 65
e-mail: sales@excel-solutions.co.uk
Web: www.excel-solutions.co.uk

Products
Passenger transport management systems integrated into accounting software by Sage Enterprise Solutions for business management.

Freeway Fleet Systems

Unit 3 Dock Offices, Surrey Quays Road, London, SE16 2XU, UK
Tel: (+44 844) 884 30 33
Fax: (+44 20) 76 81 15 25
e-mail: info@fleetmanage.com
Web: www.fleetmanage.com

Other offices
Africa
PO Box 6251, Cresta 2118, South Africa
Tel: (+27 11) 678 24 57

Street address
104 Eva Office Park, Block C, Cnr Beyers Naude and Judges, Blackheath, South Africa

Products
Computerised transport systems.

Contracts
Recent contract is for a pc-based management system for Midland Metro's light rail which uses 16 trams, running a six minute service, operating between Wolverhampton and Birmingham, UK.

Goal Systems

Julio Camba 1, 3 Ofic 2, E-28028 Madrid, Spain
Tel: (+34 91) 725 30 00
Fax: (+34 91) 725 56 08
e-mail: goal@goalsystems.com
Web: www.goalsystems.com

Key personnel
Research and Development Team Leader: *Pasquale Iannelli*

Products
IT solutions for bus and rail transport resource planning and optimisation. Software products include:

GoalBus, with basic modules covering generation of bus timetables and services and optimum assignment of drivers to shifts;

GoalDriver, with basic modules covering drivers' timetable planning and replanning of drivers' timetable periods, including responses to incidents;

GoalRail, with basic modules covering timetable planning and rolling stock utilisation, driver and supervisor planning, allocation of rolling stock, drivers and supervisors, replanning of rolling stock, drivers and supervisors.

Supplementary modules are available for each product to expand the scope of the system.

Contracts
In May 2008 Goal Systems was appointed by Renfe Operadora as the successful bidder of the project for the design, development, implementation and integral maintenance of a computer tool for optimisation of productive

resources of the general department of high-speed/longer distance services.

Inversiones Alsacia and Express of Santiago de Chile, are the two main operators in the Transantiago plan to modernise public transport in Santiago, set up by the government in October 2005. GoalBus® has been put into operation as a system for planning bus and shift timetables; GoalDriver® as a system for allocation of resources, and GoalReports as a system of integration and the generation of reports.

Hansen Information Technologies, Inc

Transit and Rail Business Unit
595 Market Street, 4th Floor, San Francisco, California 94105, US
Tel: (+1 415) 593 29 99
Fax: (+1 415) 593 32 07
e-mail: sales@hansen.com
Web: www.hansen.com

Key personnel
Business Unit Director: *Peter Morris*
Business Unit Sales Manager: *Bill Adams*

Background
Formerly Spear Technologies Inc, the company was acquired by Hansen Information Technologies in April 2006.

Products
Hansen provides the Spear 4i™ Enterprise Asset Management (EAM) software solutions for rail operators. The Spear 4i system assists rail operators to improve service, safety and economic performance and is designed specifically for commuter and freight rail fleets, facilities and maintenance of way.

Developments
Hansen's Spear 4i was newly released in 2007.

ICG Transport Systems

Level 1, 139 Frome Street, Adelaide, South Australia PO Box 369, Rundle Mall SA 5000, Australia
Tel: (+61 8) 74 21 12 00
Fax: (+61 8) 74 21 12 20
e-mail: sales@vizirail.com.au
Web: www.vizirail.com.au

Products
ICG Transport Systems (ICG) is a developer of advanced train scheduling and monitoring software and is ISO 9001 certified.

ViziRail, the flagship product, is an integrated suite of software modules covering the train operating business cycle from long-term scheduling through to historical reporting on actual train performance. The customer can add functionality and customise the interface to their specific needs. The modular nature of ViziRail enables it to be implemented in stages, either as a complete system or by modules required to meet specific requirements.

ViziRail modules include: ViziRail base module; ViziRail Data Exchange; ViziRail Long Term Planner; ViziRail Short Term Planner; ViziRail Train Notices; ViziRail Train Grapher; ViziRail Schematic Path Selector; ViziRail Train Builder; ViziRail Train Running; ViziRail Train Incidents.

Contracts
ICG's clients include Australian Railroad Group, Australian RailTrack Corporation, Freight Australia, Public Transport Authority of Western Australia, Queensland Rail, RailCorp, Tasrail and WestNet Rail.

The IKI Group

IKI Portable Solutions Ltd
Grosvenor House, Telford, Shropshire, TF2 9TW, UK
Tel: (+44 1952) 21 61 81
Fax: (+44 1952) 21 61 31
e-mail: info@ikigroup.com
Web: www.ikigroup.com

Background
Established in 1987.

Products
Portable mobile data capture solutions using hand-held computers.
TouchPCFalcon: Rugged, touch-screen, hand-held device manufactured by TouchStar Technologies Limited with IKI Portable Solutions' software.

Indra Sistemas SA

Headquarters
Avenida de Bruselas 35, E-28108 Alcobendas, Madrid, Spain
Tel: (+34 91) 480 50 00-1
Fax: (+34 91) 480 50 57-8
Web: www.indra.es

Key personnel
Chairman: *Javier Monzón*
Vice-Chairman: *Humberto Figarola*
Managing Director: *Regino Moranchel*
Deputy Managing Director: *Josep María Vilá*
Chief Financial Officer: *Juan Carlos Baena*
General Managers for Operations: *Rafael Gallego, Javier Piera, Joaquin Uguet*
Resources and Corporate Management Chief Officer: *Ángel Lucio*

Products
Computer-based simulator systems for train drivers, station masters, traffic controllers and maintenance staff. Driver simulators can be supplied in fixed or moving positions, with a 45 to 180° field of view and specific or generic driving cabs and visual databases. Traffic control simulators can be supplied to train staff in the handling of individual station traffic, operating in local or remote mode, and as a CTC post, and can be configured to feature signals, track circuits, levers, points and level crossings. Integrated simulator systems combining driving and traffic control can also be supplied.

In collaboration with Madrid bus operator EMT, Indra has also developed an urban bus driver simulator system. Features include a driving position with interchangeable elements for eight different vehicle types, ticket vending machine and operational help systems, a motion system, surround field of more than 180° with exterior and interior rear-view mirrors, virtual city features, varying traffic, passenger and pedestrian models, environmental sound generation and an instructor station.

Contracts
In May 2006, the company announced that it had been awarded various contracts to introduce and renew the ticket sales and access control systems on several zones of the Madrid Metro underground network, together with a ticketing system for the new light metro line that will be coming into operation in the northern sector of Madrid. The contracts were valued at a total of EUR13.6 million.

InfodevEDI Inc

Infodev Electronic Designers International Inc
1995 rue Frank-Carrel, Bureau 202, Québec G1N 4H9, Canada

Postal address
PO Box 1222 HV, Quebec QC, G1R 5A7, Canada
Tel: (+1 418) 681 35 39
Fax: (+1 418) 681 12 09
e-mail: info@infodev.ca

Key personnel
Chief Executive Officer: *Alain Miville de Chêne*
Chief Technical Officer: *Pierre Deslauriers*
North American Transit Sales: *Sandra Howlett*
Director of European Sales: *Patrick Vidal*

Other offices
Infodev USA
7373 Newcrest Circle, Las Vegas, Nevada 89147, USA
Tel: (+1 702) 889 67 01
Fax: (+1 702) 889 03 80
e-mail: info@infodev.ca
Director of US Sales: Walter Frye

Infodev Europe
Tel: (+1 418) 681 35 39
Fax: (+1 418) 681 12 09
e-mail: pvidal@infodev.ca
Director of European Sales: Patrick Vidal

Products
Production of Automatic Passenger Counting systems (APC) and Automatic Vehicle Location systems (AVL) using directional optical sensors and also a GPS satellite positioning system applied to vehicles in order to identify and track their positions.
Infodev is ISO 9001 certified.

INIT Innovative Informatikanwendungen in Transport-, Verkehrs-und Leitsystemen GmbH

Kaeppelstrasse 4-6, D-76131 Karlsruhe, Germany
Tel: (+49 721) 610 00
Fax: (+49 721) 610 03 99
e-mail: postmaster@init-ka.de
Web: www.init-ka.de

Subsidiaries
Australia
INIT Pty Ltd
Level 5, Toowong Tower, 9 Sherwood Road, Toowong Qld, 4066 Australia
Tel: (+61 7) 33 10 88 18
Fax: (+61 7) 33 10 88 00

US
Innovations in Transportation Inc
1420 Kristina Way, Suite 101, Chesapeake, Virginia 23320
Tel: (+1 757) 413 91 00
Fax: (+1 757) 413 50 19

Canada
INIT Innovations in Transportation (Eastern Canada) Inc/INIT Innovations en Transport (Canada Est) Inc
14 Place du Commerce, suite 360, Île-des-Soeurs, Montréal, Québec H3E 1T7, Canada
Tel: (+1 514) 766 28 36
Fax: (+1 514) 766 15 78
INIT, Innovations in Transportation (Western Canada) Inc
949 West 41st Avenue, Vancouver, BC V5Z2N5, Canada
Tel: (+1 778) 995 04 93

United Arab Emirates
Init Innovation in Traffic Systems FZE
Dubai Airport Free Zone, Office 6EB 244, Dubai, UAE
Tel: (+971) 47 01 72 86

Key personnel
Chief Sales Officer: *Dr Jürgen Greschner*

Products

Fixed-route and flexible on-demand/paratransit vehicle operation, Geographical Information Systems (GIS) and map display. Depot management software. Scheduling and runcutting software. Technical interfaces to third-party scheduling and paratransit scheduling and dispatch systems.

Real-time passenger information.

Terminal management systems.

Inovas Ltd

1 Glenbervie Business Park, Larbert, Falkirk, Scotland FK5 4RB, UK
Tel: (+44 1324) 68 22 68   Fax: (+44 1324) 68 22 69
e-mail: info@inovas.co.uk
Web: www.inovas.co.uk

Products

Inovas Ltd specialises in providing driver training and route risk assessment solutions to the global transport market. The company's innovative software is utilised by leading transport operators and local authorities worldwide.

Route video footage, audio training voice commentary and mapping, PC-based VideoRoute Trainer (VRT) are the methods by which bus transport operators can train their drivers on route familiarisation and hazard identification. Through additional G-Force and fuel management linkages, driving patterns can also be analysed.

Built upon the same software used in VRT, Videoroute Analyst has been specially developed for local authorities, providing fleet service operators with a fully auditable risk assessment software tool to assess the operation of waste refuse routes. Through linking front and back video footage of refuse collection routes to mapping and operational data, the system allows for automatic, fully documented and audible route risk assessment; hazard identification; accident investigation; driver route learning; new route planning/route revision; reduction of costs on accident and insurance; indication of travel speeds and delays caused by traffic congestion; the measurement of route times, bin counts, operating payloads and reversing time.

Contracts

VRT is used by major transport operators throughout the UK, Europe and North America. VideoRoute Analyst is currently used by Fife Council in Scotland.

Inovex Digital Training

Giesshübelstrasse 64, CH-8045, Zürich, Switzerland
Tel: (+41 43) 255 57 00
Fax: (+41 43) 255 57 01
e-mail: gehlert@inovex.net
Web: www.inovex.net

Key personnel

Chief Executive Officer: *Dr Urs Guggenbuehl*
Chairman: *Fritz Schaerer*
Managing Director: *Peter Imboden*
Sales Director: *Heinz Schiesser*

Products and services

Inovex designs and develops training solutions including computer-based training (CBT) and e-learning programmes employing software-based simulation techniques. The company has wide experience working with the Swiss rail industry including driver training on the new advanced train control systems ERTMS, where it developed a computer-based course simulating the man/machine interface employing a series of typical user scenarios.

IVU Traffic Technologies AG

Bundesallee 88, D-12161 Berlin, Germany
Tel: (+49 30) 85 90 60
Fax: (+49 30) 85 90 61 11
e-mail: post@ivu.de
Web: www.ivu.de

Key personnel

Chairman: *Ernst Denert*
Head of Corporate Communications: *Renate Bader*
    Staff: Approximately 300

Other offices

With its headquarters in Berlin, the company also has offices in Aachen, Germany, Birmingham, UK, Rome, Italy and Veenendaal in the Netherlands.

Products

Software development for planning and scheduling of public transport including timetables, quality management, fleet management, passenger information, ticketing, demand-response systems and depot and strategic operations management.

The IVU.plan, IVU.vehicle, IVU.crew database systems are used by municipal and regional

public transport companies as well as railway, commuter train, light rail operators and ferries, are currently being used in more than 15 countries and are available in different local languages. IVU.fleet is an automatic Vehicle Location (AVL) and information system for public transport which optimises operations through reliable disruption management and allows realtime passenger information. The IVU.box family is a user-friendly onboard computer system combined with a reliable software. The software is for communication between the AVL, drivers and vehicle (IVU.cockpit) and for selling tickets (IVU.ticket). IVU also offers a fare management system and a tool for statistics, quality control and account settlement.

Laser Rail Ltd

Fitology House, Smedley Street East, Matlock DE4 3GH, UK
Tel: (+44 1629) 76 07 50
Fax: (+44 1629) 76 07 51
e-mail: info@laser-rail.co.uk
Web: www.laser-rail.co.uk

Key personnel

Chief Executive Officer: *David M Johnson*
Executive Director: *Alison B Stansfield*
Managing Director: *Steve Ingleton*
Non-Executive Director: *Hugh Fenwick*

Background

Laser Rail, established in 1989, is a technical consultancy supplying complete turnkey projects for rail infrastructure and metro networks. It combines experienced engineers with the latest high-technology laser-gauging systems and software to measure and analyse clients' infrastructure and provide new and innovative vehicle designs. Laser Rail is part of Balfour Beatty Rail Technologies, itself part of the Balfour Beatty Rail group. The recent acquisition of Laser Rail has extended Balfour Beatty's technology base with expertise in gauging technologies, analysis and data management and a specialist team engaged in the area of track geometry measurement and evaluation. As part of Balfour Beatty, Laser Rail is now able to include design and implementation of schemes providing their clients with the possibility of turnkey solutions.

Products

Measuring systems: Laser Gauging Vehicle (LGV), a road-rail vehicle for measuring structure profiles accurately and at speed. Laser Profiling Trolley (LaserPeT), a portable version of the LGV used at walking speed and designed to measure metro infrastructure. LaserFleX™ structure profile measuring systems, LaserSweep™, a portable measuring device for measuring structure profiles in areas where larger systems are uneconomical to use. Product approval received from Network Rail and London Underground.

Software: ClearRoute™, Stress Route™, DesignRoute™ software for vehicles and infrastructure management, 3-Dimensional databases and advanced change detection software, which provides new tools for the catalogue and management of assets.

Services: Track geometry measurement and design, route assessment for existing and new rolling stock, interoperability, feasibility studies for existing and new routes, design of new rolling stock. Risk assessment.

Laser Rail has a formal research and development group to develop core technologies associated with its activities. Projects being undertaken include infrastructure measurement, monitoring and analysis, vehicle/track interaction technology and intelligent video systems. Laser Rail also provides software training and certification to various levels of competency and

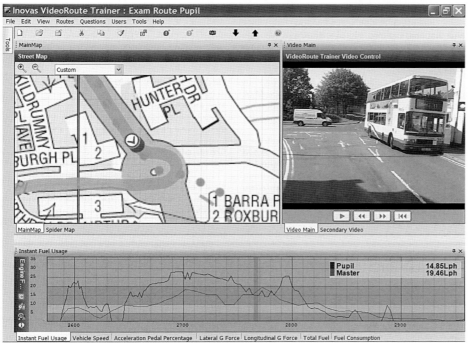

Inovas system screenshot   1174944

this can be supplied as part of the overall support package. Laser Rail operates in the UK, Europe and Australasia.

March Networks Corporation

Corporate headquarters
555 Legget Drive, Tower B, Ottawa, Ontario,
Canada K2K 2X3
Tel: (+1 613) 591 81 81
Web: www.marchnetworks.com

Key personnel
President and Chief Executive Officer: *Peter Strom*
Chief Financial Officer: *Kenneth Taylor*
Chief Operating Officer: *Steve Nicolle*

Other offices
March Networks has regional offices in the US, Mexico, UK and Italy.

Products
March Networks provides bus, passenger rail and other fleet operators around the world with complete video surveillance systems. The company's transportation solutions cover both mobile and wayside environments, including stations, depots and park-and-rides. They enable transport authorities to enhance passenger and staff safety and respond quickly to emergency situations. They also help authorities manage and reduce risk, deter theft and vandalism and improve maintenance and operational efficiency.

Key transportation partners include Bombardier Transportation and Wabtec Railway Electronics. March Network and Bombardier jointly developed the advanced video surveillance provided as part of Bombardier's SEKURFLO intelligent rail security solution. Wabtec's VideoTrax DVR for freight opertors was also jointly developed by the two companies.

Contracts
March Networks transportation customers include: the Toronto Transit Commission; French National Railways (SNCF); the Gautrain Rapid Rail Link in Gauteng Province, South Africa; London Underground's sub-surface lines; Singapore MRT; Helsinki City Transport and US based bus authorities in Miami-Dade Florida, Orange County California, Palm Beach County Florida and San Francisco, California.

Nexala

Headquarters
288 Bishopsgate, London EC2M 4QP, UK
Tel: (+44 20) 79 59 30 48
Fax: (+44 20) 79 59 30 30
Web: www.nexala.com

Key personnel
Chief Executive Officer: *Dr Karl O'Connell*
Chief Finance Officer: *John O'Sullivan*
Chief Technology Officer: *Dr Marcus O'Connell*
Vice-President Business Development: *Paul Lowry*
Account Director: *Liam Brennan*
Professional Services Director: *Shane Lillis*

Background
Nexala was established in 2002 following the acquisition of a number of technology organisations and has operations in Ireland, the UK, France and North America.

Products and Services
Nexala provides a suite of integrated products for asset and maintenance management, planning and real-time service management.

Contracts
In July 2007 Northern Rail selected Nexala to manage the performance of their assets. Nexala is used to monitor incidents and analyse the performance of their fleet.

In November 2006 One Railway selected Nexala to monitor and analyse maintenance regimes and the performance of their fleet. Also in November 2006, Nexala was selected by Hitachi to provide maintenance management, decision support and performance analysis systems to support the maintenance of the new Hitachi Class 395 electric train fleet for the Integrated Ken Franchise (IKF).

NICE Systems Ltd

International Corporate Headquarters
8 Hapnina Street, PO Box 690, 43107 Ra'anana, Israel
Tel: (+972 9) 775 37 77   Fax: (+972 9) 743 42 82
Web: www.nice.com

Key personnel
President: *Dr Shlomo Shamir*
Chief Executive Officer: *Haim Shani*
Corporate Vice-President and Chief Financial Officer: *Ran Oz*

Subsidiaries
NICE CTI Systems UK Ltd
UK
Tel: (+44 8707) 22 40 00

NICE Systems GmbH
Germany
Tel: (+49 69) 97 17 70

NICE Systems Inc
North America
Tel: (+1 201) 964 26 00

NICE Switzerland AG
Switzerland
Tel: (+41 41) 784 19 00

Products
Command control solutions for the transport sector including mass transit operators through a digital video recording platform and automatic detection tools.

Contracts
In August 2008 NICE Systems was awarded a project from Norfolk Southern Corporation to more broadly capture, manage and analyse rail communications at a further five sites to augment systems recently installed at 16 other sites, including major classification rail yards and dispatch centres. Norfolk Southern will use the NICE solutions to streamline investigations and incident reconstructions relating to railway safety.

In November 2006 NICE Systems, in partnership with Siemens, was selected by MTA New York City Transit to implement a solution for the capture and analysis of communications for MTA's Rail Control Center (RCC).

In October 2006 NICE Systems was selected by Intelligent Systems Co, Inc to supply advanced digital video surveillance and monitoring solutions as part of a large scale upgrade project for the Massachusetts Bay Transportation Authority (MBTA) new Automated Fare Collection (AFC) system.

Pallas Informatik A/S

Allerød Stationsvej 2D, DK-3450 Allerød, Denmark
Tel: (+45) 48 10 24 10
Fax: (+45) 48 10 24 01
e-mail: pallas@pallas.dk
Web: www.pallas.dk

Key personnel
Chairman of the Board: *Svend Vitting Andersen*
Managing Director: *Karsten Funder*

Products
Fleet Management, an Internet-based software programme developed to provide detailed information to management, station and workshop personnel. The system provides a real-time overview of trains in service, a parameterised view of train characteristics and a parameterised selection of trains requiring attention. A change of detail level enables the user to retrieve data pertaining to a specific train and the system can be integrated with existing vehicle workshop systems.

PC-Soft GmbH

Adolf Hennecke Strasse 37, D-01968 Senftenberg, Germany
Tel: (+49 3573) 707 50   Fax: (+49 3573) 70 75 19
e-mail: info@pcsoft.de
Web: www.pcsoft.de

Key personnel
Consultant: *Christoph Baum*

Products
Provision of software engineering and consultancy services in the field of railway systems.

The product software suite vips® consists of different modules, providing solutions for computer-based management of transport processes, vehicles and infrastructure. As an open system, vips® provides interfaces that can be integrated with other software systems such as ERP-systems like SAP/R3. The vips® software suite includes vips®/d – which supports the logistics process by centralised planning, controlling and monitoring the flow of information and goods. VIPS® Carsis supports planning, controlling and monitoring of all activities of maintenance, diagnostics as well as warranty management.

vips® supports monitoring of straining and condition of all tracks, overhead contact lines as well as the safety features and equipment. It includes the following features: detailed reports of inspection data, generating trends and prospects, controlling of critical values, exposure analysis for every single rail or switch.

These software products are available as client/server systems and run on various operating systems, including Unix and Windows platforms.

PSI Transcom GmbH

Dircksenstrasse 42-44, D-10178 Berlin, Germany
Tel: (+49 30) 28 01 16 10
Fax: (+49 30) 28 01 10 32
e-mail: info@psitrans.de
Web: www.psitranscom.de

Other office
Transcom has offices in Hamburg and Dusseldorf.

Key personnel
Chief Executive Officer: *Dipl Ing Peter Kursawe*
Business Unit Manager Sales and Marketing: *René Rothe*
Business Unit Manager, Telematics Systems: *Torsten Vogel*
Business Unit Manager, Safety: *Alexander Baer*

Background
PSI Transportation GmbH is a subsidiary of PSIAG.

Products
PSI Transcom provides Automatic Vehicle Location Systems as well as solutions for

---

real-time passenger information, depot mangement, train dispatching and safety. The basis of these solutions is its integrated and economical telematics platform which was developed on the basis of event-controlled and object-orientated technologies.

Contracts

PSI Transcom has supplied software systems to Rhätische Bahn Sihweiz, DVB, Dresden, ZOB GmbH, operator of Hamburg's central bus station, the Hamburg S-Bahn, Rostocker Strassenbahn AG, Rostock, the Süd-Thüringen-Bahn and GVB, Amsterdam.

S&A Systems Inc

PO Box 1928, Rockwell, Texas 75087-2028, US
Tel: (+1 972) 722 10 09   Fax: (+1 972) 722 10 33
e-mail: don.srygley@fleetwatch.com
Web: www.fleetwatch.com

Key personnel
President: *Don Srygley*
Chief Executive Officer: *Jim Srygley*
Vice-President of Software Development: *Cookie Stokes*
Vice-President of Engineering: *John Elliott*

Products
Fleetwatch electronic trip recorder system based on a bus hub-mounted unit that automatically transmits vehicle identification and mileage to either a fixed-mount or mobile receiver. This can be integrated with the Fleetwatch Fluid Management System which additionally captures data on fuel, oil, coolant and transmission fluid dispensed.

Southern Vectis plc

Nelson Road, Newport PO30 1RD, UK
Tel: (+44 1983) 52 24 56   Fax: (+44 1983) 52 49 61

Key personnel
Managing Director: *Stuart Linn*

Capabilities
Drawing on the company's bus and coach experience, its consultancy section offers expertise in commercial, management, marketing and ticketing aspects of bus and tramway operation, including network design/assessment and commercial franchising.

Projects
The successful joint venture with Kalisz, Poland, has celebrated four years and is now joined by one with Chelm, near the Ukrainian border. Other work has included Moldova and France.

SYSTRA Consulting Inc

150 Clove Rd Little Falls, New Jersey 07424, US
Tel: (+1 973) 873 97 00   Fax: 973-873-9701
e-mail: systra@systra.com
Web: www.systraconsulting.com

Key personnel
President and Chief Executive Officer: *Charles Stark, PE*
Chief Financial Officer/Secretary: *Garry Hartwig*
Vice-President Business Development: *Lucia DiMeglio*
Vice-President Human Resources: *Marcia Coleman*
Senior Vice-President Northeast Regional Director: *Ruby Siegel*
Senior Vice-President Mid-Atlantic Regional Director: *Dominic Sabatini*

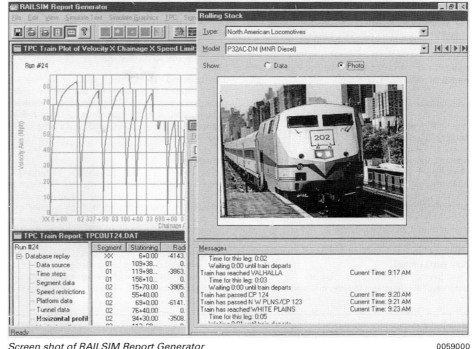
Screen shot of RAILSIM Report Generator   0059000

Vice-President Western Regional Director: *James C Fea*
Vice-President Construction Management: *Joseph Sais*
Vice-President Rail Operations Analysis and RAILSIM®: *F William Lipfert, Jr*

Background
Systra Consulting, Inc (also operating as Systra Engineering) is a full service, multidisciplinary firm offering planning, engineering, design and construction management services for transportation systems and associated facilities. Part of the Systra Group, Systra Consulting serves clients from a network of offices throughout the US.

Products
RAILSIM® Simulation Software Suite, simulation/engineering package – Systra's RAILSIM suite is a family of rail network modelling and analysis applications that run on Windows 2000 and XP. RAILSIM packages are customised according to the licensee's needs. For example, the Simulation/Engineering package contains: RAILSIM Network Simulator, RAILSIM Editor, RAILSIM Track Profile Generator, RAILSIM Train Performance Calculator (TPC), RAILSIM Rolling Stock Libraries, RAILSIM Headway Calculation, Safe Braking Distance Calculation and Signal Design Add-Ons. RAILSIM output includes graphical plots and text reports compatible with any Windows plotter or printer. Reports can be stored in AutoCAD® DXF file or comma-delimited text format, ready for incorporation into reports, spreadsheets and engineering drawings. Typical RAILSIM license packages include: Base License, LFA package, simulation/engineering package.

Trapeze Software Group

Head office
5800 Explorer Drive, 5th Floor, Mississauga, Ontario, Canada L4W 5L4
Tel: (+1 905) 629 87 27
Fax: (+1 905) 238 84 08
e-mail: info@trapezegroup.co.uk
Web: www.trapezegroup.co.uk

Other offices
Suite 7, 1st Floor, Alderley House, Alderley Road, Wilmslow, Cheshire, UK
Tel: (+44 1625) 54 53 70
Fax: (+44 1625) 54 53 88

Products
Integrated modular IT systems for:

Planning: bus/train scheduling, block planning, duty planning.
Operation: day-to-day operations, rosters and duties, wage calculation.
Administration and statistics: passenger information, contract administration, management information.

Trivector System AB

Åldermansgatan 13, SE-227 64 Lund, Sweden
Tel: (+46 42) 38 65 00   Fax: (+46 42) 38 65 25
e-mail: info@trivector.se
Web: www.trivector.se

Key personnel
Managing Director: *Klas Odelid*
Marketing Manager: *Ola Fogelberg*
Project Manager: *Anders Månsson*

Products
VEMOS (Vehicle Monitoring System) is a comprehensive information system for a public transportation system. It works in real time and contains a traffic control system, a central system and a depot system. The complete system is in operation in the city of Karlstad, Sweden and is to be in operation in the Dalarna region in the future. RAPP (Route Analysis Programme Package) is a system for analysing route-time data.

Verint Systems Inc

Worldwide Headquarters
330 South Service Road, Melville, New York 11747, US
Tel: (+1 631) 962 96 00
Fax: (+1 631) 962 93 00
Web: www.verint.com

Key personnel
President, Chief Executive Officer and Director: *Dan Bodner*
Chief Financial Officer: *Doug Robinson*
Chief Strategic Officer and Director: *Peter Fante*

Background
Founded in 1994, Verint is headquartered in Melville, New York, with offices in 18 countries and a staff of 2,500 professionals around the world.

Products

CCTV security and surveillance systems including mobile DVR's, cameras and monitors; management software for reviewing and configuration; wireless connectivity from vehicle to station or control centre; Internet Protocol (IP) based transmission of video.

Vigil Systems Pty Ltd

AMC Building, Brisbane Technology Park, Clunies Ross Court, Eight Mile Plains, Queensland 4113, Australia
PO Box 4172, Eight Mile Plains, Queensland 4113, Australia
Tel: (+61 7) 33 64 06 10   Fax: (+61 7) 33 64 07 88
e-mail: info@vigilsystems.com
Web: www.vigilsystems.com

Key personnel

Chief Executive Officer: *Ian Haynes*
Business Development Manager: *Leesa Hubbard*

Subsidiaries

Vigil Systems Inc, US Office
Tel: (+1 213) 341 17 44 (+1 877) 293 70 05
Fax: (+1 213) 652 19 63
President: *Dave Norstrom*

Background

Vigil Systems specialises in the development of advanced driver training and improvement systems and provides solutions to large transit organisations across Australia, Asia and North America.

Products

VigilVanguard is an advanced 'behind-the-wheel' driver training system used to improve the safety and performance of transit operators. The system offers consistent, high quality and unbiased 'real world' training and uses custom assessment forms, generating custom reports which describe sensor-detected and trainer-generated events. VigilPassenger is a lower cost alternative, providing a powerful tool designed for in-service check rides which allows instructors to assess bus operators in service and also produce a custom report on the operator's performance.

VIPS AB

Heurlins Plats 1, SE-413 01 Gothenburg, Sweden
Tel: (+46 31) 743 75 75   Fax: (+46 31) 701 73 20
e-mail: vips@vips.se
Web: www.ptv-scandinavia.se/vips

Key personnel

Managing Director: *Bo Sahlström*

Background

VIP AB is a subsidiary of the German management software developer, PTV Group.

Products

Supplier of PC-based strategic planning systems mainly for public transport but also for private transport.

More than 70 VIPS systems are installed worldwide with bus, tram, metro and heavy rail operators.

CONSULTANCY SERVICES

Company listing by country

AUSTRALIA
Asia Pacific Rail
Ranbury Management Group
TTG Transportation Technology (TTG TT)

AUSTRIA
RTA Rail Tec Arsenal Fahrzeugversuchsanlage
    GmbH

BELGIUM
Stratec SA
Transurb Technirail SA

CANADA
CANAC Railway Services Inc
Canarail Consultants Inc
CPCS Transcom
Delcan Corporation
Giro Inc
McCormick Rankin Corporation

DENMARK
COWI Consulting Engineers and Planners AS
Ødegaard & Danneskiold-Samsøe A/S

FINLAND
Creadesign Oy

FRANCE
AREP
Certifer
Egis Rail
Equival
EurailTest
SEMTCAR
Systra SA

GERMANY
DB International GmbH
ETC Transport Consultants GmbH
HaCon Ingenieurgesellschaft mbH
Lahmeyer International GmbH
Light Rail Transit Consultants GmbH
LogoMotive GmbH
Metroconsult
Pöyry Infra (Hannover) GmbH
SCI Verkehr GmbH
Socialdata
TTK – TransportTechnologie-Consult Karlsruhe
    GmbH

GREECE
Doxiadis Associates SA

HONG KONG
MTR Corporation Consultancy Services

HUNGARY
Uvaterv Engineering Consultants Ltd

INDIA
Pallavan Transport Consultancy Services Limited
RITES Ltd

IRELAND
CIE Consult

ITALY
Italcertifer
Italferr SpA

JAPAN
Japan Railway Technical Service (JARTS)

NETHERLANDS
DHV BV
Lloyd's Register Rail BV
NEA Transport Research and Training

SINGAPORE
SMRT Engineering Pte Ltd (SMRTE)

SPAIN
Ardanuy Ingeneria SA
INECO-TIFSA
Intraesa

SWEDEN
Banverket Consulting

SWITZERLAND
ENOTRAC AG
Prose Ltd

UNITED KINGDOM
WSP Policy & Research Unit
Accent
Amey
Arup Group Ltd
Atkins Rail
Babcock Rail
Balfour Beatty Rail Technologies Limited
Best Impressions
BMT Reliability Consultants Ltd
Capita Symonds Ltd
Capoco Design
Colin Buchanan
Corus Rail Technologies
Creactive Design
DCA Design International Ltd
Design and Projects Int Ltd
Design Triangle
FaberMaunsell
Hodgson and Hodgson Group Ltd
Hyder Consulting
IBIS Transport Consultants Ltd
Interfleet Technology Ltd
Jacobs
Joint Mobility Partnership

LEK Consulting LLP
Lend Lease
Listavia International Consultants Ltd
Lloyd's Register Rail Limited
Millbrook Proving Ground Limited
Mott MacDonald Group
MVA Consultancy
Newbus Technology Limited
Peter Davidson Consultancy
Prima Services Group Ltd
Ptarmigan Transport Solutions Ltd
QinetiQ Rail
Roundel Ltd
Scott Brownrigg
Scott Wilson Railways Ltd
Serco Raildata
Southdowns Environmental Consultants Ltd
Southern Vectis plc
Steer Davies Gleave
TAS Partnership Ltd
The Nichols Group
The QSS Group Ltd
The Railway Consultancy Ltd
Transportation Management Solutions
Transys Projects Ltd
TRL Limited (Transport Research Laboratory)
Urban Initiatives
URS Corporation Ltd

UNITED STATES
Bechtel Corporation
Berger/Abam Engineers Inc
Booz, Allen & Hamilton Inc
CRA International, Inc
Delon Hampton & Associates
Earth Tech Inc
Hatch Mott MacDonald Inc
Hill International Inc
ICF International
Jakes Associates, Inc
Laramore, Douglass and Popham
Lea+Elliott Inc
Lemna International, Inc
LTK Engineering Services
Modjeski & Masters Inc
Parsons Brinckerhoff
RailWorks Corporation
STV Group
TERA International Group, Inc (TERA)
The Corradino Group
The Harbor Consultancy International (THCI)
Thomas K Dyer, Inc
Transportation Technology Center Inc (TTCI)
Urbitran
Wilbur Smith Associates
Wilson, Ihrig & Associates
ZGF – Zimmer Gunsul Frasca Partnership

Accent

Gable House, 14-16 Turnham Green Terrace, Chiswick, London W4 1QP, UK
Tel: (+44 20) 87 42 22 11   Fax: (+44 20) 87 42 19 91
e-mail: info@accent-mr.com
Web: www.accent-mr.com

Key personnel
Managing Director: *Rob Sheldon*
Marketing Director: *Rachel Risely*
Business Development Manager: *Scott Hinton*

Capabilities
Accent is a full service research agency, with offices in London, Bristol, Edinburgh and Munich and the resources and equipment to undertake both qualitative and quantitative studies of significant size.

Accent is an expert in research using trade-off techniques and has been instrumental in the introduction and development of the technique in the UK, having conducted many studies using these methods for high-profile clients.

Accent's research in the rail industry includes: customer priorities, estimating demand, real-time information, strategy and policy, ticketing, value of time and vehicle design.

Amey

Amey, The Sherard Building, Edmund Halley Road, Oxford OX4 4DQ, UK
Tel: (+44 1865) 71 31 00
e-mail: enquiry@amey.co.uk
Web: www.amey.co.uk

Key personnel
Chief Executive: *Mel Ewell*

Background
Amey is part of Ferrovial, one of Europe's largest infrastructure and services groups.

Capabilities
Amey is one of the UK's leading support service partners working in partnership with customers across a number of sectors including: rail and strategic highways, central government, defence, education and local government.

Ardanuy Ingeneria SA

Avenida Europa 34, Edificio B, E-28023 Madrid, Spain
Tel: (+34 91) 799 45 00
Fax: (+34 91) 799 45 01
e-mail: madrid@ardanuy.com
Web: www.ardanuy.com

Key personnel
President: *Josep-Maria Ribes*
General Manager: *Carlos Alonso*
International Manager: *Alberto Gonzalez*

Other offices
Ardanuy Ingeniería, SA operates mainly in Spain, where it has offices in Madrid, Barcelona, Valencia, Seville, Tenerife, Bilbao. The company currently has two subsidiary companies, in Lithuania (UAB Ardanuy Baltic) and in Poland (Ardanuy Polska Sp zoo). It also has operations in South America: Argentina, Chile, Cuba, Puerto Rico, US; Africa: Egypt, Morocco, South Africa; and central and eastern Europe: Poland, Romania, Hungary, Bulgaria, Czech Republic, Latvia, Lithuania.

Capabilities
Feasibility studies, planning, projects, (cost benefit analysis, tender documentation, technical specifications, detailed projects) and design, work supervision, technical assistance, procurement management, project management and other consultancy services for railways; metros and tramway (signalling, communications, catenary,

power substations, track, rolling stock) and tunnels.

Projects
Ardanuy has successfully carried out more than 600 transportation projects in Europe, America, Africa and Asia. Examples include: high-speed line Barcelona- Madrid, Madrid-Toledo, Madrid-Valladolid; the Guadarrama tunnel (27 km) and the railway station in Cádiz.

In the field of urban transport, the company has led numerous projects for lines and underground stations, trams and transport by cable in a number of cities including: Barcelona, Madrid, Valencia, Bilbao, Seville, Málaga, Alicante, Tenerife, San Juan de Puerto Rico and Valparaíso (Chile).

AREP

163 bis, avenue de Clichy, Impasse Chalabre, F-75847 Paris, Cedex 17, France
Tel: (+33 1) 56 33 05 08   Fax: (+33 1) 53 42 02 86
e-mail: contact@arep.fr
Web: www.arep.fr

Key personnel
President: *Jean Marie Duthilleul*
General Manager: *Etienne Tricaud*
Director, International Projects: *Etienne Tricaud*

Background
AREP is part of the SNCF Group and a subsidiary of SNCF Participations.

Capabilities
AREP is a multidisciplinary engineering and consulting firm that designs and builds urban transport centres and exchange hubs and public spaces. It makes its competencies available to carriers, decision-makers and investors in different sectors through nine departments covering: urban planning and layout; design, engineering and site supervision; international projects; programming; interior layouts and design; structures; building engineers; design and installation of utility systems and economic viability studies.

Arup Group Ltd

13 Fitzroy Street, London W1T 4BQ, UK
Tel: (+44 20) 76 36 15 31   Fax: (+44 20) 77 55 24 51
Web: www.arup.com

Key personnel
Chairman: *Terry Hill*
Transport Director: *Ed Humphreys*

Background
Founded in 1946, Arup Group Ltd comprises around 120 professional and technical staff operating through a network of UK offices including Birmingham, Bristol, Cardiff, Coventry, Edinburgh, London, Leeds, Manchester and Newcastle.

It has specialist staff in Australia, Hong Kong, Singapore, Johannesburg and New York and a network of offices throughout Europe, Asia, Australasia and North America.

Capabilities
Transport planning, environmental, economics, acoustics, geotechnical, civil, mechanical and electrical engineering, structural and building engineering services. Planning and design of urban and interurban transport systems; business case appraisal, specialists in rail, light rail and bus planning and appraisal, strategic transport planning studies, demand forecasting and modelling, information technology, bus priority and network planning, rail and LRT operations, traffic control systems, feasibility studies, design of infrastructure including bus and rail stations, station capacity, rail and road construction management; traffic engineering

including parking control and strategy work; pedestrian movement and flow modelling.

Projects
Victoria Transport Interchange, Central London Congestion Charging, King's Cross Central, MEDA (European Mediterranean Transport Project), SYPTE framework projects, TERFFS extension; gauge corner cracking control strategy development; rail freight grant regime review and industry consultation; King's Cross rail and station planning, including the detailed design of the new western concourse and associated buildings; Channel Tunnel rail link; rail freight avoidable cost review, Manchester – crewe layout remodelling; level crossing signalling renewals for Railtrack LNE (Network Rail); Sunderland extension Metro-Railtrack signalling interface specification and implementation; Welwyn-Hitchin upgrade feasibility.

Asia Pacific Rail

Head Office
Level 2, 60 Collins Street, Melbourne, Victoria, Australia, 3000
Tel: (+61 3) 96 50 14 44
e-mail: enquiries@asiapacific.com.au
Web: www.asiapacificrail.com.au

Key personnel
Chief Executive Officer: *Alan Burns*
Principal Consultants: *Alan Carey, Henry van Ginkel, Howard Ellis, Marc Chadwick*

Background
Asia Pacific Rail is an Australian rail engineering consultancy and a wholly owned subsidiary of Coffey International Limited.

Capabilities
Involved and experienced in both private and government sectors Asia Pacific's specialisations include: track engineering and design; signal and communications engineering and design; civil engineering and design; power and overheads engineering and design; planning, feasibility studies and concept development; tender specification, evaluation and award; project management; contract administration and legal advice; financial and cost management; design and documentation; construction and installation; testing and commissioning, as well as operations, safety and maintenance.

Projects
Current projects include: Victorian Level Crossings Upgrade Project for the Victorian Rail Track Corporation (VicTrack), track management for the Tasmanian Department of Infrastructure, Energy and Resources, Train Control Monitoring System Project for the Victorian Department of Transport, route alignment and track design for Gindalbie Metals in the Pilbara.

Other recent projects include: the Geelong Rail Access Improvement project for the Victorian Department of Transport, the Train Control Consolidation project for the Australian Rail Track Corporation and the Eltham to Hurstbridge Rail Safety Improvement project for Connex, Melbourne's metropolitan rail operator.

Atkins Rail

Euston Tower, 286 Euston Road, London NW1 3AT, UK
Tel: (+44 20) 71 21 20 00
Fax: (+44 20) 71 21 21 11
e-mail: rail@atkinsglobal.com
Web: www.atkinsglobal.com/rail

Key personnel
Chairman: *Ed Wallis*
Chief Executive: *Keith Clarke*
Group Finance Director: *Robert MacLeod*

Commercial and Marketing Director: *Graham Clench*
Managing Consultant, Transport Planning: *Abhi Bhasin*
Director, Rail Vehicles: *Dave Saunders*
Head of Press Office: *Ben Thompson*
Director of Civil Engineering: *Steve Ashton*
Director of Electrification: *Bob Ducksbury*
Director of Control and Systems: *Dr Rob Davis*

Regional offices

Atkins Rail UK regional office locations: Birmingham, Chippenham, Crewe, Croydon, Daventry, Derby, Epsom, Glasgow, London, Manchester, Orpington, Swindon, Waterloo and York.

Overseas offices

Atkins office locations: China, Copenhagen, Denmark, Ireland, Hong Kong, Sweden and UAE.

Capabilities

Atkins Rail can take a project through its complete life-cycle from feasibility studies, planning, conceptual design and detailed design to safety, reliability and risk assessments, project and contract management, life-cycle costing, design implementation and whole life asset management support. Experience includes work undertaken for main line, freight, suburban, metro and light rail systems in the UK and worldwide.

Projects

Atkins Rail is engaged on a number of significant alliances with players within the industry. Its partnership with Carillion and Network Rail together forms the North Staffs Alliance, which has enabled the completion of the GBP75 million modernisation of the West Coast Main Line (WCML). Atkins is also a member of the alliance with Network Rail, Balfour Beatty and Carillion to deliver the GBP600 million upgrade and renewal of the West Coast Main Line electrification system including 2,130 miles of re-wired overhead line equipment together with 22 new electrical substations.

The company is a partner in the equity consortium Metronet Rail BCV Limited, incorporating the London Underground Bakerloo, Central, Victoria and Waterloo and City lines, and Metronet Rail SSL Limited, incorporating the Metropolitan, District, Circle, Hammersmith and City and East London lines.

Babcock Rail

Head office
Kintail House, 3 Lister Way, Hamilton International Park, Blantyre G72 0FT, UK
Tel: (+44 845) 000 30 05   Fax: (+44 845) 30 06
Web: www.babcock.co.uk

Key personnel

Chief Executive: *Andrew Pearson*
Commercial Director: *Bobby Forbes*
Key Account Director: *Meirion Thomas*

Background

Previously called First Engineering, the company is part of Babcock International Group plc. It has regional offices located in London, York, Birmingham, Manchester and Hamilton.

Capabilities

Railway infrastructure and civil engineering consultancy.

Balfour Beatty Rail Technologies Limited

Head Office
Room A108, Midland House, Nelson Street, Derby DE1 2SA, UK
Tel: (+44 1332) 26 24 24   Fax: (+44 1332) 26 20 27
e-mail: info.bbrt.uk@bbrail.com
Web: www.bbrail.com

Key personnel

General Manager: *Neil Andrew*
Head of Signalling Systems: *Stephen Cox*
Director Laser Rail Technologies: *Stephen Ingleton*
Technical Services Director: *Andy Curzon*

Services

Balfour Beatty Rail Technologies Limited specialises in decision support of railway maintenance and renewal operations, and in the creation of new technology to perform these operations in a cost-effective manner. Technologies, part of the worldwide Balfour Beatty Rail group, operates on the areas of track, structures and signalling where it develops new technology and software, and also provides consultancy services in support of these.

The company is organised into three divisions, signalling systems, laser rail technologies and technical services. Signalling systems develop technology which enhances the performance of conventional railway signalling through 'intelligent infrastructure' – systems and software which monitor the performance of signalling, points and interlocking and advises of incipient problems. Laser Rail Technologies develops measuring systems and analytical software which can be used to monitor track geometry and infrastructure gauge – maximising capacity and durability. Technical services provide support consultancy covering use of its own systems and emerging new technology such as new trackforms, track stabilisation, novel techniques and production methods.

Banverket Consulting

Industridivisionen
SE-781 85 Borlänge, Sweden
Tel: (+46 243) 44 61 00
Fax: (+46 243) 44 61 10
e-mail: consulting@hk.banverket.se
Web: www.banverket.se

Key personnel

Director: *John-Olof Hermanson*
Area Directors: *Sture Åberg, Rolf Ericsson, Leif Malm, Lars Moberg, Lennart Eldh and Jan Nilsson*

Background

Banverket Consulting is a consultancy unit within Banverket (the Swedish National Rail Administration). Banverket Consulting has run its operation since 1998 and is based in Borlänge, with area offices in six locations throughout Sweden.

Capabilities

Banverket Consulting offers a range of services and products: services in railway research, project planning, and project and construction management within the railway sector. Its operations are IT-intensive with technical planning tools integrated in common computer and CAD environments. Also expertise within the areas of marshalling technology, carrying capacity, power supply simulations and track geometry.

Projects

Botniabanan AB has been commissioned by the Swedish government to build the Bothnia Line, a railway running from Nyland, north of Kramfors, via Örnsköldsvik, to Umeå. The new railway will be 190 km long, with 140 bridges and 25 km of tunnels.

Bechtel Corporation

Corporate Headquarters
50 Beale Street, San Francisco, California 94105-1895, US
Tel: (+1 415) 768 12 34
Fax: (+1 415) 768 90 38
Web: www.bechtel.com

Key personnel

Chairman and Chief Executive Officer: *Riley Bechtel*
President and Chief Operating Officer: *Adiran Zaccaria*
Executive Vice-President and Deputy Chief Operating Officer: *Jude Laspa*

Capabilities

Bechtel offers a broad spectrum of services including feasibility and environmental studies, architectural/engineering design, project management, engineering management, construction management, start-up and operations, and financial planning in addition to engineering, procurement and construction.

Bechtel's transportation experience includes over 20 urban rapid transit systems and more than 5,600 miles of railways. The company has been involved in most new transit projects in the USA (Washington metro; Boston rapid transit; San Diego light rail; Sacramento light rail; Atlanta MARTA; San Francisco BART; Baltimore rapid transit; MTA/LIRR East Side Access in New York; and the Los Angeles metro), in domestic main line projects, including the Alameda Corridor-East (ACE) freight corridor upgrade in California, and in key international transit and rail projects, such as the Caracas metro, the São Paulo metro, Taipei rapid transit, Attika Metro in Athens, South Korea high-speed rail, the Western Corridor Railway linking Kowloon (Hong Kong) with northwest New Territories, and the Channel Tunnel Rail Link, Thameslink 2000 and Jubilee Line Extension in the UK.

Bechtel was retained by London Underground Ltd to provide a fast-track push to the commissioning and completion of the Jubilee Line Extension in time to support the official opening of the Millennium Dome in Greenwich. The system was commissioned in three phases culminating in the provision of through passenger services from Stanmore to Stratford on 20 November 1999. The final passenger station, Westminster, opened on 22 December 1999.

Contracts

Bechtel is working with Cross London Rail Links (CLRL), a joint-venture company between Transport for London and the Department for Transport, that is leading the Crossrail project to build a high-capacity east-west heavy rail line across the UK's capital. Bechtel is managing a team of design and cost consultants to help produce a reference design for the Crossrail line which will connect Maidenhead to Shenfield and Abbey Wood.

Berger/Abam Engineers Inc

Suite 300, 33301 Ninth Avenue South, Federal Way, Washington 98003-2600, US
Tel: (+1 206) 431 23 00   Fax: (+1 206) 431 22 50
e-mail: info@abam.com
Web: www.abam.com
A member of the Berger Group

Key personnel

President and CEO: *Arnfinn Rusten*
Chairman of the Board: *Alexander Popoff Jr*
Finance Director: *Milo Clancy*
Marketing Director: *Kimberly D Hinckley*
Technical Directors: *James S Guarre, Robert Griebenow*
Operations Director: *Michael Lallier*

Capabilities:

Planning, civil and structural engineering, construction management, highways, bridges, mass transit facilities, site analysis, corridor selection, impact studies, alignment and alternative studies, aerial structure design, condition surveys, seismic assessment and design, repair/modernisation.

Projects:

Bangkok Mass Transit System Bangkok, Thailand: Berger/Abam provided a review of the transit system design.

The Seattle Monorail plan, led by Berger/A bam, evaluates the feasibility of extending the existing monorail route.

Best Impressions

15 Starfield Road, London W12 9SN
Tel: (+44 20) 87 40 64 43   Fax: (+44 20) 87 40 91 34
e-mail: talk2us@best-impressions.co.uk
Web: www.best-impressions.co.uk

Key personnel
Director: *Ray Stenning*

Capabilities
Leaflets, maps, brochures, liveries, branding and brand development, corporate identity, websites, marketing and vehicle styling.

Projects
Design and marketing work for a range of public transport operators and local authorites, including: Stagecoach UK Bus, South West Trains, London Midland, East Midlands, Trent Barton Buses, Oxford Bus Company, Wilts & Dorset Bus Company, Bluestar, Southern Vectis, First Group, Cambridgeshire County Council and Buckinghamshire County Council.

BMT Reliability Consultants Ltd

Trading as BMT Rail
12 Little Park Farm Road, Fareham PO15 5SU, UK
Tel: (+44 1489) 55 31 00   Fax: (+44 1489) 55 31 01
e-mail: messages@bmtrcl.com
Web: www.bmtrcl.com

Key personnel
Managing Director: *Jim Lambert*
Rail Business Director: *Jacque Reynolds*
Marketing Director: *Stuart Duffin*

Capabilities
BMT's fields of expertise include specialist services, depot and infrastructure divisions. Engineering consultancy services to reduce risk and improve reliability, safety and through-life economics of railway assets and processes. The company develops and applies techniques which assist infrastructure suppliers and operators to assess and optimise rolling stock reliability, maintenance, safety, risk and cost.

Projects
Independent Safety Assessor for the dmus for Northern Irelenad Railways (Translink); risk assessment programme management for the Class 465 modification programme; strategic maintenance review on both the Class 465 and Class 91 locomotive; GNER high-speed train (HST) impact minute reduction programme; project management of both the BT 41 bogie overhaul and the Silverlink Class 508 refurbishment; reliability and safety of the Heathrow Express train for Siemens and CAF; independent safety assessment of the Networker Classic for Bombardier Transportation (formerly Adtranz); maintenance optimisation of the Swanley Junction switched diamonds for Balfour Beatty Rail Maintenance; through-life cost model development for ALSTOM; risk analysis in support of the East London Line extension private finance initiative application for London Underground; corrosion management of Classes 313 and 321 for HSBC Rail (UK) Ltd.

Booz, Allen & Hamilton Inc

Transportation Consulting Division
101 California Street, Suite 3300, San Francisco, California 94111-5855, US
Tel: (+1 415) 391 19 00   Fax: (+1 415) 627 42 83
Web: www.boozallen.com

Key personnel
Senior Vice-Presidents: *Ghassan Salameh, Jürgen Ringbeck, Joe Saddi, Justin F Zubrod*
Vice-Presidents: *Chris Manning, Robert J Williams, Edward C Tse, Dieter Schneiderbauer, Alexander Niehues, Fadi Majdalani*

Capabilities
Booz, Allen & Hamilton conducts assignments for passenger and freight railways spanning a broad range of functional areas and issues: vehicle engineering; operations and productivity improvement; strategic planning and reliability, maintainability and safety systems.

Projects
Include Netherlands high-speed rail, Croydon Tramlink, Attiko Metro, Channel Tunnel Rail Link, St Louis Metrolink, Bay Area Rapid Transit, Los Angeles Metro Rail, Hudson-Bergen Light Rail, San Francisco Municipal Railway, and State Rail Authority of New South Wales.

CANAC Railway Services Inc

3950 Hickmore Street, St Laurent, Québec H4T 1K2, Canada
Tel: (+1 514) 734 47 10   Fax: (+1 514) 734 48 64
Web: www.canac.com

Key personnel
President and Chief Executive Officer: *Allen Alexander*
Executive Vice-President, Chief Financial Officer, Finance and Administration: *Benson Lewis*
Senior Vice-President and General Manager – Rail Services: *Michel Robitaille*
Vice-President, Planning: *Graham Pengelley*
Manager, Training Solutions: *Kristian Raphaelsen*
Project Manager, International: *Nathalie Bourque*
Director, Finance and Administration: *Robert Conyers*

Background
A subsidiary of Savage Companies, CANAC was established in 1971 and has completed over 800 major projects in all areas of railway operations and engineering.

Capabilities
CANAC Railway Services Inc provides services to industrial rail users; freight, passenger and commuter railroads; and investor and government authorities.

Capabilities include planning and engineering using the latest technology, in-plant rail logistics where services range from yard design and optimisation studies to full contract switching and a rail technical training capability incorporating instructors/trainers and subject matter experts with a wide-ranging railroad operations course inventory.

Canarail Consultants Inc

1140 de Maisonneuve Boulevard West, Suite 1050, Montreal, Quebec H3A 1M8, Canada
Tel: (+1 514) 985 09 30   Fax: (+1 514) 985 09 29
e-mail: inbox@canarail.com
Web: www.canarail.com

Key personnel
President: *Jim D Spielman*
Executive Vice-President, Mechanical Engineering: *Harry Aghjayan*
Vice-President and Chief Engineer: *Donald R Gillstrom*
Vice-President, Business Development and Human Resources: *Elizabeth Tadgell*

Capabilities
Consulting services for the urban and railway transportation sectors. Providing expertise in civil and mechanical engineering, light rail transit systems, railway operations, signalling and telecommunications, financial, economic, marketing, training, institutional and environmental disciplines. Studies carried out by Canarail include feasibility studies, transportation planning, human resources, financial and economic services, and asset valuation. Training services include needs analysis, programme development, testing and certification of railway personnel and the delivery of technical training courses for the railway industry. Management services provide assistance to clients with the restructuring, commercialisation and the divestiture of government-owned railways to the private sector, including the preparation of enabling regulatory and legislative policies for private sector development.

Engineering services include conceptual and detailed design, environmental assessment, preparation of bid documents, procurement and tendering services, construction supervision and start-up assistance.

Projects
Algeria: Double tracking study.
Bangladesh: Flood rehabilitation project.
Bosnia-Herzegovina: Equipment and software procurement assistance for a management information system.
Cambodia: Restructuring of the Cambodian railway.
Canada: Railway feasibility study of iron ore project on Baffin Island. Study on catenary electrical power grid.
Croatia: Croatian Railways modernisation and restructuring project, double-tracking and fibre-optic study.
Guinea: Engineering, operational and technical assistance services.
Mauritania: Railway capacity study.
Saudi Arabia: Detailed design of a new 2,400 km rail line between Riyadh and the port of Daman. Construction supervision of the North South Railway project.
Uganda/Kenya: Transaction advisor to the Government of Uganda with regard to the privatisation of the Uganda Railways. Joint concessioning with Kenya Railways has been included in this process.
Uzbekistan: Assistance to Uzbekistan Railways with the procurement and technical aspects of locomotive re-powering and foundry workshops modernisation.

Capita Symonds Ltd

Railways (Engineering and Operations)
Capita Symonds House, Wood Street, East Grinstead RH19 1UU, UK
Tel: (+44 1342) 32 71 61
Fax: (+44 1342) 31 59 27
Web: www.capita.co.uk

Rail Division
24-30 Holborn, London EC1N 2LX
Tel: (+44 20) 78 70 93 00   Fax: (+44 20) 78 70 93 99

Key personnel
Director (Rail Engineering and Operations): *Drew Bradley*
Senior Associate Director (Projects): *John M Mayne*
Associate Director (Operations): *Steve Sharp*
Division Director (Rail): *David Young*

Capabilities
Multi-disciplinary consultants engaged in a comprehensive range of services covering rail engineering, management and policy, evaluation, design and commissioning of major infrastructure projects, cost and commercial management and train planning. Providing advice and technical support to rail operators, banks and governments.

Projects
Capita Symonds Ltd is providing permanent way design skills to the Thameslink project and has carried out a number of permanent

way projects throughout the UK. The company has provided advice to many developers who wish to build on or around the railway and obtained approvals from the rail authorities. The company continues to assist various train operating companies in developing the proposals in their passenger franchise bids; work has involved both operational aspects and infrastructure enhancements. The company has recently completed the project management of the construction of a new station on the West London Line. It has been commissioned by Irish Rail to carry out structural design work (bridges and culverts) for two rail re-openings: Glounthaune-Middleton, and Dunboyne (M3) Commuter Rail. It also continues to advise UK and international funders on a wide variety of rail projects including, during 2007/2008, Tel Aviv metro and Rheims Tramway. The company also acts as an advisor to the Department for Transport on freight facilities grants applications (for rail and waterways) and is engaged to carry out assessment of individual cases.

Capoco Design

Stone Cross, Chicksgrove, Salisbury SP3 6NA, UK
Tel: (+44 1722) 71 67 22
Fax: (+44 1722) 71 62 26
e-mail: alanp@capoco.co.uk
Web: www.capoco.co.uk

Key personnel
Design Director: *Alan Ponsford*

Capabilities
Design and analysis of buses, coaches and specialist trucks across five continents. Whole vehicle design covering exterior form, internal packaging and complete structural solution. The majority of these design processes are computer based. The layout work uses 2D and 3D CAD modelling using AutoCad, Microstation and Solid Edge software. The FEA work uses ANSYS and DYNA-3D. The styling modelling is based on 3D rendering in Rhino plus specific graphical output software to achieve a virtual design studio result. The powertrain optimisation is a combination of 3D CAD packaging with ADVISOR software for the VPS (Vehicle Performance Simulation) work. These studies cover both conventional mechanical drives and electric drives for hybrid and fuel cell projects.

Projects
Single- and double-deck bus chassis, bus body and integral bus. Many other bus and coach projects, notably in North America and Asia, have been completed. These have included diesel hybrid, fuel cell and alternative fuel city buses.

Developments
Recent developments have included the Bus Rapid Transit system (BRT) produced in lengths from 10.5 m to 24.5 m. This integral vehicle uses a structure of riveted aluminium with single tyre on all axles. The drive system is electric with a range of energy source options. These include diesel hybrid, fuel cell hybrid, overhead 'trolleybus' line and EV battery models. The design offers high passenger capacity at both low initial and low operating costs. In addition, further benefits include flexible operational control and rapid deployment using existing roadways.

Another recent development project is a transport system called 'mobilicity', which integrates a new automated vehicle with an

Capoco Designs US diesel transit bus   1066871

Capoco Designs US hydrogen fuel cell hybrid bus   1066872

intelligent operational control system. The vehicles are called PPT (Personalised Public Transport).

Certifer

Agence de Certification Ferroviaire
BP 45, 154 boulevard Harpignies, F-59300 Valenciennes, France
Tel: (+33 3) 27 28 35 00   Fax: (+33 3) 27 28 35 09
e-mail: contact@certifer.fr
Web: www.certifer.asso.fr

Background
Certifer was founded in 1997 by French National Railways (SNCF), the Paris Public Transport Authority (RATP), the French Railway Industries Federation (FIF) and the National Research Institute for Transport and Transport Safety (INRETS). In 1998, the Union of Public Transport (UTP) and the French Railways Infrastructure Authority (RFF) became members.

Capabilities
Certifer assesses the compliance of railway products and services with statutes and regulations, technical specifications and standards. It also carries out audits, inspections, expert evaluations and evaluations for authorisation. Its competences cover rolling stock, signalling and control systems and infrastructure.

CIE Consult

Heuston Station, Dublin 8, Ireland
Tel: (+353 1) 703 47 00
Fax: (+353 1) 886 05 13
e-mail: barry.collins@cieconsult.ie
Web: www.cieconsult.ie

Key personnel
Acting Chief Financial Officer, CIE: *Roddy Connolly*
General Manager: *Barry Collins*

Background
The Irish Government is currently the sole owner of CIÉ, the Government's representatives are the Minister for Transport and his Department.

Capabilities
CIE Consult draws on the resources and expertise of CIE Group of operating companies, Iarnród Éireann (the Irish state rail network), Bus Atha Cliath (the Dublin City bus operator) and Bus Éireann (operator of all other bus services) to provide transport-related consultancy service across the world.

Projects
Examples of recent contracts include:
Botswana: Supervising engineer for a new railway signalling system; strategic concessioning advisor.
Bulgaria: Railway organisational restructuring and management development of the railway infrastructure company.
Lithuania: Support to Lithuanian Railways for restructuring and privatisation.
Macedonia: Assistance with restructuring study of transport investment needs in Macedonia.
Romania: FIDIC engineer for supervision and co-ordination of works for interlocking systems in four main railway stations. Design of rehabilitation programme for Romanian Railways.
Tanzania: Privatisation and concessioning of Tanzania Railways Corporation.
Zambia: Development of new legislative framework, post concessioning and strengthening the Ministry of Transport and Communications.
Zimbabwe: Concessioning of Zimbabwe Railways.
Various: Support to the Phare PMU in Bulgaria and Slovakia; Central Asia Railways restructuring studies; Pakistan Railways corporatisation; rail privatisation study in Georgia; and Russian Railways MIS study.

For details of the latest updates to *Jane's Urban Transport Systems* online and to discover the additional information available exclusively to online subscribers please visit
juts.janes.com

Others:
Hungary: Study of investment needs of BKV, the Budapest urban transport operator, financed by the World Bank.
Kazakstan: Development of national transport strategy.
Kyrgyzstan: Study of urban passenger and urban roads for the three cities of Bishkek, Osh and Djalalabad for the World Bank.
Latvia: Public transport master plan study. EU Phare funded.
Mongolia: Urban transport components of the World Bank transport sector rehabilitation project. World Bank funded.
Poland: Gdansk Urban Transport Project financed by EBRD.
Romania: Bucharest urban transport study. EU phare funded.
Russian cities: Improving urban passenger transport in Russian cities, as a model for other former Soviet Union cities, with the World Bank.
Uzbekistan: World Bank-funded study of urban transport in five cities to identify World Bank investment opportunities.

Colin Buchanan

10 Eastbourne Terrace, London W2 6LG
Tel: (+44 20) 70 53 13 00   Fax: (+44 20) 70 53 13 01
e-mail: enquiries@buchanan.co.uk
Web: www.colinbuchanan.com

Other offices
Belfast, Birmingham, Bristol, Cardiff, Dublin, Edinburgh, Galway, Glasgow, Newbury and Manchester.

Key personnel
Chairman: *Malcolm Buchanan*
Director, Development: *Andreas Markides*
Director, Public Transport: *Hugh Chaplain*
Director, Traffic: *Kevan Weaver*
Economics Director: *Paul Buchanan*
Director, Transport Planning: *Atholl Noon*
Planning, Regeneration and Urban Design Director: *Hugh Roberts*
Transport Modelling Director: *Chris Pyatt*
Director: *Paul McTernan*
Director of Finance and Operations: *Alan Power*

Background
Colin Buchanan is a transport, planning, urban design and economics consultancy founded by Sir Colin Buchanan in 1964.

Capabilities
The services Colin Buchanan offers encompass all of those necessary to research, design and implement transport and planning measures for a wide range of clients. These include transport planning, economics, development planning, land use planning, demand management, urban design, sustainable travel, regeneration, public transport, market research and surveys, traffic engineering, consultation and participation, highway safety and parking.

COWI Consulting Engineers and Planners AS

Parallelvej 15, DK-2800 Lyngby, Denmark
Tel: (+45) 45 97 22 11   Fax: (+45) 45 97 22 12
e-mail: cowi@cowi.dk
Web: www.cowi.dk

Key personnel
Managing Director: *Klaus H Ostenfeld*
Head of Department: *Preben Juul Mikkelsen*
Communications Manager: *John Jørgensen*
Director, Rail, Metro and Tunnel: *Arne Steen Jacobsen*

Other offices
Also in Norway (Oslo), Germany (Berlin), Belgium (Brussels), Spain (Madrid), Lithuania (Vilnius), Poland (Warsaw), Russia (Moscow), USA (San Francisco), Canada (Vancouver), Tanzania (Dar es Salaam), Nigeria (Lagos), Kenya (Nairobi), Uganda (Kampala), Ghana (Accra), Burkina Faso (Tenkodogo), South Africa (Johannesburg), Bahrain (Manama), United Arab Emirates (Dubai), Oman (Qurum), Qatar (Doha), Saudi Arabia (Dammam), Philippines (Manila), Thailand (Bangkok), China (Beijing) and Vietnam (Hanoi).

Background
Founded in 1930, COWI is privately owned with the COWI Foundation as the majority shareholder.

Capabilities
COWI offers consulting services at all stages of multi-disciplinary large-scale railway projects from initial planning and engineering design to construction management and supervision and advice on operation and maintenance. COWI's services range from professional advice on a particular problem to total coverage of services required by public and private clients from idea to realisation of railway systems. Feasibility studies, development of tender solutions and contract documents, managing of tender procedures, contracting, authority approval management, contract administration, environmental management, risk management, system certification management and maintenance management, analysis for the maintenance and reinvestment of railway infrastructure and administration.
Recent contracts have included: the development of a maintenance management system for the Danish and Norwegian railway agencies; project management and consultant on civil works design for the 21 km driverless metro system, worth £600 million, in Copenhagen; consultant for the conceptual design and outline design of the 6.5 km Malmo City Railway tunnel linking Malmo Central Station to Copenhagen, worth £550 million; for EU PHARE railway upgrading projects in eastern Europe, and in Denmark, COWI was project manager for the S-train ring line running around the centre of Copenhagen and design of the Flintholm station, the largest in Denmark.

The Corradino Group

200 South Fifth Street, Suite 300 North, First Trust Centre, Louisville, Kentucky 40202, US
Tel: (+1 502) 587 72 21   Fax: (+1 502) 587 26 36
e-mail: louisville@corradino.com
Web: www.corradino.com

Key personnel
Chief Executive Officer: *Joe C Corradino*
President: *Burt J Deutsch*
Chief Operating Officer: *Fred P Pool*
Vice Presidents: *Joe M Corradino, Stephen B Sullivan, Ed Perez de Morales*

Head Office
First Trust Centre – 300N, 200 South Fifth Street, Louisville, Kentucky 40202, US
Tel: (+1 502) 587 72 21   Fax: (+1 502) 587 26 36
e-mail: louisville@corradino.com
Web: www.corradino.com

Projects
Construction Program Manager of I-95 Reconstruction in Palm Beach County, Florida; HOT Lanes Study of I-95 in Dade and Broward Counties, Florida; Multimodal Plan for Ann Arbor, Michigan.

Corus Rail Technologies

Headquarters
Swinden Technology Centre, Moorgate, Rotherham, South Yorkshire S60 3AR, UK
Tel: (+44 1709) 82 52 64   Fax: (+44 1709) 82 53 46
e-mail: railtechnologies@corusgroup.com
Web: www.corusrailtechnologies.com

Key personnel
Principal Consultant: *Gareth Evans*
Senior Consultant Light Rail: *Paul Norbury*
Commercial Manager: *David Coleman*

Capabilities
Corus offers expertise and experience in fields such as asset management, condition monitoring, track inspection, failure analysis, rail welding, laboratory testing and computer modelling. Its consultants have in-depth knowledge of metallurgy and track product design, manufacture and performance and work in collaboration with network operators and maintenance and renewal contractors on a range of projects.
Corus also manufactures and supplies rail products from facilities in the UK and France.

CPCS Transcom

72 Chamberlain Avenue, Ottawa, Ontario K1S 1V9, Canada
Tel: (+1 613) 237 25 00   Fax: (+1 613) 237 44 94
e-mail: ottawa@cpcstrans.com
Web: www.cpcstrans.com

Branch office
4 Lansing Square, Ontario M2J 1T1, Canada
Tel: (+1 416) 499 26 90   Fax: (+1 416) 499 29 29

Key personnel
Chairman: *Douglas Young*
President: *Peter R Kieran*

Capabilities
CPCS Transcom is a privately owned international consulting firm specialising in transportation, telecommunications and commercialisation/ privatisation. It provides technical, advisory and training services to governments and the private sector in the planning, engineering, operating, marketing and maintenance of transportation and telecommunications systems. Since its establishment in 1969, CPCS Transcom has successfully completed over 700 projects in over 60 countries around the world.

CRA International, Inc

John Hancock Tower, 200 Clarendon Street, Boston, Massachusetts 02116-5092, US
Tel: (+1 617) 425 30 00   Fax: (+1 617) 425 31 32

Key personnel
President: *James C Burrows*
Director of Transportation Projects: *Steven C Grundman*
Vice-Presidents: *Steven C Grundman, Daniel Brand, Michael Kemp, George Eads, Nils Von Hinton Reed*
Other Senior Staff: *Jon Bottom, Harry Foster, Mark Kiefer, Masroor Hasan, David Cuneo*

Background
Previously called Charles River Associates, CRA International, Inc was established in 1965 and has a staff of 1,000.

Offices
London, UK; Sydney, Canberra and Melbourne, Australia; Brussels, Belgium; Bahrain; Hong Kong; Wellington and Auckland, New Zealand; Toronto, Canada; and in the US: Atlanta, Silicon Valley; Boston, New York, Washington, Philadelphia, Chicago, Dallas, Houston, College Station, Salt Lake City, Oakland, Palo Alto, Pasadena.

Capabilities
All aspects of transport planning and evaluation, including ridership and revenue forecasting, capital investment planning and budgeting, major investment studies, financing and pricing,

management and operations planning, mergers and acquisitions, and market research. Specialist work is undertaken in travel demand and revenue forecasting for new systems, project and programme evaluation including ITS, travel surveys, transport economics and urban planning.

Projects

Include planning for the initial and subsequent capital programmes for upgrading the New York City metro, bus and commuter rail systems, and the Chicago RTA's long-range capital plan. Has also undertaken high-speed ground transport studies in several intercity corridors, both North American and overseas, and various highway toll studies.

CRA's policy analysis work has included developing analytical tools and studying the impact of federal policies on the transit industry. Comprehensive fare policy studies have been undertaken for several transit agencies.

For the US, DoT has provided information for formulation of federal policy concerning strategy studies, major capital investments, privatisation, and productivity improvements. Benefits and costs attributed to new starts, extensions, modernisation projects and vehicle purchase programmes have been examined.

Work has also been undertaken to evaluate existing and proposed ground access modes to a number of airports. Has also examined air quality regulations and impact of alternative fuels.

Creactive Design

22 New Street, Leamington Spa CV31 1HP, UK
Tel: (+44 1926) 83 31 13   Fax: (+44 1926) 83 27 88
e-mail: info@creactive-design.co.uk
Web: www.creactive-design.co.uk

Key personnel
Directors: *Neil Bates, Tony Hume*

Capabilities
Specialising in design for rail vehicles and transport infrastructure, Creactive Design provides resources through a team of designers, engineers and ergonomists. The company offers interior and exterior design for new and refurbished rolling stock, stations and associated furniture, safety design, mock-ups, prototypes and feasibility studies.

Projects
Recent projects include: design and supply of cab cooling systems for Class 319 and two London Undergruond lines; emergency feasibility study and station equipment rooms for LUL; interio design for new intercity trains for Mitsui-Rotem and Ilarnród Éireann; refurbishments for Chiltern Railways and Wrexham Shropshire and Marlybone Railway; branding, vehicle stop and landscape design for Nottingham Express Transit.

Creadesign Oy

Köydenpunojankatu 2 a D 5 krs, FIN00180, Helsinki, Finland
Tel: (+358 9) 25 12 10 18   Fax: (+358 9) 60 58 32
e-mail: info@creadesign.fi
Web: www.creadesign.fi

Key personnel
Managing Director: *Hannu Kähönen*

Capabilities
Industrial design, including rolling stock styling and interiors, from strategic concept design to product launch; corporate image; marketing communication.

Projects
Projects include interior and exterior design of the Variotram built by Bombardier Transportation

and Talgo for HKL, Helsinki. Design work has also been undertaken for VR Ltd (Finnish Railways) and Talgo.

DCA Design International Ltd

19 Church Street, Warwick CV34 4AB, UK
Tel: (+44 1926) 49 94 61
Fax: (+44 1926) 40 11 34
e-mail: transport@dca-design.com
Web: www.dca-design.com/transport

Key personnel
Chairman and Managing Director: *Rob Woolston*
Directors: *Rob Bassil, John Daly, Nick Mival*

Capabilities
DCA's has been creating transportation design solutions for more than 30 years. Its team of over 70 researchers, designers, mechanical engineers, electronics engineers and modelmakers provides a unique integrated design and prototypying service. The company is ISO 9001/2000 approved.

Projects
These have included designs for new rolling stock for London Underground Ltd's Central Line; visual and driver ergonomic aspects of the British Rail Class 90 and 91 locomotives; design of the Tangara double-deck commuter trainset for the State Rail Authority of New South Wales, Australia; Channel Tunnel shuttle wagons and locomotives for European and Canadian members of the ESCW and ESCL consortia; refurbishment of London Underground Ltd's Metropolitan Line trainsets; design of the British Rail Class 341 emu for the proposed CrossRail line; the Class 365 'Networker Express' trainset; Class 371 Thameslink 2000 trains; train and corporate design work for the new cross-border train services between Belfast and Dublin; new and refurbishment concepts for MTRC in Hong Kong; M6 double-deck cars for SNCB, Belgium; and mockups and detailed design of Virgin CrossCountry demus; Transport for London (TfL) PPP ITT support; and Eurostar refurbishment seating design and interior detail design and specification. Finite element analysis on freight vehicle bogie; design and prototyping of dashboard assembly for Cushman electric vehicle; design and ergonomics study of an electric four-wheel drive tourist vehicle set for Harrison Caves, Barbados; modular seating design and supplier liason for the LUL D stock; emergency passenger egress system design for two separate sets of UK-based underground rolling stock; and climatic control system integration into underground rolling stock; new livery design for Translink.

DB International GmbH

Bornitzstrasse 73-75, D-10365 Berlin, Germany
Tel: (+49 30) 29 76 99 01   Fax: (+49 30) 29 76 99 09
Web: www.db-international.de

Business Department
International
Oskar-Sommer-Strasse 15, D-60596 Frankfurt am Main
Tel: (+49 69) 631 90   Fax: (+49 69) 631 93 56
e-mail: info@db-international.de
Web: www.db-international.de

Key personnel
Supervisory Board Chairman: *Dr Otto Wiesheu*
Board of Managing Directors
  Chair: Martin Bay, Andreas Wegerif
  Head of Marketing and Business: *Martin Hagen*

Background
Formerly DE-Consult Deutsche Eisenbahn-Consulting GmbH, DB International is a wholly owned subsidiary of DB Mobility Logistics AG (DB ML AG), itself the wholly owned mobility and

logistics services provision arm of Germany's national railway company, DB AG. DB ML AG was created in June 2008 ahead of a partial privatisation by the German government that will see 24.9 per cent of its shares offered for public subscription.

Capabilities
Range of advisory services including planning and management of complex infrastructure projects involving long-distance and urban passenger and freight transport, rolling stock and workshops, management consultancy, operations planning, transport economics, finance and marketing, manpower development and training.

Projects
DB International has been involved in over 1,000 projects internationally. High-speed projects in Germany, Korea, Taiwan, Spain and Italy; suburban transport systems projects in Thailand, Greece, Netherlands and Germany; rehabilitation projects in Eastern Europe, Africa, America and the Far East; freight transport projects in Germany, South America, Eastern Europe and Africa; training projects in South America, Eastern Europe, Africa and Asia.

Delcan Corporation

625 Cochrane Drive, Suite 500 Markham, Ontario L3R 9R9, Canada
Tel: (+1 905) 943 05 00   Fax: (+1 905) 943 04 00
e-mail: info@delcan.com
Web: www.delcan.com

Key personnel
Chief Executive Officer: *Jim Kerr*
President, Systems Business, National Operations: *Lester Yoshida*
President, Infrastructure Business, Canada & International Operations: *Charles Orolowitz*
President, Systems Business, Canada & International Operations: *Joe Lam*
President, Infrastructure Business, National Operations: *Brian Stearman*

Overseas offices
Barbados, Hong Kong, US (Atlanta, Chicago, Austin, TX, Coral Springs, Fl, Denver, Colorado, La Mirada, CA, Washington, DC), UK and Venezuela.

Background
The DHV Group holds a 40 per cent interest in Delcan Corporation.

Capabilities
A full range of consulting services ranging from studies to the overall design and construction supervision of large railway infrastructures. Project management, feasibility studies, engineering, compliance auditing, implementation, operations and maintenance for urban transit, commuter, intercity passenger and freight railways.

Delon Hampton & Associates

900 Seventh Street, NW – Suite 800 Washington, DC 20001, US
Tel: (+1 202) 898 19 99
Fax: (+1 202) 371 20 73
e-mail: dhadc@delonhampton.com
Web: www.delonhampton.com

Key personnel
Chairman: *Delon Hampton*
President and Chief Executive Officer: *Jeffrey L Humber*
Vice-President and Chief Financial Officer: *Tracy S Harris*

Capabilities
Design, planning and inspection of rapid transit and light rail systems and other transportation structures; programme and construction

management services; planning, design and construction support services and construction inspection services.

Design and Projects Int Ltd

No 2 Manor Farm, Flexford Road, North Baddesly SO52 9DF, UK
Tel: (+44 23) 80 27 79 10   Fax: (+44 23) 80 27 79 20
e-mail: dpil@msn.com
Web: www.railwaymaintenance.com

Key personnel
Managing Director: *Colin Brooks*
Operations Director: *Stuart Blyth*

Capabilities
Design, supply and setting to work of equipment needed to overhaul, maintain, repair and clean rail vehicles and their components for metro, main line and suburban railway systems. This includes all depot/workshop, track and overhead catenary system maintenance equipment.

While the company normally executes contracts on a turnkey basis, projects can also be undertaken for equipment and supplier studies, and the design of one-off specialist equipment. The company can also provide other engineering and management support in relation to railway maintenance facilities, purpose equipment, design and supply of diagnostic test equipment for rail vehicles; supply of maintenance equipment for track work, signalling and all fixed systems.

Projects
In January 2007, Design and Projects Int Ltd were responsible for the design of the facilities and the supply of the maintenance equipment for Mitsubishi Heavy Industrie for the Dubai Metro Red Line. D&P are continuing with the design of the two depots for the Red Line in Dubai.

Design Triangle

The Maltings, Burwell, Cambridge CB5 0HB, UK
Tel: (+44 1638) 74 30 70   Fax: (+44 1638) 74 34 93
e-mail: mail@designtriangle.co.uk
Web: www.designtriangle.com

Key personnel
Partners: *Siep Wijsenbeek, Andrew Crawshaw, Andy Clark*

Capabilities
Design Triangle specialises in the design of rail vehicles: interiors, exteriors, cabs and components. An integrated team of industrial designers and engineers provides innovative concepts and develops them through to manufacturing drawings and data.

Services include: research to improve understanding of customer needs; innovative concepts for competitive new products; 3-D CAD visualisation and animation, allowing effective communication of ideas; engineering development through design-for-manufacture, analysis and the refinement of forms; prototypes, allowing the testing and approval of designs prior

CAD design for Heathrow Express by Design Triangle   0016444

to manufacture; and consultancy. Clients include service operators, major vehicle manufacturers and component manufacturers.

Projects
Exterior and interior design of the Heathrow Express train; exterior and interior design of 67 new carriages for Irish Rail Intercity for CAF as part of an ongoing collaboration; tender designs for Melbourne Hillside for ALSTOM; Spoornet 9E loco cab interior refurbishment for ALSTOM; consultants to STIB, Brussels for the Tramway 2000; exterior design and cab design of the Hong Kong Airport Express train for the MTR Corporation, including detrainment device; development of exterior styling for the TKE train, also for the MTR Corporation; consultancy for London Underground planning standards; capacity and passenger flow studies for Docklands Light Railway, UK; modular seating prototypes for KAB Seating; design and engineering for BAE Systems and Kawasaki for Maryland double-deck cars; interior and exterior design of RET Rotterdam metro; design of new rolling stock for Metro de Madrid and many light rail vehicles.

DHV BV

Environment and Transport
PO Box 1132, NL-3800 BC Amersfoort, Netherlands
T +31 33 468 28 37   F +31 33 468 30 30
E rail@dhv.com
Tel: (+31 33) 468 37 00   Fax: (+31 33) 468 30 30
e-mail: rail@dhv.nl
Web: www.dhv.com

Key personnel
President: *Bertrand van Ee*
Vice-President: *Piet W Besselink*
Communications Manager: *Maurice Voestermans*

Background
Founded in 1917, DHV is an international consultancy and engineering group that provides services and sustainable solutions.

Over 3,700 DHV professionals develop innovative concepts in the fields of consultancy and engineering.

Capabilities
Management consultancy, advice, design and engineering, project management, contract management and operational management.

Projects
As a partner in the Dutch HSL-South Project Organisation, DHV developed noise barriers, which in addition to limiting the noise nuisance for the surrounding area, can also be used for the sustainable generation of electricity. The company has also been closely involved in the planning and design of the five tunnels required for the high-speed link.

DHV is also conducting research into techniques of laying track beds on the soft terrain found in delta areas.

Other recent projects include transport and infrastructure in China and South Africa.

Integrated safety case for Dutch HSL-South: passenger services on the HSL-Zuid high-speed rail link.

Traffic management and information systems for British Colombia. The insurance company ICBC has requsted DHV's Canadian partner, Delcan, to identify ways in which Intelligent Transport Systems (ITS) can help resolve congestion and improve road safety.

Doxiadis Associates SA

13 Aegidon & Seneka str, GR-145 64 Nea Kifissia, Athens, Greece
Tel: (+30 210) 624 63 00   Fax: (+30 210) 624 63 99
e-mail: doxiadis@doxiadis.com
Web: www.doxiadis.com

Key personnel
Managing Director: *Elias Xanthakos*
Vice-Chairman, Business Development: *Anastasios C Antonopoulos*

Other offices
Doxiadis Associates SA
PO Box 1574, Riyadh, 11441 Riyadh, Saudia Arabia
Tel: (+966 1) 476 28 00
e-mail: doxiadis@zajil.net

Background
Doxiadis Associates SA was established in 1951 by the architect, Constantinos A Doxiadis. The majority shareholding was acquired by Metrotech in 1999 through an increase of the company's capital.

Capabilities
Transport planning and engineering design, traffic management, analysis and design, urban planning, project management, highway engineering, construction supervision and maintenance. Also participates in study teams for preparation of comprehensive development, regional and urban plans.

Since it was established, the company has been awarded major development projects in over 60 countries worldwide by clients that include governments, private developers and international organisations.

Earth Tech Inc

Corporate headquarters
300 Oceangate, Suite 700, Long Beach, California 90802, US
Tel: (+1 562) 951 20 00   Fax: (+1 562) 951 21 00
e-mail: transportation@earthtech.com
Web: www.earthtech.com

Key personnel
President: *Alan P Krusi Edward C Regan, Charles F Van Cook, Ronald H Axelrod, Brian J O'Connor*
Principals: *Edward C Regan, Charles F Van Cook, Ronald H Axelrod, Brian J O'Connor*

Background
Earth Tech is a Tyco International Ltd company.

Capabilities
Architecural, engineering, construction and operations services.

Contracts
In May 2007 The Florida Department of Transportation (FDOT) awarded Earth Tech with a 15-month contract to plan, design, and prepare construction documents for the Central Station at the Miami Intermodal Centre (MIC) which will consolidate Tri-Rail and Amtrak passenger services under one location. The design will also accommodate a potential Florida high-speed rail terminus.

Egis Rail

Headquarters
25 Cours Emile Zola, F-69625 Villeurbanne, France
Tel: (+33 4) 72 69 60 00   Fax: (+33 4) 78 89 68 57
e-mail: contact.egis-rail@egis.fr
Web: www.egis-rail.eu

Key personnel
Chairman: *Nicolas Jachiet*
Chief Executive Officer: *Hervé Chaine*
Managing Director: *Hubert Magnon-Pujo*
Deputy Managing Director: *Olivier Bouvart*
Technical Director: *Pascal Forte*
Business Development Director: *André Marchand*

Background
Egis Rail was formed as a result of a merger between Semaly and Scetauroute's rail transport

department. The new entity will combine within a single company, all Semaly's divisions and Scetauroute's rail activity. Egis Rail is a subsidiary of the Caisse des Dépôts, its second shareholder is the US engineering company BECHTEL.

Capabilities

From conceptual design to start up of services, Egis Rail, as an urban and railway transport engineering company, undertakes financial and economic studies, feasibility studies, preliminary and detailed design, construction management, testing and commissioning for public transport and rail systems.

Projects

Recent projects include:

France: Maréchaux East line, Paris new LRT tramway project, a second section of tramway line that will circle Paris; for Paris Airport (ADP) Egis Rail, in conjunction with Setec, is in charge of assisting the prime contractor in the supervision of the construction of an automatic passenger transport system for Roissy-Charles de Gaulle airport. The people mover project network comprises a main line (Line 1) of 3.3 km connecting airport terminals 1 and 2 (five stations, line sections on overpasses, in tunnels and overhead, a workshop garage, the OCC), also the Line 1 extensions (a short line named LISA links terminal 2,3 and 2E satellite terminals). General project management (on equipment aspects) of the Rhine/Rhone high-speed line; the project consists in building a high-speed train line between Dijon and Mulhouse. Toulouse's tramway line E (project management); the extension of Montpellier's LRT network (tramway Line 2 and 3); Marseille's tramway lines (project management); Marseille's metro extensions (tunnelling etc); Lyon: assistance to the owner in the design and construction of Leslys. Lyon's commuter tram connecting the city centre and Lyon Saint-Exupery Airport.

Ireland: Studies and technical assistance for Dublin's first light rail line in the final phase of the works, reception and tests.

Le Reunion Island: The tram-train project will involve the crossing of nine towns, both through the town centres and the outskirts, as well as the boring of a 10 km long tunnel.

Morocco: Rabat's light rail project's management and Casablanca mass transit network projects (assistance to the city of Casablanca).

Poland: Advisory and technical assistance for Krakow 'Fast Tram'.

Saudi Arabia: Egis Rail and its partner Dar Al-Handasah will handle the feasibility study and preliminary design of the Light Rail Transit project in Riyadh. Mecca: preliminary studies of a 12 km metro line (in partnership with Systra). Egis Rail will be responsible for the equipment studies.

US: In the framework of the 2nd Avenue project and Staten Island Metro project, Egis Rail is handling the implementation of the new signalling and remote transmissions metro systems.

ENOTRAC AG

Seefeldstrasse 8, CH-3600 Thun, Switzerland
Tel: (+41 33) 346 66 11
Fax: (+41 33) 346 66 12
e-mail: info@enotrac.com
Web: www.enotrac.com

Key personnel

Executive: *Heinz Voegeli*

Subsidiaries

ENOTRAC UK Ltd
Times House, Throwley Way, Sutton SM1 4AF, UK
Tel: (+44 20) 87 70 35 01   Fax: (+44 20) 87 70 35 02
e-mail: ziad.mouneimne@enotrac.com
Executive: Dr Ziad S Mouneimne

Capabilities

ENOTRAC provides consulting services covering systems engineering, feasibility studies, planning,

technology evaluation, tender preparation and evaluation, asset replacement strategy, equipment specification, procurement support, software development, field tests, quality assurance, reliability and safety assessments, signalling compatibility studies and operational procedures.

For rolling stock, the services encompass performance evaluation, energy consumption, comparative assessment of traction equipment, rehabilitation and maintenance management.

For fleet management, ENOTRAC provides VIPSCARSIS, the software system for configuration, warranty, maintenance and modification management including LCC- and RAM-calculations, tailor-made for rolling stock and fixed installations. The services include process studies and consulting, workshops, training and full user support.

Power supply services include rating of equipment (substations, catenary), optimum substation spacing, reinforcement requirements, short-circuit calculations and protection, earthing, step and touch voltages, and energy, active and reactive power requirements and magnetic field computation. Optimised design is achieved by a powerful software suite developed in-house for multitrain simulation of complex AC and DC-supplied networks.

Equival

LAC A318,54, Quai de la Rapée, F-75012 Paris, France
Tel: (+33 1) 58 78 24 39   Fax: (+33 1) 58 78 22 37
e-mail: equival87@transdev.eu
Web: www.equival.fr,
    www.ratp-developpement.com

Key personnel

Chairman and Chief Executive Officer, RATP Développement: *Jean-Marc Janaillac*

Background

Equival was created in 2004 by RATP Développement SA (75 per cent owned by RAT and 25 per cent cent by Transdev) and Transdev. Both companies have an equal shareholding.

Capabilities

Consultants in the field of intermodal passenger mobility, covering: the management of intermodal fare collection; the management of transport interchanges, including information provision, ticket retailing, management of passenger flows, security and maintenance; and the development and management of services to promote intermodality, such as multimodal Internet sites, telephone enquiry services, on-demand public transport, cycle hire and passenger information centres.

Projects

Assisted in the creation of multimodal fare collection systems in several regions of France. It also manages and co-ordinates operations at Rennes bus station.

ETC Transport Consultants GmbH

Am Karlsbad 11, D-10785 Berlin, Germany
PO Box 303150, D-10729 Berlin, Germany
Tel: (+49 30) 25 46 50   Fax: (+49 30) 25 46 51 01
e-mail: info@etc-consult.de
Web: www.etc-consult.de

Key personnel

Managing Directors: *Dipl Ing Gernot Steinbrink, Dr Ing Christian Gleue*
Key Consultants: *Dipl Ing Hinrich Brümmer, Dipl Oec Klaus Kupec, Dipl Ing Francois Reisenberger*

Background

Established in 1967 as a division of Berliner Verkehrsbetreibe (BVG) (Berlin Transport

Corporation) and founded as an independent company jointly by BVG and BC Berlin Consult in 1974, in 1995 the firm was renamed as ETC Transport Consultants GmbH, having merged with its subsidiary Ingenieurgesellschaft Verkehrs Berlin GmbH (IVB). ETC's shareholder is COWI A/ S, Denmark.

Capabilities

Feasibility studies and network planning; traffic and transport engineering; preliminary and detailed design (structural, mechanical, signalling, electrical and safety); management and financial studies, operational planning, training and start-up operation, project management of turnkey projects, DP management, and Management Information Systems (MIS).

Projects

Austria: Consulting services to Österreichische Bundesbahn (ÖBB, Austrian Federal Railways) regarding assessment of the existing and introduction of a new system of technical services in the field of maintenance of rolling stock.

Chile: Study regarding the development and optimisation of regional rail passenger transport in the Santiago de Chile region, pre-feasibility study on the introduction of an urban rail system, using an existing railway corridor in Santiago de Chile.

China: For Shanghai Metro Corporation (SMC), benchmarking study on large metro systems; organisation of a ten-year train overhaul for Shanghai Metro and supervision of execution as a training measure for metro workshop personnel; planning support to Quingdao municipality regarding the introduction of an MTR system; assistance to the Chinese government regarding the introduction of a technical standards system for metro and light rapid transport networks in Chinese cities; setting up a training centre for metro operational personnel including a simulator and training programmes; advisory services for the introduction of Metro and LRT systems; preliminary and detailed design of workshops in Shanghai, metro network studies in Chengdu, Quingdao and Shanghai.

Germany: Studies on and introduction of systems for the apportionment of revenue between the participating transport companies belonging to large integrated transport systems; traffic forecasts and network planning; LRT and regional rail network studies, development of MIS and marketing concepts for the integrated transport systems in the Rhein-Main and Halle/Leipzig regions; studies on the development of tourism including outline marketing strategies; studies regarding simulators for staff training; studies on freight transport and logistics; for example, logistics for the Elbe bridge construction site near the city of Wittenberg; infrastructure and engineering projects for DB AG and S-Bahn Berlin; preliminary and final design for the upgrading of railway signalling systems in passenger transport services (PZB90, about 4,300 signals in about 1,100 stations) and in goods transport services (G_PZB90: about 1,900 signals in approximately 300 stations); project management for planning and construction works for the rehabilitation and upgrading of the Berlin-Rostock railway section (approximately 200 km); preliminary and detailed design of metro-, LRT- and urban workshops in Berlin.

Greece: Operational assistance for the establishment of the Athens tram system; training programmes for operational personnel of Athens metro, preliminary and detailed design of workshops for Athens metro.

Lithuania: Drafting of a strategic national rail transport development plan 2005-2015; feasibility study on high-speed non-stop trains.

Mexico: Pre-feasibility studies on the introduction of urban rail-based passenger transport in Monterrey (using existing railway infrastructure) and Cancún (servicing tourist areas).

Mongolia: Feasibility study, project management and supervision of construction for the Zamyn Uud transhipment facility for oil products at the Mongolian-Chinese border.

Switzerland: Development and improvement of the infrastructure access charge system and a train path sales strategy for Swiss Federal Railways (SBB) and some connecting private railways.

Turkey/Germany: Training of management personnel at Izmir metro.

Vietnam: Traffic forecast, financial and economic evaluation for rolling stock modernisation.

EurailTest

GIE EurailTest
Head office
1, Boulevard Saint-Martin, 75003, Paris, France
Tel: (+33 1) 44 61 93 20   Fax: (+33 1) 44 61 93 21
e-mail: eurailtest@eurailtest.com
Web: www.eurailtest.com

Key personnel

Director: *Olivier Brun*
Deputy Director: *Pascal Corcelle*
Personal Assistant: *Joëlle de Courrèges*
Consulting Engineers:
Rolling Stock: Catherine Dine, Vincent Dziepak
Rolling Stock Components: *Frédéric Harrang*
Infrastructure and Environment: *Cyril Charbonnet*
Urban Systems Transport: *Jean Baranger*

Capabilities

Eurailtest provides a fully qualified comprehensive technical testing service for: rolling stock (characterisation of interaction wheel/track, pantograph/catenary and traction or brake performance); infrastructure (control/command systems (classical and ERTMS) and associated software), signalling equipment, track (electrical parameters and geometry); railway environment (acoustic, electromagnetic fields (EMF) and compatibility (EMC) with trackside installations).

A wide variety of services have been provided in Europe, both conventional rail and high-speed railways, freight and urban transport systems, from basic assessment to complete qualification testing for a global rail system.

Eurailtest is able to provide testing services for every stage of the life cycle of a product or complete system.

Projects

Major projects: all wagons: tank, containers, cars or trucks, combined rail and road transport. All locomotives: electric or diesel locomotives such as FRET SNCF, BR185 Railion, MaK 1000 by Vossloh Locomotives; emus or dmus: AGC (F), TER 2Nng (F), Silicio (P), Super Voyager (UK), automotive high speed: ICE3; TGV: AVE (Madrid Seville), KTX (Korea), TGV Duplex, TGB POS, ETR500. Urban transport systems: MF77, MF2000, Val de Rennes, M° Santiago and tramway including Bordeaux, Orléans, Caen, Nantes and Marseille. Tram-train: testing before commissioning (HSL in France, Eurotunnel, CTRL, Paris-Brussels, HSL in Korea). Acoustic and EMC for all types of rolling stock and infrastructures.

FaberMaunsell

Marlborough House, Upper Marlborough Road, St Albans, AL1 3UT, UK
Tel: (+44 20) 87 84 57 84   Fax: (+44 20) 87 84 57 00
Web: www.fabermaunsell.com

Key personnel

Chief Executive (International): *Ken Dalton*

Background

FaberMaunsell is part of AECOM Technology Corporation and is the result of the merger of Oscar Faber, Maunsell Europe and Metcaf & Eddy UK.

The company is an international consultancy employing over 2,500 people through a network of over 30 office locations across the UK and Europe.

UK offices

Aberdeen, Altrincham, Beckenham, Belfast, Birkenhead, Birmingham, Bradford, Bristol, Cardiff, Coventry, Darlington, Durham, Edinburgh, Exeter, Glasgow, Leeds, Leicester, Liverpool, London, Newcastle-upon-Tyne, Norwich, Redhill, St Albans, St Mellion, Warrington, Witham and York.

International offices

Athens, Brussels, Bucharest, Copenhagen, De Bilt, Dublin, Warsaw.

Capabilities

FaberMaunsell provides specialist advice, amongst other areas related to airport projects, for transportation access through rail infrastructure, rapid transit/light rail facilities and has undertaken a wide range of professional services in connection with airports and their surrounding infrastructure. The company has planned, appraised and designed surface access transport systems supporting major airports. Planning and design has included new roads, light rail, metro and bus systems. The company has extensive experience in the UK and also worldwide experience through its parent company, AECOM.

FaberMaunsell's experience in urban transportation systems ranges from: light rail systems; new concepts such as Bus Rapid Transit; strategic traffic management including red routes; groundbreaking policy and implementation including congestion charging; advanced UTMC; development of transport strategy whether encompassing all modes, a single mode or a specific management regime, such as parking.

FaberMaunsell is currently enhancing its traditional capabilities with new services covering issues such as Homeland Security which is increasingly important in the context of strategic transport networks and their vulnerability to attack. This work is also being progressed in close co-operation with its parent company, AECOM.

Giro Inc

75, rue de Port-Royal est, bureau 500, Montréal, Québec Canada H3L 3T1
Tel: (+1 514) 383 04 04   Fax: (+1 514) 383 49 71
e-mail: info@giro.ca
Web: www.giro.ca

Key personnel

President: *Paul Hamelin*
Vice-President, Marketing: *Marc Dupont*
Vice-President, Business Development: *Pierre Trudeau*

Capabilities

Software for transport authorities, including vehicle and crew scheduling, passenger information and automated scheduling for demand-responsive transport.

HaCon Ingenieurgesellschaft mbH

Lister Strasse 15, D-30163 Hannover, Germany
Tel: (+49 511) 33 69 90   Fax: (+49 511) 336 99 99
e-mail: info@hacon.de
Web: www.hacon.de

Key personnel

Managing Directors: *Michael Frankenberg, Marian Gaidzik, Werner Sommerfeld, Werner Kretschmer, Volker Sustrate, Peter Talke*

Capabilities:

HAFAS program system: timetable information on local intercity and air traffic routes and connections; UX-SIMU program system;

interactive timetable planning and simulation; RASIM program system; simulation of marshalling operations and Radis program system; online information and scheduling management system.

The Harbor Consultancy International (THCI)

165 Beal Street, Hingham, Massachusetts 02043, US
Tel: (+1 781) 749 00 78
Fax: (+1 781) 749 00 78
e-mail: ferryboat@compuserve.com

Key personnel

Principal: *Martha A R Bewick*

Background

The Harbor Consultancy International was established in 1987 and provides a wide range of ferry transit system consultancy to both government and private clients worldwide.

Capabilities

Specialises in national ferry policy; feasibility studies for new routes and services; ferry system plans, design issues and performance criteria and urban ferry systems.

Hatch Mott MacDonald Inc

Head office
27 Bleeker Street, Millburn, New Jersey 07041, US
Tel: (+1 973) 379 34 00
Fax: (+1 973) 376 10 72
e-mail: railtransit@hatchmott.com; corporate@hatchmott.com
Web: www.hatchmott.com

Key personnel

President and Chief Executive Officer: *Peter Wickens*

Capabilities

Engineering consulting services, project and construction management and planning and architectural services for rail and transit systems. Services include: planning, route selection and environmental assessment; civil engineering, including alignment, trackwork, structures, bridges and elevated guideways; tunnels in soft ground or rock, including planning, architecture and safety; building services; systems engineering including signalling, telecommunications, traction power and distribution, tunnel ventilation; programme and project management; and construction management.

Projects

Recent projects include: programme management services for Toronto Transit Commission's Rapid Transit Expansion Programme; design, project management and construction management for CN North America's St Clair River Tunnel between Sarnia, Canada and Port Huron, US; construction management services for the construction of the Denver LRT system; application engineering services for the installation of an enhanced speed enforcement system at priority locations systemwide for New York City Transit Authority; detailed design of Ocean Parkway interlocking as part of the Brighton Beach Line resignalling programme for New York City Transit Authority; construction management services for the traction power system for the Montréal-Deux Montagnes route modernisation; and consulting and oversight services to Santa Clara County Transportation Agency on the design of trackwork, signals and telecommunications for the 12 mile Tasman Corridor LRT extension.

Hill International Inc

1 Levitt Parkway, Willingboro, New Jersey 08046 US
Tel: (+1 609) 871 58 00   Fax: (+1 609) 871 12 61
Web: www.hillintl.com

Key personnel
Chairman: *Irvin E Richter*
President and Chief Executive Officer: *David L Richter*
Senior Vice-President and Chief Financial Officer: *John Fanelli III*
Vice-President of Marketing and Corporate Communications: *John P Paolin*

Capabilities
Engineering consultancy; project and construction management; project management supervision; construction claims analysis; expert witness testimony; claims prevention and dispute resolution.

Projects
Projects include: MTA Capital Improvement Program, New York, NY, US for New York Metropolitan Transportation Authority; World Trade Center Transportation Hub, New York, NY, US for Port Authority of New York & New Jersey; Los Angeles Metro Rail, Los Angeles, US for Federal Transit Administration; Attiko Metro, Athens, Greece for Coopers & Lybrand; Twin Cities Transitway-Hiawatha Corridor Light Rail Project, Minneapolis/St. Paul, MN, US for Federal Transit Administration; St Pancras Station, Location, UK for Manhattan Loft Corporation.

Hodgson and Hodgson Group Ltd

Crown Business Park, Old Dalby, Melton Mowbray LE14 3NQ, UK
Tel: (+44 1664) 82 18 10
e-mail: info@hodgsongroup.co.uk
Web: www.acoustic.co.uk

Key personnel
Chairman: *G Balshaw-Jones*
Managing Director: *J Roberts*
Technical Director: *N Grundy*

Services
Acoustic consultancy services for bus and railway traction units, rolling stock and associated buildings.

Projects have included Waterloo Eurostar Terminal (buildings), St Petersburg Rail Terminal (buildings), Barratt Housing Project (railside development), Eurotram (complete vehicle), Europa Transrapid (complete vehicle), MTRC Hong Kong (complete vehicle), Arlanda, Stockholm (complete vehicle), Juniper, Turbostar and Electrostar and West Coast Main Line (rolling stock), Brush Engines (traction units), First Bus, Mellor Vancraft, Optare and Marshalls (engine/exhaust jacketing and moulded internal and external lining panels).

Hyder Consulting

Head office
29 Bressenden Place, London SW1E 5DZ, UK
Tel: (+44 20) 73 16 60 00   Fax: (+44 20) 73 16 61 25
e-mail: corp.marketing@hyderconsulting.com
Web: www.hyderconsulting.com

Key personnel
Director, Transportation Planning: *John Spiers*
Director, Urban Design and Transportation: *Geoff Webber*

Associated companies
Hyder Consulting Middle East
PO Box 2774, Abu Dhabi, United Arab Emirates
Tel: (+971 2) 633 34 00   Fax: (+971 2) 633 07 46

Hyder Consulting (Australia) Pty Ltd
Level 5, 116 Miller Street, North Sydney, New South Wales 2060, Australia
Tel: (+61 2) 89 07 90 00   Fax: (+61 2) 89 07 90 01

Hyder Consulting (Hong Kong) Ltd
47th Floor, Hopewell Centre, 183 Queens Road East, Wanchai, Hong Kong
Tel: (+852) 29 11 22 33   Fax: (+852) 28 05 50 28

Capabilities
Management and advisory services including: economic and financial appraisal; operations and research management; tariff negotiation; public transportation planning, traffic modelling and forecasting; operations audits; technical audits; quality audits; maintenance management, environmental impact assessment; safety and reliability audits, training and certification, and value engineering.

Project planning and design including: design management; concept design and system selection; feasibility studies; outline designs and specification for legislative approval; funding applications; operations and system planning; highway and traffic engineering; road safety engineering and audits; alignment and permanent way engineering; signalling and control systems; rolling stock; and freight terminal and depot design.

Project implementation including: preparation of contract documents; preparation of specifications; tender invitations and adjudication; project management and cost control; construction supervision; monitoring and quality control of procurement contracts; testing and commissioning; and operations and maintenance management.

Areas of activity include: main line, regional and suburban rail services; metros and urban transit systems including light rail and people movers; bus priority routes; freight logistics; bimodal and multimodal interchanges.

Projects
Recent projects include: the Bahrain traffic model and strategic plan; technical consultancy for Croydon Tramlink; Old Palace Yard, Westminster; Dubai parking control system; electronic road user charging projects in Hong Kong, New Zealand and UK; Western Sydney Bus Transitway; Melbourne City Link; London Bus Red Routes and London Bus Priority Network; London Congestion Charging, Project Evergreen (Chiltern Line, UK); technical consultancy for the London Underground PPP, and Transport for London framework contracts for consultancy services, project management and management consultancy.

Typical rail projects completed or in hand are:
Project Evergreen (Chiltern Line UK).
Technical consultancy for the London Underground PPP.
UK GNER, East Coast Main Line upgrade review.
Edinburgh Cross – rail feasibility.
Chiltern Railways, infrastructure upgrade feasibility. Railtrack Midlands – structure design. Railtrack North West, station improvements. Great Western – signalling design. West Coast Mainline – upgrade geotechnics study. Stratford Station Redevelopment (Western and Eastern Concourse) – structural and services design for new station concourse.
Istanbul metro, Turkey: electrical and mechanical systems design: supervision of implementation: commissioning and acceptance.
Thailand SRT Freight railway proposal: Feasibility study.
LAR Lai King Station, Hong Kong: detailed design of all E&M services and civil and structural aspects for the Lai King station, which is the interchange station of the Tsuen Wan line and Lantau Airport line.
Ankara LRT, Turkey: supervision of supply and installation of rolling stock, E&M subsystems, commissioning and acceptance.
Kuala Lumpur LRT system, Malaysia: checking engineer for the contracting consortium on Line 1, Stage 2.
New Southern Railway, Sydney, Australia: comprehensive review of technical aspects

including contractual construction and environmental issues and tunnelling concepts. Krakow, Poland: project appraisal of the financing and technology option.
West Rail, Hong Kong – Sham Shi Po section.
Guangzhou Metro China – civil, mechanical, electrical design and environmental services. Operations and maintenance advice.

IBIS Transport Consultants Ltd

12 High Street, Chalfont St Giles, HP8 4QA, UK
Tel: (+44 1494) 87 60 58
e-mail: ibistc@btinternet.com

Key personnel
Managing Director: *Ian Barrett*
Operations Director: *Graham Fletcher*

Capabilities
IBIS Transport Consultants is a management consultancy specialising in the planning, regulatory and operational aspects of urban passenger transport in developing and transition countries. Its corporate experience is based on the operation of more than 4,500 buses in Africa, the Caribbean, East Asia, the Middle East, the South Pacific, as well as the UK. This practical experience has been developed and marketed for the last 17 years in these regions as well as in Eastern Europe and Central and South Asia.

Areas of specialisation include: metropolitan sector and modal studies, and preparation of transport master plans; identification of priority sector investments and their financial and economic appraisal; economic and technical regulatory policy, with supporting institutions and enforcement capacity; enterprise restructuring, including private-sector participation and contract management; business process restructuring, covering development of business plans and information systems; fleet asset management, from specification and procurement through to financing and life-cycle maintenance; environmental improvement measures, involving appropriate technologies and monitoring; operational infrastructure, including public transport priority and bus rapid transit; vehicle and crew productivity, including computerised scheduling and rostering techniques; revenue optimisation, based on marketing, ticketing technologies and protection of its integrity; human resource development, from job specification through to targeted training delivery.

Projects
Selected projects: Urban transport development and BRT: Lagos, Nigeria; Accra, Ghana. Transport policy and strategy: Bucharest, Romania; Lagos, Nigeria. Regulatory and institutional frameworks: Tbilisi, Georgia; Accra, Ghana; Gdansk, Poland; Lagos, Nigeria. Investment identification: Bucharest, Romania; Budapest, Hungary; Togliatti, Russia. Business efficiency measures: Gdansk, Poland; Sarajevo, Bosnia; Ulaan Baatar, Mongolia. Private sector participation: Blantyre, Malawi; Colombo, Sri Lanka; Lahore, Pakistan. Privatisation: Addis Ababa, Ethiopia; Durban, South Africa; Dar es Salaam, Tanzania. Vehicle technology and specification: Mumbai, India; Samarkand, Uzbekistan. Fleet financing: Dakar, Senegal; Lagos, Nigeria.

Work has also been undertaken in the passenger transport sector in: Australia; Barbados; Fiji; Hong Kong; Ireland; Indonesia; Jamaica; Kenya; Kyrgyzstan; Latvia; Palestine; Saudi Arabia; Uganda; Vietnam and the UK.

ICF International

9300 Lee Highway, Fairfax, Virginia 22031-1207, US
Tel: (+1 703) 934 36 03   Fax: (+1 703) 934 37 40
e-mail: info@icfi.com
Web: www.icfi.com

Other offices

Rio de Janeiro, Brazil; Toronto, Canada; New Delhi, India; Moscow, Russian Federation; London, UK; Albany, Arlington, Baton, Charleston, Dallas, Dayton, Fairfax, Houston, Lexington, Los Angeles, Middletown, Ogden, Oklahoma City, Orange County, Research Triangle Park, Rockville, San Francisco, Seattle, Washington, DC.

Key personnel

Chairman and Chief Executive Officer: *Sudhakar Kesavan*
Chief Financial officer: *Alan Stewart*
Executive Vice-President and Chief Operating officer: *John Wasson*
Executive Vice-President and General Counsel: *Judith Kassel*

Background

Since 1969 ICF has been serving government at all levels, major corporations, and multinational institutions. More than 3,000 employees serve these clients worldwide.

Capabilities

ICF International partners with government and commercial clients to deliver consulting services and technology solutions in the energy, climate change, environment, transportation, social programs, health, defence, and emergency management markets.

INECO-TIFSA

Ingeniería y Economía del Transporte, SA
Tecnología e Investigación Ferroviaria, SA
Paseo de la Habana 138, E-28036 Madrid, Spain
Tel: (+34 91) 452 12 00   Fax: (+34 91) 452 13 00
e-mail: ineco@ineco.es
tifsa@tifsa.es
Web: www.ineco.es

Key personnel

Chairman: *Antonio Fernández Gil*
General Director, Advisor to the Chairman: *Juan Barrón Benavente*
General Directors: *Juan Torrejón, Javier Cos, Marcos García Cruzado, Juan Batanero, José María Urgoiti*

Capabilities

Railway engineering (track, electrification, signalling, telecommunications); consultancy (concessions, privatisations, demand analysis, feasibility studies); monitoring and supervision of railway works, technical assistance on site, integrated project management, railway planning and operations, rolling stock engineering (design, vehicle dynamics, quality control); railway maintenance (infrastructure, bridges, tunnels); intermodal transport, road and motorway engineering. Urban distribution and logistics and rail access to urban centres.

Projects

Overseas: Participation in SAMRAIL (Safety Management on Railways); development of a common safety management systems (SMS) for European railways.

Technical and economic feasibility study for a high-performance line in the Buenos Aires-Rosario corridor (Argentina).

SUR project – CPTM Brazil: INECO-TIFSA provides management and technical support to CPTM (Companhia Paulista de Trenes Metropolitanos).

National: High-speed railways programme in Spain: studies, infrastructure and superstructure, installation and telecommunications, railway systems, new stations, management of maintenance on existing lines, new technologies, environmental impact studies, control of assembly works, quality supervision and monitoring of track elements, prior to running.

Technical advice in the project and supervision during construction of 20 regional high-speed trainsets.

INECO-TIFSA has continued to work closely with different RENFE business units in many studies, projects and assistance assignments.

Consultancy and technical assistance for the control and supervision of the works in the Mediterranean Railway Corridor.

Master plan for the network railway access of Madrid; demand and mobility analysis studies for the suburban networks of Madrid, Bilbao, Seville and Cádiz.

Adaptation of Spanish railway legislation to EU directives.

Interfleet Technology Ltd

Interfleet House, Pride Parkway, Derby DE24 8HX, UK
Tel: (+44 1332) 22 30 00   Fax: (+44 1332) 22 30 01
e-mail: info@interfleet.co.uk
Web: www.interfleet-technology.com

Key personnel

Managing Director: *David Rollin*
Regional Director, UK: *Jonathan Wragg*
International Business Director: *Peter Dudley*
Technology Director: *Neil Wilson*
Knowledge Director: *David Curtis*
Finance Director: *Richard Tapping*

Subsidiaries

Interfleet Technology Pty Ltd
Australia
Interfleet Technology NZ Ltd
New Zealand
Interfleet Technology AS
Norway
Interfleet Technology AB
Sweden
Interfleet Technology Aps
Denmark
Interfleet Technology Inc
US
Interfleet Technology GmbH
Germany

Background

Interfleet Technology works with worldwide clients on rail engineering and business solutions. Interfleet was created from the engineering arm of British Rail to become one of the world's first privatised rail technology consultancies.

The company has over 500 staff with a worldwide client base.

In September 2008, the company established a strategic co-operation with German engineering firm, k+v Ingenieurgesellschaft mbH, with the objective to jointly market and expand their business segments.

Capabilities

Provision of engineering support for all vehicle types, from light to heavy rail, from commuter to high-speed and from passenger to freight, at every stage of traction and rolling stock life, for all types of projects. Total rail systems, encompassing all aspects of infrastructure and the physical railway environment. Interfleet is able to assist with infrastructure projects at both a strategic and a detail level. As business consultants and partners, Interfleet works with clients worldwide to implement new products, develop new processes and achieve maximum impact from investment programmes. Interfleet brings resources from all business disciplines, including contracting, finance, marketing, strategy and railway operations.

Intraesa

Edificio Numancia 1, Calle Viriato 47, E-08014 Barcelona, Spain
Tel: (+34 93) 366 21 10
Fax: (+34 93) 439 17 69
e-mail: intraesa.bcn@intraesa.com
Web: www. intraesa.com

Key personnel

Managing Director: *Félix Boronat*

Offices

Alicante, Madrid, Tarragona

Capabilities

Feasibility, route and engineering studies, project and works management for high-speed main line, suburban and urban rail projects.

Italcertifer

Italcertifer scpa
(Italian Institute for Railway Research and Certification)
via Alamanni 2/A, I—50123 Florence (I), Italy
Tel: (+39 055) 510 03 47   Fax: (+39 055) 510 03 53
e-mail: commercial@italcertifer.com
Web: www.italcertifer.com

Key personnel

Chief Executive Officer: *Dr Ing Carlo Carganico*
Technical Director: *Dr Ing Raffaele Mele*
Marketing Director: *Dr Ing Giovanni Florio*

Capabilities

Certification of railway systems and components, including: laboratory tests on rolling stock and components, on-track tests of rolling stock and components; tests on infrastructure components; tests on operational and functional characteristics of components and systems; research and technological development, research and development and personnel training.

Italcertifer works in partnership with Rete Ferroviaria Italiana SpA, Trenitalia SpA, the Polytechnic University of Milan and the universities of Florence, Naples Federico II and Pisa.

Italferr SpA

Via Marsala 53/67, I-00185 Rome, Italy
Tel: (+39 06) 49 75 22 98   Fax: (+39 06) 49 75 22 09
e-mail: a.damico@italferr.it
Web: www.italferr.it

Key personnel

Chairman: *Mauro Moretti*
Managing Director and Chief Executive: *Renato Casale*
Production: *Renato Bianco*
Procurement, International Activities and Operating Control: *Claudio Collinvitti*
Engineering: *Michele Del Principe*

Capabilities

Founded in 1984, Italferr SpA is the consulting engineering company of Italian Railways (FS Group) and has permanent staff of about 2,000. Italferr has an average turnover of EUR190 million and currently supervises and controls projects and investments for a total value of EUR79 billion. Italferr is active in traditional and high-speed line railways, metropolitan transit, other transportation systems and complementary sectors. Activities cover: guided transport systems; main line upgrade and design; high-speed systems; inter-regional connections; Alpine crossings; main line and urban area interconnections; urban junction redesign and technology upgrade; passenger stations and urban planning; freight marshalling systems; rolling stock/maintenance and repair facilities; intermodal terminals; innovative technology systems.

Services include supply/demand forecast and traffic analysis; transport development plans; feasibility studies/financial and economic evaluation; conceptual design and system definition; environmental impact appraisal; design of mono and multi-modal transport systems; preliminary and detailed designs; cost estimates, technical specifications, tender documents; maintenance manuals/construction site safety plans; preparation and evaluation of tenders; project management; supervision of works, testing, inspection, start-up assistance; procurement services; technical assistance, training and technology transfer; organisation and management studies; BOT and project financing assistance.

Italferr plays a strategic role in the upgrading and development of the Italian railway system. The company is in charge of engineering, management and works supervision of major infrastructure and technology works financed by FS investment plans involving the principal lines and urban junctions of the national network.

Projects

Examples: Italferr has been invested by the Italian Railways and TAV SpA with the responsibility for the development and realisation of the Italian high-speed railway system, a project which will link Turin with Venice, Milan with Naples and Genoa with Milan for a total of about 1,300 km and will be an integral part of the trans-European high-speed railway network.

Abroad Italferr has successfully executed railway development projects for international funding agencies, central and local governments and private clients in a number of countries in Europe, Asia, Africa and Latin America.

Other examples include: technical assistance for preparation of detailed designs and tender documents for the improvement on line section Mezotur-Gyoma, Hungary (EU/Phare); technical assistance for the modernisation of signalling and safety devices on the railway line Divaca Bratislava Raca, Trnava, Slovak Republic (EU/Phare); review of the feasibility study for the railway section from the Hungarian Border to Simeria, Romania; technical assistance for the preparation of the rail project for the Cohesion Fund, Romania; application of directive 2001/16/EC on the interoperability of railways in the Czech Republic (EU/Phare); review of railway rehabilitation project in Central Asia (EU/Tacis); Central Asia Railway telecommunications (EU/Tacis); preparation of detailed design and tender preparation for Zezely bridge reconstruction project in Novi Sad, Serbia; upgrading of the Frejus-Modane line section, France; technical study and railway operations scheme for the new high-speed Turin-Lyon railway line, Italy/France; transport master plan for Iraq on behalf of the Coalition Provisional Authority; surveying, updating of design and tender maintenance and repair centre, Syria; new Puerto Cabollo-La Encrucijada railway line, Colombia; executive design of two maintenance plants for high-speed trainset in Ankara and Istanbul; technical assistance to the Algerian Railways, for the management of the railways investment plan, Algeria.

Italferr operates under a Quality Management System certified by the internationally accredited DNV (Det Norske Veritas) meeting UNI EN ISO 9001/2000 standards.

Jacobs

95 Bothwell Street, Glasgow G2 7HX, UK
Tel: (+44 141) 204 25 11   Fax: (+44 141) 226 31 09
e-mail: marketing-glasgow@jacobs.com
Web: www.jacobs.com

Key personnel
Group Vice-President: *Mike Higgins*
Vice-Presidents: *Bob Duff, Gordon Masterton, David Coultas, David Baird, Ross Barr*

Background
Jacobs is one of the world's largest, and diverse providers of professional technical services.

Services
Railways:
Jacob's teams work with clients within the UK, Ireland and overseas to deliver rail infrastructure and operations within the areas of: heavy rail, light rail, metro, maintenance and training facilities, stations and interchanges.

Clients are offered complete project management services, a comprehensive multi-disciplinary railway engineering and planning capability across the project life cycle and extensive operational expertise.

Transportation:
Jacob's skills cover railways, highways, airports, public transport networks, ports and canals. Planning capability includes market research, strategic transport modelling, economic appraisals, feasibility and procurement strategies, pre-investment financial auditing, environmental impact assessments, training, value engineering and risk assessment, cost and contract consultancy, local transport plans.

Skills in construction methods, programming and value engineering include:
• tunnelling and ground engineering
• bridge design
• docks, ports and harbour design
• highway design, traffic control and telematics
• railway system engineering
• station and depot design
• airports, pavement and ground lighting design
• busways and light rail infrastructure
• project management and cost consultancy.

Projects
A sample of projects include: part of the consortium advising Government on the Channel Tunnel Rail Link; multidisciplinary design services on numerous heavy rail schemes including elements of West Coast Main Line; feasibility and detailed design of major interchanges including Stratford Regional Sation and the gateway to the London 2012 Olympics, also feasibility and detailed design of light rail schemes including Croydon Tramlink, elements of West London Tram, Nottingham, Leeds and Edinburgh; depot design and fit out including new Bedford Light Maintenance Depot in advance of the Thameslink blockade in late 2005; auditing of rail industry safety cases including Network Rail safety case; Disability Discrimination Act 1995 step free access programmes for Metro and heavy rail clients.

Jakes Associates, Inc

Jakes Plaza, 1940 The Alameda, Suite 200, San Jose, California 95126-1456, US
Tel: (+1 408) 249 72 00
Fax: (+1 408) 249 72 96
e-mail: jakes@jakesassociates.com
Web: www.jakesassociates.com

Key personnel
President: *David Mori, PE*
Finance Director: *Linda Rose*
Technical Director: *Steven Castaneda*
Operations Director: *Dean Hurst*

Capabilities
Consulting in transport technologies, including rail, automated guideway transit and bus systems; procurement and project management; specification development and design review; feasibility and engineering studies; maintenance analyses; business development services.

Projects
Recently completed projects include: Hong Kong Airport Transit Systems; Tel Aviv Elevated Transit Engineering; BART-Oakland, CaliforniaConnector Project; Santa Clara, California Light Rail system; Las Vegas, Nevada development of five people mover systems; Sacramento, California strategic plan for a citywide bus system; Indianapolis, Indiana City centre transit.

Japan Railway Technical Service (JARTS)

Taiyokan Building, 27-8 Hongo 2-chome, Bunkyo-ku, Tokyo 113-0033, Japan

Tel: (+81 3) 56 84 31 71; 31 79
Fax: (+81 3) 56 84 31 70; 31 80
e-mail: jarts-kaigai@tiger.odn.ne.jp
Web: www.jarts.or.jp

Key personnel
President: *Hiroshi Komori*
Senior Executive Vice-President: *Kazuo Notake*
Director Marketing: *Katsushige Takahashi*

Capabilities
Studies, surveys, design, planning specifications, preparation of contract documents, and project control and supervision of railway, high-speed rail, metro, monorail and advanced guided transit; construction of new lines; modernisation and improvement of track; electrification; modernisation of rolling stock; restructuring of railway management.

Joint Mobility Partnership

105 Judd Street, London WC1H 9NE, UK
Tel: (+ 4420) 73 91 20 02   Fax: (+4420) 73 87 71
e-mail: info@jmuaccess.org.uk
Web: www.rnib.org.uk/jmu

Other offices
Edinburgh, Cardiff, Leeds

Capabilities:
Services include: design consultancy, infrastructure, interchanges, information systems, vehicles and streets; staff training, disability awareness and technical skills; research and development partnerships and wayfinding systems; disability policy and strategy advice; publications; mobility audits; advice and information.

Lahmeyer International GmbH

Friedberger Strasse 173, D-61118 Bad Vilbel, Germany
Tel: (+49 6101) 55 0   Fax: (+49 6101) 55 22 22
e-mail: info@lahmeyer.de
Web: www.lahmeyer.de

Key personnel
President: *Henning Nothdurft*
Managing Director: *Burkhard Neumann*
Manager: *Rainer Bothe*
Transportation Division: *Joachim Neumann; Heinz Saxer*
Offices in Berlin, Frankfurt, Munich, Stuttgart

Capabilities
The Lahmeyer International Group, with its 10 associated companies, is an independent engineering consultancy covering a spectrum of planning and consulting services in the fields of transportation, energy, hydropower and water resources, civil engineering and project management, technology and environmental sectors. The transportation division offers engineering services concerning transportation technology, railways and regional transport systems, tunnels and underground installations, bridges, roads, motorways, airports and specialised transportation facilities. The range of consultancy services encompasses studies, design and planning, tendering, project management, supervision and commissioning for high-speed railways, line-upgrading, stations, marshalling yards, intermodal terminals, depots and workshops, integrated transportation systems, suburban fast trains and feeder systems, underground and metro systems, tramways and light rail systems as well as maglev systems. Lahmeyer International possesses expertise and experience in specialised areas such as Life-Cycle Costing (LCC) in relation to rail traffic through observations and analyses in the RAMS sector (reliability, availability, maintainability and safety). For privately financed projects (BOT, PPP) it offers advisory and consultancy services to prospective owners or bidding consortia.

Laramore, Douglass and Popham

332 South Michigan Ave, Suite 400, Chicago, Illinois 60604, USA
Tel: (+1 312) 427 84 86
Fax: (+1 312) 427 84 74
e-mail: postmaster@ldpgroup.com
Web: www.ldpgroup.com

Key personnel
President: *Richard T Harvey*
Senior Vice-President: *H Saxena*

Capabilities
Design and project management for electrified rapid transit and electric railway traction power supply and distribution systems.

Lea+Elliott Inc

1009 West Randol Mill Road, Arlington, Texas 76012, US
Tel: (+1 817) 261 14 46
Fax: (+1 817) 861 32 96
Web: www.leaelliott.com

Key personnel
President : *Jack Norton*

Capabilities
Transportation system planning, analysis and design, as well as system procurement. Experience in automated people movers, metro, LRT, buses, monorails, cable-propelled and magnetic levitation systems.

Specialises in planning control systems, cost estimation, market analysis, microprocessor hardware and software design, multimodal transport planning, operations and maintenance, project management and oversight, propulsion systems, safety analysis, simulations, technical assessment, vehicle design and valuation.

Projects
Recent contracts include: Phoenix Sky Harbor International Airport Automated Train; Washington Dulles International Airport Aerotrain; Doha West Bay People Mover; New Doha International Airport Aerotrain; Doha West Bay People Mover; New Doha International Airport APM; Dulles Metrorail Corridor and MIC-Earlington Heights Connector.

LEK Consulting LLP

40 Grosvenor Place, London SW1X 7JL, UK
Tel: (+44 20) 73 89 72 00
Fax: (+44 20) 73 89 74 40
Web: www.lek.com

Other offices
Auckland, Bangkok, Beijing, Boston, Chicago, London, Los Angeles, Melbourne, Milan, Mumbai, Munich, New Delhi, New York, Paris, San Francisco, Shanghai, Singapore, Sydney, Tokyo.

Key personnel
Directors: *J I Goddard; J Simmons; A H Allum; P S Debenham; A J Scott*

Background
Founded in London in 1983, LEK Consulting employs over 850 staff across 19 offices in Europe, North America and Asia-Pacific.

Capabilities
LEK is an international firm that specialises in strategy, transaction services and performance improvement consulting. It advises large private and public sector organisations, private equity companies and smaller, more entrepreneurial businesses. Engaged by a broad range of transport-related clients, the company is experienced in public sector reform in the UK,

Europe and Australia. It has advised passenger, freight, infrastructure and rolling stock organisations on key strategic and commercial issues. It offers advice on strategic, economic, financial and operational issues, including privatisation and commercialisation, competition policy, traffic and financial forecasting, mergers and acquisitions and new technology impact assessments.

Lemna International, Inc

2445 Park Avenue, Minneapolis 55404-3790, US
Tel: (+1 612) 20 00   Fax: (+1 612) 253 20 03
e-mail: intlsales@lemna.com
Web: www.lemna.com

Key personnel
President and Chief Executive Officer: *Viet Ngo*

Background
Lemna International, Inc is a subsidiary of the Lemna Corporation holding company that was incorporated in Minnesota, US.

Products/Services
Lemna Intenational provides services in both heavy and light rail (urban transport) including, greenfield development, electrification and upgrades and rehabilitation.

Contracts
A contract was signed with the Lagos State Metropolitan Transit Authority (LAMATA), for first light rail in West Africa.

Other projects have included the signing of a general agreement with Uzbek Railways Company to provide turnkey services to implement the electrification and rehabilitation of the two rail segments, including arranging financing for the project.

Lend Lease

142 Northolt Road, Harrow HA2 0EE, UK
Tel: (+44 20) 82 71 80 78
Fax: (+44 20) 82 71 80 26
Web: www.lendlease.com
www.bovislendlease.com

Key personnel
Chief Executive Officer, Lend Lease: *Ross Taylor*
Chief Executive Officer, Lend Lease Europe: *Murray Coleman*
Chief Executive Officer, Lend Lease Asia Pacific: *Des Marks*
Chief Executive Officer, Lend Lease Americas: *Charles Bacon*
Business Development: *Mike Temple*
Director, Lend Lease (Projects): *David Sutton*
Operations Director, Lend Lease (Transport): *Richard Crossland*

Capabilities
Lend Lease's projects business offers property-related services to clients involved in the creation, improvement or management of real estate assets. This includes expertise in development and capital raising, programme management, project and construction management, design and engineering, as well as facilities and asset management. The business includes Bovis Lend Lease. In the transport sector, Lend Lease works for government agencies, railway operators, developers and commercial entities on main line, suburban, metro and light railway projects in the UK, Europe, the Americas and Asia Pacific. Lend Lease is currently managing over GBP2,500 million worth of railway projects. Services provided to the rail industry cover feasibility, project development, strategic planning and pre-construction phases through to development of procurement strategies, cost plans, construction planning and the tendering process – and to construction phase management, co-ordination

and control, including quality, value, risk and safety management.

Projects
UK
Department for Transport: Appointed to a panel of consultants providing project and commercial management services and currently involved in a range of enhancement programmes, all of which are vital to the DfT's strategy for transport. Current commissions include CTRL depots and Franchise management duties.
Network Rail: Involved in infrastructure and property asset contracts.
National Express: Project management work on C15 for Central Trains and Centro Metronet; project management teams for PPP upgrades on stations.

Asia Pacific
Involved in track and station maintenance and upgrade and capital works programme management. Projects have included: Parramatta Rail Link, Sydney; Ultimo-Pyrmont Light Rail Transit Project, Sydney; Kuala Lumpur Central Station, Malaysia; and Auckland Rail Transit System, Auckland, New Zealand.

The Americas
Involved in track and maintenance and upgrade and capital works programme management. Projects have included: Long Island Railroad (on-call services), New York; rehabilitation of Times Square Station, New York; Grand Central Terminal modernisation, New York; New Jersey Transit (on-call services)/Rail Control Centre; and Newark International Airport, New Jersey.

Light Rail Transit Consultants GmbH

Fritz-Vomfelde-Strasse 6, D-40547 Dusseldorf, Germany
Tel: (+49 211) 52 30 51 0   Fax: (+49 211) 523 05 61
e-mail: mail@lrtc.de
Web: www.lrtc.de

Key personnel
Managing Directors: *Dipl Ing Gerhard Kühr, Dieter Wolff, Dipl Ing Ulrich Lüdtke*

Background
LRTC is owned by: PB-Consult Planungs- und Betriebsberatungsgesellschaft mbH, Nürnberg (25 per cent); Rail & Bus Consultants GmbH, Düsseldorf (50 per cent) and Spiekermann Beratende Ingenieure GmbH, Düsseldorf (25 per cent).

Capabilities
Consulting and planning, design and engineering, operation and maintenance assistance for mass transit systems. LRTC provides expertise in all fields of urban transit, has access to experts of transit authorities, takes part in worldwide know-how transfer and is independent of products and suppliers.

Projects
LRTC has been active in a number of light rail-based projects in European cities and other parts of the world. These include most recently: LRT Standards, Taiwan (2004–05); LRT Kaohsiung, Taiwan (2005-); passenger transport systems at Frankfurt International Airport, Germany (2005-); a bus transit system in Ryadh, Saudi Arabia (2007-); a bus privatisation project in Ryadh, Saudi Arabia (2007-) and a bus system in Dubai, UAE (2006–2007).

Listavia International Consultants Ltd

13 Woodmancourt, Mark Way, Godalming GU7 2BT, UK
Tel: (+44 1483) 42 89 32   Fax: (+44 1483) 42 89 32

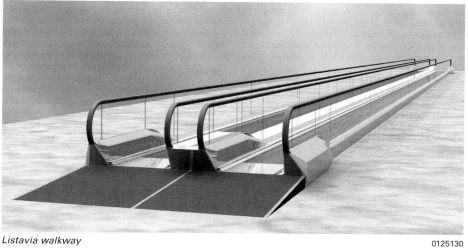

Listavia walkway 0125130

e-mail: listerw@listavia.co.uk
Web: www.listavia.co.uk

Key personnel
Principals: *Warren S Lister, G T Lister*

Background
Listavia Limited was established in 1970. Recently Listavia International Consultants Ltd (LICON) was set up to produce innovative transport systems.

Capabilities
Feasibility studies, route surveys, tender evaluation, contract administration, detailed design of innovative city and airport transport systems.

Moving walkways: Listavia has introduced low-profile moving walkways which are installed by placing them on top of existing floors. Floor pits and trenches are eliminated. Extensions can be added at will and the walkways can be extended or relocated quickly and easily.

Developments
LICON developed the Service Tunnel Transport System for the Channel Tunnel project.

Lloyd's Register Rail BV

PO Box 2016 – KTT 6, NL-3500 GA, Utrecht, Netherlands
Tel: (+31 30) 300 47 00   Fax: (+31 30) 300 48 00
Web: www.nedtrain.nl

Key personnel
Managing Director: *A J M Spaninks*
Deputy Managing Director: *Teun Cosijn*

Background
Previously part of NedTrain, in October 2006 the company was acquired by Lloyd's Register Rail and changed its name from NedTrain Consultancy to Lloyd's Register Rail BV.

The company supports operators and owners of rolling stock during the entire life cycle of their fleet, supports manufacturers developing their products and helps infra managers on the wheel-rail interface.

Capabilities
Consultancy geared towards support of rolling stock during all phases of the life cycle; strategic fleet management decisions, procurement support, tender evaluation, production monitoring, quality management, testing and commissioning, vehicle acceptance, reliability engineering and trouble shooting, design of vehicle modifications.

Projects
Recent projects include procurement support and project management for some major rolling stock projects (500 units), acceptance of light rail vehicles on the Dutch rail network, vehicle acceptance of BR189 with Siemens and DB, production monitoring for HSBC, RET and GVBA, safety cases for Virgin's Voyager, noise reduction projects for ProRail, NS Reizigers and various government departments and the business process redesign of the quality management department of a leading manufacturer.

Operation efficiency and cost reduction projects. Monitoring of rolling stock-infrastructure interference. Development and sales of rolling stock safety systems in co-operation with Bombardier.

Lloyd's Register Rail Limited

Davidson House, 2 Forbury Square, Reading RG1 3EU, UK
Tel: (+44 118) 900 07 12   Fax: (+44 118) 900 07 11
e-mail: enquiries@lrrail.com
Web: www.lr.org
Lloyd's Register Rail Limited Registered office 71 Fenchurch Street, London EC3M 4BS, UK

Key personnel
Business Development Director: *Martin Hayhoe*

Offices
Lloyd's Register Rail operates from offices in Birmingham, Belper, Bristol, Crewe, Derby, Glasgow, London, Preston and York in the UK, and Rotterdam and Utrecht in the Netherlands. Offices also in Dubai, Hong Kong, Singapore, Sydney and Melbourne. The management consulting arm, BSL Management Consultants, has offices in Hamburg and Berlin, Germany.

Background
Lloyd's Register Rail Limited is a wholly owned subsidiary of the Lloyd's Register Group. The most recent developments have been the acquisition of BSL Management Consultants (Germany) and NedTrain Consulting (the Netherlands) in 2006. The company provides services to the transportation sector through companies branded Lloyd's Register Rail for technical activities and BSL Management Consultants for economic and strategic activities.

Capabilities
Services are provided by over 500 personnel to help improve rail systems safety, quality and asset management worldwide. Lloyd's Register Rail specialises in rail systems integration, risk management and safety assurance founded on core rail skills in all key rail disciplines, including rolling stock, signalling, telecommunications, civil engineering, power systems and operations. Key areas of experience include business support, risk assessment, system assurance, safety case preparation and independent safety assessment.

Services in economic and strategic disciplines are provided by BSL Management Consultants, the transportation management consultants in the Lloyd's Register Group. BSL Management Consultants focus on the economic, organisational and corporate governance issues in the public transport sector.

Contracts
Safety cases for Virgin Cross Country tilting rolling stock for Bombardier Transportation Group and ALSTOM Transport.

Notified Body for Network Rail West Coast Route Modernisation (WCRM) and Great Western Main Line (GWML).

Railway safety case audit for several train operating companies.

Risk management framework for RailCorp, New South Wales.

RAMS assurance for the Palm Jumeirah Monorail system in Dubai.

Performance review of MRT in Hong Kong.

LogoMotive GmbH

Dr Carlo Schmid Strasse, 93a, D-90491 Nuremberg, Germany
Tel: (+49 911) 95 52 8-0   Fax: (+49 911) 955 28 19
e-mail: info@logomotive.eu
Web: www.logomotive.eu

Key personnel
Managing Director: *Ulrich Hachmann*

Capabilities
Services for the design, development and innovation of vehicles, systems and components for railways, automotive systems, special machines and plant construction. Specialising in acoustics, dynamics, structural mechanics, testing and overall systems. CAD design of complex structures such as carbodies, bogies and components. Concept design, detailed design, drawings, parts lists, including calculation (dynamics, acoustics, structural mechanics) to the relevant standards.

LTK Engineering Services

A member of the Klauder Group
100 West Butler Avenue, Ambler, Pennsylvania 19002, USA
Tel: (+1 215) 542 07 00
Fax: (+1 215) 542 76 76
Web: www.ltk.com

Key personnel
President: *George N Dorshimer*
Vice-Presidents: *F H Landell, J S Gustafson, F W Frandsen, T B Furmaniak, C M Lawlor, C A Woodbury, J M Ronalter*
Director, Business Development: *David H Oglevee*
Established: *1921*
Staff: *230*

Capabilities
Planning, engineering and design for urban transport, including design of passenger rail vehicles, communications and signalling systems, traction power systems, fare collection systems and rail vehicle maintenance facilities.

Projects
Portland Tri-Met: Systems Engineer for Banfield, Westside, Hillsboro and interstate extensions.

Amtrak: Rail vehicle engineering services for Northeast Corridor High Speed Rail Programme.

New York City Transit: Rail vehicle engineering services for R142, R142A, R143 and R160 programmes.

Seattle ST Link: Systems Engineer for the new light rail system.

Long Island Rail Road: Rail vehicle engineering services for M-7 emu programme.

New Jersey Transit: Engineering services for the Comet II overhaul and multi-level coaches.

Tren Urbano: Engineering services for new rapid transit car fleet.

Los Angeles County MTA: Rail vehicle engineering services for the LA Red, Blue, Green, Standard and Pasadena cars.

Sacramento RT: Engineering services for LRV1 and LRV3 programmes.

Dallas Area Rapid Transit: Engineering services for two LRV programmes.

Boston MBTA: Engineering services for the Green line routes 7 and 8, Red line No 3, Blue line No 4 and 5, and Orange line No 12 cars.

Philadelphia: Engineering services for SEPTA's M4 rapid transit car procurement.

Washington, DC: Engineering services for WMATA's original 766-car fleet.

McCormick Rankin Corporation

2655 North Sheridan Way, Mississauga, Ontario L5K 2P8, Canada
Tel: (+1 905) 823 85 00   Fax: (+1 905) 823 85 03
e-mail: mrc@mrc.ca
Web: www.mrc.ca

Key personnel
Chairman and Chief Executive Officer: *Ian Williams*
Senior Transit Personnel
  Manager, Public Transit Services (Canada): Dale Turvey
  President: *Reno Radolli*
  Rail Rapid Transit Planning, Design and Construction: *Dennis R Callan*
  Manager, McCormick Rankin Cagney Pty Ltd (Brisbane): *Neil Cagney*
  Transitway Planning/ITS Applications: *Steve Schijns*
  Operational Planning: *Sean Rathwell*

Other offices
Ottawa, Kingston, Kitchener, Halifax, Brisbane and Auckland.

Subsidiaries
MR International (MRI)
McCormick Rankin Pty Ltd
MRC McLean Hazel
McCormick Rankin Cagney Pty Ltd (Brisbane, Auckland)
Ecoplans Ltd (Environmental)

Capabilities
Expertise in planning, design and construction services for the full range of rapid transit technologies including busways, LRT, heavy rail, commuter rail and people mover systems; organisation and operation reviews of conventional transit systems serving urban populations from 15,000 to 500,000+; and development of stations, bus transit operations centres, transit ITS and specialised transit operations.

Projects
Initiation of first transportation project in India, working closely with Canadian firm SENES. The study is funded by the Canadian International Development Agency Industrial Cooperation (CIDA Inc). The Greater Hyderabad Municipal Corporation has requested assistance in carrying out a feasibility study for developing a Bus Rapid Transit System with emphasis on improving the traffic and consequently improving public transit, reducing private vehicle use and improving air quality.

Completion of the Environmental Assessment Study (MIS) for the 31 km North-South LRT Line in Ottawa, Canada.

Complete design of the Bayview Station and ancillary facilities on the Toronto Transit Commission's new Sheppard Subway.

Environmental assessment for a 13 km Yonge-Spadina extension (loop) of the existing Toronto subway including ridership demand analysis, impact assessment and preliminary engineering. Planning and preliminary design of 30 km busway in Brisbane, Australia, including detailed design manuals and ITS applications for service

monitoring, passenger information systems and the security network.

Development of a GO Transit interregional Bus Rapid Transit network, fully integrated with the existing Toronto TTC rapid transit and GO commuter rail networks.

Assessment of the business case for the introduction of rail link between Pearson International Airport and Union Station in downtown Toronto.

Preparation of GO Transit's (Toronto) Georgetown Corridor Commuter Rail Upgrade study.

Introduction of BRT facilities for the City of Winnipeg within two corridors totalling 19 km in length. Consulting services include preparation of design manual, the preliminary design of guideway, design of ITS application for passenger system and service monitoring and control, operation design of routes and schedules for the transitway and feeder services.

Metroconsult

Helene-Weber-Allee 15, D-80637 Munich, Germany
Tel: (+49 89) 157 68 66   Fax: (+49 89) 157 24 73
e-mail: info@metroconsult.de
Web: www.metroconsult.com

Key personnel
Managing Director: *Dr Ing Jürgen Rauch*

Capabilities
Design of metro, railway stations and consultancy mainly to public transportation system owners; planners and industry; methods of increasing capacity of metros and commuter railway systems; design of innovative platform screen door systems for metro stations; planning of buildings for public infrastructure; integration of metro systems into the transportation system of a city, technically and by means of architectural design; design of innovative parking systems in cities and within limited space; design of commuter parking systems; development of materials of fire protection in confined spaces as there are tunnels and underground stations; technology development support to manufacturers; support for innovative concepts of railway vehicles for public transport.

Additional developments include planning and consulting for building and operating stations and systems of public transport, development and management of innovations for the operation of public transport and stations including: passenger information systems; automatic passenger guidance; optimisation of operation; optimisation of weak points of operations; development of timetables/schedules, especially during peak hours for large commuter rail and metro systems; development of real time steering methods for driverless passenger transport.

Consulting for public transport operators, public authorities, supervising the transport market, consulting for the owner of the technical infrastructure (passenger information, communication, built structures), developing new solutions with the industry for rail vehicles and for information technology.

Parking guidance systems; conception of modern intermodal station with park-and-ride; station operation technology, industrial developments, new developments such as flexible platform doors. Planning for automated passenger counting for metros, train, buses; passenger guidance systems for metro; automated parking facilities; fire safe tunnel building and lining technology; planning camera surveillance – anti-terrorism measures in public transport and large public facilities; new card and fare collection technology modules and system modules for terrorism prevention to be combined with the transportation guidance system.

City and regional transportation planning, energy and land area saving solutions, infrastructure planning.

Projects
Passenger guidance system for the commuter railway network of Munich, Germany; several metro stations and parking systems in south Germany; vehicle parking related to public transport; development of fire protection materials in confined spaces, such as tunnels and underground stations, for better orientation in daily operation and emergency situations; consultancy to several city authorities and to manufacturers in the public transport industry; development of platform door systems for metros; development of concepts for a light rail train with energy systems not yet used in railway technology. As well, architectural practise for metro stations and solutions for integrating platform doors into existing station, both technically and architectonically,

In 2004 Metroconsult redeveloped the passenger guidance system into a transportation guidance system. Passenger counting, gained either by automatic passenger counting systems or by image processing software, combined with a camera surveillance system of metro trains and stations, automatically produces direct information to the dispatching system of a metro. This calculates real time the necessary number of trains, headway and train length needed for operation.

Developments
In 2006 and 2007, Metroconsult continued working in the field of increasing capacity and efficiency of highly congested railway stations and lines. Additionally, consulting to public authorities/politics for questions of organising public transportation.

During 2005 Metroconsult continued its development of automatic safety systems for railways, based on CCTV surveillance from various installation points.

Millbrook Proving Ground Limited

Millbrook, Bedford MK45 2JQ, UK
Tel: (+44 1525) 40 84 08   Fax: (+44 1525) 40 84 68
e-mail: info@millbrook.co.uk
Web: www.millbrook.co.uk

Key personnel
Head of Business Development: *Jerome Cretet*

Products
Millbrook Technology Park provides test and development solutions for the automotive and rail industries. Millbrook has a unique combination of world class tracks and laboratories and its areas of expertise include crashworthiness, systems durability, vehicle emission and fuel economy. In addition to the laboratories, the wide range of tracks available includes off road for passenger cars and military specifications, high-speed circuit, hill route and a full range of structural inputs.

Modjeski & Masters Inc

4909 Louise Drive, Mechanicsburg, Pennsylvania 17055, US
Tel: (+1 717) 790 95 65   Fax: (+1 717) 790 95 64
Web: www.modjeski.com

Key personnel
Principals: *J M Kulicki, D F Sorgenfrei, BT Martin, L K Huang, Z Prucz, T B McMeans, M F Britt*
Senior Associates: *T Y Soong, L V Borden, M C Irwin, R A Little, J L McKenney, R A Martino, S R Eshenaur, B E Peterson, R J Eppehimer, M L Sternitzke, W G Wassef, D W Petermeier*
Project Development: *M F Britt*

Other offices
New Orleans, Louisiana
Poughkeepsie, New York

Moorestown, New Jersey
Charleston, West Virginia
Edwardsville, Illinois
St Louis, Missouri

Capabilities

Rail structures; design, rehabilitation, maintenance inspections and instrumentation of fixed and movable bridges.

Mott MacDonald Group

St Anne House, Wellesley Road, Croydon CR9 2UL, UK
Tel: (+44 20) 87 74 20 00   Fax: (+44 20) 86 81 57 06
e-mail: richard.williams@mottmac.com,
    martyn.wallwork@mottmac.com
Web: www.mottmac.com

Key personnel

Group Board Directors: *M O Blackburn (Chairman) K J Howells (Managing), K J Stovell, P J Wickens, Baroness T Blackstone (non-executive) J P Brooks (non-executive)*
Transportation Managing Director: *Richard Williams*
Transportation Directors: *N Bristow, C Davis, J Martin, A Powderham, M Wallwork, R F Davies*
Key Directors: *J D Corrie, M G Simpson, A R Walker, R Staniforth, A West, R Carter, J Hughes, R N Dumolo, C Chalk, T O'Neill, D A Hand*

International offices

Australia, Bahamas, Bahrain, Bangladesh, Bulgaria, Canada, Chile, China, Czech Republic, Egypt, Ethiopia, Hungary, Iceland, India, Indonesia, Ireland, Kazakhstan, Kenya, Libya, Malaysia, Netherlands, New Zealand, Nigeria, Norway, Oman, Pakistan, Philippines, Poland, Portugal, Qatar, Romania, Russian Federation, Saudi Arabia, Singapore, South Africa, Taiwan, Thailand, Trinidad, Uganda, Ukraine, United Arab Emirates, US, Uzbekistan, Venezuela, Zambia.

Capabilities

Mott MacDonald is an independent multi-disciplinary engineering, management and development consultancy with a turnover approaching GBP600 million and over 10,000 staff worldwide including chartered engineers, systems and safety engineers, transportation planners, computer specialists, environmental scientists and support staff operating throughout 140 countries.

Planning, design and implementation of urban public transport systems; comprehensive service in transport planning, civil and structural engineering and mechanical and electrical engineering; traffic engineering and highway planning; tunnel and station ventilation; train control, signalling and communications; studies of electromagnetic compatibility and safety from traction interference; rolling stock and traction power supply performance; rolling stock procurement advice.

Projects

Canada: Sheppard Subway Project: Programme managers for the Toronto Transit Commission's 6.4 km rapid transit subway project.
Czech Republic: PRaK, Czech Republic: feasibility study for rail link to Prague airport.
Denmark: Copenhagen Metro, Denmark: tunnel ventilation studies.
Holland: Support work on the Infraspeed Consortium's HSL-Zuid railway in Holland.
Hungary: Budapest Metro Line 4, Hungary: railway authorisation design.
India: Delhi Metro: Southern Section-civil, architectural and M&E design for contract MC1B.
Indonesia: Jakarta Monorail: finalising a feasibility study into providing a mass transit monorail system.
    Jakarta North-South integrated toll road and LRT project, Indonesia (transport planning and conceptual design)

Ireland: DART Ireland: power supply design for Greystones extension.
Luas: alignment and system design.
Malaysia: Putrajaya Light Rail, Malaysia: design and project management.
    Kuala Lumpur Monorail, Malaysia: independent checking engineer.
Portugal: Linha do Norte upgrading, Portugal.
    Porto Metro, Portugal: resident engineering services in joint venture with Geodata of Italy for Transmetro, 70 km of track and 66 stations.
Singapore: North East Line, Singapore: overhead catenary system design.
    Marina Line, Singapore: concept design and performance specifications.
Sweden: Banverket, Sweden: signalling and ATP design services.
Taiwan: Taipei Department of Rapid Transit Systems: consultancy services, for mechanical and electrical commissioning.
    Kaohsiung Metro, Taiwan: technical audit.
    Lead consultant to monitor and audit the design, construction and commissioning of the GBP10 billion BOT railway for Taiwan High-Speed Rail Corporation (as part of the IREG consortium).
Thailand: Bangkok MRTA, Thailand: project management for 20 km underground metro system.
UK: Automatic Train Operation System (ATO), Glasgow, UK: Design and development of a replacement ATO system for the Glasgow underground.
    Crossrail, UK: multi-disciplinary design services for line 1 for Crossrail, the 50/50 joint venture between Transport for London (TfL) and the Strategic Rail Authority (SRA).
    Dorset Coast resignalling in partnership with Siemens on Railtrack's GBP20 million new signalling system.
    Edinburgh Light Rail, Edinburgh, UK.
    Heathrow Terminal 5: systems integrated assurance services for Heathrow Express and Piccadilly Line extensions into the new tunnel.
    London Underground, UK: asset and condition survey of earth structures, technical advice to London Underground Ltd's Chief Engineer's Directorate under a 5-year framework agreement covering a diverse range of support including knowledge, risk and programme management.
    Manchester Airport: Ground Transport Interchange, UK: lead consultant for new bus, rail interchange.
    Manchester Light Rail.
    LTS Rail: procurement of new rolling stock.
    Merseyside Light Rail Transit, Liverpool, UK: proposals for progression of planned line 1, 2 and 3 of LRT network in Merseyside.
    Nottingham Light Rapid Transit, Nottinghamshire, UK: review and refinement of existing LRT alignment options for extension of network.
    OPRAF, UK: tilting train studies and specifications for West Coast Main Line.
    Programme manager (in a joint venture with Fluor) for Railtrack's East Coast Main Line upgrade.
    Railtrack, UK: safety of dual-voltage earthing arrangements on the North London line.
    West Coast Main Line upgrade for Railtrack as consultant for feasibility and detailed design for whole route.
    West Coast Route Modernisation, UK: multi-functional consultant:
US: LA Metro, US (construction management for Red Line North Hollywood extension).
    Long Island Rail Road East Side Access, New York: technical tunnel consultant to Bechtel/URS Greiner.

MTR Corporation Consultancy Services

MTR Tower, Telford Plaza, 33 Wai Yip Street, Kowloon Bay, Hong Kong
Tel: (+852) 29 93 23 17   Fax: (+852) 29 93 77 74
e-mail: jjdring@mtr.com.hk
Web: www.mtr.com.hk

Key personnel

General Manager, International Business:
    Jonathan J Dring

Capabilities

MTR offers consultancy services to the railway industry in operating management, engineering management and maintenance fields. Based on its experience gained over 25 years in building and operating MTRC's urban rail system and Airport Express line, assistance can be given in: project preliminaries – financial proposals, feasibility studies, project definition and concept planning; project planning, design and construction – detailed planning, programming, design, system assurance, system integration, project management, construction management, inspections, testing and commissioning, operational readiness; railway operation and maintenance – station operation, train operation, central control, incident management, revenue services, documentation, infrastructure maintenance, railway system maintenance, asset management, management information systems; railway support services – safety management, quality management, environmental management, training, procurement, contract administration, inspection services, performance management; other related services – non-fare revenue, integrated property development, project financing, privatisation.

Projects

Projects in progress include: Beijing Metro Line 4; Shenzhen Metro Line 4; Shanghai Metro Line 9; Skyplaza; additional Tung Chung Line trains; Lantau Airport Railway noise barriers; major pedestrian links; Tseung Kwan O Extension (Phase 2).

MVA Consultancy

First Floor Dukes Court Duke Street Woking GU21 5BH
Tel: (+44 1483) 72 80 51
Fax: (+44 1483) 75 52 07
e-mail: mail@mva.co.uk
Web: www.mvaconsultancy.com

Key personnel

Chief Executive Officer: *Nigel Ash*
Directors: *Mick Roberts, Steve Williamson, Richard Crossley*
Technical Director: *Richard Hancox*
Finance Director and Company Secretary: *Brian Sheriff*
Managing Consultant for Smarter Travel: *Jon Foley*
Managing Consultant: *John Landels*

Other offices

MVA Consultancy has offices in Bangkok, China, France, Hong Kong, Singapore, and UAE.

Background

MVA was established in 1968 and is a member of the Systra Group, international consulting engineers for rail and urban transport.

Capabilities

MVA provides sustainable transport solutions to clients across the transport sector. Clients include governments, operators, agencies, developers and financiers. MVA delivers practical solutions in multi-modal planning, traffic engineering, public transport appraisal, demand and revenue forecasting, information management, intelligent transport systems, payment strategies, and social and market research.

Contracts

Recent contracts include the major modelling and economic appraisal for a GBP80 million busway scheme between Luton and Dunstable, advice on appraisal issues to Nottingham Express Transit, development of the business case for the Fastway guided bus system, public consultation and Transport and Works Act advice for Luton

Translink, appraisal of options for reopening the Stirling-Alloa railway line, development of the North East Regional Planning Assessment for the Strategic Rail Authority, advice on smartcard ticketing to the NoWcard Parnership of local authorities in the north west of the UK and customer satisfaction monitor for GNER.

Overseas contracts include demand forecasting for Hanoi tram, China cross boundary public transport study, Dubai light rail forecasting, advice to TransitLink on public transport integration, restructuring and fares issues in Singapore, Ho Chi Minh City Metro feasibility study, patronage and revenue studies for Bangkok Skytrain, advice on Taiwan high-speed railway, Beijing airport express line patronage and revenue study and preliminary design study for Shenzhen Metro Line 4.

NEA Transport Research and Training

Postal address: PO.Box 276, NL2700 AG Zoetermeer, Netherlands
Tel: (+31 79) 322 22 21   Fax: (+31 79) 322 22 11
e-mail: email@nea.nl
Web: www.nea.nl

Key personnel
Managing Director: *Menno M Menist*
Traffic and Transport Policy Studies: *Jan Kiel*
Passenger Transport: *Bert Schepers*

Capabilities
NEA is an independent knowledge provider operating in the field of traffic, transport, infrastructure and logistics. NEA's activities encompass the economic and social aspects of both passenger and freight transport for all modes. In the field of research and consultancy, NEA has experience in modelling, forecasting and evaluation of international freight flows, including simulation, scenario building, economic impact analysis, socio-economic research, market research and mobility studies. Training experience includes development of course materials and case studies, training needs assessments, institutional strengthening, legal harmonisation and legal reform.

Projects
Research, training and consultancy assignments have been undertaken for governments, international agencies and organisations. Clients include the World Bank, Asian Development Bank, Commission of the European Communities, the Netherlands government, international branch organisations and the private sector.

Newbus Technology Limited

Stone Cross, Chicksgrove, Salisbury, SP3 6NA, UK
Tel: (+44 1722) 71 67 22   Fax: (+44 1722) 71 62 26
e-mail: technology@newbus.com
Web: www.newbus.com

Key personnel
Design Director: *Alan Ponsford*
Director: *Mike Kellaway*

Capabilities
Design and development of next-generation, electric traction and auxiliary systems, together with the related smart onboard controls for bus and coach applications. These products are a range of technical solutions for innovative future city transport systems.

Projects
Current projects include the design and development of a series hybrid electric drive for a 10.5 and 11.0 m midibus. This work includes the specification of the complete drive system, including motor and generator, NiMh battery and

system controls. The auxiliary options include electrically driven systems for power steering and compressed air supply.

New projects underway include a diesel series hybrid drive for a lightweight aluminium 9 m integral bus. On larger vehicles, the drives are being developed for multi-axle BRT systems. These again offer the advantages of high efficiency and a flexible source of energy. These would include diesel hybrid, fuel cell hybrid and trolleybus overhead line.

The Nichols Group

2 Savile Row, London W1S 3PA, UK
Tel: (+44 20) 72 92 70 00   Fax: (+44 20) 72 92 52 00
7-9 North St David Street, Edinburgh EH2 1AW
Tel: (+44 13) 15 24 94 50   Fax: (+44 13) 15 24 94 51
e-mail: info@nichols.uk.com
Web: www.nicholsgroup.co.uk

Key personnel
Chairman and Chief Executive: *Mike Nichols*
Executive Team: *Kathryn Nichols (Company Secretary and Corporate Services)*
  Frances Nichols (Creative Director)
  Debra Rymer (Financial and Public Sector Services)
  Bill McElroy (Transport Services)

Capabilities
The Nichols Group is an independent management consultancy specialising in advising on and managing large scale, complex and rapid changes covering both major capital investments and business change programmes. The group uses its expertise in project and programme management to initiate, develop and manage investments to maximise benefits for its clients. Since 1975 the Nichols Group has played a crucial role in many major transport schemes in the UK and southeast Asia.

Capabilities include strategic planning, programme management, project delivery and major project reviews, systems integration, risk management and training and development services.

Projects
Managed strategic planning Network Rail – West Coast Route Modernisation; programme management for Strategic Rail Authority Southern Region New Trains programme; strategic planning and project delivery for Metronet; project delivery for Tube Lines; risk management review for Union Railway (North); systems development for Rail Safety and Standard Board by creating the industry plan of ERTMS; project management, sponsorship training and development for London Underground Ltd; project management for Transport Initiatives Edinburgh.

Ødegaard & Danneskiold-Samsøe A/S

Titangade 15, DK-2200 Copenhagen N, Denmark
Tel: (+45) 35 31 10 00
Fax: (+45) 35 31 10 01
e-mail: ods@lr-ods.com
Web: www.lr-ods.com

Key personnel
Managing Director: *John Ødegaard*
Business Manager, Industry and Transportation: *Kurt Jager Sørensen*
Senior Consultants: *Henrik W Thrane, Uffe Degn, Claus M Myllerup, Ulrik Møller Rasmussen, Morten Theill Jensen*

Subsidiaries
Ødegaard & Danneskiold-Samsøe Norge AS
Ørsnesalléen 17, N-3120 Tønsberg, Norway
Tel: (+47) 33 35 22 70
Fax: (+47) 33 35 22 71
Manager: *Frank W Trulsen*

Background
Ødegaard & Danneskiold-Samsøe A/S is a member of the Lloyd's Register Group.

Capabilities
Consulting engineers, specialising in noise and vibration control of trains and other modes of transport. The company's services apply to all phases of the life of a rail vehicle, from design through to operation. Services offered include: design advice, noise and vibration analyses and troubleshooting.

Pallavan Transport Consultancy Services Limited

No 2, Central Depot, Pallavan Salai, Chennai 600 002, Tamilnadu, India
Tel: (+91 44) 25 36 16 78
Fax: (+91 44) 25 38 41 00
e-mail: ptcs@md5.vsnl.net.in

Key personnel
Managing Director: *R Krishnamurthy*
Senior Consultant (Systems): *G Marthandan*

Background
PTCS is a wholly owned company of the government of Tamil Nadu, established in 1984.

Capabilities
Consultancy services; undertakes turnkey projects and renders technical and managerial assistance in all facets of public transit and highway engineering. PTCS has the support of seven sister transport corporations operating a fleet of over 16,000 buses and the Institute of Road Transport (Research Institute) in the state of Tamilnadu. It also provides system design and software development.

Projects
Recently completed projects include household interview survey for corridor identification of Metro Rail for Chennai; traffic signs proposed in Chennai Port Area; traffic study at Lalapet ROB; traffic revalidation study for Chennai-Ennore Port connectivity; Koyambedu truck terminal studyl; Sathangadu truck terminal study; traffic studies at Coimbatore Byepass and Athupalam; traffic studies at Methanagar for proposed bridge connecting NMM road and Harrington Road and identification of corridors for Monorail Transit Systems for Chennai City.

Ongoing projects include route rationalisation study for Amalgamated Transport Corporation of Tamilnadu, traffic improvements in Ennore Port Area, traffic study for connecting NH-4 with Chennai Port, proposed maritime complex at Chennai for National Institute of Port Management and proposed bus stand at Tambaram.

Parsons Brinckerhoff

One Penn Plaza, New York, New York 10119, US
Tel: (+1 212) 465 50 00
Fax: (+1 212) 465 54 77
e-mail: info@pbworld.com
Web: www.pbworld.com

Key personnel
Chief Executive Officer: *Keith Hawksworth*
Chairman: *James L Lammie*
Chief Financial Officer: *Richard Schrader*

Major Operating Managers
Chief Operating Officer, PB International: *Stuart Glenn*
Managing Director, Europe/Africa: *Gregory R Ayres*
Managing Director, Asia: *Patrick T W Lun*
Managing Director, Middle East: *Stuart L Wallace*
Managing Director, Australia-Pacific: *Jim Mantle*
Chief Operating Officer, Americas: *George Pierson*
President, PB Facilities: *William S Roman*

Corporate offices

Australia, Argentina, Belgium, China, India, Indonesia, Japan, Kuwait, Malaysia, New Zealand, Philippines, Poland, Qatar, Saudi Arabia, Singapore, South Africa, South Korea, Spain, Switzerland, Taiwan, Thailand, United Arab Emirates, UK and US.

Capabilities

Parsons Brinckerhoff (PB) is one of the leaders in developing and operating infrastructure around the world, with 12,000 employees dedicated to meeting the needs of clients and communities in the Americas, Europe/Africa, the Middle East, Asia and Australia-Pacific regions. PB offers skills and resources in strategic consulting, planning, engineering, program/construction management, and operations for all modes of infrastructure, including transportation, power, community development, water and the environment.

PB provides multidisciplinary planning, engineering, program and construction management, and operations and maintenance services for all modes of rail transport – heavy rail and light rail, commuter and freight rail, automated people mover, and maglev and high-speed rail. PB is also equipped to respond to the industry's current critical needs in intermodal and multimodal transportation; track, structures and facility design and inspection; signal and communications systems; electrification; equipment analysis; rolling stock; maintenance facilities and management of assets. It provides clients with a full range of support, including alternatives evaluation, systems design, fire/life/safety programmes, systems assurance, environmental health and safety, operations and maintenance plans, simulations, procurement support, and testing and start-up.

Projects

Australia: Epping to Chatswood Rail Line: the 12.5 km rail line will provide a direct link between Epping and Chatswood, with three new stations, including one at Macquarie University. Construction began in 2002 and was scheduled for completion in 2008. PB has been involved in the project since the initial planning studies in 1996. More recently, as a subconsultant to the design-build contractor, Thiess Hochtief Joint Venture, PB provided structural design of the running tunnels and stations as well as construction-phase services.

China: Shenzhen Metro Line 3: Line 3 is the latest addition to the new Shenzhen metro network. When completed in 2009 it will have a total length of 32.7 km (6.9 km underground section and 25.8 km above ground section). It will run in an east-west direction from Lo Wu to Longgang with 19 stations planned (six underground and 13 above ground) plus one depot at Wanggang and a stabling yard at Longtung. PB is the lead consultant and is working in association with STEDI, a local Chinese Design Institute (DI), to provide project management consultancy and design supervision services for the client – Shenzhen Metro No 3 Line Investment Co Ltd.

Zhengzhou to Xi'an High Speed Passenger Dedicated Line PRC: The Zhengzhou to Xi'an line is a 458-km high-speed rail line between Zhengzhou in Henan province and Xi'an in Shannxi province in east-central China. It is the middle segment of a major program by the Chinese Ministry of Railways to build a high speed rail line specific for passenger travel from Xuzhou in Jiangsu province to Lanzhou in Gansu province, a distance of 1,400 km. The trains will travel at speeds of up to 350 km/h. As part of a joint venture consortium PB was awarded a contract to provide project management, system assurance, safety and risk management, and construction supervision services for the China Ministry of Railways.

Shijiazhuang -Taiyuan High Speed Passenger Dedicated Line PRC: scheduled for completion in December 31, 2008, the Shi-tai passenger dedicated high speed rail line runs from Shijiazhuang (capital of Hebei province) to Taiyuan (capital of Shanxi province), passing through Luquan, Xingjing, Yuxian, Shouyang, and Yangqu. It has an overall length 190 km and is designed for speeds of 200-250km/h. The alignment passes through mountainous terrain, through low foothills, then through Taihang Mountain, finally into the Jinzhong basin. The project involves the construction of the 27.8 km Taihangshan tunnel and the 11.5 km Nanling tunnel. PB is part of consortium providing construction supervision services to the Shi-Tai PDL Co.Ltd (with exception of the Shijiazhang and Taiyuan stations).

India: Delhi Metro (Phase I and II): Phase I of the Delhi Metro project was completed in April 2007 with the opening of the 6.3 km extension into Dwarka City which forms part of the 64 km project. Design began in July 2006 for Phase II of the system which will add more than 100 km of rail, extending it eastward to Noida and westward to Gurgeon by 2010. PB as part of a consortium is providing general engineering services to the Delhi Metro Rail Corporation.

Mumbai Metro: PB is the lead in a joint venture to provide project management, construction management and engineering services for the 11.5 km metro rail line with 12 elevated stations and a depot. Construction began in December 2006 with project completion expected by late 2009.

Singapore: MRT Circle Line (CCL) – The CCL, which is set to be fully complete in 2010, will cut travelling time and allow commuters to bypass busy interchanges like City Hall and Raffles Place. CCL will be a fully underground orbital line linking all radial lines leading to the city. The line will interchange with the North-South Line, East-West Line and North-East Line. The CCL will be 33.3 km long with approx 29 stations. The project will be implemented in five stages. PB is providing the detailed architectural C/S and mechanical/electrical engineer design service for stages 4 and 5. PB is also providing the M/E design services for the CCL Kim Chuan Depot and serving as independent checker for Contract 825 of Stage 1 CCL. Apart from providing consultancy services to the Land Transport Authority of Singapore, PB is also providing design services to three construction contracts for different contractors on CCL Stage 3.

Taiwan: Taiwan High-Speed Rail – The Taiwan High Speed Rail (THSR) opened on schedule in January 2007. The THSR extends 345 km from Taipei in the north to the southern port of Kaohsiung. The two-track system includes 48 kilometers of tunnels, 260 km of viaducts and bridges, and 40 km of cut and fill, plus eight stations, four main depots and stabling yards. The project used Japanese-built trains and high-speed Shinkansen technology in its first application outside Japan.

PB has been involved with the project since 1990, when it performed a feasibility study and preliminary alignment study. PB also assisted Taiwan High Speed Rail Corporation (THSRC), the private company formed to build, finance, operate and maintain the system, in preparing the concession proposal. PB was subsequently selected by THSRC to provide a range of multidisciplinary services, including project management and design technical support. PB was also awarded contracts for the design of the tunnel environmental system, station building services and detailed design and technical support of the main workshop and depots.

Turkey: Marmaray Project – The USD3 billion Marmaray Project includes a rail tunnel under the Bosphorus Strait and 76 km of new and upgraded commuter railway on both sides of the strait. There are 9.8 km of bored tunnels, 2.4 km of cut-and-cover tunnels, four new underground stations, and 37 new or upgraded surface stations. Construction on the project began in 2004 and is scheduled to be completed in 2011.

PB is engineer to a joint venture of four firms, called Avrasyaconsult, which has a contract for design, tender preparation and construction supervision of the Marmaray Project on behalf of the General Directorate of Railways, Harbours and Airports Construction of the Turkish Ministry of Transportation and Communication.

When completed in 2011, the new commuter rail system created by the Marmaray Project will offer dramatic improvements in mobility to the 14 million residents of metropolitan Istanbul.

UAE: Dubai Metro Purple Line – The 49-km Purple Line is the third of four public transit lines being developed by Dubai's Roads and Transport Authority and will extend from Dubai International Airport to the new Jebel Ali International Airport. The mostly elevated route will include six intermediate stations in addition to the terminal stations at each airport. Trains will average 100 km/h, reaching maximum speeds of 160 km/h. PB prepared the initial design of the system in 2007. The project was expected to be put to tender for construction in April 2008. Construction is expected to begin in January 2009 and be completed by December 2012. PB is responsible for delivery of the complete railway, including rolling stock; railway systems; civil and structural works; architectural and builder's works; mechanical and electrical systems; start-up, testing and commissioning; and defects liability. PB will carry out feasibility studies, develop the preliminary design and prepare EPC (engineer-procure-construct) contract documents for tender. The firm will tender the project for supply and construction, evaluate the returned tenders, and supervise construction of the new line on behalf of the RTA.

US: Bay Area Rapid Transit (BART) Extensions, San Francisco, California – PB has participated in several recent and ongoing extensions of San Francisco's Bay Area Rapid Transit (BART) system. Currently, PB is systems designer on an extension of BART to San Jose and the Norman Y. Mineta San Jose International Airport. In earlier assignments, PB was general engineering consultant for the extension of BART to Warm Springs and for the extension to San Francisco International Airport. PB has been involved with BART since its inception, serving in joint venture as GEC for the original 120-km system that opened in 1972.

California High-Speed Rail (Statewide-California) – The California High Speed Rail Authority is developing a 1,100-km high-speed rail network connecting San Diego, Los Angeles, Sacramento and San Francisco. PB has been involved with the project since the mid-1990s and prepared the first business plan and a program-level environmental impact report/environmental impact statement. Currently, as program manager, PB is responsible for planning, design, construction, testing and commissioning of the project, overseeing 75 other consulting firms.

CSX North Bergen Yard Reconfiguration, North Bergen, New Jersey – PB was responsible for track, civil and structural design as well as environmental and permitting work.

METRA Circumferential Rail Alternative Study, Chicago, Illinois – PB performed feasibility studies for providing service on two existing freight rail lines that travel around the Chicago metropolitan region.

Minnesota Intermodal Rail Terminal Study – PB undertook a three-part study to determine the rail operating parameters, develop an operating plan and conceptual designs of the proposed rail terminal and create a pro forma business plan for a new intermodal terminal facility to be shared by Burlington, Northern Santa Fe, Union Pacific, and the Canadian Pacific Railroads in the Minneapolis-St. Paul Twin Cities area.

Railtran Commuter Rail and Intermodal Transportation Center, Fort Worth, Texas – PB provided project management, project controls, systems engineering, and construction management services to the Fort Worth Transportation Authority (the T) for extension of service from South Irving to downtown Fort Worth.

MARC Commuter Rail Master Plan – PB provided railroad planning and operations services to address growth options for the 300 km system between northern portions of West Virginia and Maryland and the Baltimore and Washington, D.C. business districts.

UK: Network Rail – PB provided programme management support for West Coast Route Modernisation, train protection and warning system, and southern zone power supplies upgrade.

Network Rail (Southern) – PB provided programme management support for West Coast route modernisation, train protection and warning system, and southern zone power supplies upgrade.

Network Rail (Southern) – PB is providing multidisciplinary design (permanent way, signalling, telecoms, civils, M&E, E&P) and track re-modelling support in association with the station capacity improvement programme in the southern region (including West Croydon and Gatwick Airport).

Thameslink – PB is supporting the client with permanent way, signalling and platform extension enhancement packages. PB has also recently won a framework contract to support further enhancements to the recently announced GBP5.2bn Thameslink project.

Transport for London, London Underground Ltd – PB is providing programme assurance capability in support of the implementation of the PPP projects on London Underground and also technical support to Chief Engineer's group on power supply and tunnel ventilation modelling. PB is also undertaking independent engineering reviews of TfL project management processes, and providing programme management to TfL on the East London and North London Lines, which are the key arterial routes for the 2012 Olympics.

Union Rail – For the Channel Tunnel Rail Link Project (CTRL), PB is providing mechanical and electrical services design, tunnel ventilation design, safety assurance and RAMS for Contract 588 on the GBP2.5 billion project.

TIE – PB is providing comprehensive systems design services for the Edinburgh Tram. Responsibilities include delivering a fully detailed design and specifications for overall system functionality, technical requirements for system components and the infrastructure to support the system.

Greater Manchester Passenger Transport – GMPTE has selected PB as delivery partner for the implementation of its seven year development and enhancement programme for Metrolink, Manchester's tram system. PB will support GMPTE on a range of projects including the expansion and refurbishment of the existing system.

Vietnam: Ho Chi Minh City Urban Railway Construction Project, BenThanh-SuoiTien Section (Line1): the HCMC Management Authority for Urban Railways (MAUR) Line 1 project extends from downtown Ben Thanh Market to Suoi Tien in District 9. The route is approximately 20 km long with three underground and 11 elevated stations and a depot. The system includes a major balanced cantilever bridge crossing the Saigon River.

The system is heavy rail, powered by a 1.5 kV dc overhead catenary system and is based on the Japanese Standard Urban Railway System for Asia (STRASYA) specification with a top design speed of 110 km/h.

PB in joint venture, was appointed by MAUR in December 2007 to be the general consultant responsible for design, procurement, construction, commissioning and operation and maintenance of HCMC Line 1.

Peter Davidson Consultancy

Brownlow House, Ravens Lane, Berkhamsted HP4 2DX, UK
Tel: (+44 1442) 87 90 75
Fax: (+44 1442) 87 97 76
e-mail: mail@peter-davidson.co.uk
Web: www.peter-davidson.co.uk

Key personnel
Managing Director: *Peter W Davidson*

Capabilities
Specialist expertise in transport modelling, market research, railway planning and computer software for transport applications; computer-aided stated preference experimentation, disaggregate modelling techniques and geographical information systems using in-house software.

Projects
Previous projects have included the Taunton Transport Strategy which developed a sustainable transport strategy capable of meeting the travel needs of Taunton into the next century.

Research into the contribution of individual elements of a quality bus service to the overall perception of the service using stated preference techniques to identify passengers' willingness to pay for each element. Elements included low-floor buses, real-time information, friendly drivers, bus lanes and other similar criteria.

Research into perception of different forms of public transport for park-and-ride for Merseytravel, UK, including bus, road train, ultra-light rail and LRT.

European research into strategic trip matrices for the Trans-European network.

Pöyry Infra (Hannover) GmbH

Calenberger Esplanade 3, D-30169 Hanover, Germany
Tel: (+49 511) 929 75 70   Fax: (+49 511) 929 75 77
e-mail: infra.hannover.de@poyry.com
Web: www.transtec-consult.de

Key personnel
Managing Director: *Rainer Johannsmeier*

Background
Formerly TransTec Consult, Pöyry Infra (Hannover) GmbH is an independent consulting firm for planning, design, implementation and operation of public transport systems and is part of the Pöyry Group.

Capabilities
Organisational and financing including: preparing operators and authorities for competitive market participation; development of institutional solutions; elaboration of procurement schemes and contract documents; life-cycle-cost estimation; cost-benefit analyses; funding and financing concepts; operating and investment cost evaluation. Planning and operation including: transport master plans, multimodal studies; patronage forecasting; planning of public transport supply; operational planning; system appraisals; marketing concepts; project management and institutional support. Systems and technology including: feasibility studies; operation and maintenance concepts; rolling stock, civil and technical infrastructure design; tender specification documents; support of transit system procurement and implementation; system acceptance and staff training and certification.

Projects
Argentina: Buenos Aires, project management support and trackwork quality control for metro refurbishment.
Germany: Bremen, project management of regional LRT system; Brunswick, introduction of a regional LRT (RegioStadtBahn) in the Greater Brunswick area; Hanover, support of authorities in preparing procurement of passenger rail services, priority system for traffic signals; Kiel, concept for further development of regional rail authority; Neckar-Alb, operation concept for the introduction of a regional LRT (RegioStadtBahn) in the Neckar-Alb region.
Greece: Athens, conceptual design of tramway.
Israel: Haifa, feasibility study on guided buses for upgrading public transport in Haifa.
Kazakhstan: Astana, assessment of transit system options for new capital.

Netherlands: Utrecht, detailed design for expansion of Bus Rapid Transit System.
Norway: Bergen, light rail rolling stock tender specification and procurement support.
Poland: Wroclaw, preparation of suburban rail services in lower Silesia for competitive tendering.
Romania: Krasnodar, economic assessment of tramway and tramcar refurbishment programme.
Venezuela: Valencia, quality control of metro alignment design and trackwork supply.

Prima Services Group Ltd

Prima House, 2 Roebuck Place, 110 Roebuck Road, Chessington, Surrey KT9 1TL, UK
Tel: (+44 20) 83 97 81 11   Fax: (+44 20) 83 97 81 19
Web: www.psgl.com

Key personnel
Managing Director: *Don Clarke*
Director: *Graham Jones*
Financial Director: *Steve Clark*

Associated company
Atlas Stirling Rail BV

Capabilities
Recruitment, training and contracting services to the heavy rail, mass transit and light rail industries. ISO 9002, Network Rail, SNCB, NS and London Underground approved. Permanent way and signal testing.

Projects
Installation of approximately 250 S&C units following gauge corner cracking initiative; plain line renewals and excess drainage; signalling maintenance and new works; re-signalling schemes; points renewals; correlation surveys; installation, testing and commissioning works; complimentary works, fencing, bridge repairs, anti-vandal screens.

Prose Ltd

Zürcherstrasse 41, CH-8400 Winterthur, Switzerland
Tel: (+41 52) 262 74 00
Fax: (+41 52) 262 74 01
e-mail: info@prose.ch
Web: www.prose.ch

Key personnel
General Manager: *Stefan Bühler*

Background
Founded in 1982, Prose acquired in 2001, the measuring and testing department of Bombardier Transportation (Switzerland), formerly SLM.

Capabilities
Consulting, project management, development and design of rolling stock, in particular, bogies. Measuring and testing of railway vehicles. Prose is an accredited test laboratory for railway rolling stock.

Ptarmigan Transport Solutions Ltd

Arran House, Arran Road, Perth PH1 3DZ, UK
Tel: (+44 1738) 45 92 68
Web: www.ptarmigansolutions.co.uk

Key personnel
Managing Director: *Stuart Newing-Davis*
Finance Director: *Sarah Newing-Davis*
Marketing Manager: *Aaron Goodrum*
Training Consultants: *Brian Raven, Kevin Wood, Simon Bales, David Cavander, Andrea Dilks, Milo Newing, Donna Lythgoe*

Capabilities

Ptarmigan Transport Solutions provides commercial and operations training services to the rail and bus industries. It offers ticket training in Fujitsu Star, Tribute, Shere SMART, Cubic FASTIS and Avantix ticket formats, RJIS, Successful Presentation of Evidence (SPOE), penalty fares, revenue protection, conflict avoidance, induction training, disability awareness, customer excellence, up-selling, rail geography, health and safety and barrier management. The company provides operational training for conductor guards, platform staff and managers and personal track safety training. The company also provides temporary training staff and ticket office staff to the railway industry.

QinetiQ Rail

Cody Technology Park, Ivey Road, Farnborough GU14 0LX, UK
Tel: (+44 8700) 10 09 42
Web: www.qinetiq.com

Key personnel
Chief Executive Officer: *Sir John Chisholm*
Chief Financial Officer: *Graham Love*

Background
Formerly DERA, the UK's defence research agency, QinetiQ has 50 years of experience in transport research and development for military and government bodies.

In March 2007 Nomad Digital, providers of specialist mobility networks, acquired QinetiQ Rail for 8.6 per cent of Nomad's ordinary share capital.

Capabilities
System engineering, human sciences, asset management and project management. These cover the fields of: traffic control; rail safety; infrastructure management; management services; rolling stock engineering; and passenger services.

Developments
QinetiQ Rail is currently working with leading train operators, train builders and infrastructure owners across Europe on a number of projects relating to its Connected Carriage™ system for delivering broadband services to moving trains.

Security services include CCTV linked to onboard recording equipment, displayed on the train manager's PDA, or uplinked to the train company's operations centre. Public Internet access via Wi-Fi enabled laptops, media content delivered to laptops or onboard display screens and customer information services, including real-time location and timetable information. Onboard voice over Wi-Fi communications to keep the train manager in constant contact with the driver, management information (uplinking of on-train monitoring and recording equipment data and GPS location), EPOS for ticket and catering sales to reduce credit card fraud and stock control for catering items. The Connected Carriage system comprises of the on-train components, the 'train-to-shore' links, and the back-office systems which are hosted in QinetiQ Rail's carrier-grade Network Operations Centre.

The QSS Group Ltd

2 St George's House, Vernon Gate, Derby DE1 1UQ, UK
Tel: (+44 1332) 22 14 00   Fax: (+44 1332) 22 14 01
e-mail: enquiries@theqssgroup.co.uk
Web: www.theqssgroup.co.uk

Key personnel
Managing Director: *Kenneth Mee*
Operations Director : *Peter Abbott*

Capabilities
The QSS Group Ltd offers customers practical assistance, training, consultancy and assessment services in management systems development (safety, quality, engineering and environmental management), risk assessment and performance improvement.

The Railway Consultancy Ltd

1st Floor South Tower, Crystal Palace Station, London SE19 2AZ, UK
Tel: (+44 20) 86 76 03 95   Fax: (+44 20) 87 78 74 39
e-mail: info@railcons.com
Web: www.railcons.com

Key personnel
Managing Director: *Dr Nigel G Harris*
Senior Analysts: *Matthew Smith; Luke Ripley*

Capabilities
Planning, economics and management for metros and railway systems; demand estimation; train service planning and simulations; timetable preparation; contingency planning; transport policy and management advice; business planning; accessibility and energy issues.

Projects
Recent projects have included: franchise bidding support; option assessment for British Government's railway High Level Output Statement; project appraisal for station upgrades at Salford Central (for GMPTE) and Bletchley (for English Partnerships); train service modelling of infrastructure enhancements for London Underground Ltd; train service performance and station audits of the suburban railway system in the Oslo area for NSB; database population for Network Rail; operational research into the optimum door width of refurbished suburban rolling stock for South West Trains: a study on crowding and train service planning for an international group of metro; demand estimation for a proposed station at Carr Mill, for Merseytravel; industrial research for equipment suppliers; a major study on the impacts of the privatisation of British Rail; an operational feasibility study into one of the proposed options for London's Crossrail project for London Underground Ltd.

Key in-house tools available for projects include the GCOST™ model for estimating the passenger demand, revenue and time-saving impact of new stations, and the TRAKATTK train service simulation.

RailWorks Corporation

Corporate Office, 5 Penn Plaza, New York, New York 10001, US
Tel: (+1 212) 502 79 00
e-mail: ksimpson@railworks.com
Web: www.railworks.com

Key personnel
Chairman: *Ray List*
President and Chief Executive Officer: *Jeffrey M Levy*
Executive Vice-President: *John August*

Subsidiaries
CPI Concrete Products, Inc
HSQ Technology
LK Comstock & Company, Inc
Pacific Northern Rail Contractors, Inc
PNR Railworks Inc
PNR Leasing, Ltd
RailWorks Canada, Inc
RailWorks Track Services, Inc
RailWorks Track Systems, Inc
RailWorks Track – Texas, Inc
RailWorks Transit, Inc

Capabilities
Integrated rail system services and products, active in new construction, rehabilitation, track repair and maintenance, signalling, communications, electrical and other track-related systems, and rail products manufacturing and supply.

Ranbury Management Group

Level 15, 344 Queen Street, Brisbane, Queensland 4000, Australia
Tel: (+61 7) 32 11 23 00   Fax: (+61 7) 32 11 29 13
e-mail: ranburymgmt@ranbury.com.au
Web: www.ranbury.com.au

Key personnel
Directors: *Nic Tilley (Chairman), David Porter (Joint Managing Director), Scott Kennelly (Joint Managing Director), Ross Hunter*

Capabilities
A multidisciplinary rail, property and infrastructure consultancy with management and engineering expertise in rolling stock design and manufacture; systems, signalling and communication; and the redevelopment of railway property. Ranbury's services also include business process management of assets including information systems, financial systems, accounting systems, compliance and strategic planning.

Projects
Projects include: infrastructure for Queensland Rail; heritage activities for Queensland Rail; alliance managers and project management services; design, manufacture and commission of the Cairns Tilt Train (Queensland Rail and EDI Rail); project management of the design, manufacture, commission and finance of the Sydney Millennium Train (EDI Rail); rail infrastructure construction interface Lang Park Redevelopment (Watpac/Multiplex); software project management, train operational systems (Queensland Rail); Port Botany Freight Project review (Rail Infrastructure Corporation); Cairns Transit Centre Development (Queensland Transport).

RITES Ltd

Rites Bhawan, Plot No 1, Sector 29, Gurgaon, Haryana, 122 001, India
Tel: (+91 124) 257 16 66   Fax: (+91 124) 257 16 60
e-mail: info@rites.com
Web: www.rites.com

Key personnel
Chairman: *Rajkamal Rao*
Managing Director: *V K Agarwal*
Technical Director: *Anil Madan*
Projects Director: *B K Makhija*

Background
RITES, a Government of India Enterprise, was established in 1974 under the aegis of the Indian Railways. Over the last three decades, RITES has grown and diversified from being a rail consultant to a company of consultants, engineers and project managers. RITES is a multi-disciplinary ISO 9001: 2000 certified consultancy organisation in the fields of transportation, information and related technologies and provides a comprehensive array of services from one location. RITES, with recognition from multi-lateral funding agencies, has experience in 62 countries in Africa, Europe, Middle East, Latin America, South East Asia, UK and US.

Capabilities
Engineering consultancy and project management services in the field of transportation, infrastructure and related technologies. It provides comprehensive consultancy services from concept to commissioning in the fields of railways, urban transport, urban development and urban

engineering, roads and highways, airports, ropeways, inland waterways, ports and harbours, information technology and export packages of rolling stock and railway related equipment.

RITES diversified service packages include feasibility, design and detailed engineering, multi-modal transport studies, project management and construction supervision, quality assurance and management, ISO-9000/ISO-14000, material management, workshop management, operation and maintenance, system engineering, economic and financial evaluation, financing plan and privatisation, railway electrification, signalling and telecommunication, environmental impact assessment, training and human resource development. RITES employs nearly 2,200 staff including 1,200 specialists of high professional standing in the fields of engineering, management and planning.

Projects

Recent projects include:

Afghanistan: Procurement facilitation services to Afghanistan Reconstruction Development Services (ADRS) under World Bank funded Public Administration and capacity building project.

Angola: Technical assistance and supply of locomotives, coaches, pick-up vehicles and buses, rail-cum road vehicles.

Bangladesh: Integrated export packages for broad-gauge (BG) diesel locomotives and maintenance of metre-gauge (MG) diesel locomotives, training of railway officials.

Colombia: Maintenance management services for rolling stock for Atlantic Railway.

India (domestic): Major member of the international consortium commissioned as 'general consultants' for the Mass Rapid Transit System (MRTS) for Delhi. Major urban/regional planning assignments in Delhi and National Capital region; Detailed project reports of MRTS in Delhi Phase II, Cuttack and Bhubaneshwar, Chandigarh, Vadodara, Bangalore; Project management consultancy for high capacity bus system (HCBS) Delhi; ROB in Punjab; feasibility study for rail link in Noida, Greater Noida and Ghaziabad; Engineering consultancy service for dedicated multi-modal high axle load freight corridors (Eastern and Western corridors) for Indian Railways; Multi-modal transport study for Planning Commission; Development of crash-worthy design of passenger coaches, development of self-steering freight bogies, frame-less tank wagons; Design and construction supervision of 12 km long tunnel in J&K rail link; Design of rail-cum road bridges over Brahmaputra and Ganga rivers; Operation and maintenance management of railway track infrastructure and rolling stocks of power plants and other industries; EIA studies for hydro-electric projects in Chattisgarh and for State Electricity Board, Central Water Commission, National Frontier Railway, and various railway lines; Environmental and social impact assessment for Delhi Metro Corridor Phase II, Indo-Nepal ICD, Ahmedabad Metro. ADB funded EIA, SIA and RAP studies for Ministry of Railways; Bid process management of the ADB financed accounting reforms project for Indian Railways.

Malaysia: Expert services for engineering design, construction and project management for railway track and electrification together with traffic and consultancy on route management system to Malaysian Railways.

Mozambique: One of the consortium members of the Beira Rail Corridor project and providing project management services.

Myanmar: Supply of locomotives and coaches to the Myanmar Railways (MR).

Senegal: Feasibility study for a new railway link between Zinginchor and Dhakar, Republic of Senegal. Supply of in-service diesel locomotives and MG day coaches to PTB, Senegal.

Sharjah: Signalling and design project and civil design for permanent way project for WS Atkins.

Sri Lanka: Training of railway personnel.

Sudan: Supply of in-service and new locomotives, rehabilitation of locomotives, wagon spares and rehabilitation of traction motors.

Tanzania: Lead partner in concession of the Tanzania Railway Corporation and technical advisory services.

Uzbekistan: Consultancy services for computerisation of financial system of Uzbekistan Railways, services of a chief document specialist for Tashguzar-Kum Kurgan new railway line project.

Roundel Ltd

7 Rosehart Mews, Westbourne Grove, Notting Hill, London W11 3TY, UK
Tel: (+44 20) 72 21 19 51   Fax: (+44 20) 72 21 18 43
e-mail: info@roundel.com
Web: www.roundel.com

Key personnel

Directors: *Tony Howard, Michael Denny, Ian St John*

Capabilities

Corporate identity design for transport systems and operators including service branding, livery design, signing and information design, branded environments and corporate communications.

Projects

Branding, livery design, environments and passenger information for Kowloon-Canton Railway; livery designs for Royal Train locomotives and Class 92 Channel Tunnel locomotives; branding and livery design for Railfreight, Great Western, Finnish State Railways and Southern; signing and information design for Docklands Light Railway and for all CTRL stations including St Pancras International; Light Rail system brands, environments and information design for Amey/Bechtel; design guidelines for London Underground and corporate communication design for ABB.

RTA Rail Tec Arsenal Fahrzeugversuchsanlage GmbH

Paukerwerkstrasse 3, A-1210 Vienna, Austria
Tel: (+43 1) 25 68 08 10   Fax: (+43 1) 25 68 08 16 00
e-mail: contact@rta.eu
Web: www.rta.eu

Key personnel

Managing Director: *Franz Hrachowitz*
Technical/Scientific Director: *Gabriel Haller*

Background

Rail Tec Arsenal is an internationally active, neutral and independent research and testing institute for rail and road vehicles, new transport systems and technical facilities that are subject to extreme climatic conditions.

Rail Tec Arsenal operates two modern climatic wind tunnels designed to optimise thermal comfort in public transport vehicles (rail and road vehicles) and to investigate and improve the availability and safety of systems in sensitive industrial areas.

Rail Tec Arsenal was founded by Arsenal Research and the international rail vehicle industry in order to safeguard the facilities and specific expertise necessary for the performance of climatic tests on a long-term basis. The consortium comprises: Innovative Science Solutions (26 per cent); ALSTOM Transport (14.8 per cent); Bombardier Transportation (29.6 per cent); Siemens Transportation Systems (14.8 per cent); Ansaldobreda and Firema Trasporti (together 14.8 per cent).

Capabilities

The Vienna Climatic Wind Tunnel , claimed by the company to be the world's largest, commenced operation on 1 January 2003. The testing facility consists of two separate climatic wind tunnels (CWT) for the testing of vehicles under extreme weather conditions. The large CWT is 100 m, long

enough to accommodate a train consisting of a power car and two carriages. At 31 m, the test section of the small CWT is long enough for a carriage, a trailer truck or a bus. The maximum air speed here is 120 km/h; the dynamometer (for road vehicles) has a maximum power rating of 250 kW. The air flow to the front of the test object can be shut off completely by means of flaps installed at the head of the test section, in order to simulate, for example, a stop and go cycle with doors opening. A soak room is directly attached to the smaller CWT. This can be used for temperature conditioning of vehicles (adaptation of material temperatures) but also for climatic cycling tests (for example, thermal simulation of train passage through a tunnel in winter). Two separate preparation halls with controlled access provide room for setup, development and changeover.

SCI Verkehr GmbH

Schanzenstrasse   117,   D-20357   Hamburg, Germany
Tel: (+49 40) 507 19 70   Fax: (+49 40) 50 71 97 20
e-mail: hamburg@sci.de
Web: www.sci.de

Main office

Vor den Siebenburgen 2, D-50676 Cologne, Germany
Tel: (+49 221) 931 78 20   Fax: (+49 221) 931 78 78
e-mail: koeln@sci.de

Project office

Novalisstrasse 7, D-10115 Berlin, Germany
Tel: (+49 30) 283 45 40   Fax: (+49 30) 28 44 54 20
e-mail: berlin@sci.de

Background

SCI Verkehr has established itself in the railway market as an independent and consultant specialist having begun its activities as a business field in the company SCI Engineering Consulting. SCI Verkehr employs over 30 staff.

Services

SCI Verkehr offers a strategic management consultancy service, including market analysis and feasibility studies for manufacturers of rail vehicles, transport equipment and transfer facilities, public and private transport companies, port authorities, interest groups and trade unions, authorities responsible for public transport as well as for traffic and economic departments of the federation, federal states and local authorities. SCI Multi Client Studies provide analyses and future prospects for the railway market.

Scott Brownrigg

Tower House, 10 Southampton Street, London WC2E 7HA, UK
Tel: (+44 20) 72 40 77 66   Fax (+44 20) 72 40 24 54
e-mail: enquiries@scottbrownrigg.com
Web: www.scottbrownrigg.com

Key personnel

Chairman: *Jonathan Hill*
Director: *Martyn Stutchbury*
Marketing and Communications Manager: *Penny Brash*

Background

Previously called Design Research Unit, the company became part of Scott Brownrigg in August 2004.

Capabilities

Station planning, architecture, interior design, graphic design, wayfinding and urban planning.

Projects

Architectural and planning work has been undertaken for many transport authorities including projects for rail/light rail and metro systems in Bangkok, Copenhagen, Hong Kong, London and Nottingham (UK). Completed works include metro and rail systems in Athens, Baghdad, Birmingham, Kuala Lumpur, Singapore, Taipei and Toronto. Graphic design and wayfinding for Network Rail, Docklands Light Rail, South West Trains and Centro in UK.

Scott Wilson Railways Ltd

Tricentre 3, Newbridge Square, Swindon SN1 1BY, UK
Tel: (+44 1793) 50 85 00
Fax: (+44 1793) 550 85 01
e-mail: rail.marketing@scottwilson.com
Web: www.scottwilson.com

Key personnel
Chief Executive: *Keith Wallace*
Director of Operations: *Richard Jones*
Director of Projects: *Mark Jackson*
Human Resources Manager: *Richard Oldham*
Technical Director, Signalling and Communications: *David Nye*
Head of Civil and Engineering and Construction: *David Lickiss*
Technical Director, Permanent Way: *Selwyn Dixon*
Head of Railway Consultancy: *David Coles*
Head of Railway Electrification and Power Engineering: *Rob Tidbury*
International Projects Director: *Derek Holden*
Finance Manager: *Pat Forde*
Head of Facilities Management: *Peter Crane*
Commercial Manager: *Martin Pickup*
Group Health and Safety Advisor: *Dave Sutton*
Computing Manager: *Mick Fry*
CADD Development Manager: *Mike Clarke*
Marketing Manager: *Lorraine Floyd*

Other offices
The company has offices in Glasgow, Birmingham, Bradford-Upon-Avon, Crewe, Glasgow, London, Plymouth, Swindon and York in the UK and also in Brisbane, Australia.

Background
Scott Wilson provides multi-disciplinary services to the railway sector and currently employs almost 600 staff. The company opened its first international base in Brisbane, Australia in September 2007.

Capabilities
The company provides consultancy services that cover all aspects of rail infrastructure planning, design, project management, construction supervision and rail maintenance. The range of services encompasses over 20 disciplines including: civil and structural engineering, construction management; environmental services; geotechnical services; permanent way; project management; railway electrification and power engineering; safety training, signalling and telecommunications; track-bed investigations; tunnelling, railway consultancy and operational modelling.

With its working relationships with strategic partners, Scott Wilson is able to offer further specialist services as required.

SEMTCAR

Société anonyme d'Économie Mixte des Transportes Collectifs de l'Agglomération Rennaise
1 rue Geneviève de Gaulle Anthonioz, CS 80827, 35208 Rennes, Cedex 2, France
Tel: (+33 2) 99 85 89 30
Fax: (+33 2) 99 65 11 51
e-mail: info@semtcar.fr
Web: www.semtcar.fr

Key personnel
President and Director General: *Daniel Delaveau*
Managing Director: *Guy Malbrancke*

Background
Created in 1992, SEMTCAR (Société anonyme d'Économie Mixte des Transportes Collectifs de l'Agglomération Rennaise) is a semi-public company with capital held by Rennes Métropole (68.7 per cent) and Transdev (30 per cent).

Capabilities
Project control, studies, advice, setting up complex operations, project management, risk management. SEMTCAR specialises in the following areas in both public and private contracts: civil engineering, geotechnical engineering, road systems, networks, transportation systems, electromechanical equipment, urbanism, architecture and communications.

Contracts
Successful management of the construction project (studies and constructing) of Rennes first light rail metro line on behalf of Rennes Metropole urban community and is currently studying and preparing the second line of exclusive lane transportation. SEMTCAR is also providing its services to other national and overseas projects in the framework of project control assistance contracts for Paris airports, ADP and Turin.

Serco Raildata

Derwent House, rtc Business Park, London Road, Derby DE24 8UP, UK
Tel: (+44 1332) 26 35 84
Fax: (+44 1332) 26 24 38
e-mail: srds@serco.railtest.co.uk;
    kfretwell@serco.railtest.co.uk
Web: www.serco.com

Key personnel
Chief Executive: *Christopher Hyman*
General Manager: *Kevin Fretwell*

Background
Serco Raildata is the specialist print and data management division of Serco Railtest Ltd.

Capabilities
Serco Raildata offers professional information management services, certified to BS EN ISO 9001: 2000 quality assurance standards. These include electronic delivery systems for rapid retrieval of structural text and graphics, database management services, parts cataloguing, document, drawing and parts management, data packaging, electronic delivery systems and archiving services.

SMRT Engineering Pte Ltd (SMRTE)

300 Bishan Road, 579828, Singapore
Tel: (+65) 54 85 35   Fax: (+64) 53 76 45
e-mail: EngDivProject@smrt.com.sg
Web: www.smrt.com.sg

Key personnel
Managing Director: *Harry Tan Chuan Huat*
President and Chief Executive Officer, SMRT Corporation Ltd: *Saw Phaik Hwa*

Background
SMRTE was set up in August 1999 and is a subsidiary of SMRT Corporation Ltd.

Services
Operations and maintenance services, engineering consultancy and project management, as well as providing communication infrastructure through the leasing of fibre-optic cables and related services.

Developments
In October 2005, the Singapore Land Transport Consortium was formed with SMRTE's participation. The consortium, supported by International Enterprise (IE) Singapore, utilises collective capabilities in regional business opportunities relating to land transport systems.

Socialdata

Institut für Verkehrs- und Infrastrukturforschung GmbH
Hans-Grässel-Weg 1, D-81375, Germany
Postfach 701629, D-81375 Munich, Germany
Tel: (+49 89) 710 81   Fax: (+49 89) 71 64 20
e-mail: socialdata@socialdata.de
Web: www.socialdata.de

Key personnel
Managing Director: *Werner Brög*

Other offices
Socialdata has other offices in Austria, Australia, Netherlands, UK and US.

Capabilities
Preparation of information and options for marketing and planning; travel surveys, cycle, pedestrian and parking studies; urban and interurban transport; price effect and tariff modelling; travel demand management; travel marketing.

Southdowns Environmental Consultants Ltd

Suite A3, 16 Station Street, Lewes, East Sussex BN7 2DB, UK
Tel: (+44 1273) 48 81 86   Fax: (+44 1273) 48 81 87
e-mail: prw@southdowns.eu.com
Web: www.southdowns.eu.com

Key personnel
Directors: *Patrick Williams, Rick Methold, Dr R Hood*

Capabilities
Southdowns Environmental Consultants Ltd specialises in the measurement, calculation, evaluation and mitigation of environmental noise and vibration from railways.

Projects
Channel Tunnel Rail Link (2006); West Coast Main Line (2003); Docklands Light Rail (2006); Crossrail (2007); Southern Railway (2006); Croydon Tram Link Extension (2007).

Southern Vectis plc

Nelson Road, Newport PO30 1RD, UK
Tel: (+44 1983) 52 24 56   Fax: (+44 1983) 52 49 61
Managing Director: *Stuart Linn*

Capabilities
Drawing on the company's bus and coach experience, its consultancy section offers expertise in commercial, management, marketing and ticketing aspects of bus and tramway operation, including network design/assessment and commercial franchising.

Projects
Recent projects have included the group's public transport database and access system, Xephos, which was successfully trialled in South Wales and drives the nationally backed Great Britain Bus Timetable, other printed material and the national multimode user-pays telephone enquiry service, Travel Call.

Steer Davies Gleave

Headquarters
28-32 Upper Ground, London SE1 9PD, UK
Tel: (+44 20) 79 10 50 00   Fax: (+44 20) 79 10 50 01
e-mail: sdginfo@sdgworld.net
Web: www.steerdaviesgleave.com

Key personnel

Chairman: *Colin Rowland*
Non-Executive Directors: *Jim Steer, Andy Costain*
Chief Executive: *Stephen Crouch*
Sales and Marketing Director: *Fred Beltrandi*
Operations and Staff Director: *Tim Ryder*

Other offices

Steer Davies Gleave has offices in Canada, Chile, Colombia, Italy, Germany, Spain and the UK.

Background

In April 2007 Steer Davies Gleave completed the final stage of the transfer of ownership to its employees with a reorganisation of its board of directors.

Capabilities

Policy; business development; strategic planning; advice on privatisation and open access regimes; economic regulation; passenger and freight demand and revenue forecasting; feasibility studies for new and/or reopened lines and stations; rolling stock procurement; franchise evaluation; performance indicators; project finance; public funding case development; operational analysis; marketing and market research; civil engineering, multi-modal freight interchanges, business strategy and policy, market research and insight, consultation and participation, modelling and forecasting, transport planning and regeneration, feasibility and design, environment, appraisal, project management, travel behaviour, tourism, visual communications, transport technology, freight and logistics.

Projects

Argentina: Business case for Buenos Aires suburban railways
Australia: Sydney-Canberra high-speed rail
Chile: Santiago-Valparaiso high-speed link; business case for passenger rail services, Santiago
Colombia: Transmilénio; Fenoco freight rail business case
EU: Rail liberalisation impact study for European Commission; track charging systems, EU
Italy: High-speed rail business model; rail feasibility study for Siracusa-Gela line, Sicily; light rail feasibility study for Alghero-Sassari line, Sardinia; rolling stock procurement and strategy for Trenitalia
South Africa: Audit of Gautrain high-speed link, Johannesburg
Spain: Business case for Perpignan-Figueras high-speed line
Sweden: Arlanda airport rail link
UK: Franchise advice to Virgin Rail Group, First Group, Serco and Chiltern Railways; Mersey Electrics franchise evaluation; Thameslink 2000 transportation; business case for Network Rail (Railtrack at the time) and Strategic Rail Authority; Crossrail business case for Strategic Rail Authority; East Coast Main Line business case review; UK high-speed rail development study for the Commission for Integrated Transport; Scottish Strategic Rail Study for Scottish Executive; East-West Rail Link, Ebbw Vale rail strategy, Welsh Development Agency
US: Concession bid support for urban rail services, Boston

Stratec SA

Avenue Adolphe Lacomble 69-71, Box 8, B-1030 Brussels, Belgium
Tel: (+32 2) 735 09 95   Fax: (+32 2) 735 49 17
e-mail: stratec@stratec.be
Web: www.stratec.be

Key personnel

Managing Director: *Hugues Duchateau*

Capabilities:

Transport planning and engineering; regional and urban development planning; environmental management; public service management; business strategy; travel demand management programmes.

STV Group

205 West Welsh Drive, Douglassville, Pennsylvania 19518, US
Tel: (+1 610) 385 82 00   Fax: (+1 610) 385 85 01
e-mail: info@stvinc.com
Web: www.stvinc.com

STV Incorporated
225 Park Avenue South, New York, New York 10003, US
Tel: (+1 212) 777 44 00
Fax: (+1 212) 529 52 37

Key personnel

Chairman and Chief Executive Officer: *D M Servedio*
Key Rail Staff: *W F Matts, M Gagliardi, D Borger, C Holliday, M Boyle, M Lam, N Altebrando, A Venturato, B Jabbonsky*

Capabilities

Transport planning; system and facility design; rolling stock engineering; operations and maintenance analysis.

Systra SA

5 avenue du Coq, F-75009 Paris, France
Tel: (+33 1) 40 16 61 00
Fax: (+33 1) 40 16 61 04
e-mail: systra@systra.com
Web: www.systra.com

Key personnel

Chairman: *Michel Cornil*
Managing Director: *Philippe Citroën*
Senior Vice-President, Engineering: *Eric Leca*
Senior Vice-President, Europe: *André Ohnheiser*
Senior Executive Vice-President, Asia Pacific: *Jean-Christophe Hugonnard*
Senior Executive Vice-President, Americas, Africa and Middle-East: *Arnaud Valranges*
Senior Executive Vice-President, France: *Gérard Chaldoreille*
Senior Vice-President Vice-President, Human Resources: *Anne-Geneviève Gariel*

Subsidiaries

MVA Consultancy Ltd, UK
MVA, Hong-Kong
Systra Consulting, US
CANARAIL, Canada
SOTEC Ingénierie, France

Other subsidiaries

Citilabs, UK/US
Systra Sotecni, Italy
Systra Ingeneria, Spain
Mexistra, Mexico
Systra Venezuela, Venezuela
Systra Maroc, Morocco
Systra Philippines, Inc (SPI), Philippines
Systra Taiwan Branch, Taiwan
Systra Asia Pacific Ltd, Hong Kong
Systra Shanghai Consulting Co, China
Systra MVA Consulting, India

Background

Systra SA is a transport consultancy and engineering company dedicated to the optimisation of transportation systems and infrastructure worldwide. Systra's activities cover a full range of expertise in urban and rail transport, from design to construction: high-speed trains, tramways, combined road-rail transport, conventional passenger rail and rail freight, commuter services, regional fast rail networks, metros, bus rapid transit, automatic driverless systems, guided bus systems. Systra has 50 years experience in over 140 countries and 350 cities.

SNCF and RATP own 72 per cent of shares equally; 28 per cent of shares are held by the following banks: Calyon, BNP-Paribas, Paribas Participations, Natixis, Etoile ID, CIC, Société Générale.

Capabilities

Systra offers consulting and engineering services for all rail and urban transport infrastructure and systems (high-speed trains, conventional rail, mass transit, metro, light rail, automatic guided transit systems and buses). Capabilities include: transport planning and organisation, from master plan development to system feasibility analysis; project management; institutional organisation; design engineering; general building engineering; construction management; equipment manufacture supervision; operation and maintenance organisation; training; testing and commissioning; start-up and pre-revenue service operations; transport planning software.

Projects

High-speed rail projects
China: assistance to the Ministry of Railways for the Beijing-Tianjin high-speed line, design review and supervision of works for Tianxingzhou Bridge.
France/Spain: technical assistance to the concessionnaire of Perpignan-Figuères high-speed line.
Spain: supervision of works and commissioning for Cordoba-Malaga high-speed line.
Morocco: design of the Settat-Marrakech and Kenitra-Tanger high-speed lines.
US: program manager (in a joint venture) of the California high-speed rail project.
Other projects
Middle-East and Africa: project management of the Dubai metro project, of the Algiers metro and eastern tramline projects, supervision of works of Cairo metro line 3, assistance to the owner of the Rabat-Salé tramway lines, consultant for Dubai Al Safooh tramline, supervision of the construction of the North-South rail line in Saudi Arabia.
Europe: a number of LRT projects in France (Bordeaux, Toulon, Marseille, Lyon, Reims, Brest, Ile de France). Assistance to the Bilbao metro for the extension of Line 2, supervision of line 2 of the Sofia metro.
Asia: Busan-Gimhae and Uijeongbu LRT projects in Korea, commissioning and launch of Shanghai metro line 10, project management of Mumbai and Bangalore metros, detailed design of Lahore metro green line, general consultant for Hanoi first metro line.

TAS Partnership Ltd

Guildhall House, Guildhall Street, Preston PR1 3NU, UK
Tel: (+44 1772) 20 49 88   Fax: (+44 1772) 56 20 70
e-mail: info@tas-part.co.uk
Web: www.tas-part.co.uk

Key personnel

Directors: *Chris Cheek, John Taylor, Adrian Grant, Brian Cox, Peter Huntley*

Capabilities

Passenger transport research; network planning; market analysis; funding mechanisms; demand evaluation and business case development; concessionary fares, cost improvement projects with local authorities through integrating transport, unconventional and community transport advice.

Projects

Patronage evaluation and bidder support for Croydon Tramlink; Nottingham LRT; Manchester Metrolink, Leeds Supertram, Dublin LUAS. Bus network design for operators throughout the UK; guided bus studies in Oxford, Crawley, Birmingham, Edinburgh, Leeds.

TERA International Group, Inc (TERA)

107 E. Holly Avenue, Suite 12, Sterling, Virginia 20164-5405, US
Tel: (+1 703) 406 44 00   Fax: (+1 703) 406 15 50
Web: www.teraus.com

Key personnel
President: *Asil Gezen*
Marketing Director: *Natalia Douma*

Other offices
TERA Beijing
Sunshine 100, Suite C-3609, No. 2, Guanghua Road, Chaoyang District
Beijing 100026, China
Tel: (+86 10) 51 00 09 00
Fax: (+86 10) 51 00 09 01

TERA Sofia
Gotze Delchev Quarter, Block 108, En A F1, 3 Apt 7
Sofia 1404, Bulgaria
Tel: (+359 2) 958 20 40
Fax: (+359 2) 958 20 41

TERA Manila
41 Premium Street, GSIS Village Proj. 8, Quezon City, Metro Manila, Philippines
Tel: (+ 63 2) 929 59 67

TERA Hawaii
5324 Kalaniana'ole Hwy, Honolulu, Hawaii 96821, US
Tel: (+1 808) 946 94 46
Fax: (+1 808) 946 94 47

Capabilities
TERA is a respected contract research and consulting firm founded in 1976.

Capabilities include: restructuring, concessioning, privatisation analyses, socioeconomic/poverty impact assessments, management information systems, strategic planning and analyses, infrastructure evaluations, organisational and management reviews, trade/traffic forecasting, operational assessments, economic/financial analyses, freight and passenger traffic tarrifs/market analyses, accounting and traffic costing, regulatory and institutional analyses.

Projects
TERA has successfully completed various projects in railway transportation in the US, Central and Eastern Europe, Africa, the Middle East, Latin America and Central and Southern Asia. Project experience covers rail car ferry service operations, metro and light and heavy urban rail projects, computer simulation of freight and passenger traffic, locomotive workshop and other facility evaluations, financial and feasibility analyses including technical, environmental, poverty, institutional considerations; rail restructuring, commercialisation, concessioning and privatisation studies; and intermodal corridor transportation studies including double-stack, piggyback and trailer-truck on flat car operations.

TERA's railway project experience includes technical assessments of railway signalling and communications in Albania, Brazil, Bulgaria, China, Guatemala, Macedonia, Poland and Romania; track laying and maintenance machinery and equipment in Brazil, Egypt, Kazakhstan; locomotive and wagon workshops in Bulgaria, Malaysia, Thailand and 10 countries in Southern and Eastern Africa; market assessments for wheels and bogies, couplers, power components as well as rolling stock. Infrastructure evaluations, trade/traffic forecasting, operational and financial assessments and feasibility studies have been conducted in more than 50 countries worldwide.

Intermodal rail car ferry service for passenger and freight operations have been analysed around the world including the Caspian Sea, the Baltic Sea and Lake Michigan. TERA conducted regional rail corridor assessments for the Balkans and a feasibility study for a regional locomotive workshop and centralised part warehouse with unit exchange in Eastern and Southern Africa for the Union of African Railways. Metro/light rail system evaluations in India, Indonesia, Philippines, Romania, Singapore, Thailand, Turkey and Venezuela have been undertaken.

Thomas K Dyer, Inc

HNTB Corporation
1762 Massachusetts Avenue, Lexington, Massachusetts 92420, USA
Tel: (+1 781) 862 20 75   Fax: (+1 781) 861 77 66
e-mail: dwoodbury@hntb.com
Web: www.hntb.com

Key personnel
Vice-President: *Douglas J Woodbury*
Marketing: *Kimberley Durkee*

Other offices
Over 60 offices throughout the US.

Background
Established in 1914, Thomas K Dyer became part of HNTB Corporation in June 2001.

Capabilities
Planning, engineering and architecture services for transport and environmental engineering.

Transportation Management Solutions

PO Box 15174, Glasgow G3 6WB, UK
Tel: (+44 141) 332 47 33   Fax: (+44 141) 354 00 76
e-mail: tramsol@aol.com
Web: www.transformscotland.org.uk

Key personnel
Principals: *Dave Holladay, Josephine Nevoh*

Capabilities
Transport management solutions (Intermodal & TDM).

Projects
Include studies and application of bike/public transport issues including fitting cycle-carrying facilities on buses in UK and on secure storage/locker systems for bus and train passengers.
Cycle parking for PT Interchange.

Transportation Technology Center Inc (TTCI)

A subsidiary of the Association of American Railroads (AAR)
PO Box 11130, Pueblo, Colorado 81001, US
Tel: (+1 719) 584 07 50   Fax: (+1 719) 584 07 11
e-mail: marketing@ttci.aar.com
Web: www.ttci.aar.com

Subsidiaries
TTCI (UK) Ltd
13 Fitzroy Street, London W1T 4BQ, UK
e-mail: barrie_brickle@aar.com
Web: www.ttciuk.co.uk
General Manager, TTCI (UK) Ltd: *Dr Barrie Brickle*

Key personnel
President: *Roy A Allen*
Vice-President Commercial Projects: *Dr Albert J Reinschmidt*
Vice-President Research and Development: *Semih Kalay*
Senior Assistant Vice-President Strategic Planning Capabilities: *Dr James R Lundgren*
Assistant Vice-President Communications and Train Control Technologies: *Alan L Polivka*

Background
The Transportation Technology Center Inc (TTCI) was formed on 1 January 1998 as a wholly owned subsidiary of the Association of American Railroads (AAR). TTCI employs approximately 250 engineers, technicians and support personnel.

TTCI (UK) Ltd was incorporated in June 2004 as a wholly owned subsidiary of the Transportation Technology Center Inc. TTCI (UK) Ltd is supported by its parent organisation with extensive testing facilities and is a professional engineering consulting company that provides services to the European Union.

Capabilities
Full-scale vehicle on-track testing and specialised laboratory testing are available at the 33 km (52 sq-mile) Transportation Technology Center (TTC) located near Pueblo, Colorado, US. The site provides over 77 km (48 miles) of specialised railroad test track, extensive track facilities for electric and dual-mode high-speed passenger, transit, commuter and freight testing. In addition, TTC is a one-of-a-kind test environment that provides highly specialised, full-scale and component laboratories in addition to on-track testing.

Consulting services include vehicle dynamics, train operations, train energy, asset management (wear, degradation and life cycle costing), engineering economics, communication-based train control systems. TTCI has expertise in on-board and wayside test instrumentation and data collection systems. TTCI provides a full compliment of instrumentation coaches and portable data collection systems.

Technical training includes vehicle dynamics, fundamentals of track engineering, non-destructive flaw detection technologies in vehicles and infrastructure components, effects of increasing axle loads, and emergency response training to hazardous materials transport emergencies.

Products include: instrumented wheelsets (wheel/rail load measurement axles fitted to vehicles); NUCARS® (vehicle dynamics model); Train Energy Model – TEM™; Railway Track Life-Cycle Model – RTLM™; Wheel/Rail Tolerance – WRTOL™; Performance Based Track Geometry – PBTG™; Simulation of Train Action to Reduce Cost of Operations – STARCO™; Truck Performance Detector (TPD); Trackside Acoustic (Bearing) Detection Systems – TADS®; Fully Automated Car Train Inspection System – FactIS®; Integrated Railway Remote Information Service – InteRRIS®.

As a wholly owned subsidiary of the Association of American Railroads , TTCI provides all of the research and development needs of the North American rail industry.

TTCI (UK) capabilities include vehicle dynamics, train operations, train energy, asset management (wear, degradation and life-cycle costing), engineering economics, and communication-based train control systems. It has expertise in on-board and wayside testing instrumentation and data collection systems and provides a full compliment of instrumentation coaches and portable data collection systems.

Technical training includes vehicle dynamics, fundamentals of track engineering, non-destructive flaw detection technologies in vehicles and infrastructure components, effects of increasing axle loads, and emergency response training to hazardous materials transportation emergencies.

Projects
The passenger rail industry has been supported by TTCI in the performance of consulting and testing of vehicles and passenger rail system components to specification and regulatory compliance.

Other projects include: positive train control (communication-based train control) related studies for fitment and track possession; CA Metro de Caracas, Venezuela, bogies retrofit programme; New York City Transit R124 crash testing; Acela high-speed train testing; Railway Technical Research Institute, Japan, gauge change train testing; Amtrak Express car performance testing; wheel spalling investigation; official AAR new car performance testing; Electro-Motive diesel locomotive testing; Companhia Vale do Rio Doce (CVRD) heavy axle load implementation testing. Recent consulting projects have been related to wheel/rail interface issues experienced by transit agencies.

Current and recently completed TTCI projects involving specification and compliance testing have included: MotivePower locomotive

Aerial view of the TTCI rail facility at Pueblo, Colorado, US   1114355

testing; qualification of the DOT's new track geometry car; Long Island RR's new M-7 emu passenger rail cars; New Jersey diesel locomotive PL 42-AC; New Jersey electric locomotive ALP – 46; Puerto Rico – Tren Urbano heavy rail subway vehicles; light rail operations consulting in Boston for the MBTA; heavy rail operations for Washington, DC Metro (WMATA) and testing of existing VIA (Canadian) passenger vehicle for dynamic performance characteristics.

Examples of some of TTCI (UK) Ltd projects include: Network Rail framework contract for a set of projects to provide business focused results in vehicle rack optimisation and asset whole life-cycle reductions. – review of variable usage and electrification asset usage charges, cost issues for the Office of Rail Regulations (ORR); Network Rail and EWS in the UK; wheelset condition monitoring – assessment for the RSSB in the UK; wheel wear and RCF model for the RSSB in the UK; assessment of a global quality assurance program for the UIC; TTCI (UK) Ltd and Lulea of Sweden reviewed the use of condition monitoring equipment on the Swedish railways in 2007; investigation of rolling contact fatigue (Hatfield incident, UK); support to ORR sponsored review of Network Rail's business plan; application of advanced acoustic bearing technology to conduct a field survey of the condition of the wheel roller bearings for a series of UK rolling stock.

Transurb Technirail SA

60 rue Raveinstein, Bte 18, B-1000 Brussels, Belgium
Tel: (+32 2) 548 53 40   Fax: (+32 2) 513 94 19
e-mail: a.willaert@transurb.com
Web: www.transurb.com

Key personnel
Chief Executive: *Patrick Steyaert*
Commercial Director: *Etienne Deblon*
Marketing Manager: *Andy Willaert*
Technical Manager: *Yannick Gilis*

Subsidiaries
TUC Rail, Belgium
Belgorail, Belgium
Transurb, Argentina
Transurb, France
Transurb International Ltd, Russian Federation
Technirail, Manila
Sobetra, Slovakia
Transurb, Algeria

Background
Transurb Technirail is a semi-public company and a subsidiary of SNCB/NMBS and also a daughter company of STIB (the urban transport company of Brussels) as well as of Belgian private transport-engineering consultants.

Capabilities
Transurb Technirail has been, since its creation in 1973, an expert company in railway and mass urban transit projects, for both transport of persons and freight.

Transurb Technirail offers a diversified range of services to customers, worldwide (including design, build, operation, maintenance, upgrade) of project cycles relating to rolling stock.

Projects
The most significant projects include: the complete maintenance of Light Rail Transit System 1 in Manila, the maintenance, by way of a concession, of the Gabonese railway, the maintenance of bogies, brakes, wheels and air-conditioning systems on behalf of Eurotunnel, assistance to the operation of Ferrovias (Belgrano Norte Line) and Metrovías (Buenos Aires underground) franchise holders in Argentina, the design and manufacture of many railway-driving simulators, the rehabilitation of 650 wagons for the Romanian railway and a BOT project for a bus terminal in Kingston, Jamaica.

Supervision of signalling and railway infrastructure construction works in Romania and Algeria.

Transys Projects Ltd

2 Priestley Wharf, Holt Street, Aston Science Park, Birmingham B7 4BN, UK
Tel: (+44 121) 359 77 77   Fax: (+44 121) 359 18 11
e-mail: info@transysprojects.ltd.uk
Web: www.transysprojects.ltd.uk

Key personnel
Managing Director: *Kevin Lane*
Sales and Marketing Manager: *Andy Colver*
Engineering Director: *Karl J Barras*
Financial Director: *Emma Stamps*

Background
Transys Projects Ltd is an independent company.

Capabilities
Multidisciplined engineering consultancy and project management organisation, covering all aspects of passenger rail vehicles and their related support services. This covers mass transit vehicles, LRVs and tramcars as well as main line dmus, emus, and passenger coaches.

Certified to BS EN ISO 9001 with 'Link-Up' accreditation in 26 relevant areas.

Specific capabilities include:

Design Engineering
- Design of complete rail vehicles or discrete areas
- Concept to production drawings/schedules
- Bodyshells, underframes, cabs, interiors
- Assembly, component and system design
- Mockups, modular design

Engineering Services
- Optimisation of design
- FEA, classical calculations, kinematics, dynamics
- Specification and management of structural testing
- Tender/tender response documents and purchase specifications

Electrical and Mechanical Systems, Engineering and Integration
- Ability to project engineer a complete range of equipment, systems and services through design, testing and validation.
- Vehicle mechanical equipment, systems, diesel drivelines, etc
- Electrical/electronic systems including control and traction auxiliaries
- Material choice, fire safety and testing
- Vehicle performance, simulation on specified routes
- Vehicle acceptance and safety case issues
- Fault finding, trouble shooting

Project Support
- Project management and planning
- Selection and monitoring of subcontractors and/or product performance
- Vehicle maintenance, efficiency and reliability improvement
- Development of technical literature and support information
- Modification and upgrade work

Projects
Recent projects include engineering and design of many vehicle enhancements including GSM-R (cab radio), OTMR passenger information systems for UK and international markets.

Design engineered and project managed Class 323 and Malaysian emus plus Glasgow Underground trailer cars.

Complex underframe installation designs covering complete diesel drivelines, fuel tanks, brake frames, electric traction drives and auxiliary equipment cases. Interior finish design/engineering for several new multiple unit packages in the UK.

General engineering consultancy, detailed structural design, safety and maintenance support for Fiat Ferroviaria on their joint UK contract with Alstom Transport for Virgin's West Coast high-speed tilting trains.

Design support for Alusuisse Road and Rail. Various other contracts for engineering consultancy and maintenance support activities.

Turnkey provision including design, engineering, installation and commissioning of automatic sanding systems on more than 700 existing multiple-units in the UK. These cover various classes of dmus and emus to improve adhesion performance during braking and traction during the leaf-fall season.

TRL Limited (Transport Research Laboratory)

Crowthorne House, Nine Mile Ride, Wokingham, RG45 3GA, UK
Tel: (+44 1344) 77 31 31
Fax: (+44 1344) 77 08 80
e-mail: enquiries@trl.co.uk
Web: www.trl.co.uk

Key personnel

Chief Executive: *Dr Susan Sharland*
Director of Marketing and Communications: *Nick Anderson*

Capabilities

Internationally recognised,TRL provides research, consultancy, advice and testing. Generating and applying science, knowledge and understanding to develop solutions for its customers worldwide, TRL has extensive experience in safety, 3D laser scanning of accident sites, crash investigation and reconstruction, testing and simulation, strategic planning, asset management, development of cost models, the use of sustainable products, risk management, environmental impact assessment and real-time passenger information.

TTK – TransportTechnologie-Consult Karlsruhe GmbH

Gerwigstrasse 53, D-76131 Karlsruhe, Germany
Tel: (+49 721) 62 50 30
Fax: (+49 721) 625 03 33
e-mail: info@ttk.de
Web: www.ttk.de

Key personnel

Managing Director: *Udo Sparmann*
Contact: *Gertrud Westermann*

Background

TransportTechnologie-Consult Karlsruhe GmbH (TTK) is an international engineering company which was founded in 1996 as a subsidiary of Albtal-Verkehrs-Gesellschaft mbH, Karlsruhe (AVG) and of PTV AG. AVG is a private public transport organisation and is the regional public transport operator of the city of Karlsruhe.

The company has staff in Germany and France.

Capabilities

Include: evaluation of tram-train solutions including track sharing by light and heavy rail; studies on railbound public transport; infrastructure planning; economic assessments; feasibility studies; infrastructure planning and design; research projects; rolling stock studies; tariff and marketing; as well as transport and operational concepts.

Projects

TTK carried out projects for LRT, tramtrain and regional railway in the following countries over the last 10 years: Austria, Germany, Finland, France, Italy, Luxembourg, Norway, Slovenia, Spain, Switzerland, UK and US.

Urban Initiatives

1 Fitzroy Square, London W1T 5HE, UK
Tel: (+44 20) 73 80 45 45
Fax: (+44 20) 73 80 45 46
e-mail: info@urbaninitiatives.co.uk
Web: www.urbaninitiatives.co.uk

Key personnel

Directors: *Kelvin Campbell, John Dales, Mike Morris, Simon Carne, Jonathan Bore*

Capabilities

Planning and design consultancy specialising in urban planning and design; transport planning and traffic engineering; infrastructure planning and environmental assessment; development planning and economics.

Projects

Projects have included: Railtrack (now Network Rail): development opportunities and pedestrian links around London Bridge station; development of scheme options for bus interchange at Cardiff station; survey of Thameslink passengers (with OPRAF) for Thameslink 2000 project; analysis of pedestrian movements in Liverpool Street station, London.

London Underground: validation of station planning guidelines; appraisal of station designs for CrossRail and East London line, development of central London station strategy for proposed Chelsea-Hackney line; and computer modelling of stations across London.

Centro, Birmingham: preparation of design guidelines for Line 2 of the LRT system.

LT Planning: creation of database on trip information for London rail network; assessment of local access arrangements for Jubilee line extension; projection of demand at Paddington station, London, for next 15 years.

Greater Manchester PTE: proposals for regeneration of Piccadilly station and surrounding area.

Vauxhall Interchange Study for Vauxhall Regeneration Company, looking at improvement options for the underground and rail stations situated in a major traffic gyratory scheme.

Urbitran

71 West 23rd Street, 11th Floor, New York, New York 10010, US
Tel: (+1 212) 366 62 00
Fax: (+1 212) 366 62 14
e-mail: transit@urbitran.com
Web: www.urbitran.com

Key personnel

Chairman and Chief Executive Officer: *Michael Horodniceanu*
President and Chief Operating Officer: *Mac Ismail*
Senior Vice-President: *David Sampson*

Offices

New Haven, Connecticut; Holyoke, Massachusetts; Edison, New Jersey; Albany, New York.

Subsidiaries

Urbitran/Rosenbloom Architects (New York, New York)
Urbitran/Garmen (Montville, New Jersey)
UA Construction (New York, New York)

Capabilities

In the transit services sector: bus and rail operations studies, transit development plan preparation, origin and destination studies, paratransit planning, marketing and survey research, management performance reviews, welfare-to-work planning, public and community outreach and ridership forecasting.

Projects

Include: Connecticut DOT statewide bus system study; Baltimore regional transit study; Buffalo Intermodal Transportation Center ridership demand development; Rockingham County, Virginia, transportation development plan; Charlottesville, Virginia, transit development plan; Albany Corridor study; comprehensive review of transit services for Santa Clarita, California; North Carolina statewide technical assistance or transit planning services.

URS Corporation Ltd

Transportation Operations, URS House, Horn Lane, Bedford MK40 1TS, UK
Tel: (+44 1234) 34 96 41   Fax: (+44 1234) 21 62 68
Web: www.urscorp.com

Head office
600 Montgomery Street, San Francisco, California 94111, US
Tel: (+1 212) 768 11 55

Key personnel

Chairman and Chief Executive Officer: *Martin M Koffel*
Business Lines Director: *K Holloway*
Divisional Directors: *R Pollock; M Horsfall; S Ashton; R Welsford*
UK Managing Director: *D J Bennison*
Finance Director: *Andrew Elliott Frey*
UK Transportation Service Line Director: *A Wakeman*

Background

The company operates in more than 30 countries with approximately 56,000 employees.

In November 2007, URS Corporation acquired Washington Group International, a provider of integrated engineering construction and management services based in Boise, Idaho and integrated it into its operations as the URS Washington division.

Capabilities

The URS Corporation UK transportation service line planning is active in the following areas: transport research; transport policy; transport planning; transport modeling; transport evaluation; transport infrastructure design and maintenance; transport implementation; transport communications and marketing.

Projects

Extensively in the UK and most recently in: London (Hackney, Barking and Dagenham, Woolwich, Wimbledon, Westminster, City of London), Leeds, Liverpool, Manchester, Sheffield, Bristol, Luton, Milton Keynes, Bedford, Cambridge, Cardiff, Glasgow, Edinburgh and Dunstable.

Keynote projects include airport surface access work at London-Luton and Belfast airports, parking studies in Ashby and Market Harborough, accessibility studies in Hackney and Tower Hamlets, bus priority studies for TfI, highway corridor studies and schemes in Luton and a range of highway improvement studies and schemes for the Highways Agency. Key framework commissions include the multi-disciplinary panel for English Partnerships, Leed CC regeneration and Merseytravel transport and environment panel and the Network Rail Professional Services Framework.

Uvaterv Engineering Consultants Ltd

PO Box 453/421, H-1537 Budapest 114, Hungary
Tel: (+36 1) 204 29 67   Fax: (+36 1) 204 29 69
e-mail: info@uvaterv.hu
Web: www.uvaterv.hu

Key personnel

President-Director General: *Gyula Bretz*
Deputy Director General and Division Director, Transportation Infrastructure: *Frigyes Kovácsházy*
Division Director, Bridges, Structures: *Zsolt Kovács*
Director, Metro and Architecture: *Imre Juhász*
Established: 1948

For details of the latest updates to *Jane's Urban Transport Systems* online and to discover the additional information available exclusively to online subscribers please visit

juts.janes.com

Capabilities

Engineering and general consultancy services for rail, metro and road systems; network planning, architectural design, structural and electrical engineering, signalling systems, traffic management.

Wilbur Smith Associates

1301 Gervais Street, 16th Floor, Columbia, South Carolina 29201-3356, US
Tel: (+1 803) 758 45 00   Fax: (+1 803) 251 29 26
e-mail: intl@WilburSmith.com; dgadow@
 WilburSmith.com
Web: www.WilburSmith.com
Postal address
PO Box 92, Columbia, South Carolina 29202-0092, US

Key personnel

President: *Hollis A Walker Jr*
Executive Vice-President, Chief Operating Officer –
 International Operations: *James Hamann*
Vice-President National Public Transportation
 Practice Leader: *Peter Sklannik*
Director, Intercity Passenger Rail Services: *Justin Fox*
Associate-in-Charge, Salt Lake City, UT: *Barry Banks*
Director of Corporate Communications: *Danielle M Gadow*
Senior Vice-President and Corporate Director of
 Business Development: *Richard H Ward*

Capabilities

Transportation consulting services covering rail, road, air and water systems, extending from planning, pre-feasibility and preliminary engineering through development of final design, contract documents, construction and maintenance services, training and technical assistance and field supervision. Management consultation services include planning, programming, budgeting and supervision of contractors and subcontractors. Services also include transit vehicle/station/facility design, design of architectural graphics and related visual communications systems, and interior space planning.

Projects

High Speed Rail: studies in California; Florida; Chicago, Illinois to Milwaukee, Wisconsin; Chicago, Illinois to St Louis, Missouri; the Pacific Northwest High Speed Rail Corridor; Oregon high speed rail capacity analysis; the Southeast high speed rail corridor improvement study.

Commuter Rail Studies: Ashtabula-Cleveland commuter rail study, Ohio; Virginia Railway Express capacity analysis; Contra Costa County commuter rail plan, California; Anchorage Metropolitan Area commuter rail study, Alaska; Florida Tri-County commuter rail extension study; Santa Clarita rail corridor study, California; Lincoln to Omaha rail passenger study, Nebraska.

Rail Freight Studies and Designs: State rail plans, grade crossing improvements, rail access to ports and industrial plants, track and structure evaluations, Intermodal Rail Yards; joint use evaluations, light density live evaluations; performance evaluations; merger studies.

Urban Rail Transit: feasibility studies; alternatives analysis; preliminary engineering

and environmental studies; alternative financing plans; economic impact assessments.

Other Services/Experience: intermodal planning; geographic information systems; bridge inspection and rehabilitation; environmental services; underwater bridge inspections; highway/railway grade crossing surveys/closures; rail consolidation studies; and Public Private Partnerships.

Wilson, Ihrig & Associates

5776 Broadway, Oakland, California 94618, US
Tel: (+1 510) 658 67 19
Fax: (+1 510) 652 44 41
Web: www.wiai.com

Key personnel

President: *Steven L Wolfe*
Marketing Manager: *Kash Gill*

Capabilities

Acoustical design and vibration consulting with extensive experience in acoustical design of stations, line sections and facilities; vehicle noise, vibration and ride quality evaluation; assessment and prediction of ground-borne vibration; track fastener design, testing and specification; noise and vibration criteria development.

TTG Transportation Technology (TTG TT)

Level 3, 225 Clarence Street, Sydney, New South Wales 2000, Australia
Tel: (+61 2) 92 49 01 00   Fax: (+61 2) 92 62 42 31
Web: www.ttgtransportationtechnology.com

Key personnel

Managing Director: *Dale Coleman*

Background

TTGTT is a new company formed in October 2007 to take over the marketing, sales and development of the former TMG International Group's railway technology and products business.

Capabilities

System modelling and simulation, timetable planning and development, operational and infrastructure planning, energy efficient train regulation, condition monitoring and dynamic analysis systems, maintenance analysis and planning, safety and risk analysis, operations and infrastructure benchmarking, asset management systems and support.

WSP Policy & Research Unit

49-51 High Street, Trumpington, Cambridge CB2 2HZ, UK
Tel: (+44 1223) 84 07 04   Fax: (+44 1223) 84 03 84
Web: www.meap.co.uk

Key personnel

Managing Director: *Ian Williams*
Executive Directors: *Lynn Devereaux*
Non-Executive Directors: *Jose Luis Burgos,
 Prof David Newbery, Richard Stibbs*

Background

In 2001, WSP Group acquired the business of Cambridge based Marcial Echenique & Partners Limited, a specialist transport, land use and economic planning consultancy with European associates in Finland, Italy and Spain.

Capabilities

Integrated land use and transport planning, covering infrastructure investment; road pricing/demand management, public transport fares and services, traffic generation, urban and regional regeneration; economic evaluation of transport policies; custom software for computer modelling; urban design and development feasibility studies.

ZGF – Zimmer Gunsul Frasca Partnership

320 SW Oak, Suite 500, Portland, Oregon 97204, US
Tel: (+1 503) 224 38 60
Fax: (+44 503) 224 24 82
e-mail: jmitchell@zgf.com
Web: www.zgf.com

Key personnel

Principals: *Ronald R Stewart*
Partners: *Gregory S Baldwin, Margaret W DeBolt, Mark M Foster, Robert J Frasca, Daniel J Huberty, Ted A Hyman, Doss Mabe, Robert G Packard, Eugene B Sandoval, Karl R Sonnenberg, Allyn B Stellmacher, Jan Carl Willemse, Larry S Bruton, Joseph A Collins, Robert L Zimmerman*

Capabilities:

Zimmer Gunsul Frasca Partnership, recipient of the 1991 AIA Architecture Firm Award, is an architecture, planning and interior design firm. With a total staff of 480, ZGF represents a diverse mix of projects, ranging from regional transportation systems to institutional and corporate campuses, urban mixed-use developments and civic and cultural facilities.

Projects:

In the last 40 years, ZGF has managed and designed nationally recognised projects, representing a broad range of project types. The firm has been responsible for architecture and urban design on a number of light rail systems in the US, including Portland's MAX Light Rail System; Seattle's Sound Transit Link and Commuter Light Rail Systems; the Minneapolis/St Paul International Airport Tunnel Station and Hiawatha Corridor Light Rail Transit System; and the Mission Valley East Light Rail Transit Project in San Diego. ZGF has also been involved in the planning and design of new streetcar systems in Portland, Seattle and Washington DC. Other transit malls, multimodal facilities, street improvements, pedestrian corridors and transit-supportive development have been designed for communities around the country including Portland, Seattle, Denver, Los Angeles, Chicago, Boise, Houston and San Francisco.

INDEX

N

NABI Inc *buses – chassis/integrals/bodies* (United States) ... 684
Nabtesco Corporation *rail and bus components/ subassemblies* (Japan) ... 587
Nabtesco Corporation *revenue collection systems/station equipment* (Japan) ... 776
Nagasaki Denki Kido *urban transport systems and operators* (Japan) ... 210
Nagasaki Electric Tramway Co Ltd *urban transport systems and operators* (Japan) ... 210
Nagasaki-Ken Kotsu Kyoku *urban transport systems and operators* (Japan) ... 209
Nagasaki Motor Bus Co Ltd *urban transport systems and operators* (Japan) ... 210
Nagasaki Transportation Bureau *urban transport systems and operators* (Japan) ... 209
Nagoya City Transport Bureau *urban transport systems and operators* (Japan) ... 210
Nagoya Railroad Company Ltd *urban transport systems and operators* (Japan) ... 212
Nagoya Tetsudo *urban transport systems and operators* (Japan) ... 212
Nagoya-shi Kotsu Kyoku *urban transport systems and operators* (Japan) ... 210
Nangoku Kotsu Transport Co Ltd *urban transport systems and operators* (Japan) ... 203
Nanjing Metro Corporation *urban transport systems and operators* (China) ... 81
Nankai Denki Tetsudo *urban transport systems and operators* (Japan) ... 217
Napa County Transportation Planning Agency *urban transport systems and operators* (United States) ... 470
Narita Manufacturing Ltd *rail and bus components/ subassemblies* (Japan) ... 587
Narita Manufacturing Ltd *revenue collection systems/ station equipment* (Japan) ... 776
Nashville Metropolitan Transit Authority *urban transport systems and operators* (United States) ... 434
NAT *urban transport systems and operators* (Egypt) ... 97, 99
National Authority for Tunnels *urban transport systems and operators* (Egypt) ... 97, 99
National Bus Company Pty Ltd *urban transport systems and operators* (Australia) ... 14
National Express East Anglia *urban transport systems and operators* (United Kingdom) ... 372
National Express West Midlands Ltd *urban transport systems and operators* (United Kingdom) ... 346
National Transport Corporation *urban transport systems and operators* (Mauritius) ... 239
Nationale Maatschappij der Belgische Spoorwegen *urban transport systems and operators* (Belgium) ... 27, 28, 30, 31
NBC *urban transport systems and operators* (Australia) ... 14
NCDOT *urban transport systems and operators* (United States) ... 397
NCTD *urban transport systems and operators* (United States) ... 462
NEA Transport Research and Training *consultancy services* (Netherlands) ... 852
Nederlandse Spoorwegen *urban transport systems and operators* (Netherlands) ... 247, 249, 250, 252
NedTrain *vehicle maintenance equipment/services* (Netherlands) ... 789
NedTrain Consulting *consultancy services* (Netherlands) ... 849
Nencki AG *vehicle maintenance equipment/services* (Switzerland) ... 789
NEOPLAN Ghana Limited *buses – chassis/integrals/ bodies* (Ghana) ... 681
Nepal Department of Transport and Management *urban transport systems and operators* (Nepal) ... 244
NET *urban transport systems and operators* (United Kingdom) ... 385
Netherlands Railway *urban transport systems and operators* (Netherlands) ... 252
Netherlands Railways *urban transport systems and operators* (Netherlands) ... 247, 249, 250
Nettbuss AS *urban transport systems and operators* (Norway) ... 260
NEU International Railways *permanent way components/ equipment/services* (France) ... 809
NEU International Railways *vehicle maintenance equipment/services* (France) ... 789
Neu Systèmes Ferroviaires *rail and bus components/ subassemblies* (France) ... 587
Neuero Technology GmbH *vehicle maintenance equipment/services* (Germany) ... 789
New Flyer Industries *buses – chassis/integrals/bodies* (Canada) ... 681
New Jersey Transit *urban transport systems and operators* (United States) ... 435
New Lantao Bus Co (1973) Ltd *urban transport systems and operators* (China) ... 75
New Orleans Regional Transit Authority *urban transport systems and operators* (United States) ... 436
New World First Bus Services Ltd *urban transport systems and operators* (China) ... 75
New World First Ferry Services Limited *urban transport systems and operators* (China) ... 80
New York City Department of Transportation *urban transport systems and operators* (United States) ... 442
Newag Spólka Akcyjna *rail vehicles* (Poland) ... 530
Newbury Data Recording Ltd *revenue collection systems/station equipment* (United Kingdom) ... 776
Newbus Technology Limited *consultancy services* (United Kingdom) ... 852
Newcastle Upon Tyne *urban transport systems and operators* (United Kingdom) ... 380, 381
Newlands Coach Services Limited *urban transport systems and operators* (New Zealand) ... 255
Nexala *information technology* (Ireland) ... 832
NextEnergy *new technology/innovative transit systems* (United States) ... 629
Nexus *urban transport systems and operators* (United Kingdom) ... 382
NFT Metro *urban transport systems and operators* (United States) ... 396
Niagara Frontier Transit Metro System Inc *urban transport systems and operators* (United States) ... 396
NICE Systems Ltd *information technology* (Israel) ... 832
Nicosia Buses Co Ltd *urban transport systems and operators* (Cyprus) ... 88
Nieaf-Smitt BV *rail and bus components/subassemblies* (Netherlands) ... 585
Niederrheinische Versorgong und Verkehr AG (NVV) – MöBus *urban transport systems and operators* (Germany) ... 153
Nigerian Railway Corporation (NRC) *urban transport systems and operators* (Nigeria) ... 256
Niigata Transys Co Ltd *rail vehicles* (Japan) ... 531
Nippon Sharyo Ltd *rail vehicles* (Japan) ... 531
Nippon Sharyo Ltd – Vehicles Of New Age *new technology/innovative transit systems* (Japan) ... 630
Nippon Signal Co Ltd *revenue collection systems/station equipment* (Japan) ... 777
Nippon Signal Co Ltd *signalling/communications/traffic control* (Japan) ... 747
Nishi Nihon Ryokaku Tetsudo *urban transport systems and operators* (Japan) ... 201, 202, 207, 209, 213, 216
Nishi Tokyo Bus Co Ltd *urban transport systems and operators* (Japan) ... 221
Nishi-Nippon Coach Industry Co Ltd *buses – chassis/ integrals/bodies* (Japan) ... 684
Nishi-Nippon Railroad Co Ltd *urban transport systems and operators* (Japan) ... 199, 204
Nishitetsu *urban transport systems and operators* (Japan) ... 199, 204
Nissan Motor Co Ltd *buses – chassis/integrals/bodies* (Japan) ... 684
Nissan Motor España SA *buses – chassis/integrals/bodies* (Spain) ... 684
Nizhegorodelektrotrans *urban transport systems and operators* (Russian Federation) ... 285
Nizhnedneprovsky *rail and bus components/subassemblies* (Ukraine) ... 587
NJ Transit *urban transport systems and operators* (United States) ... 435
NMB – Minebea UK Ltd *rail and bus components/ subassemblies* (United Kingdom) ... 588
NMBS *urban transport systems and operators* (Belgium) ... 27, 28, 30, 31
NMBS-Holding *urban transport systems and operators* (Belgium) ... 27
Noge SL *buses – chassis/integrals/bodies* (Spain) ... 684
Nokia *signalling/communications/traffic control* (Finland) ... 747
Nomix Enviro *permanent way components/equipment/ services* (United Kingdom) ... 809
Norges Statsbaner AS *urban transport systems and operators* (Norway) ... 260
Norsk Hydro ASA *rail and bus components/subassemblies* (Norway) ... 588
Nortel Networks Germany GmbH & Co *signalling/ communications/traffic control* (Germany) ... 747
North American Bus Industries Inc *buses – chassis/ integrals/bodies* (United States) ... 684
North Carolina Railroad Company *urban transport systems and operators* (United States) ... 398
North Eastern Railway *urban transport systems and operators* (India) ... 174
North Milan Railway *urban transport systems and operators* (Italy) ... 189
North San Diego County Transit Development Board – North County Transit District *urban transport systems and operators* (United States) ... 462
Northeast Illinois Regional Commuter Railroad Corporation *urban transport systems and operators* (United States) ... 400
Northern Busway Project Office *urban transport systems and operators* (New Zealand) ... 253
Northern Rail Ltd *urban transport systems and operators* (United Kingdom) ... 379, 380, 383, 387
Northern Railway *urban transport systems and operators* (India) ... 171, 174
Northern, North Central and North Eastern Railways *urban transport systems and operators* (India) ... 173
Northstar Corridor Development Authority *urban transport systems and operators* (United States) ... 432
Norwalk Transit System *urban transport systems and operators* (United States) ... 425
Norwegian State Railways *urban transport systems and operators* (Norway) ... 260
Nottingham City Transport *urban transport systems and operators* (United Kingdom) ... 384
Nottingham Express Transit *urban transport systems and operators* (United Kingdom) ... 385
Nova Bus *buses – chassis/integrals/bodies* (Canada) ... 686
Novosibirsk Metro *urban transport systems and operators* (Russian Federation) ... 285
Novosibirsk Metropolitena Municipal Enterprise *urban transport systems and operators* (Russian Federation) ... 285
NS-Groep NV *urban transport systems and operators* (Netherlands) ... 247, 249, 250, 252
NSK-Coach *buses – chassis/integrals/bodies* (Japan) ... 684
NTA *urban transport systems and operators* (Israel) ... 183
NTA – Metropolitan Mass Transit System Ltd *urban transport systems and operators* (Israel) ... 183
Nuevo Tren de la Costa SA *urban transport systems and operators* (Argentina) ... 4
Nu-Metrics *signalling/communications/traffic control* (United States) ... 748

O

ÖAF *buses – chassis/integrals/bodies* (Austria) ... 689
OASA SA *urban transport systems and operators* (Greece) ... 161
ÖBB *urban transport systems and operators* (Austria) ... 24
OC Transpo *urban transport systems and operators* (Canada) ... 54
OCTA *urban transport systems and operators* (United States) ... 472
Odakyu Bus Co Ltd *urban transport systems and operators* (Japan) ... 221
Odakyu Dentetsu *urban transport systems and operators* (Japan) ... 223
Odakyu Electric Railway Co Ltd *urban transport systems and operators* (Japan) ... 223
Ødegaard & Danneskiold-Samsøe A/S *consultancy services* (Denmark) ... 852
Offenbacher Verkehrs-Betriebe GmbH *urban transport systems and operators* (Germany) ... 141
Okaden *urban transport systems and operators* (Japan) ... 213
Okayama Denki Kido *urban transport systems and operators* (Japan) ... 213
Okayama Electric Tramway Co Ltd *urban transport systems and operators* (Japan) ... 213
Oleo International Ltd *rail and bus components/ subassemblies* (United Kingdom) ... 588
Omega Electronics SA *passenger information systems* (Switzerland) ... 764
Omnibusverkehr Franken GmbH *urban transport systems and operators* (Germany) ... 155
Omron Corporation *revenue collection systems/station equipment* (Japan) ... 777
On Track Innovations (OTI) *revenue collection systems/ station equipment* (Israel) ... 777

juts.janes.com Jane's Urban Transport Systems 2009-2010

T

W

X

Y

Z

For details of the latest updates to ***Jane's Urban Transport Systems*** online and to discover the additional information available exclusively to online subscribers please visit

juts.janes.com

NOTES

NOTES

NOTES